This b

THE COMMON LAW LIBRARY

ARLIDGE, EADY & SMITH
ON
CONTEMPT

OTHER VOLUMES IN THE COMMON LAW LIBRARY

Chitty on Contracts
Clerk & Lindsell on Torts
Chitty & Jacob's Queen's Bench Forms
Bullen & Leake's Precedents of Pleadings
Charlesworth on Negligence
Bowstead on Agency
Gatley on Libel and Slander
McGregor on Damages
Phipson on Evidence
Jackson & Powell on Professional Negligence
Goff & Jones, The Law of Restitution

AUSTRALIA
Law Book Co—Sydney

CANADA and USA
Carswell—Toronto

HONG KONG
Sweet & Maxwell—Asia

NEW ZEALAND
Brookers—Wellington

SINGAPORE and MALAYSIA
Sweet & Maxwell Asia—Singapore and Kuala Lumpur

THE COMMON LAW LIBRARY

ARLIDGE, EADY & SMITH ON CONTEMPT

Third Edition

by

SIR DAVID EADY, M.A., LL.B.
*A Judge of the High Court, Queen's Bench Division;
Bencher of the Middle Temple*

and

PROFESSOR A. T. H. SMITH, LL.D
*Barrister, 5 Raymond Buildings, and Honorary Bencher of the
Middle Temple; Barrister and Solicitor of the High Court of
New Zealand; Professor of Criminal and Public Laws and
Fellow of Gonville and Caius College, University of
Cambridge*

LONDON
SWEET & MAXWELL
2005

First Edition	(1982)	A. Arlidge and D. Eady
Second Edition	(1999)	D. Eady and A. T. H. Smith
Third Edition	(2005)	D. Eady and A. T. H. Smith

Published by
Sweet & Maxwell Limited, of
100 Avenue Road, Swiss Cottage,
London NW3 3PF
(http://www.sweetandmaxwell.co.uk)
Typeset by
Interactive Sciences,
Gloucester
Printed in Great Britain by
Bath Press, Bath

A catalogue record for this book is available from the British Library

ISBN 0 421 883405

All rights reserved. UK statutory material in this publication is acknowledged as Crown copyright.

No part of this publication may be reproduced or transmitted in any form or by any means, or stored in any retrieval system of any nature without prior written permission, except for permitted fair dealing under the Copyright, Designs and Patents Act 1988, or in accordance with the terms of a licence issued by the Copyright Licensing Agency in respect of photocopying and/or reprographic reproduction. Application for permission for other use of copyright material including permission to reproduce extracts in other published works shall be made to the publishers. Full acknowledgment of author, publisher and source must be given.

©
Sweet & Maxwell
2005

PREFACE

SINCE the last edition of this work was published in December 1998, there have been many significant developments north and south of the border. In order to try and keep pace, we issued three supplements in 2001, 2002 and 2003 and in each of the prefaces attempted to summarise events as they were taking place. In England and Wales there has been a great deal of relevant legislative activity and we, like other commentators, have found difficulty in locating the changes and tracking down when (if ever) they were to take effect. Because lay persons and their advisers have been confronted with an uncertain and shifting scene, there are concerns as to whether we are paying sufficient regard to the requirements of Art.7 of the European Convention. As was emphasised long ago in *Sunday Times v United Kingdom* (1979) 2 EHRR 245, citizens should be able to regulate their conduct with a reasonable degree of certainty, if necessary with the benefit of legal advice, and to predict the legal consequences of their proposed actions. Yet some legislation has been on the statute book for years without a date ever being appointed or readily available information about ministerial intentions.

As to strict liability contempt (which we deal with in Chapter 4), there has been relatively little activity. The Law Officers have preferred to warn and offer "guidelines" to the media rather than institute proceedings, even in respect of comments on high profile criminal cases which in the past would almost certainly have been sat on by in-house lawyers. There has been a marked reluctance to apply to the Divisional Court following the rejection of the Attorney's submissions in such cases as *Att-Gen v Unger* [1998] 1 Cr.App.R. 308 and *Att-Gen v MGN Ltd* [1997] 1 All E.R. 456. What has particularly given pause for thought is the so-called "fade factor". Courts have been readily persuaded that media comment is so ephemeral that any prejudicial effect will soon be forgotten. Also there is the increasing acceptance by judges, not only in England and Scotland but also in other jurisdictions such as Canada and New Zealand, that jurors should be treated as robust and independent of mind. "Juries are healthy bodies. They do not need a germ free atmosphere": *Cox, Petitioner* (1998) S.L.T. 1172, 1178, *per* Lord Prosser.

Counter to the trend, however, was the notable example of *Att-Gen v Express Newspapers* [2004] EWHC 2859 (Admin). There had been a great deal of coverage and media speculation for nearly a month following allegations of gang rape involving professional footballers in a London hotel. The *Daily Star* then, uniquely, identified two individuals and published photographs despite repeated warnings from the Attorney-General and the Metropolitan Police to the effect that identification was likely to be an issue. Criminal proceedings at that stage had not been launched, but "the publication was precisely what might cause a prosecution to be abandoned because of the tainting of the principal witness' evidence". The "systemic failure" within the newspaper meant that the guidelines had been "overlooked". This was regarded as an aggravating aspect of the case and a fine of £60,000 was imposed. (It was subsequently announced that there was insufficient evidence and no criminal proceedings were instituted.)

Preface

Naturally, as in the field of defamation, the rapid development of the Internet has had to be considered and, especially, the implications of the continuing availability of potentially prejudicial or unlawful allegations via media archives: *HMA v Beggs (No.2)* (2002) S.L.T. 139 and *Att-Gen v Greater Manchester Newspapers* (2001) 145 S.J.L.B. 279. It would seem that it is a question of making a practical assessment of risk against the likelihood of access to the database by relevant persons.

Other aspects of the law have loomed larger in the past seven years in the consideration of appellate courts. First, there is the recurring issue of injunctions against the media (Chapter 6). As to prior restraint, it now seems reasonably clear that the strict common law tests hitherto applied in the context of apprehended libel or contempt will survive, notwithstanding the approach of the House of Lords in *Cream Holdings v Banerjee* [2004] UKHL 44, [2005] 1 A.C. 253, where the full implications of s.12 of the Human Rights Act 1998 were considered. It would appear from this case, when considered with the decision of the Court of Appeal in *Martha Greene v Associated Newspapers Ltd* [2004] EWCA Civ 1462, [2005] 3 W.L.R. 281, [2005] 1 All E.R. 30, that the statutory intervention was intended to set a minimum standard rather than to lower the higher pre-existing thresholds established in, for example, *Bonnard v Perryman* [1891] 2 Ch. 269 and *Coe v Central Television Plc* [1994] E.M.L.R. 433

A different aspect of the law, which has become of fundamental importance over the last 20 years, is the jurisdiction to grant *contra mundum* injunctions. There has been a fresh analysis of the public policy considerations underpinning it in *Re S (FC)* [2004] UKHL 47, [2005] 1 A.C. 593. The distinction carved out by the Court of Appeal in *Re Z* [1997] Fam 1, between the "custodial" and "protective" jurisdictions, is largely of historic interest. Questions will be resolved on a case by case basis and, where competing rights under the Convention are held to be engaged, they are to be balanced in the light of the public interest and proportionality. Most commonly this will arise in relation to the Art.10 rights of the media versus the Art.8 rights of a child or other vulnerable person. Sometimes, however, Art.10 rights may come into conflict also with the rights of an adult under Articles 2 and 3: see *e.g. Venables & Thompson v News Group Newspapers Ltd* [2001] Fam 430; *X (A Woman formerly known as Mary Bell) v O'Brien* [2003] EWHC 1101 (QB); *Carr (Maxine) v News Group Newspapers Ltd* [2005] EWHC 971 (QB).

Finally, on the subject of injunctions, the validity of and justification for the controversial *Spycatcher* doctrine has been reconsidered by the House of Lords in *Att-Gen v Punch Ltd* [2002] UKHL 50, [2003] 1 A.C. 1046 and reaffirmed.

The House of Lords has also had to address (no less than three times) the topic of jury secrecy and the role of s.8 of the Contempt of Court Act (Chapter 11): see *R. v Mirza* [2004] UKHL 2, [2004] 1 A.C. 1118; *R. v Smith (Patrick)* [2005] UKHL 12, [2005] 1 W.L.R. 704; *Att-Gen v Scotcher* [2005] UKHL 36, [2005] 1 W.L.R. 1867, [2005] 3 All E.R. 1. These matters have now been clarified generally and, particularly, as to how far (if at all) it is appropriate for the court to encroach upon such delicate issues, whether before or after verdict, for the purpose of avoiding possible miscarriages of justice.

We have always been mindful of the distinction between civil and criminal contempt and the extent to which it any longer matters (Chapter 3). That distinction has now been blurred in a potentially far-reaching way. In recent years, the law of civil contempt, relating to the enforcement of injunctions and undertakings, came most frequently before the courts in the context of family law and, specifically, in that of non-molestation orders (Chapters 12 and 14). It has been provided by the new s.42A of the Family Law Act 1996 that such a breach is to become a criminal offence. The purpose was to bring greater effectiveness to that protective jurisdiction in the interests of the victims of domestic violence (both partners and children). It means that a greater range of penalties becomes available than for civil (or for that matter criminal) contempt. Hitherto, in such a case the options have been effectively limited to a fine or custody. In the future, once there is a conviction under s.42A, community penalties become available also. Another consequence is that attaching a power of arrest will be confined to Housing Act cases. It will be prevented (and unnecessary) for non-molestation orders. Parliament has also sought to limit the circumstances in which the court may accept an undertaking where there has been actual or threatened violence. This is likely to mean that there will have to be more contested hearings in situations where an undertaking is offered without an admission of liability.

Another area of rapid change has been the law of ASBOs and especially with regard to the recent concept of a "bolt-on ASBO". Here again the boundary between civil and criminal contempt has become fuzzy.

One of the principal targets for statutory intervention has been that of court reporting (Chapters 7 and 8). This has been addressed in various ways, particularly by the Youth Justice and Criminal Evidence Act 1999, of which s.46 is already in force but s.45 not. The former is directed towards the protection of victims and vulnerable witnesses; the latter primarily to taking criminal proceedings out of the reach of s.39 of the Children & Young Persons Act 1933, which would henceforth apply only to civil litigation. There is still a degree of policy shift, and thus uncertainty, on the issue of "naming and shaming" younger criminals since the clear statements of Lord Bingham in *McKerry v Teesdale and Wear Valley Justices* [2001] E.M.L.R. 127: see *e.g.* the discussion by Elias J. in *Chief Constable of Surrey v JHG and DHG* [2002] EWHC 1129.

Further guidance has also been given by the Privy Council in *Independent Publishing Co Ltd v Att-Gen of Trinidad & Tobago* [2004] UKPC 26, [2005] 1 A.C. 190 on the test to be applied before granting postponement orders under s.4(2) of the Contempt of Court Act 1981. Lord Brown endorsed the approach of the Court of Appeal in *Ex parte Telegraph Group* [2001] EWCA Crim 1075, [2001] 1 W.L.R. 1983. It was also made clear that there is no *inherent* power to order the postponement of reporting (for which *R. v Clement* (1821) 4 B. & Ald. 218 had hitherto been thought to provide some foundation).

PREFACE

There have been interesting developments on the protection of journalists' sources (Chapter 9) in *Interbrew SA v Financial Times Ltd* [2002] EWCA Civ 274, [2002] 2 Lloyd's Rep.229, *Ashworth Hospital Authority v MGN Ltd* [2002] UKHL 29, [2002] 1 W.L.R. 2033 and *Mersey Care NHS Trust v Ackroyd* [2003] EWCA Civ 663.

The Human Rights Act 1998 has had less prominence in relation to the subject of strict liability than in some other areas covered in the book, such as journalists' sources and injunctions against the media. This is largely because the statutory criteria were formulated in the 1981 Act specifically with a view to achieving compliance with the Convention following the analysis of the European Court in the *Sunday Times* case. Moreover, there has been no finding that the summary jurisdiction in contempt is, in itself, inconsistent with the requirements of the Convention: see *e.g. Wilkinson v S* [2003] EWCA Civ 95, [2003] 2 All E.R. 185. The sanction of immediate committal is only needed in circumstances of genuine urgency and, as for the formalised "summary" procedure under Ord.52, that has many effective safeguards built into it.

The other major innovation since the last edition, the advent of the CPR, has made little difference in the field of contempt since the previous rules governing practice and procedure (RSC Ord. 52 in the High Court and CCR 29 in the County Court) have been scheduled to the CPR and to a large extent continue in effect as before (Chapters 12 and 15). But things have not stood still. There is an important new Practice Direction which supplements High Court and County Court practice in this regard (which appears in Appendix 5A). Also, CPR Part 39 has emphasised the need for open justice following on from Lord Woolf's discussion in *Hodgson v Imperial Tobacco Ltd* [1998] 1 W.L.R. 1056 (Chapter 7). In the spirit of the times, there has been more recently a move towards greater openness in family courts.

As in other areas of the law, there has of course in the Access to Justice Act 1999 been a fundamental overhaul of public funding with regard to contempt cases (Chapter 15).

As we have already noted in the preface to one of our supplements, there is a useful summary of developments in Scotland in "Scottish Contempt since 1998: Brave New World?" by Alistair Bonnington and Rosalind McInnes in *The Yearbook of Copyright and Media Law 2001–2002*. They identified an "overall trend" in the case law up to that time, which seems to have been confirmed in the intervening years, in favour of less restriction upon the media (Chapter 16). Following the enactment of the Human Rights Act in Scotland in May 1999, they draw attention to three aspects of the law in particular. The common theme, however, would appear to be the greater confidence in jurors illustrated by Lord Prosser's remarks cited above from *Cox, Petitioner*. Other cases demonstrating the same approach are *BBC, Petitioners*, 2001 S.C.C.R. 440 and *HMA v Wilson*, June 15, 2001, H.C.J. It has manifested itself (1) in the context of more scrutiny before the grant of s.4(2) orders, (2) in a "more critical and stringent" attitude to the assessment of a "substantial risk of serious prejudice" for the purposes of s.2 of the 1981 Act, and (3) in a phenomenon seen also in England—the trend

Preface

"decisively away from the 'double-speak' of an earlier judicial generation" in respect of the tension between a readiness to make findings of "serious risk of prejudice" arising through media coverage and a reluctance, on the other hand, to abort trials or allow appeals because of the perceived robustness of jurors.

It thus appears to have come about, as was surely foreseeable following the absorption of the values of the European Convention in both jurisdictions, that there is now a much closer approach adopted towards these matters by English and Scottish judges, based on common experiences—and perhaps less reluctance to cite each others' case law.

We should also explain why in this edition we have not included a separate section on Northern Ireland. It seemed to consist mainly of a list of statutory exceptions or other specific provisions contained in the Contempt of Court Act 1981 (as amended). These can readily be checked nowadays on line, and we felt it would not be of great value to readers. We hasten to add that we have tried to take full account in the body of the text of relevant decisions from that jurisdiction (*e.g.* in relation to *Lord Saville of Newdigate v Harnden* [2003] NICA 6).

As before, we would like to record our gratitude to the staff of the Squire Law Library at Cambridge, always ready with a rapid response to any query, and to the Master and Fellows of Caius College for their assistance and many indulgences. There are also a number of friends and colleagues, in various jurisdictions, who have freely volunteered information and advice—to them too we express our thanks. Our publishers have yet again shown considerable forbearance in understanding our other time commitments, and they have given us support that has been much appreciated.

Nevertheless, we make clear once more that all errors and omissions are down to us alone. As we go to press, we should say that we have tried to give as accurate a picture of the law as was possible at the date below.

DE & ATHS
Cambridge
August 10, 2005

PREFACE TO THE SECOND EDITION

THE first edition of this work, published in November 1982, had been required to be delivered in manuscript only three months after the Contempt of Court Act 1981 came into effect. The publishers on this occasion have shown considerably greater indulgence in that 16 years have elapsed in which to make a more leisurely assessment of how the Act has been implemented. There has also been an opportunity to observe how the law of contempt, more generally, has adapted itself to a rapidly changing environment, and not least to the increasing influence of the European Convention on Human Rights. As we go to press, the Bill which will incorporate the Convention into English law is about to receive the Royal Assent.

During this period there has been a vast body of case law, in this jurisdiction and elsewhere, that would have been quite unforeseeable at the time of the 1981 enactment. So much so, it is probably fair to say now that most significant judicial decisions in this field post-date the Act, and that it is only rarely that one needs to go back to any earlier case law for enlightenment on the principles to be applied. Indeed, there are many pitfalls for the unwary in so doing.

One consequence of these rapid developments has been that, in updating the history of contempt (Chapter 1), we have consigned to it a number of themes that might have seemed to be of burning topicality in 1982. We conclude that section with an account of the current controversies that may be regarded as requiring resolution in the near future. We take here but two examples, one specific and the other general. First, if there is a need to deal with "chequebook journalism", it is desirable that this should be achieved by some means that will enable people to know where they stand and is clear in its definitions, particularly with regard to those who are to be treated as "potential" witnesses. Secondly, there is the persistent problem of what is the required *mens rea* for the various categories of "criminal contempt", both in relation to media publication and other forms of misconduct. Unfortunately, we have had to return to the theme over and over throughout the book, because of the uncertainty, especially with reference to the blurring in the authorities between objective and subjective tests of intention.

Since 1981 there have been no fewer than a dozen cases in which this branch of the law has received the attention of the House of Lords. There had been very few in the past, largely because there was no right of appeal in cases of criminal contempt (even to the Court of Appeal) prior to the Administration of Justice Act 1960. There had therefore been little opportunity, at the highest level, for a measured assessment or analysis of the principles. It is only in modern times that a clear and consistent pattern has begun to emerge.

Our editing process over the last three years has afforded a valuable chance to stand back and identify the broad principles now recognised. These must be culled from the multiplicity of reported cases emanating from so many apparently disparate contexts (ranging, for example, from prejudicial media comments touching pending criminal trials to the enforcement of non-molestation orders). Yet they appear to provide a common underlying theme, in their insistence that resort should only be had to the summary contempt jurisdiction where it can be demonstrated *necessary* to do so for the protection or to be vindication of the fair administration of justice. It may be, for example, that the final obsequies of "technical contempt", the concept nurtured by the House of Lords in the *Thalidomide* case of 1973, are to be found in the judgment of Lord Bingham C.J. in *Att-Gen v Newspaper Publishing plc* [1997] 1 W.L.R. 926.

In this field it is so often the case that a decision will have implications for more than one aspect of the law or practice. *Where* to deal with particular authorities has sometimes proved surprisingly problematic, but we have grouped our consideration of the law in what we hope is a logical and readily accessible order. On occasion, however, it has been necessary to include a good deal of cross-referencing in order to show all the ramifications of a particular case.

We thought it worthwhile to include a new chapter on what we have called "the constitutional dimensions" of contempt (Chapter 2). This seeks to explain the continuing need for a summary jurisdiction to protect the due administration of justice while acknowledging that, in modern conditions, some of the traditional concerns could be addressed more appropriately through the mechanism of a conventional criminal trial, provided there are sufficiently well-defined offences.

This consideration focuses closely on the disciplines imposed by the European Convention in respect of such matters as open trial, the right to legal representation, the need for certainty and clarity in the criminal law, the right to privacy, and the importance of freedom of communication. In particular, we have noted the rapidly developing recognition by the courts of a formal role in a modern democratic society for the media. In that context, there are also new sections devoted specifically to court reporting (Chapters 7 and 8). This is an area that may prove to have been revolutionised in the light of recent decisions, declaring a right to report not only judgments given in chambers but also the hearings themselves. Most significant is the judgment of Lord Woolf M.R. in *Hodgson v Imperial Tobacco Ltd* [1998] 1 W.L.R. 1056.

Another part of the book records the burgeoning jurisprudence on the need to protect the confidentiality of journalists' sources (Chapter 9). In a remarkably short space of time, there have been the decisions of *Goodwin v United Kingdom* (1996) 22 E.H.R.R. 123, *Chief Constable of Leicestershire v Garavelli* [1997] E.M.L.R. 543, *Camelot Group plc v Centaur Communications Ltd* [1998] 1 All E.R. 251 and *Saunders v Punch Ltd* [1998] 1 All E.R. 234.

So far as the press are concerned, however, one of the most significant developments in recent years has been the apparently increasing readiness of the courts to have resort to the grant of injunctions restraining publication by the media. This might be thought to be something of a paradox, having regard to the growing recognition accorded to the Fourth Estate. In reality, it seems that it is no more than an aspect of the ever difficult balancing exercises which must be carried out, as acknowledged even by the Convention itself, between competing priorities of public policy.

Preface to the Second Edition

Most notably perhaps, there was in 1987 the acknowledgement of what tends to be called the *"Spycatcher* principle", although it was by no means as revolutionary as it was then portrayed, and has its origins in much older case law. There is also the relatively new jurisdiction assumed by the Family Division in the *Mary Bell* case in 1984, and in later cases such as *Re W* [1992] Q.B. 100, and *Re Z* [1997] Fam. 1, whereby the court will restrain certain forms of publication about minors (or indeed patients) protected by the *parens patriae* jurisdiction. It has to be remembered that the protection of young persons, and in particular their privacy, is recognised by the European Convention as a legitimate factor to weigh in the scales even against freedom of speech. At all events, we have devoted a new section to discussing these important recent developments (Chapter 6).

The media undoubtedly have also been dismayed to discover how far, despite Parliament's adoption of the "strict liability" regime in 1981, the restraints of common law publication contempt continue to operate in circumstances where the criteria of that regime do not apply. This is illustrated by such cases as *Att-Gen v Sport Newspapers Ltd* [1991] 1 W.L.R. 1194 and *Coe v Central Television plc* [1994] E.M.L.R. 433. The operation and reconciliation of these two distinct sets of principles is considered extensively in successive sections of the book (Chapters 4 and 5), particularly with reference to the nature of the *mens rea* now required for common law contempt.

In relation to media contempts, one of the most interesting problems to have arisen recently is the relationship between the law of contempt itself and that governing abuse of process in circumstances in which a judge is called upon to stay proceedings for reasons of irremediable media prejudice. The question has sometimes to be considered how the two interrelate and, what is more, how these principles tie in with the Court of Appeal's approach to setting aside convictions as being unsafe on similar grounds. The issues have been starkly presented in such cases as *Taylor and Taylor* (1993) 98 Cr.App.R. 361, *Att-Gen v MGN Ltd* [1997] 1 All E.R. 456, *Att-Gen v Unger* [1998] E.M.L.R. 280, *Att-Gen v Morgan* [1998] E.M.L.R. 294 and *Att-Gen v Associated Newspapers Ltd* (October 31, 1997, unreported). These principles have now been carefully analysed and clarified in the judgments of the Divisional Court in *Att-Gen v Birmingham Post & Mail Ltd* [1998] 4 All E.R. 49.

The increasingly comprehensive coverage by *Lexis* means that we have been able to refer in detail to judgments of some significance that are not otherwise fully reported. Frequent reference will therefore be found in the footnotes to *Lexis,* which is now so much more readily accessible to practitioners. It was useful, for example, in considering such cases as *Att-Gen v Martin* (April 18, 1986), *Leary v BBC* (September 29, 1989) and *Att-Gen v Associated Newspapers Ltd* (October 31, 1997). The advantage is that one has a complete and accurate report of what the court actually said, whereas some of the long established but attenuated reports, although accepted for citation in court, prove on close inspection to be inaccurate by omission.

Despite this, it is necessary to bear in mind the *Practice Note* [1996] 3 All E.R. 382, emphasising that leave to cite unreported cases will not usually be granted.

Preface to the Second Edition

Unfortunately, media law generally tends to be under-reported, with the consequence that undoubtedly important cases have to be cited to the court in the form of dog-eared Photostats (often not readily available to practitioners outside the specialist coteries). It is difficult to see why such faith should be placed in the judgment of non-specialist editors, often no doubt governed by commercial or financial constraints, as to what may or may not be worth reporting. It is fair to recognise, however, that much progress has been made as a result of the recent appearance of the *Entertainment & Media Law Reports,* to which we have made frequent reference. Indeed, it is probably now true that this series of reports is cited before the Jury List judges, in the defamation context, more than any other.

We have also had to give more detailed consideration to non-publication criminal contempts in the light of modern authority. We have divided the treatment into two sections (Chapters 10 and 11), the first being devoted to "contempt in the face of the court" (now to a large extent statutory so far as the lower courts are concerned). Much light has been thrown on the need to afford proper safeguards to those who are at risk of committal for such conduct by *Griffin* (1988) 88 Cr.App.R. 63 and by *Schot and Barclay* [1997] 2 Cr.App.R. 283. The latter case (as do others) throws into relief the persistent question of whether it is right to cast so impenetrable a curtain over jury discussions for all puposes, and whether there may be a case for some relaxation of the provisions of section 8.

There is much expanded treatment of the law of civil contempt, in respect of which there have also been a large number of important decisions, in widely differing fields such as restrictive trade practices, *Mareva* injunctions and non-molestation orders (Chapter 12). There was also the introduction of R.S.C. Ord. 24, r.14A, by way of government response to the reference of the decision of the House of Lords in *Harman v Home Office* [1983] 1 A.C. 280 to the European Commission on Human Rights. Furthermore, although it may be thought a little eccentric in the light of the many calls for the wholesale abandonment of the distinction between civil and criminal contempt, we have devoted a whole section to reviewing the many facets of that very distinction (Chapter 3). This is partly because we found that the authorities in this field throw useful light on the underlying policy considerations affecting the law of contempt in general, and partly because there is still sometimes a tendency to confusion in relation to important points of principle where the two areas of law operate rather differently (for example, in relation to *mens rea* and to the complicated issues raised by the extraterritorial effect of court orders).

There has naturally been a good deal of academic writing on contempt and closely related issues in the last two decades, and we have tried to include extensive reference to this store of material. Especially in those areas that are developing or unclear, so far as the law of England is concerned, we have also found great assistance in the careful reviews of the common law to be found in decisions of the higher courts in Canada, Australia and New Zealand. This accounts for our extensive citation from Commonwealth authorities.

Preface to the Second Edition

We have spent a good deal of time considering Scottish law in this field for a number of reasons. In particular, Lord Hailsham L.C. made it plain, at the time when the Bill was going through Parliament, that one of the main objects of the 1981 Act was to unify the application of the law regulating media contempt as between Scotland and England. There has, however, been a significantly different approach adopted subsequently by the Scottish courts, in a number of respects, from that to be found in England. These issues are considered in the section on Scotland (Chapter 16). Not only did we find this an interesting comparative exercise in its own right, but it is intended to be of assistance particularly to those who face the problems of cross-border media publication or broadcasting. We should like to express our thanks in this context to Craig Sandison, and to Alistair Bonnington, who between them probably know more about contempt in Scotland than anyone. We are very grateful to them for their generosity with their valuable time and experience. There remains a substantial bedrock of material representing the contribution made in this area for the last edition of Herbert Kerrigan and Janet Parkes.

We should also like to record our gratitude to Brenda Moss who typed parts of the new material, and to Manuel Barca who did a good deal of research in the early stages of the preparation of this edition. Thanks are due to Sarah Clover and Rupert Elliott in the context of research into Commonwealth authorities. We are grateful also to Jaclyn Moriarty for allowing us to see and discuss with her some of the work she has done for her doctoral thesis, relating particularly to the use of injunctions for the protection of children.

Needless to say, in this context as in all others, the howlers are our responsibility and ours alone. (It is perhaps worth saying that this is a joint responsibility, in the sense that we have edited the book together, rather than allocating separate tasks to one another. This was intended to achieve a uniform style and consistency of approach, particularly with regard to matters such as cross-referencing.)

We were sorry that Anthony Arlidge, without whom neither of us would be here, was unable to participate in the second edition because of his many commitments.

Our publishers have been remarkably patient over many years, and indeed over several generations of staff, and we thank them somewhat sheepishly for their forbearance. Over several years, too, there has been unfailing support, in various ways, from the Master and Fellows of Gonville and Caius, as well as from the librarians of the Cambridge Law Library. A special word of thanks is due to them. It was Professor John Spencer, also at Cambridge, who originally put us in touch with one another with a view to our collaboration on this project. We, at least, wish to thank him for setting us on a course that has provided us with a good deal of innocent entertainment.

The attempt has been made to state the law, or at least to identify the unresolved issues, applying at July 31, 1998. This was in fact the date of the decision of Laddie J. in *Re Swaptronics, The Times,* August 17, 1998. He raised the issue of whether the courts or the legislature should now review the traditional approach adopted in civil litigation toward contemnors, which tends to preclude them from being heard further in the proceedings until the relevant contempt has been purged (see, for example, *Hadkinson v Hadkinson* [1952] P. 285 and *X Ltd v Morgan-Grampian Publishers Ltd* [1991] A.C. 1). This is an important matter of controversy, not least because of the requirements of the Convention that there should be access to the courts. We discuss this in Chapter 12. No doubt there may soon be interesting developments in this area, as in other aspects of contempt, but the line has to be drawn somewhere and we thought the end of the summer term as good a time as any. The happy consequence is that the last word goes, as it so often does, to Laddie J.

D.E., A.T.H.S.
Cambridge
August 1998

CONTENTS

Preface v
Second Edition Preface x
Table of Cases xlix
Table of Statutes cxxix
Table of International Legislation cxlv
Table of Statutory Instruments cxlvii
Table of Rules of the Supreme Court cli
Table of Civil Procedure Rules cliii

PARA.   PAGE

Chapter 1

HISTORY OF THE LAW OF CONTEMPT

1–1   I.   The Common Law Courts   1

1–1   A. Early Contempt: hindrance or obstruction 1
1–5   B. Contempt by words 3
1–7   C. Early procedure 3
1–24   D. The jurisdiction over officers of the court 8

1–26   II.   Influence of the Star Chamber   8

1–26   A. Introduction 8
1–27   B. The role of the King's Council 9
1–30   C. Star Chamber procedure 10
1–38   D. Abolition of the Star Chamber 12

1–41   III.   The Court of Chancery: The Development of   13
                            Civil Contempt

1–42   A. Criminal contempts 13
1–47   B. Civil contempt 15

1–51   IV.   Summary Procedure in the Eighteenth Century   16

1–51   A. The recognition of summary powers 16

[xvii]

PARA.		PAGE
1–57	B. Contempt by publication in the eighteenth century..................	18
1–64	C. Strict liability for contempt in the eighteenth century	20

1–71	V. THE RULE AGAINST *EX PARTE* STATEMENTS	23

1–74	VI. OTHER NINETEENTH CENTURY DEVELOPMENTS	24

1–74	A. The appellate jurisdiction	24
1–76	B. Discouraging the use of the summary process	24
1–78	C. Technical contempts..	25
1–84	D. The gradual demise of attachment	27
1–85	E. Attempts to legislate in respect of the judges' arbitrary power ...	27

1–86	VII. BACKGROUND TO THE CONTEMPT OF COURT ACT 1981	27

1–86	A. The Phillimore Committee	27
1–87	B. *Att-Gen v Times Newspapers Ltd*	28
1–99	C. The Phillimore Committee's reaction to the House of Lords..	31
1–104	D. *Sunday Times v United Kingdom*	33

1–114	VIII. THE CONTEMPT OF COURT ACT 1981	36

1–114	A. The occasion of the enactment..	36
1–115	B. The purposes of the 1981 Act...	37
1–116	C. The strict liability "rule"	37
1–119	D. Some "miscellaneous amendments"	38
1–124	E. Civil contempt left untouched by the Act...............................	39

1–126	IX. DEVELOPMENTS SINCE THE 1981 ACT: A SUMMARY	40

1–126	A. Developments in the law of contempt.....................................	40
1–128	B. Surviving forms of common law contempt: residual uncertainties..	41
1–132	C. The influence of the European Convention	42
1–135	D. The *Spycatcher* litigation	43
1–137	E. The use of contempt and sequestration in politically sensitive disputes	44

PARA.		PAGE
1–138	F. Prominence of contempt in the family law cases.....................	45
1–141	G. Contempt and the Crown..	46
1–142	H. Developments in other common law jurisdictions	46
1–145	I. Technological developments	48
1–151	J. Other legislative developments...................................	50
1–153	K. A changing climate in the context of free press versus fair trial .	51

1–161	ISSUES CURRENTLY REQUIRING ATTENTION IN THE LAW OF CONTEMPT	54

1–161	A. Reassessing priorities..	54
1–164	B. Public statements by legal representatives and the police	55
1–172	C. "Cheque-book journalism"	58
1–173	D. Reporting court proceedings......................................	58
1–174	E. Privacy	59
1–177	F. Non-publication contempts and the general criminal law.........	60
1–179	G. The implications of the world wide web..............................	60

CHAPTER 2

CONTEMPT OF COURT: THE CONSTITUTIONAL DIMENSIONS

2–1	I. THE CONTINUING ROLE OF THE CONTEMPT JURISDICTION	63

2–1	A. The purpose of the summary jurisdiction..............................	63
2–3	B. The broad categories of contempt..	63
2–4	C. "Summary" procedures	64
2–6	D. The underlying rationale of the contempt jurisdiction	64
2–10	E. The misleading implications of the word "contempt"	66
2–13	F. The overlap between contempt and the general criminal law ..	66
2–17	G. The missing safeguards	68
2–26	H. Factors justifying the use of the summary procedure	71

2–32	II. FREEDOM OF INFORMATION AND THE LAW OF CONTEMPT	73

2–32	A. The competing rights	73
2–38	B. The law of contempt as a fetter on freedom of speech	74

[xix]

Contents

PARA.		PAGE
2–45	C. Vilification of those punished by the courts	77
2–48	D. Media pressure upon the Home Secretary	79
2–49	E. The "constitutional" role of the press	79
2–64	F. Provision in the Criminal Procedure Rules	85
2–67	G. A continuing tension	86
2–70	III. FREE PRESS AND FAIR TRIAL	87
2–71	A. The issues of principle	88
2–79	B. The traditional approach	91
2–99	C. Developments in other common law jurisdictions	96
2–102	D. Minimising the risk of prejudice without restricting free speech	98
2–122	IV. THE IMPACT OF THE EUROPEAN CONVENTION	105
2–123	A. "Incorporation" into United Kingdom law	106
2–124	B. A survey of the influence of the European Convention between 1981 and 2000	106
2–142	C. The relevance of the Convention to the law of contempt	112
2–147	D. Constitutional protection of rights: the common law approach	115
2–155	E. A matter of balance? Contrasting approaches to rights adjudication	117
2–161	F. Open justice: Articles 6 and 10	119
2–163	G. Comparison with the common law	120
2–165	H. Maintaining the authority and impartiality of the judiciary	121
2–166	I. The significance of the right of individual petition	121
2–168	J. The so called "margin of appreciation"	122
2–169	K. Developing the law of contempt judicially: Article 7	123
2–179	L. "Principles" contrasted with "rules" in criminal law	126
2–183	M. The problem illustrated in *Dobson v Hastings*	127
2–191	N. The need to confine judicial law-making in the criminal context	129
2–192	O. Contempt cases in which reliance was placed upon the European Convention	130
2–198	P. The enactment of the Human Rights Act 1998	132
2–199	V. THE ROLE OF THE ATTORNEY-GENERAL	133
2–199	A. The initiation of contempt proceedings	133
2–203	B. Section 7 of the Contempt of Court Act 1981	135
2–207	C. Doubts as to the *locus standi* of other persons	136

PARA.		PAGE
2–208	D. *Locus standi* to obtain an injunction	136
2–209	E. Considering the public interest	136
2–220	F. The Attorney's role in relation to civil contempts	139
2–221	G. The Court's power to act of its own initiative	140
2–222	VI. CONTEMPT OF COURT AND THE CROWN	140
2–223	A. Contempt by Ministers of the Crown: *Re M*	140

CHAPTER 3

THE DISTINCTION BETWEEN CRIMINAL AND CIVIL CONTEMPT

3–1	I. THE DISTINCTION EXPLAINED	143
3–1	A. The essence of the distinction	143
3–12	B. Illustrations of the dual nature of civil contempts	146
3–25	C. Points of comparison between civil and criminal contempts: an overview	149
3–47	D. Phillimore's suggestion for abandoning the distinction altogether	154
3–48	E. Continuing criticisms of the distinction	154
3–51	F. An attempted reformulation	155
3–55	II. THE JURIDICAL NATURE OF CONTEMPT	157
3–55	A. Criminal contempt and the general criminal law framework	157
3–69	B. The nature of civil contempt	161
3–73	C. The adoption of some criminal safeguards for civil contempt	163
3–76	D. To what extent is the purpose of the law of civil contempt "remedial"?	164
3–78	E. Civil contempts as "misdemeanours"	165
3–85	F. Is contempt of court a wrong *sui generis*?	167
3–88	G. The practical importance of the distinction gradually minimised	168
3–92	H. How do the contempts created by the 1981 Act fit into the framework?	170
3–107	I. Breaches classified as criminal at common law	174

PARA.		PAGE
3–115	J. Orders relating to wards of court	176
3–119	K. Contempts by third parties in relation to court orders	177
3–130	III. POINTS OF COMPARISON BETWEEN CIVIL AND CRIMINAL CONTEMPTS	181
3–130	A. Scheme of discussion	181
3–131	B. Appeals	181
3–141	C. Privilege from arrest and imprisonment	183
3–157	D. Waiver	188
3–169	E. Institution of proceedings	192
3–176	F. Sanctions	193
3–179	G. Release *ex debito justitiae* no longer available	194
3–184	H. Execution	196
3–185	I. Exercise of the Royal prerogative	197
3–188	J. The privilege against self-incrimination	198
3–209	K. *Autrefois acquit* and *convict*	207
3–223	L. Extra-territorial jurisdiction	210
3–227	M. Hearsay evidence	211
3–238	N. Fresh evidence on appeal	215
3–241	O. The standard of proof	216
3–247	P. The approach to *mens rea* as between civil and criminal contempt	217
3–250	Q. A possible distinction as to the relevance of duress	218

CHAPTER 4

THE STATUTORY REGIME FOR STRICT LIABILITY

4–1	I. THE STRICT LIABILITY RULE	221
4–1	A. The nature of "the strict liability rule"	221
4–4	B. The scheme of the Act	222
4–5	C. The uncertain scope of strict liability at common law	223
4–15	D. The statutory terminology further examined	226
4–51	E. Intention to publish required	239
4–52	II. RESTRICTIONS ON THE *ACTUS REUS* OF STRICT LIABILITY CONTEMPTS	239
4–52	A. The statutory means of confinement	239

PARA.		PAGE
4–54	B. The concept of "risk": when is a risk "substantial"?...........	240
4–60	C. The relationship between "risk" and "prejudice"	242
4–84	D. The principles summarised	249
4–90	E. The application of the common law when section 2(2) does not apply...	252
4–92	F. The nature of "prejudice" generally...	253
4–96	G. What amounts to serious prejudice?	254
4–97	H. "Impeded"...	254
4–110	III. CATEGORIES OF PERSONS THOUGHT SUSCEPTIBLE TO INFLUENCE	257
4–110	Who is thought susceptible to influence?	257
4–148	IV. STRICT LIABILITY CONTEMPT AND ABUSE OF PROCESS	269
4–148	The interrelationship between strict liability contempt and abuse of process	269
4–174	V. WHEN ARE PROCEEDINGS "ACTIVE"?	277
4–174	A. Schedule 1 of the 1981 Act..	277
4–175	B. The general scheme	277
4–183	VI. SECTION 7 AND THE ATTORNEY-GENERAL	281
4–183	Role of the Attorney-General under the strict liability rule..........	281
4–191	VII. WHO MAY BE LIABLE FOR PUBLICATION AND UPON WHAT BASIS?	283
4–191	A. Liability under section 2 of the 1981 Act	283
4–193	B. Scheme of the following discussion...	284
4–194	C. Candidates for liability..	284
4–195	D. The basis of liability of proprietors and publishers.................	284
4–199	E. The traditional approach to the vicarious liability of proprietors	286
4–204	F. Vicarious liability in the corporate context..............................	287
4–212	G. Editorial responsibility..	290
4–216	H. Other journalists..	291

Contents

PARA.		PAGE
4–224	I. The analogy with the law of libel	293
4–230	J. Printers	294
4–234	K. "Distributors"	295

4–236	VIII. Innocent Publication or Distribution	296

4–236	A. Innocent publication and distribution: section 3	296
4–238	B. The history of section 3	297
4–242	C. The standard of care expected	298
4–254	D. Vicarious liability and section 3	300
4–261	E. The burden of proof	302

4–263	IX. The Right to Report Court Proceedings	303

4–263	A. Contemporaneous reporting of court proceedings: the general principle	303
4–265	B. Section 4(1)	303
4–274	C. The requirement that the report be contemporaneous	306
4–282	D. proceedings in private	308
4–283	E. The requirement of good faith	308
4–286	F. Fair and accurate reporting	309
4–289	G. Legal proceedings	310
4–292	H. The interrelationship between section 4(1) and section 4(2)	311

4–293	X. Discussing Public Affairs	311

4–293	A. Discussion of public affairs: section 5	311
4–294	B. The common law background to section 5	311
4–300	C. The issues addressed in *Attorney-General v English*	313
4–315	D. Section 5 inapplicable to intentional contempts	317
4–316	E. Injunctions and section 5	318
4–318	F. The burden of proof	318

4–319	XI. What Are the "Defences" Preserved by Section 6?	319

4–319	A. The statutory context	319
4–323	B. Possible candidates	320

CHAPTER 5

CONTEMPTS BY PUBLICATION AT COMMON LAW

PARA.		PAGE
5–1	I. QUESTIONS UNRESOLVED BY THE 1981 ACT	326
5–1	A. Introduction: the outstanding questions	326
5–5	II. THE *ACTUS REUS*	327
5–5	A. The impact of the Act on the common law test	327
5–12	B. Possible formulations of the *actus reus*	330
5–13	C. Private publications	330
5–14	D. Creating a less than "substantial risk" of serious prejudice	331
5–18	E. Creating a risk of less than "serious" prejudice	332
5–62	F. Publication when proceedings are pending but not "active"	346
5–67	G. Proceedings "imminent" but not yet pending	348
5–96	H. Where proceedings are merely "on the cards"	356
5–100	I. Intentional contempts before the commencement of an appeal	357
5–104	J. Some examples of the *actus reus* at common law	359
5–120	III. THE MENTAL ELEMENT IN COMMON LAW PUBLICATION CONTEMPT	363
5–120	A. The mental element in crime: some general propositions	363
5–129	B. The concept of recklessness generally in criminal law	366
5–132	C. The nature of *mens rea* in publication contempt	367
5–171	D. Is an intention to create a risk of prejudice sufficient?	378
5–195	E. Practical difficulties in differentiating intention and recklessness	383
5–200	F. Conclusions as to the modern law of *mens rea*	385
5–201	IV. IS THERE A GENERAL DEFENCE OF FAIR COMMENT/PUBLIC INTEREST?	386
5–204	V. SCANDALISING THE COURT	387
5–204	A. Introduction	387
5–210	B. The residual need for such protection	389
5–220	C. Origins of the modern law: eighteenth century developments	391

PARA.		PAGE
5–223	D. Later developments	392
5–232	E. The need to protect the right of legitimate criticism	394
5–235	F. The *actus reus* of scandalising contempts	395
5–239	G. Allegations of bias or improper motive	397
5–242	H. Publication	398
5–244	I. The requisite state of mind for scandalising contempt	399
5–250	J. Knowledge of contents	400
5–251	K. Lack of good faith	400
5–252	L. Special defences available in scandalising	401
5–260	M. Other jurisdictions	403

Chapter 6

COURT ORDERS AFFECTING THE MEDIA

6–1	I. *Quia Timet* Injunctions to Restrain a Contempt	409
6–1	A. A jurisdiction to be sparingly exercised	409
6–5	B. The traditional reluctance to grant prior restraint	410
6–11	C. The relevance of section 12 of the Human Rights Act 1998	412
6–20	D. The approach of the Strasbourg jurisprudence towards prior restraint	416
6–21	E. A comparison with the Canadian Charter	417
6–22	F. Who may claim an injunction?	417
6–30	G. What must an applicant prove?	420
6–36	H. The need to avoid any appearance of censorship	421
6–38	I. The standard of proof	422
6–39	J. To which court should an application be made?	422
6–41	II. The Inherent (or *Parens Patriae*) Jurisdiction	423
6–41	A. Injunctions *contra mundum*	423
6–53	B. The history of the *parens patriae* (or "inherent") jurisdiction generally	428
6–56	C. The distinction between the "custodial" and "protective"	429
6–61	D. The focus in *Re Z* upon the "custodial" aspect of the jurisdiction	431
6–74	E. How media rights were addressed before the Human Rights Act	436
6–82	F. The "protective" aspect of the jurisdiction	439
6–97	G. Could such a media ban restrict the reporting of criminal proceedings?	446

PARA.		PAGE
6–108	H. The impact of the Children Act 1989 upon practice and procedure	451
6–110	I. The uncertainty over where the balance of free speech was to be struck	452
6–114	J. A brief summary of developments since the Human Rights Act..	453
6–115	III. INJUNCTIONS AFFECTING PERSONS WHO ARE NOT DIRECTLY BOUND	454
6–115	A. Injunctions intended to bind non-parties	454
6–124	B. Injunctions indirectly affecting third parties	456
6–126	C. The nature of the liability of persons not directly bound by an order	457
6–148	D. Applying the principles	466
6–149	E. The possible opportunities for avoiding the difficulty	466

CHAPTER 7

COURT REPORTING I: RESTRICTIONS UNDER THE 1981 ACT

7–1	I. THE COMMON LAW BACKGROUND	468
7–1	A. Open justice	468
7–16	B. The right of the public to be informed	474
7–21	C. Arbitration: a limited qualification to the principle of open justice	476
7–27	D. The limited power to confer privacy on proceedings	478
7–36	E. The distinction between public and private hearings: a change of practice	481
7–56	F. The traditionally recognised exceptions to the openness principle	488
7–68	G. The residual discretion: deterrence of witnesses by publicity	492
7–76	H. Circumstances justifying the withholding of particular items of information in open court	495
7–82	I. The continuing relevance of the common law	497

PARA.		PAGE
7–83	II. SECTION 11 OF THE CONTEMPT OF COURT ACT	498
7–83	A. The terms of section 11	498
7–87	B. The consequences of breaching a section 11 order	500
7–89	C. The 2005 Consolidated Criminal Practice Direction	501
7–91	D. *Mens rea* for breach of section 11 orders	501
7–95	E. Decisions in the light of section 11	502
7–109	III. POSTPONEMENT ORDERS UNDER SECTION 4(2) OF THE 1981 ACT	507
7–109	A. Postponing publication: the common law background	507
7–111	B. Section 4(2): reporting restrictions	509
7–113	C. The limitations of the section 4(2) power	510
7–115	D. Teething problems	511
7–119	E. Subsequent calls for restraint	512
7–123	F. The principal issues raised by section 4(2) of the Act identified	513
7–126	G. The factual background to the *Horsham Justices* case	514
7–129	H. The relationship of section 4(2) to the existing common law powers, and to the strict liability rule	515
7–132	I. Is breach of a section 4(2) order *ipso facto* a contempt?	517
7–137	J. The "proceedings" contemplated under section 4(2)	518
7–142	K. What "publications" may be postponed?	519
7–143	L. When are proceedings "pending or imminent" under section 4(2)?	520
7–146	M. For how long may a publication be postponed?	521
7–149	N. Are journalists restrained even when no order is made?	522
7–153	O. The practical implementation of section 4(2) orders	523
7–164	P. The tests to be applied before making an order	526
7–203	Q. What is the required mental element in the case of the breach of a section 4(2) order?	538
7–228	R. Who has the power to punish a breach?	545
7–235	S. Is a journalist alleged to be in breach entitled to challenge the validity of the order itself?	548
7–244	T. The recognition of journalists' *locus standi* in relation to such orders	550
7–258	U. Appeals against section 4(2) orders: section 159 of the 1988 Act	554
7–265	V. Appeals in respect of "spent" orders	556
7–266	W. Procedure on section 159 appeals	556
7–270	X. Provision for costs on section 159 appeals	557

Chapter 8

COURT REPORTING II: OTHER STATUTORY RESTRICTIONS

PARA.		PAGE
8–1	I. Judicial Proceedings (Regulation of Reports) Act 1926	560
8–1	A. The relevant provisions of the Statute	560
8–13	B. Extension of the 1926 Act to other proceedings	564
8–15	II. Restrictions on Publication Under the Criminal Justice Act 2003	565
8–15	A. Prosecution appeals	565
8–16	B. Retrials following the quashing of an appeal	565
8–17	III. Statutory Anonymity for Victims of Sexual Offences	566
8–17	A. Legislative history	566
8–18	B. Anonymity extended to victims of other sexual offences	566
8–19	C. The time when protection begins	567
8–20	D. Power to displace the restrictions	567
8–21	E. Offences	567
8–24	F. Anonymity for the accused	569
8–25	IV. Protection for Juveniles (Children and Young Persons): the 1993 Act	569
8–25	A. Introduction	569
8–26	B. Youth court proceedings: section 47 of the 1933 Act	570
8–27	C. The reporting restrictions: the current terms of section 49	570
8–32	D. The power to lift the statutory restrictions	572
8–39	E. The proceedings to which the section 49 restrictions apply	574
8–42	F. The statutory changes in the context of anti-social behaviour orders	575
8–47	G. The duty to announce that the section applies	577
8–48	H. Does section 12 of the Administration of Justice Act 1960 apply?	577

PARA.		PAGE
8–50	I. Protection for children or young person in adult proceedings: section 39 of the 1933 Act	578
8–51	J. The anomalies and the residual role of the inherent jurisdiction	578
8–53	K. The amendments contained in the Youth Justice and Criminal Evidence Act 1999	579
8–55	L. Guidance from the courts on the exercise of the section 39 discretion	580
8–71	M. The power to clear the court: section 37	586
8–72	N. The problem of "jigsaw identification"	586
8–74	V. ANONYMITY FOR WITNESSES: SECTION 46 OF THE YOUTH JUSTICE AND CRIMINAL EVIDENCE ACT 1999	587
8–76	VI. PROTECTION FOR FAMILY PROCEEDINGS	588
8–76	A. Section 65(1) of the Magistrates' Courts Act 1980	588
8–78	B. The hybrid status of family proceedings: restrictions on attendance	590
8–80	C. Newspaper reports of family proceedings	591
8–83	D. Privacy under section 97(2) of the Children Act 1989	592
8–87	VII. CRIMINAL PROCEEDINGS BEFORE MAGISTRATES	594
8–87	A. Committal proceedings: Magistrates' Courts Act 1980, section 8	594
8–89	B. Constraints upon reporting where restrictions are lifted	596
8–91	C. The comparable restrictions under the Criminal Justice Act 1987, section 11 (transfers for trial)	597
8–92	D. Transfers in child witness cases: Criminal Justice Act 1991, section 53	597
8–95	VIII. DEROGATORY REMARKS IN MITIGATION	598
8–95	A. The mischief	598
8–96	B. Difficulties of application	598
8–97	IX. DISCLOSURES RELATING TO PROCEEDINGS IN PRIVATE	599
8–97	A. The provisions of section 12 of the Administration of Justice Act 1960	599
8–100	B. Section 12 does not in itself provide a defence	601

PARA.		PAGE
8–102	C. The meaning of "publication" in section 12	601
8–108	D. The relevant Practice Directions	604
8–111	E. Disclosures by CAFCASS	605
8–117	F. What can be published about proceedings in private?	606
8–123	G. The underlying policy	609
8–128	H. The discussion of section 12 in *Clibbery v Allen*	611
8–129	I. Does section 12 create a strict liability contempt?	611
8–141	X. EMPLOYMENT AND OTHER TRIBUNALS	615
8–141	A. Employment tribunals: restrictions on reporting	615
8–147	B. Other tribunals	617

CHAPTER 9

PROTECTION OF SOURCES

9–1	I. THE COMMON LAW CONTEXT	618
9–1	A. Introduction: the significance of journalists' sources	618
9–4	B. The common law background	620
9–13	C. The discretionary or "balancing" approach of the common law	623
9–16	D. Competing policy considerations: the role of the media	624
9–24	E. Whistleblowing	627
9–32	F. Reconciling source protection with the rule of law	629
9–42	G. Judicial discretion at common law	633
9–50	H. Experience in other common law jurisdictions	635
9–52	II. THE GENERAL SCOPE OF SECTION 10	636
9–52	A. Section 10 of the 1981 Act	636
9–54	B. The meaning of " . . . for which he is responsible"	637
9–55	C. The introduction of the words "interests of justice"	637
9–58	D. Does section 10 apply to Internet website operators?	638
9–59	E. The meaning of "publication"	638
9–60	F. Information "contained in a publication"	639
9–63	G. Information contained in photographs	640
9–64	H. Where the information does not fall within the Act	640
9–66	I. Does the Act supplement or supersede the common law?	641

PARA.		PAGE
9–83	J. The elusive concept of "necessary"	645
9–86	K. Attempts to define the word "necessary"	646
9–90	L. The onus of proof	648
9–92	M. Factors to be considered in determining "necessity"	648
9–107	N. Necessity and proportionality	653
9–108	O. The problem of establishing necessity at the interlocutory stage	653
9–111	P. Waiver	654
9–113	Q. Statutory exclusion of section 10	654
9–119	R. Duress and the journalist	656
9–126	III. THE FOUR STATUTORY EXCEPTIONS FURTHER ANALYSED	657
9–126	A. Necessity "in the interests of justice": two views	657
9–141	B. The significance of "public interest"	663
9–147	C. "Interests of justice" considered by the European Court of Human Rights	665
9–154	D. The government's response to the ruling of the European Court of Human Rights	667
9–155	E. Later judicial developments	668
9–177	F. National security	674
9–182	G. "Prevention of crime"	675
9–193	H. "The prevention of disorder"	678
9–194	IV. WHEN DOES A JOURNALIST'S REFUSAL BECOME CONTEMPT?	678
9–194	A. The nature of the problem	678
9–200	B. The need to reconcile two lines of authority	679
9–202	C. The "void" and "voidable" distinction	680
9–203	D. Orders made "without jurisdiction"	680
9–205	E. The rule that courts must be implicitly obeyed	681
9–224	F. Authorities suggesting an exception in relation to journalists' sources	685
9–232	G. The problem of reconciling *DPP v Channel Four*	688
9–236	H. The lack of any right of appeal	689
9–239	V. SHOULD THE ATTORNEY-GENERAL HAVE A ROLE TO PLAY?	689
9–239	A. The Attorney-General and the public interest	689
9–243	B. The unresolved question	690

PARA.		PAGE
9–245	VI. A GENERAL SUMMARY OF THE PRINCIPLES	691

CHAPTER 10

CONTEMPT IN THE FACE OF THE COURT

10–1	I. INTRODUCTION	694
10–1	A. The common thread..	694
10–5	B. The significance of contempt "in the face".............................	695
10–11	C. What constitutes the "face of the court"?...............................	697
10–29	D. Procedure to be used sparingly...	702
10–36	II. THE REQUIREMENTS OF NATURAL JUSTICE: ARTICLE 6	704
10–36	A. The contempt jurisdiction as "rough justice".........................	704
10–38	B. The need for safeguards...	705
10–85	C. Safeguards in other common law jurisdictions.......................	722
10–88	III. DISTURBING PROCEEDINGS IN COURT	723
10–88	A. The historical background..	723
10–90	B. The Treason Act 1351...	723
10–93	C. Assaulting a judge or other participants in the legal process..	724
10–97	D. Insults offered to the court...	725
10–98	E. The modern approach to disturbances in court.......................	726
10–106	F. Disobeying an order for the control of proceedings................	728
10–109	G. Effecting an arrest in the precincts of the court.....................	729
10–112	IV. STATUTORY CONTEMPTS IN THE FACE	729
10–112	A. Contempt in face of the magistrates' court: section 12..........	729
10–126	B. *Mens rea*: "willfully" equated to "recklessly".......................	733
10–130	C. County Courts Act 1984...	734
10–131	V. IMPROPER CONDUCT OF A CASE	735
10–131	A. Litigants..	735
10–135	B. Professional advocates...	736

PARA.		PAGE
10–157	VI. CONTEMPT COMMITTED BY WITNESSES	743

10–157	A. Examples of contempt by witnesses	743
10–159	B. Putting forward false evidence	744
10–162	C. Refusing to answer questions or prevarication	745
10–165	D. Witnesses and duress	745
10–173	E. Witness who may claim privilege	748
10–175	F. Judicial discretion	749

10–176	VII. CONTEMPT COMMITTED BY JURORS	750

10–176	A. The importance of jury service	750
10–177	B. Confidentiality of a jury's deliberations	750
10–178	C. Statutory summary offences	751
10–179	D. Misconduct in relation to deliberations or verdict	751

10–190	VIII. UNAUTHORISED RECORDING OF COURT PROCEEDINGS	755

10–190	A. Use of tape recorders in court: Section 9	755
10–196	B. Leave to use tape recorders	756
10–197	C. Granting leave: The Practice Direction	757
10–198	D. The Home Office Circular	757
10–199	E. The *mens rea* requirement	758
10–201	F. Sketching or taking photographs in court	758
10–206	G. Televising court proceedings	760

10–208	IX. *MENS REA* FOR CONTEMPT IN THE FACE OF THE COURT	761

10–208	A. The present uncertainty	761
10–220	B. The possible scope for recklessness	765

CHAPTER 11

DIRECT INTERFERENCE WITH THE ADMINISTRATION OF JUSTICE

11–1	I. GENERAL CONSIDERATIONS	767

11–1	A. The diminished role for the summary process	767
11–3	B. The necessary elements of the *actus reus*	768

PARA.		PAGE
11–4	C. Omissions	768
11–7	D. Can a neutral act be converted into contempt as a result of intent?	769
11–14	E. Is it possible to be guilty of attempted contempt?	771
11–21	II. THE MENTAL ELEMENT IN NON-PUBLICATION CONTEMPTS	773
11–21	A. Uncertainty as to the nature of the *mens rea* required	773
11–23	B. Differing strands of modern authority	773
11–29	C. The foreseeability of consequences	775
11–32	D. Conclusions as to the present state of the law	775
11–34	III. SUBVERTING THE ORDERS OR PROCEDURES OF THE COURT	776
11–34	A. The general principle	776
11–35	B. The Master of the Rolls' hypothetical examples in *Spycatcher* ..	777
11–39	C. Destroying the subject matter of an action	778
11–40	D. The principle applicable even in the absence of an order	778
11–46	E. Freezing orders	780
11–47	F. Search and seizure orders	780
11–48	IV. ABUSING THE COURT'S PROCEDURES	780
11–48	A. Forging a court document	780
11–51	B. Putting forward a false case	781
11–56	C. A false statement of truth: CPR 32.14	783
11–58	D. A false disclosure statement: CPR 31.23	784
11–59	E. The treatment of vexatious claims	784
11–61	F. Improper collusion	785
11–64	G. Abuse of the privilege attaching to court proceedings	785
11–66	H. Misconduct by solicitors	786
11–79	I. Gaining improper access to court documents	790
11–82	J. The statutory duty of confidentiality for defendants in criminal proceedings	791
11–84	I. Destroying documents which might be disclosable for court proceedings	792
11–88	V. FAILURE TO ATTEND COURT	794
11–88	A. Advocates	794
11–90	B. Witnesses: compelling attendance	795

Contents

PARA.		PAGE
11–91	C. The High Court and county court procedure	795
11–116	D. Crown Court: compelling attendance under the 1965 Act	803
11–129	E. Crown Court: breach of bail	807
11–130	F. Magistrates' court: attendance of witnesses	807
11–134	G. Production of "documents or things" in criminal proceedings	808
11–138	H. Attendance by jurors: section 20 of the Juries Act 1974	810
11–144	I. Coroner's court	813
11–145	VI. THE STATUTORY PROVISIONS AGAINST INTIMIDATION	813
11–145	A. Criminal Justice and Public Order Act 1994, section 51	813
11–148	B. The relationship of the provision to the common law	816
11–150	C. Protection for civil proceedings	816
11–151	D. *Prima facie* lawful actions and intimidation	817
11–152	E. *Mens rea* under the Act	817
11–155	VII. INTERFERENCE AT COMMON LAW: THE GENERAL PRINCIPLES	818
11–155	A. The underlying policy	818
11–160	B. The general requirement for *mens rea* at common law	819
11–168	C. Guidance from the old arrest cases	822
11–172	D. The principles exemplified in the old cases on serving civil process	823
11–173	VIII. COMMON LAW: JUDGES, JURORS AND LEGAL ADVISERS	824
11–173	A. Judges	824
11–178	B. Interference with the jury system	825
11–190	IX. COMMON LAW: INTERFERENCE WITH WITNESSES	828
11–190	A. The mischief	828
11–197	B. Reprisals against witnesses	830
11–216	C. The persuasion of witnesses (actual or potential)	835
11–259	D. Payment of witnesses (whether actual or potential)	847
11–264	E. "Cheque-book" journalism	848
11–276	X. COMMON LAW: LITIGANTS AND PARTIES	852
11–278	A. The considerations of public policy	853
11–280	B. Pressurising or intimidation	853

PARA.		PAGE
11–289	C. The threat to exercise legal rights against a party	856
11–296	D. The approach of the Phillimore Committee	858
11–300	E. Hindering access to the courts	859
11–307	F. Picketing the courts	861
11–310	G. Interference with legal advisers	862
11–311	XI. INTERFERENCE WITH OFFICERS OF THE COURT	862
11–311	A. Common law and statute	862
11–313	B. The provisions of the County Courts Act	863
11–315	C. Obstruction of enforcement officers and court officers executing process	864
11–316	D. The common law relating to officers of the court	864
11–331	XII. INTERFERENCE WITH THE WARDSHIP OR PARENS PATRIAE JURISDICTION	869
11–331	A. Interference with the court's inherent protective jurisdiction	869
11–332	B. Such interference treated as a criminal contempt	869
11–337	C. Publications relating to persons under the court's protection	870
11–339	D. Is *mens rea* required in relation to the inherent jurisdiction?	871
11–349	XIII. THE SECRECY ATTACHED TO JURY DELIBERATIONS	874
11–349	A. Disclosing the deliberations of a jury: the background	874
11–353	B. The origins of section 8	875
11–354	C. The text of section 8	876
11–355	D. The compatibility of jury secrecy with the European Convention	876
11–361	E. A comparison with the Canadian Charter	879
11–362	F. Possible exceptions to the general exclusionary rule	879
11–365	G. The meaning of "discloses" in section 8	880
11–367	H. Offering to disclose	881
11–368	I. The meaning of "deliberations"	881
11–371	J. Statutory exceptions: section 8(2)	882
11–378	K. *Mens rea* and section 8	884
11–385	L. Jury counselling	886
11–386	M. Jury secrecy and possible miscarriages of justice	886

CHAPTER 12

CIVIL CONTEMPT

PARA.		PAGE
12–1	I. GENERAL PRINCIPLES	892
12–1	A. The nature of civil contempt	892
12–5	B. The public and private aspects of civil contempt	893
12–8	C. The jurisdiction to be kept separate from criminal proceedings	894
12–15	D. The "arbitrary" nature of court's jurisdiction	897
12–18	E. Committal and sequestration to be sparingly used	897
12–24	F. Committal as a matter of "very last resort" in family proceedings	899
12–33	G. Procedural steps to be rigidly enforced	902
12–34	H. The safeguard of personal service of the notice of committal proceedings	903
12–35	I. Preliminary requirements as to service of the judgment or order	904
12–43	J. The criminal standard of proof: a further safeguard	906
12–48	K. Ambiguous or vague orders or undertakings	907
12–59	L. The possibility of approaching the court for clarification	911
12–64	M. Further analogies with criminal procedure	912
12–66	N. The Court's discretion not to hear a contemnor until the contempt is purged	912
12–80	II. THE MENTAL ELEMENT FOR CIVIL CONTEMPT	919
12–80	A. The traditional approach to *mens rea* in civil contempt	919
12–88	B. An apparent policy shift: the doubtful case of *Irtelli v Squatriti*	922
12–94	C. State of mind relevant to penalty	924
12–96	D. The relevance of CPR Sch.1, Ord.45.5: absence of "willfully"	925
12–99	III. WHO CAN BE LIABLE FOR CIVIL CONTEMPT?	926
12–99	A. Vicarious liability for civil contempt	926
12–101	B. Corporations	926
12–104	C. "Servants or agents"	927
12–109	D. Directors	929
12–116	E. Trade unions	931
12–118	F. Vicarious liability of unincorporated bodies generally	932
12–123	G. Ministers of the Crown	934

CONTENTS

PARA.		PAGE
12–124	IV. BREACHES OF COURT ORDERS GENERALLY	934

12–124	A. Disobedience to a judgment or order requiring a positive act.	934
12–136	B. Disobedience to a judgment or order to abstain from doing any act	938
12–139	C. Cases in which a judgment or order has been wrongly obtained.	939

| 12–144 | V. FREEZING AND SEARCH AND SEIZURE ORDERS | 940 |

12–144	A. Freezing orders	940
12–175	B. Search and seizure orders	950
12–181	C. Persons not directly bound	952

| 12–182 | VI. BREACHES OF UNDERTAKINGS | 953 |

12–182	A. Undertakings are equivalent to injunctions	953
12–201	B. The implied undertaking given upon disclosure of documents...	958
12–240	C. Breach of undertakings given by strangers	972
12–248	D. Undertakings given by solicitors	974
12–261	E. Failure by a solicitor to comply with a written undertaking in admiralty proceedings	978

CHAPTER 13

JURISDICTION

| 13–1 | I. GENERAL PRINCIPLES | 980 |

13–1	A. The two aspects of jurisdiction	980
13–3	B. The effect of the 1981 Act	981
13–6	C. Difficulties of ascertaining which inferior tribunals are covered by the law of contempt	981
13–7	D. Distinctions in jurisdiction between superior and inferior courts	982

| 13–8 | II. SUPERIOR COURTS OF RECORD | 982 |

| 13–8 | A. Superior courts of record: generally | 982 |

Contents

PARA.		PAGE
13–12	B. House of Lords	984
13–13	C. Court of Appeal	984
13–16	D. Courts Martial Appeal Court	985
13–17	E. High Court	985
13–21	F. Employment Appeal Tribunal	986
13–22	G. The jurisdiction of the Divisional Court over contempt of the Crown Court	986
13–34	H. The Crown Court's own jurisdiction	990
13–43	I. Inferior tribunals: the Divisional Court's role	994
13–44	J. What is an "inferior court"	994
13–48	K. *Att-Gen v BBC*	995
13–62	L. Employment tribunals	999
13–66	M. Mental health review tribunals	1000
13–70	N. The remaining uncertainty as to tribunals	1002
13–77	O. Jurisdiction conferred on the Queen's Bench Division by statute	1004

13–79	III. OTHER COURTS OF RECORD	1005

13–79	A. The general principle	1005
13–80	B. County Courts	1005
13–100	C. Coroners	1013
13–103	D. Miscellaneous other courts of record	1014

13–104	IV. MAGISTRATES' COURTS	1014

13–104	A. The nature of magistrates' courts	1014
13–112	B. Means of exercising the section 12 powers	1016
13–116	C. Disobedience to orders of the magistrates' court	1018
13–117	D. Jurisdiction in relation to witnesses	1018

13–118	V. APPELLATE JURISDICTION	1018

13–118	A. The Administration of Justice Act 1960	1018
13–125	B. Appeals to the High Court	1021
13–133	C. The prescribed appellate tribunals	1023

PARA.		PAGE

CHAPTER 14

SANCTIONS AND REMEDIES

14–1	I. CUSTODIAL PENALTIES	1026
14–1	A. Outline	1026
14–5	B. Historical use of imprisonment	1027
14–7	C. Imprisonment for civil contempt	1028
14–8	D. Section 14(1) of the 1981 Act	1029
14–10	E. Guidance as to nature and length of custodial penalty: criminal contempt	1030
14–11	F. Relating a sentence for contempt to other penalties imposed	1031
14–12	G. The application of section 14 to civil contempt	1031
14–14	H. What is the "occasion" referred to in section 14?	1032
14–18	I. Guidance as to custodial penalties in family or domestic cases	1033
14–21	J. Imprisonment: powers of magistrates' courts	1035
14–24	K. The county court: powers of imprisonment	1036
14–28	L. The power to discharge: superior courts	1037
14–30	M. The power to discharge: "inferior" courts	1039
14–32	N. Automatic release	1039
14–36	O. No provision for deducting time spent on remand	1040
14–37	P. The application of the Prison Rules	1041
14–39	Q. Pardons	1042
14–40	R. The power to suspend	1042
14–45	S. The implementation of suspended sentences	1043
14–49	T. Postponement of sentence	1045
14–55	U. Consecutive sentences	1047
14–58	V. No one should be punished twice over	1048
14–59	W. The need for the presence of the alleged contemnor	1048
14–60	X. Custodial sentences in respect of persons under 21	1048
14–65	Y. Attendance centres	1050
14–67	Z. Pre-sentence information	1050
14–71	II. ATTACHING A POWER OF ARREST	1052
14–71	A. The jurisdiction in family proceedings to attach a power of arrest	1052
14–72	B. The difficulties of application	1052
14–77	C. The 1996 reforms	1054
14–85	D. Bail	1056
14–86	E. The Practice Directions	1056
14–89	F. The provisions of the Housing Act 1996	1057
14–96	G. The reforms of 2004	1060

Contents

PARA.		PAGE
14–97	III. NON-CUSTODIAL SENTENCES	1061

14–97	A. Orders under the Mental Health Act 1983	1061
14–98	B. Community sentences	1061
14–101	C. Fines: superior courts	1062
14–102	D. Is there a power to suspend?	1062
14–103	E. Fines: inferior courts	1063
14–106	F. The standard scale	1063
14–107	G. Coroners	1064
14–108	H. Indemnifying as to payment of fines	1064
14–109	I. The enforcement of fines imposed by superior courts	1064
14–110	J. Binding over	1065
14–111	K. Sequestration	1066
14–132	L. Injunctions	1072
14–135	M. Costs	1073

14–142	IV. THE UNAVAILABILITY OF FINANCIAL COMPENSATION	1076

14–142	A. Possible sources of compensation	1076
14–150	B. The older cases on compensation	1079

CHAPTER 15

PRACTICE, PROCEDURE AND PUBLIC FUNDING

15–1	I. COMMITTAL: THE SUPREME COURT	1083

15–1	A. Criminal contempts: the role of the Attorney-General	1083
15–2	B. Contempt of Court Act 1981, section 7	1083
15–4	C. Committal	1084
15–9	D. Applications to the Divisional Court	1085
15–12	E. Application to a court other than the Divisional Court	1086
15–15	F. Special provisions relating to applications in the Family Division	1087
15–19	G. The contents of the notice or claim form	1088
15–20	H. The need to show prior service of the order on the respondent	1089
15–22	I. Dispensing with service of a mandatory order	1090
15–24	J. The need for a penal notice	1090
15–25	K. Recommended wording for penal notices	1091

Contents

PARA.		PAGE
15–27	L. Enforcement of undertakings	1092
15–28	M. The power to sit in private	1092
15–32	N. Procedural safeguards at committal hearings	1093
15–43	O. Must the respondent be put to his election?	1097
15–45	P. Form of committal order	1098
15–48	Q. The effect of a committal order	1099
15–51	II. COMMITTAL IN THE COUNTY COURT	1100
15–51	A. The changes in the rules	1100
15–57	B. Applications to commit without notice: exceptional circumstances required	1103
15–64	C. The need for strict compliance with the rules	1105
15–67	D. Contents of committal order	1106
15–70	E. Can a defective order be corrected on appeal?	1107
15–77	F. Enforcing the county court's statutory jurisdiction	1109
15–78	III. APPLICATIONS FOR SEQUESTRATION	1110
15–78	A. Mode of application	1110
15–79	B. Hearing usually in open court	1110
15–80	C. Function of the court at hearing	1110
15–81	D. Formalities following the grant of permission	1111
15–83	E. Duration of validity	1111
15–84	F. Sequestration will not lie against the Crown	1112
15–85	G. The property sequestered	1112
15–87	H. Discharge of sequestration	1112
15–88	IV. APPEALS PROCEDURE	1113
15–88	A. Introduction	1113
15–89	B. The terms of section 13 of the Administration Act 1960	1113
15–90	C. Appeals to the Court of Appeal	1114
15–103	D. Appeals to the House of Lords	1118
15–107	V. LEGAL SERVICES COMMISSION: ADVICE, ASSISTANCE AND REPRESENTATION	1119
15–107	A. The desirability of legal representation	1119

PARA.		PAGE
15–110	B. The Access to Justice Act 1999	1120
15–117	C. Limitations as to Criminal Defence Service funding	1121

CHAPTER 16

SCOTLAND

16–1	I. CONTEMPT IN SCOTS LAW BEFORE 1981	1122
16–1	A. The principles underlying the jurisdiction	1122
16–2	B. Upholding the authority of the court	1122
16–6	C. The relationship between "dignity" and "authority"	1124
16–11	D. The "domestic" jurisdiction common to all courts	1125
16–17	E. Contempts amounting also to crimes	1127
16–21	F. The law supplemented by statute	1128
16–22	G. To what extent is contempt itself "criminal"?	1129
16–29	H. Is contempt "quasi-crime"?	1131
16–39	I. Contempt as *sui generis*	1133
16–41	J. The Lord Justice-General's Memoranda on Contempt	1134
16–44	K. Summary jurisdiction to be used with restraint and discretion	1137
16–54	L. The continuing need for a summary procedure	1140
16–61	M. Procedure in non-summary cases	1141
16–64	N. The role of the Lord Advocate	1142
16–65	O. The distinction between direct and constructive contempts	1142
16–69	P. The approach to "*mens rea*" or "dole" at common law	1144
16–84	II. DIRECT CONTEMPTS INVOLVING JUDGES	1148
16–84	A. Assaulting judges	1148
16–85	B. Abusing or "murmuring" judges	1149
16–87	C. The history of murmuring	1149
16–101	D. The right to criticise the judiciary	1153
16–104	E. Seeking to influence judges by criticism	1154
16–105	F. Recognition of the limits of the summary power	1154
16–106	G. Protection for complaints to the proper authority	1155
16–109	III. MISBEHAVIOUR IN COURT	1156
16–109	A. Cases of intoxication in court	1156
16–112	B. Insults in court: the common law	1157
16–114	C. Non-attendance: the common law supplemented	1157
16–117	D. Other forms of misbehaviour at court	1159

PARA.		PAGE
16–118	IV. PREVARICATION	1159

16–118	A. Prevarication upon oath	1159
16–124	B. Prevarication as a constructive contempt	1161
16–128	C. Prevarication and perjury distinguished	1162
16–129	D. Statutory prevarication	1162
16–131	E. Procedural aspects of prevarication	1163

16–135	V. INTERFERENCE WITH EVIDENCE	1164

16–135	A. The rule stated	1164
16–136	B. Contempt involving physical evidence or documents of process	1164
16–140	C. Intimidation	1165
16–141	D. Interference with an accused in criminal proceedings	1166

16–142	VI. MEDIA CONTEMPTS	1166

16–142	A. Trial by newspaper: the common law approach	1166
16–146	B. Early cases	1167
16–158	C. The common law criteria before the 1981 Act	1170
16–164	D. The vexed question of the *terminus a quo*	1171
16–184	E. Police press announcements	1176
16–187	F. The remaining uncertainty	1177
16–191	G. When were proceedings treated as concluded?	1178
16–192	H. Discussion of public affairs: *Atkins v London Weekend Television Ltd*	1179
16–200	I. Reporting court proceedings	1180
16–224	J. Prohibiting the publication of prejudicial material	1187
16–230	K. Statutes prohibiting or restricting publication	1189
16–231	L. Attempting to pervert the course of justice	1190

16–234	VII. BREACH OF INTERDICT OR UNDERTAKING	1191

16–234	A. Breach of a court order	1191
16–237	B. Breach of an undertaking	1192
16–241	C. The mental element in breach of interdict	1193
16–244	D. Is breach of interdict properly described as "contempt"?	1194
16–249	E. Breach of interdict as "quasi-criminal"	1196
16–258	F. The impact of the quasi-criminal nature of the jurisdiction	1198

PARA.		PAGE
16–260	G. Breach of interdict: procedure	1199
16–264	H. Presence of defendant required	1200
16–265	I. Breach of orders *ad factum praestandum*	1200

16–268	VIII. THE PHILLIMORE RECOMMENDATIONS FOR SCOTLAND	1201

16–268	A. The recommendation for uniformity with England and Wales	1201
16–271	B. Scottish courts with contempt jurisdiction	1202
16–273	C. Contempts in court	1202
16–275	D. The right to be heard	1203
16–276	E. The point in proceedings from which the law of contempt is to apply	1204
16–278	F. The "open record" in Scotland	1205
16–280	G. Defence of innocent publication	1205
16–281	H. Reprisals against witnesses or jurors	1206
16–284	I. Scandalising the court	1206
16–288	J. Sentencing powers	1208
16–291	K. Procedure in Scotland	1209
16–294	L. Appeals	1209

16–301	IX. THE CONTEMPT OF COURT ACT 1981: APPLICATION TO SCOTLAND	1211

16–301	A. Closing the gap between Scotland and England	1211
16–336	B. The provisions relating specifically to Scotland	1223
16–351	C. The provisions of the 1981 Act which do not apply in Scotland	1227

16–352	X. CONTEMPT OF COURT ACT 1981: A COMMENTARY	1228

16–352	A. Introduction	1228
16–353	B. The Act in the framework of the common law	1228
16–354	C. The "strict liability rule" interpreted in Scotland	1228
16–360	D. Applications relating to prejudicial reports to be made promptly	1230
16–361	E. The statutory defences	1231
16–368	F. Reporting court proceedings	1233
16–383	G. Disclosure of sources	1236
16–387	H. Jury room secrecy: section 8	1237
16–397	I. Contempt barring trial	1239

PARA.		PAGE
16–410	J. Photographs of suspected persons	1244
16–413	K. Photography, sound recordings and television in the vicinity of the court	1245
16–420	L. Penalties for contempt after the Act	1248
16–427	M. Lack of a specific appeals procedure	1250

APPENDICES

17–1	The Contempt of Court Act 1981	1252
18–1	Forms and precedents	1271
19–1	Examples of penalties imposed since 1981	1323
20–1	Phillimore Committee: England and Wales	1353
21–1	Practice Direction—Committal Applications	1359
21–2	Family Division—Practice Direction—(Family Proceedings: Committal)	1365
21–3	Queen's Bench Division—Practice Direction—(Magistrates' Courts)—Contempt	1367

Index 1371

TABLE OF CASES

(References are to paragraph numbers)

A (A Minor) (Appeal by Party in Contempt), Re [1980] 1 F.L.R. 140, CA 12–68
A v A (Ancillary Relief); B v B (Ancillary Relief) [2000] 1 F.L.R. 701; [2000] 1 F.C.R. 577;
    [2000] Fam. Law 470, Fam Div 12–239
A v B Ex p. News Group Newspapers Ltd [1998] I.C.R. 55 7–109
A v B Plc; sub nom. A v B (A Firm); B and C v A [2002] EWCA Civ 337; [2003] Q.B. 195;
    [2002] 3 W.L.R. 542; [2002] 2 All E.R. 545; [2002] E.M.L.R. 21; [2002] 1 F.L.R.
    1021; [2002] 2 F.C.R. 158; [2002] H.R.L.R. 25; [2002] U.K.H.R.R. 457; 12 B.H.R.C.
    466; [2002] Fam. Law 415; (2002) 99(17) L.S.G. 36; (2002) 152 N.L.J. 434; (2002)
    146 S.J.L.B. 77; *The Times*, March 13, 2002; *Independent*, March 19, 2002; *Daily
    Telegraph*, March 11, 2002, CA (Civ Div) 6–114, 9–145
A v D (Contempt: Committal) (1993) Fam. Law 519 12–15
A v M (Family Proceedings: Publicity) [2000] 1 F.L.R. 562; [2000] 1 F.C.R. 1; [2000] Fam.
    Law 26, Fam Div 4–30, 6–56, 6–91, 6–94, 7–68
A v N (Committal: Refusal of Contact); sub nom. Re N (A Minor) [1997] 1 F.L.R. 533;
    [1997] 2 F.C.R. 475; [1997] Fam. Law 233; (1997) 161 J.P.N. 698, CA (Civ Div) 2–10,
    12–27, 12–28
A v Secretary of State for the Home Department; sub nom. X v Secretary of State for the
    Home Department [2004] UKHL 56; [2005] 2 W.L.R. 87; [2005] H.R.L.R. 1; 17
    B.H.R.C. 496; (2005) 155 N.L.J. 23; (2005) 149 S.J.L.B. 28; *The Times*, December 17,
    2004; *Independent*, December 21, 2004, HL 2–168
A v Times Newspapers Ltd; C v Times Newspapers Ltd [2002] EWHC 2444; [2003] 1 All
    E.R. 587; [2003] 1 F.L.R. 689; [2003] 1 F.C.R. 326; [2003] Fam. Law 228; (2003)
    100(6) L.S.G. 25; (2002) 152 N.L.J. 1895; *The Times*, December 11, 2002; *Independ-
    ent*, December 5, 2002, Fam Div 7–65, 7–155, 8–116
A v United Kingdom (1997) 25 E.H.R.R. C.D. 159 6–73
A-A v B-A [2001] 4 F.L.R. 1 19–2
Abdi v Jama [1996] 1 F.L.R. 407; [1996] 2 F.C.R. 658; [1996] Fam. Law 276, CA (Civ
    Div) 14–55, 15–46
Aberdonia Cars Ltd v Brown, Hughes Strachan Ltd (1915) 59 S.J. 598 .... 12–35, 12–40
Aberforthe v Hall and Paramore (1598) Sanders, *Chancery Orders* 1–43
Abodi Mendi, The [1939] P. 178 12–146
Abraham, Comb. 141, 90 E.R. 393 1–38
Abraham v Jutsun [1963] 1 W.L.R. 658; [1963] 2 All E.R. 402; 107 S.J. 357, CA 10–155
Acrow (Automation) Ltd v Rex Chainbelt Inc [1971] 1 W.L.R. 1676 ...... 6–1, 6–137, 12–171, 14–132
Adam v Fisher (1914) 110 L.T. 537; (1914) 30 T.L.R. 288 9–4
Adam v Ward (1915) 31 T.L.R. 299 4–49
Adam Phones Ltd v Goldschmidt [1999] 4 All E.R. 486; [2000] C.P. Rep. 23; [2000] F.S.R.
    163; (1999) 22(11) I.P.D. 22110; *The Times*, August 17, 1999; *Independent*, July 22,
    1999, Ch D 12–23, 12–93, 14–136
Adams, Petr, 1987 S.C.C.R. 650 .... 16–361, 16–408, 16–425
Adams v Hughes (1819) 1 Brod. & B. 24; (1819) 129 E.R. 632 11–317
Adams v Walsh [1963] N.Z.L.R. 158 .... 11–199, 11–216
Adcock v Normand, unreported, January 22, 1992 16–43
Adlard v Smith (1819) 6 Price 231; (1819) 146 E.R. 822 14–28
Advocate (HM) v Airs, 1975 J.C. 64; 1975 S.L.T. 177, HCJ 9–51, 16–39, 16–41, 16–118, 16–384
Advocate (HM) v Baxter (1867) 3 Irv. 351 16–122

Table of Cases

Advocate (HM) v Beggs (No.1), 2002 S.L.T. 135; 2001 S.C.C.R. 869; 2001 G.W.D. 34–1330, HCJ 1–150, 4–160, 4–168, 7–138
Advocate (HM) v Beggs (No.2), 2002 S.L.T. 139; 2001 S.C.C.R. 879; 2001 G.W.D. 34–1327, HCJ 1–149, 1–150, 1–180, 4–27, 6–94, 16–319
Advocate (HM) v Bell, 1936 J.C. 89; 1936 S.N. 74 16–114
Advocate (HM) v Caledonian Newspapers Ltd, 1995 S.C.C.R. 330 .... 16–313, 16–333, 16–358
Advocate (HM) v Carr (1854) 1 Irv. 464 .... 16–97, 16–108
Advocate (HM) v Danskin, 2000 S.C.C.R. 101, Sh Ct 16–302
Advocate (HM) v Dewar (1842) 1 Broun 233 16–122
Advocate (HM) v George Outram & Co Ltd, 1980 J.C. 51; 1980 S.L.T. (Notes) 13, HCJ 16–163, 16–184, 16–269, 16–311
Advocate (HM) v Hunter, 1989 S.L.T. 113 16–406
Advocate (HM) v Keating, unreported, August 1987, Edinburgh HC 16–316
Advocate (HM) v McCook, 1986 S.C.C.R. 491 16–372
Advocate (HM) v McGill and Strain, unreported, March 3, 1987, Glasgow High Court 16–315
Advocate (HM) v Machie (1844) 2 Brown 293 16–123
Advocate (HM) v McLean and McGillivray (1838) 2 Swin. 185 16–109
Advocate (HM) v Mitchell, 1993 S.C.C.R. 793 .... 16–313, 16–403
Advocate (HM) v News Group Newspapers; sub nom. HM Advocate v Scottish Express Newspapers, 1989 S.C.C.R. 156, HCJ ... 16–303, 16–304, 16–333, 16–356, 16–357, 16–402
Advocate (HM) v Pollock, unreported, December 3, 1984, Airdrie High Court 16–314
Advocate (HM) v Robertson (1842) 1 Broun 152 16–40
Advocate (HM) v Robertson (1870) 1 Coup. 404 .... 16–88, 16–90, 16–98, 16–106, 16–108
Advocate (HM) v Scotsman Publications Ltd, 1999 S.L.T. 466; 1999 S.C.C.R. 163; 1998 G.W.D. 21–1060, HCJ Appeal 1–163, 16–319, 16–405
Advocate (HM) v Scottish Daily Record & Sunday Mail (1986) Ltd, 1997 G.W.D. 20–937; (1997) 9 *Media Lawyer* 28, HCJ 16–302, 16–317
Advocate (HM) v Scottish Media Newspapers Ltd, 1999 S.L.T. 331 16–404
Advocate (HM) v Smith (1954) 1 Irv. 378 16–126
Advocate (HM) v Sweeney, unreported, 1975, Glasgow HC 16–413
Advocate (HM) v Tarbett, 2003 S.L.T. 1288; 2003 G.W.D. 29–807, HCJ 10–138, 11–88
Advocate (HM) v The Daily Record and The Sun (1997) *Media Lawyer* 28(9) 1–115, 2–76
Advocate (HM) v Trainer, unreported, August 28, 1997 16–408
Advocate (HM) v Wilson, unreported, June 15, 2001, HCJ 16–319, 16–379
Advocate (HM) v Yates (1847) Ark. 238 .... 16–109, 16–111
Advocate (Lord) v Galloway (1839) 2 Swin. 465 16–136
Advocate (Lord) v Hay (1822) 1 S. 288 (N.E. 267) 16–94, 16–148
Advocate (Lord) v Jamieson (1822) 1 S. 285 (N.E. 264) 16–94
Advocate (Lord) v Prentice (1822) 1 S. 385 16–53
Advocate (Lord) v Scotsman Publications Ltd [1990] 1 A.C. 812, HL; affirming 1988 S.L.T. 490; [1989] 1 F.S.R. 310; *The Times*, April 25, 1988, IH (2 Div) 2–52, 2–170, 16–226, 16–303, 16–319, 16–335
AGBC v Bezanson (1983) 50 B.C.L.R. 275, SCBC 12–80
Agricultural Industries Ltd, Re [1952] 1 All E.R. 1188 7–41
Ahnee v DPP [1999] 2 A.C. 294; [1999] 2 W.L.R. 1305; (1999) 143 S.J.L.B. 149, PC (Mau) 2–174, 5–245, 5–248, 5–258, 5–271
Aiden Shipping Co Ltd v Interbulk Ltd (The Vimeira) (No.2) [1986] A.C. 965; [1986] 2 W.L.R. 1051; [1986] 2 All E.R. 409; [1986] 2 Lloyd's Rep. 117; (1986) 130 S.J. 429, HL 7–273, 7–274, 7–275
Air Canada v Secretary of State for Trade (No.2) [1983] 2 A.C. 394; [1983] 2 W.L.R. 494; [1983] 1 All E.R. 910, HL 12–209
Aitchison v Bernardi, 1984 S.L.T. 343; 1984 S.C.C.R. 88, HCJ Appeal 4–118, 16–409
Aitken v Carmichael, 1993 S.C.C.R. 889 16–83
Aitken v Preston; Aitken v Granada Television Ltd [1997] E.M.L.R. 415; *The Times*, May 21, 1997, CA (Civ Div) 2–22, 10–176
Al-Megrahi (Abdelbasset Ali) v Times Newspapers Ltd; sub nom. Megrahi v Times Newspapers Ltd, 2000 J.C. 22; 1999 S.C.C.R. 824; 1999 G.W.D. 29–1367, HCJ 4–2, 4–95, 4–122, 4–186, 4–187, 4–272, 5–101, 16–206, 16–222, 16–302, 16–303, 16–331, 16–332, 16–409
Aldridge v Warwickshire Coal Co Ltd (1925) 133 L.T. 439, CA 11–142

TABLE OF CASES

Alexander v Rayson [1936] 1 K.B. 169, CA 15–44
Allan (1826) Shaw 172 .... 16–109, 16–110
Allardice and Boswell v Robertson (1830) 4 W. & S. 102 16–107
Allason v Random House (UK) Ltd (No.2) [2002] EWHC 1030, Ch D 14–3
Allen v Dingley (1576) Choyce, p.114 1–49
Allenet de Ribemont v France (A/308); sub nom. Allenet de Ribemont v France (15175/89)
    (1995) 20 E.H.R.R. 557, ECHR 1–112, 2–70, 2–145
Alliance and Leicester Building Society v Ghahramani [1992] 32 V.R. 198; (1992) 142 New
    Law Jo. 313 11–82
Alliance Building Society v Austen [1951] 2 All E.R. 1068 11–328
Alliance Perpetual Building Society v Belrum Investments Ltd [1957] 1 W.L.R. 720; [1957]
    1 All E.R. 635; 101 S.J. 406, Ch D 7–44, 8–97, 11–75
Almon, *Wilmot's Notes* (1765) 243, 97 E.R. 642 .... 1–60, 1–70, 5–221, 5–244
Almon (1770) 5 Burr. 2686; (1770) 98 E.R. 411 4–200
Alterskye v Scott [1948] 1 All E.R. 469; 92 S.J. 220, Ch D 3–198, 11–75, 11–76, 12–201
AM v Ryan (1996) 143 D.L.R. (4th) 1 9–16
Ambard v Att-Gen of Trinidad and Tobago [1936] A.C. 322; [1936] 1 All E.R. 704; [1936]
    2 W.W.R. 252, PC (Trin) 2–51, 5–139, 5–232, 5–240, 5–251, 5–256, 16–47, 16–101
American Cyanamid Co v Ethicon Ltd [1975] A.C. 396; [1975] 2 W.L.R. 316; [1975] 1 All
    E.R. 504; [1975] F.S.R. 101; [1975] R.P.C. 513; 119 S.J. 136, HL 6–7, 6–9, 6–12, 6–13,
                                                                    6–14, 6–15, 6–35, 6–36, 6–37
American Exchange in Europe (Ltd) v Gillig, Re (1889) 58 L.J. Ch. 706 .... 1–72, 4–232
Amery v Solicitor-General [1987] 2 N.Z.L.R. 292 2–212
Ames v Birkenhead Docks (1855) 20 Beav. 332; (1855) 52 E.R. 630 .... 11–318, 11–319, 11–320,
                                                                                                              14–132
AMIEU v Mudginberri Station Pty Ltd (1986) 161 C.L.R. 98 14–102
Amor v Scott, 1992 G.W.D. 5–260 .... 23–1300, 16–79
Anderson, Petr (1971) 35 J.C.L. 55 16–60
Anderson v Bank of British Columbia (1876) 2 Ch. D. 644 12–107
Anderson v Connacher (1850) 13 D. 405 16–249
Anderson v Douglas, 1998 S.L.T. 379; 1997 S.C.C.R. 632; 1997 G.W.D. 32–1611, HCJ
    Appeal 16–51, 16–79
Anderson v Moncrieff, 1966 S.L.T. (Sh. Ct) 28 16–241
Anderson v Stoddart, 1923 S.C. 755 16–262
Anderton v Ryan; sub nom. Chief Constable of Greater Manchester v Ryan [1985] A.C. 560;
    [1985] 2 W.L.R. 968; [1985] 2 All E.R. 355; (1985) 81 Cr. App. R. 166; (1985) 149
    J.P. 433; [1985] Crim. L.R. 503; (1985) 82 L.S.G. 2241; (1985) 135 N.L.J. 485; (1985)
    129 S.J. 362, HL; reversing [1985] 2 W.L.R. 23; [1985] 1 All E.R. 138; (1985) 80 Cr.
    App. R. 235; (1985) 149 J.P. 79; [1984] Crim. L.R. 483; (1984) 148 J.P.N. 429; (1984)
    81 L.S.G. 1676; (1984) 128 S.J. 850, QBD 4–127
Andrew v Raeburn (1874) L.R. 9 Ch. App. 522 7–57
Andrews v Chapman (1853) 3 C. & K. 286; (1853) 175 E.R. 558 .... 4–288, 12–213
Angel v Smith (1804) 9 Ves. Jun. 335; (1804) 11–321, 11–323
Anglo-French Co-operative Society, Re (1880) 14 Ch.D. 533 3–145
Anon. (1521) Rastell. Ent. 267b 10–188
Anon. (1586) Gouldsb. 30; (1586) 75 E.R. 974 11–59
Anon. (1642) March 81; (1642) 82 E.R. 421 11–188
Anon. (1677) 1 Ventr. 298; (1677) 86 E.R. 192 3–145
Anon. (1702 1 Anne) 7 Mod. 31, 87 E.R. 1076 1–53
Anon. (1710) 1 Salk. 84; (1710) 91 E.R. 79 .... 1–52, 11–317
Anon. (1731) 2 Bar. K.B. 43, 94 E.R. 345 .... 1–59, 5–250
Anon. (1745) 3 Atk. 219; (1745) 26 E.R. 928 11–317
Anon. (1758) 2 Keny. 372; (1758) 96 E.R. 1214 11–55
Anon. (1808) 15 Ves. Jun. 174; (1808) 33 E.R. 720 3–159
Anon. (1907), quoted in Oswald, *Contempt* (3rd ed., 1910), p.68 10–183
Anon. 34 E. III, quoted in Vaughan 151, 124 E.R. 1006 10–183
Ansah v Ansah [1977] Fam. 138 .... 12–15, 12–24, 12–28, 12–32
Anton Piller KG v Manufacturing Processes Ltd [1976] Ch. 55; [1976] 2 W.L.R. 162; [1976]
    1 All E.R. 779; [1976] F.S.R. 129; [1976] R.P.C. 719; (1975) 120 S.J. 63; *The Times*,
    December 9, 1975, CA (Civ Div) 12–175

TABLE OF CASES

Apple Corp Ltd v Apple Computer Inc [1992] 1 C.M.L.R. 969 12–204
Applin v Race Relations Board [1975] A.C. 259; [1974] 2 W.L.R. 541; [1974] 2 All E.R. 73;
    72 L.G.R. 479; 118 S.J. 311, HL 4–43, 4–48
Apted v Apted and Bliss [1930] P. 246 .... 10–157, 10–161
Arab Monetary Fund v Hashim, unreported, March 21, 1997 .... 9–223, 12–70
Arding v Flower (1800) 8 T.R. 534; (1800) 101 E.R. 1531 .... 3–141, 3–146
Argyle (Duke of) v McArthur (1861) 23 D. 1236 .... 16–67, 16–263
Argyll (Duchess of) v Duke of Argyll [1967] Ch. 302; [1965] 2 W.L.R. 790; [1965] 1 All
    E.R. 611, Ch D 8–5, 8–12
Arif (Mohamed) (An Infant), Re; Re Nirbhai Singh (An Infant); Re S(N) (An Infant); Singh
    v Secretary of State for Home Affairs; sub nom. A (An Infant), Re; Hanif v Secretary
    of State for Home Affairs [1968] Ch. 643; [1968] 2 W.L.R. 1290; [1968] 2 All E.R.
    145, CA (Civ Div) 6–55
Armstrong, Re Ex p. Lindsay [1892] 1 Q.B. 327 .... 3–109, 3–110, 3–143
Armstrong v Strain [1952] 1 K.B. 232 12–146
Arrow Nominees Inc v Blackledge, *The Times*, December 8, 1999 12–79
Artico v Italy (1980) 3 E.H.R.R. 1 11–88
Ashurst v Mason (1875) L.R. 20 Eq. 225 11–59
Ashworth Hospital Authority v MGN Ltd; sub nom. Ashworth Security Hospital v MGN Ltd
    [2002] UKHL 29; [2002] 1 W.L.R. 2033; [2002] 4 All E.R. 193; [2002] C.P.L.R. 712;
    [2002] E.M.L.R. 36; [2002] H.R.L.R. 41; [2002] U.K.H.R.R. 1263; 12 B.H.R.C. 443;
    [2003] F.S.R. 17; (2002) 67 B.M.L.R. 175; (2002) 99(30) L.S.G. 37; (2002) 146
    S.J.L.B. 168; *The Times*, July 1, 2002; *Independent*, July 3, 2002, HL; affirming [2001]
    1 W.L.R. 515; [2001] 1 All E.R. 991; [2001] E.M.L.R. 11; [2001] F.S.R. 33; (2001) 61
    B.M.L.R. 48; (2001) 98(6) L.S.G. 46; (2001) 145 S.J.L.B. 20; *The Times*, January 10,
    2001; *Independent*, January 18, 2001; *Daily Telegraph*, January 9, 2001, CA (Civ
    Div) 1–126, 1–158, 7–4, 9–1, 9–2, 9–9, 9–26, 9–105, 9–106, 9–108, 9–126, 9–138, 9–139,
                    9–145, 9–146, 9–148, 9–149, 9–152, 9–170, 9–176, 9–245, 10–175
Aslam v Singh [1987] 1 F.L.R. 122; [1986] Fam. Law 362, CA (Civ Div) 15–37
Associated Newspapers Ltd v London (North) Industrial Tribunal [1998] I.C.R. 1212 7–109
Associated Provincial Picture Houses Ltd v Wednesbury Corp [1948] 1 K.B. 223; [1947] 2
    All E.R. 680; 63 T.L.R. 623; 112 J.P. 55; 45 L.G.R. 635; [1948] L.J.R. 190; 177 L.T.
    641; 92 S.J. 26, CA 2–140
Astro Exito Navegacion SA v Southland Enterprise Co (The Messiniaki Tolmi) (No.1)
    [1981] 2 Lloyd's Rep. 595, CA (Civ Div) 12–33, 12–66, 12–68, 12–73
Atholl (Duke of) v Dalgaish (1823) 2 S. 422 16–257
Atholl (Duke of) v Robertson (1872) 10 Macph. 298 .... 16–235, 16–259, 16–264
Atkins v London Weekend Television Ltd, 1978 J.C. 48; 1978 S.L.T. 76, HCJ ... 16–143, 16–145,
                    16–185, 16–189, 16–190, 16–192, 16–193, 16–199, 16–224, 16–225,
                    16–269, 16–308, 16–311, 16–338, 16–355, 16–365, 16–410
Atlantic Capital Corporation v Sir Cecil Denniston Burney, CA Civil Div, Transcript 1142 of
    1994, September 15, 1994 12–70
Att-Gen v Associated Newspapers Group Plc; Att-Gen v English; Att-Gen v Oakley [1989]
    1 W.L.R. 322; [1989] 1 All E.R. 604; [1989] C.O.D. 256; (1988) 138 N.L.J. Rep. 305;
    (1988) 132 S.J. 1639; *The Times*, October 21, 1988; *Independent*, October 21, 1988;
    Guardian, October 21, 1988; *Daily Telegraph*, November 4, 1988, QBD 1–127, 2–193,
                    13–66
Att-Gen v Associated Newspapers Ltd (1992) [1994] 2 A.C. 238; [1994] 2 W.L.R. 277;
    [1994] 1 All E.R. 556; (1994) 99 Cr. App. R. 131; [1994] Crim. L.R. 672; [1994]
    C.O.D. 275; (1994) 144 N.L.J. 195; (1994) 138 S.J.L.B. 52; *The Times*, February 4,
    1994; *Independent*, February 9, 1994; *Guardian*, February 7, 1994, HL 1–126, 2–128,
                    2–130, 2–131, 2–165, 2–194, 4–223, 6–9, 11–365, 11–366, 11–367,
                    11–382
Att-Gen, Ex p.; Re Goodwin (1969) 70 S.R. (N.S.W.) 413, NSW CA 5–242
Att-Gen v Associated Newspapers Ltd, unreported, October 31, 1997, Kennedy L.J. 1–155, 2–75,
                    2–105, 4–60, 4–61, 4–74, 4–107, 4–109, 4–114, 4–151, 5–115, 19–1
Att-Gen v Barker (Worldwide Injunction) [1990] 3 All E.R. 257; *Independent*, August 24,
    1990, CA (Civ Div) 11–204

[lii]

TABLE OF CASES

Att-Gen v BBC; sub nom. Dible v BBC [1981] A.C. 303; [1980] 3 W.L.R. 109; [1980] 3 All
 E.R. 161; 78 L.G.R. 529; 124 S.J. 444, HL 1–133, 2–52, 2–103, 2–122, 2–157, 2–175,
 2–193, 4–17, 4–19, 4–20, 4–21, 4–119, 4–120, 5–22, 5–215, 6–9, 6–39,
 6–114, 7–5, 11–176, 12–214, 13–1, 13–2, 13–3, 13–4, 13–26, 13–44,
 13–45, 13–46,13–47, 13–48, 13–52, 13–54, 13–56, 13–57, 13–58, 13–63,
 13–64, 13–71, 13–73, 13–103, 14–107, 16–330
Att-Gen v BBC [1992] C.O.D. 264; *Independent*, January 3, 1992; *Guardian*, December 18,
 1991, DC 4–104, 4–148, 4–149, 4–152, 5–114, 19–1
Att-Gen v BBC; Att-Gen v Jones, December 1, 1995, DC (Lexis) 4–104, 4–149, 4–152
Att-Gen v BBC; Att-Gen v Hat Trick Productions Ltd [1997] E.M.L.R. 76; *The Times*, July
 26, 1996, DC 2–43, 4–25, 4–70, 4–86, 4–149, 4–150, 4–313, 7–171, 19–1
Att-Gen v Birmingham Post and Mail Ltd [1999] 1 W.L.R. 361; [1998] 4 All E.R. 49; [1999]
 E.M.L.R. 39; [1998] C.O.D. 432; (1998) 95(37) L.S.G. 36; *The Times*, August 31,
 1998, DC 1–162, 2–76, 2–98, 2–106, 2–109, 2–218, 4–53, 4–60, 4–107, 4–108, 4–109,
 4–114, 4–150, 4–170, 16–309, 16–318, 16–359, 16–401, 19–1
Att-Gen v Blomfield (1913) 33 N.Z.L.R. 545 5–242
Att-Gen v Blundell [1942] N.Z.L.R. 287 5–268
Att-Gen v Boyle (1864) 10 Jur. (N.S.) 309 12–182
Att-Gen v Butler [1953] N.Z. L.R. 944 5–268
Att-Gen v Butterworth; sub nom. Att-Gen's Application, Re [1963] 1 Q.B. 696; [1962] 3
 W.L.R. 819; [1962] 3 All E.R. 326; 106 S.J. 610, CA 2–171, 2–177, 4–238, 5–139, 5–268,
 7–93, 10–213, 11–3, 11–7, 11–23, 11–157, 11–165, 11–187, 11–197,
 11–199, 11–202, 11–207, 11–208, 11–211, 11–213, 11–217, 11–241,
 11–295, 13–9, 14–149, 16–281
Att-Gen v Channel 4, unreported, June 19, 1996, CA 6–40
Att-Gen v Channel 4 Television Co Ltd. *See* Att-Gen v Channel Four Television Co Ltd
Att-Gen v Channel Four Television Co Ltd; sub nom. Att-Gen v Channel 4 Television [1988]
 Crim. L.R. 237, CA (Civ Div) 4–271, 4–272, 4–273, 5–103, 6–1, 13–14
Att-Gen v Clough [1963] 1 Q.B. 773; [1963] 2 W.L.R. 343; [1963] 1 All E.R. 420; 107 S.J.
 96, QBD 9–43, 10–162, 13–78
Att-Gen v Colney Hatch Lunatic Asylum (1868) 4 Ch. App. 146 12–22
Att-Gen v English [1983] 1 A.C. 116; [1982] 3 W.L.R. 278; [1982] 2 All E.R. 903; (1982)
 75 Cr. App. R. 302; [1982] Crim. L.R. 743; (1982) 79 L.S.G. 1175; 126 S.J. 511, HL;
 reversing [1982] 2 W.L.R. 959; [1982] Crim. L.R. 429; 126 S.J. 206, QBD 1–101, 1–126,
 2–43, 4–52, 4–53, 4–56, 4–57, 4–72, 4–86, 4–96, 4–98, 4–149, 4–300,
 4–303, 4–305, 4–309, 4–312, 4–318, 4–320, 5–12, 5–15, 5–24, 5–149,
 5–200, 7–173, 7–176, 9–143, 11–225, 16–323, 16–327, 16–358, 16–365,
 16–367
Att-Gen v Express Newspapers [2004] EWHC 2859; [2005] E.M.L.R. 13, QBD (Admin) 3–41,
 3–228, 4–155, 5–112, 19–1
Att-Gen v Foster and Mulholland. *See* Att-Gen v Mulholland
Att-Gen v Greater Manchester Newspapers Ltd. *See* Venables v News Group International
 (Breach of Injunction)
Att-Gen v Guardian Newspapers Ltd (Contempt) [1999] E.M.L.R. 904; *Independent*, July
 30, 1999, QBD 2–35, 2–145, 2–197, 2–199, 4–59, 4–107, 4–109, 4–149, 4–171, 4–172,
 4–314, 5–10, 5–23, 5–200, 7–164, 9–107, 9–19
Att-Gen v Guardian Newspapers Ltd (No.1); Att-Gen v Observer Ltd; Att-Gen v Times
 Newspapers; sub nom. Spycatcher: Guardian/Observer Discharge [1987] 1 W.L.R.
 1248; [1987] 3 All E.R. 316; [1989] 2 F.S.R. 81; (1987) 84 L.S.G. 2689; (1987) 137
 N.L.J. 785; (1987) 131 S.J. 1122, HL 1–110, 2–52, 2–133, 2–153, 2–160, 2–196, 5–238,
 7–5, 16–330
Att-Gen v Guardian Newspapers Ltd (No.2); Att-Gen v Observer Ltd (No.2); Att-Gen v
 Times Newspapers Ltd (No.2) [1990] 1 A.C. 109; [1988] 3 W.L.R. 776; [1988] 3 All
 E.R. 545; [1989] 2 F.S.R. 181; (1988) 85(42) L.S.G. 45; (1988) 138 N.L.J. Rep. 296;
 (1988) 132 S.J. 1496; *The Times*, October 14, 1988; *Independent*, October 14, 1988,
 HL ... 1–136, 1–144, 2–50, 2–53, 2–138, 2–158, 4–30, 6–6, 6–49, 6–91, 7–3, 7–111, 9–7, 9–77
Att-Gen v Guardian Newspapers Ltd (No.3) [1992] 1 W.L.R. 874; [1992] 3 All E.R. 38;
 [1992] C.O.D. 338; *The Times*, February 28, 1992; *Independent*, March 4, 1992;
 Guardian, March 4, 1992, QBD 1–145, 2–50, 2–53, 2–57, 4–58, 4–77, 4–86, 4–223, 7–118,
 7–136, 7–145, 7–154, 7–159, 7–205, 7–252, 8–70, 11–225

TABLE OF CASES

Att-Gen v Guardian Newspapers Ltd (Public Libraries Case); Att-Gen v Observer Ltd; Application by Derbyshire CC, Re [1988] 1 All E.R. 385; [1989] 2 F.S.R. 163; *The Times*, October 20, 1987, Ch D 2–194, 4–27, 5–28, 6–126, 6–131, 11–5
Att-Gen v Hislop [1991] 1 Q.B. 514; [1991] 2 W.L.R. 219; [1991] 1 All E.R. 911; *Independent*, August 3, 1990, CA (Civ Div) 1–128, 4–187, 5–3, 5–17, 5–43, 5–45, 5–46, 5–73, 5–116, 5–169, 5–170, 5–176, 5–182, 11–280, 12–97, 15–91, 15–93, 19–1
Att-Gen v Independent Television News Ltd [1995] 2 All E.R. 370; [1995] 1 Cr. App. R. 204; [1994] C.O.D. 370; *The Times*, May 12, 1994; *Guardian*, May 16, 1994, QBD 2–106, 4–25, 4–30, 4–71, 4–74, 4–76, 4–86, 5–10, 5–115, 7–164, 7–177, 7–183, 16–401
Att-Gen v Jackson [1994] C.O.D. 171 .... 11–159, 11–202, 19–1
Att-Gen v James [1962] 2 Q.B. 637; [1962] 2 W.L.R. 740; [1962] 1 All E.R. 255; 106 S.J. 245, DC 3–185, 14–5, 14–28
Att-Gen v Judd [1995] C.O.D. 15; *The Times*, August 15, 1994, QBD 5–177, 5–194, 10–224, 11–3, 11–31, 11–187, 11–258, 11–379, 11–382, 13–26, 19–1
Att-Gen v Kissane (1893) 32 L.R. Ir. 220 .... 3–137, 11–326
Att-Gen v Leather Sellers Company (1844) 7 Beav. 157; (1844) 49 E.R. 1023 3–146
Att-Gen v Leveller Magazine Ltd; Att-Gen v National Union of Journalists; Att-Gen v Peace News Ltd [1979] A.C. 440; [1979] 2 W.L.R. 247; [1979] 1 All E.R. 745; (1979) 68 Cr. App. R. 342; [1979] Crim. L.R. 247; 123 S.J. 129, HL 1–67, 1–97, 2–10, 2–65, 2–179, 2–189, 3–105, 3–107, 5–139, 7–9, 7–36, 7–60, 7–61, 7–76, 7–77, 7–78, 7–84, 7–87, 7–93, 7–99, 7–100, 7–204, 7–205, 7–212, 8–131, 9–201, 9–228, 9–229
Att-Gen v Limbrick [1996] T.L.R. 186; *The Times*, March 28, 1996, QBD 2–193, 11–79
Att-Gen v Lingle [1995] 1 S.L.R. 696 .... 5–245, 5–270
Att-Gen v London Weekend Television Ltd [1973] 1 W.L.R. 202; [1972] 3 All E.R. 1146; [1973] Crim. L.R. 40; (1972) 116 S.J. 902, QBD 3–64, 4–14, 4–25, 4–96, 5–35
Att-Gen v Lundin (1982) 75 Cr. App. R. 90; [1982] Crim. L.R. 296, DC 2–67, 7–236, 7–242, 7–243, 9–14, 9–47, 9–83, 9–98, 9–160, 9–197, 9–201, 9–224, 9–227, 9–233, 9–241, 9–245, 10–162, 10–174, 10–175
Att-Gen v Mantoura (1993) 157 J.P. 317; [1993] Crim. L.R. 279; [1993] C.O.D. 9; (1993) 157 J.P.N. 234; *The Times*, August 26, 1992; *Independent*, August 7, 1992, DC 3–52, 13–25
Att-Gen v Martin (Peter), *The Times*, April 23, 1986 .... 4–135, 4–137, 4–145, 4–330, 11–3, 11–71, 11–217, 11–222, 11–229, 11–241, 11–244, 11–254, 11–282, 11–286, 11–289, 11–293, 11–294
Att-Gen v MGN Ltd; sub nom. Mirror Group Newspapers, Re [1997] 1 All E.R. 456; [1997] E.M.L.R. 284, DC 1–115, 1–154, 1–160, 1–162, 1–163, 2–52, 2–71, 2–74, 2–75, 2–76, 2–96, 2–106, 2–121, 2–194, 2–218, 4–28, 4–29, 4–30, 4–53, 4–84, 4–86, 4–109, 4–114, 4–155, 4–156, 4–163, 4–165, 4–170, 4–173, 5–200, 7–180, 11–225, 14–136, 15–106, 16–302, 16–303, 16–309, 16–317, 16–318, 16–319, 16–328, 16–330, 16–359, 16–401
Att-Gen v Mirror Group Newspapers Ltd [2002] EWHC 907 19–1
Att-Gen v Morgan; Att-Gen v News Group Newspapers Ltd [1998] E.M.L.R. 294; *Independent*, July 17, 1997 ..... 1–155, 2–75, 4–56, 4–76, 4–79, 4–109, 4–151, 5–94, 5–115, 16–169, 19–1
Att-Gen v Mulholland; Att-Gen v Foster [1963] 2 Q.B. 477; [1963] 2 W.L.R. 658; [1963] 1 All E.R. 767; 107 S.J. 154, CA 2–67, 9–14, 9–15, 9–38, 9–42, 9–43, 9–44, 9–86, 9–98, 9–126, 9–241, 10–162, 10–173, 10–175, 13–78
Att-Gen v New Statesman and Nation Publishing Co [1981] Q.B. 1; [1980] 2 W.L.R. 246; [1980] 1 All E.R. 644; (1980) 70 Cr. App. R. 193; [1980] Crim. L.R. 236; 124 S.J. 101, DC 11–353
Att-Gen v News Group Newspapers Ltd (1982) 4 Cr. App. R. (S.) 182, DC 19–1
Att-Gen v News Group Newspapers Ltd (1984) 6 Cr. App. R. (S.) 418, QBD 7–222, 19–1
Att-Gen v News Group Newspapers Ltd [1987] Q.B. 1; [1986] 3 W.L.R. 365; [1986] 2 All E.R. 833; (1986) 83 L.S.G. 1719; (1986) 136 N.L.J. 584; (1986) 130 S.J. 408, CA (Civ Div) 2–38, 2–86, 2–106, 3–28, 4–2, 4–58, 4–71, 4–72, 4–86, 4–327, 5–10, 5–65, 5–121, 6–32, 6–40, 6–133, 6–135, 7–164, 7–173, 7–177, 7–183

[liv]

Table of Cases

Att-Gen v News Group Newspapers Ltd [1989] Q.B. 110; [1988] 3 W.L.R. 163; [1988] 2 All
E.R. 906; (1988) 87 Cr. App. R. 323; (1988) 138 N.L.J. Rep. 55; (1988) 132 S.J. 934,
QBD 1–128, 1–135, 1–159, 2–22, 2–40, 2–172, 3–66, 3–90, 3–97, 3–192, 5–45, 5–68,
5–77, 5–96, 5–97, 5–98, 5–99, 5–123, 5–126, 5–163, 5–165, 5–166, 5–171,
5–177, 5–182, 5–188, 5–196, 5–246, 5–249, 6–34, 6–151, 7–94, 7–140,
7–143, 7–144, 7–214, 7–221, 7–222, 8–137, 8–138, 8–139, 10–83,
10–223, 11–21, 11–86, 11–218, 11–258, 11–271, 11–347, 12–87, 13–9,
16–82, 19–1
Att-Gen v News Group Newspapers Ltd, February 9, 1996, DC 16–363
Att-Gen v News Group Newspapers [1999] C.O.D. 190 19–1
Att-Gen v News International Plc and McKenzie, July 5, 1994 (Lexis) 19–1
Att-Gen v News UK Ltd and Stott, unreported, December 1995, Potts J. 1–136, 4–30
Att-Gen v Newspaper Publishing Plc [1988] Ch. 333; [1987] 3 W.L.R. 942; [1987] 3 All E.R.
276; [1989] 2 F.S.R. 27; (1987) 137 N.L.J. 686; (1987) 131 S.J. 1454; *Independent*,
July 16, 1987, CA (Civ Div) ... 1–66, 1–118, 1–122, 1–128, 1–133, 1–135, 1–136, 1–159, 2–3,
2–32, 2–73, 2–103, 2–158, 2–174, 2–189, 2–194, 2–209, 3–51, 3–89, 3–91,
3–97, 3–116, 3–117, 3–119, 3–121, 3–126, 4–2, 4–3, 4–85, 4–181,
4–321, 4–328, 4–329, 5–3, 5–20, 5–45, 5–121, 5–123, 5–135, 5–139,
5–141, 5–145, 5–146, 5–147, 5–165, 5–166, 5–184, 5–193, 5–198, 5–249,
6–47, 6–108, 6–110, 6–116, 6–117, 6–118, 6–120, 6–122, 6–125, 6–126,
6–128, 6–130, 6–132, 6–133, 6–148, 6–149, 7–58, 7–92, 7–93, 7–94,
7–115, 7–129, 7–135, 7–214, 7–221, 8–137, 9–17, 9–210, 10–83, 10–107,
10–216, 10–218, 10–223, 11–12, 11–21, 11–23, 11–33, 11–34, 11–35,
11–36, 11–37, 11–39, 11–271, 11–345, 11–347, 12–2, 12–6, 12–33,
12–87, 12–90, 12–104, 12–109, 12–145, 12–157, 12–181, 12–241,
12–243, 14–112, 14–123, 15–21, 15–96, 15–117, 16–82, 16–328, 16–335
Att-Gen v Newspaper Publishing Plc [1989] 1 F.S.R. 457 .... 1–128, 1–135, 2–22, 2–194, 3–66, 3–90,
3–98, 3–192, 5–45, 5–121, 5–196, 7–221, 7–222, 7–225, 11–12, 19–1
Att-Gen v Newspaper Publishing Plc [1990] T.L.R. 158, CA (Lexis) 2–175, 2–194, 5–45, 5–128,
5–135, 5–153, 6–135, 6–151, 7–214, 10–137, 11–15, 11–225, 11–258,
12–90, 14–123
Att-Gen v Newspaper Publishing Plc, *The Times*, February 28, 1990, CA 12–87
Att-Gen v Newspaper Publishing Plc; sub nom. R. v Blackledge (William Stuart) [1997] 1
W.L.R. 926; [1997] 3 All E.R. 159; [1997] E.M.L.R. 429; (1997) 147 N.L.J. 757; *The
Times*, May 2, 1997; *Independent*, April 29, 1997, CA (Crim Div) 1–156, 1–159, 1–177,
2–196, 3–66, 4–90, 5–44, 5–45, 5–59, 5–60, 5–194, 5–198, 5–246, 7–92,
7–187, 7–93, 7–214, 7–221, 10–9, 10–217, 10–218, 10–224, 11–2, 11–3,
11–34, 11–233, 11–238, 13–14, 16–330
Att-Gen v Observer Ltd. *See* Att-Gen v Guardian Newspapers Ltd (Public Libraries Case)
Att-Gen v Observer Ltd: Re an Application by Derbyshire CC. *See* Att-Gen v Guardian
Newspapers Ltd (Public Libraries Case)
Att-Gen v Pang Cheng Lian [1975] 12 M.L.J. 69 5–269
Att-Gen v Pelling [2004] EWHC 2568 (Admin) 15–41, 15–113
Att-Gen v Pelling [2005] EWHC 414, QBD (Admin) 6–76, 6–108, 7–63, 7–64, 8–83, 8–98,
8–122, 13–120, 15–28, 15–36, 15–41, 15–115
Att-Gen v Punch Ltd; sub nom. Steen v Att-Gen [2002] UKHL 50; [2003] 1 A.C. 1046;
[2003] 2 W.L.R. 49; [2003] 1 All E.R. 289; [2003] E.M.L.R. 7; [2003] H.R.L.R. 14;
The Times, December 13, 2002; *Independent*, December 17, 2002, HL 1–126, 2–6, 2–11,
6–122, 6–124, 6–141, 6–142, 6–145, 6–147, 11–34, 12–48, 16–334
Att-Gen v RSPCA; sub nom. Att-Gen v Royal Society for the Prevention of Cruelty to
Animals; *The Times*, June 22, 1985, DC 11–198, 19–1
Att-Gen v Scotcher [2005] UKHL 36; [2005] 1 W.L.R. 1867; [2005] 3 All E.R. 1; (2005) 155
N.L.J. 828; *The Times*, May 20, 2005, HL ... 1–126, 2–44, 2–101, 11–373, 11–378, 11–387,
11–392, 11–393, 16–392, 16–396
Att-Gen v Scriven, CO/1632/99, CO/3563/98, DC 5–204, 5–207
Att-Gen v Shield (1849) 11 Beav. 441; (1849) 50 E.R. 888 3–159
Att-Gen v Sillem (1864) 10 H.L. Cas. 704 12–48
Att-Gen v Skinners' Co (1837) C.P. Coop. 1; (1837) 47 E.R. 372 3–146
Att-Gen v South China Morning Post [1989] 2 F.S.R. 653 1–136

TABLE OF CASES

Att-Gen v Sport Newspapers [1991] 1 W.L.R. 1194; [1992] 1 All E.R. 503; [1992] C.O.D. 9; (1991) 135 S.J. 28; *The Times*, June 6, 1991; *Independent*, June 6, 1991; *Guardian*, June 19, 1991, DC 1–128, 2–3, 2–27, 2–40, 2–175, 2–194, 3–28, 3–66, 5–44, 5–51, 4–71, 5–76, 5–77, 5–79, 5–81, 5–88, 5–89, 5–97, 5–98, 5–99, 5–115, 5–145, 5–152, 5–163, 5–172, 5–173, 5–175, 5–176, 5–177, 5–178, 5–181, 5–188, 5–190, 5–246, 6–34, 6–151, 7–140, 7–143, 7–144, 7–227, 10–83, 10–218, 10–223, 11–30, 11–86, 11–218, 11–223, 11–258, 11–380, 13–9, 16–82, 16–301

Att-Gen v Steadman, unreported, February 7, 1994 .... 2–43, 4–111, 4–313, 5–106, 7–171

Att-Gen v Stott, unreported, December 1995, Potts J 19–1

Att-Gen v Times Newspapers Ltd [1974] A.C. 273; [1973] 3 W.L.R. 298; [1973] 3 All E.R. 54; 117 S.J. 617, HL; reversing [1973] Q.B. 710; [1973] 2 W.L.R. 452; [1973] 1 All E.R. 815; 117 S.J. 188, CA (Civ Div); reversing [1972] 3 W.L.R. 855; [1972] 3 All E.R. 1136; [1973] Crim. L.R. 38; 116 S.J. 885, QBD 1–83, 1–87, 1–88, 1–92, 1–94, 1–99, 1–100, 1–102, 1–104, 1–106, 1–109, 2–6, 2–8, 2–9, 2–11, 2–25, 2–39, 2–200, 2–201, 3–28, 3–64, 3–68, 3–89, 3–157, 3–173, 3–174, 4–14, 4–92, 4–96, 4–97, 4–112, 4–116, 4–121, 4–135, 4–138, 4–141, 4–142, 4–143, 4–144, 4–272, 4–294, 4–298, 4–312, 4–319, 4–325, 4–329, 4–333, 4–335, 5–8, 5–9, 5–10, 5–12, 5–16, 5–19, 5–26, 5–27, 5–30, 5–35, 5–36, 5–37, 5–38, 5–40, 5–41, 5–44, 5–47, 5–49, 5–52, 5–55, 5–64, 5–65, 5–66, 5–86, 5–115, 5–116, 5–200, 5–201, 5–268, 6–1, 6–4, 6–27, 6–39, 9–240, 10–1, 11–216, 11–222, 11–231, 11–241, 11–277, 11–279, 11–294, 11–300, 12–6, 14–132, 14–136, 16–82, 16–308

Att-Gen v Times Newspapers Ltd, *The Times*, February 12, 1983 (Lexis) ... 2–47, 4–66, 4–99, 4–127, 4–137, 4–314, 11–278, 11–286, 16–221

Att-Gen v Times Newspapers Ltd; Att-Gen v Newspaper Publishing Plc; Att-Gen v Growfar; Att-Gen v Sunday Telegraph; sub nom. Att-Gen v Observer and Guardian Newspapers [1992] 1 A.C. 191; [1991] 2 W.L.R. 994; [1991] 2 All E.R. 398; (1991) 141 N.L.J. 528; (1991) 135 S.J.L.B. 508; *The Times*, April 12, 1991; *Independent*, April 23, 1991; *Guardian*, April 12, 1991, HL; affirming *The Times*, February 28, 1990, CA (Civ Div); affirming [1989] 1 F.S.R. 457; *The Times*, May 9, 1989; *Independent*, May 9, 1989; *Guardian*, May 9, 1989, Ch D ... 1–126, 1–135, 2–177, 2–194, 3–50, 3–66, 3–90, 3–98, 3–118, 3–119, 3–123, 3–248, 5–45, 5–111, 5–150, 5–160, 5–161, 6–121, 6–125, 6–136, 6–139, 6–148, 7–87, 7–93, 7–204, 7–222, 7–225, 8–137, 10–107, 11–33, 11–34, 11–40, 11–45, 12–48, 12–82, 12–087, 12–90, 12–145, 12–150, 12–181, 12–243, 14–112, 14–123

Att-Gen v Times Newspapers Ltd; sub nom. Att-Gen v Kelsey; Att-Gen v Leppard [2001] EWCA Civ 97; [2001] 1 W.L.R. 885; [2001] E.M.L.R. 19; (2001) 98(9) L.S.G. 38; (2001) 145 S.J.L.B. 30; *The Times*, January 31, 2001; *Independent*, January 30, 2001, CA (Civ Div) 1–136, 6–94, 6–141

Att-Gen v TVS Television Ltd; Att-Gen v H W Southey; *The Times*, July 7, 1989; *Independent*, July 7, 1989, DC 4–307, 19–1

Att-Gen v Unger [1998] 1 Cr. App. R. 308; [1998] E.M.L.R. 280, *Independent*, July 8, 1997, DC .... 1–155, 1–160, 2–38, 2–47, 2–96, 2–98, 4–53, 4–60, 4–61, 4–67, 4–76, 4–78, 4–86, 4–100, 4–102, 4–114, 4–127, 4–137, 4–160, 4–166, 4–169, 4–172, 4–173, 5–104, v

Att-Gen v Wain (No 1) [1991] 2 M.L.J. 525 .... 4–232, 5–269

Att-Gen v Walthamstow UDC (1895) 11 T.L.R. 533 .... 12–022, 12–126

Att-Gen v Westminster City Council [1924] 2 Ch. 416 2–214

Att-Gen v Wheatley & Co Ltd (1903) 48 S.J. 116 12–199

Att-Gen's Reference (No.1 of 1988), Re [1989] A.C. 971; [1989] 2 W.L.R. 729; [1989] 2 All E.R. 1; (1989) 5 B.C.C. 625; [1990] B.C.L.C. 172; [1989] P.C.C. 249; (1989) 89 Cr. App. R. 60; [1989] Crim. L.R. 647; (1989) 139 N.L.J. 541; *Independent*, April 14, 1989, HL 2–129

Att-Gen's Reference (No.33 of 1996), Re; sub nom. R. v Latham (Daniel George) [1997] 2 Cr. App. R. (S.) 10; [1997] Crim. L.R. 140; *The Times*, November 15, 1996; *Independent*, November 12, 1996, CA (Crim Div) 5–101

TABLE OF CASES

Att-Gen's Reference (No.1 of 1999), Re [2000] Q.B. 365; [1999] 3 W.L.R. 769; [1999] 2 Cr. App. R. 418; (1999) 163 J.P. 769; (1999) 163 J.P.N. 1010; (1999) 96(26) L.S.G. 27; *The Times*, July 6, 1999; *Independent*, July 12, 1999 (C.S.), CA (Crim Div) 11–145, 11–154, 11–182

Att-Gen's Reference (No.2 of 1999), Re [2000] Q.B. 796; [2000] 3 W.L.R. 195; [2000] 3 All E.R. 182; [2001] B.C.C. 210; [2000] 2 B.C.L.C. 257; [2000] 2 Cr. App. R. 207; [2000] I.R.L.R. 417; [2000] Crim. L.R. 475; (2000) 97(9) L.S.G. 39; *The Times*, February 29, 2000, CA (Crim Div) 4–211

Att-Gen's Reference (No.1 of 2002), Re [2002] EWCA Crim 2392; [2003] Crim. L.R. 410, CA (Crim Div) 11–21, 11–167

Att-Gen's Reference (No.3 of 2003), Re [2004] EWCA Crim 868; [2005] Q.B. 73; [2004] 3 W.L.R. 451; [2004] 2 Cr. App. R. 23; *The Times*, April 22, 2004, CA (Crim Div) 5–130

Att-Gen for England and Wales v Tomlinson [1999] 3 N.Z.L.R. 722 .... 3–40, 3–223, 6–128, 9–209, 12–77

Att-Gen for New South Wales v John Fairfax & Sons Ltd (1985) 6 N.S.W.L.R. 695 .... 4–58, 4–68, 4–77, 5–14

Att-Gen for New South Wales v Mundey [1972] 2 N.S.W.L.R. 887 .... 5–239, 5–245

Att-Gen for New South Wales v Truth and Sportsman (1957) 75 W.N. (N.S.W.) 70 .... 4–67, 5–265

Att-Gen of Tuvalu v Philatelic Distribution Corp Ltd [1990] 1 W.L.R. 926; [1990] 2 All E.R. 216; [1990] B.C.C. 30; [1990] B.C.L.C. 245; (1990) 134 S.J. 832; *The Times*, October 24, 1989; *Independent*, October 25, 1989; *Financial Times*, November 1, 1989; *Daily Telegraph*, November 6, 1989, CA (Civ Div) 12–36, 12–98, 12–112, 16–243

Att-Gen for United Kingdom v Heinemann Publishers (1988) 78 A.L.R. 449 1–136

Att-Gen for United Kingdom v Wellington Newspapers Ltd [1988] 1 N.Z.L.R. 129 1–136

Austin Rover Group Ltd v Amalgamated Union of Engineering Workers (AUEW) (Technical, Administrative and Supervisory Section) (TASS) [1985] I.R.L.R. 162 .... 12–141, 14–109

Australian Capital Television Pty Ltd v The Commonwealth (1992) 177 C.L.R. 106, HC 2–99

Australian Consolidated Press Ltd v Morgan (1965) 112 C.L.R. 483 14–121

Australian Meat Industry Employees' Union v Mudginberri Station Pty Ltd (1986) 161 C.L.R. 98 3–15

Avory v Andrews (1882) 30 W.R. 564 11–34

B, Ex p., February 17, 1994, Scott Baker J. 2–86

B (A Child) (Court's Jurisdiction), Re; sub nom. B v B (Residence Order: Jurisdiction) [2004] EWCA Civ 681; [2004] 2 F.L.R. 741; [2004] 2 F.C.R. 391; [2004] Fam. Law 788, CA (Civ Div) 9–222

B (A Child) (Disclosure), Re. *See* Kent CC v B (A Child)

B (A Child) v DPP [2000] 2 A.C. 428; [2000] 2 W.L.R. 452; [2000] 1 All E.R. 833; [2000] 2 Cr. App. R. 65; [2000] Crim. L.R. 403; (2000) 97(11) L.S.G. 36; (2000) 144 S.J.L.B. 108; *The Times*, February 25, 2000; *Independent*, April 10, 2000 (C.S.), HL 7–206

B (A Minor) (Contempt of Court: Affidavit Evidence), Re [1996] 1 W.L.R. 627; [1996] 1 F.L.R. 239; [1996] 1 F.C.R. 158; [1996] Fam. Law 147; (1995) 92(44) L.S.G. 30; (1996) 140 S.J.L.B. 12; *The Times*, November 15, 1995; *Independent*, December 4, 1995 (C.S.), Fam Div 1–44, 2–21, 3–64, 3–75, 3–81, 3–89, 3–192, 3–207, 3–208, 15–15, 15–18, 15–28, 15–32, 15–35, 15–44

B (JA) (An Infant), Re [1965] Ch. 1112; [1965] 3 W.L.R. 253; [1965] 2 All E.R. 168; 109 S.J. 556, Ch D 3–117, 5–139, 11–216, 11–225, 11–238, 11–244, 11–256, 11–281, 11–332, 14–6, 15–19

B (Minors) (Wardship: Power to Detain), Re [1994] 2 F.L.R. 479; [1994] 2 F.C.R. 1142; [1994] Fam. Law 607; *The Times*, May 24, 1994; *Independent*, July 25, 1994 (C.S.), CA (Civ Div) 14–6

B v Auckland District Law Society; sub nom. Russell McVeagh McKenzie Bartleet & Co v Auckland District Law Society [2003] UKPC 38; [2003] 2 A.C. 736; [2003] 3 W.L.R. 859; [2004] 4 All E.R. 269; (2003) 100(26) L.S.G. 38; (2003) 147 S.J.L.B. 627; *The Times*, May 21, 2003, PC (NZ) 9–13

B v B (Contempt: Committal) [1991] 2 F.L.R. 588; [1991] F.C.R. 386; [1992] Fam. Law 58, CA (Civ Div) 3–221, 14–58, 15–47, 15–63, 15–64, 15–67, 15–74

[lvii]

TABLE OF CASES

B v B and F (No.2); sub nom. B (BPM) v B (MM); B (B) v B (M) [1969] P. 103; [1969] 2 W.L.R. 862; [1969] 1 All E.R. 891; (1968) 133 J.P. 245; 112 S.J. 985; *The Times*, December 7, 1968, DC 13–133

B v United Kingdom (36337/97); P v United Kingdom (35974/97) [2001] 2 F.L.R. 261; [2001] 2 F.C.R. 221; (2002) 34 E.H.R.R. 19; 11 B.H.R.C. 667; [2001] Fam. Law 506; *The Times*, May 15, 2001, ECHR 7–25, 7–64, 8–76, 8–126

B (BPM) v B (BMM). *See* B v B and F (No.2)

B (L) (Otherwise P) v Att-Gen [1967] P. 119; [1966] 2 W.L.R. 58; [1965] 3 All E.R. 253; 109 S.J. 536, PDAD 7–74

BAT Australia Services Ltd v Cowell [2003] VSCA 43 11–86

BBC, Petitioners (No.1), 2000 J.C. 419; 2000 S.L.T. 845; 2000 S.C.C.R. 533; 2000 G.W.D. 11–383; *The Times*, April 11, 2000, HCJ 16–417

BBC, Petitioners (No.2), 2000 J.C. 521; 2000 S.L.T. 860; 2000 S.C.C.R. 533; [2000] H.R.L.R. 423; 2000 G.W.D. 15–584; *The Times*, June 13, 2000, HCJ 16–419

BBC, Petitioners (No.3), 2002 J.C. 27; 2002 S.L.T. 2; 2001 S.C.C.R. 440; 2001 G.W.D. 17–671 .... 7–156, 7–201, 7–205, 16–319, 16–377, 16–378

BBC v Law Officers of the Crown, unreported, November 18, 1988, Guernsey Court of Appeal (Civ. Div.) 4–90, 5–6, 5–52

BBPM v BMM DC 14–7, 14–40

BCGEU v Att-Gen for British Columbia (1988) 44 C.C.C. (3d) 289; (1988) 53 D.L.R. (4th) 1; [1988] 2 S.C.R. 214 11–309

B-J (A Child) (Non Molestation Order: Power of Arrest), Re [2001] Fam. 415; [2001] 2 W.L.R. 1660; [2001] 1 All E.R. 235; [2000] 2 F.L.R. 443; [2000] 2 F.C.R. 599; [2000] Fam. Law 807; *Independent*, July 4, 2000, CA (Civ Div) 14–75, 14–81

BK v R. (1995) 129 D.L.R. (4th) 500 .... 10–36, 10–85

Babanaft International Co SA v Bassatne [1990] Ch. 13; [1989] 2 W.L.R. 232; [1989] 1 All E.R. 433; [1988] 2 Lloyd's Rep. 435; [1989] E.C.C. 151; (1988) 138 N.L.J. Rep. 203; (1989) 133 S.J. 46; *The Times*, July 2, 1988; *Independent*, June 30, 1988; *Financial Times*, July 6, 1988, CA (Civ Div) 12–159

Bache v Essex CC [2000] 2 All E.R. 847; [2000] I.C.R. 313; [2000] I.R.L.R. 251; (2000) 97(5) L.S.G. 33; (2000) 150 N.L.J. 99; *The Times*, February 2, 2000; *Independent*, March 13, 2000 (C.S.), CA (Civ Div) 10–136, 10–137

Badische Anilin & Soda Fabrik v Levinstein (1883) 24 Ch.D. 156 7–57

Badry v DPP of Mauritius; sub nom. Lutchmeeparsad Badry v DPP [1983] 2 A.C. 297; [1983] 2 W.L.R. 161; [1982] 3 All E.R. 973; 126 S.J. 819, PC (Mau) 13–75

Bahama Islands, Re [1893] A.C. 138 .... 4–20, 4–21, 9–4, 14–6, 14–101

Baker v Baker (1860) 2 Sw. & Tr. 380; (1860) 164 E.R. 1043 12–129

Baker v Baker (No.2) [1997] 1 F.L.R. 148, CA 7–195, 12–71

Baldry v Jackson [1976] 1 N.S.W.L.R. 19 11–305

Baldwin v Rusbridger [2001] E.M.L.R. 47; *The Times*, July 23, 2001, QBD 2–22

Ball v Coutts (1812) 1 V. & B. 292; (1781) 35 E.R. 114 11–334

Balogh v St Albans Crown Court [1975] Q.B. 73; [1974] 3 W.L.R. 314; [1974] 3 All E.R. 283; 118 S.J. 582, CA (Civ Div) ... 2–5, 2–28, 2–30, 2–209, 3–67, 3–87, 3–113, 7–231, 7–232, 7–234, 10–4, 10–15, 10–16, 10–26, 10–30, 10–31, 10–36, 10–49, 10–103, 11–16, 11–17, 11–18, 11–163, 13–9, 13–11, 13–26, 13–28, 13–30, 13–31, 13–32, 13–35, 13–38, 13–41, 13–119, 15–5, 15–96

Baltic Shipping Co v Translink Shipping Ltd [1995] 1 Lloyd's Rep. 673, QBD (Comm) 12–165, 12–166

Bangoura v Washington Post (2004) 235 D.L.R. (4th) 564, SC Ont. 1–181

Bank Mellat v Kazmi [1989] Q.B. 541; [1989] 2 W.L.R. 613; [1989] 1 All E.R. 925; (1989) 133 S.J. 185, CA (Civ Div) 12–148

Bank of China v NBM LLC [2001] EWCA Civ 1933; [2002] 1 W.L.R. 844; [2002] 1 All E.R. 717; [2002] 1 All E.R. (Comm) 472; [2002] 1 Lloyd's Rep. 506; [2002] C.P. Rep. 19; [2002] C.L.C. 477; (2002) 99(9) L.S.G. 29; (2002) 146 S.J.L.B. 22; *The Times*, January 10, 2002, CA (Civ Div) 12–166

Bank of Western Australia Ltd v Anchorage Investments (1992) 10 W.A.R. 59 12–48

Banks v Vannet, 1998 G.W.D. 36–1853, HCJ Appeal 16–51

Barber (1721) 1 Str. 444, 93 E.R. 624 .... 1–52, 1–59

Barclays De Zoete Wedd Securities Ltd v Nadir, *The Times*, March 25, 1992; *Independent*, March 16, 1992, Ch D 3–207, 15–43

[lviii]

TABLE OF CASES

Barfod v Denmark (1989) 13 E.H.R.R. 393 5–240
Barings Plc (In Liquidation) v Coopers & Lybrand (No.1); sub nom. Barings Futures
    (Singapore) PTE Ltd (In Liquidation) v Mattar (No.1) [2000] 1 W.L.R. 2353; [2000]
    3 All E.R. 910; [2000] Lloyd's Rep. Bank. 225; (2000) 150 N.L.J. 681; *The Times*,
    May 17, 2000; *Independent*, May 10, 2000, CA (Civ Div) 7–19
Barker v Shepherd (1633) Toth. 102; (1633) 21 E.R. 136 11–317
Barlee v Barlee (1822) 1 Add. 301; (1822) 162 E.R. 105 3–160
Barlow Clowes Gilt Managers Ltd v Clowes [1990] T.L.R. 82 7–178
Barnardo v McHugh [1891] A.C. 388 6–55
Barnes v Williams (1832) 1 Dowl. 615 11–100
Barnet LBC v Hurst [2002] EWCA Civ 1009; [2003] 1 W.L.R. 722; [2002] 4 All E.R. 457;
    [2002] C.P. Rep. 74; [2003] H.L.R. 19; (2002) 99(36) L.S.G. 39; (2002) 152 N.L.J.
    1275; (2002) 146 S.J.L.B. 198; [2002] N.P.C. 99; *The Times*, August 12, 2002, CA
    (Civ Div) 12–10, 12–12, 12–13, 13–121, 13–133, 15–88, 15–89, 15–95
Barrell Enterprises, Re [1973] 1 W.L.R. 19, CA (Civ Div) 3–176, 12–7, 14–137
Barrister (Wasted Costs Order) (No.1 of 1991), Re; sub nom. Ex p. H (A Barrister) [1993]
    Q.B. 293; [1992] 3 W.L.R. 662; [1992] 3 All E.R. 429; (1992) 95 Cr. App. R. 288;
    (1992) 142 N.L.J. 636; (1992) 136 S.J.L.B. 147; *The Times*, May 6, 1992; *Independent*,
    April 23, 1992; *Guardian*, May 6, 1992, CA (Crim Div) 11–54
Barrow v Humphreys (1820) 3 B. & Ald. 598; (1820) 106 E.R. 780 .... 11–100, 11–101
Bartrum v Healeswood [1973] 10 F.S.R. 585, CA (civ Div) 3–246, 11–20, 12–43, 12–44
Basset v Lumley, *The Times*, July 24, 1959 11–75
Bathurst v Murray (1602) 8 Ves. Jun. 74; (1602) 32 E.R. 279 11–342
Batt v Rookes (1577) Cary 61; (1577) 21 E.R. 33 11–100
Battersby's Estate, Re (1892) 31 L.R. Ir. 73 9–201
Baxter (Adam) (1867) 5 Irv. 351 16–118
Bayer AG v Winter (No.2) [1986] 1 W.L.R. 540; [1986] 2 All E.R. 43; (1985) 130 S.J. 373,
    Ch D 3–201
Bayly v Went (1884) W.N. 197 .... 11–320, 14–132
Beattie v Rodger (1835) 14 S. 6 16–247
Becker v Noel; sub nom. Practice Note (CA: Inherent Jurisdiction to Revoke Leave Given
    Ex parte) [1971] 1 W.L.R. 803; [1971] 2 All E.R. 1248, CA (Civ Div) 15–63
Bedford (Duke of) v Ellis [1901] A.C. 1, HL 12–120
Beecher's Case (1608) 8 Co. Rep. 58a 13–79
Beeston Shipping Ltd v Babanaft 12–34
Beggs v Scottish Ministers S.L.T. 305, 2005 2–225
Beggs v Scottish Ministers (Prisoners: Privileged Correspondence) (No.2), 2005 S.L.T. 305;
    2005 G.W.D. 10–145, IH (1 Div) 14–2, 16–239, 16–242, 16–243
Belgolaise v Purchandani, 142 Sol. Jo. L.B. 252; *The Times*, July 30, 1998 12–18
Bell v Gow (1862) 1 M. 84 .... 16–254, 16–255
Bell v Stewart (1920) 28 C.L.R. 419 .... 4–119, 10–129
Bell v Tuohy; sub nom. Tuohy v Bell [2002] EWCA Civ 423; [2002] 1 W.L.R. 2703; [2002]
    3 All E.R. 975; [2002] C.P. Rep. 46; [2003] B.P.I.R. 749; (2002) 152 N.L.J. 587;
    (2002) 146 S.J.L.B. 109; [2002] N.P.C. 50; *Independent*, May 27, 2002 (C.S.); VAC 13–91,
                                                                              14–118, 15–24, 15–52, 15–76, 15–78
Bell and Moncrieff v Jameson (1848) 10 D. 1413 16–255
Benabo v W Jay Ltd [1941] Ch. 52 15–26
Benham v United Kingdom (19380/92) (1996) 22 E.H.R.R. 293; *The Times*, June 24, 1996;
    Independent, June 19, 1996, ECHR 3–4, 3–75, 3–247, 13–89, 15–115, 16–40
Bennett v Normand, 1993 G.W.D. 24–492 16–112
Bennett v Southwark LBC [2002] EWCA Civ 223; [2002] I.C.R. 881; [2002] I.R.L.R. 407;
    (2002) 146 S.J.L.B. 59; *The Times*, February 28, 2002, CA (Civ Div) 5–207, 10–135,
                                                                                                  10–137, 13–65
Bensaid v United Kingdom (2001) 33 E.H.R.R. 10 7–106
Benson v Richards [2002] EWCA Civ 1402; (2002) 146 S.J.L.B. 231; *The Times*, October
    17, 2002, CA (Civ Div) 15–57, 13–15, 15–23
Berezovsky v Forbes Inc (No.2) [2001] EWCA Civ 1251; [2001] E.M.L.R. 45, CA (Civ
    Div) 1–144, 2–164, 7–4, 9–9
Bergens v Tidende (2000) E.H.R.R. 430 9–2

[lix]

TABLE OF CASES

Berry Trade Ltd v Moussavi (No.1) [2002] EWCA Civ 477; [2002] 1 W.L.R. 1910; [2002]
  C.P.L.R. 427; [2002] B.P.I.R. 881; (2002) 99(18) L.S.G. 36; (2002) 146 S.J.L.B. 83;
  The Times, April 10, 2002; *Independent*, April 23, 2002, CA (Civ Div) 3–75, 3–238, 15–41
Best v Gompertz (1837) 2 Y. & C. Ex. 582; (1837) 160 E.R. 528 3–159
Best Training Ltd v URO Properties Ltd [2002] All E.R. (D) 364 14–40
Bestobell Paints v Bigg [1975] F.S.R. 421; (1975) Sol. Jo. 678 6–7
Bettinson v Bettinson [1965] Ch. 465 12–66
Bevan v Hastings Jones [1978] 1 W.L.R. 294; [1978] 1 All E.R. 479; 122 S.J. 146, Ch D 15–14
Bhamjee v Forsdick [2003] EWCA Civ 1113; [2004] 1 W.L.R. 88; [2003] C.P. Rep. 67;
  [2003] B.P.I.R. 1252; (2003) 100(36) L.S.G. 41; *The Times*, July 31, 2003; *Independent*, July 29, 2003, CA (Civ Div) 14–134
Bhimji v Chatwani (No.1) [1991] 1 W.L.R. 989; [1991] 1 All E.R. 705, Ch D 12–94, 12–146,
  12–175, 12–176, 12–179, 12–181, 15–43
Bhimji v Chatwani (No.2); sub nom. Chatwani v Bhimji [1992] 1 W.L.R. 1158; [1992] 4 All
  E.R. 912; [1992] B.C.L.C. 387, Ch D 3–80, 3–83, 3–191
Biba Ltd v Stratford Investments Ltd [1973] Ch. 281; [1972] 3 W.L.R. 902; [1972] 3 All E.R.
  1041; [1972] F.S.R. 511; [1973] R.P.C. 799; 116 S.J. 728, Ch D 12–111, 12–182, 12–200
Bibby Bulk Carriers v Cansulex [1989] Q.B. 155; [1989] 2 W.L.R. 182; [1988] 2 All E.R.
  820; [1988] 1 Lloyd's Rep. 565; [1988] 1 F.T.L.R. 113; (1988) 132 S.J. 1640, QBD
  (Comm) 12–220
Bickerton [1985] Can. Curr. Law 10774 11–88
Billing v Pate (1580) Choyce, p.133 1–47
Birch v Birch (1883) 8 P.D. 163 14–120
Birch v Walsh (1846) 10 I Eq. R. 9 1–51
Bird v Hadkinson [1999] B.P.I.R. 653 12–93
Bird v Jones (1846) 7 Q.B. 742; (1846) 115 E.R. 668 10–110
Birmingham Post and Mail v Birmingham City Council (1994) 17 B.M.L.R. 116 .... 7–30, 7–89,
  7–106
Bishop v Willis (1749) 5 Beav. 83n; (1749) 49 E.R. 508 11–50
Black v McGlennan, 1995 G.W.D. 2–85 16–81
Blackburn v Bowering [1994] 1 W.L.R. 1324; [1994] 3 All E.R. 380, CA 6–127, 11–160, 13–86
Blackshaw v Lord [1984] Q.B. 1; [1983] 3 W.L.R. 283; [1983] 2 All E.R. 311, CA (Civ Div) 4–49,
  4–338
Blackwell v Tatlow (1833) 2 My. & K. 321 11–329
Bladet Tromsø v Norway (2000) E.H.R.R. 125 2–50
Blair-Wilson, Petr, 1997 S.L.T. 621, HCJ Appeal 10–142, 16–50, 16–132
Blake v Blake (1844) 7 Beav. 514; (1844) 49 E.R. 1165 9–201
Blake v Macdonald (1890) 2 White 447 .... 16–129, 16–28, 16–44
Blandford v De Tastet (1813) 5 Taunt. 259; (1813) 128 E.R. 689 .... 11–111, 11–114
Blantyre (Lord) v Dunn (1845) 9 D. 299 16–257
Bloom v Illinois, 391 U.S. 194 (1968) 3–59
Bloomsbury County Court Judge Ex p. Brady, *The Times*, December 16, 1987, CA 13–80
Bluffield v Curtis [1988] 1 F.L.R. 170; [1988] Fam. Law 20, CA (Civ Div) 14–46, 14–47
Bobolas v Economist Newspaper [1987] 1 W.L.R. 1101; [1987] 3 All E.R. 121; (1987) 84
  L.S.G. 2536; (1987) 131 S.J. 1064, CA (Civ Div) 7–69
Bodden v Commissioner of Police of the Metropolis [1990] 2 Q.B. 397; [1990] 2 W.L.R. 76;
  [1989] 3 All E.R. 833; (1990) 154 J.P. 217; (1990) 154 J.P.N. 45; (1990) 87(5) L.S.G.
  39; (1989) 139 N.L.J. 1526; (1990) 134 S.J. 342, CA (Civ Div) 10–121, 10–126, 10–219,
  10–222, 13–27, 13–106
Bokhari v Blessed, *Independent*, January 16, 1995, CA 14–103
Bolton v Bolton [1891] 3 Ch. 270 11–338
Bonnar v Simpson (1836) 1 Swin. 39 16–117
Bonnard v Perryman [1891] 2 Ch. 269; [1891–94] All E.R. Rep. 965, CA 2–150, 4–2, 4–181,
  4–324, 4–325, 4–326, 4–328, 4–329, 6–7, 6–17, 6–18, 6–131, 6–132,
  6–133
Bonzel (T) v Intervention Ltd (No.2) [1991] R.P.C. 231, Ch D (Patents Ct) 12–224
Borre, The [1921] P. 390 12–261
Bosch v Simms Manufacturing 12–197
Boswell's Trs v Pearson (1886) 24 S.L.R. 32 16–67
Botibol, Re [1947] 1 All E.R. 26 11–319

TABLE OF CASES

Bourns Inc v Raychem Corp (No.3) [1999] 3 All E.R. 154; [1999] C.L.C. 1029; [1999] 2
    Costs L.R. 72; [1999] F.S.R. 641; (1999) 22(7) I.P.D. 22063; *The Times*, May 12, 1999;
    Independent, May 24, 1999 (C.S.), CA (Civ Div) 3–199
Boutet: Re Bernheim; Re CBC (1983) 35 CR (3d) 302, CS Qué 3–86, 16–39
Bowden v Russell (1877) 46 L.J. Ch. 414 .... 1–72, 11–65
Bowen v Bowen (1986) CA Transcript No.6775 15–47
Bowen v Bowen [1990] 2 F.L.R. 93; [1989] Fam. Law 73, CA (Civ Div) 14–71
Bowles v Johnson (1748) 1 W. Black 36; (1748) 96 E.R. 19 .... 11–103, 11–104
Boylan v Boylan (1980) 11 Fam. Law 76, CA (Civ Div) 14–73
Bramblevale, Re [1970] Ch. 128; [1969] 3 W.L.R. 699; [1969] 3 All E.R. 1062; 113 S.J. 775,
    CA (Civ Div) 3–89, 3–188, 3–241, 3–244, 12–33, 12–43, 12–44, 12–52, 12–53, 12–190
Brandon v Knight (1752) Dick. 160; (1752) 21 E.R. 230 11–334
Brantschen, Ex p., *The Times*, December 7, 1970 11–305
Branzburg v Hayes, 408 U.S. 665 (1972) 9–15, 9–51
Brasyer v Maclean (1875) L.R. 6 P.C. 398 11–329
Bread Manufacturers Ltd, Ex p. (1937) S.R. (N.S.W.) 242 ... 1–103, 4–295, 4–298, 4–305, 7–110,
    16–145, 16–192, 16–193, 16–198, 16–366
Brendan v Spiro [1938] 1 K.B. 176 .... 11–67, 11–68
Brewer v Brewer [1989] 2 F.L.R. 251; [1989] F.C.R. 515; [1989] Fam. Law 352, CA (Civ
    Div) 19–2
Briffett v DPP; sub nom. Briffett v Crown Prosecution Service; Briffet v DPP [2001] EWHC
    Admin 841; (2002) 166 J.P. 66; [2002] E.M.L.R. 12; (2002) 166 J.P.N. 92; *The Times*,
    November 26, 2001, DC 8–68
Briggs' Case (1615) 1 Roll. Rep. 336; (1615) 81 E.R. 526 15–48
Brill v Television One [1976] 1 N.Z.L.R. 683 .... 2–51, 9–5
British Concrete Pipe Association's Agreement, Re; sub nom. Re Agreement between
    Members of the British Concrete Pipe Association [1983] 1 All E.R. 203, CA (Civ
    Div); affirming [1982] I.C.R. 182; *The Times*, December 18, 1980, Ch D (RPC) 12–182,
    19–2
British Steel Corp v Granada Television Ltd [1981] A.C. 1096; [1980] 3 W.L.R. 774; [1981]
    1 All E.R. 417; 124 S.J. 812, HL 2–152, 4–270, 9–4, 9–5, 9–6, 9–23, 9–45, 9–48,
    9–126, 9–129, 9–139, 10–175, 11–85
Broad v Wickham (1831) 4 Sim. 511; (1831) 58 E.R. 191 .... 11–320, 11–321
Broadcasting Corp of New Zealand v Alex Harvey Industries [1980] 1 N.Z.L.R. 163 .... 2–51, 9–4,
    9–5, 9–23
Broadcasting Corp of New Zealand v Att-Gen [1982] 1 N.Z.L.R. 120 .... 7–7, 7–16
Brocas v Lloyd (1856) 23 Beav. 129; (1856) 53 E.R. 51 .... 11–103, 11–104
Bromilow v Phillips (1891) 8 T.L.R. 168 .... 11–216, 11–244, 11–287
Brompton County Court Judge [1893] 2 Q.B. 195 13–80
Brook v Evans (1860) 29 L.J. Ch. 616 .... 4–288, 6–1
Brook v Montague (1606) Cro. Jac. 90; (1606) 79 E.R. 77 10–150
Brown (William) (1832) B.N. 255 16–123
Brown v Bennett (Wasted Costs) (No.1) [2002] 1 W.L.R. 713; [2002] 2 All E.R. 273; [2002]
    Lloyd's Rep. P.N. 155; [2002] P.N.L.R. 17; (2002) 99(2) L.S.G. 27; (2001) 151 N.L.J.
    1733; (2001) 145 S.J.L.B. 267; *The Times*, November 21, 2001, Ch D 11–54
Brown v Crowley (No.1) [1963] 1 W.L.R. 1102; [1963] 3 All E.R. 655; 107 S.J. 650, CA 15–99,
    15–101
Brown v Crowley (No.2) [1964] 1 W.L.R. 147, CA 13–120
Brown v United Kingdom (Admissibility) (44223/98) (2002) 35 E.H.R.R. CD197, ECHR 8–23
Brownlow, Ex p. *See* R. v Sheffield Crown Court Ex p. Brownlow
Bruce v Linton and McDougall (1861) 24 D. 184 16–32
Brutus v Cozens [1973] A.C. 854; [1972] 3 W.L.R. 521; [1972] 2 All E.R. 1297; (1972) 56
    Cr. App. R. 799; [1973] Crim. L.R. 56; 116 S.J. 647, HL 10–113, 13–107
Bryan (Lloyd) [1998] 2 Cr. App. R. (S) 109 19–1
Brydges v Brydges and Wood [1909] P. 187 6–137
Bryson v Carmichael, 1993 G.W.D. 24–1493 .... 16–79, 16–43
Bucknell v Bucknell [1969] 1 W.L.R. 1204; [1969] 2 All E.R. 998; 113 S.J. 586, PDAD 14–120,
    14–123, 14–136, 15–86
Buenos Ayres Gas Company Ltd v Wilde (1880) 29 W.R. 43 .... 4–264, 4–280, 7–52
Bullen v Ovey (1809) 16 Ves. Jun. 141 12–98

TABLE OF CASES

Burdett v Abbott (1811) 14 East 1; (1811) 104 E.R. 501 .... 3–184, 15–48
Burdett's Case (1680) 8 St. Tr. 14 .... 1–58, 1–59
Burmah Oil Co Ltd v Bank of England [1980] A.C. 1090; [1979] 3 W.L.R. 722; [1979] 3 All
E.R. 700; 123 S.J. 786, HL 9–181
Burris v Azadani [1995] 1 W.L.R. 1372; [1995] 4 All E.R. 802; [1996] 1 F.L.R. 266; [1996]
1 F.C.R. 618; [1996] Fam. Law 145; (1995) 145 N.L.J. 1330; *The Times*, August 9,
1995, CA (Civ Div) 9–33
Burrows v Iqbal [1984] F.L.R. 844 15–74
Burton v Earl of Darnley (1869) L.R. 8 Eq. 576n 11–336
Burton v Winters [1993] 1 W.L.R. 1077; [1993] 3 All E.R. 847, CA (Civ Div) 12–7, 12–171
Bush v Green [1985] 1 W.L.R. 1143; [1985] 3 All E.R. 721; (1985) 82 L.S.G. 2818; (1985)
135 N.L.J. 827; (1985) 129 S.J. 654, CA (Civ Div) 10–130, 13–80
Bushell's Case (1670) 6 St. Tr. 999; (1670) Vaughan 135; (1670) 124 E.R. 1006 ... 10–82, 10–83,
10–179, 10–180, 10–188, 11–142
Butler v Butler (1888) 13 P.D. 73 11–261
Butler v Freeman (1756) Amb. 301 6–53
Butler's case (1696) 2 Salk. 586; (1696) 91 E.R. 504 6–126
Butterworth v Herron, 1975 S.L.T. (Notes) 56 16–427
Byne, Ex p. (1813) 1 Ves. & B. 316; (1813) 35 E.R. 123 11–304
Byrne v Herbert [1966] 2 Q.B. 121 13–92
Byrne v Ross, 1993 S.L.T. 307; 1992 S.C.L.R. 898 .... 16–248, 16–252, 16–254, 16–256

C (A Minor) (Care Proceedings: Disclosure), Re; sub Nom. Re EC (A Minor) (Care
Proceedings: Disclosure); Re EC (Disclosure of Material) [1997] Fam. 76; [1997] 2
W.L.R. 322; [1996] 2 F.L.R. 725; [1996] 3 F.C.R. 521; [1997] Fam. Law 160; *The
Times*, October 22, 1996, CA (Civ Div) 11–81
C (A Minor) (Contempt), Re [1996] 1 F.L.R. 578 .... 15–64, 15–67, 15–70
C (A Minor) (Wardship: Contempt), Re [1986] 1 F.L.R. 578; [1986] Fam. Law 187, CA (Civ
Div) 12–44, 14–47, 15–17
C (A Minor) (Wardship: Medical Treatment) (No.2), Re [1990] Fam. 39; [1989] 3 W.L.R.
252; [1989] 2 All E.R. 791; [1990] 1 F.L.R. 263; [1990] F.C.R. 229; [1990] Fam. Law
133; (1990) 154 J.P.N. 11; (1989) 139 N.L.J. 613; *The Times*, April 27, 1989;
Independent, April 27, 1989; *Guardian*, April 27, 1989, CA (Civ Div) 2–194, 6–47, 6–54,
6–84, 6–87, 6–90, 6–94, 6–108, 11–337
C (Adult Patient: Restriction of Publicity after Death), Re [1996] 2 F.L.R. 251; [1996] 1
F.C.R. 605; [1996] Fam. Law 610, Fam Div 6–54
C (An Infant), Re, *The Times*, June 18, 1969 11–337
C (Contempt: Committal Order), Re [1989] 1 F.L.R. 288, CA (Civ Div) 15–31
C (Minors) (Contempt Proceedings), Re; sub nom. Re C v C (Contempt: Evidence); C
(Minors) (Hearsay Evidence: Contempt Proceedings) [1993] 4 All E.R. 690; [1993] 1
F.L.R. 220; [1993] 1 F.C.R. 820; [1993] Fam. Law 223, CA (Civ Div) 3–233, 3–235, 3–237
C (A Minor) v DPP; sub nom. Curry v DPP [1996] A.C. 1; [1995] 2 W.L.R. 383; [1995] 2
All E.R. 43; [1995] 2 Cr. App. R. 166; (1995) 159 J.P. 269; [1995] R.T.R. 261; [1995]
1 F.L.R. 933; [1995] Crim. L.R. 801; [1995] Fam. Law 400; (1995) 159 J.P.N. 248;
(1995) 145 N.L.J. 416; *The Times*, March 17, 1995; *Independent*, March 21, 1995,
HL 2–173, 2–191
C v C (Access Order: Enforcement) [1990] 1 F.L.R. 462; [1990] F.C.R. 682; [1990] Fam.
Law 220, CA (Civ Div) 12–24
C v C (Application for Non Molestation Order: Jurisdiction) [1998] Fam. 70; [1998] 2
W.L.R. 599; [1998] 1 F.L.R. 554; [1998] 1 F.C.R. 11; [1998] Fam. Law 254; (1997)
94(47) L.S.G. 30; (1997) 141 S.J.L.B. 236; *The Times*, December 16, 1997;
Independent, November 27, 1997, Fam Div 12–57
CBS (UK) Ltd v Manoli (1985) New L.J. 555, CA 15–47, 15–67
CCSU v Minister for the Civil Service. *See* Council of Civil Service Unions v Minister for
the Civil Service
CR Smith Glaziers (Dunfermline) Ltd v Anderson, 1993 S.L.T. 592, OH 16–257
CT Bowring & Co (Insurance) v Corsi and Partners Ltd [1994] 2 Lloyd's Rep. 567 7–62
Caldwell v Normand, 1994 S.L.T. 489; 1993 S.C.C.R. 624, HCJ Appeal 16–43, 16–79, 16–81
Caledonian Rly Co v Hamilton etc. (1850) 7 Bell's App. 272 .... 16–67, 16–242, 16–249

TABLE OF CASES

Callow v Young (1886) 55 L.T. 543 .... 12–36, 12–191, 12–244, 15–5, 15–8, 15–27
Cambell Mussels v Thompson (1984) Law Soc. Gaz. 2457, CA 12–70
Cambridge Nutrition Ltd v BBC [1990] 3 All E.R. 523; *The Times*, December 5, 1987, CA
    (Civ Div) 6–94
Cambridgeshire County Council v D [1999] 2 F.L.R. 42 19–2
Cambridgeshire and Isle of Ely CC v Rust [1972] 2 Q.B. 426; [1972] 3 W.L.R. 226; [1972]
    3 All E.R. 232; 70 L.G.R. 444; [1972] Crim. L.R. 433; 116 S.J. 564, DC 2–187
Camden LBC v Alpenoak Ltd (1985) 135 New L.J. 1209 .... 12–191, 12–196
Camelot Group Plc v Centaur Communications Ltd [1999] Q.B. 124; [1998] 2 W.L.R. 379;
    [1998] 1 All E.R. 251; [1998] I.R.L.R. 80; [1998] E.M.L.R. 1; (1997) 94(43) L.S.G.
    30; (1997) 147 N.L.J. 1618; (1998) 142 S.J.L.B. 19; *The Times*, October 30, 1997;
    Independent, October 28, 1997, CA (Civ Div) 1–158, 2–52, 2–67, 2–160, 2–166, 2–180,
                            9–2, 9–3, 9–8, 9–9, 9–10, 9–21, 9–22, 9–29, 9–35, 9–68, 9–103, 9–126,
                            9–135, 9–141, 9–151, 9–152, 9–155, 9–156, 9–164, 9–168, 9–175, 9–184,
                                                      9–196, 9–245, 11–257
Cameron v Lightfoot (1777) 2 Bl. W. 1190; (1777) 96 E.R. 701 14–152
Cameron v Normand, 1993 G.W.D. 40–2639 16–79
Campbell (1673) Hume ,Vol.II, p.139 16–92
Campbell v Mackay, 1959 S.L.T. (Sh. Ct) 34 .... 16–243, 16–256
Campbell v Mirror Group Newspapers Ltd; sub nom. Campbell v MGN Ltd [2004] UKHL
    22; [2004] 2 A.C. 457; [2004] 2 W.L.R. 1232; [2004] 2 All E.R. 995; [2004] E.M.L.R.
    15; [2004] H.R.L.R. 24; [2004] U.K.H.R.R. 648; 16 B.H.R.C. 500; (2004) 101(21)
    L.S.G. 36; (2004) 154 N.L.J. 733; (2004) 148 S.J.L.B. 572; *The Times*, May 7, 2004;
    Independent, May 11, 2004, HL 6–106, 9–63
Campbell v O'Brien, 1993 G.W.D. 8–562 16–112
Campbell v Tameside MBC [1982] 2 All E.R. 791 9–14
Campbell and Fell v United Kingdom (A/80) (1985) 7 E.H.R.R. 165, ECHR 7–16
Canada (Human Rights Commission) v Taylor (1990) 75 D.L.R. (4th) 577 12–141
Canadian Broadcasting Corp v Lessard [1991] 3 S.C.R. 421 .... 9–1, 9–51
Canadian Broadcasting Corp v New Brunswick (Att-Gen) (1996) 110 C.C.C. (3rd) 193 9–51
Canadian Imperial Bank of Commerce v Bhattesa, Court of Appeal, Transcript No.694, April
    21, 1993 12–170
Canadian Newspapers Co v Canada (Att-Gen) (1988) 43 C.C.C. (3d) 24, 52 D.L.R. (4th) 690,
    [1988] S.C.R. 122 2–49
Canadian Union of Public Employees, Local 301 v Montreal (City) [1997] 1 S.C.R. 793 1–137
Cann v Cann; sub nom. Anon. (1754) 2 Ves. Sen. 520; (1754) 28 E.R. 332 .... 1–51, 14–6
Caprice v Boswell (1986) Fam. Law 52, CA 12–8
Carl Zeiss Stiftung v Rayner & Keeler Ltd (Letter: Contempt of Court); sub nom. Trade
    Mark No.249457, Re [1960] 1 W.L.R. 1145; [1960] 3 All E.R. 289; [1961] R.P.C. 1;
    104 S.J. 869, Ch D 1–83, 5–9, 11–74
Carla Homes (South) Ltd v Chichester DC, *The Times*, October 15, 1999 12–33
Carlion's Case (1345) 2 Dyer 188b; (1345) 73 E.R. 416 11–157
Carmichael, Complainer, 1992 S.C.C.R. 553 16–115
Carr v News Group Newspapers Ltd [2005] EWHC 971, QBD 6–44, 6–49, 6–56, 6–87, 6–92,
                                               6–108, 6–116, 6–146, 7–31, 7–102
Carus Wilson's Case (1845) 7 Q.B. 984 3–132
Cassidy v Howcroft [2001] C.P. Rep. 49; [2000] C.P.L.R. 628, CA 12–202
Cassidy v Steuart (1841) 2 Man. & G. 437; (1841) 133 E.R. 817 3–145
Castells v Spain (1992) 14 E.H.R.R. 445 2–50
Cave v Borax Europe Ltd [2002] All E.R. (D) 287 (May) 14–136
Cavendish v Cavendish and Rochefoucauld (1866) 15 W.R. 182 12–66
Central Independent Television Plc, Re [1991] 1 W.L.R. 4; (1991) 92 Cr. App. R. 154 7–111,
                                       7–114, 7–116, 7–177, 7–192, 7–262, 7–265, 7–271
Century Insurance Co v Larkin [1910] I.R. 91 15–22
Chahal v United Kingdom (22414/93) (1997) 23 E.H.R.R. 413; 1 B.H.R.C. 405; *The Times*,
    November 28, 1996; *Independent*, November 20, 1996, ECHR 7–55
Chamberlain v Stoneham (1889) 24 Q.B.D. 113 11–103
Chambers v Hudson Dodsworth & Co [1936] 2 K.B. 595 .... 1–83, 5–9

[lxiii]

Table of Cases

Chan U Seek v Alvis Vehicles Ltd; sub nom. Re *Guardian* Newspapers Ltd (Court Record: Disclosure) [2004] EWHC 3092; [2005] 3 All E.R. 155; [2005] E.M.L.R. 19; *The Times*, December 14, 2004, Ch D 12–220, 12–225
Chandler v Florida, 449 U.S. 560 (1981) 10–207
Chandler v Horne; sub nom. Roberts v Garratt (1842) 2 M. & Rob. 423; (1842) 174 E.R. 338; 6 J.P. 154 10–158
Chandler v Metropolitan Police Commissioner. *See* R. v Chandler (Terence Norman) (No.2)
Chanel Ltd v FGM Cosmetics [1981] F.S.R. 471, Ch D 15–12, 15–19, 15–32
Chang Hang Kiu v Pigott [1909] A.C. 312, PC 2–18, 10–50, 10–143
Channel 4 Television v United Kingdom, D.R. 56/156 7–248
Chapman v Davis (1841) 3 Man. & G. 609; (1841) 133 E.R. 1284 .... 11–106, 11–111
Chapman v Honig [1963] 2 Q.B. 502; [1963] 3 W.L.R. 19; [1963] 2 All E.R. 513; 107 S.J. 374, CA 3–76, 11–199, 11–203, 11–214, 11–217, 14–149, 14–150, 14–153, 14–159
Chapman v Pointon (1741) 2 Strange. 1150; (1741) 93 E.R. 1093 .... 11–103, 11–104, 11–111
Charder v Charder [1980] C.L.Y. 1837 14–130
Charles Marsden & Sons Ltd v Old Silkstone Colliers Ltd (1914) 13 L.G.R. 342 15–80
Charter v Race Relations Board [1973] A.C. 868; [1973] 2 W.L.R. 299; [1973] 1 All E.R. 512; 117 S.J. 125, HL 4–41, 4–42, 4–45, 4–50
Chechi v Bashier [1999] 2 F.L.R. 489; [1999] 2 F.C.R. 241; [1999] Fam. Law 528; (1999) 143 S.J.L.B. 113; *The Times*, March 25, 1999, CA (Civ Div) 14–77
Chelsea Man Menswear Ltd v Chelsea Girl (No.2) Ltd; sub nom. Chelsea Man Plc v Chelsea Girl Ltd [1988] F.S.R. 217, Ch D 12–52, 12–103
Cheltenham and Swansea Railway Carriage and Wagon Co. (1869) L.R. 8 Eq. 580 1–72
Chester Corp v Rothwell (1940) 7 L.J. C.C.R. 58 11–175
Chief Constable of Leicestershire v Garavelli [1997] E.M.L.R. 543, QBD 1–157, 2–50, 2–52, 2–67, 2–154, 2–193, 2–207, 2–211, 6–28, 7–118, 7–236, 7–243, 9–2, 9–003, 9–12, 9–17, 9–22, 9–34, 9–41, 9–42, 9–96, 9–107, 9–111, 9–155, 9–163, 9–168, 9–197, 9–201, 9–214, 9–226, 9–243, 9–245, 11–97, 16–385, 16–386
Chief Constable of Surrey v JHG. *See* R. (on the application of T) v St Albans Crown Court
Childerston v Barrett (1809) 11 East 439; (1809) 103 E.R. 1073 .... 3–146, 11–304
Childs v McLeod, 1981 S.L.T. (Notes) 27, HCJ Appeal 16–44, 16–127
Chiltern DC v Keane [1985] 1 W.L.R. 619; [1985] 2 All E.R. 118; 83 L.G.R. 573; (1985) 82 L.S.G. 1567; (1985) 129 S.J. 206, CA (Civ Div) 12–34, 15–47, 15–67
Chippeway; sub nom. Bunn [1994] 10 W.W.R. 153; 94 C.C.C. (3d) 57 11–88
Chisholm v Black and Morrision (1871) 2 Coup. 49 16–254
Christie v Leachinsky [1947] A.C. 573 10–110
Christie Miller v Bain (1879) 6 R. 1215 .... 16–31, 16–37, 16–249, 16–258, 16–262
Chuck v Cremer (1846) 1 Coop. temp. Cott 338; (1846) 47 E.R. 884 .... 9–201, 12–66
Church's Tr v Hibbard [1902] Ch. 784 3–222
Churchard v Churchard [1984] F.L.R. 635 12–26
Churchman v Joint Shop Stewards Committee of the Workers of the Port of London; sub nom. Churchman v Port of London Joint Shop Stewards Committee [1972] 1 W.L.R. 1094; [1972] 3 All E.R. 603; [1972] I.C.R. 222; 13 K.I.R. 123; 116 S.J. 617, CA (Civ Div) ... 3–89, 3–170, 3–181, 3–241, 12–35, 12–39, 12–43, 12–48, 12–190, 12–191, 13–119, 15–20
Cinderby v Cinderby, CA, Transcript No.272, April 26, 1978 15–70
Cinema Morano Ltée v Co-op de Logement et de Production Culturelle Inc (1984) 58 N.B.R. (2d) 72, QB 12–80
Citadel Management Inc v Equal Ltdub nom. Citadel Management Inc v Thompson [1999] 1 F.L.R. 21; [1998] Fam. Law 738; (1998) 95(36) L.S.G. 32; (1998) 142 S.J.L.B. 253; *The Times*, September 25, 1998, CA (Civ Div) 12–250, 19–2
City Trust Ltd v Levy [1988] 1 W.L.R. 1051 13–98
Civil Aviation Authority v Australian Broadcasting Corporation (1995) 39 N.S.W.L.R. 540 1–156
Clark (1829) Shaw 215 16–112
Clark v Gill (1854) 1 K. & J. 19; (1854) 69 E.R. 351 11–104
Clark v Molineux (1677) 1 Lev. 159; (1677) 83 E.R. 348 10–109

TABLE OF CASES

Clark v Stirling, Presbytery of Dunkeld, Henderson (1839) 1 D. 955 .... 16–247, 16–263
Clark v United States, U.S. 1 (1993) 11–350
Clarke v Chadburn [1985] 1 W.L.R. 78; [1985] 1 All E.R. 211; [1984] I.R.L.R. 350; (1984)
    81 L.S.G. 3094; (1984) 128 S.J. 767, Ch D 1–137, 2–9, 2–220, 2–221, 3–69, 3–86, 3–89,
                                                                                                3–158, 3–171, 13–11
Clarke v Clarke [1990] 2 F.L.R. 115; [1990] F.C.R. 641; (1990) 154 J.P.N. 742, CA (Civ
    Div) 15–46, 15–67, 15–74
Clarke v Heathfield (No.1) [1985] I.C.R. 203 .... 12–69, 14–126, 14–128
Clarke v Heathfield (No.2) [1985] I.C.R. 606 .... 12–69, 14–126
Clarke v Law (1855) 2 K. & J. 28; (1855) 69 E.R. 680 15–35
Claydon v Finch (1873) L.R. 15 Eq. 266 14–120
Cleese v Clark [2003] EWHC 137; [2004] E.M.L.R. 3, QBD 5–111
Clements, Re; Republic of Costa Rica v Erlanger (1877) 46 L.J. Ch. 375 ...... 1–76, 1–82, 11–311,
                                                                                                            12–15, 12–18
Clements v Williams (1836) 2 Scott 814 11–224
Clibbery v Allan; sub nom. Cliberry v Allan [2002] EWCA Civ 45; [2002] Fam. 261; [2002]
    2 W.L.R. 1511; [2002] 1 All E.R. 865; [2002] 1 F.L.R. 565; [2002] 1 F.C.R. 385;
    [2002] U.K.H.R.R. 697; [2002] Fam. Law 260; (2002) 99(11) L.S.G. 37; (2002) 152
    N.L.J. 222; (2002) 146 S.J.L.B. 38; *The Times*, February 5, 2002; *Independent*,
    February 5, 2002, CA (Civ Div); affirming [2001] 2 F.L.R. 819; [2001] 2 F.C.R. 577;
    [2001] Fam. Law 654; (2001) 98(27) L.S.G. 40; (2001) 151 N.L.J. 969; (2001) 145
    S.J.L.B. 160; *The Times*, July 2, 2001; *Independent*, July 30, 2001 (C.S.), Fam Div 1–174,
                                                                        7–65, 7–107, 8–76, 8–128, 12–57, 15–16
Clipper Maritime Co Ltd of Monrovia v Mineral Import-Export (The Marie Leonhardt)
    [1981] 1 W.L.R. 1262; [1981] 3 All E.R. 664; [1981] 2 Lloyd's Rep. 458, QBD
    (Comm) 12–147
Coats (J & P) v Chadwick [1894] 1 Ch. 347, Ch D 1–72, 4–95
Cobb, Re [1924] N.Z.L.R. 495 5–268
Cobra Golf Inc v Rata [1996] F.S.R. 819 .... 3–190, 3–199, 12–175
Coca-Cola Co v Aytacli [2003] EWHC 91; (2003) 26(3) I.P.D. 26016; (2003) 100(11) L.S.G.
    31; *The Times*, February 11, 2003, Ch D 3–5, 3–58, 3–75, 3–202, 3–207, 3–250, 3–251,
                                                                                                                    12–95
Coca-Cola Co v Gilbey; Schweppes Ltd v Gilbey [1996] F.S.R. 23, CA (Civ Div) 3–250, 12–95,
                                                                                                                    19–2
Cochrane, Ex p. (1875) L.R. 20 Eq. 282 .... 11–319, 11–321
Cocker v Tempest (1841) 7 M. & W. 502; (1841) 151 E.R. 864 10–22
Coco v AN Clark (Engineers) Ltd [1968] F.S.R. 415; [1969] R.P.C. 41, Ch D 4–30, 6–49
Coe v Central Television Plc [1994] E.M.L.R. 433; *Independent*, August 11, 1993, CA (Civ
    Div) 3–66, 5–45, 5–99, 5–152, 5–173, 5–183, 5–184, 5–188, 5–200, 6–9, 6–18, 6–22, 6–30,
                                                                                    6–33, 6–38, 7–142, 8–30
Cohen v Cowles Media Co, 111 S.Ct 2513 (1991) 9–51
Colbatch (1723) K.B. Easter, George I 1–59
Colbeck v Ferguson, January 1, 2002 12–231
Cole v Hawkins (1738) Andrews 275; (1738) 95 E.R. 396 .... 11–157, 11–172, 11–304, 11–305
Coleman v West Hartlepool Ry Co (1860) 8 W.R. 734 6–1
Coles v Coles [1957] P. 68; [1956] 3 W.L.R. 861; [1956] 3 All E.R. 542; 100 S.J. 842,
    PDAD 15–87
Colledge (1681) 8 St. Tr. 714 10–88
Collett, Ex p., unreported, October 10, 1952, QBD 15–9
Collins v Godefroy (1831) 1 B. & Ad. 950; (1831) 109 E.R. 1040 .... 11–103, 11–259
Columbia Pictures Industries v Robinson [1987] Ch. 38; [1986] 3 W.L.R. 542; [1986] 3 All
    E.R. 338; [1986] F.S.R. 367; (1986) 83 L.S.G. 3424; (1986) 130 S.J. 766, Ch D 12–66,
                                                                                        12–146, 12–175, 12–176, 12–177
Comet Products (UK) Ltd v Hawkex Plastics Ltd, [1971] 2 Q.B. 67; [1971] 2 W.L.R. 361;
    [1971] 1 All E.R. 1141; [1971] F.S.R. 7; [1972] R.P.C. 691; 114 S.J. 975; *The Times*,
    December 9, 1970, CA (Civ Div) 3–21, 3–71, 3–89, 3–188, 3–192, 3–208, 3–241, 12–33,
                                                                                            12–43, 15–35, 16–44
Commissioner of Police of the Metropolis v Caldwell. *See* R. v Caldwell (James)
Commissioner of Water Resources v Federated Engine Drivers' and Firemen's Association
    of Australasia [1988] 2 Qd R. 385 .... 12–44, 12–55

[lxv]

TABLE OF CASES

Company, A, Re, *The Times*, December 27, 1983, Nourse J. 3–74, 12–64
Company, No. 001424 of 1983, Re, *The Times*, June 21, 1984 .... 11–281, 15–35
Con Mech (Engineers) v Amalgamated Union of Engineering Workers (Engineering Section)
  (No.1) [1973] I.C.R. 620; [1974] I.R.L.R. 2; (1973) 117 S.J. 813, NIRC 3–170, 12–5,
  14–108, 14–121, 14–123
Condliffe v Hislop [1996] 1 W.L.R. 753; [1996] 1 All E.R. 431, CA 7–62
Connolly v Dale [1996] Q.B. 120; [1995] 3 W.L.R. 786; [1996] 1 All E.R. 224; [1996] 1 Cr.
  App. R. 200; *The Times*, July 13, 1995; *Independent*, July 27, 1995, DC 2–222, 6–22,
  10–184, 10–215, 10–216, 11–23, 11–28, 13–10
Consolidated Press, Re, Ex p. Auld (1936) 36 S.R.N.S.W. 596 5–112
Consolidated Press v McRae (1955) 93 C.L.R. 325 11–7
Const v Ebers (1816) 1 Madd. 530; (1816) 56 E.R. 194 3–159
Controller-General of Patents [1898] 1 Q.B. 909 2–214
Cook v Alexander [1974] Q.B. 279; [1973] 3 W.L.R. 617; [1973] 3 All E.R. 1037; 117 S.J.
  618, CA (Civ Div) 4–268
Cooke v United States, 267 U.S. 517 (1925) 3–59
Cooper v Asprey (1863) 32 L.J. Q.B. 209 11–328
Corcoran v Corcoran [1950] 1 All E.R. 495; 94 S.J. 226, PDAD 3–23, 3–89, 3–162, 3–167, 3–170
Cordiner, Petr, 1973 J.C. 16; 1973 S.L.T. 125, HCJ 16–60, 16–237, 16–262, 16–274
Cornish, Re; Staff v Gill (1894) 9 T.L.R. 196 .... 4–134, 5–77
Costa v Costa, 1929 S.N. 62 16–262
Costa Rica Republic v Erlanger (1877) 46 L.J. Ch. 375 11–311
Cotroni v Quebec Police Commission and Brunet (1977) 80 D.L.R. (3d) 490 SCC 9–32, 10–85
Cotton's Case (1733) 2 Barn. K.B. 313; (1733) 94 E.R. 523 13–105
Couche v Lord Arundel (1802) 3 East 127; (1802) 102 E.R. 545 3–145
Couling v Coxe (1848) 6 C.B. 703; (1848) 136 E.R. 1424; (1848) S.C. 6 D. & L. 399 14–156,
  14–157
Coulson & Sons v James Coulson & Co (1887) 3 T.L.R. 846, CA 4–324, 6–8
Council of Civil Service Unions v Minister for the Civil Service; sub nom. CCSU v Minister
  for the Civil Service [1985] A.C. 374; [1984] 1 W.L.R. 1174; [1984] 3 All E.R. 935;
  [1985] I.C.R. 14; [1985] I.R.L.R. 28; (1985) 82 L.S.G. 437; (1984) 128 S.J. 837,
  HL 2–216
County Court Judge of Lambeth (1887) 36 W.R. 476 15–6
Couzens v Couzens [2001] EWCA Civ 992; [2001] 2 F.L.R. 701; [2001] 3 F.C.R. 289;
  [2001] Fam. Law 729, CA (Civ Div) 15–66, 15–74
Cowan, March 17, 1998, HCJ 5–103
Coward v Stapleton (1953) 90 C.L.R. 573 .... 2–18, 10–56, 10–164
Cowie v George Outram & Co, 1912 1 S.L.T. 248; (1912) 6 Adam 556 .... 16–162, 16–229, 16–145
Cox, Petr; sub nom. Cox and Griffiths, Petrs (Contempt of Court), 1998 J.C. 267; 1998 S.L.T.
  1172; 1998 S.C.C.R. 561; 1998 G.W.D. 28–1400, HCJ 4–114, 16–302, 16–303, 16–305,
  16–331
Cox v Bennett (1874) 31 L.T. 83 11–334
Cox and Griffiths, Petrs. *See* Cox, Petr
Coxe v Phillips (1736) Cas. t. Hard. 237; (1736) 95 E.R. 152 .... 11–52, 11–54
Craig v Craig [1896] P. 171 .... 14–112, 14–123
Cream Holdings Ltd v Banerjee [2004] UKHL 44; [2005] 1 A.C. 253; [2004] 3 W.L.R. 918;
  [2004] 4 All E.R. 617; [2005] E.M.L.R. 1; [2004] H.R.L.R. 39; [2004] U.K.H.R.R.
  1071; 17 B.H.R.C. 464; (2005) 28(2) I.P.D. 28001; (2004) 101(42) L.S.G. 29; (2004)
  154 N.L.J. 1589; (2004) 148 S.J.L.B. 1215; *The Times*, October 15, 2004, HL 2–198, 4–324,
  6–13, 6–16, 6–18, 6–19, 8–23
Crédit Suisse Fides Trust SA v Cuoghi [1998] Q.B. 818; [1998] 1 W.L.R. 474; [1997] 3
  W.L.R. 871; [1997] 3 All E.R. 724; [1997] C.L.C. 1187; [1998] I.L.Pr. 41; *The Times*,
  July 3, 1997, CA (Civ Div) 12–167, 12–168
Crepps v Durden (1772) 2 Cowp. 640; (1772) 98 E.R. 1283 3–209
Crest Homes Plc v Marks [1987] A.C. 829; [1987] 3 W.L.R. 293; [1987] 2 All E.R. 1074;
  [1988] R.P.C. 21; (1987) 84 L.S.G. 2362; (1987) 137 N.L.J. 662; (1987) 131 S.J. 1003,
  HL 3–71, 3–188, 3–189, 3–192, 3–194, 3–195, 3–196, 3–198, 3–199, 3–201, 12–59,
  12–201
Cretynge's Case, Y.B. 17 Edward III (R.S.) 276 1–22
Crewe v Field (1896) 12 T.L.R. 405 .... 14–154, 14–158

[lxvi]

TABLE OF CASES

Croissant v Germany (A/237B) (1993) 16 E.H.R.R. 135, ECHR 15–42
Cronmire v The Daily Bourse (1892) 9 T.L.R. 101 .... 4–326, 14–136
Crook, Ex p., *The Times*, November 8, 1984 2–193
Crook (Tim), Re (1989) 93 Cr. App. R. 17 2–51
Crowe v Price (1889) 22 Q.B.D. 429 14–120
Crown Bank, Re; sub nom. O'Malley, Re (1890) L.R. 44 Ch. D. 649, Ch D 1–72, 5–77
Crown Prosecution Service v Tweddell; sub nom. DPP v Tweddell [2001] EWHC Admin
  188; [2002] 1 F.L.R. 400; [2002] 1 F.C.R. 438; [2001] A.C.D. 83; [2002] Fam. Law
  502, DC 12–12
Crowther v Appleby (1873) L.R. 9 C.P. 23 11–115
Crump (An Infant), Re [1963] Crim. L.R. 777; (1963) 107 S.J. 682; *The Times*, August 22,
  1963 .... 3–89, 3–117, 3–174, 11–334, 11–335, 14–6
Cullen v Rose [1985] CA Transcript No.804 15–47
Cullin's Case (1653) Sty. 395; (1653) 82 E.R. 807 11–304
Cunningham v Essex CC [1997] T.L.R. 182 12–203
Cunningham v The Scotsman Publications Ltd, 1987 S.C. 107; 1987 S.L.T. 698; 1987
  S.C.L.R. 314 .... 12–220, 16–210, 16–212, 16–220
Curran, Petr, 1996 G.W.D. 36–2093 16–127
Currie, December 9–10, 1799; Hume, Vol.II, ch.VI, p.140 16–122
Currie v Chief Constable of Surrey [1982] 1 W.L.R. 215; [1982] 1 All E.R. 89 11–97
Curtis v Curtis (1845) 5 Moo. P.C. 252; (1845) 13 E.R. 487 12–66
Cutbush (1867) L.R. 2 Q.B. 379 14–55
Cuthell (1799) 27 St. Tr. 641 1–69
Cutler v Wandsworth Stadium Ltd [1945] 1 All E.R. 103, CA 12–59, 12–188

D (Protection of Party Anonymity), Re (1997–98) 1 C.C.L. Rep. 1909; (1999) 45 B.M.L.R.
  191 7–104
D v A & Co [1900] 1 Ch. 484 .... 12–182, 12–191, 12–244, 15–8
D v D [1993] 2 F.L.R. 802 13–92
D v D (Access: Contempt: Committal) [1991] 2 F.L.R. 34; [1991] Fam. Law 365, CA (Civ
  Div) 15–24
DE Normanville v Hereford Times Ltd (1936) 79 S.J. 796; (1936) 80 S.J. 423, CA 4–288
Dag v Penkevill (1605) Moo. K.B. 770: (1605) 72 E.R. 895 11–48
Dagenais v Canadian Broadcasting Corp (1994) 120 D.L.R. (4th) 12; (1994) 94 C.C.C. (3d)
  289 .... 1–144, 1–145, 2–32, 2–35, 2–71, 2–100, 2–101, 2–102, 2–103, 4–103, 4–114, 4–161,
                                              6–1, 6–21, 7–6, 7–177, 7–198, 7–200, 16–313
Dallas v Ledger (1888) 52 J.P. 328; (1888) 4 T.L.R. 432 .... 5–102, 5–103
Daltel Europe Ltd (In Liquidation) v Makki (No.3) [2005] EWHC 749, Ch D 3–75, 3–237
Danchevsky v Danchevsky (No.1) [1975] Fam. 17 .... 12–15, 12–17, 12–133, 13–93, 14–58
Danchevsky v Danchevsky (No.2) (1977) 121 S.J. 796; Transcript, November 10, 1977, CA
  (Civ Div) 3–67, 3–80, 3–83, 3–210, 3–221, 15–63
Dando v Anastassiou [1951] V.L.R. 235 7–38
Daniel v Drew [2005] EWCA Civ 507; *The Times*, May 18, 2005, CA (Civ Div) 4–145, 11–284,
                                                                                                              11–293
Danskin v HM Advocate, 2002 S.L.T. 889; 2001 G.W.D. 26–1025, HCJ Appeal 16–305
Danson v Le Capelain & Steele (1852) 7 Exch. 667; (1852) 155 E.R. 1116 11–317
Darby v Love (1796) Mor. 7907 16–26
Dastoines v Apprice (1580) Cary 131 1–43
Davies, Re (1888) 21 Q.B.D. 236 .... 3–23, 3–185, 12–15, 14–7
Davies v Davies [1960] 3 All E.R. 248 11–68
Davis v Barlow (1911) 18 W.L.R. 238 6–126
Davis v Johnson [1979] A.C. 264; [1978] 2 W.L.R. 553; [1978] 1 All E.R. 1132; 122 S.J.
  178, HL 14–72
Davis v Lovell (1839) 4 M. & W. 679; (1839) 150 E.R. 1593 14–155
Davis v Rhayader Granite Quarries Ltd (1911) 131 L.T.J. 79 14–122
Davis's Case (1461) 2 Dyer 188; (1461) 73 E.R. 415 .... 1–2, 1–16
Davis's Case (1560) Dy. 188b;(1560) 73 E.R. 415 10–96
Davy International Ltd v Tazzyman; Davy International Ltd v Durnig [1997] 1 W.L.R. 1256;
  [1997] 3 All E.R. 183; *The Times*, May 9, 1997, CA (Civ Div) 15–23, 15–57

TABLE OF CASES

Daw v Eley (No.3) (1868–69) L.R. 7 Eq. 49, Ct of Chancery 5–110, 11–73
Dawes v Cardle, 1987 S.C.C.R. 135 16–423
Dawson, Ex p. [1961] S.R. (N.S.W.) 573 4–298
Dawson v Princeps (1795) 2 Anstr. 521; (1795) 145 E.R. 954 12–241
Day v Longhurst (1843) 62 L.J. Ch. 334 12–22
Day v Longhurst (1893) 41 W.R. 283 11–34
De Beaujeu's Application for Writ of Attachment Against Cudlipp, Re [1949] 1 Ch. 230 8–120,
8–125, 11–347
de Brewse (William) (1305) Mich. 33 & 34 E 1 Coram Rege, Rot. 75 11–159
de Court, Re [1997] T.L.R. 601 .... 11–26, 11–145, 11–207, 11–312, 11–316, 13–82, 14–133
De Haes and Gijesels v Belgium (19983/92) (1998) 25 E.H.R.R. 1, ECHR 5–218
De Libellis Famosis (1605) 5 Co. Rep. 125, 77 E.R. 250 .... 1–29, 1–32
de Sadington's Case (1293) Plac. Abbrev., p.291, rot.7 1–3
De Vries v Kay, *The Times*, October 7, 1978 15–14
De Vries v National Westminster Bank Plc; *The Times*, August 16, 1984, QBD 2–13, 10–157
Deacon v Deacon (1827) 2 Russ. 607, 38 E.R. 463 1–72
Dean v Dean [1987] 1 F.L.R. 517; [1987] 1 F.C.R. 96; [1987] Fam. Law 200; (1987) 151
    J.P.N. 254, CA (Civ Div) 3–80, 3–246, 4–1, 12–43, 12–44, 12–52, 12–53
Dean's Case (1598) Cro. Eliz. 689; (1598) 78 E.R. 925 .... 1–23, 10–2
Deborah Building Equipment Ltd v Scaffco Ltd, *The Times*, November 5, 1986 ...... 3–246, 12–43
Defries v Creed (1865) 34 L.J. Ch. 607 .... 11–318, 11–319
Delaney v Delaney [1996] Q.B. 387; [1996] 2 W.L.R. 74; [1996] 1 All E.R. 367; [1996] 1
    F.L.R. 458; [1996] 2 F.C.R. 13; [1996] Fam. Law 207; *The Times*, November 2, 1995;
    Independent, November 27, 1995 (C.S.), CA (Civ Div) 3–111, 3–181, 14–9, 14–36, 14–40,
14–50
Dendron GmbH v University of California (Parallel Proceedings: Use of Evidence) [2004]
    EWHC 589; [2005] 1 W.L.R. 200; [2004] I.L.Pr. 35; [2004] F.S.R. 42; (2004) 27(6)
    I.P.D. 27063; *The Times*, May 24, 2004, Ch D (Patents Ct) 3–203, 12–226
Denison v Harding (1867) 15 W.R. 346 11–317
Dent v Dent (1867) L.R. 1 P. & D. 366 .... 14–120, 14–125
Dent v Dent and Hall [1962] P. 187; [1962] 2 W.L.R. 793; [1962] 1 All E.R. 746; 106 S.J.
    200, PDAD 14–44
Dentice v Valuers Registration Board [1992] 1 N.Z.L.R. 720 11–200
Deodat v Deodat, unreported, June 9, 1978, CA 12–56
Department of Economic Policy and Development of the City of Moscow v Bankers Trust
    Co; sub nom. Moscow City Council v Bankers Trust Co; Department of Economics,
    Policy and Development of the City of Moscow v Bankers Trust Co [2004] EWCA
    Civ 314; [2005] Q.B. 207; [2004] 3 W.L.R. 533; [2004] 4 All E.R. 746; [2004] 2 All
    E.R. (Comm) 193; [2004] 2 Lloyd's Rep. 179; [2004] 1 C.L.C. 1099; [2004] B.L.R.
    229; (2004) 148 S.J.L.B. 389, CA (Civ Div); reversing in part [2003] EWHC 1377;
    [2003] 1 W.L.R. 2885; *The Times*, September 1, 2003, QBD (Comm) 7–25
Deputy Coroner for Middlesex, Ex p. (1861) 6 H. & N. 501; (1861) 158 E.R. 206 3–146
Derby & Co Ltd v Weldon, The *Independent*, November 2, 1988 12–232
Derby & Co Ltd v Weldon (Nos.3 and No.4) [1990] Ch. 65; [1989] 2 W.L.R. 412; [1989] 1
    All E.R. 1002; [1989] E.C.C. 322; (1989) 139 N.L.J. 11; (1989) 133 S.J. 83; *The
    Times*, December 26, 1988; *Independent*, December 20, 1988, CA (Civ Div) 12–160,
12–164, 12–167
Derby & Co Ltd v Weldon (No.6) [1990] 1 W.L.R. 1139; [1990] 3 All E.R. 263; [1991]
    I.L.Pr. 24; (1990) 140 N.L.J. 1001; (1990) 134 S.J. 1041; *The Times*, May 14, 1990;
    Independent, June 1, 1990; *Financial Times*, May 16, 1990, CA (Civ Div) 12–171
Derbyshire CC v Times Newspapers Ltd [1993] A.C. 534; [1993] 2 W.L.R. 449; [1993] 1 All
    E.R. 1011; 91 L.G.R. 179; (1993) 143 N.L.J. 283; (1993) 137 S.J.L.B. 52; *The Times*,
    February 19, 1993; *Independent*, February 19, 1993; *Guardian*, February 19, 1993,
    HL; affirming [1992] Q.B. 770; [1992] 3 W.L.R. 28; [1992] 3 All E.R. 65; 90 L.G.R.
    221; (1992) 4 Admin. L.R. 469; [1992] C.O.D. 305; (1992) 142 N.L.J. 276; *The Times*,
    February 20, 1992; *Independent*, February 21, 1992; *Guardian*, March 11, 1992, CA
    (Civ Div) 1–110, 1–132, 1–144, 2–38, 2–54, 2–126, 2–127, 2–133, 2–138, 2–158, 2–164,
4–90, 5–5, 5–93, 6–6, 7–3, 7–187, 9–7, 9–19, 9–77
Devon CC v B [1997] T.L.R. 6, CA 13–92
Dewar (1842) 1 Broun 233 16–118

TABLE OF CASES

Dewar, Petr, unreported, September 5, 1944 16–406
Diane (Stockport), Re; Re Grosvenor Garage; Re Lane Garage; Re Tennant W; *The Times*,
 July 15, 1982 .... 3–176, 19–2
Dicas v Lawson (1835) 1 C. M. & R. 934; (1835) 149 E.R. 1359 11–106
Diennet v France (1996) 21 E.H.R.R. 554 7–1
Dilworth v Commissioner of Stamps; Dilworth v Commissioner for Land and Income Tax
 [1899] A.C. 99, PC (NZ) 4–31, 4–50
Dingle v Turner [1972] A.C. 601; [1972] 2 W.L.R. 523; [1972] 1 All E.R. 878; 116 S.J. 195,
 HL 4–47
Dingwall Magistrates v Mackenzie (1831) 5 W. & S. 351; (1829) 7 S. 899 16–252
Dinnis v Morgan, *Cary's Causes in Chancery*, p.121 1–48
Director-General of Fair Trading v Buckland; sub nom. Agreements Relating to the Supply
 of Ready-Mixed Concrete, Re [1990] 1 W.L.R. 920; [1990] 1 All E.R. 545; (1989) 5
 B.C.C. 817; [1990] B.C.L.C. 162; *Independent*, July 20, 1989; *Daily Telegraph*,
 August 24, 1989, Ch D (RPC) 12–111, 12–112
Director-General of Fair Trading v Pioneer Concrete (UK) Ltd; sub nom. Supply of Ready
 Mixed Concrete (No.2), Re [1995] 1 A.C. 456; [1994] 3 W.L.R. 1249; [1995] 1 All
 E.R. 135; [1995] I.C.R. 25; (1995) 92(1) L.S.G. 37; (1995) 145 N.L.J. 17; [1995] 139
 S.J.L.B. 14; *The Times*, November 25, 1994; *Independent*, November 30, 1994, HL 1–126,
 3–97, 3–129, 3–176, 3–247, 4–206, 12–80, 12–91, 12–92, 12–93, 12–99,
 12–103, 12–106, 12–178, 16–243, 19–2
Director-General of Fair Trading v Proprietary Association of Great Britain; sub nom.
 Medicaments and Related Classes of Goods (No.2), Re [2001] 1 W.L.R. 700; [2001]
 U.K.C.L.R. 550; [2001] I.C.R. 564; [2001] H.R.L.R. 17; [2001] U.K.H.R.R. 429;
 (2001) 3 L.G.L.R. 32; (2001) 98(7) L.S.G. 40; (2001) 151 N.L.J. 17; (2001) 145
 S.J.L.B. 29; *The Times*, February 2, 2001; *Independent*, January 12, 2001, CA (Civ
 Div) 5–239, 10–49
Director-General of Fair Trading v Smiths Concrete Ltd; Director-General of Fair Trading v
 Hulett; sub nom. Re Supply of Ready Mixed Concrete [1992] Q.B. 213; [1991] 3
 W.L.R. 707; [1991] 4 All E.R. 150; [1992] I.C.R. 229; *The Times*, July 26, 1991;
 Independent, August 2, 1991, CA (Civ Div) 6–127
DPP v Channel Four Television Co Ltd [1993] 2 All E.R. 517; [1993] Crim. L.R. 277; [1993]
 C.O.D. 6; (1992) 142 N.L.J. 1412; *The Times*, September 14, 1992; *The Times*,
 September 1, 1992; *Independent*, August 5, 1992; *Guardian*, August 12, 1992, QBD 2–210,
 7–118, 7–242, 9–29, 9–72, 9–114, 9–119, 9–125, 9–201, 9–232, 9–242,
 10–29, 10–49, 12–22, 13–29, 13–33, 13–35
DPP v Mills; sub nom. R. v Mills [1997] Q.B. 300; [1996] 3 W.L.R. 1093; [1997] 2 Cr. App.
 R. 6; [1996] Crim. L.R. 746; [1996] C.O.D. 352; (1996) 160 J.P.N. 482; *The Times*,
 April 2, 1996, DC 11–146
DPP v Smith (Jim); sub nom. R. v Smith (Jim) [1961] A.C. 290; [1960] 3 W.L.R. 546; [1960]
 3 All E.R. 161; (1960) 44 Cr. App. R. 261; (1960) 124 J.P. 473; 104 S.J. 683, HL 5–156
DPP v Tweddell. *See* Crown Prosecution Service v Tweddell
Distillers Co (Biochemicals) Ltd v Times Newspapers Ltd; Distillers Co (Biochemicals)
 Ltdv Phillips [1975] Q.B. 613; [1974] 3 W.L.R. 728; [1975] 1 All E.R. 41; 118 S.J.
 864, QBD 12–201
Dixon v Dixon [1904] 1 Ch. 161 .... 11–320, 11–321, 14–132
Dixon v Lee (1834) 3 Dowl. 259 .... 11–101, 11–104
Dixon v Rowe (1876) 35 L.T. 548 .... 14–120, 14–121
Dobson v Hastings [1992] Ch. 394; [1992] 2 W.L.R. 414; [1992] 2 All E.R. 94; (1992) 89(8)
 L.S.G. 27; (1991) 141 N.L.J. 1625; *The Times*, November 18, 1991; *Independent*,
 November 12, 1991; *Guardian*, November 13, 1991, Ch D 2–183, 2–184, 2–189, 2–194,
 2–207, 3–66, 6–28, 9–243, 11–1, 11–27, 11–29, 11–80, 11–257
Dockers' Labour Club and Institute v Race Relations Board; sub nom. Race Relations Board
 v Dockers Labour Club and Institute [1976] A.C. 285; [1974] 3 W.L.R. 533; [1974] 3
 All E.R. 592; 118 S.J. 738, HL 4–43, 4–45
Dodd and Briggs (1736) Sanders, Chancery Orders, pp. 539–542 1–60
Dodington v Hudson (1824) 1 Bing. 410; (1824) 130 E.R. 165 .... 12–21, 12–33, 12–98
Dodwell, Re, in Seton, *Judgements and Orders* (7th ed., 1912), p.457 10–95
Dolman v Pritman (1670) 3 Ch. R. 64; (1670) 21 E.R. 730 11–100
Donaldson v Linton (1861) 4 Irv. 115 16–123

[lxix]

TABLE OF CASES

Doncaster and Retford Cooperative Societies Agreement (Practice Note), Re; sub nom.
 Practice Note (RPC: Evidence) (1960) L.R. 2 R.P. 129 4–130
Dorrell v Dorrell [1985] F.L.R. 1089, CA 15–61
Douglas v Hello! Ltd (No.1) [2001] Q.B. 967; [2001] 2 W.L.R. 992; [2001] 2 All E.R. 289;
 [2001] E.M.L.R. 9; [2001] 1 F.L.R. 982; [2002] 1 F.C.R. 289; [2001] H.R.L.R. 26;
 [2001] U.K.H.R.R. 223; 9 B.H.R.C. 543; [2001] F.S.R. 40; *The Times*, January 16,
 2001; *Daily Telegraph*, January 9, 2001, CA (Civ Div) 6–16, 6–106, 9–39
Douglas v Hello! Ltd (No.3) [2003] EWHC 55; [2003] 1 All E.R. 1087 (Note); [2003]
 E.M.L.R. 29; (2003) 100(11) L.S.G. 34; (2003) 153 N.L.J. 175; *The Times*, January 30,
 2003, Ch D 11–86
Dove Group Plc and Jaguar Cars Ltd v Hynes [1993] C.O.D. 174 11–280
Dow Jones & Co Inc v Gutnick [2002] H.C.A. 56; (2002) 210 C.L.R. 575 4–191
Dow Jones & Co Inc v Jameel. *See* Jameel v Dow Jones & Co Inc
Downie and Arrindell, Re (1841) 3 Moo. P.C. 414; (1841) 13 E.R. 168 10–143
Drewry v Thacker (1819) 3 Swan 529; (1819) 36 E.R. 963 9–201
Driver-Davidson v Cullen, unreported, November 2, 1993, CA 3–229
Drummond v Haywood, 1994 G.W.D. 5–260 16–79
Dubarry v Dubarry [2002] EWCA Civ 1808 19–2
Dudgeon v Thomson and Donaldson (1876) 3 R. 974 .... 6–41, 16–67, 16–236, 16–247, 16–252,
 16–263
Dummer v Chippenham Corp (1807) 14 Ves. Jun. 245; (1807) 33 E.R. 515 .... 6–117, 12–107
Dun, in Hume, Vol.II, p.140 16–136
Duncan, Re [1958] S.C.R. 41; (1958) 11 D.L.R. (2d) 616 10–141
Duncan v Jones [1936] 1 K.B. 218, KBD 2–151
Duncan v Ramsay (1853) 1 Irv. 208 16–251
Duncan v Sparling (1894) 10 T.L.R. 353 .... 4–288, 5–30
Duncan Practice Home Co Ltd v Provost, Magistrates and Councillors of the Burgh of
 Dunoon, 1921 S.C. 908 16–261
Dundass v Lord Weymouth (1777) Cowp. 665; (1777) 98 E.R. 1296 11–54
Dunkley's Case, in Hudson, *Collect Jurid.* ii, 118 1–32
Dunlop Pneumatic Tyre Co v Rose (1901) 3 F. 635 .... 16–249, 16–259
Dunn, Aspinall, Re (1906) V.L.R. 493 .... 11–179, 11–180
Dunn v Bevan; Brodie v Bevan[1922] 1 Ch. 276, Ch D 4–268
Dunoon Picture House Co v Magistrates of Edinburgh, 1921 S.C. 908 16–235
Duo v Osborne (formerly Duo) [1992] 1 W.L.R. 611; [1992] 3 All E.R. 121; [1992] 2 F.L.R.
 425; [1992] 2 F.C.R. 583, CA (Civ Div) 14–76, 15–38, 19–2
Dyce Sombre, Re (1849) 1 Mac. & G. 116; (1849) 41 E.R. 1207 11–175
Dyson v Att-Gen (No.2) [1912] 1 Ch. 158, CA 9–240

E (A Minor) (Access), Re [1987] 1 F.L.R. 368; [1987] Fam. Law 90, CA (Civ Div) 12–24
E (by her litigation friend the Official Solicitor) v Channel Four [2005] EWHC 1144, Fam
 Div 6–114
EC (A Minor) (Care Proceedings: Disclosure), Re. *See* Re C (A Minor) (Care Proceedings:
 Disclosure)
EMI Ltd v Pandit [1975] 1 W.L.R. 302; [1975] 1 All E.R. 418; [1975] F.S.R. 111; [1976]
 R.P.C. 333; (1974) 119 S.J. 136, Ch D 12–175
Eagleson v Cardle, 1994 G.W.D. 5–259 16–134
Eastern Trust Co v McKenzie, Mann & Co Ltd [1915] A.C. 750 9–201
Eccles & Co v Louisville and Nashville Railroad Co [1912] 1 K.B. 135 .... 3–137, 11–115, 12–181
Eckman v Midland Bank Ltd; sub nom. Goad, Re; Goad v Amalgamated Union of
 Engineering Workers (Engineering Section) (Sequestration: Costs) [1973] Q.B. 519;
 [1973] 3 W.L.R. 284; [1973] 1 All E.R. 609; [1973] 1 Lloyd's Rep. 162; [1973] I.C.R.
 71; (1972) 117 S.J. 87; *The Times*, December 8, 1972, NIRC 6–126, 14–123, 14–127
Edes v Brereton (1738) West temp. Hard. 348; (1738) 25 E.R. 974 11–335
Edgar v Fisher's Trs (1893) 21 R. 59; (1893) 1 S.L.T. 301 .... 16–234, 16–267
Edward Grey Ltd v Greys (Midlands) Ltd [1952] R.P.C. 25 12–19
Edwards v Leith (1843) 15 Sc. Ju. 375 16–248
Edwards v United Kingdom (1993) 15 E.H.R.R. 417 .... 11–143, 13–118

TABLE OF CASES

Egger v Viscount Chelmsford; sub nom. Egger v Davies [1965] 1 Q.B. 248; [1964] 3 W.L.R. 714; [1964] 3 All E.R. 406; 108 S.J. 619, CA 4–215, 4–258
El Capistrano SA v ATO Marketing Ltd [1989] 1 W.L.R. 471; [1989] 2 All E.R. 572; (1989) 133 S.J. 693. CA (Civ Div) 3–83, 3–214, 3–229
Elder or Smith (1827) Syme 71 16–223
Elliot v Halmarnock (1816) 1 Mer. 302; (1816) 35 E.R. 839 11–317
Elliot v Klinger [1967] 1 W.L.R. 1165; [1967] 3 All E.R. 141; 111 S.J. 635, Ch D 12–125, 12–198, 12–242, 14–113, 14–132
Ellis, Petr, unreported, February 1965, HCJ 16–100
Ellis v Deheer [1922] 2 K.B. 113, CA 3–93, 10–82, 11–349, 11–386, 11–392
Ellis v Earl Grey (1833) 6 Sim. 214; (1833) 58 E.R. 574 2–225
Elsam, Re (1824) 3 B. & C. 597; (1824) 107 E.R. 855 .... 11–52, 11–54
Emerson v Dallison (1660) 1 Ch. R. 194; (1660) 21 E.R. 547 11–54
Emery v Bowen (1836) 5 L.J. Ch. 349 11–317
Emond (1829) Shaw 299 .... 16–224, 16–227
Enfield LBC v Mahoney [1983] 1 W.L.R. 749; [1983] 2 All E.R. 901; (1983) 127 S.J. 392, CA (Civ Div) 3–181, 14–9
Entick v Carrington (1765) 19 St. Tr. 1030 2–225
Esso BHP v Plowman (1995) 128 A.L.R. 391 7–21
Esso Petroleum v Kingswood Motors [1974] Q.B. 142 .... 6–1, 12–171, 14–132
Estes v Texas, 381 U.S. 532 (1965) 10–207
Etherington v Big Blow Gold Mines [1897] W.N. 21 15–85
European Asian Bank AG v Wentworth (1986) 5 N.S.W.L.R. 445 .... 10–26, 10–29
European Pacific Banking Corp v Fourth Estate Publications Ltd [1993] 1 N.Z.L.R. 559, CA 9–5
European Pacific Banking Corp v Television New Zealand Ltd [1994] 3 N.Z.L.R. 43 9–96
Eutectic Welding Alloys Co Ltd v Whitting, 1969 S.L.T. (News) 79 .... 16–256, 16–265
Evans, Re; Evans v Noton [1893] 1 Ch. 252 .... 3–137, 10–162, 11–100, 15–6
Evans v Amicus Healthcare Ltd; Hadley v Midland Fertility Services Ltd [2004] EWCA Civ 727; [2005] Fam. 1; [2004] 3 W.L.R. 681; [2004] 3 All E.R. 1025; [2004] 2 F.L.R. 766; [2004] 2 F.C.R. 530; (2004) 78 B.M.L.R. 181; [2004] Fam. Law 647; (2004) 148 S.J.L.B. 823; *The Times*, June 30, 2004; *Independent*, June 29, 2004, CA (Civ Div) 2–168
Evans v Evans (1893) 67 L.T. 719 12–129
Evelyn v Lewis (1844) 3 Hare 472; (1844) 67 E.R. 467 .... 11–319, 11–320, 14–132
Evening Star, Re (1884) N.Z.L.R. 3 S.C. 8 16–211
Everet v Williams (1725), unreported, referred to in Lindley and Banks, *Partnership* (18th ed., 2002) 11–54, 11–59
Ewan v Macewan, Hume, Vol.II, p.139 16–151
Express Newspapers Plc, Petrs, 1999 J.C. 176; 1999 S.L.T. 644; 1999 S.C.C.R. 262; 1999 G.W.D. 11–494, HCJ 16–55, 16–300, 16–343, 16–427, 16–429, 16–430, 16–426
Eyre v Countess of Shaftsbury (1722) 2 P. Wms. 103; (1722) 24 E.R. 659 11–334

F (A Minor) (Publication of Information), Re; sub nom. A (A Minor), Re [1977] Fam. 58; [1976] 3 W.L.R. 813; [1977] 1 All E.R. 114; 120 S.J. 753; *The Times*, October 15, 1976, CA (Civ Div) 4–2, 4–16, 5–139, 6–85, 7–211, 7–212, 8–99, 8–118, 8–120, 8–122, 8–123, 8–132, 8–135, 8–136, 8–139, 11–337, 11–339, 11–346, 11–348, 15–17
F (Mental Patient: Sterilisation), Re. *See* F v West Berkshire HA
F (Minors) (Wardship: Police Investigation), Re; sub nom. Re FS (Minors: Wardship: Publication of Transcript) [1989] Fam. 18; [1988] 3 W.L.R. 818; [1989] 1 F.L.R. 39; [1989] F.C.R. 752; 87 L.G.R. 63; [1989] Fam. Law 18; (1990) 154 J.P.N. 105; (1988) 132 S.J. 1324, CA (Civ Div) 7–47, 8–102
F (Orse A) (A Minor) (Publication of Information), Re. *See* Re F (A Minor) (Publication of Information)
F v West Berkshire HA; sub nom. Re F (Mental Patient: Sterilisation) [1990] 2 A.C. 1; [1989] 2 W.L.R. 1025; [1989] 2 All E.R. 545; [1989] 2 F.L.R. 376; (1989) 139 N.L.J. 789; (1989) 133 S.J. 785, HL 6–54
Fairclough v Manchester Ship Canal Co (No.1) (1896) 13 T.L.R. 56 4–123

TABLE OF CASES

Fairclough & Sons v Manchester Ship Canal Co (No.2) (1897) 41 S.J. 225; [1897] W.N. 7, CA 12–15, 12–94, 12–96, 12–103, 14–124, 16–243
Fakih Bros v P Moller (Copenhagen) Ltd [1994] 1 Lloyd's Rep. 103 12–70
Family of Derek Bennett v Officers A and B and HM Coroner and Commissioner of Metropolitan Police. *See* R. (on the application of A) v HM Coroner for Inner South London
Fanshaw v Knowles [1916] 2 K.B. 538 10–187
Farrah v Kent (1838) 6 Dowl. 676 11–114
Favard v Favard (1896) 75 L.T. 664 .... 12–33, 15–13
Fawcett v Garford (1789) unreported, cited in Oswald, *Contempt* (3rd ed.), p.62 11–50
Federal Bank of the Middle East v Hadkinson (Stay of Action); Hadkinson v Saab (No.1) [2000] 1 W.L.R. 1695; [2000] 2 All E.R. 395; [2000] C.P.L.R. 295; [2000] B.P.I.R. 597; (2000) 97(12) L.S.G. 42; (2000) 150 N.L.J. 393; (2000) 144 S.J.L.B. 128; *The Times*, March 16, 2000; *Independent*, March 14, 2000, CA (Civ Div) 12–48, 12–70, 12–153, 15–40
Felkin v Herbert (1864) 33 L.J. Ch. 294 .... 4–202, 14–6
Fenlon v Lowther (1787) 1 Cox Eq. Cas. 315 14–123
Fenn (1835) 3 Dowl. 346 .... 11–100, 11–101
Fenner v Wilson & Co (Barnsley) Ltd (1893) 10 R.P.C. 283 11–74
Fennings v Humphrey (1841) 4 Beav. 1; (1841) 49 E.R. 237 9–201
Ferguson v Normand, 1994 J.C. 260; 1994 S.L.T. 1355; 1994 S.C.C.R. 812, HCJ Appeal 16–51, 16–79
Ferguson's CB, Petr (1905) 7 F. 898 16–267
Fernandez, Ex p. (1861) 10 C.B. (N.S.) 3; (1861) 142 E.R. 349 .... 3–132, 3–185, 10–162, 13–7, 14–5, 14–101
Finance Union, Re (1895) 11 T.L.R. 167 .... 5–31, 5–105
Finnerty v Smith (1835) 1 Bing. N.C. 649; (1835) 131 E.R. 1267 11–48
First Express, Re [1991] B.C.C. 782 12–163
Fisher (1811) 2 Camp. 563 4–111
Fitzgibbon v Barker (1992) 111 F.L.R. 191 5–266
Flint v Pike (1825) 2 B. & C. 473; (1825) 107 E.R. 1136 10–150
Flynn v HM Advocate, unreported, 1990 16–79
Forbes v Forbes, 1993 S.L.T. 16 .... 16–260, 16–262
Forbes v Samuel [1913] 3 K.B. 706 11–115
Forbes v Smith [1998] 1 All E.R. 973; [1998] 1 F.L.R. 835; [1998] 2 F.C.R. 342; [1998] F.S.R. 295; [1998] Fam. Law 256; *The Times*, January 14, 1998, Ch D ... 7–43, 7–50, 7–52, 8–126, 8–128, 11–75, 11–81
Forkes v Weir, 1897 5 S.L.T. 194 16–140
Forrest v Wilson, 1993 S.C.C.R. 631; 1994 S.L.T. 490 .... 16–115, 16–420
Fortescue v McKeown [1914] 1 I.R. 30 3–15
Foster v Hawden, 2 Lev. 205; 2 Hawk P.C., c.22, s.17 10–181
Foster v Jackson (1616) Hob. 52; (1616) 80 E.R. 201 3–145
Fox v Bannister, King & Rigbeys [1988] 1 Q.B. 925, CA 12–255
Fox v Wheatley (1893), Oswald, *Contempt* (3rd ed., 1910), p.53 10–89
Francome v Mirror Group Newspapers Ltd [1984] 1 W.L.R. 892; [1984] 2 All E.R. 408; (1984) 81 L.S.G. 2225; (1984) 128 S.J. 484, CA (Civ Div) 1–102, 2–48, 4–335, 6–7, 9–19, 9–33, 9–110
Fraser v Evans [1969] 1 Q.B. 349; [1968] 3 W.L.R. 1172; [1969] 1 All E.R. 8; 112 S.J. 805, CA (Civ Div); reversing *The Times*, September 26, 1968 .... 2–150, 6–18
Fraser v The Queen; Meredith v The Queen (1984) 3 N.S.W.L.R. 212 .... 10–24, 10–25
Fraser's Trs v Cran (1879) 6 R. 451 16–243
Freston, Re (1883) 11 Q.B.D. 545 ..... 3–53, 3–71, 3–89, 3–141, 3–143, 3–146, 3–148, 3–150, 3–152, 3–153, 3–154, 3–179, 3–180, 3–184, 11–67
Freudiana Holdings Ltd, Re [1995] T.L.R. 635 11–54
Friel v Scott, 2000 J.C. 86; 1999 S.L.T. 1384; 1999 G.W.D. 30–1413, HCJ 8–12
Fripp v Bridgewater Canal Co (1845) 3 W.R. 356 11–320
Fuller v Prentice, 1 H. Bl. 49; 126 E.R. 31 .... 11–103, 11–104
Furniss v Cambridge News Ltd (1907) 23 T.L.R. 705, CA 2–51, 7–16, 9–23, 12–222

Table of Cases

G (A Child) (Contempt: Committal Order), Re; sub nom. PG v LMR [2003] EWCA Civ 489; [2003] 1 W.L.R. 2051; [2003] 2 F.L.R. 58; [2003] 2 F.C.R. 231; [2003] Fam. Law 470; (2003) 100(24) L.S.G. 35; *The Times*, May 5, 2003, CA (Civ Div) 13–83, 19–2

G (A Child) (Litigants In Person), Re; sub nom. G (A Child) (Disclosure: Prohibition), Re [2003] EWCA Civ 1055; [2003] 2 F.L.R. 963; [2003] Fam. Law 808; *The Times*, July 31, 2003; *Independent*, October 8, 2003, CA (Civ Div) 4–194, 4–224, 8–102, 8–104

G (A Minor), Re. *See* Re G (Chambers Proceedings: McKenzie Friend)

G (Adult Patient: Publicity), Re [1996] 1 F.C.R. 413; [1995] 2 F.L.R. 528; [1995] Fam. Law 677, Fam Div 6–54

G (Chambers Proceedings: McKenzie Friend), Re; sub nom. Re G [1999] 1 W.L.R. 1828 (Note); [1999] 2 F.L.R. 59; [1999] Fam. Law 454, CA (Civ Div) 7–47

G (Minors), Re [1982] 1 W.L.R. 438; [1982] 2 All E.R. 32; 80 L.G.R. 596; (1982) 12 Fam. Law 119; 126 S.J. 135, CA (Civ Div) 14–9

G (Minors) (Celebrities: Publicity), Re [1999] 1 F.L.R. 409; [1999] 3 F.C.R. 181; [1999] Fam. Law 141; *The Times*, October 28, 1998, CA (Civ Div) 1–102, 2–58, 6–55, 6–64, 6–77, 6–81, 6–127, 6–140, 8–140

G v C (Residence Order: Committal); sub nom. C v G [1998] 1 F.L.R. 43; [1998] 1 F.C.R. 592; [1997] Fam. Law 785; *The Times*, October 14, 1996, CA (Civ Div) 19–2

G's Application for a Committal Order, Re [1954] 1 W.L.R. 1116 15–14

GCT (Management) Ltd v Laurie Marsh Group Ltd [1972] F.S.R. 519; [1973] R.P.C. 432, Ch D 12–125, 15–80

GIO Personal Investment Services Ltd v Liverpool and London Steamship Protection & Indemnity Association Ltd [1999] 1 W.L.R. 984; (1999) 96(6) L.S.G. 35; *The Times*, January 13, 1999, CA (Civ Div) 2–62, 7–18, 12–211

Gagnon v McDonald, *The Times*, November 14, 1984 12–33

Galbraith v HM Advocate (No.1), 2001 S.L.T. 465; 2000 S.C.C.R. 935; 2000 G.W.D. 31–1223, HCJ 7–138, 7–139, 7–156, 7–205, 16–376

Gallagher v Durack (1983) 152 C.L.R. 238; (1983) 57 A.L.J.R. 191; 45 A.L.R. 53, H Ct (Aus) 5–205, 5–264

Galloway (Earl of) v Nixon (1877) 5 R. 28 16–257

Galvanised Tank Manufacturer's Association Ltd's Agreement, Re [1965] 2 All E.R. 1003 12–102

Gammon (Hong Kong) Ltd v Att-Gen of Hong Kong [1985] A.C. 1; [1984] 3 W.L.R. 437; [1984] 2 All E.R. 503; 26 B.L.R. 159; (1985) 80 Cr. App. R. 194; [1984] Crim. L.R. 479; (1984) 81 L.S.G. 1993; (1984) 128 S.J. 549, PC (HK) 7–206

Gandolfo v Gandolfo [1981] Q.B. 359, CA 13–92

Garage Equipment Association's Agreement, Re (1964) L.R. 4 R.P. 491 12–102

Garden v Cresswell (1837) 2 M. & W. 319; (1837) 150 E.R. 778 11–100

Garibaldo v Cagnoni (1703) 6 Mod. 90; (1703) 87 E.R. 848 .... 5–139, 11–160, 11–169, 11–304

Garnett v Ferrand (1827) 6 B. & C. 611 13–100

Garstin v Garstin (1865) 4 Sw. & Tr. 73; (1865) 164 E.R. 1443 12–66

Garvin v Domus Publishing Ltd [1989] Ch. 335; [1988] 3 W.L.R. 314; [1989] 2 All E.R. 344; (1988) 85(33) L.S.G. 44; (1988) 132 S.J. 1091, Ch D 3–191

Gaskell and Chambers Ltd v Hudson Dodsworth & Co [1936] K.B. 595 11–65

Gaunt v Johnson (1848) 6 Hare 551; (1848) 67 E.R. 1283 11–105

Gay v Hancock (1887) 56 L.T. 726 12–15

Gee v BBC, unreported, June 8, 1984, CA 13–76

General Medical Council v BBC [1998] 1 W.L.R. 1573; [1998] 3 All E.R. 426; [1998] E.M.L.R. 833; (1998) 43 B.M.L.R. 143; (1998) 95(25) L.S.G. 32; (1998) 148 N.L.J. 942; (1998) 142 S.J.L.B. 182; *The Times*, June 11, 1998; *Independent*, June 17, 1998, CA (Civ Div) 4–117, 7–109, 13–76

Gent-Davis v Harris, Re (1892) 40 W.R. 267 11–322

Gentile v State Bar of Nevada [1991] 500 1 U.S. 1030, 111 S.C.R. 2720 1–164

George v George [1986] 2 F.L.R. 347; [1986] Fam. Law 294, CA (Civ Div) 12–28, 15–51

George Outram & Co Ltd v Lees, 1992 J.C. 17; 1992 S.L.T. 32; 1992 S.C.C.R. 120, HCJ 16–55, 16–427, 16–429

Gertrud, The [1927] W.N. 265; [1927] 44 T.L.R. 1; [1927] 29 Lloyd's Rep. 5 12–262

Gibbons v Registrar, Stroud CC, *Independent*, October 8, 1990, CA 11–313

Gibbs v Phillipson (1829) 1 Russ. & My. 19; (1829) 39 E.R. 8 3–146

Giles v Lackington (1584) Ch. Cas. Ch. 177; (1584) 21 E.R. 103 11–317

[lxxiii]

TABLE OF CASES

Giles v Venson (1728) 1 Barn. K.B. 56; (1728) 94 E.R. 39 11–317
Gilfillan v Ure (1824) 3 S. 15 .... 16–144, 16–215
Gilham (1828) 1 M. & M. 165; 173 E.R. 1118 4–25
Gilkie, Hume, Vol.II, p.139 16–150
Gilpin v Cohen (1869) L.R. Ex. 131 3–146
Gisborne Herald Co Ltd v Solicitor-General [1995] 3 N.Z.L.R. 563 ..... 1–142, 1–144, 2–34, 2–35,
             2–100, 2–101, 2–107, 2–144, 4–68, 4–69, 4–74, 4–88, 5–200
Glasgow International Exhibition v Sosnowski (1901) 39 S.L.R. 28 .... 16–261, 16–67
Glasner (1994) 119 D.L.R. (4th) 113; 93 C.C.C. (3d) 226, SCC 11–88
Glendinning v Browne (1854) 3 Ir. C.L.R. 115 3–146
Glendinning v Thomas (1862) 6 L.T. 251 11–111
Globe and Mail v Boland [1960] S.C.R. 203; (1960) 22 D.L.R. (2d) 277 2–99
Goad v Amalgamated Union of Engineering Workers (Engineering Section) (Continued
   Failure to Comply: Fine); sub nom. Goad v Amalgamated Union of Engineering
   Workers (Engineering Section) (No.3) [1973] I.C.R. 108; *The Times*, December 9,
   1972, NIRC 3–21
Goad v AUEW (No.3). *See* Goad v Amalgamated Union of Engineering Workers
   (Engineering Section) (Continued Failure to Comply: Fine)
Gobbey v Dewes (1833) 10 Bing. 112; (1833) 131 E.R. 848 11–329
Goby v Weatherill [1915] 2 K.B. 674 10–182
Godfrey v Demon Internet Ltd (Application to Strike Out) [2001] Q.B. 201; [2000] 3 W.L.R.
   1020; [1999] 4 All E.R. 342; [1999] E.M.L.R. 542; [1998–99] Info. T.L.R. 252; [1999]
   I.T.C.L.R. 282; [1999] Masons C.L.R. 267; (1999) 149 N.L.J. 609; *The Times*, April
   20, 1999, QBD 1–179, 4–28, 4–191
Godwin, Ex p. *See* R. v Southwark Crown Court Ex p. Godwin
Godwin, Re. *See* R. v Southwark Crown Court Ex p. Godwin
Goff v Goff [1990] F.C.R. 10; [1989] Fam. Law 276; (1990) 154 J.P.N. 121, CA (Civ Div) 12–24,
                                              19–2
Goff v Mills (1844) 13 L.J.Q.B. 227 .... 11–100, 11–101, 11–105, 11–114
Gohohas v Lintas Export Advertising Services, *The Times*, January 21, 1964 10–103
Golder v United Kingdom [1975] 1 E.H.R.R. 524 11–302
Goldsmith v Pressdram Ltd [1988] 1 W.L.R. 64; [1987] 3 All E.R. 485, CA (Civ Div) 10–176
Gompers v Bucks's Stove and Range Co, 221 U.S. 418 (1911) 3–2, 3–59, 3–245
Goodall v Harris (1730) 2 Eq. Ca. Abr. 756; (1730) 22 E.R. 641 11–338
Goodwin v United Kingdom (17488/90) (1996) 22 E.H.R.R. 123; 1 B.H.R.C. 81; *The Times*,
   March 28, 1996, ECHR 1–110, 1–157, 1–158, 2–38, 2–50, 2–52, 2–67, 2–69, 2–193, 2–211,
         3–187, 5–262, 7–118, 7–236, 9–1, 9–2, 9–3, 9–7, 9–8, 9–12, 9–22, 9–35,
         9–87, 9–96, 9–107, 9–137, 9–150, 9–151, 9–153. 9–154, 9–155, 9–162,
         9–163, 9–165, 9–167, 9–172, 9–174, 9–244, 9–245, 10–163, 16–385
Goodwin v West (1638) Jones W. 430; (1638) 82 E.R. 226 14–155
Goose v Sandford & Co [1998] T.L.R. 85 5–238
Gordon v Fiddler (1823) 2 S. 486 16–243
Gordon v Gordon [1903] P. 1417 15–13
Gordon v Gordon [1904] P. 163, CA 12–66
Goudy v Duncombe (1847) 1 Exch. 430; (1847) 154 E.R. 183 3–145
Gouriet v Union of Post Office Workers; sub nom. Att-Gen v Gouriet [1978] A.C. 435;
   [1977] 3 W.L.R. 300; [1977] 3 All E.R. 70; 121 S.J. 543, HL; reversing [1977] Q.B.
   729; [1977] 2 W.L.R. 310; [1977] 1 All E.R. 696; 121 S.J. 103, CA (Civ Div) 2–209, 2–214,
                                2–215, 3–89, 6–27, 9–240
Government of Sierra Leone v Davenport. *See* Sierra Leone v Davenport (No.2)
Gradinger v Austria (A/328) (1995) 33/1994/480/562 .... 3–209, 12–14
Graham (1876) 3 Coup. 217 16–141
Graham v Farquhar, 1893 1 S.L.T. 63 16–220
Graham v Robert Younger Ltd, 1955 J.C. 28; 1955 S.L.T. 250 .... 12–182, 16–237, 16–238, 16–239,
                                          16–242
Grant (1820) Shaw 50 16–123
Grantham Wholesale Fruit, Vegetable and Potato Merchants Ltd, Re [1972] 1 W.L.R. 559;
   116 S.J. 332, Ch D 3–10, 3–89, 3–164, 3–170, 14–101
Gray (James) (1831) B.N. 165 16–122
Gray v McNair (1826) 4 S. 785 16–260

[lxxiv]

Table of Cases

Gray (Lord) v Petrie (1848) 10 D. 718 16–260
Gray (Lord) v Petrie (1849) 11 D. 1021 16–264
Great Future International Ltd v Sealand Housing Corp (No.7) [2004] EWHC 124; *The Times*, March 1, 2004, Ch D 3–75, 3–238
Greaves, Re (1827) 1 C. & J. 374; (1827) 148 E.R. 1466 12–255
Green (A Bankrupt), Re [1958] 2 All E.R. 57 7–41
Green v Smith, 1987 S.C.C.R. 686; 1988 S.L.T. 175 16–128
Greenberg (1919) 12 L.T. 288 11–216
Greene v Associated Newspapers Ltd [2004] EWCA Civ 1462; [2005] 1 All E.R. 30; [2005] E.M.L.R. 10; (2004) 101(45) L.S.G. 31; (2004) 148 S.J.L.B. 1318; *The Times*, November 10, 2004; *Independent*, November 9, 2004, CA (Civ Div) 2–198, 6–19, 6–131
Greenway v Att-Gen (1927) 44 T.L.R. 124 7–74
Greenwood v Leather Shod Wheel Co [1900] 1 Ch. 421, CA 4–129
Gregory v United Kingdom (1997) 25 E.H.R.R. 577 .... 11–355, 11–360, 11–389
Gregson v Grant (1910) 48 S.L.T. 6; 1910 2 S.L.T. 16 16–137
Grey, Re 1892 12–248
Gribben v Gribben, 1976 S.L.T. 266, IH (1 Div) 16–235, 16–248, 16–254, 16–256
Griesley's Case (1588) Co. 8 Rep. 38a, 77 E.R. 530 .... 1–35, 11–140
Griffin (Paul), Re [1996] T.L.R. 619 11–28
Griffin v Griffin [2000] C.P.L.R. 452; [2000] 2 F.L.R. 44; [2000] 2 F.C.R. 302; [2000] Fam. Law 531; (2000) 97(20) L.S.G. 42; (2000) 144 S.J.L.B. 213; *The Times*, April 28, 2000, CA (Civ Div) 14–47
Groenvelt v Burwell (1700) 1 Ld Raym. 454; (1700) 91 E.R. 1065 13–105
Grupo Torras SA v Sheik Fahad Mohammed Al Sabah, *The Times*, March 30, 1999 ..... 12–70, 12–72, 12–73
Guardian Newspapers Ltd, Ex p., Re [1999] 1 W.L.R. 2130; [1999] 1 All E.R. 65; [1999] 1 Cr. App. R. 284; (1998) 95(39) L.S.G. 34; (1998) 148 N.L.J. 1514; (1998) 142 S.J.L.B. 255; *The Times*, October 9, 1998; *Independent*, October 8, 1998, CA (Crim Div) 2–66, 7–32, 7–33, 7–34
Guardian Newspapers Ltd, Re. *See* Chan U Seek v Alvis Vehicles Ltd
Gugenheim v Ladbroke & Co Ltd [1947] 1 All E.R. 292 11–52
Guildford BC v Valler; sub nom. Guildford BC v Smith [1993] T.L.R. 274 ...... 3–19, 3–49, 3–68, 3–76, 3–193, 14–149, 16–252
Gutch (1829) M.& M. 433; (1829) 173 E.R. 1214 4–201

H (A Minor) (Injunction: Breach), Re (1986) Fam. Law 139 12–9
H (A Minor) (Wardship: Applications), Re; sub nom. Re H (A Minor) [1985] 1 W.L.R. 1164; [1985] 3 All E.R. 1; [1986] 1 F.L.R. 132; [1986] Fam. Law 26; (1985) 82 L.S.G. 2997; (1985) 129 S.J. 622, CA (Civ Div) 8–110
H (Minors) (Public Interest: Protection of Identity), Re; sub nom. HS v HS; Re H-S [1994] 1 W.L.R. 1141; [1994] 3 All E.R. 390; [1994] 1 F.L.R. 519; [1994] 3 F.C.R. 90; [1994] Fam. Law 251; *The Times*, December 27, 1993; *Independent*, January 12, 1994, CA (Civ Div) 1–139, 1–174, 2–37, 6–56, 6–87, 6–90, 6–96
H (Minors) (Sexual Abuse: Standard of Proof), Re; sub nom. Re H (Minors) (Child Abuse: Threshold Conditions); Re H and R (Child Sexual Abuse: Standard of Proof) [1996] A.C. 563; [1996] 2 W.L.R. 8; [1996] 1 All E.R. 1; [1996] 1 F.L.R. 80; [1996] 1 F.C.R. 509; [1996] Fam. Law 74; (1995) 145 N.L.J. 1887; (1996) 140 S.J.L.B. 24; *The Times*, December 15, 1995; *Independent*, January 17, 1996, HL 3–245
H v C (Contempt and Criminal Proceedings) [1993] 1 F.L.R. 787, CA 12–9, 12–10
H v Ministry of Defence [1991] 2 Q.B. 103; [1991] 2 W.L.R. 1192; [1991] 2 All E.R. 834; (1991) 141 N.L.J. 420; *The Times*, April 1, 1991; *Independent*, March 22, 1991; *Guardian*, March 27, 1991; *Daily Telegraph*, April 1, 1991, CA (Civ Div) ... 7–104, 7–108, 8–8, 8–9
H (falsely called C) v C (1859) 29 L.J. (P. & M.) 29 8–128
H's Settlement, Re; H v H [1909] 2 Ch. 260 .... 11–334, 11–339, 12–94
H-S, Re. *See* Re H (Minors) (Public Interest: Protection of Identity)
H v H (Breach of Injunction) [2001] EWCA Civ 653; [2001] 3 F.C.R. 628 19–2
HM Coroner for Kent v Terrill, CO/1384/00; [2001] A.C.D. 27, May 8, 2000 ..... 11–105, 11–144, 13–102, 19–1

[lxxv]

TABLE OF CASES

HPSI Ltd v Thomas and Williams (1983) 133 New Law Jo. 598 12–94
HTV Cymru (Wales) Ltd, Ex p. [2002] E.M.L.R. 11, Crown Ct (Cardiff) 4–104, 6–2, 6–18, 6–38,
    10–7, 13–26, 13–37, 14–43
Hadkinson v Hadkinson [1952] P. 285 .... 9–201, 9–209, 12–66, 12–67, 12–70, 12–71, 12–73
Hadmore Productions Ltd v Hamilton [1983] 1 A.C. 191 7–195
Haire (1829) Hume, Vol.II, S.N. 165 16–227
Halcon International Inc v Shell Transport and Trading Co (Discovery: Confidential
    Documents) [1979] R.P.C. 97; 122 S.J. 645, CA (Civ Div) 3–201, 12–201
Hale v Castleman (1746) 1 W. Bl. 2; (1746) 96 E.R. 2 11–48
Hale v Tanner [2000] 1 W.L.R. 2377; [2000] 2 F.L.R. 879; [2000] 3 F.C.R. 62; [2000] Fam.
    Law 876; (2001) 165 J.P.N. 184; (2000) 164 J.P.N. 861; *The Times*, August 22, 2000,
    CA (Civ Div) 12–7, 14–18, 14–20, 14–45, 14–47, 14–58, 14–75, 14–79, 15–15, 15–63,
    19–2
Hall (1776) 2 W. Bl. 1110 .... 11–268, 11–304
Hall v Associated Newspapers, 1979 J.C. 1; 1978 S.L.T. 241, HCJ 5–81, 5–109, 16–39, 16–49,
    16–55, 16–65, 16–71, 16–76, 16–160, 16–164, 16–165, 16–166, 16–172,
    16–178, 16–182, 16–184, 16–185, 16–190, 16–214, 16–232, 16–269,
    16–276, 16–279, 16–280, 16–306, 16–308, 16–311, 16–338, 16–355
Hallam-Eames v Merrett Syndicates [1995] T.L.R. 346 7–27
Hallet v Mears (1810) 13 East 15n; (1810) 104 E.R. 271 .... 11–103, 11–104, 11–111
Halsam, Ex p. (1740) 2 Atk. 49; (1740) 26 E.R. 427 .... 11–216, 11–287
Hamilton v Anderson (1856) 18 D. 1003 .... 16–30, 16–48
Hampden v Wallis (1884) 26 Ch. D. 746 15–24
Hampshire CC v Gillingham, unreported, June 22, 2000 .... 13.120, 13–122, 13–133, 15–88
Handmade Films (Production) Ltd v Express Newspapers [1986] F.S.R. 463 .... 9–5, 9–20, 9–63,
    9–85, 9–97, 9–110, 9–132, 9–226, 9–245
Handyside v United Kingdom (A/24) (1979–80) 1 E.H.R.R. 737, ECHR 1–107, 1–110, 1–112,
    2–168, 8–7
Hannes v Waugh (1713) 2 Eq. Cas. Abr. 754; (1713) 22 E.R. 639 .... 11–338, 11–342
Harb v Aziz [2005] EWCA Civ 632; *The Times*, June 6, 2005, CA (Civ Div) 1–174
Harby, Re (1739) Sanders, *Chancery Orders*, p.545 11–48
Harley v McDonald [2001] UKPC 18; [2001] A.C. 678, PC; reversing [1999] 3 N.Z.L.R.
    545 .... 10–139, 11–67
Harman v Secretary of State for the Home Dept. *See* Home Office v Harman
Harman v United Kingdom (1985) 7 E.H.R.R. 146 12–218
Harmsworth v Harmsworth [1987] 1 W.L.R. 1676; [1987] 3 All E.R. 816; [1988] 1 F.L.R.
    349; [1988] Fam. Law 169; (1987) 131 S.J. 1625, CA (Civ Div) 13–134, 15–19, 15–32,
    15–74
Harrington v North London Polytechnic [1984] 1 W.L.R. 1293; [1984] 3 All E.R. 666;
    (1984) 81 L.S.G. 3341; (1984) 128 S.J. 800, CA (Civ Div) 1–137, 3–129, 6–117, 12–107,
    12–108
Harris (An Infant), Re, *The Times*, May 21, 1960 .... 11–336, 12–94
Harris v Harris (Contempt of Court: Application to Purge) [2001] EWCA Civ 1645; [2002]
    Fam. 253; [2002] 2 W.L.R. 747; [2002] 1 All E.R. 185; [2002] 1 F.L.R. 248; [2001]
    3 F.C.R. 640; [2002] Fam. Law 93; (2002) 99(2) L.S.G. 27; (2001) 145 S.J.L.B. 270;
    The Times, November 19, 2001; *Independent*, November 14, 2001, CA (Civ Div);
    reversing in part [2001] Fam. 502; [2001] 3 W.L.R. 765; [2001] 2 F.L.R. 955; [2001]
    Fam. Law 730; (2001) 98(29) L.S.G. 39; (2001) 145 S.J.L.B. 163; *The Times*, August
    6, 2001, Fam Div 3–11, 3–181, 12–185, 14–6, 14–42, 14–54
Harris v Harris; sub nom. Att-Gen v Harris [2001] 2 F.L.R. 895; [2001] 3 F.C.R. 193; [2001]
    Fam. Law 651; [2001] Fam. 502, Fam Div 5–237, 6–10, 6–42, 6–64, 6–94, 12–54, 12–55,
    13–91, 14–9, 14–53
Harrison v Goodhall (1852) Kay 310; (1852) 69 E.R. 131 11–336
Harrison v Harrison (1842) 4 Moo. P.C. 96; (1842) 13 E.R. 238 .... 3–161, 12–66
Harrison v Lewis; sub nom. R. v S [1988] 2 F.L.R. 339; [1989] F.C.R. 765; [1988] Fam. Law
    477; (1989) 153 J.P.N. 768, CA (Civ Div) 14–76
Harrison's Case (1638) Cro. Car. 503; (1638) 79 E.R. 1034 .... 1–18, 1–19, 1–37, 10–144
Harrods Ltd v Dow Jones & Co Inc [2003] EWHC 1162, QBD 1–179, 1–181

TABLE OF CASES

Harrow LBC v Johnstone [1997] 1 W.L.R. 459; [1997] 1 All E.R. 929; [1997] 1 F.L.R. 887; [1997] 2 F.C.R. 225; (1997) 29 H.L.R. 475; [1997] Fam. Law 478; (1997) 161 J.P. Rep. 580; [1997] E.G.C.S. 41; (1997) 94(15) L.S.G. 26; (1997) 147 N.L.J. 413; [1997] N.P.C. 40; *The Times*, March 14, 1997, HL 1–126, 3–97, 3–118, 3–139, 5–198, 6–136, 11–42, 11–45
Harvey, In the Estate of [1907] P. 239 .... 11–104, 12–132
Harvey v Harvey (1884) 26 Ch. D. 644 .... 3–89, 3–184, 15–48
Harvie v Ross (1886) 24 S.L.R. 58; (1886) 14 R. 71 .... 6–41, 6–126, 16–234, 16–236, 16–263
Hashman and Harrup v UK (2000) 30 E.H.R.R. 241; [2000] Crim. L.R. 185 14–110
Haskell Golf Ball Co v Hutchison & Main (1904) 21 R.P.C. 497 11–74
Hassneh Insurance Co of Israel v Steuart J Mew [1993] 2 Ll. Rep. 243 12–201
Hastings, Re (1892) 67 L.T. 334 14–121
Hastingwood Property Ltd v Saunders Bearman Anselm [1991] Ch. 114; [1990] 3 W.L.R. 623; (1990) 140 N.L.J. 817; (1990) 134 S.J. 1153, Ch D 12–258
Hatch v Blissett (1714) Gilb. 308; (1714) 93 E.R. 338 3–146
Haughey v Prendeville and Penfield Enterprises Ltd [1996] N.I. 367 9–16
Hawkins v Gathercole (1852) 1 Drew 12; (1852) 61 E.R. 355 11–319
Haydon v Haydon [1911] 2 K.B. 191, CA 15–22
Haynes v Davis [1915] 1 K.B. 332 3–216
Haywood, Ex p. (1881) W.N. 115 11–320
Head v Orrow [2004] EWCA Civ 1691 .... 14–19, 14–20
Hearn v Tennant (1807) 14 Ves. Jun. 136; (1807) 33 E.R. 473 12–38
Heathcote v Crackles [2002] EWCA Civ 222 19–2
Heatons Transport (St Helens) Ltd v Transport and General Workers Union; Craddock Bros v Transport and General Workers Union (Non-Payment of Fine: Accountability of Union); Panalpina Services Ltd v Transport and General Workers Union [1973] A.C. 15; [1972] 3 W.L.R. 431; [1972] 3 All E.R. 101; [1972] I.C.R. 308; [1972] I.R.L.R. 25; 14 K.I.R. 48; 116 S.J. 598, HL 3–150, 3–247, 11–111, 12–80, 12–90, 12–94, 12–96, 12–97, 12–99, 12–118, 16–243
Hector v Att-Gen of Antigua and Barbuda [1990] 2 A.C. 312; [1990] 2 W.L.R. 606; [1990] 2 All E.R. 103; (1990) 87(10) L.S.G. 34; (1990) 134 S.J. 316, PC (Ant) 2–50, 2–54
Hegarty v O'Sullivan (1985) 135 N.L.J. 557; *The Times*, May 8, 1985, CA (Civ Div) 15–67, 15–74
Heirs of the line of Towie v Barclay of Auchredy (1669) Mor. 7417 16–121
Hellewell v Chief Constable of Derbyshire [1995] 1 W.L.R. 804; [1995] 4 All E.R. 473; (1995) 92(7) L.S.G. 35; (1995) 139 S.J.L.B. 49; *The Times*, January 13, 1995, QBD 9–63
Helmore v Smith (No.2) (1887) L.R. 35 Ch. D. 449, CA 2–171, 11–321
Hendale's Case (1714) Hil. 12 Anne 1–58
Henderson v Laing (1824) 3 S. 271 .... 16–144, 16–149
Henderson v Maclellan (1874) 1 R. 920 .... 16–241, 16–249
Hennegal v Evance (1806) 12 Ves. Jun. 201; (1806) 33 E.R. 77 10–158
Hennessy v Wright (1888) 21 Q.B.D. 509 9–4
Henry Pound, Son & Hutchins, Re (1889) 42 Ch. D. 402 11–323
Herbert's Case (1731) 3 P. Wms. 116; (1731) 24 E.R. 992 .... 1–65, 11–338, 11–339, 11–344, 11–347
Herrett v Reynolds (1860) 2 Giff. 409; (1860) 66 E.R. 170 3–159
Hewitt v Grunwald [2004] EWHC 2959, QBD 1–179, 4–50
Hickman v Clarke (1615) 2 Fowler's Exch. Prac. 407 11–54
Higg's Mortgage, Re (1894) 29 W.N. 73 11–328
Higgens v Sommerland (1614) 2 Bulstr. 68; (1614) 80 E.R. 965 11–59
Hill (1603) Cary 27 11–54
Hill Samuel & Co Ltd v Littaur (1985) 82 L.S.G. 2248; (1985) 135 N.L.J. 556; (1985) 129 S.J. 433; *The Times*, April 13, 1985, CA (Civ Div) 15–23, 15–70, 15–74
Hillfinch Properties v Newark Investments, *The Times*, July 1, 1981 .... 11–301, 16–281
Hill (1976) 73 D.L.R. (3d) 621 11–88
Hills v Ellis [1983] Q.B. 680; [1983] 2 W.L.R. 234; [1983] 1 All E.R. 667; (1983) 76 Cr. App. R. 217; [1983] Crim. L.R. 182; (1983) 80 L.S.G. 153; (1983) 133 N.L.J. 280; 126 S.J. 768, DC 10–216, 11–23
Hinch v Att-Gen (Victoria) (1987) 164 C.L.R. 15 .... 4–66, 4–74, 11–384
Hinde, Re; Thornhill v Steel Morris (1911) 56 S.J. 34 .... 4–131, 5–116
Hipgrave v Hipgrave [1962] P. 91 12–34

TABLE OF CASES

Hipkin v Hipkin [1962] 1 W.L.R. 491 14–125
Hitachi Sales (UK) v Mitsui Osk Lines [1986] 2 Lloyd's Rep. 574, CA (Civ Div) 12–128
Hoare, Re Ex p. Nelson (1880) 14 Ch. D. 41, CA 14–120
Hodgson v Imperial Tobacco Ltd (No.1) [1998] 1 W.L.R. 1056; [1998] 2 All E.R. 673;
    [1998] 1 Costs L.R. 14; [1999] P.I.Q.R. Q1; (1998) 41 B.M.L.R. 1; (1998) 95(15)
    L.S.G. 31; (1998) 148 N.L.J. 241; (1998) 142 S.J.L.B. 93; *The Times*, February 13,
    1998; *Independent*, February 17, 1998, CA (Civ Div) ... 1–164, 1–166, 1–171, 1–173, 2–50,
                            2–62, 4–282, 5–6, 7–36, 7–43, 7–45, 7–46, 7–49, 7–50, 7–51, 7–52, 7–109,
                                           7–253, 8–124, 8–126, 8–128, 11–73, 11–75, 11–81
Hodgson, Woolf Productions and NUJ and Channel 4 v United Kingdom (1987) 10 E.H.R.R.
    503 .... 2–193, 7–248
Hogarth's Trs v Hope (1824) 2 H.L. Shaw's App. Cas. 125 16–107
Holbrooke's Case (1329) Y.B. 33–5, 3 Edward III, rot. 116 1–22
Holden & Co v Crown Prosecution Service (No.2). *See* Steele Ford & Newton v Crown
    Prosecution Service (No.2)
Hole & Pugsley v Sumption [2002] Lloyd's Rep. P.N. 419; [2002] P.N.L.R. 20; (2002)
    99(10) L.S.G. 32; (2001) 151 N.L.J. 1851; (2002) 146 S.J.L.B. 44; *The Times*, January
    29, 2002, Ch D 12–251, 12–256
Holgate v Grantham (1576) *Cary's Causes in Chancery*, p.82 1–47
Holley v Smyth [1998] Q.B. 726; [1998] 2 W.L.R. 742; [1998] 1 All E.R. 853; [1998]
    E.M.L.R. 133; (1998) 95(2) L.S.G. 23; (1998) 142 S.J.L.B. 35; *The Times*, December
    20, 1997, CA (Civ Div) 2–150, 4–324, 6–7
Holliday v Pitt (1734) 2 Str. 985 3–145
Holtby v Hodgson (1889) 24 Q.B.D. 103 12–146
Home Office v Harman; sub nom. Harman v Home Office; Harman v Secretary of State for
    the Home Dept [1983] 1 A.C. 280; [1982] 2 W.L.R. 338; [1982] 1 All E.R. 532; 126
    S.J. 136, HL 2–152, 2–193, 3–114, 3–157, 3–187, 3–198, 3–201, 5–20, 7–18, 11–76,
                                                              12–182, 12–201, 12–205, 12–224
Hood's Case (1892) 147 H.C. Journal 167 11–198
Hooker (Patricia), Re [1993] C.O.D. 190; C/2478/92, DC 10–37, 10–65, 10–116, 10–119, 10–120,
                                           10–127, 10–194, 10–199, 13–109, 13–126, 13–130, 13–133
Hooley, Re. *See* R. v Hooley
Hope, Re (1845) 9 Jur. 856 3–146
Hope v Carnegie (1869) 4 Ch. App. 264; (1868) 7 Eq. 254 12–99
Horgan v Horgan [2002] EWCA Civ 1371, CA (Civ Div) 14–36, 14–87, 15–55, 19–2
Horne v Smith (1815) 6 Taunt. 9; (1815) 128 E.R. 935 .... 11–104, 11–259
Horner v Horner [1982] Fam. 90; [1982] 2 W.L.R. 914; [1982] 2 All E.R. 495; (1983) 4
    F.L.R. 50; (1982) 12 Fam. Law 144, CA (Civ Div) 12–57, 14–72
Horrocks v Lowe [1975] A.C. 135; [1974] 2 W.L.R. 282; [1974] 1 All E.R. 662; 72 L.G.R.
    251; 118 S.J. 149, HL 4–284, 4–285, 4–310, 5–153
Horton v Scott, 1994 G.W.D. 8–467 16–79
Hoskins v Lloyd (1823) 1 Sim. & Sty. 393; (1823) 57 E.R. 157 3–159
Howitt Transport Ltd v Transport and General Workers Union [1973] I.C.R. 1; [1972]
    I.R.L.R. 93, NIRC 14–124
Hoye v Bush (1840) 1 Man. & G. 775; (1840) 133 E.R. 545 15–54
Hubbard v Pitt [1976] Q.B. 142; [1975] 3 W.L.R. 201; [1975] 3 All E.R. 1; [1975] I.C.R.
    308; 119 S.J. 393, CA (Civ Div) 1–137
Hubbard v Woodfield (1913) 57 Sol. Jo. 729 .... 6–1, 6–126, 12–171, 14–132
Huddart Parker & Co Proprietary v Moorehead; Appleton v Moorehead [1909] 8 C.L.R.
    330 4–19
Hudson, Re; Hudson v Hudson [1966] Ch. 209 .... 12–7, 12–187, 12–188
Hudson v Hudson (1995) [1995] 2 F.L.R. 72; [1996] 1 F.C.R. 19; [1995] Fam. Law 550; *The
    Times*, March 23, 1995; *Independent*, April 18, 1995 (C.S.), CA (Civ Div) 19–2
Huggins (1730) 2 Ld. Raym. 1574 4–199
Hughes, Ex p. (1822) 5 B. & Ald. 482; (1822) 106 E.R. 1267 12–255
Hughes v Carmichael, 1993 G.W.D. 12–805 16–81
Hulbert v Cathcart [1896] A.C. 470 15–80
Humble v Malbe (1559) Cary 41; (1559) 21 E.R. 22 11–114
Hungerford v Aylmer (1664) Sanders, *Chancery Orders*, p.317 11–48

TABLE OF CASES

Hunt, Re; sub nom. Hunt v Allied Bakeries (No.3) [1959] 2 Q.B. 69; [1959] 2 W.L.R. 686; [1959] 2 All E.R. 252; 103 S.J. 372, CA 3–146, 3–179, 3–180, 3–89, 3–141, 14–28
Hunt v Clarke (1889) 58 L.J.Q.B. 490 ...... 1–74, 1–79, 1–80, 3–135, 5–9, 5–29, 5–38, 5–39, 5–77
Hunter v Wilson (1848) 10 D. 893 .... 11–20, 16–236
Hussain v Hussain [1986] Fam. 134; [1986] 2 W.L.R. 801; [1986] 1 All E.R. 961; [1986] 2 F.L.R. 271; [1986] Fam. Law 269; (1986) 83 L.S.G. 1314; (1986) 136 N.L.J. 358; (1986) 130 S.J. 341, CA (Civ Div) 12–36, 12–48, 12–182, 12–188, 12–191, 12–193, 12–244, 15–27
Husson v Husson [1962] 1 W.L.R. 1434; [1962] 3 All E.R. 1056; 106 S.J. 737, PDAD 12–38, 12–81
Hutchinson v Amalgamated Engineering Union; Re the Daily Worker, *The Times*, August 25, 1932 .... 4–131, 5–104, 5–116
Hutchison and Harper v HM Advocate, 1983 S.C.C.R. 504; 1984 S.L.T. 233 16–133
Hyam v DPP; sub nom. R. v Hyam (Pearl Kathleen) [1975] A.C. 55; [1974] 2 W.L.R. 607; [1974] 2 All E.R. 41; (1974) 59 Cr. App. R. 91; [1974] Crim. L.R. 365; 118 S.J. 311, HL 5–120, 5–191

I v D (Access Order: Enforcement) [1989] F.C.R. 91; [1988] Fam. Law 338 .... 12–15, 19–2
IBM United Kingdom Ltd v Prima Data International Ltd [1994] 1 W.L.R. 719; [1994] 4 All E.R. 748, Ch D 3–191
Iberian Trust Ltd v Founders Trust & Investment Co Ltd [1932] 2 K.B. 87 ..... 12–48, 12–115, 2–128, 15–24, 15–26
Ibis VI, The [1921] P. 255 11–259
Ilkley Local Board v Lister (1895) 11 T.L.R. 176 14–6
Imperial Tobacco Ltd v Att-Gen [1981] A.C. 718; [1980] 2 W.L.R. 466; [1980] 1 All E.R. 866; 124 S.J. 271, HL 12–60
Imutran Ltd v Uncaged Campaigns Ltd [2001] 2 All E.R. 385; [2001] C.P. Rep. 28; [2001] E.C.D.R. 16; [2001] E.M.L.R. 21; [2001] H.R.L.R. 31; [2002] F.S.R. 2; (2001) 24(5) I.P.D. 24031; (2001) 98(14) L.S.G. 40; *The Times*, January 30, 2001, Ch D 4–324, 6–12, 6–13
Independent Commission Against Corruption v Cornwall (1993) 116 A.L.R. 97 9–50
Independent Publishing Co Ltd v Att-Gen of Trinidad and Tobago; Trinidad and Tobago News Centre Ltd v Att-Gen of Trinidad and Tobago [2004] UKPC 26; [2005] 1 A.C. 190; [2004] 3 W.L.R. 611; [2005] 1 All E.R. 499; [2004] E.M.L.R. 28; 17 B.H.R.C. 661; (2004) 101(26) L.S.G. 27; (2004) 148 S.J.L.B. 757; *The Times*, June 24, 2004, PC (Trin) 7–77, 7–78, 7–82, 7–84, 7–109, 7–110, 7–130, 7–172, 7–201, 9–83, 16–223
Ingles (1740) Sanders, *Chancery Orders*, p.552 1–60
IRC v Hoogstraten [1985] Q.B. 1077; [1984] 3 W.L.R. 933; [1984] 3 All E.R. 25; (1984) 81 L.S.G. 1368; (1984) 128 S.J. 484, CA (Civ Div) 9–222, 11–318, 14–115, 14–127
Innes (1831) Shaw 238 16–117
Inquiry under the Company Securities (Insider Dealing) Act 1985 (No.1), Re [1988] A.C. 660; [1988] 2 W.L.R. 33; [1988] 1 All E.R. 203; (1988) 4 B.C.C. 35; [1988] B.C.L.C. 153; [1988] P.C.C. 133; (1988) 85(4) L.S.G. 33; (1987) 137 N.L.J. 1181; (1988) 132 S.J. 21; *Independent*, December 11, 1987, HL 1–126, 2–67, 2–193, 7–170, 7–186, 9–17, 9–42, 9–65, 9–72, 9–79, 9–86, 9–100, 9–116, 9–143, 9–182, 9–191, 9–245, 11–133
Insurance Co v Lloyd's Syndicate [1995] 1 Ll. Rep. 272 12–201
Interbrew SA v *Financial Times* Ltd [2002] EWCA Civ 274; [2002] 2 Lloyd's Rep. 229; [2002] E.M.L.R. 24; (2002) 99(16) L.S.G. 37; *The Times*, March 21, 2002; *Independent*, March 12, 2002; *Daily Telegraph*, March 14, 2002, CA (Civ Div); affirming [2002] 1 Lloyd's Rep. 542; (2002) 99(9) L.S.G. 28; *The Times*, January 4, 2002, Ch D 1–158, 9–127, 9–146, 9–176
International Forest Products Ltd v Kern (2001) 94 B.C.L.R. (3d) 67, BCCA 1–137
International Union, United Mine Workers v Bagwell, 114 S. Ct 2552 (1994) 2–220, 3–78, 3–88, 3–171
Irtelli v Squatriti [1993] Q.B. 83; [1992] 3 W.L.R. 218; [1992] 3 All E.R. 294; (1992) 136 S.J.L.B. 100; *The Times*, March 2, 1992, CA (Civ Div) 3–140, 3–239, 3–249, 12–22, 12–35, 12–65, 12–80, 12–82, 12–88, 12–90, 12–92, 12–93, 12–94, 15–32, 15–100

TABLE OF CASES

Isaacs v Robertson [1985] A.C. 97; [1984] 3 W.L.R. 705; [1984] 3 All E.R. 140; (1984) 81
L.S.G. 2769; (1984) 134 N.L.J. 745, PC (StV) 9–202, 9–225
Isbey v Broadcasting Corp of New Zealand (No.2) [1975] 2 N.Z.L.R. 237 .... 2–51, 9–5
Iveson v Harris (1802) 7 Ves. Jun. 251; (1802) 32 E.R. 102 .... 6–41, 6–49, 6–115, 12–241, 16–226
Izuora v Queen, The [1953] A.C. 327; [1953] 2 W.L.R. 700; [1953] 1 All E.R. 827; 97 S.J.
224, PC (West Africa) 3–139, 10–136, 10–145, 11–68, 11–89

J v C; sub nom. Re C (An Infant) [1970] A.C. 668; [1969] 2 W.L.R. 540; [1969] 1 All E.R.
788; 113 S.J. 164, HL 6–61
J.P. v MacMillan Bloedel Ltd; Att-Gen of Canada Intervener (1996) 130 D.L.R. (4th) 385 1–137,
3–86
J. & R.'s Case (1367) Y.B. Lib. Ass. 40 Edw. III, pl.10 10–179
J Barber & Sons v Lloyd's Underwriters; J Barber & Sons v Toplis Harding Inc [1987] Q.B.
103; [1986] 3 W.L.R. 515; [1986] 2 All E.R. 845; [1987] E.C.C. 154; (1986) 83 L.S.G.
3253; (1986) 136 N.L.J. 658; (1986) 130 S.J. 730, QBD 10–190, 10–206
Jackson v Seager (1844) 2 Dowl. & L. 13 11–114
Jacobs, Re (1835) 1 Har. & W. 123 11–114
Jacobs, Re, *The Times*, June 13, 1874 11–48
Jademan (Holdings) Ltd v Wong Chun-Loong [1990] 2 H.K.L.R. 577 12–70
Jaggard v United Kingdom (1997) 24 E.H.R.R. 39 .... 1–109, 2–168
Jameel v Dow Jones & Co Inc; sub nom. Dow Jones & Co Inc v Jameel [2005] EWCA Civ
75; [2005] 2 W.L.R. 1614; [2005] E.M.L.R. 16; (2005) 149 S.J.L.B. 181; *The Times*,
February 14, 2005; *Independent*, February 10, 2005, CA (Civ Div) 1–179, 11–59
Jameel v Wall Street Journal Europe SPRL (No.3) [2005] EWCA Civ 74; [2005] 2 W.L.R.
1577; [2005] E.M.L.R. 17; [2005] H.R.L.R. 10; (2005) 102(15) L.S.G. 33; *The Times*,
February 14, 2005; *Independent*, February 9, 2005, CA (Civ Div) 1–181
James v Cliffe, *The Times*, June 16, 1987, CA (Civ Div) 3–10
James v Robinson (1963) 109 C.L.R. 593 .... 1–129, 5–76, 5–89, 7–143, 11–223, 11–269
Jarlinn, The [1965] 1 W.L.R. 1098 12–146
Jarvis v Islington BC (1909) 73 J.P.J. 323 11–320
Jefferson v Bhetcha [1979] 1 W.L.R. 898; [1979] 2 All E.R. 1108; 123 S.J. 389, CA (Civ
Div) 12–10
Jeffes, Cro. Car. 175, 79 E.R. 753 1–37
Jelson (Estates) Ltd v Harvey [1983] 1 W.L.R. 1401; [1984] 1 All E.R. 12; (1983) 127 S.J.
697, CA (Civ Div) 3–80, 3–213, 3–215
Jendell Australia Pty Ltd v Kesby [1983] 1 N.S.W.L.R. 127 .... 3–245, 12–44
Jennison v Baker [1972] 2 Q.B. 52; [1972] 2 W.L.R. 429; [1972] 1 All E.R. 997; (1971) 115
S.J. 930, CA (Civ Div) 2–9, 3–9, 3–12, 3–14, 3–24, 3–48, 3–69, 3–78, 3–89, 3–158, 3–164,
3–170, 12–5, 14–7, 15–5
Jewison v Dyson (1842) 9 M. & W. 540 13–100
Jewitt, Re (1864) 33 Beav. 559; (1864) 55 E.R. 486 3–146
Jockey Club v Buffham [2002] EWHC 1866; [2003] Q.B. 462; [2003] 2 W.L.R. 178; [2003]
C.P. Rep. 22; [2003] E.M.L.R. 5; (2002) 99(40) L.S.G. 32; *The Times*, October 4,
2002, QBD 6–141, 6–145
John v Express Newspapers [2000] 1 W.L.R. 1931; [2000] 3 All E.R. 257; [2000] E.M.L.R.
606; (2000) 97(21) L.S.G. 38; (2000) 150 N.L.J. 615; (2000) 144 S.J.L.B. 217; *The
Times*, April 26, 2000; *Independent*, May 2, 2000, CA (Civ Div) 9–90, 9–106, 10–175
John v MGN Ltd [1997] Q.B. 586; [1996] 3 W.L.R. 593; [1996] 2 All E.R. 35; [1996]
E.M.L.R. 229; (1996) 146 N.L.J. 13; *The Times*, December 14, 1995, CA (Civ Div) 1–132
John Fairfax & Sons Ltd v Cojuango (1988) 165 C.L.R. 364; (1988) 82 A.L.R. 1, HC 9–4
John Fairfax & Sons Ltd v Police Tribunal of New South Wales (1986) 5 N.S.W.L.R. 465 7–84
John Fairfax and Sons Pty Ltd v McRae (1955) 93 C.L.R. 351 3–86
John Fox (A Firm) v Bannister King & Rigbeys (A Firm) [1988] Q.B. 925n 13–98
John Reid Enterprises Ltd v Pell [1999] E.M.L.R. 675, Ch D 9–54, 9–141
Johnes v Claughton (1822) Jac. 573; (1822) 37 E.R. 966 .... 11–320, 14–132
Johnson, (1686) Comb. 36, 90 E.R. 328 1–38
Johnson, Re (1888) 20 Q.B.D. 68 .... 1–3, 2–28, 3–135, 6–1, 10–21, 10–97, 11–72, 11–156, 11–157,
11–158, 11–194, 11–201, 11–310

[lxxx]

TABLE OF CASES

Johnson v Grant, 1923 S.C. 789; 1923 S.L.T. 501, IH (1 Div) ... 2–11, 3–11, 3–22, 3–180, 5–207, 5–209, 12–27, 16–67, 16–234, 16–244, 16–247
Johnson v Leicestershire Constabulary; *The Times*, October 7, 1998, DC 4–115
Johnson v Walton [1990] 1 F.L.R. 350; [1990] F.C.R. 568; [1990] Fam. Law 260; (1990) 154 J.P.N. 506; *The Times*, January 2, 1990, CA (Civ Div) ... 3–76, 9–201, 9–208, 12–7, 12–22, 12–57, 14–149
Johnston v Scot and Small, WS (1829) 7 S. 234 16–67
Johnston and Drummond (1793) Hume, Vol.II, p.139 .... 16–147, 16–155
Jokai Tea Holdings, Re [1992] 1 W.L.R. 1196; [1993] 1 All E.R. 630; *Financial Times*, February 24, 1989, CA (Civ Div) 12–79
Jolly v Brown (1828) 6 S. 872 .... 16–259, 16–262
Jolly v Governor of Wandsworth Prison, Transcript 1/TLQ/0404, QBD 15–55
Jolly v Hull; Jolly v Jolly; sub nom. Jolly v Circuit Judge of Staines [2000] 2 F.L.R. 69; [2000] 2 F.C.R. 59; [2000] Fam. Law 399; *The Times*, March 10, 2000, CA (Civ Div) 14–152, 15–23, 15–57
Jolly v Staines County Court Circuit Judge. *See* Jolly v Hull
Jones, Ex p. (1806) 13 Ves. Jun. 237; (1806) 33 E.R. 283 .... 4–7, 4–12, 14–6, 11–174
Jones (1719) 1 Str. 185; (1719) 93 E.R. 462 .... 1–58, 11–317
Jones v Jones [1993] 2 F.L.R. 377; [1993] 2 F.C.R. 82; [1993] Fam. Law 519; *The Times*, March 23, 1993, CA (Civ Div) 12–28, 19–2
Jordan, (1888) 36 W.R. 589 and 797 10–144
Jordan v Jordan [1993] 1 F.L.R. 169; [1992] 2 F.C.R. 701; [1993] Fam. Law 264; *The Times*, June 22, 1992, CA (Civ Div) 12–15, 15–107
Joshua Stubbs Ltd, Re [1891] 1 Ch. 475 11–323
Juby v Miller [1991] 1 F.L.R. 133; [1991] F.C.R. 52; [1991] Fam. Law 97; (1990) 154 J.P.N. 754; *The Times*, May 9, 1990, CA (Civ Div) 15–47, 19–2

K (Children) (Contact: Committal Order), Re; sub nom. Re K (Children) (Committal Proceedings) [2002] EWCA Civ 1559; [2003] 1 F.L.R. 277; [2003] 2 F.C.R. 336; [2003] Fam. Law 11, CA (Civ Div) 15–41, 15–115
K (Minors) (Disclosure of Privileged Material), Re; sub nom. Kent CC v K [1994] 1 W.L.R. 912; [1994] 3 All E.R. 230; [1994] 1 F.L.R. 377; [1994] 2 F.C.R. 805; [1994] Fam. Law 247; *Independent*, November 23, 1993, Fam Div 6–54
Kabushiki Kaisha Sony Computer Entertainment Inc v Ball (Contempt of Court) [2004] EWHC 1984; (2004) 27(10) I.P.D. 27087, Ch D 11–56, 19–2
Kane v Carmichael, 1993 S.C.C.R. 626, HCJ Appeal 16–79
Kangol Industries Ltd v Bray (Alfred) & Sons Ltd [1953] 1 All E.R. 444 .... 12–16, 12–190
Katchis (John), In the matter of, February 17, 2000 12–93
Kavanagh v Kavanagh, CA transcript No.166 of 1978 13–93
Keane v HM Advocate, 1986 S.C.C.R. 491 16–374
Keeber v Keeber [1995] 2 F.L.R. 748; [1996] 1 F.C.R. 199; [1996] Fam. Law 24; (1995) 159 J.P.N. 778; *The Times*, July 14, 1995, CA (Civ Div) 12–8, 12–10
Keegstra v One Yellow Rabbit Theatre Association (1992) 91 D.L.R. (4th) 532 .... 2–110, 4–25, 4–111
Keeley v Brooking (1979) 143 C.L.R. 162; (1979) 53 A.L.J.R. 526 .... 9–43, 13–30
Keller, Re, 22 L.R. Ir. 158 10–162
Kelly v BBC [2001] Fam. 59 .... 1–136, 2–195, 6–6, 6–42, 6–59, 6–64, 6–75, 6–78, 6–80, 6–94, 6–113, 8–84, 8–86, 8–120, 11–337, 12–79
Kelly v O'Neill and Brady [2000] 1 I.R. 354, S Ct (Ire) 2–47, 4–120, 5–101, 11–176, 16–206, 16–409
Keltie v Wilson (1828) 7 S. 208 16–243
Kemp, Petr, 1982 J.C. 29; 1982 S.L.T. 357; 1982 S.C.C.R. 1, HCJ Appeal 16–55, 16–162, 16–300, 16–429
Kemp v Glasgow Corporation, 1918 S.C. 639; 1918 2 S.L.T. 2; (1918) 55 S.L.R. 553 ...... 16–205, 16–102
Kemp v Neville (1861) 10 C.B. (N.S.) 523; (1861) 142 E.R. 556 13–105
Kemsley v Foot [1952] A.C. 345, HL; affirming [1951] 2 K.B. 34; [1951] 1 All E.R. 331; [1951] 1 T.L.R. 197, CA 2–49, 2–51

TABLE OF CASES

Kenny v Preen [1963] 1 Q.B. 499; [1962] 3 W.L.R. 1233; [1962] 3 All E.R. 814; 106 S.J. 854, CA 13–123
Kent CC v B (A Child); sub nom. B (A Child) (Disclosure), Re [2004] EWHC 411; [2004] 2 F.L.R. 142; [2004] 3 F.C.R. 1; [2004] Lloyd's Rep. Med. 303; [2004] Fam. Law 493; (2004) 154 N.L.J. 498, Fam Div 4–194, 4–224, 6–37, 8–103, 8–104, 8–105, 8–109, 8–119, 8–121
Kent CC v Batchelor (No.1) (1976) 75 L.G.R. 151; (1977) 33 P. & C.R. 185; (1976) 242 E.G. 287; [1976] J.P.L. 754, CA (Civ Div) 3–140, 3–246, 12–43, 12–44, 15–100
Kent Free Press v National Graphical Association (NGA) [1987] I.R.L.R. 267, HC 1–137, 3–176, 19–2
Ker of Crummock v Orr and Fulton (1744) Mor. 7419 16–25
Kerly Son & Verden, Re [1901] 1 Ch. 467 12–94
Kerr (1822) Shaw 68 16–118
Kerr's Factor v Kerr and Milligan (1868) 6 M. 1125 16–267
Khazanchi v Faircharm Investments Ltd. *See* McLeod v Butterwick
Kilbane v HM Advocate, 1989 S.C.C.R. 313 .... 16–313, 16–403, 16–
Kimber v Press Association Ltd [1893] 1 Q.B. 65, CA 1–73, 4–288
King, Ex p. (1802) 7 Ves. Jun. 312; (1802) 32 E.R. 127 3–146
King v Dopson (1911) 56 Sol. Jo. 51 11–321
King v Lees, 1993 S.C.C.R. 28 16–81
King v Lewis; sub nom. Lewis v King [2004] EWCA Civ 1329; [2005] I.L.Pr. 16; [2005] E.M.L.R. 4; (2004) 148 S.J.L.B. 1248; *The Times*, October 26, 2004; *Independent*, November 11, 2004, CA (Civ Div) 1–181
King v Read; sub nom. Read v King [1999] 1 F.L.R. 425; [1999] Fam. Law 90, CA (Civ Div) 13–85, 13–121, 13–122, 15–108
Kingston's Case (Duchess of) (1716) 20 St. Tr. 355 9–14
Kirby v Webb (1887) 3 T.L.R. 763 .... 11–72, 11–158
Kirkcaldy Magistrates v Dougal (1679) Mor. 1984 16–93
Kitcat v Sharpe (1882) 52 L.J. Ch. 134 .... 6–1, 14–132
Knight v Clifton [1971] Ch. 700; [1971] 2 W.L.R. 564; [1971] 2 All E.R. 378; 115 S.J. 60, CA (Civ Div) 12–80, 12–94, 14–137
Knill v Dumergue [1911] 2 Ch. 199 14–120
Knuller (Publishing, Printing and Promotions) Ltd v DPP; Keen (Graham) v DPP; Stansill (Peter) v DPP; Hall (David) v DPP; sub nom. R. v Knuller (Publishing, Printing and Promotions) Ltd [1973] A.C. 435; [1972] 3 W.L.R. 143; [1972] 2 All E.R. 898; (1972) 56 Cr. App. R. 633; [1975] Crim. L.R. 704; 116 S.J. 545, HL 2–172, 12–63
Kopyto (1988) 47 D.L.R. (4th) 213, Ont CA 5–261
Kumari v Jalal; sub nom. Kumara v Jalal [1997] 1 W.L.R. 97; [1996] 4 All E.R. 65; [1996] 2 F.L.R. 588; [1997] 1 F.C.R. 422; [1997] Fam. Law 13; (1996) 146 N.L.J. 1349; *The Times*, October 15, 1996, CA (Civ Div) 3–74, 3–212, 3–222
Kwan Cheuk-Yin and Lam Wong Fai [1973] H.K.L.R. 335 11–259
Kyprianou v Cyprus (Admissibility) (73797/01) (2002) 35 E.H.R.R. CD102, ECHR 5–239, 10–36, 10–48, 10–49, 10–52, 10–135, 10–146, 10–155, 10–156, 13–42

L (A Minor) (Police Investigation: Privilege), Re; sub nom. Re L (Minors) (Disclosure of Medical Reports); Re L (Minors) (Police Investigation: Privilege) [1997] A.C. 16; [1996] 2 W.L.R. 395; [1996] 2 All E.R. 78; [1996] 1 F.L.R. 731; [1996] 2 F.C.R. 145; (1996) 32 B.M.L.R. 160; [1996] Fam. Law 400; (1996) 160 L.G. Rev. 417; (1996) 93(15) L.S.G. 30; (1996) 146 N.L.J. 441; (1996) 140 S.J.L.B. 116; *The Times*, March 22, 1996, HL 6–108, 9–13, 10–173
L (A Minor) (Wardship: Freedom of Publication), Re; sub nom. Re L (A Ward) (Publication of Information) [1988] 1 All E.R. 418; [1988] 1 F.L.R. 255; (1987) 137 N.L.J. 760; *The Times*, July 4, 1987, Fam Div ... 1–139, 6–41, 6–90, 6–110, 6–148, 8–119, 8–120, 11–337, 12–85
L (A Ward) (Publication of Information), Re. See Re L (A Minor) (Wardship: Freedom of Publication)
L (An Infant), Re [1968] P. 119; [1967] 3 W.L.R. 1645; [1968] 1 All E.R. 20; 111 S.J. 908, CA (Civ Div) 6–54
Labouchere, Re Ex p. Columbus Co Ltd (1901) 17 T.L.R. 578 5–116

TABLE OF CASES

Lacon v De Groat (1893) 10 T.L.R. 24 11–328
Ladd v Marshall [1954] 1 W.L.R. 1489; [1954] 3 All E.R. 745; 98 S.J. 870, CA ... 3–239, 12–65, 15–100
Lakah Group and Lakah v Al Jazeera Satellite Channel and Mansour [2002] EWHC 2500, QBD 1–181, 3–40, 3–224
Lamb v Lamb [1984] F.L.R. 278; [1984] Fam. Law 60, CA (Civ Div) 3–210, 14–58, 14–59, 15–64
Lamont v Crook (1840) 6 M. & W. 615; (1840) 151 E.R. 558 11–101
Lane v Sterne (1862) 3 Giff. 629; (1862) 66 E.R.559 .... 11–320, 11–321
Lange v Atkinson [1997] 3 N.Z.L.R. 22 2–34
Lange v Atkinson [2000] NZCA 95; [2000] 3 N.Z.L.R. 385 2–180
Lange v Australian Broadcasting Corp (1997) 71 A.L.J.R. 818, HC 2–99
Langdell v Sutton (1737) Barnes 32; (1737) 94 E.R. 791 10–181
Langley, Ex p. (1879) 13 Ch.D. 110 .... 12–39, 12–99
Larkman v Lindsell, *The Times*, November 30, 1985, CA 13–93
Launder, Re; Launder v Richards (1908) 98 L.T. 554 .... 12–191, 12–196, 12–244, 15–27
Laurie v Raglan Building Co Ltd [1942] 1 K.B. 152 15–44
Lawford v Spicer (1856) 2 Jur. (N.S.) 564 .... 3–146, 12–182
Lawley (1731) Mich. 5 George II 1–59
Lawrie v Roberts & Linton (1882) 4 Coup. 606 .... 10–34, 16–44, 16–99
Lawson (1937) 81 S.J. 280 .... 16–189, 16–197
Lawson's Case (1713) Hil. 11 Anne 1–58
Lea's Case (1586) Gouldsb. 33; (1586) 75 E.R. 976 .... 11–157, 11–169, 11–304
Leake v Marrow (1576) *Cary's Causes in Chancery*, p.75 1–47
Leary v BBC, September 29, 1989 (Lexis) 2–43, 2–86, 2–208, 4–86, 4–316, 6–3, 6–22, 6–24, 6–25, 6–26, 6–028, 6–31, 6–32, 6–38, 6–151, 7–142, 7–177, 7–180, 8–5, 12–62, 16–322, 16–334, 16–367
Lechmere Charlton's Case. *See* Re Ludlow Charities
Leck v Epsom RDC [1922] 1 K.B. 383 11–139
Lecointe v Court's Administrator of the Central Criminal Court, February 8, 1973, Bar Library Transcript 10–17
Lee v Aylesbury UDC (1902) 19 T.L.R. 106 12–126
Lee v Walker [1985] Q.B. 1191; [1985] 3 W.L.R. 170; [1985] 1 All E.R. 781; [1985] Fam. Law 164; (1985) 82 L.S.G. 2996; (1985) 129 S.J. 484, CA (Civ Div) 3–80, 12–33, 14–44, 14–45, 14–55, 15–66, 15–74
Leicester University v A [1999] I.C.R. 701; [1999] I.R.L.R. 352; *The Times*, March 23, 1999, EAT 8–146
Leigh, Re; Leigh v Leigh (1888) 40 Ch. D. 290 11–334
Lennard's Carrying Co Ltd v Asiatic Petroleum Co Ltd; sub nom. Asiatic Petroleum Co Ltd v Lennard's Carrying Co Ltd [1915] A.C. 705, HL 4–210
Lennon v Scottish Daily Record & Sunday Mail Ltd [2004] EWHC 359; [2004] E.M.L.R. 18, QBD 1–136
Leonard v Attwell (1810) 17 Ves. Jun. 385 12–98
Levison v Jewish Chronicle Ltd, 1924 S.L.T. 755 .... 16–136, 16–138
Lewes v Morgan (1818) 5 Price 518; (1818) 146 E.R. 681 11–34
Lewis v James (1887) 3 T.L.R. 527 .... 11–216, 12–242
Lewis v Levy (1858) 27 L.J. Q.B. 282 1–73
Lewis v Lewis [1991] 1 W.L.R. 235; [1991] 3 All E.R. 251; [1991] 2 F.L.R. 43; [1991] Fam. Law 469, CA (Civ Div) 15–52, 15–57
Lewis v Ogden (1983) 153 C.L.R. 682, HC 4–239
Lewis v Ogden (1984) 58 A.L.J.R. 342 .... 10–50, 10–128, 10–129, 10–133, 10–135
Lewis v Owen [1894] 1 Q.B. 102 11–316
Lewis v Pontypridd, Caerphilly and Newport Ry Co (1895) 11 T.L.R. 203 12–150
Levy v Victoria (1997) 189 C.L.R. 579 2–99
Leys v Leys (1886) 13 R. 1223; (1886) 23 S.L.R. 834 .... 16–63, 16–234, 16–267
Liebrand, Ex p. [1914] W.N. 310 15–14
Lightfoot v Cameron (1776) 2 W. Bl. 1113; (1776) 96 E.R. 658 3–141
Lightfoot v Lightfoot [1989] 1 F.L.R. 414; [1989] F.C.R. 305; (1989) 153 J.P.N. 372; *The Times*, December 12, 1988; *Independent*, December 12, 1988 (C.S.), CA (Civ Div) 3–111, 3–181, 12–7, 14–9, 19–2

TABLE OF CASES

Lilly ICOS Ltd v Pfizer Ltd (No.2); sub nom. Lilly ICOS LLC v Pfizer Ltd (No.2); Lily ICOS Ltd v Pfizer Ltd (No.2) [2002] EWCA Civ 2; [2002] 1 W.L.R. 2253; [2002] 1 All E.R. 842; [2002] F.S.R. 54; (2002) 25(3) I.P.D. 25016; (2002) 99(10) L.S.G. 33; (2002) 146 S.J.L.B. 29; *The Times*, January 28, 2002, CA (Civ Div) 12–224, 12–226, 12–239
Lincoln's Case (Bishop of) (1637) 3 State Trials 770 11–261
Lingens v Austria (1986) 8 E.H.R.R. 407 2–50
Linkleter v Linkleter [1988] 1 F.L.R. 360; [1988] Fam. Law 360, CA (Civ Div) 15–67, 15–70, 15–74
Linnett v Coles [1987] Q.B. 555; [1986] 3 W.L.R. 843; [1986] 3 All E.R. 652; (1987) 84 Cr. App. R. 227; (1986) 136 N.L.J. 1016; (1986) 130 S.J. 841, CA (Civ Div) 13–134, 14–7, 14–63, 15–46, 15–62, 15–67, 15–72
Linton v Mackenzie, *The Times*, October 31, 1893 12–246
Linwood v Andrews (1888) L.T. 612 10–159
Lion Laboratories Ltd v Evans [1985] Q.B. 526; [1984] 3 W.L.R. 539; [1984] 2 All E.R. 417; (1984) 81 L.S.G. 1233; (1984) 81 L.S.G. 2000; (1984) 128 S.J. 533, CA (Civ Div) 2–150, 6–16, 9–28
Lister, Re (1894) 70 L.T. 812 12–130
Little Sisters Book and Art Emporium v Canada (Minister of Justice) (2000) 193 D.L.R. (4th) 193; [2000] 2 S.C.R. 1120 6–21
Littler v Thomson (1839) 2 Beav. 129; (1839) 49 E.R. 1129 5–116
Locabail (UK) Ltd v Bayfield Properties Ltd (Leave to Appeal); Locabail (UK) Ltd v Waldorf Investment Corp (Leave to Appeal); Timmins v Gormley; Williams v Inspector of Taxes; R. v Bristol Betting and Gaming Licensing Committee Ex p. O'Callaghan [2000] Q.B. 451; [2000] 2 W.L.R. 870; [2000] 1 All E.R. 65; [2000] I.R.L.R. 96; [2000] H.R.L.R. 290; [2000] U.K.H.R.R. 300; 7 B.H.R.C. 583; (1999) 149 N.L.J. 1793; [1999] N.P.C. 143; *The Times*, November 19, 1999; *Independent*, November 23, 1999, CA (Civ Div) 5–239
Local Authority (Inquiry: Restraint on Publication), Re A; sub nom. Local Authority v Health Authority (Disclosure: Restriction on Publication) [2003] EWHC 2746; [2004] Fam. 96; [2004] 2 W.L.R. 926; [2004] 1 All E.R. 480; [2004] 1 F.L.R. 541; [2004] 1 F.C.R. 113; [2004] B.L.G.R. 117; (2004) 7 C.C.L. Rep. 426; (2004) 76 B.M.L.R. 210; [2004] Fam. Law 179; (2004) 101(3) L.S.G. 33; *The Times*, December 5, 2003, Fam Div 6–54, 6–87, 6–90, 6–93, 6–96
Local Authority, A v W [2005] EWHC 1564, Fam 6–106
Lock International Plc v Beswick [1989] 1 W.L.R. 1268; [1989] 3 All E.R. 373; [1989] I.R.L.R. 481; (1989) 86(39) L.S.G. 36; (1989) 139 N.L.J. 644; (1989) S.J. 1297, Ch D 12–175
Logan v Procurator Fiscal for Kilmarnock, 1999 S.C.C.R. 584 16–115
Lomas v Parle [2003] EWCA Civ 1804; [2004] 1 W.L.R. 1642; [2004] 1 All E.R. 1173; [2004] 1 F.L.R. 812; [2004] 1 F.C.R. 97; [2004] Fam. Law 243; *The Times*, January 13, 2004, CA (Civ Div) 12–7, 14–19
Lombard North Central Plc v Pratt (1989) 139 N.L.J. 1709; *The Times*, November 27, 1989, CA (Civ Div) 2–62, 7–18, 12–211
London & Birmingham Ry v Grand Junction Canal Co (1835) 1 Ry. Ca. 224 12–182
London Borough of Barnet v Hurst [2002] EWCA Civ 1009; W.L.R. 722; [2002] 4 All E.R. 457 19–2
London CC v Att-Gen; sub nom. Att-Gen v London CC [1902] A.C. 165, HL 2–214
Long v Elways (1729) Mosely 249; (1729) 25 E.R. 378 11–335
Long Wellesley's Case (1831) 2 Russ. & My. 639 .... 11–333, 14–6
Long's Case (1677) 2 Mod. 181; (1677) 86 E.R. 1012 .... 11–170, 11–304
Lonrho Plc (Contempt Proceedings), Re; sub nom. Lonrho Plc and Observer, Re [1990] 2 A.C. 154; [1989] 3 W.L.R. 535; [1989] 2 All E.R. 1100; (1989) 139 N.L.J. 1073; (1989) 133 S.J. 120, HL 1–126, 2–14, 2–28, 2–194, 3–67, 3–86, 3–139, 3–170, 4–58, 4–91, 4–95, 4–125, 4–127, 4–189, 5–27, 5–45, 5–199, 5–212, 5–239, 6–130, 7–230, 7–232, 10–50, 11–10, 11–15, 11–176, 13–12, 13–35, 13–41, 13–94
Lord v Thornton (1614) 2 Bulstr. 67; (1614) 80 E.R. 965 11–51
Lorenzo Halcoussi, The [1988] 1 Lloyd's Rep. 180 .... 11–99, 11–110

TABLE OF CASES

Loseby v Newman [1995] 2 F.L.R. 754; [1996] 1 F.C.R. 647; [1996] Fam. Law 24, CA (Civ Div) 12–163, 14–46, 14–47, 15–47, 15–67, 15–70
Loughran (1839) 1 Cr. & D. 79 11–216
Loutchansky v Times Newspapers Ltd (No.2) [2001] EWCA Civ 1805; [2002] Q.B. 783; [2002] 2 W.L.R. 640; [2002] 1 All E.R. 652; [2002] E.M.L.R. 14; [2002] Masons C.L.R. 35; (2002) 99(6) L.S.G. 30; (2001) 145 S.J.L.B. 277; *The Times*, December 7, 2001; *Independent*, December 11, 2001, CA (Civ Div) 1–179, 4–191
Lovat (Lord) v Macdonnell (1868) 6 M. 330 16–256
Lubrizol Corp v Esso Petroleum Co Ltd (No.2) [1993] F.S.R. 53, Ch D (Patents Ct) 12–237
Luca v Italy (2003) 36 E.H.R.R. 46 3–238
Lucas & Son (Nelson Mail) Ltd v O'Brien [1978] 2 N.Z.L.R. 289 .... 16–200, 16–211
Ludlow Charities, Re; Lechmere Charlton's case (1837) 2 My. & Cr. 316; (1837) 40 E.R. 661 .... 11–7, 11–175, 3–157, 3–173
Ludlow's Case (1594) Q.B. Crown Side, Rule Book I, fo. 41 Mich. 36, 37 Elizabeth   1–32
Lukoviak v Unidad Editorial SA [2001] E.M.L.R. 46 1–136
Lyle-Samuel v Odhams Ltd [1920] 1 K.B. 135 9–5

M, Re. *See* M v Home Office
M (A Child) (Children and Family Reporter: Disclosure), Re; sub nom. M (A Child) (Disclosure: Children and Family Reporter), Re [2002] EWCA Civ 1199; [2003] Fam. 26; [2002] 3 W.L.R. 1669; [2002] 4 All E.R. 401; [2002] 2 F.L.R. 893; [2002] 3 F.C.R. 208; [2003] Fam. Law 96; (2002) 99(39) L.S.G. 37; *The Times*, August 23, 2002; *Independent*, October 2, 2002, CA (Civ Div) 4–194, 4–224, 8–103, 8–111, 8–112
M (A Minor) (Contempt of Court: Committal of Court's Own Motion), Re. *See* Re M (Minors) (Breach of Contact Order: Committal)
M (Minors) (Access: Contempt: Committal), Re; sub nom. Re M (Minors) (Breach of Undertaking) [1991] 1 F.L.R. 355; [1991] F.C.R. 272; [1991] Crim. L.R. 265, CA (Civ Div) 12–5, 12–29, 12–58, 12–192, 12–196, 15–74
M (Minors) (Breach of Contact Order: Committal), Re; sub nom. Re M (A Minor) (Contempt of Court: Committal of Court's Own Motion) [1999] Fam. 263; [1999] 2 W.L.R. 810; [1999] 2 All E.R. 56; [1999] 1 F.L.R. 810; [1999] 1 F.C.R. 683; [1999] Fam. Law 208; (1999) 96(6) L.S.G. 33; (1999) 143 S.J.L.B. 36; *The Times*, December 31, 1998; *Independent*, January 14, 1999, CA (Civ Div) 12–5, 12–27, 12–32, 13–11, 13–94, 15–61
M v H.M Advocate, 1974 S.L.T. (Notes) 25 .... 6–54, 6–87, 6–88, 6–89, 6–90, 6–108, 16–407
M v Home Office; sub nom. Re M [1994] 1 A.C. 377; [1993] 3 W.L.R. 433; [1993] 3 All E.R. 537; (1995) 7 Admin. L.R. 113; (1993) 90(37) L.S.G. 50; (1993) 143 N.L.J. 1099; (1993) 137 S.J.L.B. 199; *The Times*, July 28, 1993; *Independent*, July 28, 1993, HL; affirming [1992] Q.B. 270; [1992] 2 W.L.R. 73; [1992] 4 All E.R. 97; [1992] C.O.D. 97; (1991) 141 N.L.J. 1663; *The Times*, December 2, 1991; *Independent*, December 3, 1991; *Guardian*, December 4, 1991, CA (Civ Div)9 1–126, 1–141, 2–222, 2–224, 2–227, 2–228, 2–230, 3–247, 3–248, 3–249, 7–242, 9–198, 9–201, 9–203, 9–207, 9–211, 9–227, 9–230, 12–80, 12–90, 12–123, 12–142, 12–195, 14–111, 16–240
M v M (Contempt: Committal) [1997] 1 F.L.R. 762; [1997] 3 F.C.R. 288; [1997] Fam. Law 321, CA (Civ Div) 12–9, 12–10
M v P (Contempt of Court: Committal Order); Butler v Butler [1993] Fam. 167; [1992] 3 W.L.R. 813; [1992] 4 All E.R. 833; [1993] 1 F.L.R. 773; [1993] 1 F.C.R. 405; [1993] Fam. Law 467; (1992) 142 N.L.J. 1339; *The Times*, August 4, 1992, CA (Civ Div) 12–33, 15–37, 15–45, 15–46, 15–70, 15–75
M v Vincent [1998] I.C.R. 73, EAT 8–146
M v W (Non-Molestation Order: Duration) [2000] 1 F.L.R. 107 14–82
M and N (Minors), Re [1990] Fam. 211; [1989] 3 W.L.R. 1136; [1990] 1 All E.R. 205; [1990] 1 F.L.R. 149; [1990] F.C.R. 395; [1990] Fam. Law 22; (1990) 154 J.P.N. 345; (1990) 87(1) L.S.G. 32; (1989) 139 N.L.J. 1154; (1990) 164 S.J. 165; *The Times*, July 14, 1989, CA (Civ Div) 1–139
M. Michaels (Furriers) Ltd v Askew (1983) 134 New Law Jo. 655; (1983) 127 Sol. Jo. 597 12–120

TABLE OF CASES

MGN Pension Trustees Ltd v Bank of America National Trust and Savings Association and
    Credit Suisse [1995] 2 All E.R. 355; [1995] E.M.L.R. 99; *The Times*, December 21,
    1994; *Independent*, December 15, 1994, Ch D 2–43, 3–96, 4–313, 7–171, 7–186, 7–194,
    12–1
MM and HM, Re (1933) 1 I.R. 299 10–182
MPC v Caldwell. *See* R. v Caldwell (James)
MacAlister v Associated Newspapers Ltd, 1954 S.L.T. 14, HCJ Appeal 16–143, 16–144, 16–158,
    16–178
Macara v MacFarlane, 1980 S.L.T. (Notes) 26, HCJ Appeal 16–60, 16–274
Macarthur v Carlaway Estate Ltd (1943) S.L.C.R. 45 16–110
MacDonald (1993) 70 A. Crim. R. 478 11–310
MacDougall v Knight (1889) L.R. 14 App.Cas. 194, HL 4–264, 4–286
Macgill's Case (1748) 2 Fowler's Exch. Prac. (2nd ed.), p.404 11–174
M'Gregor v Barrett (1848) 6 C.B. 262; (1848) 136 E.R. 1251 11–61
Mackay v Ross (1853) 1 Irv. 288 16–251
Mackenzie and Munro v Magistrates of Dingwall (1839) 1 D. 487; (1839) 14 Fac. 535 16–24,
    16–251, 16–252
Mackett v Herne Bay Commissioners (1876) 24 W.R. 845 6–1
Mackinnon v Donaldson Lufkin & Jenrette Securities Corp [1986] Ch. 482; [1986] 2 W.L.R.
    453; [1986] 1 All E.R. 653; [1987] E.C.C. 139; [1986] Fin. L.R. 225; (1986) 83 L.S.G.
    1226; (1985) 130 S.J. 224; *Financial Times*, November 12, 1985, Ch D 3–225, 12–161,
    12–162
Maclachlan v John W. Bruce & Company, 1912 S.L.T. 129; 1912 S.C. 440; (1912) 49 S.L.R.
    433 .... 16–37, 16–262
MacLauchlan v Carson (1826) 5 S. 147 (N.E. 133) 16–144
Macleay v Macdonald and Maclennan, 1928 S.C. 776 .... 16–246, 16–260, 16–261
MacLeod v Lewis Justices of the Peace (1892) 20 R. 218 .... 16–202, 16–216, 16–220
MacMillan Bloedel Ltd v Simpson (1994) 90 B.C.L.R. (2d) 24; (1994) 89 C.C.C. (3d) 217;
    (1994) 113 D.L.R. (4th) 368 .... 3–71, 16–39
MacMillan Inc v Bishopsgate Investment Trust Plc [1993] 1 W.L.R. 1372, CA 11–110
MacPherson v McLeod, 1994 G.W.D. 6–325 16–79
Maddison v Shore (1703) 5 Mod. 355; (1703) 87 E.R. 701 15–155
Magistrates' Court at Prahan v Murphy [1997] 2 V.R. 186 .... 10–50, 10–87, 10–135, 10–145
Magnay v Burt (1843) 5 Q.B. 381; (1843) 114 E.R. 1293 ... 5–139, 11–160, 11–171, 11–304, 14–152
Maharaj v Att-Gen for Trinidad [1977] 1 All E.R. 411 .... 10–50, 10–147
Mahfouz v Brisard [2004] EWHC 1735, QBD 1–181
Mahon v Rahn (No.1) [1998] Q.B. 424; [1997] 3 W.L.R. 1230; [1997] 3 All E.R. 687; [1997]
    E.M.L.R. 558; *The Times*, June 12, 1997, CA (Civ Div) 2–163, 11–82, 12–203, 12–231,
    12–232, 12–233, 12–236
Maidstone Palace of Varieties, Re [1909] Ch. 283 .... 11–320, 14–132
Malcolm v Day (1819) 3 Moo. C.P. 579; (1819) 21 R.R. 730 .... 11–106, 11–113
Malgar Ltd v RE Leach (Engineering) Ltd [2000] C.P. Rep. 39; [2000] F.S.R. 393; (2000)
    23(1) I.P.D. 23007; *The Times*, February 17, 2000, Ch D 11–56
Manchester City Council v McCann [1999] Q.B. 1214; [1999] 2 W.L.R. 590; (1999) 31
    H.L.R. 770; (1998) 95(48) L.S.G. 31; *The Times*, November 26, 1998; *Independent*,
    November 20, 1998, CA (Civ Div) 2–173, 10–125, 13–7, 13–79, 13–107
Manchester City Council v Worthington [2000] 1 F.L.R. 411; [2000] Fam. Law 238, CA (Civ
    Div) 14–90, 15–64, 15–71
Manda (Wardship Documents) (Disclosure), Re [1993] Fam. 183; [1993] 2 W.L.R. 161;
    [1993] 1 All E.R. 733; [1993] 1 F.L.R. 205; [1993] Fam. Law 217; (1992) 142 N.L.J.
    1233; 136 S.J.L.B. 253; *The Times*, October 6, 1992; *Independent*, August 26, 1992,
    CA (Civ Div) 6–90, 7–56, 8–106
Mander v Falcke [1891] 3 Ch. 488 .... 12–34, 15–13
Manning v Hill (1995) 126 D.L.R. (4th) 129 2–99
Mansell v Jones [1905] W.N. 168, CA 12–137
Manson, Petr (1977) S.C.C.R. Supp. 176 .... 16–122, 16–128
Marcel v Commissioner of Police of the Metropolis; Anchor Brewhouse Developments v
    Jaggard [1992] Ch. 225; [1992] 2 W.L.R. 50; [1992] 1 All E.R. 72; (1992) 4 Admin.
    L.R. 309; (1991) 141 N.L.J. 1224; (1991) 135 S.J.L.B. 125; *The Times*, August 7,
    1991; *Independent*, July 24, 1991; *Guardian*, August 28, 1991, CA (Civ Div) 11–110

[lxxxvi]

TABLE OF CASES

Marckx v Belgium (1979) 2 E.H.R.R. 330 2–36
Marengo v Daily Sketch and Sunday Graphic [1948] 1 All E.R. 406; 64 T.L.R. 160; (1948)
    65 R.P.C. 242; [1948] W.N. 92; [1948] L.J.R. 787, HL 1–127, 6–120, 6–137, 12–104,
   12–105
Markt Intern Verlag GmbH v Germany (A/164); sub nom. Markt Intern Verlag GmbH v
    Germany (10572/83); Markt Intern and Beermann v Germany (1990) 12 E.H.R.R. 161;
    The Times, November 23, 1989, ECHR 6–20
Marlborough (Duke of), Ex p. (1844) 5 Q.B. 955; (1844) 114 E.R. 1508 10–144
Marlwood Commercial Inc v Kozeny. *See* Omega Group Holdings Ltd v Kozeny
Marsden and Sons Ltd v Old Silkstone Collieries Ltd (1914) 13 L.G.R. 342 .... 14–132, 14–136
Marsh v Joseph [1897] 1 Ch. 213 12–253
Marshall v Marshall (1966) 110 Sol. Jo. 112 12–15
Marshall v York, Newcastle and Berwick Ry Co (1831) 11 C.B. 398; (1831) 138 E.R. 527 11–100
Marsham v Brookes (1863) 32 L.J. P. 95 12–129
Martin's Case (1747) 2 Russ. & My. 674n; (1747) 39 E.R. 551 11–174
Martindale, Re [1894] 3 Ch. 193 .... 8–125, 11–347
Mason v Lawton [1991] 1 W.L.R. 322; [1990] 2 All E.R. 784; [1991] 2 F.L.R. 50; [1991]
    F.C.R. 507; [1992] Fam. Law 416; *The Times*, December 11, 1990; *Daily Telegraph*,
    January 18, 1991, CA (Civ Div) 9–205, 14–13, 14–63, 19–2
Masterman v Judson (1832) 8 Bing. 224 14–155
Mathesis, The (1844) 2 Wm. Rob. 286 12–146
Maville Hose, Re [1939] Ch. 32 11–115
Maxwell v DPP [1935] A.C. 309; (1934) 24 Cr. App. R. 152, HL 4–81
Maxwell v Pressdram [1987] 1 W.L.R. 298; [1987] 1 All E.R. 656; (1987) 84 L.S.G. 1148;
    (1987) 131 S.J. 327; *The Times*, November 12, 1986, CA (Civ Div) 9–64, 9–88, 9–89, 9–95,
  9–160, 9–245
Maynard v Maynard [1984] F.L.R. 85, CA 12–66
McAlley's JF, Petr (1900) 2 F. 1198 16–267
McAulay v McKenzie (1830) 9 S. 48 16–254
McCadden v HM Advocate, 1985 J.C. 98; 1986 S.L.T. 138; 1985 S.C.C.R. 282, HCJ
    Appeal 11–354, 16–390, 16–393, 16–395, 16–407
McCann v Wright [1995] 1 W.L.R. 1556; [1996] 1 All E.R. 204; [1995] 2 F.L.R. 579; [1996]
    1 F.C.R. 90; [1996] Fam. Law 25; (1995) 92(28) L.S.G. 41; (1995) 139 S.J.L.B. 166;
    The Times, July 10, 1995; *Independent*, July 17, 1995 (C.S.), CA (Civ Div) 14–75, 14–76
McCartan Turkington Breen v Times Newspapers Ltd; sub nom. Turkington v Times
    Newspapers Ltd [2001] 2 A.C. 277; [2000] 3 W.L.R. 1670; [2000] 4 All E.R. 913;
    [2000] N.I. 410; [2001] E.M.L.R. 1; [2001] U.K.H.R.R. 184; 9 B.H.R.C. 497; (2000)
    97(47) L.S.G. 40; (2000) 150 N.L.J. 1657; (2000) 144 S.J.L.B. 287; *The Times*,
    November 3, 2000; *Independent*, November 7, 2000, HL (NI) 2–50, 4–49, 4–338
McConnick v Normand, 1991 G.W.D. 22–1285 16–81
McDermott v Judges of British Guiana (1869) L.R. 2 P.C. 341 3–132
McDonald's Corp v Steel (No.1) [1995] 3 All E.R. 615; [1995] E.M.L.R. 527; *The Times*,
    April 14, 1994; *Independent*, April 22, 1994, CA (Civ Div) 9–65
McDonald's Corp v Steel (No.4); sub nom. Steel v McDonald's Corp (*Locus Standi*),
    Independent, May 10, 1999 (C.S.), CA (Civ Div); reversing in part unreported, June
    19, 1997, QBD 10–131
McDowell v Standard Oil Co (New Jersey) [1927] A.C. 632, HL 5–28
McEwan and McLeod (1829) Shaw 213 .... 16–118, 16–120, 16–122
McGeary v O'Brien, 1993 G.W.D. 36–2315 16–79
McGoldrick v Citicorp Finance Pty Ltd [1990] V.R. 494 9–43
McGrath v Chief Constable of the Royal Ulster Constabulary [2001] UKHL 39; [2001] 2
    A.C. 731; [2001] 3 W.L.R. 312; [2001] 4 All E.R. 334; [2001] N.I. 303; *The Times*,
    July 13, 2001; *Independent*, October 29, 2001 (C.S.), HL (NI) 15–54
McGuinness v Att-Gen of Victoria (1940) 63 C.L.R. 73 .... 9–5, 9–50
McIlraith v Grady [1968] 1 Q.B. 468; [1967] 3 W.L.R. 1331; [1967] 3 All E.R. 625; 111 S.J.
    583, CA (Civ Div) 12–033, 15–47, 15–67
McIntyre (1831) Shaw's Just. Cases 220 16–95
McIntyre v Annand, 1989 G.W.D. 20–833 16–115
McIntyre v Sheridan, 1993 S.L.T. 412 .... 16–243, 16–254, 16–257, 16–263
McKeown v The Queen (1971) 16 D.L.R. (3d) 390 .... 2–23, 10–13, 10–20, 11–88

TABLE OF CASES

McKerr v Armagh Coroner [1990] 1 All E.R. 865, HL 11–144
McKerry v Teesdale and Wear Valley Justices; sub nom. McKerry v DPP (2000) 164 J.P.
    355; [2001] E.M.L.R. 5; [2000] Crim. L.R. 594; [2000] C.O.D. 199; (2000) 97(11)
    L.S.G. 36; (2000) 144 S.J.L.B. 126; *The Times*, February 29, 2000; *Independent*,
    March 27, 2000 (C.S.), DC 2–58, 8–36, 8–37, 8–41, 8–54, 8–67
McKinnon v Douglas, 1982 S.L.T. 375; 1982 S.C.C.R. 80, HCJ Appeal 16–79
McKnight v Northern [2001] EWCA Civ 2028, CA (Civ Div) 14–36, 19–2
McLauchlan v Carson (1826) 5 S. 147 .... 16–149, 16–200
McLaughlin v Douglas & Kidston (1863) 4 Irv. 273 16–117
McLean v Nugent [1980] 1 F.L.R. 26; 123 S.J. 521, CA (Civ Div) 14–76
McLeod (1820) Shaw (J.) 3 .... 16–154, 16–191
McLeod v Butterwick; sub nom. Khazanchi v Faircharm Investments Ltd [1998] 1 W.L.R.
    1603; [1998] 2 All E.R. 901; (1999) 77 P. & C.R. 29; [1998] 3 E.G.L.R. 147; [1999]
    R.V.R. 190; [1998] E.G.C.S. 46; (1998) 95(17) L.S.G. 31; (1998) 148 N.L.J. 479;
    (1998) 142 S.J.L.B. 142; [1998] N.P.C. 47; (1998) 76 P. & C.R. D8; *The Times*, March
    25, 1998, CA (Civ Div) 3–184, 15–48
McLeod v HM Advocate, 1998 S.L.T. 60 16–406
McLeod v St Aubyn [1899] A.C. 549, PC (StV) 4–51, 4–226, 4–232, 5–139, 5–204, 5–209, 5–250
McLeod v Speirs (1884) 5 Coup. 387; (1884) 11 R. (J.) 26; (1884) 21 S.L.R. 530 .... 16–27, 16–33,
                16–67, 16–109, 16–118, 16–120, 16–122, 16–124, 16–125, 16–128,
                                                                                                                                16–130
McManus v Beckham [2002] EWCA Civ 939; [2002] 1 W.L.R. 2982; [2002] 4 All E.R. 497;
    [2002] E.M.L.R. 40; (2002) 99(35) L.S.G. 36; (2002) 146 S.J.L.B. 183; *The Times*,
    July 11, 2002; *Independent*, July 12, 2002, CA (Civ Div) 4–50, 4–51, 4–228
McMillan v Carmichael, 1994 S.L.T. 510; 1993 S.C.C.R. 943, HCJ Appeal 16–51, 16–82, 16–83
McMillan Graham Printers Ltd v RR (UK) [1993] T.L.R. 152; [1993] 21 L.S. Gaz. R. 40; *The
    Times*, March 19, 1993, CA (Civ Div) 12–114, 14–101, 14–108
McNeilage v HM Advocate, 1999 S.C.C.R. 471 .... 16–115, 16–125
McNeill v Scott (1866) 4 Macph. 608 .... 16–235, 16–249, 16–254
McPherson v Heywood, 1993 G.W.D. 15–990 16–81
McPherson v McPherson [1936] A.C. 177, PC 2–37, 7–38
McPherson v Thorne (1844) 6 D. 422 16–261
Mead v Cross (1580) Cary 137 1–43
Medcalf v Mardell (Wasted Costs Order); sub nom. Medcalf v Weatherill [2002] UKHL 27;
    [2003] 1 A.C. 120; [2002] 3 W.L.R. 172; [2002] 3 All E.R. 721; [2002] C.P. Rep. 70;
    [2002] C.P.L.R. 647; [2002] 3 Costs L.R. 428; [2002] P.N.L.R. 43; (2002) 99(31)
    L.S.G. 34; (2002) 152 N.L.J. 1032; (2002) 146 S.J.L.B. 175; [2002] N.P.C. 89; *The
    Times*, June 28, 2002, HL 11–54
Medicaments and Related Classes of Goods, Re. *See* Director General of Fair Trading v
    Proprietary Association of Great Britain
Medway Council v BBC [2002] 1 F.L.R. 104; [2001] Fam. Law 883, Fam Div 6–79
Meekins v Smith (1791) 1 H. Bl. 629; (1791) 126 E.R. 359 .... 3–141, 3–146
Mellor v Thompson (1885) 31 Ch. D. 55 7–41
Memory Corp Plc v Sidhu (No.2) [2000] Ch. 645; [2000] 2 W.L.R. 1106; [2000] 1 All E.R.
    434; (2000) 97(4) L.S.G. 33; (2000) 144 S.J.L.B. 51; *The Times*, December 3, 1999,
    Ch D 3–204
Menzies v Macdonald (1864) 2 M. 652 16–256
Meridian Global Funds Management Asia Ltd v Securities Commission [1995] 2 A.C. 500;
    [1995] 3 W.L.R. 413; [1995] 3 All E.R. 918; [1995] B.C.C. 942; [1995] 2 B.C.L.C.
    116; (1995) 92(28) L.S.G. 39; (1995) 139 S.J.L.B. 152; *The Times*, June 29, 1995, PC
    (NZ) 4–204, 4–211
Merrick v Heathcoat-Amory [1955] Ch. 567 2–224
Mersey Care NHS Trust v Ackroyd; sub nom. Ackroyd v Mersey Care NHS Trust [2003]
    EWCA Civ 663; [2003] E.M.L.R. 36; [2003] Lloyd's Rep. Med. 379; (2003) 73
    B.M.L.R. 88; (2003) 100(28) L.S.G. 30; (2003) 147 S.J.L.B. 595; *The Times*, May 21,
    2003; *Independent*, May 22, 2003, CA (Civ Div) 9–127, 9–140, 9–145, 9–170
Mesham v Clarke [1989] 1 F.L.R. 370; [1989] F.C.R. 782; (1989) 153 J.P.N. 768, CA (Civ
    Div) 12–28, 15–102, 19–2

TABLE OF CASES

Messenger Newspaper Group v National Graphical Association (NGA) [1984] 1 All E.R. 293; [1984] I.C.R. 345; (1984) 134 N.L.J. 257, CA (Civ Div); affirming [1984] I.R.L.R. 397 .... 1–137, 3–176, 6–126, 14–123, 14–127, 19–2
Messiniaki Tolmi, The. *See* Astro Exito Navegacion SA v Southland Enterprise Co (The Messiniaki Tolmi) (No.1)
Meters Ltd v Metropolitan Gas Meters Ltd (1907) 51 S.J. 499 .... 12–98, 15–81
Metropolitan Music Hall v Lake (1889) 58 L.J. Ch. 513 .... 4–9, 4–12
Metzler v Gounod (1874) 30 T.L.R. 264 5–103
Michael O'Mara Books Ltd v Express Newspapers Plc [1998] E.M.L.R. 383; [1999] F.S.R. 49; (1998) 21(7) I.P.D. 21070; *The Times*, March 6, 1998, Ch D 9–108
Michigan (Great Britain) Ltd v Mathew (1966) R.P.C. 47 .... 12–94, 14–136
Mid-Bedfordshire DC v Brown [2004] EWCA Civ 1709; [2005] 1 W.L.R. 1460; (2005) 102(4) L.S.G. 31; *The Times*, January 3, 2005; *Independent*, January 12, 2005, CA (Civ Div) 3–70, 9–201
Mid East Trading Ltd, Re; sub nom. Lehman Bros Inc v Phillips; Phillips v Lehman Brothers [1998] 1 All E.R. 577; [1998] B.C.C. 726; [1998] 1 B.C.L.C. 240; (1998) 95(3) L.S.G. 24; (1998) 142 S.J.L.B. 45; *The Times*, December 20, 1997, CA (Civ Div) 12–162
Middlebrook Mushrooms v Transport and General Workers Union [1993] I.C.R. 612; [1993] I.R.L.R. 232; *The Times*, January 18, 1993, CA (Civ Div) 2–134
Middleton v Chichester (1871) L.R. 6 Ch. 152 3–148
Midland Bank Trust Co Ltd v Green (No.3) [1982] Ch. 529, CA (Civ Div); affirming [1979] Ch. 496; [1979] 2 W.L.R. 594; [1979] 2 All E.R. 193; 123 S.J. 306, Ch D 12–66
Midland Marts Ltd v Hobday [1989] 1 W.L.R. 1143; [1989] 3 All E.R. 246; (1989) 86(27) L.S.G. 41; (1989) 133 S.J. 1109; *The Times*, April 25, 1989, Ch D 14–148, 14–149
Milburn, 1946 S.C. 301; 1946 S.L.T. 219, IH (1 Div) 10–34, 16–31, 16–44, 16–45, 16–49
Milburn v Newton Colliery Ltd (1908) 52 S.J. 317 .... 12–182, 12–183, 12–200
Mileage Conference Group of the Tyre Manufacturers' Conferences' Agreement, Re [1966] 1 W.L.R. 1137; [1966] 2 All E.R. 849; 110 S.J. 483, Ch D (RPC) 3–249, 12–80, 12–90, 12–94, 15–80
Miller v Huddlestone (1883) 22 Ch. D. 233 .... 14–120, 15–86
Miller v James (1823) 8 Moo. C.P. 208 12–261
Miller v Knox (1838) 4 Bing. (N.C.) 574; (1838) 132 E.R. 910 .... 10–21, 11–326
Miller v Mitchell (1835) 13 S. 644 16–215
Miller v Scorey; Miller v Forrest [1996] 1 W.L.R. 1122; [1996] 3 All E.R. 18; *The Times*, April 2, 1996, Ch D 12–80, 12–86, 12–94, 12–182, 12–201
Millet v Rowse (1802) 7 Ves. Jun. 419; (1802) 32 E.R. 169 11–334
Milne v Davidson (1829) 8 S. 223 .... 16–235, 16–264
Milne v Express Newspapers Ltd (No.1) [2004] EWCA Civ 664; [2005] 1 W.L.R. 772; [2005] 1 All E.R. 1021; [2004] E.M.L.R. 24; (2004) 148 S.J.L.B. 696; *Independent*, June 11, 2004, CA (Civ Div) 4–237, 8–21, 16–363
Milsom v Bevan, unreported, November 1977, Pain J. 11–317
Minister for Justice v West Australian Newspapers Ltd [1970] W.A.R. 292 4–287
Mir v Mir; sub nom. M v M (Sequestration: Sale of Property) [1992] Fam. 79; [1992] 2 W.L.R. 225; [1992] 1 All E.R. 765; [1992] 1 F.L.R. 624; [1992] 1 F.C.R. 227; [1992] Fam. Law 378; (1992) 89(4) L.S.G. 33; (1992) 136 S.J.L.B. 10, Fam Div 14–130, 15–85
Mirror Group Newspapers v Harrison, unreported, November 7, 1986 .... 1–137, 19–2
Moerman-Lenglet v Henshaw, *The Times*, November 23, 1992 15–24
Monckton, Re (1837) 1 Moo. P.C. 455; (1837) 12 E.R. 887 10–143
Monroe v Robertson's Trs (1834) 12 S. 788 16–247
Monson v Tussauds Ltd; Monson v Louis Tussaud; sub nom. Monson v Louis Tussaud [1894] 1 Q.B. 671, CA 4–25
Montgomery v HM Advocate; Coulter v HM Advocate; sub nom. HM Advocate v Montgomery [2003] 1 A.C. 641; [2001] 2 W.L.R. 779; 2001 S.C. (P.C.) 1; 2001 S.L.T. 37; 2000 S.C.C.R. 1044; [2001] U.K.H.R.R. 124; 9 B.H.R.C. 641; 2000 G.W.D. 40–1487; *The Times*, December 6, 2000, PC (Sc) 4–114, 4–117, 16–305, 16–400
Mordaunt v Clarke (1869) 1 P. & D. 592 12–130
More v Clerk of Assize, Bristol [1972] 1 W.L.R. 1669; [1972] 1 All E.R. 58 11–159
More v More (1741) 2 Atk. 157 11–335
More v Woreham (1580) Cary 99; (1580) 21 E.R. 53 .... 11–104, 11–114
Morgan v Jones (1745) in Dick. 91; 21 E.R. 202 11–317

TABLE OF CASES

Morgan v Morgan [1977] Fam. 122 11–109
Morris v Crown Office; sub nom. Morris v Master of the Crown Office [1970] 2 Q.B. 114;
    [1970] 2 W.L.R. 792; [1970] 1 All E.R. 1079; 114 S.J. 151, CA (Civ Div) 2–10, 3–86,
        10–11, 10–34, 10–100, 11–85, 13–119, 14–40, 14–48, 14–49, 14–55, 14–60,
                                                            14–110, 14–143, 16–39
Morrison v Jessop, 1989 S.L.T. 86, HCJ Appeal 16–43
Moscow City Council v Bankers Trust. *See* Department of Economic Policy and Development of the City of Moscow v Bankers Trust Co
Motorola Credit Corp v Uzan (No.2). *See* Motorola Credit Corp v Uzan (No.6)
Motorola Credit Corp v Uzan (No.6); sub nom. Motorola Credit Corp v Uzan (No.2) [2003]
    EWCA Civ 752; [2004] 1 W.L.R. 113; [2003] C.P. Rep. 56; [2003] 2 C.L.C. 1026;
    (2003) 100(32) L.S.G. 34; (2003) 147 S.J.L.B. 752; *The Times*, June 19, 2003;
    Independent, July 23, 2003 (C.S), CA (Civ Div) 2–195, 9–216, 12–66, 12–79, 12–168,
                                                                       12–169, 12–176
Mowbray v Lowe, 1990 G.W.D. 10–529 16–115
Mowbray v Valentine, 1991 S.C.C.R. 494 .... 16–112, 16–113
Moyna v Secretary of State for Work and Pensions; sub nom. Moyna v Secretary of State for
    Social Security [2003] UKHL 44; [2003] 1 W.L.R. 1929; [2003] 4 All E.R. 162;
    (2003) 73 B.M.L.R. 201; *The Times*, August 11, 2003; *Independent*, October 2, 2003,
    HL 10–113
Moynihan v Moynihan (Nos 1 and 2); sub nom. Re Moynihan [1997] 1 F.L.R. 59; [1997]
    Fam. Law 88; *Independent*, October 7, 1996 (C.S.), Fam Div 8–5, 8–10, 8–12
Moysa v Alberta (Labour Relations Board) (1989) 60 D.L.R. (4th) 1 .... 9–1, 9–51
Mubarak v Mubarak (No.1); Mubarak v Wani; Mubarak v Dianoor International Ltd;
    Mubarak v Dianoor Jewels Ltd; sub nom. Mubarak v Mubarik; Murbarak v Murbarak
    [2001] 1 F.L.R. 698; [2001] 1 F.C.R. 193; [2001] Fam. Law 178; *Daily Telegraph*,
    January 23, 2001, CA (Civ Div) 13–89, 15–52, 15–56
Mucklow's Case, Welcden v Elkington (1578) Plowd. 516; (1578) 75 E.R. 763 10–188
Muir v BBC, 1997 S.L.T. 425; 1997 S.C.C.R. 584 ...... 16–322, 16–324, 16–326, 16–328, 16–331,
                                                                       16–367
Muir v Milligan (1868) 6 M. 1125 16–234
Muirhead v Douglas, 1979 S.L.T. (Notes) 17; [1981] Crim. L.R. 781, HCJ 11–88, 16–65, 16–74,
                                                                       16–78
Muller v Switzerland (A/133) (1991) 13 E.H.R.R. 212, ECHR 8–7
Mullett v Hunt (1833) 1 C. & M. 753 14–155
Mullins v Howell (1879) 11 Ch.D. 763 12–189
Mulock, Re (1864) 33 L.J. P.M. & A. 205 11–280
Munster v Lamb (1883) 11 Q.B.D. 588 10–150
Murdanaigum v Henderson, April 24, 1996; 1996 G.W.D. 19–1079, HCJ 16–81
Murphy (1969) 4 D.L.R. 289 5–261
Murray (1820) Shaw's J.C. 16–144
Mustafa v Mustafa, *The Times*, September 11 and 13, 1967 11–336
Myers v Elman [1940] A.C. 282 .... 12–248, 12–253, 14–140
Myers v Wills (1820) 4 Moo. C.P. 147 11–317

N (A Minor) (Access: Penal Notice), Re [1992] 1 F.L.R. 134; [1991] F.C.R. 1000; [1992]
    Fam. Law 149; *The Times*, July 23, 1991, CA (Civ Div) 15–24
N (Infants), Re [1967] Ch. 512; [1967] 2 W.L.R. 691; [1967] 1 All E.R. 161; 110 S.J. 924,
    Ch D 6–54
N v N (Contempt: Committal), Re [1992] 1 F.L.R. 370; [1992] 1 F.C.R. 362; [1992] Fam.
    Law 286; *The Times*, August 13, 1991, CA (Civ Div) 3–17, 3–219, 12–11, 16–254
NLRB v Local 825, International Union of Operating Engineers, 430 F. 2d 1225 (3rd Cir.
    1970), cert. denied, 401 U.S. 976 (1971) 3–76
NSW Egg Corporation v Peek (1987) 10 N.S.W.L.R. 72 .... 3–245, 12–44
Naf Naf SA v Dickens (London) Ltd [1993] F.S.R. 424, Ch D 3–201
Nairn and Ogilvy (1765) Hume, Vol.II, p.139 16–146
Nanan v The State. *See* Nanan (Lalchan) v Trinidad and Tobago

TABLE OF CASES

Nanan (Lalchan) v Trinidad and Tobago; sub. nom. Nana v The State [1986] A.C. 860; [1986] 3 W.L.R. 304; [1986] 3 All E.R. 248; (1986) 83 Cr. App. R. 292; (1986) 83 L.S.G. 1995; (1986) 130 S.J. 592, PC (Trin) 11–389
National Bank of Greece v Constantinos Dimitriou, *The Times*, November 16, 1987 12–70
National Federated Electrical Association's Agreement, Re [1961] L.R. 2 R.P. 447 12–182
Nationwide News Pty Ltd v Wills (1992) 177 C.L.R. 1, H Ct (Aus) 2–99, 5–225, 5–254, 5–255, 5–259, 5–267
Neath Canal Co v Ynisarwed Resolven Colliery Co (1875) 10 Ch. App. 450 .... 12–182, 15–27
Neckles v Yorkshire Rider Ltd (t/a First Huddersfield) [2002] All E.R. (D) Jan; [2002] UKEAT 1267/01 .... 10–194, 13–65
Needham v Dowling (1845) 15 L.J. C. P. 9 10–150
Needham v Frazer (1845) 14 L.J. C.P. 256 14–158
Neil v Ryan [1998] 2 F.L.R. 1068; [1999] 1 F.C.R. 241; [1998] Fam. Law 728, CA (Civ Div) 13–119, 14–46, 15–88, 19–2
Neish v Stevenson, 1969 S.L.T. 229 16–81
Nelson v Nelson, 1988 S.C.L.R. 663 16–265
Neville v Neville, 1924 S.L.T. (Sh. Ct) 43 16–241
Nevitt, Re, 117 F. 448 (8th Cir. 1902) 3–22, 3–179
New Brunswick Broadcasting Co v Nova Scotia (1991) 80 D.L.R. (4th) 11 9–1
New Brunswick Co v Muggeridge (1859) 4 Drew. 686; (1859) 62 E.R. 263 12–254
New Gold Coast Exploration Co, Re [1901] 1 Ch. 860, Ch D 5–30
New York Times Co v Sullivan (1964) 376 U.S. 254 .... 2–38, 2–54, 9–7
Newfoundland (Treasury Board) v Newfoundland Association of Public Employees (1986) 59 Nfld & P.E.I.R. 93 12–70
Newham LBC v Jones [2002] EWCA Civ 1779; (2002) 146 S.J.L.B. 269, CA (Civ Div) 14–91
Newlands v Newlands (1741) Mor. 7331 .... 16–89, 16–138
Newman (t/a Mantella Publishing) v Modern Bookbinders Ltd [2000] 1 W.L.R. 2559; [2000] 2 All E.R. 814; *Independent*, February 3, 2000, CA (Civ Div) 2–195, 3–4, 13–89, 15–108
News Group Newspapers, Ex p. [2002] E.M.L.R. 160 7–121
Newton v Harland (1840) 1 Man. & G. 956; (1840) 133 E.R. 619; (1839) 8 Scott 70 .... 3–146, 11–104, 11–105
Newton v North-Western Provinces Court Judge (1871) L.R. 4 P.C. 18 10–143
Nguyen v Phung [1984] F.L.R. 773 .... 12–33, 15–47, 15–58, 15–64, 15–67, 15–69
Nicholls v DPP [1994] 61 S.A.S.R. 31; [1994] 66 A. Crim. R. 517 9–50
Nicholls v Nicholls [1997] 1 W.L.R. 314; [1997] 2 All E.R. 97; [1997] 1 F.L.R. 649; [1997] 3 F.C.R. 14; [1997] Fam. Law 321; (1997) 147 N.L.J. 61; *The Times*, January 21, 1997, CA (Civ Div) 3–69, 12–79, 14–45, 14–63, 15–67, 15–75, 15–76
Nicholson v Squire (1809) 16 Ves. Jun. 259; (1809) 33 E.R. 983 .... 11–335, 11–342
Nicol, Re (1954) 3 D.L.R. 690 5–261
Nicol v Caledonian Newspapers Ltd, 2002 S.C. 493; 2003 S.L.T. 109; 2002 G.W.D. 13–417, OH 8–12
Nimmo (1839) 2 Swin. 338 16–118
Norman v Beaumont (1744) Willes 484; (1744) 125 E.R. 1281 11–188
North Cheshire and Manchester Brewery Co Ltd v Manchester Brewery Co Ltd; sub nom. Manchester Brewery Co Ltd v North Cheshire and Manchester Brewery Co Ltd [1899] A.C. 83, HL 5–28
Northern Counties Securities Ltd v Jackson & Steeple Ltd [1974] 1 W.L.R. 1133 12–182
Northumberland (Duke of) v Harris, Bell (1832) 10 S. 366 16–254
Northwest Territories Public Service Association v Commissioner of the Northwest Territories (1980) 107 D.L.R. (3d) 458 12–48
Norwich (Bishop of) v Earl of Kent (1500) Y.B. T. 14 Hen. 7, pl. 4 10–182
Norwich Pharmacal Co v Customs and Excise Commissioners; sub nom. Morton-Norwich Products Inc v Customs and Excise Commissioners [1974] A.C. 133; [1973] 3 W.L.R. 164; [1973] 2 All E.R. 943; [1973] F.S.R. 365; [1974] R.P.C. 101; 117 S.J. 567, HL; reversing [1972] 3 W.L.R. 870; [1972] 3 All E.R. 813; [1972] F.S.R. 405; [1972] R.P.C. 743; 116 S.J. 823, CA (Civ Div); reversing [1972] Ch. 566; [1972] 2 W.L.R. 864; [1972] 1 All E.R. 972; [1972] F.S.R. 1; (1971) 116 S.J. 315, Ch D 1–148, 3–192, 9–129, 9–147, 9–148, 12–108

TABLE OF CASES

Nottingham City Council v October Films Ltd [1999] 2 F.L.R. 347; [1999] 2 F.C.R. 529; [1999] Fam. Law 536; (1999) 163 J.P.N. 929; (1999) 96(23) L.S.G. 33; *The Times*, May 21, 1999, Fam Div 6–72, 6–87
Nwogbe v Nwogbe [2000] 2 F.L.R. 744; [2000] 3 F.C.R. 345; [2000] Fam. Law 797; *The Times*, July 11, 2000, CA (Civ Div) 15–56

O (A Minor) (Contact: Imposition of Conditions), Re [1995] 2 F.L.R. 124; [1995] Fam. Law 541; (1995) 159 J.P.N. 540; *The Times*, March 17, 1995; *Independent*, June 26, 1995 (C.S.), CA (Civ Div) 12–27, 15–24
O (Infants), Re [1962] 2 All E.R. 10 11–336
O (Minors) (Contempt: Committal), Re [1995] 2 F.L.R. 767; [1996] 2 F.C.R. 89; [1996] Fam. Law 26, CA (Civ Div) 19–2
Oberschlick v Austria (1995) 19 E.H.R.R. 389 .... 2–50, 2–168
O'Brennan v Tully (1935) 69 I.L.T. 115 10–162
O'Brien v The Queen (1888) 16 S.C.R. 197 16–66
Observer and *Guardian* v United Kingdom (A/216) (1992) 14 E.H.R.R. 153, *The Times*, November 27, 1991; *Independent*, November 27, 1991; *Guardian*, November 27, 1991, ECHR 1–135, 2–194, 6–20
O'Connell, Whelan and Watson, Re [2005] EWCA Civ 759 7–48
O'Connor, Re; Chesshire v Strauss (1896) 12 T.L.R. 291 4–213
O'Donovan v O'Donovan [1955] 1 W.L.R. 1086; [1955] 3 All E.R. 278 (Note); 99 S.J. 709, PDAD 12–34, 15–13
Official Solicitor v News Group Newspapers Ltd [1994] 2 F.L.R. 174; [1994] 2 F.C.R. 552; [1994] Fam. Law 499, Fam Div 1–135, 2–22, 2–194, 3–66, 4–16, 4–213, 5–121, 5–169, 5–196, 6–85, 6–151, 7–223, 7–224, 8–99, 8–118, 8–120, 8–125, 8–127, 8–138, 8–140, 11–258, 12–87, 16–82, 19–1
Oldfield v Cobbett (1845) 1 Ph. 557; (1845) 41 E.R. 744 3–159
Oliveira v Switzerland (1999) 28 E.H.R.R. 289; [1998] H.R.C.D. 755, ECHR 3–209, 12–14
Olk v Olk [2001] EWCA Civ 1075, CA (Civ Div) 15–47, 15–67, 15–76, 19–2
Omega Group Holdings Ltd v Kozeny; Marlwood Commercial Inc v Kozeny [2004] EWCA Civ 798; [2005] 1 W.L.R. 104; [2004] 3 All E.R. 648; [2004] 2 C.L.C. 166; (2004) 148 S.J.L.B. 822, CA (Civ Div) 11–82, 12–205, 12–239
Omond v Lees, 1994 S.L.T. 1265; 1994 S.C.C.R. 389, HCJ Appeal 16–43, 16–44, 16–134
Open Door Counselling Ltd v Ireland (A/246); Dublin Well Woman Centre v Ireland (A/246); sub nom. Open Door Counselling Ltd v Ireland (14234/88, 14253/88) (1993) 15 E.H.R.R. 244; *The Times*, November 5, 1992; *Independent*, November 3, 1992; *Guardian*, November 3, 1992, ECHR 6–20, 8–7
O'Riordan v DPP [2005] EWHC 1240; *The Times*, May 31, 2005, QBD (Admin) 8–19, 8–21, 8–22
Orr Ewing's JF, Petr (1884) 11 R. 682 16–267
O'Sullivan, Re; Ex p. O'Sullivan v Commonwealth Bank of Australia [1995] 129 A.L.R. 295 11–305
Osborne v Tuthell (1583) Ch. Cas. Ch. 168; (1583) 21 E.R. 98 11–317
O'Shea v O'Shea and Parnell Ex p. Tuohy (1890) 15 P.D. 59 .... 3–28, 3–135, 3–138
Oswald v Heywood, 1991 G.W.D. 36–2182 16–81
Oullet, Re (1976) 67 D.L.R. (3d) 73 5–245
Overseas League v Taylor, 1951 S.C. 105 16–262
Oxfordshire CC v L and F [1997] 1 F.L.R. 235; [1997] 3 F.C.R. 124; [1997] Fam. Law 249, Fam Div 1–140, 6–55, 6–65, 6–68, 6–69, 6–96, 6–108, 7–58, 8–99, 10–173, 11–337

Oxfordshire CC v P [1995] Fam. 161 10–173
P, Ex p. [1988] T.L.R. 204 .... 7–8, 8.145
P (Minors) (Custody Order: Penal Notice), Re [1990] 1 W.L.R. 613; [1990] 2 F.L.R. 223; [1990] F.C.R. 909; (1990) 154 J.P.N. 754; (1990) 87(12) L.S.G. 40; (1990) 134 S.J. 661; *The Times*, February 27, 1990; *Independent*, March 13, 1990 (C.S.), CA (Civ Div) 14–118, 15–24, 15–52, 15–78
P (Minors: Wardship) (Access: Contempt), Re; sub nom. Re P (Minors) [1991] 1 F.L.R. 280; [1991] F.C.R. 283; [1991] Fam. Law 274; (1991) 155 J.P.N. 138; *The Times*, November 1, 1990, CA (Civ Div) 12–68

TABLE OF CASES

P v Liverpool Daily Post and Echo Newspapers Plc. *See* Pickering v Liverpool Daily Post and Echo
P v P (Contempt of Court: Mental Capacity) [1999] 2 F.L.R. 897; [1999] 3 F.C.R. 547; [1999] Fam. Law 690; *The Times*, July 21, 1999, CA (Civ Div) 12–83
PA Thomas & Co v Mould [1968] 2 Q.B. 913 12–48
P-B (A Minor) (Child Cases: Hearings in Open Court), Re; sub nom. Re PB (Hearings in Open Court); Re PB (A Minor) (Hearing in Private); Re P-B (Children Act: Open Court) [1997] 1 All E.R. 58; [1996] 2 F.L.R. 765; [1996] 3 F.C.R. 705; [1996] Fam. Law 606; (1996) 160 J.P.N. 1046; *Independent*, July 9, 1996, CA (Civ Div) 1–174, 6–108, 7–63, 7–65, 8–76
PB (Hearings in Open Court), Re. *See* Re P-B (A Minor) (Child Cases: Hearings in Open Court)
Padfield v Minister of Agriculture, Fisheries and Food [1968] A.C. 997; [1968] 2 W.L.R. 924; [1968] 1 All E.R. 694; 112 S.J. 171, HL 2–225
Page, Ex p. (1810) 17 Ves. Jun. 59; (1810) 34 E.R. 23 11–317
Pall Mall Gazette, Re; Jones v Flower (1894) 11 T.L.R. 122 .... 4–131, 4–274, 5–116
Palmer v Maynard (1598) Sanders 79a 1–43
Palser v Grinling; Property Holding Co v Mischeff [1948] A.C. 291; [1948] 1 All E.R. 1; 64 T.L.R. 2; [1948] L.J.R. 600; 92 S.J. 53, HL 4–56
Parker v Pocock (1874) 30 L.T. 458 11–320
Parker (t/a NBC Services) v Rasalingham (t/a Micro Tec) [2000] All E.R. (D) 912; *The Times*, July 12, 2000 .... 12–94, 14–148, 14–149
Parkinson v Thornton (1868) 37 L.J. P. 3 12–129
Parra v Rones [1986] Fam. Law 262, CA (Civ Div) 15–47, 15–67
Parsons v Nasar [1990] 2 F.L.R. 103; (1991) 23 H.L.R. 1; *The Times*, November 19, 1988, CA (Civ Div) 14–38
Partridge v Partridge (1639) Tothill 40; (1639) 21 E.R. 117 11–216
Paston's Case (1465) Y.B. (Long Quinto) 5 Edw. IV 5 1–36
Patel v Daybells [2001] EWCA Civ 1229; [2002] P.N.L.R. 6; [2001] 32 E.G.C.S. 87; *Daily Telegraph*, September 11, 2001, CA (Civ Div) 12–256
Patel v Patel [1988] 2 F.L.R. 179, CA 14–135
Pater, Ex p. (1864) 5 B. & S. 299; (1864) 122 E.R. 842 ... 3–132, 10–146, 10–150, 10–153, 11–8
Paterson v Kilgour (1865) 3 Mor. 1119; (1865) 385 J. 5 .... 16–66, 16–67
Paterson v Robson (1872) 11 M. 76 16–254
Pattison v Fitzgerald (1823) 2 S. 536 .... 16–226, 16–234
Paul Magder Furs Ltd v Att-Gen (Ontario) (1991) 85 D.L.R. (4th) 694 .... 12–70, 12–76
Pavlova v Harvey, *The Times*, November 27, 1911 11–280
Payne v Cooper [1896] 1 Q.B. 577 1–81
Peach Grey & Co v Sommers [1995] 2 All E.R. 513; [1995] I.C.R. 549; [1995] I.R.L.R. 363; (1995) 92(13) L.S.G. 31; (1995) 139 S.J.L.B. 93; *The Times*, February 16, 1995; *Independent*, March 13, 1995 (C.S.), DC 1–127, 4–17, 4–20, 7–109, 10–6, 10–136, 13–63
Peacock v London Weekend Television (1986) 150 J.P. 71; (1986) 150 J.P.N. 47, CA (Civ Div) 2–39, 2–208, 4–270, 5–106, 6–1, 6–22, 6–23, 6–25, 6–26, 6–29, 6–40, 7–142, 8–5, 13–36, 13–101, 15–3
Pearce v Pearce, *The Times*, January 30, 1959 13–34
Peart v Stewart; Whitter v Peters [1983] 2 A.C. 109; [1983] 2 W.L.R. 451; [1983] 1 All E.R. 859; [1984] Fam. Law 54; (1983) 127 S.J. 206, HL; reversing [1982] 1 W.L.R. 389; [1982] 2 All E.R. 369; [1983] 4 F.L.R. 8; (1982) 12 Fam. Law 84; 126 S.J. 100, CA (Civ Div) 1–124, 1–125, 1–126, 3–22, 3–95, 3–178, 12–86, 13–92, 14–12, 14–25, 14–26, 14–56, 15–5, 19–2
Peck v United Kingdom (2003) 36 E.H.R.R. 41 6–73
Pelham (Lord) v Duchess of Newcastle (1712) 3 Swan 289n; (1712) 36 E.R. 865 11–323
Pell v Daubeny (1850) 5 Exch. 955; (1850) 155 E.R. 416 11–119
Pelling v Bruce-Williams [2004] EWCA Civ 845; [2004] Fam. 155; [2004] 3 W.L.R. 1178; [2004] 3 All E.R. 875; [2004] 2 F.L.R. 823; [2004] 3 F.C.R. 108; [2004] Fam. Law 784, CA (Civ Div) 1–174, 7–63, 7–67
Pelling v Hammond, C/00/2363, September 22, 2000 .... 2–207, 3–174, 15–9

TABLE OF CASES

Pepper (Inspector of Taxes) v Hart [1993] A.C. 593; [1992] 3 W.L.R. 1032; [1993] 1 All E.R. 42; [1992] S.T.C. 898; [1993] I.C.R. 291; [1993] I.R.L.R. 33; [1993] R.V.R. 127; (1993) 143 N.L.J. 17; [1992] N.P.C. 154; *The Times*, November 30, 1992; *Independent*, November 26, 1992, HL 1–115, 4–57
Perera (Arthur Reginald) v The King [1951] A.C. 482; [1951] 1 T.L.R. 829; 95 S.J. 333, PC (Cey) 5–139, 5–233, 5–251, 5–257
Peteranna v McClory, 1991 G.W.D. 10–575 16–79
Peters v Bradlaugh (1888) 4 T.L.R. 414 5–105
Petrie v Angus (1889) 2 White 358; (1889) 17 R. (J.) 3; (1889) 27 S.L.R. 197 .... 3–71, 16–34, 16–35, 16–59, 16–62, 16–107, 16–109, 16–137, 16–235
Phillips v Hedges (1736) Cooke C.P. 132; (1736) 125 E.R. 1004 11–317
Phillips v Nova Scotia (Westray Inquiry) (1995) 98 C.C.C. (3d) 20 .... 1–144, 2–100
Phillips v Symes; Harland v Symes [2003] EWCA Civ 1769; (2003) 147 S.J.L.B. 1431, CA (Civ Div) 3–192, 15–39
Phipps v Lord Anglesea (1721) 1 P. Wms. 696; (1721) 24 E.R. 576 11–334
Phonographic Performance Ltd v Amusement Caterers (Peckham) [1964] Ch. 195; [1963] 3 W.L.R. 898; [1963] 3 All E.R. 493; 107 S.J. 853, Ch D 3–8, 3–13, 3–71, 3–89, 3–176, 12–1, 12–5, 12–125, 12–126, 14–101, 15–80
Phonographic Performance Ltd v Inch [2002] All E.R. (D) 253 15–32
Phonographic Performance Ltd v Tierney [2003] EWHC 2416; [2003] All E.R. (D) 08; (2004) 27(1) I.P.D. 27006, Ch D 14–47
Phonographic Performance Ltd v Tsang (1985) 82 L.S.G. 2331; *The Times*, May 17, 1985, CA (Civ Div) 12–34
Pickering v Liverpool Daily Post and Echo; sub nom. P v Liverpool Daily Post and Echo [1991] 2 A.C. 370; [1991] 2 W.L.R. 513; [1991] 1 All E.R. 622; (1991) 3 Admin. L.R. 397; [1991] 2 Med. L.R. 240; (1991) 141 N.L.J. 166; 135 S.J.L.B. 166, HL; reversing [1990] 2 W.L.R. 494; [1990] 1 All E.R. 335; (1990) 2 Admin. L.R. 403; (1990) 87(14) L.S.G. 44; 134 S.J. 786, CA (Civ Div) 1–126, 1–127, 2–193, 2–207, 2–208, 3–49, 3–67, 3–68, 4–17, 4–20, 4–282, 6–3, 6–004, 6–22, 6–26, 6–30, 6–40, 6–150, 7–58, 7–109, 7–135, 7–142, 8–5, 8–48, 8–117, 8–120, 8–130, 8–131, 8–133, 8–134, 8–135, 9–243, 10–6, 13–44, 13–54, 13–66, 13–68, 13–106, 14–1, 14–132, 16–39, 16–252, 16–334
Pidduck v Molloy [1992] 2 F.L.R. 202; [1992] Fam. Law 529; *The Times*, March 9, 1992, CA (Civ Div) 14–47, 14–76
Pirie v Hawthorn, 1962 J.C. 69; 1962 S.L.T. 291, HCJ Appeal 16–51, 16–73, 16–75
Pitcher v King (1845) 5 Nev. & Man. 431; (1845) 1 Car. & Kir. 655 11–100
Pitt v Coombs (1834) 3 Nev. and M. K.B. 212 3–146
Plant, Re; Plant v Hayward (1881) 45 L.T. 326 11–321
Plating Co v Farquharson (1881) L.R. 17 Ch. D. 49, CA 1–62, 1–77, 4–134, 5–30, 14–136
Plumbe v Plumbe (1844) 2 L.T. Jo. 439 .... 3–159, 11–72, 11–261
Pojé v Att-Gen of British Columbia [1953] 2 D.L.R. 785 .... 3–15, 3–18, 3–124, 3–157, 3–158, 3–167, 3–170
Polanski v Condé Nast Publications Ltd [2005] UKHL 10; [2005] 1 W.L.R. 637; [2005] 1 All E.R. 945; [2005] C.P. Rep. 22; [2005] E.M.L.R. 14; [2005] H.R.L.R. 11; (2005) 102(10) L.S.G. 29; (2005) 155 N.L.J. 245; *The Times*, February 11, 2005; *Independent*, February 16, 2005, HL 12–70, 12–75, 12–79
Police v O'Connor [1992] 1 N.Z.L.R. 87 .... 2–68, 7–7, 7–16, 7–84
Pollard, In re (1868) L.R. 2 P.C. 106 .... 2–18, 10–50, 10–144, 10–150
Pollard, Re [1903] 2 K.B. 41 .... 14–120, 14–121
Pool v Sacheverel (1720) 1 P. Wms. 676; (1720) 24 E.R. 565 .... 1–61, 4–134, 11–72, 11–261
Poole v Gould (1856) 1 H. & N. 99; (1856) 156 E.R. 1133 11–304
Porteous (Peter) (1832) 5 Deas and Anderson 53 .... 16–91, 16–96
Porter v Magill; Weeks v Magill; Hartley v Magill; England v Magill; Phillips v Magill; sub nom. Magill v Porter; Magill v Weeks [2001] UKHL 67; [2002] 2 A.C. 357; [2002] 2 W.L.R. 37; [2002] 1 All E.R. 465; [2002] H.R.L.R. 16; [2002] H.L.R. 16; [2002] B.L.G.R. 51; (2001) 151 N.L.J. 1886; [2001] N.P.C. 184; *The Times*, December 14, 2001; *Independent*, February 4, 2002 (C.S.); *Daily Telegraph*, December 20, 2001, HL 5–239, 10–49
Pott v Stuteley [1955] W.N. 140 3–15
Prager and Oberschlick v Austria (1996) 21 E.H.R.R. 1 2–50

TABLE OF CASES

Pratt v Inman (1889) 43 Ch. D. 175 .... 14–112, 14–114
Preston (1691) 1 Salk. 278; (1691) 91 E.R. 243 10–158
Preston, Re (1883) 11 Q.B.D. 545 14–28
Price v Hutchinson (1869) 9 L.R. Eq. 534 .... 11–316, 11–317
Price v United Kingdom (2002) 34 E.H.R.R. 53; [2001] Crim. L.R. 916 14–70
Pritchard Englefield (A Firm) v Steinberg [2005] EWCA Civ 288; (2005) 149 S.J.L.B. 300,
  CA (Civ Div) 1–181
Proctor v Smiles (1886) 55 L.J.Q.B. 527, CA 9–13
Prothonotary, The v Collins (1985) 2 N.S.W.L.R. 549 ..... 4–50, 4–111, 10–26, 11–12, 11–13, 11–308
Prudential Assurance Co Ltd v Fountain Page Ltd [1991] 1 W.L.R. 756; [1991] 3 All E.R.
  878, QBD 12–201
Purdin v Roberts (1910) 74 J.P. Jo. 88 .... 5–139, 10–18, 10–96, 11–157, 11–158, 11–164, 11–195
Pyke v National Westminster Bank Ltd, *The Times*, December 9, 1977 12–79

Quality Pizzas v Canterbury Hotel Employees' Industrial Union [1983] N.Z.L.R. 612 14–124
Quartz Hill & Co Ex P. Young, Re (1881) 21 Ch. D. 642 15–35

R (A Minor) (Contempt: Sentence), Re [1994] 1 W.L.R. 487; [1994] 2 All E.R. 144; [1994]
  2 F.L.R. 185; [1994] 2 F.C.R. 629; [1994] Fam. Law 435, CA (Civ Div) 14–17, 14–33
—— (A Minor) (Wardship: Restrictions on Publication), Re [1994] Fam. 254; [1994] 3
  W.L.R. 36; [1994] 3 All E.R. 658; [1994] 2 F.L.R. 637; [1994] 2 F.C.R. 468; [1994]
  Fam. Law 623; *The Times*, April 25, 1994, CA (Civ Div) 6–55, 6–74, 6–85, 6–86, 6–88,
                                    6–97, 6–99, 6–100, 6–113, 7–56, 11–337
—— (Court of Appeal: Order Against Identification), Re [1999] 2 F.L.R. 145; [1999] 3
  F.C.R. 213 7–66
—— (MJ) (A Minor) (Publication of Transcript), Re; sub nom. Re R (MJ) (An Infant)
  (Proceedings: Transcripts: Publication) [1975] Fam. 89; [1975] 2 W.L.R. 978; [1975]
  2 All E.R. 749; (1975) 5 Fam. Law 154; 119 S.J. 338, Fam Div 8–102, 15–17
—— v H [2003] EWCA Crim 485; *The Times*, March 10, 2003 .... 7–18, 12–211
—— v R [1979] Fam. 56 12–15
—— & T. Thew Ltd v Reeves (No.2) [1982] Q.B. 1283; [1982] 3 W.L.R. 869; [1982] 3 All
  E.R. 1086; 126 S.J. 674, CA (Civ Div) 12–253
—— v Abdulaziz [1989] Crim. L.R. 717 .... 11–107, 11–122, 11–125, 11–126, 11–128, 11–139
—— v Adomako (John Asare); R. v Sullman (Barry); R. v Prentice (Michael Charles); R.
  v Holloway (Stephen John) [1995] 1 A.C. 171; [1994] 3 W.L.R. 288; [1994] 3 All E.R.
  79; (1994) 99 Cr. App. R. 362; (1994) 158 J.P. 653; [1994] 5 Med. L.R. 277; [1994]
  Crim. L.R. 757; (1994) 158 J.P.N. 507; (1994) 144 N.L.J. 936; *The Times*, July 4,
  1994; *Independent*, July 1, 1994, HL 3–80
—— v Alcindor (Herald of Free Enterprise), June 11, 1990, Turner J.—2–75
—— v Ali (Mumtaz) (1995) 16 Cr. App. R. (S.) 692; [1995] Crim. L.R. 303, CA (Crim
  Div) 9–124
—— v Andrews (Tracey) [1999] Crim. L.R. 156 .... 2–118, 2–119
—— v Anomo (Taiye Olokun) [1998] 2 Cr. App. R. (S.) 269; [1998] Crim. L.R. 356; *The
  Times*, February 26, 1998; *Independent*, February 18, 1998, CA (Crim Div) 3–80, 3–178,
                                                        14–9, 14–56
—— v Aquarius (Jesus) (1974) 59 Cr. App. R. 165; [1974] Crim. L.R. 373, CA (Crim Div) 10–4,
                                    10–104, 10–132, 10–213, 14–11, 14–57
—— v Argent (Brian) [1997] 2 Cr. App. R. 27; (1997) 161 J.P. 190; [1997] Crim. L.R. 346;
  (1997) 161 J.P.N. 260; *The Times*, December 19, 1996, CA (Crim Div) 3–64
—— v Armstrong (1951) 35 Cr. App. R. 72 .... 2–81, 2–83
—— v Arnold (Kenneth) [2004] EWCA Crim 1293; [2005] Crim. L.R. 56; (2004) 148
  S.J.L.B. 660, CA (Crim Div) 3–238
—— v Arradi [2003] 1 S.C.R. 280; (2003) 173 C.C.C. (3d) 1; (2003) 244 D.L.R. (4th) 301 10–37,
                                                        10–85
—— v Arundel Justices Ex p. Westminster Press [1986] 1 W.L.R. 676; [1985] 1 W.L.R. 708;
  [1985] 2 All E.R. 390; (1985) 149 J.P. 299; (1985) 82 L.S.G. 1781; (1985) 129 S.J.
  274, DC 7–81

TABLE OF CASES

R v Ashley (Phillip Martin) [2003] EWCA Crim 2571; [2004] 1 W.L.R. 2057; [2004] 1 Cr. App. R. 23; (2003) 167 J.P. 548; [2004] Crim. L.R. 297; (2003) 167 J.P.N. 854, CA (Crim Div) 9–183, 11–129
—— v Associated Newspapers Ex p. Fisher [1941] S.R. (N.S.W.) 272 4–289
—— v Aston [1948] W.N. 252 .... 10–34, 14–11
—— v Astor Ex p. Isaacs (1913) 30 T.L.R. 19 5–114
—— v Att-Gen Ex p. BBC and Jones, December 1, 1995 (Lexis) 19–1
—— v Att-Gen Ex p. Edey, unreported, February 26, 1992 .... 2–214, 2–215
—— v Att-Gen Ex p. Ferrante [1995] C.O.D. 18, Popplewell J. 2–214, 2–215
—— v Ayres (1994) 15 C.C.C. (3d) 208 .... 9–119, 10–166
—— v B (Sharon Kristine) (1994) 15 Cr. App. R. (S.) 815, CA (Crim Div) 5–101
—— v Baines [1909] 1 K.B. 258 11–111
—— v Baker (1891) 113 C.C.C. Cas. 374 11–179
—— v Baldwin, *The Times*, May 3, 1978 3–89
—— v Balfour (1895) 11 T.L.R. 492 5–106
—— v Banham, 95/3049/Z3, November 2, 1995, Kennedy L.J. 10–29, 10–39
—— v Barnardo (1889) L.R. 23 Q.B.D. 305, CA 3–136, 3–137
—— v Barlow [1996] 2 N.Z.L.R. 116 2–212
—— v Barraclough [2000] Crim. L.R. 325 .... 2–84, 2–121, 11–189, 11–351
—— v Barry Ex p. Grey (1939) 83 S.J. 872 5–115
—— v Bashir (Mohammed); R. v Azam (Mohammed) (1988) 10 Cr. App. R. (S.) 76, CA (Crim Div) 19–1
—— v Baxter [1974] Crim. L.R. 611, CA (Crim Div) 14–108
—— v Beaconsfield Justices Ex p. Westminster Press Ltd (1994) 158 J.P. 1055; (1994) 158 J.P.N. 587; [1994] T.L.R. 350; *The Times*, June 28, 1994, QBD 7–120
—— v Bean [1991] Crim. L.R. 843 .... 10–83, 11–350
—— v Beaverbrook Newspapers and Associated Newspapers [1962] N.I. 15 ...... 4–254, 5–87, 5–104, 5–115
—— v Beck Ex p. *Daily Telegraph* Plc [1993] 2 All E.R. 177; (1992) 94 Cr. App. R. 376, CA (Crim Div) 2–43, 2–56, 7–164, 7–168, 7–183, 7–184, 7–185, 7–190, 7–192, 7–193, 7–200,7–245, 7–259
—— v Bedfordshire Coroner Ex p. Local Sunday Newspapers Ltd (2000) 164 J.P. 283; (2000) 164 J.P.N. 370, QBD 7–86
—— v Bjarnson Ex p. The Official Receiver, The Jarlinn [1965] 1 W.L.R. 1098 11–325
—— v Blackwell (Jody Ann); R. v Farley (Neil); R. v Adams (Ian) [1995] 2 Cr. App. R. 625; [1996] Crim. L.R. 428; *The Times*, March 2, 1995; *Independent*, April 24, 1995 (C.S.), CA (Crim Div) 11–351, 11–392
—— v Bloomsbury County Court Ex p. Brady, *The Times*, December 16, 1987, DC 10–130
—— v Bolam Ex p. Haigh; sub nom. Bolam and Ors Ex p. Haigh (1949) 93 S.J. 220, DC 4–202, 5–104, 5–108
—— v Border Television Ex p. Att-Gen (1978) 68 Cr. App. R. 375 .... 7–129, 7–150, 7–152
—— v Bottomley, *The Times*, December 19, 1908 .... 4–129, 5–104
—— v Bow County Court Ex p. Pelling (No.1) [1999] 1 W.L.R. 1807; [1999] 4 All E.R. 751; [1999] 2 F.L.R. 1126; [1999] 3 F.C.R. 97; [1999] Fam. Law 698; (1999) 96(32) L.S.G. 33; (1999) 149 N.L.J. 1369; *The Times*, August 18, 1999; *Independent*, October 1, 1999, CA (Civ Div) 7–47
—— v Bow Street Magistrates' Court Ex p. Choudhury [1991] 1 Q.B. 429; [1990] 3 W.L.R. 986; (1990) 91 Cr. App. R. 393; [1990] Crim. L.R. 711; [1990] C.O.D. 305; (1990) 87(24) L.S.G. 40; (1990) 140 N.L.J. 782, QBD 2–138, 2–172
—— v Bow Street Metropolitan Stipendiary Magistrate Ex p. DPP (1992) 95 Cr. App. R. 9; [1992] Crim. L.R. 790; [1992] C.O.D. 267; *Independent*, January 31, 1992; *Guardian*, January 29, 1992, QBD 2–105
—— v Bow Street Metropolitan Stipendiary Magistrate Ex p. Mirror Group Newspapers Ltd; R. v Bow Street Metropolitan Stipendiary Magistrate Ex p. BBC [1992] 1 W.L.R. 412; [1992] 2 All E.R. 638; [1992] C.O.D. 15, QBD ... 7–119, 7–249, 7–272, 7–275, 7–276
—— v Box (1951) 35 Cr. App. R. 72 2–112
—— v Box (John); R. v Box (Neville Austin) [1964] 1 Q.B. 430; [1963] 3 W.L.R. 696; [1963] 3 All E.R. 240; (1963) 47 Cr. App. R. 284; 127 J.P. 553; 107 S.J. 633, CCA 2–84, 10–182

TABLE OF CASES

R v Brackley (Roger); R. v Weller (Colin Edward), 199902062/Y5, 199902053/Y5, November 3, 2000, CA (Crim Div) 2–114, 11–355
—— v Brandon (1969) 53 Cr. App. Rep. 466 11–361
—— v Briggs (1883) 47 J.P. 615 13–88
—— v Broadcasting Complaints Commission Ex p. Barclay [1997] E.M.L.R. 62; (1997) 9 Admin. L.R. 265; [1997] C.O.D. 57; *The Times*, October 11, 1996; *Independent*, October 14, 1996 (C.S.), QBD 1–115, 2–132
—— v Broadcasting Complaints Commission Ex p. Granada Television Ltd [1995] E.M.L.R. 163; [1995] C.O.D. 207; (1995) 92(7) L.S.G. 36; (1995) 139 S.J.L.B. 48; *The Times*, December 16, 1994; *Independent*, February 20, 1995 (C.S.); *Guardian*, December 19, 1994, CA (Civ Div) 1–136, 4–30, 6–49, 6–91
—— v Bromell [1996] T.L.R. 67, CA (Crim Div) 10–37, 10–60, 11–195, 11–262, 15–107
—— v Brooks, unreported, July 31, 1992, Buckley J. 7–192
—— v Brown (Anthony Joseph); R. v Laskey (Colin); R. v Jaggard (Roland Leonard); R. v Lucas (Saxon); R. v Carter (Christopher Robert); R. v Cadman (Graham William) [1994] 1 A.C. 212; [1993] 2 W.L.R. 556; [1993] 2 All E.R. 75; (1993) 97 Cr. App. R. 44; (1993) 157 J.P. 337; (1993) 157 J.P.N. 233; (1993) 143 N.L.J. 399; *The Times*, March 12, 1993; *Independent*, March 12, 1993, HL 1–109
—— v Brown [1907] 7 N.S.W. St. Rep. 290 .... 10–83, 11–350
—— v Brown (Winston) [1995] 1 Cr. App. R. 191 11–136
—— v Brownell (1834) 1 Ad. & E. 598; (1834) 119 E.R. 1335 .... 11–97, 13–43
—— v Bulgin, Ex p. BBC; *The Times*, July 14, 1977, DC 4–121
—— v Bull and Schmidt (1845) 1 Cox 281 11–154
—— v Burke (Alisdair David) [1991] 1 A.C. 135; [1990] 2 W.L.R. 1313; (1990) 91 Cr. App. R. 384; (1990) 154 J.P. 798; (1990) 22 H.L.R. 433; [1990] Crim. L.R. 877; (1990) 154 J.P.N. 546; (1990) 154 L.G. Rev. 637; (1990) 87(24) L.S.G. 43; (1990) 140 N.L.J. 742; (1990) 134 S.J. 1106, HL 5–122
—— v Butt (1884) 15 Cox 565 11–154
—— v Butt (Reginald Dennis) (1957) 41 Cr. App. R. 82, CCA 10–34, 14–11
—— v Byas (Vincent) (1995) 16 Cr. App. R. (S.) 869; (1995) 159 J.P. 458; [1995] Crim. L.R. 439; (1995) 159 J.P.N. 406, CA (Crim Div) 14–61
—— v Caldwell (James); sub nom. Commissioner of Police of the Metropolis v Caldwell [1982] A.C. 341; [1981] 2 W.L.R. 509; [1981] 1 All E.R. 961; (1981) 73 Cr. App. R. 13; [1981] Crim. L.R. 392; 125 S.J. 239, HL 5–130, 7–204, 10–220, 10–221
—— v Cambridge DHA Ex p. B (No.2); sub nom. R. v Cambridge and Huntingdon HA Ex p. B (No.2); Re B (A Minor) (No.2); Re B (A Minor) (Reporting Restrictions) [1996] 1 F.L.R. 375; [1996] 1 F.C.R. 661; (1996) 30 B.M.L.R. 101; [1996] Fam. Law 146; *The Times*, October 27, 1995, CA (Civ Div) 8–86
—— v Canadian Broadcasting Corp (2001) 52 O.R. (3d) 757 9–51
—— v Cannan (John David) (1991) 92 Cr. App. R. 16; [1990] Crim. L.R. 869, CA (Crim Div) 2–96, 4–114, 4–160, 7–177, 16–309, 16–313
—— v Cannings (Angela) [2004] EWCA Crim 1; [2004] 1 W.L.R. 2607; [2004] 1 All E.R. 725; [2004] 2 Cr. App. R. 7; [2004] 1 F.C.R. 193; [2005] Crim. L.R. 126; (2004) 101(5) L.S.G. 27; (2004) 148 S.J.L.B. 114; *The Times*, January 23, 2004, CA (Crim Div) 8–105, 8–106
—— v Cardiff Crown Court Ex p. M [1998] T.L.R. 264 8–50
—— v Carr-Briant [1943] K.B. 607, CCA 4–262
—— v Carroll (1799) 1 Wils. K.B. 75; (1799) 95 E.R. 500 .... 11–280, 11–281
—— v Carter and Nailor (1994) 16 Cr. App. R. (S) 434 19–1
—— v Castro (Thomas) (Contempt of Court); Onslow's Case; sub nom. R. v Orton; Skipworth's Case (1873–74) L.R. 9 Q.B. 219, QB 3–172, 4–25, 5–104, 5–106, 5–244, 14–101, 14–110
—— v Central Criminal Court Ex p. Bright; R. v Central Criminal Court Ex p. Alton; R. v Central Criminal Court Ex p. Rusbridger; sub nom. R. v Central Criminal Court Ex p. Observer; R. v Central Criminal Court Ex p. *Guardian*; R. (on the application of Bright) v Central Criminal Court [2001] 1 W.L.R. 662; [2001] 2 All E.R. 244; [2001] E.M.L.R. 4; [2000] U.K.H.R.R. 796; [2002] Crim. L.R. 64; (2000) 97(38) L.S.G. 43; *The Times*, July 26, 2000, DC 9–31
—— v Central Criminal Court Ex p. Crook, *The Times*, November 8, 1984, DC 2–55, 7–244, 7–245, 7–249

Table of Cases

R v Central Criminal Court Ex p. Crook; sub nom. Crook, Ex p.; R. v Central Criminal Court Ex p. Godwin [1995] 1 W.L.R. 139; [1995] 1 All E.R. 537; [1995] 2 Cr. App. R. 212; (1995) 159 J.P. 295; [1995] 1 F.L.R. 132; [1995] 2 F.C.R. 153; [1995] Crim. L.R. 509; [1995] Fam. Law 73; (1995) 159 J.P.N. 249; (1994) 91(39) L.S.G. 39; (1994) 138 S.J.L.B. 199; *The Times*, August 16, 1994; *Independent*, September 5, 1994 (C.S.), CA (Crim Div) 2–56, 8–55, 8–056, 8–62, 8–065, 8–68
—— v Central Criminal Court Ex p. Godwin and Crook. *See* R. v Central Criminal Court Ex p. Crook
—— v Central Criminal Court Ex p. S; R. v Central Criminal Court Ex p. P (1999) 163 J.P. 776; [1999] 1 F.L.R. 480; [1999] Crim. L.R. 159; [1999] Fam. Law 93; *The Times*, October 26, 1998; *Independent*, October 26, 1998 (C.S.), DC 6–94, 6–113, 8–25, 8–65
—— v Central Criminal Court Ex p.Telegraph Plc; R v Central Criminal Court Ex p. BBC; R v Central Criminal Court Ex p. Newspaper Publishing; R v Central Criminal Court Ex p. Slater; R v Central Criminal Court Ex p. C; R v Central Criminal Court Ex p. H; R v Central Criminal Court Ex p. M; R v Central Criminal Court Ex p. P; sub nom. R v Central Criminal Court Ex p. the Telegraph Plc [1993] 1 W.L.R. 980; [1993] 2 All E.R. 971; (1994) 98 Cr. App. R. 91; (1993) 143 N.L.J. 475; (1993) 137 S.J.L.B. 107; *The Times*, March 16, 1993; *Independent*, April 28, 1993, CA (Crim Div) 16–309, 16–313
—— v Central Independent Television Plc [1994] Fam. 192; [1994] 3 W.L.R. 20; [1994] 3 All E.R. 641; [1994] 2 F.L.R. 151; [1995] 1 F.C.R. 521; [1994] Fam. Law 500; *The Times*, February 19, 1994; *Independent*, February 17, 1994, CA (Civ Div) 1–139, 2–158, 6–46, 6–55, 6–76, 6–85, 6–86, 6–88, 6–90, 6–120, 7–182, 7–193, 7–200, 11–337
—— v Chancellor of the Chichester Consistory Court Ex p. News Group Newspapers Ltd [1991] T.L.R. 340 13–103
—— v Chancellor of the Chichester Consistory Court Ex p. News Group Newspapers Ltd [1992] C.O.D. 48; *The Times*, July 15, 1991; *Independent*, September 11, 1991, DC 7–72
—— v Chandler (Terence Norman) (No.2); sub nom. Chandler v Commissioner of Police of the Metropolis [1964] Crim. L.R. 404, HL; [1964] 2 Q.B. 322; [1964] 2 W.L.R. 689; [1964] 1 All E.R. 761; (1964) 48 Cr. App. R. 143; (1964) 128 J.P. 244; [1964] Crim. L.R. 305; 108 S.J. 139; *The Times*, February 6, 1964, CCA 2–114
—— v Chapman (1838) 8 C. & P. 558 3–89
—— v Cheltenham Justices Ex p. Secretary of State for Trade [1977] 1 W.L.R. 95; [1977] 1 All E.R. 460; (1977) 121 S.J. 70, DC 11–135
—— v Cheshire County Court Judge [1921] 2 K.B. 694 13–92
—— v Chief Constable of the West Midlands Ex p. Wiley; R. v Chief Constable of Nottinghamshire Ex p. Sunderland [1995] 1 A.C. 274; [1994] 3 W.L.R. 433; [1994] 3 All E.R. 420; [1995] 1 Cr. App. R. 342; [1994] C.O.D. 520; (1994) 91(40) L.S.G. 35; (1994) 144 N.L.J. 1008; (1994) 138 S.J.L.B. 156; *The Times*, July 15, 1994; *Independent*, July 15, 1994, HL 11–136
—— v Chief Metropolitan Magistrate Ex p. Choudhury. *See* R. v Bow Street Magistrates' Court Ex p. Choudhury
—— v Chief Registrar of Friendly Societies Ex p. New Cross Building Society [1984] Q.B. 227; [1984] 2 W.L.R. 370; [1984] 2 All E.R. 27, CA (Civ Div) 7–10, 7–21
—— v Chignell and Walker [1990–2] 1 N.Z.B.O.R.R. 179 6–33
—— v Ching (Yap Chuan) (1976) 63 Cr. App. R. 7; [1976] Crim. L.R. 687, CA (Crim Div) 4–270
—— v Chowdhury; R. v Crone, *The Times*, March 29, 1984 .... 11–121, 11–126
—— v CICB Ex p. A [1992] C.O.D. 379 7–105
—— v City of London Magistrates' Court Ex p. Green; sub nom. Green v Staples [1997] 3 All E.R. 551; [1998] I.T.C.L.R. 42; [1998] Crim. L.R. 54; *The Times*, March 13, 1997, QBD 12–35, 15–20
—— v Clark (Sally) (Appeal against Conviction) (No.2) [2003] EWCA Crim 1020; [2003] 2 F.C.R. 447; (2003) 147 S.J.L.B. 473, CA (Crim Div) 8–105
—— v Clarke Ex p. Crippen (1910) 103 L.T. 636, DC 5–81, 5–109
—— v Clarke (Christopher Henry Tollemache) [1969] 1 W.L.R. 1109; [1969] 2 All E.R. 1008; (1969) 53 Cr. App. R. 438; 133 J.P. 546; 113 S.J. 428, CA (Crim Div) 11–128, 11–139
—— v Clement (1821) 11 Price 68; (1821) 4 B. & Ald. 218; (1821) 106 E.R. 918 ... 1–54, 7–77, 7–78, 7–109, 7–130, 11–138, 14–101, 16–223

[xcviii]

TABLE OF CASES

R v Clerkenwell Metropolitan Stipendiary Magistrates' Court Ex p. Telegraph Plc [1993] Q.B. 462; [1993] 2 W.L.R. 233; [1993] 2 All E.R. 183; (1993) 97 Cr. App. R. 18; (1993) 157 J.P. 554; [1993] C.O.D. 94; (1992) 142 N.L.J. 1541; *The Times*, October 22, 1992; *Independent*, October 16, 1992, DC 2–38, 2–56, 7–16, 7–244
—— v Clowes (Peter) (No.1) [1992] 3 All E.R. 440; [1992] B.C.L.C. 1158; (1992) 95 Cr. App. R. 440, Central Crim Ct 11–135
—— v Coghill [1995] 3 N.Z.L.R. 651, CA 2–108
—— v Colbatch (1723) K.B. Easter 9, George I 5–220
—— v Cole (Anthony) [1997] 1 Cr. App. R. (S.) 228, CA (Crim Div) 14–10, 19–1
—— v Collins [1954] V.L.R. 46 5–243
—— v Colsey (1931) 37 L.Q.R. 315; *The Times*, May 9, 1931 .... 5–231, 5–239, 5–240
—— v Comerford (Thomas Anthony) [1998] 1 W.L.R. 191; [1998] 1 All E.R. 823; [1998] 1 Cr. App. R. 235; [1998] Crim. L.R. 285; (1997) 94(45) L.S.G. 28; (1997) 141 S.J.L.B. 251; *The Times*, November 3, 1997; *Independent*, October 31, 1997, CA (Crim Div) 7–79, 11–182
—— v Commissioner of Police of the Metropolis Ex p. Blackburn (No.2) [1968] 2 Q.B. 150; [1968] 2 W.L.R. 1204; [1968] 2 All E.R. 319; 112 S.J. 191, CA (Civ Div) 5–139, 5–234, 5–236, 5–241, 5–251, 5–256, 10–145, 16–47, 16–102
—— v Connor and Mirza. *See* R. v Mirza (Shabbir Ali)
—— v Cooke (1824) 1 C. & P. 321; (1821) 171 E.R. 1213 .... 11–119, 11–138
—— v Coolledge [1996] Crim. L.R. 748, CA (Crim Div) 10–165, 11–121
—— v Corbett (1988) 41 C.C.C. (3d) 385 .... 2–86, 4–114, 4–161, 7–177, 16–313
—— v Cosgrave, *The Times*, March 17, 1877 10–93
—— v Cotter (Christopher James); R. v Clair (Surjit Singh); R. v Wynn (Craig Alan) [2002] EWCA Crim 1033; [2003] Q.B. 951; [2003] 2 W.L.R. 115; [2002] 2 Cr. App. R. 29; [2002] Crim. L.R. 824; (2002) 99(25) L.S.G. 34; (2002) 146 S.J.L.B. 137; *The Times*, May 29, 2002; *Daily Telegraph*, May 16, 2002, CA (Crim Div) 11–87
—— v Coughlan (Martin); R v Young (Gerard Peter) (1976) 63 Cr. App. R. 33; [1976] Crim. L.R. 628, CA (Crim Div) 2–86, 2–96, 4–114, 4–160, 7–177, 16–313
—— v Coughton (1976) 63 Cr. App. R. 33 16–309
—— v Coventry City Council Ex p. Phoenix Aviation; R. v Dover Harbour Board Ex p. Peter Gilder & Sons; R. v Associated British Ports Ex p. Plymouth City Council; sub nom. R. v Coventry Airport Ex p. Phoenix Aviation [1995] 3 All E.R. 37; [1995] C.L.C. 757; (1995) 7 Admin. L.R. 597; [1995] C.O.D. 300; (1995) 145 N.L.J. 559; *The Times*, April 17, 1995; *Independent*, April 13, 1995, DC 2–151
—— v Coventry Magistrates' Court Ex p. Perks [1985] R.T.R. 74 11–135
—— v Cowan (Donald); R. v Gayle (Ricky); R. v Ricciardi (Carmine) [1996] Q.B. 373; [1995] 3 W.L.R. 818; [1995] 4 All E.R. 939; [1996] 1 Cr. App. R. 1; (1996) 160 J.P. 165; [1996] Crim. L.R. 409; (1996) 160 J.P.N. 14; (1995) 92(38) L.S.G. 26; (1995) 145 N.L.J. 1611; (1995) 139 S.J.L.B. 215; *The Times*, October 13, 1995; *Independent*, October 25, 1995, CA (Crim Div) 3–64
—— v Craddock, *The Times*, March 17, 1875 11–216
—— v Crawford (1849) 13 Q.B. (N.S.) 613 14–5
—— v Crook (Timothy) [1992] 2 All E.R. 687; (1991) 93 Cr. App. R. 17; (1989) 139 N.L.J. 1633; (1989) 133 S.J. 1577, CA (Crim Div) 7–32, 7–33, 7–253, 7–262
—— v Crowley, *The Times*, March 2, 1973 10–94
—— v Cunningham (Roy) [1957] 2 Q.B. 396; [1957] 3 W.L.R. 76; [1957] 2 All E.R. 412; (1957) 41 Cr. App. R. 155; 121 J.P. 451; [1957] Crim. L.R. 326; 101 S.J. 503, CCA 5–131, 7–204, 7–209, 10–222
—— v D (Contempt of Court: Illegal Photography); sub nom. R. v D (Vincent) [2004] EWCA Crim 1271; *The Times*, May 13, 2004, CA (Crim Div) 10–190, 10–201, 10–203
—— v D (Ian Malcolm) [1984] A.C. 778; [1984] 3 W.L.R. 186; [1984] 2 All E.R. 449; (1984) 79 Cr. App. R. 313; [1984] Crim. L.R. 558; [1984] Fam. Law 311; (1984) 81 L.S.G. 2458, HL ... 2–14, 2–19, 3–67, 3–80, 3–86, 3–117, 4–1, 5–212, 7–228, 10–7, 11–15, 11–336, 13–25
—— v Daily Herald Ex p. Bishop of Norwich; R. v Empire News Ex p. Bishop of Norwich [1932] 2 K.B. 402, KBD 3–49, 3–67, 5–104, 14–136
—— v Daily Herald Ex p. Rouse (1931) 75 Sol. Jo. 119 .... 4–25, 5–107
—— v Daily Mirror Ex p. Smith [1927] 1 K.B. 845, KBD 5–82, 5–112, 16–189, 16–197, 16–410
—— v Daily Worker Ex p. Goulding (1934) 78 Sol. Jo. 860 4–288

TABLE OF CASES

R v Dammaree (1710) 15 St. Tr. 522 2–111
—— v Danga (Harbeer Singh) [1992] Q.B. 476; [1992] 2 W.L.R. 277; [1992] 1 All E.R. 624; (1992) 94 Cr. App. R. 252; (1992) 13 Cr. App. R. (S.) 408; (1992) 156 J.P. 382; [1992] Crim. L.R. 219; (1992) 156 J.P.N. 382; *The Times*, November 1, 1991, CA (Crim Div) 14–66
—— v David Syme and Co Ltd [1982] V.R. 173 4–232
—— v Davidson (1821) 4 Barn. & Ald. 329; (1821) 106 E.R. 958 10–34
—— v Davies (David) [1906] 1 K.B. 32, KBD 5–80, 5–81, 5–86, 5–104, 13–23, 13–43, 13–81
—— v Davies (1909) 150 C.C.C. Cas. 736 11–179
—— v Davies Ex p. Delbert-Evans [1945] 1 K.B. 435 .... 4–123, 5–100, 12–222
—— v Davis (Seaton Roy) (1986) 8 Cr. App. R. (S.) 64, CA (Crim Div) 8 19–1
—— v Davison (1821) 4 B. & Ald. 329; (1821) 106 E.R. 958 .... 3–113, 10–106, 10–131, 10–132,
10–133, 10–135, 14–101
—— v Daye [1908] 2 K.B. 333 .... 11–100, 11–111
—— v Denbigh Justices Ex p. Williams; R v Denbigh Justices Ex p. Evans [1974] Q.B. 759; [1974] 3 W.L.R. 45; [1974] 2 All E.R. 1052; [1974] Crim. L.R. 442; 118 S.J. 478, QBD 7–37, 7–40
—— v Denyer (Percy Ingram) [1926] 2 K.B. 258, CCA 11–299
—— v Derby Crown Court Ex p. Brooks (1985) 80 Cr. App. R. 164; [1985] Crim. L.R. 754; (1984) 148 J.P.N. 573; *The Times*, August 3, 1984, QBD 2–77, 4–148
—— v Derby Magistrates' Court Ex p. B [1996] A.C. 487; [1995] 3 W.L.R. 681; [1995] 4 All E.R. 526; [1996] 1 Cr. App. R. 385; (1995) 159 J.P. 785; [1996] 1 F.L.R. 513; [1996] Fam. Law 210; (1995) 159 J.P.N. 778; (1995) 145 N.L.J. 1575; [1995] 139 S.J.L.B. 219; *The Times*, October 25, 1995; *Independent*, October 27, 1995, HL 9–13,
9–126, 11–132, 11–134, 11–136
—— v DPP Ex p. Kebilene; R. v DPP Ex p. Boukemiche (Farid); R. v DPP Ex p. Souidi (Sofiane); R. v DPP Ex p. Rechachi (Fatah); sub nom. R. v DPP Ex p. Kebelene [2000] 2 A.C. 326; [1999] 3 W.L.R. 972; [1999] 4 All E.R. 801; [2000] 1 Cr. App. R. 275; [2000] U.K.H.R.R. 176; (2000) 2 L.G.L.R. 697; (1999) 11 Admin. L.R. 1026; [2000] Crim. L.R. 486; (1999) 96(43) L.S.G. 32; *The Times*, November 2, 1999, HL 2–168
—— v Director of the Serious Fraud Office Ex p. Smith; sub nom. Smith v Director of the Serious Fraud Office [1993] A.C. 1; [1992] 3 W.L.R. 66; [1992] 3 All E.R. 456; [1992] B.C.L.C. 879; (1992) 95 Cr. App. R. 191; [1992] Crim. L.R. 504; [1992] C.O.D. 270; (1992) 89(27) L.S.G. 34; (1992) 142 N.L.J. 895; (1992) 136 S.J.L.B. 182; *The Times*, June 16, 1992; *Independent*, June 12, 1992; *Financial Times*, June 17, 1992; *Guardian*, July 1, 1992, HL 3–192
—— v DJX, SYC, GCZ (1989) 91 Cr. App. R. 36 7–69
—— v Dodd (1981) 74 Cr. App. R. 50 11–182
—— v Dodds (Raymond) [2002] EWCA Crim 1328; [2003] 1 Cr. App. R. 3; [2002] Crim. L.R. 735, CA (Crim Div)10–55, 11–143, 13–118
—— v Dover Justices Ex p. Dover DC (1992) 156 J.P. 433; [1992] Crim. L.R. 371; (1992) 156 J.P.N. 172; *The Times*, October 21, 1991; *Independent*, October 21, 1991 (C.S.), DC 7–98
—— v Duckenfield and Murray, T991569 7–117
—— v Duffy Ex p. Nash [1960] 2 Q.B. 188; [1960] 3 W.L.R. 320; [1960] 2 All E.R. 891; 104 S.J. 585, DC 1–83, 4–118, 5–9, 5–10, 5–33, 5–38, 5–103, 7–137, 7–140
—— v Duffy, February 9, 1996 (Lexis) 4–206, 4–214, 4–223, 4–242, 4–243, 4–255, 4–262
—— v Dunbar (Ronald Patrick) [1958] 1 Q.B. 1; [1957] 3 W.L.R. 330; [1957] 2 All E.R. 737; (1957) 41 Cr. App. R. 182; 121 J.P. 506; 101 S.J. 594, CCA 4–262
—— v Dunbabin Ex p. Williams (1935) 53 C.L.R. 434, HC (Aus) 264
—— v Dyson (1943) 29 Cr. App. R. 104 .... 2–82, 2–83
—— v Ealing Justices Ex p. Weafer (1982) 74 Cr. App. R. 204 .... 7–27, 7–28
—— v Editor of New Statesman Ex p. DPP (1928) 44 T.L.R. 301 .... 5–229, 5–245, 5–268, 5–270
—— v Editor, Printer and Publishers of Daily Herald Ex p. Bishop of Norwich [1932] 2 K.B. 402 13–43
—— v Edmonton Sun Publishing Ltd (1981) 62 C.C.C. (2d) 318 4–25
—— v Edwards (1933) 49 T.L.R. 383 13–43
—— v Edwards (Errington) [1975] Q.B. 27; [1974] 3 W.L.R. 285; [1974] 2 All E.R. 1085; (1974) 59 Cr. App. R. 213; [1974] Crim. L.R. 540; 118 S.J. 582, CA (Crim Div) 12–170

[c]

TABLE OF CASES

R v Edwards Ex p. Welsh Church Temporalities Commissioners (1933) 49 T.L.R. 383 13–81
—— v Electricity Commissioners Ex p. London Electricity Joint Committee Co (1920) Ltd [1924] 1 K.B. 171 13–55
—— v Evans (Dorothy Gertrude) [2004] EWCA Crim 3102; [2005] 1 W.L.R. 1435; [2005] 1 Cr. App. R. 32; (2005) 169 J.P. 129; (2005) 169 J.P.N. 222; (2005) 102(7) L.S.G. 26; *The Times*, December 10, 2004, CA (Crim Div) 10–113
—— v Evening News Ex p. Campbell, *The Times*, October 27, 1925 4–25
—— v Evening News Ex p. Hobbs [1925] 2 K.B. 158, KBD 4–288
—— v Evening Standard Co Ltd Ex p. Att-Gen [1954] 1 Q.B. 578; [1954] 2 W.L.R. 861; [1954] Crim. L.R. 135, CA 4–10, 4–53, 4–98, 4–202, 4–213, 4–215, 4–217, 4–258, 4–286, 5–114, 5–200, 13–23, 13–43, 16–306
—— v Evening Standard Co Ltd Ex p. DPP (1924) 40 T.L.R. 833 ..... 4–213, 5–115, 16–188, 16–306
—— v Evesham Justices Ex p. McDonagh and Berrows Newspapers Ltd; sub nom. R v Evesham Justices Ex p. Mcdonagh [1988] Q.B. 553; (1988) 87 Cr. App. R. 28, QBD 7–96, 7–98, 7–104, 7–108
—— v Felixstowe Justices Ex p. Leigh [1987] Q.B. 582; [1987] 2 W.L.R. 380; [1987] 1 All E.R. 551; (1987) 84 Cr. App. R. 327; (1987) 151 J.P. 65; [1987] Crim. L.R. 125; (1987) 151 J.P.N. 31; (1987) 84 L.S.G. 901; (1986) 136 N.L.J. 988; (1986) 130 S.J. 767, QBD 2–52, 7–16, 7–17, 7–36, 7–85, 7–118
—— v Fields (1987) Can. Curr. Law 2193 13–79
—— v Fisher (1811) 2 Camp. 563, 170 1253 .... 1–73, 2–81
—— v Fitzpatrick [1977] N.I.L.R. 20, CCA (NI) 9–123, 9–125
—— v Fleet (1818) 1 Bar. & Ald. 379, 106 E.R. 140 1–73
—— v Ford (Royston James) [1989] Q.B. 868; [1989] 3 W.L.R. 762; [1989] 3 All E.R. 445; (1989) 89 Cr. App. R. 278; [1989] Crim. L.R. 828, CA (Crim Div) 2–114
—— v Foster Ex p. Isaacs (1941) V.L.R. 77 2–18
—— v Fox Ex p. Mosley; *The Times*, February 17, 1966; *Guardian*, February 17, 1966, DC 5–65
—— v Freeman, *The Times*, November 18, 1925 5–228
—— v G; R. v R [2003] UKHL 50; [2004] 1 A.C. 1034; [2003] 3 W.L.R. 1060; [2003] 4 All E.R. 765; [2004] 1 Cr. App. R. 21; (2003) 167 J.P. 621; [2004] Crim. L.R. 369; (2003) 167 J.P.N. 955; (2003) 100(43) L.S.G. 31; *The Times*, October 17, 2003, HL 5–130, 10–220
—— v Galbraith (George Charles) [1981] 1 W.L.R. 1039; [1981] 2 All E.R. 1060; (1981) 73 Cr. App. R. 124; [1981] Crim. L.R. 648; 125 S.J. 442, CA (Crim Div) 10–180
—— v Galbraith (Kim). *See* Galbraith v HM Advocate (No.1)
—— v George (Barry Michael) [2002] EWCA Crim 1923; [2003] Crim. L.R. 282; (2002) 99(38) L.S.G. 33; *The Times*, August 30, 2002; *Daily Telegraph*, August 1, 2002, CA (Crim Div) 1–162, 7–181
—— v Ghafoor (Imran Hussain) [2002] EWCA Crim 1857; [2003] 1 Cr. App. R. (S.) 84; (2002) 166 J.P. 601; [2002] Crim. L.R. 739; (2002) 166 J.P.N. 744, CA (Crim Div) 14–64
—— v Giscombe (Michael George) (1984) 79 Cr. App. R. 79; (1983) 5 Cr. App. R. (S.) 151, CA (Crim Div) 10–83, 10–211, 11–157, 11–160, 11–183, 19–1
—— v Glennon (1992) 173 C.L.R. 592 2–86
—— v Glynn, unreported, December 8, 1998, CA (Crim Div) 11–129
—— v Goldman [1968] 3 N.S.W.L.R. 325 .... 11–157, 11–201
—— v Gossip, *The Times*, February 18, 1909 4–129
—— v Gough (Robert) [1993] A.C. 646; [1993] 2 W.L.R. 883; [1993] 2 All E.R. 724; (1993) 97 Cr. App. R. 188; (1993) 157 J.P. 612; [1993] Crim. L.R. 886; (1993) 157 J.P.N. 394; (1993) 143 N.L.J. 775; (1993) 137 S.J.L.B. 168; *The Times*, May 24, 1993; *Independent*, May 26, 1993; *Guardian*, May 22, 1993, HL 2–118, 10–48, 10–83, 11–351
—— v Goult (Raymond Arthur) (1983) 76 Cr. App. R. 140; (1982) 4 Cr. App. R. (S.) 355; [1983] Crim. L.R. 103, CA (Crim Div) 10–4, 11–183, 19–1
—— v Governor of Lewes Prison Ex p. Doyle [1917] 2 K.B. 254, KBD 7–27, 7–36
—— v Governor of Pentonville Prison Ex p. Fernandez; sub nom. Fernandez v Singapore [1971] 1 W.L.R. 987; [1971] 2 All E.R. 691; 115 S.J. 469, HL 7–86
—— v Gray (1865) 10 Cox C.C. 1–73
—— v Gray (1903) 23 N.Z.L.R. 52 11–216
—— v Gray (Howard Alexander) [1900] 2 Q.B. 36; 82 L.T. 534; 64 J.P. 484, QBD 5–204, 5–223, 5–227, 10–57, 10–141, 13–23

TABLE OF CASES

R v Green (Bryan Gwyn) [1993] Crim. L.R. 46; (1992) 136 S.J.L.B. 260; *The Times*, July 14, 1992, CA (Crim Div) 3–17, 3–218, 12–11, 16–254
— v Griffin (Joseph) (1989) 88 Cr. App. R. 63; [1988] Crim. L.R. 680; *The Times*, March 1, 1988, CA (Crim Div) 2–4, 2–17, 2–19, 2–24, 2–29, 3–49, 3–56, 3–67, 3–85, 7–228, 7–234, 10–6, 10–12, 10–32, 10–40, 10–51, 11–195, 13–26, 13–32, 16–39
— v Griffin [1996] T.L.R. 619 11–310
— v Griffiths Ex p. Att-Gen [1957] 2 Q.B. 192; [1957] 2 W.L.R. 1064; [1957] 2 All E.R. 379; 101 S.J. 447, DC 3–224, 4–219, 4–231, 4–235, 4–239, 4–252, 5–268, 13–23
— v Grimes (Joseph Patrick) [1968] 3 All E.R. 179 (Note), Crown Ct 11–225
— v Guardian Newspapers Ltd [1994] Crim. L.R. 912 7–266
— v Guildford Crown Court Ex p. Siderfin [1990] 2 Q.B. 683; [1990] 2 W.L.R. 152; [1989] 3 All E.R. 73; (1990) 90 Cr. App. R. 192; [1990] Crim. L.R. 417; [1990] C.O.D. 13; (1989) 86(42) L.S.G. 39; (1989) 139 N.L.J. 827; (1989) 133 S.J. 1406, QBD 10–82, 10–83
— v Gunn Ex p. Att-Gen (No.2) [1954] Crim. L.R. 53, DC 11–7, 13–50
— v Gurney (1867) 10 Cox C.C. 550 11–174
— v H [2003] EWHC Crim. 485; *The Times*, March 10, 2003 2–62
— v H; R. v C [2004] UKHL 3; [2004] 2 A.C. 134; [2004] 2 W.L.R. 335; [2004] 1 All E.R. 1269; [2004] 2 Cr. App. R. 10; [2004] H.R.L.R. 20; 16 B.H.R.C. 332; (2004) 101(8) L.S.G. 29; (2004) 148 S.J.L.B. 183; *The Times*, February 6, 2004; *Independent*, February 10, 2004, HL 9–181
— v H (L) [1997] 1 Cr. App. R. 176 11–135
— v Hall (1776) 2 Wl. Bl. 1110 11–85
— v Hammond [1914] 2 K.B. 866 12–125
— v Hancock (Reginald Dean); R. v Shankland (Russell) [1986] A.C. 455; [1986] 2 W.L.R. 357; [1986] 1 All E.R. 646; (1986) 82 Cr. App. R. 264; (1986) 150 J.P. 203; [1986] Crim. L.R. 400, HL 5–120, 5–126
— v Hardwick, November 2, 2000, CA (Crim Div) 14–11, 19–1
— v Hargreaves Ex p. Dill (No.2) [1954] Crim. L.R. 54, DC 2–199, 2–200, 3–173
— v Harris (1762) 3 Burr. 1330 2–107
— v Hart [1998] Crim. L.R. 417 10–83
— v Hart and White (1808) 30 St. Tr. 1131; 1193 1 Camp. 359n, 170 E.R. 985 5–222
— v Harvey and Osborne, 95/5658/Z2, March 5, 1996 10–167
— v Harwood (1672) 2 Lev. 32; (1672) 83 E.R. 439 11–342
— v Hasan (Aytach); sub nom. R. v Z [2005] UKHL 22; [2005] 2 W.L.R. 709; (2005) 149 S.J.L.B. 360; *The Times*, March 21, 2005; *Independent*, March 22, 2005, HL 3–253, 3–254, 9–119, 9–121, 9–124, 10–166, 10–168
— v Haslam (Jermaine Colin) [2003] EWCA Crim 3444, CA (Crim Div) 10–47, 10–53
— v Havant Justices Ex p. Palmer; sub nom. R. v Havant Magistrates' Court and Portsmouth Crown Court Ex p. Palmer (1985) 149 J.P. 609; [1985] Crim. L.R. 658; (1985) 149 J.P.N. 479; *The Times*, May 15, 1985, DC 10–114, 10–116, 10–118, 10–124, 13–107, 13–129, 13–133, 14–144
— v Hemming [1985] Crim. L.R. 395 2–88
— v Highbury Corner Magistrates Court Ex p. O'Donoghue (1997) 161 J.P. 161; (1997) 161 J.P.N. 334; *The Times*, February 24, 1997, QBD 7–118, 7–242, 9–201, 9–223
— v Hill (1977) 73 D.L.R. 621 5–139
— v Hill [1986] Crim. L.R. 457, CA (Crim Div) 10–8, 10–37, 10–40, 10–41, 10–46, 10–52, 10–97, 10–194, 10–209, 10–218
— v HM Coroner for Inner London West District Ex p. Dallaglio; R. v HM Coroner for Inner London West District Ex p. Lockwood-Croft [1994] 4 All E.R. 139; (1995) 159 J.P. 133; (1995) 7 Admin. L.R. 256; [1995] C.O.D. 20; *The Times*, June 16, 1994; *Independent*, June 17, 1994, CA (Civ Div) 10–49
— v HM Coroner for West Yorkshire Ex p. Smith (No.2) [1985] Q.B. 1096; [1985] 2 W.L.R. 332; [1985] 1 All E.R. 100; (1985) 149 J.P. 97; (1985) 129 S.J. 131; *The Times*, October 3, 1984, DC 4–37, 4–290, 13–127, 14–107
— v Hollis (1819) 2 Stark 536; (1819) 171 E.R. 728 9–229
— v Holsworthy Justices Ex p. Edwards [1952] 1 All E.R. 411 13–88
— v Holt and Bird (1996) 161 J.P. 96 .... 10–169, 10–170
— v Hooley; sub nom. Re Hooley (1898) 79 L.T. 306 .... 11–216, 11–262, 11–287, 12–125

TABLE OF CASES

R v Horsham Justices Ex p. Farquharson [1982] Q.B. 762; [1982] 2 W.L.R. 430; [1982] 2 All E.R. 269; (1983) 76 Cr. App. R. 87; 126 S.J. 98, CA (Civ Div) 2–86, 3–95, 4–292, 7–84, 7–111, 7–114, 7–115, 7–125, 7–129, 7–137, 7–139, 7–145, 7–149, 7–150, 7–152, 7–153, 7–177, 7–202, 7–217, 7–226, 7–227, 7–228, 7–235, 7–240, 7–249, 8–90, 9–201, 9–224, 16–376
—— v Hoser and Kotabi Pty Ltd [2001] V.S.C. 443 .... 5–254, 5–258
—— v Hubbert (1975) 29 C.C.C. (2d) 279 2–87
—— v Hudson (Linda); R. v Taylor (Elaine) [1971] 2 Q.B. 202; [1971] 2 W.L.R. 1047; [1971] 2 All E.R. 244; (1972) 56 Cr. App. R. 1; 115 S.J. 303, CA (Crim Div) 3–253, 3–254, 3–255, 9–119, 10–168
—— v Hudson (Terence) [1966] 1 Q.B. 448; [1965] 2 W.L.R. 604; [1965] 1 All E.R. 721; (1965) 49 Cr. App. R. 69; 129 J.P. 193; 109 S.J. 49; *Guardian*, December 19, 1964, CCA 4–262
—— v Hunt (Richard Selwyn) [1987] A.C. 352; [1986] 3 W.L.R. 1115; [1987] 1 All E.R. 1; (1987) 84 Cr. App. R. 163; [1987] Crim. L.R. 263, HL 4–262, 12–170
—— v Huntley and Carr, T 20029158/9 10–204
—— v Hutchinson Ex p. MacMahon [1936] 2 All E.R. 1514 4–25
—— v Hutton [1990] Crim. L.R. 875, CA (Crim Div) 7–160
—— v Ingrams Ex p. Goldsmith [1977] Crim.L.R. 40; (1977) 120 S.J. 606 .... 5–2, 5–16, 5–25
—— v IRC Ex p. Kingston Smith [1996] S.T.C. 1210; 70 T.C. 264; *The Times*, August 15, 1996, QBD 2–221, 2–222, 3–69, 3–158, 3–166, 12–5, 13–11
—— v Inner London Crown Court Ex p. Barnes (Anthony); sub nom. R. v Inner London Crown Court Ex p. B [1996] C.O.D. 17; *The Times*, August 7, 1995; *Independent*, September 11, 1995 (C.S.), DC 8–62, 8–065
—— v J [2003] EWCA Crim 3268, CA (Crim Div) 7–104
—— v James (1822) 5 B. & Ald. 894; (1822) 106 E.R. 1418 14–5
—— v James (Alan Michael) (1988) 10 Cr. App. R. (S.) 392, CA (Crim Div) 19–1
—— v Jameson (1896) 12 T.L.R. 551 11–372
—— v Jardine (Michael Anthony) (1987) 9 Cr. App. R. (S.) 41, CA (Crim Div) 10–166, 14–10, 19–1
—— v Jermy (1752) Sayer 47; (1752) 96 E.R. 799 11–317
—— v Johnson (1678) 2 Show. K.B. 1; (1678) 89 E.R. 753 11–229
—— v Jones (Paul Andrew) [1996] Crim. L.R. 806, CA (Crim Div) 3–61, 3–85, 10–7, 13–27, 16–39
—— v Jones Ex p. McVittie [1931] 1 K.B. 664, KBD 5–139, 11–157, 11–172, 11–195, 11–305
—— v Judge Ex p. Isle of Ely Justices [1931] 2 K.B. 442 .... 11–90, 11–97, 13–43
—— v Justices of Portsmouth [1892] 1 Q.B. 491 3–220
—— v K (1984) 78 Cr. App. R. 82; (1984) 148 J.P. 410; [1983] Crim. L.R. 736, CA (Crim Div) 3–252, 3–255, 9–119, 10–61, 10–166
—— v K (1997) 129 D.L.R. (4th) 500 13–42
—— v Karakaya (Adem) [2005] EWCA Crim 346; [2005] 2 Cr. App. R. 5; *The Times*, February 28, 2005, CA (Crim Div) 1–179
—— v Keane [1994] 1 W.L.R. 746; (1994) 99 Cr. App. R. 1 11–136
—— v Kellett (Alan Rex) [1976] Q.B. 372; [1975] 3 W.L.R. 713; [1975] 3 All E.R. 468; (1975) 61 Cr. App. R. 240; [1975] Crim. L.R. 576; 119 S.J. 542, CA (Crim Div) 4–135, 4–330, 11–192, 11–217, 11–219, 11–222, 11–227, 11–228, 11–229, 11–231, 11–233, 11–235, 11–238, 11–241, 11–244, 11–245, 11–248, 11–250, 11–254, 11–262, 11–291, 16–140
—— v Kendrick (1754) Sayer 114; (1754) 96 E.R. 822 11–317
—— v Ketteridge [1915] 1 K.B. 467, CCA 2–112, 10–183
—— v Khan (Sultan) [1997] A.C. 558; [1996] 3 W.L.R. 162; [1996] 3 All E.R. 289; [1996] 2 Cr. App. R. 440; [1996] Crim. L.R. 733; (1996) 93(28) L.S.G. 29; (1996) 146 N.L.J. 1024; (1996) 140 S.J.L.B. 166; *The Times*, July 5, 1996; *Independent*, July 11, 1996, HL 2–136
—— v King (Hugo Allen); R. v Chinn (Brian Leonard); R. v Webley (Peter John); R. v Neads (William Bernard); R. v Cunningham (Anthony Kenneth) [1992] Q.B. 20; [1991] 3 W.L.R. 246; [1991] 3 All E.R. 705; (1991) 93 Cr. App. R. 259; [1991] Crim. L.R. 906; (1991) 141 N.L.J. 1071; (1991) 135 S.J.L.B. 76; *The Times*, June 26, 1991; *Guardian*, June 26, 1991, CA (Crim Div) 5–130
—— v Klein, September 23, 1996 (Lexis), CACD 5–101

TABLE OF CASES

R v Kohli (Brij Lal) (1983) 5 Cr. App. R. (S.) 175; [1983] Crim. L.R. 634, CA (Crim Div) 19–1
—— v Kray (Ronald) (1969) 53 Cr. App. R. 412, Central Crim Ct 2–86, 2–115, 2–118, 2–120,
4–113, 6–32, 7–110, 7–130, 7–144, 7–177
—— v Kylsant [1932] 1 K.B. 442 5–28
—— v Lalani [1999] Crim. L.R. 992, CA (Crim Div) 11–166
—— v Lambert (Steven); R. v Ali (Mudassir Mohammed); R. v Jordan (Shirley) [2001]
UKHL 37; [2002] 2 A.C. 545; [2001] 3 W.L.R. 206; [2002] 1 All E.R. 2; [2001] 3 All
E.R. 577; [2001] 2 Cr. App. R. 28; [2001] H.R.L.R. 55; [2001] U.K.H.R.R. 1074;
[2001] Crim. L.R. 806; (2001) 98(33) L.S.G. 29; (2001) 145 S.J.L.B. 174; *The Times*,
July 6, 2001; *Independent*, July 19, 2001; *Daily Telegraph*, July 17, 2001, HL 1–144, 4–261
—— v Lane & Ross (1970) 1 C.C.C. 196 .... 4–114, 4–162
—— v Lawley (1731) Mich 5, George II 5–220
—— v Lawrence (Stephen Richard) [1982] A.C. 510; [1981] 2 W.L.R. 524; [1981] 1 All
E.R. 974; (1981) 73 Cr. App. R. 1; [1981] R.T.R. 217; [1981] Crim. L.R. 409, HL 5–130
—— v Lawson Ex p. Nodder (1937) 81 Sol. Jo. 280 .... 2–199, 5–113, 16–410
—— v Lee (1804) 5 Esp. 123, 170 E.R. 759 1–73
—— v Lee (Anthony William) (A Minor) [1993] 1 W.L.R. 103; [1993] 2 All E.R. 170;
(1993) 96 Cr. App. R. 188; (1993) 157 J.P. 533; [1993] Crim. L.R. 65; (1992) 156
J.P.N. 746; *The Times*, July 21, 1992, CA (Crim Div) 7–254, 8–58, 8–59, 8–60
—— v Lee Kun (1916) 11 Cr. App. R. 293 11–121
—— v Lefroy (1873) L.R. 8 Q.B. 134 .... 10–130, 11–120, 13–79, 13–80
—— v Legal Aid Board Ex p. Kaim Todner; sub nom. R. v Legal Aid Board Ex p. T (A Firm
of Solicitors) [1999] Q.B. 966; [1998] 3 W.L.R. 925; [1998] 3 All E.R. 541; (1998)
95(26) L.S.G. 31; (1998) 148 N.L.J. 941; (1998) 142 S.J.L.B. 189; *The Times*, June 15,
1998; *Independent*, June 12, 1998, CA (Civ Div) 7–7, 7–27, 7–103
—— v Leicester City Justices Ex p. Barrow [1991] 2 Q.B. 260; [1991] 3 W.L.R. 368; [1991]
3 All E.R. 935; (1991) 155 J.P. 901; [1991] R.A. 205; [1991] Crim. L.R. 556; (1991)
155 J.P.N. 736; (1991) 141 N.L.J. 1145; *The Times*, August 5, 1991; *Independent*,
August 7, 1991; *Guardian*, August 14, 1991, CA (Civ Div) 7–47, 10–131
—— v Leicester Crown Court Ex p. S (A Minor) [1993] 1 W.L.R. 111; [1992] 2 All E.R.
659; (1992) 94 Cr. App. R. 153; [1991] Crim. L.R. 365; [1991] C.O.D. 231; (1991) 155
J.P.N. 139; *The Times*, December 19, 1990; *Independent*, December 12, 1990;
Guardian, December 13, 1990; *Daily Telegraph*, December 10, 1990, QBD 8–57, 8–62
—— v Leicester Guardians (1899) 81 L.T. 559 12–128
—— v Lennock (1993) 97 Cr. App. R. 228; (1993) 157 J.P. 1070 .... 11–120, 11–122, 11–124,
11–128
—— v Leonard (Robert Grieve) (1984) 6 Cr. App. R. (S.) 279, CA (Crim Div) 14–10, 19–1
—— v Less [1993] T.L.R. 186 .... 10–189, 11–395
—— v Levy (1916) 32 T.L.R. 238 11–188
—— v Lewis (1992) 96 Cr. App. R. 412 10–166
—— v Lewis, *The Times*, November 4, 1999, CA (Crim Div) 10–105
—— v Lewis (Patrick Arthur) [2001] EWCA Crim 749; *The Times*, April 26, 2001, CA
(Crim Div) 10–83, 11–389
—— v Ling [1987] Crim. L.R. 495 11–182
—— v Little; R. v Miller [1926] 2 W.W.R. 762 13–100
—— v Littlewood [2002] All E.R. (D) 328 (Feb), CA (Crim Div) 7–264
—— v Liverpool City Council Ex p. May [1994] C.O.D. 144, QBD 11–54
—— v Liverpool City Magistrates Court Ex p. DPP (1997) 161 J.P. 43; [1997] C.O.D. 92;
(1997) 161 J.P.N. 8, QBD 7–69, 7–78
—— v Logan [1974] Crim. L.R. 609, CA (Crim Div) 14–11, 10–34, 10–35, 10–98
—— v London (North) Industrial Tribunal Ex p. Associated Newspapers Ltd; sub nom.
Associated Newspapers Ltd v London (North) Industrial Tribunal [1998] I.C.R. 1212;
[1998] I.R.L.R. 569; (1999) 1 L.G.L.R. 20; *The Times*, May 13, 1998, QBD 8–146
—— v Lord Saville of Newdigate Ex p. A. *See* R. v Lord Saville of Newdigate Ex p. B
(No.2)
—— v Lord Saville of Newdigate Ex p. B (No.2); sub nom. R. v Lord Saville of Newdigate
Ex p. A [2000] 1 W.L.R. 1855; [1999] 4 All E.R. 860; [1999] C.O.D. 436; (1999) 149
N.L.J. 1201; *The Times*, July 29, 1999, CA (Civ Div) 2–195, 7–31, 7–86
—— v Lubega (1999) 163 J.P. 221, CA (Crim Div) 10–54, 11–129
—— v Lucas [1991] Crim. L.R. 844, CA (Crim Div) 11–350

TABLE OF CASES

R v Luntley (1833) 1 C. & M. 579; (1833) 149 E.R. 530 3–146
—— v Luton Magistrates' Court Ex p. Sullivan [1992] 2 F.L.R. 196; [1992] F.C.R. 475; [1992] Fam. Law 380; (1992) 156 J.P.N. 426 .... 14–22, 14–23, 14–27, 15–38
—— v McCann, Cullen and Shanahan (1990) 92 Cr. App. R. 239 .... 2–73, 2–91, 2–93, 2–108, 2–114, 2–121
—— v McClure [2001] S.C.R. 445 9–14
—— v McDaniel (Cliff) (1990–91) 12 Cr. App. R. (S.) 44, CA (Crim Div) 10–8, 19–1
—— v Machin (Lawrence) [1980] 1 W.L.R. 763; [1980] 3 All E.R. 151; (1980) 71 Cr. App. R. 166; [1980] R.T.R. 233; [1980] Crim. L.R. 376; 124 S.J. 359, CA (Crim Div) 11–21
—— v MacLeod (Calum Iain) [2001] Crim. L.R. 589; *The Times*, December 20, 2000, CA (Crim Div) 3–58, 10–36, 10–43, 10–46, 10–48, 19–1
—— v McMichael, *The Times*, January 14 and 17, 1961 10–100
—— v McNaughten (Gary Stephen); sub nom. R. v M (Stephen); R. v McNaghten (Stephen) [2003] EWCA Crim 3479; *The Times*, January 15, 2004, CA (Crim Div) 14–20
—— v Macrae, *The Times*, November 18 and 19, 1892 .... 10–182, 10–184, 10–185, 10–218
—— v Madge Ex p. Isaacs (1913) 30 T.L.R. 10 8–124
—— v Magee, unreported, January 23, 1997, Woolwich Crown Court 2–105
—— v Maguire [1997] 1 Cr. App. R. 61, CA (Crim Div) 10–160, 16–132
—— v Maloney (Grant) (1986) 8 Cr. App. R. (S.) 123, CA (Crim Div) 19–1
—— v Malvern Justices Ex p. Evans; R. v Evesham Justices Ex p. McDonagh and Berrows Newspapers Ltd; sub nom. R. v Malvern Justices Ex p. Evans and Berrows Newspapers Ltd [1988] Q.B. 540; [1988] 2 W.L.R. 218; [1988] 1 All E.R. 371; (1988) 87 Cr. App. R. 19; (1988) 152 J.P. 65; [1988] Crim. L.R. 120; [1988] Crim. L.R. 181; (1988) 152 J.P.N. 30; (1988) 85(2) L.S.G. 36; (1987) 137 N.L.J. 757; (1987) 131 S.J. 1698, QBD 7–40, 7–69
—— v Manchester Crown Court Ex p. H (A Juvenile); sub nom. Re D (A Minor) (Reporting Restrictions); Re H (A Minor) (Reporting Restrictions) [2000] 1 W.L.R. 760; [2000] 2 All E.R. 166; [2000] 1 Cr. App. R. 262; *The Times*, August 13, 1999, QBD 8–60, 8–66
—— v Manley (1844) 1 Cox 104 11–154
—— v Mantoura [1993] Crim. L.R. 279 12–240
—— v Martin (1848) 5 Cox C.C. 356 .... 11–157, 11–158, 11–178, 11–187, 11–201, 11–383
—— v Martin (1985) 19 C.C.C. (3d) 248 13–42
—— v Martin (Peter), *The Times*, April 23, 1986 10–154
—— v Martin [1996] Crim. L.R. 589 10–165
—— v Mason Ex p. DPP, *The Times*, December, 17, 1932 4–232
—— v Mason (Vincent) [1981] Q.B. 881; [1980] 3 W.L.R. 617; [1980] 3 All E.R. 777; (1980) 71 Cr. App. R. 157; 124 S.J. 645, CA (Crim Div) 2–114
—— v Matthews (Darren John); R. v Alleyne (Brian Dean) [2003] EWCA Crim 192; [2003] 2 Cr. App. R. 30; *The Times*, February 18, 2003, CA (Crim Div) 5–120, 5–127
—— v Maxwell, unreported, March 6, 1995, Phillips J 2–43, 2–77, 2–116, 4–148, 4–164, 4–313, 16–359
—— v Mayberry [2003] EWCA Crim 782 11–72
—— v Meissener (1995) 130 A.L.R. 547 11–167
—— v Mentuck, 2001 S.C.C. 76 6–21
—— v Miah (Badrul); R. v Akhbar (Showkat) [1997] 2 Cr. App. R. 12; [1997] Crim. L.R. 351; *The Times*, December 18, 1996, CA (Crim Div) 10–83, 11–350, 11–360, 11–368, 11–389, 11–390, 11–392
—— v Miah (Otherwise Ullah). *See* Waddington v Miah
—— v Middlesex Guildhall Crown Court Ex p. Salinger [1993] Q.B. 564; [1993] 2 W.L.R. 438; [1993] 2 All E.R. 310; (1993) 97 Cr. App. R. 34; [1992] Crim. L.R. 812; [1992] C.O.D. 358; (1992) 89(20) L.S.G. 37; *The Times*, March 30, 1992; *Independent*, March 26, 1992; *Guardian*, April 22, 1992, DC 9–197
—— v Miller [1977] C.L.Y. 477 .... 10–82, 10–183, 11–140
—— v Mills. *See* DPP v Mills
—— v Millward [1999] 1 Cr. App. R. 61 11–387

TABLE OF CASES

R v Mirza (Shabbir Ali); R. v Connor (Ben); R. v Rollock (Ashley Kenneth) [2004] UKHL 2; [2004] 1 A.C. 1118; [2004] 2 W.L.R. 201; [2004] 1 All E.R. 925; [2004] 2 Cr. App. R. 8; [2004] H.R.L.R. 11; 16 B.H.R.C. 279; (2004) 101(7) L.S.G. 34; (2004) 154 N.L.J. 145; (2004) 148 S.J.L.B. 117; *The Times*, January 23, 2004, HL; affirming [2002] EWCA Crim 1235; [2002] Crim. L.R. 921, CA (Crim Div) 1–126, 2–44, 2–101, 3–93, 10–83, 11–349, 11–353, 11–355, 11–356, 11–357, 11–358, 11–360, 11–362, 11–365, 11–369, 11–373, 11–377, 11–387, 11–391, 11–392, 16–392, 16–396
—— v Misra (Amit); R. v Srivastava (Rajeev) [2004] EWCA Crim 2375; [2005] 1 Cr. App. R. 21; (2004) 101(41) L.S.G. 35; (2004) 148 S.J.L.B. 1213; *The Times*, October 13, 2004, CA (Crim Div) 3–80, 10–177
—— v Mitchell; sub nom. Anon; Re Justices of the Court of Common Pleas in Antigua (1741) 2 Atk. 173; (1741) 26 E.R. 508; (1830) 1 Kn. 267 10–143
—— v Mitchell-Crinkley (William) [1998] 1 Cr. App. R. (S.) 368, CA (Crim Div) 19–1
—— v Mitzakis Ex p. Rivers, *The Times*, January 19, 1910 11–317
—— v Mohan [1976] Q.B. 1 11–241
—— v Moloney (Alistair Baden) [1985] A.C. 905; [1985] 2 W.L.R. 648; [1985] 1 All E.R. 1025; (1985) 81 Cr. App. R. 93; (1985) 149 J.P. 369; [1985] Crim. L.R. 378, HL 5–120, 5–124, 5–125, 5–146, 5–166, 5–198
—— v Momodou (Henry); R. v Limani (Beher) [2005] EWCA Crim 177; [2005] 2 All E.R. 571; [2005] 2 Cr. App. R. 6; (2005) 169 J.P. 186; (2005) 169 J.P.N. 276; (2005) 149 S.J.L.B. 178; *The Times*, February 9, 2005; *Independent*, February 11, 2005, CA (Crim Div) 11–72
—— v Montgomery (James) [1995] 2 All E.R. 28; [1995] 2 Cr. App. R. 23; (1995) 16 Cr. App. R. (S.) 274; [1994] Crim. L.R. 869; (1994) 144 N.L.J. 1445; *The Times*, July 19, 1994; *Independent*, July 25, 1994 (C.S.), CA (Crim Div) 10–163, 10–165, 10–172, 14–6, 14–10, 14–28, 14–29, 19–1
—— v Moore (Peter Oliver) (Costs) [2003] EWCA Crim 1574; [2003] 1 W.L.R. 2170; [2003] 2 Cr. App. R. 31; [2003] Crim. L.R. 717; (2003) 100(26) L.S.G. 35; (2003) 147 S.J.L.B. 596; *The Times*, May 15, 2003, CA (Crim Div) 7–275, 13–118, 14–138, 15–89
—— v Moran (Kevin John) (1985) 81 Cr. App. R. 51; (1985) 7 Cr. App. R. (S.) 101, CA (Crim Div) 2–17, 2–31, 10–33, 10–40, 10–43, 10–59, 10–65, 11–196, 15–107, 19–1
—— v Morin (1992) 71 C.C.C. (3d) 2–105
—— v Morrisey and Staines [1997] 2 Cr. App. R. 426, CA (Civ.Div.) 2–125, 2–136, 2–137
—— v Mulvaney (David) (1982) 4 Cr. App. R. (S.) 106; [1982] Crim. L.R. 462, CA (Crim Div) 19–1
—— v Muraglia, *The Times*, July 29, 1997 10–95
—— v Murray [1982] 1 W.L.R. 475 11–14
—— v Neal [1949] 2 All E.R. 438 2–112
—— v Nedrick (Ransford Delroy) [1986] 1 W.L.R. 1025; [1986] 3 All E.R. 1; (1986) 83 Cr. App. R. 267; (1986) 8 Cr. App. R. (S.) 179; (1986) 150 J.P. 589; [1986] Crim. L.R. 792; (1986) 150 J.P.N. 637, CA (Crim Div) 5–120
—— v Neve (Leonard Henry) (1986) 8 Cr. App. R. (S.) 270, CA (Crim Div) 19–1
—— v Newbury Justices Ex p. Pont; sub nom. R v Newbury Justices Ex p. du Pont (1984) 78 Cr. App. R. 255; (1984) 148 J.P. 248; [1984] Crim. L.R. 230, DC 3–60, 10–62, 10–64, 10–100, 14–143
—— v Newcastle upon Tyne Magistrates' Court Ex p. Still (1997) C.L.Y. 86 10–160
—— v Newton (1885) 24 L.J.Q.B. 246 2–214
—— v Newton (1903) 67 J.P. 453 .... 3–157, 11–62
—— v Newtownabbey Magistrates' Court Ex p. Belfast Telegraph Newspapers Ltd [1997] N.I. 309 .... 7–97, 7–102
—— v Nicholls (1911) 12 C.L.R. 280 .... 5–225, 5–241, 5–258, 5–272
—— v Normanton [1998] Crim. L.R. 220 11–145
—— v Odhams Press Ex p. Att-Gen [1957] 1 Q.B. 73; [1956] 3 W.L.R. 796; [1956] 3 All E.R. 494, QBD 1–115, 4–11, 4–12, 4–50, 4–202, 4–213, 4–218, 4–219, 4–231, 4–238, 5–108, 5–268
—— v Oke [1997] Crim. L.R. 898 .... 11–351, 11–392
—— v Oliver [1996] 2 Cr. App. R. 514 2–112
—— v Opie (1670) 1 Wms. Saund. 301; (1670) 85 E.R. 418 11–179
—— v Orgles [1994] 1 W.L.R. 108 11–392

TABLE OF CASES

R v Osbourne (Patrick Fenton) (1993) 14 Cr. App. R. (S.) 265, CA (Crim Div) 19–1
—— v Osmanioglu (Mustafa) [2002] EWCA Crim 930, CA (Crim Div) 11–387, 11–388
—— v O'Toole (Michael) [1987] Crim. L.R. 759, CA (Crim Div) 5–123
—— v Owen (Norman) [1976] 1 W.L.R. 840; [1976] 3 All E.R. 239; (1976) 63 Cr. App. R. 199; [1976] Crim. L.R. 753; 120 S.J. 470, CA (Crim Div) 11–180, 11–181, 14–10
—— v Palache (Theresa) (1993) 14 Cr. App. R. (S.) 294, CA (Crim Div) 19–1
—— v Palmer (1856) 5 E. & B. 1024; (1856) 119 E.R. 762 2–109
—— v Palmer (Jane Veronica) [1992] 1 W.L.R. 568; [1992] 3 All E.R. 289; (1992) 95 Cr. App. R. 170; (1992) 13 Cr. App. R. (S.) 595; (1992) 156 J.P. 667; (1992) 156 J.P.N. 284; (1992) 136 S.J.L.B. 70; *The Times*, February 5, 1992, CA (Crim Div) 3–60, 3–86, 14–10, 14–98, 14–143
—— v Pan; R. v Sawyer [2001] S.C.C. 41; [2001] S.C.R. 344 11–361
—— v Panayiotou (Andreas); R. v Antoniades (Agis) [1973] 1 W.L.R. 1032; [1973] 3 All E.R. 112; (1973) 57 Cr. App. R. 762; [1973] Crim. L.R. 445; 117 S.J. 464, CA (Crim Div) 11–221, 11–222
—— v Parke [1903] 2 K.B. 432, KBD 3–86, 5–78, 5–81, 5–86, 5–104, 5–115, 7–137, 7–140, 7–145, 13–123
—— v Pateley Bridge Justices Ex p. Percy [1994] C.O.D. 453 ..... 10–37, 10–66, 10–106, 10–114, 10–132, 13–129, 15–107
—— v Patrascu (Andrew) [2004] EWCA Crim 2417; [2004] 4 All E.R. 1066; [2005] 1 Cr. App. R. 35; (2004) 168 J.P. 589; (2004) 168 J.P.N. 897, CA (Crim Div) 4–145, 11–14, 11–147, 11–153, 11–234, 11–299
—— v Payne; sub nom. R. v Payne and Cooper [1896] 1 Q.B. 577, QBD 4–202, 5–33, 5–107
—— v Perviaz, unreported, March 26, 1999 10–166
—— v Peterborough Magistrates' Court Ex p. Willis and Amos (1987) 151 J.P. 785 11–135
—— v Peters, No.96/4112/Y5, September 8, 1996 .... 10–52, 10–57
—— v Pettigrew, *The Times*, June 1, 1965 11–140
—— v Phelan (1881) 14 Cox 579 2–109
—— v Phillips (Peter Anthony) (1984) 78 Cr. App. R. 88; (1983) 5 Cr. App. R. (S.) 297; [1983] Crim. L.R. 822, CA (Crim Div) 10–166, 14–10, 19–1
—— v Pittendrigh (William) (1985) 7 Cr. App. R. (S.) 221, CA (Crim Div) 19–1
—— v Ponting [1985] Crim. L.R. 318, Central Crim Ct 7–248
—— v Poplar MBC Ex p. London CC (No.2); R. v Poplar MBC Ex p. Metropolitan Asylum District Managers [1922] 1 K.B. 95, CA 12–80, 15–8, 15–19
—— v Poulson, *The Times*, January 4, 1974 7–130
—— v Powell (1977) 65 Cr. App. R. 174 11–14
—— v Powell (1993) 98 Cr. App. R. 224 .... 2–29, 2–190, 10–3, 10–7, 10–29, 10–99, 10–101, 13–109
—— v Qureshi (Sajid) [2001] EWCA Crim 1807; [2002] 1 W.L.R. 518; [2002] 1 Cr. App. R. 33; [2002] Crim. L.R. 62; *The Times*, September 11, 2001, CA (Crim Div) 10–83, 11–387, 11–390, 11–391
—— v R (Rape: Marital Exemption); sub nom. R. v R (A Husband) [1992] 1 A.C. 599; [1991] 3 W.L.R. 767; [1991] 4 All E.R. 481; (1992) 94 Cr. App. R. 216; (1991) 155 J.P. 989; [1992] 1 F.L.R. 217; [1992] Crim. L.R. 207; [1992] Fam. Law 108; (1991) 155 J.P.N. 752; (1991) 141 N.L.J. 1481; (1991) 135 S.J.L.B. 181; *The Times*, October 24, 1991; *Independent*, October 24, 1991; *Guardian*, October 30, 1991, HL 2–191
—— v Rafique (Mohammed Zubair); R. v Sajid (Mohammed); R. v Rajah (Nasir Aslam) [1993] Q.B. 843; [1993] 3 W.L.R. 617; [1993] 4 All E.R. 1; (1993) 97 Cr. App. R. 395; [1993] Crim. L.R. 761; (1993) 143 N.L.J. 581; (1993) 137 S.J.L.B. 119; *The Times*, April 9, 1993, CA (Crim Div) 5–84, 11–87
—— v Rankine [1997] Crim. L.R. 757 11–370
—— v Reade, unreported, October 15, 1993 2–75
—— v Reader (1987) 84 Cr. App. R. 294 11–129
—— v Reading Justices Ex p. Berkshire CC [1996] 1 Cr. App. R. 239 .... 11–127, 11–135, 11–136
—— v Redditch Justices (1885) 2 T.L.R. 193 13–60
—— v Redman (1744) in R. Carroll (1799) 1 Wils. K.B. 75; (1799) 95 E.R. 500 11–280
—— v Regal Press Pty [1972] V.R. 67 4–67
—— v Reid (John Joseph) [1992] 1 W.L.R. 793; [1992] 3 All E.R. 673; (1992) 95 Cr. App. R. 391; (1994) 158 J.P. 517; [1992] R.T.R. 341; (1994) 158 J.P.N. 452; (1992) 89(34) L.S.G. 40; (1992) 136 S.J.L.B. 253, HL 5–130

TABLE OF CASES

R v Reigate Justices Ex p. Argus Newspapers (1983) 147 J.P. 385 7–69
—— v Renshaw [1989] Crim. L.R. 11 .... 10–65, 10–163, 10–165
—— v Revel (1719) 1 Str. 420; (1719) 93 E.R. 609 10–144
—— v Rhuddlan Justices Ex p. HTV Ltd [1986] Crim. L.R. 329 ..... 6–1, 6–23, 7–114, 7–116, 7–142,
13–36, 14–132
—— v Richards (1999) 163 J.P. 246 .... 7–11, 7–13, 7–27, 7–68
—— v Robbins Ex p. Green (1891) 7 T.L.R. 411 4–220
—— v Roberts (John Marcus) (1985) 80 Cr. App. R. 89, CA (Crim Div) 3–89
—— v Rowland, unreported, February 14, 1991 .... 9–183, 11–129
—— v Runting (Simon) (1989) 89 Cr. App. R. 243; [1989] Crim. L.R. 282, CA (Crim Div) 1–153,
10–208, 10–217, 11–157, 11–194
—— v Russell Ex p. Beaverbrook Newspapers [1969] 1 Q.B. 342; [1968] 3 W.L.R. 999;
[1968] 3 All E.R. 695; (1968) 133 J.P. 27; 112 S.J. 800, DC 7–126
—— v Ruzic (2001) 1555 C.C.C. (3d) 1 9–119
—— v S. *See* R. v Salih
—— v Salih; sub nom. R. v S [1995] 2 Cr. App. R. 347; (1995) 92(10) L.S.G. 37; (1995)
139 S.J.L.B. 49; *The Times*, December 31, 1994, CA (Crim Div) ... 7–254, 7–258, 7–264, 8–59
—— v Samuda (Stephen) (1989) 11 Cr. App. R. (S.) 471; *The Times*, October 11, 1989, CA
(Crim Div) 14–10, 19–1
—— v Sanders [1995] 3 N.Z.L.R. 545 .... 2–117, 16–407
—— v Santiago (Steven Anthony) [2005] EWCA Crim 556; *The Times*, March 16, 2005, CA
(Crim Div) 5–239, 10–43, 10–46
—— v Saunders [1990] Crim. L.R. 597, CA (Crim Div) 7–192, 7–239, 7–254, 7–255, 7–256,
7–258, 7–261, 8–59
—— v Savundranayagan (Emil); R. v Walker (Stuart de Quincy); sub nom. R. v Savundra
(Emil) [1968] 1 W.L.R. 1761; [1968] 3 All E.R. 439; (1968) 52 Cr. App. R. 637; 112
S.J. 621, CA (Crim Div) 1–129, 2–80, 4–25, 5–85, 5–115, 7–143, 16–166, 16–171
—— v Saxon [1984] W.A.R. 283 4–221
—— v Scalley [1995] Crim. L.R. 504, CA (Crim Div) 5–127
—— v Scarlett (1818) 1 B. & Ald. 232; (1818) 106 E.R. 86 10–150
—— v Schot (Bonnie Belinda); R. v Barclay (Carol Andrea); sub nom. R. v Schott [1997]
2 Cr. App. R. 383; (1997) 161 J.P. 473; [1997] Crim. L.R. 827; (1997) 161 J.P.N. 628;
(1997) 141 S.J.L.B. 119; *The Times*, May 14, 1997; *Independent*, May 16, 1997, CA
(Crim Div) 1–153, 1–159, 2–5, 2–17, 2–31, 2–190, 3–189, 5–166, 5–194, 7–233, 10–9,
10–37, 10–49, 10–52, 10–57, 10–71, 10–72, 10–176, 10–179, 10–181,
10–217, 11–233, 11–376, 11–386, 13–119, 15–107, 16–396
—— v Scott [1994] Crim. L.R. 947, CA (Crim Div) 2–106
—— v Scott and Downland Publications Ltd [1972] V.R. 663 4–232
—— v Secretary of State for Health Ex p. Wagstaff; R. v Secretary of State for Health Ex
p. Associated Newspapers Ltd; sub nom R. (on the application of Wagstaff) v
Secretary of State for Health; R. (on the application of Associated Newspapers Ltd) v
Secretary of State for Health [2001] 1 W.L.R. 292; [2000] H.R.L.R. 646; [2000]
U.K.H.R.R. 875; (2000) 56 B.M.L.R. 199; [2001] A.C.D. 24; (2000) 97(37) L.S.G. 39;
(2000) 144 S.J.L.B. 249; *The Times*, August 31, 2000; *Independent*, October 30, 2000
(C.S.), DC 2–63, 7–20
—— v Secretary of State for the Home Department Ex p. Bhajan Singh [1976] Q.B. 198;
[1975] 3 W.L.R. 225; [1975] 2 All E.R. 1081; 119 S.J. 441, CA (Civ Div) 2–127
—— v Secretary of State for the Home Department Ex p. Brind [1991] 1 A.C. 696; [1991]
2 W.L.R. 588; [1991] 1 All E.R. 720; (1991) 3 Admin. L.R. 486; (1991) 141 N.L.J.
199; (1991) 135 S.J. 250; *The Times*, February 8, 1991; *Independent*, February 8, 1991;
Guardian, February 8, 1991, HL 2–124, 2–125, 2–126, 2–127, 2–139, 2–140, 2–141
—— v Secretary of State for the Home Department Ex p. Doody; R. v Secretary of State for
the Home Department Ex p. Pierson; R. v Secretary of State for the Home Department
Ex p. Smart; R. v Secretary of State for the Home Department Ex p. Pegg [1994] 1
A.C. 531; [1993] 3 W.L.R. 154; [1993] 3 All E.R. 92; (1995) 7 Admin. L.R. 1; (1993)
143 N.L.J. 991; *The Times*, June 29, 1993; *Independent*, June 25, 1993, HL 2–48, 2–214

[cviii]

TABLE OF CASES

R v Secretary of State for the Home Department Ex p. Hindley [2001] 1 A.C. 410; [2000] 2 W.L.R. 730; [2000] 2 All E.R. 385; [2000] C.O.D. 173; (2000) 97(15) L.S.G. 39; (2000) 144 S.J.L.B. 180; *The Times*, March 31, 2000, HL; affirming [2000] Q.B. 152; [1999] 2 W.L.R. 1253; (1998) 148 N.L.J. 1673; *The Times*, November 6, 1998; *Independent*, November 10, 1998, CA (Civ Div); affirming [1998] Q.B. 751; [1998] 2 W.L.R. 505; [1998] C.O.D. 171; (1998) 148 N.L.J. 49; *The Times*, December 19, 1997, DC 2–46, 11–265
—— v Secretary of State for the Home Department Ex p. Main [2000] 2 A.C. 115; [1999] 3 W.L.R. 328; [1999] 3 All E.R. 400; [1999] E.M.L.R. 689; 7 B.H.R.C. 411; (1999) 11 Admin. L.R. 961; [1999] C.O.D. 520; (1999) 96(30) L.S.G. 28; (1999) 149 N.L.J. 1073; (1999) 143 S.J.L.B. 212; *The Times*, July 9, 1999, HL 2–50, 2–59
—— v Secretary of State for the Home Department Ex p. Northumbria Police Authority [1989] Q.B. 26; [1988] 2 W.L.R. 590; [1988] 1 All E.R. 556; (1988) 152 L.G. Rev. 308; *The Times*, November 19, 1987, CA (Civ Div) 11–327
—— v Secretary of State for the Home Department Ex p. Pierson; sub nom. Pierson v Secretary of State for the Home Department [1998] A.C. 539; [1997] 3 W.L.R. 492; [1997] 3 All E.R. 577; (1997) 94(37) L.S.G. 41; (1997) 147 N.L.J. 1238; (1997) 141 S.J.L.B. 212; *The Times*, July 28, 1997; *Independent*, July 31, 1997, HL 2–46
—— v Secretary of State for the Home Department Ex p. Simms; R. v Secretary of State for the Home Department Ex p. O'Brien; R. v Governor of Whitemoor Prison Ex p. Main; sub nom. R. v
—— v Secretary of State for the Home Department Ex p. Venables; R. v Secretary of State for the Home Department Ex p. Thompson [1998] A.C. 407; [1997] 3 W.L.R. 23; [1997] 3 All E.R. 97; [1997] 2 F.L.R. 471; (1997) 9 Admin. L.R. 413; [1997] Fam. Law 789; (1997) 94(34) L.S.G. 27; (1997) 147 N.L.J. 955; *The Times*, June 13, 1997; *Independent*, June 18, 1997, HL; affirming [1997] 2 W.L.R. 67; [1997] 1 All E.R. 327; (1997) 9 Admin. L.R. 281; [1997] C.O.D. 100; *The Times*, August 7, 1996, CA (Civ Div) 2–46, 2–48, 2–75, 2–77, 8–61
—— v Secretary of State for the Home Department Ex p. Westminster Press (1992) 4 Admin. L.R. 445; [1992] C.O.D. 303; *The Times*, December 18, 1991; *Independent*, January 21, 1992; *Guardian*, February 12, 1992, DC 2–53, 2–194, 4–237, 4–246, 4–247
—— v Secretary of State for Transport Ex p. Factortame Ltd (No.1) [1990] 2 A.C. 85; [1989] 2 W.L.R. 997; [1989] 2 All E.R. 692; [1989] 3 C.M.L.R. 1; [1989] C.O.D. 531; (1989) 139 N.L.J. 715; *The Times*, May 19, 1989; *Independent*, May 26, 1989; *Financial Times*, May 23, 1989; *Guardian*, May 25, 1989; *Daily Telegraph*, June 5, 1989, HL 2–224
—— v Sehitoglou and Ozakan [1998] 1 Cr. App. R. (S) 89 7–69
—— v Selby Justices Ex p. Frame; sub nom. R v Selby Magistrates Court Ex p. Frame [1992] Q.B. 72; [1991] 2 W.L.R. 965; [1991] 2 All E.R. 344; (1990–91) 12 Cr. App. R. (S.) 434; (1991) 155 J.P. 333; [1991] C.O.D. 179; (1991) 155 J.P.N. 76; *The Times*, October 3, 1990, DC 10–52, 10–70, 13–109, 14–67, 14–68, 15–107
—— v Sellick (Santino); R. v Sellick (Carlo) [2005] EWCA Crim 651; *The Times*, March 22, 2005, CA (Crim Div) 3–238
—— v Selvage (Pauline Ann); R. v Morgan (Dennis John) [1982] Q.B. 372; [1981] 3 W.L.R. 811; [1982] 1 All E.R. 96; (1981) 73 Cr. App. R. 333; [1981] R.T.R. 481, CA (Crim Div) 5–84, 11–21
—— v Sergiou (George) (1983) 5 Cr. App. R. (S.) 227; (1983) 147 J.P. 702; [1983] Crim. L.R. 686, CA (Crim Div) 19–1
—— v Shafiq, 95/8194/January 12, 1996, CA (Crim Div) 10–58
—— v Sharp (David Bruce) [1987] Q.B. 853; [1987] 3 W.L.R. 1; [1987] 3 All E.R. 103; (1987) 85 Cr. App. R. 207; (1987) 151 J.P. 832; [1987] Crim. L.R. 566; (1987) 151 J.P.N. 825; (1987) 84 L.S.G. 1491; (1987) 131 S.J. 624, CA (Crim Div) 9–124, 10–168
—— v Sharpe and Stringer (1938) 26 Cr. App. R. 122; [1938] 1 All E.R. 48 .... 5–82, 5–83, 5–93
—— v Shayler (David Michael) [2002] UKHL 11; [2003] 1 A.C. 247; [2002] 2 W.L.R. 754; [2002] 2 All E.R. 477; [2002] H.R.L.R. 33; [2002] U.K.H.R.R. 603; [2002] A.C.D. 58; (2002) 99(17) L.S.G. 34; (2002) 146 S.J.L.B. 84; *The Times*, March 22, 2002; *Independent*, March 26, 2002, HL 2–50
—— v Sheffield Crown Court Ex p. Brownlow [1980] Q.B. 530; [1980] 2 W.L.R. 892; [1980] 2 All E.R. 444; (1980) 71 Cr. App. R. 19; [1980] Crim. L.R. 374; 124 S.J. 272, CA (Civ Div) 2–114, 2–117
—— v Shepherd (1910) 74 J.P.J. 605 10–182

TABLE OF CASES

R v Shepherd (1988) 86 Cr. App. R. 47 9–124
—— v Sheppard (James Martin); R. v Sheppard (Jennifer Christine) [1981] A.C. 394; [1980]
3 W.L.R. 960; [1980] 3 All E.R. 899; (1981) 72 Cr. App. R. 82; [1981] Crim. L.R. 171;
124 S.J. 864, HL 7–209
—— v Shivpuri (Pyare) [1987] A.C. 1; [1986] 2 W.L.R. 988; [1986] 2 All E.R. 334; (1986)
83 Cr. App. R. 178; (1986) 150 J.P. 353; [1986] Crim. L.R. 536; (1986) 150 J.P.N. 510;
(1986) 83 L.S.G. 1896; (1986) 136 N.L.J. 488; (1986) 130 S.J. 392, HL 4–127, 11–11,
11–147, 11–238
—— v Shokoya [1992] T.L.R. 284; *The Times*, June 10, 1992; *Independent*, May 22, 1992,
CA (Crim Div) 3–227
—— v Shumiatcher (1967) 64 D.L.R. (2d) 24 10–142
—— v Silverman (1908) 17 O.L.R. 248 11–253
—— v Singh (Baldev); R. v Singh (Chamkaur); R. v Singh (Jarnail) [2000] 1 Cr. App. R.
31; [1999] Crim. L.R. 681, CA (Crim Div) 11–147
—— v Skegness Magistrates' Court Ex p. Cardy [1985] R.T.R. 49 11–135
—— v Skinner (1772) Lofft 55; (1772) 98 E.R. 529 10–150
—— v Smith (Martin) [1975] Q.B. 531 14–140
—— v Smith (Patrick); R. v Mercieca (Joseph) [2005] UKHL 12; [2005] 1 W.L.R. 704;
[2005] 2 All E.R. 29; *The Times*, February 17, 2005; *Independent*, February 23, 2005,
HL 1–126, 2–44, 2–101, 11–386, 11–387, 11–388, 11–392
—— v Smith (Wallace Duncan) (No.4) [2004] EWCA Crim 631; [2004] Q.B. 1418; [2004]
3 W.L.R. 229; [2004] 2 Cr. App. R. 17; *The Times*, March 29, 2004, CA (Crim Div) 12–155
—— v Smith (William Henry) (1989) 11 Cr. App. R. (S.) 353, CA (Crim Div) 19–1
—— v Smith [2005] UKHL 12; [2005] 1 W.L.R. 704 .... 16–392, 16–396
—— v Smithers (Graham); R. v Bowen (Leslie) (1983) 5 Cr. App. R. (S.) 248; [1983] Crim.
L.R. 756, CA (Crim Div) 10–8, 10–210, 10–225, 11–193, 19–1
—— v Socialist Worker Printers & Publishers Ltd Ex p. Att-Gen [1975] Q.B. 637; [1974]
3 W.L.R. 801; [1975] 1 All E.R. 142; [1974] Crim. L.R. 711; 118 S.J. 791, DC 3–105, 7–69,
7–78, 7–87, 7–93, 9–229
—— v Solicitor General Ex p. Taylor and Taylor [1996] 1 F.C.R. 206; [1996] C.O.D. 61; *The
Times*, August 14, 1995; *Independent*, August 3, 1995, DC 2–94, 2–212, 2–213, 2–216,
2–217, 2–219, 4–190, 13–14, 16–320, 16–401
—— v Soper (1825) 3 B. & C. 857; (1825) 107 E.R. 951 9–229
—— v Southampton Industrial Tribunal Ex p. INS News Group Ltd and Express
Newspapers Ltd [1995] I.R.L.R. 247; *The Times*, April 22, 1995, QBD 7–72, 7–109, 8–142
—— v Southwark Crown Court Ex p. Godwin; R. v Southwark Crown Court Ex p. *Daily
Telegraph*; R. v Southwark Crown Court Ex p. MGN Ltd; R. v Southwark Crown
Court Ex p. Associated Newspapers; R. v Southwark Crown Court Ex p. Newspaper
Publishing; sub nom. Ex p. Godwin; Re Godwin [1992] Q.B. 190; [1991] 3 W.L.R.
689; [1991] 3 All E.R. 818; (1992) 94 Cr. App. R. 34; (1992) 156 J.P. 86; [1991] Crim.
L.R. 302; (1991) 155 J.P.N. 834; (1991) 141 N.L.J. 963; (1991) 135 S.J.L.B. 28; *The
Times*, May 30, 1991; *Independent*, July 9, 1991; *Guardian*, June 6, 1991, CA (Civ
Div) 2–65, 7–81, 8–55
—— v Southwark Juvenile Court Ex p. J [1973] 1 W.L.R. 1300; [1973] 3 All E.R. 383; 71
L.G.R. 473; [1973] Crim. L.R. 511; 117 S.J. 633, DC 8–26
—— v Sparks (Seth Joseph); R. v Kingsnorth (Glyn Kevin) (1995) 16 Cr. App. R. (S.) 480,
CA (Crim Div) 19–1
—— v Stafforce Personnel Ltd, 00/2285/Z2, November 24, 2000, CA (Crim Div) ... 3–57, 10–31,
11–162, 11–186, 15–96
—— v Stafford County Court Judge; sub nom. R. v Jordan (1888) 57 L.J.Q.B. 483; (1888)
36 W.R. 797 .... 3–132, 3–134, 10–134, 10–144
—— v Starkey (Darren) (1994) 15 Cr. App. R. (S.) 576; [1994] Crim. L.R. 380, CA (Crim
Div) 14–66
—— v Steadman, unreported, February 1994, Bell J. 4–25
—— v Steen, unreported, January 26, 2004 10–182
—— v Stevens and Holness, *Independent*, June 9, 1997 14–50
—— v Stone (Michael John) [2001] EWCA Crim 297; [2001] Crim. L.R. 465; (2001) 98(11)
L.S.G. 43; (2001) 145 S.J.L.B. 68; *The Times*, February 22, 2001, CA (Crim Div) 1–162,
2–109, 2–119
—— v Stredder (Nicholas Michael) [1997] 1 Cr. App. R. (S.) 209, CA (Crim Div) 14–57, 19–1

TABLE OF CASES

R v Surrey Coroner Ex p. Campbell; sub nom. R. v HM Coroner for Surrey Ex p. Campbell
[1982] Q.B. 661; [1982] 2 W.L.R. 626; [1982] 2 All E.R. 545; 126 S.J. 209; *The Times*,
December 10, 1981, DC 13–100
—— v Sussex Justices Ex p. McCarthy [1924] 1 K.B. 256, KBD 10–49
—— v Tamworth Justices Ex p. Walsh [1994] C.O.D. 277; *The Times*, March 3, 1994, QBD 2–17,
10–33, 10–37, 10–114, 10–140, 10–146, 11–68, 13–109, 13–129, 15–107
—— v Taylor [1912] A.C. 347 11–48
—— v Taylor (Gary) [1994] T.L.R. 484 7–69
—— v Taylor and Taylor (1993) 98 Cr. App. R. 361 .... 2–73, 2–92, 4–269, 16–320
—— v Teesside Crown Court Ex p. Gazette Media Co Ltd [2005] EWCA Crim 1983 .... 6–101, 7–81,
8–55
—— v Telford Justices Ex p. Badhan [1991] 2 Q.B. 78; [1991] 2 W.L.R. 866; [1991] 2 All
E.R. 854; (1991) 93 Cr. App. R. 171; (1991) 155 J.P. 481; [1991] Crim. L.R. 526;
[1991] C.O.D. 323; (1991) 155 J.P.N. 139; *The Times*, January 1, 1991; *Independent*,
February 15, 1991; *Daily Telegraph*, January 21, 1991, QBD 2–105
—— v Tharakan [1995] 2 Cr. App. R. 368 11–368
—— v The National Post (2004) 236 D.L.R. (4th) 551 .... 9–1, 9–14, 9–31, 9–51, 9–96
—— v Thompson (Timothy Morgan) [1962] 1 All E.R. 65; (1962) 46 Cr. App. R. 72 10–83,
11–350, 11–362, 11–368, 11–386, 11–392
—— v Thomson Newspapers Ex p. Att-Gen; sub nom. R. v Thomson Newspapers Ltd
[1968] 1 W.L.R. 1; [1968] 1 All E.R. 268; 111 S.J. 943; *The Times*, November 28,
1967, QBD 4–13, 4–208, 4–213, 4–222, 4–223, 4–232, 4–241, 4–257, 5–104, 5–115
—— v Tibbits; sub nom. R. v Tibbits and Windust [1902] 1 K.B. 77, Crown Cases
Reserved 3–139, 4–116, 11–250
—— v Tibbits and Windust. *See* R. v Tibbits
—— v Toney (Ivan); R. v Ali (Tanveer) [1993] 1 W.L.R. 364; [1993] 2 All E.R. 409; (1993)
97 Cr. App. R. 176; [1993] C.O.D. 397; (1993) 157 J.P.N. 282; (1993) 143 N.L.J. 403;
(1993) 137 S.J.L.B. 46; Times, December 15, 1992; *Independent*, January 4, 1993
(C.S.), CA (Crim Div) 11–229, 11–230, 11–243
—— v Toronto Star Newspapers Ltd, 2005 S.C.C. 41 6–21
—— v Tower Bridge Magistrates' Court Ex p. Osborne (1987) 88 Cr. App. R. 28 7–90
—— v Twiss [1918] 2 K.B. 853 2–112
—— v Tyne Tees Television Ltd [1997] T.L.R. 515; *The Times*, October 20, 1997, CA (Crim
Div) 8–50, 13–25, 15–107
—— v Uddin (1991) 13 Cr. App. R. (S) 114 19–1
—— v Unger [1998] 1 Cr. App. R. 308; [1998] E.M.L.R. 280 16–403
—— v Unitt (1723) 1 Str. 567; (1723) 93 E.R. 705 11–317
—— v Vallières and Gagnon (1974) 47 D.L.R. (3d) 378 .... 10–19, 10–50, 16–66
—— v Vano [1996] R.T.R. 15 .... 1–164, 2–45, 2–47, 5–101
—— v Vaughan (1769) 4 Burr. 2494; (1769) 98 E.R. 308 11–174
—— v Vermette (1988) 41 C.C.C. (3d) 523 .... 2–78, 2–86
—— v Vidal, *The Times*, October 14, 1922 5–227
—— v Vincent; R v Daley; R v Warren [1968] Crim. L.R. 405; (1968) 112 S.J. 541, DC 2–107
—— v Von Einem (1990) 55 S.A.S.R. 199 .... 2–94, 2–212
—— v Vreones [1891] 1 Q.B. 360, Crown Cases Reserved 5–84, 11–21
—— v W (G); R. v W(E) [1996] T.L.R. 412, CA (Crim Div) 11–137
—— v Wandsworth County Court Ex p. Munn (1994) 26 H.L.R. 697; [1994] C.O.D. 282,
QBD 15–26
—— v Wang 2005 .... 10–176, 10–180
—— v Ward (1867) 17 (N.S.) L.T. 220 10–183
—— v Wason and Walter (1868) L.R. 4 Q.B. 73 1–73
—— v Waterfield (David) [1975] 1 W.L.R. 711; [1975] 2 All E.R. 40; (1974) 60 Cr. App.
R. 296; [1975] Crim. L.R. 298; 119 S.J. 300, CA (Crim Div) 2–51, 7–253
—— v Watford Magistrates Court Ex p. Lenman [1993] Crim. L.R. 388; [1992] C.O.D. 474;
The Times, June 10, 1992, DC 7–69, 7–85
—— v Watson (1990) 12 Cr.App.R.(S) 227 19–1
—— v Weaver (1967) 51 Cr. App. R. 77 7–161
—— v Webb Ex p. Hawkers, *The Times*, January 24, 1899 .... 10–106, 10–112, 10–133, 13–104
—— v Wedlock (Jason) [1996] 1 Cr. App. R. (S.) 391, CA (Crim Div) 19–1

[cxi]

TABLE OF CASES

R v Weisz Ex p. Hector MacDonald Ltd [1951] 2 K.B. 611; [1951] 2 All E.R. 408; [1951] 2 T.L.R. 337; 95 S.J. 433, KBD 11–48, 11–51, 11–66, 11–78, 12–119
—— v West (Rosemary Pauline) [1996] 2 Cr. App. R. 374; *The Times*, April 3, 1996, CA (Crim Div) 1–172, 2–61, 4–159, 11–267, 11–272, 11–385
—— v West Yorkshire Coroner Ex p. Smith (No.2) [1985] 1 Q.B. 1096 ...... 10–6, 10–34, 13–100
—— v Westminster City Council Ex p. Castelli (No.1); R. v Westminster City Council Ex p. Tristan Garcia (No.1) [1996] 1 F.L.R. 534; [1996] 2 F.C.R. 49; (1996) 28 H.L.R. 125; (1995) 7 Admin. L.R. 840; (1996) 30 B.M.L.R. 123; [1995] C.O.D. 375; [1996] Fam. Law 81; *The Times*, August 14, 1995, QBD 2–163, 6–73, 7–30, 7–90, 7–99, 7–106
—— v Westminster City Council Ex p. Ermakov [1996] 2 All E.R. 302; [1996] 2 F.C.R. 208; (1996) 28 H.L.R. 819; (1996) 8 Admin. L.R. 389; [1996] C.O.D. 391; (1996) 160 J.P. Rep. 814; (1996) 140 S.J.L.B. 23; *The Times*, November 20, 1995, CA (Civ Div) 2–219
—— v Westminster City Council Ex p. L; sub nom. Re Lawlor; Re L [1992] 1 W.L.R. 253; [1992] 1 All E.R. 917; [1991] Crim. L.R. 633; [1991] C.O.D. 202, DC 7–40, 8–40
—— v Wiatt (1723) 8 Mod. 123, 88 E.R. 96—5–220
—— v Wigand [1913] 2 K.B. 419 12–34
—— v Wigley (1835) 7 C. & P. 4; (1835) 173 E.R. 3 ..... 10–18, 10–21, 11–157, 11–158, 11–201
—— v Wilkin (1722) K.B. Easter 8 George I 5–220
—— v Wilkinson, *The Times*, July 16, 1930 5–230
—— v Williams and Romney (1823) 2 L.J. (O.S.) K.B. Mich. Term. 30 .... 4–25, 5–106
—— v Willmont (1914) 10 Cr. App. R. 173 10–182
—— v Winchester Crown Court Ex p. B (A Minor) [1999] 1 W.L.R. 788; [1999] 4 All E.R. 53; [2000] 1 Cr. App. R. 11; (1999) 96(5) L.S.G. 35; (1999) 143 S.J.L.B. 31; *The Times*, January 8, 1999, DC 8–59, 8–60
—— v Windham (1776) 1 Cowp. 377; (1776) 98 E.R. 1139 12–125
—— v Winter; sub nom. Winter v R. (1986) Alberta L.R. (2d) 393; (1986) 72 A.R. 163; (1986) 53 C.R. (3d) 372 13–42
—— v Wood (Vincent Joseph) [1996] 1 Cr. App. R. 207; [1995] Crim. L.R. 222; [1995] 139 S.J.L.B. 179; *The Times*, July 11, 1995; *Independent*, July 31, 1995 (C.S.), CA (Crim Div) 2–73, 2–95
—— v Woods (Arthur Andrew) (1989) 11 Cr. App. R. (S.) 551; [1990] Crim. L.R. 275, CA (Crim Div) 19–1
—— v Woollin (Stephen Leslie) [1999] 1 A.C. 82, HL; reversing [1997] 1 Cr. App. R. 97; [1997] Crim. L.R. 519; *The Times*, August 12, 1996, CA (Crim Div) 5–120
—— v Worcester Corporation (1903) 98 J.P. 130 12–128
—— v Wright [2000] Crim. L.R. 510 9–121
—— v Young (1801) 2 East 16; (1801) 102 E.R. 274 11–179
—— v Young (Stephen Andrew) [1995] Q.B. 324; [1995] 2 W.L.R. 430; [1995] 2 Cr. App. R. 379; (1995) 92(6) L.S.G. 38; (1995) 139 S.J.L.B. 32; *The Times*, December 30, 1994; *Independent*, January 16, 1995 (C.S.), CA (Crim Div) 10–83, 10–181, 11–356, 11–362, 11–368, 11–372, 11–391
—— v Young and Coughlan. *See* R. v Coughlan (Martin); R v Young (Gerard Peter)
—— v Yusuf (Mohammed); sub nom. R. v Yusef (Mohammed) [2003] EWCA Crim 1488; [2003] 2 Cr. App. R. 32; [2003] Crim. L.R. 877; *The Times*, May 12, 2003; *Independent*, June 11, 2003, CA (Crim Div) 10–45, 11–120, 11–122, 11–128
—— v Z. *See* R. v Hasan (Aytach)
—— (on the application of A) v HM Coroner for Inner South London; sub nom. A v Inner South London Coroner; Bennett v A; Family of Derek Bennett v Officers A and B and HM Coroner and Commissioner of Metropolitan Police [2004] EWCA Civ 1439; [2005] U.K.H.R.R. 44; (2004) 148 S.J.L.B. 1315; *The Times*, November 11, 2004, CA (Civ Div) 7–86
—— (on the application of A) v Lord Saville of Newdigate. *See* R. (on the application of A) v Lord Saville of Newdigate (Bloody Sunday Inquiry)
—— (on the application of A) v Lord Saville of Newdigate (Bloody Sunday Inquiry); sub nom. R. (on the application of Widgery Soldiers) v Lord Saville of Newdigate; Lord Saville of Newdigate v Widgery Soldiers; R (on the application of A) v Lord Saville of Newdigate [2001] EWCA Civ 2048; [2002] 1 W.L.R. 1249; [2002] A.C.D. 22; *The Times*, December 21, 2001; *Independent*, January 11, 2002; *Daily Telegraph*, January 11, 2002, CA (Civ Div) 7–86

TABLE OF CASES

R (on the application of Al-Fawwaz) v Governor of Brixton Prison; R. (on the application of Abdel Bary) v Governor of Brixton Prison; R. (on the application of Eidarous) v Governor of Brixton Prison; sub nom. Al-Fawwaz v Governor of Brixton Prison; Re Al-Fawwaz; Abdel Bary v Governor of Brixton Prison; Eidarous v Governor of Brixton Prison; Re Abdel Bary; Re Eidarous; Re Eiderous [2001] UKHL 69; [2002] 1 A.C. 556; [2002] 2 W.L.R. 101; [2002] 1 All E.R. 545; *The Times*, December 18, 2001; *Daily Telegraph*, January 11, 2002, HL 7–78, 10–165

—— (on the application of Anderson) v Secretary of State for the Home Department; R. (on the application of Taylor) v Secretary of State for the Home Department; sub nom. R. v Secretary of State for the Home Department Ex p. Anderson; R. v Secretary of State for the Home Department Ex p. Taylor [2002] UKHL 46; [2003] 1 A.C. 837; [2002] 3 W.L.R. 1800; [2002] 4 All E.R. 1089; [2003] 1 Cr. App. R. 32; [2003] H.R.L.R. 7; [2003] U.K.H.R.R. 112; 13 B.H.R.C. 450; (2003) 100(3) L.S.G. 31; (2002) 146 S.J.L.B. 272; *The Times*, November 26, 2002; *Independent*, November 27, 2002, HL 2–48

—— (on the application of Bempoa) v Southwark LBC [2002] EWHC 153; [2002] N.P.C. 23, QBD (Admin) 12–101, 12–125, 14–2, 14–134

—— (on the application of D) v Camberwell Green Youth Court; R. (on the application of R) v Balham Youth Court; R. (on the application of N) v Camberwell Green Youth Court; R. (on the application of DPP) v Camberwell Green Youth Court; R. (on the application of G) v Camberwell Green Youth Court [2005] UKHL 4; [2005] 1 W.L.R. 393; [2005] 1 All E.R. 999; [2005] 2 Cr. App. R. 1; (2005) 169 J.P. 105; [2005] 1 F.C.R. 365; [2005] H.R.L.R. 9; 17 B.H.R.C. 625; (2005) 169 J.P.N. 257; (2005) 102(13) L.S.G. 27; (2005) 149 S.J.L.B. 146; *The Times*, February 1, 2005, HL 7–13, 7–69, 7–77

—— (on the application of Green) v City of London Magistrates [1997] 3 All E.R. 551 2–225

—— (on the application of Mahfouz) v General Medical Council; sub nom. Mahfouz v General Medical Council [2004] EWCA Civ 233; [2004] Lloyd's Rep. Med. 377; (2004) 80 B.M.L.R. 113; (2004) 101(13) L.S.G. 35; *The Times*, March 19, 2004, CA (Civ Div); reversing in part [2003] EWHC 1695, QBD (Admin) 4–117

—— (on the application of Matara) v Brent Magistrates' Court [2005] All E.R. (D) 263 15–113

—— (on the application of Mersey Care NHS Trust) v Mental Health Review Tribunal [2004] EWHC 1749; [2005] 2 All E.R. 820, QBD (Admin) 7–77, 7–81, 7–84, 7–108, 7–109, 13–67

—— (on the application of ProLife Alliance) v BBC; sub nom. ProLife Alliance v BBC; R. (on the application of Quintavalle) v BBC [2003] UKHL 23, HL; reversing [2002] EWCA Civ 297; [2002] 3 W.L.R. 1080; [2002] 2 All E.R. 756; [2002] E.M.L.R. 41; [2002] U.K.H.R.R. 1096; (2002) 152 N.L.J. 433; *The Times*, March 19, 2002; *Daily Telegraph*, March 21, 2002, CA (Civ Div) 2–198

—— (on the application of Rusbridger) v Att-Gen; sub nom. Rusbridger v Att-Gen [2003] UKHL 38; [2004] 1 A.C. 357; [2003] 3 W.L.R. 232; [2003] 3 All E.R. 784; [2003] H.R.L.R. 32; (2003) 153 N.L.J. 1029; (2003) 147 S.J.L.B. 812; *The Times*, June 27, 2003, HL 10–92, 12–60

—— (on the application of S) v S. *See* R. (on the application of Sevketoglu) v Sevketoglu

—— (on the application of S) v Waltham Forest Youth Court [2004] EWHC 715; [2004] 2 Cr. App. R. 21; (2004) 168 J.P. 293; (2004) 168 J.P.N. 438, QBD (Admin) 7–13, 7–69, 7–77

—— (on the application of Sevketoglu) v Sevketoglu; sub nom. Sevketoglu v Sevketoglu; R. (on the application of S) v S [2003] EWCA Civ 1570; *The Times*, November 27, 2003, CA (Civ Div) 14–36

—— (on the application of Sezek) v Secretary of State for the Home Department (Bail Application); sub nom. Sezek v Secretary of State for the Home Department (Bail Application) [2001] EWCA Civ 795; [2002] 1 W.L.R. 348; [2001] Imm. A.R. 657; [2001] I.N.L.R. 675; (2001) 98(31) L.S.G. 36; *The Times*, June 20, 2001, CA (Civ Div) 15–102

—— (on the application of Stanley) v Commissioner of Police of the Metropolis [2004] EWHC 2229; (2004) 168 J.P. 623; [2005] E.M.L.R. 3; [2005] U.K.H.R.R. 115; [2005] H.L.R. 8; [2005] Crim. L.R. 292; [2005] A.C.D. 13; (2004) 168 J.P.N. 937; (2004) 101(40) L.S.G. 28; (2004) 154 N.L.J. 1525; *The Times*, October 22, 2004, QBD (Admin) 8–43

TABLE OF CASES

R (on the application of T) v St Albans Crown Court; Chief Constable of Surrey v JHG
   [2002] EWHC 1129, QBD (Admin) 8–42, 8–67
—— (on the application of Telegraph Group Plc) v Sherwood; sub nom. R. v Sherwood Ex
   p. Telegraph Group Plc; Telegraph Group Plc, Ex p. [2001] EWCA Crim 1075; [2001]
   1 W.L.R. 1983; [2002] E.M.L.R. 10; (2001) 98(28) L.S.G. 42; (2001) 145 S.J.L.B.
   159; *The Times*, June 12, 2001, CA (Crim Div) 2–86, 2–97, 4–60, 4–76, 4–86, 4–114,
                     4–160, 6–94, 7–141, 7–172, 7–177, 7–184, 7–186, 7–189, 7–192, 7–199,
                                                           7–200, 7–201, 7–237, 7–239, 7–261
—— (on the application of von Brandenburg) v East London and the City Mental Health
   NHS Trust; sub nom. R. v Tower Hamlets Healthcare NHS Trust Ex p. von
   Brandenburg; R. v East London and the City Mental Health NHS Trust Ex p. von
   Brandenburg [2003] UKHL 58; [2004] 2 A.C. 280; [2003] 3 W.L.R. 1265; [2004] 1
   All E.R. 400; [2004] H.R.L.R. 6; (2004) 7 C.C.L. Rep. 121; [2004] Lloyd's Rep. Med.
   228; (2004) 76 B.M.L.R. 168; (2004) 101(5) L.S.G. 28; (2003) 147 S.J.L.B. 1366; *The
   Times*, November 14, 2003; *Independent*, November 19, 2003, HL 13–66
Racal Communications Ltd, Re; sub nom. Re Company (No.00996 of 1979) [1981] A.C.
   374; [1980] 3 W.L.R. 181; [1980] 2 All E.R. 634, HL 9–211
Radley's Case (1680) 7 St. Tr. 701 1–20
Raffique v Muse [2000] 1 F.L.R. 820. 19–2
Rainy v Sierra Leone Justices (1853) 8 Moo. P.C. 47; (1853) 15 E.R. 19 .... 3–132, 3–185, 10–143,
                                                                                                        10–144
Raja v Van Hoogstraten (Application to Strike Out) [2004] EWCA Civ 968; [2004] 4 All
   E.R. 793; [2005] C.P. Rep. 6; *The Times*, July 27, 2004; *Independent*, July 27, 2004,
   CA (Civ Div) 3–75, 3–238, 10–49, 10–53, 10–147
Ramage v Steele (1843) 6 D. 146 .... 16–235, 16–261
Ramsay, Re (1870) L.R. 3 P.C. 427 .... 3–132, 3–185, 12–33
Ramsbotham v Senior (1869) L.R. 8 Eq. 575 11–336
Randfield v Randfield (1860) 1 Dr. & Sm. 310; (1860) 62 E.R. 398 11–319
Rank Film Distributors Ltd v Video Information Centre [1982] A.C. 380; [1981] 2 W.L.R.
   668; [1981] 2 All E.R. 76; [1981] Com. L.R. 90; [1981] E.C.C. 365; [1981] F.S.R. 363;
   The Times, April 9, 1981, HL 3–191
Ranson v Platt [1911] 2 K.B. 291 6–137
Rantzen v Mirror Group Newspapers (1986) Ltd [1994] Q.B. 670; [1993] 3 W.L.R. 953;
   [1993] 4 All E.R. 975; (1993) 143 N.L.J. 507; *The Times*, April 6, 1993; *Independent*,
   April 1, 1993, CA (Civ Div) 1–132, 2–127, 2–164, 7–187
Rantzen v Rothschild (1865) 13 L.T. 399 .... 6–126, 12–99
Ravnsborg v Sweden (1994) 18 E.H.R.R. 38 (3) 2–23, 11–143
Raymond v Honey [1983] 1 A.C. 1; [1982] 2 W.L.R. 465; [1982] 1 All E.R. 756; (1982) 75
   Cr. App. R. 16, HL 2–193, 11–302
Raymond v Tapson (1882) 22 Ch. D. 430, CA 11–109
Redding's Case (1680) 1 Sid. 40; (1680) 82 E.R. 957 .... 10–143, 10–144
Redfern v Redfern [1891] P. 139, CA 3–188
Redwing Ltd v Redwing Forest Products Ltd (1947) 177 L.T. 387 ...... 12–48, 12–54, 12–190, 12–192
Refco Inc v Eastern Trading Co [1999] 1 Lloyd's Rep. 159, CA (Civ Div) 12–168, 12–169
Regan v Taylor [2000] E.M.L.R. 549; (2000) 150 N.L.J. 392; *The Times*, March 15, 2000;
   Independent, April 17, 2000 (C.S.), CA (Civ Div) 1–167, 11–73
Registrar of the Court of Appeal v Collins [1982] 1 N.S.W.L.R. 682, CA of NSW 10–15, 10–20,
                                                                                    10–22, 10–23, 10–25, 11–308
Registrar of the Court of Appeal v Willesee (1980) 2 N.S.W.L.R. 143 4–67
Registrar of the Supreme Court, Equity Division v McPherson [1980] N.S.W.L.R. 688 5–14,
                                                                                    11–25, 11–85, 11–202
Reichmann v Toronto Life Publishing Co (1988) 28 C.P.C. (2nd) 11 9–4
Rejfek v McElroy (1965) 112 C.L.R. 517; (1965) 39 A.L.R. 177 12–44
Remli v France (1996) 22 E.H.R.R. 253 11–355
Renner, Ex p. [1897] A.C. 218, PC (Gold Coast) 10–143
Rex v Bishop of Lincoln (1637) 3 State Tr. 770 11–228
Rex v Flower (1799) 8 Durn. & E. 314 13–12
Reynolds v Meston, unreported, February 24, 1986, QBD 11–104

Table of Cases

Reynolds v Times Newspapers Ltd [2001] 2 A.C. 127; [1999] 3 W.L.R. 1010; [1999] 4 All E.R. 609; [2000] E.M.L.R. 1; [2000] H.R.L.R. 134; 7 B.H.R.C. 289; (1999) 96(45) L.S.G. 34; (1999) 149 N.L.J. 1697; (1999) 143 S.J.L.B. 270; *The Times*, October 29, 1999; *Independent*, November 3, 1999, HL 2–50, 2–180, 4–49, 4–338
Rhoder, *The Times*, November 19, 1894 10–183
Riaviz v Howdle, 1996 S.C.C.R. 20 16–115
Richardson v Richardson (1989) [1989] Fam. 95; [1989] 3 W.L.R. 865; [1989] 3 All E.R. 779; [1990] 1 F.L.R. 186; [1990] F.C.R. 232; (1990) 154 J.P.N. 233, Fam Div 14–124, 14–130, 15–85
Richardson v Schwarzenegger [2004] EWHC 2422, QBD 1–181
Richardson v Wilson (1879) 2 R. 237; (1879) 17 S.L.R. 122 .... 16–202, 16–217, 16–218
Richers v Stilman (1558) *Cary's Causes in Chancery*, p.57 1–48
Richmond upon Thames LBC v H; sub nom. Re X (A Child) (Injunctions Restraining Publication) [2001] 1 F.C.R. 541; *The Times*, October 20, 2000, Fam Div 6–6, 6–42, 6–80, 6–87, 6–90, 6–96, 9–17
Richmond upon Thames LBC v Holmes, *The Times*, October 20, 2000 6–6
Riddell and Raeside v The Clydesdale Horse Society (1885) 12 R. 976 .... 16–192, 16–368
Riddick v Thames Board Mills [1977] Q.B. 881; [1977] 3 W.L.R. 63; [1977] 3 All E.R. 677, CA (Civ Div) 3–198, 3–201, 11–76, 12–201, 12–228
Ridehalgh v Horsefield; Allen v Unigate Dairies Ltd; Antonelli v Wade Gery Farr (A Firm); Philex Plc v Golban; Roberts v Coverite (Asphalters) Ltd; Watson v Watson (Wasted Costs Orders) [1994] Ch. 205; [1994] 3 W.L.R. 462; [1994] 3 All E.R. 848; [1994] B.C.C. 390; [1994] 2 F.L.R. 194; [1955–95] P.N.L.R. 636; [1994] Fam. Law 560; [1994] E.G.C.S. 15; (1994) 144 N.L.J. 231; [1994] N.P.C. 7; *The Times*, January 28, 1994; *Independent*, February 4, 1994, CA (Civ Div) 11–54
Riepan v Austria [2001] Crim. L.R. 230, ECHR 7–39
Ring, The [1931] P. 58 12–262
Ritchie (Alex) v Stewart, Brown (1797) Hume, Vol.II, p.141 16–152
Rivers' Case (Countess) (1650) Sty. 252; (1650) 82 E.R. 687 3–145
Roach v Garvan; sub nom. St James's Evening Post (1742) 2 Atk. 469; 26 E.R. 683 .... 1–51, 1–60, 1–62, 1–63, 1–67, 1–69, 1–70, 1–71, 2–38, 4–5, 4–6, 4–10, 4–12, 4–202, 5–104, 5–119, 5–133, 5–220, 13–19, 14–6
Robb v Caledonian Newspapers Ltd, 1995 S.L.T. 631; 1994 S.C.C.R. 659, HCJ 4–2, 16–39, 16–61, 16–62, 16–64, 16–235, 16–253, 16–321, 16–353, 16–360, 16–375
Robbins, In re Ex p. Green (1891) 7 T.L.R. 411 5–105
Roberts v Albert Bridge Company (1873) L.R. 8 Ch. App. 753 3–159
Roberts v Bass [2002] H.C.A. 57; [2002] 194 A.L.R. 161 12–213
Roberts v J & F Stone Lighting and Radio Ltd (1945) 172 L.T. 240 .... 14–153, 14–154, 14–158
Roberts v Roberts [1990] 2 F.L.R. 111; [1990] F.C.R. 837; [1991] Fam. Law 65; (1990) 154 J.P.N. 154, CA (Civ Div) 12–184, 15–27
Roberts v Roberts [1991] 1 F.L.R. 294; [1991] F.C.R. 590, CA (Civ Div) 14–73, 14–86
Robertson v McDonald (1829) 7 S. 272 16–241
Robinson v Barton Eccles Local Board (1882–83) L.R. 8 App. Cas. 798, HL 4–31
Robinson v Robinson [2001] All E.R. (D) 144 (Feb.) 19–2
Rockwell Machine Tool Co Ltd v EP Barrus (Concessionaires) Ltd (Practice Note) [1968] 1 W.L.R. 693; [1968] 2 All E.R. 98 (Note); 112 S.J. 380, Ch D 11–86
Roddy (A Child) (Identification: Restriction on Publication), Re; sub nom. Torbay BC v News Group Newspapers; Re Angela Roddy (A Minor) [2003] EWHC 2927; [2004] E.M.L.R. 8; [2004] 2 F.L.R. 949; [2004] 1 F.C.R. 481; [2004] Fam. Law 793, Fam Div 6–37, 6–59, 6–67, 6–71, 6–114
Roddy (Angela) (A Minor), Re. See Roddy (A Child) (Identification: Restriction on Publication), Re
Roemen and Schmit v Luxembourg, App. No.51772/99 .... 9–1, 9–106
Roger Bullivant Ltd v Ellis [1987] I.C.R. 464; [1987] I.R.L.R. 491; [1987] F.S.R. 172, CA (Civ Div); *Financial Times*, April 15, 1986, Falconer J. (Lexis) 2–204, 4–1, 4–95, 4–134, 4–185, 4–187, 4–188, 5–110, 11–74
Rogers (1702) 7 Mod. Rep. 28; (1702) 87 E.R. 1074 10–144
Rollins v Gardner, unreported, May 16, 2005 19–2
Romilly v Romilly [1964] P. 22 .... 14–125, 14–130

TABLE OF CASES

Ronald A Prior & Co (Solicitors), Re. *See* Re Solicitor (Wasted Costs Order) (No.1 of 1994)
Ronson Products Ltd v Ronson Furniture Ltd [1966] Ch. 603; [1966] 2 W.L.R. 1157; [1966] 2 All E.R. 381; [1966] F.S.R. 138; [1966] R.P.C. 497; 110 S.J. 427, Ch D 12–38, 12–081, 15–20
Rooks Rider v JR Steel [1993] 4 All E.R. 716; (1993) 143 N.L.J. 1063; *The Times*, July 1, 1993, Ch D 12–255
Rooney v Snaresbrook Crown Court (1979) 68 Cr. App. R. 78; [1979] Crim. L.R. 109; *The Times*, June 17, 1978, CA (Civ Div) 10–29, 10–31, 10–40, 11–162, 11–186, 11–202, 15–96
Rose (Fanny), Re; sub nom. Rose v Laskington Ltd [1990] 1 Q.B. 562; [1989] 3 W.L.R. 873; [1989] 3 All E.R. 306; (1989) 5 B.C.C. 758; (1989) 86(39) L.S.G. 36; (1989) 139 N.L.J. 973; (1989) 133 S.J. 1033, DC 12–135, 13–97, 14–116, 15–78
Rose v Laskington Ltd. *See* Re Rose (Fanny)
Ross v Ross (1885) 12 R. 1351; (1885) 23 S.L.R. 1 16–234
Ross v Midwest Communications, 870 F. 2d 271 6–90
Rossminster and Tucker, Re, *The Times*, May 23, 1980, CA 12–182, 13–15
Rove v West (1558) Cary 38; (1558) 21 E.R. 21 .... 1–43, 11–317
Rowden v Universities Co-operative Association (1881) 35 S.J. 886 .... 11–197, 11–241
Royal Bank of Canada v Canstar Sports Group Inc [1989] 1 W.W.R. 662 12–105
Royal Bank of Scotland Plc v Etridge (No.2); Barclays Bank Plc v Coleman; Barclays Bank Plc v Harris; Midland Bank Plc v Wallace; National Westminster Bank Plc v Gill; UCB Home Loans Corp Ltd v Moore; Bank of Scotland v Bennett; Kenyon-Brown v Desmond Banks & Co (Undue Influence) (No.2) [2001] UKHL 44; [2002] 2 A.C. 773; [2001] 3 W.L.R. 1021; [2001] 4 All E.R. 449; [2001] 2 All E.R. (Comm) 1061; [2002] 1 Lloyd's Rep. 343; [2001] 2 F.L.R. 1364; [2001] 3 F.C.R. 481; [2002] H.L.R. 4; [2001] Fam. Law 880; [2001] 43 E.G.C.S. 184; (2001) 151 N.L.J. 1538; [2001] N.P.C. 147; [2002] 1 P. & C.R. DG14; *The Times*, October 17, 2001; *Daily Telegraph*, October 23, 2001, HL 4–145, 11–284, 11–293
Royal Warrant Holders' Association v Robb, 1935 S.N. 32 16–263
Royle v Gray, 1973 S.L.T. 31, HCJ Appeal 10–34, 16–44, 16–49, 16–60, 16–274
Royson's Case (1629) 1 Cro. Car. 146; (1629) 79 E.R. 729 .... 10–157, 10–161
Rudkin-Jones v Trustee of the Property of the Bankrupt (1965) 109 Sol. Jo. 334 12–55
Ruffin v Heyward (1584) Ch. Cas. Ch. 175; (1584) 21 E.R. 102 11–317
Russell (Lord John) (1839) 7 Dowl. P.C. 693 .... 11–106, 1–111
Russell v East Anglian Ry Co (1850) Mac. & G. 104; (1850) 42 E.R. 201 ..... 9–201, 11–319, 11–320, 11–321
Russell v HM Advocate, 1992 S.L.T. 25 16–310
Rutland's Case (Countess of) (1606) 6 Co. Rep. 528; (1606) 77 E.R. 552 3–145
Rylands v Fletcher; sub nom. Fletcher v Rylands (1868) L.R. 3 H.L. 330, HL; affirming (1865–66) L.R. 1 Ex. 265; [1865–66] All E.R. Rep. 1; (1866) 4 Hurl. & C. 263, Ex Chamber; reversing (1865) 3 Hurl. & C. 774, Ex Ct 4–2

S (A Child) (Identification: Restrictions on Publication), Re; sub nom. Re S (A Child) (Identification: Restriction on Publication); Re S (FC) (A Child) [2004] UKHL 47; [2005] 1 A.C. 593; [2004] 3 W.L.R. 1129; [2004] 4 All E.R. 683; [2005] E.M.L.R. 2; [2005] 1 F.L.R. 591; [2004] 3 F.C.R. 407; [2005] H.R.L.R. 5; [2005] U.K.H.R.R. 129; 17 B.H.R.C. 646; [2005] Crim. L.R. 310; (2004) 154 N.L.J. 1654; (2004) 148 S.J.L.B. 1285; *The Times*, October 29, 2004; *Independent*, November 2, 2004, HL; affirming [2003] EWCA Civ 963; [2004] Fam. 43; [2003] 3 W.L.R. 1425; [2003] 2 F.L.R. 1253; [2003] 2 F.C.R. 577; [2003] H.R.L.R. 30; [2003] Fam. Law 818; (2003) 100(34) L.S.G. 29; (2003) 153 N.L.J. 1120; (2003) 147 S.J.L.B. 873; *The Times*, July 21, 2003; *Independent*, July 15, 2003, CA (Civ Div) 1–126, 1–140, 1–175, 1–176, 2–41, 2–146, 2–163, 6–42, 6–43, 6–52, 6–56, 6–58, 6–59, 6–60, 6–71, 6–73, 6–82, 6–85, 6–87, 6–88, 6–90, 6–93, 6–98, 6–101, 6–102, 6–105, 6–114, 7–24, 7–62, 7–67, 7–99, 7–108, 7–170, 7–193, 8–51, 8–54, 8–61

TABLE OF CASES

S (Adult Patient: Sterilisation: Patient's Best Interests), Re; sub nom. Re SL v SL; SL (Adult Patient) (Medical Treatment) [2001] Fam. 15; [2000] 3 W.L.R. 1288; [2000] 2 F.L.R. 389; [2000] 2 F.C.R. 452; [2000] Lloyd's Rep. Med. 339; (2000) 55 B.M.L.R. 105; [2000] Fam. Law 711; (2000) 97(24) L.S.G. 40; *The Times*, May 26, 2000, CA (Civ Div) 6–54
S (FC) (A Child) (Identification: Restrictions on Publication), Re. *See* Re S (A Child) (Identification: Restrictions on Publication)
S (Minors) (Child Abduction: Sequestration), Re [1995] 1 F.L.R. 858; [1995] 3 F.C.R. 707, Fam Div 14–112, 14–114, 14–131
S (Minors) (Wardship: Police Investigation), Re [1987] Fam. 199; [1987] 3 W.L.R. 847; [1987] 3 All E.R. 1076; [1988] 1 F.L.R. 1; [1988] Fam. Law 90; (1987) 151 L.G. Rev. 712; (1987) 131 S.J. 1390, Fam Div 8–102, 8–118, 8–119
S v Germany (1983) 39 D.R. 43 .... 3–209, 12–13
S v McC (orse S) and M (DS Intervener); W v W. *See* S (An Infant) v S
S v S (Judgment in Chambers: Disclosure); sub nom. S v S (Disclosure of Material) (No.2); S v S (Disclosure to Revenue); S v S (Inland Revenue: Tax Evasion) [1997] 1 W.L.R. 1621; [1997] S.T.C. 759; [1997] 2 F.L.R. 774; [1997] 3 F.C.R. 1; 69 T.C. 313; [1997] B.T.C. 333; [1997] Fam. Law 659, Fam Div 8–102, 11–81
S (An Infant) v S; W v W; W v Official Solicitor (acting as *Guardian* ad Litem for a Male Infant named PHW); sub nom. S v McC (formerly S); S v McC (orse S) and M (DS Intervener) [1972] A.C. 24; [1970] 3 W.L.R. 366; [1970] 3 All E.R. 107; 114 S.J. 635, HL 6–82, 6–85
S & A Conversions, Re (1988) 4 B.C.C. 384; (1988) 138 N.L.J. Rep. 169, CA (Civ Div) 14–14, 19–2
SC v United Kingdom (60958/00) [2005] 1 F.C.R. 347; (2005) 40 E.H.R.R. 10; 17 B.H.R.C. 607; [2005] Crim. L.R. 130; *The Times*, June 29, 2004, ECHR 8–36
SCF Finance Co Ltd v Masri (No.1); sub nom. Masri v SCF Finance Co Ltd (No.1) [1985] 1 W.L.R. 876; [1985] 2 All E.R. 747; [1985] 2 Lloyd's Rep. 206; (1985) 82 L.S.G. 2015; (1985) 129 S.J. 450, CA (Civ Div) 12–151, 12–152
Saif Ali v Sydney Mitchell & Co [1980] A.C. 198; [1978] 3 W.L.R. 849; [1978] 3 All E.R. 1033; [1955–95] P.N.L.R. 151; 122 S.J. 761, HL 10–155
St Andrews, Heddington, Re [1978] Fam. 121 .... 10–201, 13–103
St Edmundsbury and Ipswich Diocese (Chancellor of) Ex p. White [1948] 1 K.B. 195 13–103
St James's Evening Post. *See* Roach v Garvan
Salisbury DC v Le Roi; sub nom. Salisbury DC v Williams [2001] EWCA Civ 1490; [2002] 1 P. & C.R. 39; [2002] J.P.L. 700, CA (Civ Div) 9–208, 14–46, 19–2
Salles v Savignon (1801) 6 Ves. Jun. 572; (1801) 31 E.R. 1201 11–342
Saltman Engineering Co v Campbell Engineering Co (1948) p1963] 3 All E.R. 413 (note) 6–49
Sander v United Kingdom (2001) 31 E.H.R.R. 1003; (2000) 8 B.H.R.C. 279 .... 11–355, 11–389
Sansom v Sansom (1879) 4 P.D. 69 14–120
Sarbadhicary, Re (1906) 23 T.L.R. 180 .... 5–226, 10–134, 10–143
Saunders v Melhuish (1703 M. 2 Anne) 6 Mod. 73, 87 E.R. 831 1–53
Saunders v Punch Ltd [1998] 1 W.L.R. 986; [1998] 1 All E.R. 234, Ch D 9–16, 9–90, 9–91, 9–105, 9–106, 9–107, 9–126, 9–155, 9–171
Saunders v United Kingdom (19187/91) [1997] B.C.C. 872; [1998] 1 B.C.L.C. 362; (1997) 23 E.H.R.R. 313; 2 B.H.R.C. 358; *The Times*, December 18, 1996; *Independent*, January 14, 1997, ECHR 2–136, 2–137
Saville of Newdigate (Lord) v Harnden [2003] N.I. 239; [2003] NICA 6, CA (NI) 3–3, 3–27
Savings & Investment Bank Ltd v Gasco Investments (Netherlands) BV (No.2) [1988] Ch. 422; [1988] 2 W.L.R. 1212; [1988] 1 All E.R. 975; (1987) 137 N.L.J. 1088; (1988) 132 S.J. 790, CA 3–120, 3–199, 3–229, 3–237, 3–241, 15–43
Schellenberg v BBC [2000] E.M.L.R. 296, QBD 11–59
Schering Chemicals Ltd v Falkman Ltd [1982] Q.B. 1; [1981] 2 W.L.R. 848; [1981] 2 All E.R. 321; 125 S.J. 342, CA (Civ Div) 2–38, 4–122, 4–272, 4–63, 6–9
Schiavo v Anderton (1986) 83 Cr. App. R. 228 11–129
Schlesinger v Flersheim (1845) 14 L.J.Q.B. 97 11–192
Scholes v Hilton (1842) 10 M. & W. 15; (1842) 152 E.R. 362 .... 11–106, 11–114
Schreiber v Lateward (1781) 2 Dick. 592; (1781) 21 E.R. 401 11–334
Schuler-Zgraggen v Switzerland (A/263) [1994] 1 F.C.R. 453; (1993) 16 E.H.R.R. 405; *The Times*, October 21, 1993, ECHR 7–16

TABLE OF CASES

Scott v Moxon (1900) 81 L.T. 774 12–189
Scott (otherwise Morgan) v Scott [1913] A.C. 417, HL; reversing [1912] P. 241, CA 1–87, 2–37,
2–51, 2–65, 2–163, 3–21, 3–71, 3–82, 3–99, 3–102, 3–115, 3–122, 3–137,
3–141, 4–263, 6–55, 6–83, 6–116, 7–6, 7–8, 7–9, 7–12, 7–21, 7–27,
7–36, 7–46, 7–56, 7–70, 7–74, 7–75, 7–95, 7–104, 7–130, 7–209, 8–6,
8–8, 8–17, 8–122, 8–124, 8–127, 8–128, 10–22, 11–332, 12–242, 14–28
Scottish Criminal Cases Review Commission, Re, 2001 S.C.R. 775 11–368
Scottish Daily Record & Sunday Mail Ltd, Petitioners, 1999 S.L.T. 624; 1998 S.C.C.R. 626;
1998 G.W.D. 35–1785, HCJ Appeal 7–259, 16–377
Scriven, Re (No.2); sub nom. R. v Scriven [2004] EWCA Civ 683; [2004] B.P.I.R. 972;
(2004) 148 S.J.L.B. 757, CA (Civ Div) 15–76
Sea Rose Ltd v Sea Train UK Ltd [1981] 1 W.L.R. 894 12–146
Seaward v Paterson [1897] 1 Ch. 545 .... 3–89, 3–119, 3–127, 3–128, 3–157,
3–172, 3–185, 6–137, 6–144, 6–146, 11–115, 12–15, 12–104, 12–109, 12–198,
12–242, 14–6, 15–117
Secretary for Justice v Apple Daily Ltd [2002] 2 H.K.C. 739 .... 3–191, 12–108
Secretary for Justice v Oriental Press Group Ltd [1998] 2 HKC 627 5–273
Secretary of State for Defence v Guardian Newspapers Ltd [1985] A.C. 339; [1984] 3 W.L.R.
986; [1984] 3 All E.R. 601; (1984) 81 L.S.G. 3426; (1984) 128 S.J. 571, HL 1–66, 1–118,
1–122, 1–126, 2–51, 2–149, 2–193, 3–108, 3–113, 4–33, 5–204, 9–15, 9–19,
9–21, 9–34, 9–37, 9–39, 9–41, 9–56, 9–59, 9–60, 9–61, 9–66, 9–70,
9–80, 9–85, 9–91, 9–93, 9–101, 9–108, 9–111, 9–112, 9–129, 9–133,
9–141, 9–142, 9–170, 9–177, 9–179, 9–189, 9–195, 9–224, 9–225, 9–233,
9–245, 14–12
Secretary of State for Defence v Percy [1999] 1 All E.R. 732; *The Times*, May 11, 1998, Ch
D 9–209, 14–40, 14–48, 14–100, 19–2
Secretary of State for Defence v Times Newspapers Ltd, unreported, March 28, 2001,
Blofeld J. 7–55
Secretary of State for Employment v Mann [1996] I.C.R. 197 7–109
Secretary of State for Home Affairs v O'Brien; sub nom. R. v Secretary of State for Home
Affairs Ex p. O'Brien [1923] A.C. 603, HL 2–225
Secretary of State for Trade and Industry v Crane and Burton (No.2), CH/2000/APP/553,
February 11, 2001 12–10
Securities and Investments Board v Pantell SA (No.1) [1990] Ch. 426; [1989] 3 W.L.R. 698;
[1989] 2 All E.R. 673; [1989] B.C.L.C. 590; (1989) 139 N.L.J. 754, Ch D 12–160
Selden's Case, 3 St. Tr. 267 1–23
Seldon v Wilde [1911] 1 K.B. 701 .... 3–55, 3–71, 3–137, 3–152, 3–154, 3–180
Selous v Croydon Local Board (1885) 53 L.T. 209 12–137
Semayne's Case (1604) 5 Co. Rep. 91a; (1604) 77 E.R. 194 3–184
Semayne's Case (1604) Cro. Eliz. 909: (1604) 78 E.R. 1131 15–48
Semple (Andrew) (1586) 16–89
Senior v Holdsworth Ex p. *Independent* Television News [1976] Q.B. 23; [1975] 2 W.L.R.
987; [1975] 2 All E.R. 1009; 119 S.J. 393, CA (Civ Div) 9–66, 11–109
Septimus Parsonage, Re [1901] 2 Ch. 424 14–6
Seraglio, The (1885) 10 P.D. 120 .... 11–325, 12–146
Seven Bishops, Trial of the (1688) 12 St. Tr. 183 2–111
Shalson v Russo (Contempt: Application to Purge) [2002] EWHC 399, Ch D; [2002] All
E.R. (D) 13, Mar 14–13
Shamdasani v King Emperor [1945] A.C. 264, PC (Ind) 3–223, 10–31, 10–34, 10–96, 10–106,
10–136, 10–144, 10–145, 10–146, 11–2
Sharland v Sharland (1885) 1 T.L.R. 492 11–280
Shaw v Shaw (1862) 2 Sw. & Tr. 517; (1862) 164 E.R. 1097 .... 11–216, 11–244, 11–287
Shedden v Patrick (1869) L.R. 1 H.L. Sc. 470 10–131
Sheldrake v DPP; Att-Gen's Reference (No.4 of 2002), Re [2004] UKHL 43; [2005] 1 A.C.
264; [2004] 3 W.L.R. 976; [2005] 1 All E.R. 237; [2005] 1 Cr. App. R. 28; (2004) 168
J.P. 669; [2005] R.T.R. 2; [2004] H.R.L.R. 44; [2005] U.K.H.R.R. 1; 17 B.H.R.C. 339;
(2005) 169 J.P.N. 19; (2004) 101(43) L.S.G. 33; (2004) 148 S.J.L.B. 1216; *The Times*,
October 15, 2004, HL 4–261, 4–262
Shell Co of Australia Ltd v Federal Commissioner of Taxation [1931] A.C. 275 13–55
Shipley's Case (1783) 21 St. Tr. 847 1–69

TABLE OF CASES

Shopee v Nathan & Co [1892] 1 Q.B. 245 12–94
Shrewsbury's Case (Earl of) (1611) 9 Co. Rep. 46b; (1611) 77 E.R. 798 4–145
Sierra Leone v Davenport (No.2); sub nom. Government of Sierra Leone v Davenport [2002]
    EWCA Civ 230; [2002] C.P.L.R. 236, CA (Civ Div) 13–120, 13–122, 15–88, 15–91, 15–95
Silkman v Heard, February 28, 2001, QBD 5–253
Silver & Drake (A Firm) v Baines [1971] 1 Q.B. 396 ... 12–248, 12–250, 12–257, 12–258, 13–98
Simmons v Dean (1858) 27 L.J. O. 103 12–129
Singh (Tejendra) v Christie. *See* Tejendrasingh v Metsons
Sir John Moore Gold Mining Co (1877) 37 L.T. 242 1–72
Sittingbourne & Sheerness Railway Co v Lawson (1886) 2 T.L.R. 605 11–67
Skeen v Farmer, 1980 S.L.T. (Sh. Ct.) 133, Sh Ct (Glasgow) 16–70, 16–233
Skelton v Castle (1837) 6 J.P. 154n 10–158
Sloman (1832) 1 Dowl. 618; (1832) 36 R.R. 827 .... 11–100, 11–114
Smith (1854) 1 Irv. 378 16–118
Smith, Petr, 1987 S.C.C.R. 726 16–424
Smith v Blofield (1813) 2 Ves. & Beam. 100; (1813) 35 E.R. 257 3–159
Smith v Bond 10–157, 10–159, 10–161
Smith v Campbell (1830) 1 Russ. & My. 323; (1830) 39 E.R. 124 3–159
Smith v Forbes. *See* Forbes v Smith
Smith v John Ritchie & Co. (1892) 3 White 408; (1892) 20 R. (J.) 52 .... 16–144, 16–177, 16–178,
                                                                16–224, 16–229, 16–328, 16–329, 16–331
Smith v Justices of Sierra Leone (1841) 3 Moo. P.C. 362; (1841) 13 E.R. 147 10–144
Smith v Justices of Sierra Leone (1848) 7 Moo. P.C. 174; (1848) 13 E.R. 846 .... 10–144, 10–159
Smith v Lakeman (1856) 26 L.J. Ch. 305 .... 11–281, 11–287
Smith v Mitchell (1835) 14 S. 172 16–228
Smith v Smith [1988] 1 F.L.R. 179; [1988] F.C.R. 225; [1988] Fam. Law 21; (1988) 152
    J.P.N. 15, CA (Civ Div) 12–30, 12–31, 14–27, 15–34, 15–71, 19–2
Smith v Smith [1992] 2 F.L.R. 40, CA 15–64, 15–70, 15–74
Smith v Smith (Contempt: Committal) [1991] 2 F.L.R. 55; [1991] F.C.R. 233; [1991] Fam.
    Law 412; (1991) 155 J.P.N. 138; *The Times*, October 8, 1990, CA (Civ Div) 12–11, 12–45
Smith-Barry v Dawson (1891) 27 L.R. Ir. 558 6–137
SmithKline Beecham Biologicals SA v Connaught Laboratories Inc (Disclosure of Docu-
    ments) [1999] 4 All E.R. 498; [1999] C.P.L.R. 505; [2000] F.S.R. 1; (2000) 51
    B.M.L.R. 91; (1999) 22(10) I.P.D. 22092; *The Times*, July 13, 1999; *Independent*, July
    15, 1999, CA (Civ Div) 12–223, 12–224
SmithKline Beecham Plc v Generics (UK) Ltd; BASF AG v SmithKline Beecham Plc [2003]
    EWCA Civ 1109; [2004] 1 W.L.R. 1479; [2003] 4 All E.R. 1302; [2003] C.P. Rep. 66;
    [2004] F.S.R. 8; (2003) 26(11) I.P.D. 26071; (2003) 100(34) L.S.G. 31; *The Times*,
    August 25, 2003, CA (Civ Div) 3–203, 3–208, 11–76, 12–205, 12–226
Sofroniou v Szigetti [1991] F.C.R. 332; *The Times*, September 19, 1990, CA (Civ Div) 15–20
Solicitor, Re a [1996] 1 F.L.R. 40 .... 11–135, 12–250, 12–257
Solicitor (Disclosure of Confidential Records), Re [1997] 1 F.L.R. 101; [1997] 2 F.C.R. 316;
    [1997] Fam. Law 162, Fam Div 7–68, 12–122, 19–1
Solicitor (Wasted Costs Order) (No.1 of 1994), Re; sub nom. Re Ronald A Prior & Co
    (Solicitors) [1996] 1 Cr. App. R. 248; [1996] 1 F.L.R. 40; [1996] 3 F.C.R. 365; [1996]
    Fam. Law 83; (1996) 160 J.P.N. 514; (1995) 92(28) L.S.G. 40; (1995) 139 S.J.L.B.
    157; *The Times*, June 27, 1995, CA (Crim Div) 11–54
Solicitor-General v Henry and News Group Newspapers Ltd [1990] C.O.D. 307, DC 4–246,
                                                                                                    4–247, 19–1
Solicitor-General v Radio Avon Ltd [1978] 1 N.Z.L.R. 225, CA 4–213, 5–205, 5–235, 5–245,
                                                                                                    5–246, 5–268
Solicitor-General v Radio New Zealand [1994] 1 N.Z.L.R. 48, HC Full Ct 2–33, 2–44, 11–29,
                                                                                     11–350, 11–353, 11–384
Solicitor-General v Smith [2004] 2 N.Z.L.R. 540 .... 2–47, 4–120, 5–101, 5–256, 5–269
Solicitor-General v W & H Specialist Publications [2003] N.Z.A.R. 118 ..... 1–170, 2–101, 4–108,
                                                                                                    6–32
Solicitor-General v Wellington Newspapers Ltd [1995] 1 N.Z.L.R. 45 .... 5–94, 5–200
Solicitors, Re (1916) 11 W.W.R. 529 12–250

[cxix]

TABLE OF CASES

Sony Corp v Anand; Kabushika Kaisha Hattori Tokeiten v Domicrest (Fancy Goods) Ltd; Seiko Time (UK) Ltd v Domicrest (Fancy Goods) Ltd [1981] Com. L.R. 55; [1981] F.S.R. 398, Ch D 3–201
Sotham v Smout [1964] 1 Q.B. 308 13–88
Soutar and Brown v Stirling and Ferguson (1888) 2 White 19 ..... 16–28, 16–120, 16–126, 16–128
South Shields (Thames Street) Clearance Order 1931, Re (1932) 173 L.T. 76 4–141
Southam v Smout [1964] 1 Q.B. 308; [1963] 3 W.L.R. 606; [1963] 3 All E.R. 104; 107 S.J. 513, CA 11–311, 15–48
Southwark LBC v Areola, unreported, March 3, 2005, Lewison J. 19–2
Spalding v Lawrie (1836) 14 S. 1102 16–52
Sparks v Martyn (1669) 1 Vent. 1; (1669) 86 E.R. 1 10–96
Special Hospitals Service Authority v Hyde (1994) 20 B.M.L.R. 75 .... 7–236, 9–70, 9–77, 9–85, 9–101, 9–103, 9–104, 9–107, 9–214, 9–226, 9–245, 10–175
Special Reference from the Bahama Islands, Re [1893] A.C. 138, PC (Bah) 3–185, 5–209
Spectravest Inc v Aperknit Ltd [1988] F.S.R. 161, Ch D 12–49, 12–82, 12–90, 12–94
Speight v Gosnay (1891) 60 L.J.Q.B. 231 .... 4–50, 4–228
Spence, Re (1847) 2 Ph. 247; (1847) 41 E.R. 937 6–55
Spencer v Newton (1837) 6 Ad. & E. 623; (1837) 112 E.R. 239 3–146
Spencer v Sillitoe [2002] EWCA Civ 1579; [2003] E.M.L.R. 10; (2002) 146 S.J.L.B. 237, CA (Civ Div) 11–59
Sphere Drake Insurance Plc v Denby [1991] T.L.R. 595 11–109
Spink v HM Advocate, 1989 S.C.C.R. 413 16–408
Spokes v Banbury Board of Health (1865) L.R. 1 Eq. 42 .... 9–201, 12–94, 12–98
Spurrell v De Rechberg (1895) 11 T.L.R. 313 4–132
Stafford BC v Anderson [2003] All E.R. (D) 200 (Jan) 14–92
Stancombe v Trowbridge UDC [1910] 2 Ch. 190 .... 3–97, 3–247, 12–022, 12–80, 12–90, 12–91, 12–92, 12–98, 12–99, 12–103, 12–126, 14–122, 16–242, 16–243
Staple (Mayor of) (1319) Coram Rege roll, T. 13 Edw. II, m.14 1–3
Stark's Trs v Duncan (1906) 8 F. 429 .... 16–234, 16–247, 16–249, 16–258, 16–263, 16–264
Starrs v Ruxton; sub nom. Ruxton v Starrs, 2000 J.C. 208; 2000 S.L.T. 42; 1999 S.C.C.R. 1052; [2000] H.R.L.R. 191; [2000] U.K.H.R.R. 78; 8 B.H.R.C. 1; 1999 G.W.D. 37–1793; *The Times*, November 17, 1999, HCJ 16–302
State v Van Niekerk 1970 (3) S.C.A. 655(T) 5–247
Steel v United Kingdom (24838/94) (1999) 28 E.H.R.R. 603; 5 B.H.R.C. 339; [1998] Crim. L.R. 893; [1998] H.R.C.D. 872; *The Times*, October 1, 1998, ECHR 3–4, 14–110
Steel v United Kingdom (68416/01); Morris v United Kingdom (68416/01) [2005] E.M.L.R. 15; *The Times*, February 16, 2005, ECHR 10–131, 11–88, 15–41, 15–115
Steele v Carmichael, 1993 G.W.D. 11–729 16–81
Steele Ford & Newton v Crown Prosecution Service (No.2); Bradburys v Crown Prosecution Service (No.2); Robin Murray & Co v Crown Prosecution Service (No.2); McGoldrick & Co v Crown Prosecution Service (No.2); sub nom. Holden & Co v Crown Prosecution Service (No.2) [1994] 1 A.C. 22; [1993] 2 W.L.R. 934; [1993] 2 All E.R. 769; (1993) 97 Cr. App. R. 376; [1994] C.O.D. 102; (1993) 143 N.L.J. 850; (1993) 137 S.J.L.B. 152; *The Times*, May 28, 1993; *Independent*, June 10, 1993, HL; reversing [1992] 1 W.L.R. 407; [1992] 2 All E.R. 642; (1992) 89(14) L.S.G. 32; (1991) 141 N.L.J. 1626; 135 S.J.L.B. 196; *The Times*, November 14, 1991, CA (Civ Div) 7–119, 7–274, 7–275, 7–276, 14–138
Steinberg v Pritchard Englefield. *See* Pritchard Englefield (A Firm) v Steinberg
Steiner Products Ltd v Willy Steiner Ltd [1966] 1 W.L.R. 986; [1966] 2 All E.R. 387; [1966] F.S.R. 144; [1966] R.P.C. 369; 110 S.J. 272, Ch D 3–8, 12–20, 12–98, 12–125, 14–101, 14–114, 14–122, 14–124, 15–80
Stephens v Bawden (1581) *Cary's Causes in Chancery*, p.147 1–47
Stephens v Cribb (1991) 4 P.R. N.Z. 337 12–77
Stephens v Hill (1842) 10 M. & W. 28; (1842) 152 E.R. 368 12–248
Stephens v West Australia Newspapers Ltd (1994) 68 A.L.J.R. 765 2–99
Stern v Piper [1997] Q.B. 123; [1996] 3 W.L.R. 715; [1996] 3 All E.R. 385; [1996] E.M.L.R. 413; (1996) 93(22) L.S.G. 27; (1996) 140 S.J.L.B. 175; *The Times*, May 30, 1996; *Independent*, June 17, 1996 (C.S.), CA (Civ Div) 8–124, 11–75, 16–200
Steventon (1802) 2 East 362; (1802) 102 E.R. 407 11–216
Stilwell v Williamson, *The Times*, September 1, 1986, CA 11–313

TABLE OF CASES

Stirling, Petr v Associated Newspapers Ltd, 1960 J.C. 5; 1960 S.L.T. 5; [1960] Crim. L.R. 265, HCJ 5–112, 5–115, 16–71, 16–76, 16–159, 16–166, 16–167, 16–168, 16–175, 16–176, 16–177, 16–182, 16–200, 16–203, 16–269, 16–276, 16–306, 16–307
Stone (1796) 6 T.R. 527 10–89
Storer v British Gas Plc [2000] 1 W.L.R. 1237; [2000] 2 All E.R. 440; [2000] I.C.R. 603; [2000] I.R.L.R. 495; *The Times*, March 1, 2000; *Independent*, March 8, 2000, CA (Civ Div) 7–38
Storey v Storey [1961] P. 63; [1960] 3 W.L.R. 653; [1960] 3 All E.R. 279; 124 J.P. 485; 104 S.J. 825, CA 15–43
Stourton v Stourton [1963] P. 302; [1963] 2 W.L.R. 397; [1963] 1 All E.R. 606; 106 S.J. 960, PDAD 3–110, 3–141, 3–142, 3–143, 3–145
Stow v Maddock (1580) *Cary's Causes in Chancery*, p.115 1–48
Strang v Annan, 1991 S.L.T. 676 16–116
Stroble v California (1951) 343 U.S. 181 4–67
Stuart v Balkis (1884) 50 L.T. 479; (1884) 32 W.R. 676 .... 10–162, 11–98
Stuurman v HM Advocate, 1980 J.C. 111; 1980 S.L.T. (Notes) 95, HCJ Appeal 16–64, 16–161, 16–310, 16–397, 16–399, 16–400, 16–407
Suarez, Re [1918] 1 Ch. 176; (1918) 88 L.J. Ch. 10 .... 12–34, 14–128
Sunday Times v United Kingdom (No.1) (A/30) (1979–80) 2 E.H.R.R. 245; (1979) 76 L.S.G. 328, ECHR 1–104, 1–115, 1–132, 2–32, 2–42, 2–70, 2–74, 2–103, 2–122, 2–125, 2–138, 2–145, 2–157, 2–174, 4–2, 4–14, 4–58, 4–85, 4–91, 4–92, 4–319, 4–330, 5–5, 5–9, 5–22, 5–23, 5–26, 5–44, 5–61, 5–66, 5–136, 5–193, 5–262, 6–6, 6–9, 6–56, 6–87, 6–87, 6–114, 7–165, 7–170, 7–193, 7–227, 7–261, 8–8, 9–17, 9–80, 9–188, 10–37, 11–257, 12–214, 16–328
Sunday Times v United Kingdom (No.2) (A/38) (1981) 3 E.H.R.R. 317, ECHR 5–262, 6–6, 6–136, 9–245
Sunday Times v United Kingdom (A/217) (1992) 14 E.H.R.R. 229, ECHR 2–50
Supply of Ready Mixed Concrete, Re. *See* Director General of Fair Trading v Smiths Concrete Ltd
Surrey (Sheriff), Re (1860) 2 F. & F. 234; (1860) 175 E.R. 1038 .... 10–100, 10–106
Sutherland v Sutherland, *The Times*, April 19 and May 6, 1893 14–28
Swan River, Re; The Pas Transfer Ltd (1975) 51 D.L.R. (3d) 292 12–140
Swaptronics Ltd, Re (1998) 95(36) L.S.G. 33; *The Times*, August 17, 1998, Ch D (Companies Ct) 2–195, 12–79
Sweet v Parsley [1970] A.C. 132; [1969] 2 W.L.R. 470; [1969] 1 All E.R. 347; (1969) 53 Cr. App. R. 221; (1969) 133 J.P. 188; 113 S.J. 86, HL 7–206
Sybron Corp v Barclays Bank Plc [1985] Ch. 299; [1984] 3 W.L.R. 1055; (1984) 81 L.S.G. 1598; (1984) 128 S.J. 799, Ch D 3–198, 3–201, 12–201
Sykes v Beadon (1879) 11 Ch. D. 170 11–59
Symes v Phillips (Costs) [2005] EWCA Civ 663, CA (Civ Div) 14–137
Symonds v Symonds and Harrison (1872) L.R. 2 P. & D. 447 11–336
Systematica Ltd v London Computer Centre Ltd [1983] F.S.R. 313, Ch D 12–175
Szczepanski v Szczepanski [1985] Fam. Law 120; [1985] 6 F.L.R. 468, CA (Civ Div) 3–218, 12–8, 12–9
Sze v Wilson, 1992 S.L.T. 560 16–116

T (AJJ) (An Infant), Re [1970] Ch. 688; [1970] 3 W.L.R. 315; [1970] 2 All E.R. 865; 68 L.G.R. 709; 114 S.J. 550, CA (Civ Div) 11–337
T v United Kingdom (24724/94); V v United Kingdom (24888/94) [2000] 2 All E.R. 1024 (Note); (2000) 30 E.H.R.R. 121; 7 B.H.R.C. 659; 12 Fed. Sent. R. 266; [2000] Crim. L.R. 187; *The Times*, December 17, 1999, ECHR 8–36
TDK Tape Distributors (UK) Ltd v Videochoice Ltd; sub nom. TDK Tape Distributors (UK) Ltd v MS Tak Ltd [1986] 1 W.L.R. 141; [1985] 3 All E.R. 345; (1985) 82 L.S.G. 2818; (1985) 135 N.L.J. 828; (1985) 129 S.J. 574, QBD 11–71, 12–173
THQ/Jakks Pacific LLC v WWF. *See* World Wide Fund for Nature (formerly World Wildlife Fund) v World Wrestling Federation Entertainment Inc (Third Party Application)
TSB Private Bank International SA v Chabra [1992] 1 W.L.R. 231 .... 6–1, 12–171, 14–132
Tabone v Seguna [1986] 1 F.L.R. 591; [1986] Fam. Law 188, CA (Civ Div) 15–61
Taff Vale Ry v Amalgamated Society of Railway Servants [1901] A.C. 426 12–120

[cxxi]

TABLE OF CASES

Tait v Gordon (1828) 6 S. 1056 16–241
Tanfern Ltd v Cameron-MacDonald [2000] 1 W.L.R. 1311; [2000] 2 All E.R. 801; [2001]
　C.P. Rep. 8; [2000] 2 Costs L.R. 260; (2000) 97(24) L.S.G. 41; *The Times*, May 17,
　2000; *Independent*, May 16, 2000, CA (Civ Div) 9–196, 9–245, 13–120, 15–88
Tarlton v Fisher (1781) 2 Doug. 671; (1781) 99 E.R. 426 14–152
Tate Access Floors Inc v Boswell [1991] Ch. 512; [1991] 2 W.L.R. 304; [1990] 3 All E.R.
　303; (1990) 140 N.L.J. 963; (1990) 134 S.J. 1227; *The Times*, June 14, 1990;
　Independent, June 22, 1990, Ch D 3–191, 12–201
Taylor v Att-Gen [1975] 2 N.Z.L.R. 675 .... 5–268, 7–60
Taylor, Re [1912] A.C. 347 11–60
Taylor v Director of the Serious Fraud Office; sub nom. Taylor v Serious Fraud Office [1999]
　2 A.C. 177; [1998] 3 W.L.R. 1040; [1998] 4 All E.R. 801; [1999] E.M.L.R. 1; *The
　Times*, November 4, 1998; *Independent*, November 3, 1998, HL 2–163, 11–76, 11–82,
　　　　　　　　　　　　　　　　　　　　　　　　　　　　　　　　　　　　　　　12–203, 12–236
Taylor v Kilgour (1844) 17 Sc. Ju. 89 .... 16–241, 16–248, 16–251
Taylor v NUM (Yorkshire Area) [1984] I.R.L.R. 445; *The Times*, November 20, 1985 1–137,
　　　　　　　　　　　　　　　　　　　　　　　　　2–220, 6–126, 14–121, 14–126, 14–127
Taylor v Persico, *The Times*, February 12, 1992 15–19
Taylor v Ribby Hall Leisure Ltd [1998] 1 W.L.R. 400; [1997] 4 All E.R. 760; *The Times*,
　August 6, 1997, CA (Civ Div) 12–249, 12–253, 14–149
Taylor v Roe [1893] W.N. 14 15–19
Taylor v Topping [1990] T.L.R. 110 (Lexis); February 9, 1990, Lexis; *The Times*, February
　15, 1990, DC 2–30, 2–205, 4–184, 13–31, 13–33
Taylor v Williams (1830) 4 Moo. & P. 59 11–106
Taylor and Foulstone v National Union of Mineworkers (Yorkshire Area); sub nom. Taylor
　v National Union of Mineworkers [1984] I.R.L.R. 445; *The Times*, November 20,
　1985, HC 3–249
Taylor Made Golf Co Inc v Rata & Rata [1996] F.S.R. 528; (1996) 19(6) I.P.D. 19050, Ch
　D 3–176, 3–191, 3–200, 3–203, 3–208, 12–175, 14–101, 14–135, 19–2
Tejendrasingh v Metsons; Tejendrasingh v Ginn & Co; Tejendrasingh v Pickwell; sub nom.
　Tejendrasingh v Christie; Singh (Tejendra) v Christie [1997] E.M.L.R. 597, CA (Civ
　Div) 12–228, 12–236
Telegraph Group, Ex p. *See* R. (on the application of Telegraph Group Plc) v Sherwood
Television New Zealand Ltd v Quinn [1996] 3 N.Z.L.R. 24 .... 1–144, 2–34
Temple Ex p. (1814) 2 V. & B. 391; (1814) 35 E.R. 367 3–146
Temporal v Temporal [1990] 2 F.L.R. 98, CA 12–128
Tesco Supermarkets Ltd v Nattrass [1972] A.C. 153; [1971] 2 W.L.R. 1166; [1971] 2 All
　E.R. 127; 69 L.G.R. 403; 115 S.J. 285, HL 4–206, 4–209
Thanet's (Earl of) Case (1799) 27 St. Tr. 822 10–88
Theakston v MGN Ltd [2002] EWHC 137; [2002] E.M.L.R. 22, QBD 6–16
Theophanous v Herald & Weekly Times Ltd (1994) 68 A.L.J.R. 713, HC 2–99
Thomas v Churton (1862) 2 B. & S. 475 13–100
Thomas v Gwynne (1845) 8 Beav. 312; (1845) 50 E.R. 123 11–288
Thomas v News Group Newspapers Ltd; sub nom. Thomas v Hughes; Thomas v News
　Group International Ltd [2001] EWCA Civ 1233; [2002] E.M.L.R. 4; (2001) 98(34)
　L.S.G. 43; (2001) 145 S.J.L.B. 207; *The Times*, July 25, 2001; *Independent*, November
　12, 2001 (C.S); *Daily Telegraph*, July 24, 2001, CA (Civ Div) 12–57
Thomason v Thomason [1985] F.L.R. 214, CA 12–15, 12–25
Thompson v Goold & Co [1910] A.C. 409 7–279
Thompson v Gordon (1846) 15 M. & W. 610; (1846) 153 E.R. 993 12–248
Thompson v Mitchell [2004] EWCA Civ 1271; (2004) 148 S.J.L.B. 1032; *The Times*,
　September 13, 2004, CA (Civ Div) 14–34
Thompson's Case (1680) 8 St. Tr. 1 11–317
Thomson v Times Newspapers [1969] 1 W.L.R. 1236; [1969] 3 All E.R. 648; 113 S.J. 549,
　CA (Civ Div) 2–150, 4–181, 4–324, 4–327
Thorgeirson v Iceland (1992) 14 E.H.R.R. 843 2–50
Thorne v Motor Trade Association [1937] A.C. 797 11–299
Thorne Rural DC v Bunting (No.2) [1972] 3 All E.R. 1084; 71 L.G.R. 111, CA (Civ Div) 6–137,
　　　12–182
Thorpe v Gisbourne (1825) 11 Moo. C.P. 55 11–100

[cxxii]

TABLE OF CASES

Thorpe v Thorpe [1998] 2 F.L.R. 127; [1998] 2 F.C.R. 384; [1998] Fam. Law 320, CA (Civ Div) 19–2
Three Rivers DC v Bank of England (Disclosure) (No.4) [2004] UKHL 48; [2005] 1 A.C. 610; [2004] 3 W.L.R. 1274; (2004) 101(46) L.S.G. 34; (2004) 154 N.L.J. 1727; (2004) 148 S.J.L.B. 1369; *The Times*, November 12, 2004; *Independent*, November 16, 2004, HL; reversing [2004] EWCA Civ 218; [2004] Q.B. 916; [2004] 2 W.L.R. 1065; [2004] 3 All E.R. 168; (2004) 101(11) L.S.G. 36; (2004) 154 N.L.J. 382; (2004) 148 S.J.L.B. 297; *The Times*, March 3, 2004; *Independent*, March 10, 2004, CA (Civ Div) 9–13
Thynne v United Kingdom (A/190); Wilson v United Kingdom (11978/86); Gunnell v United Kingdom (12009/86); sub nom. Thynne v United Kingdom (11787/85) (1991) 13 E.H.R.R. 666; *The Times*, December 10, 1990; *Independent*, November 2, 1990; *Guardian*, November 2, 1990, ECHR 2–48
Tilco Plastics Ltd v Skurjat (1966) 57 D.L.R. (2d) 596, Gale C.J.H.C. 6–137
Tink v Rundle (1847) 10 Beav. 318; (1847) 50 E.R. 604 .... 11–320, 14–132
Tinley v Porter (1837) 5 Dowl. 744 11–106
Tito v Waddell (No.2) [1977] Ch. 106 12–254
Tole, Re Ex p. Tole (1933) 50 W.N. (N.S.W.) 216 11–305
Tolstoy Miloslavsky v Aldington [1996] 1 W.L.R. 736; [1996] 2 All E.R. 556; [1996] P.N.L.R. 335; (1996) 93(1) L.S.G. 22; (1996) 140 S.J.L.B. 26; *The Times*, December 27, 1995; *Independent*, January 3, 1996, CA (Civ Div) 1–132, 11–54
Tombling v Universal Bulb Co [1951] 2 T.L.R. 289; [1951] W.N. 247; 95 S.J. 399, CA 10–155
Torney, Ex p. [199] HCA 57 5–264
Totalise Plc v Motley Fool Ltd [2001] EWCA Civ 1897; [2002] 1 W.L.R. 1233; [2003] 2 All E.R. 872; [2002] C.P. Rep. 22; [2002] E.M.L.R. 20; [2002] F.S.R. 50; [2002] Masons C.L.R. 3; (2002) 99(9) L.S.G. 28; (2002) 146 S.J.L.B. 35; *The Times*, January 10, 2002, CA (Civ Div); reversing in part [2001] E.M.L.R. 29; [2001] E.B.L.R. 44; [2001] Masons C.L.R. 87; (2001) 98(19) L.S.G. 37; (2001) 151 N.L.J. 644; (2001) 145 S.J.L.B. 70; *The Times*, March 15, 2001, QBD 1–148, 9–58, 9–105, 9–132
Townend v Townend (1905) 93 L.T. 680 11–104
Townend v Townend [1907] P. 239 .... 12–33, 12–132
Townsend (Marquis), Re (1906) 22 T.L.R. 341 .... 4–9, 4–12
Trustor AB v Smallbone (No.1) PTA 1999/6807/3, CA (Civ Div); [2000] 1 All E.R. 811, Ch D 7–29
Tub v Paul Raymond Organisation Ltd, unreported, May 11, 1993 3–229
Tuck, Re [1906] 1 Ch. 692 15–22
Tudhope v Glass, 1981 S.C.C.R. (Sh. Ct) 336 16–409
Turner v Naval, Military & Civil Service Co-operative Society of South Africa, *The Times*, January 21, 1903 .... 12–142, 12–194
Turner v Sullivan (1862) 6 L.T. (N.S.) 130 4–288
Turner v Turner (1978) 122 Sol. Jo. 696 15–23
Tweedie (1829) Shaw 223 16–117

UKAPE v AUEW [1972] I.C.R. 151 12–118
Udall v Capri Lighting Ltd (In Liquidation) [1988] Q.B. 907 .... 12–248, 12–252, 12–253, 12–254, 12–256, 13–98
Unicargo v Flotec Maritime S de RL (The Cienvik) [1996] 2 Lloyd's Rep. 395; [1996] C.L.C. 434; *Independent*, January 1, 1996 (C.S.), QBD (Admlty) 3–225, 12–161
United Bank of Kuwait v Hammond [1988] 1 W.L.R. 1051, CA 13–98
United Kingdom Central Council for Nursing, Midwifery and Health Visiting v Gifford [1991] C.O.D. 436 11–125
United Kingdom Nirex Ltd v Barton, *The Times*, October 14, 1986, Henry J. 6–137
United Mining and Finance Corp v Becher [1910] 2 K.B. 296 .... 12–248, 12–253, 12–255, 12–257
United Nurses of Alberta v Att-Gen for Alberta (1992) 89 D.L.R. (4th) 609 ... 1–137, 3–71, 3–78, 3–124
United Steelworkers of America, Local 9332 *et al.* and Phillips *et al.*, Re; Att-Gen *et al.*, interveners (1995) 98 C.C.C. (3d) 20, SCC 1–137
United Telephone Co v Dale (1884) 25 Ch. D. 778 12–38
Universal City Studios Inc v Mukhtar & Sons [1976] 1 W.L.R. 568; [1976] 2 All E.R. 330; [1976] F.S.R. 252; 120 S.J. 385, Ch D 12–175

[cxxiii]

Table of Cases

Urquhart v Hamilton, 1996 S.C.C.R. 217, HCJ Appeal 16–80
Usher and Cunningham v Magistrates and Council of Edinburgh and Boyd and Hatton (1839) 1 D. 639 .... 16–235, 16–254
Usill v Hales (1878) L.R. 3 C.P.D. 319 1–73

VDU Installations Ltd v Integrated Computer Systems & Cybernetics Ltd [1989] 1 F.S.R. 378; *The Times*, August 13, 1988, Ch D 3–198, 3–247, 11–71, 11–76, 12–81, 12–179
VgT Verein gegen Tierfabriken v Switzerland (24699/94) (2002) 34 E.H.R.R. 4; 10 B.H.R.C. 473, ECHR 6–20
Vaise v Delaval (1785) 1 T.R. 11; (1785) 99 E.R. 944 .... 10–181, 11–362
Valiant v Dodomede (1743) 2 Atk. 592; (1743) 26 E.R. 754 11–100
Van v Price (1743) Dick. 91; (1743) 21 E.R. 202 11–317
Van Houten v Foodsafe Ltd (1980) 124 Sol. Jo. 277 12–128
Vandervelde v Lluellin (1662) 1 Keb. 220 ; (1662) 83 E.R. 910 .... 11–304, 14–152
Vaughan v Vaughan [1973] 1 W.L.R. 1159; [1973] 3 All E.R. 449; (1973) 4 Fam. Law 123; 117 S.J. 583, CA (Civ Div) 14–29
Vaughton v Brine (1840) 1 Man. & G. 359; (1840) 133 E.R. 373 11–100
Venables v News Group International (Breach of Injunction); Thompson v News Group International; sub nom. Att-Gen v Greater Manchester Newspapers Ltd (2002) 99(6) L.S.G. 30; (2001) 145 S.J.L.B. 279; *The Times*, December 7, 2001; *Daily Telegraph*, December 13, 2001, QBD 1–150, 12–54, 15–29
Venables v News Group Newspapers Ltd; Thompson v News Group Newspapers Ltd [2001] Fam. 430; [2001] 2 W.L.R. 1038; [2001] 1 All E.R. 908; [2001] E.M.L.R. 10; [2001] 1 F.L.R. 791; [2002] 1 F.C.R. 333; [2001] H.R.L.R. 19; [2001] U.K.H.R.R. 628; 9 B.H.R.C. 587; [2001] Fam. Law 258; (2001) 98(12) L.S.G. 41; (2001) 151 N.L.J. 57; (2001) 145 S.J.L.B. 43; *The Times*, January 16, 2001; *Independent*, January 17, 2001; *Daily Telegraph*, January 16, 2001, Fam Div 2–41, 6–47, 6–49, 6–50, 6–51, 6–90, 6–92, 6–94, 6–108, 6–116, 6–146, 6–147, 7–31, 7–102, 8–61, 15–29
Vernon v Bosley (No.2) [1999] Q.B. 18; [1997] 3 W.L.R. 683; [1997] 1 All E.R. 614; [1997] R.T.R. 275; [1998] 1 F.L.R. 304; [1997] P.I.Q.R. P326; (1997) 35 B.M.L.R. 174; [1997] Fam. Law 476; (1997) 94(4) L.S.G. 26; (1997) 147 N.L.J. 89; (1997) 141 S.J.L.B. 27; *The Times*, December 19, 1996; *Independent*, January 21, 1997, CA (Civ Div) 10–134, 10–155
Vicars v Colcough (1779) 5 Bro. Parl. Cas. 31; (1779) 2 E.R. 514 14–120
Vice v Anson (1827) 3 C. & P. 19; (1827) 172 E.R. 304 11–104
Vickers Sons & Maxim Ltd v Evans [1910] A.C. 444 7–279
Victoria v Australian Building Construction Employees' Federation (1982) 152 C.L.R. 25 .... 4–76, 4–120
Vidéotron Ltée v Industries Microlec Produits Electroniques Inc (1993) 96 D.L.R. (4th) 376 ..... 3–19, 3–193
Vidler v Unison [199]] I.C.R. 746 13–63
Vidyasagara v Queen, The [1963] A.C. 589; [1963] 2 W.L.R. 1033; 107 S.J. 337, PC (Cey) 5–239, 10–144, 10–149, 11–78
Villiers v Villiers [1994] 1 W.L.R. 493; [1994] 2 All E.R. 149; [1994] 1 F.L.R. 647; [1994] 2 F.C.R. 702; [1994] Fam. Law 317; (1994) 144 N.L.J. 159; *Independent*, December 27, 1993 (C.S.), CA (Civ Div) 14–14, 14–15, 14–55
Vine Products Ltd v Green. *See* Vine Products Ltd v Mackenzie & Co Ltd (No.1)
Vine Products Ltd v Mackenzie & Co Ltd (No.1); sub nom. Vine Products Ltd v Green [1966] Ch. 484; [1965] 3 W.L.R. 791; [1965] 3 All E.R. 58; [1965] R.P.C. 538; 109 S.J. 793, Ch D 1–83, 4–93, 4–122, 5–9, 5–34, 5–36, 5–38, 5–40, 11–216
Von Hannover v Germany [2004] E.M.L.R. 379; (2005) 40 E.H.R.R. 1 6–73

W (A Minor) (Wardship: Freedom of Publication), Re. *See* Re W (A Minor) (Wardship: Restrictions on Publication)

TABLE OF CASES

W (A Minor) (Wardship: Restrictions on Publication), Re; sub nom. Re W (A Minor) (Wardship: Freedom of Publication) [1992] 1 W.L.R. 100; [1992] 1 All E.R. 794; [1992] 1 F.L.R. 99; [1992] F.C.R. 231; [1992] Fam. Law 69; (1992) 156 L.G. Rev. 350; *The Times*, August 13, 1991; *Independent*, September 3, 1991; *Guardian*, August 7, 1991, CA (Civ Div) 1–139, 2–133, 2–194, 6–85, 6–87, 6–88, 6–90, 6–93, 6–113, 8–63
W (Minors) (Continuation of Wardship), Re [1996] 1 F.C.R. 393, CA (Civ Div) 6–75, 6–86, 6–88, 6–90, 11–337
W (Minors) (Surrogacy), Re [1991] 1 F.L.R. 385; [1991] Fam. Law 180 6–87
W (Wards) (Publication of Information), Re; sub nom. Re W (Minors) (Wardship: Contempt) [1989] 1 F.L.R. 246; [1989] Fam. Law 17; *The Times*, April 30, 1988, DC ... 1–139, 3–192, 6–112, 8–120, 11–337, 12–84, 12–102, 15–35, 15–43
W (Wardship: Discharge: Publicity), Re [1995] 2 F.L.R. 466; [1995] Fam. Law 612, CA (Civ Div) 6–62, 6–67
W v W. *See* S (An Infant) v S
WB v H Bauer Publishing ltd [2002] E.M.L.R. 145 6–49
WEA Records Ltd v Visions Channel 4 Ltd [1983] 1 W.L.R. 721; [1983] 2 All E.R. 589; [1984] F.S.R. 404; (1983) 127 S.J. 362; *The Times*, April 18, 1983, CA (Civ Div) 12–140, 12–176
Waddington v Miah (Otherwise Ullah); sub nom. R. v Miah (Moyna); Waddington v Miah alias Ullah [1974] 1 W.L.R. 683; [1974] 2 All E.R. 377; (1974) 59 Cr. App. R. 149; 118 S.J. 365, HL 2–173
Wade v Broughton (1814) 3 V. & B. 172; (1814) 35 E.R. 444 11–334
Waite v Waite [2001] EWCA Civ 1186, CA (Civ Div) 12–78
Waldie v Duke of Roxburghe (1822) 1 S. 367 16–243
Walker v Junor (1903) 5 F. 1035 16–264
Walker v Wishart (1825) 4 S. 302 16–243
Wallace, Re (1867) L.R. 1 P.C. 106 .... 10–134, 10–143
Wallace v O'Brien, 1994 G.W.D. 9–524 16–122
Wallace's Curator v Wallace, 1924 S.C. 212 16–267
Waller (1633) Cro. Car. 373, 79 E.R. 926 1–37
Wallersteiner v Moir (No.1); sub nom. Moir v Wallersteiner (No.1) [1974] 1 W.L.R. 991; [1974] 3 All E.R. 217; 118 S.J. 464, CA (Civ Div) 4–181, 4–324
Wallis v Valentine [2002] EWCA Civ 1034; [2003] E.M.L.R. 8; (2002) 99(37) L.S.G. 39; *The Times*, August 9, 2002, CA (Civ Div) 11–59
Walter (1799) 3 Esp. 21; (1799) 170 E.R. 524 .... 1–69, 4–200
Ward v Booth (1872) L.R. 14 Eq. 195 14–120
Ward v Swift (1848) 6 Hare 309; (1848) 67 E.R. 1184 11–320
Wardle Fabrics Ltd v G Myristis Ltd [1984] F.S.R. 263, Ch D 9–203, 12–66, 12–140, 12–146, 12–176
Warwick Corp v Russell [1964] 1 W.L.R. 613; [1964] 2 All E.R. 337; 108 S.J. 318, Ch D 15–60
Wason v Walter (1868) L.R. 4 Q.B. 73 .... 2–150, 4–334
Waters v Berd (1580) *Cary's Causes in Chancery*, p.104 1–48
Watkins v AJ Wright (Electrical) Ltd [1996] 3 All E.R. 31; *The Times*, July 15, 1996, Ch D 12–182, 12–201, 12–260
Watson v Watson, unreported, August 10, 1970, Elizabeth Lane J. 3–89, 3–165
Watson and Murray (1820) Shaw (J.) 9 16–154
Watson's Case (1788) 2 T.R. 199 5–222
Watt v Ligertwood (1874) L.R. 2 Sc. & Div. 361; (1874) 1 R. 21 ...... 3–112, 10–106, 16–136, 16–137
Watts v Brains (1600) Cro. Eliz. 695; (1600) 78 E.R. 930 .... 10–179, 10–181
Wealdstone News and Harrow News (1925) 41 T.L.R. 508 5–111
Webb v Page (1843) 1 Car. & Kir. 23; (1843) 174 E.R. 695 .... 11–104, 11–259
Webb v Times Publishing Co Ltd [1960] 2 Q.B. 535 .... 7–16, 9–23, 12–213, 12–222
Webster v Bakewell RDC [1916] 1 Ch. 300 .... 11–71, 11–199, 11–217, 11–289, 11–290
Webster v Southwark LBC [1983] Q.B. 698; [1983] 2 W.L.R. 217; 81 L.G.R. 357; (1983) 127 S.J. 53; *The Times*, November 13, 1982, QBD 12–1, 14–117, 15–78
Weeks v Whiteley (1835) 3 Dowl. P.C. 536; 1 Har. & W. 218 11–317
Welby v Still (1892) 66 L.T. 523; (1892) 8 T.L.R. 202 .... 11–72, 11–216, 11–236, 11–240, 11–244, 11–253. 11–281
Wellesley v Duke of Beaufort (1827) 2 Russ. 1; (1827) 38 E.R. 236 6–53

[cxxv]

Table of Cases

Wellesley v Duke of Beaufort (1831) 2 Russ. and My. 639, 39 E.R. 538 ..... 3–117, 3–141, 3–144, 3–145, 11–332
Wellesley (Lord) v Earl of Mornington (No.2) (1848) 11 Beav. 181; (1848) 50 E.R. 786 .... 6–137, 9–210, 11–34
Welsbach Incandescent Gas Light Co Ltd v M'Mann (1901) 4 F. 395 16–264
Welsh v Steuart (1818) 1 Mur. 397 16–241
Wemyss (1840) Bell's Notes 165 .... 16–109, 16–110
West Oxfordshire DC v Beratec Ltd, *The Times*, October 30, 1986 .... 3–246, 12–94
Westcott v Westcott [1985] Fam. Law 278, CA (Civ Div) 14–38, 15–50
Weston v Central Criminal Court Courts Administrator [1977] Q.B. 32; [1976] 3 W.L.R. 103; [1976] 2 All E.R. 875; 120 S.J. 283, CA (Civ Div) 10–33, 10–140, 10–146, 10–161, 10–214, 11–1, 11–69, 11–78, 11–88, 13–30, 14–139, 15–96
Wettenhall v Wakefield (1833) 10 Bing. 335; (1833) 131 E.R. 934 10–143
Wheeler (1761) 3 Burr. 1256; (1761) 97 E.R. 819 11–54
White v Magistrates of Dunbar, 1915 S.C. 395 .... 16–228, 16–255
White v White [1983] Fam. 54; [1983] 2 W.L.R. 872; [1983] 2 All E.R. 51; (1983) 13 Fam. Law 149, CA (Civ Div) 14–76
Whiteland v Grant (1840) 4 Jur. 1061 11–104
Whitfield v United Kingdom (46387/99); Pewter v United Kingdom (48906/99); Gaskin v United Kingdom (57410/00); Clarke v United Kingdom (57419/00), *The Times*, April 27, 2005, ECHR 11–88
Whitlock v Marriott (1686) 1 Dick. 16; (1686) 21 E.R. 172 11–50
Whitter v Peters. *See* Peart v Stewart
Whitworth v Duncan, *The Times*, January 14, 1893 11–317
Whyte v Whyte, 1913 2 S.L.T. 85 16–267
Wiatt (1723) 8 Mod. 123, 88 E.R. 96 1–59
Wiebalck v Told (1913) 29 T.L.R. 741 15–86
Wilde, Re (1910) W.N. 128 15–8
Wilkes v Wood (1769) 19 St. TR. 1406 .... 2–225, 14–55
Wilkin (1722) K.B. Easter, George I 1–59
Wilkinson v Gordon (1824) 2 Add. 152; (1824) 162 E.R. 250 11–72
Wilkinson v Lord Chancellor's Department; sub nom. Wilkinson v Official Solicitor; Wilkinson v S [2003] EWCA Civ 95; [2003] 1 W.L.R. 1254; [2003] 2 All E.R. 184; [2003] C.P. Rep. 37; [2003] 1 F.C.R. 741; (2003) 100(12) L.S.G. 29; (2003) 147 S.J.L.B. 178; *The Times*, February 7, 2003; *Independent*, February 12, 2003, CA (Civ Div) 5–239, 10–44, 10–45, 10–49, 10–96, 13–120, 15–88
Wilkinson v S. *See* Wilkinson v Lord Chancellor's Department
Willcock v Terrell (1878) 3 Ex. D. 323 .... 14–120, 15–86
William Thomas Shipping Co Ltd, Re; sub nom. HW Dillon & Sons Ltd v William Thomas Shipping Co Ltd; Thomas, Re [1930] 2 Ch. 368, Ch D 4–123, 4–140
Williams v Clark, 2001 S.C.C.R. 505; 2001 G.W.D. 20–758, HCJ Appeal 16–51
Williams v Fawcett [1986] Q.B. 604; [1985] 1 W.L.R. 501; [1985] 1 All E.R. 787; [1986] Fam. Law 52; (1985) 135 N.L.J. 227; (1985) 129 S.J. 224, CA (Civ Div) 15–47, 15–58
Williams v Johns (1773) Dick. 477; (1773) 355 11–317
Williams v Lyons (1723) 8 Mod. R. 189; (1723) 50 E.R. 123 11–287
Williams v Wolman, January 30, 1990, CA 4–324, 6–8
Williamson's case, Chester Docket Book 603–52 fo.166 10–93
Willshire-Smith v Votino Bros Pty Ltd (1992) 67 A. Crim. R. 261 .... 11–72, 11–161, 11–261, 11–281
Wilsher v Wilsher [1989] 2 F.L.R. 187; [1989] Fam. Law 353; *Independent*, March 13, 1989, CA (Civ Div) 14–27, 19–2
Wilson, Petr, 1991 S.C.C.R. 957 16–428
Wilson v John Angus & Sons, 1921 2 S.L.T. 139 .... 16–109, 16–110
Wilson v Metcalfe (1839) 1 Beav. 263 14–120
Wilson v Raffalovich (1881) 7 Q.B.D. 553 12–15
Wilson v Rastall (1792) 4 Term Rep. 758; (1792) 100 E.R. 1283 9–13
Wilson v Sheriffs of London (1620) 1 Brownl. & G. 15; (1620) 123 E.R. 635 ... 10–109
Wilson v Webster [1998] 1 F.L.R. 1097 13–119
Wilson & Whitworth Ltd v Express & *Independent* Newspapers Ltd [1969] R.P.C. 165 12–48
Wilson's case (1843) 7 Q.B. 984; (1843) 115 E.R. 759 10–145
Wilton, Ex p. (1842) 1 Dowl. N.S. 805 .... 11–72, 11–157, 11–158

TABLE OF CASES

Wingfield, Cro. Car., 251, 79 E.R. 819 1–20
Wingrove v United Kingdom (1996) 24 E.H.R.R. 1 6–20
Wiseman, Re [1969] N.Z.L.R. 55 .... 5–243, 10–134
Witham v Holloway (1995) 183 C.L.R. 525 .... 3–245, 12–44, 12–46
Witham v Witham (1668) 3 Ch. Rep. 41; (1668) 21 E.R. 723 11–317
Witten, Re (1887) 4 T.L.R. 36 .... 11–339, 12–35, 12–81
Wong Yeung Ng v Secretary for Justice [1999] HKCFA 50 5–274
Wood (1832) 1 Dowl. 509 11–100
Woodgate v Ridout (1865) 4 F. & F. 202; (1865) 176 E.R. 531 12–213
Woodward v Hutchins [1977] 1 W.L.R. 760; [1977] 2 All E.R. 751 .... 6–18, 11–204
Woodward v Lincoln (Earl of) (1674) 3 Swan. App. 626; (1674) 36 E.R. 1000 .... 9–201, 12–22
Woodward v Twinaine (1839) 9 Sim. 301; (1839) 59 E.R. 373 3–159
Woolley v Woolley, *The Times*, July 17, 1974 15–61
Woolmington v DPP [1935] A.C. 462, HL 4–9
Worboys v Worboys [1953] P. 192; [1953] 2 W.L.R. 901; [1953] 1 All E.R. 857; 97 S.J. 301, PDAD 15–13
Working Men's Mutual Society, Re (1882) 21 Ch. D. 831 .... 11–103, 11–104, 13–96
World Wide Fund for Nature (formerly World Wildlife Fund) v World Wrestling Federation Entertainment Inc (Third Party Application); sub nom. World Wide Fund for Nature v THQ/Jakks Pacific LLC; THQ/Jakks Pacific LLC v WWF [2003] EWCA Civ 401; [2004] F.S.R. 10; (2003) 26(7) I.P.D. 26044; (2003) 147 S.J.L.B. 385, CA (Civ Div) 3–127, 12–104
Worm v Austria (22714/93) (1998) 25 E.H.R.R. 454; 3 B.H.R.C. 180, ECHR 5–23, 5–61
Worthington v Ad-Lib Club [1965] Ch. 236; [1964] 3 W.L.R. 1094; [1964] 3 All E.R. 674; 108 S.J. 801, Ch D 9–201, 12–98, 14–122
Wraynham's Case (1618) 2 St. Tr. 1060 1–19
Wright v Jess [1987] 1 W.L.R. 1076; [1987] 2 All E.R. 1067; [1987] 2 F.L.R. 373; [1987] Fam. Law 380; (1987) 84 L.S.G. 1241; (1987) 131 S.J. 942, CA (Civ Div) 15–13, 15–22, 15–45, 15–58, 15–59, 15–61, 15–62
Wright v Wilkin (1858) 6 W.R. 643 11–72
Wyat v Wingford (1729) 2 Ld. Raym. 1528; (1729) 92 E.R. 491 11–100
Wylam v Wylam & Roller (1893) 69 L.T. 500 11–317
Wylie v HM Advocate, 1966 S.L.T. 149; [1967] Crim. L.R. 422, HCJ Appeal 16–55, 16–57, 16–60, 16–300, 16–429

X (A Child) (Injunctions restraining Publication), Re. *See* Richmond upon Thames LBC v H
X (A Minor) (Wardship: Injunction), Re; sub nom. X County Council v A; X (A Minor), Re; X CC v A [1984] 1 W.L.R. 1422; [1985] 1 All E.R. 53; [1985] Fam. Law 59; (1984) 81 L.S.G. 3259, Fam Div 3–117, 6–48, 12–85, 16–226
X (A Minor) (Wardship: Jurisdiction), Re; sub nom. Re X (A Minor) (Wardship: Restriction on Publication) [1975] Fam. 47; [1975] 2 W.L.R. 335; [1975] 1 All E.R. 697, CA (Civ Div) 6–41, 6–55, 6–85, 6–89, 6–116, 6–121, 6–127, 11–337
X v Dempster [1999] 1 F.L.R. 894; [1999] 3 F.C.R. 757; [1999] Fam. Law 300, Fam Div 8–120, 8–140, 19–1
X v Sweeney, 1982 S.C.C.R. 161 .... 16–310, 16–312, 16–400, 16–402
X v United Kingdom (A/46); sub nom. X v United Kingdom (6998/75) (1982) 4 E.H.R.R. 188, ECHR 2–193, 13–68
X v Z Ltd [1998] I.C.R. 43; *The Times*, April 18, 1997, CA (Civ Div) 8–145
X (A Woman formerly Known as Mary Bell) v O'Brien. *See* X (formerly known as Mary Bell) v SO
X CC v A. *See* Re X (A Minor) (Wardship: Injunction)
X (formerly known as Mary Bell) v SO [2003] EWHC 1101; [2003] E.M.L.R. 37; [2003] 2 F.C.R. 686; [2003] A.C.D. 61, QBD 6–49, 6–92, 6–108, 6–116, 6–146, 7–31, 7–102
X (HA) v Y [1988] 2 All E.R. 648; [1988] R.P.C. 379; (1987) 137 N.L.J. 1062, QBD 7–28, 9–60, 9–130, 9–189, 9–192

[cxxvii]

TABLE OF CASES

X Ltd v Morgan Grampian (Publishers) Ltd [1991] 1 A.C. 1; [1990] 2 W.L.R. 1000; [1990]
    2 All E.R. 1; (1990) 87(17) L.S.G. 28; (1990) 140 N.L.J. 553; (1990) 134 S.J. 546,
    HL 1–126, 2–67, 2–193, 7–236, 7–238, 9–17, 9–18, 9–21, 9–26, 9–33, 9–57, 9–60, 9–67,
                9–69, 9–75, 9–81, 9–82, 9–87, 9–91, 9–94, 9–96, 9–97, 9–126, 9–128,
                9–133, 9–134, 9–137, 9–139, 9–142, 9–147, 9–150, 9–151, 9–163, 9–164,
                9–165, 9–173, 9–175, 9–195, 9–203, 9–214, 9–226, 9–245, 12–67, 12–70,
                                                                12–72, 12–73, 12–78, 12–79

Yager v Musa [1961] 2 Q.B. 214; [1961] 3 W.L.R. 170; [1961] 2 All E.R. 561; 105 S.J. 568,
    CA 14–52
Yanish v Barbour, 232 F. 2d 939 (9th Cir.) 1956 3–76
Yates v Carlisle (1761) 1 Bl. W. 270; (1761) 96 E.R. 150 11–54
Yianni v Yianni [1966] 1 W.L.R. 120; [1966] 1 All E.R. 231 (Note); 110 S.J. 111, Ch D 3–71,
                                                                3–89, 3–188, 3–244, 12–23
Young v Armour, 1921 1 S.L.T. 211 .... 16–219, 16–221
Young v United States ex rel. Vuitton et Fils SA, 481 U.S. 787 (1987) 3–59, 3–175

Z (A Minor) (Freedom of Publication), Re; sub nom. Re Z (A Minor) (Identification:
    Restrictions on Publication) [1997] Fam. 1; [1996] 2 W.L.R. 88; [1995] 4 All E.R. 961;
    [1996] 1 F.L.R. 191; [1996] 2 F.C.R. 164; [1996] Fam. Law 90, CA (Civ Div) 1–140, 2–41,
                2–158, 2–194, 4–334, 6–41, 6–54, 6–55, 6–58, 6–61, 6–62, 6–65, 6–67,
                6–68, 6–73, 6–77, 6–82, 6–83, 6–86, 6–108, 6–109, 6–113, 11–337,
                                                                                        11–331
Z (A Minor) (Identification: Restrictions on Publication). See Re Z (A Minor) (Freedom of
    Publication)
Z Bank v D1 [1994] 1 Lloyd's Rep. 656, QBD (Comm) 12–44, 12–45, 12–94, 12–171
Z v Finland (1998) 25 E.H.R.R. 371; (1999) 45 B.M.L.R. 107, ECHR 2–164, 7–107
Z Ltd v A-Z and AA-LL; sub nom. Mareva Injunction, Re [1982] Q.B. 558; [1982] 2 W.L.R.
    288; [1982] 1 All E.R. 556; [1982] 1 Lloyd's Rep. 240; [1982] E.C.C. 362; 126 S.J.
    100, CA (Civ Div) 1–66, 3–26, 3–97, 3–117, 3–127, 6–126, 6–137, 7–92, 7–205, 11–343,
                12–81, 12–86, 12–98, 12–102, 12–104, 12–145, 12–146, 12–198, 14–123,
                                                                                        14–127
Zubelake v UBS Warburg LLC, WL 22410169 11–86

TABLE OF STATUTES

(References are to paragraph numbers)

1449 (c.17)	....	16–88		
1457 (c.76)	....	16–88		
1469 (c.26)	....	16–88		
1487 (c.103)	....	16–88		
1487 (c.105)	....	16–88		

1449 (c.17) 16–88
1457 (c.76) 16–88
1469 (c.26) 16–88
1487 (c.103) 16–88
1487 (c.105) 16–88
1540 Statute of the 7th Parliament of James V of Scotland (c.104) (Judges Act) 16–87, 16–286
1331 Unlawful Attachment Act (5 Edw.3) 1–85
1351 Treason Act (25 Edw.3 c.2) 10–91
1619 Lord Chancellor Bacon's Ordinance 1–50
1640 Act for the Abolition of the Star Chamber (16 Car. 1 c.10) ... 1–38
1688 Bill of Rights (1 Will. & Mar. Sess.2 c.2) Art.9 4–334
1693 Court of Session Act (5 & 6 Will. & Mar. c.27) 16–204
1792 Fox's Libel Act (32 Geo.3 c.60) 1–69
1805 Writ of Subpoena Act (45 Geo.3 c.92) 11–119
1814 Treason Act (54 Geo.3 c.146) s.1 10–92
1825 Juries Act (6 Geo.4 c.50) s.38 11–140
s.61 11–179
1828 Licensing (Scotland) Act (9 Geo.4 c.58) 16–32
1830 Contempt of Court Act (11 Geo.4 & 1 Will.4 c.36) 1–85
1832 Contempt of Court Act (2 & 3 Will.4 c.58) 1–85
1832 Reform Act 1–69
1833 Fines Act (3 & 4 Will.4 c.99) 14–109, 17–1
1843 Libel Act (Lord Campbell's Act) (6 & 7 Vict. c.96) s.7 1–69
1848 Indictable Offences Act (11 & 12 Vict. c.42) s.17 1–73
1850 Police Act (13 & 14 Vict. c.33) s.360 16–129

1853 Evidence Act (16 & 17 Vict. c.20) s.3 16–258
1853 Licensing (Scotland) Act (16 & 17 Vict.66) 16–32
1856 Police and Improvement (Scotland) Act s.360 16–129
1860 Court of Chancery Act (23 & 24 Vict. c.149) 1–85
1861 Forgery Act (24 & 25 Vict. c.98) s.30 11–49
1861 Offences Against the Person Act (24 &25 Vict. c.100) s.18 4–156
s.20 6–107
s.47 12–12
1862 Public Houses Acts Amendment (Scotland) Act (25 & 26 Vict. c.35) 16–27
s.27 16–129
1867 Vaccination Act (30 & 31 Vict. c.84) s.31 3–220
1869 Debtors Act (32 & 33 Vict. c.62) 12–110, 12–124, 12–136, 12–199, 13–123, 15–52
s.4 .... 3–148, 15–8, 15–56
s.4(4) 3–148, 3–150
s.5 .... 13–118, 15–52
1870 Juries Act (33 & 34 Vict. c.77) 2–111
1871 Regulation of Railways Act (34 & 35 Vict.c.78) s.7 8–150
1873 Supreme Court of Judicature Act (36 & 37 Vict. c.66) ... 5–80, 12–259
ss 4, 6 3–133
s.19 3–133
s.47 .... 3–88, 3–103, 3–133
s.47(1) 1–74, 3–30, 13–119
1878 Debtors Act (41 & 42 Vict. c.54) 12–110, 12–124, 12–136, 12–199, 15–52

Table of Statutes

1879	Edinburgh Municipal and Police Act	
	s.97	16–129
	s.341	16–99
1887	Sheriffs Act (50 & 51 Vict. c.55)	
	s.8(1) 11–326,	11–327
	s.8(2)	11–326
	s.39(1)(d)	11–327
1887	Coroners Act (50 & 51 Vict. c.71)	
	s.19(1), (2)	17–1
	s.23	17–1
1888	Law of Libel Amendment Act (51 & 52 Vict. c.64)	4–274
	s.3 .... 4–287, 7–17,	7–112
1889	Public Bodies Corrupt Practices Act (52 & 53 Vict. c.69)	9–190
1890	Supreme Court of Judicature Act (53 & 54 Vict. c.44)	
	s.5 7–277,	7–278
1892	Witnesses (Public Inquiries) Protection Act (55 & 56 Vict. c.64)	
	s.2	**16–282**
	s.4	14–148
1897	Juries Detention Act (60 & 61 Vict. c.18)	
	s.1	10–185
1906	Prevention of Corruption Act (6 Edw.7 c.34)	9–190
1907	Criminal Appeal Act (7 Edw.7 c.23) 3–105, 3–139,	13–119
1907	Sheriff Courts (Scotland) Act (7 Edw.7 c.51)	
	s.3	16–262
	s.13	16–285
	s.27	16–262
1908	Costs in Criminal Cases Act (8 Edw.7 c.15)	
	s.6	3–152
1908	Summary Jurisdiction (Scotland) Act (8 Edw.7 c.65)	
	s.36	16–129
1911	Perjury Act (1 & 2 Geo.5 c.6)	
	s.7	2–13
1911	Small Landholders (Scotland) Act (1 & 2 Geo.5 c.49)	16–110
	s.25(2)	16–47
1914	Bankruptcy Act (4 & 5 Geo.5 c.59)	14–121
1920	Maintenance Orders (Facilities for Enforcement) Act (10 & 11 Geo.5 c.33)	8–77
1920	Official Secrets Act (10 & 11 Geo.5 c.75)	
	s.8(4)	7–61
1921	Tribunals of Inquiry (Evidence) Act (11 & 12 Geo.5 c.7) 8–148, 13–77,	17–1
1921	Tribunals of Inquiry (Evidence) Act —*cont.*	
	s.1(2)	4–21
	s.1(2)(c)	13–73
	s.20	16–344
	s.20(2)	16–344
1925	Supreme Court of Judicature (Consolidation) Act (15 & 16 Geo.5 c.49)	
	s.18 13–17,	13–23
	s.31(1)(a) 3–133,	13–119
	s.61	7–36
1925	Criminal Justice Act (15 & 16 Geo.5 c.86)	
	s.41 .... 2–61, 2–222,	10–206
	s.41(1) 10–190,	**10–202**
	s.41(2)(c)	**10–202**
1926	Criminal Appeal (Scotland) Act (16 & 17 Geo.5 c.15)	16–300
	s.13	16–428
1926	Judicial Proceedings (Regulation of Reports) Act (16 & 17 Geo. 5 c.61) 7–71, 8–1, 8–128,	16–230
	s.1 .... **8–2**, 8–8,	8–10
	s.1(1)(a), (b)	8–3
	s.1(1)(b) 8–5, 8–10, 8–13,	8–14
1933	Children and Young Persons Act (23 &24 Geo.5 c12)	8–93
	s.37 8–25,	8–71
	s.39 .... 2–56, 6–97, 6–100, 6–101, 6–102, 7–67, 7–81, 8–22, 8–25, 8–42, 8–45, 8–50, 8–51, 8–53, 8–55, 8–57, 8–58, 8–59, 8–60, 8–61, 8–62, 8–68, 8–86,	13–25
	s.39(1) 8–52,	8–68
	s.39(2)	8–53
	s.39(3)	8–53
	s.44(1)	8–65
	s.45 8–26,	8–35
	s.45(2)	8–35
	s.46 8–41,	8–53
	s.47 .... 7–40, 8–25, 8–26,	8–41
	s.47(2) 7–6,	8–26
	s.49 .... 1–145, 8–25, 8–26, 8–32, 8–45, 8–46, 8–53, 8–63,	8–66
	s.49(1) 8–27,	8–58
	s.49(2)	8–39
	s.49(4A) 8–25, 8–35,	8–37
	s.49(4B) 2–58, 8–25,	8–35
	s.49(5) 8–25, 4–29, 8–32, 8–33,	8–35
	s.49(8)	8–34
	s.49(9)	8–27
	s.49(10)	8–47
	s.107(1)	8–28
1933	Administration of Justice (Miscellaneous Provisions) Act (23 & 24 Geo.5 c.36)	
	s.2(2)(b)	11–146

Table of Statutes

1933 Administration of Justice (Scotland) Act (23 & 24 Geo 5 c.41)
s.6 16–261
s.6(4) 16–235
1936 Public Order Act (1 Edw.8 & 1 Geo.6 c.6)
s.5 10–125
1940 Law Reform (Miscellaneous Provisions) (Scotland) Act (3 & 4 Geo.6 c.42)
s.1 16–265
s.1(1) 16–265
1945 Criminal Justice Act (Northern Ireland)(c.15)
s.35 17–1
1947 Crown Proceedings Act (10 & 11 Geo.6 c.44) 16–240
s.2(2) 2–223
Sch.2 2–223
1948 Local Government Act (11 & 12 Geo.6 c.26)
s.44(1) 13–52
1948 National Assistance Act (11 & 12 Geo.6 c.29) 10–113
s.43 8–77
1948 Criminal Justice Act (11 & 12 Geo.6 c.58) 14–60
s.19 17–1
s.35(4) 2–111
1949 Marriage Act (12, 13 & 14 Geo.6 c.76)
s.3 8–77
1950 Shops Act (14 Geo.6 c.28)
s.47 2–215
1950 Maintenance Orders Act (14 Geo.6 c.37)
Pt II 8–77
1952 Customs and Excise Act (15 & 16 Geo.6 & 1 Eliz. c.44)
s.56(2) 7–126
1952 Magistrates' Courts Act (15 & 16 Geo.6 & 1 Eliz. c.55)
s.54(3) 14–7
1952 Defamation Act (15 & 16 Geo.6 & 1 Eliz.2 c.66)
s.7 .... 1–51, 4–287
Sch. 4–287
1954 Summary Jurisdiction (Scotland) Act (2 & 3 Eliz.2 c.48)
s.3 16–290
s.33 .... 16–129, 16–290
s.33(2) 16–130
s.33(3) 16–19
1954 Landlord and Tenant Act (2 & 3 Eliz.2 c.56)
s.16(2) 12–134
s.16(2)(a), (b) 12–134

1955 Army Act (3 & 4 Eliz.2 c.18)
s101 13–77
1955 Air Force Act (3 & 4 Eliz. c.19)
s.101 13–77
1957 Naval Discipline Act (5 & 6 Eliz.2 c.53)
s.65 13–77
1958 Maintenance Orders Act (6 & 7 Eliz.2 c.39)
Pt I 8–77
1959 Coroners Act (Northern Ireland) (c.15)
s.20(1), (2) 17–1
1959 County Courts Act (7 & 8 Eliz.2 c.22)
s.74 14–25
1959 Mental Health Act (7 & 8 Eliz.2 c.72) 8–98, 8–131
1960 Indecency with Children Act (c.33) 8–19
1960 Mental Health (Scotland) Act (c.61) 16–288
1960 Administration of Justice Act (c.65) 1–75, 1–85, 3–130, 4–16, 11–129
s.1(2)–(4) 15–103
s.1(2) 13–133, 15–104
s.2 15–103
s.2(1) 4–236, 15–106
s.2(3) 15–106
s.9 4–236
s.11 ..... 4–236, 4–238, 4–241, 4–254, 4–257, 16–171, 16–362, 17–1
s.11(1) 5–88, **16–280**
s.12 .... 2–62, 4–260, 4–282, 6–55, 6–69, 6–75, 7–44, 7–58, 7–62, 7–63, 7–74, 7–135, 7–223, 8–48, 8–97, 8–98, 8–100, 8–101, 8–103, 8–104, 8–106, 8–107, 8–117, 8–119, 8–120, 8–123, 8–125, 8–128, 8–129, 8–131, 8–135, 8–136, 8–138, 11–81, 12–227, 13–68, 13–69, 15–16
s.12(1) 7–43, 7–46, 7–51, 8–48, 8–102, 8–135
s.12(1)(a)–(d) 8–117
s.12(1)(a)–(e) 8–134
s.12(1)(a) 8–106
s.12(1)(b) 8–133, 13–67
s.12(1)(e) 7–84
s.12(2) 8–120
s.12(4) ... 8–99, 8–107, 8–134, 8–135, 8–136

[cxxxi]

Table of Statutes

1960 Administration of Justice Act
—*cont.*
s.13 .... 1–126, 3–30, 3–139, 3–185,
9–237, 10–65, 10–73, 10–116,
10–118, 11–120, 11–143, 13–87,
13–120, 13–122, 13–130, 13–132,
14–63, 15–88, 15–89, 15–90,
15–96, 15–98, 15–101, 15–104,
15–111
s.13(1) 12–116, 12–117, 12–118,
13–118, 14–144, 15–91
s.13(2) 9–236, 13–119, **13–125**,
15–88, 15–93, 15–95
s.13(2)(a) ... 10–115, 13–127, 13–133
s.13(2)(b) ... 13–120, 13–126, 13–133
s.13(2)(bb) 13–126
s.13(2)(c) 13–133
s.13(3) 13–85, 13–118, 13–134,
15–38, 15–45, 15–46, 15–62,
15–70, 15–72
s.13(4) 15–103, 15–105
s.13(5) 13–118, 13–123, 15–133
s.17(1)(b) 13–119
s.19 4–236
1961 Mental Health Act (Northern
Ireland) (c.15)
s.48 17–1
1963 Betting, Gaming and Lotteries
Act (c.2) 13–60
1963 Children and Young Persons Act
(c.37)
s.57(1) 8–50
s.64(3) 8–50
Sch.5 8–50
1963 Ecclesiastical Jurisdiction Measure (m.1)
Pt IV 7–72
s.28(f) 7–72
1964 Magistrates' Courts Act (Northern Ireland) (c.21)
s.122 17–1
s.161 .... **17–1**
1964 Public Libraries and Museums
Act (c.75)
s.7 11–6
1964 Diplomatic Privileges Act
(c.81) 3–146
1965 Backing of Warrants (Republic
of Ireland) Act (c.45) ... 7–40, 8–41
Sch., para.2 8–40
1965 Criminal Procedure (Attendance
of Witnesses) Act (c.69) 10–171,
11–116, 11–142
s.2 11–134
s.2(1) 11–118
s.2A 11–120, 11–134
ss 2C, 2E 11–116
s.2C 11–127
s.2C(1)(c) 11–127
s.3 .... 11–116, 11–120, 11–139

1965 Criminal Procedure (Attendance
of Witnesses) Act—*cont.*
s.3(1A) 11–120
s.8 .... 11–116, 13–34
Sch.2, Pt I 11–119
1967 General Rate Act (c.9)
s.39 13–48
1967 Parliamentary Commissioner
Act (c.13)
s.7 13–77
s.9(1) 13–77
1967 Legal Aid (Scotland) Act
(c.43) 16–347
1967 Criminal Law Act (c.58)
ss 4, 5 11–222
s.10 11–179
s.10(2) 11–326, 11–327
Sch.3, Pt III 11–326, 11–327
Sch.3, Pt IX 11–179
1967 Criminal Justice Act (c.80) 8–87,
14–60
s.1(1) 3–67
s.3 .... 2–81, 16–307
s.8 5–155
s.8(b) 5–156
1968 Criminal Appeal Act (c.19)
s.2(1) 4–172
s.7 5–103
s.17 11–146
s.23 .... 3–42, 3–239
s.23(1) 3–239, 11–373, 12–65
1968 Courts-Martial (Appeals) Act
(c.20) 13–16
1968 Trade Descriptions Act (c.29) 4–206
1968 Domestic and Appellate Proceedings (Restriction of
Publicity) Act (c.63) 8–11
s.1(1) 7–41
s.2 .... **8–13**
s.2(1)(c)8–14
s.2(1)(d) 8–14
1968 Children and Young Persons Act
(Northern Ireland) (c.34)
s.72 17–1
1968 Civil Evidence Act (c.64)
Pt I 3–191
s.11 3–191
s.14 3–191
s.14(1)(a) 3–191
s.18(1)(a) 3–120
1968 Gaming Act (c.65) 13–60
1968 Race Relations Act (c.68)
s.2(1) 4–43
1968 Justices of the Peace Act (c.69)
s.1(7) 14–110
1969 Children and Young Persons Act
(c.54)
s.10(1), (2) 8–39
s.10(2) 8–47

Year	Statute	Reference
1970	Administration of Justice Act (c.31)	
	s.4(4)	11–99
	s.11	15–56
	s.41	14–22
	Sch.3, para.1(c)	11–99
	Sch.3, para.5	11–99
1970	Matrimonial Proceedings and Property Act (c.45)	
	s.42(1)	8–14
	Sch.2, para.3	8–14
1971	Courts Act (c.23)	7–228, 7–278, 13–23
	s.4(1)	13–24
	s.56(1), (4)	13–126
	Sch.8, Pt II, para.40(1)	13–126
	Sch.11, Pt II	13–126
1971	Attachment of Earnings Act (c.32)	
	s.23(1A)	17–1
1971	Misuse of Drugs Act (c.38)	16–397
1971	Criminal Damage Act (c.48)	5–130
1971	Sheriff Courts (Scotland) Act (c.58)	
	Sch.2	16–285
1971	Industrial Relations Act (c.72)	
	s.154	12–118
1972	Maintenance Orders (Reciprocal Enforcement) Act (c.18)	
	Pt I	8–77
1972	Land Charges Act (c.61)	
	s.6(1)(a), (b)	14–120
	s.6(4)	14–120
1973	Matrimonial Causes Act (c.18)	
	s.8(2)	8–11
	s.22	8–14
	s.27	8–14
	s.35	8–77
	Sch.2, para.7(1)	8–13
1973	Statute Law (Repeals) Act (c.39)	16–286
1973	Powers of Criminal Courts Act (c.62)	14–143
	s.2(1)	3–60, 14–98, 14–143
	s.14	14–100
	s.19(1)	14–60, 17–1
	s.21	3–60, 10–63
	s.21(1)	10–63, 13–108
	ss 21, 22	14–143
1974	Local Government Act (c.7)	
	s.26	13–77
	s.29(8)	13–77
1974	Juries Act (c.23)	
	s.2(5)	10–178, 11–139
	s.4	11–139
	s.8	11–139
	s.9(1)	10–82
	s.9(4)	10–83
	s.9A	10–75, 10–82, 10–83, 11–139
	s.9A(3)	11–141
1974	Juries Act—cont.	
	s.9B	11–141
	s.9B(2)	11–141
	s.13	10–186, 10–187
	s.17	10–83, 10–179
	s.20	11–138, **11–139**, 11–140
	s.20(1)	2–14, 11–143
	s.20(1)(b)	10–188, 11–140
	s.20(2)	10–178
	s.20(5)	10–178
	Sch.1, Pt 2	11–139
1974	Solicitors Act (c.47)	
	s.40(2)	11–71
	s.45(1)	11–97
	s.47(2)(a)	11–68
	s.50	7–274, 7–277
	s.50(1), (2)	11–67
	s.50(2)	**12–259**
	s.51(3)	11–67, 12–259
1974	Rehabilitation of Offenders Act (c.53)	5–253
1975	District Courts (Scotland) Act (c.20)	16–299
1975	Criminal Procedure (Scotland) Act (c.21)	
	s.145(4)	16–21
	s.207	17–1
	s.208	17–1
	ss 219	4–177, 17–1
	s.252	16–391
	s.252(d)	16–391
	s.230	16–427
	s.344	16–422
	s.344(2)	16–115
	s.415	17–1
	s.416	17–1
	s.432	4–177, 17–1
	Sch.10	16–130
1975	Employment Protection Act (c.71)	
	s.87	13–21
	Sch.6, para.10	13–21
1976	Fatal Accident and Sudden Deaths Inquiry (Scotland) Act (c.14)	
	s.4(4)	16–230
1976	Adoption Act (c.36)	8–79, 8–80
	s.34	8–77
	s.66(5)	8–77, 8–107
1976	Domestic Violence and Matrimonial Proceedings Act (c.50)	1–125, 11–42, 12–57, 14–73, 14–86
	s.1	9–205
	s.2(1), (2)	14–71
	s.2(2)	14–76
1976	Bail Act (c.63)	
	s.6	11–129
	s.6(5), (7)	11–129
	sch.1, Pt I	11–185

Table of Statutes

Year	Act	Reference
1976	Supplementary Benefits Act (c.71)	
	s.18	8–77
1976	Sexual Offences (Amendment) Act (c.82)	8–17
	s.6	8–24
1977	Protection from Eviction Act (c.43)	
	s.1(1)	5–122
1977	Criminal Law Act (c.45)	
	s.10	11–315, 11–326, 13–88
	s.10(1)	11–326
	s.10(6)	11–326
1978	Domestic Proceedings and Magistrates' Courts Act (c.22)	
	Pt I	8–77
	s.60	8–77
1978	Interpretation Act (c.30)	7–278
1978	Protection of Children Act (c.37)	8–93
1978	Employment Protection (Consolidation) Act (c.44)	
	s.128	13–64
	s.131	13–64
	Sch.9	13–64
	Sch.11, para.23(1)	17–1
1980	Employment Act (c.42)	
	Sch.1, para.30	17–1
1980	Magistrates' Courts Act (c.43)	13–117, 16–351
	s.1	11–146
	s.7	2–108
	s.8	1–73, 7–120, 7–128, 8–87, **8–88**, 8–90, 16–230, 16–307
	s.8(2)	7–126
	s.8(3)	4–277, 7–112
	s.8(10)	8–102
	s.36	10–113, 17–1
	s.51	13–112
	s.53(1), (2)	13–112
	s.54	13–112
	s.55	13–112
	s.55(1), (2)	13–113
	s.55(3)	13–115
	s.63(3)	3–178, 12–3, 13–116, 13–123, 13–133, 17–1
	s.65(1), (2)	8–77
	s.69	7–6, **8–79**
	s.69(2)(b)	8–26
	s.71	8–80
	s.71(3), (4)	8–81
	s.71(5)	8–82
	ss 75–91	10–113, 17–1
	s.77(2)	14–23
	s.93	14–22
	s.97	11–130, 14–21, 14–22
	s.97(1)	11–134, 13–112
	s.97(2)	11–130
	s.97(3)	10–171, 11–131
	s.97(4)	10–158, 11–132, 17–1
1980	Magistrates' Courts Act—*cont.*	
	s.101	13–112
	s.108	10–113, 13–124, 13–128, 13–133, 17–1
	s.121(1)	13–112
	s.121(3)(a)	13–112
	s.121(4)	7–36
	s.123	13–112
	s.123(1), (2)	13–113, **13–114**
	s.127	13–114
	ss 128, 129	14–88
	s.136	17–1
	s.142(1)	10–113, 17–1
	s.143	13–108
	s.144	8–76
	s.145(1)(ga)	8–77, 8–107
	s.154	13–133
	Sch.6A	13–108
	Sch.7, para.36	13–133
1980	Criminal Justice (Scotland) Act (c.62)	
	s.2	16–339
	s.42	16–420
	s.45	17–1
	Sch.2, para.16	16–391
1981	Criminal Justice (Amendment) Act (c.27)	7–126
1981	Forgery and Counterfeiting Act (c.45)	11–48
1981	Criminal Attempts Act (c.47)	11–11, 11–147, 11–220
	s.1(1), (4)	11–15
	s.1(1)	11–367
	s.6(1)	11–15
1981	Contempt of Court Act (c.49)	1–85, 1–86, 1–114, 1–115, 1–126, 1–135, 1–167, 1–180, 2–32, 2–40, 2–70, 2–73, 2–145, 2–155, 2–161, 2–194, 3–24, 3–156, 3–167, 4–85, 4–272, 5–132, 5–186, 5–193, 7–78, 8–1, 8–30, 10–112, 10–223, 11–266, 16–257, 16–339, 16–361
	ss 1–3	14–141
	ss 1–5	4–191
	ss 1–6	16–338
	ss 1–7	2–123
	ss1, 2	1–101, 4–1, 4–185, 4–186, 4–188, 4–194, 5–1, 5–25, 5–27, 5–135, 6–23, 7–91, 7–208, 9–59, 10–192, 11–344, 11–378, 12–86, 16–331
	s.1	1–118, 4–1, 4–16, 11–345, **17–1**
	s.1(1)	4–15, 4–234
	s.1(3)(a)	4–5, 4–234
	s.1(3)(d)	4–5
	s.1(3)(e)	4–5

Table of Statutes

1981 Contempt of Court Act—*cont.*
    s.2 .... 3–92, 4–32, 4–37, 4–48, 4–89, 4–90, 4–155, 4–182, 4–191, 5–13, 5–57, 5–75, 6–75, 16–189, 16–338, 16–354, 16–356, **17–1**
    s.2(1) 4–24, 4–31, 4–33, 4–34, 4–50, 5–12, 6–31, 8–102, 9–59
    s.2(2) 1–127, 4–54, 4–90, 4–96, 4–97, 4–105, 4–107, 4–149, 4–150, 4–151, 4–153, 4–172, 4–320, 5–8, 5–15, 5–134, 7–134, 7–165, 7–174, 7–175, 7–196, 16–303, 16–331, 16–402
    s.2(3) 4–120, 4–175, 5–62
    s.2(5) 4–24
    s.3 .. 2–53, 4–4, 4–51, 4–223, 4–236, 4–238, 4–242, 4–249, 4–254, 4–255, 4–256, 4–260, 4–318, 4–320, 4–337, 14–141, 16–182, 16–280, 16–362, 16–363, **17–1**
    s.3(1), (2) 4–232, 4–238
    s.3(2) 4–234, 4–235, 4–252
    s.3(3) 4–261
    s.4 .. 1–73, 2–57, 4–4, 4–188, 7–112, 7–190, 16–370, **17–1**
    s.4(1) 2–53, 4–265, 4–268, 4–278, 4–283, 4–285, 4–286, 4–291, 4–292, 4–320, 4–337, 7–17, 7–112, 7–149, 7–150, 7–151, 7–159, 7–178, 7–180, 8–89, 8–100, 16–211, 16–368, 16–369, 16–371, 16–373
    s.4(2) 1–127, 2–5, 2–38, 2–40, 2–56, 2–61, 2–62, 2–135, 3–52, 3–94, 3–106, 3–107, 4–77, 4–168, 4–290, 4–292, 5–92, 6–2, 6–97, 6–98, 7–84, 7–93, 7–109, 7–111, 7–113, 7–115, 7–116, 7–117, 7–119, 7–122, 7–123, 7–124, 7–127, 7–128, 7–129, 7–130, 7–131, 7–132, 7–133, 7–134, 7–135, 7–136, 7–137, 7–138, 7–139, 7–142, 7–143, 7–145, 7–147, 7–148, 7–149, 7–152, 7–153, 7–155, 7–156, 7–157, 7–159, 7–160, 7–163, 7–165, 7–168, 7–171, 7–172, 7–174, 7–176, 7–178, 7–183, 7–191, 7–196, 7–199, 7–200, 7–201, 7–205, 7–206, 7–208, 7–210, 7–214, 7–217, 7–218, 7–221, 7–223, 7–225, 7–226, 7–228, 7–234, 7–235, 7–237, 7–238, 7–239, 7–240, 7–241, 7–243, 7–244, 7–245, 7–248, 7–253, 7–254, 7–257, 7–258, 7–265, 7–272, 8–16, 8–49, 8–59, 8–90, 9–83, 9–215, 9–216, 9–220, 9–221, 9–238, 10–107,

1981 Contempt of Court Act—*cont.*
    s.4(2)—*cont* 12–1, 13–25, 13–36, 16–201, 16–319, 16–371, 16–373, 16–374, 16–376, 16–377, 16–378, 16–379, 16–380
    s.4(3) 4–277, 4–278, 4–280, 8–89
    s.4(4) 8–88
    s.5 .... 1–96, 1–119, 1–127, 2–43, 2–53, 2–181, 2–182, 4–4, 4–147, 4–188, 4–293, 4–294, 4–300, 4–303, 4–306, 4–310, 4–312, 4–314, 4–315, 4–316, 4–317, 4–320, 4–331, 4–337, 5–189, 5–203, 6–31, 7–172, 9–144, 14–141, 16–192, 16–199, 16–322, 16–324, 16–331, 16–364, 16–365, 16–367, **17–1**
    s.6 .... 4–321, 5–1, 5–9, **17–1**
    s.6(a) 4–4, 4–321, 4–327, 4–329
    s.6(b) 7–132, 7–133
    s.6(c) 1–128, 4–90, 4–91, 4–129, 4–266, 5–7, 5–46, 5–67, 5–70, 5–73, 5–74, 5–92, 5–138, 5–144, 5–145, 5–150, 11–11
    s.7 .... 2–203, 3–33, 3–170, 4–183, 4–184, 4–189, 6–22, 8–5, 13–10, 13–31, 13–36, **15–2**, 15–3, 16–64, 16–253, 16–320, 16–321, 16–336, 16–351, 16–353, 16–389, **17–1**
    s.8 .... 1–119, 2–44, 2–131, 3–92, 3–93, 4–16, 7–135, 10–82, 10–177, 10–181, 10–189, 11–353, **11–354**, 11–355, 11–356, 11–357, 11–358, 11–367, 11–369, 11–370, 11–373, 11–378, 11–382, 11–385, 11–390, 11–391, 11–393, 16–390, 16–393, 16–396, **17–1**
    s.8(1) 2–128, 2–129, 10–83, 11–355, 11–372, 11–373, 11–377, 11–382, 11–387, 16–351, 16–387, 16–393
    s.8(2) 11–371, 11–375, 16–351, 16–387, 16–388, 16–393
    s.8(2)(a) 10–83, 11–372, 16–396
    s.8(3) 11–367, 16–336, 16–351, 16–388
    s.9 .... 1–119, 3–94, 9–59, 10–197, 13–65, 16–414, **17–1**
    s.9(1) 10–65, 10–197
    s.9(1)(a) 10–192, 10–193, 10–194, 10–199, 10–200
    s.9(1)(b) 10–192, 10–195, 10–196, 10–197, 10–200, 16–414
    s.9(2) 10–196
    s.9(3) 10–193, 16–414
    s.9(4) 10–192, 16–414

Table of Statutes

1981 Contempt of Court Act—*cont.*
    s.10 .... 1–119, 1–127, 1–148, 2–53,
        2–67, 7–186, 9–1, 9–3, 9–15,
        9–18, 9–35, 9–36, 9–38, 9–41,
        9–43, 9–52, 9–54, 9–56, 9–58,
        9–61, 9–62, 9–65, 9–66, 9–86,
        9–88, 9–91, 9–104, 9–108,
        9–110, 9–112, 9–114, 9–116,
        9–117, 9–126, 9–132, 9–133,
        9–138, 9–139, 9–154, 9–164,
        9–177, 9–181, 9–184, 9–185,
        9–186, 9–187, 9–191, 9–196,
        9–197, 9–215, 9–216, 9–218,
        9–220, 9–221, 9–224, 9–226,
        9–227, 9–231, 9–234, 9–235,
        9–245, 10–162, 10–163, 11–133,
        16–383, **17–1**
    s.11 .. 1–120, 2–5, 2–40, 2–55, 2–62,
        2–164, 3–94, 3–105, 3–106,
        3–107, 6–2, 6–97, 7–30, 7–82,
        7–83, 7–86, 7–88, 7–89, 7–90,
        7–93, 7–97, 7–99, 7–104, 7–113,
        7–153, 7–181, 7–244, 7–248,
        7–258, 8–8, 8–49, 8–60, 9–75,
        9–81, 9–238, 9–245, 10–107,
        13–25, 16–381, 16–383, **17–1**
    s.12 .... 1–121, 2–190, 3–60, 4–16,
        10–62, 10–70, **10–113**, 10–115,
        10–117, 10–118, 10–126, 10–127,
        10–130, 10–194, 10–199, 10–222,
        13–27, 13–36, 13–80, 13–109,
        13–110, 13–112, 13–124, 13–130,
        13–133, 14–21, 14–98, 15–111,
        16–336, 16–351, **17–1**
    s.12(1) **13–106**
    s.12(1)(a) 10–33, 10–124, 10–125
    s.12(1)(b) ... 10–122, 10–124, 10–126,
        10–127
    s.12(2) 13–108, 13–129, 14–105
    s.12(4) 3–183, 13–108
    s.12(5) 10–114, 10–116, 12–119,
        13–110, 13–124, 13–128, 13–129,
        13–133
    s.13 .... 15–110, 17–1
    s.13(1)–(3) 16–336, 16–351
    s.13(4) 16–347
    s.14 .... 1–122, 1–124, 1–125, 3–22,
        3–34, 3–35, 3–95, 3–111, 3–211,
        10–95, 10–164, 10–171, 10–201,
        11–129, 11–132, 11–182, 14–12,
        14–49, 14–55, 14–56, 14–58,
        14–104, 16–336, 16–351, **17–1**
    s.14(1) ... 1–125, 3–177, **14–8**, 14–13,
        14–14, 14–17, 14–25
    s.14(2) 14–107
    s.14(2A) 14–65
    s.14(4) 14–1, 14–97
    s.14(3) 14–60
    s.14(4A) 14–26, 14–69
    s.14(5) 13–99

1981 Contempt of Court Act—*cont.*
    s.15 .... 16–115, 16–420, 16–422,
        16–423, **17–1**
    s.15(1), (2) 16–348
    s.15(2) 16–424
    s.15(3) 16–349, 16–423
    s.15(5) 16–350
    s.16 ... **14–109**, 16–336, 16–351, **17–1**
    s.17 .... 3–178, 13–112, 13–113,
        16–336, 16–351, **17–1**
    s.17(1), (2) 13–112
    s.18 .... 16–336, 16–351, **17–1**
    s.19 .... 4–17, 4–289, 5–215, 7–109,
        7–142, 9–59, 10–191, **13–3**, 13–5,
        13–47, 13–63, 13–66, 13–67,
        13–76, 14–25, 16–337, **17–1**
    s.20 .... 4–21, **13–77**, 13–78, **17–1**
    s.21 .... **17–1**
    s.21(4) 16–336, 16–351
    Sch.1 ..... 4–120, 4–174, 4–176, 5–62,
        7–143, 16–166, 16–214, 16–276,
        17–1
    Sch.1, paras 3, 4 16–341
    Sch.1, para.4, 4A 4–177
    Sch.1, para.5 5–100
    Sch.1, para.10(a), (b) 16–343
    Sch.1, para.11 16–341
    Sch.1, paras 12, 13 5–62
    Sch.1, para.12 .... 13–101, 16–344
    Sch.1, para.15 .... 5–100, 16–345
    Sch.1, para.16 8–16
    Sch.2 .... **17–1**
    Sch.2, Pts I, II 16–336
    Sch.2, Pt III 14–21
    Sch.2, Pt III, para.4 13–99
    Sch.2, Pt III, para.7 ... 10–164, 11–132
    Sch.3 .... 3–178, 12–3, 13–112,
        16–336, 16–351, **17–1**
    Sch.3, para.1(2) 13–113
    Sch.3, para.2 13–114
    Sch.4, ... 16–336, 16–351, **17–1**
1981 Supreme Court Act (c.54)
    s.1 .... 3–182, 10–7
    s.1(1) 13–34
    s.8(1) 13–34
    s.15(3) 15–102
    s.18(1)(h)(iii) ... 9–196, 9–236, 9–245
    s.19 13–17
    s.28(1) 7–263
    s.28(2)(a) 7–263
    s.29(3) 8–50, 8–60, 13–24
    s.36 11–99
    s.36(4) 11–104
    s.37 .... 6–2, 6–6, 9–216, 9–219,
        13–20, 13–36
    s.39 12–17
    s.42(1A)(b) 13–63
    s.43ZA 14–23
    s.45(1) 13–8, 13–24, 13–34

Table of Statutes

1981 Supreme Court Act—*cont.*
    s.45(4) 6–2, 6–98, 8–61, 13–24, 13–26, 13–34, 13–36, 13–37
    s.47(1) 14–57
    s.51 .... 7–274, 7–277
    s.51(1) 7–272, 7–273
    s.51(6) 11–67, 14–140
    s.53 15–96
    s.53(2)(b) 13–133
    s.61 7–63
    s.61(1), (3) 13–133
    s.67 .... 7–36, 7–42
    s.69 2–22
    s.72 .... 3–196, 3–208
    s.72(3), (4) 3–196
    s.74 13–34
    s.75(1) 2–108
    s.75(2) 13–34
    s.76(1) 2–108
    s.76(3), (4) 2–108
    s.82(2) 15–49
    s.90(1) 6–96
    s.147 12–259
    s.152(4) 12–259, 14–109
    s.154 13–17
    Sch.1 7–63
    Sch.1, para.3(d) 13–133
    Sch.7 .... 12–259, 13–17, 14–109

1982 Civil Jurisdiction and Judgments Act (c.27)
    Pt I 8–77
    s.15(4) 8–77
    Sch.12, Pt I, para.7 8–77

1982 Criminal Justice Act (c.48)
    s.1(1) 14–60
    s.2 14–67
    s.9 14–63
    s.9(1) 14–67
    s.16(3) 8–35
    ss 37, 38, 46 8–2
    s.37 ..... 8–81, 11–313, 13–84, 13–88, 14–104
    s.37(2) 14–106
    s.37(3) 11–139
    s.48 14–106
    s.77 14–65
    s.78 .... 10–113, 14–60, 17–1
    Sch.7 16–421
    Sch.14, para.60 14–65
    Sch.16 .... 10–113, 14–60, 17–1

1982 Mental Health (Amendment) Act (c.51)
    s.65(1) 14–1, 14–69, 14–97
    Sch.3, para.59 .... 14–1, 14–97
    Sch.3, para.60 14–69

1983 Representation of the People Act (c.2)
    s.123(2) 13–103

1983 Mental Health Act (c.20) ... 7–56, 8–131, 13–68
    Pt VII 8–98
    s.1(2) 14–97, 15–28
    s.35 17–1
    s.37 .... 14–1, 17–1
    s.38 .... 14–1, 17–1
    s.51(5) 17–1
    s.65(1) 14–1
    s.110(2) 13–127
    s.123(2) 13–127
    s.148 .... 4–177, 14–69, 14–97
    Sch.3, para.59 14–1
    Sch.4, para.57 ... 4–177, 14–97, 17–1
    Sch.4, para.57(6) 14–69

1983 County Courts (Penalties for Contempt) Act (c.45) 1–126, 15–90
    ss 1, 2 17–1
    s.1 .... 14–26, 14–69

1983 Medical Act (c.54)
    Sch.4, para.2(1) 11–97

1984 Dentists Act (c.24)
    Sch.3, para.4(1) 11–97

1984 County Courts Act (c.28)
    s.14 .... 11–158, 11–173, 11–330, 13–80, 13–85, 13–87, 13–123, 13–124, 15–77, 15–89, 15–99
    s.14(1) 11–313, **13–84**, 14–104
    s.14(2) 3–183, 13–85
    s.38 .... 12–135, 13–92, 13–123, 14–25, 14–55, 14–116, 15–79, 15–90
    s.38(1) 13–94
    s.55 .... 10–158, 10–164, 11–92, 11–94, 13–96, 13–99
    s.55(1) **13–95**
    s.55(2) 13–95
    s.55(3) 13–96
    s.55(4A), (5) 11–95, 13–95
    s.55(5) 13–96
    s.89(1) 14–120
    s.92 .... 11–313, 11–315, 11–330, 13–80, 13–123, 14–104, 15–77, 15–89
    s.92(1) ... 3–4, 13–88, 13–89, 15–108
    s.110 .... 13–96, **13–99**
    ss 118–121 13–80
    s.118 .... 2–173, 7–135, 10–124, 10–125, 10–130, 11–158, 11–173, 11–313, 11–314, **13–90**, 13–91, 13–107, 13–123, 14–124, 15–77, 15–89
    s.118(1) 14–103
    s.118(2) 3–183
    s.119(2) 15–54, 15–55
    s.124 15–77
    s.142 .... 11–67, 12–259, 13–98, 13–123
    s.147 11–313

Table of Statutes

1984 County Courts Act—*cont.*
    s.148(1) 13–87
    s.148(3) 17–1
    Sch.2, Pt V, para.25 13–87
    Sch.4 17–1
1984 Mental Health (Scotland) Act
    (c.36) 16–288
    s.17(2) 17–1
    s.73(1) 16–343, 17–1
    s.127(1) 4–177, 17–1
    Sch.3, para.48 .... 4–177, 17–1
1984 Matrimonial and Family Proceedings Act (c.42)
    s.32 7–63
    s.40(4)(aa) 8–77, 8–107
    s.44 8–77
1984 Police and Criminal Evidence
    Act (c.60) 3–62
    s.9 9–31
    s.10 2–51
    s.11(2), (3) 9–37
    s.13 .... 2–51, 9–66
    s.24 11–185
    s.24(1)(b) 11–185
    s.78 .... 2–136, 2–137, 3–63
    Sch.1 9–31
1985 Companies Act (c.6)
    s.436 13–77
    ss 694A, 695, 725 15–26
1985 Prosecution of Offences Act (c.23)
    s.23 .... 4–177, 17–1
    s.31(5) 4–177, 17–1
    Sch.1, Pt I 4–177
    Sch.1, Pt I, paras 4, 5 17–1
1985 Transport Act (c.67)
    s.117 13–103
    Sch.4, para.1 .... 13–103, 13–127
1985 Housing Act (c.68) 7–99
1986 Insolvency Act (c.45)
    s.134(1) 13–77
    s.248 14–121
    s.290(5) 13–77
1986 Company Directors Disqualification Act (c.46)
    s.20 12–10
1986 Legal Aid (Scotland) Act
    (c.47) 16–347
    s.45(3) 17–1
    Sch.5 17–1
1986 Family Law Act (c.55)
    Pt III 8–14
    s.55A 8–77
1986 Financial Services Act (c.60)
    s.177 9–182
    s.177(6) 2–136
    s.178 .... 7–135, 9–183, 9–186
    s.178(2) 9–116, 9–184
    s.178(2)(a) 9–183

1986 Public Order Act (c.64)
    s1(1) 4–87
    s.3(2) 4–87
    ss 4, 5 13–107
1987 Banking Act (c.22)
    s.81 7–22
    s.82(1), (2) 7–19
1987 Criminal Justice Act (c.37) 7–112
    ss 4–11 8–91
    s.4(2) 8–91
    s.6 8–91
    s.9 7–254
    s.9(3)(c) 7–256
    s.11 8–91
    s.11(13) 8–91
1987 Family Law Reform Act (c.42)
    s.33(1) 8–13
    s.33(4) 8–77
    Sch.4 8–77
    Sch.2, para.19(b) 8–13
1988 Coroners Act (c.8)
    s.8(3)(a), (b) 13–100
    s.10(1)–(3) 14–107
    s.10(3) 13–127
    s.13 2–215
1988 Criminal Justice Act (c.33) 13–119
    s.23 .... 10–165, 10–170
    s.23(3)(b) 10–169
    s.43(1) 5–103
    s.118 2–114
    s.120 11–139
    s.158 .... 8–19, 8–24
    s.159 ..... 2–62, 2–193, 7–116, 7–118,
        7–124, 7–136, 7–169, 7–235,
        7–250, 7–254, 7–258, 7–261,
        7–263, 7–265, 7–266, 7–268,
        7–271, 8–59, 9–221, 9–238,
        16–377
    s.159(1) 7–33, 7–262, 7–264
    s.159(1)(b) 7–32
    s.159(4) 7–266
    s.159(5) 7–260
    s.159(5)(c) 7–271
    s.159(6) 7–266
    s.170(2) 5–103
    Sch.16 5–103
1988 Legal Aid Act (c.34)
    s.29 .... 3–45, 10–59, 15–108
    s.29(1), (2) 15–110
    s.29(1) 15–111
    s.45 17–1
    Sch.6 17–1
1988 Court of Session Act (c.36)
    s.47(1) 16–235, 16–262
1989 Prevention of Terrorism (Temporary Provisions) Act (c.4)
    s.14 9–197
    s.18 .... 9–115, 9–117
    Sch.7, para.3 .. 2–210, 9–113, 9–232,
        9–242, 13–33

TABLE OF STATUTES

1989 Prevention of Terrorism (Temporary Provisions) Act —cont.
  Sch.7, para.4(5)(b) 9–113, 9–117, 9–118, 9–234
1989 Official Secrets Act (c.6)
  s.5 5–143
  s.8(4)(a) 9–56
  s.8(5) 9–56
  s.11(4) 7–61
1989 Children Act (c.41) 6–54, 6–108, 6–115, 8–76, 8–120, 8–122, 8–138
  Pts IV, V 10–173
  s.1 ... 1–139, 2–158, 6–52, 6–86, 7–65
  s.1(1) 6–63, 6–68, 6–77, 6–79, 6–80, 6–92, 6–113
  s.3(1) 6–66
  s.7 8–111
  s.8 .... 8–84, 14–119, 15–24
  s.8(1) 6–66
  s.8(3)(a) 8–84
  s.10(1) 8–84
  s.12 8–98
  s.12(1)(a)(ii), (iii) 8–49
  s.49(1) 8–49
  s.92 .... 8–77, 8–79, 8–80
  s.92(11) 8–77, 8–79, 8–80
  s.97 .... 6–76, 8–103
  s.97(2) 6–75, 7–48, 8–83, 8–84, 8–107, 8–120
  s.97(4) 8–84
  s.97(5) 8–83
  s.98 10–173
  s.100 .... 6–73, 6–109
  s.100(3) 6–109
  s.100(4) 6–79, 6–109
  s.108(6) 8–77
  s.108(7) 8–77
  Sch.11, para.8 .... 8–77, 8–79, 8–80
  Sch.11, Pt II, para.8(a)–(c) 8–77
  Sch.11, Pt II, para.8(c) ... 8–79, 8–80
  Sch.13, para.14 7–63
  Sch.15 8–77
1990 Human Fertilisation and Embryology Act (c.37)
  s.30 8–77
1990 Courts and Legal Services Act (c.41)
  s.3 14–25
  s.12 11–96
  s.14(3) 13–85, 14–24
  s.15(2) 14–120
  s.25 13–77
  s.74 .... 13–85, 13–90, 14–24
  s.74(6) 11–95, 13–95
  s.116(2) 8–77
  s.125(3) 8–79
  s.125(7) 8–77
  Sch.16, Pt II, para.40 8–77

1990 Courts and Legal Services Act —cont.
  sch.18, para.25(1), (6) 8–79
  Sch.20 8–77
1990 Broadcasting Act (c.42) 8–80, 8–83, 8–88
  s.201 16–230
  s.203(1) 4–24, 8–80, 17–1
  Sch.20, para.29(2) 8–80
  Sch.20, para.31(1) 4–24
  Sch.20, para.31(1)(a), (b) 17–1
1991 Child Support Act (c.48)
  ss 20, 45 8–77
1991 Criminal Justice Act (c.53) 7–112
  s.3(a) 10–164
  s.17(2) 8–2, 11–139, 14–106
  s.17(3) 10–113, 11–132, 13–90, 14–106, 14–107
  s.17(3)(a) 13–95, 13–116
  s.53 .... 8–92, 8–93
  s.53(6) 8–94
  s.70(1) 8–26
  s.72 8–26
  s.76(1) 11–313
  s.78(1), (2) 11–313
  s.100 .... 8–26, 10–113
  s.101(2) 14–67
  Sch.4 .... 10–164, 11–94, 11–314, 13–88, 13–90, 14–104
  Sch.4, Pt I 10–113, 10–164, 11–132, 13–95, 13–116, 14–106, 14–107
  Sch.4, Pt IV 13–108
  Sch.4, Pt V 10–113
  Sch.6, para.6 8–92
  Sch.11, para.29 10–113
  Sch.11, para.40(1) 8–26
  Sch.11, para.40(2)(a) 8–26
  Sch.13 14–67
1992 Social Security Administration Act (c.5)
  s.106 8–77
1992 Social Security (Consequential Provisions) Act (c.6)
  ss 3, 4 8–77
  Sch.1, para.60 8–77
1992 Local Government Finance Act (c.14)
  s.136 13–52
  Sch.11 13–52
1992 Sexual Offences (Amendment) Act (c.34) 2–53, 7–105, 8–18
  s.1 .... 8–21, 8–55
  s.1(1) 8–19
  s.3 8–20
  s.3(1)(a) 8–20
  s.3(2), (3) 8–20
  s.3(2)(b) 8–63
  s.5 8–21
  s.5(1) 8–20

[cxxxix]

1992	Sexual Offences (Amendment) Act—*cont.*		1995	Criminal Appeal Act—*cont.*	
	s.5(2), (3), (5)	8–21		s.4	3–42, 3–239
	s.5(5A)	8–21, 8–22	1995	Children (Scotland) Act (c.36)	
1992	Friendly Societies Act (c.40)			Pt II	16–230
	s.67(6)	13–77		s.44	16–230
1992	Trade Union and Labour Relations (Consolidation) Act (c.52)			s.44(5)	16–231
				s.45(8)(b)	16–114
				s.45(9)	16–114
	s.12(2), (3)	14–129		s.57	16–230
	s.23	14–129		s.60(7)	16–230
	s.15(1)(a)	14–108		s.65(7), (9)	16–230
	ss 20–22	12–117		s.76(1)	16–230
	s.20	**12–116**		s.85(1)	16–230
	s.21	12–116		s.93(1)	16–230
1993	Charities Act (c.10)		1995	Civil Evidence Act (c.38)	3–191
	s.88	13–77		ss 1, 4	3–237
1993	Criminal Justice Act (c.36)			s.1(1)	3–232, 3–236
	s.65(3), (4)	10–113		s.2(1)	3–232
	Sch.3, para.6(4)	10–113	1995	Criminal Procedure (Consequential Provisions) (Scotland) Act (c.40)	
1993	Health Service Commissioners Act (c.46)				
	s.13	13–77		s.5	16–348, 16–349, 17–1
1993	Pensions Schemes Act (c.48)			Sch.4, para.36	16–423
	s.150(4)	13–77		Sch.4, para.36(2)	16–348
1994	Finance Act (c.9)			Sch.4, para.36(3)	16–349, 17–1
	s.7	13–61		Sch.4, para.36(4)	16–350, 17–1
1994	Criminal Justice and Public Order Act (c.33)	11–191		Sch.4, para.50(7)(a)	16–343
				Sch.4, para.99	16–348
	s.3(7)	8–35	1995	Criminal Procedure (Scotland) Act (c.46)	16–300
	ss 17, 18	7–135			
	ss 34–37	9–13		s.3(2)	16–406
	s.34	3–64, 3–188		s.7(9), (10)	16–350, 17–1
	s.35	3–64, 3–188		ss 14, 15	16–340
	s.35(4)	3–64, 10–162		s.17	16–180
	s.40	11–139		s.19	16–180
	s.41	11–141		s.35	16–180
	s.43	2–112, 10–186		s.47	16–230
	s.44	7–112, 8–88		ss 58–61	16–349
	s.49	2–56, 8–27, 8–32, 8–33, 8–39, 8–47		s.58(1)	16–350, 17–1
				s.59	17–1
				s.61	17–1
	s.51	1–151, 2–14, 2–171, 11–1, 11–145, **11–146**, 11–150, 11–151, 11–182, 11–183, 11–185, 11–226, 11–234, 11–299, 11–384, 14–146		s.65(4)(b)	16–304
				s.67	16–379
				ss 91–99	16–116
				s.104(1)	16–391
	s.51(1)	11–147, 11–150, 11–152		s.118(1)(c)	5–103
	s.51(1)(a)	11–153		s.130	16–427
	s.51(1)(c)	11–147		s.135(3), (4)	16–180
	s.51(2)	11–152, 14–142		s.150	16–114
	s.51(5)	5–122		s.155	16–115, 16–139, 16–272
	s.51(6)(a)	11–182		s.155(1)	16–117
	s.51(7)	11–149, 11–152, 11–153		s.155(1)(d)	16–421
	s.51(8)	11–149, 11–152		s.155(2)	16–130
	s.51(11)	11–146, 11–182		s.155(3)	16–123
	s.168(3)	8–47		ss 176–184	16–298
	Sch.4, Pt II, para.50	7–112		s.207	16–349, 16–423
	Sch.11	8–47		s.291	16–115
1995	Criminal Appeal Act (c.35)	3–240, 4–172		s.307(1)	16–115
				s.321(3)	16–180
	s.2	4–150		Sch.7	16–21

Table of Statutes

1995	Disability Discrimination Act (c.50)	
	s.8	8–146
1996	Police Act (c.16)	
	s.49(2)	8–149
1996	Employment Tribunals Act (c.17)	13–64
	s.11	7–109, 8–143, 8–146, 13–62
	s.11(6)	8–146
	s.12	7–109, 8–143, 8–146, 13–62
	s.20(3)	10–6, 13–8, 13–21
	s.29(2)	11–91
	s.37	13–133
	s.45	14–110, 17–1
	Sch.3, Pt I	14–110, 17–1
1996	Employment Rights Act (c.18)	
	s.43M	11–163
1996	Arbitration Act (c.23)	7–21
	s.43	11–99
	s.45	7–23
	s.45(2)(b)	7–23
	s.69	7–23
	s.69(2)(b)	7–23
1996	Criminal Procedure and Investigations Act (c.25)	7–78, 8–88
	ss 1–21	11–136
	ss 17, 18	1–151, 12–203
	s.17	7–36, 11–82
	s.18	11–82
	s.29	16–307
	ss 44, 47	1–73
	s.47	11–134
	s.54	4–177, 7–112, 17–1
	s.57(3)	7–112
	ss 58–60	8–95
	s.58(4)(b)	8–96
	s.58(5)	8–96
	s.58(7), (8)	7–258
	s.61(6)	2–62
	s.66	11–116, 11–120, 11–134
	s.80	11–134
	Sch.1, Pt 1, paras 1, 7	11–134
	Sch.5(10)	11–134
1996	Family Law Act (c.27)	1–173, 17–1
	Pt II	8–2
	Pt IV	8–77, 13–93, 14–86, 14–90
	Pt V, Ch.III	14–88
	s.33	14–77
	s.40	15–56
	s.40(1)(a)(ii)	15–56
	s.42	14–18, 14–19, 14–77
	s.42A	12–186, 14–48, 14–58, 14–96
	s.42A(1)	1–152
	s.42A(3), (4)	3–218, 14–96
	s.45(3)	14–87
	s.46	12–186, 14–96
	s.46(1)–(3)	14–77
	s.46(2)	12–185
	s.46(3A)	14–96

1996	Family Law Act—cont.	
	s.46(4)	14–96
	s.47	**14–78**, 14–88
	s.47(2)–(4)	14–80
	s.47(2)	14–80, 14–96
	s.47(3)	14–96
	s.47(6)	14–71
	s.58	13–93
	s.62(3)	14–83
	s.63(1)	13–93, 14–84
	s.66(1)	8–2, 8–77, 13–115
	s.66(3)	7–14
	s.68(1), (2)	8–14
	Sch.1, para.9(a)	8–14
	Sch.2	8–14
	Sch.5, para.2(2), (5)	14–88
	Sch.8, Pt I, para.2	8–2
	Sch.8, Pt III, para.49	8–77
	Sch.8, Pt III, para.50	13–115, 17–1
	Sch.10	8–14
1996	Sexual Offences (Conspiracy and Incitement) Act (c.29)	
	s.2	8–19
1996	Defamation Act (c.31)	4–233, 4–234, 4–252
	s.1	1–147, 1–149, 4–5, 4–50, 4–191, 6–131
	s.1(1)	4–230, 16–363
	s.1(1)(c)	4–237
	s.1(2)	4–50, 4–194, 4–196, 4–212, 4–230, 4–236, 4–257
	s.1(3)	4–191
	s.1(3)(a)	4–230
	s.1(4)	4–229
	s.2	4–198
	s.3	4–193
	s.3(1)	4–193
	s.3(2)	4–191, 4–193
	s.5	4–50
	s.13	4–334
	s.14	1–51, 4–287, 7–17
	s.15	4–287
	Sch.1	4–287
	Sch.2	4–277, 7–112, 17–1
1996	Armed Forces Act (c.46)	13–16
1996	Housing Act (c.52)	14–89
	s.152, 153	14–89, 14–91
	s.152	14–92
	s.152(3)	14–90, 15–71
	ss 153A–153E	14–92
	s.153A	14–94, 14–95
	s.153A(4)	14–94, 14–95
	s.153B	14–95
	s.153C, A53D	14–95
	s.153E(7)	14–94
	s.153E(12)	14–95
	s.154	14–93
	s.155	14–91, 14–93
	Sch.15	14–91

Table of Statutes

1997	Civil Procedure Act (c.12)	
	s.7 .... 3–204, 3–205	
	s.7(7) 3–205, 12–175	
1997	Building Societies Act (c.32)	
	s.14(13) 13–77	
1997	Protection from Harassment Act	
	(c.40) 1–152, 14–147	
	ss 3–5 14–19	
	s.3 14–58	
	s.3(6) 1–152	
	s.3(7) 3–218	
	s.3(8) 3–218	
1997	Crime (Sentences) Act (c.43) 8–35, 8–66	
1997	Special Immigration Appeals Commission Act (c.68)	
	s.1(3) 13–8	
1998	Employment Rights (Dispute Resolution) Act (c.8) 13–64	
	s.1 .... 4–17, 10–6	
	s.1(1) 8–140, 13–21, 13–62	
	s.1(2) 8–146, 13–8, 13–21	
1998	Public Interest Disclosure Act	
	(c.23) 9–27	
1998	Crime and Disorder Act (c.37)	
	s.1 .... 6–79, 8–42	
	s.1(10D) 8–46	
	s.1C 8–45	
	s.9C 8–45	
	ss 11, 12 8–77	
	s.36 10–92	
	s.51 1–73	
	s.52A 1–73, 8–88	
	s.52A(6) 4–277, 7–112	
	s.119 8–77	
	Sch.3, para.3(5), (7) 4–277, 7–112	
	Sch.8, para.42 8–77	
1998	Human Rights Act (c.42) 1–131, 1–132, 1–134, 1–140, 1–161, 2–52, 2–122, 2–123, 2–124, 2–138, 2–164, 2–166, 2–191, 2–192, 2–198, 4–261, 5–2, 5–5, 6–43, 6–48, 7–5, 7–99, 9–3, 9–9, 11–389, 12–12, 13–42, 13–89, 16–40	
	s.2 2–198	
	s.3 .... 2–198, 11–357, 11–394	
	s.4 2–198	
	s.6 .... 2–139, 2–198	
	s.12 .... 2–135, 2–198, 4–324, 6–11, 6–16, 6–47, 9–214, 13–20	
	s.12(1) 6–17	
	s.12(2) 1–145, 6–96	
	s.12(3) 6–12, 6–13, 6–14, 6–15, 6–17, 6–35, 6–38, 6–131	
	s.12(4) 9–39	
1998	Scotland Act (c.46) 16–240	
	Sch.6, para.9 16–419	
1999	Access to Justice Act (c.19) 6–76, 8–120	
	s.12 .... 3–45, 15–111, 15–117	
	s.12(2) 11–313	
	s.12(2)(a) 15–111	
	s.12(2)(f) 10–10, 15–108, 15–111	
	s.24 8–88	
	s.54 15–94	
	s.56 15–88	
	s.57 13–121	
	s.62 14–23	
	s.64 .... 13–120, 13–125, 13–131, 13–133, 13–134	
	s.108(3)(b) 8–83	
	Sch.3, para.2 .... 15–112, 15–119	
	Sch.4, paras 15, 16 8–88	
	Sch.14, Pt VI, para.18 8–83	
	Sch.15, para.1 15–108	
	Sch.15, Pt III 13–125	
1999	Youth Justice and Criminal Evidence Act (c.23) 7–80, 8–21, 11–145	
	ss 16–33 10–165	
	ss 16,17 7–13	
	s.24 8–53	
	s.25(3) 2–51	
	s.45 ... 6–97, 6–100, 8–52, 8–53, 8–67	
	s.45(3) 8–54, 8–64	
	s.45(4) 8–54, 8–63	
	s.45(5) 8–54, 8–63, 8–64, 8–65	
	s.45(7) 8–54	
	s.46 .... 6–97, 7–78, 8–74, 10–165	
	s.46(4), (5) 8–75	
	s.48 8–53	
	s.67(1) 8–26	
	Sch.2, para.2(1), (2) 8–53	
	Sch.4, para.2(1), (3) 8–26	
2000	Powers of Criminal Courts (Sentencing) Act (c.6) 14–142	
	s.1 .... 4–177, 17–1	
	ss 41–44 14–98	
	s.44 14–100	
	s.60 .... 14–65, 17–1	
	ss 75–91 13–110	
	s.83 .... 10–63, 13–108	
	s.89 14–60	
	s.89(1) 14–61	
	s.108 .... 13–110, 13–111, 14–61	
	s.108(1) **14–61**, 14–67	
	s.108(3) **14–62**, 14–67	
	s.108(4) 13–111, **14–62**	
	s.130 .... 14–145, 14–146	
	s.130(1)(a) **14–143**	
	s.132 14–143	
	s.135 ...... 13–110, 17–1 s.1363–110	
	ss 139, 140 .... 14–109, 17–1	
	s.142(1) 13–110	
	s.155 11–143	
	s.165(1) 13–110, 14–65	
	Sch.7 .... 8–39, 8–47	

Table of Statutes

Year	Statute	Reference
2000	Powers of Criminal Courts (Sentencing) Act—*cont.*	
	Sch.9, para.83	13–110
	Sch.9, para.83(a)	17–1
	Sch.9, para.84	14–65, 17–1
	Sch.9, para.85	14–109, 17–1
	Sch.9, para.86	17–1
2000	Terrorism Act (c.11)	2–210, 9–118, 9–234, 9–242
	s.19(3)	9–115
	Sch.5, para.8(1)(b)	9–118
2000	Child Support, Pensions and Social Security Act (c.19)	
	s.83(5)	8–77
	s.85	8–13, 8–77
	Sch.8, para.2(1)–(2)	8–77
	Sch.9, Pt IX	8–13, 8–77
2000	Criminal Justice and Court Services Act (c.43)	8–111
	s.74	8–33, 14–61
	s.75	13–111
	Sch.7, Pt II, para.5	8–33
2002	Employment Act (c.22)	9–27
2002	Police Reform Act (c.30)	
	s.64	8–45
2001	Criminal Justice and Police Act (c.16)	
	ss 39, 40, 41	11–150
2001	Anti-terrorism, Crime and Security Act (c.24)	
	s.35	13–8
2002	Adoption of Children Act (c.38)	
	s.101(2)	8–98
	s.101(3)	8–83
	s.139(1)	8–77, 8–79, 8–80
	s.141(6)	8–77, 8–107
	Sch.3, paras 36, 37	8–77
	Sch.3, paras 36, 38	8–79
	Sch.3, para.36, 39(b)(i)	8–80
2003	Clergy Discipline Measure (No.3)	
	s.18(3)	7–72
2003	Licensing Act (c.17)	13–60
2003	Anti-social Behaviour Act (c.38)	14–89, 14–93
	s.13	14–93
	s.13(4), (5)	14–93
	s.86(3)	8–45
	Sch.3	14–93
2003	Courts Act (c.39)	
	s.76(2A)	8–77, 8–107
	s.86	2–108
	s.109(1)	8–77, 11–315
	Sch.8, para.214(1), (2)	8–77
2003	Extradition Act (c.41)	7–40
2003	Sexual Offences Act (c.42)	7–105, 8–93
	s.139	8–18
	Sch.6	8–18
2003	Criminal Justice Act (c.44)	3–41, 5–104, 8–91, 12–155, 16–230
	Pt 2	3–41
	Pt 2, Ch.1	4–61
	Pt 3	1–151, 11–136
	Pt 9	4–179, 8–15
	Pt 10	8–15
	Pt 11	2–38
	s.41	1–73, 2–108, 4–277, 7–112, 8–88, 16–307
	ss 51–56	10–165
	s.58	8–15
	s.62	8–15
	s.71(1)	8–15
	ss 82, 83	4–179
	s.82(1), (5), (6)	8–16
	ss 114–136	3–228
	s.114	3–41
	s.116(2)(e)	10–169
	s.116(3)	10–169
	s.134	3–41
	ss 137, 138	10–165
	ss 147–151	14–98
	s.147	3–86, 14–98
	s.151(1)(a)	3–60
	s.177	14–98
	s.177(1)	14–100
	s.199	14–100
	s.213	14–98
	s.258	3–182, 14–4, 14–13
	s.280(2), (3)	8–2, 13–84, 13–88
	s.321	10–82, 11–139
	s.332	2–108, 7–112, 8–93
	Sch.3	1–73, 16–307
	Sch.3, Pt 1, paras 15, 19(1)	8–88
	Sch.3, Pt 2, para.51(1), (3)	2–108
	Sch.3, Pt 2, para.53	7–112
	Sch.5	3–209
	Sch.26, para.7	8–2
	Sch.26, para.33(1), (2)	13–84
	Sch.26, para.33(1), (3)	13–88
	Sch.33	11–139
	Sch.33, para.11	11–141
	Sch.37, Pt 4	2–108, 7–112, 8–93
2004	Statute Law Repeals Act (c.14)	
	s.1	11–96
	Sch.1, Pt 1	11–96
2004	Employment Relations Act (c.24)	11–163
	s.40	11–1
2004	Domestic Violence, Crime and Victims Act (c.28)	14–18, 14–83, 14–96
	s.1	1–152, 3–218
	s.58(1), (2)	14–78, 14–80
	Sch.10, para.37	12–186
	Sch.10, para.38	1–152
	Sch.10, para.38(1)–(3)	14–78
	Sch.10, para.38(1),(4)	14–80

TABLE OF STATUTES

2004	Domestic Violence, Crime and Victims Act—*cont.*	
	Sch.11	14–78
2004	Children Act (c.31)	8–102
	s.62	7–223, 8–98, 8–109
	s.62(1)	8–83
2004	Civil Partnership Act (c.33)	
	s.58	8–14
	s.261(1)	8–2, 8–13
	Sch.27, para.8(1), (2)	8–2
	Sch.27, para.29(1), (3)	8–13
2005	Mental Capacity Act (c.9)	
	s.45	7–56
	s.45(1)	13–8
	s.47	7–56
	s.51	7–56

2005	Mental Capacity Act—*cont.*	
	s.51(2)(h)	7–56
	s.67(1)	8–98
	s.68(1)	7–56
	Sch.6, para.10	8–98
2005	Inquiries Act (c.12)	8–149, 16–344
	s.19	4–22
	s.21	4–22, 4–23
	s.35	4–23
	s.35(1)	4–23
	s.36	4–22, 13–78
2005	Serious Organised Crime and Police Act (c.15)	
	s.110	11–185
	s.141	8–46

TABLE OF INTERNATIONAL LEGISLATION

(*References are to paragraph numbers*)

1945	Courts Ordinance (preserved by the Mauritius Independence Order 1968)		1950	European Convention on Human Rights and Fundamental Freedoms (Rome, November 4, 1950; TS 71 (1953); Cmd 8969 —*cont.*
	s.15 5–271			
1950	European Convention on Human Rights and Fundamental Freedoms (Rome, November 4, 1950; TS 71 (1953); Cmd 8969 ...... 1–131, 1–134, 2–52, 2–152, 2–153, 9–80			Art.10 .. 1–104, 1–111, 1–113, 1–140, 1–176, 2–32, 2–44, 2–127, 2–131, 2–133, 2–134, 2–138, 2–141, 2–142, 2–146, 2–153, 2–154, 2–161, 2–162, 2–163, 2–164, 2–168, 2–194, 2–199, 4–91, 4–253, 4–268, 4–273, 4–315, 5–2, 5–5, 5–22, 5–76, 5–138, 5–262, 6–6, 6–43, 6–44, 6–52, 6–59, 6–67, 6–87, 6–90, 6–106, 7–1, 7–5, 7–8, 7–64, 7–81, 7–108, 7–170, 7–201, 7–268, 8–1, 8–23, 8–127, 9–2, 9–35, 9–59, 9–126, 9–127, 9–138, 9–140, 9–150, 9–164, 9–188, 9–245, 10–156, 11–22, 11–394, 14–141, 16–164, 16–419
	Art.2 .... 6–47, 6–57, 7–31, 7–102			
	Art.5(4) 13–68			
	Art.6 .... 1–174, 1–24, 2–32, 2–36, 2–37, 2–136, 2–143, 2–162, 2–163, 2–164, 2–195, 2–199, 3–4, 3–58, 3–84, 3–238, 3–251, 4–261, 4–315, 6–20, 6–57, 7–1, 7–30, 7–53, 7–61, 7–64, 7–97, 7–106, 7–108, 7–170, 7–201, 8–1, 9–139, 10–28, 10–36, 10–156, 10–177, 11–143, 11–300, 11–355, 11–357, 12–12, 13–42, 13–118, 13–120, 14–141, 15–115, 16–379			
				Art.10(1) 6–6, 6–8, 6–20
				Art.10(2) 1–106, 1–107, 1–110, 2–158, 2–159, 4–273, 5–23, 5–42, 5–216, 5–237, 6–6, 6–8, 6–9, 6–20, 6–56, 6–57, 6–90, 6–96, 7–106, 7–115, 7–165, 7–187, 7–200, 7–268, 8–7, 8–8, 8–23, 8–125, 9–32, 9–126, 9–139, 9–151, 9–193, 11–273, 16–1, 16–371
	Art.6(1) 1–104, 2–144, 2–163, 3–58, 3–238, 7–2, 7–39, 7–64, 8–25, 10–131, 15–42, 16–400			
	Art.6(2) 2–145, 3–5			
	Art.6(3) ... 2–144, 3–5, 3–238, 10–36, 10–52, 15–41			Art.13 .... 7–268, 7–269, 9–238
	Art.6(3)(b) 3–58, 16–275, 16–347			Art.25 2–122
	Art.6(3)(c) 15–41, 15–42, 15–108, 16–275			Protocol 7, Art.4 12–14
			1958	County Court Act (Vic.)
	Art.6(3)(d) 3–238			s.54A(1) 10–128
	Art.7 ..... 1–97, 2–169, 2–173, 2–190, 5–23, 5–76, 10–28, 10–92, 12–53, 14–64, 15–23, 16–1		1961	Crimes Act (New Zealand)
				s.9 5–268
	Art.8 ..... 1–140, 1–174, 1–176, 2–36, 2–37, 2–136, 2–146, 2–163, 2–194, 6–16, 6–17, 6–20, 6–43, 6–44, 6–56, 6–59, 6–67, 6–76, 6–90, 6–102, 6–104, 7–99, 7–107, 7–108, 8–1, 8–36, 8–44, 8–51, 15–115		1966	International Covenant on Civil and Political Rights 2–167
			1968	Constitution of Mauritius (replaced in 1992) 5–271
				ss 5, 12 5–271
	Art.8(1) 6–91, 6–105			s.10(4) 2–174
	Art.8(2) 6–105			s.76(1) 5–271

[cxlv]

TABLE OF INTERNATIONAL LEGISLATION

1970	Supreme Court Act (New South Wales)		1988	Industrial Relations Act (Cth)
	s.48(4) 10–24			s.299(1)(d)(ii) 5–267
1970	Supreme Court Rules (New South Wales)		1989	Convention on the Rights of the Child
	Pt 55, Div.2 10–24			Art.3.1 .... 8–25, 8–36
1980	Evidence Amendment Act (No.2) (New Zealand)			Arts 17 6–105
				Art.40 8–36
	s.35 9–50			Art.40.2(vii) 6–105
1982	Charter of Rights and Freedoms (Canada) 1–143, 6–21		1989	Whistleblower Protection Act (United States) 9–27
			1990	Bill of Rights (New Zealand) 1–143, 2–33, 2–100, 5–269
	s.1 13–42		1990	Criminal Code (Canada)
	s.2(b) .. 2–103, 5–261, 9–1, 9–2, 9–51			s.9(1) 10–50
	s.7 11–361		2000	Council Regulation (EC) No.44/2001 of 22 December 2000 on jurisdiction and the recognition and enforcement of judgments in civil and commercial matters 8–77
	s.11 13–42			
	s.11(b) 2–105			
	s.11(d) 1–103			
	s.11(f) 4–161, 11–361			

TABLE OF STATUTORY INSTRUMENTS

(References are to paragraph numbers)

1860	Consolidated Chancery Orders (now abrogated)		
	Ord.42, r.2 11–316		
1923	Shipping Casualties and Appeals and Rehearing Rules (SR&O 1923/752)		
	r.11 8–150		
1936	County Court Rules (SR&O 1936/626)		
	Ord.25, r.67 15–5		
1958	Independent Schools Tribunal Rules (SI 1958/519) 8–150		
1964	Prison Rules (SI 1964/388)		
	rr 33, 37A 11–302		
1966	Gas (Underground Storage) (Inquiries Procedure) Rules (SI 1966/1375) 8–150		
1968	Criminal Appeal Rules (SI 1968/1262)		
	r.16A 7–266		
	r.16B 7–33, 7–266		
	r.16B(6), (7) 7–267		
1969	Civil Aviation (Investigation of Accidents) Regulation (SI 1969/833) 8–150		
1971	Rent Assessment Committees (England and Wales) Regulations (SI 1971/1065) 8–150		
1974	National Health Service (Service Committees and Tribunal) regulations (SI 1974/455) ... 8–150		
1976	Treatment of Offenders (Northern Ireland) Order (SI 1976/226)		
	art.14 .... 4–177, 17–1		
1977	Lands Tribunal (Amendment) Rules (SI 1977/1820) 8–150		
1978	Agricultural Lands Tribunal (Rules) Order (SI 1978/259) 8–150		
1979	Rules of the Supreme Court (Amendment No.2) (SI 1979/402) 12–39		
1980	County Courts (Northern Ireland) Order (SI1980/397)		
	art.55 17–1		
1980	Criminal Justice (Northern Ireland) Order (1980/ 704)		
	Sch.1, para.26 17–1		
1981	Legal Aid, Advice and Assistance (Northern Ireland) Order (SI 1981/228)		
	Pt III 17–1		
	arts 29, 32, 33, 36, 40 17–1		
1981	County Court Rules (SI 1981/1687)		
	Ord.29 2–198		
	Ord.29, r.1(3) 14–118		
1982	Crown Court Rules (SI 1982/1109)		
	r.24A 7–32, 7–33, 7–34		
	r.24A(1) 2–66, 7–33, 7–34		
	r.25 11–141		
1983	Maintenance Orders (Backdating) Order (SI 1983/623)		
	art.3 8–77		
	Sch.2 8–77		
1983	Mental Health Review Tribunal Rules (SI 1983/942)		
	r.21(5) 8–130, 8–133		
1984	Coroners' Rules (SI 1984/552)		
	r.37 7–18		
1986	Mental Health (Northern Ireland) Order (SI 1986/595)		
	art.136(1) 4–177, 17–1		
	Sch.5, Pt II 4–177, 17–1		
1986	Costs in Criminal Cases (General) Regulations (SI 1986/1335)		
	regs 3E–3I 14–141		
	reg.3F(2)–(4) 14–141		
	reg.3H 14–141		
1986	Social Security (Adjudication) Regulations (SI 1986/2218) 8–150		
1987	Rules of the Supreme Court (Amendment) (SI 1987/1423) 12–218		
1989	Valuation and Community Charge Tribunals Regulations (SI 1989/439) 8–150		

[cxlvii]

Table of Statutory Instruments

1991 Children (Admissibility of Hearsay Evidence) Order (SI 1991/1115)
art.2 3–234
1991 County Courts Remedies Regulations (SI 1991/1222) 13–92
reg.2 13–92
1991 Family Proceedings Rules (SI 1991/1247) 14–71
r.2.28(1) 3–235
r.3.9(6) 14–75
r.3.9A(1) 14–75
r.3.10 14–85
r.4.1(1) 8–111
r.4.16(7) 7–63, 7–65, 7–66, 8–76
r.4.21A 14–119, 15–24
r.4.23 8–113
r.7.2 15–28
r.7.2(1) 15–15, 15–16
r.8.2(4) 13–133
r.8.3 13–133
r.9.5 13–94
r.10.15(6) 11–81
r.10.20(3) 11–81
1991 Family Proceedings (Children Act 1989) Rules (SI 1991/1395)
r.14 8–76
r.16(7) 8–76
1992 Transfer of Functions (Magistrates' Courts and Family Law) Order (SI 1992/709)
art.3(2) 8–84
Sch.2 8–84
1992 Family Proceedings (Amendment No.2) Rules (SI 1992/2067) 14–119, 15–24
1992 Prisons (Amendment) (No.2) Rules (SI 1992/2080) 3–34
1993 Children (Admissibility of Hearsay Evidence) Order (SI 1993/621) 3–234
1993 Maintenance Orders (Backdating) Order (SI 1993/623)
art.3 8–77
Sch.2, para.2 8–77
1993 Industrial Tribunal (Constitution and Rules of Procedure) Regulations (SI 1993/2687)
r.8(2) 7–38
r.13(2)(e) 13–65
Sch.I 7–38, 13–64
1994 Rules of the Court of Session (SI1994/1443)
r.14.2(d) 16–262

1994 Prison and Young Offenders Institutions (Scotland) Rules (SI 1994/1931)
r.50 16–240
r.50(3) 16–239
1995 Criminal Justice and Public Order Act 1994 (Commencement No.5 and Transitional Provisions) Order (SI 1995/127) 8–39, 8–47
1995 County Court Remedies (Amendment) regulations (SI 1995/206) 13–92
reg.2(b) 14–25
reg.3(3) 14–25
1997 Family Proceedings (Amendment No.2) Rules (SI 1997/1056) 3–235
1997 Family Proceedings (Amendment No.3) Rules (SI 1997/1893) 14–75, 14–85
1997 Family Law Act 1996 (Modification of Enactments) Order (SI 1997/1898)
art.2 8–77
1999 Prison Rules (SI 1999/728)
rr 34–39 11–302
2000 Access to Justice Act 1999 (Destination of Appeals) Order (SI 2000/107) 15–88
art.1(2)(c) 13–121
art.3(2) 13–121
art.5 13–121
2000 Civil Procedure (Amendment) Rules (SI 2000/221) 12–121
2001 Employment Tribunals (Constitution and Rules of Procedure) Regulations (SI 2001/1171)
r.15(2)(d) 10–194, 13–65
2001 Criminal Defence Service (General) (No.2) Regulations (SI 2001/1437) 15–114
2001 Civil Jurisdiction and Judgments Order (SI 2001/3929)
art.1(b) 8–77
2001 Civil Procedure (Amendment No.5) Rules (SI 2001/4015) 7–23, 15–56, 15–83
2002 Civil Procedure (Modification of Enactments) Order (SI 2002/439) 13–99, 15–52
2003 Anti-social Behaviour Act 2003 (Commencement No.1 and Transitional Provisions) Order (SI 2003/3300)
art.2(f)(ii) 8–45

Table of Statutory Instruments

2004 Civil Procedure (Amendment) Rules (SI 2004/1306) 14–89
2004 Employment Tribunals (Constitution and Rules of Procedure) Regulations (SI 2004/1861) ... 7–35, 8–141, 10–194, 13–64
    Sch.1, r.16 .... 7–109, 8–141
    Sch.1, r.26(3) 7–109
    Sch.1, r.50 8–143
    Sch.2 8–141
2004 Youth Justice and Criminal Evidence Act 1999 (Commencement No.10) (England and Wales) Order (SI 2004/2428) 8–74
2005 Criminal Procedure Rules (SI 2005/384)
    Pt 67 7–33
    Pts 67.1, 67.2 7–267
    r.16.10 ..... 2–64, 2–66, 7–32, 10–165
    r.68.1.3 7–33

TABLE OF RULES OF THE SUPREME COURT

(References are to paragraph numbers)

1965 Rules of the Supreme Court (SI 1965/1776)
- Ord.15, r.12 12–121
- Ord.22, r.7 5–111
- Ord.24, r.8 9–4
- Ord.24, r.14A .. 2–193, 3–187, 11–76, 11–77, 12–218, 12–228, 12–229, 12–231, 12–232, 12–237, 12–238
- Ord.25, r.67 1–84
- Ord.38, rr 14–18 11–91
- Ord.41, r.5(2) 3–232
- Ord.42, r.2 12–137
- Ord.42, r.2(2) 12–18, 12–130
- Ord.42, r.3(1) 12–146
- Ord.42, rr 6, 7 12–138
- Ord.42, r.31 .... 12–96, 12–115, 12–138, 12–200
- Ord.43, rr 6, 7 12–138
- Ord.44, r.2 15–8
- Ord.44, r.2(2) 7–228
- Ord.45, r.1 14–131
- Ord.45, r.5 12–111

1965 Rules of the Supreme Court —cont.
- Ord.45, r.5(1)(b) 1.120
- Ord.47, r.7 .... 1–84, 15–7
- Ord.52 .... 1–84, 2–19, 2–23, 2–28, 2–198, 2–210, 3–55, 4–158, 7–228, 7–230
- Ord.52, r.1 13–51
- Ord.52, r.2 .... 3–174, 9–228
- Ord.52, r.6 15–28
- Ord.52, r.7(1) 3–181, 14–53
- Ord.52, r.8 3–182
- Ord.52, r.8(1) 3–185, 14–53
- Ord.59, r.20 13–134
- Ord.62, r.11 11–67
- Ord.63, r.4 11–27
- Ord.63, r.4(1)(a) 11–75, 11–79
- Ord.65, r.2 .... 11–100, 12–35
- Ord.75, r.9 12–261
- Ord.79, r.10 11–134
- Ord.80, r.2 14–133
- Ord.82, r.6 9–4
- Ord.109, rr 1–3 13–134
- Ord.109, r.2(1) 13–133

TABLE OF CIVIL PROCEDURE RULES

(References are to paragraph numbers)

1998 Civil Procedure Rules (SI 1998/3132)
r.1.4 15–33
r.2.3 14–24
PD2.5(1) 15–13
PD2.5(2) 15–12, 15–19, 15–32
PD2.5(3) 15–19, 15–33
PD2.6(1) 15–13
PD2.6(2) 15–12, 15–19, 15–32
PD2.6(3) 15–19, 15–33
r.3.1(2)(a) 12–124, 12–127
r.3.2(2)(a) 12–18, 12–127
r.3.4 .... 11–1, 11–59
r.3.10 15–31
r.5.4(2) 11–27, 11–75, 11–79, 15–12
r.5.4(5)(b) 12–225
Pt 6 .... 15–26, 15–52
r.6.4(3) 12–35, 12–39, 15–11
r.6.8 ... 12–34, 12–37, 12–175, 15–13, 15–78
Pt 8 15–12
PD9 .... 15–28, 15–30
r.21.2 14–133
PD21 14–133
Pt 22 11–56
Pt 23 .... 12–127, 15–78
Pt 25 6–6
r.25.13 7–62
PD25, para.8.4 .... 3–196, 9–13
Pt 31 .... 12–205, 12–226
r.31.5(2) 9–4
r.31.17 .... 3–203, 12–226
r.31.19 9–4
r.31.22 .... 2–193, 3–187, 3–203, 11–76, 11–77, 12–205,**12–219**, 12–227, 12–228, 12–237
r.31.22(2) 11–77, 12–224, 12–226, 12–239
r.31.23 11–58
r.32.1 11–1
r.32.1(2) 3–237
r.32.14 .... 11–56, 11–57
PD32, para.4.2 3–232
Pt 34 .... 11–92, 11–93, 11–99, 13–95
r.34.2 .... 11–91, 11–100
r.34.3 11–91

1998 Civil Procedure Rules—*cont.*
r.34.4 11–97
r.34.6 11–100
r.34.7 .... 11–102, 13–96
r.34.8 11–98
r.35.9 3–206
r.34.10 11–98
r.35.9 15–35
Pt 36 4–124
r.36.19(2) 4–124, 5–111
Pt 39 .... 1–171, 1–173
r.39.2 .... 7–23, 7–54
r.39.2(3)(b) 7–61
PD39, para.1.11 11–81
PD39, para.2 .... **11–96**
r.40.7 .... 12–127, 12–130
r.40.7(1) 12–137
r.40.11 .... 12–127, 12–130
r.44.3 .... 1–148, 14–137
r.48.3 1–148
r.48.7 11–67
r.49(1) 12–261
r.49(2)(a) 12–261
PD49 12–261
Pt 52 ..... 9–245, 13–134, 15–95, 15–97
r.52.1(4) 15–95
r.52.3 15–94
r.52.3(1)(a)(i) 13–120, 15–88, 15–95
r.52.4(3) 15–98
r.52.13 13–121
r.52.14 13–121
PD52, para.21.4 .... 15–88, 15–98
r.53.3 9–4
PD61 12–261
r.62.10 .... 7–23, 7–25
r.62.10(1) 7–24, 7–26
Pt 65 14–89
PD70, para.1.2(2) 15–78
Sch.1 1–23
Sch.1, Ord.15.13A 12–121
Sch.1, Ord.45 .... 14–114, 15–84
Sch.1, Ord.45.1 ...... 14–111, 14–112, 14–124, 14–131
Sch.1, Ord.45.3 12–133
Sch.1, Ord.45.3(1) 12–18
Sch.1, Ord.45.3(2) 12–133

Table of Civil Procedure Rules

1998 Civil Procedure Rules—*cont.*

Sch.1, Ord.45.3(3)	12–133
Sch.1, Ord.45.3(3)(b)	12–134
Sch.1, Ord.45.4	12–135
Sch.1, Ord.45.4(1)(b), (c)	12–135
Sch.1, Ord.45.4(2)(b), (c)	12–131
Sch.1, Ord.45.5	12–18, 12–41, 12–42, 12–96, 12–110, 12–124, 12–127, 12–199, 13–97, 15–20
Sch.1, Ord.45.5(1), (2)	12–41
Sch.1, Ord.45.5(1)	12–135, 12–136, 14–122
Sch.1, Ord.45.5(3)	12–131, 12–135
Sch.1, Ord.45.6	12–18, 12–127, 12–131, 12–133
Sch.1, Ord.45.6(1)	12–41, 12–127
Sch.1, Ord.45.6(2)	12–42, 12–135
Sch.1, Ord.45.7	12–40, 12–175, 12–191
Sch.1, Ord.45.7(2)	12–37
Sch.1, Ord.45.7(3)(b)	12–40
Sch.1, Ord.45.7(4)	12–39, 12–40, 15–24
Sch.1, Ord.45.7(5)	12–41, 12–42
Sch.1, Ord.45.7(6), (7)	12–37, 15–26
Sch.1, Ord.45.7(6)	15–20, 15–24
Sch.1, Ord.45.7(7)	15–2, 15–23
Sch.1, Ord.45.8	12–17
Sch.1, Ord.46	15–84
Sch.1, Ord.46.3	11–328
Sch.1, Ord.46.5	14–111, 14–124
Sch.1, Ord.46.5(1)–(3)	15–78
Sch.1, Ord.46.5(4)	15–79
Sch.1, Ord.46.6(1)–(3)	15–81
Sch.1, Ord.46.6(4)	15–81
Sch.1, Ord.46.6(6)	15–82
Sch.1, Ord.46.8(1)–(5)	15–83
Sch.1, Ord.52	2–210, 3–55, 10–7, 10–27, 10–38, 10–193, 10–195, 11–92, 11–367, 13–24, 15–4, 15–9, 15–51, 15–84, 15–105
Sch.1, Ord.52.1	7–228, 10–136, 13–13, 13–23, 13–27, 13–28, 11–51
Sch.1, Ord.52.1(2)	10–7, 13–17
Sch.1, Ord.52.1(2)(a)(i)	13–17
Sch.1, Ord.52.1(2)(a)(ii)	10–7, 10–136, 13–13, 13–23, 13–25, 13–27
Sch.1, Ord.52.1(2)(a)(iii)	13–43
Sch.1, Ord.52.1(3)	13–17
Sch.1, Ord.52.1(4)	13–77
Sch.1, Ord.52.2	15–9, 15–32
Sch.1, Ord.52.2(2)	15–9
Sch.1, Ord.52.2(3)–(5)	15–10
Sch.1, Ord.52.3(1),(2)	15–10
Sch.1, Ord.52.3(3)	15–11
Sch.1, Ord.52.3(4)	12–34

1998 Civil Procedure Rules—*cont.*

Sch.1, Ord.52.4(1)	15–12
Sch.1, Ord.52.4(2), (3)	15–13
Sch.1, Ord.52.5	7–228, 12–125, 13–14, 13–19
Sch.1, Ord.52.6	15–16
Sch.1, Ord.52.6(1)	15–16, 15–28, 15–79
Sch.1, Ord.52.6(2)	15–16, 15–30
Sch.1, Ord.52.6(3)	15–16, 15–32, 15–33
Sch.1, Ord.52.6(4)	15–35
Sch.1, Ord.52.7	14–54, 15–102
Sch.1, Ord.52.8	3–182, 3–185, 15–102
Sch.1, PD52, paras 2.1, 2.2	15–12
Sch.1, Ord.77.15	14–111
Sch.1, Ord.77.15(1)	15–84
Sch.1, Ord.109	13–132, 13–133
Sch.1, Ord.109, rr 1–3	13–134
Sch.1, Ord.109, r.2(1)	13–133
Sch.1, Ord.109, r.2(4)	13–132
Sch.1, Ord.109, r.2(5)	13–132
Sch.1, Ord.113	6–117, 12–133
Sch.1, Ord.113.7(1)	12–133
Sch.2, Ord.13, r.3	14–74
Sch.2, Ord.26	12–133
Sch.2, Ord.26.17(4), (5)	11–328
Sch.2, Ord.27.7B	13–99
Sch.2, Ord.27.8	13–99
Sch.2, Ord.28	13–89, 13–96, 15–56
Sch.2, Ord.28.2(3), (4)	13–89
Sch.2, Ord.28.4	13–89, 13–99
Sch.2, Ord.28.4(2)	13–99
Sch.2, Ord.28.5(2)	13–89
Sch.2, Ord.29	10–38, 11–67, 13–92, 15–24, 15–51
Sch.2, Ord.29.1	12–34, 13–97, 15–52, 15–65, 15–66
Sch.2, Ord.29.1(1)	15–56
Sch.2, Ord.29.1(3)	14–118
Sch.2, Ord.29.1(4)	15–58, 15–59, 15–60, 15–67
Sch.2, Ord.29.1(5)	15–77
Sch.2, Ord.29.1(6)	15–58
Sch.2, Ord.29.1(7)	15–57
Sch.2, Ord.29.2	13–98
Sch.2, Ord.34	11–92
Sch.2, Ord.34.1	13–84, 14–24, **15–77**
Sch.2, Ord.34.1A	**15–77**
Sch.2, Ord.34.3	13–96
Sch.2, Ord.34.4	13–96
Sch.2, Ord.35, r.5	14–24
Sch.2, Ord.47, r.8(7)	14–71
Sch.2, PD49	14–91

CHAPTER 1

HISTORY OF THE LAW OF CONTEMPT[1]

		PARA
I.	The Common Law Courts	1–1
II.	Influence of the Star Chamber	1–26
III.	The Court of Chancery: the Development of Civil Contempt	1–41
IV.	Summary Procedure in the Eighteenth Century	1–51
V.	The Rule Against *Ex Parte* Statements	1–71
VI.	Other Nineteenth Century Developments	1–74
VII.	Background to the Contempt of Court Act 1981	1–86
VIII.	The Contempt of Court Act 1981	1–114
IX.	Developments Since the 1981 Act: a Summary	1–126
X.	Issues Currently Requiring Attention in the Law of Contempt	1–161

I. THE COMMON LAW COURTS

A. Early contempts: hindrance or obstruction

From earliest legal history the courts have assumed the power to coerce those who obstruct the administration of justice. The authors of *Glanville*, writing in the late part of the twelfth century, refer on several occasions to *contemptus curiae*, by which they seem to mean the contempt shown by a party to a suit who fails to appear before the court. They say, of an action concerning a freehold, that if the Demandant and Tenant are both absent the King or his justices may at their pleasure punish both parties, the one for his contempt of court and the other for his false claim.[2] Bracton, writing in the middle of the thirteenth century, thought there was "no greater crime than Contempt and Disobedience, for all persons within the Realm ought to be obedient to the King and within his Peace".[3]   1–1

Certainly from about 1250 onwards, the Rolls and Year Books contain references to contempt of court.[4] These usually relate to some disturbance or   1–2

---

[1] This chapter relies heavily upon *The History of Contempt of Court*, Oxford University Press (1927) by Sir John Fox, which was based to a large extent on his articles published in the *Law Quarterly Review*, as follows: "The King v. Almon" (1908) 24 L.Q.R. 184 and 266; "The Summary Process to Punish Contempt" (1909) 25 L.Q.R 238 and 354; "Eccentricities of the Law of Contempt of Court" (1920) 36 L.Q.R 394; "The Nature of Contempt of Court" (1921) 37 L.Q.R 191; "The Practice in Contempt of Court Cases" (1922) 38 L.Q.R. 185; "The Writ of Attachment" (1924) 40 L.Q.R. 43. Some of Sir John's own work was based upon the article by F. Solly-Flood Q.C, "The Story of Prince Henry of Monmouth and Chief-Justice Gascoign" (1886) Vol. 3, *Transactions of the Royal Historical Society*, N.S. 47, and the unpublished manuscript, also by Solly-Flood, *Abridged History of the Writ of Habeas Corpus* (1887). We have not been able to consult the latter manuscript. Sir John Fox referred to these works as "m" and "M.S." respectively, and we have adopted the same practice.
[2] *Tractatus de Legibus et Consuetudinibus Regni Angliae*, i, 33; iii, 6; xiii, 10.
[3] *ibid.*, fos.1b, 127b.
[4] Contained in the Appendix to Fox, which is a compilation of references from the works of Solly-Flood. Above, n.1.

1–2 CHAPTER 1—HISTORY OF THE LAW OF CONTEMPT

hostile reaction in or near the court affecting its business, or to some violent or insulting reaction to service of the court's process. It was also recognised as a contempt to draw a sword to strike a judge,[5] or to assault in open court the Attorney General,[6] one of the King's clerks,[7] a juror,[8] a witness,[9] or an opposing party.[10] It seems, however, that the element of assault was not regarded as essential, for sometimes it was simply alleged that the contemnor had hindered proceedings in court.[11]

1–3 Moreover, the relevant act did not necessarily have to be committed actually in the presence of the court, though in the few available cases the conduct was treated as constructively in the presence of the court. So it was held to be a contempt to assault a person connected with the business of the court in its immediate precincts, for example in Westminster Hall.[12] Similarly, an assault on a litigant[13] or an officer of the court[14] on the way to court. This is an early instance of the principle enunciated by Bowen L.J. in *Re Johnson*[15] that:

> "those who have duties to discharge in a court of justice are protected by the law, and shielded on their way to the discharge of such duties, while discharging them, and on their return therefrom, in order that such persons may safely have resort to courts of justice."

1–4 In 1317 a clerk of the King's Court brought an action for an assault on him when coming from Fleet Street to transact the business of the King. Again, however, the assault was alleged to have occurred in the presence of the court.[16] In 1365 an assault on a man before the gates of Winchester Castle as he was coming to the court to prosecute an assize of novel disseisin was alleged to have occurred in the presence of the justices.[17] No such artifice appears to have been necessary when the offence complained of was resistance to the execution of a writ. Such an act would be clearly an interference with the business of the court.[18]

---

[5] (1348) Y.B., 22 Edw. III, p.13, pl. 26.
[6] Coram Rege roll, M. 30 Edw. III, m. 113 (Solly-Flood).
[7] (1253) Curia Regis roll, M. 37–8 Henry III, m. 12d; Placit. Abbrev., p.132, rot. 12.
[8] Coram Rege roll, H. 22 Edw. III, m. 103.
[9] *Davis's Case* (1461) 2 Dyer 188, 73 E.R. 415.
[10] Coram Rege roll, T. 30 Edw. I, m. 9d.
[11] (1254) Curia Regis roll, M. 38–9 Henry III, m. 22d; (1289) Rot. Parl., i, 33b; (1323) Coram Rege roll, M. 17 Edw. II, m. 16d, Plac. Abbrev., p.342, rot. 16.
[12] See *William de Sadington's Case* (1293) Plac. Abbrev., p.291, rot. 7; *Mayor of Staple* (1319) Coram Rege roll, T. 13 Edw. II, m. 14.
[13] (1323) Coram Rege roll, M. 17 Edw. II, m. 16d; (1398) Cal. Pat. Rolls, 22 Rich. II, 427.
[14] (1317) Coram Rege roll, T. 11 Edw. II, m. 48 (which suggests the assault was on a juror) and Plac. Abbrev., p.331, rot. 48 (which suggests it was on a clerk of the King's Court).
[15] (1887) 20 Q.B.D. 68, 74.
[16] Plac. Abbrev., p.331, rot. 48; and see Cal. Pat. Rolls, 22 Rich. II, 427 where an assault in Fleet Street was alleged to have occurred in the presence of the King and the whole Parliament.
[17] Y.B., Lib. Ass., 39 Edw. III, pl. 1. The continuing problem, albeit of diminishing significance, of defining what is "in the face of the court" is discussed in chap.10.
[18] Curia Regis roll, H. 38, Henry III, m. 8d. See also Coram Rege roll, P. 4 Edw. I, minus r., m. 4.; Coram Rege roll, P. 4 Edw. I, majus r., m. 6; Coram Rege roll, M. 7 & 8 Edw. I, m. 27; Coram Rege roll, T. 21 Edw. I, m. 28d.

B. Contempt by words

It appears to have been recognised at an early stage that a contempt could consist merely in words. It was a contempt to insult a judge in open court[19] or in the presence of his fellow judges as they were going to hold pleas,[20] or to abuse a jury[21] or party to a suit[22] in open court. Similarly it was a contempt to speak insultingly of the King's writ which the King's bailiff was attempting to execute.[23] Moreover, it seems that publication out of court of matter scandalising the court was treated as contempt by the fourteenth century. In 1344 John de Northampton, an attorney, confessed that he had written a letter to one of the King's Council reflecting on the judges of the King's Bench. It was adjudged by that court that the letter was a scandal upon the court and John was committed to the Marshal before sureties were found for his good behaviour.[24]

1–5

In 1345 Robert Hovel[25] sued by petition to the King alleging that an assize was awarded against him contrary to law in the King's Bench and that some of the justices awarded the assize contrary to the unanimous opinion of their fellows. The bill of petition was sent in a letter under the privy seal to Sir William Scot C.J., who said this suit was a slander on the court.

1–6

C. Early procedure

The early history of the contempt process reveals a greater variety of procedural means of dealing with alleged contemnors than is found today.

1–7

1. *Writ of attachment*

Where the alleged contemnor was not already before the court, he was brought there by the writ of attachment. In the twelfth and thirteenth centuries this writ appears to have been a general preliminary process to compel appearance in the common law courts.[26] The writ, directed to the Sheriff, took two forms—*per vadium et plegios* (by security and sureties) and *per corpus suum* (by imprisonment).[27] By the end of the thirteenth century, attachment by imprisonment appears to have been the correct process in the case of contempts against the King and his officers.[28] In the course of time it became a process applicable only

1–8

---

[19] (1293) Coram Rege roll, P. 21 Edw. I, par. i., m. 95 (Solly-Flood), William de Bereford J.; (1305) Coram Rege roll, M. 33 & 34 Edw. I, m. 75 (Solly-Flood); Plac. Abbrev., pp.256–7, rot. 75, Baron Roger de Hegham.
[20] (1340) Y.B. 14 Edw. III (Rolls Series), 324–31.
[21] Coram Rege roll, P. 10 Edw. III, m. 15d.
[22] Coram Rege roll, M. 17 Edw. II, m. 16d.
[23] Coram Rege roll, T. 21 Edw. I, m. 28d.
[24] Coram Rege roll, M. 18 Edw. III; 2 Co. Inst. 174.
[25] (1345) Y.B. 19 Edw. (R.S.) III, 138, 19 *Lib. Ass.*, pl. 5.
[26] Glanvill I, 14, 21, 30, 31; III, 6; VI, 10. VIII, 5; X, 3, 15, 16; Bracton fo. 149.
[27] Bracton fo. 149. And see F. Pollock and F.W. Maitland, *History of English Law* (2nd ed., 1898) Vol. 2, p.185n., and Fox, *op. cit.*, p.60.
[28] Britton I, xxxvii; Fox, *op. cit.*, pp.64–6.

to such contempts and, as the form *per vadium* fell into abeyance, the words *per corpus suum* were omitted from the writ of attachment.[29]

2. Complaint

1–9 On occasion contempts appear to have been brought to the notice of the court by a simple complaint. In 1293, for instance, William de Sadington appeared covered in blood before the court of King's Bench and complained that the defendant had struck him in Westminster Hall. William was awarded 20s damages assessed by the court and the defendant was committed to the Marshal.[30] In the following year two members of a jury complained that the defendant had falsely accused them of making a false oath. The defendant denied the words. A jury was empanelled instantly, and they found that the defendant spoke the words in contempt of the King. The defendant was committed to the Marshal and ordered to pay the complainants 6s 8d damages.[31] It can be seen that the two aspects of contempt, public and private, were being recognised and addressed.[32] The wrong to the complainant was compensated by damages; the wrong to the King was a separate matter, to be dealt with initially by committal to the Marshal.

3. Remedial claims[33]

1–10 It was quite common for a person adversely affected by a contempt to bring an action for damages, although essentially by way of an action for trespass or assault. Under the early writs of trespass it was usual for a losing defendant to pay not only damages to the plaintiff, but also an amount to the King for the breach of his peace.[34]

1–11 Contempt of court was a breach of the peace which would touch the King more closely than an ordinary trespass. Hence again the proceedings were serving a dual purpose. In 1319, for example, the Mayor of the Staple brought an action of trespass against the defendant for abusing and assaulting him in Westminster Hall. The matter was tried by a jury and there was a verdict for the plaintiff with damages of £100. The defendant was committed to the Marshal at the King's will.[35] In 1332 an action was brought for contempt (*de placito contemptu*) in assaulting the plaintiff in open court.[36] In 1353 an action was brought for trespass in the Palace at Westminster in the presence of the King and his justices.[37] In 1352 an action was brought by one of a jury for violent assault in open court. Damages were adjudged at £10 of which 120s were awarded to the King.[38]

---

[29] Fox, p.64.
[30] Plac. Abbrev., p.291 rot. 7.
[31] Coram Rege roll, P. 22 Edw. I, m. 39 (Solly-Flood). Plac Abbrev., p.291, rot. 39.
[32] See paras 3–6 *et seq*.
[33] For the modern law, see paras 14–142 *et seq*.
[34] See F.W. Maitland, *The Constitutional History of England* (1908) p.114.
[35] Coram Rege roll, T. 13 Edward II, m. 14 (Solly-Flood). Plac. Abbrev., p.336, rot. 14.
[36] Coram Rege roll, M. 6 Edward III, m. 30d.
[37] Y.B., Lib. Ass., 27 Edward III, pl. 49.
[38] Coram Rege roll, P. 26 Edward III, m. 60 (Solly-Flood).

There are also instances of an action for abusing a party to a suit in court[39] and for hindering proceedings in court.[40] Officers of the Crown such as sheriffs[41] or bailiffs[42] brought actions for resistance to the execution of a writ. Sometimes in such cases the action was brought at the suit of the King.[43]

4. Bill in the King's Bench

There was also a more formal process of a suit by a bill in the King's Bench. Hale writing in the seventeenth century refers to this process as anciently practised, but long disused.[44] The complainant filed a bill in the King's Bench, informing that court of the alleged contempt, and suing for damages for himself and a penalty for the King. In 1309, for example, such a bill was filed alleging that the defendant, on being served with a writ of prohibition, threw it to the ground and trampled it underfoot, in contempt of the King to the extent of £1,000 and to the damage of the plaintiff £100. The defendant pleaded not guilty, but was tried and found guilty by a jury. It was adjudged that the plaintiff recover his damages and the defendant was committed (*capiatur*—be taken or imprisoned), although it may be that no other financial penalty was imposed.[45]

In the case where the plaintiff brought proceedings for an assault on him before the gates of Winchester Castle, proceedings were initiated by a bill.[46] The defendant was found guilty by inquest of a jury, and £10 damages was awarded to the plaintiff. The defendant was also committed, and the justices were "to consult with the Council what should be done as to the fine and with regard to the King for the assault made in the presence of the Justices".

In 1356 Seton J. appears to have brought a bill in the Exchequer against a defendant for openly calling him a traitor in the presence of the Treasurer and Barons of the Exchequer, in contempt of the King and to the slander of the court. This may indicate that the procedure was available in all the common law courts. The defendant pleaded not guilty and the issue was tried by attorneys of the Common Bench and Exchequer. He was found guilty with 100 marks damages to the plaintiff and also imprisoned to abide the King's will.[47]

5. Indictment

Contemnors appear also to have been indicted. In 1345 one N. was indicted in the King's Bench, that in the presence of the justices he threatened and struck the

---

[39] *ibid.*, M. 17 Edward II, m. 63.
[40] *ibid.*, M. 38–9 Henry III, m. 22d.
[41] Coram Rege roll, H. 38 Henry III, m. 8d; Coram Rege roll, P. 4 Edward I, majus, r., m. 6.
[42] Coram Rege roll, M. 7 & 8 Edward I, m. 27.
[43] *ibid.*, P 12 Edward II, m. 114d; Coram Rege roll, T. 21 Edward I, m. 28d.
[44] "Discourse concerning the courts of King's Bench and Common Pleas", in F. Hargrave, *A Collection of Tracts relative to the Law of England* (1787) at p.363.
[45] Coram Rege roll, M. 3 Edward II, m. 35 (Solly-Flood M.S., p.420).
[46] (1365) Y.B., Lib. Ass., 39 Edward III, pl. 1. See para.1–4. The role of the King's Council is considered further at para.1–27.
[47] *ibid.*, 30 Edward III, pl. 19.

1–16   CHAPTER 1—HISTORY OF THE LAW OF CONTEMPT

jurors of an inquest. He confessed and was severely punished.[48] In 1348 a knight and esquire were indicted for raising strife before Thorpe C.J., where the esquire had actually drawn his sword to strike the judge. They too were convicted and punished.[49] In 1461 a man was indicted for striking a witness in the presence of the court and threatening to hang him if he gave evidence.[50]

1–17   Indeed, Fox was unable in his researches to find any example of summary committal for contempt committed out of the presence of the judges, apart from offences committed by officers of the court. There are authorities which show that, even where the contempt was committed in their presence, the judges were reluctant to deal with the matter summarily. In one early case, a conviction for contempt in the face of the King's Bench in Ireland was reversed by writ of error because the contempt was not tried by a jury.[51] In 1340 certain defendants were attached by bill to answer a justice of the King's Bench for insulting him in the presence of his fellow judges as they were going to hold the pleas. The plaintiff prayed that inasmuch as the offence was committed in the presence of the justices they should take the inquest immediately. This was refused and a writ was sent to the sheriff to cause 12 men to come from the neighbourhood of Westminster.[52]

1–18   In 1631, a prisoner who threw a brickbat at Richardson C.J.C.P. in court and narrowly missed was indicted for his offence.[53] As late as 1638 a clergyman who rushed to the bar of the Common Bench when the courts were sitting and openly accused one of the presiding judges of high treason was also indicted.[54]

1–19   In 1565 one Welch was indicted for saying "My Lord Chief Justice Catlyne is incensed against me; I cannot have justice nor can be heard, for that Court now is made a court of conscience."[55] And in 1629 there was an indictment for a libel upon Sir Edward Coke and upon the King's Bench.[56] A contempt in the court of Common Pleas could be dealt with on indictment in the King's Bench.

6. *Information*

1–20   Informations were certainly used in the seventeenth century as a means of bringing contempts before the courts; for example, in 1632 for an assault upon

---

[48] Y.B. (Rolls Series), 19 Edward III 452. The punishment was that the offender's right hand be struck off and his land and chattels forfeited, and that he be imprisoned for life; but the execution was stayed until the King had signified his pleasure.
[49] Y.B., 22 Edward III, p.13, pl. 26.
[50] *Davis's Case* (1461) 2 Dyer, 188, 73 E.R. 415.
[51] (1331) Coram Rege roll, M. 5 Edward III, m. 128.
[52] Y.B. 14 Edward III (R.S.) 324–31.
[53] *Anon.*, cited in a note to 2 Dyer 188b, 73 E.R. 415. Discussed by J.H. Baker, "Le Brickbat Que Narrowly Mist" (1984) 100 L.Q.R. 544.
[54] *Harrison's Case* (1638) Cro. Car. 503, 79 E.R. 1034.
[55] Cited in *Wraynham's Case* (1618) 2 St.Tr. 1060: the court referred to is the King's Bench.
[56] *Harrison's Case* (1638) Cro. Car. 503, 79 E.R. 1034.

the Sheriff of Middlesex while levying execution[57] and in 1680 for speaking scandalous words of Chief Justice Scroggs.[58]

7. *Reluctance to use the summary process even in early times*

Generally, the alleged contemnor, unless he confessed, seems to have been put on trial by jury. It was clearly recognised, however, that the remedy for contempt must be swift. There are several examples of a jury being empanelled *instanter*. In 1317 a clerk of the King's Court brought an action against two men for an assault upon him in Fleet Street on his way to court. The Marshal was ordered to summon 12 men of the court and the sheriff 12 men of the neighbourhood of Fleet Street instantly.[59] In 1368 when an assault was alleged to have occurred on a litigant in Westminster Hall a jury of stall-keepers in Westminster Hall was empanelled.[60] We have already seen that when Seton J. brought a bill in the Exchequer alleging that a defendant had called him a traitor, the issue was tried by attorneys of the Common Bench and Exchequer.[61]

1–21

It seems probable that the common law courts did have power to deal summarily with contempt committed in their presence.[62] Fox quotes two cases which he suggests demonstrate that this was so. In 1306 the parties to a suit, being asked several times by the court by what right they claimed, would not answer. They were committed to the Fleet.[63] In *Holbrooke's* case (1329) the defendant raised a clamour before the Commissioners of Oyer and Terminer and was ordered to be committed.[64] There are certainly *dicta* indicating that a distinction was drawn between acts in the presence of the judges and those elsewhere.[65] In 1343 Shareshull J. said that a justice of *nisi prius* might punish a trespass committed in his presence which sounded in contempt of the King.[66]

1–22

It may be that summary committal occurred more often than the reported cases indicate, for in 1452 Fortescue, Chief Justice of the King's Bench, said that many were committed to custody for some offence committed at Court of which no record was kept.[67] It seems that the court of Common Pleas may have adopted a similar course. Brooks, Chief Justice of that Court, wrote in about 1558 in his *Abridgement* that justices of the Bench could adjudge anything done before themselves without trial or jury.[68] In *Dean's* case[69] it was urged before the

1–23

---

[57] *Wingfield* Cro. Car., 251, 79 E.R. 819.
[58] *Radley's Case* (1680) 7 St. Tr. 701.
[59] Plac. Abbrev., p.331 rot. 48.
[60] Y.B., Lib Ass., 42 Edward III, pl. 18.
[61] Edward III, pl. 19.
[62] Fox, pp.50–1.
[63] Y.B. 33–5 Edward I (R.S.) 316.
[64] *ibid.*, 3 Edward III, rot. 116.
[65] See also chap.10.
[66] *Cretynge's Case*, Y.B. 17 Edward III (R.S.) 276.
[67] Y.B., 31 Henry VI, p.10, pl. 5.
[68] Bro. Abr., 'Judges', 21.
[69] (1598) Cro. Eliz. 689, 78 E.R. 925.

Common Pleas that a justice of the peace could by custom commit a person who had publicly abused an alderman and who failed to find sureties for his good behaviour, but the court could not see how the custom could be maintained and discharged the prisoner. Anderson C.J.C.P. added that "a man may be imprisoned for a contempt done in court, but not for a contempt out of court."[70] In 1629 counsel arguing in *Selden's* case[71] before the King's Bench also made the distinction, expressly saying that contempts were punishable only on conviction, unless committed in the face of the court.

D. The jurisdiction over officers of the court

1–24 Officers of justice seem to have been regarded as being in a special position, such that they could be dealt with summarily even for offences out of court.[72] Fox suggests that they may have been presumed to be always in the presence of the court, but the court naturally would have special disciplinary power over its own officers.[73] There are reported examples of summary proceedings against officers of the court. In 1346, a clerk accused of forging a writ was brought before the King's Bench, sworn and examined secretly by the justices.[74] In 1310 Stanton J. appears to have proceeded summarily against an attorney who had not issued a writ and so had delayed a woman from her dower.[75]

1–25 There are, on the other hand, cases in the reign of Henry III, Edward I and Edward II, in which an attorney was proceeded against by action or information.[76] Hence, if a *sui generis* jurisdiction over officers of the court did exist, it was by no means always used. From 1402 to 1640 a number of statutes were passed giving the superior courts powers to proceed summarily in certain cases against officers of the court, which also embraced jurors.[77]

II. INFLUENCE OF THE STAR CHAMBER

A. Introduction

1–26 So far we have been considering the powers of the common law courts to punish contempt. From the earliest times, however, the King's Council took an interest in such offences and in time its jurisdiction passed to the Star Chamber. That court dealt with contempt not by the common law procedure, but by its own

---

[70] A distinction has been drawn since at least the sixteenth century between contempts in the face of the court, and other forms of interference with the administration of justice. Contempts in the face are more fully discussed in ch.10.
[71] St. Tr. 267.
[72] See Fox, pp.156–63.
[73] And see Hawkins, *Pleas of the Crown* (1721) Bk. II. Ch. 22, s.12.
[74] Fox, p.73; Y.B. 20 Edward III (R.S.), Part ii, Introduction, p.50.
[75] Fox, p.161, Y.B. (Selden Society), 3 & 4 Edward II, p.194.
[76] Fox, p.158.
[77] Fox, p.82. Style's *Practical Register* published in 1657 shows that certainly by the middle of the seventeenth century the King's Bench was proceeding summarily against its officers; Titles "Attachment".

summary process. The alleged contemnor was summoned by a writ which stated merely that he had committed a contempt without specifying its nature. Once before the court, he was examined either by interrogatories on oath or, if he confessed, orally but without the need of sworn testimony. Once his guilt was established, he could be both fined and imprisoned. When the Star Chamber was abolished, it appears that much of its jurisdiction was assumed by the common law courts; it may well be that the summary method of dealing with contempt, which developed in the eighteenth century, owed much to the earlier process of the Star Chamber.

B. The role of the King's Council

As early as 1293, Bereford J. petitioned the King and his Council in Parliament against two men for assaulting him with words of contumely in court for contempt of the King. The respondents acknowledged their fault and were imprisoned at the King's will.[78] In 1305 Hegham B. brought an information before the King and his Council against William de Brewes for abusing him in open court. William confessed and was sentenced to ask pardon in court and to be imprisoned at the King's will.[79]

1-27

When a man had been found guilty of contempt in the common law courts, the judges would sometimes consult the Council as to the appropriate punishment, in so far as the contempt touched the King. Conversely, if a contemnor brought before the Council did not confess, he might be referred to the judges for trial. In 1315 certain justices of the King complained to the Parliament at Lincoln that while on the business of the King at Bristol the commonalty of that city assaulted and imprisoned them. Six men of the commonalty were summoned to attend before the Council at Westminster. A writ was issued to summon a jury and some justices of the King were assigned to hear and determine the contempts. The jury found mainly against the commonalty and fines of 4,000 marks were imposed.[80]

1-28

In the sixteenth and seventeenth centuries the Star Chamber, itself an offshoot of the Council, punished contempts of the common law courts. Hudson in his treatise on the court, written early in the seventeenth century, recorded that for a misdemeanour committed in any court the Star Chamber might punish it as well as the judges of the relevant court.[81] He gave examples such as unlawful alteration of a pleading in the Common Pleas, extortions, bribery and corruption of officers.[82] The Star Chamber also had jurisdiction over criminal libels.[83] This covered both written and spoken words, and it included some libels which could be regarded as contempts. Coke in his report of the case *De Libellis Famosis*[84]

1-29

---

[78] Coram Rege roll, P. 21 Edward I, par. i, m. 95 (Solly-Flood). Rot. Parl., i, 95a.
[79] Coram Rege roll, M 33 & 34 Edw. I, m. 75; Plac. Abbrev., pp.256–7, rot. 75; 3 Inst., 142.
[80] Rot. Parl., 9 Ed. II, i 359b.
[81] W. Hudson, *Treatise of the Court of Star Chamber: Collectanea Juridica*, ii 117 at 118.
[82] ibid. See also *Att-Gen v Browne*, Star Chamber Reports (Camden Society) 148 and *Att-Gen v Casen*, ibid. at 116., quoted in Fox, p.184.
[83] See T.F.T. Plucknett, *A Concise History of the Common Law* (5th ed., 1956) p.485.
[84] (1605) 5 Co. Rep.125, 77 E.R. 250.

observed that a libel against a private man deserved severe punishment, but if it be against a magistrate, or other public person, it was a greater offence. A libeller (called *famosus defamator*) was to be punished either by indictment at common law or by bill, if he denied it, or *ore tenus* on a confession in the Star Chamber. The Star Chamber also punished contempts of the Court of Chancery.

C. Star Chamber procedure

1–30 We must now consider the summary procedure of the Star Chamber and its possible influence on the common law.

1. General writs

1–31 Writs of attachment at common law originally stated the nature of the alleged contempt.[85] In the Star Chamber, however, a contemnor was summoned to answer concerning a certain contempt alleged to have been committed by him, without the offending conduct being specified.[86] The earliest form of a common law writ of attachment of this kind is found in the *Thesaurus Brevium* in 1687.[87] A similar writ to compel attendance for contempt in the Court of Chancery appeared in the same year in the *Registrum Brevium*.[88] Since the Star Chamber was abolished less than 50 years before this date, it is possible that this form of general writ was derived from that court.[89]

2. Interrogatories on oath

1–32 The King's Council interrogated persons on oath from the time of Edward II.[90] This process was adopted by the Star Chamber.[91] That court also adopted the procedure of examination *ore tenus* in private and not on oath, but this could only be used when the accused person confessed.[92] It might be used to obtain further admissions. There is some evidence that in the late sixteenth and early seventeenth centuries the common law courts attempted to adopt the procedure of examining alleged contemnors on oath. In *Ludlow's* case[93] Ludlow was attached with others for contempt and it was ordered by the Queen's Bench that they should be examined by interrogatories concerning that and all other contempts. It may be that the court of Common Pleas adopted a similar course in *Dunkley's* case[94] in 1621.

1–33 In 1630 Commissioners appointed to enquire into the offices and fees of the King's Bench certified that "For examination upon attachments of contempt we

---

[85] See Fox, chap. VI and the examples there given.
[86] Hudson, *Collect. Jurid.*, ii 147.
[87] Fox, p.67.
[88] ibid.
[89] See para.1–8.
[90] J.F. Baldwin, *The King's Council in England During the Middle Ages* (1913), pp.296–7.
[91] Hudson, *Collect. Jurid.*, ii 169.
[92] ibid., 127, 8. And see Coke C.J. in the case *De Libellis Famosis*, para.1–29.
[93] (1594) Q.B. Crown Side, Rule Book I, fo. 41 Mich. 36, 37 Elizabeth, quoted in Fox, p.86.
[94] Hudson, *Collect Jurid.* ii, 118, 119.

do not know what hath been anciently taken by reason of the fewness of them, but of late there hath been taken the fee of 3s 4d."[95] This may indicate that the common law courts were beginning to cover the jurisdiction of the Star Chamber.

In the introduction to *Vidian's Entries*, it was stated,[96] of the practice of the King's Bench, that if any contemnor despised any rule of court, an attachment might issue to arrest the offender. He had to appear personally, in court and enter into recognisances and be sworn to answer interrogatories, which should be exhibited against him, and examined on oath by the Master. If he acquitted himself, he might be discharged on motion to the court, but if not, he was fined for contempt at the discretion of the court. How far this was a general process on contempt is not clear, but by Blackstone's time examination by interrogatories in cases of contempt had become part of the regular process of the King's Bench.

3. *Fine and imprisonment*[97]

In the early common law the judgment of the court not only gave or refused relief, but also declared that the losing party either be in *misericordia regis* (in the King's mercy) or *capiatur* (be taken or imprisoned).[98] In the former case he was amerced; that is he had to make a money payment to the Crown which was fixed provisionally by the court and later affeered by a local Justice of Assize and jury.[99] If he failed to pay, the immediate consequence was that his goods would be distrained. The payment of an amercement was enforceable by distress but not by imprisonment.[1] In such a case, although he was ultimately liable to be imprisoned, he could always avoid imprisonment by "making fine"[2] with the Crown, that is paying a sum fixed by the court in lieu of imprisonment.[3] Only if he did not pay would he go to prison.[4] Which sanction was used depended on the form of proceeding. In contempt, amercement applied to parties to proceedings; the order in relation to third parties was *capiatur*.[5] The result was that a contemnor could not both be imprisoned *and* forced to pay a pecuniary penalty.

---

[95] *Jus Filizarii*.
[96] A.Vidian, *The Exact Pleader: A Book of Entries of Choice, Select and Special Pleadings in the court of Kings-Bench in the Reign of His Present Majesty King Charles II* (1684).
[97] Fox deals with this subject in great detail in ch. VIII. This did not form the subject of one of his *Law Quarterly Review* articles.
[98] Fox, pp.118 *et seq.*
[99] For examples see Fox, pp.134–6.
[1] Fox, p.118; *Griesley's* Case (1588) Co. 8 Rep.38a, 77 E.R. 530.
[2] *Finem fecit*—literally he made an end of the matter; the form of the judgment was that he be imprisoned for his fine—*capiatur pro fine*, see Fox, p.137.
[3] In cases of contempt the Council often fixed the sum to be forfeited ("amercement"—the original distinction between a fine and an amercement was that the former was a fixed sum, and there was no power to enforce its payment by imprisonment).
[4] Fox, pp.137–9, 164–77; it should be remembered that in the centuries following the Conquest royal justice was an important source of royal revenue.
[5] See Fox, pp.119, 136.

1-36 Again, however, officers of justice appear to have fallen into a special category. The sum they had to pay for a contempt was fixed finally by the court and not by a jury. In addition to paying such a sum, they could be imprisoned until the court or the Council saw fit to discharge them, without the right to avoid imprisonment by making fine.[6] In the course of the sixteenth century a change seems to have occurred.[7] Gradually we find the modern phrase "to be fined" replacing the older "to make fine".[8] A fine was no longer a voluntary payment to avoid imprisonment, but a compulsory payment in default of or in addition to which an offender might be imprisoned.

1-37 Certainly by 1630 the King's Bench had assumed the power to imprison and fine for the same offence. In that year *Jeffes*,[9] who was indicted for a libel on Sir Edward Coke, put in a scandalous plea and was fined £1,000 and imprisoned. The cases of *Waller*[10] and *Harrison*[11] were similarly dealt with. The Star Chamber had always exercised a power to fine *and* imprison; indeed the ordinary form of punishment in that Court was a pecuniary penalty and committal to the Fleet or Tower.[12] Sir Thomas Smith in his *Commonwealth of England* referred to the sentences of the Star Chamber as often consisting of both imprisonment and fine.[13] *Jeffes* shows that the King's Bench had also assumed this power before the abolition of the Star Chamber, but again it may be that the King's Bench was imitating or even deliberately encroaching on the powers of the Star Chamber. In any event, it seems clear that after the abolition of that Court, the common law courts exercised the power to combine fine and imprisonment for contempt.

D. Abolition of the Star Chamber

1-38 In 1640 the Act for the Abolition of the Star Chamber was passed and it recited that all matters previously determinable in that Court would henceforth have their proper remedy and redress by the common law of the land and in the ordinary course of justice.[14] In 1686 Herbert C.J.K.B. is reported as saying that the reason for dispensing with the Star Chamber was because their authority had been, and was yet again, vested in the King's Bench; consequently that Court was no longer necessary.[15] In 1689 Holt C.J.K.B. stated that the King's Bench had acquired all the lawful power that had been vested in the Star Chamber.[16]

1-39 In the next century Blackstone wrote:

"Upon the dissolution of the Star Chamber the old common law authority of the court of King's Bench as *custos morum* of the nation, being found necessary to reside

---

[6] Fox, p.136 and *Paston's* Case (1465) Y.B. (Long Quinto) 5 Edw. IV 5.
[7] See Fox, pp.164–95.
[8] See Fox, p.130.
[9] Cro. Car. 175, 79 E.R. 753.
[10] (1633) Cro. Car. 373, 79 E.R. 926.
[11] (1638) Cro. Car. 503, 79 E.R. 1034.
[12] Fox, p.165.
[13] (1589) Bk. III ch. 4.
[14] 16 Charles I c.10.
[15] *Johnson*, Comb. 36, 90 E.R. 328.
[16] *Abraham*, Comb. 141, 90 E.R. 393.

somewhere for the peace and good government of the kingdom, was again revived in practice."[17]

A great deal of the Star Chamber's law of misdemeanours and in particular its law of libel passed into the common law.[18]

1–40 It may also be that its summary contempt procedure passed into the common law. We have already noted that soon after the abolition of the Star Chamber examples appear in the King's Bench of general writs of attachment and examination on interrogatories. Style's *Practical Register* shows that contempts were punished summarily in the King's Bench after 1640, but the examples cited are mostly those committed by officers of the court or parties to suits.[19] No instance is given of any contempt being punished summarily when committed out of court by a stranger to proceedings. The wider application of the summary process in contempt cases does not appear to have been established until the eighteenth century, but Blackstone's words cited above suggest that it may have derived from the Star Chamber.

III. THE COURT OF CHANCERY: THE DEVELOPMENT OF CIVIL CONTEMPT

1–41 In the seventeenth century an important development in the law of contempt took place in the court of Chancery. The writ of attachment began to be used not merely in the case of those flagrant abuses of the administration of justice which the common law courts were wont to punish, but also to compel performance as between parties in a particular suit. The writ of attachment and its summary process became part of the ordinary procedure of the court. This development led eventually to the uneasy assimilation of the procedural means of dealing with the two forms of misconduct which came to be called criminal and civil contempts. While the following treatment is categorised in accordance with this terminology, it should be remembered that in the seventeenth and eighteenth centuries the distinction was not made as clearly as it was from the nineteenth century.

A. Criminal contempts

1–42 The Chancellor's aid was invoked in a case of contempt as early as 1397. Reginald Bernewell in his petition recited how the Lord Chancellor granted a writ directed to Thomas Barton, Marshal of the Marshalsea, commanding him that he should not maintain a quarrel between Reginald and one John Glam in the Court of the Marshalsea. Whereupon Thomas avowed his intention to continue to maintain the quarrel and lay in wait for and assaulted Reginald's counsel. Reginald prayed the Chancellor to grant a writ by virtue of which Thomas might be arrested and brought before him

---

[17] *Commentaries*, (1769) Vol. iv, 310.
[18] See Plucknett, *A Concise History of the Common Law* (5th ed., 1956), pp.459 and 497–9.
[19] (1657) Titles "Attachment" and "Contempt"; see Fox, p.93.

"to answer as well to our Lord the King for the contempt, as to the said suppliant for the said torts and grievances, and to find sufficient surety for the peace towards the said suppliant."[20]

1-43 In another early petition John Swelle complained that a writ issued by the Lord Chancellor at his request to John Hawkin was vilely trampled upon by Hawkin when he received it. Swelle was not quite certain of his remedy for he asked the Chancellor to issue "such writ as to you shall seem reasonable."[21] In course of time, however, this seems to have been a form of contempt with which the court often dealt. The sixteenth century reports contain a number of examples of summary process against persons using violence on a process server.[22] Lord Chancellor Bacon in his Ordinances of 1619 details the procedure in such matters: "In case of contempts granted upon force or ill words upon serving of process, or upon words of scandal of the court, proved by affidavit, the party is forthwith to stand committed." When he had been sufficiently punished he might be discharged as a matter of grace.[23]

1-44 Later Ordinances altered the procedure slightly, requiring two affidavits for an immediate committal; if there was only one then the alleged contemnor was examined on interrogatories.[24] It should be remembered that the Court of Chancery as well as the Star Chamber was accustomed to using interrogatories, and they were used as a matter of course in dealing with civil contempts. These Chancery Ordinances appear to treat words scandalising the court as in themselves a contempt. Some of the early petitions were concerned with abuse of judicial officials,[25] but the case books of the sixteenth and seventeenth centuries do not appear to contain any example of a publisher of such scandal being punished, except where the words were spoken on service of process.

1-45 Certain contempts were dealt with by the Court of Chancery itself. In other and perhaps more serious cases, it seems to have referred the matters elsewhere. There are a number of examples of the Star Chamber punishing contempts of the Court of Chancery.[26] For example, in 1594 one Fysher, who threatened counsel with a pistol, forged an order of the court and filed a libellous affidavit, was ordered by the Lord Keeper to be taken to the Star Chamber to be informed against *ore tenus* by Her Majesty's counsel.[27]

---

[20] *Select Cases in Chancery*, Selden Society (1896) Vol. X, Case 22: "pur respondre sibien a nostre seignur le Roy du contempt come al dit suppliant dez tortz et greuauncez suisditz, et pur trouer suffisaunt seurte de pees as ditz suppliant". And see Cases 58 and 69.
[21] ibid., Case 58.
[22] *Rove v West* (1558) Cary 54; *Dastoines v Apprice* (1580) Cary 131; *Mead v Cross* (1580) Cary 137; *Aberforthe v Hall and Paramore* (1598) Sanders, *Orders Of the High Court of Chancery and Statutes of the Realm Relating to Chancery* (1845), 76; *Palmer v Maynard* (1598) Sanders 79a.
[23] Sanders, *Chancery Orders*, p.119. In J. Spedding and D.D. Heath, *The Works of Francis Bacon* (1859) Vol. VII, p.170, the word "granted" is given as "grounded".
[24] ibid., 240–1. For a discussion of the modern practice in family proceedings, see *Re B (Contempt: Evidence)* [1996] 1 F.L.R. 239, discussed at paras 15–32 *et seq*.
[25] *Select Cases*, 108 (1395–6) and 111 (1413–1414).
[26] G. Spence, *Equitable Jurisdiction of the court of Chancery* (1846–49), i 351, 354, 689–91.
[27] ibid., p.354.

After the abolition of that Court there may have been some doubt as to the correct procedure. In 1663 the Attorney-General prayed the court to punish one Hungerford for forging subpoenas and the imprint of the Great Seal; conduct he described as a misdemeanour, abuse and contempt of court. The Master of the Rolls ordered a search of the register for precedents.[28] In 1700 a person called Hatcher was accused of forging writs and the imprint of the Great Seal and, on receiving affidavits in the matter, the Master of the Rolls ordered that an information be brought against Hatcher by the Attorney-General in the King's Bench.[29] In 1707, leave was given to prosecute a tipstaff of the court in the Petty Bag, that is the common law side of Chancery, for falsely executing a warrant.[30] It may be, therefore, that the jurisdiction of the Court of Chancery to deal summarily with *all* such forms of contempt was not established until the eighteenth century.

1-46

B. Civil contempt

If the general jurisdiction of the Court of Chancery remained in doubt at the end of the seventeenth century, one particular aspect of its jurisdiction was clear; namely the power to deal summarily with what we now call civil contempts. The common law courts in general offered litigants the remedy of damages with distress as the ultimate sanction. The Court of Chancery, however, was ready to compel obedience to its orders and decrees, and indeed its general process, by imprisonment. Those who disobeyed were brought before the court by writ of attachment and were regarded as contemnors.[31] In Cary's *Causes in Chancery*, which covers the period 1557–1604, there are examples of attachment being issued against those who failed to comply with an order of the court,[32] or failed to perform one of its decrees,[33] or disobeyed an injunction.[34]

1-47

Moreover, the appearance of a defendant was enforced by subpoena served on him and, if he failed to appear, attachment was granted.[35] The full process is illustrated by the case of *Richers v Stilman*.[36] "An attachment was awarded against the defendant for his not appearance upon oath; he was served with a subpoena, who now appeared gratis, and would have excused himself, that he had no notice of the subpoena, but he that served the subpoena deposed, he did hang the same upon the defendant's door, and within half an hour after, saw him abroad with a writ in his hand which he supposed to be the subpoena; therefore he is committed to the prison of the Fleet."

1-48

---

[28] Sanders, *Chancery Orders*, 317.
[29] *ibid.*, pp.414–5.
[30] *ibid.*, p.432.
[31] See Holdsworth, *A History of the English Law*, Vol. 1, (7th ed., 1956), p.458 and Vol. 5. (3rd ed., 1945), p.335; and generally Plucknett, *A Concise History of the Common Law* (5th ed., 1956) p.678, and F.W. Maitland, *The Constitutional History of England* (1908) p.226.
[32] *Stephens v Bawden* (1581) p.147.
[33] *Leake v Marrow* (1576) p.75.
[34] *Holgate v Grantham* (1576) p.82.
[35] See, *e.g. Waters v Berd* (1580) p.104; *Stow v Maddock* (1580) p.115; *Dinnis v Morgan* p.121.
[36] (1558) *Cary's Causes in Chancery*, p.57.

1-49 The pattern is repeated in *Choyce's Cases in Chancery* covering the same period. There are examples of attachment used to prevent persons litigating in other courts.[37] In *Billing v Pate,* attachment was awarded against the defendant for proceeding in the court of the Manor of Bersted contrary to the order of the court.[38] In *Allen v Dingley* an injunction was issued restraining proceedings at common law. Although Serjeant Poutrel moved the King's Bench for judgment for the defendant, the plaintiff was called before the Court of Chancery for the contempt in breaching the injunction. He was there enjoined in the sum of £100 not to depart out of the town until he should be licensed thereunto by the Lord Keeper.[39]

1-50 Lord Chancellor Bacon in his Ordinance of 1619 set out the procedure for this class of contempt.[40] In case of disobedience to orders or decrees of the court, on affidavit evidence, attachment would issue against the alleged contemnor. He was then examined on interrogatories and witnesses might also be examined. If he confessed, or the contempt was proved, he might be committed to prison and ought not to be discharged until he obeyed the order of the court. It seems that here, unlike the case of criminal contempts, it was the usual practice to interrogate before committal, and also that, once the order of the court was performed then the contemnor was entitled to his release *ex debito justitiae*.[41] The procedure of the Court of Chancery in the case of such contempts was not finally settled until the eighteenth century.[42] In any event, it was not until the early nineteenth century that an attempt was made to distinguish clearly between criminal and civil contempts.

IV. Summary Procedure in the Eighteenth Century

A. The recognition of summary powers

1-51 The jurisdiction of the Court of Chancery to deal summarily with all types of contempt was placed beyond doubt when Lord Hardwicke L.C. summarily committed the printers of *The Champion* and *The St. James's Evening Post* for publishing matter calculated to prejudice the fair trial of pending proceedings.[43] He adopted a similar course in *Cann v Cann,*[44] a decision which aroused strong criticism of the arbitrary exercise of power by the courts in matters of contempt. One writer likened the proceedings to "the monstrous tyranny which first disgraced, and at length overwhelmed the Star Chamber."[45] But, however it

---

[37] And see Holdsworth, *A History of the English Law,* Vol. V (1924), 335–6.
[38] (1580) Choyce, p.133.
[39] (1576) Choyce, p.114.
[40] Sanders, *Chancery Orders,* p.119.
[41] See the later history of this in paras 3–179 *et seq.*
[42] Holdsworth, *A History of English Law* Vol. IX (3rd ed., 1944), pp.348–53 where it is set out in detail.
[43] *The St. James's Evening Post (Roach v Garvan)* (1742) 2 Atk. 469, 26 E.R. 683.
[44] (1754) 2 Ves. Sen. 520, (*sub nom. Anon.*) 28 E.R. 332.
[45] Hargrave, in Turner and Venables *Chancery Practice,* 5th ed., at 231, cited in *Birch v Walsh* (1846) 10 I. Eq. R. 9.

might be exercised in future, the jurisdiction of the court no longer seemed in doubt.

1-52 The Court of King's Bench also adopted the summary mode of proceeding on contempts. Blackstone in his *Commentaries* gave a full account of the procedure.[46] For contempts out of the court, if the judges saw sufficient ground on affidavit to suspect a contempt had been committed, they made a rule on the suspected party to show cause why attachment should not issue against him; if he could not show sufficient cause to discharge the rule it was made absolute. In flagrant cases attachment issued in the first instance without a rule *nisi*.[47] The process of attachment was merely intended to bring the party into court. When there, he either stood committed or on bail, to answer interrogatories on oath with respect to the circumstances of the contempt. Interrogatories had to be exhibited (shown to the defendant) within four days. The defendant could move the court to strike out any that were improper.[48] Those remaining he had to answer, and if he refused or answered in an evasive manner he was guilty of contempt.

1-53 Blackstone pointed out an important procedural distinction between interrogatories administered in the courts of equity and those administered on attachment in the common law courts: in the former the answers on oath could be contradicted and disproved by affidavits of the adverse party[49]; in the latter, if the defendant cleared himself on oath, his answers could not be disproved and he had to be discharged, but he was open to prosecution for perjury.[50] Blackstone commented that the "admission of the party to purge himself on oath is more favourable to his liberty, though perhaps not less dangerous to his conscience."[51] He added that the process of making the defendant answer on oath to a criminal charge, though not agreeable to the common law in any other instance, by long immemorial usage was now become the law of the land in cases of contempt. Once the defendant was found in contempt the court would pass judgment on him.

1-54 This summary process in the King's Bench was challenged in *Almon's Case*.[52] The Attorney-General moved the court on affidavit to grant an attachment against Almon for publishing a pamphlet entitled "A letter concerning Libels, Warrants, Seizure of Papers &c," which allegedly contained libels on the Court of King's Bench and in particular on Lord Mansfield C.J. A rule *nisi* issued and the case was argued, but owing to a defect in the wording of the rule, judgment was not delivered and the matter was not taken further. Wilmot J., however, prepared his judgment and this was preserved and published in 1802.[53] It was cited by

---

[46] *Commentaries*, Vol. IV, pp.283–8.
[47] See *Anon* (1710) 1 Salk. 84, 91 E.R. 79.
[48] *Barber* (1721) 1 Str. 444, 93 E.R. 624.
[49] Tothill, *Transactions of the Court of Chancery* (1649), p.33.
[50] Holt C.J. in *Saunders v Melhuish* (1703 M. 2 Anne) 6 Mod. 73, 87 E.R. 831 and *Anon* (1702 1 Anne) 7 Mod. 31, 87 E.R. 1076.
[51] *Anon*, Vol. IV, p.288.
[52] *Wilmot's Notes* (1765) 243, 97 E.R. 94 at 99. For a modern account of the background to the decision, see D. Hay, "Contempt by Scandalising the Court: A Political History of the First Hundred Years" [1987] 25 Osgoode Hall L.J. 433.
[53] Last note.

Holroyd J. in *R. v Clement*[54] and since then has been regarded as a leading authority and regularly cited.[55]

1–55 Counsel for Almon argued that in all the circumstances of the case the court ought not to proceed by way of attachment, but should leave the offence to be prosecuted and punished by indictment or information. Wilmot J. dismissed the argument in these terms:

> "The power, which the courts in Westminster Hall have of vindicating their own authority, is coeval with their first foundation and institution; it is a necessary incident to every Court of Justice, whether of record or not, to fine and imprison for a contempt to the court, acted in the face of it, *1 Vent. 1*. And the issuing of attachments by the Supreme Courts of Justice in Westminster Hall, for contempts out of court, stands upon the same immemorial usage as supports the whole fabrick of the common law; it is as much the *lex terrae*, and within the exception of Magna Charta, as the issuing any other legal process whatsoever.
>
> I have examined very carefully to see if I could find out any vestiges or traces of its introduction, but can find none. It is as ancient as any other part of the common law; there is no priority or posteriority to be discovered about it, and therefore cannot be said to invade the common law, but to act in an alliance and friendly conjunction with every provision which the wisdom of our ancestors has established for the general good of society. And though I do not mean to compare and contrast attachments with trials by jury, yet truth compels me to say, that the mode of proceeding by attachment stands upon the very same foundation and basis as trials by jury do,—immemorial usage and practice; it is a constitutional remedy in particular cases, and the Judges, in those cases, are as much bound to give an activity to this part of the law as to any other part of it."

1–56 The recognition of a summary procedure for contempt in the common law courts may have been of more recent origin than Wilmot J. supposed, but nevertheless his views expressed in *Almon's* case have become accepted as establishing the jurisdiction of the common law courts to deal summarily with all types of contempt.

B. Contempt by publication in the eighteenth century

1–57 It was in the eighteenth century that the press and the pamphleteers flourished, and it was in that period that it became clearly established that contempt could be committed by publishing matter calculated to interfere with the due administration of justice. It developed in three stages. First, there are examples of persons being punished for speaking disrespectfully of the court on service of process. Then the stage was reached where matter scandalising the court constituted a contempt whenever published. Finally the courts began to punish persons who published matter calculated to prejudice the fair trial of a pending case.

---

[54] (1821) 4 B. & Ald. 218, 233, 106 E.R. 918 at 923. But see *Independent Publishing Co Ltd v Att-Gen of Trinidad and Tobago* [2003] 1 A.C. 190 discussed at para.7–110.
[55] See Fox, pp.30–1.

Speaking disrespectfully of the court on service of process had been a long-established form of contempt. There are certainly a number of examples early in the eighteenth century.[56] There seems to have been no need, however, to treat such contempts as having occurred constructively in the presence of the court. It may also be that publication of matter scandalising the court had been recognised as contempt for a much longer period, but few examples appear in the reports.[57]

1-58

The courts in the early eighteenth century recognised a jurisdiction to punish this type of conduct. There are a number of such cases, commencing in 1721, and in most the defendant was examined on interrogatories and fined or committed and compelled to undertake his good behaviour for a period.[58]

1-59

In *The St. James's Evening Post*,[59] Lord Hardwicke recognised that scandalising the court was an identifiable category of contempt. There had been two recent examples of the Court of Chancery punishing such contempts.[60] In the Court of the King's Bench, the facts considered in the (undelivered) judgment in *Almon*[61] provided an example of a libel on the court and its judges.

1-60

Thus there could by then be no doubt that the courts could punish contempts even though committed out of court by strangers to proceedings. Indeed, Lord Hardwick recognised the importance of preventing any prejudice against parties to litigation "before the cause is finally heard." Even as early as 1720 in *Pool v Sacheverell*,[62] Lord Parker L.C. had committed a person who advertised for witnesses in a particular cause, because the advertisement was "a means of preventing justice in a cause now depending." The decision in this case has since been questioned,[63] but it is nevertheless of historical interest.

1-61

The clearest statement of principle, however, in relation to the various categories of publication contempt is to be found in *The St. James's Evening Post*,[64] which became the leading case on the subject. A motion was brought to commit the printers of *The Champion* and *The St. James's Evening Post* for publishing a libel on certain executors and a testator's widow concerned in pending proceedings. Lord Hardwicke L.C. had no doubt that the publication was libellous, but agreed with the Solicitor-General that the court had no cognisance

1-62

---

[56] *Lawson's Case* (1713) Hil. 11 Anne; *Hendale's Case* (1714) Hil. 12 Anne; *Jones* (1719) 1 Str. 185, 93 E.R. 462—these are all to be found in the Appendix to the Report of the Select Committee on *Burdett's Case* (1680) 8 St. Tr. 14.
[57] See para.1–5.
[58] *Barber* (1721) 1 Str. 444, 93 E.R. 624; *Wilkin* (1722) K.B. Easter, George I; *Colbatch* (1723) K.B. Easter, George I; *Wiatt* (1723) 8 Mod. 123, 88 E.R. 96; *Anon* (1731) 2 Barn K.B. 43, 94 E.R. 345; *Lawley* (1731) Mich. 5 George II are all contained in the Appendix to the Report of the Select Committee on *Burdett's Case* (1680) 8 St. Tr. 14; and see also Fox, pp.112–3.
[59] (1742) 2 Atk. 469, 26 E.R. 642.
[60] *Dodd and Briggs* (1736) Sanders, *Chancery Orders*, pp.539–42, *Ingles* (1740) *ibid.*, p.552.
[61] (1765), para.1–54.
[62] 1 P. Wms.675, 24 E.R. 565.
[63] By the Court of Appeal in *The Plating Company v Farquharson* (1881) 17 Ch. D. 49.
[64] (1742) 2 Atk. 469, 26 E.R. 642.

1-62 of the matter unless it was also a contempt, in which case it would become possible to invoke its inherent jurisdiction.[65] He held that[66]:

> "Nothing is more incumbent upon courts of justice, than to preserve their proceedings from being misrepresented; nor is there any thing of more pernicious consequence, than to prejudice the minds of the publick against persons concerned as parties in causes, before the cause is finally heard."

1-63 Later he added[67]:

> "There are three different sorts of contempt. One kind of contempt is, scandalizing the court itself. There may be likewise a contempt of this court, in abusing parties who are concerned in causes here. There may be also a contempt of this court, in prejudicing mankind against persons before the cause is heard. There cannot be anything of greater consequence, than to keep the streams of justice clear and pure, that parties may proceed with safety both to themselves and their characters."

C. Strict liability for contempt in the eighteenth century

1-64 It was in the Court of Chancery that the question of the requisite state of mind appears first to have been considered. In relation both to wardship and to the publication of prejudicial matter, defences were raised that the alleged contemnor, although he had committed the act alleged, did not know or understand its import. In both cases the defence was rejected and strict liability upheld.

1-65 In *Herbert's* case,[68] a ward of court married a servant without the court's consent, she being older than himself and of no fortune. The person who conducted the ceremony and one Williams, who purported to be the guardian of the infant and consented to the marriage, were brought before Sir Joseph Jekyll; both pleaded ignorance that Herbert was a ward of court. The Master of the Rolls held this to be no defence:

> "With regard to what is alleged by way of excuse, that the parson and the pretended guardian had no notice of the infant's being a ward of court; it is to be observed, that the commitment of the wardship to Sir Thomas Clarges was an act of the court, and in a cause then depending, of which every one at his peril is concerned to take notice, in the same manner as of a *lis pendens*. Surely it may be as well presumed every one is apprised of the proceedings of this court, as that all executors should be presumed to take notice of all judgments even in the inferior courts of law, and therefore are not to pay bonds before such judgments, but at their peril. In the case of a writ of ravishment of ward brought by any subject, it is no excuse for the defendant to say, he did not know the party was a ward of the plaintiff's: and if this be so in a private case, *a fortiori* will it hold, where the public justice of the court is concerned. Besides, where the marriage of an infant is encouraged without the concurrence of his real guardians or relations, the

---

[65] For a discussion of the development of the inherent jurisdiction of the courts generally, see I.H. Jacob, "The Inherent Jurisdiction of the court" (1970) 23 C.L.P. 23; K. Mason, "The Inherent Jurisdiction of the Court" (1983) 57 A.L.J. 449. See also M.S. Dockray, "The Inherent Jurisdiction to Regulate Civil Proceedings" (1997) 113 L.Q.R. 120.
[66] At 469, 26 E.R. 683.
[67] At 471, 26 E.R. 684.
[68] (1731) 3 P. Wms. 115, 24 E.R. 992.

consequences of such marriage ought to be at the peril of all those that are instrumental therein—if actual notice of the infant's being a ward of the court were necessary, then these offences would be continually practised with impunity: for it would be an easy matter to put other people not really privy to the acts of the court (in committing the guardianship of the infant) to transact and bring about the marriage; for which reason, if the circumstances of the marriage are suspicious (as in the present case they unquestionably are, where one acts as guardian of the infant who never appears to have known him before, and acts too not for the benefit, but to the prejudice and probably to the ruin, of the infant) in such case (I say) all the parties ought to be severely censured for example sake, and to deter others from the like offences."

Eveleigh L.J. in *Z Ltd v A-Z and AA-LL*[69] assumed that Sir Joseph Jekyll's remarks were still valid in relation to wardship proceedings. This approach has subsequently been confirmed by, for example, Sir John Donaldson M.R. in *Att.-Gen. v Newspaper Publishing Plc.*,[70] and by Lord Diplock, in *Secretary of State for Defence v Guardian Newspapers Ltd*.[71] The 1981 Act would have made no inroad upon this principle, since its restrictions upon strict liability were concerned only with contempt by publication in the media.

The decision concerning publication contempt was *The St. James's Evening Post*[72] itself, which continued to bedevil the coverage of court proceedings by journalists until the 1981 reforms. Lord Hardwicke L.C. held that it was no defence that a person publishing matter calculated to prejudice the fair trial of a pending cause had no knowledge of the contents of the publication, stating:

" . . . though it is true, this is a trade, yet they must take care to do it with prudence and caution[73]: for if they print anything that is libellous, it is no excuse, to say, the printer had no knowledge of the contents and was ignorant of its being libellous: and so is the rule at law, and I will always adhere to the strict rules of law in these cases."

It would appear from the context that Lord Hardwicke was making a direct reference to the law of libel, and in particular criminal libel. Criminal libels had been punished by the Court of Star Chamber. When that Court was abolished, its jurisdiction in this respect was assumed by the Court of King's Bench, which

---

[69] [1982] Q.B. 558 at 579C–E.
[70] [1988] Ch. 333 at 374C.
[71] [1985] 1 A.C. 339 at 346G–H HL.
[72] (1742) 2 Atk. 469 at 472, 26 E.R. 683 at 685.
[73] The apparent lack of empathy in relation to those who publish in the course of business continued until just before the enactment of the 1981 Act. See, *e.g.* Lord Edmund-Davies in *Att-Gen v Leveller Magazine Ltd* [1979] A.C. 440, 466B–D: where he referred to "people controlling or connected with powerful organs of publicity who, for reasons of their own (one of which may be no more than the desire to boost sales), decide to take the course of defiant dissemination of matter which ought to be kept confidential". He went on to say that it was incumbent upon "such people" to ascertain what had happened in court; they had the means of doing so, and could not be heard to complain that they were ignorant of what had taken place. See also the Phillimore Report (1974) Cmnd. 5794, at para.153. Echoes of this approach are to be found even after the 1981 Act, in the last paragraph of *Consolidated Criminal Practice Direction* [2002] 1 W.L.R. 2870 set out at para.7–153. For the latest version of the Direction see www.courtservice.gov.uk/docs/cpd/consol_criminal_pd_220305.doc.

certainly punished criminal libels in the eighteenth century. On a trial for criminal libel the only questions for the jury were (i) did the accused publish the words complained of? (ii) if so, were they libellous?

1–69   In *Shipley's* case[74] Lord Mansfield rejected Erskine's argument that on a trial for criminal libel the jury were entitled to consider whether the accused acted with a mischievous intention. The House of Lords subsequently confirmed that a criminal intention in the *writer* was not a requirement at common law. In 1792, Fox's Libel Act reversed the decision in *Shipley's* case by making it open to the jury on all trials on indictment or information for libel to give a general verdict of guilty or not guilty upon the whole matter put in issue, including the intention of the accused. This was held, however, not to affect the rule that a *publisher or bookseller* could be criminally liable for publishing a libel even though ignorant of the contents of his publication.[75] Lord Campbell's Libel Act of 1843[76] alleviated the position by providing that it would be competent for the defendant to prove "that such publication was made without his authority, consent, or knowledge, and that the said publication did not arise from want of due care or caution on his part". In any event, after the 1832 Reform Act there were very few prosecutions for criminal libel.[77]

1–70   Although Lord Hardwicke's judgment in *The St. James's Evening Post* appears to have assumed that strict liability applied in cases of scandalising the court,[78] Wilmot J. appeared to take a different view in the Court of King's Bench in his undelivered judgment in *Almon's* case.[79] He said in answer to an argument that summary proceedings by attachment were inappropriate to determine the state of mind of the contemnor:

> "If an attachment is a constitutional mode of proceeding for libels upon Courts of Justice, they must be competent to the question of 'quo animo' they are published; . . . It is the intention which, in all cases, constitutes the offence. '*Actus non facit reum, nisi mens sit rea.*' It would be a contradiction in terms to admit Courts to have a cognizance of the offence, and yet not admit them to be Judges of the only ingredient which makes it so."

---

[74] (1783) 21 St. Tr. 847. Although this case was decided after *The St. James's Evening Post*, it would appear that it only confirmed existing law. See *Walter* (1799) 3 Esp.21, 170 E.R. 524, where Kenyon C.J. stated that it was old and received law for above a century that in criminal libel the proprietor of a newspaper was liable for the acts of his servants even if he had no personal guilt in the matter. For a discussion of the modern application of the rules of vicarious liability in this context, see para.4–191 *et seq.*
[75] *Cuthell* (1799) 27 St. Tr. 641.
[76] s.7.
[77] Generally on criminal libels see J.F. Stephen, *A History of the Criminal Law*, (1883) Vol. II, ch. XXIV. For later developments, see J.R. Spencer, "Criminal Libel—A Skeleton in the Cupboard" [1977] Crim.L.R. 383 and 465, and in ed. P.R. Glazebrook, *Reshaping the Criminal Law* (1978), "The Press and the Reform of Criminal Libel". The Supreme Court Procedure Committee Report on Defamation (the Neill Report) recommended in July 1991 that criminal libel should be abolished.
[78] (1742) 2 Atk. 469 at 471–2, 26 E.R. 683 at 685.
[79] *Wilmot's notes* (1765) 243 at 263, 97 E.R. 94 at 102. And see para.1–54.

Thus, it is not possible to state definitively whether *mens rea* was indeed required in order to establish, at common law, the offence of scandalising the court through media publications.[80]

V. THE RULE AGAINST *EX PARTE* STATEMENTS

It was not merely in relation to the alleged offender's state of mind that the courts in the eighteenth century adopted a strict test. They also applied a rigid and technical approach to what might constitute the *actus reus* of contempt. So Lord Hardwicke, in *The St. James's Evening Post*, referred to the (unreported) case of one Captain Perry "who printed his brief before the cause came on" and was held in contempt for "prejudicing the world with regard to the merits of the cause before it was heard." It became well-established in the nineteenth century, more generally, that it was a contempt to publish any *ex parte* statement as to the issues in litigation before trial.

1–71

Thus, in accordance with this reasoning, it was held that it was a contempt to publish the following: statements made at the examination of a person by the liquidator of a company[81]; a report of proceedings on *ex parte* application for an injunction[82]; a statement of claim, even if unaccompanied by additional comment[83]; a winding-up petition[84]; a circular to fellow shareholders dealing with a pending liquidation of the company[85]; a circular by a party to trade mark proceedings for the purpose of warning the trade generally[86]; and indeed simply a one-sided account of a case.[87] The policy underlying this rule is closely allied to that which governs qualified privilege in relation to media reporting of court proceedings; it is necessary for such reports to be "fair and accurate", and a one-sided or distorted picture of the issues may well fall outside that category.

1–72

At the beginning of the century a series of cases established the proposition that to publish any account of the evidence given before committing justices was a contempt, because it would inevitably be a one-sided statement of the case.[88] At that time, however, the accused had no right to be present at committal proceedings. The Indictable Offences Act 1848, s.17 conferred that right. It was established thereafter that it was not a libel to publish a fair and accurate report of such proceedings.[89] It also became accepted that it was not a contempt, and by

1–73

---

[80] See the discussion of later developments in paras 5–244 *et seq*.
[81] *Re the American Exchange in Europe (Ltd) v Gillig* (1889) 58 L.J. Ch. 706.
[82] *Deacon v Deacon* (1827) 2 Russ 607. 38 E.R. 463.
[83] *Bowden v Russell* (1887) 46 L.J. Ch. 414.
[84] *Re The Cheltenham and Swansea Railway Carriage and Wagon Co.* (1869) L.R. 8 Eq. 580.
[85] *Re Sir John Moore Gold Mining Co* (1877) 37 L.T. 242.
[86] *J & P Coats v Chadwick* [1894] 1 Ch. 347.
[87] *Re Crown Bank* (1890) 44 Ch. D. 649.
[88] *R. v Lee* (1804) 5 Esp.123, 170 E.R. 759; *R. v Fisher* (1811) 2 Camp. 563 at 570, 170 E.R. 1253 at 1255, Lord Ellenborough; *R. v Fleet* (1818) 1 Bar. & Ald. 379, 106 E.R. 140.
[89] See *Lewis v Levy* (1858) 27 L.J. Q.B. 282; *R. v Gray* (1865) 10 Cox C.C.; *R. v Wason and Walter* (1868) L.R. 4 Q.B. 73; *Usill v Hales* (1878) L.R. 3 C.P.D. 319; *Kimber v Press Association* [1893] 1 Q.B. 65.

1-73   CHAPTER 1—HISTORY OF THE LAW OF CONTEMPT

the first half of the twentieth century it had become common to publish such reports in the newspapers.[90] Now the matter is governed by statute.[91]

VI. OTHER NINETEENTH CENTURY DEVELOPMENTS

A. The appellate jurisdiction

1-74   Prior to 1875 the law of contempt had developed piecemeal in the different common law courts and in the Court of Chancery. The Judicature Acts of that year unified the structure of the courts and provided for appeals in cases other than in any criminal cause or matter[92] to the Court of Appeal. This court could therefore consider decisions made by judges of the High Court on an application for leave to issue an attachment or committal, including in some cases which would nowadays be classified as concerning criminal contempt.[93] This jurisdiction afforded the court an opportunity to soften the rigour of some of the older contempt cases. However, the tentative manner in which the court sought to discriminate between them led to a confusing distinction between technical and real contempts, which long bedevilled the definition of the *actus reus* of contempt.

1-75   One of the other main sources of confusion over the next century was that the Court of Appeal strained the definition of civil contempt to a considerable extent in order to ensure that they had jurisdiction to hear a case. Since 1960 when the Administration of Justice Act gave a right of appeal in criminal cases also, such strained constructions are no longer necessary. In the result, the courts began to stress the quasi-criminal nature of most civil contempts to the point where the distinction between the two kinds of contempt has sometimes been said to have disappeared.[94]

B. Discouraging the use of the summary process

1-76   When the Court of Appeal was established in 1875, and began to consider the law of contempt, it became apparent that it had been applied too inflexibly.

---

[90] See generally J. Knelman, "Trial by Newspaper in Nineteenth-Century England" (1994) 15 Med. Law and P. 106.

[91] For committal proceedings, the matter is for the time being governed by s.8 of the Magistrates' Courts Act 1980, as amended by the Criminal Procedure and Investigations Act 1996, ss.44 and 47; and see s.4 of the Contempt of Court Act 1981, which is discussed at paras 4–265 *et seq.* and paras 7–111 *et seq.* Committal proceedings are in the process of being phased out, and s.8 is to be repealed (by the Criminal Justice 2003) and replaced by a process known as the "allocation and sending" of offences. The Criminal Justice Act 2003, s.41, Sch.3, makes numerous amendments to the existing statutory framework. Allocation and sending are to be governed by the Crime and Disorder Act 1998, s.51, and the consequent reporting restrictions are to be found in s.52A of that Act from a date to be appointed (believed at the time of writing to be September 2006). For a useful overview, see R. Taylor, M. Wasik and R. Leng, *Blackstone's Guide to the Criminal Justice Act 2003* (2004), chap.5. See para.8–87 *et seq.*

[92] Supreme Court of Judicature Act 1873, s.47(1) (repealed).

[93] See, *e.g. Hunt v Clarke* (1889) 58 L.J.Q.B. 490, for the facts of which see below para.1–79 and the discussion at paras 3–130 *et seq.*

[94] The continuing distinctions between civil and criminal contempt are nevertheless discussed in detail in ch.3.

Distinctions began to be drawn between conduct which merited the attention of the court and that which did not, and a degree of sensitivity emerged as to the arbitrary nature of the jurisdiction. In *Re Clements, Republic of Costa Rica v Erlanger*,[95] Sir George Jessel M.R. warned:

> "It seems to me that this jurisdiction of committing for contempt being practically arbitrary and unlimited should be most jealously and carefully watched, and exercised, . . . with the greatest reluctance and the greatest anxiety on the part of Judges to see whether there is no other mode which is not open to the objection of arbitrariness and which can be brought to bear upon the subject."

Later, in *The Plating Company v Farquharson*,[96] the Court of Appeal stressed that motions to commit should be brought only where there was a real case for committal, and not simply to make a point, where no other remedy was sought beyond the payment of costs.

1–77

C. Technical contempts

When the Court of Appeal came to consider some of the earlier cases in which disapproval had been expressed of *ex parte* statements, it might have been said simply that they had been wrongly decided and that, in order to establish a contempt, it ought to be necessary to show at least a risk of real prejudice. Instead the court preferred to rely upon the fact that a court might dismiss an application for committal without costs, or even with costs against the applicant, notwithstanding that a contempt had been technically established.

1–78

In the leading case of *Hunt v Clarke*,[97] the Court of Appeal refused to punish the publishers of the *Star* newspaper for contempt. While an action for fraudulent misrepresentation was pending, the paper had published an article naming the parties and stating that the plaintiff claimed £1,800 on the ground of fraudulent misrepresentation in connection with certain companies, including one called the Moldacot Company. It was said that the case was expected to present features of especial interest to investors and that "mourners over the Moldacot fiasco are likely to hear a little inside history of the business." The court construed the article as suggesting that the defendants were mixed up with doubtful companies and that hidden things of darkness would be brought to light. It was thus technically a contempt, and the contemnors therefore had to bear their own costs. Nevertheless the contempt was not such as would ever justify an order for committal and the motion should never have been brought.

1–79

In an important passage, Cotton L.J. adverted to the notion of "technical" contempt:

1–80

> "It does technically become a contempt if pending a cause or before a cause even had begun, any observations are made or published to the world which tend in any way to prejudice the parties in the case . . . where the offence complained of is of a slight and

---

[95] (1877) 46 L.J. Ch. 375 at 383.
[96] (1881) 17 Ch. D. 49.
[97] (1889) 58 L.J.Q.B. 490.

trifling nature and not likely to cause any substantial prejudice to the party in the conduct of the action or the due administration of justice, the party ought not to apply."

1–81 This same distinction between technical and substantial contempts was made in *R. v Payne and Cooper*,[98] where the Divisional Court followed the lead of the Court of Appeal. The sub-editor of a newspaper was charged with attempting to set fire to the newspaper's premises. An article appeared in a newspaper stating that the property of the newspaper company was for sale and that the sub-editor had been arrested and charged with attempted arson. It was also stated that the newspaper had been the victim of an elaborate and prolonged system of fraud. The charge of attempted arson was subsequently dismissed, but further charges of larceny and embezzlement were made against the sub-editor. While he was awaiting trial at Assizes, another article appeared in the newspaper. It stated that the newspaper was under new management, referred to the troubles previously reported and stated that further information would probably become public after the Assizes. Later a report was published of proceedings before a committee of the local authority when a resolution was passed confirming the action of the Chief Constable in obtaining legal assistance to prosecute the sub-editor.

1–82 The court held that no contempt was established. The first article was a reasonable explanation to shareholders of the company's position; the second was innocuous; and the third was a fair report of the proceedings of a public body. Russell commented that in relation to certain cases in the Chancery Division cited, as authorities in support of the application, that he would not refer to those decisions "further than to say that, in my opinion, in some instances, the courts have gone rather too far". He expressed agreement with the view of Jessel M.R. in *Re Clements, Republic of Costa Rica v Erlanger*.[99] Such applications were being made too frequently. The court should only exercise its summary jurisdiction where there was a real contempt. So far as the proceedings before the local authority were concerned he said: "No doubt in the course of those proceedings certain statements were made which were necessarily *ex parte*, but it seems to be perfectly ridiculous that the publication of these statements would prejudice the trial which was pending." Even though a contempt was technically established on the facts of that case, the court concluded that it was so trifling that it left the applicant to bear his own costs.

1–83 Some later decisions appeared to depart from this approach, and inclined towards the view that unless there was a serious risk of prejudice to the administration of justice no contempt would be established.[1] In due course, however, in *Att-Gen v Times Newspapers Ltd*,[2] this unsatisfactory concept of technical contempt found favour with the House of Lords.

---

[98] [1896] 1 Q.B. 577.
[99] (1877) 46 L.J. Ch. 375 at 383, cited at para.1–76.
[1] See, *e.g. Chambers v Hudson Dodsworth & Co* [1936] 2 K.B. 595; *R. v Duffy Ex p. Nash* [1960] 2 Q.B. 188; *Carl-Zeiss-Stiftung v Rayner & Keeler Ltd* [1960] W.L.R. 1145; *Vine Products Ltd v Green* [1966] Ch. 484.
[2] [1974] A.C. 273, fully discussed at paras 1–87 *et seq.*

D. The gradual demise of attachment

Prior to the establishment of the Supreme Court, committal and attachment were exclusive remedies. Order 47, r.7 of the Rules of the Supreme Court provided that in certain cases they were equally available procedures, but there still remained other situations where only committal was appropriate. The distinction between the two remedies was highly technical and it became customary to ask for both in the alternative. In 1965 the Rules were amended and Order 52 made committal the only remedy in the High Court and Court of Appeal. Attachment survived in the county court (Order 25, r.67) until 1978[3] when consistency was achieved with the High Court procedure, and committal became the only appropriate mechanism.

E. Attempts to legislate in respect of the judges' arbitrary power

The intervention of statute in the history of the law of contempt has been relatively minimal,[4] even when the Contempt of Court Act 1981 is taken into consideration.[5] In 1906 and 1908, resolutions were passed in the House of Commons[6] to the effect that "the jurisdiction of Judges in dealing with contempt of court is practically arbitrary and unlimited and calls for the action of parliament with a view to its definition and limitation". Despite these concerns, when in the years 1883, 1892, 1894, 1896 and 1908, bills for the amendment of the law were brought in, they failed to be enacted.[7]

VII. Background to the Contempt of Court Act 1981

A. The Phillimore Committee

On June 8, 1971 Lord Hailsham L.C. appointed a committee under the chairmanship of Lord Justice Phillimore to consider whether any changes were required in the law relating to contempt of court. The Committee reported in December 1974[8] making a number of important recommendations for change. Some of these were to find their way on to the statute book in the Contempt of

---

[3] See para.15–6.
[4] Fox, *op. cit.* pp.76–83 notes that from 1402 to 1640, a number of statutes gave the common law courts power to punish summarily certain specified forms of conduct—primarily breaches of duty by officers of the court—which had much in common with what would now be described as contempt.
[5] According to E. Harnon, "Civil and Criminal Contempts of Court" (1962) 25 M.L.R. 179 at n.49, the Contempt of Court Acts of 1830 and 1832, the Unlawful Attachment Act 1331 and the court of Chancery Act 1860 appeared to be the only statutes dealing with the subject before the Administration of Justice Act 1960.
[6] *Hansard*, 4th series, Vol. 155, 614 (April 4 1906); Vol. 185, 1432 (March 10, 1908).
[7] Fox, *op. cit.*, p.3. See also the passage cited at para.2–15.
[8] *Report of the Committee on Contempt of Court* (1974) Cmnd. 5794. For early commentary, see R. Dhavan, "Contempt of Court and the Phillimore Committee Report" (1976) Anglo-American Law Rev. 186–253; G. Borrie, "The Phillimore Report" [1975] Crim.L.R. 123.

1–86 CHAPTER 1—HISTORY OF THE LAW OF CONTEMPT

Court Act 1981. A summary of the recommendations is set out in an Appendix.[9]

B. *Att-Gen v Times Newspapers Ltd*

1–87 In the course of the Phillimore Committee's deliberations the House of Lords delivered their speeches in *Att-Gen v Times Newspapers Ltd*.[10] This was (apart from the decision in *Scott v Scott*[11] which was on a relatively narrow issue) the first time that the House of Lords had considered the contempt jurisdiction in any depth.

1–88 An action was pending between the parents of children seriously affected by the drug thalidomide and the Distillers Company which manufactured it. On September 24, 1972 the *Sunday Times* published an article designed to put moral pressure on Distillers to settle the action on terms favourable to the children. No action was taken in relation to that article. Subsequently, the newspaper proposed to publish a further article discussing the issues involved in the litigation, and suggesting that there was a strong case in negligence against Distillers. The editor of *The Sunday Times* sent the article to the Attorney-General prior to publication and the Attorney-General applied for an injunction restraining its publication, which was granted by the Divisional Court on November 17, 1972 on the basis that it raised a serious risk of interference with the administration of justice. On February 16, 1973 the Court of Appeal lifted the injunction, mainly upon the ground that the history of litigation was such that it could properly be regarded as dormant and therefore no longer pending.[12]

1–89 The House of Lords restored the injunction, holding that any publication which pre-judged the issues in pending proceedings was a contempt, even if it was merely a technical offence which involved no more than a small likelihood of prejudice. The House clearly rejected the view of the Court of Appeal that the litigation could be treated as dormant at the time the injunction was granted.[13]

1–90 The conclusion that any pre-judgment amounted to contempt was criticised by the Phillimore Committee in their Report.[14] They recommended that the pre-judgment test should be replaced by a requirement that, to qualify as contempt, a publication would have to create a risk of serious prejudice to the course of justice.

1–91 Because of its significance for various aspects of the modern law of contempt, it is necessary to identify each of the issues which were addressed by their Lordships.

---

[9] Appendix 4.
[10] [1974] A.C. 273.
[11] [1913] A.C. 417.
[12] [1973] Q.B. 710 at 727.
[13] Lord Reid at 301, Lord Diplock at 312, Lord Simon at 317 and Lord Cross at 324.
[14] para.111.

1. Pre-Judgment

Lord Reid explained the vice of pre-judgment in the following terms[15]:

1–92

"I think that anything in the nature of pre-judgment of a case or of specific issues in it is objectionable, not only because of its possible effect on that particular case but also because of its side effects which may be far reaching. Responsible 'mass media' will do their best to be fair, but there will also be ill-informed, slapdash or prejudiced attempts to influence the public. If people are led to think that it is easy to find the truth, disrespect for the process of law could follow, and, if mass media are allowed to judge, unpopular people and unpopular causes will fare badly. Most cases of pre-judging of issues fall within the existing authorities on contempt. I do not think that the freedom of the press would suffer, and I think the law would be clearer and easier to apply in practice if it is made a general rule that it is not permissible to pre-judge issues in pending causes."

Lord Cross concurred in this reasoning.[16] Lord Morris also agreed saying[17]:

"Not only is it from the public point of view unseemly that in respect of a cause awaiting the determinations of a court there should be public advocacy in favour of one particular side or some particular point of view but also the courts, I think, owe it to the parties to protect them either from the prejudices of pre-judgment or from the necessity of having themselves to participate in the flurries of pre-trial publicity. In this connection I agree with Lord Denning M.R. when he said at 460:

'We must not allow trial by newspaper or trial by television or trial by any other medium than the courts of law'."

All three Law Lords took the view that the article complained of could be distinguished from earlier *Sunday Times* material, because it specifically sought to pre-judge the issue of negligence between the Distillers company and the parents of the thalidomide children. Lords Reid and Cross distinguished the article of September 24, because that was no more than a moral exhortation to the Distillers to pay more.

1–93

2. Pressurising a party to litigation

Lord Diplock considered however that it was also a contempt to hold a litigant up to public obloquy in a manner calculated to deter him from exercising his established legal rights or to usurp the functions of the courts[18]:

1–94

"The due administration of justice requires: first that all citizens should have unhindered access to the constitutionally established courts of criminal or civil jurisdiction for the determination of disputes as to their legal rights and liabilities; secondly, that they should be able to rely upon obtaining in the courts the arbitrament

---

[15] [1974] A.C. 273, 300.
[16] At 322.
[17] At 304. And see at 307 ("It was avowedly written with the purpose and object of arousing public sympathy with and support for the claims that were being made and in order to bring pressure upon Distillers to pay more").
[18] At 309–10.

of a tribunal which is free from bias against any party and whose decision will be based upon those facts only that have been proved in evidence adduced before it in accordance with the procedures adopted in courts of law; and thirdly that, once the dispute had been submitted to a court of law, they should be able to rely upon there being no usurpation by any other person of the function of that court to decide it according to law. Conduct which is calculated to prejudice any of these three requirements or to undermine the public confidence that they will be observed is contempt of court . . . My Lords, to hold a party up to public obloquy for exercising his constituted right to have recourse to a court of law for the ascertainment and enforcement of his legal rights and obligations is calculated to prejudice the first requirement for the due administration of justice: the unhindered access of all citizens to the established courts of law. Similarly 'trial by newspaper', i.e. public discussion or comment on the merits of a dispute which has been submitted to a court of law or on the alleged facts of the dispute before they have been found by the court upon the evidence adduced before it, is calculated to prejudice the third requirement: that parties to litigation should be able to rely upon there being no usurpation by any other person of the function of that court to decide that dispute according to law. If to have recourse to civil litigation were to expose a litigant to the risk of public obloquy or to public and prejudicial discussion of the facts or merits of the case before they have been determined by the court, potential suitors would be inhibited from availing themselves of courts of law for the purpose for which they are established."

1–95 Lord Simon[19] and Lord Morris[20] concurred in this view. Thus, they considered that even the article of September 24 had been a contempt. Lord Diplock added that, whilst public moral pressure was impermissible, private moral pressure was permissible within certain limits.[21] Yet, Lord Simon had reservations as to the extent to which even private moral pressure would be legitimate. This aspect of the matter will be considered in detail later.[22]

3. *Debating matters of public interest*

1–96 The House unanimously took the view that litigation should not prevent discussion of issues of general legal or other public interest (such as whether negligence is a proper basis for liability or whether the law of damages is sufficient to compensate a class of litigants adequately) even though such general issues might bear upon the particular litigation.[23] They considered that even where particular matters were already under public discussion when litigation commenced that discussion could continue, provided it was not exploited as a particular means of putting pressure on the litigants.[24] It was partly for the purpose of addressing such matters that Parliament eventually enacted s.5 of the Contempt of Court Act 1981.

---

[19] At 314. And see 320.
[20] At 302 and 307.
[21] See also Lord Reid at 295G: ("Why would it be contrary to public policy to seek by fair comment to dissuade Shylock from proceeding with his action?").
[22] See paras 11–278 *et seq.*
[23] *per* Lord Morris at 306, Lord Diplock at 312; Lord Cross at 323.
[24] See Lord Reid at 296 and Lord Simon at 321.

4. The need for certainty

In approaching the definition of contempt in the context of the newspaper article complained of, the House of Lords stressed the need for certainty. A clear and simple rule was required to enable editors and others who had to decide what could be published to make the right decision. Lord Reid said: "The main objection to the law of contempt is its uncertainty. I think we must try to remove that reproach at least with regard to those parts of the law with which the present case is concerned."[25] Similarly Lord Simon made the observation that:

> "To attempt to strike anew in each case the balance between the two public interests involved in the instant appeal—in freedom of discussion and in due administration of justice—would not be satisfactory. The law would then be giving too uncertain a guidance in a matter of daily concern, and its application would tend to vary with the length of the particular judge's foot. The law must lay down some general guide lines."[26]

It is to be noted that certainty is also a consideration to which importance is attached by the European Convention.[27]

Unfortunately, this factor led the House to adopt a wide definition of contempt, broad enough to include many technical contempts which carry no serious risk to the administration of justice. Thus, it was held that any public pre-judgment of a case would be treated as contempt. This rule, while it had the advantage of certainty, had the disadvantage that it caught within its net many publications of which the impact was likely to be relatively trivial. This was offset sufficiently, in their Lordships' view, by the power of the court to dismiss an application for committal with costs in circumstances where the contempt complained of was established but adjudged trivial.

C. The Phillimore Committee's reaction to the House of Lords

The Phillimore Committee was still considering the law of contempt when the speeches in *Att-Gen v Times Newspapers Ltd* were delivered, and it considered the implications. The Committee recommended that strict liability should apply to publications liable to affect particular proceedings, subject to certain statutory defences.[28] It recognised the obvious dangers of trial by newspaper and stated:

> "It would be unfortunate if the high reputation enjoyed by the courts of this country for impartiality and fairness in hearing and decision were lessened or undermined in this way."[29]

---

[25] At 294.
[26] At 319. This is to be contrasted with the approach of Lord Edmund-Davies in *Att-Gen v Leveller Magazine Ltd* [1979] A.C. 440, 465D–E: " ... intelligent anticipation of what would be fair and what would be unfair can go a long way to ease the burden of the disseminators".
[27] See Art.7, set out below at para.2–169. And see para.2–69, n.41.
[28] para.74.
[29] para.110.

While acknowledging the problems which the House of Lords had sought to address, it proposed rather different solutions.

1. Pre-judgment rejected: a new test for contempt advocated

1–100   First, it was critical of the pre-judgment test, as being not easy to define and spreading a net which was too wide.[30] Accordingly, the Committee recommended a new test based on the formula adopted in the Divisional Court in *Att-Gen v Times Newspapers Ltd*,[31] namely whether the words complained of created a serious risk that the course of justice might be interfered with. The Committee stated[32]:

> "The Divisional Court's formula would be improved in our view by three modifications. The first is that the words 'interfered with' are too imprecise. The definition should make it clear that the interference has to be undesirable. What the law is aiming at is prejudice and obstruction: those or words like them, are the words which should be used. Secondly, the law should aim at preventing serious prejudice, not serious risks. It has been emphasised many times by the courts that trivial cases ought not to be brought before the courts, and the triviality relates to the degree of prejudice. On the other hand, the creation of a risk of serious prejudice should always be prohibited unless the risk is so slight as to fall within the ordinary *de minimis* rule. This change would thus have the advantage of doing away with the unsatisfactory concept of 'technical' contempt which still appears to persist. Finally, the test would be tightened further by substituting 'will' for 'may'. *We recommend in relation to publications which are alleged to affect particular proceedings a statutory definition on the following lines–*
>
> > '*The test of contempt is whether the publications complained of creates a risk that the course of justice will be seriously impeded or prejudiced.*'
>
> This test, as the Divisional Court went on to point out, must be applied in the light of all the surrounding circumstances existing at the time of publication."

1–101   It was largely this test which found its way in to ss.1 and 2 of the 1981 Act. Although the word "substantial" was inserted in the course of the Bill's passage through Parliament to qualify the word "risk", it later emerged in the House of Lords' decision in *Att-Gen v English*[33] that it really had added nothing to the *de minimis* criterion proposed by the Phillimore Committee.[34]

2. A defence of public benefit?

1–102   The Committee went on to consider whether a general defence of public benefit should be created but rejected the idea, observing that "public benefit is notoriously difficult to define".[35] They also felt that it would be extremely

---

[30] para.111.
[31] [1973] 1 Q.B. 710 at 725.
[32] para.113.
[33] [1983] 1 A.C. 116.
[34] For further consideration, see paras 4–53 *et seq.*
[35] paras 143–145. See also the warning by Sir John Donaldson M.R. in *Francome v Mirror Group Newspapers Ltd* [1984] 1 W.L.R. 892, 898: "The media . . . are peculiarly vulnerable to the error of confusing the public interest with their own interest."

difficult for editors to decide in advance whether a defence of public benefit could be successfully raised in any particular case. The creation of such a defence would introduce a fresh area of uncertainty into the law. Moreover, it is difficult to reconcile a conclusion that there is created a significant risk of prejudice to pending proceedings with the proposition that this might be for the public benefit. As Lord Morris observed in *Att-Gen v Times Newspapers Ltd*,[36] "There can be no such thing as a justifiable contempt of court". The Committee considered the argument that in particular cases the public interest in publication might be said to outweigh that in ensuring the accused had a fair trial, but they concluded "that is not an argument that commends itself to us".[37]

They recognised, however, that argument to the effect that a publication had been intended for the public benefit might be relevant in mitigation of penalty. Where there was an existing public debate and litigation was commenced bearing on the subject matter of the debate, the debate should not automatically be guillotined. Such discussion should be permitted to continue, even if likely to cause an incidental but unintended risk of prejudice to a person who happened to be involved in court proceedings at the time.[38] In due course, Parliament sought to address these considerations by the introduction of the special defence in s.5 of the 1981 Act.[39]

D. Sunday Times v United Kingdom

The respondents referred the decision of the House of Lords to the European Court of Human Rights complaining of a breach of Articles of the European Convention.[40] The court had to consider various competing provisions of the European Convention.[41] *The Sunday Times* claimed that the decision of the House of Lords in *Att-Gen v Times Newspapers Ltd* was a breach of certain provisions of the Convention and in particular of Article 10 which provides:

"1. Everyone has the right to freedom of expression. This right shall include freedom to hold opinions and to receive and impart information and ideas without influence by public authority and regardless of frontiers.

2. The exercise of these freedoms, since it carries with it duties and responsibilities, may be subject to such formalities, conditions, restrictions or penalties as are prescribed

---

[36] [1974] A.C. 273 at 302D. See also *Re G (Celebrities: Publicity)* [1999] 1 F.L.R. 409 at 415. The Court of Appeal granted an injunction in family proceedings against two well-known parents from communicating with the media. A proviso was sought for the protection of the media such that , if either of the parents breached the order, the media would then be entitled to publish what would have come into the public domain. The court declined to grant this exemption for the very reason that, if the newspaper published comments made in breach of the order, with knowledge of the order, there would be on the face of it a criminal contempt. It would thus be inappropriate for the court to purport to exempt the newspaper or, in effect, to license a contempt.
[37] para.144.
[38] para.142. See also *Ex p. Bread Manufacturers* (1937) 37 S.R. (N.S.W.) at 249, Jordan C.J.
[39] Discussed in paras 4–293 *et seq.*
[40] *Sunday Times v United Kingdom*, Series A, No.30. (1979) 2 E.H.R.R. 245. For a highly critical account of the decision, see F.A. Mann, note, (1979) 95 L.Q.R. 349, who pointed out, *inter alia*, that a law of contempt was not known in the jurisdictions of the judges who constituted the majority.
[41] For further discussion, see paras 2–142 *et seq.*

by law and are necessary in a democratic society, in the interests of national security, territorial integrity or public safety, for the prevention of disorder or crime, for the protection of health or morals, for the protection of the reputation or rights of order, for preventing the disclosure of information received in confidence, or for maintaining the authority and impartiality of the judiciary."

1–105 The Court also had to consider the provisions of Art.6(1):

"In the determination of his civil rights and obligations or of any criminal charge against him everyone is entitled to a fair and public hearing within a reasonable time by an independent and impartial tribunal established by law . . . ".

1–106 It was argued for *The Sunday Times* that the restriction imposed upon them was not "prescribed by law" because the law of contempt of court was too uncertain in its application. Yet only two of the 20 judges agreed. There was also debate as to how far the wording of Art.10(2), "maintaining the authority and impartiality of the judiciary", actually extended. The Court explained its breadth in the following passage[42]:

"Insofar as the law of contempt may serve to protect the rights of litigants, this purpose is already included in the phrase 'maintaining the authority and impartiality of the judiciary': the rights so protected are the rights of individuals in their capacity as litigants, that is, as persons involved in the machinery of justice, and the authority of that machinery will not be maintained unless protection is afforded to all those involved in or having recourse to it."

1–107 Nevertheless, on the facts of the particular case before them, a majority of eleven held that the restriction imposed on *The Sunday Times* by the House of Lords was not necessary in a democratic society for maintaining the authority and impartiality of the judiciary even in this wide sense. A minority of nine dissented. A crucial difference between the majority and the minority was the extent to which it was proper for the European Court to express an opinion on the judgments of national courts. In the earlier case of *Handyside v United Kingdom*,[43] the court had underlined that the initial responsibility for securing the rights and freedoms enshrined in the Convention lay with the individual Contracting States. Article 10(2) left domestic judicial bodies a "margin of appreciation" in interpreting and applying domestic law. When a domestic court held, for example, that a particular restriction on free speech was necessary to protect morals, the European Court of Human Rights should be slow to interfere because the domestic court was best placed to judge what was required in that regard at a particular place or time.

1–108 The minority in the *Sunday Times* case held that exactly the same principle applied in regard to restrictions considered necessary by domestic courts for the maintenance of the authority and impartiality of the judiciary.[44] This led them to take the view that the European Court should not find there was a breach of the Convention in the *Sunday Times* case, where there were grounds upon which the

---

[42] Majority judgment, para.56.
[43] (1976) Series A, No. 24, 22, para.48, 1 E.H.R.R. 737 at 753.
[44] para.9 of the minority dissenting judgment, 2 E.H.R.R. at 289.

House of Lords *could* properly find the restriction necessary within the margin of appreciation.

The majority of the judges, however, distinguished between a restriction imposed to protect morals, where there was a wide margin of domestic appreciation,[45] and a restriction designed to maintain the authority of and impartiality of the judiciary where the margin was narrower.[46] Issues relating to the maintenance of the authority of the judiciary could be judged more objectively by the European Court of Human Rights than questions of morality. Domestic law and practice of Contracting States revealed a fairly substantial measure of common ground in this area. It was also observed to be relevant that the decisions of the various English courts dealing with *Att-Gen v Times Newspapers Ltd* had shown a considerable variety of judicial reasoning; that subsequently the Phillimore Committee had proposed that the pre-judgment test be replaced by an alternative; and that the Government's Green Paper on Contempt[47] did not call that recommendation in question.

1–109

In *Handyside v United Kingdom*,[48] the European Court had also considered the meaning of the word "necessary" in Art.10(2) of the Convention, and held that it implied the existence of a pressing social need.[49] Accordingly, in the *Sunday Times* case the majority asked themselves this question: did the injunction imposed on *The Sunday Times* by the House of Lords correspond to a pressing social need and was it proportionate to the legitimate aim pursued?[50] They concluded that the answer was in both cases in the negative. They pointed out that it was inappropriate to regard the domestic court as seeking to maintain a *balance* between freedom of speech and the due administration of justice; the Convention laid down a general right of freedom of speech subject to a number of exceptions which must be narrowly interpreted.[51]

1–110

The Court concluded that the perceived interference with the administration of justice did not correspond to a social need sufficiently pressing to outweigh the public interest in freedom of expression. The restraint was not necessary in a democratic society for maintaining the authority of the judiciary, and thus Art.10 had been violated.

1–111

It is plain that this decision was based upon a number of factors taken together. It involved weighing the public interest in the issues involved in the particular

1–112

---

[45] Confirmed by later developments—see in particular the judgment of the European Court of Human Rights arising from the decision of the House of Lords in *R. v Brown* [1994] 1 A.C. 212, to the effect that consent was no defence to sado-masochistic assault: *Jaggard v United Kingdom* (1997) 24 E.H.R.R. 39.
[46] para.59 of the majority judgment, 2 E.H.R.R. at 275.
[47] *Contempt of Court: A Discussion Paper* Cmnd. 7145 (1978).
[48] (1976) Series A, No.24, 1 E.H.R.R. 737.
[49] para.48, 1 E.H.R.R. 753–4.
[50] para.62, 2 E.H.R.R. 277–8. See also *Goodwin v UK* (1996) 22 E.H.R.R. 123; *Att-Gen v Guardian Newspapers Ltd* [1987] 1 W.L.R. 1248 at 1296–7 and 1307, Lords Templeman and Ackner; *Derbyshire County Council v Times Newspapers Ltd* [1992] Q.B. 770 at 812C, Balcombe L.J., CA.
[51] para.65, 2 E.H.R.R. 280–1. See now the discussion of *Re S(FC) (A Child)* [2004] UKHL 47, [2005] 1 A.C. 593 at paras 6–43 *et seq.*

litigation; the extent of public discussion apart from the article complained of; the stage which the relevant litigation had reached; its likely future course; and the general tenor of the article. Moreover, while it rejected the view that *any* pre-judgment of the issues in a pending case must be prohibited, the Court nevertheless recognised that attempts to pre-judge cases, in many instances, would be undesirable[52]:

> "The speeches in the House of Lords emphasised above all the concern that the process of the law may be brought into disrespect and the functions of the courts usurped either if the public is led to form an opinion on the subject matter of litigation before adjudication by the courts or if the parties to the litigation have to undergo 'trial by newspaper'. Such concern is in itself 'relevant' to the maintenance of the 'authority of the judiciary' as that expression is understood by the court ... if the issues arising in litigation are ventilated in such a way as to lead the public to form its own conclusion thereon in advance, it may lose its respect for and confidence in the courts. Again it cannot be excluded that the public's becoming accustomed to the regular spectacle of pseudo-trials in the news media might in the long run have nefarious consequences for the acceptance of the courts as the proper forum for the settlement of legal disputes."

1–113 In effect, the court recognised as a matter of principle that trial by newspaper is undesirable, but felt that such a principle might have to give way if public interest in the subject matter was sufficiently great, particularly if the relevant litigation was protracted. However, the Court rejected the view expressed in the House of Lords that a simple wide pre-judgment test was desirable for the sake of certainty, and adopted the approach that:

> "The Court has to be satisfied that the interference [i.e. with the exercise of the right to freedom of information guaranteed by Art.10] was necessary having regard to the facts and circumstances prevailing in the specific case before it".[53]

VIII. THE CONTEMPT OF COURT ACT 1981[54]

A. The occasion of the enactment

1–114 By the end of 1979 the Government was faced with a pressing need to reform the law of contempt. None of the recommendations of the 1974 Phillimore Committee's Report had been enacted. There was now a requirement to bring United Kingdom law into line with the decision of the European Court of Human Rights, and so to repair the breach of the European Convention of Human Rights.

---

[52] para.63, 2 E.H.R.R. 245 at 278–9. And see *Allenet de Ribemont v France* (1995) 20 E.H.R.R. 557, discussed below para.2–145.
[53] para.65, at 281.
[54] For early commentaries on the Act, see S. H. Bailey, "The Contempt of Court Act 1981" (1982) 45 M.L.R. 301–16; C.J. Miller, "The Contempt of Court Act 1981" [1982] Crim.L.R. 71; N. V. Lowe, "Contempt of Court Act 1981" [1982] P.L. 20; P. J. Cooke, "Contempt, the strict liability rule and the Contempt of Court Act 1981" (1983) 5 The Liverpool Law Review 35–55.

B. The purposes of the 1981 Act

On December 9, 1980[55] Lord Hailsham L.C. moved the second reading in the House of Lords of the Contempt of Court Bill which had been introduced in that House. The Bill was intended as a reforming exercise, described by the Lord Chancellor as a liberalising measure (his "little ewe lamb"). As he explained, the Bill had three principal purposes: it sought to put into effect the bulk of the recommendations of the Phillimore Committee, with some minor differences; it attempted to harmonise the law of England and Wales with the European Court's judgment in the *Sunday Times v United Kingdom*[56]; and it sought to bring consistency in the law of contempt applying, particularly with regard to media publication, in different parts of the United Kingdom.[57] These were not intended to be comprehensive reforms of the law of contempt. It does not, perhaps, go too far to say that the reforms were seen at the time as a holding operation, awaiting *inter alia* the outcome of the deliberations of the Law Commission on offences against the administration of justice.[58] Be that as it may, the Contempt of Court Act 1981 came into effect on August 27 of that year, and subject to minor amendments, remains in force today.

1–115

C. The strict liability "rule"

Prior to the 1981 Act there was authority to the effect that strict liability (whereby a person might be guilty of a criminal offence, notwithstanding the lack of *mens rea* in relation to one or more of the elements of the *actus reus*) attached to certain forms of criminal contempt; notably that of publishing matter calculated to interfere with the fair conduct of legal proceedings, and perhaps also for contempts relating to wards of court. In publication cases, all the complainant had to prove was that the alleged contemnor had published matter which *in fact* tended to prejudice pending proceedings; it mattered not, for purposes of liability,

1–116

---

[55] *Hansard*, H.L., Vol. 415, (5th series), col. 660. Since it is now permissible to have recourse to Parliamentary history for purposes of interpretation more readily than hitherto, as a result of the decision of the House of Lords in *Pepper v Hart* [1993] A.C. 593, we record that the Bill was further considered as follows: in the House of Lords, Vol. 416, cols.179, 351, 362 (Comm.); Vol. 417, cols.142 (R); 582 (3R); House of Commons, H.C. Vol. 1000, col. 28 (2R); Standing Committee A, seven sittings beginning April 28, 1981; Vol. 6, cols.880, 951 (R); H.L. Vol. 422, col. 235 (H.C. Amnds); H.C. Vol. 9, col. 410 (H.L.Amnds.). As to the use that was made of the European Convention of Human Rights where there was a possible conflict with what has been said in Parliament, see *R. v Broadcasting Complaints Commission Ex p. Barclay* (1996) 9 Admin L.R. 265.
[56] (1979) 2 E.H.R.R. 245.
[57] The law in Scotland is considered in ch.16. It seems reasonably clear that judges north of the border for a time took a sterner stance towards prejudicial pre-trial publicity; see A.J. Bonnington, "Press and Prejudice" (1995) 145 New L.J. 1623; and by the same author, (1996) 146 New Law Jo. 1312. See also *HMA v The Daily Record and The Sun* (1997) part 9, Media Lawyer 28, where Mr. Bonnington reports a decision in which the Scottish High Court appeared unwilling to follow the English decision in *Att-Gen v MGN Ltd* [1997] 1 All E.R. 456. It was a case in which a defendant's picture had been shown in *The Daily Record*, together with an account of his previous convictions, and the appellation "sex beast". Cp. *R. v Odhams Press Ltd Ex p. Att-Gen* [1957] 1 Q.B. 73: "Arrest this Beast".
[58] Law Commission Report No.96, *Criminal Law: Offences Relating to Interference With the Course of Justice* (1979), H.C. 213.

that the contemnor did not know the proceedings were pending, or that he failed to appreciate the prejudicial nature of his publication.

1–117   *Mens rea* was required in other forms of criminal contempt. It was not clear, however, how far strict liability extended; where the dividing line lay between contempts for which liability was strict and those which required *mens rea*.

1–118   The 1981 Act appears at first sight, in s.1, to define an existing rule of law. In truth, prior to the passing of the Act, there was no strict liability "rule" as such, though it was undoubtedly true that in the case of some contempts liability could be established in the absence of proof of intention. The draftsman appears to have coined a "rule"[59] for the purpose of setting limits to the application of strict liability. That is, by providing that no *mens rea* is required in cases of media contempt where the publication creates a substantial risk that the course of justice in the proceedings in question will be seriously impeded or prejudiced. But the "rule" applies only at the stage when those proceedings have become "active".

D. Some "miscellaneous amendments"[60]

1–119   The Contempt of Court Act is not a comprehensive restatement of the law of contempt. It reformed the law in certain specific areas by, for example, attempting to set relatively clear limits to the points in time at which publishers are at risk of committing the strict liability offence, providing for a defence in respect of the discussion of public affairs,[61] and also for the protection of journalists' sources.[62] It regulated the law relating to the disclosure of the secrets of the jury room,[63] and the use of tape recorders in court.[64]

1–120   Section 11 gives a court the power to control publication of details relating to names or other matters withheld from the public in proceedings, but *only* in cases where the court already had a recognised power to withhold the relevant information.[65] While much of the common law still applies after the Act, the relationship between the statute and the common law, particularly in the context of publication contempt, was not addressed by Parliament but was left to be worked out by the courts.

---

[59] See, *e.g. Att-Gen v Newspaper Publishing plc* [1988] Ch. 333 at 374A: "The Act of 1981 did not seek to systematise the approach of the courts. It simply defined by section 1 a term of art, namely, 'the strict liability rule' ": *per* Sir John Donaldson M.R. The significance of this point is discussed further at para.4–1.
[60] A phrase used by Lord Diplock in *Defence Secretary v Guardian Newspapers Ltd* [1985] 1 A.C. 339 at 346G–H, HL.
[61] See s.5, paras 4–293 *et seq.*
[62] See s.10, discussed in ch.9.
[63] See s.8, which is discussed at para.11–349.
[64] See s.9, para.10–190.
[65] Para.7–83.

Large areas of the law of contempt were untouched. Apart from the question 1–121
of penalty, for example, civil contempt remains a matter for the common law. The
law of contempt in the face of the court was not formalised by the Act,[66] despite
the fact that it is this problem which arguably provides the principal justification
for having a "summary" jurisdiction at all, while giving rise also to particular
problems for trial judges. Statutory guidance might have been valuable.

A general assessment of the Act was given by Lord Diplock in *Secretry of* 1–122
State for Defence v Guardian Newspapers Ltd[67]:

> "My Lords, save that the subject matter of the Act of 1981 is limited to contempt of
> court, as its long title shows, there is no consistent theme that can be identified as being
> common to all its sections. It consists of a number of miscellaneous amendments to the
> previous law of contempt of court both criminal and civil[68]; and all that can be
> predicated as an aid in giving a purposive construction to a particular section is that it
> presupposes the existence of . . . 'particular legal proceedings' ".[69]

Thus, far from codifying or replacing the common law of contempt of court, 1–123
the Act merely grafted certain rules on to the pre-existing law. When it is
necessary to determine, for example, whether or not any particular form of
contempt does or does not require proof of *mens rea*, it is still necessary to
consider the common law cases that might have a bearing on the point.

E. Civil contempt left untouched by the Act

In *Whitter v Peters*,[70] the Court of Appeal recognised there was a strong 1–124
argument that the 1981 Act was not intended to affect civil contempt at all. It was
pointed out that, apart from s.14 of the Act (which deals with penalties for
contempt), the various sections read in context plainly referred only to criminal
contempts. Moreover, the sub-heading "penalties" might suggest that even s.14
was not intended to apply to civil contempt. The court nevertheless left the matter
undecided as it was unnecessary for the immediate purpose.

In the House of Lords[71] it was held that the county court was an "inferior 1–125
court" within the ordinary meaning of that term, and therefore also within s.14(1)
of the Act; it was thus limited as to the period of committal to one month. The
context was committal in respect of *civil* contempt, namely breach of an
exclusion order under the Domestic Violence and Matrimonial Proceedings Act

---

[66] Except in the face of the magistrates' court: see s.12.
[67] [1985] 1 A.C. 339 at 346G–H, HL.
[68] The Act only affected civil contempt with respect to the maximum penalty: see s.14.
[69] See also Sir John Donaldson M.R. in *Att-Gen v Newspaper Publishing plc* [1988] Ch. 333 at 374B–C.
[70] [1982] 1 W.L.R. 389.
[71] *Sub nom. Peart v Stewart* [1983] 2 A.C. 109.

1–125 CHAPTER 1—HISTORY OF THE LAW OF CONTEMPT

1976.[72] Save in this limited respect, however, the law of civil contempt was untouched by the 1981 Act.

IX. DEVELOPMENTS SINCE THE 1981 ACT: A SUMMARY

A. Developments in the law of contempt

1–126 The law of contempt was, at the time of the enactment of the Contempt of Court Act 1981, still undeveloped in certain respects. One reason was that the right of appeal in cases of criminal contempt had existed only since 1961,[73] so that there was no body of case law in the appellate courts around which a consistent and integrated jurisprudence could evolve.[74] Since 1981, the law has developed at a remarkable pace. The House of Lords, in particular, has had to consider the law of contempt on several occasions.[75]

1–127 The drafting of the statute posed some fairly obvious questions which were going to require the consideration of higher courts. What constitutes a "substantial risk" of serious prejudice, and when is prejudice "serious"?[76] When is it "necessary" to make an order postponing a report of court proceedings?[77] When can it be said that the risk of prejudice is "merely incidental" to the discussion of a matter of public importance?[78] In what circumstances might it be "necessary for the... prevention of disorder or crime"[79] that a journalist should reveal his or her source? What is a "court" for the purposes of the law of contempt?[80] These problems of statutory interpretation have been, in some measure, resolved

---

[72] The special problems raised by s.14 are considered paras 14–8 *et seq.* See also the County Courts (Penalties for Contempt) Act 1983, considered at para.14–26.
[73] Administration of Justice Act 1960, s.13. See D.G.T. Williams, [1961] Crim.L.R. 87.
[74] The point is true of the jurisprudence of the criminal law more generally, since, until the Administration of Justice Act 1960, it was extremely rare for a criminal appeal to be heard by the House of Lords. See A.T.H. Smith, "Criminal Appeals in the House of Lords" (1984) 47 M.L.R. 133.
[75] *Att-Gen v English* [1983] 1 A.C. 116; *Peart v Stewart* [1983] 2 A.C. 109; *Secretary of State for Defence v Guardian Newspapers Ltd* [1985] A.C. 339; *Inquiry under the Company Securities (Insider Dealing) Act 1985, In Re* [1988] A.C. 660; *Re Lonrho plc* [1990] 2 A.C. 154 (albeit not in an appellate capacity); *X Ltd v Morgan Grampian (Publishers)* [1991] 1 A.C. 1; *P v Liverpool Daily Post and Echo Newspapers plc* [1991] 2 A.C. 370; *Att-Gen v Times Newspapers Ltd* [1992] 1 A.C. 191; *Re M: M v Home Office* [1994] 1 A.C. 377; *Att-Gen v Associated Newspapers Ltd* [1994] 2 A.C. 238; *Director General of Fair Trading v Pioneer Concrete (UK) Ltd* [1995] A.C. 456; *Harrow London Borough Council v Johnstone* [1997] 1 W.L.R. 459, [1997] 1 All E.R. 929; *Ashworth Hospital Authority v MGN Ltd* [2002] UKHL 29, [2002] 1 W.L.R. 2033, [2002] 4 All E.R. 193; *Att-Gen v Punch Ltd* [2002] UKHL 50, [2003] 1 A.C. 1046; *R. v Mirza* [2004] UKHL 2; *Re S (FC) (A Child)* [2004] UKHL 47, [2005] 1 A.C. 593; *R. v Smith* [2005] UKHL 12, [2005] 1 W.L.R. 704; *Att-Gen v Scotcher* [2005] UKHL 36, [2005] 1 W.L.R. 1867, [2005] 3 All E.R. 1.
[76] As required by s.2(2); see paras 4–55 *et seq.*
[77] Under s.4(2), paras 7–164 *et seq.*
[78] As required by s.5; see paras 4–293 *et seq.*
[79] Under s.10; see paras 9–182 *et seq.*
[80] *Att-Gen v Associated Newspapers Group plc* [1989] 1 All E.R. 604, D.C.; *P v Liverpool Daily Post and Echo Newspapers plc* [1991] 2 A.C. 370; *Peach Grey & Co (A Firm) v Sommers* [1995] I.C.R. 549, [1995] 2 All E.R. 513; see ch.13.

DEVELOPMENTS SINCE THE 1981 ACT: A SUMMARY   1–131

by the courts, and they are considered in detail in later chapters. Quite apart from interpreting the Act itself, there has been a good deal of judicial attention devoted to the continuing impact of the common law of contempt, especially in the field of media publications.

B. Surviving forms of common law contempt: residual uncertainties

One of the purposes of the 1981 Act was to introduce certainty into this area of the law.[81] In so far as journalists can now at least ascertain *when* they are at risk of proceedings under the strict liability rule, the Act has accomplished its objective. There are, however, some important residual uncertainties. Intentional contempt by publication is preserved by s.6(c). The Attorney-General was therefore enabled to rely in a number of cases following the 1981 Act upon the old principles of common law contempt, to a greater extent than might have been expected.[82]   1–128

In the light of these developments, it has become important to clarify (1) what is contemplated by "intention" in this context, and (2) the time at which the law begins to bite for common law purposes, irrespective of when proceedings may become "active" under the statutory regime. Does it apply to what might be termed "prospective" or "contingent"[83] proceedings generally, or only where proceedings are "virtually certain" to be commenced? There are questions as to the significance of "imminence", so that ironically the possibility of liability at common law may actually inhibit news coverage at an even earlier stage than when *R. v Savundranayagan*[84] was decided (apparently the opposite of what Parliament intended).[85]   1–129

There is the further difficulty that the *actus reus* of the common law contempt is by no means certain either. Is it the same as that enshrined in the Act (*i.e.* substantial risk of serious prejudice), or would something less suffice? We address these difficult, interrelated questions in the chapter on common law contempt by publication.[86]   1–130

So far as non-publication contempt is concerned, important questions remained unanswered for a time. Must there be an intention to interfere with the administration of justice, or would something less (recklessness perhaps) suffice?   1–131

---

[81] See para.1–97.
[82] *Att-Gen v Newspaper Publishing plc* [1988] Ch. 333; *Att-Gen v News Group Newspapers plc* [1989] 1 Q.B. 110, discussed at para.5–163; *Att-Gen v Newspaper Publishing plc* [1989] F.S.R. 457, Morritt J.; *Att-Gen v Hislop* [1991] 1 Q.B. 514; *Att-Gen v Sport Newspapers Ltd* [1991] 1 W.L.R. 1195, [1992] 1 All E.R. 503, discussed paras 5–51 *et seq.* and 5–174 *et seq.*; *Att-Gen v Newspaper Publishing plc* [1997] 1 W.L.R. 926, [1997] 3 All E.R. 159.
[83] The expression is one apparently coined by Windeyer J. in *James v Robinson* (1963) 109 C.L.R. 593 at 618.
[84] [1968] 1 W.L.R. 1761.
[85] See paras 5–96 *et seq.*
[86] See paras 5–5 *et seq.*

1-131 CHAPTER 1—HISTORY OF THE LAW OF CONTEMPT

Or might it be unnecessary in such contexts to address at all the state of the alleged contemnor's mind towards the *consequences* of his conduct for the administration of justice? Since the Act did not touch upon any of these issues, there were uncertainties both as to what constituted the *actus reus*[87] and the requisite *mens rea*.[88]

C. The Influence of the European Convention[89]

1-132 There can be little doubt that between 1980 and 2000 the decision of the European Court of Human Rights in *Sunday Times v UK*[90] had a considerable impact on the development of the English law,[91] in at least two respects. First, it alerted the press and the legal representatives of the media to the fact that it was possible to level effective challenges to English law and practice, particularly with regard to the treatment of freedom of speech.[92] No longer could Westminster be regarded as having the final word as to the priorities to be accorded to competing policy considerations in that field.

1-133 Secondly, the English judges themselves became more receptive to legal arguments based on the European Convention.[93] An early example was that of Lord Scarman in *Att-Gen v BBC*[94] who expressed considerable inhibition about extending the protection of the law of contempt to "administrative courts and tribunals" other than the established courts of law. As he put it,

> "If we are to make the extension, we have to ask ourselves, if the United Kingdom is to comply with its international obligations, whether the extension is necessary in our democratic society. Is there a 'pressing social need' for the extension? For that, according to the European Court of Human Rights, (1979) 2 E.H.R.R. 245, 275, is what the phrase means. It has not been demonstrated to me that there is."

---

[87] See para.11-3.
[88] See paras 10-208 *et seq.* and paras 11-21 *et seq.*
[89] Convention for the Protection of Human Rights and Fundamental Freedoms (Rome, November 4, 1950) T.S. 71 (1953); Cmd. 8969. The Labour government coming into office in May 1997 indicated its intention to introduce legislation to "incorporate" the European Convention into British Law; *Hansard*, H.C. Vol. 294, col. 42, May 14, 1997. In due course, the Human Rights Act came into force on October 2, 2000.
[90] (1979) 2 E.H.R.R. 245.
[91] The status of the European Convention of Human Rights in English law in the twenty years prior to the enactment of the Human Rights Act 1998 is more fully considered in ch.2. Whatever its technical status during that period, the Convention had an enormous effect upon English legal thinking and practice since the early eighties.
[92] This proposition is true not simply for the law of contempt, but has had ramifications elsewhere, particularly in the law of defamation: *Derbyshire County Council v Times Newspapers Ltd* [1992] Q.B. 770 (although the House of Lords reached the same conclusion without express reliance upon the Convention): [1993] A.C. 534; *Rantzen v Mirror Group (1986) Ltd* [1994] Q.B. 670, CA; *John v MGN Ltd* [1997] Q.B. 568; *Tolstoy-Miloslavsky v Lord Aldington* [1996] 1 W.L.R. 736, [1996] 2 All E.R. 556.
[93] See the discussion at paras 2-122 *et seq.* See however paras 16-301 *et seq.* for a comparison with the approach of the Scottish judiciary.
[94] [1981] A.C. 303 at 362C-D.

Developments since the 1981 Act: A Summary   1–135

This willingness to consider the Convention has had a fundamental influence on the law and practice of contempt in particular, following the Contempt of Court Act, not least because lawyers have been obliged to recognise that it was largely to give effect to the European Court's decision that Parliament enacted the principal provisions.[95]

The United Kingdom government that came in to office in May 1997   1–134
committed itself to the "incorporation" of the European Convention on Human Rights into the domestic law of the United Kingdom.[96] On October 2, 2000 the Human Rights Act 1998 came into effect. Naturally, as in so many other areas of the law, its terms will have been considered in most if not all cases in which the contempt jurisdiction has been relevant and these are mentioned at the appropriate juncture in this book.[97]

D. The *Spycatcher* litigation

By no means all of the important decisions have been concerned with the   1–135
interpretation of the Contempt of Court Act 1981. Much of the learning on the law of contempt in the late nineteen-eighties sprang from the *Spycatcher* litigation, in the course of which the then United Kingdom government was seeking to prevent the further publication of the memoirs of a former security officer, primarily on the basis of breach of confidence. The decision of the Court of Appeal in *Att-Gen v Newspaper Publishing plc*.[98] has had considerable influence by reason of its confirmation that those who deliberately interfere with the administration of justice by undermining judicial orders may be guilty of contempt, even though not directly bound. This has had important implications for journalists,[99] not least because of the readiness with which judges have shown themselves in a number of decisions as being prepared to infer the relevant intention from the surrounding circumstances.[1]

---

[95] See Lloyd L.J. in *Att-Gen v Newspaper Publishing plc* [1988] Ch. 333 at 382D–F.
[96] *Hansard*, H.C. Vol. 294, col. 42, May 14, 1997. There had already been significant support for such a course among members of the judiciary. Whereas Lord Justice Scarman (as he then was) was something of a lone judicial voice when he delivered his Hamlyn Lectures, *English Law—The New Dimension* (1974), he was subsequently joined by others of his brethren. See for example, Lord Browne-Wilkinson, "The Infiltration of a Bill of Rights" [1992] P.L. 397; Sir Thomas Bingham, "The European Convention on Human Rights: Time to Incorporate" (1993) 109 L.Q.R. 390; Sir John Laws, "Law and Democracy" [1995] P.L. 72; Lord Woolf, "Droit Public—English Style" [1995] P.L. 57; Sir Stephen Sedley, "Human Rights: a Twenty-First Century Agenda" [1995] P.L. 386. Lord Lester Q.C., in "The Mouse that Roared: The Human Rights Bill 1995" [1995] P.L. 198, n.1 stated that his Bill had the support of most Law Lords, both serving and retired. As has been pointed out, this was "an entirely new and very significant development": M. Zander, *A Bill of Rights?* (4th ed., 1997).
[97] See also the general observations on the consequences of the enactment at paras 2–198 *et seq*.
[98] [1988] Ch. 333. See *Observer, Guardian and Sunday Times (No.2) v United Kingdom* (1992) 14 E.H.R.R. 153, 299. See also P. Duffy, "Spycatcher in Europe" (1991) 141 New Law Jo. 1703.
[99] See the discussion in ch.6.
[1] See *Att-Gen v News Group Newspapers plc* [1989] Q.B. 110; *Att-Gen v Newspaper Publishing plc* [1989] F.S.R. 457, Morritt J.; *Att-Gen v Times Newspapers Ltd* [1992] 1 A.C. 191; *Official Solicitor v News Group Newspapers plc* [1994] 2 F.L.R. 174.

1-136 Yet the government's attempts to stifle *Spycatcher* proved ultimately to be futile since the relevant information became known world wide.[2] In a succession of cases, Commonwealth courts[3] declined to accord to the United Kingdom government the degree of protection sought, and the purpose of the interim order was defeated. So far as the law of confidence is concerned, however, and especially as it applies to personal lives rather than to government, this factor does not necessarily mean that any restraining order made by an English court can be regarded automatically as superseded merely because the relevant confidential information has been published elsewhere.[4] Undoubtedly, however, these uncertainties have led to confusion on the part of journalists and their advisers.[5]

E. The use of contempt and sequestration in politically sensitive disputes

1-137 Another development of significance was the resort to the law of contempt in the field of industrial relations law. " 'Contempt of court' . . . was rarely found in labour law studies before the 1980s but . . . it is now a crucial part of the subject."[6] The law of contempt was put under strain for a considerable period, particularly during the coal miners' strike of 1984–5, where attempts were made to use the process of contempt to deal with breaches of orders made in relation to conduct forming part of the strategy of the strikers in the course of industrial disputes.[7] So too the process of contempt has been used in connection

---

[2] See the more realistic practical approach of the Court of Appeal in *Att-Gen v Times Newspapers Ltd* [2001] EWCA Civ 97, [2001] 1 W.L.R. 885 where the realities of the global village were acknowledged. For other examples of the court acknowledging the practicalities of living in a "global village", see also *Lukoviak v Unidad Editorial SA* [2001] EMLR 46; *Kelly v BBC* [2001] Fam. 59 at 78; *Lennon v Scottish Daily Record* [2004] EWHC 359 (QB).

[3] *Att-Gen for United Kingdom v Heinemann Publishers* (1988) 78 A.L.R. 449 (Australia): *Att-Gen for UK v Wellington Newspapers Ltd* [1988] 1 N.Z.L.R. 129 (New Zealand); *Att-Gen v South China Morning Post* [1989] 2 F.S.R. 653 (Hong Kong).

[4] See, e.g. Lord Keith in *Att-Gen v Guardian Newspapers Ltd (No.2)* [1990] 1 A.C. 109 at 260E–H; *R. v Broadcasting Complaints Commission Ex p. Granada TV* [1995] E.M.L.R. 16.

[5] For example, in *Att-Gen v News UK Ltd and Stott*, December 1995, Potts J. imposed heavy fines upon the publishers and editor of the (by then defunct) newspaper *Today* because an in-house lawyer had assumed that extracts from the memoirs of a Royal housekeeper could be published in England, following their publication in the United States, despite the fact that an injunction remained in force against the housekeeper which had been granted by Steel J. the previous January. This is an illustration of the real practical difficulties in which such advisers find themselves in trying to reconcile, on the one hand, the approach of the Court of Appeal in *Att-Gen v Newspaper Publishing plc* [1988] Ch. 333 and, on the other, the approach of the House of Lords in *Att-Gen v Guardian Newspapers Ltd (No.2)* [1990] 1 A.C. 109. The essence of the distinction turns upon the difference between personal rights and government secrets: see Lord Keith at 255–6. The lesson to be learned is that it should never be assumed that an order has been superseded until an application has been made to the court for it to be discharged in the light of changed circumstances.

[6] Lord Wedderburn, Commentary, "Contempt of Court: Vicarious Liability of Companies and Unions" (1992) 21 I.L.J. 51.

[7] See G. Lightman, "A Trade Union in Chains" (1987) C.L.P. 25; C. O'Regan, "Contempt of Court and the Enforcement of Labour Injunctions" (1991) 54 M.L.R. 385. For cases arising directly out of the miners' strike, see *Taylor v NUM, The Times*, November 20, 1985; *Clarke v Chadburn* [1985] 1 W.L.R. 78. And see, in the context of other industrial disputes, the decisions in *Messenger Group Newspapers Ltd v National Graphical Association* (1982) [1984] I.C.R. 345; *Kent Free Press v NGA* [1987] I.R.L.R. 267.

Developments since the 1981 Act: A Summary   1–140

with other forms of demonstration.[8] Within this jurisdiction, at least, in recent years, the pursuit of injunctions, and the contempt remedies available in respect of a breach, have been less prominent in the context of industrial disputes or protest demonstrations. By contrast, it still seems that these weapons have continued to be utilised in Canada.[9]

F. Prominence of contempt in the family law cases

In the field of civil contempt much of the case law in recent years has derived from family disputes, and in particular in the context of non-molestation injunctions and that of disobedience to orders relating to children. This is despite the fact that the courts have frequently insisted that the use of the contempt jurisdiction should be a matter of "last resort".[10]   1–138

Perhaps one of the most significant developments, however, for the media has been the increasing resort to the inherent jurisdiction of the Family Division for the purpose of making wide-ranging injunctions restraining reference to minors or patients. It became necessary also to resolve the apparent conflict between two quite different strands of authority. On the one hand, there is the principle (confirmed by s.1 of the Children Act 1989) that the court should treat the interests of a child as paramount. On the other hand, a number of authorities in the Court of Appeal had given priority to the demands of freedom of speech, even in cases where the welfare of a minor might be damaged through media coverage.[11]   1–139

The balance for a time seemed to be struck, at least in principle, in accordance with the guidelines contained in the judgment of Ward L.J. in *Re Z (A Minor) (Identification: Restrictions on Publication)*.[12] Priority was to be accorded to a   1–140

---

[8] *Hubbard v Pitt* [1976] Q.B. 142; *Harrington v North London Polytechnic* [1984] 1 W.L.R. 1293, 3 All E.R. 666. See by way of background P. Wallington, "Injunctions and the Right to Demonstrate" (1976) C.L.J. 82; *Messenger Group Newspapers Ltd v NGA* [1984] I.R.L.R. 397 (union fined £675,000 in respect of a series of prohibited demonstrations); *Kent Free Press v NGA* [1987] I.R.L.R. 267; *Mirror Group Newspapers v Harrison*, (unreported) November 7, 1986.
[9] As in *United Nurses of Alberta v Att-Gen for Alberta* (1992) 89 D.L.R. (4th) 609; *J.P. v MacMillan Bloedel Ltd; Attorney General of Canada Intervener* (1996) 130 D.L.R. (4th) 385; *Re United Steelworkers of America, Local 9332 et al. and Phillips et al.; Attorney General et al., Interveners* (1995) 98 C.C.C. (3d) 20, SCC; *Canadian Union of Public Employees, Local 301 v Montreal (City)* [1997] 1 S.C.R. 793; *International Forest Products Ltd v Kern* (2001) 94 BCLR (3d) 67, BCCA. See Also A. Attaran, "Mandamus in the Enforcement of the Criminal Law: Ending the Anti-Protest Injunction Habit—Issues Arising from MacMillan Bloedel" (1999) 33 U.B.C.L. Rev. 181; J. Lawn, "The John Doe Injunction in Mass Protest Cases" (1998) 56 U. of T. Fac. Law Rev. 101; J. Berryman, "Injunctions—The Ability to Bind Non-Parties" (2002) Can Bar Rev. 207.
[10] See para.12–24.
[11] See generally ch.6, and, *e.g. Re L (A Minor) Wardship: Freedom of Publication* [1988] 1 All E.R. 418 at 421, Booth J.; *Re W (Wards) (Publication of Information)* [1989] 1 F.L.R. 246, Sir Stephen Brown P.; *Re M & N (Minors) (Wardship: Publication of Information)* [1990] Fam. 211, CA *Re W (A Minor) (Wardship: Restrictions on Publication)* [1992] 1 W.L.R. 100, [1992] 1 All E.R. 794; CA; *R. v Central Independent Television plc* [1994] Fam. 192, CA; *Re H-S* [1994] 3 All E.R. 390 at 398c, CA.
[12] [1997] Fam. 1. See also *Oxfordshire County Council v L and F* [1997] 1 F.L.R. 235, Stuart-White J.

1-140   CHAPTER 1—HISTORY OF THE LAW OF CONTEMPT

minor's welfare in circumstances when the order that the court was asked to make involved the taking of a quasi-parental decision, by the court itself, in the exercise of what was traditionally known as the inherent or *parens patriae* jurisdiction. By contrast, where it was sought to restrain publicity relating to a minor or patient which was only likely to arise incidentally in the coverage of some topic of genuine public interest, then normally freedom of speech was likely to prevail. Subsequently, however, the matter was addressed by the House of Lords in *Re S (FC) (A Child)*,[13] in the light of which it seems unlikely that there will be so much focus on the supposed distinction between what had been referred to as the "custodial" and "protective" jurisdictions. The emphasis now, in the light of the Human Rights Act 1998, is more likely to be upon balancing the competing considerations of the rights under Arts 8 and 10 of the European Convention having regard to the facts of the individual case.

G. Contempt and the Crown

1-141 A decision of considerable constitutional importance was that of the House of Lords in *Re M: M v Home Office*,[14] to the effect that a minister of the Crown, acting in his official capacity, could be made the subject of an injunction, enforceable, if necessary, by way of proceedings for contempt. Given the history of governmental compliance with rulings of the court, even though believed not to be obligatory, it may be that the practical consequences of the decision will not prove to be very far-reaching. But had the decision in the House of Lords gone the other way, and ministers were held *not* bound by such orders, this might have had serious long-term consequences for the rule of law.[15]

H. Developments in other common law jurisdictions

1-142 The common law of contempt still governs in Australia, Canada and New Zealand. In areas of English law where the Contempt of Court Act does not bite, therefore, the developments in the higher common law courts, in particular the High Court of Australia, the Supreme Court of Canada and the New Zealand Court of Appeal, continue to offer valuable guidance. Caution is needed, however, in placing reliance on the case law of other jurisdictions, since there may well be significant differences, political, social, legislative and constitutional. As Sir Ivor Richardson J. put it in *Gisborne Herald v Solicitor-General*[16]:

> "First, the complex process of balancing the values underlying free expression and fair trial rights may vary from country to country, even though there is a common and genuine commitment to international human rights norms. The balancing will be

---

[13] [2004] UKHL 47, [2005] 1 A.C. 593, considered at paras 6–43 *et seq*.
[14] [1994] 1 A.C. 377, discussed more fully at paras 2–223 *et seq*.
[15] See H.W.R. Wade (1992) 108 L.Q.R. 173.
[16] [1995] 3 N.Z.L.R. 562, 573.

influenced by the culture and values of the particular community... The result of the balancing process will necessarily reflect the court's assessment of society's values."

Potentially, one of the most significant developments in the protection of civil liberties in common law countries has been the enactment of bills of rights. This occurred in Canada in 1982,[17] and in New Zealand in 1990.[18]

1–143

Experience in the other jurisdictions shows that entrenched rights to freedom of information tend to come into conflict with other such rights, and especially the right to a fair trial. The resolution of such conflicts can have a destabilising effect upon the pre-existing law. A bill of rights would not necessarily demand solutions that are any different from those arrived at by the common law.[19] Yet in Canada the judiciary appear to have treated the Charter as requiring a fundamentally different balance to be struck between these competing policy considerations.[20] By contrast, despite the fact that the corresponding provisions are very similar, New Zealand judges have come to the conclusion that the traditional priority afforded by the common law to ensuring a fair trial should still prevail.[21]

1–144

---

[17] Canadian Charter of Rights and Freedoms 1982. See generally eds. P. Anisman and A. Linden, *The Media, The Courts and the Charter* (Toronto: Carswell, 1986); R.J. Sharpe, K.E. Swinton and K. Roach, *The Charter of Rights and Freedoms* (2002). See also the literature cited in R. Penner, "The Canadian Experience with the Charter of Rights: Are there Lessons for the United Kingdom?" [1996] P.L. 104; B. McLachlin, "The Canadian Charter and the Democratic Process", in eds. C. Gearty and A. Tomkins, *Understanding Human Rights* (1996); J.B. Kelly, "The *Charter of Rights and Freedoms* and the Rebalancing of Liberal Constitutionalism in Canada, 1982–1997" (1997) 37 Osgoode Hall Law Jo. 625; P.J. Monahan, "Constitutional Cases 2000: An Overview" (2001) 14 Supreme Court Law Rev. 1; P.W. Hogg and A. Thornton, "Reply to 'Six Degrees of Dialogue' " (1999) 37 Osgoode Hall L.J. 529; J. Clements, "Introducing Canadian Rights Jurisprudence" (2004) Juridical Review 159 and 207.

[18] Bill of Rights Act 1990. For a discussion of the impact of this Act on the law of contempt, see J.F. Burrows and U. Cheer, *Media Law in New Zealand* (5th ed., 2005) at p.644ff; G. Huscroft in ed. P. Rishworth, *The New Zealand Bill of Rights* (2003) ch. 12; J.F. Burrows, "Freedom of the Press Under the New Zealand Bill of Rights Act 1990" in ed. P.A. Joseph, *Essays on the Constitution* (1995), p.285. See also G. Huscroft and P. Rishworth, *Rights and Freedoms: The New Zealand Bill of Rights Act 1990 and The Human Rights Act 1993* (1995). A note of caution is sounded in A.S. Butler, "The Bill of Rights Debate: Why the New Zealand Bill of Rights Act 1990 is a Bad Model for Britain" (1997) 17 O. J. L.S. 323. A. Geddis, "The Horizontal Effects of the NZBORA, as Applied in Hosking v Runting" [2004] N.Z. Law Rev. 681. See also Sir I.L.M. Richardson, "The New Zealand Bill of Rights: Experience and Potential, Including the Implications for Commerce" [2004] 10 Canta L.R. 259.

[19] See, *e.g.* Lord Goff in *Att-Gen v Guardian (No.2)* [1990] 1 A.C. 109 at 284A: "I have no reason to believe that English law, as applied in the courts, leads to any different conclusion". See also Lord Keith in *Derbyshire County Council v Times Newspapers Ltd* [1993] A.C. 534 at 551F–G. With the benefit of hindsight such observations are perceived in some quarters as being a little complacent: see, *e.g.* the observations of Sedley L.J. in, *e.g. Berezovsky v Forbes Inc* [2001] EWCA Civ 1251, [2001] EMLR 1030 at [10] urging a readiness "to cull sacred jurisprudential cows" borrowing a metaphor from Lord Slynn in the House in *R. v Lambert* [2001] UKHL 37, [2002] 2 A.C. 545, at [6].

[20] *Dagenais v Canadian Broadcasting Corp* (1994) 120 D.L.R. (4th) 12; *Phillips v Nova Scotia* (Westray Inquiry) (1995) 98 C.C.C. (3d) 20.

[21] *Gisborne Herald v Solicitor-General* [1995] 3 N.Z.L.R. 563. And see *Television New Zealand Ltd v Quinn* [1996] 3 N.Z.L.R. 24 at 45: "I am not persuaded that the Bill of Rights has the result of putting media freedoms above the right to one's reputation", *per* McKay J.

1-145   CHAPTER 1—HISTORY OF THE LAW OF CONTEMPT

I. Technological developments[22]

1-145 At least so far as imposing restrictions upon the reporting of legal proceedings is concerned, technological developments and the speed of communication have had a considerable impact upon the ability of the courts to impose wide-ranging restraints upon the media at short notice.[23] On the other hand, the development of satellite television and its relay by cable networks, and even more recently emerging technologies such as the Internet, pose difficulties for would-be regulators of public speech and discussion.[24] This was recognised by, for example, Lamer C.J.C. in *Dagenais v Canadian Broadcasting Corp*.[25]:

> "It should also be noted that recent technological advances have brought with them considerable difficulties for those who seek to enforce bans. The efficacy of bans has been reduced by the growth of interprovincial and international television and radio broadcasts available through cable television, satellite dishes, and short wave radios. It has also been reduced by the advent of information exchanges available through computer networks. In this global electronic age, meaningfully restricting the flow of information is becoming increasingly difficult. Therefore, the actual effect of bans on jury impartiality is substantially diminishing."

---

[22] See Katch, "Rights, Camera, Action" (1995) 104 Yale L.J. 1681; C. Sunstein, "The First Amendment in Cyberspace" *ibid.*, 1757; Volokh, "Cheap Speech and What it Will Do", *ibid.*, 1805. See also Hon. Justice M. Kirby, "The Globalisation of Media and Judicial Independence" (1996) 1 Communications Law 115. See Donald F. Theall, "Canada, Censorship and the Internet" in Klaus Petersen and Alan C. Hutchinson eds, *Interpreting Censorship in Canada* (1999), University of Toronto Press. The occasion for the writing of the article was the Homolka-Bernardo case in 1994, where in the course of a prosecution for murder the trial judge sought to prevent publication of reports of the proceedings for fear that a later trial of a co-defendant might be jeopardised. The matter was however readily available on American websites, although attempts were made to prevent access to those websites by certain Internet service providers.

[23] See in particular *Att-Gen v Guardian (No.3)* [1992] 1 W.L.R. 874 at 882, Mann L.J.; 885, Brooke J. For the text of what was said, see para.7-154. For some time, the existence of s.4(2) orders has been notified on the Scottish courts website. On March 18, 2005 the then President of the Family Division handed down a President's *Practice Direction (Applications for Reporting Restriction Orders)* [2005] 2 F.L.R. 120, and *Practice Note (Official Solicitor: Deputy Director of Legal Services: Cafcass: Applications for Reporting Restriction Orders)* [2005] 2 F.L.R. 111, setting out guidance on applications for reporting restrictions orders affecting national media organisations. The object was to put in place a secure system for advance notice where an applicant wishes to apply for a reporting restriction against the media. This appears to have been prompted by the demands of s.12(2) of the Human Rights Act 1998 which we consider in para.6-11.

[24] An example is provided by the problem which arose in relation to the then Home Secretary's son who was involved in December 1997 in an allegation of supplying a controlled drug. The Attorney-General obtained an injunction to prevent the identity of the person concerned, who was 17 years of age, from being revealed, although the precise basis of the application remained obscure. It was not clear whether it was perceived that such a publication would have involved a breach of the Children and Young Persons Act 1933, s.49 (discussed at paras 8–39 *et seq.*), or whether it was being suggested that the revelation of the name in conjunction with other detailed accounts of the incident which had already been highly publicised might give rise to a substantial risk of serious prejudice. At all events, the injunction was lifted in due course, not before the matter had been pre-empted by the posting of the name on the Internet. The Home Office has considered whether fresh legislation is needed to deal with such problems; *The Times*, February 2, 1998.

[25] (1994) 120 D.L.R. (4th) 12, 44a–c. For the problems associated with the "global village" see the cases at para.1–136, n.2.

One commentator[26] suggested that the commonplace risks that have always 1–146
beset parties to litigation, including police and defence in criminal cases:

" . . . are compounded in the case of new audio-visual technologies by reference to
their instantaneous and especially their transnational nature. This new factor means that
national arrangements which may have been worked out over many years and represent
a careful compromise, may be breached, wittingly or unwittingly, by externally-sited
media organisations with neither the intimate knowledge of local rules or cultures nor
the willingness to abide by them."

Although attempts have been made by piecemeal statutory provisions to adjust 1–147
the law to the changes brought about by these technological developments, they
have not really kept pace, and it may be argued that the "penny numbers"
approach has led to gaps, anomalies and inconsistencies.[27] There is a clear need
for a degree of consistency in media law, and to regulate liability for contempt on
the part of editors, publishers, journalists and distributors in a similar way. The
present system means that there are two separate regimes for media lawyers to
address, depending upon whether they are advising on the risks of libel or those
of contempt.

In *Totalise plc v Motley Fool Ltd*,[28] Owen J. had to consider the position of 1–148
website operators.[29] He was specifically concerned with an issue of statutory
construction, as to whether s.10 of the Contempt of Court Act 1981 afforded such
persons privilege as to their contributors, but he indicated that as a matter of
discretion he would have ordered the identity to be disclosed because of the ease
with which contributors could otherwise use the Internet for wrongdoing without
fear of detection. The decision came before the Court of Appeal but only on the
issue of costs, the judge having ordered the web-site operator to pay the costs of
the application for the *Norwich Pharmacal* order, as to which they had taken a
neutral stance.[30] The general rule that the unsuccessful party should pay the
costs[31] did not fit *Norwich Pharmacal* applications which were not really *inter
partes* disputes. Moreover, on the facts, the judge had failed to take into account
the neutral stance of the operator or the effect upon it if it had revealed the
confidential details. *Norwich Pharmacal* applications were more akin to those
made for pre-action disclosure, where the costs were governed by CPR 48.3.
Normally the person required to give the disclosure should recover costs.

---

[26] C. Walker, "Fundamental Rights, Fair Trials and the New Audio-Visual Sector" (1996) 59 M.L.R. 517 at 521, and see, by the same author, "Cyber Contempt: Fair Trials and the Internet" [1997/8] Y.E.M.L. 3. See also M.R. Chesterman, "O.J. and the Dingo: How Media Contempt is Dealt with in Australia and America" (1997) 45 Am. Jo. Comp. Law 801; "Satellite Avoids Ban in Bulger Case" (1993) J. Media Law and Practice 157.
[27] See, *e.g.* the Defamation Act 1996, which by s.1 was intended *inter alia* to protect computer network service operators and providers from primary responsibility for publication, by the means in effect of an extended defence of innocent dissemination. It also uses the same device to limit the categories of persons who may be considered the author, editor or publisher of a statement in the context of defamation law. See generally M. Collins, *The Law of Defamation and the Internet* (2nd ed., 2005) Oxford University Press.
[28] [2001] E.M.L.R. 750.
[29] See para.9–58 below.
[30] [2002] 1 W.L.R. 1233.
[31] See CPR 44.3.

1-149 These problems were considered in *HMA v Beggs (No.2)*.[32] Lord Osborne highlighted the distinction, so far as service providers are concerned, between the law of contempt and the provisions specifically made for their protection in s.1 of the Defamation Act 1996.

1-150 It is potentially an important aspect of the continuing availability of material on the world wide web that prejudicial publications may not be so readily discounted as ephemeral, and the "fade factor" may be less easily invoked.[33] The similar, and vexed, question of whether that which can be accessed via the internet should be characterised as "in the public domain" was considered in *Att-Gen v Greater Manchester Newspapers Ltd*.[34] On the particular facts, it was held that the information had not entered the public domain because accessibility of government statistical information *via* a government department website was "theoretical" and it was therefore not generally accessible to the public. This was because a member of the public would need "some degree of background knowledge and persistence for it to become available". Such flexible concepts give rise to problems of classification and thus to undesirable uncertainty for those seeking or giving pre-publication advice.

J. Other legislative developments

1-151 Increasingly, Parliament legislates for specific situations which hitherto would have fallen within the scope of the general law of contempt. We discuss elsewhere the overlap between the law of contempt and some of the modern statutory offences.[35] The Criminal Justice and Public Order Act 1994, s.51, makes provision for specific offences of intimidation of witnesses, jurors and others, and reprisals against them. This reduces the role for the law of contempt, consistently with the recommendations of the Phillimore Committee,[36] although little if any consideration was then given to the Report of that Committee, or to what was to become of the traditional functions of the law of contempt with regard to jurors and witnesses. On the other hand, ss.17 and 18 of the Criminal Procedure and Investigation Act 1996,[37] which regulate the disclosure process in criminal proceedings, employ specifically the contempt sanction[38] in the case of wrongful use of disclosed material.

1-152 A more recent development, however, has been the making of specific provision, particularly in the field of domestic violence, introducing the criminal law and penalties into an area which was previously thought to fall exclusively within the domain of civil contempt. It has long been recognised that conduct

---

[32] 2002 S.L.T. 139, S.C.C.R. 879 at [11], High Court of Justiciary.
[33] See, *e.g. HMA v Beggs (No.1)*, 2002 S.L.T. 135, discussed at para.4–168 and para.7–138 below, and also *HMA v Beggs (No.2)*, considered at para.1–149 and para.4–27.
[34] [2001] All E.R. (D) 32 (Dec) (2001) 145 S.J.L.B. 279, at paras 28–33.
[35] At para.2–13.
[36] Cmnd. 5794 (1974), para.21, recommending that the contempt jurisdiction should only be invoked where (a) the offending act does not fall within the definition of any other offence, or (b) where urgency or practical necessity require a summary disposal. See also para.2–16.
[37] Supplemented by the Criminal Justice Act 2003, Pt 3.
[38] For a list of statutes which incorporate references to the penal sanctions associated with the law of contempt, see para.13–77, n.45.

constituting a breach of an injunction might also form the subject matter of a criminal offence. Judicial attention has therefore been focused on the avoidance of double jeopardy in this context. What is new is that now a breach of an injunction in the context of "non-molestation" has itself been treated as constituting a criminal offence.[39] Also it is provided in the Protection from Harassment Act 1997 that breach of an injunction or restraining order granted under its provisions shall be a criminal offence.[40] The power of arrest, on the other hand, which was available for attachment to a non-molestation order is to be removed and retained only in the context of an "occupation order".[41]

K. A changing climate in the context of free press versus fair trial

There were several decisions suggesting greater inhibition on the part of the courts in sanctioning resort to the summary process of contempt, or at least a willingness to apply a more analytical discrimination to the process of determining in which circumstances it should be used. This was so in relation to non-publication contempt as well as in cases to which Art.10 of the European Convention is relevant. For example, in *R. v Runting*[42] Lord Lane C.J. with reference to the *actus reus* of contempt (relating to an allegation of molestation of a defendant on his way from court by a press photographer) commented that there is " . . . a dividing line between trivial acts, which no one would say could on any account amount to unnecessary interference, and serious acts which might amount to unnecessary interference". Also in *R. v Schot and Barclay*,[43] where two jurors were sentenced to 30 days' imprisonment for failing to reach a verdict, the Court of Appeal made it plain that the use of the summary power to commit for contempt in the face should be used only with the utmost caution.

1–153

In *Att-Gen v MGN Ltd*,[44] where a trial had been aborted because of potentially prejudicial pre-trial publicity on the part of several newspapers, the Divisional Court held that there had nevertheless been no contempt, on the facts of that case, where there had been a six month delay between the publications and the anticipated trial. It was recognised that there were bound to be cases where, even though it was right to abandon a trial (or to allow an appeal against conviction), it would not be possible to establish contempt in respect of any particular newspaper to the required criminal standard.

1–154

A cautious approach was also taken by the Divisional Court in *Att-Gen v Unger*,[45] where Simon Brown L.J. admitted overcoming his "strong initial view"

1–155

---

[39] Family Law Act s.42A(1), as amended by the Domestic Violence, Crime and Victims Act 2004, s.1 which is to come in to force from a date to be appointed: the section says that " . . . a person who without reasonable excuse does anything that he is prohibited from doing by a non-molestation order is guilty of an offence".
[40] s.3(6).
[41] See the discussion in paras 14–71 *et seq.* and the provisions of the Domestic Violence, Crime and Victims Act 2004, Sch.10, para.38.
[42] (1989) 89 Cr.App.R. 243 at 245.
[43] [1997] 2 Cr.App.R. 383, (1997) 161 J.P. 473, more fully discussed at paras 10–72 *et seq.* and 10–176.
[44] [1997] 1 All E.R. 456.
[45] [1998] 1 Cr.App.R. 308, [1998] E.M.L.R. 280, discussed at para.4–166.

1-155 that the articles in question constituted a plain contempt of court, amounting as they did to the clearest possible statements that a home-help was guilty of theft from an elderly woman at a time when proceedings for such offences were active. He further commented "if ever there was a case of trial by newspaper, this surely was it." He nevertheless came to the view that this was a simplistic and no longer permissible view of the law, especially in the light of the careful analysis of the competing considerations contained in the judgment of Schiemann L.J. in *MGN Ltd*. Nonetheless there have also been a number of examples of findings of contempt by newspapers in circumstances where the court was satisfied that a fair trial has genuinely been rendered impractical.[46]

1-156 In another case, the Divisional Court has re-emphasised the importance of not invoking the summary jurisdiction of contempt except where it can be demonstrated that such a restriction is "truly necessary in a democratic society"[47] and, moreover, that it should not be used in circumstances where conduct by a third party (in that case the publishers of a newspaper) is inconsistent with a court order in a way that could be described as "trivial or technical".[48]

1-157 The decision of the European Court of Human Rights in *Goodwin v United Kingdom*,[49] with its insistence that a journalist should be required to reveal sources only where the circumstances are such that the revelation would fulfil the criterion of being "necessary in a democratic society", was followed very positively by the Divisional Court in *Chief Constable of Leicestershire v Garavelli*.[50]

1-158 Nor is there any indication that the different emphasis the Court of Appeal in *Camelot Group plc v Centaur Communications Ltd*[51] has reversed the trend. That was a case in which the court *did* order disclosure of documents in circumstances which might lead to the identification of a source. It was one of a number of instances of alleged breach of confidence by an employee. There was the apprehension of further leaks if this step were not taken for the employer's protection. In *Goodwin v United Kingdom*[52] the European Court had been strongly influenced by the fact that the legitimate interests of the employer in that case were, on the particular facts, adequately protected by an existing injunction against further disclosure by the publishers. In *Camelot*, however, the Court of Appeal did not find this to be a sufficient protection of the employer's legitimate business interests, and accordingly ordered that the documents should be handed over. In two further cases, disclosure has been ordered on the "interests of justice" ground for the purpose of identifying the employees who had apparently

---

[46] *Att-Gen v Morgan* [1998] E.M.L.R. 294, discussed at para.4–79; *Att-Gen v Associated Newspapers Ltd*, October 31, 1997 (Lexis), discussed at paras 4–60 *et seq*.
[47] *Att-Gen v Newspaper Publishing plc* [1997] 1 W.L.R. 926, 3 All E.R. 159. See also *Civil Aviation Authority v Australian Broadcasting Corporation* (1995) 39 N.S.W.L.R. 540, where the "pre-judgment test" was disapproved.
[48] [1997] 1 W.L.R. at 936C.
[49] (1996) 22 E.H.R.R. 123.
[50] [1997] E.M.L.R. 543, discussed para.9–156.
[51] [1999] Q.B. 124.
[52] (1996) 22 E.H.R.R. 123.

revealed confidential information.[53] Nevertheless, full weight was given in arriving at these decisions to the public policy considerations embodied in the European position.

Another important trend is revealed by the courts' consistent theme in recent years that, for common law contempts of whatever kind, there is required proof of a positive intention to interfere with the administration of justice. As subsequent discussion of the case law will demonstrate,[54] there is some residual doubt about precisely what this entails. But on a number of occasions when they have been called upon to consider the matter, both the Divisional Court[55] and the Court of Appeal[56] have insisted that nothing less than such an intention will suffice. This declared aspiration, however, needs to be contrasted with the willingness of the courts to disbelieve editors who depose to the absence of any such intention. This difficult problem is discussed in chapter 5 more fully, where we draw attention to the very fine line between recklessness (which the courts have disavowed as being the appropriate test) and an actual intention to interfere with the administration of justice, which can nonetheless be readily inferred from surrounding circumstances *including the obviousness of the risk*.

1–159

It is now apparent how significant cases such as *Att-Gen v MGN Ltd* and *Att-Gen v Unger* actually were. In particular, the court's awareness of the "fade factor" discussed in those cases led in practice to a considerable downturn in the number of cases launched against the media by the Law Officers. There was a disinclination to risk public funds and incur media criticism by taking proceedings in which there could be no assurance that the court would find a substantial risk of serious prejudice proved to the criminal standard. For a number of years, therefore, those advising media clients on the risks attaching to stories touching upon pending criminal proceedings were in a state of considerable uncertainty. In some cases, which would previously have been perceived as giving rise to a significant risk of contempt proceedings, no action was taken by the Attorney-General and gradually the conclusion was reached that this form of contempt was in abeyance. After a time the Attorney-General adopted the novel approach of issuing "guidelines" as to how certain pending cases should be covered by the media.[57] Their legal status was uncertain and did little to reassure practitioners advising media organisations.[58] Several of them concerned a notorious case in which it was alleged that a group of professional footballers had raped a young

1–160

---

[53] See *Ashworth Hospital Authority v MGN Ltd* and [2002] UKHL 29, [2002] 1 W.L.R. 2033 and *Interbrew v Financial Times Ltd* [2002] 1 Lloyd's Rep. 542, Lightman J. and [2002] EWCA Civ 274, [2002] 2 Lloyd's Rep. 229, CA (discussed below at para.9–127 and para.9–146).
[54] Paras 5–120 *et seq.* (publication contempts) and para.10–208 and paras 11–21 *et seq.* (non-publication).
[55] *Att-Gen v News Group Newspapers plc* [1989] Q.B. 110; *Att-Gen v Newspaper Publishing plc* [1997] 1 W.L.R. 926, 3 All E.R. 159.
[56] *Att-Gen v Newspaper Publishing plc* [1988] Ch. 333, discussed at paras 5–141 *et seq*. See also *R. v Schot and Barclay* [1997] 2 Cr.App.R. 383, (1997) 161 J.P. 473, CACD.
[57] Initially these guidelines were available to the press through the Attorney's website, but the practice then developed of highlighting the subject on the website, but inviting those interested to contact the Law Officers' Department for a copy of the relevant document.
[58] See P. Hoult, "Restraining Influence" (2003) Law Soc Gaz 24; M. Dodd, "Attorney-General Faces Confrontation with Media Over Contempt" (2003) Criminal Lawyer 3–5.

woman in an hotel room. It was accepted by the publishers of the *Daily Star* that they had failed to heed the guidelines, requests and advice repeatedly issued in relation to the case for three weeks, by the Attorney-General and the Metropolitan Police. These stated that identification was in issue and requested that the suspects should not be named or any photograph published. The guidelines were "overlooked" and counsel apologised for "a bad mistake". A fine of £60,000 was imposed. This was such a clear case, therefore, that the Attorney-General no doubt came to the conclusion that he could proceed with confidence.

X. Issues Currently Requiring Attention in the Law of Contempt

A. Reassessing priorities

1-161   It may be appropriate here to offer some tentative conclusions about the state of the law of contempt, and a judgment about the extent to which it succeeds in accomplishing its objectives. There is no doubt that it can be used to protect important public interests. But it would be wrong to be complacent about the state of the law. Indeed, it has even been suggested that the law governing publication contempts is in such an unsatisfactory state that it is necessary to set up a Royal Commission to consider it.[59] Whilst we agree that the law governing publication contempt is in important respects regrettably obscure, we do not think these obscurities are yet beyond resolution by the courts themselves. Indeed, the judicial pronouncements in the field give reason to hope that such uncertainties as remain could soon be clarified in a consistent and balanced way, so as to reconcile the need to protect the administration of justice with the disciplines of the Human Rights Act 1998.

1-162   Nevertheless, it was worrying that, in the 1980s and 1990s, trials were aborted and convictions quashed as a result of what was perceived to be prejudicial publicity. English law was apparently having considerable difficulty in accommodating the conflicting demands of, on the one hand, freedom of information as enshrined in the European Convention, and the demands of an impartial trial by jury on the other.[60] It appears to be gradually emerging as a matter of policy that priority is nowadays to be accorded to the *desideratum* of freedom of information and open justice, and that it has to be accepted with reluctance that the price to be paid will on some occasions be the abandonment of a trial, or the quashing of a conviction[61]:

---

[59] J. Caplan Q.C., (1996) 146 New Law Jo. 1497.
[60] See the fuller discussion in ch.2. And see, for example, J. Cooper, (1997) 147 New Law Jo. 963, where complaint was made by the author, counsel in a much publicised manslaughter case, arising from death through drug taking, that it was particularly difficult to ensure that a fair trial ensued. Other articles—*e.g.* M. Mansfield Q.C., "Fair Trials Endangered" in *Counsel*, December 2002) p.12; D. Corker, "Threat to Justice or 'Tomorrow's Firelighter?" (2003) 153 New Law Jo. 1853, commenting on *R. v Stone* [2001] EWCA Crim 297, [2001] Crim. L.R. 465. And see *George* [2002] EWCA Crim 1923.
[61] *per* Schiemann L.J. in *Att-Gen v MGN Ltd* [1997] 1 All. E.R. 456 at 466g–h. See too the detailed analysis of the Divisional Court in *Att-Gen v Birmingham Post and Mail Ltd* [1998] 4 All E.R 49, discussed in ch.4.

"A consequence of the need in contempt proceedings, in which respondents face imprisonment or a fine, to be sure and to look at each publication separately and the need in trial proceedings to look at risk of prejudice created by the totality of publications can be that it is proper to stay proceedings on the ground of prejudice albeit that no individual is guilty of contempt. One may regret that situation or one may take the view that this is the best answer to a difficult problem."

As we have pointed out above,[62] this rigorous approach to the standard of proof appears to have led to a downturn in committal applications against the media in the intervening years. For a time it seemed as though this increasingly robust attitude in the courts of England and Wales would give rise to inconsistencies with the policy adopted in Scotland, thus rendering more elusive Lord Hailsham's objective of achieving uniformity between English and Scottish law in this area.[63] More recently, however, and in the period after the previous edition of this work, the courts in the separate jurisdictions seem to have been following converging paths. It has even been noted that there has been a degree of cross-fertilisation—to the extent that reference has been made to the judgment of Schiemann L.J. in *Att-Gen v MGN Ltd.*[64]

1–163

B. Public statements by legal representatives and the police

There are occasions when media comment is recognised as undesirable and irresponsible, even though it falls outside the law of contempt[65]; and even though few people would wish to see such restrictions extended. Nor is it the media alone who are criticised for such indiscretions. The Lord Chancellor's Advisory Committee on Legal Education and Conduct, which is concerned with the standards to be observed by professional advisers, concluded in 1997[66]:

1–164

> "The law of contempt does not constitute an effective control on the media, the police *or the defence*, especially in the pre-trial stage of criminal proceedings, either with regard to prejudice to the outcome of judicial proceedings or to public recognition of the principle that the issues in criminal cases are to be determined exclusively by the courts ... The court normally achieves effective control during the trial through co-operation with the media, although there remains a sense of unease about lapses from that norm ... This control does not extend either to the pre-charge stage or, apparently, after conviction ... " (emphasis added).

---

[62] At para.1–160.
[63] See the discussion at paras 16–301 *et seq.*
[64] [1997] 1 All E.R. 456. In *HMA v Scotsman Publications* 1999 S.L.T. 466, it was said that the English case "provides a particularly useful index of the various matters which should be borne in mind in a case of this sort."
[65] *Vano* [1996] R.T.R. 15, Lord Taylor C.J.
[66] *Lawyers' Comments to the Media*, p.24. S. Stapley, *Media Relations for Lawyers* (2nd ed., 2003). And see *Hodgson v Imperial Tobacco Ltd* [1998] 1 W.L.R. 1056, 2 All E.R. 673, where Lord Woolf M.R. invoked the observations of Chief Justice Rehnquist in *Gentile v State Bar of Nevada* [1991] 500 1 U.S. 1030, 111 S.C.R. 2720 to the effect that "extra-judicial statements by legal representatives can be especially unhelpful since they are likely to be received by the media as specially authoritative even if they are inaccurate." See now also articles in (1998) Legal Ethics, Vol. 1, No. 2; D.A. Ipp, "Talking to the Media: An Australian Perspective", at p.123 and "Lawyers and the Media", *ibid.* at p.109, by L. Austen, B. Gilbert, J. Heath and R. Mitchell; D.M. Brown, "What Can Lawyers Say in Public?" (1999) 78 Can. Bar Rev. 283.

1–165 If this is correct, it would appear that there may be two reasons why the law of contempt is not effective in this context. First, the strict liability threshold of "substantial risk of serious prejudice"[67] is very high. For common law contempt by publication, on the other hand, it may be too difficult to establish the required *mens rea*, which seems to be nothing less than an intention to interfere with the administration of justice.[68]

1–166 In relation to professional lawyers, restraints were by convention imposed upon public comment upon pending court proceedings in which clients are involved, solely deriving from ethical obligations ultimately enforceable by disciplinary proceedings. While recognising the legitimate interests of the press and public in following court proceedings, Lord Woolf M.R. in *Hodgson v Imperial Tobacco Ltd*[69] nonetheless emphasised that lawyers ought not to become engaged in *commenting* about such proceedings to the press (as opposed to communicating facts).

1–167 In a relatively short space of time, however, this approach towards professional obligations seems to have undergone significant change. Solicitors are much more inclined to make public comment on the merits, or supposed merits, of their clients' cases (sometimes presenting them as being of wider significance for the public interest). It is possible perhaps to detect a growing tendency in England in high profile criminal cases for solicitors, and sometimes other representatives of those involved, to issue "media statements" setting out their clients' case by way of detailed rebuttal of the Crown's or an alleged victim's allegations even during the period when proceedings would be considered "active" within the meaning of the Contempt of Court Act 1981.[70] There are some signs that the courts are recognising this somewhat extended function of the solicitor's traditional role. In *Regan v Taylor*,[71] the Court of Appeal (by a majority, Chadwick L.J. dissenting) upheld a defence of qualified privilege for a solicitor's comments to the media when acting on behalf of a client. It was recognised that it has become increasingly part of the functions of a solicitor to represent a client for the purposes of communicating with the media. The privilege was even held to extend to remarks made on the solicitor's initiative, drawing on his own experience of litigation rather than on the basis of direct instructions from the lay client.

1–168 So far as barristers are concerned, it is provided in the Code of Conduct[72] that "a barrister must not in relation to any anticipated or current proceedings or mediation in which he is briefed or expects to appear or has appeared as an advocate express a personal opinion to the press or other media or in any other public statement upon the facts or issues arising in the proceedings". This

---

[67] Considered more fully in ch.4.
[68] But see the discussion at paras 5–120 *et seq.*
[69] [1998] 1 W.L.R. 1056, 2 All E.R. 673.
[70] For a discussion of this increasing reliance in the United States context upon public relations, and the ethical implications, see Jonathan M. Moses, Note "Legal Spin Control: Ethics and Advocacy in the Court of Public Opinion" (1995) 95 Colum. L. Rev. 1811
[71] [2000] E.M.L.R. 549.
[72] Paras 709.1 and 709.2.

provision, however, is not to be regarded as preventing the expression of an opinion in an educational or academic context.

A salutary lesson is to be noted for lawyers (and especially for prosecutors) who are tempted to leak or spin about cases they are handling from the "Bakaly debacle."[73] Charles G. Bakely III was a former spokesperson for Kenneth Starr, the Independent Counsel enquiring into alleged wrongdoing by President Clinton. He was tried for criminal contempt on the basis that he lied in court filings when he denied talking to a *New York Times* reporter. This is because it was alleged that there had been a violation of the Federal Rule of Criminal Procedure 6(e) which required attorneys for the government to maintain the secrecy of "matters occurring before the Grand Jury".

It is of some interest to note also that in New Zealand Elias C.J. commented in *Solicitor-General v W&H Specialist Publications*[74] that expressions of innocence by those accused of crime and by people close to them will not usually constitute contempt. She was not impressed by the argument that proclamations of innocence were the "flip side" of an attack on the prosecution case or the complainant's character, since it did not accord with experience. "There is no basis for believing that jurors are so credulous".[75] She was of the view that the point would be made more vividly at trial by the very fact of a plea of not guilty. She was concerned with a magazine article which included the statement that a man accused of rape was supported by his girlfriend, who was "standing by him". Elias C.J. thought that this fact too was likely to be obvious to the jurors when she attended trial and sat in court.

Lord Woolf referred in *Hodgson* to the need for discretion on the part of lawyers in the context of increasing media coverage of court proceedings. He observed that the traditional "chambers culture" whereby lawyers respect the confidentiality of what occurs in chambers, should continue to be honoured; indeed "For the majority of lawyers to treat what happens in chambers in any other way would not be in accord with proper professional behaviour."[76] How this was to be reconciled with the acknowledgment in the same case that "justice should be administered in a manner which is as open as is practical in the particular circumstances" was unclear for a while. Over the intervening period it is perhaps fair to say that the "chambers culture" has withered on the vine because very few hearings now take place in private in any meaningful sense. A distinction now drawn in the daily cause list is not between "chambers" and "open court" so much as "unrobed" or "robed". In itself this is now regarded as neutral so far as media access and court reporting are concerned. On the few

---

[73] See J.R. O'Sullivan "The Bakaly debacle: the role of the press in high profile criminal investigations" (2001) Maryland Law Review, Vol. 60 at 149 and John Q. Barrett, "The Leak and the Craft: a Hardline Proposal to stop unaccountable disclosures of law enforcement information" (1999) 68 Fordham L. Rev. 613; Daniel C. Richman, "Grand Jury Secrecy: Plugging the Leaks in an Empty Bucket" (1999) 36 A. Crim. L. Rev 339; Ronald D. Rotunda, "Independent Counsel and the Charges of Leaking: a Brief Case Study" (1999) 68 Fordham L. Rev. 869.
[74] [2003] N.Z.A.R. 118 at [23].
[75] *ibid*. at [27] and [34].
[76] [1998] 1 W.L.R. 1056 at 1071, [1998] 2 All E.R. 673 at 686e–f.

1–171 occasions when the court thinks it appropriate to protect privacy by restricting access, the position will be made expressly clear, for example in accordance with the provisions of CPR Pt 39[77] where the terms of an infant settlement or the address of the family needs to be withheld to discourage prurient attention or the sending of begging letters.

C. "Cheque-book journalism"

1–172 Another area where the state of the current law and practice gives cause for disquiet is in relation to so-called "cheque book journalism". Rosemary West's unsuccessful appeal cited the prejudice that might have arisen from cheque-book journalism,[78] and this in turn prompted the Lord Chancellor's Department to promote a Discussion Paper, *Payments to Witnesses*.[79] Another consultation paper was issued by the Lord Chancellor on the same subject in March 2002, with a view to discussing the detail, rather than the principle, of proposed legislation to prevent payments to witnesses or potential witnesses. Yet on August 29 of the same year, following strong representations by media organisations, it was announced once again that the matter would be left to self-regulation, and the Press Complaints Commission has altered its Code accordingly.[80]

D. Reporting court proceedings

1–173 So far as the reporting of court proceedings is concerned, a Lord Chancellor's Department Consultation Paper[81] concluded that "there is a need for rationalisation of the law and practice relating to access to and reporting of family proceedings to remove unnecessary complexity and inconsistency and to establish provisions which are as clear and simple as possible while retaining flexibility where necessary".[82] However, the Report also said that there was no "need for change for its own sake". So far, it would appear, there have been no legislative steps to implement the recommendations of the Committee, and in particular, the opportunity presented when the Family Law Act 1996 was going through Parliament was missed. More generally, however, without the need for legislation, the scope for reporting "chambers" hearings (other than in the traditionally protected areas of children, national security and trade secrets) has been considerably widened by the decision of the Court of Appeal in *Hodgson v Imperial Tobacco Ltd*[83] and the subsequent introduction of the CPR, including the provisions for open justice contained in Pt 39.[84]

---

[77] Set out at para.7–54.
[78] *R. v West* [1996] 2 Cr.App.R. 374.
[79] October 20, 1996. In November, 1997, the Government announced that it was intended to introduce legislation. See paras 11–264 *et seq*.
[80] The new code is set out below, at para.11–266. See L. Blom-Cooper, "Cheque-Book Journalism on Display" [2003] P.L. 378 referring to the Press Complaints Commission's "consistently successful struggle to fend off governmental moves to impose statutory regulations on the newspaper industry".
[81] *Review of Access to and Reporting of Family Proceedings* (1993).
[82] para.5.9.
[83] [1998] 1 W.L.R. 1056, 2 All E.R. 673, discussed at paras 7–43 *et seq*.
[84] Set out at para.7–54.

E. Privacy

The familiar problem of reconciling the conflicting requirements of open justice **1–174** and privacy[85] has also loomed large, particularly in the context of family law. The right to privacy received the attention of the Court of Appeal in *Re PB (Hearings in Open Court)*,[86] in the context of the Family Proceedings Rules. It was confirmed that, even though there is a discretion to hear proceedings in open court, it is only rarely that the court will go in to open court when the interests of the child are under consideration. Here, it might appear that there is no need to change practice specifically because of the European Convention; Art.6 expressly recognises an exception to the requirements of open justice in cases "where the interests of juveniles or the protection of the private life of the parties so require". Yet even the accommodation of priorities within this area of law has been in a state of flux because of the increasing imperative recognised in the Family Division (and the Court of Appeal)[87] that the principles of open justice apply in that context also, so that restrictions upon attendance and reporting should only be imposed when strictly necessary for the purpose of protecting the rights of privacy—usually those of children or other vulnerable persons.

As we discuss more fully elsewhere,[88] the importance of privacy rights has **1–175** been emphasised also by the House of Lords in *Re S (FC) (A Child)*[89] in the context of court reporting. That discussion is also of general importance when the court is called upon to consider the grant of a *contra mundum* injunction, a jurisdiction which has been regularly invoked since the coming into effect of the Human Rights Act.

Article 8 of the Convention has become increasingly important in the context **1–176** of media publication and its interrelation with Art.10.[90] Its terms are as follows:

"1. Everyone has the right to respect for his private and family life, his home and his correspondence.

2. There shall be no interference by a public authority with the exercise of this right except such as is in accordance with the law and is necessary in a democratic society in the interests of national security, public safety or the economic well-being of the country, for the prevention of disorder or crime, for the protection of health or morals, or for the protection of the rights and freedoms of others."

It impacts upon the law of contempt, potentially at least, in two particular contexts. It is now recognised that it must come to the fore whenever the court

---

[85] See also *Re H-S* [1994] 3 All E.R. 390 at 398c, one of the earlier cases, where specific reference was made to Art.8 of the European Convention.
[86] [1996] 2 F.L.R. 765. See also Karen Rhodes, "Open Court Proceedings and Privacy Law: Re-Examining the Bases for the Privilege" (1996) 74 Texas Law Review 881.
[87] "There is a discernible move in the Family Justice system towards greater openness": *per* Thorpe L.J. in *Harb v King Fahd Bin Abdul Aziz* [2005] EWCA Civ 632 at [22]. See also *Clibbery v Allan* [2002] EWCA Civ 45, [2002] Fam. 261 discussed at para.8–128, and *Pelling v Bruce-Williams (Secretary of State for Constitutional Affairs as an Interested Party)* [2004] EWCA Civ 845, [2004] Fam. 155.
[88] See, *e.g.* para.2–146 and the discussion in ch.6, Pt II.
[89] [2004] UKHL 47, [2005] 1 A.C. 593.
[90] See para.2–36 and para.2–37.

1-176

is called upon to exercise its recently recognised power to restrict publicity *contra mundum*, whether under the traditional *parens patriae* jurisdiction or otherwise. Secondly, there is the possibility that it may sometimes be used as a basis, when demonstrated to be necessary for the purpose and only in exceptional circumstances, for restricting the reporting of court proceedings. "The duty of the court is to examine with care each application for a departure from the rule [of open justice in criminal proceedings] by reason of rights under article 8".[91]

F. Non-publication contempts and the general criminal law

1-177 With regard to non-publication contempts (other than those occurring in the face of the court), a provisional view may be offered that in the United Kingdom, at least, it may not be practical or desirable to abandon the notion of contempt and to substitute for it a battery of individual criminal offences or other provisions intended to cover all possible eventualities, as was recommended in Australia.[92]

1-178 Another view is, however, that it would be sensible to implement the stated objective of successive governments to reduce the criminal law of England and Wales into a codified form,[93] and to include provision for protecting the administration of justice within it. There remain uncertainties both as to what constitutes the *actus reus* of the offence,[94] and the *mens rea*.[95] It might therefore be said that the time has come, at least in this area, for the law and practice relating to interference with the administration of justice to be reformed, in line with the recommendations of the Phillimore Committee[96] and the Law Commission.[97]

G. The implications of the world wide web

1-179 A matter which has given rise to uncertainty and to a flurry of judicial decisions in the area of media law is the growing impact of electronic communications and

---

[91] *Re S (FC) (A Child)* [2004] UKHL 47, [2005] 1 A.C. 593 at [18]. This is discussed fully in paras 6–43 *et seq*.
[92] By the Australian Law Reform Commission Report No.35, *Contempt* (1987), para.113 (contempts in the face); para.168 (non-publication contempts not being contempts in the face of the court); para.267 (publication contempts). And see M.R. Chesterman (1997) 45 Am. Jo. Comp. Law 801.
[93] See a summary of the arguments and developments in A.T.H. Smith, "The Case for a Code" [1986] Crim.L.R. 285 and [1992] Crim.L.R. 396. And see the Law Commission Report No.218, *Legislating the Criminal Code* (1993); Lord Bingham C.J., "A Criminal Code: Must We Wait For Ever?" [1998] Crim. L.R. 694, reprinted in his collected essays, *The Business of Judging* (2000), Oxford University Press; White Paper, "Criminal Justice: the Way Ahead" (2001) Cm 5074; Sir Robin Auld, *Criminal Courts Review* (2001), paras 35–36; White Paper, *Justice for All* (July, 2002), Civ 5563, ch.7.16.
[94] See paras 11–3 *et seq*.
[95] See para.11–21.
[96] *Report of the Committee on Contempt of Court* Cmnd. 5794 (1974). See, *e.g.* para.72, to the effect that " . . . conduct intended to pervert or obstruct the course of justice should only be capable of being dealt with summarily as a contempt of court if the proceedings to which the conduct relates have started and have not been completed." and also at para.157, that " . . . to take or threaten reprisals against a witness after the proceedings are concluded should no longer be a contempt, but that it should instead be made an indictable offence".
[97] See in particular the recommendations of the Law Commission Report No.96, *Criminal Law: Offences Relating to Interference With the Course of Justice* (1979), H.C. 213.

especially the implications of the world wide web.[98] There are problems which need to be grappled with, preferably by way of international agreement, and which are relevant to the law of contempt as well as to defamation and breach of confidence. So far, most of the authorities have been focussed upon the law of defamation in the context of cross-border publication.[99] It is easy to see, on the other hand, that complications may arise for the law of contempt in at least two respects. First, there is an inability to control access within the jurisdiction to prejudicial material emanating from elsewhere. This is unlikely to present problems very often because essentially it would be a question of asking whether a substantial risk has arisen of serious prejudice being caused by jurors or potential jurors accessing material from the Internet. But in one case,[1] after a defendant had been convicted, material was found in the jury retiring room which had clearly been downloaded from the Internet and which contained prejudicial material which was not and could not have been introduced in evidence. The Court of Appeal held that "the material obtained by the juror from the internet after the jury had retired, contravened the principles which prohibit the use of information, potentially relevant to the outcome of the case, privately obtained out of court by a juror". The Court quashed the conviction on the grounds that it was unsafe.

There is also the fact that the "fade factor" is to some extent undermined by the continuing availability of prejudicial material on readily accessible archives.[2] The Attorney-General therefore issued a general warning to newspapers that there might be occasions when it would be appropriate for them to remove archived material from a website because of a risk of prejudice to pending proceedings. It is easy to envisage circumstances, for example, in which there was prominent and one-sided coverage of a high profile crime prior to the point at which any proceedings had become "active" for the purposes of the Contempt of Court Act 1981. This would be unobjectionable in itself, but if it continued to be available after that cut-off point, obvious difficulties could arise.

Furthermore, there is likely to be a significant difficulty over policing compliance with injunctions granted by English courts against litigants based abroad. In practical terms, there may be very little that a court can do to enforce compliance with an injunction in respect of a party or an activity outside the

---

[98] *Godfrey v Demon Internet* [2001] Q.B. 201; *Gutnick v Dow Jones* (2002) HCA 56, (2002) 210 C.L.R. 575.
[99] M. Collins, *The Law of Defamation and the Internet* (2nd ed., 2005), Oxford University Press; *Loutchansky v The Times Newspapers (Nos 2 to 5)* [2001] EWCA Civ 1805, [2002] (QB) 783; *Harrods v Dow Jones & Co. Ltd* [2003] EWHC 1162; *Jameel (Yousef) v Dow Jones and Co Inc* [2005] EWCA Civ 75, [2005] 2 W.L.R. 1614 (QB); *Hewitt v Grunwald* [2004] EWHC 2959 (QB).
[1] *R. v Karakaya* [2005] EWCA Crim 346; [2005] 2 Cr.App.R. 5; see also the Law Commission, Scoping Study No.2, *Defamation and the Internet* (December 2002), where the Commission came to the conclusion (at para.1.19) that there was no need for a change in the law relating to potentially prejudicial archival material, saying that there are "already sufficient safeguards in the existing law to ensure that internet publishers are protected against inappropriate, arbitrary or trivial prosecution (for contempt)."
[2] *HMA v Beggs (No.2)*, 2002 S.L.T. 139, S.C.C.R. 879, High Court of Justiciary, discussed at para.1–149 and para.4–27.

1–181   CHAPTER 1—HISTORY OF THE LAW OF CONTEMPT

jurisdiction.[3] It is frequently argued, in such cases, that for this reason it is inappropriate to make any such order at all. On the other hand, there are sometimes tangible advantages for a litigant in obtaining such an order even though it cannot be enforced directly. The question particularly arises in the context of libel actions brought within England and Wales, against a party or parties served outside the jurisdiction, where the object is not primarily to enforce a money judgment or an injunction against further publication, but rather to have the benefit of a reasoned judgment for the purposes of vindication.[4]

---

[3] *Lakah Group and Lakah v Al Jazeera and Mansour* [2002] EWHC 2500 (QB).
[4] *Harrods v Dow Jones & Co Ltd* [2003] EWHC 1162 (QB); *Mahfouz v Brisard* [2004] EWHC 1735 (QB); *Steinberg v Pritchard Englefield* [2005] EWCA Civ 288; *Richardson v Schwarzenegger* [2005] EWCA Civ 28; *Jameel (Mohammed Abdul Latif) v The Wall Street Journal Europe SPRL* [2005] EWCA Civ 74, [2005] 2 W.L.R. 1577, [2003] EWHC 2945 (QB); *King v Lewis* [2004] EWCA Civ 1, [2005] E.M.L.R. 4. See also *Bangoura v Washington Post* (2004) 235 D.L.R. (4th) 564, S.C.Ont.

Chapter 2

CONTEMPT OF COURT: THE CONSTITUTIONAL DIMENSIONS

I.	The Continuing Role of the Contempt Jurisdiction	2–1
II.	Freedom of Information and the Law of Contempt	2–32
III.	Free Press and Fair Trial	2–70
IV.	The Impact of the European Convention	2–122
V.	The Role of the Attorney-General	2–199
VI.	Contempt of Court and the Crown	2–222

I. The Continuing Role of the Contempt Jurisdiction

A. The purpose of the summary jurisdiction

The existence of a special "summary" jurisdiction, suggesting as it does a somewhat peremptory method of dealing with contempts, may seem to call for some justification. Given that there is a considerable overlap between the general law protecting the administration of justice and the law of contempt,[1] it may be asked why it is necessary to preserve the jurisdiction in its summary form.[2]   2–1

There are two issues: first, whether there should be a specific branch of the law grouping together the disparate matters conventionally labelled "contempt" at all (instead of leaving the differing categories of mischief, to which it is directed, to be addressed by separate criminal offences); and, if so, whether it is desirable or necessary to use summary procedures to accomplish the required objectives. At the outset, we propose to summarise the scope of the substantive law of contempt, and then to consider how appropriate is the word "summary" to describe its specific procedures.   2–2

B. The broad categories of contempt

It has frequently (and rightly) been said that contempt is "Protean" in character.[3] But, for the purpose of analysis (and discussion in this work), it is convenient to subdivide the principal categories of contempt as follows: 2–3

1. publication contempts, both under the 1981 Act, and at common law,

---
[1] See paras 2–13 *et seq*.
[2] R.B. Kuhns, "The Summary Contempt Power: A Critique and a New Perspective" (1978) 88 Yale Law Jo. 39. See also R.L. Goldfarb, *The Contempt Power*, New York, Columbia University Press (1963); D.B. Dobbs, "The Contempt Power: A Survey" (1971) 56 Cornell Law Rev. 183.
[3] See, *e.g.* J. Moskovitz, "Contempt of Injunctions, Civil and Criminal" (1943) 43 Col. L.R. 780; see also the use of the term by Sir John Donaldson M.R. in *Att-Gen v Newspaper Publishing plc* [1988] Ch. 333 at 362B–C, and by Hodgson J. in *Att-Gen v Sport Newspapers Ltd* [1991] 1 W.L.R. 1194 at 1230C, [1992] 1 All E.R. 503 at 536g.

2. other forms of criminal contempt, whether committed in the face of the court, or consisting of some other interference with the administration of justice,[4]

3. civil contempt, consisting in non-compliance with court orders, or undertakings, in the course of civil litigation.

C. "Summary" procedures

2–4 Although the jurisdiction to punish for contempt is frequently referred to as "summary", the term has to be approached with some caution. Each of the categories of contempt described in the previous paragraph is made the subject of a different procedure. Where a possible publication contempt has been referred to the Attorney-General for consideration,[5] for example, any proceedings may take several months to come on for a hearing; the description "summary" is appropriate only in the sense that the trial is by judge alone, and that some of the safeguards that would attend the hearing of a criminal prosecution are absent.[6]

2–5 Where a person is punished for contempt in the face of the court,[7] however, it may truly be said that the punishment is "summary" in the sense both that it is relatively[8] immediate, and that the court generally acts of its own motion. So too, if a judge were to seek to exercise jurisdiction in respect of a breach of a s.4(2) or s.11 order in the course of a trial.[9]

D. The underlying rationale of the contempt jurisdiction

2–6 The court's jurisdiction in contempt has been described as "an essential adjunct of the rule of law".[10] Lord Morris summarised the necessity for this branch of the law in *Att-Gen v Times Newspapers Ltd*[11]:

> "In an ordered community courts are established for the pacific settlement of disputes and for the maintenance of law and order. In the general interests of the community it is imperative that the authority of the courts should not be imperilled and that recourse to them should not be subject to unjustifiable interference. When such unjustifiable interference is suppressed it is not because those charged with the responsibilities of administering justice are concerned for their own dignity: it is because the very

---

[4] For a list of statutes in which the penal sanctions associated with contempt of court are employed, see para.13–77, n.45.
[5] See paras 2–199 *et seq.*, where the desirability of referring the matter to the Attorney-General is considered. See also paras 15–1 *et seq.*
[6] See the elaboration of the point by Mustill L.J. in *R. v Griffin* (1989) 88 Cr.App.R. 63, cited at para.2–17.
[7] As to which, see ch.10.
[8] 'Relatively', because the Court of Appeal has insisted upon the need for reflection in these circumstances, opportunities for advice and, where appropriate, legal funding. See paras 10–41 *et seq.* and paras 15–107 *et seq.*; *Balogh v St. Albans Crown Court* [1975] Q.B. 73, and *R. v Schot and Barclay* [1997] 2 Cr.App.R. 383, (1997) 161 J.P. 473.
[9] As to the question whether a judge has the power to do this, see the discussion in paras 7–228 *et seq.*
[10] *per* Lord Nicholls in *Att-Gen v Punch Ltd* [2002] UKHL 50, [2003] 1 A.C. 1046 at [2].
[11] [1974] A.C. 273 at 302.

The Continuing Role of the Contempt Jurisdiction 2–9

structure of ordered life is at risk if the recognised courts of the land are so flouted and their authority wanes and is supplanted."

This is similar to the terms of the Phillimore Committee's observation that[12]:

2–7

"The law relating to contempt of court has developed over the centuries as a means whereby the courts may act to prevent or punish conduct which tends to obstruct, prejudice or abuse the administration of justice either in relation to a particular case or generally."

In *Att-Gen v Times Newspapers Ltd*,[13] Lord Diplock set out more fully what he took to be elementary requirements for the due administration of justice:

2–8

"... *first* that all citizens should have unhindered access to the constitutionally established courts of criminal or civil jurisdiction for the determination of disputes as to their legal rights and liabilities; *secondly*, that they should be able to rely upon obtaining in the courts the arbitrament of a tribunal which is free from bias against any party and whose decision will be based upon those facts only that have been proved in evidence adduced before it in accordance with the procedure adopted in courts of law; and *thirdly* that, once the dispute has been submitted to a court of law, they should be able to rely upon there being no usurpation by any other person of the function of that court to decide it according to law. Conduct which is calculated to prejudice any of these three requirements or to undermine the public confidence that they will be observed is contempt of court."

Quite apart from the support that it affords to the individual litigant, the law relating to civil contempt (consisting typically in the breach of an order or undertaking in civil proceedings) is explained also by reference to the need to uphold the authority of the court.[14] As Lord Diplock explained in *Att-Gen v Times Newspapers Ltd*,[15] in relation to "civil contempts":

2–9

"The order is made at the request and for the sole benefit of the other party to the civil action. There is an element of public policy in punishing civil contempt, since the administration of justice would be undermined if the order of any court of law could be disregarded with impunity."

In short, it is the need to protect the rule of law that is the common factor underlying the contempt jurisdiction generally.[16]

---

[12] *Report of the Committee on Contempt of Court*, Cmnd. 5794 (1974), para.1.
[13] [1974] A.C. 273 at 309.
[14] A fuller discussion is to be found in ch.3 of the comparison between the notions of criminal and civil contempt, as well as upon the overlap between the public and private interests which the law is intended to protect. See also paras 12–5 *et seq*.
[15] [1974] A.C. 273 at 307–8.
[16] See also Megarry V.-C. in *Clarke v Chadburn* [1984] I.R.L.R. 350, [1985] 1 W.L.R. 78, [1985] 1 All E.R. 211; *Jennison v Baker* [1972] 2 Q.B. 52.

CHAPTER 2—CONTEMPT OF COURT: CONSTITUTIONAL DIMENSIONS

E. The misleading implications of the word "contempt"

2–10 The use of the term "contempt" was regarded as a matter of some regret by Salmon L.J. in *Morris v Crown Office*[17]:

> "The archaic description of these proceedings as 'contempt of court' is in my view unfortunate and misleading. It suggests that they are designed to buttress the dignity of the judges and to protect them from insult. Nothing could be further from the truth. No such protection is needed. The sole purpose of proceedings for contempt is to give our courts the power effectively to protect the rights of the public by ensuring that the administration of justice shall not be obstructed or prevented."

2–11 Lord Cross of Chelsea made a similar point in *Att-Gen v Times Newspapers Ltd*[18]:

> " 'Contempt of court' means an interference with the administration of justice and it is unfortunate that the offence should continue to be known by a name which suggests to the modern mind that its essence is a supposed affront to the dignity of the court. Nowadays when sympathy is readily accorded to anyone who defies constituted authority the very name of the offence predisposes many people in favour of the alleged offender. Yet the due administration of justice is something which all citizens, whether on the left or the right or in the centre, should be anxious to safeguard."

In *Att-Gen v Punch Ltd*[19] Lord Nicholls described contempt of court as the "established, if unfortunate, name given to the species of wrongful conduct which consists of interference with the administration of justice".

2–12 These remarks may perhaps be especially apposite in the context of publications about the administration of justice or the behaviour of particular judges.[20] Even in this context, the purpose of the jurisdiction is not the protection of judicial dignity,[21] but the prevention of interference with the administration of justice, or the maintenance of the court's authority and the effectiveness of its orders. The Phillimore Committee addressed the vexed question of terminology, but was unable to offer any suggestions for reform.[22]

F. The overlap between contempt and the general criminal law

2–13 The law of contempt and the general criminal law will inevitably overlap, in the sense that misconduct may amount to contempt of court while, at the same time, constituting another specific criminal offence, either at common law or under

---

[17] [1970] 2 Q.B. 114, 129. See also Lord Diplock in *Att-Gen v Leveller Magazine Ltd* [1979] A.C. 440 at 449: "It is justice itself that is flouted by contempt of court, not the individual court or judge who is attempting to administer it". And see *A v N (Committal: Refusal of Contact)* [1997] 1 F.L.R. 533 at 542.
[18] [1974] A.C. 273 at 322. See also the passage cited at para.2–6, in the speech of Lord Morris, and *Johnson v Grant*, 1923 S.C. 789 at 790, Lord President Clyde, cited at para.16–6.
[19] [2002] UKHL 50, [2003] 1 A.C. 1046 at [2].
[20] See the discussion of "scandalising" in English law at paras 5–204 *et seq.* and of "murmuring" in Scottish law at para.16–85.
[21] See the discussion of "dignity" in the Scottish context at para.16–6.
[22] *Report of the Committee on Contempt of Court*, Cmnd. 5794 (1974), para.12.

statute. For example, there are common law offences of interference with the administration of justice, conspiracy to pervert the course of justice, subornation of witnesses,[23] and embracery.[24]

Parliament has supplemented the common law by provisions which make it an offence to tamper with witnesses and other participants in the legal process before, during and after the trial.[25] So too, persons called for jury service may commit offences under the Juries Act 1974, s.20(1); while the same conduct could be proceeded against by way of committal for contempt. When the overlap occurs, the Crown (or as it may be, the judge) is presented with a series of options as to how best to proceed in respect of the conduct in question, and has a choice between proceedings on indictment[26] or the summary procedure under the contempt jurisdiction.

Concerns have long been expressed over the readiness of judges in some cases to resort to the inherent summary jurisdiction in circumstances when it was not strictly necessary. For example, as long ago as 1874, an article appeared in the *Solicitors' Journal & Reporter*[27] where it was observed:

"It has been of late frequently said by those whose opinion is entitled to respect, and we believe it is not without foundation, that the bench is becoming too strong, and that even the bar cannot anywhere point to leaders on whose moral courage it could thoroughly rely to defend its privileges. It seems to us that this is not the time to allow of a jurisdiction growing up and extending itself unopposed, which is silently withdrawing from the protection of trial by jury an important and considerable part of criminal law, and handing over to judges a paternal administration of fine and imprisonment."

Eventually, the Phillimore Committee recommended that as a matter of principle[28] the summary contempt jurisdiction should not be invoked except where:

---

[23] Inducing a witness to commit perjury, or seeking to do so. The common law offence has been superseded by the Perjury Act 1911, s.7. Where a witness has committed perjury, there will also generally be a contempt. But the better course, the Divisional Court has said, is to deal with the perjury after the proceedings in question have been completed: *De Vries v National Westminster Bank*, The Times, August 16, 1984. It is an offence in relation to which it may be necessary to examine with some care the state of the alleged offender's mind and knowledge. The summary procedure associated with contempt in the face would hardly be appropriate.
[24] See para.11–179.
[25] Criminal Justice and Public Order Act 1994, s.51, discussed at para.11–145. The government has expressed an intention to legislate to prevent payments to witnesses in criminal proceedings, with a defence to the effect that there was good reason not to know that the person concerned was a witness. See paras 11–274 *et seq.*
[26] This is not to suggest that proceedings on indictment will be brought for contempt *eo nomine*. In *Re Lonrho plc* [1990] 2 A.C. 154 at 177C, Lord Keith said that the practice of proceeding by way of indictment "ought not to be revived". But the circumstances may require prosecution for a specific offence on indictment rather than the invoking of the contempt jurisdiction. See, *e.g. R. v D* [1984] A.C. 778 at 806, where Lord Brandon suggested that a parent ought to be prosecuted for kidnapping his or her own child only when ordinary citizens would truly regard the conduct as "criminal". If that (somewhat impressionistic) test is not fulfilled, then a contempt application through disobedience to a court order would generally suffice.
[27] June 27, 1874, at 642–3.
[28] *Report of the Committee on Contempt of Court*, Cmnd. 5794 (1974), para.21.

2–16   CHAPTER 2—CONTEMPT OF COURT: CONSTITUTIONAL DIMENSIONS

"(a) the offending act does not fall within the definition of any other offence; or
(b) where urgency or practical necessity require that the matter be dealt with summarily".

G. The missing safeguards

2–17   The "safeguards" missing when the contempt jurisdiction is exercised summarily were succinctly summarised by Mustill L.J. in *R. v Griffin*[29]:

> "We are here concerned with the exercise of a jurisdiction which is *sui generis* so far as English law is concerned. In proceedings for criminal contempt there is no prosecutor, or even a requirement that a representative of the Crown or of the injured party should initiate the proceedings. The judge is entitled to proceed of his own motion. There is no summons or indictment, nor is it mandatory for any written account of the accusation made against him to be furnished to the contemnor. There is no preliminary enquiry or filtering procedure, such as a committal. Depositions are not taken. There is no jury. Nor is the system adversarial in character. The judge himself enquires into the circumstances, so far as they are not within his personal knowledge. He identifies the ground of complaint, selects the witnesses and investigates what they have to say (subject to a right of cross-examination), decides on guilt and pronounces sentence. This summary procedure, which by its nature is to be used quickly if it is to be used at all, omits many of the safeguards to which an accused is ordinarily entitled, and for this reason it has been repeatedly stated that the judge should choose to adopt it only in cases of real need."

2–18   Some additional reasons why caution should be exercised were articulated by the High Court of Australia in *Coward v Stapleton*[30]:

> " . . . it is a well-recognised principle of law that no person ought to be punished for contempt of court unless the specific charge against him be distinctly stated and an opportunity of answering it given to him: *In re Pollard* (1868) L.R. 2 P.C. 106, at p.120; *R. v Foster; Ex parte Isaacs* (1941) V.L.R. 77, at p.81. The gist of the accusation must be made clear to the person charged, though it is not always necessary to formulate the charge in a series of specific allegations: *Chang Hang Kiu v Piggott* (1909) A.C. 312, at p.315 . . .
> Resting as it does upon accepted notions of elementary justice, this principle must be rigorously insisted upon".

2–19   The remarks of Mustill L.J. in *R. v Griffin*[31] were directed principally at cases of contempt in the face of the court. But even in the more formalised procedure of the former RSC Ord.52 some of the more traditional safeguards of the criminal

---

[29] (1989) 88 Cr.App.R. 63, following *R. v Moran* (1985) 81 Cr.App.R. 51, which emphasises the virtue of reflection by all concerned; see para.10–59 where the full text of Lawton L.J.'s remarks is cited. The expression "calm reflection" has frequently been used: see, *e.g.* McCowan L.J. in *R. v Tamworth Justices Ex p. Walsh* [1994] C.O.D. 277 and Rose L.J. in *R. v Schot and Barclay* [1997] 2 Cr.App.R. 383 at 339A-B, (1997) 161 J.P. 473. Phillimore also emphasised the importance of reflection, particularly in matters of sentencing, where the " . . . powers . . . should only be exercised and be seen to be exercised after due deliberation, and without their exercise appearing to be influenced by the heat or exasperation of the moment": Cmnd. 5794, para.33.
[30] (1953) 90 C.L.R. 573 at 579–80.
[31] (1989) 88 Cr.App.R. 63, cited at para.2–17.

process were always, and still are, absent. For example, evidence is by affidavit.[32] As was observed by Watkins L.J. in the Court of Appeal in *R. v D*[33]:

> "For a very long time now, decisions in all contempt cases have been made by judges who are best equipped to tell whether a contempt has been committed and may very well be able to do so on affidavit evidence alone."

The result is that there is no opportunity for the accused to observe the witness giving evidence in chief; nor will there normally be an opportunity to cross-examine and test the strength of the "prosecution" case by this means. But this objection is perhaps less formidable than might appear at first sight, for a number of reasons.

2–20 Generally in such applications against media respondents, the affidavit is sworn by an official in the Law Officers' Department who will exhibit, for example, a newspaper article, and set out certain propositions of law, together with evidence as to the state of the proceedings in respect of which prejudice is said to have arisen. It is unlikely that the deponent's demeanour would cast much light on the situation; nor indeed that much would be yielded through cross-examination. In any event, there is always the possibility of applying for leave to cross-examine witnesses where appropriate.

2–21 The respondent might be called upon, both in cases of criminal and civil contempt, to serve affidavits before the case against him has been tested through submissions to the court.[34] There is difficulty in reconciling this with the privilege against self-incrimination that is a feature of the criminal process. On the other hand, as has been made clear by Wall J.,[35] an applicant in a civil contempt case cannot pray in aid any admissions contained in an affidavit unless and until the respondent elects to place reliance upon it.

2–22 There is no possibility of jury trial for the determination of disputed questions of fact; for example, as to the intention with which an editor or publisher acted.[36] This is a somewhat sensitive area, and there has in recent times been a strong feeling amongst some journalists (particularly in the context of libel actions)[37] as to the importance of jury trial where proceedings are brought against journalists or publishers.

---

[32] See *Practice Direction*, at para.3.1, set out at Appendix 5A.
[33] [1984] 1 A.C. 778 at 792D–E.
[34] The privilege against self-incrimination in the context of contempt is considered in paras 3–188 *et seq.*, and the problems specific to civil contempt in para.15–35.
[35] *Re B (A Minor) (Contempt: Evidence)* [1996] 1 W.L.R. 627, [1996] 1 F.L.R. 239.
[36] This was the issue resolved, adversely, by Morritt J. in *Att-Gen v Newspaper Publishing plc* [1989] F.S.R. 457. See also *Att-Gen v News Group Newspapers plc* [1989] 1 Q.B. 110, and *Official Solicitor v News Group Newspapers plc* [1994] 2 F.L.R. 174, in both of which the court found *mens rea* against the then editor of *The Sun* newspaper despite sworn denials.
[37] Supreme Court Act 1981, s.69; *Aitken v Preston* [1997] E.M.L.R. 415. For example, the commentary in *The Guardian* which argued, following the discontinuance of Jonathan Aitken's libel action against that newspaper that the laws "should be reformed and never again should a defendant be denied the fundamental right to a jury": The *Guardian*, June 21, 1997, p.1. But contrast the attitude displayed by the same newspaper editor when a jury's decision went against him: *Baldwin v Rusbridger* [2001] E.M.L.R. 47.

2–23 It is nonetheless possible to justify the use of the so-called summary procedure embodied in the former RSC Ord.52[38] because it has become so formalised as to be summary in name only.[39] Such safeguards have been built into the rules that it is difficult to identify any injustice to alleged contemnors, and in effect the only advantage that they do not have which is associated with criminal proceedings generally is that of jury trial. That disadvantage is unlikely to be held in itself to amount to an infringement of the European Convention, since a significant number of signatory states do not regard jury trial as a matter of fundamental right.[40] Moreover, the need for a summary procedure was expressly recognised in *Ravnsbourg v Sweden*.[41]

2–24 As to contempts in the face of the court, there is a danger that the process may be thought to offend against the requirement in Art.6 for an impartial tribunal; the judge might be perceived to be not only a judge in his own cause, but also to be acting as witness and prosecutor.[42] Against this, it might be argued that "the power is healthy, and if the offence is recent and clear the punitive and deterrent effect is multiplied if it is exercised on the spot".[43] Furthermore, the safeguards increasingly insisted upon by the courts[44] are adequate to rescue the law and practice of contempt from the charge that it inadequately respects the rules of natural justice.

2–25 The courts have, with increasing frequency, stressed the need for the contempt jurisdiction to be used with caution. Lord Diplock[45] explained:

"The remedy for contempt of court after it has been committed is punitive; it may involve imprisonment yet it is summary; it is generally obtained on affidavit evidence and it is not accompanied by those special safeguards in favour of the accused that are a feature of the trial of an ordinary criminal offence. Furthermore, it is a procedure which if instituted by one of the parties to litigation is open to abuse, particularly in relation to so-called gagging writs issued for the purpose of preventing repetition of statements that are defamatory but true. The courts have therefore been vigilant to see

---

[38] Currently forming part of Sch.1 to the CPR.
[39] See, *e.g.* the comments of Laskin J. (dissenting) in *McKeown v The Queen* (1971) 16 D.L.R. (3d) 390 at 398: "Practice over the years has purified any historically-based misgivings about the regularity of summary procedures as alternatives to ordinary trial by jury . . . There has been, and my view properly so, a continuing concern by Courts and Judges about the magnitude of the power to punish contempt by summary process. Statutory controls have been introduced in some common law jurisdictions, and rules of Court in others have given some form and precision to the time-honoured procedures of committal and attachment."
[40] For a survey of the laws relating to (*inter alia*) lay participation in the criminal justice process, in at least some of the signatory states of the European Convention, see ed. C. Van Den Wyngaert, *Criminal Procedure Systems in the European Community* (1993) Butterworths; ed. N. Vidmar, *World Jury Systems* (2000) Oxford University Press.
[41] (1994) 18 E.H.R.R. 38.
[42] See D. Feldman, *Civil Liberties and Human Rights in England and Wales* (2nd ed., 2002) at 964 Oxford University Press. This was also recognised in the words of Staughton L.J. in *R. v Powell* (1994) 98 Cr.App.R. 224 at 226: "The court is the victim; the court is the witness; the court is the prosecutor, and the court is the judge . . . . Nevertheless, it is right that in many cases the matter should be dealt with by the judge then and there."
[43] *R. v Griffin* (1989) 88 Cr.App.R. 63 at 70.
[44] See paras 2–17 *et seq.* and paras 10–38 *et seq.*
[45] *Att-Gen. v Times Newspapers Ltd* [1974] A.C. at 311–2.

that the procedure for committal is not lightly invoked in cases where although a contempt has been committed there is no serious likelihood that it has caused any harm to the interests of any of the parties to the litigation or to the public interest."

H. Factors justifying the use of the summary procedure

The principal justification for resorting to a summary procedure, and the concomitant by-passing of the traditional safeguards of criminal proceedings, would therefore appear to be that of "urgency or practical necessity".[46]

Hodgson J. said in *Att-Gen v Sport Newspapers Ltd*[47]:

"It seems to me that the principle underlying the arrogation to themselves by the judges of a right to deprive a person of the right he would otherwise have to trial by jury and, by a summary procedure, punish him, lies in the need for them to have available machinery by which, speedily and effectively, they can protect the proceedings over which they have control".

This criterion might be fulfilled, for example, where there is a need to bring the proceedings to a dignified conclusion. In the words of Lawton L.J. in *Balogh v St. Albans Crown Court*[48]:

"The fact that judges, whether of the High Court or the Crown Court, have this summary jurisdiction does not mean that they should use it whenever opportunity offers. It is an unusual jurisdiction which has come into being to protect the due administration of justice. In Blackstone's words, it applies to any conduct which

'demonstrates a gross want of that regard and respect, which when once the courts of justice are deprived of, their authority (so necessary for the good order of the kingdom) is entirely lost among the people.': see *Commentaries*, p.285.

In my judgment this summary and Draconian jurisdiction should only be used for the purpose of ensuring that a trial in progress or about to start can be brought to a proper and dignified end without disturbance and with a fair chance of a just verdict or judgment. Contempts which are not likely to disturb the trial or affect the verdict or judgment can be dealt with by a motion to commit under RSC, Ord.52, or even by indictment."[49]

Lawton L.J. was there clearly treating the Ord.52 procedure as not being truly "summary" at all, and therefore not requiring to be justified by reference to

---

[46] See the observations of the Phillimore Committee, cited at para.2–16. For the position in the USA, see R.B. Kuhns, "The Summary Contempt Power: A Critique and a New Perspective" (1978) 88 Yale Law Jo. 39.
[47] [1991] 1 W.L.R. 1194 at 1225G–H, [1992] 1 All E.R. 503 at 532h–j. For a discussion of the court's need for a summary power to preserve control in the courtroom itself, see M. Chesterman, "Disorder in the court: the Judge's Response" (1987) 10 U.N.S.W.L.J. 32–46.
[48] [1975] Q.B. 73 at 92–3.
[49] This reference to "indictment" probably means, in the context in which it was uttered, by indictment for some other statutory or common law offence, such as perverting the course of justice. The use of the indictment for proceeding in respect of contempt as such is now obsolete: *Re Lonrho plc* [1990] 2 A.C. 154 at 177C, *per* Lord Keith.

2–28 CHAPTER 2—CONTEMPT OF COURT: CONSTITUTIONAL DIMENSIONS

urgency. What he was contemplating as the "summary and Draconian jurisdiction" would seem to be that of punishing *"brevi manu"*[50] for contempt in the face of the court.[51]

2–29 Another factor might be the need to save delay and expense, for example where there is no dispute as to the facts[52] and no wider question of public interest involved. In *R. v Powell*,[53] the appellant had disrupted proceedings by wolf-whistling loudly at a juror from the rear of the court. Later the same day (after he had received legal advice from a barrister who was present in the court, representing a different client), he was sentenced to 14 days' imprisonment. Although the sentence was varied, the Court of Appeal held that the trial judge had been correct to employ the summary procedure. In the words of Staughton L.J.:

> "There are some cases which, although serious, do not justify the cumbersome procedure of reporting the matter to the Attorney-General, waiting for him to consider it, prepare affidavits and possibly oral evidence, and then have a Motion before the Divisional Court. In such cases, it seems to us that it is right for the judge to deal with the matter then and there."

2–30 Sometimes, it happens to be convenient for respondents themselves to accept the exercise by the judge of his inherent jurisdiction,[54] rather than undergoing the expense and delay of a reference to the Attorney-General and the subsequent deliberations of the Divisional Court. For example, in March 1996, News Group Newspapers plc consented to have a complaint in relation to their coverage of certain criminal proceedings in the *Sun* newspaper dealt with by Judge Cotran at the Southwark Crown Court. Having heard submissions from counsel, he imposed a fine of £10,000.

2–31 There is, in addition, the point made in *R. v Moran*[55] as to the difficulty for persons who were not present of assessing the situation, and especially after considerable delay. As Lawton L.J. observed in the Court of Appeal: "These situations are always difficult for judges to deal with. The trial judge is in a much better situation to assess what is required to be done than this court some months afterwards." It is necessary, however, to recognise the risks involved, and in particular of giving an impression of bias; it is now generally thought desirable for a judge to at least consider referring a case of apparent contempt in the face of the court for determination by another tribunal.[56]

---

[50] The phrase used in *Re Johnson* (1887) 20 Q.B.D. 68 at 74 by Bowen L.J.
[51] For contempt in the face, see generally ch.10.
[52] The Court of Appeal in *R. v Griffin* (1989) 88 Cr.App.R. 63 noted that where issues were to be contested, the informal summary procedure was not well suited to resolving them.
[53] (1993) 98 Cr.App.R. 224.
[54] That there remains such a residual jurisdiction was confirmed by Lawton L.J. in *Balogh v St. Albans Crown Court* [1975] Q.B. 73 at 93, and by the Divisional Court in *Taylor v Topping* [1990] T.L.R. 110 (Lexis), but its exercise should normally be confined to circumstances calling for the summary jurisdiction, *e.g.*, when it is necessary for controlling the trial or bringing it to a proper conclusion. Once the trial is over, the trial judge is *functus officio*: see *Taylor v Topping*.
[55] (1985) 81 Cr.App.R. 51 at 53.
[56] See the discussion of *R. v Schot and Barclay* [1997] 2 Cr.App.R. 383, (1997) 161 J.P. 473 at paras 10–83 *et seq.*

II. Freedom of Information and the Law of Contempt

A. The competing rights

The common law of contempt has gradually evolved in a way that reveals a continuing struggle to reconcile competing rights and interests. In the process, judge-made law has been supplemented from time to time by statute. The rights most obviously relevant are, perhaps, those articulated in Arts 6 (the right to a fair and public trial) and 10 (freedom of speech and information) of the European Convention on Human Rights. The common law has long recognised both of those rights, and attempted its own reconciliation between them. But the Contempt of Court Act 1981, enacted under the spur of the European Convention, and as a result of *Sunday Times v United Kingdom*,[57] was intended to effect a "permanent shift in the balance of public interest away from the protection of the administration of justice and in favour of freedom of speech".[58]

By contrast, in New Zealand, it has been said that the right to freedom of expression guaranteed in the Bill of Rights Act 1990 must be balanced against all other affirmed freedoms and rights, including minimum standards of criminal procedure[59]:

"The right to a fair and impartial trial, one in which the onus of proof is on the prosecution and the accused is presumed innocent until proved guilty, is at least as fundamental and as important as the right to freedom of speech. At the heart of the criminal trial is the jury's impartiality and its freedom from any constraint from outside."

The right to freedom of expression is qualified by the necessity to preserve and protect those fundamental features of the jury system. The need to give weight to both considerations was emphasised by a Full Court of Appeal in *Gisborne Herald Co. Ltd v Solicitor-General*[60]:

"The common law of contempt is based on public policy. It requires the balancing of public interest factors. Freedom of the press as a vehicle for comment on public issues is basic to our democratic system. The assurance of a fair trial by an impartial Court is essential for the preservation of an effective system of justice. Both values have been affirmed by the Bill of Rights. The public interest in the functioning of the courts invokes both these values".

Collins J. in *Att-Gen v Guardian Newspapers Ltd*[61] observed that "the New Zealand approach . . . tends in the forbidden direction of the House of Lords' decision in *Att-Gen v Times Newspapers*" [*i.e.* the thalidomide case]. In the same

---

[57] (1979) 2 E.H.R.R. 245.
[58] *per* Lloyd L.J. in *Att-Gen v Newspaper Publishing plc* [1988] Ch. 333 at 382D–F. A similar shift has occurred in Canada, as a result of the enactment of the Canadian Charter of Rights and Freedoms: *Dagenais v Canadian Broadcasting Corp.* (1994) 120 D.L.R. (4th) 12.
[59] *Solicitor-General v Radio New Zealand* [1994] 1 N.Z.L.R. 48 at 60, H.C. Full Ct.
[60] [1995] 3 N.Z.L.R. 563 at 571, *per* Richardson J. See also *Television New Zealand Ltd v Quinn* [1996] 3 N.Z.L.R. 24, and *Lange v Atkinson* [1997] 3 N.Z.L.R. 22.
[61] [1999] E.M.L.R. 904 at 918–19 at [46].

case, however, Sedley L.J. noted that Richardson J. (as he then was) in *Gisborne Herald* had cited with approval the words of McLachlin J. in *Dagenais v Canadian Broadcasting Corp.*[62] observing that the most serious consideration needs to be given both to the need for a fair trial and to freedom of expression. This suggests that there is perhaps a risk of attaching undue significance to differences of emphasis as between common law jurisdictions and seeing distinctions of principle or of priority which are more theoretical than real.

2–36 Another factor which needs to be taken into account in the equation, when striking the balance according to the priorities of any particular society, is the right to personal privacy. Thus, for example, there is a tension between Art.6 of the European Convention, which ensures that justice must be open, and Art.8, intended to protect privacy. It is true that when originally conceived, shortly after the second world war, its purpose was primarily to protect citizens against official interference or, in the words of Sir Gerald Fitzmaurice, "... the whole gamut of fascist and communist inquisitorial practices ... ".[63] At that stage it was not apparently contemplated as a threat to privacy that journalists might intrude upon personal lives, or that citizens might be vulnerable to long-distance photography or bugging devices.

2–37 Although there was for a long time little jurisprudence on Art.8, and particularly in English case law,[64] the protection of "private life" was catered for to some extent through the medium of Art.6, where it was recognised that media coverage of court proceedings might on occasion be restricted for this purpose. The problem of reconciling competing interests is one with which the common law has long been familiar,[65] and the subject is discussed more fully below in the context of the *parens patriae* jurisdiction,[66] and also that of court reporting where there arises a conflict with the need for personal privacy.[67]

B. The law of contempt as a fetter on freedom of speech[68]

2–38 It is plain that the law of contempt of court can operate as a fetter on the exercise of the right to free speech, and upon the general right of the public to be informed,[69] and thus gives rise to what is frequently referred to as a "chilling

---

[62] (1994) 120 D.L.R. (4th) 12, (1995) 94 C.C.C. (3rd) 289 at 370–1.
[63] *Marckx v Belgium* (1979) 2 E.H.R.R. 330.
[64] See however a passing reference by Ward J. in *Re H-S* [1994] 3 All E.R. 390 at 398c, CA.
[65] *Scott v Scott* [1913] A.C. 417; *McPherson v McPherson* [1936] A.C. 177, P.C.
[66] See in particular paras 6–82 *et seq*.
[67] para.7–96.
[68] E. Barendt, *Freedom of Speech*, (Oxford: Clarendon Press, 2nd ed., 2005); F. Schauer, *Free Speech: A Philosophical Enquiry* (Cambridge, Cambridge University Press, 1982); Sally Walker, "Freedom of Speech and Contempt of Court: The English and Australian Approaches Compared" (1991) 40 I.C.L.Q. 583; C. Walker, "Fundamental Rights, Fair Trials and the New Audio-Visual Sector" (1996) 59 M.L.R. 517. See also Sir Charles Gray, "The Bastion of Freedom of Expression—Is It Threatened by the Laws of Confidentiality, Privacy or Contempt?" in M. Saville and R. Susskind eds, *Essays in Honour of Sir Brian Neill: The Quintessential Judge*, Butterworths (2003), p.173.
[69] Lord Denning M.R. in *Schering Chemicals v Falkman Ltd* [1982] Q.B. 1 at 22, pointed out that these are two somewhat distinct rights: "Freedom of the press is of fundamental importance in our society. It covers not only the right of the press to impart information of general interest or concern, but also the right of the public to receive it." See also *per* Mann L.J. in *R. v Clerkenwell Stipendiary Magistrate Ex p. The Telegraph plc* [1993] Q.B. 462 at 469F: "The public has a legitimate and

effect".[70] Fundamentally, this is because journalists are required to abide by the principle that anything prejudicial to the issues, or relating to the character of defendants in criminal proceedings, must not be publicised, for fear that a jury might be tainted by an inappropriate source of information.[71] Even in those civil proceedings where a jury is likely to be involved, reporting or comment may have to be restrained for similar reasons.[72] As long ago as in 1742, these concerns were being articulated by Lord Hardwicke L.C.[73]:

> "Nothing is more incumbent upon courts of justice, than to preserve their proceedings from being misrepresented; nor is there any thing of more pernicious consequence, than to prejudice the minds of the publick against persons concerned as parties in causes, before the cause is finally heard".

A more modern statement to similar effect is that of Watkins L.J. in *Peacock v London Weekend Television*[74]: 2–39

> "In our land we do not allow trial by television or newspaper. Until the well recognized institution of this country for the doing of justice, namely the courts, have worked their course, then the hand of the writer and the voice of the broadcaster must be still."

Despite the attempt of the Contempt of Court Act 1981 to limit these restraints by introducing the "strict liability" regime, this obligation can still hinder press reporting even prior to the commencement of proceedings, at least where such proceedings are "virtually certain" to take place,[75] and even possibly before that stage is reached.[76] 2–40

Similar constraints may sometimes be imposed on the reporting of court proceedings themselves, if a later related trial may itself be prejudiced. Indeed, 2–41

---

important interest in legal proceedings held in public and is accordingly entitled to reports of all such proceedings".

[70] This phrase has been used in the context of media inhibitions arising from the law of defamation. See, *e.g.* Lord Keith in *Derbyshire County Council v Times Newspapers Ltd* [1993] A.C. 534 at 548D, who speaks of the "chilling effect" of restrictive laws, citing *New York Times Co v Sullivan* (1964) U.S. 254. Recognition of the "chilling effect" is also to be found in the judgment of the European Court of Human Rights, in the context of contempt of court, in *Goodwin v United Kingdom* (1996) 22 E.H.R.R. 123. For a general survey, see Barendt, Lustgarten, Norrie and Stephenson, *Libel and the Media* (1997).

[71] See generally ch.4, and in particular Simon Brown L.J. in *Att-Gen v Unger* [1998] 1 Cr.App.R. 308 at 317a–b and the discussion at paras 4–61 *et seq*. It should be noted that, despite the provisions contained in the Criminal Justice Act 2003, Pt 11, for admitting in certain circumstances previous convictions of defendants in criminal proceedings, the Attorney-General warned the media on December 1, 2004 that this did not give "... a green light to report matters such as previous convictions before a trial". As he pointed out, there is to be no automatic admission of such evidence. It will be for the trial judge to decide. Journalists should not anticipate what is to happen in this respect at the point of arrest or in the period leading up to trial.

[72] See, *e.g. Att-Gen v News Group Newspapers Ltd* [1987] Q.B. 1, CA. It would be commonplace, for example, for a s.4(2) order to be made in preliminary hearings in high profile libel actions, where unrestrained submissions could be made which it would not be appropriate for potential jurors to read about before hearing the evidence.

[73] *The St. James's Evening Post (Roach v Garvan)* (1742) 2 Atk. 469, 26 E.R. 683.

[74] (1985) 150 J.P. 71 at 80. A much cited passage is the statement of Lord Reid in *Att-Gen v Times Newspapers Ltd* [1974] A.C. 273 at 300: "There has long been and there still is in this country a strong and generally held feeling that trial by newspaper is wrong and should be prevented."

[75] *Att-Gen v News Group Newspapers plc* [1989] 1 Q.B. 110 at 135A. See the discussion at para.5–67.

[76] See Bingham L.J. in *Att-Gen v Sport Newspapers Ltd* [1991] 1 W.L.R. 1194, [1992] 1 All E.R. 503, and the discussion of that case at paras 5–71 and paras 5–96 *et seq*.

2–41 CHAPTER 2—CONTEMPT OF COURT: CONSTITUTIONAL DIMENSIONS

Parliament has sanctioned a statutory jurisdiction to postpone reporting for that reason.[77] Care has also to be taken not to publish material which might bring improper influence to bear upon litigants in civil proceedings, those concerned directly in criminal proceedings, or witnesses generally. Other interests such as the need to protect privacy, whether of a child or a patient,[78] or of others such as a witness who is a blackmail victim, can also be protected by an order preventing identification[79] such that, if breached with knowledge of its existence, those responsible may find themselves committed for contempt. A similarly wide-ranging order was also made for the protection of life and physical well-being in *Venables and Thompson v News Group Newspapers Ltd.*[80]

2–42 An attempt was made in the 1981 Act to reconcile the public interest in ensuring, so far as possible, that citizens are able to have a fair trial and unrestricted access to the judicial process, on the one hand, with that of permitting freedom of communication, and particularly of informing the public about criminal or anti-social activities on the other. It had been intended to resolve these tensions definitively by the strict liability framework, drafted to take account of the concerns of the European Court of Human Rights[81] and those of the Phillimore Committee. Yet it has not proved to be capable of finally disposing of the problem, and much of the discussion in chapter 5 is concerned with how far the traditional common law restraints continue to apply, and how they interrelate with the statutory rules.

2–43 Another device by which Parliament sought to achieve a reconciliation between the demands of free public discussion within a democratic society, especially with regard to matters of public interest, and the need to protect those undergoing the criminal process, was the formulation of the defence afforded by s.5 of the 1981 Act. As a matter of policy, the decision was taken that a risk of prejudice would be regarded as acceptable provided it arose incidentally to a discussion on a matter of public interest. In some cases, the courts have shown themselves sensitive to the need not to restrict public debate despite the currency of criminal proceedings.[82] By contrast, despite the notoriety and scale of his activities, the public were significantly deprived of the opportunity to discuss the conduct of Robert Maxwell by the constraints which the law of contempt imposed in respect of the pending proceedings against his sons.[83]

---

[77] Contempt of Court Act 1981, s.4(2), the operation of which is considered at para.7–111.
[78] The Family Division, in particular, often grants wide-ranging injunctions against the media under its *parens patriae* jurisdiction. See in particular the discussion of *Re Z (A Minor) (Identification)* [1997] 1 Fam. 1, at paras 6–58 *et seq.*; and *Re S (FC) (A Child)* [2004] UKHL 22, [2004] 2 A.C. 457, discussed at paras 6–43 *et seq.*
[79] By virtue of s.11, considered at paras 7–83 *et seq.*
[80] [2001] Fam. 430.
[81] *Sunday Times v United Kingdom* (1979) 2 E.H.R.R. 245.
[82] *Att-Gen v English* [1983] 1 A.C. 116; *R. v Beck Ex p. Daily Telegraph plc* [1993] 2 All E.R. 177, 94 Cr.App.R. 367. See also *Leary v BBC* (Lexis), September 29, 1989, discussed at paras 6–31 *et seq.* There is not as much authority on s.5 as might have been expected over the intervening years. On the other hand, it is possible that it has had a restraining influence behind the scenes, in the sense of inhibiting applications which might otherwise have been made for restraint by injunction.
[83] *R. v Maxwell* (unreported), March 6, 1995, Phillips J.; see also *Att-Gen v BBC, Hat Trick Productions* [1997] E.M.L.R. 76, and *Att-Gen v Steadman* (unreported) February 7, 1994 in which Bell J. granted an injunction restraining the respondent from staging "Maxwell: The Musical" on the basis that the musical would be in breach of the strict liability rule. See Sir Charles Gray "The

A further restriction imposed by the law of contempt upon the free flow of 2–44
information arises from the fact that jurors cannot be questioned about what
occurred in the confines of the jury room, and the public is deprived of valuable
research material as to the workings of the judicial system and improvements that
could be made to it.[84] It was expressly acknowledged in *Att-Gen v Scotcher*[85] that
the Art.10 rights of the appellant, who had been imprisoned for a breach of s.8
of the Contempt of Court Act 1981, had been engaged but the objective of
protecting jury confidentiality was sufficiently important to justify limiting a
juror's freedom of expression. Moreover, the provision was rationally connected
to its aim and the means adopted no more than reasonably necessary, because the
restriction would not apply to *bona fide* disclosures to the court authorities. There
being no comparable restriction in New Zealand, research was carried out by the
New Zealand Law Commission the results of which suggested that the adverse
impact in that jurisdiction of potentially prejudicial press coverage has in fact
been minimal.[86] Sir Robin Auld has recommended that in England and Wales the
restrictions imposed by s.8 should be relaxed so as to permit, where appropriate,
enquiry by the trial judge and/or the Court of Appeal into alleged impropriety by
a jury, whether in the course of its deliberations or otherwise.[87]

C. Vilification of those punished by the courts

Because it is generally recognised that tribunals consisting solely of professional 2–45
judges are unlikely to be influenced by what appears in the media, there is
sometimes a tendency to throw caution to the winds and to vilify a convicted
person at the appellate stage, thus adding an element of extra-judicial condemnation or punishment to that which the courts might choose to impose. For example,
in *R. v Vano*,[88] a driver entered a pedestrian crossing when a child stepped from
the central reservation and was struck by his car, suffering injuries from which
she died. He was convicted of causing death by dangerous driving, and was
remanded in custody pending a pre-sentence report. He was sentenced in due
course to 28 days' imprisonment (as well as being disqualified for three years and

---

Bastion of Freedom of Expression—Is It Threatened by the Laws of Confidentiality, Privacy or Contempt?" in M. Saville and R. Susskind eds, *Essays in Honour of Sir Brian Neill: The Quintessential Judge*, Butterworths (2003) p.218. By contrast, Lindsay J. took a more relaxed view as to the coverage of the Chancery proceedings which were happening in parallel, largely because the press took less interest: *MGN Pension Trustees Ltd v Bank of America National Trust and Savings Association and another (Serious Fraud Office Intervening)* [1995] 2 All E.R. 355.

[84] s.8, considered at paras 11–349 *et seq*. For the common law position in New Zealand, see *Solicitor-General v Radio New Zealand Ltd* [1994] 1 N.Z.L.R. 48.

[85] [2005] UKHL 36, [2005] 1 W.L.R. 1867, [2005] 3 All E.R. 1 at [29]–[31].

[86] Young, and Tinsley, *Juries in Criminal Trials: Part 2* (November 1999). See also Law Commission Report, *Juries in Criminal Trials* (February 2001); W. Young, "Summing up to Juries in Criminal Cases: What Jury Research Says About Current Rules and Practice" [2003] Crim. L.R. 665.

[87] *Review of Criminal Courts of England and Wales* (2001), ch.5, para.98. This recommendation was referred to by the House of Lords in *R. v Mirza* [2004] UKH.L. 2, [2004] 1 A.C. 1118 at [24] where Lord Steyn, having said that his view was that the jurisdiction already existed (although he was "in a minority of one"), added that " . . . the importance and urgency of the recommendation cannot be overstated". See *R. v Smith (Patrick)* [2005] UKHL 12, [2005] 1 W.L.R.704; *Att-Gen v Scotcher* [2005] UKHL 36, [2005] 1 W.L.R. 1867, [2005] 3 All E.R. 1. See also the Department of Constitutional Affairs Consultation Paper, *Jury Research and Impropriety*, published January 21, 2005, (CP 04/05).

[88] *Att-Gen's Ref No.34 of 1994* (1995) 16 Cr.App.R. (S) 785, [1996] R.T.R. 15.

2–45 CHAPTER 2—CONTEMPT OF COURT: CONSTITUTIONAL DIMENSIONS

ordered to retake his driving test), but because he had spent 14 days on remand, the effect of the sentence was that he was to be released immediately.

2–46 On an Attorney-General's reference, the Court of Appeal (Criminal Division) declined to increase the sentence and, towards the end of the judgment, Lord Taylor C.J. referred to the impact upon the man concerned of a press campaign[89]:

> "We would like to stress that, whilst the press are the guardians of the public interest, to pursue a campaign of vilification of someone who has been before the court, in a way which causes hate mail to be sent, which causes his family to be under the need to move house, which causes his children to be shunned by other children in the neighbourhood, is doing no public service. Furthermore, if it is intended to bring pressure to bear on the courts, then it is wholly misguided."

2–47 This illustrates how some aspects of the relationship between the media and the judicial system were left quite untouched by Parliament in the 1981 Act. Such pressures may not amount to contempt of court, because the individual before the court may by that stage have no choices left to make, and thus be impervious to any influence such press coverage might bring to bear.[90] Nonetheless, the remarks of Lord Taylor highlight what may sometimes be the unfairness of the double jeopardy involved when the press (who may be only partially informed as to the facts of the case) seek to impose an additional set of penalties upon those already punished by the tribunals duly charged by society with the responsibility of administering justice. On the other hand, the courts sometimes wish to demonstrate that they are in fact responsive to public opinion, which it may be difficult to assess other than through media coverage.[91]

---

[89] And see Lord Taylor's address, "Justice in the Media Age", a paper presented to the Commonwealth Judges' and Magistrates' Association at the University of Hertfordshire, April 15, 1995, where he expressed similar concerns. See *R. v Secretary of State for the Home Department Ex p. Thompson and Venables* [1998] A.C. 407, where the House of Lords held that natural justice requires the Home Secretary to ignore as irrelevant public petitions or public opinion as expressed in the media in the exercise of his discretion. See also *R. v Secretary of State for the Home Department Ex p. Hindley* [2000] Q.B. 152, [2001] 1 A.C. 401; *R. v Pierson* [1998] A.C. 539; *R. v B* (1994) 15 Cr.App.R. (S) 815. For a general discussion, see S. Shute, "The Place of Public Opinion in Sentencing Law" [1998] Crim. L.R. 465; A.J. Ashworth and M. Hough, "Sentencing and the Climate of Opinion" [1996] Crim. L.R. 776; see also A.T.H. Smith, "Free Press and Fair Trial : Challenges and Change" in eds J. Beatson and Y. Cripps, *Freedom of Expression and Freedom of Information* (Oxford University Press 2000), p.123. The difficult problem of ill-informed media pressure upon the courts and the legislature continues to be topical and arose acutely in the context of Mr Tony Martin who was convicted of murder by a jury at Norwich after shooting an intruder in his home. See, *e.g.* S. Yeo, "Killing in Defence of Property" (2000) 150 New L.J. 730.

[90] See the discussion of *Att-Gen v Times Newspapers Ltd*, February 12, 1983 (Lexis) at paras 4–99 *et seq.* and *Att-Gen v Unger* [1998] 1 Cr.App.R. 308 at paras 4–166 *et seq.*

[91] See the discussion of *R. v Vano* [1996] R.T.R. 15 at para.5–101, and the cases cited in note 54 thereto. In this jurisdiction too, it seems that there is an increasing perception that lawyers may legitimately press their clients' cases through the media while keeping a weather eye on the law of contempt, because "it is going to be tried by human beings". See S. Stapley, *Media Relations for Lawyers* (2nd ed, 2003). See too Bar News (The Journal of the New South Wales Bar), Spring/Summer 1994, p.26, for an unusually frank account of a barrister's strategic manipulation of the media: "It was a sensational case and the accused could easily have been portrayed as a monster. Our aim was to get the best coverage possible of our client's version of events—also we hoped for a sentence less than life . . . . Some cases get into the collective conscience of the community so that the eventual outcome may well be affected by . . . the folklore surrounding a particular matter". This is cited by the Hon. D.A. Ipp in "Talking to the Media: An Australian Perspective" (1998) 1 Legal

D. Media pressure upon the Home Secretary

At one stage further removed from the law of contempt is media pressure brought to bear upon the Home Secretary, who formerly exercised a number of quasi-judicial powers, some by way of what was left of the Royal Prerogative, and others pursuant to statute.[92] It would be even more difficult to contend that a member of the executive should in any way be shielded from the influence of the media, even though he was taking decisions affecting the lives and liberty of citizens as part of the criminal justice system. Nonetheless, it has been emphasised in the House of Lords that the Secretary of State should not take such considerations into account when exercising that discretion.[93] These considerations are likely to cease to have any further practical significance in the light of the acknowledgment by the legislature that politicians in general, and the executive in particular, ought to refrain from exercising what should be the judicial function of imposing penalties or fixing tariffs in individual cases.

2–48

E. The "constitutional" role of the press[94]

Traditionally, the courts have been slow to acknowledge that the press occupies an especially protected role within the common law system.[95] Yet there have

2–49

Ethics 123. In *Kelly v O'Neill and Brady* [2000] 1 I.R. 354, a decision of the Irish Supreme Court, it seems actually to have been recognised that media coverage might affect the minds of professional judges. Also, in *Solicitor-General v Smith* [2004] 2 N.Z.L.R. 540 at 557, it was observed in the High Court of New Zealand that "Judges, despite their training and experience are only human and not entirely aloof from pressure".

[92] These powers have been narrowed in recent years as a result of views expressed in the European Court of Human Rights: see, *e.g. Thynne, Wilson and Gunnell v United Kingdom* (1990) 13 E.H.R.R. 666; *V v United Kingdom* (1999) 30 E.H.R.R. 121. See also *R. v Secretary of State for the Home Department Ex p. Doody* [1994] 1 A.C. 531; *R. (Anderson) v Secretary of State for the Home Department* [2003] A.C. 837; See now Criminal Justice Act 2003, Chapter 7, "Effect of Life Sentence", ss.269–277 and *The Consolidated Criminal Practice Direction (Amendment No.2) (Mandatory Life Sentences)* [2004] 1 W.L.R. 2551, [2005] 1 Cr.App.R. 8.

[93] *R. v Secretary of State for the Home Department Ex p. Thompson and Venables* [1998] A.C. 407, CA and HL.

[94] See the discussion of "Journalists' special rights" in G. Robertson and A. Nicol, *Media Law* (4th ed., 2002), pp.17–18; L. Lustgarten and I. Leigh, *In From the Cold* (1994), ch. 10. Extra-judicially, Lord Denning described the media as the "watchdog of justice", in "A Free Press" (1984) 17 Bracton Law Jo. 13. See also Lord Denning, *The Road to Justice* (1955), p.64. Lord Taylor C.J. in *Vano* itself, cited at para.2–46, recognised that: "the press are the guardians of the public interest"; likewise Sir John Donaldson M.R. in *Francome v Mirror Group Newspapers Ltd* [1984] 1 W.L.R. 892 at 898A: "The media ... are an essential element of any democracy. In exposing crime, anti-social behaviour and hypocrisy and in campaigning for reform and propagating the views of minorities, they perform an invaluable function". However, he also went on to observe that "The media ... are peculiarly vulnerable to the error of confusing the public interest with their own interest." See A.T.H. Smith, "The Press, The Courts, and the Constitution" (1999) 52 C.L.P. 126. See also Recommendation No.R(2000) 7 of the Committee of Ministers to member States on the right of journalists not to disclose their sources of information, adopted by the Committee of Ministers on March 8, 2000 at the 701st meeting of the Ministers' Deputies.

[95] G. Robertson and A. Nicol, *Media Law* (4th ed., 2002) defend this approach on the basis of a "principle that journalism is not a profession, but the exercise by occupation of the citizen's right to freedom of expression" (p.274). To accord any special protection is therefore in their view contrary to principle. Similar views were expressed by the Court of Appeal in *Kemsley v Foot* [1951] 2 K.B. 34 at 46–7, Birkett L.J.: "It is the right of every man to comment freely, fairly and honestly on any matter of public interest, and this is not a privilege which belongs to particular persons in particular circumstances. It matters not whether the comments are made to the few or to the many, whether they

2–49 CHAPTER 2—CONTEMPT OF COURT: CONSTITUTIONAL DIMENSIONS

been signs that this attitude is changing. It is increasingly common to encounter sentiments such as those of Lamer C.J.C. in *Canadian Newspapers Co v Canada (Attorney-General)*[96]:

> "Freedom of the press is, indeed, an important and essential attribute of a free and democratic society, and measures which prohibit the media from publishing information deemed of interest obviously restrict that freedom".

2–50 Free speech, including the freedom of the press, plays an important role in the functioning of any democratic society.[97] The free flow of information should enable its readers to make better informed judgments about the conduct of government and the workings of the institutions of their society. A good deal has been said, not only in the European Court of Human Rights[98] but also in the higher courts of England and Wales[99] to emphasise just how fundamental a role and status the media must be accorded in a modern society.

2–51 It has become apparent that the courts (and indeed Parliament) are now willing to accord to the press a "constitutional" significance that was largely unrecognised at common law.[1] It is true that the role of the press was always recognised by the courts up to a point,[2] but the function of journalism has become

---

are made by a powerful newspaper or by an individual, whether they are written or spoken: the defence ... is open to all".

[96] (1988) 43 C.C.C. (3d) 24 at 29, 52 D.L.R. (4th) 690 at 695, [1988] S.C.R. 122.

[97] See F. Schauer, *Free Speech: A Philosophical Inquiry* (1982), ch.3; E. Barendt, *Freedom of Speech* (1987); G. Marshall, "Press Freedom and Free Speech Theory" [1992] P.L. 40; C. Walker, "Fundamental Rights, Fair Trials and the New Audio-Visual Sector" (1996) 59 M.L.R. 517.

[98] See, *e.g. Lingens v Austria* (1986) 8 E.H.R.R. 407; *Sunday Times v United Kingdom (No.2)* (1991) 14 E.H.R.R. 229; *Castells v Spain* (1992) 14 E.H.R.R. 445; *Thorgeirson v Iceland* (1992) 14 E.H.R.R. 843; *Oberschlick v Austria* (1995) 19 E.H.R.R. 389; *Prager & Oberschlick v Austria* (1996) 21 E.H.R.R. 1; *Goodwin v United Kingdom* (1996) 22 E.H.R.R. 123; *Bladet Tromsø v Norway* (2000) E.H.R.R. 125.

[99] See, *e.g. Att-Gen v Guardian Newspapers Ltd (No.2)* [1990] 1 A.C. 109, 183F, Sir John Donaldson M.R. himself; *Hector v Att-Gen of Antigua* [1990] 2 A.C. 312, 318, Lord Bridge; *Att-Gen v Guardian Newspapers Ltd (No.3)* [1992] 1 W.L.R. 874, [1992] 3 All E.R. 38, Q.B.D.; *Chief Constable of Leicestershire v Garavelli* [1997] E.M.L.R. 543, Q.B.D.; *Hodgson v Imperial Tobacco Ltd* [1998] 1 W.L.R. 1056, [1998] 2 All E.R. 673, CA; *Reynolds v Times Newspapers Ltd* [2001] 2 A.C. 127 (H.L.); *R. v Shayler (David)* [2002] UKHL 11, [2002] 1 A.C. 247 (Lord Bingham); *R. v Secretary of State for the Home Department Ex p. Simms* [2000] 2 A.C. 115 at 126E; *McCartan Turkington Breen v Times Newspapers Ltd* [2001] 2 A.C. 277 at 290G–91B.

[1] See, *e.g.* the passage in the speech of Lord Scarman in in *Secretary of State for Defence v Guardian Newspapers Ltd* [1985] A.C. 339 at 361E–F, cited at para.9–80. Parliament too has recognised the importance of the journalist's role in various statutes. Special provision is made for, and protection given to, "journalistic material" in the Police and Criminal Evidence Act 1984, s.13. See also the position of the journalist under s.10 (protection of sources), discussed at paras 9–53 *et seq.*, whereby Parliament has acknowledged the importance in a democratic society that a journalist should be able to protect sources.

[2] *Scott v Scott* [1913] A.C. 417. See also *Furniss v Cambridge News Ltd* (1907) 23 T.L.R. 705, as discussed at para.7–16, and the protection afforded to journalists through qualified privilege, both at common law and under successive statutory regimes, for the reporting of the courts, Parliament and an ever wider range of activities: cp. the Defamation Act 1952, s.7 with the Defamation Act 1996, s.14. Furthermore, there has always been a measure of protection for sources at the discovery stage in libel actions through the so-called "newspaper rule". It has been held that the basis of the rule is the public interest in protecting the media's sources of information, because of the need to encourage a free flow of information: *Broadcasting Corporation of New Zealand v Alex Harvey Industries* [1980] 1 N.Z.L.R. 163. See also *Isbey v Broadcasting Corporation of NZ (No.2)* [1975] 2 N.Z.L.R. 237; *Brill v Television One* [1976] 1 N.Z.L.R. 683.

increasingly formalised by Parliament and its importance ungrudgingly acknowledged by the judiciary. The traditional approach was that journalists were ordinary citizens with no greater rights than any other.[3] As Lord Lane C.J. observed in *Re Crook (Tim)*[4]:

" ... while giving full recognition to the importance of the role of the press, it would not be right as a general rule to distinguish between excluding the press and other members of the public. If exclusion of the public is necessary, applying the strict standard required to justify it, it would not usually[5] be right to make an exception in favour of the press. There will often be other members of the public, such as the family of a defendant, victims of the alleged crime and others having a direct concern in the case with as much interest in the proceedings and as good a claim to be present as the press. It could cause a real sense of grievance if they were excluded while representatives of the press were allowed to be present."

By articulating the reasons why free speech and freedom of the press are so fundamental to a democracy, and reflecting upon the way in which the law of contempt conflicts with such *"desiderata"*,[6] the courts began to develop well before the Human Rights Act 1998 a role for the fourth estate that the common law would not have recognised so overtly without the influence of the European Convention. The influence is increasingly acknowledged directly,[7] as in the speech of Lord Templeman in *Att-Gen v Guardian Newspapers Ltd*[8]:

"My Lords, this appeal involves a conflict between the right of the public to be protected by the Security Service and the right of the public to be supplied with full information by the press. This appeal therefore involves consideration of the Convention for the Protection of Human Rights and Fundamental Freedoms (1953) (Cmd. 8969) ("the Convention") to which the British Government adheres ...

---

[3] See, *e.g. Ambard v Att.-Gen* [1936] A.C. 322, 337 and the comments of Birkett L.J. in *Kemsley v Foot* [1951] 2 K.B. 34 at 46–7 cited above at para.2–49, n.95.
[4] (1989) 93 Cr.App.R. 17 at 24.
[5] Lord Lane referred to the exceptional example of *R. v Waterfield* [1975] 1 W.L.R. 711, (1975) 60 Cr.App.R. 296, where the press had been permitted to be present when the general public were excluded. This concerned the importation of indecent films, and the reason for excluding the public in general was said to be "the atmosphere that might be created by persons with no more interest than a taste for the nasty." It may not be easy to draw a distinction, however, between evidence of a salacious kind contained in film or video format and such evidence when adduced from a distressed victim in a rape or indecency case. Indeed, it may be thought *more* desirable to exclude the "dirty mac" brigade when live evidence is being given by a victim than when films are being displayed. Now there is a statutory discretion whereby a court may order the general public to be excluded when a vulnerable witness is giving evidence while permitting an identified press representative to be present: Youth Justice and Criminal Evidence Act 1999, s.25(3).
[6] The expression used by Schiemann L.J. in *Att-Gen v MGN Ltd* [1997] 1 All E.R. 456 at 458h.
[7] See, *e.g.* the direct adoption of the test set out in Art.10(2) of the European Convention ("necessary in a democratic society") in *Att-Gen v Guardian Newspapers Ltd* [1987] 1 W.L.R. 1248 at 1296F–G, Lord Templeman and 1307, Lord Ackner. See also Lord Scarman in *Att-Gen v BBC* [1980] A.C. 303 at 362D; Lord Templeman in *Lord Advocate v Scotsman Publications Ltd*, 1989 S.L.T. 705, [1989] 2 All E.R. 852 at 858; *Chief Constable of Leicestershire v Garavelli* [1997] E.M.L.R. 543, (where the court adopted *inter alia* the test of "overriding public interest" from *Goodwin v United Kingdom* (1996) 22 E.H.R.R. 123). But see *Camelot Group plc v Centaur Communications Ltd* [1999] Q.B. 124, discussed at paras 9–164 *et seq.*
[8] At 1296F–G.

2–52 CHAPTER 2—CONTEMPT OF COURT: CONSTITUTIONAL DIMENSIONS

The question is therefore whether the interference with freedom of expression constituted by the Millett [interim] injunctions was, on 30 July 1987 when they were continued by this House, *necessary in a democratic society* in the interests of national security, for protecting the reputation or rights of others, for preventing disclosure of information received in confidence or for maintaining the authority and impartiality of the judiciary having regard to the facts and circumstances prevailing on the 30 July 1987 and in the light of the events which had happened. The continuance of the Millett injunctions appears to me to be necessary for all these purposes" (emphasis added).

2–53 Sometimes, however, the influence of the Convention was less overt.[9] For example, Watkins L.J. in *R. v Felixstowe Justices Ex p. Leigh*[10] said:

"No one nowadays surely can doubt that his [the journalist's] presence in Court for the purpose of reporting proceedings conducted therein is indispensable. Without him, how is the public to be informed of how justice is being administered in our Courts?"

In a similar vein, Brooke J. in *Att-Gen v Guardian (No.3)*[11] referred to "the status of the news media as the trustees of the general public, whose eyes and ears they are".

2–54 Judges have also readily acknowledged that there is a public interest in the survival of a press which is free to probe, and to publicise suspicions of wrongdoing or incompetence, especially on the part of public bodies.[12] In the words of Lord Bridge in *Hector v Att-Gen of Antigua*[13]:

"In a free democratic society it is almost too obvious to need stating that those who hold office in government and who are responsible for public administration must always be open to criticism. Any attempt to stifle or fetter such criticism amounts to political censorship of the most insidious and objectionable kind".

2–55 The point is well illustrated by considering the shifting approach adopted towards the press in relation to the coverage of court proceedings, and the higher priority accorded to freedom of information. In *R. v Central Criminal Court Ex p. Crook*,[14] as recently as 1984, it was said in the Divisional Court that:

---

[9] Including, *e.g.* through the enactment of statutory provisions, such as in the Contempt of Court Act 1981, ss.3, 4(1), 5 and 10 and the Sexual Offences (Amendment) Act 1992, where steps were taken to protect the privacy of those alleged to be the victims of sexual offences.
[10] [1987] 1 Q.B. 582 at 591H. But see *R. v Home Secretary Ex p. Westminster Press Ltd* (1991) 4 Admin. L.R. 445 at 456, from which it is clear that the view of Watkins L.J. was strictly confined to the role of the press in covering trials and did not extend to obtaining information in advance: "... I do not accept the press has any kind of right to know from the police the name of a person being investigated or who has been charged with a criminal offence. Their rights of acquiring knowledge of matters of public interest are no greater than those possessed by any other member of the public."
[11] [1992] 1 W.L.R. 874 at 886H, citing Sir John Donaldson M.R. in *Att-Gen v Guardian Newspapers Ltd (No.2)* [1990] 1 A.C. 109 at 183F.
[12] *Derbyshire County Council v Times Newspapers Ltd* [1993] A.C. 534 at 547, Lord Keith, echoing what was said by the United States Supreme Court in *New York Times Co v Sullivan* (1964) U.S. 254.
[13] [1990] 2 A.C. 312 at 318.
[14] *The Times*, November 8, 1984, DC. The occasion for the making of these remarks was a challenge (unsuccessful) to the making of an order under s.11 of the Contempt of Court Act, as to which see para.7–83.

"... any attempt by counsel acting on behalf of a witness to make representations to the court should be firmly resisted; likewise applications sought to be made by journalists or any other lay persons".

Within less than a decade, in *R. v Clerkenwell Stipendiary Magistrate Ex p. Telegraph*,[15] the Divisional Court (Mann L.J. and Leonard J.) was taking a very different stance. The magistrate had declined to hear representations from members of the press before making an order forbidding the publication of court proceedings. The Divisional Court, however, referred to the balancing exercise to which the Court of Appeal referred in *Beck*,[16] and Mann L.J.[17] spoke positively of the role of journalists in such judicial deliberations:

2–56

"I regard it as implicit in the enactment of s.4(2) that a court contemplating its use should be enabled to receive assistance from those who will, if there is no order, enjoy the right of making reports of the proceedings before the court. They are in particular the best qualified to represent that public interest in publicity which the court has to take into account when performing any balancing exercise which has to be undertaken."

The change in approach was also evident in the judgments in *Att-Gen v Guardian Newspapers Ltd (No.3)*,[18] where Brooke J. indicated that the "courts should be diligent and understanding in accommodating the legitimate interests of the press",[19] and Mann L.J, who suggested that the terms of all s.4 orders should be faxed to the Press Association:

2–57

"... to answer newspaper inquiries about them. Adoption of the practice by other courts would have the advantage that a source of information about the precise terms of orders would be available to press at such times as the late afternoon or early evening, when articles are prepared, but court officials are not necessarily available to answer queries."

It was observed by Thorpe L.J. in the context of injunctions granted in the Family Division in *Re G (Celebrities: Publicity)*[20]: "Those who are to be bound by *contra mundum* orders have no opportunity to make submissions as to where the boundaries should be drawn nor to contribute their expertise in the drafting. In my opinion consideration should be given to establishing a procedure to meet this deficit." Shortly afterwards, in a criminal context, in *McKerry v Teesdale and Wear Valley Justices*,[21] Lord Bingham C.J. commented[22] that while s.49(4B) of the Children and Young Persons Act 1933 only required the court to afford the *parties* an opportunity to make representations, there is nothing which precludes

2–58

---

[15] [1993] Q.B. 462. And see *R. v Central Criminal Court Ex p. Crook and Godwin* [1995] 2 Cr.App.R. 212, CA. The judge or magistrate has a complete discretion to allow representatives of those whom he considers to have a legitimate interest in the making of, or opposing the making of, orders under s.39 of the Children and Young Persons Act 1933. See now the Criminal Justice and Public Order Act 1994, s.49.
[16] [1993] 2 All E.R. 177 at 181b–c, Farquharson L.J.
[17] [1993] Q.B. 462 at 471E–F.
[18] [1992] 1 N.L.R. 874, [1992] 3 All E.R. 38.
[19] *ibid.* at 50.
[20] [1999] 1 F.L.R. 409 at 418.
[21] [2001] E.M.L.R. 127, (2000) 164 J.P. 355.
[22] At [28].

2–58 CHAPTER 2—CONTEMPT OF COURT: CONSTITUTIONAL DIMENSIONS

the court from receiving submissions from a representative of the press orally or in writing. The prosecution will be expected to take a neutral stance on such matters, whereas the defence is unlikely to do anything but oppose an application. In such circumstances, submissions from the media may help to prevent the court from falling into error.

2–59 The recognition of the legitimate role of the media was extended beyond the matter of court reporting in the House of Lords' decision in *R. v Secretary of State for the Home Department Ex p. Simms*.[23] It was there accepted that a prisoner has a fundamental and basic right to seek through oral interviews to persuade a journalist to investigate the safety of his conviction and to publicise the findings in an effort to gain access to justice. In the context of paras 37 and 37A of the Prison Service Standing Order 5A, it was held that such a fundamental right could not be overridden by general or ambiguous words.

2–60 Where it is known that there is going to be considerable press interest, the Lord Chancellor's Department took to making available press packs containing general information about the proceedings in question, and the personnel involved, and these would generally include details as to any orders or requests which judge may have made in relation to the restriction of press coverage. In the notorious Soham murder case at the end of 2003, there were issued a number of facility notes (not for publication) dealing with matters such as passes to the courtroom and media seating.[24]

2–61 Similarly, in the case of *R. v West*[25] the *Media Court Guide* (which ran to some 14 pages) contained a map of Winchester, a plan of the court layout, potted biographies of the judge and counsel, arrangements about parking, telephone and broadcasting facilities, security passes, and also a section headed "orders to the media". This related to anything said in the absence of the jury, harassment of witnesses or of the defendant's or victims' family members, and the definition of "precincts" at the Winchester combined court centre (for the purposes of s.41 of the Criminal Justice Act 1925).[26] There was also a section headed "reporting restrictions"; this dealt with s.4(2) orders and also contained verbatim extracts of comments which had passed between the judge and counsel as to the way in which the press should approach certain aspects of the trial (for example, that "it would be dangerous for anything to be published" in relation to an application for a stay, other than the bare fact of its having been refused).

2–62 This is only one development in the evolving general relationship between the press and the courts. Earlier, the press had been given a right to appeal against

---

[23] [2000] 2 A.C. 115.
[24] See, *e.g.* 167/03 (April 15); 353/03 (September 17), 431/03 (November 3), 436/03 (November 6), 428/03 (October 31) and 444/03 (November 7).
[25] Tried at Winchester before Mantell J. during the autumn of 1995, and subsequently the subject of an unsuccessful appeal: [1996] 2 Cr.App.R. 374.
[26] See para.10–202.

orders restricting court reporting.[27] Lord Donaldson M.R. had also directed that counsel should make copies of skeleton arguments available to the press.[28] This process culminated in the judgment of Lord Woolf M.R. in *Hodgson v Imperial Tobacco Ltd*[29] where it was held that all judgments, even those given in chambers, must be made available to the press if required, and also that it will generally be appropriate to admit media representatives to chambers hearings (except those in the categories defined in s.12 of the Administration of Justice Act 1960).[30]

In relation to the enquiry by Dame Janet Smith into the circumstances in which the former general practitioner, Harold Shipman, had killed a large number of his patients, the Divisional Court upheld submissions as to the form the enquiry should take from an interest group representing not only families of his victims but also the press. It was held, in particular, that the evidence should be taken in public with a view to informing the public and maintaining public confidence.[31]

F. Provision in the Criminal Procedure Rules

The Criminal Procedure Rules 2005 now effectively make provision for notice to be given to the press when it is intended to sit *in camera*, and this is clearly a further vehicle through which the legitimate functions of the press are being accommodated. Rule 16.10 provides:

> "Where a prosecutor or a defendant intends to apply for an order that all or part of a trial be held in camera for reasons of national security or for the protection of the identity of a witness or any other person, he shall not less than 7 days before the date on which the trial is expected to begin serve a notice in writing to that effect ... ".

The notice is then to be displayed in prominent parts of the court premises. Furthermore, it was held in *Re Godwin*[32] that a judge does not have an inherent power to override the rules and order evidence to be heard *in camera* in a case where there has been no attempt to comply with them. Such a power would

---

[27] Under s.4(2) and s.11, by the Criminal Justice Act 1988, s.159, discussed more fully at para.7–258. Similar protection has been accorded subsequently in the Criminal Proceedings and Investigations Act 1996, s.61(6), in respect of an order under that statute restricting publication of derogatory remarks in mitigation: see paras 8–95 *et seq.*
[28] *Lombard North Central v Pratt* (1989) 139 New L.J. 1709, *The Times*, November 27, 1989 (fourth copy of skeleton argument required for journalists). The decision does not appear to have been incorporated in to any of the *Practice Directions* relating to the preparation and filing of skeleton arguments, and in practice such skeletons would only be made available if a journalist showed particular interest. See *R. v Howell* [2003] EWCA Crim 486, *The Times*, March 10, 2003 where it was affirmed by the Criminal Division of the court of Appeal that the principle of open justice requires that skeleton arguments should be disclosed if and when a request to do so is received. See also *GIO Personal Investment Services Ltd v Liverpool and London Steamship Protection and Indemnity Association Ltd* [1999] 1 W.L.R. 984.
[29] [1998] 1 W.L.R. 1056, 2 All E.R. 673. See also *Forbes v Smith* [1998] 1 All E.R. 973.
[30] para.8–97.
[31] *R. v Secretary of State for Health Ex p. Wagstaff* [2000] 1 W.L.R. 292.
[32] [1991] Crim.L.R. 302, CACD.

2-65 effectively frustrate the purpose underlying the rules; namely, to give the public and the press an opportunity to object. On the facts of that case, there had been ample opportunity to comply, but no effort to do so, and the judge was therefore not entitled to side-step the rules. It was recognised, however, that there might sometimes be circumstances of urgency which precluded the possibility of compliance, and when it might be legitimate to have resort to the inherent powers identified in such cases as *Scott v Scott*[33] and *Att-Gen v Leveller Magazine Ltd*.[34]

2-66 Careful consideration was given by the Court of Appeal in *Ex p. Guardian Newspapers Ltd*[35] to the protection of the interests of the media in relation to the giving of notice under r.24A(1) of the Crown Court Rules 1982[36] when an application was made for a hearing *in camera* in respect of a criminal trial or proceedings ancillary to such a trial. It was observed that the seven day notice period would ordinarily enable "word to get round the media" so that any challenge could be mounted by any objector with full knowledge of the grounds relied upon. No argument was heard on the question of whether a judge had power to abridge the period of notice; nevertheless, even if such a power existed, any judge should be very slow to exercise it. It was added that the judge "has to take into account the interests of all the media, and not merely those of a watchful representative of the press who happens to have spotted an application for an *in camera* hearing of which short notice was given."[37]

G. A continuing tension

2-67 Nonetheless, at least until recently, the relationship between the media and the courts has been in some respects in an awkward state of transition. An especially thorny problem was that of how to handle questions to a journalist about sources.[38] There was a mutual distrust evident between the courts and investigative journalists in particular, which might to some extent be inevitable, but there was reason to hope that their respective responsibilities may be more readily defined in the light of the guidance given by the European Court of Human Rights in *Goodwin v United Kingdom*.[39]

---

[33] [1913] A.C. 417.
[34] [1979] A.C. 440.
[35] [1999] 1 W.L.R. 2130.
[36] See now r.16.10 of the Criminal Procedure Rules 2005.
[37] At 2147-8.
[38] See the discussion of s.10 at paras 9–53 *et seq*. See also *Goodwin v United Kingdom* (1996) 22 E.H.R.R. 123; *Chief Constable of Leicestershire v Garavelli* [1997] E.M.L.R. 543; *Att-Gen v Lundin* (1982) 75 Cr.App.R. 90. Contrast the more traditional approach in *Att-Gen v Mulholland; Att-Gen v Foster* [1963] 2 Q.B. 477, and more recently *Re an Inquiry Under the Companies (Insider Dealing Act 1985)* [1988] A.C. 660; *X Ltd v Morgan Grampian (Publishers) Ltd* [1991] 1 A.C. 1.
[39] (1996) 22 E.H.R.R. 123. It is clear that this approach towards the press, exemplified in that decision, was being followed very positively by the Divisional Court in *Chief Constable of Leicestershire v Garavelli* [1997] E.M.L.R. 543. But see the discussion of *Camelot Group plc v Centaur Communications Ltd* [1999] Q.B. 124 at paras 9–164 *et seq*. and *Interbrew SA v Financial Times Ltd* [2002] EWCA Civ 274, [2002] 2 Lloyd's Rep. 229, discussed at para.9-127.

There remains, however, a degree of scepticism, or at any rate caution. As 2–68
Thomas J. commented in the New Zealand case of *Police v O'Connor*[40]:

" . . . because the power of the press is great, a free press must be a responsible press. It must not abuse its power.
No responsible reporter or editor would cavil with such a requirement. Nonetheless, when exulting the concept of freedom of expression it is probably prudent to reiterate this caution lest the right be confused with an unlimited licence. The selection of which proceedings, or part of a proceeding, to report may be based on criteria and considerations which are largely unrelated to any wider notion of representing to the public the overall administration of justice. Sensationalism is not unknown. Moreover, in practice Court proceedings are sometimes misreported. At times the slant or angle taken may even appear mischievous. However, this only reinforces the need to ensure that the right of freedom of expression is exercised responsibly. Occasional shortcomings in the practice do not impair the right itself and, by and large, are to be accepted in the interests of securing a free and vigorous press".

To the process of news gathering and dissemination, the media can bring 2–69
enormous resources of manpower and money, reaching a huge audience or readership (sometimes international in scale). They can, depending on the extent to which they are uncontrolled, also exert a corresponding influence on what the public see and hear, quite possibly in a partisan way. Editors and journalists may sometimes behave irresponsibly. In circumstances where there is temptation to sensationalise at the expense of individual citizens whose rights are being in some way violated, it is the task of the law to give clear guidance as to what is and what is not permitted.[41]

III. FREE PRESS AND FAIR TRIAL

The tension between the two competing interests of freedom of communication 2–70
and of the right to a fair trial[42] has been conveniently summarised in the European Court of Human Rights[43]:

"Again it cannot be excluded that the public's becoming accustomed to the regular spectacle of pseudo-trials in the news media might in the long run have nefarious consequences for the acceptance of the courts as the proper forum for the settlement of legal disputes."

---

[40] [1992] 1 N.Z.L.R. 87 at 99. An order for the suppression of details of the punishment of a repeat offender who was using the courts to secure publicity for his cause could not be justified as "necessary" in the interests of justice.
[41] "The Court reiterates that, according to its case law, the relevant national law must be formulated with sufficient precision to enable the persons concerned—if need be with appropriate legal advice—to foresee, to a degree that is reasonable in the circumstances, the consequences which a given action may entail": *Goodwin v United Kingdom* (1996) 22 E.H.R.R. 123 at 140.
[42] More fully discussed in ch.4.
[43] *Sunday Times v United Kingdom* (1979) 2 E.H.R.R. 245 at para.63.

A similar point was made in *Allenet de Ribemont v France*[44] where it was said that "Art.6(2) cannot therefore prevent the authorities from informing the public about criminal investigations in progress, but it requires that they do so with all discretion and circumspection necessary if the presumption of innocence is to be respected".

A. The issues of principle[45]

2-71   There is a balance to be struck between the two "*desiderata*"[46] of fair and unencumbered trial, on the one hand, and the freedom of journalists to report and comment upon matters of public interest, on the other. In *Dagenais v Canadian Broadcasting Corp*,[47] Lamer C.J.C. rejected what he called the "clash model", a reference to the "clash between two titans—freedom of expression for the media versus the right to a fair trial for the accused." Amongst the positive advantages of media publicity that he identifies are that it may:

— "maximise the chances of individuals with relevant information hearing about a case and coming forward with new information;
— prevent perjury by placing witnesses under public scrutiny;
— prevent state and/or court wrongdoing by placing the criminal justice process under public scrutiny;
— reduce crime through the public expression of disapproval for crime; and
— promote the public discussion of important issues".

2-72   It must be said, however, that most of these advantages accrue to the public rather than to the accused, and that they relate to the reporting of court proceedings themselves rather than to pre-trial publicity. Historically, the scales under English law came down heavily in favour of seeking to ensure a fair trial.[48] It imposed liability strictly in the event of any prejudicial comment, or even pre-

---

[44] (1995) 20 E.H.R.R. 557.
[45] Mark R. Stabile, "Free Press-Fair Trial: Can they be Reconciled in a Highly Publicized Criminal Case?" (1990) 79 Georgetown Law Jo 337; A.W. Bradley, "Press Freedom, Governmental Constraints and the Privy Council" [1990] P.L. 453. For a suggestion that similar provisions to those of the Contempt of Court Act 1981 might be adopted in the United States of America, see S.J. Krause, "Punishing the Press: Using Contempt of Court to Secure the Right to a Fair Trial" [1996] 76 Boston Law Rev. 537. See also J. Watson, "Badmouthing the Bench: is There a Clear and Present Danger? To What?" (1992) 56 Saskatchewan Law Rev. 113. And see the discussion at para.2-122 of the same difficulties in the context of the European Convention. See also J. Godard, "*Contempt of court* en Angleterre et en Ecosse ou le controle des médias pour garantir le bon fonctionnement de la justice", *Revue de science criminelle et de droit pénal comparé* (April–June 2000); C.H. Whitebread and D.W. Contreras, "Free Press v Fair Trial: Protecting the Criminal Defendant's Rights in a Highly Publicized Trial by Applying the *Sheppard-Mu'Min* Remedy" (1996) 69 S. Cal. Law Rev. 1587; F. Robinson, "No, No! Sentence First—Verdict Afterwards. Freedom of the Press and Contempt by Publication" (2001) 23 Sydney L.R. 261 and the New South Wales Law Reform Commission, *Contempt by Publication* Discussion Paper No.43 (2000).
[46] *Att-Gen v MGN Ltd* [1997] 1 All E.R. 456 at 458h, Schiemann L.J.
[47] (1994) 120 D.L.R. 12 at 40–1.
[48] See paras 2–38 *et seq*. See also A.L. Goodhart, "Newspapers and Contempt of Court in England" (1935) 48 Harv. L.R. 885; A. Boyle, "Freedom of Expression as a Public Interest in English Law" [1982] P.L. 574.

judgment, where proceedings were pending or imminent. This gave rise to considerable concern in the years leading up to the 1981 enactment.[49]

There has been a gradual shifting of the balance in favour of freedom of the press in the courts, which is consistent with the purposes of Parliament in constructing the strict liability framework of the Contempt of Court Act 1981.[50] One almost inevitable countervailing consequence of this greater reluctance to impinge upon freedom of information has been that trials have had to be abandoned, or convictions quashed, as a result of media coverage; yet without necessarily any corresponding remedy or resort by means of the contempt jurisdiction against those responsible.[51]

2–73

This must be regarded as in some respects an unwelcome development, but it may be that it is the price that has to be paid.[52] In a prescient commentary on the decision of the European Court in *Sunday Times v United Kingdom*, F.A. Mann warned against precisely this consequence[53]:

2–74

"It is important to realise that a far-reaching inroad into the traditional law of contempt of court has been made. In a potentially wide variety of cases the European Court may assume a revising function and impose continental standards or, perhaps one should say, abuses upon this country which, in the name of freedom of the press and discussion, are likely to lower English usages by the substitution of trial by media for trial by courts. It is a matter for legislative concern whether this country is prepared to assume the risk to which it is now exposed. If the answer is in the negative a change of English law so as to comply with the standards of the Strasbourg judgment, yet to avoid trial by newspaper is unlikely to prove workable."

There have been a number of cases in which the courts have stayed proceedings because of prejudicial pre-trial publicity or unfair court reporting.[54] Issues were thus prevented from being canvassed which the public interest, and

2–75

---

[49] JUSTICE, *Report on Contempt of Court* (1959); JUSTICE, *Report on Law and the Press* (1965); Phillimore, *Report of the Committee on Contempt of Court*, Cmnd. 5794 (1974).
[50] Lloyd L.J. in *Att-Gen v Newspaper Publishing plc* [1988] Ch. 333 at 382D–F, cited at para.2–32.
[51] *R. v Cullen, McCann and Shanahan* (1990) 92 Cr.App.R. 239; *R. v Taylor and Taylor* (1993) 98 Cr.App.R. 361; *R. v Wood* [1996] 1 Cr.App.R. 207. See also B. Naylor, "Fair Trial or Free Press: Legal Responses to Media Reports of Criminal Trials" [1994] C.L.J. 492; D. Corker and M. Levi, "Pre-trial Publicity and its Treatment in the English Courts" [1996] Crim.L.R. 622.
[52] *Att-Gen v MGN Ltd* [1997] 1 All E.R. 456 at 466h, Schiemann L.J.
[53] (1979) 95 L.Q.R. 348 at 352.
[54] In *Att-Gen v MGN Ltd* [1997] 1 All E.R. 456, the court was informed by the Solicitor-General that no fewer than three cases in the previous six months had been halted as a result of prejudicial publicity. Over some years such applications had become more common. See also the cases cited at para.2–73, n.51 above. For another well publicised example, see *R. v Reade*, October 15, 1993, *The Independent*, October 19, where Garland J. stayed proceedings brought against policemen who were involved in the Birmingham Six case, publicity being a factor in his decision to stay. But see *R. v Alcindor* (Herald of Free Enterprise), June 11, 1990, Turner J. (application for stay refused); *R. v Thompson and Venables* (the Bulger case), November 1, 1993, Morland J. (application for stay refused). See also *Att-Gen v Morgan* [1998] E.M.L.R. 294; *Att-Gen v Associated Newspapers Ltd*, October 31, 1997 (Lexis).

perhaps in particular the interests of the "victims", required to be thoroughly investigated.[55]

2–76 *Att-Gen v MGN Ltd*[56] was an illustration of the considerable gap which exists between the law relating to abuse of process, whereby a judge may abandon criminal proceedings on the basis that media publicity has rendered it impossible to hold a fair trial, and the law of contempt. Schiemann L.J. explained[57]:

> "A consequence of the need in contempt proceedings, in which respondents face imprisonment or a fine, to be sure and look at each publication separately and the need in trial proceedings to look at the risk of prejudice created by the totality of publications can be that it is proper to stay proceedings on the grounds of prejudice albeit that no individual is guilty of contempt. One may regret that situation or one may take the view that it is the best answer to a difficult problem."

2–77 Even though the media as a whole might, in a particular case, create a barrage of prejudice, the contribution of any individual respondent has in contempt proceedings to be considered separately. Moreover, each case of alleged contempt has to be proved according to the criminal standard; this is not so with an application for stay on the grounds of abuse of process, where the civil standard will suffice. Phillips J. in *Maxwell*[58] expressed the test to be applied as follows:

> "It seems to me that the court will only be justified in staying a trial on the ground of adverse pre-trial publicity, if satisfied *on balance of probabilities* that if the jury return a verdict of guilty, the effect of the pre-trial publicity will be such as to render that verdict unsafe and unsatisfactory." (emphasis added).

2–78 The point at which a judgment has to be made as to whether it is going to be possible to have a fair trial is that when the trial is due to take place. In *R. v Vermette*,[59] the Supreme Court of Canada took the view that it had been premature to stay the trial prior to jury selection. Highly prejudicial remarks had been made by the Premier in the National Assembly in the course of a trial, as a result of which the trial was discontinued and a new trial ordered. Motions were

---

[55] B. Naylor, "Fair Trial or Free Press: Legal Responses to Media Reports of Criminal Trials" [1994] C.L.J. 492.

[56] [1997] 1 All E.R. 456. Discussed more fully at paras 4–155 *et seq*. But see paras 16–301 *et seq*. for the position in Scotland, discussing *inter alia*, *HMA v The Daily Record and The Sun* (1997) 9 Media Lawyer 28. There may be a detectable trend in more recent Scottish decisions towards an approach more consistent with that in England and Wales—not least a willingness to take into account the factors identified in *Att-Gen v MGN Ltd*. This is hardly surprising given that the judges in both jurisdictions have been striving to comply with the values of the European Convention.

[57] *ibid*. at 466g–h. See too the detailed discussion in *Att-Gen v Birmingham Post and Mail Ltd* [1998] 4 All E.R. 49.

[58] March 6, 1995, unreported. Phillips J. cited Sir Roger Ormerod in *R. v Derby Crown Court Ex p. Brookes* (1984) 80 Cr.App.R. 164 at 168–9: "It may be an abuse of process if . . . on the balance of probability the defendant has been, or will be, prejudiced in the preparations or conduct of his defence . . . ": transcript p.72. He also cited Morland J. in *R. v Thompson and Venables*, November 1, 1993: "No stay should be imposed unless the defendant shows on the balance of probabilities that owing to the extent and the nature of the pre-trial publicity he will suffer serious prejudice to the extent that no fair trial can be held."

[59] (1988) 41 C.C.C. (3d) 523.

successfully brought, before the retrial, seeking to quash the information, and also seeking a stay of the pending proceedings on the ground of abuse of process. The appeal by the Crown was allowed. The test for abuse of process was not confined to whether there was an actual interference with the applicant's guaranteed rights, but would extend also to an apprehended interference at a future trial. Yet the question whether it would be possible for the accused to be tried by an impartial jury arose only at the time when the jury were to be selected rather than in advance.

B. The traditional approach

Notwithstanding that a finding of contempt in cases of prejudicial publicity necessarily involves also a finding that a real risk of prejudice has been created, the courts were until recently reluctant to follow through the apparent logic to quashing convictions. The willingness to acknowledge retrospectively that a criminal trial might have been tainted by prejudicial media publicity is a relatively recent development; formerly the courts were generally reluctant to accept that the process had been adversely affected. 2–79

This was true in *R. v Savundranayagan*,[60] for example, one of the cases that prompted the establishment of the Phillimore Committee. The Court of Appeal was quite satisfied that, in the particular circumstances, there had been no real risk of the jury's being influenced by the pre-trial publicity. Salmon L.J. also observed that the case for the Crown was "so overwhelming that no jury could conceivably have returned any different verdicts against Savundra". 2–80

In former times, prejudice could be caused by the perfectly fair and accurate reporting of preliminary hearings at which, typically, only the evidence for the prosecution was presented.[61] Similarly, bail applications used to take place in open court, and thus inevitably there were occasions when a defendant's record could find its way into the newspapers. Nevertheless, in *Armstrong*,[62] the Court of Criminal Appeal held that, although such a disclosure in the press was undesirable, it was not in itself a ground for quashing the conviction in the case where the evidence of the defendant's guilt was clear. Lynskey J. added, somewhat sweepingly, " . . . the fact that such information is given is no ground for this Court to infer either that the jurors who tried the case had read it or that, 2–81

---

[60] [1968] 1 W.L.R. 1761, 3 All E.R. 439. In addition, the court took the view that, by agreeing to appear on television, the appellant was to some extent the author of his own misfortune: "It hardly lies in his mouth to complain".
[61] See, *e.g. R. v Fisher* (1811) 2 Camp. 563 at 570, 170 E.R. 1253 at 1255, Lord Ellenborough. Restraints were first imposed by the Criminal Justice Act 1967, s.3. See G.J. Webber, "Trial by Newspaper" (1958) C.L.P. 37. The modern law governing restrictions placed upon the reporting of committal proceedings (and the new procedures of "allocation and sending") is discussed in ch.8.
[62] (1951) 35 Cr.App.R. 72. See the comment by Glanville Williams, (1952) 15 M.L.R. 98 who maintained that all commentators accepted that this was an area of the law that cried out for reform.

2–81 if they had read it, ... they were unfit to try the case or biased against the prisoner for the purpose of the trial".

2–82 It would appear that *Dyson*[63] was the first case in which a conviction was quashed on the ground of prejudicial publicity. The evidence in the case was described as "very short, and really overwhelming". It was a shoplifting case in which an assistant had seen the appellant put a number of pairs of socks under his coat, and he was caught red-handed outside the shop. Nevertheless, the point was taken that at the committal hearing his 40 previous convictions had been read out and reported in the local newspaper. Not surprisingly, this was described as "a most unfortunate complication". The appeal was allowed and the conviction quashed "in the special circumstances of this particular case."

2–83 These words were fixed upon in the later case of *Armstrong*, where Lynskey J. emphasised that the court had not been laying down any rule to the effect that merely because a newspaper, either local or national, discloses what has happened at the magistrates' court, any conviction should be quashed on that ground alone. Thus, the example of *Dyson* remained something of a *rara avis* for many years.

2–84 A typically robust approach was taken in *R. v Box*,[64] where it emerged upon a reference by the Home Secretary that, over the short adjournment during a criminal trial, after the evidence had been completed, the foreman of the jury had commented to two non-jurors, in a local hotel, that he did not need to hear the evidence, and would see that the defendants got 10 years. The Court of Criminal Appeal declined to hear the evidence of the two non-jurors but received that of the foreman himself *de bene esse*. He revealed to the court that he had known of the defendants before the trial and had heard, in particular, that they were ex-burglars, villains, and associates of prostitutes. Moreover he knew that one of the two defendants had recently come out of prison. Nevertheless, although he admitted that he was biased against the defendants, he claimed to have formed his view of their guilt only as the case went on.

2–85 It was held that knowledge of a defendant's character or previous convictions by a member of the jury was not an automatic disqualification for fitness to serve; and that, there being no evidence that the foreman had failed to observe his oath or to give the defendants a fair trial, the court was of the view that there had been no miscarriage of justice. It would have been desirable, however, for the foreman to have asked the clerk of the court to be excused, stating the reasons and thus to be made exempt from sitting. Indeed, the view was expressed by Lord Parker C.J. that it was quite improper for the foreman not to have done so in that case. Despite this, the appeals were dismissed.

---

[63] (1943) 29 Cr.App.R. 104.
[64] [1964] 1 Q.B. 430. The case was referred to in *R. v Barraclough* [2000] Crim. L.R. 325 discussed at para.2–121 and, rather surprisingly in the then climate, relied upon to support the proposition that knowledge of previous convictions did not necessarily lead to a real danger of bias. See the remarks on the case by Professor Birch [2000] Crim.L.R. at p.326.

In a similar vein, Lawton J. in *R. v Kray*[65] indicated that a robust direction to 2–86
the jury could cure any potential miscarriage of justice:

"It is . . . a matter of human experience, and certainly a matter of experience of those who practice in the Criminal Courts, first, that the public's recollection is short, and, secondly, that the drama, if I may use that term, of a trial almost always has the effect of excluding from recollection that which went before".[66]

The practical problem for the courts is how far it is sensible to give jurors 2–87
credit for an ability to set prejudice to one side in compliance with their oaths.
This was recognised by the Ontario Court of Appeal in *R. v Hubbert*[67]:

"In this era of rapid dissemination of news by various media, it would be naive to think that in the case of a crime involving considerable notoriety, it would be possible to select 12 jurors who had not heard anything about the case. Prior information about a case and even the holding of a tentative opinion about it, does not make partial a juror sworn to render a true verdict according to the evidence".

In *R. v Hemming*,[68] a potentially prejudicial photograph of the defendant was 2–88
published in the course of the trial. Counsel drew the photograph to the attention
of the trial judge and asked that the jury be discharged. The jury were brought
back in to court and asked by the judge whether any of them had been prejudiced
by the publication. When the jury indicated that they had not, the judge refused
the application. The appeal against conviction was dismissed, but the court said
that the proper course in such circumstances was for the judge to make his own
assessment as to likelihood of prejudice and then either discharge the jury or
instruct them to put the incident out of their minds.

As to the susceptibility of jurors to extraneous influence, there seem to have 2–89
been two apparently conflicting strands of thought among the judiciary. Sometimes there was an apparent readiness to restrain or punish media publications on

---

[65] (1969) 53 Cr.App.R. 413 (on an application to poll the jury as to their prior knowledge of the events that they were about to consider in the course of trial). And see Lawton L.J. in *R. v Young and Coughlan* (1976) 63 Cr.App.R. 33, 37; Lord Denning M.R. in *R. v Horsham Justices Ex p. Farquharson* [1982] 1 Q.B. 672, 795A; Sir John Donaldson M.R. in *Att-Gen v News Group Newspapers plc* [1987] 1 Q.B. 1, 16; *Ex p. The Telegraph plc* [1993] 1 W.L.R. 980 at 987, Taylor C.J.; *Ex p. B*, February 17, 1994, Scott Baker J.: "Increasingly these days publicity is advanced as a reason why it is impossible for the defendants to have a fair trial in a particular place or sometimes anywhere. In most cases, one day's headline is the next day's firelighter. Most members of the public do not remember in any detail what they have seen on television, heard on the radio or read in the newspaper except for a very short period of time." See also Lord Donaldson M.R. in *Leary v BBC*, September 29, 1989 (Lexis): "It is idle to think that the courts can cocoon juries against all outside influences, and I agree with Lawton J. in the case of *R. v Kray* (1969) 53 Cr.App.R. 412 in which he said that they do show a remarkable ability to ignore outside comment. That is truer in long cases where the jury has become more and more—I will not say 'mesmerised' by the evidence—but has become more and more involved in the evidence than it has in the shorter cases, but even in the shorter case juries do, by and large, conscientiously follow that warning".
[66] See, *e.g. R. v Young and Coughlan* (1976) 63 Cr.App.R. 33, 37; *Ex p. The Telegraph plc* [1993] 1 W.L.R. 980 at 987, (1994) 98 Cr.App.R. 91 at 98, Lord Taylor C.J. In Canada, the same approach was adopted by the Supreme Court in *R. v Corbett* (1988) 41 C.C.C. (3d) 385, [1988] 1 S.C.R. 670 and in *R. v Vermette* (1988) 41 C.C.C. (3d) 523. In Australia, see *R. v Glennon* (1992) 173 C.L.R. 592.
[67] (1975) 29 C.C.C. (2d) 279, 291. See also the robust remarks of Addy J. cited at para.4–162.
[68] [1985] Crim.L.R. 395.

2–89 CHAPTER 2—CONTEMPT OF COURT: CONSTITUTIONAL DIMENSIONS

the basis that the material in question was likely to influence jurors. On the other hand, a more robust approach was taken when it came to challenging convictions on appeal. In that context, it seems to have been readily accepted that possible prejudice would have been overcome with the help of directions by the trial judge.

2–90 In a series of cases more recently, however, the courts have acknowledged that particularly prejudicial material might indeed have rendered a conviction unsafe, or been such as to make the conduct of a fair trial impossible.

2–91 This is illustrated by *R. v McCann, Cullen and Shanahan*[69] where a former Master of the Rolls,[70] the then Home Secretary, had both made adverse comments about the right to silence, even as it was being exercised by persons on trial at Winchester. Convictions for conspiracy to murder, and 25 year gaol sentences, were quashed. The court took the view that the prejudicial impact of the publicity was such that "the only way in which justice could be done and be obviously seen to be done was by discharging the jury and ordering a retrial."[71] Since that had not been done, the verdict of the jury was unsafe, and the convictions were quashed.

2–92 Similarly, in *R. v Taylor and Taylor*[72] where the press coverage, purportedly of the trial itself, was couched in language endorsed by the Court of Appeal as being "unremitting, extensive, sensational, inaccurate and misleading". It included such headlines as "The Killer Mistress who was at Lover's Wedding," and "Love Crazy Mistress Butchered Rival Wife Court Told". The court had been told no such thing. Purported coverage of the trial was illustrated with a still photograph taken from a video tape of the victim's wedding (which "had no relevance to the trial and was not played at it"), showing one of the defendants kissing the groom (her lover). "They froze the frame so that the peck on the cheek was made to appear a mouth-to-mouth kiss". McCowan L.J. concluded[73]:

> "What, in fact, they did was not reporting at all; it was comment, and comment which assumed guilt on the part of the girls in the dock. But the Press is no more entitled to assume guilt in what it writes during the course of a trial, than a police officer is entitled to convince himself that a defendant is guilty and suppress evidence, the emergence of which he fears might lead to the defendant's acquittal".

2–93 The court took the view that it was "impossible to say that the jury were not influenced in their decision by what they read in the press", and acted upon the principle, enunciated in *R. v McCann*, that "if the media coverage at trial has created a real risk of prejudice against the defendants, the conviction should be

---

[69] (1991) 92 Cr.App.R. 239.
[70] Lord Denning's own account of the incidents giving rise to the appeal is to be found in [1990] Crim.L.R. 535.
[71] (1991) 92 Cr.App.R. at 253.
[72] (1993) 98 Cr.App.R. 361.
[73] *ibid.* at 369.

regarded as unsafe and unsatisfactory."[74] Despite the judge having given the jury several warnings to decide the case on the evidence alone, and repeated that in the course of his summing up, the convictions were quashed on the ground *inter alia* of possible prejudice. Furthermore, because of the prejudice, no retrial was ordered.

It would seem to follow that, since the offending material fell outside anything that could be called "a fair and accurate report", this would not have come within the good faith reporting formula under s.4(1).[75] Notwithstanding this, and despite the fact that the court ordered the papers to be sent to the Attorney-General for his consideration, no proceedings for contempt were brought against the newspapers concerned, and the High Court declined to grant judicial review of his refusal to do so.[76] **2–94**

A retrial was, however, ordered in *R. v Wood*.[77] There was held to have been a possibility of prejudice as a result of pre-trial reporting. One of the articles might well have led potential jurors to conclude that there was evidence of guilt which could not be produced in court. On the ground of this possible prejudice, combined with another ground of appeal, a retrial was ordered. The court recognised that it would be for the trial judge in due course to consider afresh any application based on lingering prejudice. **2–95**

More recently judges have begun to recognise the apparent inconsistency between the two strands of thought on jurors' supposed susceptibility, and have accepted the need for reconciliation. In *Att-Gen v MGN Ltd*[78] the Divisional Court was ready to adopt, on a contempt motion, the same robust attitude towards the independence and objectivity of jurors, or potential jurors, as had been taken in the past in cases involving appeals against conviction.[79] **2–96**

This was consistent with the approach taken in *Ex p. The Telegraph plc*,[80] where Lord Taylor C.J. had said that "a court should credit the jury with the will and ability to abide by the judge's direction to decide the case only on the evidence before them", and referred to the limited staying power of media publicity, even in cases of notoriety. In *R. v Cannan*,[81] he had pointed out that **2–97**

---

[74] At 369.
[75] Considered at paras 4–265 *et seq.*
[76] *R. v Solicitor-General Ex p. Taylor* [1995] C.O.D. 61 (Lexis). The refusal of the court to interfere has been criticised, on the ground that it appears to exempt the Law Officers alone from the ambit of judicial review: J. Miller and D. Feldman, note, (1997) L.Q.R. 36. Compare the position in South Australia, where the Attorney-General's prosecutorial discretion is regarded as not reviewable: see, e.g. *R. v Von Einem* (1990) 55 S.A.S.R. 199.
[77] [1996] 1 Cr.App.R. 207.
[78] [1997] 1 All E.R. 456, considered at paras 4–155 *et seq*. See in particular the important comment of Simon Brown L.J. in *Att-Gen v Unger* [1998] 1 Cr.App.R. 308 at 318E–F, E.M.L.R. 280 at 291, cited at para.2–98 and para.4–169. See now J.M. Oliveira, "Speaking with two voices: The tension between strict liability contempt and abuse of process in the context of adverse pre-trial publicity" [2001] H.K.L.J. 459.
[79] e.g. *R. v Coughlan* (1976) 63 Cr.App.R. 33 at 37; *R. v Cannan* (1990) 92 Cr.App.R. 16.
[80] [1993] 1 W.L.R. 980 at 987E.
[81] (1990) 92 Cr.App.R. 16.

2–97 CHAPTER 2—CONTEMPT OF COURT: CONSTITUTIONAL DIMENSIONS

juries are trusted to do justice in cases of sexual offences, where the risk of prejudice is self-evidently greater.

2–98 The apparent dichotomy between the two lines of authority was expressly referred to by Simon Brown L.J. in *Att-Gen v Unger*,[82] where he made the following significant comment:

> "It seems to me important in these cases that the courts do not speak with two voices, one used to dismiss criminal appeals with the court roundly rejecting any suggestion that prejudice resulted from media publications, the other holding comparable publications to be in contempt, the courts on these occasions expressing grave doubts as to the jury's ability to forget or put aside what they have heard or read.
>
> I am certainly not saying that in respect of one and the same publication there cannot be both a contempt (of the present, outcome, sort) and a safe conviction. Plainly there can, most obviously perhaps in cases where the trial has had to be moved or delayed to minimise the prejudice occasioned by some publication. But generally speaking it seems to me that unless a publication materially affects the course of trial in that kind of way, or requires directions from the court well beyond those ordinarily required and routinely given to juries to focus their attention on evidence called before them rather than whatever they may have heard or read outside court, or creates at the very least a seriously arguable ground for an appeal on the basis of prejudice, it is unlikely to be vulnerable to contempt proceedings under the strict liability rule."

C. Developments in other common law jurisdictions

2–99 The law of contempt being a creature of the common law, it is important to take account of developments in other jurisdictions. Some countries, including Canada and New Zealand, now have a Charter or Bill of Rights,[83] which includes protection for freedom of speech. The High Court of Australia has held, in the absence of legislative intervention, that there is an implied constitutional right to communicate on political and governmental matters.[84]

2–100 In *Dagenais v Canadian Broadcasting Corp*[85] the Supreme Court of Canada, by a majority came closer to an American/European approach to the protection of rights, and refused to censor the media's coverage of an impending trial. New

---

[82] [1998] 1 Cr.App.R. 308 at 318–19, [1998] E.M.L.R. 280 at 291, D.C. These remarks were re-visited by Simon Brown L.J. in *Att-Gen v Birmingham Post and Mail Ltd* [1998] 4 All E.R. 49, discussed in ch.4.

[83] More generally, see S. Kentridge Q.C, "Bills of Rights—the South African Experiment" (1996) 112 L.Q.R. 237; Sir R. Cooke, "Brass Tacks and Bills of Rights" (1995) 25 H.K.L.J. 64.

[84] The litigation has been, for the most part, in the context of the law of defamation. But there is no reason why, in principle, similar considerations would not extend to the law of contempt. See, *e.g. Australian Capital Television Pty Ltd v The Commonwealth* (1992) 177 C.L.R. 106, HC; *Nationwide News Ltd v Wills* (1992) 177 C.L.R. 1, HC; *Theophanous v Herald & Weekly Times Ltd* (1994) 68 A.L.J.R. 713, HC; *Stephens v West Australia Newspapers Ltd* (1994) 68 A.L.J.R. 765, HC; *Lange v Australian Broadcasting Corp* (1997) 71 A.L.J.R. 818, HC; *Levy v Victoria* (1997) 189 C.L.R. 579. See generally M. Chesterman, *Freedom of Speech in Australian Law: A Delicate Plant* (2000). Contrast the position in Canada. See, *e.g. Manning v Hill* (1995) 126 D.L.R. (4th) 129, SCC, which points out that allowing the free speech principle too free a rein is a disincentive to people to engage in the democratic process, *e.g.* by standing for election. And see *Globe and Mail v Boland* [1960] S.C.R. 203, (1960) 22 D.L.R. (2d) 277.

[85] (1994) 120 D.L.R. (4th) 12; see also *Phillips v Nova Scotia (Westray Inquiry)* (1995) 98 C.C.C. (3d) 20.

Zealand, by contrast, which has now to reconcile the free speech requirements of the Bill of Rights Act 1990 with the right to a fair trial, appears to have reaffirmed the classical[86] common law approach, the Court of Appeal having declined to follow the Supreme Court of Canada.[87]

The Court in *Gisborne Herald Co Ltd v Solicitor General*[88] acknowledged that the law of contempt made certain long-held assumptions about how jurors might behave if exposed to potentially prejudicial material. Richardson J. explained why the New Zealand Court of Appeal was unwilling to adopt the reasoning of the Supreme Court of Canada in *Dagenais*:

2–101

> "First, the complex process of balancing the values underlying free expression and fair trial rights may vary from country to country, even though there is a common and genuine commitment to international human rights norms. The balancing will be influenced by the culture and values of the particular community.... The result of the balancing process will necessarily reflect the court's assessment of society's values.
> ... Second, there is a lack of data on which the courts could confidently rely as justifying a change in the balancing of free expression/fair trial values.
> ... absence of current empirical data to support a long-standing assumption in public policy is not, in our view, adequate justification for shifting policy ground in favour of another approach which is also deficient in supporting policy data and analysis. The present rule is that, where on the conventional analysis freedom of expression and fair trial rights cannot both be fully assured, it is appropriate in our free and democratic society to temporarily curtail freedom of media expression so as to guarantee a fair trial.
> Third, and again in the absence of any adequate empirical data, we are not persuaded that the alternative measures suggested by Lamer C.J.C.[89] in *Dagenais* should be treated as an adequate protection in this country against the intrusion of potentially prejudicial material into the public domain."

The "lack of data" has to an extent been remedied by the content of a New Zealand Law Commission paper published in November 1999, which suggests that the impact of potentially prejudicial material in the media is very slight.[90] Nonetheless, in the later case of *Solicitor-General v W&H Specialist Publication*[91] Elias C.J., having re-emphasised that the burden always lies on the Crown to establish a real risk of prejudice, went on to state:

---

[86] That is, giving priority to fair trial over freedom of information, and requiring reporting to be postponed. See paras 2–38 and para.2–72.

[87] *Gisborne Herald Co Ltd v Solicitor-General* [1995] 3 N.Z.L.R. 563. See also John McGrath Q.C. "Contempt and the Media: Constitutional Safeguard or State Censorship" (1998) N.Z.L. Rev. 371. Mr McGrath was then the Solicitor General for New Zealand and later (2000) became a member of the New Zealand Court of Appeal, and in 2005 of the Supreme Court.

[88] [1995] 3 N.Z.L.R. 563.

[89] See para.2–102.

[90] Law Commission, preliminary paper No.37, Young, Cameron and Tinsley, *Juries in Criminal Trials, Part Two*. This has been supplemented by the Law Commission Report, *Juries in Criminal Trials* (February 2001). This research has been referred to in *Montgomery v HMA* [2003] 1 A.C. 641 (P.C.). Such research would still be precluded in England and Wales by reason of s.8 of the Contempt of Court Act 1981. See the discussion at paras 11–349 *et seq.* and *R. v Connor, R. v Mirza* [2004] UKH.L. 2, [2004] 1 A.C. 1118; *R. v Smith (Patrick)* [2005] UKHL 12, [2005] 1 W.L.R.704; *Att-Gen v Scotcher* [2005] UKHL 36, [2005] 1 W.L.R. 1867, [2005] 3 All E.R. 1. See now the Consultation paper CP04/05, *Jury Research and Impropriety* (January 21, 2005) prepared by the Department for Constitutional Affairs.

[91] [2003] N.Z.A.R. 118 at [19].

2–101 CHAPTER 2—CONTEMPT OF COURT: CONSTITUTIONAL DIMENSIONS

"On the other hand, where there is a real risk of trial prejudice, a temporary restraint on freedom to publish is preferable to the uncertain countermeasures available such as a firm direction from the judge that such pre-trial publicity is to be ignored or changes of venue (where publication is local)".

D. Minimising the risk of prejudice without restricting free speech

2–102 There are various devices of which the courts could, in theory, avail themselves if it was thought appropriate to try and avoid or reduce the prejudicial impact of media communication, short of imposing an outright ban. Some of these have been explored in other common law jurisdictions. For example, in *Dagenais v Canadian Broadcasting Corp.*,[92] where the court was considering the possibility of enjoining the broadcast of a "docudrama", Lamer C.J.C. suggested a number of alternative measures:

"Possibilities that readily come to mind, however, include adjourning trials, changing venues, sequestering jurors, allowing challenges for cause and *voir dires* during jury selection, and providing strong judicial direction to the jury."

2–103 The need to investigate these possibilities arose from the fact that the adoption of the Canadian Charter of Rights and Freedoms had altered the traditional balance as between free press and fair trial. Lamer C.J.C. explained[93]:

"The pre-Charter common-law rule governing publication bans emphasised the right to a fair trial over the free expression interests of those affected by the ban. ... the balance this rule strikes is inconsistent with the principles of the Charter, and in particular, the equal status given by the Charter to ss.2(b)[94] and 11(d).[95] It would be inappropriate for the courts to continue to apply a common-law rule that automatically favoured the rights protected by s.11(d) over those protected by s.2(b). A hierarchical approach to rights, which places some over others, must be avoided, both when interpreting the Charter and when developing the common law. When the protected rights of two individuals come into conflict, as can occur in the case of publication bans, Charter principles require a balance[96] to be achieved that fully respects the importance of both sets of rights.
... the common-law rule must be adapted so as to require a consideration both of the objectives of a publication ban, and the proportionality of the ban to its effect on protected Charter rights. The modified rule may be stated as follows:

'A publication ban should only be ordered when:

---

[92] (1994) 94 C.C.C. (3d) 289, 317, (1994) 120 D.L.R. (4th) 12, 40d–e.
[93] (1994) 12 D.L.R. at 37–8. For a comparable shift within this jurisdiction, see Lloyd L.J's remarks in *Att-Gen v Newspaper Publishing plc* [1988] Ch. 333 at 382D–F, cited at para.2–32.
[94] Which provides that "everyone has the following fundamental freedoms: ... (b) freedom of thought, belief, opinion and expression, including freedom of the press and other media of communication."
[95] Any person charged with an offence has the right " ... (d) to be presumed innocent until proven guilty according to law in a fair and public hearing by an independent and impartial tribunal".
[96] The terminology of "balancing" might be contrasted with that of the European Court of Human Rights, as explained in *Sunday Times v United Kingdom* (1979) 2 E.H.R.R. 245 at 281. See the observations of Lord Fraser in *Att-Gen v BBC* [1981] A.C. 303 at 352B–F, cited at para.2–157. But see *Re S(FC) (A Child)* [2004] UKHL, [2005] 1 A.C. 593 at para.6–44 and para.6–87.

(a) Such a ban is *necessary* in order to prevent a real and substantial risk to the fairness of the trial, because reasonably available alternative measures will not prevent the risk; and
(b) The salutary effects of the publication ban outweigh the deleterious effects to the free expression of those affected by the ban.'

... To assess the validity of the order in the case at bar, it is necessary to consider the objective of the order, to examine the availability of reasonable alternative measures that could achieve this objective, and to consider whether the salutary effects of the publication ban outweigh the deleterious impact the ban has on freedom of expression."

It is proposed to examine *seriatim* the suggestions made by Lamer C.J.C.[97] as to the ways in which the possibilities of prejudice might be minimised using the traditional methods available at common law.

1. *Postponement of the trial*

The first possibility for avoiding prejudice suggested by Lamer C.J.C. was that the trial might be postponed. But delay[98] may cause prejudice to the defendant; summarised in the truism that "justice delayed is justice denied." Furthermore, Art.6(1) of the European Convention provides that "everyone is entitled to a fair and public hearing within a reasonable time".[99] The result of a postponement may mean that a defendant is subjected to a further, perhaps prolonged period of pre-trial imprisonment; memories fade, and there is a risk that relevant evidence may be lost or deteriorate.[1] Any of these factors may lead to prejudice to one side or the other.

2. *Change of venue*[2]

It may be the case that prejudice caused by publicity is relatively local,[3] and the jury selection, taken as it is from the electoral roll, is also local. One of the factors that is taken into account in assessing the risk of prejudice is the locality in which

---

[97] See para.2–102.
[98] See generally, *Archbold 2005*, paras 4–66 *et seq.*; A. L.-T. Choo, *Abuse of Process and Judicial Stays of Criminal Proceedings* (1993) Oxford University Press, particularly ch.3, "Delay".
[99] The Canadian Charter, s.11(b) considered in *R. v Morin* (1992) 71 C.C.C. (3d) 1 is similarly phrased.
[1] See *R. v Telford Justices Ex p. Badhan* [1991] 2 Q.B. 78, D.C. In *R. v Bow Street Metropolitan Stipendiary Magistrate Ex p. DPP* (1992) 95 Cr.App.R. 9, it was considered that a delay of some 18 years would not necessarily prevent the respondents from securing a fair trial, even though the court recognised that they would inevitably suffer some prejudice as a result of the lapse of time. In *R. v Magee* (unreported), January 23, 1997 (Woolwich Crown Court), Maurice Kay J. concluded that, apart from prejudice caused by an *Evening Standard* feature article, there had been so much delay that it was causing unfairness. There was also medical evidence that some of the defendants were beginning to deteriorate mentally; see also for the consequent contempt proceedings *Att-Gen v Associated Newspapers Ltd*, October 31, 1997 (Lexis), Kennedy L.J. cited at paras 4–60 *et seq.*
[2] N. Vidmar and J.W.T. Judson, "The Use of Social Science Data in a Change of Venue Application: A Case Study" (1981) 59 Can. Bar Rev. 76.
[3] *Att-Gen v News Group Newspapers plc* [1987] Q.B. 1; *Att-Gen v Independent Television News Ltd* [1995] 2 All E.R. 370, 1 Cr.App.R. 204; *Att-Gen v MGN Ltd* [1997] 1 All E.R. 456; *Att-Gen v Birmingham Post and Mail Ltd* [1998] 4 All E.R. 49 (case transferred from Birmingham to Leicester).

the case is to be heard: "To declare in a speech at a public meeting in Cornwall that a man about to be tried in Durham is guilty of the offence charged and has many previous convictions for the same offence may well carry no substantial risk of affecting his trial . . . ".[4] One possible solution might therefore be to move the trial from the place where the prejudice is said to have occurred. The decision whether or not to transfer a particular case is pre-eminently a matter for the discretion of the trial judge.[5]

2–107 A transfer may cause logistical difficulties; there may well be considerable inconvenience to witnesses and defendants. In addition, it is thought desirable that a person should be tried in the area where the offence took place.[6] In *R. v Vincent*,[7] an application was made to the High Court to change the venue of a trial where reporting restrictions of committal proceedings had been lifted against the wishes of two of the three co-defendants. The applicants contended that there was considerable local feeling and that pre-trial publicity materially prejudiced the prospect of a fair and impartial trial in Hampshire. Granting the application, the court said that, but for the Criminal Justice Act of 1967 which first imposed reporting restrictions upon committal proceedings, the application would not have stood a chance. In imposing reporting restrictions upon committal proceedings, Parliament must be presumed to have acted because of an apprehension that jurors might be influenced.

2–108 Historically, the initial determination as to place of the trial of either way offences has been taken by "examining magistrates", who were obliged to consider the convenience of witnesses and the expediting of the trial. No mention was specifically made of the need to guard against local prejudice. Section 7 of the Magistrates' Courts Act 1980[8] did, however, provide that the magistrates' court must also have regard to any directions given by the Lord Chief Justice under s.75(1) of the Supreme Court Act 1981.[9] Yet again, no specific provision has been made in any Practice Direction to deal with local prejudice. By contrast, s.76(1) of the Supreme Court Act does provide that the Crown Court may itself give directions altering the place of any trial on indictment. If a party was dissatisfied with a place of trial fixed by the magistrates or by the Crown Court, he had to apply for a direction varying the place of trial in open court before a

---

[4] [1987] 1 Q.B. 1, 15, *per* Donaldson M.R.
[5] *R. v Scott* [1994] Crim. L.R. 947.
[6] See Richardson J. in *Gisborne Herald Co Ltd v Solicitor-General* [1995] 3 N.Z.L.R. 563 at 575. The rule is one of some antiquity, and there are old authorities to the effect that there must be a clear and solid foundation for an application for change of venue; in *R. v Harris* (1762) 3 Burr. 1330, 1334, 97 E.R. 858 at 860, for example, Wilmot J. is reported as follows: " . . . there was no rule better established, he said, than, 'that all causes shall be tried in the county, and by the neighbourhood of the place, where the fact is committed'. And therefore that rule ought never to be infringed, unless it plainly appears that a fair and impartial trial cannot be had in that county." Denison and Foster JJ. made remarks to very similar effect.
[7] [1968] Crim.L.R. 405.
[8] The section is to be repealed by the Criminal Justice 2003, ss.41, 332, Sch.3, Pt 2, para.51(1),(3), Sch.37, Pt 4 from a date to be appointed.
[9] Now governed by *Practice Direction: (Criminal Proceedings: Consolidation)* [2002] 1 W.L.R. 2870, Pt III.21 and IV.31–33 (as amended by Amendment No.12). For the latest version of the *Direction* see www.courtservice.gov.uk/docs/cpd/consol_criminal_pd_220305.doc.

judge of the High Court.[10] These restrictions have now been removed by the Courts Act 2003, s.86, which came in to force on May 1, 2004.

The Act does not indicate any specific factors to be taken into account, but there is older authority to the effect that local prejudice is regarded as relevant. In *R. v Phelan*,[11] it was held that a change of venue should be ordered where it is clearly shown that the circumstances in the intended place of trial are such that it is unlikely that a fair and impartial trial could be held there.

2–109

3. *Sequestering the jurors*

Another suggestion made by Lamer C.J.C.[12] was that of censoring what the jury can see whilst the case is actually in progress. If necessary, this could be done by keeping the members of the jury together. There are difficulties with this suggestion. Such a practice would add considerably, perhaps intolerably, to the burden of being a member of a jury.[13]

2–110

At common law, the jurors were not permitted to separate once a trial had begun. Indeed, at one time members of the jury had no right to food, drink or light.[14] This was conducive to the making of speedy judgments. There was also an assumption that, if the jury were permitted to separate, they might engage in improper communication with other persons. The harshness of this treatment has been gradually relaxed, and a greater willingness to trust the jury to honour the oath has slowly emerged.[15]

2–111

A somewhat crude distinction was drawn. The fact that a juror might have discussed the case with outsiders before the summing up would not normally render the trial abortive unless it appeared that the discussion had been such as

2–112

---

[10] Supreme Court Act 1981, s.76(3), (4) as amended. It may be noted in passing that in *R. v McCann, Cullen and Shanahan* (1990) 92 Cr.App.R. 239, one of the cases in which convictions were quashed for possible prejudice, an application for change of venue had been refused. In *R. v Coghill* [1995] 3 N.Z.L.R. 651 at 662, CA, it was said that a defendant who has not sought a change of venue to avoid allegedly prejudicial effects on the trial, such as the effect of adverse pre-trial publicity, will rarely be able to raise a claim after conviction that such factors produced a miscarriage of justice.
[11] (1881) 14 Cox 579. See also *R. v Palmer* (1856) 5 E. & B. 1024, 119 E.R. 762; and for modern examples, *Att-Gen v Birmingham Post and Mail Ltd* [1998] 4 All E.R. 49; *R. v Stone* [2001] EWCA Crim 192, [2001] Crim. L.R. 465.
[12] para.2–102.
[13] In *Keegstra v One Yellow Rabbit Theatre Association* (1992) 91 D.L.R. (4th) 532, 536–7, Kerans J.A. in the Alberta Court of Appeal responded to counsel's suggestion of sequestering a jury, as an alternative to banning production of a play, as a "monstrous suggestion". He continued that "No citizens presently offer a greater contribution to the enforcement of the right to a fair trial . . . than the jurors. Why should they suffer more? Why should the potential audience of the appellant's production not instead be patient for a month or two as *their* contribution to the protection of constitutional rights in our society?"
[14] *The Trial of the Seven Bishops* (1688) 12 St. Tr. 183 at 430; *R. v Dammaree* (1710) 15 St. Tr. 522, 610. The Juries Act 1870 permitted the jury to have "reasonable refreshment". See generally, G. Williams, *Proof of Guilt* (3rd ed., 1963), pp.253ff.
[15] Criminal Justice Act 1948, s.35(4) provided that the court could permit separation in any trial on indictment, at least until the jury began to consider their verdict.

2-112 to prejudice its fairness.[16] Yet after summing up, the mere fact that a juror separated himself and, not being under the control of the court, conversed or was in a position to converse with outsiders might be enough to abort the trial.[17] It has now been provided that a trial judge should have a discretion to permit the jurors to separate even after summing up and before the verdict.[18] This is what generally happens.

2-113 For a judge to order that a jury should be sequestered, therefore, on the ground of prejudicial publicity in the course of the trial, would be running against the tide.

4. *Jury vetting and selection by the use of a* voir dire[19]

2-114 Normally, the selection of a jury is subject to certain rules as to challenges for (and formerly without) cause.[20] The general principle was stated by Lord Denning M.R. in *Ex p. Brownlow*[21]: "Our philosophy is that the jury should be selected at random from a panel of persons who are nominated at random . . . the parties must take them as they come".[22] Any suggestion that there might be routine vetting of prospective jurors in the light of what is perceived as potentially prejudicial publicity (or with a view to discovering the individual's pre-conceived opinion, or other prejudice) is likely to be met with considerable resistance. The general rule was that questions might not be put to potential jurors unless a foundation of fact had first been laid to justify such a course.[23] The practice has become more common in recent years, in circumstances where it is thought that there is a risk of members of the jury panel knowing a party or witness. Indeed, in certain parts of the country (*e.g.* on the Western Circuit) it has become routine to make enquiries of the jury panel for this purpose. The is because of the perception that in communities with relatively low population resident within a particular catchment area may more easily acquire knowledge

---

[16] *R. v Twiss* [1918] 2 K.B. 853. See also *R. v Box* (1951) 35 Cr. App. R 72, discussed at para.2–84.
[17] *R. v Ketteridge* [1915] K.B. 467; *R. v Neal* [1949] 2 All E.R. 438.
[18] Criminal Justice and Public Order Act 1994, s.43. In *R. v Oliver* [1996] 2 Cr.App.R. 514, Blofeld J. gave guidance as to the directions that should be given when separation is permitted. See Judicial Studies Board *Model Direction* No.59.
[19] For an early account of the effects of pre-trial publicity upon potential jurors, see E. Costantini and J. King, "The Partial Juror" (1981) 15 Law and Soc. Rev. 9; see also N. Vidmar and J. Melnitzer, "Juror Prejudice: An Empirical Study of A Challenge for Cause" [1984] Osgoode Hall L.J. 487; P. Horwitz, "Jury Selection After *Dagenais*: Prejudicial Pre-Trial Publicity" (1996) 42 C.R. 220.
[20] See R. Buxton, "Challenging and Discharging Jurors—1" [1990] Crim.L.R. 225; "Challenging and Discharging Jurors—2" [1990] Crim.L.R. 284. Peremptory challenge was abolished by the Criminal Justice Act 1988, s.118.
[21] [1980] Q.B. 530 at 541. In *R. v Ford (Royston)* [1989] Q.B. 868, the court rejected the notion of seeking to achieve a racial balance in the composition of the jury. See also *Tarrant* [1998] Crim.L.R. 342, [1997] T.L.R. 708.
[22] See, however, A. Sanders and R. Young, *Criminal Justice* (1994, Butterworths), p.353ff as to the limitations of the powers available to the defence to affect the composition of the jury. The powers of the Crown, the existence of which was confirmed by *R. v Mason* [1981] Q.B. 881 and *R. v McCann* (1990) 92 Cr.App.R. 239, are regulated by *Attorney-General's Guidelines on the Exercise by the Crown of its Right of Stand By* [1988] 3 All E.R. 1086, 88 Cr.App.R. 123.
[23] *Chandler (No.2) v Metropolitan Police Commissioner* [1964] 2 Q.B. 322.

or preconceptions of local people and events. In *R. v Brackley and Weller*,[24] the court recognised that:

> "... in some rare cases it would be inappropriate for an individual with knowledge of a place where a crime was committed to serve on a jury. It might be that the crime was so notorious that anyone living in the immediate vicinity would have become emotionally involved, or an innocent, or a deliberate, participant in rumour and gossip. It might also be that the geography of the locality would be so crucial to the outcome of the case, that a juror with personal knowledge might believe himself to be, or be treated by the other jurors as, an expert on the locality, whose knowledge was to be preferred to the evidence of any other witness called on the subject".

Nevertheless, the practice of vetting the potential members of a jury specifically with an eye to the possibility of prejudice arising from media publicity is not entirely without precedent. In *Kray*,[25] Lawton J. said that usually no vetting should be necessary or permitted, although he recognised a material difference:

> "... when newspapers, knowing that there is going to be a later trial, dig up from the past of the convicted who have to meet further charges discreditable allegations which may be either fact or fiction and those allegations are then publicised over a wide area. This does, in my judgment, lead to a prima facie presumption that anybody who may have read that kind of information might find it difficult to reach a verdict in a fair-minded way."

It followed that, in the particular circumstances, a challenge for cause might be founded upon the sort of adverse publicity that had surrounded the Kray brothers, and defence counsel was entitled to apply to be allowed to examine the jurors as they came in to the box to be sworn.

Sir Nicholas Phillips has described the procedure that he adopted in another sensitive case[26]:

> "... I adopted a course that was without precedent. I settled, with the help of counsel, a questionnaire designed to identify those potential jurors who might be prejudiced as the result of the media coverage. Each member of the panel from which the jury would be selected was required to complete this questionnaire. The potential jurors were kept out of court when the selection ballot took place. As each juror was selected I considered his or her questionnaire with counsel and then questioned the juror to explore any possibility of prejudice suggested by the questionnaire. In the light of the answers I received, and with the express or tacit approval of counsel, I excused from serving close on 50% of those selected."

---

[24] November 3, 2000, CACD, at [98], *per* Judge L.J.
[25] (1969) 53 Cr.App.R. 412, CCC.
[26] "Challenge for Cause" (1996) 26 V.U.W.L.R. 479 at 483. The case in question was the prosecution in *R. v Maxwell* (unreported), 1995. Quite apart from the problem of adverse publicity, the collapse of the Maxwell group of companies was on a large scale, and there was a real possibility that potential jurors (or their relatives) might have had some indirect financial involvement in the case.

2–117 CHAPTER 2—CONTEMPT OF COURT: CONSTITUTIONAL DIMENSIONS

2–117 As the citation from *Ex p. Brownlow*[27] demonstrates, this is at variance with the traditions of the common law. The New Zealand Court of Appeal firmly rejected any such approach. In *R. v Sanders*[28] Cooke P., after considering a list of seven questions propounded by counsel, for the purpose of testing the extent to which any juror might have been prejudiced, came to this conclusion:

"It is hardly necessary to do more than to reproduce that list to bring out the intrusive, inconclusive, and time-consuming inquiries which an inquisition of that kind would introduce into jury balloting. New Zealand law should not go down that road. Moreover, the quality of a jury obtained after such a process as is suggested would be questionable."

2–118 The Court of Appeal in England considered the matter of jury vetting or questioning in *R. v Andrews (Tracey).*[29] The appellant had been convicted of stabbing the victim to death. Her defence had been that another motorist had killed the victim in a fit of "road rage". There had been extensive press coverage and a number of false stories had circulated (including, for example, that a knife had been found in the petrol tank of the car in which she and the victim had been travelling). The trial judge had rejected a defence submission that potential jurors should, for this reason, be required to answer a questionnaire. He was content to direct the jury to put out of their minds any pre-trial publicity and require the Crown, prior to the opening, to refute the story about the knife in the petrol tank specifically. The Court of Appeal rejected the complaint (for which leave had not been given) that the judge had erred in refusing to put the questionnaire. It was emphasised that the principle of random juries meant that there was, in general, no jury vetting or questioning. It would only be in exceptional circumstances that the court would intervene; in particular, if there was a real danger of bias. The trial judge would be in the best position to assess whether such an exceptional course was required.[30]

2–119 The Court of Appeal adverted to *Andrews* in *R. v Stone*[31] when considering whether a re-trial should be held in the case of a successful appellant who had been convicted of two highly publicised offences of murder and one of attempted murder. The Court's task was to decide on a balance of probabilities whether the publicity had been such as to lead it to conclude, then and there, that no fair trial could thereafter be held. The risk of prejudice would be reduced if the retrial were held away from Maidstone, where the first trial had taken place, because the impact of the crimes was perceived as being at its greatest locally. It might be that further safeguards could be achieved if a few careful enquiries were made of the jury panel, but this would obviously be for the trial judge. The Court had in mind that such questioning should only take place in exceptional circumstances, as highlighted in *Andrews*. Yet it was an option that the trial judge would be free to

---

[27] See para.2–114.
[28] [1995] 3 N.Z.L.R. 545, consisting of a strong five-judge court: Cooke P., Richardson, Casey, Hardie Boys and McKay JJ.
[29] [1999] Crim. L.R. 156.
[30] See, *e.g. R. v Gough* [1993] A.C. 646; *Att-Gen's Guidelines on the Exercise of the Crown of its Right of Stand-by* (1989) 88 Cr.App.R. 123; *R. v Kray* (1969) 53 Cr.App.R. 412.
[31] [2001] EWCA Crim 192, [2001] Crim. L.R. 465.

consider. The Court was not at that stage satisfied, to the required standard, that any conviction upon a re-trial would be found (by the hypothetical future appellate court) unsafe by reason of the publicity.

5. The effectiveness of strong judicial direction

The remarks of Lawton J. in *R. v Kray*[32] represent a classic statement of the willingness of the judges to trust the jury not to take account of irrelevant and prejudicial material. But this must be balanced against a willingness to recognise that, if a newspaper has created a serious risk of prejudice, this fact must be acknowledged when the reliability of the conviction of an appellant is being considered. There are two sides to the coin. If it really is true, for the purposes of the law of contempt, that a publication has created a real risk of serious prejudice, then that fact must be acknowledged when the safety of a conviction is being considered by an appellate court. The need for a consistency of approach is one that the judges have been increasingly willing to acknowledge.[33]

2–120

In *R. v Barraclough*[34] a jury was discharged after having been told of a defendant's previous convictions. The judge clearly felt that a strong judicial direction was required and warned them, "Do not talk to a soul about this case", having in mind the possibility that potential jurors for the retrial might also be contaminated by the information. The Court of Appeal held, partly for this reason, that there was no significant risk when asked to address the safety of his subsequent conviction.

2–121

IV. THE IMPACT OF THE EUROPEAN CONVENTION

The decision of the European Court of Human Rights in the *Sunday Times* case alerted the press and its legal advisers to the potential relevance of the European Convention in this area of the law.[35] Although the Convention had been signed and come into force many years prior to that litigation, it was not until 1966[36] that the right of individual petition was first granted. Since that time, there has

2–122

---

[32] (1969) 53 Cr.App.R. 412, cited at para.2–86.

[33] In *R. v McCann, Cullen and Shanahan* (1991) 92 Cr.App.R. 239, the court concluded that the impact which the prejudicial statements might have had upon the jury "could not be overcome by any direction to the jury". A similar conclusion seems to have been reached by the trial judge in *Att-Gen v MGN Ltd* [1997] 1 All E.R. 456, discussed at paras 4–156 *et seq*. See too the observations of Simon Brown L.J. cited at para.4–169.

[34] [2000] Crim. L.R. 325.

[35] Lord Scarman had shown, at an early stage, his awareness of the significance of the Convention for the law contempt, in *Att-Gen v BBC* [1980] A.C. 303, 362D, cited at para.1–133. See also Lord Fraser at 352B–F.

[36] Technically, the United Kingdom government made a declaration under Art.25 of the Convention that the right of individual petition was to be recognised in respect of events occurring after January 14, 1966. See *Declarations recognising the competence of the European Commission of Human Rights to receive individual petitions and recognising as compulsory the jurisdiction of the European Court of Human Rights*, Cmnd. 2894. The background to this development is described by Lord Lester Q.C., "UK Acceptance of the Strasbourg Jurisdiction: What Really went on in Whitehall in 1965" [1998] P.L. 237 and (with L. Kapinska) "Human Rights and the British Constitution" in eds. D. Oliver and J. Jowell, *The Changing Constitution* (5th ed., 2004).

been an increasing flow of litigation in which the Convention has played a significant part.[37] Eventually, the Human Rights Act came into effect on October 1, 2000.

A. "Incorporation" into United Kingdom law

2-123 The government coming into office in May 1997 indicated its intention to introduce legislation "to give further effect to" the European Convention in United Kingdom domestic law.[38] A Bill to accomplish this objective, the Human Rights Bill 1998, was introduced into the House of Lords on October 23, 1997. Eventually the Human Rights Act 1998 came into effect on October 1, 2000. In the meantime, however, the Convention had been playing an increasingly significant part in the development of the law within the United Kingdom (both common law and statutory) and especially in the interpretation of rights afforded in respect of freedom of communication and of fair and impartial court hearings—both of which are plainly relevant to the subject of this work. In any event, it is important to bear in mind that one of the principal objectives in the enactment of the Contempt of Court Act 1981, and especially with regard to ss.1 to 7, was to achieve compliance for Scottish and English law with the Convention in so far as it was necessary to restrict media coverage. The impact of the Convention over the following 20 years leading up to the enactment of the Human Rights Act 1998 thus remains of significance.

B. A survey of the influence of the European Convention between 1981 and 2000[39]

2-124 Until the enactment of the Human Rights Act 1998, the European Convention, having the status of an international treaty, could not be applied directly as Sir John Laws explained extra-judicially:

---

[37] See in particular Murray Hunt, *Using Human Rights Law in English Courts* (1997). See also paras 2–192 *et seq.* for the impact of the Convention specifically in the field of contempt.

[38] *Hansard*, H.C. Vol. 294, col. 42, May 14, 1997. See the White Paper, *Rights Brought Home: The Human Rights Bill*, Cm. 3782, (1997). A consultation paper was published in December 1996, by Jack Straw M.P. and Paul Boateng M.P., "Bringing Rights Home: Labour's plans to incorporate the European Convention on Human Rights into UK Law" [1997] E.H.R.L. Rev. 71. For comment, see J. Wadham, [1997] P.L. 75. And see [1997] E.H.R.L. Rev. generally: Lord Lester, "Towards a Constitutional Bill of Rights", *ibid.*, 124; Sir Nicholas Lyell, Q.C., M.P., "Whither Strasbourg? Why Britain Should Think Long and Hard Before Incorporating the European Convention on Human Rights", *ibid.*, 132; J. Wadham, "Bringing Rights Half-Way Home", *ibid.*, 141; K.D. Ewing and C.A. Gearty, "Rocky Foundations for Labour's New Rights", *ibid.*, 146; D. Beyleveld, "The Concept of a Human Right and Incorporation of the European Convention on Human Rights" [1995] P.L. 577; T.H. Jones, "The Devaluation of Human Rights Under the European Convention" [1995] P.L. 430; Rt. Hon. Sir Thomas Bingham, "The European Convention on Human Rights: Time to Incorporate" (1993) 109 L.Q.R. 390. More generally, see D Feldman, *Civil Liberties and Human Rights in England and Wales* (2nd ed., 2002) ch.17, Oxford University Press.

[39] See D. Harris, M. O'Boyle and C. Warbrick, *Law of the European Convention on Human Rights* (1995); S. Farran, *The United Kingdom Before the European Court of Human Rights* (1996); F.G. Jacobs and R.C.A. White, *The European Convention on Human Rights* (2nd ed., 1996); M.W. Janis, R.S. Kay and A.W. Bradley, *European Human Rights Law* (1995); L.J. Clements, *European Human Rights: Taking a Case Under the Convention* (1994); Murray Hunt, *Using Human Rights Law in English Courts* (1997).

" . . . since a treaty is made by the Executive, generally as an act of prerogative power, it cannot have the force of law for the very good reason that the Crown is not a source of law: the only sources of law under our constitution are the other two arms of government, the Judiciary and the Legislature. Thus the rule about treaties should appeal particularly to libertarians: it means that the government cannot impose laws on the people by entering into international agreements, any more than by any other means save by command of a majority in the elected Parliament, where the law proposed becomes, of course, an act of Parliament".[40]

Nevertheless, the Convention imposed obligations in the international arena.[41] In addition, it provided an increasingly significant yardstick against which domestic law came to be measured. Where English or Scottish rules did not conform to the requirements of the Convention, there was an obligation in international law[42] that the municipal law or practice should be changed in order to achieve compliance.[43] It was at least from the mid-sixties a special feature also, however, of the European Convention that there was a right of individual petition, the significance of which is explained below.[44] This period cannot be set to one side as being of no more than historical interest, since the Convention and the Strasbourg jurisprudence played a significant part in the development of the law.

The precise status of the Convention at this intermediate stage was fully considered judicially by the Court of Appeal in *Derbyshire County Council v Times Newspapers Ltd*,[45] where the issue was whether a local authority, as opposed to individual councillors or officers, could bring a libel action in relation to words said to reflect upon its governing, administrative and statutory functions. Balcombe L.J. identified three different ways in which the Convention might be relevant in English law.[46] These related to the interpretation of statutes, the exercise of judicial discretion, and the resolution of any uncertainties in the scope of the common law. Each will be considered in turn. The application of the Convention to the exercise of ministerial discretion, which was the subject of decision in the House of Lords in *R. v Secretary of State for the Home Department Ex p. Brind*,[47] will also be discussed.

---

[40] Sir John Laws, "Is the High Court the Guardian of Fundamental Constitutional Rights?" [1993] P.L. 59 at 61–2. See also the passages from *R. v Secretary of State for the Home Department Ex p. Brind* [1991] 1 A.C. 696, discussed at paras 2–140 to 2.141.
[41] The leading statement of the position of the Convention in English law was in *R. v Secretary of State Ex p. Brind* [1991] 1 A.C. 696. See *R. v Morrisey and Staines* [1997] 2 Cr.App.R. 426, CACD; see also C. Warbrick, "Rights, The European Convention on Human Rights and English Law" [1994] 19 European Law Rev. 34.
[42] As to which, see I.D. Brownlie, *Principles of Public International Law* (4th ed., 2003), pp.542 *et seq*.
[43] In *Sunday Times v United Kingdom* (1979) 2 E.H.R.R. 245, for example, three members of the European Court ruled that the United Kingdom's law of contempt was insufficiently certain in its scope to be acceptable as a restriction "prescribed by law".
[44] para.2–166.
[45] [1992] Q.B. 770. Although the House of Lords reached their conclusion without reliance upon the Convention, nothing was said to cast doubt upon the general analysis of Balcombe L.J.
[46] At 812C.
[47] [1991] 1 A.C. 696.

1. Statutory interpretation

2-127 The courts were under a self-imposed obligation to give effect to the Convention (as with any other treaty) when resolving ambiguity in statutes, since it is presumed that Parliament does not intend to legislate at variance with international obligations.[48] "(1) Art.10 may be used for the purpose of the resolution of an ambiguity in English primary or subordinate legislation".[49]

2-128 The application of this rule was considered in the context of contempt by the House of Lords in *Att-Gen v Associated Newspapers Ltd*,[50] where it was held that the provisions of s.8(1) of the Contempt of Court Act 1981[51] making it contempt of court to "disclose" jury deliberations were not sufficiently "ambiguous" to justify resort to the Convention. The question was whether the word "disclose" referred exclusively to disclosure of information *by a juror* or was wide enough to embrace publication by a newspaper.

2-129 The appellants had published an article which included accounts of three jurors of how they had arrived at their decisions in a long fraud trial. The Divisional Court held on an application for committal brought by the Attorney-General that the publication was in breach of s.8(1). It was conceded on behalf of the appellants that what they had done amounted to a disclosure "in the ordinary sense of that word", but it was contended that, in accordance with principle, where in a criminal case a provision was ambiguous, it should be given the narrower meaning.[52]

2-130 The House held that this was not an example of ambiguity that would attract the operation of the rule[53]:

> "The appellants say that the word is ambiguous because it can refer either to disclosure by a juror or to disclosure through newspaper publication or by some other means. The true view is that 'disclose' describes and includes both (or all) kinds of disclosure. The question being whether it describes merely A or A and B together, the answer, having regard to all the points that I have discussed is 'A and B,' using the plain and natural meaning."

2-131 To the argument that s.8 imposed a restriction upon freedom of expression, which was protected by Art.10 of the Convention guaranteeing freedom of speech, Lord Lowry responded[54]:

---

[48] *R. v Secretary of State for the Home Department Ex p. Bhajan Singh* [1976] Q.B. 198 at 207D–208B, CA; *R. v Home Secretary Ex p. Brind* [1991] A.C. 696; *Derbyshire County Council v Times Newspapers Ltd* [1992] 1 Q.B. 770, Balcombe L.J., CA; *Rantzen v Mirror Group Newspapers (1986) Ltd* [1994] Q.B. 670.
[49] Balcombe L.J. at [1992] 1 Q.B. at 812B–C, citing *R. v Secretary of State for the Home Department Ex p. Brind* [1991] 1 A.C. 696, at 747–8, 749–50, 760, Lord Bridge, Lord Roskill and Lord Ackner.
[50] [1994] 2 A.C. 238, HL.
[51] For the text of which, see para.11–354.
[52] Citing *Att-Gen's Reference (No.1 of 1988)* [1989] A.C. 971.
[53] [1994] 2 A.C. 238 at 260C–D, *per* Lord Lowry.
[54] [1994] 2 A.C. at 262F–H.

"I cannot think that the argument is sound which says that it can be in the interests of freedom of expression, and not harmful to the authority and impartiality of the court system, to allow the publication and discussion of matters that a law which is for the sake of argument assumed to be acceptable has forbidden jurors to reveal to anyone. Secondly, if it is legitimate, on the ground that disclosure by a juror will be harmful to the authority and impartiality of the court system, to enact, 'in response to a pressing social need,' an absolute prohibition against such a disclosure, I do not see how it can be wrong also to prohibit a potentially more harmful further disclosure by way of publication. It seems to me that either both prohibitions are justified or neither is. On this basis the appellants' Convention-based argument in favour of the narrow construction rather than the wide one would disappear."

A somewhat more obscure point arose in *R. v Broadcasting Complaints Commission Ex p. Barclay*,[55] relating to the use of aids to statutory construction. Where both *Hansard* and the European Convention are relevant to a point of statutory interpretation, and *Hansard* discloses a clear intention to take a course which is contrary to the Convention, the Convention must then yield. But where *Hansard* discloses that the promoter of the legislation took the view that the Bill conformed to the Convention, the respective roles of *Hansard* and the Convention are likely to be more complex, and the court would not be assisted by a "doctrinal ranking" of one source above the other.

2. *The exercise of judicial discretion*

Balcombe L.J. in *Derbyshire County Council v Times Newspapers Ltd* explained that, secondly[56]:

"Art.10 may be used when considering the principles upon which the court should act in exercising a discretion, e.g. whether or not to grant an interlocutory injunction; *per* Lord Templeman and Lord Ackner in *Attorney-General v Guardian* [1987] 1 W.L.R. 1248, 1296, 1307; *In re W (A Minor)(Wardship: Restrictions on Publication)* [1992] 1 W.L.R. 100, 103 in the court of Appeal;"

In *Middlebrook Mushrooms Ltd v Transport and General Workers Union*,[57] an employer sought an injunction to restrain a trade union from organising a picket to boycott one of its shops. Neill L.J. said[58]:

"Though counsel for the defendants did not place any specific reliance on article 10 of the European Convention of Human Rights and Fundamental Freedoms (1953) Cmd. 8969 it is relevant to bear in mind that in all cases which involve a proposed restriction on the right of free speech the court is concerned, when exercising its discretion, to consider whether the suggested restraint is necessary."

The grant of an injunction is a discretionary matter,[59] and where it might inhibit a guaranteed right, as in the case of preventing a media publication, this

---

[55] (1996) 9 Admin L.R. 265.
[56] [1992] Q.B. 770 at 812C–D.
[57] [1993] I.C.R. 612, CA.
[58] *ibid*. at 620C.
[59] For a discussion of applications for injunctions to restrain a contempt, see ch.6.

would have naturally been a factor to be carefully weighed, and subsequently the legislature sought to formalise these considerations in s.12 of the Human Rights Act 1998.[60] There are other powers, both statutory and at common law, in the field of contempt which require the exercise of discretion; for example, that of making postponement orders under s.4(2) of the 1981 Act,[61] and other restrictions permitted under s.11.[62]

2–136 On the other hand, it emerged from the case of *R. v Morrissey and Staines*,[63] that there was a limit to the extent to which the courts could resort to the notion of discretion for the purpose of applying the provisions of the Convention. In order to explain the background, it is necessary to refer to the decision of the European Court of Human Rights in *Saunders v United Kingdom*.[64] Section 177(6) of the Financial Services Act 1986 expressly provided that "A statement made by a person in compliance with a requirement imposed by virtue of this section may be used against him". The court held, however, that there had been a breach of Art.6 of the Convention by the United Kingdom when the prosecuting authorities were permitted to introduce such evidence against Mr Saunders.

2–137 In *R. v Morrisey and Staines*, the appellants sought to argue that their convictions should be quashed on the ground that evidence compulsorily acquired from them in the course of an investigation under statutory powers should not have been used against them. It was argued in the light of *Saunders* that the court could exclude the evidence so obtained, in the exercise of a discretion to exclude evidence under the Police and Criminal Evidence Act 1984, s.78.[65] Lord Bingham C.J. said that[66]:

> "If the Court were to exclude the evidence in the present appeals, the court would be obliged to exclude such evidence in all such cases. That would amount to a repeal at least partially of an English statute in deference to a ruling in the European Court of Human Rights which, as a matter of strict law, was irrelevant."

3. *Resolving uncertainties in the scope of the common law*

2–138 As to uncertainty in the common law, the position before the Human Rights Act 1998 took effect was that the courts were entitled to take the Convention into account, but were not obliged to do so.[67] Again, in the words of Balcombe L.J. in *Derbyshire County Council v Times Newspapers Ltd*[68]:

---

[60] Discussed at paras 6–11 *et seq.*
[61] See paras 7–109 *et seq.*
[62] See paras 7–83 *et seq.*
[63] [1997] 2 Cr.App.R. 426. See also *R. v Khan (Sultan)* [1997] A.C. 558, H.L., where it was held in the context of the discretion arising under s.78 of the Police and Criminal Evidence Act 1984 that a trial had been fair, as a whole, notwithstanding that the evidence may have been obtained in breach of Art.8 of the European Convention.
[64] (1997) 23 E.H.R.R. 313.
[65] See generally *Archbold 2005*, paras 15–452 *et seq.*
[66] [1997] 2 Cr.App.R. 426 at 442C–D.
[67] *Derbyshire County Council v Times Newspapers Ltd* [1992] 1 Q.B. 770.
[68] [1992] Q.B. 770 at 812D–813H.

"Article 10 may be used when the common law (by which I include the doctrines of equity) is uncertain. In *Attorney-General v Guardian Newspapers Ltd (No.2)* [1990] 1 A.C. 109 the courts at all levels had regard to the provisions of Article 10 in considering the extent of the duty of confidence. They did not limit the application of Article 10 to the discretion of the court to grant or withhold an injunction to restrain a breach of confidence.

Even if the common law is certain, the courts will still, when appropriate, consider whether the United Kingdom is in breach of Article 10; *R. v Chief Metropolitan Magistrate, Ex p. Choudhury* [1991] 1 Q.B. 429, . . .

This approach of English law to Article 10 is wholly consistent with the jurisprudence of the European Court of Human Rights. That Court has, on more than one occasion, held that a decision of the English courts has violated a litigant's rights under Article 10 and this on occasion has led to Parliament having to change the substantive law. Thus *Sunday Times v United Kingdom* (1979) 2 E.H.R.R. 245 was in part responsible for the Contempt of Court Act 1981 . . .

In my judgment, therefore, where the law is uncertain, it must be right for the court to approach the issue before it with a predilection to ensure that our law should not involve a breach of Article 10 . . . .The law on this very important point is, in my view, uncertain . . . .This court is in a position to define the extent of this common law tort in such a way as not to require a positive amendment of the law by Parliament. In my judgment we can and should consider the effect of Article 10."

4. *The exercise of ministerial discretion*

It would seem that, as a matter of strict law, ministers of the Crown were free in the era prior to the Human Rights Act to take account of or ignore the Convention at their own discretion. The courts were not permitted to resort to the sanction of judicial review so as to insist that ministers *must* take account of the Convention.[69] Nor could they hold that any decision, appearing to have been inconsistent with a principle embodied in the Convention, was for that reason alone *Wednesbury* unreasonable.[70]

The argument against *requiring* ministers to take specific account of the Convention was that, being a treaty, it was a creature of the exercise of the prerogative power. It should not be possible for the executive to change the common law in such a wholesale way.[71] The logical implications were spelt out in the House of Lords in *R. v Home Secretary Ex p. Brind*[72] by Lord Bridge:

"When confronted with a simple choice between two possible interpretations of some specific statutory provision, the presumption whereby the courts prefer that which avoids conflict between our domestic legislation and our international treaty obligations is a mere canon of construction which involves no importation of international law into

---

[69] *R. v Secretary of State for the Home Department Ex p. Brind* [1991] A.C. 696. Now, following the enactment of the Human Rights Act 1998, ministers would be regarded as "public authorities" within s.6 and would thus be obliged to do so.
[70] That is, in breach of the principles articulated in *Associated Provincial Picture Houses Ltd v Wednesbury Corporation* [1948] 1 K.B. 223 at 229, Lord Greene M.R. See H.W.R. Wade and C.F. Forsyth, *Administrative Law* (9th ed., 2004), p.363ff.
[71] See the argument put by Sir John Laws, para.2–124.
[72] [1991] 1 A.C. 696 at 748A–F.

the domestic field. But where Parliament has conferred on the executive an administrative discretion without indicating the precise limits within which it must be exercised, to presume that it *must* be exercised with Convention limits would be to go far beyond the resolution of an ambiguity. It would be to impute to Parliament an intention not only that the executive should exercise the discretion in conformity with the Convention but also that the domestic courts should enforce that conformity by the importation into domestic administrative law of the text of the Convention and the jurisprudence of the European Court of Human Rights in the interpretation and application of it . . . . When Parliament has been content for so long to leave those who complain that their Convention rights have been infringed to seek their remedy in Strasbourg, it would be surprising suddenly to find that the judiciary had, without Parliament's aid, the means to incorporate the Convention into such an important area of domestic law and I cannot escape the conclusion that this would be a judicial usurpation of the legislative function." (our emphasis)

2–141 Lord Ackner expressed the same point slightly differently:

"The fallacy of this submission is however plain. If the Secretary of State was obliged to have proper regard to the Convention, i.e. to conform with article 10, this inevitably would result in incorporating the Convention into English domestic law by the back door. It would oblige the courts to police the operation of the Convention and to ask themselves in each case, where there was a challenge, whether the restrictions were 'necessary in a democratic society' . . . applying principles enunciated in the decisions of the European Court of Human Rights. The treaty, not having been incorporated in English law, cannot be a source of rights and obligations . . . ".

C. The relevance of the Convention to the law of contempt

2–142 It is necessary at this point to set out the Articles of the European Convention directly relevant to the development of the law of contempt.[73] Art.10 of the Convention provides as follows:

"(1) Everyone has the right to freedom of expression. This right shall include freedom to hold opinions and to receive and impart information and ideas without interference by public authority and regardless of frontiers. This Article shall not prevent states from requiring the licensing of broadcasting, television or cinema enterprises.

(2) The exercise of these freedoms, since it carries with it duties and responsibilities, may be subject to formalities, conditions, restrictions or penalties as are prescribed by law and are necessary in a democratic society, in the interests of national security, territorial integrity or public safety, for the prevention of disorder or crime, for the protection of health or morals, for the protection of the reputation or rights of others, for preventing the disclosure of information received in confidence, or for maintaining the authority and impartiality of the judiciary."

2–143 Mention must also be made of Art.6 of the Convention. Because it seeks to guarantee fair trial, it shares one of the objectives of the law of contempt. It provides:

---

[73] For discussion of the Articles of the Convention relevant to media law in this area, see Lord Lester Q.C. and N. Schiffrin, "The European Human Rights Convention and Media Law" in *The Yearbook of Media and Entertainment Law* (1995), p.241; and *ibid.* (1996) p.299; and *ibid.* (1997–8) p.265.

"1. In the determination of his civil rights and obligations or of any criminal charge against him, everyone is entitled to a fair and public hearing within a reasonable time by an independent and impartial tribunal established by law. Judgment shall be pronounced publicly but the press may be excluded from all or part of the trial in the interests of morals, public order or national security in a democratic society, where the interests of juveniles or the protection of the private life of the parties so require, or to the extent strictly necessary in the opinion of the court in special circumstances where publicity would prejudice the interests of justice.

2. Everyone charged with a criminal offence shall be presumed innocent until proved guilty according to law.

3. Everyone charged with a criminal offence has the following minimum rights:

(a) to be informed promptly, in a language which he understands and in detail, of the nature and cause of the accusation against him;
(b) to have adequate facilities and time for the preparation of his defence;
(c) to defend himself in person or through legal assistance of his own choosing or, if he has not sufficient means to pay for legal assistance, to be given it free when the interests of justice so require;
(d) to examine or have examined witnesses against him and to obtain the attendance and examination of witnesses on his behalf under the same conditions as witnesses against him;
(e) to have the free assistance of an interpreter if he cannot understand or speak the language used in court."

This article is relevant to the law of contempt in at least three distinct ways:

1. Art.6(1) guarantees a "public hearing", subject to the specified exceptions. The implications of this for the reporting of legal proceedings are more fully considered in chapter 7.

2. It also guarantees a fair trial to (in particular) a defendant in criminal proceedings. He is entitled to have his case considered by an "independent and impartial tribunal", which means one free from improper influences, including prejudicial press comment. The difficulty for the courts in the context of the law of contempt was expressed by Richardson J. as follows[74]:

"Freedom of the press as a vehicle for comment on public issues is basic to our democratic system. The assurance of a fair trial by an impartial Court is essential for the preservation of an effective system of justice. Both values have been affirmed by the Bill of Rights. The public interest in the function of the Courts invokes both these values. It calls for free expression of information and opinions as to the performance of those public responsibilities. It also calls for determination of disputes by Courts which are free from bias and which make their decisions solely on the evidence judicially brought before them".

---

[74] *Gisborne Herald Co Ltd v Solicitor-General* [1995] 3 N.Z.L.R. 563 at 571. And see further paras 2–99 *et seq.*

3. Art.6(3) affords certain rights that might be at variance with the use of the summary procedure, as recognised in this jurisdiction, especially in connection with contempt in the face of the court.[75]

2–145 *Allenet de Ribemont v France*[76] is an important decision of the European Court of Human Rights in the context of guaranteeing a fair trial. The background was that a French Minister and a number of police officers, shortly after the applicant's arrest, publicly named him as one of the instigators of the murder of a French politician. The European Court held that the making of those statements, carrying a clear implication of guilt, violated the presumption of innocence protected by Art.6(2). The public statements "encouraged the public to believe him guilty and, secondly, *prejudged* the assessment of the facts by the competent judicial authority" (emphasis added). It is perhaps ironic that reference should be made to what is, in effect, a "prejudgment" test in the light of the fact that one of the objectives of the United Kingdom Parliament when enacting the Contempt of Court Act 1981 was to eliminate such a test from English and Scottish law for the purpose of achieving compliance with the European Convention.[77]

2–146 Article 8 of the Convention has become increasingly important in the context of media publication and its interaction with Art.10. [78] Its terms are as follows:

"1. Everyone has the right to respect for his private and family life, his home and his correspondence.
  2. There shall be no interference by a public authority with the exercise of this right except such as is in accordance with the law and is necessary in a democratic society in the interests of national security, public safety or the economic well-being of the country, for the prevention of disorder or crime, for the protection of health or morals, or for the protection of the rights and freedoms of others."

It impacts upon the law of contempt, potentially at least, in two particular contexts. It is now recognised that it must come to the fore whenever the court is called upon to exercise its recently-recognised power to restrict publicity *contra mundum*, whether under the traditional *parens patriae* jurisdiction or otherwise. Secondly, there is the possibility that it may sometimes be used as a basis, when demonstrated to be necessary for the purpose and only in exceptional circumstances, for restricting the reporting of court proceedings. "The duty of the

---

[75] See the objections of D. Feldman, *Civil Liberties and Human Rights in England and Wales* (2nd ed., 2002), p.963, Oxford University Press. The objections are more fully considered in paras 10–36 *et seq.*
[76] (1995) 20 E.H.R.R. 557.
[77] See Lord Hailsham, who said "It puts an end, of course, to the pre-judgment criterion which was adopted by your Lordships' House in the *Sunday Times* case": *Hansard*, H.L. Vol. 415 (5th series), col. 660, December 9, 1980). See also the remarks of Collins J. In *Att-Gen v Guardian Newspapers Ltd* [1999] E.M.L.R. 904 at 918–19 cited at para.2–35.
[78] See paras 2–36 and 2–37.

court is to examine with care each application for a departure from the rule [of open justice in criminal proceedings] by reason of rights under article 8".[79]

D. Constitutional protection of rights: the common law approach[80]

"The 'rule of law', lastly, may be used as a formula for expressing the fact that with us the law of the constitution, the rules which in foreign countries naturally form part of a constitutional code, are not the source but the consequence of the rights of individuals, as defined and enforced by the courts; that, in short, the principles of private law have with us been by the action of the courts and Parliament so extended as to determine the position of the Crown and of its servants; thus the constitution is the result of the ordinary law of the land."

2–147

This passage from Dicey's *Introduction to the Study of the Law of the Constitution*,[81] has exerted a significant influence on the development of the common law, and the perception of judges as to how rights should be defined and protected. The approach has been that "rights" are thought of as being "residual". A person can do or say what he pleases, unless and until the law provides otherwise. This was considered by Dicey (and others before him, such as Bentham) as the most efficacious method of protecting rights. Written constitutions and bills of rights were considered to be capable of being all too readily suspended or set aside. The common law, weaving as it does a whole fabric of liberties, protected through a system focusing on remedies rather than rights, is much more difficult comprehensively to suspend.

2–148

"To say that the 'constitution guaranteed' one class of rights more than the other would be to an Englishman an unnatural or a senseless form of speech".[82] A consequence of this *laissez faire* tradition has been that the protection of rights has proved spasmodic and patchy.[83] Through want of articulation some rights have perhaps failed to receive the acknowledgment they might deserve.

2–149

The importance of free speech has nonetheless been widely recognised by the common law. In *Bonnard v Perryman*,[84] for example, the court declined to grant an injunction against a threatened libel on the explicit ground that: "The right of free speech is one which it is for the public interest that individuals should

2–150

---

[79] *Re S (FC) (A Child)* [2004] UKHL 47, [2005] 1 A.C. 593 at [18]. This is discussed fully in paras 6–43 *et seq.*
[80] For a spirited defence of the methodology of the common law, see T.R.S. Allan, *Law, Liberty and Justice* (1993), especially ch.6, "Constitutional Rights and Common Law".
[81] The passage is cited from the 10th ed., (1959), p.203. The first edition was published in 1885.
[82] Dicey, *op. cit.* at p.201. Cp. Lord Scarman in *Secretary of State for Defence v Guardian Newspapers Ltd* [1985] A.C. 339 at 361E–F, cited para.9–80.
[83] A point made by D. Feldman in the first edition of, *Civil Liberties and Human Rights in England and Wales* (1993), para.2.6. See also A. Boyle, "Freedom of Expression as a Public Interest in English Law" [1982] P.L. 574; J.F. Burrows, "Freedom of the Press under the New Zealand Bill of Rights Act 1990" in ed. P. Joseph, *Essays on the Constitution* (1995), p.286.
[84] [1891] 2 Ch.D. 269 at 284, Lord Coleridge C.J. The words were quoted with approval by Lord Denning M.R. in *Fraser v Evans* [1969] 1 Q.B. 349 at 361F, who spoke of the "importance in the public interest that the truth should out". See also *Thomson v Times Newspapers Ltd* [1969] 1 W.L.R. 1236, 3 All E.R. 648 (no gagging writs), discussed at para.4–324. See also *Holley v Smyth* [1998] Q.B. 726.

possess, and indeed, that they should exercise without impediment, so long as no wrongful act is done". Similarly, in *Wason v Walter*,[85] Lord Cockburn C.J. acknowledged "the full liberty of public writers to comment on the conduct and motives of public men", although he observed that "it has only in very recent times been recognised". The public interest in being informed was expressly considered as a counterweight to obligations of confidence in *Lion Laboratories Ltd v Evans*.[86]

2–151   There was, sometimes, a tendency to treat the concept of rights somewhat dismissively. Lord Hewart, C.J. in a much-criticised[87] case concerning freedom of speech in public observed[88]:

"There have been moments during the argument in this case when it appeared to be suggested that the court had to do with a grave case involving what is called the right of public meeting. I say 'called' because English law does not recognise any special right of public meeting for political or other purposes. The right of assembly, as Professor Dicey puts it, is nothing more than a view taken by the court of the individual liberty of the subject".

2–152   A similarly dismissive approach was adopted by Lord Diplock in *Harman v Secretary of State for The Home Department*[89]:

"My Lords, in a case which has attracted a good deal of publicity it may assist in clearing up misconceptions if I start by saying what the case is *not* about. It is *not* about freedom of speech, freedom of the press, openness of justice or documents coming into 'the public domain'; nor, with all respect to those of your Lordships who think the contrary, does it in my opinion call for consideration of any of those human rights and fundamental freedoms which in the European Convention for the Protection of Human Rights and Fundamental Freedoms (Rome, 4 November 1950; TS 71 (1953); Cmd 8969) are contained in separate articles each starting with a statement in absolute terms but followed immediately by very broadly stated exceptions."

2–153   Gradually, however, judges became willing to acknowledge the notion of "rights" in a less inhibited way.[90] A striking example was provided by the speech of Lord Bridge (albeit dissenting) in *Att-Gen v Guardian Newspapers Ltd*[91]:

"Having no written constitution, we have no equivalent in our law to the First Amendment to the Constitution of the United States of America. Some think that puts

---

[85] (1868) L.R. 4 Q.B. 73 at 93–4.
[86] [1985] Q.B. 526.
[87] See, *e.g.* T.C. Daintith, "Disobeying a Policeman: A Fresh Look at *Duncan v Jones*" [1966] P.L. 248; ed. M. Supperstone, *Brownlie's Law of Public Order and National Security* (2nd ed., 1981), pp.111–13; A.T.H. Smith, *Offences Against Public Order* (1987), pp.174–6.
[88] *Duncan v Jones* [1936] 1 K.B. 218. The decision has been described by a Divisional Court as not involving "any penetrating analysis of the legal principles in play": *R. v Coventry City Council Ex p. Phoenix* [1995] 3 All E.R. 37 at 59a, Simon Brown L.J.
[89] [1983] 1 A.C. 280 at 299E–F. See also Lord Wilberforce in *British Steel Corp v Granada Television Ltd* [1981] A.C. 1096 at 1168, cited at para.9–6.
[90] M. Beloff Q.C. and H. Mountfield, "Unconventional Behaviour? Judicial Uses of the European Convention in England and Wales" [1996] E.H.R.L.R. 5. See also F. Klug and K. Starmer, "Incorporation Through the Back Door?" [1997] P.L. 223.
[91] [1987] 1 W.L.R. 1248 at 1286B–C.

freedom of speech on too lofty a pedestal. Perhaps they are right. We have not adopted as part of our law the European Convention for the Protection of Human Rights and Fundamental Freedoms to which this country is a signatory. Many think that we should. I have hitherto not been of that persuasion, in large part because I have had confidence in the capacity of the common law to safeguard the fundamental freedoms essential to a free society including the right to freedom of speech which is specifically safeguarded by article 10 of the Convention. My confidence is seriously undermined by your Lordships' decision . . . ".

A "right" to withhold sources was acknowledged by Beldam L.J. in *Chief Constable of Leicestershire v Garavelli*[92] to have been accorded by s.10:   **2–154**

"This it seems to me gives a journalist, in Miss Garavelli's position, the right to refuse to disclose the source of her information until it is established that it is in the interests of justice for disclosure to be made."

E. A matter of balance? Contrasting approaches to rights adjudication

The contempt jurisdiction is in origin a creature of the common law, having no counterpart in jurisdictions emanating from the civil law.[93] The practical compromise that it represents, between the conflicting "*desiderata*" of freedom of information and the right to a fair trial, is by no means to be dismissed, although it is perhaps something of an exaggeration to claim that " . . . contempt of court is undoubtedly one of the great contributions the common law has made to the civilised behaviour of a large part of the world beyond the continent of Europe where the institution is unknown".[94]   **2–155**

In this jurisdiction, the law of contempt, in so far as it concerns the media, has in the past been seen to require a balancing of the right to freedom of speech with the interests of justice.[95] This may be contrasted with other systems that accord a higher priority to the importance of freedom of speech: for example, the constitution of the United States of America, of which the First Amendment provides that "Congress shall make no law . . . abridging the freedom of speech, or of the press" and to a lesser extent the European Convention, which asserts a right to freedom of speech that can be curtailed only in certain, closely defined circumstances.   **2–156**

It was expressly recognised in this context that the approach of the English courts might in the past have been at variance with that of the European Court. Speaking in the House of Lords in *Att-Gen v BBC*,[96] Lord Fraser said: **2–157**

---

[92] [1997] E.M.L.R. 543 at 552.
[93] See M. Chesterman, "Contempt: in the Common Law, but not the Civil Law" [1997] 46 I.C.L.Q. 521. See also C. Cremonini, "An Italian Lawyer Looks at Civil Contempt—From Rome to Glastonbury" (1984) 3 Civil J.Q. 133.
[94] (1979) 95 L.Q.R. at 348–9 (note), F.A. Mann. There has even been a suggestion that the United States of America might usefully adopt some of the protections afforded by the Contempt of Court Act 1981. See Stephen J. Krause, "Punishing the Press: Using Contempt of Court to Secure the Right to a Fair Trial" (1996) 76 Boston U. L. Rev. 537.
[95] See particularly A. Boyle, "Freedom of Expression as a Public Interest in English Law" [1982] P.L. 574; *Att-Gen v BBC* [1981] A.C. 303 at 352B–F, Lord Fraser.
[96] [1981] A.C. 303 at 352B–F.

2–157 CHAPTER 2—CONTEMPT OF COURT: CONSTITUTIONAL DIMENSIONS

"I agree that in deciding this appeal the House has to hold a balance between the principle of freedom of expression and the principle that the administration of justice must be kept free from outside interference. Neither principle is more important than the other, and where they come in to conflict, as they do in this case, the boundary has to be drawn between the spheres in which they respectively operate. That is not the way in which the European Court of Human Rights would approach the question, as we see from the following passage in the report of *Sunday Times v United Kingdom* (1979) 2 E.H.R.R. 245, 281:

> 'Whilst emphasising that it is not its function to pronounce itself on an interpretation of English law adopted in the House of Lords, the court points out that it has to take a different approach. The court is faced not with a choice between two conflicting principles, but with a principle of freedom of expression that is subject to a number of exceptions which must be narrowly interpreted.'

It is, therefore, not to be expected that decisions of this House on questions of this sort will invariably be consistent with those of the European Court."

2–158 This European priority was increasingly to be found within this jurisdiction. For example, Hoffmann L.J. in *R. v Central Television plc*[97] said:

> "It cannot be too strongly emphasised that outside the established exceptions, or any new ones which Parliament may enact in accordance with its obligations under the Convention, there is no question of balancing freedom of speech against other interests. It is a trump card[98] which always wins".

2–159 Yet it is undeniable that the development of the common law method has been perceived by judges as being a task of balancing one consideration against another, over an infinite variety of factual circumstances. Article 10(2) itself recognises a number of specific exceptions, which signatory states may take into account when deciding whether to restrict freedom of speech. It is difficult to see what this process entails if it is not the weighing of competing considerations, and the recognition that the balance is to be set within the recognised margin of appreciation.

---

[97] [1994] Fam. 192 at 203D. And see Lloyd L.J. in *Att-Gen v Newspaper Publishing plc* [1988] Ch. 333 at 382D–F, who spoke of a "permanent shift in the balance of public interest away from the protection of the administration of justice and in favour of freedom of speech". By contrast, see Lord Goff in *Att-Gen v Guardian (No.2)* [1990] 1 A.C. 109 at 284A: "I have no reason to believe that English law, as applied in the courts, leads to any different conclusion". See also Lord Keith in *Derbyshire County Council v Times Newspapers Ltd* [1993] A.C. 534 at 551F–G.

[98] The notion of rights as "trumps" is associated in particular with the jurisprudence of R. Dworkin. The expression "a trump over utility" appears in (1981) 1 O.J.L.S. 177 at 199. But the broad terms of Art.10(2) make its stark invocation somewhat simplistic in this context, and Hoffmann L.J's statement has to be qualified in the light of the development, shortly after it was uttered, in *Re Z (A Minor) (Identification: Restrictions on Publication)* [1997] Fam. 1: see paras 6–58 *et seq*. There, it was recognised that in the context of the *parens patriae* jurisdiction the interests of the child may prove to be the trump card. Section 1 of the Children Act 1989 requires that the rights of the child be treated as paramount in some circumstances. Furthermore, in the context of court reporting, Art.6 of the Convention itself permits the exclusion of the press "where the interests of juveniles or the protection of the private life of the parties so require". See now *Re S(FC) (A Child)* [2004] UKHL 47, [2005] 1 A.C. 593.

It may be observed that, while Lord Bridge and Lord Templeman disagreed 2–160 fundamentally in their conclusions over the "Millett injunctions",[99] both regarded consideration of the European Convention, and justification of a decision in its terms, as essential requirements in their determination because rights (specifically freedom of speech and information) were in issue. It is significant that despite having resort to the "precise terms" in which it is couched, they nonetheless were able to reach such diametrically opposite conclusions on the facts of the case. As was observed by the Schiemann L.J. in the Court of Appeal in *Camelot Group plc v Centaur Communications Ltd*[1] it is not altogether surprising that different judges should come to different conclusions on the same facts, even though applying directly the principles expressed in the Convention.

F. Open Justice: Articles 6 and 10

One of the main objectives of the Contempt of Court Act 1981 was to bring 2–161 English law into compliance with the treaty obligations undertaken by the United Kingdom as a signatory to the European Convention on Human Rights.[2] There are apparently separate provisions of the Convention which nonetheless interact in the context of the right of journalists to report, and of the public to be informed about, judicial proceedings. Article 10[3] provides for freedom of information subject to certain limited exceptions which include restrictions which can be shown to be necessary, in a democratic society, for the purpose of maintaining the authority and impartiality of the judiciary, or that of protecting health and morals.

There is obvious scope for tension between Art.10 and Art.6,[4] which is 2–162 intended to ensure free access to the judicial process and in particular to *open justice*:

> "Everyone is entitled to a fair and *public* hearing within a reasonable time by an independent and impartial tribunal established by law. Judgment shall be pronounced *publicly* but the press may be excluded from all or part of the trial in the interests of *morals*, public order or national security in a democratic society, where the *interests of juveniles* or the protection of the *private life of the parties* so require, or to the extent strictly necessary in the opinion of the court in special circumstances where publicity would prejudice the interests of justice"[5] (emphases added).

---

[99] *Att-Gen v Guardian Newspapers Ltd* [1987] 1 W.L.R. 1248 at 1296F–G, *per* Lord Templeman cited at para.2–52. But see Lord Bridge, at 1286B–C, cited at para.2–153.
[1] [1999] Q.B. 124 at 135G, cited at para.9–152.
[2] See the explanation of Lord Hailsham L.C.: *Hansard*, H.L., Vol. 415, (5th series) col. 660, December 9, 1980.
[3] See para.2–142.
[4] para.2–143.
[5] It is not perhaps surprising that the language of the Convention mirrors that of the common law, since the Convention was drafted in large measure by British draftsmen. See G. Marston, "The United Kingdom's Part in the Preparation of the European Convention on Human Rights, 1950" (1993) 42 I.C.L.Q. 796.

CHAPTER 2—CONTEMPT OF COURT: CONSTITUTIONAL DIMENSIONS

G. Comparison with the common law

2–163 It is clear that there are many parallels in the wording of Art.6(1) with the common law principles[6] expounded particularly by the House of Lords in *Scott v Scott*.[7] Also, in *Re S (FC) (A Child)*[8] it was observed by Lord Steyn "on a historical note that ... the approach adopted in the past under the inherent jurisdiction was remarkably similar to that to be adopted under the ECHR." On the other hand, in England and Wales the matter of "private life" was conventionally regarded as being unlikely to justify the withholding of information[9] unless some statutory provision were expressly made (such as, for example, was suggested by the Committee on Privacy and Related Matters as to the names and addresses of victims of crime).[10] On the face of it, therefore, in this respect the English common law would appear to lean more in favour of open reporting rather than less. It is of some interest that, apart from the reference to "private life" in Art.6, there is another article of the Convention devoted in its entirety to the protection of privacy (*i.e.* Art.8), and this gives rise to further possibilities for conflict with both Arts 6 and 10.[11]

2–164 It is reasonable to suppose that the undefined common law powers of restriction referred to in (although not conferred by) s.11 of the Contempt of Court Act 1981 would now have to be construed, at least in circumstances of any doubt or ambiguity, in the light of the principles underlying Arts 6 and 10 of the European Convention. It was established well before the Human Rights Act 1998 was enacted that such reference could be made as an aid to interpretation of statutes[12] and to resolve uncertainties in the common law.[13] Nevertheless, there may be considerable doubt as to whether this would have the effect of leading to any different approach on the part of modern judges from that adopted since *Scott v Scott* was decided,[14] especially in the light of what appear to be genetic links between that case and the wording of Art.6 itself.

---

[6] The principles are more fully considered in paras 7–1 *et seq.*
[7] [1913] A.C. 417.
[8] [2004] UKHL 47, [2005] 1 A.C. 593 at [23].
[9] See *R. v Westminster City Council Ex p. Castelli and Tristran-Garcia* [1996] 1 F.L.R. 534, at paras 7–99 *et seq.*
[10] (1990) Cm. 1102, at para.10.15. See also the Lord Chancellor's Department Consultation Paper on Infringement of Privacy, 1993; the House of Commons National Heritage Committee, *Privacy and Media Intrusion* (March 1993), Fourth Report, H.C. 294–1 and the Government's response, White Paper, *Privacy and Media Intrusion*, Cm. 2198 (1995).
[11] In *Mahon v Rahn* [1998] Q.B. 424 at 450F–G, Otton L.J. prayed in aid Art.6 in rejecting the notion of an implied undertaking in criminal proceedings, as to disclosed documents, by analogy with that in civil proceedings. See now however, *Taylor v Director of the Serious Fraud Office* [1999] 2 A.C. 177.
[12] See, *e.g. Rantzen v Mirror Group Newspapers (1986) Ltd* [1994] Q.B. 670.
[13] *Derbyshire County Council v Times Newspapers Ltd* [1992] Q.B. 770, CA.
[14] See the citation from Lord Keith in *Derbyshire County Council v Times Newspapers Ltd* cited at para.7–3. But see now *Z v Finland* (1997) 25 E.H.R.R. 371 and comments by Sedley L.J. in *Berezovsky v Forbes Inc (No.2)* [2001] EWCA Civ 1251, [2001] E.M.L.R. 1030 at [9], to the effect that it will no longer do to rest on the laurels of such "earlier judicial statements, albeit of high authority, that the English common law already conforms with Article 10".

H. Maintaining the authority and impartiality of the judiciary

It was recognised by the European Court of Human Rights that it is necessary to adopt a broad interpretation of the expression "maintaining the authority and impartiality of the judiciary"[15]:

2–165

> "In so far as the law of contempt may serve to protect the rights of litigants, this purpose is already included in the phrase 'maintaining the authority and impartiality of the judiciary': the rights so protected are the rights of individuals in their capacity as litigants, that is as persons involved in the machinery of justice, and the authority of that machinery will not be maintained unless protection is afforded to all those involved in or having recourse to it."

I. The significance of the right of individual petition[16]

It is unusual in an instrument such as the European Convention that there should be a right of individual petition, because it is a treaty, and normally only the sovereign states themselves have standing in international law. It was suggested[17] that decisions of the European Court (and by implication the provisions of the Convention itself) had a standing similar to persuasive Commonwealth authorities, or for that matter decisions of other similar jurisdictions such as the Supreme Court of Israel. Since there is, however, an individual right of petition to Strasbourg, it was argued that there was a greater obligation to comply with decisions of the European Court of Human Rights than in the case of other persuasive authority, such as that afforded by the superior Commonwealth courts.[18] A disappointed individual within England and Wales obviously cannot appeal to the Supreme Court of Israel or the High Court of Australia, but he can take proceedings directly to Strasbourg from a ruling of the English Courts. The jurisdiction of the European Court has as a result "come to resemble more that of a domestic supreme court than an international tribunal",[19] and it was argued that its judgments were entitled to a greater weight than the other sources to which reference has traditionally been made in the English common law. The value of the European Court's judgment has, however, been described in less formal terms by the Court of Appeal in *Camelot Group plc v Centaur Communications Ltd* where it was said merely that "that court has unrivalled experience in this field and it would be foolish not to take advantage of that

2–166

---

[15] Majority judgment, para.56, (1979) 2 E.H.R.R. 245, 274. See also the Divisional Court in *Att-Gen v Associated Newspapers Ltd* [1994] 2 A.C. 238 at 243D–E, Beldam L.J.
[16] C. Warbrick, "Rights, The European Convention on Human Rights and English Law" [1994] 19 European Law Rev. 34.
[17] By Sir John Laws in his article "Is the High Court the Guardian of Fundamental Constitutional Rights?" [1993] P.L. 59.
[18] See, *e.g.* Warbrick, above, n.16. Since Eleventh Protocol to the Convention became operational in November 1998, it is no longer necessary (or indeed possible) to ratify the existence of the right at five-yearly intervals.
[19] See C. Gearty, "The European Court of Human Rights and the Protection of Civil Liberties" [1993] C.L.J. 89 at p.93.

2-166 CHAPTER 2—CONTEMPT OF COURT: CONSTITUTIONAL DIMENSIONS

experience".[20] Since the Human Rights Act came into effect in October 2000, the status and authority of Strasbourg jurisprudence is governed by s.2 of the statute which requires the courts of the United Kingdom to "take into account" any judgment, decision, declaration or opinion of the relevant Strasbourg institutions.[21]

2-167 It is perhaps significant that, although the International Covenant on Civil and Political Rights[22] carries the option of individual petition, that is not one of which the United Kingdom government has availed itself. Perhaps partly as a consequence, it has had very little influence in the domestic law.

J. The so called "margin of appreciation"

2-168 In the previous chapter,[23] it was noted that the doctrine of a "margin of appreciation"[24] was of critical importance in the different conclusions reached by the judges in *The Sunday Times* decision. Thus contracting states always had a certain amount of discretion, subject to "European supervision", when taking legislative, administrative or judicial action in the area of a Convention right.[25] The doctrine is controversial,[26] since the recognition of a margin of appreciation opens up the possibility that rights will be differentially treated as between member states. A further complicating feature is that the degrees of latitude permitted to members states depend on the right in issue. A state may be allowed considerable latitude in deciding how far to protect public morals, for example.[27] But "the margin of appreciation is reduced almost to vanishing point in certain

---

[20] [1999] Q.B. 124 at 137A–C, Schiemann L.J., cited at para.9–3.
[21] For a discussion, see R. Masterman, "Section 2(1) of the Human Rights Act 1998: Binding Domestic Courts to Strasbourg" [2004] P.L. 725.
[22] See D. Feldman in eds. D. Harris and S. Joseph, *The International Covenant on Civil and Political Rights and United Kingdom Law*, "Freedom of Expression" (ch.12).
[23] para.1–107.
[24] In *Evans v Amicus Healthcare Ltd* [2005] Fam. 1 at [63] Sedley L.J. made the point that "the margin of appreciation (a solecism originating in the literal rendering in the English text of the decision in *Handyside v United Kingdom* (1976) 1 E.H.R.R. 737 of the French phrase 'marge d'appréciation', meaning margin of appraisal or judgment) is a tool by which the Strasbourg court gauges the relationship of a state's act to the Convention. It has no direct relevance to the process by which a court adjudicates, within a state, on the compatibility of a measure adopted by the executive or the legislature . . . ".
[25] See D.J. Harris, M. O'Boyle and C. Warbrick, *Law of the European Convention on Human Rights* (1995), p.12. See generally R. Clayton and H. Tomlinson, *The Law of Human Rights* (2000) and supplements, at paras 6–31—6–39; D. Feldman in ed. D. Feldman, *English Public Law* (2004) at paras 7–31—7–34. The doctrine has been the subject of consideration in the House of Lords in *R. v DPP Ex p. Kebilene* [2002] 2 A.C. 326 at 380–1, Lord Hope; *A v Secretary of State for the Home Department* [2004] UKHL 56, [2005] 2 W.L.R. 87, discussed by M. Dwyer, "Rights Brought Home" (2005) 121 L.Q.R. 359. And see P. Sales and B. Hooper, "Proportionality and the Form of Law" (2003) 119 L.Q.R. 426.
[26] See P. Mahoney, "Human rights: Universality versus subsidiarity in the Strasbourg case law on free speech: explaining some recent judgments" [1997] E.H.R.L.R. 364 and the reply by Lord Lester at [1998] E.H.R.L.R. 73.
[27] *Handyside v United Kingdom* (1976) Series A, No.24, 1 E.H.R.R. 737; *Jaggard v United Kingdom* (1997) 24 E.H.R.R. 39.

areas, as where the justification for a restriction is the protection of the authority of the judiciary".[28]

K. Developing the law of contempt judicially: Article 7

Art.7 of the Convention provides: 2–169

"(1) No one shall be held guilty of any criminal offence on account of any act or omission which did not constitute a criminal offence under national or international law at the time when it was committed. Nor shall a heavier penalty be imposed than the one that was applicable at the time the criminal offence was committed.
(2) This Article shall not prejudice the trial and punishment of any person for any act or omission which, at the time when it was committed, was criminal according to the general principles of law recognised by civilised nations."

This clearly has important implications in restricting the scope for judges to extend the law of contempt to new situations, even where it is being justified by reference to "principles".

This was a problem to which Lord Templeman, in *Lord Advocate v Scotsman* 2–170
Publications Ltd,[29] was clearly alive when he urged caution over the need to safeguard the respective roles of the courts and Parliament:

"In my opinion it is for Parliament to determine the restraints on freedom of expression which are necessary in a democratic society. The courts of this country should follow any guidance contained in a statute. If that guidance is inconsistent with the requirements of the convention then that will be a matter for the convention authorities and for the United Kingdom government. It will not be a matter for the courts."

Until 1960, there was no right of appeal in criminal contempt cases, and 2–171
therefore the scope for exposition or principled development of the law in this field was inevitably limited. Nevertheless, it is arguable that the scope for development in such a jurisdiction, being criminal in character, ought in any event to be narrowly confined. This is despite judicial remarks such as that of Lord Denning M.R. in *Att-Gen v Butterworth*[30]: "It may be that there is no authority to be found in the books, but if this be so, all I can say is that the sooner we make one the better."

---

[28] D.J. Harris, M. O'Boyle and C. Warbrick, *Law of the European Convention on Human Rights* (1995), p.14. In *Oberschlick v Austria* (1997) 25 E.H.R.R. 357, the Commission " . . . recalls that the adjective 'necessary' within the meaning of Article 10 implies the existence of a 'pressing social need'. The Contracting States enjoy a certain margin of appreciation in determining whether such a need exists, but this goes hand in hand with a European supervision, embracing both the legislation and the decisions applying it . . . ": para.48.
[29] [1989] 2 All E.R. 852 at 859g.
[30] [1963] 1 Q.B. 696. The conduct complained of in that case, namely the victimisation of a witness *after* giving evidence, would probably not constitute an offence under the Criminal Justice and Public Order Act 1994, s.51; see para.11–145. And see *Helmore v Smith (No.2)* (1886) 35 Ch.D. 449, where Cotton L.J. said "It is true that the exact case is a novel one. Counsel on neither side have been able to discover a case at all like it in its facts . . . though the case is a new one, [it] amounted to a contempt of Court", at 454–5, and Bowen L.J. observed, at 457, that "Where it is necessary for the protection of its officers . . . the court must shew that it has a long arm."

2-172 In the view also of Watkins L.J. in *Att-Gen v News Group Newspapers plc*,[31] a judicial extension of the common law could sometimes be justified:

> "The common law is not a worn out jurisprudence rendered incapable of further development by the ever increasing incursion of Parliamentary legislation. It is a lively body of law capable of adaption and expansion to meet fresh needs calling for the exertion of the discipline of the law".

No reference was made to the fact that the law of which expansion was contemplated is criminal in character, nor to the self-denying ordinance that the courts are no longer[32] free to re-define criminal offences as they see fit, as Watkins L.J. had himself acknowledged when invited to extend the law of blasphemy in *R. v Chief Metropolitan Magistrate Ex p. Choudhury*.[33] Nor was it made clear what "fresh needs" (as opposed to simply unforeseen circumstances) had manifested themselves, since 1981, as requiring an extension of the law.

2-173 So open a willingness to extend the scope of the criminal law might now be in peril of a challenge as being in breach of Art.7 of the Convention.[34] Moreover, the flexible approach towards development of the common law is difficult to reconcile with the specific attention given by Parliament in 1981 to this area of the law,[35] which was "intended to shift the balance permanently in favour of freedom of speech".[36]

2-174 An argument based on uncertainty was developed before the Privy Council, in relation to the Constitution of Mauritius, in *Ahnee v DPP*.[37] It was accepted that there was to be implied in s.10(4) a requirement that in criminal matters any law must be formulated with sufficient precision to enable the citizen to regulate his conduct. Reference was made to *Sunday Times v United Kingdom*.[38] Their Lordships rejected the argument that this provision was inapplicable for the reason that scandalising should not be regarded as truly criminal in character. Such a restrictive interpretation would mean, in the field of contempt, that retrospective or hopelessly vague legislation would not be unconstitutional. The

---

[31] [1989] Q.B. 110.
[32] *Knuller (Publishing, Printing and Promotions) Ltd v DPP* [1973] A.C. 435. For discussion see A.T.H. Smith, "Judicial Law Making in the Criminal Law" (1984) 100 L.Q.R. 46.
[33] [1991] 1 Q.B. 429.
[34] See, e.g. *R. v Miah* [1974] 1 W.L.R. 683 at 690H–691A, CA; 694C–E, HL. In *Manchester City Council v McCann* [1999] Q.B. 1214. Lord Woolf M.R. made the comment in the context of determining whether "insults" includes "threatens" within the meaning of s.118 of the County Courts Act 1984: "True, the statute is penal, but a *purposive* construction clearly points to the wider construction, which in our judgment is the right one". Although the language of purposive construction is unusual in the criminal law, the consequence of this interpretation seems unobjectionable on policy grounds.
[35] In *C v DPP* [1996] 1 A.C. 1, 28A–B, Lord Lowry warned that courts should be wary of venturing into judicial law-making in areas which had received specific attention of the legislature.
[36] Lloyd L.J. in *Att-Gen v Newspaper Publishing plc* [1988] Ch. 333 at 382D–F.
[37] [1999] 2 A.C. 294. The provision under consideration corresponded to Art.7 of the ECHR.
[38] (1979) 2 E.H.R.R. 245.

implied guarantee of certainty was indeed applicable to the contempt jurisdiction but there was no breach because the meaning of "scandalising" was sufficiently explained in the case law.

The expansive or creative approach adopted in some cases[39] may be contrasted with the words of Hodgson J. in *Att-Gen v Sport Newspapers Ltd*[40]: 2–175

"I do not think that the ambit of the summary procedure for publication contempt should be widened. The criminal law should be left to deal with offences of perverting the course of justice. Judges should not find guilt and punish unless it is necessary for the effective control of active proceedings. If contempt be the Proteus of the common law then for my part I would hope that his repertoire will not be increased."

Yet the matter is by no means straightforward. The traditional approach of the English common law (even in the context of crime) appears to be that, while general principles of the law of contempt can readily be stated, there is scope for the application of those principles in new and diverse circumstances, and that this process should not be regarded as judicial law-making at all. 2–176

Lord Ackner addressed the issue in *Att-Gen v Times Newspapers Ltd*,[41] in response to the proposition that "It is for Parliament and not the courts to extend the concept of criminal contempt": 2–177

"I do not accept that your Lordships are being asked by the Attorney-General to widen the law of criminal contempt. The submission of the Attorney-General is based upon established principles, to which I have made detailed reference. The issue in this case is whether, in applying those established principles to novel facts, the offence has been established. I agree with the view expressed by Sir John Donaldson M.R. [1988] Ch. 333, 368D in his judgment on the preliminary issue that the application of the established principle to novel circumstances, for example to the punishment of a witness *after* he has given evidence (*Attorney-General v Butterworth* [1963] 1 Q.B. 696) is not a case of *widening* the principle. It is merely a new example of its application".

This suggests that it is permissible to argue that the categories of contempt are not closed for ever. To what extent should it be open to the courts to continue to extend the law (especially the criminal law) while purporting to do no more than apply a principle? 2–178

---

[39] See the discussion of Nicholls L.J.'s judgment in *Att-Gen v Newspaper Publishing* in the Court of Appeal at [1990] T.L.R. 158 (Lexis) and his reference to a "broad, flexible approach" at para.5–160.
[40] [1991] 1 W.L.R. 1198 at 1230C, [1992] 1 All E.R. 503 at 536g. See also Lord Scarman in *Att-Gen v BBC* [1981] A.C. 303 at 362A–C: "Neither the meagre authorities available in the books nor the historical origins of contempt of court require the House to extend the doctrine to administrative courts and tribunals... If Parliament wishes to extend the doctrine to a specific institution which it establishes, it must say so explicitly in its enactment".
[41] [1992] 1 A.C. 191 at 215.

L. "Principles" contrasted with "rules" in criminal law

2–179 Lord Ackner speaks of a "principle", by which he appears to be referring to the proposition that any conduct that is intended to interfere with the due administration of justice amounts to a contempt of court.[42] But it may be said that the law, especially the criminal law, consists primarily of rules rather than principles.[43] Principles tend (1) to be general and sometimes vague or uncertain in their formulation and (2) to come into conflict with one another, so as to give rise to a need for reconciliation.

1. Vagueness

2–180 To take each in turn: vagueness is a vice in the formulation of the criminal law, since it prevents any citizen from knowing what the law requires, permits or prohibits.[44] It is not so much that the person at risk *does not* know, but that he genuinely *cannot* know until the court has decided how the law is to be applied to the situation confronting him. This, particularly in a context where freedom of expression is at issue, is objectionable. Intelligent guesswork or anticipation cannot be a substitute in such situations for knowledge.[45] Resort to one "principle" may often be met by reference to another, apparently inconsistent, and detailed rules or sub-principles are thus required in order to achieve a reconciliation.

2. The tendency to conflict

2–181 Secondly, since principles tend to conflict, their application may call for the making of policy judgments on issues of priority, by reference to detailed and ascertainable rules, which ideally in a democracy ought to be made by the legislature.[46] For example, the defence afforded by s.5 of the 1981 Act[47] (that even prejudicial publication is permitted if it is incidental to the discussion in good faith of public affairs or other matters of general public interest) reflects a compromise, worked out by Parliament, between the competing principles of free speech and fair trial. Yet Parliament cannot in practice resolve all conflicts that

---

[42] His Lordship had cited a passage from the Phillimore Committee, Cmnd. 5794, para.1, and also some words of Lord Diplock in *Att-Gen v Leveller Magazine Ltd* [1979] A.C. 440 at 449 and concluded that "it has accordingly been common ground throughout this appeal that the aim and purpose of the law of contempt is to prevent interference with the due administration of justice."

[43] The distinction between rules and principles was discussed by R. Dworkin, "The Model of Rules" (1967) Univ. of Chicago Law Rev.

[44] J. Jeffries, "Legality, Vagueness and the Construction of Penal Statutes" (1985) 71 Va. L.R. 189. Vagueness may in certain circumstances constitute a ground for judicial review of statutes in the United States. The classic article on the issue is A. Amsterdam, "The Void-for-Vagueness Doctrine in the Supreme Court" (1960) 109 U. Pa. L. Rev. 67.

[45] Compare the commentary on *Camelot Group plc v Centaur Communications Ltd* [1999] Q.B. 124, at para.9–11. It may be noted that the New Zealand Court of Appeal declined, in the context of freedom of speech, to adopt the House of Lords' exposition of qualified privilege in *Reynolds v Times Newspapers Ltd* [2001] 2 A.C. 127 because of the "chilling effect" of its perceived vagueness and uncertainty: *Lange v Atkinson* [2000] NZCA 95, [2000] 3 N.Z.L.R. 385.

[46] See the passage cited from Lord Templeman in para.2–170.

[47] para.4–293.

may arise, and therefore judges will need to effect the reconciliation between principles themselves. This requires them to make policy decisions, or else to resort to some higher or more general principle for that purpose. This has happened with increasing frequency now that the European Convention has taken its place in English law.

3. *The advantages of "rules"*

By contrast, the advantage of rules is that there is less scope for conflict. Rules can be refined and qualified. Where a rule is being applied, it is likely to yield a conclusion much more easily. Section 5 itself contains a rule, which states that "a publication made as or as part of a discussion in good faith of public affairs or other matters of general public interest is not to be treated as contempt of court under the strict liability rule if the risk of impediment or prejudice to particular proceedings is merely incidental to the discussion." Although a rule may sometimes be difficult to apply, because it too may be in some respects vague and imprecise, at least there should be no difficulty of having to reconcile it with a conflicting rule. It is purely a question of ascertaining whether the wording covers the situation in hand.

2–182

M. The problem illustrated in *Dobson v Hastings*

This difficulty of having to *apply* principles to uncharted factual situations, and the potentially serious consequences for investigative journalism, required consideration by Sir Donald Nicholls V.-C. in *Dobson v Hastings*.[48] The case concerned a journalist who visited the office of the Registrar of Companies to inspect an originating summons relating to the disqualification of company directors. She was made aware that she needed leave to inspect the court file, but assumed that this was a formality and took advantage of the fact that the file had been left with her meanwhile, in order to make notes with a view to incorporating the information in a newspaper article. One of the matters she explored was the Official Receiver's report. In fact she should have made a written application, supported by an affidavit. This was subsequently explained by the Registrar when he telephoned the newspaper office. The editor formed the impression from the conversation that it was a matter of balancing ethical considerations, rather than one of legal restraint, and he decided to go ahead with the publication of a story based upon the information which she had obtained.

2–183

On the facts, it was held that all the respondents (the editor, the individual journalist, the managing director and the company) lacked the necessary *mens rea*. It was recognised that "the court system was at fault far more than she was."[49] Nevertheless, the difficulty of applying principles to new situations was expressly recognised by the Vice-Chancellor[50]:

2–184

---

[48] [1992] Ch. 394.
[49] At 408H.
[50] At 404B–C.

[127]

"I am very conscious of the need for the court to take great care, and exercise much caution, when confronted with an apparently novel application of the established principles relating to contempt of court."

2–185   In the particular case, the rules were not widely known, and they did not in any event provide a sanction against someone who obtained or published information without the necessary leave. This left only the court's jurisdiction in contempt as the means of securing compliance with the rules. The central question was therefore whether a person committed a contempt of court (or, in the language preferred by the Vice-Chancellor, an interference with the administration of justice) if he or she inspected a court file without having obtained leave when it was *known* to be necessary. The Vice-Chancellor was obliged to go back to first principles, in circumstances where the authorities gave no specific guidance.

2–186   He found as a matter of fact that there was no trickery or dishonesty on the part of the journalist, and that she had been given the file to take to the Registrar herself (a practice which was subsequently changed). She could not be blamed for concluding in those circumstances that, if they really were confidential, the documents would not have been entrusted to her. He decided that the boundary should be drawn where information was taken from documents in the custody of the court with knowledge that leave was needed and that it had not been obtained. The necessary *mens rea* was held to be lacking, on the facts, because the "key feature is the need for knowledge that the inspection in question is a contravention of the rules". There would be such knowledge in the case of a person who was fully aware that a court officer was acting under a mistake, just as much as in a case where the mistaken belief was induced by deception.

2–187   At first sight, it might be thought that this approach conflicts with the general principle in the criminal law that ignorance is no excuse.[51] On the other hand, the Vice-Chancellor was not deciding a charge of failing to comply with the rules as such, but rather determining whether the journalist had intended to interfere with the court's process; her understandable failure to appreciate the breach of the rules would clearly be material in arriving at a conclusion on *that* issue.

2–188   Quite often, where a person is accused of interfering with the course of justice, it will be obvious to all concerned that the conduct in question can be so characterised. In the circumstances of this case, the Vice-Chancellor was dealing with a somewhat arcane set of rules, requiring non-parties who wished to inspect documents to obtain leave from the court. These formed but "a small part of the whole framework the law has created for the just and convenient resolution of disputes and claims". Yet, even in this somewhat obscure area, a person who acted in breach of the rules could be described as "setting at nought one of the court's procedures devised to strike a balance between the various factors which pull in different directions in all court processes."[52] He concluded therefore that,

---

[51] *Cambridgeshire and Isle of Ely County Council v Rust* [1972] 2 Q.B. 426, where the person convicted had been actively misled by the officials responsible for administering the legislation.
[52] [1992] Ch. 394 at 404A.

provided there was knowledge, such conduct could amount to the *actus reus* of contempt of court.

This case illustrates how infinitely varied the circumstances are in which a person might be said to be interfering, knowingly or otherwise, with the administration of justice. Sir John Donaldson M.R. in *Att-Gen v Newspaper Publishing plc*[53] had referred to the contempt jurisdiction as being "Protean"; just as Lord Diplock[54] had referred to criminal contempt as taking a "variety of forms". Although flexibility has advantages for the protection of the administration of justice, as *Dobson v Hastings* illustrates,[55] there is bound to be a degree of corresponding and undesirable uncertainty.

2–189

Another illustration of the difficulty of applying general principles to novel factual situations is provided by the case of *R. v Powell*.[56] The Court of Appeal recognised the problem of coping with the general principle that the purpose of proceedings for contempt was to ensure the due administration of justice without interference, but sought guidance in carrying that principle into effect from s.12 of the Contempt of Court Act 1981, which deals with wilful insults or interruption in magistrates' courts, even though the facts before them concerned proceedings in the Crown Court. Nonetheless, Staughton L.J. expressed the view that it "must have been intended by Parliament to reflect the sort of behaviour which would, at the very least, constitute contempt in the face of the court at common law." There was clearly a wariness of appearing to step outside that which had been clearly established. It is necessary now to have particular regard for the restrictions imposed by Art.7 of the European Convention on Human Rights, which identifies retrospectivity in criminal law matters as being undesirable.

2–190

N. The need to confine judicial law-making in the criminal context

In *C v DPP*,[57] Lord Lowry tried to set the boundaries to judicial law-making:

2–191

"(1) if the solution is doubtful, the judges should beware of imposing their own remedy; (2) caution should prevail if Parliament has rejected opportunities of clearing up a known difficulty or has legislated while leaving the difficulty untouched;(3) disputed

---

[53] [1988] Ch. 333 at 362B–C.
[54] *Att-Gen v Leveller Magazine Ltd* [1979] A.C. 440 at 449E–F: "... they all share a common characteristic: they involve an interference with the due administration of justice, either in a particular case or more generally as a continuing process."
[55] Nicholls L.J. also appeared to commend the advantages of flexibility in *Att-Gen v Newspaper Publishing* 1990 T.L.R. 158, CA (Lexis). See the discussion at paras 5–160 *et seq*.
[56] (1994) 98 Cr.App.R. 224 (wolf-whistling at a juror). The facts are more fully discussed at para.10–99. See also *R. v Schot and Barclay* [1997] 2 Cr.App.R. 383, (1997) 161 J.P. 473, para.10–72, where the application of principle was also required in an unprecedented situation involving jurors.
[57] [1996] 1 A.C. 1. The decision altering the marital rape immunity *R v R* [1992] 1 A.C. 599, was challenged in the European Court of Human Rights, but the European Court ruled that there was no breach of Art.7; [1996] 1 F.L.R. 434. See P.R. Ghandhi and J.A. James, "Marital Rape and Retrospectivity—the Human Rights Dimension at Strasbourg" (1997) 9 Ch. and F.L.Q. 17.

2–191 CHAPTER 2—CONTEMPT OF COURT: CONSTITUTIONAL DIMENSIONS

matters of social policy are less suitable areas for judicial intervention than purely legal problems; (4) fundamental legal doctrines should not lightly be set aside; (5) judges should not make change unless they can achieve finality and certainty."

This guidance was given in the context of a criminal case but could be construed as expressing a policy of broader application. Nonetheless, since the advent of the Human Rights Act and the need to take account of European Court jurisprudence, it is probably fair to say that these observations are less authoritative in the context of civil cases.

O. Contempt cases in which reliance was placed upon the European Convention

2–192 It may be of some interest to list the English contempt cases in which the Convention was cited prior to the Human Rights Act 1998. The extent to which it was influential in the decision-making process is, to some extent, a matter of conjecture, but that it had already become a regular feature of the jurisprudence is undeniable.

2–193 The Convention has on several occasions been seen to be relevant to the question what qualifies as a "court" for the purposes of contempt of court.[58] It was also relevant in determining the continuing effect of the implied undertaking given upon discovery when documents have been read in open court,[59] and to the right to inspect pleadings in advance of a hearing in open court.[60] It has also been considered on such miscellaneous matters as the power of a prison governor to censor correspondence,[61] the right of newspapers to appeal against the making of orders restricting court reporting or the withholding of other information from the public,[62] and the protection of journalists' sources.[63]

---

[58] *Att-Gen v BBC* [1981] A.C. 303 at 352, 354A–F, 362D; *Att-Gen v Associated Newspapers Group plc* [1989] 1 W.L.R. 322 at 325G, 328B–G, CA, Mann L.J.; overruled in *P v Liverpool Daily Post and Echo Newspapers plc* [1991] 2 A.C. 370, where the Convention was again prayed in aid, at 380H–381C, 391C, CA, Lord Donaldson M.R. and Farquharson L.J.; 413A–B, HL, Lord Bridge. See also *X v The United Kingdom* (1981) 4 E.H.R.R. 188.
[59] *Harman v Secretary of State for the Home Department* [1983] 1 A.C. 280 at 299F, 311C, 315D, 316H, 317G, 318D. See the former RSC Ord.24, Rule 14A and now CPR 31.22. The present law is discussed paras 12–201 *et seq*.
[60] *Att-Gen v Limbrick, The Times* [1996] T.L.R. 186, Garland J. (Lexis).
[61] *Raymond v Honey* [1983] 1 A.C. 1 at 10F–G, 15B–C; see para.11–302.
[62] *Ex p. Crook, The Times*, November 8, 1984; *Hodgson, Woolf Productions and N.U.J. and Channel 4 v United Kingdom* (1987) 10 E.H.R.R. 503 at 510; Criminal Justice Act 1988, s.159.
[63] *Secretary of State for Defence v Guardian Newspapers Ltd* [1985] A.C. 339 at 361E–F; *Re an Inquiry under the Company Securities (Insider Dealing) Act* [1988] A.C. 660 at 684C, CA, Lloyd L.J, 705F–706E, HL, Lord Griffiths. By contrast, the Convention does not appear to have been specifically addressed by the House in *X Ltd v Morgan-Grampian (Publishers) Ltd* [1991] 1 A.C. 1, although Lord Templeman does allude to the European Court of Human Rights' interpretation of "necessary", at 49. *Goodwin v UK* (1996) 22 E.H.R.R. 123 contains the judgment of the European Court of Human Rights arising from that decision. And see *Chief Constable of Leicestershire v Garavelli* [1997] E.M.L.R. 543.

THE IMPACT OF THE EUROPEAN CONVENTION 2–196

The Convention was also important in the *Spycatcher* litigation.⁶⁴ It is 2–194
pertinent to ascertaining the scope of restrictions upon publication for the
protection of children,⁶⁵ and the interpretation of the provisions of the Contempt
of Court Act 1981 against invading the secrecy of the jury room.⁶⁶ The scope of
the common law of contempt, whether by publication,⁶⁷ or otherwise,⁶⁸ and the
scope of the strict liability rule itself,⁶⁹ have all been determined in the light of
the Convention, as has the availability or otherwise of judicial review of a Home
Office circular on police obligations to alert the press as to whether or not a
suspect has been arrested.⁷⁰

Other relevant cases in which reference was made to the European Convention 2–195
on Human Rights prior to October 2000 include *R. v Lord Saville of Newdigate*⁷¹
(anonymity sought for witnesses at the "Bloody Sunday" Inquiry in the context
of protecting their right to life); *Newman v Modern Bookbinders Ltd*⁷² (the need
to inform an alleged contemnor of the right to legal aid, as it then was); *Re
Swaptronics*,⁷³ (where the potential difficulties were pointed out, in the light of
Art.6, for the continuance of the judicial discretion not to hear a litigant for so
long as he or she remains in breach of a court order); *Kelly v BBC*.⁷⁴

Quite apart from the cases in which the European Convention was expressly 2–196
prayed in aid in support of a judicial decision, it was also having an indirect
impact. The language and thinking that infuse the European jurisprudence have
become part of the common law. This is well illustrated by the judgment of Lord

---

⁶⁴ *Att-Gen v Newspaper Publishing plc* [1988] Ch. 333, 382, Lloyd L.J.; *Att. Gen. v Observer Ltd: Re an Application by Derbyshire County Council* [1988] 1 All E.R. 385 at 396b–c, 398e–g; *Att-Gen v Newspaper Publishing plc* [1989] 1 F.S.R. 457 at 475–6, Morritt J.; *Att-Gen v Newspaper Publishing plc* [1990] T.L.R. 158, CA (Lexis); *Att-Gen v Times Newspapers Ltd* [1992] 1 A.C. 191 at 225C–F, Lord Oliver; *The Observer and Guardian v United Kingdom* (1992) 14 E.H.R.R. 153.
⁶⁵ *Re Z (A Minor) (Identification)* [1997] Fam. 1. Guidance was also given in *Re C (Wardship: Treatment) (No.2)* [1990] Fam. 39, and in *Re M & N (Minors)* [1990] Fam. 211, and the principal considerations were extracted from those authorities and helpfully listed by Neill L. J. in *Re W (A Minor)* [1992] 1 W.L.R. 100 at 103. See also *Official Solicitor v News Group Newspapers plc* [1994] 2 F.L.R. 174 at 183A–D, Connell J.; *Re H-S* [1994] 3 All E.R. 390 at 398a–d, where the Court of Appeal drew attention to the need to take account not only of Art.10 but also of Art.8 of the Convention ("right to respect for private and family life") in deciding the scope of an order prohibiting the identification of children whose father was seeking to publicise his experiences as a transsexual.
⁶⁶ *Att-Gen v Associated Newspapers Ltd* [1994] 2 A.C. 238 at 242C–243F, 246G–H, 247B–248E, D.C.; HL, 258E–G, 261H–262H, Lord Lowry. See further paras 11–349 *et seq.*
⁶⁷ *Att-Gen v Sport Newspapers Ltd* [1991] 1 W.L.R. 1194 at 1206B–E, [1992] 1 All E.R. 503 at 514e–j, Bingham L.J.; *Re Lonrho plc* [1990] 2 A.C. at 208G–H where Lord Bridge expressed the view that prejudgment cannot any longer *per se* be a contempt in the light of Art.10.
⁶⁸ *Dobson v Hastings* [1993] Ch. 394 at 405D–406A, para.2–183.
⁶⁹ *Att-Gen v MGN Ltd* [1997] 1 All. E.R. 456 at 459, Schiemann L.J.
⁷⁰ *R. v Secretary of State for the Home Department Ex p. Westminster Press Ltd* (1992) 4 Admin.L.R. 445 at 453C, D.C., Watkins L.J.
⁷¹ [2000] 1 W.L.R. 1855, [1999] 4 All E.R. 860.
⁷² [2000] 1 W.L.R. 2559, [2000] 2 All E.R. 814.
⁷³ *The Times*, August 17, 1998, 95 (36) L.S.G. 33. (But see *Motorola Credit Corporation v Uzan (No.2)* [2003] EWCA Civ 752, [2004] 1 W.L.R. 113 at [56]–[58], where some of Laddie J.'s observations were considered and doubts expressed).
⁷⁴ [2001] Fam. 59.

2–196 CHAPTER 2—CONTEMPT OF COURT: CONSTITUTIONAL DIMENSIONS

Bingham C.J. in *Att-Gen v Newspaper Publishing plc*,[75] who, in rejecting the notion of technical contempts, emphasised " . . . that the restraints upon freedom of expression should be no wider than are truly necessary in a democratic society . . . ".[76]

2–197 In *Att-Gen v Guardian Newspapers Ltd*,[77] the Divisional Court considered an article in *The Observer*, published in the course of a trial, which suggested that one of the defendants was a necrophile with a perverted personality. He was charged with stealing body parts and the only live issue at the time was whether he and his co-defendant had behaved dishonestly. The test was applied, at least as a cross-check, whether the right to a fair trial rendered it necessary and proportionate in a democratic society that the respondent should not publish the article at the relevant time. The application was dismissed on the basis that there was no substantial risk of serious prejudice.

P. The enactment of the Human Rights Act 1998

2–198 It is now almost inevitable, since the coming into effect of the Human Rights Act 1998, that reference will be made to the European Convention in contempt proceedings. Moreover, the Practice Direction[78] supplementing RSC Ord.52 and CCR Ord.29 emphasises the need to address "Convention rights". There is, of course, a wealth of material by way of judicial pronouncements and academic writing as to the significance generally of the Human Rights Act 1998, which came in to effect in October 2000.[79] It is not within the scope of this work to rehearse it save inasmuch as it has a direct bearing, as it plainly must, in the field of contempt. In general terms, however, as is well known, the following general principles apply:

---

[75] [1997] 1 W.L.R. 926 at 936C, 3 All E.R. 159 at 168j.
[76] See also the European formulation used by Lord Templeman in *Att-Gen v Guardian Newspapers Ltd* [1987] 1 W.L.R. 1248 at 1296: "the question is therefore whether the interference with freedom of expression constituted by the Millett injunction was . . . necessary in a democratic society in the interests of national security, for protecting the reputation or rights of others, for preventing the disclosure of information received in confidence or for maintaining the authority and impartiality of the judiciary . . . ".
[77] [1999] E.M.L.R. 904.
[78] Set out in Appendix 5A.
[79] See by way of example Desmond Browne Q.C., "Article 10 ECHR and freedom of expression: What has it added to the common law?" and Sir Charles Gray, "The bastion of freedom of expression—is it threatened by the laws of confidentiality, privacy or contempt" in eds M. Saville and R. Susskind, *Essays in Honour of Sir Brian Neill: The Quintessential Judge* (Butterworths, 2003) at pp.17 and 173 respectively. See also C. Gearty, *Principles of Human Rights Adjudication* (Oxford University Press 2004) 54–59. The author is critical of the decision of the House of Lords in *R (ProLife Alliance) v BBC* [2002] EWCA Civ 297, [2003] UKHL 23, [2004] 1 A.C. 185, also discussed by A. Scott, "A Monstrous and Unjustifiable Infringement? Political Expression and the Broadcasting Ban on Advocacy Advertising" (2003) 66 M.L.R. 224; A. Geddis, "What Future for Political Advertising on the United Kingdom's Television Screens" [2002] P.L. 615; L. Wildhaber, "The Right to Offend, Shock or Disturb?—Aspects of Freedom of Expression under the European Convention on Human Rights" (2001) 36 The Irish Jurist 17; M. Amos, "Can We Speak Freely Now? Freedom of Expression under the Human Rights Act" [2002] E.H.R.L.R. 750; I. Hare, "Method and Objectivity in Free Speech Adjudication: Lessons from America" (2005) 54 I.C.L.Q. 49.

1. Convention rights (including of course, freedom of expression, open justice and privacy) became enforceable in the courts of the United Kingdom;
2. The Strasbourg jurisprudence must be taken into account by domestic tribunals when issues engaging Convention rights arise (s.2);
3. Legislation *must* be interpreted compatibly with Convention rights so far as it is possible to do so (s.3);
4. Courts as "public authorities" must act compatibly with Convention rights in their actions—unless prevented by primary legislation (which might give rise to the need for a declaration of incompatibility) (ss.4 and 6);
5. Specific provision is made in s.12 with regard to the grant of injunctions affecting freedom of expression. This seems to have been somewhat hastily drafted, but its general effect now seems reasonably clear in the light of the House of Lords' decision in *Cream Holdings v Banerjee*[80] and that of the Court of Appeal in *Martha Greene v Associated Newspapers*.[81]

The consequences for the grant of injunctions to restrain a contempt are addressed in chapter 6 (England and Wales) and chapter 16 (Scotland).

V. THE ROLE OF THE ATTORNEY-GENERAL

A. The initiation of contempt proceedings

It has long been recognised that the Attorney-General is the "appropriate officer" to safeguard the public interest,[82] and that he has a considerable discretion as to when it may be appropriate to initiate proceedings,[83] and in particular contempt proceedings, for the purpose of vindicating that interest. In *R. v Hargreaves Ex p. Dill*[84] the Divisional Court had dismissed a motion for attachment against the editor of *Lilliput* in connection with an article which appeared to attribute responsibility over a racing fraud, then currently the subject of criminal proceedings. Lord Goddard C.J. expressed the view that such motions should only be made by the Law Officers.[85]

2–199

---

[80] [2004] UKHL 44, [2005] 1 A.C. 253.
[81] [2004] EWCA 1462, [2005] 3 W.L.R. 281, [2005] 1 All E.R. 30.
[82] Sedley L.J. in *Att-Gen v Guardian Newspapers Ltd* [1999] E.M.L.R. 904 has expressed the view that the Attorney-General would not be regarded as a "victim" for the purposes of Art.6 of the E.C.H.R. The only person who has a *right* to a fair criminal trial is the accused; the press on the other hand enjoy an express right to freedom of expression under Art.10.
[83] See the Law Commission's paper, *Consents to Prosecution*, Law Com. No.149 (1997). For a discussion of the possible role of the Attorney-General in connection with the protection of journalists' sources, see paras 9–239 *et seq*.
[84] [1954] Crim.L.R. 54, *The Times*, November 4, 1953.
[85] He had made a similar point in *R. v Lawson Ex p. Nodder* (1937) 81 Sol. Jo. 280.

2–200 Subsequently, in *Att-Gen v Times Newspapers Ltd*[86] Lord Diplock (who had been counsel for the successful respondent in *Hargreaves*), expressed approval of the practice which had thereafter been adopted in the light of Lord Goddard's remarks, whereby the Attorney had accepted responsibility for receiving complaints of alleged contempt, and of making an application in his official capacity if he considered that course to be justified in the public interest. He continued:

> "He is the appropriate public officer to represent the public interest in the administration of justice. In doing so he acts in constitutional theory on behalf of the Crown, as do Her Majesty's judges themselves; but he acts on behalf of the Crown as 'the fountain of justice' and not in the exercise of its executive functions. It is in a similar capacity that he is available to assist the court as amicus curiae and is a nominal party to relator actions. Where it becomes manifest, as it had by 1954, that there is a need that the public interest should be represented in a class of proceedings before courts of justice which have hitherto been conducted by those representing private interests only, we are fortunate in having a constitution flexible enough to permit of this extension of the historic role of the Attorney-General.
>
> ... Where complaint is made to the Attorney-General of an alleged contempt, in deciding whether to move the court for committal of the contemner *(sic)* he is concerned, not with whether the conduct is a technical contempt but whether it falls into the category of contempts which the court would regard as deserving of some punishment. Since this involves anticipating the way in which the court would exercise its own wide discretion, there is clearly a considerable field for the exercise of his personal judgment."

2–201 Lord Cross[87] described the role of the Attorney-General in carefully chosen words, differing from the views expressed in the Court of Appeal by Lord Denning M.R. and Phillimore L.J. as to his function in cases of alleged contempt of court:

> "If he takes them up he does not do so as a Minister of the Crown—'putting the authority of the Crown behind the complaint' [1973] Q.B. 710, 738— but as 'amicus curiae' bring to the notice of the court some matter of which he considers that the court shall be informed in the interests of the administration of justice. It is, I think, most desirable that in civil as well as in criminal cases anyone who thinks that a criminal contempt of court has been or is about to be committed should, if possible, place the facts before the Attorney-General for him to consider whether or not those facts appear to disclose a contempt of court of sufficient gravity to warrant his bringing the matter to notice of the court. Of course, in some cases it may be essential if an application is to be made at all for it to be made promptly and there may be no time for the person affected by the 'contempt' to put the facts before the Attorney before moving himself. Again the fact that the Attorney declines to take up the case will not prevent the complainant from seeking to persuade the court that notwithstanding the refusal of the Attorney to act the matter complained of does in fact constitute a contempt of which the court should taken notice. Yet again, of course, there may be cases where a serious contempt appears to have been committed but for one reason or another none of the parties affected by it wishes any action to be taken in respect of it. In such cases if the

---

[86] [1974] A.C. 273, 311. And see J. Ll. Edwards, *The Attorney-General, Politics and the Public Interest* (1984) 168 at 174.
[87] [1974] A.C. at 326–7.

facts come to the knowledge of the Attorney from some other source he will naturally himself bring the matter to the attention of the court."

These passages illustrate why it is generally inappropriate to refer to the initiation of contempt proceedings by the Attorney-General as being a "prosecution".[88] In deciding whether or not to initiate proceedings against a newspaper publisher or editor, the Attorney-General makes a practice of writing to the editor responsible for the offending publication, asking whether there is any reason why contempt proceedings should not be brought, but pointing out that the editor is under no obligation to give any explanation should he choose not to do so. 2–202

B. Section 7 of the Contempt of Court Act 1981

Prior to the passing of the Contempt of Court Act 1981, private individuals could initiate contempt proceedings although, in the case of contempts by publication, the usual practice was to refer the complaint to the Attorney-General. Where, however, it is now contemplated that proceedings should be brought under "the strict liability rule", s.7 provides: 2–203

"Proceedings for a contempt of court under the strict liability rule (other than Scottish proceedings) shall not be instituted except by or with the consent of the Attorney General or on the motion of a court having jurisdiction to deal with it."

Thus, it is clear that in this respect the words of Lord Cross[89] have now to be qualified, in the sense that if the Attorney declines to take up a strict liability case that fact *will* prevent a complainant from seeking to persuade the court[90] that there has been a contempt. If it is alleged that *mens rea* is present and a common law contempt has been committed, private parties will not require his consent.[91] 2–204

Where anyone alleges that a publication falls within the strict liability rule, consent must be obtained. For example, in *Taylor v Topping*,[92] a circuit judge having directed the acquittal of the applicant,[93] and instructed that a recently published book, in which the applicant was described as a person "who associated regularly with people believed to be involved in serious organised crime", should be referred to the Attorney-General with a view to seeing whether he might wish to bring proceedings for contempt. The Attorney declined, but the applicant brought proceedings to commit nevertheless. 2–205

The court took the view, however, that since there was no evidence before it of any specific intention to affect the proceedings, the matter could only be dealt 2–206

---

[88] See the discussion as to the extent to which it is appropriate to employ the language of the criminal law, in paras 3–67 and 3–78 *et seq.*
[89] See para.2–201.
[90] It will be noted that the court's jurisdiction to proceed of its own motion is expressly preserved.
[91] But see the discussion of *Roger Bullivant v Ellis*, Falconer J., *Financial Times*, April 15, 1986 (Lexis) at paras 4–185 *et seq.*
[92] [1990] T.L.R. 110 (Lexis).
[93] The transcript does not disclose the nature of the charge.

with, if at all, under the strict liability rule. The Attorney-General was entitled to decline to proceed under that rule, and the application was accordingly dismissed.

C. Doubts as to the *locus standi* of other persons

2–207   Outside this context, however, there remains a degree of uncertainty as to the limits of the *locus standi* of individual litigants or other interested parties to initiate proceedings for contempt; not least because sometimes there is an overlap between the public interest and the need to protect the private interests of an individual litigant. The matter has been left open in three recent cases.[94]

D. *Locus standi* to obtain an injunction

2–208   Even in relation to the obtaining of an injunction, the matter is by no means free from doubt. It appeared to be the law that s.7 did not prevent someone other than the Attorney-General from bringing proceedings for an injunction to prevent the commission of an apprehended contempt.[95] Later, this question, described as "both difficult and important", was left open by the House of Lords for future consideration.[96]

E. Considering the public interest

2–209   Normally, even where it is the rights or interests of an individual citizen that are primarily in issue, because contempt of court arises there will also be an element of public interest involved. In *Gouriet v UPOW*,[97] it was recognised that individuals may have a role to play when seeking to enforce private rights through public law remedies. On the other hand, it was for the Law Officers exclusively to represent the *public* interest.[98] In the words of Lord Wilberforce,[99] "That it is the exclusive right of the Attorney General to represent the public interest . . . is not technical, not procedural, not fictional. It is constitutional."

2–210   A more recent example, in the context of journalists' sources, is provided by *DPP v Channel 4*,[1] where an officer in the Metropolitan Police Special Branch

---

[94] *Dobson v Hastings* [1992] Ch. 394 at 411, Sir Donald Nicholls V.-C.; *P v Liverpool Daily Post and Echo Newspapers plc* [1991] 2 A.C. 370 at 425, HL, Lord Bridge; *Chief Constable of Leicestershire v Garavelli* [1997] E.M.L.R. 543. See also the remarks of Laws L.J. in *Pelling v Hammond* (C/00/2363), September 22, 2000, cited at para.3–174, n.91 below.
[95] *Peacock v London Weekend Television* (1985) 150 J.P. 71, (1985) 150 J.P.N. 47 CA; *Leary v BBC*, September 29, 1989, unreported, CA (Lexis), although Ralph Gibson L.J. preferred to leave the question of *locus standi* open.
[96] *P v Liverpool Daily Post and Echo Newspapers plc* [1991] 2 A.C. 370 at 425A–C, Lord Bridge.
[97] [1978] A.C. 435 at 482–3.
[98] *ibid.*, at 483D–484B, Lord Wilberforce; 495E–F, Viscount Dilhorne; 499G–500F, Lord Diplock; 518–519, Lord Fraser. See also *Att-Gen v Newspaper Publishing plc* [1988] Ch. 333 at 362D, 367H–368A, Sir John Donaldson M.R.; *Balogh v St. Albans Crown Court* [1975] 1 Q.B. 73 at 88F–G, Stephenson L.J.
[99] At 481A–B.
[1] [1993] 2 All E.R. 517 at 519c–d, 523g–h.

had made an application[2] for documents to be produced by Channel 4 and also by a production company. Orders were made, and the respondents refused to comply, in particular, with an order that material which had been removed abroad should be returned to the jurisdiction. This was because they did not wish to disclose their source. The matter was referred to the Attorney-General, and an application was made on his behalf under RSC Ord.52[3] for the imposition of fines or orders of sequestration against the companies.

Shortly afterwards, in *Chief Constable of Leicestershire v Garavelli*,[4] the Divisional Court found it unnecessary to consider whether applications to enforce orders for the disclosure of a journalist's source should *only* be made on behalf of the Law Officers. The argument raised was to the effect that, since the European Court of Human Rights in *Goodwin v United Kingdom*[5] had emphasised the need for an "overriding *public* interest" before such orders should be made, the Attorney was the appropriate person to assess and protect any such public interest.

A decision by the Attorney-General not to commence proceedings is sometimes a matter of controversy. Increasingly, the legal representatives of persons about to be placed on trial are inclined to criticise such decisions.[6] Nevertheless, it has been held in *R. v Solicitor-General Ex p. Taylor*[7] that the decision of the Law Officers not to institute proceedings under the strict liability rule is not amenable to judicial review.

The sequence of events was as follows. In *R. v Taylor and Taylor*,[8] the convictions of two sisters had been quashed on the ground that the newspaper coverage of their trial for murder was "unremitting, extensive, sensational, inaccurate and misleading". In spite of this, the Law Officers declined to bring proceedings for contempt.[9] The refusal of the court to interfere has been criticised,[10] on the ground that it appears to exempt the Law Officers alone from

---

[2] Under the Prevention of Terrorism (Temporary Provisions) Act 1989, Sch.7, para.3. Repealed by the Terrorism Act 2000.
[3] See now CPR, Sch.1, Ord.52.
[4] [1997] E.M.L.R. 543.
[5] (1996) 22 E.H.R.R. 123.
[6] See, *e.g.* the remarks attributed to solicitors acting for Colin Stagg and Rosemary West, two particularly well-publicised prosecutions, by D. Conn, "Attorney-General Under Pressure Over Media Reporting" (1995) Sol Jo. 79. See also the Lord Chancellor's Advisory Committee on Legal Education and Conduct, *Lawyers Comments to the Media* (May 1997). It has been suggested that English law should be altered so as to permit the right of private action: Borrie and Lowe, *The Law of Contempt* (3rd ed., 1996), at pp.vi and 483.
[7] [1996] C.O.D. 61 (Lexis). See *Amery v Solicitor-General* [1987] 2 N.Z.L.R. 292, where it was stated by Cooke P. that a decision of the New Zealand Law Officer might be reviewable. But see *R. v Barlow* [1996] 2 N.Z.L.R. 116, where the High Court held that although arguably it could review a Law Officer's decision to stay a prosecution, there was no precedent for the proposition that it could review a decision *not* to intervene. And see *R. v Von Einem* (1990) 55 S.A.S.R. 199 for the position in South Australia.
[8] (1994) 98 Cr.App.R. 361 at 368.
[9] [1996] C.O.D. 61.
[10] J. Miller and D. Feldman, "The Law Officers, Contempt and Judicial Review" note, (1997) 113 L.Q.R. 36. For a more general account of the case law, see S. Hilson, "Discretion to Prosecute and Judicial Review" [1993] Crim. L.R. 739.

2–213 CHAPTER 2—CONTEMPT OF COURT: CONSTITUTIONAL DIMENSIONS

the ambit of judicial review, and that this stands out against the developments in the law of judicial review more generally.

2–214 Two decisions fell to be considered. On the one hand, there was the decision of the Law Officers not to institute proceedings for contempt in the first place. Secondly, their failure to give any, or any adequate, reasons for the first decision was alleged to be unfair in the light of recent authority on the general duty to give reasons.[11] It was argued on behalf of the Solicitor-General that the authorities supported the proposition that decisions of the Law Officers were immune from review.[12]

2–215 In *Gouriet v UPOW* at the Court of Appeal stage,[13] although Lord Denning M.R. dissented in this respect, the majority[14] had decided that the Attorney was accountable to Parliament rather than the courts, on the ground that his duty to act in accordance with public policy considerations was one which the courts were ill-equipped to review. (The plaintiff in that case abandoned this point by the time it reached the House of Lords.) The view of the majority was treated as binding by a later Court of Appeal in *Att-Gen Ex p. Edey*,[15] when it was sought to challenge a decision not to prosecute for Sunday trading.[16] Similarly, in *Att-Gen Ex p. Ferrante*,[17] Popplewell J. took the view that it was not possible to challenge by way of judicial review the Attorney's decision to withhold his authority for an application for a new inquest.[18]

2–216 It was argued in *R. v Solicitor-General Ex p. Taylor*[19] that this longstanding approach required reconsideration following developments in public law, in the light of changes in 1978 to the procedure for judicial review. It was contended that every exercise of public power ought to be reviewable unless the nature of the power, or the circumstances giving rise to it, meant that the matter should not be regarded as justiciable.[20] Despite this, the Divisional Court regarded the Law Officers as having a "unique constitutional position", because of their role in giving effect to policy considerations as to the safeguarding of the public interest. "Parliament must be taken to know the law as stated in *Gouriet* and the previous authorities; if it had intended the Attorney-General's discretion to be reviewable by the court in this instance, it would have said so".[21]

---

[11] See, *e.g. Secretary of State for the Home Department Ex p. Doody* [1994] 1 A.C. 531.
[12] *R. v Newton* (1885) 24 L.J.Q.B. 246 at 247; *Controller General of Patents* [1898] 1 Q.B. 909, 913; *LCC v Att-Gen* [1902] A.C. 165 at 168–9; *Att-Gen v Westminster City Council* [1924] 2 Ch. 416; *Gouriet v UPOW* [1977] Q.B. 729, 768 and [1978] A.C. 435; *Att-Gen Ex p. Edey*, February 26, 1992, Lexis, CA; *Att-Gen Ex p. Ferrante* [1995] C.O.D. 18, Popplewell J.
[13] [1977] 1 Q.B. 729.
[14] Ormrod and Lawton L.JJ.
[15] February 26, 1992, unreported, CA.
[16] Under the Shops Act 1950, s.47.
[17] [1995] C.O.D. 18. The decision was upheld by the Court of Appeal which nevertheless was prepared to assume that the Attorney's decision was in principle renewable: *Independent*, April 3, 1995.
[18] Under the Coroners Act 1988, s.13.
[19] [1996] C.O.D. 61 (Lexis).
[20] *CCSU v Minister for the Civil Service* [1985] 1 A.C. 374.
[21] *per* Stuart-Smith L.J. [1996] C.O.D. 61 at 62.

As to the refusal to give reasons, it was held that no criticism could be made 2–217
of the Law Officers' refusal to give more detailed reasons than had been given
to the applicants' solicitors in a letter from the legal secretariat, in the following
terms:

> "I can confirm that the decision taken by the Solicitor-General accorded with the advice received from counsel. It is the practice of this office not to make public the detailed reasons for decisions. Suffice it to say the Solicitor-General concluded that proceedings for contempt of court were unlikely to succeed in respect of any individual item or newspaper report. I am not able to provide you with a copy of counsel's advice."

A further comment was made in the Divisional Court, to the effect that no 2–218
criticism could be made of the refusal to give more detailed reasons, even though
the Solicitor-General's decision appeared, as a matter of first impression, to differ
from the view taken by the Court of Appeal at the stage when the convictions
were quashed. It may be doubted, however, whether there was indeed any
inconsistency. As is made clear by the subsequent decision of the Divisional
Court in *Att-Gen v MGN Ltd*,[22] circumstances may very well arise where it is
appropriate on an abuse of process application, or appeal against conviction, to
conclude that a fair trial became impossible as a result of prejudicial media
coverage, even though it may not be possible to establish to the criminal standard
of proof that any individual publisher has committed contempt of court.

A fuller explanation for the decision not to proceed in the *Taylor* case was 2–219
apparently offered to the Divisional Court on the hearing of the application for
judicial review, and in the light of that it was said that, even if the decision had
been reviewable, and the reasons given inadequate, then as a matter of discretion
leave would have been refused.[23]

F. The Attorney's role in relation to civil contempts

Where the contempt consists of a failure to comply with a court order, it is usual 2–220
for contempt proceedings to be initiated at the behest of the party in whose favour
the order was made. Even where the party takes the view that no further action
is necessary, the court may, if it chooses to do so, draw the matter to the attention
of the Attorney-General for action. The reasons for this were explained by
Megarry V.-C. in *Clarke v Chadburn*[24] as follows:

> "The order is made so as to assist the litigant in obtaining his rights, and he may consult his own interests in deciding whether or not to enforce it. If he decides not to, there may

---

[22] [1997] 1 All E.R. 456 at 466, Schiemann L.J., discussed at para.4–165. See also the detailed analysis of the Divisional Court in *Att-Gen v Birmingham Post and Mail Ltd* [1998] 4 All E.R. 49, discussed in paras 4–150 *et seq.*
[23] But see *R. v Westminster City Council Ex p. Ermakov* [1996] 2 All E.R. 302 where the Court of Appeal indicated that, in cases where the reasons stated were shown to be manifestly flawed, relief should be refused only in very exceptional cases on the strength of matters adduced after the commencement of proceedings.
[24] [1984] I.R.L.R. 350, [1985] 1 W.L.R. 78, [1985] 1 All E.R. 211. It appears that in *Taylor v NUM (Yorkshire Area)* [1984] I.R.L.R. 445, the Attorney-General agreed to underwrite the costs of the sequestrators in tracing the assets. See *Hansard*, H.C., 6th series, Vol. 69, col. 929, December 11, 1984. See also *International Union, United Mine Workers v Bagwell* 114 S. Ct. 2552 (1994).

in some cases be a public element involved, and the Attorney General will judge whether the public interest requires him to intervene in order to enforce the order."

G. The Court's power to act of its own initiative

2–221 As to the court's power to act of its own motion, the Vice-Chancellor went on in *Clarke* to say:

> "If neither the litigant nor the Attorney General seeks to enforce the order, the court will act of its own volition in punishing the contempt only in exceptional cases of clear contempts . . . ".

There may, however, be cases where the court itself has to be alert to the public interests involved. This arose, for example, in *R. v Commissioners of Inland Revenue Ex p. Kingston Smith*,[25] where the representatives of the Inland Revenue Commissioners acted in breach of an interim injunction (not to continue with a search of an accountant's premises) for some hours after the order was made. The judge pointed out that the accountants "understandably" did not wish to pursue the matter, but he emphasised that it was open to the court of its own motion to initiate proceedings for contempt. The plain breach of the court's order was one that he felt compelled to regard with considerable gravity.

VI. CONTEMPT OF COURT AND THE CROWN

2–222 The Crown cannot be guilty of contempt, any more than it can be said to be guilty of a criminal offence.[26] Some individual officers or representatives of the state, including police officers,[27] and in particular officers of government departments such as the Inland Revenue,[28] are nevertheless susceptible to the coercive and punitive disciplines of the law of contempt.

A. Contempt by Ministers of the Crown: Re M[29]

2–223 There has been a long-standing distinction between the Crown and its officers. The Crown itself is indeed immune from coercive judicial orders. In addition, the Crown Proceedings Act 1947 provides that no injunction or order should issue

---

[25] [1996] 2 S.T.C. 1210.
[26] See Glanville Williams, *Textbook of Criminal Law* (2nd ed., 1983), p.637. Consistently with this principle, it would appear that when certain proceedings were experimentally filmed in November 2004, the view was taken that there would be immunity from liability under the Criminal Justice Act 1925, s.41 which prohibits photography in court. See paras 10–202 *et seq*.
[27] *Connolly v Dale* [1996] Q.B. 120.
[28] *R. v Inland Revenue Commissioners Ex p. Kingston Smith* [1996] 2 S.T.C. 1210.
[29] [1994] 1 A.C. 377. See R. Brazier, *Ministers of the Crown* (1997), especially p.222ff; R. Brazier, "Ministers in Court: The Personal Legal Liability of Ministers" (1993) 44 N.I.L.Q. 317. See also Law Commission Report No.226, *Administrative Law: Judicial Review and Statutory Appeals* (1994) para.6.13, which recommends legislation enshrining the principle derived from the decision in *Re M*.

against an *officer* of the Crown if the *effect* would be to give a remedy against the Crown which could not have been obtained in proceedings directly.[30]

For some time after this enactment, it was supposed that this conferred immunity on ministers of the Crown from injunctive relief.[31] This was despite the recognition in the eighteenth century that ministers were not immune, and indeed that ministers and civil servants "like any other citizen, are subject to the law, the rule of law, and the full jurisdiction of the courts."[32]

2–224

In the leading cases of *Wilkes v Wood*[33] and *Entick v Carrington*[34] this proposition was clearly established. "The law makes no difference between great and petty officers, thank God they are all amenable to justice."[35] Moreover, in *Ellis v Earl Grey*[36] an injunction had been granted against a minister, in *Home Secretary v O'Brien*[37] habeas corpus and in *Padfield v Minister of Agriculture*[38] an order of *mandamus*.

2–225

A distinction must be drawn between the situation where the Crown acts on the advice of a minister,[39] and where the minister has been authorised to act personally. In the latter situation, there is no reason why ministers of the Crown should be free to disregard court orders in either their personal or official capacities. In a decision of considerable constitutional importance,[40] the House of Lords ultimately confirmed this to be so.

2–226

In *Re M: M v Home Office*[41] the Home Secretary permitted the deportation of an illegal immigrant in breach of an undertaking given to a judge. It was held that the Home Secretary had been in contempt of court in failing to comply with a judge's order to return a Zaire citizen to this jurisdiction following his

2–227

---

[30] Crown Proceedings Act 1947, s.2(2) and Sch.2.
[31] The source of this misunderstanding was the decision in *Merrick v Heathcoat-Amory* [1955] Ch. 567. For an exposition of the problem, see Sir H.W.R. Wade, "Injunctive Relief against the Crown and Ministers" (1991) 107 L.Q.R. 4. Lord Bridge in the House of Lords had said, in *R. v Secretary of State for Transport Ex p. Factortame Ltd* [1990] 2 A.C. 85, that injunctive relief is not available against the Crown or an officer of the Crown, when acting as such, in judicial review proceedings. In *Re M* this was held to be incorrect.
[32] Lord Donaldson M.R. in *Re M: M. v Home Office* [1992] Q.B. 270 at 302G.
[33] (1769) 19 St. Tr. 1406.
[34] (1765) 19 St. Tr. 1030.
[35] *per* Wilmot C.J. in *Entick v Carrington* (1765) 19 St.Tr. 1406. In *R. (on the application of Green) v City of London Magistrates* [1997] 3 All E.R. 551, it was held that there was no distinction between a Minister of the Crown in this context and the Director of the Serious Fraud Office. In an appropriate case, therefore, proceedings could be taken against the Director for contempt. See too *Beggs v The Scottish Ministers* [2005] CSIH 5—March 15, 2005.
[36] (1833) 6 Sim. 214, 58 E.R. 574.
[37] [1923] A.C. 603.
[38] [1968] A.C. 997.
[39] As, for example, in the exercise of the prerogative of mercy or the appointment of the judiciary.
[40] Sir H.W.R. Wade described the decision as giving rise to "perhaps the most important question of constitutional law to arise for more than two centuries" (1992) 108 L.Q.R. 173. For a more sceptical account, see Carol Harlow, "Accidental Loss of an Asylum Seeker" (1994) 57 M.L.R. 620.
[41] [1994] 1 A.C. 377. See G. Marshall, "Ministerial responsibility, the Home Office and Mr. Baker" (1992) P.L. 7; C. Harlow, note, (1994) 57 M.L.R. 620.

unsuccessful attempt to seek political asylum. An application had been made to the judge in chambers for leave to apply a second time for judicial review of the decision of the Home Secretary that the applicant should be removed. An order was made that "the application for leave to move for judicial review be adjourned on the undertaking by counsel for the Home Office... that the applicant would not be removed from the United Kingdom to Zaire". Counsel for the Home Office was apparently unaware of the precise terms of this order, and was under the impression that the judge had made no more than an informal request that the applicant should not be removed.

2–228 As a result of misunderstandings about the scope of the order, the applicant was removed. The judge then made a further order that the applicant should be returned, and arrangements were made for the applicant's return. The Home Secretary received advice that the order had been made, as against the Crown, without jurisdiction and that an application would be made to have it set aside. The return travel arrangements were accordingly cancelled, the Home Secretary being apparently under the impression that he could postpone compliance with the order even though, in the words of Lord Donaldson M.R. in the Court of Appeal, "non-compliance could have had irremediable and even fatal consequences for [the applicant], for whose protection the order was made."[42]

2–229 Proceedings were commenced against the Home Office and the Secretary of State for failing to comply with the second order. Simon Brown J. held that the judge had had no jurisdiction to make the order. The Court of Appeal and the House of Lords held, however, that there had indeed been jurisdiction to make such an order against a minister of the Crown, and his failure to comply was accordingly held to be in contempt.

2–230 It was contended on behalf of the Home Office and the Secretary of State that neither the Crown, nor a department of state, nor yet a minister of the Crown acting in that capacity should be amenable to proceedings in contempt; for the reason that there was no power in the courts to grant injunctions against such persons. In the words of Lord Woolf,... "the issue is of constitutional importance since it goes to the heart of the relationship between the executive and the court. Is the relationship based, as [counsel] submits, on trust and co-operation or ultimately on coercion?"[43] It appears that it is the latter.

---

[42] [1992] 2 Q.B. 270 at 305.
[43] [1994] 1 A.C. 377 at 405D.

Chapter 3

THE DISTINCTION BETWEEN CRIMINAL AND CIVIL CONTEMPT

		Para
I.	The Distinction Explained	3–1
II.	The Juridical Nature of Contempt	3–55
III.	Points of Comparison Between Civil and Criminal Contempts	3–130

I. The Distinction Explained

A. The essence of the distinction

Contempts of court have traditionally been classified as being either criminal or civil. In England, the general approach has been that a criminal contempt is an act which so threatens the administration of justice that it requires punishment from the public point of view; whereas, by contrast, a civil contempt involves disobedience of a court order or undertaking by a person involved in litigation. In these cases, the purpose of the imposition of the contempt sanction has been seen as primarily coercive or "remedial".

3–1

In an American Supreme Court decision on the nature of the distinction, it was said:

3–2

"It is not the fact of punishment, but rather its character and purpose, that often serve to distinguish between the two classes of cases. If it is for civil contempt the punishment is remedial, and for the benefit of the complainant. But if it is for criminal contempt the sentence is punitive, to vindicate the authority of the court".[1]

The distinction thus described, however, has never been rigidly maintained, and the desire to retain flexibility to cope with a variety of circumstances continued to give rise to difficulties of classification, not only in England but also in other common law jurisdictions.[2]

3–3

---

[1] *Gompers v Bucks's Stove and Range Co* 221 U.S. 418 (1911), at 441. For the position in the United States, see further R.L. Goldfarb, *The Contempt Power* (1963). Two important articles on more recent developments in the United States are by Earl C. Dudley, "Getting Beyond the Civil/Criminal Distinction: A New Approach to the Regulation of Indirect Contempts" (1993) 79 Va. L. Rev. 1025, and by P.A. Hostak, "International Union, United Mine Workers v Bagwell: A Paradigm Shift in the Distinction Between Civil and Criminal Contempt" (1995) 81 Cornell Law Rev. 181.

[2] J.H. Beale, "Contempt of Court, Criminal and Civil" (1908) 21 Harv. L.Rev. 161; H. Fischer, "Civil and Criminal Aspects of Contempt of Court" (1956) 34 Can. Bar Rev. 121; E. Harnon, "Civil and Criminal Contempts of Court" (1962) 25 M.L.R. 179; Robert J. Martineau, "Contempt of Court: Eliminating the Confusion Between Civil and Criminal Contempt" (1981) 50 U. of Cincinnati L. Rev. 677. The first three paragraphs of this chapter were cited by the Northern Ireland Court of Appeal in *Lord Saville of Newdigate v Toby Harnden* [2003] NICA 6.

3–4 CHAPTER 3—THE DISTINCTION BETWEEN CRIMINAL/CIVIL CONTEMPT

3–4   Proceedings for civil contempt are sometimes described as "quasi-criminal" because of the penal consequences that can attend the breach of an order. The European Court of Human Rights does not regard itself as being bound by the domestic characterisation of proceedings as being either civil or criminal; the language of Art.6, which accords protection in cases of persons "charged with a criminal offence", is said to be "autonomous".[3] There may come a time, therefore, when the European Court of Human Rights would categorise such proceedings as truly "criminal", and as requiring the traditional safeguards referred to in Art.6. Meanwhile, in *Newman v Modern Bookbinders Ltd*[4] it was observed in the context of s.92(1) of the County Courts Act 1984 that "What matters, especially in a legal system which is about to be required to accommodate the standards of the European Convention on Human Rights, is that this is a penal process". It was concluded that a charge of rescue of goods was, for Convention purposes, a criminal charge, and reference was made to *Benham v UK*.[5]

3–5   By contrast, in *The Coca-Cola Company v Aytacli*[6] a distinction was drawn between civil and criminal proceedings for contempt in that the burden of proving duress in the case of civil contempt was held to be on the alleged contemnor; what is more, that it would only go to mitigation rather than constitute a defence. The judge added[7]:

> "I do not see that [Article 6(2) and 6(3) of the European Convention] should be read as extending to someone who is not charged with a criminal offence but who is subject to civil proceedings with criminal sanctions".

It is suggested that these observations (at first instance) should be treated with caution. The question of a possible distinction in the context of duress between civil and criminal contempt is discussed below.[8]

3–6   Although the distinction between civil and criminal contempt continues to be made, and has to be considered carefully, the two categories have rather more in common than their traditional separation would imply. The considerations of public policy underlying the contempt jurisdiction generally are the protection of the administration of justice and the maintenance of the court's authority. There lies at the heart of both civil and criminal contempt the need for society both to protect its citizens' rights and to maintain the rule of law.

3–7   Thus, although "civil contempt" is concerned with breaches of court orders or undertakings in civil litigation, which were originally for the benefit of one or other of the parties, the court may wish in such cases to coerce parties into

---

[3] See *Benham v UK* (1996) 22 E.H.R.R. 293, where the decision of magistrates to impose imprisonment for non-payment of poll tax was held to be "criminal", notwithstanding the fact that such proceedings are classified as civil under English law. See also *Steel v UK* (1999) E.H.R.R. 603, [1998] Crim. L.R. 893 (binding over is criminal in character under the Convention).
[4] [2000] 1 W.L.R. 2559, [2000] 2 All E.R. 814, CA.
[5] (1996) 20 E.H.R.R. 293.
[6] [2003] EWHC 91, (Ch.)
[7] At [49].
[8] See paras 3–250 *et seq.*

compliance with its orders; or alternatively, even in this context, it may be primarily concerned to punish disobedience (where the time for compliance has passed). In such circumstances as these, deterrence clearly has a role to play. It is therefore possible, in many examples of civil contempt, to discern these various policy considerations in operation alongside one another.

This was explained by Cross J., for example, in *Phonographic Performance Ltd v Amusement Caterers*.[9] A company and its directors were restrained by injunction from playing certain gramophone records on its juke boxes. The records continued to be played. The judge took the view that the directors of the company were deliberately defying the court:

3–8

> "Where there has been wilful disobedience to an order of the court and a measure of contumacy on the part of the defendants, then civil contempt, what is called 'contempt of procedure', bears a twofold character implying as between the parties to proceedings merely a right to exercise and a liability to submit to a form of civil execution, but as between the party in default and the state, a penal or disciplinary jurisdiction to be exercised by the court in the public interest."

Similarly, in *Jennison v Baker*[10] Salmon L.J. made the important point that:

3–9

> "The public at large no less than the individual litigant have an interest and a very real interest in justice being effectively administered".

So too the duality was emphasised by Megarry J. in *Re Grantham Wholesale Fruit, Vegetable and Potato Merchants Ltd*[11]:

3–10

> "In this type of case a motion for committal is, of course, a means of putting pressure on the contemnor to obey the order, but it is not this alone: it is also a means of imposing any penalty thought proper in respect of the contempt that has already been committed."

In the context of a breach of interdict Lord President Clyde in *Johnson v Grant*[12] drew a similar distinction:

3–11

> " . . . not only has no one the power to purge himself of a deliberate offence by saying he is sorry, but the mere circumstance that he presents a belated expression of contrition has, with regard to the public aspect of the matter, almost no importance at all . . . The appeal is simply to the clemency of the Court; there is no palliative of the offence at all; and the idea must not be harboured that a person who has wilfully committed a breach of interdict can obtain remission of sentence by coming to the court and saying, 'I realise my transgression and apologise for it'—however sincerely such an apology may be made."

---

[9] [1964] Ch. 195 at 198–9. See also *Steiner Products Ltd v Willy Steiner Ltd* [1966] 1 W.L.R. 986, [1966] 2 All E.R. 387.
[10] [1972] 2 Q.B. 52 at 61F.
[11] [1972] 1 W.L.R. 559 at 565F. And see *James v Cliffe*, The Times, June 16, 1987 (punishment of three months' imprisonment imposed on appeal even though contemnor had disappeared, and there was no immediate prospect of enforcing the order).
[12] 1923 S.C. 789 at 790. The notion of "purging" was described by Thorpe L.J. in *Harris v Harris* [2001] EWCA Civ 1644, [2002] Fam. 253 at [21] as "rooted in quasi-religious concepts of purification, expiation and atonement".

B. Illustrations of the dual nature of civil contempts

1. *Jennison v Baker*

3–12   In some cases the court when dealing with the breach of an order is simply punishing the contemnor, and there is no element of coercion at all. In *Jennison v Baker*[13] the defendant had bought a house divided into flats. She then embarked on a policy of evicting the existing tenants. They commenced proceedings for breach of a covenant for quiet enjoyment and sought injunctions to prevent the defendant evicting or attempting to evict them. Interim injunctions were granted and served on the defendant. She committed serious breaches of the injunctions, harassing the plaintiffs to the point where all of them had left the house. At the hearing no perpetual injunction was sought because the plaintiffs no longer wished to live in the house. The county court judge nevertheless issued an order of attachment committing the defendant to prison for her contempts.

3–13   The Court of Appeal upheld that order, Edmund-Davies L.J. approving and adopting the passage quoted above[14] from the judgment of Cross J. in *Phonographic Performance Ltd v Amusement Caterers*.[15] The damage that had been done could not be undone and there was no likelihood of any repetition. Nevertheless the contempts were so flagrant that the court felt bound to punish the contemnor.

3–14   In the words of Salmon L.J.[16]:

> "An injunction is granted and enforced for the protection of the plaintiff. The defendant who breaches it is sent to prison for contempt with the object of vindicating (a) the rights of plaintiffs (especially the plaintiff in the action) and (b) the authority of the court. The two objects are in my view inextricably intermixed."

2. *Tony Pojé v the Att-Gen of British Columbia*

3–15   A similar factual situation confronted the Supreme Court of Canada in *Tony Pojé v the Att-Gen of British Columbia*,[17] although in that case the court seems to have been particularly affected in its treatment of the contemnors by the fact that the defiance of the order in question took place on the public stage.[18] Members of the International Woodworkers of America were picketing a dock so as to prevent longshoremen loading a cargo of timber on to the plaintiff's ship. The plaintiff obtained an injunction restraining the defendants from besetting the ship or preventing or interfering with the loading. They then received public warnings from the sheriff that they were acting in contempt of court, but maintained their defiance. The plaintiff moved to commit those who had disobeyed the order, but

---

[13] [1972] 2 Q.B. 52.
[14] para.3–8.
[15] [1964] Ch. 195.
[16] In *Jennison v Baker* [1972] 2 Q.B. at 64G.
[17] [1953] 2 D.L.R. 785.
[18] For a similar approach in Australia, see *Australian Meat Industry Employees' Union v Mudginberri Station Pty Ltd* (1986) 161 C.L.R. 98 at 108.

before the motion was heard the parties composed their differences and the plaintiff agreed to discontinue the motion.

When the matter came before the Chief Justice of British Columbia, he ordered that writs of attachment should issue. Pojé was subsequently fined and sentenced to three months' imprisonment, and the other defendants were also fined. The Supreme Court of Canada upheld this decision. The analysis applied by the court went so far as to classify the misconduct in question, although it consisted in the breach of an injunction, as *criminal* contempt.

This is not an approach which has commended itself to English courts. Even though sometimes confronted with circumstances in which the punitive element will predominate, the court does not approach the issue of liability by applying the criteria appropriate to criminal contempt. Breaches of injunctions are always traditionally addressed as falling within the category of civil contempt, even though the conduct itself may assume a criminal character and, accordingly, the court's consequential orders may be correspondingly punitive. A striking example is provided by the case in which a husband, being the subject of a non-molestation order, commited a breach by raping his wife.[19] Even so, the court focuses upon the civil contempt consisting in the breach of the court order, rather than treating the act as a crime.

Nevertheless, it is possible to recognise in the judgment of Kellock J., delivering the majority judgment in the Supreme Court of Canada in the *Tony Pojé* case, the very factors which underline the dual nature of the civil contempt jurisdiction. He approved the statement in *Oswald on Contempt of Court*[20] that "where the contempt involves a public injury or offence, it is criminal in its nature, and the proper remedy is committal—but where the contempt involves a private injury only it is not criminal in its nature." He then went on to say:

> "The context in which these incidents occurred, and the large number of men involved and the public nature of the defiance of the order of the court transfer the conduct here in question from the realm of a mere civil contempt, such as an ordinary breach of injunction with respect to private rights in a patent or trade mark, for example, into the realm of a public depreciation of justice, . . . the character of the conduct involved a public injury amounting to criminal contempt."

In the more recent case of *Vidéotron Ltée v Industries Microlec Produits Electroniques Inc*,[21] it was held in the Supreme Court of Canada that the imposition of penalties for contempt of court, even when used to enforce a purely private order, still involves an element of "public law" because "respect for the role and authority of the courts, one of the foundations of the rule of law, is always at issue".

---

[19] See, *e.g. N v N (Contempt: Committal)* [1992] 1 F.L.R. 370 at 375B-C, Russell L.J. See also *R. v Green (Bryan)* [1993] Crim.L.R. 46. See also the discussion at paras 12–8 *et seq.*
[20] (3rd. ed., 1910), p.36.
[21] (1993) 96 D.L.R. (4th) 376 at 398, Gonthier J., with whom Lamer C.J.C. and La Forest J. concurred (L' Heureux-Dubé J. dissenting). For comparable dicta in this jurisdiction, see *Guildford Borough Council v Valler* [1993] T.L.R. 274, 275, referred to at para.3–49.

3–20 To an extent the discussion may be arid. The fact that disobedience to a court order is widespread and takes place in the glare of publicity may well justify the imposition of a penalty, or perhaps a heavier penalty, than would otherwise be the case. Nonetheless, this would not logically justify a change of classification in the nature of the jurisdiction being exercised. Sir John Laws, in addressing the factors identified by Kellock J. in the passage cited above, has commented that "... surely the difference is not of kind but of degree."[22]

3. Breaches treated in England as civil contempt

3–21 In England, the approach of the courts appears to be that even though a civil contempt may take on characteristics which are sometimes said to be "criminal" in its nature,[23] breaches of court orders and undertakings are nonetheless still classified as civil.[24] As Lord Atkinson noted in *Scott v Scott*[25]:

> "... if a person be expressly enjoined by injunction, a most solemn and authoritative form of order, from doing a particular thing, and he deliberately, in breach of that injunction, does that thing, he is not guilty of any crime whatever, but only of a civil contempt of Court."

3–22 On some occasions, by contrast, the sanction of the court may be primarily coercive in purpose, even though involving a lengthy sentence of imprisonment. In the days before the Contempt of Court Act 1981 imposed a maximum period of imprisonment, which applies to both civil and criminal contempts,[26] the court would sometimes imprison a contemnor who was in defiance of a court order indefinitely, with the object of compelling compliance; "in such cases, according to the overly worn saw, civil contemnors are said to 'carry the keys to their prison in their own pockets'".[27] The traditional expression used in this context was release "*ex debito justitiae*," which implied a virtual right to be released once the contempt was purged.

3–23 The case of *Maria Annie Davies*[28] is the best known example of a contemnor who spent a long time in prison solely because of her continuing refusal to obey an order. She had brought an action for the recovery of certain property, but it was decided that she had no title. She then tried to take possession by force, and

---

[22] (2000) 116 L.Q.R. 156 at 161.
[23] See Lord Denning M.R. in *Comet Products UK Ltd v Hawkex Plastics Ltd* [1971] 2 Q.B. 67, 73F: "Although this is a civil contempt it partakes of the nature of a criminal charge. The defendant is liable to be punished for it."
[24] See, *e.g. Goad v AUEW (No.3)* [1973] I.C.R. 108 at 111, NIRC, Sir John Donaldson.
[25] [1913] A.C. 417 at 456.
[26] See now s.14, discussed at para.14–8. See *Whitter v Peters; Peart v Stewart* [1982] 1 W.L.R. 389, CA; *Peart v Stewart* [1983] 2 A.C. 109, HL, which hold that the maximum applies to both civil and criminal contempt.
[27] P.A. Hostak, (1995) 81 Cornell L.Rev. at 183; see also *Re Nevitt* 117 F. 448 at 461 (8th Cir. 1902). There is strictly speaking no such "right". The matter has to be considered by the court in the exercise of its discretion against all the circumstances of the individual case: see the observations of Lord President Clyde in *Johnson v Grant* 1923 S.C. 789 at 790, cited at para.3–11.
[28] (1888) 21 Q.B.D. 236. For another example, see *Corcoran v Corcoran* [1950] 1 All E.R. 495, discussed at para.3–162.

an injunction was obtained restraining her from further molesting the owner and tenants of the estate. She again tried to take possession and was committed for contempt. She was informed that she would be released upon promising to give up her idle and vexatious claim and undertaking to abstain from further attempts to enter upon the property. She refused to give any such promise and remained in prison for 18 months.

Where proceedings perform these functions simultaneously, with the balance shifting from one objective to another, problems of classification become more difficult. The only rationale behind punishing criminal contemnors is protecting the administration of justice in general. Yet Salmon L.J. made it clear in *Jennison v Baker*[29] that it is precisely the same rationale which lies behind the punitive element in civil contempt. Despite this, the courts have preferred not to amalgamate both forms of contempt, and the distinction continues to be made. No opportunity was taken, in particular, to abolish the distinction at the time of the Contempt of Court Act 1981, even though this had been recommended by the Phillimore Committee.[30]

C. Points of comparison between civil and criminal contempt: an overview

Although the two types of contempt thus overlap to a considerable degree, the classification retains some importance, since it may lead to rather different procedural consequences even today. While the principles of contempt represent a body of substantive law, this depends for its effectiveness upon the flexible procedural rules which account for the unique "summary" character of this jurisdiction. The purpose of this chapter is to explore the extent to which the distinction still persists as a matter of law, to evaluate its continued significance, and to consider recommendations for change.

It is not easy to make a valid general classification of contempts because there are so many different manifestations. As Eveleigh L.J. pointed out[31]:

> "contempt of court may take a wide variety of forms and the fact that it is regarded as an absolute offence in one form does not necessarily require it to be so treated in another form. It is very much a matter of public policy".

Despite the cogency of this observation, and the flexibility which would obviously be appropriate to such a range of disparate activities, it is clear that, for largely historical reasons, different forms of contempt have been allocated to one or other of the two traditional broad categories. Most examples of conduct classified as contempt have been characterised as "criminal". They include contempts in the face of the court; publication of matter scandalising the court; acts calculated to prejudice the fair trial of a pending case (criminal or civil); reprisals against those who participate in legal proceedings for what they have

---

[29] [1972] 2 Q.B. 52.
[30] *Report of the Committee on Contempt of Court*, Cmnd. 5794 (1974), para.169.
[31] *Z Ltd v A-Z and AA-LL* [1982] Q.B. 558 at 579 D–F.

done; impeding service of, or forging, the process of the court; and also most contempts in relation to wards of court.[32]

3–28 Such conduct is regarded as criminal contempt even if committed in relation to civil proceedings. For example, disruption of court proceedings is regarded as criminal contempt irrespective of whether the proceedings are civil or criminal. The unlawful publication of matter calculated to prejudice the fair trial of a pending case is a criminal contempt even if the case affected is itself civil litigation.[33]

3–29 A number of points of distinction between criminal and civil contempts evolved gradually as the common law developed, whereas others have emerged more recently as problems requiring to be addressed in the light of general principle. The extent to which these distinctions continue to have any significance will be more fully considered below.[34]

1. Appeals

3–30 From 1873[35] to 1960 an appeal lay against orders in respect of contempt in connection with civil proceedings but not where committed with regard to proceedings on indictment. Now,[36] the Court of Appeal has power to entertain appeals in both cases.

2. Privilege

3–31 Privilege from arrest and imprisonment might be pleaded successfully only where the contemnor was arrested in respect of a civil contempt, and only then if the court was satisfied that the order sought to be executed was purely coercive in nature, rather than punitive or disciplinary.

3. Waiver

3–32 A civil contempt might sometimes be waived by the party for whose benefit the order was made, but only if there was no public interest element such as to justify intervention for the purpose of vindicating the authority of the court (either of the court's own motion or at the instance of the Attorney-General): a criminal contempt could never be waived by the party adversely affected.

---

[32] The paragraph in the text was cited by the Northern Ireland Court of Appeal in *Lord Saville of Newdigate v Toby Harnden* [2003] NICA 6 at [12].

[33] *O'Shea v O'Shea and Parnell Ex p. Tuohy* (1890) 15 P.D. 59; *Att-Gen v Times Newspapers Ltd* [1974] A.C. 273; *Att-Gen v News Group Newspapers plc* [1987] 1 Q.B. 1. See however the *obiter* remark of Hodgson J. in *Att-Gen v Sport Newspapers Ltd* [1991] 1 W.L.R. 1194 at 1211C, [1992] 1 All E.R. 503 at 519a: "If the proceedings were criminal proceedings the publication could amount to a criminal contempt; if civil, to a civil contempt."

[34] In Pt III of this chapter.

[35] Supreme Court of Judicature Act 1873, s.47(1).

[36] As the result of the Administration of Justice Act 1960, s.13, discussed at paras 13–118 *et seq.* and paras 15–88 *et seq.*

4. *Institution of proceedings*

Proceedings in respect of a criminal contempt could be commenced by the court of its own motion or by the Attorney-General, and in practice also by an interested party (except where this is prohibited by s.7 of the Contempt of Court Act 1981)[37]: proceedings for civil contempt would normally be commenced by the party aggrieved.

5. *Sanctions*

In general, imprisonment for a criminal contempt was for a fixed term or alternatively until the court ordered the release of the contemnor. In the case of a civil contempt the appropriate order, with the purpose of coercion, was generally imprisonment for an unspecified period until the order of the court was obeyed.[38] A fine could always be imposed for a criminal contempt, sometimes in addition to a sentence of imprisonment. It is only in very recent times that fines for so-called civil contempts have been imposed. Now, all sentences of imprisonment, whether for criminal or civil contempt, must be for a fixed period.[39]

6. *Release* ex debito justitiae

Once a civil contemnor had purged his contempt by demonstrating a willingness to comply with the relevant order, or by giving satisfactory undertakings, he was treated as virtually entitled to his release *ex debito justitiae*. This is no longer possible, as a result of s.14 of the Contempt of Court Act 1981, which imposes both a maximum period of imprisonment and the requirement that any such sentence shall be for a fixed term.[40] A contemnor is nonetheless free to apply for release, whether his contempt be civil or criminal.

7. *Execution*

Those executing a writ of attachment issued in respect of a criminal contempt might in some circumstances adopt more extreme measures (for example, breaking open an external door) than in the case of a writ issued in respect of a civil contempt.

---

[37] Considered at paras 2–203 and paras 4–183 *et seq*. No such statutory restriction applies in Scotland.
[38] Persons imprisoned for contempt were formerly dealt with differently from, and more favourably than other prisoners in matters of clothing, correspondence and prison visits: Halsbury's *Laws of England*, 4th ed. Vol. 36(2), paras 699 *et seq*. This was true of both criminal and civil contempts. This distinction, however, ceased in 1992 (SI 1992/2080), probably because of the improvements in the treatment of prisoners more generally which followed the recommendations of the Report, *Prison Disturbances* (1990), Cm. 1456, by Lord Woolf.
[39] Contempt of Court Act 1981, s.14.
[40] Discussed more fully at paras 14–8 *et seq*.

8. The Royal Prerogative

3-37   The prerogative of mercy could be exercised in respect of criminal but not civil contempt.

9. The privilege against self-incrimination

3-38   Although the privilege against self-incrimination is essentially a criminal law concept, it has been to an extent applied by the courts, and with the intervention of Parliament, to cover proceedings for civil contempt in certain situations. Here too, the distinction between the two categories of contempt has thus lessened in its significance.

10. Autrefois acquit *and* convict *in civil contempt*

3-39   The principle of double jeopardy, that a person should not be punished twice for the same offence, has long applied to criminal contempt. The recognition of the penal consequences of proceedings for civil contempt has been relatively more recent. But it is clear that the courts have extended the double jeopardy principles to punishment for civil contempt.

11. Extra-territorial jurisdiction

3-40   One of the difficulties about dealing with breaches of court orders which take place abroad concerns the question of whether the alleged contemnor can be deemed to be before the court (as in the case of a litigant who has been duly served, including by way of substituted service). Once such a person is, in that sense, truly before the court, there seems to be no reason why a breach would not be susceptible to the law of contempt.[41] By contrast, when the act in question is done by a person who is *not* regarded as before the court, even in the artificial sense, there can only be an act of criminal contempt. In that context, the court would have no jurisdiction in respect of acts done abroad, in the absence of specific statutory provision.[42]

12. Hearsay evidence

3-41   There has been no conclusive decision on the question whether hearsay evidence is admissible in the case of criminal contempt.[43] In civil contempt, by contrast,

---

[41] The first two sentences of this paragraph were cited and apparently accepted as valid in the High Court of New Zealand in by Gendall J. in *Att-Gen for England and Wales v Tomlinson* [1999] 3 N.Z.L.R. 722 at 729.

[42] See, *e.g. Lakah Group and Lakah v Al Jazeera and Mansour* [2002] EWHC 2500, (QB).

[43] In *Att-Gen v Express Newspapers* [2004] EWHC 2859 (Admin), Rose L.J. proceeded on the basis that hearsay was inadmissible. He expressed the view, however, that there was a respectable argument that it should be admissible and left for the court to assess as a matter of weight in the circumstances of the particular case. He bore in mind *inter alia* the fact that hearsay would become admissible in criminal proceedings generally when s.114 of the Criminal Justice Act 2003 came into force (which it did on April 4, 2005).

it was on occasion held that applications for committal were to be regarded as interlocutory proceedings,[44] thus permitting a relatively relaxed evidence regime, and that such evidence was therefore treated as admissible for that reason. The hearsay rules in both the criminal[45] and civil contexts have undergone important changes; it would seem that hearsay evidence may now also be admitted in cases of criminal contempt in accordance with the principles set out in chapter 2 of the Criminal Justice Act 2003.

13. *Fresh evidence on appeal*

The Court of Appeal has held that, because of the penal consequences attaching to committal for contempt, evidence should be admitted on appeal according to the stricter criteria applied in a criminal case; even in cases of civil contempt, it would seem, the provisions of the Criminal Appeal Act 1968, s.23,[46] should apply.

14. *The standard of proof*

After some hesitation, it has been held in modern cases that the applicable standard of proof in both types of contempt is the criminal one; that is to say, beyond reasonable doubt.

15. *The extent to which* mens rea *is required*

In the case of criminal contempts not falling within the strict liability rule, it would appear that an intention to interfere with the administration of justice is required, at least for publication contempts. For other types of criminal contempt, the mental element is less clear. In the case of civil contempt, all that is generally required is knowledge of the existence of the relevant order, although in one case the Court of Appeal has suggested that rather more than this may be required.

16. *The availability of public funding*

The provisions of s.29 of the Legal Aid Act 1988 only applied in respect of certain forms of criminal contempt. The section had no application to civil contempt, where a breach has occurred of an order or undertaking. Nor would it apply, for example, to publication contempts whether under the strict liability rule or the common law; such contempts could not be classified as being "in the face of the court".[47] There has been a fundamental overhaul of public funding arrangements, and the matter is now governed by s.12 of the Access to Justice Act 1999.[48]

---

[44] See paras 3–229 *et seq.*
[45] "Criminal proceedings" are defined for the purpose of Pt 2 of the Criminal Justice Act 2003, in s.134 as "criminal proceedings in relation to which the strict rules of evidence apply".
[46] As amended by the Criminal Appeal Act 1995, s.4.
[47] For a discussion of which, see ch.10.
[48] See paras 15–110 *et seq.*

17. *Duress*

3–46 In the light of the authorities as they stand, it may be that there is a distinction to be drawn between civil and criminal contempt so far as the availablity of a defence of duress is concerned. In the criminal context, it would appear that duress operates as a complete defence. There is some authority to suggest that in cases of civil contempt it would only have relevance by way of mitigation.

D. Phillimore's suggestion for abandoning the distinction altogether

3–47 By the time the Phillimore Committee reported, a series of cases had whittled down the practical distinctions between criminal and civil contempt to such an extent that the Committee recommended[49] that those remaining should be abolished. They did not seek to abolish the classification of civil and criminal contempt as such, but merely to amend the law (relating to privilege, waiver, sanctions, execution, the prerogative of mercy and the standard of proof) so that there would remain no practical differences between the two kinds of contempt. The 1981 Act only gave effect to the Committee's recommendations on sanctions, so that the distinction between civil and criminal contempt continues to require close scrutiny.

E. Continuing criticisms of the distinction

3–48 The distinction between the two forms of contempt certainly has evoked criticism both from the bench[50] and otherwise. For example, the view has been expressed that[51]:

> "... the distinction between civil and criminal contempt not only lacks utility: I believe it also lacks principle. An assertion of principle must rest in the proposition that civil contempt consists in a wrong done to the beneficiary of the court order which is breached, whereas criminal contempt consists in an interference with the administration of justice, whether generally or specifically. But this is not a principled distinction. It will be seen at once that any example of the first is also an example of the second: if the court has made a peremptory order, its breach is necessarily an interference with the way in which the court has expressly determined to administer the course of justice."

3–49 A similar line of reasoning was pursued by Sedley J. in *Guildford Borough Council v Valler*,[52] where he accepted that the distinction between civil and criminal contempt was historically important and might be analytically useful. But as to substantive law, it had become today in his view "academic". He said that he was unable to accept that committal on the motion of an antagonist in civil

---

[49] Cmnd. 5794, para.169.
[50] See, *e.g.* Salmon L.J. in *Jennison v Baker* [1972] 2 Q.B. 52, 61G: "I think that, at any rate today, this is an unhelpful and almost meaningless classification."
[51] John Laws, "Current Problems in the Law of Contempt" (1990) 43 C.L.P. 99 at 101.
[52] [1993] T.L.R. 274, 275 (Lexis), *sub nom. Guildford Borough Council v Smith*.

proceedings was in any admissible sense the private law right which the "older *dicta*"[53] suggested it was. To all intents and purposes it was a form of private prosecution.[54]

Despite such criticism, the terminology continues to be used and a valuable summary of the differing factors applying in civil and criminal contempt can be found in the speech of Lord Oliver in *Att Gen v Times Newspapers Ltd*[55]: **3–50**

"A distinction (which has been variously described as 'unhelpful' or 'largely meaningless') is sometimes drawn between what is described as 'civil contempt', that is to say, contempt by a party to proceedings in a matter of procedure, and 'criminal contempt.' One particular form of contempt by a party to proceedings is that constituted by an intentional act which is in breach of the order of a competent court. Where this occurs as a result of the act of a party who is bound by the order or of others acting at his direction or on his instigation, it constitutes a civil contempt by him which is punishable by the court at the instance of the party for whose benefit the order was made and which can be waived by him. The intention with which the act was done will, of course, be of the highest relevance in the determination of the penalty (if any) to be imposed by the court, but the liability here is a strict one in the sense that all that requires to be proved is service of the order and the subsequent doing by the party bound of that which is prohibited. When, however, the prohibited act is done not by the party bound himself but by a third party, a stranger to the litigation, that person may also be liable for contempt. There is, however, this essential distinction that his liability is for criminal contempt and arises not because the contemnor is himself affected by the prohibition contained in the order but because his act constitutes a wilful interference with the administration of justice by the court in the proceedings in which the order was made. Here the liability is not strict in the sense referred to, for there has to be shown not only knowledge of the order but an intention to interfere with or impede the administration of justice—an intention which can of course be inferred from the circumstances."

F. An attempted reformulation

Sir John Donaldson M.R. in *Att-Gen v Newspaper Publishing Ltd*[56] expressed the view that the standard classification into civil and criminal contempt should be replaced: **3–51**

"Despite its protean nature, contempt has been classified under two heads, namely 'civil contempt' and 'criminal contempt'. I venture to think that it now tends to mislead rather

---

[53] The full judgment (Lexis) does not disclose what *dicta* the learned judge had in mind.
[54] By contrast, however, it has also been argued that the language of "prosecution" is altogether inappropriate to describe the process of invoking the summary contempt jurisdiction. See *e.g.* the argument of counsel in *P v Liverpool Daily Post and Echo Newspapers plc* [1991] 2 A.C. 370, 412A, and his reference to the case of *R. v Daily Herald Editor, Printers and Publishers Ex p. the Bishop of Norwich* [1932] 2 K.B. 402 at 411–12. See also Mustill L.J. in *R. v Griffin* (1989) 88 Cr.App.R. 63 at 67 (" . . . there is no prosecutor").
[55] [1992] 1 A.C. 191 at 217–18.
[56] [1988] Ch. 333 at 362B–C.

3–51 CHAPTER 3—THE DISTINCTION BETWEEN CRIMINAL/CIVIL CONTEMPT

than assist, because the standard of proof is the same, namely, the criminal standard, and there are now common rights of appeal. Of greater assistance is a re-classification as (a) conduct which involves a breach, or assisting in the breach, of a court order and (b) any other conduct which involves an interference with the due administration of justice, either in a particular case or, more generally, as a continuing process, the first category being a special form of the latter, such interference being a characteristic common to all contempts."

3–52 This attempt at re-classification has much to commend it, in particular because it identifies the gist of the wrongdoing in each case. But it gives rise to a number of difficulties. There are some orders (such as for example, under s.4(2) of the Contempt of Court Act,[57] and those made by judges in the course of a court hearing requiring a witness to answer a question,[58] where disobedience would appear to be treated as being criminal in character.[59] In such cases, it may be quite inappropriate for a party to activate the summary procedure, and yet necessary for the interests of justice to be protected in a way that goes beyond the interests of those individuals.

3–53 Another example which would perhaps fall outside Sir John Donaldson's formulation may be found in the case of disobedience to a court order by a solicitor acting in his capacity as an officer of the court[60]; again, such a contempt is regarded as criminal in character, even though taking the form of disobedience to an order. Furthermore, there remain certain practical differences that are of continuing importance, and which depend upon whether the contempt is of a type traditionally classified as civil or criminal.[61]

3–54 The assimilation of disobedience to court orders with other acts categorised as contempt may have arisen historically for procedural reasons, in that the same remedy (attachment) had been used for two different purposes. The writ of attachment was used by the common law courts to bring before them for punishment those persons who interfered with their proceedings: the court of Chancery used the same writ not only for that purpose but also to secure obedience to its orders made in a particular suit. It was not until the process of statutory rationalisation in the middle of the nineteenth century that the true nature of the historical link between civil and criminal contempt came to be analysed. Some of the points of distinction had no apparent rational basis and could be explained purely in procedural terms, whereas it became gradually apparent that others had more substance.

---

[57] Postponement of reporting court proceedings; see paras 7–111 *et seq.*
[58] Discussed at para.10–162, and in relation to journalists, see ch.9.
[59] See also *Att-Gen v Mantoura* [1993] Crim.L.R. 279 where a father failed to comply with an undertaking to a judge of the Crown Court to pay £25,000 compensation to the victim of a fraud committed by his son, and this was treated as a criminal contempt "well suited for disposal by the Divisional Court".
[60] *Re Freston* (1883) 11 Q.B.D. 545; as particularly, for example, while executing a search and seizure (formerly called "*Anton Piller*") order.
[61] In particular, extra-territorial jurisdiction para.3–223, and hearsay evidence para.3–227.

II. THE JURIDICAL NATURE OF CONTEMPT

A. Criminal contempt and the general criminal law framework

There is no doubt that contempt of court is in some of its manifestations appropriately described as criminal[62] because of the threat which is implied to the administration of justice. The purpose the law serves in this context, as with other criminal offences, is to protect a public interest, and to punish its violation. Yet the law of criminal contempt has certain procedural attributes which appear to distinguish it from other forms of criminal offence. These primarily relate to the summary nature of the procedure, which was evolved at common law and subsequently refined by rules of court.[63]

3–55

A useful summary of these unique characteristics was given by Mustill L.J. in *R. v Griffin*[64]:

3–56

"In proceedings for criminal contempt there is no prosecutor, or even a requirement that a representative of the Crown or of the injured party should initiate the proceedings. The judge is entitled to proceed of his own motion. There is no summons or indictment, nor is it mandatory for any written account of the accusation made against him to be furnished to the contemnor. There is no preliminary enquiry or filtering procedure, such as a committal. Depositions are not taken. There is no jury. Nor is the system adversarial in character. The judge himself enquires into the circumstances, so far as they are not within his personal knowledge. He identifies the grounds of complaint, selects the witnesses and investigates what they have to say (subject to a right of cross-examination) decides on guilt and pronounces sentence. This summary procedure, which by its nature is to be used quickly if it is used at all, omits many of the safeguards to which an accused is ordinarily entitled, and for this reason it has been repeatedly stated that the judge should choose to adopt it only in cases of real need".

Another aspect of the summary procedure which was addressed by the Court of Appeal in that case was the question whether a finding of contempt by a judge, in the exercise of that jurisdiction, would render him *functus officio*. On the facts it was not necessary to come to a conclusion whether such a finding was equivalent to the return of a verdict by a jury; yet the view was expressed that "the dignity of the law, which the judge is engaged upon upholding, can scarcely be enhanced if it is seen publicly that the judge is constrained to punish conduct as a contempt which he no longer believes to be such."[65] Thus, the procedure being *sui generis*, a judge would seem not to be bound by what must be regarded as a provisional view that a contempt had been committed, and could, where appropriate, revise that view later in the proceedings in the light of further evidence or submissions.

3–57

---

[62] See the discussion of Buckley L.J. in *Seldon v Wilde* [1911] 1 K.B. 701.
[63] Principally, RSC Ord.52; see paras 15–9 *et seq*. See now CPR, Sch.1, Ord.52: see too the supplemental Practice Direction now governing committal applications in the High Court and county court, set out in Appendix 5A.
[64] (1989) 88 Cr.App.R. 63 at 67.
[65] *per* Mustill L.J. at 70. This passage was cited and followed in *R. v Stafforce Personnel Ltd*, November 24, 2000, CACD.

3–58 CHAPTER 3—THE DISTINCTION BETWEEN CRIMINAL/CIVIL CONTEMPT

3–58 The extent to which these exceptional procedures are consistent with the "fair and public hearing" requirements of Art.6 of the European Convention on Human Rights[66] may fall to be determined at some future date.[67] Meanwhile, it is necessary to consider some of these characteristics in slightly more detail.

1. Absence of jury trial

3–59 Notwithstanding that the available penalty is two years' imprisonment, there is no right to a trial by jury, even though an offence carrying such a penalty would ordinarily be triable "either way" under the general criminal law.[68] This is to be contrasted with the position in the United States, where the Supreme Court has granted the constitutional protection of trial by jury for "serious contempts".[69]

2. The variable application of general sentencing provisions to contempt cases

3–60 It is frequently unclear whether legislation of general application in the criminal law is to be taken as applying in the context of contempt. Only with some hesitation was it held, for example, that a committal by justices under s.12 of the Contempt of Court Act 1981[70] did *not* amount to a "summary conviction" for the purposes of s.21 of the Powers of Criminal Courts Act 1973,[71] and that there was accordingly no statutory entitlement to legal representation before a period of imprisonment was imposed,[72] although it would in practice generally granted.[73] Similarly, a person found guilty of criminal contempt was not thereby "convicted of an offence" for the purposes of s.2(1) of the 1973 Act, and could not therefore be placed on probation.[74] The same reasoning would apply to the wording of the Criminal Justice Act 2003, s.151(1)(a) of which states that only those "convicted

---

[66] Art.6 is more fully considered at paras 2–143 *et seq.*
[67] At least one writer takes the view that the summary contempt procedure "contravenes both the right to be tried by an independent and impartial tribunal, under Art.6(1) of the European Convention on Human Rights, and the right to have adequate legal assistance, under Art.6(3)(b) and (c)". See D. Feldman, *Civil Liberties and Human Rights in England and Wales* (2nd ed, 2002), p.963, citing *R. v Macleod (Calum Ian)* [2001] Crim. L.R. 509, which is discussed at paras 10–36 *et seq.* See also *The Coca-Cola Company v Aytacli* [2003] EWHC 91 (Ch) discussed at para.3–5.
[68] That is to say, an offence which, if committed by an adult, is triable either on indictment or summarily. See generally ed. D. Ormerod, Smith and Hogan, *Criminal Law* (11th ed., 2005), ch.3.
[69] *Bloom v Illinois* 391 U.S. 194 (1968). The decision represented the culmination of a process in which the Supreme Court acknowledged that criminal contempt is a "crime in the ordinary sense" warranting trial by jury. The court had earlier accorded a number of constitutional protections to those charged with contempt: see, *e.g. Cooke v United States* 267 U.S. 517 (1925) (notice of charges and assistance of counsel); *Gompers v Buck's Stove & Range Co* 221 U.S. 418 (1911) (privilege against self-incrimination and proof beyond reasonable doubt); *Young v United States ex rel. Vuitton et Fils, SA* 481 U.S. 787 (1987) (the recognition of a need for a disinterested prosecutor). See P. A. Hostak, (1995) 81 Cornell Law Rev. 181 at 191.
[70] See further paras 10–112 *et seq.*
[71] See now the Criminal Justice Act 2003, s.151(1)(a). The availability of non-custodial sentences in the context of contempt is more generally considered at paras 14–97 *et seq.*
[72] *R. v Newbury Justices Ex p. Pont* (1984) 78 Cr.App.R. 255.
[73] For further discussion, see para.10–53.
[74] *R. v Palmer* (1992) 95 Cr.App.R. 170, [1992] 3 All E.R. 289.

of an offence" may be made the subject of community sentence orders, as they are now called.

3. *The applicability of PACE*

The question has also arisen as to the extent to which the ordinary rules governing police powers apply in proceedings for criminal contempt. The question was considered by the Court of Appeal in *R. v Jones*,[75] where it was held that, at least in some respects, they do not. The appellant and a co-accused, who had been in the public gallery at a criminal trial, had been heard to utter remarks to a member of the jury, including "definitely not guilty". As a result of these remarks, which the trial judge construed as threatening, the jury was discharged, and the two men ordered to be arrested, because the judge considered that they might have committed a contempt. He dealt with the conduct himself on the day after he had discharged the jury. One of the witnesses against Jones was a police officer who had overheard incriminating remarks made as he was escorting them to the cells.

It was contended on behalf of the appellant that the officer had failed to comply with Code of Practice C (dealing with the conduct of interviews), made pursuant to the Police and Criminal Evidence Act 1984. This required a contemporaneous record to be made, and an opportunity afforded to the suspect to challenge its accuracy. It was argued before the Court of Appeal that the trial judge had erred in exercising his discretion to admit this evidence.

It was held that the judge had not erred in ruling as he did. Contempt proceedings were *sui generis*,[76] and there was no need therefore always to follow procedures to be found in other areas of the criminal law. Nevertheless, s.78 of the Police and Criminal Evidence Act, governing the exercise of discretion to exclude evidence, could be applicable to contempt proceedings in some circumstances, since it expressly applies to evidence "in any proceedings".[77] Similarly, the PACE Codes of Practice could be relevant and invoked in certain (unspecified) circumstances. The Court was however satisfied that there was no *obligation* under statute or otherwise to invoke any such procedure.

4. *The "right to silence"*

Sections 34 and 35 of the Criminal Justice and Public Order Act 1994 modify the "right to silence" in criminal cases. The Act itself does not say whether its

---

[75] [1996] Crim.L.R. 806.
[76] See further paras 3–85 *et seq.*
[77] Which gives rise to the question: could s.78 be raised in cases of civil contempt? There is no authority on the point, but the Act applies solely to criminal proceedings, and it may be assumed that it could not.

provisions apply to contempt proceedings.[78] Section 35(4), which deals with the effect of the accused's silence at trial, provides that the "section does not render the accused compellable to give evidence on his own behalf, and he shall accordingly not be guilty of contempt of court by reason of a failure to do so." Presumably, nevertheless, it is still open to the court to draw adverse inferences from the accused's silence in a contempt case, as in any other criminal proceedings, where it seems appropriate to do so.[79]

5. *The relevance of general principles of criminal liability*

3–65   Another unanswered question is the extent to which the characteristic principles of criminal liability apply in the law of contempt. How far, for example, do the ordinary principles of accessorial liability apply?[80] Can there be proceedings for conspiracy to commit contempt? How, if at all, does the law of attempts apply in this context?[81] To what extent does liability arise on a vicarious basis for criminal contempt?[82]

3–66   In a number of recent decisions, the courts have insisted that the requirements of *mens rea* applying in the criminal law generally should also operate in this context. Specifically, the mental element required in those forms of criminal contempt not falling within the scope of the strict liability rule has been held to be an intention to interfere with the administration of justice.[83] On the other hand, the court has been very ready to infer an intention from the surrounding circumstances.[84]

---

[78] In *Re B (A Minor) (Contempt of Court: Affidavit Evidence)* [1996] 1 W.L.R. 627, 1 F.L.R. 239, Wall J. held, in family proceedings, that it was open to a court to require respondents in civil contempt proceedings to swear affidavits, or to produce witness statements upon which they might rely, at a convenient time before the hearing so as to permit the proper preparation of evidence in reply (although they could not be cross-examined upon the contents, unless and until they chose to place reliance upon such evidence). This goes beyond anything that could be done in the criminal law context. For a discussion of the contents of affidavits in the context of criminal contempts, see *Att-Gen v London Weekend Television* [1972] 3 All E.R. 1146 at 1152 where the Divisional Court acknowledged that, in the *Sunday Times* case (*Att-Gen v Times Newspapers Ltd* [1972] 3 All E.R. 1136), the evidence of intention was found in the editor's affidavit.
[79] The circumstances in which it is appropriate to draw such inferences were dealt with originally by the Court of Appeal (Crim. Div.) in *R. v Cowan* [1996] Q.B. 373 and *R. v Argent* (1996) 161 J.P. 190: see generally paras 3–188 *et seq*. For the current position see *Archbold 2005* at paras 15–415 *et seq*.
[80] See generally paras 4–191 *et seq*.
[81] The question is addressed further at paras 11–14 *et seq*.
[82] paras 4–199 *et seq*.
[83] See for example, *Dobson v Hastings* [1992] Ch. 394; *Coe v Central Television plc* [1994] E.M.L.R. 433; *Att-Gen v Sport Newspapers Ltd* [1991] 1 W.L.R. 1195, [1992] 1 All E.R. 503; *Att-Gen v Newspaper Publishing plc* [1997] 1 W.L.R. 926, [1997] 1 All E.R. 159.
[84] *Att-Gen v News Group Newspapers plc* [1989] Q.B. 110; *Att-Gen v Newspaper Publishing plc* [1989] F.S.R. 457; *Att-Gen v Times Newspapers Ltd* [1992] 1 A.C. 191 (and in particular the passage from Lord Oliver at 218, cited above at para.3–50; *Official Solicitor v News Group Newspapers plc* [1994] 2 F.L.R. 174. See also paras 5–146 *et seq*.

6. Criminal contempts as "misdemeanours"

Before 1967, it could be said with some confidence that a criminal contempt was 3–67
a misdemeanour. The distinction between felonies and misdemeanours was
abolished in that year,[85] but it thereafter remained common for judges to refer to
criminal contempt as a "misdemeanour".[86] It is a somewhat anachronistic usage,
and moreover one which might give the impression that contempt is simply a
common law criminal offence, with the usual characteristics and procedural
safeguards, rather than being in some respects *sui generis*. Even if it is possible
to assimilate criminal contempt into the general body of substantive criminal law,
the procedural distinctions to which Mustill L.J. drew attention in *R. v Griffin*[87]
are so important that it is undesirable to use language which has the effect of
blurring the very real distinctions that remain; not least because, in *Re Lonrho
plc*,[88] it was made expressly clear that the traditional criminal process of
prosecution on indictment should not be used for contempt. Moreover, it is
doubtful whether even the terminology of "prosecution" is apt in the context of
contempt.[89]

It seems that counsel's argument in *P v Liverpool Daily Post and Echo* 3–68
Newspapers plc[90] was to the effect that whenever contempt proceedings are
launched, whether by the Attorney General or otherwise, what is happening is
that the court is being invited to exercise its inherent jurisdiction rather than try
a criminal offence. Lord Cross in *Att-Gen v Times Newspapers Ltd*[91] took the
view that the Attorney-General acts as "'amicus curiae' bringing to the notice of
the court some matter of which he considers that the court should be informed in
the interests of the administration of justice".

B. The nature of civil contempt

Traditionally civil contempt is regarded as consisting in disobedience to an order 3–69
of the court made, or breach of an undertaking given, in civil litigation. Whereas
the administration of justice as a whole is threatened by a criminal contempt, in
most cases of civil contempt less attention needs to be paid to considerations of
public interest; those concerned to pursue a breach of a court order will ordinarily

---

[85] Criminal Law Act 1967, s.1(1).
[86] *Balogh v St. Albans Crown Court* [1975] Q.B. 73 at 87B, Stephenson L.J. and 91E, Lawton L.J., CA; indeed, the term "misdemeanour" has from time to time been applied even to civil contempts: *Dean v Dean* [1987] F.L.R 517, which cites *Danchevsky v Danchevsky (No.2)* (1977) 121 S.J. 796; see further paras 3–77 *et seq.*
[87] (1989) 88 Cr.App.R. 63 at 67, cited fully at para.3–56.
[88] [1990] 2 A.C. 154, 177. See also *R. v D* [1984] 1 A.C. 778 at 792C–E, Watkins L.J., CA.
[89] See again Mustill L.J. in *Griffin* at 67 ("... there is no prosecutor"); see also *P v Liverpool Daily Post and Echo Newspapers plc* [1991] 2 A.C. 370 at 412A; particularly the argument of counsel, relying upon *R. v Daily Herald Editor, Printers and Publishers Ex p. the Bishop of Norwich* [1932] 2 K.B. 402 at 411–12. In fact, no reference was made by the court in this case to the use of the term "prosecution", but Lord Hewart C.J. did refer to "a long and interesting argument on the question of [the court's] jurisdiction", and concluded that there was no doubt that there was an inherent jurisdiction both to correct and protect inferior courts. But see *Guildford Borough Council v Valler* [1993] T.L.R. 274, 275 (Lexis), where Sedley J. said that civil contempts are a form of "private prosecution".
[90] [1991] 2 A.C. 370 at 412A.
[91] [1974] A.C. 273 at 326E.

3–69 CHAPTER 3—THE DISTINCTION BETWEEN CRIMINAL/CIVIL CONTEMPT

be the parties to the litigation in which the contempt arose. Historically, civil contempts as a class tended to be regarded as less grave. Nevertheless, there has been a growing recognition of the dual nature of civil contempt, in the sense that circumstances can indeed arise when the courts may wish to address the impact, from the public interest point of view, of a failure to comply with a court order or an undertaking.[92] As Lord Woolf M.R. observed in *Nicholls v Nicholls*[93]:

> "Today it is no longer appropriate to regard an order for committal as being no more than a form of execution available to another party against an alleged contemnor. The court itself has a very substantial interest in seeing that its orders are upheld."

3–70 The public policy considerations were explained by Lord Phillips M.R. in *Mid-Bedfordshire District Council v Brown (Thomas)*.[94] He was addressing a situation where a judge had suspended an injunction ordering gypsies to vacate land occupied in breach of planning control and an existing court order:

> "The practical effect of suspending the injunction has been to allow the defendants to change the use of the land and to retain the benefit of occupation of the land with caravans for residential purposes. This was in defiance of a court order properly served on them and correctly explained to them. In those circumstances there is a real risk that the suspension of the injunction would be perceived as condoning the breach. This would send out the wrong signal, both to others tempted to do the same and to law-abiding members of the public. The message would be that the court is prepared to tolerate contempt of its orders and to permit those who break them to profit from their contempt.
>
> The effect of that message would be to diminish respect for court orders, to undermine the authority of the court and to subvert the rule of law. In our judgment, those overarching public interest considerations far outweigh the factors which favour a suspension of the injunction so as to allow the defendants to keep their caravans on the land and to continue to reside there in breach of planning control".

3–71 Although civil contempt has been referred to in general terms in some of the older cases as an "offence",[95] this language would not really be regarded as appropriate nowadays.[96] On occasion, reference has also been made to the imprecise concept of civil contempt being "quasi-criminal".[97] It has long been

---

[92] See *Jennison v Baker* [1972] 2 Q.B. 52, CA discussed at para.3–12, and paras 12–5 *et seq*. See also *Clarke v Chadburn* [1984] I.R.L.R. 350, [1985] 1 W.L.R. 78, [1985] 1 All E.R. 211, discussed more fully at para.2–220 and paras 3–171 *et seq*.; *R. v Commissioners of Inland Revenue Ex p. Kingston Smith* [1996] 2 S.T.C. 1210.
[93] [1997] 1 W.L.R. 314 at 326B–C.
[94] [2004] EWCA Civ 1709, [2005] 1 W.L.R. 1460.
[95] See *Re Freston* (1883) 11 Q.B.D. 545 at 553, Brett M.R.; *Seldon v Wilde* [1911] 1 K.B. 701 at 708, Buckley L.J.
[96] In *Crest Homes plc v Marks* [1987] 1 A.C. 829 at 856E, Lord Oliver observed that " . . . 'offence' hardly seems an appropriate word to describe a civil contempt . . . ".
[97] See, *e.g.* Buckley L.J. in *Seldon v Wilde* [1911] 1 K.B. 701 at 705; *Phonographic Performance Ltd v Amusement Caterers* [1964] Ch. 195; Cross J. in *Yianni v Yianni* [1966] 1 W.L.R. 120; and Cross L.J. and Lord Denning M.R. in *Comet Products UK Ltd v Hawkex Plastics Ltd* [1971] 2 Q.B. 67. For discussion of parallel developments in Scotland, see *Petrie v Angus* (1889) 2 White 358, 17 R. (J.) 3, 27 S.L.R. 197, para.16–29.

recognised, however, that civil contempts do not necessarily, or even generally, entail criminality.[98]

In the context of civil contempt, also, a summary form of contempt procedure is employed. It is, however, only one of a number of enforcement mechanisms available; other methods include attachment of earnings and substituted performance. If such alternatives are available, the courts take the view that they should normally be used, and that recourse to the summary contempt jurisdiction should be regarded as a matter of last resort.[99]

C. The adoption of some criminal safeguards for civil contempt

Some cases of civil contempt may merit imprisonment for a period of up to two years, and others can attract very high financial penalties.[1] Because of the potentially serious consequences of findings of civil contempt (particularly where the conduct is held to be "contumacious"), there has been a tendency towards assimilating the two categories of contempt; this is partly because of concern that the safeguards that would normally be thought appropriate to criminal contempts should apply also to civil contempt, at least in serious cases.

Because the liberty of the subject is at stake, one might expect to find the courts insisting upon the greater safeguards normally associated with the criminal trial process.[2] In certain respects, this expectation has been fulfilled; most notably in relation to the standard of proof required,[3] the opportunities afforded for legal representation and the right to be properly heard.[4] It has also been held that,[5] in the hearing of a motion in which two parties are joined, there is a discretion as to whether the two applications should be heard together or separately. Where, as in that case, there was a risk that one of the parties might be prejudiced by the joint hearing (even taking into account that the hearing would be before a judge alone), the hearing should be severed. The judge applied the ordinary principles that obtain in criminal law cases, which he found in the pages of *Archbold*.[6]

Despite this general tendency, the courts appear careful to maintain the summary procedure for civil contempt as well as criminal, and to resist its full assimilation into the framework of criminal safeguards.[7] As Wall J. observed[8]:

---

[98] *Scott v Scott* [1913] A.C. 417 at 460, Lord Atkinson. But see the different approach adopted in Canada: *United Nurses of Alberta v Att-Gen for Alberta* (1992) 89 D.L.R. (4th) 609, where there appears to be a greater willingness to apply the term "criminal" to breaches of court orders in cases of defiance, especially, perhaps, where it is overt. In *Macmillan Bloedel Ltd v Simpson* (1994) 90 B.C.L.R. (2d) 24, 89 C.C.C. (3d) 217, 113 D.L.R. (4th) 368, the "open, continuous and flagrant" defiance of a court order was treated as a criminal contempt.
[99] See further para.12–18.
[1] See the list of fines in Appendix 3.
[2] See, *e.g. Kumari v Jalal* [1997] 1 W.L.R. 97, [1996] 4 All E.R. 65, CA.
[3] See paras 3–241 *et seq.*
[4] For a discussion of the judicial development of such safeguards, see paras 15–32 *et seq.*
[5] *Re a Company, The Times*, December 27, 1983, Nourse J.
[6] 41st ed., at paras 1–70—1–74; see now, *Archbold 2005*, paras 1–164 *et seq.*
[7] See also para.12–8.
[8] *Re B (A Minor) (Contempt of Court: Affidavit Evidence)* [1996] 1 W.L.R. 627 at 639A, 1 F.L.R. 239 at 251E.

3–75 CHAPTER 3—THE DISTINCTION BETWEEN CRIMINAL/CIVIL CONTEMPT

"I respectfully agree . . . that the analogy with criminal proceedings can be taken too far and that in civil proceedings for contempt the court will introduce those safeguards which are necessary for the protection of alleged contemnors but will not import criminal procedure wholesale or indiscriminately".

This passage was relied on in *The Coca-Cola Company v Aytacli*.[9] The judge took the view that this was relevant to the application of the Human Rights Act in civil proceedings. He concluded that, where duress was raised as a defence in civil contempt proceedings, the burden did *not* lie on the applicant to disprove duress and that Wall J.'s comments provided support for that conclusion. Article 6(2) and 6(3) related to persons charged with criminal offences, as the judge pointed out, but it is important to remember that the general approach of the European jurisprudence is to concentrate on substance rather than form in this respect. Thus, even though the domestic English law may regard certain proceedings as civil in character, nevertheless if there is a possibility of penal consequences, the safeguards habitually associated with criminal cases may to that extent be applicable.[10]

D. To what extent is the purpose of the law of civil contempt "remedial"?

3–76 The purpose underlying the law of civil contempt is for the most part either coercive or punitive. There is a question whether the contempt jurisdiction can ever, in addition, afford a restitutionary remedy to an individual litigant.[11] A remedial function is recognised to some extent in the United States, where in appropriate cases the court levies a fine "keyed to a determination of the aggrieved party's damages and payable to that party".[12] This has never been accepted in modern times in England, where the courts have taken the view that damages are not available for contempt.[13] In the words of Lord Donaldson M.R., proceedings for contempt "are not intended to provide solace or compensation to the plaintiff. If the plaintiff wants compensation, she must seek it in other forms".[14]

3–77 The purpose of the law of contempt is the protection of the administration of justice, and therefore only in a very limited sense "remedial"; its principal purposes are coercive (which may in a limited sense be described as "remedial", so far as the applicant is concerned), and punitive. In the former case the primary object is to protect the interests of the litigant in whose favour the order has been

---

[9] [2003] EWHC 91 (Ch.).
[10] *Benham v United Kingdom* (1996) 22 E.H.R.R. 293; see also *Berry Trade Ltd v Moussavi* [2002] 1 W.L.R. 1910; *Great Future International Ltd v Sealand Housing Corporation* [2004] EWHC 124 (Ch); *Raja v Hoogstraten* [2004] EWCA Civ 968, [2004] 4 All E.R. 793; *Daltel Europe Ltd (in liquidation) v Makki* [2005] EWHC 749 (Ch). See para.3–4.
[11] See Sedley J. in *Guildford Borough Council v Valler* [1993] T.L.R. 274 at 275. See also para.3–49: civil contempt should not be regarded as giving rise to a "private law right".
[12] See Hostak, (1995) 81 Cornell Law Rev. 181 at 183, citing *NLRB v Local 825, International Union of Operating Engineers*, 430 F. 2d 1225 at 1229 (3rd Cir. 1970), cert. denied, 401 U.S. 976 (1971); *Yanish v Barber*, 232 F. 2d 939 at 944 (9th Cir.) 1956.
[13] See *Chapman v Honig* [1963] 2 Q.B. 502, discussed at paras 14–159 *et seq*. But see the medieval practice referred to at paras 1–10 *et seq*.
[14] *Johnson v Walton* [1990] 1 F.L.R. 350 at 353D–E.

made or the undertaking given; in the latter case, the *only* object is the vindication of the court's authority.

E. Civil contempts as "misdemeanours"

Although coercion is an important element in the law of civil contempt, the jurisdiction is often exercised also with a view to punishment or deterrence.[15] In Canada, it has been held that[16]:

3–78

> "[a] person who simply breaches a court order is viewed as having committed a civil contempt. However, when the element of public defiance of the court's process in a way calculated to lessen societal respect for the courts is added to the breach *it becomes criminal*" (emphasis added).

An intentional flouting of the court's authority, or hindrance to the due administration of justice, can be just as objectionable from the public point of view, albeit in the context of civil contempt, as would be deliberate interference by a contemnor in one or other of the categories traditionally grouped under "criminal contempt". It is for this reason that a person who is found to be deliberately in civil contempt is at risk of being sent to prison for a lengthy period.

3–79

Indeed, the potential gravity of civil contempt has been recognised from time to time by the somewhat anachronistic application of the term "misdemeanour", for example in *Danchevsky v Danchevsky (No.2)*[17] by Lawton L.J. This has been described as the "vexed and largely historical question whether a civil contempt is, strictly speaking, a misdemeanour under our criminal law"[18]; The problem in using such terminology is, however, that it may be construed as entailing certain

3–80

---

[15] *Jennison v Baker* [1972] 2 Q.B. 52 at 61F and 64G, Salmon L.J. which are quoted at para.3–9 and para.3–14.
[16] *United Nurses of Alberta v Att-Gen for Alberta* (1992) 89 D.L.R. (4th) 609 at 636, McLachlin J. The process of formal incorporation into the criminal law can be observed in the American jurisprudence, with the result that traditional procedural safeguards (such as jury trial) have become available: see *International Union, United Mine Workers v Bagwell* 114 S. Ct. 2552 (1994).
[17] (1977) 121 Sol. Jo. 796, CA; *Dean v Dean* [1987] F.L.R 517. See by contrast *R. v D* [1984] A.C. 778 at 806 where Lord Brandon purported to draw a distinction between civil contempt and the commission of a criminal offence, expressing the opinion that parents who snatched their own children in defiance of a court order ought to be dealt with by way of the contempt jurisdiction, rather than a prosecution for kidnapping, except where the conduct of the parent concerned has been so bad that the ordinary right-thinking person would immediately regard it as criminal in nature. The conceptual difficulties of applying this test are similar to those encountered in the area of manslaughter by negligence, where it has been said that " . . . The essence of the matter which is supremely a jury question is whether having regard to the risk of death involved, the conduct of the defendant was so bad in all the circumstances as to amount in their judgment to a criminal act or omission": see, *e.g. R. v Adomako* [1995] 1 A.C. 171 at 187, where Lord Mackay L.C. also acknowledged that the test " . . . involves an element of circularity." It was later held in *R. v Misra* [2004] EWCA Crim 2375, [2005] 1 Cr.App.R. 328 that this formulation did not offend the requirements of certainty as guaranteed by Art.7 of the E.C.H.R.
[18] *Bhimji v Chatwani (No.3)* [1992] 4 All E.R. 912, 925 at 928, *per* Knox J. (a question he saw no need to embark upon for the purposes in hand).

3–80 procedural and jurisdictional consequences. This appears to be the conclusion drawn by Cumming-Bruce L.J. in *Jelson (Estates) Ltd v Harvey*[19]:

> "Lawton L.J. in *Danchevsky* said that civil contempt of court in the form of a breach of an undertaking or injunction is a common law misdemeanour, and so it would follow that the civil court could not do anything that a criminal court could not have done".

3–81 This reasoning might appear to suggest that all the safeguards that protect a criminal defendant should be available to one who is alleged to have been guilty of civil contempt. The analogy can only be pressed so far,[20] however; indeed, the ultimate protection of trial by jury is plainly precluded in cases even of criminal contempt. The limited extent of the protection that the Lord Justice had in mind in that case was the application of the twin principles of *autrefois acquit* and *convict*.[21]

3–82 This "misdemeanour" characterisation is rather surprising on two counts. Not only was the distinction between the two forms of criminal wrong (felonies and misdemeanours) itself abolished in 1967, but it was a characteristic of misdemeanours that they were triable only on indictment. Yet it is plain that civil contempt was *never* proceeded against by way of indictment.[22] Perhaps it is even more misleading to use the term because of the fact that, notwithstanding the reforms of 1967, "misdemeanour" may legitimately still be used in the modern criminal law to refer to certain common law offences.[23]

3–83 Moreover, it is clear that not all judges have regarded that terminology as appropriate. For example, in *El Capistrano SA v ATO Marketing Ltd*[24] Balcombe L.J. cavilled at the usage "misdemeanour":

> "This appeal turns on the question: How far should the analogy of the criminal law be applied in dealing with a civil contempt of court? In this connection I would not, without further argument, be prepared to accept the dictum of Lawton L.J. in *Danchevsky v Danchevsky (No 2)* 121 S.J. 796, that any contempt of court is a common law misdemeanour."

3–84 What emerges from the authorities is that there is inconsistency as to the application of terminology, as well as a degree of confusion as to substance. What matters is not so much the labelling of the wrongful conduct in question, but rather the recognition that, where the liberty of the subject is at stake, appropriate evidential and procedural safeguards should be made available to the

---

[19] [1983] 1 W.L.R. 1401, [1984] 1 All E.R. 12 at 20. And see *Lee v Walker* [1985] Q.B. 1191 at 1201D, where Cumming-Bruce L.J. again characterised civil contempts as "misdemeanours". See also the discussion in *R. v Anomo, The Independent*, February 18, 1998 (Lexis).
[20] *Re B (A Minor) (Contempt of Court: Affidavit Evidence)* [1996] 1 F.L.R. 239 at 251E, Wall J.
[21] See further paras 3–209 *et seq*.
[22] See, *e.g.* the remarks of Lord Atkinson in *Scott v Scott* [1913] A.C. 417 at 460–1.
[23] For example, the offences of interfering with the or perverting the administration of justice. See generally *Archbold 2005*, ch.28. Incitement too is an offence at common law, but attempts are now the subject of statute: Criminal Attempts Act 1981.
[24] [1989] 1 W.L.R. 471 at 485H, 2 All E.R. 572 at 584.See also *Bhimji v Chatwani (No.3)* [1992] 4 All E.R. 912 at 925, 928.

accused person, provided that they do not defeat the need to maintain the flexibility which the summary procedure was intended to afford.[25] The availability of such safeguards may become especially important in the light of the discipline of Art.6 of the European Convention which provides that "everyone is entitled to a fair and public hearing within a reasonable time by an independent and impartial tribunal[26] established by law".

F. Is contempt of court a wrong *sui generis*?

Writers on the nature of crime are generally driven to the conclusion that there is no such entity as a "crime" independently of the procedure by which it is pursued.[27] That being so, the question whether the substantive law of contempt is directed towards misconduct which may itself be classified as *sui generis* becomes illusory, since it is clear that it does attract *sui generis* procedures. Indeed, it may be doubted whether the Court of Appeal was intending to say anything to the contrary when Mustill L.J. made the observation in *Griffin* that[28]: "We are here concerned with the exercise of a jurisdiction which is *sui generis* so far as English law is concerned."

3–85

In *Morris v The Crown Office*[29] the Attorney-General, Sir Elwyn Jones Q.C., argued that contempt of court was to be regarded as a wrong *sui generis*.[30] The Court of Appeal, however, preferred to base its decision on the proposition that contempt of court was a misdemeanour, but one for which the *procedure* is *sui generis*. Criminal contempt of court seems at one time to have been regarded as in itself capable of prosecution by way of indictment,[31] although it was also susceptible to the alternative summary procedure of committal, which was not

3–86

---

[25] See Wall J., cited at para.3–75.
[26] Which would by no means necessarily require jury trial, since that is not a common feature in the legal systems of other signatory countries. See C. van den Wyngaert, *Criminal Procedure Systems in the European Community* (1993) for a survey of, *inter alia*, the role of lay persons in the criminal justice systems of some signatory states to the European Convention. See also ed. N. Vidmar, *World Jury* Systems (2000) Oxford University Press.
[27] See Glanville Williams, "The Definition of Crime" (1955) 8 C.L.P. 107: "Crimes, then, are wrongs which the judges have held, or Parliament has from time to time laid down, are sufficiently injurious to the public to warrant the application of criminal procedure to deal with them". See also ed. D. Ormerod, Smith and Hogan, *Criminal Law* (11th ed., 2005) ch.2. It may be observed, in the light of Glanville Williams' sophisticated definition of what constitutes criminality, how unsatisfactory is the test suggested by Lord Brandon (cited at n.17 above). It should not be for laymen to decide, especially on an *ad hoc* basis, what is "criminal", but the courts or the legislature.
[28] (1989) 88 Cr.App.R. 63 at 67. See also *R. v Jones* [1996] Crim.L.R. 806, CA.
[29] [1970] 2 Q.B. 114.
[30] *Morris* was applied in *R. v Palmer* (1992) 95 Cr.App.R. 170, [1992] 3 All E.R. 289, where it was held that the court had no power to make a probation order in a contempt case. What was formerly called probation is now included within a "community sentence"order by virtue of the Criminal Justice Act 2003, s.147. The availability of non-custodial sentences for contempt more generally is considered at paras 14–97 *et. seq.* For the position in Scotland, see para.16–39. The contempt jurisdiction has also been referred to in Canada as *"sui generis"*; see *Boutet: re Bernheim; re CBC* (1983) 35 CR (3d) 302, CS Que; *J.P. v MacMillan Bloedel Ltd; Att-Gen of Canada, Intervener* (1996) 130 D.L.R. 385, SCC, 385 at 395, Lamer C.J.C.
[31] *R. v Parke* [1903] 2 K.B. 432, 442. See also *John Fairfax and Sons Pty Ltd v McRae* (1955) 93 C.L.R. 351 at 364; J.C. McCruer "Criminal Contempt of Court Procedure: A Protection to the Rights of the Individual" (1951) 30 Can. Bar Rev. 225 at 236–7.

available for other criminal wrongs. Indeed, it is the summary method that is nowadays recognised as the only legitimate means of proceeding.[32] It is submitted that, while it is obvious that much of the contempt procedure is *sui generis*, it would be wrong to minimise the criminal characteristics and consequences of any conduct which is held to be contempt of court (at least so far as criminal contempt is concerned).[33]

3–87   It was recognised in *Balogh v St. Albans Crown Court*[34] that contemnors should not be dealt with "on the spot", except where necessary "for the purpose of ensuring that a trial in progress or about to start can be brought to a proper and dignified end without disturbance and with a fair chance of a just verdict or judgment." The Court was saying no more than that contempt cases should be disposed of with due consideration, either by allowing for a cooling off period or by referring the matter to the Attorney-General. It has not so far been suggested (by contrast with the position in the United States)[35] that the criminal character of contempt requires the safeguards of trial by jury on indictment.

G. The practical importance of the distinction gradually minimised

3–88   The labelling distinction, criminal or civil, became especially significant in the years following 1873, when appeals to the Court of Appeal were made available in civil cases,[36] but not for criminal contempts. It is not surprising, therefore, to find that the matter of labelling tended to dominate much of the subsequent judicial discussion of contempt. The courts were sometimes conscious of conflicting considerations of public policy. On the one hand, it might often seem desirable that the right of appeal should not be restricted by a narrow definition of civil contempt: on the other hand, certain examples of defiant civil contempt were so serious in nature, from the public point of view, that it seemed inappropriate to accord the contemnor the benefits of such traditional incidents of civil contempt as privilege, waiver and release *ex debito justitiae*.

3–89   Since 1960 there has been a right of appeal in the case of both civil and criminal contempt, and accordingly no temptation to label examples of contempt as civil rather than criminal purely for that reason. Moreover, even before 1960, there had been a gradual blurring of the distinctions regarding the incidents of civil and those of criminal contempt. For example, it had been held in relation to at least some forms of civil contempt, as well as in relation to criminal, that a plea of privilege might not be relied upon[37]; the breach of an order could not always

---

[32] See *Re Lonrho plc* [1990] 2 A.C. 154 at 177 where it was said that the procedure by way of indictment is now obsolete and "ought not to be revived".
[33] In the context of civil contempt, Lord Brandon in *R. v D* [1984] 1 A.C. 778 at 806 appears to have graded disobedience to a court order as only meriting the attention of the criminal law when the conduct in question was so bad that an ordinary citizen would unhesitatingly characterise it as criminal in nature. There seems to be no other authority to support this elusive test and it is to be noted that his remarks just pre-date the convergence of the public policy considerations to which the coal strike gave a particular focus: cp *Clarke v Chadburn* cited at para.3–171.
[34] [1975] 1 Q.B. 73 at 92–3, Lawton L.J., CA.
[35] See *International Union, United Mine Workers v Bagwell*, 512 U.S. 821 (1994).
[36] Supreme Court of Judicature Act 1873, s.47.
[37] *Re Freston* (1883) 11 Q.B.D. 545; *Re Hunt* [1959] 2 Q.B. 69.

be waived by a party[38]; the court could proceed of its own motion[39]; it would be possible, where the public interest required, for the Attorney-General to intervene[40]; a civil contemnor would not invariably be entitled to his release *ex debito justitiae*[41]; a sheriff was permitted on a writ of attachment for contempt to break open outer doors, even though it was in respect of non-compliance with an order for delivery of documents, despite the fact that this is not permitted "in a merely civil process at the suit of a subject (such as the execution of a writ of *fieri facias*)"[42]; a fine could be imposed[43]; the standard of proof is beyond reasonable doubt[44]; the alleged contemnor has a right to silence and cannot be compelled to give evidence[45]; and the judge may call a witness whom neither side proposes to call, which would not ordinarily happen in civil litigation,[46] although rarely it may happen in criminal proceedings.[47]

Indeed, even the enduringly separate approaches towards the requirements as to the state of mind of alleged contemnors might nowadays be construed as more apparent than real; particularly having regard to the court's willingness, in the context of common law criminal contempts, to *infer* the presence of any requisite intent.[48]

All of these developments tend to support the views of, *inter alios*, the Phillimore Committee,[49] Lord Donaldson M.R.,[50] and Sir John Laws,[51] that this

---

[38] *Seaward v Paterson* [1897] 1 Ch. 545 at 560, Rigby L.J.; *Corcoran v Corcoran* [1950] 1 All E.R. 495; *Re Grantham Wholesale Fruit, Vegetable and Potato Merchants Ltd* [1972] 1 W.L.R. 559; *Jennison v Baker* [1972] 2 Q.B. 52; *Watson v Watson*, August 10,1970, Elizabeth Lane J. unreported; the subject of waiver is discussed more fully at paras 3–157 *et seq.*
[39] *Churchman v Joint Shop Stewards' Committee of the Workers of the Port of London* [1972] 1 W.L.R. 1094, Lord Denning at 1100. See also the words of Megarry V.-C. in *Clarke v Chadburn* [1984] I.R.L.R. 350, [1985] 1 W.L.R. 78, cited at para.3–171.
[40] He did intervene in *Re Crump* (1963) 107 Sol. Jo. 682, [1963] Crim. L.R. 777, *The Times*, August 22, 1963, a case of disobedience to an order restraining a ward of court from marrying, but on the basis that this was a criminal contempt. See also *Clarke v Chadburn* [1984] 1 I.R.L.R. 350, [1985] 1 W.L.R. 78 at 82G, quoted fully at para.2–220 and para.3–171. For the role of the Law Officers more generally, see *Att-Gen v Times Newspapers Ltd* [1974] A.C. 273 at 311, 326; *Gouriet v UPOW* [1978] A.C. 435 at 481A–B, 483–484, 495E-F, 499–500, 518; *Att-Gen v Newspaper Publishing plc* [1988] Ch. 333 at 362D, 367H–368A.
[41] *Re Hunt* [1959] 2 Q.B. 69.
[42] *Harvey v Harvey* (1884) 26 Ch.D. 644 at 655, Chitty J.
[43] *Phonographic Performance Ltd v Amusement Caterers* [1964] Ch. 195.
[44] *Re Bramblevale* [1970] 1 Ch. 128; for discussion, see para.3–241.
[45] *Comet Products UK Ltd v Hawkex Plastics Ltd* [1971] 2 Q.B. 67. See further para.3–188. In addition see *Re B (A Minor) (Contempt of Court: Affidavit Evidence)* [1996] 1 W.L.R. 627 at 639A, 1 F.L.R. 239, Wall J., which is discussed at para.15–15 and para.15–35.
[46] *Yianni v Yianni* [1966] 1 W.L.R. 120.
[47] *R. v Chapman* (1839) 8 C. & P. 558, 173 E.R. 617; *Baldwin, The Times*, May 3, 1978; *Roberts (JM)* 80 Cr.App.R. 89, CA. This jurisdiction should only be used most sparingly and when it is necessary in the interests of justice.
[48] For a discussion, see paras 5–146 *et seq.*; *Att-Gen v News Group Newspapers plc* [1989] Q.B. 110; *Att-Gen v Newspaper Publishing plc* [1989] F.S.R. 457; *Att-Gen v Times Newspapers Ltd* [1992] 1 A.C. 191.
[49] Cmnd. 5794 (1974), ch.8.
[50] As Sir John Donaldson M.R. in *Att-Gen v Newspaper Publishing plc* [1988] Ch. 333, 362E-C, quoted at para.3–51.
[51] para.3–48, n.51.

3-91 CHAPTER 3—THE DISTINCTION BETWEEN CRIMINAL/CIVIL CONTEMPT

fundamental distinction, serving no apparently useful purpose, might itself be consigned to history. As we have explained, however, so many practical distinctions between the two categories have emerged, that it would not serve any useful purpose simply to abolish the traditional labelling, without at the same time making it clear what was to happen to these disparities.

H. How do the contempts created by the 1981 Act fit into the framework?

1. Introduction

3-92 Although the 1981 Act did not abolish the distinction between civil and criminal contempts, the draftsman nowhere specified whether the statutory contempts identified within it are to be classified as civil or criminal in character. In the absence of statutory guidance, the matter must be approached from principle. Plainly, a contempt within the strict liability rule[52] is criminal in character, since it involves, *ex hypothesi*, the creation of a risk that the administration of justice will be impeded or prejudiced. But other forms of contempt, both those coming into existence by virtue of the Act and those left untouched by it, require careful consideration.

2. The secrecy of jury deliberations: section 8

3-93 Section 8[53] of the 1981 Act makes it expressly a "contempt" (as opposed merely to an offence) to "obtain, disclose or solicit any particulars of statements made, opinions expressed, arguments advanced or votes cast by members of a jury in the course of their deliberations". The Act does not state specifically that this is to be categorised as a criminal contempt. Indeed, it does not advert to the distinction in any of its provisions. Yet it is difficult to see that this could be anything other than criminal in character. The section was intended to implement, as a matter of public policy, Parliament's purposes of preserving jurors from harassment, and their verdicts from being undermined[54] (as for example, by the exposure of faulty reasoning).[55]

---

[52] s.2 of the Act, discussed in ch.4 *passim*.
[53] The section is considered more fully at para.11–349.
[54] Lord Hailsham L.C., *Hansard*, H.L., Vol. 415, (5th series), cols.663–4, December 9, 1980. No exception was made for *bona fide* research into the workings of the jury system, although subsequently this was the very first recommendation of the *Royal Commission on Criminal Justice: Report* (1993), Cm. 2263, ch.1, para.8. One of the rare examples of an English jury's deliberations emerging into the light of day, subsequent to the 1981 Act, is provided by the publication in the *Irish Sunday Independent* on November 24, 1996, of a detailed account of the jury's reasoning at the conclusion of a libel action brought by Albert Reynolds (the former Irish Taoiseach—Prime Minister). See Sir Robin Auld, *Review of Criminal Courts of England and Wales* (2001), ch.5, para.98 who thought the prohibition in s.8 "indefensible and capable of causing serious injustice" and *R. v Connor and Mirza* [2004] UKHL 2, [2004] 1 A.C. 1118. See now the Department of Constitutional Affairs Consultation Paper CP 04/05, *Jury Research and Impropriety*, January 21, 2005.
[55] See, *e.g Ellis v Deheer* [1922] 2 K.B. 113 at 121, Atkin L.J.

3. Tape recording in court: section 9

Section 9[56] of the Act also makes it a "contempt" to use a tape recorder in court **3–94** without leave of the court, or to publish a tape recording of legal proceedings. Again this would appear to be a statutory form of *criminal* contempt.

4. Breaches of section 4(2) and section 11 orders

Failing to comply with a s.4(2)[57] or s.11[58] order (postponing the reporting of **3–95** court proceedings, and withholding a name or other matter, respectively) might appear *prima facie* to be civil contempts, since the essence of the offence would be disobedience to an order. The Contempt of Court Act 1981 gives no clue as to which species of contempt is intended.[59] Although Ackner L.J. in *Horsham Justices* recognised that a breach of a s.4 order would constitute contempt of court, he did not address the question of whether it should be classified as civil or criminal.[60]

Such orders are, however, in form and substance usually addressed to the **3–96** world at large rather than to a party to the proceedings in question. This is true even where such orders are made in civil proceedings.[61] The purpose of such orders is the protection of the administration of justice from people in general (mainly journalists), rather than to direct the conduct of any individual litigant. In this respect, therefore, they differ from the kinds of orders traditionally regarded as the subject of "contempt in procedure".

Nevertheless, it may be significant that in practice the court tends to adopt a **3–97** uniform approach towards breaches of court orders, so far as the requisite state of mind is concerned, whether they be classified as criminal or civil. It is true that in principle a clear distinction is drawn. On the one hand, for criminal contempt outside the strict liability rule, it is necessary to demonstrate an intention to interfere with the administration of justice[62]; no such requirement, on the other hand, applies to breaches of court orders. It is generally thought to be enough that the alleged contemnor should know of the existence of the order and that he

---

[56] See para.10–190.
[57] See para.7–111.
[58] para.7–83.
[59] The Act does not at any point make reference to the notion of civil contempt; nor does it appear to contain provisions relating to the types of conduct normally categorised as civil contempt (although it has been held that the restrictions on sentencing imposed by s.14 apply to penalties imposed in respect of civil contempts: *Peart v Stewart* [1983] 2 A.C. 109).
[60] *R. v Horsham Justices Ex p. Farquharson* [1982] Q.B. 762 at 804–7.
[61] See *MGN Pension Trustees Ltd v Bank of America National Trust and Savings Association and another (Serious Fraud Office Intervening)* [1995] 2 All E.R. 355 (where an order was in fact refused).
[62] *Att-Gen v Newspaper Publishing plc* [1988] Ch. 333; *Att-Gen v News Group Newspapers plc* [1989] Q.B. 110; *London Borough of Harrow v Johnstone* [1997] 1 W.L.R. 459 at 468F–G and 469D–F, Lord Mustill.

3–97 CHAPTER 3—THE DISTINCTION BETWEEN CRIMINAL/CIVIL CONTEMPT

should be aware of what he is doing.[63] He does not have to be shown specifically to intend either to breach the order itself or to interfere with the administration of justice in any broader sense.

3–98 In practice, however, the court has proved in recent years to be so ready to infer an intention to interfere with the administration of justice, even in those cases where the conduct relied upon would be classified as criminal,[64] from the alleged contemnor's knowledge of the relevant order and from the conduct itself, that the clear distinction of principle has little practical effect.

5. Guidance from the common law: Scott v Scott

3–99 In so far, however, as the distinction between civil and criminal contempt continues to have significance in respect of breaches of court orders, it is necessary to have regard to the way the matter was approached at common law, and in particular to the House of Lords decision in *Scott v Scott*,[65] even though that does not entirely resolve the issue.

3–100 Mrs Scott filed a petition in the High Court seeking that her marriage be declared null and void by reason of her husband's impotence. She applied for the matter to be heard *in camera* and an order was made accordingly. After decree absolute, she obtained through her solicitor three copies of the transcript of evidence, of which she and her solicitor sent one to the respondent's father, one to his sister and one to a third party. The respondent moved for the petitioner and her solicitor to be committed for contempt. Mrs Scott, in an affidavit in opposition to the motion, stated that she had sent the copies of the transcript to the three persons in consequence of reports sent to them by the respondent reflecting upon her sanity, and had done so in defence of her reputation.

3–101 Bargrave Deane J. held that the petitioner and her solicitor were in contempt and ordered them to pay the costs of the motion. They appealed and the preliminary objection was taken by the respondent that there was no jurisdiction to hear the appeal, since the judge's order had been made in the course of criminal proceedings. The Court of Appeal upheld this objection by the unusual majority of four to two.

3–102 In the Court of Appeal[66] Buckley L.J., who held that it was a criminal contempt, reasoned as follows:

> "An order for hearing in camera a civil suit such as this is not an order to enforce any civil right arising as between the parties. It is an order which the court thinks proper to

---

[63] *Stancomb v Trowbridge Urban District Council* [1910] 2 Ch. 190; *Director General of Fair Trading v Pioneer Concrete (UK) Ltd* [1995] 1 A.C. 456; see para.12–80. And see Eveleigh L.J. in *Z Ltd v A-Z and AA-LL* [1982] Q.B. 558, holding that banks must be shown to have knowledge of the existence of a *Mareva* injunction (freezing order).
[64] *Att-Gen v Newspaper Publishing plc* [1989] 1 F.S.R. 457; *Att-Gen v Times Newspapers Ltd* [1992] 1 A.C. 191.
[65] [1913] A.C. 417, HL.
[66] [1912] P. 241 at 293.

make for two reasons, first, that the parties may not be deterred from coming forward to seek relief and giving their evidence in the matter (a consideration which proceeds upon the necessity of ensuring the proper administration of justice); and secondly, that upon grounds of morality and public decency a public hearing, resulting in a publication of details such as are relevant in such a suit, shall be excluded ... the order in short is not an order in aid of any civil right of the parties but an order of the court the breach of which is an offence not inter partes, but against the order of the court in a matter affecting the administration of justice."

The House of Lords, however, held that the proceedings were civil in character, because the order had been made in the course of a nullity suit, which was not a "criminal cause or matter" within the meaning of s.47 of the Judicature Act 1873, and that an appeal therefore lay.

This decision appears therefore to have been based not so much upon the nature of Mrs Scott's conduct or upon the kind of order she breached, but rather upon the character of the original nullity proceedings in which Bargrave Deane J. had resolved the issue of contempt and made his order for costs. The matter turned upon the wording of the particular statutory provision which excluded any appeal in respect of a criminal cause or matter.[67] The case nonetheless gives some guidance as to general principle.

6. *Conclusion*

A number of possibilities have to be considered. If an order breached has been made in criminal proceedings, or an order made in civil proceedings has been breached by a non-party, there can be little doubt that any such breach would be treated as criminal in character. This conclusion is supported by the approach of the court in *R. v Socialist Worker Ex p. Att-Gen*,[68] since the nature of the order there made was closely analogous to orders which would now fall within s.11 of the 1981 Act. There the Divisional Court held that it was a contempt to disclose the identity of a blackmail victim where the court had ordered that his evidence be given anonymously, and apparently treated it as a criminal contempt. As has been pointed out,[69] such orders are directed to the world in general, and are intended to protect the purposes of the administration of justice.

Suppose, on the other hand, that an order under s.4(2) or under s.11 has been made in the course of civil proceedings, and it is subsequently breached by someone who happens to be a party to the proceedings. It is difficult to see why (*pace* the decision of the House of Lords in *Scott v Scott*) such a breach should be classified differently purely because the conduct happens to be that of a party. In practice, perhaps, the labelling is unlikely to make very much difference to the way in which the court treats the breach in most cases that can be foreseen.

---

[67] There was no appeal in criminal cases at all until the Criminal Appeal Act 1907, which created the Court of Criminal Appeal. But the right of appeal in respect of contempt (because it did not involve a conviction on indictment) did not arise until 1960: see para.3–30.
[68] [1975] Q.B. 637. See also *Att-Gen v Leveller Magazine* [1979] A.C. 440.
[69] paras 3–95 *et seq.*

3-107 CHAPTER 3—THE DISTINCTION BETWEEN CRIMINAL/CIVIL CONTEMPT

I. Breaches classified as criminal at common law

1. Orders made under the common law for the restriction of court reporting

3–107   We have come above to the conclusion that breaches of orders made under the provisions of ss.4(2) and 11 of the 1981 Act would probably be classified as criminal contempts. Indeed, prior to the enactment of s.11, disobedience to orders made under the common law jurisdiction in the course of criminal proceedings had been regarded as criminal contempt. In *Att-Gen v The Leveller Magazine*[70] it was alleged that the defendants had breached an order of the court not to reveal the identity of a witness who, on grounds of national security, had been allowed to refer to himself as Colonel B. Their Lordships held that if an order *had* been made it had been waived or invalidated by subsequent disclosures in the course of proceedings. However, they plainly proceeded on the basis that in such circumstances a breach would have been a criminal contempt.[71]

2. Failing to answer questions when ordered to do so

3–108   Failure to answer questions while giving evidence in court, when required to do so by a judge, would also be treated as criminal. Lord Diplock in *Secretary of State for Defence v Guardian Newspapers Ltd*[72] said expressly that "a refusal to answer the question if ordered to by the judge to do so would constitute a contempt committed in the face of the court and thus a criminal contempt". Thus, it seems clear that such a failure on the part of a witness would not assume the character of civil contempt merely because it consists in breach of a court order, even in civil proceedings.

3–109   *Re Armstrong Ex p. Lindsay*[73] might appear at first sight to be inconsistent with this proposition. There a witness refused to submit himself for examination in Scottish bankruptcy proceedings, and the judge said " ... I think that any imprisonment ordered in the present case would be by way of civil process and would determine *ex debito justitiae* as soon as the person committed yielded obedience to the order of the court and paid the costs."

3–110   The context is, however, important. The witness in question was a member of Parliament on whose behalf a claim for privilege from arrest was made. In judging whether or not such a claim is legitimate, the test appears to be whether the order for committal (or, in some of the older cases, attachment) had as its purpose punishment of the offender or merely coercion. It was in the latter context only that privilege might be claimed.[74] The judge in *Re Armstrong* was concerned with whether he could coerce the witness to attend for the purposes of giving evidence, rather than dealing with a refusal in the face of the court. In the

---

[70] [1979] A.C. 440; and see discussion at para.7–76.
[71] *e.g.* Lord Diplock at 449, Lord Edmund-Davies at 461, Lord Scarman at 469.
[72] [1985] A.C. 339 at 347C–E.
[73] [1892] 1 Q.B. 327.
[74] Discussed further paras 3–141 *et seq*. The authorities appear to suggest that privilege was precluded in cases where the purpose was punitive rather than coercive: *Stourton v Stourton* [1963] P. 302.

light of this analysis, there is in truth no inconsistency with Lord Diplock's proposition of law.[75]

When a person, having come to court, refused to answer questions, he would have been unlikely to be granted the benefit of what used to be regarded as release *ex debito justitiae*. The court would be seeking to punish him for past refusals to answer, rather than seeking to coerce him. (In any event, since the enactment of s.14 of the 1981 Act,[76] *no one* can be said to be entitled to be released *ex debito justitiae*, because of the requirement of a fixed term of imprisonment. Although it has been recognised that an application to the court can be made for release on the basis that the contempt has been purged, this is no longer regarded as in any sense a matter of "right". It is a matter for the judge's discretion.)[77] 3–111

3. *Cases where the existence of the order is incidental to the contempt*

A striking instance of disobedience of an order having been treated as a criminal contempt (virtually, it seems, a contempt in the face of the court) is provided by the Scottish case of *Watt v Ligertwood*.[78] The facts were described as being "unprecedented" and such that "none of the Judges nor anybody else, ever heard of anything of this kind before". A sheriff-substitute had decided that a petition presented for an interdict should be rejected and that, in those circumstances, the respondent was entitled to have a deliverance written upon the petition. He handed it to the clerk for the purpose of having his interlocutor written upon it. While the sheriff was proceeding to dictate the interlocutor, the advocate took the petition and, in defiance of the specific order of the sheriff, put it in his pocket and left the court. He was dealt with summarily for contempt. In the words of Lord Cairns L.C.: " . . . the dignity of the court would not have been vindicated if some proceeding of this kind had not been taken."[79] 3–112

This language is very similar to that used by the Court of Appeal in *Balogh v St. Albans Crown Court*,[80] and tends to show that their Lordships were in reality dealing with defiance in the face of the court, and that the case was not analysed by them in terms of a breach of order *simpliciter*. This would accord with the reasoning of Lord Diplock in the *Secretary of State for Defence v Guardian Newspapers Ltd.*[81] Similarly, in other cases, persistence in a course of conduct by an advocate which the court had already ruled improper has been treated as criminal in character.[82] 3–113

---

[75] para.3–108.
[76] Discussed at para.14–8.
[77] *Lightfoot v Lightfoot* [1989] 1 F.L.R. 414 at 417, Lord Donaldson M.R. See also *Delaney v Delaney* [1996] Q.B. 387, CA.
[78] (1874) L.R. 2 Sc. & Div. 361, HL.
[79] At 364.
[80] [1975] 1 Q.B. 73, CA.
[81] [1985] 1 A.C. 339 at 347C–D, cited at para.3–108.
[82] See, *e.g. R. v Davison* (1821) 4 B. & Ald. 329, 106 E.R. 958; *Parashuram v King-Emperor* [1945] A.C. 264. For discussion of contempt by advocates, see para.10–135.

3–114 This is to be contrasted with the situation in *Harman v Secretary of State for the Home Department*.[83] Although, once again, it was the conduct of a party's solicitor that was in issue (in that she had communicated documents obtained on discovery to a journalist), this behaviour was *not* treated as a criminal contempt. She was acting in breach of the undertaking impliedly given by all litigants, including her client, to treat such documents confidentially and to use them only for the purposes of the litigation in hand. There was no defiance in the face of the court; breach of an undertaking to the court, whether express or implied, is one of the classic instances of "contempt in procedure". Indeed, Lord Scarman expressed the opinion that the misconduct in question was capable of being waived[84]; this would clearly not apply to a criminal contempt, such as that committed by Mr Watt in the Scottish case cited above, or to that of a witness refusing to answer a question in the witness box.

J. Orders relating to wards of court

3–115 In *Scott v Scott*,[85] Lord Atkinson stated that the wardship jurisdiction was in a special category because judges in those cases "act as representatives of the Sovereign as *parens patriae*, and exercise on his behalf a paternal and quasi-domestic jurisdiction over the person and property of the wards for the benefit of the latter." He therefore concluded that the authorities on wardship were of no help in resolving any of the issues arising on the facts then before the House.

3–116 The question thus remains whether breach of an order relating to a ward, or made under the inherent jurisdiction of the court (even though not specifically under the wardship jurisdiction), is to be treated as criminal or civil. Anyone who acts inconsistently with such an order, knowing of its existence, is likely to be held to have had the requisite state of mind to justify a finding of criminal contempt. Thus, if a father who knows that an order has been made that the ward should reside with her mother takes her away without permission, he would appear to be deliberately subverting the purpose of the court. This would be consistent with the reasoning of the Court of Appeal in *Att-Gen v Newspaper Publishing plc*,[86] to the effect that anyone who knowingly subverts an order of the court is guilty of a criminal contempt.

3–117 Moreover, it seems to have been a principle of long standing that any contempt in relation to a ward, whether there is a specific order in effect or not, is treated

---

[83] [1983] 1 A.C. 280 discussed in detail at paras 12–201 *et seq*.
[84] [1983] 1 A.C. 280 at 310.
[85] [1913] A.C. 417 at 462.
[86] [1988] Ch. 333. See in particular Lloyd L.J. at 380E–F quoting from the 1st edition of this work as follows: "'Since the test of contempt is not breach of the order but interference with the administration of justice, it follows that *at common law* a contempt may be committed even if no specific order has been made by the court affecting anyone other than those involved in the proceedings. At common law, if the court makes an order regulating its own procedure and the purpose of the order is plainly to protect the administration of justice, then anyone who subverts that order will be guilty of contempt'. In my judgment that represents an accurate statement of the law."

as a criminal contempt.[87] "Any action which tends to hamper the court in carrying out its duty [to protect its wards] is an interference with the administration of justice and a criminal contempt".[88] As Sir John Donaldson M.R. pointed out in *Att-Gen v Newspaper Publishing plc*[89]:

" . . . knowledge of how the court is administering, or intends to administer, justice is of the essence of the unlawfulness of conduct which interferes with that administration, whether or not that conduct consists of disobedience to an order."

This point has also been emphasised in the House of Lords in the speeches of Lord Oliver in *Att-Gen v Times Newspapers Ltd*[90] and of Lord Mustill in *London Borough of Harrow v Johnstone*.[91] It happens, however, that in many instances it is a court order which is the vehicle through which the purpose of the court is made manifest.

K. Contempts by third parties in relation to court orders[92]

1. *The basis of liability of parties compared to that of strangers to the litigation*

There is clear authority that persons aiding and abetting or inciting disobedience to an order of the court are guilty of criminal contempt, even though disobedience of the principal contemnor would amount only to a civil contempt.[93] This reflects the fact that civil contempt has always been treated as "contempt in procedure", which can generally only be committed by someone who is a party to civil litigation.

The position relating to enforcement of an order against company directors under RSC Ord.45, r.5(1)(b) is a special case. In *Savings Bank v Gasco BV (No.2)*,[94] the Court of Appeal held that since a committal application had been made to enforce an order ancillary to the main proceedings, seeking to preserve assets pending trial, the judge had ruled wrongly that the proceedings to commit the directors for procuring, aiding and abetting the company's breach of its undertaking (not to dispose of its assets beyond a certain value) were a separate *lis* unconnected with the action. The enforcement of an interlocutory order was a civil proceeding for the purposes of the Civil Evidence Act 1968, s.18(1)(a).

---

[87] *Wellesley v Duke of Beaufort* (1831) 2 Russ. and My. 639, 39 E.R. 538; *Re Crump* (1963) 107 Sol. Jo. 682, [1963] Crim.L.R. 777, Faulks J.; *Z Ltd v A-Z and AA-LL* [1982] Q.B. 558 at 579, Eveleigh L.J. *R. v D* [1984] A.C. 778 at 791, Watkins L.J., CA. See also *Re X (A Minor)(Wardship: Injunction)* [1984] 1 W.L.R. 1422, Balcombe J., and the explanation given by Sir John Donaldson M.R. in *Att-Gen v Newspaper Publishing plc* [1988] Ch. 333 at 369–70.
[88] *Re B (JA) (An Infant)* [1965] Ch. 1112 at 1117, *per* Cross J.
[89] [1988] Ch. 333 at 370D–E.
[90] [1992] 1 A.C. 191 at 224.
[91] [1997] 1 W.L.R. 459 at 468F–G.
[92] For fuller discussion of the point, see paras 6–124 *et seq*. See also in relation to non-publication criminal contempts, discussed at para.11–34.
[93] *Seaward v Paterson* [1897] 1 Ch. 545; *Att-Gen v Newspaper Publishing plc* [1988] Ch. 333; *Att-Gen v Times Newspapers Ltd* [1992] 1 A.C. 191. See paras 6–124 *et seq*. for a fuller discussion of the role of third parties in the context of court orders affecting the media.
[94] [1988] Ch. 422. See now CPR Sch.1, Ord.45.5(1).

Nonetheless it is clear that basis for committing the directors was that their conduct was treated as criminal contempt.

3–121 The apparent inconsistency of this classification has been challenged. In *Att-Gen v Newspaper Publishing plc*,[95] for example, Lloyd L.J. commented that:

> "... it does not make sense that a stranger to the order, who aids and abets a breach should be criminally liable while the person to whom the order is directed and who himself commits a breach, should only be liable for a civil contempt. That is the sort of nonsense which does no credit to the law."

3–122 This echoes remarks made in the House of Lords by Lord Atkinson in *Scott v Scott*,[96] who referred to the apparent inconsistency that one who aids and abets a civil contempt is himself guilty of *criminal* contempt:

> "It would appear to me to be almost inconceivable that the law should tolerate such an absurd anomaly as this: that a principal who does an act he is expressly prohibited by injunction from doing should only be guilty of a civil contempt of Court, while a person not expressly or at all prohibited who aids and abets the principal in doing that very act should be held guilty of a crime, a criminal contempt of Court, with the result that the more flagrant transgressor of the two, the principal, would have a right to appeal to the Court of Appeal against any order punishing him for his misdeed, while the accessory would have no right of appeal from the order punishing him for aiding and abetting the principal to commit the forbidden act. The disrespect to the court which made the order that was disobeyed, and the defiance of its authority, would seem to be greater in the case of the principal than in that of the accessory. The interference with the course of justice if that resulted would probably be the same in both. It can hardly be that the fact that the principal was named in the order he has disobeyed is to palliate rather than aggravate his guilt ... "

3–123 There is clearly some force in these critical observations, but it is important to remember the context of Lord Atkinson's remarks; namely, that he was primarily addressing the disparity which then existed between civil and criminal contemnors as to rights of appeal. Moreover, the distinction, from the public policy perspective, is by no means as absurd as might at first sight appear. The mental element in cases of criminal contempt at common law consists in an intention to interfere with the administration of justice.[97] It is at least arguable that, so long as this requirement is resolutely insisted upon, it makes perfect sense to say that a person who deliberately acts in such a way as to frustrate the order of a court should be guilty of a criminal contempt.

3–124 Where, perhaps, the position appears to be less satisfactory is in those cases where there is a deliberate or public flouting of a court order (or undertaking) by a person who *is* a party to the proceedings. Whereas in some jurisdictions the damage to the administration of justice caused by such conduct may regarded as

---

[95] [1988] Ch. 333 at 362.
[96] [1913] A.C. 417 at 456; and see paras 3–99 *et seq.*
[97] *Att-Gen v Times Newspapers Ltd* [1992] 1 A.C. 191; *London Borough of Harrow v Johnstone* [1997] 1 W.L.R. 459 at 468F–G, 469D–F, Lord Mustill. See further paras 11–21 *et seq.*

criminal,[98] in England it is still labelled as civil contempt.[99] The rationale of the distinction drawn in England between civil and criminal contempt does not appear to be based upon any assessment or comparison of the moral blameworthiness involved on the part of the relevant contemnors, but rather upon the procedural consequences of their conduct. However, if in any given case the court truly regards the civil contemnor (or "principal", to use Lord Atkinson's term) as being more blameworthy than a third party associated with his contempt, then there is no reason why he should not attract a more severe penalty. Moreover, in appropriate circumstances, a party to civil litigation who manifests an *intention* to subvert the purposes of the court, over and above the mere fact of non-compliance with an order, could also be held (at least in theory) to be in criminal contempt.

2. *Third parties and primary liability*

In a case where the third party is aiding and abetting the person who is the subject of the court order in carrying out his breach, or perhaps conspiring with or inciting him to bring it about, there are theoretical questions, which also arise generally in the criminal law, relating to accessorial liability; for example, whether or not the liability of the third party would depend upon the fact of a contempt having been committed by a "principal".[1]   **3–125**

In some cases, however, such as that which was before Lloyd L.J. in *Att-Gen v Newspaper Publishing plc*,[2] the third party may be guilty of a wholly independent criminal contempt, which is in no way derivative from any breach on the part of the party bound by the order. For example, where a newspaper editor decides to publish a confidential document, knowing of a restriction imposed upon a rival editor in respect of the same document, he may well be held to be deliberately flouting the purpose and authority of the court. Meanwhile, the editor against whom the order was originally made may be quite content to abide by its terms; but this would in no way detract from the criminality of the other's behaviour. In these circumstances, it would seem that it is nowadays unrewarding to enter into any debate (of the kind that engaged Lord Atkinson in the passage quoted)[3] as to the relative blameworthiness of a civil contemnor who is in breach of an injunction and that of a third party who commits some criminal contempt in relation to the same order (save in relation to sentence). Such conduct on the part of a non-party is simply a sub-category of contempt intended to interfere with the administration of justice.   **3–126**

---

[98] See in particular, the position in Canada, *Tony Pojé v the Att-Gen of British Columbia* [1953] 2 D.L.R. 785; *United Nurses of Alberta v Att-Gen for Alberta* (1992) 89 D.L.R. (4th) 609.
[99] For which, however, a penalty of some severity is still available, by way of *punishment*.
[1] Increasingly, it has been argued, the courts in the criminal law generally are treating those who would formerly have been classed as accessories as principal offenders. Liability would now appear to turn upon what it is that the third party has himself done, rather than upon the guilt of the principal. For a discussion, see A.J. Ashworth, *Principles of Criminal Law* (4th ed., 2003), ch.10.6.
[2] [1988] Ch. 333, discussed at paras 6–115 *et seq*.
[3] para.3–122.

3. The liability of non-parties named in an order

3–127 An injunction may expressly extend to persons who are not parties to the action in which it was made. The order, for instance, may apply in terms to the "servants or agents"[4] of the party directly bound, but this constitutes "nothing other than a warning against wrongdoing to those persons who may by reason of their situation be thought easily to fall into the error of implicating themselves in a breach of the injunction by the defendant".[5] It should not be thought that the injunction can be enforced against such persons as though they were simply in breach, and strictly speaking they could only be liable on the basis of assisting a breach or thwarting the intention of the court, provided they had the necessary knowledge of the existence of the order.[6]

3–128 In *Seaward v Paterson*,[7] an injunction was granted to restrain one Paterson, his servants or agents, from breaking a covenant not to interfere with the quiet enjoyment of neighbouring premises by holding boxing matches attended by the public on premises leased to him by the plaintiff. In breach of the injunction boxing matches were held and the court was moved to commit Paterson and also Shepherd and Murray, who had assisted him at the matches well knowing the terms of the injunction. Shepherd was a servant of Paterson and so, apparently, directly within the terms of the injunction, but North J. appears to have dealt with him on the same basis as Murray, namely as knowingly assisting in the breach.

3–129 If, however, a servant or agent who is *named* in a court order, and has been served with it,[8] merely fails to comply with its terms without any element of deliberate defiance or even any intention, it may be difficult to fix him with criminal responsibility, but the court would probably feel no inhibition about classifying him as a civil contemnor. It will be remembered that for the purposes of establishing civil contempt there is no need to prove any intention to flout the terms of the court's order, but only knowledge of its existence (which may indeed be purely constructive knowledge, based upon the fact of having been served).[9] In practice, the difference is likely to be more significant to issues of sentencing rather than liability.

---

[4] This term was contrasted in *THQ/Jakks Pacific LLC v World Wide Fund for Nature* [2003] EWCA Civ 401 with "licensees", and it was made clear that the insertion of such a term in the wording of an injunction was not such as to impose liability upon the relevant person for the acts of third parties.
[5] *Marengo v Daily Sketch and Sunday Graphic Ltd* [1948] 1 All E.R. 406 at 407c, HL.
[6] North J. in *Seaward v Paterson* [1897] 1 Ch. 545 at 551–2. But see the criticism of this decision by Lord Uthwatt in *Marengo v Daily Sketch and Sunday Graphic Ltd* [1948] 1 All E.R. 406 at 407E–F. See also *Z Ltd v A-Z and AA-LL* [1982] Q.B 558 at 579–80, for the position of banks in the context of "freezing orders". While it is often appropriate to notify a defendant's bank that such an order has been granted, the bank itself will only be liable for contempt in relation to a breach of the order if it was aware that any act on its part was facilitating the breach.
[7] Last note.
[8] See, *e.g.* the circumstances which arose in relation to members of the polytechnic staff in *Harrington v North London Polytechnic* [1984] 1 W.L.R. 1293, 3 All E.R. 666. See para.12–107.
[9] See the discussion at paras 12–80 *et seq.* and in particular of the House of Lords' decision in *Director General of Fair Trading v Pioneer Concrete (UK) Ltd* [1995] 1 A.C. 456.

III. Points of Comparison between Civil and Criminal Contempts

A. Scheme of discussion

We must now consider in more detail the areas of actual or potential distinction between criminal and civil contempt. They were listed above,[10] and we shall address them in the same sequence.

3–130

B. Appeals

The Administration of Justice Act 1960 provides in matters of contempt a general right of appeal to the Court of Appeal. From 1873 to 1960, however, one of the most important distinctions between civil and criminal contempts was that in the case of the former an appeal lay to the Court of Appeal, but against a finding of criminal contempt there was no right of appeal at all.

3–131

Before 1873 there was no recourse against an order made by a court of record fining or imprisoning a person for contempt, except for error on the face of the record.[11] Attempts were made to question such orders by the writ of *habeas corpus*, but if the return to the writ was good on its face the Queen's Bench would not interfere.[12] An order of an inferior court of record, such as a county court or Quarter Sessions, might be brought before the Queen's Bench by *certiorari*, but not in circumstances where the inferior court had jurisdiction and there was evidence upon which it could reasonably have found a contempt to have been committed.[13] Yet in neither the case of *habeas corpus* nor that of *certiorari* was the court of Queen's Bench acting as a true court of appeal.

3–132

In 1873, however, the Supreme Court of Judicature Act established the Court of Appeal.[14] Section 19 of the Act provided that the court should have jurisdiction to determine appeals from any judgment or order of the High Court, but this section was expressly subject to the subsequent provisions of the Act. These included s.47, which provided *inter alia* that "no appeal shall lie from any judgment of the said High Court in any criminal cause or matter."[15]

3–133

It was not, however, until 1888 in *R. v Stafford County Court Judge*[16] that doubt was first expressed whether an appeal might lie against a finding of

3–134

---

[10] At paras 3–29 *et seq.*
[11] See *Rainy v Justices of Sierra Leone* (1852) 8 Moo. P.C. 47, Lord Cranworth at 54, 14 E.R. 19 at 22, and *McDermott v Judges of British Guiana* (1869) L.R. 2 P.C. 341. See also *Ex p. Fernandez* (1861) 10 C.B. (N.S.) 1, Erle J. at 25–6, 142 E.R. 349 at 358; *Re Ramsay* (1870) L.R. 3 P.C. 427.
[12] See *Ex p. Fernandez* (1861) 10 C.B. (N.S.) 1, and *Carus Wilson's Case* (1845) 7 Q.B. 984, 115 E.R. 759.
[13] *Ex p. Pater* (1864) 5 B. & S. 299 at 311–312, 122 E.R. 842 at 847, Blackburn J. See also *R. v Jordan* (1888) 36 W.R. 797.
[14] By ss.4 and 6.
[15] The Act was subsequently replaced by the Supreme Court of Judicature Act 1925, s.31(1)(a) of which also excluded appeals in any "criminal cause or matter". Although the Court of Criminal Appeal had been established in 1907, its jurisdiction was confined to appeals relating to trials upon indictment.
[16] (1888) 57 L.J.Q.B. 483, *sub nom. R. v Jordan* (1888) 36 W.R. 797.

criminal contempt. In that case the Court of Appeal dismissed an appeal from the Divisional Court, in respect of a county court judge's order committing a solicitor to prison for "wilful insult",[17] but subsequently, upon enquiry, there was appended to the report the following comment of Lindley L.J.: "It is doubtful whether this was not a criminal matter, upon which we could not have heard an appeal. At any rate, this must not be taken as a precedent for hearing such appeals."

3–135 In a number of cases at about that time the Court of Appeal did hear and determine on the merits appeals against findings of criminal contempt, but no point as to jurisdiction seems to have been taken.[18] The point was finally settled by *O'Shea v O'Shea and Parnell Ex p. Tuohy*.[19] This concerned an application on behalf of Captain O'Shea for a writ of attachment against the manager of a newspaper office in London, in respect of comments upon his character at a time when he was the petitioner in pending divorce proceedings, on the ground that the publication was calculated to prejudice a fair trial.

3–136 The Court of Appeal held on the preliminary jurisdiction point that such a criminal contempt did indeed fall within the statutory notion of "criminal cause or matter", and hence no appeal lay. A clear distinction was drawn between that situation, where the contempt application was "entirely outside the divorce action, and its object was only to obtain that fair trial to which every suitor has a right,"[20] and proceedings in which the contempt jurisdiction had been invoked for the purpose of seeking to enforce an order made in civil proceedings against one of the parties.[21]

3–137 There are in the reports a number of other cases[22] in which it was important for the court to determine whether or not the proceedings in which orders for committal had been made were to be categorised as a "criminal cause or matter". For example, in *R. v Barnardo*,[23] a mother had given a child into the custody of the defendant to place in one of his homes for destitute children. The mother later wrote to him asking for the child back, but he handed her over to a third party who took her abroad. A writ of *habeas corpus* was then issued directing the defendant to produce the child. He returned to the writ that the child was no longer in his custody or control, but out of the jurisdiction. Attachment was granted against the defendant for his contempt in disobeying the writ.

3–138 On appeal, the point was taken that no appeal lay for the reason that the order appealed against was made in a criminal cause or matter. The Court of Appeal

---

[17] Then under s.113 of the County Courts Act 1846.
[18] See, *e.g. Hunt v Clarke* (1889) 58 L.J.Q.B. 490; *Re Johnson* (1887) 20 Q.B.D. 68.
[19] (1890) 15 P.D. 59.
[20] *Per* Cotton L.J. at 63–4.
[21] The example given by each of the Lords Justices was that of *Barnardo* (1889) 23 Q.B.D. 305.
[22] See *Re Evans, Evans v Noton* [1893] 1 Ch. 252; *Eccles and Co v Louisville and Nashville Railroad Co* (1911) 28 T.L.R. 36; see also *Att-Gen v Kissane* (1893) 32 L.R. Ir. 220, where it was held that an order made by the Queen's Bench Division attaching a constable for refusing to come to the aid of a sheriff, in the execution of a writ, was a judgment in a criminal cause or matter.
[23] (1889) 23 Q.B.D. 305. See also *Scott v Scott* [1913] A.C. 417 and *Seldon v Wilde* [1911] 1 K.B. 701.

held that the relevant proceeding was to obtain the doing of an act required in the Queen's Bench proceedings.[24] The order was merely to enforce the performance of an act, namely delivery up of the child, in the course of civil proceedings. An appeal therefore lay.

The Criminal Appeal Act 1907, which established the Court of Criminal Appeal, gave a right of appeal, but only from conviction on indictment.[25] Although a finding by a judge that a person has committed a criminal contempt is sometimes termed a conviction,[26] no contempt has in modern times been proceeded against by way of indictment.[27] Hence the 1907 Act did not give a general right of appeal against findings of criminal contempt. The anomalous situation was finally remedied by the Administration of Justice Act 1960.[28]

Although in civil cases such an appeal will take place in the Civil Division of the Court of Appeal, it has been held that the court will hear the case, in some respects at least, as though it were a criminal appeal, and an order will be set aside if the evidence makes it unsafe to sustain it.[29] Furthermore, it appears that a similar approach will be adopted towards the admission of new evidence to that of the Court of Appeal (Criminal Division).[30]

C. Privilege from arrest and imprisonment

1. *The principle stated*

Although it may be of little practical significance nowadays, it is necessary to note the relevance of the continuing distinction between civil and criminal contempt in the context of privilege from arrest. A claim of privilege will not be effective against arrest on criminal process, including a criminal contempt of court, but should succeed in respect of arrest on civil process.[31] The test which is to be applied, however, apparently turns on what is the court's objective in making the order to which the arrest relates. It would seem that if the true purpose of the process is punitive or disciplinary (as opposed to merely coercive)

---

[24] See also *O'Shea v O'Shea and Parnell Ex p. Tuohy* (1890) 15 P.D. 59 at 63, Cotton L.J.
[25] s.3.
[26] See *Izuora v R.* [1953] A.C. 327 where the West African Court of Appeal Ordinance gave a right of appeal against conviction generally and not merely convictions on indictment. See also the use of the word "convict" (in the context of intention) in *London Borough of Harrow v Johnstone* [1997] 1 W.L.R. 459 at 470.
[27] It is sometimes said that the last case of contempt to have been brought against a newspaper by way of indictment was *R. v Tibbits and Windust* [1902] 1 K.B. 77; see, *e.g.* D.G.T. Williams, [1961] Crim.L.R. at 93, n.19, and also Lord Keith in *Re Lonrho plc* [1990] 2 A.C. 154 at 177. But the case was in fact an indictment for offences of perverting the course of justice, and attempting and conspiring to do so.
[28] s.13. The JUSTICE Report, *Contempt of Court* (1959), had recommended the change.
[29] *Kent County Council v Batchelor* (1976) 75 L.G.R. 151.
[30] *Irtelli v Squatriti* [1993] Q.B. 83, discussed at paras 12–88 *et seq.*
[31] *Wellesley v Duke of Beaufort* (1831) 2 Russ. & My. 639, 39 E.R. 538. See also *Lightfoot v Cameron* (1776) 2 W. Bl. 1113, 96 E.R. 658; *Meekins v Smith* (1791) 1 H. Bl. 629, 126 E.R. 359; *Arding v Flower* (1800) 8 T.R. 534, 101 E.R. 1531; *Re Freston* (1883) 11 Q.B.D. 545.

3–141 CHAPTER 3—THE DISTINCTION BETWEEN CRIMINAL/CIVIL CONTEMPT

then a claim of privilege is unlikely to succeed,[32] even though the proceedings giving rise to the application to commit might themselves ordinarily be classified as civil.

3–142 Such punishment will normally only be appropriate if the judge has come to the conclusion that the contemnor's conduct "has about it some degree of criminality, some defiance of the general law".[33] This is a question that can only be answered by reference to the facts of each case.[34] When the issue of privilege arises, the court will have to investigate whether, as a matter of fact, the purpose of the order included the imposition of a penalty. This may emerge from the terms of the judgment, or it may have to be inferred from the surrounding circumstances. Normally, no difficulty should arise, because the likelihood is that the judge who is asked the determine the matter of privilege will be the same judge who imposed the order giving rise to the claim. Thus, it is clear that there is no simple touchstone for deciding whether privilege may be claimed, depending purely on whether the contempt sought to be punished consists of disobedience to an order or of conduct in one of the traditional categories of criminal contempt. It is always the *purpose* of the warrant that has to be considered.

3–143 These principles were explained in *Stourton v Stourton*,[35] where Scarman J. held that a husband, who was entitled to sit in the House of Lords, was able to claim privilege in circumstances where his wife had issued a summons for leave to issue a writ of attachment against him because of his failure to comply with an earlier order (to deliver certain items of property to the wife, and to file a schedule within a certain time). The judge held that the purpose for which the writ of attachment was sought was to compel the performance of acts required by civil process rather than to punish.

3–144 Scarman J. went on however, at the end of his judgment, to make it clear that it did not follow that, because the claim to privilege had succeeded on those facts, such a plea of privilege would avail in the case of disobeying an injunction against molestation or removal of a child out of the jurisdiction.[36] This view was expressed *obiter*, but there are obviously good reasons of public policy why a claim of privilege should not succeed in such circumstances.

2. *To whom is a plea of privilege available?*

3–145 It is not within the compass of this work to discuss fully all those who are entitled to claim privilege, but it may be helpful to identify some particular examples.

---

[32] *Re Freston* (1883) 11 Q.B.D. 545—and see the comments upon the case by Lord Atkinson in *Scott v Scott* [1913] A.C. 417; see also *Re Hunt* [1959] 2 Q.B. 69; *Stourton v Stourton* [1963] P. 302.
[33] *Stourton v Stourton* [1963] P. 302 at 310.
[34] *ibid.* at 310, Scarman J.
[35] [1963] P. 302, following *Re Freston* (1883) 11 Q.B.D. 545, which is considered in greater detail at paras 3–147 *et seq.* See also *Re Armstrong Ex p. Lindsay* [1892] 1 Q.B. 327.
[36] See also *Wellesley v Duke of Beaufort* (1831) 2 Russ. & M. 639, 39 E.R. 538.

POINTS OF COMPARISON BETWEEN CIVIL AND CRIMINAL CONTEMPTS 3–146

Peers of the realm can at all times claim privilege from arrest on civil process.[37] So can peeresses in their own right or by marriage.[38] Members of Parliament can claim a similar privilege from arrest[39] for a period lasting from 40 days before, and until 40 days after, a session of Parliament.[40]

Certain persons in the diplomatic service of foreign countries whilst in England may also claim privilege from arrest on civil process.[41] All persons who are engaged in a suit in a court of law are privileged from arrest on civil process on their way to court, at court and on their return from court.[42] This protects persons acting in a judicial capacity such as magistrates[43] or coroners,[44] as well as officers of the court. It also protects parties,[45] barristers[46] and solicitors,[47] jurors[48] and witnesses.[49] The privilege, however, upon a proper analysis is not that of the individuals concerned. It is that of the court. Thus, it is for the courts to determine whether or not it is proper to have the person arrested.[50]

3–146

---

[37] *Stourton v Stourton* [1963] P. 302; *Earl of Shrewsbury's Case* (1611) 9 Co Rep.46b at 49a, 77 E.R. 798 at 803; *Foster v Jackson* (1616) Hob. 52 at 61, 80 E.R. 201 at 210; *Couche v Lord Arundel* (1802) 3 East 127, 102 E.R. 545; *Cassidy v Steuart* (1841) 2 Man. & G. 437, 133 E.R. 817. And see *Wellesley v Duke of Beaufort* (1831) 2 Russ & My. 639, 39 E.R. 538. For a discussion of a modern instance where the claim to privilege was disallowed, however, see P.M. Leopold, "The Freedom of Peers from Arrest" [1989] P.L. 398.

[38] *Countess of Rutland's Case* (1606) 6 Co Rep.52b, 77 E.R. 332; *Countess Rivers' Case* (1650) Sty. 252, 82 E.R. 687; *Anon.* (1677) 1 Ventr. 298, 86 E.R. 192.

[39] See generally *Erskine May's Treatise on the Law, Privileges, Proceedings and Usage of Parliament* (23rd ed., 2004), ch.7.

[40] See *Wellesley v Duke of Beaufort* (1831) 2 Russ & My 639, 39 E.R. 538; *Goudy v Duncombe* (1847) 1 Exch. 430, 154 E.R. 183; *Holiday v Pitt* (1734) 2 Str. 985, 94 E.R. 984; *Cassidy v Steuart* (1841) 2 Man. & G. 437, 133E.R. 817; *Re the Anglo-French Co-operative Society* (1880) 14 Ch.D. 533.

[41] See in particular the Diplomatic Privileges Act 1964; Halsbury's *Statutes of England*, Vol. 10, p.746.

[42] See *Re Freston* (1883) 11 Q.B.D. 545; *Meekins v Smith* (1791) 1 H. Bl. 636, 126 E.R. 363; *Arding v Flower* (1800) 8 T.R. 534, 101 E.R. 1531; *Ex p. King* (1802) 7 Ves. Jun. 312, 32 E.R. 127; *Gilpin v Cohen* (1869) L.R. Ex. 131; as to the interpretation of *eundo, morando et redeundo*, see *Childerston v Barrett* (1809) 11 East 439, 103 E.R. 1073; *Hatch v Blissett* (1714) Gilb. 308, 93 E.R. 338; *Ex parte Temple* (1814) 2 V. & B. 391, 35 E.R. 367; *Gibbs v Phillipson* (1829) 1 Russ. & My. 19, 39 E.R. 8; *Spencer v Newton* (1837) 6 Ad. & E. 623, 112 E.R. 239; *Att-Gen v Leather Sellers Company* (1844) 7 Beav. 157, 49 E.R. 1023; *Re Jewitt* (1864) 33 Beav. 559, 55 E.R. 486.

[43] Com. Dig. tit. Privilege; *Glendinning v Browne* (1854) 3 Ir. C.L.R. 115.

[44] *Ex p. Deputy Coroner for Middlesex* (1861) 6 H. & N. 501, 158 E.R. 206.

[45] *Pitt v Coombs* (1834) 3 Nev. and M. K.B. 212. They are regarded as being "*substantially* privileged from arrest, whilst returning home from the court, both for the dignity of the court and the orderly proceeding of its business": *per* Denman C.J. at 213.

[46] *Meekings v Smith* (1791) 1 H. Bl. 636, 126 E.R, 363; this was referred to in *Newton v Harland* (1839) 8 Scott 70, where Tindal C.J. observed that "The privilege of counsel is for the benefit of the client". See also *Luntly* (1833) 1 C. & M. 579, 149 E.R. 530, where it was held that a practising barrister, being privileged from arrest in his professional attendance at Quarter Sessions, did not lose his privilege by going into a picture shop on his way from session, although it might have been otherwise if he had stayed in the shop "an unreasonable time".

[47] *Re Hope* (1845) 9 Jur. 856; *Att-Gen v Skinners' Co* (1837) C.P. Coop.1, 47 E.R. 372; *Att-Gen v Leather Sellers Co* (1844) 7 Beav. 157, 49 E.R. 1023; *Re Jewitt* (1864) 33 Beav. 559, 55 E.R. 486.

[48] *Gilpin v Cohen* (1869) L.R. 4 Ex. 131 at 134.

[49] *Lawford v Spicer* (1856) 2 Jur. N.S. 564.

[50] *Re Hunt* [1959] 2 Q.B. 69 at 77, Romer L.J.

CHAPTER 3—THE DISTINCTION BETWEEN CRIMINAL/CIVIL CONTEMPT

3. Disciplinary control over officers of the court

3–147 A person who is an officer of the court (a solicitor, for example), or acting under the supervision of the court (such as a trustee or a liquidator), is subject to a disciplinary jurisdiction. If this jurisdiction is exercised by the imposition of punishment, this too will preclude such a person from relying upon any privilege that he might otherwise enjoy.

3–148 This is clear from the case of *Re Freston*.[51] A solicitor represented to another firm of solicitors that he was acting for the person whom they wished to execute a deed of conveyance. He said his client would execute the deed if the client received £5 and he (Freston) also received £5. The deed and the money were sent to him but nothing more was heard from him. Proceedings were taken against him to recover the debt of £10. The Debtors Act 1869 had abolished imprisonment for debt save in certain exceptional cases. One of these was identified in s.4(4), which exempted a default by an attorney or solicitor in the payment of costs when ordered to pay costs for misconduct, as such, or in the payment of any other sum of money which he was ordered to pay *qua* officer of the court. Persons whose conduct fell within this description could be proceeded against by attachment and imprisoned.[52] Denman J. ordered that a writ of attachment should be drawn up, but should not issue if Freston paid back the £10 and the costs of the proceedings within a week. He did pay the £10, but failed to pay the costs.

3–149 The writ was issued and Freston was arrested as he was returning from Bow Street, where he had been acting in certain criminal proceedings. He pleaded privilege from arrest, as a solicitor returning from court where he had been acting in a professional capacity. The Court of Appeal held that he was *not* entitled to privilege. Privilege could only be pleaded successfully when a person was arrested on civil process, but here Freston had been arrested on process which was punitive or disciplinary in its purpose.

3–150 This conclusion was based on the disciplinary jurisdiction and the provisions of s.4(4) of the Debtors Act 1869. In the words of Lindley L.J.[53]:

> "All contempts are not the same; they are of different kinds; some contempts are merely theoretical, but others are wilful, such as disobedience to injunctions[54] or to orders to deliver up documents—in those cases there is no privilege from arrest. In this case the attachment was granted for something more than a mere theoretical contempt, and therefore it was something more than merely civil process: there was therefore no privilege."

---

[51] (1883) 11 Q.B.D. 545.
[52] See also *Middleton v Chichester* (1871) L.R. 6 Ch. 152 at 156–7. The case concerned the third exemption under s.4 of the Debtors Act 1869, which relates to trustees who are ordered to pay sums of money within their possession or control. Lord Hatherley analysed the various exceptions and remarked that "in every case there is something of the character of delinquency."
[53] (1883) 11 Q.B.D. 545 at 556.
[54] It should not be assumed that all cases of disobedience to an injunction are "wilful": for a discussion of the significance of the term in this context, see Lord Wilberforce in *Heatons Transport (St. Helens) Ltd v TGWU* [1973] A.C. 15 at 108–10.

For similar reasons, the court also expressed the view that, even if Freston paid the money he owed, he would not be entitled to his release from prison *ex debito justitiae*, as he would if the process had merely been coercive; he had to apply to the court in any event for his release.

Re Freston was later considered in *Seldon v Wilde*.[55] In that case, the plaintiff and the defendant were both solicitors, the plaintiff being the defendant's agent. The plaintiff obtained an order for the taxation of the defendant's costs and accordingly for the delivery of the defendant's bill of costs. The defendant made default in delivery and the plaintiff moved to attach him for contempt. At the hearing the defendant was ordered to pay the taxed costs of the motion against him. The plaintiff then sued the defendant following taxation for those costs. Counsel for the defendant argued that the action was not maintainable, because it sought to enforce an order for costs being made in criminal proceedings in circumstances where no relevant statute conferred jurisdiction.[56]

The Court of Appeal held by a majority that the order for the delivery of the bill of costs was not made in the course of criminal proceedings and that the action lay. Buckley L.J. expressed the view that the contempt in *Re Freston* was not a criminal contempt. "The ratio decidendi was that privilege extends to protect from attachment in that which is simply in the nature of civil process, but does not extend to protect from attachment which is punitive or disciplinary."[57] As he explained, the question in *Re Freston* was not whether the process was criminal or quasi-criminal, but whether it was *merely* civil.

Kennedy L.J. concurred with Buckley L.J., although expressing the view that the proceedings in *Re Freston* partook of a criminal nature, and that if the proceedings in the instant case were similar then no action would lie. But he went on:

> "In my judgment the true view is that where, as in *Re Freston*, the order for attachment has been made, under which the solicitor may be imprisoned and cannot claim release *ex debito justitiae* upon doing the acts commanded, the disciplinary process has ceased to be merely civil, but has so far acquired a criminal nature that a civil action, based upon part of the order of attachment, cannot be maintained by the party to whom money, in the shape of costs or otherwise, has become payable under that order. But, until that stage has been reached, proceedings against a solicitor, whether to strike him off the rolls or to order him to deliver a bill of costs, although of a truly disciplinary character, inasmuch as they supply a peculiar method of redress wherein the jurisdiction of the court is invoked against a solicitor as an officer of the Court, remain essentially civil proceedings, so that an order of the court for the payment of costs is an order which may be enforced by a civil action."

Vaughan Williams L.J., dissenting, held that the order to deliver up the bill of costs was made in the course of proceedings of a criminal nature and no action lay for the costs. He took the view that the proceedings were of a disciplinary character, and pointed out that this jurisdiction might be put in motion not only

---

[55] [1911] 1 K.B. 701.
[56] Such as under s.6 of the Costs in Criminal Cases Act 1908.
[57] [1911] 1 K.B. 701 at 706.

by the person to whom the money had been ordered to be paid, but by any other person.[58] It seemed to him to be improbable that the rules were intended to allow anyone to enforce by action an order not intended to compel or enforce payment but to punish for non-payment. He went on to add that he could see no difference, in this context, between the case where there was an order made for payment of the costs of a contempt motion and a case in which attachment had actually been ordered. It may be, however, that the majority would not have accepted the proposition that *any* order made on such a motion should be regarded as punitive. It is quite possible to decide to inflict no punishment and yet order the party concerned to pay costs.

3–156   The Phillimore Committee had recommended that the rule whereby privilege could apply to civil contempts should be abolished,[59] although no steps were taken to include any such provision in the Contempt of Court Act 1981.

D. Waiver

1. The nature of the issue

3–157   A criminal contempt cannot be waived by a person aggrieved by the conduct,[60] or disposed of between the parties for pecuniary consideration.[61] There is some authority to suggest that a civil contempt may be waived.[62] For example, Lord Diplock in the *Att-Gen v Times Newspapers Ltd* makes the point that[63]:

> " ... there is an element of public policy in punishing civil contempt, since the administration of justice would be undermined if the order of any court of law could be disregarded with impunity; but no sufficient public interest is served by punishing the offender if the only person for whose benefit the order was made chooses not to insist on its enforcement ... "

3–158   The matter is not entirely straightforward, since in some cases the public interest may come into play and require that the court's authority be vindicated irrespective of the wishes of the parties.[64] There is little recent authority on the significance of waiver in the context of civil contempts. It would seem that it will not normally be possible to waive a civil contempt if the breach constitutes a deliberate defiance of the authority of the court (especially in cases of public

---

[58] At 716.
[59] Cmnd. 5794 (1974), para.170.
[60] *Lechmere Charlton's Case* (1836) 2 My. & Cr. 316, 40 E.R. 661; *Seaward v Paterson* [1897] 1 Ch. 545 at 560; *Tony Pojé v Att-Gen for British Columbia* [1953] 2 D.L.R. 785.
[61] *Newton* (1903) 67 J.P. 453.
[62] See Lord Diplock in *Att-Gen v Times Newspapers Ltd* [1974] A.C. 273 at 308; Lord Scarman in *Harman v Secretary of State for the Home Department* [1983] 1 A.C. 280 at 310; moreover, it seems to have been *assumed* for a long time that a civil contempt may be waived; see, *e.g.* the cases cited above, at n.60.
[63] [1974] A.C. 273 at 307–8.
[64] As in *Jennison v Baker* [1972] 2 Q.B. 52; *Clarke v Chadburn* [1984] 1 I.R.L.R. 350, [1985] 1 W.L.R. 78, Sir Robert Megarry V.-C.; *R. v Commissioners of Inland Revenue Ex p. Kingston Smith* [1996] S.T.C. 1210, Buxton J.

defiance),[65] or requires to be punished or otherwise pursued from the public point of view.

2. Early examples of waiver

Examples of waiver are to be found in the old Court of Chancery; namely, failure to put in an answer in time would be treated as being waived by the opposite party if he took a further step in the action, such as accepting and replying to an answer put in out of time,[66] amending the bill[67] or filing a cross-bill for discovery of facts.[68] Contempt in failing to pay the costs of a receiver could also be waived.[69]

3–159

There are authorities from the time when matrimonial proceedings were under the jurisdiction of the ecclesiastical courts appearing to support the proposition that breaches of court orders could be waived. In *Barlee v Barlee*,[70] the Arches Court of Canterbury decreed that Mrs Barlee should return to her husband. She failed to do so and was committed. She later sought her release, but Sir John Nicoll, clearly treating the contempt as civil in nature, held that she could only be released on undertaking to comply with the order or if her husband waived his right of cohabitation.

3–160

In *Harrison v Harrison*,[71] the Privy Council on appeal from the Court of Arches allowed the husband's appeal to be heard in a nullity suit despite the contention that the husband had placed himself in contempt by refusing to undergo an inspection. It appears from Lord Brougham's intervention in the course of argument that this was on the basis of waiver.

3–161

3. Public interest can exclude waiver

In *Corcoran v Corcoran*,[72] a wife obtained a decree absolute against her husband and he was ordered to deliver the child of the marriage to her custody. He failed to comply with the order and was committed for contempt. The child was in Eire and the wife instituted proceedings in the High Court of Eire, but that court refused to make an order granting her custody. After the husband had been in prison for a year, application was made for his release on the grounds that he had undergone a long period of detention and that the wife by taking proceedings in

3–162

---

[65] *Tony Pojé v Att-Gen for British Columbia* [1953] 2 D.L.R. 785; see also the words of Megarry V.-C. in *Clarke v Chadburn* [1984] I.R.L.R. 350, cited at para.2–220.
[66] *Anon* (1808) 15 Ves. Jun. 174, 33 E.R. 720; *Smith v Blofield* (1813) 2 Ves. & Beam. 100, 35 E.R. 257; *Const v Ebers* (1816) 1 Madd. 530, 56 E.R. 194; *Hoskins v Lloyd* (1823) 1 Sim. & Sty. 393, 57 E.R. 157; *Oldfield v Cobbett* (1845) 1 Ph. 557, 41 E.R. 744; *Roberts v Albert Bridge Company* (1873) L.R. 8 Ch.App.753. And see *Woodward v Twinaine* (1839) 9 Sim. 301, 59 E.R. 373; *Att-Gen v Shield* (1849) 11 Beav. 441, 50 E.R. 888; *Herrett v Reynolds* (1860) 2 Giff. 409, 66 E.R. 170.
[67] *Smith v Campbell* (1830) 1 Russ & My. 323, 39 E.R. 124.
[68] *Best v Gompertz* (1837) 2 Y. & C. Ex. 582, 160 E.R. 528.
[69] *Plumbe v Plumbe* (1844) 2 L.T. Jo. 439.
[70] (1822) 1 Add. 301, 162 E.R. 105.
[71] (1842) 4 Moo. P.C. 96, 13 E.R. 238.
[72] [1950] 1 All E.R. 495.

3–162 CHAPTER 3—THE DISTINCTION BETWEEN CRIMINAL/CIVIL CONTEMPT

Eire had waived his contempt in the English courts. Willmer J. took the view that the husband could not be released until he complied with the order of the court. Hence his imprisonment was primarily to compel performance of an order of the court rather than punitive in character.

3–163 Willmer J. nevertheless held that the doctrine of waiver could not apply. "I do not think that anybody can possibly do anything in regard to waiving the rights of a child in such circumstances as those of this case." The court clearly took the view that the child's welfare was a separate factor to be weighed by the court in determining whether to invoke the contempt jurisdiction, independently of the wishes of the parties.

3–164 In *Re Grantham Wholesale Fruit, Vegetable and Potato Merchants Ltd*,[73] the liquidator of a company failed over a prolonged period to comply with an order of the court. The Department of Trade and Industry moved to commit him for contempt, but meanwhile the order was obeyed. At the hearing the Department merely sought an order for costs. Megarry J. took the view that the fact that a complainant in such circumstances confined itself to seeking an order for costs, without pressing for committal, did not fetter the powers of the court, which could commit of its own motion. He nevertheless recognised that the complainant's attitude was a factor to be weighed in the exercise of his discretion. The reasoning is similar to that in *Jennison v Baker*,[74] where there had been flagrant breaches of the orders of the court, and the Court of Appeal proceeded of its own motion to deal with the landlady's contempt irrespective of the fact that her campaign of harassment had succeeded in emptying the property, and that there was accordingly no longer any purpose to be served by the original order which she had flouted.

3–165 In *Watson v Watson*,[75] where a husband's disobedience to a non-molestation injunction had twice been the subject of applications for committal, Elizabeth Lane J. concluded, even though at the hearing the wife decided no longer to press for committal, that the court had to come to an independent decision as to whether imprisonment was appropriate in the light of clear and repeated acts of disobedience.

4. *Recommendations for clarification and reform on waiver*

3–166 The Phillimore Committee pointed out that there are three classes of case in which it is desirable that the court should have power to take action against a contemnor regardless of the aggrieved party's wishes[76]:

"The first is the case in which an order has been made in respect of a child for that child's benefit. The parents or guardian of the child may agree together to make

---

[73] [1972] 1 W.L.R. 559.
[74] [1972] 2 Q.B. 52. See especially Salmon L.J. at 64, who said that a plaintiff cannot waive the order, but also considered it appropriate to take into account the wishes of such a party.
[75] Unreported, August 10, 1970.
[76] Cmnd. 5794 (1974), para.171.

arrangements other than those directed by the court, and which are not for the child's benefit. In that event the court should clearly have power to intervene if the facts come to its notice, perhaps by way of the court welfare officer. (The courts already have this power in relation to wards of court.) Secondly, the person in whose favour the order was made may for one reason or another be nervous of attempting to enforce it. In order to ensure that justice is done, the court must have power to deal with any breach itself.[77] Thirdly, in particularly flagrant cases it is necessary that the court should have power to vindicate its authority and the rule of law without waiting for an application by the aggrieved party."

3–167 It was observed that the courts might well have power to deal with such situations, in any event, on the authority of *Corcoran v Corcoran*[78] and *Tony Pojé v Att-Gen for British Columbia*.[79] However, the Committee recommended that to clarify the position the court should be given statutory power to act of its own motion against a person who disobeys its order, whenever it thinks fit to do so, and for this purpose it should be empowered to require any breach to be reported to it by the party in whose favour the order was made or, in appropriate cases, by a court official.[80] This recommendation was not implemented by the Contempt of Court Act 1981.

3–168 In the Report of the Australian Law Reform Commission,[81] it was also recommended that statutory provision should be made to cover those circumstances in which it was appropriate for action to be taken, in respect of the flouting of a court order, contrary to the wishes of the party for whose benefit the order had been obtained. It was in favour of retaining the "doctrine of waiver", because neither the interest of a successful party in litigation, nor the interest of the community, was furthered by the continuance of proceedings against, and the imposition of punitive sanctions upon, a disobedient party. The qualification was entered that, where there was a flagrant challenge to the court's authority, the matter should fall within a specified criminal offence, irrespective of any waiver by the successful party; it also suggested a qualification for the purpose of covering the special requirements of family law.[82]

3–169 As Sir John Laws has observed extra-judicially, "There is no need for any statutory change; the courts have only to make it clear that waiver as a distinct doctrine has no place in the law of contempt, while recognising that where the aggrieved party chooses to make no complaint the court may well decide that no action is necessary"[83]: He had observed that a true doctrine of waiver would involve the proposition that the court has *no power* to act if the aggrieved party "waives" the breach of the order. This is surely not the position.

---

[77] Buxton J. in the *R. v Revenue Commissioners Ex p. Kingston Smith* [1996] S.T.C. 1210. noted that the respondents might have been "understandably" reluctant to pursue the law to its limits.
[78] [1950] 1 All E.R. 495.
[79] [1953] 2 D.L.R. 785.
[80] Cmnd. 5794 (1974), para.171.
[81] Law Reform Commission, *Report No.35; Contempt*, (1987), para.534.
[82] *ibid.* para.609.
[83] (2000) 116 L.Q.R. 156 at 161.

E. Institution of proceedings

3–170 The general principle is that, whereas the institution of proceedings in relation to criminal contempts is primarily a matter for the Attorney-General, or for the court of its own motion,[84] it is generally for the parties themselves to invoke the jurisdiction of the courts in cases of civil contempt. However, as the Phillimore Committee pointed out,[85] it may well be that the court has the power to protect its own process and authority by proceeding of its own motion in cases where the court's authority has been flouted.[86] Alternatively, the court may choose to refer the matter to the Attorney-General for his consideration.

3–171 It seems from *Clarke v Chadburn*[87] that there has to be an "open flouting" before proceedings on the motion of the court are appropriate. The point was considered by Sir Robert Megarry V.-C.:

"It is perhaps not generally realised that where the party who has obtained an order from the court is content that it should not be performed, the court, generally speaking, has no interest in interfering so as to enforce what the litigant does not want enforced. The order is made so as to assist the litigant in obtaining his rights, and he may consult his own interests in deciding whether or not to enforce it. If he decides not to, there may in some cases be a public element involved, and the Attorney General will judge whether the public interest requires him to intervene in order to enforce the order. If neither the litigant nor the Attorney General seeks to enforce the order, the court will act of its own volition in punishing the contempt only in exceptional cases of clear contempts . . .

There seems to me to be a clear case for considering whether there should be some relaxation by the courts of their present restraint on themselves in enforcing their orders in cases where these are being openly flouted and the administration of justice is being brought into disrespect. For the courts to say, as they often say, that 'Orders of the court must be obeyed,' becomes idle if there are daily instances of open and notorious disobedience remaining unpunished. If the courts became more ready to enforce orders of their own motion, no doubt consideration should be given to the machinery by which this might be done. But I have to apply the law as it stands".

3–172 While this may be so as a matter of general policy, there could arise circumstances in which orders have been granted in a context which is highly charged politically (for example, in another industrial dispute); in such a case the

---

[84] As in *Re Lonhro* [1990] 2 A.C. 154. It is to be noted that the court's power to act of its own motion in relation to strict liability contempts is expressly preserved by s.7 of the Contempt of Court Act 1981: para.2–203. That provision otherwise leaves questions of "strict liability" contempt under the Act to the Attorney-General (although there is no corresponding provision for Scotland).
[85] Cmnd. 5794 (1974), para.171, and the discussion at paras 3–173 *et seq*. See also *Corcoran v Corcoran* [1950] 1 All E.R. 495; *Tony Pojé v Att-Gen for British Columbia* [1953] 2 D.L.R. 785.
[86] *Churchman v Joint Shop Stewards' Committee of the Workers of the Port of London* [1972] 1 W.L.R. 1094, Lord Denning M.R. at 1100; cf. *Re Grantham Wholesale Fruit, Vegetable and Potato Merchants Ltd* [1972] 1 W.L.R. 559; *Jennison v Baker* [1972] 2 Q.B. 52 and the wording of RSC Ord.52, r.5. See now CPR Sch.1, Ord.52.5. See also *Con-Mech (Engineers) Ltd v AUEW* [1973] I.C.R. 620 at 626, *per* Sir John Donaldson; *Re M (A Minor) (Contempt of Court: Committal of Court's own Motion)* [1999] Fam. 263.
[87] [1984] I.R.L.R. 350 at 353, [1985] 1 W.L.R. 78 at 82F–H, [1985] 1 All E.R. 211 at 215b–c. See also *International Union, United Mine Workers v Bagwell* 114 S. Ct. 2552 (1994).

court would need to weigh carefully whether the public interest required resort to the contempt jurisdiction if there was a risk of exacerbating the dispute itself.

Proceedings for criminal contempt may be instituted by the court of its own motion, notwithstanding that any person aggrieved may not wish to take the matter further.[88] Although s.7 of the 1981 Act provides that proceedings for a contempt of court under the strict liability rule should not be instituted other than with the consent of the Attorney-General,[89] the section expressly preserves the court's inherent jurisdiction. In other cases of criminal contempt relating to criminal proceedings it is at least preferable that the Attorney-General should institute proceedings, being the "appropriate officer" to consider and protect the public interest.[90]

Where a criminal contempt relates to civil proceedings, and is outside the provisions of s.7, it is therefore desirable that the aggrieved party should place the facts before the Attorney-General prior to instituting proceedings himself.[91] Sometimes, however, urgency may render this impracticable, as where an injunction is sought to prevent the publication of an apprehended contempt.[92] In any event, the Attorney-General may institute proceedings for a criminal contempt relating to civil proceedings, where the contempt is serious and the party aggrieved does not wish to proceed.[93]

In the United States, the Supreme Court has held[94] that a person charged with contempt has a right to a disinterested prosecutor, which "prohibits a successful litigant in a civil action from prosecuting the opposing party for criminal contempt for violation of an injunction won in the underlying civil proceeding".[95]

F. Sanctions

Formerly, one of the principal distinctions between the purposes underlying criminal and civil contempt was reflected in the sanctions applied. Criminal

---

[88] *Lechmere Charlton's Case* (1836) 2 My. & Cr. 316, 40 E.R. 661; *Castro, Skipworth's Case* (1873) L.R. 9 Q.B. 219; *Seaward v Paterson* [1897] 1 Ch. 545 at 559–560.
[89] The Attorney-General's role is considered in paras 2–199 *et seq.*, and paras 4–183 *et seq.*
[90] *Regina v Hargreaves Ex p. Dill* [1954] Crim.L.R. 54, *The Times*, November 4, 1953; *Att-Gen v Times Newspapers Ltd* [1974] A.C. 273 at 311.
[91] *Att-Gen v Times Newspapers Ltd* [1974] A.C. 273 at 311, 326. See the remarks of Laws L.J. in *Pelling v Hammond* (C/00/2363), September 22, 2000, on an application for permission to appeal the refusal of the Divisional Court to grant an application to bring proceedings for contempt under RSC Ord.52, r.2. Because the allegation was one of criminal contempt, he commented that he had considerable doubts as to the applicant's standing and said that it was "certainly desirable and perhaps necessary for the Attorney-General to be approached to see whether he should bring contempt proceedings". In any event, the application was "totally without merit and entirely barren".
[92] Ch.6, Pt I.
[93] *Re Crump* (1963) 107 Sol. Jo. 682, [1963] Crim.L.R. 777, *The Times*, August 22, 1963; see also Lord Reid [1974] A.C. at 293 and Lord Cross at 326.
[94] *Young v United States ex rel. Vuitton et Fils, SA* 481 U.S. 787 (1987).
[95] This summary of the decision is taken from Joan Meir, "The 'right' to a Disinterested Prosecutor of Criminal Contempt: Unpacking Public and Private Interests" [1992] 70 Wash. U.L.Q. 85 at 87.

3–176 CHAPTER 3—THE DISTINCTION BETWEEN CRIMINAL/CIVIL CONTEMPT

contempts were punished by imprisonment for a fixed term and/or a fine. Civil contempts were dealt with by imprisonment for an indefinite period; the contemnor was released when he had purged his contempt. Normally this would be by remedying the wrong, when he was entitled to release *ex debito justitiae*. If he continued to refuse to remedy his wrong for a long period, he could nonetheless be released if the court took the view that he had been sufficiently punished.[96] Although it seems that fines were not historically imposed for civil contempts,[97] it is now clearly established that they may be, whether in respect of companies,[98] trades unions[99] or individuals.[1]

3–177   The Contempt of Court Act 1981 provides in s.14(1):

"In any case where a court has power to commit a person to prison for contempt of court and (apart from this provision) no limitation applies to the period of committal, the committal shall (without prejudice to the power of the court to order his earlier discharge) be for a fixed term, and that term shall not on any occasion exceed two years in the case of committal by a superior court, or one month in the case of committal by an inferior court."

3–178   Hence imprisonment for an indefinite period is no longer possible even in the case of a superior court, whether for civil or criminal contempt.[2] However, s.63(3) of the Magistrates' Courts Act 1980 gives a magistrates' court power in relation to certain civil contempts to commit a contemnor to custody until he has remedied his default or for a period not exceeding two months.[3]

G. Release *ex debito justitiae* no longer available

3–179   In the days before Parliament introduced this maximum period of imprisonment, which applies to both civil and criminal contempts, the court would sometimes imprison a civil contemnor indefinitely, with the object of compelling compliance with an outstanding order; "in such cases, according to the overly worn saw, civil contemnors are said to 'carry the keys to their prison in their own pockets' ".[4] The traditional expression used in this context was release "*ex debito*

---

[96] See, *e.g. Re Barrell Enterprises* [1973] 1 W.L.R. 19.
[97] Lord Selborne L.C., H.L. *Deb.*, 3rd series, Vol. 276, col. 1709, March 8, 1883.
[98] *Phonographic Performance Ltd v Amusement Caterers* [1964] Ch. 195; *Re British Concrete Pipe Association's Agreement* [1982] I.C.R. 182; *Director General of Fair Trading v Pioneer Concrete (UK) Ltd* [1995] 1 A.C. 456 (£2,225,000 fine); *Taylor Made Golf Co Inc v Rata & Rata* [1996] F.S.R. 528.
[99] *e.g. Messenger Group Newspapers Ltd v NGA* [1984] I.R.L.R. 397; *Kent Free Press v NGA* [1987] I.R.L.R. 267.
[1] *Re Diane (Stockport) Ltd, The Times*, August 4, 1982.
[2] *Peart v Stewart* [1983] 2 A.C. 109, HL, which held that s.14 applies to both civil and criminal contempts. This case appears not to have been referred to in *Anomo, The Independent*, February 18, 1998 where it was argued (albeit unsuccessfully) that a sentence imposed in the Crown Court could not be imposed consecutively to a period of imprisonment in respect of civil contempt, on the basis that such a sentence would not necessarily be for a fixed period.
[3] And see Contempt of Court Act 1981, s.17 and Sch.3 to Contempt of Court Act 1981.
[4] P.A. Hostak, (1995) 81 Cornell L.R. at 183; see also *Re Nevitt* 117 F. 448 at 461 (8th Cir. 1902).

justitiae,"⁵ which implied a virtual right to be released once the contempt was purged.

This indulgence was, however, not permitted to a contemnor in cases where the court had imposed the sentence for a punitive or disciplinary purpose, rather than merely with the objective of compelling compliance. For example, in *Re Hunt*⁶ where a contemnor failed to attend an appointment before an examiner of the court Pearce L.J. stated: **3–180**

> "The appellant was guilty of wilful disobedience to the order of the court. The committal was a punishment for that disobedience and not merely, as the appellant asserts, an inducement to him to comply with the order and he could not by complying with the order claim to be released at once *ex debito justitiae*."

This distinction has lost its significance, since the need for a fixed sentence means that a contemnor can only be released, before the expiry of the relevant term, if the court exercises a discretion in his favour.⁷ Plainly, however, one of the factors which the court would weigh when asked to exercise that discretion⁸ would be the extent to which there had been an element of defiance in the contemnor's behaviour. While it seems to be the case that the court will generally look for a change of circumstances to justify early release, it does not appear to be a necessary requirement that there shall have been a change of heart on the part of the contemnor, such as to qualify as a "purging" of the contempt. "There must be many circumstances in which [the] court, in reviewing the order of the **3–181**

---

⁵ See, *e.g. Re Freston* (1883) 11 Q.B.D. 545 at 554, Brett M.R.; *Re Hunt* [1959] 2 Q.B. 69.
⁶ [1959] 2 Q.B. 69 at 78. For a "disciplinary" example, see *Re Freston* (1883) 11 Q.B.D. 545 at 554–5, Brett M.R.; see also *Seldon v Wilde* [1911] 1 K.B. 701 at 715, Vaughan Williams L.J. and compare the words of Lord President Clyde in *Johnson v Grant* 1923 S.C. 789 at 790 cited at para.3–11.
⁷ In *Lightfoot v Lightfoot* [1989] 1 F.L.R. 414 at 417, Lord Donaldson M.R., and *Delaney v Delaney* [1996] Q.B. 387, CA, it was suggested that the appropriate solution was to impose the maximum sentence permitted under the 1981 Act, leaving the remedy in the contemnor's hands. He can come back to the court and apply for release on the basis that he has purged his contempt. Later, in *Harris v Harris* [2001] Fam. 502 Munby J. cited these two cases as instances of the Court of Appeal's being "prepared to manipulate the sentencing powers of the court . . . in such a way as to give the court flexibility in meeting the difficulties of the particular type of case in question". He was speaking in the context of the court's inability to predict how a contemnor is likely to behave in the future and the extent to which the court's purpose of coercing compliance with its orders is likely to prove successful. He was determined to maintain flexibility "so as to maximise the court's capacity to secure compliance with its orders, that is, its capacity to persuade contemnors, whether by punishment, deterrence or coercion, or a mixture of all three, to behave themselves in future". (What he decided to do was to order immediate release on terms that the execution of the remaining part of the sentence be suspended for nine months on condition that the applicant obeyed the terms of the injunctions. His decision was reversed: [2001] EWCA Civ 1644, [2002] Fam. 253. The Court of Appeal held that the only power to suspend was that accorded by RSC Ord.52, r.7(1) and that the choice between immediate execution and suspension of the warrant had to be made at the time of sentencing for the relevant breach).
⁸ On application either by the contemnor himself, or by the Official Solicitor on his behalf, as in *Enfield LBC v Mahoney* [1983] 2 All E.R. 901. See also *Churchman v Joint Shop Stewards' Committee of the Workers of Port of London* [1974] 1 W.L.R. 1094 at 1095, [1972] 3 All E.R. 603 at 604.

3–181 CHAPTER 3—THE DISTINCTION BETWEEN CRIMINAL/CIVIL CONTEMPT

judge below to keep a contemnor in prison, will come to the conclusion that they compel the court to order release."[9]

3–182 In a superior court, a contemnor who has been sentenced to a fixed term may be able to apply for his release before its expiry under the terms of Ord.52, r.8 of the Rules of the Supreme Court.[10] The rule applies to "any contempt of court," which would embrace both civil and criminal contempt; although clearly it would only apply to "the Supreme Court" (which is defined to include the Crown Court).[11]

3–183 Statutory provision is made for early release from imprisonment in cases of county and magistrates' courts.[12]

H. Execution[13]

3–184 In executing a writ of attachment on a criminal contempt, the sheriff may break open an outer door to secure an arrest, but doubt was expressed as to whether he might do so in the case of a civil contempt.[14] The principle, of ancient origin, appears to be that if the officer was proceeding on the King's business, as opposed to pursuing the interest of a private citizen, it was lawful to break open the door.[15] A criminal contempt would apparently come within that principle. Yet it was held in *Harvey v Harvey*[16] that the sheriff was entitled to break open the outer door even in respect of a writ of attachment which had been issued against a party because of non-compliance with an order for delivery of deeds and documents, despite the fact that this would ordinarily be classified as a civil contempt. The conclusion Chitty J. drew from a review of the authorities was that the restriction upon sheriffs in this respect related to what he described as "merely civil process at the suit of a subject".[17]

---

[9] *Enfield LBC v Mahoney* [1983] 2 All E.R. 901 at 906g–h, Tasker Watkins L.J. The change of circumstances perceived by the Court of Appeal to be sufficient to justify release was that the contemnor "because of his eccentricity and stubborness" (*sic*) appeared to be taking satisfaction from his predicament and the attention it was receiving from the press and television. "But prison is not to be used for such a purpose; neither are orders of the court to be abused for such a purpose . . . it is high time that the prison service was rid of this man".

[10] See now CPR Sch.1, Ord.52.8.The rule dates from 1965. The county court and High Court powers to order early discharge are considered at para.14–30 and para.14–28 respectively, and the automatic early release provisions of the Criminal Justice Act 2003, s.258 are set out at para.14–35.

[11] Supreme Court Act 1981, s.1.

[12] See the County Courts Act 1984, s.14(2) and s.118(2), and s.12(4) of the Contempt of Court Act 1981, set out at para.14–30.

[13] See para.15–48.

[14] *Burdett v Abbott* (1811) 14 East 1 at 154–8, 104 E.R. 501 at 560–1, Lord Ellenborough C.J.; 14 East 1 at 162–3, 104 E.R. 501 at 562–3, Bayley J. See also *Semayne's case* (1604) 5 Co Rep.91a, 77 E.R. 194.

[15] See generally R. Stone, *The Law of Entry, Search and Seizure* (4th ed., 2005); *McLeod v Butterwick* [1998] 1 W.L.R. 1603, [1998] 2 All E.R. 901, CA.

[16] (1884) 26 Ch.D. 644, Chitty J.

[17] The example he gave, at 655, was that of a writ of *fieri facias*. For the phrases "*merely* subject to civil process", and "*merely* for the purpose of enforcing judgments in civil disputes", see also Brett M.R. in *Re Freston* (1883) 11 Q.B.D. 545 at 554.

I. Exercise of the Royal prerogative[18]

One distinction which may still remain is that the Crown's power to pardon is confined to those punished for criminal contempt.[19] Under the prerogative power, exercised nowadays by the Home Secretary, it would be possible in such cases to remit sentences of imprisonment[20] and fines,[21] either wholly or in part.[22] In *Att-Gen v James*,[23] Lord Parker C.J. was confronted with a situation where a contemnor had been committed by the Divisional Court for criminal contempt (obstructing a county court bailiff who had been seeking to arrest him), and who had returned to the Divisional Court seeking an order that he be discharged on the ground that his contempt had been purged. It was held that the court had no jurisdiction to release him. It was not as though the court had merely committed him for an indefinite period until the contempt had been purged, as used to happen in the case of a judge seeking to coerce someone into complying with a court order in civil proceedings. He observed:

3–185

> "It is, accordingly, in my judgment, settled law that, in the case of criminal contempt, the period of imprisonment should be for a fixed term as for punishment for a criminal offence. In those circumstances, the court, once that has been done, is functus officio, and, apart from appeal,[24] the remedy would be an application to the Home Secretary. Having said that, I, for my part, would feel that the proper course in the present case would be for the court to communicate with the Home Office saying that the court had no jurisdiction in the matter, but felt that this was a case in which the Crown might well exercise the power of discharge."

The Court did communicate with the Home Office, as directed by the Lord Chief Justice. Shortly afterwards, by the revision of the Rules of the Supreme Court in 1965, a power was conferred upon the court to discharge a prisoner at any time in cases of criminal as well as civil contempt.[25]

In the context of civil contempt, in cases where the court's purpose was to coerce a contemnor to perform or abstain from performing a particular act, in order to achieve compliance with a pre-existing order, the issue of a pardon would completely frustrate that purpose. Lord Selborne L.C. was asked in Parliament in 1883[26] why the Home Secretary had not been able to release a prisoner who was refusing to comply with an order of the Ecclesiastical Court. He explained (as reported in indirect speech) that:

3–186

---

[18] See A.T.H. Smith, "The Prerogative of Mercy, the Power of Pardon and Criminal Justice" [1983] P.L. 398 at 411–12.
[19] *The case of the Rev Mr Green*, Hansard, H.L. Deb., 3rd series, Vol. 276, cols.1710 and 1714, March 8, 1883; *Re the Bahama Islands* [1893] A.C. 138, Sir Charles Russell, Attorney-General, arguendo, at 145; *Seaward v Paterson* [1897] 1 Ch. 545 at 559.
[20] *Re the Bahama Islands* [1893] A.C. 138; *Ex p. Fernandez* (1861) 10 C.B.(N.S.) 3 at 25, 39; 142 E.R. 349 at 358. See also *Re Davies* (1888) 21 Q.B.D. 236 at 238.
[21] *Re Ramsay* (1870) 3 L.R. P.C. 47.
[22] *Rainy v The Justices of Sierra Leone* (1853) 8 Moo. P.C. 47, 14 E.R. 19.
[23] [1962] 2 Q.B. 637.
[24] Passing reference was made to the right of appeal recently given by the Administration of Justice Act 1960, s.13.
[25] RSC Ord.52, r.8(1), discussed at paras 14–28 *et seq*. See CPR Sch.1, Ord.52.8.
[26] H.L. *Deb.*, 3rd series, Vol. 276, cols.1713 and 1714, March 8, 1883.

"... the Crown had been advised that, though it had an undoubted power to pardon criminal and ecclesiastical offences, yet that mere contempt of Court did not come within that power. No authority, that he was aware of, could be found for the exercise of any such prerogative. He was bound to say that so long as the party guilty of the contempt persisted in his offence, and was unwilling to give any promise of obedience, there would be a difficulty in the exercise of such a prerogative, even if it were clearly established."

3–187   It has been suggested[27] that the power of pardon would enable the government to comply with the spirit of the decision of the European Court of Human Rights in *Goodwin v The United Kingdom*.[28] This may provide a convenient answer in the case of a criminal contempt, but the problem could not be so easily solved when the conduct in question falls clearly within the category of civil contempt, as for example in *Harman v Secretary of State for the Home Department*.[29] (In that instance, what was done was to amend the Rules of the Supreme Court by the addition of RSC Ord.24, r.14A.)[30] It might be possible on policy grounds, however, to draw a distinction between a penalty imposed purely by way of punishment in respect of a past incident of disobedience, and an order which was directed instead at coercion to achieve compliance with a continuing obligation. There would appear to be some support for such a distinction in Lord Selborne's reasoning in the passage cited above, since he referred specifically to a contemnor who "was unwilling to give any promise of obedience".

J. The privilege against self-incrimination

3–188   It appears from a number of authorities, mainly concerned directly with allegations of civil contempt,[31] that there has developed a recognition of a *prima facie* privilege against self-incrimination in respect of proceedings for contempt. In *Comet Products UK Ltd v Hawkex Plastics Ltd*,[32] Lord Denning M.R. acknowledged that this could not be reconciled with the procedures that had prevailed in cases of criminal contempt in the time of Blackstone.[33] Citing relatively modern authorities,[34] he came to the conclusion that since civil contempt partakes of the nature of a criminal charge, "the rules as to criminal charges have always been applied to such a proceeding."[35] He added:

"I am prepared to accept that such a rule [compulsory interrogation] did exist in the days of Sir William Blackstone. But I do not think it exists any longer today. The genius of the common law has prevailed. I hold that a man who is charged with contempt of

---

[27] By Geoffrey Robertson Q.C. in (1996) 146 New Law Jo. 472.
[28] (1996) 22 E.H.R.R. 123.
[29] [1983] 1 A.C. 280, discussed at para.12–201.
[30] See now CPR 31.22.
[31] Cited at nn.34 and 39 below.
[32] [1971] 2 Q.B. 67 at 74–5.
[33] See para.1–52.
[34] *Yianni v Yianni* [1966] 1 W.L.R. 120; *In re Bramblevale Ltd* [1970] Ch. 128. He also quoted from Bowen L.J. in *Redfern v Redfern* [1891] P. 139 at 147: "no one is bound to criminate himself".
[35] [1971] 2 Q.B. at 73F.

court cannot be compelled to answer interrogatories or to give evidence himself to make him prove his guilt. I reject the submission that the defendant is a compellable witness in the contempt proceedings against him".

This reasoning would perhaps lead to the conclusion that the policy underlying the Criminal Justice and Public Order Act 1994[36] relating to the inferences that may properly be drawn from a defendant's silence in criminal cases is applicable in this context. These provisions apply to "proceedings for an offence" a term which is not apt to cover a committal application, particularly in the context of civil contempt.[37]

3–189 More recently, specifically in the context of a possible criminal contempt, the Court of Appeal in *R. v Schot and Barclay*[38] criticised the judge's questioning of the jury, *inter alia*, because he had given no warning that the jurors concerned were not obliged to answer questions that might incriminate them.

3–190 As a matter of general practice, whenever a letter is written from the Law Officers' Department to anyone in respect of whom contempt proceedings are being contemplated, an opportunity is always afforded to give an explanation, although it is made clear that there is no obligation to answer.

3–191 It has been expressly held by Rimer J. in the Chancery Division that "proceedings for civil contempt are proceedings for the 'recovery of a penalty' in respect of which there is a privilege against self-incrimination."[39] This was with reference to the Civil Evidence Act 1968, s.14, which provides expressly for the privilege against self-incrimination in civil proceedings. Thus it would appear that in civil proceedings a person has *prima facie* privilege against self-incrimination if he is asked a question which might expose him to proceedings for civil contempt.

3–192 We have noted above that in general terms a person is not a compellable witness in proceedings against him for contempt. Nor can he be required to

---

[36] ss.34 and 35. For the current position see *Archbold 2005* at paras 15–415 *et seq*. (failure to mention facts when questioned or charged) and para.4–305 (silence at trial) respectively, although in the context of civil contempt the former section would have no relevance in any event.
[37] See, *e.g. Crest Homes plc v Marks* [1987] 1 A.C. 829 at 856.
[38] [1997] 2 Cr.App.R. 383, (1997) 161 J.P. 473.
[39] *Cobra Golf Inc v Rata* [1998] Ch. 109. Rimer J. reviewed a number of authorities, including *Rank Film Distributors Ltd v Video Information Centre* [1982] A.C. 380, Ch D, CA, HL; *Crest Homes plc v Marks* [1987] A.C. 829; *IBM United Kingdom Ltd v Prima Data International Ltd* [1994] 1 W.L.R. 718; *Tate Access Floors Inc v Boswell* [1991] Ch. 512. See also *Bhimji v Chatwani (No.3)* [1992] 4 All E.R. 912, Knox J., not following *Garvin v Domus Publishing* [1989] Ch. 335, Walton J. (who had held that proceedings for contempt of court were not proceedings for the purpose of s.14(1)(a) of the Civil Evidence Act 1968 and therefore that privilege against self-incrimination did not apply to documents obtained under an *Anton Piller* order). Section 14 of the 1968 Act remains in force following the enactment of the Civil Evidence Act 1995, which repeals only Pt I of the earlier statute (up to s.11).

3–192 CHAPTER 3—THE DISTINCTION BETWEEN CRIMINAL/CIVIL CONTEMPT

answer interrogatories.[40] On the other hand, leave can be given to cross-examine a respondent, in relation to the contempt, if he chooses to put in evidence,[41] whether the proceedings are in respect of civil or criminal contempt.[42] Furthermore, even if not cross-examined, a respondent may find that factual assertions made in the affidavit evidence are disbelieved on the basis that the Court is not bound to accept such evidence.[43] In *Phillips v Symes*[44] it was held by the Court of Appeal that a judge had misdirected himself in permitting "post judgment" cross-examination of a defendant in so far as it was aimed at establishing either a breach of the conditions governing a suspended sentence for a particular contempt or the committing of further contempt.

3–193   The Supreme Court of Canada[45] has held that the right to protection against self-incrimination, including in respect of civil contempt, is guaranteed by s.11(c) of the Charter of Rights and Freedoms. This was because there are characteristics common to all types of contempt which may be unduly masked by too great an insistence on the distinction between civil and criminal contempt. In particular, a penalty imposed in respect of civil contempt involves an element of "public law",[46] because respect for the role and authority of the courts is always at issue.

3–194   Within this jurisdiction, however, the matter is not entirely free from doubt. It seems to have been considered mainly in the context of intellectual property disputes and the execution of *Anton Piller* (now called "search and seizure") orders. In *Crest Homes plc v Marks*,[47] Lord Oliver referred to the uncertain state of the law:

---

[40] *Comet Products UK Ltd v Hawkex Plastics Ltd* [1971] 2 Q.B. 67 and 74A–B, Lord Denning M.R., cited at para.3–188. This judgment was cited in the court of First Instance in Hong Kong, and Lord Denning's dicta followed, in a criminal context: *Secretary for Justice v Apple Daily Ltd* [2000] 2 HKC 739. An attempt was made to obtain the identity of the journalist who had written an article which led to the jury being discharged in a murder trial. It had, following the first day of the hearing, made references to the defendant in terms which did not reflect any allegation so far made in the proceedings (including to the effect that he was a paedophile). The court rejected an attempt to obtain a *Norwich Pharmacal* order against the newspaper proprietor and editor. Gall J., having considered the authorities including *Director of Serious Fraud Office Ex p. Smith* [1993] A.C. 1, 30 (*per* Lord Mustill), held that such an order "would cut across the basic principles of the criminal law" in forcing them to divulge details pertaining to "the offence".

[41] See *Crest Homes plc v Marks* [1987] A.C. 829 at 858G–859A, Lord Oliver; *Comet Products UK Ltd v Hawkex Plastics Ltd* [1971] 2 Q.B. 76. But see *Re B (A Minor) (Contempt of Court: Affidavit Evidence)* [1996] 1 F.L.R. 239, discussed at paras 15–32 *et seq.*

[42] See *Re W (Wards) (Publication of Information)* [1989] 1 F.L.R. 246; *Att-Gen v Newspaper Publishing plc* [1989] F.S.R. 457, Morritt J.

[43] *Att-Gen v News Group Newspapers plc* [1989] 1 Q.B. 110 at 127D.

[44] [2003] EWCA Civ 1769, (2003) 147 S.J.L.B. 1431.

[45] *Vidéotron Ltée v Industries Microlec Produits Electroniques Inc* (1993) 96 D.L.R. (4th) 376. L'Heureux-Dubé J., dissenting, expressed the view that it is essential to bear in mind the distinction between criminal contempt and civil contempt; the essence of the latter lying primarily in the protection of private interests.

[46] See also Sedley J. in *Guildford Borough Council v Valler* [1993] T.L.R. 274, (where the view was expressed that committal in civil proceedings was not " . . . in any admissible sense the private law right which the older *dicta* suggested it was. To all intents and purposes it was a form of private prosecution").

[47] [1987] 1 A.C. 829 at 859E–F.

"Should the point arise for decision it may be necessary in relation to the production of relevant documents essential to the conduct of proceedings—I say nothing about interrogatories—to reconsider the extent of the privilege against self-incrimination where it is prayed in aid solely on the ground of liability to a motion for civil contempt in those proceedings."

There is a danger that the ends of justice would be defeated, especially in the context of the use of the search and seizure procedure, if pleas of privilege too readily prevail. As Lord Oliver pointed out, 3–195

" . . . logically a defendant who, in response to an order for verification of his list of documents by affidavit, makes inadequate discovery can thereafter resist any application for discovery of particular documents on the ground that to comply would demonstrate that he had been in breach of the earlier order and thus in contempt."

Supreme Court Act 1981, s.72

Parliament sought to achieve a proper balance between the traditional protection against self-incrimination and, on the other hand, the rights of those who wish to defend intellectual property rights by the flexible procedure of search and seizure. It is provided in s.72 of the Supreme Court Act 1981, which was said by Lord Oliver to be "far from easy to construe",[48] as follows: 3–196

"(1) In any proceedings to which this subsection applies a person shall not be excused, by reason that to do so would tend to expose that person . . . to proceedings for a related offence or for the recovery of a related penalty -

(a) from answering any question put to that person in the first mentioned proceedings; or
(b) from complying with any order made in those proceedings.

(2) Subsection (1) applies to the following civil proceedings in the High Court, namely—

(a) proceedings for infringement of rights pertaining to any intellectual property or for passing off;
(b) proceedings brought to obtain disclosure of information relating to any infringement of such rights or to any passing off; and
(c) proceedings brought to prevent any apprehended infringement of such rights or any apprehended passing off.

(3) Subject to subsection (4), no statement or admission made by a person—

(a) in answering a question put to him in any proceedings to which subsection (1) applies; or
(b) in complying with any order made in any such proceedings,

shall, in proceedings for any related offence or for the recovery of any related penalty, be admissible in evidence against that person or (unless they married after the making of the statement or admission) against the spouse of that person.

(4) Nothing in subsection (3) shall render any statement or admission made by a person as there mentioned inadmissible in evidence against that person in proceedings for perjury or contempt of court."

---

[48] [1987] 1 A.C. at 856C.

3-196 CHAPTER 3—THE DISTINCTION BETWEEN CRIMINAL/CIVIL CONTEMPT

Because of this statutory intervention to limit the scope of the privilege against self-incrimination, the Practice Direction to CPR Pt 25 warns that the standard form of search and seizure order requires amendment so that the recipient of the order shall not be misled into thinking that he can refuse to answer on this ground in an intellectual property case.[49]

3-197   Lord Oliver expressed the view that s.72(4) was probably inserted from an abundance of caution to forestall any argument that s.72(3) afforded protection in cases of contempt or perjury (whether or not either of these could be described as a "related offence").[50] In any event, he regarded it as peripheral to the issue which had to be determined in the case before their Lordships. This was whether or not leave should be given to rely upon material obtained in the course of *Anton Piller* proceedings, for the purpose of demonstrating non-compliance with earlier orders of the court, notwithstanding the implied undertaking to use material so obtained solely for the purposes of the instant litigation.

3-198   It is certainly the case that those who obtain documents or information by way of search and seizure proceedings are subject to the same *prima facie* obligation not to use such material for purposes outside the scope of the litigation as always applied in the context of documents disclosed on discovery.[51] The obligation applies not only to physical material,[52] such as documents or video tapes, but also to information derived from such material.[53] There is a discretion in the court, however, to release or modify that obligation in appropriate circumstances. In *Crest Homes plc v Marks*[54] there were two actions, and what was sought was leave to refer to material obtained in the second action for the purpose of civil contempt proceedings arising out of the first. It was purely adventitious that there happened to be two actions rather than one; it was thus held that the plaintiffs should be released from the implied undertaking, since no injustice would be done.

3-199   It remains important to preserve the integrity of undertakings given to the court as the price of disclosure. If what had been in issue was the revelation in the seized material of a civil contempt in some other "wholly unrelated proceeding",[55] it seems unlikely that leave would have been given. In *Crest Homes plc v Marks*, what determined the matter was the special circumstance that the two actions could be treated as being in substance a single set of proceedings. If the material is sought to be relied upon for the purpose of contempt committed in the very same proceedings, then it would be artificial to regard the contempt aspect as being outside the use which is traditionally permitted within the terms of the

---

[49] See para.8.4 of 25PD.12.
[50] [1987] 1 A.C. at 855B and 856G–H.
[51] *Crest Homes plc v Marks* [1987] 1 A.C. 829; see also *Alterskye v Scott* [1948] 1 All E.R. 469; *Riddick v Thames Board Mills Ltd* [1977] Q.B. 881; *Harman v Secretary of State for the Home Department* [1983] 1 A.C. 280.
[52] See *VDU Installations Ltd v Integrated Computer Systems and Cybernetics Ltd* [1989] 1 F.S.R. 378.
[53] *Sybron Corporation v Barclays Bank plc* [1985] Ch. 299, as approved in *Crest Homes plc v Marks* [1987] 1 A.C. 829 at 854A, Lord Oliver.
[54] [1987] 1 A.C. 829.
[55] An expression used by Lord Oliver in [1987] 1 A.C. 829 at 859H.

implied undertaking. In other words, proceedings for civil contempt should not be regarded as being in some way apart from or collateral to the primary civil proceedings. This is because the proper policing and enforcement by the court of orders made, and undertakings given to the court, are as much an integral part of the proceedings to which they relate as any other steps in the prosecution of the claim.[56] Lord Oliver's observations were held not to be applicable to the particular facts in *Bourns v Raychem Corporation*.[57] In that case, there had been an express undertaking to the court not to use documents for contempt proceedings without permission.

The approach of the House of Lords to the possible use of seized material for the purpose of establishing contempt in some "other wholly unrelated proceeding" had an inhibiting effect on the court in *Cobra Golf Inc v Rata*.[58] An application was made in one action for leave to use material obtained under the procedure in another unrelated action. Both claims concerned Rata & Rata, a firm engaged in copying the distinctive get-up of various kinds of golfing equipment, but each had been brought by a different plaintiff. The objective was to save time and money in duplicating search and seizure proceedings by making use of the information obtained in the other action.

3–200

Laddie J. reviewed a number of authorities including *Crest Homes plc v Marks*,[59] and helpfully summarised the factors to be taken into account when the court is asked to exercise its discretion to permit the use of discovery (now "disclosure") obtained in one action for the purposes of another:

3–201

" (1) Documents may not be used for a collateral purpose without leave of the court or the party from whom they came.
(2) That restriction on collateral use covers not only the documents themselves but also copies of them and the information they contain.
(3) In this context collateral purpose means some purpose not reasonably necessary for the proper conduct of the action in which the discovery was given.
(4) Strictly speaking, asking for release of the documents for use outside the proceedings in which they were disclosed is itself a collateral use, since it is a use of knowledge of the contents of the documents for a purpose collateral to those proceedings. However, this must be taken to be a necessary exception to the otherwise all-embracing effect of the undertaking.
(5) The unsanctioned collateral use constitutes an abuse of process or contempt of court. Whether it gives rise to a civil cause of action is not clear.
(6) The existence of the implied undertaking means that an application to release the party from restraint must be made before there is collateral use.
(7) Normally the application will be made first to the other party and only after refusal will it be made to the court.

---

[56] [1987] 1 A.C. at 860E–G, Lord Oliver. See also *Savings Bank v Gasco BV (No.2)* [1988] 1 Ch. 422 at 443, Nicholls L.J.
[57] [1999] 3 All E.R. 154, [1999] F.S.R. 641.
[58] [1996] F.S.R. 819.
[59] [1987] 1 A.C. 829. Also referred to were *Riddick v Thames Board Mills Ltd* [1977] Q.B. 881, CA; *Halcon International Inc v The Shell Transport and Trading Co* [1979] R.P.C. 97, CA; *Sony Corporation v Anand* [1981] F.S.R. 398, Browne-Wilkinson J.; *Sybron Corporation v Barclays Bank plc* [1985] Ch. 299, Scott J.; *Bayer AG v Winter (No.2)* [1986] F.S.R. 357, Hoffmann J.

3–201 CHAPTER 3—THE DISTINCTION BETWEEN CRIMINAL/CIVIL CONTEMPT

(8) In exceptional cases, such as ones in which notice to the party of the intended use to which the documents may be put are [*sic*] likely to defeat the ends of justice, the application for release from the undertakings may be made *ex parte*.

(9) When made *ex parte*., the court should normally impose an *inter partes* return date in the near future when the affected party will be able if he so wishes to argue that the documents should not be used.[60]

(10) On any application to relax the undertaking, the court has a discretion which must be exercised to achieve justice on the basis of all the circumstances of the case.

(11) The circumstances which may be taken into account include the following:

(a) The extent to which relaxation of the undertaking will cause injustice to the party which provided the discovery.

(b) Whether the proposed collateral use is in court proceedings or outside litigation (e.g. for disclosure to the press as in *Harman*). *Prima facie* if it is for use outside litigation, it is not the court's function to release for that purpose.

(c) Whether, if the collateral use is in aid of criminal or civil proceedings, those proceedings are in this country or abroad.

(d) In so far as the satellite proceedings are in this country:

  (i) If they are criminal proceedings, the court must take into account the possibility of the application being a method of by-passing the privilege against self-incrimination.

  (ii) If the collateral use is for civil proceedings, the court should take into account:

   (a) whether the hub proceedings and the satellite proceedings are similar in character;
   (b) whether the parties in the two sets of proceedings are the same;
   (c) the extent to which the party seeking relaxation of the undertaking would be able to obtain discovery by another route and, if so, which route is likely to be cheaper or quicker;
   (d) whether the effect of the relaxation of the undertaking will have the effect of generating new proceedings or whether it will merely help in pursuing a claim or defence which already exists or could be run anyway;
   (e) prima facie it is not in the interests of justice to hinder a party from advancing a good claim or defence in other proceedings;
   (f) prima facie it is not in the interests of justice to allow discovery in the hub action to be released for the purpose of supporting the initiation of contempt proceedings in the satellite action, at least if the two proceedings are 'unrelated'.

  (iii) In so far as the documents are to be used in proceedings abroad,

   (a) Whether those proceedings are criminal or civil.
   (b) If the satellite proceedings are criminal, the court here should be wary of doing anything in this country which may subject the disclosing party to an unfair disadvantage in those proceedings.
   (c) If the satellite proceedings are civil, the court should take into account whether the disclosure would put the disclosing party at a significant disadvantage in those proceedings—for example by forcing it to produce in the public domain documents which, under the local procedure, would not otherwise be made public.

---

[60] *Naf SA v Dickens (London) Ltd* [1993] F.S.R. 424.

(e) There does not appear to be any reason in principle why documents properly obtained as a result of an *Anton Piller* order should be treated differently to any other discovery documents. Once disclosed they are no more nor less protected by the implied undertaking."

Laddie J. would have been inclined to give leave on the facts before him, were it not for the views expressed in the House of Lords in the words of Lord Oliver (albeit *obiter*)[61] to the effect that it should be at least a significant factor in the exercise of the court's discretion that the application for leave was for the purpose of using the material obtained on discovery in one action for the purposes of civil contempt proceedings in another.

3–202

The guidance given by Laddie J. in the *Cobra Golf* case has been described as "useful", but it is now important under the CPR to have in mind the overriding principles when considering whether to lift an order made under CPR 31.22. A material consideration must be whether the documents could have been obtained under CPR 31.17, which enables a court to order disclosure from third parties if necessary to dispose fairly of a claim.[62] Laddie J. stated in *Dendron GmbH v University of California*[63] that he had considered again what he said in *Cobra Golf* and said that among the factors which should be taken into account, although not previously mentioned, was whether the release of the material from the restriction would serve a purpose; for example, it would not serve the ends of justice to release material for use before a foreign court or tribunal which would not admit it in evidence or pay any attention to it.

3–203

In *Memory Corporation plc v Sidhu*,[64] Arden J. considered the question whether there was some specific exception from the privilege against self-incrimination where the alleged contempt arose out of actions in the case before the court. She took the view that there was not. It followed from the fact that the defendant was not a compellable witness in any contempt proceedings that he should be entitled to the privilege, particularly as it was sought to cross-examine him on an affidavit sworn pursuant to an order of the court. There was no valid reason for drawing the distinction between the facts before her and a case where committal proceedings had already been initiated.

3–204

The provisions of section 7 of the Civil Procedure Act 1997

A further statutory intervention in this context is to be found in s.7 of the Civil Procedure Act 1997, which governs the power of courts to make "orders for preserving evidence etc". These include the context of search and seizure orders. It is expressly provided in s.7(7) that the section does not affect any right of a person to refuse to do anything on the ground that to do so might tend to expose

3–205

---

[61] [1987] 1 A.C. 829 at 859.
[62] *Smithkline Beecham plc v Generics (UK) Ltd* [2003] EWCA Civ 1109, [2004 1 W.L.R. 1479 at [37], *per* Aldous L.J.
[63] [2004] EWHC 589 (Pat), [2005] 1 W.L.R. 200 at [42].
[64] [2000] Ch. 645.

him or his spouse or civil partner to proceedings for an offence or the recovery of a penalty.

3. *The provisions in CPR 35.9*

3–206 Under CPR 35.9, the court has the power to direct a party who has access to information which is not reasonably available to the other party to prepare and file a document recording the information and to serve a copy on the other party. The Practice Direction on committal,[65] however, expressly excludes that power for the purpose of committal applications.

4. *The need to file evidence notwithstanding the privilege*

3–207 Another issue which has brought into focus the question of whether the privilege against self-incrimination will protect someone in the context of civil contempt is that of whether such an alleged contemnor can be required to file evidence in advance of an application to commit him. This was addressed by Wall J. in *Re B (A Minor) (Contempt of Court: Affidavit Evidence)*,[66] where he held that while there may be an obligation imposed to serve evidence in advance of the hearing, no use may be made of it unless and until the respondent chooses to place reliance upon it. This represents a compromise. "The court will introduce whatever safeguards may be necessary for the protection of alleged contemnors but will not import criminal procedures wholesale or indiscriminately."[67]

5. *Conclusions*

3–208 It is possible, therefore, to draw the following conclusions. While it seems now to be clearly established that there is a privilege against self-incrimination in respect of allegations of civil contempt,[68] the likelihood is that the problem is going to arise primarily in cases of intellectual property disputes and specifically in the context of document disclosure or search and seizure cases. The authorities considered above would appear to suggest that any question which arises is likely to be resolved not so much by reference to any common law principle relating to self-incrimination, but rather by the exercise of discretion, now to be determined

---

[65] Appendix 5A, Pt I, para.6.
[66] [1996] 1 F.L.R. 239. This is more fully considered at paras 15–32 *et seq.*
[67] *ibid.* at 251E, Wall J. See also *Barclays de Zoete Wedd Securities Ltd v Nadir* [1992] T.L.R. 141 where Knox J. held that it did not follow, purely because the standard of proof in civil contempt proceedings was the criminal one, that criminal procedure should be adopted in civil proceedings generally and that, accordingly, there was no reason to conclude that a respondent in civil contempt proceedings was entitled to make a submission of no case without making an election as to whether he would call evidence.
[68] *Cobra Golf Inc v Rata* [1998] Ch. 109, Rimer J.; *Comet Products UK Ltd v Hawkex Plastics Ltd* [1971] 2 Q.B. 67.

in the light of the guidance given by Laddie J. in *Cobra Golf Inc v Rata*.[69] It is clear that, although weight will undoubtedly be given to the possibility of exposure to civil contempt proceedings, this will not necessarily be an absolute bar to the granting of leave to use the disclosed material. This clearly accords with the policy of the legislature as embodied in s.72 of the Supreme Court Act 1981.[70]

K. *Autrefois acquit* and *convict*

3–209 The principle that a person may not be punished twice for the same wrong is of ancient origin.[71] Its application to the law of contempt has, however, occasioned some difficulties. Anyone committed for contempt through failure to comply with a court order might appear, if he continues to decline to comply during his period of imprisonment and afterwards, to be at risk of being re-committed for continuing failure upon release from prison. Care must be taken, however, to avoid offending against the criminal law doctrines of *autrefois convict* and, sometimes, *autrefois acquit*, which apply in this context because of the penal nature of committal, even where the contempt is civil in character. Although inroads have been made into the double jeopardy principle by the Criminal Justice Act 2003, the relevant list of offences to which the operative provisions apply[72] does not include contempt.

3–210 In *Lamb v Lamb*,[73] a judge made an *ex parte* order committing a husband to prison for 14 days for breach of an ouster injunction. Shortly afterwards, there was an *inter partes* hearing at which the judge sentenced the husband to be detained for three months. The appeal against the second of these orders was allowed, there having been no evidence at the second hearing of any further acts amounting to a breach of the injunction. The Court of Appeal held that the judge had no jurisdiction to act as he did since " . . . it is clearly wrong that a man should be sentenced twice for what is, in substance, the same offence".[74] It was wrong to treat the *ex parte* hearing as giving rise to an interim order that the judge was free to extend at the later hearing.

---

[69] [1996] F.S.R. 819 at 830–832, considered at paras 3–200 *et seq*. It is necessary now also to bear in mind the words of Aldous L.J. in *Smithkline Beecham plc v Generics (UK) Ltd* [2003] EWCA Civ 1109, [23004] 1 W.L.R. 1497 at [37], where it was emphasised that it is necessary to have regard to the overriding principles of the CPR, and in particular the need to establish where the interests of justice lie having regard to the interests of both parties. And see *Re B (A Minor) (Contempt of Court: Affidavit Evidence)* [1996] 1 W.L.R. 627, 1 F.L.R. 239, Wall J.
[70] See para.3–196.
[71] An early authority is *Crepps v Durden* (1772) 2 Cowp. 640, 98 E.R. 1283. For an extended study, see M. Friedland, *Double Jeopardy* (Clarendon, 1969). See also D.S. Rudstein, "Double Jeopardy and Summary Contempt Prosecution" (1994) 69 Notre Dame Law Rev. 691. The principle of *ne bis in idem* is also recognised in European jurisprudence: *S v Germany* (1983) 39 D.R. 43; *Gradinger v Austria* (1995) A/328, 33/1994/480/562; *Oliveira v Switzerland* (1998) 28 E.H.R.R. 289. Art.4, Protocol 7 of the European Convention, which guarantees freedom from double jeopardy, is discussed at para.12–14.
[72] See Sch.5.
[73] [1984] F.L.R. 278, following *Danchevsky v Danchevsky (No.2)* (1977) 121 S.J. 796.
[74] *Per* Oliver L.J. at 283A.

3–211 CHAPTER 3—THE DISTINCTION BETWEEN CRIMINAL/CIVIL CONTEMPT

3–211   The application of these doctrines should have been rendered simpler since the enactment of s.14 of the Contempt of Court Act 1981, requiring all committals for contempt to be for a specified period, rather than for a period pending compliance with the court order. The warrant for committal should always specify the period for which the contemnor is committed. If beyond that date the contemnor has still not complied with the order, the proper course is to secure a fresh order and then, if there is another refusal, to move for a fresh committal.

3–212   This was the course advocated by the Court of Appeal in *Kumari v Jalal*,[75] where a county court judge had sentenced a recalcitrant husband, who continued to refuse to return certain specified items of property to his wife after his release, to a further term of imprisonment (six months). He appealed to the Court of Appeal on the basis that the failure to comply with the order within the time specified was a single breach which was now spent and that, since the principles of *autrefois convict* applied, he could not be again committed for the failure to comply. The court agreed with this contention. The continued failure to comply was not a new breach and it followed that the judge had no power to commit the husband to prison again on the basis of the first order.

3–213   Where an application to commit for contempt is dismissed, a question arises as to whether fresh proceedings can be instituted in respect of the same incident. The point arose in *Jelson (Estates) Ltd v Harvey*,[76] where the Court of Appeal affirmed that the criminal law doctrines of *autrefois acquit* and *autrefois convict* do apply in the context of civil contempt. Nevertheless the question to be determined in each case is whether or not the alleged contemnor was genuinely in peril of punishment on the first application. The judge had there merely dismissed the application because of a defect in the notice of motion, refusing to consider the merits. On the facts, therefore, the "defendant" had never been acquitted on the merits, and it followed that the judge had been right to proceed upon the second motion.

3–214   The issue fell for consideration again in *El Capistrano SA v ATO Marketing Ltd*,[77] where the judge dismissed applications for committal and sequestration on the ground that the evidence in support of the notice of motion was inadmissible. The plaintiffs issued a fresh motion to commit which complied with the rules, although they relied on the same facts as in the first motion. When the defendants pleaded *autrefois acquit*, because they claimed to have been in peril of punishment on the hearing of the previous motion, the judge upheld that contention and dismissed the motion. On appeal, it was held that the dismissal of civil process for procedural irregularity was not necessarily to be equated to an acquittal in criminal proceedings for the purposes of the doctrine. Accordingly, the appeal was allowed.

3–215   It had been sought to distinguish *Jelson (Estates)* on the basis that in that case the notice of motion was itself invalid whereas, in the instant case, the

---

[75] [1997] 1 W.L.R. 97, [1996] 4 All E.R. 65, CA.
[76] [1984] 1 All E.R. 12.
[77] [1989] 1 W.L.R. 471 at 485, [1989] 2 All E.R. 572 at 584.

proceedings could have been amended (the court spoke of the "plaintiffs' right to get their tackle in order and to start again").[78] The court took the view that this was a "narrow procedural distinction", and that it was appropriate to view such cases on "a broad basis of justice". There was no authority requiring a narrow interpretation of "on the merits" or more generally of the doctrine of double jeopardy as applied in the law of civil contempt. Even though there may have been no defect in the proceedings, there had been no determination on the merits.

The Court cited, with approval, the minority judgment of Lush J. in *Haynes v Davis*,[79] to the effect that the defendant in that case had never been in jeopardy because the magistrate had no jurisdiction. In his view,[80] there were three conditions which had to be fulfilled before a plea of *autrefois acquit* could be successfully raised: 3–216

(1) the court had to be competent to try the defendant for the offence in question;

(2) the trial had to be upon a good indictment, on which a valid judgment of conviction could be entered;

(3) the acquittal had to be upon the merits, followed by a judgment or order of acquittal.

The essential point appears to be that the doctrines can have no application, in the context of civil contempt, unless there has been a genuine determination upon the merits. 3–217

It is possible that one act might amount both to a contempt and to a criminal offence under the general law. In such cases, the principle of *autrefois* (whether *acquit* or *convict*) would not operate in such a way as to protect someone committed for contempt from proceedings for the other offence. In *R. v Green (Bryan)*[81] a husband committed an assault. This constituted both a criminal offence in its own right, and contempt, because it had occurred in breach of an injunction. It was held that the committal for contempt did not give rise to the plea of *autrefois convict* in later proceedings for assault.[82] 3–218

This would be consistent with the court's approach in *N v N*,[83] where a breach of a non-molestation order, consisting of rape, resulted in a sentence directed 3–219

---

[78] [1989] 1 W.L.R. at 481, [1989] 2 All E.R. at 580ff.
[79] [1915] 1 K.B. 332. He differed from the majority, Ridley and Avory JJ.
[80] In reliance upon *Russell on Crime* (7th ed., 1909), Vol. 2, p.1982.
[81] [1993] Crim.L.R. 46 (Lexis), (1992) Sol. Jo. L.B. 260; following *Szczepanski v Szczepanski* [1985] 6 F.L.R. 468.
[82] In the Protection from Harassment Act 1997, specific provision is made to deal with the problem. It is provided first that if a person is convicted of an offence of breaching an injunction granted under the Act, that conduct is not punishable as a contempt of court: s.3(7). Conversely, where a person has been punished in respect of any conduct as a contempt of court, he or she cannot be convicted of an offence under the Act: s.3(8). Analogous provision is contained in s.42A(3) and (4) of the Family Law Act 1996, inserted by s.1 of the Domestic Violence, Crime and Victims Act 2004.
[83] [1992] 1 F.L.R. 370.

solely towards the element of civil contempt. Had there been subsequent proceedings for rape, which would ordinarily attract a much higher penalty than the statutory maximum for contempt, it would not have availed the defendant to pray in aid in his defence the finding of contempt (although no doubt the contempt penalty would be a relevant factor in determining sentence).

The application of these principles to orders of continuing effect

3–220　In *R. v Justices of Portsmouth*[84] the Divisional Court was concerned with two separate fines imposed in respect of the same court order. The order had been made under s.31 of the Vaccination Act 1867 whereby a parent could be directed to have a child vaccinated within a certain time. The order was disobeyed and on information of the vaccination officer the parent was fined, the amount being recovered under a distress warrant. A month later further proceedings were taken in relation to a continuing failure to comply with the original direction. A further fine was imposed and the amount recovered by the same means. It was held that the conviction should be quashed since there was no statutory basis for treating disobedience as a continuing offence. Once the initial fine had been imposed, there would have to have been a second application to the magistrates, so that they could exercise their discretion afresh whether or not to make a further order.

3–221　This principle of the criminal law would presumably apply in relation to a penalty imposed in respect of a contempt. Even in relation to a civil contempt, a committal order is a "criminal or quasi-criminal sentence" and therefore no one should be sentenced to two such penalties in respect of one breach.[85]

3–222　As Vaughan Williams L.J. observed in *Church's Trustee v Hibbard*,[86] " . . . you cannot punish twice in respect of the same offence, or give two sentences in respect of the same offence. I say nothing about what you might or might not do in some cases of continued offences." It may be important to distinguish between orders of two different kinds. In the Vaccination Act case, the act was ordered to be carried out within a certain time.[87] But an injunction, and especially one in prohibitory form, may be framed in terms that impose a continuing obligation. In such a case, it could be appropriate to impose a separate penalty for a continuing breach, even though no fresh order has been made, on the basis that a separate breach has occurred of the existing order.[88]

L. Extra-territorial jurisdiction

3–223　The court has jurisdiction over parties who have been served with proceedings, including those who have been properly served outside the jurisdiction (with

---

[84] [1892] 1 Q.B. 491.
[85] *B v B (Contempt: Committal)* [1991] 2 F.L.R. 588. See also *Danchevsky v Danchevsky (No.2)*, November 10, 1977, Lawton L.J.
[86] [1902] 2 Ch. 784 at 791.
[87] Cp *Kumari v Jalal* [1997] 1 W.L.R. 97, [1996] 4 All E.R. 65, CA, where the order in question had to be carried out within a specified time. The case is discussed at para.3–212.
[88] See *B v B (Contempt: Committal)* [1991] 2 F.L.R. 588 at 601, Purchas L.J.

permission of the court).[89] Thus, if any party disobeys an order or breaches an undertaking to the court there will be a *prima facie* contempt which the court will have jurisdiction to punish. In a case, however, where a third party outside the jurisdiction becomes involved in thwarting the purpose of an order of the English court, whether by encouraging or assisting a party to do so, or by any other means, such conduct could be classified only as criminal contempt.

The court does not have criminal jurisdiction outside the boundaries of England and Wales,[90] subject to any specific exceptions, at common law or by statute, and therefore the court would seem to be powerless to deal with any such third party through the processes of the contempt jurisdiction. This is a situation which can arise in many circumstances, although examples occur particularly in relation to the treatment of children who have been taken abroad or are kept there in breach of an English court order, or in the context of freezing orders.[91]

3–224

The issue was touched upon in a decision of Clarke J.[92] where he said:

3–225

"Even though . . . a defendant out of the jurisdiction who is not served with but is given notice of the terms of an order out of the jurisdiction may not strictly be in contempt of Court because it is not yet a party to the proceedings and the alleged 'contempt' will have taken place out of the jurisdiction, I can see no reason why the court should not take into account a refusal to obey the order without first applying to set it aside when considering how to exercise any subsequent discretion which the court may have".

The judge appeared to recognise the difficulty in attempting to punish any such thwarting of the court's order, while at the same time being prepared to take into account such conduct as a factor weighing in the scales when the court was called upon to exercise any discretion subsequently in relation to the alleged miscreant. There is no inconsistency here, since the court may always weigh any relevant person's conduct in the context of a discretion, whether or not it would be possible to exercise the summary jurisdiction in contempt.

3–226

M. Hearsay evidence

1. *Criminal contempts*

The decision of the Court of Appeal in *R. v Shokoya*[93] concerned the failure of a witness to attend trial to give evidence. Another witness, a policeman, deposed that he had told the mother of another witness and that she had confirmed that she had told appellant of the date of the hearing. It was held that, in reaching his conclusion that the appellant had been aware of the date of the hearing and had chosen not to attend, the judge had referred to inadmissible evidence. The finding

3–227

---

[89] See also the discussion in *Att-Gen for England and Wales v Tomlinson* [1999] 3 N.Z.L.R. 722.
[90] See generally *Archbold 2005*, paras 2–33, 2–34, and *R. v Griffiths Ex p. Att-Gen* [1957] 2 Q.B. 192. See also *Lakah Group and Lakah v Al Jazeera and Mansour* [2002] EWHC 2500 (QB).
[91] *Mackinnon v Donaldson, Lufkin and Jenrette Corp* [1986] 1 Ch. 482, Hoffmann J. The matter is considered more fully in the context of freezing orders at para.12–155.
[92] *Unicargo v Flotec Maritime S de RL, The "Cienvik"* [1996] 2 Lloyd's Rep.395 at 399.
[93] [1992] T.L.R. 284.

of contempt, and the sentence of 14 days in a young offender's institution, were quashed.

2. Reform of hearsay law in criminal cases

3–228 The Law Commission made recommendations for the reform of the hearsay law governing criminal proceedings generally.[94] The matter is now governed by chapter 2 of the Criminal Justice Act 2003, ss.114 to 136. In that context, "criminal proceedings" is defined to mean "criminal proceedings in relation to which the strict rules of evidence apply". Even before these provisions came into force (in April 2005), Rose L.J. expressed the view that there was a "respectable argument" that hearsay should be admissible in the criminal contempt proceedings before the court in that case.[95] He expressed no concluded view, but identified three factors which lent support to the admissibility of hearsay. One point was that contempt proceedings are regarded as *sui generis*.[96] Secondly, there had been a progressive relaxation of the old exclusionary rule in relation to hearsay so far as civil proceedings were concerned. Thirdly, the fundamental changes incorporated in the Criminal Justice Act 2003 were, at that time, shortly to come into force with regard to criminal proceedings generally. Since this Act came into force, there is no decision on the extent to which the hearsay provisions apply to committal applications in respect of criminal contempt, but since these are heard by judge alone the likelihood is that courts would be at least as ready to admit hearsay in that context as in criminal proceedings tried on indictment.

2. Civil contempts

3–229 The law governing civil contempts is somewhat more complicated in this respect. Until comparatively recently, it was generally assumed that hearsay evidence was not admissible.[97] But in *Savings and Investment Bank Ltd v Gasco Investments (Netherlands) BV (No.2)*,[98] the Court of Appeal held that in certain circumstances hearsay evidence could indeed be admitted in support of a committal motion in respect of civil contempt.

3–230 The court was there faced with the question whether the proceedings before them were to be classified as interlocutory, and thus within the provisions of the former RSC Ord.41, r.5(2) which provided that:

---

[94] Law Com. Consultation Paper No.138, *Evidence in Criminal Proceedings: Hearsay and Related Topics* (1995). Discussed by A.A.S. Zuckerman [1996] Crim.L.R. 4, David C. Ormerod [1996] Crim.L.R. 16 and J.R. Spencer [1996] Crim.L.R. 29. See now P. Roberts and A. Zuckerman, *Criminal Evidence* (2004), ch.12; R. May and S. Powles, *Criminal Evidence* (5th ed., 2004), ch.8; *Cross and Tapper on Evidence* (10th ed., 2004), ch.XII.
[95] *Att-Gen v Express Newspapers* [2004] EWHC 2859 (Admin) at [7].
[96] See the discussion at paras 3–85 *et seq*. For the position in Scotland, see para.16–39.
[97] *e.g.* by Harman J. at first instance in *El Capistrano SA v ATO Marketing Ltd* [1989] 2 All E.R. 572, before whom the decision in *Savings and Investment Bank Ltd*, discussed immediately below, had not been cited.
[98] [1988] Ch. 422. See also *Driver-Davidson v Cullen*, CA (unreported), November 2, 1993 (Lexis); *Tub v Paul Raymond Organisation Ltd*, CA (unreported), May 11, 1993 (Lexis).

"An affidavit sworn for the purpose of being used in interlocutory proceedings may contain statements of information or belief with the sources and grounds thereof".

This enabled the giving of what would otherwise be inadmissible hearsay. It was held that committal proceedings could be either final or interlocutory, depending on the circumstances in which the application was made (but not on the nature of the penalties sought). Purchas L.J. considered that the judge may have fallen into error in attempting to place committal proceedings as a genus into a single category, namely either interlocutory or final.

Frequently, for example, in matrimonial proceedings, orders are made for the exclusion of one or other party from the home; such orders are intended to further the resolution of the main issues, or to preserve the *status quo* pending final determination. The fact that breach of such an order may result in committal proceedings does not render the proceedings themselves a free standing *lis* (still less criminal in character). On the other hand, there may be committal proceedings arising after final determination of the main suit, and in those circumstances they could clearly not be described as interlocutory. 3–231

This debate as to the distinction between whether proceedings were interlocutory or final is now mainly of historical interest only, since there is no direct equivalent to RSC, Ord.41, r.5(2) in the CPR. It would be unnecessary now, in the light of the Civil Evidence Act 1995.[99] 3–232

The decision of the Court of Appeal in *Re C (Minors) (Hearsay Evidence: Contempt Proceedings)*[1] must be approached with some caution, since it would seem at least possible that the law as articulated in that case has been altered by the Civil Evidence Act 1995.[2] Contempt proceedings had been commenced in respect of an alleged breach of a non-molestation injunction. A husband had been observed committing breaches of the order by his children, who made statements to a minister of the church, which were contained in the report of the court welfare officer. 3–233

The judge declined to admit the evidence, on the ground that it was hearsay. He rejected the argument that it came within the scope of the exception provided for in Art.2 of the Children (Admissibility of Hearsay Evidence) Order.[3] This provided that: 3–234

"In civil proceedings before the High Court or a county court and in family proceedings in a magistrates' court, evidence given in connection with the upbringing, maintenance or welfare of a child shall be admissible notwithstanding any rule of law relating to hearsay."

---

[99] See ss.1(1) and 2(1) and CPR Pt 32, PD para.4.2.
[1] [1993] 4 All E.R. 690.
[2] paras 3–236 *et seq.*
[3] SI 1991/1115 (subsequently replaced by SI 1993/621). The treatment of hearsay evidence in family proceedings now takes account of the Civil Evidence Act 1995: see SI 1997/1056, and r.2.28(1) of the Family Proceedings Rules 1991, as amended thereby.

3–235 The judge took the view that the proposed evidence could not be said to have been tendered in connection with any of the relevant purposes, and the Court of Appeal agreed. In the words of Butler-Sloss L.J.,

> "It will be a matter of the facts of each case as to whether the connection is sufficiently substantial to justify the hearsay evidence being admitted. For example, if the injunction said to have been breached was designed to protect the child, evidence of its breach coming from the child himself would be likely to be in connection with the welfare of the child. But, in a dispute between the parents where the purpose of the injunction is to protect one parent, the evidence of a child who was not himself directly affected by it would be unlikely to demonstrate other than an insubstantial connection."[4]

3. *The Civil Evidence 1995*

3–236 Following the recommendations of the Law Commission,[5] Parliament enacted the Civil Evidence Act 1995, which greatly modifies the hearsay law. The Act provides that "In civil proceedings evidence shall not be excluded on the ground that it is hearsay".[6] Safeguards surround the introduction of such evidence. Notice of any proposal to adduce hearsay evidence must be given, and there is a power by rules of court to make provision for calling the maker of the hearsay statement if he is not called as a witness by the party introducing the hearsay.[7] "Civil proceedings" are defined by s.11 to mean " . . . civil proceedings, before any tribunal, in relation to which the strict rules of evidence apply, whether as a matter of law or by agreement of the parties." It is clear that civil contempt proceedings would be treated as "civil proceedings" for the purpose of this legislation.[8]

3–237 It was the provisions of ss.1 and 4 of the 1995 Act which led David Richards J. in a civil contempt case[9] to reject the argument that he should exclude hearsay evidence under CPR Pt 32.1(2). In view of the court's duty under s.4 to consider and decide the weight of such evidence in civil proceedings, there was no need to exclude it and it was held inappropriate to do so. He regarded Pt 32.1(2) as "primarily a case management power".

3–238 The judge also considered the extent to which Art.6 of the European Convention impacted upon the question he had to decide. He proceeded on the basis that Art.6 applied in its entirety notwithstanding the fact that the proceedings were treated under domestic law as "civil".[10] The argument was raised that no hearsay evidence should be admitted in the light of Art.6(3) if the defendant did not have the opportunity to cross-examine the maker of the

---

[4] At 693–4.
[5] Law Com. Report No.216, 1993.
[6] Civil Evidence Act 1995, s.1(1).
[7] *ibid*. s.3.
[8] *Savings and Investment Bank Ltd v Gasco Investments (Netherlands) BV (No.2)* [1988] Ch. 422; *Re C (Minors) (Hearsay Evidence: Contempt Proceedings)* [1993] 4 All E.R. 690.
[9] *Daltel Europe Ltd (in liquidation) v Makki* [2005] EWHC 749 (Ch) at [52]–[56] and [66].
[10] Citing *Berry Trade Ltd v Moussavi* [2002] 1 W.L.R. 1910; *Great Future International Ltd v Sealand Housing Corporation* [2004] EWHC 124, Ch; *Raja v Hoogstraten* [2004] EWCA Civ 968, [2004] 4 All E.R. 793.

statement.[11] The argument was rejected in the light of earlier domestic authorities on Art.6(3) and in particular *R. v Sellick*.[12] It was there held *inter alia* that it was not necessarily incompatible with Art.6(1) and (3)(d) for depositions to be read—even if there has been no opportunity to cross-examine. The approach taken was that Art.6(3)(d) was simply an illustration of matters to be taken into account in determining the overall question of whether a fair trial has been held. It will clearly be an important factor in deciding that issue in any particular case to what extent the hearsay evidence was "the sole or determinative element against the accused".[13] In the case before him, David Richards J. decided that Art.6 did not require a blanket exclusion of the evidence, particularly having regard to the fact that the relevant evidence was by no means the sole evidence against the defendant; nor would it be the case that findings against him on the relevant issues would necessarily be based on the evidence to a decisive degree. Moreover, it would be open to him to call other witnesses himself on those matters.

N. Fresh evidence on appeal

The rules regulating the production of fresh evidence on appeal in civil contempt cases are the relevant rules of criminal evidence and not those of the civil law. This was finally established by the Court of Appeal in *Irtelli v Squatriti*,[14] which noted that there was no authority as to the proper approach to be adopted in such cases. The court addressed the matter from first principles. Noting that the appellants "stand to lose their liberty", the court concluded that "where the subject is in danger of losing his liberty it is desirable that the wider terms of s.23(1) of the [Criminal Appeal] Act of 1968 should by analogy be applied".[15] The court expressly disclaimed reliance upon the rules formulated in *Ladd v Marshall*.[16]

3–239

The section was amended to implement a recommendation of the Royal Commission[17] relating to the conditions upon which fresh evidence might be admitted on hearing an appeal. The Commissioners were of the view that too high a threshold was set by the test "likely to be credible". It was thought that greater scope for doing justice would be afforded if the supposedly lower threshold "capable of belief" were to be adopted.[18]

3–240

---

[11] See, *e.g. Luca v Italy* (2003) 36 E.H.R.R. 46,.
[12] [2005] EWCA Crim 651; [2005] 2 Cr.App.R. 15.
[13] See also *R. v Arnold* [2004] EWCA Crim 1293.
[14] [1993] Q.B. 83. The relevant rules are now to be found in the Criminal Appeal Act 1968, s.23 as amended by the Criminal Appeal Act 1995, s.4, for the text of which, see *Archbold 2005*, para.7–208.
[15] At 88H.
[16] [1954] 1 W.L.R. 1489, [1954] 3 All E.R. 745.
[17] *Royal Commission on Criminal Justice* (1993) Cm. 2263.
[18] For comment, see Sir J.C. Smith, "The Criminal Appeal Act 1995: Appeals Against Conviction" [1995] Crim.L.R. 920, who argues, at p.928 that the language by which the alteration to the law was intended to be effected is unlikely to achieve its purpose of making the evidence more readily admissible.

O. The standard of proof

3–241 It was established in *Re Bramblevale Ltd*[19] that the standard of proof for civil contempt is proof beyond reasonable doubt. In the words of Lord Denning M.R.:

> "A contempt of court is an offence of a criminal character. A man may be sent to prison for it. It must be satisfactorily proved. To use the time-honoured phrase, it must be proved beyond reasonable doubt."

3–242 The contemnor had failed to produce books of account when required to do so and was committed to prison after a hearing in which he gave an account of the destruction of the books which the judge (Megarry J.) regarded as a lie. Some three weeks later, he applied for release on the ground that he no longer had the books, but Megarry J. declined to release him, taking the view that the only two possibilities were that he still had the books, in which case the continuance of the committal might induce him to produce them, or that he had destroyed them, in which case he would have committed an offence under the Companies Act, "but that he should in any event give a proper account of what had happened".[20]

3–243 Without referring to any authorities cited,[21] the Court of Appeal allowed the appeal, taking the view that the mere fact that the applicant might be thought to have told lies was not, without further evidence, sufficient to discharge the burden. As Cross L.J. pointed out, the judge himself had referred to the possibility that the books were no longer in existence, which meant that the inference that he was still in possession of them could not be justified even on the balance of probabilities, let alone beyond reasonable doubt.

3–244 Winn L.J. took a slightly different view. He rested his decision on the

> "... simple ground ... that unless the guilt of the appellant was proved with such strictness of proof as is consistent with the test 'beyond reasonable doubt'; or, as my Lord (Lord Denning) has more than once put it, consistent with such standard as the court, with its responsibility, regards as consistent with the gravity of the charge—a test which I personally prefer—the decision that he should be imprisoned for contempt of court cannot be sustained."[22]

3–245 This statement was open to the interpretation that there should be some sort of sliding scale to be applied, according to the nature of the case that the complainant is seeking to bring. Where the purpose of the proceedings is punitive, the scale is the criminal one, but where the purpose is coercive or

---

[19] [1970] 1 Ch. 128. And see *Comet Products UK Ltd v Hawkex Plastics Ltd* [1971] 2 Q.B. 67; *Churchman v Joint Shop Stewards' Committee of the Workers of the Port of London* [1972] 1 W.L.R. 1094 at 1098, Lord Denning; *Savings and Investment Bank Ltd v Gasco Investments (Netherlands) BV (No.2)* [1988] Ch. 422. See further para.12–43.
[20] The words are cited from the headnote; *quaere* whether such a requirement is consistent with the privilege against self-incrimination, considered paras 3–188 *et seq*.
[21] Although Cross L.J. had earlier decided in *Yianni v Yianni* [1966] 1 W.L.R. 120 that the appropriate standard was the criminal one.
[22] *ibid.* at 137F–H.

remedial, the lesser standard might apply.[23] This view obtains in some United States jurisdictions,[24] and until recently,[25] in some of the Australian States.[26]

English law on the point was, however, firmly established by the Court of Appeal in *Dean v Dean*.[27] The judge in the court below had sentenced the appellant to three months' imprisonment, having expressly applied the civil standard of proof.[28] The Court of Appeal was in no doubt that he had misdirected himself. In the words of Dillon L.J.:

3–246

> "I have no doubt that he was wrong . . . It has long been recognised that the procedure in contempt is of a criminal nature and that the case against the alleged contemnor must be proved to the criminal standard of proof."

This is consistent with European jurisprudence. The fact that the court has the power to impose a penalty, notwithstanding that the proceedings are regarded as "civil" for some purposes (such as hearsay) would mean that the safeguard of the criminal standard of proof would be required.[29]

P. The approach to *mens rea* as between civil and criminal contempt

A distinction is still to be drawn as to the mental element that must accompany the act of contempt. Whereas, in cases of criminal contempts, whether publication contempt falling outside the strict liability rule,[30] or non-publication contempts through interfering with the administration of justice,[31] there has been an increasing insistence that only an intention to interfere with the administration of justice will suffice. By contrast, in civil contempt, it is sufficient that the alleged contemnor be proved to have deliberately done the relevant act.[32]

3–247

The point was very clearly articulated by Lord Oliver in *Att-Gen v Times Newspapers Ltd*[33]:

3–248

---

[23] Compare the law in connection with the claim to privilege; see paras 3–141 *et seq*. As to the civil standard of proof and the notion of sliding scales, see generally the exposition of Lord Nicholls in *Re H* [1996] A.C. 563.
[24] Following *Gompers v Buck's Stove & Range Co* 221 U.S. 418.
[25] See now *Witham v Holloway* (1995) 183 C.L.R. 525.
[26] *Jendell Aust Pty Ltd v Kesby* [1983] 1 N.S.W.L.R. 127; *NSW Egg Corporation v Peek* (1987) 10 N.S.W.L.R. 72, both disapproved by the High Court of Australia in *Witham v Holloway*, last note.
[27] [1987] 1 F.L.R. 517 at 521 Dillon L.J., 522, Stephen Brown L.J., CA; see also *Bartrum v Healeswood* [1973] 10 F.S.R. 585, CA; *Kent County Council v Batchelor* (1977) L.G.R. 151, CA; *Deborah Building Equipment Ltd v Scaffco Ltd*, The Times, November 5, 1986, Potts J.
[28] Basing himself upon a recent decision of Hutchison J., *West Oxfordshire District Council v Beratec Ltd*, The Times, October 30, 1986, in which it had been held that the civil standard was sufficient.
[29] *Benham v UK* (1996) 22 E.H.R.R. 293.
[30] See paras 5–132 *et seq*.
[31] See paras 11–21 *et seq*. and the discussion of *mens rea* there.
[32] *Stancomb v Trowbridge Urban District Council* [1910] 2 Ch. 190, affirmed by the House of Lords in *Heatons Transport (St. Helens) Ltd v TGWU* [1973] A.C. 15 at 109, Lord Wilberforce; in *Director of Fair Trading v Pioneer Concrete (UK) Ltd* [1995] 1 A.C. 456 at 479–81, Lord Nolan; and in *Re M: M v Home Office* [1994] 1 A.C. 377. See also *VDU Installations Ltd v Integrated Computer Systems & Cybernetics Ltd* [1989] F.S.R. 378. For a fuller discussion, see paras 12–80 *et seq*.
[33] [1992] 1 A.C. 191 at 217–18. The passage was followed by Lord Woolf in *Re M: M v Home Office* [1994] 1 A.C. 377 at 427.

3-248 CHAPTER 3—THE DISTINCTION BETWEEN CRIMINAL/CIVIL CONTEMPT

"A distinction (which has been variously described as 'unhelpful' or 'largely meaningless') is sometimes drawn between what is described as 'civil contempt,' that is to say, contempt by a party to proceedings in a matter of procedure, and 'criminal contempt'. One particular form of contempt by a party to proceedings is that constituted by an intentional act which is in breach of the order of a competent court. Where this occurs as a result of the act of a party who is bound by the order or of others acting at his direction or on his instigation, it constituted a civil contempt by him which is punishable by the court at the instance of the party for whose benefit the order was made and which can be waived by him. The intention with which the act was done will, of course, be of the highest relevance in the determination of the penalty (if any) to be imposed by the court, but the liability here is a strict one in the sense that all that requires to be proved is service of the order and the subsequent doing by the party bound not by the party bound of that which is prohibited. When, however, the prohibited act is done not by the party bound himself but by a third party, a stranger to the litigation, that person may also be liable for contempt. There is, however, this essential distinction that his liability is for criminal contempt and arises not because the contemnor is himself affected by the prohibition contained in the order but because his act constitutes a wilful interference with the administration of justice by the court in the proceedings in which the order was made. Here the liability is not strict in the sense referred to, for there has to be shown not only knowledge of the order but an intention to interfere with or impede the administration of justice—an intention which can of course be inferred from the circumstances."

3-249   The mere breach of an order is a contempt even in a case where the act or omission is *bona fide*, and based on legal advice.[34] Indeed, circumstances might arise in which not only would the client be unable to escape liability on the basis of reliance upon legal advice, but also the solicitors themselves would be liable for encouraging or inducing such a breach. This would be a criminal contempt, but only if the solicitors were in a position to know that they were assisting in a course of conduct which would constitute such a breach.[35]

Q. A possible distinction as to the relevance of duress

3-250   A judge in *The Coca-Cola Company v Aytacli*[36] has expressed the opinion that, in civil proceedings for contempt, the factor of duress could only serve as mitigation rather than as a defence. This followed, in his view, from the Court of Appeal's decision in *Coca-Cola Company & Schweppes Ltd v Peter John Gilbey*.[37] Whether this is a correct interpretation of this decision is perhaps open to question, since the Court of Appeal appeared to do little more than acknowledge that there might arise a situation in which a person failing to comply with a court order through personal fear might persuade the court on that ground to vary or discharge the order as a matter of discretion. The concept of

---

[34] *Re the Mileage Conference Group of the Tyre Manufacturers' Conference Ltd's Agreement* [1966] 1 W.L.R. 1137. See also *Re M: M v Home Office* [1994] 1 A.C. 377 at 397D and 426–7, HL. But see the discussion of *Irtelli v Squatriti* [1993] Q.B. 83 at para.12–88.
[35] See Nicholls J. in *Taylor v NUM, The Times*, November 20, 1985, in the context of those who had given professional or other advice to the NUM during its period of sequestration arising from the miners' strike of 1984–5.
[36] [2003] EWHC 91 (Ch).
[37] [1996] F.S.R. 23.

duress was not expressly addressed, although no doubt on a committal application the exercise of the court's discretion as to the appropriate disposal *might* be tempered by convincing evidence of conduct which could be considered as tantamount to duress.

The judge in the *Aytacli* case also expressed the view that there is a distinction between civil and criminal contempt as to where the burden of proof lies for the purpose of establishing duress. He posited the doubtful proposition[38] that Art.6 applies only to criminal cases, and that in a civil case it was not for the applicant to prove that duress did not apply. This distinction was also said to be based on the earlier decision. Again, this may be reading too much into those judgments. One cannot find any statement to the effect, for example, that one who is alleged to be in breach of a court order will necessarily have a "defence" provided only that he establishes the familiar ingredients of the criminal concept of duress; nor yet was the question addressed, in terms, as to whether an applicant for committal in such circumstances will ever need to adduce evidence on the allegation of duress. Nevertheless, it is probably fair to say that the applicant will generally need to prove no more than a breach of the order (or undertaking) to the criminal standard. Once that is established, then there is a contempt. Whether committal (or indeed any penalty) is appropriate will be for the court to decide in all the circumstances of the case. The contemnor may establish threats or pressure on him (not necessarily fulfilling the criteria of duress in a criminal context) which would so engage the sympathies of the court as to justify taking a lenient course. What does emerge, however, from the Court of Appeal judgment is that this is likely to occur only "in the very most exceptional set of circumstances".[39]

3–251

In the case of criminal contempt, by contrast, it is clear that the defence is in theory available. In *R. v K*,[40] the appellant had been committed for contempt for refusing to give evidence against a person accused of wounding him in prison. Having given a witness statement and agreed to give evidence, the appellant changed his mind, claiming that threats had been made that grave harm would be done to him and his family if he were to give evidence. At the trial, he was summarily sentenced to three months imprisonment for failing to testify (with the result that the prosecution collapsed). It was held that this was a plain case of the appellant's mind being overborne by duress, as to which he should have been permitted (with the assistance of proper legal advice) to testify, and since this had not been allowed by the trial judge the finding of contempt could not stand.

3–252

The precise circumstances in which duress will be available as a defence, however, are not entirely clear. In *R. v Z (Hasan)*,[41] the House of Lords emphasised the importance of the limitation that the defendant must have had no opportunity to avoid the threat save by complying with it, and disapproved the decision of *R. v Hudson and Taylor*.[42] In that case, two young women (17 and 19)

3–253

---

[38] See para.3–5.
[39] *per* Simon Brown L.J. at 32.
[40] (1984) 78 Cr.App.R. 82, 148 J.P. 410. The case appears not to have been cited to the House of Lords in *R. v Hasan* [2005] UKHL 22; [2005] 2 W.L.R. 709 considered below.
[41] [2005] UKHL 22; [2005] 2 W.L.R. 709.
[42] [1971] 2 Q.B. 202.

had been convicted of perjury. Their defence to that charge was that they had been threatened with violence should they give truthful evidence at a trial (the person threatening being present in court when they were due to give evidence). The appeal was allowed on the basis that the facts were capable of giving rise to a plea of duress, which the jury had not been permitted to consider by the trial judge.

3–254   At issue were the two questions, namely whether the threat of violence was sufficiently immediate and whether any effective police protection would have been available. So far as the first was concerned, the Court of Appeal in *Hudson and Taylor* had taken the view that it was enough that the execution of the threat was merely imminent—it did not have to be immediate. So far as official protection was concerned, the court took the view that it was necessary to distinguish situations where the police protection would have been adequate from those situations where it would not be. This aspect of the decision was commented upon adversely by Lord Bingham in *Hasan* who said that whilst he understood why the court in *Hudson* " . . . had sympathy with the predicament of the young appellants", he nevertheless could not consistently with principle "accept that a witness testifying . . . has no opportunity to avoid complying with a threat incapable of execution then or there".[43]

3–255   This dilemma is likely to arise with increasing frequency, but how far the decision in *Hasan* will have effect in the field of contempt where the witness refuses to answer through fear (rather than telling lies, as in *Hudson and Taylor*) is problematic. Lord Bingham's remarks in *Hasan* are strictly *obiter*, since the decision turned on the fact that the appellant there had voluntarily associated with the people who subsequently subjected him to duress, the House holding that a defendant is "not entitled to rely on the defence of duress where as a result of his voluntary association with known criminals he had foreseen or ought reasonably to have foreseen the risk of being subjected to any compulsion by threats of violence". Given his incarceration at the time, the appellant in *R. v K* could hardly be taken to task for "associating" with persons of a violent disposition. That being said, judges contemplating use of the contempt sanction to punish a failure or refusal to testify might now be expected to scrutinise with great care any claim that a witness acted out of fear (especially perhaps in the light of witness protection schemes[44] that have become available since *Hudson and Taylor* was decided).

---

[43] At [27].
[44] See paras 10–165 *et seq*.

CHAPTER 4

THE STATUTORY REGIME FOR STRICT LIABILITY

		PARA
I.	The Strict Liability Rule	4–1
II.	Restrictions on the *Actus Reus* of Strict Liability Contempts	4–52
III.	Categories of Persons Thought Susceptible to Influence	4–110
IV.	Strict Liability Contempt and Abuse of Process	4–148
V.	When Are Proceedings "Active"?	4–174
VI.	Section 7 and the Attorney-General	4–183
VII.	Who May Be Liable For Publication and Upon What Basis?	4–191
VIII.	Innocent Publication or Distribution	4–236
IX.	The Right to Report Court Proceedings	4–263
X.	Discussing Public Affairs	4–293
XI.	What Are the "Defences" Preserved by Section 6?	4–319

I. THE STRICT LIABILITY RULE

A. The nature of "the strict liability rule"

Since a finding of contempt of court may have serious consequences for the liberty of the subject,[1] it would accord with general criminal law principles to require the applicant to prove *mens rea* on the part of the alleged contemnor, in relation to each element of the *actus reus*. However, s.1 of the Contempt of Court Act 1981 renders this unnecessary in cases to which the "strict liability rule" applies. The section provides that:

4–1

> "In this Act, 'the strict liability rule' means the rule of law whereby conduct may be treated as a contempt of court as tending to interfere with the course of justice in particular legal proceedings regardless of intent to do so."[2]

It is couched in terms that purport to describe an existing rule of law without defining it, and it is sometimes supposed that there was indeed such a pre-

4–2

---

[1] Including in the quasi-criminal context of civil contempt: see, *e.g.* Neill L.J. in *Dean v Dean* [1987] F.C.R. 86, 1 F.L.R. 517 and *R. v D* [1984] A.C. 778 at 806, *per* Lord Brandon. The general question as to whether contempts can be classified as "misdemeanours" is discussed para.3–67 (criminal contempts) and para.3–78 (civil contempts).

[2] This phrase "regardless of intent to do so" was considered by Falconer J. in *Roger Bullivant Ltd v Ellis*, *Financial Times*, April 16, 1986 (Lexis), discussed at paras 4–185 *et seq.*

4–2 Chapter 4—The Statutory Regime for Strict Liability

existing rule[3]; but it may be doubted whether such a "rule" could truly be said to have come into being prior to this statutory formulation. In the many common law cases prior to the Act determining the scope of *mens rea* in the law of contempt, there appears to be no mention of a "strict liability rule",[4] and the Phillimore Committee does not characterise the relevant law in such terms.[5] By contrast, there *is* a strict liability rule in the law of torts, more generally referred to as "the rule in *Rylands v Fletcher*".[6]

4–3 The true nature of the "strict liability rule" in the context of contempt is, it is suggested, a term of art[7] coined by the draftsman as the basis of a statutory framework, set out in the first seven sections of the Act under the cross-heading "Strict Liability". The Act was intended to confine the impact of strict liability, in the context of publication contempt, because of the risk of interfering with freedom of communication when it may not be necessary. The "rule" is essentially a convenient drafting formula for so limiting the scope of strict liability. This was an integral part of the attempt to effect a "permanent shift"[8] in emphasis away from protecting the administration of justice in the direction of protecting freedom of speech, and thereby to achieve compliance with Art.10 of the European Convention on Human Rights.[9]

B. The scheme of the Act

4–4 The Act narrowly defines the *actus reus* of the relevant publication contempts, and then goes on to make provision for a number of escape mechanisms that are available even in respect of publications which give rise to a substantial risk of serious prejudice. These are:

(1) innocent publication or distribution (s.3)[10];

(2) contemporary reporting of proceedings (s.4(1))[11];

---

[3] See, *e.g.* Sir John Donaldson M.R. in *Att-Gen v News Group Newspapers plc* [1987] 1 Q.B. 1, 12F: "In the years immediately before the passing of the Act, the courts were engaged in the exercise of reconciling the rule in *Bonnard v Perryman* [1891] 2 Ch. 269 with the strict liability rule". And see Lloyd L.J. in *Att-Gen v Newspaper Publishing plc* [1988] Ch. 333, 381B where he appears also to take it for granted that there was such a rule. See also *Al Megrahi and Fhima v Times Newspapers Ltd*, 1999 S.C.C.R. 824 (High Court of Justiciary), where the Lord Justice Clerk commented that "... sections 1 and 2 of the Contempt of Court Act 1981 ... *restate in statutory form* what is described as the strict liability rule" (emphasis added) and *Robb v Caledonian Newspapers Ltd*, 1995 S.L.T. 631 at 634.

[4] An electronic search through Lexis and the Law Reports, for example, discloses no reference to "the strict liability rule" in pre-Act cases. The modern rule is discussed at paras 4–15 *et seq*.

[5] Lord Scarman in *Re F (Orse A) (A Minor) (Publication of Information)* [1977] Fam. 58 at 96D refers to "a rule of strict liability", but it is clear in the context that he means no more than to acknowledge that there were cases where no *mens rea* needed to be proved as to one or more elements in certain types of contempt.

[6] See *Clerk and Lindsell on Torts* (18th ed., 2001), ch.20.

[7] Sir John Donaldson M.R. in *Att-Gen v Newspaper Publishing plc* [1988] Ch. 333 at 374A refers to the strict liability rule as "a term of art".

[8] *Att-Gen v Newspaper Publishing plc* [1988] Ch. 333 at 382D–E, *per* Lloyd L.J.

[9] Following the decision in *Sunday Times v United Kingdom* (1979) 2 E.H.R.R. 245.

[10] See paras 4–236 *et seq.*

[11] paras 4–265 *et seq.*

(3) discussion of public affairs in good faith (s.5).[12]

In addition, s.6(a) preserves any existing defence[13] at common law under "the strict liability rule".

C. The uncertain scope of strict liability at common law

Prior to the Act there was clear authority that the publication of matter calculated to prejudice the fair trial of a pending cause was in certain respects what would now be described as an "absolute" or "strict liability"[14] offence. As to printers or publishers, notwithstanding that they might be unaware of the contents of what they printed, this was established by at least 1742. In *St. James's Evening Post*[15] Lord Hardwicke L.C. found that an edition of a journal contained material which was in contempt, and that the authors of the article intended to prejudice the course of justice. It was argued for the publisher that she was not aware of the nature of the journal, and that her trade was merely that of printing. Her argument was analogous to the defence of "innocent dissemination" long recognised in the law of libel for carriers and newsagents,[16] but not until recently for printers.[17] It is not made clear in the report of the case whether her lack of knowledge was of the details of the particular publication or of the fact that they were calculated to prejudice pending proceedings.

Lord Hardwicke nevertheless committed the publisher to the Fleet saying[18]:

" ... though it is true, this is a trade, yet they must take care to do it with prudence and caution; for if they print any thing that is libellous, it is no excuse to say that the printer had no knowledge of the contents, and was entirely ignorant of its being libellous; and so is the rule at law, and I will always adhere to the strict rules of law in these cases."

The reference to "the rule at law" appears to relate to the law of criminal libel, which was then a strict liability offence so far as the content of the publication was concerned.

---

[12] paras 4–293 *et seq*.
[13] There is considerable doubt as to what defences the draftsman might have had in mind. See the discussion at paras 4–319 *et seq*.
[14] ed. D. Ormerod, Smith and Hogan, *Criminal Law* (11th ed., 2005) p.139 prefer the terminology of "strict liability" rather than "absolute" offences, the latter perhaps suggesting that absolutely no proof of any element of *mens rea* is required. There are very few offences of which this is true. Usually, to describe an offence as a "strict liability offence" is to do no more than recognise that no proof is required as to one or more of the elements of the *actus reus* of the offence.
[15] *Roach v Garvan* (1742) 2 Atk. 469, 26 E.R. 683. See paras 1–60 *et seq*.
[16] See, *e.g. Gatley on Libel and Slander* (10th ed., 2004) see para.6–18.
[17] See the Defamation Act 1996, s.1, which extends the principle for which she was contending much more widely, by excluding from liability a person who is considered not to be an "author, editor or publisher". This would protect a printer (s.1(3)(a)), broadcaster (s.1(3)(d)) or provider of computer network services (s.1(3)(e)). See *Gatley on Libel and Slander* (10th ed., 2004) paras 6–19 *et seq*. It is arguable that the law should be the same for contempt in this respect, since similar policy considerations arise in relation to freedom of communication. It would appear that Lord Hardwicke saw no reason to distinguish libel from contempt in this respect: see the passage cited at para.4–6.
[18] (1742) 2 Atk. 469 at 472, 26 E.R. 683 at 685.

4–7 CHAPTER 4—THE STATUTORY REGIME FOR STRICT LIABILITY

4–7   In *Ex p. Jones*,[19] one of the defendants had printed a pamphlet which was intended by its author "to procure a different species of judgment from that, which would be administered in the ordinary course; and by flattering the Judge to taint the source of justice". This was held to be a contempt, not only on the part of the author, but also on that of the printers, of whose position Lord Erskine L.C. said:

> "the maxim *actus non facit reum, nisi mens sit rea* cannot be made applicable to this subject in the ordinary administration of justice as the effect would be, that the ends of justice would be defeated by contrivance."

4–8   It should be noted, however, that Lord Erskine declined to exercise his jurisdiction in respect of three of the printers who were apparently unaware of what had been written. But a fourth printer, having apparently at first said that the pamphlet ought not to be published, nonetheless did print it. Lord Erskine continued, " . . . though the *locus penitentiae* was afforded to him, and he was called upon not to print any more, he proceeded, until he had notice of this Petition".

4–9   Two later cases, one at first instance[20] and one in the Court of Appeal,[21] appeared to suggest that *mens rea* had become a necessary constituent of this form of contempt. In both, the defence was raised that the authors and publishers were unaware that the relevant legal proceedings had been commenced, and in each case the application to commit was dismissed. Yet in neither case were the earlier authorities expressly distinguished. For a considerable period of time, therefore, it was perceived that there was a rule that those responsible for publishing prejudicial material would have a defence[22] if either they did not know that legal proceedings were concurrent with the publication, or they were unaware that legal proceedings were imminent at all; it was never suggested that mere ignorance of the content of a publication would afford protection.

4–10   Two mid-twentieth century decisions appeared to impose upon publishers and journalists a more burdensome form of strict liability without clearly defining its rationale or scope. In *R. v Evening Standard Co Ltd*,[23] a reporter sent in a report of what had purportedly taken place in court but which was seriously in error and contained matter that had been ruled inadmissible. The Divisional Court held that the report was calculated to prejudice the fair trial of the case. The court further found, however, that the reporter had not deliberately set out to misrepresent the evidence. Although the reporting was made the subject of adverse comment by the court, no moral blame was seen to attach to the editor of the newspaper which published the report, because he had no reason to suppose the report inaccurate.

---

[19] (1806) 13 Ves. Jun 237 at 239, 33 E.R. 283 at 284.
[20] *Metropolitan Music Hall v Lake* (1889) 58 L.J. Ch. 513.
[21] *In Re the Marquis Townsend* (1906) 22 T.L.R. 341.
[22] The cases preceded the landmark decision of the House of Lords in *Woolmington v DPP* [1935] A.C. 462, which held that the burden of proof rests on the prosecution, and so it is probably not inaccurate to express the matter in terms of "defence".
[23] [1954] 1 Q.B. 578.

Nevertheless, relying on *St. James's Evening Post*, the court held that both were liable in contempt. The underlying reason would seem to be that the only *mens rea* required was as to the act of publication itself.[24]

Shortly afterwards, a newspaper published a report calling in sensational terms for the prosecution of an alleged brothel keeper, who had already been arrested and charged with precisely that offence. The terms of the report were such that they were held to have been calculated to prejudice the trial. Neither the editor nor the reporter knew that the case was pending, although the court in *R. v Odhams Press Ltd*[25] was critical of both. In the case of the editor, "he seemed to think this was no concern of his, and that he was entitled to rely on his reporter without more". The response to this was that "the tradition of English journalism [is] that the editor takes responsibility for what is published in his paper". As to the reporter, "the evidence falls far short of showing that standard of care which persons indulging in this sort of journalism are bound to take". They and the publishing company were held in contempt and all were fined. Thus, in this instance at least, it did not prove to be a sufficient reason for escaping liability that the person accused of contempt was unaware of the pending proceedings. The court seems to have assumed that there was a duty find out the facts.

4–11

The court considered that the two later cases,[26] which stated in very general terms that *mens rea* was required in cases of contempt, could not be taken to detract from the principles established in *St. James's Evening Post* and *Ex parte Jones*.[27] Yet it seems clear that the court was influenced by the carelessness of the journalist and editor, saying that "in matters of the description with which we are now dealing and which urge the prosecution of an alleged criminal, the publication is at the risk of those responsible for it".[28] In short, although the court did not use the terminology of negligence, it was principally concerned to punish want of care.[29]

4–12

In 1968, the same approach was still being followed. The *Sunday Times* made reference to previous convictions of one Michael X[30] at a time when criminal proceedings were pending against him at Reading. The reporter who wrote the article knew that proceedings were pending but showed lack of care in failing to appreciate the possible effect of the article on the proceedings. No proceedings were taken against him, but the printers, the publishing company and editor were brought before the Divisional Court. The editor did not know proceedings were

4–13

---

[24] The court declined to impose any penalty upon the reporter, albeit with some hesitation: " . . . he made an honest mistake, that is to say, he did not deliberately send up that which he knew to be untrue; but, perhaps owing to ill-health or other reasons, he had a confused idea in his mind". As to the editor, it was said: " . . . he had no reason to suppose that the report telephoned to him by the reporter was otherwise than accurate".
[25] [1957] 1 Q.B. 73.
[26] *Metropolitan Music Hall v Lake* (1889) 58 L.J. Ch. 513, and *Re the Marquis Townsend* (1906) 22 T.L.R. 341.
[27] See the discussion at paras 4–5 *et seq*.
[28] *R. v Odhams Press Ltd* [1957] 1 Q.B. 73 at 83, Lord Goddard.
[29] See Glanville Williams, *Criminal Law: The General Part* (2nd ed., 1961), para.85 ("responsibility for contempt of court").
[30] *R. v Thomson Newspapers Ltd Ex p. Att-Gen* [1968] 1 W.L.R. 1, [1968] 1 All E.R. 268.

4-13 pending and had sought to devise an efficient system to prevent matter of this nature being published. In this case it had broken down. All three were held to be in contempt, but no fine was imposed upon the printers "having regard to the relation between the parties", nor upon the editor, in view of the care that he had taken.

4-14 There was thus a degree of uncertainty as to the basic principles to be applied, which inevitably had a "chilling effect" upon reports and investigative journalists. It is thus ironic that the law was described during this period by Brabin J. in *Att-Gen v LWT Ltd*[31] in the following terms: "the law of contempt of court is old, free of conflicting decisions and therefore certain. It is to be expected since it concerns a power described as being coeval with the foundation and institution of the courts." Eventually, in *Att-Gen v Times Newspapers Ltd*,[32] the House of Lords resolved any doubts in favour of the more restrictive approach, and confirmed the continuing vitality of "technical contempt". As a result of the subsequent decision of the European Court of Human Rights,[33] however, it became clear that strict liability could not survive without clear restrictions or confinement.

D. The statutory terminology further examined

4-15 It is now necessary to examine the individual elements of s.1(1), with a view to showing how the Act is intended to confine the ambit of the strict liability rule.

1. *"Particular legal proceedings"*

4-16 Section 1 of the 1981 Act[34] is concerned with interference with the administration of justice in "particular legal proceedings". Thus, publications which interfere with the course of justice in a wider sense, without reference to any specific proceedings, are outside "the strict liability rule"; for example, the publication of matter "scandalising" the court, or in breach of a permanent reporting restriction (*e.g.* in relation to the identity of a witness) after the proceedings had been completed,[35] or details of a jury's deliberations.[36] Such publications may often relate to particular proceedings, in a loose sense, but they are punished not for their interference with those proceedings but for the effect on the administration of justice more generally.

---

[31] [1972] 3 All E.R. 1146 at 1149c.
[32] [1974] A.C. 273, discussed more fully at paras 1–87 *et seq.*
[33] *Sunday Times v United Kingdom* (1979) 2 E.H.R.R. 245.
[34] The text of which is set out at para.4–1.
[35] See, *e.g. Official Solicitor v News Group Newspapers plc* [1994] 2 F.L.R. 174 where the editor and publishers of a daily newspaper were held in contempt under s.12 of the Administration of Justice Act 1960 because of disclosure of information received by the court in confidence in connection with contested Children Act proceedings. See also *Re F (Orse A) (A Minor)* [1977] Fam. 58.
[36] See now s.8 of the Act, considered more fully at paras 11–349 *et seq.*

2. "Court"

The contempt contemplated by the Act has to relate to the proceedings of a "court". Section 19 defines the terms "court" and "legal proceedings". "Court" includes any tribunal or body exercising the judicial power of the state,[37] and "legal proceedings" are to be construed accordingly.[38] The phrase "the judicial power of the state" is taken from the speech of Lord Scarman in *Att-Gen v BBC*.[39] The decision in that case indicates that the phrase includes (a) tribunals which have inherent or statutory jurisdiction to deal with contempts themselves, and also (b) those which only the Divisional Court of the Queen's Bench Division can protect as part of its jurisdiction over inferior courts.

The position may be summarised for present purposes as follows. A tribunal cannot be protected unless it is a court. It may be a court if it is described as such, whether traditionally (*e.g.* the High Court of Justice) or by statute (*e.g.* the county court or the Crown Court), or if it adopts procedures normally associated with courts. Yet this latter characteristic would not *necessarily* mean that any particular tribunal was exercising the judicial power of the state; the critical question is whether the decision it seeks to reach is a judicial rather than an administrative determination.

Indeed, not even every "court" conducts legal proceedings. Many courts carry out administrative rather than judicial functions. A judicial power means the power which every sovereign authority requires in order to decide controversies between its citizens, or between itself and its citizens, whether in relation to life, liberty or property. The exercise of such a power cannot begin until a tribunal which has the jurisdiction to give a binding and authoritative decision (whether subject to appeal or not) is called upon to take action.[40] The application of these principles is not always easy.[41] It has been demonstrated, both before and after the Act, that the borderline is unclear.

The case of *Att-Gen v BBC*[42] concerned a local valuation tribunal which was hearing an appeal on the question whether premises belonging to a religious organisation were exempt from rates because they were used for public religious meetings. Lord Scarman took the view that the tribunal merely had power to

---

[37] Contempt of Court Act 1981, s.19.
[38] The meaning of "court" and "legal proceedings" is more fully considered under the head of jurisdiction. See paras 13–2 *et seq.*
[39] [1981] A.C. 303 at 359. More fully discussed at paras 13–45 *et seq.* Tribunals to which the law of contempt applies have been held to include, for example, mental health review tribunals and industrial tribunals (now "employment tribunals": Employment Rights (Dispute Resolution) Act 1998, s.1). See respectively *P v Liverpool Daily Post and Echo Newspapers plc* [1991] 2 A.C. 370, HL; *Peach Grey & Co (a Firm) v Sommers* [1995] I.C.R. 549, [1995] 2 All E.R. 513.
[40] See Lord Scarman in *Att-Gen v BBC* at 359, approving Griffith C.J. in *Huddart, Parker & Co v Moorehead* [1909] 8 C.L.R. 330 at 357.
[41] See the discussion in ch.13.
[42] [1981] A.C. 303.

4–20 correct the valuation list. It imposed no tax, nor any liability on citizens to pay money or to do anything else.[43]

4–21 Modern statutory tribunals would appear to fall within the ambit of contempt only if statute so provides.[44] Section 20 of the 1981 Act[45] made it clear, for example, that the provisions of the Act (which would include the strict liability rule) applied to any tribunal to which the Tribunals of Inquiry (Evidence) Act 1921 applied. It was provided in s.1(2) of that statute that if any person did anything which would, if the tribunal had been a court of law having power to commit for contempt, have been contempt of that court the High Court, or in Scotland the court of Session could punish that person in like manner as if he had been guilty of contempt of the court. At the time the 1921 Act was passed the draftsman would have had in mind the common law of contempt. Perhaps from an abundance of caution, the 1981 draftsman thought it necessary to ensure that these provisions would extend to the statutory law of contempt embraced within the 1981 Act.

4–22 The provisions of the Inquiries Act 2005 follow a different pattern. Although there is still provision[46] for enforcement by the High Court or Court of Session following certification by the chairman of the inquiry, this is limited to circumstances where there has been failure to comply with a notice under s.19 (restricting attendance at an inquiry or disclosure or publication of evidence or documents) or s.21 (requiring a person to attend to give evidence or produce documents), or an order made by an inquiry, or where a person threatens to do so. In such circumstances, the court may make such an order by way of enforcement or otherwise as it could make if the matter had arisen in proceedings before the court.

4–23 There is also a regime of criminal offences,[47] which include doing anything intended to have the effect of distorting or altering any evidence or document that is given, produced or provided to the inquiry panel, preventing evidence or documents being so provided and intentionally suppressing, concealing, altering or destroying a relevant document. Failure to do anything that a person is required to do by a notice under s.21 is also included[48] within the category of criminal offences, as well as being capable of enforcement through the court.

---

[43] This decision will be considered under the head of jurisdiction, along with a number of cases subsequent to the Act at paras 13–1 *et seq.*: *Badry v DPP of Mauritius* [1983] 2 A.C. 297; *P v Liverpool Daily Post and Echo Newspapers plc* [1991] 2 A.C. 370, HL (mental health review tribunals); *Peach Grey & Co (A Firm) v Sommers* [1995] I.C.R. 549, 2 All E.R. 513 (industrial tribunals).
[44] *Att-Gen v BBC* [1981] A.C. 303 at 337, Lord Dilhorne, 342 Lord Salmon. See also *Badry v DPP of Mauritius* [1983] 2 A.C. 297 at 307.
[45] At the time of writing s.20 itself has not been repealed although the 1921 Act with which it is concerned was repealed and replaced with effect from June 2005 by the Inquiries Act 2005.
[46] s.36.
[47] s.35.
[48] s.35(1).

3. "Publications"

The Act having described the strict liability rule then provides that it applies only in relation to "publications"; a concept which, in the context of defamation at common law, embraces any act whereby information is communicated from one person to another. Section 2(1) of the 1981 Act provides:

> "The strict liability rule applies only in relation to publications, and for this purpose 'publication' includes any speech, writing, [programme included in a programme service][49] or other communication in whatever form, which is addressed to the public at large or any section of the public."

This wide approach to the concept of publication is consistent with the common law. Before the Act, for example, there had—apart from the newspaper cases—been instances of contempt proceedings (just as there had been instances of defamation) in cases where the publication had been oral,[50] by way of cartoons,[51] placards,[52] theatrical performance,[53] a captioned news film,[54] television broadcast[55] and even in waxworks.[56]

The broad language of the section ("communication in whatever form") clearly suggests that the statute was by no means intended to limit the application of the strict liability rule to any particular category such as, for example, media publications. The need for restriction or confinement, arising from the policy of Art.10, is intended to be fulfilled by the last words of the subsection, which indicate the importance attached to establishing communication "to the public at large or any section of the public". This aspect of the wording is separately considered below.[57]

---

[49] The words in square brackets were substituted by the Broadcasting Act 1990, s.203(1) Sch.20, para.31(1). It is provided by s.2(5) of the Contempt of Court Act, also added by the same provisions, that "programme service" is to have the same meaning as in the Broadcasting Act 1990.

[50] *R. v Castro, Onslow's and Whalley's Case*; *Skipworth and the Defendant's case* (1873) L.R. 9 Q.B. 219.

[51] *R. v Evening News Ex p. Campbell*, *The Times*, October 27, 1925; *R. v Edmonton Sun Publishing Ltd* (1981) 62 C.C.C. (2d) 318 at 323.

[52] *R. v Daily Herald Ex p. Rouse* (1931) 75 Sol. Jo. 119 ("Another blazing car murder").

[53] *R. v Williams and Romney* (1823) 2 L.J. (O.S.) K.B. Mich Term. 30. See also *R. v Steadman*, February 1994, where Bell J. granted an injunction restraining the performance of a play, "Maxwell—the Musical" while proceedings were pending *inter alia* against the two sons of Robert Maxwell. Compare *Keegstra v One Yellow Rabbit Theatre Association* (1992) 91 D.L.R. (4th) 532, where the Alberta Court of Appeal declined to interfere with the exercise of discretion by a judge who had granted a *quia timet* injunction to restrain production of a play during the trial of criminal proceedings. This was on the basis that "he was not obviously wrong in deciding that a real and substantial risk existed that a juror might be influenced".

[54] *R. v Hutchinson Ex p. MacMahon* [1936] 2 All E.R. 1514 (film of arrest, with the misleading caption, "Attempt on the King's life").

[55] See *Att-Gen v BBC, Hat Trick Productions* [1997] E.M.L.R. 76; *Att-Gen v ITN Ltd* [1995] 2 All E.R. 370; *Att-Gen v LWT Ltd* [1972] 3 All E.R. 1146 at 1152a–b, Brabin J.; see also *R. v Savundranayagan* [1968] 1 W.L.R. 1761.

[56] *Gilham* (1828) 1 M. & M. 165, 173 E.R. 1118. See also *Monson v Tussauds* [1894] 1 Q.B. 671.

[57] paras 4–34 *et seq*.

4–27 CHAPTER 4—THE STATUTORY REGIME FOR STRICT LIABILITY

4. *"Publication" on the internet*

4–27 The concept of "publication" needs to be carefully addressed in the light of communications made *via* the internet.[58] The matter was considered in the Scottish case of *HMA v Beggs (No.2)*.[59] Very striking and prejudicial allegations about a man accused of murder were published in the media in 1999 but still remained available on the Internet in 2001 both as archive newspaper material and on other websites.[60] These included, for example, details of previous convictions (including one in England for murder, later quashed on appeal) and a description of him as the "gay ripper". It seems that the accused found the material at the end of the first day of the trial and complained of contempt. It was submitted by the Advocate Depute that the 1981 Act contemplates criminal sanctions only in respect of "conduct" consisting of "publication" at a particular time and, specifically, at a time when proceedings are active. A distinction should thus be drawn between "publishing", as such, and the archiving of material. An analogy was drawn in argument between having to search on the Internet and approaching a librarian for access to stored back copies of national newspapers. Availability, it was submitted, is not the same as "publication". It was recognised, however, that criminal behaviour could on occasion consist in a failure to take action.[61]

4–28 In the circumstances, it was argued first that the availability of the allegations for access did not constitute publication at a time when the proceedings were active; alternatively, that availability on the web did not create a substantial risk of serious prejudice—not least because it should not be supposed that a juror would be likely to pursue such research, especially where the court has directed him or her to focus only on the evidence. Lord Osborne concluded that material communicated on the internet, during the period when proceedings were active, was such that s.2 of the Contempt of Court Act *could* apply. He found some support for that view in the English case of *Godfrey v Demon Internet*.[62] On the other hand, he decided on the facts of the case before him, and the nature of the archive material, that it had not been demonstrated that there was a substantial risk of prejudice. In that context, he derived assistance from the observations of Schiemann L.J. in *Att-Gen v MGN Ltd*.[63]

---

[58] See generally M. Collins, *Defamation and the Internet* (2nd ed. 2005) Oxford University Press.
[59] 2002 S.L.T. 139, S.C.C.R. 879, High Court of Justiciary.
[60] The Attorney-General warned media organisations on November 25, 2004 that they must be prepared to remove archive material when it gives rise to a substantial risk of serious prejudice, *Media Lawyer*, January 2005, p.4. The Lord Chancellor, however, has pointed out that the retention of online archive material is not necessarily contempt. In an address to the Fleet Street Lawyers' Society, Lord Falconer is reported as saying that there was a need to " . . . look for something special to make it a risk" and that " . . . there must be additional factors that make the risk substantial": see *Media Lawyer Online*, April 27, 2005. But see the discussion of the significance of the word "substantial" at paras 4–54 *et seq*. See also the conclusions of the Law Commission in its paper, *Defamation and the Internet: A Preliminary Investigation*, Scoping Study No.2 (December 2002) that no legal change was required, at [1.18]–[1.19].
[61] See the discussion in the context of contempt in *Att-Gen v Observer Ltd* [1988] 1 All E.R. 385, 399 at para.5–28 n.50.
[62] [1999] 4 All E.R. 342.
[63] [1997] 1 All E.R. 456 at 461–2; see para.4–86.

5. Re-publication

Suppose that a prejudicial piece of information has been made public by the media; would there be a defence for someone who republished that information, to the effect that he had not been the *original* publisher? It is submitted that it could not be a defence merely to assert that one was not the first to place the relevant information before the public. It would always depend whether what was published was, at the time of publication, such as to create a substantial risk of serious prejudice. It is true that it may sometimes prove difficult to establish that any individual publication will, in the light of an existing climate, in itself cause any tangible or marginal risk.[64] All will depend upon the circumstances.

4–29

It would be wrong to assume, however, that the fact that some piece of information is already in the public domain will prevent a finding of contempt.[65] In this respect, the law of contempt might appear to differ to some extent from that relating to commercially confidential information. The general approach in that context is that information should be regarded as either confidential or not; once it is in the public domain, it can no longer be treated as confidential.[66] Where, on the other hand, the information is of a personal character, tending to infringe the privacy of an individual, it seems that the courts may be less inclined to adopt this "once and for all" approach.[67]

4–30

6. "Includes" is equivalent to "means"

Whenever the word "includes" appears in a definition section,[68] one needs to ask the question whether "includes" indicates that the examples thereafter set out are intended to be exhaustive. The issue arose in *Dilworth v Commissioner of Stamps*[69] in the context of a statute defining charitable purposes as "including" various categories of act. The House of Lords took the view it was an exhaustive definition. Lord Watson said[70]:

4–31

> "The word 'include' is very generally used in interpretation clauses in order to enlarge the meaning of words or phrases occurring in the body of the statute; and when it is so used these words or phrases must be construed as comprehending, not only such things as may signify according to their natural import, but also those things which the interpretation clause declares they shall include. But the word 'include' is susceptible of another construction, which may become imperative, if the context of the Act is sufficient to show that it was not merely employed for the purpose of adding to the natural significance of the words or expressions defined. It may be equivalent to 'mean

---

[64] See, *e.g.* Schiemann L.J. in *Att-Gen v MGN Ltd* [1997] 1 All E.R. 456 at 463g–j.
[65] *Att-Gen v ITN Ltd* [1995] 2 All E.R. 370 at 381b–d, Leggatt L.J. and *Att-Gen v MGN Ltd* [1997] 1 All E.R. 456 at 460b–d. See also *Att-Gen v News UK Ltd and Stott*, unreported, December 1995, Potts J. The facts are given at para.1–136, n.5.
[66] See, *e.g. Coco v Clark (AN) (Engineers) Ltd* [1969] R.P.C. 41.
[67] See *Att-Gen v Guardian Newspapers Ltd (No.2)* [1990] 1 A.C. 109 at 260E–H, Lord Keith; *R. v Broadcasting Complaints Commission Ex p. Granada TV* [1995] E.M.L.R. 163; *A. v M (Family Proceedings: Publicity)* [2000] 1 F.L.R. 562 at 570E–F, Charles J.
[68] As it does in s.2(1); see para.4–24.
[69] [1899] A.C. 99.
[70] At 105; cf. *Robinson v Barton-Eccles Local Board* (1883) 8 App. Cas. 798 at 801.

4–31 and include' and in that case it may afford an exhaustive explanation of the meaning which, for the purpose of the Act, must invariably be attached to these words or expressions."

4–32 In the present statute, the question is whether publications outside the categories listed fall inside or outside the strict liability rule. Notwithstanding the language in which it is couched, the definition appears to be exhaustive. The additional words in s.2 of the 1981 Act ("includes any speech, writing, [programme included in a programme service] or other communication in whatever form") all obviously fall within the description of "publication" itself. They cannot have been inserted for the avoidance of doubt. There would have been no point in including them unless Parliament intended thereby to emphasise that only *private* communications were to be excluded from the ambit of the strict liability rule.

4–33 The point was addressed by the House of Lords in *Secretary of State for Defence v Guardian Newspapers Ltd*,[71] where Lord Diplock appears to have had no doubt from its context that s.2(1) was "intended as a complete and comprehensive definition of the term". In any event, the meaning here is surely effectively put beyond doubt by the phrase "in whatever form". Accordingly one can conclude with some confidence that "includes" in s.2(1) is equivalent to "means"; *any* act that can be classified as a "communication" falls within the ambit of the Act.

7. *"... addressed to the public at large ..."*

4–34 In order for the publication to fall within the strict liability rule it must be addressed to the public at large "or any section of the public".[72] It is, however, possible to create a substantial risk that the course of justice will be seriously impeded or prejudiced by communicating to a small number of persons, or even on occasion one person. Thus a communication to a juror or a witness in a case could easily be more prejudicial than a general publication.

4–35 Yet such a limited publication would not fall within the wording of the section, and in such a case Parliament must have intended that it would be necessary to demonstrate *mens rea* before liability would attach. This would presumably have been on the basis that it could not be justified as "necessary in a democratic society" to criminalise private communications[73] in general, even if they may be viewed, objectively, as tending to create prejudice in relation to pending proceedings.

---

[71] [1985] A.C. 339 at 348.
[72] s.2(1). *Cp* the wording of the Children Act 2004, s.62, discussed at paras 8–83 and 8–107.
[73] See Phillimore Committee, para.80 and the comments of Lord Gardiner during the passage of the Contempt of Court Bill; *Hansard*, H.L., Vol. 416, (5th series), col. 182, January 15, 1981.

8. "... or any section of the public"

(a) Introduction

A person who communicates to a class or grouping of persons large enough to be classified as a "section of the public" was intended by Parliament to be caught by the strict liability rule. There would clearly be some potential difficulties of classification even if the statute had been confined to "the public at large", since some small-scale publications might not perhaps be held to be sufficiently "public" even if unrestricted. Further such problems arise, however, because of the introduction of the concept of "section of the public".

4–36

Exceptionally an outburst in open court[74] might create a substantial risk of serious prejudice and fall within the strict liability rule. A possible example of this might be accusing a witness of murder in open court and before the press,[75] or shouting out that the defendant already has a prior conviction, thus putting the continuation of the trial in jeopardy. Indeed, juries are sometimes discharged following the introduction of inadmissible evidence or mistaken references by counsel or witnesses to prejudicial matters which should have been kept from them.

4–37

The Phillimore Committee recommended a definition of "publication" similar to that later contained in the 1981 Act but omitting the words "section of the public."[76] The Committee wished by their definition to exclude publications intended only for private circulation. On the other hand they did intend to include words "addressed to a public meeting or any function or entertainment to which the public is invited, as well as to private meetings to which the press is invited, but not an address to a private meeting to which the press is not invited."

4–38

They continued:

4–39

"If in the latter case a person present at the meeting communicated what was said to the press, he and the publisher should be liable to contempt proceedings, but the speaker should only be liable if his conduct were shown to be intended to cause prejudice as described in the previous chapter."

This recommendation is confusing, because it appears to conflate two fundamentally different concepts. On the one hand, there is the test to be applied in the case of common law publication contempts; that is to say, whether the alleged contemnor intended to cause prejudice.[77] On the other hand, by contrast,

4–40

---

[74] "Publication" is defined in s.2 of the 1981 Act to include, *inter alia*, "any speech".
[75] As happened in the case of *R. v West Yorkshire Coroner Ex p. Smith (No.2)* [1985] 1 Q.B. 1096.
[76] paras 80, 216(8); and see the Report of the Law Commission No.96, *Offences Relating to Interference with the Course of Justice* (1979), paras 3–69 and 3–78. The wisdom of adding the words "any section of the public" to the Committee's recommendation was questioned by Lord Gardiner, because he anticipated that this would have the effect of enlarging the area of contempt "beyond Phillimore". He thought that it was undesirable to extend the risk of the penal consequences of strict liability to communications which could be classified as being "only for private circulation"; H.L. *Hansard*, Vol. 416, (5th series) col. 182, January 15, 1981.
[77] paras 5–120 *et seq*.

there is the test applied generally in cases of strict liability, which requires no more than an intention to do the act in question. (In a case of this type of contempt, what matters is whether or not a person intended the act of publication, and not whether he had any regard to its likely consequences.) Surely in the present context, in drawing a distinction between the potential liability of the original speaker and that of the journalist, what matters from the speaker's point of view is whether or not he or she intended or authorised the republication by the journalist to the public, or to a section of the public.

(b) *Comparable legislation using the same phrase*

4–41 The words "section of the public" have been judicially considered in other areas of the law, and it may be instructive to consider these in attempting to construe the 1981 Act. One should be wary of attaching too much weight to interpretations of similar wording from a different statutory context. As Lord Simon pointed out in *Race Relations Board v Charter*[78]:

> "A decision on even the same phraseology in a different branch of the law can be of value in only two ways. [1] It is of direct significance if it seems likely that the draftsman of the provisions under instant interpretation had in mind the other phrase and its judicial interpretations and intended the court to invoke them ... [2] interpretation of a similar phrase in a different statute or from a different branch of the law may be indirectly of value by showing how a legal phrase has struck different judicial minds: the value, though, will vary directly with the closeness of the context."

4–42 The Race Relations legislation had provided that it was unlawful for any person, concerned with the provision to the public or a section of the public of any goods, facilities or services, to discriminate against anyone seeking to obtain them. It went on to give examples of the types of services intended. In *Race Relations Board v Charter*[79] the House of Lords held that a local Conservative Club, which had a genuine personal selection procedure for choosing members and also met in private, was *not* a section of the public.

4–43 In *Dockers' Labour Club & Institute Ltd v Race Relations Board*[80] a working men's club had a genuine selection procedure which made it a private club. It was part of a union of working men's clubs, each club having the right to select associate members who were permitted to enter any club in the union. There were a million associates in all. On a normal day in the particular club where discrimination occurred about one in twelve of those present were associates. The House of Lords held the club was not, purely for that reason, providing services to a section of the public because (a) the associates themselves were subject to a selection procedure by other clubs and (b) the numbers of them actually attending the particular club did not take it from the private to the public sphere.

---

[78] [1973] A.C. 868 at 901; see also Lord Reid at 887. A similar note of caution was sounded by the Phillimore Committee at para.80.
[79] [1973] A.C. 868.
[80] [1976] A.C. 285. See also *Applin v Race Relations Board* [1975] A.C. 259, where foster children in the care of a particular local authority were held to constitute a section of the public within s.2(1) of the Race Relations Act 1968.

In contrasting the words of the Contempt of Court Act and the Race Relations **4–44**
Acts, it is worthy of note that the latter:

(a) do not draw an express distinction between the public at large and "a section of the public";

(b) do not include the word "addressed";

(c) qualify the words "section of the public" by the limiting description " ... not consisting exclusively of members of an association of which the person publishing or distributing is a member";

(d) serve a different social purpose from the provisions under consideration.

Subject to such caveats, however, some general assistance may be derived **4–45**
from these cases. The House of Lords:

(a) construed the words "section of the public" as words of limitation[81];

(b) contrasted "public" with private (Lord Hodson observing "The antithesis of 'public' is 'private' and the enquiry must therefore be as to who is fitted by the cap 'private' ")[82];

(c) indicated that the application of a purely numerical test would not be conclusive, although it could illuminate one relevant factor: thus in the *Dockers' Labour Club and Institute Ltd v Race Relations Board*[83] the fact that a million associate members *might* choose to come to the club did not alter its private nature. Lord Reid, however, reserved for future consideration the situation where so many non-members *habitually* attend at a club that it loses its character as a private meeting place[84];

(d) held that the crucial test in the club cases was the basis of selection of those attending; that is to say, where there was operated a genuine selection procedure, then the club was private rather than public[85];

(e) acknowledged that the *purpose* of the grouping might also be relevant.

Thus Lord Simon said in *Charter's* case[86]:

"We all have, we hope, a spark of unique personality. But every one of us plays a number of roles in life. We are children, husbands or wives, mothers or fathers, members of some association, passengers in a bus, cinemagoers, workers with varying status in industry or commerce or profession, adherents of a religious denomination,

---

[81] See, *e.g.* Lord Reid in *Race Relations Board v Charter* [1973] A.C. 868 at 885 and Lord Hodson at 897.
[82] *ibid.* at 897: and see Lord Reid at 886 and Lord Cross at 906. But contrast Lord Morris at 892, who points out that a private group may also be a section of the public.
[83] [1976] A.C. 285.
[84] *ibid.* at 292.
[85] Lord Reid in the *Dockers' Club* case gave the example of a golf club which allowed anyone to play who offered to pay the green fee. That in his view was a service to the public or a section of it.
[86] [1973] A.C. at 901.

parliamentary or local government electors, nationals of a state, together with countless other personae in the course of a lifetime—many in the course of a day—some, indeed, simultaneously. Certain of these roles lie in the public domain; others in the private or domestic. When the draftsman used the words 'provision to the public or a section of the public' he was contemplating, I think, provision to persons aggregated in one or other of their public roles."

4–46   Suppose a communication is made (say in a newsletter or house journal) to a group of persons who happen to be members of a genuinely private club, but their membership of that club is merely incidental, in the sense that it is immaterial to the subject matter of the relevant part of the communication. The right analysis in such a case could well be that they were being addressed on that occasion as a section of the public.

(c) *The context of the communication*

4–47   It may be deduced from the Lord Simon's reasoning in the passage just cited that the *purpose* for which people gather or are addressed may be crucial to the question whether they constitute a "section of the public". By way of analogy, the courts sometimes have to consider whether the purposes of a charity are public or private. In *Dingle v Turner*[87] Lord Cross said:

"No doubt some classes are more naturally describable as sections of the public than as private classes while other classes are more naturally describable as private classes than as sections of the public. The blind, for example, can naturally be described as a section of the public; but what they have in common—their blindness—does not join them together in such a way that they could be called a private class. On the other hand, the descendants of Mr. Gladstone might more reasonably be described as a 'private class' than as a section of the public, and in the field of common employment the same might well be said of the employees in some fairly small firm. But if one turns to large companies employing many thousands of men and women most of whom are quite unknown to one another and to the directors the answer is by no means so clear. One might say that in such a case the distinction between a section of the public and a private class is not applicable at all or even that the employees in such concerns as I.C.I. or G.E.C. are just as much 'sections of the public' as the residents in some geographical area. In truth the question whether or not the potential beneficiaries of a trust can fairly be said to constitute a section of the public is a question of degree and cannot be by itself decisive of the question whether the trust is a charity. Much must depend on the purpose of the trust."

4–48   So too the context of the communication may provide a useful test in relation to s.2 of the 1981 Act. For example, communication might be to a group of people who had a special interest in particular litigation, such as a class action. Participants in such litigation might be regarded as a section of the public (just as foster children in the care of a local authority were),[88] but a communication to them discussing the merits of the litigation affecting their interests would probably be different in character from a communication on matters of general public interest, and may well in consequence be regarded as private. In any event,

---

[87] [1972] A.C. 601 at 623.
[88] *Applin v Race Relations Board* [1975] A.C. 259.

discussions as to the merits of civil litigation are unlikely to give rise to a risk of serious prejudice.

(d) *A comparison with the common law of qualified privilege*

It is recognised in the context of defamation that journalists and broadcasters may sometimes be able to plead qualified privilege in respect of communications to the world at large, provided that (a) the subject matter is of genuine public interest and (b) there is a duty (whether legal, social or moral) to impart the defamatory information in question to the general public.[89] On the other hand, in that context a duty owed to "a section of the public" is not enough.[90] 4–49

(e) *General conclusions on the meaning of "section of the public"*

It remains then to sum up the position on the meaning of "section of the public" in the 1981 Act: 4–50

(1) What is a section of the public must always be a matter of fact and degree.[91]

(2) The word "public" in its ordinary meaning must have been intended to contrast with private communications.[92]

(3) The words "section of the public" were apparently inserted to make it clear that limited circulation would not in itself be sufficient to exclude a communication from the description "public". Thus to publish prejudicial matter in a local or specialist journal could be a public communication for strict liability purposes; a company house magazine, for example, or a journal distributed only to members of a particular political party[93] *might* also be a publication to a section of the public, depending on a number of factors (including the number of people involved). It may ultimately depend on whether the recipients of the communication can be shown (presumably by the Attorney-General, who will be seeking to

---

[89] *Reynolds v Times Newspapers Ltd* [2001] 2 A.C. 127 where the "classical duty/interest test" was reaffirmed: *per* Lord Cooke in *McCartan Turkington Breen v Times Newspapers Ltd* [2001] 2 A.C. 277, 300. See, *e.g. Adam v Ward* (1915) 31 T.L.R. 299 at 304, Buckley L.J.; *Blackshaw v Lord* [1984] 1 Q.B. 1.
[90] *Blackshaw v Lord* [1984] 1 Q.B. at 26, Stephenson L.J. But it may be that privilege could attach to publications on the Internet to a particular group of persons because of a common and corresponding interest or a duty owed specifically to that group, notwithstanding the fact that the material may be accessed incidentally by others: see, *e.g.* the discussion in *Hewitt v Grunwald* [2004] EWHC 2959 (QB).
[91] See Lord Cross in *Dingle v Turner* [1972] A.C. 601 at 623.
[92] See Lord Hodson in *Race Relations Board v Charter* [1973] A.C. 868 at 897.
[93] So far as publications of this kind are concerned a distinction is now implicitly drawn between the law of libel and the law of contempt as to who may be responsible for an offending publication. Section 1 of the Defamation Act 1996 would appear to exclude defamation proceedings against a "publisher" (the definition of which in s.1(2) of the Act is confined to a "commercial publisher" who issues material in the course of a business) in respect of such a journal. It is less clear however whether an editor would be similarly protected. In any event, the traditional common law approach towards editorial responsibility, even in respect of limited publications, would presumably still apply so far as contempt is concerned: see *R. v Odhams Press Ltd* [1957] 1 Q.B. 73, discussed at paras 4–11, 4–218.

prove strict liability) to have been "aggregated"[94] and in what capacity.

(4) The number of people addressed would not be decisive; *prima facie* the greater the numbers involved, the greater the likelihood that the communication will be held to have been "public". However, if six persons selected for jury service were to become the object of a prejudicial communication, as they waited to see if they would be impanelled for a particular case,[95] they would be likely to be classified as a section of the public. (In such circumstances, it might not be too difficult to establish intention in any event, and thus bypass the statutory hurdle for strict liability.)

(5) A critical question will often be, "what is the context of the communication?" Thus a distinction might be drawn between a meeting of a trade union branch, or a meeting of Lloyd's names, at which members discussed the merits of a pending action concerning their own affairs and such a meeting which happens to be discussing the merits of some controversial pending case of wider significance. A special interest in the litigation on the part of those present could take the communication outside the statutory notion of "section of the public". To use Lord Simon's words,[96] those present would be aggregated in their private rather than their public roles.

(6) Also important may be the manner in which the communication is controlled. Thus a communication to a meeting at which attendance is controlled by genuine personal selection may be private; if the press are invited that same meeting would surely become a public one. Moreover, a meeting which was originally private may be turned into a public one by the arrival of outsiders.

(7) Both (5) and (6) above are based upon the test, "to whom is the communication addressed?" This is the true test under the Act.

(8) Difficulty may arise where there is conflict between the criteria set out in (5) and (6) above. What is the position of persons who are present at a meeting controlled by genuine personal selection and in the course of the evening they discuss potentially prejudicial matters relating to an action in which they have no special interest? Suppose a political club, whose members are genuinely personally selected, holds such a discussion about a case concerning paedophile activity in the vicinity. There may be amongst their members potential jurors. Are they for this purpose a section of the public because they have assumed a public persona within a private gathering, or merely private persons discussing an issue which

---

[94] Lord Simon in *Charter* [1973] A.C. 868 at 901.
[95] See, *e.g. The Prothonotary v Collins* (1985) 2 N.S.W.L.R. 549 at 563 where McHugh J.A. observed: "As long as the law of contempt and trial by jury retain their present forms, the distribution to jurors of extraneous material which tends to influence their verdicts can only be regarded as a serious contempt calling for severe punishment".
[96] para.4–45.

happens to be public? In such a situation the context of the communication could prove to be the decisive factor, so that within the meaning of the statute there may be a "public" communication at a private meeting. Such general discussions, however, may very well be subject to a defence under s.5 of the Act, because any element of prejudice would be likely to be "merely incidental".[97]

(9) A person who repeats to the public at large a communication that was intended to be private will, by his republication, be making a communication within the contemplation of s.2(1).[98] A communication to even one journalist, however, might be classified as being made to the public at large. It is difficult to see why a communication to someone who is known to be a journalist should not ordinarily be taken as authorising the passing of the information to his readership, unless perhaps the information has been passed in such a way as to negate any such authorisation.[99] The release of such material to a journalist, being inherently prejudicial to the conduct of active proceedings, could create a risk that it will reach potential jurors.

E. Intention to publish required

Liability under the statute is strict in the sense that it will be imposed even where there is no intention to interfere with the administration of justice. Strict liability may also apply[1] even where the editor, publisher or distributor is unaware of the contents of the publication, or that particular relevant proceedings are active. But it would appear that there must still be proved in such situations at least an intention to publish.[2] If a person were to supply information to a journalist, being truly unaware that the reporter intended to repeat the remarks, he would not be liable for the subsequent re-publication to the public at large.[3]

4–51

II. RESTRICTIONS ON THE *ACTUS REUS* OF STRICT LIABILITY CONTEMPTS

A. The statutory means of confinement

There was always obscurity as to what constituted the *actus reus* in this form of criminal contempt at common law.[4] One can only rarely demonstrate tangible

4–52

---

[97] para.4–293.
[98] See para.4–24.
[99] See, *e.g. Gatley on Libel and Slander*, (10th ed., 2004) paras 6–36 *et seq.* and the principles expounded in *Speight v Gosnay* (1891) 60 L.J.Q.B. 231; *McManus v Beckham* [2002] EWCA Civ 939, [2002] 1 W.L.R. 2982, [2002] 4 All E.R. 497, [2002] E.M.L.R. 40.
[1] Subject to certain statutory defences under the Contempt of Court Act 1981, s.3, discussed paras 4–236 *et seq.*
[2] See, *e.g. McLeod v St. Aubyn* [1899] A.C. 549 at 562 (Lord Morris). "A printer and publisher intends to publish, and so intending cannot plead as a justification that he did not know the contents. The appellant in this case never intended to publish."
[3] See also *McManus v Beckham* [2002] EWCA Civ 939, [2002] 1 W.L.R. 2982, [2002] 4 All E.R. 497, [2002] E.M.L.R. 40 cited above.
[4] See Sir John Smith's commentary on *R. v Ingrams* in *Ex p. Goldsmith* [1977] Crim. L.R. 40, 41, quoted para.5–2, n.92.

prejudice or impediment as a result of publication, and therefore it has always been recognised that in order to make the law effective it is necessary to treat the creation of some degree of *risk* as itself constituting the *actus reus*. It is to this somewhat elusive "noumenon"[5] that the Phillimore Committee and the Parliamentary draftsman thus directed their attention when seeking to limit the scope of strict liability for the purpose of achieving compliance with the disciplines of Art.10.

4–53 The Act confines the sort of conduct that will give rise to strict liability by a number of means, including the need to establish a "substantial risk" of prejudice that is itself required to be "serious". Whether these criteria are fulfilled upon the facts of any given case is a matter which has to be judged by reference to the circumstances prevailing at the date of publication. It is thus irrelevant, for example, what subsequently transpires as to the outcome of the proceedings to which the alleged prejudice is said to relate. It is not relevant for this purpose whether an accused person is convicted or acquitted[6]; nor would it be determinative that the assigned trial judge might have concluded that the publicity in question has rendered a fair trial impossible.[7]

B. The concept of "risk": when is a risk "substantial"?

4–54 Section 2(2) of the Act provides that:

"The strict liability rule applies only to a publication which creates a *substantial risk* that the course of justice in the proceedings in question will be seriously impeded or prejudiced."

4–55 This section contained one apparently significant difference from the recommendations of the Phillimore Committee, namely the insertion of the word "substantial" before "risk" in the course of the Bill's passage through Parliament.[8] Phillimore stated at para.113:

"The law should aim at preventing serious prejudice not serious risks. It has been emphasised many times by the courts that trivial cases ought not to be brought before the courts, and the triviality relates to the degree of prejudice. On the other hand the risk of serious prejudice should always be prohibited unless the risk is so slight as to fall within the ordinary *de minimis* rule."

4–56 Parliament might appear to have intended to go beyond Phillimore and confine the strict liability rule even further by the use of the word "substantial". The

---

[5] The word used by Lord Diplock in *Att-Gen v English* [1983] 1 A.C. 116 at 142A.
[6] *Att-Gen v English* [1983] 1 A.C. 116, 141: "That the risk that was created by the publication when it was actually published does not ultimately affect the outcome of the proceedings is, as Lord Goddard C.J. said in *R. v Evening Standard Co Ltd* [1954] 1 Q.B. 578 at 582 'neither here nor there.'", *per* Lord Diplock, who also observed that "The public policy that underlies the strict liability rule in contempt of court is deterrence". See also *Att-Gen v Unger* [1998] 1 Cr.App.R. 308, [1998] E.M.L.R. 280.
[7] *Att-Gen v MGN Ltd* [1997] 1 All E.R. 456; nevertheless, it now seems clear from *Att-Gen v Birmingham Post and Mail Ltd* [1998] 4 All E.R. 49 that it will sometimes be regarded as a "telling pointer": *per* Simon Brown L.J.
[8] See *Hansard*, H.L. Vol. 416, (5th series), col. 182, (Lord Elwyn-Jones).

restriction generated a certain amount of semantic debate which was shortly afterwards disposed of by the decision of the House of Lords in *Att-Gen v English*.[9] Their Lordships, like the Divisional Court, rejected the argument that substantial meant "large" or "great".[10] Lord Diplock (with whose speech the remainder concurred) held that the word "substantial" is to be equated with "not remote"[11]:

> "Next for consideration is the concatenation in the subsection of the adjective 'substantial' and the adverb 'seriously', the former to describe the degree of risk, the latter to describe the degree of impediment or prejudice to the course of justice. 'Substantial' is hardly the most apt word to apply to 'risk' which is a noumenon.[12] In combination I take the two words to be intended to exclude a risk that is only remote."

It is doubtful if Lord Diplock would have come to any different conclusion on the matter if he had the opportunity to consult the Parliamentary Debates in accordance with the modern practice.[13] The conclusion of Lord Hailsham in the course of debate was that the insertion of the word "substantial" would not make much difference in practice.[14] Despite this change of wording, it seems in the light of the House of Lords' conclusion in *Att-Gen v English*[15] that in this respect the purpose of the Phillimore Report has been achieved.

Lord Diplock was indicating that only *de minimis* risks were to be excluded from the strict liability provisions. Thus, it may be assumed that Parliament only deemed it "necessary" to legislate against the creation of risks that are *not* trivial or remote. Lord Diplock's analysis is therefore consistent with the reasoning of the European Court in *Sunday Times v United Kingdom*.[16] There are limits to the assistance that may be derived from semantic analyses in an area where the facts can vary infinitely and there is inevitably large scope for subjective judgment and difference of opinion.[17] What seems clear, however, is that "the risk must be a practical risk and not a theoretical risk".[18]

---

[9] [1983] A.C. 116 (discussed at paras 4–300 *et seq.*).
[10] Contrast *Palser v Grinling* [1948] A.C. 291 at 317: "One of the primary meanings of the word is equivalent to considerable, solid or big. It is in this sense that we speak of a substantial fortune, a substantial meal, a substantial man, a substantial argument or ground of defence".
[11] [1983] A.C. 116 at 141–2. This passage was cited and followed in *Att-Gen v Morgan* [1998] E.M.L.R. 294, Pill L.J.
[12] *i.e.* a purely intellectual concept to which physical descriptions were thought by Lord Diplock to be inappropriate. That is to say, something which may be contrasted with a *phenomenon* (*i.e.* that which is apparent or tangible) because it is a mental or abstract concept only.
[13] Sanctioned by the House of Lords in *Pepper v Hart* [1993] A.C. 593.
[14] *Hansard*, H.L., Vol. 417, (5th series), col. 143: " . . . if it makes no difference, and if persons of such eminence support it and want it, why not give in?—and so I am doing."
[15] [1983] 1 A.C. 116.
[16] (1979) 2 E.H.R.R. 245.
[17] See, *e.g.* the citation from *Re Lonrho* [1990] 2 A.C. 154, para.4–95.
[18] *Att-Gen v Guardian Newspapers Ltd (No.3)* [1992] 1 W.L.R. 874 at 881, Mann L.J. citing *Att-Gen v News Group Newspapers Ltd* [1987] Q.B. 1, 16C at 19D; *Att-Gen for New South Wales v John Fairfax & Sons Ltd* (1985) 6 N.S.W.L.R. 695 at 708C and F.

4–59 In *Att-Gen v Guardian Newspapers Ltd*[19] Sedley L.J. focussed, unusually, on the matter of 'substantial risk' in rejecting the Attorney's application. He was of the view that the risk was undoubtedly one of serious prejudice to the course of justice but decided that he could not be sure that there was a substantial risk that jurors, properly directed to disregard their own sentiments and any media comment, would nevertheless have their own thoughts or value judgments reinforced by the article to a point where it influenced the verdict.

C. The relationship between "risk" and "prejudice"

4–60 The assessment of risk may depend on many factors, and will turn in each case on the particular facts. The risk may be at its height when the trial, at the moment of publication, is about to begin or is actually in progress.[20] At such a moment it is often unrealistic to expect jurors, however conscientious, to shut out strikingly prejudicial material and in particular information about an accused person's criminal record. The danger is that such a publication will "have loaded the scales in favour of the prosecution in a way in which no judicial warning could redress".[21] In *Att-Gen v Associated Newspapers Ltd*, Kennedy L.J. made the following general comment[22]:

> "So long as it is accepted that the interests of justice require that in general jurors should not be told about the antecedents of an accused it must follow that a publication like this during the course of a trial will be in danger of being regarded by this court as creating a substantial risk that the course of justice in the proceedings will be seriously prejudiced. With potential jurors receiving information in so many different ways, high profile cases would become impossible to try if jurors could not be relied on to disregard much of the information to which they may have been exposed, but that does not mean that they can be expected to disregard any information, whenever and however it is received, otherwise there would be no point in withholding from them any relevant information however prejudicial in content or presentation, hence the need for the law of contempt which we are required to enforce."

4–61 There is clearly a sliding scale into which the facts of any particular case have to be slotted. At one extreme, as Simon Brown L.J. pointed out in *Att-Gen v Unger*,[23] is the publication of inadmissible material (such as previous convictions)[24] at the time of the trial. A particularly striking example is presented by the

---

[19] [1999] E.M.L.R. 904 at 927.
[20] As, for example, in *Att-Gen v Associated Newspapers Ltd*, October 31, 1997 (Lexis), Kennedy L.J. See also *Att-Gen v Unger* [1998] 1 Cr.App.R. 308, [1998] E.M.L.R. 280, discussed at para.4–166, Simon Brown L.J.; *Att-Gen v Birmingham Post and Mail Ltd* [1998] 4 All E.R. 49.
[21] *Att-Gen v Associated Newspapers Ltd*, October 31, 1997 (Lexis) *per* Kennedy L.J.
[22] *ibid*. This passage was cited and followed in *Ex p. Telegraph Group* [2001] EWCA Crim 1075, [2001] 1 W.L.R. 1983. See also Simon Brown L.J. in *Att-Gen v Unger* [1998] 1 Cr.App.R. 308, [1998] E.M.L.R. 280.
[23] [1998] 1 Cr.App.R. 308 at 317A–B, [1998] E.M.L.R. 280 at 292.
[24] This was traditionally seen as the paradigm case of prejudicial material, but sometimes previous convictions may now be admitted by the trial judge in accordance with the provisions of the Criminal Justice Act 2003, Pt 11, ch.1. That does not, however, necessarily affect the restriction imposed by the law during the period when the proceedings are active and before the convictions are admitted.

facts of *Att-Gen v Associated Newspapers Ltd*.[25] The background was the escape in September 1994 from Whitemoor Prison of six prisoners, of whom five were convicted IRA terrorists. There was from time to time a good deal of media publicity about the circumstances, not least because the Home Secretary appointed an enquiry into the security arrangements at the prison.

Eventually the six prisoners came to trial in September 1996 on charges *inter alia* of breaking prison. Two unsuccessful applications had been made for a stay on the grounds of pre-trial publicity. In rejecting those applications the trial judge had recognised that there was an unavoidable prejudicial element in such a case; in particular, the jury would have to know that the accused were already convicted prisoners who were regarded as presenting such a security risk that it was necessary to house them in a special unit. It had been agreed, however, between counsel, that there was no need to mention the nature of the offences of which they had been convicted. As soon as that trial started, that information was widely published in national newspapers, and a third application for a stay was partly successful. The jury was discharged and the trial stayed for a few months. The judge (Maurice Kay J. as he then was) recognised an "enormous difference" between publicity in advance of a trial and "publicity that arises during and particularly at the very outset of the trial".

The delayed trial began at Woolwich Crown Court in January 1997, and on the second day a further application for a stay was refused. The judge in the absence of the jury reminded the media representatives of the unfortunate history of the proceedings and urged them to confine their coverage to what was said in court in the presence of the jury. A week later a two-page feature article appeared in the *Evening Standard*, in which three of the defendants' photographs were published and they were described as having committed serious terrorist offences. The newspaper in question circulates widely in London and the south east of England, the area in which the trial was taking place.

A fresh application was granted, and the proceedings were permanently stayed. The judge concluded that the jury had probably seen the article, that there was a significant risk that they would be prejudiced, and that the defendants' right to a fair trial had thus been undermined. The Divisional Court subsequently rejected the submission that there had been no substantial risk of serious prejudice. It was accepted that the case was unusual, in that the jury knew from the outset that the defendants must have been convicted of serious crimes, and indeed some of them may have recalled from pre-trial publicity that they were members of the IRA. Although the jury could reasonably be expected to put such recollections or inferences to one side when deliberating about the issues in the trial, "the article in question was something different", since no juror who saw it could fail to be gripped by it. It revealed that three of the defendants were indeed members of the IRA and that one of them was a double murderer, while the other two had been convicted of conspiring to cause explosions.

---

[25] October 31, 1997 (Lexis).

4–65 Naturally, a long gap between publication and an anticipated trial date may significantly reduce any risk of contamination. Also, the fact that publication takes place in local media, outside the anticipated area of trial, would be a major consideration in reducing the risk of prejudice.

4–66 On the other hand, some facts are so striking, even when published some time in advance of a hearing, as to render it impossible to be confident that the conscientiousness of jurors, or the directions of a trial judge, would prevent a substantial risk that the course of justice in the trial would be seriously impeded or prejudiced. Such factors may arise because of the memorable facts of the case itself (as for example in *Att-Gen v Times Newspapers Ltd*,[26] which concerned the person who broke into the Queen's bedroom), or because the facts disclosed in the media coverage about the accused will themselves stay in the mind. This is perhaps especially so in the case of the revelation of a criminal record.[27]

4–67 The difficulties of addressing the sliding scale, and marrying risk with prejudice, can be illustrated by reference to a number of cases where the principles have been applied in a wide variety of circumstances. It is true that the cases are only illustrations of principles being applied to unique factual situations, but reference to past experience can often be helpful as there is no touchstone which can offer unerring and precise guidance. As Frankfurter J. observed in *Stroble v California*[28]:

> "Science with all its advances has not given us instruments for determining when the impact of such newspaper exploitation has spent itself or whether the powerful impression bound to be made by such inflaming articles as here preceded the trial can be dissipated in the mind of the average juror by the tame and often pedestrian proceedings in court."

4–68 Given the absence of either statutory prescription or reliable empirical data, judges have to rely on their professional expertise and general experience of life in determining where to draw the line. Inevitably, this means that there are difficulties for editors in predicting the likely judicial response as each new set of circumstances presents itself.[29] Although there are in many reported decisions vigorous pronouncements on the robust common sense of juries, it is by no means uncommon to find equally strong statements to the effect that no juror could be expected to put certain information out of mind.[30] Such statements cannot be given the status of legal principles, and in truth they are no more than

---

[26] *The Times*, February 12, 1983 (Lexis).
[27] Mason C.J. in *Hinch v Att-Gen for Victoria* (1987) 164 C.L.R. 15 at 28 commented that courts have always taken a serious view of any published disclosure of a prior conviction, because it would be inadmissible evidence and likely to prejudice a jury, and such publication is usually regarded as sufficient to invalidate the trial. See also *Registrar of the Court of Appeal v Willesee* (1980) 2 N.S.W.L.R. 143 at 149; *Att-Gen of NSW v Truth and Sportsman* (1957) 75 W.N. (N.S.W.) 70; *R. v Regal Press Pty* [1972] V.R. 67; *Att-Gen v Unger* [1998] 1 Cr.App.R. 308 at 317A–B, [1998] E.M.L.R. 280 at 292, Simon Brown L.J.
[28] (1951) 343 U.S. 181 at 201.
[29] See, *e.g. Gisborne Herald Co Ltd v Solicitor General* [1995] 3 N.Z.L.R. 563 at 570, Richardson J.
[30] See paras 4–148 *et seq.* for a discussion of the reconciliation of these contrasting strands of opinion.

the reflections of individual judges based upon experience and common sense. Samuels J.A. noted in *Att-Gen for NSW v John Fairfax & Sons Ltd*[31]:

"There lie at the speculative core of many legal doctrines assumptions about the conduct and capacity of ordinary men and women to whom a disparate array of characteristics are attributed, ranging from extreme obtuseness to almost divine prescience depending on the interest to be advanced or protected. Assessments of the possible or probable conduct and responses of juries fall within much the same category and are equally speculative. It was suggested, however, that jurors, as ordinary members of the community, have developed defences or analytical filters by which to repel or dilute the remorseless assaults of the media. I have no idea whether this is so or not."

When judges make the necessary assessment of the likely impact of information upon a range of unidentifiable people, every such decision is bound to reflect the culture and values of the particular society; matters plainly relevant to where the balance may be struck from time to time as to the weight given, respectively, to freedom of expression and the right to a fair trial.[32] Moreover, it is necessary to have regard to geographical circumstances, because what may pass unnoticed in the impersonal surroundings of a large conurbation may have a much more immediate and lasting impact in a smaller community.

4–69

When analysing the cases that follow, it is also important to heed the warning of Auld L.J. in *Att-Gen v BBC and Hat Trick Productions Ltd*[33]:

4–70

"Much depends on the combination of circumstances in the case in question and the court's own assessment of their likely effect at the time of publication. This is essentially a value judgment for the court, albeit that it must be sure of its judgment before it can find that there has been contempt. *There is little value in making comparisons with the facts of other cases*" (emphasis added).

All these factors have to be borne in mind when considering the following examples of how the strict liability test has been applied in England since the provisions were enacted.

1. *Att-Gen v News Group Newspapers plc*

The relationship between degree of risk and degree of prejudice was considered, in the context of civil proceedings, in the case of *Att-Gen v News Group Newspapers plc*,[34] a decision involving the cricketer Ian Botham. A newspaper published two articles alleging misbehaviour on his part in the course of a foreign tour. Mr Botham sued for libel. After the case had become active, he learnt that another newspaper was intending to publish similar allegations and obtained an injunction prohibiting publication. On appeal the injunction was discharged, the Court of Appeal taking the view that the risk of prejudice was not substantial,

4–71

---

[31] (1985) 6 N.S.W.L.R. 695 at 699D–E.
[32] *Gisborne Herald Co Ltd v Solicitor General* [1995] 3 N.Z.L.R. 563 at 573.
[33] [1997] E.M.L.R. 76 at 81.
[34] [1987] Q.B. 1. See also *Att-Gen v Independent Television News Ltd* [1995] 2 All E.R. 370, [1995] 1 Cr.App.R. 204 discussed at para.4–74.

4-71 CHAPTER 4—THE STATUTORY REGIME FOR STRICT LIABILITY

having regard to the interval of time that would elapse before the anticipated trial. It was expected that some 10 or 11 months would elapse between publication and trial.

4-72 Sir John Donaldson M.R. explained the scheme of the Act. It is surprising to note that the House of Lords' decision in *Att-Gen v English*[35] is not listed as having been cited in this case. Nevertheless, it does not appear that there is any inconsistency between Lord Diplock's approach to "substantial risk" and that of the Master of the Rolls, who put the matter as follows[36]:

> "There has to be a *substantial* risk that the course of the proceedings in question will be *seriously* impeded or prejudiced. This is a double test. First, there has to be some risk that the proceedings in question will be affected at all. Second, there has to be a prospect that, if affected, the effect will be serious. The two limbs of the text can overlap, but they can be quite separate. I accept that submission of counsel for the defendants that 'substantial' as a qualification of 'risk' does not have the meaning of 'weighty', but rather means 'not insubstantial', or 'not minimal'. The 'risk' part of the test will usually be of importance in the context of the width of the publication. To declare in a speech at a public meeting in Cornwall that a man about to be tried in Durham is guilty of the offence charged and has many previous convictions for the same offence may well carry no substantial risk of affecting his trial, but, if it occurred, the prejudice would be most serious. By contrast, a nationwide television broadcast at peak viewing time of some far more innocuous statement would certainly involve a substantial risk of having some effect on a trial anywhere in the country and the sole effective question would arise under the 'seriousness' limb of the test. Proximity in time between the publication and the proceedings would probably have a greater bearing on the risk limb than on the seriousness limb, but could go to both".

4-73 To publish prejudicial comments in a local newspaper in Cornwall about a Durham case might, however, raise a risk of serious prejudice if a potential juror happened to be visiting Cornwall. Yet this would normally not be perceived as raising any such risk for the reason that the likelihood of a potential juror reading it would be small. What has to be addressed is what is sometimes referred as the "leakage" argument; that is to say, whether there is anything more on the facts of the particular case than a minimal risk or "an outside chance" of a local newspaper being read adventitiously by a juror outside its normal catchment area.

2. *Att-Gen v ITN Ltd*

4-74 The point is well illustrated by the decision of the Divisional Court in *Att-Gen v ITN Ltd*,[37] where a television news company in reporting the arrest of two men for murder of a special constable, and also for attempted murder, stated that one of the men was a convicted terrorist who had earlier escaped from gaol in

---

[35] [1983] 1 A.C. 116.
[36] [1987] 1 Q.B. 1 at 15C–F.
[37] [1995] 2 All E.R. 370; see also *Gisborne Herald Co Ltd v Solicitor-General* [1995] 3 N.Z.L.R. 563; *Hinch v Att-Gen of Victoria* (1987) 164 C.L.R. 15, HC.

Belfast[38] where he had been serving a life sentence for the murder of an SAS officer. A poor photograph of the arrested man was also shown.

The second to fifth respondents to the proceedings for contempt brought by the Attorney-General were the publishers of newspapers which had given an account of the incident, including details of the defendant's associations with the IRA, his previous conviction for murder, his gaol break and his period on the run. Only one of the newspapers omitted the fact that the defendant had been convicted of the murder. The articles appeared in the first editions of each newspaper, and the total numbers distributed in London were 2,485, 1,000, 1,850 and 146 respectively. The trial of the two accused took place in London nine months after publication. 4–75

The court took the view that, if at the trial the previous conviction had come to the attention of the jury, the prejudice suffered would have been very serious. But a question also to be determined was whether the risk was substantial. In assessing that, the court should ask whether, *at the time of the publication*, there was a substantial risk that the course of justice would be prejudiced. It was necessary to take into account the brevity of the broadcast and its ephemeral nature,[39] the relatively small circulation of the offending articles in London (where the trial took place), and the all-important factor of the time lapse between publication and the likely date of trial. The court was not satisfied that there had been, on those facts, a substantial risk. As Leggatt L.J. observed[40]: 4–76

"When the long odds against the potential juror reading any of the publications is multiplied by the long odds against any reader remembering it, the risk of prejudice is, in my judgment, remote".

3. *Att-Gen v Guardian Newspapers Ltd (No.3)*

A further illustration is provided by *Att-Gen v Guardian Newspapers Ltd (No.3)*,[41] where an editor and publisher were made subject of contempt applications by the Attorney-General, for having written and published respectively an article criticising the use by trial judges of their powers to impose reporting restrictions. Mention had been made of the fact that one of the defendants in a major fraud trial in Manchester was also involved in other proceedings, described as "a quite separate trial which may one day come to court in the Isle of Man". In order to avoid prejudice to the future proceedings, reporting restrictions under s.4(2) of the 1981 Act were imposed in respect of the 4–77

---

[38] The same escaper was also one of the defendants in the Whitemoor case referred to at paras 4–60 *et seq.*
[39] Sometimes referred to as "the fade factor"; see, *e.g.* Simon Brown L.J. in *Att-Gen v Unger* [1998] 1 Cr.App.R. 308, [1998] E.M.L.R. 280; *Ex p. The Telegraph plc* [1993] 1 W.L.R. 980 at 987E; *Victoria v Australian Building Construction Employees' Federation* (1982) 152 C.L.R. 25 at 136, Wilson J. ("What is news today is no longer news tomorrow"); *Att-Gen v Morgan* [1998] E.M.L.R. 294.
[40] [1995] 2 All E.R. 370 at 383g.
[41] [1992] 1 W.L.R. 874, [1992] 3 All E.R. 38, D.C. Reference was made to *Att-Gen for New South Wales v John Fairfax and Sons Ltd* (1985) 6 N.S.W.L.R. 695.

4-77 CHAPTER 4—THE STATUTORY REGIME FOR STRICT LIABILITY

first Manchester trial. As a result of the publication of the critical article, revealing to the Manchester jury the existence of the other pending proceedings, the judge discharged the jury and ordered a retrial, resulting in substantial wasted costs and delay.

4-78 Notwithstanding this, when the Attorney-General launched proceedings for strict liability contempt, the Divisional Court held that the publication of the article need not necessarily have created a substantial risk that the course of justice would be seriously impeded. It was said that the question to be determined was not whether an article is inherently likely to cause prejudice, but whether, in the particular case, there had been created a substantial risk that the course of justice would be seriously impeded or prejudiced.[42] The publication of the fact that one unidentified defendant was to be involved in a separate trial in the Isle of Man gave rise to no significant practical risk of engendering bias in a juror of ordinary good sense.

4. *Att-Gen v Morgan*[43]

4-79 The *News of the World* published in September 1994 an article headed "We smash £100m fake cash ring," although at the time criminal proceedings were "active" in connection with an alleged conspiracy to deliver a counterfeit currency note. The arrest, which had taken place the day before publication, arose out of an investigation by one of the newspaper's reporters. The article contained a detailed description of the investigations and of the alleged conspiracy. There was agreed to be a likely time-lapse of some eight months between arrest and trial. When the matter came on for trial ten months after publication, in July 1995, the judge ordered a stay of the proceedings because of the prejudice.

4-80 A second article was published in the same newspaper in August 1995 under the heading "New terror gang take on Triad thugs". Nearly three months earlier two people had been arrested and charged with offences of blackmail, the prosecution case being that they were members of a gang operating an extortion racket to the detriment of Chinese restaurants in Birmingham. As at the date of publication, it was agreed that there was likely to be an interval before trial of about seven months. In the event, at a directions hearing in June 1996 the judge refused applications for the proceedings to be stayed. The indictment having been severed, the two defendants were convicted in November and December 1996 respectively. Although one of them appealed, no reliance was placed upon pre-trial publicity.

4-81 The Divisional Court concluded, in respect of the first article, that it constituted a strict liability contempt. It was accepted that the publication of many sensational articles, and not only in the respondents' newspapers, made it less likely that a reader would remember any one of them. The particular article

---

[42] See also Simon Brown L.J. in *Att-Gen v Unger* [1998] 1 Cr.App.R. 308 at 314A, [1998] E.M.L.R. 280 at 286.
[43] [1998] E.M.L.R. 294.

had been presented in a skilful manner and was well designed to make a big impact on the readers. It made reference to the bad character of the relevant defendants, which was a striking feature of the article and one likely to be remembered by readers. Having concluded that there was a substantial risk of a juror or jurors recollecting the substance of the article, Pill L.J. found little difficulty in also holding that there was a substantial risk that the course of justice would be seriously prejudiced. It was regarded as important in England that previous convictions should not be disclosed.[44] The contents of the article were considered to be such that neither the conscientiousness of jurors nor the directions of the trial judge could avoid the risk of prejudice.

In relation to the second article, the court concluded that several of the features criticised in respect of the first article were either not present at all or were present to a more limited extent. In particular, there was not the same assumption or assertion of guilt. Nor was there any reference to previous convictions. Although a potential juror might have remembered reading allegations that vicious Vietnamese criminals were operating in Birmingham, he or she would be unlikely to remember those named. The general impression created by the article, if it remained, would be unlikely to influence a juror's approach to the trial of the two defendants, especially bearing in mind the juror's oath and the directions that would be given by the trial judge. **4-82**

The comparison between the two cases thus highlights the importance, when assessing the likely impact over a delay of many months between publication and trial, of such factors as: **4-83**

(1) striking or sensational presentation;

(2) reference to a criminal background on the part of the accused, including in particular past convictions;

(3) any assumption or assertion of guilt in the publication in question.

D. The principles summarised

In *Att-Gen v MGN Ltd*,[45] an attempt was made by Schiemann L.J. in the light of the authorities to summarise the principles to be applied on any application for committal based on the strict liability provisions. Before doing so, he identified the conflicting public interest considerations which always come into play: **4-84**

> "The present application focuses, as these applications usually do, on the tension between two desiderata—
>
> 1. the desire that a person facing trial should face a tribunal which is not prejudiced against him by reason of matters which have not been proved in evidence and
>
> 2. the desire that newspapers should be free to publish what they please.

---

[44] Reference was made to the speech of Viscount Sankey L.C. in *Maxwell v DPP* [1935] A.C. 309, 317, where he referred to "one of the most deeply rooted and jealously guarded principles of our criminal law".

[45] [1997] 1 All E.R. 456, discussed also at paras 4–156 *et seq.*

4–84 CHAPTER 4—THE STATUTORY REGIME FOR STRICT LIABILITY

This tension is particularly strong in cases which are of widespread public interest because of the notoriety of the persons or deeds involved. The problems posed by this tension are real and recurring.

The Solicitor General has drawn our attention to no less than three cases in the last 6 months where, to the Attorney General's knowledge, a prosecution has been stayed indefinitely because of pre-trial publicity. Clearly that seriously prejudices the course of justice. There must be many others where a trial has had to be delayed or moved to a less convenient place and where it could be submitted that the course of justice has been seriously impeded".

4–85 Reference was made to the decision of the European Court of Human Rights in *Sunday Times v United Kingdom*,[46] and to the observation of Lloyd L.J. in *Att-Gen v Newspaper Publishing plc*,[47] that the statutory purpose behind the Contempt of Court Act 1981 was to effect a "permanent shift" in favour of freedom of speech.

4–86 Schiemann L.J. went on to set out the principles governing assessment of the risk of prejudice, in the application of the strict liability rule, which he described as being not the subject of serious dispute[48]:

"1. Each case must be decided on its own facts[49];

2. The court will look at each publication separately[50] and test matters as at the time of publication[51]; nevertheless, the mere fact that, by reason of earlier publications, there is already some risk of prejudice does not prevent a finding that the latest publication has created a further risk[52];

3. The publication in question must create some risk that the course of justice in the proceedings in question will be impeded or prejudiced by that publication;

4. That risk must be substantial[53];

5. The substantial risk must be that the course of justice in the proceedings in question will not only be impeded or prejudiced but seriously so;

6. The court will not convict of contempt unless it is sure that the publication has created this substantial risk of that serious effect on the course of justice;

---

[46] (1979) 2 E.H.R.R. 245.
[47] [1988] Ch. 333 at 382E–F.
[48] [1997] 1 All E.R. 456 at 461–2.
[49] See *Att-Gen v News Group Newspapers Ltd* [1987] 1 Q.B. 1 at 18A, Parker L.J. and *Att-Gen v BBC and Hat Trick Productions* [1997] E.M.L.R. 76, Auld L.J., cited at para.4–70.
[50] But see the recommendation of the National Heritage Committee that the law be amended, referred to in the Parliamentary answer given by the Lord Chancellor on February 27, 1998, at para.4–155.
[51] See *Att-Gen v English* [1983] 1 A.C. 116 at 141F–G (*per* Lord Diplock) and *Att-Gen v Guardian Newspapers Ltd (No.3)* [1992] 1 W.L.R. 874 at 885E.
[52] See *Att-Gen v Independent Television News Ltd* [1995] 2 All E.R. 370 at 381b–d, where Leggatt L.J. accepted that, if several newspapers published prejudicial material, they could not escape from liability by contending that the damage has already been done. Each could have caused its own additional risk of prejudice, or, as it might be said, each could exacerbate and increase that risk.
[53] For the meaning of "substantial" see *Att-Gen v English* [1983] 1 A.C. 116 and the discussion by Sir Charles Gray, "The Bastion of Freedom of Expression—Is It Threatened by the Laws of Confidentiality, Privacy or Contempt?" M. Saville and R. Susskind eds, *Essays in Honour of Sir Brian Neill: The Quintessential Judge* (Butterworths, 2003), p.218.

7. In making an assessment of whether the publication does create this substantial risk of that serious effect on the course of justice the following amongst other matters arise for consideration:

   (a) The likelihood of the publication coming to the attention of a potential juror;
   (b) The likely impact of the publication on an ordinary reader at the time of publication;
   (c) The residual impact of the publication on a notional juror at the time of trial.

   It is this last matter which is crucial.[54]

   One must remember that in this, as in any exercise of risk assessment, a small risk multiplied by a small risk results in an even smaller risk.[55]

8. In making an assessment of the likelihood of the publication coming to the attention of a potential juror the court will consider amongst other matters:

   (a) whether the publication circulates in the area from which the jurors are likely to be drawn, and
   (b) how many copies circulated.

9. In making an assessment of the likely impact of the publication on an ordinary reader at the time of publication the court will consider amongst other matters:

   (a) the prominence of the article in the publication, and
   (b) the novelty of the content of the article in the context of likely readers of that publication.

10. In making an assessment of the residual impact of the publication on a notional juror at the time of trial the court will consider amongst other matters:

    (a) the length of time between publication and the likely date of trial,[56]
    (b) the focusing effect of listening over a prolonged period to evidence in a case,[57]
    (c) the likely effect of the judge's directions to a jury."

One of the most significant aspects of the decision is that the Divisional Court declined to adopt the approach of considering the various respondents' publications compendiously. The submissions on behalf of the Attorney-General were framed in general terms addressing "the articles" or "the respondents' publications" together. Schiemann L.J. expressly recognised that each publication had to be looked at separately. This clearly accords with the general approach in the criminal law that responsibility is individual and personal. In those rare cases where public policy requires the conduct of persons to be aggregated, specific statutory provision is needed to achieve that objective; for example, in ss.1(1) and 3(2) of the Public Order Act 1986, which deal respectively with riot and affray.

Furthermore, the Divisional Court differed in its approach from that adopted in *Gisborne Herald Co Ltd v Solicitor-General*,[58] where the New Zealand Court

---

[54] This seventh proposition of Schiemann L.J. was further discussed, and followed, in *Att-Gen v Unger* [1998] 1 Cr.App.R. 308, [1998] E.M.L.R. 280.
[55] *Att-Gen v Independent Television News Ltd* [1995] 2 All E.R. 370 at 383g, Leggatt L.J.
[56] *Att-Gen v News Group Newspapers Ltd* [1987] Q.B. 1 at 17–18, Parker L.J.; *Att-Gen v Independent Television News Ltd* [1995] 2 All E.R. 370 at 382–83, Leggatt L.J.
[57] *Ex p. The Telegraph plc* [1993] 1 W.L.R. 980 at 987, Lord Taylor C.J., CA. See also Lord Donaldson M.R. in *Leary v BBC*, September 29, 1989 (Lexis) cited at para.6–32.
[58] [1995] 3 N.Z.L.R. 563.

4–88   CHAPTER 4—THE STATUTORY REGIME FOR STRICT LIABILITY

of Appeal seems to have been prepared to find contempt even though "the information published added little to what was already in the public domain". The Divisional Court made it clear that what is required in such circumstances is to demonstrate that the respondent in question has made an independent contribution which adds to the risk of prejudice already subsisting.

4–89   The rejection of the Attorney-General's approach led the National Heritage Committee to recommend a change to s.2 of the 1981 Act so as to cover the situation where trials appear to have been prejudiced by the collective or cumulative effect of pre-trial publicity.[59]

E. The application of the common law when section 2(2) does not apply

4–90   Section 2 does not expressly say that publications which carry either (a) a less than substantial risk of serious prejudice or (b) a substantial risk of less than serious prejudice are *ipso facto* incapable of constituting contempt. The wording thus leaves open the theoretical possibility that conduct falling outside the statutory criteria, in either of these respects, may amount to contempt under pre-existing common law,[60] subject to the proviso that *mens rea* would have to be proved. The continuing scope of the common law will be considered in the next chapter. We there explain our reasons for doubting that a different test for the *actus reus* of common law contempt can have survived the passage of the 1981 Act, especially in view of the need to justify *any* restriction on freedom of speech, which has to be "prescribed by law", by reference to what is "necessary in a democratic society".[61] Also, it is increasingly recognised that it is inappropriate to invoke the law of contempt in cases where the supposed mischief is technical or theoretical in character.[62]

4–91   It is necessary to construe the Act in the light of Article 10 of the European Convention and the decision in the *Sunday Times v United Kingdom*.[63] Accordingly the "prejudgment" test, for assessing the *actus reus*, cannot be held to have survived the passing of the 1981 Act whether for the purposes of common law or strict liability.[64] Nevertheless, when considering common law contempt, it is necessary perhaps to focus primarily on the issue of *mens rea*, and to bear in mind the rather different public policy factors that may be relevant. It may be entirely consistent with the policy underlying the Convention to permit member states to provide by law for the punishment of those who act with the *intention*

---

[59] See para.4–155.
[60] As preserved by s.6(c); para.5–144.
[61] Article 10 of the European Convention. See *Derbyshire County Council v Times Newspapers Ltd* [1992] 1 Q.B. 770, CA; *BBC v Law Officers of the Crown* (unreported), November 18, 1988, discussed at paras.5–52. And see paras 2–122 *et seq.* for a discussion of the impact of the European Convention on the common law.
[62] *Att-Gen v Newspaper Publishing plc* [1997] 1 W.L.R. 926, [1997] 1 All E.R. 159.
[63] (1979) 2 E.H.R.R. 245.
[64] See *Hansard*, H.L., Vol. 415, (5th series), col. 660, December 9, 1980, Lord Hailsham. See also the discussion of how it came about that the older pre-judgment authorities are no longer applicable, paras 1–99 *et seq.* See also *Re Lonrho (Contempt Proceedings)* [1990] 2 A.C. 154 at 209 and 213.

of creating a risk of or causing prejudice.⁶⁵ In practice, such a person is unlikely, when forming the relevant intention, to distinguish mentally between prejudice and serious prejudice.

F. The nature of "prejudice" generally

"Prejudice" is defined in the *Shorter Oxford English Dictionary* as "injury, detriment or damage caused to a person by a judgment or action in which his rights are disregarded" and "a previous judgment; a particular hasty judgment; bias favourable or unfavourable." The Act might thus at first sight seem to be adopting the pre-judgment test, when its real purpose was to replace just such a test as had been contemplated in *Att-Gen v Times Newspapers Ltd*.⁶⁶ The point, however, is that strict liability *can* apply in cases of prejudgment, but only if the prejudgment creates a substantial risk of serious prejudice to particular proceedings.

4–92

Strict liability no longer applies to what can conveniently be described as "technical contempts".⁶⁷ The publication criticised in *Vine Products Ltd v Green*⁶⁸ could now be treated as contempt only if it had been truly intended to prejudice the hearing of the case.

4–93

Moreover, although the two words are closely related etymologically, in the present context it is clear that "prejudice" goes wider and can embrace other forms of "injury, detriment or damage" than merely those caused by "prejudgment".

4–94

Anything that might have a deleterious impact on the conduct or outcome of legal proceedings could be regarded as impeding or prejudicial to the course of justice. "Prejudice" in this context probably equates to "improperly affecting" the course of the proceedings. Lord Bridge offered some examples in *Re Lonrho (Contempt Proceedings)*⁶⁹:

4–95

"Whether the course of justice in particular proceedings will be impeded or prejudiced by a publication must depend primarily on whether the publication will bring influence to bear which is likely to divert the proceedings in some way from the course which they would otherwise have followed. The influence may affect the conduct of witnesses, the parties or the court. Before proceedings have come to trial and before the facts have been found, it is easy to see how critical public discussion of the issues and criticism of the conduct of the parties, particularly if a party is held up to public obloquy, may impede or prejudice the course of proceedings by influencing the conduct of witnesses

---

⁶⁵ See s.6(c); see para.5–144. It is clear that mere intention is not enough: see para.11–12.
⁶⁶ [1974] A.C. 273. See Lord Hailsham, *Hansard*, H.L., (5th series), Vol. 415, col. 660; "It puts an end, of course, to the prejudgment criterion which was adopted by your Lordships' House in the *Sunday Times* case". And see the Attorney-General, Sir Michael Havers, *Hansard*, H.C., Vol. 1000, col. 30.
⁶⁷ paras 1–78 *et seq.*
⁶⁸ [1966] Ch. 484; see para.5–34.
⁶⁹ [1990] 2 A.C. 154, 209. This passage was cited by the Lord Justice Clerk in *Al Megrahi and Fhima v Times Newspapers Ltd*, 1999 S.C.C.R. 824 (High Court of Justiciary) in the context of alleged prejudice in the conduct of the Lockerbie bombing trial in the Netherlands.

4–95 CHAPTER 4—THE STATUTORY REGIME FOR STRICT LIABILITY

or parties in relation to the proceedings.[70] If the trial is to be by jury, the possibility of prejudice by advance publicity directed to an issue which the jury will have to decide is obvious."

G. What amounts to serious prejudice?

4–96 It appears that, prior to the enactment of the Contempt of Court Act 1981, the courts applied the test of a serious risk of *any* prejudice.[71] It thus became important to establish how much difference the introduction of the word "serious" would make in practice. Lord Diplock in *Att-Gen v English*[72] addressed the question of "serious prejudice" for the purposes of s.2(2).[73] He proceeded on the basis that the adverb "seriously" in the wording was intended to apply to "prejudiced" as well as to "impeded", and suggested the following analysis:

"With regard to the adverb 'seriously' a perusal of cases cited in *Att-Gen v Times Newspapers*[74] discloses that the adjective 'serious' has from time to time been used as an alternative to 'real' to describe the degree of risk of interfering with the course of justice, but not the degree of interference itself. It is, however, an ordinary English word that is not intrinsically inapt when used to describe the extent of an impediment or prejudice to the cause of justice in particular legal proceedings . . . If, as in the instant case and probably in most other criminal trials on indictment, it is the outcome of the trial or the need to discharge the jury without proceeding to a verdict that is put at risk, there can be no question that that which in the course of justice is put at risk is a serious as anything could be".

H. "Impeded"

4–97 The words "impeded or prejudiced" in s.2(2) require some further consideration. To "impede" is defined in the *Shorter Oxford English Dictionary* as "to obstruct in progress or in action, to hinder; to stand in the way of." The Phillimore Committee suggested that the statutory definition should avoid the use of such words as "interfered with", to be found for example in the judgments of the Divisional Court in *Att-Gen v Times Newspapers Ltd*,[75] because of the need to "make it clear that the interference has to be undesirable. What the law is aiming at is prejudice and obstruction."[76]

4–98 The use of the word "impeded", as recommended by the Phillimore Committee, makes it clear that if a publication is likely to have the effect of slowing down the stream of justice, or of diverting its flow even temporarily, that may in itself be treated as "undesirable" as a matter of public policy and punishable as

---

[70] As was alleged in *Roger Bullivant v Ellis*, Financial Times, April 15, 1986 (Lexis); see para.4–185. See also *J & P Coats v Chadwick* [1894] 1 Ch. 347.
[71] *Att-Gen v LWT Ltd* [1972] 3 All E.R. 1146 at 1149–50, Brabin J.
[72] [1983] A.C 116, at 142A–B.
[73] Which provides: "The strict liability rule applies only to a publication which creates a substantial risk that the course of justice in the proceedings in question will be seriously impeded or prejudiced."
[74] [1974] A.C. 273, discussed at paras 1–87 *et seq.*
[75] [1973] 1 Q.B. 710 at 725.
[76] para.113. The words "interfered with" were there said to be "too imprecise".

contempt. It does not appear to be necessary to go so far as to demonstrate that the conduct is likely to affect the outcome of the proceedings.[77]

For example, in *Att-Gen v Times Newspapers Ltd*,[78] Oliver L.J. said: 4–99

"The course of justice is not just concerned with the outcome of proceedings. It is concerned with the whole process of the law, including the freedom of a person accused of a crime to elect, so far as the law permits him to do so, the mode of trial which he prefers and to conduct his defence in the way which seems best to him and to his advisers. Any extraneous factor or external pressure which *impedes or restricts* that election or that conduct, or which impels a person accused to adopt a course in the conduct of his own defence which he does not wish to adopt, deprives him to an extent of the freedom of choice which the law confers upon him and is, in my judgment, not only a prejudice but a serious prejudice" (emphasis added).

These remarks were cited by Simon Brown L.J. in *Att-Gen v Unger*.[79] The *Daily Mail* published still photographs taken from a video recording of a home help taking money from her employer's hiding place, under the heading "The home help who was busy helping herself". At the time of publication, proceedings were "active" because she had been arrested and charged with two offences of theft. Proceedings for contempt were taken on the basis of possible prejudice to the outcome of proceedings. 4–100

The Divisional Court, however, raised the possibility of a different form of interference with the legal proceedings, namely that such a publication might influence the conduct of the accused herself. The only reported authority cited to the court on this aspect of the case was the judgment of Oliver L.J., which had been delivered in the course of contempt proceedings involving various newspaper respondents over their coverage of Michael Fagan, the intruder who was found in the Queen's bedroom. He had come to the conclusion that the *Sunday Times* in particular had been "gunning for" Fagan and took into account his solicitor's evidence that he had been forced to opt for trial on indictment, with consequential delay, as a result of the *Sunday Times* article. 4–101

In *Unger*, the court came to the conclusion that, on the facts, no contempt was made out, on either basis, but there seems to be no reason in principle why such influence upon a litigant or a defendant in criminal proceedings should not fall within the mischief contemplated by s.2(2). Even though the matter would not be directly relevant to the outcome of the proceedings, but only to their conduct, the consequences could be classified as either "impediment" or "prejudice". 4–102

It has sometimes been suggested that it is not "necessary in a democratic society" to criminalise conduct in circumstances where any adverse impact could be addressed by other means, such as careful directions by the ultimate trial judge 4–103

---

[77] See, *e.g.* the remarks of Lord Diplock in *Att-Gen v English* [1983] A.C. 116 at 141G and of Lord Goddard C.J. in *R. v Evening Standard Co Ltd* [1954] 1 Q.B. 578 at 582.
[78] *The Times*, February 12, 1983 (Lexis).
[79] [1998] 1 Cr.App.R. 308, [1998] E.M.L.R. 280, discussed more fully at para.4–166.

4–103 CHAPTER 4—THE STATUTORY REGIME FOR STRICT LIABILITY

or by jury vetting.[80] However, the use of the word "impede" might suggest that the very creation of a need to take such precautions, or avoiding measures, is inherently "undesirable".

4–104 This is borne out to an extent by the approach of Tasker Watkins L.J. in *Att-Gen v BBC*[81] where he, in the course of counsel's submission, indicated that it would be appropriate to impose a fine which reflected the proportion of the day's proceedings taken up, and public money wasted. A judge in the Crown Court at Shrewsbury had had to spend several hours considering a broadcast news item and minimising its prejudicial impact. Four members of the jury had seen the programme which, in purporting to summarise prosecution counsel's opening speech, included a number of matters which he had deliberately omitted, and which had come from an earlier police briefing.

4–105 In the Divisional Court, attention was focused on the wording of s.2(2), and the relationship between "impeding" and "prejudice". Tasker Watkins L.J. pointed out that the two separate risks may not always be mutually exclusive. On the facts, the matters published seemed to give rise to the possibility of impeding the course of justice rather than that of prejudicing the defence. The fact that the jury were *not* discharged did not assist in deciding whether, immediately following the broadcast, there had been a substantial risk of seriously impeding or prejudicing the course of justice. The Attorney-General had been right in submitting that there was a serious risk of the course of justice being seriously impeded. It was on the cards that the jury would have to be discharged; there was also the risk that if they were not discharged, and the defendants were convicted, the failure to discharge would found a ground of appeal.

4–106 Despite the fact, as the court had acknowledged, that the conduct has to be "viewed objectively at the time of publication", it nevertheless remains difficult, in practice, to argue in such a case that there has been no "impeding", or that there should be no finding of contempt. A respondent may be placed in the invidious position of having to argue that the trial judge had overreacted to the relevant publication, in taking steps to mitigate some perceived risk.

4–107 In fact, however, the tendency of the most recent authorities has been to concentrate primarily on the statutory notion of "prejudice" in construing s.2(2) of the Act and to relegate that of "impeding" to a lesser importance.[82] The two

---

[80] See the discussion in *Dagenais v Canadian Broadcasting Corp* (1994) 120 D.L.R. (4th) 12 at 42–7, (1995) 94 C.C.C. (3d) 289 at 322–7: "The judge must consider all other options besides the ban and must find that there is no reasonable and effective alternative available" at 327, Lamer C.J.C.; see also at 354–8, Gonthier J.

[81] [1992] C.O.D. 264. See also *Att-Gen v BBC and Jones*, December 1, 1995 D.C. (Lexis). And now see the decision of Aikens J. in *Ex p. HTV Cymru (Wales) Ltd*, [2002] E.M.L.R. 11, Cardiff Crown Court. The judge took into account, in deciding whether to grant a *quia timet* injunction, the risk of the instant murder trial being diverted by having to make enquiries into the consequences of an interview that HTV was proposing to hold with a prosecution witness (and ultimately to broadcast).

[82] *Att-Gen v Associated Newspapers Ltd*, October 31, 1997, DC (Lexis); *Att-Gen v Birmingham Post and Mail* [1998] 4 All E.R. 49. See also *Att-Gen v Guardian Newspapers Ltd* [1999] E.M.L.R. 904.

CATEGORIES OF PERSONS THOUGHT SUSCEPTIBLE TO INFLUENCE 4–110

are not true alternatives, and there is room for confusion if the attempt is made to give equal weight to each. There is a danger also of finding contempt proved where there is truly no risk of prejudice, and thus setting the threshold lower than Parliament intended.

It is submitted that just because time may have been taken at the trial arguing about whether the publication constitutes contempt, that ought not necessarily in itself to count as impeding the trial (not least because the submissions that a contempt had been committed might not be upheld). The true question might appear to be whether the trial has been diverted because the jury reasonably requires to be brought back on course by the judge. Even applying the European Convention test of "necessity", it is difficult to see why it should be thought impermissible to impose sanctions in respect of conduct which leads to trial judges having to take up time in setting the process of justice back on course. Yet, it seems clear from the judgment of Simon Brown L.J. in *Att-Gen v Birmingham Post and Mail Ltd*[83] that the mere need to give a direction to the jury would be an unsatisfactory basis on which to find contempt. Relevant here are the observations of Elias C.J. in *Solicitor-General v W&H Specialist Publications*[84]:   4–108

"The fact that the trial was postponed because of the publication is not sufficient to demonstrate that a real risk of prejudice existed. It is appropriate for a Judge dealing with an application for adjournment because of pre-trial publicity to be risk averse, particularly when the application is not opposed... The adjournment of the trial, although unfortunate, is not however the test for contempt."

It is important to emphasise that where a trial judge decides that prejudice has been occasioned to the particular proceedings by reason of media coverage, perhaps even to the point of staying proceedings for abuse of process, any such conclusion would in no way bind a tribunal charged with the responsibility of determining whether a contempt of court has been established.[85] While any rulings by the trial judge would be entitled to respect, the court hearing a committal application must come to its own view on the separate, though related, question as to whether or not there was created a substantial risk of serious prejudice.[86]   4–109

III. CATEGORIES OF PERSONS THOUGHT SUSCEPTIBLE TO INFLUENCE

Who is thought susceptible to influence?

Older authorities may be useful in considering the various categories of persons involved in the judicial process who are thought capable of being influenced by   4–110

---

[83] [1998] 4 All E.R. 49.
[84] [2003] N.Z.A.R. 118 at [31].
[85] *Att-Gen v MGN Ltd* [1997] 1 All E.R. 456; *Att-Gen v Morgan* [1998] E.M.L.R. 294. But it could be a "telling factor": *per* Simon Brown L.J. in *Att-Gen v Birmingham Post and Mail* [1998] 4 All E.R. 49. See too the remarks of Elias C.J. cited above.
[86] See, *e.g.* Pill L.J. in *Att-Gen v Morgan* [1998] E.M.L.R. 294 at 301. See also *Att-Gen v Associated Newspapers Ltd*, October 31, 1997, DC Kennedy L.J. (Lexis); *Att-Gen v Guardian Newspapers Ltd* [1999] E.M.L.R. 904.

4–110 CHAPTER 4—THE STATUTORY REGIME FOR STRICT LIABILITY

prejudicial publication. These must all be read now, however, in the light of the restrictions imposed by the strict liability rule.

1. *Jurors*

4–111 Jurors have, at least until recently,[87] been treated as being particularly vulnerable to prejudicial publications because of their lack of legal training and experience. In *R. v Fisher*[88] Lord Ellenborough C.J. said:

> "If anything is more important than another in the administration of justice, it is that jurymen should come to the trial of those persons on whose guilt or innocence they are to decide, with minds pure and unprejudiced."

4–112 In *Att-Gen v Times Newspapers Ltd*[89] Lord Diplock stated that the due administration of justice requires that all citizens should be able to rely upon obtaining in the courts the arbitrament of a tribunal which is free from bias against any party and whose decision will be based upon those facts only that have been proved in evidence adduced before it in accordance with the procedure adopted in courts of law. He went on to point out that in the decided cases the judges had sought to protect laymen including jurors from any influence or pressure which might impair their impartiality or cause them to form preconceived views as to the facts of the dispute (clearly a lower threshold than now sanctioned by the 1981 Act).

4–113 Whilst it is important that justice should not only be done but also be seen to be done, it would be wrong to take too fastidious a view of jurors' susceptibilities. In *R. v Kray*[90] two men were convicted of serious offences and their trial had been widely publicised. Immediately afterwards they stood trial on further charges. Lawton J. observed that:

> "I have enough confidence in my fellow-countrymen to think that they have got newspapers sized up and they are capable in normal circumstances of looking at a matter fairly and without prejudice even though they have to disregard what they may have read in a newspaper."

In the event the jury in the second trial acquitted the accused on some of the charges.

4–114 Increasingly, both in England and in other common law jurisdictions, there is a trend towards treating jurors as responsible and capable of resisting extraneous influences in the discharge of their duties, whether the matter arises in the context

---

[87] See paras 4–159 *et seq.*
[88] (1811) 2 Camp.563 at 570, 170 E.R. 1253. For modern examples, see *The Prothonotary v Collins* (1985) 2 N.S.W.L.R. 549 at 563, McHugh J.A.; *Keegstra v One Yellow Rabbit Theatre Association* (1992) 91 D.L.R. (4th) 532, where it was said that there was a real and substantial risk that a juror might be prejudiced in relation to pending criminal proceedings as a result of seeing a play; *Att-Gen v Steadman* (unreported) February 7, 1994, in which Bell J. also granted an injunction against the production of a play, "Maxwell, the Musical".
[89] [1974] A.C. at 309.
[90] (1969) 53 Cr.App.R. 412.

CATEGORIES OF PERSONS THOUGHT SUSCEPTIBLE TO INFLUENCE   4–116

of an appeal against conviction, or an application to stay for abuse of process, or upon an application to commit for contempt.[91] In Scotland, the trend is in the same direction, where it has been said[92]:

> "Juries are healthy bodies. They do not need a germ free atmosphere. Even when articles in the press do contain germs of prejudice, it will rarely be appropriate, in my opinion, to bring these to the attention of the court, far less for specific directions to have to be given, far less for the issue to be treated as even potentially one of contempt".

In *Montgomery v HMA*,[93] Lord Hope commented that the entire system of jury trial is based upon the assumption that the jury will follow the instructions which they receive from the trial judge and that they will return a true verdict in accordance with the evidence. The effect of prejudicial material had to be considered in the context of the proceedings as a whole, including the likely impact of oral evidence. There are occasionally, however, exceptional circumstances which render it impossible to be sure that all risk of prejudice can be eliminated however conscientious the jurors may be, and however forcefully they may be directed.[94]

2. *Lay magistrates*

There are few cases where the court has had to consider specifically the matter of potential prejudice occurring in relation to a trial before lay justices.[95] This is perhaps because in the case of an offence "triable either way" the court will, on any application based on contempt, assess whether a risk of prejudice has been created in the light of the fact that the accused person may opt for trial by jury. The court would be confined to addressing the issue of justices themselves being prejudiced only if the relevant offence is triable summarily, or, if triable either way, when the publication took place after the accused has already elected summary trial.   4–115

Lay magistrates, although not legally qualified, have collective experience of the legal process greater than that of the ordinary layman. The traditional view of the judiciary was expressed by Lord Diplock in *Att-Gen v Times Newspapers Ltd*,[96] when he commented that laymen, whether acting as jurymen or witnesses (or, for that matter, as magistrates), were regarded as being vulnerable to influence or pressure which might impair their impartiality or cause them to form   4–116

---

[91] *R. v Cannan* (1990) 92 Cr.App.R. 16; *R. v Corbett* (1988) 41 C.C.C. (3d) 385 at 400–3. See also *Dagenais v Canadian Broadcasting Corp* (1994) 120 D.L.R. (4th) 12, 94 C.C.C. (3d) 289, 322, Lamer C.J.C.; *Ex p. The Telegraph plc* [1993] 1 W.L.R. 980 at 987; *R. v Coughlan* (1976) 63 Cr.App.R. 33 at 37; *R. v Lane & Ross* (1970) 1 C.C.C. 196; *Att-Gen v MGN Ltd* [1997] 1 All E.R. 456; *Att-Gen v Unger* [1998] 1 Cr.App.R. 308, [1998] E.M.L.R. 280, Simon Brown L.J. See also the judgments of the Divisional Court in *Att-Gen v Birmingham Post and Mail* [1998] 4 All E.R. 49. These decisions are discussed at paras 4–148 *et seq.*
[92] *Cox, Petr.* 1998 S.L.T. 1172 at 1178 (*per* Lord Prosser).
[93] [2003] 1 A.C. 641, 2000 S.C.C.R. 1044 at 1107B.
[94] See, *e.g. Att-Gen v Associated Newspapers Ltd*, discussed at paras 4–61 *et seq.*
[95] But see, *e.g. Johnson v Leicestershire Constabulary*, *The Times*, October 7, 1998.
[96] [1974] A.C. 273 at 309.

4–116 preconceived views as to the issues before them.[97] If the matter were to be addressed nowadays, the court would be wary of expressing such an apprehension, especially in the light of the training which magistrates nowadays undergo, and the increasingly robust attitude towards possible prejudice on the part of jurors.

4–117 Reference was made to the relevance of lay justices' experience in this context in the case of *R. (Mahfouz) v General Medical Council*.[98] The question was raised of prejudicial newspaper coverage having been read by members of the professional conduct committee of the GMC. Having referred to *Montgomery v HMA*, Carnwath L.J. referred to a spectrum with the jury being at one end, with no previous experience of court procedures, and lay justices being "further along the line because they should be better able to put out of mind irrelevant matters by virtue of training and experience." On the facts, it was held that there was no basis for questioning the committee's ability to decide the case fairly on the evidence before it. The court was concerned with allegations both of prejudice and bias. The important difference between the two concepts was that bias or apparent bias could not be corrected. As to prejudice, however, the impact of prejudicial material had, as explained in *Montgomery*, to be assessed in the context of the proceedings as a whole and the availability of legal advice. Just as a judge by a strong direction to a jury could often be taken to have effectively countered any prejudice, so too the legal assessor could give the professional committee legal advice (presumably as to the importance of ignoring extraneous material).

3. Professional judges generally

4–118 Professional judges by reason of their legal and professional experience are generally expected to be unaffected by reading prejudicial matter. In *R. v Duffy Ex p. Nash*[99] Lord Parker C.J. said:

> "A judge is in a very different position to a juryman. Though in no sense a superhuman, he has by his training no difficulty in putting out of his mind matters which are not in evidence in the case. This indeed happens daily to judges on Assize. This is all the more so in the case of a member of the Court of Criminal Appeal, who in regard to an appeal against conviction is dealing almost entirely with points of law and who in the case of an appeal against sentence is considering whether or not the sentence is correct in principle."

---

[97] In the case of *R. v Tibbits and Windust* [1902] 1 K.B. 77, the view was expressed that whilst it was a contempt to try to pervert the mind of a magistrate it was not as serious as attempting to pervert that of a juror.
[98] [2004] EWCA Civ 431, *The Times* March 19, 2004 CA. This was not a contempt case, and indeed it could not be, having regard to the fact that the General Medical Council is not a body that exercises the judicial power of the state and hence is not a "court" within the meaning of s.19 of the Contempt of Court Act 1981: *GMC v BBC* [1998] 3 All E.R. 426.
[99] [1960] 2 Q.B. 188 at 198. For the position in Scotland, see *Aitchison v Bernadi*, 1984 S.C.C.R. 88, at para.16–409.

CATEGORIES OF PERSONS THOUGHT SUSCEPTIBLE TO INFLUENCE   4–121

By contrast, however, in *Att-Gen v BBC*[1] Viscount Dilhorne said: 4–119

"It is sometimes asserted that no judge will be influenced in his judgment by anything said by the media and consequently that the need to prevent the publication of matter prejudicial to the hearing of a case only exists where the decision rests with laymen. This claim to judicial superiority over human frailty is one that I find some difficulty in accepting. Every holder of a judicial office does his utmost not to let his mind be affected by what he has seen or heard or read outside the court and he will not knowingly let himself be influenced in any way by the media, nor in my view will any layman experienced in the discharge of judicial duties. Nevertheless it should, I think, be recognised that a man may not be able to put that which he has seen, heard or read entirely out of his mind and that he may be subconsciously affected by it."

Yet in the same case Lord Salmon expressed the more traditional view[2]:   4–120

"I am and have always been satisfied that no judge would be influenced in his judgment by what may be said by the media. If he were, he would not be fit to be a judge."

The decision of the Irish Supreme Court in *Kelly v O'Neill and Brady*[3] is of interest in this context. It was recognised that, notwithstanding their professional training and solemn declaration on taking office, it could not be said that professional judges were incapable of being prejudiced by unnecessary exposure to media material. The case concerned the publication of information based on police sources but not adduced in evidence; this took place between conviction and sentence. It was thought necessary to guard against a public perception that the court was responding to media pressure in sentencing, even if unjustifiable, since the perception could in itself be damaging to the administration of justice. In England and Wales, perhaps for similar reasons, criminal proceedings remain "active" and thus as not "concluded", for the purposes of s.2(3) and Sch.1 of the Contempt of Court Act 1981, until sentence has been passed.[4]

There will be few occasions when a publication will raise a substantial risk of   4–121
serious prejudice to a trial to be conducted by a judge alone.[5] Lord Reid in *Att-Gen v Times Newspapers Ltd* said[6]:

---

[1] [1981] A.C. 303 at 335. See also *Bell v Stewart* (1920) 28 C.L.R. 419, 433 (Isaacs and Rich JJ. dissenting). See also para.5–101, and the cases cited in n.54 thereto.
[2] [1981] A.C. 303 at 342. See also *Victoria v Australian Building Construction Employees' and Builders Labourers' Federation* (1982) 152 C.L.R. 25 at 136, Wilson J.
[3] [2000] 1 I.R. 354. See also *Solicitor-General v Smith* [2004] 2 N.Z.L.R. 540 at 557: "Judges, despite their training and experience are only human and not entirely aloof from pressure".
[4] See paras 4–175 *et seq*. Cp. the remarks of Lord Hobhouse of Woodborough in (2001) 117 L.Q.R. 496 at 498, cited at para.11–307.
[5] Occasionally, judges may sit with lay assessors. For example, in *R. v Bulgin Ex p. BBC, The Times*, July 14, 1977, the Divisional Court was considering an article in *West Indian World* headed "B.B.C. is guilty of racial discrimination". It was argued that this might cause prejudice to proceedings then pending in the county court between the Race Relations Board and the BBC, and in particular that it might affect the two lay assessors sitting with the county court judge. Lord Widgery C.J. said that he did not believe for a moment that they would be affected or that they would carry forward any impression created by an article appearing several months beforehand. Nor could any inference be drawn as to any such adverse impact upon potential witnesses.
[6] [1974] A.C. 273 at 301.

4–121 CHAPTER 4—THE STATUTORY REGIME FOR STRICT LIABILITY

"It is scarcely possible to imagine a case when comment could influence judges in the Court of Appeal or noble and learned Lords in this House. And it would be wrong and contrary to existing practice to limit proper criticism of judgments already given but under appeal."

Lord Simon although indicating that appellate proceedings might in principle be the subject-matter of contempt, expressed similar views to Lord Reid.[7]

4–122 Since the old pre-judgment test has now gone, it is reasonable to assume, in a case to be tried by judge alone,[8] that it would be most unlikely that any discussion of the merits would be held to create a substantial risk of serious prejudice. This point was discussed by the High Court of Justiciary in *Al Megrahi and Fhima v Times Newspapers Ltd*.[9] The case concerned the Lockerbie bombing. Two Libyan citizens were being tried according to Scottish law in the Netherlands by professional judges without a jury. The case concerned a leading article in the *Sunday Times* commenting upon the merits of the criminal prosecution and expressing the opinion under the headline "The Guilt of Gadaffi" that "it would be an odd sort of justice that found his cat's-paws guilty of murder and let the real villain off the hook". The article went on to state that "... even if the suspects are convicted (and it is conceivable that a verdict in Scottish law of not proven or even not guilty might be found after all this time), what will the Government do then? Lift sanctions against a regime convicted of mass murder". The court emphasised the difference between trial by judge alone and trial by jury and concluded that, in the absence of a jury in that case, there was no substantial risk of serious prejudice.

4–123 A separate matter, in relation to trial by judge alone, was mentioned in the much earlier case of *Davies Ex p. Delbert-Evans*.[10] Humphreys J. expressed the view that it was wrong to publish matter which might embarrass a judge and make it more difficult for him to do his work. In the absence, however, of substantial risk of serious prejudice any such publication would be treated as contempt only if *mens rea* is present.

4–124 A possible further instance in which a publication might be held to be a contempt under the strict liability rule, even though it potentially affected a judge sitting alone, would be disclosure in a newspaper of an amount of money paid into court or the content of an offer made under CPR Pt 36.[11] Such a publication might cause a trial to be abandoned, and in such circumstances the course of justice would plainly be impeded.

---

[7] *ibid.* at 321.
[8] Such as, *e.g. Vine Products Ltd v Green* [1966] Ch. 484. See also *Schering Chemicals Ltd v Falkman Ltd* [1982] Q.B. 1 at 29F, Shaw L.J., 40E, Templeman L.J.
[9] 1999 S.C.C.R. 824.
[10] [1945] 1 K.B. at 442; cf. *Fairclough v Manchester Ship Canal Co* (1896) 13 T.L.R. 56 and *Re William Thomas Shipping* [1930] 2 Ch. 368.
[11] CPR 36.19(2) stipulates that a payment shall not be communicated to the trial judge until all questions of liability and the amount of money to be awarded have been decided.

4. The Judicial Committee of the House of Lords

In *Re Lonrho (Contempt Proceedings)*,[12] proceedings were instigated against Lonrho plc, named directors, and the publishers and editor of *The Observer* (a newspaper owned by Lonrho) for contempt of the House of Lords. The Secretary of State for Trade and Industry had commissioned a report in response to allegations of misconduct in relation to the circumstances of a takeover, and it was forwarded to the Serious Fraud Office. He declined to publish the report because of potential prejudice in the event of criminal prosecutions.

Proceedings were brought to have this decision quashed by way of judicial review. This was unsuccessful in the Court of Appeal, and the matter went to the House of Lords. At this point, a copy of the report came into Lonrho's possession, and it was decided to publish extracts in *The Observer*. Copies (as well as other campaign literature) were sent to members of the House, including those who were to be hearing the appeal and the question was raised on the motion of their Lordships whether lobbying the House in this way might not amount to a contempt, either under the 1981 Act or at common law.

The first committee which heard the matter recused itself for possible bias, on the ground of natural justice, and a fresh committee expressed the view that the "possibility that a professional judge will be influenced by anything that he has read about the issues in a case which he has to try is very much more remote" than would be the case with a juror. It was also observed that, by the time a case reaches the House of Lords, the possibility that the parties could be adversely influenced was also "remote". Lord Bridge commented[13]:

> "So far as the appellate tribunal is concerned, it is difficult to visualise circumstances in which any court in the United Kingdom exercising appellate jurisdiction would be in the least likely to be influenced by public discussion of the merits of a decision appealed against or of the parties' conduct in the proceedings".

He continued:

> "Discussion and criticism of decisions of first instance or of the Court of Appeal which are subject to pending appeals are a commonplace in legal journals,[14] but on matters of more general public interest examples also readily spring to mind of criticism in the general press directed against, for example, criminal convictions, sentences imposed, damages awarded in libel actions and other court decisions which arouse public controversy. No case was drawn to our attention in which public discussion of the issues

---

[12] [1990] 2 A.C. 154, HL.
[13] *ibid.* at 209. And see *Att-Gen v Times Newspapers Ltd* (*The Times*, February 12, 1983) (Lexis), and *Att-Gen v Unger* [1998] 1 Cr.App.R. 308, [1998] E.M.L.R. 280, paras 4–99 *et seq.*, for cases where the possibility of contempt arising through the press bringing pressure to bear upon defendants in criminal proceedings is discussed.
[14] See also his speech in *R. v Shivpuri* [1987] A.C. 1 at 23E–G: "... I have had the advantage, since the conclusion of the argument in this appeal, of reading an article by Professor Glanville Williams entitled 'The Lords and Impossible Attempts, or Quis Custodiet Ipsos Custodes?' [1986] C.L.J. 33. The language in which he criticises the decision in *Anderton v Ryan* is not conspicuous for its moderation, but it would be foolish, on that account, not to recognise the force of the criticism and churlish not to acknowledge the assistance I have derived from it".

4–127 CHAPTER 4—THE STATUTORY REGIME FOR STRICT LIABILITY

arising in, or criticism of the parties to, litigation already decided at first instance has been held to be a contempt on the ground that it was likely to impede or prejudice the course of justice in proceedings on appeal from that decision."

4–128 The House also had to consider the proposition that, in publishing the report, the respondents had been pre-empting the outcome of the appeal to the House. Again, the committee applied the statutory formula and came to the conclusion that there was no substantial risk of serious prejudice.[15]

5. *Witnesses*[16]

4–129 In so far as witnesses could be deterred from coming forward to give evidence by the publication of material in the media, this was regarded at common law as being capable of constituting contempt.[17] Such deterrence may now afford an example of strict liability contempt, provided there is a substantial risk of serious prejudice.

4–130 Potential witnesses may be deterred by direct public intimidation. In *Re Doncaster and Retford Co-operative Societies Agreement*,[18] an article appeared in the *Co-operative News* which strongly disparaged officials of the Co-operative movement who might decide to give evidence against boundary agreements in a case pending before the Restrictive Practices Court.[19] Diplock J. took the view that the article was an attempt to intimidate witnesses and to influence evidence, and thus a serious contempt of court.

4–131 Even an implied or indirect threat to potential witnesses, for example through attacks upon a party to the relevant litigation, can constitute contempt.[20] When *The Daily Worker* commented that the members of a trade union " . . . will no doubt have no mercy upon those who seek to upset working class decisions in the capitalist courts", Goddard J. found that although the article was disparaging of the plaintiff it was a contempt because of its deterrent effect upon witnesses who might otherwise come forward to offer their assistance. So too, where a local newspaper criticised the motives of a plaintiff in pending proceedings, in a political context, it was held that this was likely to deter witnesses from

---

[15] It was also held that there was no contempt at common law. This was not very fully discussed, but the House concluded that there was no intent to impede or prejudice the course of justice, so that s.6(c) of the Contempt of Court Act 1981, which preserves liability for an intentional contempt, could not apply.
[16] For discussion of contempt in relation to witnesses otherwise than by publication, see paras 11–190 *et seq*.
[17] See, *e.g. Greenwood v The Leather Shod Wheel Co Ltd* (1898) 14 T.L.R. 241; *R. v Bottomley, The Times*, December 19, 1908; *R. v Gossip, The Times*, February 18, 1909.
[18] [1960] L.R. 2 R.P.C. 129.
[19] What was said was that "One of the most disturbing aspects of this case was the probability that the chief officials of a number of societies will give evidence for the State against boundary agreements which in practice means against the Co-operative union, which is carrying out Congress policy on this matter."
[20] See *Hutchinson v Amalgamated Engineering Union, Re The Daily Worker, The Times*, August 25, 1932.

Categories of Persons Thought Susceptible to Influence   4–135

supporting him with their evidence.[21] It is by no means certain that such conduct would be categorised as contempt today, and a court might be expected to take a more robust view.

In *Spurrell v De Rechberg*,[22] allegations were made in a newspaper, in the context of pending proceedings in the Probate, Divorce and Admiralty Division, about the validity of a will, to the effect that the testator was acting under "undue influence". The President observed that no such allegation had been made by the defendants in the litigation, and it was such as to deter witnesses from coming forward. He therefore held that the article constituted a contempt.   4–132

Apart from deterrence, potential witnesses may also be affected by media publications in the sense that their evidence could be coloured by what they have read or seen.   4–133

It is not a contempt to advertise for witnesses even if the advertisement offers a reward to those who come forward,[23] provided the advertisement is a *bona fide* attempt to find witnesses and not merely intended to put pressure on parties to litigation.[24] Care should be taken to see that the advertisement does not contain generally prejudicial matter.[25]   4–134

6. Parties in criminal or civil proceedings

A distinction has been drawn as a matter of policy between the court's approach to influence brought to bear, whether by media publication or otherwise, upon witnesses or potential witnesses and any such pressures exerted upon parties to civil litigation.[26] In *Att-Gen v Times Newspapers Ltd*[27] Lord Reid said: 4–135

> "I think that there is a difference between direct interference with the fair trial of an action and words or conduct which may affect the mind of a litigant. Comment likely to affect the minds of witnesses and of the tribunal must be stopped for otherwise the trial may well be unfair. But the fact that a party refrains from seeking to enforce his full legal rights in no way prejudices a fair trial, whether the decision is or is not influenced by some third party. There are other weighty reasons for preventing improper influence being brought to bear on litigants, but they have little to do with interference with the fairness of a trial. There must be absolute prohibition of interference with a fair trial but beyond that there must be a balancing of relevant considerations."

---

[21] *Re Hinde, Thornhill v Steel Morris* (1911) 56 S. J. 34; *Re Pall Mall Gazette* (1894) 11 T.L.R. 122.
[22] (1895) 11 T.L.R. 313.
[23] *Plating Co v Farquharson* (1881) 17 Ch. D. 49 overruling *Pool v Sacheverall* (1720) 1 P. Wms.676, 24 E.R. 565.
[24] *Cornish v Gill* (1894) 9 T.L.R. 196.
[25] See, *e.g.* *Roger Bullivant v Ellis*, *Financial Times*, April 15, 1986 (Lexis).
[26] See, *e.g.* *R. v Kellett* [1976] Q.B. 372 and *Att-Gen v Martin (Peter)*, *The Times*, April 23, 1986, discussed at para.11–282.
[27] [1974] A.C. 273 at 296.

4–136 CHAPTER 4—THE STATUTORY REGIME FOR STRICT LIABILITY

4–136 There may be publications which exert influence upon litigants, but which nevertheless fall outside the strict liability rule, either because they do not raise a substantial risk of serious prejudice or because they are private and not public communications. Private communications may often be more effective in bringing pressure to bear than publications to the world at large.[28] The subject is addressed in chapter 11. However, since media publications may well create a substantial risk of serious prejudice or impediment in particular legal proceedings, the subject is appropriately addressed also in this chapter.

4–137 The considerations of policy applying to litigants in civil litigation do not necessarily have relevance to those involved in criminal proceedings as defendants. They would not normally have a great deal of choice as to the commencement or continuance of such proceedings. Nevertheless, it is not permitted to bring influence to bear upon defendants, whether by publication or otherwise, so as to deprive them of options relating, for example, relating to a proposed plea or to mode of trial.[29] As to private prosecutors, however, it appears that it may be legitimate to exert fair and reasonable pressure with a view to persuading the person concerned not to continue with the prosecution,[30] as is the case with claimants involved in civil litigation.

4–138 *Att-Gen v Times Newspapers Ltd*[31] remains the leading case in this field, although it is now necessary to bear in mind the constraints imposed by the 1981 Act so far as strict liability is concerned. The *Sunday Times* published an article concerning litigation between the Distillers Company and the parents of children seriously injured by the thalidomide drugs sold by that company. The article, published on September 24, 1972, suggested that the Distillers were in a morally indefensible position. A second article, publication of which was restrained by injunction, would have canvassed, and thus sought to prejudice, the merits on the issue of negligence.

4–139 The House held unanimously that the second article would have constituted a contempt. Lords Simon and Diplock (and also by implication Lord Morris) decided that to hold a litigant up to public obloquy, so as to influence his conduct in the course of litigation, would be a contempt.

4–140 Differing views were also expressed as to the effect of the article actually published on September 24. Lords Reid and Cross took the view that it did not constitute contempt; Lords Diplock and Simon concluded that it did. Lord Morris was content to observe that in his view the Attorney-General had been right in deciding not to refer that article to the court.

4–141 Lord Reid considered that it was in principle permissible to seek to dissuade a litigant from proceeding with an action including, apparently, by threatening to cease trading, or by actually doing so. He chose the illustration of Shylock's

---

[28] See para.11–276.
[29] See, *e.g. Att-Gen v Times Newspapers Ltd*, February 12, 1983 (Lexis), Oliver L.J., discussed at paras 4–95 *et seq*; *Att-Gen v Unger* [1998] 1 Cr.App.R. 308, [1998] E.M.L.R. 280.
[30] *Att-Gen v Martin (Peter)*, The Times, April 23, 1986 (Lexis), discussed at para.11–282.
[31] [1974] A.C. 273. See para.1–87.

claim to the pound of flesh, thus implying that such pressure would be legitimate in the case of a claim perceived to be morally or legally indefensible. Any fair and temperate criticism of a litigant, falling short of actually pre-judging the issues, would in his view have been permissible, although he drew a distinction between criticism of that kind and, on the other hand, "injurious misrepresentation".[32] His view of the article of September 24 was that it had *not* gone beyond fair and temperate criticism of the Distillers' moral position and therefore, although it clearly helped to persuade the Distillers to increase their offer of settlement, that it did not amount to contempt.

Lord Cross concurred in the view that fair and temperate criticism of a litigant was permissible, even if intended to influence a litigant's conduct of a case, and indeed even if it was successful in doing so. He also concluded that the article of September 24 was not a contempt. He expressed the distinction in the following terms[33]:

4–142

> "To say that there must be no prejudging of the issues in a case is one thing. To say that no one must in any circumstances exert any pressure on a party to litigation to induce him to act in relation to the litigation in a way in which he would otherwise not choose to act is another and a very different, thing. A layman who reflected on the matter might well be prepared to agree that a rule that the issues in pending proceedings should not be prejudged by discussions in the media was justifiable; but I am sure that he would consider that a rule prohibiting the publication of any statement likely to influence a party in the conduct of litigation, even though it did not relate to the issues in the action, was an unwarranted interference with freedom of expression. 'Surely,' he would say, 'it ought to depend on the way in which the influence is exerted.' That is, I think, in fact the legal position. To seek to dissuade a litigant from prosecuting or defending proceedings by threats of unlawful action, by abuse, by misrepresentation of the nature of the proceedings or the circumstances out of which they arose and such like, is no doubt a contempt of court; but if the writer states the facts fairly and accurately, and expresses his view in temperate language the fact that the publication may bring pressure—possibly great pressure—to bear on the litigant should not make it a contempt of court".

Lord Morris observed:

4–143

> "... I see no reason why a temperate and reasoned appeal might not have been expressed inviting Distillers to consider whether, quite regardless as to whether they were in law in any way liable, they should make generous payments on the basis that it was as the result of purchases of that which they had sold that such unfortunate consequences had resulted."[34]

This is clearly very close to the reasoning of Lords Reid and Cross.

---

[32] [1974] A.C. 273 at 297D (a phrase echoing the judgment of Maugham J. in *Re William Thomas Shipping Co* [1930] 2 Ch. 368, 374). Lord Reid also referred to *Re South Shields (Thames Street) Clearance Order 1931* (1932) 173 L.T. 76 as an example of published criticism of litigants which did not exceed the bounds of "fair and temperate comment".
[33] [1974] A.C. at 325–6.
[34] *ibid.* at 307.

4–144 Lord Diplock came to a different conclusion as to the first article. He had no doubt that it was a contempt to hold a party to litigation up to public obloquy, since that might inhibit potential claimants in general from bringing cases before the court. He nevertheless concluded that it was permissible to bring private pressure to bear on a litigant to change his conduct of litigation. In his view the article of September 24 fell on the wrong side of the line. Private persuasion could in his view extend to threats to cease trading with a litigant unless he withdrew his legal proceedings. He stated the principle in the following words[35]:

> "In my opinion, a distinction is to be drawn between private persuasion of a party not to insist on relying in pending litigation on claims or defences to which he is entitled under the existing law, and public abuse of him for doing so. The former, so long as it is unaccompanied by unlawful threats, is not, in my opinion, contempt of court, the latter is at least a technical contempt, and this whether or not the abuse is likely to have any effect upon the conduct of that particular litigation by the party publicly abused."

4–145 In *Att-Gen v Martin (Peter)*,[36] Glidewell L.J. expressed the opinion that, since Lord Diplock had been in all material respects in agreement with the remainder of their Lordships' House, he was not to be understood by the phrase "unlawful threats" as meaning threats to do something inherently illegal. He was referring to "improper"[37] threats; that is to say going beyond that which was "fair, reasonable or moderate".

4–146 Lord Simon agreed[38] that the holding of a litigant up to execration, with the object of preventing his vindicating a legal right through negotiations, must be equally capable of being an interference with the due course of justice as conduct intended to deter pursuit of the same right at the trial itself. In his view the article of September 24 did hold Distillers up to public execration. He felt that in certain narrowly confined circumstances private interference with a litigant was permissible, for example, if there were a "genuine, unofficious and paramount concern for the real welfare of the litigant".

4–147 The key to this debate may be found in Lord Cross' conclusion that it ought to, and does, depend on the way the influence is exerted.[39] All their Lordships appear to have agreed with Lord Cross that abuse or misrepresentation would generally be regarded as impermissible. Any such pressure would not, in order to be classified as contempt of court, have to be shown either to fall within what is now the definition of strict liability contempt or be accompanied by an intention to interfere with the administration of justice. In the case of a *prima facie* strict

---

[35] *ibid.* at 313D–E.
[36] *The Times*, April 23, 1986 (Lexis), discussed para.11–282.
[37] See the use of the word "improper" in *R. v Patrascu* [2004] EWCA Crim 2417, [2004] 4 All E.R. 1066; and, on the circumstances in which "threats" to enforce one's legal rights might amount to "improper pressure", *Daniel v Drew* [2005] EWCA Civ 507, applying *Royal Bank of Scotland v Etridge (No.2)* [2001] UKHL 44, [2002] A.C. 773.
[38] [1974] A.C. at 317.
[39] At 326.

IV. STRICT LIABILITY CONTEMPT AND ABUSE OF PROCESS

The interrelationship between strict liability contempt and abuse of process

liability contempt, there might still be room for a defence under s.5[40] of the 1981 Act, but if the publication in question was directed towards the conduct of particular proceedings, it is unlikely that any prejudice created would be classified as "incidental".

A question arises as to cases where a publication, relied upon as a strict liability contempt, has already led to the abandonment of a trial; or where, even though a trial has gone ahead, the Court of Appeal has subsequently set aside a conviction as unsafe for the very reason of adverse publicity before or during the trial. Even in cases where the perceived prejudice has been caused by one publication, it seems that those responsible would be entitled to argue that they should not *ipso facto* be regarded as in contempt. The test of contempt is objective[41]; moreover the standard of proof is quite different in cases where a judge has to ask whether a fair trial is still possible.[42]

4–148

On the other hand, if one attributes too much significance to the differing standards of proof, one may be tempted to argue that the s.2(2) criteria could never be established by the Attorney-General *unless* the trial judge had stayed the proceedings. That this is not the law is illustrated clearly by *Att-Gen v English*,[43] *Att-Gen v BBC*,[44] *Att-Gen v BBC and Jones*,[45] and *Att-Gen v BBC and Hat Trick Productions*.[46] Nor is it the case that contempt can only be established in such circumstances if a defendant who has been found guilty would be able to succeed on appeal in showing his conviction to be unsafe.

4–149

One and the same publication may well constitute a contempt and yet, even though not substantially mitigated in its effect by a temporary stay and/or change of venue, not so prejudice a trial as to undermine the safety of any subsequent conviction. Reconciliation is required between the tests variously applied by (a) trial judges, (b) the Divisional Court hearing contempt applications, and (c) the Court of Appeal determining whether a conviction is unsafe. An answer was

4–150

---

[40] Considered at para.4–293.
[41] See, *e.g. Att-Gen v BBC* [1992] C.O.D. 264 where Tasker Watkins L.J. said that it was "... enough if the conduct complained of, viewed objectively at the time of publication, can surely be said to create a substantial risk that the course of justice in the proceedings to which the publication relates will be seriously impeded or prejudiced".
[42] Phillips J. in *R. v Maxwell*, March 6, 1995 held that the standard of proof is on the balance of probabilities, citing *R. v Derby Crown Court Ex p. Brookes* (1984) 80 Cr.App.R. 164. See para.4–164. Abuse of process stay applications are now governed by the 2002 consolidation of existing practice directions [2002] 1 W.L.R. 2870, [2002] 3 All E.R. 904 at [36]. For the latest version of the Direction see *www.courtservice.gov.uk/docs/cpd/consol_criminal_pd_220305.doc*.
[43] [1983] 1 A.C. 116.
[44] [1992] C.O.D. 264 (Lexis).
[45] December 1, 1995 (Lexis).
[46] [1997] E.M.L.R. 76.

4–150 CHAPTER 4—THE STATUTORY REGIME FOR STRICT LIABILITY

supplied by the Divisional Court in *Att-Gen v Birmingham Post and Mail Ltd*,[47] namely:

" ... section 2(2) postulates a lesser degree of prejudice than is required to make good an appeal against conviction. Similarly it seems to me to postulate a lesser degree of prejudice than would justify an order for a stay. In short, section 2(2) is designed to avoid (and where necessary punish) publications even if they merely risk prejudicing proceedings, whereas a stay will generally only be granted where it is recognised that any subsequent conviction would otherwise be imperilled, and a conviction will only be set aside (at all events now, since section 2 of the Criminal Appeals Act 1995) if it is actually unsafe. Whilst, therefore, it is correct to say that the Attorney General has to prove a contempt application beyond reasonable doubt, one must also bear in mind, as Auld L.J. observed in *Hat Trick Productions*, that 'the threshold of risk is not high' ".

4–151 In that case, a trial had been abandoned in Birmingham and the case transferred to Leicester where a new trial began ten days afterwards. The case focused primarily on the relationship in s.2(2) of the 1981 Act between "seriously impeding" and "seriously prejudicing". For the respondents, it was submitted that the word "impeded" added little to the scope of the strict liability rule, and that the Divisional Court should simply address the question whether objectively the publication had given rise to a substantial risk that the Birmingham trial would be prejudiced, paying little regard to the decision of the trial judge to discharge the jury and change the venue. This was consistent with the approach adopted in *Att-Gen v Morgan*[48] and *Att-Gen v Associated Newspapers Ltd*.[49] There were advanced three policy considerations to justify such an analysis:

(a) There is a different standard of proof governing a trial judge's decision whether to stay a criminal trial from and that relevant to the Divisional Court's determination of a committal application.

(b) Any other approach would require publishers to take advice on whether the proposed publication would create a substantial risk that a judge would, unnecessarily but reasonably, decide to stay proceedings.

(c) Publishers would on that basis need routinely to be represented before the trial judge to prevent their arguments on prejudice not being pre-empted.

4–152 By contrast, for the Attorney it was argued that a stay would obviously impede a trial and that the statutory criteria would thus be fulfilled where it could be demonstrated that there was created a substantial risk of such an order. Support was to be found for this in *Att-Gen v BBC*[50] and in *Att-Gen v BBC and Jones*.[51]

---

[47] [1998] 4 All E.R. 49; see also *Att-Gen v Guardian Newspapers Ltd* [1999] E.M.L.R. 904, discussed at para.4–171.
[48] [1998] E.M.L.R. 295.
[49] October 31, 1997 (Lexis).
[50] [1992] C.O.D. 264 (Lexis).
[51] December 1, 1995 (Lexis).

Simon Brown L.J. observed that "at first blush" these rival approaches appeared irreconcilable. Either s.2(2) is satisfied whenever it is "on the cards" that a jury would have to be discharged (*a fortiori* whenever they have been "reasonably" discharged); or the court should put that issue to one side and focus on the question whether there was a substantial risk of serious prejudice *had the proceedings continued*. He concluded that the significance of the distinction was more apparent than real.

As a matter of juridical analysis, the Divisional Court was of the view that the grant of a stay does not of itself prove contempt (still less would the Attorney establish contempt by merely showing that a stay was "on the cards"). Nevertheless, in practice, at least where a publication occurs during a trial, it would be difficult to envisage a publication which has caused the judge sufficient concern to discharge the jury and yet would not properly be regarded as a contempt. Simon Brown L.J. added:

> "I conclude that the only situation in which realistically that is likely to arise is where, analysed with the benefit of argument from the publishers' counsel, the publication is seen to have been so little prejudicial as not even to have given rise to a seriously arguable ground of appeal had the trial been allowed to continue and proceeded to conviction. I venture to doubt whether many stays will have been granted in these circumstances. Rather, as the cases show, it is altogether more likely that a stay will have been refused (or perhaps not even sought) and yet the publication nevertheless be in contempt."

The situation becomes more problematic where the perceived prejudice has been caused by a general climate, hostile to a defendant, and created by more than one newspaper or by the media in general. It seemed clear in the light of the Divisional Court's decision in *Att-Gen v MGN Ltd*[52] that, for the purposes of a committal application, the responsibility of each individual publisher must be addressed separately.[53] Yet on an application for the stay or abandonment of a criminal trial on the grounds of abuse of process a general climate of prejudice may be taken into account. This distinction clearly had potentially serious implications for the accountability of media proprietors and journalists. Some thought it necessary to take steps to neutralise the effect of the ruling. It was noted by the government in February 1998[54] that the National Heritage Committee had made a recommendation to the following effect:

> "... that Section 2 of the Contempt of Court Act 1981 should be strengthened so that it covers the collective or cumulative effect of pre-trial publicity in risking prejudicing a trial, as well as the effect of individual articles. This means that newspapers could not escape liability, as one case held they could, because a number of them had acted in a similar way and together had caused the prejudice."

In the House of Lords, Lord Irvine L.C. stated that the government accepted the recommendation for "strengthening" and that legislation would be brought

---

[52] [1997] 1 All E.R. 456.
[53] para.4–88. See the observations on this problem by Pitchford J. In *Att-Gen v Express Newspapers* [2004] EWHC 2859 (Admin).
[54] Lord Chancellor's Department, Press Notice 48/98.

4-155   CHAPTER 4—THE STATUTORY REGIME FOR STRICT LIABILITY

forward when a suitable opportunity could be found.[55] Yet to date no such measure has been introduced.[56] This is no doubt largely because of difficulties in both principle and definition.

4-156   The factual background to *Att-Gen v MGN Ltd* was as follows. On April 16, 1995 the partner of a well known television actress was arrested for assaulting her and her driver, following an incident outside their home address. The next day, he was charged with wounding the driver with intent, contrary to s.18 of the Offences Against the Person Act 1861. He appeared before magistrates on April 18 and was granted bail.

4-157   On April 18, and 22, 1995, the first, second, third and fourth respondents published articles concerning these events. On May 12 and 13, 1995 further articles were published by, respectively, the third and fifth respondents. On June 13, 1995, the defendant was committed to stand trial at the Crown Court, and shortly afterwards a provisional trial date was fixed for October 16, 1995.

4-158   At the end of September 1995, counsel for the defendant obtained a stay of proceedings on the basis that the pre-trial press coverage of the case had made a fair trial impossible. After this, the Attorney-General obtained leave to launch committal proceedings under RSC Ord.52, relying on the strict liability rule.

4-159   The Divisional Court considered, in determining the allegations of contempt, a number of appellate decisions addressing the capacity of jurors to resist the influence of media publications, but from the somewhat different context of appeals based upon the contention *ex post facto* that publicity had caused actual prejudice to criminal trials. In *R. v West*,[57] for example, Lord Taylor C.J. recognised that there had indeed been, in advance of the trial, press coverage that was extensive and hostile to the Wests; yet he continued:

> "However lurid the reporting, there can scarcely ever have been a case more calculated to shock the public who were entitled to know the facts. The question raised on behalf of the defence is whether a fair trial could be held after such intensive publicity adverse to the accused. In our view it could. To hold otherwise would mean that if allegations of murder are sufficiently horrendous so as inevitably to shock the nation, the accused cannot be tried. That would be absurd. Moreover, providing the Judge effectively warns the Jury to act only on the evidence given in Court, there is no reason to suppose that they would do otherwise."

4-160   The court also referred to other such cases, including *R. v Coughlan*,[58] where Lawton L.J had made the point that juries are regularly expected to disregard what one accused says about another in his absence, and that accordingly they should be expected to be able to disregard what they read in the newspapers. So

---

[55] *Hansard*, H.L. Vol. 586, (5th series), col. WA 117, February 27, 1998.
[56] On February 21, 2005 the Parliamentary Under-Secretary at the Department of Constitutional Affairs told the House of Commons that "The law of contempt plays a vital role in safeguarding the administration of justice, and there are no plans to reform it": *Hansard*, H.C. Vol. 431 (6th series) col. 447.
[57] [1996] 2 Cr.App.R. 374.
[58] (1976) 63 Cr.App.R. 33 at 37.

too, in *R. v Cannan*⁵⁹ Lord Lane C.J. had pointed out that juries are trusted to do justice in cases of sexual offences, where the risk of prejudice is self-evidently greater. He had also commented in *Ex p. The Telegraph plc*⁶⁰ that "a court should credit the jury with the will and ability to abide by the judge's direction to decide the case only on the evidence before them", and referred to the limited staying power of media publicity, even in cases of notoriety.⁶¹

The Divisional Court was also impressed by the approach adopted towards the responsibilities of jurors in the Canadian case of *R. v Corbett*,⁶² where attention had been drawn to the role of juries entrenched in the Canadian Charter of Rights and Freedoms. The matter was there considered by Dickson C.J.C. in the following terms: **4–161**

"It is, of course, entirely possible to construct an argument disputing the theory of trial by jury. Juries are capable of egregious mistakes and they may at times seem to be ill adapted to the exigencies of an increasingly complicated and refined criminal law. But until the paradigm is altered by Parliament, the court should not be heard to call into question the capacity of jurors to do the job assigned to them. The ramifications of any such statement could be enormous. Moreover, the fundamental *right* to a jury trial has recently been underscored by s.11(f) of the Charter. If that right is so important, it is logically incoherent to hold that juries are incapable of following the explicit instructions of a judge."

Both Dickson C.J.C. and Schiemann L.J. in *Att-Gen v MGN* cited the robust words of Addy J. in *R. v Lane & Ross*⁶³: **4–162**

" . . . I do not feel that, in deciding questions of this kind, one must proceed on the assumption that jurors are morons, completely devoid of intelligence and totally incapable of understanding a rule of evidence of this type or of acting in accordance with it. If such were the case, there would be no justification at all for the existence of juries, and what had been regarded for centuries as a bulwark of our democratic system and a guarantee of our basic freedoms under the law would in fact be nothing less than a delusion".

In the light of these authorities, the Divisional Court in *Att-Gen v MGN Ltd* came to the conclusion that the Attorney-General's application for committal should be dismissed in respect of all the respondent newspaper groups; and this was despite the decision of the Crown Court judge to abandon the trial in the light of the same publicity. The court was not called upon to rule upon the correctness of that decision. It seems clear that the Crown Court judge had taken into account, as he was entitled to do, the overall effect of the pre-trial publicity, **4–163**

---

⁵⁹ (1990) 92 Cr.App.R. 16.
⁶⁰ [1993] 1 W.L.R. 980 at 987.
⁶¹ See also the judgment of Simon Brown L.J. in *Att-Gen v Unger* [1998] 1 Cr.App.R. 308, [1998] E.M.L.R. 280, D.C., where this was described as the "fade factor". But see now *HMA v Beggs (No.1)*, High Court of Justiciary, 2002 S.L.T. 135, S.C.C.R. 869, which highlights the problems that may be caused by the continuing availability of prejudicial allegations on the internet, *e.g.* in the form of newspaper archive material.
⁶² (1988) 41 C.C.C. (3d) 385 at 400–3. See also *Dagenais v Canadian Broadcasting Corp.* (1994) 120 D.L.R. (4th) 12 at 42, (1994) 94 C.C.C. (3d) 289 at 322, Lamer C.J.C.
⁶³ (1970) 1 C.C.C. 196 at 201.

without distinguishing between one newspaper and another. He had also taken into account articles closer in time to the anticipated trial, in respect of which the Attorney-General had not moved to commit.

4–164 Crucial was the fact that the standard of proof in the contempt proceedings was such that the Divisional Court was required to be satisfied, in respect of each respondent,[64] beyond reasonable doubt. By contrast, a judge who is considering whether or not a fair trial is possible is entitled to apply the different test described by Phillips J. in *R. v Maxwell*[65]:

> "The court will only be justified in staying a trial on the ground of adverse pre-trial publicity, if it is satisfied *on the balance of probabilities* that if the jury return a verdict of guilty, the effect of the pre-trial publicity will be such as to render that verdict unsafe and unsatisfactory" (emphasis added).

4–165 It was pointed out by Schiemann L.J. that these differences in the criteria to be adopted, depending on the standpoint of the court in question, inevitably lead to a gap in the provision which the law makes for the protection of criminal trials from adverse publicity. It may be proper to stay proceedings on the ground of prejudice albeit that no individual is guilty of contempt. He went on to observe, "One may regret that situation or one may take the view that this is the best answer to a difficult problem".[66]

4–166 The judgment of Schiemann L.J. was cited and followed in the Divisional Court in *Att-Gen v Unger*.[67] Two articles had been published, in the *Manchester Evening News* and the *Daily Mail* respectively, referring to the fact that a home help had been stealing from her employer, and to the recording on video film of her taking money from the refrigerator in the kitchen. Proceedings were "active"[68] at the time of publication, because she had been arrested and charged with two offences of theft. Although Simon Brown L.J. commented that his initial reaction had been that the publications constituted contempt of court, amounting as they did to the clearest possible statements that the accused was guilty, he was persuaded that this was "a simplistic and no longer permissible view of the law".[69]

4–167 Although the respondents had no business assuming that there would be no trial, the court was not satisfied to the required standard that there had arisen a substantial risk of serious prejudice. There would have been a significant "fade factor" because of the interval before any jury trial and, unlike some other cases, there was no question of any inadmissible material having been published, such as previous convictions. He also focused on the "presumption that jurors will

---

[64] But see the government announcement as to proposals to change the law in this respect, in February 1998, cited at para.4–155, but which so far shows no signs of being implemented.
[65] Unreported, March 6, 1995, Phillips J.
[66] [1997] 1 All E.R. 456 at 466h.
[67] [1998] 1 Cr.App.R. 308, [1998] E.M.L.R. 280, Simon Brown L.J.
[68] Discussed at paras 4–174 *et seq.*
[69] [1998] 1 Cr.App.R. at 312.

decide cases solely according to the evidence put before them and the directions they are given, a presumption central to the whole criminal process."

So far as the "fade factor" is concerned, the development of the Internet has given rise to significant practical difficulties. The matter was discussed in the Scottish case of *HMA v Beggs (No.1)*, in the High Court of Justiciary.[70] It concerned a murder trial where the previous convictions and lifestyle of the accused had been discussed in the media in 1999 and 2000 in dramatic and lurid terms (he being called, for example, "the gay ripper"), but much of the published material remained available for public scrutiny on a number of web-sites, including the archives of individual newspapers and broadcasting organisations but also on other sites such as "Scottish Media Monitor". By the time the matter came before the court in September 2001, there had already been opinions by Lord Wheatley and (on appeal) Lord Coulsfield rejecting a plea in bar of trial which were based, at least in part, upon the proposition that the risks of prejudice "could be managed". That issue was not being reopened but Lord Osborne did address the practicalities of risk management given the continuing availability on the Internet of material in respect of which it was submitted that "the jury ought not to have access". A motion was therefore made under s.4(2) of the Contempt of Court Act 1981 to restrict the reporting of the trial until after verdict. This was on the basis that "even responsible, contemporaneous, fair and accurate reporting of the trial proceedings would be likely to start ... a 'feeding frenzy'". In particular, websites were not easily susceptible to control. This motion was rejected,[71] but the facts of the case illustrate how it has become more difficult to dismiss the effect of prejudicial material as spent, or faded, after the lapse of weeks or months following the original publication.

The courts must not "speak with two voices"

More significantly, Brown L.J. referred in *Unger* to the two distinct lines of authority on the susceptibility of jurors, which had been carefully considered by Schiemann L.J., and added his own comment on the point of principle[72]:

"It seems to me important in these cases that the courts do not speak with two voices, one used to dismiss criminal appeals with the court roundly rejecting any suggestion that prejudice resulted from media publications, the other holding comparable publications to be in contempt, the courts on these occasions expressing grave doubts as to the jury's ability to forget or put aside what they have heard or read.

I am certainly not saying that in respect of one and the same publication there cannot be both a contempt (of the present, outcome, sort) and a safe conviction. Plainly there can, most obviously perhaps in cases where the trial has had to be moved or delayed to minimise the prejudice occasioned by some publication. But generally speaking it seems to me that unless a publication materially affects the course of trial in that kind of way, or requires directions from the court well beyond those ordinarily required and

---

[70] 2002 S.L.T. 135, S.C.C.R. 869.
[71] For the reasons discussed at para.7–138.
[72] [1998] 1 Cr.App.R. 308 at 318E–F, [1998] E.M.L.R. 280 at 291. See also the discussion by J.M. Oliveira, "Speaking with two voices: The tension between strict liability contempt and abuse of process in the context of adverse pre-trial publicity" [2001] H.K.L.J. 459.

4–169 CHAPTER 4—THE STATUTORY REGIME FOR STRICT LIABILITY

routinely given to juries to focus their attention on evidence called before them rather than whatever they may have heard or read outside court, or creates at the very least a seriously arguable ground for an appeal on the basis of prejudice, it is unlikely to be vulnerable to contempt proceedings under the strict liability rule."

4–170 The Lord Justice re-visited this passage in *Att-Gen v Birmingham Post and Mail Ltd*,[73] and expressed himself still satisfied (although the mere creation of a need for a trial judge to give the jury a special direction "would perhaps be a debatable basis for a finding of contempt") that to give rise to a "seriously arguable ground of appeal" would be a sufficient basis for establishing strict liability contempt. A decision to grant or refuse a stay will not necessarily be determinative of whether contempt is proved. Nevertheless, the grant of a stay is likely to be a "telling factor" on a contempt application in a case where the publication has occurred during the trial, and where there is no question of other prejudicial publications complicating the position, as in *Att-Gen v MGN Ltd*.[74]

4–171 The problem was considered yet again in *Att-Gen v Guardian Newspapers Ltd*[75] where the Divisional Court re-emphasised that the court should not speak with different voices when considering criminal appeals and when considering contempt cases. There should be a single standard (*i.e.* a substantial risk of prejudicing the fairness of the criminal trial) although it would be applied differently in the two contexts. In contempt cases the matter had to be gauged prospectively and without regard to the outcome of the trial; whereas on a criminal appeal the matter would obviously have to be addressed following and in the light of a conviction. It was recognised that the reaction of the trial judge was of "high relevance" but that it would not be determinative—not least because the judge's concern would be that the integrity of an ongoing trial should be unassailable, and he would thus rightly incline to caution. Sedley L.J. suggested[76] that one way to ensure that the courts speak with a single voice was to test an accusation by assuming:

(a) that jurors have read the publication,

(b) that an application to discharge the jury has been made and refused,

(c) that the judge has given the jury a proper direction to disregard anything they have read,

(d) that a conviction was not inevitable, and

(e) that the jury have convicted.

4–172 He continued:

"If in such a situation an appeal on the ground of prejudice would not succeed, no more should the publisher be guilty of contempt. The prospective risk of serious prejudice cannot be any greater than the actual possibility, in the assumed situation, that it has

---

[73] [1998] 4 All E.R. 49.
[74] [1997] 1 All E.R. 456.
[75] [1999] E.M.L.R. 904.
[76] At 924.

occurred. By parity of reasoning, a case in which an appeal would on the assumed events succeed will ordinarily be a case where contempt is made out, provided always that the court is sure that the facts meet the test.

This formulation differs, I accept, from that of Simon Brown L.J. in *Unger*: it looks to the existence of grounds for allowing or dismissing an appeal against conviction rather than for granting or refusing leave to appeal. This is because, the test on appeal now being the safety of the conviction (Criminal Appeal Act 1968, s.2(1), as amended by the Criminal Appeal Act 1995), any substantial risk (cf. s.2(2) of the 1981 Act) that a conviction has been contributed to by a prejudicial publication will ordinarily make it unsafe. To reduce this threshold to the leave stage, requiring only an arguable case of risk, may be to set the threshold of contempt unduly low, at a level where there is not a demonstrable risk of prejudice but only an arguable case of it".

4–173
There can be little doubt that the prominence given, especially in *Att-Gen v MGN*[77] and *Att-Gen v Unger*,[78] to (1) the "fade factor", (2) the "presumption central to the whole criminal process" that jurors will decide cases solely on the evidence before them and (3) the need to prove a causal link between the individual article(s) and the risk of prejudice (as opposed to relying upon a general climate of prejudice) have contributed significantly to the reluctance of the Law Officers in the intervening years to institute proceedings for strict liability contempt.

V. WHEN ARE PROCEEDINGS "ACTIVE"?

A. Schedule 1 of the 1981 Act

4–174
By comparison with the position at common law, when the question was whether or not proceedings were "pending or imminent", it is now a relatively straightforward matter for reporters, publishers and editors to ascertain whether or not proceedings are "active", and therefore likely to involve liability under the strict liability rule. This is because the Act makes specific provision for the point of time at which proceedings become "active", and when they cease to be so. That is not to say, however, that potential liability for contempt can be put out of mind as easily as had been expected by the legislators. There still remains the threat of common law contempt, even in cases where proceedings cannot yet be said to have become "active".[79]

B. The general scheme

4–175
Section 2(3) provides that:

"The strict liability rule applies to a publication only if the proceedings in question are active within the meaning of this section at the time of publication."

4–176
Schedule 1 to the Act determines the times at which proceedings are to be treated as active. The Schedule provides as follows:

---

[77] [1997] 1 All E.R. 456.
[78] [1998] 1 Cr.App.R. 308, [1998] E.M.L.R. 280.
[79] See the discussion at paras 5–62 *et seq*.

4-176 CHAPTER 4—THE STATUTORY REGIME FOR STRICT LIABILITY

"**Preliminary**

1. In this Schedule "criminal proceedings" means proceedings against a person in respect of an offence, not being appellate proceedings or proceedings commenced by motion for committal or attachment in England and Wales or Northern Ireland; and "appellate proceedings" means proceedings on appeal from or for the review of the decision of a court in any proceedings.

2. Criminal, appellate and other proceedings are active within the meaning of section 2 at the times respectively prescribed by the following paragraphs of this Schedule; and in relation to proceedings in which more than one of the steps described in any of those paragraphs is taken, the reference in that paragraph is a reference to the first of those steps.

4-177 *Criminal proceedings*

3. Subject to the following provisions of this Schedule, criminal proceedings are active from the relevant initial step specified in paragraph 4 [or 4A] until concluded as described in paragraph 5.

4. The initial steps of criminal proceedings are—

(a) arrest without warrant;
(b) the issue, or in Scotland the grant, of a warrant for arrest;
(c) the issue of a summons to appear, or in Scotland the grant of a warrant to cite;
(d) the service of an indictment or other document specifying the charge;
(e) except in Scotland, oral charge.

[4A Where as a result of an order under section 54 of the Criminal Procedure and Investigations Act 1996 (acquittal tainted by an administration of justice offence) proceedings are brought against a person for an offence of which he has previously been acquitted, the initial step of the proceedings is a certification under subsection (2) of that section; and paragraph 4 has effect subject to this.]

5. Criminal proceedings are concluded—

(a) by acquittal or, as the case may be, by sentence;
(b) by any other verdict, finding, order or decision which puts an end to the proceedings;
(c) by discontinuance or by operation of law.

6. The reference in paragraph 5(a) to sentence includes any order or decision consequent on conviction or finding of guilt which disposes of the case, either absolutely or subject to future events, and a deferment of sentence under [section 1 of the Powers of Criminal Courts (Sentencing) Act 2000], section 219 or 432 of the Criminal Procedure (Scotland) Act 1975 or Article 14 of the Treatment of Offenders (Northern Ireland) Order 1976.

7. Proceedings are discontinued within the meaning of paragraph 5(c)—

(a) in England and Wales or Northern Ireland, if the charge or summons is withdrawn or a nolle prosequi entered;
[(aa) in England and Wales if they are discontinued by virtue of section 23 of the Prosecution of Offences Act 1985;][80]
(b) in Scotland, if the proceedings are expressly abandoned by the prosecutor or are deserted simpliciter;
(c) in the case of proceedings in England and Wales or Northern Ireland commenced

---

[80] Added by the Prosecution of Offences Act 1985, s.31(5), Sch.1, Pt I. Sections 4A and 7(aa) were added by the relevant statute.

by arrest without warrant, if the person arrested is released, otherwise than on bail, without having been charged.

8. Criminal proceedings before a court-martial or standing civilian court are not concluded until the completion of any review of finding or sentence.

9. Criminal proceedings in England and Wales or Northern Ireland cease to be active if an order is made for the charge to lie on the file, but become active again if leave is later given for the proceedings to continue.

[9A. Where proceedings in England and Wales have been discontinued by virtue of section 23 of the Prosecution of Offences Act 1985, but notice is given by the accused under subsection (7) of that section to the effect that he wants the proceedings to continue, they become active again with the giving of that notice.][81]

10. Without prejudice to paragraph 5(b) above, criminal proceedings against a person cease to be active—

(a) if the accused is found to be under a disability such as to render him unfit to be tried or unfit to plead or, in Scotland, is found to be insane in bar of trial; or
(b) if a hospital order is made in his case under [section 51(5) of the Mental Health Act 1983][82] or [Article 57(5) of the Mental Health (Northern Ireland) Order 1986][83] or, in Scotland, where a transfer order ceases to have effect by virtue of [section 73(1) of the Mental Health (Scotland) Act 1984],[84]

but become active again if they are later resumed.

11. Criminal proceedings against a person which become active on the issue or the grant of a warrant for his arrest cease to be active at the end of the period of twelve months beginning with the date of the warrant unless he has been arrested within that period, but become active again if he is subsequently arrested.

Other proceedings at first instance 4–178

12. Proceedings other than criminal proceedings and appellate proceedings are active from the time when arrangements for the hearing are made or, if no such arrangements are previously made, from the time the hearing begins, until the proceedings are disposed of or discontinued or withdrawn; and for the purposes of this paragraph any motion or application made in or for the purposes of any proceedings, and any pre-trial review in the county court, is to be treated as a distinct proceeding.

13. In England and Wales or Northern Ireland arrangements for the hearing of proceedings to which paragraph 12 applies are made within the meaning of that paragraph—

(a) in the case of proceedings in the High Court for which provision is made by rules of court for setting down for trial, when the case is set down[85];
(b) in the case of any proceedings, when a date for the trial or hearing is fixed.

14. In Scotland arrangements for the hearing of proceedings to which paragraph 12 applies are made within the meaning of that paragraph—

(a) in the case of an ordinary action in the court of Session or in the Sheriff court, when the Record is closed;
(b) in the case of a motion or application, when it is enrolled or made;
(c) in any other case, when the date for a hearing is fixed or a hearing is allowed.

---

[81] Added by the Prosecution of Offences Act 1985, s.31(5), Sch.1, Pt I.
[82] Added by Mental Health Act 1983, s.148, Sch.4, para.57.
[83] Substituted by SI 1986/595, art.136(1), Sch.5, Pt II.
[84] Substituted by Mental Health (Scotland) Act 1984, s.127(1), Sch.3, para.48.
[85] This terminology is no longer apt because the appropriate stage of proceedings would now be either the fixing of a trial window or the giving of a date within that window for the trial.

4–179 *Appellate proceedings*

15. Appellate proceedings are active from the time when they are commenced—

(a) by application for leave to appeal or apply for review, or by notice of such an application;
(b) by notice of appeal or of application for review;
(c) by other originating process,

until disposed of or abandoned, discontinued or withdrawn.

16. Where, in appellate proceedings relating to criminal proceedings, the court—

(a) remits the case to the court below; or
(b) orders a new trial or a *venire de novo*, or in Scotland grants authority to bring a new prosecution,

any further or new proceedings which result shall be treated as active from the conclusion of the appellate proceedings."[86]

4–180 Certain general comments may be made upon these provisions. First, the subsection merely restricts the application of the strict liability rule to proceedings which are "active". It does not provide that prejudicial publications outside the active period cannot be contempts at all, though *mens rea*[87] would be necessary in such cases. Secondly, the Act departs from the Phillimore Committee's recommendation[88] in relation to the starting point of the active period for criminal cases. The Act provides that arrest can be the starting point, whereas Phillimore had recommended that the "active" period should commence upon charge. It is to be noted, however, that para.4(e) of the schedule also contemplates "oral charge" as the starting point in certain circumstances. This might apply, for example, to the situation that arises where a person is in a police station voluntarily, without arrest, and is then subsequently charged.

4–181 Thirdly, the provisions of the Schedule, in so far as they relate to civil proceedings, reduce the temptation to issue a "gagging writ"; that is to say, a writ issued in libel proceedings without the intention of prosecuting the action further, but with the purpose of preventing repetition.[89] The strict liability rule will not apply until arrangements are made for the hearing. This is unlikely to have much significance except in those civil proceedings in which there is trial by jury, such as defamation and actions against the police involving, for example, false imprisonment and malicious prosecution. The terminology of "setting down" is obsolete since the implementation of the CPR in 1999. The modern equivalent would be either the fixing of a trial window or, within that window, a trial date.

---

[86] Additional provision is made in ss.82 and 83 of the Criminal Justice Act 2003 for the restriction of publishing "any matter in a publication" if it would give rise to a substantial risk of prejudice in a retrial ordered following a prosecution appeal under Pt 9 of the statute.
[87] See paras 5–133 *et seq*.
[88] Cmnd. 5794 (1974), para.123.
[89] In *Thomson v Times Newspapers Ltd* [1969] 1 W.L.R. 1236, 3 All E.R. 648, Salmon L.J. said that it was a "widely held fallacy" to suppose that the issue of a writ would automatically stifle further comment. Since no injunction would ever be granted against a defendant who intended to justify in such circumstances, in accordance with the principle in *Bonnard v Perryman* [1891] 2 Ch. 269, it would obviously be wrong to suppose that re-publication would necessarily constitute contempt. See also *Wallersteiner v Moir* [1974] 1 W.L.R. 991 and Sir John Donaldson M.R. in *Att-Gen v Newspaper Publishing plc* [1988] Ch. 333 at 371B–E, and the general discussion at paras 4–324 *et seq*.

SECTION 7 AND THE ATTORNEY-GENERAL

Again, it should be noted that if the libel is repeated with the *intention* of prejudicing the trial then the publication may yet be a contempt at common law.[90]

Finally, where there is a gap between the conclusion of proceedings at first instance and the commencement of appellate proceedings (whether civil or criminal), the publication of matter otherwise falling within the definitions in s.2 would not apparently be a contempt within the strict liability rule, because no provision was made to bridge the gap between the conclusion of the period of "activity" for the purposes of the trial, and the commencement of the corresponding period for any appeal.[91]

4–182

VI. SECTION 7 AND THE ATTORNEY-GENERAL

A. Role of the Attorney-General under the strict liability rule

Section 7 of the Act provides:

4–183

"Proceedings for a contempt of court under the strict liability rule (other than Scottish proceedings) shall not be instituted except by or with the consent of the Attorney-General or on the motion of a court having jurisdiction to deal with it."

While the role of the Attorney-General is considered in greater detail in other chapters,[92] it is right to mention s.7 here also, so as to give its place in the overall context of the statutory code. The fact that the Attorney-General's consent is required in the case of strict liability publication contempts was clearly intended to serve as an additional safeguard in the light of the strictures of the European Court. It was also intended to secure a degree of consistency in the application of the strict liability rule. It does not apply in Scotland, and there is no provision that the Lord Advocate's leave is required there for the initiation of such proceedings. This may seem curious in view of the declared aim of bringing uniformity of application as between England and Scotland.[93]

4–184

It was argued in *Roger Bullivant v Ellis*[94] that, if the contempt alleged in any given case would otherwise fall within the scope of ss.1 and 2 of the 1981 Act, it would be necessary to obtain the consent of the Attorney even in those cases where it was alleged that *mens rea* was present (so as to fulfil the requirements of a common law publication contempt). Reliance was placed especially on the words "regardless of intent to do so" in s.1.[95] The case did not concern a media publication but a circular letter, widely distributed and arguing the merits of

4–185

---

[90] See the examples cited in *Att-Gen v Newspaper Publishing plc* [1988] Ch. 333 at 371B–E.
[91] Sch.1, paras 15 and 16.
[92] See mainly paras 2–199 *et seq*. See paras 2–205 *et seq*. for a discussion of *Taylor v Topping* [1990] T.L.R. 110 (Lexis), and para.9–239 for a consideration of a possible role for the Attorney-General in connection with the protection of journalists' sources.
[93] See Lord Hailsham, *Hansard*, H.L. Vol. 415, (5th series), col. 660, December 9, 1980, and the discussion at para.16–301.
[94] Falconer J., *Financial Times*, April 15, 1986 (Lexis).
[95] For the text of which, see para.4–1.

4–185 CHAPTER 4—THE STATUTORY REGIME FOR STRICT LIABILITY

litigation pending in the Chancery Division. The case concerned allegations of breach of confidence, infringement of copyright and infringement of two of the plaintiff's patents. The letter was sent *inter alios* to potential witnesses and it was said that there was an intention to change their minds.

4–186 The submission seems to have been upheld by Falconer J. that the statute leaves no room for a common law jurisdiction, operating in parallel to the statutory regime, in respect of situations falling within the carefully defined scope of ss.1 and 2. A similar analysis was applied by the Lord Justice Clerk in the Scottish case of *Al Megrahi and Fhima v Times Newspapers Ltd*,[96] where he observed,

> "On any view it could hardly be supposed that, in regard to the possible effect of a publication on the course of justice in particular proceedings which are 'active', a publisher is exposed to liability according to one test under the statute and another test according to the common law".

4–187 Yet the Court of Appeal in *Att-Gen v Hislop*[97] saw no difficulty in concluding that there had been contempt both at common law and under the statutory strict liability rule. The court did not need to address, however, what would have happened in a case where the Attorney-General had neither initiated the contempt proceedings himself nor been asked to give his consent. Would any interested party have been able to proceed, without such consent, in respect of an alleged media contempt solely by virtue of reliance upon an allegation of *mens rea*? It would appear not—if the reasoning in *Roger Bullivant* and *Al Megrahi and Fhima* is correct.

4–188 The other argument canvassed in *Roger Bullivant*, which was also upheld by Falconer J., was that, if there truly were co-existing these two parallel jurisdictions in respect of any *actus reus* falling within ss.1 and 2, Parliament's intentions over the statutory "escape routes" in ss.3 to 5 of the Act would have been stultified. It was suggested that these "defences" would not be available to a respondent in circumstances in which the complainant stated that he was proceeding under the common law alone. But s.4 is concerned with a "fair and accurate report of legal proceedings" published "in good faith"; s.5 also presupposes "good faith" in the discussion of public affairs. This concept would appear to be incompatible with the intention to interfere with the administration of justice, which is required for liability at common law.[98]

4–189 The court can proceed of its own motion, as expressly recognised in s.7. This is what happened, for example, in the case of *Re Lonrho*.[99] It could hardly be arguable in such a case that the court was precluded from considering common law contempt as an alternative to a finding of strict liability. Indeed, the House of Lords did so in the *Lonrho* case. There seems to be no logical reason why, in a similar case where the court is not proceeding of its own motion, the common

---

[96] 1999 S.C.C.R. 824.
[97] [1991] 1 Q.B. 514.
[98] See ch.5.
[99] [1990] 2 A.C. 154.

law should be automatically excluded from consideration despite evidence of an intention to interfere with the administration of justice.

In the case of *R. v Solicitor-General Ex p. Taylor*,[1] where a challenge was mounted to the Solicitor-General's decision not to institute committal proceedings under the strict liability rule in respect of prejudicial newspaper coverage, the question does not seem to have been addressed whether the complainants might have themselves instituted proceedings with a view to establishing common law contempt. The answer may be that funds were not available to take such steps, or that there was no sufficient confidence in their ability to establish the necessary *mens rea*.

4–190

VII. WHO MAY BE LIABLE FOR PUBLICATION AND UPON WHAT BASIS?

A. Liability under section 2 of the 1981 Act

The way in which the statutory code is set out in ss.1 to 5 of the Act is unhelpful to the extent that it fails to address the various categories of individuals and corporations who would *prima facie* be liable for publications to "the public or any section of the public". In the ordinary way, those who are likely to fall foul of the law of contempt will be journalists, proprietors, publishers, printers, distributors of printed matter and the equivalents in broadcasting. The Act has not as yet been amended to make provision for modern means of communication, such as e-mail and the internet. Should the question arise, it will be necessary to determine whether it can fairly be said that any person who is responsible for placing material in the public domain by such means is publishing it.[2] In the libel context it has been held that a publication takes place where the allegations are downloaded and that those responsible for the communication may be held liable accordingly.[3] By contrast with s.1 of the Defamation Act 1996,[4] no attempt is made to provide specifically for attributing liability in respect of any or all of these categories of people, save for distributors.[5]

4–191

It is unsatisfactory that such closely related areas of the law as defamation and contempt, both of them vitally important to those concerned in the day-to-day business of media communication, should have to be approached from different standpoints. It may be that Parliament will wish to harmonise the two in order to avoid inconsistency. Unless and until such steps are taken, however, it is necessary to approach the matter from the general principles applying in the

4–192

---

[1] [1996] C.O.D. 61 (Lexis).
[2] Under the Defamation Act 1996, s.1(3), a person is not to be considered as the "author, editor or publisher of a statement if he is only involved ... (e) as the operator of or provider of access to a communications system by means of which the statement is transmitted, or made available, by a person over whom he has no control".
[3] *Godfrey v Demon Internet* [2001] Q.B. 201; *Loutchansky v Times Newspapers Ltd (No.2)* [2002] Q.B. 783 at [58] and [59]; *Dow Jones & Co Inc v Gutnick* [2002] H.C.A. 56, (2002) 210 C.L.R. 575.
[4] See *Gatley on Libel and Slander* (10th ed., 2004), ch.6.
[5] In s.3(2).

4–192   CHAPTER 4—THE STATUTORY REGIME FOR STRICT LIABILITY

criminal law. It is reasonable to suppose that the same approach to such questions would be adopted in relation both to strict liability and to common law publication contempt.

B. Scheme of the following discussion

4–193 It is confusing that the draftsman addresses the distinction between two (only) categories of potential contemnors, namely "publishers" and "distributors", only at the stage of affording defences under s.3.[6] For this reason, it is necessary in our discussion to depart from the format of the statute itself, because logic requires that the subject of who may be held *prima facie* responsible for a publication contempt needs to be addressed *before* discussing any possible defences. Even in strict liability cases, the state of mind may become material, and the underlying nature of responsibility on the part of proprietors and publishers (usually corporate entities) becomes of real significance, when a respondent wishes to pray in aid an innocent publication defence under s.3(1).[7] In the case of distributors, similarly, state of mind may become material for the purposes of a defence of innocent dissemination, under s.3(2).[8] For ease of exposition, however, it is desirable to consider the legal basis of liability at the outset.

C. Candidates for liability

4–194 Traditionally the concept of publication involved, at common law, no more than communicating information from one or more persons to at least one other.[9] However, before a media publication is communicated to "the public at large or any section of the public", various individuals may be involved at different stages of the production process. By the time it has reached the public, a news item will already have been communicated incidentally to many different people. At least some of these communications will have been made with the intention that eventually the item will be communicated to the public at large, and thus could be construed as entailing participation in the ultimate publication contemplated in ss.1 and 2 of the 1981 Act.

D. The basis of liability of proprietors and publishers

4–195 In discussing the theoretical basis for liability in the law of contempt, whether at common law or under the strict liability regime, it is necessary to remember that the courts regularly hold the proprietors and publishers of newspapers and journals liable and impose individual penalties, without a close analysis of the juridical basis for doing so. It could hardly be disputed that the publishers are responsible for a contempt published in one of their journals and, in so far as state of mind becomes relevant either under the common law or by reason of one of

---

[6] See paras 4–236 *et seq.*
[7] *ibid.*
[8] *ibid.*
[9] See paras 4–24 *et seq.* But see the Defamation Act 1996, s.1(2) where the word "publisher" is used in a narrower sense. See also *Re B (A Child) (Disclosure)* [2004] EWHC 411 (Fam), [2004] 2 F.L.R. 142 at [68] to [72]; *In Re M (A Child)* [2002] EWCA Civ 1199, [2003] Fam. 26; *Re G (Litigants in Person)* [2003] EWCA Civ 1055, [2003] 2 F.L.R. 963.

Who May Be Liable For Publication and Upon What Basis? 4–198

the statutory "escape routes", then the relevant company will be fixed with responsibility for (say) an intention, or any lack of good faith, on the part of a relevant employee.

In the case of a newspaper group, the proprietors and publishers are generally one and the same. It would be exceptional to draw a distinction between them, although Robert Maxwell used to describe himself as "the publisher" of *The Daily Mirror* and of other titles within the group. The responsibility of "publishers" for the publication of defamatory words is now formally recognised in s.1(2) of the Defamation Act 1996, which defines the term exclusively by reference to a "commercial publisher", a term defined as:

4–196

" . . . a person whose business is issuing material to the public, or a section of the public, who issues material containing the statement in the course of that business."

The Act makes no separate reference to "proprietors", since almost certainly the distinction was thought to be of no significance.

There are three different but overlapping concepts to be addressed:

4–197

(1) strict liability—liability under the statute of a person for his own act irrespective of *mens rea*;

(2) vicarious liability—the liability of one person for the act of another, even in circumstances where *mens rea* may be an essential requirement and the employer or principal lacks any independent intention;

(3) corporate liability and the doctrine of identification—whereby there is imputed to a company direct responsibility for the acts or omissions of employees.

The distinction between the doctrine of identification and that of vicarious liability is that in the former case the corporate entity is deemed to responsible on its own account, and not made to assume responsibility for acts or omissions of another. This is considered more fully below, under the heading of "vicarious liability in the corporate context".[10] It is necessary also to bear in mind the principles governing corporate responsibility for civil contempt, which have developed along rather different lines.[11] The potential importance of making these distinctions arises in considering (a) the categories of person who may be responsible for publishing a contempt, and in particular, in strict liability contempt under s.2, and (b) those who may wish to avail themselves of the defence of innocent publication or dissemination under s.3. The matter needs to be addressed particularly in the context of the publication of newspapers and periodicals.

4–198

---

[10] para.4–204.
[11] These are discussed at para.12–101.

4-199 CHAPTER 4—THE STATUTORY REGIME FOR STRICT LIABILITY

E. The traditional approach to the vicarious liability of proprietors

4-199 Whilst vicarious liability is central to civil litigation, judges have been reluctant to import the concept into the general criminal law.[12] However, it was recognised specifically in the context of criminal libel (including seditious and blasphemous libel). The historical origins of the law of contempt[13] suggest that it is appropriate to consider it as something of a special case, separate and apart in certain respects from general common law principles.[14]

4-200 At first there seems to have been no more than a presumption that a person in whose name a periodical was published was the responsible publisher.[15] However, in *R. v Walter*[16] the proprietor of *The Times* gave evidence that he had nothing to do with its day-to-day running, that he resided in the country, and that his son had been given a wide discretion. Lord Kenyon C.J. held this to be no defence; the proprietor of a newspaper was answerable under the criminal law.

4-201 In *R. v Gutch*[17] Lord Tenterden C.J. said:

" . . . it is said that this is a different principle from that which prevails in all other criminal cases; but this does not appear to me to be so, the rule seems to me to be comfortable to principle and to common sense; surely a person who derives profit from, and who furnishes means for carrying on the concern, and entrusts the conduct of the publication to one who he selects, and in whom he confides, may be said to cause to be published what actually appears, and ought to be answerable, although you cannot shew that he was individually concerned in the particular publication."

In these two cases the proprietors were private individuals. If they had been companies, what is now called the doctrine of identification might come into play. But this analysis has never been applied in the law of contempt. Companies have been treated as liable on the same basis as were the individual proprietors long ago.

4-202 In *R. v Evening Standard Co Ltd*,[18] which is perhaps the leading modern case, Lord Goddard C.J. commented:

"Sir Hartley Shawcross said that while his clients desired to abide by the well understood rule of journalism that the editor and proprietor of papers must in a case such as this take responsibility, he would suggest to the court that vicarious liability, as it is called, ought not in law to be visited upon them and that they ought not to be made vicariously liable for the mistake or misconduct of the reporter. I do not think we can possibly agree with that submission."

---

[12] *R. v Huggins* (1730) 2 Ld. Raym. 1574, 92 E.R. 518. See generally ed. D. Ormerod, Smith and Hogan, *Criminal Law* (11th ed., 2005), ch.10.
[13] See paras 1–26 *et seq.*
[14] See Glanville Williams, *Criminal Law: The General Part* (2nd ed., 1961) cited at para.4–206.
[15] *Almon* (1770) 5 Burr. 2686, 98 E.R. 411. The surrounding facts were said to be "sufficient *prima facie* evidence of its being published by him".
[16] (1799) 3 Esp. 21, 170 E.R. 524.
[17] (1829) M. & M. 433 at 437, 173 E.R. 1214 at 1216.
[18] [1954] 1 Q.B. 578 at 585: cf. *Felkin v Herbert* (1864) 33 L.J. Ch. 294; *Bolam Ex p. Haigh* (1948) S.J. 220; *R. v Odhams Press Ltd* [1957] 1 Q.B. 73.

In support of that proposition he cited *R. v Payne*,[19] which was decided on the basis that what was published was not calculated to prejudice the fair trial of a pending case, and *St. James's Evening Post*.[20]

4–203 Since the introduction of defences of innocent publication and dissemination, in the 1981 Act, it has become more important to focus upon the true nature of the liability of each of those who can be held responsible for strict liability contempt. So long as there was no defence of innocent publication or dissemination, it mattered not whether a person was held liable on a vicarious or personal basis. Under these provisions, it may be crucial to determine the basis of liability. Either an editor or a proprietor might seek to rely on the defence of innocent publication under s.3.[21]

F. Vicarious liability in the corporate context

4–204 Generally, proprietors (and indeed distributors) are now likely to be limited companies. The artificiality of companies sometimes leads to difficulty in determining whether liability in a particular legal context is intended to be attributed to the corporate entity itself. As Lord Hoffmann observed in *Meridian Global Funds Management Asia Ltd v Securities Commission*[22]:

> "Any proposition about a company necessarily involves a reference to a set of rules. A company exists because there is a rule (usually in a statute) which says that a *persona ficta* shall be deemed to exist and to have certain of the powers, rights and duties of a natural person. But there would be little sense in deeming such a *persona ficta* to exist unless there were also rules to tell one what acts were to count as acts of the company. It is therefore a necessary part of corporate personality that there should be rules by which acts are attributed to the company. These may be called 'the rules of attribution'".

4–205 He went on to explain that there are primary rules of attribution (deriving either from the articles of association or from the rules of company law), although these will not cover every situation that arises. Therefore it is necessary to supplement these *primary* rules of attribution by reference to *general* rules of attribution which are equally available as in the case of natural persons. Thus the general principles of agency will apply also to corporate entities, including those relating to estoppel and ostensible authority, in the law of contract, and those governing vicarious liability in tort.

4–206 Generally these principles will provide the answer to any given problem, but in the criminal law context a rule will often be stated in language primarily applicable to a natural person. It becomes necessary to determine from the context, which will usually be statutory, whether the legislative purpose was to embrace corporate persons or not. One has therefore to beware of taking judicial

---

[19] [1896] 1 Q.B. 577.
[20] (1742) 2 Atk. 469, 26 E.R. 683.
[21] See paras 4–236 *et seq*.
[22] [1995] 2 A.C. 500 at 506B–C, PC. See G.R. Sullivan, "The Attribution of Culpability to Limited Companies" [1996] 55 C.L.J. 515.

4–206 CHAPTER 4—THE STATUTORY REGIME FOR STRICT LIABILITY

decisions from one statutory context as applicable to another. For example, the decision of the House of Lords in *Tesco Supermarkets Ltd v Nattrass*[23] was specifically made against the policy considerations applying to the Trade Descriptions Act 1968. On the other hand, that in *Director General of Fair Trading v Pioneer Concrete (UK) Ltd*[24] was concerned with the breach of an undertaking relating to restrictive practices. What is necessary to decide is whether any given set of rules was intended, as a matter of policy, to apply to companies. In the context of strict liability contempt under the 1981 Act, there can be little doubt that Parliament did intend to fix corporate publishers with liability. Since the vast majority of publishers are now corporate, the law would otherwise prove ineffective. In any event, the common law background upon which the statutory framework was constructed, and as to which a number of assumptions were clearly made by the legislature (in particular, as to the existence of a "strict liability rule"), is such that the liability of corporate publishers as well as of editors was clearly intended. Indeed, Glanville Williams classified the law of contempt as being an established "exception" to the general rule in criminal law that there is no vicarious liability.[25] Moreover, the approach of applying vicarious liability has more recently been accepted, in the context of strict liability, with reference to the statutory defence under s.3.[26] It is in that context that state of mind is most likely to be material under the strict liability regime.

4–207 Questions may arise as to how a limited company can acquire the knowledge that particular legal proceedings are active; and as to what would amount to negligence in that regard. The problem is, however, likely to be more central in cases of common law publication contempt, since it is there necessary to prove intention, and the question arises of how the relevant *mens rea* can be attributed to a proprietor or publisher. The traditional answer is that the publisher is fixed with liability on a vicarious basis. This was justified as a matter of policy in the Report of the Phillimore Committee, in the following terms[27]:

> "At present the proprietors of a newspaper are also held liable for contempt. This is usually expressed as a penalty imposed upon 'the newspaper'. Unlike editorial liability, this is an example of ordinary vicarious liability, and we believe it to be right in principle. The proprietors are ultimately responsible for the enterprise as a whole. It is they who seek to obtain profits or other benefits from publishing. Liability for contempt and other infringements of the law is the other side of this coin".

4–208 This is why in the context of contempt questions of this kind rarely if ever seem to arise in practice. Points do not seem to be taken as to individual responsibility within the organisation,[28] and the proprietors generally stand

---

[23] [1972] A.C. 153.
[24] [1995] 1 A.C. 456. See the discussion at paras 12–80 *et seq.*, in the context of civil contempt.
[25] *Criminal Law: The General Part* (2nd ed., 1961), para.92.
[26] *R. v Duffy*, February 9, 1996 (Lexis), discussed at paras 4–242 *et seq.*
[27] para.153.
[28] See, *e.g. R. v Thomson Newspapers Ltd Ex p. Att-Gen* [1968] 1 W.L.R. 1, [1968] 1 All E.R. 268.

without demur behind whichever individuals have actually caused the offending publication.

More generally in the criminal law, liability is attributed to corporations either vicariously or according to the doctrine of identification. This latter doctrine owes its origin to rather different circumstances from those under consideration here. In *Tesco Supermarkets Ltd v Nattrass*[29] Lord Reid expressed the view that, where a person hands over to another responsibilities and discretion so completely that the other in effect stands in the principal's shoes, then the principal becomes liable personally rather than vicariously. That was, however, a case where the House of Lords sought to identify, for the purposes of s.24(1) of the Trade Descriptions Act 1968, at which level of seniority within the organisation an employee's knowledge became attributable directly to a corporate employer.

4–209

This conceptual problem was highlighted long ago in *Lennard's Carrying Co Ltd v Asiatic Petroleum Ltd*.[30] Nevertheless, the likelihood is, in the context of contempt where the principles of vicarious liability have been applied for so long, that there will be no need to introduce the doctrine of identification. The case law on innocent dissemination (discussed below) appears to demonstrate that vicarious liability, even though transplanted from elsewhere, should serve to provide answers to all questions of "attribution" in the corporate context. In Lord Tenterden's words, "this still seems to be comfortable to principle and to common sense".

4–210

The general problem of corporate liability was briefly addressed by Sir John Smith in his commentary[31] on *Attorney-General's Reference (No.2 of 1999)*[32] where the Court of Appeal answered the question "Can a defendant be properly convicted of manslaughter by gross negligence in the absence of evidence as to that defendant's state of mind?" in the affirmative and the question "Can a non-human defendant be convicted of the crime of manslaughter by gross negligence in the absence of evidence establishing the guilt of an identified human individual for the same crime?" in the negative. Sir John observed that the court's conclusion on the second question was apparently assumed to reflect a general principle of corporate liability at common law. He submitted that there is in fact no such principle. Gross negligence, he pointed out, is concerned with conduct rather than with anyone's state of mind. He emphasised that the case of *Meridian Global Funds Management Asia Ltd v Securities Commission*[33] had nothing whatever to say about liability for negligence in cases not requiring proof of a state of mind. In the *Att-Gen's Reference* case, the Court of Appeal had referred to the views of the Law Commission, but Sir John concluded that the Law Commission and, through it, the Court of Appeal had been misled by the supposition that the "identification principle" lies at the root of *all* corporate

4–211

---

[29] [1972] A.C. 153.
[30] [1915] A.C. 705 at 713, Viscount Haldane L.C.
[31] [2000] Crim. L.R. 475.
[32] [2000] 3 All E.R. 182.
[33] [1995] 2 A.C. 500.

4-211 CHAPTER 4—THE STATUTORY REGIME FOR STRICT LIABILITY

liability. That is not the case. As was pointed out above, so far as the law of contempt is concerned, the *Meridian* case is relevant because the attribution of corporate responsibility in this field appears by long tradition to be founded upon vicarious liability for the acts of individuals.

G. Editorial responsibility

4-212 Almost invariably the proprietors and publishers entrust editorial responsibility for the contents of the journal to one individual, the editor. That individual too bears responsibility for what appears in the newspaper. This primary responsibility has recently been confirmed in the context of defamation by s.1(2) of the Defamation Act 1996, which provides that " 'editor' means a person having editorial or equivalent responsibility for the content of the statement or the decision to publish it."

4-213 An editor's responsibility is special to the profession of journalism, in the sense that editors have accepted responsibility for what appears in their journals even when they have not been directly involved in the composition of an article or in the decision to publish it,[34] and they are expected to do so.[35]

4-214 Although editorial responsibility has traditionally been treated as primary rather than vicarious, in *R. v Duffy*[36] the Divisional Court held that, at least in the context of a s.3 defence, the legal responsibility on the part of the editor (and indeed of the proprietors) for the actions of the individual reporter was vicarious. This decision was not based upon any detailed or theoretical analysis of the authorities on criminal responsibility but rather, it seems, upon the injustice that would have arisen on the facts of that case if, notwithstanding the entitlement of the reporter to pray in aid a s.3 defence, the other respondents were to be held primarily responsible nevertheless.

4-215 It is possible that, on fuller argument, there would be a distinction to be drawn between editors and publishers. It is true that in *R. v Evening Standard Co Ltd*[37] Lord Goddard C.J. rejected counsel's argument that vicarious responsibility was inappropriate.[38] There appears to have been no argument as to a possible distinction of principle between editors and proprietors; furthermore, the court was not there concerned with the assessment of individual states of mind in the way that is now contemplated by s.3. If a reporter were malicious, there would be no compelling reason of policy why his employers should not bear

---

[34] *Re O'Connor, Chesshire v Strauss* (1896) 12 T.L.R. 291, Day J.; *R. v Evening Standard Ex p. DPP* (1924) 40 T.L.R. 833 at 836, Lord Hewart C.J.; *R. v Thomson Newspapers Ltd Ex p. Att-Gen* [1968] 1 W.L.R. 1 at 6, 1 All E.R. 268 at 271, Lord Parker C.J. And see *Solicitor-General v Radio Avon Ltd* [1978] 1 N.Z.L.R. 225 at 241, CA and the "debate as to how, if at all, the principle of editorial responsibility fits in with general legal principles". The court found it unnecessary to resolve the point on the facts before them.
[35] *R. v Evening Standard Co Ltd* [1954] 1 Q.B. 578; *R. v Odhams Press Ltd* [1957] 1 Q.B. 73 at 80, Lord Goddard C.J. See also *Official Solicitor v News Group Newspapers plc* [1994] 2 F.L.R. 174. For the similar approach in Scotland see paras 16–163 *et seq.*
[36] February 9, 1996 (Lexis). See para.4–242.
[37] [1954] 1 Q.B. 578.
[38] para.4–202.

responsibility for that state of mind, on a vicarious basis, as happens in the law of defamation.[39] Yet it is by no means obvious why an innocent editor in such circumstances, being no more than a fellow employee, should be fixed with responsibility for the reporter's state of mind.

H. Other journalists

Apart from the editor, other journalists will generally also participate in an *actus reus* of communicating "to the public at large or any section of the public". The question is to what extent they may in so doing become personally liable for any strict liability contempt contained within that ultimate publication. It is true that the internal communication of their material would not of itself be to the public or a section of the public. Nor would that act, of itself, create a substantial risk of serious prejudice, sufficient to satisfy the statutory requirements. But the nature of the business is such that a journalist would anticipate, and indeed hope, that his copy would find its way into the newspaper or journal. He would thus surely be authorising its communication to the public at large. It would appear that the only *mens rea* required for strict liability contempt under the Act is that of intending to publish the relevant material.[40]

4–216

These principles are illustrated by *R. v Evening Standard Co Ltd*,[41] where a reporter had telephoned an account of a trial which inaccurately attributed to a witness evidence which had not, in fact, been given at all, and which was highly prejudicial to the accused. This was held to be a contempt on the part of *inter alios* the reporter, although, since he had no intention to interfere with the administration of justice, no separate penalty was imposed upon him.

4–217

A sterner view was taken, however, in *R. v Odhams Press Ltd Ex p. Att-Gen*.[42] A newspaper published an article alleging that a man was purveying vice and managing "street women". At the time of the publication the man had in fact been committed for trial on a charge of brothel-keeping. Neither the proprietors, the editor nor the experienced reporter knew of this. The newspaper had made arrangements with court reporters, for the supply of reports of cases relating to prostitutes and brothel-keeping, and especially those relating to the activities of individuals about whom the reporter had been writing over a period of some weeks, but no information relating to this particular defendant had reached them. The court expressed the view that it was "certainly remarkable . . . that an experienced crime reporter . . . should not have known that one of the men he was so actively pursuing had not only been arrested and charged but actually committed for trial". The court also concluded that "the evidence fell far short of showing that standard of care which persons indulging in this kind of journalism are bound to take", and fined the journalist himself £500.

4–218

---

[39] See, *e.g. Egger v Chelmsford* [1965] 1 Q.B. 248.
[40] See para.4–51.
[41] [1954] 1 Q.B. 578.
[42] [1957] 1 Q.B. 73.

4–219   CHAPTER 4—THE STATUTORY REGIME FOR STRICT LIABILITY

4–219   In *R. v Griffiths Ex p. Att-Gen*[43] Lord Goddard C.J. remarked that "it has never yet been held that a reporter who supplied objectionable matter to his editor or employer, which the latter published, is himself guilty of contempt." The apparent inconsistency may be explicable on the basis that, in *Odhams Press* to which the Lord Chief Justice expressly adverted, the journalist had himself written the story eventually published. By contrast, Griffiths' usual role was merely that of a collector of material, which he transmitted to the publishers in New York where it was decided what use, if any, was to be made of it. Sometimes, he also wrote stories. In this case, however, he had not even supplied any material upon the basis of which the offending article was published. In those circumstances, even though he was described as the "chief European correspondent", it was held that no responsibility for the article or its publication could be imposed:

> "This respondent seems to be the representative of the magazine in this country, but that is not enough. While this jurisdiction to punish for improper comment on pending proceedings is absolutely necessary for the proper and impartial administration of justice, it is one which must be used with caution, and ought not to be vicariously extended because the real offenders are outside the jurisdiction."

4–220   Suppose, however, that he had supplied the material from which a story was compiled. It may be difficult to draw a distinction between reporters supplying information to their editors and the manager of a news agency who transmits stories to his subscribers for re-publication, if they so choose, in their newspapers. In *R. v Robbins Ex p. Green*[44] the manager of the Press Association Ltd was held responsible for material which had been disseminated by his staff. This represented that the defendants in a slander action had no case, and that they did not intend to contest the claim at trial, the sole remaining issue for the jury being the amount of damages. This story was completely untrue and, it was held, calculated to interfere with the administration of justice because of its possible effects on potential jurors. The manager was held personally responsible, although it would clearly be unlikely that the limited publication to subscribers, for which his staff were *directly* responsible, would itself have an impact on potential jurors. In that case, at least the story was complete, and its possible impact on the administration of justice could have been ascertained by the manager. If, however, the contribution of the journalist lies in doing no more than supplying the material from which somebody else compiles an article, it could be argued that he does not thereby necessarily publish or cause to be published a final form of wording.

4–221   In *R. v Saxon*,[45] where an article was written by a journalist on the basis of his long investigation, he was held personally liable despite the fact that he had submitted the article to his paper's legal advisers and substantial amendments had been made prior to publication. The outcome might well be different in a

---

[43] [1957] 2 Q.B. 192 at 202.
[44] (1891) 7 T.L.R. 411.
[45] [1984] W.A.R. 283.

case where the changes were sufficient to convert that which would otherwise have been innocent into a contempt.

In *R. v Thomson Newspapers Ltd Ex p. Att-Gen*[46] some of those involved in the offending publication, including the editor, did *not* know of the criminal proceedings pending against Michael X. Nevertheless, he was held liable, presumably in accordance with the traditional principle of editorial responsibility. All relevant personnel, however, had an intention to publish the material that was ultimately held to be in contempt. 4–222

Proceedings are not invariably brought against journalists, even in those cases where they appear in accordance with these principles to have been in some degree at fault. In *R. v Thomson Newspapers Ltd Ex p. Att-Gen*, no proceedings were instituted in respect of the reporter who had produced the offending story. By contrast, the journalist was proceeded against in *Att-Gen v Associated Newspapers Ltd*,[47] and *Att-Gen v Guardian Newspapers Ltd (No.3)*.[48] Similarly in *R. v Duffy*,[49] although in that case reliance was placed upon the defence under s.3 of the 1981 Act. 4–223

I. The analogy with the law of libel

There is, perhaps, a useful analogy to be drawn with the principles of defamation, where the law also has to grapple with different levels of publication. The width of the notion of "publication" in the civil law of libel is conveniently illustrated by the Porter Committee[50]: 4–224

"Where defamatory matter is contained in a book, periodical or newspaper, there are normally a series of publications each of which constitutes a separate tort. First, there is a publication by the author to publisher for which the author is solely liable. Secondly, there is the publication by the author and publisher to the printer, for which author and publisher are jointly liable. Thirdly, there is the publication of reprinted work to the trade and the public, for which the author and publisher are jointly liable."

Although in some ways it is illuminating to compare the law of defamation with that of contempt, in the context of responsibility for publication, it has to be remembered that there are important distinctions in the nature of the respective wrongs, not least because liability for publication contempt is criminal in character. 4–225

While it is true that an internal defamatory communication by one journalist to another would constitute a sufficient publication to give rise to a cause of action in libel, in the case of an internal communication it is unlikely that circumstances 4–226

---

[46] [1968] 1 W.L.R. 1, [1968] 1 All E.R. 268, discussed at para.4–13.
[47] [1994] 2 A.C. 238.
[48] [1992] 1 W.L.R. 874, [1992] 3 All E.R. 38.
[49] February 9, 1996 (Lexis), discussed at para.4–243.
[50] *Report of the Committee on the Law of Defamation* (1948), para.116. Compare the discussion of the meaning of "publication" in *Re B (A Child) (Disclosure)* [2004] EWHC 411 (Fam), [2004] 2 F.L.R. 142 at [68] to [72]; *In Re M (A Child)* [2002] EWCA Civ 1199, [2003] Fam. 26; *Re G (Litigants in Person)* [2003] EWCA Civ 1055, [2003] 2 F.L.R. 963.

would have arisen, even before the 1981 Act, in which there would thereby have been created a substantial risk of serious prejudice to the administration of justice. By contrast, in the now largely outmoded form of contempt known as "scandalising the court",[51] even a technical publication would have sufficed because it was not of the essence of the offence that the words should necessarily have been communicated to a large number of persons.[52]

4–227　The critical question is which individuals in the chain of causation, leading to the ultimate publication of an article, can be identified as bearing responsibility for the *actus reus* of that publication. It is in this area that the traditional approach of the common law, in the field of defamation, can give some assistance.

4–228　A journalist who filed copy would certainly be held liable for the ultimate publication unless he had expressly or impliedly made it clear that the communication was for internal purposes only. More generally, it is recognised in the law of defamation that a person who publishes defamatory words is liable for their onward re-publication where he or she authorised or intended that re-publication.[53]

4–229　An attempt was made in the Defamation Act 1996, s.1(4), to shed some light on the scope of responsibility of subordinates in the publication process, but in the result the wording provides little illumination:

> "Employees or agents of an author, editor or publisher are in the same position as their employer or principal to the extent that they are responsible for the content of the statement or the decision to publish it."

What does perhaps emerge is that Parliament wished in the context of defamation to exclude from liability those who merely play the role of a conduit, without applying any judgment or making any decision regarding content or the act of publication itself. Yet at common law responsibility for defamation could be placed upon even those who played such minor roles in the publication process as printers and distributors.[54] It may well be that a similar statutory test should be introduced in relation to strict liability contempts in order to achieve consistency.

J. Printers

4–230　Although a defence of innocent dissemination has long been recognised in respect of distributors, in the law of defamation,[55] it was only relatively recently

---

[51] See paras 5–204 *et seq*.
[52] In *McLeod v St. Aubyn* [1899] A.C. 549, the alleged "publication" consisted of handing over an unread copy of a newspaper to a librarian, for return the following day. No point was taken that this was not a relevant publication at common law.
[53] *Speight v Gosnay* (1891) 60 L.J. Q.B. 231; 7 T.L.R. 239; *McManus v Beckham* [2002] EWCA Civ 939, [2002] 1 W.L.R. 2982, [2002] 4 All E.R. 497, [2002] E.M.L.R. 40; *Gatley on Libel and Slander* (10th ed., 2004), paras 6.31 to 6.41.
[54] *Gatley on Libel and Slander* (10th ed., 2004), ch.6, especially paras 6.15 to 6.17.
[55] *ibid.* para.6–18.

Who May Be Liable For Publication and Upon What Basis? 4–234

that the Lord Chancellor decided to extend protection of this kind to printers.[56] It appears that, were it not for the express exclusion of those " ... only involved ... in printing, producing, distributing or selling printed material containing the [defamatory] statement", persons playing such peripheral roles in the publication process *would* be considered to be embraced within the broad concept of a "publisher". That term is defined in s.1(2) of the Defamation Act 1996 to mean "a person whose business is issuing material to the public, or a section of the public ... ".

According to Lord Goddard C.J. in *R. v Griffiths Ex p. Att-Gen*,[57] cases of contempt " ... stand in a class of their own and are not truly analogous to cases of defamation"; a defence of innocent dissemination would not be available to distributors who put such offending matter into circulation in the course of their trade.[58]   4–231

Since the Contempt of Court Act, by contrast, does not have any exclusion in respect of printers, or indeed any other such peripheral participants, it is reasonable to suppose that they would *prima facie* be liable for any contempt which they published, provided either (a) they had the necessary *mens rea* for the purposes of common law contempt, or (b) they did not have available one of the defences available under s.3(1) or (2) of the Contempt of Court Act 1981. For example, in *McLeod v St. Aubyn*[59] Lord Morris said that: 4–232

"A printer and publisher intends to publish, and so intending cannot plead as a justification that he did not know the contents."

Thus, since the Defamation Act 1996 came into effect, the anomalous position appears to have arisen that printers would escape liability for defamation without needing to establish any particular mental state, whereas in the field of contempt it would appear to be necessary for them to show that they did not know and had no reason to suspect that any relevant proceedings were active.   4–233

K. "Distributors"

"Distributors", although mentioned in s.3(2),[60] are not defined in the Contempt of Court Act. The term would appear to cover anyone who disseminates material   4–234

---

[56] ss.1(1) and 1(3)(a) of the Defamation Act 1996; see also the *Supreme Court Procedure Committee Report on Practice and Procedure on Defamation* (July 1991), commonly known as "The Neill Report". (On this subject of innocent dissemination, an interim report had also been submitted, which was included in the final Report in virtually identical terms.)
[57] [1957] 2 Q.B. 192 at 204.
[58] See also *R. v Odhams Press Ltd* [1957] 1 Q.B. 73.
[59] [1899] A.C. 549 at 562. See also *R. v Mason Ex p. DPP*, *The Times*, 17 December, 1932. In *Re The American Exchange in Europe (Ltd) v Gillig* (1889) 58 L.J. Ch. 706 at 707–8, Stirling J. said of a foreman printer, who was held out to the public as the publisher: "I apprehend that under these circumstances he is answerable for publishing the article complained of although he be entirely ignorant of its contents"; see also *R. v Thomson Newspapers Ltd Ex p. Att-Gen* [1968] 1 W.L.R. 1, 1 All E.R. 268; *Att-Gen v Wain (No.1)* [1991] 2 M.L.J. 525; *R. v Scott and Downland Publications Ltd* [1972] V.R. 663; *R. v David Syme and Co Ltd* [1982] V.R. 173.
[60] The text of which is set out in para.4–236.

4–234 CHAPTER 4—THE STATUTORY REGIME FOR STRICT LIABILITY

after it has left the hands of the publisher. As in the case of printers, the Defamation Act 1996 seeks to exclude distributors from liability for defamation, by providing that a person shall not be considered as a publisher if he is only involved in distributing.[61] Even before this, however, the common law had recognised a defence of innocent dissemination,[62] to which it will no longer presumably be necessary to have resort, because the distributor is excluded from *prima facie* liability (although, rather curiously, this is expressed to be a "defence"[63]).

4–235 The common law afforded no corresponding defence to distributors in the field of contempt. In *R. v Griffiths Ex p. Att-Gen*[64] a magazine published in America was distributed by booksellers in England. The booksellers were found in contempt because they authorised publication in this country. They would now have a defence under the Contempt of Court Act 1981, s.3(2).[65]

VIII. INNOCENT PUBLICATION OR DISTRIBUTION

A. Innocent publication and distribution: Section 3

4–236 Section 3 of the 1981 Act (which replaces s.11 of the Administration of Justice Act 1960)[66] provides as follows:

"(1) A person is not guilty of contempt of court under the strict liability rule as the publisher[67] of any matter to which that rule applies if at the time of publication (having taken all reasonable care) he does not know and has no reason to suspect that relevant proceedings are active.[68]

(2) A person is not guilty of contempt of court under the strict liability rule as the distributor[69] of a publication containing any such matter if at the time of distribution (having taken all reasonable care) he does not know that it contains such matter and has no reason to suspect that it is likely to do so.

(3) The burden of proof of any fact tending to establish a defence afforded by this section to any person lies upon that person."

4–237 The phrase used in this statute is "no reason to suspect", whereas in the Defamation Act 1996, s.1(1)(c), there is a significant departure in the use of the

---

[61] s.1(3)(a).
[62] *Gatley on Libel and Slander* (10th ed., 2004), para.6.18.
[63] s.1(1).
[64] [1957] 2 Q.B. 192.
[65] Considered at paras 4–236 *et seq.*
[66] The terms of which are set out at para.16–280.
[67] There is no express definition contained within the Act of the word "publisher". It is necessary, however, to bear in mind that the verb "publish" is to be construed (except in the context of s.9) in the light of the meaning assigned to "publication" in s.2(1) by virtue of s.19. That word was defined by reference to any communication "addressed to the public at large or any section of the public". It will presumably embrace anyone who must be taken as responsible for a communication to the public or any section of the public. It does not have the restricted meaning attributed by the Defamation Act 1996, s.1(2), set out at para.4–196.
[68] See paras 4–174 *et seq.* for the meaning of "active".
[69] See para.4–234 for the position generally in relation to distributors.

words "reason to believe". This clearly affords somewhat greater protection for the categories of persons sought by Parliament to be excluded from liability.[70]

B. The history of section 3

It was largely in response to two significant cases, that the protection now afforded by s.3 of the Contempt of Court Act 1981 was first introduced.[71] In *R. v Odhams Press Ltd*[72] the Divisional Court took the view that the respondents, who included the proprietors, the editor and the journalist, had not taken all reasonable precautions. It was irrelevant to their liability that they had all made a mistake.

4–238

The case of *R. v Griffiths Ex p. the Att-Gen*[73] may similarly be regarded as a precursor to the enactment of subsection (2). Two English companies had distributed an American magazine (*Newsweek*) on a wide scale in the United Kingdom. One of the companies had distributed it for eight years and the other (W.H. Smith and Co) for 20 years. Before the latter company undertook to distribute it, the directors had read (apparently, some 20 years earlier) three editions of the magazine and concluded that it was unlikely to contain prejudicial matter, and they had continued to distribute the magazine subsequently, without complaint. The trial for murder of Dr. Bodkin Adams, which took place in London, evoked world-wide interest. The American magazine printed an article which was likely to cause prejudice to that trial, and the English companies distributed it.

4–239

They were both held to have been in contempt. As the law then stood, the Divisional Court was not called upon to consider the question of "reasonable care", but commented (having regard to the "gossipy nature"[74] of the magazine the wide interest in the particular trial and the notorious fact that the restraints of the English law of contempt are not imposed in America) that greater care might have been taken.

4–240

For a long time after the enactment of s.11, however, it appears (at least from the law reports) that no editor or proprietor sought to rely upon it. In *R. v*

4–241

---

[70] See the facts of *Secretary of State for the Home Department Ex p. Westminster Press* (1991) 4 Admin L.R. 445 [1994] C.O.D. 303, which provide a good illustration of the distinction between "reason to suspect" in ss.3(1) and (2) and "reason to believe" in the Defamation Act, s.1(1)(c). The journalist who had enquired of the police as to whether an arrest had taken place could hardly hope to escape the conclusion that he or she had reason to suspect, whereas it would be more difficult to support "reason to *believe.*" See E. Griew, "Consistency, Communication and Codification—Reflections on Two Mens Rea Words" in ed. P.R. Glazebrook, *Reshaping the Criminal Law* (1978), p.57. See also *Milne v Express Newspapers Ltd* [2004] EWCA Civ 664, [2005] 1 W.L.R. 772, [2005] 1 All E.R. 1021, [2004] E.M.L.R. 461, on the distinction between "reason to believe" and "reason to suspect".
[71] By the Adminstration of Justice Act 1960, s.11. See Lord Denning M.R.'s comments in *Att-Gen v Butterworth* [1963] 1 Q.B. 696 at 722, to the effect that *Odhams Press* was "reversed" by s.11.
[72] [1957] 1 Q.B. 73, more fully discussed at para.4–11 and para.4–218.
[73] [1957] 2 Q.B. 192.
[74] *ibid.* at 204.

4–241   Chapter 4—The Statutory Regime for Strict Liability

Thomson Newspapers Ltd Ex p. Att-Gen[75] an article containing prejudicial material appeared in a newspaper, owing to the carelessness of a reporter. The editor did not know that the proceedings which were likely to be prejudiced were pending and had personally shown all reasonable care, in the sense that he had devised so far as was humanly possible a system to prevent contempt. He did not rely on s.11 of the 1960 Act and neither did the proprietors. Both were held to have been in contempt, but the proprietors alone were fined.

C. The standard of care expected

4–242   In *R. v Duffy*,[76] the Divisional Court considered in general terms the requirements of journalists imposed by s.3 of the Act:

> "Section 3 expects of journalists a high standard of care before they are in a position to avail themselves of that defence, not least because, as [counsel] has pointed out, the results of an article being published at the wrong time can be so disruptive of the course of justice. It will be rare, indeed, for a journalist, who writes an article suggesting that an identifiable person has committed a criminal offence, to be able to avail himself of the statutory defence without specifically asking those in a position to know if there are any active criminal proceedings but, as this case shows, even that rule cannot be absolute."

4–243   The facts of *Duffy* were as follows. An experienced investigative journalist with the *News of the World*, aware of the provisions of the 1981 Act, habitually tried to work in co-operation with the police so far as possible. He received information about the wide-spread cultivation of skunk cannabis in Cleveland, and also to the effect that one of the main people involved was Christopher Duffy.

4–244   He contacted a detective inspector whose name he had obtained from an earlier article in *The Sun* as having been involved in police raids in connection with that drug. He was not aware that there were proceedings pending against Duffy at that time, and the police officers he met did not apprise him of that fact. He entered into a deal with them to the effect that he would let them have information obtained by him for an article, but only at the point where it was ready to print. On November 20, 1994 such an article was indeed published, referring to "The Mr Big who sets up new superdrug farms" and claiming that the newspaper had "smashed a nation-wide drugs ring". The journalist argued, and the court accepted, that no such claim would have been made if he had truly known of the pending proceedings, as he would have realised that it would have made him a laughing stock.

4–245   The article gave rise to a substantial risk of serious prejudice, there being at that stage the real possibility of a trial before the following Easter. The court, in considering the s.3 defence, accepted that the journalist had no actual knowledge of the pending proceedings. The argument was advanced on behalf of the Attorney that he was only ignorant because he had not taken all reasonable care

---

[75] [1968] 1 W.L.R. 1, the facts of which are given at para.4–13.
[76] February 9, 1996 (Lexis).

when he had reason to suspect that proceedings might be "active". The court accepted that the only relevant information he had been given by the police officers was that Duffy was "known to the police". It was argued that he could have expressly asked if criminal proceedings were pending of the police officers themselves, or of the Crown Prosecution Service, or of the Crown Courts in the area.

On the particular facts of the case, since the deal he had proposed to the police officers would have been "unreal or at least very difficult" if proceedings were pending, he was entitled to assume that the officers would have told him. The court commented that one of the officers could have said something like: "How can you possibly publish this article before we get this Crown Court trial at Leeds out of the way?" There was no need to have gone to the CPS or to the courts, because he had gone already to "the horse's mouth"; that is to say, to the senior officer in the drugs squad for the relevant area. He was therefore entitled to say "that he had no reason to suspect that criminal proceedings were active, that he did not know of any, and that he had taken all reasonable care." It is true that there is no obligation on police officers in such cases to provide information to the press,[77] but it is difficult to see what more a journalist could have done to ascertain the facts. **4–246**

By contrast, in another case concerning the *News of the World*,[78] a defence under s.3, although ultimately abandoned, had been advanced on the basis that police officers could be counted on to volunteer information without actually being asked. **4–247**

A young woman had disappeared in Bristol and, three weeks later, a man was arrested following an armed robbery in Leamington Spa. It was after his arrest for this offence that police discovered him to be in possession of the missing woman's car and driving licence. Against this background, the newspaper published a front page headline "Bride Quiz Man Is Rapist", and the man being questioned over the Bristol abduction was described as "A convicted sex beast". **4–248**

The respondents were not in a position to resist the conclusion that the publication gave rise to a *prima facie* strict liability contempt, but they did seek to place reliance on s.3. In this respect too their options were strictly limited, because they knew at the material time that the man had been arrested for the robbery (and therefore that criminal proceedings were "active"). It was accepted, **4–249**

---

[77] *R. v Home Secretary Ex p. Westminster Press Ltd* (1991) 4 Admin. L.R. 445. The Divisional Court refused to grant judicial review of a Home Office circular giving advice and guidance to the effect that police interviews should not be given to the press regarding the investigation, questioning, arresting and charging of suspects, except for giving a brief statement. The court held that the press and public have no right to know who has been investigated, questioned, arrested or charged. The case is also referred to at para.2–53, n.10. See also *Solicitor-General v Henry*, March 20, 1990 (Lexis) discussed at para.4–247.

[78] *Solicitor-General v Henry*, March 20, 1990 (Lexis), [1990] C.O.D. 307. The case was argued nearly two years before the decision in *R. v Secretary of State for the Home Department Ex p. Westminster Press* (1991) 4 Admin L.R. 445.

4–249 however, that they were unaware that proceedings were also "active" in relation to the abduction. The journalist concerned had been told by Bristol police that the man was being questioned, but had not yet been charged. These facts were both true, but the police did not volunteer that he had actually been arrested on the Friday before the date of publication. In those circumstances, it was said by Mustill L.J. that reliance on s.3 was "always likely to be a difficult defence to maintain", but in any event it was abandoned part way though the hearing.

4–250 It may be that the distinction between these facts and those of *Duffy* is obvious. In this later case the police officers led an experienced journalist by their actions to believe that there were no active criminal proceedings. It was thus not surprising that his doubts were dispelled and that he was exonerated, despite the fact that he had not asked the direct question whether proceedings were "active". As Kennedy L.J. pointed out, however, it will be rare to succeed under the statutory defence without making that specific enquiry.

4–251 As long ago as 1959, it was suggested that[79]:

> "distributors should be regarded as having reason to suspect contemptuous matter in well-known disreputable types of publication, and even in reputable foreign publications whenever a trial in England or Wales is of so sensational a nature as to excite the interest of the world".

4–252 In the context of s.3(2), it is unlikely nowadays (and is certainly contrary to the approach of Parliament to distributors in the Defamation Act 1996) that such a person would be deprived of the defence merely because a magazine is thought to be in some way "gossipy"[80] or in some way generally "disreputable".

4–253 The nature of society has changed so much in the last 50 years, and there could no longer be said to be a general recognition as to appropriate standards in such matters. The community within this jurisdiction is less homogeneous, and greater priority is given to freedom of communication, not least because of the influence of the Art.10 of the European Convention. On the other hand, the fact that distributors are required to take "all reasonable care" will oblige them to show in practice that they have put in place some system of scrutiny to prevent the publication of prejudicial material.

D. Vicarious liability and section 3

4–254 The Phillimore Committee recommended that the principle of editorial responsibility ought to be maintained,[81] but do not seem to have addressed specifically the problems raised by s.11 of the 1960 Act. The Committee analysed the basis of liability of the editor as being strict.[82] While recognising that "liability without fault should not be lightly imposed, especially where it is a liability for the act

---

[79] JUSTICE Report, *Contempt of Court* (1959).
[80] The phrase used by Lord Goddard C.J. in *R. v Griffiths Ex p. the Att-Gen* [1957] 2 Q.B. 192, para.4–240.
[81] paras 147–153.
[82] See, *e.g. R. v Beaverbrook Newspapers* [1962] N.I. 15.

or neglect of another", the Committee found there to be compelling reasons for maintaining this form of liability because the editor's position is "a very special one"[83]:

> "It is because of the doctrine of editorial responsibility that many newspapers set up a system designed to prevent the publication of offending material. A deterrent which caught only the individual reporter would be virtually no deterrent at all. We are sure that it is necessary to retain responsibility at a higher level."

They did not indicate whether in their view an editor should be able to rely upon the statutory defence.

4–255 While Kennedy L.J. made clear in *Duffy*[84] that nothing said in that case should be taken as anything more than a decision upon its own facts, he did accept the submission that the responsibility of the editor and publishers was vicarious rather than primary. Thus, if the individual journalist who had made the enquiries of the police was entitled in the circumstances to rely upon the s.3 defence, there would be no finding of contempt against the editor and publishers either.

4–256 The logical conclusion of the reasoning of Kennedy L.J. is that, if the individual journalist were *not* able to avail himself of a s.3 defence, the editor would similarly fail. The matter has yet to be tested, however, in that situation, when further argument might be required. It is by no means clear as a matter of principle that an editor should be fixed with responsibility for the state of mind of another who has in law merely the status of a fellow-employee. Furthermore, the principle of editorial responsibility that has been recognised for so long does not in itself entail that the editor should be made vicariously liable for the wrongdoing of others, should he or she wish to advance an individual defence.

4–257 The editor in *R. v Thomson Newspapers Ltd Ex p. the Att-Gen* did not seek to rely on s.11 of the 1960 Act, notwithstanding his having taken all reasonable care in setting up a system of scrutiny. An editor would appear to be a "publisher" for the purposes of s.3,[85] and the section does provide an escape mechanism for anyone falling within that description. If the editor has taken reasonable care by setting up a system it is difficult to see why he should not be able to take advantage of the terms of the section.

4–258 The answer may be that editors and proprietors seem to be treated similarly in the law of contempt, in the sense that both are regarded as vicariously liable for the errors or state of mind of reporters.[86] This seems not to fit comfortably with the general principle of *respondeat superior* since the editor and the reporter will often be fellow employees of the same newspaper company. It is curious that the notion of editorial responsibility should be taken to entail vicarious responsibility. It would be difficult to imagine an editor (as opposed to an employing

---

[83] paras 147–153.
[84] February 9, 1996 (Lexis).
[85] Cf. the Defamation Act 1996, s.1(2), where "editor" and "publisher" are separately defined.
[86] See, *e.g.* Lord Goddard C.J. in *R. v Evening Standard Co Ltd* [1954] 1 Q.B. 578.

proprietor) being held responsible for malice for one of his reporters in the context of defamation.[87]

4–259 It will be noted that the defence available to a publisher is more confined than that provided for distributors; the former can only plead ignorance that proceedings were active, while the latter can additionally rely upon lack of knowledge as to the contents of the publication itself.

4–260 It is important to note that the scope of the s.3 defence is confined to strict liability contempts, and has no application, for example, to the revelation of material relating to private proceedings contrary to s.12 of the Administration of Justice Act 1960.[88]

E. The burden of proof

4–261 In s.3(3) of the 1981 Act,[89] which provides the defence of innocent publication or dissemination, Parliament clearly places the burden of proving such a defence upon the alleged contemnor. The advent of the Human Rights Act 1998 (the fair trial guarantees under Art.6 of the ECHR), and the body of case law that this has generated, makes the issue somewhat less straightforward than might hitherto have been supposed. Even the fact that Parliament may have intended to impose a legal burden on the defendant is not now to be regarded as conclusive.[90] The courts are now required to ask the rather broader question whether the imposition of a legal burden is a legitimate and proportionate legislative response to the conduct that Parliament is seeking to deter, in this instance preventing the publication or distribution of material that creates a substantial risk of serious prejudice to the process of justice.

4–262 Two questions need to be addressed in these situations: first, in precisely what circumstances does a burden of proof lie upon a defendant? And, secondly, is it a fully probative burden, or merely an evidential burden that must be discharged?[91] If there is to be a legal burden, that standard of proof will presumably be upon the balance of probabilities.[92] It is probably fair to say that the court proceeded both in the *Duffy* case and the *Henry* case as though Parliament had clearly intended to impose a legal burden in s.3.

---

[87] *Egger v Chelmsford* [1965] 1 Q.B. 248. See generally *Gatley on Libel and Slander* (10th ed., 2004), para.8.29.
[88] See paras 8–97 *et seq*.
[89] The subsection provides: "(3) The burden of proof of any fact tending to establish a defence afforded by this section to any person lies upon that person".
[90] See *R. v Lambert* [2001] UKHL 37, [2002] 2 A.C. 545; *Sheldrake v DPP; Att-Gen's Reference No.4 of 2002* [2004] UKHL 43, [2005] 1 A.C. 264.
[91] For a discussion of the distinction between the two burdens, see *Sheldrake*, last note, at [1], Lord Bingham. "An evidential burden is not a burden of proof. It is a burden of raising, on the evidence in the case, an issue as to the matter in question fit for consideration by the tribunal of fact".
[92] *R. v Duffy*, February 9, 1996 (Lexis). Kennedy L.J. states as much, though without citing authority. This is consistent with such authorities as *R. v Carr-Briant* [1943] K.B. 607; *R. v Dunbar* [1958] 1 Q.B. 1. *R. v Hudson* [1966] 1 Q.B. 448; *R. v Hunt* [1987] 1 A.C. 352 at 374 (Lord Griffiths).

THE RIGHT TO REPORT COURT PROCEEDINGS 4–265

IX. THE RIGHT TO REPORT COURT PROCEEDINGS

A. Contemporaneous Reporting of Court Proceedings: the general principle[93]

The importance attached to open justice in cases such as *Scott v Scott*[94] requires that newspapers should be able to attend and report upon court proceedings. The underlying justification for this principle is that it is only by this means that the vast majority of citizens will be able to observe and understand what takes place in the course of the administration of justice. They are entitled to be placed as far as possible in the same position, by following proceedings through the media, as if they had attended in person. Justice must not only be done, but must manifestly be seen to be done. This is why it has long been recognised in the context of defamation that there should be a defence of privilege for those who report court proceedings.[95]

4–263

There was also authority before the 1981 Act that publication of a report of court proceedings should not be treated as being in contempt, provided it was fair and accurate. In *Buenos Ayres Gas Company Ltd v Wilde*,[96] Malins V.-C. refused to commit a man who had published an accurate report of court proceedings, alleged to constitute a contempt. The respondent had undertaken in court not to publish a certain advertisement, pending the outcome of litigation. These preliminary proceedings were misreported by a national newspaper. In order to set the record straight, he caused to be published an account of the preliminary proceedings, and included the terms of the very advertisement that he had undertaken not to publish. It was alleged that this was merely a device to enable him to publish the forbidden advertisement. Malins V.-C. rejected that argument, on the basis that the publication was no more than a fair representation of what had taken place in court saying: "As I understand the law it is this, that any fair representation of what takes place in a court of justice is justifiable, provided it is accurate."

4–264

B. Section 4(1)

The right to report court proceedings is now also correspondingly protected by statute in the context of contempt of court. Section 4(1) of the Contempt of Court Act 1981 provides:

4–265

---

[93] D. Brogarth and C. Walker, "Court Reporting and Open Justice" (1988) 138 New Law Journal 909; C. Walker, I. Cram, D. Brogarth, "The reporting of Crown Court proceedings and the Contempt of Court Act 1981" (1992) 55 M.L.R. 647; Michael Beloff, "Fair Trial—Free Press? Reporting Restrictions in Law and Practice" [1992] P.L. 92; Martin, Robert, "An open legal system" (1985) 23 University of Western Ontario Law Review 169; James Michael, "Open Justice: Publicity and the Judicial Process" [1993] Crim.L.J. 190.
[94] [1913] A.C. 417, HL. See generally paras 2–161, 7–61 *et seq.*
[95] The similar reasoning justifying qualified privilege in court reporting is referred to at para.7–17. See also *Gatley on Libel and Slander* (10th ed., 2004), at para.14–102 and para.15–8.
[96] (1880) 29 W.R. 43; see also Lord Halsbury in *MacDougall v Knight* (1889) 14 App. Cas. 194, 200.

4–265

"Subject to this section a person is not guilty of contempt of court under the strict liability rule in respect of a fair and accurate report of legal proceedings held in public,[97] published contemporaneously and in good faith."

4–266 This provision is part of the statutory code relating to strict liability contempt. It would not appear to provide, for example, any protection for someone who is alleged to be in breach of an injunction (granted, say, in a libel action) not to publish certain material. The section cannot have any relevance to an allegation of contempt at common law since the "strict liability rule" is entirely a creation of the statute and, in any event, since intention is a necessary ingredient in common law contempt,[98] either the respondent would have no need of such a defence or, if *prima facie* in contempt, he would fail to come within the requirement for "good faith" reporting.

1. Burden of proof

4–267 Presumably the Attorney-General would have to show, once the point is raised, that the publication was not a report, not contemporaneous or not in good faith. If he is unable to establish any of these points, then the alleged contemnor would have a defence to a charge of strict liability contempt.

2. *What is a report?*

4–268 There is no reason to suppose that the court would apply too strict a definition of "report", especially in the light of Art.10. Again, some assistance may be derived from the law of defamation.[99] On the other hand, it is necessary to remember that different policy considerations arise in the law of contempt, and that the protection of s.4(1) does not need to be invoked at all unless the material would *prima facie* give rise to a substantial risk of serious prejudice.[1] Where a trial is by judge alone, therefore, an inaccurate report is most unlikely to give rise to a contempt, even if published during the currency of the proceedings.

4–269 It appears that the status of "report" will not necessarily be lost if it contains slight inaccuracy.[2] If there is a substantial inaccuracy, the protection may be lost.[3]

---

[97] For discussion of the distinction between proceedings held in public and in private, see paras 7–36 *et seq.*
[98] See s.6(c) of the Act, discussed more fully at para.5–144.
[99] See *Gatley on Libel and Slander* (10th ed., 2004) para.13.37, n.7. In *Cook v Alexander* [1974] Q.B. 279, for example, it was held that an article taking the form of a "parliamentary sketch" could nonetheless constitute a report provided it gave a fair account of the impression made upon listeners.
[1] The misreporting of proceedings, after they have been completed, and for the purpose of injuring one of the parties, could not give rise to prejudice to the proceedings, although it may give rise to an action for defamation. The element of malice may destroy any privilege: see *Dunn v Bevan* [1922] 1 Ch. 276.
[2] *Gatley on Libel and Slander* (10th ed., 2004), para.13.38.
[3] *Gatley on Libel and Slander* (10th ed., 2004), para.13.39. In *R. v Taylor and Taylor* (1993) 98 Cr.App.R. 361, the Court of Appeal observed that the newspaper coverage of criminal proceedings was such that it could not be classified as "reporting" at all: see para.2–92.

A contemporaneous account of court proceedings, even though it might appear as part of a feature article, would almost certainly qualify as a report.[4]

In the light of the significance of television nowadays, it is quite possible that a "docudrama" or reconstruction of a court hearing *might* be classified as a report, if appropriately treated. Yet this would represent a new departure, as the traditional view of judges has been that any form of television coverage should broadly be classified as "entertainment" rather than informing the public.[5] 4–270

In *Att-Gen v Channel 4 Television Co Ltd*,[6] it was proposed to broadcast daily dramatised summaries of proceedings in the Court of Appeal, during one of the "Birmingham Six" appeals. It was held that the programme was not analogous to press reports, since witnesses (as well as counsel and the court) were to be portrayed by actors. The comment and judgment of viewers would be conditioned by the way in which the witness was portrayed, and this in turn might affect the public's view of the court's judgment. 4–271

The reasoning of this case was criticised in the High Court of Justiciary in *Al Megrahi and Fhima v Times Newspapers Ltd*,[7] on the basis that the Lord Chief Justice appeared to be applying a pre-judgment test deriving partly from Lord Diplock in *Att-Gen v Times Newspapers Ltd*,[8] and partly from the judgment of Shaw L.J. in *Schering Chemicals Ltd v Falkman Ltd*.[9] This was regarded by the judges as being inconsistent with the terms of the Contempt of Court Act 1981. The Lord Justice Clerk concluded, "Accordingly I do not consider that the judicial statements which were relied upon by the Court of Appeal in *Att-Gen v Channel 4 Television* could still be regarded as authoritative at the time of its decision." 4–272

The *Channel 4* case had been referred to the European Commission.[10] It was held that the case failed to disclose an arguable claim of violation of Art.10. This was on the basis that the restriction imposed had been prescribed by law and pursued the legitimate aims of protecting the rights of others and of maintaining the authority and impartiality of the judiciary. It was justified by a pressing social need for purposes of Art.10(2). 4–273

---

[4] See *Gatley on Libel and Slander* (10th ed., 2004), paras 13.35 *et seq.* and para.14.102.
[5] See, *e.g. Peacock v London Weekend Television* (1985) 150 J.P. 71, 83, Croom-Johnson L.J. Indeed, he said in relation to a proposed reconstruction of events about to be investigated at a coroner's inquest: "It certainly cannot be regarded as a programme which is reporting events. The mere fact that it is a reconstruction and a re-enactment gives the lie to that." See also *British Steel Corp. v Granada Television Ltd* [1981] A.C. 1096 at 1116–7, Megarry V.-C. ("with television, entertainment predominates over the news"); *R. v Yap Chuan Ching* (1976) 63 Cr.App.R. 7 at 9, Lawton L.J. (" . . . one of the popular forms of entertainment nowadays on television is a series of reconstructed trials which have a striking degree of realism").
[6] [1988] Crim. L.R. 237.
[7] 1999 S.C.C.R. 824.
[8] [1974] A.C. 273.
[9] [1982] Q.B. 1, 30.
[10] See the decision of April 13, 1989 (Appn. No.14132/88).

C. The requirement that the report be contemporaneous

4–274   Just as Parliament in 1888 took the view that only contemporaneous reports required the protection of absolute, as opposed to qualified, privilege in the law of defamation, so too it is not unreasonable to suppose that Parliament intended in the 1981 Act (which after all expressly referred to the 1888 Act)[11] to provide a defence to a *prima facie* strict liability contempt only for contemporaneous reports made in good faith. Although the Act does not use the terminology of privilege, it affords in effect a defence analogous to qualified rather than absolute privilege.

4–275   Because of the need for the public to be informed about the administration of justice,[12] it is reasonable that statutory protection should be given to those who have to cope with the exigencies of immediate reporting. Where it is intended to discuss or refer to proceedings at some later date, those pressures no longer apply and it is not unreasonable that the authors and publishers should be expected to take additional precautions to ensure accuracy. There is no urgency about reporting proceedings other than contemporaneously, and non-contemporaneous reports can reasonably be required to wait until after the risk of prejudice has dissipated.

4–276   It could hardly be argued that the public interest was being served by informing the public about past proceedings in circumstances where they had become of interest only because of fresh criminal proceedings launched against the same individual. The journalists concerned would presumably be left to bear the consequences of any prejudice created.

4–277   While the statute does not afford a definition of the word "contemporaneous", s.4(3) makes provision for two specified situations where the right to report has been postponed:

> "For the purposes of subsection (1) of this section[13] . . . a report of proceedings shall be treated as published contemporaneously—
>
> (a) in the case of a report of which publication is postponed pursuant to an order under subsection (2) of this section, if published as soon as practicable after that order expires;
> (b) in the case of a report of committal proceedings of which publication is permitted by virtue only of subsection (3) of section 8 of the Magistrates' Courts Act 1980, if published as soon as practicable after publication is so permitted.
> [(b) in the case of a report of allocation or sending proceedings of which publication is permitted by virtue only of subsection (6) of section 52A of the Crime and Disorder Act 1998 ("the 1998 Act"), if published as soon as practicable after publication is so permitted;

---

[11] It was held in *Re Pall Mall Gazette, Jones v Flower and Hopkinson* (1894) 11 T.L.R. 122 that the protection of the 1888 Act was inapplicable to contempt.
[12] See paras 7–16 *et seq.*
[13] The omitted words were repealed by the Defamation Act 1996, Sch.2, with effect from April 1, 1999.

(c) in the case of a report of an application of which publication is permitted by virtue only of subparagraph (5) or (7) of paragraph 3 of Schedule 3 to the 1998 Act, if published as soon as practicable after publication is so permitted]".[14]

4–278 It is reasonable to suppose, however, that where there has been no such postponement, publication would be regarded as contemporaneous if it takes place "as soon as practicable" after the hearing in question. Thus, although no express reference is made to practicability in s.4(1) itself, it would be wrong to assume that any greater degree of elasticity was intended than under subsection (3). It would appear that, for a daily newspaper, it would generally be practicable to report the proceedings within twenty four hours. In the case of a weekly publication, it would be anticipated that the report should occur in the first publication after the hearing had taken place.

4–279 Some guidance may be sought by reference to the use of the same concept in the law of privilege in defamation.[15] *Gatley on Libel and Slander*[16] suggests that the word means "as nearly at the same time as the proceedings as is reasonably possible, having regard to the opportunities for preparation of the report and the time of going to press or of making the broadcast". No doubt a weekly or fortnightly journal would still be able to avail itself of the defence even if a week or ten days were to elapse before the report was published.

4–280 Under s.4(3), where the right to report is postponed, the report is treated as contemporaneous if made as soon as practicable after the right to publish arises. For example, if the court orders that certain evidence shall not be reported until the conclusion of a trial, or some other related proceedings, the subsequent reporting could not be criticised as not being "contemporaneous". There is nothing in *Buenos Ayres Gas Co Ltd v Wilde*[17] to suggest that report had to be contemporaneous at common law, although in that case the report was in fact contemporaneous.

4–281 The qualified privilege in the context of defamation would be destroyed by malice; correspondingly, in relation to contempt, if a report (possibly better referred to as an "account") of court proceedings was published in bad faith, in the sense of being intended to interfere with the administration of justice, the fact that the publication consisted of a report of court proceedings would surely not enable the author or publisher to escape from a finding of common law contempt. Suppose, for example, that a man were being questioned about his possible involvement in a rape, and a newspaper were to publish an account of much earlier proceedings in which he was acquitted, with the intention of ensuring his conviction on this occasion. This would be a classic example of a common law contempt, and even the most scrupulously accurate account of what had happened on the previous occasion ought not to enable the editors or publisher

---

[14] Paragraphs (b) and (c) in square brackets were inserted by the Criminal Justice Act 2003, s.41 and are to come in to force from a date to be appointed.
[15] For a discussion of the contemporaneity requirement in the law of defamation, see *Gatley on Libel and Slander* (10th ed., 2004), para.13.36.
[16] *ibid.*
[17] (1880) 29 W.R. 43.

4–281 CHAPTER 4—THE STATUTORY REGIME FOR STRICT LIABILITY

to escape liability. This would correspond to an absence of "good faith" in the context of s.3.

D. Proceedings in private

4–282 The Act provides protection only for reports of proceedings "in public". It would therefore appear that if a report is published of proceedings which took place in private, and which would create a substantial risk of serious prejudice either to those or to other "particular proceedings", no reliance could be placed upon the fact that it was a report of court proceedings made in good faith. It is true that publication of private proceedings is not necessarily a contempt, and this is confirmed by the provisions of s.12 of the Administration of Justice Act 1960.[18] The distinction between proceedings in private and those held in public no longer has the significance attributed to it in the past.[19] Most proceedings are now open to the public.

E. The requirement of good faith

4–283 Guidance may be obtained from common law decisions in construing the notion of "good faith", and determining in any given circumstances whether a person can bring himself within that protection. It is suggested that for this purpose, it is helpful to focus upon the underlying purpose for which the s.4(1) protection is intended, namely, the entitlement of the public to be informed about current legal proceedings.

4–284 This would certainly accord with the approach of Lord Diplock towards the analysis of the concept of malice, in the context of defamation, in *Horrocks v Lowe*,[20] where he said:

> "Even a positive belief in the truth of what is published on a privileged occasion—which is presumed unless the contrary is proved—may not be sufficient to negative express malice if it can be proved that the defendant misused the occasion *for some purpose other than that for which the privilege is accorded by law*" (emphasis added).

4–285 It is likely that the court would apply a similarly generous test to assessing a person's "good faith" under s.4(1) to that adopted by Lord Diplock when distinguishing malice from other states of mind. He warned that the protection of qualified privilege would prove illusory if too stringent a test were applied, and emphasised that the privilege afforded to local councillors was justified because[21]:

> "... those who represent the local government electors should be able to speak freely and frankly, boldly and bluntly, on any matter which they believe affects the interests

---

[18] Discussed at paras 8–97 *et seq*. See also the consideration of its provisions in *P v Liverpool Daily Post and Echo Newspapers plc* [1991] 2 A.C. 370.
[19] See the discussion of *Hodgson v Imperial Tobacco Ltd* [1998] 1 W.L.R. 1056, 2 All E.R. 673, at paras 7–41 *et seq*.
[20] [1975] A.C. 135 at 150.
[21] *ibid*. at 152A–B.

or welfare of the inhabitants. They may be swayed by strong political prejudice, they may be obstinate and pig-headed, stupid and obtuse; but they were chosen by the electors to speak their minds on matters of local concern and so long as they do so honestly they run no risk of liability for defamation of those who are the subjects of their criticism."

In the light of such warnings, it is not easy to prove malice in defamation proceedings, where the civil standard of proof applies. In the law of contempt, where it is the criminal standard that is relevant, it would be very difficult to prove that a person has not been acting in good faith in reporting court proceedings.

F. Fair and accurate reporting

Under s.4(1) the report must be both fair and accurate. A misreport may give rise to a substantial risk of serious prejudice and thus constitute a strict liability contempt.[22] So too the reporting of proceedings only in part, if the consequences are that overall the proceedings are unfairly misrepresented.[23] For example, it is common practice for the media to report counsel's opening speech in a criminal trial or other proceedings, and then to give far less coverage, if any, to the other side's case. In the Report of the Australian Law Reform Commission,[24] the point was considered in the following terms: **4–286**

"It has been pointed out to the Commission that due to the pronounced emphasis placed in modern times on delivering news to the public as quickly and as frequently as possible, court reporters often produce piecemeal, if not significantly distorted, accounts of legal proceedings for speedy transmission to the public... The Commission does not, however, view current practice in disseminating news quickly as any sort of excuse for failing to report fairly and accurately."

The phrase "fair and accurate" has been judicially considered in the context of the privilege in respect of court reports afforded by s.3 of the Law of Libel Amendment Act 1888.[25] The distinction between the two concepts was highlighted in *Minister for Justice v West Australian Newspapers Ltd*,[26] where it was said by Jackson C.J. that: **4–287**

"The authorities show that one essential requirement to avoid a finding of contempt is that the report should be a fair one. A report may be accurate as far as it goes, but unfair either in its mode of presentation or in stressing unfavourable aspects of the proceedings or in accurately reporting some parts but omitting other parts of the proceedings".

---

[22] For a case prior to the 1981 Act, see *R. v Evening Standard Co Ltd* [1954] 1 Q.B. 578.
[23] See Lord Halsbury in *MacDougall v Knight* (1889) App. Cas. 194.
[24] Report No.35, *Contempt* (1987) p.186, para.322.
[25] Now replaced by the Defamation Act 1996, s.14. See also the requirement of fairness and accuracy as conditions for qualified privilege under the Defamation Act 1996, s.15, and Sch.I, and the discussion as to the similar conditions imposed under its predecessor (*i.e.* the Defamation Act 1952, s.7 and the Schedule), in *Gatley on Libel and Slander* (10th ed., 2004), paras 13.37 *et seq.*
[26] [1970] W.A.R. 202 at 207.

4–288 CHAPTER 4—THE STATUTORY REGIME FOR STRICT LIABILITY

4–288   Fairness and accuracy were in the context of defamation regarded as questions of fact for the jury.[27] The assessment of fairness and accuracy in the context of contempt will be determined by the Divisional Court, but they are nonetheless judges of fact for this purpose. The report need not be accurate in every detail, provided it is substantially fair and accurate.[28] The court will not wish to punish as contempt every report that is inaccurate.[29]

G. Legal proceedings

4–289   The section applies to reports of legal proceedings. These are effectively defined in s.19 as proceedings before any tribunal or body exercising the judicial power of the state. This phrase has already been considered earlier in this chapter.[30] In the Australian case of *Re Associated Newspapers Ex p. Fisher*,[31] it was held that the publication of a *bona fide* and substantially accurate report of anything that occurs in a court of justice, while it is performing its official duties, is exempt from being treated as contempt. This is provided that the incident arises out of, and is substantially connected with, the matter which the court is investigating. The fact that an attempt had been made to demonstrate against an accused, on his way to or from court, and any steps taken by the proper authorities to suppress such demonstrations, were held to be matters so intimately associated with the proceedings in the courtroom itself that a fair and accurate report of those matters stood on the same footing as a report of actual disorder during the course of the hearing itself.

4–290   On the other hand, it is difficult to see why some truly extraneous abuse shouted in court, or some other misuse of the public forum which court proceedings afford, should be reported under the same protection as that given to truly judicial proceedings.[32] It might at first be thought that such problems could be sufficiently addressed by the judge exercising the court's power to postpone reporting under s.4(2). The statutory wording, however, refers to a "report of legal proceedings" and it might be argued that such extraneous material does not truly form part of legal proceedings. In practice, however, the court would be likely to give a sufficiently broad construction to the wording to enable a judge in such circumstances to maintain control of the court's process.

4–291   If such matters are not to be taken as forming part of "legal proceedings", the primary protection afforded by s.4(1) would not avail media reporters in any event. If, however, they can be so classified, then the judge would have a corresponding power to restrict reporting.

---

[27] *Turner v Sullivan* (1862) 6 L.T. (N.S.) 130. See also *Gatley on Libel and Slander* (10th ed., 2004), paras 13.48 and 34.16.
[28] *Andrews v Chapman* (1853) 3 C. & K. 286, 175 E.R. 558; *Kimber v Press Association* [1893] 1 Q.B. 65 at 72–3; *De Normanville v Hereford Times Ltd* (1936) 79 S.J. 796; 80 S.J. 423, CA.
[29] *R. v Daily Worker Ex p. Goulding* (1934) 78 Sol. Jo. 860, Lord Hewart C.J.; see also *Brook v Evans* (1860) 29 L.J. Ch. 616; *Duncan v Sparling* (1894) 10 T.L.R. 353, and *R. v Evening News Ex p. Hobbs* [1925] 2 K.B. 518.
[30] See para.4–17.
[31] [1941] S.R. (N.S.W.) 272.
[32] See *R. v West Yorkshire Coroner Ex p. Smith (No.2)* [1985] Q.B. 1096.

H. The interrelationship between section 4(1) and section 4(2)

The fundamental principle of open justice, reflected in s.4(1), is subject to the discretionary power conferred by s.4(2) of the Act which enables courts in certain circumstances to impose restrictions on reporting even of aspects of proceedings which have taken place in open court.[33] It is possible that a person who breaches such an order will thereby create a substantial risk of serious prejudice. In such circumstances, the question arises whether he would be able to rely upon his report being fair and accurate under s.4(1) so as to provide him with a defence in respect of that kind of contempt. The answer may well be that if he knew of the order he would hardly be acting in good faith. If not, he might have a defence in respect of the s.4(2) order anyway.[34] Since it appears that a person who, at least knowingly, breaches an order made under s.4(2) will be thereby committing a contempt, irrespective of whether the publication creates a substantial risk of serious prejudice,[35] s.4(1) would not be of any assistance in those circumstances.[36]

X. Discussing Public Affairs

A. Discussion of public affairs: Section 5

Section 5 of the Act provides:

> "A publication made as or as part of a discussion in good faith of public affairs or other matters of general public interest is not to be treated as a contempt of court under the strict liability rule if the risk of impediment or prejudice to particular legal proceedings is merely incidental to the discussion."

B. The common law background to section 5

Prior to this enactment, there was some authority to support the view that, where public discussion was already taking place at the time when litigation began, then the discussion could continue provided (a test which would require an investigation into motives) that it was not exploited as a covert way of prejudicing the outcome of the relevant dispute. In *Att-Gen v Times Newspapers Ltd*[37] Lord Reid posited a hypothetical situation:

> " . . . suppose that there is in the press and elsewhere active discussion of some question of wide public interest, such as the propriety of local authorities or other landlords ejecting squatters from empty premises due for demolition. Then legal proceedings are begun against some squatters, it may be by some authority which had already been

---

[33] The general jurisdiction to impose restrictions on reporting is considered in ch.7.
[34] paras 7–203 *et seq.*
[35] See also paras 7–132 *et seq.*
[36] See now *R. v Horsham Justices Ex p. Farquharson* [1982] Q.B. 762, discussed at paras 7–125 *et seq.*
[37] [1974] A.C. 273 at 296. Lord Cross concurred in Lord Reid's general approach and adopted his example of the squatters.

4–294   CHAPTER 4—THE STATUTORY REGIME FOR STRICT LIABILITY

criticised in the press. The controversy could hardly be continued without likelihood that it might influence the authority in its conduct of the action. Must there then be silence until that case is decided? And there may be a series of actions by the same or different landlords. Surely public policy does not require that a system of stop and go shall apply to public discussion."

4–295   Lord Reid went on to approve the following passage in the judgment of Jordan C.J. in the Australian case of *Ex p. Bread Manufacturers*[38]:

> "The discussion of public affairs and the denunciation of public abuses, actual or supposed, cannot be required to be suspended merely because the discussion or the denunciation may, as an incidental but not intended by-product, cause some likelihood of prejudice to a person who happens at the time to be a litigant. It is well settled that a person cannot be prevented by process of contempt from continuing to discuss publicly a matter which may fairly be regarded as one of public interest, by reason merely of the fact that the matter in question has become the subject of litigation or that a person whose conduct is being publicly criticised has become a party to litigation either as plaintiff or as defendant, and whether in relation to the matter which is under discussion or with respect to some other matter."

4–296   Jordan C.J. made it clear that he was addressing the possibility of prejudice such as might be created as an incidental by-product but which was "not intended". It is to be assumed that Lord Reid, in expressing approval of this passage, was also alive to the different policy considerations that could be said to apply to *deliberate* attempts to interfere with the course of justice and those which are concerned with the protection of *bona fide* discussion of public affairs. This distinction is reflected in s.5 itself by the adoption of the condition that any discussion, in order to be protected, is required to be conducted in good faith.

4–297   Lord Simon disagreed with Lord Reid, and in his view there was an absolute prohibition on all discussion of the merits of a case, even of a party's moral position in litigation, until the close of the case. Despite this, he recognised one exception[39]:

> "There is one particular situation where the law might strike the balance between the competing interests either way, but in fact strikes it in favour of freedom of discussion. This is where a matter is already under public debate when litigation supervenes which the continuance of the debate might interfere with. The situation of public debate involves that there is probably at stake some matter of which the public has a legitimate interest to be informed; and the law, in pragmatic judgment, says that conditionally the debate may continue."

4–298   Lord Simon went on to approve the principle set out in the judgments in the Australian cases of *Ex p. Bread Manufacturers* and *Ex p. Dawson*.[40] He also stressed that a contempt would be committed if the publication was *intended* to prejudice the pending proceedings.[41]

---

[38] (1937) S.R. (N.S.W.) 249.
[39] At 321.
[40] [1961] S.R. (N.S.W.) 573 at 575.
[41] [1974] A.C. 273 at 321.

Lord Reid did not specifically address the important question of whether there could be any justifiable basis for prohibiting, by contrast, the *commencement* of a discussion of general issues prompted by a particular scandal which happened to be the subject of court proceedings.[42] In explaining the point by reference to "pragmatic judgment", Lord Simon also failed to provide any principled distinction between public discussion launched *prior* to commencement of litigation and general debate occasioned by the *casus belli* of the litigation itself. In the light of the statutory test, subsequently adopted, of "incidental" prejudice, it is not easy to see how that apparently arbitrary distinction depending upon the genesis of the public discussion can be supported. The question will need to be considered at some stage, in the light of the importance attached to freedom of information by Art.10 of the European Convention.

C. The issues addressed in *Attorney-General v English*

1. *The background to the House of Lords' decision*

In *Att-Gen v English*[43] the Divisional Court considered the effect of s.5 of the 1981 Act. In August of 1981 publicity was given to a case in the Court of Appeal, in which the issue was raised whether an operation should be performed to save the life of a baby suffering from Down's Syndrome. The parents were opposed to the operation, but the court ordered that it should take place. In October of the same year, a woman who had been born without arms was nominated as a "Pro-Life" candidate in a Parliamentary by-election, and a journalist prepared an election address supporting her candidature. These controversial matters had therefore become the subject of a good deal of attention and public discussion.

Against this background, a trial opened a week later, in which a doctor was charged with murdering a baby. The baby suffered from various handicaps including Down's Syndrome. The allegation against the doctor was not merely that he had allowed the child to die, but that he had caused or accelerated his death by the administration of drugs and by the regime of medical care adopted (described as "nursing care only").

On the third day of the trial, the journalist's election address was published (with some modifications) in the form of an article in *The Daily Mail*, which included the following statements:

> "Today the chances of such a baby surviving would be very small indeed. Someone would surely recommend letting her die of starvation, or otherwise disposing of her... With the developing skills of modern medicine the human race could be pruned and carefully tended until only the perfect blooms—the beauty queens, the Mensa I.Q.s, the athletes remain."

---

[42] Cp. the remarks of Lord Simon cited at para.4–297.
[43] [1983] A.C. 116. For a note critical of the decision, see G. Zellick, [1982] P.L. 343. See also A. Ward, (1983) 46 M.L.R. 85; M. Redmond [1983] C.L.J 9.

4–303 The Divisional Court held in contempt proceedings[44] that the statements in the article were capable of prejudicing jurors, no matter how carefully a judge might direct them, and that:

(1) the article did create a substantial risk that the course of justice in the proceedings in question would be seriously impeded or prejudiced, and that "substantial" in this context did not mean "large" or "great" but denoted a risk that was simply "real;"

(2) The burden of establishing a defence under s.5 lay on the alleged contemnor on the balance of probabilities;

(3) the article could be described as part of a discussion of a matter of general public interest, but it also contained "assertions or insinuations";

(4) it was published in good faith;

(5) the risk of prejudice to the pending trial was *not* merely incidental to the public discussion;

(6) the newspaper's proprietors and the editor were accordingly in contempt (the proprietors being fined £500).

When the matter came before the House of Lords, the separate strands in the statutory provisions were individually analysed.

2. What is a "discussion"?

4–304 The House of Lords in *English* held that it had been inappropriate for the Divisional Court to seek to distinguish between "accusations" and "discussions", since there is no warrant to be found within the statute for doing so. Lord Diplock rejected their approach which involved an attempt to confine "discussion" to "the airing of views and the propounding and debating of principles and arguments". He pointed out that[45] that if the newspaper article was not permitted to contain the accusation that it was a common practice among some doctors to allow hopelessly handicapped babies to die, then:

> "The article would be emasculated into a mere contribution to a purely hypothetical problem appropriate, it may be, for debate between academic successors of the medieval schoolmen, but remote from all public affairs and devoid of any general public interest to readers of the 'Daily Mail'."

3. What is merely incidental?

4–305 Jordan C.J. in *Ex p. Bread Manufacturers*[46] posed the question whether the apprehended prejudice can be described as "an incidental but not intended by-product." To answer this question the court should focus upon the discussion

---

[44] [1983] 1 A.C. 116.
[45] At 143.
[46] (1937) S.R. (N.S.W.) 249.

rather than on the trial which it is thought may be prejudiced. The statute does not require judges to try, as the Divisional Court in *English* sought to do, to strike "a sensible balance between on the one hand the maintenance of an unimpeded and unprejudiced justice to every litigant and defendant and on the other hand the preservation of the freedom of discussion of matters of general public interest." Parliament attempted to strike that balance in framing the terms of s.5 itself. Moreover, it has to be remembered that the approach adopted by the European Court of Human Rights is not that of striking a balance so much as recognising a fundamental right (in this case, that of free speech), to which certain limited exceptions may be permitted where necessary.

The Divisional Court interpreted the substance of s.5 too narrowly, in arriving at the conclusion, on the particular facts before them, that the defence was not established. They found that the passages complained of were not a "necessary" part of the general theme of the discussion. The Act, however, provides no such test. Lord Diplock addressed the matter as follows[47]:

4–306

"I have drawn attention to the passages principally relied upon by the Divisional Court as causing a risk of prejudice that was not 'merely incidental to the discussion'. The Court described them as 'unnecessary' to the discussion and as 'accusations'. The test, however, is not whether an article could have been written as effectively without these passages or whether some other phraseology might have been substituted for them that could have reduced the risk of prejudicing Dr Arthur's fair trial; it is whether the risk created by the words actually chosen by the author was 'merely incidental to the discussion,' which I take to mean: no more than an incidental consequence of expounding its main theme."

4. *Later developments*

This question arose again in *Att-Gen v TVS Television Ltd*,[48] in relation to a local newspaper publication and regional television broadcast. These had admittedly given rise to a substantial risk of seriously prejudicing Crown Court proceedings then taking place in the relevant area. The programme was entitled "The New Rachmans". It concerned an exposure of landlords who were alleged to be misusing the bed and breakfast provisions and obtaining public money by deception. The direct result of these publications was that a trial had to be aborted, in which one of the landlords faced a charge of conspiracy to defraud. The cost of the aborted trial was estimated to be £215,000. There was a later trial resulting in a conviction.

4–307

The only issue was whether the prejudice had been "merely incidental" to the discussion within the meaning of section. It was accepted in relation to the television broadcast that there was an attempt to analyse the causes of a new wave of Rachmanism in southern England generally, but the thrust of the discussion was held to be more narrowly focused upon a small number of landlords in the particular locality. Indeed, it was possible to recognise the

4–308

---

[47] At 143B.
[48] *The Times*, July 7, 1989 (Lexis).

4–308 CHAPTER 4—THE STATUTORY REGIME FOR STRICT LIABILITY

defendant in one of the still photographs shown, in which he was outside the main post office.

4–309 The test applied was based upon that of Lord Diplock in *Att-Gen v English*,[49] namely whether the risk created was merely an incidental consequence to the expounding of the main theme. It was held to be unhelpful to treat these words as though they were to be found in the statute, and it was necessary to look at the subject matter of the discussion and see how closely it related to the proceedings. The closer the relationship, the easier it would be for the Attorney to show a correspondingly increased seriousness of risk.

4–310 Whether a particular passage is "necessary" or not may go to the *bona fides* of the discussion of public affairs.[50] It may also go to *mens rea*. A person who intentionally seeks to prejudice a pending trial, using a public discussion as a device to achieve that end, may be guilty of contempt quite apart from the strict liability rule. On the other hand, it is to be observed that if the offending passages had been omitted there would presumably have been no risk of prejudice and, it would follow, no need to rely on the statutory defence. Before s.5 comes into play at all, the Act envisages that there shall have been a publication which does create a substantial risk of serious prejudice. It was clearly contemplated by Parliament that there may be some circumstances in which some risk of prejudice has to be accepted because of countervailing considerations of freedom of communication and expression. It is how that balance is to be struck that is so important. In this context, the questions which arise under s.5 are:

(1) Is that publication part of a discussion of public affairs?

(2) Is that part of the publication which creates the prejudice merely incidental to the discussion?

4–311 One matter that the court may wish to enquire into is whether the prejudicial passage dealt with a topic which had already been publicly discussed or was a justified extension of a continuing debate. It is clear from what Lord Reid[51] and Jordan C.J.[52] have said that if a particular issue is being aired as a matter of public debate *before* the relevant proceedings began, it can more readily be concluded that any prejudice arising from a continuation of that discussion was merely incidental.

4–312 The Act, however, does not make it a requirement that the public discussion should *already* be under way. Thus the pending case itself may, at least theoretically, legitimately spark off consideration of general public issues. In *Att-*

---

[49] [1983] 1 A.C. 116 at 143.
[50] This would be consistent with Lord Diplock's approach to malice in *Horrocks v Lowe* [1975] A.C. 135 at 151 which was that the relevance of including unnecessary material on an occasion of qualified privilege was that it should be weighed on the issue of malice, rather than affecting whether there was an occasion of privilege at all.
[51] para.4–294.
[52] para.4–295.

Gen v Times Newspapers Ltd[53] the House considered that the pending hearing of the action against the Distillers Company should not have inhibited a discussion as to whether manufacturers of drugs should be absolutely liable for injuries caused by their products. Similarly, it should not have prevented discussion as to the adequacy of the legal principles of compensation, nor even a discussion of the adequacy of awards of damages to other thalidomide children in earlier settled proceedings. Moreover, in *Att-Gen v English*, Lord Diplock concluded by saying[54]:

> "Such gagging of bona fide discussion in the press of controversial matters of general public interest, merely because there are in existence contemporaneous legal proceedings in which some particular instance of those controversial matters may be in issue, is what section 5 of the Contempt of Court Act 1981 was in my view intended to prevent."

None of this sits comfortably with the approach adopted by the courts towards the controversial affairs of Robert Maxwell. Despite the manifest public importance of the issues raised by his misconduct, public discussion was severely restricted[55] by reason of the pendency of criminal proceedings against his two sons, although a more open approach was adopted by the judge presiding over contemporaneous proceedings in the Chancery Division.[56]

The Divisional Court in *Att-Gen v Guardian Newspapers Ltd*[57] considered s.5 briefly although it was not a matter essential for their decision. Collins J. referred to the widespread discussion of the Queen's security in 1982 in the aftermath of an intruder (Mr Fagan) finding his way into her bedroom. The prejudice to the fairness of Mr Fagan's trial could truly be classified as incidental.[58] He drew a contrast between those circumstances and the situation he was addressing, where the subject matter of *The Observer* article related to the very fact on which the prosecution was based.

D. Section 5 inapplicable to intentional contempts

If prejudice to a pending trial is *intended*, then the publication may be a contempt quite apart from the strict liability rule.[59] Moreover, the degree of risk of prejudice required, for intentional contempt, may be lower than under the strict liability test.[60] Although there seems to have been a defence at common law

---

[53] [1974] A.C. 273.
[54] [1983] A.C. 116 at 144.
[55] *R. v Maxwell* (unreported), March 6, 1995, Phillips J.; see also *Att-Gen v BBC, Hat Trick Productions* [1997] E.M.L.R. 76, and *Att-Gen v Steadman* (unreported), February 7, 1994, in which Bell J. granted an injunction restraining the respondent from staging "Maxwell: The Musical" on the basis that the musical would be in breach of the strict liability rule.
[56] Lindsay J. took a more relaxed view as to the coverage of the Chancery proceedings which were happening in parallel, largely because the press took less interest: *MGN Pension Trustees Ltd v Bank of America National Trust and Savings Association and another (Serious Fraud Office Intervening)* [1995] 2 All E.R. 355.
[57] [1999] E.M.L.R 904.
[58] *Att-Gen v Times Newspapers, The Times*, February 12, 1983 (Lexis).
[59] See ch.5.
[60] para.5–18.

4–315

similar to that provided by s.5, it would not appear (if the exposition of Jordan C.J. is to be followed) to have applied to those *intending* prejudice. The provisions of Art.10 of the European Convention do not, as a matter of public policy, protect people who deliberately set out to upset the administration of justice. Indeed, such persons would be undermining the very object of Art.6 of the Convention, which protects the right to a fair trial. The 1981 Act is intended to restrict the impact only of *strict* liability.[61]

E. Injunctions and section 5

4–316 Where an injunction is sought to restrain a publication, and the publisher (or broadcaster) intends to assert that the proposed discussion falls within the terms of s.5, it is for the person seeking the injunction to establish that the protection is inapplicable. This was established by the decision of the Court of Appeal in *Leary v BBC*,[62] where an injunction was sought to prevent the transmission of a television programme concerning *inter alia* the events that gave rise to the disbandment of the West Midlands Serious Crimes Squad. A theme of the programme was to be that "some members of the Squad seem to have committed repeated acts of serious misconduct over periods of years, in particular by fabricating evidence of confessions by innocent people".[63]

4–317 The court took the view that, even if it had been established to the requisite standard[64] that the proposed programme would create a substantial risk of serious prejudice, there would be no contempt. Section 5 was applicable, since the programme undoubtedly constituted a discussion of a matter of general public interest. There being no allegation of bad faith, and provided that the creation of a risk through the broadcast was no more than "an incidental consequence of expounding" or discussing the material in the programme relevant to the matter of general public interest, the programme would not infringe the strict liability rule.

F. The burden of proof

4–318 Section 3 of the 1981 Act, which provided the defence of innocent publication or dissemination, specifically stipulates that the burden of establishing such a defence lies on the alleged contemnor. There is no such provision in s.5, but it was confirmed in *Att-Gen v English*[65] in the House of Lords that the burden rested upon the Attorney-General to show that the publication was *not* "merely incidental" to the discussion. It is no doubt for the alleged contemnor to raise the issue, and there will be an evidential burden on him; once there is evidence upon which the court can consider the defence, however, it is for the Attorney to show that it has not been established.

---

[61] See paras 5–1 *et seq.*
[62] September 29, 1989 (Lexis), discussed at paras 6–31 *et seq.*
[63] *ibid.*, *per* Nicholls L.J., concurring with Lord Donaldson M.R. and Gibson L.J.
[64] See paras 5–184, 6–38.
[65] [1983] 1 A.C. 116, reversing the decision of the Divisional Court.

XI. What Are the "Defences" Preserved by Section 6?

A. The statutory context

Hitherto, in this chapter, we have been addressing the terms of the statutory framework enacted by Parliament, which was intended to confine the scope of strict liability for contempt of court in respect of publications. This was apparently intended[66] to remove from our law the old "prejudgment" test expounded in *Att-Gen v Times Newspapers Ltd*,[67] in order to achieve compliance with the requirements of the European Convention on Human Rights,[68] and also to implement the recommendations of the Phillimore Report.

We have also considered the "escape routes" specifically provided in the statute, whereby liability may be excluded in situations giving rise to a *prima facie* case of strict liability contempt. The provisions in s.3[69] are described in the Act, albeit only in the cross-heading, as giving rise to a "defence", although in *Att-Gen v English*[70] Lord Diplock does not seem to have thought this an appropriate description of the protection afforded in s.5 to the discussion of public affairs. Nor would it be especially apt either as applying to contemporaneous reports of court proceedings.[71] Nevertheless, these provisions can at least be construed and applied by reference to the statutory context in which they appear.

When one turns, however, to the "saving" provisions of s.6(a) of the 1981 Act, the implications are less readily comprehensible.[72] It is clear from s.6 that no conduct was intended to be classified as contempt under the Act which would not have been so classified previously. Nor was it intended to remove any defences that would have been available under the common law " ... to a charge of contempt of court under the strict liability rule". Since the "strict liability rule" seems, as such, to have been a creature of draftsman of the 1981 Act itself, this wording is somewhat uncertain of scope. It may best be construed to mean that where a person would have had a defence at common law, in respect of a publication giving rise *prima facie* to strict liability, then any such defence would still be available, if needed, after the coming into effect of the Act.

This requires one to posit a publication that creates a substantial risk that particular legal proceedings will be seriously impeded or prejudiced. It also

---

[66] See the explanation of Lord Hailsham L.C. in Parliament: *Hansard*, H.L. Vol. 415 (5th Series) col. 660, December 9, 1980.
[67] [1974] A.C. 273.
[68] *Sunday Times v United Kingdom* (1979) 2 E.H.R.R. 245.
[69] See paras 4–236 *et seq*.
[70] [1983] 1 A.C. 116 at 141C–E. He described the section as standing on an equal footing with s.2(2). "It does not set out exculpatory matter. Like s.2(2) it states what publication shall *not* amount to contempt of court despite their tendency to interfere with the course of justice in particular proceedings".
[71] As provided in s.4(1).
[72] See generally the useful discussion of s.6 in the judgment of Lloyd L.J. in *Att-Gen v Newspaper Publishing plc* [1988] 1 Ch. 333 at 381–3.

4–322 CHAPTER 4—THE STATUTORY REGIME FOR STRICT LIABILITY

requires one to suppose that none of the other escape routes expressly contemplated by the statute would be available. Also, since we are considering here strict liability, it must be assumed that there was no *intention* to interfere with the course of justice; if there were, then there could well be a publication contempt at common law. It is not easy to identify what defences, if any, the draftsman may have had in mind (other than, perhaps, the lack of intent itself).

B. Possible candidates

4–323 There are a number of possible candidates which need to be addressed. Such escape routes as were recognised piecemeal by the common law, prior to the 1981 Act, may represent attempts to mitigate in deserving cases the rigours of the strict prejudgment test applied at that time. It is arguable, however, that since those concerns have been addressed by the European Court of Human Rights, and subsequently by an Act of Parliament, there is no longer room for similar but differently expressed defences to be formulated by judicial development. Nevertheless, it is necessary to consider some of the common law principles in order to see how they fit in with the statutory framework.

1. *Protection from "gagging" writs*

4–324 One respect in which the English common law has long accorded a high priority to freedom of speech is in its unwillingness to grant interlocutory injunctions by way of "previous restraint"[73] for the prevention of defamatory publications. What is now generally known as the rule in *Bonnard v Perryman*[74] means that an injunction will always be refused in such circumstances, where the defendant swears that he will prove the truth of what he intends to say, *unless* the applicant can demonstrate that the mooted plea of justification is bound to fail.[75] In *Thomson v Times Newspapers Ltd*, Salmon L.J. said[76]:

> "It is a widely held fallacy that the issue of a writ automatically stifles further comment. There is no authority that I know of to support the view that further comment would amount to contempt of court. Once a newspaper has justified, and there is some prima facie support for the justification, the plaintiff cannot obtain an interlocutory injunction to restrain the defendants from repeating the matters complained of. In these circumstances it is obviously wrong to suppose that they could be committing a contempt by doing so. It seems to me equally obvious that no other newspaper that repeats the same sort of criticism is committing a contempt of court. They may be publishing a libel, and if they do so, and they have no defence to it, they will have to pay whatever may be the appropriate damages; but the writ does not, in my view,

---

[73] See Blackstone, *Commentaries on the Laws of England* (1765), Book IV, pp.151–2. See now also the provisions of s.12 of the Human Rights Act 1998 addressed in *Imutran Ltd v Uncaged Campaigns Ltd* [2001] 2 All E.R. 385 and *Cream Holdings Ltd v Banerjee* [2004] UKHL 44, [2005] 1 A.C. 253.
[74] [1891] 2 Ch. 269.
[75] *Coulson v Coulson* (1887) 3 T.L.R. 846; *Holley v Smyth* [1998] Q.B. 726; *Williams v Wolman* January 30, 1990 (Lexis) CA, where it was said that the plaintiff needed to show that the words were "manifestly untrue", *per* Stocker L.J.
[76] [1969] 1 W.L.R. 1236. See also *Wallersteiner v Moir* [1974] 1 W.L.R. 991 at 1005.

What Are the "Defences" Preserved by Section 6? 4–327

preclude the publication of any further criticism; it merely puts the person who makes the further criticism on risk of being sued for libel".

Salmon L.J. appears to have made the leap from *Bonnard v Perryman* to the conclusion that publication of a libel, in circumstances where an injunction would be refused, *could* not amount to a contempt of court. As Lord Denning M.R. observed in *Att-Gen v Times Newspapers Ltd*[77]: 4–325

> "Our law of contempt does not prevent comment before the litigation is started, nor after it has ended. Nor does it prevent it when the litigation is dormant and is not being actively pursued. If the pending action is one which, as a matter of public interest, ought to have been brought to trial long ago, or ought to have been settled long ago, the newspapers can fairly comment on the failure to bring it to trial or to reach a settlement. No person can stop comment by serving a writ and letting it lie idle: nor can he stop it by entering an appearance and doing no more. It is active litigation which is protected by the law of contempt, not the absence of it."

Consistent with this approach is the case of *Cronmire v The Daily Bourse*.[78] The defendants had published a number of paragraphs which were allegedly defamatory of the plaintiff. He issued a writ in respect of these, and on the day after it was issued the defendants published a further article, stating that the plaintiff had not the slightest intention of bringing an action and had merely served the writ to shut the mouth of the defendants. The article went on to repeat defamatory statements about the plaintiff. A Divisional Court held that this subsequent article was not a contempt. In the course of argument counsel had admitted that there was no precedent for an application to commit in a case of libel. Lord Coleridge C.J. observed, also in the course of argument, that " . . . if the defendant may summarily be sent to prison merely because a writ in an action for libel has been issued that may be made the means of restraining a very valuable right of comment and free discussion on matters of public interest".[79] Lord Coleridge and Wills J. appear to have been troubled by the apparent inconsistency, that would arise from committing such a person for contempt, with the principle recently established in *Bonnard v Perryman*. 4–326

It may be therefore that these principles would fall within the contemplation of s.6(a) of the Contempt of Court Act 1981. Yet it is undoubtedly the case that the repetition of a libel, during the period when a libel action was active, *could* create circumstances whereby there was indeed a substantial risk that potential jurors could be seriously prejudiced against the plaintiff. In *Att-Gen v News Group Newspapers plc*[80] it so happened that the court was not satisfied that such prejudice would arise, largely because of the anticipated time lapse before trial. Suppose, however, there had been a trial of the issues in that case, concerning the allegations of drug-taking, and a newspaper had, much closer to its commencement, re-published similar allegations (while lacking any state of mind that could be characterised as *mens rea* for the purposes of common law contempt). Could 4–327

---

[77] [1973] Q.B. 710 at 740A–B.
[78] (1892) 9 T.L.R. 101.
[79] *ibid*. at 102.
[80] [1987] 1 Q.B. 1.

such a journalist or publisher have prayed in aid the words of Salmon L.J. in *Thomson v Times Newspapers Ltd*.[81]

4–328 Sir John Donaldson M.R. in *Att-Gen v Newspaper Publishing plc*[82] explained why the publication of defamatory words in such circumstances would not ordinarily be a contempt. Yet he pointed out that there are circumstances in which the law of contempt, or more accurately the public interest in protecting the right to a fair trial, should take priority over even the *Bonnard v Perryman* principle.

4–329 It is necessary to bear in mind that what Salmon L.J. was saying was in the context of the so-called "gagging writ". He was making it clear that *merely* by the issue of a writ one could not stifle further comment by, as it were, activating the law of contempt. This appears to be reconcilable with what Sir John Donaldson M.R. said in *Att-Gen v Newspaper Publishing plc*[83] The test is really whether the publication actually would create a substantial risk of serious prejudice in particular legal proceedings. If so, it is submitted, no special defence along these lines would enable the publisher to escape from the finding of strict liability. Our conclusion would be, therefore, that the principle expounded in *Bonnard v Perryman* and *Thomson v Times Newspapers Ltd* cannot be categorised as giving rise to a special defence such as the draftsman of s.6(a) had in mind.

2. *Fair and temperate criticism of a litigant*

4–330 Private persuasion of a litigant does not arise for consideration here,[84] because we are now concerned with communications made "to the public at large or any section of the public." If a litigant is criticised publicly the possibility of strict liability arises; it has to be considered therefore whether some special protection is afforded in that context where a prejudicial publication could nonetheless be characterised as fair and temperate criticism of a litigant. This was the nature of the proposed newspaper article which came before the European Court in *Sunday Times v United Kingdom*.[85] The criticism there was directed at the attitude being taken by defendants in negligence proceedings, which would have been tried by judge alone. There was unlikely to be a substantial risk of serious prejudice.

4–331 Suppose, however, that the criticism were directed at a newspaper defending itself in a libel action, or at the Metropolitan Police Commissioner in respect of pending proceedings for false imprisonment. In either case, there could well be a jury. If the criticism, or the canvassing of the merits, were such as to give rise to a substantial risk of serious prejudice, and yet did not fall within the special defence provided for public discussion in s.5 of the 1981 Act, it is difficult to see

---

[81] Cited at para.4–324.
[82] [1988] Ch. 333 at 371C–E.
[83] See also Lord Diplock in *Att-Gen v Times Newspapers Ltd* [1974] A.C. at 312.
[84] See *Att-Gen v Martin (Peter)*, *The Times*, April 23, 1986 (Lexis), discussed para.11–282; *R. v Kellett* [1976] 1 Q.B. 372, CA, discussed para.11–241.
[85] (1979) 2 E.H.R.R. 244.

that the publisher could avoid a finding of contempt on the basis of claiming only to have criticised the litigant fairly and temperately. The more measured, reasonable and persuasive the criticism, the more effective may be the prejudice created in the minds of potential jurors who read it. An overtly abusive article may be more easily dismissed as likely to be ineffectual.

3. Parliamentary privilege

Although, once a *contra mundum* order has been made, any publication inconsistent with it is likely to be treated as a contempt of court, an interesting question arises as to a possible defence in relation to reporting material appearing to be a *prima facie* breach—but for the fact that it was uttered in Parliament.

This seems to have been envisaged by Lord Denning M.R., in *Att-Gen v Times Newspapers Ltd*,[86] where he said:

" ... as soon as matters are discussed in Parliament, they can be, and are, reported at large in the newspapers. The publication in the newspapers is protected by the law. Whatever comments are made in Parliament, they can be repeated in the newspapers without any fear of an action for libel or proceedings for contempt of court. If it is no contempt for a newspaper to publish the comments made in Parliament, it should be no contempt to publish the self-same comments made outside Parliament."

This problem arose when more recently, in spite of the order of Cazalet J., subsequently affirmed by the Court of Appeal in *Re Z (A Minor) (Identification: Restrictions on Publication)*,[87] a member of Parliament proceeded some months afterwards to announce the name of the protected child in an early day motion in the House of Commons. There can be little doubt that the M.P. would be protected in so doing by the terms of Art.9 of the Bill of Rights 1688[88]; or that journalists reporting such remarks fairly and accurately would themselves be protected on the usual principles that protect Parliamentary reporting.[89] In the event, the Official Solicitor applied to Cazalet J. in the light of this exposure for permission to publish the terms of the injunction itself.

4. *No defence of public good or benefit*

The Act significantly omits any *general* defence that a publication complained of as contempt was for the public benefit. In this respect the statute followed the recommendation of the Phillimore Committee.[90] The Committee concluded (as did the House of Lords in *Att-Gen v Times Newspapers Ltd*) that certainty in the

---

[86] [1973] Q.B. 710 at 741.
[87] [1997] Fam. 1.
[88] Even after the hasty amendment to those provisions contained in the Defamation Act 1996, s.13.
[89] See, *e.g. Wason v Walter* (1868) L.R. 4 Q.B. 73, and the full discussions contained in *Gatley on Libel and Slander* (10th ed., 2004) at para.13.29 *et seq.*, and in Erskine May, *Treatise on the Law, Privileges, Proceedings and Usage of Parliament* (23rd ed., 2004), ch.6. See P.M. Leopold, "Parliamentary Free Speech, Court Orders and European Law" (1998) Jo. Leg. Studies 53.
[90] para.145.

4–335 CHAPTER 4—THE STATUTORY REGIME FOR STRICT LIABILITY

law of contempt was of greater importance, particularly so far as newspapers were concerned. Editors should know where they stood[91]:

> "To decide whether, in respect of a particular matter, a defence of public benefit could be successfully advanced would on the contrary be extremely difficult. Public benefit is notoriously difficult to define; the creation of a defence on that basis would introduce a fresh area of uncertainty into the law. Moreover, the ventilation of a misconceived defence on these lines could well exacerbate the risks of prejudice."

4–336 These views were expressed before the judgment of the European Court of Human Rights. That court asked itself the question whether grant of the injunction imposed upon the *Sunday Times* corresponded to a social need so pressing as to supplant the priority accorded to freedom of speech.[92] In effect, therefore, they were asking whether the injunction could be justified by reference to some other public interest or benefit. This involved balancing a variety of considerations, an exercise which Phillimore and the House of Lords rejected in the interests of certainty.

4–337 In the statute, the balancing exercise has been carried out by narrowly defining the *actus reus* of strict liability contempt, and the provision of specific escape routes. If no substantial risk of serious prejudice or impediment is created, the problem does not arise. If such a risk can be established, then a defence to committal proceedings would need to be established by demonstrating that the situation fell within one of the conditions prescribed by s.4(1), s.3 or s.5. It is submitted that "public benefit" could not be prayed in aid if otherwise the circumstances did not so qualify.

4–338 It is possible to imagine circumstances in which proceedings are not "active" and yet it may be virtually certain that a wanted man will be captured. Suppose a newspaper publishes matter about the suspect which may enable him to be caught, but which will almost inevitably lead to prejudice to his trial following capture. It may be said by way of defence that there was no intention to prejudice the administration of justice, and that the dominant motive was to assist in his capture. Nevertheless, it may have been recognised overtly that prejudice could arise. It is recognised in the law of defamation that there may sometimes be exigencies justifying the publication of damaging material in the wider public interest, and indeed that there may be a social or moral duty to publish such material.[93]

---

[91] *ibid*. See also the words of Sir John Donaldson M.R. in *Francome v Mirror Group Newspapers Ltd* [1984] 1 W.L.R. 892 at 898.
[92] See paras 1–104 *et seq*.
[93] See, *e.g. Blackshaw v Lord* [1984] 1 Q.B. 1, 27A, *per* Stephenson L.J.: "There may be extreme cases where the urgency of communicating a warning is so great, or the source of the information so reliable, that publication of suspicion or speculation is justified; for example, where there is danger to the public from a suspected terrorist or the distribution of contaminated food or drugs". Since the House of Lords decision in *Reynolds v Times Newspapers Ltd* [2001] 2 A.C. 127 it may confidently be said that the "classic interest/duty test" is adaptable to a great variety of circumstances: *per* Lord Cooke in *McCartan Turkington Breen v Times Newspapers Ltd* [2001] 2 A.C. 277 at 300.

It might at first sight seem strange that there should be a duty recognised in one area of the law, and yet there appears to be no corresponding defence in proceedings for common law contempt. Nevertheless, although both principles are fundamentally important to the media in their coverage of crime and other matters of public interest, there are different policy considerations that come into play. The position would appear to be that the law as formulated by Parliament in the 1981 Act regards it as necessary to prevent adverse publicity if, objectively judged, it creates a substantial risk of serious prejudice and yet the circumstances do not fall within any of the prescribed escape routes. Moreover, as we shall consider in the following chapter concerning common law contempt, the dominant intention in our hypothetical example will not avail a journalist in circumstances where a court may ultimately conclude that the relevant risk must have been obvious.

CHAPTER 5

CONTEMPTS BY PUBLICATION AT COMMON LAW

I.	Questions Unresolved by the 1981 Act	5–1
II.	The *Actus Reus*	5–5
III.	The Mental Element in Common Law Publication Contempt	5–120
IV.	Is There a General Defence of Fair Comment/Public Interest?	5–201
V.	Scandalising the Court	5–204

I. QUESTIONS UNRESOLVED BY THE 1981 ACT

A. Introduction: the outstanding questions

5–1 Most applications to commit for contempt in respect of media publications are based upon the strict liability provisions contained in ss.1 and 2 of the Contempt of Court Act 1981. Nonetheless, it was clear that Parliament intended to retain the application of the common law of contempt not only generally, but also in the area of media publication, provided that there was present an element of *mens rea*. This much was apparent from the terms of s.6,[1] which provide *inter alia*:

"Nothing in the foregoing provisions of this Act—

. . .

(c) restricts liability for contempt of court in respect of conduct intended to impede or prejudice the administration of justice."

5–2 What is less clear is how the conduct is to be characterised which constitutes the *actus reus*,[2] and the precise nature of the *mens rea* required.[3] It is the purpose of this chapter to consider these questions. This exercise will require some attention to be given to the common law authorities before 1981; the extent to which those principles may need to be modified in the light of Art.10 of the European Convention, as interpreted by decisions of the European Court of Human Rights and especially having regard to the coming into effect of the Human Rights Act 1998 in October 2000; and the handful of English decisions on this subject in the light of the 1981 Act.

---

[1] Discussed more generally at paras 5–144 *et seq*.
[2] In his commentary upon *R. v Ingrams Ex p. Goldsmith* [1977] Crim.L.R. 40 at 41, Sir John Smith observed in relation to common law contempt that "There must be an *actus reus* as well as *mens rea*. The exact nature of the *actus reus* is obscure. Is it the actual prejudice of the proceedings? Clearly not, otherwise there could be no completed offence of contempt until the proceedings were completed. It would seem that the offence is complete when a real risk of prejudice is created."
[3] See paras 5–120 *et seq*. See also Richard Stone, " 'Intentional' contempt and press freedom" (1988) 138 New Law Jo. 423–4.

In the context of publication contempt, there is clearly a tension between two 5–3 public policy objectives. On the one hand, as Nicholls L.J. observed in *Att-Gen v Hislop*,[4] "... the Act left untouched, and outside the strict boundaries set for the strict liability rule, cases ... where the conduct was intended to impede or prejudice the administration of justice". There is, however, on the other hand the crucial consideration, acknowledged by the Court of Appeal in *Att-Gen v Newspaper Publishing plc*,[5] that one of the primary purposes of the 1981 Act was to effect a permanent shift in the balance between freedom of speech and the protection of the administration of justice.

The matter of *actus reus* and that of *mens rea* are considered separately, but the 5–4 two issues are inevitably interrelated, and it is necessary to address some general questions of policy, and to have regard to the considerations which underlay the decision of Parliament to retain the application of the common law of contempt to publications outside the strict liability framework—yet alongside the new regime.

II. THE *ACTUS REUS*

A. The impact of the Act on the common law test

The provisions of the 1981 Act left unaffected the *actus reus* of publication 5–5 contempts falling outside the strict liability rule. For guidance in this context, one has to look to the common law. But one possible view is that it is unrealistic to suppose that the common law has remained static; it may have been affected, quite apart from the limited steps that Parliament took in the 1981 Act, in particular by the adverse comments upon the jurisprudence of the law of contempt in *Sunday Times v United Kingdom* in the European Court of Human Rights,[6] and by the increasing significance of Art.10 of the European Convention. Even before the advent of the Human Rights Act 1998, it had become accepted that reference could and should be made to the Convention in situations where the common law was unclear.[7]

Thus, the argument would run, the *actus reus* for common law contempt 5–6 should now equate with the creation of a substantial risk of serious prejudice.[8] It is sometimes assumed, accordingly, that the effect of the statute extends more widely, albeit indirectly, than publications falling within the definition of strict liability contempt. Lord Woolf M.R. made the comment, for example, in

---

[4] [1991] 1 Q.B. 514 at 532F.
[5] [1988] Ch. 333 at 386, Lloyd L.J.
[6] (1979) 2 E.H.R.R. 245.
[7] See, *e.g. Derbyshire County Council v Times Newspapers Ltd* [1992] Q.B. 770. See also Lord Lester and N. Schiffrin, "The European Human Rights Convention and Media Law" in *The Yearbook of Media and Entertainment Law* (1995), p.241; "The European Human Rights Convention and Media Law" in *The Yearbook of Media and Entertainment Law* (1996) p.299. And see paras 2–124 *et seq.*
[8] See the discussion of *BBC v The Law Officers* (Guernsey Court of Appeal) at paras 5–52 *et seq.*

Hodgson v Imperial Tobacco Ltd,[9] that "the Act clearly reveals the intention of Parliament as to where the line should be drawn if there is a conflict between the interests of the administration of justice and freedom of expression." Although he expressed himself in general terms, he may not have intended to be taken as given a considered view on common law contempts specifically.

5–7 It is clear that the essential factor in common law contempts now is the requirement by Parliament of the presence of intention. There may be some doubt as to the nature of the *mens rea* required,[10] but it was intentional conduct to which Parliament was specifically directing its attention in s.6(c) of the Act. An alternative view, therefore, to those addressed in the preceding paragraph is that there is no corresponding policy imperative to modify the approach to *actus reus* in such cases. If a person is setting out deliberately to interfere with the administration of justice, it is by no means clear that the public policy underlying s.6(c) requires that such a contemnor shall have gone so far down the road as to have created a substantial risk of serious prejudice. He will clearly have to have perpetrated some act on the route to achieving his objective, and that may well be sufficient to attract the operation of the law, even though it falls short of the statutory threshold for the *actus reus*. It is submitted that it is this latter approach which has prevailed in the authorities.

5–8 In restricting the cases to which strict liability attaches, the 1981 Act in effect defines the *actus reus* of publication contempts for the purposes of "the strict liability rule". The wording confines strict liability to publications which create a substantial risk that the course of justice in particular proceedings will be seriously impeded or prejudiced.[11] Prior to 1981, the *actus reus* of publication contempt was more loosely and broadly interpreted, and would include any act calculated to interfere with the due administration of justice. "Calculated" at common law generally meant no more than "tending" or "likely to"; that is to say, the act or omission complained of had to create a real risk of prejudice,[12] but not necessarily of *serious* prejudice.

5–9 We must therefore focus carefully on those acts which Parliament (or the draftsman) must be taken to have contemplated, in the context of s.6, as being within the *actus reus* of common law publication contempt. Before the House of Lords decision, there were a number of cases which appeared to adopt the higher test of a *serious* risk of prejudice.[13] However, the House of Lords in *Att-Gen v Times Newspapers Ltd*[14] reaffirmed the application of the law to "technical

---

[9] [1998] 1 W.L.R. 1056, 2 All E.R. 673.
[10] Discussed at paras 5–120 *et seq.*
[11] s.2(2).
[12] *Att-Gen v Times Newspapers Ltd* [1974] A.C. 273. "Real" probably connoted nothing more than that the risk itself had to qualify as being something more than *de minimis*.
[13] *Chambers v Hudson Dodsworth & Co.* [1936] 2 K.B. 595, 603; *R. v Duffy Ex p. Nash* [1960] 2 Q.B. 188 at 200; *Carl-Zeiss-Stiftung v Rayner & Keeler Ltd* [1960] 1 W.L.R. 1145; *Vine Products Ltd v Green* [1966] Ch. 484.
[14] [1974] A.C. 273.

contempts".[15] It is now clear from the decision of the European Court of Human Rights in *Sunday Times v United Kingdom*[16] that the scope of the *actus reus* of contempt had been set too wide by the House in that case, and that it was not legitimate to impose strict liability for anything less than the creation of a risk of *serious* prejudice.

Since the enactment of the strict liability provisions in the 1981 Act, it is natural to focus on the dichotomy between the two limbs of "substantial risk" and "serious prejudice", and this is clearly helpful in considering cases brought under those provisions.[17] Nevertheless, discussion of such matters prior to the Act was not focused on quite the same terminology, and judges tended to concentrate more upon what is now regarded as the first "limb", namely the degree of risk.[18] Although we have broken down the discussion that follows, and in particular included sections dealing separately with "risk" and "prejudice", it is important to remember that this division is not always reflected in the earlier common law cases. In particular, we have found it convenient to address the rather vague but nonetheless significant notion of "technical contempt" (which continued to bedevil any discussion of media contempts up to and beyond the decision of the House of Lords in *Att-Gen v Times Newspapers Ltd*)[19] under the heading of "less than serious prejudice".[20]

5–10

The quite distinct problem also remains, despite Parliament's efforts to introduce clarity and certainty, of the point in time at which the common law of contempt should begin to impact upon journalists' freedom to canvass issues arising in forthcoming court proceedings. Once proceedings are "active", within the meaning of the Schedule to the Act, this problem disappears. In cases where no intention is present on the part of a journalist to cause prejudice or impediment, his exposure to strict liability is capable of ready ascertainment. The provisions may be arbitrary in where the line is drawn, but they are broadly speaking unobjectionable and at least have the virtue of certainty. Yet, as to liability at common law, in cases where there are grounds for alleging or inferring an intention, journalists are left to assess the consequences of their future conduct while labouring the same handicaps as beset them before the 1981 Act (subject to such guidance as may be gleaned from the subsequent authorities).

5–11

---

[15] [1974] A.C. 273. See, *e.g.* Lord Simon at 321, and for the treatment of "technical contempt", see paras 1–78 *et seq.* and paras 5–19 *et seq.* The meaning of the term "technical contempt" was also discussed in *Hunt v Clarke* (1889) 58 L.J.Q.B. 490.
[16] (1979) 2 E.H.R.R. 245.
[17] See, *e.g.* the discussion of Sir John Donaldson M.R. in *Att-Gen v News Group Newspapers plc* [1987] 1 Q.B. 1 at 15C–G, and Parker L.J. at 17–18; *Att-Gen v ITN Ltd* [1995] 2 All E.R. 370 at 375–8, Leggatt L.J.; *Att-Gen v Guardian Newspapers Ltd* [1999] E.M.L.R. 904 at 927, Sedley L.J.
[18] See, *e.g.* the speech of Lord Reid in *Att-Gen v Times Newspapers Ltd* [1974] A.C. 273 at 298–9: "The question whether there was a serious risk of influencing the litigant is certainly a factor to be considered in deciding what course to take by way of punishment . . . "; Lord Diplock at 311–2 (" . . . no serious likelihood that it has caused any harm . . . "); Lord Parker C.J. in *R. v Duffy Ex p. Nash* [1960] 2 Q.B. 188 at 200 (" . . . there must be a real risk as opposed to a remote possibility of interference").
[19] [1974] A.C. 273.
[20] paras 5–18, *et seq.*

B. Possible formulations of the *actus reus*

5–12 Against this background, therefore, there are a number of categories of conduct which have to be considered as possible candidates for defining the *actus reus* of common law publication contempt. The issues raised in some instances relate primarily to the degree of risk or gravity of prejudice; others are more concerned with the point of time at which liability might arise. These hypothetical situations include:

1. Private publications: which would include communications of prejudicial material to people falling outside the statutory category of "the public at large or any section of the public."[21]

2. Creating a less than "substantial" risk of serious prejudice: although in the light of the House of Lords' decision in *Att-Gen v English*,[22] it appears that anything less than "substantial" in this context would be discounted as *de minimis*.

3. Creating a risk of less than "serious" prejudice: such conduct would certainly have been embraced within the mischief addressed by the House of Lords as amounting to "technical contempt" in *Att-Gen v Times Newspapers Ltd*.[23]

4. Creating a risk in relation to proceedings which are not "active" but are nonetheless pending.

5. Creating a risk in relation to proceedings which are "imminent", in the sense of virtually certain to take place, although not yet formally begun.

6. Creating a risk in relation to proceedings which are "on the cards" but which cannot yet be categorised as "virtually certain" to happen.

7. Creating a risk in relation to a possible appeal prior to the commencement of any appellate proceedings.

C. Private publications

5–13 As a result of s.2 of the Act, the strict liability rule applies now only to those publications which are made to the public at large or a section of it. No one can now be liable strictly in respect of a private communication. One may be liable, however, if one *intended* to prejudice or impermissibly interfere with proceedings. We have already discussed the meaning of publication to "the public at large or any section of the public".[24] If what is said at a private meeting is intended to prejudice proceedings then a contempt may be committed. To take an example; if a speaker were to say "Anyone present who gives evidence for X will be boycotted," that would obviously be intended to deter witnesses in the audience

---

[21] s.2(1), which is considered more fully at para.4–34.
[22] [1983] 1 A.C. 116.
[23] [1974] A.C. 273.
[24] See paras 4–34 *et seq*.

from coming forward to give evidence and would thus be a contempt, if only because it would constitute a threat of reprisal. Another example would be that of a person who spoke to members of a jury panel before selection, for example about the merits of the case or the previous convictions of the person about to stand trial.

D. Creating a less than "substantial risk" of serious prejudice

In some jurisdictions there appears to have been little inhibition about holding journalists or publishers in contempt, assuming the presence of a relevant intention, in circumstances where there is only a remote risk of interference with the administration of justice. For example, it was commented in the New South Wales Court of Appeal that[25]:

5–14

> "There is ... another class of case where a publication will constitute contempt, even though the possibility of interference is remote or theoretical. These are cases where matter is published with the intention of interfering with the due administration of justice in the particular case."

Here, s.2(2)[26] of the Act confines the application of the strict liability rule to publications which create a "substantial risk" of serious prejudice. In *Att-Gen v English*,[27] Lord Diplock explained that "substantial" serves no other purpose than to exclude a *de minimis* risk. Although the word "substantial" was inserted during the course of Parliamentary consideration of the proposed strict liability test, the consequence of the House of Lords' decision is that the test to be applied in this respect is no different from that proposed by the Phillimore Committee, who were concerned to prohibit any risk (provided it was a risk of "serious prejudice") unless it was so slight as to fall within the ordinary *de minimis* rule.[28]

5–15

Indeed, it may be that there is no significant distinction between the judicial approach to the degree of risk (as opposed to the gravity of the prejudice) after the statute and that in operation beforehand. For example, the view was expressed by the Divisional Court in *R. v Ingrams Ex p. Goldsmith*[29] that the test to be applied was whether there was "a real risk of prejudicing the fair and proper trial of pending legal proceedings".[30]

5–16

This would appear to accord with the test applied in one passage by the Court of Appeal in *Att-Gen v Hislop*,[31] long after the statute came into effect, namely

5–17

---

[25] *Att-Gen (NSW) v John Fairfax and Sons Ltd* [1980] 1 N.S.W.L.R. 362 at 369; see also *Registrar of the Supreme Court, Equity Division v McPherson* [1980] N.S.W.L.R. 688 at 697.
[26] For a discussion of the scope of the statute, see paras 4–52 *et seq*.
[27] [1983] 1 A.C. 116.
[28] para.113.
[29] [1977] Crim.L.R. 40, (1977) 120 S.J. 606.
[30] See also for example, the discussion of the requisite degree of risk contained in *Att-Gen v Times Newspapers Ltd* [1974] A.C. 273 at 300–1, and in particular where Lord Reid acknowledged that "there is no contempt if the possibility of influence is remote", although he was clearly of the view that even a small likelihood of prejudice was sufficient.
[31] [1991] 1 Q.B. 514 at 525D–E.

5–17 CHAPTER 5—CONTEMPTS BY PUBLICATION AT COMMON LAW

whether there had been proved "a real risk of a fair trial being prejudiced".[32] Thus, in seeking to define the difference between the statutory test and that obtaining at common law, it is probably wise to concentrate not so much upon the degree of risk, but rather upon the gravity of prejudice required.[33]

E. Creating a risk of less than "serious" prejudice

5–18 As already explained,[34] discussion of what constituted the *actus reus* of contempt at common law prior to the 1981 Act did not focus upon what are now regarded as the two critical "limbs" of substantial risk and serious prejudice. Nevertheless, we consider that it is helpful to do so, and it is therefore in the context of the degree of prejudice that we discuss now the notion of "technical contempt" and the attempts to eliminate it, which culminated in the enactment of the strict liability provisions of the 1981 Act. Unfortunately, the question still retains some importance in identifying what is necessary to constitute the *actus reus* of common law publication contempts, and it may be that some guidance can be derived from the earlier law.

1. "Technical contempts" and the "pre-judgment" test

5–19 In *Att-Gen v Times Newspapers Ltd*,[35] the House of Lords refused to discharge an injunction granted by the Divisional Court of the Queen's Bench Division restraining publication of a certain article in the *Sunday Times*. There was pending an action between the parents of children seriously affected by the drug thalidomide and the Distillers Company which manufactured it. On September 24, 1972, the *Sunday Times* published an article designed to put moral pressure on the Distillers to settle the action on terms favourable to the children. No action was taken over that article. Subsequently the newspaper proposed to publish a further article, discussing the issues involved in the litigation, and suggesting that there was a strong case in negligence against Distillers. An injunction was granted restraining its publication.

5–20 The House of Lords held that any pre-judgment of the issues in a pending case was a contempt even if it only created a small risk (excluding *de minimis*) that the proceedings would be prejudiced. Indeed, Lord Cross went so far as to suggest that any publication amounting to a pre-judgment would constitute contempt even if there were no actual risk of prejudice to the proceedings in question, and justified this by reference to the requirements of public policy.[36] The details of the case and its subsequent treatment by the European Court of

---

[32] But compare [1991] 1 Q.B. 514 at 526D–E, where the test is stated in terms corresponding to the statutory wording for strict liability, "Was there a substantial risk that the course of proceedings would be seriously impeded or prejudiced by inducing Mrs Sutcliffe to settle?".
[33] For a discussion of the priorities of the Phillimore Committee, (para.113), see para.5–44.
[34] para.5–10.
[35] [1974] A.C. 273.
[36] See, *e.g* Lord Cross of Chelsea at 322–3. The nature of the "risk" required by the Act is more fully discussed at paras 4–52 *et seq*.

Human Rights are considered earlier in this work.[37] Suffice it to say here that the Phillimore Committee and the European Court concluded that the test was too stringent, and then the 1981 Act itself sought to effect a "permanent shift in the balance of public interest away from the protection of the administration of justice and in favour of freedom of speech".[38]

Pre-judging the outcome of a pending case, in a media publication, may not cause any actual prejudice, or even a risk of prejudice, but such a case would provide one example of what used to be classified as a "technical contempt"; that is to say, conduct which the House of Lords was prepared to contemplate as unlawful even though not in fact interfering with or impeding the administration of justice. There are difficult questions of policy here, and what does seem clear is that since 1973 there has been a considerable shift in the balancing of competing interests.

2. *The competing policy considerations*

A number of factors have combined in this process; in particular, the Phillimore Committee's recommendations, the increasing awareness of the importance of Art.10 of the European Convention, and thus the need for rigorous justification of any limitations to be placed on freedom of communication, together with the decision of the European Court of Human Rights itself in the thalidomide case.[39] Although there is a margin of appreciation[40] for individual signatory states, all restrictions aimed at upholding the integrity of the judicial process need to be justified by reference to a "pressing social need".[41] It is difficult to establish a pressing social need to restrain or punish conduct which is "technical", in the sense that it is not possible to demonstrate at least a risk of interference with or impeding of the administration of justice.

It is a matter of aiming at a satisfactory definition of that which is considered to overstep the mark; a definition which is workable and brings a sufficient degree of certainty (having regard to Art.7 of the European Convention) and which is not unduly restrictive of freedom of speech, given the need to establish necessity (Art.10(2)). It would appear that the margin of appreciation will permit conduct to be treated as unlawful, even if it in fact succeeds in having little or no impact, provided the ingredient of *intention* to interfere with the administration

---

[37] paras 1–87 *et seq.*
[38] *Att-Gen v Newspaper Publishing plc* [1988] Ch. 333 at 382D–F, *per* Lloyd L.J. An early warning that the test should not be too stringent is provided by Lord Roskill in *Harman v Secretary of State for the Home Department* [1983] 1 A.C. 280 at 366: "I would be reluctant to countenance a rule which would in principle at least involve a commonplace occurrence being contempt of court even though in practice such contempt might be ignored."
[39] *Sunday Times v United Kingdom* (1979) 2 E.H.R.R. 245.
[40] See paras 2–168 *et seq.*
[41] See, *e.g.* Lord Scarman in *Att-Gen v BBC* [1981] A.C. 303 at 362, citing the decision of the European Court in *Sunday Times v United Kingdom* (1979) 2 E.H.R.R. 245 at 275.

of justice is present.[42] One can more readily justify, as a matter of public policy, the criminalising of conduct *intended* to interfere with the administration of justice, even if it is not successful. That seems to have been the approach of the Phillimore Committee.[43]

5–24   Where no intention is present, however, it becomes critical, before imposing criminal sanctions, to set up a filtering process so that *only* such conduct is caught which can reasonably be considered as impeding or interfering with the judicial process. At the heart of this process, however, lies the inherent difficulty that one is not solely concerned with preventing tangible interference (such as the obvious examples of an aborted trial or a conviction based on inadmissible evidence). It can also be legitimate to regard as "necessary" the discouragement of that which is not tangible but, in Lord Diplock's word, merely a "noumenon".[44]

5–25   It appears that what Lord Diplock had in mind was the creation of a *risk* (an intangible and purely intellectual construct)[45]; namely, that the flow of justice will be contaminated by the injection of impermissible influences. Such influences could take many forms, but concern arises particularly from the introduction of extraneous advocacy or evidence, which ought not to play a part in the tribunal's deliberations. The classic example would be to inform a jury prematurely of a defendant's previous convictions.[46] In setting up the filter, however, those who frame or implement such criminal sanctions need carefully to address such factors as how likely it is that such impermissible material will reach the tribunal in the first place and, if it does, whether it would be likely to have any significant impact on the determination of the issues. It is with these conceptual difficulties that the draftsman of ss.1 and 2 of the 1981 Act had to grapple.

5–26   The discussion of technical contempts in *Att-Gen v Times Newspapers Ltd* was very much concerned with the concept of pre-judgment, but "technical contempt" could have application beyond this context. The Phillimore Committee[47] expressed the view that any conduct intended to prejudice the administration of justice should be a contempt, even if ineffective. If the relevant *mens rea* is present, together with an act which goes some way towards achieving the

---

[42] See *Sunday Times v United Kingdom* (1979) 2 E.H.R.R. 245 at 271–2, paras.50–51 of the judgment, especially in the context of the so-called "pressure principle", where it was recognised that English law was formulated with sufficient precision to enable people to know that a *deliberate* attempt to influence the settlement of pending proceedings, by bringing public pressure to bear on a party, was unacceptable. See also *Worm v Austria* (1997) 25 E.H.R.R. 454, where it was held that there had been no violation of the applicant's Convention rights in relation to his conviction under Austrian law for having published an article during the trial of a politician on a charge of tax evasion, asserting his guilt. One of the factors mentioned by the court as being "relevant and sufficient", among the reasons given by the Austrian Court in support of the applicant's conviction, was that the article had been *intended* to influence the outcome of the proceedings. *Worm v Austria* was cited by the Divisional Court in *Att-Gen v Guardian Newspapers Ltd* [1999] E.M.L.R. 904.
[43] See the Report, Cmnd. 5794, at para.66.
[44] *Att-Gen v English* [1983] 1 A.C. 116, 142A.
[45] See the description given by Sir John Smith in his commentary to *R. v Ingrams Ex p. Goldsmith* [1977] Crim. L.R. 40–1, quoted at para.5–2, n.2.
[46] For other examples, see para.5–104.
[47] Report, Cmnd. 5794, para.66.

objective, then it is reasonable to suppose that the ingredients of contempt at common law will be deemed to be present, even if the statutory test of "substantial risk" of "serious prejudice" could not be satisfied. It is perhaps worth remembering, however, that the Committee considered[48] that its proposals, for identifying the degree of risk required for strict liability, would eliminate the risk of journalists being found guilty of "technical" contempt. It was probably believed that a contempt which had been *intended* could not be classified as technical. Thus, it may be that the publication of opinions which merely prejudge *could* still amount to contempt, but only if accompanied by an intention to exert some extraneous influence upon the course of justice.

For the reasons we have considered above, it remains necessary to consider the historical context of "technical contempt" against which these legislative reforms were introduced. Nevertheless, a warning note should be sounded as to the weight now to be attached to judicial pronouncements prior to the Act, and, in particular, to the formulation of principles to be found in the speeches of the House of Lords in *Att-Gen v Times Newspapers Ltd*, which was the leading case in this field until the enactment of the strict liability rule. In *Re Lonrho plc*,[49] Lord Bridge commented:

5–27

> "How far these passages from the speeches of their Lordships may still be relied upon as accurate expressions of the law is extremely doubtful, certainly in relation to the kind of contempt which is the subject matter of the strict liability rule under ss.1 and 2 of the Act of 1981."

3. *The historical context*

The nature of contempt as understood at common law was that it consisted in an act (or possibly an omission)[50] calculated to interfere with the due administration of justice. "Calculated" in ordinary parlance may import a notion of intention or premeditation. This was no part of its meaning in the common law. Indeed, in the context of contempt, publication calculated to prejudice the fair trial of a pending case was treated at common law as an offence of strict liability.[51] In the eighteenth and early nineteenth centuries the word "calculated" was used as

5–28

---

[48] Report, Cmnd. 5794, para.113. Moreover, in the House of Lords, Lord Hailsham L.C. said, on introducing the Bill on Second Reading, after describing it as a "liberalising" provision, that "It puts an end, of course, to the prejudgment criterion which was adopted by your Lordships' House in the *Sunday Times* case": *Hansard*, H.L., Vol. 415, (5th series), col. 660, December 9, 1980.

[49] [1990] 2 A.C. 154 at 208C–D (not an appellate authority, because of the unique circumstances giving rise to the contempt proceedings).

[50] It is difficult to think of an example whereby publication contempt could be committed by omission, although occasionally a material omission has been held to give rise to criminal liability: see, *e.g. R. v Kylsant* [1932] 1 K.B. 442 (a case of fraud). In the context of contempt, one might envisage circumstances where a misleading and prejudicial report of court proceedings was published, as a result of an omission of (say) the defendant's case, but in such a case contempt would naturally be said to arise by virtue of the positive act of publication (of a misleading report). See also the discussion of the possibility of omission constituting the *actus reus* of contempt by Knox J. in *Att-Gen v Observer Ltd* [1988] 1 All E.R. 385 at 399a–b. What was there relied upon was a failure to ascertain prior to display whether a library's selection of newspapers, magazines and periodicals contained information obtained by the author of *Spycatcher* while he was a member of the Security Service.

[51] See para.1–64.

5–28 CHAPTER 5—CONTEMPTS BY PUBLICATION AT COMMON LAW

meaning no more than "tending or likely to."[52] In the result the net of contempt was spread wide, and this prevented, for example, virtually all *ex parte* statements[53] about a case, and any discussion of the merits of pending litigation.

5–29 This seems to have been recognised, with some reluctance, in the Court of Appeal in *Hunt v Clarke*.[54] Cotton L.J. there stated that:

"... it does technically become a contempt if pending a cause, or before a cause even has begun, any observations are made or published to the world which tend in any way to prejudice the parties in the case."

5–30 In so saying he acknowledged that the scope of contempt was widely spread, but he made some attempt to limit its practical effect. In his view a committal order should only be made where the summary jurisdiction of the court was needed to enable justice to be administered without any interruption or interference. Indeed, no application to the court should be made unless the publication was likely to cause substantial interference. In the particular case the Court of Appeal took the view that there had been a technical contempt only, and held that the proper order was to dismiss the application to commit without costs.[55] Unfortunately, in subsequent cases, discussion of technical contempt becomes confused by a failure to distinguish between conduct which does not require to be punished and conduct which ought not to be classified as contempt at all.[56]

5–31 Wright J. in *Re Finance Union*[57] stated that the "special" jurisdiction of the courts "ought to be based on the necessity of securing [a] fair trial, and it ought not to be exercised except when there is a case made out showing that it is probable that the publication will substantially interfere with a fair trial". He added that it was no part of the functions of the court to see that articles that were merely "reprehensible" should not be published in the press.[58] From this brief judgment, it appears that Wright J. at least was against the notion of what has subsequently been described as "technical contempt", and would require that there should be a "substantial" risk of interference.

5–32 He referred to the word "reprehensible" because it had been used by a brother judge in the same case (Wills J.), who had described the conduct before the court

---

[52] See, *e.g. The North Cheshire and Manchester Brewery Co Ltd* [1899] A.C. 83 at 86; *McDowell v Standard Oil Co* [1927] A.C. 632 at 637.
[53] See para.1–71.
[54] (1889) 58 L.J.Q.B. 490.
[55] See also *Plating Co v Farquharson* (1881) 17 Ch. D. 49 at 56; *Re New Gold Coast Exploration Co* [1901] 1 Ch. 860 at 863.
[56] See, *e.g.* the comments of Lord Diplock in *Att-Gen v Times Newspapers Ltd* [1974] A.C. at 311–2, and of Lord Simon at 321. See also the remarks of Mathew J. in *Duncan v Sparling* (1894) 10 T.L.R. 353 at 355.
[57] (1895) 11 T.L.R. 167.
[58] *ibid*., at 169. (He observed that the fine of £10 was not too severe, although it appears that he might well have come to the conclusion that there was no contempt proved, but for the fact that "the defendant has pleaded guilty".)

as "a most reprehensible attempt to interfere with the course of justice", although he was not disposed to deal with it severely. What he seems to have focused on primarily was the element of *mens rea* which he perceived to be present, rather than the lack of actual interference with the process of justice (this being what led him to propose only a modest penalty). He emphasised "the general principle that such attempts to influence or interfere with the course of justice are improper and ought not to be allowed." He added that " . . . there appeared to be on the part of some portion of the newspaper Press a great desire to substitute the new mode of trial—trial by newspaper—for the old mode of trial".

The Divisional Court in *R. v Payne and Cooper*[59] held that the summary jurisdiction in contempt should only be exercised where there was a real possibility of interference with a fair trial. Similarly, Lord Parker in *R. v Duffy Ex p. Nash*[60] observed that for the court to act there had to be a real risk, as opposed to a remote possibility of interference. **5–33**

The last significant pre-Act case to consider the point was *Vine Products Ltd v Green*,[61] where Buckley J. held that there had to be a real and grave risk that the proper administration of justice would be interfered with. The question had arisen as to which wines could properly be called sherry. There had been an earlier action in which the use of the word champagne had been confined, and a national newspaper published a leading article suggesting that the use of the word sherry should be similarly restricted. The article thus pre-judged the issue at the heart of the case, although it was to be tried by judge alone. Buckley J. held there was no contempt because it did not raise a serious risk of prejudice. **5–34**

It seemed at this stage that the notion of a technical contempt might be abandoned, and a positive attempt made to preclude findings of contempt in a technical sense. Indeed, this approach appeared to be endorsed in *Att-Gen v Times Newspapers Ltd* before the matter reached the House of Lords. The Divisional Court,[62] as in the associated case of the *Att-Gen v London Weekend Television Ltd*,[63] adopted the view that for a contempt to be established there had to be a serious risk of interference with the due administration of justice. The Court of Appeal in the *Att-Gen v Times Newspapers Ltd* also considered that there had to be a real or substantial danger of prejudice.[64] Although it was sought to emphasise the degree of risk, rather than the degree of prejudice, as the Parliamentary draftsman subsequently chose to do, it was at least clear that courts at this time were trying significantly to raise the threshold for a finding of liability. However, the House of Lords unanimously reversed this process and reaffirmed that a publisher could be held liable for even a "technical contempt". **5–35**

---

[59] [1896] 1 Q.B. 577.
[60] [1960] 2 Q.B. 188 at 200.
[61] [1966] Ch. 484.
[62] [1972] 3 All E.R. 1136.
[63] [1973] 1 W.L.R. 202, [1972] 3 All E.R. 1146.
[64] [1973] Q.B. 710.

5–36 In *Att-Gen v Times Newspapers Ltd*, it was held that Buckley J. in *Vine Products* had been wrong to exonerate the journalist, albeit that the contempt was technical. The motion to commit the editor should have been dismissed, but without costs. In Lord Reid's view the consequences of the article were so trifling that it would have been wrong to impose punishment or even to order the contemnor to pay costs, but it was technically a contempt nonetheless[65]; the editor ought to have withheld his judgment until the case had been decided.

4. The House of Lords: "real" or "serious" risk

5–37 Lords Reid and Diplock concluded that the law of contempt should embrace any act creating real (including small) risk of interference with the due administration of justice. Lord Diplock expressed it in this way[66]:

> "Since the court's discretion in dealing with a motion for committal is wide enough to entitle it to dismiss the motion with costs despite the fact that a contempt has been committed if it thinks that the contempt was too venial to justify its being brought to the attention of the court at all, the distinction between conduct which is within the general concept of 'contempt of court' and conduct included within that general concept, which a court regards as deserving of punishment in the particular circumstances of the case, is often blurred in the judgments on the reported cases. The expression 'technical contempt' is a convenient expression which has sometimes been used to describe conduct which falls into the former but outside the latter category; and I agree with my noble and learned friend, Lord Reid, that given conduct which presents a real risk as opposed to a mere possibility of interference with the due administration of justice, this is at very least a technical contempt. The seriousness of that risk is relevant only to the question whether the contempt is one for which the court in its discretion ought to inflict any punishment, and, if so, what punishment it should inflict."

5–38 Lord Reid commented as follows[67]:

> "I think, agreeing with Cotton L.J. in his judgment in *Hunt v Clarke* (1889) 58 L.J.Q.B. 490 that there must be two questions; first, was there any contempt to all, and, secondly, was it sufficiently serious to require, or justify the court in making, an order against the respondent? The question whether there was a serious risk of influencing the litigant is certainly a factor to be considered in deciding what course to take by way of punishment, as is the intention with which the comment was made. But it is, I think, confusing to import this into the question whether there was any contempt at all or into the definition of contempt.
>
> I think the true view is that expressed by Lord Parker C.J. in *R. v Duffy, Ex parte Nash* [1960] 2 Q.B. 188, 200 that there must be a 'real risk, as opposed to a remote possibility.' That is an application of the ordinary *de minimis* principle. There is no contempt if the possibility of influence is remote. If there is some but only a small likelihood, that may influence the court to refrain from inflicting any punishment. If there is a serious risk some action may be necessary. And I think that the particular comment cannot be considered in isolation when considering its probable effect. If

---

[65] [1974] A.C. 273 at 300–1.
[66] *ibid.* at 312B–E.
[67] *ibid.* at 298G–299B and 300H–302A.

others are to be free and are likely to make similar comments that must be taken into account.

... In my opinion the law was rather too narrowly stated in *Vine Products Ltd v Green* [1966] Ch. 484. There the question was what wine could properly be called sherry, and a newspaper published an article which clearly prejudged the issue. In my view that was technically in contempt of court. But the fault was so venial and the possible consequences so trifling that it would have been quite wrong to impose punishment or, I think, even to require the newspaper to pay the costs of the applicant. But the newspaper ought to have withheld its judgment until the case had been decided."

5. *"Tendency to interfere"*

Lord Simon of Glaisdale appears to have adopted an approach closer to that of Cotton L.J. in *Hunt v Clarke*,[68] who referred to a tendency to interfere with the due administration of justice. He referred to an earlier article published in the *Sunday Times*, in respect of which the Attorney-General had decided to take no action and which was not before the House. Their Lordships nevertheless considered this article and were divided as to whether it might have constituted a contempt had proceedings been brought in respect of it.[69]

In speaking of "technical contempt", Lord Simon said:

"The publication in *Vine Products Ltd v Green*[70] was, in my view, a technical contempt... ; On the other hand, I think that the article of September 24, 1972, was more than a technical contempt; since ... it was intended to interfere with the terms of settlement by holding Distillers up to execration."

This comment may be important in assessing what is required for the *actus reus* in common law contempt by publication after 1981. Lord Simon appeared to recognise that an otherwise trivial act, or at least one what was not worthy of being drawn to the court's attention, might be rendered a significant contempt if accompanied by a positive intention to interfere with the course of justice (even to the extent of interfering with negotiations between the parties to civil litigation).

6. *Pre-judgment and the risk of escalation*

Lord Cross expressed general agreement with Lord Reid. He went on to seek to justify, by reference to public policy considerations, the retention of pre-judgment as a sufficient condition for activating the law of contempt. Although this passage cannot now be held to be authoritative in the light of later developments, it is nonetheless illuminating for the purpose of assessing the *actus reus* in common law contempt. He explained[71]:

---

[68] (1889) 58 L.J.Q.B. 490.
[69] This aspect of the case is discussed at paras 5–117 *et seq*.
[70] [1966] Ch. 484.
[71] [1974] A.C. 273 at 322–3.

5-41

"It is easy enough to see that any publication which pre-judges an issue in pending proceedings ought to be forbidden if there is any real risk that it may influence the tribunal—whether judge, magistrate or jury, or any of those who may be called upon to give evidence when the case comes to be heard.

But why, it may be said, should such a publication be prohibited when there is no such risk? The reason is that one cannot deal with one particular publication in isolation. A publication pre-judging an issue in pending litigation which is itself innocuous enough may provoke replies which are far from innocuous but which, as they are replies, it would seem unfair to restrain. So gradually the public would become habituated to, look forward to and resent the absence of preliminary discussions in the 'media' of any case which aroused widespread interest. An absolute rule—though it may seem to be unreasonable if one looks only to the particular case—is necessary in order to prevent a gradual slide towards trial by newspaper or television."

5-42 It is difficult now to envisage this reasoning being upheld in the European Court of Human Rights, since it is unlikely to be held to be "necessary in a democratic society" to restrict debate of the kind he was contemplating unless there were created at least *some* degree of risk of prejudice. Under the Convention, publications can only be treated as contempts if there is a pressing social need "for maintaining the authority and impartiality of the judiciary."[72] There will rarely be a pressing social need that a publication which raises only a small likelihood of prejudice should be treated as a contempt. On the other hand, if there were a concerted effort on the part of journalists to create a climate such that the outcome of proceedings would actually be influenced, it is by no means certain that it would be held to be unacceptable to employ the law to proscribe such conduct. Once again, therefore, one can see that the presence of intention may be crucial.

5-43 Lord Cross stressed that in assessing the degree of risk it is legitimate to look beyond the particular act complained of to see what reactions it is likely to produce in others. Even if, upon such an assessment, it were not possible to establish a risk of prejudice such as to satisfy the statutory strict liability test, it may be that the presence of intention would nonetheless justify the intervention of the law, even after the 1981 Act.[73]

7. Criticisms of the House of Lords decision

5-44 The Phillimore Committee[74] had criticised the pre-judgment test propounded by the House of Lords in *Att-Gen v Times Newspapers Ltd*[75] as being too wide in some respects, and too narrow in others. Moreover, they considered that pre-judgment was no clearer than risk of prejudice as a workable criterion. Accordingly they proposed[76] the test of "a risk that the course of justice will be seriously impeded or prejudiced". The Committee observed that the law should

---

[72] Art.10(2).
[73] See the discussion of *Att-Gen v Hislop* [1991] Q.B. 514, discussed at para.5–169.
[74] Report, Cmnd. 5794, para.111.
[75] [1974] A.C. 273.
[76] Report, Cmnd. 5794, para.113.

aim at "preventing serious prejudice, not serious risks."⁷⁷ All that should be required in relation to the risk is to show that it was not so slight as to fall within the *de minimis* rule. Subsequently the European Court of Human Rights held that the decision of the House of Lords contravened the provisions of the European Convention on Human Rights.⁷⁸

8. Guidance from authorities after the 1981 Act

(a) *Re Lonrho*

While it is true that the question of *mens rea* in common law contempt by publication has been specifically addressed in a number of decisions since the 1981 Act came into effect,⁷⁹ it is less easy to obtain guidance from such cases on how the issue of *actus reus* should now be approached.⁸⁰ As has been pointed out already, doubt was cast upon the authority of the observations in *Att-Gen v Times Newspapers Ltd*⁸¹ by Lord Bridge in *Re Lonrho*,⁸² who went on to express the view that "the only safe course" was to apply the test imposed by the statutory language according to its ordinary meaning, and without any preconception derived from the earlier case. It is to be noted, however, that this remark was made in the context of considering allegations of strict liability contempt. The subject of common law contempt was also raised in *Re Lonrho*, but this was dealt with very briefly, and principally on the basis of absence of *mens rea*. It is submitted therefore that it would be unwise to infer from Lord Bridge's remarks any implication that the common law test for *actus reus* should be approached differently as a result of the statutory wording.

5–45

(b) *Att-Gen v Hislop*

Another case which is less than helpful is the decision of the Court of Appeal in *Att-Gen v Hislop*,⁸³ which concerned pressure brought to bear by the editor and publishers of *Private Eye* upon a litigant shortly before the hearing of her libel action against them. Reliance had been placed by the Attorney-General both

5–46

---

⁷⁷ This is to be contrasted with the way in which Bingham L.J. in *Att-Gen v Sport Newspapers Ltd* [1991] 1 W.L.R. 1195 at 1208D–E, [1992] 1 All E.R. 503 at 516f–g expressed himself: " . . . the applicant cannot, I accept, show a certainty of prejudice, and in the event there may have been none. But the law of contempt is concerned with a real *risk* of prejudice to the due administration of justice, and that such a real risk existed on the facts here I am in no doubt at all". It is doubtful, however, whether any difference of substance was intended: see especially the remarks of Lord Bingham C.J. in *Att-Gen v Newspaper Publishing plc* [1997] 1 W.L.R. 926 at 936F–G, [1997] 3 All E.R. 159 at 169d.
⁷⁸ *Sunday Times v United Kingdom* (1979) 2 E.H.R.R. 245. See also the discussion of the case at paras 1–104 *et seq.*
⁷⁹ *Att-Gen v Newspaper Publishing plc* [1988] Ch. 333; *Att-Gen v News Group Newspapers plc* [1989] Q.B. 110; *Att-Gen v Newspaper Publishing plc* [1989] 1 F.S.R. 457; *Att-Gen v Newspaper Publishing plc* [1990] T.L.R. 158, CA (Lexis); *Re Lonrho* [1990] 2 A.C. 154; *Att-Gen v Hislop* [1991] 1 Q.B. 514; *Att-Gen v Times Newspapers Ltd* [1992] 1 A.C. 191; *Coe v Central Television plc* [1994] E.M.L.R. 433.
⁸⁰ But see *Att-Gen v Newspaper Publishing Plc* [1997] 1 W.L.R. 926, discussed at paras 5–59 *et seq.*
⁸¹ [1974] A.C. 273.
⁸² [1990] 2 A.C. 154 at 208C–D, quoted at para.5–27.
⁸³ [1991] 1 Q.B. 514.

upon strict liability contempt and, in the alternative, upon the common law contempt jurisdiction preserved by s.6(c) of the 1981 Act. The respondents were held liable on the Attorney's appeal under both heads. The judge at first instance had dismissed the application, on the basis that there had been no improper pressure placed on the litigant, and no risk of prejudice to the jury in the forthcoming trial. The Court of Appeal took the view that these conclusions were unsustainable.

5–47   It was necessary to address issues of *mens rea* and *actus reus*, so far as common law contempt had been raised, and the case therefore provided a good opportunity for guidance to be given on any distinctions that should be drawn between the test for the *actus reus* in statutory contempt and that obtaining at common law. Unfortunately, it is not possible to derive any definitive conclusions on these issues from the judgments delivered. For example, Parker L.J., in dealing with common law contempt specifically, posed the test as follows: "had [the Attorney] shown, ... by the standard of the criminal law, that there was a real risk of a fair trial being prejudiced?"[84] This language is reminiscent of the approach adopted prior to the 1981 Act, for example by the House of Lords in *Att-Gen v Times Newspapers Ltd.*[85] It is notable that not only is there no reference to "substantial risk", but far more importantly, there is none to "*serious* prejudice" either.

5–48   A little further on in the judgment, however, the Lord Justice referred to the question having been posed by the judge below, "Was there a substantial risk that the course of proceedings would be seriously impeded or prejudiced by inducing [the litigant] to settle?" He did so without any comment to suggest either that the learned judge had there been concerning himself only with strict liability, or that the question posed was inappropriate for determining the issue of common law contempt. On the facts of the case, since the Court of Appeal appeared to take the view that this was a serious case of contempt, there was perhaps no need for them to address the possibility of the publication having given rise to a risk of less than serious prejudice. Nevertheless, it is somewhat confusing for the reader to find these two quite different tests set out so close to one another, and both under the heading "common law contempt".

5–49   Moreover, there is nothing in the other two judgments to shed further light on any possible distinction. For example, Nicholls L.J. simply elided the two tests[86]: "Was there a real risk of prejudicing a fair trial or, to use the statutory language, was there a substantial risk that the course of justice in the proceedings would be seriously impeded or prejudiced?" This tends to confirm the view that the court did not consider it necessary to draw any distinction, in the light of their conclusion as to the facts. McCowan L.J. also took the view that "the course of justice in the proceedings would be seriously impeded or prejudiced", both in

---

[84] *ibid*. at 525D–E.
[85] [1974] A.C. 273.
[86] *ibid*. at 531D.

relation to the potential deterrent effect upon the litigant and with regard to possible impact on potential jurors.[87]

It is possible, however, to imagine circumstances in which it might become important to focus on whether there is indeed a different test to be applied as to *actus reus*. Suppose that a journalist writes a powerful article proclaiming the merits of a pending case, intending to influence the decision of the trial judge; or, following upon the reasoning of Lord Cross in *Att-Gen v Times Newspapers Ltd*,[88] suppose that a wide ranging debate upon the merits were to develop in the press with the intention of creating a climate in which the judge was driven to come to a particular conclusion. In such circumstances, it would be difficult to argue that there was a substantial risk of serious prejudice or impediment, since the court would be unlikely to acknowledge that the judge *could* be influenced by any such publication. It would on the other hand be surprising, given the posited intention of the hypothetical journalist, if such conduct were not held to fall within the ambit of common law of contempt which Parliament specifically preserved in the 1981 Act. There is no doubt that the Attorney-General would have a considerable burden to discharge in establishing that any such journalist *intended* to influence the trial judge in the circumstances posited, because his defence would undoubtedly include the argument that it never occurred to him that the judge would be influenced by newspaper articles; and that all he was intending to do was to canvass issues of topical interest. That is no reason, however, to avoid addressing the important point of principle as to the *actus reus*.

5–50

(c) *Att-Gen v Sport Newspapers Ltd*

It seems to have been accepted by the Divisional Court in *Att-Gen v Sport Newspapers Ltd*[89] that it would not be necessary to establish, in addition to an intention to interfere with the administration of justice, a substantial risk of serious prejudice. For example, there seems to have been no dispute of substance between counsel that what was necessary was to show that the publication created "a real risk of prejudice to the due administration of justice"; that is to say, it was not suggested or held by the court that it was necessary to approach the statutory threshold of strict liability (*i.e.* a risk of *serious* prejudice).[90]

5–51

(d) *BBC v Law Officers of the Crown*

It is perhaps of some interest to consider how the common law was approached by the Guernsey Court of Appeal (Civil Division) in the unreported decision of *BBC v Law Officers of the Crown*.[91] The Corporation had been found guilty earlier the same year by the Royal Court, sitting as an Ordinary Court and made

5–52

---

[87] *ibid.* at 535G–H and 536C–D.
[88] See the passage quoted at para.5–41.
[89] [1991] 1 W.L.R. 1194, [1992] 1 All E.R. 503.
[90] [1991] 1 W.L.R. 1194, [1992] 1 All E.R. 503. See in particular Bingham L.J. at 1199–1200, 508h–j and 1208A–E, 516b–f, Hodgson J. at 1210F, 518f and 1229H–1230B, 536e–g.
[91] November 18, 1988. The Court consisted of John Collins Q.C. (President), David Calcutt Q.C. and John Chadwick Q.C. (now Chadwick L.J.).

up of the Deputy Bailiff and three Jurats. Although fined only £200, the BBC appealed as a matter of principle, and on one of the grounds succeeded.

5–53   The proceedings related to a morning broadcast by Radio Guernsey, alleged to have included a comment which not only pre-judged issues pending before the Royal Court, but also was likely to influence the outcome of proceedings. In fact, even at first instance, the matter proceeded solely on the basis of the allegation of prejudice. A motor vessel had put into the harbour where it was abandoned by the Master. He fled the island leaving the vessel and Sri Lankan crew "to their fate". The crew were owed wages and were left without any support. Proceedings were instituted *in rem* against the vessel on behalf of some members of the crew; she was sold by the Sheriff who received the proceeds of sale, which proved insufficient to satisfy the claims of the crew and of others. It was therefore necessary for the Royal Court to distribute the proceeds.

5–54   The broadcast took place prior to the effective start of the proceedings before the Commissioner appointed by the court. The offending comments included reference to "an expert on British maritime law" who had apparently said that the three crew members should be paid their £12,000 back pay before any other claims were settled. It was no part of the Law Officers' case that the publication constituted an intentional or deliberate contempt, and the Court of Appeal therefore proceeded on that basis.

5–55   The difficulty was to identify what was the relevant test to apply in Guernsey, where there had apparently been no previous instance of a case of publication contempt, and where the 1981 Act had no application. Ordinarily, the practice in Guernsey would be to follow the approach of the English common law. The English common law, however, minus the principles enshrined in the 1981 Act, might be thought to be found embodied primarily in the decision of the House of Lords in *Att-Gen v Times Newspapers Ltd*,[92] with its (by then) outmoded espousal of the pre-judgment test and the notion of technical contempt.

5–56   This gave rise to an apparently insoluble problem because, even though Guernsey did not have the benefit of the 1981 Act, it was accepted on all sides that the European Convention on Human Rights was applicable. The exercise upon which the Court of Appeal therefore embarked, in order to cut the Gordian knot, was the artificial one of determining how the common law of England might be deemed to have changed in order to accommodate the provisions of the European Convention if it had not been supplemented by the 1981 Act. Before undertaking its analysis, the court emphasised that its observations would have no application to any case where it was alleged that the person concerned had intended to prejudice current proceedings. They were thereby tacitly acknowledging the problem now under consideration; that is to say, the possibility that the *actus reus* might have to be differently assessed in such circumstances.

5–57   The conclusion arrived at was that regard might be had to the 1981 Act, not on the basis that the statute extended to Guernsey, but rather because it provided

---

[92] [1974] A.C. 273.

a model which gave recognition to the treaty obligations arising under the European Convention, and which the court might find to be of assistance in its own formulation of the law to be applied in Guernsey. The court proceeded by analogy with the terms of s.2 of the Act, observing that there were no special "local requirements" affecting the application of the Convention within the Island. In these circumstances, they concluded that the Deputy Bailiff had erred in his directions to the Jurats when he omitted to direct their minds to the issue of "*serious* prejudice".

It may be legitimate to apply a similar process of reasoning, in England, in order to determine whether the obligations imposed by the European Convention give rise to a comparable imperative for change in relation to the *actus reus* of common law publication contempts. It might be argued that, as a matter of principle, the *actus reus* of common law contempt should now be regarded as including only those acts which actually cause serious prejudice or, at least, create a risk of such prejudice.[93] This would in effect mean that the approach to be adopted towards the *actus reus* of common law publication contempt would be identical to that applying under the strict liability regime.

(e) *Att-Gen v Newspaper Publishing plc*

An important statement of principle is to be found in the judgment of Lord Bingham C.J. in *Att-Gen v Newspaper Publishing plc*.[94] Although it happened to be concerned with an alleged breach of a court order, for the regulation of its own proceedings, the alleged *actus reus* before the Criminal Division of the Court of Appeal was that of a newspaper publication (of a reproduction of a document). Had contempt been proved, it would have been classifiable, in so far as it matters,[95] as criminal in character. The judgment therefore is clearly relevant in the present context.

The Lord Chief Justice recognised that since:

" ... restraints upon freedom of expression should be no wider than are truly necessary in a democratic society, we do not accept that conduct by a third party which is inconsistent with a court order in only a trivial or technical way should expose a party to conviction for contempt."

This passage occurred in that part of his judgment labelled *"The actus reus of contempt"*, and thus may be construed perhaps as finally disposing of the notion of "technical contempt". The court also found, as a matter of fact, that the requisite *mens rea* was not established. This approach is clearly consistent with the policy of the Human Rights Act.

---

[93] But see our conclusion at para.5–61.
[94] [1997] 1 W.L.R. 926 at 936C, [1997] 3 All E.R. 159 at 168j.
[95] For a discussion of the continuing significance of the distinction between civil and criminal contempt, see ch.3.

9. Conclusion as to the demise of technical contempt

5–61 When dealing with allegations of common law contempt by way of publication, the court is unlikely to require, in addition to an intention to interfere with the administration of justice,[96] an *actus reus* which fulfils the statutory criteria for strict liability; that is to say, a substantial risk that the course of justice in the proceedings in question will be "*seriously* impeded or prejudiced". That wording was directed at protecting journalists from being held strictly liable for contempt, and as a matter of public policy it would appear that there is no need to afford this protection to a respondent who positively *intends* to interfere with the administration of justice. Nor, it seems, would the European Court of Human Rights consider that such a decision would fall outside the margin of appreciation permitted to signatory states.[97] Clearly, however, something more than *de minimis* will be required. Indeed, in the light of Lord Bingham's judgment cited above, it is clear that nothing "trivial or technical" will suffice.

F. Publication when proceedings are pending but not "active"

5–62 Section 2(3) of the Act confines the application of the strict liability rule to the period when the relevant proceedings are active.[98] In the case of criminal proceedings they are active from one of the steps specified in Sch.1 of the Act[99] (broadly, the time of arrest, the issue of a summons or warrant, service of the indictment or oral charging); in the case of civil proceedings they are active from the time "when arrangements for the hearing are made" (in the High Court, this will be either when a trial window has fixed or a trial date within it, and in the case of other proceedings when a date is fixed).[1]

5–63 At common law the restraints of contempt applied once proceedings had been formally commenced, and at least in relation to criminal proceedings even before formal commencement, when they could be described as merely "imminent". In a civil case there may be a considerable period between formal commencement and arrangements for a hearing being made. Prejudicial publications in this period, when the proceedings may truly be said to be "pending", may still constitute contempt at common law provided *mens rea* is present. Nevertheless, it no doubt remains the case that " . . . the court should not be anxious to accept submissions that discussions of a pending action must necessarily be unseemly or harmful to the administration of justice."[2] As to criminal proceedings, broadly the statutory points at which such proceedings become "active" will correspond to the commencement of their being "pending".

---

[96] The requisite degree of *mens rea* is discussed at paras 5–132 *et seq*.
[97] *Sunday Times v United Kingdom* (1979) 2 E.H.R.R. 245 at 271–2, paras 50–51 of the judgment. See also *Worm v Austria* (1997) 25 E.H.R.R. 454, referred to at para.5–23, n.142.
[98] See paras 4–174. *et seq*.
[99] para.4.
[1] Sch.1, paras 12 and 13. See para.4–174. The Contempt of Court Act has not been amended so far to take account of the fact that the notion of "setting down" in the High Court is no longer used after the coming into effect of the CPR in April 1999.
[2] *Schering Chemicals Ltd v Falkman* [1982] Q.B. 1 at 40E–F, *per* Templeman L.J.

1. *The notion of "dormant" civil litigation*

It was possible to argue at common law that if proceedings had remained **5–64** dormant for some time prior to setting down, they would at some stage cease to be regarded as pending for the purposes of contempt. This problem is perhaps less likely now to arise, given the stricter time limits in operation in civil litigation, and the imperative towards speedy justice. In *Att-Gen v Times Newspapers Ltd*[3] the court was concerned with a history of litigation over a period of 10 years. Although negotiations between the parties had been carried on during that period, the Court of Appeal held that the action had become dormant and therefore comments on the merits of the action were not to be treated as in contempt.[4] This view was rejected by the House of Lords on the ground that negotiations towards a settlement had been going on for many years and were still continuing.

However, there was no conclusion that it was impossible, as a matter of **5–65** principle, for an action to become dormant and, for that reason, for the restrictions on public discussion to be relaxed. Lord Reid, for example, said[5]:

"So if there is no undue procrastination in the negotiations for a settlement I do not see how in this context an action can be said to be dormant ... if things drag on indefinitely so that there is no early prospect either of a settlement or of a trial in court then I think that there will have to be a reassessment of the public interest in a unique situation."

This implies that in his view an action *could* in theory at least become dormant in the sense intended by the Court of Appeal.[6] It is not without relevance, perhaps, that even during the "active" period of civil proceedings, the court may take the view that there is a long enough period before trial to reduce the risk of prejudice below the statutory threshold.[7] The degree of risk is probably what matters—rather than any arbitrary status of "dormancy".

The subject of the appeal in *Att-Gen v Times Newspapers Ltd* was an **5–66** injunction restraining publication of an article, and it would have been open to the newspaper concerned to apply for discharge of the injunction if circumstances changed. An example of such a change would be provided by a loss of interest in the litigation by the parties, or a failure to prosecute it expeditiously. One of the reasons why the European Court of Human Rights disagreed with the House of Lords' decision was the fact that the case had gone into a legal cocoon.[8]

---

[3] [1974] A.C. 273.
[4] [1973] Q.B. 210.
[5] [1974] A.C. 273 at 301.
[6] See *Fox Ex p. Mosley*, *The Times*, February 17, 1966, *Guardian*, February 17, 1966.
[7] *Att-Gen v News Group Newspapers plc* [1987] 1 Q.B. 1.
[8] (1979) 2 E.H.R.R. 245 at 281, para.66 of the judgment.

G. Proceedings "imminent" but not yet pending

1. *The uncertainty left by s.6(c) of the Act*

5–67   Before the 1981 Act, one of the difficulties confronting journalists was to ascertain at which point in time the application of the law of contempt began to restrict the right to cover matters connected with possible future legal proceedings. When the schedule to the Act identified in detail the moments at which variously defined "proceedings" were to be regarded as active, for the purposes of the strict liability rule, it was generally assumed that these uncertainties had been removed. The impact of s.6(c) was not fully realised for some time, even though it clearly preserved existing rules of common law contempt in the context of media publications.

5–68   Then came the decision of the Divisional Court in *Att-Gen v News Group Newspapers plc*.[9] The facts were most unusual. After the Crown Prosecution Service had decided not to prosecute a doctor suspected of sexually molesting a young girl, *The Sun* newspaper offered to finance a private prosecution, and then ran a series of articles whose headlines included the following: "He's a real swine", "Beast must be named says M.P." and "Doc groped me, says girl". Not surprisingly, the court held that such acts of publication amounted to common law contempt, even though the proceedings were not "active" at the time of publication. Proceedings were held to be "virtually certain" to be commenced, and were therefore imminent.

5–69   The court was inevitably driven back to applying the old common law tests of "pending or imminent", despite the vagueness that Parliament had sought to eradicate by the introduction of the "active proceedings" framework for strict liability. Watkins L.J. went further than this, however, and expressed the *obiter* view that, if necessary, the common law might be extended to cover a situation where proceedings were as yet not even pending or imminent, but merely "in contemplation".[10]

5–70   It may be that Parliament did not intend the ambit of the common law of contempt to continue to be applied so widely, but the problem springs from the wording of s.6(c) of the 1981 Act. It is vague in itself, but it is not easy to derive any assistance from the contents of the Parliamentary debates so as to identify the scope of the mischief which the section was intended to address. It is possible that Parliament's purpose was that, once intention to interfere with the administration of justice could be proved in any given case, the requirements for *actus reus* would be only minimal. (Perhaps it was contemplated that the test would be similar to the requirements in the criminal law for an attempt; that is to say, an act which has gone beyond being merely preparatory.)

---

[9] [1989] Q.B. 110.
[10] *ibid*. at 133. This aspect of the case is discussed more fully in relation to proceedings which are merely "on the cards"; para.5–96.

5-71 These uncertainties troubled the Divisional Court again in *Att-Gen v Sport Newspapers Ltd*.[11] A 15 year-old girl disappeared and the police (without, apparently, seeking a warrant for arrest) held a news conference at which the newspapers were invited to help discover a named missing person, but they were requested not to publish the fact that the suspect had previous convictions for serious sexual offences. The respondent did not receive the Press Association's communication inviting the press to refrain from publishing the wanted man's record. It published a description of the suspect describing him as a "vicious evil rapist" and "sex monster". Two days after the report, a warrant was issued for the arrest of the suspect who was eventually found (in France), returned to the jurisdiction and convicted of murder. At the end of the trial (no application having been made to hold the trial elsewhere, or for a stay on the ground of prejudicial publicity), proceedings for contempt were brought against the publishers, the editor and the journalist concerned.

5-72 On the facts, it was held that it had not been shown to the required standard of proof that there was a specific intention to prejudice the fair conduct of the proceedings, and indeed it was recognised that the editor at the time regarded the possibility of proceedings as speculative and remote.[12]

5-73 Hodgson J. expressed some doubt whether it had been intended to retain the availability of summary contempt procedures in the case of publications prejudicing *specific* proceedings at all, outside the strict liability rule. He nevertheless concluded that the necessary implication of the wording of s.6(c) was that such procedures *must* have been so retained.[13]

5-74 Bingham L.J.[14] rejected an argument that the purpose of the provision was to retain liability for intentionally prejudicial publications *after* proceedings were in existence, since it was unnecessary for that purpose. His view was that s.6(c) would serve no other sensible purpose than to preserve what had been understood to be the existing law; namely, that one could be liable for an intentionally prejudicial publication at a time when proceedings were "imminent".[15]

5-75 He may, however, not have sufficiently distinguished between proceedings being "in existence" and their being "active". While his point would have been valid in respect of strict liability contempt, the relevant wording in s.2 would not bite in all circumstances where proceedings were in existence; for example, where (i) proceedings (particularly civil proceedings) were pending but not "active", or (ii) proceedings in respect of which a risk of less than serious prejudice had been created, or (iii) improper pressure has been brought to bear on a litigant, even if no other prejudice arises.

---

[11] [1991] 1 W.L.R. 1194, [1992] 1 All E.R. 503.
[12] For a discussion of the significance of the decision so far as *mens rea* is concerned, see paras 5–174 et seq.
[13] See also *Att-Gen v Hislop* [1991] 1 Q.B. 514.
[14] [1991] W.L.R. at 1206–7.
[15] See also (1964) 80 L.Q.R. 166, where A.L. Goodhart referred to a lecture by Lord Parker C.J. in Baltimore on June 28, 1963 and expressed agreement with his view that contempt could be committed even before proceedings were in existence.

5-76 Because it now seems that the *actus reus* in such cases has to be assessed in accordance with the common law authorities, despite their vagueness and inconsistency, it is necessary still to have regard to that background. It is important, however, to recognise that to acknowledge the possibility of contempt at the stage of "imminence" imports a contingency into the *actus reus* of a criminal offence.[16] Since it is generally accepted that the risk of prejudice has to be assessed as at the time of publication, such a doctrine would permit findings of contempt in respect of notional proceedings which may never materialise. Such a principle is not easy to reconcile with the requirements of Arts 7 and 10 of the European Convention.

2. The older authorities

5-77 Before the 1981 Act it was by no means undisputed that contempt could be committed when proceedings were imminent but not yet pending. In *Hunt v Clarke*[17] Cotton L.J. recognised the possibility in an *obiter* remark that publication of prejudicial matter before a case has even begun could be a contempt: "In my opinion, it does technically become a contempt if pending a cause, *or before a cause even has begun*, any observations are made or published to the world which tend in any way to prejudice the parties in the case" (emphasis added). However, the view was expressed by North J. in *Re Crown Bank*[18] that publication before proceedings had been formally commenced could *not* be punished as contempt.[19] The same judge in *Re Cornish, Staff v Gill*[20] gave as a reason for making no order against an alleged contemnor that she had published matter alleged to be prejudicial before proceedings had commenced (his primary ground for rejecting the application being that the publication was not in any event likely to prejudice a fair trial).

5-78 In *R. v Parke*[21] a line of reasoning was adopted by the Divisional Court which appeared to extend the meaning of "pending." Whilst an accused was waiting to appear before committing magistrates, but before his committal, an article was published which was calculated to prejudice his trial at Assizes. It was argued that this could not be a contempt of the Assize Court since at the time of publication there were no proceedings pending before that court. Wills J. delivering the judgment of the Divisional Court met the argument thus:

---

[16] See *James v Robinson* (1963) 109 C.L.R. 593 at 618, *per* Windeyer J. and the discussion of that case by Hodgson J. in *Att-Gen v Sport Newspapers Ltd* [1991] 1 W.L.R. 1194 at 1220, [1992] 1 All E.R. 503 at 525–7.
[17] (1889) 58 L.J.Q.B. 490 at 491–2 (apparently not cited in either *Att-Gen v Sport Newspapers Ltd* [1991] 1 W.L.R. 1194, [1992] 1 All E.R. 503 or in *Att-Gen v News Group Newspapers plc* [1989] 1 Q.B. 110).
[18] (1890) 44 Ch.D. 649.
[19] This was the only English authority in which the distinction had to be clearly made between pending proceedings and proceedings which were merely imminent. As was pointed out by Hodgson J. in *Att-Gen v Sport Newspapers* [1991] 1 W.L.R. 1194 at 1212, [1992] 1 All E.R. 503 at 520, the judge's remarks were accordingly not *obiter*.
[20] (1892) 9 T.L.R. 196.
[21] [1903] 2 K.B. 432.

"The reason why the publication of articles like these with which we have to deal is treated as a contempt of Court is because their tendency and sometimes their object[22] is to deprive the court of the power of doing that which is the end for which it exists—namely to administer justice duly, impartially, and with reference solely to the facts judicially brought before it. Their tendency is to reduce the court which has to try the case to impotence, so far as the effectual elimination of prejudice and prepossession is concerned . . . if it be once grasped that such is the nature of the offence, what possible difference can it make whether the particular Court which is thus sought to be deprived of its independence, and its power of effecting the great end for which it is created, be at that moment in session or even actually constituted or not? It is perfectly certain that by law it will and must be constituted, and that when constituted it and it alone can take cognizance of the particular offence which is the subject of the preliminary enquiry . . . Great stress has been laid by Mr. Danckwerts upon an expression which has been used in the judgments upon questions of this kind—that the remedy exists when there is a cause pending in the court. We think undue importance has been attached to it. It is true that in very nearly all the cases which have arisen there has been a cause actually begun, so that the expression, quite naturally under the circumstances, accentuates the fact, not that the case has been begun, but that it is not at an end. That is the cardinal consideration. It is possible very effectually to poison the fountain of justice before it begins to flow. It is not possible to do so when the stream has ceased."

At that time a Court of Assize was not constituted until the Commission of Assize had been issued. That being so, the reasoning could be applied to the publication of prejudicial matter before proceedings in any court had been formally commenced. Yet, in a case where a man was merely a suspect there would be no "certainty" that there would be a case at all; in *R. v Parke* there were preliminary proceedings already in existence which in the ordinary course would lead to a trial before the court of Assize.[23] Thus, there was no question of a mere contingency.

Whilst the passage quoted formed the *ratio* of the judgment, when a similar problem arose in *R. v Davies*[24] the Divisional Court based its reasoning on the general supervisory jurisdiction by which it protected inferior courts. The case concerned a person charged at the Petty Sessions with an indictable offence, triable at either the Assizes or Quarter Sessions, and the court's jurisdiction was held to apply notwithstanding that, at the time of the offending publication, it was uncertain whether the person charged, if committed at all, would go to the Assizes or the Quarter Sessions.[25] By virtue of the Judicature Act 1873, the Assizes had been made a part of the High Court, and therefore had original jurisdiction. The Quarter Sessions had no such jurisdiction. The court held that the mischief to be suppressed in the case of the inferior courts is the same as that which exists when the jurisdiction of the superior courts is made the subject of interference. Just as it had jurisdiction to control the inferior court, it also had

---

[22] Although Wills J. appeared from these words not to think that it made any difference whether intention was present or not, clearly in this respect he can no longer be followed; if no intention was present, there can only be liability now if the criteria for strict liability are fulfilled.
[23] See *Att-Gen v Sport Newspapers Ltd* [1991] 1 W.L.R. at 1213H, [1992] 1 All E.R. 521e, Hodgson J.
[24] [1906] 1 K.B. 32.
[25] *ibid.* at 35.

5-80 CHAPTER 5—CONTEMPTS BY PUBLICATION AT COMMON LAW

jurisdiction to protect the inferior courts through the law of contempt, by ensuring that the misdeeds of others should be corrected.

5-81   In *Att-Gen v Sport Newspapers Ltd*,[26] Hodgson J. said that neither *Parke* nor *Davies* was authority for the proposition that "publication contempt" can be committed before the curial process has begun at all. Both were cases where proceedings were pending (albeit at the material time before magistrates only). So too, in the case of *Clarke Ex p. Crippen*,[27] it was held that contempt could be committed during the period when Dr Crippen was being brought back from Canada to England, before he had been formally charged; but the curial process had begun, because a judicial act had been performed by the magistrate when he had issued the warrant. Crippen was regarded as being within the protection of the court[28] from that time. Moreover, in any event, it could clearly be seen that proceedings were virtually "certain" to take place.

5-82   The next decision of significance[29] in this context was that of the Court of Criminal Appeal in *R. v Sharpe and Stringer*[30] where the two accused were charged with a conspiracy to pervert the course of justice. The particulars were that they had conspired to conceal and destroy evidence of the commission of a crime; attempted to suborn a person to give perjured evidence; and attempted to mislead police officers investigating the crime, by making statements which they knew to be untrue. Some of these acts could perhaps be regarded as constituting also contempt of court, notably the destruction of evidence and the attempt to persuade a person to commit perjury. It was argued that the offence could not be committed until proceedings were pending or commenced.

5-83   The court rejected this argument[31]:

> "Public justice requires not only that people should not take steps to conceal a crime or destroy evidence once a summons has been served upon somebody, but also that every crime should be suitably dealt with, and a man who obstructs public justice as soon as a crime is committed and endeavours to avoid the consequences of his wrongdoing by conspiracy with others is just as much guilty of an offence as if he waits until after proceedings are actually pending."

Nevertheless, it may be material that "the course of justice" is a wider concept, which would include such preliminary matters as the process of investigating the crime prior to charging. The same reasoning cannot necessarily be applied to the narrower concept of contempt.

---

[26] [1991] 1 W.L.R. 1194, [1992] 1 All E.R. 503.
[27] (1910) 103 L.T. 636, DC.
[28] Very similar language was used in Scotland, in *Hall v Associated Newspapers Ltd*, 1978 S.L.T. 241, cited at para.16–178.
[29] Meanwhile, in the *Daily Mirror Ex. p. Smith* [1927] 1 K.B. 845, 851, Lord Hewart C.J. had expressly left open the question of the application of the law of contempt to proceedings which were merely imminent.
[30] (1938) 26 Cr.App.R. 122, [1938] 1 All E.R. 48.
[31] *ibid.* at 126 and 51, *per* Du Parcq J.

A similar approach was adopted in *R. v Vreones*.[32] A cargo of wheat had been sold subject to an arbitration clause. The defendant as agent for the sellers took samples of the wheat in sacks, but later substituted wheat of a better quality in order to deceive any arbitrators that might be appointed. In fact no individuals had been appointed, but he was held to have attempted to pervert the course of justice, notwithstanding that no arbitration had been commenced at the time of his wrongful act.

5–84

The question was specifically considered again in the case of *R. v Savundranayagan*.[33] The appellant had been convicted on charges of fraud. Shortly before his arrest he had been interviewed in a television programme, and on his appeal against conviction it was argued that the effect of the interview had been so prejudicial as to preclude a fair trial. This was rejected but Salmon L.J. made some general observations upon the law of contempt. He expressed the view that at the time of the television interview it must have been obvious to everybody that Savundranayagan was about to be arrested:

5–85

"It must not be supposed that proceedings to commit for contempt of court can be instituted only in respect of matters published after proceedings have actually been begun. No one should imagine he is safe from committal for contempt of court, if, knowing or having good reason to believe that criminal proceedings are imminent, he chooses to publish matters calculated to prejudice a fair trial."

In *Att-Gen v Times Newspapers Ltd*[34] Lord Diplock said that:

5–86

"To constitute a contempt of court that attracts the summary remedy, the conduct complained of must relate to some specific case in which litigation in a court of law is actually proceeding or known to be imminent."

(It is perhaps worth observing that this statement would be entirely consistent with such cases as *R. v Parke* and *R. v Davies*, discussed above, and Lord Diplock need not necessarily be taken to have endorsed the notion of "contingent contempt" prior to the curial process having begun.) Lords Reid,[35] Simon,[36] and Cross[37] also apparently accepted that a contempt could be committed when proceedings were imminent.

---

[32] [1891] 1 Q.B. 360. See also *R. v Rafique* [1993] Q.B. 843. But cf. *R. v Selvage* [1982] Q.B. 372 (where the Court of Appeal described the facts of *Vreones* as being "as close to if not on the very boundary itself of the offence", and held that an act could not have a tendency to pervert the course of justice unless proceedings of some kind were in being or imminent, or an investigation was in progress which might bring about proceedings, so that a course of justice had been embarked upon).
[33] [1968] 1 W.L.R. 1761.
[34] [1974] A.C. 273 at 308.
[35] *ibid.* at 301.
[36] *ibid.* at 322.
[37] *ibid.* at 323.

3. *The lack of precision in the word "imminence"*

5–87 There are two cases which need to be considered (albeit outside England and Wales) where the problem of "imminence" has arisen directly, but in which differing conclusions were reached. In *R. v Beaverbrook Newspapers*[38] a man was suspected of a recent murder. He was surrounded in a house by police. A reporter gained access and interviewed him. The reporter's newspaper published the interview before the accused was arrested but when it was obvious that he shortly would be. The article contained a denial of guilt by the accused, but also details of his previous convictions which he himself supplied. The article was held to be in contempt. This is not surprising in view of the fact that proceedings were virtually "certain" to take place.

5–88 The principal ground, however, was the conclusion that s.11(1) of the Administration of Justice Act 1960, which provided a defence of innocent publication where proceedings were "pending *or imminent* at the time of publication", had by the use of those words made clear that the law of contempt was to cover proceedings which were merely imminent. Yet surely the mere fact that Parliament had provided such a defence would not necessarily mean it intended to extend existing law.[39] Clearer words would have been needed.

5–89 It is obvious that the publication of a man's previous convictions at a time when he is about to be arrested could prejudice his trial, especially in a high profile case. This was the issue addressed in *James v Robinson*[40] by the High Court of Australia. Two persons having been shot dead and their assailant having escaped, a newspaper published the name of the killer, together with his photograph and accounts from eye witnesses of what was described as murder. It was conceded that the articles were calculated to prejudice the trial, but argued that there was no contempt, for the reason that proceedings were not pending at the time of publication. This reasoning was accepted. The court concluded (a) that the person aggrieved must be aggrieved in his capacity as a party to proceedings, and (b) that it would be astonishing if the publisher were to be found guilty or not guilty according to the fortuitous circumstance of whether or not proceedings were *subsequently* commenced. In that case, Windeyer J.[41] described "imminent" as " . . . an imprecise word by which to mark out a period of time".

4. *The continued chilling effect of the "imminence" test*

5–90 As has already been pointed out, much of the discussion preceding the 1981 Act centred on the proper starting point for the application of the law of contempt. Objection was taken to the "imminence" test because of its lack of precision.

---

[38] [1962] N.I. 15.
[39] This was also the view expressed by Hodgson J. in *Att-Gen v Sport Newspapers Ltd* [1991] 1 W.L.R. 1194 at 1215H, [1992] 1 All E.R. 503 at 523d.
[40] (1963) 109 C.L.R. 593.
[41] *ibid.* at 618. See also *Att-Gen v Sport Newspapers Ltd* [1991] 1 W.L.R. 1194 at 1206, [1992] 1 All E.R. 503 at 515a.

Unfortunately, in the light of the post-Act authorities, there are still uncertainties which will continue to inhibit journalists and particularly the investigation of wrongdoing.

It was acknowledged in the statute, by the s.3 defence of "innocent publication", that there are good grounds for refusing to apply strict liability when a publisher "does not know and has no reason to suspect that relevant proceedings are active". Conversely, it may not be unreasonable to conclude, as a matter of policy, that liability for contempt should be established where such a person (i) *does* know that proceedings are "virtually certain" to be commenced, and (ii) intends to have some impact upon the outcome of such proceedings.

5–91

Moreover, it is clear that Parliament was concerned with the problem of prejudice to "imminent" proceedings, not only from the terms of s.6(c) but also because the word appears in s.4(2). In this latter context, a discretion was being provided for, to enable the court to postpone reports of proceedings for such period as might be thought necessary for the purpose of avoiding prejudice *inter alia* to the administration of justice in "other proceedings pending or imminent".[42] The use of the notion of imminence in that context is not as problematic, since it concerns the making of temporary restraint orders rather than the imposition of criminal liability.

5–92

Despite the fact that findings against journalists of an intention to interfere with imminent proceedings are likely to be relatively rare, the shadow which common law contempt continues to cast may very well have an inhibiting or "chilling" effect[43] upon journalists. It might have been better if Parliament had addressed the question whether the public interest required such behaviour to be the subject of the summary procedures, associated with contempt of court, or whether it might have been preferable to bring it expressly within the law governing attempts to pervert the "course of justice"[44] (accompanied by the traditional safeguards associated with a criminal trial).

5–93

The fact that common law contempt can still be committed when proceedings are merely imminent may cause practical difficulties for investigative journalism, notwithstanding the requirement to prove *mens rea*. This is perhaps especially so in view of the absence of any s.5 protection as to the discussion of matters of general public interest.[45] There are instances where a newspaper investigates a

5–94

---

[42] See the discussion in paras 7–111 *et seq*.
[43] An expression found with increasing frequency within this jurisdiction. See, *e.g.* Lord Keith in *Derbyshire County Council v Times Newspapers Ltd* [1993] A.C. 534 at 548D.
[44] See *Archbold 2005*, ch.28. See also paras 2–13 *et seq*. and the discussion of the case of *R. v Sharpe and Stringer* (1938) 26 Cr.App.R. 122, [1938] 1 All E.R. 48, para.5–82.
[45] See *Solicitor-General v Wellington Newspapers Ltd* [1995] 1 N.Z.L.R. 45, where the High Court emphasised that once it has been established that there is a real risk, as distinct from a remote possibility, of interference with a fair trial, there are no countervailing public policy considerations. See also the discussion of a possible "public interest" defence at paras 5–201 *et seq*.

crime of which the police know nothing.⁴⁶ Once the details of the investigation are published it may transpire that proceedings become imminent. The details may be highly prejudicial. Could the publication of such prejudicial details unearthed during such an investigation support a finding of contempt? Only, nowadays, if there was an intention to interfere with the administration of justice. It may be difficult to prove such an intention, since the journalist's answer would be that his intention had been to unearth the wrongdoing and, in so far as he was concerned with the possibility of contingent judicial proceedings at all, he had no other intention than that justice should take its proper course. Even so, it is unsatisfactory that such investigators should be left in uncertainty when trying to assess the legality of their proposed publications.

5-95   It might be said that the newspaper should make its material available to the police before publication. The Phillimore Committee considered this point, and recognised that investigative journalism served a worthwhile function and was a legitimate means of obtaining copy; it concluded that such an obligation would be a disincentive.⁴⁷

H. Where proceedings are merely "on the cards"

5-96   Watkins L.J. in *Att-Gen v News Group Newspapers plc*⁴⁸ was prepared to acknowledge that the public interest might require the law of contempt to come into play even where proceedings could not be described as "imminent", or (in the phrase he adopted) "virtually certain to be commenced", provided there was "a specific intent to interfere with the course of justice accompanied by a real risk that the published matter would impede a fair trial". He did not need to come to such a conclusion on the facts of the case before him, because it was found that the proceedings were indeed "imminent", and that the relevant intention was present. Nevertheless, in responding to the wider submission, he expressed the view that it was a "formidable contention". He went on to make the comment that⁴⁹:

> "The common law is not a worn out jurisprudence rendered incapable of further development by the ever increasing incursion of Parliamentary legislation. It is a lively body of law capable of adaption and expansion to meet fresh needs calling for the exertion of the discipline of the law".

5-97   In *Att-Gen v Sport Newspapers Ltd*⁵⁰ Bingham L.J. also came to the conclusion that the common law of contempt is indeed capable of applying to publications which may give rise to prejudice in respect of contingent proceedings which would not even qualify as "imminent":

---

⁴⁶ This situation arose in *Att-Gen v Morgan* [1998] E.M.L.R. 294, DC; the newspaper company was fined £50,000.
⁴⁷ paras 97 to 99.
⁴⁸ [1989] 1 Q.B. 110 at 133.
⁴⁹ *ibid*. 133D. See also para.2–169.
⁵⁰ [1991] 1 W.L.R. 1194 at 1207D–G, [1992] 1 All E.R. 503 at 515g–j.

"... I accordingly have no doubt that a publication made with the intention of prejudicing proceedings which, although not in existence, are imminent may be contemptuous and punishable as such if they give rise to the required risk.

If the question were at large, I would be much more hesitant whether that proposition could hold if proceedings were not imminent. *A-G v News Group Newspapers Ltd* is, however, a very clear decision on the point, and in making it this court expressly recognised that it was extending the boundaries of contempt as previously understood. It is a decision with very serious implications in those cases, perhaps increasingly common, where reporters are concerned to highlight an alleged crime, to point an accusing finger at an identified culprit and to stimulate a demand for prosecution. It also has the effect of enlarging a quasi-criminal liability in a field very recently considered by Parliament . . . In a matter of this nature it is very highly desirable that the law should be clear so that it may be understood and observed. I am quite satisfied that we should not be justified in departing from the rule so recently and unambiguously laid down in this court."

By contrast, in the same case, Hodgson J. expressed the view that the earlier decision in *Att-Gen v News Group Newspapers plc* was wrong in so far as it supported the proposition that publication of material even prior to proceedings being *pending* can amount to publication contempt. He also considered that the ambit of the summary procedure should not be widened, and added: 5–98

"... the criminal law should be left to deal with offences of perverting the course of justice. Judges should not find guilt and punish unless it is necessary for the effective control of active proceedings. If contempt be the Proteus of the common law then for my part I would hope that his repertoire will not be increased."

The somewhat unsatisfactory state of the authorities is further illustrated by the comments of the Court of Appeal in *Coe v Central TV*,[51] who were prepared simply to proceed on the basis that the decision in *Att-Gen v News Group Newspapers plc* was correctly decided and that the appropriate test was that adopted by Bingham L.J. in *Att-Gen v Sport Newspapers Ltd*, rather than following the approach of Hodgson J. It had not been necessary to hear argument on that point; meanwhile, however, it is probably wise to proceed upon the same assumption. 5–99

I. Intentional contempts before the commencement of an appeal

There may be an interval between a trial and the commencement of an appeal, during which the strict liability rule does not apply because of the wording of Sch.1 to the Contempt of Court Act 1981.[52] There is no reason why an intentional contempt cannot still be committed in that period because at common law a case is treated as pending until all possibilities of appeal have been exhausted.[53] 5–100

---

[51] [1994] E.M.L.R. 433 at 441, Glidewell L.J.
[52] See para.5, relating to the conclusion of criminal proceedings; para.12 to the conclusion of civil proceedings; and para.15 in relation to the commencement of appellate proceedings.
[53] *R. v Davies Ex p. Delbert-Evans* [1945] 1 K.B. 435.

5-101 CHAPTER 5—CONTEMPTS BY PUBLICATION AT COMMON LAW

5-101   There do not appear to have been any cases where publication between trial and appeal have in fact been treated as a contempt, though Lord Taylor C.J. has deprecated the publication of prejudicial matter during that period,[54] because it does no public service to vilify a person who has been before the court; it was also said to be wholly misguided if intended to bring pressure to bear on the courts themselves.

5-102   On the other hand, it is questionable whether it really is appropriate, as a matter of public policy, to treat such comment as contempt. While publication of prejudicial matter at such a time may be undesirable, a proper balance must be struck between the need for impartiality in the courts and the entitlement of the public to information about their workings.[55] As Field J. indicated long ago in *Dallas v Ledger*,[56] the rights of a public commentator should not be held in suspense for two or three years simply because a case may be taken to the House of Lords. Furthermore, appeals are decided by professional judges, who are most unlikely to be influenced by such extraneous material.[57] It is necessary to recall, however, that such publicity may perhaps in some circumstances, even if not capable of influencing the tribunal itself, amount to the exertion of improper pressure upon one or other of the parties to the relevant litigation.

5-103   Difficulties might arise where the appellate court has power to order a re-trial, as it does in criminal cases as well as in civil.[58] The older cases suggest, however,

---

[54] *R. v Vano* [1996] R.T.R. 15 (a press campaign had been instigated against what was perceived to be a low sentence). It would not be easy to prove in any given case an intention to bring pressure to bear on professional judges, not least because it is so often said that judges would not be susceptible, and journalists would perhaps be entitled to take that at face value. The courts may sometimes, however, find themselves in a dilemma because, on the one hand, it is proclaimed that judges are capable of setting aside what they read in the newspapers. On the other hand, courts also claim to be responsive to public opinion: *Att-Gen's Reference No.33 of 1996 (Daniel Latham)* [1997] 2 Cr.App.R. (S) 10; *R. v Klein*, September 23, 1996 (Lexis), CACD: "We are quite satisfied that the judge was right in concluding that these offences were so serious that only a custodial sentence was justified. In the present climate of public opinion and with the ever increasing use of firearms by criminals, the control of weapons is of paramount importance"; *R. v B* (1994) 15 Cr.App.R. (S) 815: "We are not obliged to act solely upon medical opinion but we are obliged to bring into the balance what the appellant actually did, knowing precisely what she was doing and to reflect public opinion when deciding what is the appropriate course to adopt." See also D.A. Ipp, "Talking to the Media: An Australian Perspective" (1998) 1 Legal Ethics 123, and his citation of the remarks of a barrister in New South Wales on a media campaign in which he participated: see above at para.2–47, n. 91. And see the various comments acknowledging the possibility of unconscious influence upon judges from media publicity in *Al Megrahi and Fhima v Times Newspapers Ltd*, 1999 S.C.C.R. 824. See also the recent discussion in the Irish Supreme Court of the problem of publicity, given between conviction and sentence, to prejudicial information apparently from police sources: *Kelly v O'Neill and Brady* [2000] 1 I.R. 354 and *Solicitor-General v Smith* [2004] 2 N.Z.L.R. 540 at [79].
[55] See para.7–16.
[56] (1888) 52 J.P. 328; 4 T.L.R. 432.
[57] See para.4–118.
[58] Criminal Appeal Act 1968, s.7, as amended by the Criminal Justice Act 1988, ss.43(1) and 170(2) and Sch.16. In Scotland, under s.118(1)(c) of the Criminal Procedure (Scotland) Act 1995, there is the possibility of an order of the High Court of Justiciary authorising a fresh prosecution: See *Forbes Duncan Cowan* March 17, 1998.

that a re-trial would not be regarded as "pending", even at common law, until the relevant order has been made.[59]

J. Some examples of the *actus reus* at common law[60]

1. "Prejudicing mankind against persons before their case is heard"[61]

When a criminal case is pending it is generally treated as a contempt to publish that the accused has previous convictions[62] or to attack his character so as to cause him prejudice at his trial.[63] To hold a witness up to public opprobrium was also regarded as contempt, because it might deter other witnesses from coming forward as well as tending to discredit the witness in the eyes of the tribunal.[64]

Predictions as to the outcome of court proceedings tended in the past to be treated somewhat indiscriminately as comprising the *actus reus* of contempt. A direct assertion that one side could or should prevail, on one or more issues, was regarded as an unacceptable form of pre-judgment. Statements that the odds in favour of one party winning were 100 to 1 and that the result of the action would be disastrous for the opposing party,[65] or that there was no defence,[66] or that there would be no issue as to liability but only as to the quantum of damages[67] have all been treated as contempt. It is no doubt significant that these cases were is concerned with pending litigation in which there was to be trial by jury. The court would be unlikely nowadays to treat such allegations as amounting to the *actus reus* of contempt but for this factor.

---

[59] *Metzler v Gounod* (1874) 30 T.L.R. 264; *Dallas v Ledger* (1888) 52 J.P. 328; 4 T.L.R. 432; *R. v Duffy Ex p. Nash* [1960] 2 Q.B. 188, 198. Since the decision in *Duffy*, the Court of Appeal (Criminal Division) has been given extended powers to order a re-trial, and the problem may thus arise more frequently. In *Att-Gen v Channel 4 Television Co Ltd* [1988] Crim.L.R. 237, the possibility of a re-trial was a factor that influenced the Court of Appeal against discharging an injunction restraining the broadcast of a television reconstruction of the Court of Appeal hearing.

[60] There is also to be found a detailed discussion in ch.4 of examples of *actus reus* in strict liability contempt.

[61] *per* Lord Hardwicke in *The St. James's Evening Post (Roach v Garvan)* (1742) 2 Atk. 469, 26 E.R. 683. The passage was cited in *R. v Bolam Ex p. Haigh* (1949) 93 Sol Jo. 220, by Lord Goddard C.J.

[62] *R. v Parke* [1903] 2 K.B. 432; *R. v Davies* [1906] 1 K.B. 32; and cf. *R. v Beaverbrook Newspapers* [1962] N.I. 15. Simon Brown L.J. in *Att-Gen v Unger* [1998] 1 Cr.App.R. 308, [1998] E.M.L.R. 280 cited revealing previous convictions as a classic example of contempt. It is true that in the light of the Criminal Justice Act 2003 previous convictions are likely to be admitted in some criminal trials, but the judge will need to decide on admissibility and that exercise of judgment and discretion should not be pre-empted by pre-trial media coverage.

[63] *R. v Thomson Newspapers Ltd Ex p. Att-Gen* [1968] 1 W.L.R. 1.

[64] *R. v Bottomley, The Times*, December 19, 1908; *R. v Castro, Onslow and Whalley's Case* (1873) L.R. 9 Q.B. 219; *Daily Herald Ex p. the Bishop of Norwich* [1932] K.B. 402; *Hutchison v Amalgamated Engineering Union, The Times*, August 25, 1932.

[65] *Re Finance Union* (1895) 11 T.L.R. 167 (libel).

[66] *Peters v Bradlaugh* (1888) 4 T.L.R. 414 (libel action removed to the High Court for trial).

[67] *In re Robbins Ex p. Green* (1891) 7 T.L.R. 411 (slander).

5-106 In a criminal case it was always treated as a contempt to state that an accused was guilty or not guilty,[68] and indeed such statements would nowadays generally qualify as meeting the test for a strict liability contempt. To give an obvious example, where a theatrical representation depicted an accused as a murderer,[69] it was held to be a contempt.

5-107 In *R. v Daily Herald Ex p. Rouse*[70] the accused had been committed for trial on a charge of murdering a man whose body was found in a burnt out car. A headline in a newspaper "Another Blazing Car Murder" was held to be a contempt because it "might well seem to suggest that the case on which Rouse was to be tried was a case of murder. That was the very issue which the jury would have to try". It was held that there was no doubt that the poster fell within the definition of contempt, given by Lord Russell of Killowen in *R. v Payne*,[71] namely, "that something has been published which either is clearly intended, or at least is calculated, to prejudice a trial which is pending".

5-108 A further blatant example is provided by *R. v Odhams Press Ltd*,[72] where it was held that contempt was committed by the publication of an article headed "Arrest this beast", and which described a man who had been charged with brothel-keeping as "up to his eyes in the foul business of purveying vice and managing street women." In *R. v Bolam Ex p. Haigh*[73] the *Daily Mirror* stated that a man who had been charged with murder had committed other murders and named his alleged victims. This was a serious contempt which resulted in the editor being imprisoned for three months, and the proprietors fined £10,000. Whilst it did not directly discuss the particular murder with which the accused had been charged, the publication of the additional information was such that "the court could only describe [it] as a disgrace to English journalism and as violating every principle of justice and fair play which it had been the pride of this country to extend to the worst of criminals."

5-109 Clearly, to publish what is alleged to be a confession on the part of a person charged with a criminal offence would be likely to be treated as a contempt.[74]

5-110 It is not only in criminal cases that such prejudice might be caused. In *Daw v Eley*[75] where a claim was pending in which the novelty of an invention was in

---

[68] *R. v Castro, Onslow and Whalley's Case* (1873) L.R. 9 Q.B. 219 (prosecution for perjury and forgery in connection with the Tichborne case); *R. v Balfour* (1895) 11 T.L.R. 492.
[69] *R. v Williams and Romney* (1823) L.J. (O.S.) K.B. 30. See also *Att-Gen v Steadman* (unreported), February 7, 1994, where an injunction was granted restraining performance of "Maxwell—The Musical" during the pendency of criminal proceedings against Robert Maxwell's sons; *Peacock v London Weekend Television* (1985) 150 J.P. 71 (the television reconstruction of a death in police custody when an inquest was pending. The facts are given at para.6–23).
[70] (1931) 75 S.J. 119, Lord Hewart C.J.
[71] [1896] 1 Q.B. at 580.
[72] [1957] 1 Q.B. 73.
[73] (1949) 93 S.J. 220.
[74] *R. v Clarke Ex p. Crippen* (1910) 103 L.T. 636. Cf. *Hall v Associated Newspapers Ltd* 1978 S.L.T. 241 discussed at paras 16–172 *et seq.*
[75] (1868) L.R. 7 Eq. Cas.49. Cp. *Roger Bullivant Ltd v Ellis, Financial Times*, April 15, 1986, Falconer J. (Lexis), discussed at para.4–185 as a modern example, where letters were sent to the customers of a business rival, the customers being potential witnesses.

issue, a newspaper was held to be in contempt for having published letters tending to disprove its novelty.

Suppose that a newspaper were to reveal the fact that a sum of money had been paid into court by a defendant in a civil action, in satisfaction of one or more causes of action.[76] This was held to be a contempt where a case was to be tried by jury[77] but it could conceivably be a contempt even where a judge is trying a case alone, for rules of court have for a long time forbidden that the judge be told before the conclusion of the trial.[78] It may be unlikely that a judge's mind would actually be prejudiced by learning of the payment, but if the necessary *mens rea* were present there could be a common law contempt in any event. In some circumstances, the court might readily infer the presence of the relevant state of mind, because it is obvious[79] that the rule is intended to protect and regulate the court's process and that its object could easily be thwarted by revealing such information. Generally, however, if the matter has been revealed by inadvertence, it will simply be a question for the judge to resolve in the light of the damage which he considers has been done. He has a discretion in deciding whether it is necessary to decline to hear the action further, or whether to continue despite the revelations.

2. *Pre-empting an issue of identification*

If identity is likely to be an issue in a pending or imminent case, then it could be a contempt to publish a photograph of the relevant person.[80] According to Lord Hewart C.J., the test of contempt in these circumstances is whether at the time of publication "it is apparent to a reasonable man that a question of identity may arise".[81] This seems an unsatisfactory test because it will often not be known until a trial starts whether identification will be an issue or not. Although the decided cases all refer to criminal trials, no doubt the principle is of general application. Though it is less common for identity to be raised as an issue in civil proceedings, the problem certainly could arise as, for example, where defendants in a libel action maintain that it was indeed the claimant who was seen to commit some form of misconduct at a certain time or place.

Where the police had issued a description of a wanted person, it was held that the publication of a photograph which did not materially differ from the police description had not been proved to amount to contempt.[82]

---

[76] *R. v Wealdstone News and Harrow News* (1925) 41 T.L.R. 508.
[77] *ibid.*
[78] RSC Ord.22, r.7. See now CPR Pt 36.19(2) and also in the context of offer of amends in defamation, *Cleese v Clark* [2003] EWHC 137 (QB), [2004] E.M.L.R. 3.
[79] See Lord Oliver in *Att-Gen v Times Newspapers Ltd* [1992] 1 A.C. 191 at 223.
[80] In *R. v Daily Mirror Ex p. Smith* [1927] 1 K.B. 845 at 850; cf. *Stirling v Associated Newspapers Ltd* 1960 S.L.T. 5. discussed at para.16–167. See also *Att-Gen v Express Newspapers* [2004] EWHC 2859 (Admin). The Attorney-General had warned newspapers in advance not to identify suspects following arrests under the Terrorism legislation; see Lord Goldsmith's letter to *The Times* on April 13, 2004 defending the decision to apply for an injunction.
[81] [1927] 1 K.B. at 850–1, where it is made clear that the test is an objective one; see also *Re Consolidated Press Ex p. Auld* (1936) 36 S.R.N.S.W. 596.
[82] *Lawson Ex p. Nodder* (1937) 81 Sol.Jo. 280.

5-114 CHAPTER 5—CONTEMPTS BY PUBLICATION AT COMMON LAW

3. Inadmissible evidence

5-114 To publish matter that is to some degree probative but which is in fact inadmissible at the trial would also be likely to be treated as contempt. In *R. v Evening Standard Co Ltd*[83] a statement to the effect that an alleged murderer had, after his wife's death, made an offer of marriage was published while the trial was in progress. This purported to be part of a report of the evidence that had been given at the trial. Although such evidence had been given before the examining justices, it was ruled inadmissible at the trial itself on the ground that it was more prejudicial than probative. This was held to be a contempt.

5-115 The publication of an accused's previous convictions pending a criminal trial would be another obvious example of communicating inadmissible material to potential jurors.[84] For a newspaper to publish the results of its own detailed investigation of a case or one of the issues in a case may be contempt.[85] To publish an interview with a party may also be so treated, at any rate if it is likely to affect his credibility or to contain inadmissible material.[86] The same reasoning would apply to a published interview with a witness.[87] To attack a witness in such a way as to discredit him may be a contempt if it would tend to affect the view of the tribunal of fact, whether judge or jury, of the credibility of that witness.[88]

4. Statements critical of persons concerned in litigation

5-116 Critical attacks upon parties to litigation may be objectionable because they may conceivably cause prejudice in the mind of the tribunal[89] especially if there is to be a jury trial, or they may deter those criticised from taking part in or continuing litigation.[90] In *Att-Gen v Times Newspapers Ltd*[91] Lord Diplock expressed the

---

[83] [1954] 1 Q.B. 578; see also *R. v Astor Ex p. Isaacs* (1913) 30 T.L.R. 10, and *Att-Gen v BBC* [1992] C.O.D. 264, DC, Tasker Watkins L.J., where a news broadcast in purporting to report counsel's opening remarks at the trial wrongly attributed to him allegations which had been derived from an earlier police briefing. Subsequently the decision had been made by counsel to make no reference to these.
[84] For an example see *R. v Parke* [1903] 2 K.B. 432; see also *R. v Thomson Newspapers Ltd* [1968] 1 W.L.R. 1; *Att-Gen v Sport Newspapers Ltd* [1991] 1 W.L.R. 1194, [1992] 1 All E.R. 503, DC; *Att-Gen v ITN Ltd* [1995] 2 All E.R. 370; and *Att-Gen v Associated Newspapers*, October 31, 1997.
[85] *Att-Gen v Times Newspapers Ltd* [1974] A.C. 273; *R. v Evening Standard Ex p. D.P.P.* (1924) 40 T.L.R. 833. See also *Att-Gen v Morgan* [1998] E.M.L.R. 294, DC.
[86] *R. v Savundranayagan* [1968] 1 W.L.R. 1761, 3 All E.R. 439; *R. v Beaverbrook Newspapers* [1962] N.I. 15; but see also *R. v Barry Ex p. Grey* (1939) 83 S.J. 872 where an interview with a party to a civil action was held not to be a contempt.
[87] *Stirling v Associated Newspapers Ltd* (1960) S.L.T. 5; and the comments on this subject of the *Interdepartmental Committee on the Law of Contempt as it Affects Tribunals of Inquiries*, Cmnd. 4078 (1969).
[88] *Re Labouchere Ex p. Columbus Co Ltd* (1901) 17 T.L.R. 578. For the position on physical attacks upon a witness, see ch.11.
[89] *Re Pall Mall Gazette, Jones v Flower* (1894) 11 T.L.R. 122; *Re Hinde, Thornhill v Steel Morris* (1911) 56 S.J. 34.
[90] See, e.g. *Att-Gen v Hislop* [1991] 1 Q.B. 514, CA, discussed at para.5–169. See also *Littler v Thomson* (1839) 2 Beav. 129, 49 E.R. 1129 ("The effect of such publications would seem to be not only to deter persons from coming forward to give evidence on one side, but to induce witnesses to give evidence on the other side alone", per Lord Langdale M.R.); *Hutchinson v Amalgamated Engineering Union, Re Daily Worker, The Times*, August 25, 1932, discussed at para.4–131.
[91] [1974] A.C. 273 at 310.

view that it was a contempt to hold up any suitor to public obloquy. Lord Simon concurred, saying that it was a contempt to hold one of the parties up to obloquy in order to cause him to abandon some position which was legitimately open to him.[92]

Lord Morris similarly categorised conduct calculated so to abuse or pillory a party to litigation, or to subject him to such obloquy as to shame or dissuade him from obtaining the adjudication of the court to which he is entitled.[93] These remarks were *obiter* because the decision in that case was based on the notion of pre-judgment.[94] However, the House went on to consider *obiter* the effect of an earlier article, which did not constitute a pre-judgment of the case but which urged in strong terms that the defendants' moral position was such that they ought to give the plaintiffs complete compensation regardless of the legal position. The article was intended to make the defendants offer more by way of settlement.

Whether that other article would itself have constituted contempt of court was a matter on which views were divided. Lords Diplock and Simon both took the view that this earlier article also constituted a contempt because it held up the defendants to public abuse or execration. Lords Reid and Cross took the view that it was permissible to comment upon a party's moral position, in contradistinction to its legal position, and that the article was therefore not a contempt. It was legitimate to criticise a party in a fair and temperate way.

There is abundant authority for the proposition that it is a contempt to *abuse* a person concerned in litigation. In *St. James's Evening Post*,[95] one of Lord Hardwicke's categories of publication contempt was the abuse of parties.

III. THE MENTAL ELEMENT IN COMMON LAW PUBLICATION CONTEMPT

A. The mental element in crime: some general propositions

Before any discussion of *mens rea* in relation to contempt, it is appropriate to consider briefly the significance of the concepts of intention and recklessness in the criminal law generally.[96] The meaning of intention has been the subject of much discussion in recent years,[97] more particularly in the context of the law of

---

[92] *ibid*. at 317.
[93] *ibid*. at 302.
[94] See paras 1–92, and 5–19 *et seq*.
[95] (1742) 2 Atk. 469 at 471, 26 E.R. 683 at 685.
[96] For the mental element in civil contempts, see paras 12–80 *et seq*.
[97] J.C. Smith, "Intention in Criminal Law" (1974) 27 C.L.P. 93; J.H. Buzzard, "Intent" [1978] Crim.L.R. 5 and J.C. Smith, *ibid*. "A Reply" at 14; J. Stannard, "Mens Rea in the Melting Pot" (1986) 37 N.I.L.Q. 61; I. Dennis, "The Mental Element for Accessories" in ed. P.F. Smith, *Essays in Honour of J.C. Smith* (1987) and the comment and counter comment by G.R. Sullivan, "Intent, Purpose and Complicity" [1988] Crim.L.R. 641; A. Duff, "Codifying Criminal Fault; Conceptual Problems and Presuppositions" in ed. I.H. Dennis, *Criminal Law and Justice* (1987) Sweet & Maxwell 93; A Duff, "The Obscure Intentions of the House of Lords" [1986] Crim.L.R. 771; G. Williams, "Oblique Intent" [1987] 46 C.L.J. 417; R. Buxton, "Some Simple Thoughts on Intention" [1988] Crim.L.R. 484; Lord Goff of Chieveley, "The Mental Element in the Crime of Murder" (1988) 104 L.Q.R. 30; M. Moore, "Intentions and Mens Rea" in ed. R. Gavison, *Issues in Contemporary Legal Philosophy* (1987) at 245; J.C. Smith, "A Note on Intention" [1990] Crim.L.R. 85; N. Lacey, "A Clear Concept of Intention: Elusive or Illusory" (1993) 56 M.L.R. 621; A.P.

5–120   Chapter 5—Contempts by Publication at Common Law

murder.[98] But the law as laid down is of general application, and should be briefly summarised.

5–121   It is necessary to have particular regard to this difficult area of the law, in the context of contempt, because there have been a number of instances where courts have held, on the one hand, that nothing short of a positive intention to interfere with the course of justice will suffice to establish the mental element in common law contempt; whereas, on the other hand, such an intention has been readily inferred from the surrounding circumstances, albeit in the teeth of sworn denials.[99]

1. *Purpose as intention*

5–122   A person is said to intend a consequence when he wills that it should come about. This is the paradigm case of intention; it is his purpose or desire that the consequence should occur. Where a person takes a step with intention of this kind, it is irrelevant to his liability that the likelihood that the consequence will occur is extremely remote. It is nonetheless a natural use of language to say that he intends that consequence. Occasionally, when the legislature uses the language of intention, only this form of *mens rea* will suffice.[1]

2. *Oblique intention*

5–123   More commonly, however, when Parliament (and the judges) use the language of intention in the criminal law, they mean to include the culpable state of mind of a person who desires to bring about one consequence, also knowing that there is, in some degree of likelihood, the possibility of a different (but not desired) consequence. In most contexts (such as the law of criminal damage, for example) the distinction between this form of intention and recklessness, which is discussed specifically below,[2] is of no great practical significance. Recklessness

---

Simester and W. Chan, "Intention Thus Far" [1997] Crim.L.R. 704; A. Norrie, "After *Woollin*" [1999] Crim. L.R. 532; A. Pedain, "Intention and the Terrorist Example" [2003] Crim. L.R. 579; M. C. Kaveny, "Inferring Intention from Foresight" (2004) 120 L.Q.R. 81.

[98] The cases that have formed the principal focus for discussion are *Hyam v DPP* [1975] A.C. 55; *R. v Moloney* [1985] A.C. 905; *R. v Hancock and Shankland* [1986] A.C. 455; *R. v Nedrick* [1986] 1 W.L.R. 1025; *R. v Woollin* [1997] 1 Cr.App.R. 97; *R. v Matthews and Alleyne* [2003] EWCA Crim. 192, [2003] Crim. L.R. 443.

[99] *Att-Gen v Newspaper Publishing plc* [1988] Ch. 333; *Att-Gen v News Group Newspapers plc* [1989] 1 Q.B. at 126A-B, 130C, DC. See also *Att-Gen v Newspaper Publishing plc* [1989] F.S.R. 457, Morritt J.; *Official Solicitor v News Group Newspapers* [1994] 2 F.L.R. 174.

[1] As for example, the intention to cause another to give up the occupation of his residential premises in the Protection from Eviction Act 1977, s.1(1); see *R. v Burke* [1991] 1 A.C. 135. The Criminal Justice and Public Order Act 1994 actually uses the word "motive" to describe one of the requisite states of mind required, in s.51(5). This use is very rare.

[2] para.5–129.

is in any event sufficient for a conviction in the case of most criminal offences.[3] But in relation to publication contempts, the Court of Appeal has held that recklessness is insufficient[4]; thus in this context it may be necessary to draw a sharp distinction between the two states of mind.

3. *Foresight of virtual certainty*

5–124 Until relatively recently, it was the law that a person might be said to intend a consequence simply because he foresaw that it was virtually certain to occur. In other words the foresight of a consequence was equated to an intention to bring it about. In *R. v Moloney*,[5] however, the House of Lords rejected this formulation, holding instead that foresight of a possible consequence was merely a matter of evidence from which a jury could *infer* an intention. The more likely it was that the consequence would come about, the more readily might the jury infer that the defendant intended that outcome.

5–125 In formulating his guidance to trial judges, charged with the task of instructing juries as to intention, Lord Bridge in *Moloney* said that the jury should be told to ask whether or not the outcome was a "natural consequence" of what the defendant was doing, and whether or not the defendant realised that it was a "natural consequence". The use of this expression was unfortunate, since a consequence may be reckoned "natural" whether it is a bare possibility or a virtual certainty; it cannot be taken to mean that the consequence has even to be very likely (which is what Lord Bridge almost certainly meant).

5–126 In the light of that, in *Hancock and Shankland*,[6] the House qualified its previous decision, saying that the jury should be told to decide whether or not the defendant realised that it was virtually certain[7] that the consequence would occur as a result of what he was doing. The jury *could* then infer that the defendant intended that consequence.

5–127 The difficulty with this formulation is that it leaves the law unclear as to just what is the additional ingredient (*i.e.* beyond the foresight) of intention in these circumstances. If a person realises that it is virtually certain that as a result of his proposed course of action a given consequence will follow, and he nevertheless decides to pursue it, in what circumstances can he be heard to say that it was *not* his intention that the outcome should occur? Sir John Smith has posed the question: suppose a puzzled jury were to return and ask the judge, "We have considered the defendant's state of mind. We believe that he did not desire the consequence, but we have come to the conclusion that he did realise that it was

---

[3] Only intention will suffice in the law of murder. See the cases cited in para.5–120, n.98. Although recklessness is sufficient on the substantive charge of criminal damage, proof of recklessness is insufficient for a charge of attempted criminal damage: *O'Toole* [1987] Crim. L.R. 759.
[4] *Att-Gen v Newspaper Publishing plc* [1988] Ch. 333, 374–5, Sir John Donaldson M.R., 382–3, Lloyd L.J. See also *Att-Gen v News Group Newspapers plc* [1989] Q.B. 110.
[5] [1985] A.C. 905.
[6] [1986] A.C. 455.
[7] See the use of this expression in *Att-Gen v News Group Newspapers plc* [1989] Q.B. 110, 135A, by Watkins L.J.

5-127 CHAPTER 5—CONTEMPTS BY PUBLICATION AT COMMON LAW

virtually certain that the result would happen if he continued with his course of conduct. Of what more must we be satisfied before we can infer that he intended to kill him?" There is no logical answer to that question, though trial judges were expected to behave as though there was.[8] In *R. v Matthews; R. v Alleyne*,[9] the Court of Appeal, having noted the criticisms of Sir John Smith, affirmed nevertheless that proof of foresight that a consequence is virtually certain to occur is no more than evidence of intention. Where such foresight is established, the jury may, but not *must*, infer that the defendant intended.

5-128 In one of the Court of Appeal contempt hearings during the *Spycatcher* litigation,[10] Nicholls L.J. pointed out that:

"To describe the issue as simply 'a jury question' or a question of evidence, or to say only that the fact-finding tribunal may, but not must, 'infer' the existence of 'intention' provides no answer. It leaves the matter obscure, and does not assist in defining, or even explaining, what is meant by 'intention' in this context."

B. The concept of recklessness generally in criminal law

5-129 It is not appropriate here to explore the detail of the debate about the scope of recklessness.[11] Suffice it to say that there were, until relatively recently, two forms of recklessness to be found in English criminal law.

1. Inadvertent recklessness

5-130 In the case of the first, known as *Caldwell* or *Lawrence* recklessness,[12] a defendant could be held to have acted recklessly, upon the application of an *objective* test, in circumstances in which he has committed an act which creates a serious risk of causing certain consequences, and without having given any thought to the possibility of such a risk, provided that the risk would have been obvious to any reasonably prudent person. The decision in *Caldwell* was overruled by the House of Lords in *R. v G*[13] in the context of its use in the Criminal Damage Act 1971. How widely this decision impacts on recklessness in other areas of the criminal law is yet to be resolved, and Lord Bingham said that he wished "to make it as plain as I can that I am not addressing the meaning

---

[8] See Sir John Smith's commentary on *R. v Scalley* [1995] Crim. L.R. 504, where the Court of Appeal reduced a conviction from murder to manslaughter because the judge had failed to direct the jury that, if they came to the conclusion that the defendant realised that it was virtually certain that his victim would sustain death or grievous bodily harm, they *might* but need not necessarily convict him. See also Sir John Laws (2000) 116 L.Q.R. 158.
[9] [2003] EWCA Crim 192, [2003] 2 Cr.App.R. 30.
[10] *Att-Gen v Newspaper Publishing plc* [1990] T.L.R. 158 (Lexis).
[11] See Glanville Williams, "Recklessness Redefined" (1981) 40 C.L.J. 252; S. Gardner, (note) (1993) 109 L.Q.R. 21.
[12] Resulting from the two decisions of the House of Lords, *MPC v Caldwell* [1982] A.C. 341; *R. v Lawrence* [1982] A.C. 510. The decisions have been followed subsequently by the Court of Appeal in *R. v King* [1992] 1 Q.B. 20. See also *R. v Reid* [1992] 1 W.L.R. 793, 3 All E.R. 673, 95 Cr.App.R. 391, HL.
[13] [2003] UKHL 50, [2004] 1 A.C. 1034. See D.J. Ibbetson, "Recklessness restored" (2004) C.L.J. 13; D. Kimel, "Inadvertent Recklessness in Criminal Law" (2004) 120 L.Q.R. 548.

of 'reckless' in any other statutory or common law context".[14] But the reasoning of Lord Bingham that " ... it is not clearly blameworthy to do something involving a risk of injury to another if ... one genuinely does not perceive the risk" would appear to be of wider application.[15] However the law develops in this respect, the second form of recklessness is unaffected by the decision in *R. v G* and it is to this form that we now turn.

2. *Advertent recklessness*

The other (and perhaps more traditional) form is the so-called *Cunningham* recklessness,[16] whereby it is said that a person is culpably reckless only when he actually foresees that a risk may eventuate but he nevertheless continues his course of conduct; or, as it is sometimes put, it is the conscious taking of an unjustified risk.

5–131

C. The nature of *mens rea* in publication contempt

After the passing of the Contempt of Court Act 1981, it was for a while unclear how far the common law of contempt continued to apply to media publications and to what extent it was likely to be invoked, especially against journalists, despite the statutory reforms. In particular, in the case of publications falling outside the statutory notion of strict liability, what was the nature of *mens rea* which would need to be proved? It is necessary, before attempting an answer to such difficult questions, to consider how the law has developed since the statute came into effect, and the common law background against which it was enacted.

5–132

1. *The effect of enacting "the strict liability rule"*

Prior to the passing of the 1981 Act there was clear authority that strict liability[17] applied at common law to certain sorts of criminal contempt. This was true particularly of cases involving publication of matter calculated to prejudice the fair trial of pending proceedings. The 1981 Act defined "the strict liability rule" in s.1 as:

5–133

"the rule of law whereby conduct may be treated as a contempt of court as tending to interfere with the course of justice in particular legal proceedings regardless of intent to do so."

---

[14] At [28].
[15] In *Att-Gen's Reference (No.3 of 2003)* [2004] EWCA Crim 868, [2005] Q.B. 73, the decision was applied in the context of the common law offence of misconduct in public office, it being held that actual awareness was required.
[16] *R. v Cunningham* [1957] 2 Q.B. 396.
[17] That is, there could be liability in the absence of proof that the alleged contemnor had *mens rea* in relation to one or more aspects of the *actus reus* of the contempt alleged. See, *e.g. St. James's Evening Post* (1742) 2 Atk. 469, 26 E.R. 642, discussed at para.1–62. See also the authorities on wardship which are discussed in paras 11–339 *et seq.*

5–134 The Act thereby confined the application of the so-called strict liability rule, in the publication context, to those communications which create a substantial risk that the course of justice in proceedings that are "active" will be seriously impeded or prejudiced.[18] As a matter of statutory interpretation, it is submitted that it would be a mistake to read s.2(2) as though it said that "*strict liability* applies only to a publication which creates a substantial risk that the course of justice in the proceedings in question will be seriously impeded or prejudiced".

5–135 At first sight, it might be thought that strict liability was henceforth to have no application at all in the law of contempt, save in so far as was specifically provided in ss.1 and 2; that is to say, solely in relation to publication contempts which tend to "interfere with the course of justice in particular legal proceedings". It is most unlikely, however, that the draftsman had in mind any other application of strict liability that might have obtained in the common law beforehand (as appears to have been the case, for example, in relation to wards of court).[19]

5–136 The statute uses the expression "the strict liability rule", which is defined in s.1; it does not refer generally to "strict liability". It would be a misreading of the Act, therefore, to assume that Parliament has made any provision against "strict liability" in any other area of the law of contempt. Had it been intended to require *mens rea* in every other category of contempt, it would have been easy so to provide expressly. Moreover, in the light of the decision in *Sunday Times v United Kingdom*,[20] and the content of the Parliamentary debates,[21] it is by no means unreasonable to assume that it was with publication contempt that the legislature was solely concerned.

5–137 The Act certainly appears to be directed primarily towards regulating the law governing publication contempts, save where express provision is made; in relation, for example, to jury secrecy, the use of tape recorders in court, and the limitations imposed upon sentencing powers.

5–138 The conclusion is that we are driven back to an (admittedly very uncertain) common law for guidance upon the ingredients of *mens rea* in the law of contempt. Some attention must also be paid to the impact of s.6(c), and where appropriate to the provisions of Art.10, at least where publication and freedom of speech are concerned.

2. *The discordant strands in the post-1981 cases*

5–139 Since 1981, the question has arisen on several occasions as to precisely what state of mind is now required for common law publication contempts. The matter

---

[18] A fuller discussion of these terms will be found in paras 4–52 *et seq.*
[19] See Sir John Donaldson M.R. in *Att-Gen v Newspaper Publishing plc* [1988] Ch. 333 at 374; see also Gibson L.J. later in the same litigation [1990] T.L.R. 158, CA (Lexis), cited at paras 5–158 *et seq.*
[20] (1979) 2 E.H.R.R. 245.
[21] The legislative history of the Act is briefly described in para.1–115, n.55.

first fell to be considered in detail by the Court of Appeal in *Att-Gen v Newspaper Publishing plc*,[22] in which Sir John Donaldson M.R. described the topic of *mens rea* in the law of contempt as "something of a minefield".[23] Unfortunately, nothing since he made that comment in July 1987 has charted any more certain path through the field, and there are some apparent inconsistencies between judicial statements on the required ingredients.

The separate lines of authority that need to be reconciled are as follows: 5–140

1. It is sometimes said that an intention to create a *risk* of prejudice or impediment to the administration of justice will be enough, without there necessarily being present an intention to create actual prejudice or impediment.

2. Other authorities suggest that it is not even necessary to go so far as to establish a positive intention to cause any consequences for the administration of justice, but that it will be sufficient for the alleged contemnor to have intended the act which, objectively judged, may be taken to have created a risk of prejudice or impediment.

Each of the relevant cases must be considered in a little detail.

(a) *The* Spycatcher *litigation*

i. *The context*

The point arose in *Att-Gen v Newspaper Publishing plc*,[24] in determining a 5–141
preliminary issue as to whether a third party *could* be liable for deliberately publishing matter that was the subject of an injunction, when not personally bound by its terms. That question was answered in the affirmative, but it was held that liability in any given case would depend in part upon whether the necessary *mens rea* was present. The significance of *mens rea* had not been appreciated at first instance, and the point was thus raised for the first time in the Court of Appeal.

---

[22] [1988] Ch. 333. In the first edition of the work reference was made at para.2–74 to a number of older authorities in an attempt to obtain guidance on what appeared to be a completely open question. Now that the matter has been specifically addressed in a number of modern decisions, there is no need to discuss the earlier cases in any detail, and it is sufficient to list them here in case the reader should wish to make further enquiry: *McLeod v St. Aubyn* [1899] A.C. 549 (lending a magazine which scandalised the court without knowledge of its contents); *Perera v R.* [1951] A.C. 482 (criticism of a procedure adopted by the court in Ceylon, in the mistaken belief that it was directed merely towards a prison regulation); *Garibaldo v Cagnoni* (1703) 6 Mod. 90, 87 E.R. 848; *Magnay v Burt* (1843) 5 Q.B. 381 at 394–5; *Purdin v Roberts* (1910) 74 J.P.Jo. 88; *Jones Ex p. McVittie* [1931] 1 K.B. 664; *Ambard v Att-Gen* [1936] A.C. 549; *Att-Gen v Butterworth* [1963] 1 Q.B. 696; *Re B (JA) An Infant* [1965] Ch. 1112; *Metropolitan Police Commissioner Ex p. Blackburn (no.2)* [1968] 2 Q.B. 150; *Re F (orse A) (A Minor)* [1977] Fam. 58; *R. v Hill* (1977) 73 D.L.R. 621, 629; *Att-Gen v Leveller Magazine* [1979] A.C. 440 at 466, 472.
[23] [1988] Ch. 333 at 373H.
[24] Last note.

5–142 The case arose out of the *Spycatcher* litigation, the court having been asked to punish the publishers of certain newspapers for publishing articles thought by the Attorney-General to be likely to thwart the effect of injunctions granted against the proprietors and editors of two *other* newspapers, namely *The Observer* and *The Guardian*. Those two newspapers had been restrained from publishing extracts from *Spycatcher*, the memoirs of a former officer of the security service.[25]

5–143 The factual background was unusual in a number of respects, but from the point of view of its place in the framework of the law of contempt, it is worth noting that, while it concerned publication in a newspaper, this was not in the usual context of considering the creation of a risk of prejudice to current proceedings. The problem was that the publications under consideration would undermine or subvert the purpose of the court in granting the Attorney-General protective injunctions to abide the outcome of his claim based on breach of confidence. The case therefore bridges both the subject of publication contempt at common law (which is considered in this chapter) and that of interference with the administration of justice more generally.[26] The analyses given by the Court of Appeal are relevant to the *mens rea* required for publication contempt, and it is therefore desirable to consider the judgments carefully in this context.

ii. *The arguments raised as to s.6(c)*

5–144 When the other newspapers published excerpts from the *Spycatcher* manuscript, it was argued that this was likely to reduce or destroy the efficacy of the injunctions. Because the proceedings against *The Observer* and *The Guardian* were not "active" within the meaning of the Act,[27] there could only be liability, if at all, at common law. Accordingly, it became necessary to consider whether the conduct was *intended* to impede or prejudice the administration of justice within the terms of s.6(c) of the Contempt of Court Act 1981, which provides as follows[28]:

"6. Nothing in the foregoing provisions of this Act—

(c) restricts liability for contempt of court in respect of conduct intended to impede or prejudice the administration of justice."

5–145 It was argued for the Attorney-General that all that was required was a general or basic intent, whereas the respondents contended that a *specific* intent was necessary. The Master of the Rolls ruled with reference to the saving provision of s.6(c) of the Act[29]:

---

[25] The cause of action relied upon was breach of confidence. The publication of such material by third parties would also now constitute an offence under the Official Secrets Act 1989, s.5, which was enacted partly by way of reaction to the ultimate failure of the proceedings in *Spycatcher*.
[26] Considered more fully in ch.11.
[27] See para.4–174.
[28] paras 5–1 *et seq.*
[29] [1988] Ch. 333 at 374G–H. See also *Att-Gen v Sport Newspapers Ltd* [1991] 1 W.L.R. 1194, [1992] 1 All E.R. 503, discussed at paras 5–174 *et seq.*

"I am quite satisfied that what is contemplated, and what is 'saved', is the power of the court to commit for contempt when the conduct complained of is specifically intended to impede or prejudice the administration of justice".

Nevertheless, such an intent could be inferred from surrounding circumstances, and it would not be necessary to demonstrate any express avowal. The foreseeability of the consequences of the conduct would be one relevant factor to be weighed in determining whether to draw such an inference.[30] Moreover, there was no need to show that the intention to impede or prejudice was the *sole* intention in the contemnor's mind; so too intent is to be distinguished from motive or desire.[31] **5–146**

Lloyd L.J. in considering the nature of the *mens rea* required,[32] identified three possible solutions: **5–147**

(1) There would be liability if (a) the respondents merely intended to do the act in question (*i.e.* on the facts before him they intended to publish the articles), even though there was no actual intent to impede or prejudice the administration of justice, and (b) the article in fact so impedes or prejudices;

(2) Liability could only arise if there was either (a) an actual intention to interfere with justice or (b) recklessness as to such interference;

(3) Recklessness would not suffice, and there could only be liability if there were demonstrated (beyond reasonable doubt) an actual intention to interfere.

Both Lloyd and Balcombe L.JJ., like the Master of the Rolls, concluded that the third of these represented the correct approach. It is perhaps unfortunate that in the three alternative solutions identified different terminology was used, but it is clear that "interference" was not intended to signify something different from "impeding or prejudicing". The explanation given was that the single concept of "interference" was being used by way of "brevity", to avoid repeating the clumsy expression "impede or prejudice" several times. **5–148**

iii. *Freedom of speech: the policy issue*

An important element in the court's reasoning was the policy underlying the 1981 Act "to effect a permanent shift in the balance of public interest away from the protection of the administration of justice and in favour of freedom of speech."[33] It would thus not be furthering the statutory purpose to admit of liability on the basis of recklessness alone. It is now possible to state the principle, therefore, with some confidence. Intention is required, and recklessness will *not* suffice to establish contempt. That is not to say, however, that all **5–149**

---

[30] See the remarks of Sir John Smith, cited at para.5–127.
[31] [1988] Ch. 333 at 375A, Sir John Donaldson M.R., and 383B, Lloyd L.J. See also *Moloney* [1985] A.C. 905 at 926.
[32] [1988] Ch. at 381D–E.
[33] *ibid.,* per Lloyd L.J. at 382D–F.

5–149 CHAPTER 5—CONTEMPTS BY PUBLICATION AT COMMON LAW

uncertainties are resolved. In particular, it may be necessary one day to focus on how one reconciles the decision that recklessness will not suffice with the inherent difficulty of the concept that the *actus reus* can often consist in the creation of what is merely a "noumenon" (*i.e.* a risk of serious prejudice in pending proceedings).[34]

iv. Later developments in the Spycatcher litigation

5–150 Subsequently, almost two years after the decision of the Court of Appeal, the matter came before Morritt J.[35] whose task it was to determine a number of issues, including whether the Attorney-General had established, as a matter of fact, that the relevant personnel on the newspapers' staff had intended to impede or prejudice the administration of justice within s.6(c) of the Act. He came to the conclusion in relation to the editor of the *Sunday Times* that he had not wished to be in contempt of court and that he had believed, albeit wrongly, that he could not be in contempt for the reason that there was no injunction against his particular newspaper. Nevertheless, the judge found himself in no doubt that it had been the intention of the editor to interfere with the administration of justice by publishing the *Spycatcher* extracts. He concluded that " . . . it is clear beyond doubt that [the editor] knew that publication . . . would inevitably damage or destroy confidentiality in . . . material which the court had sought to preserve". It was an inevitable consequence of putting the material into the public domain, which the editor both appreciated and accepted, that the confidentiality would be damaged or destroyed.

5–151 The importance of this decision is clear. It was an early demonstration of how the court is on occasion prepared to draw an inference, despite a newspaper editor's sworn denials, that the requisite intention to interfere with the administration of justice was present. This is an illustration of the well known principle that intention is not to be equated with desire. Also, however, it shows how little practical comfort journalists were able to derive from the positive statements made earlier in the Court of Appeal to the effect that recklessness would not suffice.

5–152 Yet the special context of the *Spycatcher* litigation makes it necessary to be cautious about extending the reasoning too readily to the more usual circumstances in which publication contempt arises. Normally the court is concerned with assessing whether a sufficient risk was created of interference with the process of justice, and correspondingly with whether the journalist concerned had an intention either to create that risk,[36] or actually to cause such interference.[37] Because such questions have to be determined as at the date of the relevant publication, the process involves inevitably a degree of speculation. On the facts which confronted Morritt J., however, speculation was unnecessary

---

[34] *Att-Gen v English* [1983] A.C. 116 at 141–2, Lord Diplock, discussed at paras 4–55 *et seq.*
[35] [1989] 1 F.S.R 457.
[36] As was argued in *Coe v Central TV plc* [1994] E.M.L.R. 433 at 441, discussed paras 5–184, 6–33 and 6–38.
[37] As was held to be necessary in *Att-Gen v Sport Newspapers Ltd* [1991] 1 W.L.R. 1194, [1992] 1 All E.R. 503, discussed in this context at para.5–174.

because it was obvious to anyone that, whether or not the editors were going to fall foul of the law of contempt, the publication of the *Spycatcher* extracts in whole or in part was going to nullify or at least frustrate the purpose of the court in granting the original injunction.

The next stage was that the matter wound its way back into a differently constituted Court of Appeal, where three more analytical judgments were delivered on the matter of *mens rea*.[38] The decision of Morritt J., finding both *actus reus* and *mens rea* to have been present, was upheld. Fox L.J., in considering the publication by *The Independent*, made the following significant observation:

5–153

> "My conclusion is not based upon any suggestion that [the editor] deliberately intended to interfere with the course of justice, but upon the fact that what he did inevitably had that effect".

This use of the apparently tautologous expression "deliberately intended"[39] would appear to be a reference to what was described earlier as the first type of intention recognised by the criminal law, namely where desire or purpose is present[40]; and therefore, since he excluded it, the Lord Justice must have based his conclusion upon the presence of the other form of *mens rea* (oblique intention).[41]

His approach, however, is to be contrasted with that of Lloyd L.J. in the first of the Court of Appeal hearings, in which his two brethren had concurred. It will be remembered that they concluded that what was required was *mens rea* of the third category identified by Lloyd L.J., namely where the alleged contemnor "intends to interfere with the course of justice". Fox L.J. seems to have been content with what Lloyd L.J. had identified as the *first* possible category; that is to say, " . . . the contemnor is liable if he intends to do the act in question, in this case publish the article, even though he does not intend to impede or prejudice the administration of justice." He seems to have focused upon what the editor of *The Independent* knew (*i.e.* that "what was being done . . . was what the court decided should not be done"), and then to have made the objective judgment that it was "the inevitable consequence . . . that the course of justice would be interfered with". Indeed, later in the judgment, Fox L.J. went so far as to say of the editor that "he *must be taken* to have intended the inevitable consequences of his act" (emphasis added).[42]

5–154

The implication in these words (of a possible presumption of intention) is perhaps surprising in view of the fact that it was agreed on all sides that the court was there dealing with *criminal* contempt. Section 8 of the Criminal Justice Act 1967 provides:

5–155

---

[38] [1990] T.L.R. 158, Fox, Ralph Gibson and Nicholls L.JJ., CA (Lexis).
[39] cp. the remarks of Lord Diplock in the context of "honest belief" in *Horrocks v Lowe* [1975] A.C. 135 at 150.
[40] Discussed in para.5–122.
[41] See para.5–123.
[42] And see the remarks of Bingham L.J. cited in para.5–177.

5-155 CHAPTER 5—CONTEMPTS BY PUBLICATION AT COMMON LAW

"A court or jury, in determining whether a person has committed an offence,

(a) shall not be bound in law to infer that he intended or foresaw a result of his actions by reason only of its being a natural and probable result of those actions; but
(b) shall decide whether he did intend or foresee that result by reference to all the evidence drawing such inferences from the evidence as appears proper in the circumstances."

5-156 It is thought that this enactment was intended to restore the law as it had been generally understood prior to the decision of the House of Lords in *DPP v Smith*[43]; namely, that there was no presumption of law that a man intended or foresaw the natural consequences of his acts. No reference was made to this provision by the Court of Appeal, but it is possible to reconcile it with the comment of Fox L.J. by recognising that he was addressing himself to a consequence which he perceived as "inevitable", rather than as merely "natural and probable". Moreover, he would have been entitled under s.8 (b) to draw the (proper) inference that the editor had intended to flout the purpose of the original injunction from "all the evidence", including the "inevitability" he referred to, as well as the intelligence and sophistication of the editor concerned. The use by Fox L.J. of the phrase "must be taken", against this background, probably should be construed as meaning no more than that the Lord Justice came to his own decision on the facts, that the editor did intend; and not that he felt *bound* so to conclude, as a matter of law.

5-157 As has already been pointed out, however, such a process of reasoning would not necessarily lead to an adverse conclusion in the ordinary cases of common law publication contempt, where what is relied upon is a risk to some future or even contingent legal proceedings. In such circumstances, it would not be so easy to speak of an "inevitable consequence".

5-158 The second judgment in the Court of Appeal was that of Ralph Gibson L.J., who began his analysis with the proposition that:

"It is common ground in this appeal that the necessary mental element is the specific intention to perform the acts which, if done with that intent, constitute the offence."

This, it will be observed, also savours of the first of the three categories identified by Lloyd L.J. on the earlier occasion.[44] He too appears to have ruled out the need for the Attorney-General to demonstrate an actual intention to interfere with the administration of justice. It was submitted on behalf of the editor of *The Independent* that, for proof of a specific intent to interfere in the administration of justice, it would have been necessary to prove that the editor "had the sophisticated understanding of the processes of justice necessary for a true realisation by him of the consequences of the publication which he decided should be made."

---

[43] [1961] A.C. 290.
[44] para.5-147.

Ralph Gibson L.J. rejected this proposition, on the basis that "the law makes no requirement of proof of sophisticated understanding". What *was* required was proof of the specific intent to do that which the law defines as amounting to interference with the administration of justice; in this instance, "subverting the order". It did not avail the editor either that he did not "desire" to be in contempt of court, or that he believed that he could not be in contempt (by reason of the absence of an injunction against his own newspaper). What mattered was that he had accepted in cross-examination that there was an identity between what he did and what the Court of Appeal had said should not be done. Morritt J. had therefore been entitled to conclude that the editor knew that publication would inevitably interfere in the proper administration of justice, and that therefore he had intended that it should do so. He knew that he was defeating the court's purpose in making the order; namely, to preserve confidentiality until trial.

Nicholls L.J. emphasised the need for close scrutiny of any court decision "which involves, or seemingly involves, the press being subject to a restriction not previously appreciated". He went on to grapple with the "much vexed question of what is meant by 'intention' in crimes of specific intent when the person in question foresees that his conduct will or may have a consequence", but without desiring it. Having stressed the obscurity in which the meaning of the word "intention" was shrouded by the existing authorities, he went on to say:

" . . . there are cases where the intuitive response of right-thinking people is that even though a person did not desire a particular result, his state of mind does not fall to be distinguished from that of purposive intention. The fact-finding tribunal, normally a jury, personifies right-thinking people in this regard.

It is because the courts have adopted this broad, flexible approach, that further definition is not possible".

This is, perhaps, an unusual approach in the criminal law.[45] On the other hand, when it came to the precise grounds of his decision, Nicholls L.J. founded himself upon the findings of fact which Morritt J. had made in the court below; namely, that the editor of *The Independent*

" . . . knew that he was doing precisely what the court had said should not be done. He knew and accepted that he should not knowingly frustrate the purpose of the court order against another because he would be interfering in the course of justice if he did. He knew that publishing his article would inevitably interfere in the administration of justice . . . ".

He thus concluded that the judge had been entitled to hold that the relevant intention to interfere in the administration had been duly proved. He came to a similar conclusion in relation to the editor of *The Sunday Times*.

Although the case subsequently went to the House of Lords,[46] it had been conceded for the purposes of the hearing that *mens rea* was present, and it was primarily concerned with the matter of principle originally canvassed at the first

---

[45] See para.2–169.
[46] [1992] 1 A.C. 191.

5–162   CHAPTER 5—CONTEMPTS BY PUBLICATION AT COMMON LAW

Court of Appeal hearing in 1987; that is to say, whether or not the publication by the third parties *could* constitute contempt of court.

(b) *Att-Gen v News Group Newspapers plc*

5–163   Another case where an editor's sworn disavowal of any intention to interfere with the administration of justice was rejected was that of *Att-Gen v News Group Newspapers plc*[47] There the Divisional Court was concerned with the much more common situation of a newspaper publishing allegations said to give rise to a risk of prejudice in relation to forthcoming criminal proceedings. Its importance can be gauged from the observation of Bingham L.J. in the later case of *Att-Gen v Sport Newspapers Ltd*[48] where he described it as having had "the effect of enlarging the quasi-criminal liability in a field very recently considered by Parliament".

5–164   He was satisfied that the differently constituted Divisional Court of which he was a member would not be justified in departing from the rule so recently and unambiguously laid down in that case. Although Bingham L.J. in the passage cited had in mind primarily what had been said about the impact of the law of contempt upon proceedings neither begun nor even imminent, the case is also of importance in its approach towards establishing the necessary *mens rea* in publication contempt.

5–165   It was suggested on behalf of the applicant in *Att-Gen v News Group Newspapers plc* that the statements in the first *Spycatcher* hearing[49] were *obiter dicta*, and that the argument on specific intent might at some future stage be re-opened. Watkins L.J. (with whom Mann L.J. agreed) indicated that he would be surprised, in that event, if the law were declared to be that anything less than specific intent would suffice; what was in contemplation was serious criminal misconduct and the possibility of a drastic penalty. Moreover, he regarded the remarks of Lloyd L.J. in the first *Spycatcher* case as persuasive authority to the effect that recklessness would not suffice.[50] On the facts before him, however, he came to the conclusion that the editor concerned had the specific intent required; accordingly the outcome of the case did not turn upon recklessness.

5–166   Yet the case illustrates how difficult it can be in practice for a court to draw a distinction between the two separate processes, on the one hand of making a finding of recklessness and, on the other, of inferring an intent (in the face of a sworn denial) from the surrounding circumstances, "including the foreseeability of the consequences of the conduct".[51] As Lloyd L.J. had put it in the *Spycatcher* case, " . . . the more obvious the interference with the course of justice, the more readily will the requisite intent be inferred."[52]

---

[47] [1989] 1 Q.B. 110 at 126A–B, 130C, DC.
[48] [1991] 1 W.L.R. 1194, [1992] 1 All E.R. 503 at 515g–j, quoted more fully at para.5–97.
[49] [1988] Ch. 333, considered at paras 5–144 *et seq.*
[50] [1989] 1 Q.B. at 126A–C and 128E.
[51] The words of Sir John Donaldson M.R. in *Att-Gen v Newspaper Publishing plc* [1988] Ch. 333 at 374G–375A, with which Watkins and Mann L.JJ. expressed agreement in the later case: [1989] 1 Q.B. 110 at 126C. See also *Schot and Barclay* [1997] 2 Cr.App.R. 383, (1997) 161 J.P. 473.
[52] [1988] Ch. 333 at 383. Cp. *Moloney* [1985] A.C. 905.

The facts were highly unusual in that the editor of the newspaper had authorised publication in March 1986 of articles referring to the alleged rape of an eight-year-old girl by a doctor, in respect of which the proprietors were offering to fund a private prosecution. It was held that, although such proceedings had not been commenced at the time of publication, there was nonetheless sufficient evidence of the necessary intention to prejudice the course of justice (by mentioning material about the doctor which would be inadmissible in criminal proceedings).

In the court's view it had been virtually certain at the relevant time that proceedings would be commenced, and the editor, since he was aware of the fact that his newspaper was financing the private prosecution, knew of that fact. The editor had deposed that the question of contempt had not occurred to him and that he had no intention of causing prejudice. Yet the court drew the "inescapable inference" that he *intended* to persuade his readers (and therefore potential jurors) to take a similar view to his own, namely that the doctor was guilty and ought to be prosecuted; in other words it was trial by newspaper. An editor of his experience could not have failed to foresee the possibility of prejudice.[53]

(c) *Att-Gen v Hislop*

In *Att-Gen v Hislop*,[54] the Court of Appeal was confronted by an application on the part of the Attorney-General based, in the alternative, upon an allegation of strict liability contempt under the 1981 Act, and upon contempt at common law. The case concerned two articles published in a magazine about someone who was already engaged in libel litigation against it, at a stage when the hearing of the action was imminent. It had been held at first instance that although those articles had been published in an attempt to dissuade her from continuing, there had been no improper pressure upon the plaintiff; nor had they given rise to a risk of prejudice so far as potential jurors were concerned. The appeal was allowed, on the basis that the facts disclosed liability on the part of the respondents both under the statute and at common law.

The court concluded that the editor had indeed had the necessary *mens rea* to justify a finding of contempt at common law. In so far as the appropriate test was addressed in the judgments, it seems clear that the Court of Appeal considered that what had to be shown was an intention to impede or prejudice the administration of justice,[55] either by attempting to prejudice the jury, or to "pressure" the litigant herself. The Court of Appeal had no difficulty in concluding that both elements had been made out, and indeed that "a more obvious and blatant attempt to put pressure on [the litigant] would be hard to imagine."[56]

---

[53] Compare the earlier discussion at paras 5–150 *et seq.*; see also *Official Solicitor v News Group Newspapers plc* [1994] 2 F.L.R. 174.
[54] [1991] 1 Q.B. 514.
[55] [1991] 1 Q.B. at 525D, Parker L.J., 532F, Nicholls L.J.
[56] Parker L.J. at 525G.

D. Is an intention to create a risk of prejudice sufficient?

5–171 The case of *Att-Gen v News Group Newspapers plc*[57] was an unusual one, because of the fact that the newspaper was financing the private prosecution, and the court was thus able more readily to find an intention to persuade readers of the guilt of the prospective defendant. On the basis of that finding, there would clearly be an intention to prejudice the course of justice in the particular case; there would also be an intention that the course of justice would be interfered with, in the sense that impermissible influences would be brought to bear.

5–172 Suppose that such a high degree of intentionality cannot be established. Suppose that the editor of a newspaper is in possession of information that might be suggestive of guilt (previous convictions for similar offences, perhaps, but not offences so similar that they are likely to be led in chief by the Crown, and which may therefore be inadmissible in a subsequent trial). Can the editor publish before proceedings become active? It might in that case be said that there is a risk of prejudice, even of serious prejudice; that the editor is aware that there is such a risk and, if he should go on to publish, that he intends to take that risk. Is that degree of intention sufficient? The decision of the Divisional Court in *Att-Gen v Sport Newspapers Ltd*[58] would appear to demonstrate that it would not be. It is an important decision which needs to be fully considered.

5–173 Nevertheless, it has to be assessed in the light of other statements of the law, not least those to be found in the Court of Appeal decision in *Coe v Central TV plc*.[59] Although it was about the grant of an interim injunction, this was the decision of a strong three member court, which came to the conclusion that, for an injunction to be granted, it was necessary for a court to be satisfied to the criminal standard of proof that there was a specific intention of causing a *real risk* of prejudice. Each of these authorities will be considered in turn.

1. *Att-Gen v Sport Newspapers Ltd*[60]

5–174 It was contended on behalf of the Attorney-General that it should be sufficient for an editor to be guilty of contempt if he acted with the intention of creating a risk. The newspaper had published prejudicial material before proceedings had become "active" even though the police had requested that the suspect's antecedents should not be made public. The suspect (in the case of a rape-murder) had previously been convicted of attempted rape and of the full offence, but his whereabouts were unknown at the time the article was published.

5–175 Bingham L.J. put the matter in this way[61]:

"Mr Havers, making this application on behalf of the Attorney-General, submitted that

---

[57] [1989] 1 Q.B. 110.
[58] [1991] 1 W.L.R. 1194 at 1199–1200, [1992] 1 All E.R. 503 at 508h–j, Bingham L.J.
[59] [1994] E.M.L.R. 433, considered in more detail at paras 6–33 and 6–38. See also Bingham L.J. in *Att-Gen v Sport Newspapers Ltd* [1991] 1 W.L.R. 1194 at 1208–9, [1992] 1 All E.R. 503 at 516–18.
[60] For the facts of which, see para.5–71.
[61] [1991] 1 W.L.R. 1194 at 1199–1200, [1992] 1 All E.R. 503 at 508h–j.

a contempt at common law is established if it is shown, on the criminal burden (*sic*) of proof and with reference to the date of publication (1) that publication of the material complained of created a real risk of prejudice to the due administration of justice; and (2) that the alleged contemnor published the material *with the specific intent of causing such risk*. This common law offence could be committed, Mr Havers argued, if proceedings, were imminent and even if they were not.

Mr Collins, for the respondents accepted the substance of this proposition . . . " (emphasis added).

Bingham L.J summarised his interpretation of the purpose of s.6(c) as follows[62]:

"In my view section 6(c) was intended to preserve what was understood to be the existing law, that a publisher was liable in contempt for an intentionally prejudicial publication made at a time when proceedings were imminent."

He developed the point by reference back to counsel's submissions, including that as to the requirements for *mens rea*:

"It must in my judgment follow that, if the risk and the intention referred to as (1) and (2) at the outset of this section are established, contempt may be committed even though proceedings are neither in existence nor imminent. In short, I accept Mr Havers' submission".

He later, however, expressed the *mens rea* element in quite different terms from those earlier quoted from the submissions of counsel[63]:

"The parties were agreed that the applicant must show that the respondents' publication was specifically intended to impede or prejudice the due administration of justice. Such an intent need not be expressly avowed or admitted but can be inferred from all the circumstances, including the foreseeability of the consequences of the conduct, although the probability of the consequence taken to have been foreseen must be little short of overwhelming before it will suffice to establish the necessary intent. But this need not be the sole intention of the contemnor, and intention is to be distinguished from motive or desire.[64] I base this brief and, and I hope uncontroversial, summary on the valuable discussion of this question in *Att-Gen v News Group Newspapers plc* [1989] Q.B. 110, 125–127, and the citations there made."

Although he thought that the issues were finely balanced, he came ultimately to the conclusion that intent was not proved beyond a reasonable doubt[65]:

"If proof of recklessness were enough, the answer might be different, but it is not. On the facts here I cannot be satisfied that the second respondent intended to prejudice the fair conduct of proceedings the very existence of which he regarded as speculative and remote".

---

[62] *ibid.* at 1206–7, [1992] 1 All E.R. 503 at 515c–e. See *Att-Gen v Hislop* [1991] 1 Q.B. 514, where proceedings were brought both in respect of common law and strict liability contempt, even though the proceedings were active.
[63] [1991] 1 W.L.R. 1194 at 1208F–G, [1992] 1 All E.R. 503 at 516g–h.
[64] This passage was cited and followed in *R. v Judd* [1995] C.O.D. 15 at 16, where it was said to represent the law in relation to non-publication contempts also.
[65] *ibid.* at 1209F–G.

5–179 But this exposition is not without difficulty, because Bingham L.J. seems to be approving two different propositions. The submission of Mr Havers (which had apparently been accepted) was to the effect that the intention to create a *risk* would be sufficient. So far as the editor's attitude to the interference with the course of justice is concerned, this amounts to no more than advertent recklessness.[66]

5–180 By contrast, in the final passage cited above, where recklessness was expressly rejected as a criterion, he is saying that there must be an intention as to the consequence; namely, that it must be shown that the editor realised as a matter of virtual certainty that the interests of justice would be impeded or prejudiced. Only then would it be open to a court to infer that he had the relevant intention. Moreover, he also seems to attribute this proposition to both counsel, at one point,[67] where he says that the parties were agreed on the need for the applicant to show that the publication was "specifically intended to impede or prejudice the due administration of justice".

5–181 This more stringent test appeared to find favour with Hodgson J., who identified the *mens rea* required, in the following terms:

> "intending thereby to achieve a miscarriage of justice in ... any judicial proceedings".

If this, however, really does represent the threshold that the Attorney-General had to achieve, it is not surprising that liability was not established. Indeed, it would be exceedingly difficult ever to prove contempt of this kind at common law.

5–182 It is true that an inference of intention can be drawn from the surrounding circumstances, and it need not be expressed or avowed. Yet, as Bingham L.J. had appeared to recognise (in the passage quoted above), the probability of the consequence taken to have been foreseen would have to be "little short of overwhelming". It would appear that this criterion was fulfilled in the *Spycatcher* litigation described above, because the consequences of the publications in question led "inevitably" to the frustration of the court's purpose in having granted the original injunction, and in *Att-Gen v News Group Newspapers plc*[68] because of the special factor of the intention to fund the private prosecution and the editor's awareness of that. Moreover, in *Att-Gen v Hislop*,[69] the Court of Appeal had no difficulty in concluding that there had been a blatant attempt to put pressure upon a litigant by those whom she was engaged in suing for libel. These cases were therefore most unusual, in their different ways, and need not perhaps give rise to the anxiety that courts would in more commonplace circumstances readily infer an intention to interfere in the course of justice.

5–183 There would be much more cause for concern if the right test to apply was whether the journalist concerned intended no more than the creation of a *risk* of

---

[66] Considered at para.5–131.
[67] *ibid.* at 1208F.
[68] [1989] Q.B. 110.
[69] [1991] 1 Q.B. 514, discussed paras 5–169 *et seq.*

causing such interference (in the sense of recognising and being willing to countenance such a risk as being inherent in the act of publication). Yet not only did Bingham L.J. appear at one point in his judgment to accept that submission, but it also appears to have been quite expressly adopted by the Court of Appeal in *Coe v Central TV plc*.[70]

2. Coe v Central TV plc

Although this was a case about whether an interlocutory injunction should be granted to prevent publication of an apprehended common law contempt, and certain aspects of the case were said not to have been fully argued,[71] there is no doubt that on the issue of *mens rea* the court did have cited to it relevant passages from the two Divisional Court cases already considered, as well as from the first Court of Appeal hearing in the *Spycatcher* litigation.[72]   5–184

The facts concerned the proposed broadcast of a television programme on the subject of the plaintiff's alleged activities as a distributor of computer pornography. The police executed a search warrant, accompanied by a film crew, who were filming as the police seized material in the plaintiff's possession. Part of the message of the programme was to have been the suggestion that existing laws were inadequate to deal with activities of this kind.   5–185

There was no arrest, and no criminal proceedings could be said to be "active" under the provisions of the Contempt of Court Act 1981, but the plaintiff sought an interlocutory injunction from the court (although, as Glidewell L.J. acknowledged in his judgment, in practice it would be a final order). He based himself upon the contention that such a broadcast would constitute common law contempt. The injunction was originally granted on an emergency basis, but was discharged later the same day by the Court of Appeal, who gave reasons three days later.   5–186

It was then explained that the test which the court had applied was whether or not they had been satisfied to the criminal standard of proof of the necessary elements, namely that: 5–187

"(i) the publication ... will create a real risk of prejudice to the administration of justice;
(ii) that the defendants will publish that material with a specific intent of causing that risk."

This test was not satisfied on the facts of the case, but it will be immediately recognised that the threshold is considerably lower than that identified in either of the decisions of the Court of Appeal in the course of the *Spycatcher*   5–188

---

[70] [1994] E.M.L.R. 422 at 441.
[71] In particular, it was said by Glidewell L.J. that argument was not addressed to the court on whether it was necessary to prove that proceedings were "imminent".
[72] [1988] Ch. 333.

litigation,[73] as well as that propounded by Watkins L.J. in *Att-Gen v News Group Newspapers plc*. Yet even this latter case was described by Bingham L.J. as having " . . . very serious implications in those cases, perhaps increasingly common, where reporters are concerned to highlight an alleged crime, to point an accusing finger at an identified culprit and to stimulate a demand for prosecution."[74] The *Coe v Central TV plc* case concerned exactly those circumstances, although the lower threshold may be said to give rise to even more serious implications for investigative journalism. It was fortunate from the respondents' point of view that in the particular circumstances the possibility of any criminal proceedings happened to be a matter for speculation only.

5–189 In a case where the law provided a more readily available criminal offence, the outcome might have been different. In a situation of that kind, it is not difficult to imagine that investigative journalists might be placed under a serious inhibition if all that were necessary was to demonstrate a willingness on their part, even incidentally to the main purpose of their programme,[75] to countenance some degree of risk of interference in the criminal proceedings that might well follow their investigations (especially if the prospect of such proceedings could be described as being merely "on the cards"[76] at that stage, rather than actually "imminent").

5–190 It is clear that the law on *mens rea* for common law contempt remains something of a "minefield" (to use the expression of Sir John Donaldson M.R. in the first of the *Spycatcher* hearings in the Court of Appeal). The central difficulty emerging from the review of these authorities is that of reconciling the judicial *dicta* which set a high threshold, requiring a positive intention to interfere with the course of justice, and those such as are contained in the judgment of Glidewell L.J. in *Coe* and in at least part of the judgment of Bingham L.J. in *Att-Gen v Sport Newspapers Ltd*.[77]

5–191 It is true that Lord Hailsham in the case of *Hyam v DPP*[78] seemed to think that the decision to take a risk was equivalent to an intention for the purposes of the law of murder. This does not, however, represent what is now the generally accepted approach towards the establishing of intention in the criminal law.[79]

5–192 The principal problem is to reconcile the proposition that recklessness will not suffice to establish the requisite *mens rea* for contempt at common law, at least in relation to publication in the media, with the proposition espoused in some judicial statements to the effect that an intention to create a risk of prejudice or impediment *will* suffice.

---

[73] Discussed at para.5–141, paras 5–153 *et seq.* and para.6–126.
[74] *Att-Gen v Sport Newspapers Ltd* [1991] 1 W.L.R. at 1207E–F, [1992] 1 All E.R. 503 at 515g–j.
[75] See paras 4–293 *et seq.* For discussion of the statutory protection afforded by s.5 of the Contempt of Court Act 1981 to the publication of prejudicial material which is merely "incidental".
[76] See the discussion of this term in para.5–96.
[77] [1991] 1 W.L.R. at 1200A–B and 1207G–H, [1992] 1 All E.R. 503 at 515 g–j.
[78] [1975] A.C. 55.
[79] See the cases on murder cited above, para.5–120, n.98.

Moreover, it is by no means clear to what extent the principles relevant in publication contempts are also applicable to other forms of common law contempt. For example, it was said in *Att-Gen v Newspaper Publishing plc*[80] that to hold that recklessness could found liability for contempt would be inconsistent with the purpose underlying the Contempt of Court Act 1981; and particularly with the policy of shifting the balance in favour of freedom of speech, and addressing the considerations which led to the criticisms of English common law to be found in the decision of the European Court of Human Rights in *Sunday Times v United Kingdom*.[81] Those factors do not seem to have any direct bearing upon other forms of common law contempt.

5-193

Yet there is a trend in the authorities suggesting that the test to be applied is the same for all forms of common law contempt.[82]

5-194

E. Practical difficulties in differentiating intention and recklessness

In theory the distinction between the process of finding recklessness and that of finding specific intent is clear. In practice it is not easy, in the context of experienced newspaper editors, to envisage circumstances in which such a person would be reckless without the court going on to conclude, from the obviousness of the risk, that he *must* have intended to interfere. This may be inherent in the unusual nature of the *actus reus* in contempt, involving as it sometimes can such imprecise concepts as creating a *risk* or *tending* to prejudice. If such a risk is truly obvious, it will be difficult to avoid the conclusion that the journalist in fact intended to create it.

5-195

The point is illustrated by the findings of Morritt J. in *Att-Gen v Newspaper Publishing plc*.[83] He was concerned to establish in the light of the evidence of the editor of *The Sunday Times* (Andrew Neil) whether he had formed the relevant intention at the time when he decided to publish extracts from *Spycatcher* notwithstanding the existence of an injunction against *The Guardian* and *The Observer*. He concluded that it would be an inevitable consequence of putting the material into the public domain, which Mr Neil both appreciated and accepted, that the confidentiality in it would be damaged or destroyed. Despite this, Mr Neil had told the court that whether he was interfering with the administration of justice was not a matter that ever crossed his mind. The judge analysed his thought processes as follows:

5-196

"No doubt that is what he thought when he gave his evidence but I do not accept the answer as correctly portraying his state of mind on 12 July 1987 [the date of publication]. When he gave his evidence he knew of the decision of the Court of Appeal

---

[80] [1988] Ch. 333 at 382G–H; "If we were to hold that, where the strict liability rule does not apply . . . , the publisher might nevertheless be liable if he is reckless, we would certainly not be furthering the statutory purpose."
[81] (1979) 2 E.H.R.R. 245.
[82] *Att-Gen v Judd* [1995] C.O.D. 15; *Schot and Barclay* [1997] 2 Cr.App.R. 383, (1997) 161 J.P. 473; *Att-Gen v Newspaper Publishing plc* [1997] 1 W.L.R. 926, [1997] 3 All E.R. 159.
[83] [1989] 1 F.S.R. 457. See also *Att-Gen v News Group Newspapers plc* [1989] Q.B. 110; *Official Solicitor v News Group Newspapers plc* [1994] 2 F.L.R. 174.

5–196 CHAPTER 5—CONTEMPTS BY PUBLICATION AT COMMON LAW

on the preliminary issue and was equating interference in the administration of justice with contempt of court, liability for which he had always sought to avoid. But on 12 July 1987 he thought he could not be in contempt of court whatever his intention.

I have no doubt that it was the intention of Mr Neil to interfere in the administration of justice by publishing extracts from *Spycatcher*. He did not wish to be in contempt of court and because there was no injunction against the *Sunday Times* he believed genuinely, but wrongly, that he could not be in contempt of court. But, for the reasons that I have given, that cannot in the circumstances be a defence. Likewise, his belief that publication in the United States would cause greater and more wholesale damage or destruction to the Attorney General's case and therefore a more substantial interference in the administration of justice, did not alter his intention."

5–197 It might be thought, however, that a true analysis of the editor's state of mind would lead to the conclusion that it was actually one of recklessness. In particular, his evidence was encapsulated in the sentence: "My intention was to put Wright into the public domain in Britain regardless of the consequences which were not my concern provided my legal advice was that I was not breaking the law."

5–198 Despite these conceptual difficulties, recent authority has re-emphasised the need for a specific intention to interfere with the administration of justice. In *Att-Gen v Newspaper Publishing plc*, Lord Bingham C.J. under the heading "*Mens rea*" made the following observation[84]:

"Both parties accepted the test propounded by Sir John Donaldson M.R. in *Attorney-General v Newspaper Publishing plc* [1988] Ch. 333, 374–375. To show contempt, the Attorney-General must establish, to the criminal standard of proof, that 'the conduct complained of is specifically intended to impede or prejudice the administration of justice. Such an intent need not be expressly avowed or admitted, but can be inferred from all the circumstances, including the foreseeability of the consequences of the conduct. Nor need it be the sole intention of the contemnor. An intent is to be distinguished from motive or desire: see per Lord Bridge of Harwich in *Reg. v Moloney* [1985] A.C. 905, 926.'"

5–199 This is consistent with the comments made in *Re Lonrho*[85]:

"If the publication of 'The Observer' special edition did create a risk that the course of justice in Lonrho's appeal would be impeded or prejudiced, there would be no difficulty in inferring that those responsible for the publication intended that consequence. But if the publication created no such risk, as we concluded in considering the question of statutory contempt, common law contempt ... could only be established if those responsible for the publication intended it to have consequences affecting the appellate proceedings which it neither achieved nor was ever likely to achieve."

The passage nevertheless comes close to recognising that whether or not *mens rea* can be established is an issue upon which the conclusion is likely to be conditioned largely by the decision on *actus reus*.

---

[84] [1997] 1 W.L.R. 926 at 937, 3 All E.R. 159 at 169e–g. See also *London Borough of Harrow v Johnstone* [1997] 1 W.L.R. 459 at 468–469.
[85] [1990] 2 A.C. 154 at 213G, Lord Bridge.

F. Conclusions as to the modern law of *mens rea*

While the law of *mens rea* in common law contempt cannot yet be definitively stated for the reasons discussed above, it is nevertheless possible to set out some basic propositions upon which it would be difficult to show any significant dissent in the case law:

1. The issue must be judged as at the time of publication.[86]

2. It is necessary to establish for the purpose of liability for publication contempt at common law an intention to impede or prejudice the administration of justice, either in relation to particular proceedings or more generally.

3. It is possible to find proved the presence of such an intention, even in the face of sworn denials, on the basis of inference from the surrounding circumstances.

4. A legitimate factor to take into account, in assessing those circumstances, is the extent to which adverse consequences for the administration of justice would be foreseeable at the time of the relevant publication.

5. It seems that the consequence taken to have been foreseen must be "inevitable", or perhaps the probability of it "little short of overwhelming", before the necessary intent may be taken to be established (or, as it is sometimes put, the alleged contemnor *must have* intended the consequence).

6. It is by no means the case that the alleged contemnor would have to have *only* that intention.

7. Intention in this context is to be distinguished from motive or desire.

8. Recklessness is not overtly acknowledged to be sufficient to establish the requisite *mens rea* (although if the *dicta*[87] suggesting that it will suffice for an alleged contemnor to intend merely to countenance a risk of interference are indeed correct, then it is difficult to see how this can be distinguished from advertent recklessness).[88]

9. Whereas journalists have the protection of a s.5 defence when they are at risk of a finding of strict liability under the Act, it is doubtful whether any such escape route would be available in the common law context once

---

[86] *R. v Evening Standard Co Ltd* [1954] 1 Q.B. 578, 582, Lord Goddard C.J.; *Att-Gen v English* [1983] A.C. 116, 141F–G, Lord Diplock; *Att-Gen v MGN Ltd* [1997] 1 All E.R. 567; *Gisborne Herald Co Ltd v Solicitor-General* [1995] 3 N.Z.L.R. 563; *Att-Gen v Guardian Newspapers* [1999] E.M.L.R. 904 at 915, Collins J.
[87] See, *e.g. Coe v Central TV plc* [1994] E.M.L.R. 422 at 441.
[88] See para.5–131.

mens rea and *actus reus* have been established (which may cause considerable hardship to investigative journalists if it truly is sufficient for establishing *mens rea* to demonstrate merely a willingness to countenance a *risk* of prejudice or impediment).[89]

IV. IS THERE A GENERAL DEFENCE OF FAIR COMMENT/PUBLIC INTEREST?

5–201 In the Court of Appeal in the *Distillers* case,[90] Lord Denning M.R. observed that the facts of that case were "unique" and went on to suggest that " . . . the *public interest* in having it discussed outweighs the prejudice which might thereby be occasioned to a party to the dispute" (emphasis added). He also expressed the view that when *The Sunday Times* submitted the article to the Attorney-General in draft its publication would not have amounted to a contempt of court. The reason he gave was that " . . . it dealt with a matter of the greatest *public interest* and contained comments which the newspaper honestly believed to be true"[91] (emphasis added).

5–202 It is submitted that these general words, which might taken alone suggest the existence of some general "public interest" defence in contempt at common law, should be treated with the greatest caution. It is necessary, in particular, to remember the words of Lord Morris in the same case in the House of Lords,[92] to the effect that there is no such thing as a justifiable contempt. Moreover, the context in which Lord Denning made this comment was that of matters which had been discussed in Parliament. Since the subject matter had been permitted to be raised in Parliament, notwithstanding its own *sub judice* rules, Lord Denning commented, "So why should not we in these courts also permit it?"

5–203 As has been observed already,[93] there may well be strong policy arguments for permitting material to be published in newspapers, even though it may give rise to a *prima facie* case of strict liability contempt, provided the publication consists genuinely of a report of Parliamentary proceedings. Indeed, such a report might now well attract a defence under s.5 of the 1981 Act.[94] That is a very different matter, however, from a general defence in the context of contempt of either fair comment or of public interest. It would now be unwise to proceed on the basis that any such publication of prejudicial material would attract a defence, on either basis, which fell outside the scope of the provisions of s.5.

---

[89] "There can be no such thing as a justifiable contempt of court": see Lord Morris of Borth-y-Gest [1974] A.C. 372 at 302D. See also *Solicitor-General v Wellington Newspapers Ltd* [1995] 1 N.Z.L.R. 45.
[90] *Att-Gen v Times Newspapers Ltd* [1973] Q.B. 710, [1973] 1 All E.R. 815 at 821.
[91] [1973] Q.B. at 741G.
[92] [1974] A.C. 273 at 302D.
[93] See para.4–332.
[94] Discussed paras 4–293 *et seq.*

V. SCANDALISING THE COURT[95]

A. Introduction

It is still in theory a contempt to publish matter which "scandalises" the court, although Lord Diplock in *Secretary of State for Defence v Guardian Newspapers Ltd*[96] referred to this as being "virtually obsolescent".[97] Broadly speaking what this principle would prohibit is scurrilous abuse of a judge *qua* judge, or of a court, and unwarranted attacks upon the integrity or impartiality of a judge or court. It is unclear precisely what degree of *mens rea* is required,[98] and what defences might be relevant, in particular whether those of fair comment[99] and truth[1] would be available.

5–204

The mischief is the undermining of public confidence in the administration of justice.[2] In the language of the High Court of Australia[3]:

5–205

"The authority of the law rests on public confidence, and it is important for the stability of society that the confidence of the public should not be shaken by baseless attacks on the integrity or impartiality of courts or judges".

Particular importance is nowadays attached to such attacks being "baseless" or "unwarranted". Strangely, what is more likely to undermine public confidence, on the face of it, are attacks which have some foundation in truth. In such circumstances, however, what is required is not the penalising of criticism but the removal of those who are unworthy of judicial office, so that public confidence may be maintained or restored.

5–206

Proceedings for contempt of this kind are rare, the courts within the United Kingdom preferring to ignore attacks upon themselves.[4] The modern approach to

5–207

---

[95] C. Walker, "Scandalising in the Eighties" (1985) 101 L.Q.R. 359; D. Hay, "Contempt by Scandalising the court: A Political History of the First Hundred Years" (1987) 25(3) Osgoode Hall Law Journal 431; H. Burmester, "Scandalizing the judges" (1985) 15 Melb. U.L.R. 313; Frank Bates, "Scandalising the court: Some Peculiarly Australian Developments" (1994) 13 Civil Justice Quarterly 241; D. Pannick, *Judges*, (1987), pp.109–18; O. Litaba, "Does the 'Offence' of Scandalising the court Have a Valid Place in the Law of Modern Day Australia?" (2003) 8 Deakin L.R. 113; M. Addo, "Are Judges beyond criticism under article 10 of the European Convention on Human Rights?" (1997) 47 I.C.L.Q. 425.
[96] [1985] A.C. 339 at 347A.
[97] Indeed Lord Morris in *McLeod v St. Aubyn* [1899] A.C. 549 at 561 had declared scandalising contempt to be "obsolete in this country", but ironically the jurisdiction was exercised the following year, in *R. v Gray* [1900] 2 Q.B. 36. See also *Att-Gen v Scriven*, CO 1632/99 (Smith Bernal) where Simon Brown L.J. commented "The whole question of scandalising the judiciary or the courts, or however it is put, is perhaps somewhat remote from present day life." And see M. Addo, *Freedom of Expression and the Criticism of Judges: a Comparative Study of European Legal Standards* (2000).
[98] Discussed at paras 5–244 *et seq.*
[99] para.5–256.
[1] para.5–253.
[2] *Solicitor-General v Radio Avon Ltd* [1978] 1 N.Z.L.R. 225. It must be proved that there is a real risk that public confidence will be so undermined.
[3] *Gallagher v Durack* (1983) 152 C.L.R. 238 at 234.
[4] One of the most frequently cited judgments in this context is that of Lord President Clyde in *Johnson v Grant*, 1923 S.C. 789, 790, cited at para.16–6.

5–207   CHAPTER 5—CONTEMPTS BY PUBLICATION AT COMMON LAW

what would once have been regarded as a form of scandalising, namely by way of unjustified attacks on judicial *competence*, is well encapsulated in Lord Ackner's advice to newly-appointed judges[5]:

> "I said that I thought that the soundest advice was to 'grin and bear it', that they should bear in mind today's newspaper is tomorrow's fire lighter and that this was one of the occupational hazards of being a judge".

5–208   On the other hand, where the allegations are sufficiently serious in relation to the reputation or authority of individual judges, there are civil remedies available. In recent years, there have been a significant number of libel actions over allegations of either incompetence or bias. None of these has come to trial, and settlements have always so far been reached with the judge concerned, sometimes involving the publication of an apology.[6] In addition, nowadays, judges by convention have rather greater freedom to defend themselves[7] and answer their critics, since the relaxation of the so-called Kilmuir Rules.[8]

5–209   Even when this form of contempt was more regularly invoked, the test applied was whether the criticism or attack raised a real risk of interference with the due administration of justice by seriously lowering the authority of the judge or court.[9] It was not sufficient that the publication libelled a judge, since the purpose

---

[5] "'Cet animal est mechant': One Judge's view of the Media" (1992) Holdsworth Club 1 at p.19. "A wry smile is, I think, our usual response and the more extravagant the allegations, the more ludicrous they sound": *Att-Gen v Scriven*, CO 1632/99 (Smith Bernal) *per* Simon Brown L.J. It was said, similarly, in *Bennett v London Borough of Southwark* [2002] EWCA Civ 223, [2002] I.C.R. 881 at [56], that the striking out of proceedings before an employment tribunal had been "disproportionate to the necessary metaphorical shrugging of the shoulders and getting on with it" (*per* Ward L.J.). This was in relation to an apparent allegation of bias against the tribunal by an (unqualified) advocate.

[6] For example, Garland J., in a letter to the editor, (1996) 146 New Law J. at p.1070, mentioned a "very satisfactory apology from Channel 4 . . . The judiciary too can take action when the media go too far". The *Sunday Times*, August 8, 1993, reported that it had paid damages to a judge as the result of an article describing the judge as "guilty of jarring errors of judgment, stupidity, crassness and blatant prejudice and an affront to human reason". The newspaper accepted that this was "based on an inaccurate report of his comments" and that the article "quoted selectively from, misrepresented and took out of context what he said". The article had also "wrongly stated that he had been 'active in business' while at the Bar. This would have been a clear breach of the rules of the Bar. He has, in fact, never been in business in his life".

[7] In a letter to *The Times*, October 23, 1993 Lord Woolf warned that the effects of such freedom were not wholly beneficial: "If judges feel that they will receive the same over-exposure as I have received, I fear that they may well be deterred from making a useful contribution to the discussion." In "Judges under Attack" [1994] N.Z.L.J. 359 at 366, Justice Michael Kirby describes the judge as a "shackled combatant" in self-defence against media attacks. See also the same author, "Attacks on Judges—A Universal Phenomenon" (1998) 72 A.L.J. 599. Justice Kirby was himself attacked under the cloak of Parliamentary Privilege; see E. Campbell and M. Groves, "Attacks on judges under parliamentary privilege: a sorry Australian episode" [2002] P.L. 626.

[8] The Rules were relaxed in a letter from the Lord Chancellor, Lord Mackay of Clashfern to the Lord Chief Justice, Lord Lane, on October 16, 1989. In it, he gave an explanation of his view that "it must be left to the judges themselves to decide whether, and on what conditions, they should give interviews to journalists or appear on radio or television". The text of the original Kilmuir rules may be found in A.W. Bradley, "Judges and the Media: the Kilmuir Rules" [1986] P.L. 383, 384. See also *Press reporting of judges' sentencing remarks,* L.C.D. press release (57/97) published on March 26, 1997 which was intended to provide assistance for judges dealing with media comment, perhaps especially in the context of uninformed criticism about sentencing.

[9] *Re a Special Reference from the Bahama Islands* [1893] A.C. 138.

of the jurisdiction was not the protection of an individual judge but rather the protection of the administration of justice itself.[10]

B. The residual need for such protection

1. *The recommendations of the Phillimore Committee*

Attacks upon the integrity of the judiciary and upon the administration of justice generally are perhaps not so lightly dismissed as attacks upon individual competence or judgment. The question whether there needs to be legal constraint in respect of such attacks has been considered by advisory bodies on two occasions. Both concluded that the scandalising law should be abolished. Nevertheless, it was not suggested that the law of defamation was adequate to meet all the problems which they addressed. 5–210

The Phillimore Committee concluded that some additional legal restraint was required, for two reasons[11]: 5–211

"First, this branch of the law of contempt is concerned with the protection of the administration of justice, and especially the preservation of public confidence in its honesty and impartiality; it is only incidentally, if at all, concerned with the personal reputations of judges. Moreover, some damaging attacks, for example upon an unspecified group of judges, may not be capable of being made the subject of libel proceedings at all. Secondly, judges commonly feel constrained by their position not to take action in reply to criticism, and they have no proper forum in which to do so such as other public figures may have. These considerations lead us to the conclusion that there is need for an effective remedy against imputations of improper or corrupt judicial conduct."

They were, however, of the opinion that the majority of such cases ought not to be dealt with summarily, and recommended a specific indictable offence, for which purpose legislation would be necessary.[12] Even if such an offence were created, however, the Committee's view was that there would still be a need for a judge to be able to deal summarily with a contemnor who abused him in the course of proceedings in open court.[13] 5–212

2. *Recommendations of the Law Commission*

The Law Commission recommended[14] that statute should provide for the following offence which was set out in clause 13 of a Draft Bill appended to the Report: 5–213

---

[10] *ibid.* And see *McLeod v St. Aubyn* [1899] A.C. 549 at 561; *Johnson v Grant* (1923) S.C. 789 at 790.
[11] paras 162–164. See the fuller discussion of the Phillimore recommendations at 16–284.
[12] See the comments of Lord Keith in *Re Lonrho* [1990] 2 A.C. 154 at 177C, where he made it clear that contempt ought not to be dealt with by way of indictment. See also *R. v D* [1984] A.C. 778 at 806, Lord Brandon.
[13] See the discussion in paras 10–46 *et seq.*
[14] Report, *Offences Relating to Interference with the Course of Justice*, Law. Com. No.96, 1979, H.C. 213.

5–213 CHAPTER 5—CONTEMPTS BY PUBLICATION AT COMMON LAW

"13(1) Subject to subsection (2) below, if—

(a) a person publishes or distributes a false statement alleging

(i) that a court or tribunal or such a body as is mentioned in s.2(1)(c) above is corrupt in the performance of its functions, or
(ii) that any judge, magistrate, arbitrator or person holding a statutory enquiry, any member or officer of a court or tribunal or any member of such a body as is mentioned in s.2(1)(c) above has been corrupt in the performance of his functions in relation to any judicial proceedings which have come before him and

(b) at the time when he publishes or distributes it he intends it to be taken as true but knows it to be false or is reckless whether it is false he is guilty of an offence.

(2) Publication or distribution of such a statement outside England and Wales is not an offence under this section."

5–214 This proposal was directed towards preventing an unwarranted loss of confidence by the public in the administration of justice as a whole. The Commission took the view that allegations falling short of corruption were unlikely so to impair public confidence in the administration of justice.

5–215 The reference to draft clause 2(1)(c) embraced the bodies there referred to, namely "any other body of persons having by virtue of any rule of law authority to hear, receive and examine evidence". Such a definition would appear to extend the scope of the proposed offence beyond those persons currently protected by the law of contempt.[15] These provisions did not become law.

3. *The present position*

5–216 The Phillimore Committee recommended that, if the matter were to be dealt with by way of a new statutory offence, then this should replace the common law relating to scandalising.[16] When Parliament came to enact some of the Committee's proposals, however, this suggestion was not implemented. Thus, at any rate in theory, it remains necessary to consider the pre-existing common law. There has been little modern authority in England and Wales, largely because this form of contempt has fallen into disuse. Indeed, any resort to it would now have to be justified as being necessary in a democratic society "for maintaining the authority and impartiality of the judiciary".[17]

5–217 It has been suggested[18] that the law of scandalising is incompatible with the European Convention on Human Rights, since it may be unable to meet the test that restrictions require the law to be a response to a "pressing social need":

---

[15] See *Att-Gen v BBC* [1981] A.C. 303. See also s.19 of the Contempt of Court Act 1981, set out at para.13–3, and the discussion in ch.13.
[16] para.164.
[17] European Convention on Human Rights, Art.10(2).
[18] D. Feldman, *Civil Liberties and Human Rights in England and Wales* (2nd ed., 2003), at pp.970–1.

"Is it a response to a pressing social need, in the conditions current in English society? It is hard to see any pressing social need which demands general protection for the judges against public comment. Even given the sensitivity of the European Court of Human Rights to local needs, it is hard to see how the law on scandalizing could be said to be proportionate to the aim pursued. Not only is it counter-democratic, but it is also highly unlikely to achieve its purpose: in modern English conditions, the more thoroughly expression is suppressed, the more likely it is to fuel, rather than allay, suspicions about the conduct and attitudes of the judges".

Nevertheless, that the application of such a principle can sometimes be justified is demonstrated by the case of *De Haes and Gijesels v Belgium*.[19] The European Court acknowledged that the domestic courts, as guarantors of justice whose role is fundamental in a state based upon the rule of law, must enjoy public confidence. They must accordingly be protected from *unfounded* and destructive attacks.[20]

Most of the modern authorities, however, are to be found in Commonwealth cases, which need to be construed against the political and social circumstances prevailing in the relevant jurisdiction. Nevertheless, all of these cases purport to derive their authority from the common law principles established in the eighteenth century.

C. Origins of the modern law: eighteenth century developments[21]

Following an earlier revival,[22] the jurisdiction was confirmed by Lord Hardwicke L.C. in *St. James's Evening Post*.[23] Although that decision was principally concerned with a publication calculated to prejudice the fair trial of a pending case, Lord Hardwicke remarked that "one kind of contempt is, scandalizing the court itself".

This was followed in 1765, when Almon published libels upon the Court of King's Bench and Lord Mansfield C.J., in relation to the conduct of that court in the General Warrants cases involving John Wilkes. He was proceeded against summarily, but the proceedings eventually failed on technical grounds, and judgments as to the scope of the substantive law were never formally delivered. Wilmot J., however, preserved the judgment he had prepared, and this has since been regarded as a leading authority on this aspect of the law,[24] for which the rationale was clearly explained:

---

[19] (1997) 25 E.H.R.R. 1.
[20] This was thought to be especially important in view of the fact that judges are subject to a need for discretion, which may inhibit them from replying to criticism: *ibid.*, 52–3.
[21] The early history of contempt by scandalising is dealt with at paras 1–57 *et seq.*
[22] *R. v Wilkin* (1722) K.B. Easter 8 George I; *R. v Colbatch* (1723) K.B. Easter 9, George I; *R. v Wiatt* (1723) 8 Mod. 123, 88 E.R. 96; *R. v Lawley* (1731) Mich 5, George II—all contained in the Appendix to the Report of the Select Committee on *Burdett's Case*, 8 St. Tr. 14.
[23] (1742) 2 Atk. 469, 26 E.R. 642, discussed at para.1–62.
[24] *Wilmot's Notes* 243, 97 E.R. 94. See Fox, *The History of Contempt of Court: the Form of Trial and the Mode of Punishment* (1927); D. Hay, "Contempt by Scandalising the court: A Political History of the First Hundred Years" (1987) 25 Osgoode Hall Law Journal 431.

5-221

"The arraignment of the justice of the Judges, is arraigning the King's justice; it is an impeachment of his wisdom and goodness in the choice of his Judges, and excites in the minds of the people a general dissatisfaction with all judicial determinations, and indisposes their minds to obey them; and whenever men's allegiance to the laws is so fundamentally shaken, it is the most fatal and most dangerous obstruction of justice, and, in my opinion, calls out for a more rapid and immediate redress than any other obstruction whatsoever; not for the sake of the Judges, as private individuals, but because they are the channels by which the King's justice is conveyed to the people. To be impartial, and to be universally thought so, are both absolutely necessary for the giving justice that free, open, and uninterrupted current, which it has, for many ages, found all over this kingdom, and which so eminently distinguishes and exalts it above all nations upon the earth."

5-222 This passage has been quoted frequently, but it may be doubted whether its reasoning has survived intact into an age when judges are more used to vigorous public debate. In the eighteenth century the judiciary were much exercised by the proper controls that should be set upon the newly-established press, and the tradition of the virulent seventeenth century pamphleteers was by no means dead. It is noteworthy that since Wilmot J.'s judgment was written there have been relatively few examples of such proceedings.[25]

D. Later developments

5-223 The next case of significance is that of *R. v Gray*.[26] At the commencement of a prosecution for obscene libel, Darling J. warned the press that they would have no protection in law if they reported the obscenity as part of the proceedings. He added that if his advice was not heeded he would make it his business to see that the law in that respect was enforced. After the trial had been concluded, the *Birmingham Daily Argus* published an article headlined "A Defender of Decency", in which the judge's actions were criticised.

5-224 The article was personally abusive to the judge, describing him as "an impudent little man in horse-hair" and a "microcosm of conceit and empty headedness." It concluded: "No newspaper can exist except upon its merits, a condition from which the Bench, happily for Mr. Justice Darling, is exempt. Mr. Justice Darling would do well to master the duties of his own profession before undertaking regulation of another."

5-225 Lord Russell of Killowen C.J. described the article as "personal scurrilous abuse of a judge as a judge" and the Divisional Court held the article a contempt. It most unlikely, however, that a similar view would be taken today. Abusive

---

[25] *Watson's Case* (1788) 2 T.R. 199; *R. v Hart and White* (1808) 30 St. Tr. 1131 at 1193, 1 Camp.359n, 170 E.R. 985. Fox says that the attachment procedure fell into further disrepute as a result of the imprisonment of another Wilkite supporter, William Bingley: see *Contempt of Court* (1927), pp.35–6.

[26] [1900] 2 Q.B. 36 (where, however, the offending passage is not cited); 82 L.T. 534, 64 J.P. 484 (where it is). R. Stevens, in *The Independence of the Judiciary* (1993), Oxford University Press, at p.5 says that "the idea that criticising a judge might be contempt of court was invented by the Court of Appeal in 1900 to protect Mr Justice Darling". This hardly seems right, although the incident was the occasion upon which the dormant jurisdiction was revived.

though the article was, of the judge personally, a modern court would probably conclude that there was no threat to the administration of justice itself arising from mere personal abuse.[27] If allegations of misbehaviour or unfitness for office were well-founded, however, such pressure may prove salutary, in the sense of leading to resignation. This might help to maintain confidence in the administration of justice.[28] If such allegations were false, then an apology might be extracted either as a result of the disciplines of defamation or those of the Press Complaints Commission.[29]

Scandalising was considered by the Privy Council in the case of *S.B. Sarbadhicary*.[30] The High Court of Allahabad had suspended a barrister from practice under its statutory power to do so for "reasonable cause". He had published an article which represented that the Chief Justice of that court had insufficient ability to act in court or to write his judgments alone. The Privy Council advised that "in this case a contempt of Court was undoubtedly committed (and as the evidence shows not for the first time) by an advocate in a matter concerning himself personally in his professional character". As such, the publication was sufficient cause to justify the suspension.

In two separate decisions, the law of scandalising was employed to constrain litigants who sought to embroil judges in private litigation. In *R. v Vidal*[31] a person displayed placards outside the Royal Courts of Justice accusing the President of the Probate Divorce and Admiralty Division of actively supporting a conspiracy to suppress evidence, and alleging that he had "defrauded the course of justice". His "defence" to the allegation of contempt was that he was seeking to force the judge to sue him for libel, so that he could then assert that his statements were true in substance and in fact. The court concluded, however, that this was "scurrilous abuse of the worst description", which was contempt. The court cited Lord Russell in *R. v Gray* to the effect that "Judges and Courts are alike open to criticism, and if reasonable argument or expostulation is offered against any judicial act as contrary to law or the public good, no Court could or would treat that as contempt of Court". Vidal was committed to prison for four months. It has to be said that abusive placards outside the Royal Courts of Justice, including about judges and their decision making, have become relatively commonplace in recent years and have thus attracted less and less attention.

Similarly, in *R. v Freeman*,[32] a litigant wrote a series of abusive letters to Roche J. and other persons accusing the judge of being "a liar, a coward a perjurer", and of aiding a man in a felony. Notwithstanding warnings to desist, he refused to cease publication of the letters and "announced his intention of continuing to send them at a rate of three a day". At the application to commit

---

[27] See, *e.g.* the citation from the Phillimore Committee at para.5–211.
[28] See, *e.g.* the comments of Brennan J. in *Nationwide News Pty Ltd v Wills* (1992) 177 C.L.R. 1 at 38–9, cited at para.5–259. See also *R. v Nicholls* (1911) 12 C.L.R. 280 at 286, Griffiths C.J.
[29] See para.5–208, n.6.
[30] (1906) 23 T.L.R. 180.
[31] *The Times*, October 14, 1922.
[32] *The Times*, November 18, 1925.

5–229   The principle also came into play in the context of allegations of judicial bias. In *R. v Editor of New Statesman Ex p. DPP*,[33] a journal published a leading article criticising the summing up of Avory J. in a case involving Dr. Marie Stopes, a well known advocate of birth control. The writer alleged that the judge's prejudice against Dr. Stopes' views and conduct had influenced his summing up against her and added: "The serious point in this case, however, is that an individual owning such views as those of Dr. Stopes cannot apparently hope for a fair hearing in a Court presided over by Mr. Justice Avory—and there are many Avorys." The Divisional Court held that the article did scandalise the court. "It imputed unfairness and lack of impartiality to a Judge in the discharge of his judicial duties. The gravamen of the offence was that by lowering his authority it interfered with the performance of his judicial duties."

5–230   Shortly afterwards, the *Daily Worker* published an article containing the accusation that the sentences of the courts, against serving soldiers who committed crimes to avoid military service, were:

> "violent oppression of the working classes which is rapidly becoming the hall-mark of the policy of the Labour Government. Rigby Swift, the Judge who sentenced Comrade Thomas, was the bewigged puppet and former Tory M.P. chosen to put Communist leaders away in 1926. The defending counsel, able as he was, could not do much in the face of strong class bias of the Judge and jury."

At the hearing[34] the alleged contemnors aggravated the offence by maintaining and repeating what had been said in the original article. They were held in contempt and three of them imprisoned for their offence.

5–231   A few months later, the editor of *Truth* was fined for publishing an article which alleged by implication that Slesser L.J. could not be unbiased in regard to a certain piece of legislation when he had been Solicitor-General in the government which had introduced it. That appears to be the last reported example of an English court punishing contempt of this sort.[35]

E. The need to protect the right of legitimate criticism

5–232   There has been an increasing recognition by the courts of the need to be sensitive in a democracy to the right of citizens to criticise institutions, including the administration of justice. The classic statement is to be found in *Ambard v Att-Gen for Trinidad and Tobago*,[36] where the Privy Council advised that an article

---

[33] (1928) 44 T.L.R. 301.
[34] *R. v Wilkinson*, The Times, July 16, 1930.
[35] *R. v Colsey*, The Times, May 9, 1931. See A.L. Goodhart, "Newspapers and Contempt of Court" (1935–36) 48 Harv. L.R. 883 at 903, who commented that this decision " . . . seems to carry the doctrine of constructive contempt to extreme limits". See also (1931) 47 L.Q.R. 315, cited at para.5–239.
[36] [1936] A.C. 322 at 335.

criticising apparently discrepant sentences was not a contempt, even though it contained strong criticism of the judge. Lord Atkin formulated the modern approach to scandalising:

" ... whether the authority and position of an individual judge, or the due administration of justice, is concerned, no wrong is committed by any member of the public who exercises the ordinary right of criticising, in good faith, in private or public, the public act done in the seat of justice. The path of criticism is a public way: the wrong headed are permitted to err therein: provided that members of the public abstain from imputing improper motives to those taking part in the administration of justice, and are genuinely exercising a right of criticism, and not acting in malice or attempting to impair the administration of justice, they are immune. Justice is not a cloistered virtue: she must be allowed to suffer the scrutiny and respectful, even though outspoken, comments of ordinary men."

In *Perera v R*.[37] the alleged contemnor was a member of the House of Representatives in Ceylon, and it was part of his duties to inspect prisons. A book was provided for comments by such visitors. Acting on misinformation from prisoners and a prison officer the appellant commented that "The present practice of appeals of remand prisoners being heard in their absence is not healthy. When represented by counsel or otherwise the prisoner should be present at proceedings." The alleged contemnor thought this was a criticism of a prison regulation, but in fact it was an inaccurate criticism of court procedure. Nevertheless the Privy Council advised that it was not such as seriously to undermine the authority of the court.

5–233

A similar approach was being adopted towards the law as applied in England and Wales by the time of the decision in *Metropolitan Police Commissioner Ex p. Blackburn*.[38] Vigorous criticism of the Court of Appeal's handling of recent gaming legislation was held not to be a contempt, even though based upon a mistake of fact.

5–234

F. The *actus reus* of scandalising contempts

The conflicting policy considerations, as between the protection of free speech and the upholding of the authority of the courts, have already been discussed in the broader context of common law publication contempt.[39] They are also relevant in this specific context. Scandalising contempts have normally occurred after the conclusion of proceedings. The *actus reus* is said to consist of publication that creates a real risk that public confidence in the judicial system will be undermined.[40] In evaluating this question in any particular case, the court must look at the status of the author or publisher, and the breadth of publication as well as the substance of what is alleged.

5–235

---

[37] [1951] A.C. 482.
[38] [1968] 2 Q.B. 150.
[39] paras 5–22 *et seq.*
[40] See, *e.g. Solicitor-General v Radio Avon* [1978] 1 N.Z.L.R. 225.

1. The relevance of the mode of expression: "scurrilous abuse"

5–236 The early cases seemed much concerned with the *manner* in which criticism was expressed. If the words used amounted to scurrilous abuse, then it would appear that this might of itself have rendered the publisher liable for contempt. Indeed, Lord Atkin himself acknowledged that comments about the administration of justice could be "outspoken", while appearing to stipulate that they would need to be "respectful".[41] Even in *M.P.C. Ex p. Blackburn*[42] 30 years later, Salmon L.J. stated that "no criticism of a judgment, however vigorous, can amount to contempt of court if it keeps within the limits of reasonable courtesy and good faith." Yet to draw the line between criticism strongly expressed and scurrilous abuse may not be easy.

5–237 It is difficult today to justify the notion that the maintenance of public confidence in the administration of justice should depend upon whether criticism is expressed in courteous and respectful terms rather than upon whether it is well-founded or not, especially having regard to the priorities enshrined in Art.10 of the European Convention.[43] In *Harris v Harris; Att-Gen v Harris*,[44] Munby J. observed:

> ". . . that which is lawful if expressed in the temperate or scholarly language of a legal periodical or the broadsheet press does not become unlawful simply because expressed in the more robust, colourful or intemperate language of the tabloid press or even in language which is crude, insulting and vulgar. Judges, after all, are expected to be, and I have no doubt are, men and women of fortitude, able to thrive in a hardy climate, and the vehemence of the language used cannot of itself measure the power to punish for contempt. On the contrary, so long as it does not undermine what in Art.10(2) is referred to as 'the authority and impartiality of the judiciary', such criticism is healthy. There is, I think, much to be said for the view that the judges must be kept mindful of their limitations and of their ultimate public responsibility by a vigorous stream of criticism expressed with candour however blunt. Moreover, a much more robust view must, in my judgment, be taken today than previously of what ought rightly to be allowed to pass as permissible criticism. Society is more tolerant today of strong or even offensive language. Society has in large part lost its previous habit of deferential respect. Much of what might well, even in the comparatively recent past, have been considered by the judges to be scurrilous abuse of themselves or their brethren has today, as it seems to me, to be recognised as amounting to no more than acceptable if trenchant criticism".

5–238 It is perhaps in this context more than any other that the law has been overtaken by changes in social attitudes and manners. The first decision of the House of Lords in *Spycatcher*[45] was greeted by a tabloid headline displaying pictures of members of the Committee with a caption "You fools". More recently, it has become fashionable to publish surveys purporting to measure

---

[41] para.5–232.
[42] [1968] 2 Q.B. 150. See Lord Denning M.R. at 155.
[43] See para.2–142.
[44] [2001] 2 F.L.R. 895 at [372].
[45] *Att-Gen v Guardian Newspapers Ltd* [1987] 1 W.L.R. 1248 (the interim injunction stage).

judicial performance, sometimes couched in highly critical terms. *Legal Business*, in May 1992,[46] published an article "ranking" the High Court judges, and making personal comments about the judge who proved least popular. It was never suggested that any action should be taken.[47] Subsequently it published a survey in May 2003 of Chancery judges and, in December of the same year, of Queen's Bench judges which set out league tables and comments about individual judges under different qualities, *e.g.* "courtroom management" (one judge being described variously as "detached from reality" and " . . . living on Planet Judge at the moment"), "legal and technical abilities", "fairness", "courtesy and sensitivity" and "judgments".

G. Allegations of bias or improper motive[48]

In a case note on *R. v Colsey*,[49] A.L. Goodhart stated:

> "To state that a judge is consciously biased in his judgement is obviously a grave contempt of Court, but to say, as is the natural implication of these words, that a judge may be unconsciously influenced by his political and social convictions is merely to state a fact which must be true in some cases unless judges differ from all other men".

Indeed, more recently, it has been suggested in Australia that an allegation of even conscious bias ought to escape the sanctions of the law of contempt, in at least some circumstances. Hope J.A. made the following comment[50]:

> " . . . It does not necessarily amount to a contempt of court to claim that a court or judge had been influenced, or too much influenced whether consciously or unconsciously, by some particular consideration in respect of a matter which has been determined. Such criticism is frequently made in academic journals and books,[51] and the right cannot be limited to academics . . . ".

---

[46] For comparable developments in Canada, see "Canadian Lawyers' Survey on the Provincial Court Bench: The Worst of the Provincial Court" (1991) 15 Canadian Lawyer 18; and in New Zealand, the *Independent* (NZ), September 2, 1994, discussed by J.L. Caldwell, "Is Scandalising the court a Scandal?" (1994) N.Z.L.J. 442. See also G. Chapman, "Criticism of Judges, Courts and Judicial Decisions, Especially by Politicians" (1995) N.Z.L.J. 267.

[47] Subsequently, following further criticism (including by the Court of Appeal for delay in arriving at a decision), the judge in question resigned: see the LCD press release, 40/98, February 13, 1998. The Court of Appeal granted a fresh trial: *Goose v Sandford & Co* [1998] T.L.R. 85.

[48] See R. Paterson, "Criminal Contempt of Court: Allegations of Judicial Partiality" (1978) N.Z.L.J. 21. Advocates may be under a duty to make on behalf of their clients an application that the court recuse itself because of the appearance, to reasonable onlookers, of bias or partiality: see, *e.g.* Re *Lonrho plc* [1990] 2 A.C. 154. See also *Locabail (UK) Ltd v Bayfield Properties Ltd* [2000] Q.B. 451; *In Re Medicaments and Related Classes of Goods* [2001] 1 W.L.R. 700; *Porter v Magill* [2002] 2 A.C. 357; *Wilkinson v S* [2003] EWCA Civ 95, [2003] 1 W.L.R. 1254 and *R. v Santiago* [2005] EWCA Crim 556, [2005] 2 Cr.App.R. 24. See para.10–49. For circumstances in which intemperate and direct accusations of bias might be treated as constituting contempt in the face of the court, see para.10–144. See also *Lewis v Ogden* (1983) 153 C.L.R. 682, HC; *Vidyasagara v R.* [1963] A.C. 589 at 596, Lord Guest; *Kyprianou v Cyprus*, Appn. No.73797/01, January 27, 2004.

[49] *The Times*, May 9, 1931; (1931) 37 L.Q.R. 315.

[50] *Att-Gen for NSW v Mundey* [1972] 2 N.S.W.L.R. 887 at 910.

[51] See, *e.g.* J.A.G. Griffith, *The Politics of the Judiciary* (5th ed., 1997) which was originally written as a "controversial book" advancing "the simple thesis that our judiciary cannot, under our system, act neutrally but must act politically" (preface to the 2nd ed., 1981).

5–240 It is by no means the case, however, that any allegation of bias now has to be tolerated even in the context of the European Convention. In *Barfod v Denmark*,[52] a person who made allegations of bias against two Greenland lay judges was successfully prosecuted for defamation of character. It was held by the European Court of Human Rights that the interference by the state in the defendant's right to freedom of expression was prescribed by law, and had the legitimate aim of *inter alia* protecting the authority and impartiality of the judiciary. The state was said to have a legitimate interest in protecting the reputation of the judges. In *Ambard's case* Lord Atkin recognised that it might be a contempt to ascribe improper motives to the judiciary. It may be that *R. v Colsey*[53] fell within this perceived mischief; yet overall it would seem that, even in the few cases where matter has been held to be scandalous, no great harm would have been done to the administration of justice if the particular publication had been passed over unnoticed. If, as suggested, the correct test is whether there is a risk of serious interference with the administration of justice, it may be that there will be few cases where this will be established.

5–241 Yet, if a judge's conduct of the case is truly biased to an extent that it may affect the eventual outcome, it is surely desirable that the press should be free to comment to that effect in strong terms, even falling short of being "respectful" (to use Lord Atkin's word) or "courtesy" (to use that of Salmon L.J. in *Blackburn*).[54] Indeed, in the Australian High Court Griffiths C.J. adopted the view in *Nicholls*[55] that a newspaper which commented upon a judge's lack of impartiality could successfully plead fair comment upon a matter of public interest by way of defence.[56]

H. Publication

5–242 Since the true rationale of the principle is that *public* confidence in the administration of justice should not be undermined, one would expect to find that all the cases are concerned with publication to the world at large.[57] Nevertheless, in an Australian case, it has been held that a communication was sufficiently published in this context by sending a circular letter to the Attorney General and 13 Court Registrars.[58]

5–243 So too in *Collins*,[59] the scandalous allegations were contained in an affidavit which was required to be available for inspection by members of the public, although there was no evidence that it had been widely read. In New Zealand also, a very limited publication by a solicitor[60] contained in affidavits was held to fall foul of the scandalising principle, because statements were made accusing

---

[52] (1989) 13 E.H.R.R. 393.
[53] *The Times*, May 9, 1931, the facts of which are given in para.5–231.
[54] [1968] 2 Q.B. 150, 155.
[55] (1911) 12 C.L.R. 280, cited at para.5–258.
[56] The analogy with defamation is discussed more fully at paras 5–252 *et seq*.
[57] Including in *Att-Gen v Blomfield* (1913) 33 N.Z.L.R. 545 the publication of a cartoon.
[58] *Ex p. Att-Gen; Re Goodwin* (1969) 70 S.R. (N.S.W.) 413, NSWCA.
[59] [1954] V.L.R. 46.
[60] *Re Wiseman* [1969] N.Z.L.R. 55.

judges of forgery, fabricating evidence, deliberately showing partiality, and attempting to intimidate him. It is not easy to see how the *public* confidence in the administration of justice could be undermined by such limited communications.

I. The requisite state of mind for scandalising contempt

Before the passing of the 1981 Act, there was some authority that *mens rea* was required in this form of contempt.[61] Wilmot J. in *Almon's Case*[62] clearly adopted the view that, in such situations, it was necessary to establish *mens rea*. The argument had been advanced that a jury could best decide with what intention the libels on the court were published, and that for this reason the summary procedure should not be adopted. Although he rejected this argument Wilmot J. nevertheless stated[63]:

5–244

> "It is the intention which, in all cases, constitutes the offence. 'Actus non facit reum, nisi mens sit rea.'"

On the other hand, Lord Hewart C.J. in *R. v Editor of New Statesman Ex p. DPP*,[64] observed that if intention had been proved, imprisonment would have been the appropriate penalty, and this suggests that no intention was required to establish liability. This decision has been widely influential in Commonwealth decisions.[65] He did not, however, consider in any detail the nature of the *mens rea* required.

5–245

Although the law in this respect probably remains untouched by the enactment of the strict liability rule, the question needs to be addressed in the light of the later decisions.[66] First, it would probably be regarded in England and Wales as necessary to prove an intention to interfere with the administration of justice,[67] and in this context that would mean the undermining of public confidence.[68] That might well be implicit in the content of the published allegations themselves. Nevertheless, it may be wise to apply the test put forward by Bingham L.J. in *Att-Gen v Sport Newspapers Ltd*[69] that such an inference is required to be "little short of overwhelming".

5–246

In *State v Van Niekerk*[70] proceedings were brought against a legal academic in respect of an article in which he imputed racial bias to the South African judges.

5–247

---

[61] See, *e.g. R. v Castro, Skipworth and the Defendant's Case* (1873) L.R. 9 Q.B. 219.
[62] *Wilmot's Notes* (1765) 243, 97 E.R. 94.
[63] *ibid*. at 102. The passage is set out more fully in para.1–70.
[64] (1928) 44 T.L.R. 301.
[65] See also *Att-Gen for NSW v Mundey* [1972] 2 N.S.W.L.R. 887 at 911–2; *Solicitor-General v Radio Avon Ltd* [1978] 1 N.Z.L.R. 225 at 232–4; *Re Oullet* (1976) 67 D.L.R. (3d) 73, at 92; *Att-Gen v Lingle* [1995] 1 S.L.R. 696; *Ahnee v DPP* [1999] A.C. 294.
[66] *Att-Gen v News Group Newspapers plc* [1989] 1 Q.B. 110; *Att-Gen v Sport Newspapers Ltd* [1991] 1 W.L.R. 1194, [1992] 1 All E.R. 503, DC; *Att-Gen v Newspaper Publishing plc* [1997] 1 W.L.R. 926 at 937, 3 All E.R. 159 at 169e–g.
[67] See the remarks of Lord Atkin, cited at para.5–232.
[68] It is unlikely, therefore, that an English court would follow the approach in *Solicitor-General v Radio Avon Ltd* [1978] N.Z.L.R. 225.
[69] [1991] 1 W.L.R. 1194, [1992] 1 All E.R. 503, DC.
[70] 1970 (3) S.CA. 655(T).

5–247 CHAPTER 5—CONTEMPTS BY PUBLICATION AT COMMON LAW

The language in which the article was couched was temperate. The proceedings were dismissed on the grounds that it was required to be established that the publication was[71]:

" ... made with the intention of bringing the judges in their judicial capacity into contempt or of casting suspicion on the administration of justice. For this type of intention it is sufficient if the accused subjectively foresaw the possibility of his act being in contempt of court and he was reckless as to the result ... "

5–248 The matter of *mens rea* was considered by the Privy Council in the context of an appeal from Mauritius in *Ahnee v DPP*.[72] It was held that, the publication itself being intentional, there was no additional element of *mens rea* required. If the article was calculated to undermine the authority of the court, and if the defence of fair criticism in good faith was inapplicable, then the offence would be established.

5–249 In England, the test of recklessness has been rejected for publication contempt.[73] It may nevertheless suffice, paradoxically, that a respondent had knowingly created a risk of undermining public confidence.[74]

J. Knowledge of contents

5–250 It would seem that the contemnor would have to know that his publication contained the offending matter. In *McCleod v St. Aubyn*[75] the appellant received by post a copy of a current weekly newspaper on sale in the locality. Before he had read it a friend of his borrowed the appellant's copy with his consent. Unknown to the appellant it contained scandalous matter. The Privy Council advised that the appellant was not in contempt: he had not published the matter because he had not intended to publish it. He obviously intended to publish the contents of the newspaper, but he did not know that it included scandalous matter. Some reliance was placed upon the fact that they were both private individuals.

K. Lack of good faith

5–251 A number of cases stress that the publication in order to amount to a contempt must be *mala fide*.[76] Thus, if the alleged contemnor were to make an honest mistake of fact, thinking that the publication did not relate to the courts at all, this would not be treated as contempt. Although this might seem a somewhat unlikely scenario, it was held in *Perera v R*.[77] that when someone criticised the procedures

---

[71] *ibid.* at 657, Claasen J.
[72] [1999] A.C. 294 at 307D–E.
[73] *Att-Gen v Newspaper Publishing plc* [1988] Ch. 333; *Att-Gen v News Group Newspapers plc* [1989] Q.B. 110.
[74] See paras 5–187 *et seq.*
[75] [1899] A.C. 549; the old case of *Anon* 2 Bar. K.B. 43, 94 E.R. 345, where it was held that ignorance of the contents was in itself no defence, must now be regarded as wrongly decided.
[76] *Ambard v Att-Gen for Trinidad and Tobago* [1936] A.C. 322; *Metropolitan Police Commissioner Ex p. Blackburn* [1968] 2 Q.B. 150.
[77] [1952] A.C. 482.

of the court, while under the impression that he was merely criticising a prison regulation, he was not in contempt. The Privy Council stressed that his remarks were honest criticism on a matter of public interest.

L. Special defences available in scandalising

1. *The nature of the uncertainty*

What if someone is criticising a judge knowingly for corruption or other serious misconduct, but in doing so is under a fundamental though honest misapprehension as to the facts? There would be no defence in the law of defamation, since both fair comment and justification require that the facts be truly stated. It seems unlikely that such a person would escape liability under the law of contempt either, because the common law has applied in this form of contempt principles that seem very close to those of defamation. Clearly, this is a quite separate approach from that applied in other forms of publication contempt. For example, if a newspaper were to commit a strict liability contempt, by revealing an accused's criminal record, it would be no defence that the facts had been accurately reported.

5–252

2. *Truth as a defence*

The Phillimore Committee were in favour of an offence closely related to "scandalising" at common law, but proposed that it should be defined by Parliament. It recommended that truth should not be an absolute defence where such an offence was charged, even if it consisted in pure allegations of fact (as it would be if a judge were to sue for libel). This was because the very presentation of such a defence might provide a platform for the repetition of the original assertions or allegations; it might provide a cover under which to rake up some damaging episode in a judge's past life.[78] It did, however, consider that truth should be a defence provided that the publication was for the public benefit.[79] In so far as it would be necessary to establish an *additional* ingredient of "public benefit", such a restrictive rule would hardly seem to accord with the requirements of Art.10.[80]

5–253

Nevertheless, a similar approach was taken by the High Court of Australia in *Nationwide News Pty Ltd v Wills*,[81] where the comment was made:

5–254

"It is not necessary, even if it be possible, to chart the limits of the law of contempt scandalising the court. It is sufficient to say that the revelation of truth—at all events when its revelation is for the public benefit—and the making of a fair criticism based

---

[78] para.165.
[79] para.166. Compare the Rehabilitation of Offenders Act 1974, considered in *Gatley on Libel and Slander* (10th ed., 2004), ch.17.
[80] See *Silkman v Heard*, February 28, 2001, Q.B.D. quoted in *Gatley on Libel and Slander* (10th ed.) at para.17–14, n.62.
[81] (1992) 177 C.L.R. 1, 39 at Brennan J. And see *R. v Hoser and Kotabi Pty Ltd* [2001] V.S.C. 443 at [58]–[64].

on fact do not amount to a contempt of court though the truth revealed or the criticism made is such as to deprive the court of public confidence".

This passage suggests that there might be circumstances in which it would be no defence to establish the truth of the allegations without establishing also the nebulous concept of "public benefit". As the law stands, in England, there is no reason to suppose that an alleged contemnor would have to go beyond proving that the facts were true.

5–255 In another respect, however, it appears that the approach in Australia would be the same as that in England. The use in *Wills*, when describing the basis of scandalising, of terms such as "unjustified", "baseless" and "unwarranted"[82] suggests that the test is objective, as in the law of defamation. That is to say, if a judge is accused publicly of misconduct, in such a way as to undermine public confidence in the administration of justice, it would not appear that it would be a defence to contempt proceedings that such a person *believed* the allegations to be true.

3. *Fair comment on a matter of public interest*

5–256 There is reasonably clear modern authority for the view that a person charged with scandalising the court may put forward by way of defence that his criticism was fair comment on a matter of public interest,[83] analogous to that in defamation. In *Metropolitan Police Commissioner Ex p. Blackburn*,[84] Lord Denning M.R. stated that:

> "It is the right of every man, in Parliament or out of it, in the Press or over the broadcast, to make fair comment, even outspoken comment, on matters of public interest. Those who comment can deal faithfully with all that is done in a court of justice. They can say that we are mistaken, and our decisions erroneous, whether they are subject to appeal or not."

5–257 Likewise, the Privy Council in *Perera v R*.[85] gave as its final reason for allowing the appeal that what was published was honest criticism on a matter of public interest.

5–258 In the High Court of Australia in *R. v Nicholls*[86] Griffiths C.J. drew the analogy with libel:

> "I am not prepared to accede to the proposition that an imputation of want of impartiality to a Judge is necessarily a contempt of Court. On the contrary, I think that,

---

[82] (1992) 177 C.L.R. 1 at 38.
[83] In *Solicitor-General v Smith* [2004] 2 N.Z.L.R. 540, it was held that the defence is not available where there is an intention to interfere with the administration of justice by seeking to put pressure on a tribunal with reference to pending proceedings.
[84] [1968] 2 Q.B. 150 at 155. See also the words of Lord Atkin in *Ambard v Att-Gen for Trinidad and Tobago* [1936] A.C. 322, cited at para.5–232.
[85] [1951] A.C. 482.
[86] (1911) 12 C.L.R. 280. See also *R. v Hoser and Kotabi Ltd* [2001] V.S.C. 443 at [65]–[91].

if any Judge of this Court or of any other Court were to make a public utterance of such a character as to be likely to impair the confidence of the public, or of suitors or any class of suitors, in the impartiality of the court in any matter likely to be before it, any public comment on such an utterance, if it were fair comment, would, so far from being a contempt of Court, be for the public benefit, and would be entitled to similar protection to that which comment upon matters of public interest is entitled under the law of libel."

The Privy Council expressed agreement with this approach in *Ahnee v DPP*.[87]

To similar effect were the words of Brennan J. in *Nationwide News Pty Ltd v Wills*[88]:

" . . . it has been said that it is no contempt of court to criticise court decisions when the criticism is fair and not distorted by malice and the basis of the criticism is accurately stated. To the contrary, a public comment fairly made on judicial conduct that is truly disreputable (in the sense that it would impair the confidence of the public in the competence or integrity of the court) is for the public benefit".

This would perhaps suggest that there is no *additional* requirement of establishing a public benefit over and above the mere publication of that which is true or fair comment.

M. Other jurisdictions

Modern examples of "scandalising" are to be found in other common law jurisdictions, although such applications of the principle may be less readily transferable than would be case with other aspects of the law of contempt.

1. *Canada*

In Canada, the English common law was, until comparatively recently, the basis of the scandalising jurisdiction.[89] It has been held that this area of the law might fall foul of s.2(b) of the Canadian Charter of Rights and Freedoms guaranteeing "freedom of thought, belief, opinion and expression, including freedom of the press and other media of communication". In *Kopyto*,[90] the Ontario Court of Appeal were divided as to the application of the provision in this context, although all five judges were agreed that the appeal against committal should be allowed. The case concerned a lawyer charged with scandalising over remarks made after the dismissal of a case in which he had appeared as counsel. He commented to a newspaper reporter "This decision is a mockery of justice. It

---

[87] [1999] A.C. 294 at 306D–E.
[88] (1992) 177 C.L.R. at 38–9.
[89] *Re Nicol* (1954) 3 D.L.R. 690; *R. v Murphy* (1969) 4 D.L.R. 289.
[90] (1988) 47 D.L.R. (4th) 213, Ont CA. For a discussion of the constitutional significance of the decision, so far as the independence of the judiciary is concerned, see M.L. Friedland, *A Place Apart: Judicial Independence and Accountability in Canada* (1995) Ottawa, Canadian Judicial Council. And see J. Watson, "Badmouthing the Bench" (1992) 56 Sask. L.Rev. 113; R. Martin, "Criticising the Judges" (1982) 28 McGill Law Jo. 1; Jacob S. Ziegel, "Some Aspects of the Law of Contempt of Court in Canada, England and the United States" (1959–60) 6 McGill L.J. 229.

5–261 CHAPTER 5—CONTEMPTS BY PUBLICATION AT COMMON LAW

stinks to high hell. It says it is okay to break the law and you are immune so long as someone above you said to do it." He then queried the point of appealing and " . . . continuing this charade of the courts in this country which are warped in favour of protecting the police."

5–262 Two members of the court (dissenting in this respect) took the view that contempt of court "properly understood" was not an abridgement of freedom of speech, since it could be committed only where the speaker intended to bring the administration of justice into disrepute, and that the risk that the administration might be interfered with must be shown to be "serious, real or substantial". It was, therefore, unnecessary to decide the constitutional issue. Whatever justification there may be, generally or in the particular circumstances of an individual case, for invoking the contempt jurisdiction, it is hard to understand the conclusion that it does not represent a *prima facie* abridgment of free speech. This has long been recognised by the European Court of Human Rights in the context of Art.10.[91]

5–263 Other members of the Court, however, concluded that the common law of scandalising could only be regarded as compatible with the Charter provided that it was strictly limited in its application. The difficulty with the current law was that it assumes, without requiring proof, that words which are the subject matter of the charge will bring the court in to contempt or lower its authority. There was thus no reasonable limit prescribed on the abridgment of freedom of expression, as guaranteed by the Charter.

2. Australia[92]

5–264 It has been accepted by the High Court of Australia that, whilst this head of liability persists, " . . . a procedure whereby a court deals, in a summary way, with a challenge to its own integrity and authority, should be exercised sparingly, and only when necessity demands."[93] Criticism of the High Court for having "knocked holes in the Federal Laws" was held to have constituted a contempt in *R. v Dunbabin Ex p. Williams*,[94] since it amounted to an allegation that the court exercised ingenuity to defeat legislation of great public importance. The words were calculated to lessen or discredit the authority of the court in the minds of reasonable people. A similar example is provided by *Gallagher v Durack*,[95] in which a well-known trade union leader was held to have been in contempt for

---

[91] *Sunday Times v United Kingdom* (1979) 2 E.H.R.R. 245; *Sunday Times v United Kingdom (No.2)* (1991) 14 E.H.R.R. 229; *Goodwin v United Kingdom* (1996) 22 E.H.R.R. 123.

[92] E. Campbell, "Contemptuous Criticism of the Judiciary and the Judicial Process" (1960) 34 A.L.J. 224; H. Burmester, "Scandalizing the judges" (1985) 15 Melb. U.L.R. 313; Frank Bates, "Scandalising the court: Some Peculiarly Australian Developments" (1994) 13 Civil Justice Quarterly 241; S. D. Dawson, "Judges and the media" (1987) 10 U.N.S.W. Law Jo. 17; Sally Walker, "Freedom of Speech and Contempt of Court: The English and Australian Approaches Compared" (1991) 40 I.C.L.Q. 583.

[93] *Ex parte Torney* [1999] HCA 57 at [5], Gleeson C.J. and Gummow J. The High Court of Australia rejected the argument that scandalising should be tried by a jury on indictment.

[94] (1935) 53 C.L.R. 434, HC.

[95] (1983) 57 A.L.J.R. 191, 45 A.L.R. 53, HC.

having publicly claimed that the actions of his rank and file had influenced the Full Court of the Federal Court of Australia in allowing an appeal. The allegation reflected upon the judges as individuals, but what justified the application of the law of contempt was the undermining of confidence in the independent and impartial administration of justice.

Attacks on a single judge (for having passed sentences believed to be too lenient) were also treated as an attempt to intimidate the court and to prevent it from deciding cases in a judicial atmosphere.[96] **5–265**

That common law contempt by scandalising retains some vitality is confirmed, to an extent, by a decision of the Family Court of Australia in *Fitzgibbon v Barker*.[97] A report of protesters claiming that a man had been "jailed for two years only because he wanted to see his children" was held to be calculated to lessen or discredit the authority and prestige of the court in the minds of reasonable people. As published, the material was said to be gross a distortion of the findings in the particular case (there being a history of breaching non-molestation orders) and of the role of the Family Court in general. **5–266**

In the decision of the High Court of Australia in *Nationwide News Proprietary Ltd v Wills*,[98] it was also recognised that the principles relating to contempt by scandalising are far from a dead letter, at least in respect of the traditionally recognised courts of justice. There, it was held that a statute[99] which made it an offence by writing or speech to use words "calculated to bring a member of the (Industrial Relations) Commission or the Commission into disrepute" was unconstitutional. The protection that it sought to afford to the Commission and its members went far beyond that afforded to the ordinary courts, since it did not purport to permit (as does the common law) criticism that was justifiable, fair and reasonable. This could not be regarded as reasonably necessary to attain the legitimate objective, and had adverse consequences upon "fundamental values traditionally protected by the common law, such as freedom of expression". **5–267**

3. *New Zealand*[1]

In a war-time case where there had been an allegation by a senior politician to the effect that "the workers" could not obtain justice from either the Supreme Court or the court of Arbitration, Myers C.J. held that the newspaper reports of the speech undoubtedly constituted contempt: "Such statements are calculated tor diminish the confidence of the public in the courts and they are clearly contempts **5–268**

---

[96] *Ex p. the Att-Gen—Re Truth and Sportsman Ltd* (1961) S.R.N.S.W. 484.
[97] (1992) 111 F.L.R. 191.
[98] (1992) 177 C.L.R. 1.
[99] Industrial Relations Act 1988 (Cth), s.299(1)(d)(ii).
[1] Although most criminal law in New Zealand is to be found in statutory form, the law of contempt is excepted by the Crimes Act 1961, s.9. This was enacted to confirm what was said by the Full Court in *Re Cobb* [1924] N.Z.L.R. 495 with reference to its inherent jurisdiction. See *Taylor v Att-Gen* [1975] 2 N.Z.L.R. 675. See generally J. Burrows and U. Cheer, *Media Law in New Zealand* (5th ed., 2005) at pp.383 *et seq.*

5-268 CHAPTER 5—CONTEMPTS BY PUBLICATION AT COMMON LAW

of court."[2] It has been held that the contempt may be committed even where there is no intent to undermine the administration of justice. In *Solicitor-General v Radio Avon Ltd*[3] a radio station broadcast alleged that the son of a local judge had received preferential treatment in connection with a criminal prosecution. This was held to constitute a contempt, because it is contrary to the public interest that public confidence in the administration of justice should be undermined. It was submitted that nobody could be found guilty of a scandalising contempt unless the evidence proved not only that the act complained of was calculated to lower the authority of the judge, but also that it was intended to have that effect. Citing pre-1981 English authorities,[4] the court rejected the submission, holding that no distinction was to be drawn between scandalising and other forms of contempt by publication.

5-269 That the "scandalising" aspect of the contempt jurisdiction survives in New Zealand was confirmed more recently in *Solicitor General v Smith*[5] where a Member of Parliament broadcast several statements in which he sought, using emotive language, to put pressure upon a judge of the Family Court to determine a custody dispute in favour of one of his constituents. The court found that the MP intended to put pressure on the court, and that his conduct might undermine the confidence of the public that decisions would be arrived at without reference to extraneous influences. The court also took the view that what was said would undermine confidence in the court itself, since, however the Family Court decided the case, the public perception would be affected by seeing pressure so publicly applied. The court considered that the restriction on such behaviour constituted a reasonable limit upon freedom of expression having regard to the enactment of the Bill of Rights Act 1990.

4. Singapore

5-270 The view has been taken that in Singapore it is settled law that any publication alleging bias, lack of impartiality, impropriety or any wrongdoing concerning a judge in the exercise of his judicial functions amounts to a contempt.[6] In *Att-Gen v Lingle*,[7] proceedings were instituted against the author, editor, publisher, printer and distributor of an article, which had alleged that senior politicians in Asia (and by implication Singapore) were "bankrupting" their political opponents by bringing defamation proceedings, with the assistance of a "compliant judiciary". The application succeeded against all five respondents, it being held that the right to criticise is exceeded if the publication impugns the integrity and impartiality of the court, even if not intended.[8]

---

[2] *Att-Gen v Blundell* [1942] N.Z.L.R. 287. See also *Att-Gen v Butler* [1953] N.Z.L.R. 944.
[3] [1978] 1 N.Z.L.R. 225.
[4] *R. v Editor of the New Statesman* (1928) 44 T.L.R. 301; *R. v Odhams Press Ltd* [1957] 1 Q.B. 73; *R. v Griffiths* [1957] 2 Q.B. 192; *Att-Gen v Butterworth* [1963] 1 Q.B. 696; *Att-Gen v Times Newspapers Ltd* [1974] A.C. 273.
[5] [2004] N.Z.L.R. 540.
[6] *Att-Gen v Wain* [1991] 2 M.L.J. 353, citing *Att-Gen v Pang Cheng Lian* [1975] 12 M.L.J. 69.
[7] [1995] 1 S.L.R. 696.
[8] Reliance was placed upon *R. v Editor of New Statesman Ex p. DPP* (1928) 44 T.L.R. 301.

5. Mauritius

The Privy Council had occasion to consider the question of whether the Supreme Court of Mauritius retained the power to punish for contempt of court, specifically in the context of scandalising, subsequent to the coming into force of the Constitution of Mauritius 1968 (replaced in 1992 by a new constitution in substantially the same terms). In *Ahnee v DPP*[9] it was held that, by reason of the separation of powers as entrenched in the Constitution, the primary duty of the judiciary was the maintenance of fair and effective administration of justice. The power to protect that administration against contempts calculated to undermine it was an integral part of that constitutional function. The Supreme Court constituted by s.76(1) of the 1968 Constitution was to be construed as having an inherent power to punish for contempt. Moreover, the common law power to punish contempt had not been abrogated by s.5 or s.12 of the Constitution. In any event, s.15 of the Courts Ordinance 1945 (preserved by the Mauritius Independence Order 1968), had provided that the Supreme Court should have the same powers, authority and jurisdiction as that possessed and exercised by the High Court in England.

5–271

Their Lordships noted that proceedings in respect of scandalising contempts were rare in England and that none had been successfully brought for many years. Nevertheless, the question in the light of the Constitution was whether or not such an offence could be regarded as "reasonably justifiable in a democratic society". It was legitimate in that context to take into account that on a small island the administration of justice would be more vulnerable than in the United Kingdom. The offence was narrowly defined. It did not extend to comments made about the conduct of a judge unrelated to his "performance on the bench". The purpose was solely the protection of the administration of justice rather than the feelings of individual judges. Regard should always be had to the need in a democratic society for public scrutiny of judicial conduct and for the right of citizens to comment in good faith on matters of public concern. It was no longer acceptable to regard the imputation of improper motives to a judge as *ipso facto* contempt of court. Their Lordships expressed agreement with the view of the Australian courts embodied in *Nicholls*[10] to the effect that the exposure and criticism of judicial misconduct could be in the public interest.

5–272

6. Hong Kong

In what was believed by the court to be the first case of its kind, successful proceedings for scandalising were brought against the editor and the publishers of the *Oriental Daily News*, "the most popular newspaper in Hong Kong".[11] The newspaper and its editor published a series of increasingly intemperate articles, and sought to "threaten, harass and intimidate" a judge as a result of an adverse judgment. The articles " . . . contained passages of crude and vicious abuse of the judiciary . . . with little if any reasoned argument and which alleged systematic

5–273

---

[9] [1999] A.C. 294.
[10] (1911) 12 C.L.R. 280 (cited at para.5–258).
[11] *Secretary for Justice v Oriental Press Group Ltd* [1998] 2 HKC 627.

5–273   CHAPTER 5—CONTEMPTS BY PUBLICATION AT COMMON LAW

bias and wilful abuse of power (those allegations being without any justification whatsoever)". They also contained " threats to the judiciary". The publications were said to be calculated to undermine public confidence in the administration of justice in Hong Kong. The editor was imprisoned for four months, and the newspaper fined $5m HK.

5–274   After a thorough analysis of the ingredients of the offence at common law (relying upon the laws of several Commonwealth jurisdictions), the Court of First Instance identified the proper test as being that there should be a "real risk" as opposed to a "remote possibility" that the acts complained of would undermine public confidence in the administration of justice in the minds of at least some of the persons who were likely to become aware of the acts complained of. Nevertheless, the appeal was dismissed.[12] The court held that no intention to undermine public confidence was required, it being enough that the defendant intended to do the acts said to constitute the contempt. In so far as the law involved a restriction upon freedom of speech, it was intended to protect the rule of law within the meaning of Art.16(3) of the Bill of Rights, and was necessary for the achievement of that objective, and was accordingly compliant. Subsequently, the court of Final Appeal refused leave to appeal further.[13]

---

[12] *Wong Yeung Ng v The Secretary for Justice* [1999] HKCA 66.
[13] *Wong Yeung Ng v The Secretary for Justice* [1999] HKCFA 50.

CHAPTER 6

COURT ORDERS AFFECTING THE MEDIA

		PARA
I.	*Quia Timet* Injunctions to restrain a Contempt	6–1
II.	The Inherent (or *Parens Patriae*) Jurisdiction	6–41
III.	Injunctions Affecting Persons Who Are Not Directly Bound	6–115

I. QUIA TIMET INJUNCTIONS TO RESTRAIN A CONTEMPT

A. A jurisdiction to be sparingly exercised

The High Court[1] may in appropriate circumstances grant an injunction to restrain an anticipated contempt.[2] In *R. v Rhuddlan Justices*,[3] Tasker Watkins L.J. suggested that this was the appropriate route where the contempt anticipated was likely to be by way of media publication. It is necessary to bear in mind that he had in the earlier case of *Peacock v London Weekend Television*[4] construed s.7, providing for the leave of the Attorney-General, as not restricting the right to apply for an injunction.   6–1

It is submitted that it will generally be inappropriate for trial judges in the Crown Court to entertain applications of this kind, save where the situation is governed by s.4(2) or s.11 of the Contempt of Court Act 1981.[5] It could rarely be said to be necessary, through pressure of time, to take such a step for the purpose of protecting the integrity of the trial. It is to be noted that the Supreme Court Act 1981, s.37, which currently governs the power to grant injunctions, confers jurisdiction on the "High Court", and makes no express reference to   6–2

---

[1] And in appropriate cases the Court of Appeal itself may take such an exceptional step. See, *e.g. Att-Gen v Channel 4 Television Co Ltd* [1988] Crim. L.R. 237, where, having regard to the possibility of a retrial, the court granted an injunction to restrain a televised reconstruction of proceedings that were taking place before it.
[2] *Att-Gen v Times Newspapers Ltd* [1974] A.C. 273. See also Oswald, *Contempt* (3rd ed., 1910), p.16, and the cases there cited: *Coleman v West Hartlepool Railway Co.* (1860) 8 W.R. 734; *Mackett v Herne Bay Commissioners* (1876) 24 W.R. 845; *Kitcat v Sharp* (1882) 52 L.J. Ch. 134; *Re Johnson* (1887) 20 Q.B.D. 68 at 74 (where Bowen L.J. commented that "The law has armed the High Court of Justice with the power and imposed on it the duty of preventing *brevi manu* and by summary proceedings any attempt to interfere with the administration of justice"). See also *Brook v Evans* (1860) 29 L.J. Ch. 616; *Hubbard v Woodfield* (1913) 57 Sol.Jo. 729; *Acrow (Automation) Ltd v Rex Chainbelt Inc* [1971] 1 W.L.R. 1676 at 1683; *Esso Petroleum v Kingswood Motors* [1974] Q.B. 142 at 156; *T.S.B. Private Bank International SA v Chabra* [1992] 1 W.L.R. 231 at 240.
[3] [1986] Crim. L.R. 329, DC (Lexis). In Canada, it is thought appropriate for trial judges to deal with the matter: see, *e.g. Dagenais v Canadian Broadcasting Corp* (1994) 120 D.L.R. (4th) 12, (1995) 94 C.C.C. (3d) 286.
[4] (1985) 150 J.P. 71.
[5] See ch.7, and the discussion at para.6–97.

6–2 judges of the Crown Court. There is, however, a compelling argument that s.45(4) of the same statute (conferring in relation to *inter alia* contempt "the like powers, rights, privileges and authority as the High Court") would by implication confer also the power to grant an injunction for the purpose of restraining an anticipated contempt. It may be thought that the provisions of s.37, which deal with the grant of injunctions, would have referred expressly to the Crown Court if such an intention were present. Nonetheless, Aikens J., sitting in the Crown Court at Cardiff, in *Ex p. HTV Cymru (Wales) Ltd*[6] held that there is jurisdiction to make such an order although accepting that it should only be sparingly used. He was of the clear opinion that s.37 of the Supreme Court Act 1981 does not detract from the powers conferred on the Crown Court by s.45(4) of the same statute.

6–3 This recognition of the *quia timet* jurisdiction is despite the general reluctance to restrain the commission of anticipated criminal activity,[7] which is based on the obligation upon citizens to obey the law without the need of further constraint. "The primary defence of the administration of justice from unlawful interference by the press or by broadcasters is the heavy sanction of prosecution if a contempt is committed."[8] In the words of Lord Donaldson M.R.[9]:

> "Where the contempt would consist of impeding or prejudicing the course of justice, it [a *quia timet* injunction] will rarely be appropriate for two reasons. The first is that the injunction would have to be very specific and might indirectly mislead by suggesting that other conduct of a similar, but slightly different, nature would be permissible. The second is that it is the wise and settled practice of the courts not to grant injunctions restraining the commission of a criminal act—and contempt of court is a criminal or quasi-criminal act—unless the penalties available under the criminal law have proved to be inadequate to deter the commission of the offences. Unlawful street trading and breaches of the provisions of the Shops Acts are well known examples."

6–4 The practical difficulties were emphasised by Lord Bridge in the House of Lords[10]:

> "It is not, of course, possible to determine in advance what kind of public comment on pending proceedings will create a substantial risk that the course of justice will be seriously impeded or prejudiced. That is one reason why it is not normally possible, save in such exceptional circumstances as arose in *Att-Gen v Times Newspapers Ltd*,[11] to restrain by injunction a threatened contempt in breach of the strict liability rule."

B. The traditional reluctance to grant prior restraint

6–5 "Prior restraint" has always been regarded as undesirable because it involves depriving citizens of the fundamental right of freedom of communication. In the words of Blackstone[12]:

---

[6] [2002] E.M.L.R. 184.
[7] See D. Feldman, "Injunctions and the Criminal Law" (1979) 42 M.L.R. 369.
[8] *per* Ralph Gibson L.J. in *Leary v BBC*, CA, September 29, 1989 (Lexis). The case is discussed more fully at paras 6–24 *et seq.* and 6–31 *et seq.*
[9] *P v Liverpool Daily Post and Echo Newspapers plc* [1991] 2 A.C. 370 at 381–2, CA.
[10] *ibid.* at 425F–G.
[11] [1974] A.C. 273.
[12] *Commentaries*, (1765) Book IV, pp.151–2.

"The liberty of the press is indeed essential to the nature of a free state; but this consists in laying no previous restraints on publications, and not in freedom from censure for criminal matter when published. Every free man has an undoubted right to lay what sentiments he pleases before the public; to forbid this is to destroy the freedom of the press; but if he publishes what is improper, mischievous or illegal, he must take the consequences of his own temerity".

While it is nonetheless recognised that such injunctions can be justified in certain circumstances,[13] the court will only impose such restrictions if they may truly be regarded as "necessary".[14] The common law has always inclined towards protecting freedom of speech. As Lord Keith observed in *Derbyshire County Council v Times Newspapers Ltd*[15]: **6–6**

"My Lords, I have reached my conclusion upon the common law of England without finding any need to rely upon the European Convention. My noble and learned friend, Lord Goff of Chieveley, in *Att-Gen v Guardian Newspapers Ltd (No. 2)* [1990] 1 A.C. 109, 283–4, expressed the opinion that in the field of freedom of speech there was no difference in principle between English law on the subject and Art.10 of the Convention. I agree, and can only add that I find it satisfactory to be able to conclude that the common law of England is consistent with the obligations assumed by the Crown under the Treaty in this particular field".

In the context of defamation, for example, applications for interim injunctions to restrain the anticipated publication of defamatory words are treated by the courts as being outside the usual framework laid down by the House of Lords in *American Cyanamid Co v Ethicon Ltd*.[16] It will not do for a claimant to show merely that (i) he has an arguable case, (ii) damages would not be an adequate remedy and (iii) the balance of convenience (or justice[17]) lies in his favour. The well established principles of *Bonnard v Perryman*[18] continue to be applied because of the special value attached to freedom of speech.[19] **6–7**

It is also necessary to have regard to Art.10(2) of the European Convention on Human Rights and Fundamental Freedoms, which acknowledges that one of the **6–8**

---

[13] Supreme Court Act 1981, s.37; see CPR Pt 25.
[14] *Sunday Times v United Kingdom* (1979) 2 E.H.R.R. 245; *Sunday Times v United Kingdom (No.2)* (1991) 14 E.H.R.R. 229. See also the remarks of Bracewell J in *Richmond upon Thames LBC v Holmes*, The Times, October 20, 2000. The freedom to impart information and ideas, guaranteed by Art.10(1) of the European Convention on Human Rights, would prevail unless the circumstances came within one of the defined derogations to be found in Art.10(2). An applicant has to demonstrate (i) that such a derogation is necessary to meet a pressing social need; (ii) that it is proportionate; and (iii) that the need has been established by convincing evidence: see also *Re X (A Child) (Injunctions Restraining Publication)* [2001] 1 F.C.R. 541 and *Kelly v BBC* [2001] Fam. 59 at 85A. See C. Munro, "Prior Restraint of the Media and Human Rights Law" (2002) Juridical Review 3.
[15] [1993] A.C. 534 at 551F–G. Earlier, at 548D, Lord Keith had referred to "the chilling effect" induced by the threat of civil actions for libel as being very important, and as a factor which may prevent the publication of matters which it is very desirable to make public.
[16] [1975] A.C. 396.
[17] The term for which Sir John Donaldson M.R. expressed a preference in *Francome v Mirror Group Newspapers Ltd* [1984] 1 W.L.R. 892 at 898E–F.
[18] [1891] 2 Ch. 269.
[19] *Bestobell Paints v Bigg* [1975] F.S.R. 421, (1975) 119 Sol. Jo. 678; *Holley v Smyth* [1998] Q.B. 726.

6–8 limited exceptions to the right of free expression enshrined in Art.10(1) is where it is necessary for the protection of reputation. An injunction will be refused, however, if any *prima facie* defence is raised and the claimant is unable to demonstrate by means of evidence that it is bound to fail.[20] For example, in the modern case of *Williams v Wolman*[21] Stocker L.J. said " . . . it seems to me that the plaintiffs can only be entitled to an injunction pending trial, if the court is satisfied that a plea of justification must fail if put before a jury which was not perverse".

6–9 Article 10(2) also recognises an exception for the purpose of "maintaining the authority and impartiality of the judiciary", but the test in this context also has to be applied of what is "necessary in a democratic society".[22] In the context of contempt also, therefore, the Convention exercises an inhibiting influence on the court when an injunction is sought to restrain publication. It is suggested that the test in *American Cyanamid* is inappropriate where an injunction is sought in respect of an anticipated contempt. The same considerations as to freedom of speech also apply in that context.[23] As Lord Denning observed in *Att-Gen v BBC*[24]:

> "To my mind, the courts should not award [the Attorney-General] such an injunction except in a clear case where there would manifestly be a contempt of court for the publication to take place. The same reasoning applies here as in the cases where a party seeks to restrain the publication of a libel".

6–10 More recently, and in the same vein, Munby J. in *Harris v Harris: Att-Gen v Harris*[25] stressed the delicacy of the jurisdiction:

> "The freedom to publish things which judges might think should not be published is all the more important where the subject of what is being said is the judges themselves. Any judicial power to punish such publication requires the most cogent justification. Even more cogent must be the justification for giving the judges a power of prior restraint".

C. The relevance of section 12 of the Human Rights Act 1998

6–11 These values are now reflected in s.12 of the Human Rights Act 1998:

> "(1) This section applies if the court is considering whether to grant any relief which, if granted, might affect the exercise of the Convention right to freedom of expression . . .
>
> (2) If the person against whom the application for relief is made ('the respondent') is neither present nor represented, no such relief is to be granted unless the court is satisfied—

---

[20] *Coulson v Coulson* (1887) 3 T.L.R. 846, CA.
[21] January 30, 1990, Court of Appeal, Fox and Stocker L.JJ., unreported (Lexis).
[22] *Sunday Times v United Kingdom* (1979) 2 E.H.R.R. 245 at 274, para.56. See also the Divisional Court in *Att-Gen v Associated Newspapers Ltd* [1994] 2 A.C. 238 at 243D–E, Beldam L.J.
[23] See, *e.g. Coe v Central Television plc* [1994] E.M.L.R. 433.
[24] [1981] A.C. 303 at 311, CA. In the same case at 346, the comment of Lord Denning was approved by Lord Edmund-Davies. See also *Schering Chemicals Ltd v Falkman Ltd* [1982] 1 Q.B. 1.
[25] [2001] 2 F.L.R. 895 at [368].

(a) that the applicant has taken all practicable steps to notify the respondent; or
(b) that there are compelling reasons why the respondent should not be notified.

(3) No such relief is to be granted so as to restrain publication before trial unless the court is satisfied that the applicant is likely to establish that the publication should not be allowed."

(4) The court must have particular regard to the importance of the Convention right to freedom of expression and, where the proceedings relate to material which the respondent claims, or which appears to the court, to be journalistic, literary or artistic material (or to conduct connected with such material), to—

(a) the extent to which—

   (i) the material has, or is about to, become available to the public; or
   (ii) it is, or would be, in the public interest for the material to be published;

(b) any relevant privacy code."

It was not immediately clear how much difference, if any, this statutory intervention would make to the established principles already being applied. In *Imutran Ltd v Uncaged Campaigns Ltd*,[26] Sir Andrew Morritt V.-C. compared the test under *American Cyanamid Co v Ethicon Ltd* with this statutory provision and acknowledged that theoretically "likelihood" was slightly higher in the scale of probability than "a real prospect of success", but took the view that the difference between the two was so small that there would be few, if any, cases which would have succeeded under the *American Cyanamid* test but would now fail because of the s.12(3) test. In that case, the claim was based upon alleged breach of confidence and copyright, but it is not easy to see why the cause of action should make any difference. If freedom of expression is likely to be jeopardised by the grant of an injunction, the same policy considerations would appear to come into play however the claim is framed.[27]

The word "likely" in s.12(3) was addressed later by the Court of Appeal[28] and the House of Lords[29] in *Cream Holdings Ltd v Banerjee*. It was equated by the Court of Appeal with "more probable than not". Thus the threshold test to be applied, when considering whether or not to prevent publication, was identified by all members of that court as being whether the claimant has convincingly established a real prospect of success at trial (although Arden L.J. explained that she had arrived at her construction of the statutory words through a different reasoning process from that applied by Simon Brown and Sedley L.JJ.). Simon Brown L.J. had "some difficulty with the Vice-Chancellor's views expressed in *Imutran*" to the effect that there would not be many applications that would fail because of s.12(3) if they were such as to have passed muster under the criteria applied in *American Cyanamid v Ethicon*.[30] He was of opinion[31] that "there will indeed be a number of claims for injunctive relief which now will fail when earlier they would have succeeded: they will fail because the court is required by

---

[26] [2001] 2 All E.R. 385.
[27] See, *e.g.* the discussion in paras 6–7 and 6–33 *et seq.*
[28] [2003] EWCA Civ 103, [2003] Ch. 650.
[29] [2004] UKHL 44, [2005] 1 A.C. 253; see (2005) C.L.J. 4.
[30] [1975] A.C. 396.
[31] At [56].

6-13 CHAPTER 6—COURT ORDERS AFFECTING THE MEDIA

s.12(3) to consider their merits (so as to reach a judgment on the prospects of their eventual success) ... "

6-14 It was confirmed by the House of Lords[32] that the principal purpose of s.12(3) was to buttress the protection afforded to freedom of speech at the interlocutory stage. There was thus to be a higher threshold for the grant of interlocutory injunctions against the media than the *American Cyanamid* guideline of "a serious question to be tried" or a "real prospect" of success at trial. It was argued by the defendants both in the Court of Appeal and the House of Lords that logic required the court always to construe "likely" in s.12(3) as equivalent to "more likely than not" or "probably". Their Lordships concluded, however, that this would be too inflexible an approach since Parliament was "painting with a broad brush and setting a general standard". It cannot have been the intention to preclude the grant of an injunction in all circumstances to which such a strict interpretation would apply. Lord Nicholls explained:

> "18. ... Confidentiality, once breached, is lost for ever. Parliament cannot have intended that, whatever the circumstances, section 12(3) would preclude a judge from making a restraining order for the period needed for him to form a view on whether on balance of probability the claim would succeed at trial. That would be absurd. In the present case the 'Echo' [a local newspaper which was no longer participating in the proceedings in the House of Lords] agreed not to publish any further article pending the hearing of Cream's application for interim relief. But it would be absurd if, had the 'Echo' not done so, the court would have been powerless to preserve the confidentiality of the information until Cream's application had been heard. Similarly, if a judge refuses to grant an interlocutory injunction preserving confidentiality until trial the court ought not to be powerless to grant interim relief pending the hearing of an interlocutory appeal against the judge's order.
>
> 19. The matter goes further than these procedural difficulties. Cases may arise where the adverse consequences of disclosure of information would be extremely serious, such as a grave risk of personal injury to a particular person. Threats may have been made against a person accused or convicted of a crime or a person who gave evidence at a trial. Disclosure of his current whereabouts might have extremely serious consequences. Despite the potential seriousness of the adverse consequences of disclosure, the applicant's claim to confidentiality may be weak. The applicant's case may depend, for instance, on a disputed question of fact on which the applicant has an arguable but distinctly poor case. It would be extraordinary if in such a case the court were compelled to apply a 'probability of success' test and therefore, regardless of the seriousness of the possible adverse consequences, refuse to restrain publication until the disputed issue of fact can be resolved at the trial."

6-15 Therefore, the test was so propounded as to allow for flexibility:

> "22. ... Section 12(3) makes the likelihood of success at the trial an essential element in the court's consideration of whether to make an interim order. But in order to achieve the necessary flexibility the degree of likelihood of success at the trial needed to satisfy section 12(3) must depend on the circumstances. There can be no single, rigid standard governing all applications for interim restraint orders. Rather, on its proper construction the effect of section 12(3) is that the court is not to make an interim restraint order

---

[32] At [15].

unless satisfied the applicant's prospects of success at the trial are sufficiently favourable to justify such an order being made in the particular circumstances of the case. As to what degree of likelihood makes the prospects of success 'sufficiently favourable', the general approach should be that courts will be exceedingly slow to make interim restraint orders where the applicant has not satisfied the court he will probably ('more likely than not') succeed at the trial. In general, that should be the threshold an applicant must cross before the court embarks on exercising its discretion, duly taking into account the relevant jurisprudence on Article 10 and any countervailing Convention rights. But there will be cases where it is necessary for a court to depart from this general approach and a lesser degree of likelihood will suffice as a prerequisite. Circumstances where this may be so include those mentioned above: where the potential adverse consequences of disclosure are particularly grave, or where a short-lived injunction is needed to enable the court to hear and give proper consideration to an application for interim relief pending the trial or any relevant appeal".

It was not at first readily apparent how s.12 and the subsequent judicial interpretations of it[33] would impact upon applications to restrain a publication apprehended as giving rise to a risk of contempt. The cases have concentrated on breach of confidence and infringement of privacy rights under Art.8 of the Convention. In *Cream Holdings v Banerjee* at the Court of Appeal stage[34] Arden L.J. expressly distinguished the circumstances in that case from those in *Lion Laboratories Ltd v Evans*,[35] where it was held that there had been a public interest in the publication of information that was *prima facie* confidential (for the reason that the relevant public authority, the Home Office, appeared to be dragging its feet over dealing with possible deficiencies in the Lion intoximeter upon which a large number of convictions depended in drink driving cases). Sedley L.J., by contrast, had been of opinion that the subject matter in *Cream Holdings* was indeed of public interest (and the House of Lords ultimately agreed with him).

6–16

Arden L.J. also distinguished the facts from the situation where defamation is alleged and the relevant defendant has indicated an intention to prove the truth of the words. Both she and Simon Brown L.J.[36] adverted to the well known rule in *Bonnard v Perryman*[37] and neither suggested that this long established and stringent test had been altered or qualified by s.12(3) of the Human Rights Act. Yet, on a literal reading, the section might appear to introduce the "likelihood" test for all cases falling within s.12(1) and thus for all attempts to restrain a publication. On the other hand, one could be reasonably confident that, whatever the section was intended to achieve, it cannot have been within Parliament's contemplation in any particular case to render it *easier* to restrain media publications. It may be that the object was, on a proper analysis, to introduce a minimum threshold in such cases rather than a uniform one. It is also significant to note, as Simon Brown L.J. pointed out,[38] that the then Home Secretary in July

6–17

---

[33] See also, *e.g. Douglas v Hello Ltd* [2001] Q.B. 967, CA, and *Theakston v MGN Ltd* [2002] EWHC 137, [2002] E.M.L.R. 398.
[34] [2003] EWCA Civ 103, [2003] Ch. 650 at [96].
[35] [1985] Q.B. 526.
[36] At [43].
[37] [1891] 2 Ch. 269.
[38] At [41].

6–17 1998 when explaining sub-section (3) to the House of Commons[39] particularly cited the example of those who assert rights under Art.8. He stressed that it was sought to make clear that "the courts should consider the merits of an application when it is made and should not grant an interim injunction simply to preserve the status quo ante between the parties" but rather should "protect a respondent potential publisher from what amounts to legal or legalised intimidation". That exactly reflects, of course, the public policy that underlies the *Bonnard v Perryman* test.

6–18 Following the decision of the Court of Appeal, it thus seemed that this long standing test would continue to apply in a defamation context. Moreover, when the case reached the House of Lords, none of their Lordships mentioned *Bonnard v Perryman*, or gave any reason for supposing that its high threshold had been undermined. Although none of the judges in *Cream Holdings* mentioned applications based on contempt, it would appear on a parity of reasoning that the more stringent test identified, for example, in *Coe v Central Television plc*[40] and *Ex p. HTV Cymru (Wales) Ltd*[41] should continue to be applied. Whatever the cause of action or legal principles on which an application for interim relief may be based, it is someone's freedom of communication that is under challenge. As Lord Denning M.R. pointed out on more than one occasion,[42] if an applicant is seeking to restrain publication with a view to protecting reputation, he will find it difficult to circumvent the *Bonnard v Perryman* test by framing the case under a different cause of action.

6–19 It appears to have been confirmed by the decision of the Court of Appeal in *Martha Greene v Associated Newspapers Ltd*[43] that nothing in s.12 of the Human Rights Act, or in the House of Lords' interpretation of it in *Cream Holdings v Banerjee*, should be taken as undermining the practice of the courts when invited to grant interlocutory injunctions against the media to restrain defamatory publications (or, presumably, contempt of court).

D. The approach of the Strasbourg jurisprudence towards prior restraint

6–20 It is clear that Art.10(1) of the European Convention envisages that member states are permitted to make provision for prior restraint (indeed it expressly contemplates the licensing of cinema and broadcasting). Furthermore Arts 10(2), 8 and 6 also envisage that there may be circumstances where it is proportionate and necessary to restrain publication by the media. The case law of the European Court of Human Rights establishes that prior restraint is not inherently objectionable. But the court has warned that "the dangers inherent in prior restraints

---

[39] H.C. *Deb* 6th series, Vol. 315, cols 536–7.
[40] [1994] E.M.L.R. 433.
[41] [2002] E.M.L.R. 184.
[42] See, *e.g. Fraser v Evans* [1969] 1 Q.B. 349 cited at para.2–150 above, and *Woodward v Hutchins* [1977] 1 W.L.R. 760.
[43] [2004] EWCA Civ 1462, [2005] 3 W.L.R. 281, [2005] 1 All E.R. 30 at [60]–[66].

are such that they call for the most careful scrutiny".[44] As one commentator has reluctantly conceded, "There cannot as yet be said to be a 'bright-line' rule against judicial prior restraint in ECHR law. However, it is clear that prior restraints are viewed as pernicious and that, to be upheld as justifiable, their use will have to be viewed as appropriate, proportionate, and absolutely necessary".[45]

E. A comparison with the Canadian Charter

It is perhaps useful to compare the approach adopted to "broadcast bans" in Canada, in the light of their Charter of Rights and Freedoms. In *Dagenais v Canadian Broadcasting Corp*,[46] there were differences in the views expressed within the Supreme Court. All accepted, however, that any limitation upon freedom of expression would be highly exceptional. Nevertheless, the Charter recognised not only freedom of communication but also the right to a fair trial. Some of the judges therefore acknowledged that in certain circumstances it may be necessary to impose a temporary restriction for that purpose. They saw no necessary inconsistency between such a course and the underlying values of the Charter.

6–21

F. Who may claim an injunction?

1. *The current position on locus standi (or "standing")*[47]

It has been held that it is not only the Attorney-General who has *locus standi* to apply for injunctive relief. It appears that any citizen deemed to have a sufficiently proximate interest may also apply.[48] This is so even in the case of an anticipated contempt under the strict liability rule, despite the fact that s.7 of the Contempt of Court Act 1981 provides that proceedings in respect of a contempt actually committed under that rule may not be commenced without the leave of

6–22

---

[44] *Observer Ltd and Guardian Newspapers Ltd v United Kingdom* (1991) 14 E.H.R.R. 153 at [60]. See also *Wingrove v United Kingdom* (1996) 24 E.H.R.R. 1, at [58] where it was held that because prior restraint was involved "special scrutiny by the court" was required. And see *Markt Intern Verlag GmbH and Beerman v Germany* (1989) A165, 12 E.H.R.R. 161; *Open Door Counselling and Dublin Well Woman v Ireland* (1992) 15 E.H.R.R. 244; *Ott-Preminger-Institut v Austria* (1994) A 295–A, 19 E.H.R.R. 34;*Vgt Verein Gegen Tierfabriken v Switzerland*, App. No.24699/94.

[45] C. Munro, "Prior Restraint of the Media and Human Rights Law" (2002) Juridical Rev. 1 at 23.

[46] (1994) 120 D.L.R. (4th) 12, (1995) 94 C.C.C. (3d) 289. See also *R. v Mentuck*, 2001 S.C.C. 76; *Little Sisters Book and Art Emporium v Canada (Minister of Justice)* (2000) 193 D.L.R. (4th) 193, [2000] 2 S.C.R. 1120; *R. v Toronto Star Newspapers Ltd*, 2005 S.C.C. 41.

[47] For a general discussion of the modern law on *locus standi* (standing), see P. Craig, *Administrative Law* (5th ed., 2003) ch.21; P. Cane, *Administrative Law* (4th ed., 2004) ch.4; H.W.R. Wade and C.F. Forsyth, *Administrative Law* (9th ed., 2004), pp.679–700.

[48] *Peacock v London Weekend Television* (1985) 150 J.P. 71, CA; *Leary v BBC* September 29, 1989, unreported (Lexis), CA; *P v Liverpool Daily Post and Echo Newspapers plc* [1991] 2 A.C. 370 at 381, CA; *Connolly v Dale* [1996] Q.B. 120 at 126G, D.C.; *Coe v Central Television plc* [1994] E.M.L.R. 433. But see the note of caution raised at para.6–26.

the Attorney.[49] "The most obvious example of a private citizen who has a special interest is somebody who is an accused person."[50]

6–23 In *Peacock v London Weekend Television*[51] some police officers sought an injunction to restrain the broadcast of a reconstruction of events leading up to the death of a young man in custody, in respect of which an inquest was then pending. The Court of Appeal had no doubt that the men had the necessary *locus* to seek the relief. Indeed, shortly afterwards Tasker Watkins L.J., who had been a member of that Court, held while sitting in another case[52] that, where a breach of the strict liability rule was anticipated, the "proper remedy" was to apply to the High Court for an injunction. He did not suggest that the matter would have to be referred, for this purpose, to the Attorney-General, and appears to have thought that where "a person who is affected or might be by the material which is [to be] published . . . the proper remedy for someone with a grievance in that respect . . . " would be to bring an application so that the court could consider the provisions of ss.1 and 2 of the Contempt of Court Act 1981.

2. *Leary v BBC*

6–24 This approach was accepted as valid by the Court of Appeal in the later case of *Leary v BBC*,[53] which is of some importance on the scope of this jurisdiction and is regularly cited (although unreported).

6–25 A police officer from the recently disbanded West Midlands Serious Crimes Squad (claiming to act in a representative capacity for other officers) sought an injunction to restrain the broadcast of a BBC television programme on the ground that it would create a substantial risk of serious prejudice in respect of a large number of pending proceedings in which officers from the Squad were likely to be witnesses. It was held, following *Peacock v London Weekend Television*,[54] that *locus standi* would not of itself have been a problem for the officers provided that each of them had a sufficiently close interest in the relevant proceedings. The court went on, however, to hold that Mr Leary's role was only that of a potential witness, and that this was not sufficient for the purpose.[55]

3. *A note of caution on locus standi*

6–26 Despite the court's approach to *locus standi* in such cases as *Peacock* and *Leary*, it is necessary to sound a note of caution in relation to the right of individual citizens to bring such proceedings. The following remarks were made *obiter* by

---

[49] *Peacock v London Weekend Television* (1985) 150 J.P. 71, CA.
[50] *per* Lord Donaldson M.R. in *Leary v BBC*, September 29, 1989 (Lexis).
[51] (1985) 150 J.P. 71, CA.
[52] *R. v Rhuddlan Justices* [1986] Crim.L. R. 329, DC.
[53] September 29, 1989, CA, Lord Donaldson M.R., Ralph Gibson and Nicholls L.JJ. (Lexis).
[54] (1985) 150 J.P.71.
[55] Ralph Gibson L.J. said " . . . but I prefer to reserve any decision as to whether a witness in a prosecution case can in law have standing to apply for a *quia timet* injunction, and, if 'yes', what the necessary conditions of sufficient interest on his part are".

Lord Bridge in *P v Liverpool Daily Post and Echo Newspapers plc*,[56] in whose opinion all of their Lordships concurred:

> "It is thus not necessary to decide the question whether, if the defendants had been threatening to publish... they could have been restrained by injunction from committing such a threatened contempt at the instance of the plaintiff without the intervention of the Attorney-General. The argument addressed to this issue certainly went far enough to demonstrate that the question is both difficult and important. The Attorney-General was not represented in these proceedings and since the point does not require to be resolved for the purpose of determining the appeal it would not have been appropriate to adjourn in order to give the Attorney-General the opportunity to intervene. But I consider it eminently desirable that the Attorney-General should be heard before the point is decided and I would accordingly postpone any decision on this issue until another occasion."

An argument could be developed to the effect that the Attorney-General is the "appropriate officer" to consider and protect the public interest.[57] It was observed by Lord Wilberforce in *Gouriet v Union of Post Office Workers*[58]: "That it is the exclusive right of the Attorney General to represent the public interest... is not technical, not procedural, not fictional. It is constitutional."[59]

6–27

Such an argument was advanced in two later cases (concerning applications to commit for contempt, rather than for *quia timet* relief). In *Dobson v Hastings*,[60] and in *Chief Constable of Leicestershire v Garavelli*,[61] the matter did not need to be determined in the light of the decisions arrived at on the merits of the applications to commit. In *Leary v BBC*,[62] Ralph Gibson L.J. had reserved his position on the question.

6–28

An argument in support of the view that persons with a sufficient interest, other than the Attorney-General, *do* have standing to initiate proceedings in respect of contempt or anticipated contempt (and that therefore the decision in *Peacock v London Weekend Television* is correct) is that it would otherwise have been unnecessary for Parliament to stipulate expressly in s.7 of the Contempt of Court Act[63] that only the Attorney-General may initiate proceedings for strict liability contempt. If the position were already clear at common law that *only* the Attorney is the guardian of the public interest in this context, the argument runs, no such statutory provision would have been necessary. This may, however, be a somewhat artificial approach, since it is quite often the case that statutory provisions do no more than confirm or make express that which is recognised at

6–29

---

[56] [1991] 2 A.C. 370 at 425.
[57] *Att-Gen v Times Newspapers Ltd* [1974] A.C. 273 at 311, Lord Diplock, 326, Lord Cross.
[58] [1978] A.C. 435 at 481A–B.
[59] See also *ibid.* at 495E–F, Viscount Dilhorne and 500D–F, Lord Diplock.
[60] [1992] Ch. 394 at 411, Sir Donald Nicholls V.-C.
[61] [1997] E.M.L.R. 543.
[62] See the passage quoted from his judgment in, para.6–25 at n.55.
[63] See para.2–203.

common law. The extent to which individuals might have *locus* therefore remains doubtful.

G. What must an applicant prove?

6-30 What an applicant who seeks a *quia timet* injunction will have to prove must inevitably depend upon the nature of the potential *actus reus* that he is seeking to restrain. He may anticipate a strict liability contempt, in respect of "active" proceedings; on the other hand, he may wish to restrain conduct which could only amount to a common law contempt.[64] This will be so, for example, if he anticipates a publication contempt which is only likely to affect legal proceedings not yet "active".

1. *Applying in the context of strict liability contempt*

6-31 In *Leary v BBC*[65] an injunction was refused, not only on the ground of lack of standing, but also because the applicants had not demonstrated that there was likely to be a sufficient risk of prejudice; and, in any event, there was a s.5 defence available to the BBC because any possible prejudice was likely to be incidental to the discussion of a matter of undoubted public interest.[66] In that case, it happened that at least some of the criminal proceedings alleged to be vulnerable to prejudice were "active" within the meaning of the 1981 Act. The question at issue therefore was whether or not the proposed broadcast would give rise to a substantial risk of serious prejudice.[67]

6-32 Lord Donaldson M.R. adopted a robust attitude towards the question of possible prejudice[68]:

> "It is idle to think that the courts can cocoon juries against all outside influences. Juries are always warned to ignore such influences, and I agree with Mr Justice Lawton in the case of *R. v Kray*,[69] in which he said that they do show a remarkable ability to ignore outside comment. That is truer in long cases where the jury has become more and more—I will not say 'mesmerised' by the evidence—but has become more and more 'involved' in the evidence than it has in the shorter cases, but even in the shorter cases juries do, by and large, conscientiously follow that warning."

---

[64] See, *e.g.* Lord Donaldson M.R. in *P v Liverpool Daily Post and Echo Newspapers plc* [1991] 2 A.C. 370 at 381G. For an example of an application to restrain a common law publication contempt, see the case of *Coe v Central Television plc* [1994] E.M.L.R. 433, discussed at para.6–33.
[65] 29 Sept 1989 (Lexis). Discussed at para.4–316 in the context of s.5 of the Contempt of Court Act.
[66] para.4–293. Contrast the position in Scotland, discussed at para.16–322 and para.16–364.
[67] Contempt of Court Act 1981, s.2(1). Ralph Gibson L.J. contemplated that an applicant would have to show " . . . that the programme would create a substantial risk that the course of justice in the proceedings in question will be seriously impeded or prejudiced."
[68] Court of Appeal (Lexis). It is to be noted that Lord Donaldson M.R. had taken a similar approach to the matter of prejudice in *Att-Gen v News Group Newspapers plc* [1987] 1 Q.B. 1. See paras 4–71 *et seq*. It is perhaps appropriate also to remember that "the formality and solemnity of the court process" can serve to counter the effect of media gossip: *per* Elias C.J. in *Solicitor-General v W&H Specialist Publications* [2003] N.Z.A.R. 118 at [24].
[69] (1969) Cr.App.R. 412. See para.2–86.

2. Establishing a risk of common law contempt

The Court of Appeal in *Coe v Central Television plc*[70] considered the burden facing someone who seeks to obtain an injunction when what is anticipated is a common law contempt. In the case in question the applicant had been neither arrested nor charged, and there were thus no proceedings which were "active". This was explained by Glidewell L.J. in the following terms: 6–33

> "... it is necessary for us to be satisfied, applying the criminal standard of proof:
> (i) that the publication ... will create a real risk of prejudice to the administration of justice
> (ii) that the defendants will publish ... with a specific intent of causing that risk".

The question was left open as to whether it would also be necessary to prove that proceedings were "imminent", although the court proceeded on the basis that it was not necessary to do so.[71] 6–34

As has been noted above,[72] there is no reason to suppose the nature of what has to be proved has in any way been changed by s.12(3) of the Human Rights Act 1998. It would thus seem to be as inappropriate to import the *American Cyanamid*[73] approach into the law governing prior restraint of anticipated contempts as it is in the context of defamation. 6–35

H. The need to avoid any appearance of censorship

More generally, Lord Donaldson sounded the following warning note: 6–36

> "I am very concerned that no-one should think that on a speculative basis you can go to the courts and call upon the publisher of printed material or television or radio material to come forward and tell the court exactly what it is proposed to do, and invite the court to act as a censor. That is not the function of the court. It is different, of course, if there is solid evidence as to what the content of the publication will be and that evidence leads the court to conclude that prima facie there will be a contempt of court. Then it would no doubt be right that the defendant should be invited, but not compelled, to tell the court what in fact he intends to publish, because of course if he does not and there is a prima facie case that there will be a contempt he will find himself faced with an injunction. But that is not the same thing as setting the courts up as a censorship body to which people must submit material on pain of being prohibited from publishing it."

In the same case, Ralph Gibson L.J. observed: 6–37

> "We have, of course, no system of prior examination and permission. If a case is made out to a sufficient degree of probability that an intended publication or broadcast will

---

[70] [1994] E.M.L.R. 433, 441, Glidewell, Ralph Gibson and Kennedy L.JJ. See also *R. v Chignell and Walker* [1990–2] 1 N.Z.B.O.R.R. 179 at 183, Robertson J.
[71] In this context they were prepared to assume that *Att-Gen v News Group Newspapers plc* [1989] Q.B. 110 was correctly decided and that the right approach was that of Bingham L.J. in *Att-Gen v Newspapers Ltd* [1991] 1 W.L.R. 1194 at 1207, [1992] 1 All E.R. 503 at 516. This matter is more fully discussed at paras 5–67 *et seq.*
[72] paras 6–16 *et seq.*
[73] [1975] A.C. 396, outlined at para.6–7.

6–37   CHAPTER 6—COURT ORDERS AFFECTING THE MEDIA

interfere with the administration of justice, then the court will restrain it in advance."

As Munby J. emphatically stated in *Re B (A Child) (Disclosure)*[74]:

"It is wrong in principle to require the media to give prior notice of some proposed publication or broadcast. That is, on the face of it, a wholly unacceptable form of prior restraint. Worse than that, it is, on the face of it, a wholly unacceptable attempt at censorship. That may seem a strong word, but that is in reality what was being attempted here ... The truth is that what the local authority was seeking was the opportunity to approve in advance what the BBC broadcast or, failing agreement, the opportunity to apply to the court for an injunction ....

This, I am afraid, will not do. Licensing in advance what may be published or broadcast is simply censorship under a different name. It is not for the BBC to explain or seek permission to broadcast."

I. The standard of proof

6–38   In *Leary v BBC*,[75] Ralph Gibson L.J. did not go on to develop what "sufficient degree of probability" was required. In *Coe v Central Television plc*,[76] however, the Court of Appeal did address this specifically.[77] What is required is that the applicant must establish his case to "the criminal standard of proof". Aikens J. in *Ex parte HTV Cymru (Wales) Ltd*,[78] sitting in the Cardiff Crown Court, accepted that the right test to apply was that of the criminal standard. In other words, he had to be sure that there was a threatened contempt. This entailed being sure that the alleged acts were going to be carried out and that they would create a substantial risk that the course of justice in the instant case would be seriously impeded or prejudiced. On the facts before him the evidence was that HTV was likely to interview a prosecution witness (who might need to be recalled in rebuttal of the defence case); this in turn gave rise to a risk that the evidence might be adversely affected.

J. To which court should an application be made?

6–39   Despite the procedure adopted in *Att-Gen v Times Newspapers Ltd*,[79] and in *Att-Gen v BBC*,[80] it seems that it would not ordinarily be appropriate to make application for injunctive relief to the Divisional Court. The right course would be to issue a claim form and seek a *quia timet* injunction in the action by notice of application.

---

[74] [2004] EWHC 411 (Fam), [2004] 2 F.L.R. 142 at [145]–[146]. See also *Re Angela Roddy (A Minor)* [2003] EWHC 2927 (Fam), [2004] 2 F.L.R. 949 at [88]–[89]: "It is not for the court to substitute its own views for those of the press as to what technique of reporting should be adopted by journalists."
[75] See para.6–37.
[76] [1994] E.M.L.R. 433.
[77] See the citation at para.6–33.
[78] [2002] E.M.L.R. 184 at [25]. See above at paras 6–16 *et seq*, where it is suggested that there is no reason to suppose that this principle has been eroded by the wording of s.12(3) of the Human Rights Act 1998.
[79] [1974] A.C. 273.
[80] [1981] A.C. 303.

This would be similar to what happened, for example, in *Att-Gen v Channel 4 Television Co Ltd*,[81] when a programme was banned because it was anticipated that it would create a substantial risk of serious prejudice in criminal proceedings then under way. The programme might have cast doubt on the credibility of a witness who had already given evidence for the prosecution in a closely related criminal trial. Other examples of this more usual procedure, of applying to a single judge of the High Court,[82] are provided by *Peacock v London Weekend Television*,[83] *Att-Gen v News Group Newspapers plc*,[84] *P v Liverpool Daily Post and Echo Newspapers plc*.[85]

II. THE INHERENT (OR *PARENS PATRIAE*) JURISDICTION

A. Injunctions *contra mundum*

1. Introduction

The courts have increasingly been required to consider the power to grant injunctions in the exercise of what has long been called the *"parens patriae"* jurisdiction for the protection of vulnerable persons and, at first, particularly with reference to wards of court. Unusually,[86] such injunctions can be directed beyond those who are parties and in particular so as to bind the media generally[87] and have thus been described as operating *contra mundum* or *in rem*.[88] It is now provided[89] that service of any application for reporting restriction orders on the national media can be effected via the Press Association's Copy Direct Service to which the national newspapers and broadcasters subscribe as a means of receiving notice.

---

[81] CA, June 19, 1996, unreported, Nourse, Waite and Ward L.JJ. (Lexis).
[82] As to the jurisdiction of the Crown Court, see the discussion at para.6–2.
[83] (1985) 150 J.P. 171.
[84] [1987] Q.B. 1.
[85] [1991] 2 A.C. 370.
[86] See *Iveson v Harris* (1802) 7 Ves. Jun. 251 at 256–7, 32 E.R. 102 at 103–4, and in particular Lord Eldon's *in personam* principle, discussed at para.6–115.
[87] *X County Council v A* [1985] 1 W.L.R. 1422, Balcombe J.; *Re L (A Minor) Wardship: Freedom of Publication* [1988] 1 F.L.R. 255 at 259, [1988] 1 All E.R. 418 at 421, Booth J. It is clear from both cases that no liability for contempt can arise unless the alleged contemnor has knowledge of the order's material terms. By contrast, in Scotland the court has not accepted the jurisdiction to bind the world and seems to go no further in recognising liability in contempt, on the part of third parties who are not bound by an injunction directly, than in circumstances where there has been a conspiracy: see A. Bonnington, "Interdict and Contempt of Court" (1989) S.L.T. 381. See also *Dudgeon v Thomson* (1876) 3 R. 604 and 974; *Harvie v Ross* (1886) 14 R. 71 at 73.
[88] *Re Z (A Minor) (Identification: Restrictions on Publication)* [1997] Fam. 1 at 10F, Ward L.J. This usage is no doubt intended to contrast the usual circumstance where the court's process operates *in personam*. It is a little difficult, however, to understand quite how the phrase *in rem* operates in the context of orders against the media because, unlike the situation encountered in (say) Admiralty proceedings, there is no obvious *res* to which the term could apply.
[89] By the President's Direction of March 18, 2005, *Applications for Reporting Restriction Orders* and the *Practice Note* of the same title and date issued by the Official Solicitor and the Deputy Director of Legal Services CAFCASS. For a list of those who subscribe, see *www.medialawyer.press.net/courtapplications*.

6-42   In these circumstances, although the court will generally be ready to hear applications *ex post facto* to set aside or vary, the law works in such a way that the freedom of citizens to communicate (even on matters of public interest) is sometimes restricted without any opportunity to be heard. Once he or she has knowledge of such an order, a journalist who flouts its terms may well be in contempt. It was thus considered important in the previous edition of this work to address these relatively recent developments in domestic law and the policy considerations underlying them.[90] Since the jurisdiction has now been explained in the light of the ECHR by the House of Lords in *Re S (FC) (A Child)*,[91] the significance of that history has to some extent faded into the background but it was thought premature for it to be expunged from this edition entirely. Meanwhile, we turn to consider that case.

2. *The analysis of the jurisdiction by the House of Lords in Convention terms*

6-43   Whatever terminology was used, it is fundamental that applications to restrain publication for the protection of the vulnerable in such circumstances would engage what are now more clearly seen as conflicting Convention rights and, most frequently, those guaranteed under Arts 8 and 10. The House of Lords in *Re S (FC) (A Child)* unanimously expressed the view that, since the Human Rights Act 1998 came into effect, the earlier case law about the existence and scope of the inherent jurisdiction need not be routinely considered on such applications, since the foundation of the jurisdiction to restrain publicity could thenceforth be regarded as derived from rights under the Convention. This should not be taken, however, as entailing that the reasoning in that body of case law is now always to be regarded as completely irrelevant on such applications. Not only had the approach of the domestic courts under the inherent jurisdiction been "remarkably similar" to that to be adopted under the Convention, but the authorities "may remain of some interest in regard to the ultimate balancing exercise to be carried out".

6-44   The "ultimate balancing test" was defined[92] in terms of the four important propositions emerging from the opinions of the House in *Campbell v MGN Ltd*.[93] These illustrate the "new methodology" which needs to be borne in mind whenever earlier case law is cited in the context of the interplay between the rights arising respectively under Arts 8 and 10:

---

[90] The modern development of this jurisdiction appears to have begun in the mid 1980s. See the careful analysis by Munby J. in *Kelly v BBC* [2001] Fam. 59 at 73–75 and in *Harris v Harris; Att-Gen v Harris* [2001] 2 F.L.R. 895 at [331] *et seq*. In *Re X (A Child) (Injunctions Restraining Publication)* [2001] 1 F.C.R. 541, Bracewell J. expressed her agreement with the analysis of Munby J. See generally M. Wright, "The Press, Children and Injunctions" (1992) 55 M.L.R. 857; J. Moriarty, "Children, Privacy and the Press" (1997) 9 C.F.L.Q. 217; I. Cram, "Minors' Privacy, the courts and Limits on Freedom of Expression" [1997–8] Entertainment and Media Law Yearbook 31; J. Dixon, "Children and the Statutory Restraints on Publicity" (2001) Family Law at 757 and H. Fenwick, "Clashing Rights, the Welfare of the Child and the Human Rights Act" (2004) 67 M.L.R. 889.
[91] [2004] UKHL 47, [2005] 1 A.C. 593 at [23].
[92] *ibid.* at [17].
[93] [2004] UKHL 22, [2004] 2 A.C. 457.

(1) Neither article has *as such* precedence over the other.
(2) Where conflict arises between the values under Arts 8 and 10, an "intense focus" is necessary upon the comparative importance of the specific rights being claimed in the individual cases.
(3) The court must take into account the justifications for interfering with or restricting each right.
(4) So too, the proportionality test must be applied to each.

It would thus seem that, subject to the important principles outlined in these two decisions of the House of Lords, it is still desirable in a work of this kind to consider the domestic authorities pre-dating the Human Rights Act since they may still be of some, albeit limited, relevance. Yet great care will need to be taken in the "new era" in deciding when useful guidance can be obtained from earlier decisions and when it cannot.

6–45

3. *The development of the jurisdiction in earlier case law*

In the case of *R. v Central Independent Television plc*,[94] Hoffmann L.J. stated that " . . . the courts have, without any statutory or, so far as I can see, other previous authority, assumed a power to create by injunction what is in effect a right of privacy for children." Although it is naturally now discussed by reference to Convention rights, the recognition of this jurisdiction was effectively beyond challenge well before the Human Rights Act came into effect, even though it was not always expressed directly in terms of the Convention.

6–46

In *Att-Gen v Newspaper Publishing plc*,[95] the practice of granting *contra mundum* orders in the context of wardship was treated as being an exception to the general principle that the court acts *in personam*, although Balcombe L.J.[96] was of opinion that the wardship cases represented merely one instance of a more general power in the court to make orders *contra mundum* when necessary to protect its process, and the purpose which court proceedings are intended to achieve, from the impact of unwelcome publicity.[97] While such a jurisdiction would only be exercised in exceptional circumstances, he considered that the facts before the Court of Appeal in the *Spycatcher* litigation were such as to merit an order of this kind[98]:

6–47

"I believe that there can be another exception to the general rule which would enable the court to make an order, binding on the world at large, in the circumstances of the

---

[94] [1994] Fam. 192 at 204D.
[95] [1988] Ch. 333 at 369, 370, Sir John Donaldson M.R.. The Spycatcher litigation is considered more fully at paras 6–115 *et seq*. See also paras 5–141 *et seq*. and paras 11–34 *et seq*.
[96] *ibid*., at 388–9.
[97] See also *Re C (A Minor) (Wardship: Medical Treatment) (No.2)* [1990] Fam. 39 at 53, Nicholls L.J. It seems clear that the purpose of the injunction granted in *Venables and Thompson v News Group Newspapers Ltd* (see para.6–49), extended beyond the purposes being contemplated at that time, since it would be difficult to construe it as for the protection of the court's process. It was rather about the protection of life against the background of Art.2 of the Convention.
[98] At 388. See also the discussion of these *dicta* by A.J. Bonnington in (1989) S.L.T. 381 at 384.

present case, where such an order may be appropriate to preserve the subject matter of an action pending trial."

Although expressed in 1987, this view does not seem to be inconsistent with Strasbourg jurisprudence or with the policy now embodied in s.12 of the Human Rights Act 1998.[99]

6–48   Balcombe L.J. went on to identify the *ratio decidendi* of his earlier first instance decision in *Re X (A Minor) Wardship: Injunction*,[1] as being that ". . . in the exercise of the wardship jurisdiction, there was power to make an order . . . binding on the world at large, when persons who were potentially subject to that order had not been parties to the proceedings in which the order was obtained." On the other hand, Sir John Donaldson M.R. appears to have thought that the effect of what Balcombe J. had done in that case was to announce to the world at large that he had made an order against a particular newspaper, the *News of the World*, and to warn other journalists that, if they acted inconsistently with that order, other newspaper publishers could find themselves in contempt. Had it not been for the "happenstance" that he had been enjoining the *News of the World* any way, he might not have had jurisdiction to bind the world at large. This difference of analysis is now probably of historic interest only, since the jurisdiction must be considered generally in the light of the Human Rights Act 1998 and the need to give effect to Convention rights.

6–49   The true breadth of the jurisdiction was illustrated in *Venables and Thompson v News Group Newspapers Ltd.*[2] An order *contra mundum* was made by the President of the Family Division to prevent the identification of two young men throughout their lives. Thus, effectively, permanent restrictions were imposed on the media for the protection of persons who could not be categorised as either minors or patients. The people protected by the order had been convicted of murdering a small child when they themselves were 11 years old. The case aroused continuing publicity and strong public feelings. It became clear that there was going to be a risk to life and limb following their release from a custodial environment. A key element in the court's reasoning was the need to act in a manner compatible with the European Convention. In particular, it was necessary to have regard to Art.2 and the right to life. Thus, it was not a case concerned merely with the protection of privacy; nor yet with protecting the court's own processes in connection with current litigation. In this exceptional case, it was held that the restrictions were necessary and proportionate to the legitimate aim of protecting their safety. Indeed, there was perceived to be no other way to ensure such protection. It appears that the application was not based on the *parens patriae* jurisdiction as such but principally on the law of confidence. It was frankly recognised that the jurisdiction was being used in an unprecedented manner and that it was not compatible with Lord Eldon's *dictum* in *Iveson v*

---

[99] Set out at para.6–11 above.
[1] [1984] 1 W.L.R. 1422 (where he had made such an order in the context of Mary Bell, who had been found guilty of manslaughter at the age of 11; she had grown up meanwhile and given birth to a child of her own). For subsequent developments see now *X (A Woman Formerly Known As Mary Bell) v O'Brien* [2003] EWHC 1101 (QB), [2003] 2 F.C.R. 686.
[2] [2001] Fam. 430.

Harris.³ But it was a "new era" and remedies had to be fashioned to meet the needs of the particular case in the light of the Convention.⁴ There were clearly going to be potential problems about the restricted information coming into the public domain by publication outside the jurisdiction or through the internet. In general terms, the law of confidence in a commercial context ceases to be effective once the protected information has truly entered the public domain.⁵ Nevertheless, the President added a proviso to the order to make it clear that it would still remain in force, so as to ban publication of information that might lead to the two men being found, even if the material came into the public domain abroad or became available on the Internet.⁶

The issue of "public domain" came to be tested shortly afterwards in *Att-Gen v Greater Manchester Newspapers Ltd.*⁷ The date of the President's original order was January 8, 2001 and any information in the public domain prior to that date could properly be repeated in the press, but material made public thereafter was not to be republished. The court was concerned with the question of whether certain statistical information available through public libraries, and also *via* a government department website, was "realistically" accessible to members of the public or only "in theory". On the facts, it was held not to have been in the public domain, but there can be no general rule and each case must be closely examined in the light of its own circumstances.⁸

6–50

4. *The continuing but limited role of the* parens patriae *jurisdiction*

In most instances prior to *Venables and Thompson*, the reported cases in which *contra mundum* orders had been made concerned the court's *parens patriae* jurisdiction and attempts to protect the welfare of children or patients or the integrity of the court's process in that context. In future also, the court will in practice be likely to be called upon to exercise this exceptional power of prior restraint in one, or both, of these contexts. It seems, however, that now " . . . the relevance of the [*parens patriae*] jurisdiction may simply be to provide the vehicle which enables the court to conduct the necessary balancing exercise between the competing rights of the child under article 8 and the media under article 10".⁹ Yet, where the "ultimate balancing exercise" falls to be carried out in such cases the approach adopted in the earlier authorities "may remain of

6–51

---

³ Cited at para.6–115. See also how the reasoning has been followed in *X (A Woman Formerly Known As Mary Bell) v O'Brien* [2003] EWHC 1101 (QB), [2003] 2 F.C.R. 686 and *Carr (Maxine) v News Group Newspapers Ltd* [2005] EWHC 971 (QB).
⁴ [2001] Fam. 430 at [100].
⁵ See, *e.g. Coco v Clark (AN) (Engineers) Ltd* [1969] R.P.C. 41; *Saltman Engineering Co v Campbell Engineering Co* (1948) [1963] 3 All E.R. 413 (note).
⁶ Cp the remarks of Lord Keith in *Att-Gen v Guardian Newspapers Ltd (No.2)* [1990] 1 A.C. 109 at 260E–H; see also *R. v Broadcasting Complaints Commission Ex p. Granada TV* [1995] E.M.L.R. 163 and *WB v H Bauer Publishing Ltd* [2002] E.M.L.R. 145. These cases tend to suggest that where personal privacy is concerned the court's protection need not necessarily be lost on a once for all basis, as would be the case for example with breaches of commercial confidentiality, merely by the material coming into the public domain.
⁷ [2001] All E.R. (D) 32 (Dec). Curiously, the decision seems to be otherwise unreported.
⁸ See para.4–27, n.66.
⁹ *Re S (FC) (A Child)* [2004] UKHL 47, [2005] 1 A.C. 593 at [22].

6–51 some interest".[10] It is perhaps fair to say, in the light of the House of Lords' decision that such precedents are least likely to be of value in cases where the court has adopted too rigid an approach or, to put it another way, appears to have elevated to general principles what would now be recognised merely as factors given priority on the facts of a particular case.[11]

6–52 One needs to be on guard too against decisions which would now be perceived as according, impermissibly, automatic precedence to one Convention right over another. One commentator[12] was of the view that the domestic courts had been travelling on a route that was inconsistent with Strasbourg jurisprudence with the result that their analysis, by classifying cases according to what came to be called the "protective" versus the "custodial" jurisdiction, tended to pre-empt a principled resolution of any given conflict by ensuring that one side *automatically* won depending upon the category to which it had been allocated. She was troubled that, if the case was classified as relating to the child's upbringing, this factor by reason of s.1 of the Children Act 1989 effectively "trumped" the Art.10 rights of the media. Even before her concerns were published, however, the House of Lords in *Re S (FC) (A Child)* seemed to cure the problem by emphasising the need to examine particular cases without according precedence to any one article over another. Subject to this important caveat, it now seems still to be necessary, at least for the time being, to survey the development of the jurisdiction prior to the enactment of the Human Rights Act.

B. The history of the *parens patriae* (or "inherent") jurisdiction generally

6–53 The *parens patriae* jurisdiction is of ancient origin. Lord Eldon L.C. described it in the following terms[13]:

> " ... it belongs to the King, as *parens patriae*, having the care of those who are not able to take care of themselves, and is founded on the obvious necessity that the law should place somewhere the care of individuals who cannot take care of themselves, particularly in cases where it is clear that some care should be thrown round them."

6–54 This inherent jurisdiction was not confined to children but extended to others unable to look after themselves, such as patients and other vulnerable adults[14]; nor were these powers, which had been devolved to the courts to be exercised on behalf of the Crown, restricted to the wardship jurisdiction—although in the past

---

[10] *ibid.* at [23].
[11] See, *e.g.* the debate about the protective versus custodial jurisdiction discussed at paras 6–56 *et seq.*
[12] H. Fenwick, "Clashing Rights, the Welfare of the Child and the Human Rights Act" (2004) 67 M.L.R. 889.
[13] *Wellesley v Duke of Beaufort* (1827) 2 Russ. 1 at 20, 38 E.R. 236 at 243. See also *Butler v Freeman* (1756) Amb. 301 at 302, Lord Hardwicke L.C.
[14] See, *e.g. Re F (Mental Patient: Sterilisation)* [1992] A.C. 1 at 13, Lord Donaldson M.R.; *Re C (Adult Patient: Restriction of Publicity After Death)* [1996] 1 F.C.R. 605, Sir Stephen Brown P.; *Re G (Adult Patient: Publicity)* [1996] 1 F.C.R. 413; *Re a Local Authority (Inquiry: Restraint on Publication)* [2003] EWHC 2746 (Fam), [2004] Fam. 96.

it frequently proved to be the most apt machinery for their implementation.[15] Nevertheless, for all practical purposes, so far as children were concerned, the jurisdiction in wardship and the inherent jurisdiction were regarded as one and the same and could be considered together.[16] It is true that the Children Act 1989 had curtailed the use of wardship proceedings, but it did not affect the court's inherent jurisdiction.[17]

The Crown has long had a duty to protect its subjects, particularly children,[18] and this sometimes entailed the need for an order of the court, in the exercise of that inherent jurisdiction, which affected third parties. Sometimes it would be unnecessary to go outside the scope of the general law because, for example, the minors were protected by the normal constraints upon the revelation of information connected with court proceedings.[19] On occasion, however, it was recognised as being necessary specifically to restrain publication by the media.[20] This power to restrict the media was only recognised relatively recently.[21] It was at first justified by reference to the inherent jurisdiction, although it was by no means a pre-condition for its exercise that a child whom the court sought to protect should have been made a ward of court.[22]

6–55

C. The distinction between the "custodial" and "protective" distinction

Prior to the decisions of the House of Lords in *Campbell v MGN Ltd*[23] and, more specifically, *Re S (FC) (A Child)*,[24] judges tended to break down the circumstances in which such orders were sought, and the justification for granting them, according to their jurisdiction to protect either vulnerable citizens or the integrity

6–56

---

[15] *Re C (A Minor) (Wardship: Medical Treatment) (No.2)* [1990] Fam. 39 at 46, Lord Donaldson M.R.; see also *Re M & N (Minors) (Wardship: Publication of Information)* [1990] Fam. 211 at 223, Butler-Sloss L.J.; *Re N (Infants)* [1967] Ch. 512 at 531, Stamp J.; *Re L (An Infant)* [1968] P. 119 at 156, Lord Denning M.R.
[16] *Re Z (A Minor) (Identification: Restrictions on Publication)* [1997] Fam. 1 at 14A–B, Ward L.J.; *Re S (Adult Patient: Sterilisation)* [2001] Fam 15 at 29–30, Thorpe L.J. See also, in the context of disclosure of confidential material, *Re K and others (Minors) (Disclosure)* [1994] 1 F.L.R. 377.
[17] *Re Z* (last note). See also further reference to the Children Act 1989 at para.6–62.
[18] See generally *Re Spence* (1847) 2 Ph. 247 at 252, 41 E.R. 937 at 938, Lord Cottenham L.C.; *Barnardo v McHugh* [1891] A.C. 388 at 395, Lord Halsbury L.C.; *Scott v Scott* [1913] A.C. 417, 437, Viscount Haldane, L.C., 462, Lord Atkinson, 483, Lord Shaw of Dumferline; *Re Mohamed Arif (An Infant)* [1968] Ch. 643 at 662–3, Russell L.J.; *Re X (A Minor) (Wardship: Jurisdiction)* [1975] Fam. 47 at 52, Latey J.; *Re C (A Minor) (Wardship: Medical Treatment) (No.2)* [1990] Fam. 39 at 46, Lord Donaldson M.R.; *Re R (A Minor), (Wardship, Restrictions on Publication)* [1994] Fam. 254 at 271, [1994] F.L.R. 637 at 651, Millett L.J.; *Re Z (A Minor)(Identification: Restrictions on Publication)* [1997] Fam. 1, CA.
[19] As under s.12 of the Administration of Justice Act 1960: see, *e.g. Oxfordshire County Council v L and F* [1997] 1 F.L.R. 235, where the judge needed to take no steps to impose additional restraints, and simply declined to lift the existing restrictions upon the parents.
[20] See the discussion of this jurisdiction in the articles cited in para.6–42, n.90.
[21] *Re R (A Minor)* [1994] F.L.R. 637 at 650E–F, per Millett L.J.; *R v Central Independent Television plc* [1994] Fam. 192 at 204–5, Hoffmann L.J. And see the remarks of Thorpe L.J. in *Re G (Celebrities: Publicity)* [1999] 1 F.L.R. 409 at 418, cited above at para.2–58.
[22] Sir Thomas Bingham M.R., in *Re Z (A Minor) (Identification: Restrictions on Publication)* [1997] Fam. 1 at 32D–E.
[23] [2004] UKHL 22, [2004] 2 A.C. 457.
[24] [2004] UKHL 47, [2005] 1 A.C. 593.

of the court's own process—rather than by reference to giving effect to or balancing the rights of individuals. It was possible to tease out from the authorities before the coming into effect of the Human Rights Act in October 2000 separate strands of public policy as justifying, in different circumstances, the restriction of media publication. The approach to balancing freedom of expression against the need to protect the individual varied, depending which of these principles was being applied to the case in question. Nevertheless, it will be observed that in either case the court tended to apply the test of whether any such restriction was "necessary" to achieve the relevant purpose. To that extent, therefore, the approach was already consistent with that to be adopted under the European Convention and particularly Art.10(2).[25]

6–57 Even though there is no express reference to the protection of children,[26] as one of the recognised exceptions under Art.10(2), it does refer to the protection of the "rights" of others. This would be apt to include the "right" to respect for private and family life under Art.8 and indeed the right to life under Art.2. Article 10(2) also refers expressly to upholding the authority of the judiciary, and it will be seen that in most of the cases the power to ban media publications was justified by reference not to the well-being or privacy of a child but to the protection of the integrity of the court's process, which was perhaps easier to fit directly into the framework of Art.10(2).

6–58 For a time between 1996 and 2004, there appeared to be a need for a somewhat tortuous analysis to determine which of these two aspects of the court's jurisdiction was relevant to the case in hand, rather than going directly to a balancing of competing rights. In *Re Z (A Minor) (Identification)* [27] Ward L.J. identified:

> "... two strands which may need to be kept separate, namely, that aspect of the wardship jurisdiction which seeks to protect the welfare of the child and that aspect which can also be said to be quite another facet of the court's inherent jurisdiction, namely its power to protect its own proceedings as may be necessary in the interests of the administration of justice."

Although labels can be artificial and misleading, it was thought during this period to be helpful to refer (as did Ward L.J. in *Re Z*) to the two aspects of the court's jurisdiction respectively described by Lord MacDermott in *S v McC (Orse S) and M (DS Intervener); W v W*[28] as being "custodial" and "protective" in character.

---

[25] See also *Sunday Times v UK* (1979) 2 E.H.R.R. 245 at 275 (the right to freedom of communication should only be restricted to the extent that there is "a pressing social need"); *Re H-S* [1994] 3 All E.R. 390 at 398a–d, where the Court of Appeal drew attention to the need to take account also of Art.8 of the Convention ("right to respect for private and family life"). Art.8 was also relied upon by Charles J. in *A v M (Family Proceedings: Publicity)* [2000] 1 F.L.R. 562 at 567C–D.
[26] By contrast with the open justice provisions of Art.6, for which, see para.2–143.
[27] [1997] 1 Fam. 1 at 19F–G. For general discussion, see J. Moriarty, "Children, Privacy and the Press" (1997) 9 C.F.L.Q. 217; I. Cram, "Minors' Privacy, the courts and Limits on Freedom of Expression" in eds. E. Barendt, *et al*, [1997–8] Y.B.E.M.L. 31.
[28] [1972] A.C. 24 at 48.

It remained nonetheless important to recognise that there was yet another **6-59**
category of case apart from the "custodial" and "protective" aspects of the
court's jurisdiction. As Munby J. has pointed out, one should not lose sight of
those cases which come before the courts in which the *parens patriae* jurisdiction
" ... is not exercisable at all and the child is left to whatever remedies against
the media the law would give an adult in comparable circumstances".[29] He
explained that the "protective" jurisdiction would only come in to play and give
rise to the possibility of a court order where the proposed publication was directly
about a child whose care and upbringing were already being supervised by the
court *and* was such as might threaten the effective working of the court's
jurisdiction or the ability of the child's carers to carry out their obligations to the
court. As he said in *Re Angela Roddy*,[30] a "bright-line boundary" could no longer
be drawn in the light of the Human Rights Act, as applied by the Court of Appeal
(and indeed subsequently by the House of Lords) in *Re S (FC)*.[31] It was no longer
a forensically useful exercise to analyse the facts of a particular case with a view
to establishing at the outset whether it properly fell into the category hitherto
thought to engage the "protective" jurisdiction. The emphasis now would be
upon balancing the various rights of those concerned under the European
Convention, most frequently the competing rights under Arts 8 and 10. As Hale
L.J. put it in the Court of Appeal in *Re S (FC)*,[32] the relevance of the jurisdiction
may simply be to provide the vehicle which enables the court to conduct the
necessary balancing exercise between the competing rights. The court is at least
entitled to consider the grant of an injunction even if the publicity is *not* directed
at the child or the carers, and could not be shown to have an adverse effect on
court proceedings—although that would no doubt sometimes be a significant
factor to weigh.[33]

Since the decision of the House of Lords in *Re S (FC)*, the "new method- **6-60**
ology" has to be applied of balancing rights under the European Convention, and
the emphasis is likely to be upon the comparative importance of the specific
rights being claimed in individual cases.[34] The former focus upon the supposedly
clear cut distinction between the "protective" and the "custodial" aspects of the
jurisdiction will probably now increasingly be perceived as a sterile one, but it is
perhaps worth observing that it did not appear, even at the time when it was in
fashion, to have the countervailing advantage of certainty or predictability.

D. The focus in *Re Z* upon the "custodial" aspect of the jurisdiction

The custodial aspect of the inherent jurisdiction was described by Lord **6-61**
MacDermott as[35]:

---

[29] *Kelly v BBC* [2001] Fam. 59 at 74.
[30] [2003] EWHC 2929 (Fam), [2004] 2 F.L.R. 949 at [16].
[31] [2003] EWCA Civ 963, [2003] Ch. 650, CA, [2004] UKHL 47, [2005] 1 A.C. 593.
[32] At [40]. Adopted by Lord Steyn in the House of Lords at [22].
[33] As Latham L.J. observed in the Court of Appeal at [75].
[34] But see the tension highlighted in para.6–87.
[35] *ibid.* See also *J v C* [1970] A.C. 668.

6–61 CHAPTER 6—COURT ORDERS AFFECTING THE MEDIA

" ... an aspect of the prerogative and paternal jurisdiction of the former Court of Chancery which has now passed to the several divisions of the High Court. It is derived mainly from the administrative functions of the court of Chancery in which that Court had to make a choice between conflicting claims as to the custody and upbringing of the infant or the management of his affairs, or to determine the course to be taken in such matters even when not in actual dispute."

1. The Court's resort to the Children Act 1989 and the concept of "paramountcy"

6–62 It would not, on the face of it, often happen that the exercise of this "custodial" jurisdiction would directly impinge upon media publication. Few people *in loco parentis* have to make decisions about a child's participation in such matters. Yet this was exactly the problem that arose in *Re Z*.[36] The child's parents were well known to the public and, although she was not a ward of Court, an injunction was already in place restricting publicity about her which had been obtained at the instance of both parents. A time came when the mother wished to vary the terms of the order to enable herself and her daughter to take part in a television programme about the treatment she was receiving for her educational needs at a specialised institution. The judge and the Court of Appeal declined to permit this on the ground that such an exercise would not serve the best interests of the girl herself. The wishes of a devoted and responsible parent were not lightly to be set aside, but the court had to make an independent and objective judgment of its own.[37]

6–63 Where such a decision falls to be made by the court in the exercise of its supervisory jurisdiction, acting in effect *in loco parentis*, the child's welfare would have to be treated as paramount. This is because of the terms of s.1(1) of the Children Act 1989:

"When a court determines any question with respect to—

(a) the upbringing of a child; ... the child's welfare shall be the court's paramount consideration."

6–64 In the later judgment of the Court of Appeal in *Re G (Celebrities: Publicity)*,[38] Thorpe L.J. recognised the court's closely related jurisdiction to grant an *in personam* injunction to restrain any act by a parent that in itself would or might adversely affect the welfare of a child who is the subject of proceedings. In such cases, the interests of the child would also be paramount, by contrast with the situation where it is the "protective" aspect of the *contra mundum* jurisdiction that is engaged.

---

[36] See also *Re W (Wardship: Discharge: Publicity)* [1995] 2 F.L.R. 466 at 475–6, Hobhouse L.J.
[37] *Re Z* [1997] Fam. 1, *per* Sir Thomas Bingham M.R. at 32–3.
[38] [1999] 1 F.L.R. 409 at 414H. See the discussion of the case by J. Dixon in "Children and the Statutory Restraints on Publicity" (2001) Family Law at 757. The matter was also considered by Munby J. in *Kelly v BBC* [2001] Fam. 59 at 82C and in *Harris v Harris; Att-Gen v Harris* [2001] 2 F.L.R. 895 at [335].

Although because of this statutory provision welfare had to be the paramount consideration, this did not mean that freedom of publication was not to be weighed in the scales at all. It was said (perhaps somewhat artificially) to be one of the facts and circumstances that a reasonable parent would take into account.[39] The test applied was still, however, that of necessity. As Sir Thomas Bingham M.R. pointed out in *Re Z* itself,[40] if the court judges that the welfare of the child would be significantly harmed by media reporting and comment, it is not simply entitled but obliged to restrain publicity to such an extent as is necessary to protect it. However, the case of *Re Z* placed considerable emphasis upon the need for confidentiality and a duty of confidence owed by parents to a child,[41] which the court may exercise *in loco parentis* through the means of a prohibited steps order under the Children Act 1989. (Now it would probably be more appropriate to address the child's right of privacy rather than a duty owed *to* the child.)

2. *Specific Issue Prohibited Steps Orders*

In s.8(1) of the Children Act 1989 it is provided that:

> "'A prohibited steps order' means an order that no step which could be taken by a parent in meeting his parental responsibility for a child, and which is of a kind specified in the order, shall be taken by any person without the consent of the court; ... "

The concept of "parental responsibility" is defined in s.3(1) of the Act to include:

> " ... all the rights, duties, powers, responsibilities and authority which by law a parent of a child has in relation to the child and his property."

In *Re Z*,[42] Ward L.J. expressed the view that it was an incident of the mother's parental responsibility to decide whether to preserve or to publish matters which were *prima facie* confidential to the child. He concluded that her giving permission for the making of the film about the child was an exercise of parental responsibility; and that accordingly a prohibited steps order could be made in respect of it.[43]

---

[39] *ibid.* at 28C–D, Ward L.J. It is perhaps more accurate to say, as Professor Fenwick does in her article cited above at para.6–42, n.90, at p.892, " ... where the paramountcy principle does not apply, media freedom of expression tends to win out, while where it does apply, the Article 10 rights of the media hardly weigh in the scales at all".
[40] *ibid.*, at 33E–F.
[41] [1997] Fam. 1 at 25F. See also *Oxfordshire County Council v L and F* [1997] 1 F.L.R. 235 at 250D, 253F–G, Stuart-White J.
[42] [1997] Fam. 1, 26D–E at 30C–D. See also *Re Angela Roddy (A Minor)* [2003] EWHC 2927 (Fam), [2004] 2 F.L.R. 949 at [35]–[38] and [46]–[60], where Munby J. fully discusses the right under Art.8 to maintain one's privacy and the concomitant right, both under Art.8 and under Art.10, to publicise what would otherwise be private; and also the stage of development at which a child may be deemed capable of taking such decisions personally.
[43] See also *Re W (Wardship: Discharge: Publicity)* [1995] 2 F.L.R. 466 at 475–6, where Hobhouse L.J. expressed a similar opinion. In that case, however, both Balcombe and Waite L.JJ. doubted whether decisions as to the publication of information about a child could *ever* be classified as "a step in meeting parental responsibility", and they considered that this might be a "non-parental activity". In the light of the later decision of the Court of Appeal in *Re Z*, cited above, the view of Hobhouse L.J. on this general point may be said to have prevailed. Yet each case will depend on its own circumstances.

3. *The practical difficulties of applying the distinction*

6–68 "It is not always easy to decide when a question of upbringing is being determined".[44] Some practitioners seem to have found the full implications of this analysis difficult to work out in practice. In *Oxfordshire County Council v L and F*,[45] for example, Stuart-White J. held that it had been wrongly conceded that the decision he had to make was one "with regard to upbringing and that welfare [was] therefore paramount." A degree of uncertainty was inevitable as to how broadly the court would interpret the statutory notion in s.1(1) of questions in respect of "the upbringing of a child".

6–69 It was thus by no means easy to identify, in any given case, whether the court was to perform a balancing exercise for the purposes of the protective jurisdiction or to accord paramountcy to the child's welfare under the custodial jurisdiction. This element of uncertainty, therefore, in so far as there arose a question of possible media coverage would give rise inevitably to a chilling effect. In *L and F*[46] care proceedings came before the court in relation to two different families in which it was necessary to consider allegations of injuries inflicted by a childminder. As a result of interest expressed by a journalist, injunctions were granted prohibiting publication of any matter identifying or calculated to lead to the identification of any of the children, and prohibiting the solicitation of information about them. A further injunction prohibited the parents of one child from publishing information about the proceedings.

6–70 Subsequently, they applied for variation of the injunction for a number of reasons:

(a) The parents argued that they were the only persons with parental responsibility for the child in question, and should therefore be the only persons to determine his future. But the judge said that the application also affected other children and, in any event, the court had powers to override the exercise of parental responsibility if it was about to be exercised contrary to the welfare of the child or to the law.

(b) Secondly, it was said that the experience of what had happened to that child should be publicised as a warning to parents in general. But the judge concluded that it was not in the public interest for the "tragic history" to be so publicised not least, apparently, because of the possibility that it would be given irresponsible and sensationalist treatment.[47]

(c) It was hoped by the parents that publicising the matter might achieve a degree of catharsis for themselves, as they felt bitter about what had happened not only to their child at the hands of the minder but also about their own treatment by a social worker. (It is important that by the time

---

[44] *Re Z* [1997] Fam. 1 at 28F, Ward L.J.
[45] [1997] 1 F.L.R. 235 at 254E–F.
[46] Last note. The relevant issue in the case was whether leave should be given to the parents to reveal information which would otherwise remain confidential in the light of the Administration of Justice Act 1960, s.12. The children were not wards of court or subject to any form of statutory control.
[47] Cp the discussion at paras 7–178 *et seq.*

those matters came before the court the social worker in question had been disciplined, and it was apparently already clear that she would never again be employed in the child protection world. Thus, from the public interest point of view, there was nothing left to be exposed, investigated or otherwise achieved in that respect.) That was *not* a legitimate factor for the court to take into account as justifying a publication which would otherwise not be in the public interest.

On the facts of that case Stuart-White J. held that it had been wrongly conceded (by counsel for the parents) that the decision he had to make was one with regard to upbringing and that welfare was paramount. He therefore had to carry out a "balancing exercise" and take account of a number of factors, including the welfare of *all* the children concerned, the right of the press to publish information and comment, and the public interest in the confidentiality of court proceedings concerning children.[48] On balance, he came down in favour of giving priority to the welfare of the child and to the need for confidentiality, especially having regard to the fact that no section of the press had sought to be represented or to challenge the restrictions. He emphasised that "[a]ny right of confidentiality concerning a child in respect of whom the court's jurisdiction is invoked belongs not to the child but to the court and is imposed to protect the proper functioning of the court's jurisdiction."[49] That is a proposition which would be unlikely to be expressed subsequently to the advent of the Human Rights Act. It would be necessary not only to recognise the legitimacy of protecting the court's process, in appropriate circumstances, but also to take account of a child's own right of privacy.[50]

In 1999, the then President, Sir Stephen Brown, said that it was in the public interest that the courts should discourage interference with, and exploitation of, vulnerable children by the media. Moreover, the court where possible should support the vital role of caring professionals working with delinquent children who were at risk. In *Nottingham City Council v October Films Ltd*,[51] he accepted undertakings from a film company regarding four out of five children who were the subject of originating summonses by a local authority invoking the inherent jurisdiction under s.100 of the Children Act 1989. The purpose was to restrict and prevent further filming in circumstances where the company had decided to make a documentary about runaway young people. Its representatives had approached them without parental consent and without the knowledge of any agency with statutory supervisory responsibility. It had been argued that any interference by the social services would be unduly restrictive of freedom of the press and against the public interest in free discussion. It was held that there was abundant evidence that the activities of the film crew, in encouraging the children to co-operate with them, were liable to influence their upbringing. Notwithstanding

---

[48] A factor recognised in Art.6 of the European Convention.
[49] [1997] 1 F.L.R. 235 at 253E–F, Stuart-White J.
[50] See, *e.g. Re Angela Roddy (A Minor)* [2003] EWHC 2927, (Fam), [2004] 2 F.L.R. 949 and *Re S (FC) (A Child)* [2004] UKHL 47, [2005] 1 A.C. 593.
[51] [1999] 2 F.L.R. 347, [1999] 2 F.C.R. 529.

the importance of the principle of the freedom of the press in a democratic society, it was nevertheless in the public interest to discourage such interference. In the case of the fifth child, he was living with his mother who was content that he should continue with the project. There was therefore no need for the court to intervene in that instance.

6–73   In the judgment, although it had been cited to him, the President made no express reference to the decision in *Re Z*. Since, however, the local authority had prayed in aid the provisions of s.100 of the Children Act it would seem to be clear that the court was addressing a "question of upbringing". Even if the case had not fitted the "custodial" template, and the President had been carrying out what is now called the "ultimate balancing test", it seems unlikely that a different outcome would have been reached. The case may be an illustration of how "remarkably similar" the court's approach had been, despite differences of terminology, to the rights based analysis now sanctioned by the House of Lords in *Re S (FC)*. Indeed, even the "custodial" jurisdiction, as explained in *Re Z*, would appear to be consistent with the willingness of the European Court of Human Rights to recognise exceptions to the right of the public to be informed in cases where matters of privacy or confidentiality are concerned.[52] When the mother sought to challenge the decision in *Re Z* itself before the European Court, the Commission ruled the application inadmissible as being manifestly ill founded.[53]

E. How media rights were addressed before the Human Rights Act

6–74   The consequences of *Re Z* did not appear altogether easy, at first sight, to reconcile with earlier statements to the effect that the protection of the court's inherent jurisdiction, for example in the context of wardship proceedings, did not bestow upon a child any privileges unavailable to other children. For example, in *Re R (A Minor) (Wardship: Restrictions on Publication)*,[54] Millett L.J. had said:

> "... the wardship court has no power to exempt its ward from the general law, or to obtain for its ward rights and privileges not generally available to children who are not wards of court; ... the wardship court can seek to achieve for its ward all that wise parents or guardians acting in concert and exclusively in the interests of the child could achieve, but no more."[55]

---

[52] See, *e.g. Von Hannover v Germany* [2004] E.M.L.R. 379, (2005) 40 E.H.R.R 1; *Peck v United Kingdom* (2003) 36 E.H.R.R. 41, and more generally the discussion at para.6–68 and para.6–126. And see *R. v Westminster City Council Ex p. Castelli and Tristran-Garcia* [1996] 1 F.L.R. 534 discussed below paras 7–99 *et seq.*
[53] *A v United Kingdom* (1997) 25 E.H.R.R. C.D. 159.
[54] [1994] Fam. 254 at 271C–D.
[55] Yet an ordinary parent would not generally have been able (at least at that time) to restrain the media from publishing material, purely on the ground of protecting his or her child's privacy or general well-being, and without reference to established causes of action such as defamation or breach of confidence.

It would not be a contempt of itself to interview a ward; nor would it appear 6–75
to be necessary in the absence of any specific order to obtain the court's
permission to do so.[56] As Munby J. observed in *Kelly v BBC*[57]:

> "It makes no difference for this purpose that the child is known by those conducting,
> publishing or broadcasting the interview to be a ward of court. In publishing or
> broadcasting the media will of course have to take care to avoid any breach of the
> restraints imposed by s.12 of the Administration of Justice Act 1960 and s.97(2) of the
> Children Act 1989 (and, for that matter, by s.2 of the Contempt of Court Act 1981), but,
> so long as they do, no contempt as such is, in my judgment, committed by the media
> interviewing a child who is known to be a ward of court or publishing or broadcasting
> such an interview".

In *R. v Central Independent Television plc*,[58] it was also said that a child does 6–76
not have, simply by virtue of being a child, a right of privacy or confidentiality.
That statement would doubtless now require some clarification, since a child
would today be regarded as having rights under the Convention—not least as to
privacy under Art.8—albeit not by virtue of childhood as such. Nevertheless, in
the light of what thus appeared by that time to be a well established principle,
some consternation was caused in media circles by the implications for such
proceedings brought about by the amendment to s.97 of the Children Act 1989,
which was effected by the Access to Justice Act 1999.[59] The extension of the
publishing restrictions to children involved in High Court proceedings would on
its face appear to prevent, for the first time, the identification of a ward *qua*
ward.

Was there truly any inconsistency between the position at common law, 6–77
whereby wards were not to be accorded, as such, any greater right to privacy than
anyone else, and the recognition of the paramountcy principle where the
custodial jurisdiction was to be exercised? Ward L.J. in *Re Z*[60] did not find this
difficult to reconcile with his own approach, since he construed "confidentiality"
in this context as equivalent to "anonymity". In other words, the court did then
seem prepared to recognise a duty of confidentiality towards some children (even
though it would not be easy for the average parent to enforce who cares for a
child without the court in the background), and to have accorded it a priority
which would not be easy to detect in the earlier cases. This would seem to be
simply a question of deciding where the paramountcy principle, as enshrined in
s.1(1) of the Children Act 1989, comes in to play. The statutory provisions in
themselves do not appear to be incompatible with Convention rights. Accordingly, the issue would be likely to turn upon whether the court is determining a
question with respect to upbringing, which may occur in relation to an *in*

---

[56] See *Kelly v BBC* [2001] Fam. 59 at 75, 78, [2000] 3 F.C.R. 509 at 531 and *Re W (Minors) (Continuation of Wardship)* [1996] 1 F.C.R. 393.
[57] Last note at 75.
[58] [1994] Fam. 192 at 207A.
[59] See para.8–83 below. The provisions of s.97 have been held to be Convention compliant in *Att-Gen v Pelling* [2005] EWHC 414 (Admin).
[60] [1997] Fam. 1 at 24D.

personam order, as in *Re G (Celebrities): Publicity)*,[61] as well as in the case of a *contra mundum* order.

6–78 Munby J. took the view in *Kelly v BBC*[62] that the proposed broadcast of an interview with a 16 year-old did not engage the "custodial" jurisdiction (as opposed to the "protective" jurisdiction). The comment was made that in this age of media saturation one would not expect a media interview to be a "major" or "important" step in a ward's life—however exciting it might be for him.[63] His Lordship emphasised that it is only the taking of an important step that requires the court's consent. To undertake or facilitate such a step *without* that consent will be treated as a contempt of court subject to proving that the person concerned knew of the wardship. For this purpose, "major" or "important" steps would include for example marriage, removal from the jurisdiction, making a material change in the ward's education, residence or whereabouts, or subjecting the ward to significant medical treatment (such as sterilisation or abortion).

6–79 In *Medway Council v BBC*[64] the court was considering an interview with a boy aged 13 who was subject to an anti-social behaviour order under s.1 of the Crime and Disorder Act 1998. It was proposed by the BBC to broadcast a 30 second interview as part of a programme on *South East Today* discussing the new but then little known provisions of the 1998 Act. Three weeks after the interview was recorded, the boy became the subject of an interim care order in favour of the applicant local authority. It sought an injunction to restrain the broadcast of the interview, arguing that there was reasonable cause to believe that otherwise he would suffer "significant harm" within the meaning of s.100(4) of the Children Act 1989. Wilson J. rejected the application because he had been unable to find any such reasonable cause, or any other ground to restrict the BBC's freedom of communication. In considering *Re Z*, he also held that the paramountcy principle did not apply on the facts of the case and emphasised that s.1(1) of the Children Act needed to be construed in a way that was consistent with the broadcasters' right to freedom of expression.

6–80 The "custodial" jurisdiction was held *not* to be engaged in *Re X (A Child) (Injunctions Restraining Publication)*.[65] The court was asked to vary the terms of an injunction *contra mundum* so as to permit discussion, in the media, of the fostering and care policies of a London Borough and particularly with regard to matters of race. The judge held that the "upbringing" of a child connoted a process whereby the parents or substitute parents were the "subject" and the child the "object". Unless this was so, the welfare of the child would not be paramount since s.1(1) of the Children Act 1989 would have no application.[66]

6–81 Where the court is exercising the *in personam* jurisdiction to restrain "any act by a parent that if unrestrained would or might adversely affect the welfare of the

---

[61] [1999] 1 F.L.R. 409.
[62] [2001] Fam. 59.
[63] *ibid.* at 76.
[64] [2002] 1 F.L.R. 104, Wilson J. See the commentary by H. Brayne, (2002) 152 New Law Jo. 1253.
[65] [2001] 1 F.C.R. 541 (Bracewell J.).
[66] See also the similar remarks of Munby J. in *Kelly v BBC* [2001] Fam. 59 at 82.

THE INHERENT (OR *PARENS PATRIAE*) JURISDICTION 6–84

child the subject of the proceedings", then the interests of the child are paramount. An example is to be found in *Re G (Celebrities: Publicity)*.[67]

F. The "protective" aspect of the jurisdiction

1. *Introduction*

It had been positively stated in a number of decisions *prior* to *Re Z*[68] that a child's welfare would *not* be the paramount consideration where the court was exercising the "protective" jurisdiction. In such circumstances, s.1 of the 1989 Act would not be of direct relevance. In the words of Lord MacDermott[69]:

6–82

> "There is, first of all, the duty to *protect* the infant, particularly when engaged or involved in litigation ... It recognises that the infant, as one not sui juris, may stand in need of aid. He must not be allowed to suffer because of his incapacity. But the aim is to ensure that he gets his rights rather than to place him above the law and make his rights superior to those of others ... In exercising what I have called the ancillary jurisdiction in relation to infants the court must also observe and, if need be, exercise its protective jurisdiction."

Lord MacDermott was by "ancillary jurisdiction" referring to the court's power to take such steps as may be necessary to ensure that the administration of justice is not rendered impracticable by the presence of people who might prevent the effective trial of a case or cause parties to be deterred from seeking justice. He referred[70] to the court's jurisdiction to make interlocutory orders for the purpose of protecting a fair and satisfactory trial, and went on:

6–83

> "I do not think there is now any question about the existence of this jurisdiction, which I shall refer to as the 'ancillary jurisdiction'. It may be procedural in character, but it is much more than that. It is a jurisdiction which confers power, in the exercise of a judicial discretion, to prepare the way by suitable orders or directions for a just and proper trial of the issues joined between the parties".[71]

This "protective" jurisdiction is closely linked to the court's powers to protect the administration of justice itself. This was explained by Nicholls L.J. in the case of *C (A Minor) (Wardship: Medical Treatment) (No.2)*[72]:

6–84

> " ... the public identification of the parties, or even the hearing of the matter in public at all, may be attended by a real risk that such publicity would defeat the purpose which the court proceedings are properly intended to achieve. In such cases the court has an inherent power to conduct its process in such a way as will prevent that result. Proceedings relating to the welfare of minors are an example of this. The court is

---

[67] [1999] 1 F.L.R. 409: see paras 6–64 *et seq*.
[68] [1997] Fam. 1.
[69] *S v McC (orse S) and M (DS Intervener); W v W* [1972] A.C. 24 at 48. This language is similar to and consistent with that of Lord Steyn more than 30 years later in *Re S (FC) (A Child) (Identification: Restrictions on Publication)* [2004] UKHL 47, [2005] 1 A.C. 593 both in addressing the child's "rights" and in eschewing any intention to make those rights automatically superior to those of others: see para.6–44.
[70] At 46D–E.
[71] See also the justification for hearings *in camera* in *Scott v Scott* [1913] A.C. 417 at 439 (Lord Haldane L.C.) and 446 (Lord Loreburn).
[72] [1990] Fam. 39 at 53, CA.

concerned to see that the welfare of the child which the court is seeking to promote is not jeopardised by publicity."

6–85   It was thought necessary sometimes, for example, to prevent publication of information about a ward or the ward's family circumstances. It had been emphasised, however, in a number of cases, that this jurisdiction should only be exercised where considered "necessary" for the protection of the ward in the context of the subsisting wardship.[73] It should not be invoked merely because it may be thought desirable or convenient to do so. Moreover, the jurisdiction was not to be invoked to exempt a ward from the effects of the general law, or to obtain rights or privileges not generally available to other children.[74] Still less would it be legitimate to use the jurisdiction to protect the privacy of parents or carers, save in so far as necessary for them to carry out their proper functions and responsibility towards the child.

6–86   A principle seemed clearly to be emerging that the jurisdiction to restrain publication should only be used to protect a ward from adverse publicity if it would threaten the effective working of the court's jurisdiction. It appeared that the only legitimate objective of any such restraining order would be the protection of the administration of justice, and for example the integrity of its own wardship jurisdiction.[75] The "custodial" function of the court had not been given the significance later attached to it in *Re Z (Identification)*; nor had it apparently been appreciated what opportunities might arise for engaging the statutory paramountcy principle, to be found in s.1 of the Children Act 1989, when the court was exercising that function.

2. *The approach to a "balancing exercise" in wardship cases prior to the overt recognition of privacy rights*

6–87   Indeed, in accordance with these priorities, it was clearly asserted that the welfare of a child was *not* the paramount consideration. When considering this "protective" aspect of the court's jurisdiction.[76] This was because the court would carry out a "balancing exercise"[77] in which there was to be weighed, on

---

[73] *Re W (A Minor)* [1992] 1 W.L.R. 100 at 103, CA, per Neill L.J.; see also *R. v Central Independent Television plc* [1994] Fam. 192 at 202A, [1994] 3 All E.R. 641 at 651a.
[74] *S v McC (orse S) and M (DS Intervener); W v W* [1972] A.C. 24 at 48, per Lord MacDermott, cited at para.6–82; *Re X (A Minor) (Wardship: Restriction on Publication)* [1975] Fam. 47 at 60E, Roskill L.J.; *Re F (A Minor)* [1977] Fam. 58 at 99, Scarman L.J.; *R. v Central Independent Television plc* [1994] Fam. 192 at 200D–E, Neill L.J., 207A, Waite L.J.; *Re R (A Minor)* [1994] 3 All E.R. 658 at 672–3, [1994] 2 F.L.R. 637 at 651d–g, Millett L.J.; *Official Solicitor v News Group Newspapers plc* [1994] 2 F.L.R. 174 at 181F–G, Connell J.
[75] *R. v Central Independent Television plc* [1994] Fam. 192 at 200E, Neill L.J. and 207A, Waite L.J.; *Re R (A Minor)* [1994] 3 All E.R. 658 at 672b–c, [1994] F.L.R. 637 at 650E–F, Millett L.J. And see *Re W (Minors) (Continuation of Wardship)* [1996] 1 F.C.R. 393.
[76] *Re M & N (Minors) (Wardship: Publication of Information)* [1990] Fam. 211 at 223, CA, Butler-Sloss L.J. and 228–9 Lord Donaldson M.R.; *Re W (A Minor)* [1992] 1 W.L.R. 100 at 103; *Re H-S* [1994] 3 All E.R. 390 at 398a–d, CA.
[77] (1979) 2 E.H.R.R. 245 at 281. See in this context also the judgment of Bracewell J. in *Re X (A Child) (Injunctions Restraining Publication)* [2001] 1 F.C.R. 541 at 547–9; *Re a Local Authority (Inquiry: Restraint on Publication)* [2003] EWHC 2746 (Fam), [2004] Fam. 96.

the one hand, the need to protect the ward directly or indirectly,[78] as against, on the other hand, the need to safeguard the freedom of the press, or indeed any other citizen, to publish information or comment on matters of legitimate public interest.[79] When considering the terminology of "balancing", it was appropriate to have an eye to the following passage in the report of *Sunday Times v United Kingdom*:

"The court is faced not with a choice between two conflicting principles, but with a principle of freedom of expression that is subject to a number of exceptions which must be narrowly interpreted."

It seems reasonably clear now, however, especially in the light of the House of Lords decisions in *Campbell v MGN* and *Re S (FC) (A Child)*, that this should not be construed as according automatic priority to Art.10 rights over those contained in any other Article. It has to be admitted, however, that this more recent analysis is not easy to reconcile with the earlier statement, since it appeared to be implicit that other rights must be "narrowly interpreted" in so far as they might impinge on freedom of expression.

Any such act of balancing can be a delicate and sensitive exercise, and inevitably to some extent subjective, since it is likely to involve value judgments and sometimes an element of discretion. Thus the approach of appellate courts is generally that such decisions may only be challenged if the judge has misdirected himself in law or gone "plainly wrong"; then, as in *Re W (A Minor) (Wardship: Restrictions on Publication)*,[80] an appellate court could substitute its own discretion. At that time, however, no such "balancing act" was thought appropriate unless and until there was threatened a publication which would touch upon matters of direct concern to the court in its supervisory role over the care and upbringing of the ward.[81] That narrow approach is clearly no longer the correct one to adopt, not least because the court has a duty to examine with care each application for a departure from the principle of open justice by reason of a claim under Art.8; where the values under the two Articles are in conflict, "an intense focus on the comparative importance of the specific rights being claimed in the individual case is necessary".[82] It is important to bear this significant shift of policy in mind when considering the Court of Appeal's guidance on how the

---

[78] The protection of a ward or patient may require that carers be protected from harassment which might affect the quality of their care. For example, in *Re C (A Minor) (Wardship: Treatment) (No.2)* [1990] Fam. 39, CA, the ward's medical condition was such that she could never know anything about the media coverage; and yet identification of or enquiries about the carers could have added significantly to the stress to which *they* were subject. See also *Re W (Minors) (Surrogacy)* [1991] F.L.R. 385, when the identity of the doctors involved in the surrogacy was also protected, and the remarks of Sir Stephen Brown P. In *Nottingham City Council v October Films Ltd* [1999] 2 F.L.R. 347, 2 F.C.R. 529 as to "the vital role of caring professionals".
[79] [1992] 1 W.L.R. 100 at 103. See also *X (A Minor) (Wardship: Restriction on Publication)* [1975] Fam. 47, CA.
[80] [1992] 1 W.L.R. 100, [1992] 1 All E.R. 794. And see *Re W (Minors) (Continuation of Wardship)* [1996] 1 F.C.R. 393 at 402.
[81] *R. v Central Independent Television plc* [1994] Fam. 192 at 202A, Neill L.J., 203–4, Hoffmann L.J., 207A, Waite L.J. See also Lord Donaldson M.R. in *Re M & N (Minors)* [1990] Fam. 211, 231; *Re R (A Minor)* [1994] 2 F.L.R. 637 at 650, Millett L.J.
[82] *Re S (FC) (A Child)* [2004] UKHL 47, [2005] 1 A.C. 593 at [17]–[18].

6–88 CHAPTER 6—COURT ORDERS AFFECTING THE MEDIA

balancing exercise was to be conducted during that period. This is one of the main reasons why their Lordships in *Re S (FC)* cautioned against attaching too much weight to earlier authorities.[83]

3. Relevant considerations for the "balancing exercise" prior to the Human Rights Act

6–89 The balancing exercise inevitably varied from case to case, so that it was impossible to lay down precise rules.[84] Nevertheless, the attempt was made by the Court of Appeal to set out some guidelines, partly for the assistance of judges confronted with such problems and also partly in an effort to allay concerns on the part of the media then that the Family Division judges might have been granting such injunctions on a "common form or semi-automatic basis in the erroneous belief that the law required, as in other contexts, the welfare of the children to be treated as paramount."[85]

6–90 Guidance was given in *Re C (A Minor) (Wardship: Treatment) (No.2)*[86] and in *Re M & N (Minors)*,[87] and the principal considerations were extracted from those authorities and helpfully listed by Neill L.J. in *Re W (A Minor)*[88] in seven numbered guidelines, which we summarise below. They now need to be supplemented in the light not only of later cases but also, more generally, of the "new era" of the Human Rights Act,[89] which was re-emphasised by the House of Lords in *Re S (FC)*:

1. The court will attach great importance to safeguarding the freedom of the press.

2. The court will also take account of Art.10[90] of the European Convention.

3. These freedoms are subject to exceptions,[91] which include restrictions upon publication for the protection of children.

4. In considering whether to impose such a restriction to protect a ward, the court will carry out a balancing exercise, for the purposes of which the welfare of the child will not be treated as paramount.

5. The need to protect the ward will be weighed against the right of the press (or others) to publish or comment on matters of genuine public interest, as

---

[83] See paras 6–43 *et seq*.
[84] *Re M & N (Minors)* [1990] Fam. 211 at 229.
[85] *ibid.* at 228, *per* Lord Donaldson M.R.
[86] [1990] Fam. 39.
[87] [1990] Fam. 211.
[88] [1992] 1 W.L.R. 100 at 103.
[89] [2001] Fam. 430 at [100], the phrase used by Dame Elizabeth Butler-Sloss in *Venables and Thompson v News Group Newspapers*.
[90] See also *Re H-S* [1994] 3 All E.R. 390 at 398a–d, CA, one of the earliest cases in which it was indicated that Art.8 should also be taken into account.
[91] See especially Art.10(2), set out at para.2–142.

opposed to "cases of mere curiosity".[92] (As mentioned above, however, it was made clear by Neill L.J. in a later case,[93] that the balancing act was not then thought to become necessary unless the threatened publication touched upon matters of direct concern to the court's supervisory role.)

6. In almost every case the public interest in favour of publication can be satisfied without any identification[94] of the ward to persons other than those who already know the facts, but the risk of *some* wider identification may have to be accepted on some occasions if the story is to be told in a manner which will engage the interest of the public.[95]

7. Any restraint had to be expressed in clear terms[96] and should be no wider than is *necessary* to achieve the court's objective of protecting the ward and/or those who care for the ward[97] from the risk of harassment. It had to be recognised, therefore, that generally it would not be possible to protect the ward from such distress as may flow from reading the media coverage.

4. *The Court of Appeal guidelines overtaken by later developments*

In *A v M (Family Proceedings: Publicity)*,[98] Charles J. observed that these guidelines were not exhaustive and that, in particular, Art.8(1) of the European Convention was also a matter to be taken into account. It was a case in which the

---

[92] "Curiosity can never justify intrusion into the private lives of children": *per* Lord Donaldson M.R. in *Re M & N (Minors)* at 229. The legitimacy of press interest in wardship cases was recognised also in the *Report of the Inquiry into Child Abuse in Cleveland* 1987 (HMSO 1988), Cm. 412 (Dame E. Butler-Sloss).
[93] *R. v Central Independent Television plc* [1994] Fam. 192 at 202A, CA. But with the benefit of hindsight this would appear to be too restrictive since, as Lord Steyn observed in *Re S (FC) (A Child) (Identification: Restrictions on Publication)* [2004] UKHL 47, [2005] 1 A.C. 593 at [18], it would now be regarded as a judge's duty to examine with care each application for a departure from the open justice principle relying upon Art.8 rights.
[94] See *Re Manda* [1993] Fam. 183, [1993] 1 All E.R. 733, CA; *Re H-S* [1994] 3 All E.R. 390 at 398e, CA, where it was held, although it was a matter of genuine public interest that the court had approved of young children remaining in the care of a parent who was transsexual and who had undergone a sex change operation, that the identity of the parties did not have to be revealed for the purposes of legitimate public debate, and see *Re W (Minors) (Continuation of Wardship)* [1996] 1 F.C.R. 393. See also *A Local Authority v W* [2005] EWHC 1564 (Fam) at [74] where Sir Mark Potter P. referred to "the novelty and issues involved in the charge to which the mother is pleading guilty which render it of high interest", but added that he did not consider that reporting or discussion of the issues would be significantly inhibited if her identity was suppressed.
[95] See *R. v Central Independent Television plc* [1994] Fam. 192 at 206E–F, where Waite L.J. took note of the fact that a television company would prefer not to broadcast at all if required to blur the father's face so as to make his features unrecognisable. See also *Ross v Midwest Communications* 870 F. 2d 271 at 274 (cert. denied, 110 S.Ct. 326) ("Communicating that this particular [rape] victim was a real person with roots in the community, and showing [the publisher's] knowledge of the details of the attack upon her were of unique importance to the credibility and persuasive force of the story".) We are indebted to Ms Jaclyn Moriarty for this reference.
[96] See *Re L (A Minor)* [1988] 1 All E.R. 418 at 423, Booth J.
[97] See the considerations discussed at para.6–87, n.78 above. In *Re X (A Child) (Injunctions Restraining Publication)* [2001] 1 F.C.R. 541, it was held appropriate to protect the identities and privacy of social workers who were still involved in planning the child's care.
[98] [2000] 1 F.L.R. 562.

6-91 court restrained a mother and her partner from disclosing information about her children notwithstanding that their interests were not paramount but only a relevant factor. The court was not deciding a question with respect to the upbringing of a child but nonetheless, on the facts, the balance "pointed all one way" in favour of injunctive relief. It was in the interests of the children that there should be restraint even in respect of allegations already in the public domain.[99] Further publication could well be damaging to them.

6-92 This was an example of a Family Division judge being able to stand back from the conventional constraints then operating because he was granting an injunction which was not in form *contra mundum*. The mother had been talking to the press and the father obtained injunctive relief against her and her new partner to prevent any further similar disclosures. There were obviously implications for the media if they were to publish any of her allegations knowing of the injunction. Because of the form of the injunction sought, the judge did not need to classify the jurisdiction that he was exercising as coming within either of the labels "custodial" or "protective". He appeared overtly to be concentrating upon balancing rights of privacy against other considerations. As he put it, "... the titans in the battle comprising the balancing exercise are the relevant competing public interests". His reasoning process was thus very much in accord with what has now been called "the new era".[1] The emphasis is on greater flexibility and the need to focus on the comparative importance of the specific rights being claimed in the individual cases and, of course, upon proportionality. One has to give effect to rights both of privacy and freedom of speech without according either of the relevant ECHR Articles, as such, precedence.[2] Nevertheless, it is still necessary for courts to recognise the effect of the statutory requirement of s.1(1) the Children Act 1989 for the interest of a child to be paramount in the specified circumstances. In the new era, however, there is likely to be less temptation to strive to bring the circumstances of a case within the definition of "upbringing" purely for the purpose of acquiring jurisdiction to protect privacy.

6-93 Where it is sought to afford protection to carers,[3] it should be recognised that this will generally be a means to the end of protecting the interests of justice rather than to avoid embarrassment of the carers. Still less, of course, should an injunction be used for the purpsoe of stifling criticism. In the case of *Re a Local Authority*,[4] which was heard after the Human Rights Act came in to effect, the court was asked to consider specifically the privacy rights of a carer. A local

---

[99] Cp. the remarks of Lord Keith in *Att-Gen v Guardian Newspapers Ltd (No.2)* [1990] 1 A.C. 109 at 260E–H; see also *R. v Broadcasting Complaints Commission Ex p. Granada TV* [1995] E.M.L.R. 163.
[1] *Venables and Thompson v News Group Newspapers Ltd* [2001] Fam. 430 at [100]. See also *X (A Woman Formerly Known As Mary Bell) v O'Brien* [2003] EWHC 1101, QB, [2003] 2 F.C.R. 686; *Carr (Maxine) v News Group Newspapers Ltd* [2005] EWHC 971, QB.
[2] *Re S (FC) (A Child)* [2004] Fam. 43, [2004] UKHL 47, [2005] 1 A.C. 593.
[3] See, *e.g.* *X (A Child) (Injunctions Restraining Publication)* [2001] 1 F.C.R. 541 and guideline number 7 cited from *Re W (A Minor)* at para.6–90 above.
[4] [2003] EWHC 2746 (Fam), [2004] Fam 96 at 114 at [63]–[64].

authority was seeking permission to publish a report which had been commissioned by the area child protection committee and covered the care provided by a Ms A for children and vulnerable adults under various disabilities. Objection was taken by various parties and, in particular, on the basis that there would be an infringement of privacy rights contrary to Art.8—including those of Ms A. It was suggested that she had been treated unfairly and that there had been an attempt to "demonise" her. Dame Elizabeth Butler-Sloss P. made it clear, however, that the inherent jurisdiction could not be utilised for the protection of Ms A or, for that matter, either the local authority or the health authority. She would carry out a balancing exercise under the court's "protective" jurisdiction in order to decide whether it was necessary and proportionate to restrict publication of the report in order to protect "the rights and welfare of the children".

5. *The recognition of the need for a public domain proviso*

In *Kelly v BBC*[5] Munby J. accepted counsel's submissions to the effect that "... an injunction *in rem* or *contra mundum* should normally be qualified by a public domain proviso". Although the decision of Charles J. in *A v M* was cited to him, he preferred to follow the reasoning of Sir Stephen Brown P. in the unreported case of *Re C (A Minor)*,[6] where he commented that " ... it would be taking a very strong line indeed if a court were to seek to restrict the media from publishing information which they have lawfully published in the past and which remains on their files and is readily available to members of the public, for example in libraries ... [7] I do not think that it would be appropriate for the court to attempt to prevent the re-publication of such information, although it may deprecate the way in which that may be done. Nevertheless, there is an important principle to be borne in mind concerning the preservation of freedom of speech". In *Harris v Harris; Att-Gen v Harris*,[8] Munby J. adopted a public domain proviso modelled on that approved by the Court of Appeal in *Att-Gen v Times Newspapers Ltd*[9] (in the different context of the publication of memoirs by a former security service employee).

6. *The court's recognition of topicality as a factor*

In the context of recognising that there may be a public interest in the facts underlying certain cases involving minors or patients, one factor that the court is

---

[5] [2001] Fam. 59 at 93, [2000] 3 F.C.R. 509 at 551.
[6] March 15, 1990.
[7] For consideration of the difficulties caused by archival material on the internet, see *HMA v Beggs (No.2)* 2002 S.L.T. 139; *Att-Gen v Greater Manchester Newspapers Ltd* [2001] All E.R. (D) 33 and the discussions at paras 1–149 *et seq.* and para.4–27.
[8] [2001] 2 F.L.R. 895 at [208].
[9] [2001] EWCA Civ 97, [2001] 1 W.L.R. 885.

prepared increasingly to take into account, when asked to restrain media publications, is the need to publish when the subject matter is topical.[10]

7. Injunction cases should generally be heard in the High Court

6–96 The former President of the Family Division, through the Court of Appeal,[11] made it clear that where an injunction is sought the effect of which would be to impose a restraint upon the freedom of the media, then the matter should be transferred to the High Court and the Official Solicitor invited, where appropriate, to represent the child concerned.[12] It was emphasised in *Re X (A Child) (Injunctions Restraining Publication)*[13] that the burden is upon anyone seeking to establish that a ban is necessary and proportionate within Art.10(2) of the European Convention to do so by adducing "proper evidence". It is not appropriate to invite the court simply to make assumptions.

G. Could such a media ban restrict the reporting of criminal proceedings?

6–97 The possibility was canvassed in one case that a Family Division judge might have the power to extend such restrictions on the media as far as coverage of a criminal trial, although this was acknowledged to be a doubtful proposition; but, in any event, the need for any such restrictions should in practice be left to the judge in the criminal proceedings,[14] who should be unfettered in the exercise of any judgment as to the imposition of restrictions under such provisions as s.39 of the Children and Young Persons Act 1933 (as amended)[15] and under s.4(2) and s.11 of the Contempt of Court Act.

---

[10] See, *e.g. Cambridge Nutrition Ltd v BBC* [1990] 3 All E.R. 523 at 535, Kerr L.J. ; *R. v Central Criminal Court Ex p. S and P* [1999] 1 F.L.R. 480 at 490B–C, (1998) 163 J.P. 776 at 787E ("Delay in reporting would kill the news value of the story and it would be wrong if an unmeritorious appeal could prevent the reporting of a conviction for a significant period"); *Kelly v BBC* [2001] Fam. 59 at 90; *Att-Gen v Times Newspapers Ltd* [2001] EWCA Civ 97, [2001] 1 W.L.R. 885; *Ex p. The Telegraph Group* [2001] EWCA Crim 1075, [2001] 1 W.L.R. 1983 at [16].

[11] *Re H-S* [1994] 3 All E.R. 390 at 398h, CA. See now the President's *Practice Direction, Applications for Reporting Restriction Orders* of March 18, 2005, at [2]. This makes it clear that if the need for a *contra mundum* order arises in the course of proceedings in the county court, judges should either transfer the application to the High Court or, after consultation, arrange for it to be heard by the Urgent Applications judge of the Family Division. It is also directed at compliance with s.12(2) of the Human Rights Act 1998 and provides for notice to be given to the media via the CopyDirect service provided by the Press Association. See also the footnote to Sir Mark Potter P.'s judgment in *A Local Authority v W* [2005] EWHC 1564 (Fam).

[12] See also *Practice Note, Official Solicitor: Appointment in Family Proceedings* [2001] 2 F.L.R. 155. The Official Solicitor is appointed by the Lord Chancellor: see s.90(1) of the Supreme Court Act 1981. The functions and duties are summarised in *Civil Procedure* 2005, Vol. 2 at 9A–391 to 9A–398. See *Oxfordshire County Council v L and F* [1997] 1 F.L.R. 235 for a consideration of the role of the guardian *ad litem*.

[13] [2001] 1 F.C.R. 541 at 549.

[14] *Re R (A Minor)* [1994] F.L.R. 637 at 646, Sir Thomas Bingham M.R., 647–9, Henry L.J., 652, Millett L.J.

[15] Vulnerable witnesses in criminal proceedings are now to be protected by the provisions of Youth Justice and Criminal Evidence Act 1999. Section 46, which deals with adults, is now in force. When s.45 comes in to force, s.39 of the 1933 Act will no longer have application in criminal proceedings.

Even though not parties to such criminal proceedings, a ward or guardian *ad*   6–98
litem would almost certainly be accorded the necessary *locus standi* at the outset of the trial, to be heard on the question of reporting restrictions, and for the purpose of inviting the court's attention to any views that might have been expressed by the wardship judge on such matters.[16] It was pointed out by Hale L.J. in the Court of Appeal in *Re S (FC)*[17] that it would not be open to *any* judge sitting in the Crown Court to make an order under the inherent jurisdiction of the High Court; the matter would thus depend upon the happenstance of whether the trial judge was a High Court judge.[18] Nevertheless, in the context of exercising the various statutory powers, the attitude of a judge in family proceedings could well be relevant for the judge in the criminal court to know. For example, one of the factors judges are entitled to take into account under s.4(2) of the 1981 Act would be whether reporting restrictions were necessary to avoid a substantial risk of prejudice to "other proceedings", which could include *parens patriae* proceedings.[19]

Nevertheless, it was stressed in *Re R (A Minor)* that the criminal trial is the   6–99
responsibility of the trial judge alone, who should make all decisions relating to it. Moreover, it is easier for him to perform the balancing exercise; he will have a full appreciation of the issues in the criminal case; he will also be best placed to tighten, relax or discharge any order made as the developing circumstances may require.[20] His hands should not be tied by orders made in wardship proceedings.

Indeed, by s.39 of the Children and Young Persons Act 1933,[21] Parliament had   6–100
entrusted the question whether and, if so, to what extent the publication of fair and accurate reports of criminal proceedings may be restricted, in the interests of a child "concerned" in those proceedings, not to whichever court is concerned with the child's welfare but rather to the judge having conduct of the criminal proceedings in question.[22]

The possible tension between the narrowly defined approach of s.39, in   6–101
protecting only those "concerned", and the broader scope of the Family Division's inherent jurisdiction came under closer scrutiny in *Re S (FC) (A Child)*.[23] It was accepted by the Court of Appeal that the Family Division did indeed have jurisdiction wide enough, where necessary, to embrace the restriction of reporting information in connection with a criminal trial. Such an order

---

[16] *ibid.* at 648–9, Henry L.J.
[17] [2003] EWCA Civ 963, [2003] Ch. 650 at [28] and [61] CA.
[18] It may be worth considering on some future occasion whether the relevant powers would be conferred upon a Crown Court judge by virtue of the Supreme Court Act 1981, s.45(4) which states that "the Crown Court shall, in relation to . . . all other matters incidental to its jurisdiction, have the like powers, rights, privileges and authority as the High Court".
[19] For a fuller consideration of s.4(2), see paras 7–111 *et seq.*
[20] *Re R (A Minor)* [1994] F.L.R. 637 at 649, Henry L.J.
[21] Set out and discussed at para.8–50. The provision is to be replaced by s.45 of the Youth Justice and Criminal Proceedings Act 1999 from a date to be appointed.
[22] *Re R (A Minor)* [1994] F.L.R. 637 at 652, Millett L.J.
[23] [2004] Fam. 43, CA and [2004] UKHL 47, [2005] 1 A.C. 593. See also *R. v Teeside Crown Court Ex p. Gazette Media Co Ltd* [2005] EWCA Crim 1983.

6–101 had been made by Hedley J. to protect a small boy ("CS") whose mother had been charged with the murder of his brother. The judge at first made an order in care proceedings under the *parens patriae* jurisdiction which would have had the effect of preventing publication of the mother's name and photograph during her criminal trial as well as information likely to identify the deceased brother. It was afterwards varied by the same judge on the application of the publishers of a newspaper, who wished to give readers an informative account of the trial. The judge weighed the competing considerations of public policy, in the light of their submissions, and came to the conclusion that open justice, in the particular circumstances, prevailed over the need to protect CS' Art.8 right to respect for his private life. It was pointed out by Hale L.J. that his Art.8 rights had undoubtedly been engaged by the interference in his life by the local authority and the Family Division of the High Court and that, additionally, the criminal proceedings in themselves meant that "other public authorities" were now also encroaching upon those rights. Of course, the criminal proceedings served legitimate aims, but it became necessary to consider whether the impact upon the child's rights could be minimised—in particular by restricting reports of the trial. The judge had varied his original order so as to permit reporting of the particulars of any proceedings of a court other than one sitting in private.

6–102 The majority in the Court of Appeal decided that he was entitled to have reached that conclusion (although there was criticism of him for not expressly identifying and carrying out the balancing act required of him—which was subsequently found by the House of Lords to be unjustified). Hale L.J., however, dissented on the basis that she thought it right to accord priority to the child's Art.8 rights over the usual imperative of open justice. Nonetheless, at that stage what emerged from the case was that a judge exercising the inherent jurisdiction, and weighing the competing considerations, should not feel inhibited by according any priority to the judge at the criminal trial or to the statutory framework of s.39 of the 1933 Act. It was confirmed by the Master of the Rolls in *Re S (FC)*[24] that the inherent jurisdiction could in appropriate cases extend to imposing restrictions upon the reporting of a criminal trial—even if those circumstances fell outside those contemplated by s.39 of the Children and Young Persons Act (or any comparable statutory provisions).

6–103 He went on to offer guidance as to the policy considerations engaged when such an order is contemplated:

> "It is possible to derive the following general principles from the various provisions set out above:
>
> (i) It is an important principle that justice should be conducted in public and that judicial proceedings should be freely reported;
> (ii) by way of exception, restrictions can be justified where necessary for the due administration of justice;
> (iii) in civil and criminal proceedings reporting restrictions are usually justified in order to protect children and young persons who are involved in the proceedings as parties or witnesses;

---

[24] At [83].

(iv) in civil proceedings the court has jurisdiction to prevent the disclosure of the identity of a party or a witness in order to protect his interests".

A little later, he added that " ... the principles to be derived from the pre Human Rights Act authorities cannot be rigidly applied. It is necessary in the individual case to balance article 8 rights which are engaged against article 10 rights." These propositions were confirmed when the matter was fully considered by the House of Lords. It was held that the jurisdiction was not in doubt,[25] but in the light of their Lordships' analysis it now seems unlikely that an order will be made by a judge exercising the inherent jurisdiction which would have the effect directly of inhibiting media reporting of a criminal trial.

The position was fully explained by Lord Steyn:

"26. While Art.8.1 is engaged, and none of the factors in article 8.2 justifies the interference, it is necessary to assess realistically the nature of the relief sought. This is an application for an injunction beyond the scope of section 39, the remedy provided by Parliament to protect juveniles directly affected by criminal proceedings. No such injunction has in the past been granted under the inherent jurisdiction or under the provisions of the ECHR. There is no decision of the Strasbourg court granting injunctive relief to non-parties, juvenile or adult, in respect of publication of criminal proceedings. Moreover, the Convention on the Rights of the Child, which entered into force on 2 September 1990, protects the privacy of children directly involved in criminal proceedings, but does not protect the privacy of children if they are only indirectly affected by criminal trials: articles 17 and 40.2(vii); see also Geraldine Van Bueren, *The International Law on the Rights of the Child*, 1994, 141 and 182. The verdict of experience appears to be that such a development is a step too far.

. . .

32. There are a number of specific consequences of the grant of an injunction as asked for in this case to be considered. First, while counsel for the child wanted to confine a ruling to the grant of an injunction restraining publication *to protect a child*, that will not do. The jurisdiction under the ECHR could equally be invoked by an adult non-party faced with possible damaging publicity as a result of a trial of a parent, child or spouse. Adult non-parties to a criminal trial must therefore be added to the prospective pool of applicants who could apply for such injunctions. This would confront newspapers with an ever wider spectrum of potentially costly proceedings and would seriously inhibit the freedom of the press to report criminal trials.

33. Secondly, if such an injunction were to be granted in this case, it cannot be assumed that relief will only be sought in future in respect of the name of a defendant and a photograph of the defendant and the victim. It is easy to visualise circumstances in which attempts will be made to enjoin publicity of, for example, the gruesome circumstances of a crime. The process of piling exception upon exception to the principle of open justice would be encouraged and would gain in momentum.

34. Thirdly, it is important to bear in mind that from a newspaper's point of view a report of a sensational trial without revealing the identity of the defendant would be a very much disembodied trial. If the newspapers choose not to contest such an injunction, they are less likely to give prominence to reports of the trial. Certainly,

---

[25] At [23].

readers will be less interested and editors will act accordingly. Informed debate about criminal justice will suffer.

35. Fourthly, it is true that newspapers can always contest an application for an injunction. Even for national newspapers that is, however, a costly matter which may involve proceedings at different judicial levels. Moreover, time constraints of an impending trial may not always permit such proceedings. Often it will be too late and the injunction will have had its negative effect on contemporary reporting.

36. Fifthly, it is easy to fall into the trap of considering the position from the point of view of national newspapers only. Local newspapers play a huge role. In the United Kingdom according to the website of The Newspaper Society there are 1301 regional and local newspapers which serve villages, towns and cities. Apparently, again according to the website of The Newspaper Society, over 85% of all British adults read a regional or local newspaper compared to 70% who read a national newspaper. Very often a sensational or serious criminal trial will be of great interest in the community where it took place. A regional or local newspaper is likely to give prominence to it. That happens every day up and down the country. For local newspapers, who do not have the financial resources of national newspapers, the spectre of being involved in costly legal proceedings is bound to have a chilling effect. If local newspapers are threatened with the prospect of an injunction such as is now under consideration it is likely that they will often be silenced. Prudently, the Romford Recorder, which has some 116,000 readers a week, chose not to contest these proceedings. The impact of such a new development on the regional and local press in the United Kingdom strongly militates against its adoption. If permitted, it would seriously impoverish public discussion of criminal justice."

6–106 It was observed by Sir Mark Potter P. in *A Local Authority v W*[26] that the decision of their Lordships is "on analysis by no means easy to apply". While it was clear that there should be no presumption of priority as between Art.10 and Art.8 rights, it had been also emphasised that "the ordinary rule that the press may report everything that takes place in a criminal court can only be displaced by 'unusual or exceptional circumstances'". Nevertheless, the President ultimately came to the conclusion that Lord Steyn had nowhere indicated that the weight to be accorded to free reporting of criminal proceedings would invariably be determinative of the outcome, since it could be displaced. He did not, therefore, agree with an (unidentified) commentator who had suggested that their Lordships had "effectively restored the presumptive priority of Article 10 which they had been at pains to reject in *Campbell*."[27] The President summarised the position as follows[28]:

"The exercise to be performed is one of parallel analysis in which the starting point is presumptive parity, in that neither Article has precedence over or 'trumps' the other. The exercise of parallel analysis requires the court to examine the justification for interfering with each right and the issue of proportionality[29] is to be considered in respect of each. It is not a mechanical exercise to be decided upon the basis of rival generalities. An intense focus upon the comparative importance of the specific rights

---

[26] [2005] EWHC 1564 (Fam) at [24].
[27] [2004] UKHL 22, [2004] 2 A.C. 457.
[28] At [53].
[29] See also the observations of Sedley L.J. in *Douglas v Hello! Ltd* [2001] Q.B. 967, at [137] ("the outcome... is determined principally by considerations of proportionality").

being claimed in the individual case is necessary before the ultimate balancing test in terms of proportionality is carried out".

Although the President was carefully applying the principles expounded by Lord Steyn, he came to the conclusion on the facts before him that an injunction was appropriate. The case concerned proceedings in which a mother had pleaded guilty to a charge under s.20 of the Offences Against the Person Act 1861 of knowingly infecting the father of one of her children with the HIV virus. A local authority, supported by the guardian of her two children, sought to restrain publication of the identity of the woman herself and that of the victim in order to protect the privacy, health and well-being of the children because of widespread prejudice, which had led to local abuse and demonstrations, and which it was feared would also make it difficult to place the children. In those circumstances, the ultimate balancing exercise was resolved in favour of the children's privacy. The President also mentioned that, although the result of the order would in a sense lead to a "disembodied trial", he did not consider that the legitimate media reporting and discussion of the issues in the case would be significantly inhibited.

H. The impact of the Children Act 1989 upon practice and procedure

Since the coming into effect of the Children Act 1989, the machinery of wardship has been less frequently invoked. In *Re Z (A Minor) (Identification)*[30] Ward L.J. reported that there had been 4,791 originating summonses in wardship in 1991, but that there had been a dramatic reduction in 1992, down to 492, after the 1989 Act came into effect. He pointed out, however, also that the Act did not affect the court's inherent jurisdiction. The court's powers to restrict media publication have not been treated as confined to the wardship procedure,[31] since they derive from the inherent jurisdiction of the court to protect its own processes wherever necessary, and particularly in the context of exercising the powers of the Crown as *parens patriae*. It simply happens to be the case that wardship traditionally represented the principal machinery through which these powers were exercised.[32] Proceedings under the Children Act have been recognised in the present context as analogous to wardship proceedings.[33]

---

[30] [1997] Fam. 1 at 13C.
[31] See, *e.g. Re Z (A Minor) (Identification: Restrictions on Publication)* [1997] Fam. 1 at 32D–E, Sir Thomas Bingham M.R.
[32] *Re M & N (Minors)* [1990] Fam. 211 at 223, Butler-Sloss L.J.; *Re C (A Minor) (Wardship: Medical Treatment) (No.2)* [1990] Fam. 39 at 46, Lord Donaldson M.R. Indeed, Balcombe L.J. expressed the view in *Att-Gen v Newspaper Publishing plc* [1988] Ch. 333 that the court's powers to make such orders extended more widely than the *parens patriae* jurisdiction. That would appear to be confirmed by the grant of protective injunctions in the Queen's Bench Division to adults such as in *Venables and Thompson v News Group Newspapers Ltd* [2001] Fam. 430; *X (A Woman Formerly Known As Mary Bell) v O'Brien* [2003] EWHC 1101 (QB), [2003] 2 F.C.R. 686; *Carr (Maxine) v News Group Newspapers Ltd* [2005] EWHC 971 (QB). In each case, the court's objective was to protect the life and physical well-being of persons at risk of vigilante attack.
[33] *Oxfordshire County Council v M* [1994] Fam. 151, Sir Stephen Brown P.; *Re L (Police Investigation: Privilege)* [1996] 1 F.L.R. 731; *Re P-B (A Minor)* [1997] 1 All E.R. 58; *Att-Gen v Pelling* [2005] EWHC 414 (Admin).

6–109   CHAPTER 6—COURT ORDERS AFFECTING THE MEDIA

6–109 It is provided in s.100 of the Act that the wardship procedure should not be used without the permission of the court. This will only be granted if the child would otherwise suffer significant harm.[34] In consequence, it became more common for proceedings to be launched with the heading "In the Matter of the Inherent Jurisdiction".[35] It is less than clear when the wardship jurisdiction as such should be invoked.[36]

I. The uncertainty over where the balance with free speech was to be struck

6–110 The cases in the last decade before the advent of the Human Rights Act, particularly those concerned with the so-called "protective" jurisdiction appeared to illustrate a significant shift over a short period of time in the approach towards the balance between the demands of the judicial process and the public interest in openness and freedom of communication.[37] Indeed, it still seems strange that as recently as 1987 it could have been argued[38] that the mere fact that somebody was a ward of court entailed at common law "a prohibition on the publication of *any* information relating to her and in particular any information which identifies her as a ward."

6–111 The case concerned a 12 year-old girl whose parents and grandmother had been killed in the Herald of Free Enterprise disaster, and the Senior Registrar had sought to protect her privacy on the occasion of the family funeral. He made an order in wardship proceedings to the effect that the police were requested to prevent any photographs of her from being taken, and to warn any journalists that she was a ward of court "and no information about her may be published". Subsequently *The Daily Mail* (as it happened, being unaware of the existence of the order) published an article referring to her demeanour and to the fact that she was a ward. The local authority contended that the newspaper was in contempt. Booth J. expressed herself satisfied that there was no common law rule prohibiting publication of *any* information relating to a ward.

6–112 So too did Sir Stephen Brown P. in *Re W (Wards) (Publication of Information)*.[39] Whereas some automatic consequences of wardship had long been recognised, so that for example it would be contempt to marry a ward or to remove one from the jurisdiction without permission, there was no authority to support the proposition that there should be an automatic clampdown on information relating to wards. Each case has to be judged on its merits, and an order will only be made if the court is satisfied that it is *necessary* to do so.

---

[34] ss.100(3) and (4).
[35] See, *e.g. Re Z (A Minor) (Identification: Restrictions on Publication)* [1997] Fam. 1 at 14A–B, Ward L.J.
[36] See generally J. Dixon, "Children and the Statutory Restraints on Publicity" (2001) Family Law 757 at 761, which spoke of muddle and confusion "which does the law no credit".
[37] See the approach of the Court of Appeal in *Att-Gen v Newspaper Publishing plc* [1988] Ch. 333, which concluded that the 1981 Act itself was intended to embody Parliament's policy decision to effect a permanent shift in favour of freedom of speech.
[38] *Re L (A Minor)* [1988] 1 All E.R. 418 at 422.
[39] [1989] 1 F.L.R. 246 at 258.

THE INHERENT (OR *PARENS PATRIAE*) JURISDICTION   **6–114**

It seemed for a time after the *Re Z* case that since the willingness of the courts **6–113** to focus upon the paramountcy principle embodied in s.1 of the Children Act 1989, and upon the recognition of a child's right of confidence or privacy in relation to health and education matters,[40] the apparent policy shift in favour of free speech might recede somewhat into the background. The court might have become more willing to restrict publicity than the earlier cases[41] seemed to suggest, and to achieve this by invoking a quasi-parental duty of confidence,[42] perhaps through a prohibited steps order under the 1989 Act. Much would turn on the scope of the activities held to fall within the phrase "upbringing of a child".[43] Yet in July 2000, Munby J. pointed out in *Kelly v BBC*[44] that counsel in that case had been unable to identify any other example of the court's exercising its custodial jurisdiction in a manner analogous to that adopted in *Re Z*.

J. A brief summary of developments since the Human Rights Act

It now seems that the court will not strive in such cases to classify the **6–114** circumstances of any particular case as falling under the "protective" or "custodial" labels we have been considering; the focus is more likely to be upon reaching a correct result on the individual facts. The exercise of classification was coming to be recognised as both difficult and arid. It was eventually put to one side by the Court of Appeal and the House of Lords in *Re S (FC)* as a potential distraction from the more important circumstances of the case in hand. If the distinction has not been altogether abandoned, it is perhaps fair to say (in the words of Munby J.)[45] that there is no longer a "bright line boundary" between those two aspects of the court's jurisdiction. The peg on which the new approach was hung was the Human Rights Act 1998. The emphasis was put upon the need to "hold the balance" between the competing rights provided for in the European Convention.[46] As Latham L.J. encapsulated the test,[47] what is now required is to carry out the exercise of identifying "the extent to which refusing to grant the relevant terms of the injunction asked for would be a proportionate interference with the private life of the child on the one hand and their grant would be a proportionate interference with the rights of the press under article 10

---

[40] *Re Z (Identification)* [1997] Fam. 1 at 24–25, Ward L.J.
[41] *Re W (A Minor)* [1992] 1 W.L.R. 100; *Re R (Wardship: Restrictions on Publication)* [1994] Fam. 254; *R v Central Independent Television plc* [1994] Fam. 192.
[42] *Re Z (Identification)* [1997] Fam. 1 at 24, 25, 30–1, Ward L.J.
[43] See the Children Act 1989, s.1(1).
[44] [2001] Fam. 59 at 74.
[45] *Re Angela Roddy (A Minor)* [2003] EWHC 2927 (Fam), [2004] 2 F.L.R. 949 at [16]. See also *E (By Her Litigation Friend the Official Solicitor) v Channel Four* [2005] EWHC 1144 (Fam).
[46] See also, *e.g. A v B plc* [2003] Q.B. 195 at [6], *per* Lord Woolf C.J. The question arises whether this "balancing approach" is consistent with that of the European Court of Human Rights in *Sunday Times v UK* (1979) 2 E.H.R.R. 245 at 281 which was cited by Lord Fraser in *Att-Gen v BBC* [1981] A.C. 303 at 352B–F. See above at para.2–157. The difference may be more apparent than real since the courts recognise the importance of free speech and will only countenance exceptions to the rights under Art.10 where they are necesssary and proportionate for the protection of a countervailing Convention right.
[47] *Re S (A Child)* [2003] EWCA Civ 963, [2003] Ch. 650 at [64].

on the other hand". This was the approach adopted also by Lord Steyn in the House of Lords.[48]

III. INJUNCTIONS AFFECTING PERSONS WHO ARE NOT DIRECTLY BOUND

A. Injunctions intended to bind non-parties

6–115   In the case of *contra mundum* injunctions considered above, the order is intended to be served on and to bind persons who are not parties to the litigation in question (which had generally, prior to the coming in to effect of the Children Act 1989, taken the form of wardship proceedings) in respect of which the order has been made. This practice appears therefore to represent an encroachment upon the general principle that the court acts *in personam*, acknowledged by Lord Eldon in *Iveson v Harris*[49]:

" . . . I have no conception that it is competent to this Court to hold a man bound by injunction, who is not a party in the cause for the purpose of the cause."

6–116   The exercise of the court's *parens patriae* jurisdiction cannot be regarded as confined by the ordinary principles of *inter partes* litigation.[50] In that context the court is not merely holding the ring between litigants; it has an independent role, which may often need to be more proactive in character, for the purpose of protecting the citizens in its care. If this is put forward as the justification for the recently recognised power to grant wide-ranging injunctive relief against the media, it would perhaps be reasonable to conclude that this power is confined to the *parens patriae* jurisdiction.[51] Indeed Balcombe J., in *X County Council v A*,[52] expressed himself to be positively of this view: "Let me say at once that, if it were not an exercise of the wardship jurisdiction, I am satisfied that there would be no such power." Yet it is now necessary to accommodate within the analysis such cases as *Venables and Thompson v News Group Newspapers Ltd*,[53] *X (A Woman Formerly Known as Mary Bell) v O'Brien*,[54] and *Carr (Maxine) v News Group Newspapers Ltd*.[55] These clearly have to be justified by reasoning outside the concept of wardship.

6–117   Another possible analysis would be to treat this jurisdiction as being truly consistent with Lord Eldon's principle, since it might be said to have the effect, perhaps, of bringing those who are served with notice of the existence of the

---

[48] See the citation at para.6–105.
[49] (1802) 7 Ves. Jun. 251 at 256–7, 32 E.R. 102 at 103–4.
[50] Lord Shaw of Dunfermline referred to the jurisdiction as *"intra familiam"*: *Scott v Scott* [1913] A.C. 417 at 483.
[51] See Balcombe J. in *X County Council v A* [1985] 1 All E.R. 53 at 55h and 56g; Lloyd L.J. in *Att-Gen v Newspaper Publishing plc* [1988] 1 Ch. 333 at 377G contented himself by simply recognising wardship as the "best established" of certain very limited (but otherwise unspecified) exceptions. See also the analysis of this decision by Sir John Donaldson M.R., at 369.
[52] [1985] 1 All E.R. 53 at 55h.
[53] [2001] Fam. 430.
[54] [2003] EWHC 1101 (QB), [2003] 2 F.C.R. 686.
[55] [2005] EWHC 971 (QB).

order into the litigation, albeit on an *ad hoc* basis. There would be a ready analogy with the situation that arises under CPR Sch.1, Ord.113, where "persons unknown" are treated as being parties to the litigation,[56] or that where an order for disclosure may be made against servants or agents of a corporation personally, even though not parties to the litigation themselves.[57]

Yet neither of these analyses found favour with the Court of Appeal when they considered the jurisdiction in *Att-Gen v Newspaper Publishing plc*.[58] Balcombe L.J. expressed the view that it represents an exception to Lord Eldon's *in personam* principle, although by this time he was no longer inclined to confine the exception by reference to wardship. Lloyd L.J. accepted that Lord Eldon's principle that the courts act *in personam* is fundamental, although he also recognised that there were " . . . certain fairly limited exceptions of which the best established is wardship".[59] The court can thus apparently bind the world, and in particular the media, without needing to make them parties to the litigation.

6–118

Balcombe L.J. went on to identify the *Spycatcher* case as one which would also merit exceptional treatment, inconsistent with Lord Eldon's *in personam* principle, even though it had nothing to do with the wardship or *parens patriae* jurisdiction. He thought that it would have been justified by the court's objective in that context of seeking to protect the subject matter of pending litigation.

6–119

In *R. v Central Independent Television plc*,[60] Hoffmann L.J expressed the view that Balcombe J. "for wholly commendable reasons, was asserting a jurisdiction which did not exist". This was because, had such a jurisdiction existed, it could be exercised to restrain the identification of *any* convicted criminal with young children. He recognised, however, that recently " . . . the courts have, without any statutory or, so far as I can see, other previous authority, assumed a power to create by injunction what is in effect a right of privacy for children".[61] The question therefore remains whether, when the court chooses to exercise this recently recognised jurisdiction, it is in fact binding the world at large or merely notifying people in general that an order has been made against some particular individual. The latter analysis was the one that appealed to Sir John Donaldson M.R. in *Att-Gen v Newspaper Publishing plc*.[62]

6–120

Whatever the correct analysis may be, it now seems to be beyond dispute that orders of this kind represent an exception to the *in personam* principle. It would appear to follow that any non-party, such as a newspaper publisher or editor,

6–121

---

[56] See, *e.g.* the reference to this process in *Att-Gen v Newspaper Publishing plc* [1988] Ch. 333 at 369C, Sir John Donaldson M.R.
[57] *Dummer v Chippenham Corp* (1807) 14 Ves. Jun. 245, 33 E.R. 515, Lord Eldon; *Harrington v North London Polytechnic* [1984] 1 W.L.R. 1293, [1984] 3 All E.R. 666.
[58] [1988] Ch. 333. See generally Lord Oliver, "Spycatcher: Confidence, Copyright and Contempt" (1989) 23 Is. L.R. 409.
[59] [1988] Ch. 333 at 377G.
[60] [1994] Fam. 192 at 205B–C.
[61] *R. v Central Independent Television plc* [1994] Fam. 192 at 204D.
[62] [1988] Ch. 333 at 369. See also Lord Uthwatt in *Marengo v Daily Sketch and Sunday Graphic Ltd* [1948] 1 All E.R. 406 at 407, HL.

6–121 whom the court wished to restrain, could hardly be found liable for *civil* contempt. It was recognised by Balcombe J. in *X County Council v A*,[63] that no such person could be held in contempt without having had knowledge of the existence of the order in question. In such a case, if the order had been drawn to the attention of an alleged contemnor, and it was clear on its face that he or his newspaper was one of those to whom it was directed, there could be no room for misunderstanding. It would not be necessary to go beyond this in order to demonstrate some super-added intention to interfere with the administration of justice. It would suffice to establish liability that he had knowledge of an order of which the purpose is obvious on its face.[64]

6–122 The position has been summarised by Lord Hope in *Att-Gen v Punch Ltd*[65]:

"The power to commit for contempt ensures that acts and words tending to obstruct the administration of justice are prohibited. So a stranger is liable for contempt if his act constitutes a wilful interference with the administration of justice by the court in the proceedings in which the order was made. It has also to be shown there was an intention on his part to interfere with or impede the administration of justice. This is an essential ingredient, and it has to be established to the criminal standard of proof. But the intent need not be stated expressly or admitted by the defendant. As is the case where the question of intention, or *mens rea*, arises in criminal cases, it can be inferred from all the circumstances including the foreseeability of the consequences of the defendant's conduct: *Att-Gen v Newspaper Publishing plc* [1988] Ch. 333, 374–375, *per* Sir John Donaldson M.R.*"*

6–123 Editors or journalists who are given notice of such an order, restraining publication of details relating to (say) a minor or patient, find themselves in similar circumstances to those confronting a bank which is notified of the terms of a freezing order.[66] Such a bank is intended to be directly affected by the restrictions contained in the order, although it relates primarily to the defendant who happens to be its customer; yet the bank no more becomes a party to its client's litigation than does the newspaper editor become a party to the wardship or other family proceedings.

B. Injunctions indirectly affecting third parties

6–124 In any event, in recent years it has become apparent that there may be circumstances in which non-parties, and in particular the media, may be liable for contempt in respect of orders made against parties to civil litigation which were not even intended to be served on such non-parties nor, in form, to be binding upon them. "An interlocutory order for the non-disclosure of information is the paradigm example of the type of order where the principle is in point".[67]

---

[63] [1985] 1 All E.R. 53 at 56f–g.
[64] Compare the remarks of Lord Oliver in *Att-Gen v Times Newspapers Ltd* [1992] 1 A.C. 191 at 224.
[65] [2002] UKHL 50, [2003] 1 A.C. 1046 at [87].
[66] See the discussion at paras 12–144 *et seq.*
[67] *Att-Gen v Punch Ltd* [2002] UKHL 50, [2003] 1 A.C. 1046 at [4], Lord Nicholls.

The decision of the Court of Appeal in *Att-Gen v Newspaper Publishing plc* 6–125
itself[68] led at least for a time to a widespread but, it is submitted, misguided notion on the part of some litigants and journalists that the direct effect of an injunction can be extended once it is obtained against any other person who is served with or notified of it. For example, some libel claimants have taken the view that by obtaining an injunction to restrain, perhaps even without notice, against one newspaper, they can effectively bind the other media by faxing a copy to all concerned. Naturally, the receipt of such a document will have an inhibiting effect upon the newspapers concerned, and it would be a bold editor who chose to publish material *apparently* inconsistent with the order without knowing the full circumstances in which it was made. The potential for a "chilling effect" is thus obvious.

C. The nature of the liability of persons not directly bound by an order

It is necessary therefore to consider the true principles underlying this important 6–126
decision of the Court of Appeal, which was treated by some as though it had driven a coach and four through Lord Eldon's principle (that only parties to proceedings could be bound by orders made in the course of those proceedings). It is submitted that the decision did nothing of the kind and that neither was it intended to do so. It was no more than an illustration of the law adopted by Lloyd L.J. in the following terms[69]:

"Since the test of contempt is not breach of the order but interference with the administration of justice, it follows that *at common law* a contempt may be committed even if no specific order has been made by the court affecting anyone other than those involved in the proceedings. At common law, if the court makes an order regulating its own procedure and the purpose of the order is plainly to protect the administration of justice, then anyone who subverts that order will be guilty of contempt."

Thus, anyone who has knowledge[70] of an order made by the court, and the 6–127
purpose for which it was made, whether formally served with it or not,[71] *could* be in contempt in publishing material inconsistent with that purpose. This would

---

[68] [1988] 1 Ch. 333. The reasoning of the Court of Appeal was subsequently considered in the related case of *Att-Gen v Times Newspapers Ltd* [1992] 1 A.C. 191, considered at paras 6–136 *et seq.*
[69] [1988] Ch. 333 at 380. See also *Eckman v Midland Bank Ltd* [1973] Q.B. 519 (Sir John Donaldson M.R.); *Z Ltd v A-Z and AA-LL* [1982] 1 Q.B. 558, CA; *Messenger Group Newspapers Ltd v NGA* [1984] 1 All E.R. 293, CA, *per* Sir John Donaldson M.R.; *Taylor v NUM, The Times,* November 20, 1985 Ch. D., Nicholls J.; *Att-Gen v Observer Ltd: Re an Application by Derbyshire County Council* [1988] 1 All E.R. 385 at 397–8; *Sir James Butler's case* (1696) 2 Salk 596, 91 E.R. 504; *Rantzen v Rothschild* (1865) 13 L.T. 399; *Davis v Barlow* (1911) 18 W.L.R. 238; *Hubbard v Woodfield* (1913) 57 S.J. 729; *Harvie v Ross and Ross* (1886) 24 S.L.R. 58, 14 R 21. See also Gareth Jones, "Breach of Confidence after Spycatcher" (1989) 42 C.L.P. 49; Y. Cripps, "Breaches of Copyright and Confidence—The Spycatcher Effect" [1989] P.L. 13; and Catherine O'Regan, "Contempt of Court and the Enforcement of Labour Injunctions" (1991) 54 M.L.R. 385.
[70] Even a party intended by the court to be directly bound by such an order could not be liable for a breach unless fixed with knowledge: see, *e.g. X County Council v A* [1985] 1 All E.R. 53 at 56f–g; *Re Supply of Ready Mixed Concrete (No.2)* [1992] 2 Q.B. 213 at 239 Lord Donaldson M.R.; *Blackburn v Bowering* [1994] 1 W.L.R. 1324 at 1329, Sir Thomas Bingham M.R. See also *Re G (Celebrities: Publicity)* [1999] 1 F.L.R. 409 at 415, where Thorpe L.J. emphasised that knowledge of the order in such cases is an essential ingredient.
[71] See para.6–134.

not, however, be on the basis of having been in breach of an order to which he or she was not, *ex hypothesi*, a party; but rather because, assuming the necessary *mens rea*, such a person would come within one of the traditional categories of *criminal* contempt. Accordingly, once again we submit that this is not inconsistent with Lord Eldon's principle.

6–128 The background of *Att-Gen v Newspaper Publishing plc*[72] was a good illustration of how the situation might arise, because it concerned an interim injunction made by the court against two newspapers in a breach of confidence case, for the traditional purpose of preserving the *status quo* until the outcome of the trial. If the information alleged to be confidential were to be published before that stage the court's process would be rendered of no avail. As Sir John Donaldson M.R. put it,[73] the "ice cube" would have melted and there would have been nothing left about which to litigate. "Once a confidence is let loose, or escapes, it cannot be recaptured. Defiance of the interim order denies the process of justice as it renders nugatory the purpose of the substantive hearing".[74]

6–129 The newspapers to whom the injunction had been directed were *The Guardian* and *The Observer*, who were restrained from publishing extracts from *Spycatcher* (which purported to be an account by a former officer in the security service of his experiences, and which included confidential material). Subsequently, *The Independent* and two other newspapers also published extracts from the memoirs. It was these publications which came to the attention of the Court of Appeal after the Vice-Chancellor had ruled that their conduct in publishing, albeit with knowledge of the existence of the injunctions against *The Guardian* and *The Observer*, did *not* constitute criminal contempt, on the ground that they were not themselves subject to any such injunction. The Court of Appeal remitted the matter for it to be determined whether the respondents had the necessary *mens rea*, that is to say whether they intended to impede or prejudice the administration of justice.

6–130 Each case will naturally depend on its own facts, but if a stranger to the proceedings is aware that the court has sought to protect the purposes of the administration of justice by maintaining confidentiality of certain information pending trial, and thereafter deliberately brings that information into the public domain, he may well be held to have flouted the court's intention and subverted its protective order.[75] In that case the *actus reus* would be tantamount to the destruction of the subject matter of the action (and the argument before the Court of Appeal was refined so as to limit it to that situation).[76]

6–131 On the other hand, it is most unlikely that a distributor, newsagent or librarian, even one who knows of such an order restricting the dissemination of information, would be held to have committed the *actus reus* of contempt merely by

---

[72] [1988] Ch. 333.
[73] [1988] Ch. at 358F.
[74] *Att-Gen for England and Wales v Tomlinson* [1999] 3 N.Z.L.R. 722 at 732, Gendall J.
[75] The position might well be different where there was no such order—see the dismissal by the House of counsel's "pre-emptive" argument on these grounds, in *Re Lonrho plc* [1990] 2 A.C. 154 at 210–13.
[76] [1988] Ch. 333 at 383, Balcombe L.J.

virtue of omitting to carry out checks to see whether books, newspapers or periodicals that he was proposing to display or put into circulation contained any of the protected information.[77]

1. *The relevance of* Bonnard v Perryman[78] *in this context*

The Court of Appeal in *Att-Gen v Newspaper Publishing plc*[79] was considering a case in which the respondents did have knowledge of the relevant order. This would not necessarily matter in the typical instance where a libel claimant has obtained an interim injunction. As Sir John Donaldson M.R. explained,[80] the important question is whether the non-party's publication of the defamatory material would interfere with the administration of justice. If it did, then (subject to the necessary *mens rea*) there might well be a contempt, even if the non-party would be able to rely on *Bonnard v Perryman*[81] and depose that, if sued himself, he intended to plead justification.

6–132

It had been held already by the Court of Appeal in *Att-Gen v News Group Newspapers Ltd*[82] that the *Bonnard v Perryman* principle in defamation cases was subordinate to the rules of contempt preventing interference with the administration of justice. In most cases, however, a non-party could publish despite the terms of an interim injunction restraining defamation without being in contempt. The Master of the Rolls drew an analogy with assault[83]:

6–133

"If B is enjoined not to assault A and C then assaults A, there is no interference with the administration of justice in the action *A v B*. It is simply a further tort or crime. Similarly with defamation. The Court will prohibit a second defamatory statement (or blow) by B, but the subsequent making of the same defamatory statement by C (i.e. an additional blow) will not interfere with the administration of justice as between A and B. It is simply an independent tort if, in the end, it cannot be successfully defended."

2. *The absence of procedural safeguards*

A point that had appealed to the Vice-Chancellor in the *Spycatcher* hearing at first instance was that if a non-party, such as *The Independent*, were to be held liable in contempt it would mean that such a person would be deprived of the

6–134

---

[77] *Att-Gen v Observer Ltd: Re an Application by Derbyshire County Council* [1988] 1 All E.R. 385 at 399, Knox J. Cp. the Defamation Act 1996, s.1, intended to afford protection in the field of defamation for those who play only a subsidiary role in the communication of defamatory matter.
[78] [1891] 2 Ch. 269, discussed at paras 6–5 *et seq*. The continuing relevance of the strict test in *Bonnard v Perryman* has been re-affirmed by the Court of Appeal in *Martha Greene v Associated Newspapers Ltd* [2004] EWCA Civ 1462, [2005] 3 W.L.R. 281, [2005] 1 All E.R. 30, notwithstanding the terms of s.12(3) of the Human Rights Act 1998.
[79] [1988] Ch. 333.
[80] *ibid*. at 371.
[81] [1891] 2 Ch. 269.
[82] [1987] 1 Q.B. 1.
[83] [1988] Ch. 333 at 371.

"very elaborate procedural safeguards" applying to those against whom injunctions are sought; for example, personal service of the order and the indorsement of the penal notice. The Master of the Rolls pointed out[84] that this was to confuse two separate categories of contempt: on the one hand, that which consists in disobedience to an order, where those "safeguards" do apply, and on the other hand the general category of contempt which consists in interfering with the due administration of justice. This corresponds to the traditional distinction between civil and criminal contempt, although his Lordship suggested that this classification nowadays tends to mislead rather than assist,[85] and it would be better to concentrate more on the substantive distinction between disobedience to an order and the general category of interference with the administration of justice.

3. *Spycatcher: the appellate stages*

6–135   After the matter was remitted for the relevant facts to be found, and in particular whether there had been the necessary *mens rea*, it came before Morritt J. nearly two years later and he held that there had indeed been an intention on the part of *The Independent* and *The Sunday Times* to impede or prejudice the administration of justice.[86] He imposed heavy fines which were remitted by the Court of Appeal (Fox, Ralph Gibson and Nicholls L.JJ.)[87] although they did not overturn the rulings on liability for contempt.

6–136   Eventually, the matters of legal principle were re-opened before the House of Lords in *Att-Gen v Times Newspapers Ltd*[88] in 1991, by which time it was no longer contended that *mens rea* was absent. The only point taken by *The Sunday Times* was that their conduct in publishing the extracts in 1987 had not constituted the *actus reus* of contempt. Their Lordships dismissed the appeal[89] and applied similar reasoning to that of the Court of Appeal in the earlier hearing.[90]

6–137   It had been argued before the House that the findings of contempt were inconsistent with Lord Eldon's principle[91] that non-parties to litigation cannot be bound by holdings in the litigation, but their Lordships pointed out that there had never been any suggestion by the Attorney-General that the injunction *bound*

---

[84] *ibid.* at 372.
[85] The passage is set out in full at para.3–51.
[86] [1989] 1 F.S.R. 457.
[87] See *Att-Gen v Newspaper Publishing plc* [1990] T.L.R. 158, CA (Lexis), discussed at paras 5–153 *et seq.*
[88] [1992] 1 A.C. 191. It may be noted that these House of Lords' speeches were handed down in April 1991, some months before the European Court of Human Rights ruled on the earlier decision of the House on the matter of the *Spycatcher* injunctions and whether they could be defended as necessary in a democratic society; *Sunday Times Ltd v United Kingdom (No.2)* (1991) 14 E.H.R.R 229.
[89] [1992] 1 A.C. 191. See also the consideration of these principles by Lord Mustill in *London Borough of Harrow v Johnstone* [1997] 1 W.L.R. 459 at 468–70, discussed at paras 11–42 *et seq.*
[90] [1988] Ch. 333.
[91] See para.6–115 and paras 11–34 *et seq.* See also the discussion at para.12–241.

non-party newspapers.[92] It was also argued that the authorities[93] were only consistent with finding a non-party liable for contempt if he had aided or abetted a breach by the party enjoined. This was unanimously rejected, not least because the Court of Appeal in the case of *Z Ltd v A-Z & AA-LL*[94] had clearly demonstrated the contrary.[95]

It was also contended that it was inappropriate to found criminal liability upon conduct which the court deemed to subvert the *purpose* of the order, as opposed to the precise terms of the order, since this may not always be apparent. Yet as Lord Oliver explained,[96] any such difficulty was more apparent than real. In the *Spycatcher* instance nobody could have been in any doubt but that the purpose of the original *Guardian* and *Observer* orders was to keep confidential the information in the author's possession (a right which the Attorney-General acting in this instance on behalf of the government enjoyed against the whole world, albeit specifically threatened by those two newspapers at that time). In a hypothetical case where there was, however, genuine doubt about the court's purpose, then the party charged would be likely to escape liability for want of the requisite *mens rea* since, if the purpose was neither known nor obvious, it would be difficult to establish a positive intention on his part to frustrate it.

A related argument was to the effect that if an order can only be made *inter partes*, and not *contra mundum*, a non-party could hardly perform an act inconsistent with that limited purpose. If the courts had intended, however, to include the restriction of the non-party, that would not be a legitimate purpose. This was, said Lord Oliver,[97] to confuse the scope of an order made in private litigation with the public law question of the proper administration of justice:

"If the court has taken into its hands the conduct of the matter to the extent of ordering the interim preservation of the interest of the plaintiff so that the issue between him and the defendant can be properly and fairly tried, it has to be accepted that that is what the court had determined that the interests of justice require. The gratuitous intervention of a third party intended to result in that purpose being frustrated and the outcome of the trial prejudiced, must manifestly interfere with and obstruct what the court has determined to be the interests of justice. Those interests are not dependent upon the scope of the order."

---

[92] [1992] 1 A.C. at 203 (Lord Brandon), 211 (Lord Ackner), 217–8 (Lord Oliver), 228 (Lord Jauncey).
[93] *Marengo v Daily Sketch and Sunday Graphic Ltd* [1948] 1 All E.R. 406,407, HL; *Lord Wellesley v Earl of Mornington* (1848) 11 Beav. 180 at 181, 50 E.R. 785 at 786; *Seaward v Patterson* [1897] 1 Ch. 545; *Brydges v Brydges and Wood* [1909] P. 187 at 191, Farwell L.J.; *Ranson v Platt* [1911] 2 K.B. 291 at 307–8; *Acrow (Automation) Ltd v Rex Chainbelt Inc* [1977] 1 W.L.R. 1676 at 1682; *Thorne RDC v Bunting (No.2)* [1972] 3 All E.R. 1084 at 1087–8; *Z Ltd v A-Z & AA-LL* [1982] Q.B. 558 at 572–3, 578.
[94] See previous note. The decision is discussed in more detail at paras 12–145 *et seq.*
[95] [1992] 1 A.C. at 214, Lord Ackner; see also Lord Oliver at 220. See also *United Kingdom Nirex Ltd v Barton*, The Times, October 14, 1986, Henry J.; *Smith-Barry v Dawson* (1891) 27 L.R. Ir. 558; *Tilco Plastics Ltd v Skurjat* (1966) 57 D.L.R. (2d) 596 at 619, Gale C.J.H.C.
[96] [1992] 1 A.C. at 223.
[97] *ibid.* at 224.

6-140 Lord Oliver's speech was cited and followed by the Court of Appeal in *Re G (Celebrities: Publicity)*.[98] The background was a dispute between two well-known parents who had, in the course of family proceedings concerning residence orders, been restrained from communicating about each other or the children, and from disclosing the contents of the proceedings. Counsel for News Group Newspapers had applied for certain restrictions to be relaxed for the benefit of his clients, and in particular for the insertion of a proviso in the following terms: " . . . provided that it shall not be a contempt of court for any news medium to publish anything spoken or written by the father or mother in breach of this paragraph of this order or any information already in the public domain." Thorpe L.J. had been initially attracted by this suggestion, which was designed simply to protect the newspaper in the event of publication, with knowledge of the injunction, of a statement made by one parent concerning the other. However, in the light of Lord Oliver's analysis, it was clear that such a publication with *knowledge of the order* (quite apart from any question of aiding or abetting a parent to breach the order) would constitute a criminal contempt. Thus, if the court were to insert the proviso, it would in effect be licensing one means of committing a criminal contempt.

4. *Att-Gen v Punch Ltd*

6-141 Further consideration was given to the House of Lords decision in *Att-Gen v Times Newspapers Ltd* in *Att-Gen v Punch Ltd*.[99] Lord Phillips M.R. (from whom in this respect there seems to have been no dissent) summarised the *ratio* of their Lordships' decision as follows:

> "(a) Intentional interference with the manner in which a judge is conducting a trial can amount to a contempt of court.
>
> (b) When in the course of a trial a judge makes an order with the purpose of furthering some aspect of the conduct of the trial, a third party who, with knowledge of that purpose, intentionally acts in such a way as to defeat that purpose can be in contempt of court.
>   When a [claimant] brings an action to preserve an alleged right of confidentiality in information and the court makes an order that the information is not to be published pending trial, the purpose of the order is to protect the confidentiality of the information pending trial. A third party who, with knowledge of the order, publishes the information and thereby destroys its confidentiality will commit a contempt of court. The contempt is committed not because the third party is in breach of the order—the order does not bind the third party. The contempt is committed because the purpose of the judge in making the order is intentionally frustrated with the consequence that the conduct of the trial is disrupted".

The Court clearly had a certain difficulty in deciding to what extent their Lordships had (if at all) regarded these principles as extending beyond interim orders, intended to hold the ring between the parties until the issues are resolved,

---

[98] [1999] 1 F.L.R. 409 at 415.
[99] [2002] UKHL 50, [2003] 1 A.C. 1046 at [87].

and embracing also final orders made at the conclusion of the litigation. The matter was left over for later consideration as and when necessary.[1]

6–142 The background to the *Punch* case was that in 1997 the Attorney-General had sought injunctions against Mr David Shayler, a former officer of the security service ("MI5"), and Associated Newspapers. The purpose was to restrain the communication of information obtained by him in the course of his former employment, which was subject to the obligations of confidentiality by which all such officers are bound—and ultimately to protect national security itself. A private arrangement had then been reached between the parties and the injunctions were granted by consent. The terms agreed included a proviso, whereby both respondents would be enabled to publish information if no objection was taken to it by the security service, following referral through the Treasury Solicitor. To outsiders, of course, and especially to journalists, this arrangement appeared to have about it the aura and trappings of government censorship. Yet, so long as those parties found it convenient to themselves, it was unlikely to cause trouble. The time came, however, in 2000, when the editor of *Punch* (Mr Steen) wished to publish an article by Mr Shayler containing allegations about the circumstances underlying the Bishopsgate bomb planted some years earlier by the IRA. It was uncontroversial that the article contained at least some information deriving from Mr Shayler's time with MI5 which had not previously found its way into the public domain. The Treasury Solicitor had suggested certain amendments and invited further comments. Not all the amendments were acceptable to the editor but he went ahead and published the article, including some material that was unacceptable so far as the security service was concerned—without taking up the offer of further discussions.

6–143 The case illustrates a general difficulty about consent orders, where the parties have reached mutually satisfactory terms, and an order is then granted accordingly by a busy judge without an independent mind being applied in any analytical way to the exact purpose(s) of the order or any wider implications it may have. Moreover, such agreements may sometimes be reached by the parties through negotiations without there being anything like comparable bargaining power or equality of arms; so too, they may or may not have addressed the wider public interest in arriving at their agreed terms or considered the impact upon Convention rights such as, for example, those relating to privacy or freedom of expression; in particular, whether it can be shown that the terms and scope of the order are no wider than necessary. In such circumstances, it may not be easy to establish in any meaningful sense what "purpose(s)" *the court* actually had in granting the order placed before it in the context of later having to apply the principles explained in *Spycatcher* and particularly by Lord Oliver.[2]

6–144 In the light of the evidence the judge, applying the *Spycatcher* principles, had found contempt proved against both the editor and the proprietors of the magazine; that is to say, he found that both the *actus reus* and the necessary *mens*

---

[1] See now *Jockey Club v Buffham* [2002] EWHC 1866, [2003] Q.B. 462, discussed at para.6–145 below.
[2] [1992] 1 A.C. at 223–4.

6-144

rea had been established by the Attorney-General. The editor appealed. It seemed to be common ground between all members of the Court of Appeal that what had been done by the editor would have constituted aiding and abetting Mr Shayler in the breaching of his obligations of confidence.[3] That, however, was not the way the Attorney had put his case. The application had been framed, for whatever reason, on the basis of the more sophisticated doctrine developed in *Spycatcher*. It was in its application that there came about a "narrow but ultimately critical point" at which Simon Brown L.J. departed from the reasoning of his brethren. The majority concluded that the Attorney had failed to demonstrate *mens rea* on the editor's part, since it was by no means clear that he intended to defeat the court's object in making the 1997 order. It was at least possible that he had understood its purpose to be that of protecting national security, rather than holding the ring between the parties until trial with a view to protecting the administration of justice (as in *Spycatcher* itself). Simon Brown L.J., on the other hand, thought that the ring-holding purpose must have been obvious to the editor from the terms of the proviso—"for written clearance by the Attorney-General in respect of any particular information upon anyone's application". The case illustrates perhaps, once again, that the *mens rea* "minefield" (to use Sir John Donaldson's expression) is still to be cleared. Also, as Lord Phillips M.R. himself observed[4]:

> "This appeal demonstrates the limitations of the *Spycatcher* jurisdiction. It is not easy to draft an interlocutory injunction in terms that go no wider than is necessary to restrain the publication of material in respect of which the claimant has an arguable claim to confidentiality. It is, however, necessary to do this if the terms of the injunction are to equate with the purpose for which the injunction is ordered, namely the preservation of the confidentiality of the material in question. Even then that purpose may be destroyed if, with the passage of time, the information in question is brought within the public domain. Third parties are not directly bound by the terms of such an injunction. If they are to be held liable for the contempt of interfering with the course of justice it must be demonstrated that the disclosure made by them defeated, in whole or in part, the court's purpose in granting the injunction and that they appreciated that it would do so. This will be particularly difficult to demonstrate if the court adopts the approach of ordering injunctions in wide terms, but delegating to the claimant the role of determining what is and what is not to be restrained from publication".

6-145

The point left open for future consideration[5] as to the applicability or otherwise of the *Spycatcher* doctrine to permanent injunctions, came before Gray J. in *The Jockey Club v Buffham*.[6] Having cited Lord Phillips' judgment in *Att-Gen v Punch Ltd*,[7] his Lordship observed that although they were strictly *obiter* he accepted that the principle was indeed limited to interlocutory injunctions. That is because the underlying judicial policy of the doctrine has been perceived as that of protecting the administration of justice, in the sense of enforcing the court's objective in granting an interim injunction—most frequently that of

---

[3] See, *e.g. Seaward v Paterson* [1897] 1 Ch. 545.
[4] [2001] EWCA Civ 403, [2001] Q.B. 1028 at [124].
[5] See para.6–141 above.
[6] [2002] EWHC 1866, [2003] Q.B. 462.
[7] At [87]–[88].

protecting the confidentiality of information pending a final resolution of the issues at trial—and not the protection of confidential information as such.

Generally speaking, once proceedings have concluded with the grant of a permanent injunction, there will simply be an *inter partes* order and such parties as are directly bound by it will have to comply with it. There will not normally be any wider implications for the administration of justice such as, for example, to engage the *Spycatcher* doctrine. Of course, if a third party assists the person bound by the injunction to breach its terms, there could be a direct liability for contempt on the part of the third party, as an aider or abettor in accordance with *Seaward v Paterson*,[8] but that is quite another matter. On the other hand, there may be special circumstances in which the court grants a permanent injunction *contra mundum* when the court's purpose can be seen to extend beyond the immediate parties to the litigation. As Gray J. pointed out, the permanent injunction so granted in *Venables v News Group Newspapers Ltd*[9] would continue indefinitely to bind people generally within the jurisdiction of the court, including the media. Whether, as a matter of analysis, this would be because of the *Spycatcher* doctrine, or because it has the effect of directly binding everyone, is a moot if somewhat sterile point.[10] It is best seen as an exception to the *in personam* principle, and thus any potential liability, on the part of strangers to the litigation, would be in respect of criminal contempt with the consequences that flow from that—including particularly with regard to *mens rea*. It would be necessary to establish knowledge of the purpose of the order although in the *Venables* case, unlike any example of the *Spycatcher* doctrine, that purpose would not so much be the protection of the administration of justice as the protection of the claimants' physical safety.

6–146

When the *Punch* case reached the House of Lords, the general issue of whether a distinction should be drawn, as a matter of principle, between interlocutory and permanent injunctions was not specifically addressed. It was referred to by Lord Hope[11] but his Lordship went on to focus particularly on what was considered to have been the Court of Appeal's misunderstanding as to the "purpose" for which the injunction had been granted to restrict publication of information deriving from Mr Shayler. He held that "the only purpose that is relevant to the question whether a contempt has been committed is the purpose which the court was seeking to serve in the interests of justice" (*i.e.* to ensure that the material remained confidential until its status was determined at trial). Lord Hope thought it confusing to classify this as the "ulterior purpose", a phrase used by the Master of the Rolls to distinguish it from the "immediate purpose" (*i.e.* to restrain publication) and from the "ultimate purpose" (*i.e.* to prevent damage to the national interest). This analysis would tend to confirm that the *Spycatcher* doctrine is likely to have application, at least primarily, to interference with the administration of justice by the subverting of interlocutory injunctions. Thus the

6–147

---

[8] [1897] 1 Ch. 545.
[9] [2001] Fam. 430; see para.6–49 above. See also *X (A Woman Formerly Known As Mary Bell) v O'Brien* [2003] EWHC 1101 (QB), [2003] 2 F.C.R. 686; *Carr (Maxine) v News Group Newspapers Ltd* [2005] EWHC 971 (QB).
[10] See paras 6–116 *et seq.*
[11] At [95].

6–147   CHAPTER 6—COURT ORDERS AFFECTING THE MEDIA

"purpose" that is relevant to this doctrine is that of protecting the administration of justice. If a final injunction is granted in a case concerning confidential material, and a third party acts in a way that would constitute a breach if done by the party directly bound, then the appropriate remedy at that stage, against the third party, would seem to be for breach of confidence (or under the Official Secrets legislation, as the case may be) rather than by way of contempt—because the mischief by that time would not be the frustration of the administration of justice so much as the fact of revealing the confidential information. In the *Venables* case, considered above, any breach of the final injunction would be unlikely to constitute a separate wrong over and above the breach itself. Punishment by way of contempt would, however, be available not because of the *Spycatcher* doctrine but for the same reason as in any of the more conventional cases of a *contra mundum* injunction.

D. Applying the principles

6–148   The principles have now been analysed at the highest levels and, at least since these decisions of the House of Lords, there can be little room for doubt (save as to the general question of *mens rea* discussed elsewhere).[12] As to the practical effect, however, there may well be difficulties for the editors of newspapers which have been served with, or otherwise learnt of, an interim injunction, especially in circumstances where the purpose of the order is not clear to them. It is obviously desirable that the court making such an order, especially against publication, should make its purpose clear.[13] In the event of a genuine doubt, however, the uncertain editor may be advised that he can publish in the confidence that he is unlikely to be held in contempt because of the difficulty of establishing in such circumstances a positive intention to frustrate the court's purpose, in accordance with Lord Oliver's analysis.[14] It is perhaps especially comforting in this context for an editor or his advisers to bear in mind the authoritative statements of appellate courts that recklessness would not be sufficient.[15]

E. The possible opportunities for avoiding the difficulty

1. *Approaching the parties*

6–149   There are also the options referred to in Lord Oliver's speech[16] of (a) approaching the party who has obtained the injunction, so as to give him an opportunity of objecting or seeking relief, or (b) approaching the court itself to argue that the planned publication would not be unlawful.

6–150   As to the first, if the injunction had been obtained by the claimant in a libel action, and the editor was contemplating publishing a similar story himself, this

---

[12] paras 5–120 *et seq.* (publication contempt) and paras 11–21 *et seq.* (non-publication contempt).
[13] See, *e.g.* Booth J. in *Re L (A Minor)* [1988] 1 All E.R. 418 at 423g.
[14] See the passage in *Att-Gen v Times Newspapers Ltd*, cited at para.6–139.
[15] See *Att-Gen v Newspaper Publishing plc* [1988] Ch. 333 at 374–5, Lord Donaldson M.R., 382–3, Lloyd L.J. See the discussion of *mens rea* at paras 5–120 *et seq.*
[16] *ibid.* at 224. See also the words of Lord Donaldson M.R. at [1988] Ch. 333 at 375.

would not present too much difficulty since he would ordinarily wish to approach the claimant, as the subject of the proposed story, for a comment in any event. In cases of alleged breach of confidence, however, such an approach might not be routine, and editors may find it distasteful to give the impression of seeking clearance for publication of such a story. For example, it sometimes happens that an individual or public body will apply to restrain the publication of information about a patient or prisoner, perhaps with a record of violence, who is about to be released in to the community without the local residents being aware as to who is to join them.[17] A newspaper editor would not ordinarily wish to consult such a person, still less a public authority, before publishing such material.

2. *Approaching the court*

Moreover, Lord Oliver's second option, of making an application to the court, might well be repugnant to newspaper editors, as appearing to suggest that permission needed to be sought from the court.[18] The matter has to be left to the editor's choice. If he wishes for certainty, those options are at least available to him. If he wishes to go ahead, without taking these precautions, he will have to rely upon advice, in the circumstances of the particular case, which can now be informed by the discussion of principles in the authorities considered above. In the absence of a positive intention to prejudice or impede the administration of justice,[19] he would have little to fear unless his proposed article is likely to flout the plain and obvious intention of the court, as for example, by destroying the subject matter of the pending litigation. Then he is likely to fall foul of the readiness with which the courts seem prepared to accept that an intention can be inferred, even in the absence of desire.[20]

6–151

---

[17] *P v Liverpool Daily Post and Echo Newspapers plc* [1991] 2 A.C. 370.
[18] Which the court has recognised to be wholly inappropriate: see, *e.g.* the remarks of Lord Donaldson M.R. in *Leary v BBC*, cited at para.6–36 (no censorship).
[19] See *Att-Gen v Sport Newspapers Ltd* [1991] 1 W.L.R. 1194, [1992] 1 All E.R. 503, discussed at para.5–174.
[20] *Att-Gen v News Group Newspapers plc.* [1989] 1 Q.B. 110; *Att-Gen v Sport Newspapers Ltd* [1991] 1 W.L.R. 1194, [1992] 1 All E.R. 503, discussed at para.5–174, where however Bingham L.J. stated that the inference should only be drawn where it is "overwhelming". See also Connell J. in *Official Solicitor v News Group Newspapers plc* [1994] 2 F.L.R. 174. See also *Att-Gen v Newspaper Publishing plc* [1990] T.L.R. 158, CA (Lexis), paras 5–153 *et seq.*

CHAPTER 7

COURT REPORTING I: RESTRICTIONS UNDER THE 1981 ACT[1]

	PARA
I. The Common Law Background	7–1
II. Section 11 of the Contempt of Court Act	7–83
III. Postponement Orders Under Section 4(2) of the 1981 Act	7–109

I. THE COMMON LAW BACKGROUND

A. Open justice

7–1 The starting point, when considering the right of the media to cover court proceedings, is to identify certain fundamental principles long recognised at common law.[2] It is now necessary to consider these in the light of both modern statutory developments and the impact of at least two of the Articles contained in the European Convention on Human Rights. Article 10 is concerned with the priority given to freedom of information; Art.6 with access to judicial proceedings, and in particular to the entitlement to "a fair and public hearing within a reasonable time by an independent and impartial tribunal".[3]

7–2 There arises a need to reconcile the competing objectives of freedom of information, on the one hand, and the right to a fair trial on the other.[4] It may be that the means of achieving this reconciliation is to a large extent left to the margin of appreciation[5] permitted to signatory states. In this part of the chapter we consider in some detail the common law background, and will turn later to the relationship between those principles and the more recent statutory accretions.

---

[1] See generally A. Nicol and H. Rogers, "Annual Survey: Media Reporting Restrictions" in *The Yearbook of Media and Entertainment Law* (1995), p.295; (1996), p.349; (1997–98), p.309. A useful guide was produced for the benefit of judges and journalists covering all reporting restrictions applying in the Crown Court. It was proposed as joint initiative between the Senior Presiding Judge, the Judicial Studies Board, the Lord Chancellor's Department and media organisations: see www.ukeditors.com. There is also a guide to reporting restrictions in the magistrates' court, which can be found at www.jsboard.co.uk. but both should be treated with some caution, since they date from 2000 and 2002 respectively.

[2] For the common law background to the principles of open justice, see J. Jaconelli, *Open Justice: A Critique of the Public Trial* (2002) Oxford University Press; I. Cram, *A Virtue Less Cloistered: Courts, Speech and Constitutions* (2002) Hart Publishing. See also the discussion at paras 2–32 *et seq.*

[3] As was observed in *Diennet v France* (1996) 21 E.H.R.R. 554 at [33], "By rendering the administration of justice transparent, publicity contributes to the achievement of the aim of Art 6(1), namely a fair trial, the guarantee of which is one of the fundamental principles of any democratic society...".

[4] See the general discussion at paras 2–71 *et seq.*

[5] paras 2–168 *et seq.*

A view at one time expressed was that generally the requirements of the   7–3
Convention would add little to the protection already afforded by the common
law. In *Derbyshire County Council v Times Newspapers Ltd*[6] Lord Keith
observed:

> "My noble and learned friend, Lord Goff of Chieveley, in *Att-Gen v Guardian Newspapers Ltd (No.2)*,[7] expressed the opinion that in the field of freedom of speech there was no difference in principle between English law on the subject and article 10 of the Convention. I agree, and can only add that I find it satisfactory to be able to conclude that the common law of England is consistent with the obligations assumed by the Crown under the Treaty in this particular field".

It has since become clear that this approach is regarded by a later generation   7–4
of judges as somewhat complacent.[8] For example, Sedley L.J. in *Berezovsky v Forbes Inc*[9] commented that Lord Keith's proposition as to the general compatibility of the Convention with the existing common law can no longer be taken for granted. So too Lord Phillips M.R. in *Ashworth Hospital Authority v MGN Ltd*[10] was inclined to accept a submission that the decisions of the European Court of Human Rights demonstrated that freedom of the press has in the past carried greater weight in Strasbourg than it has in the courts of this country.

It is worthy of note, however, that some senior judges well before the   7–5
enactment of the Human Rights Act 1998 appear, with the benefit of hindsight, to have been more perceptive. As Lord Bridge observed in *Att-Gen v Guardian Newspapers Ltd*[11] (the first time that the *Spycatcher* litigation found its way to the House of Lords):

> "We have not adopted as part of our law the European Convention for the Protection of Human Rights and Fundamental Freedoms to which this country is a signatory. Many think that we should. I have hitherto not been of that persuasion, in large part because I have had confidence in the capacity of the common law to safeguard the fundamental freedoms essential to a free society including the right to freedom of speech which is specifically safeguarded by article 10 of the Convention. My confidence is seriously undermined by Your Lordships' decision ... I can see nothing whatever, either in law or on the merits, to be said for the maintenance of a total ban on discussion in the press of this country of matters of undoubted public interest and concern which the rest of the world now knows all about and can discuss freely. Still less can I approve Your Lordships' decision to throw in for good measure a restriction on reporting court proceedings in Australia which the Attorney-General had never even asked for.
> Freedom of speech is always the first casualty under a totalitarian regime. Such a regime cannot afford to allow the free circulation of information and ideas among its

---

[6] [1993] A.C. 534 at 551F–G.
[7] [1990] 1 A.C. 109 at 283–4.
[8] See also C. Warbrick, "Rights, The European Convention on Human Rights and English Law" [1994] 19 European Law Rev. 34; C. Gearty, in ed. C. Gearty, "The United Kingdom", in *European Civil Liberties and the European Convention on Human Rights* (1997), p.53.
[9] [2001] EWCA Civ 1251, [2001] E.M.L.R. 45.
[10] [2001] 1 W.L.R. 515 at 536–7, [2001] 1 All E.R. 991 at 1012a–b.
[11] [1987] 1 W.L.R. 1248 at 1286. See also Lord Scarman in *Att-Gen v BBC* [1981] A.C. 303 at 362D.

7-5 CHAPTER 7—COURT REPORTING I: RESTRICTIONS UNDER 1981 ACT

citizens. Censorship is the indispensable tool to regulate what the public may and what they may not know. The present attempt to insulate the public in this country from information which is freely available elsewhere is a significant step down that very dangerous road. The maintenance of the ban, as more and more copies of the book *Spycatcher* enter this country and circulate here, will seem more and more ridiculous. If the Government are determined to fight to maintain the ban to the end, they will face inevitable condemnation and humiliation by the European Court of Human Rights in Strasbourg. Long before that they will have been condemned at the bar of public opinion in the free world."

7-6 There is a presumption in favour of open justice, in the sense that members of the public, including the media,[12] should be able to attend court hearings as well as the parties. The burden lies upon those who seek to displace that presumption to demonstrate that circumstances render it *necessary* to restrict public access for the purpose of achieving the court's paramount objective—"to secure that justice is done".[13] There are some traditionally recognised categories of case where it is possible to discharge the onus, but it seems that the critical question always to be addressed is that formulated by Lord Loreburn in *Scott v Scott*[14]:

"In all cases where the public has been excluded with admitted propriety the underlying principle, as it seems to me, is that the administration of justice would be rendered impracticable by their presence, whether because the case could not be effectively tried, or the parties entitled to justice would be reasonably deterred from seeking it at the hands of the court."

7-7 Members of the public have the right to be present during a court hearing and to publish to others what they have heard. The reasons for this have frequently been stated, and they are encapsulated in a judgment of the New Zealand Court of Appeal[15]:

"... the principle of public access to the courts is an essential element in our system. Nor are the reasons in the slightest degree difficult to find. The Judges speak and act on behalf of the community. They necessarily exercise great powers in order to discharge

---

[12] There are special circumstances provided for by statute where, unusually, representatives of the media are allowed to attend court hearings, concerning children and young persons, whereas the general public is excluded: see s.47(2) of the Children and Young Persons Act 1933 (dealing with youth courts) and s.69 of the Magistrates' Courts Act 1980 (family proceedings). These provisions are considered in detail in the next chapter, at para.8–25 and para.8–79.

[13] *Scott v Scott* [1913] A.C. 417 at 437–8, Lord Haldane L.C. ("... the exceptions are themselves the outcome of a yet more fundamental principle that the chief object of Courts of Justice must be to secure that justice is done ... It may often be necessary, in order to attain its primary object, that the court should exclude the public ... it may well be that justice could not be done at all if it had to be done in public. As the paramount object must always be to do justice, the general rule as to publicity, after all only the means to an end, must accordingly yield".) See the discussion of these principles in the Supreme Court of Canada in *Canadian Broadcasting Corp v Att-Gen for New Brunswick* (1997) 2 B.H.R.C. 210.

[14] [1913] A.C. 417 at 446.

[15] *Broadcasting Corp of NZ v Att-Gen* [1982] 1 N.Z.L.R. 120 at 122–3, Woodhouse P.; see also *Police v O'Connor* [1992] 1 N.Z.L.R. 87; *R. v Legal Aid Board Ex p. Kaim Todner* [1999] Q.B. 966 at 976–7, Lord Woolf M.R. And see C. Baylis, "Justice Done and Seen to be Done—the Public Administration of Justice" (1991) 21 V.U.W.L.R. 177.

heavy responsibilities. The fact that they do it under the eyes of their fellow citizens means that they must provide daily and public assurance that so far as they can manage it what they do is done efficiently if possible, with human understanding it may be hoped, but certainly by a fair and balanced application of the law to facts as they really appear to be. It is a matter as well of maintaining a system of justice which requires that the judiciary will be seen day by day attempting to grapple in the same even fashion with the whole generality of cases. To the extent that public confidence is then given in return so may the process be regarded as fulfilling its purpose."

Whether or not circumstances require the public to be excluded is therefore not a matter of discretion or mere convenience. As Lord Haldane L.C. put it in *Scott v Scott*[16]:

"The question is by no means one which, consistently with the spirit of our jurisprudence, can be dealt with by the judge as resting in his mere discretion as to what is expedient. The latter must treat it as one of principle, and as turning, not on convenience but on necessity[17] ... He who maintains that by no other means than by such a hearing can justice be done may apply for an unusual procedure. He must make out his case strictly, and bring it up to the standard which the underlying principle requires. He may be able to show that the evidence can be effectively brought before the court in no other fashion ... The mere consideration that the evidence is of an unsavoury character is not enough ... and still less is it enough that the parties agree in being reluctant to have their case tried with open doors".

Similarly, in *Att-Gen v Leveller Magazine Ltd*,[18] Lord Diplock commented on the general rule and also the need for some qualification:

"As a general rule the English system of administering justice does require that it be done in public: Scott v Scott [1913] A.C. 417. If the way that courts behave cannot be hidden from the public ear and eye this provides a safeguard against judicial arbitrariness or idiosyncrasy and maintains the public confidence in the administration of justice. The application of this principle of open justice has two aspects: as respects proceedings in the court itself it requires that they should be held in open court to which the press and public are admitted and that, in criminal cases at any rate, all evidence communicated to the court is communicated publicly. As respects the publication to a wider public of fair and accurate reports of proceedings that have taken place in court the principle requires that nothing should be done to discourage this.

However, since the purpose of the general rule is to serve the ends of justice it may be necessary to depart from it where the nature or circumstances of the particular proceeding are such that the application of the general rule in its entirety would frustrate or render impracticable the administration of justice or would damage some other public interest for whose protection Parliament has made some statutory derogation from the rule".

---

[16] [1913] A.C. 417 at 438.
[17] It will be observed how closely this formulation corresponds to that now recognised in Art.10 of the European Convention on Human Rights. See also the remarks of Staughton L.J. in *Ex p. P* [1988] T.L.R. 204, cited at para.8–145, n.21.
[18] [1979] A.C. 440 at 449–50.

7-10 In *R. v Chief Registrar of Friendly Societies Ex p. New Cross Building Society*[19] Sir John Donaldson M.R., in following these fundamental principles, reaffirmed the underlying public policy considerations:

> "The general rule that the courts shall conduct their proceedings in public is but an aid, albeit a very important aid, to the achievement of the paramount objective of the courts, which is to do justice in accordance with the law. It is only if, in wholly exceptional circumstances, the presence of the public or public knowledge of the proceedings is likely to defeat that paramount object that the courts are justified in proceeding in camera. These circumstances are incapable of definition. Each application for privacy must be considered on its merits, but the applicant must satisfy the court that nothing short of total privacy will enable justice to be done. It is not sufficient that a public hearing will create embarrassment for some or all of those concerned. It must be shown that a public hearing is likely to lead, directly or indirectly, to a denial of justice".

7-11 There is sometimes a difficulty in determining where the boundary lies. If a vital witness simply says that he or she will not give evidence unless the court is cleared, the trial judge is left with an unattractive choice. Either the course of the proceedings will be prejudiced by the evidence not being available (assuming the witness's threat is genuine) or the judge will be open to the criticism that he or she complied too readily with the witness's wishes or convenience. In the last analysis the tension is incapable of resolution. In *R. v Richards*,[20] the Court of Appeal was confronted with a situation where the Crown's most important witness in a murder trial had refused to give evidence unless the public gallery was cleared. The trial judge had allowed time for consideration and mentioned the possibility of arrest if she did not voluntarily attend. She was indeed arrested and brought to court, whereupon the judge ruled that the gallery could at least be cleared for the purpose of hearing what she had to say. The witness did not put forward the reason that she was being threatened or intimidated but merely stated that she would feel uncomfortable about giving evidence in front of anyone. She said that no-one could force her to give evidence and that, if necessary, she would accept any punishment imposed. The judge decided that the administration of justice required the gallery to be cleared for her evidence.

7-12 An application for leave to appeal was made by the defendant, having been convicted of murder, on the basis that the ruling was inconsistent with Article 6 of the European Convention and the principles explained in *Scott v Scott*.[21] The application was dismissed by the Court of Appeal; the judge was entitled to exclude the public if it was strictly necessary for him to do so. He had formed the view that the witness's protestation that she would otherwise not give evidence was genuine. It was acknowledged that courts should be reluctant not to comply with the broad principle that a criminal trial should take place in public. On the other hand, the more fundamental principle was that justice should be done. If the order had not been made, the interests of justice would have been prejudiced. While it is difficult to criticise the reasoning of either the trial judge or the Court of Appeal, the case does highlight the scope for exploitation of the system

---

[19] [1984] Q.B. 227 at 235.
[20] (1999) 163 J.P. 246.
[21] [1913] A.C. 417.

available to those who, on other occasions, might wish to take advantage of it without good reason.[22]

Recent statutory encroachments on the principle

Commentators[23] have drawn attention to the difficulty of reconciling broad inherent powers of exclusion (such as that exercised in *R. v Richards*) with any need for statutory intervention in the Youth Justice and Criminal Evidence Act 1999 for the protection of vulnerable or "eligible" witnesses. It would appear that Parliament's objective was the prevention of circumstances which would adversely affect the possibility of doing justice. Various provisions are contained in the statute for the protection of witnesses (other than the accused[24]) in criminal proceedings who are perceived as vulnerable (s.16). Several categories are defined as "eligible for assistance". In particular, those under the age of seventeen at the time of the hearing; persons the quality of whose evidence is likely to be diminished by reason of mental disorder, significant impairment of intelligence *and* social functioning *or* physical disability or disorder. The "quality" of evidence is defined in this context in terms of completeness, coherence and accuracy.

7–13

Protection is also available when the court is satisfied in respect of a witness (other than the accused) that the quality of his or her evidence is likely to be diminished by reason of fear or distress in connection with testifying (s.17). This is no doubt prompted by the prevalence of witness and jury "tampering" to which reference has been made by several judges in recent years.[25] Moreover, in the case of a sexual offence, the complainant is automatically eligible for assistance "unless the witness has informed the court of the witness' wish not to be so eligible".[26]

7–14

---

[22] The *Media Lawyer* July/Aug 2002 drew attention to a case in which an employment tribunal in Cardiff declined, in response to an application by various media groups, to lift a reporting restriction order in favour of a rock star who was being accused of sexual misconduct in relation to an employee prior to her being wrongfully dismissed. He had been accorded anonymity because of concerns he had expressed about giving evidence himself if the ban was lifted. It was said by the chairman that the only reason for the refusal was the overriding necessity to ensure the due administration of justice.
[23] Professor J.R. Spencer (1999) C.L.J. 497 and Professor D. Birch [1999] Crim. L.R. 765.
[24] *S (R. on the application of) v Waltham Forest Youth Court and (1) Crown Prosecution Service (2) Secretary of State for the Home Department (Interested Parties)* [2004] EWHC 715 (Admin), [2004] 2 Cr.App.R. 335. See also the strictures of Professor Birch and Dilys Tausz in [2001] Crim. L.R. 473: "The government has been told, time and again, that this is unacceptable, but has not so far budged ... It is really something of a farce that in proceedings concerning, say, a fight between gangs of boys in which one 'side' ends up in the dock and the other in the witness box, only the latter are deemed to benefit from the live-link". It was, however, doubted by Baroness Hale in *R. (on the application of D) v Camberwell Youth Court; R. (on the application of the Director of Public Prosecutions) v Camberwell Youth Court* [2005] UKHL 4, [2005] 1 F.C.R. 365 at [63] that the Divisional Court was correct in the *Waltham Forest* case to rule out the possibility of a vulnerable accused being protected by the exercise of inherent powers.
[25] See para.11–145.
[26] s.17(4).

7-15 CHAPTER 7—COURT REPORTING I: RESTRICTIONS UNDER 1981 ACT

7-15   The route by which the court may "assist" is by means of a "special measures direction". The steps to be negotiated are somewhat complicated but most relevant for present purposes is the entitlement of the court[27] to exclude during the witness' evidence "persons of any description specified in the direction". Fortunately, the court is not permitted under these provisions to exclude the accused or his lawyers. Any direction given under s.19 (special measures directions) or s.36 (restrictions on an accused's right to cross-examine), or any order discharging or varying such a direction, is not to be included in any publication.[28]

B. The right of the public to be informed

1. Introduction

7-16   A recurring theme in the authorities relating to reports of judicial proceedings is that the public is generally entitled to be kept informed,[29] albeit by way of summary, as to what is taking place in open court proceedings. "The public has a legitimate and important interest in legal proceedings held in public and is accordingly entitled to reports of all such proceedings."[30] There would be little point in open justice, in practical terms, if the public at large were not able to be informed through the media, since only a tiny proportion of the public can and does attend court hearings.[31]

7-17   Considerations of this kind underlay the defence of qualified privilege attaching to reports of judicial proceedings, both at common law and later under the Law of Libel Amendment Act 1888, s.3.[32] The same policy prompted the protection afforded to such reports in s.4(1) of the Contempt of Court Act 1981 itself.[33] In *R. v Felixstowe Justices Ex p. Leigh*,[34] the point was made by Watkins L.J.:

---

[27] s.25, which came into effect on July 24, 2002.
[28] s.47, which also came into effect on July 24, 2002.
[29] See, *e.g. Furniss v Cambridge News Ltd* (1907) 23 T.L.R. 705, CA, and especially the words of Sir Gorell Barnes at 706: " ... as everyone could not be in Court, it was for the public benefit that they should be informed of what took place substantially as if they were present"; *Webb v Times Publishing Co* [1960] 2 Q.B. 535 at 559–62, Pearson J. For a fuller discussion of these matters see, *e.g. Gatley on Libel & Slander* (10th ed., 2004) at para.14.102. See also the passage from *Broadcasting Corporation of New Zealand v Att-Gen* [1982] N.Z.L.R. 120, cited at para.7–7. See also *Schuler-Zgraggen v Switzerland* [1994] 1 F.C.R. 453 at [58]; *Campbell v United Kingdom* (1985) 7 E.H.R.R. 165.
[30] *R. v Clerkenwell Magistrates' Court Ex p. Telegraph plc* [1993] Q.B. 462 at 469F, Mann L.J. See also *R. v Felixstowe Justices Ex p. Leigh* [1987] Q.B. 582 at 591H.
[31] For a discussion of the constitutional position of the press see paras 2–49 *et seq.* See also Marjorie Jones, *Justice and Journalism* (1974) p.24, Barry Rose, "The constant presence of newspaper men in magistrates' courts provided not only a record of the proceedings but also a means of communication with the public. Through newspaper reports magistrates had access to a wider audience beyond the justice room or the police office. Communication is particularly important for deterrent sentencing, which requires that potential offenders shall be aware of the punishment they are likely to incur." See also Thomas J. in *Police v O'Connor* [1992] 1 N.Z.L.R. 87.
[32] Now repealed, and replaced by s.14 of the Defamation Act 1996.
[33] More fully considered at para.4–265.
[34] [1987] 1 Q.B. 582 at 591H.

"No one nowadays surely can doubt that [the journalist's] presence in Court for the purpose of reporting proceedings conducted therein is indispensable. Without him, how is the public to be informed of how justice is being administered in our Courts?"

2. The need to take account of pre-reading and the diminution of "orality"

A relatively recent problem is that cases have become more difficult for the casual observer to follow because of the court's concern to speed up litigation by adopting such methods as pre-reading by judges, silent reading in court, and the conducting of argument largely through written submissions or skeleton arguments.[35] The implications for open justice rapidly became obvious, and in 1989 the Court of Appeal made it clear that, for this reason, counsel ought to provide four copies rather than three of their skeleton arguments, so that one could be given to the court associate to be made available for the press.[36]

The practical consequences of pre-reading were considered by the Court of Appeal in *Barings v Coopers & Lybrand*,[37] where it was held that the modern practices intended to ensure the efficient resolution of litigation should not be allowed adversely to affect the public's ability to follow what was happening. Where documents were placed before the court with a view to being read as part of the evidence, the onus would be on the party contending that they had not thereby entered the public domain to so demonstrate. It might be possible, for example, to show that the judge had not in fact read them, or that an order had been made legitimately for the purpose of maintaining their confidentiality. On the facts of the particular case, the court was concerned with whether documents had been "made available to the public" within the meaning of s.82(2) of the Banking Act 1987. The defendants were contending that some transcripts of interviews fell, for that reason, outside the protection against disclosure afforded by s.82(1). The judge at first instance had held that they had *not* proved that they had been made available. But, on appeal, it was held that the mere fact that there was no evidence that another judge, in earlier disqualification proceedings, had actually read the documents was not fatal to the defendants' contention. The burden was the other way about.

3. The application to public enquiries

The question of openness in the context of public enquiries was considered in *R. v Secretary of State for Health Ex p. Wagstaff*.[38] The Divisional Court had to

---

[35] See also a discussion of the case of *Harman v Secretary of State for the Home Department* [1983] 1 A.C. 280 at paras 12–201 *et seq.* in the context of documents losing the protection of confidentiality once they are read or referred to in open court. Compare, *e.g.* the Coroners' Rules 1984, r.37, which provides for a discretion to direct that evidence be tendered in writing.
[36] *Lombard North Central v Pratt, The Times,* November 27, 1989. See also *Practice Direction (Court of Appeal: Presentation of Argument)* [1989] 1 W.L.R. 281; *GIO Personal Investment Services Ltd v Liverpool and London Steamship Protection and Indemnity Association Ltd* [1999] 1 W.L.R. 984. See also *R. v Howell* [2003] EWCA Crim, *The Times,* March 10, 2003 where it was affirmed by the Criminal Division of the Court of Appeal that the principle of open justice requires that skeleton arguments should be disclosed if and when a request to do so is received.
[37] [2000] 1 W.L.R. 2353.
[38] [2000] 1 W.L.R. 292.

consider an application by an interest group as to the nature of an enquiry to be held into the background of the many murders committed by the notorious general practitioner Harold Shipman and into the possibility that there might have been other victims whose deaths had not so far been the subject of court proceedings. The enquiry was to be carried out by Dame Janet Smith. The applicants represented victims' families and also the press. One of the main issues was whether it was desirable that evidence should be taken in public, there being no established uniform practice on such matters. An important factor addressed was that of public confidence. If the enquiry were to receive evidence in private, this would interfere with the families' freedom of expression without any sufficient justification. It would curtail their right to receive information from other witnesses, or potential witnesses, and also their right to impart information to the enquiry itself. The court's conclusion was that, where an enquiry purported to be a public one, there was in effect a presumption that it would proceed in public unless there were persuasive reasons to take another course. The facts of each individual case would have to be carefully considered including such matters as the complexity of the information, any need for confidentiality, any perceived demand for public accountability, the aims of the particular enquiry, the need for a speedy result, the desirability of gaining access to material which might only be available if one form of enquiry rather than another were adopted, and the relative cost involved. On the facts of that case, the court held that the decision of the Secretary of State that evidence should be taken in private was irrational.

C. Arbitration: a limited qualification to the principle of open justice

7–21   It might appear from the citations above[39] that the principle of openness, as espoused by the European Convention, has also been an immutable feature of the English common law; yet throughout the twentieth century the resolution of disputes between citizens has increasingly been referred on a contractual basis to arbitration.[40] While it has long been recognised that the resolution of disputes between citizens in Her Majesty's courts should be open to public scrutiny, there has apparently been no corresponding imperative so far as private dispute resolution is concerned. There were always limited exceptions, such as when matters would become public in the course of court proceedings for the purpose of enforcing or challenging an award. Nonetheless, confidentiality and privacy were regarded as two of the basic tenets of English arbitration law, and to represent two of the main advantages over the traditional court procedures.[41] More recently, however, inroads have been made which suggest that public policy now acknowledges that sometimes openness may be required even in the context of arbitration hearings themselves.

---

[39] *Scott v Scott* [1913] A.C. 417; *R. v Chief Registrar of Friendly Societies Ex p. New Cross Building Society* [1984] Q.B. 227.
[40] See now the Arbitration Act 1996, and the increasing encouragement given by the Lord Chancellor's Department and later the Department of Constitutional Affairs to take advantage of what is familiarly known as "ADR" (alternative dispute resolution).
[41] See, *e.g. Esso/BHP v Plowman* (1995) 128 A.L.R. 391. See also commentary by A.W. Sheppard on the Arbitration Act 1996, in *Current Law Statutes* (1996), Vol. 2, 23–5.

The Common Law Background

7–22 It had been recommended in the departmental advisory committee, under the then chairmanship of Sir Mark Saville (as he then was), that s.81 of the Act should include specific provision in relation to "confidentiality and privacy", but this recommendation was not adopted by Parliament. Eventually, however, the committee concluded that the courts should be left to deal with matters "on a pragmatic case-by-case basis" in view of the "myriad exceptions" and the qualifications that would have to follow. Hence, when the relevant provision in the CPR came to be formulated in due course, the court's discretion was expressed in remarkably general terms.

7–23 CPR 62.10 now provides its own code of privacy[42]:

"(1) The court may order that an arbitration claim may be heard either in public or in private.
(2) Rule 39.2[43] does not apply.
(3) Subject to any order made under paragraph (1)—
  (a) the determination of—
    (i) a preliminary point of law under section 45 of the Arbitration Act 1996; or
    (ii) an appeal under section 69 of the Arbitration Act 1996 on a question of law arising out of an award will be heard in public; and
  (b) all other arbitration claims will be heard in private.
(4) Paragraph (3)(a) does not apply to—
  (a) the preliminary question of whether the court is satisfied of the matters set out in section 45(2)(b)[44]; or
  (b) an application for permission to appeal under section 69(2)(b)."

7–24 There would thus seem to be a recognition that arbitrations will continue generally to be heard in private. The rule specifically makes exceptions in respect of points of law, no doubt for the reason that they will be of general interest. As to the discretion contemplated in CPR 62.10(1), it is likely that the primary consideration will be that of the public interest. An arbitration may give rise to issues of legitimate public interest quite apart from purely legal ones. A judge is likely therefore to weigh the extent of the public interest against the legitimate interests of the parties in maintaining personal privacy or rights of commercial confidentiality. This would in some respects correspond to the balancing exercise sanctioned by the House of Lords in *Re S (FC) (A Child)*[45] in the context of *contra mundum* injunctions.

7–25 In *Moscow City Council v Bankers Trust Co*[46] Cooke J. confirmed that the presumption of open justice was not directly applicable to arbitration claims

---

[42] Civil Procedure (Amendment No.5) Rules 2001, SI 2001/4015 which came in to effect on March 25, 2002.
[43] Set out at para.7–54.
[44] Those matters being (i) that the determination of the question is likely to produce substantial savings in costs, and (ii) that the application was made without delay.
[45] [2004] UKHL 47, [2005] 1 A.C. 593.
[46] [2003] EWHC 1377 (Comm), [2003] 1 W.L.R. 2885.

7–25 since they fell within the privacy provisions of CPR 62.10, which provides its own code. An arbitration took place in private and there followed a challenge to the award under s.68 of the Arbitration Act 1996 based on serious irregularity. The hearing was also in private and, on a later occasion, the judge decided that his ruling should remain private. The Court of Appeal[47] upheld the judge but confirmed that, in exercising their supervisory functions under the 1996 Act, the courts act as a branch of the state in the public interest in order to facilitate fairness in the arbitration process. It was for the court to determine, either on application by a party or of its own motion, whether the public interest in open justice outweighed the parties' wishes to maintain privacy and confidentiality. This would depend on the circumstances of the case, but stricter standards had to be applied to the question whether the court's judgment should be produced or handed down publicly than to that of whether the underlying proceedings should themselves be private.[48] If a judgment could be given without disclosing significant confidential information, then the public interest would militate in favour of a public judgment, since there is a public interest in ensuring appropriate standards of fairness in the conduct of arbitrations. On the other hand, the Court of Appeal ruled that a Lawtel summary which, as it happened, had originally been made available by mistake could be made available to the public since there was nothing it revealed by way of confidential or sensitive information.

7–26 It is of interest that the Court of Appeal construed the words "in private" in CPR 62.10(1) as being equivalent, in modern practice, to "in secret". This is clearly because the former half-way category of "in chambers" has largely disappeared and hearings are either completely open to the public or, for some good reason, restricted either as to access or to reporting.

D. The limited power to confer privacy on proceedings

7–27 The court has an inherent power to regulate proceedings in open court. The court may be cleared or closed if such a precaution is necessary for the administration of justice. Tumult or disorder, or the reasonable apprehension of it, would certainly justify exclusion of all from whom such interruption is expected and, if discrimination is impracticable, the exclusion of the public in general.[49] Beyond this, however, there are sometimes circumstances which require that the whole or part of proceedings should be heard privately, or *in camera*, in order that the court's primary objective of doing justice between the parties shall not be frustrated. In the words of Viscount Reading C.J., " ... it is in my judgment plain that inherent jurisdiction exists in any Court which enables it to exclude the public where it becomes necessary in order to administer justice."[50]

---

[47] *Department of Economics, Policy and Development of the City of Moscow v Bankers Trust Co* [2004] EWCA Civ 314, [2005] Q.B. 204.
[48] See also *B v United Kingdom* (2000) 34 E.H.R.R. 529 at 545, [2001] 2 F.L.R.261, [2001] 2 F.C.R. 221.
[49] *per* Lord Loreburn in *Scott v Scott*, at 445–6.
[50] *Governor of Lewes Prison Ex p. Doyle* [1917] 2 K.B. 254 at 271. See also *Ealing Justices Ex p. Weafer* (1982) 74 Cr.App.R. 204; *Hallam-Eames v Merrett Syndicates* [1995] T.L.R. 346, Cresswell J.; *R. v Richards* (1999) 163 J.P. 246, and the discussion of Professor Birch in [1999] Crim. L.R. 765. See also *R. v Legal Aid Board Ex p. Kaim Todner* [1999] Q.B. 966 at 977, Lord Woolf M.R.

It is, nonetheless, a very exceptional step to take and it is one which should be 7–28
avoided if there is any other way of serving the interests of justice.[51] An example
is provided by *X v Y*,[52] where the hearing had taken place *in camera* although
judgment was subsequently given in open court. The justification for privacy in
that case was described by Rose J. as follows:

> " ... I took the very exceptional course of ordering that the proceedings, prior to
> judgment, would be heard in camera. I did so because I took the view that a public
> hearing would defeat the ends of justice; it appeared that the trial could not be properly
> conducted without reference to and disclosure of the very matters whose confidentiality
> the action was intended to protect".

A further example is provided by the decision of Rimer J. in *Trustor AB v* 7–29
Smallbone.[53] The court rejected an application for a secret hearing, which had
been sought on the basis that one of the defendants was the subject of a criminal
investigation in Sweden. He wished to avoid the possibility that evidence
adduced by him in England would come to the attention of the Swedish
authorities and encourage a prosecution. The defendant also wished to have
reporting restrictions to prevent the publication even of those parts of the
judgment which did not refer to the protected evidence. The case was complicated by certain undertakings volunteered by the applicant which had the effect
that the defendants had conducted their defence on the basis that the protected
evidence would not be disclosed to the Swedish prosecutors. The undertakings
could have been refused but they were voluntarily given and accepted by the
court. In those exceptional circumstances, the judge considered that the due
administration of justice—or at least fairness as between the parties—did require
that the court should protect the defendants from the release into the public
domain of references in his judgment to the protected evidence.

It may be that the criterion applied by the English courts,[54] in relation to the 7–30
protection of personal privacy, was in the past more stringent than that
contemplated by Art.6 of the European Convention, which acknowledges that
"the protection of the private life of the parties" may of itself provide a ground
for making an order restricting public access.

A recent development has taken place whereby the court has recognised, on a 7–31
number of occasions, that a degree of restriction upon the freedom to publish
(including the reporting of court proceedings) may sometimes become necessary
for the protection of physical safety or even the right to life. In *R. v Lord Saville*
of Newdigate,[55] it was held that anonymity for witnesses could be justified where
there was a reasonable apprehension of violence or other reprisals being taken
against them. Reference was made to the right to life protected under the terms

---

[51] *Ealing Justices Ex p. Weafer* (1982) 74 Cr.App.R. 204 at 205, Donaldson L.J.
[52] [1988] 2 All E.R. 648 at 650, Rose J.
[53] [2000] 1 All E.R. 811.
[54] See *R. v Westminster City Council Ex p. Castelli and Tristran-Garcia* [1996] 1 F.L.R. 534, where
Latham J. was dismissive of an application under s.11 of the 1981 Act because, *inter alia*, "the power
cannot be used simply to protect privacy or avoid embarrassment". See also *Birmingham Post and*
Mail Ltd v Birmingham City Council (1994) 17 B.M.L.R. 116.
[55] [2000] 1 W.L.R. 1855, [1999] 4 All E.R. 860.

7-31 CHAPTER 7—COURT REPORTING I: RESTRICTIONS UNDER 1981 ACT

of the European Convention on Human Rights, Art.2. It is this which has also justified the restrictive order made against the media in the case of *Venables and Thompson v News Group Newspapers Ltd*.[56]

The Criminal Procedure Rules 2005

7-32 There are specific provisions about how and when the Crown Court can go in to *camera*,[57] promulgated as a result of the enactment of section 159(1)(b) of the Criminal Justice Act 1988.[58] These require notice to be given of any intention to request that a trial should go into *camera*, with the apparent object of offering to the press or other interested persons a right to make representations.[59] The rule provides that:

"(1) Where a prosecutor or a defendant intends to apply for an order that all or part of a trial be held in camera for reasons of national security or for the protection of the identity of a witness or any other person, he shall not less than 7 days before the date on which the trial is expected to begin serve a notice in writing to that effect on the Crown Court officer and the prosecutor or the defendant as the case may be.

(2) On receiving such notice, the court officer shall forthwith cause a copy thereof to be displayed in a prominent place within the precincts of the court."

7-33 The Court of Appeal gave guidance in 1991 by reference to r.24A as to applications to sit *in camera*.[60] Consideration was again given to that rule in *Ex p. Guardian Newspapers Ltd*.[61] Defendants had served a notice, purportedly under r.24A(1), of their intention to apply to hold a hearing *in camera* relating to an application to stay the trial for abuse of process. The application was opposed by a journalist and the Crown took a neutral stand. The judge having heard submissions *in camera* ruled, in open court, that he would hear the abuse of process application *in camera*. The journalist's employer served a notice seeking leave to appeal against that ruling. The judge adjourned the proceedings pending appeal. The Court of Appeal held that the word "trial" in the relevant rule meant "the trial process" and was therefore apt to include any proceedings ancillary to a trial. Rule 24A(1) therefore applied to the pre-trial application for a stay. Accordingly, notice of the application by the defendants should have been served seven days before the hearing. Rule 16B of the Criminal Appeal Rules 1968[62] applied to the newspaper's application for leave to appeal made under s.159(1)

---

[56] [2001] Fam. 430; *X (A Woman Formerly Known As Mary Bell) v O'Brien* [2003] EWHC 1101 (QB), [2003] 2 F.C.R. 686; *Carr (Maxine) v News Group Newspapers Ltd* [2005] EWHC 971 (QB).
[57] Criminal Procedure Rules 2005, r.16.10. For a detailed consideration of its predecessor (Crown Court Rules 1982, r.24A), see *Ex p. Guardian Newspapers Ltd* [1999] 1 W.L.R. 2130, CACD, discussed below at paras 7–33 *et seq*. See *Archbold 2005*, para.4–7.
[58] For the text of which, see para.7–258.
[59] See, however, the decision of the Court of Appeal in *Re Crook* (1991) 93 Cr.App.R. 17 where it was held that the rules have no application to those cases not involving national security or the protection of a witness or any other person.
[60] *Re Crook* (1991) 93 Cr.App.R. 17, Lord Lane C.J.
[61] [1999] 1 W.L.R. 2130.
[62] See now r.68.1.3, *Criminal Procedure Rules 2005*. For the procedure on appeal, see Pt 67 of the 2005 *Rules* and *Archbold 2005*, paras 7–310 *et seq*.

of the Criminal Justice Act 1988. The appeal was allowed. It was observed that open justice promoted the rule of law and was a powerful deterrent to any potential abuse of power or improper behaviour.

It was held in *Ex p. Guardian* that a notice under r.24A(1) should specify whether the ground relied upon for seeking an *in camera* hearing is national security, or the protection of the identity of a witness or other person, or both. The notice in *Ex p. Guardian Newspapers* was defective in this respect. Furthermore, where reasons of national security were to be relied upon, the judge should receive relevant evidence on the subject. The court should not be left to infer, in the absence of relevant material from the Crown, whether national security would be at risk. If the issue is properly raised, and the judge has not been told the attitude of "the guardians of our national security", he should adjourn the hearing and seek the assistance of the Law Officers. In this instance, the judge had no evidence from the Crown as to whether the interests of national security would be prejudiced. The procedure was thus seriously flawed, and the order would be set aside for the matter to be considered *de novo*. The court also recommended that a notice under r.24A should be dated and that the copy displayed by the court should show the date on which it was displayed.

Employment Tribunals

The principle of open justice applies to employment tribunals, although they operate under their own regulatory system.[63]

E. The distinction between public and private hearings: a change of practice[64]

"In open court"

Most proceedings must be heard "in court", or in "open court".[65] In particular, it is provided by s.67 of the Supreme Court Act 1981[66] that:

---

[63] Employment Tribunals (Constitution and Rules of Procedure) Regulations 2004, SI 2004/1861. See paras 8–141 *et seq*.
[64] See the helpful discussion of the practice as it stood before the advent of the CPR in the Lord Chancellor's Department Consultation paper, *Review of Access to and Reporting of Family Proceedings* (August 1993), the text of which may be found at *www.bopcris.ac.uk/imgall/ref23874_1_1.html*.
[65] In *R. v Felixstowe Justices Ex p. Leigh* [1987] Q.B. 582 at 592–3, Watkins L.J. stated "It must ever be borne in mind that save upon rare occasions when a court is entitled to sit in camera, it must sit in public. The principle of open justice has been well established for a very long time"; see also *Att-Gen v Leveller Magazine Ltd* [1979] A.C. 440 at 449–50, Lord Diplock, and *Scott v Scott* [1913] A.C. 417. It has long been accepted at common law that a trial on indictment must be held in a public court with open doors. Sometimes the common law presumptions in favour of open justice are confirmed or qualified by statutory provisions, as in the Magistrates' Courts Act 1980, s.121(4) and the Criminal Procedure and Investigations Act 1996, s.17 (confidentiality of disclosed information).
[66] This was the successor to the Judicature Act 1925, s.61.

7–36 CHAPTER 7—COURT REPORTING I: RESTRICTIONS UNDER 1981 ACT

"Business in the High Court shall be heard and disposed of in court except in so far as it may, under this or any other Act, under rules of court or in accordance with the practice of the court, be dealt with in chambers".[67]

It has been recognised for many years that it would be impossible to enumerate all the circumstances which would justify an exception to this general rule that proceedings should take place in public.[68]

7–37 Although the term "open court" was generally well understood, Lord Widgery C.J. made the point that "it is not altogether easy to define in terms the characteristics which make a court open, as opposed to one which is conducted in private".[69] He went on to say that:

> "... the injunction to the presiding judge or magistrate is: do your best to enable the public to come in and see what is happening, having a proper common sense regard for the facilities available and the facility for keeping order, security and the like.
> ... the presence or absence of the press is a vital factor in deciding whether a particular hearing was or was not in open court. I find it difficult to imagine a case which can be said to be held publicly if the press have been actively excluded."

7–38 In the Supreme Court of Victoria, Dean J. has said that "if a court were to sit in an empty building in a remote part of the town, with no public intimation of any kind, it could hardly be an open court merely because the doors were kept open."[70] Similarly, when the trial of a divorce action took place in a judges' law library, with no robes worn by the judge or counsel, and with the word "private" on the entrance to the room, the Privy Council held in *McPherson v McPherson* that the hearing was not in open court.[71] This authority was followed in *Storer v British Gas plc*,[72] where the Court of Appeal quashed the decision of an Employment Appeal Tribunal. The hearing had taken place behind a door with a coded door lock and there were signs on the stairs outside forbidding the public to enter. This was only because of the absence of available court rooms, but there was nevertheless an actual physical barrier. This constituted a breach of the relevant rule.[73] It is a question of fact and degree whether a court is sitting in public, but it is always necessary to judge the matter in the light of the policy behind the rule, namely the need for justice to be seen to be done and to avoid arbitrariness in the administration of justice. The case was held to be stronger than *McPherson* because there had been no actual physical barrier on that occasion, even though there had been a "private" sign.

7–39 In *Riepan v Austria*[74] the European Court of Human Rights found a violation of Art.6(1) in circumstances in which a long term prisoner had been tried (for

---

[67] The statute continues to make reference to "chambers" anachronistically.
[68] See, *e.g. R. v Lewes Prison (Governor) Ex p. Doyle* [1917] 2 K.B. 254 at 271, Lord Reading C.J.; *Hodgson v Imperial Tobacco Ltd* [1998] 1 W.L.R. 1056 at 1071H, 2 All E.R. 673 at 687c.
[69] *R. v Denbigh Justices Ex p. Williams* [1974] Q.B. 759 at 764–5.
[70] *Dando v Anastassiou* [1951] V.L.R. 235 at 238.
[71] [1936] A.C. 177.
[72] [2000] 1 W.L.R. 1237, [2000] 2 All E.R. 440.
[73] Rule 8(2) of Sch.I to the Industrial Tribunal (Constitution and Rules of Procedure) Regs 1993, SI 1993/2687.
[74] (2000) ECtHR, 00035155/97), [2001] Crim. L.R. 228.

threatening a prison officer with violence) in a room at the prison albeit that members of the public or journalists would have been admitted on request. The hearing was early in the morning and few steps were taken to inform the public that it was to take place.

On the other hand, the Divisional Court has held[75] that the mandatory requirement of the Backing of Warrants (Republic of Ireland) Act 1965[76] that the hearing be in "open court" must be read subject to the provisions of Children and Young Persons Act 1933, s.47, which restricted access to juvenile courts to certain named groups of individuals (including "news gathering or reporting organisations"). The fact that the doors to the court had been locked shut did not prevent the requirements of open justice from being fulfilled. Here the doors were locked for fear that the juvenile for whom extradition was sought might abscond. Since no person who had the right to attend by the Children and Young Persons Act was prevented from so doing, and given the court's inherent power to restrict public access to its proceedings if the administration of justice so requires,[77] the proceedings were not invalid. The *Practice Direction (Crown Court: Young Defendants)*[78] indicates that the court should be prepared to restrict attendance at a trial to a small number, perhaps limited to some of those with an immediate and direct interest in the outcome of the trial. The court should rule upon any challenged claim to attend.

2. *"In chambers" and "in camera"*

In the past it was sometimes necessary to distinguish between the terms "in chambers" and "in camera". Although these two labels connoted different forms of hearing, they were used rather loosely, and sometimes as though they were interchangeable. In the context of the Court of Appeal's powers, however, it was observed by Sir Raymond Evershed M.R. that while in appropriate circumstances the court might sit *in camera*, there was no acknowledged power at that stage to sit "in chambers".[79] Subsequently, it was specifically provided by statute that an appellate court might sit in private during the whole or any part of proceedings on an appeal, or during an application for leave, in circumstances where the court of first instance had power to sit in private.[80]

Whether proceedings were being heard in chambers or *in camera*, it was generally thought that the public could not be admitted, and that only the parties

---

[75] *R. v Westminster City Council Ex p. L* [1992] 1 W.L.R. 253, DC.
[76] Repealed by the Extradition Act 2003, save for transitional proceedings
[77] Citing *R. v Denbigh Justices Ex p. Williams* [1974] Q.B. 759; *R. v Malvern Justices Ex p. Evans* [1988] Q.B. 540.
[78] [2000] 1 W.L.R. 659. See now the *Consolidated Criminal Practice Direction* [2002] 1 W.L.R. 2870, IV.39 (as amended). For the latest version of the *Direction* see www.courtservice.gov.uk/docs/cpd/consol_criminal_pd_220305.doc.
[79] *Re Agricultural Industries Ltd* [1952] 1 All E.R. 1188 at 1189E–G. See also *Mellor v Thompson* (1885) 31 Ch.D. 55; *Re Green (A Bankrupt)* [1958] 2 All E.R. 57.
[80] Domestic and Appellate Proceedings (Restriction of Publicity) Act 1968, s.1(1).

7–42 CHAPTER 7—COURT REPORTING I: RESTRICTIONS UNDER 1981 ACT

and their legal representatives might attend.[81] Beyond that, however, it was by no means clear where the distinction lay. For example, it was said in the notes to *The Supreme Court Practice 1997*[82] that:

> "The expression 'in Chambers' used in [s.67 of the Supreme Court Act 1981] in contrast to 'in Court', means private, secret, secluded behind closed doors, in proceedings at which only the parties and their advisers are entitled to be present and from which the public and press are excluded unless invited to be present with the consent of the parties and the court."

7–43 It was observed by Lord Woolf M.R. in *Hodgson v Imperial Tobacco Ltd*[83] that this note was attributed to the editorship of Sir Jack Jacob Q.C. and that it therefore justified great respect. Nevertheless, it was regarded by the Court of Appeal as inaccurately reflecting the position so far as an "in chambers" hearing was concerned. The judgment of Jacob J. in *Forbes v Smith*[84] was held to reflect the modern practice more accurately. He had summarised the position by saying:

> "A chambers hearing is in private, in the sense that members of the public are not given admission as of right to the courtroom. Courts sit in chambers or in open court generally merely as a matter of administrative convenience. For example, in the Chancery Division the normal practice for urgent interlocutory cases is for the matters to be heard in open court, the application being made by way of motion. Corresponding applications in the Queen's Bench Division are normally made in chambers. There is no logic or reason as to why exactly the same sort of case in one Division should be in open court and, in another Division, in chambers".

Both Jacob J. and the Court of Appeal recognised that an order or judgment made in chambers was to be treated as a public document (save in respect of the specific cases identified in s.12(1) of the Administration of Justice Act 1960).

7–44 A decision of Harman J. (dating from shortly before the 1960 Act) was cited to Jacob J., as giving a very restrictive view as to what might be published in the media concerning matters heard in chambers.[85] It went so far as to suggest that merely to report what had occurred in chambers would constitute contempt of court. Any such proposition has clearly been overtaken by the terms of s.12 of the 1960 Act but, in any event, Jacob J. made it clear that the case was not to be regarded as authority for the proposition that judgments given in chambers should not be reported.[86]

7–45 It was long thought necessary that a judge should be asked permission for any judgment given in chambers to be cited or for its contents to be revealed beyond the immediate parties and their advisers. Jacob J. expressed the view that "the

---

[81] See, *e.g.* the Law Commission, *Report on the Powers of Appeal Courts to Sit in Private and the Restrictions upon Publicity in Domestic Proceedings* (1966) Law Com. No.8, Cmnd. 3149, p.5.
[82] Vol. 2, para.5276.
[83] [1998] 1 W.L.R. 1056 at 1069C, 2 All E.R. 673 at 684g.
[84] [1998] 1 All E.R. 973 at 974e–g.
[85] *Alliance Perpetual Building Society v Belrum Investments Ltd* [1957] 1 W.L.R. 720 at 724.
[86] [1998] 1 All E.R. at 975e–j.

concept of a secret judgment is one which I believe to be inherently abhorrent". It became clear, in the light of the Court of Appeal's judgment in *Imperial Tobacco*,[87] that any judgment given in chambers could be made freely available.

Whereas proceedings which took place, wholly exceptionally, *in camera*[88] could be described as "secret", those which were heard in chambers for reasons of convention or administrative convenience were not appropriately so categorised. So too, where a chambers hearing fell within one of the specified exceptions defined in s.12(1) of the 1960 Act, involving in particular the protection of children, national security or trade secrets, the term "secret" could also be aptly ascribed. Because it was true to say, in relation to *any* hearing in chambers, that the public had no *right* to attend, the term "private" might accurately be used. It was the failure to distinguish between secrecy and privacy which primarily led the Court of Appeal to disapprove the passage cited above from *The Supreme Court Practice 1997*.

7–46

3. The court's discretion to exclude from chambers hearings

The court, when sitting in chambers, was generally regarded in the past as having an absolute discretion as to who might be permitted to be present.[89] For example, where the court was sitting in chambers, there was recognised a discretion to allow a litigant to be assisted by an unqualified person known as a "McKenzie friend". It appears from *Re G*[90] that where the proceedings were "highly confidential" the court might refuse to allow that form of representation, and that such a ruling would not be disturbed on appeal. However, where the court sat *in camera*, there was no direct authority as to whether such a discretion existed, although the position would surely be *a fortiori*. Later guidance from the Court of Appeal suggested that, in public proceedings and non-private chambers proceedings, a litigant in person should be allowed the assistance of a McKenzie friend, save where the judge is satisfied that fairness and the interests of justice do not require it. Where, however, proceedings are held truly in private, the nature of the proceedings *may* make it undesirable for a McKenzie friend to assist. The judge should give reasons for refusing to allow the assistance, but that obligation is owed to the litigant in person and not to the proposed McKenzie friend. The court is solely concerned with the interests of the litigant in person.[91]

7–47

When the matter came to be considered afresh by the Court of Appeal in *Re O'Connell, Whelan and Watson*,[92] it was reaffirmed that the presumption in

7–48

---

[87] [1998] 1 W.L.R. 1056, [1998] 2 All E.R. 673.
[88] See, *e.g. Scott v Scott* [1913] A.C. 417 at 446; *Hodgson v Imperial Tobacco Ltd* [1998] 1 W.L.R. 1056 at 1070E, [1998] 2 All E.R. 673 at 685j.
[89] See *Re G (A Minor)* [1999] 1 W.L.R. 1828 (note) (which had been heard by the Court of Appeal on July 10, 1991) referred to in *R. v Leicester City Justices Ex p. Barrow* [1991] 2 Q.B. 260. See also *Re F (Minors)(Wardship: Police Investigation)* [1989] Fam.18 at 23B–C.
[90] Last note.
[91] *R. v Bow County Court Ex p. Pelling* [1999] 1 W.L.R. 1807, [1999] 4 All E.R. 751, CA.
[92] [2005] EWCA Civ 759.

7–48 CHAPTER 7—COURT REPORTING I: RESTRICTIONS UNDER 1981 ACT

favour of allowing a McKenzie friend is a strong one and that a request should not be refused without good reason, even where the proceedings relate to a child and are being heard in private. It was, however, added that it was not good practice to exclude the proposed McKenzie friend while the application for his assistance was made. Any concerns about the friend could be ventilated in his presence and the judge could be satisfied that the person concerned understood the nature of the role and the obligations with regard to confidential documents. The court should require an assurance from both the litigant and the McKenzie friend that the documents would only be used for the purposes of the proceedings. A formal undertaking was not required—not least because publication would constitute contempt in any event.[93]

7–49 The discretion of the court to exclude members of the public more generally may now be regarded as significantly circumscribed by the guidance given in *Imperial Tobacco*.[94] There had been a remarkable lack of authority on the circumstances in which it was appropriate to admit either the press or other members of the public to chambers hearings, and also as to the extent to which it would be legitimate to reveal what took place in chambers to those not directly connected with the proceedings. This may perhaps be accounted for by one or other of two considerations. On the one hand, the vast majority of what took place in chambers was of little interest to anyone except those immediately involved. Also, a "chambers culture" had grown up over the years, in itself contributing to the efficient dispatch of the work of the courts, whereby parties and legal advisers recognised that it was desirable to treat what had taken place in a confidential manner. Indeed, it would not be regarded as behaving in accordance with proper professional standards to reveal what had taken place.

7–50 All these considerations became the subject of attention from the Court of Appeal in *Hodgson v Imperial Tobacco Ltd*[95] from which it emerged that there was to be a fundamental change in established practice. The case concerned an order which had been made in a class action about claims arising from illnesses incurred through long-term smoking. There had been a good deal of general press interest in the litigation and the judge had ordered that, although directions he had given were to made available to the press, neither party should make any comment upon them.

7–51 This order was ultimately quashed by the Court of Appeal, and in the course of his judgment Lord Woolf took the opportunity to set out some general principles of good practice governing chambers hearings[96]:

> "1. The public has no right to attend hearings in chambers because of the nature of the work transacted in chambers and because of the physical restrictions on the room available, but if requested, permission should be granted to attend when and to the extent that this is practical.

---

[93] See paras 8–83 *et seq.* for a discussion of s.97(2) of the Children Act 1989.
[94] [1998] 1 W.L.R. 1056, [1998] 2 All E.R. 673.
[95] *ibid.* See also *Forbes v Smith* [1998] 1 All E.R. 973, Jacob J.
[96] [1998] 1 W.L.R. 1056 at 1072A–C, [1998] 2 All E.R. 673 at 687d–f.

2. What happens during the proceedings in chambers is not confidential or secret and information about what occurs in chambers and the judgment or order pronounced can, and in the case of any judgment or order should, be made available to the public when requested.

3. If members of the public who seek to attend can not be accommodated, the judge should consider adjourning the proceedings in whole or in part into open court to the extent that this is practical or allowing one or more representatives of the press to attend the hearing in chambers.

4. To disclose what occurs in chambers does not constitute a breach of confidence or amount to contempt as long as any comment which is made does not substantially prejudice the administration of justice.

5. The position summarised above does not apply to the exceptional situations identified in section 12(1) of the 1960 Act[97] or where the court, with the power to do so, orders otherwise."

7-52 Traditionally, the practice had been for many years in the Chancery Division that interlocutory proceedings, including applications for interlocutory injunctions, would take place by way of motion in open court.[98] By contrast, in the Queen's Bench Division, such proceedings always took place in chambers. There was no logical explanation for this, as was pointed out by Jacob J. in *Forbes v Smith*.[99] It was made clear by Lord Woolf in *Hodgson v Imperial Tobacco Ltd* that the position would be rationalised by the new rules of court then being drafted.

4. *The provisions of CPR 39*

7-53 The relevant rules of court were subsequently implemented and reflect the provisions of Art.6 of the European Convention on Human Rights. Now the term "chambers" is rarely used and in the daily cause lists in the High Court the distinction drawn is between "robed" and "unrobed". The public generally are regularly admitted to "unrobed" hearings, which hitherto would have taken place in the Queen's Bench Division "in chambers", as freely as the traditionally open court hearings. There is no longer a "judge in chambers" and the role is now described as that of the "interim applications judge" in Court 37. (That is obviously inaccurate, since the scope of the work is much wider.) The press feel free to attend such hearings and, although they sometimes did so in the past, it was less practical because the courtroom used previously (Room 101) was smaller and more cramped.

7-54 CPR 39.2 provides:

"(1) The general rule is that a hearing is to be in public.
(2) The requirement for a hearing to be in public does not require the court to make special arrangements for accommodating members of the public.
(3) A hearing, or any part of it, may be in private if—

---

[97] Administration of Justice Act 1960, discussed at para.7–58 and para.8–98.
[98] Correspondingly, there was no restriction upon reporting what took place. See, *e.g. Buenos Ayres Gas Co Ltd v Wilde* (1880) 29 W.R. 43.
[99] [1998] 1 All E.R. 973.

7–54 CHAPTER 7—COURT REPORTING I: RESTRICTIONS UNDER 1981 ACT

    (a) publicity would defeat the object of the hearing;
    (b) it involves matters relating to national security;
    (c) it involves confidential information (including information relating to personal financial matters) and publicity would damage that confidentiality;
    (d) a private hearing is necessary to protect the interests of any child or patient;
    (e) it is a hearing of an application made without notice and it would be unjust to any respondent for there to be a public hearing;
    (f) it involves uncontentious matters arising in the administration of trusts or in the administration of a deceased person's estate; or
    (g) the court considers this to be necessary, in the interests of justice.

(4) The court may order that the identity of any party or witness must not be disclosed if it considers non-disclosure necessary in order to protect the interests of that party or witness".

7–55 In *Chahal v United Kingdom*,[1] it was made clear that domestic courts must be able to exercise effective control where it has been asserted that "national security" is involved. Submissions were made about "national security" in *Secretary of State for Defence v Times Newspapers Ltd*.[2] The Judge[3] recognised that there might be some cases where it would be appropriate for proceedings to be heard in private from the outset, but on the facts before him he saw no reason why the hearing should not have at least started in open court. Moreover, there was "an ongoing duty throughout the case to consider whether it is necessary and proportionate to continue to hear the proceedings in private".

F. The traditionally recognised exceptions to the openness principle

7–56 The categories of proceedings traditionally recognised as justifying a departure from the open justice principle included those in which the court was exercising its inherent jurisdiction, on behalf of the Crown, by way of *parens patriae*[4]; that is to say, the proceedings normally characterised in the past as relating to wardship or "lunacy" (the modern equivalent of the latter now being proceedings under the Mental Health Act 1983).[5] In the *parens patriae* cases, the court may be said to be exercising an *intra familiam* jurisdiction,[6] rather than administering justice as between contending litigants.

---

[1] (1996) 23 E.H.R.R. 413, [131].
[2] March 28, 2001, Blofeld J. (unreported).
[3] At para.6 of the transcript.
[4] See, *e.g. Scott v Scott* [1913] A.C. 417 at 483, Lord Shaw of Dunfermline, 437, Lord Haldane L.C. This jurisdiction is considered more fully, in the context of the court's power to grant injunctions, in ch.6. Also, the modern rules governing the hearing of such matters in private are considered in ch.15, which deals with Practice and Procedure.
[5] See now the Mental Capacity Act 2005, s.45 of which states that "there is to be a superior court of record known as the Court of Protection," which is to have the same powers as the High Court (s.47). Section 51 makes provision for the making of Court of Protection Rules including (s.51(2)(h)) provision "for enabling or requiring the proceedings or any part of them to be conducted in private and for enabling the court to determine who is to be admitted when the court sits in private and to exclude specific persons when it sits in public". The Act is to take effect from a date to be appointed (s.68(1)).
[6] See, *e.g. Scott v Scott* [1913] A.C. 417 at 483, Lord Shaw of Dunfermline; *Re Manda* [1993] Fam. 183 at 190, Balcombe L.J.; *In re R (Wardship: Restrictions on Publication)* [1994] Fam. 254 at 271, Millett L.J.

The Common Law Background 7-61

It was also long recognised that litigation concerning secret technical processes would need to be similarly protected, in order to avoid the fundamental objective of the court's proceedings being rendered ineffective.[7] In the case of secret processes, it is clear that proceedings to protect such information, in for example patent or copyright litigation, would be rendered useless if the proceedings themselves had to take place fully in public. The primary objective of doing justice would be undermined. Just as in cases of anticipated breach of confidence, nothing would be served if going to court inevitably led to the information being made public in any event.[8]

7-57

In some instances, this recognition has resulted in cases being *generally* heard, under provisions of rules of court, in private rather than openly. These traditional categories have received formal recognition in the provisions of s.12 of the Administration of Justice Act 1960.[9] This was considered in *P v Liverpool Daily Post and Echo Newspapers plc*,[10] where it was held that the effect was to render the public reporting of such proceedings, having taken place in private, as *prima facie* contempt.[11]

7-58

In other cases, however, where there is no such specific provision, the matter may require to be dealt with *ad hoc*, and the court will be asked to exercise its jurisdiction, on a case by case basis, in the light of general principle.

7-59

The view was expressed by Lord Scarman in *Att-Gen v Leveller Magazine Ltd*[12] that there would also be a power to sit in private in cases involving national security, yet consistently with the principle that the need for the courts to do justice is paramount. He considered that there could well be circumstances in which the due administration of justice might be endangered, in the sense that the Crown would be deterred from prosecuting in future cases when it was clearly in the public interest that action should be taken. Similar reasoning was applied by the New Zealand Court of Appeal in the case of *Taylor v Attorney General*,[13] where it was held that the trial judge had an inherent power to make an order "prohibiting the publication of anything that may lead to the identification of officers of the New Zealand Security Service".

7-60

Viscount Dilhorne, however, considered that the courts in England would have no such power unless given by statute.[14] It is, however, to be observed that Art.6

7-61

---

[7] See, *e.g. Badische Anilin & Soda Fabrik v Levinstein* (1883) 24 Ch.D. 156, Pearson J., where the defendant was given leave to decline to answer any questions which would disclose his process.
[8] See *Andrew v Raeburn* (1874) L.R. 9 Ch. App.522; *Att-Gen v Newspaper Publishing plc* [1988] Ch. 333; *X v Y* [1988] 2 All E.R. 648 at 650, cited at para.7–28.
[9] This is considered more fully in the next chapter, at paras 8–97 *et seq.*
[10] [1991] 2 A.C. 370.
[11] *ibid.* at 383E–H, 386F–H, Lord Donaldson M.R., 395F–H, Farquharson L.J., 419A–C, 421C–H and 423F–G, Lord Bridge. See also Stuart-White J. in *Oxfordshire County Council v L and F* [1997] 1 F.L.R. 235 at 249D–G.
[12] [1979] A.C. 440 at 471.
[13] [1975] N.Z.L.R. 675.
[14] *Att-Gen v Leveller Magazine Ltd* [1979] A.C. 440 at 456. See, *e.g.* Official Secrets Act 1920, s.8(4) and Official Secrets Act 1989, s.11(4) (exclusion of the public form hearings on the grounds of national safety).

7–61 CHAPTER 7—COURT REPORTING I: RESTRICTIONS UNDER 1981 ACT

of the European Convention actually does countenance "security" as a factor which may justify a restriction upon the open justice principle.[15] The matter is now expressly referred to in CPR 39.2(3)(b).[16]

7–62 The court would generally be slow to extend too freely the categories recognised by the common law by resorting to the inherent jurisdiction.[17] Where Parliament has recognised certain kinds of proceedings as requiring access and reporting to be restricted, as in s.12 of the Administration of Justice Act 1960, it is likely to be considered inappropriate to employ the court's inherent jurisdiction to introduce new general categories. For example, Lord Steyn in *Re S (FC) (A Child)*[18] commented:

> "Given the number of statutory exceptions, it needs to be said clearly and unambiguously that the court has no power to create by a process of analogy, except in the most compelling circumstances, further exceptions to the general principle of open justice".

7–63 The recognition that it is appropriate to hear cases relating to children in private has found formal expression in the amendment[19] to s.12 of the Administration of Justice Act 1960, which specifically refers to proceedings under the Children Act 1989, and also in the Family Proceedings Rules 1991.[20] In r. 4.16(7) of those rules, it is provided that a judge has a discretion, even in family proceedings involving children, to hear all or part of a case in public. In *Re P-B (A Minor)*,[21] however, the Court of Appeal held that this power should only rarely be exercised. Family proceedings involving children should generally be heard in private. It was even said that the judge in deciding whether or not to exercise the discretion ought not to feel constrained by considerations of open justice or freedom of expression.[22]

7–64 The father in that case wanted an application for a residence order (formerly known as a custody order) under the Children Act 1989 to be heard in open court, and there was no objection from the mother or the Official Solicitor. Nevertheless, the judge was held rightly to have refused the father's application.

---

[15] See para.2–143.
[16] Set out above at para.7–54.
[17] See *CT Bowring & Co (Insurance) v Corsi and Partners Ltd* [1994] 2 Lloyd's Rep.567; *Condliffe v Hislop* [1996] 1 W.L.R. 753, [1996] 1 All E.R. 431, where the Court of Appeal said that it is inappropriate to have recourse to the inherent jurisdiction of the court when Parliament and the Rules Committee had sought to provide an exhaustive code (*e.g.* in relation to ordering security for costs: see now CPR 25.13.).
[18] [2004] UKHL 47, [2005] 1 A.C. 593 at [20].
[19] Children Act 1989, Sch.13, para.14.
[20] Rule 1.2 provides that "family proceedings" has the meaning ascribed to it by the Matrimonial and Family Proceedings Act 1984, s.32; namely proceedings which are family business: that is to say, "business of any description which in the High Court is for the time being assigned to the Family Division and to no other Division . . . "; Supreme Court Act 1981, s.61 and Sch.1.
[21] [1997] 1 All E.R. 58, CA. See also *Pelling v Bruce-Williams* [2004] EWCA Civ 845, [2004] Fam. 155; *Att-Gen v Pelling* [2005] EWHC 414 (Admin).
[22] Although in the light of later developments a judge would nowadays probably be more inclined to address such an application for a hearing to be in open court on its merits in the circumstances of the particular case.

Reliance had been placed on Arts 6 and 10 of the European Convention, but the Court of Appeal took note of the fact that Art.6(1) was subject to the proviso that the press and public can be excluded from all or part of a trial "where the interests of juveniles... so require". The present procedures in family cases were thus held to be in accordance with the policy of the Convention. It was recognised that it would often be appropriate for judgment to be given in public where the court believed that there was a public interest in the case or a need to give guidance to practitioners. This legitimate public interest consideration, however, does not generally require either evidence to be revealed in public or the identities of the parties. Indeed, in *B v United Kingdom*,[23] the European Court of Human Rights recognised that there may be instances in which even the pronouncement of a judgment in public would defeat the legitimate objective of protecting not only the privacy of children or parties but also the wider interests of justice.

It was pointed out by Munby J. in *Clibbery v Allan*[24] that there was nothing to suggest that Butler-Sloss L.J. in *Re P-B* was treating r.4.16(7) as requiring a hearing to be held in *secret* as opposed to in *private*.[25] Moreover, as he demonstrated in that case, there is no reason to apply any such presumption in favour of privacy, by way of analogy, to other chambers hearings in the Family Division *not* concerning children. The decision was upheld on appeal.[26] In *A v Times Newspapers Ltd*[27] it was confirmed by Sumner J. that, as a matter of practice, the public is generally excluded from hearings relating to children, because publicity is almost invariably inimical to a child's welfare (the paramount consideration in accordance with s.1 of the Children Act 1989).

7–65

Appellate proceedings

Court of Appeal hearings will generally take place in public, but not when the appeal relates to children proceedings (to which r.4.16(7) would apply at first instance). It is the usual practice to include a provision in the order that no-one shall publish or reveal the name or address of the child who is the subject of the proceedings or publish or reveal any information which would be likely to lead to the identification of the minor. The practice enables applications to be made with regard to the circumstances of a particular child, where publicity may be advantageous, and it also has the desirable result that there is no mystery as to what is the general approach of the court.[28]

7–66

In *Pelling v Bruce-Williams (Secretary of State for Constitutional Affairs Intervening)*,[29] it was observed that the time had come for the Court of Appeal

7–67

---

[23] [2001] 2 F.L.R. 261, [2001] 2 F.C.R. 221, (2002) 34 E.H.R.R. 19. See also *Att-Gen v Pelling* [2005] EWHC 414 (Admin) where the history of Dr Pelling's application is reviewed.
[24] [2001] 2 F.L.R 819 at [76].
[25] See, *e.g.* the discussion at paras 7–41 *et seq.*
[26] [2002] EWCA Civ 45, [2002] Fam. 261. See M. Dodd, "Case Commentary: Or Scott v Scott Revisited—Clibbery v Allan" [2002] C.F.L.Q. 461; "Children, the Press—and a Missed Opportunity" (2002) C.F.L.Q. 103.
[27] [2002] EWHC 2444 (Fam), [2003] 1 All E.R. 587.
[28] *Re R (Court of Appeal: Order Against Identification)* [1999] 2 F.L.R. 145, 3 F.C.R. 213.
[29] [2004] EWCA Civ 845, [2004] Fam. 155 at [49] and [54].

7-67 CHAPTER 7—COURT REPORTING I: RESTRICTIONS UNDER 1981 ACT

to consider in each case concerning children whether a proper balance of competing rights required the anonymisation of any report of its proceedings and judgment following a hearing that was conducted in public. Moreover, the inherent jurisdiction empowered the court to impose reporting restrictions in an individual case but neither that factor nor the statutory restrictions permitted under s.39 of the Children and Young Persons Act 1933 would justify the imposition of an automatic restriction without the exercise of a specific discretion in the individual case.[30] It was also suggested that the Master of the Rolls and President of the Family Division might review the practice of the Court of Appeal to reflect the need to balance competing rights.

G. The residual discretion: deterrence of witnesses by publicity

7-68 The administration of justice may be frustrated if litigants or others are deterred from taking part in proceedings by the prospect of attendant publicity, and in some cases this consideration has been regarded as so fundamental as to justify hearing some parts of the relevant proceedings *in camera*, or withholding certain information or evidence from being referred to publicly. While, as already observed, mere embarrassment or inconvenience will not justify such a course,[31] if there is a genuine element of deterrence this could be such as to undermine the process of justice itself, unless at least some degree of limitation is imposed upon the principle. The case of *R. v Richards*[32] provides a striking example of the court indulging a witness who simply did not *want* to give evidence in public.

7-69   Blackmail victims provide an obvious example.[33] Similarly, protection might be afforded to witnesses such as "supergrasses"[34] and other police informants,

---

[30] Cp. the approach of the House of Lords in *Re S (FC) (A Child)* [2004] UKHL 47, [2005] 1 A.C. 593, where it was made clear that there should be an intense focus on the individual circumstances of the case when the court comes to balance competing rights.

[31] See paras 7–10 and 7–30. It is therefore perhaps surprising that, in *Re A Solicitor (Disclosure of Confidential Records)* [1997] 1 F.L.R. 101 at 104, despite the fact that the judge, Johnson J., set the modest level of the fine for contempt against a firm of solicitors partly by reference to "the publicity which this case will generate for this old-established and, may I say, highly regarded firm of solicitors", the report records that "the names of instructing solicitors are omitted in the interest of preserving anonymity". See also *A v M (Family Proceedings: Publicity)* [2000] 1 F.L.R. 562 at 564–5, Charles J., discussed at para.6–91 above.

[32] (1999) 163 J.P. 246. See the discussion at para.7–11 above.

[33] *R. v Socialist Worker Printers and Publishers Ltd Ex p. Att-Gen* [1975] Q.B. 637. See also A.L. Goodhart (1935) 48 Harv. L.R. 885 at 905.

[34] *R. v Reigate Justices Ex p. Argus Newspapers* (1983) 147 J.P. 385. Anonymity would not be granted automatically by any means, and it would be most unlikely that even a "supergrass" would be accorded anonymity in the role of defendant. There is no question of deterring so far as defendants are concerned. See, *e.g. R. v Sehitoglou and Ozakan* [1998] 1 Cr.App.R. (S) 89. There is a difference of treatment with regard to defendants in the Youth and Criminal Evidence Act 1999, no provision being made for even young defendants who may fall into the category of "vulnerable" witnesses: see *S (R on the application of) v Waltham Forest Youth Court and (1) Crown Prosecution Service (2) Secretary of State for the Home Department (Interested Parties)* [2004] EWHC 715 (Admin), [2004] 2 Cr.App.R. 335. But see Baroness Hale in *R. (on the application of D) v Camberwell Youth Court; R. (on the application of the Director of Public Prosecutions) v Camberwell Youth Court* [2005] UKHL 4, [2005] 1 All E.R. 999, [2005] 1 F.C.R. 365 at [63] who reserved her position on this point.

who may be unwilling to come forward for fear of reprisal, unless some measure of protection is afforded.[35]

Lord Loreburn considered the problem of deterrence in *Scott v Scott*,[36] where he was concerned with the particular problems to which nullity proceedings might give rise: **7–70**

> "Applying this principle to proceedings for nullity, if the Court is satisfied that to insist upon publicity would in the circumstances reasonably deter a party from seeking redress, or interfere with the effective trial of the cause, in my opinion an order for hearing or partial hearing *in camera* may lawfully be made. But I cannot think it may be made as a matter of course, although my own view is that the power ought to be liberally exercised, because justice will be frustrated or declined if the court is made a place of moral torture".

Subsequently, however, some measure of protection was afforded by statute to take account of the considerations addressed by Lord Loreburn in the particular context of matrimonial proceedings. These provisions, contained in the Judicial Proceedings (Regulation of Reports) Act 1926, are more fully considered below.[37]   **7–71**

In Pt IV of the Ecclesiastical Jurisdiction Measure 1963, s.28(f),[38] it is provided, in relation to Consistory Courts, that: **7–72**

> " . . . the chancellor, if satisfied that it is in the interests of justice to do so, may give directions that during any part of the proceedings such persons or classes of persons including the assessors as the court may determine shall be excluded."

In *R. v Chancellor of the Chichester Consistory Court Ex p. News Group Newspapers Ltd*,[39] the Chancellor had made an order that the press and public should be excluded from hearing evidence. While recognising that the power

---

[35] *R. v DJX, SYC, GCZ* (1989) 91 Cr.App.R. 36; *R. v Watford Magistrates Court Ex p. Lenman* [1993] Crim. L.R. 388, [1992] T.L.R. 285, DC; *R. v Taylor (Gary)* [1994] T.L.R. 484, CA. It is always a matter for the discretion of the trial judge, but an accused should only be deprived of the fundamental right to see and know the identity of his accusers in rare and exceptional circumstances: *R. v Malvern Justices Ex p. Evans* [1988] Q.B. 553; see also *R. v Liverpool Magistrates' Court Ex p. DPP* (1997) 161 J.P. 43; *S (R. on the application of) v Waltham Forest Youth Court and (1) Crown Prosecution Service (2) Secretary of State for the Home Department (Interested Parties)* [2004] EWHC 715 (Admin), [2004] 2 Cr.App.R. 335. (In *Bobolas v Economist Newspaper Ltd*, on March 24, 1987, a Russian defector was allowed by Kenneth Jones J. to give evidence behind a screen in an attempt to avoid his being recognised, even though his name was given. The case concerned allegations about a Greek newspaper being under the influence of the KGB, and the witness' evidence was as to his experience of KGB policy in relation to Greece and Turkey. Although the case is reported in [1987] 1 W.L.R. 1101 on a different point, no reference was made to this incident.)
[36] [1913] A.C. 417 at 446.
[37] See paras 8–2 *et seq*.
[38] Repealed from a date to be decided by the Clergy Discipline Measure 2003, s.18(3)(c) of which makes rather different provision namely: " . . . the hearing shall be in private, except that the tribunal or court, if satisfied that it is in the interests of justice so to do or the respondent so requests, shall direct that the hearing shall be in public in which case the tribunal or court may, during any part of the proceedings, exclude such person or persons as it may determine."
[39] [1992] C.O.D. 48, DC.

7–72 CHAPTER 7—COURT REPORTING I: RESTRICTIONS UNDER 1981 ACT

should be only sparingly exercised, the court was convinced that it would be in the interests of justice to do so, because at least one female witness was in tears in the course of giving her evidence. He had decided that the media were "intent on reporting every salacious detail of the acts of sexual congress of which evidence was to be given."[40]

7–73 The Divisional Court concluded that the tearfulness of the woman provided some material upon which the Chancellor was entitled to exercise his discretion. Moreover, he had directed himself properly, having regard to the critical question of "necessity in the interests of justice". In those circumstances, the court declined to interfere.

7–74 It is perhaps necessary to be wary of Lord Loreburn's phrase "liberally exercised", in the sense that any party seeking to restrict the principle of open justice would, in the light of subsequent authority, in practice face a considerable hurdle.[41] Beyond those cases where it was traditionally acknowledged that proceedings *in camera* may be justified, and which received recognition in s.12 of the Administration of Justice Act 1960, it is difficult to lay down any rule of general application. Indeed, in *Scott v Scott* itself, caution was expressed by Lord Halsbury[42]:

> "I wish to guard myself against the proposition that a judge may bring a case within the category of enforced secrecy because he thinks that justice cannot be done unless it is heard in secret. I do not deny it, because it is impossible to prove what cases might or might not be brought within the category, but I should require to have brought before me the concrete case before I could express an opinion upon it".

7–75 Lord Shaw also voiced his concerns[43]:

> "Granted that the principle of openness of justice may yield to compulsory secrecy in cases involving patrimonial interest and property, such as those affecting trade secrets, or confidential documents, may not the fear of giving evidence in public, on questions of status like the present, deter witnesses of delicate feeling from giving testimony, and rather induce the abandonment of their just right by sensitive suitors? And may not that be a sound reason for administering justice in such cases with closed doors? For otherwise justice, it is argued, would thus be in some cases defeated. My Lords, this ground is very dangerous ground. One's experience shews that the reluctance to intrude one's private affairs upon public notice induces many citizens to forgo their just claims. It is no doubt true that many of such cases might have been brought before tribunals if only the tribunals were secret. But the concession to these feelings would, in my opinion, tend to bring about those very dangers to liberty in general, and to society at

---

[40] Cp. *R. v Southampton Industrial Tribunal Ex p. INS News Group Ltd and Express Newspapers plc* [1995] I.R.L.R. 247, discussed at paras 8–142 *et seq*.
[41] For early examples, see, *e.g. Greenway v Att-Gen* (1927) 44 T.L.R. 124; *B (Orse P) v Att-Gen* [1967] P. 119. And for the modern law, see the discussion in paras 7–36 *et seq*.
[42] [1913] A.C. 417 at 442.
[43] *ibid.* at 484–5.

large, against which publicity tends to keeps us (*sic*) secure: and it must be further remembered that, in questions of status, society as such—of which marriage is one of the primary institutions—has also a real and grave interest as well as have the parties to the individual cause".

H. Circumstances justifying the withholding of particular items of information in open court

Where the court has power to order a hearing *in camera*, whether at common law or by statute, it may as a matter of principle make a less Draconian order if it will suffice to achieve the same end.[44] In *Att-Gen v Leveller Magazine Ltd*[45] application was made to a magistrates' court, during a preliminary hearing of charges under the Official Secrets Act, that a witness should be referred to in court as Colonel B and his true name disclosed only to the court, the defendants and their counsel. The reason for the application was stated to be that it was necessary for national security. The magistrates agreed to that course. Subsequently Colonel B gave evidence in open court from which it was comparatively easy to establish his identity. The respondents revealed his identity in their journal.

The House of Lords allowed their appeal (from a judgment of the Divisional Court which had found them in contempt) because Colonel B's evidence had effectively compromised his anonymity and thus would have destroyed the effect of any order the magistrates might have legitimately made. In considering the principles involved, however, Lords Diplock, Russell of Killowen and Scarman all concurred in the view that the greater includes the lesser,[46] and that a court has always power to adopt a device which in its view is sufficient to provide the protection required but involves less derogation from the principle of open justice

---

[44] But see the discussion at para.7–77, n.46.
[45] [1979] A.C. 440.
[46] It was observed by Beatson J. in *R. (On the Application of Mersey Care NHS Trust) v Mental Health Review Tribunal (Brady and other Interested Parties)* [2004] EWHC 1749 (Admin), [2005] 2 All E.R. 820 at [51] that the proposition that the greater includes the lesser needs to be qualified in the light of the decision in *Independent Publishing Company Ltd v Att-Gen of Trinidad and Tobago* [2004] UKPC 26, [2005] 1 A.C. 190. As he noted, "The Judicial Committee of the Privy Council held that there is no common law power [in] a court to impose such restrictions on the information released in open court proceedings". One has to be careful, however, about "qualifying" propositions of law laid down by the House of Lords. A problem may be that Beatson J. was addressing a summary by counsel of the law as stated in *The Leveller* case to the effect that " . . . a tribunal with power to sit in private will in general also have power to take the lesser step of imposing restrictions on the information released to the public". It is important to record that Lord Edmund-Davies made it clear that " . . . a court has no power to pronounce to the public at large such a prohibition against publication that all disobedience to it would automatically constitute a contempt", at 464A. The "lesser" step contemplated by the Lordships in *The Leveller* was conferring anonymity upon a witness. There is no doubt that such a power exists. What the Privy Council was declaring in *Tobago* was that the court had no common law power to restrict publication of anything which takes place in open court (despite a widespread impression that such a power could be inferred from the case of *R. v Clement* (1821) 4 B. & Ald. 218, 106 E.R. 918). Thus, on a careful reading of *The Leveller* case it is not by any means clear that the law there stated requires to be qualified by the later case.

7-77 CHAPTER 7—COURT REPORTING I: RESTRICTIONS UNDER 1981 ACT

than a hearing *in camera*.[47] Similarly, it may even be permissible on some occasions to allow a particular piece of evidence to be written down, although such a power should be used sparingly and only if it is plain that it is unlikely, because of a witness' reluctance or for some other reason, to emerge in the absence of such protection.[48]

7-78   Until the analysis by Lord Brown in *Independent Publishing Company Ltd v Att-Gen of Trinidad and Tobago*,[49] it had been believed on the authority of *R. v Clement*[50] that orders might be made in certain circumstances preventing information from being released to the public either on a permanent or a temporary basis. It is important now to recognise that this old authority cannot be regarded as supporting such a wide common law power. While it was no doubt true before the enactment of the Contempt of Court Act 1981 that there was an inherent power to postpone reporting of certain aspects of proceedings until the conclusion of those very proceedings, there was no power corresponding to that conferred by the statute to postpone reporting any further (*e.g.* until the conclusion of other proceedings). Nonetheless, there can be no doubt that witnesses are permitted to withhold an address when identifying themselves[51] at the beginning of their testimony (or when disclosure is made under the Criminal Procedure and Investigations Act 1996), if there is a sufficient reason, and it may be desirable that the court should give a warning as to the intended effect of its ruling and of the risk of proceedings for contempt if it is ignored.[52]

---

[47] The inherent jurisdiction may be ousted if Parliament has made it sufficiently clear that a particular matter is to be governed exclusively by statute: see, *e.g. S (R. on the application of) v Waltham Forest Youth Court and (1) Crown Prosecution Service (2) Secretary of State for the Home Department (Interested Parties)* [2004] EWHC 715 (Admin), [2004] 2 Cr.App.R. 235 at [19] *et seq*. But see Baroness Hale in *R. (on the application of D) v Camberwell Youth Court); R. (on the application of the Director of Public Prosecutions v Camberwell Youth Court)* [2005] UKHL 4, [2005] 1 F.C.R. 365 at [63].
[48] *per* Lord Dilhorne in *Att-Gen v Leveller Magazine Ltd*, at 458.
[49] [2004] UKPC 26, [2005] 1 A.C. 19.
[50] (1821) 4 B. & Ald. 218, 106 E.R. 918. For a fuller consideration of orders *postponing* publication, see section III below.
[51] *R. v Liverpool Magistrates' Court Ex p. DPP* (1997) 161 J.P. 43, discussed by F.G. Davies, "Preserving the Anonymity of Witnesses" (1997) 161 J.P.N. 351. The basic principle has always been that a defendant is entitled to know the identity of his accusers. Despite this, it was suggested in July 1996 by the Trials Issues Group that: "Unless it is necessary for evidential purposes, defence and prosecution witnesses should not be required to disclose their addresses in open court. Exceptionally, it will be appropriate for the defence and the prosecution to make application for the non-disclosure, in open court, of the names of witnesses": *Statement of National Standards of Witness Care in the Criminal Justice System*, para.17. As is pointed out in *Archbold 2005*, para.8–71a, this has never been published as a practice direction despite having the approval of Lord Bingham C.J. See also the recommendation of the *Committee on Privacy and Related Matters* (The Calcutt Committee) Cm. 1102 (1990), para.10.15 (for protection of privacy for victims of crime). See generally *Archbold 2005*, para.16–68, where the compatibility of witness anonymity with the requirements of the ECHR is considered.
[52] *Att-Gen v Leveller Magazine Ltd* [1979] A.C. 440, 453G–H, 456G–H, 465E–G, 469A; *R. v Socialist Worker Printers and Publishers Ltd Ex p. Att-Gen* [1975] Q.B. 637. And see *R. (Al Fawwaz) v Governor of Brixton Prison* [2001] UKHL 69, [2002] 1 A.C. 556, where factors relevant to the decision whether a judge may permit a witness to conceal his identity entirely from the defendant are outlined. The courts now have a statutory power to prohibit the identification of witnesses, by virtue of the Youth Justice and Criminal Evidence Act 1999, s.46, which is set out and considered at paras 8–74 *et seq*.

In *R. v Comerford*,[53] the Court of Appeal declined to overturn a conviction 7–79
when the appeal was based in part upon the contention that the judge at trial had
ordered that the jurors, instead of having their names read out in court in the
ordinary way, should be known only by numbers. He had taken this precaution
since an earlier trial was abandoned because the jury had to be discharged. It was
recognised that, although it was generally desirable that the usual procedure for
empanelling a jury should be followed, whereby the name of each juror selected
by ballot would be called out in open court, in cases where there was a risk of
interference with the jury, a judge was entitled to permit their names to be
withheld. He would need to satisfied, however, that the defendant's right of
challenge was preserved and that the proceedings were not rendered unfair in any
respect.

The common law has been supplemented in the Youth Justice and Criminal 7–80
Evidence Act 1999 which gives the court the power to make a "reporting
direction" for the protection of vulnerable witnesses.[54]

It seems clear, however, that once information is released to those present in 7–81
court the wider public also has a right to be informed. If something is mentioned
in open court, it will not normally be appropriate to restrain its publication in the
media outside.[55] Any such restriction would have to be justified by reference to
Art.10 of the ECHR.[56]

I. The continuing relevance of the common law

In those cases where reporting of court proceedings is governed by statute, it is 7–82
possible to set out the principles by reference to the specific provisions in
question and to any subsequent authorities. The statutory provisions are
considered in turn the later parts of this chapter and the next. The matter is not
wholly governed by statute, however, and it is necessary still to have regard to the
common law powers to restrict court reporting,[57] not least because they are
expressly preserved by s.11 of the Contempt of Court Act 1981. This provision

---

[53] [1998] 1 All E.R. 823, CA.
[54] See the fuller treatment at paras 8–74 *et seq.*
[55] *R. v Arundel Justices Ex p. Westminster Press Ltd* [1985] 1 W.L.R. 708; see also *Re Crook, The Times,* November 8, 1984 and *Ex p. Godwin* [1992] Q.B. 190; there is no power under s.39 of the Children and Young Persons Act 1933 to order that the name of the *defendant* should not be published. But see the remarks of Maurice Kay L.J. in *R. v Teeside Crown Court Ex p. Gazette Media Co Ltd* [2005] EWCA Crim 1983 set out at para.8–55. The section is set out at para.8–50. The paragraph in the text was cited with approval by Beatson J. in *R. (on the application of Mersey Care Trust) v Mental Health Review Tribunal* [2004] EWHC 1749 (Admin), [2005] 2 All E.R. 820 at [54].
[56] See *R. (on the application of Mersey Care Trust) v Mental Health Review Tribunal* [2004] EWHC 1749 (Admin), [2005] 1 W.L.R. 2469, [2005] 2 All E.R. 820 at [13].
[57] The residual common law power of courts to restrict reporting was considered by the Privy Council in *Independent Publishing Company Ltd v Att-Gen of Trinidad and Tobago* [2004] UKPC 26, [2005] 1 A.C. 190.

is considered in detail below,[58] but regard must also be had to the interrelationship between these common law principles and the European Convention on Human Rights.[59]

II. SECTION 11 OF THE CONTEMPT OF COURT ACT

A. The terms of section 11

7-83 The common law powers of withholding information in court are implicitly preserved in s.11 of the Contempt of Court Act 1981 which is in the following terms:

> "In any case where a court (having power to do so) allows a name or other matter to be withheld from the public in proceedings before the court, the court may give such directions prohibiting the publication of that name or matter in connection with the proceedings as appear to the court to be necessary for the purpose for which it was so withheld".

7-84 It will be apparent that:

(i) The section does not confer the power to withhold "a name or other matter". It simply refers to a common law jurisdiction assumed to exist, without defining it.[60] What was new was the granting of a power to give directions to prohibit publication.[61] This would appear to be based to an extent upon the recommendation of the Phillimore Report[62] that "... legislation ... should provide for these specific circumstances in which a court shall be empowered to prohibit, in the public interest, the publication of names or of other matters arising at a trial".

(ii) It refers to "prohibiting" rather than "postponing", which is the more limited power addressed in s.4(2) of the 1981 Act.[63] It should not be assumed, however, in those cases where the court *does* have a power to prohibit, that there is no power to order merely postponement of the information if that is all that is required to achieve the court's legitimate objective of protecting the administration of justice. It seems clear from

---

[58] paras 7–83 *et seq.*
[59] For a discussion of this aspect of the impact of the Convention in relation to media coverage of court proceedings, see paras 2–122 *et seq.* See also paras 6–89 *et seq.*, and para.7–30.
[60] Compare the wording of the Administration of Justice Act 1960, s.12(1)(e) where the statute also refers to, without defining, powers to prohibit publication of information which are assumed to exist.
[61] *Independent Publishing Company Ltd v Att-Gen of Trinidad and Tobago* [2004] UKPC 26, [2005] 1 A.C. 190, at [51].
[62] Cmnd. 5794 (1974), p.60, n.72. See also the remarks of Lord Edmund-Davies in *Att-Gen v Leveller Magazine Ltd* [1979] A.C. 440 at 466C–D.
[63] Considered at paras 7–111 *et seq.*

Att-Gen v Leveller Magazine Ltd[64] that the greater power effectively includes the lesser.[65]

(iii) It also refers expressly to the need for directions for the implementation of any such order and for the avoidance of uncertainty.[66]

There seems to be no doubt that magistrates were regarded as having had sufficient inherent powers to make restriction orders for the purpose of protecting the administration of justice in relation to proceedings before them.[67] For example, in *R. v Watford Magistrates' Court Ex p. Lenman*,[68] Beldam L.J. observed that:

7–85

"If a magistrate was satisfied that there was a real risk to the administration of justice, because a witness on reasonable grounds feared for his safety if his identity were disclosed, it was entirely within the powers of the magistrate to take reasonable steps to protect and reassure the witness so that the witness was not deterred from coming forward to give evidence."

Justice would no doubt require the court to balance these considerations against any prejudice caused to an accused person, particularly with regard to preparing and conducting his defence.

The matter of anonymity was considered in the context of a coroner's inquest in *R. v Bedfordshire Coroner Ex p. Local Sunday Newspapers Ltd*,[69] although apparently without express reference to s.11 of the Contempt of Court Act 1981. The deceased had been fatally injured by armed police officers and the Assistant Chief Constable had applied for the four officers concerned in the incident to remain anonymous. The coroner granted the request. A verdict of lawful killing was returned by the jury, and thereafter the proprietors of a local newspaper sought to quash the inquisition by way of certiorari and to have a new inquest with the officers identified. Later they confined themselves to seeking a declaration to the effect that the policemen should have been identified. Burton J. rejected the application, even as narrowed. He held that once a reason for granting anonymity has been established on an objective basis, the court should

7–86

---

[64] [1979] A.C. 440. See para.7–77.
[65] But see the observations of Beatson J. In *R. (on the application of Mersey Care Trust) v Mental Health Review Tribunal* [2004] EWHC 1749 (Admin), [2005] 1 W.L.R. 2469, [2005] 2 All E.R. 820 discussed at para.7–77, n.46 above.
[66] See the remarks of Lord Denning M.R. in *R. v Horsham Justices Ex p. Farquharson* [1982] Q.B. 762 at 793C: "... now it needs an order, not an implication". And see the *Practice Direction* [1983] 1 W.L.R. 1475, [1983] 1 All E.R. 64, 76 Cr.App.R. 78, discussed at para.7–153. As to the position in New Zealand, see Thomas J. in *Police v O'Connor* [1992] N.Z.L.R. 87 at 105: "The need for an explicit and precise order is self-evident. Apart from the fact that any inhibition on the right of free expression should be well-defined, the order is binding on the media, and the media is entitled to know exactly what it can and cannot publish". See also *John Fairfax & Sons v Police Tribunal of New South Wales* (1986) 5 N.S.W.L.R. 465 at 477, McHugh J.A.
[67] Such considerations would not, however, justify the adoption of a policy of withholding the identities of magistrates from the public and the press: *R. v Felixstowe Justices Ex p. Leigh* [1987] Q.B. 582.
[68] [1993] Crim. L.R. 388, [1992] T.L.R. 285, DC. But see the cases discussed at paras 7–96 *et seq.*
[69] (2000) 164 J.P. 283.

then perform a balancing exercise to determine what is in the overall interests of justice. He also commented that the grant of anonymity would be likely to have less serious repercussions at an inquest than in a criminal trial, and that accordingly a coroner may be entitled to view the scales as being less heavily weighted in favour of open justice. He held that on the facts the coroner had objective grounds to justify his carrying out such a balancing exercise. Particular factors were that the police officer who had fired the fatal shot, and his family, had already been subjected to threats following an earlier unrelated incident. He also took account of the public interest in not revealing the identities of members of sensitive units such as an armed response group. The judge concluded that the coroner had thus applied the correct test and that there was evidence upon which he was entitled to reach his conclusion. The test applied by the judge in that case was later criticised by the Court of Appeal in *Family of Derek Bennett v Officers A and B and HM Coroner and Commissioner of Metropolitan Police*[70] as setting the threshold too high. The court did not think it right to give any more definitive description of the threshold test than that "there must be reasonable grounds which show that the fears of a witness are objectively justified".

B. The consequences of breaching a section 11 order

7–87 The section does not provide that breach of any such directions is *ipso facto* a contempt. However, once the order prohibiting publication has been properly made, then anyone who knowingly acts inconsistently with it is likely to be held in contempt.[71] The cases of *Att-Gen v Leveller Magazine Ltd*[72] and *R. v Socialist Worker Printers and Publishers Ltd Ex p. Att-Gen*[73] show that wherever the court makes an order for partial secrecy it is desirable to make the following matters plain:

(a) whether a formal order not to publish is made or merely an informal request not to publish;

(b) the purpose of the order, in particular whether it is intended to protect the due administration of justice[74];

(c) the basis of the order—for instance whether it is intended merely to prevent injustice arising in the instant or linked cases or whether it is intended to protect the administration of justice as a continuing process;

(d) whether there is any specific time limit on publication;

(e) that a breach of the order will or may well constitute a contempt.

---

[70] [2004] EWCA Civ 1439, [2005] U.K.H.R.R. 44, at [29]–[30]; see also *R. v Governor of Pentonville Prison Ex p. Fernandez* [1971] 1 W.L.R. 987; *R. v Lord Saville of Newdigate Ex p. A* [2000] 1 W.L.R. 1855 [68] and again in *R. (A) v Lord Saville of Newdigate* [2002] 1 W.L.R. 1249.
[71] [1988] Ch. 333 at 380D–F, Lloyd L.J.
[72] [1979] A.C. 440 at 453G–H, Lord Diplock, 456G–H, Viscount Dilhorne, 465E–G, Lord Edmund-Davies, 469A, Lord Russell of Killowen.
[73] [1975] Q.B. 637.
[74] See Lord Oliver in *Att-Gen v Times Newspapers Ltd* [1992] 1 A.C. 191 at 223, where it was pointed out that the purpose of an order is very often obvious, quite apart from its terms.

The making of orders in this form should obviate difficulties that have 7–88
occurred in earlier cases, and the specific reference to "directions" in s.11 itself
should also serve as a reminder of the need to make the terms and purpose of
such an order explicit.

C. The 2005 Consolidated Criminal Practice Direction

Also relevant in this context is the Practice Direction which came into effect 7–89
shortly after the 1981 Act,[75] and which applies both to orders made under s.11
and to those under s.4(2). Although it plainly cannot either confer or remove
powers in itself, the object of this Direction was to reaffirm that orders have to
be made expressly and clearly, and that the purpose should be specified. In
Birmingham Post & Mail Ltd v Birmingham City Council,[76] Mann L.J. said:

> "The court wishes to emphasise how important it is that those who exercise their
> powers under s.11 of the 1981 Act should give immediate and written reasons for doing
> so (see Practice Direction (contempt: reporting restrictions)) . . . Open justice demands
> of them no less".

Applications for an order under s.11 should normally be heard *in camera* 7–90
since, if it is held that the application has merit, then the order would be rendered
ineffective and pointless.[77]

D. *Mens rea* for breach of section 11 orders

If any information, validly withheld from the jury during the course of a trial, 7–91
were to be revealed to the media before they have reached their verdict, it is
conceivable that the publication would constitute a strict liability contempt.[78] In
many cases, however, the revelation of the information (say, as to a witness'
identity) would be unlikely to create a substantial risk of serious prejudice to the
particular proceedings. In such a case, the impact of public revelation would be
more likely to be confined to the administration of justice in general terms. It
might, for example, discourage others from coming forward in the future. Thus,
it is necessary to consider what degree of *mens rea* would be required, since there
could be no strict liability contempt in such circumstances.[79]

The question arises as to whether the test should be the same as that applied 7–92
in *Att-Gen v Newspaper Publishing plc*[80]; that is to say, would an applicant have

---

[75] [1982] 1 W.L.R. 1475. The equivalent practice direction is now to be found in the *Consolidated Criminal Practice Direction* [2002] 1 W.L.R. 2870, [2002] 3 All E.R. 904, at [Pt I.3] (as amended March 22, 2005); for the latest version of which see www.courtservice.gov.uk/docs/cpd/consol_criminal_pd_220305.doc. The terms of the Direction are fully set out at para.7-153. And see para.7-219.
[76] (1994) 17 B.M.L.R. 116 at 121.
[77] *R. v Tower Bridge Magistrates' Court Ex p. Osborne* (1987) 88 Cr.App.R. 28; *R. v Westminster City Council Ex p. Castelli and Tristran-Garcia* [1996] 1 F.L.R. 534 at 539, where the judge pointed out that one reason for not making an anonymity order was that the applicants' names had been mentioned in open court on the application for leave.
[78] See ss.1 and 2 of the 1981 Act, considered in ch.4.
[79] See the discussion on *mens rea* for contempt by publication generally in ch.5.
[80] [1988] Ch. 333 at 374–5, Sir John Donaldson M.R., 381–383, Lloyd L.J. and 387, Balcombe L.J.

7-92 CHAPTER 7—COURT REPORTING I: RESTRICTIONS UNDER 1981 ACT

to show that the person concerned not only knew that the order had been made,[81] but also had additionally an intention to interfere with the administration of justice?

7-93 It was accepted by both parties in the later case of *Att-Gen v Newspaper Publishing plc*[82] that the conduct complained of had to be "specifically intended to impede or prejudice the administration of justice". Lord Bingham C.J. also reaffirmed that the necessary intent could be inferred from the surrounding circumstances. Thus, if the purpose of the order has been specified on its face (as required by the Practice Direction) or it is obvious,[83] the court is likely to proceed on the basis that a sufficient intention to interfere with the administration of justice was present for the purposes of common law contempt.[84] The court's approach is likely to be consistent as between the provisions of s.11 and those of s.4(2).[85]

7-94 It is not necessary in such circumstances to show that such an order has actually been served upon the alleged contemnor.[86] While recklessness is apparently not enough for publication contempt at common law generally,[87] journalists should, nevertheless, it appears, have regard to the warning contained in the Practice Direction as to the obligation of newspapers to check to see whether such orders have been made.[88]

E. Decisions in the light of section 11

7-95 A number of decisions after the 1981 Act came into effect have confirmed the principles applied beforehand, and in particular that the policy underlying the court's power to make such orders is that judges need sufficient authority to protect the processes of the administration of justice itself. As was made clear in *Scott v Scott*,[89] that is the paramount consideration.

---

[81] See, e.g *Z Ltd v A-Z and AA-LL* [1982] Q.B. 558; *Att-Gen v Newspaper Publishing plc* [1997] 1 W.L.R. 926, 3 All E.R. 159.

[82] [1997] 1 W.L.R. 926 at 936–7, [1997] 3 All E.R. 159 at 169f (adopting the language of Sir John Donaldson M.R. in *Att-Gen v Newspaper Publishing plc* [1988] Ch. 333 at 374–5).

[83] See *Att-Gen v Times Newspapers Ltd* [1992] 1 A.C. 191 at 223 (Lord Oliver) and *Att-Gen v Leveller Magazine Ltd* [1979] A.C. 440 at 452 (Lord Diplock) and 456 (Viscount Dilhorne).

[84] See also the approach adopted by the House of Lords in *Att-Gen v Leveller Magazine Ltd* [1979] A.C. 440, where approval was expressed of *R. v Socialist Worker Printers and Publishers Ltd Ex p. Att-Gen* [1975] Q.B. 637 and *Att-Gen v Butterworth* [1963] 1 Q.B. 696. Liability would thus appear to arise on the basis of an affront to the authority of the court and its capacity to protect witnesses, and such conduct would be calculated to prejudice the administration of justice in the wider sense (judged objectively).

[85] See paras 7–221 *et seq*.

[86] See the remarks of Sir John Donaldson M.R. in *Att-Gen v Newspaper Publishing plc* [1988] Ch. 333 at 372A–D.

[87] *Att-Gen v Newspaper Publishing plc* [1988] Ch. 333; *Att-Gen v News Group Newspapers plc* [1989] Q.B. 110.

[88] See para.7–219. See now [2002] 1 W.L.R. 2870, [2002] 3 All E.R. 904, at [3.3] (as amended March 22, 2005). For the latest version of the Direction, see www.courtservice.gov.uk/docs/cpd/consol_criminal_pd_220305.doc.

[89] [1913] A.C. 417.

SECTION 11 OF THE CONTEMPT OF COURT ACT   7–98

1. *Cases where anonymity was wrongly granted or rightly withheld*

In *R. v Evesham Justices Ex p. McDonagh*[90] magistrates prohibited publication   7–96
of a defendant's home address, because he was apparently afraid of harassment
by a former wife. It is difficult to see how that information could be of the
slightest legitimate public interest, and it would certainly not serve the underlying purpose of open justice. Indeed, the Committee on Privacy and Related
Matters[91] recommended that, in respect of *victims*, in any criminal proceedings
there should be a statutory power:

> " . . . to make an order prohibiting the publication of the name or address of any person
> against whom the offence is alleged to have been committed, or of any other matters
> likely to lead to his or her identification. This should only be exercised if the court is
> satisfied that this is reasonably necessary to protect the mental or physical health,
> personal security or security of the home of the victim. Embarrassment or grief should
> not of themselves provide grounds for an order for anonymity".

Yet even this relatively modest proposal was not enacted,[92] although greater   7–97
protection has now been accorded to victims of sexual offences.[93] Against the
background of that relatively limited protection, it would be difficult to see how
the suppression of information about *defendants*, as opposed to victims or
witnesses, could ever be justified by any of the current exceptions to the
principles of open justice. It is true that some victims, or witnesses, might be
discouraged from participating in the court's process if protection were not
afforded. The same argument would not apply to a defendant, however, since
such persons are normally before the court by reason of compulsion rather than
because they have volunteered. Not surprisingly, therefore, the Divisional Court
held that the decision of the Evesham Justices was unjustified. As Tasker Watkins
L.J. put it " . . . section 11 was not enacted for the comfort and feelings of
defendants".[94]

In that case the information sought to be suppressed was purely incidental, but   7–98
in another case, *R. v Dover Justices Ex p. Dover District Council and Wells*,[95] the
justices had gone so far (wrongly, as it was subsequently held) as to seek to
prevent the public from learning of the identity of a person charged with public
health offences. The ground relied on was apprehended economic loss. Yet that
is exactly the kind of information which the principle of open justice is intended

---

[90] [1988] 1 Q.B. 553.
[91] (1990) Cm. 1102 (the Calcutt Committee) at para.10.15.
[92] Although Art.6 of the Convention contemplates that "the private life of the parties" *can* justify
restrictions on the principle of open justice, there is obviously a margin of appreciation which enables
each contracting state to determine to what extent such provisions need to be implemented.
[93] Se the discussion at paras 8–18 *et seq.*
[94] [1988] 1 Q.B. 553 at 562. See also *R. v Newtownabbey Magistrates' Court Ex p. Belfast Telegraph
Newspapers Ltd* [1997] N.I. 309.
[95] (1991) 156 J.P. 433.

7–98 CHAPTER 7—COURT REPORTING I: RESTRICTIONS UNDER 1981 ACT

to ensure should be made available to the public. As Tasker Watkins L.J. had observed in *R. v Evesham Justices Ex p. McDonagh*[96]:

" ... I go so far as to say that in the vast majority of cases, in magistrates' courts anyway, defendants would like their identity to be unrevealed and would be capable of advancing seemingly plausible reasons why that should be so."

7–99 Again, in *R. v Westminster City Council Ex p. Castelli and Tristran Garcia*[97] reliance was placed on s.11 of the 1981 Act by two persons who were claiming that there was a duty on the part of a local authority to house them under the Housing Act 1985. They sought to be protected by anonymity because they were HIV positive and contended that some degree of stigma attached to their condition. The case is of particular interest because, with both the press and the Attorney-General being represented, the extent of s.11 was fully considered. The judge refused to make an order and, after carefully considering the principles discussed by the House of Lords in *Att-Gen v Leveller Magazine Ltd*,[98] he concluded that the claim was "no more than a plea for privacy".[99]

7–100 Latham J. was not persuaded that other HIV sufferers would be discouraged from making applications to the court, or that any such order could be justified as being necessary in any other way for the purposes of justice:

"I do not consider that a general assertion that those with this medical condition will be deterred from seeking their rights is itself a sufficient justification. The particular reason for the publicity in these cases was not so much the medical condition, but the fact that the applicants came from Italy and Spain and were seeking to obtain benefits in this country. That does not provide any basis for saying that what has in fact happened in terms of publicity for these two applicants will be a deterrent for the future for others who have the same medical condition. I have no secure information about how many, if any, other potential applicants are in the same position as these applicants. It may be that in a particular case sufficient evidence could be provided to justify the conclusion that in that case the interests of justice demanded there should be anonymity. But that is not the situation here."

7–101 He confirmed the view that the test in cases such as these is that an applicant always had to establish " ... that the failure to grant anonymity would render the attainment of justice really doubtful or, in effect, impracticable."

7–102 It seems that even "a possible attack upon the defendant by ill-intentioned persons could not be regarded as a consequence of the publication of the proceedings of the court which should influence the court in its deliberations and

---

[96] [1988] Q.B. 553 at 562.
[97] [1996] 1 F.L.R. 534, Latham J.
[98] [1979] A.C. 440.
[99] [1996] 1 F.L.R. at 538H. It may be that "privacy" could not be dismissed so lightly following the enactment of the Human Rights Act 1998. Indeed, more recent authorities recognise that where Art.8 rights are engaged an intense focus will be required in balancing the competing interests in the light of the facts of the particular case. It could therefore be an important factor to be weighed against open justice in some circumstances. See the discussion of *Re S (FC) (A Child)* [2004] UKHL 47, [2005] 1 A.C. 593 at paras 6–43 *et seq*.

the danger of its occurrence should not cause the court to depart from well-established principles".[1]

The Court of Appeal held, in a case in which solicitors applied for anonymity in their proceedings for judicial review of the Legal Aid Board's termination of their legal aid franchise, that there was no justification for singling out the legal profession for special treatment. The applicants were also refused the protection of anonymity in relation to the appeal itself.[2]   7–103

2. Cases where anonymity has been properly granted

One instance where the Court of Appeal upheld the grant of anonymity under s.11 was that of *H v Ministry of Defence*,[3] where it was alleged by the plaintiff that medical negligence had led to a distressing personal injury and that if intimate details were published, without anonymity, he would suffer grave distress and embarrassment. It was held that his identity was irrelevant to any legitimate public interest that would be served by reporting the case.[4] Yet that would be true of other cases and would certainly apply, for example, to the defendant's address in *R. v Evesham Justices Ex p. McDonagh*.[5] However, the Court of Appeal had taken into account also evidence of the plaintiff's trauma and suicide attempts. It seems that the case exemplifies the rationale for withholding information which had been given by Lord Loreburn in relation to nullity cases; namely, that "... justice will be frustrated or declined if the court is made a place of moral torture".[6]   7–104

So too, the "psychiatric and psychological interests" of the applicant were clearly a major factor in the decision to grant anonymity to a victim of sexual abuse, who was seeking judicial review of a Criminal Injuries Compensation Board decision.[7] Anonymity could perhaps be justified even without the threat to health, and this would be consonant with the public policy considerations which led Parliament to accept the recommendations of the Committee on Privacy and Related Matters[8] for anonymity for victims of sexual assault.[9]   7–105

---

[1] *per* McCollom L.J. in *R. v Newtownabbey Magistrates' Court Ex p. Belfast Telegraph Newspapers Ltd* [1997] N.I. 309, a case in which a magistrate had purported to prevent the publication of the name and address of a defendant charged with indecent assault. There are circumstances where Art.2 of the European Convention would come into play if there was perceived by the court to be a real threat to life: *Venables and Thompson v News Group Newspapers Ltd* [2001] Fam. 430; *X (A Woman Formerly Known As Mary Bell) v O'Brien* [2003] EWHC 1101 (QB), [2003] 2 F.C.R. 686; *Carr (Maxine) v News Group Newspapers Ltd* [2005] EWHC 971 (QB).
[2] *R. v Legal Aid Board Ex p. Kaim Todner* [1998] 3 All E.R. 541, where Lord Woolf M.R. rehearsed the considerations of public policy which have traditionally required the opportunity of scrutiny of judicial proceedings by the public.
[3] [1991] 2 Q.B. 103. The decision has been followed in *Re D (Protection of Party Anonymity)* (1997–98) 1 C.C.L. Rep.1909, (1999) 45 B.M.L.R. 191 and *R. v J* [2003] EWCA Crim 3268.
[4] *per* Lord Donaldson M.R. at 107.
[5] [1988] 1 Q.B. 553.
[6] *Scott v Scott* [1913] A.C. at 446.
[7] *R. v CICB Ex p. A* [1992] C.O.D. 379.
[8] Cm. 1102 (1990), para.10.13.
[9] See the Sexual Offences (Amendment) Act 1992, considered at paras 8–18 *et seq*. The protection afforded by that Act has been extended by the Sexual Offences Act 2003.

7–106 Moreover, in each of these two cases it might have been possible to argue, in the context of Art.10(2) of the European Convention on Human Rights, that the restriction was necessary "for the protection of health", at least in the context of psychological trauma. "Mental health must also be regarded as a crucial part of private life associated with the aspect of moral integrity".[10] It is clear, however, that this has not so far been recognised expressly in any English case as being in itself a justification for reporting restrictions. It has been stated that the power *cannot* be used simply to protect privacy or avoid embarrassment.[11] Latham J. in *Castelli* was quite positive in his conclusion that a mere desire to protect privacy could not be a sufficient justification as the law then stood for making an order. Yet anonymity would apparently be consistent with Art.6 of the Convention, which contemplates "protection of the private life" as a justification for such restrictions. Indeed, is now recognised that Art.8 is devoted to the protection of the privacy of individual citizens which includes "gender identification, name and sexual orientation and sexual life . . . as important elements of the personal sphere protected by [that article]".[12]

7–107 The European Court of Human Rights in *Z v Finland*[13] has held that the protection of personal data, not least medical data, is of fundamental importance to a person's enjoyment of his or her right to respect for private and family life as guaranteed by Art.8. "Respecting the confidentiality of health data is a vital principle in the legal systems of all the Contracting Parties to the Convention. It is crucial not only to respect the sense of privacy of a patient but also to preserve his or her confidence in the medical profession and in the health services in general". It is therefore necessary for domestic law to afford appropriate safeguards to prevent any communication or disclosure of health data in so far as it would be inconsistent with such guarantees. A balance has to be struck having regard to the nature and seriousness of the interests at stake and the gravity of the interference.[14] The court will always take such considerations into account but proportionality is clearly important, and matters of privacy may be outweighed by factors such as the interest of the public in the investigation and prosecution of crime and/or in the publicity of court proceedings.[15]

7–108 Article 6 of the European Convention acknowledges that it may be appropriate in certain circumstances for the press to be excluded from all or part of a trial where the "protection of the private life of the parties" so requires. It would clearly be less restrictive of press freedom to limit the publication of certain specific facts than to exclude journalists from the hearing altogether. It may be, therefore, that there would be nothing in the European Convention to prevent the United Kingdom Parliament, if it so chose within its "margin of appreciation",[16] from legislating to prevent publicity about such matters as the defendant's private

---

[10] *Bensaid v UK* (2001) 33 E.H.R.R. 10 at [47].
[11] *Birmingham Post and Mail Ltd v Birmingham City Council* (1994) 17 B.M.L.R. 116.
[12] *Bensaid v UK* at [47].
[13] (1998) 25 E.H.R.R. 371 at [95].
[14] As acknowledged by Munby J. in *Clibbery v Allan* [2001] 2 F.L.R. 819 at [133]–[141], upheld by the Court of Appeal at [2002] EWCA Civ 45, [2002] Fam. 261.
[15] See (1998) 25 E.H.R.R. 371 at [97]–[99].
[16] See paras 2–168 *et seq.*

address, which arose in *R. v Evesham Justices Ex p. McDonagh*,[17] or the personal medical details protected by the Court of Appeal in *H v Ministry of Defence*.[18] There would be no doubt an outcry from the press if any such attempt were made, but it would be difficult for such protesters to pray in aid the terms of Art.10 of the European Convention in the light of these countervailing policy considerations identified in Arts 6 and 8. Indeed, since the decision of the House of Lords in *Re S (FC) (A Child)*[19] it has become clear that there may be occasions when a balancing exercise between Art.8 rights of privacy and media rights under Art.10 *could* lead to a restriction upon canvassing personal information in open court. It would be the duty of the court to address any such application on its merits in the light of the facts of the particular case. What does seem clear, however, is that if a restriction is thought desirable information should not be revealed in open court; once that happens further publication cannot easily be restricted by an order.[20] The increasing recognition accorded to rights of privacy and the need to protect the integrity of the individual has resulted in further statutory protection for vulnerable witnesses.[21]

III. POSTPONEMENT ORDERS UNDER SECTION 4(2) OF THE 1981 ACT

A. Postponing publication: the common law background[22]

Where the court[23] sits in public it has certain powers by statute to postpone media reporting of part or all of the proceedings. It was for a long time also thought that

---

[17] [1988] 1 Q.B. 553.
[18] [1991] 2 Q.B. 103.
[19] [2004] UKHL 47, [2005] 1 A.C. 593 at [18].
[20] See Beatson J. in *R. (on the application of Mersey Care Trust) v Mental Health Review Tribunal* [2004] EWHC 1749 (Admin), [2005] 1 W.L.R. 2469, [2005] 2 All E.R. 820 discussed at para.7–77, n.46 above.
[21] See below paras 8–74 *et seq*.
[22] Michael Beloff Q.C., "Fair Trial—Free Press? Reporting Restrictions in Law and Practice" [1992] P.L. 92; C. Walker, I. Cram and D. Brogarth, "The reporting of Crown Court proceedings and the Contempt of Court Act 1981" (1992) 55 M.L.R. 647.
[23] "Court" is defined by s.19 of the Act as including any tribunal or body exercising the judicial power of the state. The phrase would not embrace a professional disciplinary body, such as the General Medical Council: *GMC v BBC* [1998] 3 All E.R. 426, CA. It has been held, however, to include an industrial (now "employment") tribunal: *Peach Grey & Co (A Firm) v Sommers* [1995] I.C.R. 549, [1995] 2 All E.R. 513; and also a Mental Health Review Tribunal: *P v Liverpool Daily Post and Echo Newspapers plc* [1991] 2 A.C. 370, HL. See also *R. (on the application of Mersey Care Trust) v Mental Health Review Tribunal* [2004] EWHC 1749 (Admin), [2005] 1 W.L.R. 2469, [2005] 2 All E.R. 820. It would thus appear at first sight that such tribunals, where the necessary conditions are fulfilled, would have the power to make a postponement order under s.4(2), and it was so suggested by A. Nicol and H. Rogers, *Media and Entertainment Law Yearbook* (1996) at 369. Yet there are specific powers granted to such tribunals, for example under the Employment Tribunals (Constitution and Rules of Procedure) Regulations 2004, SI 2004/1861. The general rule under the Employment Tribunal Rules of Procedure is that proceedings are to be in public: Sch.1, r.26(3). But there is a limited power to conduct hearings in private under Sch.1, r.16. The Employment Tribunals Act 1996 makes specific provision for the regulation of reporting in cases involving "sexual misconduct" (s.11) and in "disability cases" (s.12). It may perhaps be inferred from this that there is no more general power to prohibit publication. Furthermore, because it is a creature of statute, it has no inherent power; see *Secretary of State for Employment v Mann* [1996] I.C.R. 197 at 204F; *A v B Ex p. News Group Newspapers Ltd* [1998] I.C.R. 55. See also *R. v Southampton Industrial Tribunal Ex p. INS News Group Ltd and Express Newspapers plc* [1995] I.R.L.R. 247. This suggests

there was an inherent or residual power at common law to postpone publication. This belief was largely based on *R. v Clement*.[24] This case was however considered in *Independent Publishing Company Ltd v Att-Gen of Trinidad and Tobago*,[25] where it was held no longer to afford a sufficiently sure foundation to support the existence of an inherent power to impose reporting restrictions on matters mentioned in open court. In *R. v Clement*, where a number of closely related trials were pending (regarded by the Privy Council in retrospect as being one set of proceedings), the trial judge took the view that the publication of proceedings in one trial might prejudice the subsequent trials. He accordingly ordered that there should be no publication of the proceedings until all the trials were completed. Clement breached that order and was punished for contempt, for having acted contrary to the order of the court and to the obstruction of public justice. The jurisdiction to order the postponement was explained by Holroyd J., one of the King's Bench judges who heard the appeal, on the basis that it was within the court's inherent powers to regulate its own proceedings.[26] This would be a difficult argument to sustain nowadays, not least in the light of the principles of the European Convention, since the ability to restrict the freedom of communication of journalists, and others who are not parties, clearly goes beyond what is necessary to regulate the conduct of the proceedings themselves.[27]

7–110   Nevertheless, a similar course of action was adopted by Waller J. in the trial in Leeds of the architect Poulson,[28] where there were to be sequential corruption trials. On this occasion, the perceived problem was that Poulson had given evidence about his links with another person in respect of whom proceedings were imminent. Waller J. therefore made it clear that those allegations should not be published in the meantime because "things have been said here which might be highly prejudicial to that trial".[29] The ruling caused consternation among the press at the time, and subsequently representations were made to the Phillimore Committee as to the unsatisfactory position created. Their consideration of this case reinforced the Committee's view that "fair and accurate reporting of

---

that if there is specific provision, the tribunal cannot resort to s.4(2). In *Associated Newspapers Ltd v London (North) Industrial Tribunal* [1998] I.C.R. 1212, Keene J. stated that, having regard to the principle of the freedom of the press to report court and tribunal hearings fully and contemporaneously, the words permitting the making of restricted reporting orders should be interpreted narrowly.

[24] (1821) 4 B. & Ald. 218, 106 E.R. 918. Abbot C.J. ordered that press reports of the trial of one Thistlethwaite, who was accused with others of high treason following the Cato Street conspiracy, should be postponed until the conclusion of proceedings of against charged with the same offence. Apparently, the thinking was that witnesses in the subsequent proceedings might be tempted to adjust their evidence in the light of the Thistlethwaite coverage.

[25] [2004] UKPC 26, [2005] 1 A.C. 190.

[26] (1821) 4 B. & Ald. 218 at 232–3, 106 E.R. 918 at 923.

[27] *Hodgson v Imperial Tobacco Ltd* [1998] 1 W.L.R. 1056 at 1072A–B, 1073B, 2 All E.R. 673 at 687d–e, 688f–g.

[28] *The Times*, January 4, 1974 (unreported). There were two articles published in the newspaper on this date; the first, "Judge's statements cause confusion", at p.3 by Marcel Berlins, and a leader, at p.13, "Courts in Contempt of Each Other". This cited the robust approach of Lawton J. in *R. v Kray* (1969) 53 Cr.App.R. 412, para.2–86, and also that of Jordan C.J. in *Ex p. Bread Manufacturers Ltd, Re Truth and Sportsman Ltd* (1937) 37 S.R. (N.S.W.) 242. See also the editorial in [1974] Crim. L.R. 141.

[29] *The Times*, January 4, 1974, p.3.

proceedings in open court should in no circumstances be liable to be treated as a contempt".[30] In the light of *Independent Publishing Co Ltd v Att-Gen of Trinidad and Tobago*,[31] it now appears clear that the trial judge did not have power to make the order in any event.

B. Section 4(2): Reporting restrictions

The court's power to order postponement of the reporting of a particular case is now to be regarded as confined by s.4(2) of the 1981 Act. Open justice and freedom of the press are, Lord Denning observed in *R. v Horsham Justices Ex p. Farquharson*,[32] two fundamental legal principles. Nevertheless, there may be occasions when it is necessary[33] for the interests of justice to prevail, in the sense that reporting (even fair and accurate reporting) of legal proceedings can give rise to an unacceptable risk of prejudice. Parliament has therefore given the courts the power to postpone the reporting of their proceedings. It was observed by ministers at the Standing Committee stage of the Contempt of Court Bill's progress through Parliament that this provision was required for the codification of common law powers.[34] Nonetheless it clearly was intended to go beyond any powers recognised in the decided cases, although no attempt was made to define the precise range of circumstances in which the power might be exercised.[35]

7–111

The relevant provisions of s.4[36] of the Contempt of Court Act are couched in the following terms:

7–112

"(1) Subject to this section a person is not guilty of contempt of court under the strict liability rule in respect of a fair and accurate report of legal proceedings held in public, published contemporaneously and in good faith.

(2) In any such proceedings the court may, where it appears to be necessary for avoiding a substantial risk of prejudice to the administration of justice in those proceedings, or in any other proceedings pending or imminent,[37] order that the publication of any report of the proceedings, or any part of the proceedings, be postponed for such period as the court thinks necessary for that purpose.

(2A) Where in proceedings for any offence which is an administration of justice offence for the purposes of section 54 of the Criminal Procedure and Investigations Act 1996 (acquittal tainted by an administration of justice offence) it appears to the court that there is a possibility that (by virtue of that section) proceedings may be taken against a person for an offence of which he has been acquitted, subsection (2) of this section shall apply as if those proceedings were pending or imminent.[38]

---

[30] para.135.
[31] [2004] UKPC 26, [2005] 1 A.C. 190.
[32] *R. v Horsham Justices Ex p. Farquharson* [1982] Q.B. 762 at 793B–794G, 759B–C. See also *Att-Gen v Guardian Newspapers Ltd (No.2)* [1990] 1 A.C. 109 at 183E–G, Sir John Donaldson M.R., and *Ex p. Central Television plc* [1991] 1 W.L.R. 4, 8E, Lord Lane C.J.
[33] See the discussion on the use of the word "necessary" at para.7–185 and at paras 7–198 *et seq.*
[34] See H.C. Debs, Standing Cttee. A, (1980–81), col. 173, May 14, 1981 (Sir N. Fairbairn, Q.C., Sol-Gen for Scotland).
[35] *ibid.*, cols. 172–3.
[36] For a consideration of s.4(1), see para.4–265.
[37] For cases on the meaning of "imminent" see paras 5–67 *et seq.*
[38] Inserted by Criminal Procedure and Investigations Act 1996, s.57(3).

7-112 CHAPTER 7—COURT REPORTING I: RESTRICTIONS UNDER 1981 ACT

(3) For the purposes of subsection (1) of this section [and of section 3 of the Law of Libel Amendment Act 1888 (privilege)][39] a report of proceedings shall be treated as published contemporaneously—

(a) in the case of a report of which publication is postponed pursuant to an order under subsection (2) of this section, if published as soon as practicable after that order expires;
(b) in the case of a report of committal proceedings of which publication is permitted by virtue only of subsection (3) of section 8 of the Magistrates' Courts Act 1980,[40] if published as soon as practicable after publication is so permitted.[41]
[(b) in the case of a report of allocation or sending proceedings of which publication is permitted by virtue only of subsection (6) of section 52A of the Crime and Disorder Act 1998 ("the 1998 Act"), if published as soon as practicable after publication is so permitted;
(c) in the case of a report of an application of which publication is permitted by virtue only of subparagraph (5) or (7) of paragraph 3 of Schedule 3 to the 1998 Act, if published as soon as practicable after publication is so permitted]."[42]

C. The limitations of the section 4(2) power

7-113 The power given under s.4(2) is for the purpose of protecting the administration of justice in relation to particular proceedings; it does not give power to make an order restricting publication for the purpose of protecting the administration of justice *in general*. Where a court wishes to protect the anonymity of persons who have already given evidence (for example, in the case of blackmail victims or informants), resort should be had to the common law powers preserved under s.11 of the Act.[43]

7-114 It is to be noted that a magistrates' court can take into account possible prejudice not only to its own proceedings but also to other proceedings, for example, related proceedings due to take place in the Crown Court. It can also fix a time limit for the reporting of its own proceedings by reference to the anticipated conclusion of such other proceedings. What it cannot do is to seek to impose any restriction wider than in respect of the reporting of proceedings taking place in its own court,[44] such as, for example, the reporting of any subsequent Crown Court proceedings.[45]

---

[39] The words in square brackets were deleted by the Defamation Act 1996, Sch.2, which also repealed s.3 of the Law of Libel Amendment Act 1888 itself.
[40] The existing forms of transfer proceedings under the Criminal Justice Acts 1987 (serious fraud) and 1991 (cases involving children) continue for the time being, but the relevant provisions have been prospectively repealed and replaced by the Criminal Justice Act 2003, s.332, Sch.37, Pt 4. The relevant reporting restrictions are considered in ch.8.
[41] The amendments that were to be inserted by the Criminal Justice and Public Order Act 1994, s.44, Sch.4, Pt II, para.50 were never brought into effect. See generally Anthony Edwards, "(2) The Procedural Aspects" [1997] Crim. L.R. 321, at 322–5.
[42] Para.(b) of subsection 3 is to be substituted by subsequent paras (b) and (c), by the Criminal Justice Act 2003, s.41, Sch.3, Pt 2, para.53, from a date to be appointed.
[43] See the discussion of the common law powers at paras 7–95 *et seq.*
[44] *R. v Rhuddlan Justices Ex p. HTV Ltd* [1986] Crim. L.R. 329; *Ex p. Central Television plc* [1991] 1 W.L.R. 4, [1991] 1 All E.R. 347.
[45] See, *e.g. Horsham Justices Ex p. Farquharson* [1982] Q.B. 762 at 797, 807.

POSTPONEMENT ORDERS UNDER SECTION 4(2) OF THE 1981 ACT   7–117

D. Teething problems

There was a general tendency shortly after the Act came into effect, both on the part of Crown Court judges and magistrates, to rely upon s.4(2) more frequently than was intended, and for purposes going beyond the restricted language of the statute.[46] Indeed, for a time, it appeared that the provision was being used to *increase* the restraints upon press reporting rather than to confine them, as intended,[47] to situations of necessity. It is to be remembered that one of the spurs to the enactment of the 1981 Act was the need to comply with the requirements of the European Convention and in particular the test of "necessity" contained in Art.10(2), by reference to which any restrictions on freedom of expression have to be justified. Not only were orders being made in excess of jurisdiction, but even within the scope of the jurisdiction there was a tendency to make orders too freely and without sufficient regard to this test.   7–115

R. v Rhuddlan Justices Ex p. HTV Ltd[48] is an example of the misuse of the power. A television camera crew filmed the arrest of a man for drug offences, which was to be shown as part of a programme about drug trafficking. He pleaded guilty. His solicitor having heard of the programme that was planned obtained an order, purportedly made under s.4(2), restraining use of the film. The Divisional Court held that the magistrates had no jurisdiction to make the order. Similarly, in *Ex p. Central Independent Television plc*,[49] where a trial judge made an order prohibiting the reporting of the trial by radio or television because in the judge's view the jury ought to be free to watch television or listen to the radio without the possibility of being prejudiced by media reports. Three television and radio companies were able to take advantage of the provisions of s.159 of the Criminal Justice Act 1988, and successfully appealed the order on the ground that there was no substantial risk of prejudice to the administration of justice.   7–116

As late as June 2000, the power was still being used from time to time in circumstances that appeared to fall outside the statutory wording. In *R. v Duckenfield and Murray*,[50] some former police officers were being tried in Leeds for manslaughter in connection with the Hillsborough Stadium football disaster. With express reference to s.4(2), the judge ordered that there was to be no publication, subject to limited exceptions, of any historical film, photographs or   7–117

---

[46] I. Cram, "Section 4(2) Postponement Orders: Media Reports of Court Proceedings under the Contempt of Court Act 1981" in *The Yearbook of Media and Entertainment Law* (1996), p.111; C. Walker, I. Cram, D. Brogarth, "The reporting of Crown Court proceedings and the Contempt of Court Act 1981" (1992) 55 M.L.R. 647–6. D. Brogarth and C. Walker, "Court Reporting and Open Justice" (1988) 138 New Law Jo. 909.
[47] Lord Hailsham L.C. referred to the Bill in Parliament on several occasions as being a "liberalising Bill"; see *Hansard*, H.L., Vol. 415, (5th series), cols. 659–60. See also Lord Denning M.R. in *R. v Horsham Justices Ex p. Farquharson* [1982] Q.B. 762 at 793E: " . . . the statute is not a measure for restricting the freedom of the press. It is a measure for liberating it." And see Lloyd L.J. in *Att-Gen v Newspaper Publishing plc* [1988] Ch. 333 at 382D–F, who said that the Act was intended to effect a "permanent shift in the balance of public interest away from the protection of the administration of justice and in favour of freedom of speech".
[48] [1986] Crim. L.R. 329.
[49] [1991] 1 W.L.R. 4, [1991] 1 All E.R. 347.
[50] Case T991569. The facts of the case may be found set out in [2000] 1 W.L.R. 55.

videos relating to the Hillsborough disaster or to memorials erected in memory of the deceased. The order was to remain in force until the jury returned its verdicts or until further order. Nevertheless, provision was made for any member of the media to make an application to the judge for an exception to be made should the need arise.

7–118 Until an opportunity to appeal (conditional upon leave) was accorded in 1988,[51] there was no remedy in respect of the Crown Court orders, and there is still no remedy in respect of magistrates apart from judicial review. Indeed, until the decision in *Felixstowe Justices Ex p. Leigh*,[52] it was not entirely clear that journalists would have *locus standi* for the purpose of bringing proceedings for judicial review. Otherwise, journalists or broadcasters would have no choice but to obey such orders, even though made without jurisdiction and outside the scope of what Parliament intended, because disobeying a court order is never an option.[53] Until set aside or appealed, anyone knowing of the terms of such an order is likely to be held in contempt in so far as he or she acts inconsistently with it.[54]

E. Subsequent calls for restraint

7–119 In the years after the Act came into effect, courts were urged to exercise restraint in the use of this power, not least because of its implications for freedom of communication and the requirements of open justice. Gradually the climate has changed. In *R. v Bow Street Magistrates' Court Ex p. Mirror Group Newspapers Ltd*[55] the Divisional Court (Nolan L.J. and Auld J.) quashed a stipendiary magistrate's s.4(2) order forbidding the press to publish the reasons why he had stayed, as an abuse of process, the committal proceedings of four policemen charged with conspiracy to pervert the course of justice. It was understood that the Director of Public Prosecutions intended to apply for judicial review of the magistrate's refusal to commit the accused for trial, and that this was the real reason why the jurisdiction had been invoked. It was explained that:

> "The parties agreed that the purpose of the order was . . . to prevent prejudice to the administration of justice in the Divisional Court . . . Where was the prejudice to the administration of justice if, between the hearing of the committal proceedings and the hearing of the Director of Public Prosecutions' application for judicial review, publicity was given to the magistrate's reasons for ordering a stay? . . . In any event, it could not

---

[51] By Criminal Justice Act 1988, s.159, discussed at paras 7–258 *et seq.*
[52] [1987] Q.B. 582.
[53] *R. v Highbury Corner Magistrates' Court Ex p. O'Donoghue* (1997) 161 J.P. 217.
[54] *Att-Gen v Guardian Newspapers Ltd (No.3)* [1992] 1 W.L.R. 874 at 884H–885A, [1992] 3 All E.R. 38 at 48e–f, Brooke J.; *DPP v Channel 4 Television Co Ltd* [1993] 2 All E.R. 517. But see para.9–224 for what appears to be the one exception, namely that it appears that a journalist who does not disclose sources in spite of being ordered to do so may ultimately be held *not* to be in contempt of court if the court determining that issue comes to the conclusion that the original order to disclose was made without jurisdiction or failed to meet the strict test of necessity as construed in *Goodwin v UK* (1996) 22 E.H.R.R. 123, and in *Chief Constable of Leicestershire v Garavelli* [1997] E.M.L.R. 543.
[55] [1992] C.O.D. 15. See also [1992] 1 W.L.R. 412, 2 All E.R. 638 (where the court ordered the payment of costs from central funds, albeit subsequently overruled by the House of Lords in *Holden v CPS (No.2)* [1994] 1 A.C. 22).

be said that the order was 'necessary', for the purpose defined in it or that the risk of prejudice from it was 'substantial' as required by section 4(2) of the Act."

In *R. v Beaconsfield Justices Ex p. Westminster Press Ltd*,[56] Bell J. granted an application for judicial review of the magistrates' decision that there should be no report of committal proceedings until the trial commenced. "As a matter of general policy justices were to be slow to make orders restricting reporting which were additional to those already in force under section 8 of the 1980 Act in relation to committal."[57] He recognised that there might be reason to make an order in some cases where there had been potentially prejudicial reporting close in time to the committal proceedings, but he held that this was not appropriate where there had been a lapse of four months since any reporting of a questionable kind.

In April 1999 counsel in *Ex p. News Group Newspapers*[58] drew the attention of the Court of Appeal to the fact that orders were being made inappropriately in some parts of the country. The appeal was said by the Lord Chief Justice to have served the valuable purpose of drawing attention to "a serious problem", and he urged the necessity of giving very serious consideration to whether any such order should be made.

It was emphasised by the Lord Chief Justice that the matter of costs was always discretionary. It should not be thought that orders would *never* be made against the Crown; for example, if an order restraining publication had been applied for, and granted, where it was inappropriate to do so. Nevertheless, where such an order was made, an order for costs would not automatically follow merely because it was subsequently held to be wrong. The court would presumably need to address the question of whether counsel for the Crown had discharged the duty of giving assistance to the court on the proper principles to be applied on applications made under s.4(2) of the Act.

F. The principal issues raised by section 4(2) of the Act identified

The teething problems that arose over the implementation of s.4(2) and its apparent misuse over the years tend to show that neither Parliament's intentions nor the policy concerns underlying the section were made clear. It is possible to identify a number of questions to which the section gives rise, although by no means as easy in every case to provide the answer.

We propose to list the issues, and then to consider them in the light of such guidance as may be derived from the authorities:

(1) The relationship of the section to the existing common law powers and to the strict liability rule under the Act.

(2) Is a breach of a s.4(2) order *ipso facto* a contempt?

---

[56] [1994] T.L.R. 350.
[57] s.8 of the Magistrates' Courts Act 1980, which is prospectively repealed, is considered in ch.8.
[58] [2002] E.M.L.R. 160.

7-124   (3) What are the "proceedings" contemplated in the section?

(4) What types of publication may be postponed?

(5) When are proceedings "pending or imminent'?

(6) For how long may a publication be postponed?

(7) Are journalists restricted where no s.4(2) order is made?

(8) The effect of the 1983 Practice Direction.[59]

(9) What tests should a court apply before making an order?

(10) What, if any, is the required mental element in the case of a breach?

(11) Who has the power to act in relation to an alleged breach?

(12) Is a journalist alleged to be in breach entitled to challenge the validity of the order itself?

(13) The recognition of journalists' *locus standi* in relation to such orders.

(14) Appeals against s.4(2) orders: the 1988 Act, s.159.

(15) Appeals against "spent orders".

(16) Procedure on s.159 appeals.

(17) Provision for costs on s.159 appeals.

7-125   Some of these matters were addressed by the Court of Appeal in the important early case of *R. v Horsham Justices Ex p. Farquharson*,[60] although it did not eliminate all the uncertainties. Before turning to these specific issues *seriatim*, it is necessary to set out the background to that case.

G. The factual background to the *Horsham Justices* case

7-126   Four men were charged with offences of exporting, or attempting to export, revolvers, pistols and ammunition with intent to evade the prohibition upon them, contrary to s.56(2) of the Customs and Excise Act 1952. In June 1981 the matter was before the magistrates at Horsham as examining justices under the "old style" committal procedure. At that stage, the Contempt of Court Act 1981 had not come into force. On June 23, one of the four asked for the reporting restrictions to be lifted under s.8(2) of the Magistrates' Courts Act 1980, and this the magistrates were obliged to grant[61] because it was not until October 2, 1981 that the provisions of the Criminal Justice (Amendment) Act 1981 came into effect. This conferred upon examining justices the discretion to refuse to lift reporting restrictions, where any co-accused objected and the justices did not regard it as being in the interests of justice to do so. Arrangements were duly

---

[59] See now the Consolidated Criminal Practice Direction [2002] 1 W.L.R.2870 (as amended March 22, 2005), for the latest version of which see www.courtservice.gov.uk/docs/cpd/consol_criminal_pd_220305.doc.
[60] [1982] Q.B. 762.
[61] See *Russell Ex p. Beaverbrook Newspapers Ltd* [1969] 1 Q.B. 342.

made for a full hearing to be started on October 16 (after both of the new statutes had come into effect).

By that time the accused who had previously requested restrictions to be lifted had changed his mind, and on the first day of the resumed hearing an application was made under s.4(2) of the Contempt of Court Act that there should be no reporting, because the lawyers anticipated that some of the details to be aired would be of a highly prejudicial nature and that reports would be likely to inflame readers' feelings because of the political and social implications, in particular those relating to political assassination. In fact, these matters were not relevant to the pending charges. The application was granted and an order made in blanket terms, which prohibited reporting of any part of the proceedings until the commencement of any trial hearing.

An order in such wide terms obviously had the effect of preventing the reporting even of the matters then permitted under s.8 of the Magistrates' Courts Act 1980. It was plainly felt by the justices that the Contempt of Court Act had been intended by Parliament to give greater powers of restriction over press reports than had obtained previously.[62] The order provoked a leading article in a local newspaper which expressed anxiety about being "plunged into a frightening world of justice administered behind a lock and key." The journalists concerned then sought to challenge the justices' order in the Divisional Court by way of judicial review, which was the only avenue then open to them. On November 13, that court (Forbes and Glidewell JJ.) quashed the order and remitted the matter to the justices for them to consider, in the light of its judgment, whether an order should be made postponing publication of all or only a part of the committal proceedings. An appeal to the Court of Appeal was dismissed, and it was confirmed that while the justices had jurisdiction to make an order under s.4(2) they had been wrong to make a blanket order in such wide terms. The matter was duly remitted. Guidance was given on a number of issues, although there were some instances where the members of the court differed in their conclusions.

H. The relationship of section 4(2) to the existing common law powers, and to the strict liability rule

In *Horsham Justices Ex p. Farquharson*, Lord Denning M.R. took the view that the s.4(2) power applied only to a very limited type of case, and that the statute was not a measure for restricting the press but one for liberating it.[63] He indicated that no court was given any greater power to restrict press reports than had been

---

[62] Although in Parliament, Lord Hailsham L.C. had described the measure as a "liberalising Bill": *Hansard*, H.L., Vol. 425, (5th series) cols. 659–60. It seems that the policy underlying s.8 of the 1980 Act was to protect defendants at the beginning of proceedings likely to lead to a full trial; whereas s.4(2) was intended to protect a wider category of people including, for example, witnesses and defendants in other proceedings.
[63] Cp. Lloyd L.J. in *Att-Gen v Newspaper Publishing plc* [1988] Ch. 333 at 382E. "... the statutory purpose behind the Contempt of Court Act 1981 was to effect a permanent shift in the balance of public interest away from the protection of the administration of justice and in favour of freedom of speech".

7-129 available at common law. Moreover, it would now be necessary for a court to give an express direction rather than leave the press to infer a restriction from the circumstances, whereas in the past judges had been content often to regard it as self-evident that certain material should not be published (for example material relating to discussions in the absence of the jury).[64] In this respect, Ackner L.J. was in agreement.[65]

7-130 The situations that Lord Denning had in mind[66] (although he left open the possibility that there might be others) were:

(a) where it is necessary to postpone publication for the furthering of justice in pending or imminent proceedings as, for example, in *R. v Clement*,[67] where several defendants were charged with high treason but were to be tried successively; or

(b) a "trial within a trial", where there should be no premature publication of proceedings which take place in the absence of the jury;

(c) the "pseudonym" cases, where a judge permits anonymity for, *e.g.* a blackmail victim[68]; and

(d) cases in which two people are jointly indicted, but to be tried separately; or where there is "another case going on at the same time, such as happened in 1974 in *R. v Poulson*",[69] and the judge directs that certain items of evidence should temporarily not be published because of the risk of causing prejudice to other proceedings.

7-131 In taking such a restrictive view of s.4(2), despite the wide discretion which its express terms would appear to bestow, Lord Denning based himself[70] to a large degree upon s.6(b) of the same statute, which provides as follows:

"Nothing in the foregoing provisions of this Act . . . (b) implies that any publication is punishable as contempt of court under that rule, which would not be so punishable apart from those provisions."

---

[64] See *R. v Border Television Ex p. Att-Gen* (1978) 68 Cr.App.R. 375.
[65] [1982] Q.B. at 805.
[66] [1982] Q.B. 762 at 791–2.
[67] (1821) 4 B. and Ald. 218, 106 E.R. 918. Lord Denning's observations were disapproved in *Independent Publishing Company Ltd v Att-Gen of Trinidad and Tobago* [2004] UKPC 26, [2005] 1 A.C. 190, and the circumstances of *Clement* were analysed by the Privy Council in terms of their being one set of proceedings. The headnote in the official reports says that *Clement* was "overruled" by the Privy Council, although technically that court has no jurisdiction to overrule English authorities. See also *Scott v Scott* [1913] A.C. 417 at 438, 453.
[68] It might be thought that for this purpose an order under s.11 would be more appropriate, since Lord Denning appears to be contemplating the use of a s.4(2) order to achieve a *permanent* restriction, which is plainly not its purpose: see paras 7–146 *et seq*.
[69] *The Times*, January 4, 1974. (Although Lord Denning refers to January 2, 1974, the discussion of the postponement order is to be found in *The Times* of January 4, at pp.3 and 13). Cp. the decision of Lawton J. in *R. Kray* (1969) 53 Cr.App.R. 412, which *The Times* leader commended as the more robust approach.
[70] [1982] Q.B. 762 at 790–1.

I. Is breach of a section 4(2) order *ipso facto* a contempt?

Did the section create a new class of contempt, so that breach of an order made under the section will always be a contempt? Lord Denning M.R. apparently took the view that it did not.[71] He construed s.6(b) to be of general effect, and to entail that s.4(2) did not create any new form of contempt which had not existed prior to the Act. In this respect, however, the majority (Shaw and Ackner L.JJ.) differed from him.

Ackner L.J.[72] drew attention to the words "under that rule" which appear in s.6(b) and which could only refer to the strict liability rule. In his view the proper construction of s.4(2), notwithstanding the words upon which Lord Denning placed reliance, was that Parliament had intended to create a new head of contempt, separate and distinct from the strict liability rule, whereby a journalist would be guilty of contempt in reporting proceedings which had been made the subject of a postponement order. Thus, it would seem that a person who publishes material in breach of such an order may be liable *ipso facto* for contempt, even if that which he publishes would not, when objectively judged, give rise to a substantial risk of serious prejudice. Judges are permitted an element of subjective judgment under s.4(2), and where their orders are breached, there is provided the sanction of committal for contempt *irrespective of the strict liability rule*.[73]

This analysis is supported, perhaps, by the omission of the word "serious" from s.4(2), so that a judge has a discretion to postpone publication upon the apprehension of a risk, merely, of "prejudice". It will be recalled that, by contrast, s.2(2), in defining the strict liability rule, refers to a "substantial risk that the course of justice in the proceedings in question will be *seriously* impeded or prejudiced".

It is true, in contradistinction to s.8 of the Contempt of Court Act 1981 (dealing with disclosure of the deliberations of a jury), that s.4(2) does not specifically provide that breach of an order made under the section is a "contempt".[74] Nevertheless, since a s.4(2) order can only be made for the purpose of protecting the administration of justice, it is difficult to see how a

---

[71] [1982] 1 Q.B. 762 at 790–1.
[72] [1982] Q.B. 762 at 804–5.
[73] This approach is to be contrasted with that advocated some years earlier by the then Editor of the Criminal Law Review, following Waller J.'s order restricting press coverage of the Poulson trial, to the effect that "first no contempt action should be permitted in respect of fair and accurate reports of proceedings in open court unless the judge's warning has been given, and secondly it should not be a contempt in itself to ignore the judge's warning. It should be so only where, in addition, prejudice is likely to be caused in the other proceedings": [1974] Crim. L.R. 141 at 143.
[74] See also, *e.g.* Criminal Justice and Public Order Act 1996, ss.17 and 18; Financial Services Act 1986, s.178; County Courts Act 1984, s.118. These also provide for certain conduct to be treated as contempt. See also the discussion of s.12 of the Administration Act 1960, which was considered in *P v Liverpool Daily Post and Echo Newspapers plc* [1991] 2 A.C. 370, discussed in ch.8.

publication of prohibited material with knowledge of such an order could be other than a contempt.[75]

7-136 There is now little room for doubt on the matter, in the light of the words of Brooke J. in *Att-Gen v Guardian Newspapers Ltd (No.3)*[76] (although in that case the Attorney was not in fact relying upon a breach of a s.4(2) order, but rather upon strict liability):

> "If such an order is made, and if its scope is clear, then it is the duty of the press to comply with it. Anyone who is dissatisfied with the provisions of such an order may now appeal against it to the Court of Appeal, with the leave of that Court, pursuant to section 159 of the Criminal Justice Act 1988, but unless and until it is varied or set aside on appeal, he is liable to be committed for contempt if he acts in breach of its terms."

J. The "proceedings" contemplated under section 4(2)

7-137 The court may make an order during proceedings held in public where it appears to be necessary for avoiding a substantial risk of prejudice to the administration of justice "in those proceedings, or in any other proceedings pending or imminent." In *Horsham Justices Ex p. Farquharson*, the Court of Appeal accepted the construction of Glidewell J. as to the meaning of "those proceedings" rather than that of Forbes J., who had held below[77] that the term was meant to include as one set of proceedings both the committal proceedings and any subsequent Crown Court proceedings. "Those proceedings" can only refer to the proceedings being heard at the relevant time (that is, when the order is sought), while "other proceedings pending or imminent" would certainly have included, so far as examining justices were concerned, any Crown Court proceedings which might subsequently take place.[78] Thus, justices cannot make an order restricting the reporting of Crown Court proceedings.

7-138 Despite the statutory words "in those proceedings ... ", the comment was made by Lord Osborne in the High Court of Justiciary in *HMA v Beggs (No.1)*[79] that the Advocate Depute was unaware of any case in which a s.4(2) order had been made for the purpose of avoiding a risk of prejudice in the very proceedings in which it was made. It had been submitted that it was difficult to see how fair and accurate reporting of those current proceedings could create such a risk; and that it was plain from the opinion in *R. v Galbraith*[80] that the purpose of such an order was to deal with " ... reports of proceedings which were fair and accurate, but which should nonetheless be postponed, not with other material the publication of which might constitute a contempt of court". If inappropriate publicity were to arise in the course of the murder trial itself, this should be dealt

---

[75] Cp. *Att-Gen v Newspaper Publishing plc* [1988] Ch. 333, discussed more fully at paras 6–124 *et seq.*
[76] [1992] 1 W.L.R. 874 at 884H–885A, 3 All E.R. 38 at 49e–f, DC.
[77] [1982] 1 Q.B. at 773B.
[78] Cf. *R. v Parke* [1903] 2 K.B. 432; *R. v Duffy Ex p. Nash* [1960] 2 Q.B. 188 at 195.
[79] 2002 S.L.T. 135, S.C.C.R. 669.
[80] 2001 S.L.T. 465 at 468.

with as a contempt of court. These arguments were accepted and a s.4(2) order refused. It was conceded on behalf of the accused that he had "no problem" with fair and accurate reporting; a concession which Lord Osborne regarded as fatal to the grant of any such order.

Counsel for the National Union of Journalists and Farquharson had contended before the Court of Appeal in *Horsham Justices* that, for so long as the committal proceedings are in progress, a Crown Court trial cannot be categorised as either "pending" or "imminent".[81] His submission was thus to the effect that s.4(2) had no operation in relation to committal proceedings. This was considered by Shaw L.J.[82] to be "fallacious":   7–139

> "The words 'pending or imminent' have been held to include the possible (not necessarily the inevitable) outcome of legal process. This has nothing to do with proceedings being 'active'. That expression is used as a term of art in the Contempt of Court Act 1981 for the purpose of defining the scope and application of the strict liability rule as defined by section 1. The purpose and intent of section 4(2) is wider and different. It is designed to prevent injustice to individuals whose interests might be unduly and unjustifiably threatened or prejudiced by premature publication of matters which could adversely affect their rights or status."

Also, Ackner L.J. pointed out[83] that it had long been established that from the time a person is charged his trial is regarded as "pending", even though he may not yet have been committed.[84] Moreover, proceedings can be regarded as "imminent" even before charging.[85]   7–140

Restricting a report of appellate proceedings

Ex p. The Telegraph Group[86] provides an example of a situation in which the Court of Appeal thought it appropriate to make an order that its own proceedings should not be reported until the conclusion of sequential criminal trials then pending—save for the fact that its order had been made.   7–141

K. What "publications" may be postponed?

The power conferred by s.4(2) is limited to the restriction of *reports* of legal proceedings.[87] In *R. v Rhuddlan Justices Ex p. HTV Ltd*[88] magistrates made an   7–142

---

[81] This concept is discussed elsewhere, see paras 5–67 *et seq.*
[82] [1982] Q.B. at 797. This passage from the judgment of Shaw L.J. was considered in *Galbraith v HMA* 2001 S.L.T. 465, 2000 S.C.C.R. 935 at 940, at paras 11–12. The court noted the uncertainty as to whether it would be permissible to make a postponement order in respect of reporting appellate proceedings, with a view to protecting a possible retrial. Since the court came to the conclusion that it would not have been appropriate to do so even if the power existed, the issue did not need to be decided and was left over for later consideration.
[83] [1982] Q.B. at 807.
[84] *R. v Parke* [1903] 2 K.B. 432; *R. v Duffy Ex p. Nash* [1960] 2 Q.B. 188 at 195.
[85] See, *e.g. Att-Gen v News Group Newspapers plc* [1989] Q.B. 110; *Att-Gen v Sport Newspapers Ltd* [1991] 1 W.L.R. 1194.
[86] [2001] EWCA Crim 1075, [2001] 1 W.L.R. 1983.
[87] For the meaning of "legal proceedings", see s.19 of the 1981 Act, discussed at paras 13–3 *et seq.*
[88] [1986] Crim. L.R. 329.

order purporting to prevent a television company from showing, in a programme about drug trafficking, the arrest of a man for that very offence (to which he subsequently pleaded guilty). The Divisional Court held that the justices had exceeded their powers because the film could in no sense be said to be a report of legal proceedings. If it was suggested that the company had been about to show material that would be prejudicial to a forthcoming trial, the proper procedure was to apply to the High Court for an injunction for the purpose of restraining a strict liability contempt.[89]

L. When are proceedings "pending or imminent" under section 4(2)?

7–143   An order may be made under s.4(2) to protect proceedings which are "imminent". It is questionable whether "imminent" in this context means the same as "imminent" when used in such cases as *Att-Gen v News Group Newspapers plc*[90] and *Att-Gen v Sport Newspapers Ltd*,[91] especially since the draftsman of the 1981 Act would probably not have had that concept in mind. After all, it was widely believed for some years after the Act came into effect that it would no longer be possible to be in contempt of proceedings which were merely "imminent" in the sense contemplated by Salmon L.J. in *R. v Savundranayagan*[92] and described, illuminatingly, by Windeyer J.[93] as giving rise to "contingent contempt". It had been intended to eliminate uncertainties of that kind by instituting the statutory framework for determining when proceedings become "active" for contempt purposes.[94]

7–144   Indeed, Hodgson J. in *Sport Newspapers* would have concluded that the law of contempt was no longer intended to impinge upon proceedings not yet begun (that is to say, "contingent" proceedings), were it not for prior authority to the contrary.[95] At all events, it might have been thought at the time of the enactment that the use of the phrase "any other proceedings" contemplated *actual* proceedings, such as, for example, the proceedings under consideration by Lawton J. in *R. v Kray*,[96] rather than hypothetical or "contingent" ones. It should certainly not be assumed that Parliament intended, by what is effectively a sidewind, to prolong the *Savundra* doctrine.

7–145   Nevertheless, it would now be right to proceed on the basis that the court does have the power to make a s.4(2) order in respect of "imminent proceedings"

---

[89] See para.6–1. It is necessary to approach this matter with some caution in the light of the fact that Lord Bridge in *P v Liverpool Daily Post and Echo Newspapers plc* [1991] 2 A.C. 370 at 425, expressed a wish to reserve his position as to the *locus standi* of individuals to apply for injunctions without reference to the Attorney-General. But see *Peacock v London Weekend Television* (1985) 150 J.P. 71, CA; *Leary v BBC* (unreported) 29 September 1989, CA; *Coe v Central Television plc* [1994] E.M.L.R. 433, all discussed in ch.6.
[90] [1989] Q.B. 110. Considered in ch.5.
[91] [1991] 1 W.L.R. 1194, [1992] 1 All E.R. 503. Considered at para.5–174.
[92] [1968] 1 W.L.R. 1761.
[93] *James v Robinson* (1963) 109 C.L.R. 593 at 618.
[94] Contained in Sch.1 of the 1981 Act; para.4–174.
[95] *Att-Gen v News Group Newspapers plc* [1989] Q.B. 110 (to which Hodgson J. referred in *Sport* [1991] 1 W.L.R. 1194 at 1225F and 1229H [1992] 1 All E.R. 503 at 534c).
[96] (1969) 53 Cr.App.R. 412.

POSTPONEMENT ORDERS UNDER SECTION 4(2) OF THE 1981 ACT 7–148

which are no more than contingent at the time of the order, on the basis that "it is possible very effectually to poison the fountain of justice before it begins to flow".[97] Moreover, this would appear to be the view taken by both Ackner L.J.[98] and Shaw L.J.[99] in *Horsham Justices Ex p. Farquharson*. It would therefore logically follow that a postponement order can be made and yet the contingent proceedings never come about. In such cases, it may be necessary at some stage to apply for the order to be discharged as no longer serving any purpose. It would not be safe to assume, even once it is clear that the proceedings originally in contemplation are not to take place, that the reporting restriction can be ignored.[1]

M. For how long may a publication be postponed?

The section gives a power to postpone publication for such period as the court thinks necessary for the statutory purpose, namely the protection of particular proceedings (whether actual, pending or imminent). The question needs to be addressed whether this power could be exercised in such a way as to achieve an indefinite postponement. The Practice Direction[2] introduced by the Lord Chief Justice shortly after the Act came into effect indicates that an order should state *inter alia* "the time at which it shall cease to have effect, if appropriate". This appears to contemplate that there might be circumstances in which it was inappropriate to fix any time limit at all. 7–146

It is submitted, however, that this cannot have been intended by Parliament. (Nor, obviously, can the language of the Practice Direction affect the construction of the statute itself.) While it is true that sometimes it is necessary to make indefinite orders, with a view to protecting the administration of justice *in general*, for example, in relation to the protection of the identities of victims or witnesses, it is suggested that all of these objectives can be provided for within the terms of s.11 of the Act.[3] The scope of s.4(2) was surely intended to be more limited, and specifically because of the reference to "particular proceedings". If it had been intended to confer a power to postpone indefinitely, the section could simply have said so. 7–147

The time appointed need not be specific as to a particular date; it is regularly fixed by reference to the point when the relevant "other proceedings" are concluded. Thus, as pointed out in the previous section, if an order is made in respect of "contingent" proceedings, and those proceedings do not materialise, 7–148

---

[97] *R. v Parke* [1903] 2 K.B. 432 at 437, Wills J., cited at para.5–78.
[98] [1982] Q.B. at 807C–D.
[99] [1982] Q.B. at 797E.
[1] See, *e.g.* the words of Brooke J. in *Att-Gen v Guardian Newspapers Ltd (No.3)* [1992] 1 W.L.R. 874, [1992] 3 All E.R. 38, cited at para.7–136.
[2] [1982] 1 W.L.R. 1475, 1 All E.R. 64, 76 Cr.App.R. 78. See now [2002] 1 W.L.R. 2870 for the Consolidated Criminal Practice Direction (as amended March 22, 2005), for the latest version of which see *www.courtservice.gov.uk/docs/cpd/consol_criminal_pd_220305.doc*. The relevant section of the direction is set out and discussed at paras 7–153 *et seq.*
[3] See the discussion of s.11 at paras 7–83 *et seq.*

or come to a premature conclusion, it may be necessary to apply for the s.4(2) order to be set aside.

N. Are journalists restrained even where no order is made?

7–149 In *R. v Horsham Justices Ex p. Farquharson*,[4] the Court of Appeal took the view that in the light of the section a person who published matters heard in open court, where the court had power to postpone publication but did not exercise it, would not be in contempt. Section 4(1) of the Act[5] protects fair and accurate reporting, in good faith, of proceedings in open court, but this is expressly in the context of the strict liability rule. That protection is, however, subject to what follows in the section. It would appear that, where a s.4(2) order *is* made, a person who publishes during the period of postponement could not pray in aid the protection provided by s.4(1), on the basis that it was nevertheless a fair and accurate report of proceedings. If he is aware of the order, s.4(1) will not avail him.

7–150 If an order has *not* been made, then the s.4(1) protection might be thought inevitably to prevail, but it may be useful to follow through the consequences of that conclusion a little further. At common law there was an implicit prohibition on the publication of what passed in a "trial within a trial," or of an argument in the absence of the jury on admissibility.[6] It was well understood that what passed between the judge and the advocates should not be published, at least until after the trial. Now, it appears, in the light of the Court of Appeal's decision in *Horsham Justices Ex p. Farquharson*, an express order is required.

7–151 Yet suppose that through oversight or for some other reason no such order is made. Suppose also that information comes to light in the absence of the jury—guilty pleas, or an inadmissible confession, for example—which journalists readily appreciate would be likely to prejudice the jury if they were to find out about it. It may well be, in such circumstances, that the publication of that information would give rise to a substantial risk of serious prejudice, and thus to a *prima facie* contempt under the strict liability rule. It would seem that in principle, provided the publication took place in good faith, the s.4(1) protection would nonetheless prevail.[7] Even though the jury is absent, such proceedings take place "in open court".

7–152 Even if the journalists were conscious of the risk of serious prejudice at the time of publication, it would be difficult to infer any intention on their part to interfere with the administration of justice sufficient to found a common law contempt, since they would presumably (in accordance with the view of the majority in *Horsham Justices*) be entitled to assume that the court, having the power to order a s.4(2) postponement, knew its own business and had decided on

---

[4] [1982] Q.B. 762 at 793, Lord Denning M.R., and 804–5, Ackner L.J.: see paras 7–125 *et seq.* for fuller discussion.
[5] See paras 4–263 *et seq.* for a discussion of the interrelationship between ss.4(1) and 4(2).
[6] *Horsham Justices Ex p. Farquharson* [1982] 1 Q.B. 762 at 792A–B, Lord Denning M.R. Cp. *R. v Border Television Ex p. Att-Gen (note)* (1978) 68 Cr.App.R. 375.
[7] See para.4–265.

good and sufficient grounds to make no such order. This contrasts with the position at common law, since before the Act it had been regarded as self-evident when evidence was given in the absence of the jury, and not repeated in their presence, that it should not be reported so as to reach their attention.[8]

O. The practical implementation of section 4(2) orders

In the light of the consideration of s.4(2) by the Court of Appeal in *R. v Horsham Justices Ex p. Farquharson*, a Practice Direction was promulgated shortly afterwards, which courts are now required to follow. Its successor is now expressed in the following terms[9]:

> "I.3.1 Under section 4(2) of the *Contempt of Court Act 1981*, a court may, where it appears necessary for avoiding a substantial risk of prejudice to the administration of justice in the proceedings before it or in any others pending or imminent, order that publication of any report of the proceedings or part thereof be postponed for such period as the court thinks necessary for that purpose. Section 11 of the Act provides that a court may prohibit the publication of any name or other matter in connection with the proceedings before which (having power to do so) it has allowed to be withheld from the public.
>
> I.3.2 When considering whether to make such an order there is nothing which precludes the court from hearing a representative of the press. Indeed it is likely that the court will wish to do so.
>
> I.3.3 It is necessary to keep a permanent record of such orders for later reference. For this purpose all orders made under section 4(2) must be formulated in precise terms, having regard to the decision of *R. v Horsham Justices Ex p. Farquharson* (76 Cr.App.R. 87), and orders under both sections must be committed to writing either by the judge personally or by the clerk of the court under the judge's directions. An order must state (a) its precise scope, (b) the time at which it shall cease to have effect, if appropriate, and (c) the specific purpose of making the order. Courts will normally give notice to the press in some form that an order has been made under either section of the Act and court staff should be prepared to answer any inquiry about a specific case, but it is, and will remain, the responsibility of those reporting cases, and their editors, to ensure that no breach of any order occurs and the onus rests with them to make inquiry in any case of doubt."

Further guidance was given in *Att-Gen v Guardian Newspapers Ltd (No.3)*[10]:

> "The respondents suggested the risk of being misled would be reduced if the terms of all section 4 orders were faxed by the court to the Press Association, as is apparently the practice at the Central Criminal Court. In this regard, we have been told that the practice of the Press Association is to keep on file any such orders it may receive principally for its own reference purposes, but also to answer newspapers' inquiries

---

[8] *R. v Border Television Ex p. Att-Gen (note)* (1978) 68 Cr.App.R. 375; see also *R. v Horsham Justices Ex p. Farquharson* [1982] 1 Q.B. 762 at 805, Ackner L.J.
[9] [1982] 1 W.L.R. 1475, [1983] 1 All E.R. 64, 76 Cr.App.R. 78. See now [2002] 1 W.L.R. 2870 for the Consolidated Criminal Practice Direction (as amended March 22, 2005), for the latest version of which see www.courtservice.gov.uk/docs/cpd/consol_criminal_pd_220305.doc.
[10] [1992] 1 W.L.R. 874 at 882, Mann L.J.; and at 885, Brooke J.

about them. Adoption of the practice by other courts would have the advantage that a source of information about the precise terms of orders would be available to the press at such times as the late afternoon or early evening when articles are prepared, but court officials are not necessarily available to answer queries.

I can see the good sense of the suggestion. I hope it will be considered by circuit administrators."

7–155   The court noted that it is "desirable that wherever possible an application for such an order in relation to a Crown Court trial should be made in advance of the hearing itself so that everyone, including the press, will know where they stand before the trial starts. If this is done and if anyone is aggrieved with any order the court may make, the Court of Appeal can then accommodate the appeal in an orderly way before the trial starts."[11] The Divisional Court also reminded trial judges of the need to make plain to what extent the terms of any s.4(2) order are themselves permitted to be published.[12]

7–156   It has been held in Scotland that the courts' website would now be regarded as the obvious place for journalists to check, in order to discover if a s.4(2) order has been made.[13] It is now the practice in Scotland for s.4(2) orders to be sent immediately by e-mail to various newspapers and broadcasting organisations and to their agents. The fact that such an order has been made is also published on the Scottish Court Service website.[14]

7–157   Suppose an order is made under s.4(2) on the first day of a long trial and the judge does not reiterate the order on every occasion when the jury retires (and indeed this would be the normal position). A person who then visits the trial without knowing of the order might nonetheless find himself in contempt if he were to report any part of the proceedings which he observed in the absence of the jury. As the Practice Direction makes clear, he has an obligation to check whether such an order has been made at some stage to cover the duration of the trial. The question of the requisite *mens rea* is discussed more generally below.[15]

7–158   Apart from the Practice Direction, further guidance was provided by the Lord Chancellor's Department in Business Item B948.[16] Two illustrations were provided of potential prejudice; namely, where guilty pleas are entered as to some counts of an indictment, with a trial to take place on the remainder, and where a

---

[11] *per* Brooke J. at 885B–C. The position may be contrasted with the former approach adopted in relation to family proceedings. For example in *A v Times Newspapers Ltd* [2002] EWHC 2444 (Fam). Sumner J. explained that there is no duty on the part of CAFCASS, or for that matter on any of the parties, to engage with the media or to notify them of information about hearings involving children since these are almost invariably heard in private. Practice in the Family Division has now changed in that provision is made for notification to the media when an application founded on Convention rights to restrict freedom of expression. See the President's Direction of March 18, 2005, *Applications for Reporting Restriction Orders* and the *Practice Note* of the same title and date issued by the Official Solicitor and the Deputy Director of Legal Services CAFCASS.
[12] [1992] 1 W.L.R. at 882 and 886.
[13] *Galbraith v HMA* 2001 S.L.T. 465, [2000] S.C.C.R. 935.
[14] *BBC, Petrs*, May 2, 2001, High Court of Justiciary, para.4.
[15] See paras 7–204 *et seq.*
[16] L.C.D. No.8/81.

"trial within a trial occurs as to the admissibility of a confession." In 1986 this Business Item was replaced by B1460.[17] This contained fuller guidance and added the further example of potential prejudice to other related proceedings, pending or imminent. It also clearly suggested that most of such orders would be confined to these specified situations. Whether or not these technically remain current, they are not available through the website.

Whether to reveal the existence of a section 4(2) order

A problem which sometimes arises is whether the fact of the existence of the s.4(2) order itself is something which, if it came to the attention of the jury or potential jurors, might create a risk of prejudice. Mann L.J. in *Att-Gen v Guardian Newspapers Ltd (No.3)*[18] expressed doubt as to whether it would ordinarily be appropriate to report the fact that an order had been made on the basis that it might not be covered by the phrase "legal proceedings held in public" in s.4(1) of the 1981 Act. It is perhaps difficult to understand why such an order, if made in public, would not be so covered. Journalists very often hear such applications being made, and indeed are regularly heard as to whether the restriction is appropriate. The matter can be put beyond doubt, however, by the judge spelling out whether and to what extent the making and terms of the order can be published at the time of making it.

In *R. v Hutton*,[19] a s.4(2) order was made banning publication relating to proceedings (concerning charges of deception and obtaining credit whilst an undischarged bankrupt) pending further trials against the defendant. The order was promulgated within the Crown Court building, and was read by a juror, who was thus able to discover that the defendant awaited trial on other matters. The judge was not informed of this fact until after the jury had retired. At that stage, a defence application was made to discharge the jury, but this was resisted by the Crown on the basis, *inter alia*, that the defence case accepted that the defendant was someone who was "not averse to sharp practice", although he had not committed the offences charged. The judge refused to discharge the jury and the defendant appealed.

The appeal was allowed, and it was observed that, had the matter been brought to the judge's attention earlier, it would have been possible for him to make tactful enquiries and, if necessary, direct the jury to ignore such matters as had come to their attention.[20] Unfortunately, however, by the time the judge had given his ruling, the jury had been deliberating for well over an hour. He had accepted the Crown's argument, which was of doubtful validity, to the effect that there would be no prejudice because the fact that there was a forthcoming trial was only what the jury would have expected in the case of such a person.

---

[17] L.C.D. No.5/86.
[18] [1992] 1 W.L.R. 874, [1992] 3 All E.R. 38 at 46b–c.
[19] [1990] Crim. L.R. 875, CACD.
[20] Cp. *R. v Weaver* (1967) 51 Cr.App.R. 77 (the judge is not always obliged to discharge a jury when there has been some passing reference, in the course of a trial, to information about previous convictions).

7–162 It was true that the judge had a discretion as to whether or not to discharge the jury, and if properly exercised the Court of Appeal would not ordinarily interfere. On the facts, however, it seemed that the exercise of his discretion had been vitiated by giving his mind, in the course of argument, to alternative scenarios for avoiding a retrial, such as (i) the appellant's acquittal, which would avoid further argument; and (ii) an appeal to the Court of Appeal if he was convicted. The court came to the conclusion that there was a real possibility that the awareness of further trials might have tipped the balance against the appellant, at least in the absence of any warning from the judge; and the juror in question might well have discussed the matter with his colleagues. (As it happened, a retrial was indeed avoided, but largely because of the time which the appellant had spent in custody both in England and abroad.)

7–163 As court staff became more aware, albeit somewhat slowly, of the need to take care over s.4(2) orders and the need to make them readily available to the public, the procedures for doing so have gradually improved.[21]

P. The tests to be applied before making an order

1. *The nature of the uncertainty*

7–164 In deciding whether to make an order, a judge must consider first whether or not there is likely to be a substantial risk of prejudice to the administration of justice in the event of the material being published.[22] Only if the court is satisfied that there would be such a risk does the jurisdiction arise to make such an order at all. The second question (arguably also a matter going to the jurisdiction to make such an order) is whether or not it is "necessary" to make such an order to avoid the risk of prejudice in either those or in later proceedings. The mere fact that a defendant faces a second trial does not of itself justify the making of an order under the Act.[23]

7–165 Although the language of the section is similar to that found elsewhere in the Act,[24] there is not a precise correspondence, and the meaning may be slightly different in each context. It may be noted, for example, that although the necessary foundation for imposing a s.4(2) postponement order is a "substantial risk", it apparently need not be a risk of "serious" prejudice, as is required for the operation of the strict liability rule. It seems strange that a court can impose such an order restraining the freedom to report court proceedings, albeit only temporarily, if the prejudice in contemplation is less than serious. This would not seem to sit comfortably with the decision of the European Court of Human

---

[21] As for example, with the issue of "Media Court Guides" issued by the Lord Chancellor's Department in high profile trials. See para.2–60. For the practice of putting s.4(2) orders on the Scottish website, see para.7–156.

[22] As to the facts having a bearing on this issue, see the discussion of the "risk" limb of the strict liability rule, and such cases as *Att-Gen v News Group Newspapers Ltd* [1987] 1 Q.B. 1 and *Att-Gen v ITN Ltd* [1995] 2 All E.R. 370, paras 4–60 *et seq*. See also Sedley L.J. in *Att-Gen v Guardian Newspapers Ltd* [1999] E.M.L.R. 904, 927.

[23] *R. v Beck Ex p. Daily Telegraph plc* [1993] 2 All E.R. 177 at 181g–h, Farquharson L.J. Each case has to be weighed in the light of the facts, and in particular the nature of the charges themselves, the timing of the later trial and its location.

[24] "Substantial risk" is also to be found in s.2(2), para.4–53.

Rights in *Sunday Times v UK*[25] and the need to show that any restriction of freedom of speech under Art.10(2) of the Convention can be justified by reference to what is "necessary in a democratic society".

Nevertheless, the Act must be approached on the footing that Parliament intended the omission to have significance. It may be thought that the test of "necessity" is easier to fulfil in this context for the reason that the restriction is only temporary and that, accordingly, the greater priority can be given to the objective of achieving fair trials. It may be that this factor partly explains the frequency with which such orders seem to be made, despite the regularity with which it has been authoritatively pointed out that jurors are capable of excluding inadmissible matters from their consideration. **7–166**

On the other hand, where the prejudice apprehended is less than serious, it is likely to be more readily be outweighed in the judge's consideration by other competing interests, such as freedom of information and the entitlement of the public to be informed about court proceedings. **7–167**

In *R. v Beck Ex p. Daily Telegraph plc*,[26] the indictment against three social workers, accused of sexually abusing children in their care, was severed, so that the charges would be spread over three trials. At a preliminary hearing a s.4(2) order was made postponing media reports, specifically of the fact that the three defendants faced three indictments, until after the first had been dealt with. The purpose of this was to avoid the jury at the first trial from being prejudiced by the knowledge that the defendants in their charge were to face later criminal proceedings. This was not in itself a provision which the media found objectionable. **7–168**

At the first trial, however, the judge made a further such order forbidding *any* reporting of the first trial up to and including the verdicts; the position was then to be reviewed. The initiative for this order seems to have been that of the trial judge himself. It was apparently prompted by press and television reports. At that stage, the basis of the order was to avoid the prejudicial effect of reporting the trial upon the second and third indictments. The appellants, four national newspapers and a press agency, appealed under s.159 of the Criminal Justice Act 1988 against the order. Stressing the importance of open justice, the Court of Appeal discharged the order. **7–169**

In deciding whether or not the order was necessary, the judge had to undertake a balancing operation,[27] weighing considerations which supported the need for a **7–170**

---

[25] (1979) 2 E.H.R.R. 245.
[26] [1993] 2 All E.R. 177, 94 Cr.App.R. 367.
[27] One needs perhaps to be wary of "balancing" terminology when freedom of expression is in issue. See, *e.g. Sunday Times v UK* (1979) 2 E.H.R.R. 245 at 281: "The court is faced not with a choice between two conflicting principles, but with a principle of freedom of expression that is subject to a number of exceptions which must be narrowly interpreted". See also the remarks of Lord Griffiths in *Re an Inquiry under the Company Securities (Insider Dealing) Act 1985* [1988] 1 A.C. 660 at 703E. But it is now recognised that where two Convention rights come into conflict, as here in the case of articles 6 and article 10, it is necessary to carry out a balancing exercise in the light of the facts. See *Re S (FC) (A Child)* [2004] UKHL 47, [2005] 1 A.C. 593 at paras 6–43 *et seq.*

fair trial by an unprejudiced jury, on the one hand, and the requirements of open justice and a legitimate public interest and concern in those matters on the other. Having regard to the widespread public concern caused by the trial, and the concern over "the circumstances in which those in public service have the opportunity to commit such offences, and why, notwithstanding the complaints on the part of the victims, nothing whatever was done about it," it was not thought right for the trial to proceed without the public having an opportunity of knowing what was going on.[28]

2. The criteria analysed

7-171 Some of these matters were helpfully ventilated, and the relevant authorities canvassed, by Lindsay J. in *MGN Pension Trustees Ltd v Bank of America National Trust and Savings Association and another (Serious Fraud Office Intervening).*[29] The context was a series of civil actions in the aftermath of Robert Maxwell's activities.[30] After some 40 days of a civil action, which was going to be running in parallel with criminal prosecutions of some of the individuals whose actions were also in issue in the civil case, the Serious Fraud Office sought to persuade the court to impose reporting restrictions under s.4(2), on the ground that there might be prejudice to the defendants in the criminal trial. The concern of the Serious Fraud Office was twofold; first, that it might be impossible to ensure that those defendants received a fair trial; secondly, that lengthy and costly proceedings might be rendered ineffective.

3. A three stage test?

7-172 Lindsay J. took the view (somewhat tentatively, adopting counsel's submissions on the matter) that he should approach the making of an order in three stages. He was to ask himself (i) whether there was a substantial risk of prejudice to the administration of justice in the other proceedings (pending or imminent), (ii) whether an order would be necessary for avoiding that risk and (iii) whether the court in its discretion ought to make any and, if so, what order. He took the view that, in framing s.4(2) as it did, the legislature had recognised that a risk of prejudice that could not be described as substantial had to be tolerated, as the price of a free press[31]; and that, even if a risk could be described as substantial, it did not necessarily follow that an order had to be made. It may be that, for example, where there is a substantial risk but of only trivial or slight prejudice,

---

[28] [1993] 2 All E.R. at 182, 94 Cr.App.R. 367.
[29] [1995] 2 All E.R. 355.
[30] See T. Bower, *Maxwell: The Final Verdict* (1995); R. Greenslade, *Maxwell: The Rise and Fall of Robert Maxwell and his Empire* (1992). In addition to *MGN Pension Trustees Ltd v Bank of America National Trust and Savings Association and another (Serious Fraud Office Intervening)* (last note), the facts gave rise to *Att-Gen v Steadman* (unreported), February 7, 1994, in which Bell J. granted an injunction restraining the Respondent from staging "Maxwell: The Musical" on the basis that the musical would be in breach of the strict liability rule in respect of criminal proceedings brought against Maxwell's sons. See also *Att-Gen v BBC and Hat Trick Productions* [1997] E.M.L.R. 76.
[31] Compare the situation under s.5 of the Contempt of Court Act 1981, which also recognises that some risk of prejudice must be tolerated in the context of discussion of public affairs. See para. 4-293.

the right of the public to be informed would prevail. Matters have since moved on and the hurdles a judge should tackle have been more precisely defined in *Ex p. The Telegraph Group*[32] which was followed by the Privy Council in *Independent Publishing Company Ltd v Att-Gen of Trinidad and Tobago*.[33]

4. What is a "substantial risk of prejudice?"

The question of what constitutes a "substantial risk" has already been considered in the context of the operation of the strict liability rule.[34] Lindsay J. noted the remarks of Lord Diplock[35] that the words were intended to "exclude a risk that is only remote", and those of Sir John Donaldson M.R.,[36] who had accepted counsel's submission that:

> " 'substantial' as a qualification of 'risk' does not have the meaning of 'weighty' but rather means 'not insubstantial' or 'not minimal' ".

In both instances, however, the remarks were addressed to the meaning of the expression in s.2(2) (the strict liability rule) and not s.4(2). Even allowing that the identical words of a statute ought *prima facie* to bear the same meaning wherever they appear, there is the difference that s.4(2) does not speak of "serious" prejudice, but of "prejudice" *simpliciter*. Lindsay J. observed in relation to the word "substantial", that:

> "... the adjective is describing only the risk and not the degree of prejudice; one can plainly have a substantial or a not insubstantial risk which is of either a serious or slight prejudice or of some prejudice in between".

If therefore the meaning attributed to the expression "substantial" were the same in the context of s.4(2) as that explained in relation to the use of the word in s.2(2), Lindsay J. thought that it may well be that "to require only a 'not insubstantial' risk of prejudice would be to have a lower threshold for the operation of s.4(2) than the legislature intended".

It would clearly be unsatisfactory intellectually to treat the word "substantial" as having a different meaning in different sections of the same statute, and it is submitted that Lord Diplock's analysis of the concept in *Att-Gen v English*[37] is equally applicable to the term when used in s.4(2). It is therefore suggested that the concerns expressed by Lindsay J., as to the threshold being worryingly low, having regard to the disciplines of Art.10, are properly to be addressed at the stage (or stages) of considering whether it is "necessary" to make the order, and/or whether the discretion should be exercised in favour of such an order in any

---

[32] [2001] EWCA Crim 1075, [2001] 1 W.L.R. 1983. See the fuller discussion below at paras 7–199 *et seq.*
[33] [2004] UKPC 26, [2005] 1 A.C. 190.
[34] See paras 4–53 *et seq.*
[35] In *Att-Gen v English* [1983] A.C. 116 at 142.
[36] *Att-Gen v News Group Newspapers Ltd* [1987] Q.B. 1 at 15D–E, CA.
[37] [1983] 1 A.C. 116.

given case. It is on this important issue that the discussion should now focus, and as to the number of stages involved in the process.

5. *Stage 1: evaluating the risk*

7–177 The court has to make a determination whether, at the time when the order is sought, it can be said that there would be a "substantial risk" that subsequent legal proceedings, usually involving a jury, will be prejudiced. In a number of cases, the courts have said that the judge should credit a jury with the will and ability to abide by the judge's direction to decide the case only on the evidence before them.[38] The judge should also bear in mind the fact that the staying power of press publicity, and especially the detail of it, even in cases of notoriety, is limited,[39] and that the nature of a trial is to turn the proceedings inward, so that the jury's minds are focused on the evidence before them rather than on matters outside the courtroom.[40]

6. *It should not be assumed that coverage will be tendentious*

7–178 The judge should also approach the matter on the basis that any reporting of the relevant proceedings would, as contemplated by s.4(1) of the Act, be "fair and accurate". In *Barlow Clowes Gilt Managers Ltd v Clowes*[41] Sir Nicolas Browne-Wilkinson V.-C. had to make an evaluation of risk under s.4(2) in the following circumstances. An order had been obtained by the Serious Fraud Office from Vinelott J. in July 1989, restricting the publication of reports of legal proceedings in the Chancery Division, on the ground that such publication might invite a substantial risk of prejudice in pending criminal proceedings against Mr Clowes (not himself a party to the civil litigation).

7–179 Subsequently, the liquidators of two Barlow Clowes companies applied to the Vice-Chancellor for the appointment of a receiver of the defendant company Groverod Ltd in order to secure assets which it was *alleged* could be traced to funds which the managers of those companies had obtained in breach of duty. The order was granted in January 1990, but the Vice-Chancellor emphasised that

---

[38] *Ex p. The Telegraph plc* [1993] 1 W.L.R. 980, 987, Lord Taylor C.J. See also *R. v Corbett* (1988) 41 C.C.C. (3d) 385 at 400–1; *Dagenais v Canadian Broadcasting Corp* (1994) 120 D.L.R. (4th) 12, (1995) 94 C.C.C. (3d) 289 at 322 (Lamer C.J.C.); *R. v Coughlan, R. v Young* (1976) 63 Cr.App.R. 33, CA; *R. v Cannan* (1990) 92 Cr.App.R. 16, CA; *Leary v BBC*, September 29, 1989 (Lexis).
[39] *Ex p. The Telegraph plc* [1993] 1 W.L.R. 980 at 987; *Att-Gen v News Group Newspapers Ltd* [1987] Q.B. 1 at 16B–D, Sir John Donaldson M.R.; *Att-Gen v Independent Television News Ltd* [1995] 2 All E.R. 372.
[40] *R. v Kray* (1969) 53 Cr.App.R. 412 at 415–16, Lawton J.; *R. v Horsham Justices Ex p. Farquharson* [1982] 1 Q.B. 762 at 794, Lord Denning M.R.; *Ex p. Central Television plc* [1991] 1 W.L.R. 4 at 8B–D, Lord Lane C.J. See also Lord Donaldson M.R. in *Leary v BBC*, September 29, 1989 (Lexis), as cited at para.6–32. Evidence on this point is difficult to secure, since serious research on the issue is made impossible by the terms of s.8 of the Act, considered at para.11–349. But see the Report No.69, *Juries in Criminal Trials*, New Zealand Law Commission, February 2001. See also the Australian Report by M. Chesterman, J. Chan and S. Hampton, *Managing Prejudicial Publicity An Empirical Study of Criminal Jury Trials in New South Wales* (Law and Justice Foundation of New South Wales), February 2001.
[41] [1990] T.L.R. 82.

they were only matters of allegation and that he had made an interim order to keep the funds safe pending a decision as to their true ownership. Although he held that there was an arguable case in that context, nothing had been proved. He lifted the restriction already imposed but only in relation to his two decisions, which related (a) to the appointment of a receiver and (b) to the reasons for lifting the reporting restrictions.

In the view of the Vice-Chancellor there was nothing in his judgment that could prejudice a fair trial for Mr Clowes, since it contained only allegations. Moreover, there had already been widespread coverage in the press of the Barlow Clowes collapse and in far greater detail.[42] He was not prepared to assume that coverage of his judgment would be tendentious, and therefore not fair and accurate. If any report failed to make it clear that there had only been, thus far, unsubstantiated allegations, such a report would be neither fair nor accurate. There should be freedom of information unless there had been shown a real necessity to prevent it. The press had to show a corresponding sense of responsibility. Any coverage which was not fair and accurate would clearly risk losing the protection afforded by s.4(1) of the Contempt of Court Act 1981.

7–180

The matter of risk has to be assessed at the time the restriction is sought. In the case of *R. v George*[43] the accused had been charged with the murder of a well known TV presenter on April 26, 1999, but he was only arrested some 13 months later. At that point an order had been made by the magistrates' court under s.11 of the Contempt of Court Act 1981 prohibiting publication of any photographs of his face to protect the integrity of any identification parades. The order was lifted in February 2001, two months before the trial was due to begin. There were no further identification parades due to take place and thus no apparent reason for the ban to continue. The Crown took a neutral stance and the order was lifted. There were immediately published "lurid headlines" and information about the accused having changed his appearance from time to time. It was observed in the Court of Appeal in July 2002 that if the judge had appreciated the lack of restraint that was going to be shown by a section of the media, "he would undoubtedly have not lifted the order". That did not mean, however, that at the time the decision was made it was wrong. "It would be wrong to regard the decision of the judge unfavourably because he did not take into account the danger of the media behaving irresponsibly."

7–181

In another case, where there had been nothing in the reporting of a trial throughout its course to suggest that it would be other than fair and accurate, the Court of Appeal held that a judge had no power to order the postponement of a

7–182

---

[42] This approach to past publicity is similar to that adopted by the Divisional Court in *Att-Gen v MGN Ltd* [1997] 1 All E.R. 456 where there had been extensive coverage of a defendant's character and previous convictions prior to the publication of the articles alleged to be in contempt of the proceedings against him for assault, which had just become active: see para.4–155. So too, Lord Donaldson M.R. in *Leary v BBC*, CA, unreported, September 29, 1989: see paras 6–31 *et seq*. The Court of Appeal took into account the extensive publicity surrounding the disbandment of the West Midlands Serious Crimes Squad, earlier that year, as one factor working against restraint of a particular television programme dealing with that subject.
[43] [2002] EWCA Crim 1923 at [23].

report on television and radio of an account of proceedings, after the jury had retired to consider its verdict, and were then to spend the night in an hotel.[44] He had imposed the order "so that the jury can relax" by watching television without having to concern themselves with the case. It was held that he had thus failed to give the wording of the Act its plain meaning, and there were no grounds on which he could have come to the conclusion that there was any risk at all of prejudice to the proceedings.

7. The factor of time lapse

7–183   In evaluating whether or not there is a substantial risk of prejudice in the context of the operation of the strict liability rule, the courts have said in general terms that factors such as, in particular, the lapse of time between the publicity and the later trial should be taken into account.[45] The matter does not seem to have been expressly addressed, however, in the context of s.4(2). This factor must as a matter of principle also surely be relevant in determining whether a s.4(2) order should be made. "It depends on all the circumstances, including the nature of the charges, the timing of the second trial and the place where the second trial is to be heard."[46]

7–184   In *R. v Beck Ex p. Daily Telegraph plc*,[47] the Court of Appeal, while taking the view that such factors were relevant, did not specify whether they came into play at the stage of determining jurisdiction (that is to say, in assessing whether there was a substantial risk of prejudice) or that of exercising the discretion.[48]

8. Stage 2: The "necessity" for making an order

7–185   The Court of Appeal in *R. v Beck Ex p. Daily Telegraph plc*[49] held that the trial judge had not given sufficient weight to the principle that the media should be allowed to report criminal trials so far as possible. The court took the view that there would be a substantial risk of prejudice if the trial of the first indictment were to be reported. It decided, nevertheless, that there was widespread public concern over the circumstances in which persons in public service had apparently been able to commit the offences over a long period, without any action being taken notwithstanding complaints on the part of the victims. For those reasons, it would not be right for the trial to proceed without any public knowledge of what was going on, and the judge's order was rescinded. There was no careful

---

[44] *Re Central Independent Television plc* [1991] 1 W.L.R. 4, 1 All E.R. 347, (1991) 92 Cr.App.R. 154.
[45] See, *e.g. Att-Gen v News Group Newspapers Ltd* [1987] 1 Q.B. 1; *Att-Gen v Independent Television News Ltd* [1995] 2 All E.R. 370. (In each of these cases, there was a period of several months between the publications alleged to be in contempt and the anticipated trials.)
[46] *R. v Beck Ex p. Daily Telegraph plc* [1993] 2 All E.R. 177 at 181h.
[47] [1993] 2 All E.R. 177, discussed at paras 7–168 *et seq.*
[48] This was one of the cases which Lord Taylor C.J. identified as tending "to merge the requirement of necessity and the exercise of discretion": *Ex p. The Telegraph plc* [1993] 1 W.L.R. 980 at 984F–G.
[49] [1993] 2 All E.R. 177.

POSTPONEMENT ORDERS UNDER SECTION 4(2) OF THE 1981 ACT **7–189**

analysis, however, of the right approach to adopt as to determining "necessity".

The question whether or not it was "necessary" to make an order was considered by Lindsay J. in *MGN Pension Trustees*.[50] He noted that there was some authority as to the meaning of the same word used elsewhere in the Act; namely, in the House of Lords' discussion of s.10 in *Re An Inquiry under the Company Securities (Insider Dealing) Act 1985*.[51] In construing this latter section, the House of Lords indicated that the word "necessary" could be given a meaning somewhere between 'indispensable' on the one hand and 'useful' or 'convenient' on the other. It has also been said that the use of the word is a "statutory recognition of the principle of open justice".[52] Lindsay J. concluded that to equate the expression with mere convenience would be to undervalue the significance of freedom of the press. **7–186**

The House of Lords also made reference to the use of the word "necessary" in Art.10(2) of the European Convention. It is submitted that, in view of the implications for freedom of communication, this is the best guide in considering any ambiguities in the application of any statutory wording.[53] This is especially so perhaps in view of the role which the European Convention played in the genesis of the Contempt of Court Act. **7–187**

At all events, it was urged by counsel before Lindsay J. that the expression "necessary" had a threefold purpose. First, it was directed to ensuring that an order would not be made unless there were no other way of avoiding the prejudice; secondly, such an order if made would need to be likely to avoid the prejudice; and thirdly, the order, if made, should be no wider in its ambit than was needed to avoid the risk. The judge was attracted by this approach because it enabled the words "for avoiding" in the statute to be given their full weight[54]: **7–188**

" . . . the section does not simply say, as it could so easily have done, that the court may make a postponement order where an order is necessary by reason of a substantial risk of that prejudice but only where it appears necessary for avoiding that prejudice."

Merely because the conclusion to the first question in any particular case is that there is a substantial risk of prejudice, it does not follow that the making of an order is automatically necessary. Yet this appears to have been exactly what the trial judge did in *Ex p. The Telegraph plc*.[55] since, having decided that there was such a risk, he went on immediately to consider how it could be avoided. This **7–189**

---

[50] [1995] 2 All E.R. 355. See paras 7–171 *et seq.*
[51] [1988] A.C. 660. See at paras 9–182 *et seq.*
[52] *per* Lord Taylor C.J. in *Ex p. The Telegraph plc* [1993] 1 W.L.R. 980 at 984G–H, (1993) 98 Cr.App.R. 91 at 95.
[53] As was done by the Court of Appeal in *Derbyshire County Council v Times Newspapers Ltd* [1992] 1 Q.B. 70, [1992] 3 All E.R. 65 (the House of Lords felt no need to have resort to the terms of the Convention in the circumstances before them): see also *Rantzen v Mirror Group Newspapers (1986) Ltd* [1994] Q.B. 670, and Lord Bingham C.J. in *Att-Gen v Newspaper Publishing plc* [1997] 3 All E.R. 159.
[54] [1995] 2 All E.R. at 362c–d.
[55] [1993] 1 W.L.R. 980, 2 All E.R. 971.

was held by the Court of Appeal to have been a wrong approach. Instead, having identified the risk, "he should then have considered whether in the light of the competing public interests to which he referred it was necessary for avoiding that risk to make the order, whether in his discretion he should make it and, if so, with all or only some of the restrictions sought".[56]

9. The exercise of judicial discretion: is there a third stage?

7–190 After deciding that there is a substantial risk of prejudice, and possibly even after concluding that the making of an order would be "necessary" if the risk of prejudice is to be eliminated, the judge may still be left with a discretion as to whether or not to make an order. On the other hand, the process was described by Farquharson L.J. in *R. v Beck Ex p. Daily Telegraph plc*[57] as follows:

"The judge when contemplating the making of an order under s.4 of the 1981 Act has, once he has found that there is a substantial risk of injustice, to enter into a balancing act of the considerations which support the need for fair trial by an unprejudiced jury on the one hand and the requirement of open justice and a legitimate public interest and concern in these matters on the other."

7–191 The process thus described is not one in which discretion, as opposed to the evaluation of competing interests and factors, really arises. Thus there would be no room for the exercise of discretion in addition. It seems that the difficulty about the analysis of the decision in *Beck* is that it does not sufficiently tease out the important distinction between determining the issue of whether there is a "substantial risk of prejudice" from that of deciding whether it is on the facts necessary to make an order. It is essential not to lose sight of the recognition by Parliament, expressed in the wording of s.4(2), that the court is entitled to refuse to make such an order notwithstanding the existence of the requisite risk of prejudice.

7–192 Shortly afterwards, Lord Taylor C.J. observed[58]:

"It is noteworthy that whether the element of discretion is to be regarded as part of the 'necessity' test or as a third requirement, the courts as a matter of practice have tended to merge the requirement of necessity and the exercise of discretion".

He gave a number of examples of this, namely *R. v Saunders*,[59] *R. v Brooks*,[60] *Ex p. Central Television plc*[61] and the case of *R. v Beck Ex p. Daily Telegraph plc*[62] itself.

7–193 Furthermore, the language of "balancing", as used for example by Farquharson L.J. in *Beck*, needs to be approached with caution in the light of the

---

[56] *ibid.* at 986 *per* Lord Taylor C.J.
[57] [1993] 2 All E.R. 177 at 181a–b.
[58] *Ex p. The Telegraph plc* [1993] 1 W.L.R. 980 at 984F–G.
[59] (Unreported) February 5, 1990, Henry J.
[60] July 31, 1992, Buckley J.
[61] [1991] 1 W.L.R. 4, 8E, Lord Lane C.J.
[62] [1993] 2 All E.R. 177, 181, Farquharson L.J., cited above.

jurisprudence in the European Convention. The right to freedom of communication is sometimes referred to as being subject to certain closely defined exceptions.[63]

7–194 Thus, it was not entirely clear for a time whether the application of discretion truly represented a third, independent prerequisite for the making of an order, as was contemplated by Lindsay J. in *MGN Pension Trustees*,[64] or whether the discretion conferred on the courts by the use of the apparently permissive word "may" in s.4(2) would already have been taken into account at the second stage identified by Lindsay J.

7–195 The distinction was potentially important, not least because of the limited role of appellate tribunals generally when reviewing the exercise of a judge's discretion.[65] Yet the question (of law), as to whether or not the judge has a discretion once he has decided (a) that there is a substantial risk and (b) that the making of an order is "necessary" in the light of all the factors that he *must* take into account, remained open to some doubt.

7–196 The case for a residual discretion is to be found in the language of the Act, which provides that " ... the court *may* ... order". There may be a supplemental argument from principle arising from the wording of s.4(2), which does not refer to "serious prejudice", by contrast with s.2(2). In the absence of a discretion, the Act would have to be construed as saying that so long as the judge comes to the conclusion (a) that there is a substantial risk of *any* prejudice, and (b) that it is necessary to make an order to avoid that prejudice, he must make an order even though the potential prejudice is relatively trivial.

7–197 If this construction were right, it would have the effect that when the need for restricting court reporting is weighed against press freedom, the balance would not seem to be struck at the point that Parliament must have intended.

10. *Two uses of "necessity"*

7–198 It is perhaps desirable to consider "necessity" in two separate contexts. On the one hand, it may be necessary to make an order in order to avoid a degree of prejudice, however trivial, simply because without such an order the prejudice will occur (*i.e.* "necessity" in a purely mechanical sense).[66] That would seem to

---

[63] See *Sunday Times v UK* (1979) 2 E.H.R.R. 245 at 281. See also Hoffmann L.J.'s observation that freedom of speech is a "trump card" in *R v Central Independent Television* [1994] Fam. 192, 203D. This view has now been overtaken by events. For example, it was recognised by the House of Lords that no one convention right took automatic precedence over another: *Re S (FC) (A Child)* [2004] UKHL 22, [2004] 2 A.C. 457: see para.6–44.
[64] See para.7–172.
[65] *Hadmore Productions Ltd v Hamilton* [1983] 1 A.C. 191. See also *Baker v Baker (No.2)* [1997] 1 F.L.R. 148 at 153F–G.
[66] In *Dagenais v Canadian Broadcasting Corp* (1995) 120 D.L.R. (4th) 12, (1995) 94 C.C.C. (3d) 289, the Supreme Court of Canada held that the imposition of an order did not satisfy this test, since there were other ways in which the risk of prejudice could be avoided or eliminated. See para. 2–102.

be an assessment not involving the element of discretion. On the other hand, it may not be "necessary in a democratic society" to limit freedom of speech in order to avoid that element of prejudice because the interest in open justice, and the right of the public to be informed about court proceedings, may take precedence. This would to invest the concept of "necessity" with an element of value judgment (for example in relation to the relative importance of competing public interests and thus considerations of proportionality).

11. *The uncertainty resolved*

7–199   Illuminating guidance is to be found in the words of Lord Taylor C.J. in *Ex p. The Telegraph plc*[67] where he said of the judge in the Crown Court that:

> "... with the best intentions, he failed to keep distinct the two main requirements of section 4(2). Having satisfied himself that there would be a substantial risk of prejudice to the administration of justice in the respects that he identified, he appears to have assumed the necessity to avoid it and to have searched for a solution by tailoring the order to a form which he considered would eliminate the risk. Having identified the risk there would be, unless certain restrictions were imposed, he should then have considered whether in the light of the competing public interests to which he referred it was necessary for avoiding that risk to make the order, whether in his discretion he should make it and, if so, with all or only some of the restrictions sought. In our view, his failure to adopt this approach led him into error."

7–200   Thus, whereas there had been some confusion caused by the use of the concept of necessity in s.4(2), which in the context could easily be conflated with "necessity" in its Art.10(2) sense, matters were becoming clearer. It was suggested in the second edition of this work that it was desirable to take into account the two different meanings of "necessity"; and that the three stages could be implemented as follows:

(1) Is there a not insubstantial risk of prejudice? If not, there is no need to proceed any further.

(2) If the required risk is perceived to be present, would a s.4(2) order eliminate it? If not, again there is no need to proceed further because the condition precedent to an order would not have been fulfilled; indeed, it *could* not be necessary to make it. Even if an order *would* eliminate the risk, it may be that other (less drastic) steps could be taken to minimise or eliminate the risk; if so, it would still not be "necessary" to impose an order. In the words of Lord Lane, C.J.[68]:

---

[67] [1993] 1 W.L.R. 980 at 986B–C. See also the very full discussion in I. Cram, "Section 4(2) Postponement Orders: Media Reports of Court Proceedings under the Contempt of Court Act 1981" in *The Yearbook of Media and Entertainment Law* (1996), p.111.

[68] *Re Central Independent Television plc* [1991] 1 W.L.R. 4 at 8D–G, 1 All E.R. 347 at 350, (1991) 92 Cr.App.R. 154 at 157. In addressing the question of whether the trial judge's order in *R. v Beck Ex p. Daily Telegraph plc* [1993] 2 All E.R. 177 was "necessary", counsel for one of the defendants referred to problems about alternative measures such as relocating the second and third trials, *e.g.* as that the case had excited national interest outside the local (Leicester) area. See also *Dagenais v Canadian Broadcasting Corp* (1995) 94 C.C.C. (3d) 289, 120 D.L.R. (4th) 12.

"On the assumption that there is a substantial risk to the administration of justice if any report of proceedings is published, it is by no means always necessary to order postponement of publication . . . had it been necessary to insulate [the jury] from the media, it would in this case, and in most others where such a risk exists, have been possible to overcome it by means other than action under s.4(2). Where such an alternative is reasonably available, it should be used.

(3) Even if there is no other way of eliminating the risk than by making an order, it does not follow that an order must be made. There is still the further question whether a degree of risk might be tolerable in the light of other conflicting public considerations. It is at this stage that the judicial discretion comes into play, and only at that stage that it is appropriate for the judge to take into account the "competing public interests", as contemplated by the Court of Appeal in *Ex p. The Telegraph plc*.[69] One of those competing interests will be freedom of communication, and the judge should therefore take into account at that stage the question whether such a restriction is "necessary" in the broader sense contemplated by Art.10(2)."

This was the approach adopted by the Court of Appeal (Criminal Division) in *Ex p. The Telegraph Group*[70] and followed by the Privy Council in *Independent Publishing Company Ltd v Att-Gen of Trinidad and Tobago*[71]:

"[I]n considering whether it was 'necessary' both in the sense under section 4(2) of the 1981 Act of avoiding a substantial risk of prejudice to the administration of justice and therefore of protecting the defendant's right to a free trial under article 6 of the Convention and in the different sense contemplated by article 10 of the Convention as being 'prescribed by law' and 'necessary in a democratic society' by reference to wider considerations of public policy, the factors to be taken into account could be expressed as a three-part test; that the first question was whether reporting would give rise to a not insubstantial risk of prejudice to the administration of justice in the relevant proceedings, and if not that would be the end of the matter; that, if such a risk was perceived to exist, then the second question was whether a section 4(2) order would eliminate the risk, and if not there could be no necessity to impose such a ban and again that would be the end of the matter; that, nevertheless, even if an order would achieve the objective, the court should still consider whether the risk could satisfactorily be

---

[69] [1993] 1 W.L.R. 980 at 986B–C, Lord Taylor C.J.
[70] [2001] E.W.CA. Crim. 1075, [2001] 1 W.L.R. 1983. See also *BBC, Petrs*, May 2, 2001, High Court of Justiciary, where the court considered the notion of "necessity" in this context and Lord Taylor's words in *Ex p. The Telegraph plc* [1993] 1 W.L.R. 980. The decision was dated May 2, 2001 (as it happens, the day before the decision in *Ex p. The Telegraph* was handed down in England). Agreement was expressed by the Lord Justice General with the analysis of Lord Taylor in the 1993 case, and it was recognised that even where a publication would create a substantial risk of prejudice to the administration of justice there might be other means of eliminating or reducing the risk without resorting to a s.4(2) order. Moreover, it has to be shown that such an order would be justified by a "pressing social need". This will require appraising the competing public considerations of ensuring a fair trial and of open justice. On the facts, it was concluded that no such order was necessary because the administration of justice would be adequately protected by directions from the trial judge (*i.e.* in the later trial in respect of which protection had been sought). Thus, it can be seen that the English and Scottish courts are proceeding in this respect along parallel and consistent lines.
[71] [2004] UKPC 26 at [69], [2005] 1 A.C. 190 (Lord Brown of Eaton-under-Heywood) quoting the headnote in the report of *Ex p. The Telegraph Group* at [2001] 1 W.L.R. 1983.

7–201 CHAPTER 7—COURT REPORTING I: RESTRICTIONS UNDER 1981 ACT

overcome by some less restrictive means, since otherwise it could not be said to be 'necessary' to take the more drastic approach; and that, thirdly, even if there was indeed no other way of eliminating the perceived risk of prejudice, it still did not follow necessarily that an order had to be made and the court might still have to ask whether the degree of risk contemplated should be regarded as tolerable in the sense of being the lesser of two evils; and that at that stage value judgments might have to be made as to the priority between the competing public interests represented by articles 6 and 10 of the Convention."

7–202 It is perhaps worth observing that as long ago as in *R. v Horsham Justices Ex p. Farquharson* itself Lord Denning M.R. had identified[72] each of these issues as requiring separate consideration. He rejected a submission by counsel for one of the defendants to the effect that the magistrates could have made an order postponing *any* report of the proceedings at the outset of the committal. He took the view that it would be an impossible task to place upon them at that stage, before knowing enough about the issues and the evidence, and delineated the steps which they would have to take:

"They would have to consider, on such information as they could glean, whether, if the case were reported in the press, there would be 'a substantial risk of prejudice to the administration of justice.' They would have to consider whether it is 'necessary' to make an order. They would have to consider whether it is to be for the 'whole' or for 'part'. Then they would have to exercise a discretion. The section only says 'may ... order' ".

Q. What is the required mental element in the case of the breach of a section 4(2) order?

7–203 No indication was given in the Act as to the nature of the *mens rea* required. Questions arise whether (a) it is sufficient to know of or be reckless as to the existence of the order, and (b) if not, the nature of any intention required. It is unfortunate that the opportunity was not taken in the 1981 Act to eliminate these uncertainties once and for all.

7–204 It is convenient to isolate four separate issues for discussion:

(1) What must be proved as to the publisher's state of mind in relation to the existence of the order: actual knowledge, or will recklessness suffice?

(2) Assuming knowledge of the existence of an order, is there any additional need to establish a positive intention to interfere with the administration of justice, or is a form of strict liability then imposed?

(3) Assuming that strict liability is not imposed, will it suffice to establish a state of mind short of positive intention, such as recklessness as to the

---

[72] [1982] 1 Q.B. 762 at 789C–D.

interests of justice (either conscious recklessness[73] or being indifferent to an obvious risk[74] of which the publisher was unaware)?

(4) If the breach of the order happens also to create a substantial risk of serious prejudice, there is the possibility of a strict liability contempt under the 1981 Act in any event, and a question arises as to the interrelationship between the two.

1. Question 1: (a) Knowledge of the order

In principle, it must be a requirement that a person accused of breaching a s.4(2) order should be shown to have knowledge that publication is postponed.[75] According to Brooke J. in *Att-Gen v Guardian Newspapers Ltd (No.3)*,[76] a journalist will be liable for contempt if he acts inconsistently with the terms of a s.4(2) order, provided that its scope is clear. He was clearly contemplating the situation where an order has been brought to the attention of the media so that there is at least an opportunity to understand its purpose and effect. Indeed, the court in that case was concerned to make suggestions as to how information about such orders could most effectively be drawn to the attention of the press, and in particular through the medium of the Press Association.[77]

A conventional analysis might suggest that liability for contempt in respect of a failure to comply with a s.4(2) order cannot arise without knowledge of its existence having been established. Furthermore, the courts were traditionally inclined to construe legislation imposing criminal liability, if silent as to the question of the mental element, in such a way that some proof of *mens rea* is required.[78] This is especially so where the legislation potentially imposes heavy penalties, or where the offence may be categorised as "truly criminal" in character.[79]

---

[73] *R. v Cunningham* [1957] 2 Q.B. 396.
[74] *Commissioner of Police for the Metropolis v Caldwell* [1982] A.C. 341; the decision was not followed by the House of Lords in *R. v G* [2003] UKHL 50, [2004] 1 A.C. 1034. See the discussion of the demise of Caldwell recklessness at para.5-130. See also *Att-Gen v Leveller Magazine Ltd* [1979] A.C. 440 at 452 (Lord Diplock) and 456 (Viscount Dilhorne). As to when the purpose of the order, and the associated risk to the administration of justice might be said to be "obvious", see *Att-Gen v Times Newspapers Ltd* [1992] 1 A.C. 191 at 223 (Lord Oliver).
[75] See Eveleigh L.J. in *Z Ltd v A-Z and AA-LL* [1982] Q.B. 558 at 580B–C, 581E, and the discussion of "recklessness" at para.7-209. See also *Att-Gen v Leveller Magazine Ltd* [1979] A.C. 440 at 452 (Lord Diplock).
[76] [1992] 1 W.L.R. 874 at 884H–885A, [1992] 3 All E.R. 38 at 48e–f.
[77] See the passage cited at para.7-154. It is now the practice in Scotland for s.4(2) orders to be sent immediately by e-mail to various newspapers and broadcasting organisations and to their agents. The fact that such an order has been made is also published on the Scottish Court Service website: *BBC, Petrs*, May 2, 2001; see *Galbraith v HMA* 2001 S.L.T. 465, [2000] S.C.C.R. 935 High Court of Justiciary, para.4 (cited at para.7-156). See also *Galbraith v HMA* 2001 S.L.T. 465, [2000] S.C.C.R. 935 (cited at para.7-156). There is as yet no comparable facility south of the border.
[78] *Sweet v Parsley* [1970] A.C. 132; *B (A Minor) v DPP* [2000] 2 A.C. 428; *R. v K* [2001] UKH.L. 37, [2002] 1 A.C. 462. But see A.J. Ashworth, *Principles of Criminal Law* (4th ed., 2003) at p.164ff.
[79] See, *e.g. Gammon v Att-Gen for Hong Kong* [1985] 1 A.C. 1 at 14, Lord Scarman. See also ed. D. Ormerod, Smith and Hogan, *Criminal Law* (11th ed., 2005), p.148.

7-207 Moreover, the presumption that *mens rea* is required can normally only be displaced where the statute is concerned with an issue of social concern. The usual examples given are those of public health and safety, although it may be argued that the need to preserve the integrity of the court process, especially in relation to criminal trials, would represent another. Even where the particular statute can be said to fulfil such criteria, the presumption in favour of *mens rea* should only be displaced where it is clear that this would promote the objects of the particular statute by encouraging greater vigilance.

7-208 In the context of contempt, the careful confinement by Parliament of the scope of strict liability, in ss.1 and 2 of the 1981 Act, would suggest that it is particularly difficult in this field to argue that the presumption is displaced. Unfortunately, however, the full implication of these principles has not been addressed in the context of compliance with s.4(2) orders (or for that matter s.11 orders). For this reason, it remains necessary to consider whether recklessness as to the existence of such an order will suffice.[80]

2. Question 1: (b) Will recklessness as to the existence of the order suffice?

7-209 Before the passing of the 1981 Act, there was uncertainty as to the extent to which recklessness would suffice to found liability for acts inconsistent with court orders directed towards the restriction of publicity for matters taking place within the court process. In *Scott v Scott*[81] Lord Loreburn expressed the view that "The jurisdiction must surely be limited to wilful and malicious publications". He did not seek to define either of these terms. He may have meant that the matter had to be published with knowledge that an order had been made. On the other hand, elsewhere in the criminal law, both "malicious" and "wilful" are taken to import advertent recklessness.[82]

7-210 The issue might appear at first to be of little practical significance. Yet it may assume importance in some cases, especially when one remembers that it is sometimes directed by the court that the very fact that a s.4(2) order has been made should itself be withheld from public knowledge (perhaps especially when this information might lead to prejudice on the part of jurors).[83] Even in cases where there is no such restriction, court staff are said to be sometimes less than effective at communicating the information to the press.[84] Moreover, it is not always to be assumed that journalists attending a high profile trial, or some part of the proceedings, will be familiar with the practice of the courts in relation to press reporting restrictions. For example, in the case of Rosemary West, who was

---

[80] One commentator has expressed the view that recklessness might survive in this context: see, *e.g.* C.J. Miller, *Contempt of Court* (3rd ed., 2000), para.10-130.
[81] [1913] A.C. 417 at 448.
[82] *R. v Cunningham* [1957] 2 Q.B. 396 ("malicious") and *R. v Sheppard* [1981] A.C. 398 at 418, Lord Keith ("wilful").
[83] See the discussion at paras 7-159 *et seq.*
[84] See G. Robertson and A. Nicol *Media Law* (4th ed., 2002), pp.457-63. A case was cited in the previous edition at p.341, n.167, from the *Guardian*, January 25, 1984, where a journalist who had asked about a verdict and was not told of an order postponing its publication was held to be not guilty of contempt by a judge at Wolverhampton Crown Court.

tried on ten murder counts at Winchester in 1995, the interest was international and some of the journalists attending would certainly have been unfamiliar with these procedures.

In *Re F (Orse A) (A Minor) (Publication of Information)*,[85] the court was unanimous that *mens rea* was a necessary ingredient to establish liability for publication contempt, and founded the decision on the fact that the applicant had not established that the contemnor *knew* that the information published related to private wardship proceedings. However, Lord Denning M.R. went so far as to say that it would be sufficient if the contemnor knew that publication might be prohibited by law, but nevertheless went ahead, not caring whether it was prohibited or not. 7–211

Some members of the House of Lords in *Att-Gen v Leveller Magazine Ltd*,[86] however, stressed (in a rather different context) that a breach of an order must be deliberate. For example, Lord Scarman[87] made the following comment: 7–212

"The offence is interference, with knowledge of the court's proceedings, with the course of administration of justice: see *In re F (orse A) (A Minor) (Publication of Information)* [1977] Fam. 58. It was for this reason, no doubt, that Lord Widgery C.J. in this case stressed the element of 'flouting' the authority of the court. Though I would not have chosen the word, I think it does reflect the essence of the offence, namely that the conduct complained of, in this case the publication, must be a *deliberate* frustration of the effort of the court to protect justice from interference" (emphasis added).

Lord Edmund-Davies referred to "people controlling or connected with powerful organs of publicity who, for reasons of their own (one of which may be no more than the desire to boost sales), decide to take the course of *defiant* dissemination of matter which ought to be kept confidential." Yet, by contrast, he went on to warn that "it is incumbent upon such people to ascertain what had happened in court. They have the means of doing this, and they cannot be heard to complain that they were ignorant of what had taken place."[88] 7–213

It is therefore necessary even now at least to acknowledge the possibility that, in the context of s.4(2) orders, recklessness as to the existence of the order might suffice. This is despite the clear general statements about common law publication contempt that recklessness is insufficient, in such cases as *Att-Gen v Newspaper Publishing plc*,[89] *Att-Gen v News Group Newspapers plc*[90] and the unreported *Spycatcher* decision in the Court of Appeal, *Att-Gen v Newspaper Publishing plc*.[91] Yet again, in a third *Att-Gen v Newspaper Publishing plc* 7–214

---

[85] [1977] Fam. 58.
[86] [1979] A.C. 440.
[87] *ibid.* at 472.
[88] [1979] A.C. 440 at 466. Cp. the wording of the Practice Direction cited at para.7–219 which in effect assumes that recklessness will suffice.
[89] [1988] Ch. 333, CA.
[90] [1989] Q.B. 110, DC.
[91] [1990] T.L.R 158, CA (Lexis).

7–214 CHAPTER 7—COURT REPORTING I: RESTRICTIONS UNDER 1981 ACT

decision,[92] there was a similar general statement as to the requisite degree of *mens rea*.

7–215 All of these cases appear to require nothing less than proof of an intention to interfere with the administration of justice, but they are more directly concerned with the *mens rea* as to the consequences of publication, rather than the present issue. Here we are concerned with the extent of the knowledge required of the existence of any relevant order (and irrespective of any actual interference with the administration of justice which might be occasioned by such a breach).

7–216 In the present context, it remains uncertain whether the applicant would be required to prove (a) not only that the publisher was aware of the existence and terms of the order, but also that it was his intention to undermine the administration of justice; or (b) merely that the publisher knew that at an order had been made, and knew of its terms, without there being any additional requirement as to his also having given thought to the consequences of publication for the administration of justice in any broader sense.

7–217 Where the purpose of a court order which is clear on its face, the latter construction would probably be preferred, despite the statements made in the wider context of common law publication contempt generally. It should be remembered that Ackner L.J. in *R. v Horsham Justices Ex p. Farquharson* came to the conclusion that the effect of s.4(2) was to create the possibility of a *sui generis* form of contempt, separate and apart from the matter of creating a risk of prejudice to proceedings.[93] This factor would justify a separate treatment of the *mens rea* issue from that accorded to those common law contempts of which such a risk is an essential ingredient.

7–218 The law as to s.4(2) orders would become unworkable if it were necessary to investigate in the case of every alleged breach whether the journalist had applied his or her mind to the question of how the publication might impact upon the administration of justice. Yet if the logic of this argument is to be pursued to its conclusion, then surely nothing less than actual knowledge of the order would suffice. A person cannot be held to intend to interfere with the administration of justice by publishing in breach of an order of whose existence he is completely unaware. On the other hand, it would (if necessary) be relatively easy to draw an inference as to the presence of such an intention once it is established that the reporter in question knew of the order.

7–219 That there should be uncertainty on such a fundamental matter is unsatisfactory, but the Consolidated Criminal Practice Direction[94] contains the following ominous passage:

---

[92] [1997] 1 W.L.R. 926, [1997] 3 All E.R. 159.
[93] para.7–133.
[94] See now the Consolidated Criminal Practice Direction [2002] 1 W.L.R. 2870 at [3] (as amended March 22, 2005). For the latest version of the Direction, see *www.courtservice.gov.uk/docs/cpd/consol_criminal_pd_220305.doc*.

"... it is, and will remain, the responsibility of those reporting cases, and their editors, to ensure that no breach of any order occurs and the onus rests with them to make inquiry in any case of doubt."

Naturally, a practice direction (even though issued under the authority of the Lord Chief Justice) is unlikely to be held in itself determinative of the question of the degree of *mens rea* required, but it is impossible in these circumstances to advise newspaper editors that they will escape liability merely because they had no knowledge of a current s.4(2) order. A failure to check the lists or to make proper enquiries of court officials *may* give rise to liability.

3. *Question 2: Is there additionally a need to prove intention to interfere with the administration of justice?*

The separate question arises as to whether it is necessary to demonstrate any other element of *mens rea*, in the case of a journalist who *is* aware that an order has been made under s.4(2) and, if recklessness will yet suffice, which individual had the relevant state of mind. In particular, would it be necessary to show that he had any particular intention as to the consequences of his proposed publication for the administration of justice? In the light of such cases as *Att-Gen v Newspaper Publishing plc*,[95] *Att-Gen v News Group Newspapers plc*[96] and *Att-Gen v Newspaper Publishing plc*,[97] it does appear to be necessary to show a positive intention to interfere with the course of justice, albeit one that may be inferred, more or less readily, from the surrounding circumstances (including knowledge of any relevant order). Moreover, this trend was confirmed by Lord Bingham C.J. in the later case of *Att-Gen v Newspaper Publishing plc*.[98] It is thus reasonable to suppose that these statements truly represent the requirements for *mens rea* in relation to any publication contempt.

4. *Question 3: Will recklessness as to the consequences suffice?*

On the other hand, it has sometimes in the past been suggested that recklessness even in this regard might suffice.[99] Moreover, there is perhaps some support for this view in the decided cases. For example, in a case against the *Sun* newspaper, also reported as *Att-Gen v News Group Newspapers Ltd*,[1] Stephen Brown L.J. said: "It has to be made plain that there is a strict duty of care placed upon those who publish news items relating to trials to see that they do not run the risk of interfering with the course of justice." But this decision of the Divisional Court pre-dates the important series of authorities in the *Spycatcher* litigation, which appear to impose the more stringent requirement for a positive intention. In practice, however, the distinction may be more theoretical than real, because of

---

[95] [1988] Ch. 333.
[96] [1989] Q.B. 110.
[97] [1989] F.S.R. 457, Morritt J.
[98] [1997] 3 All E.R. 159.
[99] See, *e.g.* Miller, *op cit* (3rd ed., 2000) para.10–130.
[1] (1984) 6 Cr.App.R.(S) 418 at 420.

the courts' readiness to infer the necessary intention from the surrounding circumstances, including the obviousness of a risk.[2]

7–223   A later decision of Connell J., in *Official Solicitor v News Group Newspapers plc*,[3] appeared also to contemplate recklessness as the test. It is not clear, however, from the report whether the earlier *Spycatcher* cases were cited, although it seems likely that they would have been. Unfortunately, if they were, they were not addressed in the text of the judgment. Although the case did not directly concern s.4(2) of the 1981 Act, the subject matter of the complaint was the prohibited publication of extracts from confidential reports prepared for the purpose of what were then termed custody proceedings (relating to the children of an auxiliary nurse suffering from Munchausen's syndrome by proxy). The prohibition upon publication of these arose not from any specific order of the court but from the confidentiality attaching to all such proceedings, as recognised in s.12 of the Administration of Justice Act 1960.[4] In principle, however, it is difficult to see why there should be varying tests when assessing the liability of journalists.

7–224   In this context, Connell J. imposed fines for contempt, while expressly accepting that he was not dealing with "a case of intentional contempt in the sense that either of the respondents intended disrespect to the court or chose wilfully to ignore a direction of the court." He continued:

> "If a newspaper or other interested party wishes to publish extracts from such evidence it is always open to them to apply to the court for leave so to do, explaining to the court why they believe that the normal rule of privacy should be relaxed in the particular case. Not only was no such application made here by either of the respondents, but neither [the editor] nor his experienced legal adviser appears to have given any thought to the possibility of contempt arising, although they plainly knew that they were publishing extracts and reports produced for and used in private proceedings. I view this as a serious omission which requires the imposition of something significantly more than a nominal penalty."

He also observed that the experienced editor "should have given more careful thought to the contents of these articles". It is by no means clear how these statements could be reconciled in principle with the *mens rea* criteria applied to publication contempt in the three *Newspaper Publishing plc* cases identified above,[5] where recklessness has been disavowed as the appropriate test.

7–225   As to s.4(2) orders, there is an obligation upon the judge to make it clear what is the purpose of his order and how far it extends. Once it can be shown that a journalist has knowledge of any such order, it is clearly going to be difficult for him, having published a report inconsistent with its terms, plausibly to contend that he lacked the necessary *mens rea*. Thus, even if recklessness is ultimately

---

[2] *Att-Gen v News Group Newspapers plc* [1989] Q.B. 110; *Att-Gen v Newspaper Publishing plc* [1989] F.S.R. 457, Morritt J.; *Att-Gen v Times Newspapers Ltd* [1992] 1 A.C. 191.
[3] [1994] 2 F.L.R. 174.
[4] As amended by the Children Act 2004, s.62. See further ch.8.
[5] para.7–221.

POSTPONEMENT ORDERS UNDER SECTION 4(2) OF THE 1981 ACT   7-228

held to be insufficient to establish such a breach, there can be little doubt that the court would readily infer an intention to flout the expressed purpose of the court's order.[6]

Question 4: The relationship between section 4(2) and strict liability

There is particular difficulty in relation to s.4(2) orders, since there may often in practice, when the matter is objectively judged, be no risk to the administration of justice, or at least none which is obvious to an outside observer. It is not difficult to imagine circumstances in which a journalist might wish to write about some development in a criminal trial without being familiar with the real issues in the case. The court may, therefore, only be able to find liability for contempt, in cases where journalists have failed to spot that an order has been made and thus failed to comply with it, if there is a frank recognition that recklessness will indeed suffice.[7] It was held in *R. v Horsham Justices Ex p. Farquharson*[8] by Ackner and Shaw L.JJ. that there was created by s.4(2) the potential for a new head of contempt, quite independent of strict liability, although the nature of the *mens rea* required in such circumstances was not addressed.   7-226

It is necessary, however, to bear in mind the clear policy underlying the very restrictive approach taken to strict liability for publication contempts in the 1981 Act. Indeed, in the *Horsham Justices* case itself, it was recognised by Lord Denning M.R. and Ackner L.J. that journalists had become entitled to expect that any obligations would be spelt out expressly, rather than their being left to infer or assume them, as had previously been the case in relation to matters passing between judge and counsel in the absence of the jury. Furthermore, Art.7 of the Convention requires that people should be able to regulate their conduct by knowing where they stand.[9] It is accordingly important to promulgate such orders via recognised channels of communication readily accessible to reporters.   7-227

R. Who has the power to punish a breach?

It has already been noted that the effect of the enactment of s.4(2) gives rise to the possibility of a *sui generis* form of contempt, quite independently of any risk of prejudice to "particular legal proceedings",[10] whenever a publication occurs which is inconsistent with the terms of such an order. It is not certain whether the jurisdiction to deal with such a breach is exclusively that of the Divisional   7-228

---

[6] See, *e.g. Att-Gen v Newspaper Publishing plc* [1989] F.S.R. 457; *Att-Gen v Times Newspapers Ltd* [1992] 1 A.C. 191.
[7] As the *Practice Direction* [1982] 1 W.L.R. 1475, [1983] 1 All E.R. 64, 76 Cr.App.R. 78, might suggest. See now the consolidation of existing practice directions: [2002] 1 W.L.R. 2870, [2002] 3 All E.R. 904, (as amended March 22, 2005) at [3], for the latest version of the Direction, see www.courtservice.gov.uk/docs/cpd/consol_criminal_pd_220305.doc.
[8] paras 7–125 *et seq.*
[9] See, *e.g. Sunday Times v United Kingdom* (1997) 2 E.H.R.R. 245. See also *Att-Gen v Sport Newspapers* [1991] 1 W.L.R. 1194 at 1207G, [1992] 1 All E.R. 503 at 515j, Bingham L.J.
[10] para.7–133, Ackner L.J. in *Horsham Justices Ex p. Farquharson* [1982] Q.B. 762.

7–228 CHAPTER 7—COURT REPORTING I: RESTRICTIONS UNDER 1981 ACT

Court.[11] It has been suggested[12] that the Crown Court would also have the power to deal with the matter. Moreover, one of the exceptions identified in CPR Sch.1, Ord.52.1 to the exclusive jurisdiction of the Divisional Court (alongside contempt in the face) is contempt committed in connection with criminal proceedings and consisting of "disobedience to an order of the court."[13] On the other hand, it was observed by the Court of Appeal in *R. v D*[14] that:

> "The customary manner of proceeding in a case of disobedience to the order of a court, which is not committed in the face of the court, is by application for committal made pursuant to leave therefor to the Divisional Court of the Queen's Bench Division under R.S.C. Ord. 52".

7–229 From time to time Crown Court judges call for representatives of newspaper or broadcasting companies to attend in the course of a trial, in order to explain how a publication came to be made in circumstances giving rise to an apparent contempt. Sometimes such publications would fall within the "strict liability rule", but on other occasions the judge's concern will relate to an apparent breach of a postponement order made in connection with the pending trial. Either the judge is satisfied with the explanation given, often accompanied by an apology for an oversight, or he will conclude that the matter merits further action. In those circumstances, the complaint will generally be referred to the Attorney-General for him to consider the institution of proceedings for contempt.

7–230 If it is right that the Crown Court judge does have jurisdiction to deal with the matter personally, a question arises as to how this could most conveniently be carried out, and what procedural steps should be taken to ensure that the respondent's case can be fairly presented. It may be that it would cause unacceptable delay or interruption to the current criminal proceedings if the judge were to deal with the matter summarily. On the other hand, if it is postponed until later, this might have the effect that the judge would be seised of the contempt issue long after the trial in question has come to its natural conclusion and, indeed, he may have moved on to a different court. For these reasons, it may be more satisfactory that any such contempts should be referred to the Attorney-General. Indeed, it is to be noted that in *Re Lonrho plc*[15] Lord

---

[11] Exercising its jurisdiction under CPR Sch.1, Ord.52.1: "Where contempt of court is committed in connection with criminal proceedings".
[12] A. Nicol and H. Rogers, "Media Reporting Restrictions", *Yearbook of Entertainment and Media Law* (1996), p.357. See also in a different context *R. v Griffin* (1989) 88 Cr.App.R. 63 at 69, Mustill L.J. cited at para.3–56 and para.7–234.
[13] Although under the Courts Act 1971, the Crown Court became part of the Supreme Court, CPR Sch.1, Ord.52.5 is in the following terms: "Nothing in the foregoing provisions of this Order shall be taken as affecting the power of the High Court or Court of Appeal to make an order of committal of its own motion against a person guilty of contempt of court." Thus, although the jurisdiction of these tribunals is no longer regarded as being confined to contempts "in the face of the court" (the wording to be found in the former Ord.44, r.2(2)), the wording would not apparently be apt to cover Crown Court judges. See the discussion of the jurisdiction of the Crown Court at paras 13–34 *et seq*.
[14] [1984] A.C. 778 at 791H–792E, Watkins L.J.
[15] [1990] 2 A.C. 154 at 177B–C. (It is fair to say, perhaps, that the context of this remark was the contrast being drawn between committal proceedings on the one hand and proceedings by way of indictment, on the other, as opposed to contrasting the Ord.52 procedure with the judge proceeding of his own motion; nevertheless, the quoted words would apparently be of general application.)

Keith made the general comment that "the proper and convenient remedy in the case of alleged contempt of court by the media is by way of committal proceedings in the High Court".

Furthermore, the reasoning of the Court of Appeal in *Balogh v St. Albans Crown Court*[16] is very much in point. For example, it will rarely be the case that it can be convincingly argued that it is necessary for the Crown Court judge to deal with the breach for the purpose of bringing the proceedings before him to a dignified conclusion. Nor will there ordinarily be any urgency to deal with the respondents' alleged breach for any other reason. It may be that the consequence of the breach is serious, and one could imagine circumstances when the breach might lead to a trial having to be abandoned. This would in no way entail, however, any urgency in dealing with the contempt. Indeed, the more serious the outcome, the more important it surely would be for the media respondents to have a full opportunity of preparing and arguing their case. 7–231

Other considerations mentioned in *Balogh* were the need for a period of calm reflection before any action is taken and, more importantly, the desirability of referring the matter to be dealt with by someone other than the trial judge whose trial has been affected. This concern is clearly directed towards ensuring the avoidance of any appearance of bias,[17] and towards a compliance with the rules of natural justice generally. 7–232

A more recent object lesson in the difficulties that can arise when a Crown Court judge decides to deal with contempt of his or her own motion is provided by the decision of the Court of Appeal in *R. v Schot and Barclay*.[18] Although this was a case concerning an allegation of contempt on the part of jurors, the pitfalls are nonetheless worth remembering in this context also. 7–233

Equally pertinent are the comments of Mustill L.J. in *R. v Griffin*.[19] It had there been suggested that, in the light of some of the *dicta* in *Balogh*, the issue of jurisdiction on the part of a Crown Court judge to deal with contempt might itself depend upon the degree of urgency to which the circumstances gave rise. This he addressed in the following terms: 7–234

> "We should add that certain dicta (for example, in *Balogh*) may be read as suggesting that the court has no jurisdiction to adopt the summary process unless the matter is urgent. We doubt whether this is strictly accurate. In our view the question of urgency or no is material, not to the existence of the jurisdiction but as to whether the jurisdiction should be exercised in preference to some more measured form of process".

---

[16] [1975] Q.B. 73.
[17] See, *e.g. Re Lonrho plc* [1990] 2 A.C. 154, where the Judicial Committee recused itself.
[18] [1997] 2 Cr.App.R. 383, (1997) 161 J.P. 473, considered more fully at paras 10–72 *et seq.*
[19] (1989) 88 Cr.App.R. 63 at 69. This was not a s.4(2) case but concerned allegations of interference with witnesses.

S. Is a journalist alleged to be in breach entitled to challenge the validity of the order itself?

7–235 Is it possible, on an application to commit, to question the basis of an order under s.4(2)? The justification for the original order can be challenged directly, by following the procedure adopted in *Horsham Justices Ex p. Farquharson*[20] itself, or by the appellate procedure introduced in 1988. The question is whether, additionally, it might also be possible for an alleged contemnor to attack the basis for such an order, and to allege that it was not justified, by way of defence in contempt proceedings. This was certainly the view of Lord Denning M.R. in that case,[21] who pointed out that such an order " . . . might be made by someone or other—in some tribunal or other—out of lack of knowledge or dislike of the press or even a sense of power". He also pointed out (before the introduction of a right of appeal some years afterwards)[22] that such an order could be made which would apparently bind a newspaper without giving notice or affording any opportunity of challenge or right of appeal.

7–236 It may be appropriate to consider an analogy. In relation to orders for disclosure of journalists' sources, it is clear that no such order may be made unless it is established as a matter of fact that it is "necessary" to override the privilege on the basis of one or other of the four statutory exceptions.[23] Therefore, it is legitimate for a journalist accused of contempt to challenge the existence of the jurisdiction to make the order in respect of which he is said to be in breach. As it was put by Tasker Watkins L.J. in *Att-Gen v Lundin*[24]:

> "To defy deliberately, albeit politely as Lundin did, a proper order of a judge is a serious matter. When Lundin took this step he was fully aware of the possible consequences. So if his action was contemptuous he cannot complain if he is punished for it. However, refusal by a witness to answer a question in a criminal trial even when ordered by a judge to do so does not inevitably put that person in contempt of court."

In that case the Divisional Court went on to conclude that, although the question put to Lundin had been relevant, it could not be said objectively that the answer was necessary in the interests of justice.[25]

7–237 By contrast, it does not appear that a judge's decision, in the context of s.4(2), that " . . . it appears to be necessary for avoiding a substantial risk of prejudice . . . " can so readily be challenged, because some elements of that decision-making process involve the exercise of a discretion or subjective value judgment rather than a conclusion of fact. This appears consistent with the

---

[20] [1982] 1 Q.B. 762. See paras 7–125 *et seq.*
[21] *Horsham Justices* [1982] 1 Q.B. 762 at 790. He cited W. Shakespeare, *Measure for Measure*, Act II, Scene II, l. 117.
[22] Criminal Justice Act 1988, s.159, discussed at para.7–258.
[23] Discussed at paras 9–126 *et seq.* See also *Goodwin v UK* (1996) 22 E.H.R.R. 123; *X Ltd v Morgan-Grampian (Publishers) Ltd* [1991] 1 A.C. 1 at 43–4, Lord Bridge; see also *Special Hospitals Service Authority v Hyde* (1994) 20 B.M.L.R. 75 at 85, Sir Peter Pain.
[24] (1982) 75 Cr.App.R. 90 at 95.
[25] See also the decision of the Divisional Court in *Chief Constable of Leicestershire v Garavelli* [1997] E.M.L.R. 543.

analysis of Lord Taylor C.J. in *Ex p. The Telegraph plc*[26] where he referred expressly to the "discretion" involved in weighing "competing public interests". Moreover, even orders made without jurisdiction appear to command obedience until set aside.[27]

It may not be easy to reconcile Lord Taylor's approach with that of Lord Bridge in *X Ltd v Morgan-Grampian (Publishers) Ltd*[28] where he expressly characterised the exercise of determining "necessity" (in the context of ordering source disclosure) as one of "fact" rather than "discretion", although he did acknowledge that the process involved the application of value judgments. Nevertheless, it is possible that the earlier stages of the decision making process under s.4(2) can more readily be characterised as going to objective matters of fact rather than discretion. For example, the decision whether or not there is a genuine risk of prejudice, or that as to whether an order of postponement *could* eliminate the perceived risk, might very well be classified as decisions of fact. If so, it may be open to a court determining whether a contempt has been committed to come to a different decision on those factual questions and thus acquit the alleged contemnor on the basis that the order had been made without jurisdiction, despite the fact that discretion had a role to play at the later stages of the reasoning process.

7–238

Yet in view of the opportunity of appealing, subject to leave, now available to journalists in respect of s.4(2) orders, a court might be rather unsympathetic to such a plea if the opportunity had not been taken to test the matter by way of appeal. Also, it is necessary to bear in mind the words of Russell L.J. in *R. v Saunders*[29] to the effect that "the judicial exercise of discretion under s.4(2) . . . could only become an exercise which involved a question of law if . . . the discretion was exercised on a fundamentally flawed basis." This remark was made before Lord Taylor C.J. analysed the process of determining whether to grant a s.4(2) order into its separate stages in *Ex p. The Telegraph plc*.[30] In the light of this, it is more difficult to categorise the exercise as being one purely of discretion since, for example, a judgment as to whether or not an order is necessary (in the "mechanical" sense described above)[31] is not easily so classified.

7–239

A different point of view was put by Ackner L.J. in *R. v Horsham Justices Ex p. Farquharson*,[32] who concluded that:

7–240

"If [counsel for the applicant journalists] was right in his submissions, it would be necessary to look behind every order made under section 4(2) and not only to reconsider the very basis of the order, but to revive all the old uncertainties recognised to exist at common law as to whether the conduct complained of could have amounted to

---

[26] [1993] 1 W.L.R. 980 at 986B–C, discussed at paras 7–199 *et seq.*
[27] See in particular paras 9–200 *et seq.*
[28] [1991] 1 A.C. 1 at 44.
[29] [1990] Crim. L.R. 597. The words of Russell L.J. are more fully cited at para.7–257 below.
[30] [1993] 1 W.L.R. 980, 2 All E.R. 971.
[31] Which is the term used at para.7–198.
[32] [1982] 1 Q.B. 762, 806.

contempt. This cannot have been Parliament's intention. It would involve a section 4(2) order having *no effect* at all in regard to committal proceedings and little effect in regard to other proceedings."

7-241 He was supported in his reasoning by Shaw L.J.[33] who was also unable to accept counsel's submission, since a s.4(2) order made in relation to committal proceedings before the magistrates would be "quite futile" if newspapers were free to act in contravention of it. This approach does, however, mean that where an order has been incorrectly made the principles of open justice and freedom of communication would be subordinated to maintaining the authority of a court, however misguided the order may have been. Nevertheless, the scope for injustice is much reduced since 1982, when Lord Denning expressed his reservations. Not only is it now recognised that journalists can and should be heard before orders are made under the Act, but also there has been put in place, in respect of Crown Court proceedings, a right of appeal.[34]

7-242 Moreover, the majority view expressed by Ackner and Shaw L.JJ. is consistent with the many authorities of long standing to the effect that orders must be implicitly obeyed until duly set aside.[35] A more recent example of this line of reasoning is to be found in judgment of Woolf L.J. in *DPP v Channel 4 Television Co Ltd*[36] where he rejected an argument by analogy with the *Lundin* approach and affirmed the importance for the rule of law of implicit obedience to court orders until properly set aside. This was, however, a case in which it was recognised that the jurisdiction to make the order in question was unassailable. Even where orders are made without jurisdiction, it has been held that they need to be obeyed until set aside.[37]

7-243 In the light of these authorities, and despite the different approach adopted in relation to journalists' sources in *Lundin* and *Garavelli*, it is submitted that the validity of a s.4(2) order cannot be made the subject of challenge in contempt proceedings based upon a breach, but only by way of judicial review or a s.159 appeal, as may be appropriate.

T. The recognition of journalists' *locus standi* in relation to such orders

7-244 Courts have a discretion to hear representations from the press when considering whether to make an order under s.4(2).[38] There was, however, a traditional reluctance to allow non-parties to intervene in proceedings. For example, in *R. v*

---

[33] [1982] Q.B. 762, 798C.
[34] Under the Criminal Justice Act, s.159, considered at para.7-258.
[35] See para.7-118 and para.9-205. But see paras 9-224 *et seq.*
[36] [1993] 2 All E.R. 517 at 529. See also *R. v Highbury Corner Magistrates' Court Ex p. O'Donoghue* (1997) 161 J.P. 217: "It is not an option simply to decide that it is an order that the court should not have made and therefore to disregard it": *per* Lord Bingham C.J. at 223.
[37] See Lord Donaldson M.R. *Re M: M v Home Office* [1992] Q.B. 270 at 298, considered at para. 9-207.
[38] *R. v Clerkenwell Magistrates' Court Ex p. Telegraph plc* [1993] Q.B. 462 at 471G, Mann L.J.

Central Criminal Court Ex p. Crook,[39] it was said in the Divisional Court that:

> "... any attempt by counsel acting on behalf of a witness to make representations to the court should be firmly resisted; likewise applications sought to be made by journalists or any other lay persons".

Similarly, the magistrate in *R. v Clerkenwell Magistrates' Court Ex p. Telegraph plc*[40] had declined to hear representations from members of the press before making an order.

By this time (1992), however, the Divisional Court (Mann L.J. and Leonard J.), dealing with this magistrate's decision by way of judicial review, was taking a very different stance from its predecessors in *Ex p. Crook*.[41] The Divisional Court referred to the balancing exercise of which the Court of Appeal spoke in *Beck*,[42] and Mann L.J.[43] spoke positively of the role of press representatives in such judicial deliberations:

> "I regard it as implicit in the enactment of section 4(2) that a court contemplating its use should be enabled to receive assistance from those who will, if there is no order, enjoy the right of making reports of the proceedings before the court. They are in particular the best qualified to represent that public interest in publicity which the court has to take into account when performing any balancing exercise which has to be undertaken."

As to the exercise of the discretion to hear press representatives, he continued[44]:

> "The occasion and manner of its exercise are matters for the court invested with the power, but I expect that the power will ordinarily be exercised when the media ask to be heard either on the making of an order or in regard to its continuance. The power will ordinarily be exercised because the court can expect to find assistance in representations from the news media. In practice, it will be convenient if the press are able to present a single view, thereby avoiding any need for the court to restrain repetition."

The press were not intermeddling in the resolution of any issue between the parties to the proceedings, since reporting restrictions are a quite separate matter in which the public has its own legitimate interest. Thus, although the power to hear representation is a discretionary one, the Divisional Court then gave a strong indication that it would ordinarily be exercised in favour of the media.

---

[39] *The Times*, November 8, 1984, DC. The occasion for the making of these remarks was an appeal (unsuccessful) against the making of an order under s.11 of the Contempt of Court Act, as to which see paras 7–83 *et seq.*
[40] [1993] Q.B. 462.
[41] *The Times*, November 8, 1984, DC.
[42] [1993] 2 All E.R. 177 at 181b–c, Farquharson L.J.
[43] [1993] Q.B. 462 at 471E–F.
[44] [1993] Q.B. 462 at 471H, Mann L.J.; see also 472D, Leonard J. I. Cram, "Section 4(2) Postponement Orders: Media Reports of Court Proceedings under the Contempt of Court Act 1981" in *The Yearbook of Media and Entertainment Law* (1996), p.111, criticises the suggestion that the media should be required to present a united position, but the court's suggestions will in most circumstances represent a fair and practical approach.

7–248 Meanwhile, an application had been made to the European Commission of Human Rights by a journalist, a television production company and the National Union of Journalists in which complaint was made that there was no procedure by which the press were able to challenge orders made under ss.4(2) and 11.[45] What had been planned was the broadcast of a television programme which would cover the trial of *R. v Ponting*, an official secrets case which had attracted wide publicity and was due to begin at the Central Criminal Court. It was intended that there would be a programme called "Court Report" broadcast every evening during the trial. On the first day of the trial, the judge made an order "that a report of any part of the proceedings in the form proposed by Channel Four in their nightly half-hour Court Report be postponed until after the jury has given its verdict in this case or until further order".

7–249 The order was not opposed by counsel in the criminal trial and the judge, basing himself upon *Ex p. Crook*,[46] held that it would be inappropriate to hear counsel on behalf of Channel Four and the production company because they had no standing to make the application. The complaint was treated by the European Commission as admissible by reference to Art.13 of the Convention:

> "Everyone whose rights and freedoms as set forth in this Convention are violated shall have an effective remedy before a national authority notwithstanding that the violation has been committed by persons acting in an official capacity."

7–250 It was following this outcome that it was decided by the government to provide for a right of appeal by persons aggrieved by such orders, and this led to the enactment of s.159 of the Criminal Justice Act 1988.[47]

7–251 Since the press are held to be "persons aggrieved" for the purposes of an appeal from the making of an order by the Crown Court or High Court,[48] the current approach of the courts to journalists seems entirely sensible, and consonant with the spirit of the Convention. This is especially so since the High Court regularly accords standing to the press in applications for judicial review of any order made by magistrates.[49]

7–252 The case of *Att-Gen v Guardian Newspapers Ltd (No.3)*[50] was said by Brooke J. to provide valuable lessons for the future, not the least of which was that " . . . courts should be diligent in accommodating and understanding the legitimate interests of the press". If courts are minded to make orders which prevent the public from knowing what is going on in a public court, such orders should be drafted and made public in a way which makes it crystal clear what the press may

---

[45] *Hodgson, Woolf Productions and NUJ and Channel Four Television v UK* (1987) 10 E.H.R.R. 503. And see *Channel 4 TV v United Kingdom*, D.R. 56/156.
[46] *The Times*, November 8, 1984, DC.
[47] See para.7–258.
[48] See para.7–262.
[49] As in, for example, *Horsham Justices Ex p. Farquharson* [1982] Q.B. 762; *R. v Bow Street Metropolitan Stipendiary Magistrate Ex p. Mirror Group Newspapers Ltd* [1992] C.O.D. 15.
[50] [1992] 1 W.L.R. 874 at 886G, [1992] 3 All E.R. 38 at 50b, DC. The facts of the case are discussed at para.4–77.

or may not do, both in reporting the proceedings themselves and in reporting the terms of the order.

Although the media now generally expect to be permitted to make representations, there may be exceptional cases where matters concerning the making of a s.4(2) order have to be heard *in camera*, and therefore in the absence of the press and the public. The point arose in *Re Crook*[51] where it was held that a judge sometimes needs an opportunity to receive information in chambers so that he can decide the preliminary question whether privacy is required in the interests of justice and, if so, to what extent. In such a case a judge should only adjourn to chambers, however, if he believes that something may be said which makes the determination in private appropriate. He should be alert, in any event, to the importance of adjourning into open court as soon as it emerges that the need to exclude the public is no longer necessary. The court recognised that there may be cases in which the considerations leading to the exclusion of the public would not necessarily justify excluding the press as well.[52] Nevertheless, it held that[53]:

> " . . . it would not be right as a general rule to distinguish between excluding the press and other members of the public. If exclusion of the public is necessary, applying the strict standard required to justify it, it would not usually be right to make an exception in favour of the press."

Section 9(11) of the Criminal Justice Act 1987

Section 159 of the Criminal Justice Act 1988 only confers jurisdiction to hear appeals against orders which *do* impose a restriction.[54] An attempt was made in *R. v Saunders*[55] to challenge the *refusal* to make a s.4(2) order by resorting to s.9 of the Criminal Justice Act 1987, which so far as is relevant provides as follows:

> "(3) He [the judge at a preparatory hearing] may determine—
>
> (b) any question as to the admissibility of evidence; and
> (c) any other question of law relating to the case.
>
> . . .
>
> (11) An appeal shall lie to the Court of Appeal from any order or ruling of a judge under subsection (3)(b) or (c) above, but only with the leave of the judge or of the Court of Appeal".

---

[51] (1991) 93 Cr.App.R. 17, [1992] 2 All E.R. 687, CA.
[52] As in *R. v Waterfield* [1975] 1 W.L.R. 711, (1975) 60 Cr.App.R. 296. In a different context, it has subsequently been recognised by the Court of Appeal in *Hodgson v Imperial Tobacco Ltd* [1998] 1 W.L.R. 1056, 2 All E.R. 673 that it may sometimes be appropriate in civil proceedings taking place "in chambers", in circumstances where space is restricted, to admit a representative member of the press in acknowledgment of what is now recognised to be the right of the public to follow the course of litigation even at the interlocutory stage.
[53] (1991) 93 Cr.App.R. 17, 24, Lord Lane C.J.
[54] See *R. v S* [1995] 2 Crim App.R. 347; *R. v Lee* [1993] 2 All E.R. 170.
[55] [1990] Crim. L.R. 597 (Lexis).

7–255 The application concerned a trial arising from the Guinness share support scheme of 1986, which was to be the subject of two separate criminal trials; the second of these was to take place a considerable time after the first. Henry J. declined to make an order, sought by Mr Saunders, that there should be no publication of material relating to the first trial until the second trial had been concluded.[56] The Court of Appeal took the view that, once a judge carried out what was regarded as an exercise of discretion based upon the proper considerations, the court would not interfere unless it was shown that the decision was perverse.

7–256 It is necessary to consider briefly the statutory background of the *Saunders* appeal. The 1987 Act introduced preliminary hearings of serious fraud trials, and provided in s.9(3)(c) that in the course of such a hearing the judge "may determine any other question of law relating to the case". The Court of Appeal only had jurisdiction in respect of any order or ruling made under subs.(3)(b) or (c). Thus, it would be necessary for there to have been a determination of a "question of law" by the trial judge.

7–257 A decision under s.4(2) could not be so categorised. In the words of Russell L.J.[57]:

"The judicial exercise of discretion under section 4(2) of the 1981 Act could only become an exercise which involved a question of law if it could be demonstrated that the discretion was exercised by the judge on a fundamentally flawed basis. Once the judge carries out what is essentially a balancing exercise upon proper material, the Court of Appeal will not interfere unless it can be shown that the decision was perverse".

U. Appeals against section 4(2) orders: Section 159 of the 1988 Act

1. *The background and the terms of the section*

7–258 Following the reference to the European Commission described above,[58] Parliament enacted a right of appeal against postponement orders under s.4(2), or orders made under s.11 of the Act. It did not, however, include a right of appeal against the *refusal* to make an order.[59] The Criminal Justice Act 1988, s.159, provides that:

"(1) A person aggrieved may appeal to the Court of Appeal, if that court grants leave, against—
 (a) an order under section 4 or 11 of the Contempt of Court Act 1981 made in relation to a trial on indictment;
 (aa) an order made by the Crown Court under section 58(7) or (8) of the Criminal Procedure and Investigations Act 1996 in a case where the court has convicted a person on trial on indictment;

---

[56] *R. v Saunders* [1990] Crim. L.R. 597 (Lexis).
[57] *ibid.*
[58] paras 7–248 *et seq.*
[59] *R. v S* [1995] 2 Cr.App.R. 347. See also the predicament which faced the applicant in *R. v Saunders* considered at paras 7–254 *et seq.*

(b) any order restricting the access of the public to the whole or any part of a trial on indictment or to any proceedings ancillary to such a trial; and
(c) any order restricting the publication of any report of the whole or any part of a trial on indictment or ancillary to such proceedings."

In *Scottish Daily Record & Sunday Mail Ltd, Petrs*,[60] Lord McCluskey observed that the court was unable to reach any conclusion as to why similar provisions had not been enacted with regard to Scotland, but expressed agreement with words of Farquharson L.J., cited from *R v Beck*,[61] to the effect that the media should be allowed to report criminal trials unless, under the terms of a particular statute, it was necessary for them to be excluded.   7–259

2. The function of the Court of Appeal in section 159 appeals

The jurisdiction of the Court of Appeal is not confined to considering the trial judge's decisions on "a question of law". Section 159(5) provides that: 7–260

"On the hearing of an appeal under this section the Court of Appeal shall have power—
(a) to stay any proceedings in any other court until after the appeal is disposed of,
(b) to confirm, reverse or vary the order complained of; and
(c) to make such order as to costs as it thinks fit."

The function of the Court of Appeal on an appeal under s.159 is not simply to review the judge's ruling but to form its own view on the material put before it, and it may, in the exercise of its own independent jurisdiction, reverse, confirm or vary any order that has been made. This was held to be so in *Ex p. The Telegraph plc*.[62] There is no inconsistency with the earlier decision in *R. v Saunders*, cited above,[63] because the difference in the later statutory wording would appear to confer a wider jurisdiction upon the Court of Appeal. Section 159 is not confined to "admissibility" or "any other question of law".   7–261

3. "Person(s) aggrieved"

Any "person aggrieved" by the making of an order may bring proceedings in respect of it.[64] In view of the difficulties that this expression has generated in connection with the principles governing *locus standi* in public law,[65] this was a surprising term for the draftsman to have used. It seems to have been assumed   7–262

---

[60] 1998 S.C.C.R. 626 at 630.
[61] [1993] 2 All E.R. 177 at 181f–g, 94 Cr.App.R. 376 at 380.
[62] [1993] 1 W.L.R. 980 at 986C–D, 2 All E.R. 971 at 976, Lord Taylor C.J. See also *R. v Beck Ex p. Daily Telegraph plc* [1993] 2 All E.R. 177 at 180d–e, Farquharson L.J. and *Ex p. The Telegraph* [2001] EWCA Crim 1075, [2001] 1 W.L.R. 1983.
[63] [1990] Crim. L.R. 597. The ruling of Henry J. of February 5, 1990, appealed from in that case is cited in the Report, but not the decision of the Court of Appeal of February 8, 1990.
[64] Criminal Justice Act 1988, s.159(1).
[65] For a general discussion of the modern law on *locus standi* (standing), see P. Craig, *Administrative Law* (5th ed., 2003) ch.21; P. Cane, *Administrative Law* (4th ed., 2004) ch.4; H.W.R. Wade and C.F. Forsyth, *Administrative Law* (9th ed., 2004), pp.679–700.

7-263   that it would necessarily encompass the media, as indeed has subsequently been held to be the case.[66] It would also presumably apply to parties either in the proceedings in which the order has been made or in the proceedings sought to be protected.

7-263   The power of the court to deal with such appeals is, however, confined to the situation where a court *does* order a restriction. It is not possible for any one, however "aggrieved" he may be by the decision, to pray these provisions in aid where the judge *refuses* to make one of the relevant orders defined by s.159. Moreover, there would be no possibility of a party to the proceedings seeking to have such an order reviewed, since it would be a decision of the Crown Court relating to a trial on indictment.[67]

7-264   The point was raised in *R. v S*,[68] where the applicant was charged with importing cocaine. His defence was that he had been acting under duress. He was reluctant to give evidence in open court but the judge ruled that the only witness to be heard *in camera* would be his mother. He sought leave under s.159(1) to challenge the judge's refusal to hold the rest of the proceedings *in camera*. It was however held by the Court of Appeal (Criminal Division) that there was no jurisdiction except to deal with an order *restricting* access.

V. Appeals in respect of "spent" orders

7-265   It was held in *Re Central Independent Television plc*[69] that s.159 applies also to "spent" orders. It was enacted to provide redress for cases in which orders under s.4(2) of the Act had been wrongly made. The court took the view that the provision would not be fully effective if orders wrongly made could not be reversed simply because they had ceased to operate.

W. Procedure on section 159 appeals

7-266   Provision was made by rules of court, inserted in the Criminal Appeal Rules 1968, to deal with the new right of appeal under s.159. It was contained in rr.16A and 16B.[70] In *R. v Guardian Newspapers Ltd*[71] a challenge was made to the *vires* of r.16B. Blofeld J. had made an order that parts of a trial should be heard *in camera*, and the applicants sought leave to appeal. It was provided in s.159(4) of the 1988 Act that any party to such an appeal might give evidence orally or in writing. Section 159(6) provided that rules of court might make special provision for the practice to be followed in relation to hearings *in camera*.

---

[66] See, *e.g. Re Crook (Tim)* (1989) 93 Cr.App.R. 17 at 19, CA; *Re Central Independent Television plc* [1991] 1 W.L.R. 4, 92 Cr.App.R. 154 at 155, CA.
[67] Supreme Court Act 1981, s.28(1) and (2)(a).
[68] [1995] 2 Cr.App.R. 347. Also reported *sub nom. R. v Salih* [1994] T.L.R. 692. The case was followed in *R. v Littlewood* [2002] All E.R. (D) 328 (Feb), CACD.
[69] [1991] 1 W.L.R. 4, 92 Cr.App.R. 154, CA.
[70] See now Pts 67.1 and 67.2 respectively of the Consolidated Criminal Procedure Rules 2005; the wording of the rules has not been altered. See also *Archbold 2005*, paras 7–310—7–312.
[71] [1994] Crim. L.R. 912.

Rule 16B(6) stated that an application for leave to appeal should be determined by a judge of the court, or the court as the case may be, *without a hearing*. Furthermore, by reason of r.16B(7), where leave to appeal was granted, the appeal itself was to be determined without a hearing. It was these provisions that the applicants wished to contend were *ultra vires*. It was argued that departures from the principle of open justice should only be permitted where they could be clearly justified; and that Parliament had given no sanction to any such departure as that entailed in sub-rr.(6) and (7). In particular, nothing was said in s.159(6) about a power to dispense with submissions or an oral hearing.

7–267

Reliance was placed upon Arts 10 and 13 of the European Convention, which provide respectively for freedom of information and for an "effective remedy" before a national authority. Accordingly, s.159 should not be interpreted as granting the power to deny an oral hearing, and thus an effective remedy. In response to this, it was argued that the terms of s.159(6) were unambiguous; its width was clear from the concluding words, which demonstrated that the rules could deprive the parties of the right to give evidence, whether orally or in writing. Moreover, Art.10(2) actually made express provision for restrictions on freedom of information where it might be necessary in the interests of national security.

7–268

This argument of the respondents prevailed in the Court of Appeal (Criminal Division). Since the words of the statute were clear, there was in those days no need for assistance as to its construction by reference to the European Convention; in any event, there was no inconsistency. Article 13 did not go so far as to require an oral hearing.

7–269

X. Provision for costs on section 159 appeals

The important practical question has arisen more than once as to whether provision may be made for the costs of an "aggrieved party" who is successful in a s.159 appeal. No express provision is made for this in the 1988 Act or any other statute. This led to uncertainty and the need for the matter to be determined by the House of Lords.

7–270

Section 159(5)(c) empowers the court "to make such order as to costs as it thinks fit." The provision enables the court to order one party to pay the costs of another. In *Re Central Independent Television plc*[72] Lord Lane C.J. took the view that, although an order out of central funds was not expressly provided for, it was right to read in the power by implication for the reason that there was no other possible source for the costs. In this instance, there had been a successful appeal under s.159 of the Criminal Justice Act 1988 against an order by the Crown Court, purporting to restrict media reports of a criminal trial during the period of the jury's deliberations.

7–271

Similarly, in *R. v Bow Street Metropolitan Stipendiary Magistrate Ex p. Mirror Group Newspapers Ltd*[73] an order made by the magistrate under s.4(2) of the

7–272

---

[72] [1991] 1 W.L.R. 4 at 9.
[73] [1992] 1 W.L.R. 412.

7-272 CHAPTER 7—COURT REPORTING I: RESTRICTIONS UNDER 1981 ACT

Contempt of Court Act 1981 was quashed by way of judicial review, and the question arose as to whether the Divisional Court could award costs to a successful applicant out of central funds. Nolan L.J. held that there was jurisdiction to make the order under s.51(1) of the Supreme Court Act 1981, which at the material time provided:

> "Subject to the provisions of this or any other Act and to rules of court, the costs of and incidental to all proceedings in the Civil Division of the Court of Appeal and in the High Court . . . shall be in the discretion of the court, and the court shall have full power to determine by whom and to what extent the costs are to be paid".

7-273   The House of Lords in *Aiden Shipping Co Ltd v Interbulk Ltd; The Vimeira*[74] held that there was no warrant for confining the court's powers under s.51(1) of the Supreme Court Act to the awarding of costs against a *party* to the proceedings in question. It was held that the discretionary power was in wide terms and there was no justification for implying a limitation to that effect.

7-274   In *Holden & Co v CPS*[75] the respondent firms of solicitors had been ordered to pay the whole or part of the prosecution costs in Crown Court proceedings (in which they had represented defendants). At that time an appeal lay by virtue of s.50 of the Solicitors Act 1974 to the Court of Appeal, Civil Division. When the matter came before that court, Lord Lane C.J. said[76]:

> "Section 51 of the 1981 Act confers jurisdiction on the court to make an order for costs in the broadest terms, subject only to rules of court. Mr Laws [counsel for the Lord Chancellor's Department] invites us, in effect, to apply a limitation on the statutory jurisdiction so conferred, as a matter of construction. But this was just the error which was exposed by the House of Lords in the *Aiden Shipping* case. There is no warrant for restricting the wide words of s.51 so as to exclude the power of the court to award costs out of central funds when justice requires".

7-275   This decision was overruled, however, by the House of Lords in *Holden & Co v CPS (No.2)*.[77] It was held by Lord Bridge,[78] with whom the remaining members of the House concurred, that the Court of Appeal (and also the Divisional Court in the *Bow Street* case) had taken Lord Goff's words from *The Vimeira* out of context and applied them "to a situation far removed from the subject matter to which the original language was addressed."

7-276   The House of Lords went on to hold that both the *Bow Street* and *Central Independent Television* cases should, in so far as they related to costs, be overruled. Lord Bridge drew the following conclusion[79]:

---

[74] [1986] A.C. 965.
[75] [1992] 1 W.L.R. 407, CA.
[76] [1992] 1 W.L.R. 407 at 411.
[77] [1994] 1 A.C. 22. See also *R. v Moore* [2003] EWCA Crim 1574, [2003] 1 W.L.R. 2170, [2003] 2 Cr.App.R. 31, where the House of Lords decision was followed in the context of an order which had been mistakenly made for payment of a successful appellant's costs out of central funds in a contempt case.
[78] *ibid.* at 30–1.
[79] 1994] 1 A.C. 22 at 40.

" . . . I find it impossible to say that whenever the legislature gives a right of appeal, whether in civil or criminal proceedings, in circumstances where a successful appellant may be unable to recover his costs from any other party, that affords a sufficient ground to imply a term enabling the court to order the costs to be paid out of public funds. The strictly limited range of the legislation expressly authorising payment of costs out of central funds in criminal proceedings no more lends itself to extension by judicial implication than does the equally limited range of legislation authorising payment of costs out of the legal aid fund in civil proceedings. Some general legislative provision authorising public funding of otherwise irrecoverable costs, either in all proceedings or in all appellate proceedings, would no doubt be an admirable step in the right direction which the judiciary would heartily applaud but this does not, in my opinion, justify the courts in attempting to achieve some similar result by the piecemeal implication of terms giving a power to order payment of costs out of central funds in particular statutes, which can only lead to anomalies."

Lord Bridge explained that the wide terminology of s.51 of the Supreme Court Act 1981 had first seen light of day in s.5 of the Supreme Court of Judicature Act 1890. This identical wording might be apt to embrace an order for payment of costs by the Crown in those categories of civil proceedings in which the Crown as a party was amenable by statute to such an order, but could not have been intended to apply to the Crown as a party to any other category of proceedings—let alone to authorise payment by the Crown of the costs of civil litigation[80] to which the Crown was not a party.

Moreover, the concept of "central funds" was first introduced by the courts Act 1971, and was defined by the Interpretation Act 1978 as meaning "money provided by Parliament." Lord Bridge concluded that it was impossible to read into the wording of s.5 of the 1890 Act a power to order "payment of costs out of . . . money provided by Parliament" in anticipation of language which was first used by the parliamentary draftsman (a) many years later, and (b) only in legislation relating to criminal proceedings.

The court's power to read words into a legislative provision is extremely limited.[81] It was especially difficult to do so against the background of the constitutional convention which safeguards the exclusive control exercised by Parliament over the levying and expenditure of the public revenue.

---

[80] An appeal under s.50 of the Solicitors Act 1974 is classified as civil litigation.
[81] *Thompson v Goold & Co* [1910] A.C. 409 at 420, Lord Mersey; *Vickers Sons & Maxim Ltd v Evans* [1910] A.C. 444 at 445, Lord Loreburn L.C.

CHAPTER 8

COURT REPORTING II: OTHER STATUTORY RESTRICTIONS

		PARA
I.	Judicial Proceedings (Regulation of Reports) Act 1926..	8–1
II.	Restrictions on Publication Under the Criminal Justice Act 2003..............................	8–15
III.	Statutory Anonymity for Victims of Sexual Offences..	8–17
IV.	Protection for Juveniles (Children and Young Persons): the 1993 Act	8–25
V.	Anonymity for Witnesses: Section 46 of the Youth Justice and Criminal Evidence Act 1999............	8–74
VI.	Protection for Family Proceedings..	8–76
VII.	Criminal Proceedings Before Magistrates	8–87
VIII.	Derogatory Remarks in Mitigation	8–95
IX.	Disclosures Relating to Proceedings in Private..	8–97
X.	Employment and Other Tribunals..	8–141

I. JUDICIAL PROCEEDINGS (REGULATION OF REPORTS) ACT 1926

A. The relevant provisions of the Statute

8–1 A variety of statutes have been enacted over the years, in a piecemeal way, which impact upon the right to report and comment upon court proceedings and, therefore, upon the right of citizens generally to be informed about such matters. Clearly it is necessary to justify such restrictions as being "necessary" in a democratic society for one or more solid reasons of public policy. In particular, every such restriction needs to be considered in the light of the values enshrined in Art.6 (open and accessible justice), Art.8 (privacy) and Art.10 (freedom of communication). We have already in chapter 7 addressed the common law background and the specific provisions of the Contempt of Court Act 1981 dealing with court reporting. In this chapter we consider other miscellaneous provisions which make up the framework within which reporters and the media need to operate. The longest surviving enactment still operative in this context is the Judicial Proceedings (Regulation of Reports) Act 1926.

8–2 The relevant provisions of the 1926 Act[1] are as follows:

"**1. Restriction on publication of reports of judicial proceedings**

(1) It shall not be lawful to print or publish, or cause or procure to be printed or published—

---

[1] For the background to the Act, see S. Cretney, " 'Disgusted, Buckingham Palace . . . ' "—The Judicial Proceedings (Regulation of Reports) Act 1926" (1997) 9 Ch. and Fam. Q. 43. See also G. Savage, "Erotic Stories and Public Decency: Newspaper Reports of Divorce Proceedings in England" (1998) 41 Historical Journal 511.

(a) in relation to any judicial proceedings any indecent matter or indecent medical, surgical or physiological details being matter or details the publication of which would be calculated to injure public morals;
(b) in relation to [any proceedings under Part II of the Family Law Act 1996 or otherwise in relation to][2] any judicial proceedings for dissolution of marriage, for nullity of marriage, or for judicial separation, *or for restitution of conjugal rights*[3] [or for the dissolution or annulment of a civil partnership or for the separation of civil partners],[4] any particulars other than the following, that is to say:
  (i) the names, addresses and occupations of the parties and witnesses;
  (ii) a concise statement of the charges, defences and counter-charges in support of which evidence has been given;
  (iii) submissions on any point of law arising in the course of the proceedings, and the decision of the court thereon;
  (iv) the summing-up of the judge and the finding of the jury (if any) and the judgment of the court and observations made by the judge in giving judgment:

Provided that nothing in this part of this subsection shall be held to permit the publication of anything contrary to the provisions of paragraph (a) of this subsection.

(2) If any person acts in contravention of the provisions of this Act, he shall in respect of each offence be liable, on summary conviction, to imprisonment for a term not exceeding four months [51 weeks],[5] or to a fine not exceeding [level 5 of the standard scale],[6] or to both such imprisonment and fine:

Provided that no person, other than a proprietor, editor, master printer or publisher, shall be liable to be convicted under this Act.

(3) No prosecution for an offence under this Act shall be commenced in England and Wales by any person without the sanction of the Attorney-General.

(4) Nothing in this section shall apply to the printing of any pleading, transcript of evidence or other document for use in connection with any judicial proceedings or the communication thereof to persons concerned in the proceedings, or to the printing or publishing of any notice or report in pursuance of the directions of the court; or to the printing or publishing of any matter in any separate volume or part of any bona fide series of law reports which does not form part of any other publication and consists solely of reports of proceedings in courts of law, or in any publication of a technical character bona fide intended for circulation among members of the legal or medical professions."

It is clear that s.1(1)(a) was intended to be wider in its application than s.1(1)(b), since the former applies to "any judicial proceedings", whereas the latter is confined to proceedings within the defined categories. Even in respect of the matters which are permitted to be reported, from these specified "matrimonial

---

[2] The words in brackets were inserted by the Family Law Act 1996, s.66(1), Sch.8, Pt I, para.2.
[3] The words in italics are to be repealed from a date to be appointed: Civil Partnership Act 2004, s.261(1), Sch.27, para.8(1), (2). Section 1(1)(v) had provided for the comparable proceedings in Scotland called "an action of adherence or of adherence and aliment".
[4] Inserted from a date to be appointed: Civil Partnership Act 2004, s.261(1), Sch.27, para.8(1), (2).
[5] The words in square brackets were introduced by the Criminal Justice Act 2003, s.280(2)(3), Sch.26, para.7 to replace the specified period of four months; from a date to be appointed.
[6] Currently £5,000: see the Criminal Justice Act 1982, ss.37, 38, 46 as amended by the Criminal Justice Act 1991, s.17(2).

proceedings", any report would have to be drafted to exclude any indecent matter "calculated to injure public morals".

8–4   It is difficult nowadays to envisage proceedings being brought which would entail the prosecution having to demonstrate that material was calculated to injure public morals. Moreover, prurient detail is commonplace in daily newspapers and magazines, and there would be no guarantee of consensus among jurors or lay magistrates as to what is now regarded as "indecent".

8–5   Under s.7 of the Contempt of Court Act 1981, relating to strict liability contempt, proceedings may only be brought by or with the consent of the Attorney-General, or on the court's own initiative.[7] Similarly, the court may on its own initiative restrain publications which would be in breach of the provisions of the 1926 Act.[8] A court nowadays, however, might take a good deal of persuading to make such an order.[9] The reasoning in *Argyll v Argyll*[10] was that s.1(1)(b) was designed to protect the parties themselves, and not simply public morals.

8–6   In view of the fact that Parliament introduced a statutory provision specifically to restrain reports likely to contain "indecent material", it would be even more difficult to justify restraining court reports by reference to distress and embarrassment than it would have been, at the time of *Scott v Scott*,[11] to justify a hearing *in camera* for such reasons. It was there agreed that these would not be sufficient grounds to justify infringing the principle of open justice. Since Parliament introduced the additional test of "public morals" in the 1926 Act, anyone now seeking to restrain reporting in such circumstances would presumably have to assume that nebulous burden.

8–7   One of the exceptions recognised in Art.10(2) of the European Convention on Human Rights relates to the "protection of . . . morals".[12] There is at least therefore consistency in this respect between the terms of s.1 of the 1926 Act and the Convention; that fact makes it no easier to apply.

---

[7] Proceedings for an injunction, however, to restrain an apprehended strict liability contempt may apparently be brought *without* obtaining consent. See *Peacock v London Weekend Television* (1985) 150 J.P. 71, CA, and *Leary v BBC*, September 29, 1989, CA (Lexis). But see the reservations of Lord Bridge in *P v Liverpool Daily Post and Echo Newspapers plc* [1991] 2 A.C. 370 at 425.
[8] *Argyll v Argyll* [1967] Ch. 302.
[9] But see *Moynihan v Moynihan (No.1)* [1997] 1 F.L.R. 59, Sir Stephen Brown P., considered at para.8–10 below.
[10] [1967] Ch. 302 at 343A, Ungoed-Thomas J.
[11] [1913] A.C. 417.
[12] See *Handyside v United Kingdom* (1976) 1 E.H.R.R. 737 (ban on a publication for children including a chapter on sexual practices was justified, as being necessary for the protection of public morals); *Muller v Switzerland* (1988) 13 E.H.R.R. 212 (punishment of an artist for exhibiting obscene paintings was within the state's margin of appreciation); *Open Door Counselling and Dublin Well Woman v Ireland* (1992) 15 E.H.R.R. 244 (although it is *primarily* for signatory states to assess the content of morals, the European Court of Human Rights would scrutinise any individual claim that action taken to protect the state's own conception of morals was "necessary in a democratic society"); *Otto Preminger Institut v Austria* (1994) 19 E.H.R.R. 34. See A. Geddis, "You Can't Say 'God' on the Radio: Freedom of Expression, Religious Advertising and the Broadcast Media after *Murphy v Ireland*" [2004] E.H.R.L.R. 181.

One question that might arise in theory is to what extent it remains open to the court to restrain under s.11 of the 1981 Act the publication of material on grounds purely of embarrassment or distress, so as to avoid the court room becoming "a place of moral torture",[13] if it could also be categorised as "indecent"—unless it could also be demonstrated to present a risk to "public morals". Not only did Parliament address the matter expressly, introducing that very test in 1926, but the European Convention also requires that hurdle to be overcome. The provision of Art.10(2) relating to the protection of the judicial process, as such, is limited to the object of "maintaining the authority and impartiality of the judiciary".[14] Without the "public morals" element, it might not be so easy to justify restraint of court reporting on the footing that other litigants might be discouraged from coming forward. These considerations might perhaps raise some doubt as to the appropriateness of the decision in *H v Ministry of Defence*.[15]

As pointed out already,[16] however, if such a matter arose again it might be possible to justify the restraint, in *H v Ministry of Defence*, by reason of the individual's record of trauma and suicide attempts, since "protection of health" is one of the factors contemplated as justifying an exception to the basic right of freedom of information, *provided* the test of "necessity" can be satisfied, as well as that of "proportionality".

The terms of s.1 of the 1926 Act were considered by the court in 1996. Great press interest had been shown in the facts of a dispute in which the Queen's Proctor sought a ruling that a decree of divorce granted in 1990 to the late Lord Moynihan should be declared null and void, as having been achieved by fraud. As a preliminary question, the President was asked[17] to consider s.1(1)(b) of the 1926 Act, and whether it had the effect of preventing newspaper reporting of details given in the course of the evidence. It was made clear that nobody, including the Attorney-General, had any objection to such reports; the only issue was one of construction.

The effect of the section was held to be mandatory, since the restrictions applied to "any judicial proceedings for dissolution of marriage". Such proceedings are not concluded until any question as to the validity of any decree or order has been finally resolved.[18] The provisions of the 1926 Act had to be construed restrictively as they contained a criminal sanction. Even though the Attorney-General had indicated through counsel that there would be no enthusiasm for the institution of criminal proceedings, if the strict letter of the law was breached, the

---

[13] [1913] A.C. 417 at 446, Lord Loreburn.
[14] It was recognised in *Sunday Times v United Kingdom* (1979) 2 E.H.R.R. 245 that this phrase should have a reasonably wide interpretation; sufficiently wide, for example, to embrace the protection of the administration of justice generally.
[15] [1991] 2 Q.B. 103, CA, considered in para.7–104.
[16] See para.7–106.
[17] *Moynihan v Moynihan (No.1)* [1997] 1 F.L.R. 59, Sir Stephen Brown P.
[18] See the Domestic and Appellate Proceedings (Restriction of Publicity) Act 1968 and the Matrimonial Causes Act 1973, s.8(2).

Act would inevitably have to be construed as restricting press reports in any such case unless and until Parliament intervened to amend or revoke its provisions.

8–12   The *Moynihan* case was briefly considered in the Scottish case of *Nicol v Caledonian Newspapers Ltd*,[19] where it was submitted that since a report published in breach of the Act's provisions was by definition unlawful the publisher ought not to be entitled to the protection of qualified privilege in a claim for defamation. On this, of course, Sir Stephen Brown's decision offered no guidance. It was held by Lady Paton that the 1926 Act was not intended to restrict common law remedies or defences in such a field as defamation, to which the legislature had made no reference. It was to provide criminal sanctions and not civil remedies. Its object appeared to be the protection of the public from salacious detail rather than the privacy of litigants, in particular those involved in divorce proceedings.[20] Reference was made to *Friel v Scott*.[21] Lady Paton went on to observe that litigants were not an identifiable class of persons intended by Parliament to be protected. The case gives rise to interesting questions, and whether the same view would be taken in England is by no means clear. It might, for example, not be addressed in terms of whether the statute took away a defence of qualified privilege; but rather of whether the public interest which generally requires court reports to be protected by qualified privilege (so as to enable the general public to know what is going on in the courts) operates in a case where the public has been expressly prevented by the legislature from receiving the information in question—because, presumably, it was perceived as being *contrary* to the public interest. At all events, Lady Paton expressed doubt, on the facts, as to whether the defence would succeed in the light of the omission of important facts which were in the pursuer's favour (*e.g.* his denials of violence).

B. Extension of the 1926 Act to other proceedings

8–13   The same protection as that afforded under the 1926 Act is extended to certain other proceedings by the Domestic and Appellate Proceedings (Restriction of Publicity) Act 1968. The relevant terms of that Act (as amended)[22] are as follows:

"s.2 ... (3) Section 1(1)(b) of the Judicial Proceedings (Regulation of Reports) Act 1926 (which restricts the reporting of matrimonial causes) shall extend to any such proceedings as are mentioned in subsection (1) above subject, in the case of the proceedings mentioned in [subsection (1)(d)[23] [or (db)] ...][24] above, to the modification that the matters allowed to be printed or published by virtue of sub-paragraph (ii) of the said section 1(1)(b) shall be particulars of the declaration sought by a petition

---

[19] 2003 S.L.T. 109.
[20] *Cf.* the views of Ungoed-Thomas J. in *Argyll v Argyll* [1967] Ch. at 343A.
[21] 2000 S.L.T. 1384 at 1385 *et seq.*, Lord Justice General Rodger.
[22] See the Matrimonial Causes Act 1973, Sch.2, para.7(1). The words in square brackets were added by s.33(1) and Sch.2, para.19(b) of the Family Law Reform Act 1987.
[23] Paragraph (e) of the section was repealed by the Child Support, Pensions and Social Security Act 2000, s.85, Sch.9, Pt IX.
[24] Inserted from a date to be appointed by the Civil Partnership Act 2004, s.261(1), Sch.27, para.29(1), (3).

RESTRICTIONS ON PUBLICATION UNDER CRIMINAL JUSTICE ACT   8–16

(instead of a concise statement of the charges, defences and counter-charges in support of which evidence has been given)."

The effect of these provisions is that the limitations contained in s.1(1)(b) of the 1926 Act[25] are extended to cover also the following categories of proceedings: **8–14**

- Proceedings for maintenance pending suit under s.22 of the Matrimonial Causes Act 1973.[26]

- Proceedings for financial provision in cases of neglect to maintain under s.27 of the Matrimonial Causes Act 1973: referred to in s.2(1)(c) of the 1968 Act.[27]

- Petitions for declaration of status: Pt III of the Family Law Act 1986: referred to in s.2(1)(d).[28]

- Proceedings under s.58 of the Civil Partnership Act 2004 (declarations as to subsistence, etc of civil partnership).

II. RESTRICTIONS ON PUBLICATION UNDER THE CRIMINAL JUSTICE ACT 2003

A. Prosecution appeals

Provision is made in the Criminal Justice Act 2003 for certain restrictions upon publication in the context of prosecution appeals under Pt 9 and subsequent retrials under Pt 10. There is a general right of appeal for the prosecution in respect of rulings in relation to a trial on indictment[29] and also in respect of evidentiary rulings.[30] There is a corresponding general restriction upon a report of "anything done" under those provisions, and of such an appeal, and of any consequent appeal to the House of Lords, and of any application for leave to appeal in respect of either form of ruling.[31] **8–15**

B. Retrials following the quashing of an acquittal

Prior to an application for an order quashing an acquittal and directing a retrial, the Director of Public Prosecutions may apply for an order that any matter which would give rise to a substantial risk of prejudice to the administration of justice in a retrial be not included in any publication for so long as the order has effect. This is subject to the proviso that, since the acquittal concerned, an investigation **8–16**

---

[25] Set out at para.8–2.
[26] Prospectively repealed by the Family Law Act 1996, s.66(3), Sch.10 from a date to be appointed.
[27] Added originally by s.42(1), Sch.2, para.3, of the Matrimonial Proceedings and Property Act 1970.
[28] Added by the Family Law Act 1986, s.68(1), (2), Sch.1, para.9(a), Sch.2.
[29] s.58.
[30] s.62.
[31] s.71(1).

of the commission by the acquitted person of the qualifying offence has been commenced by officers.[32] *After* notice of application has been given, the court may make such an order for restricting publication either of its own motion or on the application of the Director.[33] It will be apparent that the jurisdiction resembles closely that under s.4(2) of the Contempt of Court Act 1981 to postpone publication of material giving rise to a substantial risk of prejudice. That provision, however, is confined to restricting the publication of court reports, and is thus relatively easy to understand and apply. The "inclusion of any matter in a publication", however, is more difficult. Where any such order is made, it would clearly be desirable for the court to define on the face of the order precisely the scope of the prohibition. Once a retrial has been ordered, those proceedings would be regarded as "active" within the meaning of the Contempt of Court Act 1981.[34]

III. Statutory Anonymity for Victims of Sexual Offences

A. Legislative history

8–17 In the Report of the Advisory Group on the Law of Rape[35] it was recommended that anonymity should be accorded to female rape complainants, in order that they should not be discouraged by the prospect of distressing publicity from coming forward to report an offence.[36] This reasoning is clearly consonant with the public policy considerations discussed by the House of Lords in *Scott v Scott*.[37] These restrictions were thus intended to serve the wider interests of society at large, and of the administration of justice in particular. The provisions were enacted shortly afterwards in the Sexual Offences (Amendment) Act 1976.

B. Anonymity extended to victims of other sexual offences

8–18 In the Report of the Committee on Privacy and Related Matters[38] it was recommended that, in England and Wales, the statutory prohibition on identifying rape victims should be extended to cover the victims of other sexual assaults, which were specifically listed at appendix H to the Report. In accordance with that recommendation, Parliament passed the Sexual Offences (Amendment) Act 1992, which came into effect in August of that year. With the enactment of the Sexual Offences Act 2003,[39] the list of offences (still contained within the framework of the 1992 Act) has been much extended.

---

[32] s.82(1) and (6).
[33] s.82(5).
[34] Sch.1, para.16.
[35] Cmnd. 6352 (1975), under the chairmanship of Dame Rose Heilbron. The Report and subsequent developments are considered by J. Temkin, *Rape and the Legal Process* (2nd ed., 2002), pp.305–315.
[36] *ibid.*, para.177.
[37] [1913] A.C. 417: see especially Lord Loreburn at 446.
[38] (1990) Cm. 1102 (the Calcutt Committee), para.10.13.
[39] s.139, Sch.6.

C. The time when protection begins

Originally, protection was afforded only from the time when a suspect was charged. This seemed to miss the point of the recommendation to a large extent. Its purpose was not limited to the actual course of criminal proceedings, but was also directed to the encouragement of victims not to hold back from making complaints. Unless they are protected during that specially vulnerable period prior to anyone being charged, the policy objective would be frustrated. Eventually, amendments were made to the Act to deal with this problem; protection is now granted from the moment "where an allegation has been made".[40] This change was effected by s.158 of the Criminal Justice Act 1988.

8–19

D. Power to displace the restrictions

Although it may not necessarily be realised by the victims themselves, the fact remains that there is a discretion in the court, both at the trial and on appeal, to lift the ban in certain circumstances[41] so that the protection of anonymity is by no means guaranteed. An application may be made before trial by the accused, or by another person against whom the complainant may be expected to give evidence at the trial. It has to be shown that it is necessary, in order to induce potential witnesses to come forward, or because the applicant's defence at the trial would otherwise be substantially prejudiced: s.3(1)(a). Also, the judge shall direct that s.1 should not apply to such matter as is specified provided the judge is satisfied that it is in the public interest to remove or relax the restriction *and* that there would otherwise be a substantial and unreasonable restriction upon reporting.[42] It is provided however that the judge shall not so direct "... by reason only of the outcome of the trial."[43]

8–20

E. Offences

The offence is defined[44] with effect from October 2004 as including matter in a publication, in contravention of s.1 of the 1992 Act, which is likely to lead members of the public to identify a person as the person against whom a relevant offence is alleged to have been committed. It is a strict liability offence[45] subject to certain defences. These are identified in s.5 as amended. There is first a defence of "written consent" from the victim.[46] This will not avail, however, if

8–21

---

[40] The provisions are now to be found in the Sexual Offences (Amendment) Act 1992, s.1(1). No doubt the legislature contemplated that such an "allegation" would ordinarily be made by the victim (perhaps to the police, a social worker or perhaps to a parent or carer), whereas in *O'Riordan v DPP* [2005] EWHC 1240 (Admin) considered below, when the abductor was being interviewed by the police a number of sexual offences came to light. When he was arrested for an offence under the Indecency with Children Act 1960, and s.2 of the Sexual Offences (Conspiracy and Incitement) Act 1996, this was said to constitute the allegation to which the prohibition upon publication in the 1992 Act applied: see the judgment at [6].
[41] *ibid.* s.3.
[42] s.3(2).
[43] s.3(3).
[44] s.5(1), as amended by the Youth Justice and Criminal Evidence Act 1999.
[45] *O'Riordan (Marie) v DPP* [2005] E.W.H.C. 1240 (Admin) at [27].
[46] s.5(2).

it is proved that any person interfered unreasonably with the peace or comfort of the person giving the consent, with intent to obtain it, or that the person was under the age of 16 at the time it was given.[47] It is also a defence for a person charged under the section to prove that at the time of the alleged offence he was not aware, and neither suspected nor had a reason to suspect, that the publication included the matter in question.[48] So too, it is open to the defendant to prove that at the time of the alleged offence he was not aware, and neither suspected nor had reason to suspect, that the allegation (*i.e.* of a relevant sexual offence) had been made.[49]

8–22   The defendant in *O'Riordan (Marie) v DPP*[50] was the editor of the magazine *Marie Claire*. The unusual feature of the case was that she had been convicted in respect of a reference contained in a review of the year's events of 2003 in the January 2004 issue. A 12-year-old girl had been abducted and taken to Germany the previous July and a man was later arrested and remanded in custody. When he appeared in court on August 22, it was not reported that there was an allegation of a sexual offence. Nevertheless there was in effect from his first appearance in the magistrates' court an order under s.39 of the Children and Young Persons Act 1933 prohibiting publication of particulars leading to her identification. In the magazine, there appeared a close up photograph of the girl, her full name was given and that of the former US marine who had abducted her. No reference was made to any offence in relation to her, although he was reported as having been accused of sexual misconduct in relation to two other girls aged under 13 in 1998. The police had issued a statement to the media by e-mail asking that future reporting be restricted. As it happened, neither *Marie Claire* nor IPC Magazines, the publishers, were on the Greater Manchester police press office contact list. The point was taken for the editor when she appeared at the magistrates' court in August 2004 that there was no case to answer. At this time the statutory defence under s.5(5A) of the 1992 Act had not come into force. Her submission seems therefore to have been based upon the proposition that there was no reason to suspect that a sexual allegation involving the child had been made.[51] This was rejected and, as it was subsequently held, rightly so, since such an argument would be "wholly removed from reality". It was pointed out that, if there was any doubt about the matter, it had been possible to make inquiries of the police in order to establish the facts.

8–23   The other argument raised on her behalf before the Divisional Court was that the statutory provisions were not necessary or proportionate to the inevitable interference with the right of the media to freedom of expression under Art.10, and that the nature of the conduct prohibited was not sufficiently clearly and precisely defined so that it could properly be said that the exemption was "prescribed by law" for the purposes of Art.10(2). These arguments were also

---

[47] s.5(3).
[48] s.5(5). For the distinction between "reason to suspect" and "reason to believe", see the discussion in *Milne v Express Newspapers Ltd* [2004] EWCA Civ 664, [2005] 1 W.L.R. 772, [2005] 1 All E.R. 1021, [2004] E.M.L.R. 461.
[49] s.5(5A). Inserted by the Youth Justice and Criminal Evidence Act 1999.
[50] [2005] EWHC 1240 (Admin).
[51] See Crane J. at [35].

rejected.[52] While it was true that the word "likely" has received a variety of different definitions,[53] it would derive its flavour and meaning from its context. Here, the phrase "likely to lead members of the public to identify that person" could not be said to be so imprecise as to fall foul of that requirement. It was finally observed that it was very little to ask of the media that they should take precautions to prevent publication which might affect a 12-year-old victim in such circumstances.

F. Anonymity for the accused

The 1988 Act also dealt with another controversial matter. When the 1976 Act was first passed, there had been included by s.6 a corresponding anonymity for men accused of rape. Rape being the grave offence it is, men often suffer from the slur even after acquittal, quite apart from during the criminal process itself. That is true, however, of other serious offences, and the 1975 Report expressed the view that it was illogical to single out persons accused of rape for this special protection. Eventually, after a good deal of public debate, Parliament came round to that view and the protection was removed by the provisions of s.158 of the Criminal Justice Act 1988.

IV. PROTECTION FOR JUVENILES (CHILDREN AND YOUNG PERSONS): THE 1933 ACT

A. Introduction

There are a number of sections of the Children and Young Persons Act 1933 that impose restrictions on court reporting.[54] The purpose is to provide some measure of protection for children who become involved in legal proceedings.[55] There is a clear distinction between the statutory provisions applying in the case of youth courts (s.49) and those operating in the case of adult courts (s.39). The emphasis is different in the sense that in the former case identification is prohibited subject to subs.(4A), (4B) and (5). In the latter case, the court *may* prohibit identification. There should always be a good reason for exercising the court's discretion, under any of these provisions, and such reason or reasons should be clearly stated. But there is no obligation to set out all the underlying detail of the reasoning or to specify matters that would have been familiar to those present in court. It was held in *Ex p. S and P*[56] that it would be wrong to constrain the exercise of the court's broad discretion. It was recognised, however, that the welfare of the

---

[52] The court was "entitled to derive sustenance" from the decision in *Brown v United Kingdom*, App. No.44223/98 in 2002.
[53] See, *e.g.* the discussion of "likely" in the context of *Cream Holdings Ltd v Banerjee* [2004] UKHL 44, [2005] 1 A.C. 253 in ch.6.
[54] ss.37, 39, 47, 49.
[55] Such provisions are in compliance with Art.6(1) of the European Convention on Human Rights: *R. v Central Criminal Court Ex p. S and P* (1998) 163 J.P. 776 at 784G, Sullivan J.
[56] *ibid.* 785.

relevant child or young person will always be a primary consideration (but not the sole consideration). This would be in accordance also with the stipulation to that effect in Art.3.1 of the United Nations Convention on the Rights of the Child.

B. Youth court proceedings: section 47 of the 1933 Act

8–26 The effect of s.47(2) of the Act is to achieve a hybrid status for youth court[57] proceedings, in the sense that while the general public is not admitted some media representatives are. Its terms so far as material are as follows:

" . . . no person shall be present at any sitting of a youth court[58] except—
(a) members and officers of the court;
(b) parties to the case before the court, their solicitors and counsel,[59] and witnesses and other persons directly concerned in the case;[60]
(c) bona fide representatives of newspapers or news agencies [news gathering or reporting organisations][61];
(d) such other persons as the court may especially authorise to be present."

C. The reporting restrictions: the current terms of section 49

8–27 The prohibitions currently governing such proceedings are contained in s.49(1)[62]:

"(a) no report shall be published which reveals the name, address or school of any child or young person concerned in the proceedings or includes any particulars likely to lead to the identification of any child or young person concerned in the proceedings; and
(b) no picture shall be published or included in a programme service as being or including a picture of any child or young person concerned in the proceedings."

---

[57] Established as juvenile courts by the Children and Young Persons Act 1933, s.45, these are magistrates' courts especially established for the purpose of dealing with criminal proceedings against those under the age of 18. They were renamed "youth courts" by the Criminal Justice Act 1991, s.70(1).
[58] This term was introduced by s.72 of the Criminal Justice Act 1991, and inserted in these provisions by s.100, Sch.11, para.40(1), (2)(a).
[59] In the Magistrates' Courts Act 1980, s.69(2)(b), the expression "solicitors and counsel" has been changed to "legal representatives", which would seem to extend beyond "solicitors and counsel": para.8–79. It appears that the expression "solicitors and counsel" remains in s.47.
[60] See *R.v Southwark Juvenile Court Ex p. J* [1973] 1 W.L.R. 1300. The expression would include, for example, a social worker. It is clear that the section is directory and not mandatory.
[61] The words in square brackets were added by the Youth Justice and Criminal Evidence Act 1999, s.67(1), Sch.4, para.2(1),(3) which is to come in to force from a date to be appointed. Pending that amendment, there does not seem to be any express provision in respect of broadcast journalists. Although they could no doubt be given authorisation under s.47(2)(d), it would seem to be anomalous that print journalists should have a *right* to attend, but not broadcasters.
[62] This was substituted by the Criminal Justice and Public Order Act 1994, s.49.

Protection for Juveniles (Children and Young Persons) 8–31

The penalties are provided for in s.49(9)[63] and the current maximum is a fine not exceeding level 5 on the standard scale.[64]

Thus, it is necessary for any report not only to avoid naming any such child or young person[65] directly but also to take care not to include any details *likely* to lead to identification. Journalists need therefore to have regard to any incidental facts which may in themselves be innocuous but which could, when combined with other knowledge that readers may have, lead to conclusions being drawn as to identity. Such facts might include, for example, details of schools attended, recent events well known in a particular locality, or facts about an adult to whom the child is known to be related.

8–28

It seems that the restrictions upon reporting can have no application before any "proceedings" have begun. The matter was highlighted in December 1997 when there was controversy over whether or not the press were restricted in identifying the son of a cabinet minister who was suspected of involvement in drug dealing. There were neither at that stage nor indeed subsequently any court proceedings. Nevertheless, a judge in chambers granted an injunction restraining any identification of the individual concerned (and thus of his father), apparently on the footing that if such proceedings were to be instituted the court would be deprived of its discretion[66] to maintain the young man's anonymity.

8–29

Eventually, the pressure of publicity was such that the dam inevitably burst. The matter nevertheless gives rise to legitimate and important questions so far as media coverage is concerned. The answer would appear to be that neither the regime of the 1933 Act nor the strict liability provisions of the Contempt of Court Act 1981 would apply, and that the only possible basis for imposing a restriction would be under the common law. That is to say, an injunction might be obtainable if it could be demonstrated, beyond reasonable doubt, that there would be prejudice to any proceedings that might be brought and, what is more, that there was an intention to bring about such prejudice.[67]

8–30

In the particular circumstances, this was by no means as outlandish a proposition as some journalists were suggesting. It so happened that all the details of the alleged drug transaction (involving a journalist in a public house) had already been published before the individual or his father were identified. As soon as the identification took place, that earlier publicity would inevitably have the effect of causing some prejudice in relation to guilt or innocence and, in particular, might well have led to closing off of his options in relation to either plea or mode of trial.[68]

8–31

---

[63] Also substituted by the 1994 Act, s.49.
[64] Currently £5,000. See para.14–106.
[65] See Children and Young Persons Act 1933, s.107(1), as amended, which provides that "'child' means a person under the age of fourteen years", and "'young person' means a person who has attained the age of fourteen and is under the age of eighteen years".
[66] See the terms of s.49(5) below.
[67] *Coe v Central Television plc* [1994] E.M.L.R. 433, discussed at para.6–33.
[68] See paras 4–97 *et seq.*

D. The power to lift the statutory restrictions

8–32 The restrictions in s.49 were not without flexibility, since it is provided by s.49(5)[69] that they may be lifted by the court,[70] but only if it is satisfied—

"(a) that it is appropriate to do so for the purpose of avoiding injustice to the child or young person; or
(b) that, as respects a child or young person to whom this paragraph applies who is unlawfully at large, it is necessary to dispense with those requirements for the purpose of apprehending him and bringing him before a court or returning him to the place in which he was in custody."

8–33 The second of these provisions was introduced in 1994, and is aimed at children or young persons who may be thought to represent a danger to the public; the publication of a photograph, for example, might help the police to track them down. Thus, subs.(5)(b) applies to any such person who is charged with or has been convicted of—

"(a) a violent offence,
(b) a sexual offence, or
(c) an offence punishable in the case of a person aged 21 [18] or over with imprisonment for 14 years or more."[71]

8–34 The court's power under subs.(5) to dispense with the reporting restrictions[72] should not be exercised—

"(a) except in pursuance of an application by or on behalf of the Director of Public Prosecutions; and
(b) unless notice of the application has been given by the Director of Public Prosecutions to any legal representative of the child or young person."[73]

8–35 Further relaxation of the provisions was introduced by the Crime (Sentences) Act 1997,[74] which provided for a restriction to be lifted where a child or young person has been convicted of an offence and the court considers that it is in the

---

[69] Also substituted by the 1994 Act, s.49.
[70] Formerly, the Secretary of State also had power to dispense with the prohibition, but this has been revoked.
[71] s.49(6), as substituted by Criminal Justice and Public Order Act 1994, s.49. The figures in square brackets were added by the Criminal Justice and Court Services Act 2000, s.74, Sch.7, Pt II, para.5 to come into force from a date to be appointed.
[72] Which may be exercised by a single justice: s.49(8).
[73] s.49(7).
[74] s.45, which adds new subs.(4A) and (4B) to s.49 of the 1933 Act. The 1997 provision applied only to offences committed after the date of commencement of the section, October 1, 1997: s.45(2). The Act implemented the proposals set out in the White Paper, *Protecting the Public—the Government's Strategy on Crime in England and Wales*, Cm. 3190 (March 1996). In a White Paper, *No More Excuses: A New Approach to Tackling Youth Crime in England and Wales*, Cm. 3809 (November 1997), the implementation of this provision was said to be a first step in reinforcing the responsibility of young persons and their parents for delinquent behaviour (p.12). It was also stated that " . . . there must . . . be more openness in youth court proceedings", and that "present practice places too much emphasis on protecting the identity of young offenders at the expense of the interests of victims and the community. Justice is best served in an open court where the criminal process can be scrutinised and the offender cannot hide behind a cloak of anonymity".

public interest to do so. This was achieved by adding new subsections to s.49. The amendment was intended to deal particularly with the problem of "one-child crime waves"[75]:

"(4A) If a court is satisfied that it is in the public interest to do so, it may, in relation to a child or young person who has been convicted of an offence, by order dispense to any specified extent with the requirements of this section in relation to any proceedings before it to which this section applies by virtue of subsection (2)(a) or (b) above, being proceedings relating to—
 (a) the prosecution or conviction of the offender for the offence;
 (b) the manner in which he, or his parent or guardian, should be dealt with in respect of the offence;
 (c) the enforcement, amendment, variation, revocation or discharge of any order made in respect of the offence;
 (d) where an attendance centre order is made in respect of the offence, the enforcement of any rules made under section 16(3) of the Criminal Justice Act 1982; or
 (e) where a secure training order is so made, the enforcement of any requirements imposed under section 3(7) of the Criminal Justice and Public Order Act 1994.
(4B) A court shall not exercise its power under subsection (4A) above without—
 (a) affording the parties to the proceedings an opportunity to make representations; and
 (b) taking into account any representations which are duly made".

It would seem that the preconditions for the lifting of reporting restrictions stipulated by s.49(5)[76] are not mirrored in the new provision.

In *McKerry v Teesdale and Wear Valley Justices*[77] Lord Bingham C.J. considered the implications of the European Convention on Human Rights for the above statutory reporting restrictions. The magistrates had in part allowed an application by the editor of the *Northern Echo* to have reporting restrictions lifted in a case concerning a 15-year-old of taking a motor vehicle without consent. This was because of his previous record and previous court appearances. His name was permitted to be published but not his photograph or address. The basis of the decision was explained as being that he was "a serious danger to the public". It was suggested on appeal by way of case stated that they had failed to take adequate account of Art.8. Lord Bingham drew attention to the European Court of Human Rights decisions in *T v United Kingdom* and *V v United Kingdom*[78] as well as the Beijing rules adopted by the United Nations General Assembly on November 29, 1985. Rule 8 provides for the protection of a juvenile's privacy to avoid harm being caused by undue publicity or by the process of "labelling". In principle, it makes clear that no information should be published that may lead to the identification of a "juvenile" offender. He also referred to the United Nations Convention on the Rights of the Child 1989, adopted by the General Assembly on November 20 of that year, and in particular

8–36

---

[75] W. Greenwood, *Media Lawyer*, September 1997.
[76] Set out in para.8–32.
[77] [2001] E.M.L.R. 127, (2000) 164 J.P. 355.
[78] (2000) 30 E.H.R.R. 121. See also now *SC v United Kingdom* (2005) 40 E.H.R.R. 10.

to Arts 3.1 and 40. Attention was also drawn to Recommendation No.R(87) 20 of the Committee of Ministers of the Council of Europe, adopted on September 17, 1987.

8–37 In the light of this wider background, Lord Bingham said[79]:

"It is, in my judgment, plain that there is in a situation such as the present some tension between competing principles. It is a hallowed principle that justice is administered in public, open to full and fair reporting of the proceedings in court, so that the public may be informed about the justice administered in their name. That principle comes into collision with another important principle, also of great importance and reflected in the international instruments to which I have made reference, that the privacy of a child or young person involved in the legal proceedings must be carefully protected, and very great weight must be given to the welfare of such child or young person. It is, in my judgment plain, that power to dispense with anonymity, as permitted in certain circumstances by s.49(4A), must be exercised with very great care, caution and circumspection. It would be wholly wrong for any court to dispense with a juvenile's *prima facie* right to anonymity as an additional punishment. It is also very difficult to see any place for 'naming and shaming'. The court must be satisfied that the statutory criterion that it is in the public interest to dispense with the reporting restriction is satisfied. This will very rarely be the case,[80] and justices making an order under s.49(4A) must be clear in their minds why it is in the public interest to dispense with the restrictions."

8–38 It will be legitimate to take into account oral or written submissions from a representative of the media. It is to be noted that, although the parties are to be heard on the issue, the prosecution will be expected to take a neutral stance, generally, and the defence to oppose an order. It may be therefore that representations from the press will assist the court and make for a balanced approach to resolving such sensitive issues.

E. The proceedings to which the section 49 restrictions apply

8–39 The scope of the reporting restrictions, including as to appeals, is now governed by s.49(2) of the Children and Young Persons Act 1933.[81] The relevant wording is as follows:

"The proceedings to which this section applies are—
(a) proceedings in a youth court;
(b) proceedings on appeal from a youth court (including proceedings by way of case stated);
(c) proceedings under Schedule 7 to the Powers of Criminal Courts (Sentencing) Act 2000 (proceedings for varying or revoking supervision orders); and
(d) proceedings on appeal from a magistrates' court arising out of proceedings under Schedule 7 to that Act (including proceedings by way of case stated)."

---

[79] At [17].
[80] But see below at para.8–44 where an apparent shift of public policy is discussed in relation to ASBOs in which context publicity will now be "the norm".
[81] As substituted by Criminal Justice and Public Order Act 1994, s.49. The section came into effect on February 3, 1995: SI 1995/127. At the same time, subsections (1) and (2) of s.10 of the Children and Young Persons Act 1969 were repealed.

PROTECTION FOR JUVENILES (CHILDREN AND YOUNG PERSONS)   8-42

The matter of openness was considered in somewhat unusual circumstances in **8-40**
R. v Westminster City Council Ex p. L.[82] Warrants had been issued in Ireland for the arrest of a 16-year-old on charges of burglary, robbery and theft. It was requested that the warrants be endorsed under the Backing of Warrants (Republic of Ireland) Act 1965 and that he be returned. It was provided in that statute[83] that such proceedings had to take place in open court. The applicant appeared before a juvenile court and, after those concerned in the case had entered, the doors were locked as a security measure. The justices endorsed the warrants and ordered that he be remanded to the care of a local authority pending deportation.

An application was made to the Divisional Court for a writ of *habeas corpus*. **8-41**
This was dismissed because, although it was mandatory, the "open court" requirement under the Backing of Warrants Act 1965 Act had to be read alongside ss.46 and 47 of the 1933 Act. The hearing of a criminal charge against a juvenile had to be heard in what was then called a juvenile court, and the restrictions on access by the public to such a court were for the protection of the juvenile concerned, and thus did not impose unacceptable restraints on the principle of open justice. In any event, a magistrates' court was entitled to take into account matters of security, public order and public safety in controlling those who were permitted to enter and attend the court hearing. In the circumstances, the fact that the doors had been locked was not contrary to law, and the proceedings before the justices had therefore been valid.

F. The statutory changes in the context of anti-social behaviour orders

There has been a considerable shift of public policy specifically with regard to **8-42**
publicity concerning juveniles who are made the subject of anti-social behaviour orders. It is perceived that the local community in such circumstances has a proper interest to know the identities of such persons. This consideration therefore generally will be given priority over protection of privacy for the offenders. There is thus clearly a tension between the rights of the public at large to receive such information and the traditional disinclination to "name and shame" articulated by Lord Bingham in *McKerry v Teesdale and Wear Valley Justices*.[84] This tension was considered by Elias J. in the context of s.39 restrictions.[85] In *Chief Constable of Surrey v JHG and DHG; R. (on the application of T) v St. Albans Crown Court*,[86] he reviewed the authorities and identified a list of factors to be taken into account when determining whether to impose or lift such restrictions. He also addressed, in particular, the issue of identifying young persons who have become the subject of anti-social behaviour orders under s.1 of the Crime and Disorder Act 1998. It is a major factor to bear in mind, when considering whether to impose or lift a s.39 order, if the person in question is subject to such an order. It may be more effectively enforced if local residents are aware of it. Secondly, the purpose of any such order is to protect the public from the individual concerned, and the public thus has an interest in

---

[82] [1992] 1 W.L.R. 253.
[83] para.2 of the Schedule.
[84] [2001] E.M.L.R. 127, (2000) 164 J.P. 355, cited at para.8-37 above.
[85] As to which see below generally at para.8-50.
[86] [2002] EWHC 1129 (Admin).

knowing who in its midst has been responsible for the relevant behaviour. Elias J. drew a fine distinction between considerations of this kind and the concept of "naming and shaming" to which Lord Bingham had referred in the *McKerry* case. He said that the local community had a proper interest in knowing who had been seriously and persistently "damaging its fabric". It was not simply publicity for the sake of satisfying public prurience.

8–43 This tension was again considered in *R (Stanley, Marshall and Kelly) v Metropolitan Police Commissioner and London Borough of Brent* by Kennedy L.J.[87]:

> "It is clear to me that whether publicity is intended to inform, to reassure, to assist in enforcing the existing orders by policing, to inhibit the behaviour of those against whom the orders have been made, or to deter others, it is unlikely to be effective unless it includes photographs, names and at least partial addresses. Not only do the readers need to know against whom orders have been made, but those responsible for publicity must leave no room for mis-identification."

8–44 It was accepted that the rights of the relevant young persons to respect for their private lives would be affected by such publicity and thus Art.8 of the ECHR was engaged. The test to be applied therefore would be whether the need for publicity, and the terms in which it was couched, could be described as "necessary and proportionate" to an identified legitimate aim. Kennedy L.J. set out a number of factors to be taken into account and suggested that further guidance from the Home Office might be helpful. Thus, on March 1, 2005, the government published *Guidance on Publicising Anti-Social Behaviour Orders*[88] which was to a large extent based on the content of Kennedy L.J.'s judgment. A case by case approach needs to be adopted which balances the human rights of the individuals against those of the community as a whole. It was emphasised that publicity should be the norm in this context rather than the exception. The relevant factors were said to include:

1. An ASBO is not in itself to be regarded as a punishment (it is rather a preventative order).

2. The publicity should not be treated as a punishment of the individual, but as a means of enabling local communities to identify relevant offenders with a view to tackling anti-social behaviour.

3. In deciding whether and what information to publish, an authority must adopt measures which constitute the least possible interference with privacy.

4. It is necessary to consider whether the terms of the publicity are proportionate to the aims of the publicity in the particular case.

8–45 With effect from January 20, 2004,[89] s.49 of the Children and Young Persons Act 1933 no longer applies following conviction in a youth court in respect of a

---

[87] [2004] EWHC 2229 (Admin) at [40].
[88] www.together.gov.uk.
[89] By virtue of s.9C of the Crime and Disorder Act 1998 (inserted by the Anti-Social Behaviour Act 2003, s.86(3): SI 2003/3300, art.2(f)(ii).

PROTECTION FOR JUVENILES (CHILDREN AND YOUNG PERSONS) 8–49

child or young person against whom a "bolt-on" ASBO[90] is made. However, s.39 of the 1933 Act continues to apply so that an adult court will retain a discretionary power to prohibit publication. It is likely that this power will be exercised only in a minority of cases and that very similar considerations will be taken into account as those identified in the Home Office Guidance cited above.

Consistently with these policy developments, it was provided in the Serious Organised Crime and Police Act 2005, s.141[91] that, at a later stage, when it is alleged that an ASBO has been breached in what will inevitably be criminal proceedings, the young people concerned will be automatically deprived (prior to conviction) of the anonymity that would otherwise be provided by s.49.

8–46

G. The duty to announce that the section applies

It is provided by s.49(10)[92]:

8–47

"In any proceedings under schedule 7 to the Powers of Criminal Courts (Sentencing) Act 2000 (proceedings for varying or revoking supervision orders) before a magistrates' court other than a youth court or on appeal from such a court it shall be the duty of the magistrates' court or the appellate court to announce in the course of the proceedings that this section applies to the proceedings; and if the court fails to do so this section shall not apply to the proceedings".

H. Does section 12 of the Administration of Justice Act 1960 apply?

A question arises because of the "hybrid" status of youth court proceedings, as we have described it above[93] whether it is necessary to have regard to s.12 of the Administration of Justice Act 1960,[94] in addition to the specified restrictions contained in the Children and Young Persons Act. In the light of *P v Liverpool Daily Post and Echo Newspapers plc*,[95] it appears to be a *prima facie* contempt to publish information, within the categories identified in s.12(1), which relates to proceedings before any court *sitting in private*.

8–48

It is submitted that this general restriction would *not* apply. It is most unlikely that youth court proceedings would fall within either of the only two categories that could be relevant, that is to say proceedings brought under the Children Act

8–49

---

[90] This weapon was introduced with effect from December 2002 by the Police Reform Act 2002, s.64, which inserted a new s.1C into the Crime and Disorder Act 1998 for that purpose. Hitherto an ASBO could only be imposed in the course of civil proceedings. It was its introduction into criminal proceedings which led to the need to reconcile the publicity demands associated with such orders with the traditional statutory anonymity afforded to juveniles in criminal proceedings by virtue of ss.39 and 49 of the 1933 Act.
[91] Which inserts a new s.1(10D) into the Crime and Disorder Act 1998 for the purpose. The section came in to force on July 1, 2005.
[92] As substituted by Criminal Justice and Public Order Act 1994, s.49. Section 10(2) of the Children and Young Persons Act 1969 was repealed by the 1994 Act, s.168(3), Sch.11, with effect from February 3, 1995: SI 1995/127.
[93] At para.8–26.
[94] The terms of which are set out at para.8–98.
[95] [1991] 2 A.C. 370, considered at para.8–130.

1989[96] and proceedings relating wholly or mainly to the maintenance or upbringing of a minor.[97] Moreover, it is clearly considered desirable, as a matter of public policy, that journalists should be permitted to attend such proceedings to inform the public about that aspect of the administration of justice. Provided they comply with the specific restrictions of s.49(1), and with any orders the court makes within its general jurisdiction,[98] it is difficult to see how it could be regarded as a contempt of court to publish what passes at such proceedings; or, for that matter, how it could be regarded as "necessary in a democratic society" to impose such restrictions.

I. Protection for children or young persons in adult proceedings: section 39 of the 1933 Act

8–50 The Act provides a discretion to any court in which a child or young person appears as a defendant[99] or a witness in an adult court. This discretion, since it is to be regarded as collateral to the issues arising between the Crown and the defendant, is amenable to judicial review even though arising in the course of a trial on indictment.[1] The provisions of s.39[2] so far as material are as follows:

"(1) In relation to any proceedings in any court . . . the court may direct that—
(a) no newspaper report of the proceedings shall reveal the name, address, or school, or include any particulars[3] calculated to lead to the identification, of any child or young person concerned in the proceedings, either, as being the person by or against, or in respect of whom the proceedings are taken, or as being a witness therein;
(b) no picture shall be published in any newspaper as being or including a picture of any child or young person so concerned in the proceedings as aforesaid;
except insofar (if at all) as may be permitted by the court."

Section 39(2) prescribes a maximum penalty of £5,000.[4]

J. The anomalies and the residual role of the inherent jurisdiction

8–51 The facts of *Re S (FC) (A Child) (Identification: Restrictions on Publication)* illustrated what were in the view of the Court of Appeal[5] some of the anomalies of confining the protection to those who fall within the categories of defendant,

---

[96] s.12(1)(a)(ii).
[97] s.12(1)(a)(iii).
[98] *e.g.* under s.4(2) or s.11 of the Contempt of Court Act 1981.
[99] For example, as co-defendant with an adult, or as a defendant in proceedings for murder. See generally J. Sprack, *A Practical Approach to Criminal Procedure* (10th ed., 2004), ch.10.
[1] *R. v Cardiff Crown Court Ex p. M* [1998] T.L.R. 264, a decision on the scope of the Supreme Court Act 1981, s.29(3).
[2] The section is printed as amended and repealed, in part, by the Children and Young Persons Act 1963, ss.57(1) and 64(3) and Sch.5. This statute extended the section to cover reports on television and by sound broadcasting.
[3] See the comments made in relation to "jigsaw identification": para.8–72.
[4] See *R. v Tyne Tees Television Ltd* [1997] T.L.R. 515, where the judge had imposed a fine of £10,000 (upon the company which had chosen not to be represented) in respect of what had been a breach of an order made by him under s.39.
[5] [2004] Fam. 43.

witness or victim. A mother was indicted for the murder of one of her children. Following that child's death, his brother CS was fostered for a year and then returned to live with his father pursuant to a care order. An order was made under s.39 prohibiting publication of any detail calculated to lead to the identification of CS, but this was discharged because he did not fall into any of the relevant classes. Another order was made, however, in the inherent jurisdiction of the Family Division by the judge hearing the care proceedings[6] which had the effect (initially) of preventing the publication of the mother's name or any photograph of her during the criminal trial and of any details of the deceased's brother. This was later modified, however, on the application of a local newspaper. Nonetheless, it was pointed out by Hale L.J.[7] that had CS been a victim of his mother his welfare would have prevailed over other considerations, such as those of open justice and the entitlement of the public to have information about those charged with murder. She added:

> "Yet his brother was also, in a very real sense, a victim of the alleged offence. He has lost his brother, his mother, and his family life, and he is at much greater risk of suffering serious psychiatric ill-health in future. If one purpose of section 39 is to protect child victims from further adverse consequences of the crimes alleged to have been committed against them, there is little logic in failing to afford such protection to a child in the unenviable position in which CS finds himself."

Later,[8] she concluded:

> "There can be no doubt that the child's article 8 rights are engaged in this application. Publication is likely to interfere with his family life, both with the father who looks after him and with his mother. It is also likely to interfere with his private life".

The case went to the House of Lords.[9] Lord Steyn, having pointed out that the terms of s.45 of the Youth Justice and Criminal Evidence Act 1999 would, when they came into force, be the same in material respects as the extant s.39(1) of the 1933 Act, went on to highlight the fact that there had been a legislative choice not to extend the right to restrain publicity to children (such as the child in question) who were not "concerned" in a criminal trial. This, he said, was "a factor which cannot be ignored". He also discussed the novelty of the order sought, restricting reporting of criminal proceedings, and the public policy arguments available to support a distinction being drawn as to the privacy of children directly involved in criminal proceedings and that of those who were only indirectly affected.[10]

K. The amendments contained in the Youth Justice and Criminal Evidence Act 1999

The statutory provisions of s.39, which are still for the moment applicable, are to be significantly amended by the provisions of the Youth Justice and Criminal

---

[6] For a consideration of this aspect of the case see para.6–101.
[7] At [39].
[8] At [49].
[9] [2004] UKHL 47, [2005] 1 A.C. 593.
[10] See the discussion at [25]–[27] and the passages cited from his speech at para.6–105.

8–53 CHAPTER 8—COURT REPORTING II: OTHER STATUTORY RESTRICTIONS

Evidence Act 1999.[11] It is intended to insert a subs.(3) to s.39 of the 1933 Act which will define "proceedings" to mean proceedings other than criminal proceedings. Thus, the section will have no further application to criminal proceedings (except in relation to those begun prior to its coming into effect).[12] The power to restrict reporting of criminal proceedings involving persons under 18 years of age is to be governed by s.45 of the 1999 Act, save in relation to proceedings to which s.49 of the Children and Young Persons Act 1933 applies (*i.e.* those in youth courts).[13] As to adult witnesses, the court's power to restrict reporting in criminal proceedings is extended by s.46.[14]

8–54 The court is to be given power under s.45(3)[15] to direct that no matter relating to a person concerned in criminal proceedings, in any court in England and Wales or Northern Ireland (other than a Service Court) and in any Service Court (wherever), shall be included in any publication while he is under 18 if it is likely to identify him as a person concerned in the proceedings. A "person concerned" will still be regarded as confined to either a defendant or a witness or a victim.[16] Once made, such a direction may be dispensed with in whole or in part, if the court (or an appellate court) is satisfied that it is necessary to make such an "excepting direction" in the interests of justice.[17] An "excepting direction" may also be given where the court (or an appellate court) is satisfied that any restrictions already imposed are "substantial and unreasonable" and that it is in the public interest to remove or relax them.[18] But this power is not to be exercised by reason of the fact that the proceedings have been determined in any way or have been abandoned. Not surprisingly, in deciding whether to make a direction under s.45(3) or an "excepting direction" under subss.(4) or (5), regard must be had to the welfare of the person concerned. These powers have to be exercised having regard to international instruments such as those identified in *McKerry v Teesdale and Wear Valley Justices*.[19]

L. Guidance from the courts on the exercise of the section 39 discretion

8–55 Sometimes it may be necessary to prevent the identification even of the defendants if the revelation of their names would have the effect inevitably of revealing the identity of the children sought to be protected. The Act does not empower a court to make such an order in terms, but it may well be an incidental consequence of a properly drawn s.39 order, simply because the identification of (say) parents or carers charged with child cruelty will almost certainly identify the children.[20] The point was explained by Maurice Kay L.J. in *R. v Teeside*

---

[11] s.48 and Sch.2, para.2(1). (For a full discussion, see *Archbold 2005* at para.4–27.)
[12] s.24 and Sch.2, para.2(2) of the 1999 Act.
[13] See para.8–25.
[14] See below para.8–74 *et seq.*
[15] At the time of writing, the provision was not in force.
[16] s.45(7). See the discussion of the problems with this definition highlighted in *Re S (FC)* at para.8–51 above.
[17] s.45(4).
[18] s.45(5).
[19] [2001] E.M.L.R. 127,(2000) 164 J.P. 355. See para.8–36.
[20] *Ex parte Godwin* [1992] Q.B. 190 at 196; *R. v Central Criminal Court Ex p. Godwin and Crook* [1995] 1 F.L.R. 132.

Crown Court Ex p. Media Gazette Co Ltd.[21] The case concerned two defendants charged with offences of making or distributing indecent photographs of an 11 year-old girl and of conspiracy to rape her. They pleaded guilty to the former and were convicted of the latter. An insupportable order purporting to be made under s.39 had to be quashed because it actually included an embargo on reporting the proceedings altogether as well as preventing identification of one of the two defendants (the father of the girl). It was assumed by counsel that once these restrictions had been removed there would be no objection to reporting his name. The court however did not regard it as "axiomatic" that such reporting would comply with a properly drafted s.39 order (or indeed with the anonymity requirements under s.1 of the Sexual Offences (Amendment) Act 1992—which applied to the conspiracy to rape). It was pointed out that offences of the kind established are frequently committed by fathers and stepfathers. It was added that:

> "If the offender is named and the victim is described as 'an 11 year-old schoolgirl', in circumstances in which the offender has an 11 year-old daughter, it is at least arguable that the composite picture presented embraces 'particulars calculated to lead to the identification' of the victim".

The court went on to record that counsel for the Attorney-General supported that view. Moreover, it was made clear that were it not for the decision in the earlier case of *Ex p. Godwin*[22] the court would have construed s.39 as enabling the court to grant an express restriction upon the naming of the defendant and would have included such an express restriction in the order.

Judges are required to weigh the interest in the full reporting of the relevant crime, including the identification of the defendants, against the need to protect the children, often victims of abuse, from harm. That is a discretionary task.[23]

8–56

It was said in one case that the discretion should normally be exercised in favour of imposing restrictions. In *R. v Leicester Crown Court Ex p. S (A Minor)*[24] Tasker Watkins L.J., in the Divisional Court, commented:

8–57

> "The mere fact that the person before the court is a child or young person will normally be a good reason for restricting reports of the proceedings in the ways permitted by s.39 and it will, in our opinion, only be in rare and exceptional cases that directions under s.39 will not be given or having been given will be discharged".

It is necessary, however, to approach this statement with some caution because in the later case of *R. v Lee*[25] the Court of Appeal drew attention to the fact that nothing in the statutory wording justified the stricture that s.39 reporting restrictions were only to be withheld "in rare and exceptional cases". Parliament had clearly intended that there should be a difference of approach, as between

8–58

---

[21] [2005] EWCA Crim 1983 at [19].
[22] [1992] Q.B. 190.
[23] *R. v Central Criminal Court Ex p. Godwin and Crook* [1995] 1 F.L.R. 132. See generally the discussion in I. Cram, "To review or not to review" (1999) 149 New Law Jo. 1468.
[24] [1992] 2 All E.R. 659 at 662.
[25] [1993] 2 All E.R. 170.

8–58 CHAPTER 8—COURT REPORTING II: OTHER STATUTORY RESTRICTIONS

youth courts and adult proceedings in the Crown Court. It is obvious that s.49(1), in respect of the former, imposes a general restriction whereas, by contrast, s.39 provides for the exercise of a judicial discretion. This could be unduly circumscribed by grafting on to the statutory wording such prescriptive criteria as those adopted by Tasker Watkins L.J.

8–59 As has been pointed out already, in connection with the statutory discretion under s.4(2) of the Contempt of Court Act 1981, the enactment of s.159 of the Criminal Justice Act 1988 was introduced to afford journalists the opportunity of challenging *restrictions* on publication; and accordingly it does not avail someone who seeks, as in the case of *Lee*, to challenge a judge's *refusal* to restrict reporting.[26] The case concerned a 14-year-old rapist whose identification the judge was willing to permit. Because he had refused to make an order under s.39, the Court of Appeal held that it had no jurisdiction, but offered to hear an application for judicial review *qua* judges of the Divisional Court. It was later stated by Simon Brown L.J. that jurisdiction had been assumed wrongly and without argument.[27] The application was granted, but relief refused.

8–60 The important matter of the court's jurisdiction to review judicial decisions under s.39 of the 1933 Act was considered in *R. v Winchester Crown Court Ex p. B*[28] and in *R. v Manchester Crown Court Ex p. H and D*,[29] In the former case the Divisional Court took the view that s.29(3) of the Supreme Court Act 1981 prevented judicial review of the trial judge's decision to discharge a s.39 order. Simon Brown L.J. reasoned that directions under s.39 were "equally integral to the administration of justice as section 11 orders [*i.e.* under the Contempt of Court Act 1981]". A few months later, however, in the *Manchester Crown Court* case, a differently constituted court (Rose L.J. and Forbes J.) declined to follow this approach and concluded that the court did indeed have the power of judicial review. The court considered itself bound by the decision of *R. v Lee*,[30] despite the fact that Simon Brown L.J. in *Winchester Crown Court* had commented that the Court of Appeal in *Lee* had merely assumed jurisdiction without argument.

8–61 Another example of a judge's refusal to invoke the power of restriction under s.39 was in connection with the case of the murder of a small boy by two 10-year-olds, when Morland J. in the Liverpool Crown Court permitted their identification.[31] He did so after their convictions, so that details of their names,

---

[26] See also *R. v Saunders* [1990] Crim.L.R. 597, considered in para.7–254. The point is made explicit in *R. v S* [1995] 2 Cr.App.R. 347, in the context of s.159.
[27] *R. v Winchester Crown Court Ex p. B* [1999] 1 W.L.R. 788, [1999] 4 All E.R. 53.
[28] [1999] 1 W.L.R. 788, [1999] 4 All E.R. 53.
[29] [2000] 1 W.L.R. 760, [2000] 2 All E.R. 166.
[30] [1993] 1 W.L.R. 103, 2 All E.R. 170, considered above at para.8–58.
[31] The case went to the House of Lords, but on a different point: *R. v Secretary of State for the Home Department Ex p. Thompson and Venables* [1998] A.C. 407, CA and HL. See also now *Venables and Thompson v News Group Newspapers Ltd* [2001] Fam. 430. It is debatable whether the decision in 1993 to permit the boys to be named in itself exacerbated the security problem which had to be addressed in 2001. It may well be that their identities were widely known in any event, especially in the Liverpool area.

backgrounds and photographs taken prior to arrest could be published. Nonetheless, he also prohibited publication of addresses or of any details which would lead to revealing their whereabouts, care or treatment. This was because the public interest required that there be a reasonable opportunity of rehabilitation. These steps were taken "by virtue of his office as a High Court judge" in the exercise of the inherent or *parens patriae* jurisdiction of the High Court.[32] That opportunity would not, it seems, have been available to any judge merely by virtue of sitting in the Crown Court.[33]

The present uncertainty

One of the difficulties of the present situation, which the approach of Tasker Watkins L.J. in *Ex p. S*[34] would at least have gone some way to alleviate, is that there is no clear guidance as to the criteria judges should apply when invited to make an order under s.39. It is true that the facts will vary infinitely, and there is need for a degree of flexibility; the other side of the coin is that there is uncertainty and unpredictability, verging on arbitrariness, in an important area of court reporting. Moreover, it seems that appellate courts will be slow to interfere with the exercise of a trial judge's discretion in this respect.[35]

This uncertainty perhaps assumes greater significance in view of social trends, leading to an apparent increase in the commission of serious crimes, of a violent or sexual nature, by younger age groups. It became therefore desirable that there should be consistency and perhaps statutory guidelines to achieve that end. There could be, for example, a statutory presumption in favour of withholding the identities of such offenders, which could only be displaced if it is shown that the public interest[36] for some reason requires the *names* of the young offenders to be published; that is different from showing, for example, that the crime committed was in itself a matter of public interest, or particularly serious or repugnant, or that it provides an example of a trend of wider significance. As was pointed out by Neill L.J. in *Re W (A Minor)*,[37] in the different context of the court's *parens patriae* jurisdiction, it will be rare that any legitimate public interest will be served by revealing the identity of a child. Some cases, however, place judges under almost irresistible pressure to give newspapers wider scope for covering

---

[32] See the discussion by Hale L.J. in *Re S* [2003] EWCA Civ 963, [2004] Fam. 43 at [28] and [61].
[33] A question may arise as to whether the relevant powers would be conferred upon a Crown Court judge by virtue of the Supreme Court Act 1981, s.45(4) which states that "the Crown Court shall, in relation to . . . all other matters incidental to its jurisdiction, have the like powers, rights, privileges and authority as the High Court".
[34] [1992] 2 All E.R. 659.
[35] *R. v Inner London Crown Court Ex p. Barnes, The Times*, August 7, 1995, (1996) C.O.D. 17. See also *R. v Central Criminal Court Ex p. Godwin and Crook* [1995] 1 F.L.R. 132, CA and the discussion by I. Cram, "Publish and damn" (1999) 149 New Law Jo. 1748.
[36] These will be to some extent covered by the terms of s.45(4) and (5) of the Youth Justice and Criminal Evidence Act 1999. Cp. the similar test to be applied under s.3(2)(b) of the Sexual Offences (Amendment) Act 1992. See also the much tighter restrictions imposed by s.49 of the Children and Young Persons Act 1933, described in paras 8–27 *et seq.*, which apply to children appearing before youth courts.
[37] [1992] 1 W.L.R. 100. This case is more fully discussed in para.6–90 in the context of the court's jurisdiction to grant injunctions.

sensational crimes. There is something to be said for Parliament laying down strict criteria rather than for judges to have to operate under the threat of any such restriction being characterised as a "cover-up". On the other hand, cases vary so much as to their facts, and it would be a pity if all elements of discretion were removed.

8–64   There will at least be some such guidance when s.45(5) of the Youth Justice and Criminal Evidence Act 1999 comes into effect in the sense that two broad (if somewhat banal) criteria are identified for the purposes of making "an excepting direction" (so as to dispense with a direction under s.45(3) restricting publication of any matter relating to a person under the age of 18 which might lead to his identification). The court needs to be satisfied:

(a) that the effect of those restrictions would be to impose "a substantial and unreasonable restriction on the reporting of the proceedings";

(b) that it is in the public interest to remove or relax the restriction.

These two criteria are clearly closely linked. The public interest would most obviously be engaged where the child or young person concerned remains at liberty and represents a continuing risk.

8–65   Detailed and important guidance was given in the Divisional Court in *R. v Central Criminal Court Ex p. S and P.*[38] Section 44(1) of the 1933 Act requires the court to have regard to the welfare of the relevant person, but not to the exclusion of all other relevant factors.[39] It is necessary, for example, to bear in mind the comment of Glidewell L.J. in *R. v Central Criminal Court Ex p. Crook and Godwin*[40] to the effect that there is "a strong and proper public interest in knowing the identity of those who have committed crimes, particularly serious and detestable crimes". The discretionary exercise involves balancing the interests of the public, in knowing as much as possible about what has happened in the court, against the desirability of not causing harm to any relevant child or young person. It will be a legitimate factor for a judge to take into account that the naming of the offender may contribute to the deterrent effect of a sentence.[41] In the case of more serious offences, also, the defendants may be sentenced to a sufficiently long period of custody for press reporting not to cause any significant damage to the prospects of rehabilitation within the community. In view of the statutory introduction of the "public interest" in s.45(5) of the 1999 Act, the judicial guidance will in due course need to be set alongside that provision, but it is likely still to be of assistance.

8–66   It was, no doubt, the public interest in receiving full information about court proceedings which led to Parliament's amendment of s.49 of the Children and Young Persons Act 1933 through the Crime (Sentences) Act 1997. What now

---

[38] (1998) 163 J.P. 776.
[39] At 783, Sullivan J.
[40] (1995) 2 Cr.App.R. 212 at 219, [1995] 1 F.L.R. 132 at 137F–G.
[41] *R. v Inner London Crown Court Ex p. Barnes* (1996) C.O.D. 17, D.C. Contrast the Home Office guidance which states that publicity is *not* to be regarded as a punishment. See para.8–44.

seems to be clear is that when the court is carrying out a balancing exercise the weight to be attributed to these various factors may shift at different stages of the proceedings. In particular, protection afforded to a defendant prior to conviction (or to a plea of guilty) may cease to be appropriate thereafter. A judge may conclude that the public interest in knowing the identity of those who have committed crimes should then prevail. The Divisional Court emphasised in *R. v Crown Court at Manchester Ex p. H*[42] that it would be a highly relevant factor that non-frivolous grounds of appeal had been lodged giving rise to the possibility that a re-trial might be ordered. This would be a matter of the greatest importance in exercising the discretion as to whether anonymity should or should not be maintained.

The practice of the courts will need to be reviewed in the light of the statutory regime to be introduced by s.45 of the Youth Justice and Criminal Evidence Act 1999 and the guidance given by the Lord Chief Justice in *McKerry v Teesdale and Wear Valley Justices*,[43] where he made reference to a number of international instruments and expressed the view that there will rarely be scope for "naming and shaming". That seems consistent with the Home Office guidance to the effect that "naming" should not be regarded as a punishment. The issue requires to be considered in the light of the public interest.

8–67

Procedure for making orders under the Children and Young Persons Act

The Court of Appeal gave guidance in *Ex p. Crook*.[44] In such cases, where an order is made, it should be reduced into writing as soon as possible and " . . . it is necessary that when an order is made its terms should be clear and readily ascertainable by those whom it affects".[45] Normally it will suffice to use the words of s.39(1), or a suitable adaptation, and to relate the order to, for example, "the child/children named in the charge/indictment". If there is any doubt as to which child or children the order relates, the court should identify them with clarity. The matter was also considered in *Briffett v DPP*.[46] It was there held that the wording must "leave no doubt, in the mind of a reasonable reader or recipient, as to precisely what it is that is prohibited". This was no more than an application of "the principle of legal certainty". The order under consideration was ambiguous in that it referred simply to "reporting restrictions" under s.39 and to the need to list the matter as *Ex p. K*. Thus even an experienced reader might be unclear as to whether the order extended to the full width of the matters expressly referred to in s.39(1) or whether it was merely intended to prohibit publication of the child's name. That order was therefore held to be ineffective. Newman J. added that although s.39 orders were regularly made in the

8–68

---

[42] [2000] 1 W.L.R. 760, [2000] 2 All E.R. 166.
[43] [2001] E.M.L.R. 127, (2000) 164 J.P. 355, considered in greater detail at para.8–36. Cp. the decision of Elias J. in *Chief Constable of Surrey v JHG and DHG; The Queen on the application of T v St. Albans Crown Court* [2002] EWHC 1129 (Admin) discussed at para.8–42 above. See also the article by Michael Todd, "Taking children out of the picture" in *The Times*, February 2, 1999.
[44] [1995] 1 W.L.R. 139, [1995] 1 All E.R. 537, [1995] 1 F.L.R. 132.
[45] [1995] 1 W.L.R. at 146C, [1995] 1 All E.R. at 544c, [1995] 1 F.L.R. at 132, 139A.
[46] [2001] EWHC (Admin) 841, [2002] E.M.L.R. 203, *per* Laws L.J.

8–68 CHAPTER 8—COURT REPORTING II: OTHER STATUTORY RESTRICTIONS

Administrative Court, especially in education cases, it had not hitherto been his experience that draft orders were presented to the judge for consideration. It should now become the practice that a draft should be submitted in every case so as to enable the judge to consider the ambit of the order and the extent of the "pressing social need" for such a restriction.

8–69 Furthermore, a written copy should be drawn as soon as possible and made available in a court office for representatives of the press to inspect. It was recommended that there should be a *pro forma* which could be adapted if necessary to special cases.

8–70 The fact that an order has been made should be communicated to those who were not present. This can perhaps best be achieved by including a short notice in the daily court list. That would alert the press to the fact that an order has been made; they could ascertain its precise terms from the court office. If such a procedure is followed, it would become more practicable for editors to devise a foolproof system for regular checks to be made.[47] The matter is now also covered in the *Consolidated Criminal Practice Direction*[48] where it is provided that "Any such order, once made, should be reduced to writing and copies should on request be made available to anyone affected or potentially affected by it".

M. The power to clear the court: section 37

8–71 In addition and without prejudice to any other powers of the court to hear proceedings *in camera*, s.37 of the Act confers a power to direct, in certain circumstances, that all or any persons (save for those directly concerned with the case) be excluded from the court during the taking of evidence from a person who is, in the opinion of the court, a child or young person. Those circumstances are where the witness is giving evidence in relation to an offence against, or any conduct contrary to, "decency or morality". This power is subject to the important proviso that it cannot authorise the exclusion of *bona fide* representatives of a newspaper or news agency.[49]

N. The problem of "jigsaw identification"

8–72 There is the possibility that readers of one news source will be able to combine information contained in it with other facts from a different publication; hence the problem of so-called "jigsaw identification". This was addressed by the Committee on Privacy and Related Matters[50]:

---

[47] The situation is perhaps akin to that addressed by Mann L.J. and Brooke J. in *Att-Gen v Guardian Newspapers Ltd (No.3)* [1992] 1 W.L.R. 874, 3 All E.R. 38.
[48] See now Pt IV.39.8, [2002] 1 W.L.R. 2870 as amended. For the latest version of the *Direction* see www.courtservice.gov.uk/docs/cpd/consol_criminal_pd_220305.doc.
[49] Cp. the similar provisions of s.47, considered at para.8–26.
[50] (1990) Cm. 1102, paras 10.16–10.19. Clive Walker,"Fundamental Rights, Fair Trials and the New Audio-Visual Sector" (1996) 59 M.L.R. at 528, considers the problem of trans-national jigsaw identification.

"The problem arises where different news organisations report different details from criminal proceedings for sexual offences. For example, one report might name a defendant but not specify the alleged offence; another might refer to an un-named father charged with abusing his children. Each report may be compiled with proper regard to the law or any court order in force. Nevertheless, when the reports are read together, it is possible to identify the victim."

Legislation was not recommended to deal with this problem because of difficulty of drafting and problems of implementation.

Attempts were made to grapple with jigsaw identification, however, in clause 7 of the Code promulgated and sponsored by the Press Complaints Commission in the context of sex offences:

"Children in sex cases

1. The press must not, even if legally free to do so, identify children under 16 who are victims or witnesses in cases involving sex offences.
2. In any press report of a case involving a sexual offence against a child—
    (i) The child must not be identified.
    (ii) The adult may be identified.
    (iii) The word 'incest' must not be used where a child victim might be identified.
    (iv) Care must be taken that nothing in the report implies the relationship between the accused and the child."

V. ANONYMITY FOR WITNESSES: SECTION 46 OF THE YOUTH JUSTICE AND CRIMINAL EVIDENCE ACT 1999

The relationship between open justice and the protection for individuals involved in the judicial process has been to an extent realigned as a result of statutory intervention. Section 46 of the Youth Justice and Criminal Evidence Act 1999[51] applies to any criminal proceedings in England and Wales or Northern Ireland (other than a Service Court) and to any proceedings in a Service Court (wherever). The court may make a "reporting direction" to the effect that no matter relating to a witness shall be included in any publication if it is likely to lead to his being identified as a witness in the proceedings. The power may be exercised in respect of a witness who is "eligible for protection" if such a direction would be likely to improve the quality of his evidence or the level of co-operation given by the witness to any party in the preparation of its case. A person is "eligible" under this section if the court is satisfied that either factor is likely to be diminished by reason of fear or distress in connection with being identified as a witness.

In making that determination, the court must take into account the matters identified in s.46, subsections (4) and (5):

---

[51] The section came into effect on October 7, 2004; SI 2004/2428 (C.104).

"(4) In determining whether a witness is eligible for protection the court must take into account, in particular—
(a) the nature and alleged circumstances of the offence to which the proceedings relate;
(b) the age of the witness;
(c) such of the following matters as appear to the court to be relevant,
  (i) the social and cultural background and ethnic origins of the witness,
  (ii) the domestic and employment circumstances of the witness, and
  (iii) any religious beliefs or political opinions of the witness;
(d) any behaviour towards the witness on the part of—
  (i) the accused,
  (ii) members of the family or associates of the accused, or
  (iii) any other person who is likely to be an accused or a witness in the proceedings.
(5) In determining that question the court must in addition consider any views expressed by the witness."

VI. Protection for Family Proceedings

A. Section 65(1) of the Magistrates' Courts Act 1980

8-76 It is necessary to consider the network of statutory provisions designed to restrict both access to and reporting of "family proceedings".[52] For example, it is provided by the Magistrates' Courts Act 1980, s.144, that rules may be made for the purpose of enabling such a court to sit in private in proceedings in which any powers under the Children Act 1989 may be exercised.[53]

8-77 A convenient starting point is to set out the terms of the Magistrates' Courts Act 1980, s.65(1) and (2)[54]:

"(1) In this Act [family proceedings][55] means proceedings under any of the following enactments, that is to say—
(a)   The Maintenance Orders (Facilities for Enforcement) Act 1920;
(b)   section 43 . . . of the National Assistance Act 1948;[56]
(c)   section 3 of the Marriage Act 1949;
(d), (e)   . . .[57]

---

[52] For the position in the High Court, see the Family Proceedings Rules 1991, r.4.16(7) and *Re P-B (a Minor) (Child Cases: Hearings in Open Court)* [1997] 1 All E.R. 58. CA, where the court took the view that its wording ("Unless the court otherwise directs, a hearing of, or directions appointment in, proceedings to which this Part applies shall be in chambers") prevailed over considerations of open justice or freedom of expression. This is discussed in para.7–63. See the judgment of Munby J. in *Clibbery v Allen* [2001] 2 F.L.R. 819, [2001] F.C.R. 577 at [76], where he observed that this would appear to connote *private* rather than *secret* hearings. See too *B v United Kingdom* [2001] 2 F.L.R. 261, [2001] 2 F.C.R. 221, (2002) 34 E.H.R.R. 19.
[53] See the Family Proceedings Courts (Children Act 1989) Rules 1991, rr.14 and 16(7).
[54] As amended on a number of occasions, *e.g.* by the Children Act 1989, ss.92,108(6) and (7), Sch.11, para.8, and the Maintenance Orders (Backdating) Order 1983, SI 1993/623, art.3, Sch.2.
[55] These words were substituted by the Children Act 1989, s.92(11), Sch.11, Pt II, para.(8)(c).
[56] The words omitted were repealed by the Family Law Reform Act 1987, s.33(4), Sch.4.
[57] para. (d) was repealed by the Family Law Reform Act 1987, s.33(4), ch.4; and para.(e) was repealed by the Children Act 1989, s.108(7), Sch.15.

[(ee)	section 35 of the Matrimonial Causes Act 1973;][58]
(f)	Part I of the Maintenance Orders (Reciprocal Enforcement) Act 1972;
(g)	...[59]
(h)	The Adoption Act 1976, except proceedings under section 34 of that Act;
[(h)	the Adoption and Children Act 2002;][60]
(i)	section 18 ... of the Supplementary Benefits Act 1976;[61]
(j)	Part I of the Domestic Proceedings and Magistrates' Courts Act 1978;
(k)	...[62]
(l)	section 60 of this Act;
[(m)	Part I of the Civil Jurisdiction and Judgments Act 1982, so far as that part relates to the recognition or enforcement of maintenance orders;][63]
[(mm)	section 55A of the Family Law Act 1986;][64]
[(n)	The Children Act 1989;][65]
[(na)	section 30 of the Human Fertilisation and Embryology Act 1990][66]
[(nb)	section 106 of the Social Security Administration Act 1992;][67]
(o)	section 20 (so far as it provides, by virtue of an order under section 45, for appeals to be made to a court) ... of the Child Support Act 1991;[68]
(p)	Part IV of the Family Law Act 1996[69]
[(q)	sections 11 and 12 of the Crime and Disorder Act 1998;][70]
[(r)	Council Regulation (EC) No 44/2001 of 22nd December 2000 on jurisdiction and the recognition and enforcement of judgments in civil and commercial matters, so far as that Regulation relates to the recognition or enforcement of maintenance orders;][71]

except that, subject to subsection (2) below, it does not include—
(i) proceedings for the enforcement of any order made, confirmed or registered under any of those enactments;
(ii) proceedings for the variation of any provision for the periodical payment of money contained in an order made, confirmed or registered under any of those enactments; or,
(iii) proceedings on an information in respect of the commission of an offence under any of those enactments.

---

[58] para.(ee) was inserted by the Matrimonial and Family Proceedings Act 1984, s.44.
[59] para.(g) was repealed by the Children Act 1989, s.108(7), Sch.15.
[60] The words in square brackets to be substituted from a date to be appointed: Adoption and Children Act 2002, s.139(1), Sch.3, paras 36, 37.
[61] The words deleted from para.(i) were repealed by the Family Law Reform Act 1987, s.33(4), Sch.4.
[62] para.(k) was repealed by the Courts and Legal Services Act 1990, ss.116(2), 125(7), Sch.16, Pt II, para.40, Sch.20.
[63] The current para.(m) was inserted by the Civil Jurisdiction and Judgments Act 1982, s.15(4), Sch.12, Pt I, para.7.
[64] Inserted by the Child Support, Pensions and Social Security Act 2000, s.83(5), Sch.8, 2(1), (2) with effect from April 2001.
[65] The first para.(n) was inserted by the Children Act 1989, s.92(11), Sch.11, Pt II, para.(8)(a).
[66] Inserted by the Courts Act 2003, s.109(1), Sch.8, para.214(1),(2).
[67] The second para.(n) was added by the Social Security (Consequential Provisions) Act 1992, ss.3, 4, Sch.1, para.60.
[68] Inserted by the Maintenance Orders (Backdating) Order 1993, SI 1993/623, art.3, Sch.2. The words in square brackets were omitted by the Child Support, Pensions and Social Security Act 2000, s.85, Sch.9, Pt IX.
[69] Added by the Family Law Act 1996, s.66(1), Sch.8, Pt III, para.49.
[70] Inserted by the Crime and Disorder Act 1988, s.119, Sch.8, para.42.
[71] Inserted by SI 2001/3929, art.1(b).

8–77 CHAPTER 8—COURT REPORTING II: OTHER STATUTORY RESTRICTIONS

(2) The court before which there falls to be heard any of the following proceedings, that is to say—
  (a) proceedings (whether under this Act or any other enactment) for the enforcement of any order made, confirmed or registered under any of the enactments specified in paragraphs (a) to (k) [(m), (n) (p) and (r)][72] of subsection (1) above;
  (b) proceedings (whether under this Act or any other enactment) for the variation of any provision for the making of periodical payments contained in an order made, confirmed or registered under any of those enactments;
  (c) proceedings for an attachment of earnings order to secure maintenance payments within the meaning of the Attachment of Earnings Act 1971 or for the discharge or variation of such an order; or
  (d) proceedings for the enforcement of a maintenance order which is registered in a magistrates' court under Part II of the Maintenance Orders Act 1950 or Part I of the Maintenance Orders Act 1958 or for the variation of the rate of payments specified by such an order;
  (e) [proceedings under] section 20 (so far as it provides, by virtue of an order under section 45, for appeals to be made to a court) . . . of the Child Support Act 1991;[73]

may if it thinks fit order that those proceedings and any other proceedings being heard therewith shall, notwithstanding anything in subsection (1) above, be treated as [family proceedings][74] for the purposes of this Act".

Statutory provision has now been made for rules to be promulgated in certain circumstances for authorising publication of information relating to proceedings held in private[75] "for the purposes of the law relating to contempt of court".

B. The hybrid status of family proceedings: restrictions on attendance

8–78 It has been noted[76] that in the case of youth court proceedings the normal policy considerations which justify the reporting of court proceedings do not apply; that is to say, since members of the general public do not have a *right* to attend, there is no pressing need for the public to be informed by the media of what takes place, so as to put them in a similar position to such persons as did in fact attend. So too, with those characterised as "family proceedings".[77]

8–79 The following provisions of the Magistrates' Courts Act 1980 are material:

"**69. Sittings of magistrates' courts for family proceedings**

---

[72] This was altered by SI 2001/3929. The additional words were inserted by the Children Act 1989, s.92(11), Sch.11, Pt II, para.(8)(b), and the Family Law Act 1996 (Modification of Enactments) Order 1997, SI 1997/1898, art.2.
[73] para.(e) was added by the Maintenance Orders (Backdating) Order 1993, SI 1993/623, art.3, Sch.2, para.2. The words in square brackets were inserted by the Child Support, Pensions and Social Security Act 2000, s.83(5), Sch.8, para.2(1), (3).
[74] These words were substituted by the Children Act 1989, s.92(11), Sch.11, Pt II, para.(8)(c).
[75] Adoption Act 1976, s.66(5); Magistrates' Courts Act 1980, s.145(1)(ga); Matrimonial and Family Proceedings Act 1984, s.40(4)(aa); Adoption and Children Act 2002, s.141(6); Courts Act 2003, s.76(2A). All of these, as amended by the Children Act 2004, s.62, make provision for the making of rules to avoid the reporting of certain matters attracting liability in the context of contempt of court.
[76] See para.8–25.
[77] See the definition in para.8–77.

[590]

(1) The business of magistrates' courts shall, so far as is consistent with the due dispatch of business, be arranged in such manner as may be requisite for separating the hearing and determination of [family proceedings][78] from other business.

(2) In the case of family proceedings in a magistrates' court other than proceedings under the Adoption Act 1976 [the Adoption and Children Act 2002],[79] no person shall be present during the hearing and determination by the court of the proceedings except—
- (a) officers of the court;
- (b) parties to the case before the court, their [legal representatives],[80] witnesses and other persons directly concerned in the case;
- (c) representatives of newspapers or news agencies;
- (d) any other person whom the court may in its discretion permit to be present, so, however, that permission shall not be withheld from a person who appears to the court to have adequate grounds for attendance.

(3) In relation to any [family proceedings][81] under the Adoption Act 1976 [the Adoption and Children Act 2002],[82] subsection (2) above shall apply with the omission of paragraphs (c) and (d).

(4) When hearing family proceedings, a magistrates' court may, if it thinks it necessary in the interest of the administration of justice or of public decency, direct that any persons, not being officers of the court or parties to the case, the parties' legal representatives, or other persons directly concerned in the case, be excluded during the taking of any indecent evidence.

(5) The powers conferred on a magistrates' court by this section shall be in addition and without prejudice to any other powers of the court to hear proceedings in camera."

C. Newspaper reports of family proceedings

The provisions of s.71 of the Magistrates' Courts Act 1980, so far as they are material, are as follows[83]:

"(1) In the case of [family proceedings][84] in a magistrates' court (other than proceedings under the Adoption Act 1976) it shall not be lawful for a person to whom this subsection applies—
- (a) to print or publish, or cause or procure to be printed or published, in a newspaper or periodical, or
- (b) to include, or cause or procure to be included, in a programme included in a programme service (within the meaning of the Broadcasting Act 1990) for reception in Great Britain,

any particulars of the proceedings other than such particulars as are mentioned in subsection (1A) below.

(1A) The particulars referred to in subsection (1) above are—

---

[78] These words were substituted by the Children Act 1989, s.92(11), Sch.11, Pt II, para.8(c).
[79] Inserted from a date to be appointed by the Adoption and Children Act 2002, s.139(1), Sch.3, paras 36 and 38.
[80] These words were substituted by the Courts and Legal Services Act 1990, s.125(3), Sch.18, para.25(1)(6).
[81] Inserted by the Children Act 1989, s.92, Sch.11, para.8.
[82] The words were inserted by the Adoption and Children Act 2002, s.139(1), Sch.3, paras 36 and 38 from a date to be appointed.
[83] Subsections (1), (1A), and (1B) were substituted by the Broadcasting Act 1990, s.203(1) Sch.20, para.29(2).
[84] These words were substituted by the Children Act 1989, s.92(11), Sch.11, Pt II, para.8(c).

(a) the names, addresses and occupations of the parties and witnesses;
(b) the grounds of the application, and a concise statement of the charges, defences and counter-charges in support of which evidence has been given;
(c) submissions on any point of law arising in the course of the proceedings and the decision of the court on the submissions;
(d) the decision of the court, and any observations made by the court in giving it.
(1B) Subsection (1) above applies—
(a) in relation to paragraph (a) of that subsection, to the proprietor, editor or publisher of the newspaper or periodical, and
(b) in relation to paragraph (b) of that subsection, to any body corporate which provides the service in which the programme is included and to any person having functions in relation to the programme corresponding to those of an editor of a newspaper.
(2) In the case of [family proceedings][85] in a magistrates' court under the Adoption Act 1976 [Adoption and Children Act 2002],[86] subsection (1A) above shall apply with the omission of paragraphs (a) and (b) and the reference in that subsection to the particulars of the proceedings shall, in relation to any child concerned in the proceedings, include—
(a) the name, address or school of the child,
(b) any picture as being, or including a picture of the child, and
(c) any other particulars calculated to lead to the identification of the child".

8–81 It is provided that any person acting in contravention of these provisions shall be liable on summary conviction to a fine not exceeding level 4 on the standard scale.[87] No prosecution for an offence under this section may be begun without the consent of the Attorney-General.[88]

8–82 It is also to be noted that provision has been made specifically to cater for the printing or publishing of matter in a newspaper or periodical of a technical character, *bona fide* intended for circulation among members of the legal or medical professions.[89]

D. Privacy under section 97(2) of the Children Act 1989

8–83 It is provided by s.97(2) of the Children Act 1989 that:

"No person shall publish[90] [to the public at large or any section of the public][91] any material[92] which is intended, or likely, to identify—

---

[85] Inserted by the Children Act 1989, s.92, Sch.11, para.8.
[86] Inserted from a date to be appointed by the Adoption and Children Act 2002, s.139(1), Sch.3, paras 36, 39(b)(i).
[87] s.71(3). See the Criminal Justice Act 1982, ss.37 (as amended). The level 4 figure is currently £2,500. See para.14–106.
[88] s.71(4).
[89] s.71(5).
[90] This includes broadcasting in a programme service (within the meaning of the Broadcasting Act 1990), and also "cause to be published": s.97(5).
[91] The words in square brackets were added by s.62(1) of the Children Act 2004 and came into effect in April 2005.
[92] "Material" includes any picture or representation: s.97(5).

PROTECTION FOR FAMILY PROCEEDINGS 8–86

(a) any child as being involved in any proceedings before [the High Court, a county court or][93] a magistrates' court in which any power under this Act [or the Adoption and Children Act 2002][94] may be exercised by the court with respect to that or any other child; or
(b) an address or school as being that of a child involved in any such proceedings."

These provisions were held in *Att-Gen v Pelling*[95] to be compliant with the demands of the European Convention on Human Rights.

It was suggested by Munby J. in *Kelly v BBC*[96] that Parliament had filled a lacuna in the law by the amendment in (a) above, and the government has also explained that the changes would achieve at least modest financial savings, for litigants and the courts, because of the consequential removal of the need to apply for an injunction for the same purpose of anonymity. In appropriate cases, the court or the Lord Chancellor[97] has the power to dispense with such publishing restrictions by virtue of s.97(4). In the view of Munby J. the combined effect of s.10(1) and s.8(3)(a) of the Children Act is that the prohibition under s.97(2) now applies to wardship and other proceedings under the *parens patriae* jurisdiction. The term "family proceedings" is so defined in s.8(3)(a) as to include proceedings under the inherent jurisdiction. Moreover, there is no doubt in the light of s.10(1) that the court can make an order under s.8[98] in *any* family proceedings (and therefore can do so in proceedings under the inherent jurisdiction). Since the making of an order under s.8 would constitute the exercising of a power under the Children Act, it must follow that the prohibition on publication applies to *parens patriae* proceedings. That was certainly the interpretation of Munby J.[99] It is not necessary, as a pre-condition for the prohibition to come into effect, that the court shall have actually exercised such a power. It would appear to be enough that the power "may be exercised". 8–84

It is a defence to prove that the accused did not know, and had no reason to suspect, that the published material was intended, or likely, to identify the child.[1] Any person contravening the section shall be guilty of an offence and liable, on summary conviction, to a fine not exceeding level 4 on the standard scale.[2] 8–85

The court or the Lord Chancellor may, if satisfied that the welfare of the child requires it, by order dispense with the requirements of subs.(2) to such extent as 8–86

---

[93] The words in square brackets were inserted by the Access to Justice Act 1999, s.108 (3)(b), Sch.14, Pt IV, para.18.
[94] Inserted from a date to be appointed by the Adoption and Children Act 2002, s.101(3).
[95] [2005] EWHC 414 (Admin).
[96] [2001] Fam. 59.
[97] See SI 1992/709, art.3(2), Sch.2.
[98] See para.6–66 above.
[99] As expressed in *Kelly* at 73A–B.
[1] *ibid.*, s.97(3). For the distinction between "reason to suspect" and "reason to believe", see para. 4–237.
[2] See para.14–106.

VII. CRIMINAL PROCEEDINGS BEFORE MAGISTRATES

A. Committal proceedings: Magistrates' Courts Act 1980, section 8

8–87   The case against a person who is to be tried upon indictment for an either way offence is first presented before justices in committal proceedings. The principal object of these proceedings is to ascertain whether there is a case to be answered against an accused. Historically, only prosecution evidence was rehearsed before the court, and the reporting of such proceedings, though entirely accurate, could give a one-sided and therefore distorted picture of the strength of the case. For this reason, restrictions upon reporting such proceedings were introduced,[5] and consolidated in the Magistrates' Courts Act 1980.

8–88   It was long intended to abolish committal proceedings.[6] It appears that two main considerations have driven this proposed reform; first, the need to make the system more efficient and avoid delay and, secondly, the need to prevent inappropriate cases going to the Crown Court for trial and taking up time and resources unnecessarily. The first legislation introduced to give effect to that intention[7] was found to be unworkable, and was never implemented. A modified system was instead introduced by the Criminal Procedure and Investigations Act 1996. Special provision was made for committals in cases involving complex and serious fraud, and for cases involving child witnesses. These too are to be embraced within the new statutory framework, but they have to a large extent paved the way for the new procedure generally. Committal proceedings are intended to be replaced by a process known as "allocation and sending" and the reporting restrictions imposed by the new legislation are broadly similar to those of the Magistrates' Courts Act 1980 which they replace.[8] In the meantime, the restrictions upon publicity continue to be found in the 1980 Act, which provides:

> "8.—(1) Except as provided by subsections (2), (3) and (8) below, it shall not be lawful to publish in Great Britain a written report, or to include in a relevant programme for reception in Great Britain a report, of any committal proceedings in England and Wales containing any matter other than that permitted by subsection (4) below.

---

[3] s.97(4). As was done by Sumner J. on July 13, 2000 with regard to the teenager who was the person concerned in *Kelly v BBC* [2001] Fam. 59.
[4] Cp. in the context of the Children and Young Persons Act 1933, s.39, the decision to lift restrictions in *R. v Cambridge District Health Authority Ex p. B (No.2)* [1996] 1 F.L.R. 375, CA on the grounds that to do so would facilitate raising money for a life-saving operation on the child.
[5] By the Criminal Justice Act 1967, following the recommendations of the Tucker Committee, Report of the *Departmental Committee on Proceedings before Examining Justices*, Cmnd. 479 (1958).
[6] Following recommendations of the Royal Commission on Criminal Justice, *Report*, 1993, Cm. 2263 (1993).
[7] Criminal Justice and Public Order Act 1994, s.44.
[8] By s.52A of the Crime and Disorder Act 1998 which is to be inserted by the Criminal Justice Act 2003, s.41, Sch.3, Pt 1, paras 15, 19(1).

(2) Subject to subsection (2A) below a magistrates' court shall, on an application for the purpose made with reference to any committal proceedings by the accused or one of the accused, as the case may be, order that subsection (1) above shall not apply to reports of those proceedings.

(2A) Where in the case of two or more accused one of them objects to the making of an order under subsection (2) above, the court shall make the order if, and only if, it is satisfied, after hearing the representations of the accused, that it is in the interests of justice to do so.

(2B) An order under subsection (2) above shall not apply to reports of proceedings under subsection (2A) above, but any decision of the court to make or not to make such an order may be contained in reports published or included in a relevant programme before the time authorised by subsection (3) below.

(3) It shall not be unlawful under this section to publish, or include in a relevant programme a report of committal proceedings containing any matter other than that permitted by subsection (4) below
- (a) where the magistrates' court determines not to commit the accused, or determines to commit none of the accused, for trial, after it so determines;
- (b) where the court commits the accused or any of the accused for trial, after the conclusion of his trial or, as the case may be, the trial of the last to be tried;

and where at any time during the inquiry the court proceeds to try summarily the case of one or more of the accused under section 25 (3) or (7) below, while committing the other accused or one or more of the other accused for trial, it shall not be unlawful under this section to publish or include in a relevant programme as part of a report of the summary trial, after the court determines to proceed as aforesaid, a report of so much of the committal proceedings containing any such matter as takes place before the determination.

(4) The following matters may be contained in a report of committal proceedings published or included in a relevant programme without an order under subsection (2) above before the time authorised by subsection (3) above, that is to say
- (a) the identity of the court and the names of the examining justices;
- (b) the names, addresses and occupations of the parties and witnesses and the ages of the accused and witnesses;
- (c) the offence or offences, or a summary of them, with which the accused is or are charged;
- (d) the names of the legal representatives engaged in the proceedings;
- (e) any decision of the court to commit the accused or any of the accused for trial, and any decision of the court on the disposal of the case of any accused not committed;
- (f) where the court commits the accused or any of the accused for trial, the charge or charges, or a summary of them, on which he is committed and the court to which he is committed;
- (g) where the committal proceedings are adjourned, the date and place to which they are adjourned;
- (h) any arrangements as to bail on committal or adjournment;
- (i) whether a right to representation funded by the Legal Services Commission as part of the Criminal Defence Service was granted to the accused or any of the accused.[9]

(5) If a report is published or included in a relevant programme in contravention of this section, the following persons, that is to say—
- (a) in the case of a publication of a written report as part of a newspaper or periodical, any proprietor, editor or publisher of the newspaper or periodical;

---

[9] Substituted by the Access to Justice Act 1999, s.24, Sch.4, paras 15 and 16.

(b) in the case of a publication of a written report otherwise than as part of a newspaper or periodical, the person who publishes it;
(c) in the case of the inclusion of a report in a relevant programme, any body corporate which provides the service in which the programme is included and any person having functions in relation to the programme corresponding to those of an editor of a newspaper,

shall be liable on summary conviction to a fine not exceeding level 5 on the standard scale.

(6) Proceedings for an offence under this section shall not, in England and Wales, be instituted otherwise than by or with the consent of the Attorney-General.

(7) Subsection (1) above shall be in addition to, and not in derogation from, the provisions of any other enactment with respect to the publication of reports and proceedings of magistrates' and other courts.

(8) For the purposes of this section committal proceedings shall, in relation to an information charging an indictable offence, be deemed to include any proceedings in the magistrates' court before the court proceeds to inquire into the information as examining justices; but where a magistrates' court which has begun to try an information summarily discontinues the summary trial in pursuance of section 25 (2) or (6) below and proceeds to inquire into the information as examining justices, that circumstance shall not make it unlawful under this section for a report of any proceedings on the information which was published or included in a relevant programme before the court determined to proceed as aforesaid to have been so published, or included in a relevant programme.

(9) [Repealed by Contempt of Court Act 1981, s.4 (4).]

(10) In this section

"publish", in relation to a report, means publish the report, either by itself or as part of a newspaper or periodical, for distribution to the public;

"relevant programme" means a programme included in a programme service (within the meaning of the Broadcasting Act 1990)."

B. Constraints upon reporting where restrictions are lifted

8–89 Once restrictions are lifted by a magistrate, any reporting will be subject to the protection of s.4(1) of the Contempt of Court Act 1981[10] in so far as the report is fair, accurate and contemporaneous. Specific provision was made to deal with committal proceedings in magistrates' courts in s.4(3).[11]

1. The relationship between the Magistrates' Courts Act and the Contempt of Court Act

8–90 In *R. v Horsham Justices Ex p. Farquharson*,[12] the Court of Appeal considered the relationship between s.4(2) of the Contempt of Court Act 1981 and the statutory framework under s.8 of the Magistrates' Courts Act 1980, in the terms applicable at that time to committal proceedings in the magistrates' court. The arguments were rejected that the provisions have no application to committal proceedings and that the statutory framework of s.8 of the Magistrates' Courts

---

[10] Set out in para.4–265.
[11] The terms of which are set out in para.4–277, together with the prospective new subsections (b) and (c) which will deal with the new system of "allocation and sending".
[12] [1982] Q.B. 762.

Act 1980 (as amended) should be looked upon as providing a comprehensive and exhaustive code. It was pointed out, however, that these provisions (and their predecessors in the 1967 Act) were directed towards the protection of the accused, and that the law of contempt is directed additionally towards wider considerations. Thus the right to publish the details expressly permitted by section 8 of the 1980 Act would always be subject to the law of contempt; for example, the name of a witness could not be published if he or she had been permitted to use a pseudonym for the sake of anonymity. Shaw L.J. also drew attention to the express reference to "committal proceedings" contained in subs.(3)(b).

C. The comparable restrictions under the Criminal Justice Act 1987, section 11 (transfers for trial)

In 1987, a procedure for by-passing committal proceedings in cases of complex and serious fraud was introduced.[13] This permits a "designated authority"[14] to issue a "notice of transfer" order. This notice, which is given to the magistrates' court in whose jurisdiction the offence has been charged, transfers the case directly to the Crown Court, for the conduct of a preparatory hearing. An accused may apply for a dismissal of the transferred charges.[15] Provision is made in s.11 for restrictions on reporting of both applications for dismissal and preparatory hearings, comparable to the provisions applying to committal proceedings in the magistrates' court. A prosecution for a contravention of the section requires the consent of the Attorney-General.[16]

D. Transfers in child witness cases: Criminal Justice Act 1991, section 53

The notice of transfer system was extended by the provisions of the Criminal Justice Act 1991, with corresponding restrictions on reporting,[17] for cases of sexual offences and offences of violence involving child witnesses. The intention was to achieve a measure of protection for child witnesses, so that at least there would be no question of their giving evidence twice over. A further objective was to achieve a speedier hearing in the Crown Court by the avoidance of committal proceedings. In such cases the Director of Public Prosecutions was the person authorised to serve a notice of transfer. He or she must be satisfied that:

(a) the evidence of the offence would be sufficient to justify committal for trial;

(b) a child alleged to be a victim, or to have witnessed the commission of the offence, will be called at trial; and

---

[13] Criminal Justice Act 1987, ss.4–11. Prospectively repealed by the Criminal Justice Act 2003.
[14] The Director of Public Prosecutions, the Director of the Serious Fraud Office, the Commissioners of Inland Revenue, the Commissioners of Customs and Excise and the Secretary of State: Criminal Justice Act 1987, s.4(2).
[15] Criminal Justice Act 1987, s.6.
[16] s.11(13).
[17] s.53, Sch.6, para.6.

8–92

(c) the case should be taken over, and proceeded with, without delay by the Crown Court, for the purposes of avoiding any prejudice to the child's welfare.

8–93 The offences at which the section is directed[18] are those involving:

(a) an assault, injury or threat of injury;

(b) cruelty to persons under 16, contrary to the Children and Young Persons Act 1933;

(c) the Sexual Offences Act 2003 and the Protection of Children Act 1978; and

(d) any attempt or conspiracy to commit, or aiding, abetting, counselling, or procuring or inciting the commission of any offence falling within the above categories.

The provisions of s.53 of the 1991 are due to be repealed from a date to be appointed by the Criminal Justice Act 2003.[19]

8–94 The meaning of "child" will vary according to the offence charged.[20] For those involving violence or cruelty, the definition is directed towards persons under 14 years of age. For sexual offences, the definition embraces those under 17. In each case, it is provided that if a video recording was made of an interview about the offence with the child witness, when below the relevant age, then the age limit is increased by one year to 15 or 18, as the case may be. Otherwise, it would appear that the relevant date for determining the person's age is the date of the notice of transfer. It is not possible, in any application for dismissal, for the judge to give leave for oral evidence to be adduced from any child witness.

VIII. Derogatory Remarks in Mitigation

A. The mischief

8–95 Sometimes, a defendant in criminal proceedings, having been found (or pleaded) guilty, seeks to mitigate by comments reflecting adversely upon others, sometimes including the victim. The person so criticised has no right of reply, but the press has a right to report the allegations. The provisions introduced by the Criminal Procedure and Investigations Act 1996, ss.58, 59 and 60 were intended to give the court in certain cases the power to prevent the media from publishing such statements.

B. Difficulties of application

8–96 The statute appears to give no guidance on how a judge is supposed to form a view that an assertion is "false"[21] in circumstances where there has been no trial,

---

[18] Criminal Justice Act 1988, s.32(2) as amended.
[19] s.332, Sch.37, Pt 4.
[20] s.53(6).
[21] Within the meaning of s.58(4)(b).

and thus no opportunity to form a personal view of the evidence. It would plainly be wrong for an advocate to advance material known to be false, or for that matter irrelevant. If the advocate is not in a position to know that the information derived from his instructions is false, it is difficult to see how the judge is to come to such a conclusion. Following a trial, say for indecent assault, if the facts which have been advanced in mitigation are inconsistent with the jury's verdict there would be no problem. In those circumstances, it would surely be inappropriate for the advocate to run the argument (for example, consent) for a second time. If, on the other hand, the jury's verdict is neutral (for example, where it is being suggested that there was consent up to the last minute), the judge can form a personal view. But s.58(5) means that the provisions would have no application to such an assertion. It provides that an order must not be made in relation to an assertion if it appears to the court that it was previously made at the trial at which the relevant person was convicted of the offence or during any other proceedings relating to the offence. The difficulty arises in circumstances where there is a plea of guilty and simply no way of telling whether the mitigation is true or false. Any investigation to ascertain the facts, in the form of a Newton hearing, would only be embarked upon with the greatest reluctance. Not only might it cause distress to the victim, but it could be self-defeating from the point of view of a defendant's mitigation.

IX. DISCLOSURES RELATING TO PROCEEDINGS IN PRIVATE

A. The provisions of section 12 of the Administration of Justice Act 1960

Prior to the enactment of s.12, the extent to which proceedings loosely described as being "in private" could be publicised was unclear. That section was said to be " ... an attempt ... to clarify the law of contempt as to proceedings in private, a sphere which the Lord Chancellor in debate has described as 'obscure' and which—so far as concerns proceedings in chambers—has elsewhere been described as 'chaotic'".[22] It had been asserted in *Alliance Perpetual Building Society v Belrum Investments Ltd*[23] that:

"Interlocutory matters before the master proceed in private; the public has no right to attend them, nor has anybody, as I conceive, any right to give any account of them while the action is pending and has not been adjourned into court".

Shortly afterwards, Parliament addressed the matter specifically in s.12 of the Administration of Justice Act 1960[24]:

"(1) The publication of information relating to proceedings before any court sitting in private shall not of itself be contempt of court except in the following cases, that is to say—
(a) where the proceedings—

---

[22] See D.G.T. Williams [1961] Crim. L.R. 87 at 100.
[23] [1957] 1 W.L.R. 720 at 724, Harman J.
[24] As amended.

8–98 CHAPTER 8—COURT REPORTING II: OTHER STATUTORY RESTRICTIONS

(i) relate to the exercise of the inherent jurisdiction of the High Court with respect to minors;
(ii) are brought under the Children Act 1989[25] [or the Adoption and Children Act 2002[26]]; or
(iii) otherwise relate wholly or mainly to the maintenance or upbringing of a minor;

(b) where the proceedings are brought *under Part VIII of the Mental Health Act 1959*[27] *or under any provision of that Act* [under the Mental Capacity Act 2005, or under any provision of the Mental Health Act 1983][28] authorising an application or reference to be made to a Mental Health Review Tribunal or to a county court;

(c) where the court sits in private for reasons of national security during that part of the proceedings about which the information in question is published;

(d) where the information relates to a secret process, discovery or invention which is in issue in the proceedings;

(e) where the court (having power to do so) expressly prohibits the publication of all information relating to the proceedings or of information of the description which is published.

(2) Without prejudice to the foregoing subsection, the publication of the text or a summary of the whole or part of an order made by a court sitting in private shall not of itself be contempt of court except where the court (having power to do so) expressly prohibits the publication.

(3) In this section references to a court include references to a judge and to a tribunal and to any person exercising the functions of a court, a judge or a tribunal; and references to a court sitting in private include references to a court sitting in camera or in chambers".

(4) Nothing in this section shall be construed as implying that any publication is punishable as contempt of court which would not be so punishable apart from this section [(and in particular where the publication is not so punishable by reason of being authorised by rules of court)].[29]

8–99 It seems clear that the statute was not intended to create any new head of contempt liability but rather to clarify.[30] "The section is not intended to enlarge the scope of the offence as it existed at common law".[31]

---

[25] This was introduced with effect from October 1991 by the Children Act 1989. It was unsuccessfully argued in *Att-Gen v Pelling* [2005] EWHC 414 (Admin) that s.12 should be confined to wardship proceedings. The express reference to the Children Act was for the purpose of assimilating the new jurisdiction under that statute with its predecessors for the purpose of contempt. It was not creating a new category of contempt.

[26] The words in square brackets were inserted by the Adoption and Children Act 2002, s.101(2) and are to come in to force on a date to be appointed.

[27] This has in fact been replaced by Pt VII of the Mental Health Act 1983.

[28] The words in italics are to be repealed and the subsequent words in square brackets substituted by the Mental Capacity Act 2005, s.67(1), Sch.6, para.10.

[29] The words in square brackets were added by the Children Act 2004, s.62 and came into effect in April 2005. See the discussion below at paras 8–107 *et seq.*

[30] s.12(4). And see *Official Solicitor v News Group Newspapers plc* [1994] 2 F.L.R. 174 at 176H, Connell J.; *Oxfordshire County Council v L and F* [1997] 1 F.L.R. 235 at 249E–G, Stuart-White J.

[31] *Re F (Orse A) a Minor* [1977] Fam. 58, 107B, *per* Geoffrey Lane L.J.

B. Section 12 does not in itself provide a defence

The effect of s.12 is to lay down that it shall not be regarded as a contempt *ipso facto* to publish information (save in the specified cases). It was not intended to provide anything analogous to the blanket protection afforded, in respect of *open court proceedings*, by s.4(1) of the Contempt of Court Act 1981. If the effect of what is published is to create a "substantial risk of serious prejudice", and this gives rise to a strict liability contempt under the 1981 Act, clearly it will be no answer to pray in aid the provisions of the 1960 Act.

It may be that it would be rare for the revelation of information from a private hearing to create such a risk in civil proceedings. One could imagine, however, circumstances in which allegations of violence or other misconduct were made in matrimonial proceedings held in private, which were of interest to journalists, and which found their way into the newspapers. Suppose that the spouse against whom the allegations were made happened to be about to stand trial for some closely related criminal offence. The revelation of the information could obviously give rise to a substantial risk of serious prejudice in relation to the pending Crown Court proceedings. The newspaper would not be able to derive any assistance from s.12 of the 1960 Act.

C. The meaning of "publication" in section 12

The scope of the notion of "publication" has been addressed in amendments introduced by the Children Act 2004, but it is necessary to understand the background. Unless it is clear from the statutory context that some other interpretation is intended,[32] it is submitted that the wide interpretation of the common law, and particularly the law of defamation, would be the natural one to adopt. That is to say, the "publication" contemplated by s.12(1) would not be confined to information communicated through the media. Thus, private communications to individuals may very well constitute contempt unless permission has previously been obtained from the court itself.[33] The court has an unfettered discretion to give leave in a proper case to reveal such information, for example, where it is sought by the police with a view to investigating the commission of a crime. In such circumstances, the court will balance the competing interests of privacy, on the one hand, and that of not obstructing the police in the pursuit of criminal investigations, on the other.[34]

In *Re M*,[35] Thorpe L.J. accepted that a conversation between two individuals might amount to "publication" within the meaning of the section. Wall J.,

---

[32] See, *e.g.* s.2(1) of the Contempt of Court Act 1981, discussed fully in para.4–24 *et seq.* See also the Magistrates' Courts Act 1980, s.8(10), set out at para.8–88.

[33] The first three sentences of this para were cited and approved by Thorpe L.J. in *Re G (Litigants in Person)* [2003] EWCA Civ 1055, [2003] 2 F.L.R. 963 at [26].

[34] *Re R (MJ) (a Minor) (Publication of Transcript)* [1975] Fam. 89, 98, Rees J; *Re S (Minors)* [1988] 1 F.L.R. 1, 4 Booth J.; *Re F (Wards) (Disclosure of Material)* [1989] 1 F.L.R. 39, CA. See also *S v S (Judgment in Chambers: Disclosure)* [1997] 1 W.L.R. 1621.

[35] [2002] EWCA 1199, [2003] Fam. 26, at [21].

however, said that the word should be given its "ordinary" and "everyday" meaning; in his view "responsible inter-disciplinary communication in proceedings relating to children is not 'publication' of that information" for the purposes of either s.12 of the 1960 Act or s.97 of the Children Act 1989. Yet the difficulty remains that there may come a time when a communication takes place of material falling within the categories defined in s.12, but which does not serve such a positive and useful purpose as a matter of public policy. It seems unnecessary to define "publication" purely in the light of these rather special facts. Thus, it may be that the greater flexibility acknowledged by Thorpe L.J. has more to commend it. With this view Munby J. concurred in *Re B (A Child) (Disclosure)*.[36] He added[37]:

"If Wall J. is correct, it means that any party could, with impunity, send the whole of the papers in a care case to a journalist, for that would not, on his approach, be a publication. Surely that cannot be right."

8–104 Indeed, in the meantime in *Re G (Litigants in Person)*[38] Thorpe L.J. adopted the first three sentences of para.8–102 above and the other members of the court expressed agreement with him. It was recognised by the Court of Appeal in that case, as indeed Munby J. later accepted in *Re B*,[39] that much will depend on the circumstances. Generally speaking, it would appear that "a communication of information by someone to a professional, each acting in furtherance of the protection of children . . . " would not be treated by the court as a publication prohibited by s.12.

8–105 The facts of *Re B (A Child) (Disclosure)* were, however, far removed from a professional "child protection" context. The background was the announcement by the Law Officers in January 2004 that the government was considering a review of possible miscarriages of justice in the family system, as well as in the criminal justice system, because of concerns about the quality of expert evidence which had been expressed in well publicised cot death cases.[40] The child in the *Re B* case was aged four and had been living in the care of her paternal grandparents in the light of findings made by Bracewell J. that she had been harmed by her mother who, she found, suffered from Munchausen's Syndrome by proxy. The judge had heard evidence from six medical experts including a total of seven reports from a Dr X and a Dr Y. The child's mother refused to accept the judge's findings and denied that she had ever harmed B. On January 18, 2004 she wrote to the Professional Conduct Committee of the GMC stating that she intended to submit a complaint about Dr X and Dr Y; a copy was sent to the Minister of State for Children.

8–106 It was on the following day that the Court of Appeal gave judgment in *R. v Angela Cannings*, and on January 20 that the Law Officers made their statements

---

[36] [2004] EWHC 411 (Fam), [2004] F.L.R. 142.
[37] At [71].
[38] [2003] EWCA Civ 1055, [2003] 2 F.L.R. 963.
[39] Curiously it would appear that Munby J. in March 2004 had not had drawn to his attention the earlier decision of the Court of Appeal on July 28, 2003.
[40] e.g. *R. v Sally Clark* [2003] EWCA Crim 1020 and *R. v Angela Cannings* [2004] EWCA Crim 1, [2004] 1 W.L.R. 2607.

to Parliament. On January 21 the *Daily Mail* carried a front page story headed "the stolen childhoods" and in the same issue a special report including a critique of the expert paediatric evidence in B's case (disguised by fictionalised names). In correspondence with the local authority the mother's solicitor confirmed that the source of the newspaper's information had been her client. It later emerged before Munby J. that the mother had over several months (and her solicitor for a somewhat shorter period) been committing contempts of court by revealing confidential documents without the court's permission, including case summaries, to politicians and journalists. These had taken place on an individual basis and none of the communications was to the world at large; they were held nevertheless by Munby J. to be publications:

> "[72] ... there is a 'publication' for the purposes of s.12 whenever the law of defamation would treat there as being a publication. I recognise that this means that most forms of dissemination, whether oral or written, will constitute a publication, but I do not shrink from that. After all, the purpose of s.12(1)(a) is surely to protect what Lord Shaw of Dunfermline called 'truly private affairs', what Balcombe LJ in *Re Manda* [1993] Fam 183, [1993] 1 FLR 205 at 195 and 215 respectively referred to as the 'curtain of privacy' imposed by the family court for the protection of the particular child.
>
> [73] In the light of what has happened in the present case I need to emphasise that there is a 'publication' for this purpose whether the dissemination of information or documents is to a journalist or to a Member of Parliament, a Minister of the Crown, a Law Officer, the Director of Public Prosecutions, the Crown Prosecution Service, the police (except when exercising child protection functions), the GMC, or any other public body or public official. Specifically, I wish to make it clear that, whatever the position of the police may be when exercising child protection functions, the Minister of State for Children cannot for this purpose be taken as exercising such functions. The Minister of State is not, within the meaning of what Thorpe LJ and Wall J had in mind, a child protection professional. Disclosure to the Minister of State cannot, therefore, be justified on the footing of the exception to the general principle."

It was directly in response to this interpretation that Parliament shortly afterwards enacted provisions in s.62 of the Children Act 2004 to provide for a much more precise definition of the circumstances in which publication of such material would be regarded as unlawful. Indeed s.12(4) of the Administration of Justice Act 1960 was amended by adding the words "(and in particular where the publication is not so punishable by reason of being authorised by rules of court)". Thus the scheme now in operation is that, from time to time, rules of court may be promulgated to address particular situations and specifically by excluding certain communications from the general concept of "publication" in s.12.[41] Other statutory provisions have also been amended.[42] For example, s.97(2) of the

---

[41] See the CP37/04 *Disclosure of Information in Family Proceedings Cases Involving Children*, published in December 2004 by the Department of Constitutional Affairs, and the Government Response, Cm 6623, July 19, 2005.
[42] Adoption Act 1976, s.66(5); Magistrates' Courts Act 1980, s.145(1)(ga); Matrimonial and Family Proceedings Act 1984, s.40(4)(aa); Adoption and Children Act 2002, s.141(6); Courts Act 2003, s.76(2A). All of these make provision for the making of rules to avoid publication of certain matters attracting liability in the context of contempt of court.

Children Act 1989 was amended so that the restriction on publication is confined to "the public at large or any section of the public".[43]

D. The relevant Practice Directions

8–108 It is necessary to have regard to three long standing practice directions, which had confirmed a more restrictive approach. In the first,[44] requirements relating to welfare officers' reports are set out:

"The following wording must be boldly indorsed on all court welfare officers' reports filed in Family Division proceedings and on all copies which are supplied to the parties or their solicitors:

'This report has been prepared for the court and should be treated as confidential. It must not be shown nor its contents revealed to any person other than a party or a legal adviser to such a party. Such legal adviser may make use of the report in connection with an application for legal aid.'"

8–109 In the second,[45] the senior registrar of the Family Division (with the concurrence of the Lord Chancellor) dealt with evidence in wardship proceedings:

"The President and judges of the Family Division wish to remind practitioners of the need in wardship cases proceeding in private to obtain leave to disclose evidential documents to persons who are not parties, e.g. psychiatrists, psychologists and medical experts or any other person. Disclosure without prior leave may be a contempt of court,[46] and this is nonetheless the case where the purpose of the disclosure is only to obtain advice from the expert concerned where relevant expert evidence would be forthcoming or would be helpful to the court".

8–110 The matter was taken further by the senior registrar, specifically to deal with the obtaining of authority for disclosure of wardship papers to prospective adopters[47]:

"1. *Advance authority for disclosure of wardship papers to prospective adopters*

Prospective adopters with whom a ward of court has been placed, with the court's authority, as long-term foster parents with a view to adoption require the further authority of the court before they can be granted access to the documents in the wardship proceedings. Requests for such authority have commonly been made, until now, at a separate and subsequent appointment before the registrar or district registrar.

In the opinion of the judges of the Family Division it will in most cases be a more suitable and convenient course for the relevant authority to be sought from the judge at the main wardship hearing, on application by the local authority for an advance

---

[43] See the discussion of s.97(2) at paras 8–83 *et seq*.
[44] [1984] 1 All E.R. 827.
[45] [1987] 3 All E.R. 640.
[46] It would indeed appear to have been regarded as a contempt of court: see Munby J. in *Re B (A Child) (Disclosure)* [2004] EWHC 411 (Fam), [2004] 2 F.L.R. 142. But see now the changes brought about by the Children Act 2004, s.62.
[47] [1989] 1 All E.R. 169.

authorisation permitting the disclosure of the wardship file (subject to conditions of safeguarding confidentiality) to the prospective adopters and their legal advisers.

Leave to disclose the wardship file should therefore normally be sought from the judge at the main wardship hearing, subject to such terms and conditions (including the exception from disclosures of any particular document or category of documents) as the judge may think fit. It will be desirable for the judge's order to indicate the stage at which disclosure is to be allowed to take place; and normally this will either be before the placement is made or when leave to commence adoption proceedings is about to be sought.

2. Procedure for obtaining any necessary leave or directions from the court following authorisation of a placement

Although it continues to be the general rule in wardship that ex parte applications are permitted only in cases of urgent necessity (*Re H (a minor)* [1985] 3 All E.R. 1, [1985] 1 W.L.R. 1164, CA), applications for routine leave or directions (*e.g.* for medical attention or holidays outside the jurisdiction), in cases where the court has already made an order authorising the placement of a minor with a view to adoption, by the person or authority having the care of the minor may be made *ex parte* and without notice to any other party (but subject to consultation with the Official Solicitor in cases where he is acting as guardian ad litem)".

E. Disclosures by CAFCASS

The Children and Family Court Advisory and Support Service (CAFCASS) came into being on April 1, 2001 pursuant to the Criminal Justice and Court Services Act 2000 (involving amendments to s.7 of the Children Act 1989). An officer of the service who is asked to report to the court on a child welfare matter is known as a children and family reporter ("CFR").[48] It is well recognised that delicate problems can arise for a CFR in the course of preparing a report if he or she comes across information or allegations suggesting a need for an investigation by social services. It emerged before the Court of Appeal in *Re M*[49] that there had been differences of opinion and practice around the country as to the appropriate steps for a CFR to take in such circumstances. According to a CAFCASS survey, permission from the court to report such concerns to social services would only be required within the counties of Hampshire, Essex and Norfolk. On the Western Circuit arrangements were being put in hand for a duty judge roster to be instituted to determine urgent applications of that kind when the contested case came before the Southampton county court which ultimately enabled the Court of Appeal to determine issues of law and to give general guidance.

8–111

The CFR in *Re M* told the court that an interview with the child's mother and aunt revealed "serious allegations ... which may need referral to the social services". She sought directions from the judge as to whether, because of her concerns as to the child's welfare, she could so refer the matter. The judge declined to allow the material to be disclosed but did give permission to appeal. He had been troubled in the light of previous experience as to "uncontrolled adverse consequences" which had flowed from an earlier referral. He came to the conclusion, as a matter of principle, that "leave is needed to disclose to third

8–112

---

[48] See r.4.1(1) of the Family Proceedings Rules 1991.
[49] [2002] EWCA Civ 1199, [2003] Fam. 26.

parties material contained in the course of investigations". On the appeal, it was CAFCASS' primary submission that there was no rule of law or practice, nor anything about the inherent relationship between the CFR and the court, which gave rise to a need to seek permission. The CFR has an independent duty to protect children and a corresponding discretion whether and what to report.

8–113 It was held by the Court of Appeal that a CFR could not be prevented from reporting concerns to social services merely because, at a later stage, those concerns would find their way into a report for the court. At that stage r.4.23 of the 1991 Family Proceedings Rules (as amended) would come into play, whereby disclosure of any such document would be restricted to specified categories of persons. Meanwhile, however, there was no comparable restriction governing information which would or might ultimately be contained in such a report.

8–114 The court also accepted the argument, contrary to the conclusion of the judge below, that there was nothing about the inherent relationship between the judge and the CFR to prevent concerns being communicated to the social services. It was emphasised that the success of the new CAFCASS service depended in part upon the support of the judiciary but that, far from always having to act under the court's direction, there is an independent discretion as to the nature and extent of his or her investigations, and as to the manner in which they are approached. The relationship between the judge and the CFR should be a collaborative one. The ultimate objective of all the disciplines involved is the protection of children and the advancement of their welfare. "In pursuit of that overriding objective each must be free to operate independently as well as collaboratively and independent operation includes the exercise of an independent discretion". Naturally, although permission is not required from the court, the CFR would be expected to report back to the judge after taking any such step.

8–115 Another factor which played a part in the court's reasoning was that the child's mother could have gone directly to the social services herself without the court's permission; it was thus difficult to see why the CFR should be any more inhibited.

8–116 The role of CAFCASS was further considered in *A v Times Newspapers Ltd*[50] where Sumner J held that there was no duty on its part to engage with or to give notice to the media in relation to hearings involving children. It is well known that there is an "almost total lack of exception" to the normal rule that such cases should be heard in private.

F. What can be published about proceedings in private?

8–117 It is clear that the publication of purely formal details about proceedings being heard in private is in itself unobjectionable, and this was confirmed in *P v Liverpool Daily Post and Echo Newspapers plc*[51] Lord Bridge pointed out[52] that

---

[50] [2002] EWHC 2444 (Fam).
[51] [1991] 2 A.C. 370 at 423D–G. See also 384A–C, Lord Donaldson M.R.
[52] *ibid.*

information as to the date, time or place when proceedings of any kind are heard is, in one sense, information relating to those proceedings. He took the view that it was necessary, however, to have regard to the mischief to which the provisions of s.12 are directed:

> "In a wardship case in which no express prohibition was imposed on publication of the name of the ward I cannot think that publication of information that there was to be or had been a hearing in the case at the Royal Courts of Justice at 10.30 am on a certain date would have been regarded as encroaching on the privacy of the proceedings which the common law of contempt protected. Again, it would surely be no contempt to publish the fact that in current litigation between two manufacturers the court was today sitting in camera to hear evidence relating to some secret process, discovery or invention which was in issue in the proceedings. The essential privacy which is protected by each of the exceptions in paragraphs (a) to (d) of section 12(1) attaches to the substance of the matters which the court has closed its doors to consider, not to the fact that the court will sit, is sitting or has sat at a certain date, time or place behind closed doors to consider those matters."

The embargo would apply not only to information given to the judge at the hearing but also to affidavits or confidential reports submitted beforehand.[53] It is surprising that the scope of these provisions should have been unclear for so long, but such was the uncertainty before the ruling by the House, that Lord Bridge found himself in this respect disagreeing with the majority in the Court of Appeal.

Although "information relating to proceedings" should not be given too narrow a construction, the term would not embrace, for example, case records of a social services department which have neither been prepared for the purpose of court proceedings nor submitted in evidence. The fact that some evidence may have been based upon them will not suffice.[54] Nor would s.12 of itself prohibit publication of the bare fact that an identified witness has given evidence for or against a particular party to the proceedings.[55]

It has already been pointed out[56] that it is not *ipso facto* a contempt to publish the fact that someone is a ward of court.[57] Nor is a child protected, in the absence of a specific order, from the publication of information about him or her just

---

[53] *Re F (Orse A) (A Minor)* [1977] Fam. 58, 90C, Lord Denning M.R.; *Re S (Minors) (Wardship: Disclosure of Material)* [1988] 1 F.L.R. 1, 6F–H, Booth, J.; *Official Solicitor v News Group Newspapers plc* [1994] 2 F.L.R. 174, Connell J.
[54] *Re S (Minors) (Wardship: Disclosure of Material)* [1988] 1 F.L.R. 1, 6, Booth J. See also *Re L (A Ward) (Publication of Information)* [1988] 1 F.L.R. 255 at 260, [1988] 1 All E.R. 418 at 422 where she said that, as the section carries the sanction of imprisonment, "It must follow ... that the words of the Act must be strictly construed."
[55] *Re B (A Child) (Disclosure)* [2004] EWHC 411 (Fam), [2004] 2 F.L.R. 142, Munby J.
[56] See paras 6–110 *et seq.*
[57] See *Re L (A Minor) Wardship: Freedom of Publication* [1988] 1 All E.R. 418; *Re F (Orse A) (A Minor) (Publication of Information)* [1977] Fam. 58 at 99, Scarman L.J.

because of being the subject of proceedings.[58] In *X v Dempster*[59] Wilson J. summarised what information relating to proceedings *can* be published, in the absence of a specific injunction, by direct reference to the mischief at which s.12 of the 1960 Act is directed:

(a) the fact, if it be the case, that a child is a ward of court and is the subject of wardship proceedings or that a child is the subject of residence or other proceedings under the Children Act 1989 or of proceedings relating wholly or mainly to his maintenance or upbringing[60];

(b) the name, address or photograph of such a child as is mentioned in (a)[61];

(c) the name, address or photograph of the parties (or, if the child is a party, the other parties) to such proceedings as are mentioned in (a)[62];

(d) the date, time or place of a past or future hearing of such proceedings[63];

(e) The nature of the dispute in such proceedings[64];

(f) anything which has been seen or heard by a person conducting himself lawfully in the public corridor or other public precincts outside the court in which the hearing in private is taking place[65]; and

(g) the text or summary of the whole or part of any order made in such proceedings.[66]

8–121   The judge also illuminated the distinction between publication of "the nature of the dispute" which is permissible, and publication of evidence, including summaries of the evidence, which is impermissible.[67] It seems, however, that to report the basic fact that a witness has given evidence for one side or the other will not offend.[68]

---

[58] *Official Solicitor v News Group Newspapers plc* [1994] 2 F.L.R. 174 at 181F–G, Connell J. See para.6–85, and the authorities there cited. It is now necessary to take account of s.97(2) of the Children Act as amended by the Access to Justice Act 1999 and the apparently automatic ban on the identification of children involved in High Court proceedings including wardship and other *parens patriae* cases: see, *e.g.* the observations of Munby J. in *Kelly v BBC* [2001] Fam. 59 (discussed at para.8–84 above).
[59] [1999] 1 F.L.R. 894 at 898–9.
[60] *Re W* [1989] 1 F.L.R. 246 at 257H.
[61] *ibid.*
[62] *Re De Beaujeu's Application for Writ of Attachment Against Cudlipp* [1949] 1 Ch. 230.
[63] *Pickering v Liverpool Daily Post and Echo Newspapers plc and another* [1991] 2 AC 370 *per* Lord Bridge of Harwich at 423D–F.
[64] *ibid.* at 423F–G.
[65] *Re W,* cited above, at 257G–H.
[66] s.12(2) of the 1960 Act.
[67] See the observations of Munby J. in *Re B (A Child) (Disclosure)* [2004] EWHC 411 (Fam), [2004] 2 F.L.R. 142 where he expressed agreement at [77] with Wilson J.'s analysis.
[68] See Munby J. in *Re B (A Child) (Disclosure)* [2004] EWHC 411 (Fam), [2004] 2 F.L.R. 142 at [76].

It was confirmed in *Att-Gen v Pelling*[69] that it was a criminal contempt to publish in a journal and on the Internet the content of a judgment given in private, albeit some years earlier, in the course of proceedings under the Children Act 1989. While it was acknowledged that the publication could have no direct impact on the conduct of proceedings, it was accepted that, especially because the child concerned had been 12 years old at the time of publication, the publication undermined the administration of justice in a broader sense. In the context of Children Act proceedings, as much as in traditional wardship cases, the doing of justice is equated with the protection of the interests of the child concerned. Because such a child was in the care of the court, it was an affront to justice that a judgment should be published which, in the interests of the child, the court has advisedly determined should be kept private. This was held to be entirely consistent with the speeches in *Scott v Scott*[70] and with the decision of the Court of Appeal in *Re F*.[71]

G. The underlying policy

The type of information that is contemplated in s.12, as being worthy of protection, would probably include matters relating to the parties, the issues, evidence and submissions or argument.[72] The policy underlying this negative enactment, that publication of such information should not of itself be contempt, must be quite separate from that discussed earlier[73] relating to reports of proceedings in open court. In that context, it is thought positively desirable that the public should be informed as to what takes place in open court, and a privilege attaches to the reports themselves.

There was traditionally no privilege attaching to reports of chambers matters, and indeed the Court of Appeal reaffirmed this principle in a case in which a newspaper report quoted from the contents of an affidavit in Chancery proceedings; it had not at that stage been read out in open court or, for that matter, in chambers. The newspaper having chosen to repeat those allegations, some of which were arguably defamatory, it was held that the defendants would only be entitled to defend themselves by proving the truth of the underlying allegations. Hirst L.J. expressed the policy in the following terms[74]:

> "The media will be free to report the issue of proceedings in both civil and criminal cases, and will have the full protection of privilege (whether absolute or qualified according to the circumstances) for fair and accurate reports of all proceedings of either kind in open court. This to my mind furnishes ample scope for keeping the public properly informed".

On the other hand, in the light of the ruling in *Hodgson v Imperial Tobacco Ltd*[75] greater public access is given to cases which formerly took place in "chambers"

---

[69] [2005] EWHC 414 (Admin).
[70] [1913] A.C. 417.
[71] [1977] Fam. 58.
[72] See, *e.g. Re F* [1977] Fam. 58, 87, Lord Denning M.R.
[73] At paras 4–265 *et seq*. See also paras 7–16 *et seq*.
[74] *Stern v Piper* [1997] Q.B. 123 at 135F, CA. See also *Scott v Scott* [1913] A.C. 417 at 452, Lord Atkinson; *R. v Madge Ex p. Isaacs* (1913) 30 T.L.R. 10 at 12–13, Scrutton J.
[75] [1998] 1 W.L.R. 1056, [1998] 2 All E.R. 673, considered in paras 7–41 *et seq*.

proceedings in the Queen's Bench Division. Nevertheless, until witness statements are actually deployed in evidence citation from them would not be protected by privilege.

8–125   The statutory provisions of s.12 are thus to be justified by specific policy considerations. In the first place, they bring a degree of certainty to the confusion which had reigned hitherto.[76] Secondly, while there are no doubt good policy reasons for restricting the flow of information about proceedings in the categories specified in s.12, it would be more difficult to contend that restrictions about other proceedings held in private are "necessary in a democratic society ... for maintaining the authority and impartiality of the judiciary".[77]

8–126   Not every "chambers" hearing was designed to achieve confidentiality or secrecy. In civil proceedings, many interlocutory hearings took place in chambers purely by convention. For example, an application for an interim injunction would be heard in chambers in the Queen's Bench Division whereas in the Chancery Division such hearings always took place in open court. In the absence of a specific order, justifiable as being necessary for the protection of the administration of justice, it would hardly be possible to say that it was necessary to criminalise the publication of such material. These quirks of procedure were highlighted by Jacob J. in *Forbes v Smith*,[78] and by Lord Woolf M.R. in *Hodgson v Imperial Tobacco Ltd*.[79] The European Court of Human Rights in *B and another v United Kingdom*[80] confirmed that proceedings concerning children constituted a prime example of the type of case in which the exclusion of the press and public might be justified by the need to protect the privacy of children and parties, as well as by the need to avoid prejudicing the interests of justice.

8–127   In the case of the specified exemptions, however, there are sound policy reasons why Parliament chose to afford the protection of privacy, and particularly in relation to children[81]:

(1) the affairs which are the subject of the proceedings are purely private or domestic;[82]

(2) it is not usually in the child's best interests for the nature of the disagreements between those close to him, and the problems which those disagreements create, to be exposed to public view;

(3) those who give evidence or who provide reports should be able to speak fully and frankly and the confidentiality attaching to those matters should be preserved, if possible.

---

[76] See, *e.g. Re Martindale* [1894] 3 Ch. 193; *Re de Beaujeu's application* [1949] Ch. 230, 236, Wynn-Parry J.
[77] See Art.10(2) of the European Convention on Human Rights and the consideration of this provision in *Official Solicitor v News Group Newspapers plc* [1994] 2 F.L.R. 174 at 183A–C.
[78] [1998] 1 All E.R. 973.
[79] See the discussion of these decisions in paras 7–41 *et seq.*
[80] [2001] 2 F.C.R. 221.
[81] *per* Connell. J. in *Official Solicitor v News Group Newspapers plc* [1994] 2 F.L.R. 174 at 181–2.
[82] See also *per* Lord Shaw in *Scott v Scott* [1913] A.C. 417 at 483.

In *Official Solicitor v News Group Newspapers plc*,[83] Connell J. saw no inconsistency between these principles and the terms of Art.10 of the European Convention.[84]

H. The discussion of section 12 in *Clibbery v Allen*

In *Clibbery v Allan*,[85] Munby J. held that the Family Division had no greater power to sit in secret (*in camera*) than any other part of the High Court. He analysed in some detail the policy considerations underlying the decision of their Lordships in *Scott v Scott*, the closely corresponding provisions of s.12 of the 1960 Act, and those recently embodied in CPR 39.2. He came to the conclusion that proceedings involving children give rise to special factors irrespective of the particular tribunal hearing them and that, despite having a different set of rules (*i.e.* the Family Proceedings Rules) from those governing the other Divisions of the High Court, the Family Division has to give effect to the same principles. He explained that the reasoning of Jacob J. in *Forbes v Smith* and of the Court of Appeal in *Hodgson v Imperial Tobacco Ltd* applied with equal validity to the Family Division. This approach is consistent with that adopted in the former Court for Divorce and Matrimonial Causes in *H (falsely called C) v C*[86] and endorsed by the House of Lords in *Scott v Scott*[87] Thus, the practice which had grown up in the meantime of hearing nullity suits in camera, for reasons of delicacy, seems to have been something of an aberration.[88] Munby J. naturally recognised that there may in appropriate circumstances have to be some restraints placed upon the reporting of chambers proceedings. He cited the obvious examples of the exceptional categories listed in s.12 of the 1960 Act and the specific provisions of the Judicial Proceedings (Regulation of Reports) Act 1926.[89] There would also be protection as necessary for materials supplied under judicial compulsion; but these are factors which may arise in any court. The most significant point about the judgment is that there cannot be said to be any unique factors operating in the Family Division as such.

I. Does section 12 create a strict liability contempt?

There are potential difficulties of construction in relation to the wording of s.12. Fortunately, however, the matter has received sufficient consideration by the higher courts to leave little room for doubt. One question was whether the publication of information within any of the specified categories would constitute contempt *ipso facto*, or whether some other statutory or common law restriction would be required.

---

[83] [1994] 2 F.L.R. 174 at 183.
[84] para.2–142.
[85] [2001] 2 F.L.R. 819, affirmed by the Court of Appeal at [2002] EWCA Civ 45, [2002] Fam. 261.
[86] (1859) 29 L.J.(P & M) 29, 30 (Bramwell B.).
[87] [1913] A.C. 417 at 434, 436, 443, 446–7, 462–3, 469, 475, 478–80.
[88] See, *e.g. D v D* [1903] P 144 at 148, Sir Francis Jeune P.
[89] Discussed at paras 8–2 *et seq.*

8–130 In *P v Liverpool Daily Post and Echo Newspapers plc*,[90] a man who had been convicted of manslaughter and detained under a restriction order was applying for a discharge to a mental health review tribunal. An earlier application had attracted a great deal of publicity to the extent of impeding the tribunal. This time, it was anticipated that the defendant newspaper proprietors and publishers would publish material prejudicial to the new application. An injunction was sought to restrain the publication of the very fact that he was making the application, of the hearing date and of the ultimate decision. It was argued that any such publication should be prohibited by the Mental Health Tribunal Rules 1983, r.21(5). The relevant provisions were:

> "21(1) The tribunal shall sit in private unless the patient requests a hearing in public and the tribunal is satisfied that a hearing in public would not be contrary to the interests of the patient . . .
> (5) Except in so far as the tribunal may direct, information about proceedings before the tribunal and the names of any persons concerned in the proceedings shall not be made public."

8–131 Lord Donaldson M.R., in the Court of Appeal, expressed the opinion[91]:

> "Notwithstanding dicta in *Att-Gen v Leveller Magazine Ltd*,[92] I cannot construe section 12 as doing other than providing that, subject to knowledge, publication of information relating to proceedings under any provision of the Mental Health Act 1959, and now under the Act of 1983, is a contempt of court. The curiously worded subsection (4):
>
>> 'Nothing in this section shall be construed as implying that any publication is punishable as contempt of court which would not be so punishable apart from this section'
>
> cannot, I think, override the plain words of subsection (1)"

8–132 Thus, in Lord Donaldson's view, it appears that the section *does* render a publication a contempt provided that the alleged contemnor *knows* that the publication was prohibited.[93]

8–133 Glidewell L.J. in the same case[94] dealt with the point in the following way:

> " . . . the effect of section 12(1)(b) of the Act of 1960 is that publication of information relating to proceedings on an application to a tribunal may be a contempt if there is some statutory provision relating to such tribunals which prohibits the publication."

It follows that the ambit of the law of contempt coincides with the ambit of r.21(5) of the 1983 Rules. Glidewell L.J., therefore, came to the conclusion that a deliberate breach of r.21(5) might well be a contempt; whereas a publication which did not offend against the rule would not.

---

[90] [1991] 2 A.C. 370.
[91] *ibid.* at 386.
[92] [1979] A.C. 440, *per* Lord Edmund-Davies at 464, and *per* Lord Scarman at 472–4.
[93] See also *Re F (A Minor) (Publication of Information)* [1977] Fam. 58.
[94] At 389G–H.

The matter was also considered by Farquharson L.J.[95]: 8–134

"The basis for saying that the section expressed the common law was the provisions of section 12(4). I do not so read the subsection. It provides that the defences normally open to an alleged contemnor remain available to him and that the section is not to be construed as saying that the fact of publishing information in one of the exceptional cases in subsection (1)(a) to (e) is, *ipso facto*, a contempt".

When the matter came before the House of Lords, Lord Bridge explained[96]: 8–135

"A helpful starting point for this inquiry is the guidance found in the judgments of the Court of Appeal in *In Re F (Orse A.) (A Minor) (Publication of Information).*[97] This was a wardship case in which the court determined a number of issues arising upon the construction of section 12 of the Act of 1960 which do not strictly arise in the instant case. They rejected the view that the effect of the exceptions in section 12(1) was to constitute the publication of information relating to proceedings in the excepted categories an absolute offence of contempt. Scarman L.J. said, at p.99:

'I cannot read the words 'of itself' in subsection (1) as implying that in the five excepted cases contempt is necessarily committed if the court sits in private. The words, in their context, need mean no more than that there is a contempt in the absence of a defence recognised by law.'

I agree with this.

The court construed the obscurely worded subsection (4) as having the effect of preserving any defence which would have been available at common law and indeed held, in relation to wardship proceedings, that no one could be guilty of contempt under the section who would not also have been guilty under the pre-existing law. I also agree with this, but, of course, in relation to proceedings before a mental health review tribunal, exercising a novel and purely statutory jurisdiction, the common law principles applicable to determine what would or would not amount to a contempt of proceedings in wardship or lunacy can only be applied by analogy."

Thus, it would appear that publication of information within the specified categories of s.12 will not *ipso facto* constitute contempt of court. If, however, there is knowledge that the information is within a prohibited category (in the sense of knowing that the proceedings were heard in private), then it is likely that there will be held to have been a contempt of court by virtue of the provisions of s.12. Any defences available at common law will nevertheless remain available, as s.12(4) makes clear. It is necessary, therefore, to consider what possible "defences" at common law might be embraced within this provision. In *Re F (Orse A) (A Minor)*[98] Scarman L.J. concluded that it would include at least the following: 8–136

(1) that the reports were of information relating to the ward, but not to the wardship proceedings;

---

[95] At 396A–C.
[96] *ibid.* at 421.
[97] [1977] Fam. 58.
[98] [1977] Fam. 58 at 100B.

(2) that, even if the report did relate to the proceedings, the publisher was unaware that the information related to those proceedings, or that the proceedings were private.

Geoffrey Lane L.J. concurred, and commented that "honest mistake is a defence providing that had the mistaken circumstances been true, no offence would have been committed."[99]

8–137   Lord Denning M.R. seemed to suggest at one point that a defence might even be available if the alleged contemnor had not realised that the publication was or might be prohibited by law.[1] Whether the burden on the applicant goes as far as this, however, may be doubted in view of the general principle that ignorance of the law is no defence; and also in the light of the way the requirement for *mens rea* has been analysed in such modern cases as *Att-Gen v News Group Newspapers plc*,[2] *Att-Gen v Newspaper Publishing plc*,[3] and *Att-Gen v Times Newspapers Ltd*.[4] It is probable that an applicant would need to show that the alleged contemnor knew that the information published was within one of the categories in fact protected by the subsection, even though unaware of the legal restrictions themselves.

8–138   An example is provided by the case of *Official Solicitor v News Group Newspapers plc*,[5] which arose in the aftermath of a well-publicised trial in which a nurse had been convicted of thirteen separate offences, including murder and attempted murder. The defendant had been suffering from Munchausen's syndrome by proxy, and following the trial the estranged husband of another nurse contacted a newspaper to offer the information that his wife too had been suffering from the disorder. When asked for proof, he produced documents relating to the custody proceedings concerning his son, which contained confidential medical reports about his wife's condition. The offending articles contained references to and quotations from the confidential medical information which had been provided to the court. Thus, there was no doubt that the respondents had published "information relating to proceedings before the High Court sitting in private, which proceedings were brought under the Children Act 1989, and related wholly or mainly to the upbringing of the three-year-old child of the nurse and her husband".[6] The issue was whether they had the necessary *mens rea*. The editor of the newspaper deposed[7] that he was unaware of the relevance of s.12, and that he had received no legal advice suggesting that the revelation of the confidential medical material would be unlawful. So did the reporter.

---

[99] *ibid.* at 107B.
[1] *ibid.* at 90A.
[2] [1989] Q.B. 110.
[3] [1988] Ch. 333. See also *Att-Gen v Newspaper Publishing plc* [1990] T.L.R. 158 (Lexis).
[4] [1992] 1 A.C. 191.
[5] [1994] 2 F.L.R. 174, Connell J.
[6] *ibid.*, at 177.
[7] As he had done in *Att-Gen v News Group Newspapers plc.* [1989] Q.B. 110. For discussion of this case, see para.5–163.

It was held by Connell J. that, even if recklessness as to the legal consequences would suffice, as Lord Denning M.R. had contemplated in *Re F (Orse A) (a Minor)*,[8] that state of mind could not be established. The very fact of employing a duty lawyer demonstrated a concern that the law should not be broken. On the other hand, the editor *did* know that the story touched upon High Court proceedings, and "must have known[9] that those proceedings were private proceedings."[10] It seems to have been accepted that in fact the editor had not given any thought to the possibility of contempt arising.[11] Nevertheless, there was held to be a sufficient basis for finding *mens rea*.

8–139

The case of *Official Solicitor v News Group Newspapers plc*[12] was not apparently cited in *X v Dempster*.[13] In the latter case, legal advice (held to be "aberrant") was given to the effect that it would not be contempt to publish, in the context of cross-applications for residence orders, comments to the effect that the mother was being portrayed as a bad parent. Nonetheless the judge held that what mattered was the knowledge of the journalist and newspaper proprietors that this information related to proceedings taking place in private. He thus found contempt proved and added that there is "no point in our having a legal system if the law is whatever people think it is".[14]

8–140

X. EMPLOYMENT AND OTHER TRIBUNALS

A. Employment tribunals: restrictions on reporting[15]

The principle of open justice applies to employment tribunals, although they operate under their own regulatory system.[16] There is express provision for making an exception in cases concerning national security or certain categories of confidential information.[17] The issues canvassed before these tribunals often attract the attention of the media, and it is therefore necessary to consider the interrelationship between the general law of contempt and these specific provisions.

8–141

---

[8] [1977] Fam. 58.
[9] See also *Att-Gen v News Group Newspapers plc.* [1989] Q.B. 110; *Att-Gen v Newspaper Publishing plc* [1989] F.S.R. 457, Morritt J. These cases are discussed in the context of the *mens rea* required for common law publication contempts in paras 5–120 *et seq*.
[10] [1994] 2 F.L.R. 174 at 180G and 181D. Cp. Lord Denning M.R. in *Re F (Orse A) (A Minor)* [1977] Fam. 58 at 90C, and Scarman L.J. at 96H.
[11] [1994] 2 F.L.R. at 183F.
[12] [1994] 2 F.L.R. 174.
[13] [1999] 1 F.L.R. 894.
[14] See also *Re G (Celebrities: Publicity)* [1999] 1 F.L.R. 409, CA.
[15] Formerly known as "industrial tribunals": see now the Employment Rights (Dispute Resolution) Act 1998, s.1(1).
[16] See the Employment Tribunals (Constitution and Rules of Procedure) Regulations 2004, SI 2004/1861.
[17] See, *e.g.* Sch.1, para.16; Sch.2, which contains the Employment Tribunals (National Security) Rules of Procedure.

8–142 It was held by the Divisional Court in *R. v Southampton Industrial Tribunal Ex p. INS News Group Ltd and Express Newspapers plc*[18] that the existence of the rules precluded the tribunal from sitting in private in situations outside those identified. It was argued that the tribunal could have resort to its general power to regulate its own procedure, but the court rejected this contention on the traditional principle of construction that the specific prevails over the general.

8–143 Furthermore, a "restricted reporting" order may be made in certain circumstances.[19] Such an order had been made in the case in question, because it concerned allegations of sexual misconduct. This was another reason why the Divisional Court found against the decision to sit in private; Parliament had expressly catered for the particular problem by providing for restrictions upon *reporting*, rather than upon access to the tribunal itself.

8–144 One reason why it had been thought necessary to take the more drastic measure was that the press had already infringed the "restricted reporting" order (by publishing photographs which enabled the persons concerned to be identified, despite their faces having been obscured). The Divisional Court's response to this was that contempt proceedings would be the appropriate way of dealing with that problem, and that it was not in itself sufficient to justify excluding the public in circumstances outside the terms of the regulations themselves.

8–145 In *X v Z Ltd*,[20] the Court of Appeal held that an employment tribunal's power to make restriction orders should never be exercised automatically, whether at the request of one party or even both,[21] but only after considering whether it was in the public interest that the media should be deprived of the right to communicate information to the public.

8–146 Highly detailed enabling provisions are contained now in the Employment Tribunals Act 1996,[22] ss.11 and 12, for restriction of publicity in cases involving, respectively, sexual misconduct and complaints under s.8 of the Disability Discrimination Act 1995.[23] The Employment Appeal Tribunal construed s.11 in such a way that the words "person affected by ... " do not embrace a body corporate.[24] Thus there was no power in a case containing allegations of sexual misconduct to make a restricted reporting order in respect of the University as opposed to individual employees. This is despite the fact that the word "person" in s.11(6) had been held[25] to be capable of including corporate or unincorporated bodies.

---

[18] [1995] I.R.L.R. 247.
[19] See the Employment Tribunals Act 1996, ss.11 and 12, and Sch.1, para.50 of the 2004 Regulations.
[20] [1998] I.C.R. 43.
[21] See, *e.g.* the remarks of Staughton L.J. in *Ex p. P* [1998] T.L.R. 204: "When both sides agreed that information should be kept from the public that was when the court had to be most vigilant".
[22] Formerly known as the Industrial Tribunals Act 1996: see the Employment Rights (Dispute Resolution) Act 1998, s.1(2).
[23] See Halsbury's *Statutes of England* 4th ed., Vol.7 for the full terms of these provisions, and see the relevant regulations SI 2004/1861.
[24] *Leicester University v A* [1999] I.C.R. 701.
[25] *M v Vincent* [1998] I.C.R. 73. See also the decision of the Divisional Court in *R.v London (North) Industrial Tribunal Ex p. Associated Newspapers plc* [1998] I.R.L.R. 569.

B. Other tribunals

It is not within the scope of this work to catalogue the detailed provisions governing procedure of the many statutory tribunals exercising jurisdiction in widely differing fields of activity. Some such tribunals are by their very nature likely to attract media attention, in particular employment tribunals, and to a lesser extent mental health review tribunals. These have already been considered.[26]

8–147

So too, although the problem rarely arose,[27] when an inquiry was set up under the Tribunals of Inquiry (Evidence) Act 1921, the subject matter would generally be of considerable public interest.[28] Such proceedings were heard in public unless the chairman considered it appropriate to exclude members of the public where "it is in the public interest expedient to do so for reasons connected with the subject-matter of the inquiry or the nature of the evidence to be given".[29] This would only rarely be done, and indeed one view is that the provision would be construed so narrowly as to apply only in cases of national security.[30] The statute was repealed and replaced by the Inquiries Act 2005 with effect from June 2005.

8–148

In recent years, inquiries have been appointed *ad hoc* rather than under the 1921 statutory regime. Whether there will be public access to the hearings depended upon the discretion of the minister setting up the inquiry.[31]

8–149

In the case of regularly constituted tribunals, however, the requirements vary widely. In some instances, there will be a statutory obligation for the hearings to be in public, subject to certain limited exceptions;[32] in others, there will be a presumption in favour of privacy,[33] or an obligation to hold hearings in private where one party requests it.

8–150

---

[26] See paras 8–130 *et seq*.
[27] Criticism has been levelled at how infrequently resort has been had to this mechanism: see Z. Segal, "Tribunals of Inquiry: a British Invention Ignored in Britain" [1984] P.L. 206.
[28] See, *e.g.* the Lynskey Tribunal (1948), the Bank Rate Tribunal (1957), the Vassall Tribunal (1962), Vehicle and General (1971), "Bloody Sunday" (1972), and the Crown Agents (1974), The second "Bloody Sunday" Inquiry (June 1999).
[29] s.2.
[30] See, *e.g.* the White Paper, Cmnd. 5313 (1973), para.38, following the Salmon Commission Report, Cmnd. 3121 (1966).
[31] See, *e.g.* the Police Act 1996, s.49(2). Enquiries of this kind have been held, for example, by Lord Scarman into the Brixton Riots (1981) and by Sir William Macpherson into the death of Stephen Lawrence (1998).
[32] See, *e.g.* Rent Assessment Committees (England and Wales) Regulations 1971; Independent Schools Tribunal Rules 1958; Agricultural Lands Tribunal (Rules) Order 1978; Valuation and Community Charge Tribunals Regulations 1989; Gas (Underground Storage) (Inquiries Procedure) Rules 1966; Social Security (Adjudication) Regulations 1986.
[33] National Health Service (Service Committees and Tribunal) Regulations 1974.

CHAPTER 9

PROTECTION OF SOURCES

	PARA
I. The Common Law Context..	9–1
II. The General Scope of Section 10..	9–52
III. The Four Statutory Exceptions Further Analysed..	9–126
IV. When Does a Journalist's Refusal Become Contempt?.............................	9–194
V. Should the Attorney-General Have a Role to Play?..................................	9–239
VI. A General Summary of the Principles..	9–245

I. THE COMMON LAW CONTEXT

A. Introduction: the significance of journalists' sources[1]

9–1 The European Court of Human Rights in *Goodwin v United Kingdom*[2] referred to freedom of expression as constituting one of the essential foundations of a democratic society, and to the importance in that context of the safeguards to be afforded to the press.[3] There was agreement on all sides in that case that any requirement of a journalist that he or she reveal the identity of a source would in itself constitute a *prima facie* interference with the journalist's freedom of

---

[1] See generally T.R.S. Allan, "Disclosure of Journalists' Sources, Civil Disobedience and the Rule of Law" [1991] C.L.J. 131; S. Palmer, "Protecting Journalists' Sources: Section 10, Contempt of Court Act 1981" [1992] P.L. 61; W.F.K. Altes, "The Journalistic Privilege: A Dutch Proposal for Legislation" [1992] P.L. 73. For a full discussion and analysis of the background to these developments, see Y. Cripps, *The Legal Implications of Disclosure in the Public Interest* (2nd ed., 1994), ch.8. See also her analysis of the terms of s.10 at p.281 ff.

[2] (1996) 22 E.H.R.R. 123. See also *Roemen and Schmit v Luxembourg*, App. No.51772/99. It was confirmed by Lord Woolf in *Ashworth Hospital Authority v MGN Ltd* [2002] UKHL 29, [2002] 1 W.L.R. 2033 at [38] that the approach of the European Court of Human Rights in *Goodwin v United Kingdom* (1996) 22 E.H.R.R. 123 at [39] was equally applicable to s.10 of the Contempt of Court Act 1981. For an American perspective on the issues that arose, see R.D. Sack, "*Goodwin v United Kingdom*: an American view of protection for journalists' confidential sources under UK and European Law" (1995) 15 Media Law at p.86. The article was adapted from submissions made by the author to the Court of Human Rights in the *Goodwin* case.

[3] Apart from the European Convention, there are other instruments seeking to crystallise the rights of the press, such as the *Resolution on Journalistic Freedoms and Human Rights*, adopted at the 4th European Ministerial Conference on Mass Media Policy, Prague, December 7–8, 1994; *Resolution on the Confidentiality of Journalists' Sources* by the European Parliament on January 18, 1994, Official Journal of the European Communities No.C-44/34. See now also Recommendation No.R(2000) 7 of the Committee of Ministers to member States on the right of journalists not to disclose their sources of information, adopted by the Committee of Ministers on March 8, 2000 at the 701st meeting of the Ministers' Deputies.

expression.[4] Any such infringement has to be justified, therefore, by showing that it has been convincingly established as being "necessary in a democratic society".[5]

Signatories to the Convention, in making their assessment of whether there is a "pressing social need" in any given context, enjoy a certain "margin of appreciation".[6] Nevertheless, in the context of journalists' sources, the domestic margin of appreciation is circumscribed by the interest of any democratic society in ensuring and maintaining a free press, and by the terms of Art.10. Limitations on the confidentiality of journalistic sources call for the most careful scrutiny by the European Court, and indeed by any domestic court called upon to determine whether, on the facts of a particular case, it is necessary for the individual journalist to identify a source.[7]

These principles were exerting considerable influence in English law before the advent of the Human Rights Act 1998, and particularly in the context of s.10 of the Contempt of Court Act 1981. Shortly after the decision of the European Court in *Goodwin*, their importance was acknowledged by the Divisional Court in the case of *Chief Constable of Leicestershire v Garavelli*.[8] It was also accepted by the Court of Appeal in *Camelot Group plc v Centaur Communications Ltd*[9]:

"In making its judgment as to whether sufficiently strong reasons are shown in any particular case to outweigh the important public interest in the press being able to protect the anonymity of its sources, the domestic court will give great weight to the judgments, in particular recent judgments, made by the European Court of Human Rights in cases where the facts are similar to the case before the domestic court.

---

[4] (1996) 22 E.H.R.R. 123 at 139, [28]. In *Moysa v Alberta (Labour Relations Board)* (1989) 60 D.L.R. (4th) 1, the Supreme Court of Canada had been invited to determine a similar constitutional question, namely whether s.2(b) of the Canadian Charter of Rights and Freedoms, guaranteeing *inter alia* "freedom of the press and other media of communication", covered the right of the press to seek and receive as well as impart information. It was argued that any other interpretation would lead to news sources "drying up". The court, however, did not regard the appeal as requiring at that time an answer to " ... these broad and important constitutional questions". See also *New Brunswick Broadcasting Co v Nova Scotia* (1991) 80 D.L.R. (4th) 11; *Canadian Broadcasting Corp v Lesard* [1991] 3 S.C.R. 421, La Forest J. The freedom of expression guaranteed under s.2(b) of the Charter " ... would be of little value if [it] did not also encompass the right to gather news and information without undue governmental interference". The media are entitled to " ... special consideration because of the importance of their role in a democratic society" (at 533). See also *R. v The National Post* (2004) 236 D.L.R. (4th) 551 concerning the special considerations which arise in applications to search media premises, or to seize materials from journalists, pursuant to police powers under the Criminal Code, and the balancing exercise to which they give rise.
[5] (1996) 22 E.H.R.R. 123 at 143, [39] and [40].
[6] These points are more fully developed in para.2-168. See also *Goodwin v United Kingdom* (1996) 22 E.H.R.R. 123 at [46].
[7] (1996) 22 E.H.R.R. 123 at 143-4, [40]. See also the judgments of the Divisional Court in *Chief Constable of Leicestershire v Garavelli* [1997] E.M.L.R. 543 and of the Court of Appeal in *Camelot Group plc v Centaur Communications Ltd* [1999] Q.B. 124; *Ashworth Health Authority v MGN Ltd* [2002] UKHL 29, [2002] 1 W.L.R. 2033 at [62] (Lord Woolf) and [72] (Lord Hobhouse) citing *Bergens v Tidende* (2000) E.H.R.R. 430 at [52] and [53].
[8] [1997] E.M.L.R. 543, more fully discussed at paras 9-156 *et seq.*
[9] [1999] Q.B. 124 at 137A-C, Schiemann L.J., considered further at paras 9-164 *et seq.*

That court has unrivalled experience in this field and it would be foolish not to take advantage of that experience. The tensions which the European Court of Human Rights has to resolve are similar to those facing the domestic court and this will often be the case even though a particular case before the European Court of Human Rights sprang from facts in a country other than England."

B. The common law background

9–4 There has long been some appreciation of the problems that arise if a court is asked to order disclosure of a journalist's sources. For example, in *Adam v Fisher*,[10] Buckley L.J. had suggested that "a newspaper stood in such a position that it was not desirable on grounds of public interest that the name of a newspaper's informant should be disclosed." This was in the context of the well established rule that a journalist was not required, in an action for defamation,[11] to name an informant at the pre-trial stage, for the purpose of interrogatories[12] or disclosure of documents.[13] The more restricted rule applied before the advent of the CPR only to preliminary proceedings; it afforded in itself no protection during a trial.[14]

9–5 The precise rationale of the rule was not entirely clear.[15] Yet the real basis is surely the public interest in protecting the media's sources of information because of the need to encourage the free flow of information.[16]

---

[10] (1914) 110 L.T. 537, 30 T.L.R. 288.
[11] See also *Reichmann v Toronto Life Publishing Co* (1988) 28 C.P.C. (2nd) 11. In *Broadcasting Corporation of NZ v Alex Harvey Industries* [1980] 1 N.Z.L.R. 163, the rule was said to extend to slander of goods.
[12] The rule was formalised in the former RSC Ord.82, r.6 which provided that, in a fair comment or privilege case, no interrogatories might be administered as to the defendant's sources or grounds of belief. This followed a recommendation of the Porter Committee on Defamation in 1949. This was revoked on February 28, 2000. The modern equivalent is CPR 53.3, but its scope is wider since it is not limited to cases where fair comment or privilege is in issue: "Unless the court orders otherwise, a party will not be required to provide further information about the identity of the defendant's sources of information." See *Gatley on Libel and Slander* (10th ed., 2004) paras 31.34 *et seq.*
[13] *Hennessy v Wright* (1888) 21 Q.B.D. 509; *British Steel Corp v Granada Television Ltd* [1981] A.C. 1096 at 1178–9; see *Re Bahama Islands Reference* [1893] A.C. 138 at 149; *Adam v Fisher* (1914) 110 L.T. 537. See generally *Gatley on Libel and Slander* (10th ed., 2004) at para.31.13. Additional protection was also afforded by RSC Ord.24, r.8, which provided that documents or parts of documents should not be ordered to be disclosed, on an application for specific discovery, unless "necessary either for disposing fairly of the cause or matter or for saving costs". See now CPR 31.5(2) and 31.19.
[14] *British Steel Corp v Granada Television Ltd* [1981] A.C. 1096. See also *John Fairfax & Sons Ltd v Cojuango* (1988) 165 C.L.R. 364, 82 A.L.R. 1, H.C.
[15] See, *e.g.* the remarks of Templeman L.J. in *British Steel Corp v Granada Television Ltd* [1981] A.C. 1096 at 1134, CA, and the discussion in the same case in the House of Lords. See also *Lyle-Samuel v Odhams Ltd* [1920] 1 K.B. 135 and *McGuinness v Att-Gen of Victoria* (1940) 63 C.L.R. 73 at 102–3, Dixon J.
[16] See the words of Browne-Wilkinson V.-C. In *Handmade Films (Production) Ltd v Express Newspapers* [1986] F.S.R. 463 at 467 cited at para.9–20 below; *Broadcasting Corporation of NZ v Alex Harvey Industries* [1980] 1 N.Z.L.R. 163. See also *Isbey v Broadcasting Corporation of NZ (No.2)* [1975] 2 N.Z.L.R. 237; *Brill v Television One* [1976] 1 N.Z.L.R. 683; *European Pacific Banking Corporation v Fourth Estate Publications Ltd* [1993] 1 N.Z.L.R. 559, CA.

It was not always the case, however, that the English courts approached 9–6
journalists' sources with a full recognition of their significance for freedom of
speech. For example, in a case shortly prior to the Contempt of Court Act, *British
Steel Corp v Granada Television Ltd*,[17] Lord Wilberforce dismissed the connection in the following terms:

"First, there were appeals, made in vigorous tones to such broad principles as the
freedom of the press, the right to a free flow of information, the public's right to know.
In Granada's printed case we find quotations from pronouncements of Sheridan in
Parliament and from declarations of eminent judges in cases where the freedom of the
press might be involved. I too would be glad to be counted among those whose voice
had been raised in favour of this great national possession—a free press: who indeed
would not? But this case does not touch upon the freedom of the press even at its
periphery. Freedom of the press imports, generally, freedom to publish without pre-
censorship, subject always to the laws relating to libel, official secrets, sedition and
other recognised inhibitions."

Hesitant recognition of the "chilling effect"

By the time of *Derbyshire County Council v Times Newspapers Ltd*,[18] it was 9–7
being recognised by the House of Lords that freedom of the press needed to be
considered in terms broader than the mere absence of "pre-censorship". Lord
Keith referred to the "chilling effect" upon the free flow of information induced,
for example, by the threat of civil actions for libel.[19] It is clear that the European
Court of Human Rights approaches the revelation of journalists' sources in a
similar way. If journalists cannot be confident of maintaining the confidentiality
of their sources, important and valuable information which ought to be made
available to the public may not be revealed.[20] Lord Keith expressed satisfaction[21]
that "the common law of England is consistent with the obligations assumed by
the Crown under the Treaty in this particular field".

As the full significance of *Goodwin v United Kingdom* came to be recognised 9–8
in the English courts, there was a convergence between English and European
jurisprudence on this subject. As Thorpe L.J. accepted in *Camelot Group plc v
Centaur Communications Ltd*[22]:

"... there is no material difference of principle underlying s.10 of the Contempt of
Court Act 1981 as applied by the courts of this jurisdiction and Article 10 of the
European Convention on Human Rights as applied by the European Court of Human
Rights."

---

[17] [1981] A.C. 1096 at 1168, discussed more fully at para.9–45.
[18] [1993] A.C. 534.
[19] At 548D–E, having referred to *New York Times Co v Sullivan* (1964) 376 U.S. 254, and to other American jurisprudence.
[20] See *Goodwin v United Kingdom* (1996) 22 E.H.R.R. 123 at 143, [39]. The relevant passage is cited at para.9–22.
[21] *ibid.* at 551F–G. See also *Att-Gen v Guardian Newspapers Ltd (No.2)* [1990] 1 A.C. 109 at 283–4, Lord Goff.
[22] [1999] Q.B. 124 at 138G. The case is more fully considered at para.9–164.

9–9 Yet since the coming into effect of the Human Rights Act 1998 English judges seem ready to express a less sanguine view.[23] Even the approach of the Court of Appeal in *Camelot* to the argument based upon the "chilling effect" may suggest that its disadvantages are not always as fully appreciated by English judges as Lord Keith appears to have suggested. We turn to consider how this problem was addressed in two of the judgments. First, Schiemann L.J.[24]:

> "There remains however an important consideration. To some extent the effect of disclosing the identity of one source who has leaked unimportant material can have a chilling effect on the willingness of other sources to disclose material which is important. If the other sources are put in the position of having to guess whether or not the court will order disclosure of their names then they may well not be prepared to take the risk that the court's decision will go against them. That is a consideration, however, which will only be met if there is a blanket rule against any disclosure. That is, however, not part of our domestic law or of the Convention. So the well informed source is always going to have to take a view as to what is going to be the court's reaction to his disclosure in the circumstances of his case."

9–10 To similar effect were the words of Thorpe L.J.[25]:

> "... I was not impressed by [counsel's] submission that his failure on this appeal would have reverberations deterring others from disclosure to the public detriment. An individual case decision would only have that consequence if it were to establish a new boundary or shift an existing boundary. An individual who contemplates giving or selling confidential material to a publisher in breach of his contract of employment knows that he will thereby risk his future security and perhaps that of his dependants. The higher his position presumably the more carefully he will weigh the risks. Surely he would be wise to inform himself as to how the courts apply s.10. If he takes from this decision the message that he is at risk I cannot myself see public detriment. There is a public interest in loyalty and trust between employer and employee."

9–11 The approach in these judgments does little to allay concerns over the impact of the chilling effect. It may be all very well to emphasise that there is no blanket rule as to disclosure, in cases of disloyal employees or other "moles" (particularly where it is sought to reveal "iniquity"), but if would-be leakers have to make an assessment of the court's likely approach in the light of the current authorities it may be thought that the chill has hardly thawed at all.

9–12 It is necessary to trace the background of these developments and the changes which have taken place in the common law, from the days when the revelation of journalists' sources was treated as being a matter of judicial discretion, to the present time where it is recognised as only being justified in circumstances of "an overriding requirement in the public interest".[26]

---

[23] See, *e.g.* the remarks of Lord Phillips M.R. in *Ashworth Hospital Authority v MGN Ltd* [2001] 1 W.L.R. 515 at 536–7, [2001] 1 All E.R. 991 at 1012a–b (noted at para.7–4 above) and of Sedley L.J. in *Berezovsky v Forbes Inc (No.2)* [2001] EWCA Civ 1251, [2001] E.M.L.R. 45 (cited at para.2–164, n.14 above).
[24] [1999] Q.B 124 at 138C–E.
[25] *ibid.* at 139B–C.
[26] *Goodwin v United Kingdom* (1996) 22 E.H.R.R. 123, [45]. See also *Chief Constable of Leicestershire v Garavelli* [1997] E.M.L.R. 543 at 555, (" ... is the need so convincingly established as to override the need to protect journalistic sources in the interest of ensuring a free press in a democratic society?" *per* Beldam L.J.).

C. The discretionary or "balancing" approach of the common law

In certain circumstances, a witness may claim to be privileged from answering a relevant and necessary question in legal proceedings.[27] For example, there is a privilege against self-incrimination.[28] Also, a lawyer must refuse to disclose professional communications between himself and a client[29] unless the client waives the privilege.[30] In such circumstances, when the privilege arises, it is absolute.

9–13

By contrast, other potential witnesses who have received information in circumstances which they and their informants might regard as giving rise to an absolute duty of confidence will not be recognised by the law as having a *right* to maintain that confidentiality. For example, the priest in the confessional,[31] the doctor in the surgery,[32] and the journalist carrying out an investigation (the principal subject of this chapter) were accorded no privilege or immunity at common law. They were not permitted to refuse to disclose either the information itself or the source from which they obtained it[33]; at common law, the matter was governed by judicial discretion in the light of the facts of the particular situation.

9–14

This practice was described by Sir John Donaldson M.R. in *Secretary of State for Defence v Guardian Newspapers Ltd*[34]:

9–15

---

[27] See generally C.H.F. Tapper, *Cross and Tapper on Evidence* (10th ed., 2004), ch.IX; R. May and S. Powles, *Criminal Evidence* (5th ed., 2004), ch.11; P. Roberts and A. Zuckerman, *Criminal Evidence* (2004), ch.9.
[28] Made the subject of a number of statutory exceptions: see, *e.g.* Criminal Justice and Public Order Act 1994, ss.34–37. Nonetheless, the privilege retains its importance and is expressly highlighted, for example, in the current precedents for freezing orders (although some qualification is required so far as intellectual property cases are concerned: see para.8.4 of 25PD.12 and the discussion in para.3–196) For the relevance of self-incrimination specifically in the context of contempt, see paras 3–188 *et seq.* See generally I. Dennis, "Instrumental Protection, Human Right or Functional Necessity? Reassessing the Privilege against Self-incrimination" [1995] C.L.J. 342; S. Nash and M. Furse, "Self-Incrimination, Corporate Misconduct and the Convention on Human Rights" [1995] Crim. L.R. 854; A. Jennings, A. Ashworth and B. Emmerson, "Silence and Safety: The Impact of Human Rights Law" [2000] Crim. L.R. 879.
[29] *R. v Derby Magistrates' Court Ex p. B* [1996] A.C. 487, HL; *Re L (A Minor) (Police Investigation: Privilege)* [1997] A.C. 16, HL; see also *B v Auckland District Law Society* [2003] UKPC 38, [2003] 2 A.C. 736; *Three Rivers District Council v Governor of the Bank of England* [2004] EWCA Civ 218, [2004] UKHL 48, [2005] 1 A.C. 610.
[30] *Wilson v Rastall* (1792) 4 Term Rep. 758, 100 E.R. 1283; *Proctor v Smiles* (1886) 55 L.J.Q.B. 527, CA.
[31] The 11th Report of the Criminal Law Revision Committee, *Evidence (General),* Cmnd. 4991 (1972), paras 272–276, rejected suggestions for conferring privilege both in respect of clergymen and doctors. See Mitchell, "Must Clergy Tell? Child Abuse Reporting Requirements Versus the Clergy Privilege and the True Exercise of Religion" (1987) 71 Min L.R. 723; *R. v McClure* [2001] S.C.R. 445 at 457, Major J.
[32] *Duchess of Kingston's Case* (1716) 20 St. Tr. 355; *Campbell v Tameside Metropolitan Borough Council* [1982] 2 All E.R. 791.
[33] *Att-Gen v Lundin* (1982) 75 Cr.App.R. 90; *Att-Gen v Mulholland* [1963] 2 Q.B. 477; *R. v The National Post* (2004) 236 D.L.R. (4th) 551 at [70]–[71]. See note C. Tapper, (1963) M.L.R. 571; A.L. Goodhart, (1963) 76 L.Q.R. 167.
[34] [1984] 1 Ch. 156 at 164A, CA. See also the words of Lord Denning in *Att-Gen v Mulholland* [1963] 2 Q.B. 477, 490 cited at para.9–44; and see Y. Cripps, "Judicial Proceedings and Refusals to Disclose the Identity of Sources of Information" [1984] 43 C.L.J. 266.

9–15   Chapter 9—Protection of Sources

"Prior to the enactment of the 1981 Act it was the practice of the courts to have regard to the conscientious objections of priests, doctors, journalists and others to breaching express or implied undertakings of confidentiality. I say 'have regard to' because the courts had to balance competing public interests."

It is necessary to see how the courts have customarily treated the various competing interests in this area, so that the impact of s.10 can be fully appreciated. Its impact in practice is confined to journalists[35] and does not affect others who may perceive themselves as being under a professional obligation of confidence, since such people do not receive the information with a view to *publication*. The right to freedom of communication is not therefore regarded in those cases as being adversely affected.

D. Competing policy considerations: the role of the media[36]

9–16   In deciding whether or not the law should compel the disclosure of information that a journalist would wish to keep secret, the common law required a "balancing exercise" to be conducted[37] as between competing public policy considerations. In particular, free speech is bound to conflict from time to time with the interests of justice; the two must then be reconciled. In the Superior Court of Ontario, for example, it has been held that there should be "case-by-case balancing of respective interests" which can be assisted by the so-called "Wigmore criteria"[38]: (1) The communication must originate in a confidence; (2) the confidence must be essential to the relationship in which the communication arises; (3) the relationship must be one which should be "sedulously fostered" in the public good; (4) if those criteria are met, the court must consider whether the interests served by protecting the communications outweigh the interest in getting at the truth for the purposes of the relevant litigation.

9–17   The "balancing" formulation may nowadays lead to some confusion in this jurisdiction, having regard particularly to the approach adopted to freedom of expression in the European Court of Human Rights.[39] What has been happening

---

[35] In *Branzburg v Hayes* 408 U.S. 665 (1972), the United States Supreme Court took the view that journalists should not be accorded an especially protected position in this respect, since " . . . the informative function asserted by representatives of the organised press . . . is also performed by lecturers, political pollsters, novelists, academics, researchers and dramatists. Almost any author may quite accurately assert that he is contributing to the flow of information to the public, that he relies on confidential sources of information, and that those sources will be silenced if he is forced to make disclosures before the grand jury".

[36] See generally L. Lustgarten and I. Leigh, *In From the Cold* (1994), ch.10 (Oxford University Press).

[37] See, *e.g.* A. Boyle, "Freedom of Expression as a Public Interest in English Law" [1982] P.L. 574. The concept of a balancing exercise is one frequently met in the common law, and not least in the context of freedom of expression. See, *e.g.* "The need for a 'balancing exercise' ", in paras 6–88 *et seq.* In *Saunders v Punch Ltd* [1998] 1 W.L.R. 986, 1 All E.R. 234, Ch.D., Lindsay J. commented that to speak of a "balancing exercise" can conjure up a rather spurious picture of a more precise and scientific exercise than is involved in the weighing of competing factors on the disclosure of sources. See also *Haughey v Prendeville and Penfield Enterprises Ltd* [1996] N.I. 367.

[38] Following McLachlin C.J. in *AM v Ryan* (1996) 143 D.L.R. (4th) 1.

[39] See, *e.g. Sunday Times v United Kingdom* (1979) 2 E.H.R.R. 245 at 281 ("The court is faced not with a choice between two conflicting principles, but with a principle of freedom of expression that is subject to a number of exceptions which must be narrowly interpreted").

in recent years is that a fundamental realignment of priorities has been taking place, although English judges tend still to resort to the metaphor of scales being balanced. The use of this language might suggest that the scales have necessarily to be set equally before the court begins its own "balancing exercise", whereas increasingly the courts have been inclined to speak of "a presumption",[40] "an assumption"[41] and "preponderating importance".[42] None of these concepts is really consistent with the scales being in equilibrium from the outset.[43]

The new judicial process seems to have been recognised, in particular, in the context of the provisions of s.10 of the 1981 Act, by Lord Bridge in *X Ltd v Morgan-Grampian (Publishers) Ltd*[44]:

9–18

> "[The judge] starts with the assumptions, first, that the protection of sources is itself a matter of high public importance, secondly, that nothing less than necessity will suffice to override it, thirdly, that the necessity can only arise out of concern for another matter of high public importance, being one of the four interests listed in the section."

The role of journalists in uncovering information (sometimes adverse to the interests of those in positions of authority)[45] is vital to what is now being perceived as the "constitutional" role of the press.[46] Its function in advancing the public interest is acknowledged by the courts in England with increasing frequency and enthusiasm.[47] Although newspapers and their proprietors are, no doubt, motivated by many considerations other than the high-minded task of

9–19

---

[40] *Re an Inquiry Under the Company Securities (Insider Dealing) Act 1985* [1988] A.C. 660 at 703, Lord Griffiths. See para.9–79.
[41] Lord Bridge in *X Ltd v Morgan-Grampian (Publishers) Ltd* [1991] 1 A.C. 1 at 41.
[42] See Lord Bridge in *X Ltd v Morgan-Grampian (Publishers) Ltd* [1991] 1 A.C. 1 at 43, cited at para.9–81; see also Beldam L.J. in *Chief Constable of Leicestershire v Garavelli* [1997] E.M.L.R. 543 at 553.
[43] Indeed, Lloyd L.J. referred to Parliament's intention, as expressed in the Contempt of Court Act 1981, to " . . . effect a permanent *shift in the balance* of public interest away from the protection of the administration of justice and in favour of freedom of speech": *Att-Gen v Newspaper Publishing plc* [1988] Ch. 333 at 382 (emphasis added). See the similar remarks (in the context of the *parens patriae* jurisdiction) by Bracewell J. in *Re X (A Child) (Injunctions Restraining Publication)* [2001] 1 F.C.R. 541 at 549.
[44] [1991] 1 A.C. 1 at 41.
[45] As Lord Keith acknowledged in *Derbyshire County Council v Times Newspapers Ltd* [1993] A.C. 534 at 547F: "It is of the highest public importance that a democratically elected governmental body, or indeed any governmental body, should be open to uninhibited public criticism".
[46] See Lord Diplock in *Secretary of State for Defence v Guardian Newspapers Ltd* [1985] 1 A.C. 339 at 345C–D who cavilled at the use of the "evocative phrase" used by counsel, "constitutional right", although in the same case at 361D–E, Lord Scarman, while acknowledging that the term "will sound strange to some" in the absence of a written constitution, nevertheless accepted that the phrase might accurately prophesy the direction in which English law had to move under the compulsion of the European Convention. See J.F. Burrows, "Freedom of the Press Under the New Zealand Bill of Rights Act 1990", in ed. P. Joseph, *Essays on the Constitution* (1995), at p.285. For a more general discussion of the constitutional position of the press, see paras 2–49 *et seq.*
[47] A similar process has taken place in the United States of America. See Justice Potter Stewart, "Or of the Press" (1975) 26 Hast. Law Jo. 631, who refers to the increasing willingness of the American Supreme Court to describe the position of the press as having a *constitutional* significance.

9–19

informing the public,[48] the public interest may nevertheless be served by the ability of the press to uncover corruption, fraud and other less serious forms of anti-social behaviour.

9–20 Furthermore, the courts have also become more willing to acknowledge that the protection of journalistic sources has a significant part to play in the performance of this function. Thus, in *Handmade Films (Production) Ltd v Express Newspapers Ltd*,[49] Sir Nicolas Browne-Wilkinson V.-C. referred to the "public interest which exists in ensuring the free flow of information to the press, one of the bastions of such free flow of information being that the source of information given in confidence is not revealed by the press".

9–21 Griffiths L.J. in *Secretary of State for Defence v Guardian Newspapers Ltd*[50] also commented:

"The press have always attached the greatest importance to their ability to protect their sources of information. If they are not able to do so, they believe that many of their sources would dry up and this would seriously interfere with their effectiveness. It is in the interests of us all that we should have a truly effective press and it seems to me that Parliament by enacting s.10 has clearly recognised the importance to the ability of the press to protect their sources."

9–22 The point was made even more emphatically by the European Court of Human Rights in the case of *Goodwin v United Kingdom*,[51] which depicted the link between the role of the press and the protection of journalistic sources as follows[52]:

"Protection of journalistic sources is one of the basic conditions for press freedom ... Without such protection, sources may be deterred from assisting the press in informing the public on matters of public interest. As a result the vital public-watchdog role of the press may be undermined and the ability of the press to provide accurate and reliable information may be adversely affected. Having regard to the importance of journalistic sources for press freedom in a democratic society and the potentially chilling effect an order of source disclosure has on the exercise of that freedom, such a measure cannot be compatible with the European Convention on Human Rights unless it is justified by an overriding requirement in the public interest".

---

[48] As Lord Donaldson M.R. observed in the Court of Appeal in *X Ltd v Morgan-Grampian (Publishers) Ltd* [1991] A.C. 1 at 18E, the journalist's view of the public interest is apt to march "hand in hand with the commercial interests of the media". In similar vein, in *Francome v Mirror Group Newspapers Ltd* [1984] 1 W.L.R. 892, he had commented that the media are "an essential foundation of any democracy. In exposing crime, anti-social behaviour and hypocrisy, and in campaigning for reform and propagating the views of minorities, they perform an invaluable function. However, they are peculiarly vulnerable to the error of confusing the public interest with their own interest. Usually these interests march hand in hand, but not always."
[49] [1986] F.S.R. 463 at 467.
[50] [1984] Ch. 156 at 167, CA. These words were cited by Lord Bridge in *X Ltd v Morgan Grampian (Publishers) Ltd* [1991] 1 A.C. 1 at 41 and by Schiemann L.J. in *Camelot Group plc v Centaur Communications Ltd* [1999] Q.B. 124.
[51] (1996) 22 E.H.R.R. 123.
[52] *ibid.* para.39. The passage was cited by the Divisional Court in *Chief Constable of Leicestershire v Garavelli* [1997] E.M.L.R. 543.

This passage was quoted by Schiemann L.J. in *Camelot Group plc v Centaur Communications Ltd*[53] as being of equal validity within our own jurisdiction.

Allied to this is the growing recognition by the courts of the significance of the public's corresponding right to be informed. Lord Salmon in *British Steel Corp v Granada Television Ltd*[54] thought that the principle had been long established:

9–23

> "A free press reports matters of general public importance, and cannot, in law, be under any obligation, save in exceptional circumstances, to disclose the identity of the persons who supply it with the information appearing in its reports.
>
> It has been accepted for over 100 years that if this immunity did not exist, the press's sources of information would dry up and the public would be deprived of being informed of many matters of great public importance: this should not be allowed to occur in any free country."

E. Whistleblowing

Prior to the coming into force of the Freedom of Information Act 2000,[55] one commentator linked the public need for information to the protection of sources[56]:

9–24

> "... the absence of a general right to freedom of information in the UK makes journalists, like police officers, rely on informants, often from inside the organizations which the journalists are investigating. If it is accepted as being in the public interest to inform the public about certain matters, those who supply information may be acting in the public interest, yet be breaching civil duties of confidence and even the criminal law ... If the public-interest role of journalists is to flourish, it is important that their informants should not be discouraged from providing information, lest the flow of information to the public should dry up."

Lord Scarman has recognised, extra-judicially, that the use of unnamed sources is sometimes an unattractive spectacle[57]:

9–25

> "One knows that if information is going to reach the public through the media of the press of misdoings or inefficiency in high places, it is more than likely (let us face it) that the channel, the agent or the messenger of that information will be some 'weasel', some pretty despicable person, and his confidence is essential if the journalist is to get the information. One does not wish to protect the 'weasel'; there is no need to protect the journalist; but there is every need to ensure that the right of the public to get the information is supported."

---

[53] [1999] Q.B. 124 at 133H–134B.
[54] [1981] A.C. 1096 at 1184. As Megarry V.-C. had observed in the same case at first instance, at 1115, "I also accept that it is in the interests of the public that there should be a regular supply of reliable news." See also *Furniss v Cambridge News Ltd* (1907) 23 T.L.R. 705, CA, and especially the words of Sir Gorell Barnes at 706: "... as everyone could not be in Court, it was for the public benefit that they should be informed of what took place substantially as if they were present"; *Webb v Times Publishing Co* [1960] 2 Q.B. 535 at 559–62, Pearson J.; *Broadcasting Corporation of NZ v Alex Harvey Industries Ltd* [1980] 1 N.Z.L.R. 163, where the court spoke of "... the benefit for society in having discussion and evaluation of affairs that is informed", at 166, Woodhouse J.
[55] In January 2005.
[56] D. Feldman, *Civil Liberties in England and Wales* (2nd ed., 2002), p.849.
[57] *Hansard*, H.L., Vol. 417, (5th series), col. 156, February 10, 1981.

9–26 For this reason, claims to withhold a journalist's source will often seem unappealing. This may perhaps be the explanation for reluctance on the part of individual judges in the past when invited to accord this protection. Ensuring the confidentiality of a source may entail the covering up of conduct which is itself inherently reprehensible or discreditable. On the other hand, it appears that such conduct on the part of the source may play a significant part in carrying out the "balancing exercise", in any given case, with a view to determining whether it is truly necessary for the source to be disclosed.[58]

9–27 Some jurisdictions[59] have long recognised the importance of whistleblowing as a mechanism for informing the public,[60] even though it may involve some breach of confidence or wrongdoing.[61] It is recognised that such a person, even though disloyal, may nevertheless be doing a public service, and the protection of the law is by no means always confined to the exposure of "iniquity". There may be a public interest in acquiring information even where there is no suggestion of illegality or wrongdoing.

9–28 This was accepted, in the context of the scope of the public interest defence to an action for breach of confidence, by Griffiths L.J. in *Lion Laboratories v Evans*[62]:

> "I believe that the so-called iniquity rule evolved because in most cases where the facts justified a publication in breach of confidence, it was because the plaintiff had behaved so disgracefully or criminally that it was judged in the public interest that his behaviour should be exposed. No doubt it is in such circumstances that the defence will usually arise, but it is not difficult to think of instances where, although there has been no wrongdoing on the part of the plaintiff, it may be vital in the public interest to publish a part of his confidential information."

Later he added[63]:

> "I think in all the circumstances that the 'Daily Express' is not to be criticised for thinking that the impact of the revelations in their newspaper would be more likely to galvanise the authorities into action than a discreet behind-doors approach".

---

[58] See, *e.g.* Lord Bridge in *X Ltd v Morgan-Grampian (Publishers) Ltd* [1991] 1 A.C. 1 at 44F–G, cited at para.9–97. But see now the observations of Laws L.J. in *Hospital Authority v MGN Ltd* [2001] 1 W.L.R. 515 at 537 [2001] 1 All E.R. 991 at 1012g (cited below at para.9–145).
[59] For a survey, see *Whistleblowing, Fraud and the European Union* (1996), published by Public Concern at Work. See G. Dehn, "Public Concern at Work" [1993] P.L. 603 for a description of the composition and objectives of Public Concern at Work.
[60] See, *e.g.* the United States Statute, Whistleblower Protection Act 1989 (Public Law 101–12). See also Boyle, "A Review of Whistleblower Protections and Suggestions for Change" (1990) Labour Law Jo. 821.
[61] See Y. Cripps, *op. cit.*, para.9–1, n.1. See also L. Vickers, "Whistleblowing in the Public Sector and the E.C.H.R." [1997] P.L. 594. See now the Public Interest Disclosure Act 1998, which is intended to achieve similar objectives. See also the Employment Act 2002 www.pcaw.co.uk.
[62] [1985] Q.B. 526 at 550, where it was acknowledged that it was in the public interest that the potentially unreliable nature of the Lion intoximeter should be made public since citizens could be wrongly convicted on the basis of its data.
[63] *ibid.* at 553C.

So far as the public interest is concerned, however, there are countervailing 9–29
considerations that must be taken into account. It must, for example, be
recognised that the anonymous source may very well have his own private
objectives[64] which may not be apparent to the general public. One potential
disadvantage of non-disclosure was described by Pill J. in *DPP v Channel Four
Television Co Ltd*.[65]

> "The public have the worst of it. They endure the distrust, fear and distress which are
> bred by the allegations without the opportunity to have the truth of the allegations
> properly investigated. The danger to society if falsehoods of this kind go uncorrected
> needs no underlining. Neither does the degree of concern to be felt if [a source] is
> telling the truth".

It is by no means in all circumstances to the advantage of a journalist that 9–30
sources remain anonymous. It might sometimes lend credibility and authenticity
to a story if the source were identified.[66]

A "whistle-blowing" argument was raised in *R. v Central Criminal Court* 9–31
Ex p. Bright.[67] The Divisional Court was there concerned with applications by
Special Branch for production of special procedure material, under s.9 and Sch.1
of the Police and Criminal Evidence Act 1984, against the editors of *The
Guardian* and *The Observer*. Maurice Kay J. was unimpressed by the argument
that to grant a production order in relation to special procedure material, not
being the subject of an obligation of confidentiality to the source of the material,
would stand as a disincentive to future whistle-blowers or other sources. He
pointed out[68] that it would usually be open to such persons to demand
confidentiality as the price of their disclosure.

F. Reconciling source protection with the rule of law

Underlying the sanctions of the contempt process is the need to uphold the rule 9–32
of law, and the authority of the court.[69] Indeed, one exception to the right of free
speech acknowledged by Art.10(2) of the European Convention itself is "for
maintaining the authority and impartiality of the judiciary." If the authority of the
court is being undermined, and its processes inhibited by a refusal to answer
relevant questions about a source, this may well redound to the disadvantage of
one or indeed all of the parties concerned in the proceedings. This is because the

---

[64] See, *e.g.* the remarks of Mummery L.J. in *Camelot Group plc v Centaur Communications Ltd*
[1999] Q.B. 124 at 139H–140A, to the effect that " ... it appears that the prior and premature
disclosure and publication of the draft accounts served a private purpose of the source or a private
purpose of Centaur Communications in securing a scoop, ahead of other publications ... ".
[65] [1993] 2 All E.R. 517 at 534e–g, the facts of which are given more fully at para.9–120. See R.
Costigan, (1992) 142 New Law J. 1417.
[66] The point is made by S. Walker in "Compelling Journalists to Identify Their Sources: the
'Newspaper Rule' and 'Necessity'" (1991) 14 U.N.S.W.L.J. 302.
[67] [2001] 1 W.L.R. 662, [2001] E.M.L.R. 79.
[68] At [152]. See also *R. v The National Post* (2004) 236 D.L.R. (4th) 551 at [80], where it was clear
that a significant consideration was that the source had been given an express promise of confidentiality.
[69] See the discussion at paras 9–205, 12–139 *et seq.* and *Cotroni v Quebec Police Commission and
Brunet* (1977) 80 D.L.R. (3d) 490 S.C.C.

9-32   CHAPTER 9—PROTECTION OF SOURCES

evidence in question (which has *ex hypothesi* been ruled to be relevant) is unavailable to them as part of the material required for the resolution of the dispute.

9-33   That court orders must be obeyed is fundamental to the rule of law,[70] and a witness who refuses to answer when ordered to do so appears to challenge head-on the authority of the court. As Lord Bridge said in *X Ltd v Morgan-Grampian (Publishers) Ltd*[71]:

> "The maintenance of the rule of law is in every way as important in a free society as the democratic franchise. In our society the rule of law rests upon twin foundations: the sovereignty of the Queen in Parliament in making the law and the sovereignty of the Queen's courts in interpreting and applying the law. While no one doubts the importance of protecting journalists' sources, no one, I think, seriously advocates an absolute privilege against disclosure admitting of no exceptions. Since the enactment of section 10 of the Act of 1981 both the protection of journalists' sources and the limited grounds on which it may exceptionally be necessary to override that protection have been laid down by Parliament ... But to contend that the individual litigant, be he a journalist or anyone else, has a right of 'conscientious objection' which entitles him to set himself above the law if he does not agree with the court's decision, is a doctrine which directly undermines the rule of law and is wholly unacceptable in a democratic society.[72] Any rule of professional conduct enjoining a journalist to protect his confidential sources must, impliedly if not expressly, be subject to whatever exception is necessary to enable the journalist to obey the orders of a court of competent jurisdiction. Freedom of speech is itself a right which is dependent on the rule of law for its protection and it is paradoxical that a serious challenge to the rule of law should be mounted by responsible journalists."

9-34   It has been argued by T.R.S. Allan that "the paradox is a product of the court's own misunderstanding",[73] in that the journalist is doing no more than asserting his "statutory right"[74] to refuse to reveal his source. He suggests that it may be a mistake "to treat the journalist's recalcitrance as a case of civil disobedience at all ... [T]he journalist's recalcitrance may ... be seen as a claim of right or justice, but one within, rather than in opposition to, the law."[75] Allan concludes that such a person is thus not, at least at the initial stage, directly challenging the authority of the court. The argument is that the journalist is not merely a recalcitrant witness who declines to answer for personal reasons.[76] He or she is explaining to the court why an answer *cannot* be given.

---

[70] See, *e.g. Burris v Azadani* [1995] 1 W.L.R. 1372 at 1381, CA.
[71] [1991] A.C. 1 at 48–9.
[72] See also Sir John Donaldson M.R. in *Francome v Mirror Group Newpapers Ltd* [1984] 1 W.L.R. 892 at 897D–E, 2 All E.R. 408 at 412h, CA.
[73] [1991] C.L.J. at 136.
[74] The expression used by Lord Diplock in *Secretary of State for Defence v Guardian Newspapers Ltd* [1985] 1 A.C. 339 at 345C. See also Beldam L.J. in *Chief Constable of Leicestershire v Garavelli* [1997] E.M.L.R. 543, 552 who speaks of the " ... right to refuse to disclose the source ... " and (*ibid.* at 556) "the right that Parliament has given to refuse to disclose his or her source".
[75] [1991] C.L.J. at 139.
[76] The position of the recalcitrant witness is generally considered in para.10–162 (contempt in the face of the court).

9–35 This would be equally true of a witness who declined to answer for fear of reprisals. Each of these examples involves an apparent defiance of the court's authority. The question in each case is whether the law acknowledges a defence or immunity[77] such as to prevent the person in question being found guilty of contempt. The witness who is afraid might have a defence of duress.[78] The journalist, on the other hand, may fall within the protection of s.10 and the presumption against having to reveal a source. It is not, however, in all circumstances that the law will enable anonymity to be protected. It is clear from Art.10 itself and from the case of *Goodwin v United Kingdom* that there will sometimes be an "overriding requirement in the public interest" in favour of disclosure.[79]

9–36 Yet journalists as a profession regard themselves as subject to a "moral obligation"[80] to disobey the court even when the highest domestic tribunal may legitimately have ruled that the answer to the question is necessary within the meaning of s.10, and even in circumstances where the European Court of Human Rights itself may have found that the tribunal's order is not incompatible with the Convention. This makes clear that the nature of the privilege asserted by journalists ultimately entails a defiance of the court's authority, and thus the rule of law. It involves arrogating to themselves a form of supra-legal right to refuse to obey court orders even in circumstances where the highest courts have determined that no such right exists, or rather that the presumption in favour of such a right has been rebutted.

9–37 The National Union of Journalists code of conduct asserts that "a journalist shall protect confidential sources of information".[81] At root, the journalist's

---

[77] A term used by Mummery L.J. in *Camelot Group plc v Centaur Communications Ltd* [1999] Q.B. 124 at 139D–E.
[78] paras 9–119 *et seq.*
[79] See (1996) 22 E.H.R.R. 123, para.5, quoted at para.9–22. See also the words of Schiemann L.J. in *Camelot Group plc v Centaur Communications Ltd* [1999] Q.B. 124 at 133G–134B.
[80] See the Press Complaints Commission Code of Practice, ratified in June 2004, para.14. The terminology of *"moral* obligation" originated in the draft code attached to the report of the Home Office *Report of the Committee on Privacy and Related Matters* (The Calcutt Committee) 1990, Cm. 1102. It makes it clear that the obligation is, and is regarded by journalists as, something separate and apart from any legal right conferred by statute or the common law.
[81] para.7. It is to be noted that the word "confidential" is not applied in s.10 to qualify the journalists' sources. (Contrast ss.11(2) and (3) of the Police and Criminal Evidence Act 1984: "subject to an express or implied undertaking to hold it in confidence, or subject to a restriction on disclosure or an obligation of secrecy contained in any enactment".) However, it is plainly only of relevance in circumstances where journalists feel under an obligation, express or implied, not to reveal what has come into their possession. This will depend to some extent upon the individual journalist's own assessment of the terms upon which the relevant information came into his possession. For example, where information is sent without the knowledge or solicitation of the journalist in question, it is by no means obvious that an obligation of confidence towards the source will inevitably arise. In *Secretary of State for Defence v Guardian Newspapers Ltd* [1985] A.C. 339, the documents sent by the civil servant came "out of the blue", and it does not appear that the then editor of the newspaper felt obliged to disobey the order for disclosure following the Court of Appeal hearing. It is fair to say, however, that the "mole" in question had already confessed, and his position might have been different had this not occurred.

9–37   CHAPTER 9—PROTECTION OF SOURCES

dilemma is that "he may keep faith with his source, by resisting the court's order to reveal his identity, only at the price of denying the rule of law".[82]

9–38   Indeed this was clear before s.10 of the Act came in to force and before the formulation of Press Complaints Commission's code of conduct. For example, in *Att-Gen v Mulholland*,[83] counsel asserted that "the press has not accepted, as have doctors and bankers, that their scruples may be overruled by the discretion of the court. It is contrary to public policy that journalists should be forced to disclose the source of their information".

9–39   It was argued by some commentators that since there is no sanction in the event of the code being disobeyed, other than peer disapproval, the courts for a time tended to minimise its importance.[84] Subsequently, the courts have been constrained in certain circumstances to take into account the requirements of professional codes, including that of the Press Complaints Commission.[85] It is easy to underestimate the weight of peer pressure, however, which can sometimes be couched in stinging terms, and have grave professional consequences. For example, when it was perceived that a journalist had breached the code by revealing a source in the course of a libel action, the *Mail on Sunday* published a strong rebuke in a leading article under the heading "A Question of Honour":

> "Welcome Adam Raphael to the Peter Preston school of journalism. After a most deplorable incident, *The Guardian* edited by Preston has been dubbed the newspaper which betrays its sources.[86] Now along comes Adam Raphael, late of *The Observer*, who in a witness box in the High Court, relates in great detail his own version of remarks, which, whether reported accurately or not, were indubitably given to him off the record. Funny isn't it that, how it's the journalists who come from the so-called quality papers which claim to uphold journalistic standards who time after time fail to understand where honour and integrity lie?"

9–40   This attack was regarded by the journalist concerned as quite unjust, since he considered himself to have been released from his obligation by virtue of the fact that the plaintiff in the libel action (Jeffrey Archer, as he then was) had chosen

---

[82] Allan, *loc cit.*, p.137.
[83] [1963] 2 Q.B. 477 at 482.
[84] D. Feldman, "Press Freedom and Police Access to Journalistic Material" in *The Yearbook of Media and Entertainment Law* (1995), pp.49–50. And see Sir H.W.R. Wade in eds. C. Forsyth and I. Hare, *Constitutional Reform in the United Kingdom: Practice and Principles* (1998), pp.64–5, who points out the shortcomings of the limited remedies available to the Press Complaints Commission, by comparison with the sanctions available to the courts.
[85] See, *e.g.* s.12(4) of the Human Rights Act 1998 which enjoins a court to have particular regard to "any relevant privacy code". See, *e.g.* *Douglas v Hello! Ltd* [2001] 1 Q.B. 967.
[86] This was a reference to *Secretary of State for Defence v Guardian Newspapers Ltd* [1985] 1 A.C. 339. *The Guardian* had complied with an order to surrender documents which had come into their possession from the Ministry of Defence, and which had been regarded by the Department as confidential; the source was identified, prosecuted and sentenced to a term of imprisonment. The "source" had sent the material to the journalist unsolicited. There, the editor (Mr Preston) was said by the House of Lords to have behaved responsibly.

to give evidence himself about the conversation. He sued for libel and the case was settled with the payment of damages and a public apology.[87]

Despite the arguments of Allan, there appears to be no avoiding the conclusion that these journalistic principles cannot, in the last analysis, be reconciled with the rule of law. They are mutually incompatible, although the law has gone some way to accommodate them. Notwithstanding the terms of s.10 of the Contempt of Court Act 1981, and the reference by Lord Diplock in *Secretary of State for Defence v Guardian Newspapers Ltd*[88] to a "statutory right",[89] the two principles still sit uneasily together. Unless journalists are given some means of challenging a judge's order to reveal a source by way of appeal, they are in danger of being held in contempt (despite the statutory immunity) whenever it is decided to disobey such an order (perhaps made in the middle of a trial).[90] At least if a right of appeal were given, it would be unlikely that any finding of contempt would be made until the appeal procedure had been exhausted. Nevertheless, if a journalist chose then to persist in disobedience, this would undoubtedly be defying the rule of law.

G. Judicial discretion at common law

By contrast with the *right* now acknowledged by s.10, however, the common law traditionally took the view that, if required by a court to answer any relevant and necessary question, the journalist, like any other witness, was under an obligation to comply. The position of such a person at common law, when required by a court[91] to disclose a source, was the subject of periodic skirmishing between journalists and the courts.

1. *Att-Gen v Mulholland*

In *Att-Gen v Mulholland*,[92] two journalists were imprisoned for periods of six months and three months respectively for declining to give evidence at a tribunal of enquiry.[93] The Court of Appeal had ruled that there was no journalistic immunity from answering questions about sources. It was held that, even if the answer would be relevant, admissible, and on the face of it necessary to the case

---

[87] For an account of these matters, see A. Raphael, *My Learned Friends* (1989, W.H. Allen).
[88] [1985] 1 A.C. 339.
[89] See also *Chief Constable of Leicestershire v Garavelli* [1997] E.M.L.R. 543 at 552, where it was said that the section gives the journalist the "right to refuse to disclose the source".
[90] For further discussion of these difficulties, see paras 9–194 *et seq.*
[91] As to the meaning of "court" in this context, see paras 4–17, 13–3, 13–44. Sometimes statute will give specific authority for disobedience in relation to the tribunal under consideration to be referred to the High Court. See, *e.g. Re An Inquiry Under the Company Securities (Insider Dealing) Act 1985* [1988] A.C. 660. Furthermore, a refusal to answer an inferior tribunal may be referred to the Queen's Bench Division with a view, ultimately, to enforcement by process of contempt in the event that a High Court order should also be disobeyed. See, *e.g. Chief Constable for Leicestershire v Garavelli* [1997] E.M.L.R. 543.
[92] [1963] 2 Q.B. 477. See also Lord Wilberforce in *British Steel Corp v Granada Television Ltd* [1981] A.C. 1096 at 1169E–1171C, and *Att-Gen v Clough* [1963] 1 Q.B. 773.
[93] *Report of the Tribunal Appointed to Inquire into the Vassall Case and Related Matters*, Cmnd. 2009 (1963).

9-43   CHAPTER 9—PROTECTION OF SOURCES

of one or other of the parties involved in proceedings, the court still had a discretion at common law[94] to decline to insist upon an answer.[95] Donovan L.J. said that, even where an answer might strictly be required[96]:

"... there may be other considerations, impossible to define in advance, but arising out of the infinite variety of fact and circumstance which a court encounters, which may lead a judge to conclude that more harm than good would result from compelling a disclosure or punishing a refusal to answer. For these reasons I think it would be wrong to hold that a judge is tied hand and foot in such a case ... and must always order an answer or punish a refusal to give the answer once it is shown to be technically admissible."

9-44   Lord Denning M.R. acknowledged[97] the special position of clergymen, bankers and doctors:

"The judge will respect the confidences which each member of these honourable professions receives in the course of it, and will not direct him to answer unless not only it is relevant but also it is a proper and, indeed, necessary question in the course of justice to be put and answered. A judge is the person entrusted, on behalf of the community, to weigh these conflicting interests—to weigh on the one hand the respect due to confidence in the profession and on the other hand the ultimate interest of the community in justice being done ... ".

2. British Steel Corporation v Granada Television Ltd

9-45   Shortly before the enactment of the Contempt of Court Act, the extent of the protection then afforded by the common law was considered by the House of Lords in *British Steel Corporation v Granada Television Ltd*.[98] Granada had made a television programme in which the chairman of the British Steel Corporation was asked a number of questions clearly based on documents that had come into Granada's possession, and apparently in breach of confidence. The corporation wished to bring proceedings against any employee who might be responsible. Disclosure was sought from Granada (which had not solicited the documents in the first place), it being argued that they were themselves unable to identify the untrustworthy and disloyal employee, and it was necessary to have the documents to prevent further misuse and to remove suspicion that might otherwise be directed at innocent staff.

9-46   The House of Lords affirmed that there was no journalistic immunity in situations where disclosure was necessary "in the interests of justice". The House acknowledged, however, that there might be cases where it would perhaps be better not to insist (in the exercise of discretion) that the journalist should

---

[94] In cases falling outside s.10 of the Contempt of Court Act 1981, presumably there is still such a discretion. This is considered in paras 9–64 *et seq*.
[95] As to what constitutes a refusal (prevarication, dissembling, telling lies, etc.), see para.10–162. See also *Keeley v Brooking* (1979) 143 C.L.R. 162, 53 A.L.J.R. 526; *McGoldrick v Citicorp Finance Pty Ltd* [1990] V.R. 494. For prevarication in Scottish law, see paras 16–118 *et seq*.
[96] [1963] 2 Q.B. 477 at 492.
[97] *ibid.* at 490.
[98] [1981] A.C. 1096.

answer, and where he or she might be permitted to protect a source, if public policy so required.

3. *Att-Gen v Lundin*[99]

Lundin was a professional journalist. A police sergeant was being prosecuted for corruption. He was employed (or at any rate paid, so it was alleged) by a casino to obtain the names of punters at rival establishments by using the police national computer record of vehicle registration numbers. Lundin had come into possession of a photocopy of a note given by the sergeant to the casino. He refused to say who had given it to him and in what circumstances, on the ground that it would be a breach of confidence to do so. The Crown sought to prove the contents of the document. They did not hold the original, but sought to put in a photostat copy. Lundin's evidence would have been relevant to establishing the source of the photostat. Before that stage was reached, however, the Crown had the preliminary hurdle to overcome of accounting satisfactorily for the absence of the original. Since counsel were unable to do this, the Divisional Court held that it was not necessary for Lundin to answer the question put to him about the source of the copy; even if he had answered, the Crown would still not have been able to put the copy in evidence.

The Divisional Court, following *Granada*, said that there were two issues to be determined:

1. Was the question relevant and necessary?
2. Was there any journalistic privilege?

The court found for Lundin on the first question; even though the question of how he came to be in possession of the document was relevant, the answer was not necessary (because other aspects of the case were too weak).

On the second question, the court affirmed the principle that there was no journalistic privilege as such. The only privilege recognised was that attaching to communications with legal advisers (belonging to the client rather than the lawyer). Nor was there any doctor-patient privilege in the medical context, or priest-confessor privilege, although any such confidences would be respected by a judge deciding whether any particular questions were necessary and relevant.

H. Experience in other common law jurisdictions

Since the position in the United Kingdom is now regulated by statute, perhaps there is less to be learned from Commonwealth experience in this area than in others where the common law continues to hold sway. In New Zealand, the matter is governed by the discretion of the court, which is itself constrained by

---

[99] (1982) 75 Cr.App.R. 90, DC.

statute.¹ The principles applied in Australia are essentially those of the common law. The courts have not yet devised as strict a rule against disclosure as is encompassed by the modern English "necessity test".²

9–51 The Supreme Court of Canada³ proved unresponsive to the argument that compelling a journalist to reveal sources might be in breach of s.2(b) of the Charter, which guarantees "freedom of the press and other media of communications". The court expressed scepticism that "it is indisputable that there is a direct relationship between testimonial compulsion and a 'drying up' of news sources as alleged by the appellant"; in the absence of any evidence of any such tie, it declined to decide the "broad and important constitutional questions". Later decisions suggest that the courts in Canada are approaching each case according to its circumstances, and carrying out a balancing exercise, giving due consideration to the role of journalism in a democratic society alongside whatever other countervailing policy considerations may be engaged on the particular facts. It has been observed, for example, that "The matter requires a balancing of the important competing societal interests: freedom of expression and investigation of crime. It involves an analysis of the Charter of Rights and Freedoms and the common law of privilege".⁴

II. THE GENERAL SCOPE OF SECTION 10

A. Section 10 of the 1981 Act

9–52 The opportunity was taken in 1981 to reduce the element of uncertainty in this area of the law by the enactment of s.10 of the Contempt of Court Act, which provides that there are circumstances in which a journalist (or indeed any person who is "responsible" for a publication) cannot now be obliged to reveal any

---

[1] Evidence Amendment Act (No.2) 1980, s.35. See J.F. Burrows and U. Cheer, *Media Law in New Zealand* (5th ed., 2005), p.564ff.
[2] See *McGuinness v Att-Gen of Victoria* (1940) 63 C.L.R. 73; *Nicholls v DPP* [1994] 61 S.A.S.R. 31, 66 A. Crim. R. 517; *Independent Commission Against Corruption v Cornwall* (1993) 116 A.L.R. 97; S. Walker in "Compelling Journalists to Identify Their Sources: the 'Newspaper Rule' and 'Necessity'" (1991) 14 U.N.S.W.L.J. 302.
[3] *Moysa v Alberta Labour Relations Board* (1989) 60 D.L.R. (4th) 1. The court noted that the Labour Relations Board had cited the decision of the United States Supreme Court in *Branzburg v Hayes* 408 U.S. 665 (1972), where it was held that the First Amendment accords a reporter no privilege against appearing before a grand jury and answering questions, as to either the identity of his or her news sources or information received in confidence. It was also observed in that case that it is not necessarily better to write about crime than to prosecute it. See also R. Pomerance, "Compelling the Message from the Medium: Media Search Warrants, Subpoenas and Production Orders" (1997) 2 Can. Crim. Law Rev. 5; C.A. Vermeule, "Confidential Media Sources and the First Amendment: *Cohen v Cowles Media Co.*", 111 S.Ct. 2513 (1991) there is something missing here; ie periodical reference. For the position in Scotland, see, *HM Advocate v Airs* 1975 S.L.T. 177, discussed in para.16–39 and para.16–383.
[4] *R. v The National Post* (2004) D.L.R. (4th) 551 at [87], Benotto J. See also *Canadian Broadcasting Corp v Lessard* (1991) 3 S.C.R. 421; *Canadian Broadcasting Corp v New Brunswick (Attorney General)* (1996) 110 C.C.C (3rd) 193; *R. v Canadian Broadcasting Corp* (2001) 52 O.R. (3d) 757.

source of information. The clause was introduced by Lord Scarman in the course of the passage of the Bill through Parliament.

In an attempt to strike a satisfactory compromise between the competing interests at stake, the legislation now provides: 9–53

"No court may require a person to disclose, nor is any person guilty of contempt of court for refusing to disclose, the source of information contained in a publication for which he is responsible, unless it be established to the satisfaction of the court that disclosure is necessary in the interests of justice or national security or for the prevention of disorder or crime."

B. The meaning of " ... for which he is responsible"

The phrase " ... a publication for which he is responsible" suggests that in some cases careful enquiry may be needed to determine the extent to which any given individual can be fixed with responsibility for the relevant publication. For example, in *John Reid Enterprises v Pell*[5] Carnwath J. held that until the facts were established he had to treat the defendant as *arguably* entitled to claim the protection of s.10. He claimed to be a freelance investigative journalist and had supplied information to journalists on the *Daily Mirror* deriving *inter alia* from an accountant's letter addressed to Elton John's management company. Thereafter, he had worked with the *Mirror* journalists to complete the story, which was published as "an amazing insight into the spending habits of superstar Sir Elton John". The applicants sought an order for disclosure of Mr Pell's own source. It was argued, in the first instance, that he did not fall within the protection of s.10 since he could not be classified as responsible for the ultimate article. This was the issue which the judge decided needed to be determined in the light of the full facts. He nevertheless was able to decide on the existing facts that the balance lay in favour of ordering the source to be disclosed. 9–54

C. The introduction of the words "interests of justice"

The draft introduced by Lord Scarman[6] was in one significant respect different from the provision ultimately enacted: it had not included the exception for the "interests of justice". That was incorporated by a subsequent amendment.[7] 9–55

When the scope of s.10 came to be considered by the House of Lords in *Secretary of State for Defence v Guardian Newspapers Ltd*,[8] the breadth of its impact became apparent. The Secretary of State was claiming delivery up of a secret document, mainly for the purpose of identifying the source of the leak. 9–56

---

[5] [1999] E.M.L.R. 675.
[6] *Hansard*, H.L., Vol. 416, (5th series), col. 210, January 15, 1981.
[7] Lord Morris, in *Hansard*, H.L., Vol. 417, (5th series), col. 153, February 10, 1981. It was introduced in the Commons rather later: Standing Committee A, Session 1980–81, col. 235, May 19, 1981. Lord Scarman's (generally approving) remarks on this amendment are to be found in *Hansard*, H.L., Vol. 417, (5th series), cols.156–158. The scope of the exception is considered further at paras 9–126 *et seq.*
[8] [1985] A.C. 339. See generally Y. Cripps, "Judicial Proceedings and Refusals to Disclose the Identity of Sources of Information" [1984] 43 C.L.J. 266.

Scott J. at first instance did not accept that s.10 was intended by Parliament to extend so widely as to curtail proprietary rights.[9] He took the view that, if an applicant for disclosure was able to assert a title in the document required, then the section had no application.

9–57 The House of Lords unanimously held this to be too narrow a construction. Although the House held, by a majority, that the Crown had discharged the burden of showing that immediate delivery up was necessary "in the interests of national security", it was nonetheless recognised that the protection afforded to journalists' sources was in principle capable of prevailing even against the assertion of clear proprietary rights. This was confirmed in *X Ltd v Morgan-Grampian (Publishers) Ltd*.[10]

D. Does section 10 apply to Internet website operators?

9–58 It was emphasised by Owen J. in *Totalise plc v Motley Fool Ltd*[11] that it was to the protection of journalists' sources *only* that s.10 was directed (despite the fact that the word "journalist" is not used in the section itself). It was held to have no application to the operators of Internet websites who, by contrast, took no responsibility for what was published on their websites, and exercised no editorial control. Such persons merely provide a facility by means of which contributors are enabled to communicate their views to the public generally. The court made a *Norwich Pharmacal* order requiring the operator to disclose the identity of an anonymous contributor who had been posting defamatory material. Owen J. took the view also that, even if he were wrong in his narrow construction of the scope of the s.10 protection, it would be right to order disclosure, as being necessary in the interests of justice. To have found otherwise would have given the clearest indication to those who wished to defame others that they could do so under the protection of the anonymity made possible by the use of websites.

E. The meaning of "publication"

9–59 "Publication" is defined in s.19 of the 1981 Act for all purposes (except those of s.9) by reference to the definition in s.2(1).[12] It is important, however, to bear in mind that the policy considerations underlying the provisions governing strict liability are different from those concerning journalists' sources. The purpose of ss.1 and 2 is to *confine* the scope of "the strict liability rule", not least in order to achieve compliance with the provisions of Art.10 of the European Convention,

---

[9] See now the Official Secrets Act 1989, s.8(4)(a) and (5), which provides for an official direction for the return of documents even though there may be no property right that avails the Crown. It is to be doubted, however, that this provision in any way weakens the protection of s.10 of the 1981 Act.
[10] [1991] 1 A.C. 1 at 40–1, Lord Bridge.
[11] [2001] E.M.L.R. 750. The case went to the Court of Appeal where the issue turned on costs only: [2002] 1 W.L.R. 1233.
[12] See para.4–24. See also Lord Diplock in *Secretary of State for Defence v Guardian Newspapers Ltd* [1985] A.C. 339 at 348.

whereas in order to give effect to its underlying policy in the context of sources a broad construction of "publication" might have been more appropriate.[13]

F. Information "contained in a publication"

The protection for sources would at first sight seem to be further limited by the fact that the section is confined in its application to sources of information "contained in a publication". But the House of Lords was prepared to interpret the section widely, and indeed purposively,[14] in *X Ltd v Morgan-Grampian (Publishers) Ltd*.[15] It was held that the information need not be contained in an actual publication, provided that it has been communicated and received by the journalist with a view ultimately to publication. Thus, the section may now be taken as protecting sources from disclosure on a wider basis than the literal meaning of the words might suggest[16]:

> "The information having been communicated and received for the purposes of publication it is clearly right to treat it as subject to the rule which the section lays down, since the purpose underlying the statutory protection of sources of information is as much applicable before as after publication".

Lord Bridge observed that it was already "clearly established" that the section is to be given a wide, rather than a narrow construction, saying that he could not do better in explaining this approach than quote from the judgment of Griffiths L.J. in *Secretary of State for Defence v Guardian Newspapers Ltd*[17]:

> "It is in the interests of us all that we should have a truly effective press, and it seems to me that Parliament by enacting section 10 has clearly recognised the importance that attaches to the ability of the press to protect their sources. . . . I can see no harm in giving a wide construction to the opening words of the section because by the latter part of the section the court is given ample powers to order the source to be revealed where in the circumstances of a particular case the wider public interest makes it necessary to do so."

It has been pointed out that this avoids anomalies[18]; a journalist to whom information had been communicated but who had not yet managed to publish it would otherwise be in a worse position than one who had actually published. Prior to publication, a person with a potential interest in disclosure is less likely

---

[13] "Publication" is generally used in a wider sense in the law of defamation, so as to include even the communication of words in a private conversation between two people. See generally *Gatley on Libel and Slander* (10th ed., 2004) ch.6. For discussion as to the meaning of "publication" in s.12 of the Administration of Justice Act 1960 see paras 8–102 *et seq*.
[14] Lord Diplock in *Secretary of State for Defence v Guardian Newspapers Ltd* [1985] A.C. 339 at 345C–D, repudiated counsel's evocative phrase "constitutional right", if it was intended to mean anything more than that in ascertaining the extent of the rights which it confers the section should be given a "purposive construction", which he appears to have accepted was appropriate. The House of Lords was unanimous on the point of construction and, in the words of Lord Scarman, "We are agreed that the section must have a wide and general application."
[15] [1991] 1 A.C. 1 at 40, Lord Bridge.
[16] Lord Bridge, at 40G–H. See also Rose J. in *X v Y* [1988] 2 All E.R. 648 at 661j.
[17] [1984] Ch. 156 at 166–7.
[18] J.G. Miller, [1990] All E.R. Review at 51.

to be aware that the journalist is in possession of the relevant information; the Act was really only drafted with the situation in mind that arises following publication. The wide interpretation of the House of Lords, however, might be thought to give journalists more confidence. They are able to contact the individual or company who is the subject of their proposed story, without the fear that an injunction can be obtained, not only restraining the publication itself, but also ordering disclosure of any source (on the argument that the protection of s.10 has not yet been triggered).

G. Information contained in photographs

9–63 In *Handmade Films (Productions) Ltd v Express Newspapers Ltd*[19] it was argued that photographs were not within the protection of the Act, not being "information contained in a publication". Sir Nicolas Browne-Wilkinson V.-C. had no difficulty in rejecting the proposition[20]:

> "... photographs are the same as oral or written communications. They are merely a different form of communicating information. Photographs communicate visually: writing does it through words. But in either case what is contained in the publication is information."

H. Where the information does not fall within the Act

9–64 Presumably the common law still applies where a journalist is asked in cross-examination about information in his possession which has neither been published nor even communicated for the purpose of being included in such a publication. For example, suppose material has been supplied to a journalist or his employers with a view to assisting, if necessary, in the pleading of a defence in libel proceedings, by way of particulars of justification or fair comment. If the journalist were asked how such information came to be pleaded, whether or not it was subsequently supported by admissible evidence at the trial, he or she would almost certainly consider that there was a professional obligation not to disclose the identity of the source.[21]

9–65 This is by no means an unlikely scenario. There may be circumstances in which it is quite proper to plead (say) the whereabouts of a claimant at certain times, and to rely upon the confirmation emerging without having to call direct evidence from the source to support the allegation. It might be assumed, perhaps, that the claimant's diary or passport would confirm the source's account, or that the claimant will make admissions in due course.[22] Without having pleaded the allegation in the first place, however, in reliance upon the source, the allegation could not have been introduced into the proceedings at all. Yet because the wording of s.10 would not apparently apply, the trial judge would be thrown back

---

[19] [1986] F.S.R. 463.
[20] *ibid.* at 468. See also as to information contained within photographs, Laws J. in *Hellewell v Chief Constable of Derbyshire* [1995] 1 W.L.R. 804, [1995] 4 All E.R. 473; *Campbell v MGN* [2004] 2 A.C. 456. See also Christina Michalos, *Law of Photography and Digital Images* (2004).
[21] See, *e.g. Maxwell v Pressdram Ltd* [1987] 1 W.L.R. 298, 1 All E.R. 656, CA.
[22] See, *e.g. McDonald's Corporation v Steel* [1995] 3 All E.R. 615, CA.

upon the common law discretion whether or not to order the journalist to answer the questions. No doubt, however, the approach to exercising that discretion would be to a large extent informed by the jurisprudence relating to s.10 and the approach adopted by domestic courts to freedom of information more generally.[23]

I. Does the Act supplement or supersede the common law?

The provisions of s.10 had the effect of substituting for the common law discretion a rule of law, subject only to specifically stated exceptions, each of which needs to be established by evidence to the satisfaction of the court.[24] A court deciding whether or not one of these exceptions has been established is thus determining an issue of fact.[25] The change brought about was described by Lord Scarman as being one "of profound significance".[26] Earlier[27] he had expressed doubts as to whether or not judicial discretion afforded an adequate means at common law of balancing the public interest in not hampering news agencies against the public and private interests in making evidence fully available for court proceedings.

As Lord Bridge explained in *X Ltd v Morgan-Grampian (Publishers) Ltd*[28]:

"Whether the necessity of disclosure in this sense is established is certainly a question of fact rather than an issue calling for the exercise of the judge's discretion, but, like many other questions of fact, such as the question whether somebody has acted reasonably in given circumstances, it will call for the exercise of a discriminating and sometimes difficult value judgment."

A question thus arises as to whether the law now requires a balancing exercise, similar to that traditionally conducted at common law, or whether that approach has been entirely superseded by a factual enquiry under the statute. It might at first sight appear that no great change has been made, since at least some of the factors that would once have governed the exercise of the discretion are weighed now in the balance to determine whether the disclosure is "necessary". The difficulty of drawing a fine distinction has been highlighted by Thorpe L.J.: "The making of a value judgment on competing facts is very close to the exercise of a discretion dependent on those facts."[29]

---

[23] Cp. the approach of the House of Lords in *Re an Inquiry Under the Company Securities (Insider Dealing) Act 1985* [1988] A.C. 660 at 703, described at para.9–187.
[24] *Secretary of State for Defence v Guardian Newspapers Ltd* [1985] A.C. 339 at 361, Lord Scarman.
[25] See Lord Diplock in *Secretary of State for Defence v Guardian Newspapers Ltd* [1985] A.C. 339 at 345.
[26] *ibid.* at 361.
[27] *Senior v Holdsworth Ex p. Independent Television News* [1976] Q.B. 23 at 43. By a similar process, the protection of journalistic material is now governed by the statutory provisions of the Police and Criminal Evidence Act 1984, s.13.
[28] [1991] 1 A.C. 1 at 44.
[29] *Camelot Group plc v Centaur Communications Ltd* [1999] Q.B. 124 at 138H.

9–69 Lord Bridge himself had observed in *X Ltd*[30]:

> "In estimating the weight to be attached to the importance of disclosure in the interests of justice on the one hand and that of protection from disclosure in pursuance of the policy which underlies section 10 on the other hand, many factors will be relevant on both sides of the scale."

1. *A two-stage process*

9–70 It seems that the true answer is that now there has to be a two-stage process. First, the court will have to be satisfied, by conducting a factual enquiry (albeit involving a value judgment), that it has jurisdiction to order disclosure. In the Court of Appeal in *Secretary of State for Defence v Guardian Newspapers Ltd*, Sir John Donaldson M.R. described the effect of the enactment in the following terms[31]:

> "Section 10 of the 1981 Act, within the scope of its application, varied this discretion or practice to the extent that, unless the exceptional circumstances were established to its satisfaction, the court was bound to refuse to require any person to disclose the source of information contained in a publication."

The court would thus appear to have no right to order disclosure unless one or other of the statutory conditions is fulfilled. This is a matter which can probably be classified as going to jurisdiction.[32]

9–71 Even if the test of "necessity" is fulfilled, at stage two there still appears to be a residual discretion as to whether an order should in fact be made. The statute does not require that a court *shall* order disclosure even in those circumstances; only that it may *not* do so unless the criterion of "necessity" is established.

9–72 Lord Griffiths in *Re an Inquiry Under the Company Securities (Insider Dealing) Act 1985*[33] described how he perceived the intention of Parliament:

> "... section 10 is not framed in language that compels a judge to order a journalist to reveal his sources and I can conceive of extreme cases in which the judge might properly refuse to do so if, for instance, the crime was of a trivial nature or, at the other end of the scale, the journalist's life might be imperilled[34] if he revealed his source."

9–73 Lord Griffiths was not, presumably, intending in this passage to give an exhaustive list of the circumstances in which the judicial discretion might be exercised against ordering disclosure. It is perhaps unfortunate that the word

---

[30] [1991] 1 A.C. 1 at 44.
[31] [1984] Ch. 156 at 164A–B.
[32] See, *e.g. Special Hospitals Service Authority v Hyde* (1994) 20 B.M.L.R. 75, discussed at para.9–77 and the difficulties described in paras 9–194 *et seq*.
[33] [1988] A.C. 660 at 703G–H.
[34] But see *DPP v Channel Four Television Co Ltd* [1993] 2 All E.R. 517, where notwithstanding evidence of a threat to the life and security of the journalist and his family the Divisional Court thought it right to order disclosure.

"extreme" was used because there is a tendency when such an expression is introduced, especially in House of Lords speeches, for judges subsequently to attach a similar degree of weight as if it appeared in a statute. It is possible to envisage a wide range of hypothetical circumstances, falling on Lord Griffiths' "scale", that might justify a refusal notwithstanding that a case of *prima facie* "necessity" had been made out.

Because of the breadth and open-endedness of the concept "interests of justice", when this is the statutory exception relied upon there is perhaps more scope for confusion arising as between stages one and two of the judicial process. There may arise a tendency to conflate the factual exercise of determining whether jurisdiction exists at all in the first place and the discretionary one, if it comes to it, of deciding whether to order disclosure in the particular circumstances.

Once a judge has decided that disclosure is necessary for the purposes of one or other of the s.10 exceptions, it is not entirely clear whether, at the stage of exercising discretion, he or she should proceed on the basis that there is a presumption still against disclosure or whether the finding of necessity creates a presumption the other way.[35] Lord Griffiths' use of the word "extreme" would suggest that the "presumption" of which he had spoken immediately beforehand,[36] in favour of the protection of sources, must by that stage have been supplanted.

Because "interests of justice" seems now to be construed very broadly,[37] it is possible to imagine "necessity" in that context being established relatively easily. Accordingly, the exercise of discretion at the second stage becomes all the more important. It may be that all the factors which could have been weighed for the purposes of discretion at common law will continue to be relevant at this stage, notwithstanding the significant changes brought about by the new statutory regime.

In *Special Hospitals Service Authority v Hyde*,[38] Sir Peter Pain held that he had no jurisdiction to make an order for disclosure, since it had not been demonstrated to be "necessary" under the terms of s.10; nonetheless he went on to address the issue of how he would have exercised his discretion had one of those criteria been fulfilled. One of the factors which he had earlier considered was the principle that a public body seeking disclosure of a journalist's source needs to show that such an order would be in the public interest.[39] That is the sort of factor that might well come in to play at the discretion stage. Even if, therefore, the criterion of necessity was satisfied according to the narrow requirements of some

---

[35] See, *e.g.* Lord Donaldson M.R. in *X Ltd v Morgan-Grampian (Publishers) Ltd* [1991] 1 A.C. 1 at 28, CA.
[36] See the citation at para.9–79.
[37] paras 9–126 *et seq.*
[38] (1994) 20 B.M.L.R. 75.
[39] *ibid.* at 78, citing *Att-Gen v Guardian Newspapers Ltd (No.2)* [1990] 1 A.C. 109 at 270–80, Lord Griffiths, and 282–4, Lord Goff, and *Derbyshire County Council v Times Newspapers Ltd* [1993] A.C. 534 at 547, Lord Keith.

9-77 CHAPTER 9—PROTECTION OF SOURCES

particular piece of litigation, the court might well conclude that the discretion should be exercised against disclosure because the wider public interest did not require it.

9-78 Because of this residual discretion, it may still be appropriate to speak of a "balancing exercise" if and when that second stage is reached. What remains unclear is the extent to which it is still appropriate to use the language of "a balancing exercise" at the *first* stage of determining whether or not there is jurisdiction to order disclosure.

9-79 In *Re an Inquiry Under the Company Securities (Insider Dealing) Act 1985*[40] Lord Griffiths said:

> "The judge in deciding whether or not a journalist has a 'reasonable excuse' for refusing to reveal his sources is not carrying out a balancing exercise between two competing areas of public interest. The judge starts with the presumption that the journalist's refusal to reveal his sources does provide a reasonable excuse for refusing to answer the inspector's questions and the burden is upon the inspectors to satisfy the judge as a question of fact that the identification of his source is necessary for the prevention of crime . . . "

9-80 In *Secretary of State for Defence v Guardian Newspapers Ltd*,[41] Lord Scarman identified a change in the judicial task that may profoundly affect the substance of the law. Observing that counsel had referred to the section as introducing into the law "a constitutional right," he went on:

> "There being no written constitution, his words will sound strange to some. But they may more accurately prophesy the direction in which English law has to move under the compulsions to which it is now subject than many are yet prepared to accept. The section, it is important to note in this connection, bears a striking structural resemblance to the way in which many of the articles of the European Convention for the Protection of Human Rights and Fundamental Freedoms (1953) (cmd 8969) which formulate the fundamental rights and freedoms protected by that Convention are framed: namely, a general rule subject to carefully drawn and limited exceptions[42] which require to be established, in case of dispute, to the satisfaction of the European Court of Human Rights."

9-81 Yet, in later cases, the courts have reverted (when plainly describing stage one) to the "balancing" metaphor that was so familiar at common law. Thus, in *X Ltd v Morgan-Grampian (Publishers) Ltd*,[43] Lord Bridge said:

> "Construing the phrase 'in the interests of justice' in this sense immediately emphasises the importance of the balancing exercise. It will not be sufficient, per se, for a party

---

[40] [1988] A.C. 660 at 703.
[41] [1985] A.C. 339 at 361E–F.
[42] See the similar description given by the European Court of Human Rights in *Sunday Times v United Kingdom* (1979) 2 E.H.R.R. 245, 281 cited in para.6–87.
[43] [1991] 1 A.C. 1 at at 43–4.

seeking disclosure of a source protected by section 10 to show that he will be unable without disclosure to exercise the legal right to avert the threatened legal wrong on which he bases his claim in order to establish the necessity of disclosure. The judge's task will always be to weigh in the scales the importance of enabling the ends of justice to be attained in the circumstances of the particular case on the one hand against the importance of protecting the source on the other hand. In this balancing exercise it is only if the judge is satisfied that disclosure in the interests of justice is of such preponderating importance as to override the statutory privilege against disclosure that the threshold of necessity will be reached".

This use of the "balancing test" has been criticised by one writer as lacking authority.[44] But it is difficult to see that any test of "necessity" can be considered in the abstract. It inevitably invites the question, "necessary for what purpose?" In answering that question, and applying the answer to any given set of facts, a judge would certainly seem, as Lord Bridge has commented, to have to exercise a value judgment.[45] Yet the context in which the exercise is to be conducted will be critically affected by whether the judge starts with the same "presumption" as Lord Griffiths (and presumably Lord Scarman).[46] That approach would seem to accord a greater weight to protecting journalists' sources than would the untrammelled exercise of discretion under the common law.[47]

9–82

J. The elusive concept of "necessary"[48]

Under the statute no court may require a person to disclose his source of information; nor is any person guilty of contempt of court for refusing to disclose that source *unless* the court is satisfied that disclosure is "necessary" for one or other of the specified reasons. Nonetheless, it was not intended by Parliament that the exercise should be a subjective one. If, for example, a judge orders a witness to answer a question on the ground that it is necessary to do so in the interests of justice, when in truth it is unnecessary, the witness will not be held in contempt merely because he fails to answer. This seems to have been the position also at common law, in light of the decision in *Att-Gen v Lundin*[49] that there was no contempt. Section 10 was intended to put the matter beyond doubt.

9–83

Yet it is no easier for a journalist to determine in any objective sense whether the answer that he or she is required to give is ultimately going to be regarded by the court as "necessary". It may depend upon which level in the judicial

9–84

---

[44] I. Cram, (1992) 55 M.L.R. at 402.
[45] See further para.9–227, where the question of jurisdiction to make the order is considered. See also the citation at para.9–67.
[46] See also Lord Donaldson M.R. in the Court of Appeal in *X Ltd v Morgan Grampian (Publishers) Ltd* [1991] 1 A.C. 1 at 27.
[47] See paras 9–13 *et seq.*
[48] Compare the discussion of "necessity" in the context of s.4(2) of the Contempt of Court Act in paras 7–185 *et seq.* and the three stage test as adopted by the Privy Council in *Independent Publishing Co Ltd v Att-Gen for Trinidad and Tobago* [2004] UKPC 26, [2005] 1 A.C. 190.
[49] See para.9–47.

9-84 hierarchy has most recently pronounced upon the matter. Even at the highest tier the issue may not always be resolved with the clarity one might wish to see.

9-85 In *Secretary of State for Defence v Guardian Newspapers Ltd*,[50] the members of the House divided (three to two) on the question whether it had been "necessary" on the facts to order disclosure in the interests of national security. The Crown sought recovery of documents in the journalists' possession, asserting breach of copyright. When countered by the argument that the documents fell within the protection afforded by s.10, the Crown asserted that "moles" in the ministry who had leaked classified documents were a threat to national security,[51] and the very fact that documents had fallen into *Guardian* hands showed that the threat was a continuing one. Lords Scarman and Fraser fastened on to the word "*necessary*" in s.10, concluding that it was not enough that an order for disclosure would have been the easiest way of identifying the mole: there had to be necessity. In fact 12 days had elapsed between publication and the government demand for the documents to be returned. In those circumstances the minority took the view that the exception had not really been established.[52]

K. Attempts to define the word "necessary"

9-86 The House in *Re An Inquiry Under the Company Securities (Insider Dealing) Act 1985*[53] also considered the notion of "necessity" appearing in s.10. Being mindful of the general proposition that much depends upon context, their Lordships were not prepared to give further guidance than to say that the meaning of the word lay somewhere between "indispensable" on the one hand and "useful" or "expedient" on the other.[54] The nearest paraphrase that Lord Griffiths could suggest was "really needed", but the individual judge would always have to make his or her own assessment on the particular facts. He encapsulated the difficulties in the following passage:

> "What then is meant by the words 'necessary... for the prevention of... crime' in section 10? I do not think that much light is thrown upon this question by an elaborate discussion of the meaning of the word 'necessary'. 'Necessary' is a word in common usage in everyday speech with which everyone is familiar. Like all words, it will take colour from its context; for example, most people would regard it as 'necessary' to do everything possible to prevent a catastrophe but would not regard it as 'necessary' to do everything possible to prevent some minor inconvenience."

---

[50] [1985] 1 A.C. 339.
[51] This aspect of the decision is considered further at para.9–177.
[52] See Lord Fraser at 358, and Lord Scarman at 366. Yet, ironically, the approach is sometimes adopted (*e.g.* in *Handmade Films (Productions) Ltd v Express Newspapers Ltd* [1986] F.S.R. 463 and *Special Hospitals Service Authority v Hyde* (1994) 20 B.M.L.R. 75) that the court should not conclude that an order has become necessary unless some time has been taken in enquiries to identify the source *before* resorting to the court.
[53] [1988] A.C. 660 at 704.
[54] This illustrates the shift in the balance since, in *Att-Gen v Mulholland* [1963] 2 Q.B. 477 at 493, Donovan L.J. expressed a preference for "useful" over "necessary".

In *X Ltd v Morgan-Grampian (Publishers) Ltd*,[55] Lord Oliver summarised the 9–87
test as follows:

> "The true question, in my opinion, is not 'is the information needed in order to serve the interests of justice?' but 'are the interests of justice in this case so pressing as to require the absolute ban on disclosure to be overridden?' "

This would certainly seem to accord with the analysis of the European Court of Human Rights, later applied to the same facts, in *Goodwin v United Kingdom*.[56]

The Court of Appeal also drew a careful distinction between "expedient" and 9–88
"necessary" in *Maxwell v Pressdram Ltd*.[57] The magazine *Private Eye* published an article which was alleged by Robert Maxwell to be defamatory of him, in that it claimed that he had financed a trip abroad by the then Leader of the Opposition in order to secure a peerage for himself. He claimed aggravated and exemplary damages. Initially, at the stage when he sought an interlocutory injunction, the defendants claimed that they had "reliable and highly-placed" sources and intended to plead justification. At trial, however, that plea was withdrawn, the explanation being given that these sources had reneged on an undertaking to give evidence. Maxwell wanted to identify the sources, contending that this might go to the amount of damages, and in particular that the claim for punitive damages might depend upon the defendants' state of knowledge.[58] The trial judge held that s.10 applied, taking the view that he could deal with point by giving a strong jury direction in the plaintiff's favour, if necessary.

The Court of Appeal declined to interfere and held that, although the 9–89
disclosure might be relevant and "expedient", the plaintiff had not demonstrated that the disclosure was "necessary". In deciding the necessity issue (particularly, perhaps, where the "interests of justice" exception is under consideration), it is essential to identify the issues for which the disclosed information is said to be necessary. As Kerr L.J. said in *Maxwell v Pressdram Ltd*[59]:

> "... it is essential first to identify and define the issue in the legal proceedings which is said to require the disclosure of sources, and then to decide whether, having regard to the nature of the issue and the circumstances of the case, it is in fact 'necessary' to make such a far reaching order."

---

[55] [1991] A.C. 1 at 53C.
[56] (1996) 22 E.H.R.R. 123.
[57] [1987] 1 W.L.R. 298, 1 All E.R. 656, CA.
[58] See the Law Commission's report, *Aggravated, Exemplary and Restitutionary Damages*, Report No.247, 1997, which recommended that punitive damages be retained for deliberately tortious conduct but also that it should be governed by a statutory code. See also the explanation given by Lord Morris to the House of Lords, Vol. 417, (5th series) cols.153–4, February 10, 1981, when he introduced the government's amendment to what is now s.10 of the Contempt of Court Act to include the "interests of justice" exception: "Particularly in cases of defamation it is both relevant and vital to the administration of justice that the source of information be disclosed; and more particularly in cases where fair comment is pleaded, the establishment of the presence or absence of malice is crucial".
[59] [1987] 1 W.L.R. 298 at 309.

L. The onus of proof

9–90 The onus of showing necessity plainly falls upon the person seeking disclosure; that being the ordinary consequence of the phrase "unless it be established to the satisfaction of the court".[60]

9–91 A person resisting an order for disclosure does not need to argue that it would inescapably point to a journalist's source. It will suffice if there is a reasonable chance that it will do so.[61] Once the point is raised that a source might be revealed, presumably it will be for the applicant to demonstrate the contrary.[62]

M. Factors to be considered in determining "necessity"

9–92 Cases will vary considerably, and in particular the test is likely to be applied differently according to which of the four statutory exceptions is under consideration. For example, what may be necessary for the interests of national security will obviously involve quite distinct policy considerations from those arising in relation (say) to the interests of justice.

9–93 The majority view in *Secretary of State for Defence v Guardian Newspapers Ltd*[63] was to the effect that any measurable risk to national security would merit the conclusion that the disclosure of a relevant source was necessary in the public interest. Lord Diplock expressed his concerns in the following passage:

" . . . the risk to national security that the Government feared lay not in the publication of the particular document of which the delivery up was sought, but in the possibility—and in so potentially catastrophic a field as nuclear warfare I regard possibility as enough—that whoever leaked that document might leak in future other classified documents disclosure of which would have much more serious consequences on national security."

9–94 It may be that a similarly robust approach would be taken where the court perceived a need to prevent public disorder or crime. Lord Bridge, for example, in *X Ltd v Morgan-Grampian (Publishers) Ltd*,[64] considered the public policy factors applying to both, and commented that:

---

[60] *Saunders v Punch Ltd* [1998] 1 W.L.R. 986 at 993C, 1 All E.R. 234 at 241d, Lindsay J., Ch.D. It was observed by Lord Woolf M.R. in *John v Express Newspapers* [2000] 1 W.L.R. 1931, [2000] 3 All E.R. 257 at [29] that "in our view it is important that when orders are made requiring journalists to depart from their normal professional standards, the merits of their doing so in the public interest are clearly demonstrated."
[61] See *Secretary of State for Defence v Guardian Newspapers Ltd* [1985] A.C. 339 at 349, Lord Diplock; *X Ltd v Morgan-Grampian (Publishers) Ltd* [1991] 1 A.C. 1 at 40, Lord Bridge; *Saunders v Punch Ltd* [1998] 1 W.L.R. 986 at 993D-E, 1 All E.R. 234 at 241d-e, Lindsay J., Ch.D.
[62] The statement to the contrary in Courtney, Newell and Rasaiah, *The Law of Journalism* (1995) that "A person seeking the protection of s.10 must show that the balance of probabilities is such that the identity of his source will be revealed if he complies with the order being sought" (p.262) seems to be unsupported by any authority.
[63] [1985] 1 A.C. 339 at 355.
[64] [1991] 1 A.C. 1 at 43A–C.

"... if non-disclosure of a source of information will imperil national security or enable a crime to be committed which might otherwise be prevented, it is difficult to imagine that any judge would hesitate to order disclosure. These two public interests are of such overriding importance that once it is shown that disclosure will serve one of those interests, the necessity of disclosure follows almost automatically; though even here if a judge were asked to order disclosure of a source of information in the interests of the prevention of crime, he 'might properly refuse to do so if, for instance, the crime was of a trivial nature:' [1988] A.C. 660, 703, *per* Lord Griffiths."

As to the "interests of justice", however, there is more scope for flexibility, in the sense that there is a need to weigh up one public interest against another.[65] One might conclude, for example, that revelation of a source would be necessary in the sense of being "really needed" for the resolution of a specific issue in court proceedings such as, in a libel action, to enable a decision to be made on a pleaded allegation of malice in the context of fair comment, or upon the motives of (say) a newspaper reporter in that of exemplary damages[66]; and yet decide to exercise the residual discretion *against* disclosure, for reasons less directly concerned with the particular case than with countervailing public interest factors.

9–95

In *X Ltd v Morgan Grampian (Publishers) Ltd*[67] an attempt was made more generally to identify some factors which would be relevant in the context of the "interests of justice" exception; in particular, whether the livelihood[68] of the person seeking disclosure was under threat, and whether the information had been obtained illegally or otherwise improperly. Both these would be considerations weighing in favour of disclosure.[69] Nonetheless, such considerations can be displaced where there is a clear public interest such as in the exposure of iniquity.[70] That these will be regarded as important factors could hardly be the subject of doubt. What is more difficult to determine is how such considerations would relate to one another, and what importance will be attached in relative terms. The guidance given by Lord Bridge[71] remains helpful, although his scale of priorities may not necessarily survive in the light of the analysis given by the European Court in *Goodwin v United Kingdom*.[72]

9–96

The approach of Lord Bridge was as follows:

9–97

"It would be foolish to attempt to give comprehensive guidance as to how the balancing exercise should be carried out. But it may not be out of place to indicate the kind of

---

[65] *ibid.* at 43C.
[66] See, *e.g. Maxwell v Pressdram Ltd* [1987] 1 W.L.R. 298, discussed at para.9–88.
[67] [1991] A.C. 1.
[68] The "livelihood" argument was raised in *Chief Constable of Leicestershire v Garavelli* [1997] E.M.L.R. 543, in respect of the police officer who was before the disciplinary tribunal, but the Divisional Court seems to have been unpersuaded.
[69] But see, *e.g. European Pacific Banking Corporation v Television New Zealand Ltd* [1994] 3 N.Z.L.R. 43 at 44 where the information sought was obtained "unlawfully, by theft and conversion"; yet disclosure was not ordered.
[70] [1991] 1 A.C. 1 at 44G. Another factor of importance would be, for example, that disclosure was required for advancing the case of a defendant being tried for a criminal offence: see *R. v The National Post* (2004) 236 D.L.R. (4th) 551 at [79], Benotto J.
[71] *ibid.* at 44.
[72] (1996) 22 E.H.R.R. 123, para.9–147.

9–97

factors which will require consideration. In estimating the importance to be given to the case in favour of disclosure there will be a wide spectrum within which the particular case must be located. If the party seeking disclosure shows, for example, that his very livelihood depends upon it, this will put the case near one end of the spectrum. If he shows no more than that what he seeks to protect is a minor interest in property, this will put the case at or near the other end. On the other side the importance of protecting a source from disclosure in pursuance of the policy underlying the statute will also vary within a wide spectrum. One important factor will be the nature of the information obtained from the source. The greater the legitimate public interest in the information which the source has given to the publisher or intended publisher, the greater will be the importance of protecting the source. But another and perhaps more significant factor which will very much affect the importance of protecting the source will be the manner in which the information was itself obtained by the source. If it appears to the court that the information was obtained legitimately this will enhance the importance of protecting the source. Conversely, if it appears that the information was obtained illegally, this will diminish the importance of protecting the source unless, of course, this factor is counterbalanced by a clear public interest in publication of the information, as in the classic case where the source has acted for the purpose of exposing iniquity. I draw attention to these considerations by way of illustration only and I emphasise once again that they are in no way intended to be read as a code."

The importance of the information "exposing iniquity" may perhaps logically go not so much to necessity, but to the exercise of the residual discretion *not* to order disclosure. It is clear, however, that this factor may require investigation at the disclosure stage or during cross-examination before a conclusion can be reached. Where such matters are raised, therefore, the court may be even more reluctant to order disclosure on written evidence alone.[73]

9–98 In any event, a judge would certainly have regard to such matters as the conscience and professional sensibilities of the journalist in the exercise of discretion, as these factors were always considered at common law.[74] Some of the factors mentioned as being relevant to the exercise of judicial discretion in *Att-Gen v Lundin*[75] may be of relevance also for the purpose of the modern statutory test.

9–99 The Divisional Court came to the conclusion that it had not been necessary for Lundin to answer the questions put to him in the course of a criminal trial. Although it was not there concerned with the concept of "prevention of disorder or crime" or with "the interests of justice" as such, it is reasonable to suppose that similar factors might nowadays be taken into account by a judge in a criminal trial addressing where the "interests of justice" might lie.

9–100 On the other hand, in the context of the 1981 statute it might be held that the factors listed below, or at any rate most of them, would only come into play at the stage when the court is called upon to exercise its residual discretion whether

---

[73] See, *e.g. Handmade Films (Productions) Ltd v Express Newspapers Ltd* [1986] F.S.R. 463 at 471, Sir Nicolas Browne-Wilkinson V-C.
[74] *Att-Gen v Mulholland* [1963] 2 Q.B. 477.
[75] For the facts of the case, see para.9–47.

or not to order disclosure once "necessity" has been established.[76] The factors identified by Watkins L.J. may be conveniently summarised as follows:

(i) the seriousness of the charges being tried[77];

(ii) whether the trial would never have occurred but for the investigations of the person refusing to answer;

(iii) whether the journalist's investigations and disclosures (apart from matters which he had refused to disclose) had led to the convictions of other persons[78];

(iv) whether the information might have been disclosed to the police at an earlier stage and, if so, whether the court would have had access to other evidence no longer obtainable.[79]

A further consideration which is from time to time mentioned, apparently in the context of the exercise of discretion, is how "responsibly" the journalist in question has behaved. This point was certainly not decisive, in the context of national security, in *Secretary of State for Defence v Guardian Newspapers Ltd*.[80] On the other hand, Sir Peter Pain in *Special Hospitals Service Authority v Hyde*[81] commented that "no important or serious disclosure" had been made by the journalist, which he attributed in part to the responsible way in which he dealt with the information. This was a matter which he identified as potentially relevant to the exercise of his discretion.

9–101

Another significant factor which would have weighed in the judge's discretion against ordering disclosure, had he concluded that he had jurisdiction to do so, was the importance, from the public point of view, of the information published. He concluded that the public had an interest in "the free supply of information about Broadmoor, a public body". He found there to be "a legitimate and very lively public interest in the security of Broadmoor." He would therefore have exercised his discretion against revealing the source of information about the escape of two convicted murderers.

9–102

By contrast, in a case where the information revealed by journalists was perceived by the court not to be serving any significant public interest, the Court of Appeal upheld a judge's decision that the relevant source should be disclosed. The "necessity" alleged and upheld in *Camelot Group plc v Centaur Communications Ltd*[82] was similar to that argued in *Hyde*, namely the need to identify

9–103

---

[76] For a discussion of the apparent need for a two-stage judicial analysis, see paras 9–70 *et seq.*
[77] See also *Re an Inquiry Under the Company Securities (Insider Dealing) Act 1985* [1988] A.C. 660 at 703, Lord Griffiths, cited by Lord Bridge in the passage cited at para.9–94.
[78] (1982) 75 Cr.App.R. 90 at 100–1 (two other people had been convicted as a result of Lundin's investigations).
[79] Reliance was placed on behalf of the Attorney-General on the fact that Lundin had written an article in *Private Eye* which alerted the wrongdoers and led to the shredding of important documents.
[80] [1985] 1 A.C. 339 at 355. It had been accepted in the House of Lords that the editor of *The Guardian* had behaved responsibly.
[81] (1994) 20 B.M.L.R. 75.
[82] [1999] Q.B. 124.

9–103 a disloyal employee, and to take steps to prevent a recurrence. Yet the public interest element in the leaked information was clearly viewed very differently by the two tribunals. There was no significant countervailing public interest *against* disclosure in the *Camelot* case. Revealing financial information a few days in advance of its public disclosure, in order to obtain a scoop, was clearly of a very different order from revealing information about the security arrangements at Broadmoor.

9–104 The *Hyde* case is of some significance because it is one of the few cases where the task of determining "necessity" within the meaning of s.10 (at stage one) has been clearly distinguished from the exercising of a discretion (stage two). One factor that does seem to be of significance at stage one is whether other independent enquiries have been carried out to establish the identity of the source before resorting to the court for an order of disclosure. This was a consideration which Sir Peter Pain expressly took into account in relation to determining the issue of "necessity" (stage one). In particular, he identified the following factors in relation to the applicants:

> "(1) the failure of . . . members of the management to make any attempt to discover the source other than making application to this court; (2) the absence of any evidence to show that inquiries, if made, would not have been fruitful . . . ".

9–105 Lindsay J. in *Saunders v Punch Ltd*[83] had taken the view that the making of such attempts could not be said to be a necessary pre-condition of the court's giving its assistance, but the absence of any such enquiries could be "a powerful, even a decisive, factor against the intervention of the court".

9–106 The approach of Lindsay J. was endorsed by the Court of Appeal in *John v Express Newspapers.*[84] The case concerned the disclosure to a journalist by an unidentified person of a confidential draft advice which had originated in counsel's chambers. At first instance, the judge ordered the journalists concerned to disclose the source. Although he regarded the omission to conduct any enquiry within the chambers concerned as a factor to be weighed in the scales in deciding upon the necessity for disclosure, he did not attach as much significance to it as had Lindsay J. in *Saunders v Punch Ltd*. The Court of Appeal concluded that a minimum requirement was that other avenues should be explored to detect the source of the leak before encroaching upon the journalist's professional obligation to protect the source.

> "It cannot be assumed that it will not be possible either to find the culprit or, at least, to narrow down the number of persons who could have been responsible. When weighing the conflicting public interests involved, it is to be remembered that there is no certainty that ordering a journalist to reveal her sources will be any more successful. If it is not successful, damage will be caused to the public interest in protecting

---

[83] [1998] 1 W.L.R. 986 at 997C–E, 1 All E.R. 234 at 245e–f. See too *Totalise plc v Motley Fool Ltd* [2001] E.M.L.R. 750, Owen J., cited at para.9–58 above. Although the *Ashworth Hospital* case later came before the House of Lords and the *Totalise* case before the Court of Appeal, neither of the later decisions affects the validity of the comments cited.
[84] [2000] 1 W.L.R. 1931, [2000] 3 All E.R. 257 at [26]–[27]. See also *Roemen and Schmit v Luxembourg,* App. No.51772/99 at [44] and [56].

confidential sources without any compensating benefit to the competing public interest of protecting professional privilege."

Given the particular context, a warning was sounded that a decision to order disclosure would be wrongly interpreted as an example of lawyers attaching a disproportionate significance to the danger to their professional privilege[85] while undervaluing the interests of journalists and thus the public. The importance of previous enquiries now seems to be beyond doubt. Lord Phillips M.R. observed in *Ashworth Hospital Authority v MGN Ltd*[86] that there is ample authority that, in order to demonstrate that disclosure of a source is necessary, a claimant must show that all other reasonable means have been employed unsuccessfully to identify the source.

N. Necessity and proportionality

It will be relevant in determining "necessity" to decide whether there is "a reasonable relationship of proportionality between the legitimate aim pursued by the disclosure order and the means deployed to achieve that aim".[87]

O. The problem of establishing necessity at the interlocutory stage

There is no question but that s.10 applies to interlocutory proceedings as well as to the trial.[88] Naturally, however, it will often be more difficult at the interlocutory stage to establish that disclosure is necessary. It may be that the issues have not fully crystallised, and following dislosure or the exchange of witness statements, for example, the position would become clearer.[89] Furthermore, where an application is made against a party to litigation for a mandatory order for disclosure it may not be possible to establish all the factual ingredients for "necessity" by written evidence alone.

One of the reasons given by Lord Fraser, who was in the minority in the *Guardian* case, was that there had been insufficient evidence on the affidavits before the judge at first instance for him to be "satisfied" that disclosure was in the interests of national security. There could have been affidavit evidence, for example, as to the significance of the security classification adopted, and the

---

[85] It would probably be thought carping to point out that the privilege in relation to counsel's advice would be that of the client rather than the lawyer.
[86] [2001] 1 W.L.R. 515 at 536 at [93], [2001] 1 All E.R. 991 at 1011e.
[87] *Goodwin v United Kingdom* (1996) 22 E.H.R.R. 123 at para.46; *Special Hospital Services Authority v Hyde* 1994) 20 B.M.L.R. 75 at 79; *Chief Constable for Leicestershire v Garavelli* [1997] E.M.L.R. 543 at 554; *Saunders v Punch Ltd* [1998] 1 W.L.R. 986 at 1001F, 1 All E.R. 234 at 249f ("out of all proportion"); *Att-Gen v Guardian Newspapers Ltd* [1999] E.M.L.R. 904; *Ashworth Hospital Authority v MGN Ltd* [2001] 1 W.L.R. 515, [2001] 1 All E.R. 991, CA and Lord Woolf in the House of Lords: [2002] UKHL 29, [2002] 1 W.L.R. 2033 at [36].
[88] See, *e.g. Secretary of State for Defence v Guardian Newspapers Ltd* [1985] 1 A.C. 339 at 345 and 347. See also the "newspaper rule" discussed at paras 9–4 *et seq.*
[89] But see *Michael O'Mara Books Ltd v Express Newspapers plc* [1998] E.M.L.R. 383, Neuberger J. This was a particularly clear case where it was held, even at the preliminary stage of an application for summary judgment in a copyright case, that the interests of justice required that the deputy editor of *The Daily Express* should disclose on oath the source of a copy of a book (*Fergie—Her Secret Life*) in his possession.

9–109 extent to which other enquiries had been made to identify the source of the leak. In the absence of such evidence, Lord Fraser was not prepared to engage in speculation.

9–110 Similarly, in *Handmade Films (Productions) Ltd v Express Newspapers Ltd*,[90] Sir Nicolas Brown-Wilkinson V.-C. took the view that, even if the correct conclusion was that it was *prima facie* "necessary in the interests of justice" to order disclosure, he would not so order at that stage, since the name once revealed would cease to be confidential, and there were facts which would require investigation before it would be appropriate to treat the case as conclusively requiring disclosure under s.10.[91]

P. Waiver

9–111 Although the journalist's limited immunity from the obligation to answer questions is sometimes referred to as a "privilege",[92] it may be a mistake to assume that this usage entails any consequences as to waiver, either express or implied. For example, if a journalist is able, compatibly with what he or she takes to be professional obligations, to assist the court by giving some answers, it cannot necessarily be held that there has been a waiver of the privilege as to other questions touching upon the same subject matter. So, for example, where a journalist felt able to say in the course of a police disciplinary hearing that the policeman whose conduct was under scrutiny was *not* the source for the story,[93] the argument was rejected that she should be held thereby to have waived the privilege in such a way the she could then be obliged to answer other questions, including in particular who *was* the source.

9–112 In any event, the statutory prohibition in s.10 would surely prevail; it would be inappropriate to consider what has been described as a "constitutional right"[94] as something capable of being waived, at least without the clearest expression of an intention to that effect. It is better, for the avoidance of confusion, to acknowledge a statutory "right" rather than use the term "privilege".

Q. Statutory exclusion of section 10

9–113 The protection afforded to sources can be cut down by other express statutory provisions, provided they too are compatible with Art.10 of the European Convention. It was provided, for example, in the Prevention of Terrorism (Temporary Provisions) Act 1989, Sch.7, para.4(5)(b) that:

---

[90] [1986] F.S.R. 463.
[91] See also *Francome v Mirror Group Newspapers Ltd* [1984] 2 All E.R. 408 at 423, 425, 426.
[92] *Secretary of State for Defence v Guardian Newspapers Ltd* [1985] A.C. 339 at 367, Lord Scarman; at 369, Lord Roskill.
[93] *Chief Constable of Leicestershire v Garavelli* [1997] E.M.L.R. 543, Beldam L.J. and Smith J.
[94] In *Secretary of State for Defence v Guardian Newspapers Ltd* [1985] A.C. 339, it was referred to as a "constitutional right", although that usage by counsel was deprecated by Lord Diplock, at 345C. But compare Lord Scarman at 361E–F, cited at para.9–80, and Lord Fraser at 359B (" . . . where there is a flavour of constitutional right of freedom of expression").

THE GENERAL SCOPE OF SECTION 10   9–117

"an order under paragraph 3 above . . . shall have effect notwithstanding any obligation as to secrecy or other restriction on the disclosure of information imposed by statute or otherwise".

The relevant power (contained in Sch.7, para.3) enabled a constable, for the purposes of a terrorist investigation, to apply to a circuit judge for an order that material be produced to a constable for him to take away or that a constable be given access to such material within a specified period. In the light of the express provision set out above, it seems clear that Parliament intended that a journalist should not be permitted to withhold such material in order to protect a source. Although it does not emerge expressly from the report of the case, it would appear that this is the explanation for no reliance having been placed upon s.10 in *DPP v Channel Four Productions and Box Productions Ltd*.[95] As Woolf L.J observed that this was "a section which was not even relied upon by the companies in this case, since, presumably, it was accepted that it provided no protection".   9–114

It was a criminal offence under the s.18[96] of the 1989 Act to fail "without reasonable excuse" to disclose information which a defendant knew or believed might be of material assistance in connection with acts of terrorism related to the affairs of Northern Ireland. There is no authority directly in point, but the question might at some stage arise as to whether a journalist charged under any comparable provision might plead as a reasonable excuse the wish to preserve the confidentiality of a source of information.   9–115

In the very different statutory context of insider dealing, the concept of "reasonable excuse" appearing in s.178(2) of the Financial Services Act 1986 was considered in *Re an Inquiry under the Company Securities (Insider Dealing) Act 1985*.[97] It was conceded that the tests applicable to making an order under s.10 of the 1981 Act were equally appropriate for determining whether in that case the journalist had a "reasonable excuse" for not complying with a request for information made by inspectors conducting an enquiry.   9–116

Whether the terrorist context would lead to a different conclusion is open to question, although it may be argued that, since Parliament made express provision[98] for the purpose of excluding the protection afforded by s.10, no comparable exclusion should be taken as implied in s.18. A court might come to a conclusion, on particular facts, that the protection of the source in question was so important as to outweigh the significance of the information sought by the officer in the context of his enquiries. In the light of the priority now given to the protection of journalists' sources, both by Parliament and by the European Convention, it would be arguable that the decision on "reasonable excuse" should be treated as a matter for the judge rather than the jury. This would   9–117

---

[95] [1993] 2 All E.R. 517 at 530g–h.
[96] See now the Terrorism Act 2000, s.19(3) which provides for a defence if the person charged proves that he had a reasonable excuse.
[97] [1988] A.C. 660 HL.
[98] Sch.7, para.4(5)(b).

9–118 obviously allow for a reasoned explanation for whatever decision was reached.

9–118 In February 2001 the Terrorism Act 2000 came into force and the 1989 Act was thereby repealed. The wording in Sch.7, para.4(5)(b) differs from that in the later provision.[99] The words " ... obligations as to secrecy or other ... " no longer appear. It is submitted that this makes little or no difference so far as s.10 of the Contempt of Court Act 1981 is concerned. The current wording would be equally effective in excluding its application. It would provide no protection against an order to disclose.

R. Duress and the journalist

9–119 It is necessary to consider the extent to which the common law principles relating to the defence of duress apply in situations now governed by s.10. It is quite clear that a recalcitrant witness who claims that he is in fear of death or grievous bodily harm has available to him a defence of duress should he refuse to answer questions on that ground.[1] It is also established that duress is available as a defence in proceedings for perjury.[2] The possible application of these principles in the context of journalists' sources was not specifically addressed in *DPP v Channel Four Television Co Ltd*.[3]

9–120 An allegation was made in the course of a television programme that members of the Royal Ulster Constabulary were colluding with loyalist terrorists, with the result that there had been over 20 sectarian murders in Northern Ireland during the previous two years. There was also an allegation that a committee which included members of the Royal Ulster Constabulary was responsible for deciding that individuals believed to be republicans would be murdered.

9–121 One of the journalists made the subject of a disclosure order explained in his affidavit that he was acting under profound fear for his own safety and that of his family.[4] For several months they had been unable to live in their family home and were living in secure accommodation. He was not prepared, however, to escalate the risks they were facing by reneging on his undertakings of confidentiality.

9–122 The Court of Appeal acknowledged sympathy for the journalist. Nevertheless the "unhappy situation" in which he and his family found themselves could not

---

[99] Contained in Sch.5, para.8(1)(b) of the 2000 Act.
[1] *R. v K* (1984) 78 Cr.App.R. 82, 148 J.P. 410. The decision appears not to have been cited in *R. v Hasan* [2005] UKHL 22, [2005] 2 W.L.R. 709. See also *R. v Ayres* (1984) 15 C.C.C. (3d) 208 at 218–22 and *R. v Ruzic* (2001) 155 C.C.C. (3d) 1, where the constitutionality of the requirements of imminence and immediacy was challenged unsuccessfully. See paras 3–250 *et seq*.
[2] *R. v Hudson and Taylor* [1971] 2 Q.B. 202. But see *R. v Hasan* [2005] UKHL 22, [2005] 2 W.L.R. 709 at [22] and [27] where that decision was criticised by Lord Bingham, since he thought that the threat in that case had not been sufficiently imminent and immediate.
[3] [1993] 2 All E.R. 517.
[4] It is reasonably clear that threats to the defendant's family or to a person for whose safety he would reasonably regard himself as responsible qualify for the purposes of the law of duress as relevant threats: *R. v Hasan* [2005] UKHL 22, [2005] 2 W.L.R. 709 at [21] citing *Wright* [2000] Crim. L.R. 510.

be a justification for failing to comply with an order of the court[5]: "If [he] is going to be involved in running a company which conducts the production of investigatory television programmes of the sort that was transmitted by Channel Four..., then he must be prepared not to hide behind the consequences which can flow from this sort of activity".

How far this response is in accordance with the general law of duress requires careful consideration. The law as explained in *R. v Fitzpatrick*[6] is to the effect that, if one joins a violent gang or some similar organisation, the defence of duress is unavailable. As the Court of Criminal Appeal (Northern Ireland) there expressed it: 9–123

> "If a person behaves immorally by, for example, committing himself to an unlawful conspiracy, he ought not to be able to take advantage of the pressure exercised on him by his fellow criminals in order to put on when it suits him the breastplate of righteousness".

In *R. v Shepherd*,[7] it was held by the Court of Appeal that the question to be asked is whether the defendant knew, when he joined, that it was a violent organisation and that he was submitting *himself* to the risk of compulsion. The question (normally for the jury) would be whether he knew of the propensity for violence on the part of those with whom he was dealing (and, for example, whether he would be likely to be required himself to commit criminal acts).[8] 9–124

There seems to be no reason in principle why, even when the criteria laid down in s.10 of the Contempt of Court Act have been fulfilled, a journalist should not pray in aid a defence of this kind in appropriate circumstances. In a situation such as that which arose in *DPP v Channel Four Television Co Ltd*, however, the argument is almost certainly going to be met with the rejoinder that the journalist has voluntarily placed himself in his predicament and cannot therefore take advantage of it. It is yet to be resolved how the court would view the argument in a case where, unlike that of *Fitzpatrick*, the investigative journalist could not be said to be behaving "immorally". 9–125

III. THE FOUR STATUTORY EXCEPTIONS FURTHER ANALYSED

A. Necessity "in the interests of justice": two views

The expression in the section "in the interests of justice" echoes language used in such earlier decisions as *Att-Gen v Mulholland*[9] and *British Steel Corporation* 9–126

---

[5] *per* Woolf L.J. at 531f.
[6] [1977] N.I.L.R. 20.
[7] (1988) 86 Cr.App.R. 47. And see *R. v Sharp* [1987] Q.B. 853. The principle was supported in the Law Commission's Report, *Legislating the Criminal Code* (Law Com. No.218, 1993) which provided that the defence of duress is not applicable to "... a person who has knowingly and without reasonable excuse exposed himself to the risk of such a threat." See now *R. v Hasan* [2005] UKHL 22, [2005] 2 W.L.R. 709.
[8] *R. v Ali* [1995] Crim. L.R. 303; *R. v Hasan* [2005] UKHL 22, [2005] 2 W.L.R. 709 at [33].
[9] [1963] 2 Q.B. 477 at 489–90, CA.

9–126   *v Granada Television Ltd.*[10] The phrase did not appear in the original draft clause moved by Lord Scarman,[11] being introduced by way of amendment.[12] It is perhaps a more elusive concept than the other exceptions, "national security" and "the prevention of disorder or crime", and it may not sit too comfortably alongside them. It has been suggested that there will generally be an almost automatic preponderance in any balancing exercise so far as those are concerned.[13] Yet "interests of justice" is more elastic and susceptible to differences of interpretation.[14] There will inevitably remain a degree of uncertainty, therefore, as to the outcome of applications for disclosure based upon this ground; for that reason it is particularly likely to have a continuing "chilling" effect.[15] Moreover, the exception in favour of "the interests of justice" is not reflected in the exceptions contained within Art.10(2) of the European Convention on Human Rights. It was pointed out by Lord Phillips M.R. in *Ashworth Hospital Authority v MGN Ltd*[16] that the courts should approach the interpretation of s.10 in such a way, so far as possible, as (i) to equate the specific purposes for which disclosure of source is permitted under s.10 with the "legitimate aims" under Art.10, and (ii) to apply the same test of necessity as that applied by the European Court of Human Rights when considering Art.10.

9–127   These words were cited and followed by the Court of Appeal in *Interbrew SA v Financial Times Ltd.*[17] Interbrew is a Belgian beer manufacturer and was seeking documents in order to help track down the person responsible for distributing false information. Someone had obtained a copy of a confidential presentation from financial advisers, containing information about a possible takeover bid, and then inserted false market-sensitive information before sending it on to various news organisations. The source was held to pose a continuing threat, so long as he remained unidentified, both to Interbrew and to the security of the market in its shares. This gave rise to a "pressing need" for Art.10 purposes. The *Norwich Pharmacal* principle was applied and an order made for the original documents to be handed over.

---

[10] [1981] A.C. 1096 at 1169E–F, 1179D, 1196B–F, 1203A–B.
[11] *Hansard*, H.L., Vol. 416 (5th series), col. 210.
[12] Lord Morris in *Hansard*, H.L., Vol. 417 (5th series), col. 153, February 10, 1981.
[13] See, *e.g.* Lord Bridge in *X Ltd v Morgan-Grampian (Publishers) Ltd* [1991] 1 A.C. 1 at 43. Compare the discussion of legal professional privilege by Lord Taylor C.J. in *R. v Derby Magistrates' Court Ex p. B* [1996] 1 A.C. 487 at 508, where he said in that context "... if a balancing exercise was ever required in the case of legal professional privilege, it was performed once and for all in the 16th century, and since then has applied across the board in every case, irrespective of the client's individual merits".
[14] See, *e.g.* the comments of Lindsay J. in *Saunders v Punch Ltd* [1998] 1 W.L.R. 986 at 994, 1 All E.R. 234 at 242, comparing the discussion of Lord Bridge on "national security" and "the prevention of crime" in *X Ltd v Morgan-Grampian (Publishers) Ltd* with what he said about "the interests of justice".
[15] See, *e.g.* the discussion of *Camelot Group plc v Centaur Communications Ltd* [1999] Q.B. 124 in paras 9–135 *et seq.*
[16] [2001] 1 W.L.R. 515 at 532–3.
[17] [2002] EWCA Civ 274, [2002] 2 Lloyd's Rep. 229. See also *Mersey Care NHS Trust v Robin Ackroyd* [2002] EWHC 2115, QB, [2003] EWCA Civ 663, [2003] E.M.L.R. 36.

The Four Statutory Exceptions Further Analysed   9–131

There are at least two possible interpretations of the expression "interests of justice",[18] each reflected in separate House of Lords decisions; it can be construed as referring only to particular proceedings pending in a court of law, or to the interests of justice more widely.   9–128

In *Secretary of State for Defence v Guardian Newspapers Ltd*,[19] Lord Diplock (*obiter*) preferred the narrower view: 9–129

> "The exceptions include no reference to the 'public interest' generally and I would add that in my view the expression 'justice', the interests of which are entitled to protection, is not used in a general sense as the antonym of 'injustice' but in a technical sense of the administration of justice in the course of legal proceedings in a court of law... [The expression 'interests of justice']... refers to the administration of justice in particular legal proceedings already in existence or, in the type of 'bill of discovery' case... exemplified by the *Norwich Pharmacal Co v Customs and Excise Commissioners* [1974] A.C. 133... a particular civil action which it is proposed to bring against a wrongdoer whose identity has not yet been ascertained. I find it difficult to envisage a civil action in which section 10 of the Act would be relevant other than one of defamation or for detention of goods where the goods, as in the instant case and in *British Steel Corporation v Granada Television Ltd* [1981] A.C. 1096, consist of or include documents that have been supplied to the media in breach of confidence."

This seems to have been the approach which was followed by Rose J. in *X v Y*.[20] The case concerned the disclosure of confidential information about general practitioners suffering from AIDS. The information, obtained from hospital records, was apparently sold to newspaper reporters by one or more employees of the plaintiff health authority. The second defendants published an article written by the first defendant headed "Scandal of Docs with AIDS", which implied that the Department of Health and Social Security wished to suppress the fact that some doctors were continuing to practise despite having contracted AIDS. The health authority, on learning that it was intended to identify the doctors concerned in a subsequent article, sought an injunction to restrain the publication and also an order for disclosure of the sources.   9–130

It was argued (albeit "somewhat faintly") that it was in the interests of justice that the identity of the source should be revealed, with a view to ensuring that there would be no further leaking of such sensitive information. The judge however cited the first sentence of the above passage from the speech of Lord Diplock and concluded that, because the identity of the source was not necessary to support the claim for an injunction preventing further publication, its disclosure was not necessary "in the interests of justice". He therefore went on to address what he considered to be the "real question", namely whether the applicants had brought themselves within the other exception relating to "the prevention of crime".[21]   9–131

---

[18] For example, at the Court of Appeal stage in *X Ltd v Morgan-Grampian (Publishers) Ltd* [1991] 1 A.C. 1 at 28, Lord Donaldson M.R. considered various possible constructions all of which were confined to "the interests of the *administration* of justice".
[19] [1985] A.C. 339 at 350B.
[20] [1988] 2 All E.R. 648 at 661–2.
[21] Further discussed in this context at para.9–189.

9–132 Similarly, in *Handmade Films (Productions) Ltd v Express Newspapers Ltd*,[22] Browne-Wilkinson V.-C. sought to give effect to the construction of Lord Diplock and, although he had some difficulty in fully working out the implications, concluded that it would be necessary to come within the "interests of justice" that the identity of the source was required for the purposes of taking legal proceedings. He held that it was " . . . not apparently any longer sufficient in order to comply with the requirements of s.10, that the purpose is merely to identify the wrongdoer against whom an action might be brought".

9–133 Later, by way of contrast, Lord Bridge in *X Ltd v Morgan-Grampian (Publishers) Ltd* preferred the wider construction[23]:

> "To construe justice as an antonym of 'injustice' in section 10 would be far too wide. But to confine it to the 'technical sense of the administration of justice in the course of legal proceedings in a court of law' seems to me, with all due respect to any dictum of Lord Diplock,[24] to be too narrow. It is, in my opinion, 'in the interests of justice', in this sense in which this phrase is used in section 10, that persons should be enabled to exercise important legal rights and to protect themselves from serious legal wrongs whether or not resort to legal proceedings in a court of law will be necessary to attain these objectives. Thus, to take a very obvious example, if an employer of a large staff is suffering grave damage from the activities of an unidentified disloyal servant, it is undoubtedly in the interests of justice that he should be able to identify him in order to terminate his contract of employment, *notwithstanding that no legal proceedings may be necessary to achieve that end*." (emphasis added)

9–134 Lord Oliver[25] supported the broader interpretation:

> "The interest of the public in the administration of justice must, in my opinion, embrace its interest in the maintenance of a system of law, within the framework of which every citizen has the ability and the freedom to exercise his legal right to remedy a wrong done to him or to prevent it being done, whether or not through the medium of legal proceedings."

9–135 It was this broader construction that was adopted by the Court of Appeal in *Camelot Group plc v Centaur Communications Ltd*.[26] This also concerned information released by a disloyal employee to journalists. The plaintiff company had been authorised to run the National Lottery pursuant to licence. A draft preliminary financial statement was prepared with a view to release shortly afterwards, and it was these draft accounts that were sent to the journalist. An article was published by him in a magazine with the heading "Camelot chiefs' pay soars as good cause funds fall". There was also reference to "huge payouts for directors," which were said to be likely to spark a "fat cats" storm.

---

[22] [1986] F.S.R. 463 at 470. But see the comments of Owen J. in *Totalise v Motley Fool* [2001] E.M.L.R. 750 who declined to follow this interpretation.
[23] At 43.
[24] In *Secretary of State for Defence v Guardian Newspapers Ltd* [1985] A.C. 339 at 350, as cited in para.9–129.
[25] [1991] 1 A.C. 1 at 54.
[26] [1999] Q.B. 124, para.9–164.

The judge and the Court of Appeal ordered that the source be disclosed 9–136
because of a continuing threat of further breaches of confidence. While it was
expressly recognised that there was no longer any threat posed by further
disclosure of the draft accounts themselves, there was said to be "unease and
suspicion amongst the employees of the company which inhibits good working
relationships". The court accepted the argument that an employee who had
proved untrustworthy in one regard might also prove disloyal in other respects;
such a person might reveal, for example, the name of a hypothetical "public
figure" who had won a huge lottery prize. Thus, it is clear that the court was
concerned to protect Camelot's legitimate interest in enforcing an obligation of
loyalty and confidentiality, even though there might be no need to bring legal
proceedings to achieve that objective.

It may be noted that even the majority in the European Court in *Goodwin v* 9–137
United Kingdom,[27] when considering the reasoning of Lord Bridge in *X Ltd*, did
not suggest that his wider interpretation of "interests of justice" would be *per se*
inconsistent with the terms of Art.10 of the Convention. They confined
themselves to concluding, *on the facts of the case*, that disclosure was not
necessary.

In *Ashworth Hospital Authority v MGN Ltd*,[28] Lord Phillips M.R. concluded 9–138
that both interpretations of 'interests of justice' are consistent with Art.10 but that
Lord Bridge's interpretation accords more happily with its scheme:

"Thus 'interests of justice' in section 10 mean interests that are justiciable. I cannot
readily envisage any such interest that would not fall within one or more of the
catalogue of legitimate aims in article 10. In the present case Ashworth could argue that
its claim for identification of the source is in the interests of the protection of health, the
protection of rights of others and preventing the disclosure of information received in
confidence".

When the *Ashworth* case was before the House of Lords,[29] Lord Woolf 9–139
highlighted that Lord Oliver in the *Morgan-Grampian* case[30] had questioned
Lord Diplock's narrower construction of "the interests of justice" and had
regarded it as imposing a limitation not easily defensible in logic. Although
MGN in the *Ashworth* case was advancing the argument that "the interests of
justice" exception should, after all, be limited to cases where disclosure was
required for existing or intended proceedings,[31] this argument did not prevail.
The so-called "section 10 issue" was thus resolved in favour of the applicants.
Lord Woolf referred to the use of the phrase in *British Steel Corporation v
Granada Television Ltd*,[32] albeit pre-dating the enactment of the Contempt of
Court Act 1981 itself, and he concluded that there was no justification for
construing the concept inconsistently with the opinions there expressed (in

---

[27] (1996) 22 E.H.R.R 123.
[28] [2001] 1 W.L.R. 515 at 533 at [80]–[84], [2001] 1 All E.R. 991 at 1008–9.
[29] [2002] UKHL 29, [2002] 1 W.L.R. 2033 at [40]–[49].
[30] [1991] 1 A.C. at 53–4.
[31] At [23].
[32] [1981] A.C. 1096.

9–139 particular, by Lords Wilberforce and Fraser of Tullybelton). Lord Woolf pointed out that the narrower construction (of Lord Diplock) would result in proceedings having to be brought for purely technical reasons. The phrase "interests of justice" is not, of course, directly reflected in the European Convention on Human Rights itself. Where there are court proceedings of some kind, the revelation of a source might in some circumstances be relevant to protecting the rights defined in Art.6 of the Convention and/or justified by reference to the specific exception in Art.10(2) relating to the maintenance of the authority and impartiality of the judiciary. Where, however, as in *Ashworth*, such an order is made in circumstances where no proceedings are in contemplation, Art.6 considerations would not be relevant. Where the court is concerned with employers who wish to guard against leaks by untrustworthy staff, it may be relevant to the Art.10(2) exception concerning the prevention of "disclosure of information received in confidence". Lord Phillips M.R. in *Ashworth* at the Court of Appeal stage had highlighted the need for the courts to reconcile the public policy considerations underlying s.10 of the 1981 Act with those of Art.10 and to achieve consistency.[33] Nevertheless, it may be supposed that the broader interpretation is unlikely to be challenged now and that it is the one which will continue to prevail. Lord Phillips himself recognised that both interpretations of "interests of justice" are consistent with Art.10.[34]

9–140 The reasoning of the appellate courts was applied by Gray J. in *Mersey Care NHS Trust v Robin Ackroyd*,[35] which bore a "striking similarity". The order made in the *MGN* case had the effect of revealing Mr Ackroyd as the intermediary in respect of the information about Ian Brady, but the original source at Ashworth Hospital was still obscure. Summary judgment was therefore sought and granted against Mr Ackroyd. The judge concluded that the balance was struck in the same way as in the *MGN* case. If the application had been refused, that earlier order would have been subverted. Nevertheless, the decision was overruled by the Court of Appeal.[36] This was because the judge had not carried out correctly the balancing exercise between s.10 of the Contempt of Court Act and Art.10 of the Convention. The case should not have been determined summarily because (a) the appellant's source might have had a public interest defence, and (b) the judge should not have brushed aside the fact that the source had received no payment. Carnwath L.J. also pointed out that the Court of Appeal on that occasion (in May 2003) had to take the position as it then stood. The *MGN* case had unfortunately proceeded all the way to the House of Lords on a mistaken assumption, namely that disclosure would produce the desired result of identifying the culprit. There was no evidence that the "cloud of suspicion" was still blighting activity at the hospital; it was by no means clear that there was still "a pressing social need" to identify the perpetrator more then three years on from the material events. It was certainly not a matter for summary judgment. Ward

---

[33] See paras 9–126, 9–245.
[34] [2001] 1 W.L.R. 515 at 533 at [80]–[84]. See para.9–138.
[35] [2002] EWHC 2115 (QB).
[36] [2003] EWCA Civ 663, [2003] E.M.L.R. 36.

L.J. said that he was left "feeling uncomfortable" that the *prima facie* case for non-disclosure should be set aside without a full investigation of the facts.

B. The significance of "public interest"

A distinction between the approach of Lord Diplock in *Secretary of State for Defence v Guardian Newspapers Ltd* and that of the Court of Appeal in *Camelot* needs to be considered. It was said in *Camelot* by Mummery L.J. that "no public interest is served in shielding this source from exposure".[37] Schiemann L.J. also asked the general question: "Is it in the public interest for people in his position to disclose this type of information?"[38] He emphasised too that the court was not considering "a case of disclosing iniquity or a whistle blowing case". In *John Reid Enterprises Ltd v Pell*,[39] a case in which Carnwath J. decided to order disclosure, one of the factors he took into account was that he was not dealing with a "case where you could suggest that there is enormous public interest in the further information coming out . . . It is difficult to suggest that Elton John's finances are a matter of major public importance". 9–141

By contrast, Lord Diplock had pointed out that there is no general exception to what he had described as the "statutory right"[40] conferred by s.10 based upon "public interest" *simpliciter*. Disclosure can only be justified if shown to be "necessary" in the interests of justice or national security, or for the prevention of disorder or crime.[41] Similarly, when in *X Ltd v Morgan Grampian (Publishers) Ltd* Lord Bridge observed that disclosure of a source can only be justified by reference to some necessity which arises out of concern for a "matter of high public importance", he made it clear that any such matter had to fall within one of the statutory exceptions identified. That being so, it is difficult to see how it can be relevant, in assessing the issue of necessity for disclosure of the source, to consider whether the information disclosed has any inherent public interest, or indeed whether protection of the particular source can in itself be shown to serve the public interest. 9–142

There is, according to Lord Bridge, a primary assumption that protection of sources is itself a matter of high public importance.[42] That is not qualified by reference to how important the information that has been revealed may be. It would appear, therefore, that the absence of public interest ought not in itself to 9–143

---

[37] [1999] Q.B. 124 at 139H.
[38] *ibid.* at 138B.
[39] [1999] E.M.L.R. 675 at 680.
[40] *Secretary of State for Defence v Guardian Newspapers Ltd* [1985] 1 A.C. 339 at 345C.
[41] In *Secretary of State for Defence v Guardian Newspapers Ltd* [1985] A.C. 339 at 368, Lord Roskill observed that he could " . . . see no reason for adding to those four specific exceptions by cutting down the natural and unqualified meaning of the section's opening words".
[42] [1991] 1 A.C. 1 at 41. See also *Re an Inquiry Under the Company Securities (Insider Dealing) Act 1985* [1988] A.C. 660 at 703, where Lord Griffiths referred to a "presumption" in the passage cited at para.9–79.

9–143 weigh in favour of disclosure in determining whether the criterion of necessity has been fulfilled.[43]

9–144 On the other hand, once it is has been established to the court's satisfaction that the interests of justice require disclosure (as the judge and Court of Appeal did conclude in *Camelot* itself), then such factors as public importance or triviality might come into play as being relevant to the exercise of a residual discretion. It might, for example, be thought in an individual case that there was a necessity for the employer to know who was leaking his information ("in the interests of justice") but, nevertheless, that there was such public importance in the information disclosed that the source ought to be protected in the wider public interest.

9–145 The potential role of "public interest" was addressed by Laws L.J.at the Court of Appeal stage in *Ashworth Hospital Authority v MGN Ltd*[44]:

> "It is in my judgment of the first importance to recognise that the potential vice—the 'chilling effect'—of court orders requiring the disclosure of press sources is in no way lessened, and certainly not abrogated, simply because the case is one in which the information actually published is of no legitimate, objective public interest. Nor is it to the least degree lessened or abrogated by the fact (where it is so) that the source is a disloyal and greedy individual, prepared for money to betray his employer's confidences. The public interest in non-disclosure of press sources is constant, whatever the merits of the particular publication, and the particular source".

9–146 A different view was expressed, however, by Sedley L.J. in *Interbrew SA v Financial Times Ltd.*[45] He drew a distinction between the source's *motive* and, on the other hand, his *purpose*. He regarded the former as "immaterial to the legal issues" (and likely to be unascertainable in any event). By contrast, he considered the "purpose" of the source to be a matter on which the court should attempt to form the best view it can. To that extent (as he put it), he did not agree with the remarks of Laws L.J. in *Ashworth* to the effect that it is of no consequence that the information "may be of no legitimate objective public interest". This passage, like some of the remarks in *Camelot*, may lead to uncertainty and confusion. It perhaps reflects the rather old fashioned tendency to "balance" factors,[46] whereas to be effective the purity of the journalist's right to withhold the source should not be diluted. It is suggested that it is always *prima facie* contrary to the public interest that press sources should be disclosed under compulsion; in any given case, the question to be considered is whether

---

[43] This is no part of the statutory formulation, any more than, for example, s.5 of the Contempt of Court Act on "discussion of public affairs" requires the court to consider whether the prejudicial material was "necessary" to the discussion in question: *Att-Gen v English* [1983] 1 A.C. 116 at 143.

[44] [2001] 1 W.L.R. 515 at 537 at [101], [2001] 1 All E.R. 991 at 1012g. These words were cited by the Court of Appeal in *Mersey Care NHS Trust v Ackroyd* [2003] EWCA Civ 663, [2003] E.M.L.R. 36 at [10]. See also the words of Lord Woolf in *A v B plc* [2002] EWCA Civ 337, [2003] Q.B. 195 at [11(iv)] of his guidelines.

[45] [2002] EWCA Civ 274, [2002] 2 Lloyd's Rep 229, E.M.L.R. 24.

[46] See paras 9–16 *et seq.*

there is an overriding public interest, amounting to a pressing social need, to which source protection must be subordinated.

C. "Interests of justice" considered by the European Court of Human Rights

The background to the case of *X Ltd v Morgan-Grampian (Publishers) Ltd*[47] was that a trainee journalist (Goodwin) was given information on an unattributable basis about the highly confidential financial affairs of a company (Tetra). This was held by Hoffmann J. to have been obtained from a secret draft corporate plan, the plan having disappeared, although Mr Goodwin maintained that he had no reason to believe that the information derived from a stolen or confidential document. He telephoned Tetra to check certain facts, but the company promptly sought, and was given, an *ex parte* injunction restraining publication, on the ground that publication would lead to a loss of confidence on the part of customers, suppliers and other creditors. An order was also made when the matter came before Hoffmann J. *inter partes* that Goodwin should disclose his notes which would identify the source of his information, on the basis of the decision in *Norwich Pharmacal Co v Customs and Excise Commissioners*.[48] Hoffmann J. ruled that it was "necessary in the interests of justice" that disclosure be made.

The Court of Appeal had declined to hear Goodwin because of his continuing failure to comply and dismissed the appeal.[49] The House of Lords held unanimously that the court had jurisdiction to make such an order. The reasoning was that the defendants were "mixed up in the tortious acts" of the source.[50] This concept was further discussed in *Ashworth Hospital Authority v MGN Ltd*[51] where it was held that this equitable jurisdiction is not confined to cases of "tortious acts" and is flexible enough to embrace other forms of wrongdoing, such as breach of confidence; it could also be employed where the defendant was not "innocently mixed up" but a wrongdoer himself.

Lord Woolf explained in the House of Lords[52] that although the Master of the Rolls was "almost certainly correct" in concluding, on the facts, that a claim for breach of confidence would lie against MGN Ltd, the intermediary and the original source of the information relating to the patient, such a finding would not be necessary for the determination of the *Norwich Pharmacal* issue:

"It is sufficient that the source was a wrongdoer and MGN became involved in the wrongdoing which is incontestably the position. Whether the source's wrongdoing was

---

[47] [1991] 1 A.C. 1, HL. See I. Cram, "When the 'interests of justice' outweigh freedom of expression" (1992) 55 M.L.R. 400.
[48] [1974] A.C. 133. On the law, procedure and practice relating to *Norwich Pharmacal* orders, see P. Matthews and H.M. Malek, *Disclosure* (2001); C. Hollander, *Documentary Evidence* (8th ed., 2003), ch.5.
[49] For a discussion of this aspect of the case, see paras 12–66 *et seq.*
[50] A phrase of Lord Reid in *Norwich Pharmacal Co v Customs and Exercise Commissioners* [1974] A.C. 133 at 175.
[51] [2001] 1 W.L.R. 515 at 529–30, [2001] 1 All E.R. 991 at [61]–[66].
[52] [2002] UKHL 29, [2002] 1 W.L.R. 2033 at [34].

9–149

tortious, or in breach of contract in my judgment matters not. If there was wrongdoing then there was no further requirement that [the journalist's] and MGN's conduct should also be wrongful. It is sufficient if ... there was 'involvement or participation' ".

The need for involvement is a "threshold requirement" but in any given case the discretion should only be exercised in favour of disclosure where it has been shown to be "a necessary and proportionate response".[53] The fact that the patient in question (Ian Brady) might already have brought some of the information into the public domain would not affect the primary issue as to whether it was necessary for the applicant authority to track any employee who had, in breach of contract, revealed confidential information—although it would clearly be a relevant factor if Brady himself were pursuing a remedy for breach of confidence.

9–150 The decision of House of Lords in *X Ltd v Morgan-Grampian (Publishers) Ltd* was challenged before the European Commission and, ultimately, the European Court of Human Rights.[54] The court held by a majority that there was indeed a breach of Art.10 of the Convention in the making of the disclosure order. The proceedings against Goodwin and his employers had two purposes: (1) to prevent dissemination of damaging information about the commercial interests of the company, whose business plan had been (in all probability) stolen by the source, and (2) "unmasking a disloyal employee or collaborator, who might have continuing access to its premises, in order to terminate his or her association with the company."[55]

9–151 So far as the first of these objectives was concerned, the courts in England had granted interim relief in the form of injunctions prohibiting Goodwin and his employers from further dissemination of the financial information, although naturally not against the source himself. The second objective was not regarded by the majority in the European Court as being a sufficient reason to order disclosure. It was not enough[56]:

" ... to show merely that he or she will be unable without disclosure to exercise the legal right or avert the threatened legal wrong on which he or she bases his or her claim in order to establish the necessity of disclosure ... In that connection, the Court would recall that the considerations to be taken into account by the Convention institutions for the review under paragraph 2 of Article 10 tip the balance of competing interests in favour of the interest of democratic society in securing a free press.[57] On the facts of the present case,[58] the Court cannot find that Tetra's interests in eliminating, by proceedings against the source, that residual threat of damage through dissemination of the confidential information otherwise than by the press, in obtaining compensation and

---

[53] See *ibid.* at [36], [61]–[62] and [73].
[54] *Sub nom. Goodwin v The United Kingdom* (1996) E.H.R.R. 123.
[55] (1996) 22 E.H.R.R. 123 at [44].
[56] *ibid.* at [45] and [46].
[57] See the speech of Lord Bridge in *X Ltd v Morgan-Grampian (Publishers) Ltd* [1991] A.C. 1, cited in para.9–33.
[58] It was emphasised in *Camelot Group plc v Centaur Communications Ltd* [1999] Q.B. 124, by Schiemann L.J. that there should not be thought to be any rule of universal application in cases concerning employers and disloyal employees; he highlighted this passage in the European Court's judgment.

in unmasking a disloyal employee or collaboration were, even if considered cumulatively, sufficient to outweigh the vital public interest in the protection of the applicant journalist's source. The Court does not therefore consider that the further purposes served by the disclosure order, when measured against the standards imposed by the Convention, amount to an overriding requirement in the public interest.

In sum, there was not, in the Court's view, a reasonable relationship of proportionality between the legitimate aim pursued by the disclosure order and the means deployed to achieve that aim. The restriction which the disclosure order entailed on the applicant journalist's exercise of his freedom of expression cannot therefore be regarded as having been necessary in a democratic society, within the meaning of paragraph 2 of Article 10, for the protection of Tetra's rights under English law, notwithstanding the margin of appreciation available to the national authorities."

It was emphasised by Schiemann L.J. in *Camelot Group plc v Centaur Communications Ltd*[59] that the different conclusions reached in the European Court and in the House of Lords did not mean that there was necessarily any distinction in the test or principles applied:

9–152

"In my judgment the tests which the European Court of Human Rights and the House of Lords applied were substantially the same. I am conscious that they reached different conclusions on the same facts but this is a no more surprising legal phenomenon than this court concluding that a particular course of conduct amounted to negligence when the court of first instance concluded that the very same course of conduct did *not* amount to negligence."

Yet, in the same case, Thorpe L.J. made the interesting comment that there had been a lapse of six years between the performance of the balancing exercise in London and that in Strasbourg. He continued: "In such a period standards fundamental to the performance of the balancing exercise may change materially." This implies that there may have been rather more to the divergence between the approach of the majority in *Goodwin* and that of the House of Lords in *X Ltd* than a mere difference of personal judgment. The implication of his remarks is that their Lordships might have reached a different value judgment on the same facts had they fallen for consideration in 1996, or later, because of a change in standards. That is to say, the influence of the Convention itself may have tipped the scales rather more heavily in favour of the protection of journalists' sources.

9–153

D. The Government's response to the ruling of the European Court of Human Rights

On several occasions since the European Court delivered judgment in the *Goodwin* case, the government has been asked through questions in the House of

9–154

---

[59] [1999] Q.B. 124 at 135F. In *Ashworth Hospital Authority v MGN Ltd* [2001] 1 W.L.R. 515 at 536 at [96]–[97], [2001] 1 All E.R. 991 at 1012a the Master of the Rolls expressed agreement with this passage in the judgment of Schiemann L.J. An argument had been advanced to the effect that the divergence between their Lordships and the European Court could not be accounted for merely on the basis of a difference of view, because the margin of appreciation would have prevented such an outcome, but this appears to have been rejected. The point does not seem to have been pursued in the House of Lords: [2002] UKHL 29, [2002] 1 W.L.R. 2033.

Lords about its intentions. What action did the government intend to take?[60] Did it intend to give legislative effect to the decision, and if not, why not?[61] Were the courts obliged to interpret the relevant provisions of English law in accordance with the judgment of the European Court of Human Rights?[62] In the Commons also, it was asked what plans the government might have to amend s.10.[63] The then government's attitude was non-committal. Since the court did not award any financial compensation, it was said that no action was required. The government's provisional view was that no change was required, and that it would be for the courts to say what weight should be attached to the judgment of the European Court.[64]

E. Later judicial developments

9–155   Although at that stage the European Convention was not part of English law, it is clear from such cases as *Chief Constable of Leicestershire v Garavelli*,[65] *Camelot Group plc v Centaur Communications Ltd*,[66] and *Saunders v Punch Ltd*[67] that the closest attention was being paid to the guidance of the European Court decisions. On the other hand, it is not easy to conclude that there was uniformity of approach in these cases towards the decision in *Goodwin v United Kingdom*,[68] and each of them needs therefore to be considered in rather more detail.

1. *Chief Constable of Leicestershire v Garavelli*

9–156   An article was published in the *Newcastle Journal* written by its chief reporter Ms Garavelli under the heading "Lost Crimes Probed", which alleged that crime figures were being "massaged". In particular, it was suggested that in one month alone 20 incidents, reported as attempted burglary and theft, were being written off in police records as "no crimes". The article quoted the local member of Parliament who said that he would be writing to the Chief Constable on the matter. Disciplinary proceedings were brought against a police superintendent by the Chief Constable of Northumbria because he was suspected of having leaked the figures upon which the article was based. The hearing was conducted by the Chief Constable of Leicestershire, who had the benefit of counsel's advice throughout.

---

[60] *Hansard*, H.L., Vol. 571, (5th series), col. 47 (W.A.), April 3, 1996.
[61] *Hansard*, H.L., Vol. 571, (5th series), col. 62, (W.A), April 16, 1996.
[62] *Hansard*, H.L., Vol. 571, (5th series), col. 121 (W.A.), April 29, 1996.
[63] *Hansard*, H.C., Vol. 276, col. 57, April 23, 1996.
[64] The answers are to be found appended to the questions annotated in the above footnotes. In reply to a further question from Lord Lester Q.C., the Lord Chancellor in the succeeding government stated that "The *Goodwin* judgment is still under consideration by the Committee of Ministers pursuant to Article 54 of the Convention": *Hansard*, H.L., Vol. 582 (5th series), col. 175, (W.A.), October 14, 1997.
[65] [1997] E.M.L.R. 543, DC.
[66] [1999] Q.B. 124.
[67] [1998] 1 W.L.R. 986, 1 All E.R. 234, Ch. D., Lindsay J.
[68] (1996) 22 E.H.R.R. 123.

Ms Garavelli had made it clear from the outset that the superintendent in question had *not* been her source, but she was asked by defence counsel in the course of the enquiry who her source had been. She declined to answer because of her obligation of confidentiality. The chairman was then advised by counsel that he had a discretion whether to require an answer, and that it was for him to decide whether it was necessary that she answer the questions "in the interests of the administration of justice". The chairman decided in the affirmative, but Ms Garavelli persisted in her refusal. The chairman having heard submissions came to the conclusion that unless she was pressed and her evidence, as he put it, "tested in cross-examination" he might never feel able to find the superintendent guilty beyond all reasonable doubt. He was satisfied that there was a *prima facie* case, but it was entirely based upon inference, against which he had to consider her unequivocal denial that the accused officer had been the source.

9–157

The two Chief Constables launched an application before the Divisional Court for Ms Garavelli to be punished for contempt of court. It was suggested that she had been in breach of an order of the High Court, although the only relevant order was the *subpoena ad testificandum* issued on the authority of the High Court to compel her attendance before the disciplinary hearing, and that she had obeyed. There was a lack of particularity, therefore, as to the nature of her contempt, but the Divisional Court proceeded to consider whether her refusal to answer the questions could itself be criticised.

9–158

One of the difficulties confronting the applicants was that those conducting the disciplinary proceedings against the superintendent had chosen not to call her to support the case against him. She was a defence witness (and thus, in any event, could not be cross-examined by the counsel who had asked her the crucial question). In those circumstances, it was difficult for them to argue that her evidence, and particularly that relating to the identity of her source, could be said to be "necessary" to the conduct of the proceedings.

9–159

The issue in the disciplinary proceedings was not, in general terms, who had been Ms Garavelli's source, but rather whether it had been proved beyond reasonable doubt that it was the superintendent. There was thus a difficulty in identifying and defining the issue for the resolution of which the disclosure was said to be necessary.[69] As Tasker Watkins L.J. had observed in *Att-Gen v Lundin*,[70] " ... that which is useless cannot conceivably be said to be necessary".

9–160

There was also the unresolved question as to whether a question going only to credit should ever be made the subject of an order for disclosure. It is submitted that it is extremely doubtful.

9–161

The Divisional Court judgment cited a number of extracts from the decision of the European Court in *Goodwin v United Kingdom* as being "helpful" even though not binding. In particular, reference was made to the need for "the most

9–162

---

[69] See *Maxwell v Pressdram Ltd* [1987] 1 W.L.R. 298 at 309A, Kerr L.J. cited at para.9–89.
[70] (1982) 75 Cr.App.R. 90 at 99.

careful scrutiny by the court", as well as to the importance of protection of sources for press freedom and the potentially chilling effect of source disclosure. Significantly the court also referred to the need for "a reasonable relationship of proportionality between the legitimate aim pursued by the disclosure order and the means deployed to achieve that aim".

9–163   Following a careful review of the principles identified in both *X Ltd v Morgan-Grampian (Publishers) Ltd* and *Goodwin v United Kingdom*, Beldam L.J. summarised the position as follows:

> "[The Chairman] therefore had to decide whether he could draw the inference beyond reasonable doubt that Superintendent Cooper had disclosed the material to someone. He apparently regarded the evidence of Miss Garavelli that Superintendent Cooper had not disclosed the information to her, nor had she obtained her information from Miss Pikett [a mutual friend of Ms. Garavelli and the Superintendent] as causing him so much doubt that he might never feel able to find guilt beyond reasonable doubt. At that stage he had not heard evidence from Superintendent Cooper whose denials might further have fuelled the doubts he expressed. [The Chairman] would eventually have had to decide the question frequently decided by juries, as a matter of common sense, whether the inference which the Second Applicant was asking him to draw could reasonably be drawn in the light of the evidence of Miss Garavelli refuting the second important factor on which it was urged he should draw the inference.
>
> It is difficult to see, at that stage of the inquiry, how the interests of justice would then be served by requiring Miss Garavelli to name the person from whom she obtained her information. Further, [the Chairman] appears to have been under the impression that because the [second] applicant could not cross-examine about the sources, the weight to be attached to her testimony was affected.
>
> Such an approach would mean that in every case the interests of justice would be, to some degree, affected if a journalist exercised the right that Parliament has given to refuse to disclose his or her sources.
>
> For these reasons I am satisfied that in directing that Miss Garavelli should answer a question directed to disclosure of her source [the Chairman] was in error. I am satisfied that it was not shown, at that time, to be sufficiently necessary in the interests of justice to override the need to protect Miss Garavelli's source of information."

2. *Camelot Group plc v Centaur Communications Ltd*

9–164   In *Camelot*[71] too, the Court of Appeal acknowledged the importance of having regard to recent jurisprudence of the European Court.[72] They expressed the view also that there is no difference of principle as between s.10 of the 1981 Act, as applied within this jurisdiction, and Art.10 of the European Convention as applied by the European Court.[73] They considered that the only matter dividing the House of Lords in *X Ltd* from the majority of the European Court in *Goodwin* was the appreciation of individual factors relevant to the balancing exercise. This is inevitably likely to vary as between different tribunals.

---

[71] [1999] Q.B. 124. See para.9–135 where the facts of the decision are set out more fully.
[72] See para.9–3.
[73] See, *e.g.* Thorpe L.J. cited at para.9–8.

They came to the conclusion on the facts that the necessity for an order of disclosure had been convincingly established and, what is more, that the reasoning of the European Court in *Goodwin* would not have led to any different conclusion. Importance was attached to a continuing threat of damage of a type which was said not to have featured significantly in *Goodwin* or in *X Ltd*, namely unease and suspicion caused among Camelot employees, which was inhibiting good working relationships. There was also the perceived risk of further breaches of confidence and, particularly, in relation to the identity of future prize winners.[74] In the earlier case the concern was said by Schiemann L.J. to have been confined to the possibility of further disclosure of the information *already* revealed to Mr Goodwin.

The court was at pains to point out that there was no rule of general application which would always determine the outcome in the case of a disloyal employee. Each case would turn on its own facts. Yet where any employer is seeking to identify a "mole" in order to protect his legitimate interests, whether with a view to dismissal or transfer, or for the purposes of prospective litigation, the same argument could be raised to the effect that some future and unrelated breach of confidence might occur.

Moreover, in *Goodwin* itself, the European Court emphasised that the employer's interests in unmasking a disloyal employee or collaborator were *not* sufficient, on the facts of that case, even when considered cumulatively with other factors (such as, for example, obtaining compensation or eliminating the residual threat of the original confidential information being further disseminated *otherwise* than through the press) to outweigh the vital public interest in the protection of the journalist's source.

The importance of the distinction drawn by the Court of Appeal between the possible threat of further disclosure of the original confidential information and that of fresh disclosures might thus be somewhat overstated. One might even apply to the Court of Appeal's reasoning in *Camelot* the comment, adopting by way of analogy the words of Beldam L.J. in *Garavelli*,[75] that "such an approach would mean that in every case the interests of justice would be, to some degree, affected if a journalist exercised the right that Parliament has given to refuse to disclose his or her sources." In these circumstances, it may be questioned whether it is quite so obvious that the European Court would have come to the same conclusion as the Court of Appeal on the facts of *Camelot*.

We have already referred to the way in which the Court of Appeal dealt with what Schiemann L.J. described as the "important consideration" of the "chilling effect".[76] It is submitted that the uncertainties involved, in leaving a potential source to assess for himself the likely reaction of a court to an application for his identity to be revealed, would be unlikely to commend their approach to the European Court. The source of the difficulty may be that some English judges

---

[74] Schiemann L.J., [1999] Q.B. 124 at 137E.
[75] [1997] E.M.L.R. 543 at 556; considered in paras 9–156 *et seq.*
[76] paras 9–9 *et seq.*

9–169 were at that stage not giving sufficient weight to the presumption in favour of non-disclosure at the outset of the balancing exercise.[77]

9–170 Furthermore, we have drawn attention to the importance attached by the Court of Appeal in assessing "necessity" to the concept of the inherent "public interest", or lack of it, in the relevant confidential information.[78] That too may be thought to introduce extraneous factors, having regard to the wording of s.10 itself, and particularly in the light of Lord Diplock's comments in *Secretary of State for Defence v Guardian Newspapers Ltd*,[79] and those of Laws L.J. in *Ashworth Hospital Authority v MGN Ltd*,[80] to the effect that "public interest" is not a separate ground of exception.

3. Saunders v Punch Ltd

9–171 The weekly magazine *Punch* published an article referring to Mr Ernest Saunders who had been convicted of various criminal offences, and had subsequently successfully argued in the European Court of Human Rights[81] that his right to a fair trial had been infringed by the Crown's reliance upon material derived from interviews with Inspectors appointed by the Department of Trade and Industry. By 1997 interest was reviving in his case because of the imminent publication of the Inspectors' report. During the previous year he had received extracts from the draft report, upon which he had taken advice from counsel and solicitors. When the *Punch* article was published, Mr Saunders suspected that some of the confidential communications with his advisers had been leaked. He therefore began proceedings against the publishers.

9–172 An immediate interlocutory injunction restraining further publication was granted. In addition, however, Mr Saunders sought an order for disclosure of the sources upon which the article had been based. This was refused by Lindsay J. in the course of a detailed judgment[82] in which he considered the implications of the European Court's decision in *Goodwin*. He commented that it was necessary for the applicant to establish that disclosure was necessary upon one or more of the four statutory grounds, and took note of the fact that Parliament can hardly have forgotten "the high importance of the very long established right which a man has to the confidentiality of his privileged communications with his solicitors". Despite this, no exception had been created specifically to meet that consideration. He concluded that there was nothing to suggest " . . . that legal professional confidence is so massive that its protection or enforcement must inevitably and always preponderate in the required balancing exercise".[83]

---

[77] See paras 9–16 *et seq.*
[78] para.9–141.
[79] [1985] 1 A.C. 339 at 350B, cited in paras 9–129 *et seq.*
[80] Cited at para.9–145. See also *Mersey Care NHS Trust v Ackroyd* [2003] EWCA Civ 663, [2003] E.M.L.R. 36 at [25], where that passage in Laws L.J.'s judgment is cited and at [66]–[67] followed.
[81] *Saunders v United Kingdom* (1997) 23 E.H.R.R. 313.
[82] [1998] 1 W.L.R. 986, [1998] 1 All E.R. 234.
[83] [1998] 1 W.L.R. at 994 and [1998] 1 All E.R. at 242h. The judge did not lose sight of the fact that none of the s.10 cases dealt in terms with legal professional privilege.

He therefore applied the tests enunciated by Lord Bridge and Lord Oliver in **9–173** *X Ltd v Morgan-Grampian (Publishers) Ltd*,[84] and in particular whether the interests of justice in the particular case were shown to be so pressing as to require the absolute ban on disclosure to be overridden. He concluded that this had not been demonstrated. He bore in mind a number of considerations, including:

1. the factor of professional privilege was "made less weighty by the relative insubstantiality of foreseeable damage and the relative unlikelihood of repetition";

2. the possible prospect (albeit improbable) that evidence could emerge at trial that the confidentiality had already been lost by the plaintiff's dealings with other persons;

3. it was not suggested that the plaintiff's whole livelihood depended upon disclosure;

4. although there was some public interest in the publication of the information in question, it could not be described as "other than peripheral";

5. there was no suggestion that the publication could have been justified by reference to the revelation of "iniquity";

6. there was no evidence to suggest that there was any likelihood of further revelation by the source;

7. although the disclosure which had taken place might give the impression that Mr Saunders had been hypocritical, it would be out of all proportion to categorise any such damage as being "severe" or "very substantial".

The judge concluded that his decision could not fairly be described as giving **9–174** the "green light" to abuse of legal professional confidence, any more than the European Court in *Goodwin* could be described as giving the green light to theft. Indeed, he regarded his decision as very much on the facts of the particular case; he described his grant of the injunction as "a clear red signal".

The reasoning of the Court of Appeal in *Camelot Group plc v Centaur* **9–175** *Communications Ltd*[85] was to the effect that a person who had infringed an obligation of confidence once might easily do so again. (Lindsay J. did not have that decision available to him since it was handed down only some two weeks later.) On the other hand, the position may be rather different in a case where a disloyal employee has continuing access to his employer's confidential material, and thus could be described as "ticking away like a time bomb".[86] If someone had access merely to the confidential communications between Mr Saunders and his legal advisers, and there was truly (as the judge held) no evidence that further

---

[84] [1991] 1 A.C. 1 at 41 and 53 respectively.
[85] [1999] Q.B. 124.
[86] The expression used by Lord Donaldson M.R. in *X Ltd v Morgan-Grampian (Publishers) Ltd* [1991] 1 A.C. 1 at 28, CA.

revelations would take place, then there may be a significant distinction between these two situations.

9–176 Thus, it can be seen in the light of the above cases that the values of the European Convention had a considerable influence on the treatment by the courts of journalists' sources. After the Human Rights Act came into effect in October 2000, similar issues were considered in *Interbrew SA v Financial Times Ltd*[87] and *Ashworth Hospital Authority v MGN Ltd*[88] which are addressed elsewhere in this chapter in their appropriate contexts.

F. National security

9–177 To date, the only decision dealing with the "national security" exception in s.10 is *Secretary of State for Defence v Guardian Newpapers Ltd*.[89] Before the case reached the House of Lords, there had in fact been compliance by the defendants with the order made for disclosure of the relevant document, so that by that stage the person leaking the information had been identified as a young grade 10 clerk employed in the Foreign Secretary's private office. The leaked document was headed "Delivery of Cruise Missiles to R.A.F. Greenham Common— Parliamentary and Public Statements".

9–178 The majority in the House of Lords held that the burden had been discharged of demonstrating that the disclosure had been necessary in the interests of national security. Lord Diplock concluded[90] that the risk to national security feared by the government lay not in publication of the particular document but in the possibility that other classified documents might be leaked in the future with more serious consequences for national security. In the context of nuclear warfare, he regarded "possibility" as sufficient.

9–179 Furthermore, by the time of the hearing in the House of Lords it had emerged that the possibility feared at the interlocutory stage had indeed become a reality. The clerk had already leaked another document dealing with "contingency security arrangements" which the newspaper editor had recognised himself as being of greater significance for national security. He had therefore decided to destroy it[91] without revealing the contents. In Lord Roskill's view[92]:

---

[87] [2002] EWCA Civ 274, [2002] 2 Lloyd's Rep 229, E.M.L.R. 24.
[88] [2002] UKHL 29, [2002] 1 W.L.R. 2033.
[89] [1985] A.C. 339.
[90] *ibid.* at 355F–H.
[91] The editor was commended for his sense of responsibility, and no criticism seems to have attached to the fact that he destroyed this document. It may be that special considerations apply to a document which represents an obvious threat to national security, but it does not seem to have been suggested that the destruction of the document would have constituted contempt of court. It was clear at least that in order to establish that destruction of documents or other evidence amounts to contempt of court an intention would have to be proved to interfere with the administration of justice. This is an issue which is of more general application, although undoubtedly relevant in the context of journalists' sources, and is therefore considered at paras 11–84 *et seq*.
[92] [1985] A.C. at 371C–D.

"The essential point is that all the evidence pointed to the offender, be his or her position high or low, as someone with access to information affecting national security, and someone who could not properly be trusted with that information."

For Lord Bridge the presence of a disloyal servant in such a position self-evidently represented a potential threat to national security.[93]

Lord Fraser, who together with Lord Scarman dissented, recognised that events subsequent to the original interlocutory application had shown that the untrustworthy servant represented a serious security risk, and that it might well have been possible to place before the judge evidence to justify such a conclusion. Nevertheless, he regarded the state of the evidence in fact put forward by the government as being inadequate to discharge the burden upon them. Lord Scarman took a similar approach.

One matter which seems to be clear from this decision of the House of Lords is that it is for the court determining whether any of the exceptions under s.10 has been established, including that relating to national security, to make its own judgment in the light of the facts established. It appears that evidence presented on behalf of the Crown in support of the proposition that national security is under threat will be viewed critically by the court; mere assertion will not suffice.[94]

G. "Prevention of Crime"

1. *Re an Inquiry*

The statutory exception relating to "the prevention of crime" came before the House of Lords in *Re an Inquiry under the Company Securities (Insider Dealing) Act 1985*.[95] Inspectors were appointed under s.177 of the Financial Services Act 1986 to investigate whether a breach had occurred of the 1985 Act. There had been a suspected leak of price-sensitive takeover information from one of three government departments. This was apparently being used by people speculating on the Stock Exchange, and the Secretary of State for Trade and Industry appointed inspectors who, in the course of their inquiry, questioned a journalist who had written articles from which it appeared that he had possession of the leaked information.

When he declined to give any answers which might identify his sources, the inspectors sought the assistance of the court pursuant to s.178 of the Financial Services Act. That section empowered inspectors to ask for such assistance and,

---

[93] *ibid.* at 373B–E.
[94] A comparison may perhaps be drawn here with public interest immunity. Even in cases where the exemption from disclosure was based upon "national security" considerations, it seems, the court was entitled to take a "judicial peep" (the phrase used by Lord Edmund-Davies in *Burmah Oil Co Ltd v Bank of England* [1980 A.C. 1090 at 1129H]. See *Archbold 2005*, para.16–85. The implications of the recent European jurisprudence were considered by the House of Lords in *R. v H* [2004] UKHL 3, [2004] 2 A.C. 134 and the importance was stressed of the court inspecting all material which the prosecution seek to withhold. See also *Archbold 2005*, para.12–80d.
[95] [1988] A.C. 660.

9–183 if anybody refused to comply with a request, inspectors might certify that fact to the court. If the court was satisfied that the person did, without a reasonable excuse, refuse to answer relevant and necessary questions, the court might "punish him in like manner as if he had been guilty of contempt of the court".[96]

9–184 The journalist contended that he had a "reasonable excuse" under s.178(2), because s.10 of the Contempt of Court Act conferred an immunity[97] unless it could be shown in the circumstances that disclosure was necessary for the prevention of crime.

9–185 Hoffmann J. held that there was a reasonable excuse in the light of s.10, but the Court of Appeal and House of Lords took a different view. They concluded that sufficient evidence had been produced on behalf of the inspectors to demonstrate that it was of real importance for the purpose of their inquiry to have the sources identified.

9–186 According to Lord Griffiths, with whom all their Lordships agreed, the question whether the journalist had a "reasonable excuse" depended on whether he was entitled to rely on the public interest in protecting his source. The test to be applied must be the same whether the question arose in judicial proceedings or in such an inquiry as that before the House. Moreover, it was pointed out that in s.178 Parliament had not, by contrast with s.10 of the 1981 Act, included a power enabling the court to order the witness to answer an inspector's questions. Under s.178, the only powers vested in the High Court were either to punish the witness as if guilty of contempt, or to direct that the Secretary of State might exercise his power to limit the witness' business activities, if appropriate.

9–187 It was "academic" whether s.10 had any direct application to a reference under the 1986 Act, but the House concluded that it did not. Nevertheless, in deciding the limit of the protection afforded to a journalist's sources, a court should still follow the guidance of Parliament as set out in s.10.

9–188 The argument was rejected that the phrase "prevention of crime" should be given a narrow construction relating to some particular identifiable future crime or crimes. Parliament had used the words in a wider meaning with reference to the containment of crime in general. This was thought to be the "natural" meaning of the phrase (there being no reference in the statute to "*a crime or crimes*"). Reference was also made to Art.10 of the European Convention and to

---

[96] s.178(2)(a). In this particular situation it is difficult to envisage a journalist, if he is refusing to answer relevant and necessary questions, *not* being held in contempt. Thus the use of the words of analogy (" . . . as if he had been guilty of contempt") are somewhat misleading. On the other hand, sometimes, where a statute refers to an analogy with contempt it may be important to bear in mind that the offending conduct is not *ipso facto* contempt: see, *e.g.* the observations of Hobhouse J. in *R. v Rowland*, February 1991 (unreported), cited in *R. v Ashley* [2003] EWCA Crim 2571, [2004] 1 W.L.R. 2057 at [7] in the context of breach of bail.

[97] This is also the word used by Mummery L.J. in *Camelot Group plc v Centaur Communications Ltd* [1999] Q.B. 124 at 139D–E.

the judgment of the European Court of Human Rights in the *Sunday Times* case.[98] In so far as it was of any assistance, Lord Griffiths regarded this as lending support to the wider construction.

2. *X v Y*

The case of *X v Y*[99] has already been considered in the context of the exception "the interests of justice".[1] Rose J. was at that stage applying the narrow definition of that phrase, deriving from Lord Diplock in *Secretary of State for Defence v Guardian Newspapers Ltd*.[2] He had therefore refused to make an order for disclosure on that ground, and the applicants sought to rely upon the alternative ground that it was necessary for the "prevention of crime". This argument was also rejected, but the statutory exception was considered in some detail.

9–189

The particular crime upon which the plaintiffs relied, and indeed of which the defendants accepted that there was *prima facie* evidence, was corruption under the Public Bodies Corrupt Practices Act 1889 and the Prevention of Corruption Act 1906. The purpose of seeking the identity of the source was, however, to try to ensure that there would be no repetition of the breach of confidence.

9–190

It was submitted that the plaintiffs only had to show that disclosure was "likely to be of substantial assistance to the hospital in preventing crime". The judge rejected the proposition that the judgment of Slade L.J. at the Court of Appeal stage in *Re an Inquiry under the Company Securities (Insider Dealing) Act 1985*[3] led to a general conclusion that the word "necessary" was to be construed as equivalent to "likely to be of substantial assistance". Not only would such an approach be contrary to Parliament's use of the word in s.10, but it would also be at variance with what was said in the House of Lords in the *Guardian* case.

9–191

In the case under consideration by Slade L.J., the disclosure might well have been of substantial assistance to the Inspectors, but it was central to that decision that those seeking disclosure in that case had been specifically charged with investigating and hence preventing criminal offences. By contrast, the health authority in *X v Y* had no such responsibility. Nor did the evidence before Rose J. disclose that criminal investigation was the intended or would be the likely consequence of disclosure. There was no suggestion that the matter had been referred to the police, and what would be regarded by the authority as appropriate

9–192

---

[98] *Sunday Times v United Kingdom* (1979) 2 E.H.R.R. 245.
[99] [1988] 2 All E.R. 648, Rose J.
[1] paras 9–129 *et seq.*
[2] Cited at para.9–129.
[3] [1988] 1 A.C. 660 at 677D–E.

deterrent action could vary from warning to dismissal, but might well not extend, for policy reasons, to criminal investigation.

H. "The Prevention of Disorder"

9–193 It is not at all clear what was contemplated by using the expression "the prevention of disorder", and there have been no decisions as yet in which the wording has been considered. It, in conjunction with "the prevention of crime", corresponds directly to the language to be found in Art.10(2) of the European Convention.

IV. When Does a Journalist's Refusal Become Contempt?

A. The nature of the problem

9–194 There is a conundrum concerning the situation arising when someone has been ordered to disclose material relating to a source and refuses to do so. On the face of it, this refusal would constitute a contempt of court. On the other hand, until the appropriateness of the order has been determined by the final appellate tribunal to which the journalist wishes to address argument, it will not be possible to define conclusively the nature and extent of the obligation. The problem might at first seem to be more apparent than real, because in the ordinary way contempt proceedings would not be launched while any appeal was pending against the order itself.

9–195 In those cases where it is possible to test the order for disclosure by way of an appeal,[4] and the relevant party ultimately decides not to comply with even an order (say) of the House of Lords, then this would undoubtedly give rise to contempt.

9–196 Much depends on the opportunities available for appealing. If the issue arises in the situation where an injunction has been granted against a party (either a journalist or, perhaps, the journalist's employer) directing disclosure of a document, this should not present too many difficulties. There used to be a right of appeal, even in the case of an interlocutory order.[5] In accordance with modern practice,[6] however, permission will be required for any appeal (either from the court making the order or from the appellate court). There is still, nevertheless, the opportunity for an appeal and where a journalist's right under s.10 is in issue permission would be likely to be granted. Occasionally, a court will specifically

---

[4] See, *e.g. Secretary of State for Defence v Guardian Newspapers Ltd* [1985] 1 A.C. 339; *X Ltd v Morgan-Grampian (Publishers) Ltd* [1991] 1 A.C. 1.
[5] See, *e.g.* the now repealed provision of the Supreme Court Act 1981, contained in s.18(1)(h)(iii). On the other hand, if the order was made by way of specific discovery, there was no *right* of appeal and leave would have been required.
[6] See the discussion contained in *Tanfern Ltd v Cameron-MacDonald* [2000] 1 W.L.R. 1311, CA.

decline to suspend the effect of an order even though an appeal, or an application for permission, may be pending.[7]

If the problem arises when a journalist, not being personally a party to litigation, but simply appearing as a witness,[8] is asked to reveal a source while in the witness box, such a person as yet has no right of appeal, or other right of review.[9] The journalist is at risk of being held in contempt as soon as an answer is refused. (The difficulties would be compounded if reliance is sought to be placed on a defence of duress.)[10]

9–197

Lord Donaldson M.R. was considering a similar point in *Re M: M v Home Office*,[11] by reference to a problem which arises in the context particularly of what were then called *Anton Piller* orders:

9–198

"The problem which arises in such cases is that compliance with the order renders the right to apply to have the order set aside nugatory. What has been done in accordance with the order can never be undone".

He commented that if a person in that situation does not immediately comply with the terms of the order, he will technically be in contempt. He also referred to the option, which would still be available in the context of a freezing or search order, of applying to have the order set aside or varied. If prompt steps were taken to preserve the situation pending such an application, no penalty would be imposed if the order were subsequently set aside. That option is not available, however, to the journalist in the situation now under consideration. On the other hand, it is difficult to reconcile the principle increasingly recognised by the courts, to the effect that s.10 confers a *prima facie* statutory "right" to refuse to disclose a source, with the conclusion that a journalist would be treated as liable to punishment for contempt forthwith.

9–199

B. The need to reconcile two lines of authority

This important problem renders it necessary to consider in a little detail the two different lines of authority which apparently come into conflict at this critical point.

9–200

---

[7] This seems to have happened, for example, following the Court of Appeal hearing in *Camelot Group plc v Centaur Communications Ltd* [1999] Q.B. 124, discussed in paras 9–164 *et seq*.
[8] See, *e.g. Att-Gen v Lundin* (1982) 75 Cr.App.R. 90; *Chief Constable of Leicestershire v Garavelli* [1997] E.M.L.R. 543.
[9] See para.9–236. See *R. v Middlesex Guildhall Crown Court Ex p. Salinger* [1993] Q.B. 564, which would suggest (in the context of an application for production of video tapes under the Prevention of Terrorism (Temporary Provisions) Act 1989, s.14) that, if an order is made on an *ex parte* basis, there is unlikely to be any finding of contempt at least until the matter is dealt with *inter partes*. The matter would be heard afresh rather than on an appellate basis, so that the original order would be open to challenge on its merits. Similarly, in the case of a witness summons (and formerly a *subpoena duces tecum*), no doubt the journalist concerned would appear if ordered to do so and argue that he is entitled to withhold documents which he seeks to protect under s.10.
[10] para.9–119.
[11] [1992] 1 Q.B 270 at 300A–B.

9–201   There is authority of long standing that, for so long as an order remains effective, disobedience to it will amount to contempt.[12] Orders of the court must be implicitly obeyed and cannot be disregarded until set aside upon a proper application.[13] On the other hand, there is also relatively recent authority, with particular reference to the disclosure of sources, and orders purporting to restrain publication in connection with court proceedings, that a person will not necessarily be in contempt by failing to comply.[14]

C. The "void" and "voidable" distinction

9–202   It seems clearly established that there is no basis for drawing a distinction between orders classified as "void" and those which are merely "voidable". In the light of the decision of the Privy Council in *Isaacs v Robertson*,[15] no such distinction is appropriate in respect of an order made by "a court of unlimited jurisdiction in the course of contentious litigation." Orders made by such a court are either regular or irregular. If the latter, such an order can be set aside by the court which made it. If the former, then it can only be set aside by an appellate court.

D. Orders made "without jurisdiction"

9–203   Questions arise, however, as to when an order may be said to have been made with jurisdiction, and when not, even in the context of courts which are classified as being of either "unlimited" or "competent" jurisdiction. It is not easy to see that disobedience to an order made without jurisdiction should lead to punishment, since such an order should logically be treated as of no effect at all. The argument generally raised is that it is necessary for sustaining the authority of the court, and thus the rule of law, that orders should be complied with unless and

---

[12] See *Woodward v Lincoln (Earl)* (1674) 3 Swan. App.626, 36 E.R. 1000; *Drewry v Thacker* (1819) 3 Swan 529 at 546, 36 E.R. 963 at 967, Lord Eldon; *Fennings v Humphery* (1841) 4 Beav. 1, 49 E.R. 237; *Blake v Blake* (1844) 7 Beav. 514, 49 E.R. 1165; *Chuck v Cremer* (1846) 1 Coop. temp. Cott. 338 at 343; 47 E.R. 884 at 885; *Eastern Trust Co v McKenzie, Mann & Co Ltd* [1915] A.C. 750 at 761, Sir George Farwell; *Hadkinson v Hadkinson* [1952] P. 285 at 288–9; *R. v Highbury Corner Magistrates' Court Ex p. O'Donoghue* (1997) 161 J.P. 217. See also the discussion of the effect of a breach of an order made under s.4(2) of the 1981 Act contained in para.7-132.
[13] *Russell v East Anglian Railway Co* (1850) 3 Mac. & G. 104 at 117, 42 E.R. 201 at 206; *Spokes v Banbury Board of Health* (1865) L.R. 1 Eq. 42 at 48, Wood V.-C.; *Re Battersby's Estate* (1892) 31 L.R. Ir. 73; *Hadkinson v Hadkinson* [1952] P. 285 at 288, Romer L.J.; *Worthington v Ad-Lib Club Ltd* [1965] Ch. 236 at 250, Stirling J; *Johnson v Walton* [1990] 1 F.L.R. 350 at 352, Lord Donaldson M.R.; *DPP v Channel 4 Television Co Ltd* [1993] 2 All E.R. 517 at 529a–b, Woolf L.J.; *Re M: M v Home Office* [1994] 1 A.C. 377; *Mid-Bedfordshire District Council v Brown (Thomas)* [2004] EWCA Civ 1709, [2005] 1 W.L.R. 1460 [25]: ("The proper course for the defendants to take, if they wished to challenge the order, was to apply to the court to discharge or vary it. If that failed, the proper course was to seek to appeal.").
[14] *Att-Gen v Leveller Magazine Ltd* [1979] A.C. 440 at 455–56, Viscount Dilhorne; *Horsham Justices Ex p. Farquharson* [1982] 1 Q.B. 762 at 790B–D, 794A, Lord Denning M.R.; *Att-Gen v Lundin* (1982) 75 Cr.App.R. 90; *Chief Constable of Leicestershire v Garavelli* [1997] E.M.L.R. 543, DC.
[15] [1985] A.C. 97 at 103, Lord Diplock.

until set aside.[16] "Were it otherwise court orders would be consistently ignored in the belief, sometimes justified, that at some time in the future they would be set aside. This would be a recipe for chaos."[17]

On the other hand, an argument could be advanced that respect for the courts is undermined by any rule of practice which appears to suggest that the court must be obeyed even when wrong, and in particular when acting contrary to limitations apparently imposed upon its jurisdiction by Parliament.

E. The rule that court orders must be implicitly obeyed

In *Mason v Lawton*,[18] the Court of Appeal was considering a non-molestation order purportedly made under the Domestic Violence and Matrimonial Proceedings Act 1976, which contained reference not only to the relevant woman and her children but also to "her mother or her father". Lord Donaldson M.R. observed that, to this extent, the orders exceeded the jurisdiction of the court, since s.1 of the Act only applied to the applicant and any children living with her. He continued[19]:

> "However, apart from helpfully drawing attention to this point, [counsel for the defendant] ... has quite rightly placed no reliance upon it, since there was no appeal from the orders, and the orders of a court have to be obeyed unless and until they are varied or set aside".

Thus Lord Donaldson M.R. expressed the clear opinion that, even where an order is made without jurisdiction, it should be obeyed until set aside by due process of law. He was dealing with an order made in a county court which is a court of limited jurisdiction, governed by statute. *A fortiori*, in relation to the High Court, which is a tribunal of unlimited jurisdiction, any orders would have to be obeyed implicitly.

The Master of the Rolls addressed the jurisdiction of the High Court in *Re M: M v Home Office*.[20] He was considering an order of Garland J. made *ex parte*, which was later set aside at an *inter partes* hearing on the footing that, since injunctive orders could not be made against the Crown, it was made without jurisdiction. He continued:

> "This is not a correct analysis. That the order should not have been made in the form in which it was made is beyond dispute, although I remain of the firm view that a writ of habeas corpus could have been issued. This is not, however, to say that it was made without jurisdiction. The High Court is a court of unlimited jurisdiction. The judges of

---

[16] See, *e.g X Ltd v Morgan-Grampian (Publishers) Ltd* [1991] 1 A.C. 1 at 20B–D, Lord Donaldson M.R., CA, 48–48, Lord Bridge, HL; *Re M: M v Home Office* [1992] Q.B. 270 at 298–9, Lord Donaldson M.R., CA. For an example where a respondent was punished for disobeying an order which was subsequently set aside for non-disclosure, see *Wardle Fabrics Ltd v G Myristis Ltd* [1984] F.S.R. 263, discussed in paras 12–140 and 12–176 *et seq*.
[17] *per* Lord Donaldson M.R. in *Re M: M v Home Office* [1992] Q.B. 270 at 299B.
[18] [1991] 2 F.L.R. 50, CA.
[19] *ibid*. at 52A.
[20] [1992] Q.B. 270 at 298.

9–207 that court, acting as such, can make any order which is not illegal, the sole question on a reconsideration of the order or an appeal being whether the order should have been made. This order was irregular and therefore should not have been made, but it was not made without jurisdiction."

9–208 Similarly in *Johnson v Walton*,[21] he commented:

"It cannot be too clearly stated that, when an injunctive order is made or when an undertaking is given, it operates until it is revoked on appeal or by the court itself, and it has to be obeyed whether or not it should have been granted or accepted in the first place."

9–209 This accords with the clear statement of principle to be found in the judgment of Romer L.J. (with whom Somervell L.J. agreed) in *Hadkinson v Hadkinson*[22]:

"It is the plain and unqualified obligation of every person against, or in respect of whom, an order is made by a court of competent jurisdiction, to obey it unless and until that order is discharged. The uncompromising nature of this obligation is shown by the fact that it extends even to cases where the person affected by an order believes it to be irregular or even void."

9–210 There was an earlier statement of Sir John Donaldson M.R. in *Att-Gen v Newspaper Publishing plc*[23] which might appear at first impression to be inconsistent with his trenchant statements quoted above: "The fact that the order was addressed to the alleged contemnor would rightly have been disregarded as done without jurisdiction".[24] When analysed, however, it seems from the context that he was saying no more than that if an order is served on a third party, who is not mentioned in the order, and subsequently an attempt is made to commit that third party *for disobedience of the order*, then the court dealing with the contempt application could rightly disregard the service of that order.[25] The application could only have been framed properly by identifying the contempt as consisting

---

[21] [1990] 1 F.L.R. 350 at 352D. Similar public policy considerations underlie the decision in *Salisbury District Council v Le Roi* [2001] All E.R. (D) 30 (Oct), where the Court of Appeal upheld a committal order for failure to comply with a demolition order in respect of a building. The contemnor argued that the demolition order should not have been made, for estoppel reasons, but that argument had already been considered and rejected. Estoppel might have been a reason for not making the original order, but it was not a reason for refusing committal once it had been disobeyed. For comment, see M. Edwards [2002] J.P.L. 700.
[22] [1952] P. 285 at 288. And see *Att-Gen for England and Wales v Tomlinson* [1999] 3 N.Z.L.R. 722 at 732 where the words cited in the text of Romer L.J. (as to the "uncompromising nature of this obligation") were cited by Gendall J. See also *Secretary of State for Defence v Percy* [1999] 1 All E.R. 732. Carnwath J. was concerned with an anti-nuclear campaigner who had trespassed on land at RAF Menwith Hill in Yorkshire in breach of an injunction. Even though he took the view that there was no legal justification for the retention of the byelaw notices which she had removed, he concluded that "There is no legal principle which entitles a member of the public to go on to private land to remove such signs, even if they are there unlawfully. Similarly, there is no principle that the public's rights to the use of a footpath are extended to include law enforcement. The public's remedy is simply to ignore the notices, or, if that is not good enough, to seek a court order."
[23] [1988] Ch. 333.
[24] At 369F–G.
[25] See, *e.g. Lord Wellesley v Earl of Mornington* (1848) 11 Beav. 180, 50 E.R. 785.

in a deliberate interference with the administration of justice.[26] Some of the statements to be found in the authorities as to the unqualified obligation to comply with any court order give rise to difficult questions of both definition and principle, which have particular significance for the journalist who is ordered to reveal a source.

In particular, some of Lord Donaldson's analyses give rise to problems of application: 9–211

(1) Where a High Court judge acts "illegally" as contemplated in the citation from *Re M: M v Home Office*,[27] is the individual concerned acting as a High Court judge at all? Is the judge acting, albeit illegally, within the jurisdiction of the High Court? It is doubtful whether Lord Donaldson was intending to convey, by using the word "illegal", that an order made by a judge in circumstances which might fulfil judicial review criteria[28] (for example, because of taking into account irrelevant matters, or *vice versa*) could be ignored or disobeyed with impunity; the general tenor of his remarks would appear to suggest that such an order should be obeyed until set aside. What he meant by "illegal", therefore, remains somewhat obscure.

(2) Does it make a difference if the judge is ordering someone to do an act (or to refrain from doing an act) and the act (or omission) would in itself be "illegal" irrespective of the order? Suppose a judge were to order a litigant to carry out a mercy killing. Surely it would make no sense, while acknowledging the act as "unlawful", *not* to accept that it had been made "without jurisdiction." 9–212

(3) Can a court of "competent jurisdiction" never act without jurisdiction? 9–213

(4) Even if the High Court is of unlimited jurisdiction, so far as the common law is concerned, Parliament can surely limit the jurisdiction by statute. Sir Peter Pain seems to have concluded in *Special Hospital Services Authority v Hyde*[29] that he would not have jurisdiction to order disclosure of a source, in the light of s.10, unless it had been demonstrated to be necessary. This is a factor which is also illustrated, in relation to the grant of injunctions, by the restrictions imposed under s.12 of the Human Rights Act 1998.[30] 9–214

(5) Particular problems arise in relation to the powers conferred, and restrictions imposed, respectively by ss.4(2) and 10 of the Contempt of Court Act 1981. It is provided by s.10, *inter alia*, that "no court may require a person to disclose ... the source of information ... unless it be 9–215

---

[26] See *Lord Wellesley v Earl of Mornington (No.2)* (1848) 11 Beav. 181, 50 E.R. 786.
[27] See para.9–207.
[28] A decision of the High Court is not susceptible to judicial review; see *In re Racal Communications Ltd* [1981] A.C. 375 at 384D–G, Lord Diplock.
[29] (1994) 20 B.M.L.R. 75.
[30] See paras 6–11 *et seq.*

9–215 established to the satisfaction of the court that disclosure is necessary . . . ". In s.4(2) it is provided that a court " . . . may, wherever it appears to be necessary for avoiding a substantial risk of prejudice . . . order that the publication of any report . . . be postponed". If the "necessity" precondition is absent, in either case, it must follow that the court may *not* make any such order.[31]

9–216 It may be useful to contrast with these very specific statutory provisions, contained in ss.4(2) and 10 of the Contempt of Court Act, the much more general wording of s.37 of the Supreme Court Act 1981, with regard to injunctions, which states the existing law and practice as it has stood for many years:

> "(1) The High Court may by order (whether interlocutory or final) grant an injunction or appoint a receiver in all cases in which it appears to the court to be just and convenient to do so".

The section does not purport to fetter the High Court's power at all.[32]

9–217 That formulation is clearly consistent with the notion of unlimited jurisdiction and does not lay down any preconditions for its exercise (although it would clearly have to be exercised "judicially"). Injunctions are often set aside on appeal, but it would generally not be appropriate to treat the judge as having acted without jurisdiction, let alone "illegally" *ab initio*, save in far-fetched examples, such as that given above of the order to carry out a mercy-killing.

9–218 There may be no point in drawing a distinction for the purposes of this discussion between orders made in this context by a High Court judge (say under s.10) and those made by courts of limited jurisdiction. When it comes to journalists' sources, Parliament chose not to make any such distinction in the statutory provisions enacted for their protection.

9–219 The answer may be that it is misleading to speak of the High Court in unqualified terms as being a court of "unlimited jurisdiction". It is clear no doubt from the terms of s.37 of the Supreme Court Act 1981, and its predecessors, that judges do indeed have a wide-ranging jurisdiction to make what orders seem to be just. This power has to be exercised, however, judicially, and thus in accordance with either precedent or statutory authority.

9–220 In certain areas, however, the powers of the court derive not from any long-standing inherent jurisdiction, but from specific modern statutory provisions designed to deal with particular problems, and to take into account the balancing of competing interests. Examples are provided by ss.4(2) and s.10 of the Contempt of Court Act, and it may be that the High Court has no greater jurisdiction than any other tribunal when exercising such statutory powers; the extent of its jurisdiction, or that of any other court, can therefore only be determined by reference to the wording of the statute.

---

[31] See, *e.g. X Ltd v Morgan-Grampian (Publishers) Ltd* [1991] 1 A.C. 1; *Chief Constable of Leicestershire v Garavelli* [1997] E.M.L.R. 543.
[32] See *Motorola Credit Corporation v Uzan (No.2)* [2003] EWCA Civ 752, [2004] 1 W.L.R. 113.

Orders made therefore in conflict with these statutory provisions need to be analysed very carefully. The journalist is given no right of appeal against an order made under s.10.[33] A journalist who fails to comply with an order to disclose a source would therefore, on Lord Donaldson's analysis, seem to be in immediate and continuing contempt of court for so long as he fails to comply with it.

9–221

This is a common theme. For example, in *IRC v Hoogstraten*[34] an order had been made, apparently without jurisdiction,[35] to sequestrate assets in anticipation of future breaches of a *Mareva* injunction, notwithstanding that the earlier contempt had by then been purged. Nevertheless, it was observed by Dillon L.J.[36] that "Even though the order should not have been made, it was made, and unless set aside it is valid as an order of the court."

9–222

Similarly, albeit in another very different context, Lord Bingham C.J. commented in *R. v Highbury Corner Magistrates' Court Ex p. O'Donoghue*[37]:

9–223

"It should not be necessary to say that there were three ways of responding to a court order: to seek to set it aside; to appeal against it, if time allowed; and to obey it.
It was not an option simply to decide that it was an order that the court should not have made and therefore to disregard it."

F. Authorities suggesting an exception in relation to journalists' sources

Other authorities, however, suggest quite clearly that this principle is not so inflexible in the context of restrictions sought to be placed upon journalists.[38] Moreover, it seems from the analysis of Lord Diplock in *Secretary of State for Defence v Guardian Newspapers Ltd*[39] that the rationale underlying this distinction does derive from lack of jurisdiction:

9–224

" . . . section 10 requires actual necessity to be established; and whether it has or not is a question of fact that the judge has to find in favour of necessity as a condition precedent to his having any jurisdiction to order disclosure of sources of information."

Earlier in his speech,[40] Lord Diplock also made the following illuminating comment:

9–225

---

[33] So far as s.4(2) is concerned, this was so until s.159 of the Criminal Justice Act 1988 conferred a right of appeal to "persons aggrieved".
[34] [1985] 1 Q.B. 1077.
[35] At 1086G. See also the observations of Arden L.J. in *Re B (Court's Jurisdiction)* [2004] EWCA Civ 681, [2004] 2 F.L.R. 741 at [68].
[36] At 1086H–1087A.
[37] (1997) 161 J.P. 217. See also his Lordship's remarks in *Arab Monetary Fund v Hashim* March 21, 1997 (unreported, Lexis) as to the paramount importance of ensuring "the prompt and unquestioning observance of court orders".
[38] See, *e.g.* Lord Denning M.R. in *R. v Horsham Justices Ex p. Farquharson* [1982] Q.B. 762 at 79B–E, and Tasker Watkins L.J. in *Att-Gen v Lundin* (1982) 75 Cr.App.R. 90 at 95: "refusal by a witness to answer a question in a criminal trial even when ordered by a judge to do so does not inevitably put that person in contempt of court".
[39] [1985] 1 A.C. 339 at 350D–E.
[40] *ibid.* at 345.

9–225

"The section is so drafted as to make it a question of fact not of discretion as to whether in the particular case a requirement for disclosure of sources of information falls within one of the express exceptions introduced by the word 'unless'. If it does not, *the statutory right to refuse disclosure of sources of information in the media is absolute.*" (emphasis added).

It is not immediately clear whether Lord Diplock would apply to disclosure orders made by a High Court judge in this context the label "regular" or "irregular" to which he referred in *Isaacs v Robertson*.[41]

9–226 A similar approach was taken by Sir Peter Pain in *Special Hospital Services Authority v Hyde*,[42] where he declined to order disclosure of information in the light of the constraints of s.10, expressly stating that he regarded himself as being without jurisdiction (notwithstanding that he was sitting in a court of "unlimited jurisdiction"). This analysis is consistent not only with the words of Lord Diplock, set out above, but also with those of Lord Bridge who in *X Ltd v Morgan-Grampian (Publishers) Ltd*[43] put it this way:

"Whether the necessity of disclosure in this sense is established is certainly a question of fact rather than an issue calling for the exercise of the judge's discretion, but, like many other questions of fact, such as the question whether somebody has acted reasonably in given circumstances, it will call for the exercise of a discriminating and sometimes difficult value judgment".

9–227 Although he did not mention the word "jurisdiction" expressly, Lord Bridge appears to have regarded the establishment of the factual substratum of "necessity" as an essential precondition of exercising the power to order disclosure. If that is not a restriction upon jurisdiction, it is difficult know how otherwise to characterise it. Moreover, if Lord Donaldson's approach in *Re M: M v Home Office*[44] is correct, and an order made by a High Court judge without having established "necessity" could not be described as "made without jurisdiction", one is driven to the conclusion that his analysis is only reconcilable with the principles in the authorities on sources, whether under s.10 or the common law discretion,[45] on the basis that such a judge must be taken to have acted "illegally", by acting inconsistently with the absolute "statutory right" accorded to journalists.

9–228 It may be that some further assistance on the matter of jurisdiction can be derived from the remarks of Viscount Dilhorne, albeit in the context of the magistrates' court, in *Att-Gen v Leveller Magazine Ltd*.[46] This related to an order made in committal proceedings in respect of defendants charged under the Official Secrets Acts. The magistrates had agreed to allow a prosecution witness

---

[41] [1985] A.C. 97 at 103.
[42] (1994) 20 B.M.L.R. 75 at 85. See also *Handmade Films (Productions) Ltd v Express Newpapers Ltd* [1986] F.S.R. 463, Browne-Wilkinson V.-C. and the decision of the Divisional Court in *Chief Constable of Leicestershire v Garavelli* [1997] E.M.L.R. 543.
[43] [1991] A.C. 1 at 44. See also at 48–9.
[44] [1992] Q.B. 270. See para.9–207.
[45] In particular *Att-Gen v Lundin* (1982) 75 Cr.App.R. 90.
[46] [1979] A.C. 440 at 455–6.

to be referred to as "Colonel B" for reasons of "national safety". His name could be deduced from certain pointers in his evidence, and when his true identity was revealed in three magazines the Attorney-General alleged contempt and moved for committal. In the statements filed on his behalf under the former RSC Ord.52, r.2, it was alleged that the magistrates had expressly ordered that no attempt should be made to disclose the identity of Colonel B. Subsequently, however, the clerk to the magistrates confirmed in an affidavit that no such explicit direction had been given, for the very reason that he had advised the justices that they had no power to do so.

The Divisional Court held that the publishers of the magazines were guilty of contempt, but this ruling was overturned in the House of Lords. It was held that the statements made by the Colonel in evidence, to which no objection had been taken by the prosecution or by the court, had rendered it impossible to prevent publication outside the courtroom. Viscount Dilhorne considered the evidence that Colonel B had given, to the effect that one had only to look at an issue of the Royal Corps of Signals magazine to find out his identity, and which had enabled *The Leveller* and *Peace News* to "deduce his identity". He went on to say[47]:

> "Unless the magistrates had power to prohibit and had prohibited it, the publication of this evidence could not be a contempt of court. It was not suggested that there had been any such prohibition or that the magistrates had power to impose one. If publication of the evidence could not be a contempt of court, was it a contempt to publish what could be deduced from that evidence, namely, the identity of 'Colonel B'? In my opinion the answer is in the negative unless the magistrates had power to prohibit and had prohibited any attempt being made to ascertain his identity and the publication of his identity... If the magistrates had power to direct and had directed that 'Colonel B's' name should not be published and such a direction was operative not only within but outside the court, then the case might be different. In *Reg. v Socialist Worker Printers and Publishers Ltd Ex parte Attorney-General* [1975] Q.B. 637 the Crown did not contend that the court had any power to make orders affecting the press or other media in their conduct outside the court and in the present case the Crown, rightly in my opinion, did not contend that examining magistrates had any such power... As there is no statutory provision which gives to a court power to make an order applying to all members of the public prohibiting the publication of information which might lead to the identification of a witness such as 'Colonel B', it follows that in my opinion the advice given by [the clerk] to his bench was right and that if the chairman had given any such direction, it would not have operated to convert conduct which otherwise did not constitute a contempt into one".

It seems to follow that Viscount Dilhorne took the view that, even in the case of a prohibitory order, if it was made without jurisdiction, it could be disobeyed with impunity so far as the law of contempt was concerned. It is true that he was considering a hypothetical order made by a magistrates' court, which is a court of limited jurisdiction. It is difficult to see, however, how a different approach could be taken in circumstances where an order of that kind, having no basis in law, was made by a High Court Judge. The mere fact that the High Court, as Lord

---

[47] *ibid.* at 455–6. This would appear to be consistent with the approach adopted to the jurisdiction of magistrates in a different context in such cases as *R. v Hollis* (1819) 2 Stark 536, 171 E.R. 728 and *R. v Soper* (1825) 3 B. & C. 857, 107 E.R. 951.

Donaldson M.R. pointed out in *Re M: M v Home Office*,[48] is in general terms a court of unlimited jurisdiction could not have the effect of undermining the reasoning of Viscount Dilhorne.

9–231 In s.10 of the Contempt of Court Act it is made clear that "no court may require a person to disclose ... the source of information." There was no comparable statute declaring that magistrates had no power to prohibit the publication of Colonel B's identity, but again it is difficult to see why this should make any difference. In neither case would the power exist to make the relevant order.

G. The problem of reconciling *DPP v Channel Four*

9–232 A difficult decision in this context is that of Woolf L.J. in *DPP v Channel Four Television Co Ltd*,[49] where it was argued for the television company, which had been ordered to disclose sources under the Prevention of Terrorism (Temporary Provisions) Act 1989, that[50]:

> " ... although there is no right of appeal in respect of the order made by the judge, on an application for committal for contempt this court, even where there is a clear breach of the order, is entitled on the application for committal to decide that the lower judge wrongly exercised his discretion under Sch 7 ... "

Woolf L.J. continued:

> "I cannot accept this contention. In my judgment, the law is clear that, until an order of the type made by the judge is set aside, it has to be obeyed. However, in this case, as I have already indicated, this point is purely academic since, in my judgment, the learned judge exercised his discretion perfectly properly".

9–233 Although it was cited to him in argument, Woolf L.J. did not offer any explanation as to how this view could be reconciled with the approach in *Att-Gen v Lundin*. Moreover, it appears that the case of *Secretary of State for Defence v Guardian Newspapers Ltd* was not cited before the Divisional Court; thus Woolf L.J. did not apparently have the benefit of reading the words of Lord Diplock.[51]

9–234 It is important also to bear in mind that Woolf L.J. was there concerned with the Prevention of Terrorism (Temporary Provisions) Act 1989, Sch.7, para. 4(5)(b).[52] In these circumstances, it is perhaps not surprising that s.10 of the Court Act was not prayed in aid. Its terms would have been overridden by the explicit language of the 1989 Act. It is also to be noted that Woolf L.J. pointed out that there would have been no chance of overturning the decision below by way of judicial review. It therefore seems to have been accepted *inter alia* that it

---

[48] [1992] Q.B. 270 at 299.
[49] [1993] 2 All E.R. 517.
[50] *ibid.* at 528–9.
[51] para.9–224 and para.9–225.
[52] The terms of which are set out in para.9–113. The 1989 Act has been repealed and replaced by the Terrorism Act 2000.

could not be challenged for illegality or irrationality. As to the jurisdiction to make the order, there would equally have been no doubt.[53]

For these special reasons, it is submitted that the uncompromising terms of the judgment of Woolf L.J. do not in fact cast doubt on the approach adopted in those cases where a journalist is recognised, especially since the enactment of s.10, as having a *right* to protect his source.

H. The lack of any right of appeal

A party ordered to disclose material which may reveal a journalist's source, by way of mandatory injunction, would ordinarily have the opportunity to appeal, even in the case of an interlocutory order,[54] if permission were granted. But a witness ordered in court to reveal a source would not at present appear to have any opportunity to appeal such an order.

Normally an order to disclose a source can only be challenged by the journalist after proceedings have actually been launched to commit for failure to comply. If the judge's order is upheld in such circumstances, the consequence would appear to be that the journalist would be held to have been in continuing contempt of the order from the time he first indicated that he was not prepared to obey it. If he chooses to appeal such a finding under s.13 of the Administration of Justice Act 1960, and is successful, this would apparently have the effect of re-writing history so that he emerges at the end of the appeal process without having been in contempt at any stage.

It would be a practical solution to legislate for a right of appeal for journalists in circumstances when an order for disclosure has been made and the journalist wishes to exercise what Lord Diplock described as his "statutory right", as has been done in relation to s.4(2) and s.11 of the 1981 Act.[55] This would do nothing, however, to resolve the conceptual difficulty.

V. Should the Attorney-General Have a Role to Play?

A. The Attorney-General and the public interest

In view of the importance now attached to the protection of journalistic sources in the context of press freedom in a democratic society,[56] and the need to justify

---

[53] See 524g–h.
[54] The former provision of the Supreme Court Act 1981, contained in s.18(1)(h)(iii), afforded an unqualified right. The matter is now subject to the general regime under the CPR which requires permission to be granted for any appeal save with very few exceptions (*e.g.* the continuing right to appeal an order for committal under s.13(2) of the Administration of Justice Act 1960).
[55] Criminal Justice Act 1988, s.159. Lack of any right of challenge may not sit comfortably with the European Convention. See the discussion in paras 7–248 *et seq.*, in relation to the genesis of that section, where the Commission ruled that the provisions of Art.13, which guarantee an "effective remedy", were violated in the absence of a right of appeal.
[56] See the general discussion at paras 9–1 *et seq.*

9–239 any order of source disclosure by showing an overriding requirement in the public interest, there is an argument to the effect that it is the Attorney-General who is the "appropriate officer"[57] to consider where the public interest lies in this context and, in particular, whether it is appropriate to institute contempt proceedings in respect of a journalist who refuses to reveal a source.

9–240 As Lord Wilberforce observed in *Gouriet v Union of Post Office Workers*[58]: "That it is the exclusive right of the Attorney General to represent the public interest . . . is not technical, not procedural, not fictional. It is constitutional". While individual citizens may have a role to play when seeking to enforce private rights through public law remedies,[59] there appeared to be agreement in the House of Lords that it was for the Attorney-General exclusively to represent the *public* interest.[60]

9–241 Thus, there is much to be said for the view that when the issue of whether to order disclosure of a journalist's source has been determined, at the highest level at which it is going to be canvassed, proceedings should only thereafter be launched for contempt on the fiat of the Attorney-General, as and when it has been concluded that the public interest so requires. This seems to have happened in such leading cases as *Att-Gen v Mulholland*[61] and *Att-Gen v Lundin*.[62]

9–242 A more recent example is provided by *DPP v Channel Four Television Co Ltd*.[63] An application had been made by an officer in the Metropolitan Police Special Branch for documents to be produced by Channel Four and by a production company.[64] The respondents refused to comply with an order that material which had been taken abroad should be returned to the jurisdiction. This was because they did not wish to disclose their source. The matter was referred to the Attorney-General and an application made on his behalf that fines be imposed and that sequestration be ordered against the company.

B. The unresolved question

9–243 In *Chief Constable of Leicestershire v Garavelli*,[65] by contrast, the contempt proceedings against a journalist were launched, without reference to the Attorney-General, by two Chief Constables who wished to compel her to give an answer as to her source for the purposes of police disciplinary proceedings. It

---

[57] *Att-Gen v Times Newspapers Ltd* [1974] A.C. 273 at 311, 326.
[58] [1978] A.C. 435 at 481A–B.
[59] *ibid.* at 483E–484B, Lord Wilberforce; 495E–F, Viscount Dilhorne; 499G–500E, Lord Diplock; 518–19, Lord Fraser. See also *Dyson v Att-Gen* [1912] 1 Ch. 158.
[60] See, *e.g.* Lord Wilberforce; *ibid.* at 483E–484B; Viscount Dilhorne at 495E–F; Lord Diplock at 500E–F.
[61] [1963] 2 Q.B. 477.
[62] (1982) 75 Cr.App.R. 90.
[63] [1993] 2 All E.R. 517 at 519c–d, 523g–h. This case is discussed at paras 9–120 and para.9–232.
[64] Under the Prevention of Terrorism (Temporary Provisions) Act 1989, Sch.7, para.3 (now replaced by the Terrorism Act 2000: see para.9–118).
[65] [1997] E.M.L.R. 543, discussed more fully at paras 9–156 *et seq.*

was held in that case[66] that, in view of the conclusion reached by the Divisional Court to the effect that disclosure had not been shown to be necessary in the public interest, no decision was required as to the possible role for the Attorney-General, and the matter was thus left open.

Nevertheless, there appear to be no other examples in the law reports of an individual moving to commit a journalist for contempt, for failing to reveal a source, without the intervention of the Law Officers. In view of the decision of the European Court in *Goodwin v United Kingdom*,[67] with its emphasis upon public interest criteria, the argument for leaving such matters to the discretion of the Attorney-General is all the more powerful.

9–244

VI. A General Summary of the Principles

From the authorities on s.10 reported so far, it is now possible to derive a number of general principles, with some degree of confidence:

9–245

(1) Provided that it is addressed to the public at large or any section of it, every publication falls within the section and sources are thus protected unless falling within one of the expressed "unless" exceptions.[68]

(2) Even before publication, there is protection against disclosure provided the information deriving from the source was supplied and received for the ultimate purpose of publication.[69]

(3) There is no requirement that the information has to be of public interest; nor is the protection of the section confined to publications by the "media", although in practice they are likely to be its chief beneficiaries.[70]

(4) The four specific exceptions are not to be interpreted as though there were an additional general exception of "public interest", such that a judge could order disclosure on the basis that it was perceived to be in the public interest, without one of the four specific criteria being fulfilled.[71]

(5) As to the "interests of justice" exception, that expression should not be construed in a technical sense, but widely, and it is not to be confined to

---

[66] See also *P v Liverpool Daily Post and Echo Newspapers plc* [1991] 2 A.C. 370 at 425, Lord Bridge; *Dobson v Hastings* [1992] Ch. 394 at 411, Sir Donald Nicholls V.-C.
[67] (1996) 22 E.H.R.R. 123. See also the Law Commission, *Consents to Prosecution*, Law Com., Consultation Paper No.149 (1997), para.7.13, which identifies the need to protect free speech as being one of the important considerations in the decision to retain the consent requirement in cases of contempt.
[68] *Secretary of State for Defence v Guardian Newspapers Ltd* [1985] 1 A.C. 339.
[69] [1985] 1 A.C. 339 at 348, Lord Diplock.; *X Ltd v Morgan-Grampian (Publishers) Ltd* [1991] 1 A.C. 1 at 40.
[70] *Secretary of State for Defence v Guardian Newspapers Ltd* [1985] 1 A.C. 339 at 348G–H, Lord Diplock.
[71] *ibid.* at 350, Lord Diplock.

the administration of justice in the course of legal proceedings in a court of law, or before a tribunal or body exercising the judicial power of the state.[72]

(6) The statutory prohibition is not qualified by the nature of the judicial proceedings or, in the case of civil proceedings, by the nature of the claim or cause of action.[73]

(7) It is not the form of the requirement that matters but whether it is the case that there is a reasonable chance (or perhaps the probability) that compliance would lead to discovery of the source's identity.[74]

(8) The most careful scrutiny by the court is required before making an order.[75]

(9) The judge starts with the assumptions, first, that the protection of sources is itself a matter of high public importance, secondly, that nothing less than necessity will suffice to override it, thirdly, that the necessity can only arise out of concern for another matter of high public importance, being one of the four interests listed in the section.[76]

(10) Having regard to importance of the protection of journalistic sources for press freedom in a democratic society and the potentially chilling effect an order of source disclosure has on the exercise of that freedom, such a measure cannot be compatible with Art.10 of the Convention unless it is justified by an overriding requirement in the public interest.[77]

(11) It is a question of fact and not discretion (albeit entailing a value judgment) whether disclosure is necessary.[78]

(12) Unless necessity has been established as a matter of fact, no court may order disclosure, and this would appear to be a matter of jurisdiction.[79]

(13) If there is held to be necessity, in relation to any of the exceptions as to national security, or the prevention of public disorder or crime, this will normally conclude the matter.[80]

---

[72] *X Ltd v Morgan-Grampian (Publishers) Ltd* [1991] 1 A.C. 1 at 43, Lord Bridge, and 54, Lord Oliver; *Camelot Group plc v Centaur Communications Ltd* [1999] Q.B. 124. Lord Phillips pointed out in the Court of Appeal in *Ashworth Hospital Authority v MGN Ltd* [2001] 1 W.L.R. 515 that s.10 of the Contempt of Court Act, and specifically its exceptions to source protection, must always be reconciled with the terms of Art.10 which does not itself include the phrase "interests of justice".
[73] [1985] A.C. 339 at 349, Lord Diplock; at 356–7, Lord Fraser; at 362–3, Lord Scarman; at 368–9, Lord Roskill; at 372, Lord Bridge.
[74] *ibid.* at 349, Lord Diplock; at 356, Lord Fraser; at 362, Lord Scarman, who preferred the test of "probability"; at 369, Lord Roskill; at 372, Lord Bridge.
[75] *Goodwin v United Kingdom* (1996) 22 E.H.R.R. 123, para.40; see also *Sunday Times v UK (No.2)* (1991) 14 E.H.R.R. 229.
[76] Lord Bridge in *X Ltd v Morgan-Grampian (Publishers) Ltd* [1991] 1 A.C. 1 at 41. See also *Re an Inquiry Under the Company Securities (Insider Dealing) Act 1985* [1988] A.C. 660 at 703E, Lord Griffiths.
[77] *Goodwin v United Kingdom* (1996) 22 E.H.R.R. 123, paras 39 and 45; *Chief Constable of Leicestershire v Garavelli* [1997] E.M.L.R. 543.
[78] *X Ltd v Morgan-Grampian (Publishers) Ltd* [1991] 1 A.C. 1 at 44.
[79] *Special Hospital Services Authority v Hyde* (1994) 20 B.M.L.R. 75, Sir Peter Pain.
[80] *X Ltd v Morgan-Grampian (Publishers) Ltd* [1991] 1 A.C. 1 at 43; *Secretary of State for Defence v Guardian Newpapers Ltd* [1985] A.C. 339.

A General Summary of the Principles 9–245

(14) In the case of the "interests of justice" exception, even if it is held to be necessary, there may sometimes still be room for the exercise of a discretion against disclosure.[81]

(15) In assessing the "interests of justice", in the context of particular proceedings, there is a need to identify the true issues in those proceedings.[82]

(16) A journalist's motives for refusing to answer a question as to his sources have no bearing on whether or not he is in contempt in so refusing.[83]

(17) If necessity, in the public interest, cannot be demonstrated under one of the four specified exceptions, then there is an absolute statutory right to refuse to reveal the relevant information, and an immunity from contempt proceedings for so doing.[84]

(18) A court hearing committal proceedings against a respondent for refusing to reveal a source may re-open the validity of the original order for disclosure.[85]

(19) If the order for disclosure takes the form of an injunction against a party in litigation, there would until recently have been a right to appeal.[86] Although there is no longer any right, as such, permission may be granted to appeal. If, however, it is simply a direction against a journalist appearing as a witness in the course of proceedings to reveal a source, there is as yet no opportunity of appeal—even with permission.

(20) The courts should approach the interpretation of s.10 in such a way, so far as possible, as (i) to equate the specific purposes for which disclosure of source is permitted under s.10 with the "legitimate aims" under Art.10, and (ii) to apply the same test of necessity to that applied by the European Court of Human Rights when considering Art.10.[87]

---

[81] *Re an Inquiry Under the Company Securities (Insider Dealing) Act 1985* [1988] A.C. 660 at 703G–H; *X Ltd v Morgan-Grampian (Publishers) Ltd* [1991] 1 A.C. 1 at 28, Lord Donaldson M.R.; *Special Hospital Services Authority v Hyde* (1994) 20 B.M.L.R. 75 at 85; *Handmade Films (Productions) Ltd v Express Newspapers Ltd* [1986] F.S.R. 463.
[82] *Secretary of State for Defence v Guardian Newpapers Ltd* [1985] A.C. 339 at 350B–C; *Maxwell v Pressdram Ltd* [1987] 1 W.L.R. 298, Kerr L.J.; *Handmade Films (Productions) Ltd v Express Newpapers Ltd* [1986] F.S.R. 463, Browne-Wilkinson V.-C.
[83] *Att-Gen v Lundin* (1982) 75 Cr.App.R. 90 at 99.
[84] *Chief Constable of Leicestershire v Garavelli* [1997] E.M.L.R. 543.
[85] *Att-Gen v Lundin* (1982) 75 Cr.App.R. 90; see also *Chief Constable of Leicestershire v Garavelli* [1997] E.M.L.R. 543.
[86] See, *e.g. Secretary of State for Defence v Guardian Newspapers Ltd* [1985] A.C. 339, and also Supreme Court Act 1981, s.18(1)(h)(iii). But the matter is now governed by the ordinary principles applying since May 2000 whereby permission to appeal is required: see CPR Pt 52 and *Tanfern Ltd v Cameron MacDonald (Practice Note)* [2000] 1 W.L.R. 1311. See also paras 13–118 *et seq*. And paras 15–88 *et seq*.
[87] *Ashworth Hospital Authority v MGN Ltd* [2001] 1 W.L.R. 515 at 532–3, Lord Phillips M.R.

CHAPTER 10

CONTEMPT IN THE FACE OF THE COURT

		PARA
I.	Introduction	10–1
II.	The Requirements of Natural Justice: Article 6	10–36
III.	Disturbing Proceedings in Court	10–88
IV.	Statutory Contempts in the Face	10–112
V.	Improper Conduct of a Case	10–131
VI.	Contempt Committed By Witnesses	10–157
VII.	Contempt Committed By Jurors	10–176
VIII.	Unauthorised Recording of Court Proceedings	10–190
IX.	*Mens Rea* for Contempt in the Face of the Court	10–208

I. INTRODUCTION

A. The common thread

10–1 In earlier chapters, we have considered the subject of media contempt, both in the context of the 1981 Act and at common law. We now turn to other forms of conduct that have in the past been characterised as criminal contempt.[1] These may seem to be a motley and disparate grouping, but the unifying thread is that any system of justice must have the means readily to hand to protect its processes, and to guarantee the unhindered access of citizens to the courts,[2] as well as to punish those who would impede or subvert that system.

10–2 More particularly, in this chapter we confine ourselves to considering what may broadly be described as contempt in the face of the court; that is to say, the category which involves some form of misconduct in the course of proceedings, either within the court itself or, at least, directly connected with what is happening in court.[3] It is in this context that the summary jurisdiction is especially valuable and can most readily be justified.

10–3 The power of immediate imprisonment is sometimes required as a ready means of discouraging and punishing conduct which impedes the flow of justice. It was observed in *R. v Powell*[4] that:

---

[1] For a discussion of the differences between criminal contempt and criminal offences under the general law, see para.3–55.
[2] *Att-Gen v Times Newspapers Ltd* [1974] A.C. 273 at 309, Lord Diplock, set out at para.2–8.
[3] This is a distinction that seems to have been recognised from early times: see *Dean's* case (1598) Cro. Eliz. 689, 78 E.R. 925, referred to at para.1–23.
[4] (1993) 98 Cr.App.R. 224 at 226, Staughton L.J.

" . . . disruption of courts is unfortunately becoming commoner. There are some cases which, although serious, do not justify the cumbersome procedure of reporting the matter to the Attorney-General, waiting for him to consider it, prepare affidavits and possibly oral evidence, and then have a Motion before the Divisional Court. In such cases, it seems to us that it is right for the judge to deal with the matter then and there."

On occasion it is necessary to have available an immediate remedy, as was explained by Lawton L.J. in *Balogh v St. Albans Crown Court*,[5] "for the purpose of ensuring that a trial in progress or about to start can be brought to a proper and dignified end without disturbance and with a fair chance of a just verdict or judgment." There is no doubt, however, that contempt in the face of the court extends more widely than can be accounted for by this reasoning.[6] Yet, once the exigencies of the moment begin to recede, the need for a special summary form of procedure becomes less obvious.

B. The significance of contempt "in the face"

The traditional distinction drawn between contempts in the face of the court and those committed outside the court may not be of any great practical significance today, and thus it is probably unnecessary to analyse too closely where the boundary lies between the two categories. It is inevitably somewhat indistinct. The continuing relevance of the distinction may broadly be summarised under the following headings:

1. *Inherent jurisdiction*

So far as inherent jurisdiction is concerned, the common law approach was that inferior courts of record were limited to dealing with contempts in the face. Since nowadays those powers Parliament has deemed necessary for such courts (in particular, the county court[7] and the magistrates' court)[8] are bestowed by statute, it is largely unnecessary to consider the limits of their inherent jurisdiction. The matter may nonetheless remain of some significance[9] in relation to coroners' courts[10] and other courts of record.[11] Such important statutory creatures as

---

[5] [1975] Q.B. 73 at 92–3. See also *R. v Jesus Aquarius* (1974) 59 Cr.App.R. 165 at 169, Roskill L.J., quoted at para.10–104.
[6] See, *e.g. R. v Goult* (1982) 76 Cr.App.R. 140, 4 Cr.App.R.(S) 355, CACD, discussed at para.11–183. This concerned a sustained campaign of intimidation of jurors, both by menacing stares in court and by threatening behaviour *outside*.
[7] para.13–90.
[8] paras 10–113, and 13–106.
[9] In *R. v Griffin* (1989) 88 Cr.App.R. 63 at 69, Mustill L.J. made the point that it could sometimes be of "crucial importance" to determine the question, but on the facts before him it did not arise since the contempt there alleged was of the Crown Court; its jurisdiction was not confined to contempt in the face.
[10] See *R. v West Yorkshire Coroner Ex p. Smith (No.2)* [1985] Q.B. 1096, and the discussion at para.13–100.
[11] See, *e.g.* para.13–103.

mental health review[12] and employment tribunals[13] have been held to be inferior courts for the purposes of protection by the Divisional Court in its supervisory jurisdiction. On the other hand, they have not been declared by statute to be courts of record (unlike, for example, the Employment Appeal Tribunal),[14] and no specific powers have been conferred by Parliament to deal even with contempts in the face of the court.

2. The scope of the jurisdiction of the Divisional Court

10–7 It is provided by CPR Sch.1, Ord.52.1(2), where contempt of court is committed in connection with certain proceedings, that an order of committal may *only* be made by a Divisional Court. One of the categories consists of "criminal proceedings"[15] and would embrace criminal proceedings in the Crown Court (itself part of the Supreme Court).[16] Nevertheless, it is expressly provided that this exclusive jurisdiction of the Divisional Court does not apply where the contempt "is committed in the face of the court or consists of disobedience to an order of the court or a breach of an undertaking to the court." Accordingly, the Crown Court would have a power to deal with contempt in the face (whereas, usually, it would not deal with a strict liability contempt committed in relation to proceedings in progress before it, or any other form of extraneous interference).[17] "The customary manner of proceeding in a case of disobedience to the order of a court, which is not committed in the face of the court, is by application for committal made pursuant to leave therefor to the Divisional Court ... under R.S.C. Ord. 52".[18] For this reason too, therefore, it may be of significance to determine on the facts of a given case upon which side of the line the relevant conduct falls. Even where there has been a contempt in the face, it may sometimes be more appropriate to refer the matter for consideration by the Attorney-General and the Divisional Court, which would have concurrent jurisdiction. On the other hand, it may be better for all concerned to deal with the disturbance promptly and more cheaply.[19]

3. The matter of mens rea

10–8 At one time, it appeared possible that there might be a distinction to be drawn as to the need for *mens rea* in the case of particular contempts, depending upon whether they could be classified as having occurred "in the face". For example,

---

[12] See *P v Liverpool Daily Post and Echo Newspapers plc* [1991] 2 A.C. 370, para.13–66.
[13] *Peach Grey & Co (A Firm) v Sommers* [1995] 2 All E.R. 513, para.13–62. Industrial tribunals became known as "employment tribunals" by virtue of the Employment Rights (Dispute Resolution) Act 1998, s.1.
[14] Employment Tribunals Act 1996, s.20(3).
[15] Subr.(2)(a)(ii).
[16] Supreme Court Act 1981, s.1.
[17] See para.13–32. See also Aikens J. in *Ex p. HTV Cymru (Wales) Ltd* [2002] E.M.L.R. 184.
[18] *R. v D* [1984] 1 A.C. 778 at 792B, Watkins L.J., CA.
[19] See, *e.g.* Staughton L.J. in *R. v Powell* (1993) 98 Cr.App.R. 224 at 226 and *R. v Jones* [1996] Crim. L.R. 806.

in *R. v Hill*[20] abuse had been directed at a judge by a woman in the public gallery (to the effect that he was biased and racist). This occurred shortly after the proceedings had adjourned, and the court was in the process of being cleared. An argument was raised on her behalf that the words uttered had not been *intended* to constitute an interference with the due administration of justice. This was rejected and the insult was described as "a classic example of contempt, palpably calculated to interfere with the administration of justice".

The use of the word "calculated" might have been thought to suggest an objective test, and thus provide some support for the view that such conduct would constitute an offence of strict liability, in the sense that it would be unnecessary to prove an intention to interfere with the course of justice (as opposed to intending to do the act in question). In the light of subsequent authorities, however, it would now appear to be firmly settled that an intention to interfere with the administration of justice has to be demonstrated irrespective of whether the conduct in question occurs in or out of court.[21] Each case will depend upon its own facts, but it may often be easier to infer the necessary intention in cases where the disruptive conduct actually occurs in court. The court is unlikely in practice to be receptive to arguments, along the lines of that in *Hill*, to the effect that there was an intention merely to insult the judge but not to interfere with the course of justice as such.

4. Public funding for legal advice and representation

Another reason for differentiating contempt in the face from other forms of contempt is that the availability of public funding varies from one species to another.[22] It is still the case that the provisions contained in the Access to Justice Act 1999 make it clear that legal funding is available for those alleged to be guilty of contempt in the face of the court, by contrast with other forms of contempt.[23]

C. What constitutes the "face of the court"?

Lord Denning in *Morris v Crown Office*[24] described the need for the summary jurisdiction in this context:

"The phrase 'contempt in the face of the court' has a quaint old-fashioned ring about it; but the importance of it is this: of all the places where law and order must be maintained, it is here in these courts. The course of justice must not be deflected or interfered with. Those who strike at it strike at the very foundations of our society. To

---

[20] [1986] Crim. L.R. 457, CACD. See also *R. v Smithers and Bowen* (1983) 5 Cr.App.R.(S) 248, CACD, discussed para.10–210; *R. v McDaniel* (1990) 12 Cr.App.R.(S) 45.
[21] See in particular *Att-Gen v Newspaper Publishing plc* [1997] 1 W.L.R. 926, [1997] 3 All E.R. 159, CACD; *R. v Schot and Barclay* [1997] 2 Cr.App.R. 383, (1997) 161 J.P. 473, and the more detailed discussions on *mens rea* both in respect of publication and non-publication contempt at paras 5–132 *et seq.* and paras 11–21 *et seq.*
[22] See the discussion at paras 15–107 *et seq.*
[23] See s.12(2)(f).
[24] [1970] 2 Q.B. 114 at 122B–C.

maintain law and order, the judges have, and must have, power at once to deal with those who offend against it. It is a great power—a power instantly to imprison a person without trial—but it is a necessary power."

10–12 There has been little discussion in English law of what does or does not constitute the "face of the court" for these purposes, perhaps partly because "interference with pending proceedings falls within the summary jurisdiction of a superior court, wherever and whenever committed".[25] Since so many of the English authorities are concerned with such courts, whose jurisdiction extends more widely than merely dealing with contempts "in the face", it is not surprising to find no attempt at a definition of the concept. In relation to inferior courts of record, as Mustill L.J. observed in *R. v Griffin*,[26] that issue can become crucial. Unless such a tribunal is satisfied that the conduct in question is in the face, there simply is no power to act without specific statutory sanction. Such authorities as there are, including in other common law jurisdictions, contain a variety of statements that are not always easy to reconcile.

10–13 In *McKeown v The Queen*, Laskin J. in the Supreme Court of Canada (dissenting) said[27]:

"Contempt in the fact of the court is, in my view, distinguished from contempt not in its face on the footing that all the circumstances are in the personal knowledge of the court. The presiding judge can then deal summarily with the matter without the embarrassment of having to be a witness to issues of fact which may be in dispute because of events occurring outside".

10–14 The rationale of this approach had been explained long before by Blackstone[28]:

"... when the fact, from its nature, must be evident to the court either from ocular or other irrefragable proof, then the law departs from its usual resort, the verdict of twelve men, and relies on the judgment of the court alone".

10–15 By contrast, in *Balogh v St. Albans Crown Court*[29] Lord Denning M.R. so defined the phrase "in the face of the court" as to include not only contempts which the judge has actually witnessed but also conduct within the precincts of the court, and even outside the building, which related to proceedings pending before him or her. This would really amount to treating such conduct as being *constructively* within the sight and hearing of the court itself. The view of Lord Denning was contrasted with that of Laskin J. by Moffitt P. in *Registrar, Court of Appeal v Collins*,[30] who described them as representing the two extremes of possible views as to the meaning of the phrase.

---

[25] *per* Mustill L.J. in *R. v Griffin* (1989) 88 Cr. App.R. 63 at 69.
[26] (1989) 88 Cr.App.R. 63.
[27] (1971) 16 D.L.R. (3d) 390.
[28] *Commentaries* (1st ed., 1769), Vol.3, p.332.
[29] [1975] Q.B. 73 at 84.
[30] [1982] 1 N.S.W.L.R. 682 at 702–3, CA of NSW.

Stephenson L.J. in *Balogh* preferred to avoid confining the jurisdiction by reference to the concept "in the face of the court". He regarded it as extending widely enough to cover all contempts relating to proceedings actually proceeding or imminent.[31] Lawton L.J. stated simply that, once there were reasonable grounds for thinking that a contempt of court had been committed, no matter where, the judge had jurisdiction to deal with it summarily.

In *Lecointe v Court's Administrator of the Central Criminal Court*[32] (referred to in *Balogh*) it seems that the personal knowledge of the judge was not thought to be necessary, since the misconduct in question (distributing leaflets in the gallery) was observed by someone else who drew it to the attention of the judge.

Similarly, in *Purdin v Roberts*,[33] it was alleged that immediately after a trial had been concluded the respondent had approached a witness and assaulted him. This took place in a corridor, and not in the presence of the judge. Notwithstanding that there was a considerable conflict as to what had happened[34] the judge, Neville J., fined the defendant £5, saying:

"It is most important the public should know that persons who attend the courts to give evidence as witnesses in any matter before the courts will be protected from assault *whilst in the precincts of the courts*" (emphasis added).

Even where the conduct has been witnessed by the judge, or it is a matter which directly affects him or her, it probably would not fall within the notion of "contempt in the face" if it occurs away from the precincts of the court building. For example, in the Canadian case of *R. v Vallieres*[35] insulting letters were written to a judge, but this was held by the Quebec Court of Appeal not to be contempt in the face of the court, and summary jurisdiction was said to be reserved for cases of genuine urgency. Deschenes J.A.[36] there observed that the description applied to contempt "committed in the face of the court", in the relevant statute, was intended to cover only " . . . events which took place in Court, in the sight and knowledge of the presiding judge".

There are three modern cases from the Court of Appeal of New South Wales which also throw some light on the boundaries of the notion "the face of the court". They each concerned the troublesome practice of handing out leaflets or other information in close proximity to courtrooms, in circumstances where such material could come into the hands of jurors or witnesses. In *Registrar, Court of*

---

[31] [1975] Q.B. 73 at 89.
[32] February 8, 1973, Bar Library Transcript.
[33] (1910) 74 J.P. Jo. 88. See also *R. v Wigley* (1835) 7 C. & P. 4; 173 E.R. 3, Coleridge J. (The defendant had been struck in the lobby of the court and the contemnor was brought before the judge who heard evidence as to what had taken place and then summarily punished the contempt with a sentence of three days' imprisonment. The power exercised was no different to that exercisable in the event of an assault in the court room itself.)
[34] See however the modern authorities which indicate that such jurisdiction should only be exercised in clear cases at paras 10–57 *et seq.*
[35] (1974) 47 D.L.R. (3d) 378.
[36] *ibid.* at 385.

10–20

Appeal v Collins,[37] in seeking to give general guidance to judges as to their jurisdiction for dealing with such problems, Moffitt P. expressed the view that the narrow construction of the phrase by Laskin J. in *McKeown* ought not to be followed because of a recognition that the jurisdiction over the years "... was enlarged by degrees, the first perhaps being where it extended to a contempt outside the court room where the facts were as certain as if seen by the judge because such facts were admitted, so no evidence of them was required."

10–21 He went on to give examples of what had long before become the practice, certainly of superior courts; namely to deal summarily with conduct calculated to interfere with current proceedings on a wider basis, so as to include conduct occurring outside the court room itself. He referred to *Miller v Knox*,[38] *R. v Wigley*[39] and *Re Johnson*.[40] All of these cases were really based upon the general inherent jurisdiction of the courts to exercise their discretionary powers, as necessary for the purpose of preventing interference (particularly with regard to witnesses and jurors) or disruption.

10–22 None of them was based upon any precise definition of the notion of "in the face of the court". It was the view of Moffitt P. that this concept, or the Latin "*in facie curiae*", should not be narrowly confined by giving the words their literal meaning, but should rather be construed in the light of the enlargement of the courts' powers over the centuries as a matter of practice. This approach was justified as a matter of policy because of the need to end the threatened disruption, to discourage such conduct in future and to establish the court's authority in the relevant proceedings[41]:

"The power is but an essential element of the jurisdiction to try the particular case then current. It is an incident of the general power and duty of any court to ensure that the case before it is duly determined according to law without improper external interference ... [42] The change of practice which has occurred over the centuries has not altered the essential character of the power or the legal foundation on which it rests, but has extended the area of its operation."

10–23 He rejected the notion that whatever happened outside the court room should be dealt with on indictment before a jury and added:

"In more modern times the disposition to deal in the same summary way with contempt without resort to trial on indictment has expanded so what is now regarded as proximate has been enlarged to encompass conduct outside the actual court room."

10–24 In the later Court of Appeal case of *Fraser v The Queen; Meredith v The Queen*[43] "respectful reservations" were expressed about certain of these observations by Kirby P. and McHugh J.A. This was in the context specifically of a

---

[37] [1982] 1 N.S.W.L.R. 682, 705, CA of NSW.
[38] (1838) 4 Bing. (N.C.) 574 at 589; 132 E.R. 910 at 916, HL.
[39] (1835) 7 C. & P. 4, 173 E.R. 3.
[40] (1887) 20 Q.B.D. 68 at 74, Bowen L.J.
[41] [1982] 1 N.S.W.L.R. at 707.
[42] Reference was made to *Cocker v Tempest* (1841) 7 M. & W. 502 at 503–4, 151 E.R. 864 at 865, Alderson B.; *Scott v Scott* [1913] A.C. 417 at 437, Viscount Haldane L.C.
[43] [1984] 3 N.S.W.L.R. 212.

statutory expression applying in New South Wales[44] defining the ambit within which a judge might deal with contempt of court. It did so by requiring that the contempt should have been committed "in the face of the court or in the hearing of the court".

It was recognised that the common law in England and Australia had extended the ambit of the phrase "in the face of the court", as a result of the application of judicial policy, in order to permit the speedy despatch of complaints not actually seen or heard by the judge but occurring in close proximity to the court in question. Nevertheless, the wording of the New South Wales provision did not permit such a generous construction:

> "If the view taken by Moffitt P. in *Registrar, Court of Appeal v Collins* is correct, and if it is possible to extend 'the face of the court' by common law techniques to the surroundings of the court, the area outside the door of the courtroom and the street for a certain distance outside the court . . . , the addition of the phrase 'in the hearing of the court' becomes entirely redundant. It cannot be assumed the legislature included the expression as a rhetorical flourish or that it was inserted without reason. On the contrary, the inclusion of the expression would appear to be designed to extend the ambit of the facility for summary procedures for contempt of the judge's court."

The same tribunal in *Prothonotary v Collins*[45] departed from other aspects of the earlier judgment of Moffitt P. but did not elaborate further on the proper construction of "in the face of the court". In *European Asian Bank A.G. v Wentworth*,[46] the Court of Appeal addressed again, however, the reasons of policy for confining the summary jurisdiction and procedures to acts actually seen, heard or otherwise sensed[47] by the court itself. Kirby P. identified four factors:

1. The summary procedure is extraordinary and exceptional involving as it does a departure from normal curial procedures and in a case criminal in nature where the penalties are at large.

2. It is appropriate to confine the jurisdiction of inferior courts (the powers of which are often defined in similar terms).

3. This approach takes the summary procedure back to its historical origin where it was confined to things seen, heard or otherwise sensed by the judge and thus evidence was not required precisely for that reason.

4. The approach avoids the difficulty of drawing a geographic boundary to the operation of the summary jurisdiction.

This is by no means an exhaustive list, and other considerations may be identified as reasons for restricting the scope of the jurisdiction, for example:

---

[44] Supreme Court Act 1970, s.48(4); Supreme Court Rules 1970, Pt 55, Div. 2.
[45] (1985) 2 N.S.W.L.R. 549, CA of NSW.
[46] (1986) 5 N.S.W.L.R. 445 at 457–8.
[47] It was pointed out, for example, by Kirby P. at 457 that the facts of *Balogh*, had the contemnor succeeded in releasing the laughing gas, might well have engaged the senses of taste and smell as well as sight and hearing.

10–27 CHAPTER 10—CONTEMPT IN THE FACE OF THE COURT

1. If something has occurred outside the immediate observation of the judge, there is inevitably scope for misinterpreting precisely what has happened.

2. If the court itself is not directly disrupted, there may well be insufficient urgency to justify the exercise of the summary jurisdiction.

3. The general criminal law, with its usual safeguards, might often suffice to meet all legitimate concerns for the protection of the administration of justice.

4. Even where only the contempt jurisdiction would meet the particular circumstances, in cases other than those where it is necessary for immediate action to be taken, the proper course of action would be to leave the matter to the Attorney-General to apply for leave in accordance with CPR, Sch.1, Ord.52.

10–28 All these factors are of relevance in considering how far the provisions of the European Convention on Human Rights might exercise a restraining influence upon any United Kingdom court's inclination to extend the summary procedures beyond the immediate vicinity of the court room.[48] It is necessary to bear in mind the constraints of Art.6 of the European Convention on Human Rights,[49] and in particular its requirement for "a fair and public hearing within a reasonable time by an *independent and impartial tribunal* established by law" (emphasis added).

D. Procedure to be used sparingly

10–29 Resort to the summary process of contempt can normally only be justified if it is necessary to protect the administration of justice, either as to particular proceedings or to the judicial process more generally. A judge may be called upon to act, in effect, as witness, prosecutor, judge and jury,[50] and may even perhaps appear in the role of victim.[51] Some of the fundamental safeguards[52] of criminal justice are jeopardised by the use of the summary procedure.

10–30 Lawton L.J. in *Balogh v St. Albans Crown Court*[53] cited *inter alia* the example of reluctant or difficult witnesses, but warned of the need to be discriminating in the application of these sanctions:

---

[48] See in particular the requirements of Art.6 in relation to the need for an "independent and impartial tribunal", and perhaps also those of Art.7 which by extension requires that the criminal law should be certain in its scope. See also paras 10–36 *et seq.*
[49] Set out at para.2–143.
[50] See Woolf L.J in *DPP v Channel Four Television Co Ltd* [1993] 2 All E.R. 517 at 521a ("the judge should not appear to be a prosecutor acting in his own cause"). In *R. v Banham*, 95/3049/Z3 (Lexis), a finding of contempt was quashed where all the questions were asked by the judge, who appeared to be acting as prosecutor in his own cause. See also the remarks of Lord Denning M.R. in *Rooney v Snaresbrook Crown Court* (1979) 68 Cr.App.R. 78 at 81: "It is very undesirable that the judge should be both prosecutor and judge". The proper procedure, now set out in *Archbold 2005*, paras 28.117 *et seq.*, should have been adopted. See also *R. v Powell* (1993) 98 Cr.App.R. 224 at 226, Staughton L.J.; *European Asian Bank v Wentworth* (1986) 5 N.S.W.L.R. 445 at 453, Kirby P.
[51] As to the position when the judge is the victim of a serious assault, see para.10–95.
[52] See paras 2–17 *et seq.*
[53] [1975] Q.B. 73 at 93.

" ... but everything will depend upon the circumstances. For example, judges from time to time have to decide what to do about a witness who refuses to answer a question, often because he cannot bring himself to state that which is obvious to both judge and jury or because the answer would cause acute personal embarrassment, as sometimes happens with doctors and ministers of religion. In many such cases a judicial admonition may be adequate if judicial comment is required at all: but when the witness refuses to answer questions because he wants to deny the court evidence which is important, the position is very different."

The judge should act of his own motion "only when it is urgent and imperative to act immediately."[54] In the words of Lord Goddard C.J. in *Parashuram Detaram Shamdasani v The King Emperor*[55]:

10–31

"Their lordships would once again emphasise what has often been said before, that this summary power of punishing for contempt should be used sparingly and only in serious cases. It is a power which a court must of necessity possess; its usefulness depends on the wisdom and restraint with which it is exercised."

A more modern recognition of the difficulties associated with the use of the summary process is to be found in *R. v Griffin*, where Mustill L.J. said[56]:

10–32

"This summary procedure, which by its nature is to be used quickly if it is used at all, omits many of the safeguards to which an accused is ordinarily entitled, and for this reason it has been repeatedly stated that the judge should choose to adopt it only in cases of real need".

In *R. v Moran*,[57] guidance was given as to the procedures generally to be adopted when considering the use of the summary power; the court stressed in particular the need to pause for reflection. Where a solicitor was arrested, following some slightly insulting remarks directed towards the administrative arrangements ("the ridiculous listing of the Clerk of the court"), the Divisional Court described the incident as a "storm in a teacup".[58] Although it was recognised that it could *not* be said that no reasonable bench of justices could have concluded that the remark was "wilfully insulting",[59] *certiorari* was granted because the applicant should have been given the opportunity to reflect and to obtain advice and representation.

10–33

Judges need to have a degree of tolerance towards emotional displays of frustration or anger, and to be aware of the problem of stress for a defendant and his family when a finding of guilty is announced, or a sentence of imprisonment

10–34

---

[54] *Balogh v St. Albans Crown Court* [1975] Q.B. 73 at 85, Lord Denning M.R.; *Rooney v Snaresbrook Crown Court* (1979) 68 Cr.App.R. 78; *R. v Stafforce Personnel Ltd*, November 24, 2000, CACD.
[55] [1945] A.C. 264 at 270.
[56] (1989) 88 Cr.App.R. 63 at 67.
[57] (1985) 81 Cr.App.R. 51. See paras 10–43 *et seq.*
[58] *R. v Tamworth Justices Ex p. Walsh* [1994] C.O.D. 277, T.L.R. 116; cp. *Weston v CCC Administrator* [1977] Q.B. 32, where similar remarks were made about the listing arrangements at the Old Bailey, although by letter rather than "in the face of the court".
[59] Within the meaning of the Contempt of Court Act 1981, s.12(1)(a), set out at para.10–113.

10–34   imposed.[60] It has to be recognised "that disappointed litigants sometimes feel aggrieved and that some of them are ill-tempered, and that they may say or write things which are foolish and reprehensible."[61] It is rather different if the integrity of witnesses or jurors is under attack, or the court's processes are being abused for some ulterior purpose such as attracting the attention of newspaper reporters.[62]

10–35   The dignity of the court[63] does not always require the exercise of what is, in many respects, a Draconian power if order and decorum can be otherwise preserved. Nevertheless, it is recognised that judges have to take quick decisions in such cases, and that the exercise of this discretionary jurisdiction will not lightly be interfered with,[64] provided that the judge's conduct does not disqualify him for bias, and also provided that he accords the person concerned the safeguards which are now regarded as elementary, even in the context of this summary jurisdiction.

II. THE REQUIREMENTS OF NATURAL JUSTICE: ARTICLE 6

A. The contempt jurisdiction as "rough justice"

10–36   The traditional requirements of natural justice are that no person should be a judge in his own cause, and that decisions affecting citizens should be taken only after affording an opportunity to be heard. These are reflected in the terms of

---

[60] See, *e.g. R. v Logan* [1974] Crim. L.R. 609. It is inappropriate, for example, that a sentencer should reflect insulting remarks in sentencing for the primary offence of which a defendant has been convicted, and any such contempt should be dealt with, if at all, by a separate penalty: see also *R. v Aston* [1948] W.N. 252; *R. v Butt* (1957) 41 Cr.App.R. 82.

[61] *per* Lord President Normand in *J. D. Milburn*, 1946 S.C. 315. See also *R. v Davidson* (1821) 4 Barn. & Ald. 329, 106 E.R. 958; *Lawrie v Roberts & Linton* (1882) 4 Coup. 606; *Royle v Gray*, 1973 S.L.T. 31. Megarry, *Miscellany at Law* (1955) 295, n.19, cites the case of the litigant who threw a dead cat at the judge; the target (the cat having missed its mark) took to heart the spirit of Lord Goddard's emollient remarks in *Parashuram*, para.10–31 above, remarking simply: "I shall commit you for contempt if you do that again". Another source for the story is Sir James Comyn, *Summing It Up* (1991), p.99, who wrote that he was counsel in the case at Lambeth County Court, and that the cat was thrown at him rather than at the phlegmatic judge, who is identified as Judge Clothier Q.C.

[62] *Morris v The Crown Office* [1970] 2 Q.B. 114; *R. v West Yorkshire Coroner Ex p. Smith (No.2)* [1985] Q.B. 1096 (where the father of the deceased shouted out, at an inquest, that one of the witnesses was a murderer). The Phillimore Committee, being conscious of this consideration, regarded it as a factor pointing in the direction of speedy disposal, and commented that "The comparatively protracted procedure of a criminal prosecution and trial would be a further opportunity to obtain publicity or cause disruption, . . . ": para.31.

[63] See paras 16–6 *et seq*.

[64] *R. v Logan* [1974] Crim. L.R. 609. The appellant upon being sentenced for offences of assault occasioning actual bodily harm and possessing dangerous drugs shouted, and used expletives, protesting that his conviction for assault had been a "carve up". A consecutive sentence of six months' imprisonment was imposed. Although it was varied on appeal to one of three months concurrent, the Court of Appeal recognised that the judge was entitled to take into account the background of the case and the appellant's record, and that he could not be criticised for his assessment of the outburst as a serious contempt.

Art.6 of the European Convention.[65] The summary nature of the proceedings for contempt in the face has been criticised by Professor D. Feldman, who argues[66] that it is in breach of Art.6, and in particular Art.6(3), which guarantees *inter alia* that an accused be informed (in a language which he understands) of the nature and cause of the allegation against him; the right to an independent and impartial tribunal; a proper opportunity and facilities for the preparation of a defence, and a right to legal assistance.[67] Inevitably, it might be thought, the contempt procedure "appears to be rough justice; it is contrary to natural justice".[68] It is important therefore that any such appearance should be countered by the adoption of procedures that minimise the impression of injustice.

Such protective measures do not necessarily require statutory implementation. There can be no doubt that the judiciary can make good any such deficiencies of domestic law and practice, so far as compliance with the Convention is concerned.[69] Furthermore, there is reason to suppose that significant progress has been made in this respect even since Professor Feldman first made his criticism in 1993.[70] Courts have insisted on various occasions upon the furnishing of specific procedural safeguards for those facing contempt proceedings.[71] We address these important rights in this chapter, as a matter of substantive law associated with "contempt in the face", rather than merely confining them to the consideration of adjectival law in chapter 15 (Practice and Procedure).

B. The need for safeguards

Various attempts have been made from time to time to provide assistance to judges on how to deal with contempt in the face of the court. Inevitably, however, the circumstances will generally be such that there is little time to consult authorities or to give detailed consideration to the appropriate course. It is important to note the terms of the *Practice Direction* (Pt II of which governs committal for contempt in the face, both in the High Court and in the county court).[72] This supplements CPR Sch.1, Ord.52 and CPR Sch.2, cc29. It embraces most of the basic principles of fairness developed in the authorities and identified

---

[65] Set out in full at para.2–143. It was held in *R. v MacLeod (Calum Iain)* [2001] Crim. L.R. 509, *The Times*, December 20, 2000, CACD that Art.6 does not add to or alter the normal requirement of English law that proceedings should be conducted fairly before an independent and impartial tribunal (*per* Kennedy L.J.).
[66] *Civil Liberties and Human Rights in England and Wales* (2nd ed., 2002) at pp.963 *et seq*. (Oxford University Press). See now the decision of the European Court of Human Rights in *Kyprianou v Cyprus*, App. No.73797/01, January 27, 2004 for a consideration of all these factors.
[67] Cp. the decision of the Supreme Court of Canada in *BK v R.* (1995) 129 D.L.R. (4th) 500, in the context of the Canadian Charter.
[68] *per* Stephenson L.J. in *Balogh v St. Albans Crown Court* [1975] 1 Q.B. 73 at 90A.
[69] This is one of the points to emerge from *Sunday Times v United Kingdom* (1979) 2 E.H.R.R. 245.
[70] See the first edition (1993) at p.740.
[71] See, *e.g. R. v Hill* [1986] Crim. L.R. 457; *Re Hooker* [1993] C.O.D. 190, CO/2478/92 (Lexis); *R. v Tamworth Justices Ex p. Walsh* [1994] C.O.D. 277, T.L.R. 116; *R. v Pateley Bridge Justices Ex p. Percy* [1994] C.O.D. 453; *R. v Bromell* [1996] T.L.R. 67; *R. v Schot and Barclay* [1997] 2 Cr.App.R. 383, (1997) 161 J.P. 473. See also *R. v Arradi* [2003] 1 S.C.R. 280, (2003) 173 C.C.C. (3d)1, (2003) 244 D.L.R. (4th) 301.
[72] The latest version of the Practice Direction is set out in Appendix 5A.

10–38   CHAPTER 10—CONTEMPT IN THE FACE OF THE COURT

in this section of the book. It also emphasises the need to take account of "Convention rights".

10–39   One example of the pitfalls confronting trial judges is to found in *R. v Banham*.[73] The girlfriend of a defendant, who was on trial for burglary, shouted one evening to a prosecution witness. While she admitted shouting "What's your problem?", there was a dispute as to whether she had shouted further abuse. When the matter was reported to the trial judge, he invited the defendant's counsel to represent the girlfriend also. The matter was interposed in the middle of the trial. Little time was given to counsel for preparation. The witness was not cross-examined, because counsel had been given the impression that the girlfriend's limited admission had been accepted, and that there was therefore no need to challenge. Nevertheless, the judge concluded that the disputed remarks *had* been uttered and punished her for contempt.

10–40   The finding of contempt was quashed. There had been no such degree of urgency that the trial judge was justified in declining to give more time to prepare her case. In any event it was unsatisfactory to have her represented by the trial defendant's counsel, since he was likely to have to cross-examine her later. Also, all the questions asked of the alleged contemnor were asked by the trial judge, who thus gave the impression of being prosecutor in his own cause.[74] The correct procedure[75] should have been carried out.

10–41   The principles need, therefore, to be expressed as clearly as possible and to be easy to apply in the exigencies likely to arise in the course of the trial. Guidance was given by the court of Appeal in *R. v Hill*[76] where it was stated that it is for the judge to:

> " . . . take steps to safeguard the court's authority. Those steps will, in appropriate cases, include (1) the immediate arrest and detention of the offender; (2) telling the offender distinctly what the contempt is stated to have been; (3) giving a chance to apologise; (4) affording the opportunity of being advised and represented by counsel and making any necessary order for legal aid for that purpose; (5) granting any adjournment that may be required; (6) entertaining counsel's submission; and (7) if satisfied that punishment is merited imposing it within the limits fixed by statute."

10–42   We now turn to some of the principal safeguards which have been identified in various authorities.

1. *The desirability of a "cooling off" period*

10–43   It has long been recognised that a balance has to be achieved between the need for judges to be able to act decisively and promptly, on the one hand, and that of

---

[73] 95/3049/Z3, November 2, 1995, Kennedy L.J. (Lexis)
[74] Cp. *Rooney v Snaresbrook Crown Court* (1979) 68 Cr.App.R. 78.
[75] As set out in *Archbold 2005*, paras 28–117 *et seq*. (based primarily upon *R. v Moran* (1985) 81 Cr.App.R. 51; *R. v Hill* [1986] Crim. L.R. 457; *R.v Griffin* (1989) 88 Cr.App.R. 63).
[76] [1986] Crim. L.R. 457, Lord Lane C.J., Leggatt and Simon Brown JJ.

guarding against over-reaction on the other. The Phillimore Committee noted[77] that a penalty was on occasion imposed with undue haste and cautioned that the "very extensive" powers should only be exercised "after due deliberation and without their exercise appearing to be influenced by the heat or exasperation of the moment". To similar effect are the remarks of Lawton L.J. in *R. v Moran*[78]:

> "The following principles should be borne in mind. First, a decision to imprison the man for contempt of court should never be taken too quickly. The judge should give himself time for reflection as to what is the best course to take. Secondly, he should consider whether that time for reflection should not extend to a different day because overnight thoughts are sometimes better than thoughts on the spur of the moment."

Although a judge may need to act promptly in the middle of a trial, for example where a witness has been intimidated, it is now recognised that it will generally be wise to postpone giving reasons until the trial has concluded. This would avoid the need to express any view about a witness who was still giving evidence on the issues in the trial itself. It would also be appropriate to defer consideration of a penalty for contempt until the trial is over. Meanwhile, the witness could sometimes be adequately protected by the withdrawal of the defendant's bail.[79] Where there is no need for the court to act immediately to restore order or to ensure that the trial comes to a dignified conclusion, there is no reason why a judge should not defer dealing with an incident of contempt until the conclusion of the trial.[80]

The court should always guard against depriving a person of his liberty for unnecessarily long. In *Wilkinson v S*,[81] the Court of Appeal addressed the question whether it was lawful to order detention for a period beyond the end of the court day before dealing with the alleged contempt. It was said to be necessary to distinguish between jurisdiction and good practice. It cannot in principle be unlawful if the delay is no longer than is necessary to arrange a summary trial with proper protection for the rights of the alleged contemnor. But there had been a delay in that case from Thursday to the following Monday (it being inferred that the respondent had not been in a fit condition to give instructions to his lawyer on the Friday). It was concluded that this would be the very limit of what was lawful or acceptable. As a matter of good practice, even if the case cannot be heard the next day, it should be mentioned in open court (if possible with the respondent present) in order to explain and record the reasons for the further delay. The question of bail should also be addressed, since the provisions of the Bail Act are applicable to all proceedings of a criminal nature.

---

[77] para.33.
[78] (1985) 81 Cr.App.R. 51 at 53.
[79] *R. v MacLeod (Calum Iain)* [2001] Crim. L.R. 509, *The Times*, December 20, 2000, CACD.
[80] *R. v Santiago* [2005] EWCA Crim 556, [2005] 2 Cr.App.R. 24 (a case concerning a physical and verbal altercation with a dock officer, and separately failing to attend for sentencing, in respect of which the judge heard proceedings for contempt eight days after the conclusion of the trial).
[81] [2003] EWCA Civ 95, [2003] 1 W.L.R. 1254, [2003] 2 All E.R. 185.

10–45 A much longer delay occurred in *R. v Yusuf*.[82] The judge issued a warrant for the attendance of an important witness who was required to give evidence in a murder trial on March 24, and he was brought to court the next day. He gave evidence for the Crown but was declared a hostile witness. The jury was later discharged and a retrial ordered for March 31. Meanwhile the appellant remained in custody. He was not called on the retrial and remained in custody until the judge was prepared to deal with him on April 4 after the jury had retired. It was held by the Court of Appeal that it was appropriate for him to be dealt with by the trial judge, who could not be criticised for leaving it so long in view of the fact that he was conducting a murder trial. It was pointed out in the Criminal Law Review commentary[83] that this was hardly consistent with the strict approach in *Wilkinson v S* and it was suggested that tighter regulation was called for. A judge should always remember to consider his possibility of granting bail.

2. Should a judge refer the proceedings to another tribunal?

10–46 The Phillimore Committee identified[84] three advantages of the summary procedure for dealing with contempt in the face of the court, whereby such matters were traditionally dealt with by the judge presiding over the court in which the incident occurred, namely: (1) the judge will be in the best position to deal with the case, since he will generally have witnessed the incident[85]; (2) A judge may deal more leniently with misconduct directed at himself than a fellow judge might be inclined to do; and (3) the threat of immediate punishment is the most effective deterrent.

10–47 Increasingly, however, the disadvantages of the summary procedure have been overtly recognised. One problem is that the judge may not have seen the entire incident of which complaint is made, particularly if the act of contempt is a fleeting and single one. Thus, before the truth can be sufficiently established, it may be necessary to hear a good deal of evidence from eye-witnesses, some of whom may have had a quite different impression from that of the judge. In such a case, inevitably, the judge would be dependent on one or more accounts of what took place out of his own vision. Whether or not there would be a reasonable

---

[82] [2003] EWCA Crim 1488, [2003] Crim. L.R. 877.
[83] At 879–80.
[84] para.30.
[85] In *R. v Hill* [1986] Crim. L.R. 457, Leggatt J. commented: "Even though another judge has jurisdiction to deal summarily with the contempt, a judge, as here, should deal with what has occurred before him for the very reason that it has." See also the commentary on this case by Professor Birch at p.458. A somewhat different approach was taken in *R. v MacLeod (Calum Iain)* [2001] Crim. L.R. 509, *The Times*, December 20, 2000, CACD; it was submitted that an allegation that a witness had been intimidated by the accused (who was on bail in the course of his trial) should be dealt with by a tribunal other than the trial judge. The Court of Appeal observed, however, somewhat paradoxically, that since the conduct was alleged to have taken place in the corridor, and thus not in the view of the judge, there was no reason why he should not be regarded as an independent and impartial tribunal. *MacLeod* was considered in *R. v Santiago* [2005] EWCA Crim 556, [2005] 2 Cr.App.R. 24 where an appeal was dismissed on the basis that the judge was not required to remit proceedings to a fellow judge, because the facts were not in dispute: it was merely a question of mitigation and sentence. Also, the summary procedure was proportionate, given that the facts were not in dispute, and the circumstances did not require the Crown to instigate separate proceedings.

apprehension of bias may turn on who the witnesses are and, for example, whether he has established a professional relationship with a member of the court's staff who saw the incident.[86]

More fundamentally, it is also important in the exercise of this jurisdiction to avoid giving the impression that the judge is biased or that the decision has been prompted by any personal animus.[87] It has been observed in one case[88] that, in order to minimise any impression of bias, it would have been wise for the judge to let counsel for the Crown take a witness through her evidence, rather than doing so himself. It was being alleged that the accused had intimidated her in the course of a trial by remarks made in the corridor outside the court.

10–48

A possible solution had been canvassed in *Balogh v St. Albans Crown Court*[89] that it may be better in some circumstances for an alleged contemnor to be dealt with by another available judge:

10–49

"I see no reason why one judge of the Crown Court or the High Court should not commit for contempt of another.... It depends on all the circumstances whether more than one judge should come in to these summary proceedings. It may be better for a presiding judge available in the same building to commit for a contempt of a circuit judge's court".

In the light of other developments, and in particular the Court of Appeal's decision in *R. v Schot and Barclay*,[90] it is probably now wiser for a judge not deal with a contempt that has arisen in his or her own court where there are any issues of fact to be resolved, or reason to suppose that there is a real danger of even unconscious bias.[91] The right test is whether a fair-minded and informed observer would conclude that there was a real possibility of bias. One should certainly not assume that there is nothing to be said by an alleged contemnor in his own defence. That would not be compatible with the proper discharge of the judicial function.[92]

---

[86] *R. v Haslam* [2003] EWCA Crim 3444, [2003] All E.R. (D) 195 Nov.
[87] See, *e.g. R. v Gough* [1993] A.C. 646 at 670, Lord Goff; see also the decision of the European Court of Human Rights in *Kyprianou v Cyprus*, App. No.73797/01, January 27, 2004.
[88] *R. v MacLeod (Calum Iain)* [2001] Crim. L.R. 509, *The Times*, December 20, 2000, CACD.
[89] [1975] 1 Q.B. 73 at 90D–E, Stephenson L.J. See also Woolf L.J. in *DPP v Channel Four Television* [1993] 2 All E.R. 517 at 521d; *R. v Schot and Barclay* [1997] 2 Cr.App.R. 383, (1997) 161 J.P. 473, discussed at paras 10–72 *et seq.*
[90] [1997] 2 Cr.App.R. 383, (1997) 161 J.P. 473, considered more fully in paras 10–72 *et seq.*
[91] The classic statement of the rule against bias was for many years that of Lord Hewart C.J. in *R. v Sussex Justices Ex p. McCarthy* [1924] 1 K.B.: "The ... question depends not upon what actually was done but upon what might appear to be done. Nothing is to be done which creates even a suspicion that there has been an improper interference with the course of justice." But see now *R. v Inner West London Coroner Ex p. Dallaglio* [1993] 4 All E.R. 139, CA; *Re Medicaments and Related Classes of Goods* [2001] 1 W.L.R. 700, at [85] and [86]; *Porter v Magill* [2001] UKHL 67, [2002] 2 A.C. 357 at [102] and [103]; *Wilkinson v S* [2003] EWCA Civ 95, [2003] 1 W.L.R. 1254, [2003] 2 All E.R. 185. See too in the context of contempt *R. v Schot and Barclay* [1997] 2 Cr.App.R. 383, (1997) 161 J.P. 473.
[92] *Raja v Van Hoogstraten* [2004] EWCA Civ 968, [2004] 4 All E.R. 793 at [94].

10-50 A striking example of a tribunal recusing itself for possible bias is provided by *Re Lonrho plc*[93] where one Committee of the House of Lords decided to refer a possible contempt for the consideration of a different Committee. This concerned the sending of a contentious publication to the individual members of the panel, and was thus not an example of contempt in the face of the court in the usual sense,[94] but nevertheless illustrates well the determination of modern judges to avoid so far as possible any impression that the rules of natural justice are being infringed.

3. The need for the charge to be formulated with precision

10-51 It was also recognised at common law that it is necessary to make plain the nature of an alleged contempt.[95] In *R. v Griffin*,[96] complaint was made that the appellant had not been informed, in precise terms, before the hearing commenced, what charges were brought against him, and that the judge had failed to state which incidents he found proved as constituting contempt. The Court of Appeal allowed the appeal, taking the view that the trial judge had been wrong to exercise the summary jurisdiction in the circumstances, for a number of reasons, not least because if time had been taken for reflection it would have emerged that four or five episodes had to be investigated; the issues could only be resolved by hearing a number of witnesses. There was held to be a "disconformity" between the acts of which the appellant was accused and the only notification he ever received of the nature of the complaint (namely, two statements from witnesses) and the acts for which the judge stated that he was being punished.

10-52 Moreover, the need for full information is at the forefront of the protection sought to be guaranteed in Article 6(3) of the European Convention,[97] and English courts have continued to emphasise this right.[98] For example, in *R. v Peters*,[99] the Court of Appeal made it clear, where a witness was to give evidence at a contempt hearing for the purpose of explaining why she feared giving evidence at a forthcoming trial, that the hearing should if necessary be adjourned and a statement taken from the witness. This was so that all involved could

---

[93] [1990] 2 A.C. 154, discussed more fully at para.4–125. Cp the decision of the European Court of Human Rights in *Kyprianou v Cyprus*, App. No.73797/01, January 27, 2004.
[94] Cp. *R. v Vallieres & Gagnon* (1973) 47 D.L.R. (3d) 378, where insulting letters were sent to a judge and it was held, in the context of s.9(1) of the Canadian Criminal Code then applicable, which permitted appeals only in respect of contempts *not* in the face, that the contempts were appealable for that reason.
[95] *Re Pollard* (1868) L.R. 2 PC. 106; *Chang Hang Kiu v Pigott* [1909] A.C. 312, P.C.; *Maharaj v Att-Gen for Trinidad* [1977] 1 All E.R. 411; *Lewis v Ogden* (1984) 58 A.L.J.R. 342 at 346B (" ... the charge of contempt should specify the nature of the contempt, *i.e.*, that it consists of a wilful insult to the judge, and identify the alleged insult"); *The Magistrates' Court at Prahan v Murphy* [1997] 2 V.R. 186.
[96] (1989) 88 Cr.App.R. 63.
[97] See *Kyprianou v Cyprus*, App. No.73797/01, January 27, 2004.
[98] See, e.g. *R v Hill* [1986] Crim. L.R. 457, CACD; *R. v Selby Justices Ex p. Frame* [1992] 1 Q.B. 72, DC.; *Peters*, September 8, 1996, No.96/4112/Y5; *R. v Schot and Barclay* [1997] 2 Cr.App.R. 383, (1997) 161 J.P. 473, CACD; see paras 10–72 *et seq*.
[99] September 8, 1996, No.96/4112/Y5.

understand the nature of her allegation, including the legal representatives of the person accused of contempt.

4. Time to prepare a defence and take legal advice

Quite apart from the need for reflection and the avoidance of bias on the part of the court, there are practical difficulties for a person who suddenly finds himself at risk of summary committal; he needs the opportunity of taking informed legal advice and preparing a reasoned response, even though it may be limited to mitigation of sentence.[1]

Where he is already represented before the court, it will normally be appropriate to allow the advocate a proper opportunity to take instructions, and to consider the law, before proceeding with a contempt point where it has arisen unexpectedly in the course of a hearing.[2]

If the alleged contemnor is unrepresented, it would be wise to explain any defence (*e.g.* a specific statutory defence) available to him. In *R. v Dodds*,[3] a man summoned for jury service was found to be in contempt for not being willing to co-operate with the security checks, but it was not explained to him that he had a potential argument based on the statutory concept of "reasonable cause". Accordingly the finding of contempt was quashed on appeal.

In *Coward v Stapleton*,[4] the High Court of Australia set out the general principle:

"The charge having been made sufficiently explicit, the person accused must then be allowed a reasonable opportunity of being heard in his own defence, that is to say a reasonable opportunity of placing before the court any explanation or amplification of his evidence, and any submissions of fact or law, which he may wish the court to consider as bearing either upon the charge itself or upon the question of punishment."

The questions that arise, even in apparently clear cases of contempt in the face of the court, may be matters of some complexity.[5] Also, the facts may not disclose a convincing case of contempt in themselves, and may require fuller investigation.[6] Lord Russell of Killowen C.J. in *R. v Gray*[7] observed that the jurisdiction to deal with contempt *brevi manu* should be exercised with scrupulous care, and only where the case is clear and beyond reasonable doubt

---

[1] *R. v Haslam* [2003] EWCA Crim 3444, [2003] All E.R. (D) 195 (Nov); *Raja v Van Hoogstraten* [2004] EWCA Civ 968, [2004] 4 All E.R. 793 at [91], [92] and [94].
[2] See, *e.g. R. v Lubega* (1999) 163 J.P. 221 at 223, CACD.
[3] [2002] EWCA Crim 1328, [2003] 1 Cr.App.R. 3, [2003] Crim. L.R. 735.
[4] (1953) 90 C.L.R. 573 at 579–80.
[5] As in *R. v Schot and Barclay* [1997] 2 Cr.App.R. 383, (1997) 161 J.P. 473, discussed at paras 10–72 *et seq.* See also R.B. Kuhns, "The Summary Contempt Power: A Critique and a New Perspective" (1978) 88 Yale Law Jo. 39.
[6] *R. v Peters*, September 8, 1996, No.96/4112/Y5.
[7] [1900] 2 Q.B. 36 at 41. Although this was a case of "scandalising", the remarks would appear to be of general significance.

10–57   "... because, if it is not a case beyond reasonable doubt, the courts will and ought to leave the Attorney-General to proceed...".

10–58   This cautious approach seems to have been overlooked in *R. v Shafiq*,[8] where a finding was quashed because the judge followed the wrong procedure, unfairly preventing the applicant from presenting his case, which was based on identification. The judge had offered to hear the matter in full in five weeks time, the applicant remaining in custody meanwhile. The court took the view that the proper course would have been for the judge to re-arrange his own schedule so that he could hear it reasonably promptly, or to refer the matter to the Attorney-General.

10–59   Even in cases where the facts underlying the contempt appear straightforward, the court should recognise that the person concerned must be offered legal advice[9] and the opportunity to reflect and apologise. Lawton L.J. in *R. v Moran*[10] said:

"... the judge should consider whether the seeming contemnor should have some advice. We do not accept the proposition which was tentatively put forward on this appeal that this contemnor had a right to legal advice. Sometimes situations arise in court when the judge has to act quickly and to pass such sentence as he thinks appropriate at once; so there cannot be any right to legal advice. Justice does not require a contemnor in the face of the court to have a right to legal advice.[11] But if the circumstances are such that it is possible for the contemnor to have advice, he should be given an opportunity of having it... Giving a contemnor an opportunity to apologise is one of the most important aspects of this summary procedure, which is in many ways Draconian".

It may be that judges today would be less willing to take such a robust attitude.[12] It is true that a judge may be required to act quickly, for example, in order to bring a disturbance to a conclusion and may need, for that purpose, to have someone removed promptly. Yet it is not so obvious that a sentence needs to be imposed "at once". Indeed, more recent authorities suggest that time for reflection is generally desirable. Also, other authorities indicate that, even though there may be no "right" to public funding, every reasonable opportunity should be given for someone alleged to be in contempt to present a defence.

10–60   In *R. v Bromell*,[13] a finding of contempt, involving an allegation of attempting to bribe a potential witness, was quashed where the applicant had not been afforded legal representation even though it would have been practicable to have

---

[8] 95/8194/W4, January 12, 1996, CACD.
[9] Public funding for legal representation is available for contempts in the face; this is discussed more fully at paras 15–109 *et seq*.
[10] (1985) 81 Cr.App.R. 51.
[11] Lawton L.J. was speaking at a time before the Legal Aid Act 1988, s.29 came into effect. Even though provision was made in this and in subsequent legislation for public funding to be provided in contempt cases in a variety of circumstances, it would still strictly be correct that there is no "right" to such assistance. See paras 15–109 *et seq*.
[12] Lawton L.J. had himself had said that time for reflection was desirable. See para.10–43 above.
[13] [1996] T.L.R. 67, CACD.

done so. The judge had rightly dealt with the matter as one of urgency, having regard to the possible effect upon the trial; nonetheless having allowed legal representation, it was wrong for the judge to have declined to hear counsel on the issue of liability and confined his submissions to the matter of sentence. It was said by Hobhouse L.J. that it should be the "almost invariable practice that a person faced with an allegation of contempt and the prospect of imprisonment should be afforded legal representation if that were practicable".

What is "practicable" will depend upon the circumstances of each case, but plainly an important factor will be whether or not there is an urgent need to restore order. For example, in *R. v K*,[14] Watkins L.J. commented that it is always wise that no action be taken in haste, but he recognised that a judge might well be called upon to take swift and sometimes punitive action when suddenly confronted with protesters bursting into court and interrupting proceedings.

The Divisional Court refused to grant *certiorari* on the ground of breach of natural justice in a case where it was held that what had taken place was a serious contempt in the face of the court. In *R. v Newbury Justices Ex p. Pont*,[15] there had been a hearing before magistrates involving three defendants of whom only one was unrepresented. A request on behalf of the two represented defendants for an adjournment had been granted, but the defendant in person objected, and an exchange of words took place between her and the chairman of the bench. When he was trying to explain the situation to her she interrupted on a number of occasions. She was ordered to be removed from the court whereupon a serious disturbance broke out and police officers were instructed to take 11 people into custody. Shortly afterwards each of the 11 was dealt with by the magistrates pursuant to the powers under s.12 of the Contempt of Court Act 1981.[16] Eight of them (including the five applicants for *certiorari*) were sent to prison for 14 days.

Before the Divisional Court it was argued that there had been a breach of the rules of natural justice and, in particular, of the provisions of the Powers of Criminal Courts Act 1973, s.21(1): "A magistrates' court on summary conviction... shall not pass a sentence of imprisonment... on a person who is not legally represented in that court...". It was held that the action taken by the magistrates did not amount to a "summary conviction", and that s.21[17] had no application to a committal for contempt. May L.J. considered nevertheless that the most meritorious of the points taken before the court was the absence of legal representation. He continued:

"I remind myself, however, that this was a serious contempt in the face of the court, preventing it from carrying on its business, which had to be dealt with swiftly and firmly. I do not think that in those circumstances the requirements of natural justice did require the magistrates to see to it that any of the alleged contemners [*sic*] were afforded

---

[14] (1983) 78 Cr.App.R. 82 at 87.
[15] (1983) 78 Cr.App.R. 255.
[16] See paras 10–113 *et seq.*
[17] The equivalent provision is now contained in s.83 of the Powers of Criminal Courts (Sentencing) Act 2000.

10–63 CHAPTER 10—CONTEMPT IN THE FACE OF THE COURT

a right to legal representation and I do not think that this application can succeed on that basis."

10–64 It is doubtful, in the light of subsequent authorities, whether such an approach would be followed today even in the case of a disruptive demonstration. The court could be cleared and order restored, even though the matter of contempt was put off to be dealt with after an opportunity for reflect and for the obtaining of legal advice. Indeed, it is to be noted that May L.J. himself added the following words, namely:

> " ... should similar circumstances arise again—which I very much hope they do not—and should there be counsel or a solicitor in the court at the time, then the justices would no doubt consider whether they might ask either counsel or solicitor to have a word with the persons taken into custody ... ".

10–65 More recently, there has been an increasing emphasis upon the need to afford the opportunity of legal representation. Ten years later, for example, the Divisional Court, in *Re Hooker*,[18] allowed an appeal under s.13 of the Administration of Justice Act 1960 in respect of an order made by a stipendiary magistrate that an experienced freelance shorthand writer should pay a substantial fine for having used a tape-recorder without leave of the court.[19] The situation should never have developed as it did. Although the ingredients of the offence had been present, it was held that "such facts did not constitute a contempt where the finding had been arrived at in a way which the appellate court considered to be wholly unsatisfactory."[20] Once again the point was made that a court should be slow to act without giving reasonable thought to the problem with which it was faced, and without giving the person concerned an opportunity to take advice and to apologise.

10–66 In yet another case,[21] in which the Divisional Court found justices to have been entitled to find that a contempt had been committed, a sentence of one month's imprisonment was quashed and one day's imprisonment substituted. There were two linked applications for judicial review relating to a health visitor who had faced two charges of causing criminal damage. She appeared before magistrates unrepresented and asked to occupy the space normally allocated to professional advocates. The court refused her request, but she persisted and was held to be in contempt. (It was unclear whether a penalty had been imposed on that occasion.)

10–67 A week later, she appeared before the justices at a hearing to fix the trial, and made a similar application. Once again, her application was refused, and again

---

[18] [1993] C.O.D. 190, CO/2478/92 (Lexis).
[19] An offence contrary to the Contempt of Court Act, s.9(1), discussed more fully at paras 10–191 *et seq*.
[20] The court cited in support *R. v Moran* (1985) 81 Cr.App.R. 51 and *R. v Renshaw* [1989] Crim. L.R. 11. The proposition as stated may not be correctly reported, since it would be odd to judge retrospectively whether or not the facts of a situation constituted contempt of court by reference to how the matter had been dealt with procedurally by the tribunal concerned. It would be another matter to conclude that a finding should be quashed for procedural irregularity.
[21] *R. v Pateley Bridge Justices Ex p. Percy* [1994] C.O.D. 453.

she persisted in remaining at the advocates' table. She was informed that she was in contempt and escorted out of court. Shortly afterwards she was brought back and placed in the dock. She then refused to plead to the charges. A solicitor agreed to act for her in the contempt proceedings, and legal aid was granted. When the case was called on again, the applicant refused to go back into court. Her solicitor stated that she was not prepared to apologise, even though she "intended no malice towards the Bench". She was fined £100 in her presence, although she later denied being there.

About a month later, the case came back before a different chairman for the hearing of an application to adjourn and for variation of bail conditions. She was asked on this occasion three times to move from the advocates' position, but again refused. She was eventually held to be in contempt and, after being given a further opportunity to move, she was sentenced to one month's imprisonment.

In the Divisional Court it was held that on the first occasion the court had followed the correct procedure consequent upon the justifiable finding of contempt. On the second occasion, however, the justices did not appear to have considered the possibility of legal representation. This in itself did not warrant criticism, in view of the particular history, but since she was not legally represented the court had a duty to give her an opportunity to apologise. It would also have been wise to point out the risk of custody. For those reasons, the challenge to the sentence of one month's imprisonment was upheld and, following an apology relayed by counsel on behalf of the applicant, the court substituted a sentence of one day.

One aspect of the "considerable feeling of unease" felt by the Divisional Court in *R. v Selby Justices Ex p. Frame*,[22] after a 16-year-old had been given a custodial sentence for causing a disturbance contrary to s.12 of the Contempt of Court Act 1981, was that the justices proceeded solely on the basis of hearing a commotion below the court. The young man was not brought up or given an opportunity to deny or admit his involvement in the disturbance and, moreover, he was not legally represented.

5. *Protection against self-incrimination*

There is a privilege against self-incrimination in cases of criminal contempt (though it is difficult to find examples of it in the reports). Nevertheless, the Court of Appeal has confirmed[23] that a person accused of contempt should be alerted to the fact that he is at risk of losing his liberty, and that he is not obliged to answer questions and in particular ones that may be incriminating. How that can be translated into practice when the contempt has occurred in the face of the court is somewhat problematic.

---

[22] [1992] Q.B. 72 at 82, DC.
[23] In *R. v Schot and Barclay* [1997] 2 Cr.App.R. 383, (1997) 161 J.P. 473.

6. *General guidance given in* R. v Schot and Barclay

10–72 More comprehensive guidance, for the avoidance of judicial pitfalls, has been given by the Court of Appeal in the case of *R. v Schot and Barclay*.[24] Such is the importance of the case that it needs to be considered in some detail. Although it was concerned with a finding of contempt against two jurors in the Crown Court, it is clear that the principles set out there would also provide valuable guidance to any judge confronted with making a difficult decision at short notice, and especially when a contempt appears to have been committed in the face of the court.

10–73 The Crown Court judge had made a finding that the two appellants were in contempt of court, and had sentenced them to 30 days' imprisonment. They appealed by right under s.13 of the Administration of Justice Act 1960.

10–74 They were among the jurors sworn for the purposes of a trial in which a number of accused were charged with having custody or control of a counterfeit note. Before the jury were empanelled, the judge explained that the trial would take more than two weeks, and asked if this would cause any difficulty. The potential jurors had also seen the terms of the jury summons, and an explanatory pamphlet and video providing information about jury service. Yet, at the conclusion of the trial, some three weeks later, a note was received after the jury's retirement to this effect:

"Your Honour,

We are unable to come to any decisions owing to some jurors conscious beliefs. Please advise".

10–75 The jury were asked to write a fuller note explaining the problem, and in particular what was meant by "conscious beliefs".[25] The response was in the following terms:

"Your Honour,

Some members of the jury cannot bring themselves to make a true judgment due to our beliefs, not religious but personal.

At the beginning of the trial, before we took the oath we felt that we could not stand up in the court and stress this fact.

We thought that our feelings may change over time. After retiring we found that we still feel the same and cannot give a true verdict to these defendants."

---

[24] [1997] 2 Cr.App.R. 383, (1997) 161 J.P. 473, CACD.
[25] Clearly a reference to "conscience" was intended, but it now appears that this would not justify excusal even if mentioned before the trial began. The statutory provisions contained in s.9A of the Juries Act 1974 as a result of the 2003 reforms significantly restrict opportunities for avoiding jury service.

It transpired that one of the appellants was indeed the (female) foreman of the jury.

In the course of discussions with counsel, in the absence of the jury, the judge referred on several occasions to the "contempt" (and on one occasion "awful contempt") which he said had been committed, and it was decided that the jury should be discharged. Before this was done, however, the jury at his request provided the names of the members referred to in the second note. Then the judge expressed his disappointment at the fact that these difficulties had not been raised earlier, and commented that the trial had cost the taxpayer "an awful lot of money". He continued:

> "I am going to say to you therefore that I am angered about it and will discharge you from further deliberating on this matter. But in so far as those two jurors are concerned whose names are Carol Barclay and Bonnie Schot I want them to come before this court for the direct contempt that they have shown to this court and show cause why they ought not to be fined substantial amounts of money and I will give them until the 24th March if they so wish to go and see solicitors, have themselves represented and be before me, on 24th March at 10.15 in the morning, okay. That is . . . show cause why you should not be fined for the deliberate contempt you have shown to this court in wasting so much of court time and leading us in to this situation."

Summonses were sent to attend, this time "to show cause why you should not be held in Contempt of Court for the said refusal to deliver a verdict". An accompanying letter indicated that legal aid had been granted for them to be represented by an advocate, and that they were to notify the court clerk on their arrival so that one could be assigned on that occasion. This is what in fact took place. Although neither of the assigned advocates applied for an adjournment, they clearly had little time to consider the matter, as the hearing was to commence at 10.15 a.m.

It was assumed that the burden upon the appellants was such that they had to "show cause" why they had not been in contempt. Moreover, no warning was given by the judge that there was no obligation on either of the appellants to give evidence or answer questions that might incriminate them.

Barclay gave evidence first and said that she had tried her best to return a verdict but was unable to make up her mind. She did not intend to disrupt the proceedings or to be disrespectful. Schot said that as the elected foreman she had initiated the jury discussions and had every intention originally of reaching a verdict. She too later found herself unable to do so, in that she could not decide. Both appellants had been questioned by the judge and, *inter alia*, denied that they had been approached by anyone seeking to persuade them to behave as they had. The judge then concluded that both appellants were guilty of contempt "because both of them in their own way have intentionally disrupted this entire trial by their refusal". Up to this point no indication had been given that the judge was contemplating a custodial sentence (having originally referred only to the possibility of a fine).

At the appeal hearing criticism was made of the shifting characterisation of the alleged contempt by the judge at different stages. He had referred (when the

[717]

second note had been delivered) to the failure to mention the problem at an earlier stage, and to the wasting of court time. The summons referred to the refusal to give a verdict. Yet the findings included an intention to disrupt "the entire trial". Also, quite apart from the impermissible intrusion upon the deliberations of the jury,[26] there were substantial defects in the contempt proceedings themselves.

10–81 The appellants relied upon the following criticisms:

1. They had been denied adequate and effective legal representation.

2. Counsel in obtaining instructions might personally be in breach of the law in seeking disclosure of jury deliberations.

3. There was no warning to the effect that they were not obliged to give evidence, or that they were not obliged to say anything that might incriminate them.

4. There was no *prima facie* case to justify a finding of contempt, in that:
    (a) there was no evidence to establish the *actus reus* of contempt, and in particular, the points were made
        (i) that the first jury note was merely a request for advice, and
        (ii) the mere fact that a jury declines to return a verdict does not entail an interference with justice;
    (b) there was nothing to justify a finding by the judge that he rejected Schot's evidence or that she had the necessary *mens rea* (even if the *actus reus* had been established).

5. Both counsel emphasised the threat to the jury system in general if jurors felt exposed to contempt proceedings in such circumstances.

10–82 The court was assisted by the following submissions from an *amicus curiae*:

1. A refusal by an individual juror to give a true verdict according to the evidence is capable of constituting the *actus reus* of contempt.[27]

2. While conscientious objection might provide a reason for being excused jury service at the outset, it would provide no answer to a charge of contempt against a juror properly sworn.[28]

---

[26] See paras 11–349 *et seq.*
[27] *Bushell's Case* (1670) 6 St. Tr. 999 at 1014, (1670) Vaughan 135 at 124 E.R. 1006, Vaughan C.J. In *R. v Miller* [1977] C.L.Y. para.477. Mars-Jones J. held a juror to have been in contempt, and in breach of his oath, in circumstances where after two weeks of a rape case he informed the clerk of the court that he would not continue as a juror, as he felt unable to make up his mind. It was said on his behalf that he had been confused by the speeches and, feeling inadequate to make a decision, had panicked. Nevertheless, this was held to be deliberate defiance and a grave contempt.
[28] Section 9(1) of the Juries Act 1974 (which dealt with excusal for certain categories of persons and discretionary excusal) has been repealed by the Criminal Justice Act 2003, s.321. Discretionary deferral of jury service is now provided for by the Juries Act 1974, s.9A, and Part IV.42.1 of the *Consolidated Criminal Practice Direction* [2002] 1 W.L.R. 2870 (as amended on March 22, 2005). For the latest version of the *Direction* see *www.courtservice.gov.uk/docs/cpd/consol_criminal_pd_220305.doc*.

3. There would have to be demonstrated an intention to interfere with the due administration of justice, although this could be established by proof of knowledge of the inevitable consequences of the conduct ("so, for example, a juror who returns to court drunk, or throws a missile at the judge, or says, when invited to retire and continue deliberating with a view to reaching a majority verdict, that he will not retire, would be in obvious contempt of court").

4. Difficulties of proving contempt arose from the common law principles relating to the sanctity of jury deliberations and s.8 of the 1981 Contempt of Court Act; in particular, this was not a case of attempting to challenge the finality of a verdict or to interfere with the substance of deliberations, and, although contempt *could* be proved in relation to defiance, any such proceedings would have to be brought with sensitivity.[29]

5. The learned judge should not have made the enquiries of the jury which he did either upon receipt of the first note, or when he received the second communication; he should have given some guidance along the lines suggested by Watkins L.J. in *R. v Guildford Crown Court Ex p. Siderfin*.[30]

6. It was highly undesirable that the individual judge concerned should deal with the contempt allegation, especially given that there was no great urgency, and in the light of his own expressed conclusion that there had been contempt.

7. As to alternative methods of procedure, a reference to the Attorney-General would be somewhat slow and cumbersome; a better course would have been to refer the matter to another Crown Court judge.

8. Having regard to the gravity, difficulty and novelty of the issues, it was particularly unfortunate that counsel was instructed only on the morning of the contempt hearing.

9. It was important that the judge should not have imposed a custodial penalty, having raised an expectation of non-custodial sentencing.[31]

10. Fundamentally the problems flowed from the enquiries made by the judge following receipt of the first jury note, and his conclusions could not be sustained because of the consequential defective procedures.

The Court concluded that the judge had fallen into a sequence of errors:

1. It was doubtful whether it was proper to seek written clarification of the terms of the first jury note, and in any event he should not have decided to discharge the jury nor, once the names had been ascertained, should he

---

[29] *Ellis v Deheer* [1922] 2 K.B. 113, Atkin L.J.
[30] [1990] 2 Q.B. 683 at 691 (emphasising the vital role of jurors in criminal justice, and the importance of the obligation imposed upon every citizen called to serve).
[31] See the authorities set out in *Archbold 2005*, para.5–16.

have ordered the discharge without hearing further submissions from counsel. If he had sought the *numbers* of jurors who were having difficulties (as opposed to their names), it would have been possible on receipt of one or other of the jury notes, and with the assistance of submissions of counsel, to decide what course to take. There was no reason to justify discharging the whole jury. He might have given them a majority direction; or instead, one that stressed, while not necessarily amounting to a full *Watson* direction,[32] the importance of the oath taken and incorporated the matters referred to by Watkins L.J. in *Ex p. Siderfin*; or he could have discharged the two relevant jurors under the Juries Act 1974, s.17.

2. The judge's requests for the jury to provide the information were in breach of the widely expressed terms of s.8(1) of the Contempt of Court Act 1981, which apply to the court as to everyone else.[33] They were, moreover, in breach of the recently reaffirmed common law principle that there is no right to enquire as to what has occurred in the jury room.[34] It is possible within the terms of s.8(2)(a) of the Act to seek clarification of a jury note with a view to "enabling the jury to arrive at their verdict," but this judge ran the risk that they would disclose material parts of their deliberations outside this wording. Moreover, in seeking the jurors' names he was taking a first step in setting in motion proceedings for contempt; whereas this might be permissible in such cases as a juror falling asleep in the jury box or talking to a witness, it was inappropriate to identify a juror in relation to something said or done *in the jury room*.

3. It was desirable that consideration be given to amending the information provided to jurors, in order to incorporate some reference to the possibility of excusal on the grounds of conscientious objection.[35] In any event, this point had no relevance to Schot, because according to her evidence she had not *refused* to give a verdict, but simply found it difficult to decide.

4. A juror can be held in contempt in respect of conduct when discharging the "ministerial" (as opposed to "judicial") aspect of their duties, for

---

[32] [1988] Q.B. 690. For the latest version of the *Watson* direction, see the JSB Model Directions (No.58); see *Archbold 2005* para.4–415.
[33] See *R. v Young* [1995] Q.B. 324, discussed at paras 11–356 and 11–373.
[34] *R. v Thompson* [1962] 1 All E.R. 65 at 66D. See also *R. v Brown* [1907] 7 N.S.W. St. Rep.290; *R. v Miah and Akhbar* [1997] 2 Cr.App.R. 12, CACD (an application by Mr Miah to the European Court of Human Rights was found unanimously by the Commission to be inadmissible: App. No.37401/97); *R. v Bean* [1991] Crim. L.R. 843; *R. v Hart* [1998] Crim. L.R. 417. The principle has been reaffirmed since the advent of the Human Rights Act 1998: *R. v Qureshi (Sajid)* [2001] EWCA Crim 1807, [2002] 1 W.L.R. 518; *R. v Lewis (Patrick Arthur)* [2001] EWCA Crim 749. For a discussion of *R. v Mirza* [2004] EWHL 2, [2004] 1 A.C. 1118 and later developments, see further paras 11.358 *et seq*.
[35] Juries Act 1974, s.9(4). Discretionary deferral of jury service is now provided for by the Juries Act 1974, s.9A, and Pt IV.42.1 of the *Consolidated Criminal Practice Direction* [2002] 1 W.L.R. 2870 (as amended on March 22, 2005). For the latest version of the *Direction* see www.courtservice.gov.uk/docs/cpd/consol_criminal_pd_220305.doc.

example for "refusing to give a verdict".[36] There is no difference in principle between a juror's physically leaving the room and withdrawing from his obligations even though remaining. Thus, contumacious refusal to reach a verdict because of a reluctance to judge another person *can* establish the *actus reus* of contempt, though it may be difficult or impossible to prove.

5. The necessary *mens rea*, namely an intention to impede or create a real risk of prejudicing the administration of justice had also to be proved,[37] although "this can be established by foreseeability of consequences".[38] The judge gave no consideration to this point, and his conclusion of "intentional disruption" could not be sustained without his having expressly rejected Schot's evidence. There were in addition questions to be addressed as to whether his decision to discharge the entire jury could be regarded as a foreseeable consequence of one or two jurors refusing (if they did so) to reach a verdict. Also, the mere seeking of advice (as in the first jury note) was unlikely to support an inference of intention to disrupt.

6. The legal representation had not been adequate, because counsel who happened to be at court for other purposes were assigned to the appellants on the morning of and shortly before the hearing. This led to a failure to cite the relevant authorities and principles, and to the appellants being called to give evidence without any appropriate warning.

7. There was no "urgent and imperative need" for the judge to deal with the question of contempt himself, and there was a real danger of bias.[39] The judge should either have referred the matter to another senior judge sitting at that, or another, Crown Court; or to the Attorney-General to apply under RSC Ord.52. It may be appropriate for a judge to deal with a possible contempt on the part of a juror, but this could only happen if no indication has been given that he has already come to a concluded view, and has not behaved in any other way to suggest the possibility of bias.

8. The judge should have addressed the case against the two appellants separately. It was impossible for him to uphold the finding of contempt against Schot without an express finding that he rejected her evidence; it *might* have been possible to conclude against Barclay that she was in contempt, on the basis that she did not want to judge other people and should have disclosed this at an earlier stage, but there would have to be

---

[36] *Bushell's* case (1670) Vaughan 135 at 152, 124 E.R. 1006 at 1014; Hawkins, *Pleas of the Crown* (1824) Vol. 2, p.213.
[37] *Att-Gen v Sport Newspapers Ltd* [1991] 1 W.L.R. 1194 at 1200, [1992] 1 All E.R 503 Bingham L.J.; *Giscombe* (1984) 79 Cr.App.R. 79 at 83, Lord Lane C.J.
[38] See the discussion as to the difference between this and recklessness, at paras 5–166 *et seq*. See also *Att-Gen v Newspaper Publishing plc* [1988] Ch. 333 at 374G–375A, Sir John Donaldson M.R., and 383B–C, Lloyd L.J.; *Att-Gen v News Group Newspapers plc* [1989] 1 Q.B. 110 at 126C, Watkins L.J.
[39] *R. v Gough* [1993] A.C. 646 at 670, Lord Goff.

evidence of an "intention to defy the court and prejudice the administration of justice". In any event, this particular judge could not have tried that issue.

9. The precise nature of the contempt relied upon was never clearly defined, which would be essential in order that there could be a proper enquiry into the circumstances.

10-84 Against this background, the findings of contempt were quashed in relation to both appellants.

C. Safeguards in other common law jurisdictions

10-85 A similar trend is to be observed in Canada, no doubt in part due to the influence of the Canadian Charter.[40] In *BK v R*,[41] the Supreme Court proceeded on the basis that requirements of natural justice must be complied with in cases of contempt in the face. Despite the "loutish and obscene behaviour of the accused",[42] there was:

" . . . no justification for foregoing the usual steps, required by natural justice, of putting the witness on notice that he or she must show cause why they would not be found in contempt of court, followed by an adjournment which need be no longer than that required to offer the witness an opportunity to be advised by counsel, and, if he or she chooses, to be represented by counsel."

10-86 Lamer C.J.C. expressly reserved the "broader issue of whether the common law rule which permits a judge to act in such a manner is constitutionally infirm" because it did not arise on the facts of the case, and it was left for another day. It is clear, however, that the Chief Justice was anticipating that some qualifications might need to be imposed upon the legitimacy of the summary or *instanter* procedure in the light of a challenge under the Canadian Charter.

10-87 So too in Australia, the Court of Appeal in Victoria held[43] that there had been undue haste and thus a denial of natural justice in proceedings for contempt taken against a barrister, for allegations of bias made in the course of his submissions. Specifically, there had been a failure to provide proper particulars of the alleged misconduct. Furthermore, the fact that the magistrate concerned had immediately announced an intention to proceed by way of the summary jurisdiction also provided grounds for an objective observer to entertain a reasonable apprehension of bias on his part.

---

[40] Although it had long been accepted in Canada that the allegation in such cases had to be formulated with sufficient precision to allow the contemnor to know the gravamen of the charge against him. In *Cotroni v Quebec Police Commission and Brunet* (1977) 80 D.L.R. (3d) 490, the Supreme Court of Canada said that "a vague charge is a fatal defect".
[41] (1995) 129 D.L.R. (4th) 500. See now *R. v Arradi* [2003] 1 S.C.R. 280, (2003) 173 C.C.C. (3d)1, (2003) 244 D.L.R. (4th) 301.
[42] *per* Major J. dissenting, at 509.
[43] *The Magistrates' Court at Prahan v Murphy* [1997] 2 V.R. 186.

III. Disturbing Proceedings in Court

A. The historical background

It is, and for centuries has been,[44] a common law contempt to disrupt court proceedings. To riot in open court[45] or to attempt to rescue a prisoner from custody while he is being tried would likewise be so regarded.[46] Instances are to be found in the law reports over the centuries. When a prisoner was convicted of treason in 1681, a great shout went up.[47] One person perceived to be a ring-leader of this disturbance was committed to gaol for that night for contempt, but the next morning having given a public apology he was discharged.

In the following century, a member of the public[48] who jumped into the middle of the court at Westminster Hall and started hallooing and waving his hat was fined £20. Similarly, in 1893, one Thomas White was observed by Lord Coleridge C.J. at the Leeds Assizes[49] to be participating in a disturbance in the public gallery. He was committed for 48 hours, the judge commenting "no court shall be disgraced whilst I sit in it", but he was released the same day with a severe caution.

B. The Treason Act 1351

Historically, judges discharging their functions were regarded as administering the King's justice, and entitled to similar protection, while doing so, as that accorded to the monarch himself. This can be seen in the language of the Treason Act 1351, which provided that it was treason:

" ... if a man slay the Chancellor, Treasurer, or the King's Justices of one Bench or the other, Justices in Eyre or Justices of Assize, and all other Justices assigned to hear and determine, *being in their places, doing their offices*" (emphasis added).

This emphasis upon the exercise of judicial functions shows that, whereas murder of an individual citizen would be serious enough, it was perceived to be especially grievous to slay those who were administering justice. It would tend to undermine the structures of society so fundamentally that it was regarded as comparable to slaying the sovereign himself. The precise scope of this provision seems, however, at various points to have been open to doubt, and gave rise to difficulties of interpretation. For example, rather surprisingly Hale thought it

---

[44] (1254) Curia Regis roll, M. 38–9 Henry III, m. 22d.; 1289 Rot. Parl., 1, 33b; (1323) Coram Rege Roll, M. 17 Edw. II, m. 16d.
[45] *Earl of Thanet's Case* (1799) 27 St. Tr. 822. See the case of the *Knight and Esquire* who were indicted for raising strife before Thorpe C.J., Y.B. 22 Edw. III, p.13. pl. 26, para.1–16; see also 3 Co. Inst. 140; 1 East. P.C. 408; 4 Bl. Comm. III; Vin. Abr. tit. contempt 443.
[46] *Earl of Thanet's Case* (1799) 27 St. Tr. 822.
[47] *Colledge* (1681) 8 St. Tr. at 714.
[48] *Stone* (1796) 6 T.R. 527 at 530.
[49] *Fox v Wheatley* (1893), cited in Oswald, *Contempt* (3rd ed., 1910), p.53.

10–91   necessary to express the opinion that "being in their places, doing their offices" included a hearing in chambers,[50] and this would seem clearly to be right.

10–92   There remains considerable uncertainty. On May 19, 1986, the then Attorney-General, Sir Michael Havers, explained to Parliament the legal difficulties of employing the charge of treason in modern conditions, in response to a question demanding to know why treason was not employed in cases of terrorism.[51] At that time the death penalty still applied in cases of treason.[52] In view of the other problems, largely of interpretation,[53] it is difficult to imagine in modern times that such an offence would be dealt with except by charging the offender with murder.[54]

C. Assaulting a judge or other participants in the legal process

10–93   There is authority from as early as 1348 that it was regarded as a contempt to draw one's sword to strike a judge in court.[55] The jurisdiction was exercised sporadically, when the need arose, in the succeeding centuries. As Malins V.-C. was rising from the bench at the close of the day's business a disappointed American litigant threw an egg at him, which narrowly missed. The offender immediately confessed the assault and the Vice-Chancellor committed him. He was discharged five months later, on his being placed on board a vessel bound for the United States.[56]

10–94   Even today, it would probably be regarded as more than a mere assault to launch a physical attack on a judge while in his place and "doing his office". It would be an assault not only on the individual but also on the integrity of the system of justice, and therefore a criminal contempt. In *Crowley*,[57] after an appellant had leapt from the dock and attacked three members of the court of

---

[50] *Pleas of the Crown*, 230.
[51] see H.C. *Deb*, Vol.98, col.14. And see A. Wharam, (1976) 126 New Law Jo. 428. In *R. (Rusbridger) v Att-Gen* [2003] UKHL 38, [2004] 1 A.C. 357 the House of Lords allowed an appeal by the Attorney-General against a decision of the Court of Appeal that it was open to the Administrative Court to grant a declaration as to the state of the law of treason in respect of publications advocating constitutional change, which might in theory constitute an offence under the Treason Felony Act 1848.
[52] Treason Act, 1814, s.1. See now, however, the Crime and Disorder Act 1998, s.36, which finally abolished the death penalty.
[53] The Treason Act 1351 (written in Norman French) would now have to be interpreted in the light of Art.7 of the ECHR.
[54] The Law Commission provisionally took the view that this form of treason "would appear to have no place in the modern law" and recommended its abolition, noting that the offence would undoubtedly be proceeded against as murder: Working Paper No.72, *Treason, Sedition and Allied Offences* (1977), paras 48 and 25 respectively. See also the case of Judge Parry, cited at para. 10–95.
[55] 1348 Y.B., 22 Edw. III, p.13, pl. 26; see also *Anon* (1631) Dy. 188b, n.; 73 E.R. 416n (the brickbat "que narrowly mist"), para.1–18. In *Williamson's case*, Chester Docket Book 603–52 fo. 166, a prisoner who threw a stone at a judge had his hand cut off and nailed to the gibbet.
[56] *Re Cosgrave, The Times*, March 17, 1877. It is said that the Vice-Chancellor had the presence of mind to observe that the egg was probably meant for his brother Bacon, sitting in an adjoining court: Oswald, *op. cit.* p.42. See also Seton, *Judgments and Orders* (7th ed., 1912), p.457.
[57] *The Times*, March 2, 1973, p.3. For assaults upon officers of the county courts, see the provisions of the County Courts Act 1984, s.14(1), the text of which is set out at para.13–84.

Appeal, Cairns L.J. in sentencing him to nine months' imprisonment commented: "An assault of this kind, wherever it happens and to whatever members of the public it has occurred, would merit punishment. The matter is the more serious because it was an attempt to interfere with the administration of justice".

Where judges are physically attacked or threatened with violence in modern times, it would be usual to resort to the general criminal law and trial on indictment rather than to the contempt jurisdiction.[58] *Oswald* quoted the case of Judge Parry who was shot and seriously injured while on the Bench.[59] The offender was dealt with in the ordinary course of law rather than by way of contempt. Moreover, since the sentencing limitation was imposed by s.14 of the 1981 Act (two years' imprisonment), the law of contempt cannot be regarded as an adequate means for dealing with the more serious cases.[60]

It is not merely judges who are protected in this way, for to assault anybody in open court is a contempt.[61] In *Purdin v Roberts*,[62] Neville J. imposed a fine upon a man who had, in a corridor outside the court, assaulted a witness attending on subpoena in a Chancery action. There was a dispute as to precisely what had happened. The judge came to the conclusion that there had been exaggeration on both sides, and was prepared to accept that there had indeed been some provocation. For this reason, he did not impose a custodial penalty, but merely a fine of £5. He observed nonetheless: "It is most important the public should know that persons who attend the courts to give evidence as witnesses in any matter before the Courts will be protected from assault whilst in the precincts of the courts".

D. Insults offered to the court

Insulting a judge while he is sitting in court has also been recognised from early times to qualify as contempt of court.[63] Such conduct was recognised as "a

---

[58] See, *e.g.* the article "Judges describe day they stared down gun barrel" in *The Times*, July 29, 1997, p.5, reporting the case of *R. v Muraglia* at the Central Criminal Court. A woman was charged with possessing an imitation firearm with intent to cause fear of violence, following an incident when she had menaced the Court of Appeal (Criminal Division) with a fake Beretta pistol. For this, she was sentenced to four years.
[59] *Contempt* (3rd ed., 1910) p.42. See also *Re Dodwell*, February 1878, cited by Seton's *Judgments and Orders* (7th ed., 1912), p.457. This was a case involving the firing of a pistol at the Master of the Rolls as he was entering the Rolls House. The offender was handed over to the police, convicted of a criminal offence and detained at Her Majesty's pleasure.
[60] See, *e.g.* the case of *Muraglia* cited, n.58 above, where the assailant was sentenced to four years' imprisonment.
[61] *Parashuram Detaram Shamdasani v The King Emperor* [1945] A.C. 264 at 269, Lord Goddard C.J.; *Sparks v Martyn* (1669) 1 Vent. 1, 86 E.R. 1; *Davis's* Case (1560) Dy. 188b, 73 E.R. 415. See also *Wilkinson v S* [2003] EWCA Civ 95, [2003] 1 W.L.R. 1254, [2003] 2 All E.R. 185 where it had taken five people to restrain the contemnor in the course of his threatening and abusive conduct. This was directed at his wife and her solicitor rather than the judge.
[62] (1910) 74 J.P. Jo. 88.
[63] See paras 1–5 *et seq*. See also the discussions of the statutory provision relating to "insults" in the County Courts Act 1984, at paras 10–124 *et seq*. and para.13–90.

10–97   CHAPTER 10—CONTEMPT IN THE FACE OF THE COURT

classic example of contempt" in *R. v Hill*,[64] where a spectator in the gallery had called out that the judge was biased and a racist. It was also said to be "palpably calculated to interfere with the administration of justice". It is on these grounds that the law intervenes in such cases, "and not on any exaggerated notion of the dignity of individuals that insults to judges are not allowed."[65]

E. The modern approach to disturbances in court[66]

10–98 Although it is in the context of disruption of court proceedings that the summary jurisdiction can most easily be justified, it is nevertheless accepted even here that discretion and restraint are required when its use is contemplated. It was pointed out in *R. v Logan*[67] that outbursts in the dock are by no means unknown, and that sometimes they arise through the stress or emotion of the moment. Although not necessarily excusable, such conduct may often be readily understood. It is certainly always desirable, even where the matter cannot simply be ignored, that there should be afforded an opportunity to explain and apologise. Nevertheless, it has to be recognised that judges and magistrates will sometimes have to take quick decisions in such cases, and due allowance will be made for this in appellate tribunals.

10–99 The principles are relatively easy to state, but there are often difficulties of application in the light of the many and varied circumstances with which judges find themselves confronted. In *R. v Powell*,[68] for example, the Court of Appeal was dealing with a situation in which a spectator in the public gallery at a Crown Court wolf-whistled at a female juror when the jury were returning to court to deliver their verdict. The judge, having granted legal aid and after hearing counsel on his behalf, sentenced him to 14 days' imprisonment. At that stage counsel's submissions were confined to the matter of penalty, but on appeal it was argued that there had been no contempt at all.

10–100 A distinction was sought to be drawn between those facts and the circumstances which arose in *Morris v Crown Office*,[69] on the basis that the latter represented a true instance of interfering with the administration of justice. There, a number of student demonstrators interrupted proceedings in the High Court by shouting slogans, scattering pamphlets and singing songs. Eleven of them refused to apologise, saying that they were acting as a matter of principle on behalf of the Welsh language. Each was sentenced to an immediate term of three months' imprisonment for contempt. The sentences were held on appeal not

---

[64] [1986] Crim. L.R. 457, CACD. This case is further discussed, in the context of *mens rea*, at para.10–209.
[65] *per* Bowen L.J. in *Re Johnson* (1888) 20 Q.B.D. 68 at 74.
[66] See generally G.J. Zellick, "The Criminal Trial and the Disruptive Defendant" (1980) 43 M.L.R. 121; M. Chesterman, "Disorder in the court: the Judge's Response" (1987) 10 U.N.S.W. Law Jo. 37.
[67] [1974] Crim. L.R. 609. For the facts see para.10–35, n.64.
[68] (1994) 98 Cr.App.R. 224 at 226, CACD.
[69] [1970] 2 Q.B. 114. See also *R. v Newbury Justices Ex p. Pont* (1983) 78 Cr.App.R. 255, DC. A similar demonstration by an individual had been punished by committal in the case of *McMichael, The Times*, January 14 and 17, 1961; and see *Re Surrey (Sheriff)* (1860) 2 F. & F. 234, 175 E.R. 1038.

to have been excessive, but because of the absence of any "violence, dishonesty or vice" on the part of the appellants, they were released and bound over for 12 months. Salmon L.J., however, warned that if anything similar should occur in the future, it would be impossible to take such an "exceptionally merciful course".[70]

The Court of Appeal in *Powell* considered, however, that the most relevant guidance in the task of carrying into effect the general principles was to be found in s.12 of the 1981 Act[71] (even though that provision is confined in its scope to proceedings before magistrates). It seemed to the court that the terms of that provision were intended by Parliament to reflect the sort of behaviour which would, at the very least, constitute contempt in the face of the court at common law. **10–101**

What mattered, the court concluded, was that the conduct was potentially an insult and potentially offensive, "and a serious interference with the administration of justice and the process of the court". Jurors are under a duty to come to court when summoned, and they do not come in order to have comments, even flattering comments,[72] publicly made on their personal appearance. The administration of justice should not be interrupted at the tense moment when the jury return with their verdict. **10–102**

In *Gohoho v Lintas Export Advertising Services*,[73] a disgruntled appellant, during the hearing of the case following his own, removed all his clothing except his shirt and lay down on a bench at the front of the court. This disturbance led the members of the court to withdraw until order was restored, which plainly amounted to an interruption of the administration of justice. For this, he was imprisoned for a week. Reference has already been made, on a number of occasions, to the well known case of *Balogh v St. Albans Crown Court*,[74] where it was held that attempting to let off a canister of laughing gas was, on the facts of the case, not a contempt; the "prankster" had not proceeded sufficiently far with his plans when he was apprehended.[75] **10–103**

In the case of *Jesus Aquarius*,[76] Roskill L.J. described the appellant as having started his disrupting efforts right at the beginning of the trial, and as having deliberately set about making the proceedings impossible. He continued: **10–104**

---

[70] [1970] 2 Q.B. 114 at 130 B–C.
[71] Considered more fully at paras 10–113 *et seq.*
[72] Apparently, the individual juror had informed the Court of Appeal that she considered the wolf-whistle as a compliment, although the court recognised that this would not be true in all cases.
[73] *The Times*, January 21, 1964. More recently, disturbances have been brought about by defendants "mooning" or presenting their buttocks to the court. For example, such an incident is recorded in *The Lawyer* magazine, January 3, 1995, the defendant having endorsed the words "Happy Christmas" upon them. A later variant occurred when a defendant called out to the judge as he was passing sentence, "Is this what you want, Wiggy?" whilst making a similar presentation: *The Times*, April 16, 1996.
[74] [1975] Q.B. 73.
[75] For a discussion as to whether the conduct might have amounted to attempted contempt, see para.11–14.
[76] (1974) 59 Cr.App.R. 65.

10–104 CHAPTER 10—CONTEMPT IN THE FACE OF THE COURT

"When that sort of thing happens, it cannot be tolerated, whatever views a particular person may hold about society or courts, or the right of society or the rights of courts or others in authority to judge others or inflict punishment. So long as there are courts, those courts have to be free to do the job entrusted to them by statute and at common law freely and without interruption. If persons seek to disrupt them and make the trial difficult or indeed impossible, then the court in the interests of the public and the interests of the free administration of justice—this is nothing whatever to do with the dignity of a particular recorder or a particular judge—has to so act as to make it plain that that sort of conduct will not be tolerated."

10–105   When there is shouting or abuse from the public gallery, it may be wise for the judge to rise with a view to ensuring that misbehaviour takes place in his absence.[77] Problems of this kind have become increasingly difficult to handle in recent years as police officers are less in evidence at most Crown Court centres.

F. Disobeying an order for the control of proceedings

10–106   All courts of law have power to order a person interrupting or hindering their proceedings to leave court, and to have him removed if he fails to leave.[78] To persist in a course of conduct or use of language which the presiding judge has ruled improper is a contempt. Another example is provided by the case in which it was held to be a contempt to remove a document when this had been specifically forbidden by the court.[79] In accordance with modern trends, it is generally preferable that any individual be specifically ordered to desist and told of the possible consequences if he continues, before the summary contempt procedure is invoked.[80]

10–107   The situation is closely analogous to that in *Att-Gen v Newspaper Publishing plc*,[81] or to the circumstances which arise when there has been disobedience to an order made under s.4(2) or s.11 of the Contempt of Court Act 1981.[82] Where it is clear from what the court has said, or the underlying purpose is obvious[83] to anyone to whose attention it may be drawn, then any such person who, knowing of such an order, flouts or disobeys it may well be held in contempt.[84] It makes no difference whether the person concerned agrees with the order or considers that the legitimate objectives of the court could have been achieved by some other means.

---

[77] *R. v Lewis*, The Times, November 4, 1999, CACD.
[78] *R. v Webb Ex p. Hawkers*, The Times, January 24, 1899.
[79] *R. v Watt v Ligertwood* (1874) 2 Sc. & Div. 361.
[80] *Davison* (1821) 4 B. & Ald. 329, 106 E.R. 958; *Re Surrey (Sheriff)* (1860) 2 F. & F. 234, 175 E.R. 1038; *Parashuram Detaram Shamdasani v King-Emperor* [1945] A.C. 264; see also *R. v Pateley Bridge Justices Ex p. Percy* [1994] C.O.D. 453.
[81] [1988] Ch. 333, discussed at paras 6–124 *et seq*.
[82] Discussed more fully in ch.7.
[83] *Att-Gen v Times Newspapers Ltd* [1992] 1 A.C. 191 at 223, Lord Oliver.
[84] [1988] Ch. 333 at 380, Lloyd L.J.

Where the disobedience occurs in court then it has always been treated as criminal even though the disobedience occurs in the course of civil proceedings.[85]

G. Effecting an arrest in the precincts of the court

It may still in theory be a contempt to arrest on civil process, in the precincts of the court, anyone who is currently fulfilling a role in pending proceedings, and who has a sound claim of privilege.[86]

Apprehending a person in connection with a criminal charge in the face of a court *may*, in certain circumstances, amount to a contempt. This was acknowledged by Viscount Simon in the leading case of *Christie v Leachinsky*,[87] who drew the conclusion, upon an examination of the authorities,[88] that the established principle went no further than that the proceedings of a court are not to be *disturbed* by the execution of an arrest.

On the facts of the case before the House of Lords, there was no finding of contempt. A charge of unlawful possession of goods had been withdrawn before a magistrate in open court, but instead of coming out from the dock into the body of the court Leachinsky was, by Detective Constable Christie's intervention, motioned to descend the steps to the cells below where he was detained for some hours pending the arrival of a policeman, who charged him with larceny. There was no such disturbance of the kind contemplated by Viscount Simon, but he made the more general observation: "The gallery at the Old Bailey is not, I presume, an Alsatia for wanted criminals, but it is certainly a better practice to carry through such detentions as the law authorises outside."

IV. STATUTORY CONTEMPTS IN THE FACE

A. Contempt in face of the magistrates' court: section 12

At common law magistrates had (and continue to have) the power to order a person interrupting or hindering their proceedings to leave the court.[89] Yet before the Contempt of Court Act 1981, it seems to have been the case that a magistrates' court could not commit an offender to custody for contempt.[90] The Phillimore Committee regarded it as unsatisfactory that magistrates should have no power to punish disruptive conduct[91]:

---

[85] See para.3–52 and para.10–162.
[86] *Wilson v The Sheriffs of London* (1620) 1 Brownl. & G. 15, 123 E.R. 635; *Clarke v Molineux* (1677) 1 Lev. 159, 83 E.R. 348. See the discussion of privilege from arrest at para.3–141.
[87] [1947] A.C. 573 at 589.
[88] In particular, *Bird v Jones* (1846) 7 Q.B. 742 at 752, 115 E.R. 668.
[89] *R. v Webb Ex p. Hawkers*, The Times, January 24, 1899.
[90] Phillimore Report, *Contempt of Court*, Cmnd. 5794 (1974), paras 25 and 36.
[91] para.36.

"These courts deal at one stage or another with about 98 per cent of all criminal cases in England and Wales, and a certain amount of civil business, sometimes in difficult conditions and crowded courts. There have been instances recently of disorderly conduct in magistrates' courts which have brought proceedings to a standstill. The offenders may sometimes be removed from court, but this represents no deterrent to those who make a practice of disruption. We find it difficult, furthermore, to reconcile the absence of such powers in England with the enjoyment of them by justices' and magistrates' courts in Scotland, which have much more limited functions."

10–113   For these reasons the Committee recommended that a power should be given to deal with contempt in the face of the court. Eventually powers were conferred by Parliament by means of s.12 of the Contempt of Court Act 1981[92]:

"**12.**—(1) A magistrates' court has jurisdiction under this section to deal with any person who—

(a) wilfully insults[93] the justice or justices, any witness before or officer of the court or any solicitor or counsel having business in the court, during his or their sitting or attendance in court or in going to or returning from the court; or

(b) wilfully interrupts the proceedings of the court or otherwise misbehaves in court.

(2) In any such case the court may order any officer of the court,[94] or any constable, to take the offender into custody and detain him until the rising of the court; and the court may, if it thinks fit, commit the offender to custody for a specified period not exceeding one month[95] or impose on him a fine not exceeding £2,500,[96] or both.

(2A) A fine imposed under subsection (2) above shall be deemed, for the purposes of any enactment, to be a sum adjudged to be paid by a conviction.[97]

---

[92] The exercise of this jurisdiction is now governed by the *Consolidated Criminal Practice Direction* [2002] 1 W.L.R. 2870 (as amended), Pt V.54. For the latest version of the *Direction* see www.courtservice.gov.uk/docs/cpd/consol_criminal_pd_220305.doc. See A. Draycott, "Contempt of Magistrates' Courts" (1983) 147 J.P. 531.

[93] In *Brutus v Cozens* [1973] A.C. 854, the House of Lords said that the meaning of the word "insulting" was a question of fact rather than law, since it was an ordinary English word. The difficulties with that proposition are considered by Glanville Williams, "Law and Fact" [1976] Crim. L.R. 472 at 532, and by D.W. Elliott, "Brutus v Cozens; Decline and Fall" [1989] Crim. L.R. 323. The continuing vitality of *Brutus v Cozens* was affirmed by the House of Lords in *Moyna v Secretary of State for Work and Pensions* [2003] UKHL 44, [2003] 1 W.L.R. 1929. See in particular Lord Hoffmann at [23]. And see *R. v Evans* [2004] EWCA Crim 3102.

[94] This phrase has been modified (by the Criminal Justice Act 1991, s.100, Sch.11, para.29) so that the reference to "officer of the court" includes a reference to any court security officer assigned to the courthouse in which the court is sitting.

[95] In "Suffering in the cause of justice", *The Times*, May 21, 1996, David Pannick Q.C. suggested that the powers of magistrates are inadequate, and that Parliament should confer a power to imprison for up to six months, because a physical attack by a defendant in a criminal trial is a serious contempt. He was considering an incident at the Croydon magistrates' court when a football supporter grabbed the prosecuting solicitor by the neck, attempted to haul him over the table and tried to kick him. He swore his innocence upon the Bible and informed the occupants of the press bench that they were "scum". In a serious case, however, it might be better to refer the matter to the prosecuting authorities, not only because a serious case requires measured consideration, but also because proceedings could be instituted before a tribunal having greater powers.

[96] Substituted by the Criminal Justice Act 1991, s.17(3), Sch.4, Pt I.

[97] Added by the Criminal Justice Act 1991, s.17(3), Sch.4, Pt V, substituted by the Criminal Justice Act 1993, s.65(3),(4), Sch.3, para.6(4).

[(3) The court shall not deal with the offender by making an order under section 19 of the Criminal Justice Act 1948 (an attendance centre order) if it appears to the court, after considering any available evidence, that he is under 17 years of age.][98]

(4) A magistrates' court may at any time revoke an order of committal made under subsection (2) and, if the offender is in custody, order his discharge.

(5) The following provisions of the Magistrates' Courts Act 1980 apply in relation to an order under this section as they apply in relation to a sentence on conviction or finding of guilty of an offence, namely: section 36 (restriction on fines in respect of young persons); sections 75 to 91 (enforcement); section 108 (appeal to Crown Court)[99]; section 136 (overnight detention in default of payment); and section 142(1) (power to rectify mistakes)."

10–114 The recommendation of the Phillimore Committee was that there should be a right of appeal to the nearest Crown Court against such a finding of contempt, and that arrangements should be made for dealing with appeals expeditiously.[1] Despite this, the only such right of appeal would appear to relate to sentence.[2] The reasoning is that s.12(5) refers only to "an order" and not to "a finding" of contempt. This may have been the result of a drafting error.[3] The only means to challenge a finding would therefore seem to be by way of judicial review.[4]

10–115 This situation is to be contrasted with that provided for under the Administration of Justice Act 1960, s.13(2)(a), which appeared to suggest that, when the magistrates were exercising a true contempt jurisdiction (as opposed to the statutory jurisdiction conferred by s.12 of the 1981 Act), *an appeal* would lie to a Divisional Court of the High Court. Upon such an appeal, no doubt, the criteria to be applied would be distinct from those relevant to judicial review.

10–116 In *Re Hooker*,[5] Kennedy L.J. in the Divisional Court stated that the appeal was brought under s.13 of the Administration Act 1960, "which provides that where a magistrates' court makes an order, an appeal shall lie from such an order to this court." It appears that no challenge was made to the court's jurisdiction to hear such an appeal, and no reference to have been made to *R. v Havant Justices Ex p. Palmer*.[6] In that case May L.J. expressly addressed the matter of jurisdiction and compared the provisions of s.13(1) of the 1960 Act with those of s.12(5) of the 1981 Act.

10–117 While he accepted that, on its face, the 1960 Act might seem to give a right of appeal against a finding of contempt under s.12, he pointed out that "the true situation is made abundantly clear by the second part of subsection (1) of section 13 of the 1960 Act". He referred in particular to the words "the provisions of this

---

[98] This subsection was repealed by the Criminal Justice Act 1982, s.78, Sch.16.
[99] Although the Act as printed originally referred to "section 198," this should be "section 108."
[1] para.37.
[2] *R. v Havant Justices Ex p. Palmer* [1985] Crim. L.R. 658, (1985) 149 J.P. 609, DC.
[3] See the comment by Professor J.C. Smith at [1985] Crim. L.R. 658.
[4] See, *e.g. R. v Pateley Bridge Justices Ex p. Percy* [1994] C.O.D. 453, discussed para.10–66; *R. v Tamworth Magistrates' Court Ex p. Walsh* [1994] C.O.D. 277.
[5] [1993] C.O.D. 190, CO/2478/92 (Lexis).
[6] (1985) 149 J.P. 609 DC.

section shall have effect in substitution for any other enactment relating to appeals in civil or criminal proceedings".

10–118   May L.J. concluded that:

> "If that provision operated or was held to operate in relation to situations covered by section 12 of the 1981 Act, the position would be this. Parliament with one hand would have given by subsection (5) of section 12 of the 1981 Act a right of appeal, albeit limited to the extent that I have indicated [i.e. as to penalty], but then would have taken it away again with its other hand by virtue of the second half of subsection (1) of section 13 of the 1960 Act."

In the light of this, the court decided that s.13 of the 1960 Act could not be taken as affording a right of appeal in respect of s.12 contempts, and that the appropriate way to deal with the liability (as opposed to sentence) was, if at all, by way of judicial review.

10–119   Another way of putting the point would be on the basis of *generalia non specialibus derogant*; that is to say, that the specific provisions of s.12(5), however poorly drafted they may be, must be taken to have priority over those of the earlier, more general provisions. At the moment, the position remains uncertain because it may be that other courts would follow the precedent of *Re Hooker*. In any event, as discussed in chapter 13, s.13 has been amended so that an appeal would be to a single judge.

10–120   Even if the court had confined itself in *Re Hooker* to exercising a judicial review function, it seems that the result would have been the same, because Kennedy L.J. on that occasion found no difficulty in holding that there had been a procedural irregularity which justified setting aside the order despite there being facts present (namely use of a tape-recorder without leave) which, on the face of them, constituted a contempt.

The geographical scope of section 12

10–121   A question arises as to the geographical scope of the offence created by the section, as is illustrated by *Bodden v Metropolitan Police Commissioner*.[7] The appellant had been using a loud hailer outside the Bow Street Magistrates' court, in such a way that a magistrate in one of the courts inside the building was unable to hear what a witness was saying. He therefore directed that he should be brought before him by two police officers. The officers arrested him and detained him for some hours. A year later, he claimed damages in the Westminster County Court for wrongful arrest, false imprisonment and assault.

10–122   The judge (sitting with a jury) was asked to decide a preliminary issue, namely whether the magistrate had jurisdiction to order the police officers to bring Bodden before the court. The judge concluded that the magistrate had no such jurisdiction, and judgment was entered for the plaintiff. The Commissioner

---

[7] [1990] 2 Q.B. 397, [1989] 3 All E.R. 833, CA.

appealed on two grounds: (1) the judge had erred in applying the restrictive words "in the court" to the concept of wilful interruption, and (2) the judge erred in holding that for an interruption to be "in court", within the meaning of s.12(1)(b), it had to emanate from inside the court.

It was held by the Court of Appeal that a magistrate did indeed have **10–123** jurisdiction to deal with such interruptions irrespective of whether they were caused by acts done inside or outside the court. It was also held that the magistrate had been entitled to have the interruptor brought before him and to enquire into the circumstances.

The view was taken in one case that the magistrates have no jurisdiction under **10–124** this section to deal with a person who threatens rather than insults.[8] In *R. v Havant Magistrates' Court and Portsmouth Crown Court Ex p. Palmer*[9] the applicant for judicial review of a decision to fine him had threatened to "get" the defendant and his solicitor, a threat being different in character from an insult (which the magistrates would have power to deal with). At first sight, it might appear that a threat would fall within the notion of "misbehaviour" under s.12(1)(b), but, unlike s.12(1)(a), this does not embrace conduct while the person concerned is "going to or returning from the court", but can be committed only in the body of the court itself ("in court"). The threat in *Palmer* was uttered outside the courtroom while justices were deliberating.

Attention was drawn to the distinction between the limited wording of s.12 **10–125** (1)(a) and that contained in s.5 of the Public Order Act 1936,[10] which addressed three types of words or behaviour, namely threats, abuse and insults. Giving it its ordinary English meaning, the court held that the justices should not have come to the conclusion that the word "insult" was wide enough to include the threat which had been made. The Court of Appeal has subsequently considered s.118 of the 1984 Act in *Manchester City Council v McCann*.[11] Lord Woolf M.R. expressly differed from the Divisional Court's interpretation and took the view that "insults", at least in that context, was wide enough to embrace "threatens".

B. *Mens rea*: "wilfully" equated to "recklessly"

It is clear that there must be proved an intention, on the part of the person **10–126** disrupting, to do the act that is said to constitute the obstruction or other misconduct. The Court of Appeal has held that Parliament meant to signify rather more than this by its use of the word "wilfully". In *Bodden v Metropolitan Police Commissioner*[12] the man using the loud hailer outside the court was protesting

---

[8] It may be that the decision in *R. v Havant Justices Ex p. Palmer* [1985] Crim. L.R. 658, (1985) 149 J.P. 609 would also be relevant to the construction of the County Courts Act 1984, s.118 which refers specifically to "insults", para.13–90.
[9] (1985) 149 J.P. 609, DC.
[10] See now ss.4 and 5 of the Public Order Act 1986.
[11] [1999] Q.B. 1214.
[12] [1990] 2 Q.B. 397 at 405, CA. The facts are set out at para.10–121.

against proceedings taking place within. In the Court of Appeal, Beldam L.J. said that the judge was correct to have concluded that:

" ... in the context of section 12, it is necessary for there to be established, in addition to the deliberate commission of the acts causing the interruption, the mental element of intending they should interrupt the proceedings of the court ... In addition to an intention to interrupt the proceedings of the court, 'wilfully' would, in my judgment, also include the state of mind of an interruptor who knew that there was a risk that his acts would interrupt the proceedings of the court but nevertheless went on deliberately to do those acts. In that sense, recklessness would be a sufficient state of mind to make the interruptor guilty of an offence under section 12(1)(b)."

10–127   In *Re Hooker*,[13] Kennedy L.J. also considered the words "otherwise misbehaves" appearing in s.12(1)(b) and commented that it would be necessary to bear in mind in construing those words that they appear in a criminal statute. "One is entitled in construing s.12 to look at the way in which the other prohibitions are qualified by the word 'wilfully'. Even insulting a justice or justices does not amount to an offence unless it is committed wilfully. Thus, when one looks at the words 'otherwise misbehaved', it seems to me that one has to postulate some element of defiance or, at least, conduct such that a court should not reasonably be expected to tolerate it".

10–128   Some assistance may be derived from a decision of the High Court of Australia construing the word "wilfully" in a similar statute.[14] In *Lewis v Ogden*,[15] counsel in his address to the jury referred to the role of the judge as a sort of umpire whom one would expect to be unbiased, making a comparison with the part played by an umpire in a football match. He drew a distinction between the judge's comments on the facts and his directions as to the law, pointing out that the jury were at liberty to disregard the judge's comments on the facts. He said that the judge's attitude was "pretty adverse" to his client. The judge concluded that this amounted to a wilful insult and, having discharged the jury, fined the appellant $500.

10–129   Allowing the appeal, the High Court of Australia said[16]:

" ... the word 'wilfully' means 'intentionally', or 'deliberately', in the sense that what is said or done is intended as an insult, threat, etc. Its presence does more than negative the notion of 'inadvertently' or 'unconsciously': *Bell v Stewart* (1920) 28 C.L.R. 419 at 427. The mere voluntary uterance (*sic*) of words is not enough. 'Wilfully' imports the notion of purpose".

C. County Courts Act 1984

10–130   The county court has no inherent jurisdiction to commit for contempt, other than for contempt in the face of the court.[17] In language very similar to that of s.12 of

---

[13] [1993] C.O.D. 190, CO/2478/92 (Lexis).
[14] County Court Act 1958, s.54A (1) (Vic.).
[15] (1984) 58 A.L.J.R. 342.
[16] *ibid.* 344B–C.
[17] *R. v Lefroy* (1873) L.R. 8 Q.B. 134; followed in *Bush v Green* [1985] 1 W.L.R. 1143; *R. v Bloomsbury County Court Ex p. Brady, The Times*, December 16, 1987.

the Contempt of Court Act, s.118 of the County Courts Act 1984 makes "wilful" interruption of proceedings an offence.[18]

V. Improper Conduct of a Case

A. Litigants

Litigants in person will generally be allowed greater latitude in conducting their cases than professional advocates.[19] Lord Donaldson M.R. said with reference to such litigants and their right to be heard in their own defence: 10–131

> "Fairness, which is fundamental to all court proceedings, dictates that they shall be given all reasonable facilities for exercising this right and, in case of doubt, they should be given the benefit of that doubt for courts must not only act fairly, but be seen to act fairly."[20]

A common difficulty with litigants in person is that they sometimes seek to adduce irrelevant evidence or to make prolix or embarrassing submissions. Where such a litigant persistently introduces matter which is both irrelevant and scandalous, then the court may treat this as contempt.[21] For example, in *R. v Aquarius*,[22] a deliberately disruptive defendant, acting in person, was shown "considerable patience" by the recorder, "in trying to get him to be sensible and to plead and, if he wanted, to exercise his right of challenge of the jury". It was said that the appellant had "quite deliberately set about making his trial as impossible as he could ... ". He was sentenced to nine months' imprisonment for contempt, to run consecutively after the six months that he received on his conviction for theft. (The court took the view that there had indeed been conduct amounting to contempt, but the sentence was "out of proportion" and it was reduced to three months consecutive.) The persistent problem which arose in *R. v Pateley Justices Ex p. Percy*[23] was the unrepresented defendant's insistence, despite a number of requests from the magistrates, upon remaining in the part of the court assigned to professional advocates. 10–132

---

[18] See para.13–90.
[19] *R. v Davison* (1821) 4 B. & Ald. 329 at 333, 335–336, 106 E.R. 958 at 959, Abbott C.J.; and see *Shedden v Patrick* (1869) L.R. 1 H.L. Sc.470 (where litigants in person were afforded considerable latitude in the House of Lords). The report discloses (at 474) that "When the case was called, it became necessary for *Miss Shedden*, her counsel being unprepared, to address the House, which she did for twenty-three days". For a modern example, see the case of *McDonald's Corp v Steel*, one of the first Queen's Bench judgments to be available on the Internet (in June 1997). This was a libel action brought against litigants in person, which lasted from May 1994 to December 1996, partly because of the latitude allowed to the defendants in conducting a complicated case. In proceedings before the European Court, *Steel and Morris v United Kingdom* [2005] E.M.L.R. 314, it was held that the length and complexity of the proceedings gave rise to an inequality of arms as between the parties and consequently a breach of Art.6(1) of the ECHR.
[20] *R. v Leicester Justices Ex p. Barrow* [1991] 2 Q.B. 260 at 285.
[21] Though it has long been recognised that it would be appropriate to warn before invoking the summary jurisdiction: *R. v Davison* (1821) 4 B. & Ald. 329, 106 E.R. 958.
[22] (1974) 59 Cr.App.R. 165.
[23] [1994] C.O.D. 453, the facts of which are discussed at paras 10–66 *et seq.*

10–133   Merely to introduce irrelevant matter would not in itself be contempt, but if an advocate, whether professional or in person, knows that it has been ruled irrelevant, and thereafter persists, he will be in contempt.[24]

10–134   Litigants, whether represented or not, owe an obligation not to mislead the court.[25] A breach of this obligation could be met with any of the procedural sanctions available to the court, including ultimately the setting aside of a judgment so obtained. It is possible to imagine circumstances where these would be of no avail, and the only sanction would be the law of contempt or, if the falsehood was contained in evidence, that of perjury. Where a professional lawyer commits a contempt as a litigant, or in some other personal role, he should be punished in that capacity if at all, though it might be possible in some cases to treat his professional position as an aggravating factor.[26]

B. Professional advocates[27]

10–135   No advocate should ever be prevented from putting forward anything truly relevant to a client's case.[28] Yet there may sometimes inevitably be a tension between the duty to a client and that owed to the court. The potential exposure of professional advocates to proceedings for contempt was explained by the High Court of Australia in *Lewis v Ogden*[29]:

> "The freedom and responsibility which counsel has to present his client's case are so important to the administration of justice, that a court should be slow to hold that remarks made during the course of counsel's address to the jury amount to a wilful insult to the judge, when the remarks may be seen to be relevant to the case which counsel is presenting to the jury on behalf of his client. This is not to say that comments made in counsel's address, apparently relevant to the client's case, may not constitute a contempt. Counsel might wilfully insult a judge 'under colour of addressing the jury', to use the words of Blackburn J. Or he might yield to the temptation of seeking to divert the jury's attention away from the issues by promoting a dispute with the judge, in the belief that this tactic would advantage his client. A deliberate manoeuvre of this kind,

---

[24] *R. v Davison* (1821) 4 B. & Ald. 329, 106 E.R. 958; and *R. v Webb Ex p. Hawkers*, The Times, January 24, 1899. See also *Lewis v Ogden* (1984) A.L.J.R. 34, discussed at para.10–128.
[25] *Vernon v Bosley (No.2)* [1999] Q.B. 18.
[26] *Re Wallace* (1867) L.R. 1 P.C. 106; *Re Sarbadhicary* (1906) 23 T.L.R. 180; *R. v Stafford County Court Judge* (1888) 57 L.J.Q.B. 483, 36 W.R. 589 and 797. See also *Re Wiseman* [1969] N.Z.L.R. 55.
[27] See P. Butt, "Contempt of Court and the Legal Profession" [1978] Crim. L.R. 463; Symposium, "Counsel, I hold you in contempt" (1990) 18 Western State Law Rev. 87–127. For a comment on recent experience in Malaysia, see "Contempt of Court: Freedom of Expression and Rights of the Accused", Chew Swee Yoke in the Malayan Law Journal: www.mlj.com.my/free/articles/sychew2.htm. In the Scottish case of *HMA v Tarbett*, 2003 S.L.T. 1288 counsel was found to be in contempt on the basis that he misled the court in explaining his non-attendance, and the matter was also referred to the Dean of the Faculty. See R.S. Shiels, 2003 S.L.T. 37 at 284 and R. McInnes, "Conflict between Bar and Bench" 2004 S.L.T. 7. See also *Kyprianou v Cyprus*, App. No.73797/01, January 27, 2004.
[28] *R. v Davison* (1821) 4 B. & Ald. 329, 106 E.R. 958; see Abbot C.J. at 334, 958, Bayley J. at 337, 961, Holroyd J. at 339, 961.
[29] (1984) A.L.J.R. 342 at 344; see also *The Magistrates' Court at Prahan v Murphy* [1997] 2 V.R. 186 and for similar remarks made recently in the Court of Appeal in England *Bennett v London Borough of Southwark* [2002] EWCA Civ 223, [2002] I.C.R. 881.

calculated to interfer (*sic*) with the due course of the trial, would amount to a contempt, even if it involves no insult to the judge ... ".

Although a tighter rein may be kept on professional advocates, there exist, both in the case of solicitors and barristers, separate disciplinary bodies to deal with any misconduct, and the court will proceed for contempt only in exceptional cases.[30] In *Bache v Essex County Council*[31] Peter Gibson L.J. was considering a hypothetical situation where a representative in an employment tribunal might persist in doing what he has been told not to do. "If the representative so acts with the knowledge and approval of the party, that may in an extreme case constitute an abuse of process such as may disentitle the party from relief or from being entitled to defend the proceedings. The conduct may in an extreme case constitute contempt, though the tribunal itself will not be able to punish for contempt but may have to cause contempt proceedings to be instigated".[32]

10–136

Reference was made to the *Bache* case in *Bennett v London Borough of Southwark*,[33] where it was suggested that, if an advocate persisted in defying a tribunal without any arguable justification, the tribunal could invite the Attorney-General to consider proceedings for contempt. It was confirmed, however, that it would not be open to the tribunal simply to refuse to hear the advocate any further.

10–137

Yet on one occasion a Crown Court judge ordered defence counsel to be arrested for contempt, and a police officer twisted his arm behind his back. The incident arose[34] at the conclusion of the judge's summing up in a theft case at the Southwark Crown Court when counsel stood up and invited the judge to correct two points regarding the unchallenged evidence in chief of the defendant. The judge told the jury to retire, but counsel indicated that he had no objection to their remaining, whereupon the judge ordered him to sit down. He declined to do so and was arrested. The jury were then discharged and the judge took time to consider what action he should take. This incident probably arose from a clash of personalities, but it highlights the tension which exists between an advocate's duty to the court and that to his client.

10–138

It was said in the New Zealand Court of Appeal in *Harley v McDonald*[35]:

10–139

"In the area of incompetence ... the remedy of contempt is most unlikely to be appropriate. Yet some sanction is necessary to ensure that barristers are accountable for breaches of the standards of conduct and competence required of them."

The decision to award costs against legal advisers personally for their negligence and dereliction of duty in pursuing a hopeless case was reversed in the Privy

---

[30] *Izuora v R.* [1953] A.C. 327; *Parashuram Detaram Shamdasani v The King Emperor* [1945] A.C. 264 at 270.
[31] [2000] 2 All E.R. 847 at 853b–c.
[32] See CPR Sch.1, Ord.52, r.52(1)(2)(a)(iii) and *Peach Grey & Co v Sommers* [1995] 2 All E.R. 513.
[33] [2002] EWCA Civ 223, [2002] I.C.R. 881.
[34] *Guardian*, May 1, 1992, Home section, p.1.
[35] [1999] 3 N.Z.L.R. 545.

10–139

Council[36] on the ground *inter alia* that whether a solicitor was liable to his client in negligence was not relevant to the court's summary jurisdiction to make a costs order and that on the facts of this case the legal advisers could not be criticised for anything worse than pursuing on the plaintiff's clear instructions an apparently hopeless case.

10–140 Where a solicitor made a remark capable of being construed as an insult to the justices' clerk and was detained until the rising of the court, the Divisional Court made the point on application for judicial review[37]:

> "If the justices had thought that the solicitor should withdraw the remark and he had refused and they judged his removal necessary for the restoration of order they could have ordered his removal from the court under their inherent powers.
>
> If they thought that he was guilty of misconduct, they could have reported him to the Law Society".

Since the justices had taken neither of those sensible options, nor adjourned the matter to another day and asked the chief clerk for advice, *certiorari* was granted.

10–141 In the Saskatchewan case of *Shumiatcher*,[38] it was held that it may be the court's duty to convict an advocate of contempt in circumstances where the judge is satisfied that there has been resort to tactics designed to lay the groundwork for a new trial by needling the court and openly accusing the judge of badgering a witness. Reference was made to the remarks of Kerwin C.J.C. in *Re Duncan*[39]:

> "There is no doubt that a counsel owes a duty to his client, but he also has an obligation to conduct himself properly before any Court in Canada . . . It has been stated by Lord Russell of Killowen, C.J. in *Regina v Gray*, [1900] 2 Q.B. 36 at p.40, that Judges and Courts are alike open to criticism, and if reasonable argument or expostulation is offered against any judicial act as contrary to law or the public good, no Court could or would treat that as contempt of court. However, Lord Russell had already pointed out that any act done calculated to bring a Court into contempt or to lower its authority is a contempt of Court and belongs to that category which Lord Chancellor Hardwicke had as early as 1742 characterized as 'scandalising a Court or a judge'".[40]

10–142 The legitimate scope of advocate for pressing vigorously on behalf of a client was explored also in the Scottish case of *Blair-Wilson, Petr*[41] where it was held that a sheriff would be entitled to find an advocate in contempt if he refused to comply with a ruling but that, on the facts, the sheriff had made no clear ruling;

---

[36] [2001] UKPC 18, [2001] A.C. 678.
[37] *R. v Tamworth Justices Ex p. Walsh* [1994] C.O.D. 277, [1994] T.L.R. 116. See also *Weston v CCC Administrator* [1977] Q.B. 32 where the exasperation with listing arrangements was expressed in a letter rather than in open court.
[38] (1967) 64 D.L.R. (2d) 24.
[39] [1958] S.C.R. 41, 11 D.L.R. (2d) 616 at 618.
[40] For a discussion of scandalising generally, see paras 5–204 *et seq*.
[41] 1997 S.L.T. 621 discussed at paras 16–50 *et seq*.

he had rather created a confusing situation which the advocate was entitled to have clarified. Nothing in his conduct therefore justified the sheriff's finding of contempt.

Barristers, unlike solicitors, are not officers of the court and the High Court has no special disciplinary jurisdiction over them.[42] There are older authorities which suggest that the High Court might have power to suspend a barrister who has been guilty of such misconduct as to render him unfit to practise,[43] but these would not now be followed. In the nineteenth century the Judicial Committee of the Privy Council made it clear that, in those colonial courts where the court had power to disbar for contempt, it should only be used in exceptional circumstances.[44]

10–143

It has been held, however, that there may be occasions when it is appropriate to deal summarily with an advocate for contempt for so conducting a case as to bring the authority of the court into disrepute or to interfere with the administration of justice,[45] or to insult the court.[46] Examples have included accusing a judge on the bench of treason,[47] calling him a rogue or a liar,[48] alleging partiality,[49] and even in one case commenting in the course of a judgment "That is a most unjust remark."[50]

10–144

The insult may be aggravated by the manner in which it is uttered.[51] The courts in recent years, however, have stressed that it is not every act of discourtesy[52] by

10–145

---

[42] *Wettenhall v Wakefield* (1833) 10 Bing. 335, 131 E.R. 934.
[43] *Redding's Case* (1680) 1 Sid. 40, 82 E.R. 957; 2 Bacon Abr. Courts (E) 399; *R. v Mitchell* (1741) 2 Atk. 173, 26 E.R. 508, *sub nom. Anon*; *Re Justices of the court of Common Pleas in Antigua* (1830) 1 Kn. 267, *per* Lord Wynford at 268, 12 E.R. 321; and cf. 2 Co. Inst. 213, 3 Bl. Comm. 29, 2 Hawk. P.C., c.22, s.30
[44] *Re Monckton* (1837) 1 Moo. P.C. 455, 12 E.R. 887; *Re Downie and Arrindell* (1841) 3 Moo. P.C. 414, 13 E.R. 168; *Rainy v Sierra Leone Justices* (1853) 8 Moo. P.C. 47, 15 E.R. 19; *Re Wallace* (1867) L.R. 1 P.C. 106; *Newton v North-Western Provinces Court Judge* (1871) L.R. 4 P.C. 18; *Ex p. Renner* [1892] A.C. 218; *Re Sarbadhicary* (1906) 23 T.L.R. 180; *Chang Hang Kiu v Pigott* [1909] A.C. 312.
[45] *Parashuram Detaram Shamdasani v The King Emperor* [1945] A.C. 264. There are a number of earlier decisions of the Judicial Committee which clearly support this view, but they turn very much on their particular facts and the Board, in giving their advice, sometimes did not give detailed reasons. See, *e.g. Rainy v The Justices of Sierra Leone* (1858) 8 Moo. P.C. 47, 14 E.R. 19; *Smith v Justices of Sierra Leone* (1841) 3 Moo. P.C. 361, 13 E.R. 147; *Smith v Justices of Sierra Leone* (1848) 7 Moo. P.C. 174, 13 E.R. 846; *Re Pollard* (1868) L.R. 2 P.C. 106.
[46] *Parashuram* [1945] A.C. 264; *Redding's case* (1680) 1 Sid 40, 82 E.R. 957; *Rogers* (1702) 7 Mod. Rep.28, 87 E.R. 1074; *Ex p. the Duke of Marlborough* (1844) 5 Q.B. 955, 114 E.R. 1508.
[47] *Harrison's Case* (1638) Cro. Car. 503, 79 E.R. 1034.
[48] *R. v Revel* (1719) 1 Str. 420, 93 E.R. 609.
[49] *Vidyasagara v R.* [1963] A.C. 589. See also *The Magistrates' Court at Prahan v Murphy* [1997] 2 V.R. 186.
[50] *R. v Stafford County Court Judge* (1888) 57 L.J.Q.B. 483 and *sub nom. Jordan* 36 W.R. 589 and 797.
[51] *Carus Wilson's case* (1843) 7 Q.B. 984, 115 E.R. 759.
[52] See the discussion relating to the relevance of "courtesy", and in particular in relation to *R. v Metropolitan Police Commissioner Ex p. Blackburn* [1968] 2 Q.B. 150, at paras 5–236 *et seq.*

an advocate that amounts to contempt.[53] Thus in *Parashuram*[54] Lord Goddard said:

"Their lordships would once again emphasise what has often been said before, that this summary power of punishing for contempt should be used sparingly and only in serious cases. It is a power which a court must of necessity possess; its usefulness depends on the wisdom and restraint with which it is exercised, and to use it to suppress methods of advocacy which are merely offensive is to use it for a purpose for which it was never intended."

10–146   For counsel to insult a member of the jury in open court could amount to a contempt.[55] It is obviously undesirable that an advocate should behave in any way discourteously, even when frustrated, but in so far as it sometimes happens it is usually best ignored, or dealt with by reference to a professional disciplinary body.[56] By contrast, falsely to accuse officers of the court of corruption might well be a contempt.[57]

10–147   In *Maharaj v Att-Gen for Trinidad and Tobago*[58] a judge insisted on cases proceeding when the counsel briefed in them was not present, and heard them without the clients having a full opportunity to present their case.[59] The counsel then applied in chambers to the judge to disqualify himself from hearing any other cases in which he (counsel) might in future appear, on the ground that the judge had acted unjudicially. The application was refused. The following day the hearing of one of the cases was resumed, with counsel then participating, but an application to re-open part of the evidence was refused. Counsel repeated in open court the accusation that the judge was guilty of unjudicial conduct. He was committed for an attack on the integrity of the court.

10–148   The Privy Council advised that his appeal should be allowed, principally upon the basis that the charge against him was insufficiently particularised. They indicated, however, that the criticism "unjudicial conduct" covers a very wide spectrum. It would include circumstances in which the judge has asked far too many questions, or by an excess of zeal for speedily disposing of his list has prevented one side or the other from properly presenting their case, and would

---

[53] *Izuora* [1953] A.C. 327.
[54] [1945] A.C. 264 at 270.
[55] *Ex p. Pater* (1864) 5 B. & S. 299, 122 E.R. 842.
[56] Cp., *e.g. Weston v CCC Administrator* [1977] Q.B. 32; See also *R. v Tamworth Justices Ex p. Walsh* (1994) C.O.D. 277, the facts of which are given at para.10–140. In both of those cases, the discourtesy was clearly as a result of frustration with administrative arrangements, and was not directed to the court itself; nor was it likely to interfere with or impede the process of justice. In *Kyprianou v Cyprus*, App. No.73797/01, January 27, 2004, the European Court of Human Rights at [41] listed a number of " . . . alternative, less drastic, measures such as a warning, reporting the applicant to his professional body, refusing to hear the applicant unless he withdrew his statements, or asking him to leave the courtroom".
[57] *Parashuram*, cited above. Much would depend on the circumstances. The real test, we suggest, would be whether or not such an accusation in itself amounted to an interference with the administration of justice.
[58] [1977] 1 All E.R. 411.
[59] Cp. *Raja v Van Hoogstraten* [2004] EWCA Civ 968, [2004] 4 All E.R. 793.

extend to instances of dishonesty or corruption. An accusation of unjudicial conduct would not necessarily in itself amount to contempt.

An advocate is responsible for his conduct in court and cannot excuse impropriety on the ground that he is acting on instructions from his client.[60] **10–149**

There are important considerations of public policy weighing in favour of allowing advocates considerable latitude in the discharge of their professional responsibilities. It must always be remembered that for reasons of public policy the law affords advocates absolute privilege in respect of anything said in court, notwithstanding that it may prove to be irrelevant to the proceedings, and even if said maliciously.[61] An advocate has a wide latitude in addressing the court on behalf of a client,[62] and it would require cogent evidence to prove that anything uttered was not *bona fide*, but rather for some improper purpose such as that of insulting the court.[63] If it could indeed be proved that an advocate had abused that privilege, this would constitute a disciplinary offence irrespective of any finding of contempt. **10–150**

It may often be counsel's duty to put allegations to witnesses that are inherently insulting or offensive, or to invite the court to come to adverse conclusions about a participant's conduct or character. Yet counsel is always required to have regard to the issue of whether a question is ethically justified. An advocate should "not make statements or ask questions which are merely scandalous or intended or calculated only to vilify, insult or annoy either a witness or some other person."[64] For example, it would be unprofessional to suggest that someone is guilty of crime or misconduct, or in particular to attribute to another person a crime of which the lay client is accused, unless such allegations (including as to the credibility of a witness)[65] are properly grounded. Also, a witness should not be accused in a speech unless there has first been afforded an opportunity in cross-examination to deal with the allegation.[66] **10–151**

Nevertheless, if these ethical criteria are satisfied, then counsel is protected in the sense that there could be no suggestion that he was acting unprofessionally, still less committing a contempt of court. Indeed, it may well be his duty to make serious and damaging allegations, and there might be legitimate criticism in such circumstances of undue squeamishness. **10–152**

---

[60] *Vidyasagara v R.* [1963] A.C. 589. See also the *Code of Conduct of the Bar of England and Wales*, 8th ed., 2004, Pt III, para.307(c) and Section 3 (Written Standards for the Conduct of Professional Work) para.5.3.
[61] See *Gatley on Libel and Slander* (10th ed., 2004) at paras 13.5 *et seq.* See also *Munster v Lamb* (1883) 11 Q.B.D. 588. The earliest authorities which indicate that only qualified privilege applies are no longer good law. See, *e.g. Brook v Montague* (1606) Cro. Jac.90, 79 E.R. 77; *Hodgson v Scarlett* (1818) 1 B. & Ald. 232, 106 E.R. 86; *Flint v Pike* (1825) 2 B. & C. 473, 107 E.R. 1136; *Needham v Dowling* (1845) 15 L.J.C.P. 9.
[62] *Re Pollard* (1868) L.R. 2 P.C. 106.
[63] *Ex p. Pater* (1864) 5 B. & S. 299; 10 L.T. 376; cf. *R. v Skinner* (1772) Lofft 55, 98 E.R. 529.
[64] *Code of Conduct of the Bar of England and Wales*, 8th ed., 2004, para.708(g).
[65] *ibid.* para.708(j).
[66] *ibid.* para.708(i).

10–153 The case of *Ex p. Pater*[67] affords an illustration of the difficulties that can arise. During a trial the foreman of the jury made improper remarks directed at the manner in which counsel for the defence conducted his case. In his final address counsel said: "I thank God that there are twelve jurymen, for if it rested with one, and that one the foreman, there could be no doubt of the result; he ought to be removed from the box and another juror put in his place." The judge swore an affidavit that the words were spoken in a loud, threatening and insulting tone; and further that, on his request to withdraw the remarks, counsel refused to do so. Cockburn C.J. delivering the judgment of the Divisional Court said[68]:

> " . . . in themselves they are words which counsel might have uttered in the honest discharge of his duty for the purpose of vindicating the interests of his client . . . but if they were uttered with the intention to insult the juryman, then they were an abuse of the privilege of counsel, and the Judge might treat the uttering of them as a contempt."

10–154 This raises a problem considered elsewhere[69] as to whether otherwise neutral conduct may be categorised as contempt by virtue of intention.[70] It would appear that the court sought to treat Pater's conduct as being such that it could have been either innocent or unlawful, depending upon whether he had an intention to insult. On the other hand, if there were an intention to interfere in some impermissible way with the administration of justice, but the words or actions deployed are judged by the court, objectively, to be harmless, there would be no *actus reus*. Whatever the intention, therefore, there could be no finding of contempt.

10–155 It will not normally be contempt for an advocate to take a bad point. On the other hand, counsel is under a duty to bring relevant authorities to the court's attention, including any which are unfavourable to his own client's case. It could therefore constitute contempt for an advocate to take a point of law, and knowingly to withhold from the court an authority which shows clearly that the point is bad.[71] A barrister must not wilfully mislead the court as to the law, nor may he actively mislead the court as to the facts; although, consistently with the rule that the prosecution must prove its case, he may passively stand by and watch the court being misled by reason of its failure to ascertain facts that are

---

[67] (1864) 5 B. & S. 299, 122 E.R. 842.
[68] *ibid.* at 310 and 846.
[69] See para.11–7.
[70] See, *e.g.* the discussion of *Martin (Peter)*, *The Times*, April 23, 1986 (Lexis) at paras 11–282 *et seq.*
[71] In *Abraham v Jutsun* [1963] 2 All E.R. 402 at 404b–c, Lord Denning M.R. observed: " . . . it was, as I understand it, his duty to take any point which he believed to be fairly arguable on behalf of his client. An advocate is not to usurp the province of the judge. He is not to determine what shall be the effect of legal argument. He is not guilty of misconduct simply because he takes a point which the tribunal holds to be bad. He only becomes guilty of misconduct if he is dishonest. That is, if he knowingly takes a bad point and thereby deceives the court". In the same case, Harman L.J., at 404e–f commented: " . . . unless a bad point be taken knowing it to be bad and concealing from the court, for instance, an authority which shows it clearly to be a bad point, then it would be a very dangerous doctrine indeed to say that the advocate ought to be mulcted in the costs . . . ".

within the barrister's knowledge.[72] There is also a duty to bring any procedural irregularity to the court's attention rather than keeping it back for use on a possible appeal.[73] Any breaches of such professional obligations would probably be better dealt with nowadays by the professional disciplinary body.[74]

The argument was raised in *Kyprianou v Cyprus*[75] that the punishment of the advocate for his remarks in the Cyprus assize court infringed not only his rights under Art.6 of the Convention (mainly because of bias on the part of the tribunal and a failure to formulate clearly the complaint against him) but also those under Art.10. It was argued on the government's behalf that because of the limited and specific functions discharged by an advocate his Art.10 rights were not engaged. But the court found it unnecessary to examine separately whether there had indeed been a violation of Art.10.[76]

10–156

VI. CONTEMPT COMMITTED BY WITNESSES

A. Examples of contempt by witnesses

Obviously a witness may commit contempt in the course of proceedings. Perjury overlaps with contempt though it is generally better left to be prosecuted on indictment.[77] It may take a fuller enquiry to establish all the necessary elements, and any possible defences, than would be possible by means of the summary contempt procedure.

10–157

It has been held to be a contempt for a witness to remain in court after the court has ordered all the witnesses out of court.[78] The fact that the witness does so remain in court is not a bar to the giving of evidence, though the fact that he has wilfully disobeyed the order of the court in this respect may affect the weight to be attached to it.[79] For a witness to refuse to be sworn without good reason could in certain circumstances be treated as contempt in the face of the court, although in so far as any action may be required it is more likely that resort would be had to a specific statutory provision if available.[80]

10–158

---

[72] *Saif Ali v Sidney Mitchell & Co (A Firm)* [1980] A.C. 198 at 220, Lord Diplock. See also *Tombling v Universal Bulb Co Ltd* [1951] 2 T.L.R. 289 at 297, Denning L.J; *Vernon v Bosley (No.2)* [1999] Q.B. 18 at 37–8, Stuart-Smith L.J., 52–4, Evans L.J., 62–4, Thorpe L.J.
[73] *Code of Conduct of the Bar of England and Wales* (8th ed., 2004, para.708(d). See also *R. v Smith* [1994] Crim. L.R. 458.
[74] See the observations of the European Court of Human Rights in *Kyprianou v Cyprus*, App. No.73797/01, January 27, 2004, at [41].
[75] App. No.73797/01, January 27, 2004.
[76] At [72].
[77] *Smith v Bond* (1845) 13 M. & W. 594, 153 E.R. 248; *Royson's Case* (1629) 1 Cro. Car. 146, 79 E.R. 729; *Apted v Apted and Bliss* [1930] P. 246. See also *De Vries v Nat West Bank, The Times*, August 16, 1984.
[78] *Chandler v Horne* (1842) 2 M. & Rob. 423, 174 E.R. 338; reported *sub nom. Roberts v Garratt*, 6 J.P. 154.
[79] *Skelton v Castle* (1787) 6 J.P. 154n.; *Chandler v Horne* (1842) 2 M. & Rob. 423, 174 E.R. 338.
[80] *Preston* (1691), 1 Salk. 278, 91 E.R. 243; *Hennegal v Evance* (1806) 12 Ves. Jun. 201, 33 E.R. 77. See also the County Courts Act 1984, s.55 and the Magistrates' Courts Act 1980, s.97(4), set out at para.11–132.

B. Putting forward false evidence

10–159 For an advocate to place affidavits before the court averring matters which he clearly knows are untrue is a contempt.[81] A witness who gives evidence on oath to the court which he knows is false would be guilty of perjury and triable on indictment for that offence. In some circumstances, it is theoretically possible that such a witness might even today be dealt with summarily for contempt, although it is unlikely that there would be sufficient urgency about the matter to justify such a course. It may sometimes happen that upon full investigation into how evidence, which appeared to be false, came to be given, there emerges an explanation which puts the matter in a different light. This is one reason why the summary disposal of such matters is best avoided.[82] Also, once a judge has disbelieved a witness, even as a matter of first impression, there is inevitably a perception that the tribunal would be biased in determining any consequential contempt proceedings.

10–160 There are a number of pitfalls to be avoided in circumstances where it appears that a witness is giving false evidence or refusing to answer proper questions. For example, it is necessary to avoid if possible introducing the threat of perjury proceedings in respect of witnesses before the conclusion of the trial for which their evidence is required.[83] Furthermore, if it is intended to deal with any such matter by way of the contempt jurisdiction, it is inappropriate that the witness should be arrested in the presence of a jury.[84]

10–161 In *Smith v Bond*,[85] Alderson B. stated in the course of the argument that persons giving false testimony were in those days frequently committed for contempt. A flagrant example is provided by *Apted v Apted and Bliss*,[86] in which Lord Merrivale P. held a petitioner in a divorce suit in contempt because he had failed to disclose full particulars of his own adultery in his discretion statement. Despite the seriousness of the matter, the President felt that if the petitioner paid the costs of the intervention of the King's Proctor in the matter it would not be necessary to impose any penalty for the contempt.[87]

---

[81] *Linwood v Andrews* (1888) L.T. 612; *Smith v Justices for Sierra Leone* (1848) 7 Moo. P.C. 174 at 180 *et seq,* 13 E.R. 846 at 849; cf. *Smith v Bond* (1845) 13 M. & W. 594, 152 E.R. 924.
[82] An example is provided by the case of Tommy Docherty, a football manager, who had abandoned a libel action after admitting in cross-examination that he had told "a pack of lies". The judge in summing the case up said that the witness box could be the loneliest place in the world and that it was possible under "fierce" cross-examination, based on erroneous instructions, to make admissions without really knowing what one was saying. Mr Docherty had said he was so terrified that he only wanted to give an answer to get out of the witness box. He was duly acquitted of both perjury charges: *The Times,* October 21, 1981, p.4.
[83] *R. v Newcastle upon Tyne Magistrates' Court Ex p. Still* (1997) C.L.Y. 86, Laws J.
[84] *R v Maguire* [1997] 1 Cr.App.R. 61, CACD.
[85] (1845) 13 M. & W. 594, 153 E.R. 248. For an even earlier example, see *Royson* (1628) 1 Cro. Car. 146, 79 E.R. 729, where a surety falsely swore as to his means. On his confession Whitlock J. committed him and he was subsequently sentenced to stand in the pillory.
[86] [1930] P. 246.
[87] See the remarks of Stephenson L.J. in *Weston v CCC Administrator* [1977] Q.B. 32 at 45G–H. as to the inappropriateness of using the sanction of costs as a penalty for contempt. This is discussed at paras 14–139 *et seq.*

C. Refusing to answer questions or prevarication

It is contempt at common law for a witness to refuse to answer an admissible and necessary question, unless he claims privilege from answering and the judge upholds that claim.[88] An accused person, however, is not compellable in criminal proceedings to give evidence on his own behalf, and "he shall accordingly not be guilty of contempt of court by reason of a failure to do so."[89]

10–162

Failure by a compellable witness to answer relevant questions is a classic form of contempt in the face of the court, and the Court of Appeal has indicated that, in principle, a sentence of imprisonment is likely to be the appropriate penalty.[90] Journalists are a special case in the light of s.10 of the Act, and the decision in *Goodwin v The United Kingdom*.[91]

10–163

Mere prevarication by a witness would not be treated as contempt unless it amounted substantially to defiance or, to put the same proposition in different words, there were present an intention to disrupt or hinder the court's process.[92] In the county court a person who, having been summoned as a witness, refuses or neglects without sufficient cause to produce any documents required, or refuses to be sworn or give evidence, may in the discretion of the judge be fined up to £1,000.[93] In a magistrates' court a witness who refuses to be sworn or give evidence, or to produce a document, may be committed for up to one month (or until he sooner gives evidence or produces the document) or fined up to £2,500, or both.[94]

10–164

D. Witnesses and duress

Increasingly, experience has shown that witnesses may be reluctant to give evidence because of fear of reprisals.[95] If this were to be routinely accepted by the courts as a valid reason for declining to give evidence, guilty persons could escape conviction because, through threats of further illegality, either on their

10–165

---

[88] *Att-Gen v Lundin* (1982) 75 Cr.App.R. 90 discussed at para.9–47; *Ex parte Fernandez* (1861) 10 C.B. (N.S.) 1; *O'Brennan v Tully* (1935) 69 I.L.T. 115; *Re Keller*, 22 L.R.Ir. 158; *Att-Gen v Clough* [1963] 1 Q.B. 173; *Att-Gen v Mulholland, Att-Gen v Foster* [1963] 2 Q.B. 477. As to the position of persons failing to attend or answer questions before an examiner, see *Stuart v Balkis* (1884) 32 W.R. 676; *Re Evans, Evans v Noton* [1893] 1 Ch. 252. But see the discussion of the law applying in this context to journalists in the light of Art.10 of the European Convention and s.10 of the Contempt of Court Act 1981, at paras 9–52 *et seq.*
[89] Criminal Justice and Public Order Act 1994, s.35(4).
[90] *R. v Montgomery* [1995] 2 All E.R. 28, [1995] 2 Cr.App.R. 23. See also *R. v Renshaw* [1989] Crim. L.R. 811 at 812.
[91] (1996) 22 E.H.R.R. 123. See paras 9–52 and 9–194 *et seq.*
[92] *Coward v Stapleton* (1953) 90 C.L.R. 573. Compare the position in Scotland, discussed at para. 16–118.
[93] County Courts Act 1984, s.55. The figure of £1,000 was inserted by the Criminal Justice Act 1991, Sch.4. Expenses must be tendered.
[94] Magistrates' Courts Act 1980, s.97(4) as amended by the Contempt of Court Act 1981, s.14 and Sch.2, Pt III, para.7, and by Criminal Justice Act 1991, s.3(a), Sch.4, Pt I.
[95] See, *e.g.* J. McEwan, "Documentary Hearsay Evidence—Refuge for the Vulnerable Witness" [1989] Crim. L.R. 629. See also *R. v Martin* [1996] Crim. L.R. 589, and the commentary of Professor Birch on *R. v Coolledge* [1996] Crim. L.R. 748 at 749.

10–165 CHAPTER 10—CONTEMPT IN THE FACE OF THE COURT

part or with their connivance, insufficient evidence is available against them. As Potter L.J. said in *R. v Montgomery*[96]:

" ... where victims or witnesses to serious crime refuse to do their duty or succumb to threats of fear of reprisals by refusing to give evidence or answer questions, the result is a failure of law and order ... ".

Various recommendations were accordingly made to protect witnesses, especially those who are perceived to be vulnerable,[97] and there is now a wide range of statutory provisions to assist such persons.[98]

10–166 Alongside these new measures, however, the common law defence of duress may still be available to the defendant upon an application to commit.[99] The leading decision on the current law of duress generally is that of the House of Lords in *R. v Hasan*,[1] which establishes that, before a foundation for such a defence is laid,[2] there must be a threat of death or grievous bodily harm, or a reasonable belief in such harm. In addition, the threat must be such that a person of reasonable firmness on the facts as he reasonably believed them to be would be likely to succumb to it, given his or her personal characteristics.[3] Furthermore, the defence is not available if the person claiming it has voluntarily associated

---

[96] [1995] 2 All E.R. 28 at 34c–d, (1995) 16 Cr.App.R.(S) 274 at 279. See also the commentary of Professor Birch on *R. v Renshaw* [1989] Crim. L.R. 811 at 812.

[97] In June 1998, the Home Office issued a paper containing proposals for affording greater protection to witnesses, *Speaking up for Justice: Report of the Interdepartmental Working Group on the treatment of Vulnerable or Intimidated Witnesses in the Criminal Justice System*. This was followed by the Home Office Report, *Action for Justice: Measures to assist vulnerable or intimidated witnesses in the Criminal Justice System* (2001).

[98] In particular, the Criminal Justice Act 1988, s.23 (giving evidence in writing, rather than orally); the Youth Justice and Criminal Evidence Act 1999, ss.16–33 (special measure directions). See also s.46 (discussed at paras 8–74 *et seq.*) affording witness anonymity; Criminal Justice Act 2003, ss.51–56 (live links) and 137–138 (evidence by video recording). Rule 16.10 of the Criminal Procedure Rules 2005 (set out at para.2–64 above) contemplates that a court may go into closed session to protect witnesses. And see *R. (Al Fawwaz) v Governor of Brixton Prison* [2002] UKHL 69, [2002] 1 A.C. 556, where are outlined factors relevant to the decision whether the judge may permit a witness who has real fears for his safety to conceal his identity entirely from the defendant.

[99] *R. v K* (1983) 78 Cr.App.R. 82; *R. v Lewis* (1992) 96 Cr.App.R. 412. See also *R. v Ayres* (1994) 15 C.C.C. (3d) 208. For a discussion of duress in the context of journalists, see para.9–119. See also *Perviaz*, March 26, 1999 (Smith Bernal) where it was confirmed that the defence of duress applied to criminal contempt. The trial judge had sought to balance the duress faced by the witness against the public interest in ensuring that material witnesses testified. He appeared, however, to have lost sight of the essential question which was whether it had been proved to the criminal standard that the defendant was not acting under duress.

[1] [2005] UKHL 22, [2005] 2 W.L.R. 709. See paras 3–252 *et seq.* for further discussion of the defence in criminal law. So far as duress might be a defence to proceedings for civil contempt, see para.3–250.

[2] There is an evidential burden upon the defence in this respect: sufficient evidence must be given by the defendant or on his behalf to raise an issue for consideration by the tribunal of fact, and it is for the prosecution to show beyond reasonable doubt that the defendant was not acting under duress. Fear of reprisals amounting to something less than death or grievous bodily harm are a factor to be taken into account in sentencing if the defendant refuses to give evidence: *R. v Phillips* (1983) 78 Cr.App.R. 88; *R. v Jardine* (1997) 9 Cr.App.R.(S) 41.

[3] See *Archbold 2005*, paras 17–120 *et seq.*; see also ed. D. Ormerod, Smith and Hogan, *Criminal Law* (11th ed., 2005) at 296 *et seq.*

with those who subsequently subjected him to threats, and he knew or ought to have known that they were likely to do so.

The cases are unclear as to how specific the threat of death must have been, but there is some authority suggesting that the threats must be quite explicit. In a case concerning the law of contempt, *R. v Harvey and Osbourne*,[4] Stuart-Smith L.J. is reported as saying that an "atmosphere of fear" was a long way from establishing duress. Since the applicants had not been the subject of "direct intimidation", the defence failed.

10–167

Some of the problems of principle affecting the availability of duress as a defence in this context are similar to those encountered in relation to the law of perjury. In *R. v Hudson and Taylor*,[5] the Court of Appeal took the view that duress is available on a perjury charge. It was suggested by the Crown that a person so threatened should alert the police to his predicament, or otherwise seek official protection. But the court considered that this would be too severe a restriction, saying that it would be enough if he were to "avail himself of some opportunity which was reasonably open to him to render the threat ineffective." That decision was, however, disapproved by the House in *Hasan*. No mention was made of the possible implications for contempt of court and it is thus not now entirely easy to determine how far the law of duress applies.

10–168

A practical compromise solution, where the defendant to an application to commit alleged fear of reprisals, was suggested in *R. v Holt and Bird*.[6] Two young women were imprisoned for periods of two and three months for refusing to give evidence against the boyfriend of one of them, who was charged with causing her grievous bodily harm with intent, with the result that the prosecution collapsed. On an appeal against sentence only,[7] the court reduced the sentences in such a way as to permit immediate release, taking the view that the prosecution (and the judge) should have contemplated a different procedure, namely the possibility that the statements previously given by the young women might in the circumstances have been admissible. Section 23(3)(b) of the Criminal Justice Act 1988 provided that a statement made by a person in a document shall be admissible if "the person who made it does not give oral evidence through fear or because he is kept out of the way".[8] Had it been possible to use the statements in this way, the significance of the oral evidence that the young women would otherwise have given in the context of the trial as a whole would have been

10–169

---

[4] 95/5658/Z2; March 5, 1996.
[5] [1972] 2 Q.B. 202. See also *R. v Sharp* [1987] Q.B. 853.
[6] (1996) 161 J.P. 96.
[7] The question of duress as a defence does not appear to have been raised as such, although it is clear from the statements of fact made by the Court of Appeal that there were further intimidatory threats made both by the initial defendant and others to the young women.
[8] See now Criminal Justice Act 2003, s.116(2)(e). Subsection (3) says that "For the purposes of subsection (2)(e) 'fear' is to be widely construed and (for example) includes fear of the death or injury of another person or of financial loss" (*i.e.* the subsection contemplates a wider definition of fear than would be applicable to a defence of duress).

10–169 CHAPTER 10—CONTEMPT IN THE FACE OF THE COURT

considerably reduced, which is a factor that should be taken into account upon sentencing.

10–170 In cases of domestic violence such as *Holt and Bird*, where it appears possible that the victim will subsequently prove unwilling to give oral evidence, guidance was to be had from the *Crown Prosecution Service Policy for Prosecuting Cases of Domestic Violence*[9]:

> "If the victim confirms that the complaint is true but wants to withdraw support the Crown prosecutor will consider the following to find out whether it is still possible to continue with the prosecution . . . . Could the victim's statement be used as evidence under section 23 of the Criminal Justice Act 1988?"

Since that time, more comprehensive statutory measures have been introduced to protect vulnerable witnesses.[10]

10–171 Ironically, perhaps, if the reluctant witness refuses or fails to come to court at all, he faces a maximum of three months' imprisonment for failing to comply with a witness order, contrary to the Criminal Procedure (Attendance of Witnesses) Act 1965.[11] If the contempt procedure is invoked, for conduct in court, the maximum would be governed by s.14 of the Contempt of Court Act 1981 (*i.e.* two years).

10–172 It might also be said that, whereas, in the case of perjury, the untruthful witness does a real disservice to the legal process by seeking to *divert* it from its course, a witness who withholds true evidence merely impedes or obstructs. But that lesser disservice is, at least, highly visible, and can sometimes now be overcome in part if a written statement would be admissible.[12]

E. Witnesses who may claim privilege

10–173 In certain circumstances a witness may claim to be privileged from answering a relevant and necessary question. Thus any witness has privilege against self-incrimination,[13] subject to any statutory exception such as that contained in s.98 of the Children Act 1989,[14] which states that a person may not refuse to give evidence or refuse to answer questions on the grounds of self-incrimination in

---

[9] See now the publication of the same title (February 2005), Pt 5.
[10] Above, n.98. The regime for dealing with vulnerable witnesses is described in *Archbold 2005* paras 8–57 *et seq.*
[11] Or in the case of a magistrates' court, the Magistrates' Courts Act 1980, s.97(3), which deals with punishment for failure to attend with imprisonment for one month.
[12] In *R. v Montgomery* [1995] 2 All E.R. 28, [1995] 2 Cr.App.R.(S) 23, it was stated that this should nevertheless not prevent the period of imprisonment for contempt from being greater than three months in the appropriate circumstances.
[13] Discussed at paras 3–188 *et seq.*, specifically in the context of proceedings for contempt.
[14] See *Oxfordshire County Council v L and F* [1997] 1 F.L.R. 235 at 241; *Oxfordshire County Council v P* [1995] Fam. 161 at 168.

proceedings for the making of care and supervision orders or in proceedings for the protection of children.[15] A lawyer may generally refuse to disclose professional communications with a client, unless the client waives the privilege.[16] Others also receive information which they regard as confidential, for example the priest in the confessional or the doctor in the surgery. Yet neither could claim a privilege, although no doubt a judge will carefully weigh the effect of such moral or professional obligations before deciding, for the purpose of the case in hand, that the witness should be required to supply the information.[17]

10–174 Nevertheless, before any witness can be held in contempt for refusing to answer a question, his answer must be both relevant and necessary to the issues in the case. This was illustrated in *Att-Gen v Lundin*[18] where the Crown sought to prove the contents of a document. The original was not available, but it was sought to put in a photostat copy. Lundin could have given evidence as to the source of the photostat. Before the Crown could put in the copy, they had to account satisfactorily for the absence of the original. This they could not do. Hence the Divisional Court held that it was not necessary for Lundin to answer the question put to him about the source of the copy; even if he had answered, the Crown would still not have been able to put the copy in evidence. Now, so far as journalists are concerned, the matter is governed by s.10 of the Contempt of Court Act, which is fully discussed in chapter 9.

F. Judicial discretion

10–175 If the answer would be relevant and admissible, and even on the face of it necessary, the court still has a discretion at common law to refuse to require the answer.[19] In *Att-Gen v Mulholland; Att-Gen v Foster*[20] it was held that even where an answer is admissible and necessary to the proceedings in question, there may be other considerations which lead a judge to conclude that it is undesirable to compel disclosure or punish a refusal to answer. The factors that might be taken into account in the exercise of such discretion have been considered in such cases as *Att-Gen v Lundin*,[21] *Special Hospitals Service Authority v Hyde*[22] and *John v Express Newspapers*.[23] The importance of the residual discretion was emphasised in the House of Lords in *Ashworth Hospital Authority v MGN Ltd.*[24]

---

[15] Under Pts IV and V of the Family Law Act 1989, respectively.
[16] But see *Re L (A Minor) (Police Investigation: Privilege)* [1997] A.C. 16 in relation to the non-application of litigation privilege in Children Act proceedings.
[17] Lord Denning M.R. in *Att-Gen v Foster and Mulholland* [1963] 2 Q.B.477.
[18] (1982) 75 Cr.App.R. 90.
[19] See in the context of journalists specifically the discussion at para.9–42.
[20] [1963] 2 Q.B. 477 at 492, cited at para.9–43: followed in *British Steel Corporation v Granada Television Limited* [1981] A.C. 1096.
[21] (1982) 75 Cr.App.R. 90, discussed at paras 9–98 *et seq.*
[22] (1994) 20 B.M.L.R. 75, discussed at para.9–77.
[23] [2000] 1 W.L.R. 1931.
[24] [2002] UKHL 29, [2002] 1 W.L.R. 2033 at [2] (Lord Slynn) and [36] (Lord Woolf C.J.).

10–176   CHAPTER 10—CONTEMPT IN THE FACE OF THE COURT

VII. CONTEMPT COMMITTED BY JURORS

A. The importance of jury service

10–176 In *R. v Schot and Barclay*[25] Rose L.J. emphasised the fundamental importance of jury trial and the unusually difficult challenges to the minds and emotions of jurors, sometimes over a considerable period. He went so far as to say that civilised society, as we know it, would not survive without jury service.[26]

He continued:

"That is why, however reluctantly and with whatever trepidation, most members of the public recognise that, if summoned for jury service and sworn to try a case, that is a job which they must do conscientiously and to the best of their ability. However, it must be recognised by all members of the public that, if they have been summoned for jury service and properly empanelled without making any reasonable objection, they are at risk of punishment by the court including, in an appropriate case, imprisonment, if they contumaciously refuse or fail to discharge the obligations which they undertook when taking the oath to 'faithfully try the defendant and give a true verdict according to the evidence'".

Times would appear to have moved on since Lord Devlin wrote[27] in 1956 " . . . Trial by jury is more than an instrument of justice and more than one wheel of the constitution: it is the lamp that shows that freedom lives". For example, although Parliament has recently limited the opportunities for avoiding jury service,[28] it has also provided that those charged with certain offences should no longer have the opportunity of this mode of trial.[29] Nonetheless, the Judicial Committee of the House of Lords in *R. v Wang*[30] gave a ringing endorsement to Lord Devlin's words.

B. Confidentiality of a jury's deliberations

10–177 It is provided in s.8 of the Contempt of Court Act 1981 that it is a contempt of court *inter alia* to disclose particulars of statements made, opinions expressed, arguments advanced or votes cast by members of a jury in the course of their deliberations in any legal proceedings. It was confirmed by the House of Lords in *R. v Mirza; R. v Connor and Rollock*[31] that neither the common law rules as

---

[25] [1997] 2 Cr.App.R. 383, (1997) 161 J.P. 473, CACD; paras 10–72 *et seq*.
[26] For a contrasting view, see Sir Louis Blom-Cooper Q.C. "Article 6 and Modes of Criminal Trial" [200] E.H.R.L.R at p.5 (" . . . a publicly unaccountable jury is a 'curiosity' in today's democratic society"), an article which Sir Robin Auld cited in his Report *Criminal Courts Review* (2001), p.139.
[27] *Trial by Jury* (1956), *Hamlyn Lectures* (8th series), p.78.
[28] Criminal Justice Act 2003, s.321 and Sch.33.
[29] Criminal Justice Act 2003, Part 7. In the civil context, as was pointed out by Lord Bingham in *Aitken v Preston* [1997] E.M.L.R. 415 at 417, the emphasis is now against trial with jury. See also *Goldsmith v Pressdram Ltd* [1988] 1 W.L.R. 49 at 68, 72 and 76, CA.
[30] [2005] UKHL 9, [2005] 1 W.L.R. 661.
[31] [2004] UKHL 2, [2004] 1 A.C. 1118.

to jury secrecy nor the terms of s.8 of the Act were incompatible with the right to a fair trial under Art.6 of the European Convention. The offence applies to jurors as much as to anyone else. This subject is addressed in detail in chapter 11,[32] because generally any breach of these provisions is unlikely to be classifiable as contempt "in the face".

C. Statutory summary offences

The Juries Act 1974, s.20(5),[33] creates various summary offences, which may be committed by jurors, such as making false representations for the purpose of evading jury service; or of enabling another to do so; failing, without reasonable excuse to answer questions as to qualifications for jury service under s.2(5); deliberately or recklessly giving false answers; and serving on a jury when ineligible, disqualified or not qualified. These are not, however, under the Act expressed to be punishable as contempts.[34] The subject is therefore separately considered in chapter 11,[35] because in most cases it would not be appropriate to classify such matters as falling within contempt "in the face".

D. Misconduct in relation to deliberations or verdict

It has been clear since *Bushell's* case[36] that for a jury to deliver a verdict which happens to conflict with the judge's view of the facts, or to have the *appearance* of perversity, is not of itself a contempt.[37] Yet, if the courts are jealous of a jury's rights, they are also quick to see that they are not abused. It would be, at least in theory, a contempt for a juror to refuse to give a verdict at all,[38] though not, of course, merely to disagree with his fellow jurors.[39] It would no doubt be a contempt for a foreman deliberately to deliver a verdict which did not in fact accurately reflect the outcome.[40]

---

[32] See paras 11–349 *et seq.*
[33] Set out at para.11–139.
[34] By contrast with the wording of s.20(2), which is set out at para.11–139 and provides for the offence to be punishable either on summary conviction or "as if it were criminal contempt of court committed in the face of the court".
[35] paras 11–138 *et seq.*
[36] (1670) Vaughan 135 at 152, 124 E.R. 1006 at 1214.
[37] See the reaffirmation of this point in *R. v Schot and Barclay* [1997] 2 Cr.App.R. 383, (1997) 161 J.P. 473, discussed at paras 10–72 *et seq.* It seems that in earlier times the court did consider itself entitled to enquire into verdicts in order to see whether they were perverse and, on occasion, to impose penalties upon the jurors in respect of such verdicts: see *Watts v Brains* (1600) Cro. Eliz. 695 at 778–9, 78 E.R. 930 at 1009. See generally Glanville Williams, *Proof of Guilt* (3rd ed., 1963); W.R. Cornish, *Trial by Jury* (1968); Lord Devlin, *Trial by Jury* (rev. ed., 1966). See also *R. v Ponting* [1985] Crim. L.R. 318.
[38] Which might well require an enquiry as to what had taken place inside the jury room; see paras 11–349 *et seq.* for consideration of s.8.
[39] *Bushell's Case* (1670) Vaughan 135 at 152, 124 E.R. 1014. See also *R. v Schot and Barclay* [1997] 2 Cr.App.R. 383, (1997) 161 J.P. 473.
[40] 2 Hawk. P.C., c.22, s.17; *J. & R.'s Case* (1367) Y.B. Lib. Ass.40 Edw. III, pl. 10; and as to majority verdicts see now Juries Act 1974, s.17.

10–180 Moreover, it may be a contempt for a jury to refuse to give a verdict of acquittal which they are directed to give by the judge as a matter of law.[41] Such directions are regularly given when judges order an acquittal, following a ruling of law at the half way stage of a trial, upholding a submission of no case.[42]

10–181 It is a contempt for a jury to reach a verdict in a capricious way as by tossing a coin,[43] or by lot.[44] In *Watts v Brains*[45] ten of the jury were for acquitting and two for convicting. They therefore resolved to give a verdict of not guilty but, if in the event the court appeared to disapprove of this verdict, then to alter it to one of guilty. For this they were fined. The change of verdict, if such a thing were ever to happen, would be apparent in open court, so that the arbitrary nature of their activities would be clear without the need for enquiries into their private deliberations.[46]

10–182 A clear example of contempt would be if a juror were to attempt to sway the minds of his fellow jurors corruptly or improperly.[47] So too for a juror knowingly to hold improper communications with any party to the proceedings,[48] or indeed to discuss a case with a member of the public.[49] Such conduct would be contrary to the oath, and moreover jurors will generally have been warned expressly by judges not to discuss the case with people outside their own number.

10–183 It may also be a contempt for a member of a jury to leave his fellow jurors, without leave of the court, after they have retired to consider their verdict, even

---

[41] See the discussion in *Bushell's Case*, (1670) Vaughan 135 at 152–3, 124 E.R. 1006 at 1014–15. Reference is there made to two obscure and poorly reported cases, *Wharton's Case* and *Southwell's Case* which appear to support the proposition in the text, although the circumstances are by no means clear. As to the possibility of directions to convict, see E.J. Griew, "Directions to Convict" [1972] Crim. L.R. 204. The House of Lords in *R. v Wang* [2005] UKHL 9, [2005] 1 W.L.R. 661, finally made it clear that no such direction could be given.

[42] In accordance with the principles set out in *R. v Galbraith* [1981] 1 W.L.R. 1039.

[43] *Langdell v Sutton* (1737) Barnes 32, 94 E.R. 791, where they hustled half-pence in a hat. The jurors were ordered to attend for the purpose of being publicly admonished "that the country may take warning". In *Vaise v Delaval* (1785) 1 T.R. 11, 99 E.R. 944, it was said that the jurors decided a verdict by the toss of a coin. This was described as a "great misdemeanour", but the affidavit of the juror describing what had occurred was nevertheless rejected. See also Oswald, *Contempt* (3rd. ed. 1910), p.67.

[44] *Foster v Hawden* 2 Lev. 205; 2 Hawk. P.C., c.22, s.17. For a modern example, where some jurors consulted an *ouija* board, see *R. v Young* [1995] Q.B. 324, discussed at paras 11–343, 11–354. These were not proceedings for contempt, but it is difficult to see how the conduct of the jurors in question would not be so classified.

[45] (1600) Cro. Eliz. 778, 78 E.R. 930.

[46] See Contempt of Court Act 1981, s.8, the discussion at paras 11–349 *et seq.* and the problems which arose in *R. v Schot and Barclay* [1997] 2 Cr.App.R. 383, (1997) 161 J.P. 473.

[47] *Re MM & HM* (1933) 1 I.R. 299.

[48] Co. Litt. 227b; 2 Hawk. P.C., c.22, s.19; and cf. *R. v Willmont* (1914) 10 Cr.App.R. 173; *Goby v Wetherill* [1915] 2 K.B. 674; *R. v Shepherd* (1910) 74 J.P.J. 605. Cp. the case of *R. v Steen*, January 26, 2004, where a conviction was unsuccessfully challenged on the basis that a "love sick juror" had sent champagne and a note to prosecuting counsel after the verdict had been reached.

[49] *Bishop of N v Earl of Kent* (1500) Y.B. T. 14 Hen. 7, pl. 4; *R. v Macrae*, *The Times*, November 18 and 19, 1892, p.10. Compare *R. v Box* [1964] 1 Q.B. 430 discussed at para.2–84.

if he departs through sickness.[50] In *R. v Ward*,[51] and in *R. v Ketteridge*,[52] the view was expressed that, where a juror absents himself without leave, the only course would be to discharge the jury. In neither case, however, did the court expressly state that such a juror would be in contempt. Since in both cases the disappearance of the juror concerned had led to expensive and time-wasting interference with the administration of justice, there can be little doubt that such conduct would at least be capable of constituting the *actus reus* of contempt.

It so happens that in each case the juror appeared not to realise the significance of what he was doing, and nowadays, with the insistence upon the need to prove a positive intention to interfere with the administration of justice, it may be that any such individual would escape for that reason a finding of contempt. It is more likely, however, that the court would be prepared to draw the inference, assuming the absence to have been voluntary (as opposed to unavoidable travel complications, for example), that the person concerned must have known[53] that it would interfere with the administration of justice. It would certainly be a contempt for a juror to leave the court while evidence was being given or the summing-up in progress.

In *R. v Macrae*,[54] while the bailiff was being sworn to take charge of the jury in a murder trial, one of the jurors separated himself from his fellows and went home. Until 1897,[55] it was regarded as necessary in all cases of felony that the jury should remain together from the time the prisoner was given into their charge at the beginning of the trial until their verdict was delivered. The juror explained to Kennedy J. that he had only been away for 20 minutes to post an important letter. Because of "the extreme gravity of the case" the matter was adjourned until next morning. Meanwhile, the jury had to be locked up. The following day the judge expressed his concern that the juror had remained outside the precincts of the court for nearly half an hour "and in communication with other persons". He did not think it appropriate to speculate on whether there had been any extraneous influence brought to bear on the juror during that interval, but concluded that the conduct was contrary to the first principles of justice and to what "must ... have been known by him to be his duty." He therefore found him to have committed a "gross contempt of Court", and fined him £50. He also discharged the jury, and remanded the defendant to the next Assizes.

---

[50] *Anon.* 34 E. III quoted in Vaughan 151, 124 E.R. 1006; *Rhoder, The Times*, November 19, 1894; *Anon.* (1907) quoted in Oswald, *Contempt*, (3rd ed., 1910), p.68 and *R. v Ketteridge* [1915] 1 K.B. 467; *R. v Ward* (1867) 17 (N.S.) L.T. 220. See also *R. v Miller* (1977) C.L.Y. 447 where a juryman refused to retire with his fellow jurors because he felt too confused to deliver a verdict.
[51] (1867) 17 (N.S.) L.T. 220.
[52] [1915] 1 K.B. 467, CCA.
[53] *R. v Macrae, The Times*, November 18 and 19, 1892, pp.11 and 10 respectively; *R. v Hill* [1986] Crim. L.R. 457; *Connolly v Dale* [1996] Q.B. 120.
[54] *The Times*, November 18 and 19, 1892, pp.11 and 10 respectively.
[55] In the Juries Detention Act 1897, it was provided in s.1 that "Upon the trial of any person for a felony other than murder, treason, or treason felony, the court may, if it see fit, at any time before the jury consider their verdict, permit the jury to separate in the same way as the jury upon the trial of any person for misdemeanour are now permitted to separate."

10–186 The old practice was to keep the jury together, even before retiring to consider their verdict. Nowadays, jurors are not required to remain together even at the stage when they have retired to consider their verdict. It is provided[56]:

> "If, on the trial of any person for an offence on indictment, the court thinks fit, it may at any time (*whether before or after* the jury have been directed to consider their verdict) permit the jury to separate" (emphasis added).

Even today, however, if a juror were to absent himself when he should be in court and performing his duties, assuming the requisite *mens rea*, contempt might still have a role to play.

10–187 The substituted provision in s.13 of the Juries Act 1974 (after a transitional period in which the judges were enabled to permit the jury to separate up to the point of retirement to consider their verdict) has now changed the position, so that the jury may be permitted to disperse at night rather than having to be compelled to stay in an hotel together.[57] Even before this, in a civil case a jury was allowed to separate at any time, even after the summing-up.[58]

10–188 In a number of old cases, jurors were punished for eating and drinking in court and even after they had retired to consider their verdict.[59] Nowadays only exceptionally could a juror's eating be treated as in contempt; for example if he were allowing himself to be distracted, or did so in such a manner as to insult or disrupt the court. It is an offence under the 1974 Act for a juror to be unfit by reason of drink or drugs to discharge his duties.[60]

10–189 It is a statutory contempt for a juror to disclose the deliberations of the jury.[61] Since publication of such disclosures is also a contempt by persons who are not jurors, including judge or counsel, this matter is considered separately.[62] In *R. v Less*,[63] letters were written by two jurors to the Court of Appeal expressing their concerns over the verdict. Quite possibly this step was taken with the best of motives, but the court declined to look at them and expressed disquiet that the letters had been written and, moreover, that they had actually been placed before them. Regrettable though this incident may have been, it is hardly likely that proceedings would be taken in such a case against them, whether for contempt at common law or for a breach of the terms of s.8 itself.

---

[56] By s.43 of the Criminal Justice and Public Order Act 1994 which substituted a new s.13 in the Juries Act 1974.
[57] The wisdom of this change was questioned by R. Card and R. Ward, *The Criminal Justice and Public Order Act 1994* (1994), para.8.23.
[58] *Fanshaw v Knowles* [1916] 2 K.B. 538.
[59] Co. Litt. 227b; *Mucklow's Case, Welcden v Elkington* (1578) Plowd. 516 at 518a, 75 E.R. 763 at 766; *Anon* (1521) Rastell, Ent. 267b at 268a. See also *Bushell's Case* (1670) Vaughan 135 at 152, 124 E.R. 1006 at 1014.
[60] Juries Act 1974, s.20(1)(b), cited at para.11–139.
[61] Contempt of Court Act 1981, s.8.
[62] paras 11–349 *et seq.*
[63] [1993] T.L.R. 186.

VIII. Unauthorised Recording of Court Proceedings

A. Use of tape recorders in court: Section 9

Of the means that might be used to record court proceedings, only tape recorders and photography[64] are specifically dealt with by legislation. No legislative provision regulates the use of, in particular, lap top computers or mobile telephones.[65] Such matters can be regulated by the judge who is entitled to control the proceedings in such a way as to avoid disruption or other interference with the smooth progress of a trial.

Section 9 of the 1981 Act restricts the use of tape recorders in court.[66] It provides:

"(1) Subject to subsection (4) below, it is a contempt of court—
(a) to use in court, or bring into court for use, any tape recorder or other instrument for recording sound, except with the leave of the court;
(b) to publish a recording of legal proceedings[67] made by means of any such instrument, or any recording derived directly or indirectly from it, by playing it in the hearing of the public or any section of the public, or to dispose of it or any recording so derived, with a view to such publication;
(c) to use any such recording in contravention of any conditions of leave granted under paragraph (a).

(2) Leave under paragraph (a) of subsection (1) may be granted or refused at the discretion of the court, and if granted may be granted subject to such conditions as the court thinks proper with respect to the use of any recording made pursuant to the leave: and where leave has been granted the court may at the like discretion withdraw or amend it either generally or in relation to any particular part of the proceeding.

(3) Without prejudice to any other power to deal with an act of contempt under paragraph (a) of subsection (1), the court may order the instrument, or any recording made with it, or both, to be forfeited; and any object so forfeited shall (unless the court otherwise determines on application by a person appearing to be the owner) be sold or otherwise disposed of in such manner as the court may direct.

(4) This section does not apply to the making or use of sound recordings for purposes of official transcripts of proceedings."

The rationale of the offence under s.9(1)(a) would seem to be that such devices are apt to distract the participants. Section 9(1)(b) prohibits the publication of recordings, subject to the specific exception in subs.(4). The meaning of "the

---

[64] Criminal Justice Act 1925, s.41(1), discussed at para.10–202. Video recording of evidence given in English courts is also not permitted: *J Barber & Sons v Lloyd's Underwriters* [1987] 1 Q.B. 103 at 105, Evans J. A consultation paper *Broadcasting Courts* CP 28/04 (November 2004) was issued by the Department for Constitutional Affairs. It was announced on June 30, 2005 that a public survey revealed that a majority of those consulted were against filming in courts other than the Court of Appeal; see www.dca.gov.uk/consult/courts/broadcasting-cp28–04.htm.

[65] The use of a mobile phone camera would fall foul of the rules relating to the taking of photographs; see *R. v D (Contempt of Court; Illegal Photography)* [2004] EWCA Crim 1271, *The Times*, May 13, 2004.

[66] See generally the criticisms by J. Young, "The Contempt of Court Act 1981" (1981) B.J.L.S. 243 at 245.

[67] For the interpretation of this expression, see Contempt of Court Act 1981, s.19.

10–192

public or any section of the public" has already been considered when construing ss.1 and 2 of the Act (relating to the "strict liability rule").[68]

10–193 Since it is specifically provided by the statute that a breach of section 9 constitutes contempt of court, the matter should be dealt with in accordance with the ordinary principles governing the summary jurisdiction. Section 9(1)(a) would appear generally to fall within the category of contempt "in the face". Thus, it would come within the inherent jurisdiction of courts of record, both superior and inferior. Nevertheless, except in cases of urgency, the contempt itself should be dealt with by way of application for permission under CPR, Sch.1, Ord.52. It may be that the judge will need to order the recording to stop forthwith, or even to exercise the power of forfeiture under s.9(3) on an urgent basis, but the resolution of any disputed issues and the imposition of a penalty could await the outcome of formal committal proceedings.

10–194 In the case of courts without any inherent jurisdiction, but governed entirely by specific statutory provisions, it is necessary to establish to what extent a s.9(1)(a) breach would fit within the relevant wording. For example, in *Re Hooker*,[69] which concerned the jurisdiction of a stipendiary magistrate, the word "misbehaves" in s.12 of the 1981 Act was held to be wide enough to embrace unauthorised tape recording. Nevertheless, the right to invoke s.12 was held to be limited by reason of the need to establish an element of defiance or "at least, conduct such that a court should not reasonably be expected to tolerate it". In *Neckles v Yorkshire Rider Ltd (t/a First Huddersfield)*[70] an unauthorised tape recording was made of part of the proceedings before an employment tribunal. It was held that the tribunal had been entitled to strike out the proceedings under r.15 (2)(d) of the Employment Rules of Procedure 2001[71] because there had been an obdurate refusal to explain what had happened or to admit it despite the overwhelming evidence.

10–195 Since a breach of s.9(1)(b) would not appear to fall within the notion of contempt in the face, it should be dealt with by a committal application before the Divisional Court in accordance with CPR, Sch.1, Ord.52.

B. Leave to use tape-recorders

10–196 Section 9(2) gives the court an unfettered discretion to allow the use of a tape recorder in court. The court's scope for granting leave is limited to that situation; the statute does not appear to confer on the court express power to give leave to *publish* a recording to the public or a section of it, since s.9(1)(b) does not refer to "leave of the court". Subsection 2 gives the court power to restrict the private use of the recording still further, but it would not seem to give power to allow public use.

---

[68] See para.4–34.
[69] [1993] C.O.D. 162, CO/2478/92 (Lexis).
[70] [2002] UKEAT 1267/01, [2002] Jan All ER (D).
[71] Now the Employment Tribunals (Constitution and Rules of Procedure) Regulations 2004.

C. Granting leave: The Practice Direction

The Lord Chief Justice in the Court of Appeal[72] handed down a practice direction authorised by himself and the other heads of division:

"(I.2.1) Section 9 of the Contempt of Court Act 1981 contains provisions governing the unofficial use of tape recorders in court. Section 9(1) provides that it is a contempt of court (a) to use in court, or bring into court for use, any tape recorder or other instrument for recording sound, except with the leave of the court; (b) to publish a recording of legal proceedings made by means of any such instrument, or any recording derived directly or indirectly from it, by playing it in the hearing of the public or any section of the public, or to dispose of it or any recording so derived, with a view to such publication; (c) to use any such recording in contravention of any conditions of leave granted under paragraph (a). These provisions do not apply to the making or use of sound recordings for purposes of official transcripts of the proceedings, upon which the Act imposes no restriction whatever.

(I.2.2) The discretion given to the court to grant, withhold or withdraw leave to use tape recorders or to impose conditions as to the use of the recording is unlimited, but the following factors may be relevant to its exercise: (a) the existence of any reasonable need on the part of the applicant for leave, whether a litigant or a person connected with the press or broadcasting, for the recording to be made; (b) the risk that the recording could be used for the purpose of briefing witnesses out of court; (c) any possibility that the use of the recorder would disturb the proceedings or distract or worry any witnesses or other participants.

(I.2.3) Consideration should always be given whether conditions as to the use of a recording made pursuant to leave should be imposed. The identity and role of the applicant for leave and the nature of the subject matter of the proceedings may be relevant to this.

(I.2.4) The particular restriction imposed by section 9(1)(b) applies in every case, but may not be present to the mind of every applicant to whom leave is given. It may therefore be desirable on occasion for this provision to be drawn to the attention of those to whom leave is given.

(I.2.5) The transcript of a permitted recording is intended for the use of the person given leave to make it and is not intended to be used as, or to compete with, the official transcript mentioned in section 9(4)."

D. The Home Office Circular[73]

Guidance was given to magistrates' courts in the form of a Home Office circular issued at about the time the Act came into force as to the circumstances in which leave might be given. In particular, sympathetic consideration was encouraged for applications on behalf of those directly concerned with proceedings and also

---

[72] *Practice Direction (Tape Recorders)* [1981] 1 W.L.R. 1526, now superseded by Pt I.2 of the *Consolidated Criminal Practice Direction* [2002] 1 W.L.R. 2870, as amended, which is of general application. For the latest version of the *Direction* see www.courtservice.gov.uk/docs/cpd/consol_criminal_pd_220305.doc.
[73] No.79/1981, August 26, 1981.

for properly accredited media representatives. It was also made clear that courts should feel free in appropriate circumstances to withdraw permission if problems were being caused by the presence of the equipment, for example, through distraction or disturbance of the hearing. Particular factors to be taken into account would be "sensitivity of the subject-matter of the proceedings", and the possibility of causing embarrassment or inhibition on the part of nervous witnesses.

E. The *mens rea* requirement

10–199   In *Re Hooker*,[74] the court concluded that for the purposes of s.12 of the Contempt of Court Act 1981 the use of the tape recorder in the magistrates' court, without leave, constituted "misbehaviour". Nevertheless in that context it was held that an element of defiance would be required, and that this was absent. It appeared that, so far as s.9(1)(a) was concerned, there was a *prima facie* breach, but for reasons of procedural irregularity even that finding was set aside. For that reason, it was not necessary to come to a definitive conclusion on the requirement, if any, for *mens rea*. Nevertheless, it was the preliminary view of Kennedy L.J. that there would be no need, in respect of this subsection, to show any intention to interfere with the course of justice or an element of defiance.

10–200   It would seem in principle to be enough for liability under s.9(1)(a) that one knowingly takes in the tape-recorder, intending to use it. In accordance with the general rule that mistake of law is no defence, it would not avail a person who was unaware of the provision; a student, for example, who went to the court and hoped to take a recording of that experience would commit the offence. But ignorance of that sort would be understandable, and should be regarded as an important matter of mitigation. Similarly, as to s.9(1)(b), all that would appear to be required is that the publication should take place knowingly.

F. Sketching or taking photographs in court[75]

10–201   At common law the control of photographing in court would simply have fallen within a general jurisdiction, at least in the case of superior courts, to regulate proceedings. Although the matter has become one of considerable interest and controversy in the context of televising court proceedings, it has generally been considered in the past inappropriate for photography or video recording to take place in court. One of the main reasons is that participants in the process might be distracted, inhibited or embarrassed by the presence of cameras or the knowledge that a visual image was being recorded.[76] For many years now, however, the matter has been largely governed by statute, except in Scotland, where it continues to depend upon the common law. Moreover, it England and Wales the common law can still be of relevance. Where a person is sentenced for common law contempt, it is possible to impose a sentence of imprisonment (up

---

[74] [1993] C.O.D. 190, CO/2478/92 (Lexis).
[75] For the historical background to this provision, see M. Dockray, "Courts on Television" (1988) 51 M.L.R. 593. The televising of court proceedings is discussed below at paras 10–206 *et seq.*
[76] See, *e.g.* the remarks of the Chancellor in *Re St. Andrews, Heddington* [1978] Fam. 121 at 125.

to the statutory maximum under s.14 of the Contempt of Court Act 1981) whereas the statutory provision contemplates only a financial penalty.[77]

The Criminal Justice Act 1925, s.41(1) provides that:

"No person shall—
(a) take or attempt to take in any court any photograph, or with a view to publication make or attempt to make in any court any portrait or sketch, of any person, being a judge of the court or a witness in or a party to any proceedings before the court, whether civil or criminal or,
(b) publish any photograph, portrait or sketch taken or made in contravention of the foregoing provisions of this section or any reproduction thereof;

and if any person acts in contravention of this section he shall, on summary conviction, be liable in respect of each offence to a fine not exceeding level 3 on the standard scale."

Section 41(2)(c) is as follows:

"a photograph, portrait or sketch shall be deemed to be a photograph, portrait or sketch taken or made in court if it is taken or made in the courtroom or in the building or in the precincts of the building in which the court is held, or if it is a photograph, portrait or sketch taken or made of the person while he is entering or leaving the courtroom or any such building or precincts as aforesaid".

It was explained by the Court of Appeal in *R. v Vincent D (Contempt of Court: Illegal Photography)*[78] that the taking of photographs using mobile phones had become a major problem in criminal and civil courts. Such conduct had to be seen in the context of the growing problem of intimidation or reprisal against jurors and witnesses. It should be borne in mind that advocates and judges could also be threatened or attacked. In the particular case, concern had been expressed about the possibility of identifying the prison officer who was photographed in the dock behind the appellant's brother. It was clear that illegal photography in court had the potential gravely to prejudice the administration of justice.

The Phillimore Committee observed[79] that:

"It was represented to us that there is considerable uncertainty as to how far the 'precincts' extend, and that this is a source of difficulty to journalists seeking photographs of persons involved in court proceedings. We have therefore considered whether it would be possible to devise some definition of general application which would remove such uncertainty as may exist. The difficulty is that court buildings vary greatly throughout the country. Sometimes a court is situated in a corner or on particular floors of a town hall or of municipal offices ... We consider that it would be impracticable to attempt to define for all purposes what are the precincts of a court. However, no doubt in many cases it may be possible by means of a map or plan

---

[77] *R. v D (Contempt of Court: Illegal Photography)* [2004] EWCA Crim 1271, *The Times*, May 13, 2004.
[78] last note.
[79] para.41.

displayed in the court premises to define the extent of what will normally be treated as the court and its precincts. We recommend that this should be done whenever practicable for the guidance and assistance of all having business in the court. This should not, however, in any way limit or prejudice the court's powers to determine and declare the limits of its own precincts, or to extend them if, for example, an actual or threatened demonstration in the highway outside should interfere with proceedings in court."

10–205   Sometimes, the court will issue guidance as to how far the precincts of the particular court complex are supposed to extend.[80] Certainly, the statutory provisions would not appear to include photographs taken away from the court building. Thus, when it is necessary for a court to travel away from the building, quite often with jurors, and defendants in custody, for the purposes of a site visit or "view", the statute itself would not appear to have any application. It remains unclear to what extent the judge would have the power to restrict the taking of photographs or video recording in or from public places. The trial judge in *R. v Huntley and Carr*[81] directed the issue of a press release specifying for the purposes of a jury site visit which particular areas would be deemed to be within the court precincts for the purposes of the Act.[82] What power he had to do this was never explained.

G. Televising court proceedings

10–206   The prohibition under s.41 is understood to include television cameras, with the result that television cameras are not yet generally permitted into English courts.[83] Proposals have from time to time been advanced for change,[84] and cameras were admitted on an experimental basis into certain appellate courts in November 2004. It was a pilot scheme organised in conjunction with six broadcasting companies, not for broadcast but for purposes of evaluation and consultation.[85] It was stated at the time by the Lord Chancellor and Lord Justice Judge that it would be unacceptable to take any step which would make it more

---

[80] See, *e.g. Media Court Guides* in the trials of Rosemary West, (October 1995); Szymon Serafinowicz (February 1996); B. Grobbelaar (January 1997), which draw attention to the provisions of s.41, and describe the scope of the "precincts" for these purposes.
[81] T 20029158/9.
[82] November 7, 2003, No.444/03.
[83] See, *e.g. J Barber & Sons v Lloyd's Underwriters* [1987] 1 Q.B. 103 at 105. For the position in Scotland, see para.16–415.
[84] Bar Council Report, *Televising the Court 1991*. See J. Caplan, "Televising the courts—case for Reform" (1992) 13 Media Law and P. 176; but against, see B. Hytner Q.C., "Televising the courts—case against reform" in the same issue at p.174; A. Biondi, "T.V. Cameras Access in the courtroom: A Comparative Note" in *Yearbook of Media and Entertainment Law* (1996), p.109. See also M. Dockray, "Courts on Television" (1988) 51 M.L.R. 593 and J. Rozenberg, "The *Pinochet* case and cameras in court" [1999] P.L. 178.
[85] A consultation paper *Broadcasting Courts* CP 28/04 (November 2004) was issued by the Department for Constitutional Affairs. It was announced on June 30, 2005 that a public survey revealed that a majority of those consulted were against filming in courts other than the Court of Appeal; see www.dca.gov.uk/consult/courts/broadcasting-cp28-04.htm.

daunting or difficult for witnesses or jurors to participate.[86] The principal concern of those who continue to resist change is that, quite apart from the distraction that the physical presence of the cameras might cause, the recording might affect the proceedings themselves. It may cause some participants to accommodate their behaviour to the cameras. Furthermore, it would render what is often a nerve-wracking occasion for witnesses even more stressful. This would be particularly true in the case of victims of violent or sexual offences. The proponents, however, might admit that such coverage will have some such disadvantages, but would contend that the benefits outweigh them; in particular, the information thereby made available to the general public about the conduct of court proceedings.[87]

The Supreme Court of the United States had held in *Estes v Texas*[88] that a defendant had been deprived of his right to a fair trial because the presence of television cameras could distract jurors and witnesses and unduly burden the judge. There was a change of heart in *Chandler v Florida*.[89] In that case, the due process argument was rejected unanimously and the defendant's convictions affirmed. It was noted[90] that technological advances meant that cameras could be made less obtrusive and distracting. Moreover, the State of Florida had provided procedural safeguards for a defendant. These included the requirement that special pains be taken to protect vulnerable witnesses. The conclusion of the Chief Justice[91] was that the states were not precluded by the Constitution from experimenting with televised trials; the matter was thus left to the states to decide the matter and to fashion such procedural rules as would give protection to the fundamental principle of due process and the right to a fair trial.

IX. *MENS REA* FOR CONTEMPT IN THE FACE OF THE COURT

A. The present uncertainty

Lord Lane C.J. in *R. v Runting*,[92] observed: "As in all criminal cases, so in contempt of court in these circumstances there are two aspects to be considered: first of all, the act, and secondly the intent with which that act is performed." He later added that some acts capable of amounting to the *actus reus* of contempt would also be such that it would be proper to infer from those acts the necessary

---

[86] In the course of his enquiry in 2003 into the circumstances surrounding the death of Dr. David Kelly, Lord Hutton declined to permit the filming or broadcasting of the evidence of witnesses (and also applications made in the course of the inquiry): www.the-hutton-inquiry.org.uk. Lord Falconer commented on June 30, 2005, in the light of the public response to the consultation on the subject of broadcasting courts that "Their input has confirmed my very strong view that victims, witnesses and jurors should not be filmed. There remain powerful reasons and arguments for protecting them, and the justice process in general, from the impact of cameras and microphones in court".
[87] See paras 7–16 *et seq*.
[88] 381 U.S. 532 (1965).
[89] 449 U.S. 560 (1981).
[90] At 576.
[91] At 583.
[92] (1989) 89 Cr.App.R. 243 at 245. On the facts of the case it was held that there were no intentional acts of a sufficient degree of gravity to amount to contempt of court.

10–208

intent. It is difficult to extract from the authorities the precise nature of the state of mind required. There is some authority which might appear to suggest that, for a contempt in the face of the court, it is sufficient that the defendant has deliberately or intentionally done an act that in fact results, as judged objectively, in some degree of interference with or disruption of the proceedings of the court.

10–209   In *R. v Hill*[93] a woman insulted the Crown Court judge from the public gallery by calling him a racist and saying that he was biased. After hearing counsel, the judge committed her to prison for seven days. The point taken on appeal was that there had been no intention to interfere with the due administration of justice. The appeal was dismissed, since the insult deliberately directed at the judge was "palpably calculated to interfere with the administration of justice". The expression "calculated" seems to have been employed by the court in the traditional objective sense, so that no specific intention to interfere with the processes of justice would be required. The use of "palpably" could mean that the interference with the administration of justice would be obvious to everyone—including the alleged contemnor.

10–210   A similar impression may have been given in the judgment of Bingham J. in *R. v Smithers and Bowen*.[94] The defendants were spectators at a trial who had directed "casual and boorish abuse" at a witness as she was leaving court, and after the court had risen. In reducing the sentence from six months' imprisonment to one of 60 days, the court took into account that " . . . it may very well be that they had no intention of any kind to affect the outcome of a current or future criminal trial, and it may even be possible to believe that they did not intend to cause [the witness] the distress which in the event they did cause her." It is to be remembered, however, that in that case the facts had been admitted, and the contempt acknowledged. All that was in issue was the matter of sentence. Yet, as expressed, these passages might be taken to suggest that there could still have been a contempt even in the absence of any of the states of mind identified.

10–211   A case which is somewhat ambivalent on the matter of *mens rea* is *R. v Giscombe*.[95] The appellant had appeared as a witness for the prosecution, having been brought to court in handcuffs and subsequently declared a hostile witness. Thereafter, he regularly attended in the public gallery and called out while a police officer was giving evidence that he was a liar. He also pestered one of the jurors (away from the court). When the judge was informed of these matters, the jury were discharged and the appellant was tried summarily for contempt.

10–212   On appeal, it was argued that the judge erred in drawing inferences as to the appellant's intention. It was held that the judge was entitled to infer an intention to interfere with the trial by talking to the juror, not least because of the circumstances of the appellant's behaviour during the trial (which the judge had no doubt himself witnessed). He had been entitled to find the contempt proved.

---

[93] [1986] Crim. L.R. 457.
[94] (1983) 5 Cr.App.R.(S) 248.
[95] (1984) 79 Cr.App.R. 79.

The conduct was described by Lord Lane C.J. as "an intentional effort to interfere with the course of a criminal trial", and he referred to threats that were made "plainly with the intention of frightening the juror into taking a course of action which, without those threats, he might not take". He also said that there had been "an interference with the process of trial ... an interference intended to be such by this man."

When it came to setting out the test for *mens rea*, however, Lord Lane observed that the judgments of Lord Denning M.R. and Donovan L.J. in *Att-Gen v Butterworth*[96] did not seem to be wholly in accord one with the other. He therefore contented himself with saying no more, for the purpose of the case before him, than "that it is contempt of court if the defendant knowingly does an act which he intends, and is calculated, to interfere with the course of justice and is capable of having that effect."[97]

In *Weston v CCC Administrator*,[98] Bridge L.J. in considering an allegation of discourtesy against a solicitor relating to the listing arrangements at the Central Criminal Court, concluded somewhat hesitantly:

"At all events, in my judgment the very least that must be shown before such an omission could be held to amount to a contempt would be that it was an omission which had certainly the effect, and *possibly* the express object, of frustrating or obstructing the legal process in question" (emphasis added).

A tentative approach was also taken more recently in *Connolly v Dale*,[99] which concerned police intervention to prevent an enquiry agent, instructed by the solicitors of a defendant who was charged with murder, from seeking to support an alibi defence by showing photographs of the accused to the staff of a hostel. The respondent was a detective superintendent who had asserted that the showing of the photographs to potential witnesses would amount to wilful obstruction under the Police Act 1964, s.51(3). An application was made to commit the officer on the ground that his action was an interference with the due administration of justice.

Balcombe L.J. had no doubt that the *actus reus* of the offence of contempt was made out. He continued[1]:

"The issue for our decision is whether the element of mens rea is also established. For present purposes we assume, without deciding, that it is necessary to prove an intent to

---

[96] [1963] 1 Q.B. 696. The two passages appear respectively at 722 and 725. They are set out at para.11–211 and para.11–207.
[97] See also the words of Roskill L.J. in *R. v Aquarius* (1974) 59 Cr.App.R. 165 at 169, where the defendant was said to have "quite deliberately set about making his trial as impossible as he could". He continued: "If persons seek to disrupt [the courts] and make the trial difficult or indeed impossible then the court in the interests of the public and the interests of the free administration of justice ... has to so act as to make it plain that that sort of conduct will not be tolerated". He had made it clear that this was so "whatever views a particular person may hold about society or courts, or the right of society or the rights of courts or others in authority to judge others or inflict punishment."
[98] [1977] 1 Q.B. 32 at 47–8.
[99] [1996] Q.B. 120, DC. See the discussion at paras 11–23 *et seq*.
[1] At 125H–126B.

interfere with the course of justice: see *Attorney-General v Newspaper Publishing plc* [1988] Ch. 333, 374, 383. In so saying, we bear in mind that, as in the case of 'wilful' obstruction[2] . . . an intention to interfere with the course of justice connotes an intention to bring about a state of affairs which, objectively construed, amounts to such interference."

While accepting that the respondent's motive had been "benign", the court held that his intent was deliberately to prevent access to potential alibi witnesses.

10-217   It is doubtful, however, that the importation of an objective test can be reconciled with the requirement for *mens rea* as described in such later cases as *R. v Schot and Barclay*,[3] and *Att-Gen v Newspaper Publishing plc*.[4] Although neither of these cases concerned contempt in the face of the court, there has been a firm trend towards insisting upon a positive intention to interfere with the administration of justice.

10-218   If *mens rea* is required, then it is reasonable to conclude that it will be readily inferred in cases where the act in question was "palpably calculated to interfere", as in the case of *Hill*.[5] Lord Bingham C.J. in *Att-Gen v Newspaper Publishing plc*[6] adopted the statement of Sir John Donaldson M.R. in the earlier case of *Att-Gen v Newspaper Publishing plc*[7] (one of the *Spycatcher* cases) that "Such an intent need not be expressly avowed or admitted, but can be inferred from all the circumstances, including the foreseeability of the consequences of the conduct." Similar were the words of Lloyd L.J.[8] to the effect that an intent to interfere with the course of justice might be inferred even though there is no overt proof: "The more obvious the interference with the course of justice, the more readily will the requisite intent be inferred." An example is provided by *Macrae*[9] where the judge observed, when a juror had absented himself to post a letter, that he "must have" known this to be in breach of his duty. This is consistent with what Lord Bingham himself had said in *Att-Gen v Sport Newspapers Ltd*[10] when he suggested that for such an inference to be drawn (in the context at least of publication contempt), it would have to be "little short of overwhelming".

10-219   The administration of justice would founder if, every time someone felt like making a contribution from the public gallery, the judge was obliged to ignore it or to attempt to enter into a reasoned dialogue with the person concerned. Usually, in such circumstances, it may be sensible to issue a warning, partly in order avoid precipitate action and unnecessary escalation, and partly to ensure that the offender is aware that his conduct is regarded as an interference. If it subsequently becomes necessary to take action it will be less easy in those

---

[2] Reference was made in that context to the judgment of McCullough J. in *Hills v Ellis* [1983] Q.B. 680 at 686B.
[3] [1997] 2 Cr.App.R. 383, (1997) 161 J.P. 473. See also *R. v Runting* (1989) 89 Cr.App.R. 243.
[4] [1997] 1 W.L.R. 926 at 936-7, [1997] 3 All E.R. 159 at 169-70.
[5] [1986] Crim. L.R. 457.
[6] [1997] 1 W.L.R. 926 at 936, [1997] 3 All E.R. 159 at 169e-g.
[7] [1988] Ch. 333 at 374-375.
[8] [1988] Ch. at 383.
[9] *The Times*, November 18 and 19, 1892, discussed at para.10-185.
[10] [1991] 1 W.L.R. 1194 at 1208F-G, [1992] 1 All E.R. 503 at 516g-j.

circumstances to argue that he lacked the necessary *mens rea*.[11] Often, the warning will be enough in itself to restore order.

B. The possible scope for recklessness

In some circumstances, the conduct alleged to constitute contempt in the face will create an obvious and serious risk that the course of justice will be impeded or prejudiced; for example, where there is shouting or disruption such as to interrupt the course of a hearing. A person who behaves in such a way is at least *Caldwell* reckless[12] as to the effects of his conduct. In the general criminal law, this is sometimes regarded as a sufficient degree of *mens rea* to attract liability. In *R. v G*,[13] however, the House of Lords reversed the decision in *Caldwell* that gave rise to this form of *mens rea*, at least so far as the law of criminal damage was concerned. Lord Bingham made it clear that he was not purporting to alter the law any more widely than was necessary for the decision in that case.[14]

It is possible that *Caldwell* recklessness might be applicable to this type of contempt, but because such an interruption of court proceedings will generally be obvious to all concerned, this may be a somewhat theoretical approach. A court would generally in such circumstances take the offending individual to be conscious of the risk to the administration of justice.

The possibility that recklessness might be sufficient appears not to have been considered in the context of common law contempt in the face, although Beldam L.J. in *Bodden v Commissioner of Police of the Metropolis*[15] concluded that "wilfully" in the context of s.12 of the Contempt of Court Act 1981 would include the state of mind that may be equated to *Cunningham* recklessness.[16]

It is true that in a number of cases concerning publication contempt recklessness has been expressly eschewed as sufficient to establish the requisite *mens rea*.[17] In theory, one could seek to distinguish that form of contempt on the basis that freedom of speech is inevitably in issue. Moreover, Parliament plainly had that factor in mind when, in the Contempt of Court Act 1981, it sought to achieve the "permanent shift" in the competing public interests.[18] Nevertheless, it is difficult to imagine, or even to justify from principle, a distinction as to *mens rea* between publication contempts and other forms of interference with the administration of justice (subject always to the statutory scheme of the 1981 Act, which makes it clear that there may be strict liability in a specified range of cases).

---

[11] See, *e.g. Bodden v Commissioner of Police of the Metropolis* [1990] 2 Q.B. 397 at 406B–E, Beldam L.J.
[12] [1982] A.C. 342 which is discussed at para.5–130.
[13] [2003] UKHL 50, [2004] 1 A.C. 1034.
[14] See [28].
[15] [1990] 2 Q.B. 397 at 405C–E. Lord Donaldson M.R. and Woolf L.J. both agreed.
[16] The passage is set out at para.10–126. *Cunningham* recklessness is discussed at para.5–131.
[17] *Att-Gen v Newspaper Publishing plc* [1988] Ch. 333, CA; *Att-Gen v News Group Newspapers plc*. [1989] 1 Q.B. 110; *Att-Gen v Newspaper Publishing plc* [1989] 1 F.S.R. 457, Morritt J.; *Att-Gen v Sport Newspapers Ltd* [1991] 1 W.L.R. 1194, [1992] 1 All E.R. 503.
[18] Lloyd L.J. in *Att-Gen v Newspaper Publishing plc* [1988] Ch. 333 at 382D–E.

10–224 Against this background, it is probably wise to proceed on the basis that the courts' approach to *mens rea* in common law contempt is likely to be very similar both in publication and non-publication cases.[19] This would have the consequence that, while insisting upon the need to show a positive intention to interfere with the administration of justice, judges will nevertheless be ready to draw the inference that such an intention was indeed present in cases where it may be thought that adverse consequences for the administration of justice would have been obvious to the person concerned.[20]

10–225 A difficulty with this conclusion (perhaps more apparent than real) is how to deal with the situation when the adverse consequences for the administration of justice may be readily perceived by the court itself while being less obvious to a lay person. A juror who temporarily absented himself, or perhaps used a mobile telephone while in the middle of the jury's deliberations, may genuinely be able to say that it did not occur to him that his conduct would carry any risk of interference with the administration of justice. The likelihood now is that in such a case the court would not be satisfied that the requisite *mens rea* had been proved to the criminal standard, unless it could be demonstrated that it had been made clear to the juror concerned either by the judge, or by the information pack now supplied to jurors, that such conduct was not permitted. As always, the state of mind will be relevant to the question of penalty.[21]

---

[19] See the summary of the position in relation to common law publication contempts at para.5–200. See also *Att-Gen v Judd* [1995] C.O.D. 15.
[20] See, *e.g. Att-Gen v Newspaper Publishing plc* [1997] 3 All E.R. 159 at 169e–g.
[21] See, *e.g. R. v Smithers and Bowen* (1983) 5 Cr.App.R.(S) 248.

CHAPTER 11

DIRECT INTERFERENCE WITH THE ADMINISTRATION OF JUSTICE

	PARA
I. General Considerations	11–1
II. The Mental Element in Non-Publication Contempts	11–21
III. Subverting the Orders or Procedures of the Court	11–34
IV. Abusing the Court's Procedures	11–48
V. Failure to Attend Court	11–88
VI. The Statutory Provisions Against Intimidation	11–145
VII. Interference at Common Law: The General Principles	11–155
VIII. Common Law: Judges, Jurors and Legal Advisers	11–173
IX. Common Law: Interference With Witnesses	11–190
X. Common Law: Litigants and Parties	11–276
XI. Interference With Officers of the Court	11–311
XII. Interference With the Wardship or *Parens Patriae* Jurisdiction	11–331
XIII. The Secrecy Attached to Jury Deliberations	11–349

I. GENERAL CONSIDERATIONS

A. The diminished role for the summary process

11–1 There are many forms of interference with the administration of justice, other than contempts committed in the face of the court. These have been treated in the past as contempt of court and dealt with under the summary jurisdiction.[1] Yet in such cases there will rarely be any pressing urgency of the kind which justifies its use in the case of contempts in the face of the court.[2] Many of the cases to be considered in this chapter are relatively old, and some misconduct addressed in the past by the law of contempt would now be covered by statutory[3] or disciplinary offences,[4] or disposed of under the supervisory or case management powers of the court.[5] Moreover, in modern times, it would be more common to deal with some forms of interference by resorting to the common law criminal offences of perverting the course of justice, or conspiring or attempting to do so. In other cases, however, the inherent contempt jurisdiction will retain a residual

---

[1] See Hawk. 2 *P.C.*, c.22, s.39 on this topic generally.
[2] See the discussion in ch.10.
[3] See, *e.g.*, the Criminal Justice and Public Order Act 1994, s.51 (interference with witnesses, jurors and others), discussed at paras 11–145 *et seq*. Another example is to be found in the Employment Relations Act 2004, s.40, which deals with the protection of employees in respect of jury service, though the consequences of breach are civil rather than criminal in nature. See also paras 2–13 *et seq*. for a discussion of the use of express statutory provision in preference to the contempt jurisdiction.
[4] See, *e.g. Weston v CCC Administrator* [1977] 1 Q.B. 32.
[5] *e.g.* by striking out for abuse of process under CPR 3.4, or the removal of inappropriate matter from an affidavit or witness statement under CPR 32.1.

11–1 CHAPTER 11—INTERFERENCE WITH ADMINISTRATION OF JUSTICE

function, and especially where there is no other specific way of dealing with the problem.[6]

11–2 In principle, it would be probably still be held to be a contempt to forge the written process of the court in any way; to plead or cause to be pleaded matter knowing it to be false; to cause evidence to be given knowing it to be false; to bring a fictitious action; to enter into a collusive bargain to defeat the ends of justice; or in any way deliberately to mislead the court. Older cases should be treated with caution, more particularly now that judges approach the contempt of court jurisdiction, in cases of abuse of process, as being one to be used only in exceptional circumstances,[7] and where there has been "some significant and adverse effect upon the administration of justice".[8]

B. The necessary elements of the *actus reus*

11–3 It is clear in the context of publication contempt, whether at common law or under "the strict liability rule", that it will often suffice to establish a contempt that there has been created a *risk* that the course of justice will be in some way, at least going beyond *de minimis*, either prejudiced or impeded (even if it turns out that no harm was done in the event).[9] This will be true also in relation to some forms of non-publication contempt; for example, where the offence consists in an attempt to interfere with a juror, witness or party.[10] In other cases, however, where proceedings have come to a conclusion, and there cannot therefore be any risk of actual interference with them, criticism of or reprisals against participants in the legal process,[11] or breaches of the confidentiality of documents or information disclosed in the course of proceedings on a restricted basis,[12] may nevertheless be inherently objectionable and punishable as contempt for that reason.

C. Omissions

11–4 While it is obvious that civil contempt will regularly consist in a failure to comply with a mandatory injunction, it is much more difficult to conceive of circumstances in which a criminal contempt could be committed, by way of interference with the administration of justice, by omission only. Normally, one would expect to find some positive act giving rise to the relevant risk or interference.

---

[6] See, *e.g. Dobson v Hastings* [1992] Ch. 394, discussed at para.2–183. See also at para.11–27.
[7] *Parashuram Detaram Shamdasani v King-Emperor* [1945] A.C. 264. For more recent cases, see the discussion at paras 10–31 *et seq.*
[8] *Att-Gen v Newspaper Publishing plc* [1997] 1 W.L.R. 926 at 936B–C, [1997] 3 All E.R. 159, 168j, Lord Bingham C.J.
[9] See paras 4–55 *et seq.* and paras 5–12 *et seq.*
[10] See Glidewell L.J. in *Att-Gen v Martin (Peter), The Times*, April 23, 1986, D.C. (Lexis) where it was said that " . . . there had to be a real risk that the conduct of the proceedings . . . would have been prejudiced". The case is more fully considered at paras 11–282 *et seq.*
[11] *Att-Gen v Butterworth* [1963] 1 Q.B. 696, discussed at paras 11–202 *et seq.*; *Att-Gen v Judd* [1995] C.O.D. 15.
[12] *Att-Gen v Newspaper Publishing plc* [1997] 1 W.L.R. 926, 3 All E.R. 159, CACD (where on the facts it was held that no contempt had occurred).

In *Att-Gen v Observer Ltd*,[13] Knox J. was confronted with a situation which had arisen in the aftermath of the *Spycatcher* litigation. Shortly after the Attorney-General had been granted injunctions restraining two newspapers from publishing confidential information from Peter Wright's book, which had apparently been obtained in the course of his employment by the security service, a local authority applied to the court to determine whether it could make available in its public libraries copies of the book itself; and also whether it could make available newspapers, magazines and periodicals if its staff omitted to ascertain whether they contained such information.

It was held that the statutory obligation imposed on local authorities to provide an efficient library service[14] was qualified by the requirement that performance of that duty should not interfere with the due administration of justice. More significantly, however, it was held that a failure on the part of such a council (not itself being bound by the terms of the injunction) to check the contents of the newspapers and other publications, which it intended to display for public readership, would not of itself constitute the *actus reus* of contempt "by reason of that omission". It was, on the other hand, recognised that the positive act of displaying such material for public consumption might, depending on the circumstances, constitute contempt of court.

D. Can a neutral act be converted into contempt as a result of intent?

Despite the apparent need to demonstrate *actus reus* in the form of either an actual interference, or the creation of a real risk of such interference, there are some authorities which appear to suggest that an act creating of itself little or no risk of prejudice to the administration of justice could nonetheless constitute contempt, provided there was an *intention* to produce such prejudice.[15] In *Re Ludlow Charities, Lechmere Charlton's case*,[16] a barrister wrote a letter apparently intended to cause a master to change his decision in a particular case. Lord Cottenham L.C. in finding contempt proved said:

> "All these authorities tend to the same point; they shew that it is immaterial what measures are adopted, if the object is to taint the source of justice, and to obtain a result of legal proceedings different from that which would follow in the ordinary course. It is a contempt of the highest order: and although such a foolish attempt as this cannot be supposed to have any effect, it is obvious that if such cases were not punished, the most serious consequences might follow. If I consulted my own personal feelings upon the subject, I should pass by these letters as a foolish attempt at undue influence; but if I were to adopt that course, I should consider myself guilty of a very great dereliction of duty."

---

[13] [1988] 1 All E.R. 385.
[14] Public Libraries and Museums Act 1964, s.7.
[15] See Lord Denning M.R. in *Att-Gen v Butterworth* [1963] 1 Q.B. 696 at 722 (cited in full at para.11–211). See also Taylor J. in *Consolidated Press v McRae* (1955) 93 C.L.R. 325 at 329; and *R. v Gunn* [1954] Crim. L.R. 53 where it was said that the *object* of a newspaper article was "to bring pressure to bear upon the confirming officer and to influence his decision," following a court martial.
[16] (1837) 2 My and Cr. 316 at 342, 40 E.R. 661 at 671.

11-8 In a later case,[17] counsel criticised one of the jury in his closing speech. Cockburn C.J. explained in the course of his judgment that:

> "... in themselves they are words which counsel might have uttered in the honest discharge of his duty for the purpose of vindicating the interests of his client... but if they were uttered with the intention to insult the juryman, then they were an abuse of the privilege of counsel, and the Judge might treat the uttering of them as a contempt."

11-9 Other cases confirm that the threat of what would otherwise be lawful action can be treated as contempt if *mens rea* is present.[18] The Phillimore Committee[19] recognised that this principle could be justified as a matter of public policy:

> "It has often been held that conduct which is intended to cause prejudice or obstruction, however ineffective it may be, is a serious contempt of court. We believe that few would quarrel with that general proposition, and we recommend that such conduct should continue to be capable of being dealt with as a contempt."

11-10 More recently, the House of Lords considered the point in *Re Lonrho plc*.[20] It was held that there was no evidence of a relevant intention, but it seems to have been acknowledged that the presence of such an intention might indeed have converted an otherwise neutral act into a punishable contempt:

> "If the publication of *The Observer* special edition did create a risk that the course of justice in Lonrho's appeal would be impeded or prejudiced, there would be no difficulty in inferring that those responsible for the publication intended that consequence. But if the publication created no such risk, as we concluded in considering the question of statutory contempt, common law contempt... could only be established if those responsible for the publication intended it to have consequences affecting the appellate proceedings which it neither achieved nor was ever likely to achieve."

11-11 If indeed it was the position at common law that neutral or ambivalent conduct could be converted into contempt by the presence of an intention to interfere with the administration of justice, however ineffectual, then that position has been preserved by s.6(c)[21] of the 1981 Act. This is consistent with the policy of the Phillimore Committee. That policy is closely allied to the reasoning which led the House of Lords ultimately to recognise that an attempt may be committed, contrary to the Criminal Attempts Act 1981, even though the ultimate objective is impossible of achievement.[22]

Mere intent will not suffice

11-12 The policy is not concerned with punishing *mere* intent, since there must be some act to which the intention can be attached.[23] For example, in *Att-Gen v*

---

[17] *Ex p. Pater* (1864) 5 B. & S. 299, 122 E.R. 842. See para.10–153.
[18] See paras 11–241 *et seq*.
[19] Report, Cmnd. 5794, paras 64 and 66.
[20] [1990] 2 A.C. 154 at 213G–H (not sitting in an appellate capacity).
[21] Considered at paras 5–144.
[22] *R. v Shivpuri* [1987] A.C. 1.
[23] See the detailed discussion of these problems in *The Prothonotary v Collins* (1985) 2 N.S.W.L.R. 549 at 550–67, 569–70, Kirby P. and McHugh J.A., CA of NSW.

Newspaper Publishing plc,[24] Sir John Donaldson M.R. readily accepted the submission of counsel for *The Independent* that, if there were no *actus reus*, then it would not matter whether there was a criminal intent. "This is quite right and perhaps fortunate. If ordinary citizens could be convicted of offences which they intended to commit, but never got round to committing, the prisons would be even fuller than they are at present." He went on, however, to observe that there was no doubt that the newspapers had interfered with the administration of justice, since they had rendered the trial of the Attorney's claim for breach of confidence less effective. That in itself was capable of constituting the *actus reus*; the separate issue of whether *mens rea* had been present was left to be determined on a later occasion.[25]

In *The Prothonotary v Collins*,[26] the New South Wales Court of Appeal were concerned with the distribution of pamphlets, said to constitute an interference with the administration of justice, which contained general allegations of police corruption but which did not impinge upon the particular facts of any of the cases pending in the courts near which they were being handed out. It was observed by McHugh J.A.:

> "In the present case the distribution of the pamphlet *even when coupled with the intention, motive or purpose of the defendant* had no capacity to interfere with the course of justice. In the proved circumstances of this case, the distribution of the pamphlet had no more likelihood of interfering with the course of justice than the distribution of blank sheets of paper or a morning newspaper to the jurors and potential jurors" (Emphasis added).

E. Is it possible to be guilty of attempted contempt?

In the light of the authorities discussed above, it would appear that one can be guilty of contempt by committing an act which in itself does not interfere with the administration of justice, provided that it is done with the *intention* that it should do so. It would therefore be curious if there were any scope left for the notion of *attempted* contempt. One difficulty is that the *actus reus* of contempt may sometimes resemble the *actus reus* of an attempt to pervert or otherwise interfere with the course of justice.[27] This is so, for example, where the *actus reus* consists merely in the creation of a *risk* of prejudice or impediment to the administration of justice.

Moreover, since 1981 the law of attempt has been governed by the specific terms of the Criminal Attempts Act. The wording is such as to apply only to "indictable offences".[28] As Ralph Gibson L.J. pointed out in *Att-Gen v*

---

[24] [1988] Ch. 333 at 373F–G. See also *The Prothonotary v Collins* (1985) 2 N.S.W.L.R. 549 at 550F, Kirby P. and 567D, McHugh J.A.
[25] As it was eventually by Morritt J. in *Att-Gen v Newspaper Publishing plc* [1989] F.S.R. 457.
[26] (1985) 2 N.S.W.L.R. 549.
[27] See, *e.g. R. v Rowell* (1977) 65 Cr.App.R. 174 at 180; *R. v Murray* [1982] 1 W.L.R. 475. See also the discussion in *R. v Patrascu* [2004] EWCA Crim 2417, [2004] 4 All E.R. 1066, cited at para.11-153.
[28] Criminal Attempts Act 1981, s.1(1) and (4). The Act also provides in s.6(1) that "The offence of attempt at common law ... [is] hereby abolished for all purposes not relating to acts done before the commencement of this Act".

11–15 CHAPTER 11—INTERFERENCE WITH ADMINISTRATION OF JUSTICE

Newspaper Publishing plc,[29] it would not, for that reason, be appropriate for an applicant to rely in proceedings brought under what is now CPR, Sch.1, Ord.52 upon the law of impossible attempts under the 1981 Act. Furthermore, it is clear from *R. v D*[30] and *Re Lonrho*[31] that it is no longer appropriate for contempt proceedings to be initiated by way of indictment.

11–16 Prior to the enactment of the Criminal Attempts Act, the concept of attempted contempt was considered in *Balogh v St. Albans Crown Court*.[32] The alleged contemnor had decided to enliven proceedings by releasing laughing gas into the courtroom. He reconnoitred the building and found he could release the gas from the roof into the ventilation system. He bought the gas and brought it to court. Before he could take it on to the roof he was intercepted. The Court of Appeal held that he had committed neither a contempt nor an attempted contempt. His acts were merely preparatory and not sufficiently proximate to amount to an attempt. His intent was insufficient to make him guilty.

11–17 Lord Denning M.R. appeared nevertheless to take the view that it was possible, under the common law as it then stood, to attempt a contempt[33]:

"Contempt of court is a criminal offence which is governed by the principles applicable to criminal offences generally. In particular, by the difference between an attempt to commit an offence and an act preparatory to it."

11–18 Lawton L.J., using the language conventionally associated with attempts at common law, observed[34]:

"Providence intervened to save him from turning his preparations into criminal action. It follows that what he was proved to have done was just, but only just, short of contempt of court."

11–19 However, Stephenson L.J. doubted if an attempt to commit contempt of court would be recognised by the law, even though it was at that time not uncommon for contempt to be described as a "misdemeanour".[35] Certainly, there appears to have been no decided case in which anyone had, in terms, been found guilty of attempted contempt.

11–20 In *Bartrum v Healeswood*,[36] a case of civil contempt, the defendants had undertaken not to pass off any chauffeur-driven car-hire service as Norwood Motor Services. Thereafter they registered a company called Norwood Motor Services Ltd. Bridge J. apparently found them guilty of attempted contempt (by reference solely to the common law, since the Criminal Attempts Act had not yet been enacted). The Court of Appeal allowed their appeal upon the basis that the

---

[29] [1990] T.L.R. 158, CA (Lexis).
[30] [1984] 1 A.C. 778 at 784C and 792D–F, CA.
[31] [1990] 2 A.C. 154 at 177C.
[32] [1975] 1 Q.B. 73.
[33] *ibid.* at 85.
[34] *ibid.* at 94.
[35] See paras 3–67 *et seq.*
[36] [1973] 10 F.S.R. 585.

act of registering the company was not sufficiently proximate to an actual breach of the undertaking. Nevertheless, it was clear that Lawton L.J. saw no difficulty in principle with the concept of an attempted contempt. Whereas it may not then have seemed strange to use criminal terminology, because it was not uncommon to refer to civil contempt as a form of "misdemeanour", this practice would be most unlikely to find favour among modern judges.[37] In any event, the Criminal Attempts Act 1981 seems to determine the question.

II. THE MENTAL ELEMENT IN NON-PUBLICATION CONTEMPTS

A. Uncertainty as to the nature of the *mens rea* required

We have considered the question of *mens rea* in the context of publications outside the strict liability regime.[38] It is clear that it is necessary to have regard to the constraints of Art.10 of the European Convention on Human Rights, since freedom of communication will inevitably be a relevant factor. Partly for this reason, it has been held expressly that recklessness will not suffice for publication contempt,[39] and that in principle what has to be demonstrated is nothing less than a positive intention to interfere with the course of justice.[40] We have pointed out the difficulty of reconciling this statement of principle, in the context of publication contempt, with the other apparently uncontroversial proposition that the necessary intention can be inferred from the surrounding circumstances (including the foreseeability of some harm occurring to the administration of justice).[41]

11–21

A question remains, however, as to the nature of the *mens rea* required for common law contempt outside the context of publication, and particularly with regard to acts of direct interference with the processes of justice. Here, since Art.10 would appear to have no direct relevance, there would not necessarily be the same inhibition about acknowledging overtly that something less than a positive intention to interfere with the administration of justice might suffice.

11–22

B. Differing strands of modern authority

That the position remains unclear may be surprising, but the lack of certainty is illustrated by the terms of the judgment of Balcombe L.J. in *Connolly v Dale*.[42] The court was only prepared to *assume* for the purposes of the case, but without deciding the issue as a matter of law, that it was necessary to go so far as to prove

11–23

---

[37] para.3–77. See also *Hunter v Wilson* (1848) 10 D. 893 ("However bad the intention might have been, it amounted only to an instruction to commit the act complained of . . . ").
[38] See paras 5–120 *et seq.*
[39] *Att-Gen v Newspaper Publishing plc* [1988] Ch. 333; see also *Att-Gen v News Group Newspapers plc* [1989] 1 Q.B. 110.
[40] It is clear that this is required in the context of perverting the course of justice: see, *e.g. R. Vreones* [1891] 1 Q.B. 360 at 369; *R. v Machin* [1980] 1 W.L.R. 763; *R. v Selvage* [1982] Q.B. 372 at 383–4. See also *Att-Gen's Reference (No.1 of 2002)* [2002] EWCA Crim 2392, [2003] Crim. L.R. 410.
[41] See para.5–195.
[42] [1996] Q.B. 120 at 125–6, DC (delivering the judgment of the court).

11–23   CHAPTER 11—INTERFERENCE WITH ADMINISTRATION OF JUSTICE

an intent to interfere with the course of justice.[43] Nevertheless, the qualification was added that such a state of mind "connotes an intention to bring about a state of affairs which, *objectively construed*, amounts to such interference"[44] (emphasis added).

11–24   The Divisional Court held that a police officer, who had sought to prevent a solicitor from showing a photograph of his client to potential identification witnesses, was in contempt. This was despite the fact that his motive had been "benign", in the sense that he was seeking to prevent contamination of an identity parade. Because his interference, objectively judged, had the effect of preventing the solicitors from having full and unimpeded access, contempt was found proved.

11–25   To similar effect was the decision of the Supreme Court of New South Wales in *Registrar, Supreme Court v McPherson*,[45] where it was held that it was not necessary to establish a wish to obstruct the court in its efforts to discover the truth. It would be sufficient to establish an intention to obstruct a litigant in his efforts to place relevant facts before the court.

11–26   In *Re de Court*,[46] Sir Richard Scott V.-C. was troubled by the question of *mens rea* in circumstances where the act in question (spitting at the Chancery Clerk of the Lists) indubitably constituted the *actus reus* of contempt. The person was suffering from a degree of "mental infirmity". Nevertheless, the Vice-Chancellor came to the conclusion that all that was required was for him to be satisfied, as indeed he was, that he had "intended to do what he had done and did it consciously". In other words, he felt no need to enquire into the matter of whether any conscious thought had been given to the significance or consequences of the act for the administration of justice.

11–27   These decisions are to be contrasted with the approach of Sir Donald Nicholls V.-C. in *Dobson v Hastings*,[47] where the journalist concerned was exonerated of any "trickery or dishonesty". She was given credit for not understanding the somewhat arcane rules as to the circumstances in which it is possible to inspect an Official Receiver's report.[48] Nevertheless, she was, upon an *objective* assessment, "setting at naught one of the court's procedures devised to strike a balance between the various factors which pull in different directions in all court processes." To that extent she was doing something (albeit not "knowingly") which interfered with the administration of justice.

11–28   It is not entirely easy to reconcile this with the approach of the Divisional Court in *Connolly v Dale*. The answer may turn upon what Sir Donald Nicholls

---

[43] On the basis of certain passages in *Att-Gen v Newspaper Publishing plc* [1988] Ch. 333 at 374, 383.
[44] Reference was made to the judgment of McCullough J. in *Hills v Ellis* [1983] Q.B. 680 at 686B. See also *Att-Gen v Butterworth* [1963] 1 Q.B. 696 at 725, Donovan L.J., and para.11–207.
[45] [1980] 1 N.S.W.L.R. 688.
[46] [1997] T.L.R. 601 (Lexis).
[47] [1992] Ch. 394. The facts are fully set out at paras 2–183 *et seq*.
[48] Contained in the former RSC Ord.63, r.4; see now CPR 5.4(2).

described as the "key feature" relating to those obscure regulations; namely, that there was a need for knowledge that inspection of the documents in question would, without permission, constitute a breach of the rules. In the particular circumstances, it was even possible that the journalist, who had been handed the file in question for the purpose of taking it down the corridor to the person authorised to give leave, might have believed that she had been given implied authority to look at the contents of the file, and that the granting of leave was a pure formality.[49] By contrast, in the case of the police officer's actions in *Connolly v Dale*, the fact of his obstruction was obviously an interference with the processes of justice, even though he had not thought through the consequences.

C. The foreseeability of consequences

The distinction emerges perhaps with greater clarity in the light of the principle applied by the Full Court of the High Court of New Zealand in *Solicitor-General v Radio New Zealand Ltd*.[50] In the absence of specific intent, contempt could only be established if (a) the conduct in question necessarily involved impeding the administration of justice, and (b) this was a "clearly foreseeable consequence". Whereas these criteria would readily be fulfilled in the case of *Connolly v Dale*, the same could not be said in relation to what was done by the journalist in *Dobson v Hastings*.

The significance of whether or not a particular consequence for the administration of justice is "clearly foreseeable" is no doubt that, if there is such a high degree of foreseeability, the court will be ready to draw the inference that the necessary intention was present. This is consistent with the approach of Bingham L.J., for example, in *Att-Gen v Sport Newspapers Ltd*,[51] where he said that for such an inference to be drawn "the probability of the consequence taken to have been foreseen must be little short of overwhelming".

This passage in the judgment of Bingham L.J. was cited by the Divisional Court, and followed as being equally applicable in a non-publication case, in *Att-Gen v Judd*.[52] This concerned an approach by a convicted defendant to a juror who had been a member of the panel that had convicted him. In the circumstances, the court was satisfied that the acts of "intimidation" had indeed been done intentionally, and that the apparently high threshold identified by Bingham L.J. had been crossed.

D. Conclusions as to the present state of the law

While no definitive answer can at present be given, it seems increasingly likely that the courts will insist as a necessary ingredient upon an intention to interfere,

---

[49] Similarly, in *Re Griffin (Paul)* [1996] T.L.R. 619, a journalist had copied photographs from counsel's bundle left in court during a short adjournment in circumstances which might have given him the impression that he had implied permission to do so.
[50] [1994] 1 N.Z.L.R. 48 at 55.
[51] [1991] 1 W.L.R. 1194 at 1208F–G, [1992] 1 All E.R. 503 at 516g–j.
[52] [1995] C.O.D. 15 at 16.

both in regard to publication contempts and other forms of interference with the administration of justice. The readiness with which that burden can be held to have been discharged will naturally vary according to the circumstances, and in particular as to how obvious is the tendency of the conduct in question to interfere with the administration of justice.[53]

11–33   It is necessary to enter the *caveat* that it is still possible that some categories of common law contempt will be treated as offences of strict liability. In particular, it was traditionally thought unnecessary to establish *mens rea* in relation to contempt committed in respect of wards of court, whether or not the contempt consisted in the breach of an order. This is probably one of the unusual characteristics of the *parens patriae* jurisdiction.[54] Also, in *Att-Gen v Newspaper Publishing plc*,[55] Sir John Donaldson M.R. recognised the possibility that a further category of strict liability contempt at common law might be that involving reprisals against witnesses.[56]

III. Subverting the Orders or Procedures of the Court

A. The general principle

11–34   Since the essence of criminal contempt is interference with the administration of justice, it follows that a common law contempt may be committed in respect of a court order by someone who is not directly bound by it or even a party to the relevant proceedings.[57] Thus, if the court makes an order regulating its own procedure and the purpose of the order is plainly to protect the administration of justice, then anyone who subverts that order will be guilty of contempt,[58] provided that the relevant *mens rea* is present.[59] It is now clear that such liability can arise whether such a third party is knowingly assisting a breach on the part of a named party[60] or acting independently.

---

[53] See, *e.g Att-Gen v Times Newspapers Ltd* [1992] 1 A.C. 191 at 223, Lord Oliver.
[54] Discussed at paras 11–339 *et seq.* specifically in the context of the supposed strict liability rule. See also paras 6–53 *et seq.*
[55] [1988] Ch. 333 at 374B.
[56] Discussed at paras 11–201 *et seq.*
[57] For a discussion of the authorities on this principle, see paras 6–124 *et seq.* The matter is discussed there mainly because of its importance to journalists, and the fact that most of the recent authorities relate to the impact of the principle upon freedom of information, but it is nonetheless of general application. See also para.3–119, where the interrelationship is discussed in this context between liability for civil and criminal contempt.
[58] See *Att-Gen v Newspaper Publishing plc* [1988] Ch. 333 at 380, Lloyd L.J.; *Att-Gen v Times Newspapers Ltd* [1992] 1 A.C. 191, and particularly at 223, Lord Oliver; *Att-Gen v Newspaper Publishing plc* [1997] 1 W.L.R. 926 at 934C–E, [1997] 3 All E.R. 159 at 166–7.
[59] See paras 6–115 *et seq.*, and also the discussion at paras 5–120 *et seq.* See also the words of Lord Hope in *Att-Gen v Punch Ltd* [2002] UKHL 50, [2003] 1 A.C. 1046 at [87], cited at para.6–122 above.
[60] *Lewes v Morgan* (1818) 5 Price 518, 146 E.R. 681; *Lord Wellesley v Earl of Mornington* (1848) 11 Beav. 180, 50 E.R. 785; *Avory v Andrews* (1882) 30 W.R. 564; *Day v Longhurst* (1893) 41 W.R. 283.

B. The Master of the Rolls' hypothetical examples in *Spycatcher*

In *Att-Gen v Newspaper Publishing plc*,[61] Sir John Donaldson M.R. in exploring the general principle considered a number of illuminating hypothetical examples. These illustrate how it is that the conduct of a third party can only constitute the *actus reus* of contempt if it has a tendency to undermine or subvert the relevant pre-existing order of the court.

1. *Assault and defamation*

In relation to assault and defamation, he gave the following example:

> "If B is enjoined not to assault A and C then assaults A, there is no interference with the administration of justice in the action *A v B*. It is simply a further tort or crime. Similarly with defamation. The court will prohibit a second defamatory statement (or blow) by B, but the subsequent making of the same defamatory statement by C (i.e. an additional blow) will not interfere with the administration of justice as between A and B. It is simply an independent tort if, in the end, it cannot be successfully defended. This is not to say that the publication by C might not constitute a contempt of court, even if C was not enjoined and even if he claimed that he was in a position to justify his defamatory statement. It would all depend upon whether it would in fact interfere with the administration of justice . . . ".

2. *Trade secrets*

He also considered the subject of trade secrets. Again, he emphasised that each case will depend on its own facts:

> "I can imagine differing scenarios in which different answers might be given and it certainly cannot be said that an injunction restraining B would automatically restrain C. Indeed, I should be surprised if it did, if only because A's claim would usually relate to trade secrets entrusted by him to B and not those entrusted by him to C, even if they were the same."

3. *Industrial disputes*

A further hypothesis was that of the industrial dispute. "An order restraining B from picketing A's premises would not render picketing by C a contempt of court, because it would not interfere with a determination of whether B was entitled to picket and the giving of remedies to A if it was unjustified." The Master of the Rolls, who was concerned on that occasion with the safeguarding of any rights which the Attorney-General might have to protect the confidentiality of information contained in *Spycatcher*, indicated that, in the industrial dispute scenario, an analogy would only begin to arise if the picketing by C were to lead to the irreparable collapse of A's business so as to render a resolution of his dispute with B impossible or irrelevant.

---

[61] [1988] Ch. 333 at 370–72.

C. Destroying the subject matter of an action

11–39 In the *Spycatcher* context, the object of the protective injunctions which the Attorney had sought was to prevent the allegedly confidential information leaking away before trial, with the result that the whole subject matter of his dispute would cease to exist. In this context, it is much easier to understand how a third party (knowing of the order) could hardly be in a position to commit "an independent tort"; that is to say, how he could release the confidential information without inevitably thwarting the purpose of the court's order. The Master of the Rolls clearly identified the mischief as follows[62]:

> "Third parties—strangers to the action—who know that the court has made orders or accepted undertakings designed to protect the confidentiality of the information pending the trial, commit a serious offence against justice itself if they take action which will damage or destroy the confidentiality which the court is seeking to protect and so render the due process of law ineffectual."

D. The principle applicable even in the absence of an order

11–40 When the matter reached the House of Lords, the issue was explained by Lord Oliver[63] on a rather more general footing:

> "If the court has taken into its hands the conduct of the matter to the extent of ordering the interim preservation in the interest of the plaintiff so that the issue between him and the defendant can be properly and fairly tried, it has to be accepted that that is what the court had determined that the interests of justice require. The gratuitous intervention of a third party intended to result in that purpose being frustrated and the outcome of the trial prejudiced, must manifestly interfere with and obstruct what the court has determined to be the interests of justice. Those interests are not dependent upon the scope of the order."

11–41 Thus it would appear that, even where there is no injunction to make explicit the importance of preserving the subject matter of an action until trial, a wanton destruction of the subject matter is capable of being a contempt of court. (It would still, of course, be necessary to demonstrate the necessary intention to interfere with the course of justice.)

11–42 This was confirmed by Lord Mustill in *Harrow London Borough Council v Johnstone*,[64] where the jurisdiction was further considered by the House of Lords. A husband and wife were joint tenants of a local authority house. The wife commenced divorce proceedings. Meanwhile the parties continued to live in the house, until eventually she left, taking the children with her. The husband obtained an order[65] restraining the wife from using or threatening violence, from harassing or interfering with him, and from excluding or attempting to exclude him from the house. The wife applied to the council for rehousing, but the council had a policy of not providing accommodation to someone with an

---

[62] At 375D–E.
[63] [1992] 1 A.C. 191 at 224.
[64] [1997] 1 W.L.R. 459 at 469A–D. See also the discussion at para.6–138.
[65] Under the Domestic Violence and Matrimonial Proceedings Act 1976.

existing tenancy, and it was accordingly suggested that she should serve notice to quit on them.

The council was unaware of the injunction, but it was drawn to its attention by the defendant when he received a copy of the notice to quit. The council brought proceedings against him for possession, but the judge dismissed the claim on the basis that the wife, through having given notice to quit, was in breach of the injunction and thus in contempt. He expressed the view that the council too was in contempt in having aided and abetted her. It was held also for these reasons that the proceedings were an abuse of the process.

11–43

Although the Court of Appeal dismissed the local authority's appeal by a majority, the House of Lords held that on its true construction the injunction had not been intended to prohibit the wife from giving notice to the council. It was directed towards the prevention of molestation and to protect the husband's rights of occupation under the joint tenancy *for so long as it existed*. Thus, neither the wife nor the council could be regarded as in contempt of court, either on the basis of any breach of the order or because of any attempt to frustrate proceedings (there being in existence no matrimonial proceedings designed to obtain proprietary relief). The fact that it might have been foreseen that the actions taken by the wife and the local authority might prejudice the husband's rights in future proceedings could not support an allegation of abuse of process. In the result, the notice of termination had been effective and there was no defence to the claim for possession.

11–44

Lord Mustill distinguished the circumstances from those obtaining in the *Spycatcher* litigation, and explained that the decision of *Att-Gen v Times Newspapers Ltd*[66] had depended on four circumstances:

11–45

(1) There were proceedings in existence between the Attorney-General and the first group of defendant newspapers which would be fruitless if anyone made public the relevant information the confidentiality of which the proceedings were brought to assert.

(2) There was in force an injunction, admittedly not directed to anyone except the first group of newspapers, but obviously intended to stop the publication by any medium of materials which would compromise the pending proceedings.

(3) The editor and publishers of *The Sunday Times* knew of the injunction and understood its purpose. Accordingly they knew that if they published extracts from the book they would frustrate both the purpose of the injunction and the purpose of the action itself.

(4) Their choice to publish was treated by the courts below (and this was no longer challenged before the House) as justifying the inference of an intention to interfere with the course of justice.

---

[66] [1992] 1 A.C. 191.

Since none of these essential ingredients was present in the *Johnstone* decision, the principle could not be applied against either the wife or the local authority.

E. Freezing orders

11–46 One of the areas in which this principle falls most frequently to be considered in modern practice is that of freezing orders. It is sometimes important to bring sanctions to bear upon third parties who, though not directly bound by the relevant order, are nonetheless in a position to affect fundamentally the efficient implementation of this protective mechanism.[67]

F. Search and seizure orders

11–47 Similarly, the principle is also relevant to the effective working of the search and seizure procedure, because so often there will be persons discovered, when the order comes to be implemented, of whom the claimant or his advisers were unaware at the time when the documents were drafted in preparation for the application, and who thus will not be directly bound by the terms of the order obtained. Nevertheless, once informed of its provisions, any such person who frustrates the purpose of the order may be vulnerable to the coercive or punitive sanctions of the summary contempt jurisdiction.[68]

IV. ABUSING THE COURT'S PROCEDURES

A. Forging a court document

11–48 Not every instance of abuse of process was treated as contempt at common law.[69] Yet, for example, to counterfeit a writ or other court document was regarded as a serious contempt.[70] Likewise it was treated as contempt fraudulently to alter such documents.[71] Tampering with a document would generally now be indictable under the Forgery and Counterfeiting Act 1981, and better dealt with by this means.[72]

11–49 Even by 1874 the use of the inherent summary procedure to deal with such cases was regarded in some quarters as unsatisfactory. Brett J. had dealt by summary means with a man called Jacobs who was alleged to have erased from the back of a summons the words "no order", thus concealing from the master the fact that the judge had already adjudicated upon it. Strong criticism appeared

---

[67] See the full discussion at paras 12–144 *et seq.*
[68] See further para.12–181.
[69] *Weisz Ex p. Hector MacDonald Ltd* [1951] 2 K.B. 611, [1951] 2 All E.R. 408 (where it is more fully reported), discussed at para.11–51.
[70] *Hungerford v Aylmer* (1664) Sanders, *Chancery Orders*, p.317.
[71] *Dag v Penkevill* (1605) Moo. K.B. 770, 72 E.R. 895; *Re Harby* (1739) Sanders *Chancery Orders*, pp.545, 547; *Hale v Castleman* (1746) 1 W. Bl. 2, 96 E.R. 2; *Finnerty v Smith* (1835) 1 Bing. N.C. 649, 131 E.R. 1267; *Re Jacobs, The Times*, June 13, 1874; *Taylor* [1912] A.C. 347.
[72] See generally A.T.H. Smith, *Property Offences* (1994), ch.23.

in an article in the *Solicitors' Journal & Reporter*,[73] on the basis that Parliament had taken the trouble to make express provision for an indictable offence under s.30 of the Forgery Act 1861 and that this would embrace the very facts. The commentary continued:

> "The penalties thus enacted seem ample and exemplary, but the remedy provided by the Legislature has unfortunately one serious defect; it requires that conviction shall be upon indictment by the verdict of a *jury*. Such laws are made for men and not for gods; and the Court of Queen's Bench, despising the tardy procedure of trial by jury, and waiving the well-meant but intrusive assistance of Parliament, prefers to protect itself and its suitors by pronouncing judgment upon the finding of the *court*... Courts of justice, it seems—that is, such of them as are superior courts of record—are too majestic to be taken under the wing of Parliament. They have too much inherent power, jurisdiction, and authority to borrow any elsewhere; and their proceedings are too swift and pressing to admit of any offence or obstruction being tried by the ordinary process of the common law."

11-50 It was regarded as a contempt to forge counsel's name on a pleading or in any way to assign his name without his authority.[74] In one case a solicitor who inserted scandalous matter in pleadings, and then attached counsel's name, was committed for contempt.[75] Nowadays, it would only be appropriate to invoke the contempt jurisdiction in an exceptional and serious case. In modern times it would not be unknown for solicitors to make alterations to pleadings (now known as "statements of case") even though settled by counsel. This would sometimes be done for reasons of urgency and on the basis that they consider themselves to have implied authority to do so. If the mark were overstepped, it is likely that the matter would find its way to a professional disciplinary tribunal rather than be disposed of under the law of contempt.

B. Putting forward a false case

11-51 It is not the case, merely because an action could be struck out as an abuse of the process of the court, that those responsible for its formulation are to be regarded as thereby in contempt. An attempt to deceive the court, however, by disguising the nature of the claim would be contempt. For example, if facts are pleaded which are known to be false, this would be classified as contempt, as where a man aged sixty-three pleaded infancy to delay an action.[76] In *Weisz Ex p. Hector MacDonald Ltd*[77] a gambler wished to recover certain gaming debts from a firm of bookmakers. Although he was aware that the action was not maintainable at law, he instructed his solicitor, who in turn instructed counsel, to commence an action for their recovery. Counsel endorsed the writ as an account stated, though in fact there never had been an account stated. Subsequently counsel settled further particulars which made the nature of the claim clear, but advised that

---

[73] Vol.18, June 27, 1874, pp.642–3.
[74] *Whitlock v Marriott* (1686) 1 Dick. 16, 21 E.R. 172; *Bishop v Willis* (1749) 5 Beav. 83n., 49 E.R. 508; *Fawcett v Garford* (1789) unreported, cited in Oswald, *Contempt* (3rd ed.), p.62.
[75] *Bishop v Willis* (1749) 5 Beav. 83n, 49 E.R. 508.
[76] *Lord v Thornton* (1614) 2 Bulstr. 67, 80 E.R. 965.
[77] [1951] 2 K.B. 611, more fully reported at [1951] 2 All E.R. 408.

11–51 CHAPTER 11—INTERFERENCE WITH ADMINISTRATION OF JUSTICE

these were in fact fatal to the claim. After some delay the action was discontinued.

11–52 The bookmakers sought to have both the gambler and his solicitor committed for contempt. Lord Goddard C.J. pointed out that it was an example of putting forward what the old cases had called a "feigned issue"; that is to say, a fictitious cause of action. He referred to two older cases[78] and emphasised the necessity of being frank with the court. The court held the solicitor[79] in contempt but regarded it as a mitigating factor that the form of endorsement had often been used in the past without it having been held to be in contempt.[80] For this reason, no penalty was imposed. The gambler himself was acquitted of contempt on the basis that he was abroad when the writ was actually issued and did not know of its terms. It was clear that he insisted on an action being brought which was an abuse of process, but it had never been held previously that merely to bring an action which was an abuse amounted in itself to contempt.

11–53 Lord Goddard pointed out the mischief underlying the practice of endorsing proceedings which were in fact for the purpose of recovering gaming debts as being for an account stated. People could be deterred from defending such claims for fear of publicity, and this may lead to default judgments being signed. If the true nature of the claim were frankly acknowledged in the endorsement upon the writ, this would not be permitted to happen. The former practice, which he said should no longer be followed, thus had the vice of leading to an "interference with or distortion of the course of justice".

11–54 In the earlier case of *Re Elsam*[81] a solicitor who prepared a special case for the opinion of the court based on fictitious facts was held in contempt, even though the court found that he was actuated by a desire to save time and was not fraudulent. There are also some old authorities which show counsel being punished for putting in prolix, frivolous, scandalous or vexatious pleadings,[82] but now such misconduct would almost certainly be dealt with either by disciplinary proceedings or possibly by the sanction of a wasted costs order.[83]

---

[78] *Coxe v Phillips* (1736) Cas. t. Hard. 237, 95 E.R. 152; *Re Elsam* (1824) 3 B & C. 597, 107 E.R. 855.
[79] In fact the matter was handled by his managing clerk.
[80] See, *e.g. Gugenheim v Ladbroke & Co. Ltd* [1947] 1 All E.R. 292.
[81] (1824) 3 B. & C. 597, 107 E.R. 855; *cf. Coxe v Phillips* (1736) Cas. t. Hard. 237, 95 E.R. 152, which turned on the wording of Stat. West. 1, c.29 (now repealed).
[82] *Hill* (1603) Cary 27; *Emerson v Dallison* (1660) 1 Ch. R. 194, 21 E.R. 547; *Everet v Williams* (1725), referred to in Lindley and Banks, *Partnership* (18th ed., 2002) para.8–07n. and (1893) 9 L.Q.R. 97; *Hickman v Clarke* (1615) 2 Fowler's Exch. Prac.407; *Dundass v Lord Weymouth* (1777) Cowp.665, 98 E.R. 1296; *Yates v Carlisle* (1761) 1 Bl. W. 270 at 271, 96 E.R. 150; *Wheeler* (1761) 3 Burr. 1256 at 1258, 97 E.R. 819 at 820.
[83] Supreme Court Act 1981, s.51(6) and (7). In criminal cases, the jurisdiction arises from the Prosecution of Offences Act 1985, s.19(A)(3). See *Re a Barrister (Wasted Costs Order No.1 of 1991)* [1993] Q.B. 293; *Ridehalgh v Horsfield* [1994] Ch. 205; *Tolstoy-Miloslavsky v Lord Aldington* [1996] 1 W.L.R. 736, 2 All E.R. 556; *Freudiana Holdings Ltd* [1995] T.L.R. 635; *R. v Liverpool City Council, Ex p. May* [1994] C.O.D. 144; *Re Ronald A Prior & Co (Solicitors)* [1996] 1 Cr.App.R. 248; *Re A Solicitor (Wasted Costs Order)* [1996] 1 F.L.R. 40; *Brown v Bennett* [2002] 2 All E.R. 273; *Medcalf v Mardell* [2003] A.C. 120. See now *Practice Direction (Criminal Proceedings: Costs)* [2004] 1 W.L.R. 2657.

A serious view was taken in a case in which the court's process was invoked fraudulently,[84] because difficulty had been encountered in executing civil process. A warrant was obtained from a justice of the peace under the pretence that there were stolen goods in a certain house. Under cover of the search warrant, the house was entered and the civil process executed, but no search was made for the goods supposedly stolen. The Court of King's Bench directed that application should be made to the Common Pleas, whence the civil writ had been issued, with a view to attachment for contempt.

C. A false statement of truth: CPR 32.14

It is provided in r.32.14 of the CPR that proceedings for contempt of court may be brought against a person if he makes, or causes to be made, a false statement in a document verified by a statement of truth without an honest belief in its truth. Proceedings may be brought under the rule, however, only by the Attorney-General or with the permission of the court. The provision was considered by Sir Richard Scott V.-C. in *Malgar Ltd v RE Leach Engineering Ltd*.[85] He held that the general imperative in the new rules was as relevant to proceedings brought under this rule as to any other. The application raised the question of how the court could police the use of statements of truth (provided for in CPR Pt 22). It would be necessary to consider in each case whether there had been shown an attempt to interfere with justice sufficient to warrant contempt proceedings. This would appear to suggest that proportionality is likely to be a major factor.[86] Where proceedings are brought other than by the Attorney-General, the court will wish to confine the proceedings to cases where there is a real prospect that the applicant can establish (a) the falsity of the statement in question, (b) that the statement has, or if persisted in, would be likely to have interfered with the course of justice in some material respect and (c) that at the time it was made there was no honest belief in the truth of the statement and the maker knew that it was likely to interfere with the course of justice.[87]

The new rule does not (indeed, could not) make any substantive change to the law of contempt. It certainly does not introduce a new category of contempt. It appears that in drafts of r.32.14 the provision was for contempt proceedings to be brought against "a party", but the final version refers to "a person" who makes or causes to be made a false statement. It would thus appear to include a solicitor or agent of a party. Proceedings for contempt, however, would only be contemplated against anyone, whether a party or not, who could be shown to have intended to mislead the court or otherwise interfere with the course of justice. This would undoubtedly be a form of criminal contempt,[88] in so far as this categorisation remains any longer of significance, but it simply provides an example of the more general principle that anyone seeking to prejudice or

---

[84] *Anon.* (1758) 2 Keny. 372, 96 E.R. 1214.
[85] [2000] F.S.R. 393.
[86] See, *e.g. Kabushiki Kaisha Sony Computer Entertainment v Ball (Gaynor David)* [2004] EWHC 1984 (Ch), Blackburne J. at [24].
[87] *ibid.*
[88] But see the observations of Blackburne J. *ibid.* where he describes proceedings under CPR 32.14 as being "civil proceedings".

interfere with the court's processes will be susceptible to sanctions by way of contempt.[89]

D. A false disclosure statement: CPR 31.23

11–58 Similarly, it is provided in CPR 31.23 that proceedings for contempt of court may be brought against a person if he makes, or causes to be made, a false disclosure statement, without an honest belief in its truth. Again, however, such proceedings may only be brought by the Attorney-General or with the permission of the court.

E. The treatment of vexatious claims

11–59 Where two highwaymen brought an action for account the one against the other for the proceeds of a robbery, the action was struck out as being "scandalous and impertinent", and "reflecting upon the honour and dignity of this court". The court ordered the attachment of the plaintiff's solicitors and fined them £50 each for contempt of court, in having been parties to the launch of such a claim.[90] According to Hawkins it was a contempt to bring an oppressive or vexatious action, as for example by bringing a second set of proceedings based on the same cause of action, while an earlier action was still pending.[91] It is most unlikely that this approach would be adopted now, since the court has other means to deal with actions that are frivolous, vexatious or an abuse of the process.[92]

11–60   In *Re Taylor*[93] an action had been brought in Sierra Leone for damages for assault by shooting. The barrister representing the plaintiff sought to obtain a warrant for the arrest of the defendant on the ground that he was about to leave the colony. This was refused. He then instituted criminal proceedings for assault with intent to murder, under which the defendant *was* arrested. At first instance, it was held that the criminal proceedings were not *bona fide*, but rather an abuse of the court. A fine was imposed for contempt of court. The Judicial Committee took the view that in commencing criminal proceedings the barrister had not acted fraudulently, but had merely sought to pursue all the remedies open to his client. There was no question of abuse or dishonesty. Accordingly he was not in contempt.

---

[89] The problem of the mental element in this form of contempt is considered at paras 11–21 *et seq*.
[90] *Everet v Williams* (1725) unreported; see Lindley and Banks, *Partnership* (18th ed., 2002), para.8–07n., and (1893) 9 L.Q.R. 197; see also *Sykes v Beadon* (1879) 11 Ch.D. 170, 195, and *Ashurst v Mason* (1875) L.R. 20 Eq. 225 at 230. For a discussion, see P. Butt, "Contempt of Court and the Legal Profession" [1978] Crim. L.R. 466.
[91] *Pleas of the Crown*, c.22, ss.41 and 42. See also *Anon*. (1586) Gouldsb. 30, 75 E.R. 974; *Higgens v Sommerland* (1614) 2 Bulstr. 68, 80 E.R. 965.
[92] See, *e.g.* CPR 3.4. See also *Schellenberg v BBC* [2000] E.M.L.R. 296; *Wallis v Valentine* [2002] EWCA Civ 1034, [2003] E.M.L.R. 8; *Spencer v Sillitoe* [2002] EWCA Civ 1579, [2003] E.M.L.R. 10; *Jameel (Yousef) v Dow Jones Inc* [2005] EWCA Civ 75, where the Court of Appeal adopted the *Schellenberg* approach.
[93] [1912] A.C. 347.

F. Improper collusion

11-61 The making of a collusive bargain intended to defeat the ends of justice could conceivably still be dealt with as a contempt, but this is a situation for which the offence of conspiracy to pervert the course of justice is better suited. In the old case of *M'Gregor v Barrett*[94] the treasurer of a loan society had been dismissed from office. An action was later brought on a promissory note he had received on behalf of the society. He had refused to indorse the note, and so the society were allowed to bring an action in his name. Thereupon he gave the defendant a discharge as to this action. The court treated this as fraudulent collusion to interfere with the process of the court and attached him for what it regarded as a "gross contempt".

11-62 In *R. v Newton*[95] a newspaper had published matter which it was alleged was calculated to prejudice the fair trial of one Dougal. Dougal's solicitor wrote to the newspaper asking for an explanation and requesting a pecuniary settlement, with the implied threat that if none were forthcoming proceedings for contempt would be taken. Contempt proceedings were in fact instituted, but they were "settled" by the solicitor for 50 guineas. A rule *nisi* for attachment of the solicitor was discharged, but without costs. The court took a lenient view, because the solicitor had acted only for what he had supposed to be the benefit of his client, and further because the mistaken idea had recently grown up that contempt proceedings could be settled without the sanction of the court, a practice which Lord Alverstone C.J. said "must cease".[96]

11-63 Nevertheless, it seems from the way the court approached the case that to commence criminal proceedings in order to intimidate a person into some form of pecuniary settlement could be treated as a contempt. Indeed, despite the lenient view which the court adopted, the conduct of the solicitor was held to constitute contempt. This would be a situation which nowadays could be treated as falling within the law of blackmail.[97]

G. Abuse of the privilege attaching to court proceedings

11-64 It may be a contempt to abuse the absolute privilege attaching to court proceedings as a vehicle for libel, though it would require a very clear case to justify nowadays the use of the summary contempt jurisdiction.

11-65 Goddard J. expressed the view that such conduct constituted a contempt in *Gaskell and Chambers Ltd v Hudson Dodsworth & Co.*[98] In support he quoted the earlier decision of Malins V.-C. in *Bowden v Russell*,[99] where a plaintiff had served a statement of claim containing grave charges, and then circulated it to friends of the defendant with the object of prejudicing them against him. In

---

[94] (1848) 6 C.B. 262 at 136 E.R. 1251.
[95] (1903) 67 J.P. 453.
[96] For a discussion of waiver, see para.3–157.
[97] See generally, A.T.H. Smith, *Property Offences* (1994), ch.15.
[98] [1936] 2 K.B. 595 at 603.
[99] (1877) 46 L.J. Ch. 414.

evaluating this decision, it should be borne in mind that until the end of the nineteenth century it was considered a contempt to publish any *ex parte* account of pending proceedings, on the ground that it involved pre-judgment, even in a case to be tried by judge alone.[1]

H. Misconduct by solicitors

11–66 The position of professional *advocates* in relation to misconduct occurring in court has already been considered in chapter 10.[2] There are other ways, however, in which solicitors can abuse or flout the administration of justice. It is possible that a solicitor may also be held vicariously liable for the contempts of subordinates in his firm.[3]

11–67 A solicitor (unlike counsel)[4] is an officer of the Supreme Court.[5] The court has an inherent disciplinary jurisdiction over solicitors in that capacity,[6] a jurisdiction which was traditionally recognised as existing for "the maintenance of their character for honour and integrity".[7] This jurisdiction covers misconduct by a solicitor as an officer of the court even though, between the date of the misconduct and commencement of disciplinary proceedings, he has ceased to be an officer of the court.[8] It also includes the power to order a solicitor personally to pay the costs incurred through misconduct,[9] and also to strike him or her off the roll.[10]

11–68 The Law Society also has the power through the Solicitors Disciplinary Tribunal to consider improper conduct by a solicitor, and to strike such a person, if found guilty, off the roll.[11] Hence the usual practice now, where the court discovers misconduct by a solicitor which cannot adequately be dealt with by the imposition of costs, is for the matter to be referred to the Law Society.[12] The

---

[1] See para.1–71.
[2] See paras 10–135 *et seq*.
[3] See, *e.g. Weisz Ex p. Hector MacDonald Ltd* [1951] 2 K.B. 611, [1951] 2 All E.R. 408. For vicarious liability in criminal contempt generally, see para.4–199.
[4] See para.10–143.
[5] Solicitors Act 1974, s.50(1). For the position in the county court, see the County Courts Act 1984, s.142, and CPR Sch.2 cc.29.2. See also the discussion at paras 2–1, 12–248 and 13–98.
[6] Solicitors Act 1974, s.50(2); see paras 2–1, 12–248 *et seq*. where the matter is fully discussed in the context of breaches of solicitors' undertakings.
[7] *Sittingbourne & Sheerness Railway Co v Lawson* (1886) 2 T.L.R. 605; *Re Freston* (1883) 11 Q.B.D. 545. The jurisdiction of the court to deal with its own officers was recognised from earliest times. See para.1–24.
[8] *Brendan v Spiro* [1938] 1 K.B. 176.
[9] See Supreme Court Act 1981, s.51(6) and the former RSC Ord.62, r.11. See now CPR 48.7. See also in the context of "wasted costs" the decision of the New Zealand Court of Appeal in *Harley v McDonald* [1999] 3 N.Z.L.R. 545 (which was reversed on the facts in the Privy Council [2001] 2 A.C. 678).
[10] Solicitors Act 1974, s.51(3).
[11] Solicitors Act 1974, s.47(2)(a).
[12] *Brendan v Spiro* [1938] 1 K.B. 176; *Davies v Davies* [1960] 3 All E.R. 248 at 253. This would have been the appropriate course for the justices' clerk to have considered in *R. v Tamworth Justices Ex p. Walsh* [1994] C.O.D. 277, [1994] T.L.R. 116, as the Divisional Court pointed out. The solicitor had been taken into custody under Contempt of Court Act 1981, s.12, and detained until the court rose, for criticising the court's listing system in somewhat insulting terms.

court also has power to deal with solicitors who commit contempt, but the existence of special disciplinary powers over solicitors, vested both in the court and the disciplinary committee, means that the contempt jurisdiction should only be exercised exceptionally.[13]

In *Weston v CCC Administrator*[14] the court at first instance decided that a solicitor's failure to attend had caused the prosecution to incur costs, on a number of unnecessary attendances, and he was ordered to pay them. On appeal Stephenson L.J. expressed the view that such an order should not have been made by way of punishment for contempt, although the solicitor could have been ordered to pay the costs of the contempt hearing itself.[15]

11–69

Some contempts committed by solicitors would equally be contempts if committed by lay persons. Other forms of contempt are specific to the profession, such as the offence of commencing or defending an action, as a solicitor, whilst in prison.[16]

11–70

Because of their regular involvement with the business of the courts, it may well be that solicitors are more likely than non-lawyers to find themselves in danger of committing certain forms of contempt.[17] Thus, it is necessary to beware of excessive zeal in the course of conducting or defending court proceedings, in circumstances which may lead to improper pressure being exerted upon the parties involved.[18] The line may often be difficult to draw. For example, it may be legitimate for a solicitor to threaten a party that his client will exercise a legal right against that party if he does not discontinue an action.[19]

11–71

Similarly, it was held in older cases to be a contempt for a solicitor to exert improper pressure upon potential witnesses, such as by seeking through threats, persuasion or prompting, to influence the testimony that they are likely to give.[20]

11–72

---

[13] See, *e.g. Izuora v R.* [1953] A.C. 327, a case concerning a barrister.
[14] [1977] 1 Q.B. 32. See para.14–139.
[15] *ibid.* at 45.
[16] Solicitors Act, 1974, s.40(2).
[17] See, *e.g. TDK Tape Distributors v Video Choice* [1986] 1 W.L.R. 141; *VDU Installations Ltd v Integrated Computer Systems and Cybernetics Ltd* [1989] 1 F.S.R. 378.
[18] *Att-Gen v Martin (Peter), The Times*, April 23, 1986 (Lexis), discussed at paras 11–282 *et seq.*
[19] *Webster v Bakewell RDC* [1916] 1 Ch. 300. See the discussion at paras 11–289 *et seq.* See also *Att-Gen v Martin (Peter), The Times*, April 23, 1986 (Lexis) where there was a threat to issue proceedings for malicious prosecution against a private prosecutor: held, by a majority in the Divisional Court *not* to be a contempt. On the other hand, the threats to report him to his Inn of Court (he happened to be a barrister) were unanimously held to constitute contempt.
[20] *Welby v Still* (1892) 66 L.T. 523 ("an endeavour to warp the minds of possible witnesses", Kekewich J.). In *Wright v Wilkin* (1858) 6 W.R. 643, Kindersley V.-C. held that to show a document out of court to a witness, under oath, for the sole purpose of enabling him to refresh his memory was not a contempt. Yet nowadays, when written statements often stand as evidence in chief in civil proceedings, it is not uncommon to find legal representatives simply presenting potential witnesses with draft statements to sign and return. Moreover, the modern phenomenon of witness training and familiarisation gives rise to obvious pitfalls. Guidance was given by the Court of Appeal in *R. v Momodou* [2005] EWCA Crim 177, [2005] 2 All E.R. 571. It is a matter of professional duty on counsel and solicitors to ensure that the trial judge is informed of any familiarisation process. Such a process should normally be supervised by a solicitor or barrister, or someone who is responsible to a solicitor or barrister with experience in the criminal justice process, and preferably by an organisation accredited for the purpose by the Bar Council or Law Society.

11–72 CHAPTER 11—INTERFERENCE WITH ADMINISTRATION OF JUSTICE

On the other hand, for a solicitor to advertise for persons to come forward and give evidence for reward is not *per se* a contempt, unless the solicitor knows that the "fact" in respect of which the evidence is sought is fictitious, or the advertisement is such as to create a real risk of prejudice.[21] A solicitor needs also to be especially aware of the dangers of interfering with people fulfilling a role in court proceedings, whether actually on court premises or on the way to or from a hearing.[22] Normally any contact with a witness under oath, and in the course of giving evidence, should be avoided unless permission has been expressly sought and obtained in open court.

11–73 Solicitors are privy to a good deal of information which will not be generally available, and they need to be especially careful in communicating through the media about cases in which their clients are involved.[23]

11–74 This, however, would not prejudice the right of a solicitor to protect a client's interest in a patent or trade mark action where he does no more than warn the trade, by suitable means, that his clients own a patent or mark alleged to have been infringed.[24] Traditionally, care had to be taken in such cases that the publication did not go beyond a legitimate warning. Even if it is unlikely today, however, that contempt proceedings would be taken in relation to such a communication (not least for the reason that intellectual property cases are not tried before a jury), there remains the possibility of contaminating the evidence of witnesses.[25]

11–75 In general, though a writ (and now a claim form) has long been recognised as a public document,[26] other pleadings in a pending action should not normally be

---

[21] *Plating Co v Farquharson* (1881) 17 Ch.D. 49, which must be taken as overruling the earlier cases of *Pool v Sacheverell* (1720) 1 P. Wms.675, 24 E.R. 565, and *Wilkinson v Gordon* (1824) 2 Add. 152 at 167, 168, 162 E.R. 250 at 256. See also *Willshire-Smith v Votino Bros Pty Ltd* (1992) 67 A. Crim. R. 261 (it is proper for a litigant to search for persons who have similar complaints). In *R. v Mayberry* [2003] EWCA Crim 782, the Court of Appeal in quashing a conviction for serious sexual offences recognised and deprecated " . . . the fact that in many cases the evidence is produced by trawling for witnesses which carries with it the risk of instilling into those who are providing the information, in effect, the indication that certain answers may be expected by those who are conducting the inquiries".
[22] *Re Johnson* (1887) 20 Q.B.D. 68; *Ex p. Wilton* (1842) 1 Dowl. N.S. 805; *Kirby v Webb* (1887) 3 T.L.R. 763.
[23] See the remarks of Lord Woolf M.R. in *Hodgson v Imperial Tobacco Ltd* [1998] 1 W.L.R. 1056, [1998] 2 All E.R. 673, and the discussion in para.1–164. See also *Daw v Eley* (1868) 7 Eq. Cas. 49 and S. Stapley, *Media Relations for Lawyers* (2nd ed., 2004). The problems are illustrated by the case of *Regan v Taylor* [2000] E.M.L.R. 549 where a solicitor had been sued over remarks made about litigation in which his client was involved but was held to have a defence of qualified privilege available as he was speaking in defence of his client's interests.
[24] *Fenner v Wilson & Co (Barnsley) Ltd* (1893) 10 R.P.C. 283; *Haskell Golf Ball Co v Hutchison & Main* (1904) 21 R.P.C. 497; *Carl-Zeiss-Stiftung v Rayner & Keeler Ltd* [1960] 1 W.L.R. 1145; see also *Roger Bullivant Ltd v Ellis*, Financial Times, April 16, 1986 (Lexis), para.4–185.
[25] See *Roger Bullivant Ltd v Ellis*, Financial Times, April 16, 1986 (Lexis), para.4–185.
[26] Under the former RSC Ord.63, r.4(1)(a), for the right of the public to inspect a copy of the writ or other originating process upon payment of the prescribed fee. See now CPR 5.4(2) and also the discussion at para.11–79.

disclosed to a stranger.[27] Since there is greater recognition today of the legitimate interest of the media in reporting court proceedings, even at the interlocutory stage and in what used to be called chambers hearings,[28] it may be that a less restrictive approach will be adopted. In order to give a fair report of such hearings, it may be necessary to have access to the pleaded issues.

Furthermore, it would also be *prima facie* a civil contempt for a solicitor to disclose to a stranger the contents of a document obtained on disclosure, because of the implied undertaking not to use such documents for purposes other than those of the litigation in hand.[29] This used to be so even where all of the relevant documents had been read in open court, but after the case of *Harman v Secretary of State for the Home Department*[30] had been considered by the European Commission on Human Rights, the rules were specifically changed to exempt disclosure in those circumstances[31] and to provide a complete code governing such matters.[32] There is a similar obligation in respect of documents disclosed in criminal proceedings. It was held in *Taylor v Serious Fraud Office*[33] that material disclosed by the prosecution in criminal proceedings is protected by an implied undertaking not to use it for a collateral purpose. This protection extends both to material intended for use at trial and unused material. Thus documents disclosed by the Serious Fraud Office to an accused's lawyers, for the purposes of a criminal trial, could not be used to support a libel action.

11–76

There has been a significant change of practice whereby media representatives and members of the public are allowed to attend interlocutory hearings. This would include for example applications for specific disclosure of documents. Thus, unless any order is made to the contrary, there could be no objection to reporting the contents of any documents discussed or referred to at the hearing; also it would presumably be legitimate for solicitors to reveal the contents of such documents, for example if a journalist requests something that caught his interest. Hitherto, the assumption had been that restraint would have to be shown in this respect until such time as the documents were read out or referred to "in open court" either at the trial or in the Court of Appeal. Now not only is there a presumption that court hearings generally will be held in public,[34] but it is also provided in the current wording of CPR 31.22 that the contents of documents may be revealed if "read to or by the court, or referred to, at a hearing which has been held in public". It has thus become necessary on occasion to have resort to

11–77

---

[27] See *Alliance Perpetual Building Society v Belrum Investments Ltd* [1957] 1 W.L.R. 720 at 725, [1957] 1 All E.R. 635 at 638, Harman J. and *Busset v Lumley, The Times*, July 24, 1959. But see the comments on the judgment of Harman J. in *Smith v Forbes* [1998] 1 All E.R. 973. See also *Stern v Piper* [1997] Q.B. 123, CA.
[28] *Hodgson v Imperial Tobacco Ltd* [1998] 1 W.L.R. 1056, [1998] 2 All E.R. 673.
[29] See the discussion at paras 12–201 *et seq.* and, *e.g. Alterskye v Scott* [1948] 1 All E.R. 469; *Riddick v Thames Board Mills* [1977] Q.B. 881; *VDU Installations Ltd v Integrated Computer Systems and Cybernetics Ltd* [1989] 1 F.S.R. 378.
[30] [1983] 1 A.C. 280.
[31] RSC Ord.24, r.14A. See now CPR 31.22, and the discussion at paras 12–201 *et seq.*
[32] *SmithKline Beecham v Generics (UK) Ltd* [2003] EWCA Civ 1109, [2004] 1 W.L.R. 1479 at [28]–[29], Aldous L.J.
[33] [1999] 2 A.C. 177.
[34] CPR 39.2.

the jurisdiction to make an order for "restricting or prohibiting the use of a document which has been disclosed" under CPR 31.22(2),[35] with a view to protecting the confidentiality in documents or classes of documents which would otherwise now fall outside the conventional protection.

11–78 The mere fact that a solicitor is in breach of his or her professional duty will not constitute contempt. In *Weston v CCC Administrator*,[36] a solicitor wrote a discourteous letter to a court administrator and failed to instruct counsel, though retained in a case, because he assumed that the hearing would inevitably be adjourned. The Court of Appeal took the view that neither act interfered with the administration of justice; thus he was not to be held in contempt. The correct course would have been to refer his conduct to the Law Society to determine whether he was in breach of his professional obligations. The court stressed also that, where a solicitor is to be summoned to attend to explain his apparent misconduct, an order should be drawn and served upon him. Unless the position was made expressly clear, it could not be suggested that a failure to attend would qualify as contempt of court. On the other hand, if a solicitor would otherwise be in contempt, it will be no defence to argue that he acted on his client's instructions.[37] Where a solicitor is to be held vicariously liable for the contempt of a subordinate, it is the *mens rea* of the subordinate that matters.[38]

I. Gaining improper access to court documents

11–79 A writ was treated as a public document to which any member of the public, including journalists, might obtain access upon payment of a fee.[39] The same is now true of the CPR equivalent (a claim form). It was held in *Att-Gen v Limbrick*[40] that the then equivalent to a writ, for county court actions when transferred to the High Court, was the county court summons. The particulars of claim enclosed or annexed could not be regarded as constituting part of an "indivisible originating process" and were, therefore, not accessible.

11–80 Except in such circumstances it is inappropriate to seek or obtain access to statements of case, affidavits or other documents involved in the court's process. Sometimes to do so will amount to the *actus reus* of criminal contempt. This was the situation which came before Sir Donald Nicholls V.-C. in *Dobson v Hastings*,[41] where a journalist had inspected an Official Receiver's report on the court file. She realised that she needed leave to inspect the file but, assuming it to be a mere formality, she took advantage of her temporary possession of file to make notes for a newspaper article. She should have made a written application, supported by an affidavit, although she did not realise it at the time. The Vice-

---

[35] The terms of which are set out in para.12–219. The wording of that provision no longer requires that the judge has to find "special reasons" to justify such an order (as was stipulated in the former RSC Ord.24, r.14A).
[36] [1977] 1 Q.B. 32.
[37] *Vidyasagara v R.* [1963] A.C. 589.
[38] *Weisz and another Ex p. Hector MacDonald* [1951] 2 K.B. 611 considered at para.11–51.
[39] Under the former RSC Ord.63, r.4(1)(a). See now CPR 5.4(2).
[40] [1996] T.L.R. 186 (Lexis).
[41] [1992] Ch. 394, the facts of which are fully set out in paras 2–183 *et seq.*

Chancellor recognised the importance of complying with such procedures, which formed part of a framework of rules intended to protect the administration of justice, but concluded that in the circumstances the necessary *mens rea* had not been proved.

It is now clear that any judgment of the court, even though delivered for interlocutory purposes, will generally also be regarded as a public document.[42] In the years following the coming into effect of the CPR in April 1999, it has become common for most judgments to be made available on various websites within hours of their being handed down. (This has been less so with judgments delivered *ex tempore*, since there have been some copyright problems relating to the transcripts produced by official transcribers.)

J. The statutory duty of confidentiality for defendants in criminal proceedings

As a result of a recommendation of the Royal Commission in 1993,[43] Parliament made provision to prevent the misuse of prosecution material disclosed under Pt I of the Criminal Procedure and Investigations Act 1996.[44] This was directed particularly to the mischief of circulating, in prison and elsewhere, pornographic material or the statements of victims of sexual offences. It was the expressed purpose of the Home Office to deter those who might be tempted to misuse disclosed material, and to reassure those who supply information to the police that it will not be used other than for the intended purpose.[45] In criminal cases, it was thought for a time that there was no implied undertaking of confidentiality analogous to that applying to documents disclosed in civil proceedings.[46] It is now clear, however, from the decision of the House of Lords in *Taylor v Serious Fraud Office*[47] that there is indeed an element of confidentiality in documents obtained for the purpose of criminal proceedings.

The provisions of the 1996 Act apply only to unused material; that is to say, there is no protection for material which has been read out or exhibited in open court. If anyone breaches the obligation of confidentiality imposed, such a contravention is expressed to be "a contempt of court".[48] Jurisdiction is

---

[42] *Hodgson v Imperial Tobacco Ltd* [1998] 1 W.L.R. 1056, [1998] 2 All E.R. 673; *Forbes v Smith* [1998] 1 All E.R. 973. It is now provided in CPR 39PD 1.11 that where a hearing takes place in public, members of the public may obtain a transcript of any judgment given or a copy of any order made, subject to the payment of the appropriate fee. This is subject to specific provisions made for protecting material of the kind recognised in the Administration of Justice Act 1960, s.12. See, *e.g.* the Family Proceedings Rules 1991, r.10.15(6) and 10.20(3); *S v S (Judgment in Chambers: Disclosure)* [1997] 1 W.L.R. 1621; *Re EC (A Minor) (Care Proceedings: Disclosure)* [1996] 3 F.C.R. 521.
[43] Cm. 2263, para.8.46.
[44] ss.17 and 18.
[45] H.C. Official Report, Standing Committee B, col.7.
[46] *Mahon v Rahn* [1998] Q.B. 424.
[47] [1999] 2 A.C. 177. See too *Marlwood Commercial Inc v Kozeny* [2004] EWCA Civ 798, [2005] 1 W.L.R. 104, [2004] 3 All E.R. 648.
[48] s.18(1).

11–83 CHAPTER 11—INTERFERENCE WITH ADMINISTRATION OF JUSTICE

conferred upon the magistrates' court and the Crown Court.[49] A person dealt with for such a contempt by the magistrates' court may be committed for a specified period not exceeding six months and/or fined up to £5,000.[50] In the Crown Court, there is the usual maximum period of imprisonment for contempt (two years) and no limit to the fine which may be imposed.[51] There are also provisions for forfeiture and destruction.

I. Destroying documents which might be disclosable for court proceedings

11–84 Sometimes, journalists or others may be concerned that documents which have come into their possession may reveal information of a confidential nature, for example the identity of a source who has handed over material belonging to his or her employers.[52] There may be a temptation therefore to destroy or mutilate such material in anticipation of court proceedings. The question arises as to whether and if so, at what stage, this would constitute contempt of court. It has been asserted that "if 'leaked' documents are destroyed before the initiation of legal proceedings, this will not constitute contempt of court."[53] To do so in circumstances where an order for disclosure, production or preservation has been made is likely to be treated as contempt, however, provided that the relevant act is done with knowledge of the order.[54] Even in the absence of such an order, however, the destruction of documents in the anticipation or knowledge of forthcoming litigation could still be treated as contempt, depending on the circumstances. Journalists are entitled to rely on s.10 of the Contempt of Court Act for the protection of their sources, but that does not entitle them to take the law into their own hands.

11–85 In *British Steel Corp v Granada Television Ltd*,[55] where a leaked document had come into the possession of television journalists, it was mutilated by them apparently with a view to protecting the identity of the source. This behaviour was criticised roundly at various stages of the court proceedings.[56] Lord Denning M.R. commented that the documents were beyond question the property of the British Steel Corporation and that they were the very subject of a pending action against Granada. He described them as "the most important evidence in the case" and made the following observation:

> "Just as it is a contempt of court to obstruct oral evidence—by preventing a witness from attending the hearing—see Rex v Hall (1776) 2 Wl.Bl. 1110 so also it is a

---

[49] s.18(2).
[50] s.18(3)(a).
[51] s.18(3)(d).
[52] As, *e.g.* in *British Steel Corporation v Granada Television Ltd* [1981] A.C. 1096, and in *Secretary of State for Defence v Guardian Newspapers Ltd* [1985] A.C. 339.
[53] Courtney, Newell and Rasaiah, *The Law of Journalism* (1995), para.11–13. No authority is cited for the proposition.
[54] See, *e.g. Alliance and Leicester Building Society v Ghahramani* [1992] 32 R.V.R. 198, (1992) 142 New Law Jo. 313 (a case concerning the destruction of computer records after they had been *subpoenaed*) and the discussion concerning search and seizure orders in paras 12–175 *et seq.*
[55] [1980] A.C. 1096.
[56] See Sir Robert Megarry V.-C. at 1105F–G, Lord Denning M.R. at 1127B–D, Watkins L.J. at 1141–2, Lord Wilberforce at 1166G–H, Lord Fraser at 1202F–G and Lord Russell at 1203E–G.

contempt of court to obstruct documentary evidence—by destroying or defacing a piece of paper—which is of importance in a pending action.... Whatever the motive, it is a contempt of court deliberately to mutilate a document which is likely[57] to be called for in a pending action."

Watkins L.J., having referred to *Morris v Crown Office*,[58] added that "To act in that way is in a civil as well as in a criminal action a contempt of court."

There seems little doubt that no formal notification is required in this context, and that the journalists in question would be treated as in contempt of court in doing what they did provided only that they *knew* of the pending proceedings and of any relevant order. It is less clear whether they would have been held in contempt if the mutilation had occurred prior to the actual commencement of proceedings, when their state of mind might have been that they were only aware of either the likelihood or the possibility of such litigation.[59] It appears, in the context of publication contempt, that it is possible to be in contempt of court (assuming the necessary *mens rea*) even prior to the commencement of proceedings, and indeed prior to the stage at which they could be described as "virtually certain" to occur.[60] There is perhaps an analogy in the obligation not to destroy documents which might have to be disclosed in litigation.[61] That duty nowadays is recognised as arising at least when the relevant parties might reasonably be expected to anticipate litigation. One cannot approach the matter rigidly by reference to the formal issue of proceedings—not least having regard to the regime of pre-action protocols.[62]

11–86

What does seem clear is that the destruction of any documents that might form part of the evidence in future criminal proceedings could well be treated as falling within the common law offence of perverting the course of justice, because that offence is concerned with matters wider than court proceedings, embracing preliminary investigations as well; the *actus reus* may indeed be

11–87

---

[57] See also *Registrar of the Supreme Court v McPherson* [1980] 1 N.S.W.L.R. 688, where certain documents were destroyed which were likely to be *subpoenaed* in proceedings brought by ordinary shareholders for relief against a company and its preference shareholders. The inference was drawn that the dominant motive of the first defendant, a corporate finance manager, in destroying the document was to prevent its production to the court. It did not matter that there were other copies of the document available.
[58] [1970] 2 Q.B. 114 at 122, where Lord Denning M.R. had stated: "The course of justice must not be deflected or interfered with. Those who strike at it strike at the very foundations of our society."
[59] The point was left undecided by Morritt V.-C. in *Douglas v Hello! Ltd* [2003] 1 All E.R. 117. See too R. Harrison, "The Duty to Retain Documents" (2004) 154 New Law Jo. 1716.
[60] See, *e.g.* the remarks of Bingham L.J. in *Att-Gen v Sport Newspapers Ltd* [1991] 1 W.L.R. 1194 at 1207D–G, [1992] 1 All E.R. 503 at 515g–j, and the discussion at para.5–97. See also Watkins L.J. in *Att-Gen v News Group Newspapers plc* [1989] Q.B. 110.
[61] See, *e.g. Rockwell Machine Tool Co v EP Barrus (Concessionaires)* [1968] 1 W.L.R. 693.
[62] Cp the position in the USA: *Zubelake v UBS Warburg LLC* WL 22410169 and in Australia: *BAT Australia Services Ltd v Cowell* [2003] V.S.C.A. 43. The Court of Appeal of Victoria applied the test of whether it would amount to an attempt to pervert the course of justice. See C. Cameron and J. Liberman, "Destruction of Documents Before Proceedings Commence: What is a Court to do?" (2003) Melb.U.L.R. 273.

11–87 CHAPTER 11—INTERFERENCE WITH ADMINISTRATION OF JUSTICE

committed at any time after the commission of the relevant offence, including prior to the commencement of any police enquiries.[63]

V. FAILURE TO ATTEND COURT

A. Advocates

11–88 Lord Denning M.R. in *Weston v CCC Administrator*[64] expressed the view that if a professional advocate *deliberately* fails to attend a hearing at which he is instructed to appear, with intent to hinder or delay the hearing, that will be a contempt.[65] It was made clear in the same case, however, that if the advocate's absence does not in fact hinder or delay proceedings it cannot be a contempt (though it may still be a breach of professional duty). Sometimes, however, the consequences can be very serious for litigants and undermine the fair administration of justice. The right of access to the courts enshrined in Art.6 of the European Convention on Human Rights recognises the need for effective legal advice and representation.[66] Even where a lawyer has been assigned, there may be an infringement by the state if he or she in the event does not appear at the right time or place and the trial goes ahead in any event.[67]

11–89 Where a judge reserved his judgment and counsel for one of the parties, without permission from the judge, absented himself on the day judgment was delivered, it was held that he was not in contempt.[68] His absence might have been discourteous, and also possibly a dereliction of his duty to his client, but it was not a contempt. Normally the relevant advocate would raise the matter with the court at the time the judge announced the decision to reserve judgment. The court will generally try to be accommodating in determining when to hand down such a judgment. Sometimes it will be accepted as appropriate to hand down with no representative on either side for the purpose of saving costs. This would normally happen where the parties are agreed as to the consequences and implementation of the judgment or where they wish to have the opportunity of a later hearing to argue about such matters which is convenient to all parties.

---

[63] *R. v Rafique* [1993] Q.B. 843; *R. v Cotter* [2002] EWCA Crim 1033, [2003] Q.B. 951.
[64] [1977] 1 Q.B. 32 at 43; *McKeown* (1971) 16 D.L.R. (3rd) 390; *Muirhead v Douglas* 1979 S.L.T. (Notes) 17, considered at para.16–74. See also *Hill* (1976) 73 D.L.R. (3d) 621, and the Ontario case of *Bickerton* [1985] Can. Curr. Law 10774 (counsel's failing to attend through double booking, albeit a matter for judicial criticism, was held not to be a contempt in the absence of a complete indifference to the judicial process). See also *Chippeway* [1994] 10 W.W.R. 153, *sub nom. Bunn* 94 C.C.C. (3d) 57; *Glasner* (1994) 119 D.L.R. (4th) 113, 93 C.C.C. (3d) 226, S.C.C.
[65] In the Scottish case of *HMA v Tarbett*, 2003 S.L.T. 1288 counsel was found to be in contempt on the basis that he misled the court in explaining his non-attendance: see R.S. Shiels, 2003 S.L.T. 37 at 284 and R. McInnes, "Conflict between Bar and Bench" 2004 S.L.T. 7.
[66] *Steel and Morris v United Kingdom* [2005] E.M.L.R. 314 (arising out of the long-running legal action brought by McDonalds against two litigants in person: inequality of arms where the defendants were not publicly funded); *Whitfield v United Kingdom*, Application No.46387/99, *The Times* April 27, 2005 (prisoners and their entitlement to legal assistance).
[67] See *Artico v Italy* (1980) 3 E.H.R.R. 1.
[68] *Izuora v R.* [1953] A.C. 327

B. Witnesses: compelling attendance

11-90 It is essential if justice is to be done that witnesses should obey orders of the court for their attendance. There are differing procedures in different courts for compelling attendance, but disobedience to any such order could constitute not only a specific statutory offence but also, at least in theory, contempt of court. It would appear that such disobedience would be classified as criminal contempt, irrespective of the nature of the proceedings in respect of which the attendance was required.[69]

C. The High Court and county court procedure

11-91 Attendance of witnesses before the High Court used to be enforced by writ of *subpoena*.[70] Now the matter is governed by CPR 34.2 and 34.3, which provide for the issue of witness summonses (a term which applied in the county court and is now used in the High Court also). The CPR apply to specialist proceedings, including those in the Technology and Construction Courts,[71] subject to any practice direction specifically governing any class of proceedings. Such a summons requires a witness to attend court to give evidence or to produce documents to the court. A separate witness summons is required for each witness. The court may order a witness to produce documents either on the date fixed for a hearing or on such other date as the court may direct. The Employment Appeal Tribunal has like powers to the High Court in relation to the attendance and examination of witnesses, and also for the production and inspection of documents.[72]

11-92 Part 34 does not deal with the consequences of non-compliance. Disobedience to a witness summons would fall to be addressed by the court under the rules now contained in CPR Sch.1, Ord.52 and the earlier case law governing *subpoenas*. Although Pt 34 governs witness summonses for High Court and county court proceedings, penalties for non-compliance with regard to the county court will still be covered by s.55 of the County Courts Act 1984 and the CPR Sch.2, cc.34.

11-93 With the convergence of the rules governing civil procedure, and the common application of the CPR to the High Court and the county court, the former distinctions in practice have largely gone. The county court is also governed in this respect by CPR Pt 34.[73] When it comes to non-compliance, however, there are still lingering differences between the two jurisdictions.

---

[69] See *R. v Judge Ex p. the Isle of Ely Justices* [1931] 2 K.B. 442 at 446, Lord Hewart C.J. and at 447, Avory J.
[70] Under the former RSC Ord.38, rr.14–18. It appears that the earliest known writ of *subpoena* was in 1364: see Fox, *Contempt of Court* (1927), p.72.
[71] *Civil Procedure* 2005, Vol.2, para.2C–1.
[72] Employment Tribunals Act 1996, s.29(2).
[73] See para.11–91 above.

11–94 Under s.55 of the County Courts Act 1984, a person who refuses or neglects, without sufficient cause, to appear or to produce any documents in pursuance of such a summons is liable to a fine not exceeding £1,000.[74]

11–95 By contrast with the attendance provisions relating to the Crown Court,[75] the offence is not described specifically by reference to "contempt". Nevertheless, the procedure is summary in character and bears a strong resemblance to the contempt sanctions applying in the Crown Court. The powers may be exercised not only by a judge but also by a district judge, assistant district judge or deputy district judge.[76] The provisions do not extend to a debtor summoned to attend by a judgment summons,[77] although if a debtor fails to attend after being ordered to do so, the judge may commit him to prison for not more than 14 days.[78]

1. *Non-attendance of parties*

11–96 Quite apart from securing the attendance of witnesses, the CPR contemplate certain specific consequences in circumstances where it is one or other of the parties who fails to attend the trial. Special provision was contemplated in the Courts and Legal Services Act 1990, s.12, for dealing with non-attendance by parties in circumstances where an appointment had been fixed for a hearing in the High Court or in any county court but the provision was repealed.[79] The matter is now covered by CPR PD39–02. which provides as follows:

"2.1 Rule 39.3 sets out the consequences of a party's failure to attend the trial.

2.2 The court may proceed with a trial in the absence of a party. In the absence of:
(1) the defendant, the claimant may—
   (a) prove his claim at trial and obtain judgment on his claim and for costs, and
   (b) seek the striking out of any counterclaim,
(2) the claimant, the defendant may—
   (a) prove any counterclaim at trial and obtain judgment on his counterclaim and for costs, and
   (b) seek the striking out of the claim, or
(3) both parties, the court may strike out the whole of the proceedings.

2.3 Where the court has struck out proceedings, or any part of them, on the failure of a party to attend, that party may apply in accordance with Part 23 for the proceedings, or that part of them, to be restored and for any judgment given against that party to be set aside.

2.4 The application referred to in paragraph 2.3 above must be supported by evidence giving reasons for the failure to attend court and stating when the applicant found out about the order against him".

---

[74] This maximum became effective on October 1, 1992, Criminal Justice Act 1991, Sch.4. For the text of the relevant part of the Act, see para.13–95.
[75] Considered in para.11–120.
[76] County Courts Act 1984, s.55(4A), as added by the Courts and Legal Services Act 1990, s.74(6).
[77] County Courts Act 1984, s.55(5).
[78] *ibid.*, s.110.
[79] Statute Law Repeals Act 2004, s.1, Sch.1, Pt 1.

2. Witness summons in aid of an inferior court or tribunal

Now the county court, as well as the High Court, can issue a witness summons in aid of any court or tribunal which does not itself have such a power in relation to proceedings before it.[80] There is no definitive list of such courts or tribunals. In some cases, however, it is apparent from statutory provisions that Parliament was contemplating that certain tribunals would be within the relevant category.[81]

11–97

3. Pre-trial depositions

It is also provided by CPR 34.8 that a party in litigation may apply for a person to be examined before the hearing takes place. Such a person is referred to as a "deponent" and the evidence taken on such an occasion as a "deposition". Where an order is made for such a hearing the deponent will be examined on oath before a judge, an examiner of the court or such other person as the court appoints. Subject to any directions contained in the order for examination, it must be conducted in the same way as if the witness were giving evidence at trial. Where the examination is to take place before the examiner, but the person served with the order fails to attend, or refuses to be sworn, to answer any lawful question, or to produce any relevant document at the examination, special provision is made to enforce attendance.[82] The examiner will sign a certificate of the failure or refusal, as the case may be, which must be filed by the party requiring the deposition. Once it has been filed, the party may apply to the court for an order requiring compliance. The service of an order for the examination of a witness under CPR 34.8 does not constitute an order that the witness should attend.[83] Once, however, an order has been obtained under CPR 34.10 non-compliance may be treated as contempt and, if necessary, an order for committal sought.

11–98

4. Special provision for attendance at arbitration

An arbitrator has power to compel the attendance of witnesses.[84] It is provided that a party to arbitral proceedings who wishes to rely upon this statutory power to secure the attendance of a witness should apply for a witness summons in accordance with CPR Pt 34[85] but a summons will not be issued until the applicant

11–99

---

[80] CPR 34.4. See also *R. v Judge Ex p. Justices of the Isle of Ely* [1931] 2 K.B. 442; *R. v Brownell* (1834) 1 Ad. & E. 598, 110 E.R. 1335. See *Currie v Chief Constable of Surrey* [1982] 1 W.L.R. 215, 1 All E.R. 89 (non-police witnesses required for police disciplinary hearing); *Chief Constable of Leicestershire v Garavelli* [1997] E.M.L.R. 543.
[81] See, *e.g.* s.45(1) of the Solicitors Act 1974 which makes it clear that a witness summons may be issued in support of a hearing before the Solicitors Disciplinary Tribunal; the Medical Act 1983, Sch.4, para.2(1); the Dentists Act 1984, Sch.3, para.4(1).
[82] CPR 34.10.
[83] *Stuart v Balkis* (1884) 50 L.T. 479, 32 W.R. 676.
[84] Arbitration Act 1996, s.43, and the Supreme Court Act 1981, s.36; see also the Administration of Justice Act, 1970, s.4(4) and Sch.3, paras.1(c) and 5. See *The Lorenzo Halcoussi* [1988] 1 Lloyd's Rep. 180, Steyn J.
[85] CPR Pt 62, PD Arbitration, 7.1.

files written evidence showing that the application is made with the permission of the tribunal or the agreement of the other parties.

5. *Disobedience to a witness summons: necessary procedural steps*

11–100 Disobedience to a *subpoena* could be treated as contempt at common law.[86] Since no new provision is made by the CPR to enforce or punish disobedience to a witness summons, these long-established principles are regarded as still applicable.[87] Before such a witness became susceptible to the contempt jurisdiction, certain requirements had to be met. First, the *subpoena* had clearly to require the attendance of the witness at the time when the evidence was in fact required.[88] It is now provided by CPR 34.2 that a witness can be required to attend, or produce documents, either on a date fixed for a hearing or on such other date as the court may direct.[89] Formerly the original *subpoena* had to be shown to the witness on service.[90] Later by virtue of RSC Ord.65, r.2 (as amended) personal service was effected by leaving a copy of the *subpoena* with the person to be served. Personal service of a witness summons is not a prerequisite of r.34.6 but in practice it is likely to be necessary to secure the attendance of a witness who has indicated his reluctance to attend.[91]

11–101 If it could clearly be shown that a witness had wilfully failed to attend, it was not regarded as a legitimate objection to committal that the potential witness was not in fact called to give evidence, or even that the case was never called on.[92] Failure to answer when called was treated as *prima facie* evidence of failure to attend.[93]

6. *The need to provide "conduct money"*

11–102 It is provided by CPR 34.7 that at the time of service of a witness summons the witness must be offered or paid—

---

[86] *Wyat v Wingford* (1729) 2 Ld. Raym. 1528, 92 E.R. 491; *R. v Daye* [1908] 2 K.B. 333. And see *Batt v Rookes* (1577) Cary 61, 21 E.R. 33; *Dolman v Pritman* (1670) 3 Ch. R. 64, 21 E.R. 730; *Valiant v Dodomede* (1743) 2 Atk. 592, 26 E.R. 754; *Barrow v Humphreys* (1820) 3 B. & Ald. 598, 106 E.R. 780; *Goff v Mills* (1844) 13 L.J.Q.B. 227. Attachment was formerly the remedy; see *Re Evans* [1893] 1 Ch. 252. Now it is committal. See paras 11–111 *et seq.* for a consideration of the requisite mental element.
[87] See *Civil Procedure* 2005, Vol.1, at 34.0.3.
[88] *Vaughton v Brine* (1840) 1 Man. & G. 359, 133 E.R. 373.
[89] Any witness summons must be in the relevant practice form (N20).
[90] *Thorpe v Gisbourne* (1825) 11 Moo. C.P. 55; *Barnes v Williams* (1832) 1 Dowl. 615; *Sloman* (1832) 1 Dowl. 618, 36 R.R. 827; *Wood* (1832) 1 Dowl. 509; *Marshall v York, Newcastle and Berwick Rail. Co.* (1831) 11 C.B. 398, 138 E.R. 527; *Fenn* (1835) 3 Dowl. 346; *Garden v Creswell* (1837) 2 M. & W. 319, 150 E.R. 778; *Pitcher v King* (1845) 5 Nev. & Man. 431, 1 Car. & Kir. 655, 174 E.R. 978.
[91] See *Civil Procedure*, Vol.1, 34.6.1 and 34.6.2.
[92] *Barrow v Humphreys* (1820) 3 B. & Ald. 598, 106 E.R. 780; *Fenn* (1833) 3 Dowl. 546; *Lamont v Crook* (1840) 6 M. & W. 615, 151 E.R. 558; *Dixon v Lee* (1834) 3 Dowl. 259; *Goff v Mills* (1844) 13 L.J.Q.B. 227.
[93] *Barrow v Humphreys* (1820) 3 B. & Ald. 598, 106 E.R. 780.

(a) a sum reasonably sufficient to cover his expenses in travelling to and from the court; and

(b) such sum by way of compensation for loss of time as may be specified in the relevant practice direction.

Persons failing to comply with a *subpoena* could not avoid a finding of contempt by pleading that they would have been out of pocket, provided it could be shown that they were offered "the whole of the necessary expense of going to the place of trial, of their return from it, and also during their necessary stay there."[94] At common law, it was held that witnesses as to fact were not entitled to compensation for loss of working time in addition. Thus, once a *subpoena* had been issued, and such proper expenses tendered, that created an obligation to attend, such that any promise of an additional payment for attendance would be regarded as "a promise without consideration".[95]

11–103

For many years, however, statutory provision has been made.[96] The full amount of the expenses which the witness is likely to incur in giving his evidence must be tendered when the *subpoena* is served.[97] The amount of the expenses must depend upon the facts of the particular case.[98] If the witness requires more expenses than are in fact tendered, this should be stated at the time of tender.[99] A professional witness called as an expert is entitled to remuneration for loss of time.[1] If conduct money is not tendered the witness will not be in contempt in failing to attend or refusing to be sworn or give evidence.[2]

11–104

---

[94] *Brocas v Lloyd* (1856) 23 Beav. 129, 53 E.R. 51, where Romilly M.R. identified the principle after consulting the taxing master, and having referred to *Chapman v Pointon* (1741) 2 Strange, 1150, 93 E.R. 1093; *Bowles v Johnson* (1748) 1 W. Black 36, 96 E.R. 19; *Fuller v Prentice* 1 H. Bl. 49, 126 E.R. 31; *Hallet v Mears* (1810) 13 East 15n, 104 E.R. 271.
[95] *Collins v Godefroy* (1831) 1 B. & Ad. 950, 109 E.R. 1040; this was distinguished in *Re Working Men's Mutual Society* (1882) 21 Ch. D. 831 and *Chamberlain v Stoneham* (1889) 24 Q.B.D. 113, where it was held that the matter was covered by express provision in the Rules by then applying.
[96] See now Supreme Court Act, 1981, s.36(4) which provides that "no court shall in any case proceed against or punish any person for having made such default [*i.e.* for failing to appear as required in a *subpoena*] as aforesaid unless it is shown to the court that a reasonable and sufficient sum of money to defray—(a) the expenses of coming and attending to give evidence and of returning from giving evidence; and (b) any other reasonable expenses which he has asked to be defrayed in connection with his evidence was tendered to him at the time when the writ was served upon him". It may be noted that the section still uses the term "*subpoena*".
[97] *ibid. Whiteland v Grant* (1840) 4 Jur. 1061 suggested that expenses could be offered within a reasonable time before trial. This appears no longer to be the law.
[98] For older examples see *Vice v Anson* (1827) 3 C. & P. 19, 172 E.R. 304 (witness gone abroad between service and trial); *Dixon v Lee* (1834) 1 Cr. M. & R. 645, 149 E.R. 1239 (nursing mother).
[99] *Horne v Smith* (1815) 6 Taunt. 9, 128 E.R. 935.
[1] See, *e.g. Webb v Page* (1843) 1 Car. & Kir. 23, 174 E.R. 695; *Clark v Gill* (1854) 1 K. & J. 19, 69 E.R. 351; *Re Working Men's Mutual Society* (1882) 21 Ch. D. 831; *Reynolds v Meston* QBD, February 24, 1986, unreported, Bingham J.
[2] Supreme Court Act, 1981, s.36(4): *More v Woreham* (1580) Cary 99, 21 E.R. 53; *Chapman v Pointon* (1741) 2 Str. 1150, 93 E.R. 1093; *Fuller v Prentice* (1788) 1 H. Bl. 49, 126 E.R. 31; *Bowles v Johnson* (1748) 1 Wm. Bl. 36, 96 E.R. 19; *Hallet v Mears* (1810) 13 East 15n, 104 E.R. 271; *Horne v Smith* (1815) 6 Taunt. 9, 128 E.R. 935; *Newton v Harland* (1840) 1 Man. & G. 956, 133 E.R. 619; *Brocas v Lloyd* (1856) 23 Beav. 129, 53 E.R. 51; *Re Working Men's Mutual Society* (1882) 21 Ch. D. 831; *Townend v Townend* (1905) 93 L.T. 680; *In the Estate of Harvey* [1907] P. 239.

11–105 A witness may waive payment of his expenses, but if he does so he cannot subsequently rely on their non-payment as a reason for not attending.[3] This principle was applied by the Divisional Court in *HM Coroner for Kent v Terrill*[4] in which the Coroner initiated proceedings for contempt in respect of two witnesses whose evidence at an inquest was considered to be potentially significant as to the circumstances in which the deceased had met his death. They had declined to attend despite having had their rail fares tendered when the summonses were served. Laws L.J. cited and followed the judgment of Wightman J. in *Goff v Mills*,[5] and concluded that there were only two inferences that could be drawn from the respondents' "blank response" to the offer of conduct money; either they had no intention of attending or they were willing to pay for themselves. Either way they could not be heard now to rely on the inadequacy of the sum offered. They were in contempt and were sentenced to four days' imprisonment.

7. Materiality of the witness' potential evidence

11–106 Some early cases suggested that it had to be shown on a motion to commit, following disobedience to a *subpoena*, that the person to whom it had been directed had material evidence to give; and also that there should be affidavit evidence to support the fact.[6] Others, however, appeared to show that a witness under *subpoena* could not excuse his non-attendance on the ground that he had no material evidence to give.[7]

11–107 It later became accepted that a party who wished to *subpoena* a witness must be left to judge in the first instance whether that witness could give material evidence. It should be assumed, until the contrary was shown upon a proper application, that the witness could contribute to the proceedings. It was not for the witness to form a separate judgment; the summoning of witnesses would be unworkable if each witness were allowed, in the absence of making such an application, or following one which was unsuccessful, to form his or her own assessment of whether to attend.[8]

11–108 Where a person who was *subpoenaed* believed that he could not give material evidence, he should apply to the court before being called, to set the *subpoena*

---

[3] *Newton v Harland* (1840) 1 Man. & G. 956, 133 E.R. 619; *Goff v Mills* (1844) 13 L.J.Q.B. 227; *Gaunt v Johnson* (1848) 6 Hare 551, 67 E.R. 1283.
[4] CO/1384/00, [2001] A.C.D. 27, May 8, 2000 (Lexis).
[5] (1844) 13 L.J.Q.B. 227.
[6] *Dicas v Lawson* (1835) 1 C. M. & R. 934, 149 E.R. 1359 (where the witness said to be in contempt was Lord Brougham); *Taylor v Williams* (1830) 4 Moo. & P. 59; *Tinley v Porter* (1837) 5 Dowl. 744; see also *Lord John Russell* (1839) 7 Dowl. P.C. 693 (non-production of documents following a *subpoena duces tecum*, but they were such that Lord Denman C.J. regarded them as inadmissible).
[7] *Scholes v Hilton* (1842) 10 M. & W. 15, 152 E.R. 362; *Chapman v Davis* (1841) 3 Man. & G. 609, 133 E.R. 1284. See also *Malcolm v Day* (1819) 3 Moo. C.P. 579, 21 R. R. 730.
[8] For a modern authority, albeit in the criminal context, see *R. v Abdulaziz* [1989] Crim. L.R. 717.

aside. The court had jurisdiction to accede to the application[9] on a number of grounds, including that the witness could not give any material evidence or that the *subpoena* was not issued *bona fide* for the purpose of obtaining relevant evidence.

The court's primary concern has been to see that parties do not abuse the privilege of summoning witnesses.[10] The court could therefore set aside a *subpoena ad testificandum* if it was oppressive, as for example by requiring the revelation of personal information from someone in proceedings to which he was not a party, and such an invasion of his privacy could not be justified.[11] So also a *subpoena duces tecum*, where it appeared to the court that the request for the information, for example in a film or video tape, was irrelevant, fishing, speculative or oppressive.[12] A *subpoena* might also be set aside if intended to obtain a document for the purpose of cross-examination as to credit only.[13]

A *subpoena duces tecum* was regarded as the "servant" of the administration of justice,[14] and a court had an inherent power to amend it in whatever form might be necessary and just.[15] There is no reason to suppose that these policy considerations are any the less apt since the formal procedure changed.

8. *The requisite* mens rea *for witnesses who fail to attend*

A number of authorities suggested that, for it to be punishable, the non-attendance had to be wilful.[16] The case of *R. v Daye*[17] is an illustration of contempt through deliberate disobedience of an order but it was accepted[18] by Lord Alverstone C.J. that there had not been any "wilful disobedience on the part of the bank". There a bank official refused to produce a document under a *subpoena duces tecum*, because it had been left at the bank in a sealed envelope with instructions that it should not be opened without the depositor's consent. In *Blandford v De Tastet*[19] Lord Mansfield C.J. expressed the view that absence even through "negligence and inattention" would constitute contempt.

---

[9] See the notes in *Civil Procedure* Vol.1, 34.3.5.
[10] *Raymond v Tapson* (1882) 22 Ch.D. 430 at 435, CA.
[11] *Morgan v Morgan* [1977] Fam. 122.
[12] See, *e.g. Senior v Holdsworth Ex p. Independent Television News Ltd* [1976] Q.B. 23.
[13] *Sphere Drake Insurance plc v Denby* [1991] T.L.R. 595. See para.9–161.
[14] *The Lorenzo Halcoussi* [1988] 1 Lloyd's Rep. 180 at 185, Steyn J.
[15] See *MacMillan Inc v Bishopsgate Investment Trust plc* [1993] 1 W.L.R. 1372, CA; *Marcel v Commissioner of Police of the Metropolis* [1992] Ch. 225, CA.
[16] *Hallet v Mears* (1810) 13 East 15n, 104 E.R. 271, citing *Chapman v Pointon* (1741) 2 Stra. 1150, 93 E.R. 1093; *Lord John Russell* (1839) 7 Dowl. P.C. 693, 696, Denman C.J. and Patteson J. (" . . . it is one thing to disobey a writ, and another to be guilty of a contempt, which implies always an intentional defiance of the process of the court"); *Chapman v Davis* (1841) 3 Man. & G. 609, 133 E.R. 1284; *Glendinning v Thomas* (1862) 6 L.T. 251; *R. v Baines* [1909] 1 K.B. 258; see also *Heatons Transport (St. Helens) Ltd v T.G.W.U.* [1973] A.C. 15, on the meaning of "wilful".
[17] [1908] 2 K.B. 333.
[18] At 339.
[19] (1813) 5 Taunt. 259 at 261, 128 E.R. 689 at 690.

11–112 CHAPTER 11—INTERFERENCE WITH ADMINISTRATION OF JUSTICE

11–112 Any witness summons is in form and substance an order of the court. Once it has been served, it must be obeyed, subject to an excuse for non-compliance being made out. It is not necessary to demonstrate on the part of the person served, for the purposes of contempt, any specific intention as to the *consequences* of his non-attendance for the administration of justice.

9. Belief in excuse no defence

11–113 Suppose, however, that the defendant in *Daye* honestly *thought* that he was entitled to refuse to obey? Where the witness is physically in court, the position can be explained to him and he can then be under no illusion. What, however, if he fails to attend because he believes rightly that he cannot give material evidence and that therefore he need not attend? He knows that the court has ordered him to attend. The non-attendance occurs deliberately and with knowledge. That, it is submitted, ought to be sufficient to establish such *mens rea* as is required.[20] This accords with the general approach to the enforcement of court orders in civil litigation.[21]

10. Reasonable excuse for non-compliance

11–114 A witness may be able to show that he had a reasonable excuse for his non-attendance.[22] Thus he will not be in contempt if he is genuinely too ill to attend,[23] or otherwise prevented from attending by means beyond his control.[24] It must be remembered, however, that the duty to attend on *subpoena* was regarded as taking precedence over other public duties.[25] Yet it was probably a sufficient answer if the solicitor of the party who had *subpoenaed* the witness had purported to give the witness leave of absence himself.[26] So too, if the witness leaves the court of his own accord on pressing business, when there is no prospect of his case being reached before his return.[27] By that time, he would have demonstrated his willingness to obey.

11–115 An employee under *subpoena duces tecum* to produce his employer's documents might excuse his non-production on the ground that he was only in possession, custody or control in his capacity as an employee, that he was not a party to the proceedings himself and that to comply would violate his contractual

---

[20] See, *e.g. Malcolm v Day* (1819) 3 Moo. C.P. 579.
[21] See paras 12–80 *et seq.*
[22] *Goff v Mills* (1844) 13 L.J.Q.B. 227.
[23] *More v Woreham* (1580) Cary 99, 21 E.R. 53; *Re Jacobs* (1835) 1 Har. & W. 123; *Scholes v Hilton* (1842) 10 M. & W. 15, 152 E.R. 362.
[24] *Humble v Malbe* (1559) Cary 41, 21 E.R. 22.
[25] *Jackson v Seager* (1844) 2 Dowl. & L. 13.
[26] *Sloman* (1832) 1 Dowl. 618; *Farrah v Kent* (1838) 6 Dowl. 676.
[27] *Blandford v De Tastet* (1813) 5 Taunt. 259, 128 E.R. 689. Compare para.16–74.

obligations to his employer.[28] The proper course in such a case was to *subpoena* the person whose documents they were.[29]

D. Crown Court: compelling attendance under the 1965 Act

Attendance of a witness before the Crown Court is secured under the Criminal Procedure (Attendance of Witnesses) Act 1965 by the issue of a witness summons.[30] A change of procedure was introduced by the Criminal Procedure and Investigations Act 1996, s.66, so far as compelling attendance at the Crown Court is concerned. This was achieved by way of substituted sections in the Criminal Procedure (Attendance of Witnesses) Act 1965. There appears, however, to be no change of substance as to the grounds upon which an application to make a summons ineffective (formerly "to set it aside") may be made.[31] Such an application should be made to the court out of which the summons was issued.[32]

11–116

The 1996 Act considerably altered the magistrates' powers in relation to committals for trial in the Crown Court.[33] In particular, the power to direct the attendance of witnesses in criminal trials was transferred to the Crown Court itself. Now, a prosecution witness is normally notified by letter following the Crown Court's endorsement of the witness list produced at the plea and case management hearing.[34]

11–117

Under s.2(1) of the 1965 Act (as substituted), a witness summons shall be issued when the court has come to the conclusion that:

11–118

---

[28] *Crowther v Appleby* (1873) L.R. 9 C.P. 23; *Eccles & Co v Louisville and Nashville Railroad Co* [1912] 1 K.B. 135: as to the position of directors of a company, see *Re Maville Hose* [1939] Ch. 32. (One of several directors of company A was ordered to attend for examination in the voluntary liquidation of company B, and to bring with him two debentures issued by company B to company A together with other documents showing the state of account between the two companies. The director moved to discharge the order as being premature and oppressive. It was held to be oppressive and whether he was to produce any and what relevant documents should only be decided after he had attended for examination. The issue was not determined whether one director of a company could properly be said to have possession or custody of the company's documents.) As to partners, see *Forbes v Samuel* [1913] 3 K.B. 706. (Scrutton J. held that a member of a firm called upon *subpoena* to produce the deed of partnership, for proceedings in which one of his partners was defendant, was bound to produce his copy. This was despite the objection that the deed was in joint possession of the partners and that his co-partners objected to the production.) See *Seaward v Paterson* [1897] 1 Ch. 546 for the position of a servant of a person who is the subject of an injunction.

[29] See *Eccles and Co v Louisville and Nashville Railroad Co* [1912] 1 K.B. 135 at 148, Buckley L.J. who expressed the view that it was for the party seeking attachment to prove that the respondent had refused to produce the documents and that they were, in his hands, documents capable of being produced. (Kennedy L.J. dissented, on the basis that there was no sufficient excuse for the employee's not producing them, since not only had he not been forbidden to do so, but he had not even sought permission from his employer.)

[30] The 1965 Act had dispensed with the *subpoena* as a method of securing attendance before the Crown Court: s.8. From the wording of s.3 it would appear that it is the Crown Court itself which has exclusive power to punish disobedience of a witness summons.

[31] See also *Archbold 2005*, ch.8, sect. I.

[32] ss.2C and 2E.

[33] See generally A. Edwards, "The Procedural Aspects" [1997] Crim. L.R. 321.

[34] See now the Practice Direction (Criminal Proceedings: Case Management) [2005] 1 W.L.R. 1491 substituting a new Pt IV.41. (See *Archbold*, 3rd Supplement 2005 at para.4–85.)

11-118 CHAPTER 11—INTERFERENCE WITH ADMINISTRATION OF JUSTICE

"(a) a person is likely to be able to give evidence likely to be material evidence, or produce any document or thing likely to be material evidence, for the purpose of any criminal proceedings before the Crown Court, and
(b) the person will not voluntarily attend as a witness or will not voluntarily produce the document or thing."

11-119 It has long been established that when a witness is required to attend a criminal trial by witness summons, he need not be offered any expenses, where the summons is served within the jurisdiction of England and Wales.[35]

11-120 Under s.3 of the Act a person who, without just excuse, disobeys a witness summons requiring attendance before any court[36] is guilty of contempt,[37] and may be punished summarily by that court " ... *as if* his contempt had been committed in the face of the court" (our emphasis),[38] though the maximum punishment is three months' imprisonment. Although the process is a summary one, it has been held that a person who is in peril of being fined or imprisoned should be given the opportunity to be legally represented before any such order is made.[39] On the other hand, the Court of Appeal has accepted that proceedings for contempt in this context are not expected to be conducted "as a formal criminal prosecution".[40]

11-121 It has been held that where it is necessary to hold an enquiry into a failure to attend on the part of a material witness, any such proceedings should be held in the presence of the trial counsel and that only "very exceptional circumstances" could justify the enquiry taking place in the absence of the accused.[41] Therefore, where a judge excluded counsel for the Crown and the defence, and was told by the witness during a chambers hearing that he had been threatened by the defendant, it was held that the trial itself was tainted because defence counsel was unable to take an informed view as to how to cross-examine the witness; there was thus potential prejudice to the interests of his client. A further criticism was levelled at the procedure because the enquiry had gone beyond investigating

---

[35] This is the effect of the Writ of Subpoena Act 1805, which was extended to witness summonses by the 1965 Act, Sch.2, Pt I. See also *R. v Cooke* (1824) 1 C. & P. 321, 171 E.R. 1213; *Pell v Daubeny* (1850) 5 Exch. 955 at 957, 155 E.R. 416; 2 Hawkins, *Pleas of the Crown* c.46, s.173; *Archbold 2005*, para.8–10.
[36] See the amendment of s.3 by the substitution of a s.3(1A) by the Criminal Procedure and Investigations Act 1996, s.66, which provides for a similar sanction in respect of disobedience, without just excuse, to an order requiring advance production of a document or thing (under s.2A as substituted).
[37] It follows that there is a right of appeal under s.13 of the Administration of Justice Act 1960: see, e.g. *R. v Yusuf* [2003] EWCA Crim 1488, [2003] Crim. L.R. 877.
[38] It had been established in *R. v Lefroy* (1873) L.R. 8 Q.B. 134 that inferior courts of record could only punish for contempts in the face of the court. For the uncertain scope of this expression, see the discussion at paras 10–11 *et seq*.
[39] *R. v Chowdhury; Crone, The Times*, March 29, 1984. See Morrish and McLean's *Crown Court Index* (25th ed 2005), pp.300 *et seq*. For other safeguards recommended in modern authorities, see paras 10–38 *et seq*.
[40] *R. v Lennock* (1993) 97 Cr.App.R. 228 at 230, 158 J.P. at 1070A–B.
[41] *R. v Coolledge* [1996] Crim. L.R. 748, CACD; see also *R. v Lee Kun* (1916) 11 Cr.App.R. 293 at 300.

the matter of statutory contempt, and the judge had counselled the witness as to how he should give his evidence when the trial started.

Any prescribed requirements as to service may be assumed by the court, in the absence of any submission to the contrary, to have been complied with.[42] In *R. v Abdulaziz*,[43] however, where notice was duly served but not received, and the witness in question had only been notified orally 48 hours before the hearing, a submission that she was entitled to a written notification was rejected. It was observed by the Court of Appeal that "the practice plainly is that witnesses very often do not receive written notification, and clear oral notification would suffice".[44]

Mens rea not required under the 1965 Act

The Act did not make it expressly clear whether any element of *mens rea* is required, but the Court of Appeal has held that the offence is one of "absolute liability",[45] subject to proof of just excuse.

"Without just excuse"

There is no definition in the Act of what constitutes a "just excuse" for non-attendance. In *R. v Lennock*,[46] the argument was rejected that disobedience had to be wilful or deliberate. It had been found by the judge below that there was no deliberate defiance of the court's order, but the Court of Appeal confirmed that "culpable forgetfulness could never amount to a just excuse". The purpose of the section would be destroyed if it were necessary to demonstrate some kind of deliberate defiance.

It would seem that the term "just excuse" is, for reasons of public policy, narrowly construed.[47] As the Court of Appeal explained in *R. v Abdulaziz*:

" ... in practice, the only sort of excuse which would be regarded as a just excuse for failure to attend would arise in a situation where a witness simply could not present himself. It was not open to a witness to make value judgments between the competing claims of the court on the one hand and his private life on another. Otherwise, the door would be open for witnesses to advance all sorts of reasons for not attending".

Pressure of work was held to be no excuse in *United Kingdom Central Council for Nursing Midwifery and Health Visiting v Gifford*.[48]

---

[42] *R. v Lennock* (1993) 97 Cr.App.R. 228 at 231, 157 J.P. at 1070–1.
[43] [1989] Crim. L.R. 717 (Lexis).
[44] *ibid*. See also *R. v Yusuf* [2003] EWCA Crim 1488, [2003] Crim. L.R. 877.
[45] *R. v Lennock* (1993) 97 Cr.App.R. 228, 157 J.P. 1068.
[46] *ibid*.
[47] See the commentary on *R. v Abdulaziz* by Sir John Smith [1989] Crim. L.R. at 718.
[48] [1991] C.O.D. 436.

11-126 On the other hand, in *Crone*,[49] the Court of Appeal had said that there was "plainly" a just excuse when, as the result of a chapter of accidents, the appellant had not been notified that his attendance was required, and could not possibly have been expected to be there. The test put forward by the Court of Appeal in *R. v Abdulaziz*[50] was "whether it was practicable for the appellant to have attended on two days' notice, or was the correct conclusion that she simply could not have presented herself in time?" It was there held to be a just excuse that the period of time between notification and the hearing was very short, and that the person notified would have to make complex travel arrangements to return to the United Kingdom.

11-127 "Just excuse" would presumably include a genuine illness, or at least one which involved some degree of incapacity, or which would lead to a risk to health if the summons were obeyed. Although a tender of expenses is not necessary when a witness summons is served within the jurisdiction, it may be that if a witness is so poor as not to be able to travel at his own cost this would be taken to be a sufficient excuse.[51] The witness's own view that he or she would not be able to give material evidence cannot be a just excuse for not attending, because the Act[52] gives the witness the right to apply to the court to make the summons ineffective. This can be done only if he satisfies the court[53] that he cannot give material evidence.

11-128 The provision for establishing just excuse for non-attendance may throw an evidential burden upon the alleged defaulter. In *R. v Lennock*,[54] the court stated that "... if there is evidence which is accepted by the Judge hearing the complaint of contempt, which may give rise to a just excuse, he will find that contempt is not proved". Nevertheless, it is clear from the judgment of the Court of Appeal in *R. v Abdulaziz*[55] that the onus of proof is on the prosecution. It was pointed out in *R. v Yusuf*[56] that the role of the courts can only properly be performed if members of the public co-operate, including by participation in the trial process when required to do so as a juror or witness. Witnesses who disobeyed a summons could expect to be punished when called upon to give important evidence. Failure to attend in such circumstances was obviously likely to disrupt the trial process and sometimes to undermine it entirely. The maximum sentence of three months was upheld because contempt was deliberate and was committed by someone who was required to give important evidence in a murder trial.

---

[49] *The Times*, March 29, 1984.
[50] [1989] Crim. L.R. 717–18.
[51] *Archbold 2005*, para.8–10.
[52] By s.2C of the 1965 Act, as amended. See also *Archbold 2005*, ch.8, Pt I.
[53] s.2C(1)(c). For the burden of proof, in the context of production of documents, see *Reading Justices Ex p. Berkshire County Council* [1996] 1 Cr.App.R. 239, Simon Brown L.J. discussed at para.11–135.
[54] (1993) 97 Cr.App.R. 228, 157 J.P. 1068.
[55] [1989] Crim. L.R. 717. See also *R. v Clarke* [1969] 1 W.L.R. 1109, CA, in the context of summoning jurors.
[56] [2003] EWCA Crim 1488, [2003] Crim. L.R. 877.

E. Crown Court: breach of bail

11–129 Absconding from bail has never been treated as contempt of court, and falls to be dealt with under s.6 of the Bail Act 1976.[57] The maximum term thereunder is 12 months.[58] There is possible room for misunderstanding because it is provided by s.6(5) that a failure to surrender shall be punishable "as if it were a criminal contempt of court". Despite this, a Crown Court judge may not sentence in accordance with the maximum prescribed for contempt under s.14 of the Contempt of Court Act 1981.[59] Unfortunately the confusion is compounded by the assumption of the learned editors of *Archbold*[60] who still seem to contemplated that a breach of bail *can* be treated as a contempt of court. This is despite the fact that the Court of Appeal in *R. v Ashley* pointed out the problem and drew attention to the case of *R. v Rowland*. Subsequent editions of *Archbold* make no mention of either *Ashley* or *Rowland* or that breach of bail must be addressed solely in accordance with the statutory provisions of s.6, and it would follow that there is no automatic right of appeal under the Administration of Justice Act 1960.

F. Magistrates' court: attendance of witnesses

11–130 Attendance of a witness before a magistrates' court is secured under s.97 of the Magistrates' Courts Act 1980. Where a magistrate is satisfied that a summons would probably not procure the attendance of the witness in question, a warrant for his arrest may be issued instead (although not where attendance is required for the hearing of a complaint).[61]

11–131 Furthermore, when a summons has been issued and the person in question has failed to attend, then if certain requirements are fulfilled a warrant for his arrest may be issued (even in respect of the hearing of a complaint).[62] Those requirements are as follows:

(a) the court must be satisfied by evidence on oath that the person is likely to be able to give material evidence or produce any document or thing likely to be material evidence in the proceedings (a requirement which would have been satisfied for the issue of a summons in the first place);

(b) it has to be proved on oath, or in such other manner as may be prescribed, that he has been duly served with the summons, and that a reasonable sum has been paid or tendered to him for costs and expenses; and

---

[57] *R. v Ashley* [2003] EWCA Crim 2571, [2004] 1 W.L.R. 2057 which cites *R. v Rowland* unreported February 14, 1991 (Russell L.J., Otton J. and Hobhouse J)
[58] Bail Act 1976, s.6(7).
[59] *R. v Reader* (1987) 84 Cr.App.R. 294. See also *Schiavo v Anderton* (1986) 83 Cr.App.R. 228; *Glynn*, December 8, 1998, CACD (Smith Bernal), and *R . v Lubega* (1999) 163 J.P. 221, CACD
[60] 2005, para.3–36.
[61] s.97(2) of the 1980 Act.
[62] s.97(3).

11–131 CHAPTER 11—INTERFERENCE WITH ADMINISTRATION OF JUSTICE

(c) it must appear to the court that there is no just excuse for the failure.

11–132 Separate provision is made by s.97(4) for a witness who, having attended, declines without just excuse[63] to be sworn or to give evidence[64]:

> "If any person attending or brought before a magistrates' court refuses without just excuse to be sworn or give evidence, or to produce any document or thing, the court may commit him to custody until the expiration of such period not exceeding one month as may be specified in the warrant or until he sooner gives evidence or produces the document or thing or impose on him a fine not exceeding £2,500, or both."

This provision does not extend to production of documents by solicitors to which legal privilege attaches.[65]

11–133 If the subsection is wide enough to embrace circumstances in which a witness is willing to give evidence in general terms, but refuses to answer a particular question, it could become relevant where a journalist refuses to identify a source. In such a situation, no doubt the exercise of the "statutory right" afforded under s.10 of the Contempt of Court Act 1981 would provide a "just cause".[66]

G. Production of "documents or things" in criminal proceedings

11–134 Where it is required that a person produce a document or thing, this can be achieved in the Crown Court under s.2 and s.2(A) of the Criminal Procedure (Attendance of Witnesses) Act 1965[67] by obtaining a witness summons from the Crown Court itself.[68] As for the magistrates' court, provision is made in s.97(1) of the Magistrates' Courts Act 1980[69]:

> "Where a justice of the peace ... is satisfied that any person in England or Wales is likely to be able to give material evidence, or produce any document or thing likely to be material evidence, at the summary trial of an information or hearing of a complaint by a magistrates' court ... and that that person will not voluntarily attend as a witness or will not voluntarily produce the document or thing, the justice shall issue a summons directed to that person requiring him to attend before the court ... to give evidence or to produce the document or thing ... "

The power to issue a witness summons does not, however, extend to compel the production of documents subject to legal professional privilege which has not been waived.[70]

---

[63] Compare the discussion at paras 11–124 *et seq.*
[64] The wording is printed as amended by the Contempt of Court Act 1981, s.14, Sch.2, Pt III, para.7 and the Criminal Justice Act 1991, s.17(3) and Sch.4, Pt I.
[65] *R. v Derby Magistrates' Court Ex p. B* [1996] A.C. 487, HL.
[66] Compare the approach of the House of Lords in *Re an Inquiry under the Company Securities (Insider Dealing) Act 1985* [1988] A.C. 660. See paras 9–186 *et seq.*
[67] As substituted by the Criminal Procedure and Investigations Act 1996, s.66.
[68] It was at one time suggested that it would be possible to obtain a summons from the High Court: see the former RSC Ord.79, r.10. This no longer applies and there is no equivalent in the CPR.
[69] As amended by the Criminal Procedure and Investigations Act 1996, ss.47, 80, Sch.1, Pt I, paras 1, 7, Sch.5(10).
[70] *R. v Derby Magistrates' Court Ex p. B* [1996] A.C. 487.

The central principles governing the production of documents to be derived **11–135**
from the Divisional Court authorities[71] may be summarised as follows:

(1) To be material evidence, documents must be not only relevant to the issues arising in the criminal proceedings, but also admissible as such in evidence;

(2) Documents which are desired merely for the purpose of possible cross-examination are not admissible in evidence and, thus, are not material for the purposes of either statute;

(3) Whoever seeks production in the magistrates' court must satisfy the justices that the documents are "likely to be material" in the sense indicated, that is to say that there is a real possibility of materiality although not necessarily a probability;

(4) In the Crown Court it is for the third party to satisfy the court that the relevant documents are *not* likely to be material;

(5) It is not sufficient that the applicant merely wishes to find out whether or not the third party has a material document, since the statutory procedure should not be used as a disguised attempt to obtain discovery.

It was argued in *R. v Reading Justices* that the fast developing law with regard **11–136**
to prosecution disclosure in criminal cases[72] must be taken to have affected the practice with regard to these statutory provisions, but it was held that quite different policy considerations applied to the production of documents by third parties. Such orders may cause witnesses to be summoned quite unnecessarily with attendant inconvenience and expense. These observations were subsequently approved by the House of Lords in *R. v Derby Magistrates' Court Ex p. B*.[73]

Where a third party applies under the 1965 Act to challenge a witness **11–137**
summons requiring a large number of documents to be disclosed, the judge is entitled to accept the assertion of the possessor of the documents that they are irrelevant to any issue in the case or, if that claim is implausible or suspect, the

---

[71] *R. v Cheltenham Justices Ex p. Secretary of State for Trade* [1977] 1 W.L.R. 95, [1997] 1 All E.R. 460; *R. v Skegness Magistrates' Court Ex p. Cardy* [1985] R.T.R. 49; *R. v Coventry Magistrates' Court Ex p. Perks* [1985] R.T.R. 74; *R. v Peterborough Magistrates' Court Ex p. Willis and Amos* (1987) 151 J.P. 785; *R. v Clowes* [1992] 3 All E.R. 440, Phillips J.; *R. v Reading Justices Ex p. Berkshire County Council* [1996] 1 Cr.App.R. 239 at 246–7; see also *Re a Solicitor* [1996] 1 F.L.R. 40; *R. v H (L)* [1997] 1 Cr.App.R. 176. It would appear that the common law principles deriving from these authorities are not abrogated by the 1996 Act.
[72] See, *e.g R. v Keane* (1994) 99 Cr.App.R. 1, [1994] 1 W.L.R. 746; *R. v Brown (Winston)* [1995] 1 Cr.App.R. 191; *R. v Chief Constable of West Midlands Police Ex p. Wiley* [1995] 1 A.C. 274. See now the Criminal Procedure and Investigations Act 1996, ss.1–21 and the Criminal Justice Act 2003, Pt 3.
[73] [1996] 1 A.C. 487 at 501, Lord Taylor of Gosforth C.J.

judge may examine the documents personally. It is also proper, in the exercise of judicial discretion, for the judge to accept an assurance from an independent competent member of the bar that the documents requested are irrelevant.[74]

I. Attendance by jurors: section 20 of the Juries Act 1974

11–138   The summoning of jurors to the High Court, Crown Court and county court is governed by the Juries Act, 1974. At common law, it would probably have been treated as a contempt for a juror, duly summoned, to fail to answer the summons.[75] It is unlikely, however, that nowadays circumstances would arise in which it would be appropriate to have resort to the summary procedure of contempt against a juror for non-attendance,[76] although the statutory procedure bears a close resemblance.

11–139   It is likely that offenders would be dealt with under the specific provisions of s.20 of the 1974 Act:

"(1) Subject to the provisions of subsections (2) to (4) below—

(a) if a person duly summoned under this Act fails to attend (on the first or on any subsequent day on which he is required to attend by the summons or by the appropriate officer) in compliance with the summons, or

(b) if a person, after attending in pursuance of a summons, is not available when called on to serve as a juror, or is unfit for service by reason of drink or drugs,

he shall be liable to a fine not exceeding level 3 on the standard scale.[77]

(2) An offence under subsection (1) above shall be punishable either on summary conviction or as if it were criminal contempt of court committed in the face of the court.[78]

(3) Subsection 1(a) above shall not apply to a person summoned otherwise than under s.6 of this Act, unless the summons was duly served on him on a date not later than fourteen days before the date fixed by the summons for his first attendance.

---

[74] *R. v W (G); R. v W (E)* [1996] T.L.R. 412, CACD.
[75] Hawk. *Pleas of the Crown.*, c.22, s.14; *R. v Clement* (1821) 4 B. & Ald. 218 at 235, 106 E.R. 918, at 923, Holroyd J.
[76] This is considered more generally in the context of contempt in the face of the court, at paras 10–72 *et seq.* See also para.2–13. And see the discussion of *R. v Ashley* [2003] EWCA Crim 2571, [2004] 1 W.L.R. 2057 in the context of breach of bail. Although the provision expressly used the phrase " . . . as if it were a contempt," the court stressed the importance of using the specific statutory procedure and adhering to its sentencing limits.
[77] Criminal Justice Act 1982, s.37(3). See now Criminal Justice Act 1991, s.17(2) (currently £1,000).
[78] Although this wording provides only for an analogy with contempt in the face, it appears that it would be sufficient to bestow jurisdiction upon the relevant courts, at least as an alternative to summary proceedings in the magistrates' court, to deal with a breach as though it were a contempt in the face. The relevant courts are the High Court, Crown Court and county court (all of which have an inherent jurisdiction to deal with contempts which are truly "in the face of the court" by virtue of being courts of record).

(4) A person shall not be liable to be punished under the preceding provisions of this section if he can show some reasonable cause[79] for his failure to comply with the summons, or for not being available when called on to serve, and those provisions have effect subject to the provisions of this Act about the withdrawal or alteration[80] of a summons, and about the granting of any excusal or deferral.[81]

(5) If any person—

(a) having been summoned under this Act makes, or causes or permits to be made on his behalf, any false representation to the appropriate officer with the intention of evading jury service; or

(b) makes or causes to be made on behalf of another person who has been so summoned any false representation to that officer with the intention of enabling the other to evade jury service; or

(c) when any question is put to him in pursuance of s.2(5) of this Act, refuses without reasonable excuse to answer, or gives an answer which he knows to be false in a material particular, or recklessly gives an answer which is false in a material particular; or

(d) knowing that he is disqualified under Part 2 of Schedule 1 to this Act, serves on a jury[82]; or

(e) knowing that he is not qualified for jury service by reason of s.40 of the Criminal Justice and Public Order Act 1994, serves on a jury,] he shall be liable on summary conviction to a fine of not more than [level 5 on the standard scale] in the case of an offence of serving on a jury when disqualified and, in any other case, a fine of not more than level 3 on the standard scale."

The Act does not seem to deal specifically with a situation where someone attends in answer to a jury summons but refuses then to serve or be sworn. It may be that the word "available" in subs.1(b)[83] would be interpreted to mean ready, able and willing to serve. Alternatively, it is conceivable that such a person could be treated as committing a common law contempt.[84] Certainly in the past a juror who protested without cause against serving on a jury could be treated as being in contempt, particularly if his protests were unseemly or persisted in despite warnings.[85] Section 38 of the Juries Act 1825 which formerly governed jury service made it a contempt for a juror wilfully to withdraw himself without leave

---

[79] Largely a question of fact: *Leck v Epsom RDC* [1922] 1 K.B. 383. It is for the prosecution to demonstrate that, once there is some evidence of an excuse, it is of no avail: *R. v Clarke* [1969] 1 W.L.R. 1109, CA. It was observed by Sir John Smith in his commentary on *R. v Abdulaziz* [1989] Crim. L.R. 717–8 that "The terms, 'reasonable excuse' and 'lawful excuse' are commonly found in statutes; 'just excuse', less so. The terms seem to be used by the draftsmen in a rather arbitrary way. 'Just excuse' is very narrowly construed by the court but that seems to be because of the context rather than the particular words . . . ". He was there referring to the fact that the term "just excuse" in the Criminal Procedure (Attendance of Witnesses) Act 1965, s.3 was construed in such a way as to excuse only those situations where it was truly not practicable for a witness to attend court in accordance with the summons or order. No doubt the same policy considerations would apply to the words "reasonable cause" appearing in the Juries Act.

[80] s.4.

[81] ss.8 and 9. The words "or deferral" were added by the Criminal Justice Act 1988, s.120, which inserted a new s.9A of the Juries Act to provide for discretionary deferral.

[82] Substituted by the Criminal Justice Act 2003, s.321, Sch.33.

[83] See para.11–139.

[84] 1 Hawk. *P.C.*, c.22, s.15; *Griesley's Case* (1588) 8 Co. Rep., 77 E.R. 530; *Pettigrew, The Times*, June 1, 1965.

[85] See *Anon.*, Law Gazette, Vol.7, p.299, quoted also in Oswald, *Contempt* (3rd ed.), p.70. See also *R. v Miller* (1977) C.L.Y. 447, the facts of which are summarised at para.10–82, n.27.

of the court. The word "wilfully" is noticeably absent from s.20 of the Juries Act. It would appear likely therefore that only accidental events, or matters otherwise truly outside the individual's control, could provide a legitimate excuse in relation to the modern statutory offences.

11–141 Due service of the summons must clearly be proved before the statutory offences can be established; moreover, the person summoned must be permitted to show that there is good reason why he should be excused from attending, or why attendance should be deferred.[86] All such applications ought to be dealt with sensitively and sympathetically,[87] and are to be made in the first instance to the "appropriate officer". Where the appropriate officer is in doubt as to whether a juror is capable on account of physical disability to act effectively,[88] the person concerned may be brought before the judge for a decision. The judge shall affirm the summons unless of opinion that the person will not, on account of his disability, be capable of acting effectively as a juror, in which case he shall discharge the summons.[89] In the event of refusal by the appropriate officer to excuse or defer attendance, an opportunity is afforded of appealing to the Crown Court.[90] It is also provided in the current Practice Direction that, whether or not an application has already been made to the jury summoning officer for deferral or excusal, it is also open to the person summoned to apply to the court to be excused.[91]

11–142 The cases on reasonable excuse for failing to attend upon *subpoena*, and those relating to "just excuse" within the meaning of the Attendance of Witnesses Act 1965, would be in point here.[92] It would seem clear under this statute that it would be no defence if the juror *thought* he had a reasonable excuse, and certainly ignorance of the provisions would provide no excuse.[93] It would be a contempt at common law for a juror to refuse to withdraw after he has been challenged at or before the moment of taking the oath.[94] Indeed, it would almost certainly involve a disruption of the proceedings, which could be treated as a contempt in the face of the court.

11–143 In *R. v Dodds*[95] the defendant had been summoned for jury service and his application for exemption refused. He had objected to participating because he

---

[86] *Practice Direction (Criminal Proceedings: Consolidation)* [2002] 1 W.L.R. 2870, as amended March 22, 2005, Part IV.42.1–42.3. For the latest version of the *Direction* see www.courtservice.gov.uk/docs/cpd/consol_criminal_pd_220305.doc.
[87] *ibid.*
[88] As contemplated by s.9B of the Juries Act 1974. This was inserted by the Criminal Justice and Public Order Act 1994, s.41 and has not been repealed or amended by the provisions of the Criminal Justice Act 2003.
[89] s.9B(2).
[90] s.9A(3) of the Juries Act 1974 as amended by the Criminal Justice Act 2003, Sch.33, para.11; Crown Court Rules 1982, SI 1982/1109, r.25.
[91] *Practice Direction (Criminal Proceedings: Consolidation)* [2002] 1 W.L.R. 2870, as amended March 22, 2005, Pt IV.42.1–42.3. For the latest version of the *Direction* see www.courtservice.gov.uk/docs/cpd/consol_criminal_pd_220305.doc.
[92] para.11–114 and paras 11–124 *et seq.*
[93] *Aldridge v Warwickshire Coal Co Ltd* (1925) 133 L.T. 439, CA.
[94] *Bushell's Case* (1670) Vaughan 135 at 152, 124 E.R. 1006 at 1014.
[95] [2002] EWCA Crim 1328, [2003] 1 Cr.App.R. 3, [2002] Crim. L.R. 735.

had no faith in the system and, if forced to take part, would only find "not guilty". When he attended court he refused to co-operate with the security arrangements. He was warned by the judge that he might be held in contempt if he did not make himself available for jury service. Nevertheless, he was not available when required. Next day, he appeared in court unrepresented when answering the allegation of contempt. He was fined and later the judge declined to vary his order pursuant to s.155 of the Powers of Criminal Courts (Sentencing) Act 2000. On appeal, pursuant to the statutory right under s.13 of the Administration of Justice Act 1960, it was argued that there was a breach of natural justice and of Art.6 of the European Convention on Human Rights. It was held, *inter alia*, that in this respect the Convention added nothing to the existing law.[96] It was also observed that he was not entitled to object to the security arrangements, and that compulsory searches were justifiable for the prevention of disorder or crime or for protecting the rights of others. On the other hand, the provisions of s.20(1) of the Juries Act had not been explained to the defendant and he had not, therefore, had the chance to argue that his alleged fear of physical searches constituted "reasonable cause". This matter was first raised after the fine had been imposed and Mr Dodds had consulted solicitors and counsel. It was possible that both he and the judge were under the impression that he simply had no defence. The finding of contempt was quashed.

J. Coroner's court

Specific provision is made to deal with the attendance of witnesses and jurors before the coroner's court.[97] Since such proceedings are inquisitorial in character, and there are no litigants or parties, it is fundamentally a matter for the coroner's discretion who should be summoned to give evidence, although subject to such restrictions as the law may impose.[98]

11–144

VI. THE STATUTORY PROVISIONS AGAINST INTIMIDATION

A. Criminal Justice and Public Order Act 1994, section 51

1. *The background*

In the Criminal Justice and Order Act 1994, s.51, Parliament supplemented the common law,[99] by making express provision for a new offence of intimidating or

11–145

---

[96] Three reasons were given: (1) The common law requirements in dealing with contempt do not fall short of European jurisprudence; (2) There is a recognition of the need under the European Convention for summary procedures: *Ravnsborg v Sweden* (1994) 18 E.H.R.R. 38; (3) There would be no breach of the Convention if defects can be rectified on appeal: *Edwards v United Kingdom* (1993) 15 E.H.R.R. 417.
[97] para.13–102. And see *H.M. Coroner for Kent v Terrill*, cited above at para.11–105.
[98] *McKerr v Armagh Coroner and others* [1990] 1 All E.R. 865, HL.
[99] See s.51(11). See the Home Office Circular 29/2001 (2001) 165 J.P.N. 828. The reservation made by this subsection means that it remains necessary to consider in some detail the scope of the common law.

11–145 CHAPTER 11—INTERFERENCE WITH ADMINISTRATION OF JUSTICE

causing harm[1] to anyone who is a juror or witness, or to a person assisting in the investigation of an offence. Particularly in relation to jurors and witnesses, this provision clearly overlaps with the common law of contempt.[2] The provisions were enacted because of increasing evidence that bullying and corruption were becoming common, especially in the context of serious criminal trials. As Henry L.J. observed in *Att-Gen's Reference No.1 of 1999*[3]: "The intimidation of jurors and witnesses and those assisting in the criminal process has been a curse of these times". It is clearly an important factor in the thinking behind the provisions to protect vulnerable witnesses in the Youth Justice and Criminal Evidence Act 1999.[4]

2. *The wording of the section*

11–146 The terms of the relevant section are as follows:

"**51**—(1) A person who does to another person—

   (a) an act which intimidates, and is intended to intimidate, that other person;
   (b) knowing or believing that the other person is assisting in the investigation of an offence or is a witness or potential witness or a juror or potential juror in proceedings for an offence; and
   (c) intending thereby to cause the investigation or the course of justice to be obstructed, perverted or interfered with,

commits an offence.

(2) A person who does or threatens to do to another person—

   (a) an act which harms or would harm, and is intended to harm, that other person;
   (b) knowing or believing that the other person, or some other person, has assisted in an investigation into an offence or has given evidence or particular evidence in proceedings for an offence, or has acted as a juror or concurred in a particular verdict in proceedings for an offence; and
   (c) does or threatens to do the act because of what (within paragraph (b)) he knows or believes,

commits an offence.

(3) A person does an act 'to' another person with the intention of intimidating, or (as the case may be) harming, that other person not only where the act is done in the presence of that other[5] and directed at him directly but also where the act is done to a third person and is intended, in the circumstances, to intimidate (or as the case may be) harm the person at whom the act is directed.

---

[1] It has been held that spitting in another's face is not "harm" within the meaning of the Act: *R. v Normanton* [1998] Crim. L.R. 220. Cp. the common law position applied in *Re de Court* [1997] T.L.R. 601 (Lexis), discussed at para.11–26.
[2] Discussed at paras 11–155 *et seq.*
[3] [2000] Q.B. 365 at 371A.
[4] Which is summarised in para.7–13 above.
[5] See *R. v Mills* [1997] Q.B. 300, where it was held that the justices had erred in dismissing proceedings under s.51(1) on the ground that the alleged threats of assault and damage had been made over the telephone and not in the presence of the victim. They had thought that s.51(3) required the victim to be present, but the Divisional Court held that s.51(3) enlarged, and did not limit, the scope of the preceding two subsections.

(4) The harm that may be done or threatened may be financial as well as physical (whether to the person or a person's property) and similarly as respects an intimidatory act which consists of threats.

(5) The intention required by subsection (1)(c) and the motive required by subsection (2)(c) above need not be the only or the predominating intention or motive with which the act is done or, in the case of subsection (2), threatened.

(6) A person guilty of an offence under this section shall be liable—

(a) on conviction on indictment, to imprisonment for a term not exceeding five years or a fine or both;
(b) on summary conviction, to imprisonment for a term not exceeding six months or a fine not exceeding the statutory maximum or both.

(7) If, in proceedings against a person for an offence under subsection (1) above, it is proved that he did an act falling within paragraph (a) with the knowledge or belief required by paragraph (b), he shall be presumed, unless the contrary is proved, to have done the act with the intention required by paragraph (c) of that subsection.

(8) If, in proceedings against a person for an offence under subsection (2) above, it is proved that he did or threatened to do an act falling within paragraph (a) within the relevant period with the knowledge or belief required by paragraph (b), he shall be presumed, unless the contrary is proved, to have done the act with the motive required by paragraph (c) of that subsection.

(9) In this section—
'investigation into an offence' means such an investigation by the police or other person charged with the duty of investigating offences or charging offenders;
'offence' includes an alleged or suspected offence;
'potential', in relation to a juror,[6] means a person who has been summoned for jury service at the court at which proceedings for the offence are pending; and
'the relevant period'—

(a) in relation to a witness or juror in any proceedings for an offence, means the period beginning with the institution of the proceedings and ending with the first anniversary of the conclusion of the trial or, if there is an appeal or reference under s.17 of the Criminal Appeal Act 1968, of the conclusion of the appeal;
(b) in relation to a person who has, or is believed by the accused to have, assisted in an investigation into an offence, but was not also a witness in proceedings for an offence, means the period of one year beginning with any act of his, or any act believed by the accused to be an act of his, assisting in the investigation; and
(c) in relation to a person who both has, or is believed by the accused to have, assisted in the investigation into an offence and was a witness in proceedings for the offence, means the period beginning with any act of his, or any act believed by the accused to be an act of his, assisting in the investigation and ending with the anniversary mentioned in paragraph (a) above.

(10) For the purposes of the definition of the relevant period in subsection (9) above—

(a) proceedings for an offence are instituted at the earliest of the following times—

---

[6] There is no corresponding definition in relation to "potential witnesses" although that term is used in s.51(1)(b). But cp the Criminal Justice and Police Act 2001, s.39(5).

11–146 Chapter 11—Interference with Administration of Justice

(i) when a justice of the peace issues a summons or warrant under s.1 of the Magistrates' Courts Act 1980 in respect of the offence;
(ii) when a person is charged with the offence after being taken into custody without a warrant;
(iii) when a bill of indictment is preferred by virtue of section 2(2)(b) of the Administration of Justice (Miscellaneous Provisions) Act 1933;

(b) proceedings at a trial of an offence are concluded with the occurrence of any of the following, the discontinuance of the prosecution, the discharge of the jury without a finding, the acquittal of the accused or the sentencing of or other dealing with the accused for the offence of which he was convicted; and
(c) proceedings on an appeal are concluded on the determination of the appeal or the abandonment of the appeal.

(11) This section is in addition to, and not in derogation of, any offence subsisting at common law."

11–147 It was held in *R. v Singh*[7] that it emerges clearly from s.51(1)(c) that there must be an investigation under way. It will not suffice for the defendant to have had a mistaken belief to that effect. The question may arise, however, whether there might be liability for an impossible attempt in such a situation.[8] It should be noted, however, that in *R. v Patrascu*[9] the Court of Appeal commented that on its construction of s.51(1) there could only rarely be an offence of attempting to intimidate. That is because it was contemplated that the full offence could be committed even if the defendant's intention to intimidate was not fulfilled in the sense that the victim was actually put in fear. On the other hand, one could envisage circumstances in which the relevant threat was included in a letter which was intercepted in the post. That no doubt could amount to an attempt.

B. The relationship of the provision to the common law

11–148 The enactment of these specific provisions would indicate that in future, where conduct falls within the terms of the Act, the appropriate route will be by way of indictment rather than the summary contempt procedure.[10]

11–149 Moreover, some of the statutory provisions render this option more attractive. First, the section provides for the use of presumptions to assist in the proof of *mens rea*.[11] Also, in serious cases, the available penalty under the Act of up to five years' imprisonment may be more appropriate than imprisonment for contempt, which is limited to two years.

C. Protection for civil proceedings

11–150 It will be observed from the wording of s.51(1) that the provisions were confined in their effect to those who are involved in either the investigation of or

---

[7] [2000] 1 Cr.App.R 31, [1999] Crim. L.R. 681, CACD.
[8] Under the Criminal Attempts Act 1981, following *R. v Shivpuri* [1987] A.C. 1.
[9] [2004] EWCA Crim 2417, [2004] 4 All E.R. 1066 at [21]. See also para.11–153 and para.11–234.
[10] See para.2–13.
[11] Subsections (7) and (8).

proceedings for "an offence". Thus, the language would appear to have no application to civil proceedings, to which therefore the existing common law alone will continue to apply. Sections 39 (intimidation) and 40 (harming witnesses) of the Criminal Justice and Police Act 2001 have supplemented the provisions of s.51. The wording is modelled closely upon it, and similar sanctions are available in respect of intimidation of witnesses in civil proceedings. Section 41 defines "relevant proceedings" as any proceedings in or before the Court of Appeal, the High Court, the Crown Court or any county court or magistrates' court which—(a) are not proceedings for an offence and; (b) were commenced after the coming into force of that section.

D. *Prima facie* lawful actions and intimidation

It is by no means clear that acts constituting intimidation under s.51 of the 1994 Act are confined to acts or threats which would in themselves be unlawful. Indeed, since the "harm" contemplated by the provisions is expressly extended to cover "financial" harm, it may be that even a threat to boycott a witness's business might fall within the terms of the offence. This would not be altogether surprising since Parliament intended to cast the net wide in order to deal with the mischief of widespread intimidation of all kinds. Even before this enactment, however, it appears that the common law recognised that in some circumstances the threat of actions that might in themselves be *prima facie* lawful could constitute either contempt or the offence of perverting the course of justice.[12]

E. *Mens rea* under the Act

Whereas the common law was somewhat unclear on the nature of the *mens rea* required where the victim was a witness or juror,[13] the 1994 Act is specific in relation to each offence. The offence of intimidation under s.51(1) requires, *inter alia*, an intention to cause the investigation or course of justice to be obstructed, perverted or interfered with; whereas the harm or threatened harm offence under s.51(2) requires that the person acts "because of what he knows or believes". It will be observed, however, that s.51[14] alters the standard burden of proof. Unless the person charged proves to the contrary, it may be assumed that he did have the requisite intention once the deliberate commission of the *actus reus* is established.

The meaning of "intimidation" was considered by the Court of Appeal in *R. v Patrascu*[15] where it was held that a person might intimidate another without the victim being intimidated. May L.J. explained:

"In our judgment, a person does an act which intimidates another person within s.51(1)(a), if he puts the victim in fear. He also does so if he seeks to deter the victim from some relevant action by threat or violence. A threat unaccompanied by violence

---

[12] See the discussion at para.11–241.
[13] para.11–160.
[14] subsections (7) and (8).
[15] [2004] EWCA Crim 2417, [2004] 4 All E.R. 1066 at [18]. See further reference to the case at para.11–147 and para.11–234.

may be sufficient, and the threat need not necessarily be a threat of violence. The act must be intended to intimidate. The person doing the act has to know or believe that the victim is assisting in the investigation of an offence or is a witness or potential witness or juror or potential juror in proceedings for an offence. He has to do the act intending thereby to cause the investigation or the course of justice to be obstructed, perverted or interfered with. If the other ingredients are established, this intention is presumed unless the contrary is proved (sub-s (7)). The intimidation does not necessarily have to be successful in the sense that the victim does not have actually to be deterred or put in fear. A person may intimidate another person without the victim being intimidated. This apparent contradiction arises from different shades of meaning of the active and passive use of the verb. An act may amount to intimidation and thus intimidate even though the victim is sufficiently steadfast not to be intimidated".

11–154 Where the act of intimidation consists of a threat, it is established that the threat need not be uttered directly to the witness concerned. If the threat is made via a third party the offence may still be committed provided that the defendant intends (a) that the messenger would pass on the threat to the witness, (b) that the witness would be intimidated by the threat and (c) thereby to cause the investigation or the course of justice to be obstructed, perverted or interfered with.[16]

VII. INTERFERENCE AT COMMON LAW: THE GENERAL PRINCIPLES

A. The underlying policy

11–155 It has long been recognised that contempt can be committed by persons who interfere with those engaged in litigation or other court proceedings. Separate consideration is given in the later sections of this chapter to the authorities dealing with various categories of persons involved in the administration of justice. At this stage, it is proposed to address the general principles.

11–156 Bowen L.J. in the leading case of *Re Johnson*[17] explained the importance of the summary jurisdiction in this context and the public policy reasons justifying its use:

> "The law has armed the High Court of Justice with the power and imposed on it the duty of preventing *brevi manu* and by summary proceedings any attempt to interfere with the administration of justice. It is on that ground and not on any exaggerated notion of the dignity of individuals that insults to judges are not allowed. It is on the same ground that insults to witnesses or to jurymen are not allowed. The principle is that those who have duties to discharge in a court of justice are protected by the law, and shielded on their way to the discharge of such duties, while discharging them, and on their return therefrom in order that such persons may safely have resort to courts of justice."

---

[16] *Att-Gen's Reference No.1 of 1999* [2000] Q.B. 365. See also *R. v Manley* (1844) 1 Cox 104; *R. v Bull and Schmidt* (1845) 1 Cox 281; *R. v Butt* (1884) 15 Cox 565.
[17] (1888) 20 Q.B.D. 68 at 74.

The principle was traditionally expressed as being that such persons are privileged *eundo, morando, redeundo*.[18] Those protected include judges,[19] jurors,[20] members of the legal profession,[21] witnesses,[22] parties,[23] and also court officers such as clerks, associates, bailiffs, and ushers.

11–157

It has long been regarded as a contempt to assault[24] such a person at, or on his way to or from, a court[25] where he has or had a duty to discharge.[26]

11–158

The law of contempt will also embrace those who take or threaten revenge, by whatever means, for what has been done in the discharge of a duty in the administration of justice.[27] This principle is of ancient origin. Sir Edward Coke when considering misprisions, which he defined as heinous offences under the degree of felony, pronounced that[28]:

11–159

"There is a great misprision when any revenge is sought against a judge, justice, officer, juror, sergeant, counsellor, minister, or clerk, for that which they do in discharge of their several duties, offices and places concerning the administration of justice."

B. The general requirement for *mens rea* at common law

In accordance with general principle, it would be necessary to prove that the person concerned knew that the "victim" was at or on the way to or from court

11–160

---

[18] See, *e.g.* the use of these terms in *Att-Gen v Butterworth* [1963] 1 Q.B. 696, and in *Daniell's Chancery Practice* (8th ed., 1914) Vol.1 at 776–7. See also the remarks of Lord Lane in *R. v Runting* (1989) 89 Cr.App.R. 243 at 245, cited at para.11–194.
[19] Bowen L.J. in *Re Johnson* (1888) 20 Q.B.D. 68 at 75. See further para.11–173.
[20] *R. v Giscombe* (1983) 79 Cr.App.R. 79; *R. v Martin* (1848) 5 Cox C.C. 356; *Carlion's Case* (1345) 2 Dyer 188b, 73 E.R. 416. (He and others followed jurors to the gate of Westminster Palace and assaulted and beat them. For this he lost his right hand and was committed to the Tower for life.) See further paras 11–178 *et seq.*
[21] *Re Johnson* (1888) 20 Q.B.D. 68 ; *Lea's Case* (1586) Gouldsb. 33, 75 E.R. 976; *R. v Goldman* [1968] 3 N.S.W.R. 325. See para.11–310.
[22] *R. v Wigley* (1835) 7 C. & P. 4, 173 E.R. 3; *Purdin v Roberts* (1910) 74 J.P.J. 88. See further paras 11–190 *et seq.*
[23] *Cole v Hawkins* (1738) Andrews 275, 95 E.R. 396; cf. *Ex p. Wilton* (1842) 1 Dowl. N.S. 805, and *Jones Ex p. McVittie* [1931] 1 K.B. 664; *R. v Runting* (1989) 89 Cr.App.R. 243. See further paras 11–276 *et seq.*
[24] In early cases assaults on the King's clerks were treated as contempts: 1253 Curia Regis Roll, M. 37–38 Henry III, m. 12d; Placit. Abbrev., p.132, rot. 12.
[25] For the position in relation to county courts, see the County Courts Act, ss.14 and 118, considered at para.13–84 and para.13–90.
[26] *Re Johnson* (1888) 20 Q.B.D. 68; *R. v Wigley* (1835) 7 C. & P. 4, 173 E.R. 3; *Purdin v Roberts* (1910) 74 J.P.J. 88; *Martin* (1848) 5 Cox C.C. 356; *Kirby v Webb* (1887) 3 T.L.R. 763; but cf. *Ex p. Wilton* (1842) 1 Dowl. N.S. 805 where Coleridge J. was reluctant to deal summarily with an assault following proceedings before a Master.
[27] *Moore v Clerk of Assize, Bristol* [1972] 1 W.L.R. 1669, 1 All E.R. 58 (it was held to be a contempt to threaten a witness with violence for evidence she had given in court). See also *Att-Gen v Jackson* [1994] C.O.D. 171 (12 months' imprisonment for a series of threatening telephone calls made from within prison).
[28] 3 *Inst.* 139. In support he cited the case of *William de Brewse* (1305) Mich. 33 & 34 E 1 Coram Rege, rot. 75. He was committed to the Tower for threatening Roger de Hegham, who as justice of oyer and terminer had decided a case against him. Coke also referred to recorded examples of abusing jurors, and asserted that it was "a great misprision" to seek revenge on any man for complaining in any of the King's courts.

in connection with legal proceedings,[29] or had at some stage been performing a function in the judicial process. What is less clear is whether it is necessary to prove, in addition, that the offending conduct was intended to relate to the relevant proceedings.[30]

1. *The role of motive*

11–161 Provided there is knowledge of the individual's status or function, it is submitted that it should not make any difference in principle whether the assault, threat or other interference with the person was directed at them specifically in that capacity. In *Willshire-Smith v Votino Bros Pty Ltd*[31] a tenant in a shopping centre was engaged in proceedings against the managing agent. When, following an advertisement, another tenant contacted him, he sent a letter vilifying a judge and also the managing agents, to whom a copy was sent by the recipient. It was held to have a tendency to bring unacceptable pressure to bear on the managing agents in the conduct of their litigation and thus to constitute contempt. This was despite the fact that the motive of the author was to assist in the prosecution of his own claim. As O'Loughlin J. observed[32]:

> "In the first place it is clear from its contents that the author of the letter has no true conception of the judicial system and the administration of justice. The composition of his letter shows a mixture of ignorance and arrogance. Secondly, it is his arrogance that I find so disturbing; he is prepared to condemn anyone who does not share his views or respond to his complaints. Thirdly, I do not think that the subject of contempt of court occurred to him when he wrote that letter; his objective was to denigrate the company in the eyes of the reader of the letter. His insular thinking would not have extended to the likely adverse consequences that could flow from the letter. It was not his intention to prevent [the managing agents] from defending these proceedings: rather he was intent on finding more ammunition with which to carry on his fight against the company. On the other hand, however, the contents of the letter, particularly the display of viciousness towards authority, would have constituted a real risk that a litigant might have been dissuaded from properly prosecuting his defence to the proceedings that Mr Willshire-Smith had instituted."

11–162 In *Rooney v Snaresbrook Crown Court*,[33] the background was that an electrical engineer, who had been called for jury service some weeks hence, applied for a post with a company of which the appellant was the managing director. He was engaged, and it apparently emerged very shortly that he was unsuitable for the work. He was given a week's money in lieu of notice only three days before he was due for jury service. When he collected his allowance at the end of the first week, he commented to a court officer that he had been dismissed from his job because of his jury service.

---

[29] *Garibaldo v Cagnoni* (1703) 6 Mod. 90, 87 E.R. 848; and see *Magnay v Burt* (1843) 5 Q.B. 381, 114 E.R. 1293. But see the case of *Blackburn v Bowering* [1994] 1 W.L.R. 1324, [1994] 3 All E.R. 380 cited at para.13–86.
[30] See *R. v Giscombe* (1984) 79 Cr.App.R. 79, which is considered at paras 10–211 *et seq.*
[31] (1992) 67 A. Crim.R. 261.
[32] *ibid.* at 271.
[33] (1979) 68 Cr.App.R. 78. See also *R v Stafforce Personnel Ltd.*, 00/2285/Z2, November 24, 2000, CACD.

INTERFERENCE AT COMMON LAW: THE GENERAL PRINCIPLES   **11–166**

The appellant was called before the Crown Court judge, who "assumed the role of prosecutor" and found him guilty of contempt at a brief hearing. His appeal was allowed and the finding of contempt was quashed, on the basis that the ingredients had not been established beyond reasonable doubt. Nevertheless, the case is a useful illustration of conduct which would, if duly established, amount to contempt of court.[34] Lord Denning M.R. referred in *Balogh v St. Albans Crown Court* to an earlier instance where an employer had been imprisoned for having threatened to dismiss an employee if he obeyed a jury summons.[35] It would not matter that the employer's motive was entirely selfish or that no thought had been given to the effect upon the administration of justice.   **11–163**

Suppose a creditor has been looking for his debtor for some time in vain. One day, he observes him on the television news emerging from having given evidence during a high profile case. He then attends himself next morning, having no interest in the case, but knowing that he will catch the debtor because he is due to continue his evidence. He then assaults or harasses him, having only been able to track him down because of his role as a witness. He has had to emerge into the glare of publicity only to perform his public duty. Such a person would possibly be within the protection of the law of contempt (quite apart from the general law of assault).[36]   **11–164**

It is necessary to bear in mind, however, other clear statements to the effect that, especially in reprisal cases, the presence of the revenge motive can determine the matter against a respondent.[37] It seems, therefore, that the role of motive will vary from case to case. It is by no means an essential ingredient in cases where conduct has been demonstrated as creating a real risk to the administration of justice, but in other cases it can be the deciding factor in converting conduct which might otherwise be thought of as neutral into a contempt of court.[38]   **11–165**

It was held in *R. v Lalani*[39] that it must be shown that there was present an intention either to pervert the course of justice or to do something which, if achieved, would pervert the course of justice. Such an intention could not be inferred on the facts of that case merely from an improper communication between the defendant (who had been a juror at a criminal trial) and one of the defendants in the criminal trial. The judge had been wrong to rule that there was sufficient evidence of intention to go to the jury simply by reason of the general proposition that any communication between a juror and a defendant, concerning   **11–166**

---

[34] Statutory protection has now been afforded by the Employment Relations Act 2004, which has inserted a new s.43M into the Employment Rights Act 1996 ("Protection of employees in respect of jury service").
[35] [1975] 1 Q.B. 73 at 84–5. See also "The Rule of Law and Jury Service" (1966) 130 J.P. 622, where the earlier incident is discussed.
[36] See *Purdin v Roberts* (1910) 74 J.P.J. 88.
[37] See, *e.g.* Donovan L.J. in *Att-Gen v Butterworth* [1963] 1 Q.B. 696 at 727; and the later discussion on reprisals against witnesses, paras 11–201 *et seq*.
[38] See, *e.g.* the citation from Lord Denning M.R. in *Att-Gen v Butterworth* [1963] 1 Q.B. 696 at para.11–211, and the discussion at paras 11–7 *et seq*.
[39] [1999] Crim. L.R. 992, CACD.

the subject matter of the trial, is capable of having a tendency to pervert the course of justice. Evidence of the relevant intent is required (in the absence of any admission). As Sir John Smith has pointed out, it is difficult to comprehend what is meant by the first of the two alternatives canvassed in the judgment. "A perversion of justice must always be an event of some kind; and the defendant must be proved to intend to bring about that event"[40]: he drew an analogy between "a perversion of the course of justice" and "grievous bodily harm". In each case the question is an objective one. It would be immaterial, for example, that the defendant had never heard the phrase "perverting the course of justice".[41] In his view, it is probably for the judge alone to decide whether the conduct or events intended amount to a perversion of justice. He considered this to be a pure question of law.

11–167 Motive came sharply into focus in one case,[42] where a police officer prepared a false statement for the victim of a burglary. It suggested that photographs of the suspected culprit had been pushed through his door by someone who had witnessed the offence but did not wish to become involved. The truth was that the police officer herself had received the photographs from a neighbour. She was charged with *inter alia* perverting the course of public justice contrary to common law. The judge having directed the jury to return a verdict of not guilty, the Attorney-General referred a point of law for the opinion of the Court of Appeal: "whether the common law offence of perverting the course of public justice is committed where false evidence is given or made, not to defeat what the witnesses believes to be the ends of justice, or not to procure what the witness believed to be a false verdict?" An affirmative answer was given. Attention was drawn to the distinction between the *ends* of justice and the *course* of justice. What mattered was the course of justice for the offence in question. The relevant intention could therefore be made out even though the motive was to achieve a just result. The judge had thus erred in withdrawing the case from the jury. As Sir John Smith commented, the jurors "left to themselves, might well have thought that [the police officer's] benevolent purpose—to procure the conviction of a guilty man while sparing a vulnerable witness from the ordeal of giving evidence—could not be an intention to pervert the course of justice but they would have been wrong".

C. Guidance from the old arrest cases

11–168 The older cases concerned with arrest may be of some assistance on the common law approach to *mens rea* generally. An arrest may be made with the intention of preventing a party from giving evidence or prosecuting a claim,[43] or even as a reprisal for what he has done in court. It may, on the other hand, be quite unconnected with the proceedings which give rise to the protection and only intended to further the personal interests of the alleged contemnor.

---

[40] See the commentary *ibid.*, at 993–4.
[41] See, *e.g. R. v Meissener* (1995) 130 A.L.R. 547.
[42] *Att-Gen's Reference (No.1 of 2002)* [2002] EWCA Crim 2392, [2003] Crim. L.R. 410.
[43] *e.g. R. v Hall* (1776) 2 W. Bl. 1110.

The case of *Garibaldo v Cagnoni*[44] appears to establish that there must be 11–169
knowledge that the person arrested is at or on his way to or from court in
connection with proceedings. The early authorities suggest that nothing further
need be shown. In *Lea's* case[45] the plaintiff sued Lea in battery. After the jury had
retired, Lea caused the plaintiff to be arrested for a battery done by the plaintiff
to Lea on a previous occasion. Lea was fined for contempt. Clearly there may
have been some element of reprisal here, but the court based its decision on the
principle that "when a man is sued here, he ought safely to come and go by the
privilege of this place without vexation elsewhere." On this reasoning, all that
would matter was whether Lea, when he "vexed" the plaintiff, knew that he was
at court engaged in litigation.

In *Long's* case[46] an attorney of the Common Pleas was arrested on civil 11–170
process, issuing out of the King's Bench, in the yard of the Palace of
Westminster, the courts being then in session. The arresting officer was
committed by the Common Pleas "that he might learn to know his distance."
There may perhaps have been involved some element of rivalry between the
courts, but there certainly seems to have been no suggestion that the arresting
officer *intended* to interfere with proceedings at the court.

In the later case of *Magnay v Burt*[47] Tindal C.J. expressed the view that the 11–171
arrest must be made maliciously and with knowledge that the witness is entitled
to claim privilege. He did not make it clear what he meant by maliciously. If the
basis of the privilege is that those who have business in the courts must have
uninterrupted access to them, and the person making the arrest knows that the
person he arrests is on the business of the courts, he will inevitably be taken to
know that the arrest would interrupt access to the courts.[48]

D. The principles exemplified in the old cases on serving civil process

In the early case of *Cole v Hawkins*[49] an attorney served a Bill of Middlesex 11–172
on a defendant in an action before the King's Bench while that Court was sitting
and his case was about to be called on. Relying on the analogy of privilege from
arrest, the court held that the attorney had committed a contempt. Lee C.J. said:
"If the serving of process upon persons attending courts were to be allowed, it
would produce much terror and great distraction of business." The case is clearly
obsolete,[50] but it tends to illustrate that the courts have never been concerned, in
implementing these broad principles, with motive.

---

[44] (1703) 6 Mod. 90, 87 E.R. 848.
[45] (1586) Gouldsb. 33, 75 E.R. 976.
[46] (1677) 2 Mod. 181, 86 E.R. 1012.
[47] (1843) 5 Q.B. 381 at 394–395.
[48] See para.11–300.
[49] (1738) Andrews 275, 95 E.R. 396.
[50] See *Jones Ex p. McVittie* [1931] 1 K.B. 664.

11–173 CHAPTER 11—INTERFERENCE WITH ADMINISTRATION OF JUSTICE

VIII. COMMON LAW: JUDGES, JURORS AND LEGAL ADVISERS

A. Judges

11–173 Judges like others involved in litigation are protected by the law of contempt on their way to and from court, as well as in court.[51] There do not seem to be any recent examples of physical intimidation of judges being so treated, but the early cases demonstrate that this would clearly be a contempt.[52] This branch of the law today, however, may be of only residual significance in relation to physical assault or intimidation. It is difficult to envisage an assault being dealt with now through the summary process of contempt. Not only might the available penalty not be adequate to the wrong done, but also there would be a need to avoid any impression that the rules of natural justice were being breached. Once the person has been arrested or restrained from further misconduct, there is unlikely to be special urgency about pursuing court proceedings, and it could be dealt with by way of indictment. A disturbance in court that is interrupting the proceedings is different; despite the relative triviality of the incident itself, the place has about it a significance (and the process that it interrupts an importance) that may require it to be dealt with immediately.[53]

11–174 It would be a serious contempt to bribe or attempt to bribe a person holding judicial office, for the purpose of influencing his or her decision in pending proceedings[54] or independence of action more generally. It would be a classic form of contempt to seek to influence a judge's decision by any improper or extraneous means.

11–175 Indeed any form of private communication with a judge with such an intention could be a contempt.[55] It is sometimes the case that misguided relatives or friends of a defendant will write to the judge in order to ask for a lenient sentence, or to give what is in effect character evidence. Ordinarily any such letter will be placed on the file, and the matter referred to in open court. There would be no need to take any further action.[56]

---

[51] para.10–93. See also the provisions in the County Courts Act 1984, ss.14 and 118, which are set out in paras 13–84 (assaulting) and 13–90 (insulting) respectively.
[52] See para.1–2.
[53] Even such interruption, if it took the form of an assault on the judge, is unlikely to be dealt with through the contempt jurisdiction. See para.10–95.
[54] *Martin's Case* (1747) 2 Russ. & My. 674n, 39 E.R. 551; *Macgill's Case* (1748) 2 Fowler's Exch. Prac. (2nd ed.), p.404; *R. v Vaughan* (1769) 4 Burr. 2494, 2500, 98 E.R. 308; *R. v Gurney* (1867) 10 Cox C.C. 550.
[55] *Ex p. Jones* (1806) 13 Ves. Jun. 237, 33 E.R. 283; *Ludlow Charities Re, Lechmere Charlton's case* (1837) 2 My. & Cr. 316, 342, 40 E.R. 661, 671; *Re Dyce Sombre* (1849) 1 Mac. & G. 116, 122, 41 E.R. 1207, 1209; *Chester Corp v Rothwell* (1940) 7 L.J. C.C.R. 58.
[56] A well publicised comment was made by a politician at one of the annual party conferences in October 1995, suggesting that members of the public might like to inundate the judiciary with letters setting out their views on matters of sentencing, either generally or with reference to particular cases. Not surprisingly, this was reported as incurring the displeasure of the then Lord Chancellor.

There must be few communications, if any, which are likely to prejudice the mind of a judge.⁵⁷ On the other hand, there may be cases where, although there is no real risk of prejudice, there is a plain intention to affect a judge's mind, and this in itself might make an otherwise innocuous act a contempt.⁵⁸

11–176

The law of contempt may be of continuing importance in relation to other possible means of influence. The Law Commission proposed⁵⁹ that there should be specific statutory provision to deal with, *inter alia*, those who improperly sought to influence a judge by using threats, or by offering any consideration or by other means with intent to affect the outcome of current or future judicial proceedings. Yet so far nothing has been done to implement this proposal.

11–177

B. Interference with the jury system

It was a contempt at common law to interfere, or to attempt to interfere, with a juror in respect of the discharge of duties in judicial proceedings.⁶⁰ The principle was explained by Pigot C.B. in *R. v Martin*⁶¹:

11–178

"It is important that there should be no interference with the administration of justice; and above all, that juries should be protected from every interference with them in reference to the discharge of their important and sacred duties; they form a portion of the tribunals by which the law of the land is administered."

1. *Embracery*

Improper interference with jurors, in an attempt to corrupt or influence a verdict, was recognised from early times as the misdemeanour of embracery.⁶² Embracery consisted in any attempt to corrupt or influence or "instruct a jury in the cause beforehand", or in any way to incline them to be more favourable to the one side than to the other, by money, promises, letters, threats or persuasions, whether the jurors on whom such an attempt was made gave any verdict or not, and whether the verdict given was true or false.⁶³

11–179

---

⁵⁷ But see the comments of Viscount Dilhorne in *Att-Gen v BBC* [1981] A.C. 303 at 335, quoted at para.4–119 and the decision of the Irish Supreme Court in *Kelly v O'Neill and Brady* [2000] 1 I.R. 354.
⁵⁸ See the discussion at paras 11–7 *et seq.* See also *Re Lonrho* [1990] 2 A.C. 154, and particularly the citation at para.11–10.
⁵⁹ Report, Law Com. No.96, *Offences Relating to Interference with the Course of Justice,* (1979), para.3–52. See generally R. Leng, "Protecting the Course of Justice" [1981] Crim. L.R. 151.
⁶⁰ See "The Rule of Law and Jury Service" (1966) 130 J.P. 622.
⁶¹ (1848) 5 Cox C.C. 356.
⁶² See, *e.g.* The Juries Act 1825, s.61, repealed by the Criminal Law Act 1967, s.10, Sch.3, Pt IX.
⁶³ *Russell on Crime* (12th ed., 1964) Vol.1, p.357. For examples see *R. v Opie* (1670) 1 Wms. Saund. 301, 85 E.R. 418; *Young* (1801) 2 East 16, 102 E.R. 274; *Baker* (1891) 113 C.C.C. Cas. 374, 589; *R. v Davies* (1909) 150 C.C.C. Cas. 736. The authorities are discussed in *Dunn, Re Aspinall* (1906) V.L.R. 493.

11–180 The considerations of public policy underlying embracery may be regarded as overlapping with those governing the law of contempt,[64] but nowadays the offence of embracery itself has become obsolescent.[65]

2. The current means of dealing with jury tampering

11–181 Such conduct would be likely now to be dealt with in one of three ways. First, in the case of one individual, it is possible still that the matter could be dealt with by resorting to the summary jurisdiction in contempt,[66] or by way of the common law offence of attempting to pervert the course of justice.[67] Secondly, if more than one person were involved, there would be the possibility of a prosecution for conspiracy to pervert the course of justice.

11–182 Thirdly, there is the modern statutory offence. Because of the increasing threat to the administration of justice from conduct of this kind,[68] Parliament made specific provision in s.51 of the Criminal Justice and Public Order Act 1994[69] (while expressly making it clear that the section does not derogate from any offence subsisting at common law).[70] It provides for a maximum term of imprisonment, following conviction on indictment, of five years.[71] It is therefore more suited to serious cases falling within its scope than the law of contempt, where the maximum term is two years.[72]

11–183 The Court of Appeal in *R. v Goult*[73] was concerned with a deliberate campaign to intimidate jurors on the part of an acquaintance of a defendant in criminal proceedings. The appellant was a very large man who had been threatening jurors, both by staring at them in court and by various menacing gestures out of court; for example, by jumping behind female jurors in the street and by driving a car slowly in front of another juror. The trial judge committed him for contempt. Although these incidents would probably now fall within the wording of s.51 of the 1994 Act, the case provides a good illustration of circumstances in

---

[64] For a discussion as to whether embracery may be treated summarily as a contempt, see the Australian case of *Re Dunn, Re Aspinall* (1906) V.L.R. 493. See *R. v Owen* (1976) 63 Cr.App.R. 199, [1976] 1 W.L.R. 840, [1976] 3 All E.R. 239, where it was said that where only one person was involved in seeking to interfere with a jury, the charge should be contempt.
[65] *Owen*, last note. See also *Archbold 2005*, para.28–47, and *Archbold 2001*, para.28–151.
[66] See *Owen* (1976) 63 Cr.App.R. 199, [1976] 1 W.L.R. 840, [1976] 3 All E.R. 239.
[67] Some commentators took the view at one time, see, *e.g. Archbold 1998* para.28–25, that "the offence of perverting the course of justice is merely contempt under another name". While this may be true in the sense that both these areas of the law are directed towards a similar mischief, the criminal offence would carry a different range of penalties; it would also entail the standard safeguards of criminal procedure.
[68] See, *e.g R. v Dodd* (1981) 74 Cr.App.R. 50 at 53–4; *R. v Ling* [1987] Crim. L.R. 495; *R. v Comerford* [1998] 1 All E.R. 823; *Att-Gen's Reference (No.1 of 1999)* [2000] Q.B. 365 at 371A, Henry L.J.
[69] Set out in para.11–146.
[70] s.51(11).
[71] s.51(6)(a).
[72] Contempt of Court Act 1981, s.14.
[73] (1982) 76 Cr.App.R. 140, (1982) 4 Cr.App.R. (S) 355. See also *R. v Giscombe* (1983) 79 Cr.App.R. 79, discussed at paras 10–211 *et seq.*

which it may still be appropriate to deal with such objectionable behaviour on an immediate and summary basis.

The court upheld the trial judge's decision to take this course (although halving the term of imprisonment), not only for the purpose of protecting the dignity and authority of the court but also for the reassurance of other jurors awaiting their call for duty. Moreover, it was not one of those cases in which it could be said that there was any doubt as to the commission of the offence,[74] since there was ample evidence upon which the judge could be satisfied to the criminal standard. There was no vice in the fact that he had not given a detailed judgment, because the basis of his finding of fact and the route by which he reached it were obvious. 11–184

Since, however, the s.51 offence carries a maximum penalty of five years' imprisonment, it would qualify as an "arrestable offence".[75] It is possible, therefore, that the legitimate objective of reassuring jurors and potential jurors could now be achieved by effecting an arrest and, if appropriate, refusing bail. It is a ground for refusing bail that the accused is suspected of being likely to interfere with witnesses or to commit other offences if left at liberty.[76] (One drawback of this route, as opposed to using the contempt jurisdiction, would be that the judge trying the case affected by the intimidation would not necessarily have any control over whether bail was granted to the person seeking to exert the improper influence.) 11–185

It would be a contempt to seek to persuade a summoned juror not to answer the summons, certainly if any intimidation were used. Likewise it would be a contempt for an employer to dismiss an employee because he has been summoned for jury service.[77] 11–186

3. Reprisals against jurors

Jurors are also protected from reprisals for what they may have done in the course of their jury service.[78] In *Att-Gen v Judd*,[79] a convicted man asked a juror to write to the trial judge and tell him that she had been mistaken about his guilt. He was committed for 42 days for contempt, the Divisional Court taking the view that his conduct was analogous to that of taking reprisals against a witness.[80] 11–187

---

[74] See paras 10–57 *et seq.*
[75] Police and Criminal Evidence Act 1984, s.24(1)(b). Prospectively repealed and replaced by the Serious Organised Crime and Police Act 2005, s.110, which adds a re-worded s.24 from a date to be appointed.
[76] Bail Act 1976, Sch.1, Pt I.
[77] *Rooney v Snaresbrook Crown Court* (1979) 68 Cr.App.R. 78, discussed at paras 11–162 *et seq.* See also *R. v Stafforce Personnel Ltd*, November 24, 2000, CACD.
[78] *R. v Martin* (1848) 5 Cox C.C. 356; and see paras 11–178 *et seq.*
[79] [1995] C.O.D. 15.
[80] See, *e.g. Att-Gen v Butterworth* [1963] 1 Q.B. 696.

4. Impersonating a juror

11–188 It was held to be a contempt to impersonate a person called as a juror, and to sit and deliver a verdict in his place.[81] One cannot, however, be taken to have "impersonated" without doing so deliberately. If a person acts in place of a juror in the mistaken belief that he himself has been called to serve, that will not be treated as contempt.[82] The Law Commission[83] proposed that the common law offences of embracery and impersonating a juror be abolished and replaced by statutory offences, but no enactment has followed. The Commission's clause 12 would have made it an offence for a juror to offer or agree to influence improperly the outcome of proceedings he is trying or may try.[84]

5. The possibility of jury B contamination following the discharge of jury A

11–189 In *R. v Barraclough*,[85] the Court of Appeal was concerned with the situation in which a jury had been discharged because of some questions which might have implied that the defendant had previous convictions. Because the jurors were in their first week of jury service, the Recorder warned them in strong terms against discussing the case with any other jurors or potential jurors, because he had explained to them the reason for the discharge—including the fact that the defendant had some convictions. It was argued on appeal that to prevent any danger of contamination of the second jury by the members of the first panel, steps should have been taken either to delay the retrial for so long as was necessary to ensure that there was a completely new panel of jurors, or to discharge the first jury from further service forthwith. The question was whether there was a real danger that the second jury were prejudiced or biased against the defendant through knowing of previous convictions. On the facts there was no such danger. The panel of jurors at any one time consisted of some 200 people. Even if a meeting took place between a member of the first jury and a member of the second, there would only be contamination if the Recorder's clear instructions had been disobeyed. In a smaller court, it might have been desirable to discharge the first jury from further attendance, or to delay the retrial, on the basis that the risk of communication would be greater. There should be no hard and fast rules.

IX. COMMON LAW: INTERFERENCE WITH WITNESSES

A. The mischief

11–190 It would be a contempt to publish matter in the media calculated to deter witnesses from coming forward, or to influence them with respect to the evidence

---

[81] *Anon.* (1642) March 81, 82 E.R. 421; *R. v Levy* (1916) 32 T.L.R. 238.
[82] *Norman v Beaumont* (1744) Willes 484, 125 E.R. 1281.
[83] Report, Law Com. No.96, *Offences Relating to Interference with the Course of Justice* (1979), para.3–132.
[84] Law Com. No.96, 1979.
[85] [2000] Crim. L.R. 325.

they might give, but this would fall to be considered either as a strict liability offence under the 1981 Act,[86] or as a common law publication contempt if *mens rea* was present.[87]

What arises in the present chapter is the distinct question of the nature of the protection afforded by the law of contempt, and under the Criminal Justice and Public Order Act 1994 (considered above),[88] to witnesses in cases *not* involving media publication. It may well be appropriate now to deal with the matter by way of indictment, on the basis that the conduct constitutes some other more specific offence, such as attempting to pervert the course of justice at common law, or under the 1994 Act.

11–191

It is immaterial whether the witness is to give evidence in civil or criminal proceedings. In *Schlesinger v Flersheim*,[89] Williams J. had sought to draw a distinction, in passing, between interfering with witnesses in criminal prosecutions where "the public is directly interested in the punishment of the supposed delinquent" and such interference in the case of civil proceedings, where "the public is at least only remotely interested in the due course of justice being upheld". He had before him in that case an example of alleged interference with a witness who was to prove publication of a letter in a civil libel action. He came to the conclusion that on the facts of the case there had been no obstruction of justice, and that the matter should be left to be dealt with by the issue of a *subpoena* against the witness. In the circumstances, it would appear that his purported distinction between civil and criminal proceedings is not one that is likely to commend itself to a modern court in a case of alleged interference with a witness. As was observed by Stephenson L.J. in *R. v Kellett*, "perversion of the course of justice is *per se* an offence against the public weal."[90]

11–192

A modern statement of the principles is to be found in the words of Bingham J.[91]:

11–193

"Generally it is essential that those who give evidence in a court of law should be protected from insults and abuse. It is not an agreeable task to give evidence at the best of times, but it is very much more disagreeable if conduct of this kind is allowed to flourish. The administration of justice depends on witnesses coming forward, and they must be confident in doing so that the law will protect them."

---

[86] Ch.4.
[87] Ch.5.
[88] para.11–145.
[89] (1845) 14 L.J.Q.B. 97 at 98.
[90] [1976] 1 Q.B. 372 at 383.
[91] *R. v Smithers and Bowen* (1983) 5 Cr.App.R. (S) 248 at 249, CACD. Since the principles are so fundamental to the effective administration of justice, it is not surprising that there are many authoritative statements to similar effect, and of greater antiquity. See, *e.g.* Hawkins, *Pleas of the Crown* (8th ed., 1824), Vol.1, c.VI, s.15; *Blackstone's Commentaries*, (15th ed.,1809), Vol.4, c.9, p.126; Sir James Fitzjames Stephen, *Digest of the Criminal Law* (9th ed., 1950), Art.191; *Russell on Crime* (12th ed., 1964), Vol.1, p.312.

11–194 CHAPTER 11—INTERFERENCE WITH ADMINISTRATION OF JUSTICE

11–194 In *R. v Runting*,[92] Lord Lane C.J. was concerned with an allegation of contempt made against a press photographer who had been pestering a defendant on his way from court in a manner which, though reprehensible, fell short of constituting the *actus reus* of contempt. In the course of his judgment, however, he took the opportunity to reaffirm the general principles:

> "It should be made clear at the outset that the law insists that a defendant and witnesses, and indeed anyone else who has a duty to perform at a Court, whether in a criminal trial or in a civil trial, is entitled to go to and from the court, that is between his home and the court, whether on foot or otherwise, without being molested or assaulted or threatened with molestation.
> There are two reasons for that, it seems to this Court. The first is, there must be nothing to create in the minds of such persons any fear such as to make them less likely to wish to come to Court to carry out their proper functions. The second reason, which is perhaps more difficult to put adequately into words, is this: that the authority and dignity of the court require that those who attend the court to carry out their duties should be allowed to do so without let or hindrance, and again without fear of molestation."

11–195 There can be no doubt that a person participating in proceedings as a witness is protected *eundo, morando et redeundo*.[93] More specifically, it has been held that it would be contempt to assault a witness at court,[94] or to attempt to offer a bribe with a view to influencing evidence.[95]

11–196 Sometimes a speedy response may be required. Even when such circumstances do arise, however, it is desirable that there should, where possible, be allowed an opportunity for reflection on the part of the court, for the person concerned to take legal advice and to avoid any impression of haste or bias.[96]

B. Reprisals against witnesses

1. *Introduction*

11–197 The protection of the law continues even after the evidence is concluded, and it is thus a contempt to take reprisal against a witness for having given evidence[97]; for example, an employer who dismisses an employee as punishment for having given evidence against the employer's interest.[98]

11–198 In *Att-Gen v RSPCA*[99] it was held to be a serious contempt for the Society to bring disciplinary proceedings against one of its officers for not appearing to be

---

[92] (1989) 89 Cr.App.R. 243 at 245. These remarks were based upon the judgment of Bowen L.J. in *Re Johnson* (1888) 20 Q.B.D. 68 at 74, fully set out at para.11–156.
[93] See para.11–157; *Jones, Ex p. McVittie* [1931] 1 K.B. 664.
[94] *R. v Griffin* (1989) 88 Cr.App.R. 63. See also *Purdin v Roberts* (1910) 74 J.P. 8.
[95] *R. v Bromell* [1996] T.L.R. 67, CACD.
[96] See para.10–47; particularly *R. v Moran* (1985) 81 Cr.App.R. 51.
[97] *Att-Gen v Butterworth* [1963] 1 Q.B. 696, para.11–202.
[98] *Rowden v The Universities Co-operative Association* (1881) 35 S.J. 886; see also *Hood's Case* where it was held to be a breach of the privileges of the House of Commons to victimise an employee for giving evidence to a select Committee of the House (1892) 147 H.C. Journal 167.
[99] *The Times*, June 22, 1985, DC.

a reluctant witness for the defence at the hearing of a private prosecution brought by the Society. A fine of £10,000 was imposed. What may sometimes be more difficult, in practice, is to demonstrate that the act in question was truly connected with the employee's function as a witness, and that it was not merely coincidental.

If an association or union deprives someone of an honorary office or threatens to do so, this may amount to contempt. The question is whether it is done as a punishment for evidence given, considered to be against the interests of the association or union.[1] Likewise, if a landlord terminates a tenancy, in the purported exercise of a lawful contractual right, although in fact for the purpose of punishing the tenant for evidence given.[2] 11–199

In a New Zealand case,[3] the High Court held that there was no contempt in circumstances where valuation witnesses were charged by the Registration Board with incompetence in the preparation of reports which had been presented as evidence in a rent review arbitration. It was claimed, *inter alia*, by the valuers that the disciplinary proceedings were a contempt of court, on the ground that they were an attempt to punish them for giving evidence. It was held, however, that any censure imposed by the Registration Board would not be in respect of the fact of giving evidence so much as for failure to achieve the minimum acceptable professional standards. 11–200

2. *The relevance of "motive" or purpose in reprisal cases*

On the one hand, an act of reprisal may be unlawful quite apart from any question of contempt, as when a person is assaulted in retaliation for what has happened in a court of law.[4] On the other hand, such an act may on the face of it be lawful, but nevertheless be rendered a contempt if done with the specific intention of punishing the person *qua* witness.[5] 11–201

Where the *actus* complained of is on the face of it lawful, the critical question would seem to be whether an intention to punish was at least partly the motive.[6] This was considered in *Att-Gen v Butterworth*.[7] A member of the National Federation of Retail Newsagents was deprived by a branch committee of offices he held in the Federation, because he had given evidence perceived to be contrary to the interests of the Federation. The Court of Appeal held that not only those members of the committee motivated predominantly by a desire to punish their 11–202

---

[1] *Att-Gen v Butterworth* [1963] 1 Q.B. 696; *Adams v Walsh* [1963] N.Z.L.R. 158.
[2] *Chapman v Honig* [1963] 2 Q.B. 502; cf. *Webster v Bakewell RDC* [1916] 1 Ch. 300, paras 11–289 *et seq.*
[3] *Dentice v Valuers Registration Board* [1992] 1 N.Z.L.R. 720.
[4] *Re Johnson* (1887) 20 Q.B.D. 68; *R. v Wigley* (1835) 7 C. & P. 4, 173 E.R. 3; *R. v Martin* (1848) 5 Cox C.C. 356; *R. v Goldman* [1968] 3 N.S.W.R. 325.
[5] para.11–7.
[6] See, albeit in the context of a juror, the difficulties that can arise in establishing the true reason for an apparently lawful act, exemplified in *Rooney v Snaresbrook Crown Court* (1979) 68 Cr.App.R. 78, at para.11–162.
[7] [1963] 1 Q.B. 696, followed in *Att-Gen v Jackson* [1994] C.O.D. 171.

11–202 CHAPTER 11—INTERFERENCE WITH ADMINISTRATION OF JUSTICE

colleague were guilty of contempt, but also those who were motivated only in part by such a desire,[8] and predominantly by lack of confidence in him as a person suitable to hold office in the Federation.

11–203   Although the court took this view on the facts, however, it recognised that it would always be a matter of enquiry in such cases whether a desire to punish had indeed played any part at all. Some members of the committee had been found not to have been motivated by a desire to punish at all, and were thus acquitted of contempt. The evidence given before the Restrictive Practices Court had consisted not only of facts but also of the witnesses' opinions on certain points. Clearly it may be that the public expression of views, even as a witness in a court of law, would render a person unsuitable to hold certain honorary or other offices, whereas it is hard to see how this could ever be so in relation to the giving of accurate evidence on matters of fact. There was no question of the witness being expelled from the union. If there had been expulsion it would have been harder to justify, since this would more obviously appear to have been an act of retaliation.

11–204   An example discussed in argument was the position of the employer. Suppose a personal assistant gave evidence about his employer's private life.[9] If the employer dismissed him immediately afterwards, it might emerge upon investigation that he was motivated by a desire to punish, or simply by the conclusion that the relationship between them had become intolerable as a result of the breach of confidence.[10] The court, it seems, would have been prepared to accept, in the latter case, that the employer would not necessarily be guilty of contempt.[11]

11–205   A further hypothetical example, given by the Restrictive Practices Court,[12] was that of a settlor, with a power of appointment among his issue, for whom (since he was descended from a long line of hunting men) the last straw in the conduct of his unsatisfactory younger son was his giving evidence against a hunt in court proceedings. Here again the settlor might cut the younger son out of the settlement not with the object of punishment, but because the relationship between the two had become intolerable through incompatibility.

11–206   It is possible that a landlord living in part of a house while his tenant occupies the remainder may, if the tenant gives evidence against him in court, terminate

---

[8] Cp. *Registrar, Supreme Court v McPherson* [1980] N.S.W.L.R. 688 at 699D: "Before a nexus can be made between the act and any interference with the administration of justice . . . 'further inquiry' has to be made. The inquiry is whether a material purpose . . . in destroying the document, was to prevent it from being produced to the court upon the compulsion of a *subpoena* in proceedings then pending".
[9] See the example given by Lord Denning M.R. in *Chapman v Honig* [1963] 2 Q.B. 502 at 513–14.
[10] Compare the situations described in *Woodward v Hutchins* [1977] 1 W.L.R. 760, [1977] 2 All E.R. 751, and *Att-Gen v Barker* [1990] 3 All E.R. 257 (both cases involving breach of confidence by employees with access to personal information).
[11] See, *e.g.* Donovan L.J. at 727: "Each had the motive of punishment, and I think it immaterial whether there were other motives of greater or less priority in their minds". This suggests that if there were *no* such motive, contempt would not be made out.
[12] L.R. 3 R.P. 1, [1962] 1 Q.B. 534.

the tenancy not so much because he wishes to punish the tenant, but because it has become for that reason intolerable for the two of them to live in the same house. It may be difficult in situations like this to prove to the required standard the motive of the alleged contemnor.

3. *Is there a need to show a positive intention to interfere with the administration of justice?*

The decision of the Court of Appeal in *Att-Gen v Butterworth*[13] may be authority for the proposition that, in cases of alleged reprisal, there is no need to prove an intention to interfere with the administration of justice.[14] Donovan L.J. expressed the view that[15]:

> "... if the taking of such revenge was calculated to interfere with the administration of justice, then it will be no answer for the respondents to say that, while intending to punish Greenlees, still they had no intention of interfering with the administration of justice."

He approached the case upon the basis that the general rule was that a contempt was committed if there had been an act inherently likely to interfere with the administration of justice, but he also took the view that the inherent effect could not be judged without establishing the motive of the alleged contemnor. This was a curious analysis since the act of reprisal might objectively deter others from giving evidence in future, even though such persons might well be unaware of what was in the mind of the contemnor. Yet if the public policy justification for punishing reprisals is to reduce the risk of others being deterred from giving evidence in future cases, it would seem that the private motives of the contemnor are almost irrelevant to that objective.

It seems that if a witness is punished *qua* witness, that will suffice; just as in civil contempt, disobedience to an order will be treated as a contempt irrespective of any motive to interfere with the administration of justice.[16]

The answer may tentatively be suggested that what matters is whether the act in question was truly one of reprisal, in the sense that the alleged contemnor intended to take the relevant action in relation to the particular individual *qua* witness. If that can be demonstrated beyond reasonable doubt, it matters not whether any thought was actually given to any broader consequences for the administration of justice.

Lord Denning M.R. also discussed the need for *mens rea*[17]:

> "... contempt of court is a criminal offence, punishable summarily by the court itself, and, like all criminal offences, it requires in general a guilty mind ... At any rate, the

---

[13] [1963] 1 Q.B. 696.
[14] See also the comments of Sir John Donaldson M.R. in *Att-Gen v Newspaper Publishing plc* [1988] Ch. 333 at 374B, and Sir Richard Scott V.-C. in *Re de Court* [1997] T.L.R. 601 (Lexis).
[15] [1963] 1 Q.B. at 726.
[16] See paras 12–80 *et seq.*
[17] [1963] 1 Q.B. at 722. See also para.11–7.

law requires a guilty mind in these cases of intimidation or victimisation of witnesses. It is easy to imagine cases where the dismissal of a witness from his employment, or his suspension or expulsion from a trade union, might well be done and justified for reasons quite apart from the evidence he has given, and that clearly would not be a contempt of court. It seems to me that the intimidation of a witness is only a contempt of court if it is done with the purpose of deterring him from giving evidence or influencing him to give it in a sense different from that in which he would otherwise have given it, and the victimisation of a witness is only a contempt of court if it is done with the purpose of punishing him for having given evidence in the sense he did."

11–212 This entails the proposition that it is sufficient that the contemnor intended to punish the witness for his actions in court, whether or not he specifically addressed his mind to any possible effect on the administration of justice as such. All that is required, it would appear, is the intention to punish.

4. Private reprisals

11–213 There remains the question whether the act of reprisal would have to be shown to be likely to become known to persons other than the victim. It could be argued as a matter of principle that this would be necessary, because the rationale put forward as justifying this species of contempt seems to be that such conduct might discourage persons in future from participating in court proceedings. In cases where a witness's evidence has been completed, or the proceedings are concluded altogether, the offending conduct could have no bearing upon the case itself. As Donovan L.J. observed in *Att-Gen v Butterworth*[18]:

" . . . in this kind of case it must be proved by the Crown that knowledge of the revenge taken upon one who has given evidence is likely to come to the knowledge of potential witnesses in future cases. I think the Crown has proved that here as a matter of reasonable inference."

This seems an unsatisfactory formulation, not least because there are conceptual difficulties about proving "likelihood", as a matter of reasonable inference, beyond reasonable doubt.

11–214 Yet a similar approach was adopted by Pearson L.J. in *Chapman v Honig*[19]:

" . . . the determining factor is not harm done to the individual but harm done to the future administration of justice. The distinction is not likely to have much practical importance in relation to criminal proceedings of the usual character for contempt of court: in any ordinary case the victimisation of a person for giving evidence would become known, and would tend to deter potential witnesses from giving evidence in other actions and so would prejudice the future administration of justice. The distinction is, however, important in relation to the question arising in this appeal as to whether there is any civil liability to pay damages to the individual concerned. It is possible to imagine a case in which there would be victimisation of a witness and yet there would be no contempt of court. The object of the court's jurisdiction to punish for contempt of court is the protection of justice and not the protection of the individual affected. The

---

[18] [1963] 1 Q.B. 696 at 726.
[19] [1963] 2 Q.B. 502 at 518–19.

adverse effect on the individual does not constitute a contempt of court unless there is the additional element of probable interference with the course of justice."

By contrast, Lord Denning M.R. (Davies L.J. concurring) pointed out in **11–215** *Chapman* that, if Pearson L.J. were right, it would follow that if the victim proclaimed his grievance from the housetops the contempt would be proved, but if he kept his suffering to himself it would not. It is submitted that their analysis is to be preferred. Contempt of court has a dual aspect: it seeks to protect both the particular individual and the administration of justice in general. It has long been established that a witness is protected *after* giving evidence, at least *redeundo*. If he were beaten up on the way home, on the reasoning of Pearson L.J. an act of contempt would only have been committed if the victim let his misfortune be widely known. This does not seem to accord with that long-standing principle; or with the more general principle of the criminal law that whether the *actus reus* has been completed must be judged at the time, rather than by reference to subsequent events.

C. The persuasion of witnesses (actual or potential)

It may also be contempt to seek to persuade a witness to stay away from court **11–216** and not give evidence,[20] or to alter the nature of the evidence,[21] or to alter evidence he or she has already given orally or in an affidavit.[22]

1. *Witnesses and litigants distinguished*

The Court of Appeal in *R. v Kellett* distinguished the position of a witness from **11–217** that of a litigant,[23] and recognised that greater latitude is permitted in seeking to bring influence or persuasion to bear upon someone who has initiated proceedings. This is illustrated in the context of civil proceedings by *Webster v Bakewell RDC*[24] and in that of a private prosecution by the decision of the Divisional Court in *Att-Gen v Martin (Peter)*.[25]

---

[20] *Partridge v Partridge* (1639) Tothill 40, 21 E.R. 117; *Steventon* (1802) 2 East 362, 102 E.R. 407; *Loughran* (1839) 1 Cr. & D. 79; *Shaw v Shaw* (1861) 2 Sw. & Tr. 517, 6 L.T. 477; *Bromilow v Phillips* (1891) 8 T.L.R. 168; *R. v Craddock, The Times*, March 17, 1875, 4th leader; *Lewis v James* (1887) 3 T.L.R. 527. *Adams v Walsh* [1963] N.Z.L.R. 158.
[21] *Ex p. Halsam* (1740) 2 Atk. 49–50, 26 E.R. 427 (menacing a wife to make her give false evidence); *R. v Hooley* (1898) 79 L.T. 306; *R. v Gray* (1903) 23 N.Z.L.R. 52; *Vine Products Ltd v Green* [1966] Ch. 484 at 496; *Att-Gen v Times Newspapers Ltd* [1974] A.C. 273.
[22] *Re B (JA) (An Infant)* [1965] Ch. 1112; *R. v Greenberg* (1919) 12 L.T. 288. See also *Welby v Still* (1892) 8 T.L.R. 202.
[23] [1976] 1 Q.B. 372 at 390G–H. A distinction was noted between the victimisation cases of *Att-Gen v Butterworth* [1963] 1 Q.B. 696 and *Chapman v Honig* [1963] 2 Q.B. 502 on the one hand, which concerned witnesses, and *Webster v Bakewell RDC* [1916] 1 Ch. 300 on the other, which related to a litigant who had started proceedings. The position of litigants is considered separately at para.11–276 *et seq.*
[24] [1916] 1 Ch. 300, discussed at paras 11–289 *et seq.*
[25] *The Times*, April 23, 1986 (Lexis), discussed at para.11–282.

2. The relevance of timing

11-218 One difficulty is whether the principle applies in relation to persons who *may* be called as witnesses either in proceedings that are already in being or in future proceedings not yet begun. In the latter case, it may be necessary to show, before the court's jurisdiction in contempt can be brought to bear, that such contingent proceedings are "virtually certain" to be commenced.[26] Alternatively, it may suffice to establish no more than that such proceedings are "on the cards".[27] This difficulty is one that arises acutely in the context of "cheque-book journalism".[28]

11-219 A separate distinction may be drawn between a witness who is yet to give evidence and one who has actually begun to testify. In *R. v Kellett*[29] Stephenson L.J. said that the limits of legitimate approach to a witness who has actually given his evidence, or some part of it, in a court of law may be stricter than approaches to a potential witness. This distinction may at first seem somewhat surprising, in the sense that once a witness has given evidence any approach or persuasion cannot impact upon the particular proceedings. On the other hand, it may be that what Stephenson L.J. had in mind was that some degree of private persuasion is regarded as legitimate whereas, once the proceedings are over, there is no apparently respectable reason for making any such approach to a witness.

11-220 It is necessary also to consider the possibility of a misconception on the part of the communicator. Suppose, for example, that he mistakenly believes that the person he is addressing is a potential witness in existing proceedings, and therefore his attempt to interfere with the administration of justice has been misdirected. This would almost certainly not qualify as contempt, since it would not appear that there is conduct sufficiently connected with the administration of justice to constitute the *actus reus* of contempt. It has already been pointed out[30] that there is no scope, at least since the Criminal Attempts Act 1981, for the concept of attempted contempt as such. Where no proceedings are actually in existence, it is perhaps more likely that any attempt to bring pressure to bear upon such a person would be dealt with as an attempt to pervert the course of justice.

11-221 The problem is illustrated by the facts of *R. v Panayiotou*,[31] where an accused person approached a rape victim with an offer of payment. The woman had made a statement to the police complaining that a man had raped her. Before he had been charged, the woman was offered money to withdraw the allegation. The Court of Appeal held that she was a potential witness, and therefore the offer of payment rendered the defendant and an accomplice guilty of the offence of conspiracy to pervert the course of justice.

---

[26] *Att-Gen v News Group Newspapers plc* [1989] 1 Q.B. 110.
[27] See *Att-Gen v Sport Newspapers Ltd* [1991] 1 W.L.R. 1194, [1992] 1 All E.R. 503, DC, and also paras 5–96 *et seq.*
[28] para.11–264.
[29] [1976] 1 Q.B. 372 at 389H.
[30] paras 11–14 *et seq.*
[31] [1973] 1 W.L.R. 1032, [1973] 3 All E.R. 112.

11–222 The fact that the witness, happening also to be the complainant, could have brought a private prosecution herself made no difference to his liability, since by the time when the alleged offer was made, it was no longer in the woman's power to decide whether or not there should be a prosecution; once she had placed the matter in the hands of the police her effective role was that of a witness.[32] There is no doubt of the public interest in detecting and punishing such conduct. Indeed, unless the law were to take action in such cases, once discovered, such activities would often go unpunished, as the individual concerned might be reluctant to take the necessary steps to complain or initiate proceedings.

11–223 Care needs to be taken with the conclusions to be drawn from this decision, since the law of contempt was not specifically considered. It is possible that different policy considerations apply, and that these two branches of the law may yield different answers. The concept of "the course of justice" for the purposes of conspiracy to pervert is wide enough to embrace preliminary enquiries by the police. The law of contempt ought not, however, at least in the view of Windeyer J.,[33] to concern itself with perceived risks to particular proceedings unless and until such proceedings come into existence. He was wary of the concept of "contingent contempt".

11–224 It is unnecessary for the purpose of establishing contempt of this kind to show that matters have progressed so far as the serving of any process compelling the witness's attendance. The "witness" and his or her evidence are embraced by this branch of the law even before that stage is reached. Thus in *Clements v Williams*[34] someone kept a potential witness out of the way so that service could not be effected, and was held to be in contempt.

11–225 In *Re B (JA) (An Infant)*[35] Cross J. was prepared to treat as being within the scope of the common law rule someone who was "very likely" to give evidence. Nor does it seem to matter that, in the event, it can be demonstrated that the witness did not give evidence,[36] because, as in all areas of the law of contempt, the conduct has to be judged as at the date of the *actus reus*.[37]

---

[32] It having been explained by Lord Diplock in *Att-Gen v Times Newspapers Ltd* [1974] A.C. 273 at 319 and Stephenson L.J. in *R. v Kellett* [1976] 1 Q.B. 372 at 390G–H that the scope for persuasion of a party is greater than in the case of someone who is merely a witness, provided the means used are in themselves not objectionable. See also *Att-Gen v Martin (Peter), The Times*, April 23, 1986 (Lexis), with regard to a private prosecutor, discussed at paras 11–282 *et seq*. The court in *R. v Panayiotou* also held that the abolition of misprision and compounding a felony by ss.4 and 5 of the Criminal Law Act 1967 had not affected the common law in relation to perverting the course of justice: [1973] 1 W.L.R. at 1035H, [1973] 3 All E.R. 112 at 116b–d.
[33] *James v Robinson* (1963) 109 C.L.R. 593. But see *Att-Gen v Sport Newspapers Ltd* [1991] 1 W.L.R. 1194, [1992] 1 All E.R. 503, DC. See too paras 5–87 *et seq*.
[34] (1836) 2 Scott 814.
[35] [1965] Ch. 1112 at 1122.
[36] *R. v Grimes* [1968] 3 All E.R. 179.
[37] See, *e.g. Att-Gen v English* [1983] 1 A.C. 116 at 141F–G, Lord Diplock and *Att-Gen v Guardian Newspapers Ltd (No.3)* [1992] 1 W.L.R. 874 at 885E. See also *Att-Gen v Times Newspapers Ltd* [1990] T.L.R. 158, CA (Lexis); *Att-Gen v MGN Ltd* [1997] 1 W.L.R. 926, [1997] 1 All E.R. 456.

3. The continuing relevance of the common law

11–226 It may be asked to what extent the common law of contempt remains of relevance in this field, given Parliament's introduction of the criminal offence under s.51 of the 1994 Act.[38] There are, however, certain respects in which these provisions will have no application. It is significant that s.51 does not apply in the following circumstances:

(a) It has no application to witnesses or potential witnesses in civil proceedings.

(b) It does not appear to apply to persuasion falling short of intimidation.

(c) It has no relevance in the context of people who may be legitimately described as "potential witnesses", even though they have not yet reached the stage of helping police with their enquiries.

4. The interrelationship of motive and means

11–227 Whether an attempt to persuade a witness will be treated as contempt may depend upon similar considerations to those addressed in *R. v Kellett*,[39] namely whether (a) the accused's purpose was that the witness should give true evidence or otherwise, and (b) the means of persuasion employed could be characterised by the rather subjective and imprecise term "improper".

11–228 The Court of Appeal considered whether it could be a defence to a charge of attempting to pervert the course of justice that the defendant was merely trying to persuade a false or mistaken witness to tell the truth. Stephenson L.J. said[40]:

> "... we do not consider it fortuitous that there is no case in the books, as far as we know, which supports the extreme view indicated by some of the textbook statements that *any* interference with a witness is an attempt to pervert the course of justice. That would make a man guilty of this offence if he went privately to a witness who had made a false statement and by reasoned argument supported by material facts and documents tried to dissuade him from committing perjury and to persuade him to retract lies and tell the truth ...
>
> There is ... no warrant in the cases for going so far. In *Rex v Bishop of Lincoln*[41] one of the charges was tampering with the King's witnesses, which the Attorney-General, Sir John Banks, summarised in this way, at p.782:
>
> > '... a heap of offences, all tending to the subversion of public justice; a labouring, tampering, suborning, seducing and sending away of the King's witnesses to

---

[38] para.11–145. But see the Criminal Justice and Police Act 2001, discussed at para.11–150.
[39] [1976] 1 Q.B. 372. Although the decision principally concerned the law governing perverting the course of justice, counsel for the Crown was said to have "conceded" that the appellant was guilty of contempt; but the court also noted that the authorities then gave little or no guidance as to the circumstances in which interference with a witness might amount to a contempt of court (see 384B).
[40] [1976] 1 Q.B. 372 at 386–8.
[41] (1637) 3 State Tr. 770.

suppress the truth, to swear against the truth, and to cause witnesses to make retraction . . .'

The speeches in the Star Chamber bear out what was there said: the truth of what the witnesses were to say was not irrelevant to the charges . . .
And Lord Coventry . . . used words which are worth quoting . . . :

'Now it may be, said he, may not a man meddle, nor question with a witness? Yes, but with certain limitations, for else, if the witnesses be made and corrupted, the jurors and judges both of them may be abused; and if that witnesses may be led and instructed by questions, or the like, it comes all to one as subornation . . . when a man shall alter the testimony of a witness, and cause him to decline from the truth, whether it be by threats, promises, or rewards, it hath ever been much disallowed, and he that attempts the same is censurable, though perhaps he effects it not . . . '

With this authority in mind we would not consider that the offence of attempting to pervert the course of justice would necessarily be committed by a person who tried to persuade a false witness, or even a witness he believed to be false, to speak the truth or to refrain from giving false evidence."

5. *"Improper" means or pressure*

Thus, it would appear in principle to constitute also a common law contempt for a person to seek to persuade a witness to give false evidence; but it would probably not be contempt to seek to persuade such a person to tell the truth, except perhaps where unlawful or improper means are used.[42]

11–229

So far as the law governing perverting the course of justice is concerned, even if the aim is to persuade the witness to tell the truth, improper means must not be used to attain that end.[43] It is not so clear to what extent the use of unlawful or improper means, in such circumstances, would necessarily also be treated specifically as a contempt.

11–230

It seems from *Att-Gen v Times Newspapers Ltd*[44] and from *R. v Kellett*[45] that greater latitude may be permitted so far as exerting influence upon litigants is concerned than is the case with those who are merely witnesses. Even in relation to litigants, however, those authorities clearly suggest that "improper pressure" (falling short of illegality) may not be used. *A fortiori*, therefore, if pressure that would count as "improper" when used against a litigant were directed towards a witness, it would seem to amount to contempt.

11–231

A question may arise at some stage as to whether it is the law that *all* unlawful means of persuasion would give rise to contempt of court. Suppose, for example, that unlawful drugs were offered to a witness with a view to persuading him or

11–232

---

[42] *R. v Kellett* [1976] 1 Q.B. 372 at 388C. See also *R. v Johnson* (1678) 2 Show. K.B. 1, 89 E.R. 753; *R. v Toney; Ali (Tanveer)* [1993] 1 W.L.R. 364, [1993] 2 All E.R. 409; *Att-Gen v Martin (Peter) The Times*, April 23, 1986 (Lexis) a case about pressure exerted upon a private prosecutor, although he might well have been a witness as well: see para.11–282.
[43] See, *e.g.* the summary of principles in *R. v Toney; Ali (Tanveer)* [1993] 1 W.L.R. 364, 2 All E.R. 409, cited at para.11–243.
[44] [1974] A.C. 273 at 313.
[45] [1976] 1 Q.B. 372.

11-232 CHAPTER 11—INTERFERENCE WITH ADMINISTRATION OF JUSTICE

her to give evidence which was believed (by the alleged contemnor) to be truthful. It would be arguable that such conduct does not require to be categorised as contempt of court, as well as being subject to the law governing the supply of drugs.

11-233 A further difficulty arises if it is sought to persuade a witness to give what is, objectively judged, false evidence in circumstances where the potential contemnor actually believes that it represents the truth. In the light of the most recent authorities on *mens rea*,[46] it would seem that what the person intended (*i.e.* persuading a witness to tell the truth) would not in itself be objectionable; the *mens rea* for contempt of court would not be present. Furthermore, at least if there were no intimidation or other improper pressure upon the person concerned, there may be no need from the point of view of public policy to proceed by way of contempt. This would appear also to be consistent with the remarks of Stephenson L.J. in *Kellett* to the effect that it would not necessarily be an attempt to pervert the course of justice for someone to try to persuade a witness he *believed* to be about to give false evidence to refrain from giving it.

11-234 The concept of "improper pressure" was also considered by the Court of Appeal, specifically in the context of s.51 of the Criminal Justice and Public Order Act 1994, in *R. v Patrascu*[47]:

"In our judgment, pressure to change evidence alone is insufficient. Pressure alone might be unexceptionable and entirely proper, at least if applied in the honest belief, for instance, that what was sought was evidence which would be truthful. Alternatively, pressure might be improper, but lack any element of intimidation, for example a bribe. For a person to intimidate another person, the pressure must put the victim in some fear, or, if it does not, there must nevertheless be an element of threat or violence such that the pressure is improper pressure. Mere pressure is insufficient".

6. *Attempts to "warp the minds" of possible witnesses*

11-235 Even where there is no element of intimidation, circumstances may arise in which attempts to persuade witnesses or potential witnesses are regarded as unacceptable and as constituting contempt. Although it was observed in *R. v Kellett*[48] that some text book writers had suggested that *any* interference with the witness would be an attempt to pervert the course of justice, the Court of Appeal regarded this as an "extreme view" and commented that there was no warrant in the cases for going so far. Thus the difficulty arises of where to draw the line.

11-236 In *Welby v Still*,[49] Kekewich J. had "not the slightest doubt or hesitation" that the facts before him constituted a serious contempt. There was a motion to commit a solicitor and his son for contempt in circumstances in which the father

---

[46] *R. v Schot and Barclay* [1997] 2 Cr.App.R. 383, (1997) 161 J.P. 473; *Att-Gen v Newspaper Publishing plc* [1997] 1 W.L.R. 926, [1997] 3 All E.R. 159.
[47] [2004] EWCA Crim 2417, [2004] 4 All E.R. 1066 at [18]. See also at paras 11-147 *et seq.*
[48] [1976] 1 Q.B. 372 at 386-7.
[49] (1892) 66 L.T. 523.

was acting as the plaintiff's solicitor in an action in which it was alleged that the defendants (another firm of solicitors) had failed to account for certain monies. The two respondents had written letters to various individuals who were likely to be called as witnesses in the action, and indeed one of them had already been *subpoenaed* by the plaintiff. The letters contained charges against the defendants including, for example, to the effect that their course of conduct had been "systematically dishonest and dishonourable" and that they had "robbed the estate".

Although Kekewich J. took the view that at least some of the recipients would be unlikely to be directly influenced in the slightest degree, he nevertheless observed that " ... one must remember that the human mind is easily influenced, and possibility, not probability, is the foundation of the principle that nothing should be said or done to interfere with the administration of justice". **11–237**

It is possible now to take issue with that statement since, in those forms of contempt where *risk* of interference forms part of the *actus reus*, a modern court would be much more likely to be concerned (even outside the context of the strict liability rule) with a substantial risk of serious prejudice rather than a mere "possibility".[50] Nevertheless, there are some forms of interference which may still be regarded, for reasons of public policy, as being inherently unacceptable even though they may have no chance of achieving the perceived objective. In some forms of contempt, the *actus* seems to become *reus* by reason of its being accompanied by an intention to affect the proceedings, and in particular those cases in which the contempt consists of interference with witnesses prior to the giving of their evidence.[51] Such activity is closely related to the notion of attempt in the criminal law generally and, as has already been observed,[52] it has been recognised in that context by the House of Lords in *R. v Shivpuri*[53] that public policy does indeed sometimes require the criminalisation of attempts to achieve that which is impossible of achievement. It has been said in the context of seeking to interfere with witnesses that the mere fact that no harm has been done " ... is neither here nor there".[54] **11–238**

It may be that underlying this branch of the law is the concern that attempts to persuade witnesses to change their evidence by unacceptable means ought to be rendered unlawful generally because, although some witnesses may have sufficient resolve to remain unmoved by the approach, others may be more vulnerable. What is more, the effect of such attempts may be very difficult to detect. There is arguably therefore a need to render the conduct unlawful largely as a matter of deterrence.[55] **11–239**

---

[50] See Lord Bingham C.J. in *Att-Gen v Newspaper Publishing plc* [1997] 1 W.L.R. 926, [1997] 3 All E.R. 159.
[51] cp. *Kellett* [1976] 1 Q.B. 373 at 392A–B (albeit not a contempt case).
[52] See para.11–14.
[53] [1987] A.C. 1.
[54] *Re B (JA) (An Infant)* [1965] Ch. 1112 at 1123, Cross J.
[55] Similar considerations may explain the principles relating to improper approaches made to judges or magistrates.

11-240 This may be what Kekewich J. had in mind in *Welby v Still*,[56] in that he was not concerned so much with the mere "possibility" of influencing the particular witnesses in the case before him, but rather with the more general possibility of influencing the "weak human mind", as "the ground of the principle upon which the court acts". He addressed the submission that the respondents concerned were merely expressing opinions and did not intend to "warp the minds" of the particular witnesses, but he rejected it. He concluded that the recipients had been selected for the very reason that they were known to be persons who were likely to be witnesses.

7. Contempt by threatening prima facie lawful action

11-241 It may be contempt to threaten to exercise a lawful right against a witness if one of the purposes[57] is to persuade him to change his evidence.[58] When Lord Diplock referred in *Att-Gen v Times Newspapers Ltd*[59] to "unlawful threats", he was not seeking to confine the principle to threats of conduct which would in itself be unlawful.[60] In *R. v Kellett*,[61] the defendant threatened to sue for slander two of his neighbours, who were potential witnesses for his wife in divorce proceedings, but before doing so he invited them to withdraw statements made to an enquiry agent. The Court of Appeal applied as analogous those cases which establish that it is a contempt to seek to exercise a legal right against a witness in order to punish him for what he had already said in court. The conviction was upheld.

11-242 Some element of pressure may nonetheless be legitimate.[62] Pressure which would be permissible at one stage of proceedings may be improper at another; what would be proper for a friend or relative may cross over into impropriety or oppression coming from a person of influence or authority. Such questions, in the context of attempting to pervert the course of justice, will generally be for the jury to determine on the facts of the particular case. In the words of Stephenson L.J.[63]:

> "The decision will depend on all the circumstances of the case, including not merely the method of interfering, but the time when it is done, the relationship between the person

---

[56] (1892) 66 L.T. 523.
[57] It is not necessary that it should be the *sole* motive: see, *e.g. Att-Gen v Butterworth* [1963] 1 Q.B. 696 at 723, Denning M.R. and 727, Donovan L.J.; *R. v Kellett* [1976] 1 Q.B. 372 at 392A–D. See also *R. v Mohan* [1976] 1 Q.B. 1.
[58] *Rowden v Universities Co-operative Association* (1881) 76 L.T.J. 373. See Lord Denning M.R. in *Att-Gen v Butterworth* [1963] 1 Q.B. at 722, cited at para.11–211, on the conversion of neutral acts into contempts by the presence of *mens rea*. See also paras 11–7 *et seq.*
[59] [1974] A.C. 274 at 313D.
[60] See Glidewell L.J. in *Att-Gen v Martin (Peter)*, *The Times*, April 23, 1986 (Lexis), discussed at paras 11–282 *et seq.*
[61] [1976] 1 Q.B. 372, CA. This was a case concerning allegations of attempting to pervert the course of justice, but the discussion is nonetheless valuable in the context of contempt. It had in fact been conceded by counsel that the defendant was guilty of contempt: *ibid.* at 386A.
[62] [1976] 1 Q.B. at 392G–393B.
[63] *ibid.*, at 392G–H.

interfering and the witness and the nature of the proceedings in which the evidence is being given."

In *R. v Toney*[64] the Court of Appeal gave a helpful summary, which, although concerned directly with perverting the course of justice, would probably be equally valid in the context of common law contempt:

11–243

"We can now summarise the position as follows. (1) In the great majority of cases of perverting the course of justice by interfering with a witness the *actus reus* will be accompanied by unlawful means such as threats, bribery or improper pressure. (2) The use of unlawful means is not however an essential ingredient in the offence. . . . (3) In cases where the defendant might otherwise have a defence of lawful excuse, for example where his purpose is to persuade a false witness, or a witness he believes to be false, not to commit perjury, he will nevertheless be liable if he employs unlawful means. (4) 'Unlawful means' in this context includes a threat to do an otherwise lawful act or to exercise a legal right. (5) In all cases the prosecution must prove the necessary intent."[65]

8. The significance of intimidation

It appears that it is the element of intimidation which is often regarded as essential in the context of attempting to pervert the course of justice, and no doubt this would also apply in that of contempt. It would be no excuse, where the conduct can be so characterised, that it was believed that the witness concerned was going to give false evidence. Reference was made by Stephenson L.J. in *R. v Kellett* to the case of *Shaw v Shaw*,[66] where the respondent to a divorce suit visited a former servant and threatened her with prosecution for perjury if she gave evidence of his cruelty to his wife.[67] It had been found as a fact that he had the intention of intimidating her and preventing her from giving evidence, and this was held to have been a contempt.

11–244

Stephenson L.J. described this conduct as being clearly not only a contempt but an attempt to pervert the course of justice. He went on to observe:

11–245

" . . . and even if the servant's evidence had been false and the respondent had believed that she might be prosecuted for perjury after giving it, the threatening language he used would, in our opinion, have been enough to convict him of the attempt."

---

[64] [1993] 1 W.L.R.364 at 370.
[65] Which, in this context, meant an intention to pervert the course of justice by persuading a witness to change his evidence.
[66] (1862) 2 Sw. & Tr. 517 at 164 E.R. 1097, 6 L.T. 477. See also *Bromilow v Phillips* (1891) 40 W.R. 220, 8 T.L.R. 168 (plaintiff approaching a witness with a uniformed police officer and questioning statements in his affidavit, "in a threatening tone of voice", and suggesting that he had in effect perjured himself). *Bromilow* was referred to as an "intimidation" case by Kekewich J. in *Welby v Still* (1892) 66 L.T. 523, 525. See also *Re B (JA) (An Infant)* [1965] Ch. 1112, where Cross J. imprisoned a man for contempt when he threatened to expose a witness in a wardship case as having given birth to an illegitimate child, with a view to having her expelled from a teacher training college.
[67] cp. *Att-Gen v Martin (Peter), The Times*, April 23, 1986 (Lexis), where the threat was to bring proceedings for malicious prosecution, and it was held by a majority *not* to be contempt.

11–246 The Court of Appeal found support for their opinion in the wording of the Witnesses (Public Inquiries) Protection Act 1892, s.2. In particular, it was thought that acts which constituted the statutory offence *after* evidence had been given might provide a guide to the kinds of conduct which make interference with witnesses illegal at common law *before* evidence is given. It was concluded that anyone who "threatens, or in any way punishes, damnifies or injures, or attempts to punish, damnify or injure any person" would be committing the offence of perverting or attempting to pervert the course of justice before the relevant witness had actually given evidence; what is more, the offence would be committed even if that with which the witness was threatened would, apart from the threat, be in itself a lawful act.

9. *Empty threats*

11–247 The Court of Appeal differed from the trial judge (Lord Widgery C.J.) in expressing the view that it made no difference whether the threat was an empty threat. The jury had been directed that they had to be sure that the defendant was not intending to bring the threatened action for slander, and that he was merely making an empty threat with the purpose of persuading the witnesses not to give evidence. In this respect, it was held that Lord Widgery's direction was too favourable to the defendant.

10. *The nature of the* mens rea *required*

11–248 It is clear from *Kellett* that *mens rea* is required, in the sense that at least one of the objectives must have been to intimidate the witness into altering or withdrawing evidence.[68] Any threat or promise, in order to constitute the offence of perverting the course of justice, must be accompanied by the intention of persuading the witness to alter or withhold the evidence.[69] What is especially difficult, therefore, is to establish the role which *mens rea* plays in determining whether, in any given case, the pressure exerted is in fact to be classified as improper.

11–249 For example, the Court of Appeal seem to have accepted that it would not constitute the offence, or for that matter contempt of court, if a person went privately to a witness who had made a false statement and by reasoned argument, supported by material facts and documents, tried to dissuade the witness from committing perjury, or to persuade him to retract lies and tell the truth.[70]

11–250 The central issue of policy, as Stephenson L.J. pointed out, is whether it is the "course of justice" which has to be protected in every case, or whether it is the justice of the *outcome* in the particular case. On the former view,[71] it would be an offence even to seek to influence a witness who was going otherwise to tell

---

[68] [1976] 1 Q.B. at 392A–D.
[69] [1976] 1 Q.B. at 393A–B.
[70] [1976] Q.B. 372 at 386G–H and 388B–C.
[71] See, *e.g.* the remarks of Oliver L.J. cited at para.11–278 below.

lies. The argument that persuasion of a witness can be justified because the particular defendant happens to have truth on his side would be to confuse the course of justice with the result arrived at.[72] Moreover, so the argument runs, the potential evidence of the witness should not be affected by influences outside the recognised means, such as by being tested upon oath in cross-examination.

The Court of Appeal concentrated in *Kellett* upon distinguishing proper from "improper" *means*. Less attention was paid to the nature of the *mens rea* required. "Even if the intention of the meddler with a witness is to prevent perjury and injustice, he commits the offence if he meddles by unlawful means".[73] This would appear to suggest that, if the means used are otherwise regarded as acceptable, an alleged contemnor may rely upon the fact that, in seeking to persuade a witness to change evidence, he had believed, albeit mistakenly, that he was seeking to prevent an injustice. If this is so, it would not matter where, objectively judged, the justice of the particular case might lie (or where, objectively judged, the truth lay). 11–251

There is no problem if the court considers that the conduct in question was itself "improper", in the sense, for example, of involving intimidation. The critical question is whether the mistaken state of mind will enable an alleged contemnor to escape liability if he has resorted to reasoned argument only. 11–252

The approach adopted in *Welby v Still* might suggest that the conduct could still be characterised as "intended to warp" the mind of the witness even though the motive might be actually to prevent an injustice. In *R. v Silverman*[74] in the Ontario Court of Appeal, however, where the potential witness had given evidence at a preliminary hearing, MacLaren J.A. said: 11–253

"Even the most desirable end cannot justify the employment of corrupt means. The fountain of justice should be kept pure and not be corrupted at its source. It was quite open to the accused, believing, as he did, in the innocence of his brother, to shew to Weller, if he could, such evidence or facts as might convince him that he had been mistaken in his previous testimony."

It is suggested in the light of this reasoning, and the decisions in *Kellett* and *Att-Gen v Martin (Peter)*,[75] that the court will indeed concentrate on the means deployed and, if the method is itself unobjectionable, the alleged contemnor will *not* be found liable for contempt despite having formed a mistaken view as to where the truth lies. 11–254

---

[72] *R. v Kellett* [1976] 1 Q.B. 372 at 387A–C. See also *R. v Tibbits and Windust* [1902] 1 K.B. 77, 88, Lord Alverstone C.J.
[73] 388C–D.
[74] (1908) 17 O.L.R. 248 at 252. See also Osler J.A. at 250. This was a decision upon s.180a of the Criminal Code, although all the judges of the Court of Appeal treated the offence as a common law misdemeanour.
[75] *The Times*, April 23, 1986 (Lexis). See para.11–282.

11. Required knowledge as to status of witness

11–255 The further question remains, however, as to what degree of knowledge the alleged contemnor must be shown to have had as to the status of the person to whom his approach is addressed; in particular, as to whether that person could be characterised, at the time of the approach, as an actual or potential witness.

11–256 In *Re B (JA) (An Infant)*[76] Cross J. was satisfied on the facts that the alleged contemnor knew that the person he threatened was to be a witness in pending proceedings. However he added:

> "Even if I were not satisfied on that, however, it would make no difference, because it is not, as I understand the law, necessary in these cases that the alleged contemnor should know that the person to whom he is uttering a threat has made a statement or made up his mind to give evidence. It is quite sufficient that he should know that he is a potential witness—a person who, unless prevented, will very likely give evidence."[77]

11–257 This statement gives rise to difficulty, especially given the criminal context and the generally acknowledged need to be clear as to what behaviour or state of mind will be required as ingredients of a criminal offence.[78] It is now also to be borne in mind that certainty is an important consideration in the criminal context in the light of Art.7 of the European Convention.[79] In some cases, it would surely require a sophisticated knowledge of the law or of the facts to be able to come to a conclusion as to whether or not a particular individual would have evidence to give that was relevant and cogent. It so happens, however, that in the case before Cross J., even if the alleged contemnor had not been expressly told that the girl in question was going to give evidence, it would have been obvious to him because of the particular circumstances of the case. It is questionable whether the broader proposition of Cross J. would necessarily be followed in circumstances where the status of the person approached, as a potential witness, was less obvious.

11–258 Attention would have to be paid to the remark of Bingham L.J. in *Att-Gen v Sport Newspapers Ltd*[80] to the effect that an inference of intention (to interfere with the administration of justice) should only be drawn from the surrounding circumstances when it was "little short of overwhelming".[81] Also, it would be important to bear in mind the cases in which newspaper editors have been disbelieved on their oaths as to their intention, in publication cases, where the

---

[76] [1965] Ch. 1112.
[77] *ibid.* at 1122–3.
[78] *Sunday Times v United Kingdom* (1979) 2 E.H.R.R. 245 at 271. For other examples of problematic formulations of *mens rea* in contempt, see also *Dobson v Hastings* [1992] Ch. 394, discussed at paras 2–183 *et seq.* and *Camelot Group plc v Centaur Communications Ltd* [1999] Q.B. 124 at paras 9–9 *et seq.*
[79] See para.2–169 *et seq.*
[80] [1991] 1 W.L.R. 1194 at 1208F, [1992] 1 All E.R. 503 at 516g–j.
[81] See also *Att-Gen v Judd* [1995] C.O.D. 15 where it was said that these words were equally applicable in cases of non-publication contempt.

court has only been prepared to come to such a conclusion on the basis that the editor concerned *must have* intended the consequences of his act.[82]

D. Payment of witnesses (whether actual or potential)

The legal implications of payments or offers of payment to witnesses require detailed consideration. A witness has for a long time been recognised as being entitled to out-of-pocket expenses incurred in attending court.[83] A further consideration that needs to be borne in mind is that, as a matter of convention, it is accepted that expert witnesses may be paid a fee for their attendance and expertise over and above their expenses.[84] It is also permissible, in principle, to offer to indemnify a witness for any loss he has suffered or will genuinely suffer by his attendance at court.[85]

Difficulty can arise, however, if the amount appears to be excessive for any of these legitimate purposes. The greater the sum, the more suspicion may be aroused on the part of a party, or the court, as to the true purpose of the payment. What would be impermissible would be the purchase of evidence, at least outside the established convention relating to experts, because of the risk that the evidence will be tailored as a result of the payment. While these generalities of public policy are relatively easy to state, what is sometimes more difficult is to decide on particular facts whether the boundary has been crossed between that which is permissible and that which is regarded as objectionable.

Some early cases appeared to suggest that *any* offer or payment of reward for giving evidence was objectionable, whether it was intended that the witness should give true or false evidence.[86] However, in *Plating Company v Farquharson*[87] an advertisement appeared offering a £100 reward to anyone who could produce documentary evidence that nickel plating was done before 1869. The Court of Appeal held that no contempt was committed, there being a *bona fide* attempt to obtain evidence.[88]

By contrast, in *Re Hooley*[89] a bribe was offered to a witness with a view to his withdrawing evidence about the offerors. Wright J. not surprisingly held this to

---

[82] See, *e.g. Att-Gen v News Group Newspapers plc* [1989] 1 Q.B. 110; *Att-Gen v Newspaper Publishing plc* [1990] T.L.R. 158, CA (Lexis); *Official Solicitor v News Group Newspapers plc* [1994] 2 F.L.R. 174.
[83] *Horne v Smith* (1815) 6 Taunt. 9, 132 E.R. 854; *Webb v Page* (1843) 1 Car. & Kir. 23, 174 E.R. 695.
[84] para.11–104.
[85] *Collins v Godefroy* (1831) 1 B. & Ad. 950, 109 E.R. 1040; *The Ibis VI* [1921] P. 255; *Kwan Cheuk-Yin and Lam Wong Fai* [1973] H.K.L.R. 335.
[86] *Bishop of Lincoln's Case* (1637) 3 State Trials 770 at 784–6 and 801; *Pool v Sacheverel* (1720) 1 P. Wms.675, 24 E.R. 565.
[87] (1881) 17 Ch. D. 49.
[88] The same principle was applied in *Butler v Butler* (1888) 13 P.D. 73, but on the facts the advertisement was held not to be a *bona fide* attempt to obtain evidence. The case has also been followed more recently in the Federal Court of Australia: *Willshire-Smith v Votino Bros Pty Ltd* (1992) A.Crim.R. 261.
[89] (1898) 79 L.T. 306, 15 T.L.R. 16. See also *R. v Bromell* [1996] T.L.R. 67.

be a contempt. Indeed, the Court of Appeal in *R. v Kellett*[90] went so far as to hold that it would be a perversion of the course of justice if a witness were persuaded to withhold or alter evidence "through affection, fear, gain, reward, or the hope or promise thereof" (in the words of the oath which used to be administered to the foreman of a grand jury). Any such acts would therefore be likely to be regarded as "improper", irrespective of the end sought to be achieved by the offeror.

11–263   Sometimes, it may not be known whether there is a witness available or, where one is known to exist, what are his whereabouts or identity. Thus, it may be necessary to advertise and to offer an inducement to come forward; this common practice is surely unobjectionable.[91] Even in those circumstances, however, the offer of a substantial reward might create the risk that a person would come forward and give false evidence. In such a case, a witness could expect to be cross-examined closely as to his motives, but it is unlikely that the placing of the advertisement would be characterised as being in contempt or as attempting to pervert the course of justice. On the other hand, where a witness's whereabouts are known, it would be more difficult to justify an offer of payment to secure attendance, since the witness can (if necessary) be compelled by the usual means.

E. "Cheque-book" journalism[92]

11–264   A separate though connected topic is that of the offer or payment of money to a witness by a newspaper, before giving evidence, for exclusive rights to the story after the trial is over. Sometimes in the past the amount to be paid was contingent upon the result of the proceedings,[93] but there is a considerable risk that such an arrangement would be construed as tainting the witness's evidence and thus creating a risk of interference with the administration of justice. In such a situation a court might readily infer the requisite *mens rea* and find the offeror in contempt.[94] Even where the payment is not expressed to be contingent, the offer of a large sum might be thought to be objectionable as creating such a risk, and the court could again infer the necessary state of mind.

11–265   The Phillimore Committee (referring to the "Moors Murders" case in 1966)[95] expressed disquiet about payment or other rewards to witnesses, commonly

---

[90] [1976] 1 Q.B. 372 at 388D–E.
[91] It is obviously important that care be taken in giving publicity to any statement obtained as a result of the advertisement, particularly if the effect of a potential witness's statement goes to a central issue in the case.
[92] See generally D. Lanham, "Payment of Witnesses and Contempt of Court" [1975] Crim. L.R. 144.
[93] See para.11 of the Lord Chancellor's Department Consultation paper, *Payments to Witnesses*, October 1996, where mention was made of the agreement by *The Sunday Telegraph*, in relation to the trial of Jeremy Thorpe in 1978, to pay a prosecution witness (Peter Bessell) an additional £25,000 if his evidence led to a conviction.
[94] Discussed further at para.11–271.
[95] For the facts of the case, see the summary contained in *R. v Secretary of State for the Home Department Ex p. Hindley* [1998] Q.B 751. The case went to the Court of Appeal and the House of Lords: [2001] 1 A.C. 410.

referred to as "cheque book journalism".[96] The Committee considered that it lacked information about the prevalence of the practice. Accordingly, it suggested that an enquiry should be carried out and consideration given to the drafting of a criminal offence. The Committee did express the view that "it would be going too far to prohibit all offers to witnesses, especially those which are not contingent upon the outcome of the case." Nor was any specific offence to be found subsequently in the Law Commission's draft proposals,[97] and there has been no enactment so far.

An attempt has been made to regulate the practice, however, in the voluntary Code sought to be implemented by the Press Complaints Commission,[98] para.15 of which provides as follows:

"Witness payments in criminal trials
i) No payment or offer of payment to a witness—or any person who may reasonably be expected to be called as a witness—should be made in any case once proceedings are active as defined by the Contempt of Court Act 1981. This prohibition lasts until the suspect has been freed unconditionally by police without charge or bail or the proceedings are otherwise discontinued; or has entered a guilty plea to the court; or, in the event of a not guilty plea, the court has announced its verdict. ii) Where proceedings are not yet active but are likely and foreseeable, editors must not make or offer payment to any person who may reasonably be expected to be called as a witness, unless the information concerned ought demonstrably to be published in the public interest and there is an over-riding need to make or promise payment for this to be done; and all reasonable steps have been taken to ensure no financial dealings influence the evidence those witnesses give. In no circumstances should such payment be conditional on the outcome of a trial. iii) Any payment or offer of payment made to a person later cited to give evidence in proceedings must be disclosed to the prosecution and defence. The witness must be advised of this requirement."

(The Commission Code recognises that there may be some exceptions to the principles set out in subparagraphs (ii) and (iii) above where they can be "demonstrated to be in the public interest".) The wording has changed significantly on a number of occasions (by way of expansion and clarification) since the rule was originally promulgated.

The problem was brought sharply into focus by concerns about payments made or offered to witnesses and potential witnesses in the Rosemary West trial at Winchester in October and November 1995.[99] There were calls for legislation, along the lines of the Code, to ban *any* payments to witnesses or potential witnesses. Later, in June 2003, a criminal trial collapsed in which five men had

---

[96] paras 56 and 78–79.
[97] Law Com. No.96, 1979.
[98] The wording quoted dates from June 2004. The Press Complaints Commission is a voluntary body set up in January 1991 following the recommendations of the Calcutt Committee on Privacy in June 1990 (Cm. 1102); see Robertson and Nicol, *Media Law* (4th ed., 2002) ch.14. For a critique of the methods of the Commission, see also Sir L. Blom-Cooper Q.C. and L. R. Pruitt, "Privacy Jurisprudence of the Press Complaints Commission" (1994) Anglo-American Law R. 133; L. Blom-Cooper, "Cheque-book Journalism on Display" [2003] P.L. 378.
[99] *R. v West* [1996] 2 Cr.App.R. 374.

been accused of plotting to kidnap the wife of a well known footballer after it was revealed that a Sunday newspaper had paid £10,000 to a convicted criminal who happened to be the main prosecution witness.[1] This was at a time when the House of Commons Culture, Media and Sport Select Committee was considering proposals on regulating the media.[2]

11–268   There are obvious difficulties about any legislative proposal banning such payments to witnesses, both of practice and principle. As the Phillimore Committee pointed out, it would be difficult to justify a blanket ban on such payments, and therefore the draftsman would need to cater for a variety of situations, which might lead to detailed and artificial distinctions having to be drawn. For example, it would be necessary to define who are "potential witnesses", and at what stage they are to be so classified. This would have caused great difficulty in the West case itself, since payment was there made long before it became apparent that some of the recipients might be witnesses in the case.

11–269   The legislature would also need to address the question of whether the proceedings were required to be "active" at the time of the offer, or whether some other *terminus a quo* would be appropriate; and whether any payments could be made *before* the evidence was to be given. A similar point can be made in relation to "imminence" as that already made with regard to the word "potential". If proceedings have not actually commenced, it would be difficult to establish liability on the basis of payments made to people who might become witnesses in potential or "contingent" proceedings.[3] Matters have to be judged at the time the putative offence was committed; it would seem unlikely that Parliament could define any offence in terms such that a payment would be illegal in circumstances in which the contingent criminal proceedings never in fact took place.

11–270   People who have suffered as victims of serious criminal offences may often be permanently damaged and unable to provide for themselves; it seems hard that they should be prevented from receiving some payment where a newspaper is willing to pay for their stories, perhaps the only means of sustenance available to them. The indiscriminate prohibition of such transactions would require to be justified by some tangible imperative of public policy. If there is no demonstrable risk to the administration of justice, it is difficult to see what other justification there could be for the intervention of the criminal law.

11–271   The perennial problem of *mens rea* would also arise. The primary purpose of the newspaper offering the payment will generally be to obtain the story on an "exclusive" basis. The contractual arrangements will often be carefully drafted so as to avoid giving the impression that there is any link between the payment and either the content of the witness's evidence or the outcome of the case. It

---

[1] *The Times*, June 6, 2003.
[2] Culture, Media and Sport Committee, *Privacy and Media Intrusion*, Fifth Report of Session 2002–03, HC 458–1 (June 16, 2003). For the Government's reply, see Cm 5785.
[3] To use a convenient term from the judgment of Windeyer J. in *James v Robinson* (1963) 109 C.L.R. 593, discussed at para.5–89.

would therefore be very difficult to show an intention to interfere with the administration of justice. Recklessness has been held by the Court of Appeal not to be sufficient to establish liability for contempt of court, at least in the context of publication contempts.[4] A question would arise therefore, to be determined by the legislature, as to whether recklessness as to any risk of interference with the course of justice should nevertheless be sufficient in the case of payments of the kind to which objection is taken.

Possible reform of "cheque-book journalism"

In October 1996, the Lord Chancellor's Department published a consultation paper,[5] prompted in particular by the remarks of Lord Taylor C.J. in *R. v West*.[6] This raised a number of issues, including whether any sanctions should be by way of specifically designed offences or by reference to the existing law of contempt of court. Other questions posed were whether it should be necessary to establish proof of actual prejudice, to require proof of a *risk* of prejudice only, or to proceed on the basis that prejudice may be assumed to be inherent, and thus that no proof of risk to any particular proceedings should be required. It was also under consideration whether the recipient of any such payment should be made liable, and as to the nature of the *mens rea* required, if any. Various possible defences were canvassed, including a so-called "public interest" defence, and the question was raised whether any such legislation should apply only in respect of payments to witnesses in criminal proceedings or in civil cases also.

11–272

One factor which would surely have to be taken into account in any such proposals for legislation would be that the accounts of witnesses to whom payments are made are generally intended for publication in magazines and newspapers. The European Court of Human Rights could easily therefore construe any such restriction as giving rise to a fetter on freedom of speech. In these circumstances, any such limitation should be justified by reference to the specific exemptions listed in Art.10(2) and, in particular, whether it could be demonstrated to be necessary in a democratic society for any such purpose.

11–273

In February 1998 the Lord Chancellor announced[7] that the government had accepted in principle a recommendation of the National Heritage Committee that "there should be legislation forbidding payments to witnesses". He added that:

11–274

"The purpose of legislation will be to help ensure that trials remain fair. Media coverage of the trial itself will be unaffected. But payments to witnesses, or potential witnesses,[8] by the media run a real risk of encouraging witnesses to exaggerate their

---

[4] See, *e.g. Att-Gen v Newspaper Publishing plc* [1988] Ch. 333 at 382, Lloyd L.J.; see also *Att-Gen v News Group Newspapers plc* [1989] Q.B. 110 at 128, Watkins L.J.
[5] *Payments to Witnesses*.
[6] [1996] 2 Cr.App.R. 374.
[7] Replying to a Parliamentary question on February 27. See also Lord Chancellor's Department Press Notice 48/98. The recommendation was contained in the National Heritage Committee's Report, *Press Activity Affecting Court Cases*, January 1997.
[8] See para.11–268 for a discussion of the difficulties of definition.

evidence to make it more newsworthy, or to withhold relevant evidence from the court and make it available as an exclusive to a newspaper.

If the existence of a media contract emerges in court, juries may wonder if the witness's evidence has been affected by the contract. This may not be the case, but suspicion that it is could be enough to cause a miscarriage of justice."

11–275 Another consultation paper was issued by the Lord Chancellor on the same subject in March 2002, with a view to discussing the detail, rather than the principle, of proposed legislation to prevent payments to witnesses or potential witnesses. Yet on August 29 of the same year, following strong representations by media organisations, it was announced once again that the matter would be left to self-regulation.[9] The Culture, Media and Sport Committee of the House of Commons deprecated the practice of making payments to police officers, and recommended that codes of practice should be altered to highlight the fact that such payments were unlawful.[10] But the government took the view that the existing law of corruption was sufficiently comprehensive to combat such practices.[11]

X. COMMON LAW: LITIGANTS AND PARTIES

11–276 Reference has already been made to the different tests applicable as between witnesses and parties, so far as pressure or persuasion is concerned.[12] There is more legitimate scope for seeking to persuade a party to litigation on such matters as whether a claim or defence should be pursued, or as to the terms upon which settlement should be reached. These factors have no application to witnesses, unless they happen also to be parties.

11–277 Media pressure brought to bear on litigants is a matter which falls for consideration in chapters 4 and 5. The Phillimore Committee expressed agreement with the views of Lord Cross of Chelsea in *Att-Gen v Times Newspapers Ltd*[13] and doubted "whether it is easy or logical to draw a distinction between public and private pressure upon litigants. The difference is only one of degree". The Committee pointed out that Shylock would probably have been more influenced by a private letter from a business associate, saying he would withdraw his business if Shylock proceeded, than by any amount of public obloquy. Nevertheless, because of the clear distinction drawn by Parliament in the 1981 Act between public and private communications, it may be convenient to treat the two issues separately. This chapter is solely concerned with pressure that is brought to bear in circumstances falling outside the strict liability rule and the common law relating to publication contempt.

---

[9] LCD 271/02. See the further press notice LCD 126/03, "Government Welcomes Tighter Media Regulation of Payments to Witnesses."
[10] *Privacy and Media Intrusion* Fifth Report of Session 2002–03, HC 458-1 (June 16, 2003).
[11] For the Government's reply, see Cm 5985, (October 2003), paras 4.35–4.39.
[12] para.11–217.
[13] [1974] A.C. 273 at 325.

A. The considerations of public policy

The same considerations of public policy would appear to be applicable whether the court is concerned with civil or criminal proceedings. Oliver L.J. in *Att-Gen v Times Newspapers Ltd* [14] said (as it happens, in a criminal context):

11–278

"The course of justice is not just concerned with the outcome of proceedings. It is concerned with the whole process of the law, including the freedom of a person accused of a crime to elect, so far as the law permits him to do so, the mode of trial which he prefers and to conduct his defence in the way which seems best to him and to his advisers. Any extraneous factor or external pressure which impedes or restricts that election or that conduct, or which impels a person accused to adopt a course in the conduct of his own defence which he does not wish to adopt, deprives him to an extent of the freedom of choice which the law confers upon him and is, in my judgment, not only a prejudice but a serious prejudice."

This broad statement of principle, however, needs to be reconciled with the recognition of the courts that some degree of persuasion is legitimate.

In *Att-Gen v Times Newspapers Ltd*,[15] Lord Reid observed:

11–279

"I think there is a difference between direct interference with the fair trial of an action and words or conduct which may affect the mind of a litigant. Comment likely to affect the minds of witnesses and of the tribunal must be stopped otherwise the trial may well be unfair. But the fact that a party refrains from seeking to enforce his legal rights in no way prejudices a fair trial, whether the decision is or is not influenced by some third party. There are other weighty reasons for preventing improper influence being brought to bear upon litigants, but they have little to do with the fairness of a trial. There must be absolute prohibition of interference with a fair trial, but beyond that there must be a balancing of interests."

It is impossible to give an exhaustive list of the situations in which persuasion may be legitimate, but advice given by family and friends or professional advisers, in good faith, would clearly be unobjectionable.

B. Pressurising or intimidation

There are obvious limits to what is regarded as legitimate pressure, even so far as parties are concerned. Accordingly, it has been held to be a contempt to threaten a party with personal violence, or exposure in some disreputable way, in order to influence the conduct of a case.[16] Other forms of molestation against parties, their directors or employees, customers or business associates, can also amount to contempt.[17]

11–280

---

[14] *The Times*, February 12, 1983 (Lexis).
[15] [1974] A.C. 273 at 296.
[16] *R. v Redman* (1744) quoted in *R. v Carroll* (1799) 1 Wils. K.B. 75, 95 E.R. 500; *Re Mulock* (1864) 33 L.J. P.M. & A. 205; *Sharland v Sharland* (1885) 1 T.L.R. 492; *Pavlova v Harvey, The Times*, November 27, 1911. Cp. in the context of publication *Att-Gen v Hislop* [1991] 1 Q.B. 514, discussed at para.5–169.
[17] See, *e.g. Dove Group plc and Jaguar Cars Ltd v Hynes* [1993] C.O.D. 174.

11-281   As with threats to witnesses,[18] what seems from the reported cases to be objectionable is the element of intimidation. It would appear that it is no defence that the party at whom the intimidation is directed has stood his ground. In *Smith v Lakeman*,[19] for example, it was held to be a contempt to threaten a party with indictment for perjury and forgery if he continued his action. Reference was made in the letter to the resulting disgrace which would descend upon his family. The mischief was identified by Stuart V.-C. as being "a threat for the purpose of intimidating him as a suitor;" it made no difference whether the threat had its intended effect.[20]

11-282   In *Att-Gen v Martin (Peter)*,[21] a solicitor acting for defendants in criminal proceedings, brought by way of private prosecution, warned the prosecutor that his clients were contemplating, *inter alia*, bringing an action for malicious prosecution. A majority in the Divisional Court were not satisfied to the required standard that such a warning constituted contempt of court.

11-283   The prosecutor was a barrister who objected to the noise created by the use of a barge on the Thames as a helicopter landing pad. He referred what he believed to be an incident of unlawful low flying to the Civil Aviation Authority, which declined to prosecute. He then laid an information and summonses were issued against the pilot and the company concerned. In a series of letters addressed to the barrister, the solicitor for the pilot and the company indicated that, if the prosecution should prove unsuccessful, his clients would (a) seek costs which, given the number of witnesses and the level of legal representation, were likely to be substantial (b) bring a civil action for malicious prosecution and (c) report the barrister to a professional body, apparently with a view to disciplinary proceedings.

11-284   Whereas the court was unanimous that threats made to report him to the disciplinary body *were* an improper means of exerting pressure (the solicitor had admitted as much in the pre-hearing correspondence) and thus constituted contempt, the reference to malicious prosecution was held by a majority to fall on the other side of the line. The threat was said to be "near the boundary

---

[18] See paras 11-244 *et seq*.
[19] (1856) 26 L.J. Ch. 305; see also *R. v Carroll* (1744) 1 Wils. K.B. 75 at 95 E.R. 500. Cp. the comments of Kekewich J., in the context of witnesses, in *Welby v Still* (1892) 66 L.T. 523, para.11-237.
[20] See *Re B (JA) (An Infant)* [1965] Ch. 1112 at 1123, Cross J.; *Willshire-Smith v Votino Bros Pty Ltd* (1992) A. Crim.R. 261, 270, O'Loughlin J. Contrast, however, the rather briefly reported decision of Vinelott J. in *Re A Company, No.001424 of 1983*, *The Times*, June 21, 1984. He appears to have ruled that a respondent, whose conduct had been underhand and dishonourable, was nevertheless *not* in contempt by virtue of having written a letter to the Home Office with the intention of prejudicing the application of an Iraqui national to reside in the United Kingdom and, in turn, of thereby causing him embarrassment in Chancery litigation. The decision was apparently based on the judge's conclusion that he was not satisfied that there was a real risk that the litigation would be seriously prejudiced. In the light of the other authorities cited in this section, and especially the words of Lord Reid cited at para.11-279, it would appear that a judgment as to risk of actual prejudice should not be decisive for this form of contempt.
[21] *The Times*, April 12, 1986 (Lexis).

between what is and what is not improper pressure"[22] and, taking into account that it was for the Attorney to establish the contempt beyond reasonable doubt, the court was not satisfied that the charge was made out.

It is perhaps ironic that the threat of civil proceedings, and their attendant costs which might very well cause anxiety to an individual, was held to be legitimate whereas a completely baseless threat of disciplinary proceedings constituted contempt. It is an illustration of how the court's interpretation of what is "improper" pressure will depend to a large extent upon the facts of the case and the terms and manner of the threat in question. The emphasis here seems to have been upon the purpose and intention of the solicitor rather than upon the actual impact upon the barrister.

11–285

The facts of *Martin (Peter)* were unusual, in that the pressure was being exerted upon a private prosecutor. The principle, however, is surely the same whether it is sought to influence a course of action in criminal or in civil proceedings. Sometimes the pressure may be exerted upon defendants in criminal proceedings, who are normally thought to be incapable of being influenced in any particular direction, because they have no choice as to their involvement in the legal process. There are circumstances, however, in which such a person may find his options closed off by pressure (in particular from the media); for example in relation to the plea to be entered, or as to mode or place of trial.[23]

11–286

It would appear to be a contempt to endeavour by intimidation or bribery to induce a party to put in a false pleading,[24] to deter a party from calling certain evidence,[25] or from giving evidence himself.[26] In *Williams v Lyons*,[27] after a plaintiff had been awarded a sum of damages, the defendant had him arrested on a false charge of murder and on another civil suit, in order to persuade him to accept a lesser sum in judgment. He was held to be in contempt because of the attempted intimidation.

11–287

Interference may be treated as contempt, notwithstanding that it is motivated by a desire to protect the party concerned. Thus in *Thomas v Gwynne*,[28] the mother of a minor, who had been ordered to execute a document within a set time after being personally served, was held to be in contempt when she hid the minor to avoid service.

11–288

---

[22] For further guidance as to the circumstances in which "threats" to enforce one's legal rights might amount to "improper pressure", see *Daniel v Drew* [2005] EWCA Civ 507, applying *Royal Bank of Scotland v Etridge (No.2)* [2002] A.C. 773.
[23] See *Att-Gen v Unger* [1998] 1 Cr.App.R. 308, [1998] E.M.L.R. 280, discussed more fully at para.4–166; *Att-Gen v Times Newspapers Ltd, The Times*, February 28, 1983 (Lexis), Oliver L.J. cited at para.11–278.
[24] *Ex p. Halsam* (1740) 2 Atk. 49–50, 26 E.R. 427.
[25] *Bromilow v Phillips* (1892) 40 W.R. 220, North J. Although the respondent plaintiff did not appear, the judge concluded that an order for committal was justified in the light of *Smith v Lakeman* (1856) 26 L.J. Ch. 305; and *Shaw v Shaw* (1862) 2 Sw. & Tr. 517, 164 E.R. 1097, 6 L.T. 477.
[26] *Re Hooley* (1898) 79 L.T. 306.
[27] (1723) 8 Mod. R. 189, 88 E.R. 138.
[28] (1845) 8 Beav. 312, 50 E.R. 123.

C. The threat to exercise legal rights against a party

11–289 There is authority illustrating how it may be permissible to exercise a legal right against a party, or to threaten to do so, even though there is present the motive or purpose of persuading that party to alter his or her conduct in relation to the case.[29] In *Webster v Bakewell RDC*,[30] a yearly tenant issued a writ against a local authority for an injunction restraining them from trespassing on the land he occupied. The landlord heard of the alleged trespass and tried to settle the matter with the local authority. Her solicitor then wrote to the tenant stating that if he did not withdraw the writ the landlord would turn him out of the premises, so that he would have no *locus standi* in the matter. This letter was written on instructions because the landlord felt that the action was prejudicial to her interests (though it was not clear exactly what form the perceived prejudice was going to take).

11–290 Neville J. held that this was not a contempt[31]:

"I think it is only this: 'I do not intend to interfere with the way you carry on the action at all, but it is injurious to me and if you do carry it on and assert what you allege to be your legal rights in that way, I on my part shall give effect to the legal rights I possess and resume possession of my cottage.' I must say I cannot think that can be considered a contempt of court. The object of turning him out of the cottage would be to deprive him of legal standing to maintain his action and to resume possession of the property in respect of which he is suing. Test it in this way. Some of the tenants on the estate are yearly tenants and some are weekly tenants. Suppose the plaintiff had been a weekly tenant and the lady said to him, 'It is against my interests that this action should proceed against the local authority in respect of this particular property. You are a weekly tenant. If you persist in this action I will determine your tenancy, and then the action will necessarily fail for want of any estate upon which you can maintain it.' A weekly tenancy could be determined before any action in respect of the property could be tried and I cannot see that there is anything to prevent a landlord exercising his legal rights in that way, if he does it honestly to protect the rights he has in the property. Again suppose two neighbouring owners have for some time committed trespass on one another's lands, either by allowing water to run or in some similar way, and this in a neighbourly spirit has been allowed to go on, then one brings an action against this neighbour in respect of the trespass he has committed. The neighbour says, 'We have allowed this to go on in a friendly way, and if you sue me in respect of my trespass I will sue you on your trespass'—obviously done to prevent the prosecution of the action by a litigious neighbour. Could that be said to be contempt of court? I think not. I cannot see any distinction in principle between that and saying 'I will assert my legal rights against you if you choose to go on with your action, which to my mind is detrimental to my interest in the property.'"

11–291 This case was distinguished by the Court of Appeal in *R. v Kellett*,[32] but upon the ground that the lawful right there was to be exercised against a witness rather

---

[29] See *Att-Gen v Martin (Peter)*, *The Times*, April 23, 1986 (Lexis), discussed para.11–282, where the threat of a claim for malicious prosecution was held not to be contempt (by a majority).
[30] [1916] 1 Ch. 300.
[31] *ibid.* at 303–4.
[32] [1976] Q.B. 372.

than a party. The court was prepared to recognise that different considerations might apply in the case of a litigant.[33]

1. *The position of claimants*

The key to the distinction may be in Neville J.'s words: "I do not intend to interfere in the way you carry on the action at all." Interfering with the evidence of a witness may affect the course which litigation takes or its ultimate outcome. Merely to persuade a party not to proceed may be unobjectionable in itself from the public policy point of view.[34] The only restraint which the law would appear to impose is that, in seeking to persuade a party not to proceed with an action, the pressure used must not be "improper".[35] Nor should one seek to obstruct a litigant's access to the courts.

A claimant is in a different position from other persons concerned in litigation, because he is involved, to a greater or lesser extent, by choice. In some cases, a claimant may choose to put the machinery of justice into action in a morally indefensible cause. Hence he ought to be open to criticism which is accurate and *bona fide*. On the other hand, even unpopular litigants ought to have the right of access to the courts. To safeguard their rights there must be limits on the degree of pressure which can be put upon them.

An example discussed in the House of Lords in *Att-Gen v Times Newspapers Ltd*[36] demonstrates how it is possible to put strong pressure upon a litigant by threatening to exercise a legal right. A threat of eviction or dismissal may be just as effective as a threat to assault, and it may even be more effective to threaten non-violent action against a litigant. In judging the effect of a threat, it may be immaterial that what is threatened is the exercise of a contractual right rather than some other power available to (say) customers or consumers. Thus, to boycott a trader's goods, in an attempt to exert pressure as to the conduct of litigation, could be as effective as a threat of dismissal to an employee. What may be difficult to determine is what acts of influence or interference are likely to be categorised as amounting to "improper" pressure,[37] and thus constitute the *actus reus* of contempt notwithstanding that they are in themselves *prima facie* lawful.

---

[33] See para.11–217.
[34] See also Lord Reid, cited at para.4–279.
[35] It appears that "improper" is a wider concept than "unlawful". See Glidewell L.J. in *Att-Gen v Martin (Peter), The Times*, April 23, 1986 (Lexis), discussed at para.11–282. See also on the circumstances in which "threats" to enforce one's legal rights might amount to "improper pressure": *Daniel v Drew* [2005] EWCA Civ 507, applying *Royal Bank of Scotland v Etridge (No.2)* [2002] A.C. 773.
[36] [1974] A.C. 273.
[37] In the sense contemplated by Lords Reid and Diplock in *Att-Gen v Times Newspapers Ltd* [1974] A.C. 273, and by the Divisional Court in *Att-Gen v Martin (Peter), The Times*, April 23, 1986 (Lexis). In the latter case, the view was expressed by Glidewell L.J. that Lord Diplock had not intended to confine conduct which was "improper" to that which was unlawful.

11-295 Some guidance may be derived from the judgments of the Court of Appeal in *Att-Gen v Butterworth*,[38] although that was a case of retribution against witnesses for evidence already given. The court concluded that, where the fact that a witness had given evidence in a case made his relationship with his employer or fellow officers of a union intolerable, then it would not be a contempt for them to dismiss him. It was expressly recognised,[39] however, that in some circumstances even the exercise of a legal right *could* amount to the *actus reus* of contempt. The court has to decide on the facts the true purpose with which the legal right is being exercised. There is no reason in principle why the same approach should not be adopted in the case of *litigants*. There are sound policy reasons why persons who have power over others (whether based on a specific contractual right or not) should not be entitled to exercise it arbitrarily.

D. The approach of the Phillimore Committee

11-296 The Phillimore Committee perhaps drew the right distinction. That is to say, fair criticism should be permitted, whether in private or public[40]; intimidation, whether by means that are *prima facie* legal or not, is objectionable. It observed that[41]:

> "... the force of a campaign of moral pressure, whether public or private, must depend to some degree upon the validity of the moral grounds upon which it is based... What lent the *Sunday Times* campaign so much strength was the fact that in the eyes of many people justice and the administration of the law in the thalidomide case were two very different things. We think there is great force in the argument that this is a legitimate matter for public comment.
>
> We are therefore clear that criticism of a litigant, whether public or private, is not something from which the law of contempt should protect him. But it is possible to envisage a situation where a person is subject to threat by another with power over him, for example an employee by an employer, a tenant by his landlord, or a worker by his trade union; or where, for example, he is threatened with physical violence or injury to his reputation. In those circumstances we think that the court should have the power to step in to protect the interests of a party who is doing no more than exercising his right to have a justiciable issue determined by the courts of his country."

11-297 The Committee recommended that[42]:

> "... conduct directed against a litigant in connection with the legal proceedings in which he is concerned, which amounts to intimidation or unlawful threats to person, property or reputation should be capable of being treated as a contempt of court; but that conduct falling short of that should not be a contempt."

11-298 It appears to have accepted the view that conduct could be characterised as intimidation in some circumstances if it involved threatening to exercise a legal right; for example, an employer against an employee, a landlord against a tenant,

---

[38] [1963] 1 Q.B. 696, discussed in the context of witnesses, at paras 11–202 *et seq.*
[39] *ibid.* at 726.
[40] For a discussion of the holding of litigants up to *public* obloquy, see paras 5–116 *et seq.*
[41] paras 61, 62.
[42] para.62.

or a trade union against a member or officer. This part of the Report was not reflected in the 1981 Act. The government's discussion paper on contempt of court[43] criticised this restrictive recommendation of Phillimore, as tipping the balance too far against the interests of justice.

Intimidation, however, in relation to jurors and witnesses (among others), is now addressed by s.51 of the Criminal Justice and Public Order Act 1994,[44] which creates an indictable offence. The likelihood is that a court, in interpreting these provisions, would take a similar view to that of the Phillimore Committee and conclude that the offence could be committed by threatening to do something which was *prima facie* lawful.[45]

E. Hindering access to the courts

A party is, like jurors and witnesses, protected from abuse or assault in court, or on the way to or from court. It is likewise a contempt to prevent a litigant having access to the court. Thus in *Att-Gen v Times Newspapers Ltd*,[46] Lord Diplock identified as the *first* of the elementary requirements for the due administration of justice, " ... that all citizens should have unhindered access to the constitutionally established courts of criminal or civil jurisdiction for the determination of disputes as to their legal rights and liabilities."

In accordance with this principle, Slade J. held in *Hillfinch Properties v Newark Investments*[47] that it would constitute contempt for a Rabbinical court to threaten to excommunicate an orthodox Jew who did not take his dispute to them rather than to the civil courts.

In *Raymond v Honey*[48] the applicant, who was serving a prison sentence, wrote a letter to his solicitors. The prison governor, having reason to believe that the correspondence contained extraneous matters, read the letter and prevented its being sent.[49] The applicant then prepared a statement, an unsworn affidavit and a letter applying to commit the governor for contempt. The governor stopped those documents too.

---

[43] *Contempt of Court: A Discussion Paper*, Cmnd. 7154 (1978), para.42. One reason for not implementing the recommendation seems to have been the fear that subtle pressure, even falling short of intimidation, could put unfair and unacceptable pressure on litigants, for example in matrimonial or race relations cases.
[44] paras 11–145 *et seq.*
[45] A similar problem arises in the law of blackmail. See, *e.g. Denyer* [1926] 2 K.B. 258; *Thorne v Motor Trade Association* [1937] A.C. 797, discussed by A.T.H. Smith, *Property Offences* (1994) para.15–03, and the Symposium proceedings, (1993) 141 U. Pa.L.R. 1565–1990. See also para.11–241 above. H.E. Smith, "Harm in Blackmail" (1997–1998) 92 Nw. U. L. Rev. 861; R.J. Scalise, "Blackmail, Legality and Liberalism" (1999–2000) 74 Tul. L. Rev. 1483. See the discussion of the intimidation offence in *R. v Patrascu* [2004] EWCA Crim 2417, [2004] 4 All E.R. 1066.
[46] At 309. See also Art.6 of the European Convention on Human Rights, set out at para.2–143.
[47] *The Times*, July 1, 1981.
[48] [1983] 1 A.C. 1, HL. The House of Lords paid regard to Art.6(1) of the European Convention on Human Rights and to the decision of the European Court on Human Rights in *Golder v United Kingdom* [1975] 1 E.H.R.R. 524.
[49] In the exercise of his powers under rr.33 and 37A of the Prison Rules 1964. See now the Prison Rules 1999, rr.34–39.

11-303 A Divisional Court held that the governor was entitled to stop the original letters because he had offered to let the applicant rewrite the letter without the offending matter. The governor also believed that the applicant was to be visited soon by his solicitor in any event so that he could have explained orally whatever might have been relevant. However, the governor was held by the Divisional Court to have committed a contempt by stopping the application to the High Court, because all citizens must have unhindered access to the courts. This decision was upheld in the House of Lords, and Lord Bridge asserted as a matter of principle that a citizen's right of unimpeded access to the courts can be taken away only by express enactment.

11-304 It is clear that to arrest someone at court, and thus hinder access, would be regarded as interference with the administration of justice. The arrested litigant or witness would have had the remedy of *habeas corpus*, and the arresting officer could well be held in contempt.[50] Later, it seems that the reasoning was extended so as to lead to the doctrine that there would also be a contempt committed by effecting service of process in the precincts of the court.[51]

11-305 In *Jones Ex p. McVittie*[52] a Divisional Court took a contrary view. A solicitor had experienced difficulty in serving a judgment summons on a debtor, but eventually served him while he was in the corridor of the Manchester Assize Court waiting for an action in which he was the plaintiff to be called on. The court held this was not a contempt, and considered that the rule in *Cole v Hawkins*[53] was obsolete.[54] Lord Hewart C.J. and MacKinnon J. acknowledged the possibility that there may be cases in which the service of process within the precincts of the court might still amount to contempt, although MacKinnon J. added[55]: "Personally I cannot conceive what those circumstances could be." In *Ex p. Brantschen*[56] the Divisional Court held that service on a person at court was in any event good service.

11-306 In any event, while the arrest of a person who has business at court would clearly be likely to delay or hinder the court proceedings,[57] the same would not necessarily be true of the mere service of process.

---

[50] *Lea's Case* (1586) Gouldsb. 33, 75 E.R. 976; *Cullin's Case* (1653) Sty. 395, 82 E.R. 807; *Vandervelde v Lluellin* (1662) 1 Keb. 220, 83 E.R. 910; *Long's Case* (1677) 2 Mod. Rep. 181, 86 E.R. 1012; *Garibaldo v Cagnoni* (1703) 6 Mod. 90, 87 E.R. 848; *Hall* (1776) 2 Bl. W. 1110, 96 E.R. 655; *Childerston v Barrett* (1809) 11 East 439, 103 E.R. 1073; *Ex parte Byne* (1813) 1 Ves & B. 316, 35 E.R. 123; *Magnay v Burt* (1843) 5 Q.B. 381, 114 E.R. 1293.
[51] *Cole v Hawkins* (1738) Andrews 275, 95 E.R. 396; *Poole v Gould* (1856) 1 H. & N. 99; 156 E.R. 1133.
[52] [1931] 1 K.B. 664.
[53] (1738) Andrews 275; 95 E.R. 396.
[54] Similar reasoning was applied by the Federal Court of Australia in *Re O'Sullivan: Ex p. O'Sullivan v Commonwealth Bank of Australia* [1995] 129 A.L.R. 295, Lindgren J. See also *Re Tole; Ex p. Tole (Re Tole)* (1933) 50 W.N. (N.S.W.) 216, Long Innes J.; *Baldry v Jackson* [1976] 1 N.S.W.L.R. 19.
[55] At 671–2.
[56] *The Times*, December 7, 1970.
[57] See paras 10–109 *et seq*.

F. Picketing the courts

Whereas considerable concern has been expressed in other jurisdictions, picketing of courts (and in particular the Royal Courts of Justice in the Strand) seems to be much more common nowadays in England and to have been accepted as part of everyday experience. The serious question is the extent to which steps should be taken to prevent such picketing, whether by means of personal approaches, notices or leaflets, where parties, jurors and witnesses are likely to be entering or leaving the building. The subject of intimidation in this context has been highlighted extra-judicially by Lord Hobhouse of Woodborough.[58] He wrote of the need to protect democratic and constitutional institutions from intimidation, and continued:

> "A feature, one might also say function, of assemblies is that they are inherently intimidating and threatening. Modern society has become increasingly tolerant of demonstrations designed to influence decisions taken by the judiciary and the legislature. Our institutions are presently sufficiently robust to withstand these pressures but this should not blind those interested in public and constitutional law to the long term danger of permitting demonstrations outside courts of justice. They can be actually intimidating and, at best, give a misleading and damaging impression that judicial decisions can be influenced by such demonstrations. Parliament is similarly but more remotely affected. Parliament is a political body making political decisions and political pressure is not inappropriate. But what is liable to be overlooked is that Parliament is a democratic institution and to be threatened by a mob or a single issue demonstration is necessarily undemocratic".

In *Prothonotary v Collins*,[59] the court took the view that distributing leaflets could amount to contempt, but only where it was established that the distribution was such that it gave rise to a real risk of interference. Even if the intention was to interfere, there could be no liability without some act objectively likely to interfere with the course of justice. Where the content of a pamphlet alleging corrupt police practices (fabricating confessions in criminal trials) was such that its distribution to the public was not likely to interfere with the administration of justice generally, the fact that it was distributed to jurors and potential jurors did not make such conduct a contempt. An earlier decision[60] was distinguished on the basis that there had been evidence given that the pamphlets in that case had been distributed in connection with two current hearings in which police evidence of oral confessions was in issue. The distribution of extraneous material to passers-by who happen to include jurors could amount to contempt if it would tend to interfere with a verdict.

Moreover, anything which directly obstructs access to a court building requires to be restrained. In a Canadian case,[61] an injunction had been granted prohibiting a union from picketing a court building because they were restricting access. The

---

[58] (2001) 117 L.Q.R. 496 at 498.
[59] [1985] 2 N.S.W.L.R. 549, the facts of which are given at para.11–13.
[60] *Registrar, Court of Appeal v Collins* [1982] 1 N.S.W.L.R. 682, NSWCA.
[61] *BCGEU v Att-Gen for British Columbia* (1988) 44 C.C.C. (3d) 289, 53 D.L.R. (4th) 1, [1988] 2 S.C.R. 214. See Hogg, *Constitutional Law of Canada* (Toronto: Carswell), 847, 984–6 (looseleaf).

Supreme Court of Canada held that the Charter of Rights applied to such an injunction, which had to be recognised as imposing a limit upon freedom of speech. Nevertheless, on the facts the injunction could be justified as going no further than was reasonable. Unimpeded access to the courts was an important objective justifying the restriction.

G. Interference with legal advisers

11–310   The principle that "those who have duties to discharge in a court of justice are protected by law . . . in order that such persons may safely have resort to courts of justice"[62] applies also to legal advisers. Thus it was held in *R. v MacDonald*[63] that two police officers who searched counsel's suitcase containing his brief committed contempt in so doing. The policemen had formed the view, possibly erroneously, that certain documents in the possession of counsel might have been improperly obtained. They searched the suitcase notwithstanding counsel's objections, and seized a number of documents. One of the police officers was the informant for the prosecution in a case in which counsel was acting. It was held that, even though the police may have been acting under a genuine mistake, their conduct was calculated to interfere with the administration of justice and amounted to contempt.

XI. INTERFERENCE WITH OFFICERS OF THE COURT

A. Common law and statute

11–311   It was a contempt at common law to interfere with an officer of the court in the execution of his duty. It does not extend to an officer at a time when he is not executing his duty[64] or when he exceeds his duty.[65] Although now, to a large extent, such matters are governed by statute, the common law remains of practical importance.

11–312   In *Re de Court*,[66] Sir Richard Scott V.-C. emphasised that:

> "The administration of justice depends not simply on the judges or upon counsel in court, it depends upon court officials, members of the court Service, discharging essential functions for the purpose of enabling cases to come to court and to be dealt with by judges and counsel in the way with which we are all familiar. In my judgment a physical interference with officers of the court while conducting their duty in furthering the administration of justice is indeed a contempt of court. How serious a contempt it is will obviously depend upon the nature of the case. But the members of

---

[62] See the full citation from Bowen L.J. in *Re Johnson* (1887) 20 Q.B.D. 68, para.11–156.
[63] (1993) 70 A. Crim.R. 478. See also *R. v Griffin* [1996] T.L.R. 619, where it was held that it might be a contempt to search through papers that counsel had left on a desk. The circumstances were such that the journalist in question might reasonably have believed that he had permission to make a search.
[64] *Re Clements and Costa Rica Republic v Erlanger* (1877) 46 L.J. Ch. 375.
[65] *Southam v Smout* [1964] 1 Q.B. 308.
[66] [1997] T.L.R. 601 (Lexis).

Court Service who stand behind the counter to issue writs, and the listing officers who deal with applications both by lawyers and by litigants in person for the fixing of dates, and the process servers who serve orders of the court on persons, are all individuals of whom it can be said that if their official discharge of their duty is physically obstructed or interfered with the administration of justice itself is being interfered with. That is sufficient to constitute the [*actus*] in questions of contempt of court.

I have no doubt that what Mr de Court did in the present case constituted the *actus reus* of contempt of court".

In that case, he was concerned with a physical assault on the Chancery clerk of the lists while he was engaged in the discharge of his official duties.

B. The provisions of the County Courts Act

1. *Assaults*

Under s.14(1) of the County Courts Act 1984,[67] it is an offence to assault an officer of a court[68] while in the execution of his duty. On summary conviction, a person is liable to imprisonment for a term not exceeding three months, or to a fine of an amount not exceeding level five[69] on the standard scale, or both. Alternatively, a bailiff of the court may take the offender into custody, with or without warrant, and bring him before the judge. In those circumstances, on an order made by the judge, he may be committed for a specified period not exceeding three months to prison, or to a similar fine, or both.[70] It is similarly an offence to assault or resist or wilfully obstruct a "court security officer"[71] in the execution of his duty,[72] but this is mainly of relevance to the Crown Court.

2. *Insults*

Under s.118 of the County Courts Act 1984,[73] any person who, *inter alia*, wilfully[74] insults any officer of the court during his attendance in court, or in going to or returning from the court, commits an offence. In such circumstances, any officer of the court, with or without the assistance of any other person, may by order of the judge take the offender into custody and detain him until the

---

[67] The text of which is set out at para.13–84.
[68] For a definition of this term, see the County Courts Act 1984, s.147, as amended: "Any district judge, deputy district judge, assistant district judge of that court, and any clerk, bailiff, usher or messenger in the service of that court."
[69] Currently up to £5,000: Criminal Justice Act 1982, s.37, as amended.
[70] When this procedure is adopted, and the allegation has been found proved, an opportunity should normally be afforded to make any comments in mitigation and to explain why he should not be committed. See the general discussion at paras 10–38 *et seq*. For the county court specifically, see also *Stilwell v Williamson*, *The Times*, September 1, 1986, CA; *Gibbons v Registrar, Stroud County Court*, *The Independent*, October 8, 1990, CA. In the context of public funding, it is provided by the Access to Justice Act 1999, s.12(2) that "criminal proceedings" includes "proceedings before any court for dealing with an individual accused of an offence". This would cover the offences defined in ss.14(1), 92 and 118 of the County Courts Act 1984.
[71] As defined by the Criminal Justice Act 1991, ss.91 and 76(1).
[72] *ibid.*, ss.78(1) and 78(2).
[73] The terms of which are set out at para.13–90.
[74] For a consideration of "wilfully", see para.10–126.

11–314 CHAPTER 11—INTERFERENCE WITH ADMINISTRATION OF JUSTICE

rising of the court. The judge may then, if thought fit, make an order committing the offender for a specified period, not exceeding one month, or impose a fine of an amount not exceeding level four on the standard scale,[75] or both. Jurisdiction is not exclusive.

C. Obstruction of enforcement officers and court officers executing process

11–315 Provision is made in s.10 of the Criminal Law Act 1977[76] to deal with those who resist or intentionally obstruct enforcement officers and court officers engaged in executing any process issued by the High Court, or by any county court, for the purpose of enforcing any judgment or order for the recovery of any premises or for the delivery of possession of any premises. For the purposes of the section, the phrase "officer of a court" embraces any sheriff, under-sheriff, deputy sheriff, bailiff or officer of a sheriff, and any bailiff or other person who is an officer of the county court. A constable in uniform or any officer of the court may arrest without warrant anyone who is, or who is suspected to be, with reasonable cause, guilty of such an offence.[77]

D. The common law relating to officers of the court

11–316 All officers of the court have traditionally been protected under the relevant statutes or orders,[78] or at common law. Most of the older decisions relate either to process servers, to persons appointed by the court to hold and manage property, or to sheriffs.[79] The general principle described by Sir Richard Scott in *Re de Court*[80] embraces all these categories. Nevertheless, the older authorities are now reviewed separately.

1. Process servers

11–317 To assault a person serving the process of the court is contempt.[81] Yet merely to snatch a writ from a process server,[82] or to tear up process which has just been

---

[75] The maximum fine was increased by Sch.4 of the Criminal Justice Act 1991 with effect from October 1, 1992, to £2,500.
[76] "Enforcement officers" were added to the protection of the Act by the Courts Act 2003, s.109(1), as from March 15, 2004.
[77] Provision is also made in the County Courts Act 1984, s.92, to deal with those who rescue or attempt to rescue seized goods. See para.13–88.
[78] *e.g.* Ord.42, r.2 of the Consolidated Chancery Orders 1860 (now abrogated), which made the use of violence or abusive language to a process server punishable by committal. For an example see *Price v Hutchinson* (1870) L.R. 9 Eq. 534.
[79] For an example of a case relating to a bailiff see *Lewis v Owen* [1894] 1 Q.B. 102.
[80] [1997] T.L.R. 601. see para.11–312.
[81] *Rove v West* (1558) Cary 38, 21 E.R. 21; *Osborne v Tuthell* (1583) Ch.Cas.Ch. 168, 21 E.R. 98; *Ruffin v Heyward* (1584) Ch.Cas.Ch. 175, 21 E.R. 102; *Giles v Lackington* (1584) Ch.Cas.Ch. 177, 21 E.R. 103; *Van v Price* (1743) Dick. 91, 21 E.R. 202; *Morgan v Jones* (1745) cited in Dick. 91, 21 E.R. 202, also reported as *Anon.*(1745) 3 Atk. 219, 26 E.R. 928); *Williams v Johns* (1773) Dick. 477, 21 E.R. 355; *Ex parte Page* (1810) 17 Ves. Jun. 59, 34 E.R. 23; *Elliot v Halmarnack* (1816) 1 Mer. 302, 35 E.R. 839; *Emery v Bowen* (1836) 5 L.J. Ch. 349; *Price v Hutchinson* (1869) 9 L.R. Eq. 534; *Whitworth v Duncan, The Times,* January 14, 1893; *Mitzakis Ex p. Rivers, The Times,* January 19, 1910.
[82] *Weeks v Whiteley* (1835) 3 Dowl. P.C. 536; 1 Har. & W. 218.

served,[83] or to cause an obstruction not leading actually to the prevention of service[84] will not necessarily amount to a contempt. To prevent service of the process of the court upon someone in one's custody[85] or employment[86] is a contempt. There are a number of early authorities which indicate that insulting the process of the court by words or action was also treated as contempt.[87] Yet other cases indicate that by no means all conduct disrespectful of the process of the court would be so treated.[88] These are really applications of the *de minimis* principle.

2. Interference with court-appointed receivers and sequestrators[89]

Where the court has appointed a receiver, and the receiver has entered into possession of the relevant property, any interference with that possession without leave of the court is a contempt.[90] In *IRC v Hoogstraten*,[91] Dillon L.J. observed that: "The rule that it is contempt of court to interfere with a receiver or sequestrator, who is an officer of the court, in the exercise of his duties ... is to ensure that the receiver or sequestrator is not molested in the course of his duties."

A person who claims to have a title paramount to that of the receiver cannot seize the property[92] or commence an action[93] without leave of the court. Even where it is alleged that the order appointing the receiver is defective, it must be tested in the court and there should be no resort to self-help.[94] Although it is generally essential to the application of the rule that the receiver be in possession

---

[83] *Myers v Wills* (1820) 4 Moo. C.P. 147. In *Milsom v Bevan* (unreported, November 1977, Pain J.) a contempt motion based upon the tearing up of a writ was dismissed, but largely through lack of a penal notice.
[84] *Giles v Venson* (1728) 1 Barn. K.B. 56, 94 E.R. 39; *Adams v Hughes* (1819) 1 Brod. & B. 24, 129 E.R. 632.
[85] *Danson v Le Capelain & Steele* (1852) 7 Exch. 667, 155 E.R. 1116 (prison governor); *Denison v Harding* (1867) 15 W.R. 346 (asylum keeper).
[86] *Wylam v Wylam & Roller* (1893) 69 L.T. 500.
[87] *Barker v Shepheard* (1633) Toth. 102, 21 E.R. 136; *Witham v Witham* (1668) 3 Ch. Rep. 41, 21 E.R. 723; cases cited in *Thompson's Case* (1680) 8 St. Tr. 1, 49, 50; *Anon.* (1710) 1 Salk. 84, 91 E.R. 79; *R. v Unitt* (1723) 1 Str. 567, 93 E.R. 705; *Phillips v Hedges* (1736) Cooke C.P. 132, 125 E.R. 1004; *Jones* (1719) 1 Str. 185, 93 E.R. 462; *Van v Price* (1743) 1 Dick. 91, 21 E.R. 202; *R. v Jermy* (1752) Sayer 47, 96 E.R. 799; *R. v Kendrick* (1754) Sayer 114, 96 E.R. 822.
[88] *Giles v Venson* (1728) 1 Barn. K.B. 56, 94 E.R. 39; *Myers v Wills* (1820) 4 Moo. C.P. 147.
[89] See generally G. Lightman, "A Trade Union in Chains" (1987) C.L.P. 25; C. O'Regan, "Contempt of Court and the Enforcement of Labour Injunctions" (1991) 54 M.L.R. 385.
[90] *Ames v Birkenhead Docks* (1855) 20 Beav. 332 at 352, 52 E.R. 630; *Defries v Creed* (1865) 34 L.J. Ch. 607.
[91] [1985] 1 Q.B. 1077 at 1093E–F.
[92] *Russell v East Anglian Railway Co* (1850) 3 Mac. & G. 104, 42 E.R. 201.
[93] *Evelyn v Lewis* (1844) 3 Hare 472, 67 E.R. 467; *Hawkins v Gathercole* (1852) 1 Drew 12, 61 E.R. 355; *Randfield v Randfield* (1860) 1 Dr. & Sm. 310, 62 E.R. 398; *Ex p. Cochrane* (1875) L.R. 20 Eq. 282; *Re Botibol* [1947] 1 All E.R. 26.
[94] *Ames v Birkenhead Docks* (1855) 20 Beav. 332, 52 E.R. 630.

of the property,⁹⁵ it applies equally where he has been appointed to receive payment of sums of money and those payments are intercepted.⁹⁶

11–320 While the court may commit a person who interferes with the receiver's possession,⁹⁷ it would sometimes be appropriate to take no further step than to order him to pay the costs of the motion to commit,⁹⁸ and any costs occasioned by the interference,⁹⁹ or to grant an injunction restraining any further interference.¹ Any application to the court by the receiver should be made promptly.² The court will not protect the receiver if he has committed a wrong which gives another the right to seize the property in his possession; for example, where distress was levied to recover a fine imposed on a company for selling adulterated milk, when the offence was committed while the receiver was in control.³

11–321 The authorities disclose a variety of means of interference such as bringing an action for possession⁴; taking forcible possession of property in the hands of the receiver,⁵ or intercepting rents, profits or other monies which he has been appointed to receive⁶; taking forcible possession of chattels⁷; levying execution upon assets in his possession, even if the execution is carried out by the sheriff⁸; interfering in the management of a business in the hands of the receiver⁹; circularising customers of such a business to the effect that it is no longer a going concern and soliciting others for its business¹⁰; inducing employees of such a business to leave the business and take employment with a competing firm.¹¹

11–322 On the other hand, it was held in one case not to be a contempt for a former manager of a business, who had been appointed by the court, to engage in a similar kind of business after having been removed from office, even though he was soliciting customers of the business which he had formerly managed.¹²

---

⁹⁵ *Defries v Creed* (1865) 34 L.J. Ch. 687.
⁹⁶ *Ames v Birkenhead Docks* (1855) 20 Beav. 332, 52 E.R. 630.
⁹⁷ *Broad v Wickham* (1831) 4 Sim. 511, 58 E.R. 191.
⁹⁸ *Lane v Sterne* (1862) 3 Giff. 629, 66 E.R. 559; *Fripp v Bridgewater Canal Co* (1845) 3 W.R. 356; *Ex p. Haywood* (1881) W.N. 115.
⁹⁹ *Russell v East Anglian Railway Co* (1850) 3 Mac. & G. 104, 42 E.R. 201; *Parker v Pocock* (1874) 30 L.T. 458.
¹ *Johnes v Claughton* (1822) Jac.573, 37 E.R. 966; *Tink v Rundle* (1847) 10 Beav. 318, 50 E.R. 604; *Evelyn v Lewis* (1844) 3 Hare 475, 67 E.R. 467; *Ames v Birkenhead Docks* (1855) 20 Beav. 332, 52 E.R. 630; *Bayly v Went* (1884) W.N. 197; *Dixon v Dixon* [1904] 1 Ch. 161; cf. *Re Maidstone Palace of Varieties* [1909] Ch. 283.
² *Ward v Swift* (1848) 6 Hare 309, 67 E.R. 1184.
³ *Jarvis v Islington Borough Council* (1909) 73 J.P.J. 323.
⁴ *Angel v Smith* (1804) 9 Ves. Jun. 335, 32 E.R. 632.
⁵ *Broad v Wickham* (1831) 4 Sim. 511, 58 E.R. 191.
⁶ *ibid.*
⁷ *Ex p. Cochrane* (1875) L.R. 20 Eq. 282.
⁸ *Lane v Sterne* (1862) 3 Giff. 629, 66 E.R. 559; and cf. *Russell v East Anglian Railway Co.* (1850) 3 Mac. & G. 104, 42 E.R. 201; see also Kerr and Hunter on *Receivers and Administrators* (18th ed, 2005), paras 6–32 *et seq.*
⁹ *Re Plant, Plant v Hayward* (1881) 45 L.T. 326.
¹⁰ *Helmore v Smith (No.2)* (1886) 35 Ch. D. 449.
¹¹ *Dixon v Dixon* [1904] 1 Ch. 161. See also *King v Dopson* (1911) 56 Sol. Jo. 51.
¹² *Re Gent-Davis v Harris* (1892) 40 W.R. 267.

11–323 A liquidator appointed in the winding up of a company, who enters into possession of the property,[13] and a sequestrator in possession of property under a writ of sequestration[14] are similarly protected in the exercise of their functions by the law of contempt.

11–324 There are possible distinctions to be drawn between sequestrators and receivers in the context of contempt.[15] Since both may be appointed by the court, and would be intended to carry out functions in fulfilment of judicial objectives, conduct intended to obstruct any of those functions could be classified as contempt. It has been suggested[16] that there is a distinction between their roles, in that the receiver has the duties of a caretaker with no greater right to information from third parties than the party to the action would have, whereas a sequestrator is a "representative of the State" in the enforcement of the rule of law, so that he must be given powers to obtain such information commensurate with the task. A sequestrator is an officer of the court. The court can issue a writ and nominate the sequestrators. Their status is, however, precisely the same whether this occurs or, as is traditionally more usual, the sequestrators are nominated by the aggrieved litigant.

11–325 It is a contempt to move a ship after the Admiralty Marshall or his substitute has arrested it.[17]

3. *Interference with a sheriff*

11–326 It has already been noted that a sheriff is included within the definition of an "officer of the court" for the purposes s.10 of the Criminal Law Act 1977.[18] There was also specific provision in s.8(2) of the Sheriffs Act 1887 that if a sheriff found any resistance in the execution of a writ he should take with him the power of the county, should go in proper person to do execution, and might arrest the resisters and commit them to prison; every such resister would be guilty of an offence.[19] The "power of the county" strictly included all able bodied adult

---

[13] *Re Henry Pound, Son & Hutchins* (1889) 42 Ch.D. 402 at 411; *Re Joshua Stubbs Ltd* [1891] 1 Ch. 475.
[14] *Angel v Smith* (1804) 9 Ves. Jun. 335, 32 E.R. 632.; *Lord Pelham v Duchess of Newcastle* (1712) 3 Swan 289n, 36 E.R. 865. See paras 14–111 *et seq.* for a more detailed discussion of the relevance of the law of contempt to the function of sequestrators.
[15] G. Lightman Q.C., "A Trade Union in Chains" (1987) C.L.P. 25.
[16] *ibid.*
[17] *The Seraglio* (1885) 10 P.D. 120; *R. v Bjarnson Ex p. The Official Receiver; The Jarlinn* [1965] 1 W.L.R. 1098.
[18] See above at para.11–315.
[19] The Sheriffs Act s.8(1) was repealed by the Criminal Law Act 1967, s.10(2), Sch.3, Pt III. The provisions of s.10(1) of the Criminal Law Act 1977 (obstruction of enforcement officers and court officers) are said to be without prejudice to s.8(2). Section 10(6) of the 1977 Act (as amended) says that a court officer includes a sheriff, under sheriff and deputy sheriff as well as a bailiff or officer of a sheriff.

males within the county,[20] but it became the practice for the sheriff to call upon the local constabulary, who were as much a part of the power of the county as ordinary citizens.[21] A person who wrongfully refused to render assistance to the sheriff in these circumstances was guilty of contempt; the extent of the assistance required was regarded as being within the discretion of the sheriff.[22]

11–327 Although s.8(1), which imposed liability to a fine on anyone who failed to respond, has been repealed,[23] it seems clear that the sheriff's common law powers and duties, including his duty to keep the peace, technically remain in existence.[24] Thus, should these powers be used in exceptional circumstances, there might in theory be a contempt on the part of anyone refusing to comply with a sheriff's instruction.

11–328 More relevant for modern purposes is the fact that it was also regarded as a contempt to rescue a person arrested, or goods or land seized by the sheriff.[25] Where a sheriff has taken possession of property under a writ of possession, and the party evicted retakes possession, this has also been treated as a contempt,[26] but in such a case it is generally preferable to use the alternative procedure of the writ or warrant of restitution.[27]

11–329 The old practice in rescue cases was for the sheriff to make a return informing the court of the rescue. This was made *ex parte* in the first instance. In the common law courts the return was treated as conclusive, and a rule absolute for attachment issued.[28] The alleged contemnor's only remedy was an action for damages against the sheriff.[29] In the Court of Chancery no affidavit was required on applying *ex parte*, but if the application was successful the offender would be brought to court on attachment and then could contest the return.[30]

---

[20] See *Dalton's Office of Sheriff*, c.95. It was said that a lower age limit for such persons was 15.
[21] *Miller v Knox* (1838) 4 Bing. N.C. 574, 132 E.R. 910; *Att-Gen v Kissane* (1893) 32 L.R. Ir. 220.
[22] See *Miller v Knox* (last note).
[23] Criminal Law Act 1967, s.10(2) and Sch.3, Pt III.
[24] See Sheriffs Act 1887, s.39(1)(d), which preserves the common law. See also *R. v Secretary of State for the Home Department Ex p. Northumbria Police Authority* [1989] Q.B. 26 at 58, Nourse L.J. See also Halsbury's *Laws of England*, 4th ed., Vol.42, para.1132, n.1.
[25] Hawk. 2 *P.C.*, c.22, s.34.
[26] *Cooper v Asprey* (1863) 32 L.J.Q.B. 209; *Lacon v De Groat* (1893) 10 T.L.R. 24; *Re Higg's Mortgage* (1894) 29 W.N. 73; *Alliance Building Society v Austen* [1951] 2 All E.R. 1068.
[27] *Alliance Building Society v Austen* [1951] 2 All E.R. 1068, Roxburgh J. A warrant of restitution may be issued in the county court in aid of a warrant of possession, provided that permission of the court has been obtained: See now CPR Sch.2, cc.24.6 (warrant of possession) and cc.26.17(4) and (5). The procedure is analogous to the writ of restitution available in the High Court: See CPR Sch.1, Ord.46.3. This is the most commonly used writ "in aid of any other writ of execution". Permission should be sought without notice supported by evidence in the form of an affidavit. The relevant form is N68.
[28] *Gobby v Dewes* (1833) 10 Bing. 112, 131 E.R. 848.
[29] *Brasyer v Maclean* (1875) L.R. 6 P.C. 398.
[30] *Blackwell v Tatlow* (1833) 2 My. & K. 321, 39 E.R. 966.

The matter is now governed by statute, and the current provision is the County Courts Act 1984, s.92, which imposes penalties in respect of the rescue of goods seized.[31]

XII. Interference with the Wardship or *Parens Patriae* Jurisdiction

A. Interference with the court's inherent protective jurisdiction

Since the Children Act 1989 came into effect, the wardship machinery is less frequently invoked[32] although the court continues to exercise the same inherent *parens patriae* jurisdiction; thus the principles worked out in the authorities relating to contempt of court in the context of wardship are potentially of continuing significance.[33]

B. Such interference treated as criminal contempt

It is long established that interference with the inherent *parens patriae* jurisdiction can amount to contempt. This will be classified as criminal contempt,[34] even though in some cases consisting in disobedience to an order of the court.[35] The reasoning appears to be that where the court represents the sovereign as *parens patriae* it is not resolving contested issues as between parties.[36]

In *Long Wellesley's* case,[37] for example, an infant daughter of Wellesley was made a ward of court, and guardians were appointed, who placed the girl in the care of relatives. Wellesley removed her from their care. He was ordered by the court to bring her to the bar of the court, but he failed to do so and refused to disclose her whereabouts. He was committed to the Fleet. He was, however, a member of Parliament and reported the matter to the Speaker of the Commons, claiming privilege. The Committee of Privileges took the view that his actions constituted a *criminal* contempt, which fell within the principle under which persons committing indictable offences were considered not to be entitled to privilege.[38] The matter then came before Lord Brougham L.C. on a motion to discharge the committal order. He held that Wellesley was not entitled to privilege, for such a claim was of no avail where the object of the process was the delivery up of a person wrongfully detained.

---

[31] For the terms of the provision, see para.13–88. Procedure under the section is the same as that under s.14 of the 1984 Act, dealing with assaults, discussed at para.11–313.
[32] See paras 6–108 *et seq.*
[33] See, *e.g. Re Z (A Minor) (Identification: Restrictions on Publication)* [1997] Fam. 1 at 14, Ward L.J. and generally the discussion of the *parens patriae* jurisdiction at paras 6–41 *et seq.*
[34] *Re B (JA) (An Infant)* [1965] Ch. 1112 at 1117, Cross J.
[35] *Wellesley v Duke of Beaufort* (1831) 2 Russ. & M.. 639, 39 E.R. 538, the facts of which are given at para.11–333. See also the discussion in paras 3–115 *et seq.*
[36] *Scott v Scott* [1913] A.C. 417, Viscount Haldane L.C. at 437, and Lord Atkinson at 462.
[37] (1831) 2 Russ. & M. 639, 39 E.R. 538.
[38] See para.3–141.

11–334 Chapter 11—Interference with Administration of Justice

11–334 Even where no order of the court is directly involved, it was recognised that it would constitute contempt to marry a ward without leave.[39] It was regarded as a contempt on the part of the ward as well as on that of the person who married her.[40] It would likewise be a contempt of the part of anyone who assisted at the marriage.[41]

11–335 In *Crump*,[42] an infant girl was made a ward of court on her parents' motion. A later order was made restraining the ward and one Kearney from marrying. In breach of this order they married. At the Register Office they produced a forged form of consent, purporting to be by the girl's parents. The parents accepted the position and took no further action, but the Attorney-General moved the court to commit the ward and Kearney for contempt. Counsel for the Attorney-General stated that it was the first time he had intervened in a wardship case, but the marriage was *ipso facto* a criminal contempt and it was therefore proper that the motions for committal should be brought in this way. Faulks J. took a similar view, and sentenced both contemnors to 28 days' imprisonment, because he felt it necessary to show that such an order of the court could not be deliberately flouted.

11–336 It was also a contempt to take a ward outside the jurisdiction without the consent of the court,[43] to refuse to deliver a ward to a guardian appointed by the court,[44] or to refuse to disclose the whereabouts of a ward.[45]

C. Publications relating to persons under the court's protection[46]

11–337 It is not of itself contempt to publish information about a person who happens to be protected under the *parens patriae* jurisdiction of the court.[47] Such persons are

---

[39] *Eyre v Countess of Shaftsbury* (1722) 2 P. Wms.103, 24 E.R. 659; *Brandon v Knight* (1752) Dick. 160, 21 E.R. 230; *Cox v Bennett* (1874) 31 L.T. 83. Indeed, some early authorities suggest that conspiracy to marry a ward of court without leave was an indictable offence: *Schreiber v Lateward* (1781) 2 Dick. 592, 21 E.R. 401; *Ball v Coutts* (1812) 1 V. & B. 292, 35 E.R. 114; *Wade v Broughton* (1814) 3 V. & B. 172, 35 E.R. 444. One case suggests that simply marrying a ward of court without leave was *indictable*: *Millet v Rowse* (1802) 7 Ves. Jun. 419, 32 E.R. 169. Marrying a ward of court without leave could be the subject of a general act of pardon: *Phipps v Lord Anglesea* (1721) 1 P. Wms.696, 24 E.R. 576.

[40] *Re Leigh, Leigh v Leigh* (1888) 40 Ch. D. 290; *Re H's Settlement, H v H* [1909] 2 Ch. 260; *Re Crump (An Infant)* (1963) 107 Sol. Jo. 682, [1963] Crim. L.R. 777.

[41] *Long v Elways* (1729) Mosely 249, 25 E.R. 378; *Edes v Brereton* (1738) West temp. Hard. 348, 25 E.R. 974; and cf. *More v More* (1741) 2 Atk. 157, 26 E.R. 499, and *Nicholson v Squire* (1809) 16 Ves. Jun. 259, 33 E.R. 983.

[42] (1963) 107 S.J 682, [1963] Crim. L.R. 777.

[43] *Harrison v Goodhall* (1852) Kay 310, 69 E.R. 131; *Symonds v Symonds and Harrison* (1872) L.R. 2 P. & D. 447; *Re Harris (An Infant), The Times,* May 21, 1906; *Re O (Infants)* [1962] 2 All E.R. 10; *R. v D* [1984] A.C. 778 at 791, CA.

[44] *Burton v Earl of Darnley* (1869) L.R. 8 Eq. 576n.

[45] ibid. See also *Ramsbotham v Senior* (1869) L.R. 8 Eq. 575; *Mustafa v Mustafa, The Times,* September 11 and 13, 1967.

[46] See the discussion at paras 6–41 *et seq.* See also the important decision of Munby J. in *Kelly v BBC* [2001] Fam. 59, discussed at para.6–75 and para.6–78.

[47] *Re L (A Minor)* [1988] 1 All E.R. 418, Booth J.; *Re W (Wards) (Publication of Information)* [1989] 1 F.L.R. 246, Sir Stephen Brown P. See also *Re C (An Infant), The Times,* June 18, 1969, Goff J.; *Re W (Minors) (Continuation of Wardship)* [1996] 1 F.C.R. 393; *Kelly v BBC* [2001] Fam. 59.

not, merely by reason of their status, exempted from the effects of the general law; nor do they obtain thereby rights and privileges not available to others. It has become increasingly clear that, where the court is concerned to protect a minor or patient from the effects of publicity, it will make an order specifically for that purpose.[48] Moreover, this jurisdiction will only be exercised where it is necessary for the protection of the person concerned in the context of the court's supervisory jurisdiction. It would appear that the only legitimate purposes of imposing such a restraint would be either the protection of the administration of justice itself, and in particular the exercise of the court's supervisory functions,[49] or the exercise of a quasi-parental function under s.8 of the Children Act 1989.[50]

There could be no contempt in anticipation of wardship, even though there had been scandalous conduct towards a person subsequently made a ward.[51] Similarly, once the wardship had ceased, there could be no contempt in relation to the former ward, and all undertakings given during the wardship would generally cease to have effect.[52] 11–338

D. Is *mens rea* required in relation to the inherent jurisdiction?

Traditionally, it was not a defence that the alleged contemnor was ignorant of the fact that the relevant person was a ward of court.[53] In *Herbert's Case*,[54] an infant of 18 years had been "drawn in to marry a common servant maid, older than himself, and of no fortune". A parson conducted the marriage ceremony, and another man pretended to be guardian to the infant and purported to give consent to the marriage. They were ordered to attend before Sir Joseph Jekyll M.R., where they sought to argue that they were unaware that Mr Herbert had been a ward of court and that they could not be guilty of contempt. 11–339

The argument was rejected, on the basis that the infant had been committed to the custody of a guardian on the order of the court "in a cause then depending, 11–340

---

[48] This would avoid, for example, the uncertainty to which the remarks of Russell L.J. gave rise in *Re T (AJJ) (An Infant)* [1970] Ch. 688 at 689, where following a hearing *in camera* he remarked that "if anyone is minded to question or interview the infant they may well be at risk of being in contempt." In *Kelly v BBC* [2001] Fam. 59 at 76, Munby J expressed 'doubts and uncertainties' as to what was intended by those remarks of Russell L.J. He drew attention to the fact that Russell L.J. was speaking in 1970, before the decisions of the Court of Appeal in *Re X (A Minor) (Wardship: Jurisdiction)* [1975] Fam. 47 and *Re F (Orse A) (A Minor) (Publication of Information)* [1977] Fam. 58, and "long before the current understanding of matters had begun to emerge in the late 1980s".
[49] See, *e.g. C (A Minor) (Wardship: Medical Treatment) (No.2)* [1990] Fam. 39 at 53, Nicholls L.J.; *R. v Central Independent Television plc* [1994] Fam. 192, 200E, Neill L.J., 207A, Waite L.J.; *Re R (A Minor)* [1994] F.L.R. 637 at 650E–F, Millett L.J.
[50] See, *e.g. Re Z (A Minor) (Identification: Restrictions on Publication)* [1997] Fam. 1; *Oxfordshire County Council v L and F* [1997] 1 F.L.R. 235. But see now the discussion of Art.8 rights in *Re S(FC) (A Child)* [2004] UKHL 47, [2005] 1 A.C. 593, considered at paras 6–43 *et seq.*
[51] *Goodall v Harris* (1730) 2 Eq. Ca. Abr. 756, 22 E.R. 641; but cf. *Hannes v Waugh* (1713) 2 Eq. Cas. Abr. 754, 22 E.R. 639 and *Herbert's Case* (1731) 3 P. Wms. 116, 24 E.R. 992.
[52] *Bolton v Bolton* [1891] 3 Ch. 270.
[53] See, *e.g. Herbert's Case* (1731) 3 P. Wms. 116, 24 E.R. 992; *Re Witten* (1887) 4 T L.R. 36; *Re H's Settlement, H v H* [1903] 2 Ch. 260; but cf. *Re F (Orse A) (A Minor)* [1977] Fam. 58.
[54] (1731) 3 P. Wms. 116, 24 E.R. 992.

of which every one at his peril is concerned to take notice, in the same manner as of a *lis pendens*." The Master of the Rolls took it for granted that everyone should be presumed to be apprised of the proceedings of the court, as indeed all executors should be presumed to take notice of all judgments, even in the inferior courts of law.

11-341 He also referred to the principle that in relation to private proceedings, brought upon a writ of ravishment, it was no excuse to argue that the defendant did not know that the party was a ward of the particular plaintiff; *a fortiori*, where the public justice of the court was concerned, as in the case before him. Furthermore, where the marriage of an infant was encouraged without the concurrence of his or her true guardians, the consequences of such a marriage ought to be at the peril of those who were instrumental in bringing it about. Indeed, if the circumstances of a marriage were suspicious, the parties to the transaction needed to be severely censured for the deterrence of others.

11-342 Following a review of the older authorities,[55] the underlying policy was expressed by the Master of the Rolls:

> "If actual notice of the infant's being a ward of the court were necessary, then these offences would be continually practised with impunity: for it would be an easy matter to put other people not really privy to the acts of the court (in committing the guardianship of the infant) to transact and bring about the marriage."

It thus appears that the crux of the doctrine was not so much the modern concept of strict liability, but rather that of constructive notice.

11-343 In *Z Ltd v A-Z and AA-LL*,[56] Eveleigh L.J. mentioned this judgment of Sir Joseph Jekyll M.R., and appeared to make the assumption (*obiter*) that it remains the law that no element of *mens rea* need be shown where contempt is alleged on the basis of interference with the court's protective power in relation to a ward.

11-344 It would appear that the introduction of the strict liability regime under the Contempt of Court Act 1981 has not affected this principle, since ss.1 and 2 are concerned to confine the application of strict liability within only a narrow range of circumstances; that is to say, conduct that tends to interfere with the course of justice in particular legal proceedings. In the light of the reasoning of Sir Joseph Jekyll in *Herbert's case*, it is by no means obvious that he would have regarded the marriage of a ward as falling outside that description. He placed considerable emphasis upon the pendency of the wardship proceedings and the principle of constructive notice. It might therefore be argued that the effect of ss.1 and 2 of the 1981 Act was, *inter alia*, to take wardship contempts out of the reach of strict liability.

---

[55] *R. v Harwood* (1672) 2 Lev. 32, 83 E.R. 439; *Hannes v Waugh* (1713) 2 Eq. Cas. Abr. 754, 22 E.R. 639; *Nicholson v Squire* (1809) 16 Ves. Jun. 259, 33 E.R. 983; 2 Ves. Jun. Supp. 439, 34 E.R. 1169; *Salles v Savignon* (1801) 6 Ves. Jun. 572, 31 E.R. 1201; 1 Ves. Jun. Supp. 626, 34 E.R. 951; *Bathurst v Murray* (1602) 8 Ves. Jun. 74, 32 E.R. 279; 2 Ves. Jun. Supp. 82, 34 E.R. 1005.
[56] [1982] Q.B. 558 at 579C–D.

INTERFERENCE WITH WARDSHIP OR *PARENS PATRIAE* JURISDICTION 11–348

On the other hand, in *Att-Gen v Newspaper Publishing plc*,[57] Sir John Donaldson M.R. considered instances of conduct which might be treated as contempt of court, regardless of intent to do so, even though not falling within the description of "the strict liability rule" as defined in s.1 of the Act. One of the examples he gave was that of marrying a ward of court, or taking a ward out of the jurisdiction, without the court's permission. His reasoning was (again *obiter*) that the gravamen of the charge in such cases does not consist in interfering with the course of justice "in proceedings".

11–345

It would seem from these remarks of both Sir John Donaldson M.R. and Eveleigh L.J. that, if such contempts were matters of strict liability at common law, the position remains unchanged. It would, however, be surprising if a modern court were to proceed on the basis that a person could be guilty of contempt in relation to a ward, or some other person under the court's supervisory jurisdiction, when he was genuinely ignorant of that status. Moreover, Lord Denning M.R., in *Re F (orse A) (A Minor)*,[58] expressed the view that it was wrong that the traditional examples of contempt in wardship cases, namely those of marriage and removal from the jurisdiction, should be regarded as matters of strict liability.

11–346

In that case, the Court of Appeal held, where confidential matter was published relating to a ward although in ignorance of her status, that the publisher was not guilty of contempt.[59] The court considered that a contempt would have been committed if the alleged contemnor had *known* that the girl concerned was a ward, or had published being reckless as to her status.[60] In this respect, the decision would accord with the policy concern of Sir Joseph Jekyll in *Herbert's Case*, where he spoke of the need to impose liability where the participants in a marriage ceremony could see that the circumstances were "suspicious".

11–347

It seems unlikely that a court would hold, if the matter arose for consideration, that the 1981 Act has directly affected the common law in relation to wardship contempts. On the other hand, in the light of the approach of the Court of Appeal in *Re F*, and the general trend towards requiring *mens rea* to be demonstrated both in relation to publication and non-publication contempts at common law, it is quite possible that such a court would now conclude that there can be no liability for contempt in such circumstances unless it can be demonstrated that the alleged contemnor had at any rate some knowledge as to the relevant status of the person concerned. It is unlikely, in particular, that Sir Joseph Jekyll's

11–348

---

[57] [1988] Ch. 333 at 374B–C.
[58] [1977] Fam. 58 at 88G.
[59] See also as to the relevance of knowledge *Re Martindale* [1894] 3 Ch. 193 at 203, North J.; *Re de Beaujeu's Application* [1949] Ch. 230 at 236; *Re R (MJ)* [1975] Fam. 89.
[60] It is now necessary to bear in mind that it has been said on a number of occasions, since the Contempt of Court Act 1981 came into effect, that recklessness will not suffice to establish the necessary *mens rea* for common law contempt (at least in the context of publication, where considerations of freedom of speech and information arise): *Att-Gen v Newspaper Publishing plc* [1988] Ch. 333 at 374–5, Sir John Donaldson M.R., 382–3, Lloyd L.J. See also *Att-Gen v News Group Newspapers plc* [1989] Q.B. 110.

analysis, based on constructive knowledge of court proceedings, would find favour today.

XIII. THE SECRECY ATTACHING TO JURY DELIBERATIONS

A. Disclosing the deliberations of a jury: the background

11-349   It was a well established principle of the common law that the secrecy of the jury room was regarded as inviolate.[61] This has been described as "essentially a judge-made rule about the admissibility of evidence".[62] In *Ellis v Deheer*,[63] Atkin L.J. explained:

> "... the court does not admit evidence of a juryman as to what took place in the jury room, either by way of explanation of the grounds upon which the verdict was given, or by way of statement as to what he believed its effect to be. The reason why that evidence is not admitted is twofold, on the one hand it is in order to secure the finality of decisions arrived at by the jury, and on the other to protect the jurymen themselves and prevent their being exposed to pressure to explain the reasons which actuated them in arriving at their verdict. To my mind it is a principle which it is of the highest importance in the interests of justice to maintain."

11-350   Similarly, in *R. v Thompson*,[64] Lord Parker C.J. said:

> "... the court is quite satisfied that they would have no right at all to inquire what did occur in the jury room. It has for long been a rule of practice, based on public policy,

---

[61] See generally E. Campbell, "Jury secrecy and contempt of court" (1985) 11 Monash University L.R. 169; S. Enright, "Unlocking the jury room" (1989) 139 New Law Jo. 655. For the position in the United States, see Note "Public Disclosures of Jury Deliberations" (1983) 96 Harv. L. Rev. 886. It was suggested that the principle of the secrecy of jury deliberations may come into conflict with the requirements of Art.6 of the European Convention because of the need for reasons to be given by a judicial tribunal: J. Gibbons, "Explaining the Verdict" (1997) 147 New Law Jo. 1454 (an article prompted by remarks of the European Court of Human Rights in *Murray v United Kingdom* (1996) 22 E.H.R.L.R. 29). See also Sir John Smith, "Is Ignorance Bliss? Could Jury Trial Survive Investigation?" (1998) 38 Med. Sci. Law 98; J.R. Spencer, "Inscrutable Verdicts—the duty to give reasons and Art.6 of the ECHR" *Archbold News* Feb 2001; J.D. Jackson, "Making Juries Accountable" (2002) 50 Am. J. Comp. Law 477; J. Tunna, "Contempt of Court: Divulging the Confidences of the Jury Room" (2003) 9 Cant. Law Rev. 79; J.R. Spencer, "Juries: The Freedom to Act Irresponsibly" (2004) C.L.J. 314; P. Ferguson, "Whistleblowing Jurors" (2004) 154 New Law Jo. 370. See also the *Review of the Criminal Courts of England and Wales* (2001), Sir Robin Auld, Ch.5, para.98, who thought the prohibition in s.8 "indefensible and capable of causing serious injustice". See also J.D. Jackson "Modes of Trial: Shifting the Balance towards the Professional Judge" [2002] Crim. L.R. 249 at 266 for a discussion of Sir Robin's treatment of s.8.

[62] *R. v Connor; R. v Mirza* [2004 UKHL 2, [2004] 1 A.C. 1118 at [78], Lord Hope. See also his useful summary of the common law history at [94]–[107].

[63] [1922] 2 K.B. 113 at 121.

[64] [1962] 1 All E.R. 65 at 66D, (1962) 46 Cr.App.R. 72 at 75. See *R. v Brown* [1907] 7 N.S.W. St. Rep. 290; *R. v Bean* [1991] Crim. L.R. 843; *R. v Lucas* [1991] Crim. L.R. 844; *R. v Miah and Akhbar* [1997] 2 Cr.App.R. 12. An application by Mr Miah to the European Court of Human Rights was found to be inadmissible by the Commission: Application No.37401/97. For the position in New Zealand, see *Solicitor-General v Radio New Zealand Ltd* [1994] 1 N.Z.L.R. 48, where it was held that the participation of jurors in deliberations should be in the certain knowledge that their own views might be expressed without fear of subsequent exposure. In the United States, the privacy of jurors has also been held to be an important consideration: *Clark v United States* U.S. 1 (1993).

that the court should not inquire, by taking evidence from jurymen, what did occur in either the jury box or the jury room".

More recently, Lord Goff has observed[65]:

11–351

" . . . there are difficulties about exploring the actual state of mind of a justice or juryman. In the case of both, such an inquiry has been thought to be undesirable; and in the case of the juryman in particular, there has long been an inhibition against, so to speak, entering the jury room and finding out what any particular juryman actually thought at the time of decision".

Whether or not the secrecy of jury deliberations should be preserved and protected by the criminal law has been the subject of much deliberation.[66] The Report of the Departmental Committee on Jury Service[67] in 1965 summarised the conflicting considerations of policy as they were then perceived:

11–352

"We recognise that it is impossible to make a proper assessment of the merits of trial by jury in the absence of the adequate knowledge of what does happen when the jury retires, but we agree with those of our witnesses who argued that if such disclosure were to be made, particularly to the Press, jurors would no longer feel free to express their opinions frankly when the verdict was under discussion, for fear that what they said later might be make public".

B. The origins of section 8

It was thus long regarded as important that jurors should not be importuned by people wanting to ascertain the details of what occurred in the jury room. Notwithstanding this, the Divisional Court had held in *Att-Gen v New Statesman and Nation Publishing Co Ltd*[68] that publication of an article by a juror about the

11–353

---

[65] *R. v Gough* [1993] A.C. 646 at 659E. *Gough* was cited in *R. v Barraclough* [2000] Crim. L.R. 325, as providing the right test to apply in the situation where jurors had been discharged after being told of a defendant's previous convictions, and there was concern as to whether the potential jurors at the retrial might have been contaminated with that information. The test was taken as being whether there was a real danger of prejudice or bias through knowing of the defendant's convictions. See also *R. v Blackwell* [1995] 2 Crim. App. R. 625, [1996] Crim. L.R. 428 (a case where the behaviour of the juror was such as to "raise the strongest suspicions"); *R. v Oke* [1997] Crim. L.R. 898 where it was held that it would have been an insult to a juror and her husband to give any special warning about discussing matters which the husband had heard, while sitting in the public gallery, in the absence of the jury.
[66] *The Report of the Departmental Committee on Jury Service*, Cmnd. 2627 (1965). See also the Criminal Law Revision Committee, 10th Report, *Secrecy of the Jury Room*, Cmnd. 3750 (1968); Glanville Williams, *The Proof of Guilt* (3rd ed., 1963); Lord Devlin, *Trial by Jury* (rev. ed., 1966); J. Baldwin and M. McConville, *Jury Trials* (1979). The general issue of jury secrecy has been discussed also by S. O'Doherty, "Juries and Bias" (2000) 164 J.P. 695; Clare Dyer, "Jurors behaving badly", The Guardian, June 25, 2002; J.R. Spencer "Did the jury misbehave? Don't ask, because we do not want to know" [2002] 61 C.L.J. 291; Chopra and Ogloff, "Evaluating Jury Secrecy: Implications for Academic Research and Juror Stress", (2002) 44 Crim. L.Q. 190. See also the Department of Constitutional Affairs, Consultation Paper, *Jury Research and Impropriety* (January 21, 2005).
[67] Cmnd. 2627, at para.355.
[68] [1981] Q.B. 1. Cp. *Solicitor-General v Radio New Zealand Ltd* [1994] 1 N.Z.L.R. 48, discussed at para.11–384. It was there held that conduct tending to undermine the jury system, or public confidence in it, might constitute contempt at common law. The protection of the jury system required the finality of jury verdicts, candour and full participation of jurors in their deliberations, and an acknowledgment of the privacy of jurors.

11–353 jury's deliberations in a highly publicised case (the trial of Jeremy Thorpe, in 1978) was not a contempt. First, it could not affect the outcome of the particular proceedings. Secondly, it did not imperil the finality of jury verdicts, or affect adversely the attitude of future jurors or the quality of their deliberations. As a direct result of that decision, Parliament enacted s.8 of the Contempt of Court Act 1981, which comprehensively prohibits disclosure of a jury's deliberations, irrespective of any potential threat to the administration of justice. In *R. v Connor; R. v Mirza*[69] Lord Hope stated that the statutory provisions are ancillary to the common law rule, their purpose being " ... to reinforce the common law by enabling proceedings for contempt to be brought in circumstances where the common law had declined to provide that remedy".

C. The text of section 8

11–354 The section provides:

"(1) Subject to subsection (2) below, it is a contempt of court to obtain, disclose or solicit any particulars of statements made, opinions expressed, arguments advanced or votes cast by members of a jury in the course of their deliberations in any legal proceedings.

(2) This section does not apply to any disclosure of any particulars—

(a) in the proceedings in question for the purpose of enabling the jury to arrive at their verdict, or in connection with the delivery of that verdict, or

(b) in evidence in any subsequent proceedings for an offence alleged to have been committed in relation to the jury in the first mentioned proceedings,

or to the publication of any particulars so disclosed.

(3) Proceedings for a contempt of court under this section (other than Scottish proceedings)[70] shall not be instituted except by or with the consent of the Attorney General or on the motion of a court having jurisdiction to deal with it."

No provision has been made for any indictable offence, and the legislature seemed content that any such incident should be dealt with under the summary jurisdiction.

D. The compatibility of jury secrecy with the European Convention

11–355 It seems that the test for bias to be applied by the European Court of Human Rights, and by the domestic courts of member states, involves both subjective and objective elements. It is necessary to ask whether a particular state provides sufficient guarantees to exclude legitimate doubts about impartiality. In *R. v Brackley and Weller*,[71] Judge L.J. explained that it had been thought in the course of preparation for the hearing that the court might have to grapple with the problem of whether s.8(1) was "compatible" with the European Convention on

---

[69] [2004] UKHL 2, [2004] 1 A.C. 1118, at [78].
[70] The scope of the Act was considered in *McCadden v HM Advocate* 1985 S.C.C.R. 282, 1986 S.L.T. 138; see para.16–390.
[71] November 3, 2000, CACD, para.6.

Human Rights, and the developing jurisprudence of the European Court,[72] but in the result this proved unnecessary. The problem was dealt with by taking evidence from jurors, some orally and others in writing, which concentrated on matters not touching upon their "deliberations". Shortly afterwards, Sir Robin Auld came to the conclusion:[73]

> "In my view, the effective bar that s.8 puts on an appellate court inquiring into and remedying possible bias or other impropriety in the course of a jury's deliberations is indefensible and capable of causing serious injustice. Recent Strasbourg case law[74] suggests that, for those reasons, it is also highly vulnerable under Art.6. If, as I shall recommend, Parliament should amend s.8 to permit the Court of Appeal to investigate such matters, it is hard to see why the scope of its investigation should not also extend to allegations of impropriety of reasoning or lack of any reasoning, for example, that some jurors ignored or slept through the deliberations or that the jury decided one way or other on some irrational prejudice or whim, deliberately ignoring the evidence."

It is now necessary to have in mind that the extent of the restriction imposed by s.8 is not as wide as Sir Robin then believed. The proposition that it put a "bar... on an appellate court enquiring into and remedying possible bias or other impropriety in the course of a jury's deliberations" was largely based on a passage in the judgment of Lord Taylor C.J. in *R. v Young*[75] which was disapproved by the House of Lords in *R. v Connor; R. v Mirza*.[76] The law has subsequently become much clearer following two further decisions of their Lordships.

In *R. v Mirza*,[77] the Court of Appeal had certified two issues as of general public importance:

> "1 Should the common law prohibition on the admission of evidence of the jury's deliberations prevail even if the Court of Appeal is presented with a statement from a juror which, if admitted, would provide *prima facie* evidence of jury partiality in breach of Art.6?
>
> 2 Does s.8 of the Contempt of Court Act 1981, when interpreted in the light of s.3 of the Human Rights Act 1998 and Art.6 of the European Convention, prohibit the admission into evidence of a statement from a juror which, if admitted, would provide *prima facie* evidence of partiality in breach of Art.6? If [so], is s.8 incompatible with Art.6 to the extent that it prohibits the admission into evidence of such a statement?"

---

[72] For a summary of the relevant Strasbourg jurisprudence, see now the speech of Lord Hope in *R. v Connor; R. v Mirza* [2004] UKHL 2, [2004] 1 A.C. 1118 at [108] *et seq*.
[73] *Review of the Criminal Courts of England and Wales* (2001), Ch.5, para.98.
[74] Sir Robin cited *Remli v France* (1996) 22 E.H.R.R. 253 and *Sander v United Kingdom* (2001) 31 E.H.R.R. 1003, (2000) 8 B.H.R.C. 279, with which he contrasted *Gregory v United Kingdom* (1997) 25 E.H.R.R. 577.
[75] [1995] Q.B. 324 at 330.
[76] [2004] UKHL 2, [2004] 1 A.C. 1118.
[77] [2002] EWCA Crim 1235, [2002] Crim. L.R. 921.

11–357

When the matter was determined by the House of Lords[78] it was held that when properly understood neither the common law principles protecting the confidentiality of a jury's deliberations nor the terms of s.8 the 1981 Act were incompatible with the right to a fair trial guaranteed under Art.6.

11–358

The appeal was heard with *R. v Connor and Rollock*. In both cases there had been a conviction by a majority of 10:2. In *R. v Mirza* a letter came to the court's attention six days afterwards alleging that some jurors had been racially prejudiced against the defendant, who was a Pakistani and had settled in England in 1988. In *R. v Connor* it was not until some time later that a juror sent a letter stating that others had not considered the case against each defendant separately but had simply convicted both (of wounding with intent) in order to save time. Their Lordships dismissed the appeals. The primary obstacle to the admission of the evidence contained in those letters was not so much the content of s.8 as the long established common law rule that the court will not investigate or receive evidence about a jury's deliberations.

11–359

The particular problem was what should happen where a juror's functions have been discharged and the problem is raised only after the trial is over. It seems to be accepted, in this jurisdiction, and in the European Court of Human Rights, that if the juror raises the possibility of bias before or during the trial it is the judge's responsibility to deal with it. The difficulty is to determine to what extent it would be legitimate, as a matter of policy, to encroach upon the principle that the secrecy of jury deliberations should be inviolate. Their Lordships observed that the system of jury trial derives its strength from collective decision-making, during which the jurors should be protected not only from outside interference but also, afterwards, from ridicule, criticism and harassment. It is sometimes suggested that public confidence in criminal justice would be eroded if this principle is undermined. There is, however, something of a mismatch between the modern approach towards openness and scrutiny, so far as judicial decisions are concerned, and the traditional secrecy as to what the amateur participants in the judicial process may do. If a judge's reasons disclosed bias or the impermissible influence of some social, racial or religious prejudice, that would rightly be criticised. Correspondingly, the maintenance of public confidence would require that such matters be corrected, so far as necessary, by an appellate process. Yet, paradoxically, where there is some evidence of such influence on the deliberations of a jury, it seems to be thought that the need for public confidence requires that it be swept under the carpet.

11–360

In *Gregory v United Kingdom*[79] it had been recognised that the common law exclusionary rule, the validity of which was reaffirmed by their Lordships in *R. v Mirza*, was a "crucial and legitimate feature of English trial law which serves... to guarantee open and frank deliberations among jurors on the

---

[78] *R. v Connor; R. v Mirza* [2004] UKHL 2, [2004] 1 A.C. 1118.
[79] (1998) 25 E.H.R.R. 577 at [44]. The case concerned a note passed by the jury to the judge, warning of "racial overtones" in relation to a black defendant, while the deliberations were still taking place. See also the rejection by the Commission in relation to *R. v Miah* [1997] 2 Cr.App.R. 12, Application No.37401/97.

evidence which they have heard". The European Court of Human Rights has not, however, had to grapple specifically with the notification of apparent misconduct after the event.

E. A comparison with the Canadian Charter

In the Canadian case of *R. v Pan; R. v Sawyer*[80] it was pointed out that the application of the rule protecting the secrecy of a jury's "deliberations" in English cases has sometimes led to "incongruous" results. For example, the contrast was highlighted between *R. v Brandon*,[81] where evidence had been admitted that a jury bailiff had revealed the accused's previous convictions to the jury, and *R. v Thompson*[82] in which evidence was *not* admitted to the effect that the foreman had revealed the previous convictions to his fellow jurors. It was recognised that the rationale behind the distinction was that in the former case the information derived from a source outside the jury room and this did not involve breaking in upon the jury deliberations. The comment was nonetheless made that in each of those cases "the information is the same and its effect upon the jury is likely the same". Despite this, however, the Supreme Court held in the cases before them that the jury secrecy rule was not incompatible with the appellants' rights under s.7 of the Canadian Charter of Rights and Freedoms. It was observed that the right to trial by jury was entrenched by reason of s.11(f) of the Charter and that the secrecy of the deliberation process, both during and after the conclusion of the trial, is a vital and necessary component of the jury system.

F. Possible exceptions to the general exclusionary rule

In *R. v Mirza*[83] Lord Hope canvassed a possible exception to the rule where there came to light evidence of matters "extrinsic to the deliberation process". He gave certain examples reflecting incidents in earlier cases such as tossing a coin[84] or consulting an ouija board.[85] Once one tries to define what is truly "extrinsic", there are difficulties. Suppose the ouija board is consulted not at an hotel but in the jury room itself, and not in the absence of some members but in the presence of all. As Lord Steyn commented[86]:

> "It must also be borne in mind that in cases involving extraneous influence on the jury the court may on established principle hear evidence about such issues. That may require the admission of evidence about how the extraneous influence was brought to bear on the jury in their deliberations. For example, adapting the facts of *R. v Young (Stephen)* [1995] QB 324, it is accepted by counsel for the Director of Public Prosecutions, that if the jury brought an ouija board into the jury room and determined the issue by consulting it, the exclusionary rule would not apply. Evidence may then be led about what actually happened. It would, of course, be absurd not to allow such evidence to be led. On the other hand, counsel for the Director of Public Prosecutions

---

[80] [2001] SCC 41, [2001] SCR 344 at [55]–[56].
[81] (1969) 53 Cr.App.Rep. 466.
[82] [1962] 1 All E.R. 65.
[83] At [123].
[84] *Vaise v Delaval* (1785) 1 T.R. 11.
[85] As in *R. v Young* [1995] Q.B. 324.
[86] In *Mirza* at [15].

felt constrained to argue that, if the foreman of a jury took a coin out of his pocket in the jury room, the evidence about the tossing of a coin in the jury room to obtain a verdict, was inadmissible. Such absurd distinctions do not reflect well on our jurisprudence. Rhetorically I would ask: What justification in logic, common sense and fairness can there then be for not admitting evidence about jury deliberations tending to establish that the verdict was the result of a fundamentally tainted process?"

11–363   The point at which influence becomes "extraneous" is not easy to discern. Bribery is likely to take place outside the jury room: racial prejudice may be applied in the course of the deliberations, consciously or unconsciously, but is equally impermissible. Both are in a real sense extraneous. To distinguish between them might seem arbitrary. As was observed by Professor Ashworth[87]:

> "It is unacceptable for the rule of confidentiality to be preserved, at the cost of miscarriages of justice, on grounds relating to such nebulous concepts as 'public confidence'".

11–364   For the time being, however, the general principle of jury confidentiality prevails, so far as deliberations are concerned, largely because any encroachment upon it is perceived as undermining the need to protect public confidence in the administration of justice. Lord Steyn thought that there was a middle way which would enable the court, even post-verdict, to enquire into jury deliberations by admitting "cogent evidence demonstrating a real risk that the jury was not impartial and that the general confidence in jury verdicts was in the particular case ill reposed". The majority did not find this compromise acceptable.

G. The meaning of "discloses" in section 8

11–365   The offence can be committed by a juror who discloses the prohibited details, as well as by an outsider who obtains or solicits them, or later discloses them. This was established by the decision of the House of Lords in *Att-Gen v Associated Newspapers Ltd*[88] in which the appellants were respectively a newspaper publisher, editor and journalist, who had published the thoughts of three jurors who had participated in a long and complicated fraud trial.[89] It was argued for the appellants that the publication was not in such circumstances a "disclosure", the suggestion being that only a member of the jury could be guilty of the offence of disclosure.

11–366   The House declined to adopt this restricted meaning of the expression and adopted the language of Beldam L.J. in the court below[90]:

> "The word 'disclose', in origin to open up or uncover, has come to mean 'to open up to the knowledge of others:' *Shorter Oxford Dictionary*. It is a word wide enough to encompass the revealing of the secrets of the jury room by a juryman to his friend or

---

[87] [2004] Crim. L.R. at 1044.
[88] [1994] 2 A.C. 238. The decision was endorsed in *R. v Mirza* [2004] UKHL 2, [2004] 1 A.C. 1118.
[89] *R. v Natwest Investment Bank*, known as the "Blue Arrow" trial.
[90] [1994] 2 A.C. 238 at 248F–G.

neighbour as well as the opening up of such knowledge to the public as a whole by someone to whom it has been revealed. And in the light of the background to which we have referred, we see every reason why Parliament should have intended the word 'disclose' to cover both situations."

For a newspaper to reveal further what a member of a jury has already told a researcher is, therefore, to "disclose" within the meaning of the Act. Presumably a disclosure would have to be a conscious act, requiring *mens rea*, and would not embrace accidental revelation, for example through dropping notes made in the course of deliberation.

H. Offering to disclose

The section does not make it an offence for a juror to *offer* to disclose what had occurred in the jury room. Such an offer might appear to constitute an attempt if it could be accounted "more than merely preparatory"[91] to a disclosure. It must be remembered, however, that the Criminal Attempts Act 1981 is confined in its application to "indictable offences",[92] and that it appears to be that case that proceedings under s.8 are to be brought under CPR, Sch.1 Ord.52.[93]

I. The meaning of "deliberations"

There appears to be little authority as to whether "deliberations" was intended by Parliament to be confined to discussions once the jury have retired, or whether any of their private communications during the course of the trial would be included.[94] The underlying policy considerations would appear to require that all such discussion should be protected. This would accord with the reasoning of Lord Parker C.J. in *R. v Thompson*. However, in *R. v Young*[95] the Court of Appeal felt entitled to receive evidence about what had taken place in the course of jury discussions in an hotel room, even after they had retired to consider their verdict, on the basis that since the whole jury were not participating in the discussions the circumstances did not fall within the Act. A similar approach was taken in Scotland, the Lord-Justice General (Rodger) stating that the court found support for its interpretation in *R. v Young*. In *Re Scottish Criminal Cases Review Commission*[96] it was held that the term "deliberations" applied to what occurred in the jury room after the trial judge had directed the jurors to retire and consider their verdicts. Accordingly the Commission in carrying out its statutory duties was entitled to make enquiries of jurors on other matters, including whether one of the jurors had visited the *locus in quo* and discussed it with other jurors; and also whether two female jurors had formed an association with one of the

---

[91] Criminal Attempts Act 1981, s.1(1).
[92] para.11–15.
[93] See, *e.g. Att-Gen v Associated Newspapers Ltd* [1994] 2 A.C. 238. Section 8(3) itself does not prescribe the procedure to be used, although it does stipulate that the consent of the Attorney-General is required.
[94] See, *e.g. R. v Miah* [1997] 2 Cr.App.R. 12 at 18 where it was held that the reasoning in *Ellis v Deheer* would extend to anything said by one juror to another subsequent to their being empannelled.
[95] [1995] Q.B. 324. See also *R. v Tharakan* [1995] 2 Cr.App.R. 368.
[96] 2001 S.C.C.R. 775 at [5].

accused. On the other hand, they could not enquire into whether the deliberations had been affected by any of these factors.

11–369 The distinction based on "deliberations" is one Sir Robin Auld thought illogical. It is difficult to justify, as a matter of policy, a less interventionist approach by the court to an incident such as that involving the ouija board should it happen in the jury room itself rather than in a hotel room. It seems repugnant to common sense that the court should hold back from investigating an allegation of something so obviously improper. Sir Robin recommended an amendment to s.8 such as to permit the Court of Appeal to enquire into any allegation of impropriety. As was pointed out, however, by Lord Rodger in *R. v Mirza*[97] Parliament has shown no inclination to change the law in this respect. He added that such a far-reaching reform would be a matter for the legislature and not for the judiciary to implement.

11–370 The question of what constitutes deliberation arose obliquely in *R. v Rankine*,[98] where the main issue was whether it was any longer permissible or wise for a judge to invite a jury to consider their verdict without retiring. It was observed that there was nothing in s.8 of the 1981 Act which affected the position one way or another. It is clear, however, from the commentary of Prof. D. Birch on the case, that the foreman had asked the jury for a show of hands and "they all eventually put their hands up, one or two after hesitating for one or two seconds". If, in such circumstances, words or gestures were exchanged between jurors, in full view of the public, it is difficult to see how this would not offend the principle sought to be protected by Parliament.

J. Statutory exceptions: section 8(2)

11–371 Subsection (2)[99] provides certain limited exceptions, namely (a) to enable the jury to arrive at its verdict and (b), in subsequent proceedings, in connection with an offence alleged to have been committed in relation to the jury in the original proceedings. Prior to the commencement of such "subsequent proceedings", however, there is no scope for making enquiries with a view to seeing whether such an offence may have been committed.

11–372 Lord Taylor C.J. observed in *R. v Young* that[1]:

" . . . s.8(2)(a) was regarded by Parliament as necessary to enable the court itself to receive notes from the jury and to ask them, for example, whether they require help on any point or in the case of a majority verdict of guilty, how many agreed and dissented. If the court were excluded from the embargo in section (1), s.8(2)(a) would not have been necessary. As a matter of principle, the object of the section is clearly to maintain the secrecy of the jury's deliberation in their retiring room. To give the court power, after verdict, to inquire into those deliberations, would force the door of the jury room

---

[97] At [173].
[98] [1997] Crim. L.R. 757.
[99] The text of which is to be found at para.11–354.
[1] [1995] Q.B. 324 at 330H. See also *R. v Jameson* (1896) 12 T.L.R. 551 at 594, Lord Russell C.J.

wide open. If one dissentient juror or sharp-eared bailiff alleged irregularities in the jury room, the court would be pressed to inquire into the jury's deliberations. We are in no doubt that s.8(1) of the Act applies to the court as to everyone else".

It is now clear, however, that these observations of Lord Taylor should not be followed in so far as they suggest that the court would itself be acting unlawfully in carrying out appropriate investigations, since this proposition was disapproved by their Lordships in *R. v Connor; R. v Mirza*[2]:

"Properly construed, s.8(1) does not apply to the court of trial or to the Court of Appeal hearing an appeal in that case. It cannot properly be read as categorising what the court does in the course of its investigations as a contempt of the court itself".

It was described in *Att-Gen v Scotcher*[3] as "a very strange notion," and in *Mirza* as an "absurdity",[4] that the court could itself be in contempt. The Court of Appeal has the power under s.23(1) of the Criminal Appeal Act 1968 to receive evidence relating to an alleged irregularity in a trial and Parliament did nothing to qualify that power when enacting s.8 of the Contempt of Court Act 1981.[5]

The court is restricted by the common law rule—*not* by s.8. The court can make enquiries and make steps to obviate problems emerging *during* the trial. But the court is restricted from probing as to deliberations after retirement. In the light of this, a *Practice Direction*[6] was promulgated which provides that jurors should be instructed to inform the court of any irregularities which come to their attention. Trial judges should ensure that the jury is alerted to the need to bring any concerns about fellow jurors to the attention of the judge at the time, and not to wait until the case is concluded. More radically, Professor J.R. Spencer has suggested that there could be no principled objection to the recording of jury deliberations.[7]

Section 8(2) does not exempt research into the working of the jury system. In 1993, the first recommendation of the Royal Commission on Criminal Justice[8] was that Parliament should amend the Act "to enable research to be conducted into juries' reasons for their verdicts", but there has been no action taken on the proposal.

Where a jury is having difficulty in arriving at its verdict, it is open to a judge to ask questions which will assist the jury in its task. In *R. v Schot and Barclay*,[9]

---

[2] [2004] UKHL 2, [2004] 1 A.C. 1118 at [57], Lord Slynn.
[3] [2005] UKHL 36, [2005] 1 W.L.R. 1867, [2005] 3 All E.R. 1 at [22].
[4] At [25], Lord Steyn. See also Lord Hobhouse at [139].
[5] See also *Scottish Criminal Cases Review Commission, Petrs*, 2001 S.L.T. 1198 at 1202.
[6] [2004] 1 W.L.R. 665. See now [2002] 1 W.L.R. 2870 (March 22, 2005), Part IV.42.6. For the latest version of the *Direction* see http://www.courtservice.gov.uk/docs/cpd/consol_criminal_pd_220305.doc.
[7] [2002] 61 C.L.J. 291 at 293.
[8] *Report* (1993) Cm. 2263, para.8. See also the *Review of Criminal Courts of England & Wales* (2001), Sir Robin Auld, Ch.5, para.98, cited at para.11–355.
[9] [1997] 2 Cr.App.R. 383, (1997) 161 J.P. 473, discussed more fully at paras 10–72 *et seq.*

where the jury initially returned to court to announce that they were "unable to come to any decisions owing to some jurors conscious beliefs", the trial judge asked the jury to write a "much fuller note explaining to the court what the problem is that you are having . . . ". The jury did as instructed, and sent a second note to the effect that "some members of the jury cannot bring themselves to make a true judgment due to our beliefs, not religious but personal." The trial judge discharged the jury but, before doing so, asked the jury to write down the names of the members of the jury to whom the second note related; the jury supplied the names of the two appellants.

11–377 The Court of Appeal entertained "considerable doubt as to whether he should have sought, in the terms which he did, clarification of the first note, and certainly he should not have asked at that stage for the names of the jurors to whom the second note related. Such requests, it seems to us, were in breach of the widely expressed terms of s.8(1) of the Contempt of Court Act 1981." This last proposition, however, would appear no longer to be correct in the light of the view taken by the House of Lords in *Mirza* as to the "absurdity" of the court being in contempt.[10]

K. *Mens rea* and section 8

11–378 Section 8 itself says nothing of *mens rea*. In the context of the Contempt of Court Act, making as it does such specific provision for strict liability in ss.1 and 2, one might expect that, if s.8 were to be treated as creating a strict liability offence, the Act would say so. It would seem that the alleged contemnor would at any rate have to be shown to have deliberately obtained, solicited or disclosed, as the case may be; and also to have been aware that what was being disclosed was one of the "particulars" identified in the section ("statements made, opinions expressed, arguments advanced or votes cast"). The subject of *mens rea* was addressed by the House of Lords in *Att-Gen v Scotcher*.[11] Lord Rodger said simply that it was not disputed that the *mens rea* for a s.8 offence was "an intention to disclose". Where deliberate disclosure takes place, therefore, as in *Scotcher*, there will be liability unless a defence can be established.[12]

11–379 Suppose that a convicted defendant, convinced of his innocence, sought to discover from a member of the jury the process of reasoning by which he was convicted. Would he have any defence that he had no intention of interfering with the course of justice? The matter of *mens rea* was addressed to a limited extent only by the Divisional Court in *Att-Gen v Judd*[13] where, in addition to harassing a juror (by inviting her to write to the trial judge to tell him that she had made a mistake in voting for his conviction), the defendant also sought details of the voting.

---

[10] See para.11–373.
[11] [2005] UKHL 36, [2005] 1 W.L.R. 1867, [2005] 3 All E.R. 1 at [12].
[12] As to possible defences, see the discussion of *Att-Gen v Scotcher* below at paras 11–392 *et seq*.
[13] [1995] C.O.D. 15.

11-380 The matters identified by the court as constituting instances of the *actus reus* of common law contempt were "the attempt to persuade [the juror] to write to the trial judge, telling her that he attended many car boot sales at which he would look for her and, generally, intimidating her by his conduct." The court was satisfied that each of these matters had been established and, what is more, that they had been done intentionally. Reference was made to the judgment of Bingham L.J. in *Att-Gen v Sport Newspapers Ltd*,[14] and his statement of the law as to the *mens rea* required, in the context of publication contempt, was adopted as fairly and accurately representing the law relevant to the case in hand.

11-381 In particular, the court cited the requirement that it was necessary to show that the conduct in question was "specifically intended to impede or prejudice the due administration of justice". It was also confirmed that the relevant intent can be inferred from the surrounding circumstances, including the foreseeability of the consequences of the conduct. Nevertheless, the probability of the consequence had to be "little short of overwhelming" before it would suffice to establish the necessary intent.

11-382 In the case of *Att-Gen v Judd*,[15] there seemed to be little doubt that he was guilty of contempt in the sense of "intimidating" a juror. It may not have been necessary to go further than this, but the Divisional Court did hold that the respondent had asked a question of the juror which had "technically" amounted to a contempt of court under s.8. No separate penalty was imposed in respect of the statutory contempt. What was not directly addressed by the court was whether any specific intention was required in the context of the s.8 contempt, over and above the knowledge that he was asking a question as to the jury's deliberations. In the course of argument in the House of Lords in *Att-Gen v Associated Newspapers Ltd*,[16] it was suggested by counsel that the wide construction of s.8(1) by the Divisional Court had created "an absolute principle of liability which was capable of discouraging open discussion of a matter of public interest and concern, namely, whether serious fraud trials should continue to be heard by juries". This description was, however, neither accepted nor rejected in Lord Lowry's speech.

11-383 Although therefore a final answer cannot yet be given, it seems unlikely that a court would require anything further than the deliberate obtaining, disclosure, or solicitation, as the case may be. Indeed, it would not be difficult for a court to draw the inference that an alleged contemnor in these circumstances had realised that there would be undesirable consequences for the administration of justice; that is to say, if jurors could be pestered with enquiries as to their confidential deliberations with impunity.[17]

---

[14] [1991] 1 W.L.R. 1194, 1208F–H, [1992] 1 All E.R. 503g–j.
[15] [1995] C.O.D. 15.
[16] [1994] 2 A.C. 238 at 251A–B.
[17] See, *e.g. R. v Martin* (1848) 5 Cox C.C. 356, Pigot C.B., cited at para.11–178.

11–384 In the New Zealand case of *Solicitor-General v Radio New Zealand Ltd*,[18] it was held that at common law approaches to jurors, following the conclusion of a trial, would amount to contempt and that it was not necessary to show an intention to interfere with the administration of justice. The reasoning was explained as follows:

" ... no meaningful distinction can be drawn between interfering with the administration of justice in relation to a pending case, or injuring the system as a whole in relation to its capacity to administer justice in the future. The latter must be regarded as of at least equal importance. Accordingly we hold that the mens rea element is satisfied by proof that the defendant knowingly carried out the act or was responsible for the conduct in question. Proof of an intention to interfere with the due administration of justice may assist the conclusion that the publication had the required tendency, and its presence or absence would also be relevant to penalty; but the absence of such an intention will not necessarily lead to a conclusion that no contempt has been committed."

If the conduct in question falls within s.51 of the Criminal Justice and Public Order Act 1994,[19] it could be dealt with under those provisions, relating to intimidation or harm, rather than the law of contempt. Nevertheless, since not all approaches to jurors would be within the statute, the unresolved question as to *mens rea* remains of some importance.

L. Jury counselling

11–385 A practice appears to have developed of offering jurors in particularly traumatic cases counselling about their jury deliberations.[20] It is clear that the greatest care needs to be taken in the course of any such exercise to avoid infringing the terms of s.8. Whereas, no doubt, welfare officers employed by the Department for Constitutional Affairs could be duly briefed on the subject, it would be virtually impossible to police private counselling or medical consultations.

M. Jury secrecy and possible miscarriages of justice

11–386 A problem arises where a juror discloses (albeit perhaps unlawfully) some incident that occurred in the jury room (whether to the press or a party's legal advisers) in such a way as to cast some doubt upon the propriety of a conviction. It would surely be undesirable if a miscarriage of justice were to go uncorrected simply because the workings of the jury must remain, even in those circumstances, inviolate and secure from the public gaze at all costs. As a matter of

---

[18] [1994] 1 N.Z.L.R. 48, High Court (Full Court). See also *Hinch v Att-Gen (Vic)* (1987) 164 C.L.R. 15 at 42, Wilson J., at 46 and 49, Deane J., at 69 and 70, Toohey J., and at 85, Gaudron J.
[19] paras 11–145 *et seq.*
[20] Following the trial of *R. v West* (tried at Winchester before Mantell J. during the autumn of 1995, and subsequently the subject of an unsuccessful appeal: [1996] 2 Cr.App.R. 374), the Lord Chancellor's Department announced that it would be offering counselling to the jury. Jurors were told that they could make use of a free-phone helpline, consult their general medical practitioners or see the Lord Chancellor's Department's own welfare officers. "Debriefings" were held in a group session with such officers. See the article "Counselling for counsel" in *The Times*, January 2, 1996.

public policy, however, the courts have long set themselves against enquiring into what passes between jurors in discussions leading to a verdict.[21] Moreover, it would clearly be a *prima facie* offence for the legal advisers of a person convicted in such circumstances to address questions to the former members of the jury in an effort to uncover what had happened in the course of their deliberations.[22]

It was said in *R. v Millward*[23] that "it would . . . set a very dangerous precedent if, save in quite extraordinary circumstances, an apparently unanimous verdict of a jury delivered in open court, and not then and there challenged by any juror, were to be reopened and subjected to scrutiny". This was said in the unusual circumstances of a foreman, having delivered what purported to be a unanimous verdict of "guilty", realising the next day that she should have replied that it was a majority verdict of 10:2. Another situation was considered in *R. v Osmanioglu*.[24] On the third day of a jury's retirement and two hours after a majority direction, a jury note was received to the following effect: " One of our jurors is feeling unwell and cannot participate in the discussion. We have reached a verdict on count one". Despite the contents of the note, a verdict was taken on count one and the appellant was convicted by a majority of 10:2. The foreman indicated to the judge that the juror concerned had not been fully concentrating before they were released early for the weekend break. No point was taken at the time by the appellant's counsel and the Court of Appeal said that if he had felt that there was any injustice occurring at that point he would have objected. Moreover, the court seems to have been satisfied that the foreman's answer to the judge about her colleague's lack of concentration was, on its face, directed towards outstanding issues—rather than to count one on which the verdict had just been delivered. Neither of these reasons seems entirely convincing. The court considered *inter alia* the terms of s.8 of the Contempt of Court Act 1981. It was observed that it reflected an underlying common law principle, although reference was made to *R. v Young* and *R. v Qureshi* which have now to be approached with caution in the light of the later House of Lords decisions of *R. v Mirza* and *R. v Smith*.[25] The general exclusionary principle was reaffirmed that

" . . . it was not proper to make any enquiries into, or to receive or have regard to any evidence about, what was said by individual jury members during their deliberations, or

---

[21] See, *e.g. Ellis v Deheer* [1922] 2 K.B. 113 at 121; *R. v Thompson* [1962] 1 All E.R. 65, (1962) 46 Cr.App.R. 72.

[22] In *R. v Schot and Barclay* [1997] 2 Cr.App.R. 383 at 396E–F the Court of Appeal affirmed the principle that "there is no right in anyone to inquire as to what occurred in the jury room . . . ", adding that a trial judge "must take care not to seek such clarification as may disclose the substance of the jury's deliberations or expose their thought processes." But see now the more detailed explanation of these principles in *R. v Smith (Patrick)* [2005] UKHL 12, [2005] 1 W.L.R. 704 at [16], set out at para.11–392.

[23] [1999] 1 Cr.App.R. 61. See the commentary by D.C. Ormerod [1999] Crim. L.R. 165. See also *R. v Qureshi (Sajid)* [2001] EWCA Crim. 1807, [2002] 1 W.L.R. 518, where the same traditional approach was followed. *Qureshi* appears not to have been cited or referred to in *R. v Smith* or *Att-Gen v Scotcher* [2005] UKHL 36, [2005] 1 W.L.R. 1867, [2005] 3 All E.R. 1. This is probably because its authority had been doubted in *Mirza* by Lord Steyn at [12].

[24] [2002] EWCA Crim. 930.

[25] See too *Att-Gen v Scotcher* [2005] UKHL 36, [2005] 1 W.L.R. 1867, [2005] 3 All E.R. 1.

indeed at any time after the jury had been empannelled before it delivered its verdict. It was a principle of the highest importance and its reasons were to secure the finality of decisions and to protect the jury themselves. Any other approach would also result in the court having to hear evidence after the event from particular jury members".

11-388 Although exceptions to this principle have subsequently been recognised,[26] the facts of *Osmanioglu* would not appear to fall within any of them, in the sense that there was no question of the jury as a whole declining to deliberate or of "a negation of the function of a jury and a trial". It is probably still correct, as the court concluded,[27] that any enquiry about the ability of a particular jury member to have participated in reaching a verdict would be impermissible.

11-389 In *R. v Lewis (Patrick Arthur)*[28] Keene L.J. referred to *Nanon v The State*[29] and to the two policy reasons underlying the principle; namely (i) finality and (ii) the need to protect jurors from inducement or pressure to reveal what has gone on in the jury room and/or to alter their views about the case. It was confirmed that the Human Rights Act 1998 has not affected the principle of jury secrecy.[30] Following the decision in *R. v Miah*,[31] there was an application to the European Court of Human Rights. It was unanimously rejected by the Commission,[32] on the basis that the rule governing the secrecy of the jury deliberations is a legitimate and crucial feature of English jury trials, which serves to reinforce the jury's role as the ultimate arbiter of fact and to guarantee open and frank deliberation among jurors on the evidence they have heard.

11-390 It has been argued by Anthony Jennings Q.C.[33] that these observations in *Miah* should not necessarily be taken as being a wholehearted and general endorsement of the particular provisions contained in s.8. In *Miah* itself, although the applicant's complaint was declared inadmissible, it has to be remembered that this was fundamentally because there was no sufficient evidence of bias on the particular facts. It is not easy, applying first principles, to understand how a domestic appellate court is in a position to carry out a review that would be sufficiently rigorous, notwithstanding the constraints of s.8, to be able to exclude in all circumstances objectively justified doubts on the question of impartiality. It seems from the observations of the Commission in *Miah* that the extent of the enquiry to be expected of a domestic court will depend on the quality of the evidence of alleged bias. There does not seem to be anything in the European jurisprudence that would justify or sanction a variable test being applied to allegations of bias depending merely upon the stage the proceedings had reached. In other words, the *general* prohibition against enquiries into jury deliberations contained in s.8 (as currently interpreted), and confined to a certain stage of the

---

[26] See the summary of principles set out below from *R. v Smith (Patrick)* [2005] UKHL 12, [2005] 1 W.L.R. 704 at [16].
[27] At [35]–[36].
[28] [2001] EWCA Crim. 749, *The Times*, April 26, 2001.
[29] [1986] A.C. 860.
[30] See also *Gregory v United Kingdom* (1998) 25 E.H.R.R. 577 and *Sander v United Kingdom* (2001) 31 E.H.R.R. 1003, (2000) 8 B.H.R.C. 279.
[31] [1997] 2 Cr.App.R. 12.
[32] Application No.37401/97.
[33] *Archbold News*, July 8, 2002.

trial, might not truly be compatible with the need for rigorous enquiry. Nevertheless, the Court of Appeal in *Qureshi*[34] seemed satisfied that the Commission's statement in *Miah* constituted an unqualified endorsement of s.8 as being compliant with Art.6. Mr Jennings disagrees with that analysis and suggests that it might be possible to re-interpret the notion of "deliberations" in such a way as to render s.8 compatible with the Convention. One could insert the fundamental qualification that deliberations should only be inviolate provided they are being conducted properly and in accordance with the evidence. Obviously that could only be established following an investigation into them and such a construction would thus mean that the inviolability intended by Parliament would in fact be rendered nugatory.

Another construction of s.8 was put forward in argument in *R. v Mirza*[35] to the effect that its scope should be limited to the activities of journalists, or others, seeking to discover the terms of a jury's deliberations, and that it was concerned with questions of contempt rather than admissibility. It was suggested that it had been too broadly construed by Lord Taylor C.J. in *R. v Young*. These submissions were rejected simply on the basis that *Qureshi* was binding, and the court thus felt unable to admit the juror's letter. However the authority of that ruling was regarded by Lord Steyn in *Mirza* as being "a questionable foothold of the rule of absolute secrecy in all circumstances".[36]

The correct approach to these problems has now been comprehensively reviewed by the House of Lords and the principles were summarised by Lord Carswell in *R. v Smith (Patrick)*.[37] This synthesis was endorsed shortly afterwards in *Att-Gen v Scotcher*.[38]

(1) The general rule is that the court will not investigate, or receive evidence about, anything said in the course of the jury's deliberations while they are considering their verdict in their retiring room.[39]

(2) An exception to the above rule may exist if an allegation is made which tends to show that the jury as a whole declined to deliberate at all, but decided the case by other means such as drawing lots or tossing a coin. Such conduct would be a negation of the function of a jury and a trial whose result was determined in such a manner would not be a trial at all.[40]

(3) There is a firm rule that after the verdict has been delivered evidence directed to matters intrinsic to the deliberations of jurors is inadmissible.[41]

---

[34] [2001] EWCA Crim 1807, [2002] 1 W.L.R. 518, [2002] 1 Cr.App.R. 33.
[35] [2002] EWCA Crim 1235, and later in the House of Lords [2004] 1 A.C. 1118.
[36] At [12].
[37] [2005] UKHL 12 at [16].
[38] [2005] UKHL 36, [2005] 1 W.L.R. 1867, [2005] 3 All E.R. 1 at [17].
[39] *Ellis v Deheer* [1922] 2 KB 113 at 117–18, Bankes LJ; *R. v Miah* [1997] 2 Cr.App.R. 12, 18, Kennedy LJ; *R. v Mirza*, at 1156, para.95, Lord Hope of Craighead.
[40] *R. v Mirza* at 1164–1165, para.123, Lord Hope of Craighead.
[41] The House so held in *R. v Mirza*, affirming a line of cases going back to *Ellis v Deheer* [1922] 2 K.B. 113 and *R. v Thompson (Timothy Morgan)* [1962] 1 All E.R. 65.

(4) The common law has recognised exceptions to the rule, confined to situations where the jury is alleged to have been affected by what are termed extraneous influences, *e.g.* contact with other persons who may have passed on information which should not have been before the jury.[42]

(5) When complaints have been made during the course of trials of improper behaviour or bias on the part of jurors, judges have on occasion given further instructions to the jury and/or asked them if they feel able to continue with the case and give verdicts in the proper manner. This course should only be taken with the whole jury present and it is an irregularity to question individual jurors in the absence of the others about their ability to bring in a true verdict according to the evidence.[43]

(6) Section 8(1) of the 1981 Act is not a bar to the court itself carrying out necessary investigations of such matters as bias or irregularity in the jury's consideration of the case. The members of the House who were in the majority in *R. v Mirza*[44] all expressed the view that if matters of that nature were raised by credible evidence the judge can investigate them and deal with the allegations as the situation may require.[45]

11–393 Matters were taken further by the House of Lords shortly afterwards in *Att-Gen v Scotcher*.[46] A juror wrote to the defendant's mother, after verdict, revealing matters which related to the jury's deliberations. The Attorney-General gave leave for proceedings to be brought against him under s.8 of the Contempt of Court Act. The Divisional Court held that there was no defence available to him on the basis that he was motivated by a desire to expose a miscarriage of justice. A sentence was imposed of two months' imprisonment, suspended for twelve months, and he was ordered to pay costs of £2,500. It was accepted that the defendant had a genuine belief that there had been a miscarriage, but it was also thought that he probably was "unreceptive to the views of others".

11–394 In the House of Lords it was argued that s.8 had to be interpreted as including a defence where there was a *bona fide* aim of preventing a miscarriage of justice. Otherwise the section would not be compatible with Art.10 of the ECHR. Such a reading was said to be required by s.3 of the Human Rights Act 1998: alternatively, there should be a declaration of incompatibility. These arguments were rejected. On the other hand, it was recognised that if a juror had genuine concerns he could communicate with the court directly, or with a jury bailiff, or the clerk of the court.[47] Moreover, such concerns could be expressed in a sealed letter to the defendant's solicitors or counsel, or even perhaps to a body such as

---

[42] See such cases as *R. v Blackwell* [1995] 2 Cr.App.R. 625 and *R. v Oke* [1997] Crim L.R. 898.
[43] *R. v Orgles* [1994] 1 W.L.R. 108.
[44] [2004] 1 A.C. 1118.
[45] See the opinions of Lord Slynn of Hadley, at 1144–5, [50]–[51]; Lord Hope of Craighead at 1155, 1161 and 1165, [92], [112] and [126]; Lord Hobhouse of Woodborough, at 1170 and 1172–4, [141] and [148]; and Lord Rodger of Earlsferry at 1176, [156].
[46] [2005] UKHL 36, [2005] 1 W.L.R. 1867, [2005] 3 All E.R. 1.
[47] *ibid.* at [27].

the Citizens Advice Bureau, with a view to onward transmission to the court. Where a juror complains to the court itself, however, about misconduct which is intrinsic to the jury's deliberations, it may be that he is tendering inadmissible evidence, but that does not necessarily mean that he has done anything improper or unlawful.[48] It was observed by Lord Rodger[49] that there was nothing to be found in Parliamentary debates on the Contempt of Court Bill to suggest that limited communications of that kind were at the time a cause of concern to the legislature. The problem that Mr Scotcher was unable to overcome was that he had deliberately chosen to pass on the jury deliberation to "a third party who had no authority to receive disclosures on behalf of the court and who might, or might not, pass the contents of the letter on to the court".[50]

In the light of this analysis, it is clear that, provided that where concerns are expressed in a letter sent to an appropriate recipient, courts should no longer take the rigid approach adopted in such earlier cases as *R. v Less*[51] where the court expressed "disquiet that such documents should ever have come into existence, let alone that they should have been placed before the court".

---

[48] *ibid.* at [19].
[49] *ibid.* at [21].
[50] *ibid.* at [28].
[51] [1993] T.L.R. 186.

CHAPTER 12

CIVIL CONTEMPT

		Para
I.	General Principles	12–1
II.	The Mental Element for Civil Contempt	12–80
III.	Who Can Be Liable for Civil Contempt?	12–99
IV.	Breaches of Court Orders Generally	12–124
V.	Freezing and Search and Seizure Orders	12–144
VI.	Breaches of Undertakings	12–182

I. General Principles

A. The nature of civil contempt

12–1 Civil contempt, or "contempt in procedure"[1] as it used sometimes to be called, may arise in a variety of circumstances during the course of civil litigation. It consists principally in disobedience to an order of the court.[2] Sometimes such disobedience may also assume other characteristics. It *may* amount to criminal contempt; for example, if the order relates to a ward of court,[3] or in the case of a *publication* in breach of an order it may also be a strict liability contempt under the Contempt of Court Act 1981.[4] Also, where an order is made in court to regulate proceedings, with reference to a particular case, as for example a s.4(2) order, breach of such an order will be regarded as a criminal contempt.[5]

12–2 Someone who is not a party to civil proceedings in which an order has been made may assist a party who *is* so bound to disobey the order. Or perhaps a third party sets out independently to subvert the effect of such an order. Such behaviour may well constitute a criminal contempt at common law.[6] In most cases, however, disobedience to an order of the court (*e.g.* an injunction) on the

---

[1] See, *e.g. Halsbury's Laws of England* (4th ed., 1998) Vol. 9(1) reissue, para.402 of which still so refers to it; *Hadkinson v Hadkinson* [1952] P. 285 at 295, Denning L.J., CA; *Phonographic Performance Ltd v Amusement Caterers (Peckham) Ltd* [1964] Ch. 195 at 198–9, Cross J.

[2] It does not embrace, however, acts or omissions which are inconsistent with a merely declaratory order, even if the acts or omissions in question are those of parties to the litigation in which the order has been made: *Webster v Southwark London Borough Council* [1983] Q.B. 698, Forbes J. See the further discussion of this case, in the context of sequestration, at para.14–117.

[3] See para.3–115.

[4] See generally ch.4.

[5] See *MGN Pension Trustees Ltd v Bank of America National Trust and Savings Association and Another (SFO intervening)* [1995] 2 All E.R. 355, discussed at para.7–171. See also the discussion of s.4(2) orders at para.7–133 and paras 6–203 *et seq.*

[6] See, *e.g. Att-Gen v Newspaper Publishing plc* [1988] Ch. 333 and the cases considered at paras 6–124 *et seq.*

part of someone who is directly bound by it will be classified as civil contempt.

Proceedings under s.63(3) of the Magistrates' Courts Act 1980 are referred to as "civil contempt proceedings".[7] They concern punishment for disobedience to an order "to do anything other than the payment of money or to abstain from doing anything".[8]

12–3

The definition of civil contempt and the difficulties involved have already been discussed in detail.[9] The object of this chapter is to set out particular examples of civil contempt, and to consider certain general principles which are specific to this type of contempt.

12–4

B. The public and private aspects of civil contempt

It is obvious that any civilised society depends upon the authority and effectiveness of orders made in its courts. There is thus a public interest in seeing that orders are enforced. Civil contempt cannot be considered therefore merely as a means by which individual litigants can enforce orders in their favour. The court has an interest, on behalf of the community at large, in ensuring that orders are not disobeyed at the option of one party, or even of both.[10] It has been said that[11]:

12–5

" ... civil contempt ... bears a two-fold character, implying as between the parties to the proceedings merely a right to exercise and a liability to submit to a form of civil execution, but as between the party in default and the state, a penal or disciplinary jurisdiction to be exercised by the court in the public interest".

The Attorney-General may, as guardian of the public interest,[12] from time to time have a legitimate role in safeguarding the authority of court orders obtained in civil litigation.[13] Nevertheless, the individual litigants are entitled to have resort to the quasi-criminal process of civil contempt in order to enforce orders made in their favour. There is thus sometimes an overlap between the public and private interests.

12–6

---

[7] In Sch.3 to the Contempt of Court Act 1981.
[8] See para.13–116.
[9] See paras 3–69 et seq.
[10] See, e.g. Phonographic Performance Ltd v Amusement Caterers (Peckham) Ltd [1964] Ch. 195 at 198–9, Cross J.; Jennison v Baker [1972] 2 Q.B. 52 at 61F, CA; Con-Mech (Engineers) Ltd v AUEW (Engineering Section) [1973] I.C.R. 620 at 625, Sir John Donaldson; Re M (Minors) (Access: Contempt: Committal) [1991] 1 F.L.R. 355 at 358H, Butler-Sloss L.J; R. v Inland Revenue Commissioners Ex p. Kingston Smith [1996] 2 S.T.C. 1210 (Buxton J.); Re M (A Minor) (Contempt of Court: Committal of Court's Own Motion) [1999] Fam. 263.
[11] Laws of England, (3rd. ed. Vol. 8, 1954), p.20. The modern equivalent is to be found in the 4th ed., Vol. 91), para.460. The summary was quoted with approval in Phonographic Performance Ltd v Amusement Caterers (Peckham) Ltd [1964] Ch. 195 at 198–9, Cross J. and in Jennison v Baker [1972] 2 Q.B. 52 at 69–70, Edmund Davies L.J. See also Salmon L.J. at 61F and 64G.
[12] paras 2–199 et seq.
[13] See, e.g. Att-Gen v Newspaper Publishing plc [1988] Ch. 333 and the remarks of Lord Cross in Att-Gen v Times Newspapers Ltd [1974] A.C. 273 at 326–7.

12–7 Another dichotomy frequently encountered in the authorities is that the function of the summary process may be either coercive in nature or punitive.[14] There will be cases where the private and public considerations are both material, and others in which coercion and punishment will both have a role to play.[15] The contempt jurisdiction is not, however, to be used as a means of providing compensation to litigants in whose favour an order has been made[16]:

> "Proceedings for contempt of court are always in a rather special category because they are intended to uphold the authority of the court and to make certain that its orders are obeyed. They are not intended to provide solace or compensation to the plaintiff. If the plaintiff wants compensation, she must seek it in other forms."

C. The jurisdiction to be kept separate from criminal proceedings

12–8 The jurisdiction in relation to civil contempt is separate from the criminal jurisdiction of any other court,[17] and it is important that such cases be dealt with swiftly and decisively, even if criminal proceedings have been commenced on the basis of the same facts. It is, for example, inappropriate generally to adjourn an application to commit for breach of an order so as to abide the outcome of a prosecution for assault arising out of the same conduct.[18]

12–9 Lord Bingham C.J. summarised the relevant principles as follows[19]:

> "The first is that there is no absolute rule that civil proceedings (including contempt proceedings) should not proceed when criminal proceedings are pending. The second is that there is a general rule that contempt proceedings should be dealt with 'swiftly and decisively' (per Stephen Brown L.J. (as he then was) in *Szczepanski* at 469). The third principle is that the test as to whether or not contempt proceedings should proceed in advance of criminal proceedings is whether there is a real risk of serious prejudice leading to injustice if the contempt proceedings go ahead. That is a summary of what

---

[14] See paras 3–12 *et seq*.
[15] See, *e.g. Burton v Winters* [1993] 1 W.L.R. 1077, 1080; *Lightfoot v Lightfoot* [1989] 1 F.L.R. 414. See also *Re Barrell Enterprises* [1973] 1 W.L.R. 19 at 27C, Russell L.J.; *Hale v Tanner (Practice Note)* [2000] 1 W.L.R. 2377 at 2381B, [2000] 2 F.L.R. 879 at 884, at [29], Hale L.J. See also *Lomas v Parle* [2003] EWCA Civ 1804, [2004] 1 W.L.R. 1642, [2004] 1 All E.R. 1173, [2004] 1 F.L.R. 812.
[16] *Johnson v Walton* [1990] 1 F.L.R. 350 at 353D–E, Lord Donaldson M.R. See also *Re Hudson, Hudson v Hudson* [1966] Ch. 209 at 213–14, Buckley J.
[17] This principle remains valid despite the blurring in recent statutory amendments between the criminal and civil jurisdiction in the context of domestic violence: see, *e.g.* the Family Law Act 1996, s.42A inserted by the Domestic Violence, Crime and Victims Act 2004. See A.J. Ashworth, "Social Control and 'Anti-Social Behaviour'; the Subversion of Human Rights?" (2004) 120 L.Q.R. 263; M. Burton, "Criminalising Breaches of Civil Orders for Protection from Domestic Violence" [2003] Crim. L.R. 301. See also M. Burton, "Coherent and effective remedies for victims of domestic violence: time for an integrated domestic violence court?" (2004) 16 C.F.L.Q. 317.
[18] *Szczepanski v Szczepanski* [1985] F.L.R. 468 at 469, CA; *Caprice v Boswell* (1986) Fam. Law 52, CA; *Keeber v Keeber* [1995] 2 F.L.R. 748; *M v M* [1997] 1 F.L.R. 762, 3 F.C.R. 288. See also Posner, "Civil Contempt and Criminal Trial" (1993) Fam. Law 385.
[19] *M v M* [1997] 1 F.L.R. 762 at 764B–D. See also *Re H (A Minor) (Injunction: Breach)* (1986) Fam. Law 139.

was said by Neill L.J. in *H v C* at 789. If the answer is that there is no real risk of serious prejudice leading to injustice, then in the ordinary way the contempt proceedings should go ahead. If, on the other hand, there is judged to be a real risk of serious prejudice leading to injustice if the contempt proceedings go ahead, the court may properly stay the contempt proceedings and would ordinarily do so."

There is thus a discretion to decide whether or not a real risk of serious prejudice would be caused by so proceeding, without waiting until any such criminal proceedings are concluded.[20] But it is not appropriate, in exercising that discretion, merely to do a balancing exercise.[21] It would not normally suffice, in order to establish a real risk of serious prejudice, to show merely that the respondent to contempt proceedings would be forced to reveal his defence in the forthcoming criminal case.[22] On the other hand in *M v M (Contempt: Committal)*[23] the Court of Appeal declined to interfere with the exercise of a judge's discretion *not* to proceed with a contempt application by a wife, on the ground that such proceedings could be prejudicial to the husband's pending criminal trial. Brooke L.J. observed in *London Borough of Barnet v Hurst*[24] that it might be necessary at some stage in the future to consider the possible effect of Art.6 of the European Convention if a defendant to criminal proceedings complains of a real risk of prejudice in the event of being required to defend himself in prior contempt proceedings. On such an occasion it would be necessary to consider the effect of such decisions as *Jefferson v Bhetcha*[25] and *Secretary of State for Trade and Industry v Crane and Burton (No.2)*.[26]

Where contempt of court involves the commission of criminal offences which are already the subject of pending criminal proceedings, it is important to avoid double punishment in respect of the same incident or offence. The court should not punish for the crime rather than the contempt. In *Smith v Smith*,[27] for example, the length of the sentence that the judge imposed suggested that he had in mind the criminal aspect rather than the disobedience of the orders of the court, and the sentence was reduced to reflect this. In another case,[28] even though the breach in question consisted of a rape, the Court of Appeal held that the

---

[20] *H v C (Contempt and Criminal Proceedings)* [1993] 1 F.L.R. 787 at 789, CA, Neill L.J. See also *Jefferson v Bhetcha* [1979] 1 W.L.R. 898, CA.
[21] *Keeber v Keeber* [1995] 2 F.L.R. 748 at 751, Butler-Sloss L.J.
[22] Last note.
[23] [1997] 1 F.L.R. 762.
[24] [2002] EWCA 1009, [2003] 1 W.L.R. 722, [2002] 4 All E.R. 457 at [17].
[25] [1979] 1 W.L.R. 898, CA.
[26] CH/2000/APP/553, February 11, 2001, Ferris J. It was decided that disqualification proceedings against two company directors should not be stayed pending the outcome of criminal proceedings because they would give rise to no unfairness. The court had particular regard to recent amendments to s.20 of the Company Directors Disqualification Act 1986, which prevented the possibility that evidence which had not been given "wholly voluntarily" in that context might be used in later criminal proceedings against the director.
[27] [1991] 2 F.L.R. 55 at 63E–F, Neill L.J., 64F–G, CA, Balcombe L.J.
[28] *N v N (Contempt: Committal)* [1992] 1 F.L.R. 370 at 375B–C, Russell L.J.; *Green (Bryan)* [1993] Crim. L.R. 46.

12–11   appropriate penalty for the element of contempt was six months' imprisonment.

12–12   The relevant authorities were summarised by Brooke L.J. in *London Borough of Barnet v Hurst*,[29] and the position considered in the light of the Human Rights Act 1998. This had also been addressed by the Divisional Court in *DPP v Tweddell*,[30] which concerned a decision to stay magistrates' court proceedings in which the defendant was charged with assault contrary to s.47 of the Offences Against the Person Act 1861. The ground for the stay was a perceived abuse of process on the basis that the defendant had already been sentenced to three months for contempt in civil proceedings in the county court in respect of the same incident of violence. The prosecutor appealed successfully, and Latham L.J. highlighted the difference of function between the two types of proceedings. It was held that Art.6 of the European Convention on Human Rights had not affected the question whether a prosecutor was to be regarded as "committing a breach of process" in pursuing criminal proceedings based on the same facts as earlier contempt proceedings.

12–13   In the *Hurst* case[31] Brooke L.J. expressed agreement in this respect with the decision of the Divisional Court. He referred to relevant Strasbourg jurisprudence and, in particular, to *S v Germany*[32] where the Commission had dismissed a German citizen's complaint in respect of a German conviction arising out of the same facts as those underlying an earlier Netherlands conviction. Although he received a longer sentence in Germany, credit had been given in respect of the Netherlands sentence. At the time, as the Commission recalled, the Convention did not guarantee expressly or impliedly the principle of *Ne bis in idem* (or double jeopardy).

12–14   Nevertheless, Brooke L.J. drew attention[33] to the potentially important provisions of Art.4 to Protocol 7 to the Convention. This expressly forbids double jeopardy in respect of criminal proceedings within the same state. It was opened for signature in 1984 but had not so far been ratified or indeed signed by the United Kingdom (or Andorra), and thus the rights conferred by it do not appear among the Convention rights scheduled to the Human Rights Act 1998. There is some Strasbourg case law germane to these double jeopardy provisions, such as *Gradinger v Austria*[34] and *Oliveira v Switzerland*.[35] In the latter case, the court held that there had been no violation where a man had been convicted of different offences on separate occasions arising out of the same road traffic accident. Once again, it was an important consideration that the first fine was taken into account and deducted from what would otherwise have been the fine imposed for the more serious offence at the second hearing.

---

[29] [2002] EWCA Civ 1009, [2003] 1 W.L.R. 722, [2002] 4 All E.R. 457.
[30] [2001] EWHC (Admin) 188, [2002] 1 F.L.R. 438.
[31] At [15].
[32] (1983) 39 D.R. 43.
[33] At [13].
[34] (1995) A/328 33/1994/480/562.
[35] (1998) 28 E.H.R.R. 289.

D. The "arbitrary" nature of court's jurisdiction

In *Re Clements*[36] Sir George Jessel M.R. said:

12–15

"It seems to me that this jurisdiction of committing for contempt being practically arbitrary and unlimited should be most jealously and carefully watched and exercised, if I may say so, with the greatest reluctance and the greatest anxiety on the part of Judges, to see whether there is no other mode which is not open to the objection of arbitrariness and which can be brought to bear upon the subject."

There are a number of means available for dealing with an alleged contempt which are "not open to the objection of arbitrariness" and which are of varying degrees of effectiveness according to the circumstances. For example, where a person has given an undertaking to the court, and it is suspected that he has failed to comply with it, but there is some doubt about it, it may be appropriate before moving for committal to apply for an order requiring him to state whether he has in fact complied,[37] although this seems rarely to be done in practice. What is more likely to happen is simply that a solicitor's letter would be sent setting out the case on non-compliance, giving an opportunity to deny it or offer an explanation.

12–16

In cases of non-compliance with a mandatory order, an injunction or an order for specific performance of a contract, resort may be had to the court's power to direct that the act required may, so far as practicable, be performed by someone else; either the party by whom the judgment or order was obtained, or some other person appointed by the court at the expense of the disobedient party.[38] In *Danchevsky v Danchevsky*,[39] Lord Denning M.R. commented:

12–17

"Whenever there is a reasonable alternative available instead of committal to prison, that alternative must be taken. In this case there was a reasonable alternative available. It was this: to enforce the order for possession by a warrant for possession, to sell the house, and to make the conveyance of the property by means of an instrument to be signed and executed by a third person on the direction of the court."[40]

E. Committal and sequestration to be sparingly used

Although tempered to some extent in modern practice by procedural and evidential safeguards, it is the summary nature of the contempt jurisdiction that

12–18

---

[36] (1877) 46 L.J. Ch. at 385. See also *Wilson v Raffalovich* (1881) 7 Q.B.D. 553 at 571; *Re Davies* (1888) 21 Q.B.D. 236 at 239, Mathew J.; *Gay v Hancock* (1887) 56 L.T. 726; *Seaward v Patterson* [1897] 1 Ch. 545 at 553, Lindley L.J.; *Fairclough and Sons v The Manchester Ship Canal Co (No.2)* (1897) 41 Sol. Jo 225; *Marshall v Marshall* (1966) 110 Sol. Jo. 112; *Danchevsky v Danchevsky* [1975] Fam. 17 at 22, Lord Denning M.R.; *Ansah v Ansah* [1977] Fam. 138 at 144; *R v R* [1979] Fam. 56; *Thomason v Thomason* [1985] F.L.R. 214, CA; *I v D (Access Orders: Enforcement)* [1988] 2 F.L.R. 286, Sheldon J.; *Jordan v Jordan* [1993] 1 F.L.R. 169, CA; *A v D (Contempt Committal)* (1993) Fam. Law 519.
[37] *Kangol Industries Ltd v Bray (Alfred) & Sons Ltd* [1953] 1 All E.R. 444. See the discussion of self-incrimination in civil contempt at paras 3–188 *et seq.*
[38] For which, see now CPR Sch.1, Ord.45.8. See also *Danchevsky v Danchevsky* [1975] Fam. 17.
[39] [1975] Fam. 17 at 22.
[40] See now Supreme Court Act 1981, s.39.

12–18

is regarded as "open to the objection of arbitrariness".[41] Its implementation through the traditional means of committal and sequestration should not be invoked unless they are truly needed. Although, for example, provision is made for enforcing a judgment or order for possession of land by means of committal or sequestration,[42] such means should only be used in exceptional circumstances and normally the appropriate means of enforcement will be by writ of possession. Since in practice a judgment or order to give possession of land customarily would not specify the time within which the act is required to be done,[43] it will not ordinarily be enforceable by order of committal or writ of sequestration.[44]

12–19 Even though the liberty of the subject is not directly involved, sequestration is regarded by the court as an extremely serious matter. In *Edward Grey Ltd v Greys (Midlands) Ltd*[45] where a company was seriously in breach of an undertaking not to use in the Birmingham area a name of which "Greys" was the only prominent word, Wynn-Parry J. decided that sequestration would have been too drastic a course, particularly in view of the fact that the company had eight other branches.

12–20 Also in *Steiner Products Ltd v Willy Steiner Ltd*[46] Stamp J. declined to make an order for sequestration, even though there was no excuse for the defendant company's failure to carry out an undertaking, mentioning as a reason that such an order would probably affect the livelihood of innocent persons. This sanction was, however, tellingly brought to bear during industrial disputes more recently, and particularly during the strike of the National Union of Mineworkers of 1984–5. These developments are considered in more detail in the chapter concerning sanctions and remedies.[47]

12–21 An illustration of the court's reluctance to resort to the process of contempt until all other avenues have been explored is provided by the old case of *Dodington v Hudson*.[48] The defendant had been ordered to carry out certain building works and it was held that attachment could not issue because there had been no oral demand for performance by the plaintiff's agent at the time when the order was served. Gifford C.J. said that the plaintiff should have requested the defendant to set about the work, since "he might then perhaps have alleged some excuse for not proceeding to immediate performance."[49]

---

[41] See Jessell M.R. in *Re Clements* (1877) 46 L.J. Ch. 375 at 385, quoted at para.12–15. See also, in the context of commercial litigation, the remarks of Colman J. in *Belgolaise v Purchandani*, The Times July 30, 1998, 142 Sol. Jo. L.B. 252.
[42] CPR Sch.1, Ord.45.3(1).
[43] The former RSC, Ord.42, r.2(2). This is no longer in effect, but it is still the case that the coercive methods of enforcement under CPR Sch.1, Ord.45.5 cannot be employed unless the act was specified to be done within a particular time in the original order or by an order extending or abridging the time under CPR 3.2(2)(a) or fixing such a time under CPR Sch.1, Ord.45.6.
[44] CPR Sch.1, Ord.45.5.
[45] [1952] R.P.C. 25.
[46] [1966] 1 W.L.R. 986 at 992.
[47] See paras 14–125 *et seq*.
[48] (1824) 1 Bing. 410, 130 E.R. 165.
[49] *ibid.* at 411.

Where there is difficulty in complying with the terms of an injunction, even though such orders should be implicitly obeyed,[50] the court will take a realistic view.[51] In appropriate cases the operation of an injunction may be suspended or varied, especially if it is made clear to the court that its terms are disproportionately burdensome.[52] Sometimes, where it might help to achieve the desired aim, the court would order a writ of sequestration to lie in the office for a period of months rather than permit it to come into immediate effect, since this last resort might prove to be unnecessary if the defendants in the meantime complied with the relevant order.[53] The court had the power to issue a *subpoena* of its own motion to ascertain the facts, and this could on occasion prove to be a useful step in bringing a contempt to light and in avoiding proceedings for committal.[54]

12–22

Inappropriate resort to the summary procedures of contempt may be met with sanctions. In *Adam Phones Ltd v Goldschmidt*,[55] Jacob J. held that, where an application for committal was a wholly disproportionate response to a trivial or blameless breach of an order, the court should dismiss the application with costs in favour of the respondent. Applications for committal should not be used tactically, in cases of mere technical breach, where a respondent had done his best to obey the order.

12–23

F. Committal as a matter of "very last resort" in family proceedings

Because of the summary and quasi-criminal nature of the jurisdiction, the courts have warned that the process of contempt should not be invoked in aid of a civil remedy where some other method of achieving the desired result is available.[56] This is especially so in the context of domestic or family proceedings. For example, in *Ansah v Ansah*,[57] it was said by Ormrod L.J. that "Committal orders are remedies of last resort; in family cases they should be the very last resort".

12–24

Similarly, in *Thomason v Thomason*,[58] Bush J. made the general observation:

12–25

---

[50] *Woodward v Lincoln (Earl)* (1624) 3 Swan. App. 626, 36 E.R. 1000; *Johnson v Walton* [1990] 1 F.L.R. 350 at 352, Lord Donaldson M.R.; *DPP v Channel 4 Television Co Ltd* [1993] 2 All E.R. 517 at 529a, Woolf L.J., cited at para.9–232, and generally the discussion at paras 9–205, 12–139.
[51] See, *e.g. Irtelli v Squatriti* [1993] Q.B. 83, CA, discussed in more detail at paras 12–88 *et seq.*
[52] See, *e.g. Att-Gen v Colney Hatch Lunatic Asylum* (1868) 4 Ch. App. 146; *Day v Longhurst* (1843) 62 L.J. Ch. 334.
[53] See, *e.g. Att-Gen v Walthamstow Urban District Council* (1895) 11 T.L.R. 533; *Stancomb v Trowbridge Urban District Council* [1910] 2 Ch. 190.
[54] *Yianni v Yianni* [1966] 1 W.L.R. 120, Cross. J. The modern procedure would be by way of witness summons: see paras 11–91 *et seq.*
[55] [1999] 4 All E.R. 486.
[56] For a discussion of the similar approach adopted in Australia, see M.R. Chesterman and P. Waters, "Contempt and the Disobeying Spouse" (1985) U.N.S.W.L.J. 106. See also M. Hayes and C. Williams, *Family Law Principles, Policy and Practice* (2nd ed., 1999), pp.412–13; S. Conneely, "Sentencing for Committal: Protection and Pride" [1998] Family Law 421.
[57] [1977] Fam. 138 at 144, CA. See also *Re E (A Minor: Access)* [1987] 1 F.L.R. 368; *Goff v Goff* [1989] 1 F.L.R. 436 at 441, Croom-Johnson L.J., 442, Purchas L.J.; *C v C (Access Order: Enforcement)* [1990] 1 F.L.R. 462 at 469C–D, Lloyd L.J.
[58] [1985] F.L.R. 214, CA.

12–25

> "Questions of punishment for past behaviour, or concepts of the damage to the dignity of the court if an order is disobeyed, should not enter into consideration in a domestic jurisdiction. The object of the exercise is to enforce the breached order for access in the sense of getting it working, or putting something more workable in its place. Whilst there may be cases where the Draconian powers of the court to imprison or fine may have to be invoked, they should be regarded as the weapon of the last resort."

12–26 Indeed, in *Churchard v Churchard*,[59] Ormrod L.J. went so far as to suggest that committal orders should never be made in respect of a breach of an order relating to access. He described such applications as "legalistic and futile" and expressed the view that the court should only be concerned with the welfare of the child and that it "ought not to trouble itself too much about its own dignity". Brandon L.J. apparently agreed.

12–27 It was made very clear, however, in *A v N (Committal: Refusal of Contact)*[60] that "those sweeping observations" of Ormrod L.J. should now be regarded as confined to the facts of the particular case, since they were inconsistent with more recent pronouncements by the Court of Appeal.[61] There must come a time when the court needs to ensure compliance with its orders. It becomes a question of preserving the due administration of justice and is not a matter of the judge's own dignity.[62]

12–28 Clearly there are times when the use of that weapon cannot be avoided if the court's authority is not to be thwarted or a victim left unprotected. In *Jones v Jones*,[63] Russell L.J. warned that the words of Ormrod L.J. should not be treated as laying down any general principle to the effect that " ... irrespective of circumstances, an immediate custodial sanction should not be imposed." Also, in the earlier case of *George v George*,[64] the Court of Appeal felt able to distinguish *Ansah v Ansah*,[65] on the ground that there had not been any opportunity given to the wife in that case to remedy her ways; whereas in the case then before them the respondent had been given the opportunity, when an earlier application to commit him had been adjourned, and he failed to grasp it.

12–29 The appropriate test to apply was suggested by Butler-Sloss L.J. in *Re M (Minors) Access: Contempt: Committal)*[66]:

> "Committal orders in family cases are remedies of last resort and should only be considered where there is a continuing course of conduct and where all other efforts to resolve the situation have been unsuccessful. The court would take that measure where

---

[59] [1984] F.L.R. 635 at 638.
[60] [1997] 1 F.L.R. 533.
[61] See, *e.g. Re O (Contact: Imposition of Conditions)* [1995] 2 F.L.R. 124.
[62] Cp. the well known words of Lord President Clyde in *Johnson v Grant*, 1923 S.C. 789 at 790 (cited at para.16-6). And see *Re M (A Minor) (Contempt of Court: Committal of Court's own Motion)* [1999] Fam. 263.
[63] [1993] 2 F.L.R. 377, CA. See also *Mesham v Clarke* [1989] 1 F.L.R. 370, CA and *A v N (Committal: Refusal of Contact)* [1997] 1 F.L.R. 533.
[64] [1986] 2 F.L.R. 347 at 350, CA.
[65] [1977] Fam. 138.
[66] [1991] 1 F.L.R. 355 at 358–9.

it was clear that there has been deliberate and persistent refusal to obey a court order."

Even where a contempt is proved, it should never be assumed that committal is the natural consequence. In *Smith v Smith*,[67] Sir John Donaldson M.R., in relation to a breach of a non-molestation order, warned those who are called upon to exercise these powers:

"It is quite correct that the orders of the court must and will be maintained. But there is nothing automatic about committal to prison. It depends upon all the circumstances. The breach might have been of a very minor character, such as being found within half a mile of the plaintiff's home. That would have been a breach of the undertaking, but by no stretch of the imagination could it have justified committal to prison unless it could be shown to be an act preparatory to some form of molestation."

In the same case, Balcombe L.J. emphasised the wide range of disposals open to the court[68]:

"In the lowest degree it can merely adjourn the application for committal to see what happens. It can make a suspended committal order. It can, in appropriate cases, impose a financial penalty. Further, of course, the length of the sentence, if it is considered appropriate to commit the contemnor to prison, must, as Sir John Donaldson M.R. says, vary according to the facts of the case."

The increasing problems of enforcing compliance in the field of family law

There has been a growing problem in the field of family law in finding the means to ensure that the court's orders are complied with. Clear and comprehensive guidance was given by Ward L.J. as to the appropriate steps to be taken in *Re M (A Minor) (Contempt of Court: Committal of Court's own Motion)*.[69] It will only rarely be appropriate for a judge to initiate contempt proceedings of his or her own motion, where urgent action is required to prevent justice from being obstructed. Before taking such a step the following factors are to be borne in mind in cases of alleged civil contempt:

"(1) The extent to which knowledge of the breach has become a matter of public concern amounting to scandal capable of diminishing the authority of the court such as might lead to an increased flouting of its orders.
(2) The extent to which some other interest than that of the litigant is in need of protection. In this case there are the interests of the child which are to be upheld and the child's welfare which is to be placed at the forefront of the judge's consideration.
(3) The contempt must be clear as well as flagrant.
(4) Pursuing a committal ex mero motu is a highly exceptional course to follow and the more so in family cases where it has been famously stated by Ormrod LJ in *Ansah*

---

[67] [1988] 1 F.L.R. 179 at 181.
[68] *ibid.* at 182D–E.
[69] [1999] Fam. 263.

v Ansah [1977] 2 All ER 638 at 643, [1977] Fam 138 at 144:'Committal orders are remedies of last resort; in family cases they should be the very last resort.' Applying to commit of the court's own motion is at a stage even further down the line of case-managing the impossible.

(5) The judge should always take time to pause for reflection. He should give an opportunity to invite the Official Solicitor to represent the child or perhaps only to report on the child's position. A generous reading of para.4(5) of the practice note ([1995] 2 FLR 479 at 480), namely that the child is 'refusing contact with a parent in circumstances which point to the need for psychiatric assessment' could bring the case within the limited sphere in which the Official Solicitor has indicated he will generally be prepared to assist. If necessary, the matter can be transferred to the High Court where by virtue of the office, not the person of the High Court judge, the seriousness of the problem is better addressed. Committal is always an exceptional course, particularly if it is being taken to uphold the court's authority by punishing open defiance, rather than as a means of coercion invoked by an aggrieved party to enforce a remedy granted to him by the court. Where the judge has any lingering doubt about the balance between the need to maintain the authority of the court and the effect of committal upon the children, he may well be assisted by inviting the Official Solicitor's help in providing an independent view of the interests of the children, if this issue has not been covered adequately already by a court welfare officer's report. He may also be able to assist by adducing evidence to clarify the nature and extent of any alleged breach. I say this with the concurrence of the Official Solicitor and the President. He may, however, consider that becoming involved in the prosecution of the committal undermines the confidence the children are to have in him. It will depend on the facts of the case. He may also see a potential conflict because of the role he has in advising all those who are committed to prison. If he is in conflict, but if the contempt is none the less clear and flagrant, then I see no reason why the Attorney General should not be asked to prosecute the committal as amicus. He would not welcome being asked to intervene save in the most exceptional case.

(6) All remedies should be exhausted before this weapon is wielded. If contact was still worthwhile, a further order could have been made or perhaps the alternative suggestion of staying contact could have been tried. Another order, again of last resort, is to change the child's residence if that is not inconsistent with the child's welfare. In this particular case, there appears to have been a huge input into the psychological and psychiatric assessment of the mother but in the papers before us there is little to show whether any attempt had been made for some family therapy which involved the father in the process. Such an approach ought to be the first port of call and committal the last.

(7) The danger in initiating a committal which the affected party does not seek is that the judge is at risk of being seen to be acting to preserve his own dignity and to punish for the affront to him. Thus the justification for this condign power will have been distorted. It exists only to serve the ends of justice and ultimately the crucial consideration remains what the interests of justice in the broadest sense demand, giving proper weight to the interests of the children even if their welfare is not strictly the paramount consideration because the court is not directly determining a question with respect to their upbringing."

G. Procedural steps to be rigidly enforced

12–33 *Because* of the risk of "arbitrariness" in applying the summary jurisdiction, and the threat to the liberty of the subject, courts have traditionally insisted upon scrupulous observation of any prescribed procedural step antecedent to the

GENERAL PRINCIPLES 12-34

exercise of that jurisdiction and that strict compliance should be insisted upon.[70] This was so because the court's powers to punish for civil contempt are quasi-criminal in nature.[71] This may be contrasted with the situation where a third party is alleged to have been involved in subverting the purpose or effect of an order made in civil proceedings. The need for such "procedural safeguards" may not be so readily prayed in aid by a respondent in such a case.[72] This is because it is not the service of the order which matters in such circumstances, so much as the proving of an intention to subvert its effect. This broad principle is still relevant but modern practice is more tolerant of purely technical breaches. It is now provided in the *Practice Direction*[73] the court may waive procedural defects if satisfied that no injustice has been caused.[74]

H. The safeguard of personal service of the notice of committal proceedings

Where committal is sought, although the court has power to dispense with service of the claim form or notice of application (as the case may be),[75] personal service will generally be insisted upon unless there is clear evidence of evasion.[76] It has even been held that the attendance of the alleged contemnor at the hearing does not *per se* waive the need for service.[77] The need for service also applies to a notice of an adjourned hearing date.[78]

12-34

---

[70] See paras 15–64 *et seq*. See also Sir Gorrell Barnes P. in *Townend v Townend* [1907] P. 239 (in the notes); Park J. in *Dodington v Hudson* (1824) 1 Bing. 410 at 412; and see *Re Ramsay* (1870) L.R. 3 P.C. 427; *McIlraith v Grady* [1968] 1 Q.B. 468 at 477, Lord Denning M.R.; *Nguyen v Phung* [1984] F.L.R. 773, CA; *Gagnon v McDonald, The Times*, November 14, 1984; *Lee v Walker* [1985] Q.B. 1191, CA; *M v P (Contempt of Court: Committal Order), Butler v Butler* [1993] Fam. 167 at 174, Lord Donaldson M.R.
[71] See paras 3–69 *et seq*. See also *Re Bramblevale* [1970] Ch. 123 at 137, Lord Denning M.R.; *Comet Products UK Ltd v Hawkex Plastics Ltd* [1971] 2 Q.B. 67 at 77, Cross L.J. and *The Messiniaki Tolmi* [1981] 2 Lloyd's Rep. 595 at 600, Brandon L.J. See also para.16–29 (Scotland).
[72] See Sir John Donaldson M.R. in *Att-Gen v Newspaper Publishing plc* [1988] 1 Ch. 333 at 372, and the discussion at para.6–134.
[73] At [10].
[74] Appendix 5A. See also *Carla Homes (South) Ltd v Chichester District Council, The Times*, October 15, 1999.
[75] See the Practice Direction on Committal Applications at Appendix 5A and CPR Sch.1, Ord 52.3(4) and CPR 6.8 and for the county court, see now CPR Sch.2, cc.29.1. See also *Hipgrave v Hipgrave* [1962] P. 91, where Scarman J. made an order for committal *ex parte* in circumstances where "any delay might well entail irreparable or serious mischief". See also *Pearce v Pearce, The Times*, January 30, 1959, Melford Stevenson J.
[76] *Mander v Falcke* [1891] 3 Ch. 488 at 493, Kekewich J.: "It would be impossible and inconceivable and contrary to common sense and justice, that a man who has rendered himself liable to committal should immediately be able to evade it by keeping out of the way." See also *Favard v Favard* (1896) 75 L.T. 664; *R. v Wigand* [1913] 2 K.B. 419; *Re Suarez* [1918] 1 Ch. 176; *O'Donovan v O'Donovan* [1955] 1 W.L.R. 1086.
[77] Last note: "I have not the slightest hesitation in holding that appearance is not a waiver of an objection on the ground of irregularity in a case affecting the liberty of the subject", Kekewich J.
[78] *Chiltern District Council v Keane* [1985] 1 W.L.R. 619 at 622–3; *Phonographic Performance Ltd v Tsang, The Times*, May 17, 1985; see also *Beeston Shipping Ltd v Babanaft International SA* [1985] 1 All E.R. 923, CA.

I. Preliminary requirements as to service of the judgment or order

12–35 It is also necessary to establish service of any order which is alleged to have been disobeyed by leaving a copy with the person to be served.[79] The importance of personal service of the order, where committal is sought, is to enable the person bound by the order, and who is alleged to be in contempt, to know what conduct would amount to a breach[80]; and before committal such notice is required to be proved beyond reasonable doubt.[81] It seems, however, that it is no excuse that a party who has been served with the relevant document failed to read it.[82] In cases of urgency, before formal service can be effected, it may with permission of the court be possible to telephone, fax or email the terms of an injunction to the appropriate person. Indeed, in an appropriate case, the court may grant permission for service to be effected by one or other of these means.[83]

12–36 Where a defendant has voluntarily given an undertaking which has been embodied in an order of the court, it has been recognised as not strictly necessary to serve on him the order containing the terms of the undertaking.[84] In such cases it is his own act which creates the liability, unlike the situation where it is an order of the court with which he has to comply and which therefore needs to be drawn to his attention. Despite this, in *Hussain v Hussain*[85] it was indicated by the Court of Appeal that:

> "(1) The undertaking should be included as a recital or preamble in an order of the court; this should be done even where the substantive part of the order is merely 'No Order'.
>
> (2) The order incorporating the undertaking should be issued and served on the person who has given the undertaking.
>
> (3) The order should be endorsed with a suitably worded notice explaining the consequences of a breach of the undertaking."

12–37 Procedural requirements are considered in chapter 15, but in illustrating the special nature of the contempt jurisdiction it is important to have regard to the strict regime which is imposed on those who seek to invoke it. Before enforcing by process of contempt, it is necessary to prove that the judgment or order which is alleged to have been disobeyed has been properly served, subject to the court's powers to dispense with service, or order substituted service in appropriate

---

[79] See the former RSC Ord.65, r.2, now CPR 6.4(3). In the case of a company it may be that service on solicitors will suffice: *Aberdonia Cars Ltd v Brown, Hughes Strachan Ltd* (1915) 59 S.J. 598.

[80] See, *e.g. R. v City of London Magistrates' Court Ex p. Green* [1997] 3 All E.R. 551.

[81] *Churchman v Joint Shop Stewards' Committee of the Workers of the Port of London* [1972] 1 W.L.R. 1094 at 1098, Lord Denning M.R.

[82] *Re Witten* (1887) 4 T.L.R. 36. This gives rise to the question whether liability for civil contempt may in some respects be treated as "strict". For a fuller discussion of *mens rea* in civil contempt, see paras 12–80 *et seq*, and the possible impact of the Court of Appeal's decision in *Irtelli v Squatriti* [1993] Q.B. 83, CA, addressed at paras 12–88 *et seq*.

[83] See, *e.g. R. v City of London Magistrates' Court Ex p. Green* [1997] 3 All E.R. 551 at 558c–d.

[84] *D v A & Co* [1900] 1 Ch. 484. See also *Callow v Young* (1886) 55 L.T. 543, Chitty J.; *Hussain v Hussain* [1986] Fam. 134; *Att-Gen for Tuvalu v Philatelic Distribution Corp* [1990] 1 W.L.R. 926 at 937, Woolf L.J.

[85] [1986] Fam. 134 at 142, CA, Neill L.J.

circumstances.[86] The general rule[87] is that no judgment or order shall be enforced by process of contempt unless:

(a) a copy of the order has been served personally on the person required to do or abstain from doing the act in question; and

(b) in the case of an order requiring a person to do an act, the copy has been so served before the expiration of the time within which he was required to do the act.

12–38 A distinction has been drawn between prohibitory and mandatory injunctions, in the sense that the court will sometimes be ready to enforce a prohibitive injunction by process of contempt if satisfied that the order has been drawn to the attention of the party, even though not formally served.[88]

12–39 Personal service of such a document is effected[89] by leaving it with the individual to be served. Formerly it was also necessary to show the original to the person to be served, if so requested, but since 1979[90] this is no longer necessary. The copy served must bear a penal endorsement.[91] It is necessary to prove service beyond reasonable doubt.[92]

12–40 Although in the case of a company service of an order may generally be effected by serving solicitors,[93] special provisions apply where it is sought to enforce a judgment or order against a corporation by means of an order for committal of an officer or sequestration of his assets. Before either of these remedies may be obtained it must be proved that personal service has been effected on the officer concerned[94] and, in the case of an order requiring the corporate body to do an act, that the order has been so served before the expiration of the time within which the body was required to do the act.[95] Moreover a penal notice must be endorsed on the copy served.[96]

12–41 In situations where the order requires a positive act to be done, it is sometimes the case that the time specified for performance will have been extended or abridged.[97] If this is so, the methods of enforcement provided by CPR Sch.1,

---

[86] See now CPR Sch.1, Ord.45.7(6) and (7) and CPR 6.8.
[87] See now CPR Sch.1, Ord.45.7(2) and CPR 6.8.
[88] *Ronson Products Ltd v Ronson Furniture Ltd* [1966] Ch. 603 at 616, Stamp J.; *Husson v Husson* [1962] 3 All E.R. 1056; *United Telephone Co v Dale* (1884) 25 Ch. D. 778; *Hearn v Tennant* (1807) 14 Ves. Jun. 136, 33 E.R. 473. See also the discussion in P.H. Pettit, "Injunctions, Service and Committal" (1977) 40 M.L.R. 220 at 220–3.
[89] CPR 6.4(3).
[90] SI 1979/402.
[91] CPR Sch.1, Ord.45.7(4). For appropriate forms of endorsement see para.15–25.
[92] *per* Lord Denning M.R. in *Churchman v Joint Shop Stewards' Committee of the Workers of the Port of London* [1972] 1 W.L.R. 1094, 1098. See also *Ex p. Langley* (1879) 13 Ch.D. 110 at 119, Thesiger L.J.
[93] *Aberdonia Cars Ltd v Brown, Hughes & Strachan Ltd* (1915) 59 S.J. 598.
[94] See now CPR Sch.1, Ord.45.7.
[95] See now CPR Sch.1, Ord.45.7(3)(b).
[96] For forms of penal notice see para.15–25. See now CPR Sch.1, Ord.45.7(4).
[97] See now CPR Sch.1, Ord.45.6(1).

Ord.45.5 will only be available if there is refusal or neglect to do the act required within the time as varied.[98] In such circumstances, it will be necessary to serve a copy of the order by which the abridgement or amendment was made before reliance can be placed for enforcement upon the process of contempt.[99]

12–42 Where under a judgment or order requiring the delivery of goods there is given the alternative of paying their assessed value, the judgment or order cannot be enforced by committal without a further application. Once an application has been made to the Master for a time to be fixed, and such an order has been made, it may be enforced by process for contempt, but only if a copy of the previous order has been served as well as that of the Master fixing the time for performance.[1] Similarly, where a judgment or order which requires someone to do an act does not specify a time for performance, but an order has subsequently been made[2] to fix the time, it is necessary to serve copies of both orders before enforcing by process of contempt under CPR Sch.1, Ord.45.5.[3]

J. The criminal standard of proof: a further safeguard

12–43 Any breach alleged to constitute contempt must itself be strictly proved.[4] Logically the appropriate punishment will be considered once the breach has been proved, and there is no reason to suppose that a judge may inflict a lesser penalty, for example by way of fine, on the basis that the complainant has only proved a breach according to a less onerous standard (say, on a balance of probabilities). It is submitted that, whenever an alleged contemnor is brought before the court, the breach must be proved beyond reasonable doubt. This certainly accords with Lord Denning M.R.'s exposition of the law in *Re Bramblevale Ltd*.[5]

12–44 Winn L.J. proposed in the same case a less satisfactory test, namely that the breach need only be proved "with such strictness of proof as is ... consistent with the gravity of the charge."[6] Such a test would appear to be too imprecise for the purposes of a quasi-criminal jurisdiction; subsequent cases in the Court of

---

[98] See now CPR Sch.1, Ord.45.5(1) and (2).
[99] See now CPR Sch.1, Ord.45.7(5).
[1] See now CPR Sch.1, Ord.45.7(5).
[2] See now CPR Sch.1, Ord.45.6(2).
[3] CPR Sch.1, Ord.45.7(5).
[4] *Re Bramblevale Ltd* [1970] Ch. 128 at 137, Lord Denning M.R.; *Churchman v Joint Shop Stewards' Committee of the Workers of the Port of London* [1972] 1 W.L.R. 1094 at 1098 (where Lord Denning held that the same strict standard of proof was required whether in the High Court or in the (defunct) National Industrial Relations Court).
[5] [1970] Ch. 128. See also *Comet Products UK Ltd v Hawkex Plastics Ltd* [1971] 2 Q.B. 67; *Churchman v Joint Shop Stewards' Committee of the Workers of the Port of London* [1972] 1 W.L.R. 1094; *Bartrum v Healeswood* [1973] 10 F.S.R. 585, CA; *Kent County Council v Batchelor* (1977) L.G.R. 151, CA; *Deborah Building Equipment Ltd v Scaffco Ltd, The Times*, November 5, 1986, Potts J.; *Dean v Dean* [1987] 1 F.L.R. 517, CA, 521 (Dillon L.J.), 522, (Stephen Brown L.J.).
[6] [1970] Ch. 128 at 137F–H. See also *Rejfek v McElroy* (1965) 112 C.L.R. 517, 39 A.L.J.R. 177; *Jendell Australia Pty Ltd v Kesby* [1983] 1 N.S.W.L.R. 127 at 137, McLelland J.; *NSW Egg Corp v Peek* (1987) 10 N.S.W.L.R. 72 at 81. These last two cases have been disapproved in *Witham v Holloway* (1995) 69 A.L.J.R. 847, HC.

Appeal such as *Bartrum v Healeswood*,[7] *Kent County Council v Batchelor*,[8] *Re C (a Minor) (Contempt)*[9] and *Dean v Dean*[10] have put the matter beyond doubt.[11] In the latter case, Neill L.J. said:

> "It is to be remembered that contempt of court, whether civil or criminal, is a common law misdemeanour. Furthermore, there are many authorities of which the decision in *Re Bramblevale Ltd* is an authoritative example, to the effect that proceedings for contempt of court are criminal or quasi-criminal in nature and that the standard of proof to be applied is the criminal standard."

Later, Neill L.J. suggested that it would be wise for a judge to make it expressly clear that the criminal standard of proof is being applied.[12] This principle also applies to the determination of facts tending to show that a breach was deliberate and contumacious, a matter which goes to penalty rather than to liability.[13]

12–45

The same standard of proof has been adopted by the High Court of Australia in *Witham v Holloway*,[14] which held that the distinctions between and civil and criminal contempt (described as "largely illusory") do not justify different standards of proof; and that all proceedings for contempt are realistically to be seen as criminal in nature, thus attracting the standard of proof beyond reasonable doubt.

12–46

Despite this weight of authority, it is necessary to sound a warning note in relation to the scope for different constructions of the wording of orders and undertakings, especially in the context of intellectual property disputes, defamation actions and, perhaps to a lesser extent, in non-molestation cases.[15]

12–47

K. Ambiguous or vague orders or undertakings

An order or undertaking will not be enforced by committal if its terms are ambiguous,[16] the rule being analogous to that which governs the interpretation of penal statutes.[17] It is to the terms of the order itself that one must look in order

12–48

---

[7] [1973] 10 F.S.R. 585, CA.
[8] (1976) 75 L.G.R. 151.
[9] [1986] 1 F.L.R. 578 at 588, Mustill L.J.
[10] [1987] 1 F.L.R. 517, CA.
[11] See also *The Commissioner of Water Resources v Federated Engine Drivers' and Firemen's Association of Australasia* [1988] 2 Qd. R. 385; *Z Bank v D1* [1994] 1 Lloyd's Rep. 656 at 660.
[12] *Smith v Smith* [1991] 2 F.L.R. 55 at 61C, Neill L.J.
[13] *Z Bank v D1* [1994] 1 Lloyd's Rep. 656 at 667.
[14] (1995) 69 A.L.J.R. 847.
[15] Discussed more fully at para.12–56.
[16] *Iberian Trust Ltd v Founders Trust & Investment Co Ltd* [1932] 2 K.B. 87; *Redwing Ltd v Redwing Forest Products Ltd* (1947) 177 L.T. 387 at 390, Jenkins J.; *PA Thomas & Co v Mould* [1968] 2 Q.B. 913 at 922, O'Connor J. See also *Wilson & Whitworth Ltd v Express & Independent Newspapers Ltd* [1969] R.P.C. 165; *Hussain v Hussain* [1986] Fam. 134 at 142, CA; *R & I Bank of Western Australia Ltd v Anchorage Investments* (1992) 10 W.A.R. 59; see *R. v City of London Magistrates' Court Ex p. Green* [1997] 3 All E.R. 551.
[17] *Att-Gen v Sillem* (1864) 10 H.L. Cas. 704. See generally F.A.R. Bennion, *Statutory Interpretation* (4th ed., 2002), Pt XVII, "Principle against doubtful penalisation".

to define the obligations imposed.[18] It was held in *Federal Bank of the Middle East v Hadkinson*[19] that the words "his assets and/or funds", appearing in the then current standard form of freezing (*Mareva*) injunction, were ambiguous—in the sense that they did not make clear that the order was to cover assets or funds of which the respondent was only the bare legal owner. His appeal against a finding of contempt was therefore allowed, since the alleged breach consisted of the transfer of funds from two accounts at a Jersey bank into accounts held in the name of his wife (in circumstances where it was being assumed by the court that the funds in question were not beneficially owned by the respondent).[20] On the other hand, in cases where one is concerned with third parties who are seeking to subvert the *purpose* of a court order,[21] the court is not confined to looking at the strict terms.[22] Even a party might be held in contempt if such an intent to subvert could be demonstrated, notwithstanding ambiguity in the wording.

12–49 One of the difficulties in framing orders or undertakings is to draft the wording sufficiently broadly to ensure that the defendant cannot escape his responsibilities by drawing unduly technical distinctions. The problem arises particularly in the contexts of preventing the publication of defamatory words and the infringing of intellectual property rights. This point was addressed by Millett J. in the context of copyright in *Spectravest Inc v Aperknit*[23]:

> "In intellectual property cases a plaintiff is concerned not only to stop exact repetition of the defendant's activity which can be described with particularity, but to prevent fresh invasions of his rights in ways which cannot be foreseen or described exactly. The ingenuity of those who infringe copyright and trade marks and engage in passing off is boundless, and plaintiffs cannot be adequately protected by orders which are cabined or confined. That is the reason for the standard forms of injunctions in such cases, with their inevitable references to 'otherwise infringing,' 'substantial part,' 'colourable imitation,' and 'otherwise passing off.' Where a defendant, faced with such an order, acts honestly and reasonably, this will mitigate and even excuse a breach of the order; but if a breach is proved, it will be for him to mitigate or justify it, and his excuse may need to be thoroughly probed if the circumstances are suspicious."

Similar problems arise in the context of defamation, where the standard wording of injunctions or undertakings includes a prohibition upon the publication of "any similar words defamatory of the claimant", or perhaps "any similar libels".

12–50 There thus arises a tension between two objectives. On the one hand, it is necessary to achieve precision and clarity in the drafting because the defendant needs to understand the full extent of his obligation, in a situation where he may

---

[18] See, *e.g. Northwest Territories Public Service Association v Commissioner of the Northwest Territories* (1980) 107 D.L.R. (3d) 458.
[19] [2000] 2 All E.R. 395.
[20] See also para.12–153 below.
[21] Such as *Att-Gen v Times Newspapers Ltd* [1992] 1 A.C. 191. See also the discussion of "purpose" by Lord Hope in *Att-Gen v Punch Ltd* [2002] UKHL 50, [2003]1 A.C. 1046 at [95], discussed at para.6–147.
[22] [1992] 1 A.C. 191, *per* Lord Oliver at 224.
[23] [1988] F.S.R. 161 at 174.

GENERAL PRINCIPLES   12–54

find himself at risk of enforcement by process of contempt; whereas, on the other hand, the complainant will not unreasonably wish to ensure that he is adequately protected by wording which is wide enough to meet all possible permutations of misconduct within the defendant's ingenuity.

Especially because in civil contempt it is unnecessary to show any particular state of mind on the part of the alleged contemnor,[24] there can be difficulties when a claimant seeks to commit a defendant on the footing that what he has done amounts to a breach, and the defendant believes (perhaps as a result of legal advice) that his conduct was quite legitimate.   **12–51**

It might be thought that the principle requiring proof beyond reasonable doubt,[25] in cases of civil contempt, would be adequate protection in these circumstances. In one passing off case,[26] however, Millett J. was faced with a submission that the court could not be satisfied beyond reasonable doubt that the logos in question were indeed an infringement, to which he responded in the following terms: **12–52**

> "In my judgment... this question is not one which requires or is susceptible of proof beyond a reasonable doubt. It is a question of impression and is for the court, not the witnesses, to decide. Direct evidence of deception is not necessary... Where it is alleged that the defendant has broken the terms of an injunction or undertaking to the court, this must be strictly proved according to the criminal standard of proof, but this requirement relates only to the allegation that the defendant has committed the acts complained of. It does not relate to the very different question whether those acts, if proved to have been committed by the defendant, constitute a breach of the injunction or undertaking. That question is often, and in intellectual property cases almost invariably, one of degree and impression."

It is perhaps worthy of note that in this case neither *Re Bramblevale* nor *Dean v Dean* appears to have been cited before the judge. Whether this would have made any difference to his conclusion is clearly a matter of conjecture, but in any event his approach seriously undermines the protection afforded to litigants by the closely related principles that proof is required beyond reasonable doubt and, correspondingly, that orders and undertakings that are enforceable by process of contempt should be carefully and clearly drafted. It is surely questionable whether a quasi-criminal liability should arise, with the possibility of loss of liberty or other penal sanctions, on the basis of "degree and impression".[27]   **12–53**

It is suggested that the words of Jenkins J. in *Redwing Ltd v Redwing Forest Products Ltd*[28] are more consonant with principle and less likely to lead to arbitrariness and injustice: **12–54**

---

[24] See the discussion on the mental element at para.12–80.
[25] See, *e.g. Re Bramblevale* [1970] Ch. 128 and *Dean v Dean* [1987] 1 F.L.R. 517, discussed at paras 12–43 *et seq.*
[26] *Chelsea Man plc v Chelsea Girl Ltd* [1988] F.S.R. 217 at 224–5.
[27] Particularly having regard to Art.7 of the European Convention of Human Rights.
[28] [1947] 64 R.P.C. 67 at 71, (1947) 177 L.T. 387 at 390. These words of Jenkins J. were cited by Munby J. in *Harris v Harris; Att-Gen v Harris* [2001] 2 F.L.R. 895 at [328].

"... a Defendant cannot be committed for contempt on the ground that upon one of two possible constructions of an undertaking being given he has broken that undertaking. For the purpose of relief of this character I think the undertaking must be clear and the breach must be clear beyond all question."

The importance of clarity was also emphasised by Dame Elizabeth Butler-Sloss P in *Att-Gen v Greater Manchester Newspapers Ltd.*[29]

12–55 The burden should thus lie upon those who seek to obtain an order, or to negotiate an undertaking, to obtain clear restrictions to the full extent required at the time when the defendant's obligation arises. An order should be clear in its terms and should not require the person to whom it is addressed to cross-refer to other material in order to ascertain his precise obligation.[30] Contempt proceedings based on such a defective order may well founder.[31] There is clearly no scope for reading implied terms into an injunction.[32]

Non-molestation orders

12–56 Another area in which problems of ambiguity have sometimes arisen is that of non-molestation orders, because it may not always be obvious whether certain types of conduct could be said to amount to molestation.[33] This is perhaps especially so in relation to approaches by one former partner to another in circumstances where there is a reluctance to accept that a relationship has broken down.

12–57 In *Johnson v Walton*,[34] for example, undertakings had been given to the court not to use violence to the plaintiff and not to molest her in any way, or encourage others to do so. Shortly afterwards, photographs of her in a partially naked state appeared in the press, which the plaintiff said had been taken by the respondent during the relationship. Lord Donaldson M.R.[35] explained that harassment includes within it an element of intent to cause distress or harm, and that "molestation" had a similar meaning, whether it was used in the specific context of the Domestic Violence and Matrimonial Proceedings Act 1976 or not. He took

---

[29] [2001] All E.R. (D) 32 (Dec).
[30] *Rudkin-Jones v Trustee of the Property of the Bankrupt* (1965) 109 Sol. Jo. 334. See also now *Harris v Harris; Att-Gen v Harris* [2001] 2 F.L.R. 895 at [289]–[295].
[31] See, *e.g. The Commissioner of Water Resources v Federated Engine Drivers' and Firemen's Association of Australasia* (1988) 2 Qd. R. 385.
[32] See, *e.g. Deodat v Deodat*, June 9, 1978 (unreported), CA; *Harris v Harris; Att-Gen v Harris* [2001] 2 F.L.R. 895, [288], Munby J.
[33] See the specimen clauses 38–41 in the Family Law Form FL404.
[34] [1990] 1 F.L.R. 350, CA. Cf. however *C v C (Non-Molestation Order: Jurisdiction)* [1998] 1 F.L.R. 554, where Sir Stephen Brown P. refused to continue a non-molestation order directed towards preventing the publication of "any account of the events which have occurred during the marriage of the applicant and the respondent in relation to their personal and/or financial affairs", saying that any such complaint could be pursued by way of defamation proceedings. Cp. *Clibbery v Allen* [2002] EWCA Civ 45, [2002] Fam 261.
[35] *ibid.*, following the decision of Ormrod L.J. in *Horner v Horner* [1982] Fam. 90.

the view that sending photographs to national newspapers, intending to cause distress, could be so categorised.[36]

"Any undertaking must be drafted in terms sufficiently clear to enable a breach to be clearly stated and, if established, to be specified with sufficient particularity to enable the party to know precisely what the court has found proved against him and has resulted in an order for his committal".[37]

L. The possibility of approaching the court for clarification

Where there is doubt as to whether or not an anticipated course of conduct will amount to a breach, it may sometimes be appropriate to approach the court with a view to seeking a release from,[38] or modification of,[39] the terms of the order or undertaking. This is sometimes, however, of little comfort because an applicant would almost certainly have to pay the costs of any such application; and there may be no justification for discharging or even varying the original obligation.

What may be required ideally from the applicant's point of view would be some form of declaratory order which would have the effect of clearing in advance the legitimacy of the proposed course of conduct. Without express liberty to apply, it is doubtful whether the court would readily entertain such an application. As Viscount Dilhorne put it in *Imperial Tobacco Ltd v Att-Gen*[40]:

"I can well see the advantages of persons being able to obtain rulings on whether or not certain conduct on which they wish to embark will be criminal and it may well be a defect in our present system that it does not provide for that".

It is possible to imagine, for example, a series of applications made to the court with a view to designing some advertising material or get-up which would serve the original purpose of the defendant, as nearly as possible, without leading to quasi-criminal sanctions. The court would not welcome such a series of experimental applications, and it could hardly be said to serve the public interest.

The present attitude of the courts is illustrated by the approach of the Court of Appeal in *Leary v BBC*,[41] where Lord Donaldson M.R. said:

"The primary responsibility for avoiding a contempt of court by actions which interfere with the course of justice lies with those contemplating the action concerned. All

---

[36] Cp. the approach of the Court of Appeal in *Thomas v News Group Newspapers* [2001] EWCA Civ 1233, [2002] E.M.L.R. 4 where it was held that newspapers could be guilty of harassment.
[37] *Re M (Minors) (Access: Contempt: Committal)* [1991] 1 F.L.R. 355 at 364G–H, Beldam L.J.
[38] *Cutler v Wandsworth Stadium Ltd* [1945] 1 All E.R. 103, CA.
[39] See, *e.g. Crest Homes plc v Marks* [1987] 1 A.C. 829 at 854B, Lord Oliver.
[40] [1981] A.C. 718. For an extended discussion, see J.L.L. Edwards, *The Attorney-General, Politics and the Public Interest* (1984), p.150. And see D. Feldman, "Declarations and the Control of Prosecutions" [1981] Crim. L.R. 25. See also A.T.H. Smith, "Clarifying the Criminal Law: Declarations in Criminal Proceedings" in ed. P.F. Smith, *Criminal Law: Essays in Honour of J.C. Smith* (1987), pp.132–47; *Regina (Rusbridger) v Att-Gen* [2004] 1 A.C. 357.
[41] September 29, 1989, CA (Lexis).

citizens, including the media and corporate bodies, have a primary responsibility for obeying the law, which happily they mostly seek to discharge."

The following passage from the judgment of Ralph Gibson L.J. was to similar effect:

"The primary defence of the administration of justice from unlawful interference by the press or by broadcasters is the heavy sanction of prosecution if a contempt is committed. We have, of course, no system of prior examination and permission."

12–63 Even stronger is the language of Lord Morris in *Knuller (Publishing, Printing and Promotions) Ltd v DPP*[42]:

" ... nor do I know of any procedure under which someone could be told with precision just how far he may go before he may incur some civil or some criminal liability. Those who skate on thin ice can hardly expect to find a sign which will denote the precise spot where he (*sic*) will fall in.
It is not the function of the court to decide how close to dangerous waters it is possible to sail without actually being shipwrecked."

M. Further analogies with criminal procedure

1. *Severance*

12–64 Analogous with criminal procedure is the court's recognition that there is a discretion to order severance of a committal motion, as there is in the case of indictments.[43]

2. *The admission of fresh evidence on appeal*

12–65 It has also been held that the criminal rules relating to the admission of fresh evidence in the Court of Appeal should be followed in a case of civil contempt concerning a breach of a Tomlin order.[44] The approach adopted was that, since the appellants stood to lose their liberty if the judge's order were upheld, the court should act by analogy with the practice in the Court of Appeal (Criminal Division) which, by s.23(1) of the Criminal Appeal 1968, permitted the adducing of fresh evidence where justice required it. For this reason, it appears that the usual *Ladd v Marshall*[45] principles do not apply to the admission of fresh evidence in contempt appeals, even where the contempt in question may be properly classified as civil.

N. The Court's discretion not to hear a contemnor until the contempt is purged

12–66 An effective sanction (deriving from canon law) was the practice that one who was in contempt might not be heard further in the same litigation, for his own

---

[42] [1973] A.C. 435 at 463.
[43] *Re A Company, The Times*, December 27, 1983, Nourse J.
[44] *Irtelli v Squatriti* [1993] Q.B. 83, CA. See the more general discussion in ch.3 on the relationship between civil and criminal contempts.
[45] [1954] 1 W.L.R. 1489, CA.

benefit, unless and until he had purged his contempt.[46] In the words of Lord Brougham,[47] "It is a general rule of all Courts, that no party shall be allowed to take active proceedings, if in contempt." This was clearly a practice primarily coercive in nature rather than punitive. It was by no means universally applied. There have always been recognised so-called "exceptions", so that for example a contemnor might be heard on an application to purge the contempt; or for the purpose of setting aside the order breach of which had put him in contempt[48]; or of appealing against the order of committal for lack of jurisdiction[49]; also, he was not precluded from defending himself in the action itself.[50] So too, it has been held that a defendant in breach of the terms of an *Anton Piller* (now known as a "search and seizure") order might seek to have the order set aside, although he could still be punished for contempt.[51]

Whether it is right to speak of "exceptions", however, depends upon whether the practice could be said to have amounted to a *rule* at all,[52] or whether the true position is that there exists a discretion only[53]; in which case it would be more appropriate to categorise the so-called exceptions simply as being situations in which the discretion will generally be exercised in favour of hearing the litigant in default.

It was suggested by Brandon L.J. in *The Messiniaki Tolmi*[54] that no opportunity to apply to the court, while in contempt, would be available where the application itself could be classified as an abuse of the court's process or in cases concerned with the welfare of minors. A more flexible approach was taken

---

[46] "They that are in contempt... specially so far as proclamation of rebellion are not to be [heard] neither in that suit, nor any other, except the court of special grace suspend the contempt": Lord Bacon in 1618 Ordinance No.78: see J. Spedding and Heath, *Works of Bacon* (1859) Vol. VII, p.770. But later the rule seems to have been confined to applications made in the same proceedings as those giving rise to the contempt. See *Chuck v Cremer* (1846) 1 Coop. *temp*. Cott. 205 at 208 (and the cases there listed), 247 and 338, 47 E.R. 820 at 821, 841, 884; *Harrison v Harrison* (1842) 4 Moo. P.C. 96, 13 E.R. 238; *Garstin v Garstin* (1865) 4 Sw. & Tr. 73, 164 E.R. 1443; *Cavendish v Cavendish and Rochefoucauld* (1866) 15 W.R. 182; *Hadkinson v Hadkinson* [1952] P. 285 at 288–91, 298, Denning L.J; *Bettinson v Bettinson* [1965] Ch. 465. See also G. Lightman Q.C., "A Trade Union in Chains" (1987) C.L.P. 25 at 35.
[47] *Curtis v Curtis* (1845) 5 Moo P.C. 252 at 256, 13 E.R. 487 at 489.
[48] It did not appear to make any difference whether the grounds of application included the contention that the order in question was irregular or made as a result of irregular proceedings: *The Messiniaki Tolmi* [1981] 2 Lloyd's Rep. 595 at 602. See now *Motorola Credit Corp v Uzan (No.2)* [2003] EWCA Civ 752, [2004] 1 W.L.R. 113.
[49] *Gordon v Gordon* [1904] P. 163, CA, *Hadkinson v Hadkinson* [1952] P. 285 at 288–91, Romer L.J., 295–6, Denning L.J., CA; *Bettinson v Bettinson* [1965] Ch. 465; *The Messiniaki Tolmi* [1981] 2 Lloyd's Rep. 595 at 601; *Maynard v Maynard* [1984] F.L.R. 85 at 90, CA.
[50] *Hadkinson v Hadkinson* [1952] P. 285 at 289–90, 296; *Midland Bank v Green (No.3)* [1979] Ch. 496 at 506, Oliver J.
[51] *Wardle Fabrics Ltd v G Myristis Ltd* [1984] F.S.R. 264; *Columbia Pictures Inc v Robinson* [1987] Ch. 38 at 71–2.
[52] As the majority appear to have thought in *Hadkinson v Hadkinson* [1952] P. 285.
[53] In the light of the House of Lords' decision in *X Ltd v Morgan Grampian (Publishers) Ltd* [1991] 1 A.C. 1, this seems now recognised to be the case. See also the view of Denning L.J. in *Hadkinson v Hadkinson* [1952] P. 285 at 298.
[54] [1981] 2 Lloyd's Rep. 595 at 602.

in *Re P (Minors) (Wardship) (Access: Contempt)*,⁵⁵ where Russell L.J. indicated a willingness to proceed because the court considered that course to be in the child's best interests.

12–69   So too, in *Clarke v Heathfield*,⁵⁶ the Court of Appeal decided to hear an appeal by trustees of the National Union of Mineworkers against an *ex parte* order appointing a receiver of the union's assets, even though the appellants themselves were in open and continuing contempt. This was because the interests of all members of the union, as beneficiaries, were affected. It was emphasised, however, that the circumstances were exceptional. Shortly afterwards, on the hearing of the *inter partes* application, Mervyn Davies J. also decided that he would in the exercise of his discretion hear counsel for the contemnors (without determining whether they had a *right* to be heard).⁵⁷

12–70   More recently, the House of Lords confirmed that the question should be approached on the basis of a *discretion* to be exercised flexibly, according to the circumstances, rather than on the basis of a *rule*.⁵⁸ The discretion will be exercised in the light of the particular facts,⁵⁹ and in particular taking into account the nature and merits of the application sought to be made.⁶⁰ "A legal principle based on public policy which ignores the consequences for the parties can itself bring the administration of the law into disrepute".⁶¹ The modern, more

---

⁵⁵ [1991] 1 F.L.R. 280 at 288, CA; see also *Re A (A Minor) (Appeal by Party in Contempt)* [1980] 1 F.L.R. 140, CA.
⁵⁶ [1985] I.C.R. 203 at 205, Stephenson L.J., and 207, O'Connor L.J.
⁵⁷ *Clarke v Heathfield (No.2)* [1985] I.C.R. 606 at 613. Lightman contends in his article "A Trade Union in Chains" (1987) C.L.P. 25 that there was a right to be heard in any event, not least because the contempt had occurred in separate proceedings, albeit related: see, *e.g.* the cases listed in n.46 above.
⁵⁸ *X Ltd v Morgan-Grampian (Publishers) Ltd* [1991] 1 A.C. 1 at 46, Lord Bridge. But see the approach adopted in Canada in *Paul Magder Furs Ltd v Ontario Att-Gen* (1991) 85 D.L.R. (4th) 694, discussed at para.12–76 where Brooke. J.A. observed that "It is a general rule that a party in contempt will not be heard in the proceedings until the contempt is purged." He cited *Hadkinson v Hadkinson* [1952] 2 All E.R. at 569, and also *Newfoundland (Treasury Board) v The Newfoundland Association of Public Employees* (1986) 59 Nfld. & P.E.I.R. 93 at 95.
⁵⁹ *Cambell Mussels v Thompson* (1984) Law Soc. Gaz. 2457, CA; *Jademan (Holdings) Ltd v Wong Chun-Loong* [1990] 2 H.K.L.R. 577.
⁶⁰ *Atlantic Capital Corporation v Sir Cecil Denniston Burney*, CA Civil Div. transcript 1142 of 1994, September 15, 1994 (Lexis). See also *Fakih Bros v P Moller (Copenhagen) Ltd* [1994] 1 Lloyd's Rep. 103 at 108. In *National Bank of Greece v Constantinos Dimitriou*, The Times, 16 November, 1987 (Lexis), a defendant was in breach of a *Mareva* injunction for non-disclosure of assets, and the Court of Appeal accordingly refused to vary the terms of the injunction in order to permit payment of his solicitors. In the words of Parker L.J., "It is an appeal by a defendant who has consistently and flagrantly misled the court and who has also been in flagrant contempt of court, for there is no doubt that he has deliberately disobeyed the order ... that he should disclose his assets. Of that there can, as it seems to me, be no possible doubt. So far as such a defendant is concerned, it would appear that the court should not assist him in any way when he is still in the position that he has not disclosed what he has been told to disclose and deliberately has not done so". See also *Federal Bank of the Middle East v Hadkinson* [2000] 1 W.L.R. 1695, [2000] 2 All E.R. 395; *Grupo Torras SA v Sheik Fahad Mohammed Al Sabah*, The Times, March 30, 1999, CA, Smith Bernal; the matter is shortly discussed by A. Srivastava and A. Keltie in "Purging the Contempt" (1999) 149 New Law Jo. 535.
⁶¹ *Per* Lord Nicholls in *Polanski v Condé Nast Publications Ltd* [2005] UKHL 10, [2005] 1 All E.R. 945 at [17].

flexible approach was reflected in the words of Lord Bingham C.J. in *Arab Monetary Fund v Hashim*[62] where he indicated that the preferable course is to ask:

"... whether, in the circumstances of an individual case, the interests of justice are best served by hearing a party in contempt or by refusing to do so, always bearing in mind the paramount importance which the court must attach to the prompt and unquestioning observance of court orders".

For example, in *Baker v Baker (No.2)*,[63] the Court of Appeal refused to interfere with the exercise of the discretion of Cazalet J., who had declined to hear a husband developing his application to reduce a periodical payments order, for the reason that he had failed to pay a lump sum which had also been ordered. It was conceded that the husband was in contempt for that reason, and if the court had not refused to hear the husband there would be no other means by which the wife could secure his compliance with the order. Moreover, it was not legitimate to allow him to continue to assert that the original orders, including that in respect of the lump sum, were unjustified. This would be a recipe for protracted litigation, and it was thus a proper exercise of the judge's discretion to conclude that the *Hadkinson* "principle" applied.

In *Grupo Torras SA v Sheik Fahad Mohammed Al Sabah (No.4)*,[64] the Court of Appeal considered the unusual circumstances in which a judge had allowed a defendant to adduce expert evidence despite the fact that he was in flagrant and continuing breach of an earlier order. The claimants had decided against applying to strike out the defence. It thus appeared to the judge that they were seeking for their own purposes a trial on the merits, while debarring the relevant defendant from calling evidence even on issues unaffected by the contempt. He had decided to exercise his discretion in the light of *X Ltd v Morgan-Grampian (Publishers) Ltd*[65] in favour of admitting the evidence because it dealt with Spanish law and as to the competence of the claimants to bring the proceedings. That was described as "very close to being an issue going to jurisdiction". On this matter the Court of Appeal declined to interfere with the judge's exercise of discretion. Since he was being asked to reach a conclusion on the merits he was entitled to admit evidence which he felt would assist him to reach a correct conclusion.

In the course of his judgment the Master of the Rolls, having referred extensively to the speeches in *X Ltd*, drew attention to the words of Lord Bridge:

"I cannot help thinking that the more flexible treatment of the jurisdiction as one of discretion to be exercised in accordance with the principle stated by Denning L.J. [in *Hadkinson v Hadkinson* [1952] P. 285, 298] better accords with contemporary judicial attitudes to the importance of ensuring procedural justice than confining its exercise within the limits of a strict rule subject to defined exceptions. But in practice in most

---

[62] Unreported, March 21, 1997.
[63] [1997] 1 F.L.R. 148, CA. See also *Leavis v Leavis* [1921] P. 219.
[64] *The Times*, March 30, CA February 19, 1999, Smith Bernal, [1999] C.L.C. 885.
[65] [1991] 1 A.C. 1.

cases the two different approaches are likely to lead to the same conclusion, as they did in *Hadkinson* itself and would have done in *The Messianiki Tolmi* [1981] 2 Lloyd's Rep. 595.

"Certainly in a case where the contemnor not only fails wilfully and contumaciously to comply with an order of the court but makes it clear that he will continue to defy the court's authority if the order should be affirmed by appeal, the court must, in my opinion, have a discretion to decline to entertain his appeal against the order".

The Master of the Rolls emphasised this passage because Lord Bridge made it clear that the discretion applied even in the case of wilful and contumacious failure. Furthermore, Lord Bridge regarded it as incongruous to entertain an appeal but not to allow the appellant to be represented.

The relevance of Article 6 of the European Convention

12–74 A question yet to be determined is the extent to which these restrictions are consistent with Art.6 of the European Convention on Human Rights, which is concerned with ensuring access to the courts. It provides that:

"1. In the determination of his civil rights and obligations or of any criminal charge against him, everyone is entitled to a fair and public hearing within a reasonable time by an independent and impartial tribunal established by law . . . "

12–75 If the true analysis is on the basis of discretion rather than of a rule, then it would be necessary in the exercise of that discretion to have regard to the very limited exceptions which are permitted under the terms of Art.6, none of which appear to justify limiting the right of access of contemnors by way of coercion.[66] While it is true that one of the exceptions under Art.10(2) to the general right of freedom of communication is that of " . . . maintaining the authority and impartiality of the judiciary", no corresponding exception is to be found in Art.6. The only recognition of the "interests of justice" in that provision is in connection with the prevention of publicity, which has no relevance to the present discussion of coercive discipline.

12–76 In this context, it may be instructive to consider the approach adopted in Canada in the light of its Charter of Rights and Fundamental Freedoms. In the case of *Paul Magder Furs Ltd v Ontario Att-Gen*[67] there was persistent disobedience of an order to refrain from Sunday trading. The respondent was not permitted to be heard so long as he remained in defiance. It was argued that this was an infringement of Magder's freedoms as guaranteed under the Charter, but the argument was rejected. In the words of Brooke J.A.[68]:

---

[66] Cp. the decision of the House of Lords in *Polanski v Condé Nast Publications Ltd* [2005] UKHL 10, [2005] 1 All E.R. 945. The issue was whether a fugitive from justice, living in France, should be denied the facility of giving evidence from there by means of video conferencing because of his status. Lord Nicholls drew an analogy with the more flexible approach now adopted towards contemnors who seek to be heard, as well as to the courts' increasing recognition of the need for proportionality. An over-rigid interpretation of the requirements of public policy may be counter-productive and may involve a breach of Art.6 rights.
[67] (1991) 85 D.L.R. (4th) 694, Ontario CA.
[68] At 698–9.

" ... the Canadian Charter of Rights and Freedoms is no licence to break the law or defy an order of the court. It is elementary that so long as a law or an order of the court remains in force it must be obeyed ...

In my opinion, it is an abuse of process to assert a right to be heard by the court and at the same time refuse to undertake to obey the order of the court so long as it remains in force."

The case was considered in the High Court of New Zealand in *Att-Gen for England and Wales v Tomlinson*.[69] It was recognised that it is an abuse of process to assert a right to be heard by the court while at the same time refusing to obey an order. It would be a very rare case for the New Zealand courts to prevent anyone from defending himself in civil proceedings. But the discretion exists to be used flexibly as circumstances require. It was not exercised against the defendant in that case, although because he was in breach he could not expect the court to grant him an indulgence. Accordingly, his application for an extension of time in which to file a protest to jurisdiction was stayed until such time as he appeared before the court to justify his actions and purge his contempt.[70]

In *Waite v Waite*,[71] a husband applied to the county court for committal of his wife for non-compliance with an order to vacate certain premises. He was, however, apparently himself in breach of an earlier order for ancillary relief made in the same proceedings. The Court of Appeal referred the committal application back to the county court to be considered in the light of a full investigation into the extent of the husband's maintenance arrears. Thorpe L.J. observed[72] that it could be said on behalf of the wife " ... that a party to proceedings himself in breach of the order should not succeed in an application to commit the other party for some other breach". Hale L.J. went further and declared[73] that it was a "fundamental principle that those who seek the assistance of the courts—and in particular those who seek to enforce orders through the most draconian means available, that is of sending somebody to prison—should themselves be scrupulous in their own obedience to what the court has required of them". The third member of the court, Astill J., expressed himself to be uneasy at the prospect of a party obtaining the benefit of an order when he was in breach of a "parallel order". But he went on to suggest that this was simply a factor for the county court judge to take into account on the committal application; whether he did so, and if he did so with what result, would be matters entirely for him. It is respectfully submitted that this is the right approach, and that it would more easily accord with their Lordships' analysis in *X Ltd v Morgan-Grampian (Publishers) Ltd*.[74] It may be appropriate to regard an applicant's non-compliance as a matter to be weighed in the exercise of discretion rather than one of "fundamental principle". The case should be read with caution, therefore, and it should not be too readily assumed that a litigant will necessarily be *barred* from making an application for that reason. Committal is not an equitable remedy

---

[69] [1999] 3 N.Z.L.R. 722 at 730–3, Gendall J.
[70] See also *Stephens v Cribb* (1991) 4 P.R. N.Z. 337.
[71] [2001] EWCA Civ 1186.
[72] At [19].
[73] At [24].
[74] See para.12–70.

12–78 requiring "clean hands" on the part of the applicant; indeed there is considerable doubt as to whether it should be regarded as a remedy of any kind.[75] Moreover, there may on occasion be a public interest in one party being made to comply with an order, or punished for its breach, notwithstanding that the other party may be in breach of an order also.

12–79 Since the decision of the House of Lords in *X Ltd v Morgan-Grampian (Publishers) Ltd*,[76] this useful discretion will possibly be confined to special circumstances in the future, and perhaps used to *postpone* a contemnor from being heard, in order to give him an opportunity for compliance, rather than to prevent him indefinitely from having access. The European Court of Human Rights might well criticise a judicial system which treated contemnors in any real sense as "outlaws".[77] Laddie J. commented in *Re Swaptronics Ltd*[78]:

> "It is only actions of the party which impede the course of justice in the cause by making it more difficult for the court to ascertain the truth which give the court the discretion to refuse to hear him until the impediment is removed or good reason is shown why it should not be removed. Where an action or inaction by a party seriously interferes with the fair conduct of a trial as well as being in contempt of an order of the court, it is the former consideration, not the latter, which justifies the court in taking the steps either of staying the proceedings or, where appropriate, striking out the party's claim or defence."

He added that the decision of Sir Nicolas Browne-Wilkinson V.-C. in *Re Jokai Tea Holdings Ltd*,[79] in so far as it appeared to be suggesting that the discretion not to hear a litigant might be exercised purely on the basis of a "contumelious" breach, should not be followed in the light of the later approach of the House of Lords in *X Ltd v Morgan Grampian (Publishers)*.[80] In this context, it is instructive to consider what Lord Nicholls had to say in *Polanski v Condé Nast Publications Ltd*[81] with reference to a fugitive from justice:

> "It may seem unattractive that a person can, at one and the same time, evade justice in respect of his criminal conduct and yet seek the assistance of the courts in protection of his own civil rights. But the contrary approach, adopted in the name of the public interest, would lead to wholly unacceptable results in practice. It would mean that for so long as a fugitive remained 'on the run' from the criminal law, his property and other

---

[75] See the discussion at paras 3–76 *et seq.* and cp. the words of Lord Woolf M.R. in *Nicholls v Nicholls* [1997] 1 W.L.R. 314 at 326, cited at para.3–69.
[76] [1991] 1 A.C. 1.
[77] A term used by Megarry V.-C. in *Pyke v National Westminster Bank Ltd, The Times*, December 9, 1977 ("It was neither the law, nor ought it to be, that a person in contempt was an outlaw, unable to take proceedings in the courts until he had purged his contempt, and liable until then to have any proceedings that he brought struck out"). See also the comment of Munby J. in *Kelly v BBC* [2001] Fam. 59 at 91C, [2000] 3 F.C.R. 509 at 549 that "Even a convicted contemnor is not an outlaw", and those of Laddie J. in *Re Swaptronics Ltd, The Times,* August 17, 1998, 95 (36) 6 L.S.G. 33. But see *Motorola Credit Corp v Uzan (No.2)* [2003] EWCA Civ 752, [2004] 1 W.L.R. 113 at [56]–[58]. And see *Arrow Nominees Inc v Blackledge, The Times,* December 8, 1999 (see Lexis and Smith Bernal) (Evans-Lombe J.); for the decision of the Court of Appeal, see *The Times* July 7, 2000.
[78] Lexis, at para.21.
[79] [1992] 1 W.L.R. 1196, [1993] 1 All E.R. 630.
[80] [1991] 1 A.C. 1.
[81] [2005] UKHL 10, [2005] 1 All E.R. 945 at [26].

rights could be breached with impunity. That could not be right. Such harshness has no place in our law. Mr Polanski is not a present-day outlaw. Our law knows no principle of fugitive disentitlement".

Nevertheless, in *Motorola Credit Corp v Uzan (No.2)*[82] it was held that it would not be necessarily a breach of Art.6 to deprive a contemnor of his right to be heard. It was perceived to be essentially a matter of proportionality on a case by case basis and it was suggested that this was reflected in the approach of the House of Lords in *X Ltd* itself. The width of the discretion there recognised was apt to allow issues of proportionality to be properly considered and applied by the court in coming to its decision whether or not to hear a contemnor.

II. THE MENTAL ELEMENT FOR CIVIL CONTEMPT

A. The traditional approach to *mens rea* in civil contempt

Warrington J. expressed the principle in *Stancomb v Trowbridge Urban District Council*[83]:   12–80

"If a person or a corporation is restrained by injunction from doing a particular act, that person or corporation commits a breach of the injunction and is liable for process of contempt, if he or it in fact does the act, and it is no answer to say that the act was not contumacious in the sense that, in doing it there was no direct intention to disobey the order."

That this expresses the true position has since been confirmed by the Court of Appeal[84] and also by the House of Lords in *Heatons Transport (St. Helens) Ltd v TGWU*,[85] in *Director General of Fair Trading v Pioneer Concrete (UK) Ltd*[86] and in *Re M: M v Home Office*.[87] Motive is immaterial to the question of liability.[88]

What was traditionally required was to demonstrate that the alleged contemnor's *conduct* was intentional (in the sense that what he actually did, or   12–81

---

[82] [2003] EWCA Civ 752, [2004] 1 W.L.R. 113 at [56]–[58].
[83] [1910] 2 Ch. 190 at 194. See also *Miller v Scorey* [1996] 1 W.L.R. 1122 at 1132, Rimer J., cited at para.12–86.
[84] *Knight v Clifton* [1971] Ch. 700 at 721, Sachs L.J.; cf. *Re Mileage Conference Group of the Tyre Manufacturers' Conference Ltd's Agreement* [1966] 1 W.L.R. 1137 at 1162 (in the latter case, the party in breach was acting on legal advice); contrast the decision of the Court of Appeal in *Irtelli v Squatriti* [1993] Q.B. 83, discussed more fully at para.12–88. For the position in Scotland, see para.16–241.
[85] [1973] A.C. 15 at 109, Lord Wilberforce. Cf. the decisions in *AGBC v Bezanson* (1983) 50 B.C.L.R. 275, SCBC; *Cinema Morano Ltée v Co-op de Logement et de Production Culturelle Inc* (1984) 58 N.B.R. (2d) 72, QB.
[86] [1995] 1 A.C. 456 at 479–81, Lord Nolan.
[87] [1994] 1 A.C. 377 (also a case where the contemnor was relying on legal advice).
[88] *R. v Poplar Borough Council (No.2)* [1922] 1 K.B. 95 at 103: "Unless and until the time comes when the law of this country is that a person may disobey an order of the court or the laws as much as he likes if he does it conscientiously the question of motive is immaterial": *per* Lord Sterndale M.R.

omitted to do, was not accidental)[89]; and secondly that he knew the facts which rendered it a breach of the relevant order or undertaking. He must be shown at least in the case of a mandatory order to know of the existence of the order[90] and, as has already been pointed out, he must be shown to have been served with the order.[91] This will not necessarily, however, in itself demonstrate that the alleged contemnor actually knows of the order. The problem was highlighted by Eveleigh L.J. in *Z Ltd v A-Z and AA-LL*[92]:

> "In the great majority of cases the fact that a person does an act which is contrary to the injunction after having notice of its terms will almost inevitably mean that he is knowingly acting contrary to those terms. However, where a corporation is concerned, it may be a difficult matter to determine when a corporation is said to be acting knowingly."

12–82 Yet there is no need to go so far as to show that the respondent *realised* that his conduct would constitute a breach,[93] or even that he had read the order.[94] This means that liability for civil contempt has been treated as though it were strict; that is to say, not depending upon establishing any specific intention either to breach the terms of the order or to subvert the administration of justice in general.[95]

12–83 The relevance of mental capacity in this context was considered by the Court of Appeal in *P v P (Contempt of Court: Mental Capacity)*.[96] A disabled husband was prohibited from returning to the former matrimonial home by various injunctions and the judge found that he had a "potentially average" I.Q., but he was suffering from Usher's syndrome and was deaf and virtually blind. It was held by the Court of Appeal that a limited degree of understanding could be sufficient to found liability for contempt. There was no need for a full understanding of the finer points of law provided the contemnor understood what he must not do and what the consequences of a breach might be. In any given case, the assessment of capacity and comprehension would be a matter for the judge. On the other hand in *Wookey v Wookey*[97] the Court of Appeal held that the

---

[89] *VDU Installations Ltd v Integrated Computer Systems and Cybernetics Ltd* [1989] 1 F.S.R. 378 at 394, Knox J. (negligence will normally give rise to liability and is unlikely to escape through being classified as "casual, accidental and unintentional").
[90] *Z Ltd v A-Z and AA-LL* [1982] Q.B. 558 at 580, Eveleigh L.J.;
[91] See para.12–35 (dealing with personal service of the order), and *Husson v Husson* [1962] 1 W.L.R. 1434, Lyell J., where a husband was committed for breach of a non-molestation injunction even though he had not been served with it (as would be required in the case of a mandatory injunction), since the judge was satisfied that he had been in court when the order was made. There is a distinction drawn between prohibitory and mandatory injunctions in this respect. In the latter case it has always been thought essential to establish personal service; see, *e.g.* the remarks of Stamp J. in *Ronson Products Ltd v Ronson Furniture Ltd* [1966] Ch. 603 at 616: "If a man be ordered to do an act, so that his failure to do it may lead him to prison, justice requires that he know precisely what he has to do and by what time he has to do it".
[92] [1982] Q.B. 558 at 580, CA.
[93] *Spectravest Inc v Aperknit* [1988] F.S.R. 161. But see *Irtelli v Squatriti* [1993] Q.B. 83, CA, discussed at para.12–88.
[94] *Re Witten* (1887) 4 T.L.R. 36.
[95] *Att-Gen v Times Newspapers Ltd* [1992] 1 A.C. 191 at 217, Lord Oliver.
[96] [1999] 2 F.L.R. 897. See G. Ashton, "Injunctions and Mental Disorder" [2000] Fam. Law 39.
[97] [1991] Fam. 121.

discretionary remedy of an injunction *in personam* should only be granted against those amenable to the court's jurisdiction. Where mental incapacity was an issue, the question would be whether the respondent in question understood the nature and requirements of the order sought. An injunction ought not to be granted against someone who was, in a *M'Naghten* sense, incapable of understanding what he was doing or that what he was doing was wrong. An injunction in those circumstances would not achieve its effect either by way of deterrence or in the sense of operating upon the person's mind so as to regulate his conduct. Furthermore, any breach of such an order could hardly be the subject of enforcement proceedings.

With the increasing use of injunctions *contra mundum*, in the exercise of the court's inherent jurisdiction in respect of patients and minors,[98] it has become apparent that mere notification to the media of the existence of the order will not in that context suffice; knowledge of its terms needs also to be shown. In *Re W (Wards) (Publication of Information)*,[99] receipt of a press release was held to be insufficient to establish the requisite degree of knowledge. The court recognised that newspapers receive many such releases every day and could not be assumed to be familiar with them all.

Moreover, the nature of contempt in such cases is criminal in character and it is not surprising that the court should reflect the difference of approach traditionally adopted towards *mens rea* in that context.[1] To establish contempt in such circumstances it is probably necessary to demonstrate more than knowledge of the mere fact that an order has been made; " . . . it must be established by those who assert that a contempt has been committed that the alleged contemnor had knowledge of all the material terms of the order".[2] This appears to recognise the realities of life in a large media organisation, where it would easily lead to injustice if the mere communication of the order to an office were deemed to entail knowledge of its terms on the part of those who publish.

There is no reason to suppose that the common law position with regard to civil contempt has in any way been qualified by the provisions of the 1981 Act. The statutory limitations placed upon the "strict liability" rule are quite separate, and it is clear from ss.1 and 2 that the form of strict liability with which Parliament is there concerned relates solely to the publication of prejudicial material.[3] There is no warrant for assuming that it was intended to deal with all aspects of strict liability in the law of contempt. The matter was addressed in *Miller v Scorey*[4] by Rimer J.:

---

[98] See paras 6–41 *et seq*.
[99] [1989] 1 F.L.R. 246.
[1] See paras 3–247 *et seq*.
[2] *Re L (A Ward)(Publication of Information)* [1988] 1 F.L.R. 255 at 259, [1988] 1 All E.R. 418 at 421h–j, Booth J. See also *X County Council v A* [1985] 1 W.L.R. 1422, Balcombe J.
[3] See generally ch.4. See also *Whitter v Peters* [1982] 1 W.L.R. 389 and the same case on appeal to the House of Lords *sub nom. Peart v Stewart* [1983] 2 A.C. 109; see too *Z Ltd v A-Z and AA-LL* [1982] 1 Q.B. 558.
[4] [1996] 1 W.L.R. 1122 at 1132.

"In my judgment, sections 1 and 2 of that Act have nothing to do with the criteria which must be satisfied before proof of a contempt in the nature of an alleged breach of an undertaking to the court is established. Those sections are concerned with alleged contempts of a different kind. The question of whether or not a contempt in the nature of a breach of an undertaking to the court has been committed involves an essentially objective test requiring the determination of whether or not the alleged contemnor has acted in a manner constituting a breach of his undertaking. If he has, then a contempt will ordinarily be established, regardless of whether or not he acted contumaciously or with the direct intention of breaking his promise, although I accept that whether any, and if so what, punishment or other consequences ought to be imposed on him will, or may be, materially dependent on considerations of this sort."

12–87   Thus, it can be seen that the approach of the courts towards the mental element necessary for establishing a civil contempt has, in the past, by no means corresponded to that adopted, since the 1981 Act, towards the *mens rea* required for criminal publication contempts falling outside the "strict liability rule".[5] In that context it has been emphasised on several occasions that a specific intent is required, for common law contempts reserved by s.6(c) of the Act, to interfere with the administration of justice. It is true, however, that such an intention may readily be inferred from the surrounding circumstances.[6]

B. An apparent policy shift: the doubtful case of *Irtelli v Squatriti*

12–88   It was possible, however, to detect in one decision a degree of apparent coalescence between the requirements for *mens rea* in civil and criminal contempt. In *Irtelli v Squatriti*,[7] the Court of Appeal decided that it was impossible, especially in the light of new evidence which had not been before the judge at first instance, to conclude that the appellants had *intentionally* breached an injunction. It was a case in which they had been restrained from "selling disposing or otherwise dealing with seeking to sell dispose or deal with" property of which they owned the freehold. Thereafter they executed a charge on the property. They were committed in their absence.

12–89   On appeal, the order was discharged; the court proceeded on the basis that, in order for the appellants to be held liable in contempt, it had to be proved, in the words of Farquharson L.J., "that they did intend to act in contempt of the court's authority"[8] or that they "had the necessary intention to act in contempt of court."[9] It was also put by the other two members of the court (Taylor L.J. and Sir Donald Nicholls V.C.) on the very similar footing that the appellants had to be shown to have "knowingly breached the court order".[10]

---

[5] See, *e.g.* *Att-Gen v Newspaper Publishing plc* [1988] Ch. 333; and *Att-Gen v News Group Newspapers plc* [1989] Q.B. 110. These are more fully discussed in paras 5–120 *et seq.*
[6] *Att-Gen v Newspaper Publishing plc* [1988] Ch. 333; *Att-Gen v News Group Newspapers plc* [1989] Q.B. 110; *Att-Gen v Newspaper Publishing plc, The Times*, February 28, 1990, CA (Lexis); *Att-Gen v Times Newspapers Ltd* [1992] 1 A.C. 191; *Official Solicitor v News Group Newspapers plc* [1994] 2 F.L.R. 174.
[7] [1993] Q.B. 83, CA.
[8] At 90G–H.
[9] *ibid.* at 91A–B.
[10] *ibid.* at 92F and 93 E.

One of the factors which exercised the court was that the appellants had 12–90
received information and advice from their solicitor,[11] which did not alert them
to the risk. Nevertheless, it is interesting to note that this language is very similar
to that employed in the context of criminal contempt.[12] It is to be contrasted with
the quasi-strict liability hitherto contemplated as applying in civil contempt in
such cases as *Stancomb v Trowbridge Urban District Council*,[13] *Heatons
Transport (St Helens) Ltd v TGWU*,[14] *Spectravest Inc v Aperknit Ltd*[15] and *Att-
Gen v Times Newspapers Ltd*.[16] None of these cases appears to have been cited,
however, to the Court of Appeal in the *Irtelli* case, and it may thus be unwise to
read too much significance into that decision by way of policy shift. Nevertheless, it would in the ordinary way be unlikely that the courts would ignore a
decision from such a strong tribunal, and it might therefore have been reasonably
assumed for a while that it would become less easy to establish civil contempt
thereafter; and, in particular, not so easy to discount pleas to the effect that the
alleged contemnor was relying on legal advice or did not intend to breach the
order.

On the other hand, since the Court of Appeal's ruling, the decision in 12–91
Stancomb[17] has been expressly approved as good law in the House of Lords.[18] In
the words of Lord Nolan:

"Given that liability for contempt does not require any direct intention on the part of the
employer to disobey the order, there is nothing to prevent an employing company from
being found to have disobeyed an order 'by' its servant as a result of a deliberate act
by the servant on its behalf. In my judgment, the decision in *Stancomb's* case is good
law and should be followed in the present case."

It is true that these words were uttered in the context of a consideration of 12–92
corporate liability, but it is difficult to see how this passage can be reconciled
with the approach of the Court of Appeal in *Irtelli*, even though the latter case
was concerned with the liability of individuals. Warrington J. in *Stancomb*[19]
referred specifically to "a person or a corporation". Despite the strength of the
court, it is respectfully submitted that the statements from *Irtelli* should be treated

---

[11] Compare the position in *Re Mileage Conference Group of the Tyre Manufacturers' Conference
Ltd's Agreement* [1966] 1 W.L.R. 1137, cited in n.84 above, and in *Re M: M v Home Office* [1994]
1 A.C. 377.
[12] *Att-Gen v Newspaper Publishing plc* [1988] Ch. 333, CA (which was apparently referred to in the
skeletons before the Court of Appeal in *Irtelli* although not further cited) and *Att-Gen v Newspaper
Publishing plc* [1990] T.L.R. 158, CA (Lexis).
[13] [1910] 2 Ch. 190 at 194, cited at para.12–80.
[14] [1973] A.C. 15.
[15] [1988] F.S.R. 161.
[16] [1992] 1 A.C. 191.
[17] [1910] 2 Ch. 190.
[18] *Director General of Fair Trading v Pioneer Concrete (UK) Ltd* [1995] 1 A.C. 456; see also
Robertson, "Corporate Liability for Contempt of Court under the Restrictive Trade Practices Act
1976" [1995] 3 E.C.L.R. 196.
[19] Cited at para.12–80.

12–92

with caution, in so far as they might be thought to express any principle beyond the facts of that case.[20]

12–93 *Irtelli v Squatriri* was considered by Neuberger J. in *Bird v Hadkinson*[21] and by Jacob J. in *Adam Phones Ltd v Goldschmidt*.[22] Both judges felt bound to follow the guidance given by the House of Lords in *Director General of Fair Trading v Pioneer Concrete (UK) Ltd*.[23] It may be noted, however, that Jacob J. observed, "Free from authority I would have sided with *Irtelli's* case".

C. State of mind relevant to penalty

12–94 What is clear, however, is that the *bona fides* of contemnors and their reasons, motives and states of mind, have long been recognised as relevant factors in mitigation.[24] It seems, for example, that[25]:

> " . . . no casual or accidental and unintentional disobedience of an order would justify either commitment or sequestration. Where the court is satisfied that the conduct was not intentional or reckless, but merely casual and accidental and committed under circumstances which negative any suggestion of contumacy, while it might visit the offending party with costs and might order an inquiry as to damages, it would not take the extreme course of issuing an order either of commitment or of sequestration."

It has on the other hand been held[26] that no weight would be attached, even by way of mitigating the effect of the breach of an injunction, to legal advice in circumstances where it was unrecorded, based on instructions for which there was no factual basis, and not such as to be believed by the contemnor in any event.

---

[20] *Irtelli v Squatriti* does not appear to have been cited before the House of Lords in *Director General of Fair Trading v Pioneer Concrete (UK) Ltd* [1995] 1 A.C. 456.
[21] [1999] B.P.I.R. 653.
[22] [1999] 4 All E.R. 486 at 494. See also *In the matter of John Katchis*, February 17, 2000, Crown Office List CJA 29/97 (Smith Bernal), Richards J.
[23] [1995] 1 A.C. 456.
[24] *Re Mileage Conference Group of the Tyre Manufacturers' Conference Ltd's Agreement* [1966] 1 W.L.R. 1137 at 1162; *Knight v Clifton* [1971] Ch. 700 at 721; *Re Kerly Son & Verden* [1901] 1 Ch. 467; *Re H's Settlement, H v H* [1909] 2 Ch. 260 at 264; *Re Harris (An Infant)*, *The Times*, May 21, 1960; *West Oxfordshire District Council v Beratec Ltd*, *The Times*, October 30, 1986; *Bhimji v Chatwani* [1991] 1 W.L.R. 989 at 1001H–1003D, Scott J.; *HPSI Ltd v Thomas and Williams* (1983) 133 New Law Jo. 598; *Spectravest Inc v Aperknit* [1988] F.S.R. 161 at 173–4; *Z Bank v D1* [1994] 1 Lloyd's Rep. 656 at 668; *Miller v Scorey* [1996] 1 W.L.R. 1122 at 1132D–E, Rimer J.
[25] *Fairclough & Sons v The Manchester Ship Canal Co (No.2)* (1897) 41 Sol.Jo. 225. (The passage immediately following in Lord Russell's judgment, which indicates that the act must be contumacious to constitute a contempt has until recently been thought to be no longer good law: but see now *Irtelli v Squatriti* [1993] Q.B. 83, CA discussed at para.12–88). Cf. *Heatons Transport (St. Helens) Ltd v TGWU* [1973] A.C. 15; *Spokes v Banbury Board of Health* (1865) L.R. 1 Eq. 42; *Shoppee v Nathan & Co* [1892] 1 Q.B. 245 (Sheriff's officers not liable to a penalty for an innocent mistake in a clerk's calculation); *Michigan Ltd v Mathew* [1966] R.P.C. 47, Lloyd-Jacob J. (contempt was found proved but the matter could be sufficiently dealt with by ordering the director concerned to pay all the costs of the proceedings, which order was described as "a monetary penalty").
[26] *Parker and another (t/a NBC Services) v Rasalingham (t/a Micro Tec) and others*, *The Times* July 25, 2000, Ch. D.

As to the significance of duress, where established in the context of civil 12–95
contempt, it would seem to be a factor operating in mitigation of penalty rather
than as a defence.[27] Thus there would be a significant distinction in this respect
between civil and criminal contempt,[28] but how principled this distinction truly
is may have to be considered in the future.

D. The relevance of CPR Sch.1, Ord. 45.5: absence of "wilfully"

CPR Sch.1, Ord.45.5 provides that where certain judgments or orders of the court 12–96
have been disobeyed they may be enforced by a writ of sequestration or an order
of committal. The corresponding but earlier Ord.42, r.31, which contained
similar provisions, had required that the disobedience be wilful. The use of the
word "wilful," however, was only intended to exclude casual, accidental or
unintentional acts such as those referred to in *Fairclough & Sons v The
Manchester Ship Canal Co.*[29] This rule was not intended to define what
constitutes a contempt, but merely describes the circumstances in which
sequestration or committal may be appropriate remedies.

Lord Wilberforce, delivering the unanimous opinion of the House of Lords in 12–97
Heatons Transport (St. Helens) Ltd v TGWU,[30] suggested that the omission of the
word "wilful" might have the effect of reducing the applicant's burden of proof
to establish a *prima facie* case; but the mere proof of the act or omission in breach
of the order constitutes a *prima facie* case that a contempt has been committed.
Although the applicant may request a particular sanction against the contemnor,
and indeed would generally specify either committal or sequestration in his
notice of motion, it would seem inappropriate to speak of him having to establish
a case *prima facie* for committal or sequestration. Penalty is a matter for the
court.[31]

At all events, it seems clear that to justify a finding of contempt the 12–98
contemnor's disobedience need not amount to "stubborn opposition" or "obsti-
nacy," nor need it be "rebellious." All that is necessary, in the context of liability,
is that the conduct should be intentional and the word "wilful" in this context
does not imply anything stronger.[32] This interpretation of the law seems to be

---

[27] See *Coca-Cola Company & Schweppes Ltd v Gilbey* [1996] F.S.R. 23, CA, and *The Coca-Cola Company v Aytacli* [2003] EWHC 91, Ch.
[28] See paras 3–250 *et seq.*
[29] (1897) 41 S.J. 225. This was the view of the House of Lords in *Heatons Transport (St. Helens) Ltd v TGWU* [1973] A.C. 15.
[30] [1973] A.C. 15 at 109.
[31] *Att-Gen v Hislop* [1991] 1 Q.B. 514 at 522–3, Parker L.J.
[32] See Warrington J. in *Stancomb v Trowbridge Urban District Council* [1910] 2 Ch. 190; Stirling J. in *Worthington v Ad-Lib Club Ltd* [1965] Ch. 236 and Stamp J. in *Steiner Products Ltd v Willy Steiner Ltd* [1966] 1 W.L.R. 986. Cf. the use of the word "contumacious" by Eveleigh L.J. in *Z Ltd v A-Z and AA-LL* [1982] 1 Q.B. 558 at 583D–E, where he said that "carelessness or even recklessness on the part of the banks ought not in my opinion to make them liable for contempt unless it can be shown that there was indifference to such a degree that was contumacious." (The liability of a bank in such circumstances would be classified as for criminal rather than civl contempt.) See also the use of the word "wilful" by Woolf L.J. in *Att-Gen of Tuvalu v Philatelic Distribution Corp Ltd* [1990] 1 W.L.R. 926, [1990] 2 All E.R. 216, where he spoke of a director "wilfully" failing to take steps. See paras 12–99 *et seq.*

quite consistent with the older reported decisions where the gravity of conduct has been measured by the court on applications for attachment or committal.[33]

III. Who Can Be Liable For Civil Contempt?

A. Vicarious liability for civil contempt[34]

12–99   Where a judgment or order is binding upon an employer or principal, and a servant or agent fails to comply with the judgment or breaches the order, this may lead to a finding of liability on the basis of vicarious liability.[35] The test in this context would appear to be whether the servant or agent was acting on behalf of and within the scope of authority conferred by the employer or principal.[36] No distinction can be drawn in principle between employees and agents in this respect.[37] Often an employee, as compared with an agent, may have a wider authority because of a more permanent status and perhaps also a wider range of duties. The agent in an ordinary case is engaged to perform a particular task on a particular occasion and only has authority to do whatever is required for that purpose.[38] If the authority of the servant or agent has been revoked before the act was done, this would in principle have the consequence that the relevant act would not be attributable on a vicarious basis.[39]

12–100   The standard form of wording for an injunction includes reference to the possibility of a breach occurring indirectly through others. In the case of a corporation a negative injunction will generally restrain the prohibited act or acts "by its directors, servants or agents or otherwise howsoever." In the case of an individual, however, the wording is generally in the form "by himself, his servants or agents or otherwise howsoever."

B. Corporations

12–101   It is necessary to consider, in accordance with general principle, in what circumstances liability may arise for a corporation on the one hand, and for any relevant employees or agents on the other. In *R. (on the application of Bempoa) v Southwark London Borough Council*,[40] Munby J. held that a local authority was undoubtedly in breach of undertakings given to the court, by reason of systems

---

[33] See, *e.g. Bullen v Ovey* (1809) 16 Ves. Jun. 141 at 144, 33 E.R. 937 at 938; *Leonard v Attwell* (1810) 17 Ves. Jun. 385 at 386 (breach of injunction not wilful and therefore no order to commit); *Dodington v Hudson* (1824) 1 Bing. 410, 130 E.R. 165 (wilful disobedience necessary for attachment); *Spokes v Banbury Board of Health* (1865) L.R. 1 Eq. 42; *Meters Ltd v Metropolitan Gas Meters Ltd* (1907) 51 S.J. 499.
[34] See paras 4–199 *et seq.* for a discussion of similar issues in relation to criminal contempt.
[35] *Ex p. Langley* (1879) 13 Ch. D. 110 at 121; *Hope v Carnegie* (1868) 7 Eq. 254, affirmed (1869) 4 Ch. App. 264; *Rantsen v Rothschild* (1865) 14 W.R. 96; *Stancomb v Trowbridge Urban District Council* [1910] 2 Ch. 190; *Heatons Transport (St. Helens) Ltd v TGWU* [1973] A.C. 15.
[36] *Heatons Transport (St. Helens) Ltd v TGWU* [1973] A.C. 15.
[37] *Director General of Fair Trading v Pioneer Concrete (UK) Ltd* [1995] 1 A.C. 456 at 481A–B.
[38] *Heatons Transport (St. Helens) Ltd v TGWU* [1973] A.C. 15 at 99D.
[39] *ibid.* at 109H–110C.
[40] [2002] EWHC 153 (Admin).

so defective as to be tantamount to "heedless indifference and recklessness", but he took the view that the imposition of a fine would not punish the individuals actually responsible.

As has already been pointed out, no one can be held liable for a breach of an order without knowledge that such an order has been made.[41] Service of the order itself is also required, unless an order has been made to dispense with service.[42] Therefore it would appear that, in order to fix a corporation with liability for contempt, it will be necessary to show that it has been properly served or that service has been dispensed with, on the basis that an appropriate officer of the company had knowledge of the order, or for some other reason. It is, however, no defence for a company to show that its officers were unaware of the terms of the order or that they failed to realise that the terms were being broken by their actions.[43]

12–102

Nor is it a defence to show that the act of disobedience was done by a servant through carelessness, neglect or even in dereliction of duty.[44] Neither would it suffice for the corporation to plead that it forbade its employees to act in breach of the order; or that it took reasonable steps to achieve compliance.[45] Because it is not necessary to show any "direct intention to disobey the order"[46] a deliberate act by an employee (that is to say, one that was not casual or accidental[47]) will give rise to liability on the part of a company if, objectively judged, it would constitute a breach of the order.[48]

12–103

C. "Servants or agents"

The question arises whether servants or agents can be liable for contempt unless, knowing of the order against the relevant company, they intentionally set out to do an act which has the effect of subverting it (which would amount to a common law criminal contempt on the part of anyone).[49] Although the standard form of

12–104

---

[41] See Eveleigh L.J. in *Z Ltd v A-Z and AA-LL* [1982] Q.B. 558 at 580–1.
[42] For a discussion on dispensing with personal service see para.12–35.
[43] *Re Garage Equipment Association's Agreement* (1964) L.R. 4 R.P. 491 at 505, Megaw J., and *Re Galvanised Tank Manufacturers' Association Ltd's Agreement* [1965] 2 All E.R. 1003, 1009, Megaw J. But compare, in the context of possible liability for criminal contempt following a *contra mundum* order *Re W (Wards) (Publication of Information)* [1989] 1 F.L.R. 246, at para.12–84 above.
[44] *Stancomb v Trowbridge Urban District Council* [1910] 2 Ch. 190 at 194, Warrington J.
[45] *Director General of Fair Trading v Pioneer Concrete (UK) Ltd* [1995] 1 A.C. 456. It is to be noted that the Court of Appeal had taken a different view: [1992] 1 Q.B. 213. See also Robertson, "Corporate Liability for Contempt of Court Under The Restrictive Trade Practices Act 1976" [1995] 3 E.C.L.R. 196.
[46] *per* Warrington J. in *Stancomb v Trowbridge Urban District Council* [1910] 2 Ch. 190 at 194; *Director General of Fair Trading v Pioneer Concrete (UK) Ltd* [1995] A.C. 456 at 481, Lord Nolan.
[47] *Fairclough & Sons v Manchester Ship Canal (No.2)* (1897) 41 Sol. Jo. 225.
[48] See, *e.g. Chelsea Man plc v Chelsea Girl Ltd* [1988] F.S.R. 217 at 224–5, Millett J; *Miller v Scorey* [1996] 1 W.L.R. 1122 at 1132C–E, Rimer J.
[49] See, *e.g. Att-Gen v Newspaper Publishing plc* [1988] Ch. 333 at 380; *Marengo v Daily Sketch and Sunday Graphic Ltd* [1948] 1 All E.R. 406. It is not permissible to seek to add together two innocent states of mind, on the part of two or more employees, with a view to constructing a composite notional corporate *mens rea*, for the purpose of fixing a corporate employer with liability: *Z Ltd v A-Z and AA-LL* [1982] 1 Q.B. at 581.

12–104

order refers to "... servants or agents", it surely cannot bind them directly as though they were themselves parties to the litigation alongside their employer. The wording merely underlines that the party bound by the order will be liable for the acts or omissions of those for whom it is responsible vicariously.[50]

12–105 In the House of Lords in *Marengo v Daily Sketch and Sunday Graphic Ltd*,[51] criticism was made of the then current form of wording referring to "the defendants their staff servants and agents" in the standard form of an injunction.[52] This formulation was misleading in so far as it suggested that a direct order had been made binding upon servants or agents. Lord Uthwatt explained the point of principle:

> "The reference to servants, workmen, and agents in the common form is nothing other than a warning against wrongdoing to those persons who may by reason of their situation be thought easily to fall into the error of implicating themselves in a breach of the injunction by the defendant. There its operation, in my opinion, ends. If they knowingly assist the defendant in a breach by him of the injunction, they may be committed for contempt of court, not because they have broken the injunction—they have not done so—but because they have so conducted themselves as to obstruct the course of justice in assisting a breach and tried to set process of the court at naught. In that respect they stand in no different position from a complete stranger who knowingly sets out to assist the defendant in committing a breach."

It was held that in the case of a limited company, which can only act through human beings, the correct form of wording would be that of restraining "the defendants *by* their servants workmen agents or otherwise." The House of Lords affirmed Lord Eldon's principle in *Iveson v Harris*[53] that it was not competent to the court "... to hold a man bound by an injunction, who is not a party in the cause for the purpose of the cause."

12–106 Thus, an order against a company might cause it to be vicariously liable for non-casual and non-accidental acts of an employee amounting to a breach of the order but, unless he has the necessary *mens rea*, the employee will not himself be liable. It is only the party bound by the order who can be liable for civil contempt in respect of the breach. This in itself, as has been pointed out above, does not require any particular state of mind for liability to be established.[54]

12–107 In *Harrington v North London Polytechnic*,[55] it was held that the court had the power to require servants or agents of a corporation to provide information or

---

[50] *Seaward v Paterson* [1897] 1 Ch. 545; *Z Ltd v A-Z and AA-LL* [1982] Q.B. 558; *Att-Gen v Newspaper Publishing plc* [1988] Ch. 333. In *THQ/Jakks Pacific LLC v World Wide Fund for Nature* [2003] EWCA Civ 401, the phrase "servants or agents" was contrasted with that of "licensees", since ordinarily a party would not be liable vicariously for those it had licensed.
[51] [1948] 1 All E.R. 406.
[52] It was said that, although the inclusion of the word "staff" was a novelty, injunctions had gone in that form as a matter of course for over a century: see *Humphreys v Roberts* (1828) 1 Setons Judgments & Orders, 7th ed., p.560; *Van Heythuysen's Equity Draftsman*, 1816 ed., p.586.
[53] (1802) 7 Ves. Jun. 251, 32 E.R. 102. See also *Royal Bank of Canada v Canstar Sports Group Inc* [1989] 1 W.W.R. 662.
[54] *Director General of Fair Trading v Pioneer Concrete (UK) Ltd* [1995] 1 A.C. 456.
[55] [1984] 3 All E.R. 666, CA.

documents in their possession,[56] even though not parties to the relevant litigation themselves. If the corporation is a party, and the servant or agent holds the information on behalf of the party, then such an order would simply provide a practical means of obtaining the appropriate remedy from the corporation. The information or documents in question would be in the possession of *the corporation* through those individuals.[57] Nevertheless, such persons should normally be given an opportunity of being heard before such an order is made, and an order made without notice would be difficult to justify save in exceptional circumstances. At all events, when such an order is made it binds the servant directly even though not a party, and disobedience to the order would constitute contempt on that basis, without the need to prove the *mens rea* required for criminal contempt.

Reference was made to the *Harrington* case in the Court of First Instance in Hong Kong in *Secretary for Justice v Apple Daily Ltd*,[58] where it was sought to obtain by a *Norwich Pharmacal* application the identity of a journalist from his or her employers, while contempt proceedings were pending against them, with a view to bringing such proceedings also against that individual. The submission was rejected. Gall J. regarded the distinction between civil and criminal contempt as still subsisting, in the light of the authorities, and he took the view that the criminal law should prevail—as to the procedure to be applied in respect of criminal contempts. "If it were possible, by civil proceedings, to obtain an order for discovery against persons known to be involved in a criminal action or criminal act, to force them to divulge details of their confederates or other matters pertaining to the offence whilst attractive to the maintenance of law and order, that procedure would cut across the basic principles of criminal law". **12-108**

D. Directors

It is necessary to consider what special factors apply to directors so as to give rise to liability on their part, in circumstances where a servant or agent would not be liable. Were it not for specific provisions contained in the CPR, there would be no need for separate consideration arising purely from their status as directors. Where a director is not a party to the litigation himself, and is thus not directly bound by an order against the company, he could be personally liable for a criminal contempt, at common law, but only on the same basis as anyone else; that is to say, if he "aided or abetted" or did an act intending thereby to subvert the effect of the order.[59] **12-109**

The impact of relevant parts of what is now CPR Sch.1, Ord.45.5, however, must also be taken into account. The rule is stated in the following terms: **12-110**

---

[56] See also *Dummer v Chippenham Corporation* (1807) 14 Ves. Jun. 245, 33 E.R. 515, Lord Eldon.
[57] *Anderson v Bank of British Columbia* (1876) 2 Ch. D. 644 at 659, Mellish L.J.
[58] [2002] 2 H.K.C. 739.
[59] See *Seaward v Paterson* [1897] 1 Ch. 545; *Att-Gen v Newspaper Publishing plc* [1988] Ch. 333.

12–110

"Where—... (b) a person disobeys a judgment or order requiring him to abstain from doing an act, then, subject to the provisions of these rules, the judgment or order may be enforced by one or more of the following means, that is to say—... (ii) where that person is a body corporate, with the permission of the court, a writ of sequestration against the property of any director or other officer of the body; (iii) subject to the provisions of the Debtors Acts 1869 and 1878, an order of committal against that person or, where that person is a body corporate, against any such officer".

12–111 These provisions were considered in *Biba Ltd v Stratford Investments Ltd*,[60] where Brightman J. held that a director did have a case to answer, despite the fact that he had not played more than a passive role in the alleged breach of undertaking. This was on the basis of what was then RSC Ord.45, r.5. It applied to a director in respect of an undertaking given by the relevant company, just as though there had been an order. He did not go on to consider, however, to what extent the director's state of mind was relevant to the question of liability.

12–112 More recently the matter came before the court in *Att-Gen for Tuvalu v Philatelic Distribution Corp Ltd*[61] where it was held[62]:

"In our view where a company is ordered not to do certain acts or gives an undertaking to like effect and a director of that company is aware of the order or undertaking he is under a duty to take reasonable steps to ensure that the order or undertaking is obeyed, and if he wilfully fails to take those steps and the order or undertaking is breached he can be punished for contempt. We use the word 'wilful' to distinguish the situation where the director can reasonably believe some other director or officer is taking those steps."

By virtue of these provisions of the rules a director can be liable for civil contempt without necessarily being in contempt under the general common law.[63]

12–113 This disciplinary regime over directors might at first seem surprising and apparently inconsistent with general principle, but the rule seems to embody a policy decision to exert pressure on individuals who have accepted responsibility as directors or officers in corporations, so as to focus minds on the fulfilment of corporate obligations. Nonetheless, it does represent in the context of a quasi-criminal jurisdiction a significant departure from the general approach.

12–114 When imposing a penalty on a company and one or more of its directors, it is necessary to keep in mind their separate legal status. In *McMillan Graham Printers Ltd v RR (UK) Ltd*,[64] it was held to be wrong in principle to impose a fine jointly and severally on a company and on one of its directors (with a sentence of imprisonment in default of payment against the director). Each

---

[60] [1973] 1 Ch. 281.
[61] [1990] 1 W.L.R. 926, [1990] 2 All E.R. 216. Cf. *Director-General of Fair Trading v Buckland* [1990] 1 W.L.R. 920, [1990] 1 All E.R. 545, Anthony Lincoln J.
[62] *per* Woolf L.J., delivering the judgment of the court, at 936E–F, 222b–c.
[63] In this respect the Court of Appeal expressed disagreement with the views of Anthony Lincoln J. in *Director-General of Fair Trading v Buckland* [1990] 1 W.L.R. 920, [1990] 1 All E.R. 545: see *per* Woolf L.J. at 938A–D, 223e–g.
[64] [1993] T.L.R. 152, CA.

defendant needs to be considered separately, not least as to their respective means.[65] The failure to consider the director's means separately would have led, on the facts of that case, almost inevitably to the default sentence of imprisonment coming into effect. It was in any event wrong in principle, in cases of contempt of court, to impose a fine on two defendants jointly and severally; but practical problems were also likely to be caused by an order in the form made by the judge, because of the different procedures for enforcement against a corporation and against an individual.

It was held in *Iberian Trust Ltd v Founders Trust and Investment Co Ltd*[66] that the remedy against directors under the rules then applicable[67] was an alternative one which could not be pursued unless the plaintiffs were in a position to pursue the primary remedy against the company. If this were not open to them, for example because of a failure to endorse a penal notice, then the subsidiary remedy against the directors would not be available either.

12–115

E. Trade unions

The matter of trade union liability for contempt of court needs now to be considered against the background of s.20 of the Trade Union and Labour Relations (Consolidation) Act 1992, of which the relevant parts are as follows:

12–116

"**20.** Liability of trade union in certain proceedings in tort

. . .

(2) An act shall be taken to have been authorised or endorsed by a trade union if it was done, or was authorised or endorsed—

(a) by any person empowered by the rules to do, authorise or endorse acts of the kind in question, or
(b) by the principal executive committee or the president or general secretary, or
(c) by any other committee of the union or any other official of the union (whether employed by it or not).

(3) For the purposes of paragraph (c) of subsection (2)—

(a) any group of persons constituted in accordance with the rules of the union is a committee of the union; and
(b) an act shall be taken to have been done, authorised or endorsed by an official if it was done, authorised or endorsed by, or by any member of, any group of persons of which he was at the material time a member, the purposes of which included organising or co-ordinating industrial action.

(4) The provisions of paragraphs (b) and (c) of subsection (2) apply notwithstanding anything in the rules of the union, or in any contract or rule of law, but subject to the provisions of section 21 (repudiation by union of certain acts).

. . .

---

[65] See the discussion at para.14–101.
[66] [1932] 2 K.B. 87.
[67] RSC Ord.42, r.31.

12-116

(6) In proceedings arising out of an act which is by virtue of this section taken to have been done by a trade union, the power of the court to grant an injunction or interdict includes power to require the union to take such steps as the court considers appropriate for ensuring—

(a) that there is no, or no further, inducement of persons to take part or to continue to take part in industrial action, and
(b) that no person engages in any conduct after the granting of the injunction or interdict by virtue of having been induced before it was granted to take part or to continue to take part in industrial action.

The provisions of subsections (2) to (4) above apply in relation to proceedings for failure to comply with any such injunction or interdict as they apply in relation to the original proceedings."

It should be noted that s.21 of the Act, referred to in subsection (4), enables certain acts to be repudiated by the executive, president or general secretary, as soon as reasonably practicable after acquiring knowledge.

12-117 Section 20 itself is headed by reference to "proceedings in tort", and indeed ss.20–22 of the Act are all headed "liability of trade unions in proceedings in tort". Furthermore, the reference to subsections (2) to (4), contained in subsection (6), means that they apply to proceedings for failure to comply with an injunction as in relation to the original proceedings. Clearly, in the context, the "original proceedings" contemplated would be proceedings in tort. It is thus by no means clear that a trade union can be treated as liable in circumstances where the alleged breach of injunction has occurred in the context of proceedings taken in relation to some other cause of action.

E. Vicarious liability of unincorporated bodies generally

12-118 Section 154 of the Industrial Relations Act 1971 provided that for the purposes of enforcement of the Industrial Court's orders an organisation of workers might be treated in the same manner as a body corporate. Hence it was held that a union could be vicariously liable for the acts of its shop stewards.[68] In the absence of such a statutory intervention, it would be difficult to fix an unincorporated body with liability for a contempt by any of its individual members or employees.[69]

12-119 In the case of a partnership or firm all the partners may be parties to an order, sued either as individuals or in the name of the firm. In such a case, each individual partner may be liable not only for his or her own breach, but also for the acts or omissions of those for whom the partners are vicariously responsible, such as employees or agents of the firm.[70]

12-120 The characteristics of an unincorporated association were considered by the Court of Appeal in *M. Michaels (Furriers) Ltd v Askew*.[71] An injunction had been

---

[68] *Heatons Transport (St. Helens) Ltd v TGWU* [1973] A.C. 15. Cf. the remarks of Sir John Donaldson in *UKAPE v AUEW* [1972] I.C.R. 151.
[69] But see Halsbury's *Laws of England*, Vol. 47, (4th ed.) paras 1125 and 1549.
[70] See, *e.g. R. v Weisz Ex p. Hector MacDonald Ltd* [1952] 2 K.B. 611.
[71] (1983) 134 New Law Jo. 655, 127 Sol. Jo. 597.

sought against the defendants, on their own behalf and on behalf of all other members of "Animal Aid", restraining them from picketing the plaintiff's shop. This relief was granted, but objection was taken on appeal that the proceedings should not have been allowed to continue against the first and eighth defendants in a representative capacity. These were respectively the "local contact" in Bristol and the "national organiser". It was argued that there might be separate defences available to the various individuals sued. But the Court of Appeal referred to Lord Lindley's having emphasised in *Taff Vale Railway Co v Amalgamated Society of Railway Servants*[72] that the rule as to representative actions should be applied flexibly to situations, as they developed, in order to achieve justice. Since the case of the national organiser was simply that Animal Aid had nothing to do with events at the plaintiff's premises, the court could see no inconsistency with any defence likely to be put forward by other members of Animal Aid.

The court's conclusion was that, where a number of unidentified persons were causing injury and damage by unlawful acts, and there was an arguable case that they belonged to an organisation which encouraged action of the type complained of, and their actions could be linked to that organisation, then the provisions of RSC Ord.15, r.12[73] enabled the court to do justice in the particular case. Thus, these procedural rules would lead to the consequence that those whom the court saw fit to have represented in the proceedings could be held liable in the event of a breach.

12–121

In *Re a Solicitor (Disclosure of Confidential Records)*,[74] a father had sought disclosure of hospital records relating to interviews conducted at the special unit at Great Ormond Street Hospital. Cazalet J. ordered photocopies of the records to be disclosed to the parties' legal and medical advisers. Through an oversight, the mother was sent copies of the records by her solicitor. Johnson J. directed the Official Solicitor to bring proceedings for contempt against the firm of solicitors, because it was imperative that those who were ordered to disclose confidential information in such circumstances could be assured that the order would be obeyed. When such orders were breached the effect was to hinder the administration of justice. A fine of £1,000 was imposed upon the firm, which was also ordered to pay the costs of the Official Solicitor and of the hospital on an indemnity basis. In the circumstances it was not thought necessary to impose a separate penalty on the individual solicitor, who had admitted that what she did was wrong. The error had occurred in the course of a busy legal aid practice. Johnson J. took a sympathetic view of "the circumstances in which solicitors have to carry on their practices" and added "I hope that nothing that has occurred or that I say in this judgment will have any adverse repercussions for her in the future."

12–122

---

[72] [1901] A.C. 426; see also *Duke of Bedford v Ellis* [1901] A.C. 1, HL.
[73] RSC, Ord.15, r.12 was revoked by the Civil Procedure (Amendment) Rules 2000, SI 2000/221. See now CPR Sch.1, Ord.15.13A.
[74] [1997] 1 F.L.R. 101.

G. Ministers of the Crown

12–123 It has been confirmed that a Minister of the Crown can be liable for civil contempt, even though it is not possible for the Crown itself to be held in contempt.[75]

IV. BREACHES OF COURT ORDERS GENERALLY

A. Disobedience to a judgment or order requiring a positive act

1. Where time for compliance is specified in the order

12–124 Where a person is required by a judgment or order to do an act within a specified time or, as the case may be, within that time as extended or abridged (under what is now CPR 3.1(2)(a)), certain specific means of enforcement are available in the event of his refusing or neglecting to do it. The three methods listed in the CPR are[76]:

(i) A writ of sequestration (subject to the permission of the court) against the property of the person so neglecting or refusing;

(ii) Where the person is a body corporate, a writ of sequestration (again subject to the permission of the court) against the property of any director or other officer of the body;

(iii) An order of committal against the person so neglecting or refusing or, in the case of a corporation, against any director or other officer. This is subject to the provisions of the Debtors Acts 1869 and 1878.[77]

12–125 In the case of disobedience by a corporation the primary remedy is to apply for sequestration, since a company itself obviously cannot be committed.[78] The company may, however, be fined,[79] although this course can it seems only be taken by the court of its own motion, either on an application for sequestration by the party entitled to the benefit of the order[80] or otherwise under the inherent jurisdiction of the court.[81] As has been pointed out earlier,[82] the judge thought it inappropriate in *R. (on the application of Bempoa) v Southwark Borough*

---

[75] See *Re M: M v Home Office* [1994] 1 A.C. 337, discussed at para.2–223.
[76] CPR Sch.1 Ord.45.5.
[77] For the text of which, see Halsbury's *Statutes of England*, 4th ed., Vol. 4 at 817 and 824.
[78] See *R. v Windham* (1776) 1 Cowp. 377, 98 E.R. 1139 and *Re Hooley Ex p. Hooley* (1899) 79 L.T. 706, two authorities concerned with attachment.
[79] See *R. v Hammond* [1914] 2 K.B. 866; *Phonographic Performance Ltd v Amusement Caterers (Peckham) Ltd* [1964] Ch. 195, 200, Cross J.; *Steiner Products Ltd v Willy Steiner Ltd* [1966] 1 W.L.R. 986 at 992, [1966] 2 All E.R. 387 at 390–1, Ch.D; see also *GCT (Management) Ltd v The Laurie Marsh Group Ltd* [1972] F.S.R. 519.
[80] *Elliott v Klinger* [1967] 1 W.L.R. 1165 at 1167, Stamp J.
[81] CPR Sch.1, Ord.52.5.
[82] At para.12–101.

BREACHES OF COURT ORDERS GENERALLY   12–129

Council[83] to fine a local authority because such a course would not punish the individuals responsible (for the breaches of undertakings).

12–126 The wording of the rule, which was introduced in 1967, makes it clear that these sanctions are cumulative and not alternative.[84] Costs may be awarded on an indemnity basis.[85]

12–127 These means are available to enforce a judgment or order to do a positive act if a time is specified for performance and the act in question has not been done within that time. The material time limit may be fixed in one of three ways. It may be set out in the original judgment or order itself[86]; or by a subsequent order extending or abridging such time[87]; or, where no time for performance is laid down in the original judgment or order, the court may subsequently, upon application, fix a time.[88]

12–128 It is possible to list examples of categories of judgments or orders for which this rule provides a means of enforcement. Clearly, it will apply to any order for a mandatory order[89] or injunction, and a judgment or order for the specific performance of a contract, since such orders should specify a time for performance.[90] This should be expressed in terms of a period after service, and not merely by a specified time.[91]

12–129 Committal was recognised to be available under this rule for failure to comply with certain probate orders, for example a subpoena to bring in a will,[92] a citation to bring in a grant[93] or an order to file an inventory.[94] Similarly, the rule would

---

[83] [2002] EWHC 153 (Admin).
[84] *Phonographic Performance Ltd v Amusement Caterers (Peckham) Ltd* [1964] Ch. 195.
[85] *Att-Gen v Walthamstow Urban District Council* (1895) 11 T.L.R. 533; *Lee v Aylesbury Urban District Council* (1902) 19 T.L.R. 106; and *Stancomb v Trowbridge Urban District Council* [1910] 2 Ch. 190 at 196, Warrington J. See also para.12–122 above.
[86] These provisions were formerly to be found in RSC Ord.42, r.2(1), (2). They imposed a general obligation to specify a time limit within which the relevant act was to be done; but there was no need to specify a time in the judgment or order where the act required to be done was the payment of money, the giving of possession of land or delivery of goods. See now CPR 40.7 and, in the case of a money judgment, CPR 40.11. Although RSC, Ord.42, r.2(2) is no longer in effect, it is still the case that the coercive methods of enforcement under CPR Sch.1, Ord.45.5 cannot be employed unless the act was specified to be done within a particular time in the original order, or by an order extending or abridging the time under CPR 3.2(2)(a) or fixing such a time under CPR Sch.1, Ord.45.6.
[87] See now CPR 3.1 (2)(a) and CPR Sch.1, Ord.45.6(1).
[88] See now CPR Sch.1, Ord.45.6. An application must be made in accordance with CPR Pt 23 and the notice served personally on the person required to do the act.
[89] See, *e.g. R. v Leicester Guardians* (1899) 81 L.T. 559; *R. v Worcester Corporation* (1903) 98 J.P. 130.
[90] CPR 40.7 See also *Hitachi Sales (UK) v Mitsui Osk Lines* [1986] 2 Lloyd's Rep. 574, CA; *Temporal v Temporal* [1990] 2 F.L.R. 98, CA.
[91] *Van Houten v Foodsafe Ltd* (1980) 124 Sol. Jo. 277. Cp. *Iberian Trust Ltd v Founders Trust & Investment Co Ltd* [1932] 2 K.B. 87 (shares to be returned "within fourteen days").
[92] *Simmons v Dean* (1858) 27 L.J. P. 103; *Parkinson v Thornton* (1868) 37 L.J. P. 3.
[93] *Evans v Evans* (1893) 67 L.T. 719.
[94] *Baker v Baker* (1860) 2 Sw. & Tr. 380, 164 E.R. 1043; *Marsham v Brookes* (1863) 32 L.J.P. 95.

also include a citation to take a grant when the citee has intermeddled in the estate.[95]

2. Where no time is specified in the order

12–130 On the other hand certain types of judgments and orders, although they may require a positive act to be done, did not traditionally have to specify a time for performance.[96] As a general practice where there was a judgment or order requiring any person to pay money to another before the coming into effect of the CPR in April 1999, no time limit would initially be specified. The sanctions of sequestration and committal used not, therefore, to be available unless steps had been taken to have a time specified. Under CPR 40.11, however, there must be compliance within 14 days of the date of the judgment or order unless a different date has been specified in the judgment or order itself, or in any applicable rule, or where there has been a stay of the judgment or order. So far as any other judgment or order is concerned, the basic rule under CPR 40.7 is that it should take effect from the day it is given or made, or upon such later date as the court may specify.[97]

3. Other restrictions on committal

12–131 It is important to note certain other respects in which there are limitations upon the use of committal. Where there is a judgment or order in the alternative form, for the delivery of goods *or* to pay their assessed value, it cannot be enforced by an order of committal,[98] although a writ of sequestration may be obtained in the usual way.[99] Nevertheless the court may[1] make an order requiring the defendant to deliver the goods within a specified time, and committal will then lie for a breach of that order.

12–132 Where an order has been made to attend for cross-examination, such an order will not be enforceable by process of contempt in accordance with these rules unless conduct money has been tendered.[2]

4. Disobedience to a judgment or order to give possession of land within a specified time

12–133 Where there is an order or judgment for the giving of possession of land, and a time is specified by the court, whether at the time of the judgment or order itself

---

[95] *Mordaunt v Clarke* (1869) 1 P. & D. 592; *Re Lister* (1894) 70 L.T. 812.
[96] See the former RSC Ord.42, r.2(2). This no longer applies. See note under para.12–127, n.86.
[97] It is noted however that Sch.1, Ord.45.6 still contemplates the possibility that an order will be made without specifying a time for compliance.
[98] See now CPR Sch.1, Ord.45.5(3).
[99] See now CPR Sch.1, Ord.45.4(2)(c). The proper course is to apply for leave to issue a writ of specific delivery under Ord.45.4(2)(b), before placing reliance on the process of contempt.
[1] On the application of the person entitled to enforce the judgment or order, under CPR Sch.1, Ord.45.5(3). The application should be to the Master.
[2] *In the Estate of Harvey* [1907] P. 239 and *Townend v Townend* [1907] P. 239. See the discussion at paras 11–103 *et seq.*

or subsequently,[3] the rules provide for enforcement by process of contempt.[4] It is, however, a general principle that this process should not be invoked in aid of any civil remedy where there is available some other method of achieving the desired result.[5] It will therefore only be in the most exceptional cases that it is an appropriate means to obtain possession of land, and generally a writ of possession will be sufficient to enforce judgment. Permission has to be obtained for the issue of such a writ unless:

(1) the judgment or order was given or made in proceedings by a mortgagee or mortgagor or by any person having the right to foreclose or redeem any mortgage, being proceedings in which there is a claim for certain specified types of relief, including payment of moneys secured by the mortgage and delivery of possession[6] or

(2) the proceedings are brought under CPR Sch.1, Ord.113.[7]

A writ of possession is available notwithstanding that no order has been made specifying the time within which possession has to be given. Permission will not be granted unless it is demonstrated that due notice has been given to every person in actual possession.[8]

If the operation of the judgment or order is suspended by s.16(2) of the Landlord and Tenant Act 1954, permission will be refused unless it is shown that the applicant has not received notice from the tenant that he desires the provisions of s.16(2)(a) and (b) to have effect.[9]

5. *Disobedience to a judgment or order for the delivery of goods within a specified time*

Where goods are ordered to be delivered within a specific time but no alternative is given of paying the assessed value, the Rules make provision for enforcement by committal and sequestration.[10] Where under a judgement or order requiring the delivery of goods, the person liable does have the alternative of paying the assessed value of the goods, the judgment or order is not enforceable by way of committal under Ord.45.5(1) but the court may on application require delivery

---

[3] Under the provisions of CPR Sch.1 Ord.45.6. Similar provisions apply in the county court: CPR Sch.2, cc.26.
[4] See now CPR Sch.1, Ord.45.3.
[5] See paras 12–15 *et seq*. See also *Danchevsky v Danchevsky* [1975] Fam. 17. For a discussion in the context of family homes, see S.M. Cretney, J.M. Masson and R. Bailey-Harris, *Principles of Family Law* (7th ed., 2003), ch.10.
[6] CPR Sch.1, Ord.45.3(2).
[7] CPR Sch.1, Ord.113.7(1) (until three months have elapsed from the date of the order, when permission *will* be required).
[8] CPR Sch.1, Ord.45.3(3).
[9] CPR Sch.1, Ord.45.3(3)(b).
[10] See now CPR Sch.1, Ord.45.4(1)(b) and (c). The remedy of sequestration was held also to be available in the county court, by reason of s.38 of the County Courts Act 1984: see *Rose v Laskington Ltd* [1990] Q.B. 562 at 570, Stuart-Smith L.J.

12–135 within a time specified.[11] Thereafter the order may be enforced by committal. Because of the general rule that resort should only be had to the process of contempt where no other means of execution is readily available or practicable,[12] the most common means for enforcing judgments or orders of this type is that of writ of specific delivery.[13] Such a writ may be issued even though no time has been specified for delivery to be made.

B. Disobedience to a judgment or order to abstain from doing any act

12–136 Where a person disobeys a judgment or order requiring him to abstain from doing an act, the three specific means of enforcement listed in the former Rules of the Supreme Court[14] were:

(1) a writ of sequestration (subject to permission of the court) against the property of that person;

(2) where the person is a body corporate, with the permission of the court, a writ of sequestration against the property of any director or other officer of the body;

(3) an order of committal against the person disobeying or, in the case of a corporation, against any director or other officer. This remedy is expressed to be subject to the provisions of the Debtors Acts 1869 and 1878.[15]

12–137 Orders which are prohibitive in character are not required to specify a time for compliance.[16] On the other hand, where a time is specified even though the order may not be mandatory in form,[17] it would clearly be inappropriate to seek to enforce it until such time has expired.

12–138 The remedies available in respect of enforcing negative orders are the same as those available in the case of positive orders. Sch.1, Ord.45.5(1) makes it clear that negative orders may be enforced by writ of sequestration, whereas under the former rules[18] this was subject to doubt.

---

[11] CPR Sch.1, Ord.45.5(3) and 45.6(2).
[12] See paras 12–15 *et seq.*, and the cases cited there.
[13] CPR Sch.1, Ord.45.4.
[14] See now CPR Sch.1 Ord.45.5(1).
[15] For the text of which, see Halsbury's *Statutes of England*, 4th ed., Vol. 4 at 817 and 824.
[16] This was expressly provided for in the former RSC Ord.42, r.2. There is no direct equivalent in the CPR, but the proposition remains valid. Under the CPR 40.7(1) any judgment or order takes effect from when it is given or made but in some circumstances a court imposing a restriction may wish to allow some leeway for compliance and thus specify a later date (as the rule specifically provides); see also *Selous v Croydon Local Board* (1885) 53 L.T. 209; *Hudson v Walker* (1894) 64 L.J. Ch. 204.
[17] See, *e.g. Mansell v Jones* [1905] W.N. 168, CA. The Court of Appeal had granted a mandatory injunction, in a negative form, to the effect that the defendants were "restrained from permitting to remain any stones, soil, or materials so as to interfere with the free access to the plaintiff's land". No time was fixed for carrying out the order, and it was held that Kekewich J. had erred in as much as he thought he lacked jurisdiction to fix a time for compliance. He had suggested that the plaintiff's proper course would be to move for an immediate order of attachment or committal.
[18] The present rule replaced the former RSC Ord.42, rr.6, 7 and 31 and Ord.43, rr.6 and 7.

C. Cases in which a judgment or order has been wrongly obtained

12-139 It is necessary to consider the consequences, for enforcement by the law of contempt, in cases where an order is made wrongly in the sense that the court in question had no power to make it, or even perhaps acted contrary to express provisions of law in purporting to make it. In order to understand the approach of the courts to this question, it is appropriate to compare the situation where a judge has erred in granting an injunction, either mandatory or prohibitory in character, with circumstances in which a court has wrongly made an order compelling a journalist to disclose sources of information. In some respects such orders would appear to be very similar, and yet there are two distinct lines of authority as to the consequences which flow from disobedience. The difficulties of reconciling these lines of authority are fully discussed in chapter 9,[19] in the context of journalists' sources, but the fundamental principle is that any order of the court should be obeyed unless and until it is stayed or set aside.[20]

12-140 Some time may be allowed to enable an application for a stay to be made, for example in the context of search and seizure orders.[21] Moreover, it would not be uncommon to order a stay pending appeal. In the absence of such a stay, however, it appears that a contempt will have been committed in the event of disobedience even in circumstances where the injunction is subsequently set aside on appeal.[22] A particularly striking illustration of the principle is that of *Wardle Fabrics Ltd v G Myristis Ltd*[23] where the order was set aside for material non-disclosure, but the defendants were nonetheless held to have been in contempt.

12-141 The rationale underlying the general principle is fairly obvious and has been stated in Canada, in the context of the Charter[24]:

> "The order of the Tribunal ... continues to stand unaffected by the Charter violation until set aside. This result is as it should be. If people are free to ignore court orders because they believe their foundation is unconstitutional, anarchy cannot be far behind. The citizens' safeguard is in seeking to have illegal orders set aside through the legal process, not disobeying them."

12-142 It will be suggested that the principle has no application where an undertaking has purportedly been given on behalf of someone, but without his knowledge or authority.[25] Since such a person could not in fact give an undertaking there is

---

[19] paras 9–194 *et seq.*
[20] See, *e.g.* the words of Lord Bingham cited above at para.12–70.
[21] *WEA Records Ltd v Visions Channel 4 Ltd* [1983] 1 W.L.R. 721 at 725–6, Sir John Donaldson M.R.
[22] See, *e.g.* the Manitoba Court of Appeal in *Re Swan River—The Pas Transfer Ltd* (1975) 51 D.L.R. (3d) 292 at 308 (where Matas J.A. said: " ... a person enjoined from doing an act cannot ignore an order of the court ... or because an appeal from the order may be pending").
[23] [1984] F.S.R. 263, discussed at para.12–176.
[24] McLachlin J. in *Canada (Human Rights Commission) v Taylor* (1990) 75 D.L.R. (4th) 577, 635. See also *Austin Rover v AUEW and others* [1985] I.R.L.R. 162 at 164, Hodgson J.
[25] para.12–194; see also *Turner v Naval, Military & Civil Service Co-operative Society of South Africa, The Times*, January 21, 1903. But see the discussion of this case by Simon Brown J. in *Re M: M v Home Office* [1992] 4 All E.R. 97 at 118.

12–142 CHAPTER 12—CIVIL CONTEMPT

nothing of which he can be in breach. The law of contempt can only come in to play in relation to undertakings by virtue of the fact that a commitment to the court has been validly given by or on behalf of an individual or corporation.

12–143 That situation, however, is to be contrasted with circumstances in which an *order* of the court, whether positive or negative, has been made, since this can come about without any input from the person to whom the order is directed.

V. FREEZING AND SEARCH AND SEIZURE ORDERS

A. Freezing orders

12–144 A breach of a freezing (formerly known as a *Mareva*) injunction or a search and seizure (formerly an *Anton Piller*) order is a civil contempt of court, as much as any other breach of a court order in civil litigation. There are a number of factors, however, that call for separate consideration.[26]

12–145 We have discussed, in the context of the media,[27] the possible impact of criminal contempt upon those who become knowingly involved in conduct which has the effect of frustrating an order made in litigation to which they are not parties. These well known principles are especially important in the context of freezing orders. Indeed, one of the most important authorities in this field arose directly out of the grant of a *Mareva* order. In *Z Ltd v A-Z and AA-LL*[28] a number of clearing banks had applied for leave to appeal certain orders, for the purpose of elucidating the position of innocent third parties who were served with notice of a *Mareva*.

12–146 The application was dismissed, but guidelines were given in relation to the principles:

> (1) The *Mareva* injunction was an established feature of English law, which should be granted where it appeared likely that a plaintiff would recover judgment for a certain or approximate sum and there were reasons to believe that the defendant had assets within the jurisdiction to meet the judgment, wholly or in part, but might deal with them in such a way that they would not be available or traceable when judgment actually came to be given. Those principles had been given statutory force by s.37(3) of the Supreme Court Act 1981:
>
>> "The power of the High Court . . . to grant an interlocutory injunction restraining a party to any proceedings from removing the jurisdiction of the High Court, or otherwise dealing with, assets located within that jurisdiction shall be exercisable in cases where that party is, as well as in cases where he is not, domiciled, resident or present within that jurisdiction".

---

[26] See generally S. Gee Q.C., *Commercial Injunctions* (5th ed., 2004.)
[27] See para.6-115. See *Att-Gen v Newspaper Publishing plc* [1988] Ch. 333; *Att-Gen v Times Newspapers Ltd* [1992] 1 A.C. 179.
[28] [1982] 1 Q.B. 558.

(2) Such an order operated *in rem* and took effect, from the moment it was granted,[29] upon every asset of the defendant which it covered. Refusal by a defendant, once served, to comply with its mandatory terms will render him in contempt, even though he may successfully apply to the court later to discharge the order.[30]

(3) Every person with knowledge of the injunction had to do what he reasonably could to preserve the assets covered by the order, and would be guilty of (criminal) contempt if assisting in their disposal, because any such act would constitute an interference with the course of justice.

(4) The situation is analogous to the principles applying to the arrest of a ship. Once the warrant of arrest has been issued, and notice has been given to the master of the ship, any movement of the ship, by him, or by anyone else with knowledge, would be "a great and grievous offence, and one which rendered him amenable to attachment of the court".[31]

(5) Thus, once a bank is given notice of a freezing order, affecting goods or money in its hands, it must not dispose of them itself, or allow the defendant or anyone else to do so, except by the authority of the court. If any of the bank staff knowingly assist in the disposal of the assets, such persons will be in contempt of court, on the basis that such an act would be calculated to obstruct the course of justice. It is, however, not legitimate in order to establish the necessary *mens rea* to add together the innocent states of mind of two or more servants in order to establish a guilty mind on the part of the corporation.[32]

(6) There is no need for the defendant to have had notice of the injunction before the sanctions can bite upon third parties.[33]

(7) It is necessary for a bank to take positive steps to "trawl" through its various branches in order to discover what assets they may have belonging to the defendant in question. The reasonable cost of carrying out this exercise will have to be borne by the claimant pursuant to the undertaking which he has to give to cover all costs, expenses or fees

---

[29] RSC Ord.42, r.3(1). See also *Z Ltd v A-Z and AA-LL* [1982] 1 Q.B. 558 at 572, Lord Denning M.R.; *Holtby v Hodgson* (1889) 24 Q.B.D. 103 at 107.
[30] *Bhimji v Chatwani* [1991] 1 W.L.R., 989 at 1000F–1001H; *Wardle Fabrics Ltd v G Myristis Ltd* [1984] F.S.R. 263; *Columbia Pictures Inc v Robinson* [1987] Ch. 38 at 71–2. Compare the discussion as to the right to challenge orders made against journalists to reveal a source, in paras 9–194 *et seq.*
[31] *The Mathesis* (1844) 2 Wm. Rob. 286 at 288, 166 E.R. 762 at 763, Dr Lushington; *The Seraglio* (1885) 10 P.D. 120 at 121, Sir James Hannen P.; *The Abodi Mendi* [1939] P.178 at 194, Scott L.J.; *The Jarlinn* [1965] 1 W.L.R. 1098.
[32] *Z Ltd v A-Z and AA-LL* [1982] 1 Q.B. 558 at 581, Eveleigh L.J. who expressed the view that even recklessness would not render the bank liable for contempt unless there was indifference to such a degree that it could be characterised as contumacious; see also *Armstrong v Strain* [1952] 1 K.B. 232. If any of the bank employees should knowingly assist in the disposal of assets, there can be little doubt that the bank would be held vicariously responsible: although the context is that of criminal contempt, and vicarious liability is not generally applied in the criminal law, it seems to be recognised that contempt is an exception; furthermore, there is no reason to suppose that a distinction can be drawn for these purposes between publication and non-publication contempts. See para.4–199.
[33] *ibid.* at 581B, Eveleigh L.J. and 586C, Kerr L.J.

12–146 incurred by such third parties in complying with the order, and also to indemnify such persons against all liabilities that may flow from such compliance.[34]

12–147 The relevant part of the current form of specimen freezing injunction[35] is as follows:

"INTERPRETATION OF THIS ORDER

14) A Respondent who is an individual who is ordered not to do something must not do it himself or in any other way. He must not do it through others acting on his behalf or on his instructions or with his encouragement.

15) A Respondent which is not an individual which is ordered not to do something must not do it itself or by its directors, officers, partners, employees or agents or in any other way".

12–148 The standard form makes provision for withdrawals from bank accounts for living expenses and legal costs, and no bank need enquire as to the application or proposed application of any money withdrawn by the defendant if the withdrawal appears to be permitted by the order. So long as the bank is not aiding or abetting, or conniving at a breach by the defendant, there is no duty imposed upon it to act as a detective. The mere withdrawal of sums from a bank account will not normally constitute an act of dealing with or disposing of assets.[36]

12–149 On the other hand, if the bank is genuinely aware of the purpose for which funds are being withdrawn, and that purpose entails disobedience of the terms of the order, the bank could well be held to have assisted or connived at the wrongful act.

12–150 Clearly, if a defendant knowing of the existence of an order disables himself, before it is served upon him, from being able to comply with it, he will be in contempt for having deliberately set out to frustrate the purpose of the court.[37] This would not be disobedience to an order, which was *ex hypothesi* not yet effective, but a criminal contempt (requiring the appropriate *mens rea*).

12–151 A question also arises as to the role of joint account holders. It is not uncommon for a freezing injunction to bind all accounts "held by or on behalf of the defendant or by or on behalf of the defendant jointly with any other persons or by nominees or otherwise howsoever".[38] If a joint holder, not being joined as a party, deals with the funds from the account while knowing of the court's order against the joint holder, there would be a real risk that he or she would be found to have set out to frustrate the purpose of the order. Much will turn on the facts of each case.

---

[34] *ibid.* at 586, Kerr L.J.; see also *Sea Rose Ltd v Sea Train UK Ltd* [1981] 1 W.L.R. 894; *Clipper Maritime Co Ltd of Monrovia v Mineralimportexport* [1981] 1 W.L.R. 1262.
[35] See *Civil Procedure*, para.2A–161, Admiralty and Commercial Courts Guide, Appendix 5.
[36] *Bank Mellat v Kazmi* [1989] Q.B. 541.
[37] *Lewis v Pontypridd, Caerphilly and Newport Railway Company* (1895) 11 T.L.R. 203; see also *Att-Gen v Times Newspapers Ltd* [1992] 1 A.C. 191 at 224.
[38] See, *e.g. SCF v Masri* [1985] 1 W.L.R. 876, CA.

Sometimes it is sought to include within the scope of a freezing injunction assets which appear on their face to belong to a third party; the court should not permit this without good reason for supposing the assets are in truth those of the defendant. In *SCF v Masri*,[39] for example, an order was made on this basis extending the existing injunction to accounts in the wife's name and, later, she was joined as a party.

12–152

The Court of Appeal held in *Federal Bank of the Middle East Ltd v Hadkinson*[40] that the words "his assets and/or funds" appearing in the standard form of freezing order were not apt to cover assets and funds belonging to someone other than the person restrained. The wording was confined to assets and funds belonging to the defendant and which should remain available to satisfy the claim against him. Nevertheless, the court can in appropriate circumstances word an order so as to cover assets which might belong beneficially to the defendant. For example, it would be legitimate to include reference to bank accounts held "in the name of" the defendant. The order could be modified or discharged if, on fuller enquiry, it emerged that the relevant funds belonged beneficially to a third party.

12–153

It is now provided in the standard form[41] as follows:

12–154

"6. Paragraph 5 [which restrains removal and disposal of "his assets"] applies to all the Respondent's assets whether or not they are in his own name and whether or not they are solely or jointly owned. For the purpose of this order the Respondent's assets include any asset which he has the power, directly or indirectly, to dispose of ordeal with as if it were his own. The Respondent is to be regarded as having such power if a third party holds or controls the asset in accordance with his direct or indirect instructions"

The effect of a freezing order abroad[42]

We have already drawn attention to the significance of the distinction between the traditional categories of civil and criminal contempt with regard to acts or omissions occurring outside the jurisdiction.[43] The effectiveness of injunctive relief is one context in which this problem needs to be carefully considered. The principles which need to be reconciled are:

12–155

(a) The English court does not have jurisdiction over criminal acts or omissions outside the national boundaries (subject to any statutory exceptions), including in respect of British citizens or English residents.[44]

---

[39] *ibid.*
[40] [2000] 1 W.L.R. 1695, [2000] 2 All E.R. 395.
[41] See *Civil Procedure*, para.2A–161, Admiralty and Commercial Courts Guide, Appendix 5.
[42] See L. Collins, "The Territorial Reach of Mareva Injunctions" (1989) 105 L.Q.R. 262. See also the full discussion of these problems in Steven Gee Q.C., *Gee on Commercial Injunctions* (5th ed., 2004), ch.14.
[43] para.3–223.
[44] See generally *Archbold 2005*, paras 2–33 *et seq.* and *R. v Smith* [2004] EWCA Crim 631, [2004] Q.B. 1418.

12–155   (b) The English court *does* have jurisdiction over those who are before the court, or who are deemed to be before the court, by reason of having been served with the court's process and thus made parties to English litigation.

(c) Orders may be made and served upon parties in English litigation, and the court will have sanctions to compel performance, or to punish the failure to perform, even where the relevant acts or omissions occur abroad (for example, in the case of a runaway parent who fails to bring back a child from abroad).

12–156   The difficulty arises, however, in relation to those who are not parties but who would, if in England, be susceptible to the court's contempt jurisdiction because of assisting a party to flout an order or otherwise consciously frustrating the court's process.

12–157   Such activities would traditionally be classified as criminal contempt, and attempts in recent times to discard the old distinction[45] have tended to confuse rather than assist the analysis of the extent to which injunctions, and in particular freezing orders, will be recognised as having extra-territorial impact.

12–158   This problem has been addressed by the insertion of a form of "proviso" in standard forms of freezing orders. For example, the following wording appears in the standard form[46]:

"19. Persons outside England and Wales
(1) Except as provided in paragraph (2) below, the terms of this order do not affect or concern anyone outside the jurisdiction of this court.

(2) The terms of this order will affect the following persons in a country or state outside the jurisdiction of this court—

   (a) the Respondent or his officer or agent appointed by power of attorney;
   (b) any person who—

      (i) is subject to the jurisdiction of this court;
      (ii) has been given written notice of this order at his residence or place of business within the jurisdiction of this court; and
      (iii) is able to prevent acts or omissions outside the jurisdiction of this court which constitute or assist in a breach of the terms of this order; and

   (c) any other person, only to the extent that this order is declared enforceable by or is enforced by a court in that country or state."

20. Assets located outside England and Wales

Nothing in this order shall, in respect of assets located outside England and Wales, prevent any third party from complying with—

   (1) what it reasonably believes to be its obligations, contractual or otherwise, under the laws and obligations of the country or state in which those assets are situated

---

[45] See, *e.g. Att-Gen v Newspaper Publishing plc* [1988] Ch. 333 at 362B–D, Sir John Donaldson M.R., discussed more fully at paras 3–51 *et seq.*
[46] See *Civil Procedure*, para.2A–161, Admiralty and Commercial Courts Guide, Appendix 5.

or under the proper law of any contract between itself and the Respondent; and

(2) any orders of the courts of that country or state, provided that reasonable notice of any application for such an order is given to the Applicant's solicitors".

12-159 In *Babanaft International Co v Bassatne*[47] the problem was spelt out by Nicholls L.J. in the following terms:

"It would be wrong for an English court, by making an order in respect of overseas assets against a defendant amenable to its jurisdiction, to impose or attempt to impose obligations on persons not before the court in respect of acts to be done by them abroad regarding property outside the jurisdiction. That self-evidently would be for an English court to claim an altogether exorbitant, extra-territorial jurisdiction."

12-160 Now the standard "proviso" is based on the thinking of the court in *Derby & Co Ltd v Weldon (Nos.3 and 4)*.[48] This involves a distinction, so far as banks are concerned, between those which have a branch or branches within the jurisdiction and those which do not. The policy appears to be that a bank which has a branch in England should recognise and support an injunction in relation to a bank account at a foreign branch.[49] Thus, the English court would regard a bank served at an English branch with a freezing order as bound to observe its effect in relation to a foreign account.

12-161 As a matter of analysis, it may be that this approach confuses the effect of service upon a party with service upon a stranger to the proceedings. The English court cannot surely invest itself with criminal jurisdiction over the acts of foreign institutions abroad merely because they happen to have a branch in England.[50] This would go well beyond the enforcement of private rights in a case where a foreigner may have submitted to the jurisdiction of the court, or has agreed to perform various acts abroad pursuant to a contract over which the court has jurisdiction.[51]

12-162 Quite apart from purely jurisdictional considerations, there are practical difficulties. Not least, it is necessary to address possible conflicts between the apparent obligation, under English law, to observe the effect of the freezing order, and duties which may arise under foreign law governing the conduct of the foreign bank account. These delicate issues of conflict and comity have traditionally been recognised in other contexts, such as applications for orders

---

[47] [1990] Ch. 13 at 44.
[48] [1990] Ch. 65 at 84C–F.
[49] See, *e.g. Securities and Investments Board v Pantell SA* [1990] Ch. 426 at 432–3.
[50] *Mackinnon v Donaldson, Lufkin and Jenrette Corp* [1986] 1 Ch. 482 at 493, Hoffmann J. See also F.A. Mann, "The Doctrine of Jurisdiction in International Law" (1964) 111 Recueil des Cours 146; "The Doctrine of International Jurisdiction Revisited After Twenty Years" (1984) 196 Recueil des Cours 9. See also the problem discussed by Clarke J. in *Unicargo v Flotec Maritime S de R.L., The "Cienvik"* [1996] 2 Lloyd's Rep. at 395–9.
[51] *Mackinnon v Donaldson, Lufkin and Jenrette Corp* [1986] Ch. 482 at 494, Hoffmann J.

12–162 under s.7 of the Bankers' Books Evidence Act 1879 or applications for the issue of a subpoena.[52]

12–163 A claimant should seek relief in the relevant foreign court as expeditiously as possible, rather than relying on the extra-territorial recognition of an English order. There is inevitably a hiatus period for the claimant between obtaining an order in England and achieving corresponding protection in the foreign court, and this is especially acute with orders not made upon notice (which are, for example, not recognised in cases governed by the Brussels and Lugano Conventions). In other contexts, and especially in family or domestic proceedings, such orders should only be granted exceptionally, where, for example, there is genuinely no time to give the defendant notice, or where there is good reason to believe that he would, if given notice, take action which would defeat the purpose of the order.[53] In *Loseby v Newman*, however, Hirst L.J. expressly indicated that the case should not be taken as disapproving the well-established practice in other Divisions to grant such orders up to trial or further order without specifying a return date, and in particular in cases of freezing orders in the Commercial Court.[54]

12–164 An attempt was made to address this difficulty in the July 1993 end of year statement by the judge then in charge of the Commercial List (Saville J.):

"The *Derby v Weldon* proviso does not seem to help as it does not apply to persons who are subject to the jurisdiction, which of course is the case with most major banks. To solve this problem of double jeopardy we would suggest in appropriate cases that something along the lines of the following provision be added to the order. 'Nothing in this Order shall, in respect of assets located outside England and Wales' (and in particular [specify if necessary the foreign country concerned]) 'prevent [the bank] or its subsidiaries from complying with:

(1) what it reasonably believes to be its obligations, contractual or otherwise, under the laws and obligations of the country or state in which those assets are situated or under the proper law of the account in question;

(2) any orders of the courts of that country or state'".

This wording states no more than that which should be obvious.

12–165 It is unfortunate that these questions have not been effectively addressed by way of treaty or statute. It seems at the moment to be a matter of rather tentative trial and error. For example, in *Baltic Shipping Company v Translink Shipping Ltd*[55] the proviso suggested by Saville J. was modified to allow the bank to pay

---

[52] *Mackinnon v Donaldson, Lufkin & Jenrette Corp*, last note, Hoffmann J. (where it was held that an order requiring a bank to produce books and other papers, held at its head office in New York, which related to an account of one of the defendants, should be discharged as being an infringement of the sovereignty of the United States). See also *Re Mid East Trading Ltd (No.2)* [1998] 1 All E.R. 577 at 590–3, CA in the context of jurisdiction to make an order under the Insolvency Act 1986, s.236.

[53] *Loseby v Newman* [1995] 2 F.L.R. 754 at 755A–B, Balcombe L.J., 758B–D, Hoffmann L.J.; *Re First Express* [1991] B.C.C. 782.

[54] [1995] 2 F.L.R. at 757.

[55] [1995] 1 Lloyd's Rep. 673, Clarke J.

from the foreign account, provided that its belief that it was so obliged under the foreign law had been formed on reasonable grounds. It is submitted that, whatever may be thought desirable as a matter of practical experience in seeking to protect foreign assets, it is difficult to justify any corporation or individual, being a stranger to the relevant litigation, being treated by an English court as guilty of criminal contempt in respect of acts or omissions abroad which are thought to subvert the effect of an English injunction such as a freezing order.

Sometimes it may be appropriate nonetheless to include under "Effect on Third Parties" wording such as to enable overseas branches of banks with offices within the jurisdiction to comply with what they reasonably believe to be required under the law of the country where the relevant assets are located, or under the proper law of any relevant contract. In *Bank of China v NBM, LLC and others*,[56] a Swiss bank had been served with a freezing order in standard form and applied for a variation to add a *"Baltic"* proviso to permit it and its subsidiaries to comply with contractual and other obligations under local law or under the proper law of the bank account. The claimant was only prepared to consent in respect of compliance with the criminal law, but the Judge held that the proviso sought *should* be included unless it could be shown to be inappropriate and, what is more, that consideration should be given to including it in the standard form. This approach was upheld by the Court of Appeal. The *Baltic* proviso only required the third party to have a reasonable belief as to what its obligations were under local law, but it was entitled to that degree of protection and it would normally be appropriate for it to be included. It should therefore be included in the standard form.[57]

Freezing orders in aid of foreign proceedings

In accordance with s.25 of the Civil Jurisdiction and Judgments Act 1982 the English court may grant a freezing injunction in aid of foreign proceedings. It is provided that the relief is available unless "the fact that the court has no jurisdiction apart from this section . . . makes it inexpedient". The impracticability of enforcing its orders would generally be a powerful reason for not granting such relief.[58] It was made clear, for example, in *Credit Suisse Fides Trust SA v Cuoghi*[59] that the court might well have refused world wide relief in aid of Swiss proceedings had it not been for the fact that the relevant defendant was domiciled within the jurisdiction. Another instance where the court thought such relief appropriate was where the defendant, although not resident here and apparently having no assets here either, had used a firm of solicitors in England for the purpose of hiding his assets.

The court was asked in *Motorola Credit Corp v Uzan*[60] to grant worldwide relief (limited to $200m US) in aid of United States proceedings. The defendants

---

[56] [2001] EWCA Civ 1916, [2002] 1 W.L.R. 844, [2002] 1 All E.R. (Comm.) 472, CA.
[57] See now para.20 of the standard form cited above at para.12–158.
[58] See, *e.g. Derby and Co Ltd v Weldon (No.2)* [1989] 1 All E.R. 1002 at 1010.
[59] [1997] 3 All E.R. 724.
[60] [2003] EWCA Civ 752, [2004] 1 W.L.R. 113.

12–168 were held in contempt for failing to disclose their assets and to attend for cross-examination. The judge imposed sentences of imprisonment. The Court of Appeal exercised its discretion to hear an appeal not withstanding the continuing breach.[61] It concluded that the English court had to exercise its judgment independently rather than accept any decision made by the foreign court. This was indeed what the judge had done. Two of the defendants indicated that they had no intention of complying with any order of the English court. They were not resident here; nor did they have assets within the jurisdiction. It followed that the court would be unlikely ever to be in a position to enforce an order. Moreover, they had obtained anti-suit injunctions in Turkey preventing the court from pursuing proceedings either in the United States or in England. The court will naturally be alert to the possibility of creating by the orders it makes "jurisdictional disharmony or confusion".[62] The Court of Appeal held that the judge had failed to give sufficient weight to these two factors. An additional consideration was that the judge had rather treated the defendants collectively and should not have justified the grant of relief against the second and third defendants by reference to the circumstances of the first and fourth, for example the fact that they had assets here and the fourth defendant was also resident here. The Court of Appeal concluded that the circumstances were such as to render it "inexpedient" to grant the relief claimed. The orders were accordingly discharged.

12–169 A significant factor to be considered is whether the foreign court, before which the litigation is proceeding, would itself grant relief of the type or scale being sought in England. It seems that what matters is whether the foreign court would acknowledge a jurisdiction to make the relevant orders. It is not simply a question of the English court attempting to second-guess how the foreign court's jurisdiction would be exercised, but rather showing a reluctance to support foreign proceedings by the grant of any order which the primary court simply *could* not make.[63]

The significance of financial limits attached to freezing injunctions

12–170 The financial limits normally imposed would have considerable implications for enforcement by process of contempt in relation to breaches of freezing injunctions. The burden rests upon the claimant to establish a breach to the criminal standard of proof.[64] A defendant might argue that the disposal of assets sought to be challenged as a breach was in fact legitimate having regard to the limit imposed. Often the claimant will have to rely upon inferences from the surrounding circumstances, as his knowledge of the full extent of the defendant's assets is likely to be partial, to say the least. In practice, however, it seems that the court will not expect a claimant to take on the burden of proving a negative; that is to say, that the defendant has no other assets than those dissipated. It will

---

[61] See the discussion at paras 12–66 *et seq.*
[62] *Credit Suisse Trust SA v Cuoghi* [1997] 3 All E.R. 724 at 734j, Bingham C.J.; see also *Refco Inc v Eastern Trading Co* [1999] 1 Ll.oyd's Rep. 159 at 174, Potter L.J.
[63] *Refco Inc v Eastern Trading Co* [1999] 1 Lloyd's Rep. 559, as explained in *Motorola Credit v Uzan (No.2)* [2003] EWCA Civ, [2004] 1 W.L.R. 113.
[64] See paras 3–241, 12–43.

thus be wise for a defendant, when challenged, to demonstrate that he did indeed have other assets, in order to rebut the inference that he has put himself in breach, notwithstanding the general principle that it is for the applicant to prove that a contempt has been committed to the criminal standard of proof.[65]

12–171 Where a defendant is in breach of a freezing order it is open to the court to impose a penalty which will be mitigated or remitted altogether on condition that assets are replaced.[66] If the assets have not been dissipated, but remain intact despite a failure to comply with the order, the court may order that they be transferred back whence they came.[67] Also, if the assets remain identifiable in form, in the hands of a third party, who received them knowing that the transfer was in breach of the order, the court would in principle no doubt have the power to order him to return them in accordance with the general principle that the court has power to restrain the commission or continuance of a contempt.[68]

12–172 Where the funds are not readily identifiable, there may be greater difficulty in obtaining a remedy by means of the contempt jurisdiction. Persons who have acted knowingly to assist the depletion of the funds may be punishable, but this does not directly avail the claimant.

12–173 Solicitors, however, are under the control of the High Court,[69] and in the exercise of that jurisdiction the court may be able to order a solicitor to restore the value of the missing fund. In *TDK Tape Distributors v Video Choice*[70] the plaintiffs had obtained a freezing order against the fourth defendant restraining him from disposing or dealing with any of his assets until further order, save that he could spend a hundred pounds a week on ordinary expenses. He negligently failed to disclose that the house he owned with his wife was the subject of an endowment policy mortgage. This was subsequently redeemed, and he received just over £4,000 under the endowment policy. The money was paid into his solicitors' client account at a time when he had been charged with a criminal offence, and counsel had been instructed. He agreed with his solicitor that the sum should be used to meet the costs of the defence. This was naturally not to be classified as a living expense.

12–174 It was held that not only the fourth defendant but also his solicitor was in contempt of court, and indeed that the solicitor was primarily responsible[71] for the breach of the injunction. An order was made that the equivalent of the sum

---

[65] *Canadian Imperial Bank of Commerce v Bhattesa*, Court of Appeal, Transcript No.694, April 21, 1993 (Lexis). The Court of Appeal rejected a submission that Harman J. had erred in relying upon *R. v Edwards* [1975] Q.B. 27 at 39, which had been affirmed by the House of Lords in *R. v Hunt* [1987] A.C. 352.
[66] *Z Bank v D1* [1994] 1 Lloyd's Rep. 656 at 668, Colman J.; see also *Burton v Winters* [1993] 1 W.L.R. 1077 at 1080.
[67] *Derby v Weldon (No.6)* [1990] 1 W.L.R. 1139.
[68] See, *e.g. Hubbard v Woodfield* (1913) 57 Sol.Jo. 729; *Acrow (Automation) Ltd v Rex Chainbelt Inc* [1971] 1 W.L.R. 1676, 1683; *Esso Petroleum v Kingswood Motors* [1974] Q.B. 142 at 156; *TSB Private Bank International SA v Chabra* [1992] 1 W.L.R. 231 at 240. See also para. 6–1.
[69] See the discussion at para.12–252.
[70] [1986] 1 W.L.R. 141.
[71] See paras 11–66 *et seq.*

thus expended should be paid by the solicitors to the plaintiff's solicitors within 14 days.

B. Search and seizure orders[72]

12–175   Important attributes of the search and seizure procedure[73] are the mandatory requirements of defendants that they should permit entry on to premises,[74] and provide disclosure of documents and other information. Laddie J. observed in *Taylor Made Golf Co Inc v Rata & Rata*[75] that " . . . defendants who are the subject of *Anton Piller* orders must be aware that they are not granted by the courts simply for fun. They are in strong terms and are meant to be complied with fully and properly". It is necessary if a claimant seeks to pray in aid the process of contempt for him to demonstrate that the defendant has been personally served with the order indorsed with a penal notice.[76] This is subject to the principles governing substituted service[77] and dispensing with service.[78]

12–176   Prohibitory orders also regularly play a part in search and seizure relief. Once notice is received of the order by the defendant, he should take steps to ensure that the material specified in the order is preserved. There is a limited opportunity for obtaining legal advice, and for making an urgent application to set the order aside. If such an application fails, respondents may find themselves liable to penalties for contempt of court. Moreover, if there is reason to suppose that, between service of the order and the time of eventual compliance, any steps have been taken inconsistent with the order (for example, by destruction of records)[79] the consequences would be of "the utmost gravity".[80] Even if the application is

---

[72] For many years known as *"Anton Piller* orders" after *Anton Piller KG v Manufacturing Processes Ltd* [1976] Ch. 551. See also the notes in *Civil Procedure* Vol. 1, 25.1.29; *EMI Records Ltd v Pandit* [1975] 1 W.L.R. 302; *Universal City Studios Inc v Mukhtar & Sons* [1976] 1 W.L.R. 568; *Lock International plc v Beswick* [1989] 3 All E.R. 373; *Systematica Ltd v London Computer Centre Ltd* [1983] F.S.R. 313. See also M. Dockray and H. Laddie, "Piller Problems" (1990) 106 L.Q.R. 601. See now the statutory provisions contained in the Civil Procedure Act 1997, s.7 governing the power of the courts to make orders for the preservation of evidence, and embracing *inter alia* the power to direct a person to provide any information or article described in the order, and to allow any person described in the order "to retain for safe keeping anything described in the order".

[73] The requirements were set out in *Columbia Picture Industries v Robinson* [1986] F.S.R. 367.

[74] Indeed, a form of order which provides that the claimant's representatives "are entitled to enter" is defective. The order must require the defendant to permit such entry. A reasonable period is permitted for the taking of legal advice, but there may be considerable practical hurdles in the way of obtaining useful guidance: see, *e.g. Bhimji v Chatwani* [1991] 1 W.L.R. 989 at 1000A–F, 1 All E.R. 705 at 710–11.

[75] [1996] F.S.R. 528 at 535. See also the discussion of Laddie J.'s guidance in relation to the principles governing self-incrimination in *Cobra Golf Inc v Rata* [1996] F.S.R. 819 in the context of search and seizure at paras 3–201 *et seq.* See also the provisions of the Civil Procedure Act 1997, s.7(7) which provides that the section ("Powers of courts to make orders for preserving evidence, etc") does not affect the right of a person to refuse to do anything on the ground that to do so might tend to expose him, his spouse or civil partner to proceedings for an offence or for the recovery of a penalty.

[76] CPR Sch.1, Ord.45.7.

[77] See now CPR 6.8.

[78] CPR Sch.1, Ord.45.7 discussed at para.15–22.

[79] See the discussion at paras 11–84.

[80] *WEA Records Ltd v Visions Channel 4 Ltd* [1983] 1 W.L.R. 721 at 725–6, Sir John Donaldson M.R.

upheld, such defendants may still be found in contempt. As Goulding J. commented in *Wardle Fabrics Ltd v G Myristis Ltd*[81]:

" ... subsequent discharge of the order as having been irregularly obtained would not in logic and principle affect the disobedient party's liability to penalties for contempt. It seems to me the system of administering justice would break down if the subjects were entitled to apply their own or their advisers' ideas to the possibilities of subsequently setting aside an order and to disobey on the strength of such private judgment and, if the judgment turns out not to have been right, be free from all penalty."

There, the plaintiffs had obtained an *Anton Piller* order. The defendant company through its managing director refused consent to entry, and applied for the order to be discharged on the ground of material non-disclosure. Goulding J. discharged the *Anton Piller* order because of inadequate disclosure but, on the plaintiffs' contempt application, found the company and its managing director in contempt. He considered imposing a fine but decided simply to impose an order for indemnity costs. In such circumstances it may be said that the liberty to apply for the order to be discharged is "of little, if any, value to the respondents."[82]

We have already discussed[83] the general principles applying to personal and vicarious liability for civil contempt, and the impact of the modern approach exemplified in *Director General of Fair Trading v Pioneer Concrete (UK) Ltd.*[84] This discussion is especially relevant to search and seizure orders because the defendant's subordinates are generally involved, as being on the premises at the time when the visit takes place, and in carrying the order into effect. As often happens, the defendant will be notified by telephone that service of his order has been effected. He should then seek to ensure that material is preserved. Otherwise he may well find that he himself is in contempt even though not personally served.

Search and seizure orders are Draconian and require to be implemented with meticulous care. "They impose on plaintiffs' solicitors the almost impossible task of describing fairly to non-lawyers the true effect and nature of the orders".[85] A solicitor who falls short of the obligation to observe the exact terms of the order and who, for example, fails to give an accurate explanation, by stating wrongly to the defendant that he is entitled to search for material going beyond the scope of the order, may be held in contempt of court. This is so even if his failure arises from incompetence rather than any deliberate intention to defy the court.[86]

---

[81] [1984] F.S.R. 263 at 271–2. The reasoning of Goulding J. was followed in *Columbia Pictures Inc v Robinson* [1987] 1 Ch. 38 at 72D, Scott J. See also *Bhimji v Chatwani* [1991] 1 W.L.R. 989 at 1001B–G and *Motorola Credit Corp v Uzan (No.2)* [2003] EWCA Civ 752, [2004] 1 W.L.R. 113.
[82] *per* Scott J. in *Columbia Pictures Inc v Robinson* [1987] 1 Ch. at 71E–F.
[83] paras 12–99 *et seq.*
[84] [1995] 1 A.C. 456.
[85] *per* Scott J. in *Bhimji v Chatwani* [1991] 1 W.L.R. 898 at 1001H.
[86] *VDU Installations Ltd v Integrated Computer Systems & Cybernetics Ltd* [1989] F.S.R. 378.

12-180 The standard form of order[87] contains the following passages:

"*THIS ORDER*
... 4. If there is more than one Respondent—

(a) unless otherwise stated, references in this order to 'the Respondent' mean both or all of them; and
(b) this order is effective against any Respondent on whom it is served or who is given notice of it.

5. This order must be complied with by—

(a) the Respondent;
(b) any director, officer, partner or responsible employee of the Respondent; and
(c) if the Respondent is an individual, any other person having responsible control of the premises to be searched.

THE SEARCH

6. The Respondent must permit the following persons—

(a) [...] ('the Supervising Solicitor');
(b) [...], a solicitor in the firm of [...], the Applicant's solicitors; and
(c) up to [...] other persons being [*their identity or capacity*] accompanying them,
(together 'the search party'), to enter the premises mentioned in Schedule A to this order and any other premises of the Respondent disclosed under paragraph 18 below and any vehicles under the Respondent's control on or around the premises ('the premises') so that they can search for, inspect, photograph or photocopy, and deliver into the safekeeping of the Applicant's solicitors all the documents and articles which are listed in Schedule B to this order ('the listed items').

7. Having permitted the search party to enter the premises, the Respondent must allow the search party to remain on the premises until the search is complete. In the event that it becomes necessary for any of those persons to leave the premises before the search is complete, the Respondent must allow them to re-enter the premises immediately upon their seeking re-entry on the same or the following day in order to complete the search."

Provision is made where the premises are likely to be occupied by an unaccompanied woman, and the supervising solicitor is a man, for at least one of the search party to be a woman. Also, none of the persons accompanying the supervising solicitor should be people who could gain personally or commercially from anything they might read or see on the premises, unless their presence is essential.

C. Persons not directly bound

12-181 It will be observed that the order is directed to the respondent and does not directly embrace "any other person having responsible control of the premises to be searched." Such a person, therefore, is not bound directly by the terms of the order to give the required permission. It follows that such an individual would

---

[87] See *Civil Procedure*, para.2A–161, Admiralty and Commercial Courts Guide, Appendix 5.

not *ipso facto* be in contempt by refusing to seek instructions, or to permit personally the applicant's representatives to enter.[88] If, however, he or she, knowing of the order, deliberately sought to frustrate its effect by, for example, destroying tapes or disks falling within its scope, the individual could be guilty of criminal contempt through subverting the order.[89] It ought not in principle to make any difference whether the individual concerned has or has not authority to grant permission for the entry and search.[90] If he steps beyond mere neutrality, however, and can be shown deliberately to have frustrated the order, the court would be likely to hold him in criminal contempt.

VI. BREACHES OF UNDERTAKINGS

A. Undertakings are equivalent to injunctions

1. *The general principle*

The typical example of a civil contempt is a breach by a litigant of an injunction granted against him in litigation to which he is a party. It was stated by Sir C. Pepys M.R. that an undertaking is equivalent to an injunction and, if violated, may be the subject of an application to the court.[91] The law has generally regarded the breach of an undertaking given to the court by or on behalf of a party to civil proceedings as tantamount to a breach of injunction[92] (although the remedies were not always identical.)[93]

12–182

---

[88] Cf. *Eccles & Co v Louisville & Nashville Railroad Company* [1912] 1 K.B. 135, CA. The majority held that a servant was not in contempt for failing to comply with an order for production of certain documents, on the basis that he was in possession of them only in the character of a servant, his master not being a party to the litigation. This was despite the fact that he had not been expressly forbidden to produce them and, what is more, he had declined to ask permission. Kennedy L.J. dissenting thought that he should at least have sought permission.
[89] See, *e.g. Att-Gen v Newspaper Publishing plc* [1988] Ch. 333; *Att-Gen v Times Newspapers Ltd* [1992] 1 A.C. 191.
[90] See, *e.g. Bhimji v Chatwani* [1991] 1 W.L.R. 989 at 997B–C.
[91] *London & Birmingham Railway v Grand Junction Canal Co* (1835) 1 Ry. Ca. 224. For modern examples of breach of the (implied) undertaking not to disclose documents obtained on discovery, see *Harman v Secretary of State for the Home Department* [1983] 1 A.C. 280, HL; *Miller v Scorey* [1996] 1 W.L.R. 1122; *Watkins v AJ Wright (Electrical) Ltd and others* [1996] 3 All E.R. 31. For Scotland see *Graham v Robert Younger Ltd* 1955 J.C. 28 at 32, Lord Justice-Clerk Thomson; 1955 S.L.T. 250, cited at para.16–238.
[92] See, *e.g. Neath Canal Co v Ynisarwed Resolven Colliery Co* (1875) 10 Ch. App.450; *Lawford v Spicer* (1856) 2 Jur. (N.S.) 564; *Att-Gen v Boyle* (1864) 10 Jur. (N.S.) 309; *D v A & Co* [1900] 1 Ch. 484; *Milburn v Newton Colliery Ltd* (1908) 52 S.J. 317; see also Diplock J. in *Re National Federated Electrical Association's Agreement* [1961] L.R. 2 R.P. 447 at 452; *Thorne RDC v Bunting (No.2)* [1972] 3 All E.R. 657; and *Biba Ltd v Stratford Investments Ltd* [1973] 1 Ch. 281; *Northern Counties Securities Ltd v Jackson & Steeple Ltd* [1974] 1 W.L.R. 1133, 1143, Ch. D.; *Re Rossminster and Tucker, The Times*, May 23, 1980, CA; *Re British Concrete Pipe Association's Agreement (Note)* [1982] I.C.R. 182, R.P.C; *Hussain v Hussain* [1986] Fam. 134 at 139–40, Sir John Donaldson M.R.
[93] See para.15–5 as to the old distinction between attachment and committal, which is no longer of practical importance.

12–183 In the words of Warrington J.[94]:

> "For the purpose of enforcing an undertaking that undertaking is equivalent to an order—that is to say, an undertaking, if broken, would involve the same consequences on the persons breaking that undertaking as would their disobedience to an order for an injunction."

12–184 More recently, this principle has been emphasised by Butler-Sloss L.J. in the context of matrimonial proceedings[95]:

> "It is important for parties in matrimonial disputes to appreciate that an undertaking has all the force of an injunction. It is equally as important as an injunction, and it has the same penalties for failure to abide by it as an injunction. It is all too easy for people to promise and all too easy for them to break that promise. Then they, quite rightly, have to face the wrath of the court for having made promises which were not worth the paper which they have signed."

12–185 The value of the court's ability to accept enforceable undertakings in civil litigation needs hardly to be stated, and their flexibility was thought to be especially useful in family proceedings (subject to the restriction contained in s.46(2) of the Family Law Act 1996 which did not permit the power of arrest to be attached to an undertaking).[96] As Munby J. has pointed out in *Harris v Harris*,[97] they have a particular utility in encouraging future compliance with court orders by contemnors who have already been committed and wish to be released on assurances as to their conduct. This is because the court is not confined to accepting undertakings in terms which it would have the power to impose without consent by way of an injunction (for example, as to undergoing medical or psychiatric treatment). Although the decision was reversed by the Court of Appeal,[98] those observations remain valid in general terms.

12–186 It appears, however, that in the context of non-molestation undertakings were frequently broken and rarely enforced. Accordingly, in the Domestic Violence, Crime and Victims Act 2004, s.46 of the Family Law Act was further amended so as to restrict the use of undertakings.[99] It now provides that the court shall not accept an undertaking instead of making an occupation order in any case where, apart from this section, a power of arrest would be attached. Also an undertaking is not to be accepted instead of making a non-molestation order in any case where it appears to the court that the respondent has used or threatened violence and, for the protection of the applicant or a relevant child, it is necessary to make a non-molestation order so that any breach may be punishable as a criminal offence

---

[94] *Milburn v Newton Colliery Ltd* (1908) 52 Sol. Jo. 317.
[95] *Roberts v Roberts* [1990] 2 F.L.R. 111 at 113D–E.
[96] See paras 14–77 *et seq.*
[97] [2001] Fam. 502 at [10].
[98] [2001] EWCA Civ 1644, [2002] Fam. 253. Although the court's common law powers could be used flexibly and imaginatively, they were not unlimited. On an application by a contemnor to purge his contempt, it was not appropriate to impose a fresh sentence; the original sentence could only be varied by ordering immediate release or deferred release at a specified future date. Once the sentence of immediate imprisonment had been partly served there was no power to suspend the remainder.
[99] Sch.10, para.37.

under s.42A. It has been pointed out[1] that it is now impossible for the court to accept an undertaking offered by a respondent on an application for a non-molestation order if he couples the offer with a denial. The court would have to carry out an enquiry which would involve the hearing of evidence and be tantamount to hearing a disputed application. The policy appears to be that the acceptance of undertakings in the past has left matters unresolved when findings of fact would have been preferable.

2. Undertakings to the court to pay money

One distinction, however, between orders and undertakings remains of significance. An undertaking to the court to pay money is not, outside the context of the law of contempt, like an *order* to pay money, since the obligation to the court imposed by an undertaking confers no right upon any other person, for example, to recover by means of levying execution or attaching a debt, unless there is a bargain between the parties alongside the undertaking to the court, such as, for example, might be incorporated in the terms of a consent order. In such a case, there are available penal sanctions against the non-paying "culprit", aimed at enforcing a promise made to the court, but they are not remedies to compensate the other party.[2]

3. Release from or variation of the terms of an undertaking

An infringement of an undertaking may be made the subject of an application to punish. Wherever possible it would be a wise precaution to incorporate any undertaking in an order and serve it upon those who have undertaken the obligation.[3] There is always a discretion in the court, upon good cause being shown, to release a person from an undertaking[4] or to modify the terms of any obligation imposed by the undertaking.[5]

It may sometimes happen that a party gives a more wide-ranging undertaking than he intended. In such a situation, the court in its discretion may decline to enforce that part of the undertaking which had been given by mistake. In *Mullins v Howell*,[6] Sir George Jessel M.R. said that this power was available even "though that mistake was on one side only, the court having a sort of general control over orders made on interlocutory applications." In another case[7] Kekewich J. gave leave to a defendant to file a defence contrary to the terms of an undertaking which had been given by his solicitors.

---

[1] Robert Hill, "Abolition of the Power of Arrest" [2005] Fam Law 474.
[2] *Re Hudson, Hudson v Hudson* [1966] 1 Ch. 209 at 213–14, Buckley J.
[3] *Hussain v Hussain* [1986] Fam. 134 at 142, Neill L.J.
[4] It seems that this discretion will not be lightly exercised, and an application for release should be supported by evidence: see, *e.g. Cutler v Wandsworth Stadium Ltd* [1945] 1 All E.R. 103. The court tended to be particularly strict in the case of a solicitor's undertaking: see *Re Kerly, Son and Verden* [1901] 1 Ch. 467, CA.
[5] *per* Buckley J. in *Re Hudson, Hudson v Hudson* [1966] 1 Ch. 209 at 214C–D.
[6] (1879) 11 Ch.D. 763 at 766–7.
[7] *Scott v Moxon* (1900) 81 L.T. 774.

4. Breaches of undertakings: similar safeguards

12–190 Just as with a breach of an order, where the court will not commit an alleged contemnor unless the breach is strictly proved,[8] so with an undertaking.[9] If there is doubt it may be appropriate, instead of invoking the process of contempt, to apply for an order requiring the alleged contemnor to state whether he has complied with his undertaking,[10] although this does not seem to be an option that is often invoked.

12–191 Where a breach of undertaking is relied upon it is not necessary to serve upon the alleged contemnor any order which may have been made incorporating that undertaking,[11] although it is nowadays recognised as desirable that this should be done.[12] In any event, it is important that those who volunteer to give undertakings—whether parties or not—[13] should have explained to them, either by their own lawyers or by the court, what duty is thereby assumed and in particular that punishment for contempt may be imposed in the event of breach. In practice the judge will stress the significance of what is being done before accepting the undertaking or ensure that if the person is represented his counsel or solicitor has done so.

12–192 Care needs to be taken in drawing up orders in which orders are to be incorporated, in order to ensure that they are drafted clearly and precisely, and to avoid wrangles as to whether a breach has in fact occurred. The significance of careful drafting was emphasised by Jenkins J. in *Redwing Ltd v Redwing Forest Products*.[14]

12–193 The added precaution should be taken, where the undertaking is incorporated in an order of the court, of inserting in that order itself a form of penal endorsement.[15]

5. Undertakings given on behalf of persons without their knowledge

12–194 Where an undertaking has been given in court purportedly on a person's behalf, but actually without his authority or knowledge (even of his being a party to the

---

[8] See, *e.g.* Lord Denning M.R. in *Churchman v Joint Shop Stewards' Committee of the Workers of the Port of London* [1972] 1 W.L.R. 1094 at 1098 and *Re Bramblevale* [1970] Ch. 128 at 137.
[9] *Redwing Ltd v Redwing Forest Products Ltd* (1947) 177 L.T. 387.
[10] *Kangol Industries Ltd v Bray (Alfred) & Sons Ltd* [1953] 1 All E.R. 444. See the discussion of self-incrimination in civil contempt at paras 3–188 *et seq.*
[11] *D v A & Co* [1900] 1 Ch. 484; see also *Launder v Richards* (1908) 98 L.T. 554; *Callow v Young* (1886) 55 L.T. 543, Chitty J.; and *Camden London Borough Council v Alpenoak Ltd* (1985) 135 New L.J. 1209 (Lexis). Contrast this position with the rule relating to injunctions, where it will generally be necessary to prove that the relevant order has been served bearing a penal notice: see para.12–35 and para.15–25; see now CPR Sch.1, Ord.45.7. See also Lord Denning M.R. in *Churchman v Joint Shop Stewards' Committee of the Workers of the Port of London* [1972] 1 W.L.R. at 1098.
[12] *Hussain v Hussain* [1986] Fam. 134 at 142, Neill L.J.
[13] See para.12–240 for a discussion of the effect of undertakings given to the court by persons who are not parties to the proceedings.
[14] [1947] 64 R.P.C. 67 at 71, 177 L.T. 387 at 390, cited at para.12–54. See also *Re M (Minors) (Access: Contempt: Committal)* [1991] 1 F.L.R. 355 at 364G–H, Beldam L.J.
[15] *Hussain v Hussain* [1986] Fam. 134 at 142, Neill L.J. For the forms of penal endorsement, see para.15–25.

litigation in question), and without being communicated to him, it should not be enforced by process of contempt.[16] In *Turner v Naval, Military and Civil Service Co-operative Society of South Africa*,[17] the undertaking was given by the respondent's solicitor in proceedings to which the respondent did not even know that he was a party, let alone that the unauthorised undertaking had been given on his behalf. It is submitted that, if such a person were to do an act in those circumstances inconsistent with the terms of the undertaking, he would not even be guilty of a technical contempt. He would not have given a genuine personal undertaking.

In *Re M: M v Home Office*,[18] Simon Brown J. rejected a submission to the effect that an undertaking would not be binding on a party unless given with *specific* authority, and irrespective of whether or not the party was aware that the undertaking had been given. As a matter of principle, the question must turn upon whether the person who purports to give the undertaking has authority to do so. If the undertaking has been given, with express or implied authority, on behalf of an individual or corporate entity, it should be treated as binding. On the other hand, if no such authority underlay the undertaking purportedly given, it should be of no effect. If a person knows that he is a party to litigation and has given a general authority to his solicitor or counsel in respect of the conduct of those proceedings, there would in the ordinary way be implied authority to give undertakings to the court.

12-195

Even where such an undertaking is communicated to the person on whose behalf it was purportedly given, it is difficult to see why he should be bound by it unless there was express or at least implied authority for it to be made on his behalf at the time when it was given.[19] It has been held that a litigant can be treated as bound by an undertaking given on his behalf, and that enforcement by process of contempt will therefore lie against him should he be in breach, without being served formally with an order containing the undertaking.[20] This does not, however, in any way detract from the principle that authority is required (whether express or implied) for the undertaking to bind the litigant.

12-196

The principle must be the same whether the undertaking in question is purportedly given on behalf of a company or of an individual. Either may have difficulty, in the light of the particular facts, in suggesting that the undertaking was truly offered without authority; but if this can be demonstrated, the mere fact of notification could hardly found liability. In *Bosch v Simms Manufacturing Co Ltd*[21] it was held by Swinfen Eady J. that a company could not be fixed with liability for any breach of undertaking, given on behalf of a different company,

12-197

---

[16] *Turner v Naval, Military and Civil Service Co-operative Society of South Africa*, The Times, January 21, 1907; *Camden London Borough Council v Alpenoak Ltd* (1985) 135 New L.J. 1209, Garland J. (Lexis).
[17] Last note.
[18] [1992] 4 All E.R. 97 at 118.
[19] See, *e.g.* Lord Donaldson M.R. in *Re M: M v Home Office* [1992] Q.B. 270 at 298B–C.
[20] *Camden London Borough Council v Alpenoak Ltd* (1985) 135 New Law Jo. 1209, Garland J. (Lexis). See also *Launder v Richards* (1908) 98 L.T. 554.
[21] (1909) 25 T.L.R. 419.

12–197   merely be reason of having taken over its assets. (It might have been different, however, if the reconstruction of the old company had been carried out "colourably" for the sake of evading the obligation.)

12–198   It is true that where a stranger to proceedings has notice of the terms of an injunction or undertaking, but nonetheless intentionally aids and abets a breach, it will sometimes be appropriate to apply to the court to invoke the contempt jurisdiction against that stranger.[22] Such a person is defying the court, or seeking to subvert one of its orders, and may be liable in contempt. By contrast, however, as a matter of principle, the mere fact of a person's being notified that an undertaking has purportedly been given on his behalf cannot bind him to obey it, if it was given without his authority, so as to give rise to liability for civil contempt.

12–199   It has been given as a reason for not committing two company directors, for breach of an undertaking given by their company, that the undertaking was not theirs, although they had known of and assented to its terms.[23] Nevertheless, there is specific provision[24] for enforcing a judgment or order made against a corporation, which has been disobeyed, by means of a writ of sequestration (only with leave of the court) against the property of any director or other officer. It is also provided[25] that (subject to the Debtors Acts 1869 and 1878) committal will lie against directors or other officers.

12–200   For this purpose, in accordance with general principle, an undertaking is equivalent to a "judgment or order."[26] Warrington J. in considering the former Ord.42, r.31 rejected an argument that sequestration would not lie for breach of an undertaking and said[27]:

> "I do not think that this rule was intended to alter the practice of the court as it existed before these rules were promulgated. The practice of the Court of Chancery was not to treat an undertaking as distinct from an injunction with regard to a breach and for the purpose of enforcing an undertaking that undertaking is equivalent to an order—that is to say an undertaking, if broken, would involve the same consequence on the persons breaking that undertaking as would their disobedience to an order for an injunction."

B. The implied undertaking given upon disclosure of documents

1. Introduction

12–201   One context in which an implied undertaking was recognised at common law was that of discovery (since the advent of the CPR the term used is "disclosure"). It

---

[22] *Elliott v Klinger* [1967] 1 W.L.R. 1165. See also Lindley L.J. in *Seaward v Paterson* [1897] Ch. 545 at 555–6 and (in the context of what are now freezing orders) *Z Ltd v A-Z and AA-LL* [1982] Q.B. 558, CA.
[23] *Att-Gen v Wheatley & Co Ltd* (1903) 48 S.J. 116.
[24] See now CPR Sch.1, Ord.45.5.
[25] *ibid.* For the Debtors Acts see Appendix 4.
[26] *Milburn v Newton Colliery Ltd* (1908) 52 S.J. 317; *Biba Ltd v Stratford Investments Ltd* [1973] Ch. 281, Brightman J.
[27] (1908) 52 S.J. 317.

was for long regarded as a contempt for a party or his legal adviser, in possession of documents disclosed in civil litigation or arbitration proceedings[28] on discovery, to publish such documents or to disclose their contents to any other person. Indeed, it was held in *Harman v Secretary of State for the Home Department*[29] that even if the documents had been read in open court, this obligation persisted, although the law has now changed in this respect. The documents should not be used for any purpose other than in connection with the litigation in which they were disclosed.[30]

Cassidy v Hawcroft[31] illustrates that no such undertaking is to be implied in circumstances where the content of a document is referred to, in whole or in part, on a voluntary basis; for example, where mention was made of a document in the course of an affidavit and the other party sought disclosure for that reason, there would be no question of an implied undertaking. Nor would it be an abuse of process to rely on the document for the purpose of raising a claim in defamation.

12–202

It was held by the Court of Appeal in *Mahon v Rahn* that no such principle applies in relation to documents disclosed to the defence, and used in open court, in the course of criminal proceedings.[32] The reasoning was that the rules of disclosure in criminal proceedings were formulated for different purposes, and the reasons for implying the undertaking in the civil context were not relevant. The Court of Appeal decision was overruled in *Taylor v Serious Fraud Office*.[33]

12–203

Sometimes, permission will be given for particular reasons to treat the undertaking as discharged, notwithstanding the fact that the documents in

12–204

---

[28] *Hassneh Insurance Co Of Israel v Steuart J Mew* [1993] 2 Ll. Rep 243; *Insurance Co v Lloyd's Syndicate* [1995] 1 Ll. Rep. 272.
[29] [1983] 1 A.C. 280. See also *Alterskye v Scott* [1948] 1 All E.R. 469 and *Riddick v Thames Board Mills* [1977] Q.B. 881 at 896, Lord Denning M.R., 901–2, Stephenson L.J., 910–11, Waller L.J.; *Prudential Assurance Co Ltd v Fountain Page Ltd* [1991] 1 W.L.R. 756, [1991] 3 All E.R. 878; See also I. Eagles, "Disclosure of Material Obtained on Discovery" (1984) 47 M.L.R. 284; N. Lowe, "Discovering Contempt" (1982) 1 Civil Justice Quart. 10; Note, (1982) 98 L.Q.R. 337–9 (J.M. Thomson). But see now the provisions CPR 31.22 described at paras 12–219 *et seq.*
[30] *Distillers Co (Biochemicals) Ltd v Times Newspapers Ltd* [1975] Q.B. 613 at 621, Talbot J.; *Riddick v Thames Board Mills Ltd* [1977] Q.B. 881 at 896, Lord Denning M.R., 901–2, Stephenson L.J., 910–11, Waller L.J.; *Halcon International Inc v Shell Transport and Trading Co* [1979] R.P.C. 97 at 121, Megaw L.J.; *Harman v Secretary of State for the Home Department* [1983] 1 A.C. 280 at 301, Lord Diplock; *Sybron Corporation v Barclays Bank plc* [1985] Ch. 299 at 320–1, Scott J.; *Crest Homes plc v Marks* [1987] A.C. 829 at 853–4, Lord Oliver; *Tate Access Floors Inc v Boswell* [1991] Ch. 512 at 526, Sir Nicolas Browne-Wilkinson V.-C.; *Miller v Scorey* [1996] 1 W.L.R. 1122, Rimer J.; *Watkins v AJ Wright (Electrical) Ltd* [1996] 3 All E.R. 31, Blackburne J.
[31] [2001] C.P. Rep. 49, [2000] C.P.L.R. 628, CA.
[32] *Mahon v Rahn* [1998] Q.B. 424. Having referred to *Cunningham v Essex County Council* [1997] T.L.R. 182, where Brooke J. at first instance in *Mahon v Rahn* had been followed, Staughton L.J. at 457G–H observed that "despite this impressive concurrence of opinion among judges at first instance, I do not consider that the defendant in a criminal trial is under any implied undertaking as to the use of the material disclosed to him as part of the prosecution case, whether or not it is read in or referred to in open court." But see the provisions of the Criminal Procedure and Investigations Act 1996, ss.17 and 18.
[33] [1999] 2 A.C. 177 (see para.12–236 below).

question have not been read out in open court. For example, in one case, the reason was that they were needed for the purpose of parallel proceedings before the European Commission.[34]

2. *The policy behind the implied undertaking*

12–205 Despite the changes subsequently implemented, it is nonetheless useful to consider how the matter was dealt with in the House of Lords in *Harman v Secretary of State for the Home Department*,[35] in order to understand the policy considerations which underlie the implied undertaking protecting disclosed documents. It might be thought that the reasoning of their Lordships is not invalidated by the change in the rules and that, unless a document falls within the wording of what is now CPR 31.22, the obligations in respect of confidentiality are the same as before.[36] It is necessary to remember, however, that in *Marlwood Commercial v Kozeny*,[37] the rule there laid down was said by Rix L.J. to supersede the common law implied undertaking. Moreover in *SmithKline Beecham plc v Generics (UK) Ltd*[38] CPR Pt 31 was described as a "complete code".

12–206 Miss Harman was a solicitor.[39] She was also employed by the National Council for Civil Liberties. She had been acting in her capacity as a solicitor on behalf of a man named Williams, who was serving a lengthy prison sentence and had been detained in a special control unit within a prison. This had been set up on Home Office instructions. Williams sought a declaration that his detention in the unit was illegal and he also claimed damages in respect of his period of confinement there. It was in this connection that Miss Harman acted as his solicitor. Discovery was sought and obtained from the Home office of some 2,800 documents. They included six which contained minutes of high level policy meetings in the Home Office.

12–207 At the trial Williams' counsel read out in open court 800 documents which had been bundled up for trial. Counsel for the Home Office objected to the admissibility of the six documents on the ground of irrelevance. The trial judge reserved his judgment including the question of admissibility. Eventually he upheld the objection and ruled the documents inadmissible. Between the time of the judge reserving his judgment and that of delivering it Miss Harman showed the six documents to a journalist. He wanted to look at them for the purpose of writing an article in a national newspaper on the subject of the special control unit. He made notes and took extracts from the documents. The material he obtained appeared in the newspaper in an article which was critical of the Home Office.

---

[34] *Apple Corp Ltd v Apple Computer Inc* [1992] 1 C.M.L.R. 969.
[35] [1983] 1 A.C. 280.
[36] See the discussion in *Marlwood Commercial Inc v Kozeny* [2004] EWCA (Civ) 798, [2005] 1 W.L.R. 104, [2004] 3 All E.R. 648, CA.
[37] Last note at [10].
[38] [2003] EWCA Civ 1109, [2004] 1 W.L.R. 1479 at [28]–[29], Aldous L.J.
[39] Later to become Solicitor-General.

It was conceded on behalf of Miss Harman that the documents disclosed to her were confidential and that she had had initially no right to reveal their contents to anyone. It was said, however, that once the documents had been read in open court their contents were "in the public domain" and that she was thereafter free to make what use she chose of them. This argument the House of Lords rejected by a majority of three to two, holding that her disclosure was a contempt. The case was decided on very particular facts. Some of the practical considerations to be borne in mind were:

(1) The proceedings had been tape-recorded, and the journalist could therefore (at considerable expense) have purchased a transcript of the recording and obtained the contents of the documents in that way. Miss Harman could have purchased a similar transcript and shown it to the journalist.

(2) It was then regarded as exceptional that counsel's opening speech had been recorded.

(3) It was also exceptional that the documents should have been read in open court virtually in their entirety. Lord Roskill in particular cited the practice whereby judges read documents out of court, or ahead of counsel, in order to speed the progress of proceedings. If this was done, the choice of documents read openly in court might be entirely haphazard or arbitrary.

(4) The documents in the instant case, although disclosable, were in fact inadmissible at trial.

The majority of their Lordships stressed that discovery was an intrusion into privacy.[40] The intrusion should be limited to what was necessary in the interests of justice for the purpose of the proceedings in question. In the words of Lord Keith[41]:

"Discovery constitutes a very serious invasion of the privacy and confidentiality of a litigant's affairs. It forms part of the English legal procedure because the public interest in securing that justice is done between parties is considered to outweigh the private and public interest in the maintenance of confidentiality. But the process should not be allowed to place upon the litigant any harsher or more oppressive burden than is strictly required for the purpose of securing that justice is done. Insofar as that must necessarily involve a certain degree of publicly being given to private documents, the result has to be accepted as part of the price of achieving justice. But the fact that a certain inevitable degree of publicity has been brought about does not, in my opinion, warrant the conclusion that the door should therefore be open to widespread dissemination of the material by the other party or his legal advisers, for any ulterior purpose whatsoever, whether altruistic or aimed at financial gain. The degree of publicity resulting from the document being read out in open court is not necessarily very great. There may be nobody present apart from the parties and their legal advisers."

---

[40] See also *Air Canada v Secretary of State for Trade (No.2)* [1983] 2 A.C. 394.
[41] [1983] 1 A.C. 280 at 308B–E.

12–210 The majority also stressed that the party who had obtained documents on discovery was, even after publication in open court, in a more informed position than the general public. He had longer to digest the contents of the documents and he has their exact wording before him without any great expenditure. Such a person is in any event under an implied undertaking given to the court not to disclose the contents of such documents. Whatever anyone else may be free to do, the majority of their Lordships took the view that the litigant was forever bound by that undertaking. He might not disclose the contents of the documents for any collateral or ulterior purpose.

12–211 The majority gave paramount importance to free and frank disclosure. The greater the publicity, the less likely litigants in general would be to give full disclosure. Lords Diplock and Roskill both felt it was permissible to show legal or lay court reporters copies of documents in order that they could produce an accurate account of what is said in court. Lord Keith, however, was not ready to accept that even this should take place without the consent of the owner of the document or documents concerned. This approach is to be contrasted with the more open policy adopted later, for example with reference to the provision of skeleton arguments for the assistance of court reporters.[42]

12–212 Lord Scarman in his minority opinion (in which Lord Simon concurred) took the view that once the documents had been read out in court the duty of confidentiality was terminated. The party who had had copies of them supplied on discovery should thereafter in his view be able to publish them to the world at large. He saw the problem as one of balancing two interests[43]:

> "A balance has to be struck between two interests of the law-on the one hand, the protection of a litigant's private right to keep his documents to himself notwithstanding his duty to disclose them to the other side in litigation, and, on the other, the protection of the right, which the law recognises, subject to certain exceptions, as the right of everyone, to speak freely, and to impart information and ideas, upon matters of public knowledge."

12–213 He referred to a clear general rule in law that when information or documents, previously confidential, became public knowledge, the duty to treat them as confidential ceases. He went on to examine and reject objections raised in favour of an exception to this general rule in the case of discovery:

> (1) The advantage of prior knowledge and ease of access: this Lord Scarman acknowledged, but he felt it was only a marginal advantage over

---

[42] *Lombard North Central v Pratt* (1989) 139 N.L.J. 1709, *The Times*, November 27, 1989. See also *Practice Direction (Court of Appeal: Presentation of Argument)* [1989] 1 W.L.R. 281 and *R. v Howell* [2003] EWCA Crim 485, *The Times,* March 10, 2003 where it was affirmed by the Criminal Division of the Court of Appeal that the principle of open justice requires that skeleton arguments should be disclosed if and when a request to do so is received. In *GIO Personal Investment Services Ltd v Liverpool and London Steamship Protection and Indemnity Association Ltd* [1999] 1 W.L.R. 984 it was held that a non-party was entitled to inspect witness statements which stand as evidence in chief (although not documents referred to therein). Also where a member of the public applies for a copy of a written opening or a skeleton argument which has been accepted in lieu of an oral opening, there is a *prima facie* entitlement.
[43] [1983] 1 A.C. at 353.

someone who could obtain a transcript of court proceedings at his own expense.

(2) The importance of full disclosure: this too he acknowledged. However, he pointed out that anyone involved in litigation and required to disclose documents knew of the risk that the documents disclosed would be read out in court and thereby become public knowledge. Even if the other side were bound by undertaking not to disclose, the party who owned the documents knew that he would be at risk that journalists would publish the contents if revealed in court.

(3) Public policy requires expeditious despatch by judges of their judicial business: Lord Scarman pointed out that a judge was also concerned to ensure that justice was not only done but seen to be done. There is a public interest that evidence and argument should be publicly known, so that society may judge for itself the quality of justice administered in its name, and whether the law requires modification.[44]

As he did in *Att-Gen v BBC*,[45] Lord Scarman also paid regard to the European Convention on Human Rights and the decision of the European Court in *Sunday Times v United Kingdom*,[46] where it was emphasised that freedom of expression should only be restricted in circumstances where it was "necessary". He concluded that[47]:

12–214

"It can hardly be argued that there is a pressing social need to exclude the litigant and his solicitor from the right available to everyone else to treat as public knowledge documents which have been produced and made part and parcel of public legal proceedings."

He further pointed out that the difficulties revealed on the facts of that case could be practically overcome. Any documents as to which there was a question of admissibility could be put into a separate bundle and the trial judge invited to rule before their being put in evidence. Also the trial judge could order that they be read in closed court. He expressed the view that documents once adduced in evidence, whether read aloud or not, were part of the public record and accordingly could be made available to the public.

12–215

If a journalist is entitled to write an article, it is best that he should do so accurately and not have to rely upon a garbled or incomplete note. If information should be available to the public, then it should be freely available. Once material has been ruled to be relevant and admissible, it is sensible that the public interest in confidentiality should yield to that in free speech.

12–216

---

[44] Cf. the five reasons considered by Pearson J. in *Webb v Times Publishing Co Ltd* [1960] 2 Q.B. 535 at 559–62, which justify the privilege for newspaper reports of judicial proceedings. See also *Roberts v Bass* [2002] H.C.A. 57, [2002] 194 A.L.R. 161; *Woodgate v Ridout* (1865) 4 F. & F. 202, 217, 176 E.R. 531, and *Andrews v Chapman* (1853) 3 C. & K. 286, 175 E.R. 558.
[45] [1981] A.C. 303 at 354, 362.
[46] [1979] 2 E.H.R.R. 245.
[47] [1983] 1 A.C. 280 at 317.

12–217 This argument is consistent with the view of Lords Diplock and Roskill that it is legitimate to disclose documents to a court reporter, although they took the view that such disclosure was not appropriate to other kinds of journalist. It was pointed out by counsel for the Attorney-General that in practice it would be sometimes impossible to know which sort of reporter was making the approach in court. In any event, if there is a public interest in open justice it is difficult to see why there should be a distinction between one kind of reporter and another. If it is important that a court reporter should give an accurate account of proceedings, when he is by and large addressing himself to trained lawyers, it may be said to be equally important, if not more so, that feature writers or news reporters who are writing primarily for a lay readership should give an accurate account.

3. *The introduction of a specific rule*

12–218 As has already been observed, the House of Lords' decision in *Harman*[48] was by a majority, there being a powerful dissenting speech from Lord Scarman in which Lord Simon of Glaisdale concurred. The unsuccessful appellant referred the matter to the European Commission,[49] and shortly afterwards the government accepted that a change in the law was appropriate. On October 1, 1987, RSC Ord.24, r.14A came in to effect[50]:

> "Any undertaking, whether express or implied, not to use a document for any purposes other than those of the proceedings in which it is disclosed shall cease to apply to such document after it has been read to or by the court, or referred to, in open Court, unless the court for special reasons has otherwise ordered[51] on the application of a party or of the person to whom the document belongs".

12–219 These principles are now embodied in CPR 31.22:

> "(1) A party to whom a document has been disclosed may use the document only for the purpose of the proceedings in which it is disclosed, except where—
>
> > (a) the document has been read to or by the court, or referred to, at a hearing which has been held in public;
> > (b) the court gives permission; or
> > (c) the party who disclosed the document and the person to whom the document belongs agree.
>
> (2) The court may make an order restricting or prohibiting the use of a document which has been disclosed, even where the document has been read to or by the court, or referred to, at a hearing which has been held in public.
> (3) An application for such an order may be made—
>
> > (a) by a party; or
> > (b) by any person to whom the document belongs".

---

[48] Last note.
[49] *Harman v United Kingdom* (1985) 7 E.H.R.R. 146.
[50] SI 1987/1423.
[51] For discussion of the present rule, see para.12–237.

Although the impact of the change in 1987 was not retrospective, the change of policy was a factor which could be taken into account on an application by a person to be released from an earlier undertaking, in respect of documents read out before the material date.[52] The words "read to *or by* the court . . . " take account of the practice in modern litigation whereby much evidence and argument[53] is presented to the court in advance of the hearing. In such circumstances it is commonplace for evidence not to be read out in court, even though it might play a significant part in the ultimate adjudication. **12–220**

The fact that judges read documents in private is an argument for, rather than against, disclosure to the public. Speed is important, but this practice can lead to undesirable consequences. The increasing tendency to put argument in writing, and for judges to read papers in private, can detract from the advantages of open justice. The public may be thought to have a legitimate interest to be fully informed about such proceedings in order to be able properly to assess judicial decisions and, if need be, to press for legislation to change their effect. The matter now has to be considered against the background of the general rule that hearings take place in public.[54] **12–221**

There has thus been something of a departure in recognising that there should be public access to material not expressly referred to in open court. For example, the underlying policy of the statutory and common law privilege afforded by the law of libel to newspaper reports of court proceedings has been that the readers should be placed so far as possible in a similar state of knowledge to those *who were present in court themselves*.[55] If the readers had been in court they would not, of course, have been able to see any document which the judge perused without its being read out. Nevertheless, the quality of judicial decisions cannot be judged unless the public and legal commentators are in a position to relate them to the whole of the evidence and submissions upon which they are based. **12–222**

The provisions of Ord.24, r.14A were considered fully in this context by the Court of Appeal in *SmithKline Beecham Biologicals SA v Connaught Laboratories Inc*.[56] It was held that they applied to any document if it had been pre-read **12–223**

---

[52] *Bibby Bulk Carriers Ltd v Cansulex Ltd* [1989] Q.B. 155.
[53] See, *e.g. Practice Direction (Court of Appeal: Presentation of Argument)* [1989] 1 W.L.R. 281 at 282C. One of the advantages of skeleton arguments was there stated to be that "judges can do really effective pre-reading and thus save a considerable amount of time which would otherwise be spent reading aloud in court". This was superseded by *Practice Direction (Court of Appeal: Presentation of Argument)* [1995] 1 W.L.R. 1188, [1995] 3 All E.R. 847 and in due course by the consolidating *Practice Direction (Court of Appeal (Civil Division))* [1999] 1 W.L.R. 1027, [1999] 2 All E.R. 490, s.3; and see now the Practice Direction to CPR Pt 52. See also the judgment of Lord Clyde in *Cunningham v The Scotsman Publications Ltd* 1987 S.L.T. 698 at 706, cited at para.16–210 and of Park J. in *Re Guardian Newspapapers Ltd* [2004] EWHC 3092, (Ch) [2005] 3 All E.R. 155.
[54] CPR 39.2(1).
[55] See, *e.g. Furniss v Cambridge News Ltd* (1907) 23 T.L.R. 705, Sir Gorrell Barnes P.: "The privilege given to reports of proceedings in courts is based upon this, that, as everyone cannot be in court, it is for the public benefit that they should be informed of what takes place substantially as if they were present." See *Davies Ex p. Delbert-Evans* [1945] 1 K.B. 435 at 446, Oliver J. and Pearson J. in *Webb v Times Publishing Co Ltd* [1960] 2 Q.B. 535.
[56] [1999] 4 All E.R. 498.

12–223 by the judge and referred to by counsel in the skeleton argument incorporated into open court submissions, or if the document had been referred to by counsel or by the court. This approach preserved the rights of the public in the modern environment where evidence was not explored document by document in open court. It was explained that judges familiarise themselves with the materials out of court, and accordingly only economic reference, falling far short of verbatim citation, is therefore necessary in open court. It was also observed that in some cases, particularly those of public interest, a judge might permit a fuller canvassing of the materials than would be necessary if economy and efficiency were the only considerations. In all cases the judgment itself ought ultimately to provide a coherent summary of the issues, the evidence and the reasons for the decision. In the case of documents referred to in open court, but not read aloud or referred to in such a way as to be comprehensible to onlookers, it may be necessary (subject to suitable safeguards) for the court to allow public access to such documents in order to avoid too wide a gap between what has passed into the public domain in theory and what has actually passed into it in practice. On the facts of the case it was held that there were no special reasons to order that the implied obligation of confidentiality should remain binding. It was acknowledged that both parties had marked most of the documents disclosed as being confidential but it was not suggested that there was any information "of a truly secret nature" or that it would have been necessary, had there been a full hearing, for any part of it to be conducted *in camera*.

12–224 Further guidance as to the correct application of the provisions (by then contained in CPR 31.22(2)) was given by the Court of Appeal in *Lilly Icos Ltd v Pfizer Ltd*.[57] This may be summarised as follows:

(1) The court should start from the principle that very good reasons are required for departing from the normal rule of publicity. Reference was made to the citation of the following words by Lord Diplock in *Home Office v Harman*[58]: "Publicity is the very soul of justice. It is the keenest spur to exertion, and the surest of all guards against improbity. It keeps the judge himself, while trying, under trial."

(2) When considering an application in respect of a particular document, the court should take into account the role that the document has played or will play in the trial, and thus its relevance to the process of scrutiny referred to by Lord Diplock. The court should start from the assumption that all documents in the case are necessary and relevant for that purpose, and should not accede to general arguments that it would be possible, or substantially possible, to understand the trial and judge the judge without access to a particular document. However, in particular cases the centrality of the document to the trial is a factor to be placed in the balance.

(3) In dealing with issues of confidentiality between the parties, the court must have in mind any "chilling effect" of an order upon the interests of

---

[57] [2002] EWCA Civ 2, [2002] 1 W.L.R. 2253: see especially at [25].
[58] [1983] 1 A.C. 280 at 303.

third parties. (The example the court appeared to have in mind[59] was that an order made under CPR 31.22(2) might have the effect of rendering a third party in contempt if he comes into possession of a relevant document protected by the order and then seeks to make use of it while knowing of the court's order. It is not clear how a consideration of this kind is likely to impact upon the court's decision in practice.)

(4) Simple assertions of confidentiality and the damage that will be done by publication, even if supported by both parties, should not prevail. The court will require specific reasons why a party would be damaged by publication of a document. Those reasons will in appropriate cases be weighed in the light of the considerations referred to in sub-paragraph (ii) above.

(5) It is highly desirable, both in the general public interest and for simple convenience, to avoid the holding of trials in private, or partially in private. In the *Pfizer* case itself, the manner in which the documents were handled, together with the confidentiality agreement during the trial, enabled the whole of the trial to be held in public, even though the judge regarded it as justified to retain confidentiality in respect of a significant number of those documents after the trial was over. The court should bear in mind that, if too demanding a standard is imposed under CPR 31.22(2) in respect of documents that have been referred to inferentially or in short at the trial, it may be necessary, in order to protect genuine interests of the parties, for more trials or parts of trials to be held in private, or for instance for parts of witness statements or skeletons to be in closed form.

(6) Patent cases are subject to the same general rules as any other cases, but they do present some particular problems and are subject to some particular considerations. Reference was made to *SmithKline Beecham Biologicals SA v Connaught Laboratories Inc*[60] and to *Bonzel (T) v Intervention Ltd (No.2)*[61] and the court recognised the "peculiar public importance" of patent litigation. This not only meant that the public had to be properly informed but also that issues had to be explored properly. The parties should not feel constrained to hold back from relevant or potentially relevant issues because of (legitimate) fears of the effect of publicity. Such considerations can be borne in mind when deciding whether to withdraw confidentiality from documents that are regarded by a party as damaging to his interests if used outside the confines of the litigation in which they were disclosed.

The case was followed in *Re Guardian Newspapers Ltd*[62] where an application was made under CPR 5.4(5)(b), whereby one can obtain from the records of the court *inter alia* a copy of any document filed by a party. The newspaper applied

---

[59] Addressed at [5] of the judgment.
[60] [1999] 4 All E.R. 498.
[61] [1991] R.P.C. 231 at 234.
[62] [2004] EWHC 3092 (Ch), [2005] 3 All E.R. 155, Park J.

12–225 for copies of pleadings, and specified defence witness statements, when settlement was reached after the case had been partially heard in open court. The first objection raised was that the "court" referred to in the rule had to be the court seised of the underlying case, but this argument was rejected. The application could be made to the High Court even after the case was over. Secondly, it was argued that the principle of open justice had no application to the particular circumstances, since the purpose of the newspaper was not to scrutinise the judicial system or to publish a fair and accurate report of the hearing. This too was rejected since the general tenor of authority was in favour of disclosure of materials which had entered into the public domain. This would include witness statements which had been confirmed in general terms and stood as evidence in chief. There was no evidence to suggest that the defendant would suffer damage if the documents were obtained and it was observed that a serious newspaper should be able to see identified documents from an earlier court file if they bear on a current story or article which it is interested in publishing.[63]

12–226 The case of *Lilly Icos* was also applied by the Court of Appeal in *SmithKlein Beecham plc v Generics (UK) Ltd*[64] in the context of the power under CPR 31.22(2) to make an order restricting or prohibiting the use of a document which had been disclosed. "Disclosure" was defined in CPR Pt 31, which indicated that a party had "disclosed" a document by stating that it existed or had existed. It was held that no distinction was drawn between documents obtained from third parties and other documents, and no limitation was placed on how a disclosure took place. A reference by a party in a witness statement was thus a statement that the relevant document existed for the purpose of Pt 31. Accordingly, that would suffice to give the court the power to make an order restricting use under CPR 31.22(2). Also, when considering whether to lift a CPR 31.22(2) order, it was important to bear in mind the overriding principles of the CPR. The "interests of justice" involved a consideration of the interest of the parties seeking to use the documents and that of the party protected by the order. A relevant consideration would be whether the documents could have been obtained under CPR 31.17. On the facts of the case it was held that there was a real argument that the relevant documents were discoverable under CPR 31.17 and that the refusal by the judge to permit them to be used in other proceedings could reflect adversely on the administration of justice. An appeal was allowed so that the documents could be used in proceedings separate from those in which they had been disclosed, but on terms that they should be dealt with in private.

4. *Hearings outside the scope of CPR 31.22*

12–227 It will be observed that the rule uses the words "a hearing which has been held in public" and therefore would not, in itself, appear to relieve parties from their

---

[63] At [42].
[64] [2003] EWCA Civ 1109, [2003] 4 All E.R. 1302. In *Dendron GMBH v University of California* [2004] EWHC 589 (Pat), [2005] 1 W.L.R. 200, Laddie J. observed at [32] that in the *SmithKline Beecham* case the Court of Appeal had described CPR Pt 31 as "a complete code". He added that there can be little doubt that the principles restricting the collateral use of material released under compulsion has been lifted out of the case law and, with certain modifications, codified.

obligations in respect of documents read out during the course of proceedings which took place *in camera*. Here, the policy considerations underlying s.12 of the Administration of Justice Act 1960[65] would also come into play. The provisions of this enactment, to the effect that the publication of material from such private proceedings should *not* (outside the specified exceptions) be treated as contempt, might avail a journalist who published material from disclosed documents, after they had been read out to a judge in such private proceedings. The answer would appear to be that the judge would need to make a specific order restricting or prohibiting the use of any document under the court's inherent power (CPR 31.22 would not apply since *ex hypothesi* the hearing has not taken place "in public"). There are still in being special constraints upon solicitors as to the wider revelation of information disclosed at such hearings.[66]

5. *Does CPR 31.22 inhibit the launch of libel proceedings?*

In *Singh (Tejendra) v Christie*,[67] Drake J. applied a restrictive interpretation to the wording of r.14A (as it then was).[68] He held that a person remained subject to the implied undertaking not to use a document for purposes other than those of the proceedings in which it was disclosed, even where he has read or referred to it in open court, unless the court ordered otherwise. He was dismissing appeals by the plaintiff against orders striking out actions for defamation against a number of solicitors. The actions arose from a telephone conversation which took place between two solicitors involved in a county court action, and which was recorded in an attendance note. That attendance note had been disclosed on discovery in a different action to which the plaintiff was a party and had been read in open court. He brought four actions for defamation against the solicitors who had represented him as well as those for the opposing party in the county court action.

12–228

The judge said that he did not find it easy to understand r.14A. On the face of it, it would appear to permit someone to launch libel proceedings upon such a document once it had been read out, although this would amount to a much greater change in the law than appeared to have been intended. He expressed the view that if the litigant himself chose to read out the attendance note in open court, and was thereafter free to sue upon it, there was scope for abuse. Moreover, it might very well be that those to be sued would be neither owners of the attendance note nor parties to the action in which the document had been disclosed. Accordingly, they would not be in a position to apply to the court under r.14A itself in order to ask that the implied undertaking should continue to have effect "for special reasons."

12–229

---

[65] The terms of which are set out and discussed at paras 8–97 *et seq.*
[66] For discussion, see para.7–49 and paras 1–164 *et seq.*
[67] [1993] T.L.R. 561. The judge had in mind the principle exemplified in *Riddick v Thames Board Mills* [1977] Q.B. 881, that libel proceedings may not be commenced when the relevant allegation has only come to a claimant's attention through disclosure in litigation.
[68] For the wording of which see above at para.12–218.

12–230 He considered that the effect of the rule was correctly summarised in a note in *The Supreme Court Practice* then current,[69] to the effect that it represented a "change in the onus of showing why there should not be release from the implied undertaking where documents have been read or referred to in open court." He concluded that the rule was not intended to bring about a change in the substantive law which would be so fundamental and, at the same time, work a considerable injustice to persons in the situation of the defendants in the cases before him.

12–231 Drake J. recognised that his interpretation of the rule was not without difficulty, because the wording expressly referred to any undertaking " . . . not to use a document *for any purpose* . . . ". It did not say merely "any undertaking not to make public the contents of" such a document. Despite this problem, he was persuaded that the drafting could not have been intended to achieve such a fundamental change in the use which could be made of such documents.[70]

12–232 The decision went to the Court of Appeal which upheld the ruling of Drake J.[71] Nevertheless, in *Mahon v Rahn*[72] Staughton L.J. concluded that the decision was not binding and ought not to be followed. Drake J. had not been referred to the decision of Browne-Wilkinson V.-C. in *Derby and Co Ltd v Weldon*[73] where it had been held that Ord.24, r.14A enabled documents to be used in other proceedings if the condition laid down by the rule was fulfilled. This reasoning was preferred by the Court of Appeal.

12–233 In *Mahon v Rahn* the decision of Drake J. was not actually disapproved, but it is clear from the judgment of Otton L.J.[74] that he was doubtful as to whether libel actions should be treated in any special way. The Court of Appeal took the view that sufficient protection was afforded in libel proceedings to those in the position of Dr Rahn by the traditional defences of absolute and qualified privilege. Although any defamatory publication made in the process of disclosure, under compulsion of the law, would itself no doubt be protected by privilege, this would not apply to any earlier publication of the same document— and which only came to the respective claimant's attention by reason of the disclosure.

12–234 Despite this, the concerns expressed by Drake J. may be readily understood, given the underlying policy of the implied obligation of confidence. If the purpose was to encourage full and frank disclosure of documents, it has to be

---

[69] Vol. 1, para.24/14A/1 See now the note at *Civil Procedure*, Vol. 1, 32.22.1.
[70] In Hollander on *Documentary Evidence* (8th ed., 2003), p.323, it is stated that when r.14A applies "the holder of the document is then completely freed from all restrictions and can use the document for any purpose whatsoever." The corresponding passage from an earlier edition was cited with approval by Staughton L.J. in *Mahon v Rahn* [1998] Q.B. 424 at 455. To the same effect were the comments of the authors of Matthews and Malek, *Discovery* (1992), paras 2.22 and 2.23. Hollander says that the "position was put beyond doubt by the Court of Appeal in *Colbeck v Ferguson*" January 1, 2002. This New Year's Day judgment has however proved impossible to trace.
[71] CA Transcript 0669 of 1994, Butler-Sloss L.J. and Sir Michael Kerr.
[72] [1998] Q.B. 424 at 455C–H See also Otton L.J. at 433–4.
[73] *The Independent*, November 2, 1988.
[74] At 452B.

recognised that the threat of being sued in respect of a defamatory document would be a powerful disincentive to disclosure. This is especially so in cases where the document would be unlikely to see the light of day other than through the disclosure obligations.

It is generally accepted also that allegations made in the course of litigation, whether by way of submission or in the process of giving evidence, oral or written, are protected by privilege. Again the policy is that parties and their legal representatives should not be inhibited in the conduct of court proceedings. The possibility of being sued for libel over documents disclosed as part of the litigation process would appear to be inconsistent also with this reasoning.

12–235

In *Taylor v Serious Fraud Office*,[75] the House of Lords overruled the decision of the Court of Appeal in *Mahon v Rahn* in the criminal law context. It was held that both the principle of an implied undertaking in relation to material produced on disclosure in civil proceedings (that it would not be used for any other purpose) and that of immunity from suit attaching to actions taken in relation to a criminal trial were concerned with public policy in securing the proper administration of justice. No reference, however, was made to *Tejendra Singh*, since it was not relevant to the task, but there is no reason to suppose that the obsrvations of the Court of Appeal are any the less valid.

12–236

6. When will an order be made for "restricting or prohibiting the use of a document"?

The wording of CPR 31.22 does not refer to a judge needing "special reasons" before restricting or prohibiting the use of a document which has been referred to at a hearing "in public." This phrase had appeared in RSC Ord.24, r.14A when it was first promulgated in 1987. An example of a case where Ord.24, r.14A was disapplied is to be found in *Lubrizol Corporation v Esso Petroleum Ltd*.[76] This was a patent infringement action in which there had been, or were contemplated, parallel proceedings in a number of other jurisdictions. The plaintiffs had obtained leave *ex parte* to join the third defendant and to serve the writ upon it outside the jurisdiction. The plaintiff's evidence in support of that application had referred to documents disclosed by the first and second defendants. The third defendant was applying to set aside the *ex parte* order, and in support of this application served affidavit evidence exhibiting some of its own internal documents. It therefore applied for an order that its application be heard *in camera* or alternatively for an order disapplying r.14A, together with an injunction to restrain the plaintiffs from using its affidavit outside the United Kingdom and otherwise than for the purposes of the proceedings. This application was resisted by the plaintiffs on the basis that the documents in question had been volunteered and not disclosed by any compulsion of law.

12–237

The deputy judge held that an order disapplying r.14A was appropriate in any case where the court believed that there were "special reasons". He held there

12–238

---

[75] [1999] 2 A.C. 177.
[76] [1993] F.S.R. 53.

12–238 were such reasons. In the first place, this was an interlocutory application well before trial. Secondly, the parties themselves had clearly considered the documents to be potentially sensitive and had agreed to treat them as such, through the means of a "confidentiality club" which had been created by a consent order. The effect of this was to provide that documents disclosed should only be inspected by certain classes of persons and should not be disclosed to others except to the extent permitted under r.14A. Thirdly, it was not appropriate to call the third defendant a "volunteer", in any real sense, because the plaintiffs had served evidence relating to disclosure documents, and it was thus inevitable that the third defendant would have to rely upon its internal documents for the purpose of setting aside service.

12–239 The court now clearly has a discretion whether to restrict or prohibit the use of a document (which is no longer inhibited by the phrase "special reasons"). It is therefore reasonable to assume that the court will on any application under CPR 31.22(2) weigh the interest in maintaining confidentiality against any countervailing public interest in disclosure.[77] The guidance given by the Court of Appeal in *Lilly Icos Ltd v Pfizer Ltd*[78] is clearly important in this context.

C. Breach of undertakings given by strangers

12–240 It is unlikely that circumstances will often arise in which an undertaking is given to the court by someone in the course of proceedings to which he is a stranger.[79] In this respect there is some difference between injunctions and undertakings.

1. Lord Eldon's principle

12–241 So far as injunctions are concerned, the general principle as to strangers was expressed by Lord Eldon[80]:

> " . . . I have no conception, that it is competent to this Court to hold a man bound by an injunction, who is not a party in the cause for the purpose of the cause. The old practice was that he must be brought into Court, so as according to the ancient laws and usages of the country (to) be made a subject of the writ."

12–242 On the other hand, it seems clear that where a stranger to proceedings knowingly aids or abets the defendant in the breach of an injunction, the court has jurisdiction to commit such a stranger for contempt or, more leniently, to

---

[77] See the discussion in *A v A (Ancillary Relief); B v B (Ancillary Relief)* [2000] 1 F.L.R. 701 and *Marlwood Commercial Inc v Kozeny* [2004] EWCA Civ 798, [2005] 1 W.L.R. 104, [2004] 3 All E.R. 648.
[78] [2002] EWCA Civ 2, [2002] 1 W.L.R. 2253: see especially at [25]. See above at para.12–224.
[79] Although it can sometimes happen even in the criminal context: see, *e.g. R. v Mantoura* [1993] Crim. L.R. 279–80.
[80] *Iveson v Harris* (1802) 7 Ves. Jun. 251 at 256–7, 32 E.R. 102 at 104. See also *Dawson v Princeps* (1795) 2 Anstr. 521, 145 E.R. 954. It was this principle that was unsuccessfully prayed in aid before the Court of Appeal in *Att-Gen v Newspaper Publishing plc* [1988] Ch. 333, on the basis that the editors of the papers not bound by the confidence injunction *could* not be in contempt. See para.6–115.

grant an injunction against the stranger himself.[81] This is not because he is in breach of the terms of an injunction which does not bind him, but because of an interference with the course of justice.[82]

Similarly, it is clear that one who has knowledge of the terms of an injunction, and sets out to subvert its purpose, is also liable for contempt, even without any involvement on the part of the person or persons directly bound by the injunction.[83]

12–243

Lord Eldon's broad principle exists for the protection of those who may find themselves compelled by an injunction; it would therefore have no direct bearing upon strangers to proceedings who volunteer to be bound. It is generally presumed that those who volunteer undertakings know what they are doing. This no doubt explains the rule, where a defendant has voluntarily given an undertaking which has subsequently been embodied in an order of the court, that it is not necessary to serve on him a copy of the order containing the undertaking[84] (although in the light of the Court of Appeal's decision in *Hussain v Hussain*[85] it is clearly wise to do so).

12–244

Accordingly it is submitted that the court can, if necessary, accept undertakings in the course of proceedings from persons who are not parties; and that, for such undertakings to be enforceable by process of contempt, it is not necessary (despite the words of Lord Eldon relating to injunctions) for them to be made parties to the proceedings.

12–245

2. *Linton v Mackenzie*

In one case[86] it was held that an undertaking given by the wife of a party to proceedings (being herself a stranger to them), to the effect that she would not molest him, was enforceable by an order for attachment against her.[87] She had obtained a decree of judicial separation unopposed, and an order of £40 a year alimony *pendente lite* was then made in her favour. When the money was sent, however, it was refused and she was maintained by her brother, who eventually brought proceedings against the husband to recover his expenses. Denman J. suggested that terms should be agreed and this was done. The wife and her brother on the one hand and the husband on the other gave cross-undertakings not

12–246

---

[81] *Elliot v Klinger* [1967] 1 W.L.R. 1165. cf. *Lewis v James* (1887) 3 T.L.R. 527, where Kay J. after hearing counsel granted an injunction against a Mr. Boyle, who was not a party to the proceedings before him, to restrain him from communicating with a witness for the purpose of obstruction.
[82] *per* Lindley L.J. in *Seaward v Paterson* [1897] 1 Ch. 545 at 555–6. As to whether such contempt is civil or criminal, see Lord Atkinson in *Scott v Scott* [1913] A.C. 427 at 456–8, and the discussion of the recent authorities in paras 6–126 *et seq.* on the liability of third parties.
[83] See the discussion of *Att-Gen v Newspaper Publishing plc* [1988] Ch. 333 and *Att-Gen v Times Newspapers Ltd* [1992] 1 A.C. 191, at paras 5–141, 6–126 *et seq.*
[84] *D v A & Co* [1900] 1 Ch. 484; see also *Re Launder* (1908) 98 L.T. 554 and *Callow v Young* (1886) 55 L.T. 543 at 544, Chitty J.
[85] [1986] Fam. 134, discussed at para.12–36.
[86] *Linton v Mackenzie*, *The Times*, October 31, 1893.
[87] It appears that the order in fact made was for committal.

12–246

to molest. When the husband sought to commit the wife for a breach of her undertaking, it was argued by her counsel that she was not a party to the action and need not have made any agreement at all. He also took the point that she had not had the benefit of legal advice before the undertaking was given.

12–247 Wills J. rejected this approach, saying that Denman J. would certainly have explained the nature of the agreement she had signed. He was of opinion that it was a plain case of contempt. It was submitted by Oswald,[88] however, that this decision was wrong, and he based himself upon the argument that the wife's undertaking was not, and was not expressed to be, given to the court: "An undertaking to be summarily enforced must be one given to the Court; and it is difficult to see how a mere bystander can give such an undertaking." Wills J. based his decision upon the presumption that the wife had explained to her the significance of the undertaking when she gave it. Whether she in fact did understand it is now impossible to discover, but, on the judge's assumption that she did, no injustice appears to have been done. Furthermore, it seems difficult to follow Oswald's argument based on procedural formality. If an undertaking is volunteered to the court, and the court accepts it, it is surely artificial to suggest that the volunteer's status will of itself prevent the undertaking from being given to the court.

D. Undertakings by solicitors

12–248 It is a contempt for a solicitor to fail to carry out an undertaking given by him in his capacity as a solicitor. This is the case whether or not that undertaking is given to the court, or in the presence of the court, to a party in litigation or to a client. The basis of this jurisdiction is to be found in these words of Lord Esher M.R.[89]:

> "... the Court has a punitive and disciplinary jurisdiction over Solicitors, as being officers of the Court, which is exercised, not for the purpose of enforcing legal rights, but for the purpose of enforcing honourable conduct on the part of the Court's own officers. That power of the Court is quite distinct from any legal rights or remedies of the parties, and cannot, therefore, be affected by any thing which affects the strict legal rights of the parties."

12–249 More recently, in *Taylor v Ribby Hall Leisure*[90] Mummery L.J. described the jurisdiction in the following terms:

---

[88] *Contempt* (2nd. ed., 1895), pp.72–3. Lord Eldon's words, cited at para.12–241, were his only authority for this proposition. The passage quoted does not appear in the subsequent edition of Oswald.

[89] *Re Grey* [1892] 2 Q.B. 440, 443. See also *Stephens v Hill* (1842) 10 M. & W. 28, 152 E.R. 368; *Thompson v Gordon* (1846) 15 M. & W. 610, 153 E.R. 993; *United Mining and Finance Corp v Becher* [1910] 2 K.B. 296, Hamilton J.; *Myers v Elman* [1940] A.C. 282 at 319, Lord Wright; *Silver and Drake v Baines* [1971] 1 Q.B. 396 at 402, Lord Denning M.R.; *Udall v Capri Lighting Ltd* [1988] 1 Q.B. 907, CA.

[90] [1997] 4 All E.R. 760 at 768g–h. A contrast was drawn with the court's powers under the contempt jurisdiction, it being noted that the necessary powers of enforcement arising from the supervisory power extend to the payment of compensation for loss suffered through a solicitor's failing to implement an undertaking given. This does not apply to the contempt jurisdiction: see para.14–142.

"The supervisory power over solicitors also stands comparison with criminal proceedings. The power is essentially a summary disciplinary one exercised by the court over its own officers to ensure their observance of an honourable standard of conduct and to punish derelictions of duty."

Where a solicitor gives an undertaking *to the court*, it can be enforced on the same footing as such an undertaking given by anyone else; but other undertakings given by or on behalf of the solicitor, *provided* he was acting in his professional capacity, may be enforced by means of the special disciplinary jurisdiction. This is separate from the contempt jurisdiction, although it is closely related. One cannot apply for committal in respect of such an undertaking straight away, since it has not *ex hypothesi* been given to the court. The contempt jurisdiction may only be invoked in such a case if an application has been made to the court for a mandatory order that the solicitor does comply with his earlier undertaking.[91] If the solicitor then fails to comply with such an order, within the time appointed, then naturally he will be susceptible to enforcement by summary process of contempt, as would anyone else who disobeys a court order. It is thus probably accurate to summarise the position by saying that this jurisdiction over solicitors simply provides one potential route, unique to them, whereby they may find themselves falling foul of the law of contempt. In *Citadel Management Inc v Equal Ltd*[92] it was held that it was no excuse for non-compliance with an undertaking that compliance was difficult or impossible by reason of circumstances not disclosed at the time when the undertaking was given. If a change of circumstances occurs the solicitor giving the undertaking should inform the recipient promptly. Leave was refused to appeal a sentence of six months' imprisonment imposed for breach of the order obtained following non-compliance with the original undertaking.

12–250

It was observed by Hart J. in *Hole & Pugsley (A Firm) v Sumption*[93] that Buxton L.J. in *Citadel* did not appear to be identifying a principle that a solicitor could rid himself of liability under an undertaking simply by invoking a change of circumstances and notifying it to the recipient. There is no reason to imply into every solicitor's undertaking a term that it would only hold good so long as circumstances remained unchanged and the recipient had not been notified to the contrary. No such term is necessary or obvious and Hart J. observed that such an implication could, as in the case before him, destroy the business efficacy of such an undertaking.

12–251

The nature of the disciplinary jurisdiction

At the risk of digression, it is desirable to consider this disciplinary jurisdiction further, in its proper context, because it can be exercised in various ways and should not be regarded merely as an ante-chamber to the contempt jurisdiction. First, it is to be observed that a solicitor's undertaking, given in his professional

12–252

---

[91] *Re A Solicitor* [1966] 1 W.L.R. 1604, Pennycuick J.; see also *Silver and Drake v Baines* [1971] 1 Q.B. 396 at 402, Lord Denning M.R.; *Re Solicitors* (1916) 11 W.W.R. 529.
[92] [1999] F.L.R. 21, CA.
[93] [2002] Lloyd's Rep. PN 419, [2002] P.N.L.R 20.

12–252 capacity, need not only be enforced through the special jurisdiction of the court. It could be pursued by litigation, for example, assuming there to be a recognised cause of action, such as breach of contract; or it could be referred to the Law Society as an instance of professional misconduct.[94]

12–253 The court's disciplinary jurisdiction, on the other hand, may sometimes provide a legitimate means of avoiding litigation, since the court, once the jurisdiction has been invoked, may in its discretion properly compensate the complainant for loss occasioned by the solicitor's conduct, because the jurisdiction is "not merely punitive but compensatory."[95] It is only possible, however, to invoke this jurisdiction where a solicitor has behaved in a way that is inexcusable and merits reproof, because "it still retains a disciplinary slant."[96] This does not entail, on the other hand, a need to go so far as to prove dishonourable conduct or "peculation or dishonesty." Indeed, the very fact of a solicitor's failing to implement his undertaking would amount *prima facie* to misconduct.[97]

12–254 The facts in *Udall v Capri Lighting Ltd*[98] were unusual. A solicitor was alleged to have given his personal undertaking, *qua* solicitor, to procure second charges on the security of the houses of two directors of his client company. Although there was a claim in contract against the solicitor, there was no note or memorandum in writing; for this reason the plaintiff invoked the court's disciplinary jurisdiction over the solicitor. Since he was held to have given his personal undertaking, and there was at that stage no evidence that it was incapable of performance,[99] the judge ordered it to be carried out. The appeal was on the basis that the undertaking was indeed impossible of performance, and that the judge had been wrong not to grant an adjournment to enable the solicitor to adduce evidence to that effect. On the first of these grounds, the appeal succeeded in the light of new evidence placed before the Court of Appeal.

12–255 Neither the fact that the undertaking had been to the effect that a third party should perform an act, nor the fact that there might be a defence at law (as, for example, under the Statute of Frauds) precluded the court from exercising its supervisory jurisdiction.[1] It was clearly inappropriate to order a solicitor or anyone else to perform an undertaking which was impossible to carry out; yet it

---

[94] See, *e.g. Udall v Capri Lighting Ltd* [1988] 1 Q.B. 907 at 916C–F, Balcombe L.J.
[95] *Myers v Elman* [1940] A.C. 282 at 319, Lord Wright; see also *Marsh v Joseph* [1897] 1 Ch. 213 at 244–5, Lord Russell of Killowen C.J.; *Udall v Capri Lighting Ltd* [1988] 1 Q.B. 907 at 916–17, Balcombe L.J.; *Taylor v Ribby Hall Leisure* [1997] 4 All E.R. 760, Mummery L.J.
[96] *Udall v Capri Lighting Ltd* [1988] 1 Q.B. 907 at 917D, Balcombe L.J.; see also *R & T Thew Ltd v Reeves (No.2) (Note)* [1982] Q.B. 1283 at 1286, Lord Denning M.R.
[97] *Myers v Elman* [1940] A.C. 282, Lord Wright; see also *United Mining & Finance Corporation Ltd v Becher* [1910] 2 K.B. 296; *Udall v Capri Lighting Ltd* [1988] 1 Q.B. 907 at 917.
[98] Last note.
[99] The court would not have made an order in vain: *New Brunswick Co v Muggeridge* (1859) 4 Drew. 686 at 699, 62 E.R. 263; *Tito v Waddell (No.2)* [1977] Ch. 106 at 326.
[1] [1988] 1 Q.B. at 917G, Balcombe L.J.; see also *Ex p. Hughes* (1822) 5 B. & Ald. 482, 106 E.R. 1267; *Re Greaves* (1827) 1 C. & J. 374, 148 E.R. 1466; *Rooks Rider v Steele* [1993] 1 W.L.R. 818, [1993] 4 All E.R. 716.

by no means followed that no order should be made for compensation.[2] On the facts of the case, the Court of Appeal remitted the matter to the court below for determination of the question whether compensation was appropriate.

Udall was followed in *Hole & Pugsley (A Firm) v Sumption*.[3] The claimant firm had given undertakings for certain payments to be made to the defendant on completion of a sale of property. The claimant sought a negative declaration in respect of the undertaking, but the defendant applied for summary enforcement of the claimant's obligations thereunder. The judge granted the application and ordered financial compensation on the usual basis for a breach of contract (*i.e.* that the defendant should be placed in the same position, so far as possible, as if the contract had been performed). The point was made in *Patel v Daybells*,[4] by the Court of Appeal that solicitors' undertakings play a central role in conveyancing practice and are regarded as unconditional and unqualified. Reference was made also to their being backed by the summary procedure for enforcement and by the Solicitors Indemnity Fund (at that time) and the Compensation Fund.

12–256

In any event, where an undertaking has been given by a solicitor in a personal rather than a professional capacity, this jurisdiction may not be relied upon for enforcement. For example, it was held by the Court of Appeal[5] that the remedy could not be invoked where a solicitor had given another firm a written undertaking to repay certain money with interest, even though it had been contained in a letter written on his principal's headed writing paper. It was held to be a mere undertaking to repay money lent, and not one given in a professional capacity, despite the fact that the money had been received by the defendant's firm for the benefit of one of his clients.

12–257

Because of its summary nature the jurisdiction will only be used sparingly, and it is necessary for the case against the solicitor to be made out beyond all reasonable doubt.[6] It will not be fatal, however, for enforcement by this means that the actual word "undertaking" has not been used. What matters is that an obligation has clearly been undertaken by a solicitor in his professional capacity.[7]

12–258

The court's powers are not confined to the inherent jurisdiction. They are confirmed by statute. Section 50(2) of the Solicitors Act 1974 provides as follows:

12–259

---

[2] [1988] 1 Q.B. at 918A–D, Balcombe L.J.; *John Fox v Bannister, King & Rigbeys (Note)* [1988] 1 Q.B. 925, CA; *United Mining & Finance Corporation Ltd v Becher* [1910] 2 K.B. 296 at 306, Hamilton J.
[3] [2002] Lloyd's Rep. P.N. 419, [2002] P.N.L.R 20.
[4] [2001] EWCA Civ 1229, [2002] P.N.L.R. 6, at [62].
[5] *Silver and Drake v Baines* [1971] 1 Q.B. 396 at 402–3, Lord Denning M.R. and Widgery L.J. For examples of cases where a solicitor has been held to be acting *qua* solicitor, see *United Mining & Finance Corporation Ltd v Becher* [1910] 2 K.B. 296, Hamilton J.; *Re A Solicitor* [1966] 1 W.L.R. 1604, Pennycuick J.
[6] *Silver and Drake v Baines* [1971] 1 Q.B. 396 at 404E, Widgery L.J. This accords with the standard of proof applied generally in contempt, see paras 3–241, 12–43.
[7] *Hastingwood Property Ltd v Saunders Bearman Anselm* [1990] 3 All E.R. 107.

"Subject to the provisions of the Act, the High Court, the Crown Court and the Court of Appeal respectively, or any division or judge of those courts, may exercise the same jurisdiction in respect of solicitors as any one of the superior courts of law or equity from which the Supreme Court was constituted might have exercised immediately before the passing of the Supreme Court of Judicature Act 1873 in respect of any solicitor, attorney or proctor admitted to practise there."

An appeal lies to the Court of Appeal from any order made against a solicitor by the High Court or the Crown Court in the exercise of the jurisdiction confirmed by s.50(2) of the 1974 Act.[8] Specific provisions are made also for the county court.[9]

12–260 In *Watkins v A J Wright (Electrical) Ltd*,[10] the judge was faced with a situation in which two parties to litigation were in breach of the implied undertaking not to use documents disclosed on discovery for purposes other than those of the proceedings in which they had been disclosed. The documents in question had been supplied to the Inland Revenue. They had been ignorant of the undertaking themselves but the solicitor, who should have advised his clients of the importance of maintaining strict observance of it, was ordered to pay the costs of the committal motion brought by the party whose documents had been disclosed, and on the indemnity basis.

E. Failure by a solicitor to comply with a written undertaking in admiralty proceedings

12–261 Traditionally, where the solicitor of a party to an action *in rem* failed to comply with a written undertaking given by him to any other party, or to the solicitor of any other party, to acknowledge issue or service of the writ in the action, give bail or pay money into court in lieu of bail, he was regarded as liable to committal.[11] An undertaking to put in bail could not be withdrawn on offering the ship within the jurisdiction for arrest. Moreover, the plaintiffs did not forfeit their rights under the undertaking merely by arresting the ship.[12]

12–262 In a case where solicitors appeared and gave bail, and the owners subsequently repudiated their authority to do so, a motion by the solicitors to remove their names from the writ to discharge their undertaking was dismissed.[13] To do so would have been to destroy the basis of an action by the plaintiffs for breach of warranty of authority. Also Bateson J. refused to discharge an undertaking by

---

[8] See s.50(3), which was added by the Supreme Court Act 1981, ss.147, 152(4), Sch.7.
[9] County Courts Act 1984, s.142, discussed at para.13–98.
[10] [1996] 3 All E.R. 31, Blackburne J.
[11] The former RSC Ord.75, r.9 (which derived from the original Ord.12, r.18). See now the provision for specialist Admiralty procedure: CPR 49(1), (2)(a); Pt 49, PD at *Civil Procedure* Vol. 2, and particularly at 2A–117 and 2A–121. For enforcing undertakings by solicitors, see *Civil Procedure*, Vol. 2, 7C–213–214; CPR 61PD, 2D–130–2D131.
[12] *The Borre* [1921] P. 390 at 398, Sir Henry Duke P. It would different if there were clear proof that the plaintiffs had elected to arrest the *Borre* and to release the solicitors from their undertaking: see, *e.g. Miller v James* (1823) 8 Moo. C.P. 208.
[13] *The Gertrud* [1927] W.N. 265, 44 T.L.R. 1, 29 Lloyd's Rep. 5, Hill J.

solicitors although the vessel had been sold and the cargo owners, who had no maritime lien, were not in a position to arrest it[14]:

> "The real bargain, as I understand it, is that the solicitor gives the undertaking that he will accept service when the writ is issued, appear, and give bail, in consideration that the ship shall not be arrested, but shall be allowed to sail as soon as she pleases. In the case of a foreign ship it is important that she shall not try to avoid service. The fact that in this case the ship got into difficulties and had to be sold makes no difference to the contract I have to construe."

---

[14] *The Ring* [1931] P. 58 at 62.

CHAPTER 13

JURISDICTION

		PARA
I.	General Principles	13–1
II.	Superior Courts of Record	13–8
III.	Other Courts of Record	13–79
IV.	Magistrates' Courts	13–104
V.	Appellate Jurisdiction	13–118

I. GENERAL PRINCIPLES

A. The two aspects of jurisdiction

13–1 As was illustrated in the decision of House of Lords in *Att-Gen v BBC*[1] whenever an allegation of contempt arises, there are two quite separate questions as to jurisdiction[2] which may have to be considered:

(1) whether the affected court or tribunal is protected by the law of contempt at all;

(2) if it is, whether it has any power to deal with the alleged contempt itself, or whether it can only be dealt with by some other court, either on reference to it or of its own motion. The answers will not always be in harmony, because there are some tribunals whose proceedings are protected by the law of contempt without their having power to take proceedings in respect of such conduct.[3]

13–2 It is the first question which is most likely to give rise to difficulty in practice, especially for those in the media. There is, as Lord Salmon described it, a "host of modern inferior courts and tribunals".[4] Although they may have to a greater or lesser extent characteristics in common with traditional courts of law, they are by no means all subject to the law of contempt. If a court or tribunal *is* so protected, however, then the second question arises. Inferior courts have at most only limited powers to deal with contempts in respect of their proceedings. The Divisional Court of the Queen's Bench Division has power to deal with contempts of certain inferior courts. That jurisdiction is not coterminous with its

---

[1] [1981] A.C. 303. See in particular Lord Scarman, where he identifies the two questions there in issue: [1981] A.C. 303 at 354. In that case it was unanimously held that a valuation court was not a tribunal to which the law of contempt applied.
[2] This chapter is not concerned with "jurisdiction" in the context of extra-territoriality, although these difficulties are discussed at paras 3–223 *et seq.* and at paras 12–155 *et seq.*
[3] As, for example, employment tribunals, and mental health review tribunals.
[4] [1981] A.C. 303 at 344.

other jurisdiction to protect and control inferior courts by judicial review, which covers a wider range of tribunals than are subject to the contempt jurisdiction.[5]

B. The effect of the 1981 Act

The Contempt of Court Act 1981 confines the impact of strict liability to certain categories of publication relating to particular legal proceedings. Section 19 of the Act provides:

> "... 'court' includes any tribunal or body exercising the judicial power of the State, and 'legal proceedings' shall be construed accordingly."

In the result, a contempt to which the strict liability rule applies can only be committed in relation to proceedings before a tribunal or body exercising the judicial power of the state. The phrase "judicial power of the state" appears to have been taken from Lord Scarman's speech in *Att-Gen v BBC*.[6]

In relation to forms of contempt outside the strict liability rule, the 1981 Act contains no similar restriction. In considering how widely the protective net of common law contempt is extended, therefore, it would in theory be necessary to seek guidance from the speeches as a whole in *Att-Gen v BBC*. Lords Dilhorne and Fraser appear to have concurred in Lord Scarman's reasoning, to the effect that the law of contempt should apply to tribunals exercising the *judicial* power of the state. On the other hand, Lord Salmon apparently took a narrower view that only those "inferior courts" that were "long-established", and traditionally protected by the law of contempt, should be subject to the contempt jurisdiction.[7]

Lord Edmund-Davies, having considered in detail a number of attributes, suggested in argument as providing some defining characteristics of a "court", concluded that there was no sure guide by which a court or inferior tribunal might be unerringly identified. He thought that it was largely a matter of impression. However, there is no reason to suppose that the common law of contempt would extend any more widely in respect of tribunals than the definition of courts to be found in s.19.

C. Difficulties of ascertaining which inferior tribunals are covered by the law of contempt

Because the Act adopted Lord Scarman's general criterion, and did not identify specifically those tribunals intended to be subject to the law of contempt, a good deal of uncertainty remained as to which tribunals were to be so protected. Both in the House of Lords and the House of Commons attempts were made to draw up such a list[8] but in the end the task was abandoned. We turn to consider the

---

[5] [1981] A.C. at 352–3, Lord Fraser.
[6] [1981] A.C. 303 at 359.
[7] *ibid.* at 342.
[8] See para.13–46.

traditional distinctions, drawn between different tiers within the judicial system, which are largely responsible for those uncertainties.

D. Distinctions in jurisdiction between superior and inferior courts

13–7 As a general rule a superior court of record has jurisdiction to deal summarily with any contempt affecting its own proceedings.[9] An inferior court of record had jurisdiction at common law only to deal with contempts committed in the face of the court.[10] Inferior courts *not* of record had no jurisdiction to deal with contempt, unless statute provided to the contrary. They had otherwise to rely on the protection of the Divisional Court of the Queen's Bench Division. These traditional and clear boundaries are likely to be changed or blurred as time passes. As Lord Woolf noted in *Manchester City Council v McCann*,[11] the county court jurisdictional limits had increased significantly and the term "inferior" seemed less and less apt with each passing year. It is in contemplation that the distinction between the High Court and the county court will at some point be abolished altogether, following the process of amalgamation in practice and procedure to be found in the CPR. There is already a unified court system so far as administrative structures are concerned,[12] and there is likely to be at some point in the near future a single unified civil court. The process may not be completed for many years since the large scale statutory changes this would entail may not be given legislative priority.

II. SUPERIOR COURTS OF RECORD

A. Superior courts of record: generally

13–8 Superior courts of record include the House of Lords, the several branches of the Supreme Court including the Court of Appeal, the Courts Martial Appeal Court, the High Court in its various divisions, the Crown Court,[13] and the Employment Appeal Tribunal.[14] The Special Immigration Appeal Commission was established by the Special Immigration Appeals Commission Act 1997 and was constituted by s.1(3)[15] a court of record: it would thus have its own powers in

---

[9] Hawk. P.C. 6.2, c.22; *Ex p. Fernandez* (1861) 10 C.B. (N.S.) 3, 142 E.R. 349. For a discussion of the development of the inherent jurisdiction of the courts generally, see I.H. Jacob, "The Inherent Jurisdiction of the Court" (1970) 23 C.L.P. 23; K. Mason, "The Inherent Jurisdiction of the Court" (1983) 57 A.L.J. 449; M.S. Dockray, "The Inherent Jurisdiction to Regulate Civil Proceedings" (1997) 113 L.Q.R. 120.
[10] *Brompton County Court Judge* [1893] 2 Q.B. 195.
[11] [1999] Q.B. 1214 at 1223–4.
[12] www.hmcourts-service.gov.uk.
[13] Supreme Court Act 1981, s.45(1).
[14] Industrial Tribunals Act 1996, s.20(3); now known as the "Employment Tribunals Act 1996", by virtue of the Employment Rights (Dispute Resolution) Act 1998, s.1(2).
[15] As amended by s.35 of the Anti-terrorism, Crime and Security Act 2001.

respect of contempt. The Mental Capacity Act 2005 provides that the Court of Protection also shall be a superior court of record.[16]

Such courts have jurisdiction to deal summarily with contempts relating to their proceedings.[17] Where the contempt relates to proceedings actually pending before a particular court, that court may enquire into the matter of its own motion.[18] In a case, however, where proceedings are not yet pending before any specific court[19] (for example, where a defendant in criminal proceedings has not yet been committed) it will be rare for proceedings for contempt to be generated except by the Attorney-General referring the matter to the Divisional Court, in the exercise of his wide-ranging jurisdiction to protect the administration of justice in the public interest.[20]

13–9

An example is provided, however, by the unusual circumstances arising in *Connolly v Dale*[21] where the Divisional Court considered an application to commit a senior police officer made by a defendant who had been charged with murder. He was complaining—well before trial—of interference by the officer with the preparations being carried out by his solicitor, and in particular with his "proper and reasonable attempts" to identify and interview potential witnesses. Publication contempt may also be brought to the attention of the relevant court by an aggrieved party, although matters covered by the strict liability rule are reserved expressly for the Attorney-General, or may be dealt with "on the motion of a court having jurisdiction to deal with it".[22]

13–10

If the court enquires into an alleged contempt of its own motion, but concludes that while a contempt may have been committed it need not be dealt with as a matter of urgency, then the appropriate course is for the court to refer the matter to the Attorney-General or to leave it to an aggrieved party so to refer it.[23] So too, if the court's attention is drawn to an alleged contempt, and it is plain from the outset that even if the contempt were established it need not be dealt with as a matter of urgency, then again the proper course would be to refer the matter to the Attorney-General. If the Law Officers declined to act, and no aggrieved party

13–11

---

[16] s.45(1).
[17] See, *e.g. Balogh v St. Albans Crown Court* [1975] Q.B. 73, Lawton L.J. at 92.
[18] [1975] Q.B. 73 at 89 and 92. This power may extend to dealing with any contempt relating to proceedings which have just been concluded, *per* Lord Denning M.R. at 84. In *Att-Gen v Butterworth* [1963] 1 Q.B. 696, L.R. 3 R.P. 327, CA, for example, the Restrictive Practices Court had dealt with contemnors who punished a witness for giving evidence in proceedings which had been concluded six weeks previously. For the report of the first instance hearing, see L.R. 3 R.P. 1.
[19] For the survival of the "imminence" test after the 1981 Act, in respect of publication contempt, see *Att-Gen v Sport Newspapers Ltd* [1991] 1 W.L.R. 1194, [1992] 1 All E.R. 503, DC; *Att-Gen v News Group Newspapers plc* [1989] 1 Q.B. 110 DC, discussed at paras 5–67 *et seq.*
[20] Lord Cross in *Att-Gen v Times Newspapers Ltd* [1974] A.C. 273 at 326. See also the treatment of this subject at paras 2–199 *et seq.* and para.9–239. For a more general discussion of the role of the Attorney-General, see J. Ll. J. Edwards, *The Attorney-General, Politics and the Public Interest* (Sweet and Maxwell 1984) pp.161–76. See too the lectures by the Attorney-General to the Liberty Annual Conference (2002) and the Law for Journalists Conference (2003) available at *www.lslo.gov.uk*.
[21] [1996] Q.B. 120.
[22] s.7, which is considered more fully in paras 4–183 *et seq.*
[23] *Balogh v St. Albans Crown Court* [1975] Q.B. 73.

came forward, then the court might in certain circumstances be inclined to exercise its inherent jurisdiction to proceed of its own motion.[24]

B. House of Lords

13–12   The House of Lords is a superior court of record and has jurisdiction (and apparently exclusive jurisdiction) to commit or to impose lesser penalties in respect of any contempt relating to proceedings before it.[25] It is not a branch of the Supreme Court and is thus not governed by its rules. As Lord Keith said in *Re Lonrho plc*[26]:

> "There are also insuperable objections in the present case to contempt proceedings taking place otherwise than in this House. It is admitted that the normal and natural forum for the hearing of contempt relating to proceedings before this House is the House itself. If any authority be required, it can be found in *Rex v Flower* (1799) 8 Durn. & E. 314, 323, per Lord Kenyon C.J. Of course, when a contempt of the House also involves a separate and independent crime, then the House may well take no action in relation to the contempt, allowing or directing the ordinary criminal process to take place. For example, in 1812 a Prime Minister, Mr. Spencer Perceval, was shot in the precincts of the House of Commons and his murderer was tried by the Assize Court. But this is not such a case; the suggested contempts are contempts of court relating to proceedings before this House and no other crime is alleged. There is no authority that vests in the Divisional Court of the Queen's Bench Division or any other court jurisdiction to deal with the present matters in dispute.
>
> That is enough to dispose of the suggested reference to the Attorney-General."

C. Court of Appeal

13–13   The Court of Appeal is a superior court of record, and as such has an inherent jurisdiction to protect its own processes. It is a branch of the Supreme Court and CPR Sch.1, Ord.52.1 provides that the power of the Court of Appeal to punish for contempt of court may be exercised by committal. The Queen's Bench Division has power to deal with contempts relating to criminal proceedings (other than in the face of the court), but the subrule goes on to make it clear that this has no application "in relation to contempt of the Court of Appeal".[27]

13–14   A contempt of the Court of Appeal (Criminal Division) should be dealt with by that court.[28] CPR Sch.1, Ord.52.5 specifically provides that "nothing in the foregoing provisions of this Order shall be taken as affecting the power of the . . . Court of Appeal to make an order of committal of its own motion against a

---

[24] That inherent jurisdiction might even be invoked in cases of civil contempt. See, *e.g. Clarke v Chadburn* [1985] 1 W.L.R. 78; *R. v Commissioners of Inland Revenue Ex p. Kingston Smith* [1996] 2 S.T.C. 1210; *Re M (A Minor) (Contempt of Court: Committal of Court's own Motion)* [1999] Fam. 263.
[25] *Re Lonrho plc* [1990] 2 A.C. 154.
[26] *ibid.* at 176–7.
[27] CPR Sch.1, Ord.52.1(2)(a)(ii).
[28] See, *e.g. Att-Gen v Newspaper Publishing plc* [1997] 1 W.L.R. 926, [1997] 3 All E.R. 159. See also *Att-Gen v Channel Four Television Co Ltd* [1988] Crim. L.R. 237, where the court, having granted an injunction to restrain a televised reconstruction of proceedings that were taking place before it, asserted its own right to hear an application to discharge the injunction.

person guilty of contempt of court." In *R. v Solicitor-General Ex p. Taylor*,[29] Stuart-Smith L.J. commented in relation to the Court of Appeal (following a decision by the Law Officers not to bring proceedings for contempt):

> "Furthermore, it seems to me apparent, that the court having jurisdiction to deal with it could itself have at least in theory, acted of its own motion if the Attorney-General declined to institute proceedings or give his consent. Thus it was open to the Court of Appeal in this case when they were notified of the Solicitor-General's decision to have taken this course."

13–15 In civil matters the practice appears to be that, if a contempt is committed with regard to an order of the Court of Appeal made at the conclusion of an appeal, application for committal should be made to the court below.[30] On the other hand, in relation to contempt of its own proceedings, the Court of Appeal would clearly have jurisdiction to deal with the matter, whether referred by one of the parties or of its own motion.[31] In *Benson v Richards*,[32] Carnwath L.J. observed that the Court of Appeal's jurisdiction to deal with a contempt as a first instance court should only be exercised "in the most exceptional circumstances, particularly where the defendant is unrepresented".

D. Courts Martial Appeal Court

13–16 By virtue of s.1(2) of the Courts Martial (Appeals) Act 1968 the Courts Martial Appeal Court is a superior court of record.[33]

E. High Court

13–17 The High Court is also a superior court of record,[34] having inherited all the jurisdiction of the former Court of Chancery, the common law courts and judges of assize.[35] A single judge of any of the divisions of the High Court may commit for a contempt relating to proceedings pending in that division.[36] The only exception is a contempt of the Divisional Court of the Queen's Bench Division itself, which can only be dealt with by that court.[37]

13–18 In addition, it has a special jurisdiction inherited from the former court of Queen's Bench and recognised by CPR Sch.1, Ord.52.1.(2) which provides that

---

[29] [1995] C.O.D. 61 (Lexis).
[30] *Fortescue v McKeown* [1914] 1 I.R. 30. See also *Pott v Stuteley* [1955] W.N. 140.
[31] In *Re Rossminster and Tucker, The Times*, May 23, 1980, officers of the Inland Revenue seized documents with a view to ascertaining whether criminal offences had been committed. The civil division of the Court of Appeal held that they had exceeded their powers and ordered the return of the documents subject to an undertaking to produce them if the House of Lords reversed the order. The House of Lords did reverse the order, but the individual concerned failed to produce some of the documents. The Court of Appeal fined him for breach of his undertaking.
[32] [2002] EWCA Civ 1402, (2002) 147 S.J.L.B. 231, *The Times*, October 17, 2002 at [3].
[33] The position is not affected by the Armed Forces Act 1996.
[34] Supreme Court Act 1981, s.19.
[35] See Supreme Court of Judicature (Consolidation) Act 1925, s.18 (now repealed by the Supreme Court Act 1981, s.154 and Sch.7).
[36] CPR Sch.1, Ord.52.1(3).
[37] CPR Sch.1, Ord.52.1(2)(a)(i).

13–18   CHAPTER 13—JURISDICTION

certain types of contempt can only be punished by a Divisional Court. This applies where a contempt is committed otherwise than in connection with any proceedings. An example (albeit now largely theoretical) would be a "scandalous" attack on a member of the judiciary but unrelated to any particular case.[38]

13–19 There do not appear to be any examples in the older cases of the Court of Queen's Bench dealing with matter scandalising any of the other common law courts or the Court of Chancery. The old Court of Chancery had power to commit in respect of matter scandalising that court.[39] Moreover, CPR Sch.1, Ord.52.5 provides:

> "Nothing in the foregoing provisions of this order shall be taken as affecting the power of the High Court or Court of Appeal to make an order of committal of its own motion against a person guilty of contempt of court."

Thus, it would appear that the Chancery Division of the High Court by succession has the residual power to commit in respect of scandalous material relating to proceedings in that Division, even if no longer pending.

13–20 The High Court also has jurisdiction in appropriate cases to grant a *quia timet* injunction to restrain conduct which would, if committed, constitute contempt of court.[40]

F. Employment Appeal Tribunal

13–21 The Employment Appeal Tribunal was created by s.87 of the Employment Protection Act 1975. It became a superior court of record by virtue of Sch.6, para.10 of that Act. The matter is now governed by s.20(3) of the Employment Tribunals Act 1996.[41]

G. The jurisdiction of the Divisional Court over contempt of the Crown Court

13–22 It is common for judges of the Crown Court confronted with a contempt problem, in the middle of a trial, to have difficulty in recognising the precise scope of their own powers; whether or not it is appropriate for them to deal with the immediate situation by an exercise of their own summary powers, or to refer the matter to the Attorney-General. This arises because of an unfortunate lack of certainty in the relevant rules which purport to define the jurisdiction of the Divisional Court

---

[38] See paras 5–204 *et seq.*
[39] *The St. James's Evening Post* (1742) 2 Atk. 469, 26 E.R. 683.
[40] See the full discussion at paras 6–1 *et seq.* See also s.37 of the Supreme Court Act 1981, and s.12 of the Human Rights Act 1998.
[41] Renamed by s.1(2) of the Employment Rights (Dispute Resolution) Act 1998. The statute also renamed the tribunals themselves as "employment tribunals": s.1(1).

in relation to criminal trials, on the one hand, and to "inferior courts" on the other. Quite where the Crown Court falls within this spectrum is curiously unclear, as is the relationship between the contempt jurisdiction of the Divisional Court and that of the Crown Court judges themselves. It is necessary to consider briefly the historical background.

Before the Courts Act 1971, the Divisional Court dealt with contempts in relation to assize courts. This was justified in part by the fact that the jurisdiction of the judges of assize was vested in the High Court by s.18 of the Supreme Court of Judicature (Consolidation) Act 1925, and in part by the fact that assizes were not continuously sitting. Thus, if matter was published which was calculated to prejudice a case committed to an assize court not yet constituted,[42] or which "scandalised" an assize court which was no longer in session,[43] only the High Court could deal with the contempt.[44] RSC Ord.52, r.1(2)(a)(ii)[45] was originally drafted to recognise this situation.

13–23

When the Crown Court was created by the Courts Act 1971, it replaced the former assizes (and incorporated the Central Criminal Court). It also replaced effectively the county and borough sessions. It was declared part of the Supreme Court and a superior court of record.[46] Moreover it was specifically given the same power as the High Court in relation to contempt.[47] Yet no amendment has been made to CPR, Sch.1, Ord.52 to meet this changed situation. This gives rise to difficulties which may be more than theoretical, as discussed in the following paragraphs.

13–24

The wording of CPR, Sch.1, Ord.52.1(2)

The CPR clearly imply that the Divisional Court has power to deal with contempt of the Crown Court. CPR, Sch.1, Ord.521(2)(a)(ii) provides that an order of committal may be made *only* by a Divisional Court of the Queen's Bench Division where a contempt is committed in connection with:

13–25

---

[42] *R. v Parke* [1903] 2 K.B. 432; *R. v Davies* [1906] 1 K.B. 32.
[43] *R. v Gray* [1900] 2 Q.B. 36.
[44] The Divisional Court did deal on occasion with contempts of an assize court whilst that court was still in commission: *R. v Griffiths Ex p. Att-Gen* [1957] 2 Q.B. 192; *R. v Evening Standard Co Ltd* [1954] 1 Q.B. 578.
[45] See now CPR Sch.1, Ord.52.1, considered below.
[46] Courts Act 1971, s.4(1). See now the Supreme Court 1981, s.45(1). Contrast s.29(3) of the same Act, which expressly confers on the Divisional Court the same jurisdiction in respect of the Crown Court as it has in the case of "an inferior court". The jurisdiction is however limited to the Crown Court's jurisdiction "other than its jurisdiction in matters relating to trial on indictment". This (sometimes unclear) distinction derives from the Courts Act 1971 when it was deemed necessary to retain the supervisory jurisdiction of the High Court in respect of the matters formerly dealt with by the Quarter Sessions. See R. Ward, "Judicial Review and Trials on Indictment: Section 29(3) of the Supreme Court Act 1981" [1990] P.L. 50. See the notes in the *Civil Procedure* Vol. 2 at para. 9A–81.1.
[47] s.4(8). See now Supreme Court Act 1981, s.45(4), discussed at para.13–34.

13–25

"... criminal proceedings, except where the contempt is committed in the face of the court or consists of disobedience to an order of the court[48] or a breach of an undertaking to the court."[49]

13–26 This would appear to contemplate a concurrent jurisdiction between the Crown Court and the Divisional Court in respect of these specifically excepted circumstances; by the same token, other aspects of criminal proceedings appear to be reserved exclusively for the Divisional Court. In the case of contempt not in the face of the court,[50] it appears that the Divisional Court would according to the above wording have exclusive jurisdiction; for example, where threats are made to a witness or a juror outside the court[51] or after proceedings are completed.[52] It is necessary, however, to remember that s.45(4) of the Supreme Court Act 1981 confers upon the Crown Court *inter alia* like powers for dealing with contempt to those vested in the High Court.[53] Moreover, the rule cannot itself detract from that statutory power.[54] It therefore appears to represent good practice in these respects rather than defining jurisdiction.[55]

13–27 There is a distinction between the wording set out above in CPR Sch.1, Ord.52.1(2)(a)(ii) and that appearing in s.12 of the Contempt of Court Act 1981, which was intended to provide similar protection for magistrates' courts.[56] Whether it accords with the intention of the legislature or not, it is thus arguable that magistrates would have a wider jurisdiction than the Crown Court in respect of contempt of this kind. It may be that the distinction is more theoretical than real, but questions sometimes arise as to whether or not a particular act takes place technically "in the face of the court". For example, in *Bodden v Metropolitan Police Commissioner*,[57] the problem arose as a result of the use of a loud-hailer outside the building, and in *R. v Jones*[58] where comments were made to jurors outside the court. It seems clear that the phrase "in the face" in CPR Sch.1, Ord.52.1 is narrower than the concept of "interrupts the proceedings

---

[48] As, perhaps, disobedience to an order made under the Contempt of Court Act 1981, s.4(2) or s.11, discussed at paras 7–109 *et seq.* and paras 7–83 *et seq.* respectively. See *R. v D* [1984] A.C. 778 at 791H–792E, Watkins L.J., cited at para.7-228. See also *R. v Tyne Tees Television Ltd* [1997] T.L.R. 515, where the Court of Appeal concluded that it would have been appropriate for an apparent breach of s.39 of the Children and Young Persons Act 1933 to be reported by a Crown Court judge, with a view to consideration for summary proceedings in the Divisional Court against a television company, rather than his dealing with the matter personally.
[49] See, *e.g. Att-Gen v Mantoura* [1993] Crim. L.R. 279 (Lexis).
[50] See the discussion of this phrase at paras 10–11 *et seq.*
[51] See, *e.g.* para.11–183.
[52] *Att-Gen v Judd* [1995] C.O.D. 15.
[53] This provision was considered by Aikens J. in *Ex p. HTV Cymru (Wales) Ltd* [2002] E.M.L.R. 184 discussed below at para.13–37.
[54] Stephenson L.J. in *Balogh v St. Albans Crown Court* [1975] Q.B. 73, 89 commented: "I do not accept the argument that the limits of the power of a superior court to imprison a contemnor are defined or restricted by the Rules of the Supreme Court. They should disclose but may disguise its true nature and extent, and if they misunderstand it they may need to be revised. The question is not what the rules of procedure which regulate it say or imply that it is but what it really is." See also Lord Edmund-Davies in *Att-Gen v BBC* [1981] A.C. at 346–7, cited at para.13–51.
[55] See, *e.g.* the judgment of Mustill L.J. in *R. v Griffin* cited at para.13–32.
[56] See para.13–106.
[57] [1990] 2 Q.B. 397.
[58] [1996] Crim. L.R. 806. These matters are discussed more fully in paras 10–11 *et seq.*

of the court". Nor would it be wide enough to embrace insults offered to those involved in proceedings on their way to and from court.

"Criminal proceedings" in the context of CPR Sch.1, Ord.52.1 can only be intended to apply to criminal proceedings in the Crown Court. This was clearly the view adopted in *Balogh v St Albans Crown Court*.[59] Furthermore, in *DPP v Channel Four Television Co Ltd*[60] it was also accepted that the jurisdiction in relation to such criminal proceedings overlaps, although in relation to certain forms of contempt the Divisional Court would represent the most appropriate forum. **13–28**

Whenever there is concurrent jurisdiction, there are likely to be problems as to which is the appropriate forum in the light of the particular circumstances. In *DPP v Channel Four Television Co Ltd*[61] Woolf L.J. had noted that the issue of how the responsibility as between the Crown Court and the Divisional Court should be apportioned was "under consideration", and said that he did not wish to anticipate the outcome. **13–29**

In the meantime the court gave guidance as to the circumstances in which it would be appropriate for the Crown Court to exercise its jurisdiction in preference to referring the matter for the attention of the Divisional Court.[62] Consistently with the approach of the Court of Appeal in *Balogh*, Woolf L.J. recognised that a Crown Court judge could only act of his or her own motion if (a) the contempt was clear, (b) it affected a trial in progress or one which was about to start, (c) it was urgent and imperative to act immediately in order to prevent justice being obstructed and undermined, and to preserve the integrity of the trial, and (d) no other procedure would do if the ends of justice were to be met. **13–30**

In *Balogh* it had been made clear that the court should only proceed instantly of its own motion where that is necessary "for the purpose of ensuring that a trial in progress or about to start can be brought to a proper and dignified end without disturbance and with a fair chance of a just verdict or judgment."[63] Lawton L.J. listed types of contempt which might justify the court in proceeding summarily of its own motion[64]: **13–31**

> " ... witnesses and jurors duly summoned who refuse to attend court; witnesses duly sworn who refuse to answer proper questions; persons in court who interrupt the proceedings by insulting the judge, shouting or otherwise making a disturbance; persons in court who assault or attempt to assault or threaten the judge or any officers of the court whose presence is necessary; persons in or out of court who threaten those about to give evidence or who have given evidence; persons in or out of court who

---

[59] [1975] 1 Q.B. 73.
[60] [1993] 2 All E.R. 517.
[61] *ibid*. at 520j.
[62] [1993] 2 All E.R. at 521b where it was recognised that there was "considerable force" in counsel's submission on these matters. See also *Weston v Courts Administrator of the Central Criminal Court* [1977] Q.B. 32, and *Keeley v Brooking* (1979) 143 C.L.R. 162, 53 A.L.J.R. 526.
[63] [1975] Q.B. 73, Lawton L.J. at 92–3.
[64] *ibid*. at 93.

13–31 threaten or bribe or attempt to bribe jurors or interfere with their coming to court; persons out of court who publish comments[65] about a trial going on by revealing a defendant's criminal record when the rules of evidence exclude it."

13–32 What seems clear, however, is that these are considerations going not to jurisdiction but to the practical wisdom of adopting one course rather than another. In *Griffin*[66] it was suggested that the jurisdiction of a Crown Court judge might depend upon the degree of urgency to which the particular circumstances gave rise. This proposition was expressly addressed by Mustill L.J.[67]:

"We should add that certain dicta (for example, in *Balogh*) may be read as suggesting that the court has no jurisdiction to adopt the summary process unless the matter is urgent. We doubt whether this is strictly accurate. In our view the question of urgency or no is material, not to the existence of the jurisdiction but as to whether the jurisdiction should be exercised in preference to some more measured form of process".

13–33 In some circumstances it would be apparent that the Divisional Court would be in practice the only proper forum, notwithstanding the theoretical concurrent jurisdiction of the Crown Court. The particular example before the Divisional Court in *DPP v Channel Four Television Co Ltd* was the power under the Prevention of Terrorism (Temporary Provisions) Act 1989, Sch.7, para.3 (now repealed). Contempt in relation to such an order (notwithstanding that it can only be made by a circuit judge in the first instance) exemplified the "type of application which should invariably be heard by the Divisional Court."[68] This question of jurisdiction was touched upon in *Taylor v Topping*[69] where, in relation to the contents of a book alleged to be prejudicial to pending Crown Court proceedings, Mann L.J. commented: "Although the learned circuit judge would undoubtedly have jurisdiction to deal with contempt occurring in his face, he does not have in my judgment jurisdiction to deal with contempt occurring in a book such as this."

H. The Crown Court's own jurisdiction

13–34 By s.1(1) of the Supreme Court Act 1981 the Crown Court is a part of the Supreme Court and by s.45(1) it is declared to be a superior court of record. Section 45(4) provides that:

"Subject to s.8 of the Criminal Procedure (Attendance of Witnesses) Act 1965 . . . and to any provision contained in or having effect under this Act, the Crown Court shall, in

---

[65] This passage was referred to by the Divisional Court in *Taylor v Topping*, February 9, 1990 (Lexis), although Brooke J. observed that: "In my judgment Parliament clearly intended [in s.7 of the 1981 Act] to preserve the power of a judge who is handling a criminal trial of his own motion either in his own court or by reference to another court in the building to act summarily and fast if the interests of justice require it. However, except in that fairly narrow range of cases, I am quite satisfied that Parliament intended that proceedings for contempt of court under the strict liability rule should not be instituted except by or with the consent of the Attorney General".
[66] (1989) 88 Cr.App.R. 63.
[67] *ibid*. at 69. The case concerned allegations of interference with witnesses.
[68] [1993] 2 All E.R. at 520.
[69] February 9, 1990 (Lexis). *The Times* February 15, 1990.

relation to the attendance and examination of witnesses, *any contempt of court*, the enforcement of its orders and all other matters incidental to its jurisdiction, have the like powers, rights, privileges and authority as the High Court" (emphasis added).

By s.8(1) of the Supreme Court Act 1981, the jurisdiction of the Crown Court can be exercised by:

"(a) any judge of the High Court; or
(b) any Circuit judge, Recorder or District Judge (Magistrates' Courts);
(c) subject to and in accordance with the provisions of sections 74[70] and 75(2),[71] a judge of the High Court, Circuit judge or Recorder sitting with not more than four justices of the peace . . . ."

Apart from such circumstances that are described in *Balogh v St Albans Crown Court*[72] and *DPP v Channel Four Television Co Ltd*,[73] any alleged contempt should be referred to the Attorney-General to decide whether to move the Divisional Court to commit (or to leave an aggrieved party to do so).[74] If the matter is referred to the Attorney-General the alleged contemnor may be remanded in custody or released on bail.[75]

1. Does the Crown Court have quia timet jurisdiction?

When it is anticipated that there may be some interference with Crown Court proceedings, whether by way of prejudicial publication or otherwise, the appropriate tribunal to grant an injunction would usually be the High Court.[76] The powers of the Crown Court to restrain prejudicial publication clearly include the matters contemplated by s.4(2) and s.11 of the Contempt of Court Act 1981.[77] Where it is contemplated, however, that prejudice is likely to be caused by publication falling outside those provisions, it is good practice for such an application to be made to a High Court judge. Yet there is an argument that at least in circumstances of urgency there is a power in the Crown Court to grant *quia timet* relief. The matter turns upon the construction of s.45(4) of the Supreme Court Act 1981 which confers *inter alia* upon the Crown Court "like powers" in relation to contempt to those exercisable by the High Court. It is by no means clear that this wording would be construed as being confined to contempts already committed.[78]

---

[70] Appeals and committals for sentence.
[71] Allocation of cases according to composition of court.
[72] [1975] 1 Q.B. 73 at 93, cited in para.13-31.
[73] [1993] 2 All E.R. 517.
[74] [1975] 1 Q.B. at 85 and 93. It should be noted that there was also reference in the judgment to the possibility of proceeding by way of indictment, but it now seems clear from *Re Lonhro plc* [1990] 2 A.C. 154 that this procedure is obsolete and "ought not to be revived" (at 177).
[75] [1975] 1 Q.B. 73 at 85 and 86.
[76] See Watkins L.J. in *R. v Rhuddlan Justices* [1986] Crim. L.R. 329, DC (Lexis), and the general discussion in paras 6–1 *et seq.* See also the statutory powers governing the grant of injunctions contained in s.37 of the Supreme Court Act 1981.
[77] Discussed at para.7–111 and paras 7–83 *et seq.* respectively.
[78] Cp. *Peacock v London Weekend Television* (1985) 150 J.P. 71, where the different wording of s.7 of the Contempt of Court Act was held *not* to embrace applications to prevent the publication of prejudicial material.

13-37 Aikens J. sitting in the Cardiff Crown Court has held[79] that, by reason of s.45(4), a Crown Court judge does indeed have the jurisdiction to grant an injunction for the purpose of preventing the publication of a contempt. He emphasised, however, that it was a power to be sparingly used. In the particular case, the order was to prevent a television from interviewing a prosecution witness who had already given his evidence. The injunction granted was not *contra mundum* but only against the specific party to which the evidence related. The judge was concerned with the possibility of the witness's evidence being changed as a result of an interview in circumstances where there was a risk of his needing to be recalled to rebut defence evidence. He did *not* base his decision on the possibility of a retrial and, indeed, there was an assurance that the interview would not be broadcast until after any retrial that might take place. Moreover, such an order was only appropriate for so long as there was the possibility of the witness giving evidence.

2. The Crown Court's power of committal to be sparingly used

13-38 All members of the Court of Appeal in *Balogh* were unanimous that the power of the court to commit summarily of its own motion ought only to be used as a matter of last resort, where its exercise was necessary to ensure the fair and dignified conclusion of a pending trial. For example, Lawton L.J. stressed that the existence of this jurisdiction did not mean that it should be exercised routinely[80]:

> "Contempt of these kinds may well justify the use of the summary jurisdiction; but everything will depend upon the circumstances. For example, judges from time to time have to decide what to do about a witness who refuses to answer a question, often because he cannot bring himself to state that which is obvious to both judge and jury or because the answer would cause acute personal embarrassment, as sometimes happens with doctors and ministers of religion. In many such cases a judicial admonition may be adequate if judicial comment is required at all: but when the witness refuses to answer questions because he wants to deny the court evidence which is important, the position is very different."

13-39 The alleged contemnor was a clerk employed by a firm of solicitors attending a trial in court two at St. Albans Crown Court. Being bored by the case he decided to release laughing gas into the court through a ventilation duct. To that end he reconnoitred the roof of the building. The next morning he placed a briefcase containing a cylinder of the gas in court one, preparatory to taking it on the roof and releasing it in the duct. He was arrested for theft of the gas and brought before a High Court judge in court one. That judge heard evidence from the police and the alleged contemnor admitted the facts set out. The judge remanded him in custody and next day sentenced him to six months' imprisonment.

---

[79] *Ex p. HTV Cymru (Wales) Ltd* [2002] E.M.L.R. 184. The judge could, as it happens, in his capacity as a High Court judge have granted an injunction to restrain a contempt in any event.
[80] *Balogh v St. Albans Crown Court* [1975] 1 Q.B. 73 at 93.

The Court of Appeal set aside the sentence (1) because the facts proved did not constitute the *actus reus* of contempt[81] and (2) because the judge ought not in any event to have proceeded to commit of his own motion. The Court took the view that upon the facts reported to him the judge had jurisdiction to enquire into the matter.[82] But there were differing views about exactly how far the jurisdiction of the court extended. Lord Denning M.R. confirmed the power of the court to commit instantly of its own motion where the contempt was committed in the face of the court. Moreover, he defined the phrase "in the face of the court" to include not only contempts which the judge actually witnessed but also contempts within the precincts of the court, and even outside court, which related to proceedings pending before him. Stephenson L.J. preferred to avoid basing the jurisdiction on the words "in the face of the court" and treated it as covering all contempts relating to a case actually proceeding or imminent.[83] Lawton L.J. stated[84] simply that, once there were reasonable grounds for thinking that a contempt of court had been committed, no matter where, the judge had jurisdiction to deal with it summarily.

There is clearly a degree of conflict between competing public interests. On the one hand, an immediate remedy needs to be available to maintain the authority of the court and to prevent or deter disruption of proceedings; while, on the other, an immediate reaction by the very judge whose court has been disturbed, and whose authority may have been undermined, can give rise to concerns as to impartiality. Even a panel of the House of the Lords was prepared on one occasion to recuse itself because of the possible appearance of bias, and to have the matter dealt with instead by a differently constituted committee.[85] Rather than a circuit judge in the Crown Court proceeding summarily for contempt, in respect of proceedings before him, it has been suggested that it might be preferable for a High Court judge sitting in the same building to deal with the matter.[86] The Phillimore Committee, however, came to the conclusion for various reasons[87] that there was no need to require the judge concerned to refer the matter to another judge. In particular, they thought the threat of immediate punishment especially valuable as a deterrent.[88]

Some caution about this manner of proceeding is perhaps required in the light of Art.6 of the European Convention and the enactment of the Human Rights Act

---

[81] para.11–16.
[82] [1975] 1 Q.B. 73, at 85 and 92.
[83] *ibid.* at 89.
[84] *ibid.* at 92.
[85] *Re Lonrho plc* [1990] 2 A.C. 154.
[86] *Balogh v St. Albans Crown Court* [1975] 1 Q.B. 73 at 90. It is perhaps confusing to refer to the status of the particular judge. It would be purely fortuitous if a High Court judge happened to be available in the same building. In any event, the matter concerned the jurisdiction of the Crown Court in which the majority would be circuit judges. If the point is essentially one of avoiding bias, this could be achieved by referring the case to another judge of equal status.
[87] (1974) Cmnd 5794 at paras 30 and 31.
[88] para.30.

13-42 1998.[89] By way of analogy, in the Ontario decision of *R. v Martin*[90] it was held to conflict with s.11 of the Charter of Rights and Freedoms for a judge to conduct summary contempt proceedings against a woman who was screaming abuse at him while he was considering the appropriate sentence following her conviction for fraud. There was held to be a reasonable apprehension of bias in those circumstances. Yet, in Alberta, it was held[91] that the shouting of an obscene remark by a defendant, as he was being taken out of court, was an exceptional circumstance justifying (under s.1 of the Charter) an *instanter* disposal for the sake of maintaining good order. A distinction should perhaps be drawn, however, between the need to *remove* such a troublemaker for the sake of good order (which power undoubtedly must be available to the court) and any supposed necessity for that offence to be *tried* summarily by the same judge, rather than at leisure after time for reflection.

I. Inferior tribunals: the Divisional Court's role

13-43 The Divisional Court of the Queen's Bench Division is heir to the old Court of Queen's Bench, which had power to punish contempts of certain inferior courts.[92] CPR Sch.1, Ord.52.1(2)(a)(iii) provides that only the Divisional Court may commit for contempts connected with proceedings in an inferior court. There are, in addition, a number of statutory provisions considered below[93] which confer jurisdiction on certain inferior tribunals (for example coroners, magistrates, and county courts) to deal with conduct which would fall within the notion of contempt.

J. What is an "inferior court"?

13-44 The term "inferior court" has been considered by the House of Lords in *Att-Gen v BBC*.[94] It was also before their Lordships in *P v Liverpool Daily Post and Echo Newspapers plc*,[95] but the case did not turn upon this general issue so much as upon the specific considerations applying to mental health review tribunals.[96] Indeed the speech of Lord Bridge did not even refer to the earlier case, although

---

[89] See D. Feldman, *Civil Liberties in England and Wales* (2nd ed., 2002), p.963 where it is said that "... the summary procedure ... seems to contravene both the right to be tried by an independent and impartial tribunal ... and the right to have adequate time and facilities for the preparation of a defence and the right to legal assistance". For consideration of these criticisms, see paras 10–36 *et seq*. See now the decision of the European Court of Human Rights in *Kyprianou v Cyprus* App. No.73797/01, January 27, 2004.
[90] (1985) 19 C.C.C. (3d) 248. See also *R. v K* (1997) 129 D.L.R. (4th) 500.
[91] *Winter* (1986) Alberta L.R. (2d) 393, 72 A.R. 164 (*sub nom. Winter v R.*) 53 C.R. (3d) 372, CA.
[92] *R. v Brownell* (1834) 1 Ad. & E. 598, 110 E.R. 1335; *R. v Davies* [1906] 1 K.B. 32; *R. v Judge Ex p. Isle of Ely Justices* [1931] 2 K.B. 442; *R. v Editor, Printer and Publishers of Daily Herald Ex p. Bishop of Norwich* [1932] 2 K.B. 402; *R. v Edwards* (1933) 49 T.L.R. 383; *R. v Evening Standard Co Ltd* [1954] 1 Q.B. 578.
[93] Part III of this chapter.
[94] [1981] A.C. 303. For an extended discussion, see N.V. Lowe and H.F. Rawlings, "Tribunals and the laws protecting the administration of justice" [1982] P.L. 418.
[95] [1991] 2 A.C. 370.
[96] Discussed more fully at paras 13–66 *et seq*.

it was cited. It is still necessary, therefore, to focus primarily upon the *BBC* case for general guidance.

Their Lordships did not set out to provide an exhaustive test. They were plainly conscious that difficult questions of public policy arise in holding the balance between freedom of expression on the one hand and the need, on the other, to protect court proceedings from any unwarranted public discussion of the issues.[97] They were also concerned not to trespass on the field of the legislature.[98] They rejected the detailed approach of Eveleigh L.J. in the Court of Appeal where he set out what he considered to be six hallmarks of a court.[99] Lord Edmund-Davies having looked at various possible defining characteristics, put forward on behalf of the Attorney-General, concluded[1]:

"At the end of the day it has unfortunately to be said that there emerges no sure guide, no unmistakable hallmark by which a 'court' or 'inferior court' may unerringly be identified. It is largely a matter of impression."

During the course of debate on the Contempt of Court Bill various attempts were made to draw up a list of tribunals to which the Divisional Court's jurisdiction would be expressly attached, Lord Hailsham L.C. dismissively referring to "Ko-Ko's little list." Lord Fraser drew up such a list in a proposed amendment,[2] but it was rejected. At one time a clause was proposed[3] which extended the supervisory jurisdiction of the High Court to:

"... the proceedings of all inferior courts, tribunals and bodies (however described and wherever established) which are constituted by law and exercise any part of the judicial power of the State."

In the event that clause was withdrawn by the Attorney-General on June 18, 1981, for the reason that he too felt unable to draw up a list of relevant tribunals. There remained the definition of a court in s.19 as a tribunal or body "exercising the judicial power of the state". This definition means that strict liability contempt can only be committed in relation to a court as so defined.[4] More generally, however, in determining the extent of the Divisional Court's jurisdiction, it is necessary to have regard to the speeches in *Att-Gen v BBC*.[5]

K. *Att-Gen v BBC*

In that case a religious sect called the Exclusive Brethren applied for exemption from rating of their meeting rooms at Andover on the ground that they were a

---

[97] [1981] A.C. 303: see, *e.g.* Viscount Dilhorne at 339; Lord Salmon at 340–3; Lord Edmund-Davies at 345.
[98] *ibid.* at 339, Viscount Dilhorne; at 353, Lord Edmund-Davies; at 362, Lord Scarman.
[99] [1981] A.C. at 316. Eveleigh L.J. considered that the particular tribunal in question, a local valuation court, possessed all of his six attributes, but nonetheless the House of Lords unanimously took the view it was not "an inferior court."
[1] *ibid.* at 351.
[2] *Hansard*, H.L., Vol. 417, (5th series) col. 163, February 9, 1981.
[3] Clause 7.
[4] See para.4–17.
[5] [1981] A.C. 303.

place of public religious worship for the purposes of s.39 of the General Rate Act 1967. The local authority and valuation officer lodged objections. Before the hearing the BBC proposed to broadcast a television programme strongly critical of the sect and alleging that they were not entitled to relief because their meetings were not open to the public. The valuation court was convened under s.88(1) of the General Rate Act 1967 to hear and determine appeals against objections to proposals for the alteration of valuation lists.

13–49   The Divisional Court held that the valuation court was a court subject to the law of contempt and within its own supervisory jurisdiction. The BBC then undertook not to broadcast the programme until after a given date. By that date it had become clear that there would in fact be no hearing in the valuation court. The Court of Appeal nevertheless heard an appeal and ruled, by a majority (Eveleigh L.J. and Sir Stanley Rees), that the valuation court was subject to the law of contempt. The House of Lords unanimously reversed that decision. In the circumstances, the House was ruling, quite exceptionally, on what had become a hypothetical issue.

13–50   Their Lordships were quite clear that courts which had been long established as part of the judicial system (such as county courts, magistrates' courts, courts-martial[6] and consistory courts) were subject to the law of contempt and the protection of the Divisional Court. Beyond that, however, their Lordships laid down no universal test which is easy of application for those, such as journalists, who are confronted with the question in practical terms. They expressly attempted, however, to give guidance and to diminish to some extent the area of uncertainty. It emerges, for example, that there are certain characteristics or criteria which their Lordships did *not* regard as determinative; in a phrase of Lord Edmund-Davies, these are the "non-tests".

The "non-tests"

13–51   In the first place, the extent of the jurisdiction did not depend upon the wording of the former RSC Ord.52, r.1.[7] That merely provided the necessary machinery. It "has nothing to do with circumscribing or defining the courts in respect of which contempt proceedings may be properly instituted."[8]

13–52   Secondly, the fact that a tribunal is called a "court" does not mean that it is necessarily subject to the contempt jurisdiction.[9] In *Att-Gen v BBC* itself, a valuation court was held *not* to be so subject.

---

[6] See, *e.g. R. v Gunn Ex p. Att-Gen* [1954] Crim. L.R. 53 (a case concerning media pressure intended to influence the decision of the confirming officer). "It was of the highest importance to the administration of justice that papers should not comment on a case while it was still *sub judice* and that was why the court would exercise its jurisdiction in the present case".

[7] See now CPR Sch.1, Ord.52.1.

[8] [1981] A.C. 303 at 347, Lord Edmund-Davies.

[9] *ibid.*, *per* Viscount Dilhorne at 339; Lord Edmund-Davies at 348; Lord Fraser at 353 and Lord Scarman at 358. The "valuation court" was so named in s.44(1) of the Local Government Act 1948; it has been replaced by a "valuation tribunal": Local Government Finance Act 1992, s.136 and Sch.11.

Thirdly, the fact that the Divisional Court traditionally could protect an inferior court or tribunal by means of the prerogative writs or orders did not necessarily make it subject to the contempt jurisdiction.[10] This is not surprising in view of the extensive and increasing reach of judicial review in modern times.

Fourthly, it is not decisive that the court acts, or is obliged to act, in a judicial or quasi-judicial manner[11]:

> "If the body under review is established for a purely legislative or administrative purpose, it is part of the legislative or administrative system of the state, even though it has to perform duties which are judicial in character."

It is the *purpose* of the tribunal that is critical. Thus the valuation court was not subject to the contempt jurisdiction, even though it had to approach its task judicially, because it was established for an administrative purpose. Hence neither the constitution of a tribunal (*e.g.* whether it has a legally qualified chairman) nor its procedures (*e.g.* whether it receives evidence on oath) would be sufficient to bring it within the contempt jurisdiction.

Fifthly, it is not decisive that the court reaches a final decision; nor conversely that it is subject to appeal to a court of law; nor yet that matters are referred to it by another body.[12]

According to Lord Scarman for an inferior court to be subject to the law of contempt, and to the protection of the Divisional Court, it must be[13]:

> " . . . a body established by law to exercise, either generally or subject to defined limits, the judicial power of the state. In this context judicial power is to be contrasted with legislative and executive (i.e. administrative) power."

Viscount Dilhorne similarly distinguished between "courts of law which form part of the judicial system of the country on the one hand and courts which are constituted to resolve problems which arise in the course of administration of the government of this country."[14]

These general statements, while giving some guidance, do not purport to define what is "judicial" and what is "administrative." Lord Scarman expressed his conclusion on a valuation court[15]:

> "At the end of the day its one power is to correct a valuation list. It imposes no tax, no liability on the citizen to pay any money or do any act. It has an important role in the

---

[10] *ibid., per* Lord Fraser at 352–353.
[11] *ibid., per* Lord Scarman at 359. See also *P v Liverpool Daily Post and Echo Newspapers plc* [1991] 2 A.C. 370 at 380F–H, Lord Donaldson M.R.
[12] Lord Scarman, *ibid.*, at 359. See also *R. v Electricity Commissioners Ex p. London Electricity Joint Committee Co (1920) Ltd* [1924] 1 K.B. 171; *Shell Co of Australia Ltd v Federal Commissioner of Taxation* [1931] A.C. 275 at 295–7, PC.
[13] [1981] A.C. 303 at 359. See also Lord Fraser at 353.
[14] *ibid.* at 339–40.
[15] *ibid.* at 360.

13–57 machinery for determining a rate, and must act judicially; but it does not determine the amount of the rate or impose liability to pay it."

Accordingly, the underlying purpose of the valuation court was, in his view, administrative.

13–58 Similarly, Viscount Dilhorne said[16]:

"It has to resolve disputes as to the valuation of hereditaments. While its decisions will affect an occupier's liability for rates, it does not determine his liability. It is just part of the process of rating. It has to act judicially but that does not make it a court of law."

As he expressly recognised, "this conclusion still leaves an area of uncertainty"; there may well be tribunals in respect of which the matter will have to be argued, in order to determine whether they can be characterised as part of the judicial system.

13–59 In one sense, no court imposes liability. It is the law, statutory or otherwise, which imposes a liability. The court interprets or applies the law. In the Exclusive Brethren case the "court" would not merely have had power to decide whether the rateable value of premises should be lowered or raised, but effectively whether the premises under consideration were liable to rating at all. Such a decision would have depended upon whether a particular building in Andover was a "place of public religious worship" within the terms of s.39 of the 1967 Act. Liability may often depend, both in civil and criminal law, upon a similar matter of the construction or application of a statute. That is the type of decision which is frequently made by courts of law. It may have been an unusual decision for this type of tribunal to make. It would more ordinarily be adjusting an assessment already made by a valuation officer, but nevertheless that was the nature of the decision which might (according to the Attorney-General) have been prejudiced by the broadcast.

13–60 This leaves the difficult task of ascertaining which tribunals fall on either side of the line dividing judicial and administrative functions. While in some cases the distinction has been clearly drawn,[17] It is not feasible to provide a clear answer in all cases because the test provided is insufficiently defined. One possible view is that all tribunals determining matters connected with the collection of taxes are to be classified as administrative in nature. This would seem to accord with Lord Scarman's view that Commissioners of Income Tax carried out an administrative

---

[16] *ibid.* at 340.
[17] For example, magistrates when exercising their historic licensing power were recognised as acting in an administrative capacity, even though such applications and any objections would be heard in public, and normally in the same room in which criminal cases are heard: see, *e.g.* Betting, Gaming and Lotteries Act 1963, and the Gaming Act 1968, and *R. v Redditch Justices* (1885) 2 T.L.R. 193. The Licensing Act 2003 introduces an integrated scheme for the supply of alcohol, the provision of various forms of entertainment (such as music and dancing) and the provision of late-night refreshment. Local authorities are now required to issue authorisation in accordance with specified licensing objectives.

function.[18] If correct, it would perhaps apply equally to Value Added Tax and Duties Tribunals.[19]

With such bodies as these a point will arise where the tribunal in question is not deciding merely the amount of a tax assessment, but whether in fact a citizen is liable to the tax at all. Social Security Commissioners also determine very similar questions. Similarly, the Lands Tribunal which hears appeals from valuation courts is habitually making the kind of decisions which a court makes. Such a tribunal might well be regarded as a court.

13–61

L. Employment tribunals[20]

The proceedings of employment tribunals sometimes attract the interest of popular newspapers,[21] and journalists have in the past been left in considerable doubt as to whether the law of contempt applies to them.[22] Such tribunals regularly decide, for example, whether one citizen was entitled to dismiss another from employment and, if not, the proper compensation. Although deriving entirely from statute, their jurisdiction is closely analogous in kind to that of the courts in cases of wrongful dismissal.

13–62

The matter of contempt jurisdiction was considered by the Divisional Court in *Peach Grey and Co v Sommers*[23] where it was held that such a tribunal was indeed a court, within s.19 of the Contempt of Court Act 1981, discharging judicial rather than administrative functions.[24] The case involved allegations of intentional interference with witnesses in connection with proceedings pending before an industrial tribunal, and the Divisional Court, accepting jurisdiction to deal with the matter, made an order for committal.

13–63

A number of reasons were given by Rose L.J. in support of this conclusion, some of which would have undoubtedly been classified by Lord Edmund-Davies as "non-tests"[25]:

13–64

---

[18] [1981] A.C. at 360.
[19] Now called "VAT and duties tribunals", as they also have jurisdiction over customs and excise duties.
[20] Formerly known as "industrial tribunals". See now the Employment Rights (Dispute Resolution) Act 1998, s.1(1).
[21] Tribunals are given powers to restrict the reporting of their procedures under the Employment Tribunals Act 1996, in cases involving "sexual misconduct" (s.11), and in disability cases (s.12). See para.8–141.
[22] See E. Ellis and John Miller, "The Victimisation of Anti-Discrimination Complainants—Is it Contempt of Court?" [1993] P.L. 80, whose principal theme was that industrial tribunals should be regarded as "courts" for these purposes.
[23] [1995] 2 All E.R. 513 at 519–21, Rose L.J. and Tuckey J.
[24] Reference was made to *Att-Gen v BBC* [1981] A.C. 303, and in particular to the speeches of Viscount Dilhorne at 339, Lord Edmund-Davies at 351 and Lord Scarman at 360. It has also been held, in a reported decision of an employment tribunal, that such tribunals fall within the term "any court" within the meaning of s.42(1A)(b) of the Supreme Court Act 1981. Accordingly, a "vexatious litigant" could not pursue proceedings before the tribunal without permission of the High Court: *Vidler v Unison* [1999] I.C.R. 746.
[25] See paras 13–51 *et seq.*

13–64

(i) By virtue of the relevant legislation[26] such a tribunal had many of the characteristics recognised in the authorities as being those of a court of law.

(ii) It was established by Parliament; had a legally qualified chairman, appointed by the Lord Chancellor, and other members drawn from panels compiled by the Secretary of State for Employment.

(iii) It sat in public, and decided cases affecting the rights of citizens.

(iv) It had the power to compel attendance of witnesses, to administer oaths, to control the parties' pleadings, by striking out, and to order disclosure of documents.

(v) There was a right to legal representation (although rights of audience were not limited to lawyers).

(vi) It had rules of procedure relating to the "calling and questioning of witnesses and addresses on behalf of the parties".

(vii) It could award costs.

(viii) It was required to give reasons for its decisions.

Apart from these considerations, however, the court considered such tribunals to qualify as courts by each of the tests propounded in *Att-Gen v BBC* by the House of Lords.

13–65 In *Bennett v London Borough of Southwark*,[27] Ward and Sedley L.JJ. both commented that the case gave rise to the need for consideration by the legislature as to whether there should be a power conferred on such tribunals to exercise discipline over those permitted to appear before them (including unqualified advocates) in respect of behaviour jeopardising the proper functioning of "this important segment of our system of justice". In that case the tribunal had exercised the discretion to strike out the proceedings[28]—a course held to have been disproportionate in the particular circumstances. It was said by Sedley L.J. not to be satisfactory that the only available sanction was to wait until the representative or advocate crossed that high threshold.

M. Mental health review tribunals

13–66 Mental health review tribunals are empowered to decide matters relating to the liberty of the subject. It would obviously be difficult to classify this as an

---

[26] Employment Protection (Consolidation) Act 1978, ss.128 and 131, Sch.9; Reg.5 of Sch.1 to the Industrial Tribunals (Constitution and Rules of Procedure) Regulations 1993, SI 1993/2687. See now the Employment Tribunals Act 1996, as amended by the Employment Rights Dispute (Resolution) Act 1998. See now the Employment Tribunals (Constitution and Rules of Procedure) Regulations 2004.

[27] [2002] EWCA Civ 223, [2002] I.C.R. 881.

[28] Under r.13(2)(e) of the Employment Tribunals Rules of Procedure 1993. See also *Neckles v Yorkshire Rider Ltd (t/a) First Huddersfield* [2002] All E.R. (D) 375 where such a proceedings were struck out under r.15(2)(d) of the Rules of Procedure 2001 and the order was upheld by the EAT. There had been "an obdurate refusal to explain to the court" on the part of the applicant and his representative how a tape-recording had come to be made, contrary to s.9 of the Contempt of Court Act 1981, of part of the tribunal's proceedings.

administrative activity. In *P v Liverpool Daily Post and Echo Newspapers plc*,[29] it was held by the House of Lords that such a tribunal was "plainly" a court to which the law of contempt applied, and that it fell within the definition of "court" contained in s.19 of the Contempt of Court Act 1981.[30] Yet the matter had to be litigated as far as their Lordships' House to be resolved and, in the process, the earlier decision of the Divisional Court in *Att-Gen v Associated Newspaper Group plc*[31] was overruled. It is perhaps an illustration of how unfortunate it was that the opportunity was not taken by Parliament to include a definitive list of tribunals in a schedule to the 1981 Act, so as to avoid this uncertainty and unnecessary expenditure.

Lord Bridge put the decision on two grounds[32]; namely, (i) that it had clearly been Parliament's intention, as expressed in the Administration of Justice Act 1960, s.12(1)(b),[33] that the law of contempt should apply to such tribunals and that they should be regarded as courts; (ii) that for the reasons advanced in the Court of Appeal by Lord Donaldson M.R.[34] such a tribunal fell within the definition of "court" contained in s.19 of the Contempt of Court Act 1981.[35]

13–67

It is to be noted, however, that in the course of setting out his reasoning Lord Donaldson M.R. had stated unequivocally (notwithstanding the terms of s.12 of the 1960 Act) that, prior to the passing of the Mental Health Act 1983, "mental health review tribunals quite clearly did *not* exercise the judicial power of the state"[36] (emphasis added). Their function had been to make recommendations which the executive branch of government had been free to accept or reject. That position was changed by the terms of the 1983 Act, which conferred upon these tribunals the power and the duty of applying statutory criteria and, on the basis of their findings, ordering or refusing to order the release of restricted patients.[37]

13–68

At least the position is now clear in relation to mental health review tribunals; on the other hand, the process of reasoning by which this clarity was achieved is itself somewhat opaque. It is difficult to see how Lord Donaldson M.R. reconciled his view that such tribunals had not been within the judicial system prior to 1983 with his other conclusion, based on s.12 of the 1960 Act, that

13–69

---

[29] [1991] 2 A.C. 370. See now *R. (Von Brandenburg) v East London and the City NHS Trust* [2003] UKHL 58, [2004] 2 A.C. 280 at [8].
[30] [1991] 2 A.C. 370 at 417F–G, Lord Bridge, with whom the other members of the panel expressed agreement.
[31] [1989] 1 W.L.R. 322.
[32] [1991] 2 A.C. at 417.
[33] Discussed at paras 8–97 *et seq.*
[34] [1991] 2 A.C. 370 at 380–1. See also *R. (on the application of Mersey Care Trust) v Mental Health Review Tribunal* [2004] EWHC 1749 (Admin), [2005] 1 W.L.R. 2469, [2005] 2 All E.R. 820 at [11].
[35] See para.13–3.
[36] This passage is to be contrasted with the view of Glidewell L.J. (at 389F–G), who took the same view as Lord Bridge that such tribunals had indeed been courts since their creation in 1959.
[37] This change was forced upon Parliament by the decision of the European Court of Human Rights in *X v United Kingdom* (1981) 4 E.H.R.R. 188, whereby the United Kingdom was called upon to honour the terms of Art.5(4) of the Convention. See Farquharson L.J. in *P v Liverpool Daily Post and Echo Newspapers plc* [1991] 2 A.C. at 391, CA.

13–69   nonetheless the law of contempt had applied to them. Presumably, it could be argued that, had it not been for s.12, they would have been *outside* the protection of the law of contempt; but surely Parliament's intention to apply the law of contempt would have indicated a similar desire for the tribunals to be treated as courts from the enactment of the 1960 statute.

N. The remaining uncertainty as to tribunals

13–70   The decision on any particular court or tribunal may therefore rest in the end on "legal policy" considerations,[38] such as whether its proceedings require the protection of the law of contempt. That will depend in turn upon balancing a number of factors, such as the extent to which citizens may be adversely or favourably affected by decisions of the tribunal; whether the tribunal is constituted in a manner which particularly requires protection; and whether the type of decision it makes is susceptible to outside pressure or lobbying.

13–71   Lord Salmon expressed the clear view, as a matter of public policy, that he would not extend the jurisdiction beyond those courts already clearly protected by it[39]:

> "There is today a plethora of such tribunals which may well resemble the old 'inferior courts.' In my view, it does not by any means follow that the modern inferior courts need the umbrella of contempt of court or that they come under it. Indeed, in my opinion, public policy requires that most of the principles relating to contempt of court which have for ages necessarily applied to the long-established inferior courts such as county courts, magistrates' courts, courts martial, coroners' courts and consistory courts shall not apply to valuation courts and the host of other modern tribunals which may be regarded as inferior courts; otherwise the scope of contempt of court would be unnecessarily extended and accordingly freedom of speech and freedom of the press would be unnecessarily contracted."

13–72   It is to be observed, however, that Lord Salmon's speech was less analytical than the others, and that he was prepared to base his decision on these general policy considerations. He appears also to have differed from his brethren in two respects. First, he did not highlight the distinction between those tribunals which serve an administrative purpose and those which exercise the judicial power of the state, as representing the true test for the application of the law of contempt. Secondly, he chose expressly to leave open the question whether "the host of modern inferior courts and tribunals" might be protected by the Queen's Bench Divisional Court if they were prevented by obstruction, while sitting, from performing their duties.[40]

13–73   It is submitted that this is not consistent with the approach of the majority, since they held that the law of contempt had no application (presumably for any purpose) to courts or tribunals which discharge an administrative function and do not form part of the judicial system. Although Lord Scarman's approach was

---

[38] See the words of Lord Scarman cited at para.13–73.
[39] [1981] A.C. 303 at 342.
[40] *ibid.* at 344.

different in these respects, he concluded his speech in terms which were very close in spirit to that of Lord Salmon[41]:

> "Neither the meagre authorities available in the books nor the historic origins of contempt of Court require the House to extend the doctrine to administrative courts and tribunals. Legal policy in today's world would be better served, in my judgment, if we refused so to extend it. If Parliament wishes to extend the doctrine to a specific institution which it establishes, it must say so explicitly in its enactment; as it has done on occasion, *e.g.* Tribunals of Inquiry (Evidence) Act 1921.[42] I would not think it desirable to extend the doctrine, which is unknown, and not apparently needed, in most civilized legal systems, beyond its historical scope, namely the proceedings of courts of judicature. If we are to make the extension, we have to ask ourselves, if the United Kingdom is to comply with its international obligations, whether the extension is necessary in our democratic society. Is there a 'pressing social need' for extension?"

Despite that invitation, Parliament failed to define the limits. It may still be arguable that no courts or tribunals, other than those traditionally recognised as being subject to the jurisdiction, are within the bounds of contempt. At any rate, a complainant who seeks to show that any given tribunal is so protected will have to satisfy the court that it is part of the judicial system, and he is likely to find a more restrictive approach being applied than that adopted by the lower courts in the Exclusive Brethren case. **13–74**

In this respect the decision of the House of Lords was described by the Privy Council as having "conclusive authority" in *Badry v DPP*[43]: **13–75**

> "In their Lordships' view it is plainly established by this authority that, in the absence of statutory provision to the contrary, the law of contempt of court applies by definition only to courts of justice properly so called and to the judges of such courts of justice."

Following these principles, the Court of Appeal held in *GMC v BBC*[44] that the General Medical Council was *not* a body which exercised the judicial power of the state. This litigation could no doubt have been avoided if clear statutory provision had been made. The background was that the GMC had sought an injunction to restrain the broadcast of a programme containing controversial interviews and comment relating to disciplinary proceedings being heard by its professional conduct committee. It was accepted that this body had to adjudicate in a formal and judicial manner on serious issues, which were not only of public importance but which might also have had the gravest effect on the individuals **13–76**

---

[41] *ibid.* at 362.
[42] See para.13–77. See the report of the *Royal Commission on Tribunals of Inquiry*, Cmnd. 3121 (1966), Ch. XIII and the *Report of the Interdepartmental Committee on the Law of Contempt as it affects Tribunals of Inquiry*, which was also chaired by Salmon L.J., Cmnd. 4078 (1969), ch.7. Both endorsed the value of the power conferred by s.1(2)(c) of the 1921 Act, which was repealed in its entirely with effect from June 2005 by the Inquiries Act of that year. See paras 4–22 *et seq.*
[43] [1983] 2 A.C. 297 at 307.
[44] [1998] 3 All E.R. 426. It was noted in passing that in an unreported decision of the Court of Appeal (*Gee v BBC*, June 8, 1984) Sir John Donaldson M.R. had inclined to the view without deciding the point that the GMC did fall within the definition of s.19 of the 1981 Act. This seems to have been a somewhat hurried hearing without investigation of the authorities.

13–76 CHAPTER 13—JURISDICTION

concerned. While it was reasonable to describe this function as "exercising a sort of judicial power", nevertheless it was not the judicial power of the state that was being exercised.

O. Jurisdiction conferred on the Queen's Bench Division by statute

13–77 In some instances,[45] where conduct would constitute contempt if related to a court of law which has the power to commit for contempt, then the matter may be certified to the Queen's Bench Division.[46] For example, by s.20 of the Contempt of Court Act 1981:

> "(1) In relation to any tribunal to which the Tribunals of Inquiry (Evidence) Act 1921 applies, and the proceedings of such a tribunal, the provisions of this Act (except subsection (3) of s.9)[47] apply as they apply in relation to courts and legal proceedings; and references to the course of justice or the administration of justice in legal proceedings shall be construed accordingly.
>
> (2) The proceedings of a tribunal established under the said Act shall be treated as active within the meaning of s.2 from the time when the tribunal is appointed until its report is presented to Parliament."

13–78 This provision was deemed necessary because "A tribunal of inquiry is not a court and proceedings before it are not judicial proceedings . . . ".[48] Thus such a body would not be protected, as exercising the judicial power of the state, unless catered for specifically. At the time of writing, s.20 had not been repealed, curiously, despite the fact that with effect from June 2005, the 1921 Act had been repealed in its entirety. The provisions in s.36 of the Inquiries Act 2005 do not

---

[45] See the Army Act 1955, s.101; Air Force Act 1955, s.101; Naval Discipline Act 1957, s.65; Parliamentary Commissioner Act 1967, ss.7 and 9(1); Local Government Act 1974, s.26 and 29(8) (which provides that if a person obstructs a Local Commissioner or any assisting officer in the performance of his functions, or is guilty of any act or omission in relation to an investigation which, if that investigation were a proceeding in the High Court would constitute contempt of court, the Local Commissioner may certify the offence to the High Court. The latter may deal with him as if he had committed the like offence in relation to the High Court); Companies Act 1985, s.436 (obstruction of D.T.I. inspectors treated as contempt); Insolvency Act 1986, ss.134(1) (which provides that a person who, without reasonable excuse, fails at any time to attend his public examination, is guilty of contempt of court and liable to be punished accordingly), and s.290(5) (rendering a bankrupt liable to punishment for contempt if he fails without reasonable excuse to attend his public examination); Courts and Legal Services Act 1990, s.25 (like powers are conferred upon the Legal Services Ombudsman to those of the High Court, in respect of attendance and examination of witnesses and the production of documents, and misconduct may be certified to the court); Friendly Societies Act 1992, s.67(6) (which provides that if an officer, employee or agent of a body under investigation by an inspector refuses to co-operate in specified ways with the investigation, the inspectors may certify the refusal to the High Court, which may punish the offender in like manner as if he had been guilty of contempt of court); Charities Act 1993, s.88 (this provides that where a person disobeys an order of the Charity Commissioners, he may on application of the Commissioners to the High Court be dealt with as for disobedience to an order of the High Court); this must be to a single judge of the Chancery Division instead of to the High Court; Building Societies Act 1997, s.14(13) (this provides for certifying to the High Court any contravention by a building society of a prohibition order).
[46] CPR Sch.1, Ord.52.1(4).
[47] Relating to forfeiture of tape recorders. See para.10–190.
[48] *per* Lord Hailsham, *Hansard*, H.L. Vol. 416, col. 389. See *Att-Gen v Mulholland* [1963] 2 Q.B. 477; *Att-Gen v Clough* [1963] 1 Q.B. 773, which were examples of misconduct alleged in relation to a Tribunal of Inquiry under the 1921 Act.

refer expressly to "contempt", but they do provide for enforcement by the High Court or Court of Session as if particular conduct had arisen in proceedings before the court. Following certification, therefore, by the chairman of the relevant inquiry, in respect of the relevant failure or breach,[49] it would appear that the contempt sanction is available.

III. OTHER COURTS OF RECORD

A. The general principle

Inferior courts of record were traditionally regarded as having inherent jurisdiction only to deal with contempts committed in the face of the court.[50] In addition some of them have statutory powers to deal with conduct falling outside that narrow definition.[51] 13–79

B. County Courts

1. Introduction

The county court is by statute a court of record.[52] Hence judges of that court have long been recognised as having inherent jurisdiction to deal with contempts in the face of the court.[53] There is also a limited statutory jurisdiction to deal with contemnors under ss.14, 92 and 118–121 of the 1984 Act. Except in these cases, however, the county court has no jurisdiction to deal with criminal contempt[54]; it is clear that the jurisdiction would not extend to contempts committed outside the defined circumstances, so as to enable a county court judge, for example, to commit a journalist in respect of media publication concerning proceedings in the court. 13–80

Such matters would have been regarded traditionally as falling exclusively within the jurisdiction of the Divisional Court to protect the proceedings of inferior tribunals.[55] In *R. v Edwards Ex p. Welsh Church Temporalities Commissioners*,[56] for example, it was confirmed that the King's Bench Division had 13–81

---

[49] See the discussion at paras 4–22 *et seq.*
[50] See, *e.g. Beecher's Case* (1608) 8 Co. Rep. 58a at 61a, 75 E.R. 559 at 567; *R. v Lefroy* (1873) L.R. 8 Q.B. 134. See also the Ontario decision to similar effect in *R. v Fields* (1987) Can. Curr. Law 2193. See further paras 10–11 *et seq.*
[51] The magistrates' courts are given such powers by the Contempt of Court Act 1981, s.12, considered paras 10–113 *et seq.* See also County Courts Act 1984, ss.14, 92 and 118, set out at paras 13–84, 13–88 and 13–90 respectively. As to the appropriateness or otherwise of using the term "inferior" with regard to the county court jurisdiction, see the remarks of Lord Woolf in *Manchester City Council v McCann* [1999] Q.B. 1214 at 1223–4, summarised at para.13–7.
[52] Currently by virtue of s.1(2) of the County Courts Act 1984.
[53] *Brompton County Court Judge* [1893] 2 Q.B. 195. For a fuller consideration of contempt in the face of the court, see ch.10.
[54] *R. v Lefroy* (1873) L.R. 8 Q.B. 134; *Bush v Green* [1985] 1 W.L.R. 1143, CA; *Bloomsbury County Court Judge Ex p. Brady, The Times*, December 16, 1987, CA. For the powers to deal with civil contempt where county court orders are breached, see paras 13–92 *et seq.*
[55] para.13–43.
[56] (1933) 49 T.L.R. 383. See also *R. v Davies* [1906] 1 K.B. 32.

13–81 jurisdiction to punish a contempt of a county court, which in that instance consisted in an obstruction of a sale under a distraint levied in pursuance of an order.

13–82 More recently, in *Re de Court*,[57] Sir Richard Scott V.-C. in his then capacity as Head of Civil Justice commented that he too had an inherent power, as well as a duty, to take steps to provide protection for court officials in the county courts in relation to a troublesome litigant suffering from "mental infirmity". He therefore granted an injunction against him sufficiently wide to achieve this objective. This was in relation to a contempt taking the form of a physical assault against the Chancery Clerk of the Lists.

13–83 Where contempt of court in connection with county court proceedings consists neither in contempt in the face nor disobedience of an order, it is punishable only by an order of committal made in the Queen's Bench Division.[58] The case concerned a father who had applied to the county court for a contact order in relation to his three-year-old child. During the hearing the judge, of his own motion, initiated contempt proceedings against the father because he had, as the judge found, been publishing details on a website sufficient to identify volunteers at a contact centre, and the child who was the subject of the contact proceedings. He was held in contempt of court and sentenced to 14 days' imprisonment suspended for six months. The appeal was allowed for lack of jurisdiction.

2. Assaults upon officers

13–84 Under s.14(1) of the 1984 Act:

"If any person assaults an officer of a court while in the execution of his duty, he shall be liable—

(a) on summary conviction, to imprisonment for a term not exceeding *3 months* [51 weeks][59] or to a fine of an amount not exceeding level 5[60] on the standard scale, or both; or
(b) on an order made by the judge in that behalf, to be committed for a specified period not exceeding 3 months to prison or to such a fine as aforesaid, or to be so committed and to such a fine,

and a bailiff of the court may take the offender into custody, with or without warrant, and bring him before the judge."

13–85 A district judge, assistant district judge or deputy district judge has the same powers as a judge.[61] Any such judge may at any time revoke an order committing a person to prison under s.14 and, if he is already in custody, order his

---

[57] [1997] T.L.R. 601 (Lexis).
[58] *Re G (A Child) (Contempt: Committal)* [2003] EWCA Civ 489, [2003] 1 W.L.R. 2051.
[59] The words in italics are prospectively repealed and replaced by the words in square brackets by the Criminal Justice Act 2003, s.280(2), (3), Sch.26, para.33(1) and (2) from a date to be appointed.
[60] Currently up to £5,000: Criminal Justice Act 1982, s.37, as amended. For the procedure, see now CPR Sch.2, cc.34.1 considered further at para.15–77.
[61] Courts and Legal Services Act 1990, s.14(3); s.74.

discharge.[62] In *King v Reed and Slack*,[63] it was held that the Court of Appeal had jurisdiction under s.13(3) of the Administration of Justice Act 1960 to hear an appeal from a district judge but that ordinarily the appropriate course would be to apply "internally" to the county court judge.

It is necessary to prove an assault as the first element of the offence; this hurdle will not be overcome if the respondent is able to avail himself of self-defence.[64] On the other hand, it will not necessarily provide a defence merely to show that the defendant was mistaken as to the status of the relevant officer. It seems clear from *Blackburn v Bowering*[65] that even an honest factual mistake, either as to whether the person assaulted is an officer of the court or as to whether he is acting in the execution of his duty, would not *ipso facto* afford a defence. The general principles of the criminal law would apply to the effect that (1) the prosecutor is required to prove an assault, and (2) *some* honest mistakes (for example, that the defendant is acting in self-defence on the facts as he believes them to be) will negate that element of the offence.[66]

Proceedings under s.14 are in the nature of proceedings for contempt of court, and an appeal lies to the Court of Appeal.[67]

3. *Rescuing seized goods*

A similar regime applies by virtue of the County Courts Act 1984, s.92(1) in the case of a person who rescues or attempts to rescue any goods seized in execution under process of a county court:

> "If any person rescues or attempts to rescue any goods seized in execution under process of a county court, he shall be liable—
>
> (a) on summary conviction, to imprisonment for a term not exceeding *one month* [51 weeks][68] or to a fine of an amount not exceeding level 4[69] on the standard scale, or both; or
> (b) on an order made by the judge in that behalf, to be committed for a specified period not exceeding one month to prison or to a fine of an amount not exceeding level 4 on the standard scale or to be so committed and to such a fine,
>
> and a bailiff of the court may take the offender into custody, with or without warrant, and bring him before the judge."

---

[62] *ibid.*, s.14(2).
[63] [1999] 1 F.L.R. 425.
[64] *Blackburn v Bowering* [1994] 1 W.L.R. 1324, [1994] 3 All E.R. 380, CA.
[65] [1994] 1 W.L.R. 1324, [1994] 3 All E.R. 380.
[66] See generally D. Ormerod, J.C. Smith and B. Hogan, *Criminal Law* (11th ed., 2005), p.540.
[67] Administration of Justice Act 1960, s.13, as amended by the County Courts Act 1984, s.148(1), Sch.2, Pt V, para.25. See also now para.15–88 for the recent decisions explaining this exception to the general requirement in civil proceedings that permission is required for an appeal. See also *Southam v Smout* [1964] 1 Q.B. 308.
[68] The words in italics are prospectively repealed and replaced by the words in square brackets by the Criminal Justice Act 2003, s.280(2), (3), Sch.26, para.33(1) and (3) from a date to be appointed.
[69] Currently up to £2,500: s.37 of the Criminal Justice Act 1982, as amended by the Criminal Justice Act 1991, Sch.4.

13–88

A person who resists or intentionally obstructs a bailiff in executing a possession warrant against a trespasser is guilty of a criminal offence; one who is guilty of such an offence, or whom the bailiff with reasonable cause suspects of being so guilty, may be arrested without warrant.[70] Furthermore, the existence of the specific statutory provisions does not mean that assaults upon officers could not be dealt with as common assault.[71]

13–89 In *Newman v Modern Bookbinders Ltd*,[72] s.92(1) of the County Courts Act 1984 was considered by the Court of Appeal. It was held that a charge of rescue of goods was, for Convention purposes, a criminal charge, and reference was made to *Benham v UK*.[73] It was largely in the light of these considerations that a new Practice Direction was promulgated for the purpose of reconciling the summary jurisdiction to punish for contempt with the demands of the Human Rights Act 1998.[74] It was confirmed in *Mubarak v Mubarak*[75] that the safeguards provided for in that Practice Direction must also apply to proceedings by way of judgment summons, for which most of the relevant rules are set out in the Family Proceedings Rules and CPR Sch.2, cc.28 (so far as the county court is concerned). It was recommended that for the avoidance of doubt a specific Practice Direction should be promulgated by the President to make clear that the provisions do indeed apply both in the High Court and in the county court.[76]

4. *Wilful insults and interruptions*

13–90 Under s.118 of the County Courts Act 1984:

"(1) If any person—
 (a) wilfully[77] insults the judge of a county court, or any juror or witness, or any officer of the court during his sitting or attendance in court, or in going to or returning from the court; or
 (b) wilfully interrupts the proceedings of a county court or otherwise misbehaves in court;

any officer of the court, with or without the assistance of any other person, may, by order of the judge, take the offender into custody and detain him until the rising of the court, and the judge may, if he thinks fit,—
 (i) make an order committing the offender for a specified period not exceeding one month to prison; or
 (ii) impose upon the offender, for every offence, a fine of an amount not exceeding £2,500[78] or may both make such an order and impose such a fine.

---

[70] Criminal Law Act 1977, s.10.
[71] *R. v Holsworthy Justices Ex p. Edwards* [1952] 1 All E.R. 411, applying *R. v Briggs* (1883) 47 J.P. 615.
[72] [2000] 1 W.L.R. 2559, [2000] 2 All E.R. 814, CA.
[73] (1996) 20 E.H.R.R. 293.
[74] See *Mubarak v Mubarak* [2001] 1 F.L.R. 698 at [48].
[75] *ibid.* at [52] and [53].
[76] See now [2001] 1 W.L.R. 1253; see Appendix 5B. The rules were changed to make the procedure Convention compliant as from March 25, 2002: see Civil Procedure (Amendment No.5) Rules 2001 and the changes made, *e.g.* to cc.28.2 (3) and (4) and cc.28.4 and 28.5(2).
[77] For a consideration of "wilfully", see para.10–126.
[78] Amended by the Criminal Justice Act 1991, s.17(3) Sch.4.

(2) The judge may at any time revoke an order committing a person to prison under this section and, if he is already in custody, order his discharge.

(3) A district judge, assistant district judge or deputy district judge shall have the same powers under this section in relation to proceedings before him as a judge".[79]

The notion of "insult" within the meaning of s.118 was considered in *Bell v Tuohy*.[80] It was held by the Court of Appeal that it was impossible to assert, as a general proposition, that a statement by a party in open court that he will not comply with a court order necessarily amounts to a "wilful insult". For example, if a defendant has been ordered to give possession of his home and he responds that he will have to be evicted, this would not amount to any more than a statement of his present intention to do what *would* amount to a contempt—especially where the remark is made in the heat of the moment. On the other hand, where there has been obstruction in the execution of a valid warrant, and the person concerned has been warned of the consequences, if he then "rudely and unambiguously" maintains in court his intention to thwart any attempt to execute the order, such conduct could amount to an "insult" because that would be an open and wilful denial of the court's authority. It is perhaps worth noting that "rudeness" was considered relevant, which may not be surprising in the specific context of what is "insulting", whereas in other forms of contempt, and especially that of "scandalising the court", the *manner* of the respondent's delivery is nowadays unlikely to be considered significant.[81] Although in *Harris v Harris; Att-Gen v Harris*,[82] Munby J. called for a much more robust view to be taken today about colourful, intemperate and offensive language, this was in the context of "permissible criticism" rather than that of "wilful denial of authority".

5. *The enforcement of injunctions in the county court*

Under s.38 of the County Courts Act 1984 every such court may, in any proceedings, make any order which could be made if the proceedings were in the High Court.[83] Thus, when the county court has jurisdiction to grant an injunction,[84] it may enforce the order by a process of contempt, and in particular

---

[79] Sub-s.3 was added by s.74 of the Courts and Legal Services Act 1990.

[80] [2002] 3 All E.R. 975 at [63], [64], [71] and [72].

[81] See, *e.g.* the discussion at paras 5–236 *et seq.* and the observations of Munby J. cited at para.5–237 above.

[82] [2001] 2 F.L.R. 895 at [372].

[83] Save for mandamus, certiorari and prohibition (as the Act still describes them) and for "prescribed relief" under the County Courts Remedies Regulations 1991, SI 1991/1222, as amended by the County Court Remedies (Amendment) Regulations 1995, SI 1995/206. Regulation 2 defines "prescribed relief" by reference to an order requiring a party to admit someone for the purpose of inspecting or removing documents or articles and also to a freezing order.

[84] The jurisdiction to grant injunctive relief used to be more limited than in the case of the High Court, in that it could only be granted if ancillary to a claim for money or for certain other relief: see, *e.g. R. v Cheshire County Court Judge* [1921] 2 K.B. 694; *Byrne v Herbert* [1966] 2 Q.B. 121. See generally *Peart v Stewart* [1983] 2 A.C. 109. These restrictions have now been removed. There remain, however, limitations upon the county court's power to grant an injunction: see previous note. There is no inherent power in the county court to grant an injunction. Its jurisdiction to do so derives purely from statute; see, *e.g. D v D* [1993] 2 F.L.R. 802; *Devon County Council v B* [1997] T.L.R. 6, CA.

by an order for committal. An undertaking given by a party to litigation may be enforced in the same manner as an injunction.[85] The CPR[86] provide expressly that orders in the nature of an injunction may be enforced, on a judge's order, by committal. So too with orders within the competence of the court which, if made in an action or matter in the High Court, could there be enforced by committal. (Until 1979 the appropriate order had been one of attachment.)

13–93 Nevertheless, as in the High Court, it is clear that resort to the contempt jurisdiction should be used sparingly, and "committal and the threat of committal [are] severe remedies in relation to family disputes".[87] If a reasonable alternative to committal is available, such as for example a warrant for possession, it should normally be used.[88] It has, however, been observed by the Court of Appeal that, where a spouse proves especially obdurate, the procedure of seeking a warrant for possession first, and then having to resort to a committal order later, can sometimes prove cumbersome.[89]

13–94 In *Re M (A Minor) (Contempt of Court: Committal of Court's own Motion)*[90] the Court of Appeal confirmed that a county court judge had power by virtue of s.38(1) of the 1984 Act and the former RSC Ord.52, r.5 to initiate committal proceedings of his own motion. However it was emphasised that such a course should be taken only when it was urgent and imperative to act immediately in order to prevent justice being obstructed. There should certainly be an opportunity to pause for reflection and, in cases concerning children, consideration should be given to inviting the Official Solicitor to represent the child or report on the child's position. The Official Solicitor may act in private law proceedings and in proceedings under the inherent jurisdiction of the High Court and r.9.5 of the Family Proceedings Rules, but his involvement should be regarded as exceptional rather than automatic.[91] Also, if the circumstances justify taking such a course, the judge concerned should not both initiate the committal proceedings and thereafter sit in judgment.[92]

6. Witnesses

13–95 Under s.55(1)[93] of the County Courts Act 1984 it is provided that any person who:

---

[85] See, e.g. *Gandolfo v Gandolfo* [1981] Q.B. 359, CA, the discussion on undertakings generally in paras 12–182 et seq.
[86] CPR Sch.2, cc.29.
[87] *Larkman v Lindsell, The Times*, November 30, 1985, CA.
[88] See, e.g. *Danchevsky v Danchevsky* [1975] Fam. 17, and the general discussion at para.12–24.
[89] See, e.g. *Kavanagh v Kavanagh*, CA transcript No.166 of 1978. See the provisions of Pt IV of the Family Law Act 1996. It is also stated in s.58 of the Act that: "The powers of the court in relation to contempt of court arising out of a person's failure to comply with an order under this Part may be exercised by the relevant judicial authority". The "relevant judicial authority" is defined in s.63(1). See generally the article by Judge Platt, "Human Rights and Part IV of the Family Law Act 1996" [2000] Family Law 905.
[90] [1999] Fam. 263.
[91] See *Practice Note, Official Solicitor: Appointment in Family Proceedings* [2001] 2 F.L.R. 155.
[92] Cp. *Re Lonhro* [1990] 2 A.C. 154.
[93] See the discussion on the attendance of witnesses at paras 11–91 et seq.

"(a) having been summoned[94] in pursuance of rules of court as a witness in a county court refuses or neglects, without sufficient cause, to appear or to produce any documents required by the summons to be produced; or

(b) having been so summoned or being present in court and being required to give evidence, refuses to be sworn or give evidence,

shall forfeit such fine as the judge[95] may direct."

But the fine shall not exceed £1,000.[96]

No person summoned in pursuance of rules of court as a witness shall forfeit a fine, under that section, unless there has been tendered at the time of service such sum as may be prescribed for the purposes of the section in respect of expenses (including, in such cases as may be prescribed, compensation for loss of time).[97] A witness may refuse to give evidence until he has been paid expenses.[98] The provisions of s.55 do not apply to a debtor summoned by a judgment summons.[99] Provision is made for enforcement of such a fine,[1] and also for remission if cause is shown.[2]

7. *Corporations*

Where any judgment or order against a corporation has been disobeyed it may, by order of a judge, be enforced by order of committal against the directors or other officers.[3] A county court has jurisdiction in appropriate cases to order sequestration of a company's assets if the company is in contempt; for example, where a company is registered abroad and has no officers or directors within the jurisdiction.[4]

8. *Undertakings of solicitors*

Solicitors are not officers of the county court, and therefore specific provision has been made in s.142 of the 1984 Act to confer on county court judges a degree of control similar to that exercisable by the High Court:

---

[94] See CPR Pt 34.
[95] The same powers were conferred upon a district judge, assistant district judge and deputy district judge by s.74(6) of the Courts and Legal Services Act 1990: see s.55(4A) of the 1984 Act.
[96] County Courts Act 1984, s.55(2), as amended by the Criminal Justice Act 1991, s.17(3)(a), Sch.4, Pt I.
[97] s.55(3). See CPR 34.7, which introduced a significant change in practice with a view to achieving consistency between the Crown Court, the High Court and the county court. The term "conduct money" is still used informally to cover travelling expenses and accommodation but now, additionally, a witness must be offered compensation for loss of time.
[98] *Re Working Men's Mutual Society* (1882) 21 Ch.D. 831.
[99] s.55(5). For the procedure under a judgment summons, see s.110, set out at para.13–99, and CPR Sch.2, cc.28.
[1] s.129. See CPR Sch.2, cc.34.3.
[2] CPR Sch.2, cc.34.4.
[3] CPR Sch.2, cc.29.1. Cp. CPR Sch.1, Ord.45.5. discussed at paras 12–110 *et seq.*
[4] *Rose v Laskington Ltd* [1990] 1 Q.B. 562.

"A county court shall have the same power to enforce an undertaking given by a solicitor in relation to any proceedings in that court as the High Court has to enforce an undertaking so given in relation to any proceedings in the High Court".

This was reflected in the County Court Rules which provide[5] that such an undertaking may be enforced upon an order of the judge by committal. The summary procedure should be used, however, only in a clear case.[6]

9. Penalty for non-attendance on a judgment summons

13–99   It is provided by s.110 of the 1984 Act that:

"(1) If a debtor summoned to attend a county court by a judgment summons fails to attend[7] on the day and at the time fixed for any hearing of the summons, the judge may adjourn or further adjourn the summons to a specified time on a specified day and order the debtor to attend at the time on that day.

(2) If—

(a) a debtor, having been ordered under subsection (1) to attend at a specified time on a specified day, fails to do so; or

[(b) a debtor who attends for the hearing of a judgment summons refuses to be sworn or to give evidence;][8]

the judge may make an order committing him to prison for a period not exceeding 14 days in respect of the failure or refusal.

(3) In any case where the judge has power to make an order of committal under subsection (2) for failure to attend, he may in lieu of or in addition to making that order, order the debtor to be arrested and brought before the court either forthwith or at such time as the judge may direct.[9]

(4) A debtor shall not be committed to prison under subsection (2) for having failed to attend as required by an order under subsection (1) unless there was paid to him at the time of the service of the judgment summons, or paid or tendered to him at the time of the service of the order, such sum in respect of his expenses as may be prescribed for the purposes of this section.[10]

(5) The judge may at any time revoke an order committing a person to prison under this section and, if he is already in custody, order his discharge."

---

[5] CPR Sch.2, cc.29.2.
[6] *Silver & Drake (A Firm) v Baines* [1971] 1 Q.B. 396; *Udall v Capri Lighting Limited (In Liquidation)* [1988] Q.B. 907; *John Fox (A Firm) v Bannister King & Rigbeys (A Firm)* [1988] Q.B. 925n; *United Bank of Kuwait v Hammond* [1988] 1 W.L.R. 1051, CA; *City Trust Ltd v Levy* [1988] 1 W.L.R. 1051. See also paras 2–1, 12–248.
[7] See CPR Sch.2, cc.27.7B (suspended committal orders) and 27.8 (maintenance orders) and CPR Sch.2, cc.28.4 (enforcement of a debtor's attendance).
[8] Omitted by the Civil Procedure (Modification of Enactments) Order 2002, SI 2002/439 from March 23, 2002.
[9] This subsection was inserted by way of amendment by s.14(5), and para.4 of Pt III of Sch.2, of the Contempt of Court Act 1981.
[10] See now CPR Sch.2, cc.28.4(2). No compensation for loss of time need be paid or tendered. Contrast the position under s.55, para.13–96.

C. Coroners

The coroner's court has long been recognised as an inferior court of record.[11] There would accordingly be an inherent jurisdiction to commit, or impose a lesser penalty by way of fine,[12] in respect of contempts committed in the face of the court.[13] The Divisional Court would deal with other forms of contempt, for example prejudice arising from media coverage. Although coroners' courts sit for the most part without a jury, statute requires a jury in certain circumstances, including where a death occurs in prison or police custody,[14] or in the case of any death resulting from injury caused by a police officer.[15]

13–100

It is established that the provisions of the Contempt of Court Act 1981 concerning strict liability apply to a coroner's inquest, which is treated as "active" for those purposes once it has been opened.[16]

13–101

In addition to its inherent powers, the coroner's court has statutory jurisdiction over those who are summoned as jurors or witnesses. It is provided by the Coroners Act 1988:

13–102

"**10**—(1) Where a person duly summoned as a juror at an inquest—

(a) does not, after being openly called three times, appear to the summons; or
(b) appears to the summons but refuses without reasonable excuse to serve as a juror,

the coroner may impose on that person a fine not exceeding £1,000

(2) Where a person duly summoned to give evidence at an inquest—

(a) does not, after being openly called three times, appear to the summons; or
(b) appears to the summons but refuses without lawful excuse to answer a question put to him,

the coroner may impose on that person a fine not exceeding £1,000.

(3) The powers conferred upon a coroner by this section shall be in addition to and not in derogation of any other power which the coroner may possess—

---

[11] See 4 *Co. Inst.* 271; *Garnett v Ferrand* (1827) 6 B. & C. 611 at 625, 108 E.R. 576 at 581, Lord Tenterden C.J.; *Thomas v Churton* (1862) 2 B. & S. 475 at 478, 121 E.R. 1150 at 1151; *Jewison v Dyson* (1842) 9 M. & W. 540 at 586, 152 E.R. 228 at 247.
[12] In *R. v West Yorkshire Coroner Ex p. Smith (No.2)* [1985] 1 Q.B. 1096, the coroner imposed a fine of £50 upon the father of the deceased, who shouted out just as the court was adjourning that one of the witnesses was a murderer. There is no statutory basis for imposing a fine in these circumstances, and the jurisdiction assumed appears to be part of the accepted inherent jurisdiction for punishing contempt in the face of the court.
[13] See the forms relating to committal in Impey, *Office of Sheriff and Coroner* (3rd ed., 1835) and in Umfreville, *Office of Coroner* (1761); *R. v Little, R. v Miller* [1926] 2 W.W.R. 762 (Manitoba). For modern authorities, see *Att-Gen v BBC* [1981] A.C. 303 at 342, Lord Salmon, at 355, Lord Scarman; *R. v Surrey Coroner Ex p. Campbell* [1982] Q.B. 661; *R. v West Yorkshire Coroner Ex p. Smith (No.2)* [1985] 1 Q.B. 1096.
[14] Coroners Act 1988, s.8(3)(a).
[15] *ibid.*, s.8(3)(b).
[16] *Peacock v London Weekend Television* (1985) 150 J.P. 71 at 81, where it was held that such proceedings fall within para.12 of Sch.1: "... from the time the hearing begins, until the proceedings are disposed of or discontinued or withdrawn".

13–102   CHAPTER 13—JURISDICTION

(a) for compelling any person to appear and give evidence before him in any inquest or other proceeding; or

(b) for punishing any person for contempt of court in not so appearing and giving evidence;

but a person shall not be fined by the coroner under this section and also be punished under any such other power."

A recent example of a coroner initiating proceedings for contempt (with leave from the single judge) is to be found in *HM Coroner for Kent v Terrill*.[17]

D. Miscellaneous other courts of record

13–103   The Transport Tribunal[18] and the Election Court[19] are by statute courts of record. Consistory courts are regarded as (inferior) courts of record.[20]

IV. MAGISTRATES' COURTS

A. The nature of magistrates' courts

1. Introduction

13–104   As there would seem to be some doubt as to whether magistrates' courts are properly to be regarded as courts of record,[21] we therefore address the magistrates' jurisdiction in contempt in this separate section. The Phillimore Committee[22] appears to have regarded magistrates' courts as *not* being courts of record. They are certainly not so constituted by statute. On this basis, they would have no inherent contempt jurisdiction, and would need to rely on the protection of the Divisional Court. They had an inherent power to keep order in their own proceedings and eject persons causing disturbance.[23]

13–105   Magistrates have by statute all such powers as they are likely to need in relation to conduct amounting to an actual interference in their proceedings. Like other inferior courts, they are subject in other respects to the protection of the Queen's Bench Division. In our submission, however, the better view is that they

---

[17] May 8, 2000, CO/1384/00 (Lexis) [2001] A.C.D. 5, cited at para.11–105.
[18] Transport Act 1985, s.117 and Sch.4, para.1.
[19] Representation of the People Act 1983, s.123(2) (conferring "the same powers, jurisdiction and authority as a judge of the High Court").
[20] *Chancellor of St. Edmundsbury and Ipswich Diocese Ex p. White* [1948] 1 K.B. 195. See also *Re St. Andrews, Heddington* [1978] Fam. 121, 124–5; *Att-Gen v BBC* [1981] A.C. at 342E–F, Lord Salmon; *R. v Chancellor of the Chichester Consistory Court Ex p. News Group Newspapers Ltd* [1991] T.L.R. 340.
[21] See, *e.g.* Halsbury's *Laws of England* (4th ed.), Vol. 10, para.709 and Vol. 29, para.286.
[22] (1974) Cmnd 5794, para.25.
[23] *R. v Webb Ex p. Hawkers, The Times*, January 24, 1899. The magistrates' jurisdiction is governed by the practice direction (originally promulgated on June 5, 2001) and now to be found in the consolidation of existing practice directions at [2002] 1 W.L.R. 2870, [2002] 3 All E.R. 904 (as amended March 22, 2005); for the latest version of the Direction, see www.courtservice.gov.uk/docs/cpd/consol_criminal_pd_220305.doc.

may properly be regarded as courts of record at common law, in accordance with the doctrine which gradually developed that any court could be so classified if it had the power to fine and imprison.[24] At all events it is the statutory powers that now matter.

2. *The statutory provisions*

Jurisdiction was conferred[25] upon magistrates' courts in England and Wales by s.12(1) of the Contempt of Court Act 1981 to "deal with" any person who:

13–106

"(a) wilfully insults the justice or justices, any witness before or officer of the court or any solicitor or counsel having business in the court, during his or their sitting or attendance in court or in going to or returning from the court; or
(b) wilfully interrupts[26] the proceedings of the court or otherwise misbehaves in court."

In *R. v Havant Magistrates' Court and Portsmouth Crown Court Ex p. Palmer*,[27] it was held that threatening the defendant and his solicitors outside court was not an "insult". It may be that this interpretation will no longer be followed in the light of the decision of the Court of Appeal in *Manchester City Council v McCann*.[28] Lord Woolf M.R. said that he had the "misfortune to differ" with the Divisional Court and concluded that the word "insults" was wide enough to embrace threats. This approach is to be contrasted with that of Parliament in the Public Order Act 1986, ss.4 and 5 of which employ the separate expressions "threatening, abusive or insulting words or behaviour".

13–107

In any such case the court may order any of its officers, or any constable, to take the offender into custody and detain him until the rising of the court. The offender may be committed to custody for a specified period not exceeding one month or fined a sum not exceeding £2,500, or both.[29] It has been held by the Divisional Court[30] that a committal to custody under this jurisdiction does not amount to a summary conviction, and there would accordingly be no right under the Powers of Criminal Courts Act 1973, s.21(1), to legal representation before

13–108

---

[24] See, *e.g.* Holdsworth's *History of English Law* (3rd ed.), Vol. 5, pp.157–61. See also *Groenvelt v Burwell* (1700) 1 Ld. Raym. 454, 91 E.R. 1065; *Cotton's Case* (1733) 2 Barn. K.B. 313 at 315, 94 E.R. 523 at 524; *Kemp v Neville* (1861) 10 C.B. (N.S.) 523, 142 E.R. 556.
[25] See *P v Liverpool Daily Post and Echo Newspapers plc* [1991] 2 A.C. 370 at 380E, where Lord Donaldson M.R. referred to this as "a new jurisdiction to deal with contempt of those courts". See A. Draycott, "Contempt of Magistrates' Courts" (1983) 147 J.P. 531.
[26] This would include "interruption" emanating from outside the court itself: see *Bodden v Metropolitan Police Commissioner* [1990] 2 Q.B. 397. The substantive offences created by s.12 are more fully discussed in para.10–113.
[27] (1985) 149 J.P. 609, [1985] Crim. L.R. 658, DC.
[28] [1999] Q.B. 1214 (albeit in the context of s.118 of the County Courts Act 1984, set out at para.13–90.
[29] s.12(2); the sum was fixed by the Criminal Justice Act 1991, Sch.4 Pt I. The amount may now be altered from time to time by an order under s.143 and Sch.6A of the Magistrates' Courts Act 1980; see the 1991 Act, Sch.4 Pt IV.
[30] *R. v Newbury Justices Ex p. Pont* (1984) 78 Cr.App.R. 255, (1983) 148 J.P. 248, DC. See para.14–143, n.42.

committal.[31] The court may at any time revoke an order of committal made under this statutory jurisdiction and, if the offender is in custody, order his discharge.[32]

13–109 Section 12 of the 1981 Act has been considered in a number of authorities, which are fully considered in the context of contempt committed in the face of the court.[33]

3. *The application of other provisions of the Magistrates' Courts Act 1980 provisions*

13–110 The Contempt of Court Act also extends[34] certain statutory provisions to any order made under s.12, as they apply in relation to a sentence following a conviction or finding of guilt of an offence:

(a) s.135 of the Powers of Criminal Courts (Sentencing) Act 2000: which restricts the imposition of fines in respect of young persons.

(b) ss.75 to 91: which are concerned with enforcement.

(c) s.108: providing for a right of appeal to the Crown Court.

(d) s.136: which provides for overnight detention in a police station in default of payment.

(e) s.142(1): which confers power to re-open cases within 28 days for the purpose of rectifying mistakes.

4. *Persons aged 18 to 20*

13–111 Specific provision is made in s.108 of the Powers of Criminal Courts (Sentencing) Act 2000[35] for dealing with persons within the relevant age group who have been committed for contempt of court or "any kindred offence", and in particular for magistrates committing a person under 21 years of age to state in open court the reason for concluding that no other method of disposal is appropriate.[36]

B. Means of exercising the section 12 powers

13–112 The means by which proceedings are to be brought under the provisions are prescribed by s.17 and Sch.3 of the Contempt of Court Act 1981. The

---

[31] But see discussion of the desirability of affording legal representation at paras 10–53 *et seq.* The provisions governing legal representation are now to be found in s.83 of the Powers of Criminal Courts (Sentencing) Act 2000.

[32] s.12(4).

[33] See paras 10–113 *et seq.*; *R. v Selby Justices Ex p. Frame* [1992] Q.B. 72, DC; *R. v Powell* (1993) 98 Cr.App.R. 224; *R. v Tamworth Justices Ex p. Walsh*, *The Times*, May 3, 1994; *Re Hooker* [1993] C.O.D. 190 (Lexis).

[34] s.12(5) as amended by the Powers of Criminal Courts (Sentencing Act) 2000, s.165(1) Sch.9, para.83.

[35] The section has already been repealed by s.75 of the Criminal Justice and Court Services Act 2000, but from a day to be appointed.

[36] s.108(4) and see paras 14–60 *et seq.*

magistrates' powers may be exercised "either of the court's own motion, or by order on complaint",[37] and certain provisions of the 1980 Act are applied[38] to the exercise of these powers when the court acts of its own motion, namely:

(a) s.51 (issue of summons).

(b) s.53(1) and (2) (procedure on hearing).

(c) s.54 (adjournment).

(d) s.55 (non-appearance of defendant).

(e) s.97(1) (summons to witness).

(f) s.101 (onus of proving exceptions).

(g) s.121(1) and (3) (a) (constitution and place of sitting of court).

(h) s.123 (defect in process).

Consequential amendments to the Magistrates' Courts Act 1980

By reason of the fact that s.17 of the 1981 Act contemplated the magistrates' court acting of its own motion, it became necessary for certain consequential amendments to be made to the wording of subsections 55(1) and (2) of the 1980 Act. These provide for magistrates to proceed in the absence of the defendant and, by way of alternative, to adjourn the matter and issue a warrant. Accordingly, para.1(2) of the third Schedule to the 1981 Act removes for this purpose the words "the complainant appears but the defendant does not" and substitutes "the defendant does not appear"; it also removes the words "if the complaint has been substantiated on oath, and" altogether from s.55(2). Similarly, in s.123(1) and (2) of the 1980 Act the words "adduced on behalf of the prosecutor or complainant" are to be omitted.[39]

These sub-sections in the 1980 Act, therefore, read as follows for the purpose of contempt proceedings:

"**123**—(1) No objection shall be allowed to any information or complaint, or to any summons or warrant to procure the presence of the defendant, for any defect in it in substance or in form, or for any variance between it and the evidence ... at the hearing of the information or complaint.

(2) If it appears to a magistrates' court that any variance between a summons or warrant and the evidence ... is such that the defendant has been misled by the variance, the court shall, on the application of the defendant, adjourn the hearing."

When proceedings are taken by way of complaint, the provisions of s.127 of the 1980 Act, governing limitation of time, do not apply.[40]

---

[37] s.17(1).
[38] s.17(2) and Sch.3 of the Contempt of Court Act 1981.
[39] para.1(3) of Sch.3 to the Contempt of Court Act 1981.
[40] para.2 of Sch.3 to the Contempt of Court Act 1981.

13–115 Whether the court proceeds of its own motion or by way of complaint, s.55(3) of the 1980 Act is to apply in the following form[41]:

"The court shall not begin to hear the complaint in the absence of the defendant or issue a warrant under this section unless either it is proved to the satisfaction of the court, on oath or in such other manner as may be prescribed, that the summons was served on him within what appears to the court to be a reasonable time[42] before the hearing or adjourned hearing or the defendant has appeared on a previous occasion to answer to the complaint".

C. Disobedience to orders of the magistrates' court

13–116 A further aspect of magistrates' jurisdiction has to be considered in connection with s.63(3) of the Magistrates' Courts Act 1980, which provides as follows for punishment by fine or committal for disobeying an order to do anything other than the payment of money or an order to abstain from doing anything:

"(3) Where any person disobeys an order of a magistrates' court made under an Act passed after 31st December 1879 to do anything other than the payment of money or to abstain from doing anything the court may—

(a) order him to pay a sum not exceeding £50 for every day during which he is in default or a sum not exceeding [£5,000][43]; or
(b) commit him to custody until he has remedied his default or for a period not exceeding 2 months;

but a person who is ordered to pay a sum for every day during which he is in default or who is committed to custody until he has remedied his default shall not by virtue of this section be ordered to pay more than £1,000 or be committed for more than 2 months in all for doing or abstaining from doing the same thing[44] contrary to the order (without prejudice to the operation of this section in relation to any subsequent default)."

D. Jurisdiction in relation to witnesses

13–117 The provisions of the Magistrates' Courts act 1980 confer jurisdiction to procure the attendance of witnesses and to punish non-compliance. These matters are fully discussed in chapter 11.[45]

V. Appellate Jurisdiction

A. The Administration of Justice Act 1960

13–118 Appellate jurisdiction now derives mainly from s.13(1) of the Administration of Justice Act 1960, which gives a right of appeal from any order or decision of a

---

[41] The words in square brackets were added by the Family Law Act 1996, s.66(1), Sch.8, para.50.
[42] A matter for the Justices to decide in the light of the circumstances: *Ex p. Williams* (1851) 2 L.M. & P. 580.
[43] This section was amended by the Criminal Justice Act 1991 s.17(3)(a), and Sch.4, Pt I. The effect of the amendment was to change the figure to £5,000. The later reference to £1000 would appear to refer to a maximum sum payable for default when ordered to pay £50 per day.
[44] paras 3–209 *et seq.* (double jeopardy).
[45] paras 11–130 *et seq.*

court[46] made or given in the exercise of its jurisdiction to punish for contempt of court. The powers of the appellate tribunal are widely drawn[47]:

"The court to which an appeal is brought under this section may reverse or vary the order or decision of the court below and make such other order as may be just; ... "

It was pointed out in *R. v Dodds*[48] that the wide terms of the provision give the court ample powers to rectify any defect on appeal so as to achieve compliance with the requirements of Art.6 of the European Convention.[49] It was, however, held in *R. v Moore*[50] that its terms could not be construed as conferring a power to pay the costs of a successful appellant out of central funds.

13–119 Appeal originally lay without leave in any case at the instance of the defendant[51] and, in the case of an application for committal, the applicant could also appeal.[52] Indeed, it has been held that an applicant might appeal in respect of penalty.[53] Where the appeal is against a penalty, the court will apply the test of whether it was "unduly lenient" by analogy with an Attorney-General's Reference under the Criminal Justice Act 1988. It will be necessary also to take into account "double jeopardy".[54] Formerly there was no right of appeal from an order of attachment or committal in the case of a criminal contempt,[55] and this was one of the principal distinctions between criminal and civil contempt.[56] For many years there was a right of appeal in respect of both civil and criminal contempt, including contempt in the face of the court,[57] in respect of both liability and penalty. Written evidence was always used on appeals both in criminal and civil contempt.[58]

13–120 Despite the change in the structure of appeals generally, following the introduction of the CPR, and the need to obtain permission in most civil cases (or

---

[46] "Court" is defined to include any tribunal or person having the power to punish for contempt: s.13(5). Orders made under s.5 of the Debtors Act 1869 are excluded.
[47] s.13(3).
[48] [2002] EWCA Crim 1328, [2003] 1 Cr.App.R. 3 at [13].
[49] See also *Edwards v United Kingdom* (1993) E.H.R.R. 417.
[50] [2003] EWCA Crim 1574, [2003] 1 W.L.R. 2170 at [24].
[51] "Defendant" is defined by s.17(1)(b). The Official Solicitor may appeal on behalf of a person committed if he does not appeal himself: *Churchman v Joint Shop Stewards' Committee of the Workers of the Port of London* [1972] 1 W.L.R. 1094, CA.
[52] s.13(2).
[53] See *Wilson v Webster* [1998] 1 F.L.R. 1097.
[54] *Neil v Ryan* [1998] 2 F.L.R. 1068.
[55] When created by the Criminal Appeal Act 1907, the Court of Criminal Appeal was given no jurisdiction in relation to cases of summary conviction. Furthermore, the Court of Appeal had never had the power to entertain an appeal in any criminal cause or matter: Judicature Act 1873, s.47(1), and s.31(1)(a) of the 1925 Act.
[56] See paras 3–131 *et seq.*
[57] See, *e.g. Morris v Crown Office* [1970] 2 Q.B. 114; *Balogh v St. Albans Crown Court* [1975] 1 Q.B. 73; *R. v Schot and Barclay* [1997] 2 Cr.App.R. 383, (1997) 161 J.P. 473.
[58] *Brown v Crowley (No.2)* [1964] 1 W.L.R. 147, CA. See *Att-Gen v Pelling* [2005] EWHC 414 (Admin) where the respondent argued unsuccessfully that his Art.6 rights were infringed by his not being entitled to cross-examine the deponents. Although the court accepted that there was a discretion to permit cross-examination in appropriate cases, there was no reason to do so on the facts. The respondent then withdrew from the proceedings.

13–120 leave in criminal cases), there remains a *right* of appeal under s.13 of the Administration of Justice Act 1960.[59] There is thus an exception to the general rule described in *Tanfern Ltd v Cameron MacDonald (Practice Note)*.[60] Section 13(2)(b) of the 1960 Act, as amended by s.64 of the Access to Justice Act 1999, retains the direct appeal as of right to the Court of Appeal. But CPR 52.3(1)(a)(i) preserves that right only in respect of "a committal order", the true meaning of which is "an order which commits a party to prison".[61] It was confirmed in *Wilkinson v S*[62] that, because a suspended committal order is "an order which commits a person to prison", no permission is required to appeal such an order. In the case where committal is refused, and permission to appeal by the applicant is therefore now required, it is necessary to bear in mind that if permission is granted the respondent will be placed in a position of double jeopardy.[63] Laws L.J. has expressed the view[64] that an *applicant* who seeks to appeal a committal order (presumably because of dissatisfaction with the penalty) would now need permission to do so. It would be anomalous that he should have a right to appeal the penalty but require permission to appeal against the refusal of committal.

13–121 There is further scope for confusion when one turns to consider appeals from orders made in this jurisdiction by district judges. After the coming into effect of the CPR, there are still two routes for a *first* appeal from a committal order made by a district judge. The issue of the correct route of appeal was addressed by the Court of Appeal in *London Borough of Barnet v Hurst*.[65] Even if the case is in the multi-track it would not be within the definition of a "final decision" in art.1(2)(c) of the Access to Justice Act 1999 (Destination of Appeals) Order 2000.[66] Thus an appeal will ordinarily lie to a circuit judge in the county court. Article 3(2) of the Order and the pre-CPR decision in *King v Read and Slack*[67] would produce the same outcome. On the other hand, an appeal may exceptionally lie to the Court of Appeal through the transfer operation contained in CPR 52.14 or s.57 of the Access to Justice Act 1999. A first appeal from any other order of a district judge (*i.e.* other than for committal) made in the exercise of the jurisdiction to punish for contempt may follow the same alternative routes, except that permission to appeal will be required. As to *second* appeals, however, the route is to the Court of Appeal.[68] The rules governing such appeals are to be found in CPR 52.13 and permission is always required.

13–122 Surprise was expressed that neither *King v Read and Slack* nor *Hampshire County Council v Gillingham* had received the attention of the editors of the White Book. It was confirmed that the right of appeal under s.13 of the 1960 Act remained in effect. A distinction has to be drawn, however, between an order for

---

[59] See Latham L.J. in *Hampshire County Council v Gillingham*, June 22, 2000.
[60] [2000] 1 W.L.R. 1311.
[61] *Government of Sierra Leone v Davenport* [2002] EWCA Civ 230 at [8].
[62] [2003] EWCA Civ 95, [2003] 1 W.L.R. 1254, [2003] 2 All E.R. 185.
[63] *Government of Sierra Leone v Davenport* [2002] EWCA Civ 230 at [31], Jonathan Parker L.J. See also the observations about double jeopardy cited at paras 12–14 *et seq*.
[64] *Government of Sierra Leone v Davenport* [2002] EWCA Civ 230 at [33].
[65] [2002] EWCA Civ 1009, [2003] 1 W.L.R. 722, [2002] 4 All E.R. 457.
[66] SI 2000/107.
[67] [1999] 1 F.L.R. 425.
[68] See the 2000 Order, art.5.

committal (no permission required) and any other order or decision made in the exercise of the court's contempt jurisdiction (where permission will be required in accordance with the general practice today).[69]

It is important to define what is for present purposes considered to be an order or decision made in the exercise of jurisdiction to punish for contempt. References to "an order or decision" include references[70]:

"(a) ... to an order or decision of the High Court, Crown Court or a county court, under any enactment enabling that court to deal with an offence as if it were contempt of court;
(b) ... to an order or decision of a county court, or of any court having the powers of a county court, under sections 14, 92 or 118 of the County Courts Act 1984[71];
(c) ... to an order or decision of a magistrates' court under subsection (3) of s.63 of the Magistrates' Courts Act 1980,

but do not include references to orders under section five of the Debtors Act 1869, or under any provision of the Magistrates' Courts Act 1980, or the County Courts Act 1984, except those referred to in paragraphs (b) and (c) of this subsection and except sections 38 ancillary jurisdiction[72] and 142 undertakings of solicitors of the last mentioned Act so far as those sections confer jurisdiction in respect of a contempt of court."

All other county court or magistrates' court orders are expressly excluded from the appeal provisions of the Administration of Justice Act. Orders made under the magistrates' jurisdiction under s.12 of the Contempt of Court Act 1981[73] are brought within[74] the terms of section 108 of the Magistrates' Courts Act 1980, which provides for an appeal to the Crown Court.

B. Appeals to the High Court

It is provided by s.13(2) of the Administration of Justice Act 1960 that[75]:

"An appeal under this section shall lie in any case at the instance of the defendant and, in the case of an application for committal or attachment, at the instance of the applicant; and the appeal shall lie

(a) from an order or decision of any inferior court not referred to in the next following paragraph, to the High Court; ... ".

The "next following paragraph" (*i.e.* s.13(2)(b)) refers to the county court and "any other inferior court from which appeals generally lie to the civil division of

---

[69] See also *Government of Sierra Leone v Davenport* [2002] EWCA Civ 230.
[70] See s.13(5) of the Administration of Justice Act 1960, as amended.
[71] See paras 13–80 *et seq.*
[72] "Ancillary" is apparently equivalent to "subservient to": *Kenny v Preen* [1962] 3 All E.R. 814 at 822, Donovan L.J.
[73] See para.10–113.
[74] s.12(5) of the 1981 Act.
[75] As amended by the Access to Justice Act 1999, s.64 and Sch.15, Pt III. Such an appeal no longer lies to the Divisional Court, but to a single judge.

13–126 the Court of Appeal . . . ". During the passage of the Bill through Parliament Viscount Kilmuir L.C.[76] indicated that one purpose of the provision was to enable appeals from Quarter Sessions to be brought before the Divisional Court of the Queen's Bench Division. By virtue of the Courts Act 1971 those courts were succeeded, as were the Assizes, by the Crown Court. So far as the Crown court is concerned, express provision is now made by s.13(2)(bb)[77] for appeals to be made to the Court of Appeal.

13–127 The question therefore arises as to which inferior courts are still embraced within the terms of s.13(2)(a). The provision would *prima facie* include magistrates' courts,[78] coroners' courts,[79] and other statutory courts of record.[80]

13–128 As to magistrates' courts, however, there remains some element of confusion.[81] It is necessary to bear in mind the express provisions of s.12(5) of the Contempt of Court Act 1981, which incorporates the provisions of s.108 of the Magistrates' Courts Act 1980 in relation to "orders made" in respect of wilful insults to the justices or interruptions of their proceedings. The effect of this is to provide for an appeal to the Crown Court in such cases.

13–129 Nevertheless, in *R. v Havant Justices Ex p. Palmer*[82] it was held that the Crown Court's jurisdiction under s.12(5) is limited to hearing appeals against any penalty imposed. The reasoning was that s.12(5) refers to an "order" (as opposed to a "decision"). This in the context must refer to an order under s.12(2); that is to say, an order that the offender be taken into custody until the rising of the court, or an order for committal (not exceeding one month) or an order imposing a fine. The implication of this is that where it is sought to challenge a finding of contempt, as such, the appropriate remedy is judicial review.[83] This may seem a somewhat restrictive interpretation of s.12(5), and the matter may be assessed differently at some stage by a higher court. There would be nothing unusual about the Crown Court hearing appeals from magistrates on questions of fact.

13–130 There remains some doubt, therefore, as to the circumstances in which it is appropriate to go to the Crown Court, or to the High Court for judicial review or to the High Court by way of appeal under s.13[84] of the 1960 Act. The answer may be that s.13 does not apply to the exercise of the jurisdiction under s.12 of the Contempt of Court Act 1981 at all, for the reason that it is a specific statutory jurisdiction which is, although analogous to the contempt jurisdiction, not in fact to be so classified.

---

[76] *Hansard*, H.L., Vol. 222, (5th Series), col. 297.
[77] Inserted by the Courts Act 1971, ss.56(1),(4) Sch.8, Pt II para.40(1) and Sch.11, Pt II.
[78] *Re Hooker (Patricia)* [1993] C.O.D. 190 (Lexis).
[79] See, *e.g. R. v West Yorkshire Coroner Ex p. Smith (No.2)* [1985] Q.B. 1096; and also s.10(3) of the Coroners Act 1988.
[80] Such as the Election Court (see the Representation of the People Act 1983, s.123(2), 110(2)) and the Transport Tribunal (Transport Act 1985, Sch.4, para.1).
[81] See the discussion at paras 10–114 *et seq.*
[82] (1985) 149 J.P. 609, [1985] Crim. L.R. 658.
[83] See also *R. v Pateley Bridge Justices Ex p. Percy* [1994] C.O.D. 453; *R. v Tamworth Magistrates' Court Ex p. Walsh* [1994] C.O.D. 277.
[84] *Re Hooker* [1993] C.O.D. 190, discussed in para.10–65.

Where an appeal to the High Court is available, the jurisdiction will be exercised by a single judge rather than by the Divisional Court.[85] **13–131**

It is still provided by CPR Sch.1, Ord.109, r.2(4), which deals specifically with orders made under s.13 of the Administration of Justice Act 1960, that (unless the court gives leave to the contrary) there should not be more than four clear days between the date on which the order or decision appealed against was made and the day named in the notice of the originating motion for the hearing of the appeal. So too, the notice must be served, and the appeal entered, not less than one clear day before the day named in the notice for the hearing of the appeal.[86] Despite the fact that the appellate jurisdiction of the High Court is now to be exercised by a single judge, the terms of Ord.109 still refer to the Divisional Court. This would seem to be anachronistic. It also, however, makes express provision[87] for the granting of bail by the High Court and the Court of Appeal. **13–132**

C. The prescribed appellate tribunals

The courts having appellate jurisdiction in respect of contempt may be conveniently set out in tabular form: **13–133**

Appellate Court	Court making the decision or order
Crown Court	magistrates' court exercising its powers under s.12 of the Contempt of Court Act 1981[88] (penalty only)[89]
Queen's Bench Division	Coroner's Court[90] possibly magistrates' court[91] and other statutory courts or record

---

[85] See Access to Justice Act 1999, s.64.
[86] RSC Ord.109, r.2(5).
[87] At rr.3 and 4.
[88] Contempt of Court Act 1981, s.12(5); Magistrates' Courts Act 1980, s.108.
[89] *R. v Havant Justices Ex p. Palmer* (1985) 149 J.P. 609, [1985] Crim. L.R. 658.
[90] See the Administration of Justice Act 1960, s.13(2)(a) and (5) as amended; RSC Ord.109, r.2(1). RSC, Ord.109 r.2(1). See now CPR Sch.1, Ord.109, but also the note relating to the changes introduced by s.64 of the Access to Justice Act 1999, contained at para.13–125 above. The words of ss.13(2)(a) have been amended by s.64 of the Access to Justice Act 1999 so as to omit the words "a Divisional Court of". Accordingly, an appeal now lies from an order or decision of some inferior courts (*i.e.* those not referred to in s.13(2)(b): see below para.13–126) to a single judge of the High Court. A minor amendment to Ord.109.4(5) is that "Clerk of … " has been replaced by "Chief Executive for … ".
[91] See *Re Hooker* [1993] C.O.D. 190, and discussion at para.10–65 and paras 13–127 *et seq.*

13–133 CHAPTER 13—JURISDICTION

Appellate Court	Court making the decision or order
Divisional Court of the Family Division	magistrates' court exercising its powers under s.63(3) of the Magistrates' Courts Act 1980[92]
Court of Appeal (Criminal Division)	Crown Court[93]
Court of Appeal (Civil Division)	A judge of the High Court,[94] Employment Appeal Tribunal,[95] county court[96] and (exceptionally) a District Judge[97]
House of Lords	Court of Appeal, Courts-Martial Appeal Court, Divisional Court[98]
The County Court	District Judge[99]

For an appeal to the House of Lords the leave of the lower court or of the House is required. A certificate from the lower court is required that a point of general public importance is involved.[1]

13–134 Section 13(3) of the Administration of Justice Act 1960 provides that the court to which an appeal is brought under the section may reverse or vary the order or decision of the court below and may make such other order as may be just.[2] The rules governing procedure are contained in CPR Pt 52. There was provision *inter alia* for bail pending appeal in RSC Ord.59, r.20. This has not been preserved in

---

[92] See Supreme Court Act 1981, s.61(1)(3), Sch.1, para.3(d) and FPR 8.3; s.13(5) of the 1960 Act, as amended by s.154 and para.36 of Sch.7 to the Magistrates' Courts Act 1980; for procedure on appeals under this section, see the Family Proceedings Rules 1991, SI 1991/1247, rr.8.2(4), 8.3 (as inserted by SI 1991/2113, r.15). See also *B (BPM) v B (MM)* [1969] P. 103.
[93] s.13(2) (bb). See also Supreme Court Act 1981, s.53(2)(b).
[94] s.13(2)(b) of the 1960 Act.
[95] Employment Tribunals Act 1996, s.37.
[96] s.13(2)(b) of the 1960 Act. The subsection has been amended by s.64 of the Access to Justice Act 1999. But the changes do not appear to alter the route of appeal from the county court. An appeal still lies as of right from a committal order to the Court of Appeal: see *Hampshire County Council v Gillingham*, cited at paras 13–120, n.59 and 15–88. But see the discussion of the two possible routes of appeal from a District Judge in para.13–121. The words "decision of a single" have been removed and in substitution there appears "decision (other than a decision of an appeal under this section) of a single". All this appears to mean is that there is no appeal from a High Court judge sitting in an appellate capacity, but an appeal lies to the Court of Appeal from such a judge exercising an original jurisdiction.
[97] See the discussion in *London Borough of Barnet v Hurst* [2002] EWCA Civ 109, [2003] 1 W.L.R. 722, [2002] 4 All E.R. 457 summarised in para.13–121.
[98] Whether in respect of a decision made under original jurisdiction or one made in its appellate capacity: s.13(2)(c) of the 1960 Act.
[99] See the discussion in *London Borough of Barnet v Hurst* [2002] EWCA Civ 109, [2003] 1 W.L.R. 722, [2002] 4 All E.R. 457 summarised in para.13–121.
[1] s.1(2) of the 1960 Act.
[2] See *Linnett v Coles* [1987] Q.B. 555, CA, and also *Harmsworth v Harmsworth* [1987] 1 W.L.R. 1676; 3 All E.R. 816, CA.

the Schedule to the CPR. Appeals are now governed by CPR Pt 52, RSC Ord.109, rr.1–3 preserved in CPR Sch.1, Ord.109 rr.1–3. It is necessary, however, to have regard to the changes introduced by s.64 of the Access to Justice Act 1999.[3]

---

[3] Contained at para.13–133, n.90.

CHAPTER 14

SANCTIONS AND REMEDIES

		PARA
I.	Custodial Penalties	14–1
II.	Attaching a Power of Arrest	14–71
III.	Non-Custodial Sentences	14–97
IV.	The Unavailability of Financial Compensation	14–142

I. CUSTODIAL PENALTIES

A. Outline

14–1 The principal sanctions for contempt of court are imprisonment, fine and seizure of the contemnor's goods under a writ of sequestration. On an application to commit, the court may imprison or fine the contemnor. In addition, the superior courts may now in appropriate cases make an order under s.37 or s.38 of the Mental Health Act 1983.[1] The court also has power to bind over a contemnor to be of good behaviour,[2] to grant an injunction restraining the repetition of the contempt[3] and to penalise the contemnor with an order to pay the costs of the committal proceedings.[4] It was eventually established that damages are not available to compensate for a contempt of court as such.[5] The court has a wide discretion as to whether to impose a sanction and, if so, what is appropriate to the circumstances.

14–2 Sometimes the court will take the view that a finding of contempt does not require the imposition of any sanction over and above the "public humiliation" perceived as attaching to the delivery of a judgment in public identifying the contemnor's reprehensible behaviour. This was exemplified in *R. (on the application of Bempoa) v Southwark London Borough Council*.[6] The case concerned the eviction of the claimant from local authority accommodation in breach of undertakings given to the court. Munby J. regarded the matter as serious. Not only did it involve an unlawful violation of a home (albeit one

---

[1] A hospital order or guardianship order may be made under s.37 of the Act, or an interim hospital order under s.38; see s.14(4) of the Contempt of Court Act 1981, as amended by the Mental Health (Amendment) Act 1982, s.65(1), Sch.3, para.59; the Mental Health Act 1983, s.148, Sch.4, para.57.
[2] See para.14–110.
[3] See para.14–132. See also the remarks of Lord Donaldson M.R. in *P v Liverpool Daily Post and Echo Newspapers plc* [1991] 2 A.C. 370 at 381–2, CA that injunctions should not be needed to restrain the commission of criminal offences, cited in para.6–3.
[4] See paras 14–135 *et seq.*
[5] See paras 14–148 *et seq.*
[6] [2002] EWHC 153 (Admin), [2002] N.P.C. 23.

admitted to be occupied unlawfully), but the eviction had come about as a result of a defective system within the council and of an approach to court orders described as "slipshod and lackadaisical". Moreover, a decision not to reinstate the claimant had been taken by the housing department with knowledge of the breach and in the teeth of legal advice that reinstatement was appropriate. Despite these factors, the judge took the view that the public interest would better be served by the public being told how badly the defendant's staff had behaved rather than by the imposition of a penalty.[7] Another factor which affected the judge's approach was that a fine would punish the employing authority rather than the individuals actually responsible.

In *Allason v Random House (UK) Ltd (No.2)*,[8] Neuberger J. referred to the dual aspect of the contempt jurisdiction,[9] and decided to give priority to coercion over punishment, because it would be more satisfactory from the applicant's point of view that the disclosure orders be obeyed. A copyright claim had been dismissed and costs ordered against the claimant. Owing to concerns about his ability to meet the costs, he was ordered to disclose his financial position and that of his service company property interests. Not only was there unjustifiable delay in compliance, but he also failed to give full disclosure. Nevertheless, he was given a final opportunity to comply. 14-3

It will be apparent in the course of the chapter that Parliament frequently fails to make specific provision for contempt when passing general sentencing legislation. An exception is to be found in the Criminal Justice Act 2003, s.258 of which caters specifically for contemnors so far as early release provisions are concerned.[10] 14-4

B. Historical use of imprisonment

Imprisonment has always been a sanction in cases of contempt. It should now be regarded, however, as a matter of last resort, and especially in cases of civil contempt.[11] Prior to the 1981 Act there was no limit upon the length of sentence which could be imposed and, in some cases, the term could be indefinite. The practice varied in different courts. The King's Bench traditionally leaned towards imprisonment for a fixed term.[12] In *Att-Gen v James*[13] the Divisional Court held that a sentence of imprisonment for a fixed term was the proper sentence for a criminal contempt; in cases of criminal (as opposed to civil) contempt, the contemnor was committed until a fixed term had expired. Once the sentence had 14-5

---

[7] Cp. *Beggs v The Scottish Ministers* 2005 S.L.T. 305 at [21] and [51].
[8] [2002] EWHC 1030, (Ch), [2002] All E.R. (D) 158 (Apr).
[9] See paras 3–12 *et seq.*
[10] See para.14–35 below.
[11] See the cases referred to in para.10–29 and paras 12–18 *et seq.*
[12] *R. v James* (1822) 5 B. & Ald. 894, 106 E.R. 1418; *R. v Crawford* (1849) 13 Q.B. (N.S.) 613, 628; *Ex p. Fernandez* (1861) 10 C.B. (N.S.) 3 at 39, 142 E.R. 349 at 362–3.
[13] [1962] 2 Q.B. 637.

been passed, the court had no further jurisdiction in the matter.[14] The Probate, Divorce and Admiralty Division followed the same practice.[15]

14-6 The early practice of the Court of Chancery in respect of breaches of its orders was to commit for an indefinite period leaving the contemnor to apply for his discharge.[16] It was said by Attorney-General, Sir Charles Russell Q.C., in the course of argument in *Re the Bahama Islands*[17] that " . . . the practice in the Court of Chancery was to commit for an indefinite period, leaving applications for release to be made again and again until the contempt was considered to be purged. If the order had been for a fixed term, that might prevent the judge interfering before the term had expired." A contemnor would generally be regarded as having "purged"[18] his contempt when he had complied with the relevant order of the court, when he was thought to have been sufficiently punished or when he had expressed contrition. In later cases, however, the Chancery Division adopted the practice of sentencing to a fixed term for criminal contempts.[19] Thus the practice became general in all divisions of the High Court to punish criminal contempts with a fixed term, save perhaps in respect of breaches of orders relating to wards of court (regarded as criminal in character),[20] where the primary object might well be coercive.[21]

C. Imprisonment for civil contempt

14-7 In the case of civil contempt, where it was desired to punish for past acts, a fixed term was generally imposed[22]; where it was sought to coerce the contemnor into obeying an outstanding order of the court, an indefinite period of imprisonment would be regarded as more appropriate. In *BBPM v B (MM) (DC)*[23] a father disobeyed the order of a magistrates' court relating to access to his children. The

---

[14] *ibid.*
[15] *Sutherland v Sutherland, The Times*, April 19 and May 6, 1893.
[16] See, *e.g. Roach v Garvan* (1742) Dick. 794, 21 E.R. 480; *Cann v Cann, sub nom. Anon* (1754) 2 Ves. Sen. 520, 28 E.R. 332; *Ex p. Jones* (1806) 13 Ves. Jun. 237, 33 E.R. 283; *Long Wellesley's Case* (1831) 2 Russ. & My. 639, 39 E.R. 538; *Felkin v Herbert* (1864) 33 L.J. Ch. 294.
[17] [1893] A.C 138 at 145.
[18] A notion said to be "rooted in quasi-religious concepts of purification, expiation and attonement": *Harris v Harris* [2001] EWCA Civ 1644, [2002] Fam. 253 at [21]. The term "purging" has been held to be "inapt" for cases of criminal contempt: *R. v Montgomery* [1995] 2 All E.R. 28 at 34h–j.
[19] *Ilkley Local Board v Lister* (1895) 11 T.L.R. 176; *Re Septimus Parsonage* [1901] 2 Ch. 424; *Seaward v Paterson* [1897] 1 Ch. 545; *Re Crump* (1963) 107 Sol. Jo. 682, [1963] Crim.L.R. 777, *The Times*, August 22, 1963; *Re B (JA) (An Infant)* [1965] 1 Ch. 1112.
[20] See para.3–116.
[21] Cf. *Long Wellesley's Case* (1831) 2 Russ. and My. 639, 39 E.R. 538; but see also *Re Crump* (1963) 107 Sol. Jo. 682, [1963] Crim.L.R. 777, *The Times*, August 22, 1963, and at para.11–335, in which Faulks J. imposed a fixed 28 day term of imprisonment in respect of a ward's having married in breach of an order, so that the object could only have been punitive and deterrent. What is not permitted is to keep someone in prison, without a finding of contempt, in order to coerce others to carry out some act which is outside the individual's power to control: see *Re B (Child Abduction: Wardship: Power to Detain)* [1994] 2 F.L.R. 479.
[22] But see *Jennison v Baker* [1972] 2 Q.B. 52, discussed in para.3–12. Judge Curtis-Raleigh made an order for attachment without specifying any term. Nine days later, Judge Leslie refused an immediate discharge but ordered that the contemnor be released on a fixed date (approximately two weeks later).
[23] [1969] P. 103.

magistrates exercised their power under s.54(3) of the Magistrates' Courts Act 1952 to commit him for his failure to obey. The committal was for a fixed term of two months. The Divisional Court of the Probate, Divorce and Admiralty Division held that they had no power to do so. The proper order would have been to commit him until he remedied his default, such imprisonment not to exceed two months. Where an indefinite committal was imposed, and the contemnor continued to refuse to obey the order of the court, difficulties could arise, as in the case of *Maria Annie Davies*[24] who spent 18 months in prison but remained defiant. Eventually the issue of imprisonment for an indefinite term was resolved by statute; first of all on a piecemeal basis in respect of inferior courts and then finally, in respect of superior courts also, by the Contempt of Court Act 1981 which ensures that, in all cases, committal must be for a fixed term[25] which must not exceed two years.

D. Section 14(1) of the 1981 Act

The use of imprisonment is now governed by s.14(1), which provides, in respect of England and Wales[26]:

"In any case where a court has power to commit a person to prison for contempt of court and (apart from this provision) no limitation applies to the period of committal, the committal shall (without prejudice to the power of the court to order his earlier discharge) be for a fixed term, and that term shall not on any occasion exceed two years in the case of committal by a superior court, or one month in the case of committal by an inferior court."

The Phillimore Committee had recommended that there be a fixed term for all cases of contempt,[27] and a maximum term of two years.[28] It was to give effect to these recommendations that the section was enacted.

Whereas in the past indefinite sentences might regularly have been imposed for coercive purposes, it may now sometimes be appropriate, in order to achieve the same objective, to impose the maximum sentence permitted under the 1981 Act and leave the remedy in the contemnor's hands. He can come back to the court and apply for release on the basis that he has purged his contempt.[29] Furthermore, in those unusual cases where a defendant would never take steps to obtain his own release, a judge might at any time call upon the Official Solicitor

---

[24] (1888) 21 Q.B.D. 236; see also para.3–23.
[25] Thus, it is wrong to commit someone "until further order": *Linnett v Coles* [1987] Q.B. 555, CA.
[26] For the position in Scotland, see para.16–348. The maximum penalties in Scotland are provided for in s.15(2). While the maximum is also two years, the corresponding figure (for a case not on indictment) in the Sheriff Court is three months and for district courts 60 days.
[27] Cmnd. 5794 (1974), para.172.
[28] Cmnd. 5794 (1974), paras 201 and 206.
[29] *Lightfoot v Lightfoot* [1989] 1 F.L.R. 414 at 417, Lord Donaldson M.R.; see also *Delaney v Delaney* [1996] Q.B. 387, CA, discussed at para.14–50 and *R. v Anomo*, *The Independent*, February 18, 1998.

for assistance in carrying out investigations as to the circumstances of persons imprisoned for contempt, or the Official Solicitor may initiate an application.[30]

E. Guidance as to nature and length of custodial penalty: criminal contempt

14-10 An attempt was made in *R. v Montgomery*[31] to give guidance, in a criminal context,[32] as to the principles which should be followed in sentencing[33] for contempt of court, particularly with regard to the vexed problem of witnesses who prove unco-operative:

(1) An immediate term of imprisonment is the only appropriate sentence to impose on a person who interferes with the administration of justice, unless the circumstances are wholly exceptional.[34]

(2) Where victims or witnesses to serious crime refuse to do their duty, or succumb to fear of reprisals, by refusing to give evidence or to answer questions, the result is a failure of law and order; thus, a custodial sentence will usually be necessary, in order to mark the gravity of the matter and to stiffen the resolve of other witnesses (in most such cases a moderate period of custody will suffice).[35]

(3) The circumstances of each case are all important, and there is no rule that higher sentences should be imposed where there has been interference with, or threats to, jurors than in the case of a witness who refuses to co-operate. Indeed, while it is legitimate to have regard to the maximum sentence of three months for failing to comply with a witness order,[36] a judge may nevertheless impose a substantially longer sentence for a blatant contempt by a witness in the face of the court.[37]

(4) Unless there are pressing reasons to do otherwise, the question of punishment is best left to the end of a trial or at least to the end of the Crown's case since, so long as the prosecution's case remains open, it is desirable that the witness should have the chance to reconsider with the benefit of legal advice. Where a witness persists in his refusal, he should nevertheless be given an opportunity to explain his reasons during any

---

[30] *Enfield London Borough Council v Mahoney* [1983] 1 W.L.R. 749, CA. By a direction made by Lord Dilhorne L.C. on May 29 1963, the Official Solicitor is required to review the cases of those committed to prison for contempt of court and to seek the release of those inappropriately committed. See also the remarks about the valuable role of the Official Solicitor by Ormrod L.J. in *Re G (Minors) (Wardship: Costs)* [1982] 1 W.L.R. 438 at 442 and by Munby J. in *Harris v Harris*; *Att-Gen v Harris* [2001] 2 F.L.R. 895 at [239]. See generally for the functions and duties of the Official Solicitor, *Civil Procedure 2005*, Vol. 2 at paras 9A-391—9A-398.
[31] [1995] 2 All E.R. 28.
[32] For guidance on custodial penalties in family cases, see para.14-18 below.
[33] The word "sentence", although inevitably used, was said to be "inappropriate" by Watkins L.J. in *R. v Phillips (Peter)* (1983) 78 Cr.App.R. 88 at 90. He preferred the word "punishment".
[34] See *R. v Owen* [1976] 1 W.L.R. 840, 3 All E.R. 329.
[35] See, *e.g. R. v Cole* [1997] 1 Cr.App.R. (S) 228.
[36] For a discussion of the summoning of witnesses in the Crown Court, see para.11-116.
[37] See *R. v Phillips (Peter)* (1983) 78 Cr.App.R. 88; *R. v Jardine* (1987) 9 Cr.App.R. (S) 41; *R. v Samuda* (1989) 11 Cr.App.R. (S) 471.

summary proceedings for contempt, which is a matter essential to a fair and reasoned sentencing decision.

(5) The principal factors affecting the length of a sentence will be:
   (a) the gravity of the offence being tried;
   (b) the effect on the trial;
   (c) the contemnor's reasons for failure to give evidence;
   (d) whether or not there was impertinent defiance, as opposed to merely a stubborn refusal to answer[38];
   (e) the scale of sentences in any comparable cases, albeit each case turns on its own facts;
   (f) the antecedents, personal circumstances and characteristics of the contemnor[39];
   (g) whether any special deterrent is required, for example at the beginning of a series of trials where it is clear that witnesses are being threatened, or where there are signs of a developing pattern of refusal in relation to certain types of offence, or in particular geographical areas.

(6) Where a witness is refusing to testify, the relative importance of his evidence needs to be taken into account.[40]

F. Relating a sentence for contempt to other penalties imposed

It is necessary for a sentencer in criminal proceedings to keep separately in mind the considerations applying to any contempt occurring in the face of the court from those governing the appropriate sentence for the primary offence for which the accused is before the court. In *R. v Aston*,[41] Lord Goddard C.J. emphasised that any insulting comments should not have the effect of increasing a sentence for the main offence, but should be dealt with, if appropriate, by the imposition of a separate penalty. In *R. v Aquarius*,[42] it was held that there was nothing wrong in principle, if the facts warranted it, in making the term of imprisonment imposed for contempt longer than that for the primary offence.

G. The application of section 14 to civil contempt

It is clear from the decision of the House of Lords in *Peart v Stewart*[43] that the imposition of maximum sentences applies also to instances of civil contempt.[44]

---

[38] *R. v Leonard* (1984) 6 Cr.App.R. (S) 279.
[39] *R. v Palmer* [1992] 1 W.L.R. 568.
[40] *R. v Phillips (Peter)* (1983) 78 Cr.App.R. 88.
[41] [1948] W.N. 252. See also *R. v Butt* (1957) 41 Cr.App.R. 82; *R. v Logan* [1974] Crim.L.R. 609.
[42] (1974) 59 Cr.App.R. 165. And see *R. v Hardwick*, November 2, 2000, (CACD) (Two months sentence for harassing a witness imposed consecutively to 28 months for theft: held to be "amply justified").
[43] [1983] 2 A.C. 109 at 118D–E.
[44] The section makes no distinction between civil and criminal contempt itself, although Parliament did not adopt the Phillimore recommendation that the distinction between civil and criminal contempt should go altogether: Cmnd. 5794 (1974), para.176.

Lord Diplock said that s.14 operated upon the powers of the county court to grant injunctions generally. In *Secretary of State for Defence v Guardian Newspapers Ltd*[45] he again acknowledged that the Act had amended the law in relation to civil contempt as well as criminal.

14–13   Section 14(1) preserves the power to release a contemnor at a point earlier than the end of the fixed term of detention required by that section. It is appropriately used where a contemnor seeks to purge his contempt and the court is convinced of his sincerity.[46] Conversely, an application for early release was refused in *Shalson v Russo (Contempt: Application to Purge)*[47] in circumstances where the respondent had been sentenced to a total of two years' imprisonment for breaches of search and disclosure orders and of undertakings to provide documents and information. The court was not yet satisfied that the coercive element of his sentence would not be effective. Nor was there any indication either as to why he might be in a better position to fulfil his undertaking if released; or that it was impossible for him to comply with the relevant orders while in prison. With effect from April 4, 2005 the early release provisions of s.258 of the Criminal Justice Act 2003 mean that a person committed to prison for contempt of court "or any kindred offence" is to be released unconditionally after having served one half of the term for which he was committed. Despite the overall criminal context, and the use of the term "offence" there can be little doubt that this obligation of the Secretary of State would apply whether the contemnor has been committed in respect of a civil or criminal contempt.

H. What is the "occasion" referred to in section 14?

14–14   It appears that " ... there is no construction of s.14(1) which will avoid every possibility of anomaly".[48] Nevertheless, the general intention of the Act is that the "occasion" referred to in the section is the hearing at which the sentence is imposed, or a suspended sentence is activated, irrespective of the number of contempts or applications with which the court is concerned.[49] It is desirable, in order to make that principle work, to try and ensure that all allegations of contempt are, so far as possible, considered on a single occasion. Otherwise, the maximum sentence available may depend upon arbitrary factors and, in particular, upon the vagaries of the court's listing system. From the respondent's point of view, therefore, it would be prudent to invite the applicant to move at the same

---

[45] [1985] 1 A.C. 339 at 346G.
[46] *Mason v Lawton* [1991] 2 F.L.R. 50, 54B-D, CA.
[47] [2002] EWHC 399, Ch, [2002] All E.R. (D) 13 (Mar).
[48] *Villiers v Villiers* [1994] 1 W.L.R. 493 at 500C, [1994] 1 F.L.R. 647 at 653B, *per* Hoffmann L.J.
[49] *ibid*. This approach is to be contrasted with that taken by the Court of Appeal in *Re S & A Conversions* (1988) 4 B.C.L.C. 384, CA, where, although it had been said that the maximum penalty "for a single case of contempt of the gravest kind" of two years should be taken into account, no criticism was made in principle of the fact that the consecutive sentences imposed exceeded two years in total. The court contented itself with reducing the sentences imposed to a total of six months, while leaving open for future consideration the question ultimately resolved in *Villiers v Villiers*.

time, or not at all, in respect of any other contempt which he thinks may have been committed.[50]

It was said by Sir Thomas Bingham M.R. in *Villiers v Villiers*[51]: 14–15

" ... where, in the ordinary course, different contempts came before the court on different occasions and without any manipulation of the timetable it may be that cumulative sentences of more than 2 years could be justified. But it is, I think, clear, as I have suggested, that a contemnor must not, on any occasion, leave the court subject to a sentence of more than 2 years. If in doubt as to whether an occasion is to be treated as a single occasion or more than a single occasion it is incumbent on any judge in such a position to bear in mind the statutory provision and the obvious object of the statutory provision and bear in mind also the duty of fairness which is owed to any contemnor".

It is thus clear that the section regulates the maximum which can be imposed on any one occasion, and if several separate contempts are being dealt with together it is necessary to bear in mind that, if the aggregated total of penalties amounts to two years' imprisonment, the court will be regarded as imposing the maximum permitted. 14–16

In *R (A Minor) (Contempt: Sentence)*,[52] a man in his thirties had formed a relationship with a 14 year-old girl, who was made a ward of court; he persisted in breaching the terms of injunctions restraining contact with her. Findings of contempt were made on 13 "counts", largely on the respondent's own admissions. Various sentences were imposed totalling two years. The judge had purported to give credit for those admissions, for an apology and for the fact that the respondent had spared the ward the need to give evidence. The Court of Appeal held, however, that since he had imposed the maximum permitted by s.14(1) he could not be taken to have done so. The overall sentence was reduced to 18 months. 14–17

I. Guidance as to custodial penalties in family or domestic cases

Hale L.J. took the opportunity in the harassment case of *Hale v Tanner*[53] to give general guidance on sentencing specifically in the context of non-molestation orders under s.42 of the Family Law Act 1996. She pointed out that the circumstances surrounding civil contempt cases are more various than in ordinary criminal cases and that the objectives underlying any penalty imposed are also likely to be more various. Her general guidance included the following points: 14–18

(a) An application to commit for contempt is the only enforcement procedure available for breach of a non-molestation order under s.42.[54]

---

[50] ibid.
[51] [1994] 1 W.L.R. 493 at 499F–G, [1994] 1 F.L.R. 647 at 652E–F.
[52] [1994] 1 W.L.R. 487, [1994] 2 F.L.R. 185, CA.
[53] [2000] 1 W.L.R. 2377.
[54] But see now the Domestic Violence, Crime and Victims Act 2004, s.42A which provides for a statutory offence of breaching a non-molestation order, punishable by a term of imprisonment of five years, or fine, or both.

(b) The full range of criminal sentencing options is not available.

(c) Custody is not automatic.

(d) There is a power to fine, and a power to suspend a custodial sentence, which should nevertheless not affect the length of the sentence, that is, "you do not make the sentence longer because you are going to suspend it."

(e) The length of the sentence depends on the court's objectives which will always include marking the court's disapproval of the disobedience of its order and securing compliance with it in the future.

(f) The length of the committal has to bear some relationship to the maximum statutory sentence of two years.

(g) The court has to bear in mind the context, which may be aggravating or mitigating.

(h) " . . . in many cases, the court will have to bear in mind that there are concurrent proceedings in another court based on either the same facts or some of the same facts which are before the court on the contempt proceedings. The court cannot ignore those parallel proceedings. It may have to take into account their outcome in considering what the practical effect is upon the contempt proceedings. They do have different purposes and often the overlap is not exact, but nevertheless the court will not want . . . the contemnor to suffer punishment twice for the same offence".

14–19 Subsequently in *Lomas v Parle*[55] the Court of Appeal gave supplementary guidance and Thorpe L.J. considered the interrelationship between the contempt jurisdiction, as it applied to injunctions granted under the 1996 Act, and the jurisdiction under the Protection from Harassment Act 1997. He said[56]:

"However effectively proceedings are managed a perpetrator may face sentence for the same act which amounts to both a breach of an injunction made in family proceedings and also a crime under the Protection from Harassment Act. Of course the sentencing courts do not share the same objective and operate in different ranges. The judge in family proceedings has to fit a custodial sentence with a range of 0–24 months. An important objective for him is to uphold the authority of the court by demonstrating that its orders cannot be flouted with impunity. Nevertheless there will be a shared deterrent objective in the punishment of domestic violence by imprisonment.

Clearly therefore the first court to sentence must not anticipate or allow for a likely future sentence. It is for the second court to sentence to reflect the prior sentence in its judgment in order to ensure that the defendant is not twice punished for the same act. It is essential that the second court should be fully informed of the factors and circumstances reflected in the first sentence . . .

Within the constraints of the two year limit on sentences for harassment in breach of protective injunctions granted under s.42 of the Family Law Act and the different scale which this necessarily involves, judges should as far as possible ensure that sentences

---

[55] [2003] EWCA Civ 1804. See also *Head (Damon) v Orrow (Carol)* [2004] EWCA Civ 1691.
[56] At [47]–[50].

passed under s.42 are not manifestly discrepant with sentences for harassment charged under ss.3, 4 or 5 of the Protection from Harassment Act 1997 . . . ".

It was pointed out that the level of sentencing under the 1997 Act had been significantly higher than for comparable incidents dealt with by way of committal for contempt. He added that domestic violence could be the subject of criminal charges varying from common assault to murder. Thus the more serious the offences the less scope there would be for maintaining the relationship between sentences imposed in the different jurisdictions. It had been observed by Hale L.J. in *Hale v Tanner* that it was rare to find reported cases[57] where a penalty as high as six months imprisonment had been imposed in respect of breaches of injunctions in the domestic context even in more serious circumstances than those before the court in *Hale* itself, which mainly concerned serious persistent and threatening telephone calls. It was emphasised however by May L.J. in *Head (Damon) v Orrow (Carol)*[58] that the level of sentencing in cases prior to the implementation of the 1997 Act no longer reflected "contemporary requirements and opinion". Domestic and other violence associated with harassment and molestation now demanded more condign deterrent punishment than formerly. As was observed by Judge L.J. on a criminal appeal, concerning domestic violence[59]:

14–20

"Although we are not enunciating any new principle, we must firmly emphasise that the seriousness of an incident of violence is not diminished merely because it takes place in a 'domestic environment'. Whenever and wherever it happens an offence of violence is an offence of violence. Indeed in some respects, given the bond of trust that should exist between people who live together or who are members of the same family, repeated violence represents a betrayal of that trust which is an aggravating feature of these offences."

J. Imprisonment: powers of magistrates' courts

Magistrates have power to commit for what is effectively contempt in the face of the court under s.12 of the Contempt of Court Act 1981. This is a jurisdiction which is fully considered in chapter 10.[60] Section 97 of the Magistrates' Courts Act 1980[61] gives magistrates powers to imprison for one month to punish those who fail to attend such a court in answer to a witness summons. This is treated in chapter 11.[62]

14–21

Committal for debt

The only other aspect of magistrates' statutory powers remaining to be addressed, as being relevant to the law of contempt, are those conferred by s.76

14–22

---

[57] See the cases listed in [35] of *Head v Orrow* [2004] EWCA Civ 1691.
[58] [2004] EWCA Civ 1691 at [37].
[59] *R. v McNaughten* [2003] EWCA Crim 3479.
[60] See paras 10–113 *et seq.* And see the Consolidated Criminal Practice Direction [2002] 1 W.L.R. 2870 (as amended) in Appendix 5C. For the latest version of the *Direction* see *www.courtservice. gov.uk/docs/cpd/consol_criminal_pd_220305.doc.*
[61] As amended by Pt III of Sch.2 to the Contempt of Court Act 1981.
[62] See paras 11–130 *et seq.*

14–22   **CHAPTER 14—SANCTIONS AND REMEDIES**

of the same statute. Section 76 of the Magistrates' Courts Act 1980 governs the power of justices to issue a warrant committing to prison someone who has made default in paying a sum adjudged to be paid by one of their orders. It is a power of extreme severity. "Indeed, it might be argued that the existence of such a power in a society which long ago closed the Marshalsea prison and abandoned imprisonment as a remedy for the enforcement of debts, is anomalous."[63] It is, however, clear that it is intended to be a sanction of the very last resort, because of the conditions to which the power is made subject.[64]

14–23   First, such a person must be in court before he can be committed, and the magistrates have a power to issue a warrant to arrest him and bring him to court (an "attendance warrant"). Secondly, the power is only exercisable if it is proved that there has been wilful refusal or culpable neglect to pay maintenance ordered. Something in the nature of a deliberate defiance or reckless disregard of the court's order is required.[65] Thirdly, the court is expressly prohibited from exercising the power unless it is satisfied that all other methods of enforcing payment have been tried or considered and either have proved unsuccessful or are likely to do so. Other methods that might be considered would include an instalment order; another might be a suspended order for committal under s.77(2) of the Magistrates' Courts Act 1980, since this enables the court to fix a term of imprisonment and postpone the issue of a warrant until such time and on such conditions, if any, as the court thinks just. Provision was made in s.43ZA of the Supreme Court Act 1981[66] for the High Court to have powers to impose or vary a sentence when quashing the committal of a person to prison or detention by a magistrates' court or Crown Court for either (a) default in paying a sum adjudged to be paid by a conviction or (b) want of sufficient distress to satisfy such a sum.

K. The county court: powers of imprisonment

14–24   There are specific provisions under the County Courts Act 1984 empowering judges to punish those who wilfully insult persons concerned in such proceedings, or who wilfully interrupt them.[67] Similar provision is made[68] to address those who assault officers of the court in the execution of their duty. There is no power to remand in custody or on bail. A district judge, assistant district judge or deputy district judge was given the same powers as a judge under these sections by virtue of the Courts and Legal Services Act 1990.[69] Now it is provided in CPR 2.3 that "judge" includes a district judge; thus no specific provision is required.[70]

---

[63] *R. v Luton Magistrates' Court Ex p. Sullivan* [1992] 2 F.L.R. 196 at 201C, Waite J.
[64] Magistrates' Courts Act 1980, s.93; Administration of Justice Act 1970, s.41.
[65] *R. v Luton Magistrates' Court Ex p. Sullivan* [1992] 2 F.L.R. 196 at 198.
[66] Inserted by s.62 of the Access to Justice Act 1999.
[67] s.118, set out at para.13–90. For the procedure, see now CPR Sch.2, cc.34.1 considered further in paras 15–77 *et seq.*
[68] s.14, set out at para.13–84.
[69] See County Courts Act 1984 ss.14(3), 74.
[70] Compare the former CCR Ord.35, r.5.

The county court's "ancillary" jurisdiction

In *Whitter v Peters* and *Peart v Stewart*[71] the Court of Appeal held that, in the light of the county court's general ancillary jurisdiction under s.74 of the County Courts Act 1959,[72] and of the broad definition of "superior court" in s.19 of the Contempt of Court Act 1981, a county court judge had the power to imprison for periods up to two years where punishing for breach of an injunction. When the matter came before the House of Lords, however, it was held[73] that the section had the effect of limiting the powers of the county court to commit for a fixed term of one month. The basis for that conclusion, in construing s.14(1) of the 1981 Act, was that there was no reason to assume that Parliament intended to distinguish between the powers of the county court in the exercise of its general ancillary jurisdiction and those in the exercise of the specific powers under the County Courts Act. Such courts were "inferior", and that term had to be given its usual construction. There is now very little distinction between the scope of the powers of the county court and that of the High Court. It was provided by the County Court Remedies Regulations 1991[74] that county courts should not make seizing orders or freezing injunctions; otherwise the powers in respect of interim injunctions would appear to have been the same. In 1995 there was an amendment so as to enable a county court to grant a freezing injunction in certain specified circumstances.[75]

14–25

The effect of this decision of the House of Lords in *Whitter v Peters* was reversed by the County Courts (Penalties for Contempt) Act 1983.[76] This expressly provides that the county court is to rank in this context as a "superior court". Parliament clearly came to the conclusion that it would be pointless to have invested the county court with equivalent powers to the High Court, in respect of its ancillary jurisdiction, without giving it also comparable powers of enforcement.

14–26

Although the court has the power to commit to prison for breaches of orders, it should never be assumed that this penalty will follow automatically or as a matter of normal course. Each case must be judged on its own circumstances.[77]

14–27

L. The power to discharge: superior courts

Section 14(1) of the 1981 Act specifically preserves the powers of the courts to discharge a person who has been committed. The old rule was that a person

14–28

---

[71] [1982] 1 W.L.R. 389.
[72] The current equivalent is the County Courts Act 1984, s.38 (as substituted by the Courts and Legal Services Act 1990, s.3).
[73] *sub nom. Peart v Stewart* [1983] 2 A.C. 109.
[74] SI 1991/1222.
[75] See regs 2(b) and 3(3) as amended by the County Court Remedies (Amendment) Regulations 1995 (SI 1995/206).
[76] s.1 of this Act inserted s.14(4A) in the Contempt of Court Act 1981.
[77] *Smith v Smith* [1988] 1 F.L.R. 179 at 181E–G, Sir John Donaldson M.R., 182D–E, Balcombe L.J., CA; *Wilsher v Wilsher* [1989] 2 F.L.R. 187 at 189, Kerr L.J.; *R. v Luton Magistrates' Court Ex p. Sullivan* [1992] 2 F.L.R. 196, Waite J., FD.

14–28

committed for a fixed term could not be discharged,[78] unlike a contemnor sentenced to an indefinite period. If he was a civil contemnor, he was entitled to release *ex debito justitiae* on compliance with the court order and following an apology.[79] However, in the case of a contumacious civil contempt the court might refuse to discharge a contemnor even if an apology had been tendered and the order complied with.[80] The power of the courts to discharge is discretionary and unfettered.[81] No doubt, however, modern practice and parlance would require a refusal to discharge to be justified by the tests of necessity and proportionality to the desired objective whether penal or coercive.

14–29   It is provided in CPR Sch.1, Ord.52.8 that[82]:

"The court may, on the application of any person committed to prison for any contempt of court, discharge him."

Where a judge purported to direct, after a series of breaches of a non-molestation order, that a husband be not entitled to apply for release until the last day of his sentence (which was six months less one day), the Court of Appeal held that this order ran directly contrary to the former RSC Ord.52, r.8(1), and should not have been made.[83] The provision applies to the High Court and Court of Appeal. The Crown Court under the Supreme Court Act 1981 has the like powers to the High Court,[84] is a part of the Supreme Court and a superior court of record.[85] Accordingly, it too would have the power to discharge a contemnor.[86]

---

[78] *Att-Gen v James* [1962] 2 Q.B. 637 (it was in that case contemplated that an application could be made to the Home Secretary: *per* Lord Parker C.J. at 640); *Sutherland v Sutherland*, *The Times*, April 19 and May 6, 1893. In *R. v Montgomery* [1995] 2 All E.R. 28 at 34h–j, it was commented in the case of a reluctant witness in the Crown Court, who thought better of his refusal to give evidence, and returned to court upon an application "to purge his contempt" that the application could not have been properly so described since he had been sentenced to a finite term of imprisonment for criminal contempt. Therefore, any analogy with committal of a civil contemnor was "inapt". Nevertheless, there was the possibility of "the power of the court to order his earlier discharge" referred to in s.14.
[79] *Adlard v Smith* (1819) 6 Price 231, 146 E.R. 822; see also para.3–179.
[80] *Re Hunt* [1959] 2 Q.B. 69; see para.3–180.
[81] *Re Preston* (1883) 11 Q.B.D. 545. And cp. Buckley L.J. in *Scott v Scott* [1912] P. 241.
[82] In a *Practice Direction* of July 25, 1983 the President of the Family Division directed that on such applications the contemnor should be present to hear the outcome save where the provisions of the Mental Health Act applied, and it was considered by the solicitor conducting the application that in the particular circumstances it would not be desirable: [1983] 1 W.L.R. 998, [1983] 2 All E.R. 1066.
[83] *Vaughan v Vaughan* [1973] 1 W.L.R. 1159.
[84] s.45(4).
[85] Supreme Court Act 1981, s.45(1).
[86] As contemplated in s.14 (1). See the law governing automatic release at paras 14–32 *et seq.* But see the remarks of Potter J. in *R. v Montgomery* [1995] 2 All E.R. 28 at 34h–j, which suggest that the Court of Appeal on that occasion at least was intending to convey that there was no right to apply for a variation in sentence (rather than merely criticising the applicant's terminology of "purging").

M. The power to discharge: "inferior" courts

Section 118(2) of the County Courts Act 1984 provides a power to the judge to revoke a committal order made under the section[87] or to discharge a contemnor in custody. A similar power is provided by s.14(2) in respect of someone committed for an assault on an officer of the court.[88] When a contemnor has been imprisoned by a county court, by way of enforcing an order made under the ancillary jurisdiction, the county court would have the same power of discharge as the High Court, in the light of the policy underlying the County Court (Penalties for Contempt) Act 1983.[89]

Section 12 of the 1981 Act gives magistrates similar powers:

"(4) A magistrates' court may at any time revoke an order of committal made under subsection (2) and, if the offender is in custody, order his discharge."

N. Automatic release

It was provided by s.45 of the Criminal Justice Act 1991 that those who were committed to prison for contempt for a period of less than 12 months had to be released after serving half the sentence. As to those committed for a period of 12 months or longer, they had to be released after serving two thirds of their sentence.[90]

Thus, whereas a person committed to prison for any criminal offence (as ordinarily understood) for a period of four years or less had only to serve half that sentence, a contemnor committed for 12 months or more was required to serve two thirds. This applied to both civil and criminal contempts. The rationale was explained by Sir Thomas Bingham M.R. as follows[91]:

"Plainly Parliament has intended that a contemnor committed to prison for 12 months or more should serve two-thirds of the sentence ... It may very well be that the difference of treatment is attributable to the fact that a contemnor has the right to return to the court to purge his contempt and seek that he should be released which is a procedure not open to the criminal defendant."

In *Thompson v Mitchell*[92] the Court of Appeal considered what was described as a "non-molestation order" where three breaches had been found proved and the judge committed the appellant for a period of 72 days, and also activated a

---

[87] See para.13–90 where the section is set out.
[88] See para.13–84.
[89] See para.14–26. The second of the two subsections (4A) inserted in s.14 of the 1981 Act states that a county court shall be treated as a superior court for the purpose of the "preceding provisions of this section" which include, in s.14(1), express reference to the power of the court to order earlier discharge.
[90] The Criminal Justice Act 1991, s.33 (entitling those serving more than 12 months, but less than four years, to be released after serving one half of the sentence of imprisonment) did not apply to contemnors: s.45.
[91] *Re R (A Minor) (Contempt: Sentence)* [1994] 1 W.L.R. 487 at 492G–H, [1994] 2 F.L.R. 185 at 189B–C.
[92] [2004] EWCA Civ 1271.

14–34 suspended sentence to run consecutively, with the result that a total of 128 days was to be served. She purported to order also that "Mr Mitchell is not to be released until 128 days have passed. Mr Mitchell is at liberty to purge his contempt, but his sentence cannot be halved". When it was drawn up the order specified that he was committed for a total period of 128 days " . . . namely until 16 September 2004". It was argued on the appellant's behalf that the judge simply had no jurisdiction to make that order, since it was inconsistent with the terms of ss.33 and 45 of the Criminal Justice Act 1991 providing for automatic release. The court had adjourned the matter to have the benefit of argument from the Attorney-General as a friend of the court. In the light of his skeleton argument the court was left in no doubt that there was no power to override the early release provisions. Accordingly, a judge who sentences a contemnor must do so for a fixed term of weeks, months or years up to the maximum of two years.[93] There is no power to direct that a contemnor should remain in prison until a specified date or should not be released before a specified date. It was confirmed that a judge who wished to take account of the early release provisions should calculate a sentence which did so—provided the sentence was commensurate with the contempt.

14–35 The position governing early release is now regulated by s.258 of the Criminal Justice Act 2003, which came in to effect on April 4, 2005.[94] The section provides:

"(1) This section applies in relation to a person committed to prison—

. . . (b) for contempt of court or any kindred offence.

(2) As soon as a person to whom this section applies has served one-half of the term for which he was committed, it is the duty of the Secretary of State to release him unconditionally . . . ".

O. No provision for deducting time spent on remand

14–36 One general sentencing issue that causes difficulty in the law of contempt has been the extent to which allowance can be made for time spent in custody on remand. Sir Thomas Bingham in *Delaney v Delaney*[95] analysed the legislation then current and came to the conclusion that "time spent in custody on remand is not deducted from a committal for contempt of court". He stated that the "basic rule" is that such time should count against sentence. An anomaly arises in the contempt context because "imprisonment" for the purposes of s.67 of the Criminal Justice Act 1967 (which embodied the basic rule) did not include "committal . . . for failure to abstain from doing anything required . . . to be left undone"[96] with the result that contemnors were excluded from the benefit of

---

[93] When the Criminal Justice Act 2003, s.181 comes in to effect, a sentence of less than one year must be specified in weeks.
[94] It would thus appear that the note as to the statutory regime governing "early release" in *Civil Procedure 2005*, Vol. 1, sc.52.8.2 has been overtaken in this respect.
[95] [1996] Q.B. 387 at 466, CA.
[96] See s.104 of the 1967 Act. See also *Horgan v Horgan* [2002] EWCA Civ 1371 at [34], [2002] All E.R. (D) 95.

the rule. Despite subsequent legislative changes,[97] this anomaly seems to have survived. As pointed out by the Court of Appeal in *McKnight v Northern*,[98] any reduction thought appropriate should be made at the time of committal. The judge had in that case not addressed the point before imposing the penalty. The Court of Appeal in *Zahide S (Mustafa) (R. on the application of) v S (Korel)*[99] again emphasised the importance of remembering that time spent on remand cannot be taken into account.

P. The application of the Prison Rules[1]

Special provision was made by the Prison Rules 1964 (r.63), so that prisoners committed for contempt could wear suitable clothing of their own (under r.20), and also send and receive as many letters as they wished, subject to such limits and conditions as the Home Secretary might direct (r.34). Similar provisions were made as to the receiving of visitors. This was true of both criminal and civil contempts. This distinction, however, ceased in 1992.[2] Persons committed to prison for contempt are subject to special treatment under r.7(3) of the Prison Rules 1999.[3] They are treated largely as unconvicted or remand prisoners. Further provision is made in s.3 of the Representation of the People Act 1983, which provides that a convicted person is legally incapable of voting at a parliamentary or local election.[4] The disqualification does not however apply to persons imprisoned for contempt of court or to those imprisoned only for default in, for example, paying a fine.[5]

It was observed by Parker L.J. in *Parsons v Nasar*[6] that "it should not be thought that I am of the view that it is open to the prison authorities, when they have been provided with an order of this sort, to decide for themselves when a defendant should be released." The proposition seems doubtful, however, and it is to be noted that relevant authorities were not cited. In *Westcott v Westcott*[7] the judge imposed a seven day sentence for breach of a non-molestation order. The practice at Dorchester prison was to release prisoners due to complete their sentence on a Sunday on the preceding Friday. On discovering this, the judge purported to amend his sentence to one of nine days' imprisonment without any further formal hearing in open court. It was held that this was wholly irregular and, once the sentence was passed, the consequences were a matter for the prison regulations and rules.

---

[97] The general provision for making allowance for time spent in prison on remand is now to be found in the Criminal Justice Act 2003, s.240, and what constitutes a "sentence of imprisonment" for these purposes is defined in s.306, in terms similar to s.104(1) of the 1967 legislation.
[98] [2001] EWCA Civ 2028 (Lexis).
[99] [2003] EWCA Civ 1570. Ward L.J's plea at [9] that this point should be reported by the law reporters "or the editors of the text books" appears not to have been heeded by the former.
[1] SI 1999/728. See also Halsbury's *Laws of England*, 4th ed. Vol.36(2), paras 699 *et seq*.
[2] SI 1992/2080 (since revoked by the 1999 Rules).
[3] See SI 1999/728, and *Civil Procedure*, sc.52.1.38.
[4] This aspect of "civic death" can be traced back to the Forfeiture Act 1870 and indeed beyond.
[5] Representation of the People Act 1983, s.3(2).
[6] [1990] 2 F.L.R. 103 at 104.
[7] [1985] F.L.R. 616, CA. See also *Lamb v Lamb* [1984] F.L.R. 278 at 283, Oliver L.J.

Q. Pardons

14–39 While it seems that pardon under the Royal prerogative is available in cases of criminal contempt, this does not appear to be so for civil contempt.[8]

R. The power to suspend

14–40 The statutory provisions giving a criminal court power to suspend a sentence of imprisonment in criminal proceedings do not apply to the summary process for contempt. Section 39 of the Criminal Justice Act 1967[9] was considered by the Court of Appeal in *Morris v Crown Office* where Lord Denning M.R. concluded[10]:

> "If you read this Act as a whole, you will find that the legislature never intended s.39 to apply to a committal for a criminal contempt ... The upshot of it is that there is no provision in this Act [the Criminal Justice Act 1967] for giving effect to a suspended sentence for contempt of court—whereas there are provisions for dealing with suspended sentences for all other criminal offences. This leads me to the conclusion that the legislature never intended that committal for contempt of court should be subject to suspension of sentence."

There is, however, an inherent or common law power to suspend an order for committal.[11] As Lord Denning later added[12]:

> "The powers at common law remain intact. It is a power to fine or imprison, to give an immediate sentence or to postpone it, to commit to prison pending his consideration of the sentence, to bind over to be of good behaviour and keep the peace, and to bind over to come up for judgment if called upon. These powers enable the judge to give what is, in effect, a suspended sentence".

14–41 The current procedure is prescribed in CPR Sch.1, Ord.52.7, which contemplates such a power in the High Court and Court of Appeal (while not conferring it):

> "(1) The Court by whom an order of committal is made may by order direct that the execution of the order of committal shall be suspended for such period or on such terms or conditions as it may specify.

---

[8] See para.3–185.
[9] Repealed. See the Powers of Criminal Courts (Sentencing) Act 2000, s.118, which was superseded by the new regime of suspended sentences provided for in the Criminal Justice Act 2003, s.189, which took effect from April 4, 2005 (SI 2005/950). This does not apply to committal since it is provided in the interpretation section (s. 195) for Chapter 3 of Pt 12 of the statute (ss. 181–195: prison sentences of less than 12 months) that a committal for contempt of court is not a "sentence of imprisonment".
[10] [1970] 2 Q.B. 114 at 124. See also *BBPM v B (MM) (DC)* [1969] P. 103.
[11] A suspended sentence was imposed, for example, by the Court of Appeal in *Delaney v Delaney* [1996] Q.B. 387 at 403E–F, Sir Thomas Bingham M.R. See also *Secretary of State for Defence v Percy* [1999] 1 All E.R. 732, Ch.D. where the judge extended the period of a suspended sentence already imposed by another judge and *Best Training Ltd v URO Properties Ltd* [2002] All E.R. (D) 364 (Feb) (Casetrack).
[12] At 125.

(2) Where execution of an order of committal is suspended by an order under paragraph (1), the applicant for the order of committal must, unless the court otherwise directs, serve on the person against whom it was made notice informing him of the making and the terms of the order under that paragraph."

It was decided by the Court of Appeal in *Harris v Harris*[13] that this is the only power to suspend in such cases, affording the court the choice between a warrant for immediate execution and a warrant to be suspended. That choice had to be exercised at the sentencing hearing and would not arise again. Thus, on an application to purge, it is not open to the judge to suspend a sentence already imposed.

CPR Sch.1, Ord.52.1 which provides that committal is the correct mode for dealing with contempt in the High Court and Court of Appeal, makes no mention of the Crown Court. Under the provisions of the Supreme Court Act 1981, s.45(4),[14] however, this Court has conferred upon it the like powers to the High Court in matters of contempt. Thus there would be a power to suspend also.

There was no express power to suspend committal in the county court or magistrates' court. It was held, however, in *Lee v Walker*,[15] that the common law jurisdiction of the High Court to suspend a committal order had never been in doubt. Thus, in view of the provisions of s.38(1)(a) of the County Courts Act 1984, and those of s.14(4A)[16] of the Contempt of Court Act 1981, the county court had the power on making a committal order to suspend it upon compliance with the stated conditions. So far as magistrates are concerned, since s.12 of the Contempt of Court Act 1981 creates a criminal offence, there is no reason to suppose that the general law regarding suspension of sentences should not apply.

S. The implementation of suspended sentences

The court may direct that the execution of an order of committal shall be suspended for such period on such terms or conditions as it may specify. The Court of Appeal in *Lee v Walker*[17] held that the inherent jurisdiction of the court to punish contempt of court, as and when the circumstances require, had not been cut down by statutes dealing generally with imprisonment for crime. For example, it would appear that the general rule that suspended sentences are not to be made in respect of persons under 21 years of age[18] does not affect the generality of the court's discretion under CPR Sch.1, Ord.52.7, which is

---

[13] [2001] EWCA Civ 1644, [2002] Fam. 253.
[14] Considered in *Ex parte HTV Cymru (Wales) Ltd* [2002] E.M.L.R. 11.
[15] [1985] Q.B. 1191; see also *Dent v Dent and Hall* [1962] P. 187, Scarman J.
[16] As inserted by the County Courts (Penalties for Contempt) Act 1983. It provided that for these purposes a county court should be treated as a superior court.
[17] [1985] Q.B. 1191.
[18] Only a prison sentence can be suspended, and no such sentence could hitherto have been passed in respect of persons in this age group but it is necessary now to have regard to the provisions of the Criminal Justice and Court Services Act 2000, s.61 which, when brought in to force, will have the effect of rendering the standard custodial sentence for persons between 18 and 21 of imprisonment rather than detention.

14–45 specifically dealing with the power to commit. Nor had the court's inherent power been affected by the fact that suspended sentences were for a time restricted to "exceptional circumstances".[19] Indeed, in *Hale v Tanner (Practice Note)*,[20] it was observed by Hale L.J. that a suspended sentence, far from being exceptional in family cases, will usually be the first port of call in attempting to secure compliance with a non-molestation order.

14–46 The decision whether to suspend will generally depend upon whether the court's objective is primarily coercion or punishment. In *Le Roi v Salisbury District Council*,[21] a committal order was suspended for four months to give the contemnor an opportunity to comply with certain planning requirements, despite his having been in flagrant breach of planning controls over a long period. But in *Neil v Ryan*[22] the Court of Appeal held it to have been wrong in principle for the judge in the county court to have suspended a sentence of one month where the breach of a non-molestation order involved visiting the former partner's home and punching and kicking her. Suspension is unlikely to be an appropriate course to take if the original order has been complied with by the time of the committal hearing.[23]

14–47 A suspended term of imprisonment must itself be for a fixed term.[24] Moreover, in accordance with good sentencing practice generally, the length of the committal period should be decided without reference to whether or not it is to be suspended.[25] The period for which the order is suspended should normally also be fixed.[26] Yet in *Griffin v Griffin*,[27] the Court of Appeal upheld the validity of a committal order suspended "until further order" even though the effect was to suspend indefinitely. Reference was made to the earlier decision of *Pidduck v Molloy*,[28] and it was observed that there is an important distinction between orders that *ought* not generally to be made and those which are actually invalid.

---

[19] Powers of Criminal Courts (Sentencing) Act 2000, s.118(4)(b). The section was repealed with effect from April 4, 2005 by the Criminal Justice Act 2003, s.303, and replaced (from the same date) by s.189 of the same statute.

[20] [2000] 1 W.L.R. 2377 at 2381. See also *Nicholls v Nicholls* [1997] 1 W.L.R. 314.

[21] [2001] EWCA Civ 1490, [2002] 1 P. & C.R. 39. See M. Edwards [2002] J.P.L. 700. The sentence of three months' imprisonment was imposed in default of compliance.

[22] [1998] 2 F.L.R. 1068 at 1070.

[23] *Bluffield v Curtis* [1988] 1 F.L.R. 170. See also *Loseby v Newman* [1995] 2 F.L.R. 754, CA.

[24] *Re C (A Minor)* [1986] 1 F.L.R. 578.

[25] *Hale v Tanner (Practice Note)* [2000] 1 W.L.R. 2377. It has been argued that it is inappropriate to apply the principles of sentencing policy from the field of criminal law in this kind of case and that the priority should always be that of protecting the relevant "victim": see R.Kay, "Guidelines on Sanctions for Breach: *Hale v Tanner*" (2001) 64 M.L.R. 595.

[26] *Pidduck v Molloy* [1992] 2 F.L.R. 202, [1992] 1 F.C.R. 418 CA; *Loseby v Newman* [1995] 2 F.L.R. 754, CA.

[27] [2000] 2 F.L.R. 44, [2000] 1 F.C.R. 302. *Griffin* was considered by Neuberger J. in *Phonographic Performance Ltd v Tierney* [2003] EWHC 2416, [2003] All E.R. (D) 08. The judge noted that it was open to the court to suspend a committal order for an indefinite period but, on the facts of the case, he decided to suspend a sentence of 35 days imprisonment for 40 months—the purpose being to ensure compliance with a court order and protect the claimant's interests. The background was an ongoing problem with the defendant playing sound recordings in his nightclub without previously having paid a licence fee, as required by an earlier order.

[28] [1992] 2 F.L.R. 202.

All conditions as to suspension should be stated.[29] Where a suspended sentence is contemplated, the period of suspension should not be disproportionate to the sentence itself or to the gravity of the conduct.[30]

The flexibility of this procedure was tailored to the particular circumstances in *Secretary of State for Defence v Percy*.[31] Carnwath J. extended the period of a suspended sentence so that it would run from the date of his judgment. Ms Percy was an intrepid anti-nuclear campaigner who had come frequently before the courts on account of her sincerely held beliefs. On an earlier occasion she had been discharged from a period of committal on an application by the Official Solicitor because of health concerns. It may be that the judge took the view that no purpose would be served by imposing an immediate custodial penalty or activating the previous suspended sentence. His decision was made partly because of the limited range of penalties available for contempt of court and in particular the lack of community service as an option.[32]

T. Postponement of sentence

Despite what Lord Denning M.R. said in *Morris v Crown Office*[33] as to the court's power at that time " . . . to give an immediate sentence or to postpone it", it now appears in the light of the carefully defined terms of s.14 of the Contempt of Court Act 1981 that there is in fact no power of postponement.

In *Delaney v Delaney*[34] it was held that (apart from contempt in the face of the court[35]) there is no power to detain a contemnor in custody, without imposing a penalty, whether for the purpose of considering reports or for any other reason. Where a judge is uncertain as to the sentence he wishes to impose, he should pass a sentence towards the top end of the appropriate bracket, whilst directing that the matter be restored for further hearing at the end of a suitable period. At that hearing the judge would have in effect three options. One would be to affirm the original order and leave the contemnor in prison, subject always to his right to make further applications to "purge"; secondly, the judge could order the immediate release of the contemnor; or thirdly, he or she could indicate a future

---

[29] *Bluffield v Curtis* [1988] 1 F.L.R. 170.
[30] *Loseby v Newman* [1995] 2 F.L.R. 754 at 757C–D, Balcombe L.J., CA. But see the special facts of *Photographic Performance Ltd v Tierney* [2003] EWHC 2416, [2003] All E.R. (D) 08 set out at para.14–47, n.27 above.
[31] [1999] 1 All E.R. 732. *Quaere* whether the extension of a suspended sentence passed by another judge was strictly permissible in the light of the views expressed by Lord Denning M.R. in *Morris v Crown Office* at 124E (" . . . there is no power for a judge of the High Court to follow up a suspended sentence passed by himself or by another judge of the High Court").
[32] Community penalties are still not available generally when imposing a penalty in contempt cases, but in the specific context of non-molestation orders, the effect of s.42A of the Family Law Act 1996 (not in force at the date of writing) will be to render the breach of a non-molestation order of itself a criminal offence and thus susceptible to the normal range of sentencing options.
[33] [1970] 2 Q.B. 114 at 125.
[34] [1996] Q.B. 387.
[35] *per* Sir Thomas Bingham M.R. at 401B–C. See the discussion in chapter 10 and also *Re Stevens and Holness*, Independent, June 9, 1997.

date at which the contemnor would be released, subject to a right to make further applications in the interim.[36]

14–51 On the other hand, where an application for committal has been adjourned, even for an indeterminate period, it may sometimes be appropriate to regard that delay as having given a respondent an opportunity to mend his ways. In *George v George*,[37] Glidewell L.J. described such an adjournment as "very similar to the deferment of the imposition of a sentence in criminal proceedings". The court in that instance concluded that a custodial penalty was appropriate because the chance had not been taken.

Judging whether a contemnor has "turned over a new leaf"

14–52 A practical difficulty which often confronts those dealing with contempts in the context of family proceedings is that of assessing whether the lesson of a custodial penalty has truly been learnt so as to ensure future compliance with continuing obligations imposed by the relevant order. The problem was identified by Devlin L.J. in *Yager v Musa*[38]:

> "[Counsel] is quite right when he says there is no way of testing the sincerity of the defendant's further protestations, unless he is allowed out; no one can take them at their face value, having regard to the fact that similar protestations have twice been ignored in the past; but, on the other hand, he cannot be kept in prison indefinitely merely because there is a danger that if he is released he might commit some further act of disobedience. I see no way of dealing with a man of this sort except in the way in which a criminal court deals with a persistent offender, such as a housebreaker, when, after a preliminary warning or probation, it has to impose a sentence of imprisonment. If immediately after he comes out of prison, the housebreaker, notwithstanding that he said he was going to turn over a new leaf, immediately goes back to housebreaking, a longer sentence of imprisonment has to be imposed, and so on."

14–53 In *Harris v Harris, Att-Gen v Harris*,[39] Munby J. was dealing with a contemnor who had been sentenced, after an unhappy history of defying the court's orders, to a term of 10 months' imprisonment. It was claimed that his contempt had been purged although in the light of the background there was doubt as to whether the assurances could or should be taken at face value. It was suggested on the contemnor's part that the court had the power to test his sincerity by releasing him from custody on the basis that the outstanding part of the sentence could be suspended. The point appeared to be free of authority, but after carefully reviewing such cases as bore upon the matter and, more significantly, the public policy considerations raised, Munby J. came to the conclusion that the court did indeed have such a power to discharge the contemnor on terms that the balance was to be suspended so as to put his sincerity to the test "without enabling him, if insincere, to avoid his just deserts".

---

[36] *Delaney v Delaney* [1996] Q.B. 387 at 400G–401A, *per* Sir Thomas Bingham M.R. And see para.14–6, n.18.
[37] [1986] 2 F.L.R. 347, CA.
[38] [1961] 2 Q.B. 214 at 218.
[39] [2001] Fam. 502 at 514 at [37].

His Lordship addressed the provisions contained in the former RSC Ord.52, r.7(1) and r.8(1),[40] and decided that there was nothing there inconsistent with the order he was proposing.

The decision was reversed by the Court of Appeal whose judgment made clear[41] that the choice whether or not to suspend a warrant for committal under CPR Sch.1, Ord.52.7 had to be exercised at the time the sentence was first imposed. On the facts of the case, since the judge had found a measure of atonement on the contemnor's part, the only realistic disposal was to substitute an order for unconditional release.

U. Consecutive sentences

The High Court has always had inherent jurisdiction to impose consecutive sentences of imprisonment where appropriate. That jurisdiction, in relation to contempt of court, has not been cut down by statutes dealing with powers of imprisonment in respect of crime generally (although on any occasion the maximum is limited by s.14 of the Contempt of Court Act 1981 to a total of two years imprisonment).[42] By virtue of s.38 of the County Courts Act 1984, those courts would therefore also have the power to impose consecutive penalties in such circumstances.[43]

In a different context, the question of consecutive sentences was addressed by the Criminal Division of the Court of Appeal in *R. v Anomo*.[44] The question arose as to whether the Crown Court has the power to order a sentence of imprisonment following a criminal conviction to be served consecutively to a term of imprisonment imposed previously by a county court for contempt. It had been submitted to the court that a committal to prison for a civil contempt would not necessarily be for a fixed period, and that it was thus wrong in principle and contrary to public policy to impose a sentence in the criminal proceedings which would be for that reason uncertain as to its commencement date. It seems to have been overlooked that the requirement for a fixed term imposed by s.14 of the Contempt of Court Act 1981 applied to committal for civil contempt.[45]

The court considered the provision in s.47(1) of the Supreme Court Act 1981 to the effect that a sentence should take effect from the beginning of the day on which it is imposed "unless the court otherwise directs", together with the common law history of the principle. It was held that, just as the High Court and county court had jurisdiction to impose consecutive sentences of imprisonment,

---

[40] Considered at para.14–40 (the power to suspend) and para.14–28 (the power to discharge) respectively.
[41] [2001] EWCA Civ 1644, [2002] Fam. 253 at [21].
[42] *Villiers v Villiers* cited at para.14–15.
[43] *Lee v Walker* [1985] 1 Q.B. 1191, 1201–2, Cumming-Bruce L.J. See also *Wilkes* (1769) 19 St. Tr. 1075 at 1133–4, Wilmot C.J.; *Cutbush* (1867) L.R. 2 Q.B. 379 at 382, Cockburn C.J.; *Morris v Crown Office* [1970 2 Q.B. 114, CA. Care needs to be taken in formulating the order to ensure tht the court's intention as to whether periods are to be served consecutively is made clear: see, *e.g. Abdi v Jama (Contempt: Committal)* [1996] 1 F.L.R. 407, discussed in para.15–46.
[44] *The Independent*, February 18, 1998 (Lexis).
[45] *Peart v Stewart* [1983] 2 A.C. 109, discussed at paras 14–12 *et seq.*

so too the Crown Court had always had power to impose a term of imprisonment for contempt to take effect consecutively to another sentence.[46] This included the power to pass a sentence of imprisonment in respect of a criminal conviction so as to make it consecutive to a county court term of imprisonment. This was said to be in accordance with good sense and the principles of good sentencing.

V. No one should be punished twice over

14-58 Due regard should be paid to the principle that no one should be punished twice for the same misconduct, in contempt as in other areas of penal policy.[47] This is sometimes made express in statutory provisions. For example, it is provided in s.3 of the Protection From Harassment Act 1997 and s.42A of the Family Law Act 1996 that no one should be punished for contempt and prosecuted in respect of the same incident. There may be significant implications for the court's sentencing powers, depending on which route is taken. For example the two year maximum under s.14 of the Contempt of Court Act would not apply if a breach is prosecuted under the Protection from Harassment Act 1997 or the Family Law Act 1996. There is in either case a maximum of six months on summary conviction or five years on indictment.

W. The need for the presence of the alleged contemnor

14-59 An application to commit for contempt should only be dealt with in the absence of the alleged contemnor in exceptional circumstances. It is a matter for the discretion of the judge.[48] It is necessary, in particular, to balance the desirability of making an immediate order, and the urgency of the matter, against the possibility that the evidence before the court may not be complete. However, if such an order is thought to be necessary, when the matter later comes before the court with the contemnor attending, it is not appropriate to impose a separate penalty without additional evidence that other contempts have been committed.[49]

X. Custodial sentences in respect of persons under 21

14-60 A question arises as to how far general sentencing provisions relating to young people can be applied in the context of contempt. In *Morris v The Crown Office*[50] the Court of Appeal took the view that the Criminal Justice Acts 1948 to 1967 did not apply to contempt proceedings. It followed that s.17(2) of the Criminal Justice Act 1948, which prohibited imprisonment in respect of persons under 17,

---

[46] Reference was made by way of example to *R. v Stredder* (1997) 1 Cr.App.R. (S) 209. See also *R. v Aquarius* (1974) 59 Cr.App.R. 165, where a defendant was sentenced to six months' imprisonment for theft with a nine month sentence for contempt to follow.

[47] *Danchevsky v Danchevsky (No.2)* CA Transcript, November 10, 1977, Lawton L.J.; *Lamb v Lamb* [1984] F.L.R. 278 at 282, Oliver L.J., 283, Kerr L.J.; *B v B (Contempt: Committal)* [1991] 2 F.L.R. 588 at 601C–D, Purchas L.J. See also the discussion at paras 3–209 *et seq.* And see *Hale v Tanner (Practice Note)* [2000] 1 W.L.R. 2377 discussed at para.14–18.

[48] *Lamb v Lamb* [1984] F.L.R. 278 at 281, CA, Oliver L.J.

[49] ibid.

[50] [1970] 2 Q.B. 114 at 126, Edmund-Davies L.J., 129 Salmon L.J.; cf. Lord Denning M.R. at 124.

did not protect young persons in cases of contempt. In turn, that section was replaced by s.19(1) of the Powers of Criminal Courts Act 1973, which at one time applied to contempt proceedings by virtue of s.14(3) of the Contempt of Court Act 1981.[51] The major changes effected by s.1(1) of the Criminal Justice Act 1982, that no offender under the age of 21 years could be sent to prison for any reason are now, however, of general application.[52]

Specific provision is made in s.108 of the Powers of Criminal Courts (Sentencing) Act 2000 for dealing with contemnors between 18 and 21 years of age. There is no power to commit a person under the age of 18 to custody for contempt.[53] It is provided by s.108(1) that:

"(1) In any case where, but for s.89(1) above, a court would have power—

(a) to commit a person aged at least 18 but under 21 to prison for default in payment of a fine or any other sum of money, or
(b) to make an order fixing a term of imprisonment in the event of such a default by such a person, or
(c) to commit such a person to prison for contempt of court or any kindred offence,

the court shall have power, subject to subsection (3) below, to commit him to be detained under this section or, as the case may be, to make an order fixing a term of detention under this section in the event of default, for a term not exceeding the term of imprisonment."

There is thus no doubt that persons aged 18 to 20 can be given a custodial sentence in a young offender institution in respect of contempt. It is necessary also to have regard, however, to the terms of subsections (3) and (4), which are to the following effect:

"(3) No court shall commit a person to be detained under this section unless it is of the opinion that no other method of dealing with him is appropriate; and in forming any such opinion, the court—

(a) shall take into account all such information about the circumstances of the default or contempt (including any aggravating or mitigating factors) as is available to it; and
(b) may take into account any information about that person which is before it.

(4) Where a magistrates' court commits a person to be detained under this section, it shall—

(a) state in open court the reason for its opinion that no other method of dealing with him is appropriate; and
(b) cause that reason to be specified in the warrant of commitment and to be entered in the register."

---

[51] Now repealed by the Criminal Justice Act 1982, s.78, Sch.16.
[52] Powers of Criminal Courts (Sentencing) Act 2000, s.89; but the minimum age for imprisonment will be reduced from 21 to 18 by reason of the Criminal Justice and Court Services Act 2000, s.74 (not in effect as at the date of writing).
[53] *R. v Byas* (1995) 16 Cr.App.R. (S) 869.

14–63 In *Mason v Lawton*,[54] a man under 21 had been committed to prison for two years for a series of breaches of non-molestation orders amounting to "outright defiance" of the court. The county court judge had overlooked the statutory provisions, and the Court of Appeal exercised the power to substitute an order correcting the error, in accordance with s.13 of the Administration of Justice Act 1960.[55] The committal order should have provided for the contemnor to "be detained under s.9 of the Criminal Justice Act 1982 for a specified period"; that is to say, in a young offender institution. In fact the court ordered early release.

14–64 As always, it is necessary to determine age for the purpose of imposing a penalty by reference to a certain date. The possible impact in this context of the European Convention was considered in *R. v Ghafoor*[56] where the court did not accede to the argument that Art.7 of the ECHR required the application of a general principle that an offender should be sentenced as a person of the age he would have been at the date of the offence. Nonetheless, the starting point will be the appropriate sentence for a person of that age at the time of the offence, and this will be a "powerful factor" which should not ordinarily be departed from.

Y. Attendance centres

14–65 Further express provision is made in the Contempt of Court Act 1981, in relation to young offenders, by s.14(2A) to the following effect[57]:

> "In the exercise of jurisdiction to commit for contempt of court or any kindred offence the court shall not deal with the offender by making an order under s.60 of the Powers of Criminal Courts (Sentencing) Act 2000 (an attendance centre order) if it appears to the court, after considering any available evidence, that he is under 17 years of age."

14–66 In this context, it is probable that the reference to age is to a person's age at the date of the finding of contempt rather than at the date when the penalty is imposed and that, accordingly, an offender who is aged 20 at the date of conviction but who attains the age of 21 between conviction and sentence, should be sentenced as a person under 21 years of age and not as an adult.[58]

Z. Pre-sentence information

14–67 The question arose in *R. v Selby Justices Ex p. Frame*[59] whether a court which was contemplating imposing a custodial sentence under the predecessor to s.108

---

[54] [1991] 2 F.L.R. 50, CA.
[55] This is considered in para.15–88. See also *Linnett v Coles* [1987] Q.B. 555; *Nicholls v Nicholls* [1997] 1 W.L.R. 314.
[56] [2002] EWCA Crim 1857, [2003] 1 Cr.App.R. (S) 84, [2002] Crim. L.R. 739.
[57] This provision was added by the Criminal Justice Act 1982, s.77, Sch.14, para.60, and amended most recently by the Powers of Criminal Courts (Sentencing) Act 2000, s.165(1), Sch.9, para.84.
[58] *R. v Danga* [1992] Q.B. 476, CA; *R. v Starkey* [1994] Crim. L.R. 380, CA.
[59] [1992] Q.B. 72.

of the Powers of Criminal Courts (Sentencing) Act 2000[60] was obliged to have regard to certain general statutory sentencing obligations.[61] These included, for example, the need to obtain and consider information about the person concerned for the purpose of determining whether there was any other method appropriate for dealing with him—unless the court thought it "unnecessary" to do so. It was held that "a free-standing and independent form of sentence was created in its own right."[62] Thus, it would follow that the only constraint to which s.108(1) of the Powers of Criminal Courts (Sentencing) Act 2000 is subject is that contained in what is now s.108(3). So far as information about the person is concerned (as opposed to information about the circumstances of the contempt), the provision is permissive rather than mandatory.

14-68 The court was therefore under no obligation to obtain a social enquiry report before committing a person under 21 years of age to be detained for contempt. There is no reason to suppose that this would make any difference in practice to the approach of the court dealing with a young person held in contempt even if the general obligations were applicable. As was contemplated in the *Selby Justices* case, the summary powers of the court to deal instantly with disorderly conduct would be fettered and delayed unless the court was free to impose, in appropriate cases, an immediate custodial penalty. Because of considerations of this sort, it is likely that a judge would generally have concluded that it was "unnecessary" to obtain such a report in any event.

14-69 By virtue of s.14(4A) of the Contempt of Court Act 1981,[63] superior courts[64] have the power to remand an accused person for reports on his mental condition when there is reason to suppose that he may be suffering from mental illness or severe impairment.

14-70 A committal order made in the county court against a disabled person, for refusing to answer questions about her financial position, was challenged before the European Court of Human Rights.[65] There was held to have been a breach of Art.3 because her physical needs had not been properly catered for. In a separate opinion, Sir Nicolas Bratza said that he could see no justification for an immediate term of imprisonment " ... without at the very least ensuring in advance that there existed both adequate facilities for detaining her and conditions of detention in which her special needs could be met". In his view, the fault lay primarily not with the prison but with the judicial authorities.

---

[60] s.9(1) of the 1982 Act.
[61] Then contained in s.2 of the Criminal Justice Act 1982, repealed by the Criminal Justice Act 1991, s.101(2), Sch.13.
[62] [1992] 1 Q.B. 72, at 81B, Otton J.
[63] Inserted by the Mental Health (Amendment) Act 1982, s.65(1), Sch.3, para.60; see also the provisions of the Mental Health Act 1983, s.148, Sch.4, para.57(6).
[64] This term now includes county courts, in this context: see the second of the two sections labelled "14(4A)", inserted by s.1 of the County Courts (Penalties for Contempt) Act 1983. (The duplication appears to be the result of oversight.)
[65] *Price v United Kingdom* (2002) 34 E.H.R.R. 53, [2001] Crim. L.R. 916.

CHAPTER 14—SANCTIONS AND REMEDIES

II. ATTACHING A POWER OF ARREST

A. The jurisdiction in family proceedings to attach a power of arrest

14–71 Because of a perceived increase in domestic violence, the time came when Parliament decided that, in some circumstances, it would be appropriate when granting an injunction to attach a power of arrest in order to protect the applicant. The terms of s.2(1) of the Domestic Violence and Matrimonial Proceedings Act 1976 provided that where, on an application by a party to a marriage,[66] an injunction was granted containing a provision restraining the other party to the marriage from using violence against the applicant, or using violence against a child living with the applicant, or excluding the other party from the matrimonial home, the judge might, if satisfied that the other party had caused actual bodily harm to the applicant, and of the view that he was likely to do so again, attach a power of arrest to the injunction. The effect of such an order was that a constable might arrest without warrant a person whom he had reasonable cause for suspecting of being in breach of such a provision of an occupation or non-molestation order.[67]

B. The difficulties of application

14–72 The exercise of this power exposed a husband to immediate arrest; it caused great problems for police officers who had to enforce it; it led to the husband being kept in custody for a period of up to 24 hours before being produced before a judge, and it often involved a committal order to prison. "Anything in this sphere which operates more or less automatically is to be deprecated."[68] It was always regarded as a serious matter, and the remedy was to be reserved as a short term measure to serve an urgent need.[69]

14–73 Even though the procedure provided for a person arrested under such a power to be brought before a judge within 24 hours, this did not preclude the court from adjourning the hearing for a suitable period if it was thought that justice required it. In *Roberts v Roberts*,[70] a husband was brought before the court, having been arrested by the police, and wished to have an adjournment to enable him to call corroborative witnesses in support of his contention that he had been living with his wife amicably for several weeks at her invitation. The assistant recorder

---

[66] This included a man and woman living with each other in the same household as man and wife; s.2(2).
[67] Family Law Act 1996, s.47(6); see also *Bowen v Bowen* [1990] 2 F.L.R. 93, CA, where a judge had purported to punish a husband for contempt under the former CCR Ord.47, r.8(7), when he had been arrested not for any conduct falling within paras (a) to (c) of s.2(1) of the 1976 Act, but for damaging the car belonging to a friend of his wife, with whom she was out for the evening. The provision was in any event revoked in October 1991 on the coming into force of the Family Proceedings Rules 1991.
[68] *Horner v Horner* [1982] Fam. 90 at 93E, Ormrod L.J. CA.
[69] *Davis v Johnson* [1979] A.C. 264 at 275, Lord Denning M.R.
[70] [1991] 1 F.L.R. 294, CA. See also *Boylan v Boylan* (1980) 11 Fam. Law 76, Ormrod L.J., for another illustration of what Bingham L.J. called "the serious omissions" in the procedural provisions of the Domestic Violence and Matrimonial Proceedings Act 1976 (see *Roberts v Roberts* at 302A–B).

refused the application, in the mistaken belief that he had to deal with the matter there and then, because of the 24 hour rule. He found breaches proved and committed the husband to prison for three months.

An appeal was allowed because the proper course would have been to adjourn the matter to a convenient date, in order to give the husband the opportunity to marshal his evidence. The wife would be protected meanwhile by a continuation of the non-molestation order with the power of arrest attached. The court had an inherent power to adjourn proceedings when thought necessary in the interests of justice, and moreover the matter would fall within the terms of the general power to adjourn contained in the former CCR, Ord.13, r.3.

Nevertheless, the object of the legislation was to protect a family partner against conduct calculated to undermine his or her security, and to strengthen the court's power to grant remedies for the protection of the partner from such conduct. The ability of the court, therefore, to tailor the protection to the circumstances of a particular case was regarded as important[71]; perhaps especially so where one party failed to come to terms with the *de facto* ending of a relationship. Thus, it was not thought to be wrong in principle to add a power of arrest for a period that is co-extensive with an injunction, even for a period as long as twelve months. In any event, an injunction had clearly to separate the parts of the order backed by the power of arrest from those concerned with forms of molestation that were not arrestable.[72]

It was unclear whether this jurisdiction extended to a case where former co-habitees no longer lived together and injury had been suffered after the date of the separation.[73] It was a matter depending upon status rather than whether the persons actually lived together at the material time. So long as a marriage subsisted, therefore, the jurisdiction was available. Since the purpose of s.2(2) of the 1976 Act was to place co-habitees in a similar position to that occupied by married couples, it may be thought that the proper test in each case should be whether the parties continued to have a relationship which, for the purposes of the section, was deemed to be equivalent to marriage.[74] It was thought to have been a serious defect in the 1976 Act that it applied only for so long as the parties were married or living together as a couple. The need for a non-molestation injunction, buttressed by a power of arrest, would often be greater once the parties separated.[75]

---

[71] *McCann v Wright* [1995] 2 F.L.R. 579 at 588, Beldam L.J., CA.
[72] Family Proceedings Rules, 1991, r.3.9(6). See now r.3.9A(1), at *Family Court Practice* (2004) at p.1705, inserted by Family Proceedings (Amendment No.3) Rules 1997, SI 1997/1893. See Forms FL 406–8. See also *Hale v Tanner (Practice Note)* [2000] 1 W.L.R. 2377; *Re B-J (A Child) (Non-Molestation: Power of Arrest)* [2001] 1 All E.R. 235.
[73] *McCann v Wright* [1995] 2 F.L.R. 579 at 586, Evans L.J.
[74] *ibid.* See also *White v White* [1983] Fam. 54; *McLean v Nugent* [1980] 1 F.L.R. 26. But see *Harrison v Lewis; R. v S* [1988] 2 F.L.R. 339, CA.
[75] *Duo v Osborne (formerly Duo)* [1992] 1 W.L.R 611 at 621D–F, [1992] 2 F.L.R. 425 at 434–5, Lord Donaldson M.R. See also *Pidduck v Molloy* [1992] 2 F.L.R. 202 where the Master of the Rolls had expressed the same opinion.

C. The 1996 reforms

14–77 By reason of the Family Law Act 1996, the emphasis shifted, in that the attachment of a power of arrest became mandatory in the specified circumstances, as opposed to merely discretionary. The court continued to have the power to accept an undertaking in any case where there was a power to make an order.[76] However, it was provided that no power of arrest might be attached to an undertaking,[77] and that the court was not to accept an undertaking where a "power of arrest would be attached to the order".[78] It seemed that it was likely that there would be more orders and fewer undertakings. It was held in *Chechi v Bashir*[79] that, when making a non-molestation order on the basis of violence used or threatened, the court had little option but to attach a power of arrest. The judge was entitled to refuse to make such an order on the basis that the power of arrest would give the applicant unacceptable power over the defendant. It was a case in which cross-undertakings or cross-injunctions would be the most suitable relief; any breach would require a court hearing to determine the facts and whether either party was in contempt.

14–78 The provisions of s.47 include:

"(1)[80] *In this section 'a relevant order' means an occupation order*[81] *or a non-molestation order.*[82]

(2) If—

(a) the court makes a *relevant order* [an occupation order][83]; and
(b) it appears to the court that the respondent has used or threatened violence against the applicant or a relevant child,

it shall attach a power of arrest to one or more provisions of the order unless satisfied that in all the circumstances of the case the applicant or child will be adequately protected without such a power of arrest."

14–79 The section contemplates a discretion as to which parts of the order should or should not attract a power of arrest. It was noted in the Court of Appeal in *Hale v Tanner (Practice Note)*[84] that there is a distinction to be drawn between cases where what is prohibited is the direct use of violence, or the face-to-face threat of violence, or "the stalking of somebody and the lurking outside their premises", on the one hand, and cases of "distance harassment", on the other, where it was less obvious that a power of arrest would need to be attached in every case.

---

[76] s.46 (1).
[77] s.46(2).
[78] s.46(3).
[79] [1999] 2 F.L.R. 489.
[80] The subsection is prospectively repealed by the Domestic Violence, Crime and Victims Act 2004, s.58(1),(2), Sch.10, para.38(1)(2), Sch.11.
[81] Family Law Act 1996, s.33.
[82] Family Law Act 1996, s.42.
[83] The words in italics are prospectively repealed and the words in square brackets substituted by the Domestic Violence, Crime and Victims Act 2004, s.58(1), Sch.10, para.38(1)(3).
[84] [2000] 1 W.L.R. 2377 . See generally on this case the article by R. Kay, "Guidelines on Sanctions for Breach: *Hale v Tanner*" (2001) 64 M.L.R. 595.

It is provided by s.47(3)[85] that the *obligation* to attach a power of arrest does not apply in any case where the relevant order is made without notice to the other party. There is, however, a *discretion* to attach such a power to one or more provisions of the order, provided that it appears that the respondent has used or threatened violence against the applicant, or a relevant child, and there is a risk of significant harm. Where the court does exercise the discretion under s.47(3), it is provided expressly by s.47(4) that the power of arrest can have effect for a shorter period than the rest of the order. There is no corresponding provision, in s.47(2), for cases where notice has been given.

14–80

This distinction of wording was considered in *Re B-J (A Child) (Non-molestation: Power of Arrest)*.[86] The judge had granted a non-molestation order against a father for an indefinite period but attached a power of arrest limited to two years' duration. It was argued on the father's behalf on appeal (i) that the non-molestation order should have been limited to a specific period, and (ii) that the power of arrest could not be fixed to last for a shorter period than the order to which it was attached. Those arguments were rejected and the appeal dismissed. While it would usually be preferable to attach a power of arrest under s.47(2) for the same duration as the non-molestation order, there was jurisdiction to specify a shorter period. This was an interpretation consistent with the obligations arising under the European Convention on Human Rights. To attach a power of arrest for longer than the court perceived to be necessary for the protection of the potential victims would lead to an injustice to the person subject to the order. There was, in any event, the long-standing principle that a statutory provision affecting the liberty of the subject should be construed restrictively. If the court were to be deterred from making a non-molestation order for the appropriate period, for the purpose of protecting a particular person or persons, or from attaching a power of arrest, by reason of feeling obliged to make the power of arrest last longer than was perceived to be necessary, that could obviously work to the disadvantage of the very class of persons the statutory framework was intended to protect. The first task is always to decide whether a non-molestation order is appropriate, and if so for how long and on what terms; only then should the court turn its mind to the power of arrest.

14–81

The earlier High Court decision in *M v W (Non-Molestation Order: Duration)*[87] was overruled, in so far as it had held that the court did *not* have the jurisdiction to impose a power of arrest of shorter duration than the order to which it was attached, and that non-molestation orders should only be made of unlimited duration in "exceptional or unusual circumstances". This was to underestimate the flexibility in the court's powers intended by the legislature.

14–82

Some of the problems which had been perceived as attaching to the 1976 legislation were thus addressed in the 1996 provisions. In particular, orders could

14–83

---

[85] The words "the relevant order" appearing in this subsection are also prospectively repealed and to be substituted by "the occupation order": see by the Domestic Violence, Crime and Victims Act 2004, s.58(1),(2), Sch.10, para.38(1)(4). The power of arrest will thenceforth apply only to an occupation order.
[86] [2001] 1 All E.R. 235, CA.
[87] [2000] 1 F.L.R. 107.

14–83   CHAPTER 14—SANCTIONS AND REMEDIES

be sought by a wider class of persons, for example, "associated persons" who were defined[88] to include, for example, those who are or have been married to each other, cohabitants or former cohabitants, relatives and engaged couples.

14–84   Where an order does not contain a power of arrest, and the respondent fails to comply with it, a warrant for his arrest can be obtained from the "relevant judicial authority".[89] This would not be necessary in a case where the order itself contains a power of arrest.

D. Bail

14–85   Provision was made[90] for an application to be made for bail by a person arrested, either under a power of arrest or a warrant of arrest. Such applications may be made either orally or in writing.

E. The Practice Directions

14–86   In a *Practice Direction* of January 23, 1980, the President of the Family Division formulated procedures in relation to orders made under the 1976 Act. As originally promulgated it contained a sentence which read "He must either be dealt with for contempt, if the evidence warrants it, or released." In the light of the decision in *Roberts v Roberts*,[91] which confirmed that there was a power to adjourn proceedings for evidence to be adduced, that sentence was omitted from the *Practice Direction* as re-issued on March 7, 1991.[92] In the light of the regime brought in to operation under Pt IV of the Family Law Act 1996, a new *Practice Direction* was brought into effect on December 1, 1997,[93] which made clear that the procedure formulated in relation to orders made under the 1976 Act was also to apply to orders under the new provisions, as follows:

"The procedure formulated in the President's directions of 23 January 1980 and 7 March 1991 (*Practice Direction (Domestic Violence: Procedure on Arrest*) [1991] 1 W.L.R. 278) in relation to orders made under the Domestic Violence and Matrimonial Proceedings Act 1976, shall apply in respect of orders made under Part IV of the Family Law Act 1996, as follows. (1) Where at a hearing which has been held in private, an occupation or non-molestation order is made to which a power of arrest is attached and the person to whom it is addressed was not given notice of the hearing and was not present at the hearing, the terms of the order and the name of the person to whom it is addressed shall be announced in open court at the earliest opportunity. This may be on either the same day when the court proceeds to hear cases in open court or where there is no further business in open court on that day at the next listed sitting of the court. (2) When a person arrested under a power of arrest cannot conveniently be brought before

---

[88] s. 62(3). Later it was found necessary to extend the definitions to include same sex couples by the Domestic Violence, Crime and Victims Act 2004, by reference to "intimate personal relationship with each other which is or was of significant duration".
[89] As defined in the Family Law Act 1996, s.63(1).
[90] Family Proceedings Rules 1991, r.3.10, as amended by SI 1997/1893.
[91] [1991] 1 F.L.R. 294.
[92] *Practice Direction (Domestic Violence: Procedure on Arrest)* [1991] 1 W.L.R. 278, 1 F.L.R. 304.
[93] [1998] 1 W.L.R. 476, 1 F.L.R. 496.

the relevant judicial authority sitting in a place normally used as a courtroom within 24 hours after the arrest, he may be brought before the relevant judicial authority at any convenient place but, as the liberty of the subject is involved, the press and the public should be permitted to be present, unless security needs make this impracticable. (3) Any order of committal made otherwise than in public or in a courtroom open to the public, shall be announced in court at the earliest opportunity. This may be either on the same day when the court proceeds to hear cases in open court or where there is no further business in open court on that day at the next listed sitting of the court. The announcement shall state (a) the name of the person committed, (b) in general terms the nature of the contempt of the court in respect of which the order of committal has been made and (c) the length of the period of committal."

14–87 Further guidance was given by Ward L.J. in the Court of Appeal in *Horgan v Horgan*,[94] where his Lordship commented that he was "disconcerted" and "troubled" by aspects of the procedure adopted at the Reading county court. An order had been made without notice to the respondent (which, it was accepted, had been just and convenient), but the restraining order and the power of arrest were to remain effective for a whole year. "Given the ease with which a power of arrest may be invoked by an applicant, the court should normally be wary about making an order of this kind for longer than is necessary to give the applicant adequate protection". It is required by s.45(3) of the Family Law Act 1996 that a respondent should be given an opportunity to make representations about the order at a full hearing as soon as just and convenient. Things should not have been "left in the air" for as long as seven weeks. Further, the better practice would be to limit the time for the injunction and the power of arrest so that they remained effective for no longer than the conclusion of the return hearing. "Those dates ought ordinarily to coincide".

14–88 The court's power to remand in custody was limited by the 1996 Act,[95] so that it became unlawful to remand for a period exceeding eight clear days. The view was expressed (although there was no ruling to that effect) by Ward L.J. that s.47 permitted remand on several occasions, albeit the power was limited to a maximum of eight days. There was indeed a power to order a "further remand".[96] Moreover, such an interpretation would be consistent with the power accorded to magistrates under ss.128 and 129 of the Magistrates' Courts Act. It had been the recommendation of the Law Commission that the court's powers under the schedule to the 1996 Act should be put on a comparable footing.

F. The provisions of the Housing Act 1996

14–89 Another means of dealing with the increasing social problems concerned with domestic violence and anti-social behaviour was addressed by Parliament in the Housing Act 1996. Provision was made for courts to attach a power of arrest for

---

[94] [2002] EWCA Civ 1371. See [5] and [6].
[95] Para.2(5) of Sch.5.
[96] Para.2(2) of Sch.5.

14-89

similar reasons to those underlying the Family Law Act. The Act[97] enabled local authorities and other social landlords to obtain injunctions against those indulging in anti-social behaviour.[98] The relevant sections as originally included were s.152 (power to grant injunctions against anti-social behaviour) and s.153 (power of arrest for breach of other injunctions against anti-social behaviour). Although these provisons have now been repealed and replaced by the Anti-social Behaviour Act 2003, the terms of the 1996 Act have been considered in a number of authorities, of which it is convenient to summarise the most significant at this point.

14-90   Section 152(3) of the Housing Act fell to be considered in *Manchester City Council v Worthington*.[99] The applicants had obtained an injunction, backed with a power of arrest, restraining the respondent from anti-social behaviour, including "violence or threats". There were repeated breaches and eventually a suspended custodial penalty was imposed. Because the respondent had been brought to court following arrest desirable procedural safeguards were by-passed. It was emphasised that it was crucial to take care to establish the relevant facts; to afford adequate time for a proper disposal; and to deliver a judgment giving the reasons for the decision reached. Although a notice to show cause is not required in such a case, it would be highly desirable to have written allegations of the breaches alleged, to be placed before the judge and made available for the contemnor.[1]

14-91   In *Newham London Borough Council v Jones*[2] the local authority had obtained an injunction under ss.152 and 153 of the Act to restrain the defendant from causing annoyance to neighbours and applied to the county court for committal following breaches. The judge continued the injunction until trial or further order backed with a power of arrest. Following a threat to kill a neighbour, he was duly arrested. The judge directed committal proceedings and considered whether to remand him in custody or grant conditional bail pursuant to s.155 and Sch.15 to the Housing Act. In view of a continuing risk to neighbours and his admission of an earlier breach, he was remanded in custody. The Court of Appeal expressed the view that this was a decision the judge had been fully entitled to make but, in any event, said that the appeal route had not been appropriate since the county court could have reviewed its own decision.[3]

14-92   It was held by the Court of Appeal in *Stafford Borough Council v Anderson*[4] (the respondents not being represented) that a county court judge had been

---

[97] Chapter III of Pt V.
[98] See now Pt 65 of the CPR which came into effect by reason of the Civil Procedure (Amendment) Rules 2004, SI 2004/1306.
[99] [2000] 1 F.L.R. 411.
[1] For the implications of this decision in the context of Pt IV of the Family Law Act 1996, see the article by Judge Platt in [2000] Fam. Law 905.
[2] [2002] EWCA Civ 1779, [2002] All E.R. (D) 271.
[3] Pursuant to CPR Sch.2, cc.PD49.
[4] [2003] All E.R. (D) 200 (Jan).

plainly wrong to adjourn a committal application following breaches of an anti-social behaviour order under s.152.

New ss.153A to 153E were inserted as amendments contained in the Anti-social Behaviour Act 2003.[5] It may be noted that ss.154 and 155 dealing with powers of arrest and remand have also been amended by the same Act.[6]

Section 153A applies to conduct capable of causing nuisance or annoyance to any person which whether directly or indirectly relates to or affects the housing management functions of a relevant landlord. A "relevant landlord" is defined by s.153E(7) to include (a) a housing action trust, (b) a local authority and (c) a registered social landlord. The "housing management function" includes (a) functions conferred by or under any enactment and (b) the powers and duties of a landlord as holder of an estate or interest in housing accommodation. The High Court or a county court may grant an "anti-social behaviour injunction" on the application of a landlord if the person against whom the relief is sought is engaging or threatening to engage in conduct (as defined above) which is capable of causing nuisance or annoyance to (a) anyone with a right to reside in or occupy the accommodation; (b) anyone with a right to reside in or occupy other housing accommodation in the neighbourhood; (c) a person engaged in lawful activity in that neighbourhood; (d) a person employed in connection with the exercise of the landlord's functions.[7]

A court may also grant an injunction against the unlawful use of premises on the application of the relevant landlord.[8] The power of arrest is provided for in two situations.[9] First, in the context of an exclusion order in circumstances where the court thinks, in the case of an injunction granted under s.153A or s.153B, that the conduct (a) consists of or includes the use or threatened use of violence and (b) there is a significant risk of harm to any of the persons mentioned in s.153A(4). "Harm" includes serious ill treatment or abuse (whether physical or not).[10] Secondly, a power of arrest may be attached to an injunction against a breach of a tenancy agreement granted under s.153D. In this context, the definition of "relevant landlord" extends to include additionally a charitable housing trust which is not a registered social landlord. The section is concerned with an application by a landlord against a tenant in respect of a breach or anticipated breach of an agreement on the grounds that the tenant is engaging or threatening to engage in conduct capable of causing nuisance or annoyance to any person or is allowing, inciting or encouraging any other person so to do. Again, the provisions are directed to the granting of an exclusion order against

---

[5] s.13, Sch.3 which came into effect separately on June 30 and September 30, 2004 for England and Wales respectively.
[6] ss.13(4) and (5). The wording of all these provisions can be found in *Civil Procedure 2005*, Vol. 2, at paras 3A–1118 *et seq.*
[7] s.153A(4).
[8] s.153B.
[9] ss.153C and 153D.
[10] s.153E(12).

14-95

a tenant where the court is satisfied that the conduct includes the use or threatened use of violence or there is a significant risk of harm to any person.

G. The reforms of 2004

14-96 After almost 30 years, it seems that Parliament concluded that the power of arrest had in significant respects failed to achieve its social objectives. Also it was decided that the use of undertakings to the court should be tightened up,[11] presumably because they were not affording sufficient practical protection for the relevant victims. Hence the major legislative reforms contained in the Domestic Violence, Crime and Victims Act 2004, the principal provisions of which may be summarised as follows:

1. Section 42A of the Family Law Act 1996 will make it a new criminal offence to breach a non-molestation order.[12]

2. Because the breach of a non-molestation order is a criminal offence, it would appear that the full range of penalties is available including community sentences.

3. Section 46(3A) provides that the court shall not accept an undertaking under s.46(1) in respect of a non-molestation order where it appears to the court that a respondent has used or threatened violence, and it is necessary to make a non-molestation order so that a breach may be punishable under s.42A as a criminal offence.

4. It is no longer possible (and indeed is not necessary) to attach a power of arrest to a non-molestation order, since the breach constitutes a criminal offence, but only to an occupation order.[13]

5. Section 46(4) is intended to enable a warrant of arrest to be issued to enforce an undertaking.[14]

6. Section 46(4) also provides that an undertaking under subsection (1) is enforceable as if the court had made an occupation order or a non-molestation order in terms corresponding to those of the undertaking. This would appear to suggest that a breach of an undertaking not to molest could be dealt with as a criminal offence.

---

[11] See s.46 of the Family Law Act 1996, as amended. Having provided expressly in s.46(1) that the court may accept an undertaking in any case where it has the power to make an occupation order or non-molestation order, the draftsman has provided thereafter a series of limitations.

[12] s.42A(3) and (4) will provide respectively that a person convicted of an offence cannot be punished for contempt in respect of the same conduct, and that a person cannot be convicted of the offence if he has already been punished for contempt in respect of the same conduct.

[13] ss.47(2) and 47(3) of the 1996 Act as amended.

[14] The Family Law Form FL407 (dealing with an application for a warrant of arrest) was drafted on the assumption that this had been possible in any event.

III. Non-Custodial Sentences

A. Orders under the Mental Health Act 1983

Section 14(4) of the Contempt of Court Act 1981 (as amended)[15] provides: **14–97**

"Each of the superior courts shall have the like power to make a hospital order or guardianship order under s.37 of the Mental Health Act 1983 or an interim hospital order under s.38 of that Act in the case of a person suffering from mental illness[16] or severe mental impairment[17] who could otherwise be committed to prison for contempt of court as the Crown Court has under that section in the case of a person convicted of an offence."

B. Community sentences

The provisions contained in ss.147 to 151 of the Criminal Justice Act 2003 concerned with community sentences do not apply to committal for contempt. This is consistent with the position prior to the Act and the language of earlier statutes. For example, it was held in *R. v Palmer*[18] that s.2(1) of the Powers of Criminal Courts Act 1973 did not apply in the case of contempt; accordingly there was no power to place a contemnor on probation.[19] The appellant had attended court for the trial of her boyfriend on a charge of aggravated burglary, and was found to be in contempt for threatening to kill witnesses and using physical violence within the precincts of the court. She was committed to prison for three months, but the Court of Appeal reduced the period of committal to allow her immediate release, on the basis that the public interest did not require her to remain in custody any longer. The court accepted the argument that there is a distinction between the phraseology of criminal statutes which use the verb "convict" and that found in relation to contempt; for example, in the wording of s.12 of the 1981 Act. Probation was, accordingly, not available since s.2(1) of the Powers of Criminal Courts Act 1973 only provided for probation in circumstances where a person was "convicted of an offence". **14–98**

Although the court took the view that it would only be rarely that a judge would wish to consider using such a power, it nevertheless was of opinion that **14–99**

---

[15] By the Mental Health (Amendment) Act 1982, s.65(1), Sch.3, para.59; the Mental Health Act 1983, s.148, Sch.4, para.57.
[16] Section 1(2) of the Mental Health Act 1983 provides that "mental disorder" means mental illness, arrested or incomplete development of mind, psychopathic disorder and any other disorder or disability of mind and "mentally disordered" shall be construed accordingly.
[17] Section 1(2) of the Mental Health Act 1983 provides that "severe mental impairment" means a state of arrested or incomplete development of mind, which includes severe impairment of intelligence and social functioning and is associated with abnormally aggressive or seriously irresponsible conduct on the part of the person concerned "severely mentally impaired" shall be construed accordingly.
[18] [1992] 1 W.L.R. 568, 3 All E.R. 289.
[19] The term "probation order" has now gone and was first replaced by "community rehabilitation order": see ss.41–44 of the Powers of Criminal Courts (Sentencing) Act 2000. That too has now been superseded since April 4, 2005, and the modern equivalent would be a "supervision requirement" as part of a community order. See ss.147, 177 and 213. Since that Act (s.177) also says that the individual must have been "convicted of an offence", there is no reason to suppose that the authority of *Palmer* has been in any way affected.

14-99 CHAPTER 14—SANCTIONS AND REMEDIES

there may well be cases in which the ability to make a probation order would be useful. The hope was expressed, therefore, that on a suitable occasion Parliament might consider whether to grant such a power expressly. This has clearly not been implemented.

14-100 By the same token, community service[20] could only be imposed under s.14 of the Powers of Criminal Courts Act 1973 in respect of a person "convicted" and thus was not available in respect of contemnors either. In *Secretary of State for Defence v Percy*,[21] Carnwath J. indicated that he would have preferred to make a community service order but, since this was unavailable, the disposal he chose was that of a suspended sentence. Section 177(1) of the Criminal Justice Act 2003 stipulates that for any community order to be available, the individual must have been "convicted of an offence".

C. Fines: superior courts

14-101 It has long been established that the courts may impose fines for criminal contempt,[22] either with or without sentences of imprisonment.[23] At one time, it was not the practice to impose a fine in civil courts because the object of punishing contempt in such circumstances was regarded at least in part as coercive.[24] It is now recognised that a contemnor may be fined for a breach of a court order, at least where committed in contumacious circumstances.[25] As with any other fine, the means of the contemnor will need to be taken into account. Where there is a reluctance to provide the necessary information, it may be appropriate for the court to make a realistic estimate.[26] The means of each contemnor must be considered individually and fines should not be imposed on a joint and several basis.[27] There is no limit upon the amount of a fine which a superior court can impose.

D. Is there a power to suspend?

14-102 It has been held in the High Court of Australia[28] that there was a power to suspend a fine pending compliance with an order. This would be to use a fine, in

---

[20] The penalty was renamed as a "community punishment order": see s.44 of the Powers of Criminal Courts (Sentencing) Act 2000. Now however the nearest equivalent would be a community order with an unpaid work requirement as defined by the Criminal Justice Act 2003, s.199.
[21] [1999] 1 All E.R. 732.
[22] *R v Clement* (1821) 4 B. & Ald. 218, 106 E.R. 918, affirmed at 11 Price 68; *R. v Davison* (1821) 4 B. & Ald. 329, 106 E.R. 958.
[23] *Ex parte Fernandez* (1861) 10 C.B. (N.S.) 3; *R. v Castro, Skipworth's Case* (1873) L.R. 9 Q.B. 219; *Re the Bahama Islands* [1893] A.C. 138.
[24] Lord Selborne L.C. speaking in Parliament, *Hansard*, H.L. Deb. (3rd series), Vol. 276, col.1709, March 8, 1883.
[25] *Phonographic Performance Ltd v Amusement Caterers Ltd* [1964] Ch. 195; *Steiner Products Ltd v Willy Steiner Ltd* [1966] 1 W.L.R. 986; *Re Grantham Wholesale Fruit, Vegetable and Potato Merchants Ltd* [1972] 1 W.L.R. 559.
[26] See, *e.g. Taylor Made Golf Co Inc v Rata & Rata* [1996] F.S.R. 528 at 536, Laddie J.
[27] *McMillan Graham Printers Ltd v RR (UK) Ltd* [1993] T.L.R. 152, [1993] 21 L.S. Gaz. R. 40, CA.
[28] *AMIEU v Mudginberri Station Pty Ltd* (1986) 161 C.L.R. 98 at 114. See also Miller, *Contempt of Court* (3rd ed., 2002), p.52, para.2-17.

E. Fines: inferior courts

The jurisdiction of the county court has been considered in chapter 13. The statutory jurisdiction for dealing with wilful insults and interruptions under s.118(1) of the County Courts Act 1984 extends further than that for contempt in the face of the court.[29] One of the powers for dealing with such offenders is that of fining an amount not exceeding £2,500.[30]   **14–103**

Under s.14(1) of the County Courts Act 1984[31] provision is made for dealing with assaults on officers of the county court in the execution of their duty. On summary conviction, a fine may be imposed not exceeding level 5 on the standard scale.[32] So too, where an order is made by the judge, the limit is level 5.[33] The other relevant statutory provision is that contained in s.92 of the County Courts Act 1984, relating to the rescue of goods seized. The corresponding limit imposed is level 4.   **14–104**

Section 12(2) of the Contempt of Court Act 1981[34] gives magistrates' courts power to fine persons who disturb their proceedings up to £2,500.[35]   **14–105**

F. The standard scale

The standard fines are: **14–106**

Level on Scale	Amount of fine
1	£200
2	£500
3	£1,000
4	£2,500
5	£5,000

The sums are prescribed by s.37(2) of the Criminal Justice Act 1982 as amended by the Criminal Justice Act 1991, s.17(2). The changes came into effect on October 1, 1992. Where there has been a change in the value of money, the Secretary of State is empowered by the Criminal Justice Act 1982, s.48 to vary the maximum amount of the fines.

---

[29] See para.13–90. See also *Bokhari v Blessed*, *Independent*, January 16, 1995, CA.
[30] Criminal Justice Act 1991, Sch.4.
[31] See para.13–84.
[32] Currently £5,000: Criminal Justice Act 1982, s.37, as amended; see para.14–106.
[33] *i.e.* greater than the maximum permitted under s.14 of the Contempt of Court Act 1981.
[34] Set out para.10–113.
[35] The original figure was £500. The present maximum was inserted by the Criminal Justice Act 1991, s.17(3), Sch.4, Pt I.

G. Coroners

14–107 It is provided by s.10(3) of the Coroners Act 1988 that the power to enforce attendance of jurors and witnesses[36] shall be in addition to and not in derogation of any other power which the coroner may possess:

"(a) for compelling any person to appear and give evidence before him in any inquest or other proceeding; or
(b) for punishing any person for contempt of court in not so appearing and giving evidence;

but a person shall not be fined by the coroner under this section and also be punished under any such other power."

Section 14(2) of the 1981 Act provides that in any case where an inferior court has power to fine a person for contempt of court, and (apart from this provision) no limit applies to the amount of the fine, the fine shall not on any occasion exceed £2,500.[37] In *R. v West Yorkshire Coroner Ex p. Smith (No.2)*[38] the Divisional Court upheld the coroner's decision to impose a fine of £50 for calling out at the rising of the court that one of the witnesses who had given evidence was a murderer.

H. Indemnifying as to payment of fines

14–108 It is not permitted to use trade union funds to pay a fine imposed upon a member of the union.[39] In the absence of such a specific prohibition, there could be no objection to the payment of fines by employers or anonymous well-wishers.[40] Where a journalist is fined, he is invariably indemnified by his employers. There is no record of this practice ever having been challenged by shareholders. The general principle in relation assessing the appropriate figure when imposing a financial penalty is that only the means of the relevant defendant should be taken into account. The assessment should not be based upon the assumption that some other person is going to pay the fine.[41] There is no reason to think that any different test should apply in the context of contempt.

I. The enforcement of fines imposed by superior courts

14–109 Section 16 of the Contempt of Court Act 1981 (as amended)[42] deals with the enforcement of certain fines in England and Wales as follows:

---

[36] Under s.10(1) and (2).
[37] Criminal Justice Act 1991, s.17(3), Sch.4, Pt I. See also *Att-Gen v BBC* [1981] A.C. 303 at 342, Lord Salmon, 355–6, Lord Scarman where it was confirmed that a coroner's court is one of those "long-established" inferior courts "of ancient origin" to which the law of contempt applies.
[38] [1985] 1 Q.B. 1096.
[39] Trade Union and Labour Relations (Consolidation) Act 1992, s.15(1)(a).
[40] As happened in well-publicised circumstances in 1973 in relation to an industrial dispute, when counsel appeared on behalf of such a person before the court and announced that the funds were available: *Con-Mech (Engineers) Ltd v AUEW* [1973] I.C.R. 620.
[41] See, *e.g. R. v Baxter* [1974] Crim.L.R. 611. See also *McMillan Graham Printers Ltd v RR (UK) Ltd* [1993] T.L.R. 152, [1993] 21 L.S. Gaz. R. 40, CA.
[42] Supreme Court Act 1981, s.152(4), Sch.7.

"(1) Payment of a fine for contempt of court imposed by a superior court, other than the Crown Court or one of the courts specified in subsection (4) below, may be enforced upon the order of the court—

(a) in like manner as a judgment of the High Court for the payment of money; or
(b) in like manner as a fine imposed by the Crown Court.

(2) Where payment of a fine imposed by any court falls to be enforced as mentioned in paragraph (a) of subsection (1)—

(a) the court shall, if the fine is not paid in full forthwith or within such time as the court may allow, certify to Her Majesty's Remembrancer the sum payable;
(b) Her Majesty's Remembrancer shall thereupon proceed to enforce payment of that sum as if it were due to him as a judgment debt[43];

(3) Where payment of a fine imposed by any court falls to be enforced as mentioned in paragraph (b) of subsection (1), the provisions of ss.139 and 140 of the Powers of Criminal Courts (Sentencing) Act 2000[44] shall apply as they apply to a fine imposed by the Crown Court.

(4) Subsection (1) of this section does not apply to fines imposed by the criminal division of the Court of Appeal or by the House of Lords on appeal from that division.

(5) The Fines Act 1833 shall not apply to a fine to which subsection (1) of this section applies.

(6) *Repealed by the Employment Tribunals Act 1996, s.45, Sch.3, Part I.*"

J. Binding over

In the case of criminal contempt the court has the power to bind over the contemnor to be of good behaviour.[45] The appropriate form of order would be to require the contemnor to be of good behaviour and not to commit any contempt of court for a specified period.[46] Nowadays, a common law bind over is unusual and such orders are normally made under the Justices of the Peace Act 1968.[47] In those circumstances, the order would specifically refer to keeping the peace. It may well be appropriate for such an order to be made in circumstances where there has been a disturbance in court. It is difficult to imagine any other situation in which such wording would be appropriate. Such a person may be bound over in his own recognisance or required to produce sureties willing to be bound in specified sums to his good behaviour.[48]

---

[43] See C. O'Regan, "Contempt of Court and the Enforcement of Labour Injunctions" (1991) 54 M.L.R. 385 at 401, where the author notes that a fine imposed on the T & GWU in *Austin Rover v AUEW* [1985] I.R.L.R. 162 was enforced by this means.
[44] Substituted by the Powers of Criminal Courts (Sentencing) Act 2000, Sch.9, para.85.
[45] See the remarks of Lord Denning in *Morris v Home Office* cited at para.14–40 above. See also *R. v Castro, Skipworth's Case* (1873) L.R. 9 Q.B. 219 at 241.
[46] *R. v Castro, Skipworth's Case* (1873) L.R. 9 Q.B. 219 at 241.
[47] s.1(7) declares that any court of record having a criminal jurisdiction has an ancillary power to bind over and can require the person concerned to enter into his own recognisances or to find sureties or both and committing him to prison if he does not comply.
[48] *R. v Castro, Skipworth's Case* (1873) L.R. 9 Q.B. 219 at 241. The jurisdiction to bind over has been challenged and criticised in the European Court of Human Rights: *Hashman and Harrup v UK* (2000) 30 E.H.R.R. 241, [2000] Crim. L.R. 185; *Steel v UK* (1999) E.H.R.R. 603, [1998] Crim. L.R. 893. Nevertheless, it appears that the government remains committed to retaining the procedure. See *Bind Over: A Power for the 21st Century* (March 2003).

K. Sequestration

1. *Introduction*

14–111 The writ of sequestration is a method of enforcing judgments or orders which either:

(a) require a person to do an act within a specified time (extended if necessary); or

(b) require a person to abstain from doing an act.[49]

14–112 The question arises whether sequestration can apply otherwise than in the case of breach of an order or undertaking.[50] It has been said that " . . . there appears to be no case in which an order was made to enforce a sequestration against third persons, who disputed their liability to the debtor, on motion, in a suit to which they were not parties."[51] In the case of a third party, liable for criminal contempt because of acting inconsistently with a court order of which he has knowledge,[52] the remedy would on the face of it not be available. A fine may be appropriate, however, and a writ of sequestration might subsequently be issued by way of enforcing the fine.[53]

14–113 It is necessary to bear in mind *dicta* which suggest that sequestration could be available even in the absence of an order binding the person concerned. For example, in *Elliott v Klinger*[54] Stamp J. pointed out that it was for the court, if appropriate, to opt for a lenient alternative to committal or sequestration, such as by choosing to grant an injunction restraining any anticipated contempt. In that context, he went on to suggest that the wronged litigant was himself confined to asking for the traditional contempt remedies of committal or sequestration. Thus, he was not specifically addressing the limits of sequestration; nor had he heard argument on the point. Nevertheless, he went on to say that such a person would have the remedy " . . . where an injunction has been disobeyed *or where there has been aiding and abetting by a third party of a breach of an injunction . . . either to move to commit, or, in the case of a company, to apply for a writ of sequestration.*" (emphasis added).

14–114 In *Re S (Abduction: Sequestration)*[55] Johnson J. made remarks to similar effect. We submit, however, that in the light of the wording of what is now CPR

---

[49] See now CPR Sch.1, Ord.45. 1 and Ord.46.5. The remedy is not available against the Crown: CPR Sch.1, Ord.77. 15. Cp. *Re M: M v Home Office* [1994] 1 A.C. 377 at 427D–E, Lord Woolf.
[50] See CPR Sch.1, Ord.45.1, 5, discussed at para.12–96, and *Pratt v Inman* (1889) 43 Ch D. 175 at 179, Chitty J.; *Craig v Craig* [1896] P. 171 at 174, Gorrell Barnes J.
[51] See, *e.g. per* Gorell Barnes J. in *Craig v Craig* [1896] P. 171 at 174. But see the discussion of *Re S (Abduction: Sequestration)* [1995] 1 F.L.R. 858, Johnson J. at para.14–131.
[52] See the discussion of such cases as *Att-Gen v Newspaper Publishing plc* [1988] Ch. 333 and *Att-Gen v Times Newspapers Ltd* [1992] 1 A.C. 191, paras 5–141, 6–126 *et seq.*
[53] C. O'Regan (1991) 54 M.L.R. 385.
[54] [1967] 1 W.L.R 1165 at 1167.
[55] [1995] 1 F.L.R. 858, discussed at para.14–131.

Sch.1, Ord.45 the better view is that sequestration would not be available except in those specified cases.[56]

Moreover, the remedy is confined to persons who are in contempt at the time when the matter comes before the court. It is not appropriate to issue a writ of sequestration where a past contempt has been purged[57]; nor where a future contempt is anticipated.[58] In such a case it might be appropriate to apply for an injunction to restrain any specifically anticipated acts, assuming that there is doubt as to whether or not any existing order or undertaking is wide enough to restrain them.[59]

14–115

The county court has a power of sequestration, for the purpose of enforcing orders or undertakings, by virtue of the jurisdiction conferred in s.38 of the County Courts Act 1984.[60] If this were not the case, the court might in some circumstances (such as where the power to fine would be inadequate) have no effective means of imposing sanctions upon a corporate entity.

14–116

2. *Enforceable order required*

In *Webster v Southwark LBC*[61] Forbes J. held that a writ of sequestration might lie to enforce compliance by a local authority with its obligations, under the law relating to elections, as defined in a declaratory order. This was despite his having held that the parties had not been in contempt of that order. The circumstances were described as exceptional, but even so it may be doubted whether the remedy of sequestration, which is part of the process of contempt, can be invoked in the absence of an order or undertaking to do, or refrain from doing, some specified act or acts. A declaration is not such an order and, as a matter of principle, it is difficult to see how one can be held to be in civil contempt without breach of an enforceable order.

14–117

So too, where a consent order for custody,[62] including a direction not to remove children from the jurisdiction, was held not to be an order in the nature of an injunction, for the purposes of the former Ord.29, r.1(3) of the County Court Rules 1981. Such an order should therefore not have a penal notice attached to it.[63] The rule referred[64] to "a judgment or order enforceable by committal order"; a custody order was not in itself so enforceable. The county court judge had indicated in a note to the Court of Appeal that it had been the

14–118

---

[56] *Pratt v Inman* (1890) 43 Ch.D. 175; *Steiner Products Ltd v Willy Steiner Ltd* [1966] 1 W.L.R. 986.
[57] *IRC v Hoogstraten* [1985] 1 Q.B. 1077 at 1086–7, Dillon L.J., CA.
[58] *ibid.*, per Dillon L.J. at 1086G.
[59] As to the power to restrain anticipated contempts, in the context of publication, see paras 6–1 *et seq*. See also para.14–132.
[60] *Rose v Laskington* [1990] 1 Q.B. 562.
[61] [1983] Q.B. 698.
[62] The current terminonology is "residence order".
[63] *Re P (Minors) (Custody Order: Penal Notice)* [1990] 1 W.L.R. 613, CA; *Bell v Tuohy* [2002] 3 All E.R. 975.
[64] See now CPR Sch.2, cc.29.1(3), which is in the same terms.

14–118   standard practice in his court for a penal notice to be attached in such cases. Yet Lloyd L.J. added to his judgment a note to the effect that "neither Booth J. [who was sitting with him] with her vast experience in this field, nor [counsel for the mother] has ever come across a case of an attachment of a penal notice to an order such as this".

14–119   The matter is now governed by r.4.21A of the Family Proceedings Rules 1991.[65] Where it is sought to enforce a s.8 order, under the Children Act 1989, which might include a "residence" order, a direction of the judge or district judge must be obtained before endorsing a penal notice in Form N77.[66]

3. *The effect of a writ of sequestration*

14–120   The writ binds real property and personal property[67] in possession from the time it is issued.[68] It will embrace the rents and profits of real property and all personal estate including pensions,[69] money received in commutation of pension rights,[70] a bank balance,[71] a rentcharge,[72] an annuity under a will,[73] and both legal and equitable choses in action.[74] In so far as it affects land, the writ will not create a charge unless it is registered.[75] The title of a sequestrator will prevail over that of a mortgagee under a mortgage if made with notice of the sequestration.[76] A *bona fide* purchaser for value without notice will be protected.[77]

14–121   The effect of such a writ once issued is to place the contemnor's property in the hands of sequestrators, who become responsible for managing the property

---

[65] Substituted by the Family Proceedings (Amendment No.2) Rules 1992, SI 1992/2067.
[66] For Form N77, see Appendix 2.
[67] But see the County Courts Act 1984, s.89(1), which was inserted by the Courts and Legal Services Act 1990, s.15(2). This imposes certain limits on the extent to which a warrant of execution issued from the county court can be levied, for example, against property required for everyday needs.
[68] *Dixon v Rowe* (1876) 35 L.T. 548, Bacon V.-C.
[69] See, *e.g. Dent v Dent* (1867) L.R. 1 P.& D. 366 (naval officer); *Willcock v Terrell* (1878) 3 Ex.D. 323 (judge); *Sansom v Sansom* (1879) 4 P.D. 69 (civil servant); *Knill v Dumergue* [1911] 2 Ch. 199 (under East India Annuity Funds Act 1874). Cf. *Birch v Birch* (1883) 8 P.D. 163 (army officer), where *Willcock v Terrell* was reluctantly distinguished on the ground that in the earlier case the pension had been assignable.
[70] *Crowe v Price* (1889) 22 Q.B.D. 429.
[71] *Miller v Huddlestone* (1883) 22 Ch.D. 233.
[72] *Wilson v Metcalfe* (1839) 1 Beav. 263.
[73] *Dixon v Rowe* (1876) 35 L.T. 548.
[74] See, *e.g. Bucknell v Bucknell* [1969] 1 W.L.R. 1204, Brandon J.; see also *Claydon v Finch* (1873) L.R. 15 Eq. 266; *Wilson v Metcalfe* (1839) 1 Beav. 263. In the case of a chose in action the mere issue of the writ and service of it upon the person indebted to the judgment debtor is not sufficient to create a charge on the chose in action: see, *e.g. Re Hoare Ex p. Nelson* (1880) 14 Ch.D. 41, CA and *Re Pollard* [1903] 2 K.B. 41.
[75] Under s.6(1)(a) and (b) of the Land Charges Act 1972: see s.6(4).
[76] See *Ward v Booth* (1872) L.R. 14 Eq. 195.
[77] *Vicars v Colclough* (1779) 5 Bro. Parl. Cas. 31, 2 E.R. 514. See also Land Charges Act 1972, s.6(4).

and receiving any rents and profits.[78] It is addressed to the four persons chosen for the purpose by the party presenting the judgment or order.[79] The property remains in their hands until the court orders what is to be done with it.[80] It remains the property of the contemnor, however, and the writ of sequestration does not confer any title upon the creditor, or even a charge upon the property in his favour.[81]

Sequestration is particularly useful perhaps in a case in which an order has been disobeyed by a corporate body, where committal would obviously not be available (although in certain circumstances both committal and sequestration may be used against directors or officers of such a body).[82] An undertaking is treated for purposes of contempt as having similar effect to an injunction, and a writ of sequestration may also issue against a corporate body for breach of an undertaking.[83]

Third parties should not take any action which will hinder compliance with the sequestrators' taking possession of the contemnor's assets in accordance with the terms of the writ.[84] If they do so, they may be held to have interfered in the administration of justice; this may of itself constitute a (criminal) contempt, provided the necessary *mens rea* is demonstrated.[85] In cases of doubt, a third party, such as a bank, could clarify the situation with the sequestrators or, if necessary, with the court.[86] On the other hand, where there is no reason to doubt either the fact of the sequestration or the contemnor's title, third parties should act accordingly and not make unnecessary applications.[87]

---

[78] *Dixon v Rowe* (1876) 35 L.T. 548. The creditor did not become a secured creditor within the Bankruptcy Act 1914, though the debtor's money may have been received by the sequestrator: see, *e.g. Re Hastings* (1892) 67 L.T. 234 and *Re Pollard* [1903] 2 K.B. 41. See now the Insolvency Act 1986, s.248, for the current interpretation of "secured creditors".
[79] See Appendix 2.
[80] *Con-Mech (Engineers) Ltd v AUEW* [1973] I.C.R. 620 at 627, Sir John Donaldson; *Australian Consolidated Press Ltd v Morgan* (1965) 112 C.L.R. 483 at 501, Windeyer J.
[81] *Re Pollard* [1903] 2 K.B. 41 at 47, Romer L.J. The person whose property had been sequestrated might be guilty of theft should he interfere with the sequestrator's possession. See A.T.H. Smith, *Property Offences*, (1994), paras 4–42 *et seq*. He would almost certainly, however, be in contempt as thereby frustrating the order of the court: see, *e.g.* Nicholls J. in *Taylor v NUM*, *The Times*, November 20, 1985.
[82] See now CPR Sch.1, Ord. 45.5 (1). See also paras 12–109 *et seq*., para.15–26 and *Worthington v Ad-Lib Club Ltd* [1965] Ch. 236.
[83] See, *e.g. Stancomb v Trowbridge Urban District Council* [1910] 2 Ch. 190; *Davis v Rhayader Granite Quarries Ltd* (1911) 131 L.T.J. 79; *Steiner Products Ltd v Willy Steiner Ltd* [1966] 1 W.L.R. 986.
[84] See, *e.g. Eckman v Midland Bank Ltd* [1973] Q.B. 519; *Z Ltd v A-Z and AA-LL* [1982] Q.B. 558, and the discussion at paras 6–115 *et seq*. of *Att-Gen v Newspaper Publishing plc* [1988] Ch. 333.
[85] See, *e.g. Att-Gen v Newspaper Publishing plc* [1988] Ch. 333; and the unreported decision of the Court of Appeal in the same case [1990] T.L.R. 158 (Lexis); *Att-Gen v Times Newspapers Ltd* [1992] 1 A.C. 191 at 224, Lord Oliver. These are all discussed at paras 5–120 *et seq*.
[86] [1992] 1 A.C. at 224 at 225, Lord Oliver. See para.6–151; *Eckman v Midland Bank* [1973] Q.B. 519 at 528 (Sir John Donaldson); *Fenlon v Lowther* (1787) 1 Cox Eq. Cas. 315; *Craig v Craig* [1896] P. 171, Gorrell Barnes J.
[87] *Bucknell v Bucknell* [1969] 1 W.L.R. 1204 at 1214, Brandon J.; *Eckman v Midland Bank* (last note); *Con-Mech (Engineering) Ltd v AUEW* [1973] I.C.R. 620 at 627, Sir John Donaldson; *Messenger Newspapers Group Ltd v NGA* [1984] I.R.L.R. 397.

14–124 Sequestration is regarded as a drastic means of execution and it should only be used in serious cases.[88] The remedy is in any event only available with permission of the court obtainable on application to a judge.[89] A relevant factor may well be the possible impact upon third parties.[90]

4. The use of sequestration in industrial disputes

14–125 Sequestration was probably most commonly to be found in matrimonial cases.[91] In modern times, however, this sanction began to assume greater prominence when used against trade unions in the course of industrial disputes, not least in the context of the strike by the National Union of Mineworkers in 1984–5.[92]

14–126 In *Taylor v NUM (Yorkshire Area)*[93] certain orders against the NUM and its president were disobeyed and fines imposed in consequence. Following non-payment Nicholls J. gave leave to issue a writ of sequestration with respect to the union's property; four accountants were duly appointed. Shortly afterwards, in proceedings launched by a group of union members, its trustees were removed from office and a receiver appointed of its income and assets, in so far as they were not under the control of the sequestrators.[94] The trustees had sought to place trust property abroad, so as to defeat the object of the sequestration, and had also placed the funds in jeopardy by subjecting them to a substantial fine and to the possibility, through their own behaviour, of further fines.

14–127 Once assets are subject to a sequestration order the officers of the relevant union or company are required to co-operate with the sequestrators, and acts or omissions, whether of parties or indeed third parties, intended to hinder the discharge of the functions attaching to their court appointment may well constitute contempt of court.[95]

---

[88] This principle has been considered in the context of civil contempt generally at paras 12–18 *et seq.* See also *Fairclough & Sons v Manchester Ship Canal Co (No.2)* (1897) 41 S.J. 225, CA; *Steiner Products Ltd v Willy Steiner* [1966] 1 W.L.R. 986; *Howitt Transport Ltd v T. & GWU* [1973] I.C.R. 1 at 11, Sir John Donaldson; *Richardson v Richardson* [1989] Fam. 95 at 101, Scott Baker J.
[89] See now CPR Sch.1, Ord.45.1, 5 and Ord.46.5. For the procedure see paras 15–78 *et seq.*
[90] *Quality Pizzas v Canterbury Hotel Employees' Industrial Union* [1983] N.Z.L.R. 612.
[91] See, *e.g. Dent v Dent* (1867) L.R. 1 P. & D. 366 and the other cases cited at para.14–120, n.69; *Hipkin v Hipkin* [1962] 1 W.L.R. 491; *Romilly v Romilly* [1964] P. 22 (when sequestered property was used for the purpose of payments to the wife because the husband had failed to pay alimony *pendente lite*).
[92] See generally G. Lightman, "A Trade Union in Chains" (1987) C.L.P. 25; Sir Jack Jacob, "Sequestration for Contempt of Court" (1986) C.L.P. 221; Lord Wedderburn, *The Worker and the Law* (3rd ed., 1986), at p.730; C. O'Regan, "Contempt of Court and the Enforcement of Labour Injunctions" (1991) 54 M.L.R. 385; R.Kidner, "Sanctions for Contempt by a Trade Union" (1986) 6 L.S. 18 at 27–30.
[93] [1984] I.R.L.R. 445.
[94] *Clarke v Heathfield* [1985] I.C.R. 203 and *Clarke v Heathfield (No.2)* [1985] I.C.R. 606.
[95] *Eckman v Midland Bank Ltd* [1973] Q.B. 519 (Sir John Donaldson); *Z Ltd v A-Z and AA-LL* [1982] Q.B. 558; *Messenger Newspaper Group Ltd v NGA* [1984] 1 All E.R. 293; *Taylor v NUM, The Times*, November 20, 1985, Nicholls J.; *IRC v Hoogstraten* [1985] 1 Q.B. 1077 at 1093E–F, Dillon L.J., cited in para.11–318. See also the general discussion on the liability of third parties in respect of the subverting of orders binding *in personam*, at para.6–115.

Such co-operation may be necessary in any event because, for example, there may be assets available for the continued day-to-day running of the organisation concerned, or because the sequestrators need, in carrying out the obligations imposed by the court order, to trace property or recover it. Naturally, however, the obligation to provide information to the sequestrators would be confined to matters which they require to know pursuant to the discharge of their duties, and it is clear that in principle the court may grant relief from compliance with any request of a sequestrator going beyond what may be regarded as properly incidental to those functions. For example, in an appropriate case they may be ordered not to inspect certain documents of a confidential character,[96] or to press questions which may lead to a risk of self-incrimination.[97]

14–128

All property belonging to a trade union is vested in trustees in trust for the union but any judgment, order or award is enforceable against the property of the union, including by way of punishment for contempt, in the same manner as if the union were a body corporate.[98] This is subject to the restrictions on enforcement of awards by way of damages, costs or expenses against "protected property".[99] This protection would not appear to extend, however, to procedures for enforcement of the payment of fines imposed, for example, for contempt of court (such as by way of sequestration).

14–129

5. Removal of children from one jurisdiction to another

The remedy of sequestration has also been found to be an increasingly useful tool in the context of family law, when a spouse has removed a child wrongfully from the jurisdiction.[1] The problem arose in two cases which came before Scott Baker J. in the Family Division. First, in *Richardson v Richardson*,[2] he was confronted with a spouse who had abducted children to Ireland. He authorised the sequestrators to let or charge the spouse's property to fund the cost of litigation in that jurisdiction for the purpose of securing their return. It had been argued that the sequestered assets could not be used other than to achieve the payment of a sum of money owing, but he concluded that the "ancient tool" of sequestration should be adapted for use in modern conditions.[3] While recognising that sequestration represented a remedy of "last resort", he decided that the whole purpose of issuing the writ would in the circumstances be defeated unless he permitted the contemnor's house to be used for that purpose. In *Mir v Mir*,[4] the same judge ordered the sale of freehold property for a similar purpose. In that case the child had been removed to Pakistan, and funds were required to pursue proceedings in that jurisdiction.

14–130

---

[96] *Re Suarez* (1918) 88 L.J. Ch. 10.
[97] See the example given by Lightman in the article (1987) C.L.P. 25 at 52, which notes that Mervyn Davies J. did not, for that reason, insist upon answers to certain requests in *Clarke v Heathfield*.
[98] Trade Union and Labour Relations (Consolidation) Act 1992, s.12(2).
[99] *ibid.*, s.12(3) and s.23.
[1] See, *e.g. Romilly v Romilly* [1964] P. 22; *Charder v Charder* [1980] C.L.Y. 1837.
[2] [1989] Fam. 95.
[3] *ibid.* at 101.
[4] [1992] Fam. 79.

14–131 Sequestration was also prayed in aid in *Re S (Abduction): Sequestration*[5] by Johnson J., although on this occasion the order had been to the effect that a child should be returned to a foreign jurisdiction. In this instance, however, leave was given to issue the writ against a third party who had, with knowledge of the court's order, sought to assist the child's mother in her attempt to frustrate it. (Although the case provides another example of the court's willingness to adapt the "ancient tool" to modern use, it has already been pointed out[6] that the weight of authority, and indeed the express provisions of the former RSC Ord.45, r.1,[7] would appear to be against the extension of the remedy to the property of a non-party.)

L. Injunctions

14–132 The court may issue an injunction restraining a threatened contempt,[8] although in practice this is a jurisdiction to be sparingly exercised, especially in the context of anticipated publications.[9] It may also on an application for committal or sequestration refuse either of these remedies, and issue instead an injunction restraining the repetition of the contempt. In *Elliot v Klinger*[10] Stamp J. appeared to take the view that whilst this could be done by the court of its own initiative, it was not a proper course for an applicant to come to court and seek such an injunction without applying for committal. If, however, it is proper to seek an injunction against a threatened contempt, it is difficult to see why there should not be an application for an injunction to restrain a repetition of an already committed contempt, if there is a real danger of repetition.[11] Such an application could be coupled with an application to commit, or be made independently; the court can always proceed to commit of its own motion, if thought appropriate.

14–133 An example is provided by the case of *Re de Court*,[12] in which Sir Richard Scott V.-C. was confronted by a contempt committed by a person who was to be regarded as being under a disability (in accordance with the former RSC Ord.80, r.2).[13] He had spat into the face of the Chancery Clerk of the Lists because he was dissatisfied with the Clerk's response to his application to fix a date. There was

---

[5] [1995] 1 F.L.R. 858.
[6] See para.14–112 *et seq*.
[7] See now CPR Sch.1, Ord.45.1.
[8] *Att-Gen v Times Newspapers Ltd* [1974] A.C. 273; see also *Kitcat v Sharpe* (1882) 52 L.J.Ch. 134; *Marsden and Sons Ltd v Old Silkstone Collieries Ltd* (1914) 13 L.G.R. 342; *Johnes v Claughton* (1822) Jac. 573, 37 E.R. 966; *Tink v Rundle* (1847) 10 Beav. 318, 50 E.R. 604; *Evelyn v Lewis* (1844) 3 Hare 472, 67 E.R. 467; *Ames v Birkenhead Docks* (1855) 20 Beav. 332, 52 E.R. 630; *Bayly v Went* (1884) W.N. 197; *Dixon v Dixon* [1904] 1 Ch. 161; *Re Maidstone Palace of Varieties* [1909] Ch. 283; *Hubbard v Woodfield* (1913) 57 Sol. Jo. 729; *Acrow (Automation) Ltd v Rex Chainbelt Inc* [1971] 1 W.L.R. 1676, 1683; *Esso Petroleum v Kingswood Motors* [1974] Q.B. 142 at 156; *TSB Private Bank International S.A. v Chabra* [1992] 1 W.L.R. 231 at 240; *R. v Rhuddlan Justices Ex p. HTV Ltd* [1986] Crim. L.R. 329.
[9] See the discussion in paras 6–1 *et seq.*, especially the remarks of Lord Donaldson M.R., and Lord Bridge in *P v Liverpool Daily Post and Echo Newspapers plc* [1991] 2 A.C. 370.
[10] [1967] 1 W.L.R. 1165.
[11] Cf. *Acrow (Automation) Ltd v Rex Chainbelt Inc* [1971] 1 W.L.R. 1676 at 1683 Lord Denning M.R.
[12] [1997] T.L.R. 601 (Lexis).
[13] See now CPR 21.2; Pt 21 PD.

a history of attempting in various courts to "institute ridiculous and incomprehensible legal proceedings", some of which were described as "simply gibberish". The evidence disclosed that, when such documents were rejected by court officials, he became angry.

Against that background, the Vice-Chancellor concluded that it would be quite inappropriate to deal with the matter by way of imprisonment, the purpose of which in such a case "would be to mark the displeasure of the court about the contempt that had been committed and to punish the perpetrator". He said that a person suffering from the mental infirmity in question did not require punishment, and the court's displeasure had been marked sufficiently by the judgments the Vice-Chancellor had given.[14] He focused therefore rather upon the need to protect court officials in the future, both in the High Court and in county courts generally, and granted injunctions restraining the bringing of any action or making any claim in an action already brought except by a next friend.[15] The person was also restrained by injunction from "entering any court premises save as may be necessary to answer subpoenas".

M. Costs

Normally, costs will follow the event, and a respondent who is held in contempt would normally be ordered to bear the costs of the proceedings, in addition to any penalty imposed.[16] On some occasions, it may be appropriate to make a forthwith order for the payment of costs, determined by the judge, without the need for taxation[17] (now "detailed assessment"). The court will naturally take into account such facts as will ordinarily weigh in the consideration of such matters; for example, if the contemnor had no sufficient income or other resources to justify making an order. This may be a relevant factor especially in those cases where the court decides to impose a custodial penalty. Also, there may be some cases where the imposition of a costs order will, in the light of the respondent's means, constitute a sufficient penalty without the imposition of a fine as well.

The court has a complete discretion whether to order one party or another to pay the costs of a contempt application. There was authority that the court could order the contemnor to pay the costs, by reference to the former terminology, on a common fund basis[18] or as between solicitor and client.[19] If thought appropriate, the court has a discretion also to order costs on an indemnity basis.[20] Alternatively, the court may make no order as to costs[21]; or order the applicant to pay the costs of the application. This would obviously be appropriate where he

---

[14] Cp. *R (On the Application of Bempoa) v Southwark London Borough Council* [2002] EWHC 153 (Admin.), (2002) N.P.C. 23, discussed at para.14–2.
[15] Cp. now the procedure for civil restraint orders discussed in *Civil Procedure*, Vol. 1 at 3.1.13 *et seq.* and *Bhamjee v Forsdick* [2003] EWCA Civ 1113, [2004] 1 W.L.R. 88.
[16] *Patel v Patel* [1988] 2 F.L.R. 179, CA.
[17] *Taylor Made Golf Co Inc v Rata & Rata* [1996] F.S.R. 528, Laddie J.
[18] *Michigan (Great Britain) Ltd v Mathew* (1966) R.P.C. 47.
[19] *Daily Herald Ex p. the Bishop of Norwich* [1932] 2 K.B. 402.
[20] See, *e.g. Marsden v Old Silkstone Collieries* (1914) 13 L.G.R. 342.
[21] *Bucknell v Bucknell* [1969] 1 W.L.R. 1204; *Att-Gen v Times Newspapers Ltd* [1974] A.C. 273.

fails to establish that a contempt has been committed.[22] But even if a technical contempt was proved, the court could order the applicant to pay the costs of the motion if the contempt had been too trivial to justify its being brought to the attention of the court.[23]

Costs on a contemnor's successful appeal

14–137 The question sometimes arises as to costs following an appeal in which a contemnor has been successful in whole or in part. In *Knight v Clifton*[24] it was expressly stated that there was no difference in principle as to the exercise of the court's discretion on costs between proceedings for civil contempt and other *inter partes* proceedings. One factor to be given special weight, however, would be the fact that "the liberty of the subject is involved". It was noted by the Court of Appeal in *Symes v Phillips*[25] that there was "little material as to whether the approach to costs on a successful appeal by the contemnor in contempt proceedings should be the same as that in any civil appeal or whether a different approach should apply . . . ". The contemnor had successfully appealed a penalty of two years imprisonment imposed in the Chancery Division. The Court of Appeal substituted a term of one year and the judge's order was modified in other respects in the contemnor's favour. The claimants were represented on the appeal in order to assist the court rather than "to press for a heavy sentence" and counsel was to that extent discharging a role akin to that of an advocate to the court (formerly an *amicus*) rather than an adversarial one. The court's discretion under CPR Pt 44.3 was, on the particular facts, exercised in favour of granting the appellant half his costs of the appeal (including of the costs issue itself). The court took in to account *inter alia* the fact that the contemnor, by his admitted contempt of court, had brought the entire proceedings on himself and was thus in a weaker position as between the parties than most litigants. The appellant in that case was publicly funded. The court referred to the earlier decision on costs in *Re Barrell Enterprises*[26] in which the contemnor had been released from custody but was ordered to pay the costs himself. Longmore L.J. commented that in the earlier case the decision on costs "was not reasoned". A factor in the court's consideration may well have been that the other parties in *Re Barrell Enterprises* were the Official Receiver and, as *amicus*, the Official Solicitor.

---

[22] See *Att-Gen v MGN Ltd* [1997] 1 W.L.R. 926, [1997] 1 All E.R. 456, D.C. where the Attorney-General was ordered to pay the costs of all the newspaper groups. The Court of Appeal in *Cave v Borax Europe Ltd* [2002] EWCA Civ 799, [2002] All E.R. (D) 287 (May) declined to interfere when the judge had ordered the applicant to pay the costs on the indemnity basis because he regarded the application as having been made mischievously.
[23] *Att-Gen v Times Newspapers Ltd* [1974] A.C. 274 at 312, Lord Diplock; see also *Cronmire v Daily Bourse Ltd* (1892) 9 T.L.R. 101; *Plating Co v Farquharson* (1881) 17 Ch D. 49. For a more modern example, see the remarks of Jacob J. in *Adam Phones Ltd v Goldschmidt* [1999] 4 All E.R. 486, where he observed that it was inappropriate to punish a "blameless" respondent through costs.
[24] [1971] Ch. 700 at 718, Sachs L.J.
[25] [2005] EWCA Civ 663.
[26] [1973] 1 W.L.R. 19.

It was confirmed in *R. v Moore*,[27] following *Holden & Co v Crown Prosecution Service (No.2)*[28] that there was no power to order a successful appellant's costs out of central funds.

Responsibility for the costs of proceedings to which one is not a party

Until recently, it was considered wrong in principle to punish a person by having to pay the costs of proceedings to which he or she was not party. In the case of *Weston v CCC Administrator*,[29] it was held that "a contempt is not punishable by payment of costs".[30] A solicitor discovered, the day before, that a criminal case in which he had been instructed was to be listed as a "floater". The case was not ready for trial, and he wrote an offensive letter to the courts administrator and sent the client to court on his own, with a view to saving costs. The trial was then fixed by the judge for the following Monday. The solicitor made a further protest, and told the client to go to court on the Monday and ask the judge to stand the case out for a date to be fixed by his counsel's clerk. He also told the prosecution that the case could not be ready in time. When the client attended, still unrepresented, a different judge who had been assigned for the trial ordered the solicitor to attend before him the following day. The solicitor did not attend, because the message came only through his client. There was no official communication from the court. The judge then issued a bench warrant, and the solicitor was brought to court when the judge granted a short adjournment for him to be represented. After a hearing, in which there were many misunderstandings on both sides, and a refusal by the solicitor to apologise for the letter, the judge informed him that he was in breach of his duty as an officer of the court. He was ordered to pay the costs *of the prosecution* thrown away by their having to attend court three times to no avail.

The first question identified by Lord Denning M.R.[31] was as to the nature of the jurisdiction the judge was purporting to exercise. Was he acting under the disciplinary power of the court over solicitors? Or under the jurisdiction to punish for contempt of court? Where costs are needlessly incurred, a court can order a solicitor to pay those costs.[32] He concluded that the judge appeared to be exercising a contempt jurisdiction, and indeed that is what he had told the solicitor he was doing. Accordingly, the order to pay the costs thrown away appeared to have been a punishment "in the nature of a fine". The Court of Appeal concluded that, on the facts, this solicitor was not in contempt in any event.[33] Nevertheless, it was made clear[34] that it had been "wholly inappropriate" and a "misuse of power" to make the costs order. Not only was there no clear proof of the costs of the prosecution having been needlessly expended

---

[27] [2003] EWCA Crim 1574, [2003] 1 W.L.R. 2170.
[28] [1994] 1 A.C. 22, discussed at para.7–274 (s.159 appeals) *et seq.*
[29] [1977] 1 Q.B. 32.
[30] *ibid.* at 45.
[31] *ibid.* at 42A–B.
[32] See, *e.g. Myers v Elman* [1940] A.C. 282 at 317–19; *R. v Smith (Martin)* [1975] Q.B. 531. For a "wasted costs" order, see Supreme Court Act 1981, s.51(6).
[33] [1977] 1 Q.B. at 44.
[34] *per* Stephenson L.J. at 45. See para.11–69.

14–140 as a result of the solicitor's failure to attend, but there was the more serious objection that the judge was purporting to exercise the court's inherent jurisdiction to punish for contempt. Had there been a contempt, the court would therefore have substituted a fine, since an order for costs should not have been used for that purpose.

14–141 This principle has now, however, to be qualified because there is, since October 18, 2004, provision for a third party costs order to be made against anyone found to have committed "serious misconduct (whether or not constituting a contempt of court)" if costs have been incurred or wasted by any party to criminal proceedings as a result of the misconduct.[35] There has thus been a significant change of policy in this respect. At the time of writing, there are no examples of the power having been exercised. It is not yet possible to say conclusively how compatible the statutory formula is with the provisions of Arts 6 and 10 of the European Convention. There is, however, provision made expressly that before making any such order the court *shall* allow the third party and any party to make representations and *may* hear evidence.[36] Such an order may be made by the court at any time during or after the relevant proceedings "on the application of any party or of its own initiative (but not otherwise)".[37] An order should be made during the proceedings if the court decides that there are good reasons to do so, and the court must notify the parties and the third party of the reasons and allow any of them to make representations.[38] Any third party against whom such an order is made has a right to appeal.[39] In the case of an order made by a magistrates' court the appeal lies to the Crown Court; where the order has been made at first instance in the Crown Court, the appeal lies to the Court of Appeal. One of the main concerns about these provisions is that the term "serious misconduct" is not defined save, as indicated above, to the extent that it is not confined to conduct which would have constituted contempt at common law or under the statutory regime governing its "strict liability" under ss.1–3 of the Contempt of Court Act 1981.Thus, it is unclear for example to what extent the conduct would need to qualify as intentional or reckless or whether either of the escape routes would be available corresponding to those in ss.3[40] and 5[41] of the Act.

IV. THE UNAVAILABILITY OF FINANCIAL COMPENSATION

A. Possible sources of compensation

14–142 A claim for compensation might theoretically arise in one of three ways—(1) under the Powers of Criminal Courts (Sentencing) Act 2000, in respect of a

---

[35] This regime is contained in regs 3E–I of the Costs in Criminal Cases (General) Regulations 1986, SI 1986/13.35 inserted by SI 2004/2408, reg.7.
[36] reg.3F(4).
[37] reg.3F(2).
[38] reg.3F(3).
[39] reg.3H.
[40] See paras 4–236 *et seq.* (innocent publication).
[41] Paras 4–293 *et seq.* (discussion of public affairs in good faith).

contempt; (2) under the 2000 Act, but following a conviction for a specific criminal offence such as under s.51(2) of the Criminal Justice and Public Order Act 1994; (3) under the Harassment Act 1997; and, possibly, (4) by an action for damages in a civil court.

1. *The statutory compensation inapplicable to summary findings of contempt*

The predecessor legislation, the Powers of Criminal Courts Act 1973 gave the court power to award compensation for damage suffered by the victims of a criminal offence. It would seem that these provisions were not intended to apply to a summary finding of contempt. Section 130(1)(a) of the 2000 Act provides:

> "(1) A court by or before which a person is convicted of an offence, instead of or in addition to dealing with him in any other way, may, on application or otherwise, make an order (in this Act referred to as a 'compensation order') requiring him—
>
> > (a) to pay compensation for any personal injury, loss or damage resulting from that offence or any other offence which is taken into consideration by the court in determining sentence; . . . "

The language of "conviction" and "offence" suggests that the section would have no application to the summary contempt procedure.[42] Furthermore, s.132 of the Act provides for an appeal against such an order made on conviction on indictment, or by a magistrates' court. Neither of these descriptions would fit a finding of contempt.

Moreover, the Administration of Justice Act 1960, s.13(1), which gives a right of appeal in cases of criminal contempt to the Court of Appeal, does so only from an "order or decision of a court in the exercise of jurisdiction to punish for contempt of court,"[43] and this would not be apt to cover compensation.

A compensation order is not an order intended to punish but to compensate. It would seem, therefore, that if s.130 of the Powers of Criminal Courts (Sentencing) Act 2000 were applied to a finding of contempt, so that a compensation order was possible, there would be no corresponding right of appeal. It can hardly be that it was intended to provide for compensation in this one area without affording a right of appeal.

2. *Compensation in respect of statutory offences*

There is, however, no reason to suppose, if an offence (say) of interfering with a witness or juror under the Criminal Justice and Public Order Act 1984, s.51

---

[42] Cp. *Morris v Crown Office* [1970] 2 Q.B. 114 (a decision holding s.22 of the 1973 Act to be inapplicable); *R. v Newbury Justices Ex p. Pont* (1983) 78 Cr.App.R. 255 (a decision holding s.21 of the 1973 Act to be inapplicable); see also *R. v Palmer* [1992] 1 W.L.R. 568, 3 All E.R. 289 (s. 2(1) of the 1973 Act inapplicable). See paras 14–98 *et seq.*
[43] For the interpretation of this wording, see *R. v Havant Justices Ex p. Palmer* (1985) 149 J.P. 609, [1985] Crim. L.R. 658.

were tried on indictment, that compensation would not be available in accordance with s.130 of the 2000 Act.

3. *The Protection from Harassment Act 1997*

14–147 Under the Protection from Harassment Act 1997 it is possible to claim damages. In some circumstances, which might otherwise be covered by the Family Law Act jurisdiction, it might be more appropriate to seek damages for harassment.[44]

4. *Damages: The modern law*

14–148 Although a recommendation was made by the Phillimore Committee[45] that compensation should be available in the specific circumstances of reprisals against witnesses or jurors, this suggestion was not implemented. It seems that an action for damages does not lie for contempt as such. On the other hand, it has been held that if an undertaking to the court has been breached, so that a contempt of court has been committed, and the breach of undertaking also constitutes a breach of contract vis-a-vis the other party to the litigation, the court may on the application for committal make a summary award of damages in respect of that wrong.[46]

14–149 That damages are unavailable as a remedy in contempt seems clear from the decision of the Court of Appeal in *Chapman v Honig*.[47] The decision was based primarily upon the notion that the court's jurisdiction in contempt is concerned with a wrong against the administration of justice rather than against an individual. The exercise of that jurisdiction in relation to civil contempt often serves to protect the interests of an individual.[48] It was observed, however, by Lord Donaldson M.R.[49] that contempt proceedings generally were not such as to afford "solace or compensation". On the other hand, it was suggested by Lord

---

[44] As District Judge Robert Hill has observed in [2005] Fam. Law 364, "the reality is that, in an appropriate case, an award of damages can be just as, or even more, effective than an injunction—a kick in the wallet can be the most painful kick of all".
[45] Cmnd 5794 (1974) at para.158. See the analogy drawn with the Witnesses (Public Inquiries) Protection Act 1892, s.4, which applied both in England and in Scotland.
[46] *Midland Marts Ltd v Hobday* [1989] 1 W.L.R. 1143. This case was followed in the Chancery Division in *Parker and another (t/a NBC Services) v Rasalingham (t/a Microtec)* [2000] All E.R. (D) 912, *The Times*, July 12, 2000. The relevant order was a negotiated consent order and it was held that it was an appropriate case in which to order an enquiry into the damages suffered as a result of the breaches. An order was also made for costs on the indemnity basis.
[47] [1963] 2 Q.B. 502. See also *Midland Marts Ltd v Hobday* [1989] 1 W.L.R. 1134 at 1145, 3 All E.R. 246 at 250; *Taylor v Ribby Hall Leisure* [1997] 4 All E.R. 760 at 768h, Mummery L.J. And see *Parker and another (t/a NBC Services) v Rasalingham (t/a Microtec)* [2000] All E.R. (D) 912, *The Times*, July 12, 2000.
[48] See paras 12–5 *et seq.* for a discussion of the dual nature of civil contempt.
[49] *Johnson v Walton* [1990] 1 F.L.R. 350 at 353D–E. See also Sedley J. in *Guildford Borough Council v Valler* [1993] T.L.R. 274 at 275.

Denning M.R. in *Att-Gen v Butterworth*,[50] in the particular context of "victimisation of a witness", " . . . that if the witness has been damnified by it he may well have redress in a civil court for damages".

B. The older cases on compensation

1. *Early examples of compensatory awards*

There is a considerable body of case law relating to claims for damages in the context of two particular categories of conduct which overlap with contempt. First, there is the case in which an officer of the court arrests a person entitled to privilege; it has long been clear that no action for damages lies even if the arrest is malicious. Secondly, it appears that a claim for damages has sometimes succeeded against a witness who fails to attend upon subpoena, although probably only on proof of special damage. It is necessary to consider the extent to which these authorities may still have a bearing upon the modern law of contempt before we turn to a more detailed examination of *Chapman v Honig*.

In early times it was quite common for damages to be awarded to the victim of a contempt by the court which punished the contemnor. In 1319, for example, the Mayor of the Staple brought an action of trespass against a defendant for abusing and assaulting him in Westminster Hall. On verdict for the plaintiff he was awarded damages of £100. At the same time the contemnor was committed to the Marshall at the King's will.[51] The action was for trespass, and under the writ of trespass it was usual for the losing defendant to pay not only damages to the plaintiff, but also an amount to the King for the breach of his peace. Thus, in 1352, a man who assaulted a juror in open court was ordered to pay £4 to the juror and £6 to the King.[52] The early cases all seem to be concerned with conduct which would have been actionable upon some other basis, apart from there having been a contempt of court. In at least one case, however, the process was headed *de placito contemptu*.[53]

2. *Arrests in breach of privilege*

By the end of the seventeenth century it was established that no action for damages lay against an officer of the court who arrested a person privileged from arrest at the time, even if the officer knew or ought to have known that the person arrested was entitled to privilege.[54]

---

[50] [1963] 1 Q.B. 696 at 719.
[51] Coram Rege roll, T. 13 Edw. II, m. 14.
[52] Coram Rege roll, P. 26 Edw. III, m. 60.
[53] Coram Rege roll, M. 6 Edw. III, m. 30d.
[54] *Vandervelde v Lluellin* (1662) 1 Keb. 220, 83 E.R. 910. See also *Tarlton v Fisher* (1781) 2 Doug. 671, 99 E.R. 426; *Cameron v Lightfoot* (1777) 2 Bl. W. 1190, 96 E.R. 701; *Magnay v Burt* (1843) 5 Q.B. 381, 114 E.R. 1293. See also *Jolly v Staines County Court Circuit Judge* [2000] 2 F.C.R. 59.

3. *Failing to comply with a subpoena or witness summons*

14–153 It seems clear, however, that a party in litigation who has obtained a subpoena for a witness to attend a trial could in theory bring an action for damages if he does not attend and give evidence.[55] There remains some doubt, however, as to the scope of such compensation. The only damages to have been recovered have been in respect of costs thrown away. The cases all support the view that actual damage must be proved, although it is unclear to what extent losses actually incurred may be recovered. An application could and should always be made by the party who has obtained the subpoena for an adjournment of the proceedings. This might well be granted if the missing witness had material evidence to give. Damages would usually be limited in practice to costs thrown away through his non-attendance.

14–154 Actions have been brought in the past to recover compensation going beyond this, so as to include the damages of which plaintiffs have claimed to have been deprived because they lost their action through the non-attendance of the witness, but such claims have failed.[56] This was not overtly on the basis that no action lay for such damages, but because the court in each case was not satisfied that the loss had in fact been occasioned through the absence of the witness. It was stressed how difficult it is to prove such an allegation although the position is in some respects similar to claims against solicitors for negligence, or perhaps claims in third party proceedings for indemnity or contribution, where the court sometimes does have to assess what would have been the outcome of litigation which did not in fact take place. There are no reported instances of an action against a witness who failed to attend criminal proceedings under subpoena or witness summons.

14–155 The weight of authority seemed to support the conclusion that actual damage must be proved. The early cases, although perhaps based on the assumption that the plaintiff must show that he would have succeeded the action had the witness attended, do not go so far as to lay this down as a rule of general application. It seems always to have been assumed that the plaintiff had a good claim in the original action.[57]

14–156 In *Couling v Coxe*,[58] Lush for the plaintiff adopted a similar argument in support of general damages:

---

[55] *Roberts v J & F Stone Lighting and Radio Ltd* (1945) 172 L.T. 240, Asquith J. See also *Chapman v Honig* [1963] 2 Q.B. at 525, Davies L.J.
[56] *Crewe v Field* (1896) 12 T.L.R. 405; *Roberts v J & F Stone Lighting and Radio Ltd* (1945) 172 L.T. 240.
[57] *Masterman v Judson* (1832) 8 Bing. 224, 131 E.R. 387; *Mullett v Hunt* (1833) 1 C. & M. 753, 149 E.R. 602; *Davis v Lovell* (1839) 4 M. & W. 679, 150 E.R. 1593; cf. *Goodwin v West* (1638) Jones W. 430, 82 E.R. 226; *Maddison v Shore* (1703) 5 Mod. 355, 87 E.R. 701 which show that on an action against a witness for a penalty of £10 under 5 Eliz. c.9 for non-attendance under subpoena special damage must be shown. They turn on the wording of the statute now repealed.
[58] (1848) 6 C.B. 703 at 718–19, 136 E.R. 1424 at 1430. See also for the argument of counsel S.C. 6 D. & L. 399 at 403.

"It is not necessary, in order to maintain such an action as this to prove that the plaintiff had a good cause of action in the original action. There is no decision precisely in point; but unless it appears that an action has been brought wantonly and with full knowledge that it was not maintainable, the court will always presume that it was brought by the plaintiff in the bona fide belief that he has a good cause of action. And in all such cases, it is reasonable that the plaintiff should have the benefit of any evidence which he may think material to his cause or action. It would be dangerous to the administration of justice to permit the witnesses of a plaintiff to obey or disobey a subpoena, according as they believed that the action was well founded or not."

14–157 Wilde C.J., delivering the judgment of the Court of Common Pleas, rejected this argument on two grounds. First, he said that the authorities showed it was necessary that the plaintiff alleged a good cause of action in the original suit. In the absence of such an allegation, the pleadings did not show that the plaintiff had suffered any particular loss or damage by the witness's non-attendance. The Chief Justice's second point was:

" . . . in an action such as this, for breach of duty,—not arising out of contract between the plaintiff and defendant, but,—for disobeying the order of a competent authority, the existence of actual damage or loss is essential to the action; and the law will not imply a loss to the plaintiff from such disobedience to the subpoena."

14–158 Wilde C.J. held in the plaintiff's favour on the narrower ground that, even if the plaintiff would not have succeeded in the original proceedings *overall*, nevertheless, even if he would have been entitled to succeed on one issue, to which the absent witness's evidence was relevant, and would have saved costs if he had attended, he would be entitled to succeed to that extent in his subsequent claim against him.[59] In the later cases, the view expressed by Wilde C.J. as to general damages is accepted without question as settled law.[60]

4. *The law clarified in* Chapman v Honig

14–159 The question whether damages may be claimed in respect of a contempt of court must now be determined in the light of *Chapman v Honig*.[61] In an action against a landlord his tenant was subpoenaed by the landlord's opponent and gave evidence against the landlord. The next day the landlord gave the tenant notice to quit and, while the tenant and his family were away from the premises, he put padlocks on the doors. After discussion with the police the padlocks were removed and the tenant allowed to enter. The tenant thereupon obtained an injunction restraining the landlord from trespassing on the premises, placing padlocks on the doors or cutting off the electricity. Because, however, his wife was so distressed at what had happened, the tenant, fearing her health might suffer, moved out of the premises. The tenant brought an action for damages on the basis that the notice to quit was invalid and that therefore the act of the

---

[59] Cf. Cresswell J. in *Needham v Frazer* (1845) 14 L.J. C.P. 256 at 260.
[60] *Crewe v Field* (1896) 12 T.L.R. 405; *Roberts v J & F Stone Lighting and Radio Ltd* (1945) 172 L.T. 240.
[61] [1963] 2 Q.B. 502.

14–159 landlord in padlocking the premises was a trespass and a breach of his covenant for quiet enjoyment.

14–160 At the trial the county court judge found that the landlord had served the notice to quit in order to punish the tenant for the evidence he had given in court. The judge then expressed the view that the service of the notice to quit was a contempt of court and that he could award general damages to the plaintiff in respect of that contempt. He accordingly awarded the plaintiff £50 without feeling it necessary to consider whether the notice to quit was invalid. If the notice to quit was invalid, then the landlord's conduct would almost certainly give rise to a claim irrespective of the element of contempt, on the basis of trespass and breach of covenant.

14–161 The Court of Appeal held by a majority that the plaintiff was *not* entitled to recover damages. Their decision turned largely on whether the notice to quit was valid. Lord Denning M.R., in his dissenting judgment, took the point that if the notice was invalid then there would be an action for trespass and breach of covenant. He did not consider in terms the question whether an action for damages lay for a contempt which was not otherwise actionable, but much of his judgment was expressed in general terms.

14–162 In the view of the majority the notice to quit was valid. It was merely the exercise of a contractual right, and where a person has a contractual right he may exercise it when he wishes, and his motive is immaterial. The position in contract was contrasted with that in tort, where in some cases an act otherwise lawful may be rendered unlawful because it is done with a particular motive. In fact the defendant here had perhaps gone further than merely exercising a contractual right with a bad motive. He had arguably exercised his contractual right in such a way as to punish a witness for what he had done[62] in the discharge of his duty at court.

14–163 Apart from whether or not the notice to quit was valid, the Court of Appeal did consider whether the contempt jurisdiction exists merely to protect the administration of justice or whether it gives in addition a private remedy, for example to persons who suffer wrongful interference as a result of discharging their public duty as witnesses in the courts. Pearson L.J. concluded: "The jurisdiction exists and is exercised *alio intuitu*, for the protection of the administration of justice and not for the protection of individuals."

14–164 Thus it seems to be settled law that no claim for damages will lie in respect of conduct *qua* contempt of court, except in the particular case of a witness who fails to obey a subpoena. Then the claim will be regarded as limited to costs thrown away.

---

[62] Pearson L.J. had some doubts whether a contempt of court had been committed because there was no evidence that other persons who might be deterred from giving evidence got to know of the notice to quit and why it was served. On this point Lord Denning and Davies L.J. disagreed. See *ibid*. at 512, 526.

CHAPTER 15

PRACTICE, PROCEDURE AND PUBLIC FUNDING

		PARA
I.	Committal: The Supreme Court	15–1
II.	Committal in the County Court	15–51
III.	Applications for Sequestration	15–78
IV.	Appeals Procedure	15–88
V.	Legal Services Commission: Advice, Assistance and Representation	15–107

I. COMMITTAL: THE SUPREME COURT

A. Criminal contempts: the role of the Attorney-General

The usual means of initiating proceedings for criminal contempt is through the Law Officers. Where it is contemplated that proceedings should be brought under the strict liability rule after a contempt has been committed, proceedings can only be commenced either on the motion of the Attorney-General, or by a court, having the power to do so, of its own motion.[1]

15–1

B. Contempt of Court Act 1981, section 7

Section 7 of the 1981 Act provides that:

15–2

"Proceedings for a contempt of court under the strict liability rule (other than Scottish proceedings) shall not be instituted except by or with the consent of the Attorney General or on the motion of a court having jurisdiction to deal with it."

In deciding whether or not to initiate proceedings against a newspaper proprietor or its editor, the Attorney-General makes a practice of writing to the editor responsible for what he considers to be the offending publication, and asking whether there is any reason why contempt proceedings should not be brought, but pointing out that the editor is under no obligation to respond.

It has been held that s.7 does not prevent an interested party, other than the Attorney-General, from bringing proceedings for an injunction to restrain an apprehended contempt by way of publication.[2]

15–3

---

[1] See paras 4–183 *et seq.*
[2] *Peacock v London Weekend Television* (1985) 150 J.P. 71, (1985) 150 J.P.N. 47 CA. But see the reservations of Lord Bridge cited in para.6–26.

C. Committal

15–4 CPR, Sch.1, Ord. 52 provides that the power of the High Court and Court of Appeal to punish for contempt of court may be exercised by an order of committal. Against the background of a trend towards the assimilation of the jurisdiction of the High Court with that of the county court, the respective provisions of the rules have been supplemented by a common Practice Direction governing the procedure for committal.[3] This provides[4] *inter alia* that the court may on its own initiative or on application strike out a committal application in the prescribed circumstances.

15–5 Until 1965 there were two methods whereby the superior courts could imprison contemnors: committal and attachment. Since 1965 the relevant rules of court have provided only for committal. Attachment survived in the county court until 1979,[5] when the terms of the former Ord.25, r.67 of the County Court Rules 1936 were changed. Under the old law the distinction between committal and attachment was highly technical, and to avoid difficulties it became customary to ask for both committal and attachment as alternative sanctions.[6] Attachment is an outmoded remedy.[7] Nevertheless, we shall attempt a brief summary of the old law.

The old distinctions between committal and attachment

15–6 The primary distinction between committal and attachment was that committal was enforced by the tipstaff, wherever the contemnor was to be found in the kingdom, whereas attachment was enforced by the sheriff for the county in which the contemnor was located.[8] The distinctions were generally considered by the Court of Appeal in *Re Evans, Evans v Noton*.[9] The court had requested Mr. Registrar Lavie to prepare a memorandum on the subject and accepted his conclusions.

15–7 He described the general principle as being that a man was committed for doing what he ought not to do, and attached for not doing what he was ordered to do. This was the policy of the Court of Chancery. In the common law courts, however, attachment was the usual remedy for all forms of contempt. When the Supreme Court was established, the original Ord.47, r.7 provided that a judgment requiring a person to do an act other than payment of money, or to abstain from doing anything, might be enforced by either remedy.

---

[3] Appendix 5A.
[4] At para.5.
[5] See, *e.g. Jennison v Baker* [1972] 2 Q.B. 52 and *Whitter v Peters* [1982] 1 W.L.R. 389 at 395, Booth J.
[6] See *Callow v Young* (1887) 56 L.T. 147.
[7] *Balogh v St. Albans Crown Court* [1975] Q.B. 73 at 88F, Stephenson L.J.
[8] See *County Court Judge of Lambeth* (1887) 36 W.R. 476, Wills J.
[9] [1893] 1 Ch. 252.

Certain types of contempt were regarded as falling outside this rule, and in the following cases committal was the normal remedy: (i) breach of an undertaking[10]; (ii) misconduct towards a ward; (iii) interference with a receiver; (iv) improper comment on pending proceedings; (v) personal contempt of the court. In certain other cases it became accepted that attachment was the correct remedy: in particular, proceedings to imprison a debtor under one of the exceptions to s.4 of the Debtors Act 1869[11]; disobedience to a writ of habeas corpus[12] or to one of the prerogative orders[13]; contempt in connection with criminal proceedings or any proceedings in the Queen's Bench Division, except where committed in the face of the court or consisting in disobedience to an order of the court; and contempts in connection with proceedings in an inferior court.

D. Applications to the Divisional Court

CPR, Sch.1, Ord.52 defines in this respect the jurisdiction of the Divisional Court of the Queen's Bench Division (and of single judges in all Divisions).[14] No application to a Divisional Court for an order of committal may be made except with permission granted on a without notice application to the court itself, or in vacation to a "judge in chambers".[15] Such applications must be supported by a statement setting out the name and description of the applicant, as well as the name, description and address of the person sought to be committed. The statement should set out the grounds on which committal is sought, and an application should also be supported by an affidavit, filed beforehand, verifying all facts relied upon.[16] Both procedures may be used by a litigant in person.[17]

Notice of an application for permission must be given by the applicant to the Crown Office not later than the preceding day, and copies of the requisite statement and affidavit should be lodged in the Office at the same time.[18] If an application made in the vacation to a judge in chambers is refused, then a fresh application for permission may be made to a Divisional Court, provided it is made within eight days of the refusal or, if a Divisional Court does not sit within that period, on the first day of sitting thereafter.[19] Once permission has been granted to apply for an order, the application itself must be made to a Divisional Court and, unless the court or judge granting permission has otherwise directed,

---

[10] *D v A & Co* [1900] 1 Ch. 484; *Callow v Young* (1887) 56 L.T. 147.
[11] See *Re Wilde* (1910) W.N. 128. For the Debtors Acts, see Halsbury's *Statutes of England*, 4th ed., Vol. 4 at 817 and 824.
[12] See the former Ord.44, r.2.
[13] See *R. v Poplar Borough Council (No.2) Ex p. London County Council* [1922] 1 K.B. 95.
[14] See paras 13–17 *et seq.*
[15] See now CPR Sch.1, Ord.52.2, 6. The rule still uses the term "judge in chambers" although "single judge" or "interim applications judge" would probably accord more accurately with current usage.
[16] CPR Sch.1, Ord.52.2 (2).
[17] *Practice Note* [1947] W.N. 218; *Ex p. Collett,* QBD (unreported) October 10, 1952. In *Pelling v Hammond*, C/00/2363, September 22, 2000, Laws L.J. heard an application for permission to appeal, by a would–be "Mackenzie friend" in person, from a decision of the Divisional Court refusing permission to commence committal proceedings (although he expressed doubt as to his standing to make such an application: see para.3–174, n.91).
[18] CPR Sch.1, Ord.52.2(3).
[19] CPR Sch.1, Ord.52.2(4) and (5).

15–10 CHAPTER 15—PRACTICE, PROCEDURE AND PUBLIC FUNDING

there must be at least 14 clear days between the service of the claim form and the day of the hearing.[20] Unless the claim form is issued within 14 days after permission being granted the permission will lapse.[21]

Personal service

15–11 The general rule is that the claim form, accompanied by a copy of the statement and affidavit used in support of the application for permission, must be personally served on the person sought to be committed even if he has an address for the service of other documents.[22] Personal service is effected by leaving a copy with the person to be served.[23] If he or she doubts whether the documents served are genuine copies, then there is an entitlement on payment of the prescribed fee to search for, inspect and take a copy of any such document from the court records.[24]

E. Application to a court other than the Divisional Court

15–12 In cases where application may be made to a court other than a Divisional Court, such an application must be made by claim form or application notice. Normally a Pt 8 claim form will be appropriate but, if the application is to be made in existing proceedings, an application should be made in those proceedings.[25] It should also be supported by written evidence.[26] No permission is required. Written evidence is support of or in opposition to a committal application must be given by affidavit.[27]

Personal service

15–13 The general rule is that the claim form or application notice, accompanied by a copy of the written evidence in support of the application, must be served personally, although the court has power to dispense with personal service if thought just to do so[28] or to order service by an alternative method,[29] provided that it appears that there is a "good reason."[30] Such steps might be appropriate,

---

[20] CPR Sch.1, Ord.52.3(1).
[21] CPR Sch.1, Ord.52.3(2).
[22] CPR Sch.1, Ord.52.3(3).
[23] CPR 6.4(3).
[24] See now CPR 5.4(2).
[25] CPR Sch.1, Ord.52, PD paras 2.1 and 2.2 (see Appendix 5A).
[26] CPR Sch.1, Ord.52.4.(1). See also *Chanel Ltd v FGM Cosmetics* [1981] F.S.R. 471, which made it clear that the notice must specify the grounds clearly. It will not suffice to do so in the evidence alone. See now PD2.5(2) and 2.6(2).
[27] PD3.1 (Appendix 5A).
[28] CPR Sch.1, Ord.52.4(2) and (3) and PD 2.5(1) and 2.6(1).
[29] CPR 6.8. The rule cannot be applied retrospectively: *Elmes v Hygrade Food Products Ltd* [2001] EWCA Civ 1351.
[30] In *Worboys v Worboys* [1953] P. 192 at 198, Davies J. observed: "On the authorities that were cited to me I am quite satisfied that for very many years it has been the practice of all Divisions of this Court, in appropriate cases and where the facts justified it, to give leave for substituted service not merely of orders such as these on which attachments may issue, but of the motion for attachment itself."

for example, where there is reason to believe that personal service is being or would be evaded.[31] Even if the alleged contemnor should appear at the hearing, the necessity for service is not thereby automatically waived.[32] Any such dispensation should be recorded in any committal order thereafter made.[33]

An application to a court other than the Divisional Court by a litigant in person[34] used not to be permitted, but there is modern authority that an applicant in person may move for committal, in the Chancery Division as well as in the Queen's Bench Division.[35]

F. Special provisions relating to applications in the Family Division

Specific reference is made to the procedure for committal applications in matrimonial proceedings in the Family Proceedings Rules 1991; it is there provided[36] that such applications are to be made by summons. Such applications may be heard in private rather than in open court, but this would be most unusual. For example, in *Re B (Contempt: Evidence)*[37] it was recognised by counsel that it would be appropriate for the evidence to be heard in open court. Even if the evidence were to be heard in private, it would usually be appropriate for the court to explain briefly in open court why it has reached the decision.[38] In particular, where an order is made for committal, the reason should be given for the length of the sentence and, if it is to be suspended, the reason for that decision also.

It is true that there is a general provision under CPR Sch.1, Ord.52.6 (1) for applications to be heard in private where the "interests of the administration of justice" require it although this would require very exceptional circumstances. There is nothing in the rules to suggest that it does not apply in the Family Division. It is also clear from the terms of r.7.2(1) that it is intended to be subject to CPR Sch.1, Ord.52.6. It may be that the correct approach is the same as in other Divisions, save that the need to protect children may lead the court more frequently to decide that a private hearing is required. This would appear to accord with the reasoning of Munby J. in *Clibbery v Allan*,[39] where he explained that the principle of open justice must apply generally in all Divisions of the High Court, save in so far as there are special exceptions provided for in s.12 of the Administration of Justice Act 1960.[40] Indeed, CPR Sch.1, Ord.52.6 reflects that provision and caters specifically for committal applications arising out of

---

[31] See Kekewich J. in *Mander v Falcke* [1891] 3 Ch. 488 at 493; *O'Donovan v O'Donovan* [1955] 1 W.L.R. 1086; *Favard v Favard* (1896) 75 L.T. 664; see also *Gordon v Gordon* [1903] P. 1417.
[32] See *Mander v Falcke* [1891] 3 Ch. 488.
[33] *Wright v Jess* [1987] 1 W.L.R. 1076, 2 All E.R. 1067.
[34] *Ex p. Liebrand* [1914] W.N. 310; *Re G's Application for a Committal Order* [1954] 1 W.L.R. 1116.
[35] *Bevan v Hastings Jones* [1978] 1 W.L.R. 294; *De Vries v Kay, The Times*, October 7, 1978.
[36] Rule 7.2(1). See also the *Practice Direction (Family Proceedings: Committal)* March 16, 2001 Appendix 5B).
[37] [1996] 1 F.L.R. 239 at 242F, Wall J.
[38] *Hale v Tanner (Practice Note)* [2000] 1 W.L.R. 2377 at 2381G.
[39] [2001] 2 F.L.R. 819. The decision was upheld on appeal: [2002] EWCA Civ 45, [2002] Fam. 261.
[40] Discussed at paras 8–97 *et seq.*

15–16   CHAPTER 15—PRACTICE, PROCEDURE AND PUBLIC FUNDING

proceedings relating to infants, to persons suffering from mental disorder and to secret processes. Where, exceptionally, a committal application is heard in private, there are certain minimum requirements as to what must be stated in public; the name of the person committed, and, in general terms, the nature of the contempt for which he is committed.[41]

15–17   It is to be remembered that the Court of Appeal had stated that the appropriate procedure was by way of motion (rather than summons).[42] Nevertheless it is unlikely to make much practical difference to the way in which applications for committal are dealt with.

15–18   Wall J. commented in *Re B (Contempt: Evidence)*[43] that in his experience most summonses for contempt issued in the Family Division turned on relatively straightforward issues of fact, and whether or not the applicant was able to discharge the burden of proof. He warned practitioners, however, that they should be alert to the procedural problems thrown up by that case.[44] He pointed out that the usual practice in Children Act cases, whereby the judge would read the evidence pre-trial or immediately after the case had been opened, did not fit proceedings for committal. He recommended that advisers to respondents in such circumstances should make their position clear in advance of trial. For example, if they file evidence in answer to the summons but do not wish to put it in before closure of the applicant's case, that fact should be made clear. The wise course, generally, would be for a respondent either to make a full and frank admission of his contempt or, if he denies contempt, to set out his case clearly and in detail.[45]

G. The contents of the notice or claim form

15–19   It is necessary to set out clearly in a notice of application or claim form the grounds of the alleged contempt.[46] The written evidence needs to be served at the same time. Moreover, the applicant is confined to the grounds set out and may not supplement them by reliance on additional matters disclosed in the evidence.[47] A respondent is entitled to know in advance of what it is that he is accused, and also the evidence relied on in support of the application to commit. In a case where service had not been effected in advance, and the respondent had no direct

---

[41] CPR Sch.1, Ord.52.6(2).
[42] *Re C (A Minor) (Contempt)* [1986] 1 F.L.R. 578. See also cases where third parties have been involved and matters proceeded by way of motion: *Re R (MJ)* [1975] Fam. 89; *Re F (Orse A)* [1977] Fam. 58. In any event, in other divisions the procedure by way of motion has gone by reason of changes in procedure in the CPR: see para.15–12 above.
[43] [1996] 1 F.L.R. 239 at 251H.
[44] See also para.15–40.
[45] [1996] 1 F.L.R. 239 at 252A–C.
[46] *Taylor v Roe* [1893] W.N. 14; *Re B (JA) (An Infant)* [1965] Ch. 1112, Cross J. See PD 2.5(2) and 2.6(2).
[47] CPR Sch.1, Ord.52.6(3). *Chanel Ltd v FGM Cosmetics* [1981] F.S.R. 471, Whitford J.; *Harmsworth v Harmsworth* [1987] 1 W.L.R. 1676 at 1683, [1987] 3 All E.R. 816, 821, Nicholls L.J. See also *R. v Poplar Borough Council (No.2) Ex p. London County Council* [1922] 1 K.B. 95. An amendment to the application notice or claim form may be made with permission but not otherwise: PD 2.5(3) and 2.6(3).

evidence of what was alleged, it was held by the Court of Appeal that the judge had erred in not granting an adjournment for service to be properly effected.[48]

H. The need to show prior service of the order on the respondent

Where the contempt relied upon is disobedience to an order of the court, as a general rule it is necessary to prove beyond reasonable doubt due service of that order upon the person sought to be committed, so that he should know what conduct would amount to a breach.[49] In the case of an order requiring a person to abstain from doing an act, such an order may be enforced under CPR Sch.1, Ord.45.5 notwithstanding that service has not been effected, provided the court is satisfied that, pending service, the person in question has had notice either by being present when the order was made or subsequently by some other means, such as by telephone and/or fax[50] or in such other manner as the court shall deem sufficient.

The position of third parties

Where the respondent is alleged to have intentionally sought to subvert an order of the court, not binding upon himself directly but upon someone else, it seems to be recognised that the sanction of contempt would be ineffective if it were necessary to prove that the order had actually been served upon the respondent. Sir John Donaldson M.R. in *Att–Gen v Newspaper Publishing plc*[51] dealt with concerns which had been expressed at first instance:

> "The Vice-Chancellor also expressed the view that if the Attorney-General's submissions were correct, third parties alleged to be in contempt would be deprived of what he described as 'very elaborate procedural safeguards' and he instanced personal service of the order, the indorsement of a penal notice on the order and the care which is taken to ensure that the conduct complained of constitutes a breach of the express terms of the order. In particular, he said that if the Attorney-General's contentions were right, the alleged contempt could consist of doing some act inconsistent, not with the terms of the order, but with the purpose of the order. This confuses the category of contempt which consists of disobeying or assisting in the disobedience of an order with the general category of contempt, namely, interfering with the due administration of justice. None of these procedural safeguards has ever been applied, or could apply, in the latter category."

---

[48] *Taylor v Persico, The Times*, February 12, 1992.
[49] See, *e.g.* Lord Denning M.R. in *Churchman v Joint Shop Stewards' Committee of the Workers of the Port of London* [1972] 1 W.L.R. 1094 at 1098.
[50] See now CPR Sch.1, Ord.45.7(6). Negative orders may often be made without notice or otherwise in circumstances of urgency, and it may be necessary to enforce compliance in cases where formal service has not been possible. See *Ronson Products Ltd v Ronson Furniture Ltd* [1966] R.P.C. 497; *Sofroniou v Szegetti* [1991] F.C.R. 332, CA; *R. v City of London Magistrates' Court Ex p. Green* [1997] 3 All E.R. 551 at 558c–d.
[51] [1988] Ch. 333 at 372.

15-22   CHAPTER 15—PRACTICE, PROCEDURE AND PUBLIC FUNDING

I. Dispensing with service of a mandatory order

15-22   There is, even in the case of an order requiring a given act to be done, a power to dispense with service.[52] This is in practice exercised only in the clearest cases; for example, where it can shown that the person has notice of the order and is evading service of it. The mere fact that he was present when the order was made is not sufficient to dispense with service.[53]

15-23   Nevertheless, it has been held by the Court of Appeal in *Davy International Ltd v Tazzyman*[54] that the former RSC Ord.45, r.7(7) was sufficiently wide to confer the power to dispense with service of a copy order, in respect of a mandatory injunction, retrospectively; that is to say, after the occurrence of the matters said to constitute the relevant breach or breaches. One of the reasons that persuaded the court to take this view was that it would otherwise be powerless to deal with a respondent who deliberately failed to comply with a mandatory order made in his presence.

J. The need for a penal notice

15-24   An order served must be endorsed on the front[55] with a penal notice as prescribed by the rules.[56] The discretion under CPR Sch.1, Ord.45.7(6) includes the power to waive the failure to incorporate the requisite penal notice, but only in the case of a prohibitory order.[57] Also, in *Moerman-Lenglet v Henshaw*,[58] Chadwick J.

---

[52] CPR Sch.1, Ord.45.7(7).
[53] *Re Tuck* [1906] 1 Ch. 692 at 696, Cozens-Hardy L.J.; see also *Century Insurance Co v Larkin* [1910] I.R. 91; *Haydon v Haydon* [1911] 2 K.B. 191, CA; *Wright v Jess* [1987] 1 W.L.R 813, CA.
[54] [1997] 1 W.L.R. 1256. See also *Turner v Turner* (1978) 122 Sol. Jo. 696; *Hill Samuel v Littaur, The Times*, April 13, 1985. The case of *Davy International Ltd v Tazzyman* [1997] 1 W.L.R. 1256 was referred to in *Jolly v Staines County Court Circuit Judge* [2000] 2 F.C.R. 59, where it was confirmed that the county court has a similar power to dispense with service. But see the comments of Judge Platt in [2000] Family Law 905 at 909 to the effect that, despite these decisions, it is "arguable that any such retrospective validation of the injunction order after arrest will contravene the respondent's rights under Art.7". *Tazzyman* was again referred to by the Court of Appeal in *Benson v Richards* [2002] EWCA Civ 1402. Carnwath L.J. described it as making clear that the discretion to dispense with service before the time fixed for compliance is "unfettered" even where it is exercised retrospectively. Nonetheless, in order to exercise the discretion, the court would need to be satisfied that the purposes of the requirements of service had been achieved, *i.e.* that the respondent knew the terms of the relevant order(s); was also aware of the consequences of disobedience; and was aware of the grounds relied upon as constituting a breach with sufficient particularity to be able to answer them.
[55] The requirement for having the endorsement on the front was introduced in 1992 by SI 1992/638. See also *Iberian Trust Ltd v Founders Trust and Investment Co. Ltd* [1932] 2 K.B. 87; *Hampden v Wallis* (1884) 26 Ch.D. 746.
[56] CPR Sch.1, Ord.45.7(4), Sch.2, cc.29. Under the Children Act 1989, a penal notice is required to be endorsed on s.8 orders: r.4.21A of the Family Proceedings Rules, 1991 as amended by the Family Proceedings (Amendment No.2) Rules 1992, SI 1992/2067; *Re N* [1992] 1 F.L.R. 134; *Re O, The Times*, March 17, 1995, CA. A similar memorandum has to be endorsed on orders in divorce proceedings requiring someone to do an act.
[57] *D v D (Access: Contempt: Committal)* [1991] 2 F.L.R. 34 at 40, Dillon L.J. See also *Re P (Minors) (Custody Order: Penal Notice)* [1990] 1 W.L.R. 613, CA; *Bell v Tuohy* [2002] 3 All E.R. 975. A penal notice is not appropriate in the case of either a residence order containing a direction not to remove a child from the jurisdiction or of a possession order.
[58] *The Times*, November 23, 1992.

held that the court had no discretion to dispense, in the case of a positive order, with the requirement that a penal notice had to be displayed prominently on the front of the copy of the order served. The copy served had been endorsed only in accordance with the previous unamended rule, and that was held to be insufficient to meet the requirements.

K. Recommended wording for penal notices[59]

In the case of a judgment or order requiring a person or body corporate to do an act within a specified time the words of the endorsement should correspond to the following:

15–25

"If you, the within named A.B. (or X.Y. Ltd) neglect to obey this judgment (*or* order) by the time stated, you may be held to be in contempt of Court and liable to imprisonment (*or* liable to sequestration of your assets)."

In the case of a judgment or order requiring a person or a body corporate to abstain from doing an act the endorsement should be to the following effect:

"If you, the within named A.B. (or X.Y. Ltd) disobey this judgment (*or* order), you may be held to be in contempt of Court, and liable to imprisonment (*or* to sequestration of your assets)."

Where a judgment or order requires a body corporate to do an act, but it is sought to take enforcement proceedings against a director or other officer of that body, the penal endorsement on the copy to be served on any such individuals should be in the following form:

"If X.Y. Ltd neglect to obey this judgment (*or* order) by the time stated you A.B. a director or officer of the said X.Y. Ltd may be held to be in contempt of Court and liable to imprisonment."

Where on the other hand it requires a body corporate to abstain from doing any act, the appropriate notice to an individual director or other officer will be as follows:

"If X.Y. Ltd disobey this judgment (*or* order) you A.B. a director or officer of the said X.Y. Ltd may be held to be in contempt of Court and liable to imprisonment."

In the case of a body corporate, the penal notice should be directed to the company even where it is sought to enforce it against individual directors. The order in question may be served upon the company as provided in section CPR Pt 6,[60] but it is generally necessary to serve personally any director or other officer against whom it is proposed to take proceedings for committal.[61] A penal

15–26

---

[59] See the prescribed wording in *Civil Procedure*, Vol. 1, sc.45.7.6.
[60] 6.2(2) or under ss.695, 694A or 725 of the Companies Act 1985.
[61] *Iberian Trust Ltd v Founders Trust and Investment Co Ltd* [1932] 2 K.B. 87; *Benabo v W Jay Ltd* [1941] Ch. 52. But see exceptions or qualifications in CPR Sch.1, Ord.45.7(6) and (7). In the case of a prohibitory order against the corporation, it may be enforced against an individual if he was present when the order was made or has been notified by telephone or otherwise. More generally, the court has a discretion to dispense with service on the individual, if it thinks it just to do so.

15–26   CHAPTER 15—PRACTICE, PROCEDURE AND PUBLIC FUNDING

notice relating to an order against a corporation may, if the judge so directs, identify the individual officer or director against whom it is intended to be enforced.[62]

L. Enforcement of undertakings

15–27 An undertaking to the court may be treated as though it were an injunction for the purpose of enforcement by process of contempt.[63] Where a party has formally given undertakings to the court it does not seem to be necessary to serve him with a copy of the order containing and recording the undertaking before enforcing.[64] Nevertheless, the Court of Appeal has clearly indicated that it is desirable to do so.[65] It is therefore suggested that there would need to be some explanation given if this requirement has not been fulfilled. There are special provisions for the enforcement of undertakings by solicitors given in their professional capacity.[66]

M. The power to sit in private

15–28 It is a general rule that applications for an order of committal shall be heard in open court, but there are limited circumstances in which the court may sit in private[67]:

(a) where the application arises out of proceedings relating to the wardship or adoption of an infant, or wholly or mainly to the guardianship, custody, maintenance or upbringing of an infant, or rights of access to an infant;

(b) where the application arises out of proceedings relating to a person suffering or appearing to be suffering from mental disorder within the meaning of the Mental Health Act 1983[68];

(c) where the application arises out of proceedings in which a secret process, discovery or invention was in issue;

(d) where it appears to the court that in the interests of the administration of justice or for reasons of national security the application should be heard in private.

---

[62] *R. v Wandsworth County Court Ex p. Munn* (1994) 26 H.L.R. 697, CA.
[63] See the general discussion in para.12–182; *Neath Canal Co v Ynisarwed Resolven Colliery Co* (1875) 10 Ch. App. 450; *Roberts v Roberts* [1990] 2 F.L.R. 111 at 113D–E, Butler-Sloss L.J.
[64] *Re Launder, Launder v Richards* (1908) 98 L.T. 554; *Callow v Young* (1886) 55 L.T. 543.
[65] *Hussain v Hussain* [1986] Fam. 134, 142, Neill L.J.
[66] paras 12–248 *et seq.*
[67] CPR Sch.1, Ord.52.6(1) and PD 9. It was suggested in *Re B (Contempt: Evidence)* [1996] 1 F.L.R. 239 by Wall J. that the wording of RSC. Ord.52, r.6 was unsatisfactory, in that the procedure did not in his view fit in with the express right given under r.6(4) for a person who is sought to be committed to give oral evidence, and suggested that the problem could usefully be drawn to the attention of the appropriate Rules Committee but no change of substance was made when the CPR were promulgated. See also the discussion in para.15–15 as to the requirements under r.7.2 of the Family Proceedings Rules 1991.
[68] "Mental disorder" is defined in s.1(2) of the Mental Health Act 1983, for which see para.14–97.

The power to sit in private was excoriated in *Att-Gen v Pelling*[69] as "a monstrous denial" of the defendant's right to defend himself in open court and as being "typically what is found in totalitarian states". The Court of Appeal was unimpressed by this argument because in some circumstances, such as those listed above, it would be a necessary and proportionate step to take for the protection of individuals concerned and ultimately of the administration of justice.

In the very unusual circumstances surrounding *Venables and Thompson v News Group Newspapers Ltd*[70] it was thought appropriate, when a breach of the injunctions was alleged, that the bulk of the hearing should take place in private because of the sensitivity of the evidence adduced. It was alleged that the publishers of the *Manchester Evening News* had revealed information likely to lead to the identification of the whereabouts of the two young men concerned whose lives were thought to be at risk.[71]

Matters to be stated in open court

Even where such a course is permitted, however, it is necessary to state certain matters in open court if it is decided in a private hearing to make an order of committal,[72] namely:

(a) the name of the person to be committed;

(b) in general terms the nature of the contempt in respect of which the committal order is being made;

(c) the penalty (if any) imposed.

Where an application for committal in connection with wardship proceedings was heard in private but, in breach of these requirements, there had been a failure to state the requisite facts in open court, the irregularity was held to be remediable by a subsequent statement.[73] This is subject to the discretion of the Court of Appeal to set aside the order in appropriate circumstances.[74]

N. Procedural safeguards at committal hearings

In civil proceedings[75] for contempt, "the court will introduce whatever safeguards may be necessary for the protection of alleged contemnors but will not

---

[69] [2005] EWHC 414.
[70] [2001] Fam. 430.
[71] *Att-Gen v Greater Manchester Newspapers Ltd* [2001] All E.R. (D) 32 (Dec) [2001] 145 S.J.L.B. 43.
[72] CPR Sch.1, Ord.52 r.6(2) and PD 9, Appendix 5A.
[73] *Re C* [1989] 1 F.L.R. 288, CA.
[74] See now CPR 3.10.
[75] For the procedural safeguards to be adopted in relation to contempt in the face of the court, particularly in the context of criminal trials, see *Archbold 2005*, para.28–117 and the discussion at para.10–38.

15–32   CHAPTER 15—PRACTICE, PROCEDURE AND PUBLIC FUNDING

import criminal procedures wholesale or indiscriminately."[76] On the hearing of any application for committal the person sought to be committed has the right to be heard.[77] In *Phonographic Performance Ltd v Inch*[78] Rimer J. expressed reluctance to make a committal order in the absence of the defendant, even though service was proved; instead a bench warrant was issued so that he would have the opportunity to defend himself. The claimant was given liberty to restore its application. No grounds may be relied on, except with permission of the court, other than those set out in the statement under CPR Sch.1, Ord 52.2 or the claim form or application notice under Ord.52.4.[79]

15–33   Nevertheless the court may at any stage, either of its own motion or upon the application of any party to the proceedings, order any document other than a judgment or order to be amended, unconditionally or upon terms.[80] This power is for the purpose either of determining the real question in controversy between the parties or of correcting any defect or error in the proceedings,[81] but clearly it would not be lightly exercised on an application for committal, particularly if any prejudice were likely to arise in relation to the person sought to be committed.

15–34   The court is not entitled to take into account any matter which has not been put to the respondent and which he has had no opportunity of answering. If it is disputed by the respondent, the judge must either accept the denial or, alternatively, give the applicant an opportunity of proving it, and the respondent an opportunity of probing the evidence adduced.[82]

15–35   A respondent to a committal application is not a compellable witness, although he is entitled to give evidence (including oral evidence) if he wishes to do so.[83] Nevertheless, the court by virtue of its power to regulate its own procedure is entitled to require respondents to swear affidavits or produce statements of witnesses as to facts upon which they may wish to rely, in advance of the hearing, so as to afford the applicant an opportunity of preparing evidence in reply.[84] It

---

[76] *Re B (Contempt: Evidence)* [1996] 1 F.L.R. 239 at 251E, Wall J. The judge agreed with the submission of counsel for the Official Solicitor that the analogy with criminal law can be taken too far. For a modern example of the analogy being applied, see the willingness on the part of the Court of Appeal to admit fresh evidence in *Irtelli v Squatriti* [1993] Q.B. 83. The procedure for committal applications is now governed by the Practice Direction supplementing CPR Sch.1, Ord.52, set out in Appendix 5A.

[77] CPR Sch.1, Ord.52.6(4). See the observations of Wall J. upon this provision in *Re B (Contempt: Evidence)* [1996] 1 F.L.R. 239.

[78] [2002] All E.R. (D) 253 (May).

[79] CPR Sch.1, Ord.52.6(3) and PD 2.5(2) and 2.6(2). See also *Chanel Ltd v FGM Cosmetics* [1981] F.S.R. 471, Whitford J.; *Harmsworth v Harmsworth* [1987] 1 W.L.R. 1676, 1683, 3 All E.R. 816 at 821, Nicholls L.J.

[80] PD 2.5(3) and 2.6(3).

[81] See generally CPR1.4. See also CPR Sch.1, Ord.52.6(3).

[82] *Smith v Smith* [1988] 1 F.L.R. 179 at 181G–H, Sir John Donaldson, M.R. Cp. the "Newton hearing" in criminal proceedings, described in *Archbold 2005*, paras 5–10 *et seq.* See *R. v Newton* (1982) 77 Cr.App.R. 13.

[83] CPR Sch.1, Ord.52. 6(4); see also *Comet Products UK Ltd v Hawkex Plastics Ltd* [1971] 2 Q.B. 67 at 74B, Lord Denning M.R., 75G, Megaw L.J.; *Re B (Contempt: Evidence)* [1996] 1 F.L.R. 239, Wall J.

[84] *Re B (Contempt: Evidence)* [1996] 1 F.L.R. 239.

remains for the applicant to prove the case beyond reasonable doubt, on the basis of the evidence filed in support. While he or she is able to supplement this by reliance upon admissions, under the ordinary rules of evidence, what may *not* be done is to make use of any evidence filed in advance by the respondent until such time as the respondent chooses to deploy it. So too, the fact that a respondent may have been ordered to swear, file and serve affidavit evidence does not expose him to the risk of cross-examination upon that material until he chooses to place reliance upon it.[85] It is provided in the current Practice Direction on committal[86] *inter alia* that CPR 35.9, concerning the court's power to direct a party to provide information, shall not apply to committal applications.[87]

An opportunity to meet the "charges"

It was argued in *Att-Gen v Pelling*[88] that there was a "common law right to cross-examine" upon the written evidence relied upon for committal applications, but it was held by the Court of Appeal that "the law has never acknowledged any automatic right in a defendant to cross-examine the Attorney's deponents". The court has a discretion to allow cross-examination, and would certainly do so if justice requires it; more particularly, if there is a relevant issue of fact disputed by the defendant or of which elucidation by cross-examination might assist the defendant's case.   **15–36**

A respondent should always have a full and fair opportunity of meeting the charges.[89] He should be given every reasonable chance to test the evidence against him. In *Aslam v Singh*[90] the judge had heard a committal summons in the county court in the absence of the respondent, not realising that he was physically unable to be present. In his absence he heard evidence, including from an expert. Next day the respondent went to court, gave evidence and was cross-examined by the applicant's counsel. The judge also asked a series of questions. At this point the respondent's counsel was not even aware that the expert evidence had already been given. The committal order, which had been made the previous day in his absence, was nonetheless confirmed. The Court of Appeal allowed an appeal because the parties had not been treated on an equal footing, since one side had been allowed to cross-examine, but not the other.   **15–37**

In *Duo v Osborne (formerly Duo)*,[91] an alleged contemnor was thought to be evading service of the committal application, but arrived at court later in the day   **15–38**

---

[85] *Clarke v Law* (1855) 2 K. & J. 28, 69 E.R. 680; *Re Quartz Hill & Co Ex p. Young* (1881) 21 Ch.D. 642; *Comet Products UK Ltd v Hawkex Plastics Ltd* [1971] 2 Q.B. 67 at 74, Lord Denning M.R., 75, Megaw L.J., 77, Cross L.J.; *Re W (Wards)(Publication of Information)* [1989] 1 F.L.R. 246, Sir Stephen Brown P.; *Re A Company, Goriee v Tahmas*, Vinelott J., June 21, 1984 (Lexis); *Re B (Contempt: Evidence)* [1996] 1 F.L.R. 239 at 251A–B, Wall J.
[86] Appendix 5A Pt I, para.6.
[87] The privilege against self-incrimination is considered more fully in paras 3–188 *et seq.*
[88] [2005] EWHC 414 (Admin).
[89] *M v P (Contempt of Court: Committal Order); Butler v Butler* [1993] Fam. 167 at 178–9, Lord Donaldson M.R.
[90] [1987] 1 F.L.R. 122.
[91] [1992] 1 W.L.R. 611, [1992] 2 F.L.R. 425. See also *R. v Luton Magistrates' Court Ex p. Sullivan* [1992] 2 F.L.R. 196, Waite J., FD.

15-38 CHAPTER 15—PRACTICE, PROCEDURE AND PUBLIC FUNDING

for an access hearing. His representative only had a quarter of an hour to take instructions on the committal matter, so that he felt unable to cross-examine. Nevertheless, the respondent was sentenced to six months' imprisonment. Despite his behaviour, the respondent was held by the Court of Appeal to be entitled to as much consideration as any other litigant. The appeal was allowed, but a retrial ordered under s.13(3) of the Administration of Justice Act 1960.

15-39 A judge was held to have misdirected himself in permitting "post-judgment" cross-examination of a defendant in circumstances where it was clear that the purpose was to establish either a breach by him of the conditions attached to a suspended sentence or further contempts.[92]

15-40 The ordinary safeguards adopted were bypassed in *Federal Bank of the Middle East v Hadkinson*.[93] The defects in procedure were identified as follows:

> "There was no motion to commit with supporting affidavit evidence. There was no evidence for Mr Hadkinson to answer. There was no evidence from Mr Hadkinson. So the judge did not have the benefit of any evidence from either side about the circumstances of the alleged breach of the freezing order. The judge was deprived of material which might well have been relevant to the exercise of the court's discretion on the treatment of the contempt. It was premature to mete out punishment for contempt on an informal application made at short notice and before all relevant facts had been put before the court."

Even though no application for an adjournment had been made by counsel, it would have been better to decline to deal with the matter of alleged continuing contempt in the informal manner put forward by the applicant; to grant an adjournment to enable the bank to issue and serve the proper application for committal supported by evidence, and to give the respondent the opportunity to serve evidence.

Legal representation: Art.6 of the Convention

15-41 It is provided by Art.6(3)(c) of the European Convention that every reasonable opportunity should be offered to an alleged contemnor to obtain legal representation of his own choosing or, if he has not sufficient means to pay for legal assistance, he should be given it free of charge when the interests of justice so require. This issue was considered by the Court of Appeal in *Berry Trade Ltd v Moussavi*.[94] The defendant was alleged to be in breach of world-wide search and seizure orders, and the claimants sought his committal for contempt. He had apparently been placed in difficulty over legal representation following his bankruptcy. He had been refused public funding at one level of the Legal

---

[92] *Phillips v Symes* [2003] EWCA Civ 1769.
[93] [2000] 1 W.L.R. 1695, [2000] 2 All E.R. 395, CA. The discretion has to be "exercised fairly and reasonably in a principled way having regard to all the relevant facts", *per* Mummery L.J. at 1711H, 411c.
[94] [2002] EWCA Civ 477, [2002] 1 W.L.R. 1910; see also *Re K (Contact: Committal Order)* [2002] EWCA Civ 1559, [2003] 1 F.L.R. 277; *Att–Gen v Pelling* [2004] EWHC 2568 (Admin); *Steel and Morris v United Kingdom* [2005] E.M.L.R. 314.

Services Commission but was awaiting consideration of his renewed application at a higher level. Therefore, no doubt feeling frustrated by the delays, the claimants offered to fund his representation by lawyers of his own choice but at the levels permitted by the Commission. The defendant did not think this acceptable and wished to have an adjournment to await the outcome of his pending application for public funding. The judge, however, refused any further adjournment in the light of the claimants' offer, but he granted permission to appeal. The Court of Appeal heard the appeal within a short space of time and took the view that the judge had misdirected himself, as it had been reasonable for the defendant to decline the claimants' offer—at least for the time being. A further short period of adjournment was granted to enable his pending application to be resolved. The matter would have to be considered afresh if assistance was refused (albeit this seemed unlikely for someone at risk of being committed).

Reference was made to *Croissant v Germany*,[95] where the European Court of Human Rights had held that the national court should pay heed to the accused's own views on the matter. In the light of that, Arden L.J. concluded that to deprive someone of his right to apply for public funding, against his wishes, would run counter to the notion of a fair trial under Art.6(1) if there was no sufficient and relevant justification. Clearly, however, the rights conferred by Art.6(3)(c) were not absolute. It might well be, therefore, that if the pending application were refused for some reason it would no longer be reasonable for the claimants to be kept from achieving a court hearing. At that stage, at least the defendant's rights in the matter would have been sufficiently respected and it might be that greater weight should then be accorded to the interests of other persons involved.

O. Must the respondent be put to his election?

It was not clear whether a respondent is entitled in committal proceedings to put forward a submission of no case to answer without being put to his election; that is to say, declaring whether he wishes to call evidence. Some authorities appeared to suggest that there was such an entitlement.[96] On the other hand, the view was expressed by Knox J. in *Barclays de Zoete Wedd Securities Ltd v Nadir*[97] that there is no absolute right to withhold evidence until after making a submission of no case. He was of the opinion that it was a matter within the discretion of the trial judge.

This uncertainty was a matter that Wall J. in *Re B (Contempt: Evidence)*[98] suggested might be referred to the Rules Committee. His own tentative view was

---

[95] (1992) 16 E.H.R.R. 135.
[96] *Re W (Wards) (Publication of Information)* [1989] 1 F.L.R. 246 at 254, Sir Stephen Brown P; *Savings & Investment Bank Ltd v Gasco Investments (Netherlands) BV* (1986) 136 New L.Jo. 657, Scott J. (who was subsequently reversed on the point as to whether committal proceedings could be classified as interlocutory for the purpose of determining the validity of hearsay, but no adverse comment was made in the Court of Appeal on the matter of submissions of no case to answer: see [1988] 1 Ch. 422); *Bhimji v Chatwani* [1991] 1 W.L.R. 989, where Scott J. (although not reported on this point) repeated his view as to the respondent's entitlement not to be put to his election.
[97] *The Times*, March 25, 1995; see also *Storey v Storey* [1961] P. 63, Ormerod L.J.
[98] [1996] 1 F.L.R. 239 at 252F.

that, where the respondent's case on the submission was to the effect that the applicant's factual case was unsatisfactory (as opposed to being prepared to make the assumption that it was wholly correct), little injustice would be done by requiring the evidence to be assessed in a one-stage process rather than two. He was thus inclined to the view that, in committal cases of that kind, it would not be unreasonable to apply the practice which operates in most civil proceedings.[99]

P. Form of committal order

15–45   A form of committal order is included in the precedents section of this work.[1] In a case where service of the initiating process (whether claim form or notice of application) has been dispensed with, that fact should be recorded in the committal order, since it is necessary to draw to the attention of the contemnor how it comes about that he has been committed without prior warning or the opportunity to be heard.[2] There is included within the general power under s.13(3) of the Administration of Justice Act 1960 authority for the Court of Appeal to perfect an invalid committal order, but this should be exercised only in exceptional cases. It will always be an important consideration in exercising such discretion whether any prejudice has been occasioned to the contemnor.[3]

15–46   In *Abdi v Jama (Contempt: Committal)*[4] there had been a number of successive breaches of a non-molestation order, and correspondingly successive committal hearings. On one of the orders it was not made clear that the judge's intention had been that the periods of imprisonment ordered should be served consecutively. A different judge at a later hearing sought to amend the order to reflect that intention (as to which he had heard evidence from a police officer). The Court of Appeal held, following *M v P (Contempt of Court: Committal Order); Butler v Butler*,[5] that the interests of the victim, and the need to maintain the authority of the court, were factors which would entitle the court to amend its order where a procedural irregularity had occurred. The court was satisfied that the contemnor had suffered no injustice on the facts of the case. Moreover, there was no need to consider the provisions of s.13(3) of the 1960 Act in the circumstances, since all that was required was to vary an existing valid order to take account of procedural defects.[6]

15–47   The order must recite with particularity what has been proved against the contemnor, and should also identify any breach of an order or undertaking which

---

[99] *Alexander v Rayson* [1936] 1 K.B. 169, CA; *Laurie v Raglan Building Co Ltd* [1942] 1 K.B. 152. And see *Re Kennedy (No.1)* [2004] 3 H.K.C. 404.
[1] See Appendix 2.
[2] *Wright v Jess* [1987] 1 W.L.R. 1076. But see at 1082A–B where it was held that the criticism would not, on the facts, justify setting aside the committal order.
[3] See, e.g. *M v P (Contempt of Court: Committal Order); Butler v Butler* [1993] Fam. 167, CA; *Linnett v Coles* [1987] Q.B. 555, CA; *Clarke v Clarke* [1990] 2 F.L.R. 115, CA.
[4] [1996] 1 F.L.R. 407.
[5] [1993] Fam. 167, CA.
[6] [1996] 1 F.L.R. 407 at 412, Wall J. See also *M v P (Contempt of Court: Committal Order); Butler v Butler* [1993] Fam. 167 at 178–9, Lord Donaldson M.R.

has been found to constitute a contempt.[7] If the court has found some allegations of contempt proved but rejected others, the order should exclude any reference to those unproved. Otherwise the committal order will be invalid.[8] It is only in exceptional circumstances that the court will permit defects in a committal order to be rectified.[9] This was, however, permitted in *Olk v Olk*.[10] The application for committal was based on a general allegation that the estranged husband had been attending the wife's home in breach of injunctions on an almost daily basis. The judge committed him for 12 months on what he apparently described as Count 1; that is to say the general allegation. But he also "sentenced" him to a further period of twelve months, to run concurrently, in respect of incidents that were really no more than two examples of conduct corresponding to the general complaint (*i.e.* Count 1). These were described by the judge as Counts 2 and 3. Moreover, the two specific "counts" had not been specifically identified in the wife's application for committal. On appeal, it was held that the two specific "counts" should be deleted from the committal order but that the twelve month period should stand in any event.

Q. The effect of a committal order

The order is executed by the tipstaff, one of his assistants or by another court official to whom the order is addressed. Now the only authority required is that a warrant is issued signed by the judge, or one of the judges, of the court making the order.[11] The tipstaff or other official will immediately take the contemnor to prison, if he is at court. Otherwise he will go to his address with the order and arrest him there. It may be necessary after giving proper notice to break open the door of his house to obtain access.[12] On the other hand, if the contemnor is not to be found at his address, the tipstaff will probably communicate with the police in the area where he is believed to be, so that they may hold him in custody until the tipstaff arrives to escort him to the prison specified in the warrant.[13]

Officers of the Crown Court have an express statutory duty of giving effect to any order or directions given in that court for taking into custody and detaining any person committing contempt of court, and of executing any order or warrant

---

[7] *Parra v Rones* [1986] Fam. Law 262, CA; *McIlraith v Grady* [1968] 1 Q.B. 468, CA; *Chiltern District Council v Keane* [1985] 1 W.L.R. 619; *Williams v Fawcett* [1986] Q.B. 604; *Bowen v Bowen* (1986) CA Transcript No.6775; *CBS (UK) Ltd v Manoli* (1985) New L.J. 555, CA; *Nguyen v Phung* [1984] F.L.R. 773.
[8] *Miller v Juby* [1991] F.C.R. 52, CA; *Cullen v Rose* [1985] CA Transcript No.804.
[9] *B v B (Contempt: Committal)* [1991] 2 F.L.R. 588, CA; *Loseby v Newman* [1995] 2 F.L.R. 754 at 757A–C, CA.
[10] [2001] EWCA Civ 1075.
[11] At one time it was the practice to issue to the tipstaff an order of the Lord Chancellor, but this ceased in 1961; Practice Note, January 30, 1961. See (1961) 111 L. Jo 109 (Practice Note) which is still in effect. For the form of warrant see Appendix 2.
[12] *Semayne's Case* (1604) Cro. Eliz. 909, 78 E.R. 1131; *Briggs' Case* (1615) 1 Roll. Rep. 336, 81 E.R. 526. It has long been recognised that execution by process of contempt is an exception to the principle, expounded in these cases, that "an Englishman's home is his castle": *Burdett v Abbott* (1811) 14 East 1, 104 E.R. 501; *Harvey v Harvey* (1884) 26 Ch.D. 644 and *Southam v Smout* [1964] 1 Q.B. 308. See also *Khazanchi v Faircharm Investments Ltd: McLeod v Butterwick* [1998] 1 W.L.R. 1603, [1998] 2 All E.R. 901, CA.
[13] See the notes at *Civil Procedure 2005* Vol. 1, sc.52.7.2 *et seq.*

duly issued for committal.[14] In London the prison named will be either Pentonville or Holloway, according to gender.

15–50 Once a person has been committed for contempt, the consequences flowing from it are a matter for the Home Office and the prison authorities. It would be irregular for a judge, upon discovering that the contemnor would in fact serve a shorter sentence than he had believed, then to purport to extend the term to comply with his original intention.[15]

II. COMMITTAL IN THE COUNTY COURT

A. The changes in the rules

15–51 There has been an increasing assimilation between the practice governing committal procedure in the county court and that in the High Court and both are now to be found in the Practice Direction supplementing CPR Sch.1, Ord.52 and Sch.2, cc.29.[16] Meanwhile, the rules continue to apply separately as set out in the two schedules.

15–52 Provision is made in CPR Sch.2, cc. 29.1 for the enforcement of a judgment to do or abstain from doing any act:

"(1) Where a person required by a judgment or order to do an act refuses or neglects to do it within the time fixed by the judgment or order or any subsequent order, or where a person disobeys a judgment or order requiring him to abstain from doing an act, then, subject to the Debtors Acts 1869[17] and 1878 and to the provisions of these rules, the judgment or order may be enforced, by order of the judge, by a committal order against that person or, if that person is a body corporate, against any director or other officer of the body.

(2) Subject to paragraphs (6) and (7), a judgment or order shall not be enforced under paragraph (1) unless—

(a) a copy of the judgment or order has been served personally on the person required to do or abstain from doing the act in question and also, where that person is a body corporate, on the director or other officer of the body against whom a committal order is sought; and

(b) in the case of a judgment or order requiring a person to do an act, the copy has been so served before the expiration of the time within which he was required to do the act and was accompanied by a copy of any order, made between the date of the judgment or order and the date of service, fixing that time.

(3) Where a judgment or order enforceable by committal order under paragraph (1) has been given or made, the court officer shall, if the judgment or order is in the nature

---

[14] Supreme Court Act 1981, s.82(2).
[15] *Westcott v Westcott* [1985] F.L.R. 616, CA. See paras 14–32 *et seq.* concerning automatic release.
[16] Set out in Appendix 5A.
[17] It was held in *Mubarak v Mubarak* [2001] 1 F.L.R. 698 that the procedure under s.5 of the Debtors Act 1869 was not compatible with the European Convention, and the statute was subsequently amended by the Civil Procedure (Modification of Enactments) Order 2002, SI 2002/439.

of an injunction,[18] at the time when the judgment or order is drawn up, and in any other case on the request of the judgment creditor, issue a copy of the judgment or order, indorsed with or incorporating a notice as to the consequences of disobedience, for service in accordance with paragraph (2).[19]

(4) If the person served with the judgment or order fails to obey it, the judgment creditor may issue a claim form or, as the case may be, an application notice seeking the committal for contempt of court of that person and subject to paragraph (7), the claim form or application notice shall be served on him personally.

(4A) The claim form or application notice (as the case may be) shall—

(a) identify the provisions of the injunction or undertaking which it is alleged have been disobeyed or broken;
(b) list the ways in which it is alleged that the injunction has been disobeyed or the undertaking has been broken;
(c) be supported by an affidavit stating the grounds on which the application is made,

and unless service is dispensed with under paragraph (7), a copy of the affidavit shall be served with the claim form or application notice.

(5) If a committal order is made, the order shall be for the issue of a warrant of committal and, unless the judge otherwise orders—

(a) a copy of the order shall be served on the person to be committed either before or at the time of the execution of the warrant; or
(b) where the warrant has been signed by the judge, the order for issue of the warrant may be served on the person to be committed at any time within 36 hours after the execution of the warrant.

(5A) A warrant of committal shall not, without further order of the court, be enforced more than 2 years after the date on which the warrant is issued.

(6) A judgment or order requiring a person to abstain from doing an act may be enforced under paragraph (1) notwithstanding that service of a copy of the judgment or order has not been effected in accordance with paragraph (2) if the judge is satisfied that, pending such service, the person against whom it is sought to enforce the judgment or order has had notice thereof either—

(a) by being present when the judgment or order was given or made; or
(b) by being notified of the terms of the judgment or order whether by telephone, telegram or otherwise.

(7) Without prejudice to its powers under Part 6 of the CPR, the court may dispense with service of a copy of a judgment or order[20] under paragraph (2) or a claim form or application notice under paragraph (4) if the court thinks it just to do so.

---

[18] In *Re P (Minors) (Custody Order: Penal Notice)* [1990] 1 W.L.R. 613, CA, it was held that a consent order for what was then called "custody", which included a direction not to remove children from the jurisdiction, was not an order "in the nature of an injunction" within the meaning of this rule. See para.14–118 and para.15–24. In *Bell v Tuohy* [2002] EWCA Civ 423, [2002] 1 W.L.R. 2703, [2002] 3 All E.R. 975, it was held that an order for possession was not "in the nature of an injunction" either. Indeed, in the absence of good and exceptional grounds, it was generally undesirable that such an order should have a penal notice endorsed upon it. If, however, there was obstruction when the bailiff came to execute a warrant for possession, and if resort became necessary to the court's jurisdiction in contempt, then it would be appropriate prior to any application to commit to serve a copy of the possession order indorsed with such a notice.

[19] This is the penal notice: see form N77 in Appendix 2.

[20] *Lewis v Lewis* [1991] 1 W.L.R. 235, 2 F.L.R. 43, CA.

15-52 CHAPTER 15—PRACTICE, PROCEDURE AND PUBLIC FUNDING

(8) Where service of the claim form or application notice has been dispensed with under paragraph (7) and a committal order is made in the absence of the respondent, the judge may on his own initiative fix a date and time when the person to be committed is to be brought before him or before the court".

15-53 Changes were made in subrule (5) with effect from May 1, 1991 which were intended to enable a contemnor committed for an immediate custodial sentence to be detained straight away, even though preparation of the committal order in Form N79[21] might take some time for the purpose of ensuring accurate completion. It is the duty of the court to achieve service upon the contemnor of the order in proper form when an immediate custodial sentence has been passed.

15-54 Practical problems have arisen recently about how a contemnor should be taken into custody by way of executing an order for committal made in the county court.[22] It is provided by s.119(2) of the County Courts Act 1984 that it is the duty of every constable within the court's jurisdiction to assist in the execution of such orders, but some chief officers of police have taken the view (inconsistent with the wording of the statute) that, since the conveying of prisoners is now largely in the hands of private contractors under contractual arrangements over which they have no control, it is no longer for their officers to become involved. There is thus something of a lacuna, since the statute does not address the role of such organisations. Judges are left in the unsatisfactory position, in some areas, of making orders for committal following breaches of court orders which no one is prepared to execute. It is submitted that the statutory duty on police officers is there to be observed, however inconvenient, and whatever budgetary constraints there may be, until Parliament decides to make some different provision.

15-55 The provisions of s.119(2) were considered by Nelson J. in *Jolly v Governor of Wandsworth Prison*.[23] The claimant had been committed for contempt in 1993 (for 14 days) and was conveyed to prison by police officers, in accordance with the usual practice at the time. After his release, he sued the governor alleging false imprisonment and negligence. It was contended *inter alia* that the process of arrest and delivery to detention was unlawful, on the basis that only the district judge and bailiffs had the power to arrest and deliver a "civil prisoner". Moreover, the warrant was said to be invalid due to certain omissions and should not have been accepted as the basis for detention. In any event, it was being argued that the governor had acted not on the basis of the warrant but on the police detention log only. The court and prison staff gave evidence as to the procedure, and the court concluded that no prisoner would be accepted into

---

[21] See N329 "notes for completion of N79"—see Appendix 2.
[22] See also *McGrath v Chief Constable of the Royal Ulster Constabulary* [2001] UKHL 39, [2001] 2 A.C. 731 and *Hoye v Bush* (1840) 1 Man & G 775, 133 E.R. 545.
[23] [2001] All E.R. (D) 408. For further discussion of the practical difficulties about conveying civil contemnors, in the light of the contractual arrangements entered into with private security firms, see also *Horgan v Horgan* [2002] EWCA Civ 1371. Problems arose because the contract required Premier Security to deliver to the Crown Court only and not to the county court (five minutes away).

custody save on the basis of a warrant. The judge confirmed also that it was legitimate for the claimant to have been conveyed by police officers and, indeed, that it was their duty under the statute to assist. The underlying order had been lawful; and the warrant sufficiently identified the claimant, the term of imprisonment and the reason for the committal. The warrant was also valid on its face.

The Debtors Act and committal: the family law context

It is important to recognise the "dead hand" effect of the Debtors Acts, expressly referred to in cc.29.1(1), with regard especially to the remedies Parliament intended to provide in the Family Law Act 1996. This was highlighted in *Nwogbe v Nwogbe*.[24] A husband had been ordered to pay the monthly rent to a housing association in respect of a property which had been the matrimonial home, and in which the wife was continuing to reside with the children. The order was based on the jurisdiction contained within s.40(1)(a)(ii) of the 1996 Act, which enables the court to impose such an obligation on either party after making an occupation order. He failed to comply and the wife applied for him to be committed for contempt. The judge refused, however, and his decision was upheld on appeal. Any order made under the s.40 jurisdiction was unenforceable by reason of s.4 of the Debtors Act 1869. This had simply abolished imprisonment for debt, and the 1996 Act contained nothing that was effective to reverse or qualify that principle. There was nothing to rebut the presumption against implied repeal.[25] The Court of Appeal described this as a "glaring omission" and "a statutory lacuna of real significance". The legislature was therefore urged to consider making specific provision. Meanwhile, the court was left in a "very unsatisfactory and unattractive situation". It is true that there is conferred by the 1869 Act a limited jurisdiction to imprison for a maximum period of six weeks but, in the light of the curtailments contained in s.11 of the Administration of Justice Act 1970, there could be no question of that jurisdiction extending to breaches of orders made under s.40 of the Family Law Act. Another problem was highlighted in *Mubarak v Mubarak*,[26] where it was held that the judgment summons procedure was not Convention compliant. The rules relating to judgment summonses were changed to remedy the situation.[27]

B. Applications to commit without notice: exceptional circumstances required

The court's power to dispense with service under the former CCR Ord.29.1(7) was held in one case to apply at the stage when the order is made, and not to be exercisable retrospectively after a breach of it has actually occurred.[28] A more recent decision of the Court of Appeal, however, suggests that this is no longer

---

[24] [2000] 2 F.L.R. 744, 2 F.C.R. 345 (Dame Elizabeth Butler-Sloss P., and Thorpe and Walker L.JJ.).
[25] See, *e.g.* F.A.R. Bennion, *Statutory Interpretation* (4th ed., 2002), p.255.
[26] [2001] 1 F.L.R. 698, CA.
[27] CPR Sched.2, cc.28, with effect from March 25, 2002 by the Civil Procedure (Amendment No.5) Rules 2001. See *Civil Procedure 2005*, 28.0.2.
[28] *Lewis v Lewis* [1991] 1 W.L.R. 235, 2 F.L.R. 43, CA.

15–57 CHAPTER 15—PRACTICE, PROCEDURE AND PUBLIC FUNDING

good law.[29] Moreover, it was emphasised by the Court of Appeal in *Benson v Richards*[30] that there should be no encouragement for a persistent offender to use technicalities to defeat the purpose of orders.

15–58 The discretion contemplated under subrule (6), in relation to prohibitive orders, can be exercised at the time when the committal application is heard. A decision to dispense with service of a notice under CPR Sch.2, cc.29.1(4) should be recorded in any committal order subsequently made.[31]

15–59 The importance of these safeguards was considered in *Wright v Jess*.[32] A husband appeared to have been in breach of a non-molestation order, and a notice was issued pursuant to r.1(4), but the enquiry agent was unable to effect personal service over a two day period. In the small hours of the third day a further breach occurred, as a result of which an *ex parte* application was made to commit him on the same day. The order was made in his absence. The following procedural arguments were raised on appeal on the husband's behalf (although he had not made any application to the judge to review the order of committal):

(1) There were no exceptional grounds, such as to justify an *ex parte* order for committal;

(2) No fresh notice to show cause under r.1(4) had ever been issued in respect of the breach occurring some two days after the issue of the original notice;

(3) The judge did not dispense with service of that original notice or, if he did, the fact was not recorded in the committal order;

(4) The husband should have been brought before the judge as soon as he was arrested.

15–60 The Court of Appeal held that the county court did in exceptional cases have jurisdiction to commit upon what was then referred to as an *ex parte* motion, but only on the basis of Ord.29. The appropriate procedure in such cases was, therefore, to issue a r.1(4) notice and to dispense with service. On the particular facts, the judge was entitled to take that exceptional course. Circumstances to be taken into account would include the gravity of the breach and any apprehension as to the respondent's achieving his impermissible objective if not checked as a matter of urgency. Anyone committed in such circumstances can always, at any time and on the shortest possible notice, apply to the court for the order to be discharged.[33]

---

[29] *Davy International Ltd v Tazzyman* [1997] 1 W.L.R. 1256, [1997] 3 All E.R. 183, where *Lewis v Lewis* was not followed, para.15–23. See also *Jolly v Staines County Court Circuit Judge* [2000] 2 F.C.R. 59.
[30] [2002] EWCA Civ 1402. See the notes at *Civil Procedure 2005*, Vol. 1 at 29.1.5.
[31] *Nguyen v Phung* [1984] F.L.R 773; *Williams v Fawcett* [1986] Q.B. 604; *Wright v Jess* [1987] 1 W.L.R. 1076 at 1082.
[32] [1987] 1 W.L.R. 107.
[33] See *Warwick Corp v Russell* [1964] 1 W.L.R. 613 at 615, Buckley J.

There was no substance to the objection that the latest breaches had not been 15–61
specified in any such notice. It was not right that the court was obliged to ignore
any breach, however grave, occurring after the issue of such a notice. Moreover,
it would be an idle administrative formality to have to issue a supplemental
notice in circumstances justifying an *ex parte* committal.[34] It is to be emphasised,
however, that those circumstances were regarded as exceptional. Normally, a
committal should only be based on matters of which the respondent has been
given notice.[35] Where a judge is contemplating taking the initiative on the
institution of civil contempt proceedings, it is important to have in mind the
guidance given by Ward L.J. in *Re M (A Minor) (Contempt of Court: Committal
of Court's own Motion)*.[36]

The Court of Appeal in *Wright v Jess*, while acknowledging that it was a valid 15–62
criticism that an order dispensing with service should be recorded in the
committal order,[37] held that this defect would not justify setting the committal
order aside.[38]

It is recognised that, if an *ex parte* order is made, the court should have an 15–63
opportunity of reviewing it so as to ensure that an injustice is not committed
against the contemnor,[39] but such an occasion should not be regarded as an
opportunity to revise the sentence *upwards*.[40] No one should be sentenced twice
over for the same breach.[41]

C. The need for strict compliance with the rules

As in the High Court, there was traditionally a need for strict compliance in 15–64
committal cases with procedural rules and safeguards.[42] This was re-emphasised
by the Court of Appeal in *Nguyen v Phung*,[43] where it was pointed out that the
county courts were regularly failing to comply with procedural arrangements.
There was said to be:

---

[34] *per* Sir John Donaldson M.R., in *Wright v Jess*, at 1081F–H.
[35] *Tabone v Seguna* [1986] 1 F.L.R. 591, CA; *Dorrell v Dorrell* [1985] F.L.R. 1089, CA; *Woolley v Woolley*, The Times, July 17, 1974. See also para.15–19 and the Practice Direction (Appendix 5A) paras 2.5(2) and 2.6(2) for similar requirements in the High Court.
[36] [1999] Fam. 263 (set out at para.12–32 above).
[37] *Wright v Jess* [1987] 1 W.L.R. 1076 at 1082 A–B.
[38] See also s.13(3) of the Administration of Justice Act 1960, which enables the court to correct any such formal irregularity and *Linnett v Coles* [1987] Q.B. 555, CA and the *Practice Direction* Appendix 5A, para.10.
[39] *Becker v Knowle* [1971] 1 W.L.R. 803; *B v B (Contempt: Committal)* [1991] 2 F.L.R. 588 at 601F–G, Purchas L.J.
[40] *B v B (Contempt: Committal)* [1991] 2 F.L.R. 588.
[41] *Danchevsky v Danchevsky (No.2)*, CA Transcript, November 10, 1977, Lawton L.J.; *Lamb v Lamb* [1984] F.L.R. 278 at 282, Oliver L.J., 283, Kerr L.J.; *B v B (Contempt: Committal* last note, at 601C–D, Purchas L.J. And see *Hale v Tanner (Practice Note)* [2000] 1 W.L.R. 2377.)
[42] Now to some extent mitigated by the Practice Direction, para.10, (Appendix 5A) which provides for the waiver of procedural defects on a committal application.
[43] [1984] F.L.R. 773 at 774, CA, Cumming-Bruce L.J.; *B v B (Contempt: Committal)* [1991] 2 F.L.R. 588; *Smith v Smith* [1992] 2 F.L.R. 40, CA. For similar remarks relating to an order made in wardship proceedings by a deputy High Court Judge, see *Re C (A Minor)* [1996] 1 F.L.R. 578. See also *Manchester City Council v Worthington* [2000] 1 F.L.R. 411.

15–64

"... an astonishing laxity or ignorance in the county courts officers' appreciation of their statutory duty as is quite clearly set out in the rules and statutory forms, with the result that, with a frequency that is as astonishing as it is outrageous, time and again orders for committal for breaches of orders made by the court and otherwise have had to be set aside and sentences quashed, with the consequence that complainants are being deprived of the proper protection of the law."

15–65 It is clear[44] that for a valid order of committal to be issued the following steps are required:

(1) service on the respondent of the judgment or order, unless service has been dispensed with;

(2) service on the respondent of the notice to show good reason, unless service has been dispensed with.

15–66 These requirements are confirmed in the standard County Court Forms N78 and N79.[45] The requirement that notices served under CPR Sch.2, cc.29.1 should be signed by a proper officer of the court are designed for the protection of the person served, and compliance should be insisted upon.[46] Such a notice which has only been signed by the claimant's solicitors would be defective. In *Couzens v Couzens*[47] a judge had purported to activate a suspended sentence of committal in circumstances where the original order had not been personally served on the contemnor in the prescribed form N79. The appeal was accordingly allowed.

D. Contents of committal order

15–67 Not only the notice under CPR Sch.2, cc.29.1(4) but also the order of committal itself must notify the respondent of the specific matters which are said to have constituted breach of the order made against him.[48]

15–68 It is required[49] that the affidavits actually considered by the judge at the committal hearing (excluding those relating to service only) should be identified in the order by providing the dates and the names of deponents. If there was oral evidence, the witnesses sworn and examined should be identified. Exact details

---

[44] CPR Sch.2, cc.29.1. set out at para.15–52.
[45] N78 ("Notice to Show Good Reason why an Order for Your Committal to Prison should not be made") and N79 ("Committal or Other Order upon Proof of Disobedience of a Court Order or Breach of an Undertaking"). These are to be found in Appendix 2.
[46] *Lee v Walker* [1985] Q.B. 1191 at 1203A–C, CA.
[47] [2001] 2 F.L.R. 701.
[48] *Nguyen v Phung* [1984] F.L.R. 773 at 778. See also *McIlraith v Grady* [1968] 1 Q.B. 468; *Chiltern District Council v Keane* [1985] 1 W.L.R. 619 at 622–3; *CBS UK v Manoli* (1985) 135 New Law Jo. 555, CA; *Re C (A Minor)* [1986] 1 F.L.R. 578; *Parra v Rones* [1986] Fam. Law 262, CA. (The defect cannot be cured by including the requisite particulars in the warrant, since that is not addressed to the respondent.) *Hegarty v O'Sullivan* (1985) 135 New Law Jo. 557 at 558, Kerr L.J., CA; *Linnett v Coles* [1987] Q.B. 555; *Linkleter v Linkleter* [1988] 1 F.L.R. 360 at 363, Mustill L.J., CA; *Clarke v Clarke* [1990] 2 F.L.R. 115, CA; *B v B (Contempt: Committal)* [1991] 2 F.L.R. 588, CA; *Loseby v Newman* [1995] 2 F.L.R. 754 at 756E–F, Balcombe L.J., CA; *Nicholls v Nicholls* [1997] 1 W.L.R. 314, which was applied in *Olk v Olk* [2001] EWCA Civ 1075.
[49] See prescribed form N79, in Appendix 2.

should be set out of, and only of, those allegations which the judge found proved.[50]

The committal order should also recite the fact that the notice to show cause has been served on the respondent. It is only where discrepancies from the prescribed form of order are quite trivial that they will not invalidate the order of committal. The test appears to be whether they could have an impact upon the respondent's understanding.[51] 15–69

E. Can a defective order be corrected on appeal?

A defect in a committal order can only be corrected in limited circumstances,[52] and certainly not by reliance upon the slip rule.[53] The court cannot simply complete the form for the applicant where it has not been properly filled in.[54] 15–70

In *Smith v Smith*,[55] a son was given three months' imprisonment for breaches of a non-molestation order protecting his mother, but the part of the N79 Form for listing details of the contempts found proved was simply left blank. The court was forced into a position where it had no alternative but to allow the appeal. 15–71

Scott L.J. clearly wished that it had been possible to correct the defects under s.13(3) of the Administration of Justice Act 1960, or the former RSC Ord.59, r.10(3). He drew attention to what Lawton L.J. had said in *Linnett v Coles*[56]: 15–72

" . . . if there has been no unfairness or no material irregularity in the proceedings and nothing more than an irregularity in drawing up the committal order has occurred, I can see no reason why the irregularity should not be put right and the sentence varied, if necessary, so as to make it a just one. On the wording of [s.13(3)] a just sentence could be a longer one."

Nevertheless, Scott L.J. felt constrained by the earlier authorities which he was unable to distinguish, observing that " . . . over-fine distinctions of apparently binding authorities do not reflect much credit on the law, or in general produce a satisfactory body of jurisprudence, and particularly that may be so in case such as the present where liberty of the subject is at stake." 15–73

---

[50] See para.15–47 above.
[51] *Nguyen v Phung* [1984] F.L.R. 773 at 779, Cumming-Bruce L.J.
[52] Under s.13(3) of the Administration of Justice Act 1960, and/or under CPR Pt 52.10; *Re C (A Minor) (Contempt)* [1986] 1 F.L.R. 578; *Smith v Smith* [1992] 2 F.L.R. 40 at 45, Scott L.J.; *M v P (Contempt of Court: Committal Order); Butler v Butler* [1993] Fam. 167; *Loseby v Newman* [1995] 2 F.L.R. 754; see also *Hill Samuel and Co v Littaur* (1985) 135 New Law Jo. 556.
[53] *Cinderby v Cinderby*, CA, Transcript No.272, April 26, 1978.
[54] *Linkleter v Linkleter* [1988] 1 F.L.R. 360 at 363, Mustill L.J.
[55] [1992] 2 F.L.R. 40, CA. See also *Manchester City Council v Worthington* [2000] 1 F.L.R. 411 where the Court of Appeal emphasised the importance of setting out written allegations of the breaches alleged even in cases of apparent urgency, such as where a power of arrest has led to a person being brought before the court without warning for breaches of an injunction granted under s.152(3) of the Housing Act 1996.
[56] [1987] Q.B. 555 at 562.

15–74 If, however, in a particular case a defect may truly be regarded as insignificant, the court may disregard it.[57] In *Burrows v Iqbal*[58] the only suggested irregularity was a failure to state the date on which the only relevant contempt was found to have been committed. The circumstances were such that the contempt could only have been committed on a particular day which was easily identifiable. Nevertheless, courts appear to be less willing to contemplate such corrections if the contemnor has actually gone to prison following the order. A defendant has a right to be properly informed as to why he has been sent to prison.[59]

The guidelines in Nicholls v Nicholls

15–75 The Court of Appeal in *Nicholls v Nicholls*[60] gave general guidance for future cases in the light of what Lord Woolf M.R. had described as "a change of emphasis in the approach of this court in recent years".[61] The guidance was summarised in the following terms:

"(1) As committal orders involve the liberty of the subject it is particularly important that the relevant rules are duly complied with. It remains the responsibility of the judge when signing the committal order to ensure that it is properly drawn and that it adequately particularises the breaches which have been proved and for which the sentence has been imposed.

(2) As long as the contemnor had a fair trial and the order has been made on valid grounds the existence of a defect either in the application to commit or in the committal order served will not result in the order being set aside except in so far as the interests of justice require this to be done.

(3) Interests of justice will not require an order to be set aside where there is no prejudice caused as a result of errors in the application to commit or in the order to commit. When necessary the order can be amended.

(4) When considering whether to set aside the order, the court should have regard to the interests of any other party and the need to uphold the reputation of the justice system.

(5) If there has been a procedural irregularity or some other defect in the conduct of the proceedings which has occasioned injustice, the court will consider exercising its power to order a new trial unless there are circumstances which indicate that it would not be just to do so."

The Court of Appeal observed that it should not be necessary to revisit the authorities prior to *M v P (Contempt of Court: Committal Order); Butler v Butler*.[62] Subsequently, it was provided in the Practice Direction governing

---

[57] *Lee v Walker* [1985] Q.B. 1191 at 1203A.
[58] [1984] F.L.R. 844.
[59] See, *e.g. Hill Samuel and Co v Littaur (No.2)* (1985) 135 New Law Jo. 556 at 557, Sir David Cairns, CA; *Hegarty v O'Sullivan* [1985] 135 New Law Jo. 557, 558, Kerr L.J.; *Harmsworth v Harmsworth* [1988] 1 W.L.R. 1676, [1988] 1 F.L.R. 349, CA; *Linkleter v Linkleter* [1988] 1 F.L.R 360 at 363, Mustill L.J.; *Clarke v Clarke* [1990] 2 F.L.R. 115, 118, Farquharson L.J., CA; *Re M (Minors) (Access: Contempt: Committal)* [1991] 1 F.L.R 355 at 359–60, Butler-Sloss L.J.; *B v B (Contempt: Committal)* [1991] 2 F.L.R. 588, CA; *Smith v Smith* [1992] 2 F.L.R. 40 at 44, Nourse L.J. And see *Couzens v Couzens* [2001] 2 F.L.R. 701.
[60] [1997] 1 W.L.R. 314 at 326–7.
[61] *ibid.* at 316.
[62] [1993] Fam. 167.

committal that the court may waive any procedural defect in the commencement or conduct of committal applications if satisfied that no injustice has been caused.[63]

15-76 Nicholls v Nicholls was applied in *Olk v Olk*.[64] It was also followed in *Bell v Tuohy*,[65] where it was held that a person in contempt could not expect to avoid committal because of some defect or defects in procedure if he had not thereby been prejudiced. The court should carefully address each and every defect and decide whether any prejudice or unfairness had been caused by such defects (taken separately or together). The case concerned an invalid warrant for possession (as held by the majority on the appeal). Defiance of the bailiff in attempting to execute it would not for that reason, be treated as a contempt. Nevertheless, the judge could have dispensed with the need for a penal notice on the possession order itself, since the respondent had been clearly warned by the judge of the risk of committal if he did not comply. Accordingly, the judge was entitled to commit him in the light of his obdurate refusal to comply with it, as expressed at a later hearing, since no prejudice had been occasioned by the omission to serve a copy endorsed with a penal notice. The *Nicholls* guidelines were again applied in *Re Scriven*[66] in the following circumstances. The appellant had appealed against his committal for six months after refusal to participate in his public examination in bankruptcy. A warrant for his arrest had been issued, but was not executed for almost two years—partly because of his "travelling lifestyle". He argued that there had been a number of procedural irregularities and, in particular, the committal order had not been served on him. While it was accepted that it had not been formally served on him, and it was possible that he might not have been given accurate information about his situation, it was nevertheless clear that even if he had been served he would still have continued with his contempt. In those circumstances, it was not appropriate to regard the committal as unlawful because of a pure technicality.

F. Enforcing the county court's statutory jurisdiction

15-77 Special provision is made in the CPR Sch. 2, cc.34.1 and 34.1A, which provide:

"1. Where—
  (a) it is alleged that any person has committed an offence under s.14, 92 or 118 of the Act[67] by assaulting an officer of the court while in the execution of his duty, or by rescuing or attempting to rescue any goods seized in execution, or by wilfully insulting a judge, juror, witness or any officer of the court, and the alleged offender has not been taken into custody and brought before the judge; or
  (b) a complaint is made against an officer of the court under s.124 of the Act for having lost the opportunity of levying execution,

---

[63] Appendix 5A para.10.
[64] [2002] EWCA 423, [2002] 1 W.L.R. 2703, [2001] EWCA Civ 1075.
[65] [2002] 3 All E.R. 975.
[66] [2004] EWCA Civ 683.
[67] County Courts Act 1984.

the court officer shall issue a summons, which shall be served on the alleged offender personally not less than 8 days before the return day appointed in the summons.

1A. Rule 1(5) of Order 29[68] shall apply, with the necessary modifications, where an order is made under s.14, 92 or 118 of the Act committing a person to prison."

III. Applications for Sequestration

A. Mode of application

15–78 An application for permission to issue a writ of sequestration must be made to a judge in accordance with CPR Pt 23.[69] Although there is a power to dispense with service or order substituted service in cases where the court thinks it just to do so,[70] the rules require that the application, stating the grounds of the application and accompanied by a copy of the witness statement or affidavit in support of the application, must be served personally on the person against whose property it is sought to issue the writ.[71] The application is to be made in the same Division of the High Court in which the judgment or order to be enforced was itself obtained. The procedure is available in the High Court[72] in respect of orders in the nature of an injunction.[73] It appears, however, that the procedure is also available in the county court by virtue of s.38 of the County Courts Act 1984[74] for the purposes of ordering the sequestration of a company's assets.

B. Hearing usually in open court

15–79 The hearing must take place in open court, except in those cases where the judge would be entitled to sit in private for the purposes of a committal application, and in those circumstances there is a like discretion for sequestration applications.[75]

C. Function of the court at hearing

15–80 It is not necessary for the applicant to show that there is property which can be seized under a sequestration.[76] The court will be concerned at the hearing to

---

[68] See para.15–52.
[69] CPR Sch.1, Ord.46.5(1).
[70] CPR Sch.1, Ord.46.5(3) and CPR 6.8.
[71] CPR Sch.1, Ord.46.5(2). See Appendix 2 for the relevant precedents.
[72] See CPR PD70, para.1.2(2).
[73] See the *Civil Procedure 2005*, Vol. 1, sc.46.5.1. For the significance of "orders in the nature of an injunction" in the context of penal notices, see para.15–24 above and *Re P (Minors) (Custody Order: Penal Notice)* [1990] 1 W.L.R. 613, CA; *Bell v Tuohy* [2002] EWCA Civ 423, [2002] 1 W.L.R. 2703, [2002] 3 All E.R. 975. See also the notes in *Civil Procedure* 2005, Vol. 1, at sc.46.5.3 See also *Webster v Southwark London Borough Council* [1983] Q.B. 698 (in the case of a declaratory order where a party knowingly adopts a policy of refusing to comply with its terms, the court may have power under its inherent jurisdiction to issue a writ of sequestration, but see para.14–117).
[74] See, e.g. *Rose v Laskington Ltd* [1990] 1 Q.B. 562, DC. And see *Civil Procedure 2005*, Vol. 1, sc.52.1.34.
[75] See now CPR Sch.1, Ord.46.5(4) and CPR Sch.1, Ord.52.6(1). See para.15–28.
[76] *Hulbert v Cathcart* [1896] A.C. 470.

determine whether a contempt has been committed, and not otherwise to declare the parties' rights against each other in relation to the facts disclosed in the evidence.[77] Once contempt has been found, it is open to the court to grant an injunction,[78] to impose a fine,[79] or simply to make an order for costs,[80] rather than to grant permission to issue a writ for sequestration.[81] So much will depend on the court's view of the particular circumstances, and as to where the public interest lies.[82]

D. Formalities following the grant of permission

If permission is granted, the issue of the writ will take place on its being sealed by a court officer of the appropriate office,[83] but beforehand a praecipe for its issue must be filed,[84] and this must be signed by or on behalf of the solicitor of the person entitled to execution or, if acting in person, by the person himself.[85]

The "appropriate office" means[86]:

"(a) where the proceedings in which execution is to issue are in a district registry, that registry;
(b) where the proceedings are in the principal registry of the Family Division, that registry;
(c) where the proceedings are Admiralty proceedings or commercial proceedings which are not in a District Registry, the Admiralty and Commercial Registry;
(ca) where the proceedings are in the Chancery Division, Chancery Chambers;
(d) in any other case, the Central Office of the Supreme Court."

E. Duration of validity

For the purpose of execution, a writ of sequestration like other writs of execution is valid in the first instance for 12 months, beginning with the date of its issue.[87] Where a writ has not been wholly executed the court may by order extend the validity of the writ, from time to time, for a period of 12 months.[88] Such extensions are not normally granted in the Chancery or Queen's Bench Divisions

---

[77] See, e.g. *Meters Ltd v Metropolitan Gas Meters Ltd* (1907) 51 S.J. 499.
[78] See para.14–132.
[79] See paras 14–101 *et seq.*
[80] See para.14–135.
[81] See, e.g. *Steiner Products Ltd v Willy Steiner Ltd* [1966] 1 W.L.R. 986; *Charles Marsden & Sons Ltd v Old Silkstone Colliers Ltd* (1914) 13 L.G.R. 342; *Phonographic Performance Ltd v Amusement Caterers (Peckham) Ltd* [1964] Ch. 195; *GCT (Management) Ltd v Laurie Marsh Group Ltd* [1973] R.P.C. 432.
[82] See *Re Mileage Conference Group Tyre Manufacturers' Conference Ltd's Agreement* [1966] 1 W.L.R. 1137 at 1162–63.
[83] CPR Sch.1, Ord.46.6(1). See also the preliminary requirements prescribed by Ord.46.6(4).
[84] CPR Sch.1, Ord.46.6(2): see the praecipe in Appendix 2 (Practice Form 87).
[85] CPR Sch.1, Ord.46.6(3).
[86] CPR Sch.1, Ord.46.6(6).
[87] CPR Sch.1, Ord.46.8(1). Amended by Civil Procedure (Amendment No.5) Rules 2003/3361.
[88] CPR Sch.1, Ord.46.8(2); for other provisions relating to the grant of extensions, see also r.8(3) (requirement for sealing), 8(4) (priority from date of original delivery) and 8(5) (evidence of validity).

15–83 CHAPTER 15—PRACTICE, PROCEDURE AND PUBLIC FUNDING

except where priority of date is important.[89] If the period of 12 months expires, the normal course would be to issue a second writ upon the certificate of a solicitor that nothing has been levied under the first. Where, however, such an application is appropriate, it should be made without notice, and supported by a witness statement or affidavit, and an explanation should be offered as to why the first writ has not been executed.

F. Sequestration will not lie against the Crown

15–84 It is provided expressly in CPR Sch.1, Ord.77.15(1) that nothing of the enforcement provisions in CPR Ord.45, 46 or 52 applies in respect of any order against the Crown. This would clearly preclude the use of sequestration against the Crown, although not against an individual minister.

G. The property sequestered

15–85 The property sequestered may be applied by the sequestrators for the purposes of the party issuing the writ, but it is necessary to obtain an order for a sale.[90] Where there is in court a fund representing the proceeds of sequestration, the court may order payment out to the judgment creditor of a sum of costs which the defendant has been ordered to pay.[91]

15–86 So as to give effect to a writ of sequestration, an injunction will lie where necessary to restrain a judgment debtor from receiving a fund.[92] A writ of sequestration will cover a bank balance belonging to the contemnor.[93] In order to make the writ effective, the court may order the relevant bank, upon application in the original action, to verify the amount by affidavit and to pay it into court.[94] Where an issue is tried to determine the sequestrators' claim to property, they may be liable for the costs of that issue if unsuccessful, even though their authority derives from the court.[95]

H. Discharge of sequestration

15–87 Where the contemnor has purged his contempt, an order may be obtained discharging the sequestration.[96] Once an order for discharge has been granted, the

---

[89] For the provisions as to priority, see CPR Sch.1, Ord.46.8.4. See also the notes in *Civil Procedure 2005* Vol. 1, sc.46.8.2.
[90] See *Civil Procedure 2005* Vol. 1, sc.46.5.12.
[91] *Etherington v Big Blow Gold Mines* [1897] W.N. 21. See also the uses to which sequestered funds were put in *Richardson v Richardson* [1989] Fam. 95 and *Mir v Mir* [1992] Fam. 79, discussed at para.14–130.
[92] *Willcock v Terrell* (1878) 3 Ex.D. 323.
[93] *Miller v Huddlestone* (1883) 22 Ch.D. 233.
[94] *ibid*.
[95] *Wiebalck v Told* (1913) 29 T.L.R. 741. See also *Bucknell v Bucknell* [1969] 1 W.L.R. 1204 at 1214 where Brandon J. held that it was not unreasonable for a bank to make an application to the court, even though he held that in fact they did not require the specific protection of a court order. In those circumstances, he did not make an order for the sequestrators' costs which would have been the usual practice.
[96] See Appendix 2 for precedent.

sequestrators may be directed to withdraw from possession and to pass their final accounts. After retaining their costs, charges and expenses, and recouping any payments which they may properly have made, they will be directed to pay the balance to the contemnor; they will thereafter be discharged from further liability.[97] Where a contemnor has committed an act of bankruptcy after having property sequestered, it has been held that the trustee was not entitled to have the writ of sequestration discharged in circumstances where the contempt had not been purged.[98]

IV. Appeals Procedure

A. Introduction

In chapter 13[99] there is set out in tabular form a list of the tribunals to which appeals lie in respect of decisions made in the exercise of the contempt jurisdiction. In this section the procedural aspects of such appeals are addressed in turn. The right to appeal in a case of contempt of court under s.13 of the Administration of Justice Act 1960 is an exception to the general rule that permission to appeal is required.[1] In *Hampshire County Council v Gillingham*,[2] this was confirmed by the Court of Appeal. Such appeals are governed by CPR Pt 52, PD para.21.4. The right of appeal formerly applied both to applicants[3] and respondents. It is to be doubted, however, since the introduction of the modern regime generally requiring permission for an appeal, whether an *applicant* has a right to appeal without permission.[4] Moreover, since the right to appeal is confined to a committal order,[5] permission is required to appeal any other order made in the course of contempt proceedings such as an order for costs.[6]

15–88

B. The terms of section 13 of the Administration Act 1960

The relevant provisions are as follows:

15–89

"(1) Subject to the provisions of this section, an appeal shall lie under this section from any order or decision of a court in the exercise of jurisdiction to punish for contempt

---

[97] See *Daniell's Chancery Practice*, p.804; *Civil Procedure 2005*, Vol. 1, sc.46.5.15.
[98] *Coles v Coles* [1957] P. 68.
[99] para.13–133.
[1] See s.56 of the Access to Justice Act 1999 and the Access to Justice Act 1999 (Destination of Appeals) Order. The exception is confirmed in CPR 52.3(1)(a)(i). See also *Tanfern Ltd v Cameron-MacDonald (Practice Note)* [2000] 1 W.L.R. 1311 for an account of the new procedure generally.
[2] June 22, 2000 (CA) (Casetrack). See also *London Borough of Barnet v Hurst* [2002] EWCA Civ 1009, [2003] 1 W.L.R. 722, [2002] 4 All E.R. 457 (paras 13–85 and 13–118 *et seq.* above). See also *Wilkinson v S* [2003] EWCA Civ 95, [2003] 1 W.L.R. 1254, [2003] 2 All E.R. 184 where it was made clear that permission is not required in respect of a suspended committal order because it is "an order which commits a person to prison".
[3] An example of an applicant exercising her right of appeal under s.13(2) is to be found in *Neil v Ryan* [1998] 2 F.L.R. 1068.
[4] *Government of Sierra Leone v Davenport* [2002] EWCA Civ 230 at [32]–[34].
[5] CPR Sch.1 52.3(1)(a)(i).
[6] *Government of Sierra Leone v Davenport* [2002] EWCA Civ 230 and *London Borough of Barnet v Hurst* [2002] EWCA Civ 1009, [2003] 1 W.L.R. 722, [2002] 4 All E.R. 457.

of court (including criminal contempt); and in relation to any such order or decision the provisions of this section shall have effect in substitution for any other enactment relating to appeals in civil or criminal proceedings.

(2) An appeal under this section shall lie in any case at the instance of the defendant and, in the case of an application for committal or attachment, at the instance of the applicant; and the appeal shall lie—

(a) from an order or decision of any inferior court not referred to in the next following paragraph, to . . . the High Court;
(b) from an order or decision of a county court or any other inferior court from which appeals generally lie to the Court of Appeal, and from an order or decision (other than a decision on an appeal under this section) of a single judge of the High Court, or of any court having the powers of the High Court or of a judge of that court, to the Court of Appeal;
(bb) from an order or decision of the Crown Court to the Court of Appeal;
(c) from a decision of a single judge of the High Court on an appeal under this section, from an order or decision of a Divisional Court of the Court of Appeal (including a decision of either of those courts on an appeal under this section), and from an order or decision of the court of Criminal Appeal or the Courts-Martial Appeal Court, to the House of Lords.

(3) The court to which an appeal is brought under this section may reverse or vary the order or decision of the court below, and make such other order as may be just[7]; and without prejudice to the inherent powers of any court referred to in subsection (2) of this section, provision may be made by rules of court for authorising the release on bail of an appellant under this section."

For the purposes of s.13 of the 1960 Act "court" is defined broadly in subsection (5) and the appeal provisions would embrace, for example " . . . (b) . . . an order or decision of a county court, under s.14, 92 or 118 of the County Courts Act 1984."

C. Appeals to the Court of Appeal

15–90 The foundation for the right of appeal to the Court of Appeal lies in s.13 of the Administration of Justice Act 1960.[8] This applies to appeals, in respect of both civil and criminal contempt, from decisions of the High Court or any court having the powers of the High Court, or a judge of that court; and also from decisions of a county court (which does have in certain respects the powers of the High Court[9]).

15–91 Section 13(1) declares that the section shall have effect in substitution for any other enactment relating to appeals in civil or criminal proceedings. It might thus appear that Parliament was, unusually, seeking in s.13(1) in a sense to entrench

---

[7] It was made clear in *R. v Moore* [2003] EWCA Crim 1574, [2003] 1 W.L.R. 2170 at [24] that the words "make such other order as may be just" are not wide or specific enough to include an order for a successful appellant's costs to be paid out of central funds.
[8] See the analysis of the Act shortly after it was introduced, D.G.T. Williams, "The Administration of Justice Act 1960" [1961] Crim.L.R. 87.
[9] See the County Courts Act 1984 s.38, and the discussion of the jurisdiction of the county court in para.13–80. See also the County Courts (Penalties for Contempt) Act 1983, discussed in para.14–26.

the right of appeal in contempt cases so that a later Parliament would need to legislate specifically if the right was intended to be abrogated or qualified; that general provisions about appeals, civil or criminal, were not to be construed as derogating from the rights accorded in contempt cases. What is more, the apparently entrenched rights given to "defendants" generally, and to "applicants" in the case of committal applications, were not confined to appealing orders of committal. After all, an applicant (including for example the Attorney-General) would hardly wish or need to appeal an order for committal (save perhaps in theory to the extent of submitting that a penalty was too lenient). It would seem clear that the legislature was contemplating in s.13(1) a right for applicants to appeal when an allegation of contempt was rejected or an order for committal refused. In *Attorney-General v Hislop*[10] the Court of Appeal not only entertained but allowed an appeal from the Attorney on whether an article in *Private Eye* constituted contempt.[11]

A right of appeal was granted in relation to "any order or decision" made in the exercise of the jurisdiction to punish for contempt. That jurisdiction may be exercised by the court either on the judge's own initiative or in response to an application to commit (whether by the Attorney-General or some interested party). When a judge hears and determines the matter it is that jurisdiction which is being exercised; it would be unreal to suggest that one can only identify the nature of the jurisdiction with the benefit of hindsight. Whatever order or decision ultimately results from the judge's determination (whether or committal or otherwise), it will have been made in the exercise of the relevant jurisdiction. **15–92**

For the purposes of s.13(2) of the Administration of Justice Act 1960, the right of appeal in contempt proceedings was not qualified by whether "committal or attachment" was in practice available in the particular proceedings as a penalty for the contempt. The purpose of the phrase "an application for committal or attachment" was merely to identify the fact that the issue of contempt has not been raised by the court of its own motion. The actual punishment referred to in the application is irrelevant. Thus, for example, in *Att-Gen v Hislop*[12] the Court of Appeal held that the Attorney-General was entitled to appeal even though he had indicated that there was no intention to press for committal against the editor. **15–93**

In the light of the wording of s.13, it might at first sight appear that these rights of appeal would in all respects have survived the institution of the new appeals regime stemming from s.54 of the Access to Justice Act 1999 and CPR 52.3. It has been held by the Court of Appeal, however, on more than one occasion that this is not the case. In order to understand why, it is necessary to focus upon the **15–94**

---

[10] [1991] 1 Q.B. 514.
[11] But see the *obiter* remarks of Laws L.J. in *Government of Sierra Leone v Davenport* [2002] EWCA Civ 230 at [32]–[34] where he discussed, but did not decide, the possible scope and limits of an applicant's right of appeal.
[12] [1991] 1 Q.B. 514.

legislative framework on which the changes were based. So far as material s.54 provided:

"(1) Rules of court may provide that any right of appeal to—

... (c) the Court of Appeal,

may be exercised only with permission".

15-95 It was subsequently decided that express limited exceptions would be included in the CPR to the general requirement that permission should be obtained for an appeal. Accordingly, CPR 52.1(4) recognises that Pt 52 is "subject to any rule, enactment or practice direction which sets out special provisions with regard to any particular category of appeal". One of the limited exceptions provided in CPR 52.3(1)(a)(i) is where the appeal is against "a committal order". As Jonathan Parker L.J. observed in *Government of Sierra Leone v Davenport*, "The natural meaning of the expression 'committal order' is an order which commits a party to prison". It therefore follows that where the order or decision sought to be appealed is of some other kind permission to appeal will be required. For example, in that case, the relevant order expressly recorded that "no order" was made on the claimant's application. This decision was followed in *London Borough of Barnet v Hurst*[13] where it was recognised that the appellant, who had been committed to prison for nine months, had an unqualified right to appeal under s.13(2) of the 1960 Act; by contrast, the London Borough sought to cross-appeal in certain respects—but that required permission. So too, it would appear that permission would be required to appeal in a case where the court has disposed of a committal appplication by merely making an order for costs.

15-96 At one time, appeals under s.13 went to the Civil Division of the Court of Appeal, even though the subject matter originated in the Crown Court.[14] It is now provided, however, by s.53 of the Supreme Court Act 1981 that:

"(2) The criminal division of the Court of Appeal shall exercise—
...

(b) the jurisdiction of the Court of Appeal under s.13 of the Administration of Justice Act 1960 (appeals in cases of contempt of court) in relation to appeals from orders and decisions of the Crown Court;"

It follows that an appeal in relation to a finding of criminal contempt where committed in relation to civil proceedings, whether in the High Court or in the county court, lies to the Civil Division.[15]

15-97 The procedure for appeals relating to contempt is governed, like other appeals to the Court of Appeal, by the terms of CPR Pt 52 and the associated Practice Direction.

---

[13] [2002] EWCA Civ 1009, [2003] 1 W.L.R. 722, [2002] 4 All E.R. 457.
[14] See, *e.g. Balogh v St. Albans Crown Court* [1975] Q.B. 73; *Weston v CCC Administrator* [1977] Q.B. 32; *Rooney v Snaresbrook Crown Court* (1979) 68 Cr.App.R. 78. In the similar case of *R v Stafforce Personnel Ltd*, November 24, 2000, CACD, the matter went to the Criminal Division by reason of s.53 of the Supreme Court Act 1981.
[15] See, *e.g. Att-Gen v Newspaper Publishing plc* [1988] Ch. 333.

CPR Pt 52, PD para.21.4 requires that the appellant's notice, in a case to which s.13 of the Administration of Justice Act 1960 applies, must be served on the court from whose order or decision the appeal is brought as well as on any person to be served under CPR 52.4(3) **15–98**

Part of the statutory contempt jurisdiction bestowed on the county court is that under s.14 of the County Courts Act 1984, which governs assaults upon court officers. Although such an assault enables the jurisdiction to be exercised, no such officer becomes a party to the proceedings. It was held in *Brown v Crowley*[16] that it was not necessary to serve such an officer as a party "directly affected" under the terms of the rule then applying.[17] **15–99**

Fresh evidence on appeal

In *Irtelli v Squatriti*,[18] the Court of Appeal held that new evidence may be admitted in accordance with the practice of the Criminal Division, where the justice of the case requires it, without applying the traditional constraints of *Ladd v Marshall*[19] applicable to most cases in the Civil Division. Although in the case of civil contempt the appeal will take place in the Civil Division of the Court of Appeal, it has been held that the court will hear the case as though it were a criminal appeal, and an order will be set aside if the evidence makes it unsafe to sustain it.[20] **15–100**

The power to grant bail

Although detailed provisions for the granting of bail[21] were made by RSC Ord.59, r.20(2) to (6) they have not been preserved in the Schedule to the CPR. It seems unlikely that the court lacks the power to grant bail to a contemnor who has been in prison and is seeking to exercise his right of appeal under s.13, but the precise basis of the jurisdiction is now more difficult to identify. It is necessary also to bear in mind that the provisions of the former RSC Ord.109 have been preserved in a schedule to the CPR. Rules (3) and (4) continue to make express provision for the granting of bail by the High Court and the Court of Appeal. **15–101**

Section 15(3) of the Supreme Court Act 1981 contemplates the Court of Appeal exercising all the powers available to the court below, and this was relied upon by Peter Gibson L.J. in *R. (Sezek) v SSHD*[22] to grant bail in civil proceedings concerning immigration because the High Court had the power in judicial review proceedings to make ancillary orders temporarily releasing an applicant from detention. But it is difficult to understand how any corresponding **15–102**

---

[16] [1963] 1 W.L.R. 1102.
[17] RSC Ord.59, r.3(5) and r.19(2).
[18] [1993] Q.B. 83.
[19] [1954] 3 All E.R. 745, CA.
[20] *Kent County Council v Batchelor* (1976) 75 L.G.R. 151.
[21] *e.g.* Pearson L.J. granted bail in *Brown v Crowley* [1963] 1 W.L.R. 1102.
[22] [2001] EWCA Civ 795.

15–102 CHAPTER 15—PRACTICE, PROCEDURE AND PUBLIC FUNDING

power to grant bail would be available to a county court or High Court judge who had exercised the power to commit for contempt. There is no express power in the rules comparable, for example, to the power to suspend a sentence[23] and to discharge a contemnor.[24] It was formerly expressed to be the practice of the Court of Appeal to hear appeals in contempt cases expeditiously; and usually within one or two days of the appeal being set down, rather than granting bail and hearing the appeal later.[25] Although this is no longer made express, it is nonetheless clear that appeals against committal to prison for contempt need to come on for hearing as soon as possible because they involve the liberty of the subject, however heavy the burden upon the courts.[26]

D. Appeals to the House of Lords

15–103 The effect of s.13(4) of the Administration of Justice Act 1960 is to apply many of the provisions of s.1(2) to (4) and s.2 of the Act, which govern criminal appeals to the House of Lords, to contempt appeals also. For example, an appeal may only be made with "leave"; such leave to be obtained either from the court below or from the House itself in the event of a refusal.

15–104 In cases where the decision of the court below is itself an appellate one, also under s.13 of the Administration of Justice Act 1960, it is necessary to have a certificate from the court below to the effect that there is a point of law of general public importance involved.[27] Where such a certificate is required, and the court below refuses to grant one, a petition for leave to appeal will not be accepted for presentation to the House.

15–105 In the case of an appeal from a court of first instance, however, it is provided by s.13(4) that there is no need for such a certificate. This would apply to appeals from the Divisional Court, in relation to a first instance hearing pursuant to CPR, Sch.1, Ord.52 and also to any such appeal from either division of the Court of Appeal when dealing with a contempt at first instance (for example, a contempt in the face of one or other of those courts). Leave is nevertheless required.[28]

15–106 An application for leave to the court below should be made within 14 days of the decision in question; and an application to their Lordships should be made, if necessary, within 14 days of the refusal to grant leave.[29] An extension can be granted by the House "upon application made at any time by the defendant."[30] Following the decision of the Divisional Court in *Att-Gen v MGN Ltd*,[31] the

---

[23] CPR Sch.1, r.52.7.
[24] CPR Sch.1, r.52.8.
[25] See *The Supreme Court Practice* 1997, para.59/20/3.
[26] *Mesham v Clarke* [1989] 1 F.L.R. 370 at 372A–B, Kerr L.J.
[27] Administration of Justice Act 1960, s.1(2).
[28] *ibid.*
[29] Administration of Justice Act 1960, s.2(1). This provision is in part of the Act headed "Appeal to the House of Lords in Criminal Cases". It is to be noted that the same restrictions apply in relation to appeals involving civil contempt; see *Practice Directions and Standing Orders Applicable to Civil Appeals* (January 1996), para.2.2.
[30] Administration of Justice Act 1960, s.2(3).
[31] [1997] 1 All E.R. 456.

Attorney-General failed to make his application within the 14 day period and, not being a defendant, was not in a position to obtain an extension.

V. LEGAL SERVICES COMMISSION: ADVICE, ASSISTANCE AND REPRESENTATION

A. The desirability of legal representation

It is clearly desirable to ensure, so far as possible, that a person charged with contempt should be afforded legal representation.[32] There may be cases where it is necessary to take immediate steps to have someone restrained from preventing or disrupting the court's business; but even here it should be possible for some legal representation to be arranged when the person is brought back into court, probably later in the day, to be dealt with for the contempt. On a number of occasions, a failure to provide for legal representation has led to penalties having to be set aside.[33] Moreover, it was held that a solicitor who considered that there were grounds of appeal should not have delayed giving notice of the appeal while waiting for legal aid to be granted.[34]

In *Newman v Modern Bookbinders Ltd*,[35] it was held that it followed from s.29 of the Legal Aid Act 1988 that a court exercising any of the powers spelled out in s.92(1) of the County Courts Act 1984 should ask any unrepresented defendant, as soon as it appears that there is an appreciable risk of imprisonment, whether he or she wishes to be represented; if the answer is yes, the court should consider whether it is desirable in the interests of justice to grant representation. It is necessary to bear in mind the principle underscored by Art.6(3)(c) of the European Convention on Human Rights that a person facing possible imprisonment who wants legal representation should have it if the interests of justice so require. Reference was made also to the remarks of Lord Woolf M.R. in *King v Read and Slack*,[36] to the effect that the relevant contemnor "should have been informed . . . of his entitlement to legal aid". In that case, the Court of Appeal had discharged committal orders against the appellant because he had not been informed of his right to be given legal aid under s.29 of the Legal Aid Act 1988 without examination of his means. These provisions have now been repealed by the Access to Justice Act 1999.[37] So far as contempt in the face of the court is concerned, the matter is now governed by s.12(2)(f) of the 1999 Act.

The Phillimore Committee detected significant gaps in the provision of legal aid for contempt cases.[38] There were nevertheless lacunae in the statutory

---

[32] *R. v Moran* (1985) 81 Cr.App.R. 51 at 53, Lawton L.J., cited at para.10–59; *R. v Schot and Barclay* [1997] 2 Cr.App.R. 383, (1997) 161 J.P. 473.
[33] *R. v Selby Justices Ex p. Frame* [1992] 1 Q.B. 72; *R. v Pateley Justices Ex p. Percy* [1994] C.O.D. 453; *R. v Tamworth Magistrates' Court Ex p. Walsh* [1994] C.O.D. 277; *R. v Bromell* [1995] T.L.R. 67; *R. v Tyne Tees Television Ltd* [1997] T.L.R. 515.
[34] *Jordan v Jordan* [1992] 2 F.L.R. 701, CA.
[35] [2000] 1 W.L.R. 2559, [2000] 2 All E.R. 814, CA.
[36] [1999] 1 F.L.R. 425.
[37] Sch.15(i), para.1.
[38] Cmnd. 5794, paras 32 and 33 and Recommendation 28(c).

15–109 CHAPTER 15—PRACTICE, PROCEDURE AND PUBLIC FUNDING

schemes subsequently devised, such that it is necessary to consider the current provisions in some detail.

B. The Access to Justice Act 1999

15–110 In accordance with the recommendation of the Phillimore Committee, Parliament provided for those at risk of penalties for contempt of court to be awarded legal aid, originally by s.13 of the Contempt of Court Act 1981. This was repealed and replaced by the provisions of s.29(1) and (2) of the Legal Aid Act 1988, which in turn has subsequently been replaced by the provisions of the Access to Justice Act 1999.

15–111 Provision was made in s.12 of the 1999 Act for a Criminal Defence Service for the purpose of securing that individuals involved in criminal investigations for proceedings have access to such advice, assistance and representation as the interests of justice require. "Criminal proceedings" are defined, so far as relevant, to include "proceedings before any court dealing with an individual accused of an offence"[39] and "proceedings for contempt committed, or alleged to have been committed, by an individual in the face of a court".[40] Section 13 provides for advice and assistance for, among others, individuals who are arrested and held in custody at a police station or other premises.

15–112 Also relevant is Sch.3 to the 1999 Act, "Criminal Defence Service: Right to Representation", in which "court" is defined to include any body before which "criminal proceedings" take place—and would thus presumably include any court before which proceedings are taking place for contempt alleged to have occurred in the face of the court. That would apparently be apt to include courts such as the High Court and county courts, which would not ordinarily be considered to be exercising a criminal jurisdiction. Paragraph 2 of Sch.3 provides that:

"A court before which any criminal proceedings take place, or are to take place, has power to grant a right to representation in respect of those proceedings except in such circumstances as may be prescribed".

15–113 The criteria for granting a right of representation, whether by the court or by the Commission, are identified[41] as including risk to liberty or livelihood, or the suffering of serious damage to reputation; the consideration of a substantial question of law; whether the individual may be unable to understand the proceedings or state his own case[42]; whether the proceedings may involve the

---

[39] s.12(2)(a). This wording would appear to be sufficiently general to embrace anyone accused of an offence in a magistrates' court under s.12 of the Contempt of Court Act 1981 or of an offence under ss.14, 92 and 118 of the County Courts Act 1984. Unlike s.29(1) of the Legal Aid Act 1988, there is no express reference to these offences in s.12 of the Access to Justice Act 1999.
[40] s.12(2)(f).
[41] Sch.3, para.5.
[42] *R (on the application of Matara) v Brent Magistrates' Court* [2005] All E.R. (D) 263 (Jul), [2005] EWHC 1829 (Admin).

tracing or interviewing of witnesses or expert cross-examination; or whether it is in the interests of another person that the individual be represented.

This is reflected in the relevant regulations[43]: **15–114**

"The court, a judge of the court, [the head of the Civil Appeal Office,] or the Registrar of Criminal Appeals may grant a representation order at any stage of the proceedings in the circumstances set out in these Regulations whether or not a application has been made for such an order".

Where a mother was committed to prison for 42 days following persistent breaches of a court order allowing contact between her children and the father, it was held in the Court of Appeal[44] that her rights under Art.6 of the European Convention had been breached. The committal order had been made at a hearing at which she did not have legal representation. The Legal Services Commission should have expedited an application for emergency funding to enable her to be represented by solicitors and counsel. Legal representation might have made a difference to the outcome: this had implications with regard to Art.8 because the rights of the mother and children to a family life together were engaged. It should be recognised, however, that Art.6 would not entitle someone to indefinite offers of legal assistance if they behave so unreasonably as to make it impossible for the funders to continue sensibly to provide legal assistance, but the appellant's misconduct could not be so classified.[45] **15–115**

The provisions for legal aid in Scotland are considered elsewhere.[46] **15–116**

C. Limitations as to Criminal Defence Service funding

The provisions of s.12 of the Access to Justice Act 1999 only apply in respect of certain forms of criminal contempt. The section has no application to civil contempts, such as where a breach has occurred of an order or undertaking. Nor would it apply, for example, to media contempts whether under the strict liability rule or the common law; such contempts could not be classified as being "in the face of the court".[47] Nor at first sight would it seem to apply to someone aiding or abetting a breach of an order or to someone who is alleged to be acting, knowingly, inconsistently with such an order,[48] although now Sch.3, para.2, would apparently enable the court to grant representation "in respect of those proceedings" because the aiding or abetting of a breach would itself be classified as a *criminal* contempt. **15–117**

---

[43] See *Archbold 2005*, paras 6–129, 6–135 and 6–154 for the Criminal Defence Service (General) (No.2) Regulations 2001, SI 2001/1437 and paras 28–123 and 28–124.
[44] *Re K (Contact: Committal Order)* [2002] EWCA Civ 1559, [2003] 1 F.L.R. 277; *Att-Gen v Pelling* [2004] EWHC 2568 (Admin); see also *Benham v United Kingdom* (1996) 22 E.H.R.R. 293 at 324; *Steel and Morris v United Kingdom* [2005] E.M.L.R. 314.
[45] *Re K* at [34], Mance L.J.
[46] See para.16–348.
[47] For a discussion of which, see paras 10–11 *et seq.*
[48] See, *e.g. Att-Gen v Newspaper Publishing plc* [1988] Ch. 333. See also the discussion of *Seaward v Patterson* [1897] 1 Ch. 545 at paras 3–119 *et seq.* and paras 6–124 *et seq.*

CHAPTER 16

SCOTLAND

		PARA
I.	Contempt in Scots Law Before 1981	16–1
II.	Direct Contempts Involving Judges	16–84
III.	Misbehaviour in Court	16–109
IV.	Prevarication	16–118
V.	Interference With Evidence	16–135
VI.	Media Contempts	16–142
VII.	Breach of Interdict or Undertaking	16–234
VIII.	The Phillimore Recommendations for Scotland	16–268
IX.	The Contempt of Court Act 1981: Application to Scotland	16–301
X.	Contempt of Court Act 1981: a Commentary	16–352

I. Contempt in Scots Law Before 1981

A. The principles underlying the jurisdiction

16–1 The law of contempt in Scotland has been developed in the exercise of the separate and distinct jurisdiction of the Scots courts. It derives primarily from ancient court decisions and statutes, collated and explained by institutional writers. Yet the distinguishing principles underlying the increasingly extensive body of case law in this field remain somewhat elusive. It is nevertheless important to identify them so far as possible, in order to understand how the law developed prior to the 1981 Act, and how it continues to apply alongside the statute. Scotland, as well as England, is subject to the obligations imposed by the European Convention on Human Rights,[1] and particularly the requirements of Art.7.[2] It is thus essential to be clear what the principles are because of the need to demonstrate that any restrictions sought to be imposed on freedom of communication can be justified as "necessary in a democratic society".[3]

B. Upholding the authority of the court

16–2 In Scotland it has long been recognised by the courts and by the institutional writers that:

---

[1] See A. Brown, "The European Convention on Human Rights in Scottish Courts" 1996 S.L.T. (News) 267; A. Grotrian, "The European Convention: A Scottish Perspective" (1996) E.H.R.L.R. 511; J. Murdoch, "Scotland and the European Convention" in ed. B. Dickson, *Human Rights and the European Convention* (1997).

[2] I.D. Willock, "The Declaratory Power: Still Indefensible" 1996 S.L.T. (News) 97, 106. And see P.R. Ferguson, "Codifying Criminal Law (1): A Critique of Scots Common Law" [2004] Crim. L.R. 49.

[3] To use the language of the European Convention, Art.10(2): set out in para.2–142.

"... every Judge however limited his jurisdiction[4] may be vested with all the powers necessary, either for supporting his jurisdiction and maintaining the authority of the court, or for the execution of his decrees."[5]

Baron Hume treats the subject rather more fully[6]:

"... every Judge, of whatever degree, has power to punish summarily, and of his own motion, all such disorders or misdemeanours, committed in Court during the progress of a trial, as are a disturbance of the Judge in the exercise of his functions, as a violation of that deference which ought to be observed towards him when proceeding in his office. The hinderance, therefore, or molestation of the officers of Court, in their duty; the use of any threatening or intimidatory speech or gesture there, with relation to the Judge or the trial; any open expression of censure or approbation of the proceedings of the Judge or the jury, as by acclamation or otherwise; nay the wilful and repeated breaking of silence in Court: All these are examples of this sort of petulant contempt, for which the magistrate may reprove the delinquent, of his own knowledge, and upon the spot. All wilful disobedience or gross neglect of the orders and precepts of Court, in matters relative to any trial, is, in like manner, necessary to be subdued without delay: Otherwise, the course of justice would be liable to be stopped by the refusal of juror to serve, or of witnesses to appear, or to answer, and in many other ways."

In *Cordiner, Petr*,[7] a litigant in the Outer House of the Court of Session had shouted continuously at the judge when his decision was being given, and was sentenced swiftly by that judge to three years' imprisonment. Cordiner petitioned the *nobile officium* of the High Court for relief, where the comment was made that the law of contempt as applied in the Scottish courts arose from "an inherent and necessary jurisdiction to take effective action to vindicate their authority and preserve the due and impartial administration of justice."[8] Much earlier, Lord Traynor had commented that "the High Court of Justiciary is a supreme Court, vested with all the powers necessary for the protection of itself and its proceedings".[9]

This is one aspect of contempt: the need for the court to be able to control its proceedings and to maintain its authority. Another aspect, and one which arises frequently in modern conditions, is that concerning prejudice caused to pending proceedings from media publication. Again, however, it is simply one category

---

[4] The Law of Scotland has not recognised the English distinction in the law of contempt between superior courts of record, inferior courts of record and courts which are not courts of record: for the distinction see ch.13 generally. And see Oswald, *Contempt* (3rd ed., 1910), pp.11 and 12, and *R. v Castro, Skipworth's Case* (1873) L.R. 9 Q.B. 219 at 233.
[5] J. Erskine, *An Institute of the Law of Scotland* (1824), Vol. I, Title II, p.8. For a general consideration of the law of contempt in Scotland, see G. Watson, *Dictionary & Digest of the Law of Scotland* (1882); Macdonald, *Criminal Law of Scotland* (5th ed., 1948), pp.215, 266–267, 296, 297; D.M. Walker, *Principles of Scottish Private Law* (4th ed., 1988), Vol. I, p.60; Renton and Brown, *Criminal Procedure According to the Law of Scotland* (looseleaf ed.); Walker, *The Scottish Legal System* (6th ed., 1992), pp.382–3; G.H. Gordon, *Criminal Law* (3rd ed., 2001), ch.50.
[6] D. Hume, *Commentaries on the Laws of Scotland Respecting Crimes* (4th ed., 1844), Vol. II, p.138.
[7] 1973 S.L.T. 125 at 126.
[8] See also *HM Advocate v Airs* 1975 S.L.T. 177 at 180; *Milburn*, 1946 S.C. 301 at 315, Lord President Normand.
[9] *Smith v John Ritchie & Co* (1892) 3 White 408 at 413, 20 R.(J.) 52, 30 S.L.R. 329.

of conduct that is liable to undermine the authority of the court and ultimately the rule of law.

C. The relationship between "dignity" and "authority"

16–6 The phrase "contempt of court" has often been explained judicially in the following terms[10]:

> "The offence consists in interfering with the administration of the law; in impeding and perverting the course of justice... It is not the dignity of the court which is offended—a petty and misleading view of the issues involved—it is the fundamental supremacy of the law which is challenged."

16–7 Judges in early cases seem not to have drawn such a specific distinction between the dignity of the court and the authority of the law in analysing the jurisdiction in contempt.[11] Lord Justice-Clerk Macdonald's textbook states simply that "all Courts have the power to enforce order, and to punish acts of contempt against their authority and dignity".[12] Speaking judicially, however, he expanded the point and placed "dignity" in its true context[13]:

> "... it is in the power and, indeed, it is the duty of the court, in order to protect the dignity, quietness, and regularity of its proceedings, and to prevent defiance of its orders, to deal with such acts of contempt, and it is the practice to do so within the proceedings in which the contempt was committed, at once, and without the necessity of any formal complaint, and this applies both to procedure in civil and criminal cases."

16–8 Indeed, dignity does have an important part to play in the conduct of court proceedings and in the upholding of the court's authority. For example, in the English case of *Balogh v St. Albans Crown Court*,[14] Lawton L.J. referred to the need from time to time to exercise the court's inherent contempt jurisdiction for the purpose of bringing proceedings to a "dignified end". In truth, it is difficult to see any conflict between that statement and the sentiments expressed by Lord President Clyde in *Johnson v Grant*. While it is true that the law of contempt is not concerned with the dignity of individuals taking part in the judicial process, or even with upholding respect for the law in any purely deferential sense,[15] the

---

[10] *Johnson v Grant* 1923 S.C. 789 at 790, Lord President Clyde.
[11] See, *e.g.* the citations from *Nairn and Ogilvy* (1765) at para.16–146; *Johnston and Drummond* (1793) at para.16–147; *Gilkie* (1777) at para.16–150 from Hume, Vol. II, pp.139–40. Indeed, in England as late as 1984, committal orders were being discouraged, in cases where "access" or "contact" orders were breached, on the basis that the welfare of the relevant child or children was of greater importance than the court's own "dignity": *Churchard v Churchard* [1984] F.L.R. 635 at 638. But this perception of the rationale underlying the summary process could hardly be expressed today: see, *e.g. A v N (Committal: Refusal of Contact)* [1997] 1 F.L.R. 533.
[12] J.H.A. Macdonald, *A Practical Treatise on the Criminal Law of Scotland* (5th ed., 1948), eds. J. Walker, D.J. Stevenson, p.266. See also *The Laws of Scotland: Stair Memorial Encyclopaedia of the Laws of Scotland*, Vol. 6, Contempt of Court, para.319.
[13] *Petrie v Angus* (1889) 2 White 358 at 363; 17 R.(J.) 3; 27 S.L.R. 197. See also the words of Lord Ardmillan, cited at para.16–48.
[14] [1975] Q.B. 73 at 93A.
[15] Although Hume referred to the need for a summary power to punish *inter alia* any violation of the deference which ought to be observed towards a presiding judge, he qualified this expressly by adding the words "when proceeding in his office". See, para.16–3.

administration of justice needs to proceed in circumstances of calm and dignity in order to be effective.

Lord Young, in *MacLeod v Speirs*,[16] ruling upon whether a sheriff who had pronounced a sentence for contempt by prevarication was the proper defender in an action seeking suspension, also referred to "dignity":

> "A sentence is indeed usually and properly defended by the party at whose instance or on whose motion it was pronounced. But if the Magistrate pronounces it at his own hands in vindication of his dignity, he is clearly the proper party to defend it if he sees fit . . . ".

It is important to note his further observation that "a Sheriff may do what is necessary to maintain order and decorum in his Court, or to enforce an order requiring to be obeyed on the instant". This is to be distinguished from mere acts of discourtesy. As Lord Young put it in *Lawrie v Roberts & Linton*[17]:

> "Contempt of Court is a disregard of the authority of the court—a despising and a setting of it at defiance. While I do not say that personal rudeness may not amount to it, yet in this case when it was pointed out to the complainer . . . that he had made an unbecoming speech, he withdrew it."

D. The "domestic" jurisdiction common to all courts

More recently in the High Court of Justiciary "contempt" was said to be "the name given to conduct which challenges or affronts the authority of the court or the supremacy of the law itself, whether it takes place in or in connection with civil or criminal proceedings."[18]

These are the factors which lie behind the flexibility and speed which are so important in the summary contempt jurisdiction, and they explain also why this branch of the law has been treated, in Scotland, as being *sui generis*. The jurisdiction to punish for contempt cuts across the normal distinctions drawn between civil and criminal courts, and may be regarded as being peculiarly within the province of the court in respect of which the contempt has occurred, whether it be of itself a criminal or a civil court.[19] The summary procedure clearly differs from that applying in other criminal cases. Thus, although the punishment for contempt appears essentially similar to any other kind of judicial punishment, this special jurisdiction is not characterised by the law as being predominantly criminal in character.[20]

---

[16] 5 Coup. 387 at 401; 11 R.(J.) 26; 21 S.L.R. 530.
[17] 4 Coup 606. See also *Aitken v Carmichael*, 1993 S.C.C.R. 889; *McMillan v Carmichael* 1993 S.C.C.R. 943.
[18] See *HMA v Airs* 1975 S.L.T. 177, discussed at para.16–17.
[19] *ibid.* The principle has also been recognised as applying to the ecclesiastical courts in Scotland: see *John G Robertson* (1842) 1 Broun 152; *Andrew Holm & Alex Fraser* (1844) 2 Broun 18.
[20] See *Petrie v Angus* (1889) 2 White 358 at 363, Lord Justice-Clerk Macdonald, Lord Rutherford Clark and Lord Lee concurring.

16–13 The practical effect of this approach may be illustrated by reference to a modern case,[21] in which a litigant had been sentenced to three years' imprisonment for contempt by the Court of Session (having shouted abuse and made threats at the conclusion of a matrimonial hearing). Although he had been punished by a civil court, he presented a petition to the High Court of Justiciary to exercise its power *nobile officium* to deal with a *casus improvisus* seeking an order for "interim liberation on caution." It was held that the High Court of Justiciary had no jurisdiction to intervene in proceedings competently within the jurisdiction of the Court of Session, and the petition was accordingly dismissed. An explanation was given in the following terms:

> "... the Court of Session is wholly independent and separate from the High Court of Justiciary and this Court has no jurisdiction to intervene in proceedings which are competently within the jurisdiction of that Court ... Both the Court of Session and this Court have an inherent and necessary jurisdiction to take effective action to vindicate their authority and preserve the due and impartial administration of justice. Neither Court has any power either at common law or under statute to interfere with the exercise by the other of this important but essentially domestic jurisdiction."

16–14 This "domestic" jurisdiction on the part of civil courts was long ago recognised by Stair,[22] when he wrote in a colourful passage:

> "... For though the Lords are not criminal judges, yet all sovereign courts have implied in their jurisdiction these penalties, without which the same cannot be explicated; and therefore all affronts or contempts of the Lords, or any of them, may be so punished. And where parties are found accessory to malversations in process they are so to be punished. Thus in prevarication or excusable accession to forgery, or false testimony, parties are frequently set upon the pillory, or have their ears nailed to the trone,[23] with papers upon their brow, showing their crime, when yet the Lords do not find reason to commit the offenders to the criminal judges."

16–15 The sheriff has a civil and a criminal jurisdiction. In *Cordiner*[24] it was held that, where it was desired to submit to appeal or review a decision on a sentence pronounced by the sheriff in the contempt jurisdiction, the competent forum would be the High Court of Justiciary or the Court of Session; which of the two would depend on whether the matter arose out of criminal or civil proceedings before the sheriff.

16–16 Two earlier cases appeared to be inconsistent with the court's conclusion. In *Graham v Robert Younger Ltd*,[25] it was expressly stated by Lord Birnam that an appeal to the High Court would be competent in relation to a contempt finding made in a civil court. In *MacLeod v Speirs*,[26] the competency of such an appeal

---

[21] *Cordiner, Petr* 1973 S.L.T. 125.
[22] *The Institutions of the Law of Scotland* (4th ed., 1826), Book IV, Title 36, p.viii. See also Erskine, *op. cit.* Vol. I, Title II, p.8; *Mackenzie and Munro v Magistrates of Dingwall* (1839) 1 D. 487 at 492, 14 Fac. 535; *James Ker of Crummock v Orr and Fulton* (1744) Mor. 7419.
[23] The "tron" or "trone" was a public weighing machine, used also (in Scotland at least) for purposes of public punishment. It was especially convenient for ear nailing.
[24] 1973 S.L.T. 125 at 126. See also *Forbes v Forbes* 1994 S.L.T. 16 at 18, Lord McCluskey.
[25] 1955 J.C. 28, 1955 S.L.T. 250.
[26] (1884) 5 Coup. 37.

Contempt in Scots Law Before 1981   16–19

had also been upheld. It was said in *Cordiner* that the court had in those earlier cases wrongly assumed competency, since the point had not been argued by counsel. Whether or not this is a satisfactory explanation,[27] it is clear that those earlier cases should no longer be regarded as affirming competency even though they were not formally overruled.[28]

E. Contempts amounting also to crimes

Some conduct may be classified as criminal, in the sense of constituting the commission of one or more offences known to the law, quite apart from its character as a contempt of court. In such circumstances, the approach of the courts is that the contemnor should not be dealt with twice over in respect of the same matter. The question was expressly considered in *HMA v Airs*,[29] which concerned a journalist who was before the High Court of Justiciary as a Crown witness in a trial of persons charged with conspiracy and other offences. He gave evidence of a meeting at which he had been present, and as to a conversation he had held with someone (who was in fact a member of an extremist organisation). He was then asked by the Advocate-Depute whether he saw that person in court. He declined to answer, and explained that before attending the meeting he was obliged to give an undertaking that on no account, at any time, would he reveal the identities of those attending. The trial judge directed the witness to answer this question but he still refused. Although he did ultimately answer, this was only after he had been released from his undertaking.   16–17

The Lord Advocate presented a petition and complaint to the High Court of Justiciary, asking that the respondent should be punished. The journalist contended that the petition was incompetent and irrelevant, and the argument was advanced that in such circumstances, where the court's inherent power was not exercised to punish the contempt at the time when it occurred, the only competent way of proceeding thereafter was by indictment or summary complaint. On this procedural matter, the court's opinion was that contempts might competently be brought to the notice of the court by petition and complaint, at the instance either of the Lord Advocate or of any other interested party.[30]   16–18

The court held that it was within the province of the court itself, whether civil or criminal, to punish contempts arising in respect of its proceedings; the judgment then continued[31]:   16–19

> "In some, but in no means all, cases the facts which constitute or may constitute contempt of court may also constitute a criminal offence and render the offender liable to prosecution, but, save as expressly authorised by s.33(3) of the Summary Jurisdiction

---

[27] Lord Birnam in *Graham v Robert Younger Ltd*, 1955 J.C. 28 at 33, appeared to be satisfied that the High Court of Justiciary had co-extensive jurisdiction in the matter because "several precedents are to be found in the reports of Justiciary cases."
[28] 1973 S.L.T. at 126.
[29] 1973 S.L.T. 177. See also para.16–39. For the protection of journalists' sources generally, see ch.9, and para.16–383.
[30] See also *Atkins v London Weekend Television Ltd* 1978 S.L.T. 76, discussed further at paras 16–192 *et seq.*
[31] 1975 S.L.T. 177, 180; see also *Manson, Petr* 1977 S.C.C.R. Supp. 176 at 178.

(Scotland) Act 1954, which permits a prosecutor in the sheriff court to proceed by 'formal complaint' against a witness for certain defined acts which are deemed to be contempts, the charge will not be of contempt of court but will be of the commission of a crime known to the law of Scotland under its appropriate nomen juris, for example, perversion of the course of justice, assault, breach of the peace and the like. Where upon a given set of facts which would constitute contempt of court as well as a crime the Lord Advocate initiates a criminal prosecution the court will very properly not exercise its power to deal with the matter as contempt."

On the other hand, where the process of petition and complaint was chosen the court was entitled to deal with the matter as a contempt (notwithstanding the availability of an alternative procedure).

16–20 When conduct occurs which may be dealt with either by the law of contempt or under the general criminal law, it is important to bear in mind the generic differences between them highlighted in *Skeen v Farmer*.[32] First, the *sui generis* jurisdiction in contempt which is intended, as *Hall v Associated Newspapers Ltd*[33] made clear, to protect the accused in pending criminal proceedings, cannot be invoked prior to their commencement. Secondly, it was unnecessary in cases of contempt to establish any positive intention to interfere with the administration of justice.[34] On the other hand, the offence of attempting to pervert the course of justice *could* be brought into play in relation to conduct before proceedings were commenced, but the relevancy of the charge would depend on whether it satisfied the requirements of the general criminal law as regards specification and the need to demonstrate an "evil intention of interfering with the administration of justice in some specified way." If this were not the case, "the startling implication would then arise, that any editor who published an article about a crime, in ignorance of the fact that the police were investigating it, would be guilty of attempting to pervert the course of justice."

F. The law supplemented by statute

16–21 The law was supplemented by the provisions of s.145(4) of the Criminal Procedure (Scotland) Act 1975 which applied to cases of crime tried by solemn procedure:

> "Any person who interrupts or disturbs the court shall be liable to imprisonment or a fine or both as the judge thinks fit."

This section appeared to confirm the position at common law. Indeed, the provision was repealed by the Criminal Justice (Scotland) Act 1995.[35] That statute was only in force, however, for one day (March 31, 1996). Thereafter the relevant law relating to Scottish Criminal Procedure was contained in the consolidating Criminal Procedure (Scotland) Act 1995. This, in turn, incorporated the 1975 Act, but as amended. Since there now appears to be nothing

---

[32] 1980 S.L.T. 133, Sheriff Marcus Stone. See also paras 16–232 *et seq.*
[33] 1978 S.L.T. 241.
[34] *Hall, ibid.* See also *MacAllister v Associated Newspapers Ltd* 1954 S.L.T. 14.
[35] Sch.7.

corresponding to the provision contained in s.145(4), it may be concluded that Parliament simply decided that in this respect the common law would suffice.

G. To what extent is contempt itself "criminal"?

In *HMA v Robertson*,[36] Lord Justice-Clerk Hope stated: "I cannot understand that ... courts can be obstructed in the discharge of their duty, without such act being a crime according to the law of the land". In *MacLeod v Speirs*,[37] Lord Young, in the context of contempt by prevarication, spoke of his extensive experience as advocate, Law Officer and Judge for over half a century, and remarked:

16-22

> "There are no doubt many recorded instances of the Lords of Justiciary having summarily sentenced witnesses in criminal cases to imprisonment and other punishments for prevarication... they have pronounced such sentences in the exercise not of civil but of criminal jurisdiction... During the present generation there has not, as far as I know, been an instance of even imprisonment so inflicted by a Judge of this Court [i.e. the High Court of Justiciary]. My own memory, and I may say experience of the Court, extend over a long period, and I have never known of one.
>
> It is not in the present day thought expedient, or even reasonably safe, to find a party guilty of a criminal offence and punish him as a criminal accordingly without a regular prosecution and charge, and the ordinary safe-guards of a trial,[38] on the fiction of a contempt of Court, for it is in truth only a fiction. Prevarication by a witness on oath... is crime, and modern ideas are against regarding it as a constructive contempt so as to warrant such punishment on the spot without trial, and I, for my part, am strongly against countenancing the introduction into Inferior Civil Courts of a high-handed summary procedure founded on a fiction, which has long been practically abandoned in the Supreme Criminal Court, where alone, so far as I know, it was ever adopted."

This gives an indication of how the need to deal with conduct interfering with the course of justice, in a wider sense, became assimilated in the contempt jurisdiction. In *Paterson v Kilgour*,[39] Lord Deas, a renowned criminal judge of the day, dealing with a case of attempted intimidation of a party to an action, remarked:

16-23

> "Contempt of Court is a criminal offence, punishable in the most summary manner by censure, fine or imprisonment. It may be either direct or constructive. It is direct when the Judges are themselves the objects of it. It is constructive when the ends of justice, as judicially administered, are unduly interfered with".

In dealing with a breach of interdict case, *Mackenzie and Munro v Magistrates of Dingwall*,[40] Lord Gillies observed[41]:

16-24

---

[36] (1842) 1 Broun 152 at 160. See also *HMA v Golm and Fraser* (1844) 2 Broun 18; G.H. Gordon, *The Criminal Law of Scotland* (3rd ed., 2001), paras 50–01 and 51–10.
[37] (1884) 21 S.L.R. 530 at 534.
[38] For a similar warning in England, see Mustill L.J. in *R. v Griffin* (1989) 88 Cr.App.R. 63 at 67, para.10–32.
[39] (1865) 3 Mor. 1119 at 1123.
[40] (1839) 1 D. 487 at 492, 14 Fac. 535.
[41] This approach to what in England would be classified as a civil contempt is very different from that adopted south of the border, and is perhaps more akin to the Canadian jurisprudence on this subject: see paras 3–15 *et seq.* for fuller discussion.

"... [the complainers] accuse the defenders of guilt, and demand that they should be punished as an example to others. This is truly a criminal case, and nothing else. The contempt of this Court is a crime. It may be tried in this civil Court, because it is a contempt of our jurisdiction; but it is not the less a crime in itself though it may be so tried."

16–25 Scots law has not traditionally classified conduct as civil or criminal in nature by reason only of the court in which it may be dealt with, or by the legal forms which attend it. There is no ancient rule or practice such that proceedings are indelibly stamped with a civil or criminal nature by reason of their being taken in the Court of Session or High Court of Justiciary respectively. In *James Ker of Crummock v Orr and Fulton*, the Lords of Session would only hold themselves to be "no otherwise judges of crimes, than as they arise *incidenter* upon cases coming before them",[42] and Lord Kames in 1776, referring to the power of civil courts to punish as accessory to their jurisdiction, maintained that the Court of Session "hath a jurisdiction in all crimes, unless where the proof depends totally or chiefly in witnesses".[43]

16–26 By the time of *Darby v Love*,[44] the Court of Session was taking the view that:

"... it is usual for the court to punish incidentally perjury or prevarication committed in the course of a process depending before them, these crimes being of the nature of a contempt of Court. When any other matter of criminal charge ... comes under their observation in the course of a civil action, it is the duty of the court to take notice of it; but the proper mode of proceeding is, to recommend to His Majesty's Advocate to inquire into the matter, and, as he shall see cause, give his instance or concurrence to a prosecution brought in proper form".

16–27 This was the orthodox approach. Yet when Lord Young made his criticisms of the law of contempt in *McLeod v Speirs*,[45] the use of summary procedure seems to have been stretched to cover all kinds of crime connected with the administration of justice. For example, it was permitted by the Public Houses Acts Amendment (Scotland) Act 1862 for a magistrate in open court, without any formal complaint, and in a summary manner, to send an offender to prison for up to 60 days, subject only to the sentence recording on its face the nature of the offence.

16–28 In *Soutar and Brown v Stirling and Ferguson*,[46] it was held to have been insufficient to describe the two witnesses who had been so convicted as having been guilty "of prevarication and wilfully concealing the truth". Lord Young, however, went on to express the view that the magistrate had perjury in mind rather than prevarication, and referred to the clear principle that the magistrate had no power to use the summary process to convict of perjury:

---

[42] (1744) Mor. 7419. Cp. Stair, *Inst.*, IV, 36, p.viii.
[43] Henry Home, Lord Kames, *Historical Law*—Tracts (3rd ed., 1776), pp.232–3.
[44] (1796) Mor. 7907.
[45] (1884) 5 Coup. 387, 11 R.(J.) 26, 21 S.L.R. 530; para.16–22.
[46] (1888) 2 White 19 at 25; *Blake v Macdonald* (1890) 2 White 477 at 479.

"It is not a light matter to send a witness from the witness-box to jail upon the impression of a Bailie. It is a serious interference with the liberty of the subject, and might destroy a man for life. This sentence is not the result of a trial where an opportunity would be afforded him of bringing forward evidence in support of his position; it is a summary procedure without any trial upon the impression of a Magistrate."

H. Is contempt "quasi-crime"?[47]

The increasing acceptance of the demands of the legalist theory of judicial action (that is to say the rule of law rather than the rule of individual persons) in the nineteenth and twentieth centuries[48] has resulted in growing unease with the summary treatment of any crime, and in particular the summary procedure associated with the law of contempt. Many theorists regard crime and procedure as inextricably linked, and determine what is "criminal" by reference to the specific forms of procedure by which it may be pursued.[49]

This approach has gradually, and in a piecemeal way, led to a retreat from recognising overtly that conduct which amounts to a crime at common law can nevertheless be disposed of summarily purely because it can be dealt with as contempt in the law of Scotland. As long ago as 1856, Lord Justice-Clerk Hope in *Hamilton v Anderson*[50] expressed mild unease at the decision of a sheriff-substitute to deal summarily with defiance of a competent order in relation to a matter of written pleadings, taking the view that, since "it was not a matter requiring repression on the spot, like a matter occurring in open Court", the better course would be to "have brought the matter at once before the sheriff-depute, that his superior authority might be interposed".

One terminological device which has assisted in lending respectability to the use of summary procedure in such cases is that of "quasi-crime",[51] which enables the apologists for the summary procedure to distance contempt to some extent from true crime, and thus excuse the absence of traditional procedural safeguards.

It may be useful to compare other examples of conduct falling between the traditional classifications of civil and criminal. There developed a miscellany of statutory transgressions of various kinds, some of them in essence criminal, but treated as only semi-criminal, and often proceeded against in the civil courts.[52]

---

[47] See para.16–249.
[48] As exemplified in Art.7 of the European Convention on Human Rights.
[49] See Glanville Williams, "The Definition of Crime" (1955) 8 C.L.P. 107; G. Hughes, "The Concept of Crime: An American View" [1959] Crim. L.R. 239 at 331. For the position in European Convention jurisprudence, see para.3–4.
[50] (1856) 18 D. 1003 at 1016.
[51] See Lord President Normand in *Milburn* 1946 S.C. 301 at 313; see also *Christie Miller v Bain* (1879) 6 R 1215 at 1216, Lord President Inglis, in the context of breach of interdict. Cp. *The Laws of Scotland: Stair Memorial Encyclopaedia*, Vol. 6, Contempt of Court, para.302.
[52] *e.g.* as discussed in *Bruce v Linton and McDougall* (1861) 24 D. 184. The case concerned a conviction and other proceedings following a complaint before a police court under two statutes (9 Geo IV, c.58; 16 and 17 Vict., c.67), for bartering or selling spirits without a licence. It was held that such a complaint was a criminal proceeding, and that the defender was therefore not competent or compellable to give evidence as a witness.

16–32 These too caused difficulties as to the appropriate procedure, and there was no satisfactory criterion for ascertaining whether statutory proceedings were of a civil or criminal character. Lord Ardmillan in *Bruce v Linton*[53] thought it important to bear in mind the old distinction between what may now be called commutative and distributive justice. He described them as follows:

" ... the first being *ad civilem effectum*, for enforcement of right, or reparation of wrong, between man and man, and the second being *in vindictam publicam, in modum poenae*, for repression and punishment of offences."

He regarded the "best definitions of crime" as consistent with that distinction, and went on to cite Baron Hume.

16–33 This distinction is blurred by the use of such terminology as "quasi-crime", and the danger therefore was that it became easy to lose sight of the need for safeguards of the kind to which Lord Young referred in *MacLeod v Spiers*.[54] The use of such terminology gave the impression that, while contempts of court might *resemble* crime, they nonetheless differed from it sufficiently to justify a summary and less rigorous mode of procedure. Other terminology which is from time to time used refers to contempts as being "more or less criminal",[55] or as "virtually a crime".[56]

16–34 On the other hand, there has been a tendency since at least the end of the nineteenth century to separate the concept of contempt from crime even more fundamentally. For example, Lord Justice-Clerk Macdonald, in a case of contempt by failure to appear as a witness, stated[57]:

"My Lords, there can be no doubt that it is a general and established principle of our common law that if a person, during a judicial proceeding, or in connection with a judicial proceeding, commits contempt of court or contempt of the jurisdiction of the court, he is liable to punishment by the judge before whom the contempt was committed. This liability to punishment is not in respect of an ordinary offence against the law, for there may be contempt of court which has nothing criminal in its nature".

The problem with this approach was that judges were inclined to be less rigorous in developing rules and other safeguards for the summary procedure, because they did not fully acknowledge the criminal nature of the jurisdiction.

16–35 It was recognised in *Petrie* that a contempt may be dealt with either incidentally to the proceedings in relation to which the contempt has arisen, and by the court itself, or in a separate proceeding by way of summary complaint within a reasonable time thereafter. The conduct in *Petrie* it was made the subject of a complaint in ordinary criminal form under the Summary Procedure

---

[53] (1861) 24 D. 184 at 192.
[54] (1884) 5 Coup. 387, 11 R.(J.) 26, 21 S.L.R. 530 at 534; see para.16–22.
[55] *e.g.* J.A. Maclaren, *Court of Session Practice* (1916), Part VIII, ch.XIII, p.914.
[56] *e.g.* G.H. Gordon, *op. cit.*, para.50–01.
[57] *Petrie v Angus* (1889) 2 White 358 at 363, 17 R.(J.) 3, 27 S.L.R. 197, Lord Rutherford Clark and Lord Lee concurring.

(Scotland) Act 1864, s.10, which provided for a statutory form of contempt, punishable by imprisonment or fine, where a person cited as a witness should neglect or refuse to appear at the time and place appointed without just excuse.

In due course in the High Court of Justiciary the finding of contempt was challenged by way of suspension. Lord Macdonald concluded that the identity of the court, or the forms involved, did not necessarily render the subject-matter criminal. His Lordship would only go far as to say that the contempt was an "offence", but was not "an ordinary case of crime".[58]

As to contempt in civil proceedings, there seems to have been no doubt that courts exercising a civil jurisdiction were able to avail themselves of the summary contempt procedure, for the purposes of controlling their process and vindicating their authority, even in cases where the conduct concerned might have a criminal flavour. In *Maclachlan v John W. Bruce & Company*,[59] the Lord Justice-Clerk quoted the words of Lord President Inglis[60] that:

"... in one sense a petition for breach of interdict is a criminal proceeding. But one cannot help seeing that in many ways it is a civil proceeding. Civil interests are often largely concerned, and therefore it is often called a *quasi*-criminal proceeding."

The position had thus been reached that, contempt being protean, some of its manifestations were recognised as crimes, or as being closely related to crime, while differing from it in some unspecified manner. One could not necessarily stamp the proceedings with either a civil or criminal character merely by reference to such factors as, for example, the court in whose proceedings the contempt occurred, the procedures adopted, or the court to which an appeal was taken.

I. Contempt as *"sui generis"*

This branch of the law has been regarded fundamentally as *sui generis*.[61] This notion was considered in *HMA v Airs*.[62] A journalist called as a witness in a criminal trial for terrorist offences declined to answer questions about a meeting and a conversation as to which he had given undertakings of confidentiality. No action was taken by the trial judge, and, after the initial steps of a criminal prosecution were taken, the Lord Advocate decided to proceed by presenting to

---

[58] See the discussion of the notion of an "offence" which is not criminal in paras 3–71 and 3–78 *et seq*.
[59] 1912 S.L.T. 129, 1912 S.C. 440, 49 S.L.R. 433. The contention that breach of interdict should thus be dealt with in the Justiciary Court, rather than the Court of Session, was rejected.
[60] In *Christie Miller v Bain* (1879) 6 R 1215 at 1216.
[61] See, *e.g. HMA v Airs* 1975 S.L.T. 177; *Robb v Caledonian Newspapers Ltd* 1994 S.C.C.R. 659 at 665; *Hall v Associated Newspapers Ltd* 1978 S.L.T. 241 at 246. The contempt jurisdiction has also been referred to in Canada as *sui generis*; see, *e.g. Boutet; Re Bernheim; Re CBC* (1983) C.R. (3d) 302 (C.S. Qué); *Macmillan Bloedel Ltd v Simpson* (1995) 130 D.L.R. 385; but cf. *Morris v Crown Office* [1970] 2 Q.B. 114. In England the courts do not classify the jurisdiction as *sui generis*, although the *procedure* is sometimes so described: see, *e.g.* Mustill L.J. in *R. v Griffin* (1989) 88 Cr.App.R. 63 at 67; *R. v Jones* [1996] Crim. L.R. 806.
[62] 1975 S.L.T. 177.

the High Court of Justiciary a petition and complaint narrating the facts. It was held that contempt of court was "sui generis"[63]:

> "It is not in doubt that where commission of a crime is alleged, the only competent forms of prosecution are prosecutions upon indictment or by summary complaint. Subject only to the single qualification we mention later contempt of court is, however, not a crime within the meaning of our criminal law. It is the name given to conduct which challenges or affronts the authority of the court or the supremacy of the law itself, whether it takes place in or in connection with civil or criminal proceedings. The offence of contempt of court is an offence sui generis and, where it occurs, it is peculiarly within the province of the court itself, civil or criminal as the case may be, to punish it under its power which arises from the inherent and necessary jurisdiction to take effective action to vindicate its authority and preserve the due and impartial administration of justice. . . . Where, however, the Lord Advocate in appropriate cases does not choose to prosecute the court may deal with the matter as a contempt at its own hands or may do so if the matter is brought to its notice by the well established and competent process of petition and complaint, which may be at the instance of the Lord Advocate or any other interested party . . . By this petition the Lord Advocate does no more than to allege the commission of an offence against the court itself and in performance of his duty and no doubt mindful of the direction of the trial judge, calls the attention of the court thereto. The petition so states and notwithstanding the use of expressions such as 'gross' contempt and 'high offence offered to the Supreme Criminal Court of Scotland' the petition is, in no sense, an attempted prosecution upon a criminal charge for it neither bears to be nor is it concerned with the matter of complaint as the subject of criminal prosecution. . . . Contempt of court as such is not a crime within the meaning of our criminal law, including the statutes governing its procedure . . . the petition, which does no more than call attention to a contempt of this court, in no sense purports to initiate any prosecution."

16–40 It would now be difficult to argue that contempt should be treated as an ordinary crime or to contradict the analysis that it should be classified as *sui generis*. Despite the wise remarks of Lord Justice-Clerk Hope in *HMA v Robertson*,[64] it now seems that the gradual retreat from acknowledging contempt to be "criminal" is complete. It is probable that this approach has been brought about because of a reluctance to accord to those accused of contempt the formalities and safeguards, and consequential delays, associated with crime generally. This approach may have to be reviewed in the light of the Human Rights Act 1998, which incorporates the European Convention on Human Rights.[65] In the European Court of Human Rights the approach is to concentrate on substance rather than form, and to classify as criminal proceedings which should truly be regarded as penal in character.[66]

J. The Lord Justice-General's Memoranda on Contempt

16–41 The formal distancing of contempt from the general criminal law was further entrenched as a result of a Memorandum issued by Lord Emslie, the Lord

---

[63] *ibid.* 177 at 179–80. See also the argument of counsel in *P v Liverpool Daily Post and Echo Newspapers plc* [1991] 2 A.C. 370, referred to at para.3–68.
[64] (1842) 1 Broun 152.
[65] For a discussion, see paras 2–122 *et seq.*
[66] See *Benham v United Kingdom* (1996) 22 E.H.R.R. 293.

Justice-General, on July 2, 1975, under his power at common law to direct procedure in the criminal courts. This was as a consequence of the decision in *HMA v Airs*.[67] The effect of its provisions was to mitigate the disadvantages of summary procedure, and to afford some measure of protection to those accused under the summary jurisdiction. It was supplemented on June 21, 1995 by a further memorandum to deal with the problem of prejudice caused by the media and the personal appearance in court by representatives of the media. Both were superseded on March 28, 2003.

The text of the current Memoranda is as follows[68]:

"**A. This part of the Memorandum provides guidance as to the procedure to be adopted when a judge is considering whether the conduct of any person during a trial constitutes a contempt of court. It supersedes the Memorandum by the Lord Justice-General on Contempt of Court dated 2 July 1975.**

1. The appropriate time to make a judicial finding of contempt will vary according to the circumstances. In the case of prevarication, before the judge considers the making of a finding of contempt he should encourage the witness to speak up while there is still opportunity to do so, such as by giving him or her, outwith the presence of the jury, a firm warning and a clear explanation of the likely consequences of continued prevarication, and affording the opportunity to reflect on the situation and return to court and purge the contempt by giving further evidence.

2. No finding of contempt should be made before the person in respect of whom the judge is considering making the finding has had the opportunity to obtain legal advice and representation (and if necessary legal aid) in regard to whether a finding of contempt should be made and, if so, with what consequences to that person.

3. In the case of contempt by a witness or by a party to the proceedings in a trial, whether civil or criminal, before a jury, it is important to avoid creating prejudice in the mind of the jury. It may be appropriate for the judge to consider dealing with the matter at the conclusion of the day's proceedings after the jury have left the court.

4. Whether the alleged contemnor should be detained in custody or released subject to appropriate conditions, and, if to be detained in custody, for how long, should be given careful consideration. It is inappropriate for detention to be longer than is necessary. It may be possible for the hearing of the question of contempt to take place in 24 hours or less. It should not be assumed that it is necessary to continue the hearing until the end of the trial. The witness should not be ordered to be detained in the presence of the jury.

5. If the offence is one of prevarication, the judge should normally ascertain whether the Crown intends to bring criminal proceedings against the offender before deciding whether to deal with the matter himself as a contempt. It may be necessary to consider the making of an order in relation to the media.

---

[67] 1975 S.L.T. 177.
[68] See *www.scotcourts.gov.uk/justiciary/memorandum/mem_contempt.asp*.

6. If the judge is of the opinion that a person has committed a contempt, a judicial finding to this effect should be made at the appropriate time and, as a matter of record, entered in the minutes.

7. It is normal for the presiding judge to decide if conduct amounts to contempt. There may, however, be circumstances in which exceptionally it would be inappropriate for him or her to do so. In these circumstances the judge should remit the case to the High Court at Edinburgh on a specified diet, either detaining or releasing the person as may be appropriate. Likewise, once a finding of contempt has been made, it is for the judge to decide whether the circumstances warrant an exception to the normal rule that the judge who makes the finding of contempt ought personally to deal with the appropriate punishment for the contempt of the court. If the judge considers that the case is of such an exceptional nature that he or she cannot properly deal with the issue of punishment, he or she should, after making the formal finding of contempt, remit the case to the High Court at Edinburgh, on a specified diet, either detaining or releasing the offender as may be appropriate.

8. Although an act of contempt should be dealt with expeditiously, it is much more important that it be dealt with - and be seen to be dealt with—fairly and objectively. When the judge has made a finding of contempt he or she should consider whether to adjourn the matter to enable the offender to consider his position. The period of adjournment will depend on the circumstances. It will be a matter for the judge to determine, in the light of the circumstances of each case, whether the offender should be detained in custody until the adjourned diet, or released subject to such conditions as the judge considers appropriate. If the offender is under 21 years of age, has never before been in prison or is under social work supervision, the judge should bear in mind the propriety of obtaining a social inquiry report.

9. At the adjourned diet the offender should be given a full opportunity to apologise for his conduct and making a statement in mitigation. If a custodial sentence is imposed, it should normally be made to run consecutively to any sentence the offender is currently serving, and this would be a factor in determining severity.

B. This part of the Memorandum offers guidance to judges as to the procedure to be adopted where prejudicial publicity is alleged against a newspaper or the broadcaster of a radio or television programme. It supersedes the Further Memorandum by the Lord Justice-General on Contempt of Court dated 21 June 1995.

1. It is the practice for representatives of the newspaper or the broadcaster to be ordered to appear in court to answer the allegation. This should be done in all cases where the information before the court is sufficient to show that there is a need to consider the question of contempt, and it should also be done where the question arises as to the appropriate punishment. But it is not necessary for the editor of the newspaper, the producer of the broadcast or others in senior positions to be ordered to appear in person in all such cases. The question will be whether the absence of that person from his other duties which his attendance in court would involve can reasonably be justified.

2. An order for the personal appearance of the editor or producer should only be made where the alleged contempt is of a kind where his appearance in person is thought to be necessary so that an adequate explanation can be given or with a view to deciding what punishment is appropriate. It will be sufficient in all other cases or order that the newspaper or broadcaster be represented at the hearing, leaving it to the discretion of

the newspaper or broadcaster as to whether the editor or producer or some other person in a senior position should be present also on its behalf."

It was suggested that the 1975 memorandum had been meant to apply only to contempt arising during a criminal trial on indictment[69] (although para.3 referred to "proceedings in a trial, criminal or *civil*"). Nevertheless, the tendency was for courts to apply the procedures there set out (with any necessary adjustments) for all cases of contempt in which the court decided to invoke the summary jurisdiction. Breach of the procedures laid down in the Memorandum had been held to provide a reason for interfering with the decision of a summary criminal court on a matter of contempt.[70]

K. Summary jurisdiction to be used with restraint and discretion

As in England, the courts particularly in modern times have emphasised that their powers in this field of law are to be used sparingly.[71] Even though the jurisdiction is not to be classified as "criminal" in itself, the power of committal clearly touches upon the liberty of the subject and thus, as we have seen,[72] the jurisdiction may be regarded at least as "quasi-criminal."[73] Lord President Normand in *Milburn*[74] pointed out that:

"It has been said over and over again that the greatest restraint and discretion should be used by the court in dealing with contempt of Court, lest a process, the purpose of which is to prevent interference with the administration of justice, should degenerate into an oppressive or vindictive abuse of the Court's powers."

The Lord President continued[75]:

"The Court should never forget that disappointed litigants sometimes feel aggrieved and that some of them are ill-tempered, and that they may say or write things which are foolish and reprehensible. The Court should be on its guard against putting an overstrained construction upon such utterances, and above all it should not be too ready to find in them an attempt to interfere with the administration of justice and to visit them with the penal consequences of contempt of Court".

A landowner whose fence was being damaged by crofters had written a letter to the principal clerk of the Land Court, in which he complained of the landlord's loss of prestige with the crofters. He commented that this loss had hardly been

---

[69] N.W. Orr, "Contempt of Court" 1993 S.L.T. (News) 361 at 363.
[70] See, *e.g.*, *Omond v Lees* 1994 S.C.C.R. 389 at 392; *Morrison v Jessop* 1989 S.L.T. 86; *Adcock v Normand* (unreported) January 22, 1992 (see 1992 G.W.D. 9–468); *Bryson v Carmichael* (unreported) April 28, 1993, G.W.D. 24–1493; and tacitly in *Caldwell v Normand* 1993 S.C.C.R. 624 at 626.
[71] See, *e.g. Lawrie v Roberts & Linton* (1882) 4 Coup. 606; *Blake v Macdonald* (1890) 2 White 447; *Royle v Gray* 1973 S.L.T. 31; *Childs v McLeod* 1981 S.L.T. (Notes) 27; *Omond v Lees*, 1994 S.C.C.R. 389.
[72] paras 16–29 *et seq.*
[73] The term is also used in England; see, *e.g. Comet Products UK Ltd v Hawkex Plastics Ltd* [1971] 2 Q.B. 67.
[74] 1946 S.C. 301 at 315. See also the words of Lord Craighill in *Lawrie v Roberts & Linton* (1882) 4 Coup. 606: "Oppression, it is said, makes even wise men mad".
[75] 1946 S.C. 301 at 315–6.

lessened by the Scottish Land Court in connection with local affairs over the last few years. He had, he said, written letters to the Scottish Home Department stating that he had reserved the right to bring the complaint before Parliament. It was in respect of this letter that he was found guilty of contempt by the Chairman of the Land Court sitting alone.

16–47 Having paid a fine, he applied to the Court of Session,[76] which acknowledged its jurisdiction to deal with the matter[77] and held that he was not guilty of contempt. His letter had not been directed towards interference with the administration of justice but merely evinced a desire for amendment of existing legislation.[78]

16–48 Many years before, in *Hamilton v Anderson*,[79] Lord Ardmillan, speaking of the use of contempt process, observed:

> " . . . the true dignity of Courts of Justice very rarely requires to be vindicated by such an exercise of authority, and is most appropriately and effectually served by the courtesy, discretion, and magnanimity which refine intercourse, engage confidence, and command respect".

16–49 These principles were followed in *Royle v Gray*,[80] where the witness in a burgh police court disagreed with the prosecutor's summing up of his evidence and shook his head. He was placed in the cells until the end of the trial. He was then fined £10 for contempt without having been given an opportunity to explain himself. He appealed to the High Court of Justiciary by bill of suspension, and the conviction was quashed. His conduct did not amount to contempt, it was held, and in any event he should have been given an opportunity to be heard. The Court referred to the Lord President's words in *Milburn*, and emphasised afresh "that the court's undoubted power, and a necessary power at that, to punish contempt should be exercised with the greatest of care and the wisest discretion."

16–50 More recently, a solicitor applied successfully to the *nobile officium* to recall a finding of contempt of court against him for refusing to continue with the conduct of a client's case in a trial for assault.[81] A special defence of self-defence had been lodged and a tape from the client's answering machine was produced by the defence, which allegedly contained the voices of the two victims, one of them uttering threats against him on the very day on which the offence was said to have occurred. The solicitor tried to cross-examine the victims using the tape,

---

[76] Under s.25(2) of the Small Landholders (Scotland) Act 1911.
[77] Notwithstanding the previous payment of the fine: the court applied the same principles which govern bills of suspension in the High Court of Justiciary.
[78] See *Ambard v Att-Gen for Trinidad & Tobago* [1936] A.C. 322 at 334 and *R. v Metropolitan Police Commissioner Ex p. Blackburn (No.2)* [1968] 2 Q.B. 150.
[79] (1856) 18 D. 1003.
[80] 1973 S.L.T. 31. See also *Hall v Associated Newspapers Ltd*, 1978 S.L.T. 241 at 246, where it was said that although the jurisdiction was of vital importance in vindicating the fair and impartial administration of justice, and for the protection of persons charged with crime, it was just as important that the summary jurisdiction should be confined within proper and necessary limits.
[81] *Blair-Wilson, Petr* 1997 S.L.T. 621.

but the sheriff objected and indicated that the matter would be reviewed at a later stage. The solicitor argued that the ruling was not sufficiently clear on the use that might be made of the tape, and sought further clarification. After the sheriff considered that he had given the necessary ruling, he adjourned the matter and found the solicitor in contempt.

16–51 The petition was granted because the solicitor had not refused to continue with the case, and he did not say or do anything to indicate an intention to challenge or affront the court's authority.[82] The solicitor had been entitled to have the matter clarified because of confusion created by the sheriff, whose objections were characterised as "pedantic and unreasonable". The solicitor was entitled to insist that the conduct of the case was a matter for him unless and until he was given a clear direction that the tape was inadmissible. Moreover, the sheriff's intervention, especially in the presence of the jury, had created a risk that the client would not receive a fair trial.

16–52 It appears that the court has long been dismissive of contempt applications when the circumstances are out of all proportion to the behaviour of the individual concerned. In *Spalding v Lawrie*,[83] a Court of Session case where an agent for a party made imputations of wrongdoing against the court's clerk, the clerk referred the matter to the Lord Ordinary, Lord Cochrane. The First Division ultimately accepted a minute of apology to the clerk and court, which had not been offered below, as sufficient to declare the affair closed.

16–53 The court adopted a similarly realistic approach in *Lord Advocate v D. Prentice*[84] where, having been found in contempt on a separate matter by the Second Division, Prentice failed to find security for good behaviour as he had been ordered. Instead he circulated an account of the contempt proceedings themselves which was alleged to defame the Lord Justice-Clerk "and to bring into contempt and hatred the dignity of the Supreme Court, and the administration of justice therein". The Lord Advocate presented a petition and complaint to both Divisions, but it was concluded that in the whole circumstances of the case it was unnecessary to pronounce upon the defences raised, and the complaint was dismissed.

---

[82] Reference was made to the cases of *McMillan v Carmichael* 1994 S.L.T. 510; *Ferguson v Normand* 1994 S.L.T. 1355. Both of these recent cases, decisions of the High Court of Justiciary, show that the court is not ready nowadays to find contempt on the part of persons taking part in proceedings without there being an intention to challenge or affront the authority of the court. The first was a case of "unrestrained yawning", with no attempt at stifling, and the second a case of a solicitor having made an error of judgment about attendance at court because of a clash of commitments in his professional appointments. See also *Anderson v Douglas* 1997 S.C.C.R. 632; *Pirie v Hawthorn* 1962 J.C. 69, discussed at para.16–73. And see *Banks v Vannet* 1998 G.W.D. 36–1853, where the High Court held that a finding of contempt should be suspended because a solicitor had been found guilty, for holding a loud conversation in the public benches, without the magistrates having properly addressed the issue of *mens rea* or having sufficiently warned her. In *Williams v Clark* 2001 G.W.D. 758, the High Court suspended a similar finding where the accused's mobile phone rang while he was in the dock being sentenced. This was because of the possibility that the sheriff might have inferred the necessary intention from other aspects of her conduct on the same day—upon which she had not had the opportunity of making submissions.
[83] (1836) 14 S. 1102.
[84] (1822) 1 S. 385.

L. The continuing need for a summary procedure

16–54 Notwithstanding that the jurisdiction must be exercised with circumspection, the summary powers of the court are still considered to be valuable and important.[85] The public policy considerations underlying the law of contempt, in so far as they are concerned with upholding and protecting the effective administration of justice, require that the means of achieving these objects shall be flexible and speedy.

16–55 This was emphasised in *Wylie v HM Advocate*[86]; a case in which two Crown witnesses in the High Court of Justiciary entered the witness box but refused either to take the oath or to give evidence. They also refused to give any explanation. At the conclusion of the trial they were each sentenced to three years' imprisonment.

16–56 They appealed to the High Court of Justiciary by way of petition, and submitted that the sentences were incompetent and excessive. The appeal was held to be a competent approach to the court to exercise its power *nobile officium*. The sentences were also held to be competent, since the presiding judge had given each witness ample opportunity to justify his conduct, and they were not considered in these circumstances to be excessive.

16–57 The summary process was defended and justified in the following words:

"It has always been recognised in Scotland that when such a situation develops at a trial the Judge should investigate the matter on the spot and if satisfied that a contempt has been committed he may award at once such punishment as he thinks fit. He is not, of course, bound to dispose of the matter right away but he is clearly entitled to do so and there is much to be said for his doing it at once. He knows exactly how the matter has arisen and is in the best position to judge how grave or flagrant the contempt is. So much depends on the demeanour and bearing of the person alleged to be in contempt. The presiding Judge before whom it has happened accordingly is in the best position to determine the matter fairly and accurately. Any other Judge of Court can only recapture the atmosphere from a perusal of the cold printed record of what was said and therefore can only be dealing with the matter at second-hand."[87]

16–58 Hume described the jurisdiction in similar terms[88]:

"2. It is equally indispensable, to repress, in the like speedy and effectual manner, all attempts which may be made with relation to any trial depending at the time, or which has recently been so, to slander the proceedings of the court, or depreciate the character,

---

[85] See, *e.g.* paras 9 and 10 of the Phillimore Report: Cmnd. 5794 (1974), and *Hall v Associated Newspapers Ltd* 1978 S.L.T. 241 at 246.
[86] 1966 S.L.T. 149. *Wylie* was followed in *Kemp and others, Petrs* 1982 J.C. 29, *George Outram & Co v Lees* 1992 J.C. 17, and *Express Newspapers plc Petr* 1999 S.L.T. 644, S.C.C.R. 262, S.C. (J.C.) 176.
[87] And see para.10–46.
[88] *Law of Scotland Respecting Crimes* (1844) Vol. II, Chap. IV, pp.139–40. The passage cited at para.16–3, refers to the need to "reprove the delinquent of his own knowledge and upon the spot."

or sully the honour, of the Judges; or to impose on their wisdom, and pollute the channels of justice, to the prejudice of a fair and impartial trial.

. . . On these several occasions, there seem to have been sufficient reasons for summary chastisement of the proceedings, though tending only in a more remote way to the injury of justice: And still less can there be any doubt of applying the like correction, in the case of any direct attempt, in the course of a trial, or the preparations for it, to detain, mislead, overawe, or corrupt the witnesses; or to alter, suppress, or destroy the written, or other articles of evidence; or to conceal or pervert the truth; or to communicate with and influence the assize; whether this be on the part of the prosecutor, or the pannel, or their friends and favourers, or of one witness with respect to another, or on the part of the witnesses themselves, in the course of their examination. Hence, the numerous instances, unhappily too numerous to be recited, of the commitment or other censure of witnesses, for prevarication on oath, or obstinate concealment of the truth . . . .".

He cited as an example the instance of William Smith who had in 1714 been sent to gaol for privately whispering, in the course of his trial, to one of the witnesses produced against him.

16–59 Where the contempt takes the form of absence from court, for example through failure to obey a citation, the case may be disposed of by summary procedure, within a reasonable time, and indeed by a judge or lay justice other than one presiding over the proceedings in respect of which the contempt was committed.[89]

16–60 In cases of summary process the alleged contemnor should always be given the opportunity to explain his behaviour.[90] It has also been common practice to detain those alleged to be guilty of contempt, for example by prevarication, until the end of the day or the end of the proceedings and to deal with them at that stage; giving a chance to explain or to purge the contempt.[91]

M. Procedure in non-summary cases[92]

16–61 It was said in *Robb v Caledonian Newspapers Ltd*[93] that where the court does not deal with a contempt at its own hand, as would generally happen with contempt in the face of the court, it may address such matters when brought to its notice by means of a petition and complaint by the Lord Advocate or by any other interested party. The essential nature of the court's jurisdiction, and the procedures appropriate to bringing such matters to its attention, remained unaffected by the Contempt of Court Act 1981. They continue to be regulated by the common law.

---

[89] *Petrie v Angus* (1889) 2 White 358 at 363, 17 R.(J.) 3, 27 S.L.R. 197.
[90] See the Memorandum, paras 1, 2 and 9 cited at para.16–42 and now Art.6 of the European Convention. And see *Royle v Gray*, 1973 S.L.T. 31; *Anderson, Petr* (1971) 35 J.C.L. 55; *Macara v MacFarlane*, 1980 S.L.T. (Notes) 27.
[91] *Wylie v HM Advocate*, 1966 S.L.T. 149; see also *Cordiner, Petr* 1973 S.L.T. 125; and para.33 of the Phillimore Report, Cmnd. 5794, (1974).
[92] See A.J. Bonnington, "Contempt of Court: A Practitioner's Viewpoint", 1988 S.L.T. (News) 33.
[93] 1994 S.C.C.R. 659 at 665.

16–62 In cases where the contempt is not dealt with on the spot, therefore, the possible sources of initiating the process are as follows:

The court: The court may order the alleged contemnor to appear at the Bar either *ex proprio motu* or on motion by a party to the case.

The Crown: The Lord Advocate may proceed (i) upon indictment,[94] (ii) by complaint, or (iii) (in accordance with the decision in *Airs*[95]) by petition.

An aggrieved individual: Such a person may proceed by petition in the Court of Session,[96] or by incidental application in the sheriff court.

16–63 The course of bringing the party before the Bar has generally been adopted when he has failed to do something which he had been ordered to do[97]; should the party in question refuse to appear at the Bar, an order for his apprehension will be granted. Whereas, in cases where the party has been ordered to abstain from doing an act or acts (such as by interdict), the procedure by petition became more common.

N. The role of the Lord Advocate

16–64 If a petition and complaint is brought by an aggrieved individual who can qualify as having a legal interest, it has been held that such a complaint "should properly be brought to the attention of the Lord Advocate in the public interest".[98] The Lord Advocate may in his discretion then bring the matter to the attention of the court if he considers that this is required in the public interest. Yet it seems[99] that there was no positive requirement at common law, or under the statutory provisions after 1981,[1] for the Lord Advocate to concur in an individual's proceedings in order to confer validity upon them.

O. The distinction between direct and constructive contempts

16–65 The broad statements of principle cited in the introduction to this chapter would indicate that any conduct may be classified as contempt which presents a challenge to "the authority of the court," to "the supremacy of the law" or to

---

[94] G.H. Gordon, *op. cit.* at para.50–01; indictment or complaint may be used where the contempt is also an ordinary crime, citing *Petrie v Angus* (1889) 2 White 358.
[95] 1975 S.L.T. 177.
[96] *Robb v Caledonian Newspapers Ltd* 1994 S.C.C.R. 659, 1995 S.L.T. 631. See generally *Mackay's Manual of Practice in the Court of Session* (1893), p.587.
[97] See, *e.g. Leys v Leys* (1886) 13 R. 1223, 23 S.L.R. 834.
[98] *Stuurman v HMA* 1980 J.C. 111.
[99] *Robb v Caledonian Newspapers Ltd*, 1994 S.C.C.R. 659, 1995 S.L.T. 631.
[1] s.7 of the Contempt of Court Act 1981 does not apply in Scotland.

"the due and impartial administration of justice."² Nevertheless, in due course it will be necessary to consider individually the broad subdivisions of contempt that have gradually emerged over the years. The general considerations of public policy underlying the law of contempt have been applied in Scotland, in practice, along lines similar to the approach of the English courts.

In addressing the categories of contempt recognised under Scottish law, however, there is no warrant for a sub-division between civil and criminal contempts, such as we have described earlier in relation to the English law.³ Nor in Scotland does the traditional distinction to be found in England and other common law jurisdictions, between contempt "in the face"⁴ and other less direct forms of contempt, find an exact parallel. The rather different classification in Scottish law is that between direct and constructive contempts.⁵

16–66

Bell drew this distinction very clearly: "Contempt of court is either direct, when the judges themselves are the objects of it; or constructive, when the administration of justice is otherwise unduly interfered with".⁶ Sheriff Mackay made the same point: " . . . contempt may be either direct, as in the case of disobedience of the orders or insult to the persons of the judges, or indirect, by other acts calculated to impede or prevent the due administration of justice",⁷ and this is reflected in Maclaren's standard work on Court of Session Practice.⁸ Lord Deas was, in *Paterson v Kilgour*,⁹ at one with Bell in this classification. The same analysis is again to be found in the speeches of Lord Young in *McLeod v Speirs*¹⁰ and Lord President Clyde in *Johnson v Grant*.¹¹ "Constructive contempt" is thus a category that broadly corresponds to conduct tending to undermine the

16–67

---

² As the Bench of Five Judges observed in *Hall v Associated Newspapers Ltd* 1978 S.L.T. 241 at 246: "The law of contempt of court covers many diverse forms of conduct one of which is conduct that is liable to prejudice the administration of justice generally or in relation to the case of a particular individual. Its source is to be found in the indispensable power which is inherent in every court to do whatever is necessary to discharge the whole of its responsibilities." See also *Muirhead v Douglas* 1979 S.L.T. (Notes) 17, 18, where Lord Cameron said: "The variety and quality of the acts or omissions which in particular cases may fall within that description [contempt of court] are not capable of precise delimitation or formulation."
³ See ch.3.
⁴ See paras 10–11 *et seq.*
⁵ See the citation from the judgment of Lord Deas in *Paterson v Kilgour* (1865) 3 Mor. 1119, 1123 in para.16–23. Cp. the use of the term "constructive" also in Canada: see, *e.g. Re O'Brien v The Queen* (1888) 16 S.C.R. 197 at 208, Strong J.; *R. v Vallieres & Gagnon* (1973) 47 D.L.R. (3d) 378 at 385. See also H.J. Laski, "Procedure for Constructive Contempt in England" (1927) 41 Harv. L.R. 1031; M. Lippman and T. Weber, "The Law of Constructive Contempt: A Comparative Perspective" [1978] 2 Crim.L.J. 198.
⁶ Bell, *Dictionary, sub voce* Contempt of Court.
⁷ See J.G. Mackay, *Manual of Practice in the Court of Session* (1893), Part Second, ch.XI, p.104.
⁸ J.A.Maclaren, *Court of Session Practice*, Pt II, ch.V, p.134.
⁹ (1865) 3 Mor. 1119 at 1123, 385 J. 5.
¹⁰ (1884) 5 Coup. 387 at 408, 11 R.(J.) 26, 21 S.L.R. 530.
¹¹ 1923 S.C. 789 at 990. See also *Dudgeon v Thomson and Donaldson* (1876) 3 R. 974, Lord President Inglis at 975; Lord Deas at 975; *The Caledonian Railway Co v Hamilton, etc* (1850) 7 Bell's App. 272 at 280, Lord Brougham (clearly recognising the constructive nature of the contempt); *Glasgow International Exhibition v Sosnowzki* (1901) 39 S.L.R. 28 at 30, Lord Moncrieff; *Boswell's Trs. v Pearson* (1886) 24 S.L.R. 32 at 33, Lord President Inglis; *Duke of Argyle v McArthur* (1861) 23 D. 1236 at 1238, Lord Koloch at 1238; *Johnston v Scot and Small*, W.S. (1829) 7 S. 234 at 240, Lord President Hope.

administration of justice, yet lacking the immediate confrontational element of directly impinging upon the judges themselves.

16–68 Although there is frequent reference to a "distinction", what is perhaps more significant is the underlying aggregation of all conduct which tends adversely to affect the administration of justice into the one category of contempt. By assimilating conduct which may not need to be treated summarily into this category, and giving it the label "constructive contempt", the courts have been able to extend the ambit of the summary procedure to cover instances which could perhaps be dealt with under the general criminal law, without having to be made susceptible to the summary procedure.

P. The approach to *"mens rea"* or *"dole"* at common law

16–69 There is little authority in Scotland on what would in England be referred to as the *mens rea* required for contempt. The old distinction between direct and constructive contempts may be material in this context.[12] Gordon seems to have taken the view that newspaper contempts were, in effect, offences of strict liability even before the 1981 Act; whereas in cases where the contempt was a "direct personal one, so to speak",[13] ordinary principles would apply as to the need for establishing a mental element in the offence.

16–70 The position so far as newspapers are concerned is well illustrated by the decision of Sheriff Marcus Stone in *Skeen v Farmer*.[14] Two journalists were charged with attempting to pervert the course of justice by publishing an article in the *Sunday People* describing an assault upon one of them by a well known comedian. This was at a time when the "victim" had complained to the police and was aware that investigations were under way. The point was taken that the complaint was irrelevant, and it was held that the averments might have been appropriate to a charge of contempt of court, had criminal proceedings been commenced; yet they lacked the essentials of the crime actually charged, in that (1) there was no suggestion of any chain of causal effect in respect of mode, and (2) there was no allegation of specific wrongful intention.

16–71 In the course of his judgment the sheriff observed, in the light of *Hall v Associated Newspapers Ltd*,[15] that publication *before* criminal proceedings had commenced could not be the subject of a charge of contempt. *Dicta* to the contrary in *Stirling v Associated Newspapers Ltd*[16] had there been expressly disapproved. He went on to describe contempt of court as "an offence *sui generis*". It was not a crime and did not require *mens rea*. It was not necessary that the publication should in fact have a prejudicial effect upon the relevant court proceedings, nor that there should be any "deliberate intention... to interfere with the course of the administration of justice". While it was true that

---

[12] On which, see generally Gordon, *op. cit.*, para.50–15; N.W. Orr, "Contempt of Court" 1993 S.L.T. (News) 361.
[13] *The Criminal Law of Scotland* (3rd ed., 2001) para.50–15.
[14] 1980 S.L.T. 133.
[15] 1978 S.L.T. 241.
[16] 1960 S.L.T. 5.

the administration of justice might suffer from press publication at an earlier stage, this was a matter to be left to the control of the general criminal law, with its requirements for specification of the charges and the need to prove the requisite *mens rea*. For the purposes of attempting to pervert the course of justice it was necessary to allege "the evil intention" of interfering with the administration of justice in some specified way.

Any discussion of this subject must take account of the fact that the Scots common law of crime is probably still more accurately described as having a mental element theory along the lines of Hume's concept of "dole", rather than as being based directly on Anglo-American notions of *mens rea*.

16–72

1. *Constructive contempts*

A significant decision on the requisite mental element for constructive contempt is *Pirie v Hawthorn*.[17] A young farm worker was cited to attend the sheriff court for trial on a criminal charge, but forgot to come on time, and was found to be in contempt. In a suspension, it was said by Lord Justice-General Clyde:

16–73

" . . . it appears to me that there was no justification at all for holding contempt to be established in the present case. There was no wilful defiance of the court at any stage and no wilful failure to appear at the proper time or to explain why appearance was not made in the morning. The essential element in contempt of court is thus absent."

The bill was therefore granted.

This decision was "explained" in *Muirhead v Douglas*,[18] in which a solicitor was treated by the sheriff as being in contempt. He was representing a client at the court which had three trials listed for hearing that day, of which his own case was listed second. The complainer left the court and proceeded to his own office which was situated at a very short distance from the court building. He had been given an estimate of two hours for the first trial by the agent involved in that case, but it came to a premature conclusion because there was a change of plea. The complainer had left "instructions" with the court officer, on an informal basis, to contact him on the conclusion of the first trial. He then took the opportunity of conducting some other professional business, involving a visit to some proposed adopters said to live close to his office. He returned to the court only to discover that the previous trial had finished some 20 minutes earlier. A message had been left with his receptionist, who did not appreciate that there was any urgency in the matter, although she had undertaken to inform him on his return that he was to contact the respondent's office.

16–74

Pirie was treated by the High Court of Justiciary as a case in which the sole allegation against the complainer had been of *wilful* disobedience to the order of the court. It was assumed that had there been an alternative allegation of

16–75

---

[17] 1962 S.L.T. 291, 1962 J.C. 69.
[18] 1979 S.L.T. (News) 17 at 18.

16-75 carelessness or reckless disregard of his citation, the finding of contempt might not have been suspended.

16-76 Authority for the view that contempt was not limited to cases of deliberate disobedience was found by the court in the publication contempt cases,[19] which were said to demonstrate that "deliberate intent to cause prejudice to the administration of justice is not an essential element in contempt".[20] The publication cases decided before the Contempt of Court Act 1981, however, do not provide a perfect analogy with disobedience cases. In the latter, the act or omission with which the court is generally concerned is that which constitutes the breach of the order. It is in relation to such acts or omissions that consideration of the mental element has been given. In newspaper cases, by contrast, the mere act of publication which is said to constitute contempt will generally have been intentional.

16-77 What has been considered by the court in such cases is whether, over and above that limited intention, there needs to be proved any additional intention to interfere with the administration of justice. The authorities establish that no such intention is required (and that in that sense publication contempt may perhaps be regarded as an offence of strict responsibility). Such decisions, however, do not necessarily throw much light on those cases involving disobedience of an order, or non-attendance at court, where there is often a genuine issue as to whether or not the primary act or omission could be said to have been intended.

16-78 The ultimate decision in *Muirhead* was that it would suffice that there should be present " . . . such a degree of carelessness or disregard of obligation leading to interference with or material disruption in the course of the administration of justice as to be equiparated with wilful or deliberate disobedience or interference". The court took the view that the lawyer had deliberately chosen to take the risk of delaying the court's business for his own professional benefit. Yet even carelessness alone, without an intention to interfere with the course of justice, *could* amount to contempt. There was certainly no authority to the contrary; the question would always be "one of fact and circumstances."

16-79 Subsequently, in a number of appeals,[21] it has been confirmed that lateness or non-attendance should not be treated as giving rise to liability automatically and that some mental element is indeed required. Doubtless a *prima facie* case is established by a failure to comply with the obligation in question but, once an excuse or explanation inconsistent with the requisite mental element has been

---

[19] The example cited was *Hall v Associated Newspapers Ltd* 1978 S.L.T. 241. Reference was also made to *Stirling v Associated Newspapers Ltd* 1960 S.L.T. 5, 1960 J.C. 5.
[20] 1979 S.L.T. (News) at 18.
[21] *e.g. McKinnon v Douglas* 1982 S.C.C.R. 80, 1982 S.L.T. 375; *Flynn v HMA* (unreported) see 1990 G.W.D. 13–645; *Bryson v Carmichael*, 1993 G.W.D. 24–1493; *McGeary v O'Brien* 1993 G.W.D. 36–2315; *Horton v Scott*, 1994 G.W.D. 8–467; *Amor v Scott* 1992 G.W.D. 23–1300; *MacPherson v McLeod* 1994 G.W.D. 6–325; *Drummond v Haywood* 1994 G.W.D. 5–260; *Caldwell v Normand* 1993 S.C.C.R. 624; *Kane v Carmichael* 1993 S.C.C.R. 626; *Cameron v Normand* 1993 G.W.D. 40–2639. And see *Peteranna v McClory* 1991 G.W.D. 10–575; *Ferguson v Normand* 1994 S.C.C.R. 812, S.L.T. 1355; *Anderson v Douglas* 1997 S.C.C.R. 632.

raised before the court, liability for contempt is unlikely to be established unless the excuse has been negated.

A not dissimilar problem was considered on a bill of suspension in *Urquhart v Hamilton*.[22] The complainer had been convicted of theft; sentence was deferred for six months during which time a supplementary social work report was to be obtained. It was not available for the deferred diet because of the complainer's failure to attend at the social work department. He pleaded lack of funds to travel the necessary distance. The sheriff took the view that he could have walked, and ordered him to perform a period of community service.[23] It was held on appeal that the sheriff had been entitled to find that he was guilty of contempt, in having wilfully defied the court and shown gross disrespect. It was treated as a serious contempt, for which a custodial penalty might well have been imposed.

16–80

The formulation in *Caldwell v Normand*[24] was to the effect that "the question was whether he was wilfully defying the court or was intending disrespect to the court or was acting in any way against the court or was attempting to pervert the course of justice". What is less easy to establish is whether a particular excuse is likely to be accepted or rejected, since so much will turn on the facts of each case.[25] There have also been cases where it seems that a heavy onus has been placed on the person accused of contempt to establish his excuse,[26] and cases where inferences of guilt have been drawn, without much consideration being given to where the burden of proof lies. There remains, therefore, some lack of clarity in modern law as to the mental element in lateness and non-attendance contempts.

16–81

2. *The mental element in direct contempt*

In *McMillan v Carmichael*,[27] a person was found in contempt for yawning visibly and unrestrainedly in court. The High Court emphasised that "an intention to

16–82

---

[22] 1996 S.C.C.R. 217.
[23] Community penalties are not, so far, available in England for contempt. See para.14–98.
[24] 1993 S.C.C.R. 624 at 625. See *Murdanaigum v Henderson*, High Court of Justiciary, April 24, 1996, G.W.D. 19–1079, where it was held that the *Caldwell* test had not been fulfilled in the case of a solicitor who failed to attend his client's trial through an administrative error, in not entering the date in his diary. The sheriff had not been entitled to take into account two previous failures to attend court (although they might have been relevant to sentence), since they could not convert the inefficiency in the instant case into a pattern of wilful conduct justifying the inference that the solicitor had acted in wilful disregard of the court's authority or in contempt of court. See also *Black v McGlennan*, High Court of Justiciary, October 11, 1995, G.W.D. 2–85, where a person who was required at court left home too late to arrive on time for the hearing. It was held that he may not have organised his affairs very efficiently, but that did not mean that he was intending disrespect to the court, or wilfully defying it; the finding was suspended.
[25] See, *e.g. Oswald v Heywood*, 1991 G.W.D. 36–2182; *McConnick v Normand*, 1991 G.W.D. 22–1285.
[26] *e.g. Hughes v Carmichael* 1993 G.W.D. 12–805; *McPherson v Heywood*, 1993 G.W.D. 15–990; *Steele v Carmichael* 1993 G.W.D. 11–729. The general rule in Scotland, as in England, is that where an Act of Parliament requires an accused to prove facts that amount to a defence to a particular charge, he has to do so only on a balance of probabilities: *Neish v Stevenson* 1969 S.L.T. 229; *King v Lees* 1993 S.C.C.R. 28.
[27] 1993 S.C.C.R. 943 at 945F, Lord Justice-General Hope.

16–82

challenge or affront the authority of the court or to defy its orders is a necessary element without which it cannot hold that a contempt of court has been committed". Yet the statement was qualified by adding these important words:

> "A finding that the conduct was wilful may, of course, be based on inference. If it is necessary to resort to inferrence (sic), the question to be considered is not whether the conduct was reckless or amounted to gross neglect but whether, in all the circumstances, it can be held to have been a wilful challenge, or a wilful failure, in defiance of the authority of the court".

This analysis has a direct parallel in England. While it has been recognised there that recklessness will not suffice to establish common law contempt by publication, nonetheless it seems that the court may readily infer the requisite intention from surrounding circumstances.[28]

16–83   In *Aitken v Carmichael*,[29] a case appealed from the same court in the same year as *McMillan*, a differently constituted court was faced with a suspension of a finding of contempt against a spectator at a summary criminal trial. On leaving court during an adjournment, he had put on a set of headphones. The court did not specifically address the mental element but concluded that the sheriff was not entitled to regard the appellant's behaviour as contempt of court for the following reasons:

> "Contempt of court is conduct which challenges or affronts the authority of the court and we are satisfied that there is nothing which the complainer did which challenged the authority of the court or affronted its authority".

II. DIRECT CONTEMPTS INVOLVING JUDGES

A. Assaulting judges

16–84   To beat, strike or insult any judge sitting in judgment, or in relation to his conduct in his judicial capacity, was at one time a capital offence.[30] Also threats of violence made against a judge in relation to his office would subject the offender to "arbitrary judgment."[31] Plainly such conduct would amount to contempt, as well as falling within the ordinary provisions of the law concerned with violence. Nowadays all such conduct would be regarded as having a dual nature as a crime and a direct contempt; the choice of procedure might depend on matters such as where the conduct occurred, the extent to which the attack was directed towards affecting the judge's discharge of his duties and, if so, whether it was in relation

---

[28] *Att-Gen v Newspaper Publishing plc* [1988] Ch. 333; *Att-Gen v News Group Newspapers plc* [1989] Q.B. 110; *Att-Gen v Times Newspapers Ltd* [1992] 1 A.C. 191; *Official Solicitor v News Group Newspapers plc* [1994] 2 F.L.R. 174. Nonetheless, it seems that the inference has to be "little short of overwhelming": *Att-Gen v Sport Newspapers Ltd* [1991] 1 W.L.R. 1194 at 1208F–G, [2002] 1 All E.R. 503 at 516g–j, Bingham L.J.
[29] 1993 S.C.C.R. 889 at 891.
[30] (1593) c.177; (1600) c.4. Cp. the position in England, para.10–90.
[31] Hume, *op. cit.* Vol. I, p.406.

to particular proceedings or to the administration of justice more generally. There is anecdotal evidence of a case involving a stipendiary magistrate in Glasgow some years ago, where an accused was prosecuted on summary complaint for an assault after he had thrown a knife in court.

B. Abusing or "murmuring" judges

Slandering (also known in Scotland as "murmuring") or threatening judges, in relation to the discharge of their duties, is an example of a direct contempt of court which may either be incidentally accompanied by disruption of the court or occur quite independently.

16–85

Hume[32] sets out concisely the rationale of the law underlying this species of direct contempt, which he described as going "to their character and fame":

16–86

" ... In which respect it is still more important to the public, to guard and protect the Judges, than even in their personal safety; considering how open the ears of the multitude to this sort of calumny; and when once raised, how speedily it spreads; and how deep and extensive the mischief of awakening the jealousy of the people, with regard to the integrity of the persons who dispense the law to them, and have the decision of their most important interests in their hands ...

Offences of this sort, if relative to any proceeding which is at the time, or has lately been depending in the Criminal Court, are punishable to a certain extent, as contempts, on summary conviction there, without the verdict of a jury: The right to do so arises in such cases, from the near contingency of the slander and the proceedings; and besides the offence is here committed against the court themselves, whose character and honour, if they are to discharge their functions to any advantage, must not for any the shortest period be allowed to be sullied or suspected".

C. The history of murmuring

1. *The Act of 1540*

The old Scots Act on this species of direct contempt, known as the Judges Act,[33] was entitled "The panis Imput to wrangous Jugis", and its text was as follows:

16–87

"ITEM It is Statute and Ordanit that fforsamekle as It hes bene hevelie murmurrit To oure souerane lord That his lieges hes bene gretlie hurt in tymes bigane be Jugis baith spirituale and temporale Quha hes nocht bene alanerlie Jugis bot plane solistaris partiale counsalouris assistaris and part takaris with sum of the partijs and hes tane grete geir And proffitt therefor IT IS Statute and ordanit in tymes cuming That all Justices schireffis lordis of Sessioune ballies of regaliteis provest and ballies of burrowis and thair deputis and all vtheris Jugis spirituale and temporale Als weill within regaliteis as rialtie sall do trew and equale Justice To all oure souerane lordis liegis without ony partiale Counsale rewardis or buddis taking forther than Is promittit of the law vnder the pane of tinsale of thair honour fame and dignitie giff thai be tentit and convictit of the

---

[32] Vol. I, p.406; see also Alison, *Principles of the Criminal Law of Scotland* (1832) Vol. I, p.575.
[33] 1540; Statute of the 7th Parliament of James V of Scotland, c.104 in Glendook's edition; c.22 in Thomson's folio edition, Vol. II.

samyn And giff ony maner of persoune murmuris ony Juge temporale or spirituale als weill lordis of the sessioune as vtheris and previs nocht the samin sufficientlie he salbe pvnist in semblable maner and sort As the said Juge or persoune quham he murmuris And sall pay ane payne arbitrale at the will of the kingis grace or his counsale for the Infamyng of sic personis Provyding alwayis geif ane spirituale man failyeis That he be callit befor his Juge Ordinar".

This statute seems to have been predicated upon the fact, or at any rate the received wisdom of the day, that judges had been partial in the performance of their duties. Its primary purpose therefore was to provide an injunction to them to do true and equal justice, before going on to set out the penalty for judges who failed to do so, namely loss of honour, good name and dignity.

2. *The making of false charges*

16–88 It was only apparently as a counterbalance to this provision (which was one of many directed at the same object by the old Scots Parliament)[34] that a penalty of comparable severity was provided for false accusers against them.[35] Thus, it appears that it would have been a defence under the statute to prove the truth of the charges. As Lord Neaves put it in *HMA v Robertson*[36]: "Even where the complaint was made in the most correct, specific, and intelligible manner, I think that the object of the statute was that, if the complaint could not be proved, the party making it did so at his own risk."

3. *The breadth of publication*

16–89 It seems arguable that the provisions against the "murmuring" of judges were meant only to apply to such accusations as were made to those set in authority over them, but it seems to have been so interpreted as to embrace publication on a wider scale (even though likely to be taken with a pinch of salt and not to result in any disciplinary proceedings). As early as 1586, the Act was applied to *Andrew Semple*,[37] a Bailie-depute of Paisley, who was ordered to be warded in the Castle of Blachness under pain of rebellion, and being "put to the horn", because of his actions in a fenced court in a Paisley tolbooth. He had in the presence of 200 persons, "by words indecent, heavily murmured, injured, blasphemed, disowned and lightlied[38] the judgment and proceedings of the Court of Session".

---

[34] See, *e.g.* the Acts 1469, c.26, "The Judge Ordinor being partial, or refusand to do Justice, sall satisfie the party, and pay an unlaw to the King"; 1457, c.76, "The punition of negligent Officers"; 1449, c.17 "of punition of Officiares trespassand in their office wilfullie"; 1487, c.103, "The Schireffe and Gauner suld thoill and arise the last day of the aire"; 1487, c.105, "That all actors first be perseared before their Judge Ordinor".

[35] See, *e.g. HMA v Robertson* (1870) 1 Coup. 404 at 422–3, Lord Neaves.

[36] (1870) 1 Coup. 404 at 424.

[37] (1586); see the discussion in *Newlands v Newlands* (1741) Mor. 7331 at 7334.

[38] Which means "spoke of contemptuously".

By the time of *HMA v Robertson*,[39] Lord Neaves held:

" 'murmuring' ... evidently could mean nothing else but dispersing complaints and murmurs against a Judge's equity and honesty, such as would destroy his usefulness if proved, and the dissemination of which ought to be punished if false."

The Act therefore would seem to have covered any false accusation of wrongdoing, whatever its context and to whomsoever it was addressed.

4. *The penalties under the Act*

Similarly, the Act's provisions as to penalty were that it should match that which the slandered judge might have faced if the allegation had been true. These were never easy to apply literally and by the early nineteenth century, in *Peter Porteous*,[40] were said by Lord Moncrieff only to signify that the crime should be regarded as a "serious" one. No cases invoking the Act were reported after *Robertson*, and it was removed from the statute book by the Statute Law (Repeals) Act 1973.

5. *The development of the common law*

False criticisms of judges appear also to have been punished at common law, quite apart from the provisions of the Act. Hume records the case of *Donald Campbell*[41]:

" ... who, in the course of a trial, when standing among the multitude by the courthouse, had openly accused the Earl of Athol, Justice-General, of gross partiality and corruption in the case: He had sentence, therefore, to stand two hours upon the cuckstool, and make public confession of his fault, and to have his tongue bored by the common executioner."

Shortly afterwards,[42] one Dougal was found by the council of the burgh to have reproached magistrates as "unjust judges" and "bankrupt rascals", and was fined 50 dollars. The Lords found that the burgh had no jurisdiction, but held nevertheless that a contempt had been committed, reducing the fine to 15 dollars. The sentence was, they said, " ... necessary for the defence of authority, and the respect of magistrates, without which they would become contemptible, and unable to serve the King in their stations."

At the beginning of the nineteenth century, a writer to the signet who wrote to the Lord President making adverse comments upon his conduct in his judicial capacity, and making insulting allegations against the court, was publicly censured and ordered to find caution for his good behaviour for five years.[43] Similarly a litigant who wrote letters defaming the judges and attacking the

---

[39] (1870) 1 Coup. 404.
[40] (1832) 5 Deas and Anderson 53.
[41] (1673) Vol. II, p.139.
[42] *Magistrates of Kirkaldy v Dougal* (1679) Mor. 1984.
[43] *Lord Advocate v Jamieson* (1822) 1 S. 285 (N.E. 264).

administration of justice was imprisoned for four months and ordered to find caution for his good behaviour, also for five years.[44]

16–95 At about the same time, doubt appears to have been expressed, at least in argument by counsel, as to the extent to which the common law on murmuring survived, and also as to whether the Act of 1540 had fallen into desuetude. In the case of *Duncan McIntyre*,[45] objection was taken to charges of slandering and defaming judges on the basis of lack of recent common law precedent, and because of doubt as to the continuing validity of the Act. The Crown deserted the diet *pro loco et tempore*.

16–96 These doubts were dispelled shortly afterwards in *Peter Porteous*,[46] where an indictment charging slander of judges, both at common law and under the statute, was found relevant in both parts. Lord Mackenzie noted:

> "This is a very unusual case, and, if not the first, is almost the first, of the kind which has come before this Court for a very long period. I have no doubt that the statute libelled on is in force. If it had not been so, there must have been a remedy at common law."

Lord Moncrieff was of the opinion that "although there had been no statute, no man can doubt that the offence stated in the minor proposition[47] would have been punishable as one of a serious nature."

16–97 In *HMA v Carr*,[48] charges of slandering, insulting and threatening a judge with reference to his official conduct or capacity were assumed to be relevant, and were dealt with by jury trial at common law.

16–98 This position was affirmed, as was the continuing validity of the 1540 Act, in *HMA v Robertson*,[49] which was the last properly reported authority on this branch of law. It concerned the making of slanderous complaints to the Home Secretary and Lord Chancellor about the conduct of a sheriff in the course of an earlier trial. Lord Neaves dismissed doubts which had been expressed both as to the common law and the statute:

> "I am of opinion that the indictment is relevant in all its parts. In the first place, with regard to the major proposition, and particularly as to the charge at common law, I cannot doubt that the slandering of a Magistrate in his official capacity is a crime. As to the statutory charge, the only matter connected with relevancy depends on the question whether the Act libelled is still in force. On that subject, I can also entertain no doubt, because I see that on various occasions it has been libelled and recognised by the court as a subsisting statute, although, no doubt, at the time it was passed, it was applicable to a state of things which does not now exist."

---

[44] *Lord Advocate v Hay* (1822) 1 S. 288 (N.E. 267).
[45] (1831) Shaw's Just. Cases 220.
[46] (1832) 5 Deas and Anderson 53 at 54.
[47] Traditionally, Scottish indictments were in the form of syllogisms and there was thus a major and a minor premise.
[48] (1854) 1 Irv. 464 at 468.
[49] (1870) 1 Coup. 404.

Another statute came into play in the case of *Lawrie v Roberts and Linton*.[50] **16–99**
A person in respect of whom a charge had been found not proven told the
magistrate that it was imprudent of him to have sat in the case. The magistrate
proceeded under s.341 of the Edinburgh Municipal and Police Act 1879, which
permitted the judge in cases of contempt to imprison or fine summarily and *ex
proprio motu*. A sentence of three days' imprisonment imposed by the Magistrate
was quashed by the High Court of Justiciary on the ground that such a sentence
was "entirely incommensurate with the offence which might be held to have
been committed". The sentence was characterised as a "harsh and oppressive
proceeding".

In the more modern unreported case of *Walter Scott Ellis*,[51] there was a charge **16–100**
of sending slanderous, insulting and threatening letters to a sheriff and prosecutor
involved in the earlier criminal trial of the accused. Perhaps because of the
element of menace and intimidation of them in the lawful discharge of their
functions, the court's jurisdiction was not challenged; an acquittal was eventually
obtained. No modern writer has doubted the principle that abuse of judges retains
its criminal character and is properly classifiable as contempt.[52] In practice, the
modern approach is only to take action against the most serious examples,
containing an element of real threat.

D. The right to criticise the judiciary

There is a risk that an excessive degree of protection for judges will stifle **16–101**
legitimate comment on their conduct and even criticism of the quality of their
legal decisions. "Justice is not a cloistered virtue: she must be allowed to suffer
the scrutiny and respectful, even though outspoken, comments of ordinary
men."[53]

Lord Skerrington expressed the view in *Kemp v Glasgow Corporation*[54] **16–102**
that[55]:

" ... anyone is entitled to criticise the law, provided that he does so in a manner which
is not disrespectful to the court and which is not calculated to interfere with the
administration of justice".

The case concerned an article in a Glasgow newspaper which criticised a
sheriff's decision after the conclusion of the case but before the appeal was heard.
It was described as "a decision which cuts at the root of our civil administration."
The "description" was held, however, not to be disrespectful to the sheriff but

---

[50] (1882) 4 Coup. 606, 9 R.(J.) 22, 19 S.L.R 625.
[51] High Court, February 1965; see Gordon, *op. cit.*, paras 50–03 and 29–62, n.75.
[52] See, *e.g.* Gordon, *op. cit.*, para.50–03; *Stair Memorial Encyclopaedia* Vol. 6, Contempt of Court, para.320.
[53] *Ambard v Att-Gen for Trinidad & Tobago* [1936] A.C. 322 at 335.
[54] 1918 S.C. 639 at 646, 1918 2 S.L.T. 2, 55 S.L.R. 553.
[55] See the English cases discussed in para.5–236; and the words of Lord Denning in *R. v Metropolitan Police Commissioner Ex p. Blackburn (No.2)* [1968] 2 Q.B. 150 at 155.

16–102

merely to consist of a fair comment on the state of the law as laid down by him.

16–103   It may be difficult to separate adequately criticism directed towards the administration of justice from attacks on an individual judge. Indeed, some of the early decisions seem hardly to distinguish between the two concepts.[56] The need to draw such a distinction has only been articulated relatively recently. Moreover, criticism of an individual judge's capacity or reasoning may be of positive benefit for the administration of justice itself (if, say, it speeds the retirement date of someone whose powers are failing).

E. Seeking to influence judges by criticism

16–104   One of the factors that clearly weighed with Lord Mackenzie in *Peter Porteous*[57] was that judges should be kept free, so far as possible, from any "undue" influence. The problem, however, is how one defines or limits that which is "undue". One approach might be to accept as a matter of policy that no judge would be capable of succumbing to such influence, in relation to any given proceedings, once he is *functus officio*. Yet it is by no means clear that if a judge were regularly held up to ridicule, in respect of his conduct and judgments even after proceedings were concluded, he would remain indefinitely uninfluenced as to his future conduct. On the other hand, if such a judge were to mend his ways as a result of such pressures, it might be thought no bad thing.[58] Where comments or criticisms are directed at a judge while proceedings are pending, it might be thought that they would be incapable of influencing the outcome. Yet in several modern cases, the possibility of unconscious influence by the media upon judges has been acknowledged in various jurisdictions.[59]

F. Recognition of the limits of the summary power

16–105   It has been expressly recognised that the contempt procedure has a potential for abuse, and that limits are necessary. In *Hamilton v Anderson*,[60] a case where a sheriff-substitute had suspended a procurator in his court for conduct in a pending case, and was sued for damages, Lord Cowan observed:

> "It is not to be supposed that every thing which mere waywardness, or caprice, or malice, may choose to designate contempt of Court, can inculpably be made by any Judge the engine of a hasty or harsh sentence inferring injury to the feelings, or, it may be, personal degradation to the party supposed to be guilty of the alleged contempt. Cases of that description may be imagined, which the protection the law casts around judicial acts will not cover. And I refer to the possibility of the occurrence of such cases only to guard myself against being supposed to give any sanction to the doctrine that

---

[56] See, *e.g. The Lord Advocate v W Jamieson, WS* (1822) 1 S. 285 (N.E. 264).
[57] (1832) 5 Deas and Anderson 53 at 54, a charge under the Judges Act 1540.
[58] Cp. the comments of Griffiths C.J. in *Nicholls* (1911) 12 C.L.R. 280, cited in para.5–258.
[59] *Kelly v O'Neill* [2000] I.R. 354 and *Al Megrahi and Fhima v Times Newspapers Ltd* 1999 S.C.C.R. 824. See also *Solicitor-General v Smith* [2004] 2 N.Z.L.R. 540.
[60] (1856) 18 D. 1003 at 1022.

a Judge can so act, and be certainly free from liability for the injurious consequences that ensue from his misconduct."

G. Protection for complaints to the proper authority

16–106 There has been some recognition that judges should be accountable in respect of the discharge of their judicial duties. This is clearly a matter of some delicacy having regard to the need for an independent judiciary exercising its functions "without fear or favour". While appeal to "the tribunal of the public, and general opinion" was frowned upon,[61] those who approach the proper authorities should be accorded a degree of privilege in doing so. As Lord Justice-Clerk Moncrieff explained in *Robertson*[62]:

" ... it is the right and privilege of every citizen of this country to make his complaint if we have one, against whomsoever it may be made, on whatever grounds, to the person who has power to redress it; and as long as that right is exercised in good faith or honesty, I do not think the exercise of it could ever form the ground of a criminal charge".

16–107 The cases are less than helpful as to which might be the appropriate body to hear such complaints. Some suggestion has been made that a supervisory role could be exercised by superior courts, although no obvious procedural means of securing this appears to be available, save by the appellate route.[63] For example, in *Petrie v Angus*,[64] Lord Justice-Clerk Macdonald, in considering the summary jurisdiction in contempt, commented that:

" ... if any inferior court of the country were to abuse this power, there can be no doubt that the Court of Justiciary has power to rectify such an abuse, and I do not doubt that if the supreme courts were to exceed their powers a remedy would be found through the State."

The issue remains unsettled at common law, and it may therefore be reasonably supposed that an extra-judicial remedy for any abuse of the contempt process, though theoretically available, would be rather difficult to obtain. Most grounds of complaint could now be addressed through an appeal.

16–108 A genuine desire to make a legitimate complaint may well be determinative of whether a contempt has been committed at all. It is also clear that state of mind will be important in deciding an appropriate disposal of the case; a rash accusation deserves a lower degree of punishment than one motivated by ill will

---

[61] *per* Lord Neaves in *HMA v Robertson* (1870) 1 Coup. 404 at 425.
[62] (1870) 1 Coup. 404 at 426.
[63] See, *e.g. Allardice and Boswell v Robertson* (1830) 4 W. & S. 102 at 116, Lord Wynsford; *Hagart's Trs v Hope* (1824) 2 H.L. Shaw's App. Cas. 125 at 135, Lord Robertson at 143, Lord Gifford.
[64] (1889) 2 White 358 at 363.

or malice.[65] Mental illness has long been regarded in Scots law as a mitigating factor in matters of penalty.[66]

III. MISBEHAVIOUR IN COURT

A. Cases of intoxication in court

16–109   If the accused,[67] a witness[68] or a juryman[69] should appear in a state of intoxication, this would appear to constitute contempt in itself.[70] It may well be that on occasion drunkenness is aggravated by disruptive behaviour.

16–110   At a sitting of the Land Court at Carlaway, Lewis,[71] a local councillor representing parties conducted himself in such a manner as to render progress in the case impossible. The hearing was adjourned and the matter reported to the chairman of the Land Court, who was by chance also on the island. He came to the scene to exercise the contempt jurisdiction conferred upon him as judge in charge of the court under the Small Landholders (Scotland) Act 1911. The councillor was detained in a police lock-up, and subsequently brought before the chairman, when he was found to have been "in an inebriated condition". The chairman, because the court had been disrupted by his conduct, found him in contempt (on that occasion and indeed at the hearing before the chairman himself) and, no explanation being offered, ordered him to be imprisoned for seven days, and fined £20.

16–111   A witness in a High Court trial was imprisoned for one month.[72] James Wemyss,[73] on trial for obstructing and defaming officers of the law, was treated similarly when he compounded his offence by appearing in court drunk. Indeed, in *HMA v Elizabeth Yates*,[74] a juryman was noticed to be drunk as soon as his name was drawn from the ballot, and before he had any chance to disrupt proceedings. Contempt was nevertheless thereby established and he was fined £20. In a civil jury case,[75] it was only after some hours that the juryman was observed not to be in a fit state, and to be distracting his fellow jurors; he was summarily fined £25 after tendering an apology.

---

[65] See *HMA v Robertson* (1870) 1 Coup. 404, at the sentencing stage: *per* Lord Neaves and the Lord Justice-Clerk at 428–30.
[66] See, *e.g. HMA v Carr* (1854) 1 Irv. 464 at 468, Lord Cowan.
[67] *HMA v McLean and McGillivray* (1838) 2 Swin. 185; the Circuit Court of the High Court of Justiciary ordered the accused to be sobered up for a week or so, "and thereafter to be set at liberty".
[68] *John Allan* (1826) Shaw 172; *Jas. Wemyss* (1840) Bell's Notes 165.
[69] *HMA v Elizabeth Yates* (1847) Ark. 238; *Wilson v John Angus & Sons*, 1921 2 S.L.T. 139.
[70] See, *e.g.* Macdonald, *op. cit.* p.266; *HMA v Elizabeth Yates* (1847) Ark. 238. See also Lord Adam in *McLeod v Speirs* (1884) 5 Coup. 387 at 398, 11 R.(J.) 26, 21 S.L.R. 530; Lord Justice-Clerk Macdonald in *Petrie v Angus* (1889) 2 White 358 at 364.
[71] *Macarthur v Carlaway Estate, Ltd* (1943) S.L.C.R. 45.
[72] *John Allan* (1826) Shaw's Just. Cases 172.
[73] *Wemyss* (1840) Bell's Notes 165.
[74] (1847) Ark. 238 at 242.
[75] *Wilson v John Angus & Sons*, 1921, 2 S.L.T. 139.

B. Insults in court: the common law

Defiant or insulting language used to a judge in court is an obvious form of direct contempt.[76] The court will nowadays be vigilant to draw a distinction between that which is truly insulting and mere lack of courtesy, especially on the part of those who are under pressure as a result of fulfilling an unfamiliar role in the administration of justice. An example is afforded by *Mowbray v Valentine*,[77] where an accused person representing himself in summary criminal procedure was found to be in contempt "in respect of his behaviour . . . in that he disrupted proceedings by delaying in asking questions, asking unnecessary questions and failing to abide by rulings of the presiding sheriff throughout the trial".

16–112

He appealed by the ordinary criminal method of stated case, and the finding was quashed. The High Court concluded:

16–113

" . . . We recognise that failing to abide by the rulings of a presiding judge during a trial may constitute contempt of court. On the other hand, when a party litigant is appearing, as was the case here, it is necessary to allow some latitude . . . we are not persuaded that in the present instance the appellant's failure to abide by the rulings of the presiding sheriff was designed to insult the court."

C. Non-attendance: the common law supplemented

Wilful failure to obey a citation as witness in criminal proceedings was held, on petition and complaint at the instance of the Lord Advocate, to constitute contempt.[78] The alleged contemnor claimed that he was threatened by the accused's friends but was nonetheless found guilty and sentenced to one month's imprisonment.

16–114

Section 155 of the Criminal Procedure (Scotland) Act 1995 now provides as follows:

16–115

"(1) If a witness in a summary prosecution—

(a) wilfully fails to attend after being duly cited; or
(b) unlawfully refuses to be sworn; or
(c) after the oath has been administered to him refuses to answer any question which the court may allow; or
(d) prevaricates in his evidence,

---

[76] *Robert Clark* (1829) Shaw 215. Modern examples include *Campbell v O'Brien* 1993 G.W.D. 8–562 where the complainer had blown "a loud raspberry noise" and *Bennett v Normand* 1993 G.W.D. 24–1492 (swearing at the magistrate).
[77] 1991 S.C.C.R. 494 at 504–50. See also para.16–45.
[78] *HM Advocate v Bell*, 1936 J.C. 89, 1936 S.N. 74. See also s.150 of the Criminal Procedure (Scotland) Act 1995, in relation to an accused who fails to appear. The Children (Scotland) Act 1995, s.45(8)(b) makes it an offence for a "relevant person" to fail to attend a hearing which he is obliged to attend. The penalty is a fine not exceeding level three on the standard scale: *ibid.*, s.45(9).

16–115 he shall be deemed guilty of contempt of court and be liable to be summarily punished forthwith[79] for such contempt by a fine not exceeding level 3 on the standard scale or by imprisonment for any period not exceeding 21 days.[80]

(2) Where punishment is summarily imposed as mentioned in subsection (1) above, the clerk of court shall enter in the record of the proceedings the acts constituting the contempt or the statements forming the prevarication.[81]

(3) Subsections (1) and (2) above are without prejudice to the right of the prosecutor[82] to proceed by way of formal complaint for any such contempt where a summary punishment, as mentioned in the said subsection (1), is not imposed.

(4) Any witness[83] who, having been duly cited in accordance with section 140 of this Act—

(a) fails without reasonable excuse, after receiving at least 48 hours' notice, to attend for precognition[84] by a prosecutor at the time and place mentioned in the citation served on him; or

(b) refuses when so cited to give information within his knowledge regarding any matter relative to the commission of the offence in relation to which such precognition is taken,

shall be liable to the like punishment as is provided in subsection (1) above."

16–116 When the act said to constitute the contempt is being minuted in accordance with subsection (2) above, care must be taken to identify in detail the nature of

---

[79] There is no necessity therefore to obtain social enquiry reports, and the punishment imposed is not a "sentence". See *Forrest v Wilson* 1993 S.C.C.R. 631, 1994 S.L.T. 490. The word "sentence" is specifically defined in s.307(1) to exclude an order for committal for contempt of court. The case is more fully discussed in para.16–420.

[80] It was held in *Forrest v Wilson* 1993 S.C.C.R. 631, that in so far as there is any inconsistency between the provisions of the Contempt of Court Act 1981, s.15 and the former statutory provisions of the 1975 Act, if the contempt fell to be dealt with under the latter, then the lower penalty there specified should apply. In *Rachel Logan v Procurator Fiscal for Kilmarnock* 1999 S.C.C.R. 584 where the sheriff had purported to pass a sentence of sixty days, this was held incompetent. An admonition was substituted because the complainer had been in fear, having been brought to court in the same prison van as the accused who had threatened her before she gave evidence. By contrast, in *McNeilage v HMA* 1999 S.C.C.R. 471, the petitioner had been held in contempt of court (through prevarication) and three months imprisonment was held not to be excessive.

[81] For decisions under the corresponding provision of the 1975 Act, s.344(2), see *McIntyre v Annand*, 1989 G.W.D. 20–833 and *Mowbray v Lowe* 1990 G.W.D. 10–529 (the requirement for contempt to be entered in the record applies to non-attendance as well as to prevarication). It was held in *Rachel Logan v Procurator Fiscal for Kilmarnock* 1999 S.C.C.R. 584 that the purpose of the statutory provision was to secure an accurate record of the relevant statements for the purpose of an appeal. It would be unreasonable for the appellate court to close its eyes to the contents of the sheriff's report when examining the facts alleged in the bill of suspension. Lord Kirkwood was following an earlier decision of Lord Justice-General Hope in *Riaviz v Howdle*, 1996 S.C.C.R. 20. That was determined under s.344(2) of the Criminal Procedure (Scotland) Act 1975. Thus, it was not a fatal objection that the clerk's minute did not contain "the statements forming the prevarication" but only the words "The Court held the accused [obviously a mistake] to be in Contempt of Court Prevarication". See also *McNeilage v HMA* 1999 S.C.C.R. 471, where the court had regard to "a very adequate report" from the sheriff.

[82] The word "prosecutor" is defined in s.307(1).

[83] The word "witness" includes "haver"; see s.307(1).

[84] The factors which justify precognition on oath are set out in *Carmichael, Complainer* 1992 S.C.C.R. 553. A Bill of Advocation followed refusal of an application to precognosce on oath. Precognition on oath applications on the part of the defence are to be dealt with in accordance with Criminal Procedure (Scotland) Act 1995, s.291 ("Precognition on oath of defence witnesses").

the misconduct.[85] The sections covering solemn trials in the Criminal Procedure (Scotland) Act 1995[86] contain no provision equivalent to those set out above, presumably because in the case of trial on indictment the matter is left to common law.

D. Other forms of misbehaviour at court

It would be a plain defiance of a judge, and of the court's authority, to refuse to be sworn or to affirm.[87] Other examples which have attracted punishment for contempt are the escape of a witness from the precincts of a court by forcing a padlocked door[88] and the granting of a false certificate of character.[89]

IV. PREVARICATION

A. Prevarication upon oath

Although it is rare for witnesses so to be punished, prevarication upon oath has always been regarded as contempt.[90] It has also been held to be a contempt to remain mute and to refuse to answer a competent question.[91] Hume described the underlying rationale[92]:

" ... it will not be amiss to add a word or two concerning prevarication upon oath, or the wilful concealment of the truth; which is next in degree to perjury, and seems chiefly to differ from it in the inferior boldness of the culprit who though desirous to mislead the Judge, and make a false impression, has rather chosen to compass his object in the way of an artful and tricking oath, than by the direct averment of affirmed falsehoods; or if he has ventured on any such, has not persisted in them till the close of his oath, and has effected ignorance and want of memory, with respect to things he cannot but know; more especially, if he is at last driven from all these shifts, and is constrained to cast a true, though, taken on the whole, an inherent and a contradictory deposition. As a scandalous contempt of the presence of the court and of the reverence of an oath, his offence may summarily be punished by the Judge before whom it happens (and it rather appears only by him and only at that time) with imprisonment or, in a more flagrant case, with infamy and pillory. Many examples of both are to be found, as well as in the books of sederunt, as of adjournal."

---

[85] *Strang v Annan* 1991 S.L.T. 676 (it was held not sufficient merely to relate that the complainer had been found guilty of contempt for prevarication); see also *Sze v Wilson* 1992 S.L.T. 569 (the exact words of the witness were not required; it was apparently sufficient for the general nature of the questions to be recorded).
[86] ss.91–99.
[87] *Tweedie* (1829) Shaw 223; *Bonnar v Simpson* (1836) 1 Swin. 39; *McLaughlin v Douglas & Kidston* (1863) 4 Irv. 273, 288. See the Criminal Procedure (Scotland) Act 1995, s.155(1), now repealed in relation to summary proceedings.
[88] *Innes* (1831) Shaw 238.
[89] *Nimmo* (1839) 2 Swin. 338.
[90] See *Robert Dewar* (1842) 1 Broun 233; *Wm Smith* (1854) 1 Irv. 378; *Adam Baxter* (1867) 5 Irv. 351; *McLeod v Speirs* (1884) 5 Coup. 387, 11 R.(J.) 26, 21 S.L.R. 530; *David McEwan & Daniel McLeod* (1829) Shaw 213.
[91] *Kerr* (1822) Shaw 68; *HM Advocate v Airs* 1975 S.L.T. 177.
[92] *Law of Scotland Respecting Crimes* (1844), Vol. I, ch.XI, p.380.

16–119 Another passage is to similar effect[93]:

> "Another article which equally concerns the witnesses on either part, is, that in case of prevarication, or obstinate concealment of the truth, they are liable to the summary and immediate censure of the court; who, either of their own proper motion, or on that of the Lord Advocate, may send the offender to gaol for a suitable time, or even, if the case require it, may apply some more severe correction. Unhappily, there has so often been occasion to apply this power of reproof, that it is needless to confirm it with particular examples".

Alison, however, does cite a number of examples.[94]

16–120 The word "prevarication" is not easily defined and may embrace various matters falling short of perjury; such as fencing with questions or otherwise demonstrating an unwillingness to be candid.[95] The vagueness of the term may lead to difficulty in the accused knowing exactly what is charged against him. In *Soutar v Stirling*,[96] for example, a sentence upon a witness found "guilty while under examination on oath of prevarication and wilfully concealing the truth" was quashed for lack of specification.

16–121 In former times, some rather quaint attempts were made to mould the punishment to fit the nature of the offence. In the case of *Robert or Thomas Ogilvie*[97]:

> "The Lords found prevarication in a witness, and ordained him to be laid in the irons in the tolbooth all night, and next day to be taken to the pillory, and stand with a paper on his face, with an inscription bearing his fault, between 10 and 12, and declared him infamous, and appointed him to continue in prison till further orders".

16–122 As late as 1799, the pillory seems still to have been used for cases of prevarication[98]; though shortly thereafter imprisonment for a definite period came to be the standard penalty.[99] Prevarication continued to be recognised as contempt at common law throughout the nineteenth century, and up to the present time.[1] The common law position is expressly preserved in the 1995 Act.[2]

---

[93] Hume, Vol. II, p.410.
[94] Alison, i, 474 ff; ii, p.549.
[95] See, *e.g. McLeod v Speirs*, (1884) 5 Coup. 387, 11 R.(J.) 26, 21 S.L.R. 530; *McEwen* (1829) Shaw 213.
[96] (1888) 2 White 19.
[97] See *The Heirs of the line of Towie v Barclay of Auchredy* (1669) Mor. 7417.
[98] See, *e.g. Robert Currie*, December 9–10, 1799, cited in Hume, Vol. II, ch.VI p.140; at a housebreaking trial, Currie "grossly prevaricated and contradicted himself on oath, was sent to gaol for eight days, and sentenced to stand on the pillory for an hour".
[99] *e.g. James Gray* (1831) B.N. 165; *HMA v Dewar* (1842) 1 Broun 233; *David McEwan and Daniel McLeod* (1829) Shaw's Just. Cas 213; *HMA v Baxter* (1867) 3 Irv. 351.
[1] See *McLeod v Speirs* (1884) 5 Coup. 387 at 393, Lord Adam, 11 R.(J.) 26; 21 S.L.R. 530; *Manson, Petr* (1977) S.C.C.R. Supp. 176 at 178; *Wallace v O'Brien* 1994 G.W.D. 9–524.
[2] See Criminal Procedure (Scotland) Act 1995, s.155(3).

One element of the law of prevarication caused the courts little difficulty. It was consistently held that a conviction based on the evidence of a witness who is found to have prevaricated was not on that ground alone to be overturned.[3]

B. Prevarication as a constructive contempt

The status of prevarication as a constructive contempt, justifying a summary penalty, has caused disquiet for many years. As Lord Young observed in *McLeod v Speirs*,[4] " ... modern ideas are against regarding it as a constructive contempt so as to warrant such punishment[5] on the spot without trial". It is in any event essential to keep a proper record of precisely what misconduct is said to have constituted the prevarication, justifying summary punishment, so that a proper opportunity may be afforded to an appellate court of assessing what conduct occurred and whether it could truly be described as amounting to prevarication. If the sentence imposed does not give the necessary information to enable the appellate court to determine whether or not the court below fell into error, that in itself would be a sufficient reason for setting the order aside.[6]

Lord Young explained the difficulties confronting appeal judges with the following *cri de coeur*[7]:

"I appreciate the difficulty of defining prevarication, and of specifying wherein it consists in any particular case. It is a loose and indefinite term, which may mean many different things short of perjury; the general idea which it conveys is manifest unwillingness candidly to tell the whole truth, fencing with questions in such manner as to show reluctance to disclose the truth, and a disposition to conceal or withhold it. So regarded, it is difficult of specification undoubtedly. But only fancy the impression or opinion of a Judge to this effect, stated as a reason for sentencing a party to a civil cause to imprisonment with hard labour! A distinct falsehood sworn to, although detected and exposed or even confessed on cross-examination, could be clearly stated without difficulty. What was the prevarication here, in the Sheriff's estimation, nobody but himself knows, or it is perhaps more accurate to say this Court has not been informed."

A further example of the problem is provided by *HMA v Smith*.[8] A witness had been imprisoned for prevarication in the course of a murder trial. Lord Justice-Clerk Hope was inclined to accept that there had been prevarication on his part. On the other hand, Lords Cowan and Handyside came to the conclusion that he

---

[3] See *Donaldson v Linton* (1861) 4 Irv. 115; *HMA v Robert Machie* (1844) 2 Brown 293; *Daniel Grant* (1820) Shaw 50; *William Brown* (1832) B.N. 255.
[4] (1884) 21 S.L.R. 530 at 534, 5 Coup. 387, 11 R.(J.) 26.
[5] The nature of the "punishment" referred to by Lord Young is indicated by the passage immediately preceding the words cited, namely " ... imprisonment with hard labour, not to speak of banishment or the pillory".
[6] *McLeod v Speirs* (1884) 21 S.L.R. 530 at 535, Lord Young 5 Coup. 387, 11 R.(J.) 26.
[7] ibid. This passage from Lord Young's judgment was cited by the Lord Justice Clerk in *McNeilage v HMA*, 1999 S.C.C.R. 471. He added that "What is prevarication depends very much on a collection of impressions derived from the content of a witness' evidence and also the manner and attitude displayed by that witness in the witness box".
[8] (1854) 1 Irv. 378 at 457.

was guilty of no more than "gross stupidity", which led to "confusion" in the evidence which he had given. He was accordingly discharged. The case was later cited by Lord Young to illustrate again the undesirability of summary procedure in such cases.[9]

16–127 Despite the reservations expressed about summary procedure over the years, it is still possible to pray it in aid in genuine cases of prevarication. For example, in *Curran, Petr*[10] a petition to the *nobile officium* was refused. The petitioner had been prevaricating as a Crown witness, for which the sheriff had sentenced him to nine months' imprisonment. He had given a series of "can't remember" and selective memory answers, but it became clear from later concessions that he had been plainly unwilling and reluctant to tell the truth. The sheriff had regarded it as one of the most blatant examples of prevarication, and the sentence was held not to be excessive (even though the petitioner had never been in prison, had two children for whom he was paying maintenance, and was in full time employment).

C. Prevarication and perjury distinguished

16–128 Although Gordon maintains that perjury too is a contempt,[11] a clear distinction has always been maintained between prevarication and perjury. Burnett notes that "*Prevarication* is distinguished from *perjury*, chiefly in this, that it is not the avowment of a plain and direct falsehood, but the concealment of the truth upon oath, or a contradictory and equivocating statement, *from an intention to falsify*".[12] The modern approach is that perjury should be dealt with by the ordinary criminal law in accordance with its more formal safeguards rather than as contempt,[13] even though it "may be regarded as a form of contempt of court".[14]

D. Statutory prevarication

16–129 Throughout the last two centuries, various pieces of legislation have sought to address prevarication, along with other minor forms of constructive contempt.[15] By s.360 of the Police Act 1850, for example, magistrates were given power to imprison for prevarication, although it was provided that "the sentence shall set

---

[9] *Soutar and Brown v Stirling and Ferguson* (1888) 2 White 19.
[10] High Court of Justiciary, October 11, 1996, G.W.D. 36–2093. This may be contrasted with the case of *Childs v McLeod*, 1981 S.L.T. (Notes) 27, where it was held that there was no evidence that the lack of recollection had been feigned.
[11] Gordon, *op. cit.*, para.50–04, citing *Manson, Petr* (unreported), High Ct., May 1977.
[12] Burnett, *A Treatise on Various Branches of the Criminal Law of Scotland*, (1811) pp.208–9 (Edinburgh). See also Lord Young in *McLeod v Speirs* (1884) 21 S.L.R. 530 at 535, 5 Coup. 387, 11 R.(J.) 26.
[13] See, *e.g. Soutar and Brown v Stirling and Ferguson* (1888) 2 White 19 at 25, Lord Young.
[14] *Green v Smith* 1987 S.C.C.R. 686 at 688, 1988 S.L.T. 175.
[15] *e.g.* Public Houses Acts Amendment (Scotland) Act 1862, s.27; Police and Improvement (Scotland) Act 1856, s.360; Edinburgh Municipal and Police Act, s.97; Summary Jurisdiction (Scotland) Act 1908, s.36; Summary Jurisdiction (Scotland) Act, 1954, s.33.

forth the nature of such offence." It was held in *Blake v Macdonald*[16] that there was no sufficient compliance with this requirement by the use of the words "having wilfully concealed the truth and having persisted in such concealment after having been duly cautioned."

More recently, the problem was addressed in s.33(2) of the Summary Jurisdiction (Scotland) Act 1954, which provided that where offenders were dealt with summarily the clerk of the court should record the act or acts constituting the contempt, and the statements comprising the prevarication. This was no doubt intended to provide an accurate record in case of appeal, with a view to overcoming the problems for appellate courts referred to by Lord Young in *McLeod v Speirs*.[17] The section was repealed by the Criminal Procedure (Scotland) Act 1975.[18] It would appear that there is no equivalent statutory provision today.[19]

16–130

E. Procedural aspects of prevarication

The appropriate procedural treatment of prevarication cases has also been a source of some difficulty.

16–131

1. *Caution to be exercised in reacting to prevarication*

A trial judge should take care in dealing with apparent prevarication on the part of a witness in order to avoid possible prejudice to the conduct of the proceedings, and the risk of a conviction being overturned. According to Renton and Brown[20]:

16–132

> "Neither the prosecutor nor the judge should say or do anything during the leading of evidence in presence of the jury to indicate their views on the behaviour of a prevaricating witness, such as asking for or ordering him to be detained until the end of the trial, or suggesting that charges will be brought against him."

This problem occurred in the trial leading to the appeal in *Hutchison and Harper v HMA*.[21] Crown witnesses prevaricated in the course of their evidence and, following convictions for assault and robbery, the appellants contended that the conduct of the advocate-depute and of the trial judge had prejudiced the jury's assessment of the credibility of witnesses whose evidence was important for the defence. The witnesses had been detained after giving their evidence, and it had been suggested in front of the jury that proceedings were to be brought

16–133

---

[16] (1890) 2 White 447.
[17] (1884) 21 S.L.R. 530 at 535, 5 Coup. 387, 11 R.(J.) 26. See the passage cited at para.16–125.
[18] Sch.10.
[19] But see para.16–115 above and s.155(2) of the 1995 Act.
[20] Renton and Brown, *op. cit.* para.18–53. See *Blair-Wilson, Petr* 1997 S.L.T. 621, discussed at para.16–50. And see *R. v Maguire* [1997] 1 Cr.App.R. 61, where a judge had told a defence witness, in the presence of the jury, that he would be arrested for contempt. The defendant's appeal was allowed on the basis that the judge had caused the witness to be arrested as he left the box, and was thus likely to have created prejudice in the jurors' minds.
[21] 1983 S.C.C.R. 504, 1984 S.L.T. 233.

16–133 against them. The judge had told the jury that they should not concern themselves with what he or counsel thought of the witnesses, or with what action might be taken against them, and said there was almost overwhelming evidence to support the charges. It was held on appeal that the conduct at the trial had indeed given rise to a risk of prejudice, but that there had not been a miscarriage of justice.

2. *The procedure for establishing prevarication*

16–134 For the purpose of establishing and dealing with prevarication summarily, it is not appropriate to adopt the procedure of a trial within a trial.[22] The matter is best left to the discretion of the presiding judge. It is so often a question of fact and degree, and the High Court is unlikely to interfere in a case where the lower court has a sufficient basis for the decision.[23]

V. Interference with Evidence

A. The rule stated

16–135 Hume[24] explained the law in this way:

> "It may be observed in the close of all, that if in the course of any criminal trial, or of the preparations for it, and relative proceedings, a discovery is made of any evil practice, tending to mislead, constrain, or corrupt the witnesses, or to destroy, suppress, or alter evidence of any kind; and whether this has taken place on the part of the prosecutor or the pannel, or even of their friends or favourers, or on the part of one witness with respect to another; any such malversation may be summarily punished with fine or imprisonment, according to the degree of the offence; and this either on a complaint to the Court, or, in some of those cases, on the knowledge and *ex proprio motu* of the court themselves. This is necessary *in poenam* of such a interference with the course of justice, as well as to deter from the completion or further prosecution of the evil purpose, pending the trial if not yet concluded."

B. Contempt involving physical evidence or documents of process

16–136 Gordon notes that "It is contempt of court for a person to dispose of a production which he has been cited to produce at precognition, or to abstract or retain unlawfully anything which has been lodged in court as a production".[25] Hume records the case of *James Dun*,[26] who was imprisoned for three months, on the complaint of the Lord Advocate, for wilfully destroying part of a sederunt-book which was called for in a precognition at the instance of the Crown. This case was held to settle the competency of a petition and complaint in *Lord Advocate*

---

[22] *Omond v Lees* 1994 S.C.C.R. 389.
[23] See, *e.g. Eagleson v Cardle* 1994 G.W.D. 5–259.
[24] Vol. I, p.384.
[25] *op. cit.*, para.50–11, citing *Lord Advocate v Galloway* (1839) 2 Swin. 465; *Watt v Ligertwood* (1874) L R 2 Sc. & D. Iv. 361 at 364, 1 R. 21 at 24, HL; *Levison v Jewish Chronicle Ltd* 1924 S.L.T. 755.
[26] Hume, Vol. II, p.140.

v Galloway,[27] in which a bank cashier cited to appear as a witness in a sheriff court criminal trial, and to bring with him a bill reputed to be forged, gave up the bill to a third party, on payment of its value, before the case.

The court will also order the return to their owners of any objects produced in an action but not returned by other parties after final judgment, and failure to obey would be treated as a constructive contempt of court.[28] The question of abstraction of documents of process is exhaustively dealt with in *Watt v Ligertwood*,[29] which contained, among others, the opinion of two Lord Chancellors (Cairns and Hatherley) to the effect that the removal of documents without the consent of the court is a clear contempt. **16–137**

The court has long exercised its powers to protect documents of process. In 1592, Sir Richard Cockburn,[30] Secretary of State, purported to order that a charter-chest, which was exhibited in court by order of the Lords, be removed. On a complaint being brought that it had been "violently spuilzied and taken away", he was ordered to enter his person in ward, in the Castle of Edinburgh under pain of rebellion and being "put to the horn". The same principle was applied, albeit less drastically, in *Levison v Jewish Chronicle Ltd*.[31] In a libel action the pursuer had lodged in process credentials, certain of which were impugned by the defenders in their pleading as being "false and fabricated". The process in the action was then borrowed by the pursuer through his agent and some of the documents abstracted. It was held that this had been done with a view to depriving the defenders of them for the purposes of their enquiries and preparations. This was calculated to prejudice their interests materially, and was held to be a contempt of court tending to pervert the course of justice. In the circumstances, neither fine nor imprisonment was deemed appropriate, and the defenders were granted *absolvitor* with expenses. **16–138**

Under s.155 of the Criminal Procedure (Scotland) Act 1995, it is contempt to refuse to produce documents in one's possession when required to do so by the court in summary criminal proceedings. **16–139**

C. Intimidation

Intimidation of witnesses is plainly calculated to interfere with the due administration of justice,[32] although such conduct could be charged as subornation or as attempting to defeat the ends of justice.[33] In modern practice the intimidation of witnesses would generally be dealt with by way of indictment. **16–140**

---

[27] (1839) 2 Swin. 465.
[28] *Gregson v Grant* (1910) 48 S.L.T. 6, 1910 2 S.L.T. 16. See also *Petrie v Angus* (1889) 2 White 358 at 364, Lord Justice-Clerk Macdonald.
[29] (1874) L.R. 2 Sc. & Div. 361 at 364, (1874) 1 R. 21, 24, HL.
[30] See *Newlands v Newlands* (1741) Mor. 7331 at 7344. The *Cockburn* case was one of the precedents discovered by the judges' research in *Newlands*.
[31] 1924 S.L.T. 755.
[32] See, *e.g. Forkes v Weir*, 1897 5 S.L.T. 194: Lord Kyllacky made the observation that it is a matter of discretion whether in any given case it is appropriate to take action.
[33] Cp. *R. v Kellett* [1976] Q.B. 372.

D. Interference with an accused in criminal proceedings

16–141 It was held in *Peter Graham*[34] to be an interference with criminal procedure to offer to a man, charged with theft, money in exchange for information as to the whereabouts of stolen property. Lord Justice-Clerk Moncrieff commented: "To tamper with a man while in custody for the purpose not of obtaining evidence which would lead to the ends of public justice but to the ends of private interests—and not only so, but substantially to offer a reward for a confession of guilt—is wholly inconsistent with the principles of our criminal procedure."

VI. MEDIA CONTEMPTS

A. Trial by newspaper: the common law approach

16–142 Contempt by media publication is nowadays an important and controversial area of the law, both in England and Scotland; not least because of the delicate balance which has to be maintained between freedom of speech (particularly the freedom of the press to inform its readers and to comment about matters of public importance) and the capacity of the courts to administer justice freely and impartially and to maintain public confidence.

16–143 The principle was explained by Hume[35] in a passage immediately following that concerned with the protection of witnesses and of evidence:

"The same law holds, and for the like reasons, with respect to all those practices, equally hostile, though in a different form, to the course of justice, and equally subversive to the principles of a fair trial, which tend to bias or preoccupy the public opinion, and by consequence that of the jury, concerning the guilt or innocence of the prisoner, the propriety of the prosecution, or the justice of the law touching the offence for which he is to be tried. It is fit, that on all these points the jurymen come into Court with their minds pure of any impression or favour or dislike, and open to the public and judicial information of those who are able and entitled to instruct them."

The underlying policy is that the court has "a paramount duty to ensure that a person indicted before the High Court shall receive a fair and impartial trial."[36]

16–144 Accordingly, it has been long established under the law of Scotland that contempt of court will be committed by the publication of material tending to prejudice the minds of potential jurors.[37] This "cannot be tolerated, for it is in our

---

[34] (1876) 3 Coup. 217.
[35] Vol. I, Ch.XII, p.384.
[36] *per* Lord Justice-General Cooper in *MacAlister v Associated Newspapers* 1954 S.L.T. 14. See also *Atkins v London Weekend Television Ltd* 1978 S.L.T. 76.
[37] See, *e.g. Watson Murray* (1820) Shaw's J.C.; *Gilfillan v Ure* (1824) 3 S. 15; *Henderson v Laing* (1824) 3 S 271.; *MacLauchlan v Carson* (1826) 5 S. 147 (N.E. 133); *Smith v John Ritchie & Co* (1892) 3 White 408; 20 R.(J.) 52.

view prejudicial to the interests of justice."[38] As was observed by Sheriff Gordon[39]: " ... the publication of any information relating to a projected criminal trial other than the bare fact of an accused's arrest and committal on a particular charge might well have been treated as contempt at common law".

On the other hand, where there was truly no prejudice created, comments made about matters of current controversy were not so treated, even though touching upon the subject-matter of pending proceedings.[40] The same principle was stated by the High Court in *Atkins v London Weekend Television Ltd*[41]: 16–145

"The discussion of public affairs and the denunciation of public abuses, actual or supposed, cannot be required to be suspended merely because the discussion or the denunciation may, as an incidental but not intended by-product, cause some likelihood of prejudice to a person who happens at the time to be a litigant."

B. Early cases

Hume reports the case of printers who published an opinion of English counsel on the circumstances of the trial of *Nairn and Ogilvy*, together with "notes highly injurious to the court and the jury". It was found[42]: 16–146

" ... that the publication of the said opinion, especially with the notes prefixed to it, was a high indignity to this Court, and a precedent dangerous to the constitution of this country; but in respect of the special circumstances of this case, and more particularly that the said printers have acknowledged their fault, and submitted themselves to the court; the said Lords, in the present case, do not proceed to inflict any punishment by fine, imprisonment, or otherwise, but dismiss them with a rebuke, which they appoint to be given them by the Lord Justice-Clerk, and which they hope will prevent the like from being done for the future".

In *Johnston and Drummond*,[43] where the facts were very similar, the court held: 16–147

" ... that the said publication is a false and slanderous representation of the proceedings in the said trial, and a gross indignity offered to this Court, calculated to create groundless jealousies and doubts of the due administration of justice by the Supreme Criminal Court of this part of the United Kingdom".

The printers were imprisoned for three months and until they found surety for their good behaviour for the future. There had been no sign of contrition.

A petition and complaint was presented in *Lord Advocate v John Hay*,[44] accusing Hay of contempt by circulating letters among judges and members of 16–148

---

[38] *MacAlister v Associated Newspapers Ltd* 1954 S.L.T. at 16, Lord Justice-General Cooper.
[39] *op. cit.*, (3rd ed.), para.50–12.
[40] See, *e.g. Cowie v George Outram & Co* 1912 1 S.L.T. 248, (1912) 6 Adam. 556.
[41] 1978 S.L.T. 76 at 79. These words are taken from the judgment of Jordan C.J. in *Ex p. Bread Manufacturers Ltd* (1937) 37 S.R. (N.S.W.) 242 at 249. See para.4–295.
[42] (1765) Hume, Vol. II, p.139.
[43] (1793) Hume, Vol. II, p.139.
[44] (1822) 1 S. 288.

16–148 Parliament relating to a civil action he was pursuing. On being cited to appear before both Divisions of the Court of Session, Hay declined to acknowledge their jurisdiction in terms which so incensed the court that they found this in itself to be a contempt and an aggravation of his slanderous publications.

16–149 *Henderson v Laing*[45] was a further example of publication calculated to influence public opinion, on this occasion in relation to a matter being litigated in the Court of Session. It was brought to the court's attention by petition and complaint at the instance of the innocent party. So too in *McLauchlan v Carson*,[46] save that in this case the Court of Session heard a petition and complaint regarding publication said to prejudice a case depending before the jury court.

Prejudgment

16–150 The notion of prejudgment was being addressed as early as 1777.[47] The agent for the prosecutor in a pending murder trial circulated comments tending to prejudice the public against the accused; he was sentenced to a month's imprisonment, and to find caution for his good behaviour:

> "... such publications are a high indignity to the court, and most dangerous to the course of justice, as tending to prepossess and inflame the minds of the country against the persons accused, and thereby obstruct the course of a fair trial".

16–151 Conversely, in *Ewan Macewan*,[48] it was the agent for the pannel "who had rashly published and circulated in the neighbourhood, a sort of narrative on his part, giving an account of the charge, and the circumstances of the case". This occurred after the service of the indictment and before trial. The agent was fined and a "censure of all such unfair practices was inserted in the record".

The distinction between public and private interests

16–152 The court clearly recognised the distinction between public and private interests in this branch of law in *Alex Ritchie v Stewart, Brown*.[49] This was a complaint by Ritchie, an agent, who had himself been the subject of a complaint by the Lord Advocate in respect of alleged corruption of witnesses, when acting in his professional capacity before a sheriff. Ritchie complained against the printers and owners of a newspaper who published what he considered to be a partial account of the Lord Advocate's complaint. Since the Lord Advocate's original complaint had been dismissed as incompetent (because the only appropriate procedure in the circumstances of the case would have been by way of indictment), Ritchie's complaint was likewise dismissed.

---

[45] (1824) 3 S. 384.
[46] (1826) 5 S. 147.
[47] *Gilkie*, Hume, Vol. II, pp.139–40.
[48] Hume, Vol. II, p.140.
[49] (1797) Hume, Vol. II, p.141.

The further point was made that "Ritchie's complaint did not conclude to have the offenders punished, as for a practice injurious to the interests of justice and a fair trial, but for damages only to himself, as injured by the more general knowledge of the charge exhibited against him". Accordingly the petition and complaint were dismissed as "incompetent". If it was appropriate for Ritchie to recover damages at all, they could only be recoverable by way of a regular action before a competent court. Thus, it was clearly recognised that the procedure for dealing with contempt of court was intended to serve a public purpose, namely the protection of "the interests of justice and a fair trial". 16–153

Two cases involving the political agitator Gilbert McLeod[50] were heard in the early nineteenth century. In the first, the Lord Advocate complained to the High Court that a firm of printers in which McLeod was a partner had circulated a publication critical of the Lord Justice-Clerk's comments in passing sentence. 16–154

Counsel for the alleged contemnors objected to the summary nature of the proceedings, given the fact that the trial was concluded, and submitted that there was therefore no legally depending proceeding which the publication could directly obstruct. He contended that in these circumstances any action by the Lord Advocate should take the form of an indictment in regular criminal process. The court repelled this objection without calling upon the Lord Advocate, and condemned McLeod and his partner in precisely the terms adopted in *Johnston and Drummond*.[51] McLeod was imprisoned for four months; the partner was to be rebuked by the judge he had criticised. 16–155

McLeod was also awaiting trial, in regular criminal form, for sedition, in respect of other publications. During that trial, Henry Cockburn, again for McLeod, complained that a newspaper had been guilty of contempt "by giving a false and aggravated statement of the nature of the charges made ... in the libel, and by making his case, though under judicial trial, a matter of public discussion, which even although the statements had been correct, would have been improper". 16–156

This complaint encapsulates different aspects of the contempt jurisdiction as it was then interpreted, as did the court's finding, that "such conduct is derogatory to the authority of this court, dangerous to parties, whether prosecutors or pannels, and subversive of the principles of a fair trial". The complaint was withdrawn after the writer and editor expressed contrition and explained that the decision to publish had been an error made in the hurry of the moment, but the court nonetheless reflected the public interest element of the case by imposing a fine and rebuking the editor, as well as sentencing the writer to one month's imprisonment. 16–157

---

[50] *McLeod* (1820) Shaw (J) 3; *Wm Watson and Alex Murray* (1820) Shaw (J) 9.
[51] (1793) Hume, Vol. 2, p.139 cited at para.16–147.

C. The common law criteria before the 1981 Act

16–158 The broad principle has continued to be applied during modern times and is easy to state. For example, in *MacAllister v Associated Newspapers Ltd*,[52] Lord Justice-General Cooper held that once a person had been committed for trial:

> " ... the public dissemination thereafter of insinuations or suggestions capable of prejudicing the public mind and the minds of prospective jurors with regard to a pending prosecution cannot be tolerated, for it is in our view prejudicial to the interests of justice".

16–159 So too in *Stirling v Associated Newspapers Ltd*,[53] Lord Justice-General Clyde spoke of the "test" as being whether "the steps that have been taken by the newspaper be such as to prejudice the impartiality of the ultimate trial". He also observed:

> " ... it is no part of our system that there should be a sort of preliminary trial of the case conducted in public by a newspaper, feeding to its readers pieces of evidence which the newspaper has unearthed, and which may ultimately be brought out in their proper setting at a trial in Court. Anything of the kind strikes at the very basis of the principle that in Scotland an accused is entitled to a fair trial by an unbiased and unprejudiced jury."

16–160 In the final stages of its application before the 1981 Act, the rationale of the jurisdiction was expressed[54] to be the " ... vital importance that the court should guard jealously, in the interests of justice, its inherent jurisdiction to vindicate the fair and impartial administration of justice and, as a corollary, to protect persons charged with crime and liable to be tried for such crime or other as may be libelled against them, from actions on the part of others which may prejudice their prospects of fair and impartial trial".

16–161 Prejudice seems to have been readily perceived and the threshold to have been low compared to that subsequently laid down by the 1981 Act. As Lord Avonside pointed out in *Stuurman v HMA*[55]:

> " ... contempt of Court arises when publication is 'liable' to interfere with the course of justice, 'liable' to prejudice an accused at his trial, 'may' prejudice prospects of fair and impartial trial".

16–162 Despite these general statements of principle it was clear, by the time the Contempt of Court Act 1981 was introduced, that the "prejudice" test was difficult to apply in such a way as to lead to consistency and predictability. It is perhaps surprising how far experienced judges could differ in their opinions as to whether or not the "test" is met in a publication case. In *Kemp, Petr; The*

---

[52] 1954 S.L.T. 14.
[53] 1960 S.L.T. 5 at 8.
[54] *Hall v Associated Newspapers Ltd* 1978 S.L.T. 241 at 246.
[55] 1980 J.C. 111 at 116.

Scotsman Publications Ltd, Petrs,[56] for example, the judge in a terrorist trial taking place in the summer of 1981 held that there was a risk that publications in newspapers describing the security arrangements made to protect particular witnesses, one of whom was known by the jury to be *socius criminis*, might influence jurors as to their credibility. Yet on appeal three judges found that they had "no hesitation" in deciding that there was "nothing in the language used which expressly or by implication constitutes a suggestion or insinuation bearing upon the question of credibility".

Editorial responsibility

In *HMA v George Outram and Co Ltd*[57] the High Court of Justiciary referred to the fact that the editor had not been on the spot at the time the critical decisions had to be made, and that when he went off duty he had understood that legal advice was to be taken on the offending article and "no doubt hoped that the legal advice given would be worth seeking". While recognising that in the normal course an editor must rely on the skill and judgment of subordinates, and upon such legal advice as the newspaper was able to obtain, the court found that he was personally liable:

16-163

"He is nevertheless, and he does not shirk this, fully responsible for what was done, and we have to add that that responsibility which the editor bears includes, in particular, his responsibility for the system ... which in its operation has proved to be so inadequate."

D. The vexed question of the *terminus a quo*

It is especially difficult to strike the right compromise between the important consideration of avoiding "trial by newspaper" and the competing public interest in maintaining freedom of information (to which more formal significance is now attached, especially in the light of Art.10 of the European Convention).[58] One of the critical factors is the point in time at which the contempt jurisdiction begins to apply. As to this issue, little help was to be derived from the institutional writers. It was observed in *Hall v Associated Newspapers Ltd*[59]:

16-164

"The language of the institutional writers is not sufficiently precise to identify with accuracy the point of time for which the court's jurisdiction in contempt by publication of prejudicial material can be exercised. All that can be deduced from their various works is that the court's twofold jurisdiction to prohibit the publication of prejudicial material, and to punish the publishers of such material, appears to require that there are before the court at the time of publication proceedings which are pending, that is to say, proceedings which can properly be said to have commenced".

---

[56] 1982 S.C.C.R. 1. Cf. the differences of opinion which emerged in *Cowie, Petrs* 1912 1 S.L.T. 248, between the Lord Justice-Clerk and Lord Guthrie.
[57] 1980 S.L.T. 13; see also the reference in the Lord Justice-Clerk's Memorandum to the circumstances in which it is appropriate to require the attendance of an editor, cited at para.16-42.
[58] Considered more fully in paras 2-142 *et seq*.
[59] 1978 S.L.T. 241 at 246.

16–165 It has for some time been recognised that it is necessary to have a fixed starting point for the court's contempt jurisdiction, so that it is apparent to everyone, and in particular to journalists, from *when* their freedom to report and to comment is to be restricted. Inevitably, any such starting point is going to be arbitrary and will not catch every instance of damaging prejudice. As the court in *Hall* noted[60]:

> "It is, of course, perfectly obvious, as has been pointed out repeatedly in earlier cases and, indeed, in other jurisdictions that the administration of justice may suffer just as much injury as the result of publication or other conduct by the Press or by any other person or agency *before* the court's jurisdiction in contempt can be invoked, as it may suffer by publication or other conduct thereafter" (emphasis added).

16–166 The point at which proceedings become "active" for the purposes of the strict liability rule is specified by Sch.1 to the 1981 Act.[61] Yet the previous common law approach continued to influence the Scottish courts in their implementation of the statutory provisions, and it is necessary to consider carefully how this problem was addressed in the years prior to the enactment. One of the main areas of controversy during this period, which exercised the Phillimore Committee, was the question when proceedings should first be regarded as "pending" and the restraints of the contempt jurisdiction thus come into operation. This point arose in England in *R. v Savundranayagan*[62] and also in two leading cases in Scotland: *Stirling v Associated Newspapers Ltd*[63] and *Hall v Associated Newspapers Ltd*.[64] Each of these two decisions requires close consideration.

1. *Stirling v Associated Newspapers Ltd*[65]

16–167 The editor and publishers of the *Scottish Daily Mail* were ordered to appear in the High Court following a petition brought by a man accused of a double murder. After he had been "detained" but before he had been arrested, charged or committed, the newspaper published a photograph of him and an article which contained statements apparently from his mother, and from other persons, who might have been called upon to give evidence at his trial. All these matters, the petitioner contended, would be likely to cause prejudice to the impartial consideration of issues at his trial.

16–168 The proprietors were fined £5,000 and the editor £500. The principle was stated by the Lord Justice-General[66]:

> " . . . once a crime has been suspected and once the criminal authorities are investigating it, they and they alone have the duty of carrying out that investigation. If

---

[60] At 249–50.
[61] Although, as is pointed out in paras 5–67 *et seq*, these provisions are not necessarily exhaustive for all purposes in the law of contempt.
[62] [1968] 1 W.L.R. 1761.
[63] 1960 S.L.T. 5, 1960 J.C. 5.
[64] 1978 S.L.T. 241.
[65] See also "Contempt of Court by Newspapers—The 'Scottish Daily Mail' Case", 1960 S.L.T. (News) 29.
[66] 1960 S.L.T. at 8.

a newspaper arranges an interview with any person in any way involved in the suspected crime and then publishes the results of the interview, or an article based upon it, the newspaper is doing something which in all probability will interfere with the course of justice and hinder a fair trial. For the person interviewed may ultimately be a witness at that trial and the members of the jury may well read the account of the interview in the press, or hear criticisms of the terms of the newspaper's story before they go into the jury-box to judge the case."

Although the case gave rise to considerable newspaper comment, the *Scots Law Times* pointed out at the time that laymen should not misconstrue the judgment on the basis of certain passages which, read in isolation, appeared to make alarming innovations in the law. Particular attention was drawn to the passage: "Once a crime has been suspected, and once the criminal authorities are investigating it, they and they alone have the duty of carrying out the investigation." Taken as it stands, that passage could be understood as restricting the right of the defence advisers themselves to investigate matters; but, since the whole tenor of the court's decision was directed towards the accused receiving a fair trial, such an interpretation would be perverse. The court appears to have been intending, in truth, to limit the practice of journalists investigating the circumstances of a crime during the pendency of the relevant charge, or charges, and then publishing their findings to the prejudice of a fair trial.[67]

16–169

There was, however, another respect in which the anxiety of the press about the decision was not so misplaced. This related to the vexed question of the *terminus a quo*: the moment when newspapers begin to be at risk under the law of contempt. It was this problem to which the Phillimore Committee later directed so much attention.[68] What alarmed journalists was the suggestion made in the case that newspaper publication could amount to contempt from the moment when the authorities have started to investigate the crime in question. This gave rise to obvious practical difficulties. Not only was there the question of definition; that is to say, what actually constitutes the commencement of an investigation. There was also the fact that investigations are frequently carried out secretly, or at least on a confidential basis. It may not be known, or even ascertainable, by newspaper reporters whether and to what extent official enquiries are under way.[69]

16–170

Similar uncertainty arose in England after the comments of the Court of Appeal in *R. v Savundranayagan*,[70] to the effect that the law of contempt might be applicable in respect of proceedings not yet begun but which could be perceived as "imminent."[71] Again, whether or not proceedings were imminent could well depend upon subjective considerations or confidential matters not

16–171

---

[67] Cp. the English decision *Att-Gen v Morgan* [1998] E.M.L.R. 294, para.4–79.
[68] Cmnd. 5794, para.84.
[69] Cp. the need to avoid naming the victim of a sexual offence from the moment a complaint is made: see para.8–19.
[70] [1968] 1 W.L.R. 1761. For further consideration of this case see para.5–85.
[71] "Imminent" was a word appearing in s.11 of the Administration of Justice Act 1960, now repealed, which had no application to Scotland. The concept of "imminence" seems to have survived in England, in relation to common law contempts, and this problem is discussed in paras 5–67 *et seq.*

available to the press. Naturally this placed editors and other journalists in practical difficulty, since they often wished to know with certainty whether a proposed story would or would not infringe the law. The approach of the Phillimore Committee was to prescribe a fixed point in respect of both civil and criminal proceedings from which the law of contempt would begin to have application.

2. *Hall v Associated Newspapers Ltd*

16–172   Between the Phillimore Report and the enactment of the statute, however, the matter was again considered by the High Court in *Hall v Associated Newspapers Ltd*.[72] In that case a bench of five judges reviewed the law of contempt and expressly disapproved certain of the *dicta* in *Stirling*.

16–173   Archibald Hall was arrested on January 16, 1978 by the police in connection with a murder enquiry, and on January 19 an article appeared on the front page of the *Daily Mail* under the heading "Six victims—and Police talk of more." This described the enquiry and revealed personal details about the person in custody (later held to be a clear example of "trial by newspaper"). Subsequently Mr Hall was charged with murder and appeared at the sheriff court several days later. He presented a petition to the High Court alleging that the publication constituted a gross interference with the course of justice. He also invited the court to consider whether the article was a contempt, and to prohibit the proprietors from publishing any further articles of a similar prejudicial character until the conclusion of his trial.

16–174   At the initial hearing on March 3, 1978 before Lord Justice-General Emslie and Lords Cameron and Robertson an order prohibiting such further publication was made by consent. It was also argued that the publication had occurred before any jurisdiction in contempt had arisen, and because the point was considered to be of some difficulty the matter was adjourned to a bench of five judges and further argued on June 13 and 14. The additional judges on that occasion were Lord Justice-Clerk Wheatley and Lord Avonside.

16–175   It was argued for the respondents that there was a material distinction, for determining when the court's contempt jurisdiction arose in relation to criminal proceedings, between a period after committal on the one hand and the period after arrest but before committal on the other; and that in this respect *Stirling* was therefore wrongly decided.

16–176   In its reserved judgment the High Court was primarily concerned with this question of identifying the moment when the contempt jurisdiction began to apply, which they regarded as being free from authority apart from *Stirling* itself. It was recognised that prejudicial publications occurring before the contempt jurisdiction arose could be just as damaging as a publication afterwards, but this was a matter which could be left to the control of the general criminal law. Such

---

[72] 1978 S.L.T. 241. See A.M. McLean, "Contempt in Criminal Process" 1978 S.L.T. (News) 257.

conduct would not constitute contempt of court as such, but might fall to be dealt with as an attempt to pervert or interfere with the course of the administration of justice (assuming the presence of the requisite state of mind).

In determining when the rules of contempt became applicable to *criminal* proceedings the court concluded that no guidance could be derived from the institutional writers,[73] except that the proceedings must have commenced. In civil proceedings there was no difficulty about this, because such proceedings may be said to have commenced from the service of the summons or petition or, in the sheriff court, by service of the initial writ. In the case of criminal proceedings, however, the authorities afforded no guidance as to whether they commenced on or prior to committal. The court expressed the view that the reasoning in *Stirling* was unsound largely because, although reliance had been placed upon the authority of *Smith v John Ritchie & Co*,[74] in that case "no question of contempt of court was considered in relation to any of the pre-committal publications." Thus, if the view of the High Court in *Stirling* was to survive, that the contempt jurisdiction could apply *prior to* committal, then it must survive for other reasons. 16–177

Certainly there was nothing in *Smith* or *MacAlister* to indicate that the jurisdiction did *not* arise prior to committal; the court in *Hall* therefore proceeded on the basis that the immediate question was free from authority. They therefore had to determine the matter *de novo* upon a proper application of the policy underlying the jurisdiction. The conclusion was that[75]: 16–178

"... the starting point of the contempt jurisdiction in the administration of criminal justice will be the moment when it can be said that proceedings have commenced so as to bring about a relationship between the court and a person charged with crime, who may ultimately stand trial, in which the person concerned has come under the care of the court and within its protection".

It was observed that anyone who has been committed for trial is entitled to protection, even though he may never be indicted or proceed to trial. That protection was directed not only to the interests of the accused but also towards the impartial administration of justice. These important considerations, however, do not suddenly arise upon committal. The process of apprehending, charging and bringing a person to trial does not begin where the person is brought before the court on petition. It will normally begin by the arrest of the accused by the police upon a specific charge. Thus there is at the stage of the arrest, just as at the stage of committal for further examination, a person accused of crime who, if the subsequent steps in the process are taken, may ultimately stand trial on the charge on which he has been arrested or on other charges. 16–179

Reference was made to other forms of protection which the law grants to such persons; in particular to s.321(3) of the Criminal Procedure (Scotland) Act 16–180

---

[73] See para.16–164.
[74] (1892) 3 White 408.
[75] 1978 S.L.T. at 248.

16–180 1975.[76] This provided that the accused must be informed of the charge on which the arrest had been made, and be brought before the court (a magistrate) not later than in the course of the first day after his arrest. Reference was also made to other rights conferred by s.19 of the 1975 Act.[77] A man in custody is protected also by the law against unlawful interrogation lest he incriminate himself, and the court commented that it would be strange if at that stage he was protected by the court against prejudicial interrogation but not against conduct on the part of others which was likely to prejudice the fairness and impartiality of his trial.

16–181 The court concluded in the light of these factors that an accused person was entitled to be protected from the moment of arrest, and that the law of contempt should thus apply from that point. Furthermore, although it was not necessary to the decision in point, the court felt it appropriate to identify a second point at which the jurisdiction would arise; namely where a petition is presented to the court for a warrant to arrest a named person and the warrant is granted. At that point the court has become seised of proceedings against an individual which, if they move through all subsequent stages of the process, will end in trial. In those circumstances the machinery of justice is set in motion by the court itself, and logically therefore the accused person is entitled to the protection of the court against any injury he may sustain from the publication of material prejudicial to a fair and impartial trial.

16–182 Although the reasoning applied in *Stirling* was said by the court to be unsound, the decision did in fact accurately reflect the law of Scotland on this important matter of the commencement of the application of the court's contempt jurisdiction. Nevertheless, in *Hall* the earlier *dicta*, which tended to suggest that the jurisdiction ran from the time when a crime was suspected and investigation by the criminal authorities began, were expressly disapproved. At that stage any question of prejudice should be left to the general criminal law. Although circumstances might arise in which journalists might not know that an arrest had taken place, or that a warrant had been granted, these were matters which should be taken into account in fixing the appropriate penalty. They would not provide a defence as such.[78]

16–183 In practice, the court took the view that the problem was unlikely to arise often since the newspapers were generally concerned with "notorious cases" attracting wide public interest. Finally, it was held, in relation to summary procedure, that the jurisdiction of the court to treat prejudicial publications as contempt would arise at the time of arrest or service of the complaint, whichever be the earlier.

E. Police press announcements

16–184 In *Hall* the court expressed the opinion that it was undesirable for police to disseminate information to the press after an arrest, since this had been to a large

---

[76] See now s.135(3) (4) of the Criminal Procedure (Scotland) Act 1995.

[77] See now ss.17 and 35 of the Criminal Procedure (Scotland) Act 1995.

[78] This is a matter which is now subject to the statutory defence under s.3 of the 1981 Act. See paras 4–236 *et seq.*

extent the source of the problem.[79] The warning was repeated in *HM Advocate v George Outram & Co Ltd*.[80] Four people had been arrested on drugs charges and an article appeared two days later on the front page of the *Glasgow Herald*, identifying the accused and describing in detail the results of the police investigations in such a way as to suggest guilt. The Lord Advocate brought a petition, and contempt was admitted. The court said that the publication of an article in those terms was "well nigh incomprehensible" and that the contents were "in the highest degree objectionable."

It was said that after *Atkins*[81] and *Hall*[82] any journalist in Scotland ought to have realised that the publication of such an article would constitute contempt of the gravest kind. In the circumstances little regard was paid to the factor, relied upon in mitigation, that the lawyer's advice had been sought by telephone in advance of publication. The source was said to have been a Press Association release based in turn upon police sources south of the border; once again the court emphasised how unwise it was for the police to provide information to the press, at least at a time when the person or persons to whom it related had been arrested on criminal charges. A fine of £20,000 was imposed upon the publisher and one of £750 upon the editor, who was regarded as being fully responsible even though he had gone off duty and had relied upon legal advice being sought.[83] He was held to be responsible for the checking system, which in the instant case had proved to be inadequate.

16–185

These cases highlight a particular area of difficulty for media which publish in both England and Scotland. In Scotland the police have never been regarded as free to make disclosures, unless specific permission is given on the instructions of the Procurator Fiscal to release information in the course of an enquiry. This would normally only arise where the police are having difficulty with some particular crime and the release of information is thought to be necessary to encourage members of the public to come forward. It would not include the details of a suspect or of an accused person who has not yet come before the court. When a person does appear before the court (generally in private before a sheriff on a serious matter) his name, address and age would be released together with the fact that he had been remanded for further examination. Thus, in circumstances where there is a Scottish aspect to an enquiry, and the police south of the border follow their practice of more open disclosure, there may well be pitfalls for editors who report those disclosures in publications in Scotland.

16–186

F. The remaining uncertainty

In none of the cases did the court attempt to lay down any specific rules or guidelines for editors to follow. The judges confined themselves to considering general principles and applying them to the facts of the individual cases before

16–187

---

[79] For a discussion of this continuing problem, see para.1–164.
[80] 1980 S.L.T. 13.
[81] 1978 S.L.T. 76. Further discussed at paras 16–192 *et seq*.
[82] 1978 S.L.T. 241.
[83] See para.16–163. For editorial responsibility in England, see paras 4–212 *et seq*.

16–187 them. The circumstances of pending cases vary infinitely, of course, and any attempt to prescribe in advance what would be acceptable behaviour on the part of the media would inevitably fail to cater for all eventualities. All the court could do was to state the principle which the law seeks to uphold, namely "that a person indicted before the High Court shall receive a fair and impartial trial."

16–188 As Lord Hewart C.J. observed in *R. v Evening Standard Co Ltd*[84]:

> "It is not possible for the court, nor has it the inclination, to suggest to the responsible editors of the newspapers what are the lines along which they ought to proceed. Any such task as that is entirely beyond the province of this or any other tribunal . . . It might be that a date, a place, or a letter or some other one thing, which considered in itself looks trivial, might prove in the end to be a matter of paramount importance. It is impossible to foresee what is of importance."

16–189 To some extent, it *is* necessary in the light of s.2 of the Contempt of Court Act 1981 to decide in advance of trial what issues are going to be of importance. The strict liability rule[85] in its application entails that the court will have to determine in advance whether a publication creates a "substantial risk" that the course of justice in the proceedings under consideration will be "seriously impeded or prejudiced." The court may be called upon, for example, to decide in advance of any public statement of the accused's case to what extent dates may be of importance, whether identification[86] is likely to be an issue, or whether an alibi defence is likely to be prejudiced.

16–190 In practice, this may not be as difficult or as speculative an exercise for the court as might at first appear. Judges will only be required to determine such questions on an application supported by evidence. Thus, at least some preliminary account will have to be given of the issues which are likely to remain live at the date of trial; it will be in the light of this account that the court will have to determine to what extent there is a risk of prejudice. (It seems, however, that the leading cases of *Atkins v London Weekend Television Ltd*[87] and *Hall v Associated Newspapers Ltd*[88] would not have been determined any differently in the light of the provisions of the 1981 Act.)

G. When were proceedings treated as concluded?

16–191 The conclusion of proceedings, civil or criminal, for the purpose of determining when the contempt jurisdiction would cease to apply, was not a matter which had been clearly decided at common law.[89]

---

[84] (1924) 40 T.L.R. 833.
[85] As to which see generally ch.4.
[86] See *Atkins v London Weekend Television Ltd* 1978 S.L.T. 76 and the cases of *Lawson* (1937) 81 S.J. 280; *R. v Daily Mirror Ex p. Smith* [1927] 1 K.B. 845.
[87] 1978 S.L.T. 76.
[88] 1978 S.L.T. 241.
[89] See *McLeod*, discussed in paras 16–154 *et seq.*

H. Discussion of public affairs: *Atkins v London Weekend Television Ltd*

The Contempt of Court Act 1981 provides for a defence in s.5[90] if the publication in question forms "part of a discussion in good faith of public affairs or other matters of general public interest . . . " and the risk of impediment or prejudice to particular legal proceedings is "merely incidental" to the discussion. Even before the Act, however, it had been recognised in Scotland,[91] as elsewhere,[92] that some protection would be required in modern conditions for the discussion of matters of public concern.

16–192

The High Court in *Atkins v London Weekend Television Ltd*[93] adopted the words taken from the judgment of Jordan C.J. in *Ex p. Bread Manufacturers Ltd*[94]:

16–193

> "The discussion of public affairs and the denunciation of public abuses, actual or supposed, cannot be required to be suspended merely because the discussion or the denunciation may, as an incidental but not intended by-product, cause some likelihood of prejudice to a person who happens at the time to be a litigant."

It so happened, however, that this principle did not avail the respondents in that case. The background was that the petitioner was a nursing sister who had been charged with assaulting a 13-year-old girl to the danger of her life, in that it was alleged that she had tried to block her air supply while she lay in the intensive care unit at the Edinburgh Royal Infirmary in February 1977, suffering from severe brain damage. On November 13, 1977, the evening prior to the commencement of her trial, the respondents broadcast a programme entitled "Weekend World" throughout the United Kingdom.

16–194

Half of the programme consisted of a feature concerned with the ethical problems facing doctors in cases of patients suffering from severe brain damage, and the extent to which they should be kept alive artificially. It was given the title "The Living Dead." Quite apart from containing general discussion with surgeons and others about the appropriateness of withdrawing life support from such patients, the programme mentioned a number of specific instances, including that of the girl to whom the pending charge of assault related. The petitioner was herself mentioned and her photograph (taken apparently without her consent) was also shown twice. Furthermore, the circumstances of the alleged offence were described, and it was said that the trial was likely to become a talking point.

16–195

The sheriff adjourned the date of trial until December 14, 1977. The diet was not called and the indictment fell, so that if the Lord Advocate decided to proceed

16–196

---

[90] For the text and discussion in the English context, see paras 4–293 *et seq.*
[91] See, *e.g. Riddell and Raeside v The Clydesdale Horse Society* (1885) 12 R. 976 at 983, Lord President Inglis at 984, Lord Shand.
[92] For example, in Australia: *Ex p. Bread Manufacturers Ltd* (1937) 37 S.R. (N.S.W.) 242, discussed in paras 4–294 *et seq.*
[93] 1978 S.L.T. 76.
[94] (1937) 37 S.R. (N.S.W.) 242 at 249.

a new indictment would have to be served. The High Court was asked by Mrs Atkins in the exercise of its power *nobile officium* to prohibit London Weekend "from broadcasting, transmitting and publishing any programme or feature or comment or any material calculated to create prejudice to, or giving rise to possible prejudice to, any future trial of the petitioner." Answers to the petition were lodged by the Lord Advocate and he appeared in order to assist the court.

16–197 On January 13, 1978 the court gave judgment, finding " . . . not the slightest doubt that the references to the petitioner in the context of this particular feature as a whole were in the highest degree likely to prejudice the petitioner's prospects of a fair and impartial trial." Indeed the court entertained the gravest doubt whether a fair and impartial trial was now possible, however carefully the trial judge might direct the jury. There was the " . . . clear insinuation that the real if not the only question which would arise out of the petitioner's trial would be whether she was medically and morally justified in committing the acts charged." Further, the identity of the person who had done the acts in question was a matter which the Crown had to establish.[95]

16–198 On the matter of "incidental risk", although the court accepted the proposition of Jordan C.J.[96] in general terms, it was said to have no application to the case in question. Specific references to an immediately pending criminal trial were made part of the commentary, and on the eve of the trial itself. Indeed, counsel had only referred to *Ex p. Bread Manufacturers Ltd* during that part of his argument in which he was considering the possible effect which the programme might have had on the hypothesis that it had been broadcast *without* reference to the petitioner.

16–199 Now such a case might well give rise to an argument that there was a defence under s.5 of the 1981 Act,[97] although it seems unlikely that the court would uphold such a defence on those facts. There are similarities between the terms of s.5 and the words of Jordan C.J. The fact that the High Court in *Atkins* so clearly found this judgment irrelevant to the facts with which they were confronted gives strong grounds to suppose that, if they were to arise in the future, the court would find the s.5 defence to be equally inapplicable.

I. Reporting court proceedings

16–200 It is important that the public should be fully informed of what takes place in court proceedings, and more generally in relation to the administration of justice.[98] Yet there are countervailing public policy considerations which require that some restrictions be imposed. In particular, it was long ago recognised in Scotland that there is no need for the public to be informed of the allegations

---

[95] Cp. *Lawson* (1937) 81 S.J. 280; *R. v Daily Mirror Ex p. Smith* [1927] 1 K.B. 845.
[96] Cited in para.16–193.
[97] For the text of s.5, see para.16–364.
[98] See the remarks of Lord Clyde in *Stirling v Associated Newspapers Ltd* 1960 S.L.T. 5, 7, quoted in para.16–203.

made by parties in the early stage of proceedings before the issue is aired in open court[99]:

> "Reports of depending cases are at all times very dangerous, and tend to interfere with the administration of justice. It may be perfectly lawful to state that an interesting point of law has arisen, and is depending in Court; but it is extremely improper to enter upon a history of the facts of a case. This ought not to be done until it is decided".

Thus, so far as the law of defamation is concerned, no privilege would be accorded to the reporting of such allegations, or to their communication by a party or his agent to the press. Moreover, the revelation of such information may in itself constitute contempt.

It was also recognised at common law that sometimes the protection of the administration of justice requires that even the right of newspapers to cover what takes place in open court may have to be postponed (a matter now expressly covered in s.4(2) of the Contempt of Court Act 1981).[1] It may be desirable to consider in a little detail, however, the common law background.

1. *Contemporaneous reports of proceedings in open court*

Once a case comes to court, there is a general freedom to publish accounts of proceedings. In *Richardson v Wilson*,[2] a defamation action, Lord President Inglis stated:

> "The publication by newspapers of what takes place in Court at the hearing of any cause is undoubtedly lawful; and if it be reported in a fair and faithful manner the publisher is not responsible though the report contain statements or details of evidence affecting the character of either of the parties or of other persons; and whatever takes place in open Court falls under the same rule, though it may be either before or after the proper hearing of the cause. The principle on which this rule is founded seems to be that, as Courts of Justice are open to the public, anything that takes place before a Judge or Judges is thereby necessarily and legitimately made public, and, being once made legitimately public property, may be republished without inferring any responsibility".

So too, in *Stirling v Associated Newspapers Ltd*,[3] Lord Justice-General Clyde observed:

> " . . . the press in this country is free, free in particular fairly to report anything that occurs in open court when a trial takes place, free to publicise anything that is said or done by a judge or a counsel or a witness, or by the jury at that trial. For in doing so the press is performing a genuine public service in enabling the public to see for

---

[99] *McLauchlan v Carson* (1826) 5 S. 147. Cp. the English decision of *Stern v Piper* [1997] Q.B. 123, CA, and the New Zealand case of *Lucas & Son (Nelson Mail) Ltd v O'Brien* [1978] 2 N.Z.L.R. 289.
[1] For our main discussion of s.4(2), see paras 7–111 *et seq.* See also paras 16–371 *et seq.*
[2] (1879) 2 R. 237, 261, 17 S.L.R. 122; see too *MacLeod v Lewis Justices of the Peace* (1892) 20 R. 218 and the English authorities considered at paras 7–16 *et seq.*
[3] 1960 S.L.T. 5 at 7.

16–203 themselves whether justice is being done. The high standard of discrimination and fairness with which this work has been done by responsible Scottish newspapers has made it unnecessary for our Courts to lay down rules in this matter. We have been content to rely on their honour, their good sense and their discrimination".

16–204 The same considerations of public policy would appear to underlie the enactment in 1693 of the Court of Session Act.[4] This provided that judges should state their opinions with open doors. Because of the importance of criminal trials it was ordained that " . . . after the Debate concerning the Relevancie of Criminall Lybells Dittays or Exculpations made by the parties and their procurators are closed that the Commissioners of Justiciary and other Criminall Judges shall advyse the same with open Doors in the presence of the Pannell and Assyse and all others . . . ". Certain exceptions were permitted, and in particular in "cases of Rapt Adulterie".

2. Criticism of judicial decisions

16–205 Although the principle of open justice, and the right to report the outcome of court proceedings, seemed to be well entrenched, sometimes an account of what has taken place may go beyond merely reporting and merge into criticism of what the court has done, or of the law as it has been interpreted.[5] For example, after a civil action against the Glasgow Corporation was dismissed by a sheriff as irrelevant, and during the period for appealing, a newspaper commented adversely on the judgment and called for an appeal.[6]

16–206 An appeal was taken to the First Division of the Court of Session, where the Corporation brought the article to the notice of the court. Lord President Strathclyde took the view that he could not "find in this article . . . anything that indicates a desire on the part of the writer of the article to influence the public administration of justice or to commit a contempt of this Court". He also recognised that since the judgment had been pronounced, and there was no appeal actually pending, it was not possible by criticising the judgment, even in strong terms, to prejudice the administration of justice, or to commit contempt of court. Had there been an appeal pending, therefore, it is conceivable that he might have taken a different view.[7]

16–207 Lord Skerrington's concurring speech expressed general disapproval of any writer who proceeded "to arrogate to himself the functions of a judicial tribunal", but he decided the case on the basis that he could find nothing disrespectful to the sheriff; nor was the particular article "calculated to interfere with the administration of justice". It may be that he went a little further than the Lord President, in the sense that he took the view that it was idle to suggest that the article could affect, or was intended to affect, an appellate decision on a pure question of law.

---

[4] 1693, c.27.
[5] See paras 16–101 *et seq.*
[6] *Kemp v Glasgow Corporation* 1918 S.C. 639; 55 S.L.R. 553, 1918 2 S.L.T. 2.
[7] Even in modern times, reference has been made to the possibility of unconscious influence upon judges: see *Kelly v O'Neill* [2000] I.R. 354 and *Al Megrahi and Fhima v Times Newspapers Ltd* 1999 S.C.C.R. 824.

Thus, it seems that even if there had been an appeal pending he would *not* have regarded the article as constituting contempt.

Lord Mackenzie remarked that the court had not been "referred to any case in which comment was made on a judgment that had been given", and where contempt had been established. He added: **16–208**

> "This is not the case of an attempt to present a view of an action which has not yet come to judgment, and it differs entirely from the class of case in which newspapers present a view of the facts of a case which is to go before a jury".

Lord Johnston, dissenting, was prepared to accept that the comment would have no effect upon the course of justice in the case at hand. Nevertheless, he characterised it as being "a style of comment which tends to obstruct the untrammelled exercise of the court's jurisdiction[8] and in principle is a form of contempt of Court which ought not to be allowed to go unnoticed". **16–209**

More recently, Lord Clyde held in a defamation case[9] that the right to report was not restricted to what was actually said or read out in court: **16–210**

> "In order to make a realistic application of the principle to the circumstances of the present case, I cannot restrict the availability of the privilege to a report of what is actually read out in court. The test in my view is not what is actually read out[10]—although all that is read out is published—but what is in the presentation of the case intended to be published and so put in the same position as if it had been read out. If it is referred to and founded upon before the court with a view to advancing the submission which is being made, it is to be taken as published".

This judgment was in the Outer House of the Court of Session, and was not a decision specifically addressing the law of contempt. However, Lord Clyde did observe that "it would be unlikely that statements which could amount to contempt of court could at the same time be the subject of privilege".[11] Another way of addressing this problem is to consider the state of mind of the relevant person. If circumstances were such that an intention to interfere with the administration of justice could readily be inferred, it may well be that malice would destroy any privilege that might exist under the law of defamation; correspondingly, as with the provisions of s.4(1) of the 1981 Act,[12] the absence of good faith could render any report vulnerable to contempt proceedings. **16–211**

The broad interpretation in *Cunningham* would appear to have extended the protection for fair reporting of the contents of documents such as the closed record, adjusted petition and answers, or a transcript of evidence taken on commission, even if these were not actually read out in court, provided that they were "taken as read". In criminal cases, where the reasoning in *Cunningham* is **16–212**

---

[8] Cp. the remarks of Viscount Dilhorne cited in para.4–119.
[9] *Cunningham v The Scotsman Publications Ltd* 1987 S.L.T. 698 at 706.
[10] Cp. the discussion in paras 12–222 *et seq.*
[11] At 707L. See also *Lucas & Son (Nelson Mail) Ltd v O'Brien* [1978] 2 N.Z.L.R. 289 at 296, Richmond P.; *Re Evening Star* (1884) N.Z.L.R. 3 S.C. 8 at 12, Williams J.
[12] para.4–265.

less directly applicable, allegations may only safely be published when made in open court.

3. *Reproducing pleadings through the media prior to a hearing*

16–213 Traditionally, the court has prevented the publication of extracts from pleadings prior to their being referred to in open court. This has been achieved either through the contempt jurisdiction or through the withholding of privilege in claims for defamation.

16–214 The justification for this principle has always been that prejudice could result from the publication of a limited or incomplete statement of either party's case. Although it is now provided by Sch.1 to the Contempt of Court Act 1981 that civil proceedings become "active" for the purposes of the strict liability rule from the close of the record, it is nevertheless thought that this principle will continue to have relevance in the context of common law contempt.[13] An intention to interfere with the proceedings would have to be established. No doubt, however, it would be difficult to persuade a court that an editor, who had published the contents of the record before it was closed, did not intend thereby to have some influence upon the course of justice. It is necessary to bear in mind the *obiter* observation of the court in *Hall v Associated Newspapers Ltd*[14] that the protection of the contempt jurisdiction would arise in civil proceedings from the service of the summons or petition or, in the sheriff court, by service of the initial writ.

16–215 In *Gilfillan and Spouse v Ure, Guthrie*,[15] a summary complaint was upheld against some of the respondents on the basis that a summons of damages "expressed in the most injurious and calumnious terms" had been raised against the complainants and a large number of copies were circulated. This was presumably a device intended to enable those responsible to publish defamatory allegations under cover of the privilege attaching to court documents.

16–216 In a later case,[16] immediately after the closing of the record, the agent for the pursuer gave a journalist a reprint of the record containing averments which were undoubtedly defamatory. The newspaper published a summary of the record, including those averments, but the defenders' denial was not published at the same time. Subsequently, however, their response was published which asserted that the defamatory allegations were "a tissue of libellous falsehoods, which have

---

[13] Certainly the Phillimore Committee was of the view that there was no need for reform: Cmnd. 5794, para.130. They recommended retaining "the confidential position of unadjusted pleadings, which will make any publication of such pleadings or any part thereof a contempt".
[14] 1978 S.L.T. 241; see paras 16–172 *et seq.*
[15] (1824) 3 S. 21; see also *Miller v Mitchell* (1835) 13 S. 644.
[16] *MacLeod v Lewis Justices of the Peace* (1892) 20 R. 218 at 222, 30 S.L.R. 186.

not the slightest foundation in fact". An application was made by the pursuer but it was held that the publication of the defenders' letter, against that background, did not constitute contempt. The Lord Justice-Clerk recognised that such a letter might amount to contempt, but each case had to be judged on its merits. In that instance the "whole matter originated in a gross irregularity on the part of the pursuer, and to the nature of the charge made on the record as published."

It was also said by Lord Trayner that he did not wish to say anything which might be construed as approving of letters being written by either party in the press while a case was pending "which might have the effect of prejudicing the mind of the court or anybody else against or in favour of either party". A party is not entitled to privilege if he sends his pleading to a newspaper for publication, even though a litigant is privileged in the statements that he makes on record.[17]

16–217

In *Richardson v Wilson*,[18] Lord President Inglis identified the principle as follows:

16–218

"Parties and their agents are entitled to have access to the summons, but they must also use proper caution. If the parties were to make its contents public at this stage, they would undeniably be subject to an action of damages if it contained statements defamatory of any other person; and if the agent of either party were guilty of publishing it in any way he would not only be liable, like his principal, but would also be answerable to the court for his misconduct".

Thus, it appears, the Lord President was addressing his mind both to defamation and, at least in respect of the agent's "misconduct", to the law of contempt also.

Young v Armour[19] was a decision arising from a breach of promise case with salacious facts, where newspapers published extracts from the open record. Counsel for both parties submitted that this had seriously interfered with the administration of justice, in that the case might otherwise have been settled on the basis that the facts would *not* be made public. Lord Blackburn ordered the editor of the newspaper which had published the accounts in Scotland to appear at the bar and explain himself. An apology and explanation were accepted. The editor said that he was aware of the rule that there should be no publication of anything in an open record, but that he had seen the article in London and Manchester newspapers and had assumed, wrongly but honestly, that the case had been heard in open court. Lord Blackburn observed that he had consulted his brother judges on the case, and all were of the opinion that, had the explanation not been satisfactory, a severe fine for contempt would have been appropriate.

16–219

---

[17] At 221, Lord Young. See also *Richardson v Wilson* (1879) 7 R. 237, 17 S.L.R. 122.
[18] (1879) 7 R. 237 at 242, 17 S.L.R. 122.
[19] 1921 1 S.L.T. 211.

16–220 Lord Wellwood had also made it clear that it was improper to publish any averments made in the pleadings before the record was closed or the facts had been mentioned in court,[20] but did not take any punitive action because the pursuer did not complain of prejudice to her case (for breach of promise of marriage). It may be important, however, to note that in *MacLeod v Lewis Justices of the Peace*[21] both Lord Young and Lord Trayner expressed the view that it was of no importance, in this context, whether the record was closed or not.

16–221 Since the test for publication contempt is now governed by the Contempt of Court Act 1981, it may be thought that there is little scope for a finding of contempt where disclosures from the pleadings have not given rise to prejudice, in the sense of pre-disposing the tribunal one way or the other. However, it is necessary (having regard particularly to what occurred in *Young v Armour*) to bear in mind that prejudice can also arise through the unacceptable pressure that may be exerted on parties through media publicity.[22]

16–222 Nonetheless, it is appropriate to have regard to the practical realities of the case. This issue of "pressure" is well illustrated (albeit in the criminal context) in the case of *Al Megrahi and Fhima v Times Newspapers Ltd*.[23] Concern had been expressed over remarks made in the *Sunday Times* to the effect that Colonel Gaddafi ordered the Lockerbie bombing himself, by way of reprisal for the United States bombing of Libya in 1986. The trial of the two Libyan citizens charged, however, was to take place in the Netherlands without a jury and therefore it could hardly be said that the article gave rise to a substantial risk of serious prejudice. It nonetheless was provided under Art.16 of the relevant agreement between the governments of the United Kingdom and the Netherlands that the accused had retained the right to opt for jury trial. It was argued that publicity of this kind might, therefore, be thought to restrict their freedom of choice as to mode of trial. The High Court held, however, that it was unrealistic to approach the matter on what could only be regarded as a theoretical possibility. One of the main planks of the case of the two accused had always been that they could not obtain a fair trial from a Scottish jury.

4. *The power to postpone reports of proceedings at common law*

16–223 It seems to have been recognised at an early stage that prejudice could be created to pending proceedings through court reporting. In *Mary Elder or Smith*,[24] the

---

[20] *Graham v Farquhar* 1893 1 S.L.T. 63. See also *Cunningham v The Scotsman Publications Ltd* 1987 S.L.T. 698 at 707L.
[21] (1892) 20 R. 218 at 221.
[22] Cp. *Att-Gen v Times Newspapers Ltd, The Times*, February 12, 1983 (Lexis); *Att-Gen v Unger* [1998] 1 Cr.App.R. 308, [1998] E.M.L.R. 280, discussed at paras 4–100 *et seq*.
[23] 1999 S.C.C.R. 824.
[24] (1827) Syme 71.

court ordered the postponement of an otherwise lawful report of court proceedings.[25] A murder trial was interrupted by the illness of a juryman, and it was decided to discharge the jury and start afresh the following week. Counsel for the pannel asked the court to protect his client in the interim from prejudicial press reporting of the evidence led for the prosecution, and Lord Justice-Clerk Boyle threatened the press with adverse consequences if they published anything more than a statement that, owing to unforeseen circumstances, the trial had been postponed.

J. Prohibiting the publication of prejudicial material

Atkins v London Weekend Television Ltd[26] is an illustration of the rule that in appropriate cases the court will by order prevent the apprehended publication of prejudicial material.[27] Naturally it would constitute contempt of court to publish in defiance of such an order.[28] Indeed *Atkins* went further, in that it was argued that there was no likelihood of repetition and that prohibition of future broadcasts would therefore not be appropriate. This was held in the circumstances not to be a sufficient answer, since the offending broadcast was said to have prejudiced the petitioner's fair and impartial trial in any criminal court in Scotland and to have interfered with the administration of justice. If established, such a complaint was sufficient to justify the making of the order. Even though the court accepted the statement of the Dean of the Faculty that there had been no intention to interfere with the administration of justice, the matter was held not to be fit to rest upon an undertaking. An order was required.

This jurisdiction may only be exercised by the Court of Session or the High Court of Justiciary. Accordingly parties concerned in litigation before the lower courts, who wish to prevent the publication of prejudicial material, should present a petition for interdict. Nor is there any need for the matter to be dealt with in the first instance by the lower court. One of the points taken in *Atkins* was that the complaint was one for the sheriff court before which the proceedings were pending, but the court said that it was difficult to see how the sheriff could deal with the matter in view of his limited jurisdiction. The judgment continued:

> "We have no hesitation in saying that when an offence of this nature is in issue this becomes at once a matter for investigation and disposal by the High Court of Justiciary, and the matter may be brought to the notice of the High Court by the Lord Advocate or any other interested party by petition and complaint or in any other competent way."

---

[25] A power which may still be exercised, although now only under the provisions of the 1981 Act. See para.7–111. It was held in the Privy Council that *R. v Clement* (1821) 4 B. & Ald. 218, 106 E.R. 918 affords no secure basis for supporting the existence of any residual common law power to postpone court reports: *Independent Publishing Company Ltd v Att-Gen of Trinidad and Tobago* [2004] UKPC 26, [2005] 1 A.C. 190.
[26] 1978 S.L.T. 76.
[27] Cp. the similar jurisdiction exercised in England, discussed at para.6–1.
[28] See also *Emond* (1829) Shaw 299, and *Smith v John Ritchie & Co* (1892) 3 White 408 at 411, 20 R (J) 52, 30 S.L.R. 329.

16–226 By contrast with the position in England,[29] however, the courts in Scotland have recognised no jurisdiction to grant an interdict binding *contra mundum*.[30] Their approach is similar to that of Lord Eldon in *Iveson v Harris*,[31] where it was held that the court could not "hold a man bound by an injunction who is not a party in the cause."

16–227 Prohibitions against publishing material allegedly prejudicial to current or pending trials were issued in *Robert Emond*[32] and *William Haire*.[33] In the latter case, the purpose was to prevent the publication of confessions made by Haire's accomplice Burke, which had been advertised in the *Edinburgh Evening Courant*, while Haire was threatened with a private prosecution for the murder of one James Wilson. The editor and publishers of that journal were prohibited from "publishing or circulating anything prejudicial to the prisoner William Haire, in the said confession, or doing any thing whereby the same may be published, till the proceedings now in dependence against the said William Haire shall be brought to a conclusion; and recommend to the publishers of all newspapers to abstain in like manner from doing so." It was recognised by Lord Justice-Clerk Alloway and Lords Meadowbank and Pitmilly that the public interest element in these cases justified proceeding on the motion without recourse to the civil process of interdict. Lord Gillies and Mackenzie, however, expressed some doubt as to the competency of pronouncing an actual order, on a simple verbal motion, and without a bill being presented for interdict.

16–228 The interdict procedure was adopted, however, in *Smith v Mitchell*.[34] In connection with the interdict, an order for destruction of points of memorial and queries for counsel, which were being circulated to the alleged prejudice of a party to civil litigation, was granted upon presentation of a petition and complaint to the Court of Session. Such a presentation for that purpose alone, however, would be regarded as incompetent.[35]

16–229 In the mid-nineteenth century, the granting of interdicts in this context does not appear to have been common. Indeed, by 1892, when an order was sought from the High Court to protect the position of a man committed for trial, the

---

[29] See, *e.g. X County Council v A* [1984] 1 W.L.R. 1422, Balcombe J., and the discussion of the principles at paras 6–41 *et seq*.
[30] See, *e.g. Pattison v Fitzgerald* 1823 2 S. 536; *Lord Advocate v The Scotsman Publications Ltd* 1988 S.L.T. 490 at 506, Lord Ross, and 514, Lord Dunpark. See also Burn-Murdoch, *Interdict in the Law of Scotland* (1933), p.1 (" . . . interdict is a purely personal remedy directed against the person who is said in the action to have violated or threatened the pursuer's rights"), and pp.99–100 (where he refers to the "four elements in precision" by which the wording of an interdict may be tested, namely "Who? Where? When? How?"). He points out that precision is required as to who is to be bound by the terms of an interdict, although recognising that it may be elastic enough to require obedience by persons not named individually ("In all such cases it is manifestly essential that the interdict shall at least be brought to the knowledge of the persons to be bound by it"). See also Scott Robinson, *The Law of Interdict*, p.3 ("The remedy is purely personal and directed against the person named"), and the valuable discussion by A.J. Bonnington, "Interdict and Contempt of Court" 1989 S.L.T. 381.
[31] (1802) 7 Ves. Jun. 251, 32 E.R. 102.
[32] (1829) Shaw 229.
[33] (1829) Hume, Vol. II, S.N. 165 at 260.
[34] (1835) 14 S. 172.
[35] *White v Magistrates of Dunbar* 1915 S.C. 395.

jurisdiction itself was thought to be open to question.[36] Even though the court held that it had power to grant the order, Lord Justice-Clerk Macdonald did " . . . not think it necessary to consider whether the application falls under the category of an application to restrain from a contempt of Court or not". His Lordship's *Treatise*, however, at least in later editions, stated that[37]:

> "It is contempt of Court for any person to publish comments on a pending trial, and a petition may be presented to the court, praying the court to prohibit the publication of any statements relative to the alleged crimes until the close of the proceedings, and the court will prohibit the publication of any prejudicial matter".

K. Statutes prohibiting or restricting publication

There are a number of statutes which have supplemented the common law in regulating the reporting of court proceedings. The main provisions may be summarised as follows:

16–230

1. The Judicial Proceedings (Regulation of Reports) Act 1926,[38] restricts the reporting of cases involving divorce and similar matters, with the aim of curbing the possibility of such reports exciting a prurient interest in readers.

2. The Fatal Accident and Sudden Deaths Inquiry (Scotland) Act 1976, s.4(4), allows the prohibition of similar publication concerning young persons involved in such inquiries.

3. The Magistrates' Courts Act 1980, s.8, imposes restrictions on publication anywhere in Great Britain of details of committal proceedings in England and Wales before any subsequent trial.[39]

4. The Criminal Procedure (Scotland) Act 1995, s.47, places restrictions on the reporting of particulars calculated to reveal the identity of most persons under 16 involved in criminal proceedings, subject to regulation by the courts and the Secretary of State.

5. The Children (Scotland) Act 1995, s.44, prohibits publication[40] of any matter in respect of proceedings at a children's hearing,[41] or before a

---

[36] *Smith v John Ritchie & Co* (1892) 3 White 408 at 411; 20 R (J) 52, 30 S.L.R. 329.
[37] Macdonald, pp.215–16: In *Cowie, Petrs*, 1912 1 S.L.T. 248, 1912 S.C. (J) 788; 9 Fac. 414, the court also focused on possible prejudice to an accused.
[38] For discussion, see paras 8–2 *et seq*.
[39] See the discussion in the English context at paras 8–87 *et seq*. The committal procedure is to be abolished and replaced by provisions contained in the Criminal Justice Act 2003, which will institute a procedure of "allocation and sending".
[40] This includes (a) publishing matter in a programme service, as defined by s.201 of the Broadcasting Act 1990, and (b) *causing* matter to be published.
[41] Defined in s.93(1).

sheriff on an application under other provisions of the Act,[42] or on any appeal under Pt II of the Act, which is intended to or is likely to identify any child concerned in the proceedings or appeal, or an address or school as being that of any such child. A person contravening these restrictions is liable on summary conviction to a fine not exceeding level 4[43] on the standard scale in respect of each such contravention. There is a discretion to dispense with these requirements on the part of the court and the Secretary of State.[44]

L. Attempting to pervert the course of justice

16–231 The crime of attempting to pervert the course of justice may be committed by a media publication (assuming it is possible to demonstrate the necessary mental element). The criteria for establishing this common law offence differ in certain respects from those applying to contempt by publication, both at common law and under the 1981 Act. There is thus a temptation on occasion to revert to this common law offence of perverting the course of justice when, for example, the temporal limits imposed by the law of contempt preclude proceedings under that *sui generis* jurisdiction.

16–232 For example, in *Skeen v Farmer*,[45] the news editor and general editor of a newspaper were so charged as a result of publishing an article describing an assault upon the news editor himself by a well known comedian, despite the fact that the news editor had made a complaint to the police which he knew they were investigating. It was recognised that the law of contempt could have no application at that stage, in the light of *Hall v Associated Newspapers Ltd*,[46] since there had been no arrest or charge. The proceedings were thus formulated on the basis of an attempt to pervert the course of justice.

16–233 Sheriff Stone identified two important requirements of the common law as follows:

" ... a charge of attempting to pervert the course of justice, must, under the general criminal law, contain proper specification of the mode of the offence and of the fact that the conduct was carried out with the evil intention of interfering with the administration of justice in some specified way ... ".

The averments were held to lack essential elements, since there was no allegation of specific wrongful intention, or of any suggestion as to how the investigation or prosecution of the complaint would be prejudiced.

---

[42] In particular, under s.57, s.60(7), s.65(7) or (9), s.76(1) or s.85(1).
[43] See para.14–106.
[44] s.44(5). See paras 8–55 *et seq.* for the position in England.
[45] 1980 S.L.T. 133 at 135. Also discussed in para.16–20; A.J. Bonnington, "Common Law Contempt: The Story So Far" 1994 S.L.T. (News) 51.
[46] 1978 S.L.T. 241.

VII. BREACH OF INTERDICT OR UNDERTAKING

A. Breach of a court order[47]

Breach of an interdict is a contempt of court,[48] for which the court may inflict a penalty within its discretion. Depending on gravity, the penalty may range from censure, through fine or payment of expenses, to imprisonment.[49] Such proceedings are not to be regarded as criminal in character, despite the nature of the penalties available, but rather as a means by which the court protects its authority from contempt.[50] Once an interdict has been granted, there will be a party with title and interest to enforce it. That private interest will exist alongside the public interest in the vindication of the court's authority.[51]

16–234

In the Court of Session the procedure is by petition and complaint, presented to the Inner House, even where the interdict was granted in the Outer House.[52] In view of the quasi-criminal nature of the proceeding, the concurrence of the Lord Advocate is necessary[53] and, in the sheriff court, that of the Procurator-Fiscal. In the case of an *interim* interdict the Division or the Lord Ordinary may deal with a breach without presentation of a petition and complaint.[54]

16–235

A breach of interdict can be committed not only directly but through others. For example, where in a patent case an interdict was obtained but the respondent continued to infringe after taking a partner, through a new firm, it was held that the patent holder had a remedy for breach of interdict by way of complaint.[55] An

16–236

---

[47] H. Burn-Murdoch, *Interdict in the Law of Scotland* (1933), chs XXVII, XXVIII; Scott Robinson, *The Law of Interdict* (1987), ch.16. See also A.J. Bonnington, "Interdict and Contempt of Court" 1989 S.L.T. (News) 381.
[48] See *Pattison v Fitzgerald* (1823) 2 S. 536; *Muir v Milligan* (1868) 6 M. 1125 (a case concerning the failure, in a custody action, to deliver a child); *Ross v Ross* (1885) 12 R. 1351, 23 S.L.R. 1; *Leys v Leys* (1886) 13 R. 1223; *Harvie v Ross* (1886) 24 S.L.R. 58, 14 R. 71; *Edgar v Fisher's Trustees* (1893) 21 R. 59, 1 S.L.T. 301.
[49] Subject now to the limitations imposed by s.15 of the 1981 Act, which are discussed at para.16-348.
[50] See paras 16–2 *et seq*. See also *Stark's Trustees v Duncan* (1906) 8 F. 429, 434. As to the appropriateness of the term "contempt of court" when applied to breach of interdict, see the remarks of Lord President Clyde in *Johnson v Grant* 1923 S.C. 789, cited at para.16-244.
[51] For an early recognition of the distinct interests involved, see *Milne v Davidson* (1829) 8 S. 223. See also the discussion in paras 3–8 *et seq*.
[52] *per* Lord Curriehill in *McNeill v Scott* (1866) 4 Macph. 608. See also *Dunoon Picture House Co v Magistrates of Dunoon* 1921 S.C. 908.
[53] *Robb v Caledonian Newspapers Ltd* 1994 S.C.C.R. 659 at 666; *Gribben v Gribben* 1976 S.L.T. 266; *Usher v Magistrates of Edinburgh* (1839) 1 D. 639; *Ramage v Steele* (1843) 6 D. 146; *McNeill v Scott* (1866) 4 Macph. 608; *Duke of Atholl v Robertson* (1872) 10 Macph. 298; *Petrie v Angus* (1889) 7 R.(J.C.) 3. See also *Mackay's Manual of Practice in the Court of Session* (1893), p.244.
[54] Administration of Justice (Scotland) Act 1933, s.6(4). See now the Court of Session Act 1988, s.47(1).
[55] *Dudgeon v Thomson* (1876) 3 R. 974; 4 R.(H.L.) 88. See also *Harvie v Ross* (1886) 14 R. 71, 24 S.L.R. 58.

allegation of *intention* to commit a breach of interdict is not, it seems, a sufficient ground for petition and complaint.[56]

B. Breach of an undertaking

16–237 Breach of an *undertaking* given to the court by a partner not to interfere in the management of licensed premises was punished with imprisonment by a sheriff, and this was upheld.[57] This is perhaps not surprising, since such undertakings often provide a way to avoid an order being made to the same effect.[58]

16–238 The matter was explained in *Graham v Robert Younger Ltd*,[59] where Lord Justice-Clerk Thomson noted that:

" . . . no authority was cited to us where breach of such an undertaking was regarded as contempt of Court. But the taking of such undertakings from parties, either personally or through their counsel, is a common and convenient step in our procedure and it would rob undertakings of any usefulness if there were no sanction and if the giver of an undertaking, the terms of which were clearly understood, could proceed immediately to ignore it. I am quite satisfied that in appropriate cases a Court has jurisdiction to treat a breach of a solemnly given undertaking as contempt".

16–239 The nature of liability for breach of an undertaking fell to be considered in *Beggs v The Scottish Ministers*.[60] Reference was made to *Graham v Robert Younger* as "the sole case concerned with breach of undertaking" and it was noted that the finding of contempt had been upheld "although the conduct could have been due to 'failure to appreciate the seriousness of his conduct or to sophistry rather than contumaciousness'". The minuter had complained by way of a petition by way of judicial review of interference with his privileged correspondence, while he was a prisoner, both from his legal advisers and from the Scottish Prisons Complaints Commission. When the matter came before the Lord Ordinary on September 5, 2003 an undertaking was tendered to the effect that correspondence would not be opened in future (in breach of r.50(3) of the Prison and Young Offenders Institutions (Scotland) Rules 1994 and paras 13 and 15 of the Scottish Prison Service Circular No.79/1994). Despite the undertaking, which had been accepted, on the very next day a prison officer partially succeeded in opening a "strictly private and confidential" letter from his legal advisers. Although the Governor briefed his management about the undertaking and emphasised the importance of observance, its terms were not disseminated to

---

[56] *Hunter v Wilson* (1848) 10 D. 893. ("However bad the intention might have been, it amounted only to an instruction to commit the act complained of . . . . The Transaction amounts to instructions to attempt to violate the interdict, but does not go the length that the court can take cognizance of": the Lord-Justice Clerk.) In the same case Lord Medwyn agreed and added that the conduct in question was "only an attempt to commit a breach of interdict, fortunately for the respondent; for, had he succeeded, it would have been a very aggravated case." See 11–14 *et seq*. (attempted contempt).
[57] *Graham v Robert Younger* 1955 J.C. 28, 1955 S.L.T. 250. This was heard by the High Court of Justiciary by means of a bill of suspension and liberation; but the procedure would now be inappropriate in the light of *Cordiner, Petr* 1973 S.L.T. 125.
[58] See the observations of Munby J. discussed at para.12–185.
[59] 1955 J.C. 28 at 32.
[60] 2005 S.L.T. 305.

other members of staff. Despite the fact that a review was carried out by the residential manager for the handling of privileged mail, he was not for some reason made aware of the undertaking or its terms.

In May 2004, the minuter was transferred to HMP Edinburgh and on 7, 10 and 15 of that month "strictly private and confidential" legal correspondence was opened in his presence. Apologies were tendered and the Governor reminded all staff of the terms of r.50. On May 24 the Scottish Prison Service issued a notice to all governors drawing attention to a circular of April 2003 making clear that all correspondence from the Commissioner bearing the Commission's logo should not be opened. The minuter was returned to Peterhead in July. On November 26 a letter from the Commissioner was opened in his presence. The residential officer believed he was entitled to open it as it was not from a solicitor. Neither he nor the residential manager was aware of the undertaking. Reference was made to the Crown Proceedings Act 1947 and the Scotland Act 1998 and it was held that the proceedings against the ministers in respect of the breach were against them as officers of the Crown and not against the Crown as such. They had a sufficiently distinct legal personality to render them, individually or collectively, amenable to proceedings for contempt. They were collectively responsible for the acts or omissions of civil servants in the Scottish Administration. The court considered the reasoning in *M v Home Office*.[61] As Lord Templeman had observed there[62] "the argument that there is no power to enforce the law by injunction or contempt proceedings against a minister in his official capacity would, if upheld, establish the proposition that the executive obey the law as a matter of grace and not as a matter of necessity, a proposition which would reverse the result of the Civil War". Although the court in *Beggs* did not rely on the reasoning in *M v Home Office*, "the result is the same".[63] "The undertaking was simply not taken seriously enough".[64] No penalty was imposed, however, the finding of contempt in itself being "of great importance".

C. The mental element in breach of interdict

The mental element in cases of breach of interdict turns on whether the existence of the interdict was known to the alleged contemnor. The court, in addressing this question, has sometimes been ready to find constructive knowledge both of the existence of an interdict and of its terms,[65] although in such circumstances there may be a readiness to impose a less severe penalty.[66]

It seems that there should be a "wilful" breach before proceedings may be taken,[67] and it is of "the essence of the offence" in cases of breach of undertaking

---

[61] [1994] 1 A.C. 377, discussed at paras 12–122 and 12–123.
[62] At 395.
[63] At [24].
[64] At [50].
[65] *Welsh v Steuar* (1818) 1 Mur. 397 at 404, Lord Gillies; *Robertson v McDonald* (1829) 7 S. 272 at 274; *Henderson v Maclellan* (1874) 1 R. 920; *Tait v Gordon* (1828) 6 S. 1056; cf. *Neville v Neville* 1924 S.L.T. (Sh. Ct.) 43, 44; *Anderson v Moncrieff* 1966 S.L.T. (Sh. Ct.) 28 at 30, Lord Emslie.
[66] e.g. *Taylor v Kilgour* (1844) 17 Sc. Ju. 89.
[67] e.g. *Caledonian Railway Co v Hamilton* (1850) 7 Bell's App. 272 at 284–5, Lord Brougham.

that the relevant act or omission should be deliberate,[68] but probably only in the sense that it is not accidental.[69] It seems that it is not necessary to demonstrate an additional element of either intention or foresight as to the consequences of any such breach for the administration of justice.

16–243   It is usual for the terms of the interdict alleged to have been breached to be construed strictly, in determining whether or not the authority of the court has been wilfully flouted.[70] On the other hand, an interpretation favourable to the alleged contemnor will not be preferred if it does violence to the ordinary meaning of the words of the interdict.[71] In *Beggs v The Scottish Ministers*,[72] extensive reference was made to English authorities because there was "a dearth of Scottish authority on the liability of a corporate body for contempt of court based on the actions of its servants or agents". Reference was made to *Heatons Transport (St. Helens) Ltd v TGWU*,[73] *Fairclough v Manchester Ship Canal Co*,[74] *Stancomb v Trowbridge UDC*,[75] *Att-Gen for Tuvalu v Philatelic Distribution Corporation Ltd*[76] and *Director General of Fair Trading v Pioneer Concrete UK Ltd (No.2)*[77] and the conclusion was drawn[78]:

> "We consider that [there] is no reason why a similar approach should not be valid in Scotland where a servant or agent of a company unknowingly does the act which is prohibited by a court order which has been served on the company or by an undertaking which has been given by the company to the court. The company would have a duty to take all reasonable steps to ensure that the relevant servants or agents were made aware of the requirement to comply with the order or undertaking and did not forget, misunderstand or overlook the requirement. Where the order or undertaking has been breached as a result of a failure in that duty, the company should be held to have committed a contempt of court".

D. Is breach of interdict properly described as "contempt"?

16–244   The appropriateness of the label "contempt of court" for describing breaches of interdict was questioned in *Johnson v Grant* by Lord President Clyde[79]:

---

[68] *Graham v Robert Younger, Ltd* 1955 J.C. 28, 33, S.L.T. 250, Lord Birnam.
[69] *Beggs v The Scottish Ministers* 2005 S.L.T. 305 at [29]–[30]. To similar effect, see the passage from *Stancomb v Trowbridge Urban District Council* [1910] 2 Ch. 190 at 194, cited at para.12–80.
[70] See, *e.g. Gordon v Fiddler* (1823) 2 S. 486; *Walker v Wishart* (1825) 4 S. 302; *Keltie v Wilson* (1828) 7 S. 208; *Fraser's Trs v Cran* (1879) 6 R. 451; *Waldie v Duke of Roxburghe* (1822) 1 S. 367.
[71] See *McIntyre v Sheridan* 1993 S.L.T. 412 at 418; *Campbell v Mackay* 1959 S.L.T. (Sh. Ct.) 34 at 36.
[72] 2005 S.L.T. 305.
[73] [1973] A.C. 15.
[74] [1897] W.N. 7.
[75] [1910] 2 Ch. 190.
[76] [1990] 1 W.L.R. 926.
[77] [1995] 1 A.C. 456.
[78] At [39].
[79] 1923 S.C. 789 at 790.

"The phrase 'contempt of Court' does not in the least describe the true nature of the class of offence with which we are here concerned, and which is presented in the civil Court by petition and complaint with the concurrence of the Lord Advocate".

He nonetheless recognised that such breaches were capable of challenging the fundamental supremacy of the law, and accordingly that "conduct of this kind is properly treated as deserving of criminal punishment; it is intolerable in any civilised and well-ordered society." The regret he expressed over the currency of the phrase "contempt of court" was not on the basis that it exaggerated the importance of breaches of interdict; but rather the contrary, because he considered that the impression might be given that a person might be led into believing that all he needed to do in order to avoid the consequences would be to apologise "as for an offence against the dignity of the court". **16–245**

In *Macleay v Macdonald and Maclennon*,[80] Lord Mackay opined that the remedy for breach of interdict "is one *in poenam*, a semi-criminal punishment; it is not as accurately described as for 'contempt of Court', but as an action taken by the court itself in aid of the fundamental supremacy of the law which is challenged by wilful breaches of interdict". **16–246**

Professor D.M. Walker[81] has commented that "breach of interdict is not properly described as a contempt of court; it is a challenge to the supremacy of the law and therefore punishable". No additional authority, however, is cited for this proposition. He continued: "Nor is it a criminal proceeding, but a method by which the court protects its own authority from contempt". This was a quotation from the speech of Lord President Dunedin in *Stark's Trs v Duncan*.[82] The court's jurisdiction to deal with breach of interdict has often been justified by reference to the vindication of the court's authority.[83] **16–247**

A more modern, straightforward statement of the law is that "a complaint of breach of interdict is a complaint of disobedience of a competent order of the court. Such disobedience constitutes contempt of court".[84] **16–248**

---

[80] 1928 S.C. 776 at 778.
[81] *The Law of Civil Remedies in Scotland* (1974), p.242, citing *Johnson v Grant* 1923 S.C. 789. Cf. Scott Robinson, *op. cit.*, p.168. See, however, *Stair Memorial Encyclopaedia*, Vol. 6, Contempt of Court, para.322; G.H. Gordon, *op. cit.*, para.50–09; MacLaren, *op. cit.*, Pt VIII, ch.XIII, p.915; Burn-Murdoch, *Interdict in the Law of Scotland* (1933), para.450.
[82] (1906) 8 F. 429 at 434.
[83] *Dudgeon v Thomson and Donaldson* (1876) 4 R. 256 at 261, Lord Deas; *Beattie v Rodger* (1835) 14 S. 6 at 7, Lord Cockburn; *Clark v Presbytery of Dunkeld, Henderson* (1839) 1 D. 955 at 986, Lord Corehurst, at 979, Lord President Hope, at 981, Lord Justice-Clerk Boyle, at 986, Lord Meadowbank; *Monroe v Robertson, Trs* (1834) 12 S. 788, Lord Justice-Clerk Boyle; *Edwards v Leith* (1843) 15 Sc. Ju. 375 at 377, Lord President Boyle; *Taylor v Kilgour* (1844) 17 Sc. Ju. 89 at 90, Lord Macintyre.
[84] *Gribben v Gribben*, 1976 S.L.T. 266 at 269, Lord President Emslie, Lord Cameron, Lord Johnston; followed in *Byrne v Ross* 1993 S.L.T. 307, 1992 S.C.L.R. 898, Lord President Hope, Lord Imrie and Lord McCluskey.

E. Breach of interdict as "quasi-criminal"

16–249 In cases of direct contempt it may be that no private interest is adversely affected or, if there is, it will not be the primary concern of the court. The private element in breach of interdict tends to predominate, and this is a factor which has contributed to the widespread use of the term "*quasi*-crime". As Lord President Inglis said in *Christie Miller v Bain*[85]:

> "In one sense a petition for breach of interdict is a criminal proceeding. But one cannot help seeing that in many ways it is a civil proceeding. Civil interests are often largely concerned, and therefore it is often called a *quasi*-criminal proceeding".

16–250 One result of the currency given to the use of the "*quasi*-crime" terminology has been the suggestion that the public interest in protecting the authority of the law is best vindicated by the use of criminal law; and that, therefore, the contempt jurisdiction must be regarded as in effect a branch of the criminal law, but one that is shorn of unnecessary procedure.

16–251 A distinction was drawn at an early stage in the law relating to breach of interdict between form and substance. Lord Mackenzie, for example, implied in *Mackenzie and Munro v Magistrates of Dingwall*[86] that the remedy for breach of interdict was in substance a criminal proceeding, albeit one which was carried out in civil form, and Lord Gillies overtly referred to contempt as crime.[87] *Duncan v Ramsay*[88] seemed to suggest that the remedy could be sought in either criminal or civil form, and *Mackay v Ross*[89] in the same year, where a case in civil form was appealed to the Circuit Court of Justiciary, does not seem inconsistent with this.

16–252 The "*quasi*-penal" nature of the action was held by Lord President Inglis in *Dudgeon v Thomson and Donaldson*[90] to be a reason for not having it tried by jury; yet there were examples of jury trial in such cases.[91] The remedy sought by way of petition and complaint or other form of action for breach of interdict is directed to punishment.[92] There is thus clearly a significant public element underlying the jurisdiction, even though it may be initiated by a private litigant.

---

[85] (1879) 6 R. 1215 at 1216; 16 S.L.R. 721. The quasi-criminal formulation is also to be seen in *McNeill v Scott* (1866) 4 M. 608 at 610, Lord Curiehill, at 610–11, Lord Deas, at 616, Lord Ardmillan; *The Dunlop Pneumatic Tyre Company Ltd v Rose* (1901) 3 F. 635 at 636, Lord President Balfour; *Stark's Trs v Duncan* (1906) 8 F. 429 at 433, Lord President Dunedin; *Caledonian Rly Co v Hamilton* (1850) 7 Bell's App 272 at 280, Lord Brougham; *Henderson v Maclellan* (1874) 1 R. 920 at 924, Lord Deas. cf. *Anderson v Connacher* (1850) 13 D. 405 at 407, Lord President Boyle; Scott Robinson, *op. cit.* p.2; Burn-Murdoch, *Interdict in the Law of Scotland* (1933) para.451; Maclaren, *Court of Session Practice*, pp.131–2; Mackay, *op. cit.*, Part Sixth, ch.LXX XVII, p.587; Part Second; ch.XI, p.103.
[86] (1839) 1 D. 487 at 491.
[87] At 492. See also Lord Fullerton in *Taylor v Kilgour* (1844) 17 Sc. Ju. 89 at 90.
[88] (1853) I Irv. 208 at 211–12, Lord Wood.
[89] (1853) 1 Irv. 288 at 292, Lord Evans.
[90] (1876) 3 R. 974 at 975.
[91] e.g. *Magistrates of Dingwall v Mackenzie* (1831) 5 W & S 351, affg. (1829) 7 S. 899. See also the *Mackenzie and Munro* case at (1839) 1 D. 487.
[92] See, e.g. *Byrne v Ross* 1993 S.L.T. 307 at 310C–D, 1992 S.C.L.R. 898 at 900.

To that extent, the action for breach of interdict is analogous to a private prosecution.[93]

The procedure used in relation to breaches of interdict serves also to underline the public element and thus the close analogy with the purposes of the criminal law; and in particular the need to obtain the concurrence of the Lord Advocate[94] or his representative, the local procurator-fiscal, for proceedings in the superior and inferior courts respectively.

16–253

This requirement was established in *Duke of Northumberland v Harris*, Bell,[95] because of the "highly penal" purpose of the action. Even where the facts complained of in an action for breach amount to a crime, in the absence of a prosecution by the public authorities the civil court will take jurisdiction.[96] An example is provided by cases in which a spouse is in breach of a non-molestation order by committing an assault or some other criminal offence.[97]

16–254

Various explanations of the petition and complaint procedure are to be found in the reports. Lord Justice-Clerk Hope in *Bell and Moncrieff v Jameson*[98] stated that "a petition and complaint brings up before the court the conduct of the party complained against, that he may be subjected to their animadversion if it should be thought necessary". A similar description was that of Lord Justice-Clerk Inglis in *Bell v Gow*[99]: "by petition and complaint I understand that form of process by which a civil court is asked to inflict punishment."

16–255

The standard of proof

The standard of proof in an action for breach of interdict, albeit an action in civil form, is closely allied to the criminal standard. The modern law is founded upon

16–256

---

[93] See the use of this terminology by Sedley J. in *Guildford Borough Council v Valler* [1993] T.L.R. 274 at 275. It may be noted however that the use of the word "prosecution" was argued by counsel to be inappropriate in *P v Liverpool Daily Post and Echo Newspapers plc* [1991] 2 A.C. 370 at 412A. The reasoning behind this was that a complainant in a contempt case is really doing no more than inviting the court's attention to the misconduct concerned, so that it may consider whether to exercise its inherent jurisdiction to punish or coerce, as the case may be.
[94] *Robb v Caledonian Newspapers Ltd* 1994 S.C.C.R. 659 at 666; *Gribben v Gribben* 1976 S.L.T. 266. But cp. the terms of the Contempt of Court Act 1981, s.7, which only require the consent of the Attorney-General for strict liability proceedings in England. There is no equivalent requirement in Scotland.
[95] (1832) 10 S. 366 at 367, Lord Justice-Clerk Boyle. Cf. *McAulay v McKenzie* (1830) 9 S. 48 at 50–1. See also *Usher and Cunningham v Magistrates and Council of Edinburgh and Boyd and Hatton* (1839) 1 D. 639 at 640; *Bell v Gow* (1862) 1 M. 84 at 85; *Paterson v Robson* (1872) 11 M. 76 at 79; *Byrne v Ross* 1993 S.L.T. 307, 1992 S.C.L.R. 898 at 901 (summarising the modern situation after *Gribben v Gribben* 1976 S.L.T. 266); Lord Deas in *McNeill v Scott* (1866) 4 M. 608 at 615. See Macphail, *Sheriff Court Practice* (1988), pp.21–85, 716.
[96] See *Gribben v Gribben* 1976 S.L.T. 266 at 269; *Chisholm v Black and Morrison* (1871) 2 Coup. 49; *McIntyre v Sheridan* 1993 S.L.T. 412 at 416, Lord Caplan; cf. Burn-Murdoch, *Interdict in the Law of Scotland* (1933) para.451.
[97] Cp. *N v N (Contempt: Committal)* [1992] 1 F.L.R. 370 at 375B–C; *Green (Bryan)* [1993] Crim. L.R. 46.
[98] (1848) 10 D. 1413.
[99] (1862) 1 M. 84, 85. And see Lord Johnston in *White v Magistrates of Dunbar* 1915 S.C. 395 at 398.

the opinion of Lord Avonside in *Eutectic Welding Alloys Company Ltd v Whitting*,[1] where the quasi-penal nature of the action was said to mean that "proof should be beyond reasonable doubt". This statement was followed by the First Division in *Gribben*,[2] and applied also in *Byrne v Ross*.[3] Although the *Eutectic Welding* case was the first in which the criminal standard of proof was adopted expressly, this was by no means an innovation. It was entirely consistent with long-standing practice.[4]

Sentencing

16–257 The sentencing restrictions imposed by the Contempt of Court Act 1981 apply to sentences for breach of interdict as for contempt generally, and the same factors are relevant to be taken into consideration in fixing a sentence.[5] In the past, however, the civil nature of the proceedings has led the court to order *restitutio in integrum* if the breach was trivial or unintended and the circumstances made it appropriate.[6] It is an aggravation of breach of interdict to attempt to avoid the due process of law in respect of that breach, or to incite others to breach the interdict.[7]

F. The impact of the quasi-criminal nature of the jurisdiction

16–258 Because of the quasi-criminal nature of the proceeding, where an application was made to a sheriff for a warrant to imprison for breach of interdict, it was held that the parties could not enter into an agreement to accept the sheriff as arbiter so as to bar appeal from his decision.[8] On the other hand, the view was taken[9] that a complaint for breach of interdict was not a "criminal proceeding" in the context of s.3 of the Evidence Act 1853, with the result that the respondent to such a complaint could competently be examined as a witness.

16–259 There are other instances of the court's reluctance to afford safeguards traditionally associated with criminal proceedings to contempts of this kind. For example, it has been argued[10] that, because of the quasi-criminal character of the proceedings, it was not competent to alter a date in a petition and complaint; but the amendment was allowed nonetheless. It has also been held, notwithstanding its quasi-criminal nature, that a petition and complaint may be joined with an application for interdict against other parties in relation to the same subject-

---

[1] 1969 S.L.T. (News) 79 at 80.
[2] 1976 S.L.T. 266.
[3] 1993 S.L.T. 307, 1992 S.C.L.R. 898.
[4] See, *e.g. Lord Lovat v Macdonnell* (1868) 6 M. 330 at 332 Lord Lucan; *Menzies v Macdonald* (1864) 2 M. 652; *Campbell v Mackay* 1959 S.L.T. (Sh.Ct.) 34.
[5] *e.g.* the means of the contemnor, as in *CR Smith Glaziers (Dumfermline) Ltd v Anderson* 1993 S.L.T. 592 at 593, Lord Morton of Shuna.
[6] See, *e.g. Lord Blantyre v Dunn* (1845) 9 D. 299; *Duke of Atholl v Dalgaish* spelling (1823) 2 S. 422; Scott Robinson, *op. cit.*, p.171; Burn-Murdoch, *Interdict in the Law of Scotland* (1933), para.454.
[7] *Earl of Galloway v Nixon* (1877) 5 R. 28; *McIntyre v Sheridan* 1993 S.L.T. 412.
[8] *Stark's Trustees v Duncan* (1906) 8 F. 429, 43 S.L.R. 288, 13 S.L.T. 737.
[9] *Christie Miller v Bain* (1879) 6 R. 1215, 16 S.L.R. 721.
[10] *Dunlop Pneumatic Tyre Co Ltd v Rose* (1901) 3 F. 635, 38 S.L.R. 442, 8 S.L.T. 454.

matter.[11] Where an order to appear at the bar for alleged breach of interdict was ignored, a warrant was granted.[12]

G. Breach of interdict: procedure

The general procedure to be applied in these cases was, in effect, settled by the mid-nineteenth century.[13] The action was served on the alleged contemnor, and, if no answers were lodged for him, he was ordered to appear. If answers were lodged, pleas to the relevancy were dealt with and, if need be, the truth of the allegations determined.

16–260

Before s.6 of the Administration of Justice (Scotland) Act 1933 came into effect, breach of interdict cases in the Court of Session had to be brought before the Inner House of the court by petition and complaint. That provision allowed a complaint for breach of interdict to be brought before the court which had granted the interdict (be it Lord Ordinary or Division) if the cause was still in dependence. This was in practice achieved by lodging a minute in the process, and in so far as these cases were brought before a Lord Ordinary, the procedure reflected a common law jurisdiction of the Lord Ordinary in the absence of the Division.[14]

16–261

The corresponding modern provisions are contained in s.47(1) of the Court of Session Act 1988, and r.14.2(d) of the 1994 Rules of the Court of Session, which made petition and complaint a matter for the Outer House. This appears to be a restoration of the common law position, probably caused by pressure of business on the Inner House rather than any reassessment of the gravity with which a breach of interdict is to be viewed. The court retains a certain flexibility in the process, as in determining the length of the *induciae* (warning interval), the proper parties to bring the complaint and to be called to answer it, and whether or not an error in the pleadings is to be regarded as fatal to the proceedings.[15] In *Forbes v Forbes*,[16] a defender in an action of divorce was imprisoned by a sheriff for breach of interdict, against disposing of matrimonial property, and appealed to the sheriff principal who refused the appeal as incompetent. On appeal to the Inner House, the defender argued (1) that the appeal to the sheriff principal was

16–262

---

[11] *Jolly v Brown* (1828) 6 S. 872.
[12] *Duke of Atholl v Robertson* (1872) 10 Macph. 298.
[13] See *Lord Gray v Petrie* (1848) 10 D. 718 and the exposition by Maxwell, *The Practice of the Court of Session* (1980), p.520. Application should be made to the court which granted the interdict in the first instance, though appeal of the interdict process itself can mean that complaint for breach should also be made at the higher level: *Gray v McNair* (1826) 4 S. 785. See also *Macleay v Macdonald and Maclennan* 1928 S.C. 776 at 777n; *Forbes v Forbes* 1993 S.L.T. 16.
[14] See, *e.g. Glasgow International Exhibition v Sosnowski* (1901) 39 S.L.R. 28; *The Duncan Practice Home Company Ltd v The Provost, Magistrates and Councillors of the Burgh of Dunoon* 1921 S.C. 908; cf. *McPherson v Thorne* (1844) 6 D. 422; *Macleay v Macdonald and Maclennan* 1928 S.C. 776 at 779, Lord Mackay. Even when the Division was the appropriate court, it was usual, though not absolutely necessary (see, *e.g. Ramage v Steel* (1843) 6 D. 146) to remit proof to a single Judge of the Division as to a Lord Ordinary, to report back with the results.
[15] See *Costa v Costa* 1929 S.N. 62; *Jolly v Brown* (1828) 6 S. 872; *Overseas League v Taylor* 1951 S.C. 105; *Anderson v Stoddart* 1923 S.C. 755.
[16] 1994 S.L.T. 16.

competent, on the basis that the sheriff's interlocutor was a final judgment within the meaning of the Sheriff Courts (Scotland) Act 1907,[17] and (2) that the sheriff had given undue weight to his failure to mitigate the damage done by the breach. It was held that proceedings by way of initial writ, following breach of an interdict, were not "civil proceedings" within the meaning of s.3 of the 1907 Act and that they were to be regarded as *sui generis*.[18] If a right of appeal had been intended by Parliament, in the light of the well understood characterisation of contempt proceedings as "quasi-criminal", express provision would have been made. The court noted that there appeared to be no record of any previous appeal from the sheriff to the sheriff principal in contempt proceedings, although there were many examples of appeals to the Court of Session.

16–263   It is accepted that it is not permissible in the general case to challenge the substantive validity of the interdict in question.[19] This issue was discussed by the court in *Clark v Stirling, Presbytery of Dunkeld, Henderson*,[20] a case involving questions of the privileges of the Church, where a minority opinion was voiced, by some respected judges, that a defect in jurisdiction, or title to seek the interdict, might be cause for an exception to the general rule. It may be that very exceptional circumstances would permit challenge to the interdict breached.[21]

H. Presence of defendant required

16–264   As in most criminal cases, the court will generally require the attendance of a party at any stage in the action where punishment may be imposed, and absence in defiance of such an interdiction will be met with the issue of an arrest warrant.[22]

I. Breach of orders *ad factum praestandum*

16–265   Section 1(1) of the Law Reform (Miscellaneous Provisions) (Scotland) Act 1940 regulates the power of the court to imprison a person who has failed to obtemper a decree *ad factum praestandum*.[23] As was pointed out in *Nelson v Nelson*,[24]

---

[17] s.27.
[18] See, *e.g. Cordiner, Petr* 1973 S.L.T. 125; *Maclachlan v Bruce* 1912 S.C. 440; *Christie Miller v Bain* (1879) 6 R 1215.
[19] See, *e.g. Harvie v Ross* (1866) 24 S.L.R. 58 at 59; *Stark's Trs v Duncan* (1906) 8 F. 429, 433; cf. *Duke of Argyle v McArthur* (1861) 23 D. 1236; 5 S. 268 at 271; *McIntyre v Sheridan* 1993 S.L.T. 412 at 416. If there is a valid interdict in force, action for breach should be taken before any final interdict on the subject will be granted: *Dudgeon v Thomson and Co* (1876) 3 R 604; *Royal Warrant Holders' Association v Robb* 1935 S.N. 32.
[20] (1839) 1 D. 955; see expressly Lord Gillies at 982, Lord Cockburn at 984, Lord Fullerton at 990; Lord Jeffrey at 1007, Lord Cuninghame at 1016.
[21] See discussion at paras 9–194 *et seq.* in the context of a journalist being permitted to challenge an order to reveal a source.
[22] *Lord Gray v Petrie* (1849) 11 D. 1021, (1849) 12 D. 85; *Walker v Junor* (1903) 5 F. 1035; *Stark's Trs v Duncan* (1906) 8 F. 429; *Duke of Atholl v Robertson* (1872) 10 M. 298; *Welsbach Incandescent Gas Light Company, Ltd v M'Mann* (1901) 4 F. 395; Scott Robinson, *op. cit.*, p.171. And see *Milne v Davidson* (1829) 8 S. 223.
[23] A judicial order to do an act, other than the payment of money, which the defender should have done pursuant to an existing legal duty; or an order to undo an act performed in breach of such a duty.
[24] 1988 S.C.L.R. 663 at 666, Sheriff Principal Caplan, Sh. Ct.

"failure to honour a decree for implement is merely the reverse equivalent of a breach of interdict", and it was held that the *Eutectic Welding* standard of proof should apply.

An application under s.1 of the 1940 Act is made by the person in right of the decree, and on wilful refusal being made out the court which granted the decree may order imprisonment for up to six months, or until compliance if that is sooner. If imprisonment is not ordered, the court may substitute a pecuniary decree for the one *ad factum praestandum*, or lend its aid in other ways to the person in right of the decree.

The 1940 Act was preceded by common law powers to order imprisonment until an order was obtempered,[25] and the court also could order the acts in question to be carried out by others (at the contemnor's expense if appropriate), or use other forms of compulsion.[26] In so far as these powers were in the exercise of the court's *nobile officium*, they may well survive any later statutory encroachments on the common law.

VIII. THE PHILLIMORE RECOMMENDATIONS FOR SCOTLAND

A. The recommendation for uniformity with England and Wales

The Committee recognised that the law of contempt was in principle the same in England and Scotland, and they commented that "the procedural and theoretical differences which exist between the two systems do not obscure the wide similarity of substance in the law of the two countries."[27] They went on, however, to draw attention to the inevitable procedural differences between the two systems and to certain differences of emphasis (which may be more theoretical than real); they came to the conclusion that "in matters of this kind the law should be the same north and south of the border."[28]

It is clearly desirable that the substantive law of contempt should be rationalised and uniform, as between the two jurisdictions, especially in the light of modern communications. Not surprisingly, in view of the relatively large part which the media have played in the application of the modern law of contempt, it appears to have been this factor which primarily motivated the Committee's recommendation for greater uniformity of approach. They drew attention (especially in the context of the uncertainties created by *Stirling v Associated*

---

[25] *e.g. Leys v Leys* (1886) 13 R. 1223; *Kerr's Factor v Kerr and Milligan* (1868) 6 M. 1125.
[26] *e.g.* where a defender has been ordered to sign a disposition or discharge. See *Whyte v Whyte* 1913 2 S.L.T. 85; *Wallace's Curator v Wallace* 1924 S.C. 212; *Ferguson's Curator Bonis, Petr* (1905) 7 F. 898; *McAlley's JF Petr* (1900) 2 F. 1198; *Orr Ewing's JF, Petr* (1884) 11 R. 682; *Edgar, Petr v Fisher's Trs* (1893) 21 R. 59, 325, (1894) 21 R. 1076.
[27] Cmnd. 5794, para.23.
[28] *ibid.*

Newspapers Ltd)[29] to the fact that those who produce any publication which is distributed nationally often felt obliged to apply one test, in relation to the law of contempt, to an article touching on English legal proceedings and another one where Scottish proceedings were concerned.[30] Naturally, the same difficulty applies to radio and television broadcasts (as the case of *Atkins v London Weekend Television Ltd* has subsequently illustrated).

16–270 Although many of the Committee's recommendations were, therefore, of general application, it may be thought to be helpful in a chapter relating to the law of Scotland to summarise the effect of the recommendations which related, for procedural or other reasons, peculiarly to that jurisdiction.

B. Scottish courts with contempt jurisdiction

16–271 In Chapter 2 of the Report the Committee commented that the powers of the Court of Session and the High Court of Justiciary, which exercise civil and criminal jurisdiction respectively, were analogous to those of the Supreme Court in England and Wales.[31] The sheriff court, on the other hand, called for special comment since it exercises a wide civil and criminal jurisdiction in Scotland, while there is no real parallel in the English judicial system. They mentioned the sheriff's unrestricted common law powers in the matter of contempt, in circumstances where he tries a criminal case on indictment with a jury, which is the "solemn" as opposed to the "summary" procedure; it was pointed out that there was room for doubt as to the extent of the sheriff's powers with reference to contempt in summary criminal proceedings, a doubt which the Committee felt it desirable to remove.[32]

16–272 In the context of considering the sheriff court, the Committee also highlighted[33] the relatively limited nature of the function of the stipendiary magistrates' courts and district courts in Scotland as compared with magistrates in England. (Notwithstanding this, however, as has been pointed out above, the district courts like other courts of summary jurisdiction have limited statutory powers to deal with contempts in the face of the court and to compel the attendance of witnesses: now under s.155 of the Criminal Procedure (Scotland) Act 1995.)[34]

C. Contempts in court

16–273 In Chapter 3 the Committee came to the conclusion that, notwithstanding the criticism of the court's summary powers, it was necessary that judges should be

---

[29] 1960 S.L.T. 5. See paras 16–167 *et seq*. Although, as explained in paras 16–177 *et seq*., some of the uncertainty was subsequently removed by the decision in *Hall v Associated Newspapers Ltd*, 1978 S.L.T. 241, yet further pitfalls were highlighted for English editors publishing in Scotland both by *Hall* itself and by *HM Advocate v George Outram & Co Ltd* 1980 S.L.T. 13. English police authorities had traditionally been freer in their comments to the press than those in Scotland, and both these cases illustrated the hazard of quoting English police officers in a Scottish publication.
[30] Cmnd. 5794, para.24.
[31] *ibid*., para.26.
[32] *ibid*.
[33] *ibid*.
[34] Set out at para.16–115.

able to deal quickly and effectively with disruptive conduct in order to enable the business of the courts to continue. They felt that it was appropriate that the existing practice whereby judges dealt themselves with contempts in the face of the court should continue.[35] They rejected the suggestion that matters should be dealt with by another judge, presumably made on the basis that the judge in whose court the offence had occurred could not himself be objective; the Committee took the view that the individual judge concerned would be in the best position to know how to deal with such a contempt. Judges were, the Committee felt, sufficiently conscious of the fact that the summary powers existed not for the preservation of their own dignity but for the protection of the administration of justice, and for the orderly running of the courts. If the power of immediate punishment were removed, it was felt that some of the deterrent effect of the contempt jurisdiction would disappear with it.[36]

It was in relation to sentencing procedure, in particular, that the Committee made reference to Scottish practice. It was pointed out that one danger resulting from the summary procedure, with the judge being able to deal with the matter on the spot, was that "on occasion a penalty is imposed with undue haste."[37] It was felt to be necessary, therefore, that the power of sentencing should be exercised only after due deliberation and that the judge should be uninfluenced "by the heat or exasperation of the moment." Accordingly, it was recommended "that in all cases in which more than a small fine is considered a period of delay should be interposed between determination of the issues of contempt and the imposition of the penalty."[38] This recommendation was made irrespective of whether the contemnor admitted responsibility or not. Because it was in line with the recommendation which the Committee were making, express reference was made to the practice recently sanctioned by the High Court of Justiciary of adjourning contempt cases for imposition of the penalty.[39] Thus, the recommendation of the Committee was, both in relation to Scotland and to England and Wales, that wherever the court considered imposing a custodial penalty there should be a power to remand in custody between finding the contempt proved and sentence.

16-274

D. The right to be heard

It was further recommended that the alleged contemnor should always be entitled to be heard in mitigation of sentence and that he should be entitled to legal representation, with legal aid if necessary, even if the charge was not denied.[40] The power to grant legal aid on an emergency basis was thought to be desirable, in view of the fact that the contemnor's liberty might be in peril as well as his

16-275

---

[35] *ibid.*, para.30.
[36] *ibid.*
[37] *ibid.*, para.33. See, *e.g. Macara v MacFarlane*, 1980 S.L.T. (Notes) 27.
[38] *ibid.*
[39] See *Royle v Gray* 1973 S.L.T. 31; *Cordiner, Petr*, 1973 S.L.T. 125.
[40] Cmnd. 5794, para.33.

16–275

pocket. Accordingly it was recommended that the relevant statutes and regulations should be amended in such a way as to achieve uniformity in England and Scotland.[41]

E. The point in proceedings from which the law of contempt is to apply

1. Criminal proceedings

16–276 This is one of the areas in which the Committee was particularly exercised, as pointed out above in the context of *Stirling v Associated Newspapers Ltd*[42] and *Hall v Associated Newspapers Ltd*.[43] Their conclusion was that in Scotland the strict liability provisions should apply from the moment when the person is first publicly charged on the petition or otherwise, or at the first calling in court of a summary complaint, as the case may be. It was felt, in relation both to England and Scotland, that the moment at which the warrant for arrest was issued was not a suitable point to choose, since its issue may not become known to the public, and the media not appreciate whether they were at risk. Furthermore, the restrictions on the media could be of indefinite duration if there was a delay in executing the warrant. The recommendation for Scotland was therefore in line with that made for England (where the moment chosen was that at which the suspected man is charged or the summons is served).[44]

2. Civil proceedings

16–277 A majority of the Committee came to the conclusion that strict liability should operate in Scotland from the date of allowance of proof or jury trial in the Court of Session and sheriff courts.[45] Mr. Robin Day, however, expressed his minority view[46] that both in England and Scotland there should be a *"sub judice* list," which would be published shortly (say one or two weeks) before the trial. Once a civil case was in this list, it would become subject to the law of contempt and the media would then know with certainty where they stood. Mr. Day came to these conclusions partly in the light of the oral evidence given to the Committee by Lords Denning and Salmon, which he quoted in his Note. Lord Denning expressed the view, in relation to English law, that the moment of "setting down"[47] was too early, since thereafter a case could still be delayed (sometimes up to two years) for one reason or another, and the period of press restraint would therefore be of uncertain duration. Lord Salmon, on the other hand, went so far

---

[41] *ibid.*, para.32: The Committee had in mind *inter alia* the provisions of Art.6(3)(b) and (c) of the European Convention on Human Rights which is set out in para.2–143.
[42] 1960 S.L.T. 5, discussed in paras 16–167 *et seq.*
[43] 1978 S.L.T. 241, discussed in para.16–172.
[44] Cmnd. 5794, para.123. The question of arrest not being known to the public did not trouble the High Court in *Hall*, and they expressed the view that in practice the newspapers would be interested generally in cases of some notoriety. See para.16–183. An earlier moment, that of arrest, was selected as the *terminus a quo* both by the High Court in *Hall* and by Parliament in the 1981 Act: see Sch.1.
[45] Cmnd. 5794, para.127.
[46] Note at p.98 of the Report.
[47] This terminology is now obsolete in England.

as to say "I would not have any contempt. I say never. Certainly never in a Judge-alone case." Mr. Day, however, took the view that some restriction on comment was required.

F. The "open record" in Scotland

16–278 Special mention was made by the Committee of the complication which arose from the practice applying to the system of written pleadings in the Court of Session and the sheriff court. For so long as the record was "open," pleadings were regarded as adjustable at will by either party. One consequence is that a defender might initially place on record a very limited or restricted statement of his case (including perhaps what was sometimes referred to in England as a "holding defence" and in Scotland a "skeleton defence").

16–279 The Committee therefore took the view that a publication of the defence at this stage "would give a very misleading view of the defender's real and ultimate case." They believed, however, that any difficulty could be met by retaining the rule that while the record is open the pleadings are regarded as confidential, and available only for the court and the parties themselves. Furthermore, they did not suggest reform of the rule whereby it was regarded in Scotland as a contempt, by reason of their confidential nature, to publish any part of the unadjusted pleadings.[48] The consequence of this rule was apparently that the press had played safe by not even publishing the nature of the claim while the record remained "open." Nevertheless, it was recommended that "it should not be a contempt to publish any information about the case which was not proved to have been derived from, or to relate directly to, the unadjusted pleadings."[49]

G. Defence of innocent publication

16–280 By s.11(1) of the Administration of Justice Act 1960 it was provided that:

"A person shall not be guilty of contempt of court on the ground that he has published any matter calculated to interfere with the course of justice in connection with any proceedings pending or imminent at the time of publication if at that time (having taken all reasonable care) he did not know and had no reason to suspect that the proceedings were pending, or that such proceedings were imminent, as the case may be."

The section did not apply to Scotland, but the Committee took the view that the essence of the defence should be retained for England and Wales and extended to Scotland. There would be consequential amendments to the specific terms of the provision, in the light particularly of their recommendations as to the point in proceedings at which the rule of strict liability should begin to apply. The Committee mentioned that in future the defence would be of limited application, because the fact that a charge has been laid or a case set down is in most cases discoverable with reasonable ease by the press, and they should not accordingly

---

[48] See paras 16–213 *et seq.* See also the obiter remarks of the court in *Hall v Associated Newspapers Ltd*, 1978 S.L.T. 241 at 248 as to the point at which civil proceedings may be regarded as having commenced for the purposes of the jurisdiction in contempt.
[49] Cmnd. 5794, para.130.

need to rely upon the statutory defence.[50] In fact, the defence has been superseded by s.3 of the 1981 Act.

H. Reprisals against witnesses or jurors

16–281 In Chapter 6 of the Report the Committee recommended that it should not be treated as contempt to take or threaten reprisals against a witness. They expressed agreement with views of Pearson L.J. in *Att-Gen v Butterworth*[51] to the effect that trial by jury would be more appropriate for determining the issue of the defendant's intention or purpose. There is in cases of that kind no pressing need for prompt disposal of the matter in the light of the fact that the relevant proceedings will have been concluded. The case in question concerned a witness who was deprived of his office of treasurer and delegate in a branch of a trade union, because his colleagues thought that, in giving evidence in court proceedings, he had acted against the interests of the union.

16–282 The Committee took the view that it would be appropriate to deal with such a matter by way of a separate criminal offence along the lines of that created by the Witnesses (Public Inquiries) Protection Act 1892, which applied both in Scotland and in England.[52] It was provided by s.2 of the Act:

> "Every person who commits any of the following acts, that is to say, who threatens, or in any way punishes, damnifies, or injures, or attempts to punish, damnify, or injure, any person for having given evidence upon any inquiry, or on account of the evidence which he has given upon any such inquiry, shall, unless such evidence was given in bad faith, be guilty of a misdemeanour, and be liable on conviction thereof to a maximum penalty of £100 or to a maximum imprisonment of three months."

16–283 It was conceded that the wording of the provision was in some respects out of date but the Committee considered that the it represented the right approach. In their view the maximum penalties should be in line with those for contempt in the superior courts. The Committee added that, although they were not aware of any cases of reprisals being taken against a juror in respect of his acting in that capacity, it would be appropriate for the new statutory provision to cover jurors as well as witnesses.[53]

I. Scandalising the court

16–284 Similarly, it was recommended that the branch of the law dealing with scandalising should be replaced by a new and strictly defined criminal offence. The offence was to be constituted by the publication of matter imputing improper or corrupt judicial conduct with the intention of impairing confidence in the administration of justice. Criticism, even if scurrilous, should only be punishable

---

[50] *ibid.*, para.133. cf. the similar comments made in *Hall v Associated Newspapers Ltd*, at para.16–183.
[51] [1963] 1 Q.B. 696. Cf. *Hillfinch Properties v Newark Investments, The Times*, July 1, 1981 (in which there was a threat by a Rabbinical court to excommunicate an orthodox Jew who did not take his dispute to them rather than to the civil courts).
[52] Cmnd. 5794, para.157.
[53] *ibid.*, para.158.

in the Committee's view if it fulfilled those two requirements. The offence should be triable only on indictment and, as the matter would relate to the administration of justice itself, prosecution in Scotland should only be at the instance of the Lord Advocate (and of the Attorney-General in England and Wales).

The Committee recommended that a defence should be available if the defender could prove not only that what he had said was true but also that the publication as such was for the public benefit. They indicated that there was a precedent for such a defence in England and Wales, in the context of the law of criminal libel, which has no application to Scotland.[54] In their view, the proper course for anyone to take who believes he has evidence of judicial corruption or lack of impartiality is to submit it to the proper authority (in Scotland, the Secretary of State). By reason of s.13 of the Sheriff Courts (Scotland) Act 1907[55] he had the power of removing judicial officers below the High Court level, and the Committee seemed to think therefore that he would also be the appropriate recipient of complaints as to the conduct of High Court judges. The Committee held that it was hard to conceive how it could be held to be for the public benefit to publish allegations imputing improper motives if the defendant had taken no steps to report the matter to the proper authority.

16–285

The practical consequences of this recommendation would not be likely to be very significant, since this aspect of the law of contempt has not been invoked for many years either in Scotland or in England. Furthermore, the Judges Act 1540, which made the abuse of judges ("murmuring") in Scotland a statutory offence was repealed in 1973 by the Statute Law (Repeals) Act, although the common law power to deal with this type of offence still remained. The recommendation to remove offences of this type from the law of contempt was only intended to apply where there is no urgent need for a summary procedure. If the conduct occurred in the face of the court, or related to particular proceedings in progress, and a risk of serious prejudice thereby arose, the Committee took the view that such conduct should be capable of being dealt with summarily as a contempt.[56] Where there is no such need of urgency, however, the new offence would provide the only means of process.

16–286

The Committee did not find it appropriate to remove such offences altogether from the ambit of the law, even allowing for the liberalisation of the courts' approach towards criticism over the past century, since "there is need for an effective remedy, both in England and Wales, and in Scotland, against imputations of improper or corrupt judicial conduct." The law of defamation is not sufficient to deal with the problem. First, the law should be concerned with the protection of the administration of justice, and especially the preservation of public confidence in its honesty and impartiality. The personal reputations of judges, which the law of defamation would in theory protect, are of only incidental concern. Secondly, judges would no doubt feel inhibited about the commencement of libel proceedings. Thus, the Committee's view was that the

16–287

---

[54] *ibid.*, para.167.
[55] Repealed by the Sheriff Courts (Scotland) Act 1971, Sch.2.
[56] Cmnd. 5794, para.163.

public interest in the protection of the reputation of the administration of justice required a public remedy in respect of conduct which undermines that reputation.[57]

J. Sentencing powers

1. Superior courts

16–288 The Committee recommended that the same limitation upon sentencing as was recommended for England and Wales should apply in Scotland.[58] The maximum limit was to be two years on sentences of imprisonment in the Court of Session and the High Court of Justiciary, but there was to be no limit on the fines that might be imposed. It was also recommended that the superior courts in Scotland should have power in appropriate cases to deal with mentally disordered contemnors by way, for example, of an order under s.55 of the Mental Health (Scotland) Act 1960.[59] Previously there was no rule of law which prescribed that any sentence of imprisonment in Scotland, in respect of contempt, should be for a determinate period. Nevertheless, the practice had grown up of imposing fixed sentences.

2. Sheriff courts

16–289 The Committee did not appear to have any strong view as to whether the same limits should be brought into effect in relation to sheriff courts, although they commented that there would seem to be force in the proposition that a lesser limit would be appropriate. In the event, they recommended that the sheriff's powers of imprisonment in all proceedings, civil or criminal, should be limited to three months, and fines to £150. They regarded it as appropriate that he should have the same powers in relation to mentally disordered contemnors. In cases where the sheriff considered his sentencing powers to be inadequate, he should be able to remit to the High Court or to the Court of Session as appropriate.[60]

3. Stipendiary magistrates and district courts

16–290 It was recommended that the powers to punish contempts in the face of the court should be the same as those recommended for magistrates' courts in England and Wales, namely seven days' imprisonment or a £20 fine. There should also be a power to certify more serious cases to the High Court of Justiciary. It was not suggested that any change should be effected in relation to the limits imposed by ss.3 and 33 of the Summary Jurisdiction (Scotland) Act 1954 (since repealed). These provisions restricted the power of imprisonment to 60 days and limited fines to £50. Witnesses could be punished for contempt by a fine of not more than £25 or by imprisonment of up to 20 days. The Committee did not recommend

---

[57] ibid., para.162.
[58] ibid., para.208.
[59] See now the Mental Health (Scotland) Act 1984, as amended.
[60] Cmnd. 5794, para.207.

that legal aid (not otherwise available in District Courts in Scotland) should be made available exceptionally in respect of contempt cases. A further limitation, in line with the proposals for England and Wales, was that the power to remand in custody before sentence should be limited to a period of 24 hours.[61]

K. Procedure in Scotland

In cases where the authority of the court has been treated with contempt or defiance (as for example by breach of interdict), or where the person aggrieved is not a party to current proceedings, then the usual procedure is by way of petition and complaint to the Court of Session for the exercise of its power *nobile officium* or to the High Court of Justiciary, as appropriate. A party to civil proceedings, or the prosecutor or accused in criminal proceedings, may at any time bring to the notice of the court an alleged contempt by simple motion.

16–291

A petition and complaint, however, can only be presented with the concurrence of the Lord Advocate. The Committee accepted that this was necessary, on the basis that the responsibility for the initiation and conduct of criminal proceedings in Scotland rests with the Lord Advocate. Also, many actions which themselves constitute contempts may also at the same time be criminal, and it is plainly desirable that there should not be duplication. Thus, it is necessary for the court to whom the petition is addressed to be satisfied that the matter is not one which is engaging, or which may engage, the attention of the criminal authorities. As a petition and complaint is addressed to the court seeking the exercise of its power *nobile officium*, it can only be presented to the court which possesses this equitable and special jurisdiction; that is to say, the Court of Session and the High Court of Justiciary (the power being exercisable only by a *quorum* of the court, *i.e.* three judges). The Committee did not receive any evidence which led them to conclude that this form of procedure was not adequate for its purpose.

16–292

There is nothing equivalent to the exercise of the power *nobile officium* in the sheriff court, and the Committee did not recommend any change to enable this court to deal with such conduct as then fell to be proceeded against by way of petition and complaint. Nevertheless, they saw no reason why, once proceedings have begun and are pending, matters of alleged contempt arising out of and in the course of those proceedings should not be dealt with in that court at the instance of a party. They recommended accordingly; but subject to the exception, where a criminal charge has been made, and where neither complaint nor indictment has yet been served, that any application should only be way of petition to the High Court of Justiciary.[62]

16–293

L. Appeals

1. *Civil proceedings*

The Committee recommended that provision should be made for a simpler avenue of appeal by way of Note or Minute, in the proceedings out of which the

16–294

---

[61] *ibid.*, para.208.
[62] *ibid.*, para.193.

contempt arose, for those who are not parties to the proceedings but who have been held guilty of contempt. This would apply, for example, to witnesses or persons refusing obedience to a court order. For such persons the Committee recommended that the procedure for appealing should be made to correspond to the means available to those who are parties to the process.

16–295   While a party to civil litigation had the ordinary rights of appeal, by means of a reclaiming motion (if the proceedings were in the Court of Session) or appeal (in the case of the sheriff court), the same right was not available to non-parties. Resort had to be made in such cases to the power *nobile officium* exercised by the Inner House of the Court of Session. The procedure was by way of petition at the instance of the party aggrieved. The object of the Committee's recommendations was to remove the necessity of applying to the court to exercise its power *nobile officium*; they wished to preserve the ordinary procedural steps in civil appeals but with adequate provision for summary disposal.[63]

2. Criminal proceedings

16–296   The Committee stated that the recognised mode of appeal was by way of Bill of Suspension. Despite the apparent illogicality of the prosecutor being required on such a procedure to become the Respondent (not being himself, as a general rule, party to the proceedings), the Committee did not advocate any change of procedure for review in cases of contempt arising out of summary criminal cases in the sheriff court. They apparently received no evidence advocating a change of procedure or suggesting any other form of review or appeal. The procedure had been followed in practice over the years (so the Committee reported) without disadvantage to the public interest.

16–297   The theoretical objection was considered by the Committee that, where there is a divergence on a question of fact between the suspender and the respondent (the prosecutor), the practice of the court was to accept the respondent's version of the facts. It was pointed out, however, that as the public prosecutor was not in such cases himself a party to the proceedings, was an official of the Crown under the supervision of the Crown Office, and had no interest in the outcome of the proceedings, it was unlikely that his version of the facts should be distorted or inaccurate.[64]

16–298   In fact it seems that the Committee's analysis is of no relevance to the current practice in the Scottish courts, since the recognised mode of appeal nowadays is by way of stated case.[65] In a number of cases the High Court of Justiciary has made it clear that a Bill of Suspension is only appropriate in certain limited circumstances. The stated case provides a more suitable means of review for findings in contempt cases, because this procedure requires the judge to state the facts found proved or admitted, and to determine the procedural steps taken and sentence imposed. He is also required to provide a note giving his reasons. These

---

[63] *ibid.*, para.195.
[64] *ibid.*, para.196.
[65] See the Criminal Procedure (Scotland) Act 1995, ss.176–184.

matters can be the subject of adjustment at the instance of the contemnor and the Procurator Fiscal. The sheriff must consider the adjustments and write his reasons for refusal of any adjustment. Thus the High Court of Justiciary will have a fuller picture than Committee contemplated.

The Committee went on to observe that although it was true, in courts of summary jurisdiction other than the sheriff court, that the prosecutor was not subject directly to the supervision of the Crown Office, he was nevertheless an independent official prosecuting in the public interest. There did not accordingly seem to be any ground for altering the existing procedure for review in such courts either.[66] For some years now, however, all prosecutors in the Stipendiary Magistrates' and District Courts have been Procurators Fiscal under the supervision of the Procurator and hence of the Crown Office. Thus, since the enactment of the District Courts (Scotland) Act 1975, this part of the Committee's report may be regarded as out of date also.

3. *Proceedings on indictment*

Where a matter of contempt arises in a case being tried on indictment, the only form of review open to anyone aggrieved is by way of petition to the *nobile officium* of the High Court of Justiciary.[67] The Committee took the view that amendment should be made where necessary to the Criminal Appeal (Scotland) Act 1926,[68] so that appeals might be made to the Court of Criminal Appeal by way of Note of Appeal, with a view to that Court being enabled to review both the merits of the finding and the sentence imposed.[69]

IX. THE CONTEMPT OF COURT ACT 1981: APPLICATION TO SCOTLAND

A. Closing the gap between Scotland and England

1. *Introduction*

When the Contempt of Court Bill was under consideration by Parliament, Lord Hailsham L.C. explained[70] that one of the objectives of the proposed legislation was to unify the law as between England and Scotland.

---

[66] *ibid.*, para.197.
[67] See, *e.g. Kemp, Petr; The Scotsman Publications Ltd, Petrs* 1982 S.C.C.R. 1 and the discussion of *Express Newspapers plc, Petr* 1999 S.L.T. 644, S.C.C.R. 262, S.C. (J.C.) 176, and *Wylie v HMA* 1966 S.L.T. 149 at 16–429.
[68] The modern equivalent is the Criminal Procedure (Scotland) Act 1995.
[69] Cmnd. 5794, para.198. Parliament has at no stage taken up the suggestion of substituting any new procedure, by way of note of appeal.
[70] *Hansard*, H.L. Vol. 415, (5th series), col. 660, December 9, 1980. See also the Phillimore Report, Cmnd. 5794, para.23, considered in paras 16–268 *et seq*. It was also observed by Hodgson J. in *Att-Gen v Sport Newspapers Ltd* [1991] 1 W.L.R. 1194 at 1227D, [1992] 1 All E.R. 503 at 534b that, as a matter of comity, it is "highly undesirable" that the law in this respect should be different in England and Scotland.

16–302 In the years after the Act came into effect it became clear that the provisions relating to strict liability contempts, and particularly with reference to media coverage of pending criminal proceedings, were being applied rather differently in England and Scotland.[71] It is an illustration of how statutory wording can be implemented along quite different lines, depending upon the value judgments and traditions that underlie or inform its interpretation. It seems that the Scottish and English courts have more recently been coming closer together in their application of public policy considerations relevant to these varied and difficult problems.[72] It would be surprising if this were not in large measure due to the need to take account of the priorities of the European Convention on Human Rights (which became operative in Scottish law on May 20, 1999, well over a year before England and Wales).

16–303 At the heart of the matter lies the notion that the statutory strict liability rule applies only to a publication "which creates a substantial risk that the course of justice in the proceedings in question will be seriously impeded or prejudiced".[73] That test has to be applied north and south of the border. This was emphasised by the Lord Justice-General in *Cox and Griffiths, Petrs*.[74] In *HMA v The Scotsman Publications Ltd*,[75] Lord Marnoch said it was common ground that the risk had to be "substantial", "material" or "greater than minimal" (a phrase adopted from Lord Emslie in *HMA v News Group Newspapers plc*).[76] He also acknowledged that the test has to be applied as at the date of publication, citing *Att-Gen v MGN Ltd*.[77] Nonetheless, whether any given publication falls foul of the strict liability rule will depend on a number of variable factors, including the extent to which the courts are prepared to regard jurors as being vulnerable to the influence of what they hear or see in the course of pre-trial publicity. This was a matter which, at least for a time, seemed to be approached rather differently depending no doubt on local context and professional experience.

16–304 Differing procedural considerations may also have some bearing. For example, the 110 day rule[78] for bringing criminal proceedings to trial in Scotland may have

---

[71] See the discussions by A.J. Bonnington in "Contempt of Court: A Practitioner's Viewpoint", 1988 S.L.T. (News) 33 at 38, where the conclusion is reached that "the same statute is interpreted so differently in England that it is almost impossible to believe that it is the same piece of legislation"; "Press and Prejudice" (1995) 145 New Law Jo. 1623: " . . . its application in Scotland is so starkly different from that in England that it is difficult to believe that the two jurisdictions are dealing with the same statutory provisions"; "Cross Borders: Cross Purposes" (1996) 146 New Law Jo. 1312: "For cross-border publications in broadcasts, the situation is quite simply a nightmare". See also *HMA v The Daily Record* (1997) part 9 Media Lawyer 28, a decision in which the Scottish High Court appeared unwilling to follow the English decision in *Att-Gen v MGN Ltd* [1997] 1 All E.R. 456. See para.16–317.
[72] See *Starrs and Chalmers v Ruxton, PF Linlithgow* 2000 J.C. 208; *Cox and Griffiths, Petrs* 1998 J.C. 267; *Al Megrahi and Fhima v Times Newspapers Ltd* 1999 S.C.C.R. 824 (High Court of Justiciary); *HMA v Danskin* 2000 S.C.C.R. 10.
[73] Contempt of Court Act 1981, s.2(2).
[74] 1998 J.C. 267 at 273, 1998 S.L.T. 1172.
[75] 1999 S.L.T. 466, 1999 S.C.C.R. 163.
[76] 1989 S.C.C.R. 156.
[77] [1997] 1 All E.R. 456. See also, for the same proposition, the remarks of the Lord Justice Clerk in *Al Megrahi and Fhima v Times Newspapers Ltd* 1999 S.C.C.R. 824.
[78] See now the Criminal Procedure (Scotland) Act 1995, s.65(4)(b).

meant that a publication contempt would be more difficult to defend on the basis of fading recollection in Scotland than south of the border.[79] The "fade factor" would appear to have played a significant part south of the border in the Law Officers' greater reluctance to initiate proceedings for contempt in media cases.

An important shift of emphasis, however, emerged in *Cox and Griffiths, Petrs*.[80] It is perhaps best illustrated in the words of Lord Prosser which seem now to be cited with regularity[81]:

> "Juries are healthy bodies. They do not need a germ free atmosphere. Even when articles in the press do contain germs of prejudice, it will rarely be appropriate, in my opinion, to bring these to the attention of the court, far less for specific directions to have to be given, far less for the issue to be treated as even potentially one of contempt".

To similar effect was a passage in the judgment of Lord Hope in *Montgomery v HMA*[82] where he observed that the entire system of jury trial is based upon the assumption that a jury will follow the instructions which they receive from the trial judge and return a true verdict in accordance with the evidence.

2. *"Bad English precedents"*

When the problem of "trial by newspaper" was being considered by Lord Clyde in *Stirling v Associated Newspapers Ltd*,[83] he told counsel for the newspaper in the course of the hearing that it was "no use quoting 'bad' English precedents".[84] This was a reference to certain English authorities which had no application in Scotland by reason of differences in English procedure.

The case which counsel had cited related to the preliminary hearing before justices which was known in England and Wales as the "committal" procedure. One of the main objects of the exercise, which does not have any parallel in Scotland, was to let the accused know in advance the case he had to meet and the evidence on which the prosecution relied. Prior to 1967 this meant that newspapers in England were free to report fully the *ex parte* statements of Crown

---

[79] The point in the text was made by the court in *HMA v News Group Newspapers plc* 1989 S.C.C.R. 156 at 163E, by Lord Justice-General Emslie.
[80] 1998 J.C. 267, 1998 S.L.T. 1172.
[81] They appeared, for example, shortly afterwards in the High Court in *Danskin v HMA* 2002 S.L.T. 889 at 892 at [10]. It was held there on appeal that it was, in the light of Lord Prosser's remarks, impossible to disagree with the trial judge's conclusion that no express direction had been required to the jury to ignore press coverage.
[82] [2003] 1 A.C. 641 at 674A–B, 2000 S.C.C.R. 1044 at 1107B.
[83] 1960 S.L.T. 5. The publication in *Hall v Associated Newspapers Ltd* was also described by the High Court of Justiciary as being "as clear an example as could be found of 'trial by newspaper.' "; 1978 S.L.T. at 250.
[84] See 1960 S.L.T. (News) 29, 30. In this commentary, the anonymous commentator appears to have thought that the bad English precedent in question was *R. v Evening Standard Ltd* (1924) T.L.R. 833. But, since the court was concerned with the English procedure of preliminary hearings before a magistrate, it must have been *Evening Standard* [1954] 1 Q.B. 578 that was under discussion.

16–307 witnesses at the preliminary hearing without any challenge or rebuttal from the defence side to balance out the report—something which simply could not arise in Scotland. This problem in England and Wales was dealt with to a large extent by s.3 of the Criminal Justice Act 1967, and subsequently by s.8 of the Magistrates' Courts Act 1980,[85] which restricted the right of newspapers to report such preliminary hearings, except on certain defined and limited matters. Nevertheless, at the time of *Stirling* in 1960 the older English practice still prevailed.

16–308 Against this background, therefore, the Lord Justice-General's remark about "bad English precedents" should not be taken as indicating any intention to draw any more fundamental distinction between the principles to be applied in Scotland to "trial by newspaper" and those applied in England. Indeed, apart from the impact of such procedural distinctions, the principles sought to be applied had been remarkably similar in both jurisdictions.[86] It is therefore perhaps surprising how far the two systems seemed for a time to be diverging after what was intended to be a unifying statute. On the other hand, more recently there has been a degree of cross-fertilisation in this field between Scottish and English judicial analyses.

3. *The robustness of jurors: the converging approaches*

16–309 The decision of the Divisional Court in *Att-Gen v MGN Ltd*[87] was significant in England not least for the readiness with which the court was prepared to apply *dicta* on the robustness of jurors, not only from contempt cases but also from appeals against conviction, based upon pre-trial publicity or adverse coverage of the trial itself. Reliance had been placed, for example, on such cases as *R. v Coughlan*,[88] *R. v Cannan*,[89] and *Ex p. The Telegraph plc*.[90] Shortly afterwards, it was emphasised in the Court of Appeal that the courts should not speak with two voices, one used to dismiss criminal appeals with the court roundly rejecting any suggestion that prejudice resulted from media publications, the other holding comparable publications to be in contempt.[91]

---

[85] As amended by the Criminal Procedure and Investigations Act 1996, s.29. This has been prospectively repealed and is due for replacement by a new system under the name of "allocation and sending" by the Criminal Justice Act 2003, s.41, Sch.3.

[86] In *Hall v Associated Newspapers Ltd* 1978 S.L.T. 241, reference was expressly made to the decision of the House of Lords in *Att-Gen v Times Newspapers Ltd* [1974] A.C. 273 and in *Atkins v London Weekend Television Ltd* 1978 J.C. 48, S.L.T. 76 the court considered the question of whether there was "a real risk of prejudice" and commented: "The Courts in England would, we understand, ask precisely the same question."

[87] [1997] 1 All E.R. 456 (following the abandonment of the trial, in the light of media coverage), discussed at paras 4–155 *et seq*. But see now *Att-Gen v Birmingham Post and Mail Ltd* [1998] 4 All E.R. 49, D.C., which suggests that, save in case of multiple publication, the court will consider whether the publication in question would give rise to a "seriously arguable" ground for an appeal.

[88] (1976) 63 Cr.App.R. 33.

[89] (1991) 92 Cr.App.R. 16.

[90] [1993] 1 W.L.R. 980 at 987, Lord Taylor C.J.

[91] See the words of Simon Brown L.J. in *Att-Gen v Unger* [1998] 1 Cr.App.R. 308 at 318E–F, cited at paras 4–169 *et seq*.

16–310 In Scotland it seems that the corresponding two lines of authority, dealing with criminal appeals on the one hand and the creation of prejudice in the context of contempt on the other, remained distinct. Indeed, it might be thought that there was an inconsistency of policy, which had indeed already been overtly recognised before the 1981 Act. It is illustrated by the circumstances of *HMA v Stuurman*.[92] In that case the High Court concluded that the publications in question had created "the gravest risk of prejudice" in respect of the trial of three Dutch citizens for criminal offences alleged against them in Scotland. Later, however, the same court rejected submissions that they could not for that reason receive a fair trial from the jury. In the words of Lord Avonside[93]:

> "In asserting that proceedings in cases of contempt of Court would necessarily, or even might, stop criminal proceedings it must be assumed that at least some jurors will disobey the direction in law communicated to them by the trial Judge. There seems no proper reason to so surmise. Such reasoning could and would apply to the reaction of any jury to any instruction in law given in any case. On the contrary it must be assumed that jurors will behave with propriety and that they will exclude from their deliberations all matters which were not given in evidence in Court in the course of a trial. If this assumption is not made then trial by jury would be meaningless in this sense, that if it were accepted that directions in law might be disregarded or disobeyed the justification for trial by jury in indictment proceedings would collapse".

16–311 In *HMA v Outram*,[94] an article appeared in the *Glasgow Herald* in October 1979 identifying four individuals arrested on drugs charges. It described the results of police investigations in some detail and referred to matters of an incriminating character. Contempt was admitted and comments were made in the High Court of Justiciary to the effect that the offence was "of the gravest character" and "in the highest degree objectionable". Indeed, in the light of guidance given in *Atkins v London Weekend Television Ltd*[95] and *Hall v Associated Newspapers Ltd*,[96] the publication was "well nigh incomprehensible". Nevertheless, the same court, a few weeks later, when the accused asked for the indictments to be dismissed on the basis of that prejudice, took the view that they would be able to receive a fair hearing from a properly directed jury.

16–312 To similar effect were the words of Lord Cameron in *X v Sweeney*[97]:

> "... I think it may be assumed that jurors, having taken an oath to return a true verdict according to the evidence and having received clear direction from the presiding judge to put from their minds everything except the evidence which they have heard in court, will be faithful to that oath and obedient to the directions of the judge."

---

[92] (1980) J.C. 111.
[93] At 116–17. See also *X v Sweeney*, 1982 S.C.C.R. 161 at 172, 173; *Russell v HMA* 1992 S.L.T. 25.
[94] 1980 S.L.T. 13.
[95] 1978 S.L.T. 76.
[96] 1978 S.L.T. 241.
[97] 1982 S.C.C.R. 161 at 173.

16–313 The sentiments expressed in these passages are reminiscent of the terms of the language used in some of the Canadian[98] and English cases.[99] On the other hand, they are not easy to reconcile with the response of Lord Justice-General Hope to the submissions made on behalf of the *Evening Times* in *HMA v Caledonian Newspapers Ltd*[1] that there was no realistic possibility of the jury being influenced if, as was to be presumed, they were to follow the directions of the trial judge to decide the case solely on the evidence. The proposition was rejected that a publisher " . . . can pray in aid steps which may be taken afterwards by the court to minimise the risk of prejudice resulting from a publication which would seriously impede or prejudice the proceedings if these steps were not taken."[2]

16–314 It is necessary also to consider two unreported cases, which threw some light on the attitude of the courts at the time towards jurors' capacity for discounting extraneous material and giving priority to the evidence which they have heard and seen in court. In the first, *HMA v Pollock*,[3] Lord Cowie was considering a BBC programme which had published the full terms of an indictment after he had separated the charges into two indictments. He had then taken the view that it would have been prejudicial to allow evidence relating to charges of perverting the course of justice to be led alongside evidence on the principal charges of moneylending. This was simply because he thought it would be prejudicial for the accused to stand trial on all charges at the same time. At the contempt hearing, he made clear that he had not ordered the separation for the reason that he did not want the jury dealing with the moneylending charges to know of the others. He expressed the view that if the jurors heard the broadcast they would recognise that there had been a mistake on the part of the reporter for the very reason that they had copies of the indictment before them (which contained no charges of perverting the course of justice).

16–315 The second unreported case is that of *HMA v McGill and Strain*,[4] in which Lord Kirkwood in a case concerning the *Evening Times* followed the approach of Lord Cowie. A councillor had been charged with fraud and the newspaper published a story which was factually inaccurate. The view was taken that the

---

[98] *R. v Corbett* (1988) 41 C.C.C. (3d) 385 at 400–1, followed by the Supreme Court of Canada in *Re Dagenais and Canadian Broadcasting Corp* (1995) 94 C.C.C. (3d) 289 at 322; 120 D.L.R. (4th) 12 at 43.
[99] See *Ex p. Telegraph plc* [1993] 1 W.L.R. 980 at 987, [1993] 2 All E.R. 971 at 978, Lord Taylor C.J.; *R. v Coughlan* (1976) 63 Cr.App.R. 33; *R. v Cannan* (1991) 92 Cr.App.R. 16, discussed in paras 2–97, 4–160 *et seq.*
[1] 1995 S.C.C.R. 330 at 342, 344.
[2] But see the conclusion of the sheriff in *Kilbane v HMA* 1989 S.C.C.R. 313 to the effect that the risk of prejudice arising from the local press in that case was such that it could be obviated by an appropriate direction to the jury; a conclusion which the High Court on appeal held he was entitled to reach. Cf. the decision in *HMA v Mitchell*, 1993 S.C.C.R. 793 at 802, where it was held on the facts of that case that the sheriff had been entitled to conclude that, despite the lapse of 12 months from the publications complained of, there was still a risk of prejudice which could *not* be expected to be removed by directions from the trial judge. It is by no means surprising that media lawyers considered the law to be in a state of unacceptable uncertainty.
[3] Airdrie High Court, December 3, 1984, discussed in A.J. Bonnington, "Contempt of Court: A Practitioner's Viewpoint" 1988 S.L.T. 33 at 36.
[4] Unreported, Glasgow High Court, March 3, 1987. See again A.J. Bonnington, "Contempt of Court: A Practitioner's Viewpoint" 1988 S.L.T. (News) 33 at 36.

jury would therefore know that the story was wrong and thus proceed on the basis of the evidence before them.

A different approach appears to have been taken by Lord Mayfield in *HMA v Keating*.[5] This was a case in which contempt was alleged against the Scottish editor of *The Sun* newspaper in the course of the trial of a man accused of trying to murder his wife by attaching explosives to her car. The story in the newspaper gave the impression that the accused had admitted putting the explosive in the car. Despite the fact that the jury knew this to be false, or could have been so reminded by the judge, Lord Mayfield regarded the publication as a very serious contempt, and imposed a fine of £5,000 upon the respondent.

In practice, it would have been difficult to imagine a Scottish court at the time, if faced with similar publications to those which formed the subject matter of *Att-Gen v MGN Ltd*, arriving at the same conclusion. Yet there are signs of the courts proceeding more recently on similar lines. The facts of *Att-Gen v MGN* were striking. When proceedings had just become active, detailed accounts were published in the newspapers of alleged assaults which were likely to comprise some part of the contested prosecution case at trial. In the light of Scottish authority, such publicity would almost certainly have been treated as creating the requisite degree of risk. The case was cited in *HMA v The Daily Record*,[6] on the basis that it appeared to have led lawyers to the conclusion that the articles would not fall foul of the law. It seemed in argument that the High Court would have been unwilling to follow the English decision. One distinguishing factor referred to by Lord Marnoch was that identification could be an important issue in the *Daily Record* case, whereas this had no application in *MGN*. The picture of the accused had been shown in *The Daily Record*, together with an account of his previous convictions, and the appellation "sex beast". In the event leading counsel for *The Daily Record* and for *The Sun* conceded that a contempt had been committed. Both newspapers were fined £5,000, and the editors £250 each.[7]

In England, it began to seem that it was easier to obtain an order for the stay of criminal proceedings, on the ground of abuse of process, than to persuade a court that the relevant media were guilty of contempt. One reason for this might be, as Schiemann L.J. suggested in *Att-Gen v MGN Ltd*,[8] that:

"A consequence of the need in contempt proceedings, in which respondents face imprisonment or a fine, to be sure and to look at each publication separately and the need in trial proceedings to look at risk of publicity created by the totality of publications can be that it is proper to stay proceedings on the ground of prejudice albeit that no individual is guilty of contempt".

---

[5] *HMA v Keating*, unreported, Edinburgh H.C., August 1987; see Bonnington, *loc. cit.*
[6] (1997) Pt 9, Media Lawyer 28.
[7] We are indebted to Mr Bonnington for his note of the proceedings.
[8] [1997] 1 All E.R. 456 at 466g. This matter was further considered in *Att-Gen v Birmingham Post and Mail Ltd* [1998] 4 All E.R. 49, DC, which tends to confirm that the fact of multiple publication in *Att-Gen v MGN Ltd* was an especially significant feature.

16–319 Nevertheless, in *HMA v The Scotsman Publications Ltd*,[9] Lord Marnoch described the Divisional Court decision in *Att-Gen v MGN Ltd*[10] as providing "a particularly useful index of the various matters which should be borne in mind in a case of this sort". The judgment of Schiemann L.J. was also referred to in the High Court in *HMA v Beggs (No.2)*.[11] The court's confidence in the robustness of jurors, and their capacity to concentrate on the evidence, the submissions of counsel and the directions of the judge, was further affirmed in *BBC, Ptrs*,[12] where the High Court of Justiciary allowed an appeal and recalled a s.4(2) order as being unnecessary. The view was taken also in *HMA v Wilson*[13] that any prejudice occasioned by the reporting of a preliminary hearing could be eliminated by suitable directions from the trial judge in due course.

4. *The differing application of section 7*

16–320 A significant difference between the two jurisdictions is that the restriction contained within s.7 of the Contempt of Court Act, whereby only the Attorney-General can institute proceedings under the strict liability rule, has no parallel in Scotland. A.J. Bonnington has suggested[14] that this would have made all the difference to the outcome of the case of the Taylor sisters. They had succeeded in having a conviction overturned because of press coverage of their trial[15] but failed to obtain a review of the Law Officers' refusal to launch contempt proceedings against the publishers or editors responsible.[16]

16–321 In Scotland, they would have been able to institute "strict liability" proceedings themselves. In *Robb v Caledonian Newspapers Ltd*[17] a Church of Scotland minister brought proceedings in respect of the *Evening Times*, notwithstanding the fact that the Lord Advocate had taken no action when the publicity had been drawn to his attention. The prejudice alleged was in respect of criminal proceedings pending against the minister for sexual offences. Lord Hope referred to the decision by Parliament not to incorporate within the 1981 Act any equivalent provision to that contained in s.7, and inferred that it had been intended to preserve the right of an accused person, long recognised in Scotland, to petition directly.

5. *The interpretation of section 5*

16–322 Another divergence relates to the interpretation of s.5 of the 1981 Act. For example, it is clear from the decision of the English Court of Appeal in *Leary v*

---

[9] 1999 S.L.T. 466, S.C.C.R. 163.
[10] [1997] 1 All E.R. 456 at 460–1.
[11] 2002 S.L.T. 139, S.C.C.R. 879.
[12] 2001 S.C.C.R. 440.
[13] High Court of Justiciary, June 15, 2001.
[14] (1995) 145 New Law Jo. 1623.
[15] *R. v Taylor and Taylor* (1993) 98 Cr.App.R. 361.
[16] *R. v Solicitor-General Ex p. Taylor* [1995] T.L.R. 477.
[17] 1995 S.L.T. 631.

BBC[18] that when an application is made for an injunction, to restrain an apprehended contempt, it is legitimate for the court to take into account the strength or otherwise of a prospective defence under s.5 of the Act (that is to say, that the publication in question will form "part of a discussion in good faith of public affairs or other matters of general public interest", and should thus not be treated as contempt if the anticipated risk of prejudice is merely incidental to the discussion). By contrast, in *Muir v BBC*,[19] it was held that consideration of s.5 did not have to be taken into account at the stage of considering whether to prohibit the broadcasting of a potentially prejudicial programme.

This case also illustrates a more general difference of approach to the interpretation of s.5. It is clear from the treatment of its provisions by the House of Lords in *Att-Gen v English*[20] that, in judging the application of the defence, it is not permitted to consider whether the publisher concerned could have framed his article or broadcast differently, by excluding the prejudicial passage. The matter has to be judged objectively on the basis of the simple question whether the apprehended prejudice can be described as "incidental" or not. In other words, it was recognised that the balance was struck by Parliament in such a way that some risk of prejudice may have to be accepted, purely on the basis that it forms part of a discussion of matters of public interest.

16–323

In *Muir v BBC*, however, the High Court of Justiciary warned (and counsel had apparently accepted) that[21]:

16–324

"... the respondents would be in very considerable difficulty, having been told of the risk of prejudice to the petitioners, or a possible risk of prejudice to the petitioners, if they went ahead in broadcasting this programme. In the face of that warning they would be in considerable difficulty in trying to invoke section 5 in any proceedings for contempt of court."

This contrasts, apparently, with the approach of the House of Lords since it is difficult to see, in statutory terms, how the objective question (as to whether the prejudice actually occasioned was or was not incidental) can be affected by any such "warning". What may underlie Lord Sutherland's reasoning is the unspoken recognition that, once a warning has been given, the broadcasters might be construed as having *intended* either to cause prejudice or, more likely, to create a risk of such prejudice. In such circumstances, it might be argued that the discussion would not qualify as being within the concept of "good faith". In view of the way Parliament chose to strike the balance between, on the one hand, freedom of expression and, on the other, the need to protect a citizen's right to a fair trial, it may be thought that such resort to the pre-1981 principles would provide too easy a method of circumventing the statutory defence.

16–325

---

[18] September 29, 1989 (Lexis).
[19] 1997 S.L.T. 425, S.C.C.R. 584. The commentary in the latter report records that it was intended to refer the decision to the European Commission on Human Rights: see at 589. Nothing appears to have come of this.
[20] [1983] 1 A.C. 116.
[21] 1997 S.L.T. 425 at 427H–I, 1996 S.C.C.R. 584.

16–326 Lord Sutherland also commented[22]:

> "There are certain situations where the media may find it necessary to broadcast or print some matter as a matter of urgent public importance and then the urgency of the matter may be one of the matters to be put on the scales in considering the balance between the public interest in having matters discussed and brought into the open, and the interests of the accused persons to have a fair trial".

16–327 He went on to observe that there was no urgency in the case before him; the only reason why the programme was sought to be broadcast that night was because it happened to be the last programme in the series of *Frontline Scotland*, and it would be inconvenient to postpone it to the autumn. There is, however, no test of "urgency" to be found in the wording of the statute, and it is submitted that the court may have therefore given less weight to the right of free speech than Parliament had intended or indeed than was accorded by the House of Lords in *Att-Gen v English*.[23]

6. The test for restraining publication

16–328 What is more, the court held in *Muir v BBC* that it has the power under the *nobile officium* to make a restraining order even if the proposed broadcast or publication would *not* amount to a contempt of court under the terms of the 1981 Act. The High Court of Justiciary has under its protection persons who have been charged and, if it considers that there is a risk of prejudice to the trial of such a person, then there is a power to prevent such prejudice from occurring by such means as are appropriate. Curiously, Lord Sutherland stated[24] that, if authority for that proposition were required, it could probably be found in *Smith v Ritchie*.[25] It may seem surprising that resort should be had to an 1892 decision in construing the 1981 statute, especially in view of the fact that the statute seems to have been intended to effect a "permanent shift"[26] in favour of freedom of communication in the light of the decision of the European Court of Human Rights in *Sunday Times v United Kingdom*.[27]

16–329 *Smith v Ritchie* was a case concerning someone who had been committed for trial on a charge of uttering forged writings as genuine manuscripts of authors, including Burns and Scott. He presented a petition to the High Court against the publishers of a newspaper seeking to prohibit the respondents from publishing any statement relating to the alleged forgeries until the close of proceedings. The test applied in that case, however, was somewhat different from the modern statutory test, since the Lord Justice-Clerk asserted[28]:

---

[22] 1997 S.L.T. 425 at 428A, 1996 S.C.C.R. 584 at 590B–C.
[23] [1983] 1 A.C. 116.
[24] 1997 SLT 425 at 427.
[25] (1892) 20 R. (J) 52: 2 White 408.
[26] Lloyd L.J. in *Att-Gen v Newspaper Publishing plc* [1988] Ch. 333 at 382D–E. See also Schiemann L.J. in *Att-Gen v MGN Ltd* [1997] 1 All E.R. 456.
[27] (1979) 2 E.H.R.R. 245.
[28] (1892) 20 R. (J) 52 at 53.

"When any person has been committed for trial, that person is necessarily under the protection of the court, and is accordingly entitled to apply to the court to prevent anything being done which *may in any way prejudice him in his trial*" (emphasis added).

It will be noted that no reference was made either to a "substantial risk" or to "serious prejudice". Indeed, the Lord Justice-Clerk made it clear that he did not think it necessary to consider whether or not the application could be described as one to restrain a contempt of court. The prisoner was said to have a right to ask the court to secure him against *anything* which may prejudice the public mind, so as to endanger the prospect of obtaining a fair trial. It seems from the High Court's reliance upon this older authority that they had no regard for the test, increasingly applied in the English courts, of deciding whether or not a particular restriction is "necessary in a democratic society"[29]; corresponding to the restrictive wording contained in Art.10(2) of the European Convention.

16–330

It is now necessary, however, to have regard to later judicial interpretation of the significance of these remarks in *Muir*, which appears to make clear that a robust approach will be applied to suggestions of anticipated prejudice. The Lord Justice Clerk in *Al Megrahi and Fhima v Times Newspapers Ltd*[30] cited the words of Lloyd L.J. about a "permanent shift," cited above, and those of the Lord Justice-General in *Cox and Griffiths, Petrs* to the effect that the same test has to be applied north and south of the border.[31] He also referred to the citation of *Smith v Ritchie*.[32] He found no difficulty in reconciling the reliance upon the 1892 case governing restraint of publication with the need to apply the terms of ss.1 and 2 of the Contempt of Court Act 1981 which now govern liability for contempt in these circumstances. He concluded: " . . . when those remarks [*i.e.* in *Muir v BBC*] are read in context, it is plain that the court was distinguishing what fell within section 2(2) of the Act from what would properly constitute contempt of court after consideration of the defence under section 5".

16–331

The Lord Justice Clerk's judgment in *Al Megrahi and Fhima v Times Newspapers Ltd* also contains a valuable statement of the criteria to be applied nowadays in the Scottish courts[33]:

16–332

"There is nothing in the Act which enjoins the court to apply as the test the perception of others as to whether the course of justice may be affected. The administration of justice has to be robust enough to withstand criticism and misunderstanding. It would, of course, be an entirely different matter if the court were faced with conduct intended to impede or prejudice the administration of justice, either in the context of particular proceedings or more generally. The court would be well justified in making an order to prevent a deliberate affront to the administration of justice, for example, where a

---

[29] See, *e.g.* Lord Scarman in *Att-Gen v BBC* [1981] A.C. 303 at 362; Lords Templeman and Ackner in *Att-Gen v Guardian Newspapers Ltd* [1987] 1 W.L.R. 1248 at 1297E and 1307D–E respectively; *Att-Gen v MGN Ltd* [1997] 1 All E.R. 456; *Att-Gen v Newspaper Publishing plc* [1997] 1 W.L.R. 926, 3 All E.R. 159. See para.16–302 above.
[30] 1999 S.C.C.R. 824.
[31] 1998 J.C. 267 at 273.
[32] (1892) 3 White 408 in *Muir v BBC* 1997 S.L.T. 425 at 427.
[33] 1999 S.C.C.R. 824.

publication was regarded as impugning the integrity of the court or attacking its authority".

7. Obtaining "clearance" in advance

16–333 In *HMA v Caledonian Newspapers Ltd*[34] the High Court of Justiciary was concerned with a petition presented by the Lord Advocate in respect of an article published in the *Evening Times*, reporting the escape from custody of a prisoner who was on remand awaiting trial on a charge of robbery. It was headlined "Danger man on the Run" and referred to the warnings of the police and the prison service that he could be dangerous; as well as to the fact that he had been freed two years earlier after standing trial twice on the same murder charge. There was also a photograph of him. It was noted that[35]:

> "... publishers and responsible editors must not only try to avoid committing contempt of court, they must succeed in doing so. In the case of doubt, the only safe way to proceed, if the photograph of an untried prisoner is to be published, is to do so only with the consent of the Lord Advocate or of the procurator fiscal on his behalf."

16–334 Although it was observed that there was no provision in the 1981 Act to the effect that the strict liability rule was "elided" just because the Lord Advocate has authorised a publication, in practice a decision taken by the Lord Advocate in the public interest to authorise the publication would remove the risk of a finding of contempt. It is difficult to imagine the Attorney-General or the Director of Public Prosecutions being willing to undertake such a role in England. The approach there seems to be that the existence of the criminal law provides a sufficient discipline upon citizens in relation to their future conduct, so that they can take steps to avoid coming into conflict with the law, if necessary with the benefit of legal advice. If the act contemplated is carried out, and is subsequently held to fall foul of the law, then the citizen must take responsibility for it. It is not the tradition to seek clearance in advance.[36]

8. Interdicts and the impact upon third parties

16–335 Another decision which requires careful consideration is that of *Lord Advocate v The Scotsman Publications Ltd*.[37] It was held to be impossible for interdicts to be enforced as against third parties, on the footing that such persons might well have

---

[34] 1995 S.C.C.R. 330.
[35] At 346, *per* Lord Justice-General Hope. See also *HMA v News Group Newspapers Ltd* 1989 S.C.C.R. 156 at 162, Lord Justice-General Emslie.
[36] See, *e.g.* Lord Donaldson M.R. in *P v Liverpool Daily Post and Echo Newspapers plc* [1991] 2 A.C. 370 at 382A–B; and both Lord Donaldson M.R. and Ralph Gibson L.J. in *Leary v BBC*, September 29, 1989 (Lexis). But see the discussion in *Att-Gen v Punch Ltd* [2002] UKHL 50, [2003] 1 A.C. 1046 of an arrangement which had been agreed between the parties for advance clearance, through the Treasury Solicitor, with regard to material that might be perceived by the security service as confidential and/or as potentially damaging to national security. This was rather deprecated by Lord Nicholls at [13] and [58]–[60].
[37] 1988 S.L.T. 490, affirmed by the House of Lords 1989 S.L.T. 705 at 711, [1989] 2 All E.R. 852. See N. Walker, "Spycatcher's Scottish Sequel" [1990] P.L. 354.

no knowledge that the order was being sought and therefore no opportunity to resist it.[38] Lord Justice-Clerk Ross did not express any concluded opinion on whether the law of contempt might be invoked in Scotland.[39] It would appear, however, that the principles set out in the English case of *Att-Gen v Newspaper Publishing plc*[40] would have equal validity in Scotland, since in this respect it is difficult to justify any distinction. Moreover, it seems that this was recognised by the House of Lords (who nevertheless came to the conclusion on the facts of the case that the fine imposed should be set aside because no one could reasonably have known at the material time that this did indeed represent the law of Scotland).

B. The provisions relating specifically to Scotland

As envisaged by the Phillimore Committee, the main provisions of the 1981 Act apply to Scotland as well as to England and Wales, and to that extent the law of contempt in the two jurisdictions has been unified. These provisions, in so far as they are of general application, have been considered in the parts of the book covering English law. While it is unnecessary to repeat the discussion in the context of Scotland, it is desirable to consider to some extent how these provisions fit within the Scottish legal framework; and particularly to summarise conveniently those parts of the statute which, for procedural or other reasons, apply uniquely to Scotland. Later we shall highlight the provisions which are expressly *exempted* from application in that jurisdiction.[41]

16–336

1. *"Scottish proceedings"*

"Scottish Proceedings" are defined[42] to mean proceedings before any court, including the Courts-Martial Appeal Court, the Restrictive Practices Court and the Employment Appeal Tribunal, sitting in Scotland, and includes proceedings before the House of Lords in the exercise of any appellate jurisdiction over proceedings in such a court. (In practice, the law of contempt is likely to arise most frequently in connection with the High Court of Justiciary, the Court of Session, sheriff courts and district courts.)

16–337

2. *Strict liability: when proceedings become active*

The strict liability rule applies in England and Scotland,[43] but for the purposes of s.2 there is a separate test in Scotland for determining whether proceedings are

16–338

---

[38] A not dissimilar approach had taken by Browne-Wilkinson V.-C. in *Att-Gen v Newspaper Publishing plc* [1988] Ch. 333 at first instance, but Sir John Donaldson M.R. concluded that the reasoning was mistaken: see 372A–D.
[39] 1998 S.L.T. at 506.
[40] [1988] Ch. 333.
[41] See s.21(4) which exempts ss.7, 8(3), 12, 13(1)–(3), 14, 16, 17 and 18 together with Sch.2, Pts I and III, and Schs 3 and 4.
[42] By the Contempt of Court Act 1981, s.19.
[43] See ss.1–6 of the Act and ch.4.

16–338 to be treated as "active." The statutory tests are very close to those laid down by the High Court in the *Hall* and *Atkins* cases.[44]

16–339 By the Criminal Justice (Scotland) Act 1980, s.2, the power of detention for a period of six hours was introduced. When the Contempt of Court Act 1981 was passed, no reference was made to this section. Thus, if a newspaper or broadcaster published during such a six hour period, the provisions of the 1981 Act would not apply, since "arrest" was the critical point for the purposes of the Act. In practice, journalists and their lawyers took the view that the detention was likely to be converted into arrest later, and they therefore did not take the risk of publishing material which otherwise would fall foul of the Act.

16–340 Under the Criminal Procedure (Scotland) Act 1995 Act, that form of detention is retained in ss.14 and 15. Under these, it is possible for a person to be detained consecutively in respect of separate allegations. If the police use these provisions regularly for more than 6 hours, this could cause further uncertainty for newspapers.

(a) Criminal proceedings

16–341 Criminal proceedings are to be treated as "active" in Scotland from[45]:

(a) arrest without warrant;

(b) the grant of a warrant for arrest[46];

(c) the grant of a warrant to cite;

(d) the service of an indictment or other document[47] specifying the charge.

(The provision for "activity" from the moment of oral charge[48] has no application to Scotland).

16–342 Such proceedings are regarded as being concluded[49]:

(a) by acquittal or, as the case may be, by sentence;

(b) by any other verdict, finding, order or decision which puts an end to the proceedings;

(c) by discontinuance or by operation of law.

16–343 The reference to "sentence" includes any order or decision consequent on conviction or finding of guilt which disposes of the case, either absolutely or subject to future events and a deferment of sentence (now under s.202 of the

---

[44] Considered in para.16–172 and para.16–192.
[45] Sch.1: paras 3 and 4.
[46] If an arrest warrant is not executed for a year, "active" status will lapse until arrest is eventually effected: para.11.
[47] *i.e.* complaint. See, *e.g.* Renton and Brown, *Criminal Procedure* (looseleaf), paras 19–02 *et seq.*
[48] para.4(e).
[49] para.5.

Criminal Procedure (Scotland) Act 1995). As to "discontinuance," in Scotland this means either that proceedings are expressly abandoned by the prosecutor or deserted *simpliciter*.[50] Desertion *simpliciter* involves the prosecutor being barred from bringing any further proceedings on the charges. It is noted in Renton and Brown, *Criminal Procedure*,[51] that there is a tendency for prosecutors to desert *pro loco et tempore* even when they have no intention of raising further proceedings. Proceedings will remain active when a diet is deserted *pro loco et tempore*.[52] Also, criminal proceedings in Scotland cease to be "active" if the accused is found to be insane in bar of trial; or where a transfer order ceases to have effect by virtue of s.73(1) of the Mental Health (Scotland) Act 1984,[53] but they become active again if the proceedings are later resumed.[54]

(b) *Other proceedings at first instance*

Proceedings other than criminal proceedings and appellate proceedings[55] are active from the time when arrangements for the hearing are made (or, if none are previously made, from the time the hearing begins). In Scotland such arrangements are made:

(a) in the case of an ordinary action in the Court of Session or in the sheriff court, when the Record is closed;

(b) in the case of a motion or application, when it is enrolled or made;

(c) in any other case when the date for a hearing is fixed or a hearing is allowed.[56]

(c) *Appellate proceedings*

For appellate proceedings, "activity" begins[57] from the time such proceedings are commenced:

(a) by application for leave to appeal or apply for review, or by notice of such an application;

(b) by notice of appeal or of application for review; and

(c) by other originating process,

until disposed of or abandoned, discontinued or withdrawn.

---

[50] para.7(b).
[51] para.21–11, n.8.
[52] See, *e.g. Express Newspapers plc, Petr* 1999 S.L.T. 644, S.C.C.R. 262, S.C. (J.C.) 176.
[53] As amended by the Criminal Procedure (Consequential Provisions) Scotland Act 1995, s.5, Sch.4., para.50(7)(a).
[54] para.10(a) and (b).
[55] Except for tribunals under the Tribunals of Inquiry (Evidence) Act 1921; see s.20(2), which provides that such proceedings become active "from the time when the tribunal is appointed until its report is presented to Parliament". The statute itself (although curiously not s.20) has been repealed and replaced by the Inquiries Act 2005, with effect from June 2005.
[56] paras 12 and 14.
[57] para.15.

16–346 Where in appellate proceedings the court remits the case to the court below or, in Scotland, grants authority to bring a new prosecution, any further or new proceedings which result shall be treated as active from the conclusion of the appellate proceedings.[58]

3. Legal Aid

16–347 Amendments were made to the Legal Aid (Scotland) Act 1967 by s.13(4) of the 1981 Act, which gave effect to the recommendation of the Phillimore Committee[59] and Art.6(3)(b) and (c) of the European Convention on Human Rights. The matter is now governed by s.30 of the Legal Aid (Scotland) Act 1986.[60] This allows the court to grant legal aid if two conditions are fulfilled; that is to say, there is undue financial hardship, and the interests of justice require it. There is a discretion to restrict the grant of legal aid to counsel only or to solicitor only, and the court may assign for the purpose any counsel or solicitor who happens to be within the precincts of the court. Provision is also made for legal aid in connection with an appeal against a decision in contempt proceedings and also for petitions to the *nobile officium* of the High Court of Justiciary and the Court of Session. Reference was made to the need for legal aid in the Lord Justice-General's Memorandum.[61]

4. Penalties in Scottish proceedings

16–348 Committal is to be for a fixed term (without prejudice to the court's power to order earlier discharge).[62] The maximum is two years' imprisonment or a fine, or both, except that[63]:

(a) where the contempt is dealt with by the sheriff in the course of or in connection with proceedings other than criminal proceedings on indictment, such penalty shall not exceed three months' imprisonment or a fine of level 4 on the standard scale[64] or both; and

(b) where the contempt is dealt with by the district court, such penalty shall not exceed 60 days' imprisonment or a fine of level 4 on the standard scale or both.

---

[58] para.16.
[59] Cmnd. 5794, paras 32 and 33. Section 13(4) was repealed and replaced by the Legal Aid (Scotland) Act 1986.
[60] See C.N. Stoddard and H.S. Neilson, *The Law and Practice of Legal Aid in Scotland* (1994), ch.23.
[61] para.16–42, at para.2.
[62] s.15(1) of the Act.
[63] s.15(2).
[64] The maximum fines under paras (a) and (b) were converted to a level on the standard scale by the Criminal Procedure (Consequential Provisions) (Scotland) Act 1995, s.5, Sch.4, paras 36(2), 99. See para.14–106.

Contempt of Court Act 1981: Application to Scotland   16–351

It is provided by s.15(3) of the Contempt of Court Act 1981, as amended[65]:   16–349

"The following provisions of the Criminal Procedure (Scotland) Act 1995 shall apply in relation to persons found guilty of contempt of court in Scottish proceedings as they apply in relation to persons convicted of offences—

(a) in every case, section 207 (restrictions on detention of young offenders);
(b) in any case to which paragraph (b) of subsection (2) above does not apply, sections 58, 59 and 61 (persons suffering from mental disorder);

and in any case to which the said paragraph (b) does apply, subsection (5) below shall have effect."

Section 15(5) of the Contempt of Court Act provides that, where a district court finds a person guilty of contempt, and it appears to the court that he may be suffering from mental disorder, he is to be remitted to the sheriff.[66] Thereupon the sheriff shall have the like power to make an order[67] as if the contemnor had been convicted by him of an offence; or in dealing with him the sheriff may exercise the like powers as the district court making the remit.   16–350

C. The provisions of the 1981 Act which do not apply in Scotland

The parts of the new Act which were expressly excluded[68] from application in Scotland, and their respective functions, are as follows: 16–351

(a) Section 7 provides that in England proceedings under the strict liability rule are not to be instituted without the consent of the Attorney-General, unless upon the motion of a court having jurisdiction to deal with the matter. No such restriction applies in Scotland.

(b) Section 8(3) provides for the same restriction in England upon the institution of proceedings for contempt[69] in respect of jury confidentiality. That again has no application in Scotland.

(c) Section 12 governs contempt in English magistrates' courts.

(d) Section 13(1) to (3) made amendments to the legal aid rules applying in England and Wales (but is prospectively repealed).

(e) Section 14 lays down restrictions on penalties in relation to proceedings in England and Wales.

(f) Section 16 provides for the enforcement of fines imposed by certain superior courts, again in England and Wales.

(g) Section 17 relates to disobedience of magistrates' orders.

---

[65] Criminal Procedure (Consequential Provisions) (Scotland) Act 1995, s.5, Sch.4, para.36(3).
[66] In the manner provided by s.7(9) and (10) of the Criminal Procedure (Scotland) Act 1995. These words were substituted by the Criminal Procedure (Consequential Provisions) (Scotland) Act 1995, Sch.4, para.36(4).
[67] Under s.58(1) of the Criminal Procedure (Scotland) Act 1995. These words were substituted by the Criminal Procedure (Consequential Provisions) (Scotland) Act 1995, Sch.4, para.36(4).
[68] By s.21(4).
[69] See s.8(1) and (2) of the 1981 Act.

16–351

(h) Section 18 is concerned with Northern Ireland only.

(i) Schedule 2: Pts I and III are concerned respectively with amendments to certain statutory provisions which apply in England and Wales, with regard to (1) legal aid, (2) certain specified penalties which may be imposed by inferior courts, and (3) attachment of earnings.

(j) Schedule 3 deals with the application of the Magistrates' Courts Act 1980.

(k) Schedule 4 applies only to Northern Ireland.

X. Contempt of Court Act 1981: A Commentary

A. Introduction

16–352 The provisions of the 1981 Act apply throughout the United Kingdom, with local variations specifically noted in this chapter, but the general framework and substantive provisions of the statute have been considered with reference to their application in England and Wales. What follows is a brief summary with particular reference to its application in Scotland.

B. The Act in the framework of the common law

16–353 Although the authors of an earlier edition of *Scots Law for Journalists*[70] were of the opinion that the Act creates a statutory offence, it is submitted that the better view is that it merely adjusts the common law of contempt in certain limited respects, particularly with reference to publication contempts. The Court in *Robb v Caledonian Newspapers Ltd*,[71] commented:

> "... in our opinion the essential nature of the court's jurisdiction and the procedures appropriate to bring such matters to its attention were not affected by that Act. Its effect, in regard to allegations of contempt such as that with which we are concerned in this case, was to restate in statutory form what section 1 describes as the strict liability rule ... procedures continue to be regulated by the common law, by which any interested party[72] may bring proceedings for contempt by bringing the facts to the attention of the court".

C. The "strict liability rule" interpreted in Scotland

16–354 Section 2 of the Act provides that the "strict liability rule", which applies only in relation to publications, and indeed only to conduct which tends to interfere with the course of justice in "particular legal proceedings", is yet further

---

[70] B. McKain, A.J. Bonnington and G.A. Watt (7th ed., 2000).
[71] 1994 S.C.C.R. 659 at 665.
[72] In England it is provided by s.7 that strict liability contempts may be pursued only with the consent of the Attorney-General or on the motion of the court itself. See also the discussion at paras 16–320 *et seq*.

confined to "a publication which creates a substantial risk that the course of justice in the proceedings in question will be seriously impeded or prejudiced."

16-355 Prior to the Act, the common law test, which had been articulated in *Atkins v London Weekend Television Ltd*,[73] was that of merely a "real" risk of prejudice (without reference specifically to *serious* prejudice). The case law since 1981 did not seem to demonstrate any significant change in the approach of the Scottish courts. Furthermore the statutory definition of when proceedings become "active", for the purposes of the strict liability rule, may be thought not to differ markedly from the approach adopted in *Hall v Associated Newspapers Ltd*.[74]

16-356 In *HMA v News Group Newspapers Ltd*,[75] it was said that:

" ... the language of section 2 means precisely what it says and it says what it means very clearly indeed. In our opinion ... there can be no contempt unless there is some risk, greater than a minimal one, that the course of justice in the proceedings in question will be seriously impeded or prejudiced. The adverb 'seriously' does not require translation. It must be given its familiar and ordinary meaning".

16-357 The rationale of the law of publication contempt was expressed in the same case as being that[76]:

" ... our system of criminal justice in Scotland depends essentially upon the proposition that jurors called to try an accused person should arrive in the jury box without knowledge or impressions of facts, or alleged facts, relating to the crime charged in the indictment".

In other words, the common law rationale largely continues to be applied under the statutory regime.

16-358 The strict liability provisions were considered by Lord Justice-General Hope in *HMA v Caledonian Newspapers Ltd*.[77] He recognised the uncontroversial principles that the question of prejudice has to be assessed as at the date of publication, without regard to subsequent events, and that the "degree of risk must be a substantial one and the degree of impediment or prejudice must be serious". He went on to make the point that, in the case of criminal proceedings, "the impediment or prejudice will be regarded as serious if it *may affect the outcome* of the trial in regard to such matters as the evidence of witnesses or the evaluation by the jury of the evidence" (emphasis added). Moreover, he cited the words of Lord Diplock from *Att-Gen v English*,[78] to the effect that:

---

[73] 1978 S.L.T. 76 (discussed more fully at paras 16–192 *et seq.*).
[74] 1978 S.L.T. 241. See M.L. Pearl, "The Contempt of Court Bill" 1981 S.L.T. (News) 141. See also, generally, J.G. Logie, "The Contempt of Court Act 1981 and the Media Reporting of Crime" (1987) J.L.S.S. 249.
[75] 1989 S.C.C.R. 156 at 161E, Lord Justice-General Emslie, Lord Grieve and Lord Brand.
[76] At 162D–E.
[77] 1995 S.C.C.R. 330 at 341–2.
[78] [1983] 1 A.C. 116 at 141F–142C.

16–358

"The public policy that underlies the strict liability rule in contempt of court is deterrence. Trial by newspaper or, as it should be more compendiously expressed today, trial by the media, is not to be permitted in this country ... If, as in the instant case and probably most other criminal trials upon indictment, it is the outcome of the trial or the need to discharge the jury without proceeding to a verdict that is put at risk, there can be no question that that which in the course of justice is put at risk is as serious as anything could be".

16–359 In England it might appear that judicial attitudes somewhat softened over the intervening years, and particularly with regard to the significance to be attached to the possibility of having to discharge a jury. Far from accepting that contempt would be established *ipso facto* by publishing material creating a risk that a jury in a criminal case might have to be discharged, Schiemann L.J. in *Att-Gen v MGN Ltd*[79] recognised "a difficult problem" in reconciling the two doctrines of strict liability contempt and abuse of process (as it is referred to in England). He observed that:

"A consequence of the need in contempt proceedings ... to be sure and look at each publication separately and the need in trial proceedings to look at risk of prejudice created by the totality of publications can be that it is proper to stay proceedings on the ground of prejudice albeit that no individual is guilty of contempt."

It is necessary now to take account of the decision of the Divisional Court in *Att-Gen v Birmingham Post and Mail Ltd*[80] from which it seems that the *MGN* case is likely to be regarded as something of a special case having regard to the multiple newspaper applications then before the court. It also appears that in future a judge's decision to discharge a jury because of media publicity is likely to be regarded as at least a "telling factor" in contempt proceedings based on the same material. The test in England which the court applies in determining whether to discharge a jury, on the basis of abuse of process, is that of "balance of probabilities".[81]

D. Applications relating to prejudicial reports to be made promptly

16–360 It has been held that complaints of prejudicial reporting should be made promptly. In *Robb v Caledonian Newspapers Ltd*,[82] an attempt had been made to commence proceedings for contempt but the High Court prevented this on the ground of delay. The Law Officers had also declined to take action. The article had been published in August 1993, but the complaint was not made until seven months later, thus putting the newspaper respondents at some disadvantage. The general point was made that:

"... the publication should be drawn to the court's attention as soon as possible so that it may be dealt with immediately. This is necessary to prevent any further interference with the course of justice in the particular proceedings which are said to have been affected by it. It is necessary also in fairness to those who are said to have been

---

[79] [1997] 1 All E.R. 456 at 466g. See paras 16–309 *et seq*.
[80] [1998] 4 All E.R. 49.
[81] *Maxwell*, March 6, 1995, Phillips J., discussed at para.4–164.
[82] 1994 S.C.C.R. 659 at 666–7, Lord Justice-General Hope, Lord Cowie and Lord Wylie.

responsible for the publication, because it is in their interests that the alleged complaint should be brought to their attention as soon as possible so that the circumstances may be fully and promptly investigated. A delay in bringing proceedings for an order to prohibit further publication is less objectionable if it emerges that there is a risk of publication being repeated while the proceedings in question are still active. But proceedings which seek punishment for alleged past contempt should be brought by the interested party as soon as practicable after the event has come to his attention. Where there is a long delay and there is no substantial risk of repetition the court will normally be disinclined to exercise its jurisdiction to examine the allegation and, if appropriate, to exact punishment".

E. The statutory defences

Summarising the limited scope of the 1981 Act, the court in *Adams, Petr*[83] noted that "under the Contempt of Court Act 1981 a contempt of court by publication, putting the matter very shortly, is an offence of strict liability subject to certain rights in the person charged with contempt to put forward certain defences ... ". It is now appropriate to consider those "defences" in the Scottish context.

1. *"Innocent publication or distribution"*

Section 3 of the 1981 Act introduces into the law of Scotland a new defence of innocent publication or distribution, although its provisions are more familiar in England, since they are similar to those which had been introduced by s.11 of the Administration of Justice Act 1960.[84] A publisher is not to be held liable under the Act's provisions:

"(1) ... if at the time of publication (having taken all reasonable care) he does not know and has no reason to suspect that relevant proceedings are active".

A distributor of a publication is not so liable:

"(2) ... if at the time of distribution (having taken all reasonable care) he does not know that it contains such matter and has no reason to suspect that it is likely to do so".

The phrase "no reason to suspect" was, at a relatively late stage, rejected for inclusion in s.1(1) of the Defamation Act 1996, in favour of "no reason to *believe*".[85] This was because the task of demonstrating the absence of "reason to suspect" was thought to be more difficult and nebulous. Nevertheless, in both instances under the 1981 Act, the burden of proof that the alleged contemnor has the benefit of the defence rests on him, although the standard will not be the same as that applying to the complainer in establishing a *prima facie* contempt. Section

---

[83] 1987 S.C.C.R. 650, Lord Justice-General Emslie, Lord Grieve and Lord Kincraig.
[84] These matters are discussed more fully in paras 4–236 *et seq*.
[85] See the discussion of these two formulations in *Milne v Express Newspapers* [2004] EWCA Civ 664, [2005] 1 W.L.R. 772, [2004] E.M.L.R. 461.

16–363 3 has not so far been the subject of any reported case in Scotland, but in *R. v Duffy*; *Att-Gen v News Group Newspapers Ltd*[86] it was said by Kennedy L.J.:

> "Section 3 expects of journalists a high standard of care before they are in a position to avail themselves of that defence.... It will be rare, indeed, for a journalist, who writes an article suggesting that an identifiable person has committed a criminal offence, to be able to avail himself of the statutory defence without specifically asking those in a position to know if there any active criminal proceedings but, as this case shows, even that rule cannot be absolute."

2. Discussions in good faith

16–364 Section 5 of the 1981 Act provides that:

> "A publication made as or as part of a discussion in good faith of public affairs or other matters of general public interest is not to be treated as a contempt of court under the strict liability rule if the risk of impediment or prejudice to particular legal proceedings is merely incidental to the discussion".

16–365 This may be compared to the common law rule, as expressed in *Atkins v London Weekend Television Ltd*,[87] that contempt will not necessarily arise merely because discussion of public affairs may "cause some likelihood of prejudice to a person who happens at the time to be a litigant," where the prejudice is an incidental or unintended by-product. It may be that the statutory provision goes considerably further, in acknowledging that there may be a defence even where there is created a substantial risk of serious prejudice. Indeed, unless such a degree of risk is created, there is no need to resort to the terms of s.5.[88]

16–366 The argument did not succeed in *Atkins*, since the principle expounded by Jordan C.J. in *Ex p. Bread Manufacturers Ltd*[89] could have no application to such circumstances. Specific references were made to a pending criminal trial, immediately prior to the commencement of that trial. Nor, almost certainly, would the statutory regime have made any difference, because the programme tended to imply the factual accuracy of the very charge which it was for the prosecution to prove.[90]

16–367 In *Muir v BBC*,[91] the court considered the relevance of s.5, but only to the extent that it was prayed in aid by way of resisting an injunction. As has been

---

[86] February 9, 1996, D.C. (Lexis), discussed in paras 4–242 *et seq*. On the facts of the case it was held that the journalist had no need to check with the Crown Prosecution Service or with the courts, because he had "gone to the horse's mouth"; that is, to the senior police officer, and he had discussed the matter to the extent that he was entitled to say that he had no reason to suspect that criminal proceedings were active, and that he had taken all reasonable care.
[87] 1978 S.L.T. 76.
[88] See *Att-Gen v English* [1983] 1 A.C. 116, HL.
[89] (1937) 37 S.R. (N.S.W.) 242 at 249.
[90] See 1978 S.L.T. 76, 1978 J.C. 48 at 55, and generally, M.L. Pearl, "The Contempt of Court Bill" 1981 S.L.T. (News) 141 at 144.
[91] 1996 S.C.C.R. 584.

pointed out already,[92] and in contrast to the position in England,[93] it was held that the statutory defence was of no relevance at that stage. Moreover, a much narrower view of the defence seems to have been adopted than that of the House of Lords in *Att-Gen v English*.[94]

F. Reporting court proceedings

1. Section 4(1)

Section 4(1) of the 1981 Act provides that a person will not be liable to be found in contempt under the Act's provisions "in respect of a fair and accurate report of legal proceedings held in public, published contemporaneously and in good faith". In that a report must be "fair and accurate" to gain such protection, the Act reflects the common law of Scotland.[95]

16–368

It is likely that if a journalist is held to have *intended* to interfere with the administration of justice, in his reporting coverage, and thus *prima facie* liable for a publication contempt at common law, he would be unable to plead "good faith" for the purposes of s.4(1).

16–369

Section 4 was not intended to protect the publication of matters specifically prohibited by other statutes. It is obvious, for example, that if a journalist were to name a rape victim on the basis that her name had been mentioned in court, he would certainly not be able to plead the protection of this provision.

16–370

2. Section 4(2)

The generality of the protection afforded to court reporting in s.4(1) is qualified by the provisions of s.4(2). These powers were no doubt considered by Parliament to be consistent with the obligations of the United Kingdom under the European Convention, and thus to be "necessary in a democratic society" for one of the reasons specified in Art.10(2). The subsection provides that the court may:

16–371

" . . . where it appears to be necessary for avoiding a substantial risk of prejudice to the administration of justice in those proceedings, or in any other proceedings pending or imminent, order that the publication of any report of the proceedings, or any part of the proceedings, be postponed for such period as the court thinks necessary for that purpose".

The strictness of this "necessity" test is illustrated, perhaps, by the case of *HMA v McCook*,[96] where a postponement order was made by Lord Mayfield. The

16–372

---

[92] para.16–322.
[93] *Leary v BBC*, 29 September 29, 1989, CA (Lexis).
[94] [1983] 1 A.C. 116.
[95] See, *e.g. Riddell and Raeside v The Clydesdale Horse Society* (1885) 12 R. 976 at 983, Lord President Inglis, at 984, Lord Shand.
[96] Unreported; see B. McKain, A.J. Bonnington and G.A. Watt *op. cit.*, p.98. See also, generally, A.J. Bonnington, "The Loudest Whisper in Lake Woebegone" (1994) J.L.S.S. 214.

first of two partners in a solicitors' firm charged with fraud and embezzlement was convicted, but the trial of the second on substantially similar evidence had yet to begin. Reports of the *McCook* trial were postponed pending the outcome of the second case, which was then delayed due to the illness of the accused. After five weeks, on the joint approval of the Crown and counsel representing the Scottish Daily Newspaper Society, Lord Allanbridge lifted the postponement order.

16–373 A report postponed pursuant to these powers will be treated as "published contemporaneously", for the purposes of the protection conferred by s.4(1), provided that it is published as soon as practicable after the s.4(2) order expires.[97]

16–374 The power to postpone is regularly used by Scottish courts, although reported cases concerning s.4(2) are few. A passing reference is made to the section in the report of *Keane v HMA*,[98] where Lord Cowie made an order postponing the reporting of a preliminary diet in a criminal case, at which reference was made to the lodging of certain unspecified special defences, some of which had been withdrawn. A "moratorium" was placed on reports, on the motion of the Crown, until the commencement of the trial proper a week later. Lord Cowie expressed some reluctance at doing so because he had chosen to criticise the Crown for incompetence in their conduct of the case, and he regarded it as unfortunate to be asked not to make that public when the whole point of his criticism was that it should be.

16–375 In *Robb v Caledonian Newspapers Ltd*,[99] the High Court postponed any reporting of the hearing of a contempt petition, brought by an accused person about to stand trial. The petition was refused because of delay. Nonetheless, publication was postponed until the conclusion of the trial. Moreover, the court also stated that it would "expect" the respondents to the petition to adhere to an undertaking not to publish further articles of the kind complained of while the proceedings in question remained active. The respondents had accepted that part of the original article was open to criticism. In these circumstances, they would have been most unwise to publish the material again, when they would be unlikely to take advantage again of the delay argument.

16–376 The question was raised in *Galbraith v HMA*[1] as to whether a s.4(2) order would or could be appropriate in relation to appellate proceedings for the protection of a possible retrial. The matter was not thought to be straightforward. The Court considered *dicta* from the *Horsham Justices* case but, since it was on the particular facts unnecessary to resolve the point, it was left open for future consideration.

---

[97] See the discussion in para.4–274.
[98] 1986 S.C.C.R. 491 at 492–3.
[99] 1994 S.C.C.R. 659 at 667.
[1] 2001 S.L.T. 465, 2000 S.C.C.R. 935. The case of *Galbraith* was considered by the High Court of Justiciary in *HMA v Beggs (No.1)*, 2002 S.L.T. 135.

In the same case, it was observed that the obvious place for journalists to check nowadays to see if any postponement orders are in effect would be the Scottish Court Service website. Attention was again drawn in *BBC, Petrs*[2] to the fact that it is now the practice in Scotland for s.4(2) orders to be sent immediately by e-mail to various newspapers and broadcasting organisations and to their agents. The fact that such an order has been made is also published on the Scottish Court Service website. On the other hand, there would appear as yet not to be any comparable mechanism for notifying journalists that such an application is about to be made—so as to afford a realistic opportunity to make submissions in opposition. If there is no chance to make objections at that stage, journalists in Scotland are left only with the possibility of a challenge by way of petition to the *nobile officium*. The question was raised by Lord McCluskey in *Scottish Daily Record and Sunday Mail, Petrs*[3] as to why comparable provisions to those in s.159 of the Criminal Justice Act 1988 had not been enacted for Scotland, so as to afford journalists the opportunity to appeal as "persons aggrieved".

The case of *BBC, Petrs*[4] was one suggesting a more sanguine view as to the capacity of a jury to resist prejudicial statements. The High Court of Justiciary expressed the view that there was no need to restrict reporting by a s.4(2) order for the reason that directions at trial would adequately deal with any risk of prejudice.

Another such case was *HMA v Wilson*,[5] where a motion for a s.4(2) order was made to Lord Reed in the following circumstances. Six men were facing charges involving the abuse of children, including of rape and penetration. Notice was given under s.67 of the Criminal Procedure (Scotland) Act 1995 that the Lord Advocate intended to examine two expert witnesses who had not been included in the list served with the indictment. One of the accused (the fourth) lodged a minute indicating an intention to raise a devolution issue. This was to the effect that the Lord Advocate would thereby violate his right to a fair trial under Art.6 of the European Convention, specifically his right to confidentiality and the right be able to prepare his case without inhibition. A second minute gave notice that he sought a preliminary diet to resolve the devolution issue. Similar minutes were thereafter lodged by the first accused also. The basis of the fourth accused's Art.6 point was that the two experts in question were consultant paediatricians who had, on the instructions of agents acting on his behalf, earlier examined some of the children who were alleged victims. One of the experts had also received instructions on behalf of the first accused. Naturally, information received from any such agent by the consultants was subject to an obligation of confidentiality. But, subject to that point, Lord Reed concluded that there was nothing in the Scottish cases to prevent such a witness being called for the Crown merely by virtue of having been instructed at some stage on behalf of an accused. Nor did the law of Scotland appear to differ in this respect from that of England and Wales. There would be no basis on which to prevent the experts from giving

---

[2] 2001 S.C.C.R. 440 at [4].
[3] 1998 S.C.C.R. 626, 1999 S.L.T. 624.
[4] 2001 S.C.C.R. 440.
[5] High Court of Justiciary, June 15, 2001.

16-379 relevant evidence for that reason; indeed, that would be contrary to the public interest in the administration of justice.

16-380 The point under s.4(2) arose because the accused wished to prevent reporting of the preliminary issues until the conclusion of the trial. If the judge indicated a disinclination to afford that degree of protection, one of the options counsel was considering was that of postponing the substantive applications until the trial. At that stage, at least, he could be confident that the arguments would be canvassed in the absence of the jury (although he recognised that it was possible that they might suspect, from the mere fact that matters were being resolved in their absence, that some form of "cover up" was taking place). The immediate concern was that potential jurors might read reports of the preliminary diet hearing and be prejudiced against the relevant accused. Lord Reed said that he would only be in a position to rule on that issue at the conclusion of the substantive argument, but expressed the view that the matters to be discussed were unlikely to be so sensitive that they would create a risk of prejudice to the administration of justice; in any event, any such risk could be eliminated by directions to the jury.

3. *Section 11*

16-381 A similar, but more restricted power to restrain publication is confirmed by s.11 of the 1981 Act. By that section, a court which has by any applicable rule of law the power to allow a name or other matter to be withheld from the public in proceedings may go further and prohibit publication of that matter in connection with the proceedings, to the extent that such a prohibition may be needed to ensure that the withholding is effective.

16-382 Before the s.11 power was made available, courts had no express power to prevent publication of a withheld name or matter if reporters obtained it from another source, although there may have been power to take action *ex post facto* to punish for contempt if circumstances permitted. Before making a s.11 order, the court should be sure that publication of the information outside the court proceedings will prejudice the purpose for which it was withheld.[6]

G. Disclosure of sources

16-383 Section 10 of the 1981 Act provides:

"No court may require a person to disclose, nor is any person guilty of contempt of court for refusing to disclose, the source of information contained in a publication for which he is responsible, unless it be established to the satisfaction of the court that disclosure is necessary in the interests of justice or national security or for the prevention of disorder or crime".

16-384 This provision may be compared with the common law as explained in *Airs*,[7] where it was observed that to refuse to answer a competent and relevant question,

---

[6] See generally paras 7–83 *et seq*.
[7] 1975 S.L.T. 177.

in any court of law, was a challenge to the rule of law[8] and a serious contempt meriting a severe penalty. It was acknowledged that Mr Airs had acted from what he conceived to be honourable professional motives; and indeed that he may have been "under the misapprehension that the questions had to be shown to be necessary or useful before he could be required to answer them." It was said that he should have recognised that the trial judge was the sole arbiter of the necessity of an answer being given. He was treated "with special leniency" in all the circumstances, being fined only £500.

This now has to be seen in the light of the decision of the European Court of Human Rights in *Goodwin*,[9] which makes it clear that journalists have a right to withhold information as to their sources except in circumstances where an overriding public interest can be demonstrated; and moreover, that the trial judge can no longer be regarded as the "sole arbiter of the necessity of an answer being given". In England, *Goodwin* has been followed in *Chief Constable of Leicestershire v Garavelli*,[10] a decision of the Queen's Bench Divisional Court.

At first sight, it might have seemed to Scots lawyers difficult to understand how a question ruled competent and relevant, by a trial judge in the context of court proceedings, could be made the subject of a lawful refusal to answer under the section. The judge's conclusion as to relevancy might in itself imply that an answer was "necessary in the interests of justice". There can be little doubt that such an argument would now be rejected, and a similar approach adopted in Scotland to that in *Garavelli*.

H. Jury room secrecy: section 8

The provisions of s.8(1)[11] make it a contempt to:

"obtain, disclose or solicit any particulars of statements made, opinions expressed, arguments advanced or votes cast by members of a jury in the course of their deliberations in any legal proceedings."

Exceptions are provided, however, by s.8(2) for any such disclosure

"(a) in the proceedings in question for the purpose of enabling the jury to arrive at their verdict, or in connection with the delivery of that verdict, or
(b) in evidence in any subsequent proceedings for an offence alleged to have been committed in relation to the jury in the first mentioned proceedings".

Where, in respect of either of these exceptions, particulars are legitimately disclosed, those particulars may also be published.[12]

---

[8] See paras 9–32 *et seq*.
[9] (1996) 22 E.H.R.R. 123, discussed in paras 9–1 *et seq*.
[10] [1997] E.M.L.R. 543, Beldam L.J. and Smith J.
[11] For the text of which, see Appendix 1.
[12] s.8(2).

16–389 Just as in the case of s.7 of the Act, proceedings under this section are only permitted to be instituted in England with leave of the Attorney-General, or on the motion of the court. No such restriction applies in Scotland.[13]

16–390 The terms of s.8 were considered by the High Court in *McCadden v HMA*.[14] This was not a contempt case but concerned an appeal against conviction, on a majority verdict, of drugs offences and a sentence of ten years' imprisonment. A late addition to the grounds of appeal concerned allegations, supported by precognitions, that one of the jurors had during the trial made statements, in a conversation in a club, to the effect that the accused had made all his money from drugs and that he (the juror) was going to find the "tarry bastard guilty". He also referred to the fact that he had obtained his Rolls Royce from the proceeds of drugs dealing and, for good measure, called him a "Fenian bastard".

16–391 The argument proceeded on the basis that the court should under the provisions of Criminal Procedure (Scotland) Act 1975[15] remit the matter to a "fit person" to inquire and report. It appeared that, on no fewer than four occasions in the preceding year, judges had seen fit to desert trials on the basis that a juror had said something to the prejudice of an accused. The court was wary of "the deep waters into which the court might be plunged in such a type of inquiry". Nonetheless, it was held that an inquiry under s.252(d) of the Act would be competent. The more general issue was addressed as to the circumstances in which resort should be had to such an inquiry. It was only after considering such matters as "the possible dangers to which the allowance of such an inquiry might expose the administration of justice" that an answer could be given in any individual case.

16–392 It was noted that there may be an important distinction between the case where the juror's conduct came to light during the trial and the situation where it only emerged subsequently. In the view of the court the trial judge could, in the former case, investigate matters and conduct an interview with the juror. He would then be able to take such steps as might be necessary (for example, by discharging the juror from service).[16]

16–393 The provisions of s.8 of the Contempt of Court Act were considered by the court:

> "... in an enquiry during the trial, it would appear that the juror and his co-jurors could be questioned by the trial judge under the provisions of section 8(2) of the Contempt of Court Act 1981, not only about the matters complained of, but about the extent, if any, to which the allegedly offending juror had influenced or sought to influence the other members of the jury on the issues in the case. These advantages

---

[13] s.8(3).
[14] 1985 S.C.C.R. 282 at 285. See also Sheriff Gordon's comments at 287–8.
[15] s.252, as substituted by the Criminal Justice (Scotland) Act 1980, Sch.2, para.16. See now the Criminal Procedure (Scotland) Act 1995, s.104(1).
[16] See now the summary of principles in the House of Lords cases of *R. v Mirza* [2004] UKHL 2; *R. v Smith* [2005] UKHL 12, [2005] 1 W.L.R. 704; *Att-Gen v Scotcher* [2005] UKHL 36, [2005] 1 W.L.R. 1867, [2005] 3 All E.R. 1.

would appear to make it much easier to deal with the problem during the trial than it is to deal with it after the trial proceedings have terminated, when the same advantages are not available. For instance, the provisions of section 8(2), supra, would not be available, and the provisions of section 8(1) of that Act might be prayed in aid by a juror who was unwilling to be questioned."

The court emphasised that the appellate tribunal would need to be satisfied of the existence of substantial, convincing and trustworthy evidence to support the allegations of prejudice. On the facts, it was thought that the precognitions were far from convincing, and in particular contained no evidence that the prejudice alleged was translated into effective action in the jury room. Accordingly, the motion to allow the additional ground of appeal to be inquired into was refused.

In the course of the judgment, reference was made to the built-in safeguards in the jury system; and particularly to the fact that the concept of a trial by jury has inherent in it the possibility that there will be conflicting personal views and prejudices amongst the jurors. It was recognised that the danger may be at its greatest when political or religious feelings run high and, indeed, it had been this factor which led to the altering of the system of jury trial in Scotland and the introduction of the "not proven" verdict. It was also observed that[17]:

"It is not to be assumed that persons with prejudices will automatically put their prejudices aside when balloted for membership of a jury, but neither is it to be assumed that they would not. It has to be realistically accepted, however, that, left to themselves, some jurors might fall into the latter category. But when they are properly directed on how they should approach and carry out their duties . . . it is not to be lightly assumed that jurors will ignore the directions and pursue their prejudices in defiance of the oath which they had taken."

Despite the finding of the High Court that s.8 would lay the foundation for such an inquiry, during the course of the trial, it appeared that English courts would not come to a similar conclusion. It was by no means accepted that the wording of s.8(2)(a) would permit such an inquiry. The kind of interrogation which the High Court had in mind was not thought to be either for the purpose of enabling the jury to arrive at their verdict or in connection with the delivery of that verdict. Nor would it be consistent with the guidance given in the English case of *R. v Schot and Barclay*.[18]

I. Contempt barring trial

The gap between a finding that publication contempt has been committed in relation to a particular case, and its impact on the conduct of relevant

---

[17] At 286.
[18] [1997] 2 Cr.App.R. 383, (1997) 161 J.P. 473, considered more fully in paras 10–72 *et seq*. But all of these cases need to be considered carefully in the light of the triptych of cases in the House of Lords which would probably be considered authoritative in Scotland: *R. v Mirza* [2004] UKHL 2; *R. v Smith* [2005] UKHL 12, [2005] 1 W.L.R. 704; *Att-Gen v Scotcher* [2005] UKHL 36, [2005] 1 W.L.R. 1867, [2005] 3 All E.R. 1.

16–397

proceedings, was discussed in *Stuurman v HMA*.[19] Prior to a trial for offences under the Misuse of Drugs Act 1971, there were repeated radio broadcasts and a Scottish national newspaper article, within the area from which potential jurors would be drawn, containing allegations concerning the arrests of various defendants and the surrounding circumstances. The newspaper editor and proprietors, and the broadcasters, admitted contempt of court and were heavily fined.

16–398 At the trial diet, the accused each maintained a plea in bar of trial. Lord Allanbridge, the trial judge, consulted Lords Avonside and Grieve. At a hearing before those three judges, counsel was heard in support of the pleas. It was said that the mere fact that the Lord Advocate had complained to the court about an alleged publication contempt in the case did not *per se* bar him from proceeding with the indictment. The court could only prevent the Lord Advocate proceeding with an indictment on the ground of "oppression", a term which could not be defined; moreover, there could be no ruling to the effect that oppressive conduct would necessarily lead to bar of trial. Each case would depend on its merits. On the facts, it was held that there was no case of oppression made out; the trials proceeded and the accused were convicted.

16–399 On application to a Full Bench for leave to appeal against their convictions on the substantive charges, it was stated by Lord Emslie[20]:

"... the High Court of Justiciary has power to intervene to prevent the Lord Advocate from proceeding upon a particular indictment but this power will be exercised only in special circumstances which are likely to be rare. The special circumstances must indeed be such as to satisfy the court that, having regard to the principles of substantial justice and of fair trial, to require an accused to face trial would be oppressive. Each case will depend on its own merits, and where the alleged oppression is said to arise from events alleged to be prejudicial to the prospects of fair trial the question for the Court is whether the risk of prejudice is so grave that no direction of the trial Judge, however careful, could reasonably be expected to remove it".

16–400 This was the test applied in *X v Sweeney*,[21] where Lord Cameron, while conceding that "the well of truth can be poisoned beyond the possibility of its water ever being purified", noted that:

"The passage of time and consequently the intervention of other events catching the minds of members of the public all tend to blur recollection, especially in matters of detail, and consequently this is in my opinion a relevant factor in balancing the public interests involved".

It is necessary now to approach Lord Cameron's remarks as to "balancing the public interests involved" with some caution in view of the comments of Lord Hope in the Privy Council in *Montgomery v HMA*.[22] He noted that in *X v*

---

[19] *Stuurman v HMA* 1980 J.C. 111. See also para.16–310.
[20] At 122.
[21] 1982 S.C.C.R. 161 at 171, 174–5, 1983 S.L.T. 48, 1982 J.C. 70. The short-lived public memory was also remarked upon by the court in *Stuurman*, 1980 J.C. 111 at 123.
[22] [2003] 1 A. C. 641, PC, 2000 S.C.C.R. 1044 at 1106.

Sweeney the right to a fair trial seemed to have been weighed against another public interest, namely that in the detection and suppression of crime. It was necessary, however, to recognise that in the application of Art.6(1) of the Convention there is no such balancing exercise: "The right of the accused to a fair trial by an independent and impartial tribunal is unqualified. It is not to be subordinated to the public interest in the detection and suppression of crime. In this respect it may be said that the Convention right is superior to the common law right". Nevertheless, subject to that important principle, the *Stuurman* test (as described in the words of Lord Justice-General Emslie above) has not been deprived of its utility in an Art.6 context.

These cases tended to underline what appeared to be an important difference between Scottish and English practice. It seemed to be easier in Scotland to establish contempt than to achieve a bar in trial; whereas in England, media respondents sometimes escaped liability for contempt even in circumstances where it can be demonstrated that their publications have led to an abandonment of trial or the quashing of a conviction.[23] But it may be that this should be confined to cases of multiple media publications,[24] and that the trial judge's decision to stay criminal proceedings will be weighed in other cases as a "telling factor".[25]

16–401

It must be remarked, however, that Scots law applies, in general, very strict time limits designed to promote the prompt trial of serious crime, especially where the accused person is in custody. This point was taken by the court in *HMA v News Group Newspapers Ltd*,[26] to counter the suggestion of counsel for the respondents that there was no substantial risk within the meaning of s.2(2) of the 1981 Act because of the time which was likely to elapse before trial (what is often referred to in England as the "fade factor").[27]

16–402

On the other hand, in *Kilbane v HMA*[28] a trial was deserted *pro loco et tempore* after revelations in the local press that two of the accused were serving prison sentences. When the case was re-indicted in the same court four months later, after an extension of the usual time-limits, a preliminary plea in bar was repelled. The accused's appeal was dismissed, on the ground that the sheriff was entitled to conclude that the passage of time would have dulled recollection of the offending article. Thus the "fade factor" seems to have been acknowledged but as working to the appellant's disadvantage. It may be thought that these cases exemplify that at the time Scottish courts may have been speaking "with two

16–403

---

[23] *R. v Solicitor-General Ex p. Taylor* [1995] T.L.R. 477; *Att-Gen v MGN Ltd* [1997] 1 All E.R. 456, discussed at paras 16–309 *et seq.*
[24] Such as in *Att-Gen v MGN Ltd* (last note) and *Att-Gen v ITN Ltd* [1994] 1 W.L.R. 1500, [1995] 2 All E.R. 370.
[25] *Att-Gen v Birmingham Post and Mail Ltd* [1998] 4 All E.R. 49, DC.
[26] 1989 S.C.C.R. 156 at 163.
[27] Cp. also the observations of Lord Cameron in *X v Sweeney* 1982 S.C.C.R. 161 at 171, 174–5, 1983 S.L.T. 48, 1982 J.C. 70.
[28] 1989 S.C.C.R. 313. See also *HMA v Mitchell* 1993 S.C.C.R. 793 (where it was held on appeal that a sheriff had been entitled in a fraud case to desert the diet *pro loco et tempore* because of prejudice created by newspaper publicity, and to extend the time limit within which the trial had to commence).

16–403 voices" or applying a double standard, as seemed also to be happening in England, at least for a time, as between criminal appeals on the one hand and contempt cases on the other.[29]

16–404 Ten years later, however, in *HMA v Scottish Media Newspapers Ltd*,[30] the Lord Justice General considered that a nine month delay after publication was likely to be a sufficient period for the impact of an article ("Big Tam in Cell over Axe Claims") to have dissipated. The court was not satisfied to the required standard that there was a substantial risk of serious prejudice. The person concerned was well known to the public from a long-running BBC Scotland comedy series. It was thought unlikely that anyone cited to serve as a juror would even recall the article. In any event, when a jury is confronted with a well known personality, the jurors may often know more about such a person's way of life and the background to a charge than would ordinarily be the case. Therefore, a judge at trial would probably "think it appropriate to give a more pointed direction about the need for the jury to reach their verdict solely on the evidence led in court." Thus, even if a juror did recall the allegations in a newspaper, there was no reason to suppose that this would diminish his or her ability to reach a proper verdict on the evidence.

16–405 The facts are to be contrasted with the situation that arose in *HMA v The Scotsman Publications Ltd*.[31] It was alleged that a contempt had been committed by virtue of the publication on the front page of *The Scotsman* of an article headed "Sarwar Charge Witnesses ask for Protection". Mr Sarwar, a Scottish member of Parliament, had been charged with election fraud and attempting to pervert the course of justice. There was a suggestion that the witnesses feared intimidation and, in context, it was held that the ordinary reader was likely to assume that the accused was ultimately the person whose intimidation was feared. "There could hardly be a more prejudicial suggestion in advance of trial ... The fact that an accused should stoop to intimidating witnesses is one which many readers, including the ordinary reader, would regard as almost tantamount to guilt". When such an allegation was applied to someone as well known as Mr Sarwar, said Lord Marnoch, the impression was likely to "stick". For those reasons he was unmoved by the submission that the effect of the article would have been spent or forgotten in the months before trial. In that case, it was also held that the ordinary directions of a trial judge would not necessarily remove the prejudice. The interesting comment was added that it could only be assumed, as at the date of publication, that the trial judge would give "ordinary directions" (that is to say, to the effect that the jurors should confine themselves to the evidence in the case). For that reason, the respondents should not be permitted to pray in aid the possibility of particular directions tailored to the facts of the case (*i.e.* to ignore entirely any suggestion of intimidation). The court did not find compelling the argument that the risk of prejudice was slight, on the footing that no more than around 12,000 copies of the paper circulated in the

---

[29] Cf. Simon Brown L.J in *R. v Unger* [1998] 1 Cr.App.R. 308 at 318e–f, [1998] EMLR 280, 291; see para.4–169.
[30] 1999 S.L.T. 331.
[31] 1999 S.L.T. 466, S.C.C.R. 163.

Strathclyde region. Lord Marnoch observed that *The Scotsman* saw itself as a national newspaper and, in his view, there would be a material risk of serious prejudice if even one juror had read the article and had been affected by it in the way envisaged.

Possible change of trial district

The possibility of a transfer of the trial to a different district was considered in *Kilbane*,[32] but in the particular circumstances this option was rejected.[33] The matter was also debated on appeal before the High Court, but it was not considered necessary for the court to come to a concluded opinion upon the question whether it would have been competent for the Lord Advocate to have raised an indictment against the appellants at another sheriff court within the sheriffdom.[34] This was because the court was quite satisfied that the sheriff had been entitled to conclude that any risk of prejudice could be removed by careful direction.[35] On the other hand, in *McLeod v HM Advocate*,[36] it was held, in a case of intense publicity in a limited local context, that the sheriff should have exercised his discretion and deserted the diet *pro loco et tempore* so that a fresh indictment could be raised in a different court. It was important that justice should be seen to be done, and that account should be taken of the public perception and that of the accused himself.

Jury vetting rejected in Scotland

It was observed in *McCadden v HMA*[37] that the practical process which may come nearest to eliminating the possibility of personal prejudices would be that of "vetting" jurors; but it was said that the law of Scotland has steadfastly closed the doors against that system. The point had also been discussed by the court in *Stuurman*, and reference made to *M v HMA*,[38] where it was held that a "vetting" of the jury by asking certain formulated questions before having them take the oath could not be countenanced in Scots law.

In *Spink v HMA*,[39] the court agreed that "it is not part of our practice in Scotland to examine the antecedent knowledge of potential jurors before the

---

[32] 1989 S.C.C.R. 313.
[33] Transfer may be possible at common law (*Dewar, Ptr*, September 5,1944, unreported: see Macdonald, *op. cit.*, p.266); or by statute—see s.3(2) of the Criminal Procedure (Scotland) Act 1995, which provides that "any crime or offence which is triable on indictment may be tried by the High Court sitting at any place in Scotland".
[34] 1989 S.C.C.R. 313 at 320. Reference was made *inter alia* to the Sheriff Court Districts Reorganisation Order 1975.
[35] See also *HMA v Hunter* 1989 S.L.T. 113 (where an application was rejected to transfer from Dundee to Edinburgh because of prejudice caused by reports in local newspapers, and indeed national newspapers, which might have given rise to speculation among potential jurors in Dundee).
[36] 1998 S.L.T. 60.
[37] 1985 S.C.C.R. 282 at 285–6. See also the rejection of this device in New Zealand: *R. v Saunders* [1995] 3 N.Z.L.R. 545, at para.2–114.
[38] 1974 S.L.T. (Notes) 25.
[39] 1989 S.C.C.R. 413 at 416, Lord Justice-General Emslie, Lord Cowie and Lord Clyde.

16–408

ballot is held". But it went on to express the view that it would be acceptable to "ask jurors at the appropriate time if there are any reasons known to them which would make it desirable that they should not take part in the particular trial". Any such questions would presumably need to be tailored to the particular circumstances. In *HMA v Trainer*,[40] where the trial was abandoned due to a publication contempt, Lord Allanbridge, in reaching that decision, on the application of defence counsel, had the jury polled to discover which of them had heard the radio broadcast in question.

Trial by judge alone

16–409 The reluctance of the courts to bar trials is especially marked where the conduct of that trial will be in the hands of a judge sitting alone. As Sheriff Kearney noted in *Tudhope v Glass*,[41] " . . . such a judge is in a position, not only, as it were, to direct himself to make due allowance for any such extraneous influences but he is also, as the tribunal of fact, in a position to ensure that such directions are carried out".[42] In *Aitchison v Bernardi*,[43] it was stated that this rationale applied also to lay justices:

> "It is a trite part of the training of a judge at any level that a verdict has to depend solely on the evidence before the court and that the decision thereon must not be affected by any extraneous considerations. It is not to be assumed that justices who have been appointed to discharge judicial duties will be incapable of exercising the self-discipline to observe these basic rules simply because they are justices."

Pleas in bar of trial on the ground of publication of prejudicial material would succeed only in the most exceptional circumstances, if at all, in the case of trial by judge alone.

J. Photographs of suspected persons

16–410 In relation to still photography, most concern has centred on the publication of photographs of accused persons, and perhaps especially prison escapers. It was accepted in *Atkins v London Weekend Television Ltd*[44] that:

> " . . . the publication of a photograph of an accused person will only constitute contempt where a question of identification has arisen or may arise and where the publication is calculated to prejudice the prospects of fair trial".

16–411 Under the statutory regime, since 1981, the test for strict liability has been whether any such photograph, viewed in its context including any caption, gives

---

[40] August 28, 1997, Paisley H.C., unreported: see A.J. Bonnington, "Contempt of Court: A Practitioner's Viewpoint" 1988 S.L.T. (News) 33 at 36. The contemnors were dealt with and these subsequent proceedings are reported: *Adams, Petr* 1987 S.C.C.R. 650.
[41] 1981 S.C.C.R. (Sh. Ct.) 336 at 339.
[42] But see the remarks in *Kelly v O'Neill* [2000] I.R. 354 and *Al Megrahi and Fhima v Times Newspapers Ltd* 1999 S.C.C.R. 824 as to the possibility of judges being influenced.
[43] 1984 S.C.C.R. 88 at 91, Lord Justice-Clerk Wheatley, Lord Dunpark and Lord McDonald.
[44] 1978 J.C. 48 at 53, 1978 S.L.T. 76 at 79; see paras 16–192 *et seq*. The court referred to the two English cases of *R. v Daily Mirror* [1927] 1 K.B. 845, and *R. v Lawson* (1937) 81 S.J. 280.

rise to a substantial risk of serious prejudice or impediment. It may be difficult for newspaper and television programme editors to know whether identification is going to be an issue. It would therefore be unwise to publish photographs of an accused person or suspect without at least making appropriate enquiries of the police or prosecuting authorities.

Indeed, on occasion, the Lord Advocate or prosecuting authorities may authorise the publication of the picture of a person sought in connection with a crime.[45] In these circumstances, a publisher is probably safe from contempt proceedings, provided the proceedings are not active. Moreover, any suggestion of common law contempt would founder on the need to prove an intention to interfere with the course of justice. Similar authority may sometimes be obtained to publish a photograph of a dangerous escaper, and it can prove unwise to take the risk of publication without such clearance, at least in the case of a prisoner awaiting trial in respect of proceedings that are active.

K. Photography, sound recordings and television in the vicinity of the court

1. *Photography*

Still photography within Scottish courts is not prohibited by any statute, but, if noticed by the judge or court officials, may form the subject of contempt proceedings on the ground of disruption to the due and solemn administration of justice.[46]

2. *Tape recorders*

Section 9 of the 1981 Act provides the first statutory regulation of the use of tape recorders in court. The section makes it a contempt to use, or bring into court for use, a sound recording instrument, without leave of the court. Leave may be granted subject to conditions as to use of the recordings, and it may be withdrawn in whole or in part at any time. Forfeiture of an instrument used in the commission of this contempt is specifically provided for.[47] It is also a contempt to publish a recording of legal proceedings made by means of any such instrument, or any recording derived from it, by playing it in the hearing of the public or any section of the public; or to dispose of it, or any recording so derived, with a view to such publication.[48] Recordings for the purposes of official transcripts are expressly excluded from the operation of the section.[49]

---

[45] See the discussion at para.16–333.
[46] See, *e.g. Sweeney*, unreported, Glasgow H.Ct. 1975: B. McKain, A.J. Bonnington and G.A. Watt, *op. cit.*, p.125. Compare the position in England, which is regulated by the Criminal Justice Act 1925, s.41.
[47] s.9(3).
[48] s.9(1)(b).
[49] s.9(4).

3. The Television Practice Direction

16–415 No specific legislation exists in Scotland prohibiting the televising of court proceedings, although its intrusive nature would undoubtedly mean that any attempt to do so without the court's permission would be treated as contempt. Because occasionally requests were being made by broadcasting authorities for permission to televise proceedings in the Court of Session and the High Court of Justice, the Lord President thought it appropriate to issue a practice direction. On August 6, 1992 the following notice was issued:

"Television in the Courts"

The Lord President has issued the following directions about the practice which will be followed in regard to requests by the broadcasting authorities for permission to televise proceedings in the Court of Session and the High Court of Justiciary.

(a) The rule hitherto has been that television cameras are not allowed within the precincts of the court. While the absolute nature of the rule makes it easy to apply, it is an impediment to the making of programmes of an educational or documentary nature and to the use of television in other cases where there would be no risk to the administration of justice.

(b) In future the criterion will be whether the presence of television cameras in the court would be without risk to the administration of justice.

(c) In view of the risks to the administration of justice, the televising of current proceedings in criminal cases at first instance will not be permitted under any circumstances.

(d) Civil proofs at first instance do not normally involve juries, but the risks inherent in the televising of current proceedings while witnesses are giving their evidence justify the same practice here as in the case of criminal trials.

(e) Subject to satisfactory arrangements about the placing of cameras and to there being no additional lighting, which would make conditions in the court room intolerable, the televising of current proceedings at the appellate level in both civil and criminal cases may be undertaken with the approval of the presiding Judge and subject to such conditions as he may impose.

(f) Subject to the same conditions, ceremonies held in a court room may also be televised for the purpose of news broadcasting.

(g) The taking of television pictures, without sound, of Judges on the Bench—as a replacement for the still photographs current in use—will be permitted with the consent of the Judge concerned.

(h) Requests from television companies for provision to film proceedings, including proceedings at first instance, for the purpose of showing educational or documentary programmes at a later date will be favourably considered. But such filming may be done only with the consent of all parties involved in the proceedings, and it will be subject to approval by the presiding Judge of the final product before it is televised."

Several documentary programmes, and news items depicting the delivery of important appellate judgments, have indeed been broadcast.[50]

16–416

The Directions of the Lord President as to "Television in the Courts" were considered in the High Court of Justiciary in *BBC, Petrs (No.1)*.[51] The BBC had applied by way of petition to the *nobile officium* of the High Court for permission to broadcast the proceedings of the Lockerbie bombing trial about to be held in the Netherlands. Permission was refused for a number of reasons, including the risk that televising the proceedings would have an adverse impact on witnesses,[52] and would give rise to a real risk of prejudice to the administration of justice. Indeed, the view was expressed by Lord Macfadyen that the risk was greater than it would be in a routine criminal trial. It was argued that the reasoning underlying para.(c) of the Directions is that broadcasting would be liable to involve a risk by way of impact upon the jury and, there being no jury in the case in hand, this consideration could be said to be irrelevant. It was concluded, however, that this factor did not afford a sufficient basis for setting aside the outright prohibition contained in para.(c). In para.(d) it was recognised that in civil proceedings at first instance there would not normally be a jury. Nevertheless, the risks in respect of witnesses were regarded in themselves as sufficient to justify adherence to the same practice of not permitting the televising of civil proofs so long as they were current. Accordingly, on a fair reading of the Directions, the potential impact of broadcasting on jurors might be seen as strengthening the case for prohibition but not as essential to it.

16–417

Lord Macfadyen addressed the possibility that he might be wrong in applying paras (c) and (h) of the Lord President's Directions according to their terms. In that event, he was of opinion that the petitioners would have the burden of proving that televising the proceedings would involve no risk to the administration of justice.

16–418

It was argued also that a devolution issue arose requiring that it be referred to a larger court in the light of para.9 of Sch.6 to the Scotland Act 1998. This was because it was contended that the Lord Advocate had acted in a way that was incompatible with the BBC's Convention rights under Art.10. He had made arrangements for transmission of the proceedings to "remote sites" for the benefit of the victims' relatives but not for general broadcasting. It was accepted that this gave rise to a devolution issue that was neither vexatious nor frivolous. Nevertheless, he declined to exercise his discretion to refer the matter to a larger court in view of his own conclusions on the merits. Lord Macfadyen's reasoning on the merits was described as "very careful and persuasive" upon the second petition of the BBC appealing to the *nobile officium* of the High Court of Justiciary, which was determined by three judges in *BBC, Petrs (No.2)*.[53] Although it was suggested that due to the nature of the remedy being sought no

16–419

---

[50] See R. Munday, "Televising the Courts: An Appraisal of the Scots Experiment" (1995) 159 J.P.N. 37.
[51] 2000 J.C. 419, 2000 S.C.C.R. 533.
[52] Compare the similar factors mentioned in the public debate about televising appellate courts in England, discussed at para.10–206.
[53] 2000 J.C. 521, 2000 S.C.C.R. 533.

appeal lay against his decision, the matter was dealt with "on the merits" without the need to resolve the various procedural issues.

L. Penalties for contempt after the Act

16–420   The requirement in s.15 for fixed sentences of imprisonment appears to reflect the approach which the courts had been developing.[54] In *Forrest v Wilson*,[55] the complainer was found guilty of contempt in the summary court, for having persistently and admittedly lied in course of his evidence. He was punished summarily by the sheriff, the minute of proceedings recording a sentence of 42 days' imprisonment. There was an appeal to the High Court by bill of suspension on the basis that the proceedings were incompetent, as being in breach of s.42 of the Criminal Justice (Scotland) Act 1980, and that the sentence was excessive. The complaint based upon s.42 was that it was necessary for the court, after having received information from an officer of a local authority or otherwise, to form the view that no other method of dealing with the person was appropriate than by custodial penalty, and to record the reason for that opinion.

16–421   The question was also raised in the course of the appeal whether the competence of the sentence was affected by the provisions of s.344 of the Criminal Procedure (Scotland) Act 1975[56] which provided that a witness prevaricating in his evidence should be deemed guilty of contempt, and be liable to be summarily punished by imprisonment *up to 21* days.

16–422   It was held, first, that the minute of proceedings had been in error in referring to the accused having been "sentenced", and there had been no need to call for reports. In that respect, the proceedings were competent. On the other hand, although a custodial penalty had not been inappropriate, s.344 of the 1975 Act had been amended by Sch.7 to the Criminal Justice Act 1982, and thus it must have been Parliament's intention that its provisions should remain in force alongside those of s.15 of the Contempt of Court Act 1981. Thus, the restrictions of s.15 should be read as dealing with all cases of contempt *except for* such behaviour on the part of a witness in a summary prosecution; this fell to be dealt with under the 1975 Act, and to that extent the sheriff had acted in excess of his powers. A sentence of 21 days was therefore substituted.

16–423   A sentencing problem had arisen in relation to a "young offender" in *Dawes v Cardle*.[57] A sheriff had been confronted with some 38 demonstrators who had been brought to court and were causing disruption, not least by "singing in the cells to his annoyance". Miss Dawes declined to plead and shouted to such an extent that it became clear that her attitude was one of "open defiance and

---

[54] See Gordon, *op. cit.*, 2nd ed., para.51–01, n.7. Having cited older authorities tending to show that punishment might take the form of a fixed sentence or an indeterminate one, the author observed that "the current practice appears to be to impose fixed sentences". It is said in the 3rd edition that punishment must be for a fixed term "although this does not prevent the court from authorising his discharge prior to the completion of that term": see para.50–01.
[55] 1993 S.C.C.R. 631.
[56] See now the Criminal Procedure (Scotland) Act 1995, s.155(1)(d), set out at para.16–115.
[57] 1987 S.C.C.R. 135.

disrespect to the bench". The sheriff regarded her behaviour as "the last straw", and decided upon an immediate sentence of detention. When she appealed by bill of suspension, his sentence of 20 days' imprisonment was quashed for incompetence, since she was under 21 and he had not obtained the necessary pre-sentencing information required by the Criminal Procedure (Scotland) Act 1975, s.415.[58] This was applied to sentences for contempt by the Contempt of Court Act 1981, s.15(3).

In *Smith, Petr*,[59] Lord Sutherland, a High Court judge, had imposed a three year sentence of imprisonment for contempt on a witness who had refused to answer questions. He reported on appeal that he accepted that: **16–424**

> " . . . in terms of section 15(2) of the Contempt of Court Act 1981 the sentence imposed was in fact incompetent in that the subsection provides for a maximum penalty of two years' imprisonment for contempt of court. I can only say that this section had not been brought to my notice and it had not occurred to me that Parliament would have imposed a statutory restriction on penalty for what remains a common law offence [of] contempt in the face of the court".

The approach to punishing contempt after 1981 was addressed by the High Court in *Adams, Petr*[60] where emphasis was placed upon the need to assess individual culpability, specifically in the context of a radio programme editor who had relied on a report sent to him by an experienced freelance reporter. In those circumstances, it was thought right to quash the penalty of £20,000 imposed below following the abandonment of a criminal trial. **16–425**

In *Express Newspapers plc, Petr*,[61] the High Court imposed a fine of £50,000 on Express Newspapers plc, where liability had been acknowledged in the following circumstances. Two men had appeared in December 1997 charged with theft by housebreaking. One pleaded guilty and the other was indicted for trial in the sheriff court. The trial diet was adjourned on April 20, 1998 when the diet was deserted *pro loco et tempore*. A witness for the Crown had been unable to attend. Four days later, an article appeared on the front page of the *Scottish Daily Express*, which dealt prejudicially with the evidence in the case, published upon the mistaken view that the proceedings were no longer "active" after the diet was deserted. Despite a warning to the opposite effect, given to a reporter over the telephone by the Procurator Fiscal, the newspaper's staff continued to act upon the erroneous legal advice. The appeal on sentence was refused. Particular factors taken into account included the prominence given to the article and the "duty" of publishers to avoid creating a substantial risk of serious prejudice. **16–426**

---

[58] See now the Criminal Procedure (Scotland) Act 1995, s.207, and the Criminal Procedure (Consequential Provisions) Act 1995, which by Sch.4, para.36, amends s.15 of the 1981 Act, so as to import *inter alia* the sentencing restrictions in respect of young offenders contained in s.207.
[59] 1987 S.C.C.R. 726 at 728.
[60] 1987 S.C.C.R. 650 at 653–4; see A.J. Bonnington, "Contempt of Court: A Practitioner's Viewpoint", 1988 S.L.T. (News) 33 at 38.
[61] 1999 S.L.T. 644, S.C.C.R. 262, S.C. (J.C.) 176.

M. Lack of a specific appeals procedure

16–427 Despite the recommendations of the Phillimore Committee,[62] the opportunity was not taken by Parliament to institute a standard appeal route with respect to findings of contempt. In *Butterworth v Herron*,[63] a bill of suspension for an appeal by a witness found in contempt, in the course of solemn proceedings in the sheriff court, was held to be competent. This was, however, overruled by five judges in *George Outram and Co v Lees*,[64] who held that the correct mode of appeal was by a petition to the *nobile officium*. The case turned upon the construction of s.230 of the Criminal Procedure (Scotland) Act 1975.[65] The corresponding provisions of the 1995 Act are as follows:

> "It shall not be competent to appeal to the High Court by bill of suspension against any conviction, sentence, judgement or order pronounced in any proceedings on indictment in the sheriff court".

16–428 The origin of the provision lies in the Criminal Appeal (Scotland) Act 1926, s.13, which had abolished appeal by suspension, although appeal by advocation from the sheriff in solemn procedure had remained competent. It was argued on behalf of the Crown in *Wilson Petr*[66] that the equivalent provision in the 1975 Act was effective to preclude an appeal by petition to the *nobile officium*. This point does not seem to have been argued in *Outram*. Sheriff Gordon in his commentary upon *Outram* suggested that Parliament might consider the position and provide a statutory routine method of appeal for those found guilty of contempt in such circumstances, other than by way of the *nobile officium* which is meant to represent a reserve of inherent powers only to be called upon in extraordinary circumstances. The suggestion was not taken up in the 1995 Act.

16–429 In *Express Newspapers plc, Petr*,[67] the court took the view that in assessing the range of the *nobile officium* in modern times it is necessary to look beyond Hume and examine more recent developments. According to Hume,[68] the High Court did not have any power to review its own sentences, or orders, by suspension or reduction or any other form of process. It is now clear, however, from *Wylie v HMA*[69] that the *nobile officium* provides a means by which a witness might appeal from a High Court trial judge's decision, whether on liability for contempt or with regard to sentence. This jurisdiction was affirmed also in *Kemp and*

---

[62] See para.16–300. See the comments by the Lord Justice-General in *Express Newspapers plc, Petr* 1999 S.L.T. 644, S.C.C.R. 262, S.C. (J.C.) 176. What was different about the facts of the *Express Newspapers* case was that the finding was made and sentence imposed in proceedings on petition in the High Court. The Full Bench, however, saw no reason why a "mere difference in the form of proceedings" should lead to a different result. Indeed, it might almost be a matter of chance whether, in a particular case, the matter was dealt with by the trial judge or by the Lord Advocate raising a petition.
[63] 1975 S.L.T. (Notes) 56.
[64] 1992 S.C.C.R. 120.
[65] Now s.130 of the 1995 Act.
[66] 1991 S.C.C.R. 957.
[67] 1999 S.L.T. 644, S.C.C.R. 262, S.C. (J.C.) 176.
[68] Commentaries ii, 463 and 508.
[69] 1966 S.L.T. 149.

others, Petitioners,⁷⁰ and *George Outram and Co v Lees*.⁷¹ These cases concerned, respectively, a finding of contempt by a trial judge in the High Court against an editor, publishers and a journalist, and a similar finding by a judge in solemn proceedings in the sheriff court.

Parliament has at no stage taken up the suggestion of substituting any new procedure, by way of note of appeal. Therefore in *Express Newspapers plc, Petr*,⁷² the High Court thought it right to proceed on the basis that the legislature had been content to leave the matter on the footing established by the court, particularly with reference to the *nobile officium*. The Lord Justice-General summarised the nature of the *nobile officium*, citing Alison, *Practice of the Criminal Law of Scotland* as follows⁷³:

16–430

> " 'The Court of Justiciary has the exclusive power of providing a remedy for all extraordinary or unforeseen occurrences in the course of criminal business, *whether before themselves*, or any inferior Court' (emphasis added)."

---

⁷⁰ 1982 S.C.C.R. 1.
⁷¹ 1992 S.L.T. 32.
⁷² 1999 S.L.T. 644, S.C.C.R. 262, S.C. (J.C.) 176 at 180.
⁷³ At 23.

APPENDIX 1

Contempt of Court Act

(1981, 49)

An Act to amend the law relating to contempt of court and related matters
[27th July 1981]

BE IT ENACTED by the Queen's most Excellent Majesty, by and with the advice and consent of the Lords Spiritual and Temporal, and Commons, in this present Parliament assembled, and by the authority of the same, as follows:—

STRICT LIABILITY

1.— The strict liability rule

17–1 In this Act "the strict liability rule" means the rule of law whereby conduct may be treated as a contempt of court as tending to interfere with the course of justice in particular legal proceedings regardless of intent to do so.

NOTES

Initial Commencement
Specified date
Specified date: 27 August 1981: see s.21(3).

LIMITATION OF SCOPE OF STRICT LIABILITY

2.—(1) The strict liability rule applies only in relation to publications, and for this purpose "publication" includes any speech, writing, [programme included in a programme service] or other communication in whatever form, which is addressed to the public at large or any section of the public.

(2) The strict liability rule applies only to a publication which creates a substantial risk that the course of justice in the proceedings in question will be seriously impeded or prejudiced.

(3) The strict liability rule applies to a publication only if the proceedings in question are active within the meaning of this section at the time of the publication.

(4) Schedule 1 applies for determining the times at which proceedings are to be treated as active within the meaning of this section.

LIMITATION OF SCOPE OF STRICT LIABILITY   17–1

[(5) In this section "programme service" has the same meaning as in the Broadcasting Act 1990.]

NOTES

Initial Commencement
Specified date
Specified date: 27 August 1981: see s.21(3).

Amendment
Subs.(1): words in square brackets substituted by the Broadcasting Act 1990, s.203(1), Sch.20, para.31(1).
Subs.(5): inserted by the Broadcasting Act 1990, s.203(1), Sch.20, para.31(1).

Defence of innocent publication or distribution

3.—(1) A person is not guilty of contempt of court under the strict liability rule as the publisher of any matter to which that rule applies if at the time of publication (having taken all reasonable care) he does not know and has no reason to suspect that relevant proceedings are active.

(2) A person is not guilty of contempt of court under the strict liability rule as the distributor of a publication containing any such matter if at the time of distribution (having taken all reasonable care) he does not know that it contains such matter and has no reason to suspect that it is likely to do so.

(3) The burden of proof of any fact tending to establish a defence afforded by this section to any person lies upon that person.

(4) . . .

NOTES

Initial Commencement
Specified date
Specified date: 27 August 1981: see s.21(3).

Amendment
Sub.s (4): repealed by the Statute Law (Repeals) Act 2004.
Date in force: 22 July 2004: (no specific commencement provision).

Contemporary reports of proceedings

4.—(1) Subject to this section a person is not guilty of contempt of court under the strict liability rule in respect of a fair and accurate report of legal proceedings held in public, published contemporaneously and in good faith.

(2) In any such proceedings the court may, where it appears to be necessary for avoiding a substantial risk of prejudice to the administration of justice in those proceedings, or in any other proceedings pending or imminent, order that the publication of any report of the proceedings, or any part of the proceedings, be postponed for such period as the court thinks necessary for that purpose.

[(2A) Where in proceedings for any offence which is an administration of justice offence for the purposes of section 54 of the Criminal Procedure and Investigations Act 1996 (acquittal tainted by an administration of justice offence) it appears to the court that

APPENDIX 1

there is a possibility that (by virtue of that section) proceedings may be taken against a person for an offence of which he has been acquitted, subsection (2) of this section shall apply as if those proceedings were pending or imminent.]

(3) For the purposes of subsection (1) of this section . . . a report of proceedings shall be treated as published contemporaneously—

(a) in the case of a report of which publication is postponed pursuant to an order under subsection (2) of this section, if published as soon as practicable after that order expires;

(b) in the case of a report of committal proceedings of which publication is permitted by virtue only of subsection (3) of section 8 of the Magistrates' Courts Act 1980, if published as soon as practicable after publication is so permitted

[(b) in the case of a report of allocation or sending proceedings of which publication is permitted by virtue only of subsection (6) of section 52A of the Crime and Disorder Act 1998 ("the 1998 Act"), if published as soon as practicable after publication is so permitted;

(c) in the case of a report of an application of which publication is permitted by virtue only of sub-paragraph (5) or (7) of paragraph 3 of Schedule 3 to the 1998 Act, if published as soon as practicable after publication is so permitted].

(4) . . .

NOTES

Initial Commencement
Specified date
Specified date: 27 August 1981: see s.21(3).

Amendment
Subs.(2A): inserted by the Criminal Procedure and Investigations Act 1996, s.57(3). Subs.(3): words omitted repealed by the Defamation Act 1996, s.16, Sch.2.
Date in force: 1 April 1999: see SI 1999/817, art.2(b).
Subs.(3): para.(b) substituted, by subsequent paras (b), (c), by the Criminal Justice Act 2003, s.41, Sch.3, Pt 2, para.53.
Date in force: to be appointed: see the Criminal Justice Act 2003, s.336(3).
Subs.(4): repealed by the Statute Law (Repeals) Act 2004.
Date in force: 22 July 2004: (no specific commencement provision).

Discussion of public affairs

5.—A publication made as or as part of a discussion in good faith of public affairs or other matters of general public interest is not to be treated as a contempt of court under the strict liability rule if the risk of impediment or prejudice to particular legal proceedings is merely incidental to the discussion.

NOTES

Initial Commencement
Specified date
Specified date: 27 August 1981: see s.21(3).

Contempt of Court Act

Savings

6.—Nothing in the foregoing provisions of this Act—

(a) prejudices any defence available at common law to a charge of contempt of court under the strict liability rule;

(b) implies that any publication is punishable as contempt of court under that rule which would not be so punishable apart from those provisions;

(c) restricts liability for contempt of court in respect of conduct intended to impede or prejudice the administration of justice.

NOTES

Initial Commencement
Specified date
Specified date: 27 August 1981: see s.21(3).

Consent required for institution of proceedings

7.—Proceedings for a contempt of court under the strict liability rule (other than Scottish proceedings) shall not be instituted except by or with the consent of the Attorney General or on the motion of a court having jurisdiction to deal with it.

NOTES

Initial Commencement
Specified date
Specified date: 27 August 1981: see s.21(3).

Extent
This section does not extend to Scotland: see s.21(4).

OTHER ASPECTS OF LAW AND PROCEDURE

Confidentiality of jury's deliberations

8.—(1) Subject to subsection (2) below, it is a contempt of court to obtain, disclose or solicit any particulars of statements made, opinions expressed, arguments advanced or votes cast by members of a jury in the course of their deliberations in any legal proceedings.

(2) This section does not apply to any disclosure of any particulars—

(a) in the proceedings in question for the purpose of enabling the jury to arrive at their verdict, or in connection with the delivery of that verdict, or

(b) in evidence in any subsequent proceedings for an offence alleged to have been committed in relation to the jury in the first mentioned proceedings,

or to the publication of any particulars so disclosed.

APPENDIX 1

(3) Proceedings for a contempt of court under this section (other than Scottish proceedings) shall not be instituted except by or with the consent of the Attorney General or on the motion of a court having jurisdiction to deal with it.

NOTES

Initial Commencement
Specified date
Specified date: 27 August 1981: see s.21(3).

Extent
Subs.(3) does not extend to Scotland: see s.21(4).

Use of tape recorders

9.—(1) Subject to subsection (4) below, it is a contempt of court—

(a) to use in court, or bring into court for use, any tape recorder or other instrument for recording sound, except with the leave of the court;

(b) to publish a recording of legal proceedings made by means of any such instrument, or any recording derived directly or indirectly from it, by playing it in the hearing of the public or any section of the public, or to dispose of it or any recording so derived, with a view to such publication;

(c) to use any such recording in contravention of any conditions of leave granted under paragraph (a).

(2) Leave under paragraph (a) of subsection (1) may be granted or refused at the discretion of the court, and if granted may be granted subject to such conditions as the court thinks proper with respect to the use of any recording made pursuant to the leave; and where leave has been granted the court may at the like discretion withdraw or amend it either generally or in relation to any particular part of the proceedings.

(3) Without prejudice to any other power to deal with an act of contempt under paragraph (a) of subsection (1), the court may order the instrument, or any recording made with it, or both, to be forfeited; and any object so forfeited shall (unless the court otherwise determines on application by a person appearing to be the owner) be sold or otherwise disposed of in such manner as the court may direct.

(4) This section does not apply to the making or use of sound recordings for purposes of official transcripts of proceedings.

NOTES

Initial Commencement
Specified date
Specified date: 27 August 1981: see s.21(3).

Sources of information

10.—No court may require a person to disclose, nor is any person guilty of contempt of court for refusing to disclose, the source of information contained in a publication for which he is responsible, unless it be established to the satisfaction of the court that disclosure is necessary in the interests of justice or national security or for the prevention of disorder or crime.

NOTES

Initial Commencement
Specified date
Specified date: 27 August 1981: see s.21(3).

Publication of matters exempted from disclosure in court

11.—In any case where a court (having power to do so) allows a name or other matter to be withheld from the public in proceedings before the court, the court may give such directions prohibiting the publication of that name or matter in connection with the proceedings as appear to the court to be necessary for the purpose for which it was so withheld.

NOTES

Initial Commencement
Specified date
Specified date: 27 August 1981: see s.21(3).

Offences of contempt of magistrates' courts

12.—(1) A magistrates' court has jurisdiction under this section to deal with any person who—

(a) wilfully insults the justice or justices, any witness before or officer of the court or any solicitor or counsel having business in the court, during his or their sitting or attendance in court or in going to or returning from the court; or

(b) wilfully interrupts the proceedings of the court or otherwise misbehaves in court.

(2) In any such case the court may order any officer of the court, or any constable, to take the offender into custody and detain him until the rising of the court; and the court may, if it thinks fit, commit the offender to custody for a specified period not exceeding one month or impose on him a fine not exceeding [£2,500], or both.

[(2A) A fine imposed under subsection (2) above shall be deemed, for the purposes of any enactment, to be a sum adjudged to be paid by a conviction.]

(3) . . .

(4) A magistrates' court may at any time revoke an order of committal made under subsection (2) and, if the offender is in custody, order his discharge.

(5) [Section 135 of the Powers of Criminal Courts (Sentencing) Act 2000 (limit on fines in respect of young persons) and] the following provisions of the Magistrates' Courts Act 1980 apply in relation to an order under this section as they apply in relation to a sentence on conviction or finding of guilty of an offence[; and those provisions of the Magistrates' Courts Act 1980 are] sections 75 to 91 (enforcement); section 108 (appeal to Crown Court); section 136 (overnight detention in default of payment); and section 142(1) (power to rectify mistakes).

NOTES

Initial Commencement
Specified date
Specified date: 27 August 1981: see s.21(3).

Amendment
Subs.(2): sum in square brackets substituted by the Criminal Justice Act 1991, s.17(3), Sch.4, Part I.
Subs.(2A): inserted by the Criminal Justice Act 1991, s.17(3), Sch.4, Part V, substituted by the Criminal Justice Act 1993, s.65(3), (4), Sch.3, para.6(4).
Subs.(3): repealed by the Criminal Justice Act 1982, s.78, Sch.16.
Subs.(5): words "Section 135 of the Powers of Criminal Courts (Sentencing) Act 2000 (limit on fines in respect of young persons) and" in square brackets inserted by the Powers of Criminal Courts (Sentencing) Act 2000, s.165(1), Sch.9, para.83(a).
    Date in force: 25 August 2000: see the Powers of Criminal Courts (Sentencing) Act 2000, s.168(1).
Subs.(5): words "; and those provisions of the Magistrates' Courts Act 1980 are" in square brackets substituted by the Powers of Criminal Courts (Sentencing) Act 2000, s.165(1), Sch.9, para.83(b).
    Date in force: 25 August 2000: see the Powers of Criminal Courts (Sentencing) Act 2000, s.168(1).

Modification
Modification: reference in subs.(2) to "any officer of the court" modified by the Criminal Justice Act 1991, s.100, Sch.11, para.29.

Extent
This section does not extend to Scotland: see s.21(4).

13 . . .
. . .

NOTES

Amendment
Repealed in part by the Legal Aid (Scotland) Act 1986, s.45(3), Sch.5.
Repealed in part by the Legal Aid Act 1988, s.45(2), (3), Sch.6.
Remainder repealed by SI 2003/435, art.49(2), Sch.5.
Date in force: to be appointed: see SI 2003/435, art.1(2).

PENALTIES FOR CONTEMPT AND KINDRED OFFENCES

Proceedings in England and Wales

14.—(1) In any case where a court has power to commit a person to prison for contempt of court and (apart from this provision) no limitation applies to the period of committal, the committal shall (without prejudice to the power of the court to order his earlier discharge) be for a fixed term, and that term shall not on any occasion exceed two years in the case of committal by a superior court, or one month in the case of committal by an inferior court.

(2) In any case where an inferior court has power to fine a person for contempt of court and (apart from this provision) no limit applies to the amount of the fine, the fine shall not on any occasion exceed [£2,500].

[(2A) In the exercise of jurisdiction to commit for contempt of court or any kindred offence the court shall not deal with the offender by making an order under [section 60 of

CONTEMPT OF COURT ACT   17–1

the Powers of Criminal Courts (Sentencing) Act 2000] (an attendance centre order) if it appears to the court, after considering any available evidence, that he is under 17 years of age.]

[(2A) A fine imposed under subsection (2) above shall be deemed, for the purposes of any enactment, to be a sum adjudged to be paid by a conviction.]

(3) . . .

(4) Each of the superior courts shall have the like power to make a hospital order or guardianship order under [section 37 of the Mental Health Act 1983] [or an interim hospital order under [section 38 of that Act]] in the case of a person suffering from mental illness or [severe mental impairment] who could otherwise be committed to prison for contempt of court as the Crown Court has under that section in the case of a person convicted of an offence.

[(4A) Each of the superior courts shall have the like power to make an order under [section 35 of the said Act of 1983] (remand for report on accused's mental condition) where there is reason to suspect that a person who could be committed to prison for contempt of court is suffering from mental illness or severe mental impairment as the Crown Court has under that section in the case of an accused person within the meaning of that section.]

[(4A) For the purposes of the preceding provisions of this section a county court shall be treated as a superior court and not an inferior court.]

(5) The enactments specified in Part III of Schedule 2 shall have effect subject to the amendments set out in that Part, being amendments relating to the penalties and procedure in respect of certain offences of contempt in coroners' courts, county courts and magistrates' courts.

NOTES

Initial Commencement
Specified date
Specified date: 27 August 1981: see s.21(3).

Amendment
Subs.(2): sum "£2,500" in square brackets substituted by the Criminal Justice Act 1991, s.17(3)(a), Sch.4, Pt I.
Date in force: 1 October 1992: see SI 1992/333, art.2(2), Sch.2.
First subs.(2A): inserted by the Criminal Justice Act 1982, s.77, Sch.14, para.60.
First subs.(2A): words "section 60 of the Powers of Criminal Courts (Sentencing) Act 2000" in square brackets substituted by the Powers of Criminal Courts (Sentencing) Act 2000, s.165(1), Sch.9, para.84.
Date in force: 25 August 2000: see the Powers of Criminal Courts (Sentencing) Act 2000, s.168(1).
Second subs.(2A): inserted by the Criminal Justice Act 1991, s.17(3), Sch.4, Part V; substituted by the Criminal Justice Act 1993, s.65(3), (4), Sch.3, para.6(5).
Subs.(3): repealed by the Criminal Justice Act 1982, s.78, Sch.16.
Subs.(4): first and final words in square brackets substituted by the Mental Health Act 1983, s.148, Sch.4, para.57; second words in square brackets inserted by the Mental Health (Amendment) Act 1982, s.65(1), Sch.3, para.59, words in square brackets therein substituted by the Mental Health Act 1983, s.148, Sch.4, para.57.
First Subs.(4A): inserted by the Mental Health (Amendment) Act 1982, s.65(1), Sch.3, para.60, words in square brackets substituted by the Mental Health Act 1983, s.148, Sch.4, para.57.
Second Subs.(4A): inserted by the County Courts (Penalties for Contempt) Act 1983, s.1.

Extent
This section does not extend to Scotland: see s.21(4).

APPENDIX 1

Penalties for contempt of court in Scottish proceedings

15.—(1) In Scottish proceedings, when a person is committed to prison for contempt of court the committal shall (without prejudice to the power of the court to order his earlier discharge) be for a fixed term.

(2) The maximum penalty which may be imposed by way of imprisonment or fine for contempt of court in Scottish proceedings shall be two years' imprisonment or a fine or both, except that—

(a) where the contempt is dealt with by the sheriff in the course of or in connection with proceedings other than criminal proceedings on indictment, such penalty shall not exceed three months' imprisonment or a fine of [level 4 on the standard scale] or both; and

(b) where the contempt is dealt with by the district court, such penalty shall not exceed sixty days' imprisonment or a fine of [level 4 on the standard scale] or both.

[(3) The following provisions of the Criminal Procedure (Scotland) Act 1995 shall apply in relation to persons found guilty of contempt of court in Scottish proceedings as they apply in relation to persons convicted of offences—

(a) in every case, section 207 (restrictions on detention of young offenders);

(b) in any case to which paragraph (b) of subsection (2) above does not apply, sections 58, 59 and 61 (persons suffering from mental disorder);

and in any case to which the said paragraph (b) does apply, subsection (5) below shall have effect.]

(5) Where a person is found guilty by a district court of contempt of court and it appears to the court that he may be suffering from mental disorder, it shall remit him to the sheriff in the manner provided by [section 7(9) and (10) of the Criminal Procedure (Scotland) Act 1995] and the sheriff shall, on such remit being made, have the like power to make an order under [section 58(1)] of the said Act in respect of him as if he had been convicted by the sheriff of an offence, or in dealing with him may exercise the like powers as the court making the remit.

[(6) . . .]

NOTES

Initial Commencement
Specified date
Specified date: 27 August 1981: see s.21(3).

Amendment
Subs.(2): fines converted to a level on the standard scale by the Criminal Procedure (Consequential Provisions) (Scotland) Act 1995, s.5, Sch.4, paras 36(2), 99.
Subs.(3): substituted, for sub-ss (3), (4) as originally enacted, by the Criminal Procedure (Consequential Provisions) (Scotland) Act 1995, s.5, Sch.4, para.36(3).
Subs.(5): words in square brackets substituted by the Criminal Procedure (Consequential Provisions) (Scotland) Act 1995, s.5, Sch.4, para.36(4).
Subs.(6): inserted with retrospective effect by the Criminal Justice (Scotland) Act 1987, s.70(1), Sch.1; repealed by the Prisoners and Criminal Proceedings (Scotland) Act 1993, s.47(3), Sch.7, Part I.

CONTEMPT OF COURT ACT   17–1

Enforcement of fines imposed by certain superior courts

16.—(1) Payment of a fine for contempt of court imposed by a superior court, other than the Crown Court or one of the courts specified in subsection (4) below, may be enforced upon the order of the court—

(a) in like manner as a judgment of the High Court for the payment of money; or

(b) in like manner as a fine imposed by the Crown Court.

(2) Where payment of a fine imposed by any court falls to be enforced as mentioned in paragraph (a) of subsection (1)—

(a) the court shall, if the fine is not paid in full forthwith or within such time as the court may allow, certify to Her Majesty's Remembrancer the sum payable;

(b) Her Majesty's Remembrancer shall thereupon proceed to enforce payment of that sum as if it were due to him as a judgment debt; . . .

(c) . . .

(3) Where payment of a fine imposed by any court falls to be enforced as mentioned in paragraph (b) of subsection (1), the provisions of [sections 139 and 140 of the Powers of Criminal Courts (Sentencing) Act 2000] shall apply as they apply to a fine imposed by the Crown Court.

(4) Subsection (1) of this section does not apply to fines imposed by the criminal division of the Court of Appeal or by the *House of Lords* [Supreme Court] on appeal from that division.

(5) The Fines Act 1833 shall not apply to a fine to which subsection (1) of this section applies.

(6) . . .

NOTES

Initial Commencement
  Specified date
  Specified date: 27 August 1981: see s.21(3).

Amendment
  Subs.(2): fines converted to a level on the standard scale by the Criminal Procedure (Consequential Provisions) (Scotland) Act 1995, s.5, Sch.4, paras 36(2), 99.
  Subs.(3): substituted, for sub-ss (3), (4) as originally enacted, by the Criminal Procedure (Consequential Provisions) (Scotland) Act 1995, s.5, Sch.4, para.36(3). Subs.(5): words in square brackets substituted by the Criminal Procedure (Consequential Provisions) (Scotland) Act 1995, s.5, Sch.4, para.36(4). Subs.(6): inserted with retrospective effect by the Criminal Justice (Scotland) Act 1987, s.70(1), Sch.1; repealed by the Prisoners and Criminal Proceedings (Scotland) Act 1993, s.47(3), Sch.7, Part I.
    Date in force: 25 August 2000: see the Powers of Criminal Courts (Sentencing) Act 2000, s.168(1).
  Subs.(4): words "House of Lords" in italics repealed and subsequent words in square brackets substituted by the Constitutional Reform Act 2005, s.40(4), Sch.9, Pt 1, para.35(1), (2).
    Date in force: to be appointed: see the Constitutional Reform Act 2005, s.148(1).
  Subs.(6): repealed by the Employment Tribunals Act 1996, s.45, Sch.3, Pt I.

Miscellaneous
  By virtue of the Employment Rights (Dispute Resolution) Act 1998, s.1(2), the Industrial Tribunals Act 1996 shall be cited as the Employment Tribunals Act 1996; references to the Industrial Tribunals Act 1996 have been changed accordingly.

APPENDIX 1

Extent
   This section does not extend to Scotland: see s.21(4).

Disobedience to certain orders of magistrates' courts

17.—(1) The powers of a magistrates' court under subsection (3) of section 63 of the Magistrates' Courts Act 1980 (punishment by fine or committal for disobeying an order to do anything other than the payment of money or to abstain from doing anything) may be exercised either of the court's own motion or by order on complaint.

(2) In relation to the exercise of those powers the provisions of the Magistrates' Court Act 1980 shall apply subject to the modifications set out in Schedule 3 to this Act.

NOTES

Initial Commencement
   Specified date
   Specified date: 27 August 1981: see s.21(3).

Extent
   This section does not extend to Scotland: see s.21(4).

SUPPLEMENTAL

Northern Ireland

18.—(1) In the application of this Act to Northern Ireland references to the Attorney General shall be construed as references to the Attorney General for Northern Ireland.

(2) In their application to Northern Ireland, sections 12, 13, 14 and 16 of this Act shall have effect as set out in Schedule 4.

NOTES

Initial Commencement
   Specified date
   Specified date: 27 August 1981: see s.21(3).

Extent
   This section does not extend to Scotland: see s.21(4).

Interpretation

19. In this Act—
   [. . .]
   "court" includes any tribunal or body exercising the judicial power of the State, and "legal proceedings" shall be construed accordingly;
   "publication" has the meaning assigned by subsection (1) of section 2, and "publish" (except in section 9) shall be construed accordingly;

"Scottish proceedings" means proceedings before any court, including the Courts-Martial Appeal Court, the Restrictive Practices Court and the Employment Appeal Tribunal, sitting in Scotland, and includes proceedings before the *House of Lords* [Supreme Court] in the exercise of any appellate jurisdiction over proceedings in such a court;

"the strict liability rule" has the meaning assigned by section 1;

"superior court" means [the Supreme Court] the Court of Appeal, the High Court, the Crown Court, the Courts-Martial Appeal Court, the Restrictive Practices Court, the Employment Appeal Tribunal and any other court exercising in relation to its proceedings powers equivalent to those of the High Court, *and includes the House of Lords in the exercise of its appellate jurisdiction.*

NOTES

Initial Commencement
Specified date
Specified date: 27 August 1981: see s.21(3).

Amendment
Definition "cable programme" (omitted) inserted by the Cable and Broadcasting Act 1984, s.57(1), Sch.5, para.39(2).
Definition "cable programme" (omitted) repealed by the Broadcasting Act 1990, s.203(1), (3), Sch.20, para.31(2), Sch.21.
In definition "Scottish proceedings" words "House of Lords" in italics repealed and subsequent words in square brackets substituted by the Constitutional Reform Act 2005, s.40(4), Sch.9, Pt 1, para.35(1), (3).
  Date in force: to be appointed: see the Constitutional Reform Act 2005, s.148(1).
In definition "superior court" words "the Supreme Court" in square brackets inserted by the Constitutional Reform Act 2005, s.40(4), Sch.9, Pt 1, para.35(1), (3).
  Date in force: to be appointed: see the Constitutional Reform Act 2005, s.148(1).
In definition "superior court" words from "and includes the House of Lords" to the end repealed by the Constitutional Reform Act 2005, ss.40(4), 146, Sch.9, Pt 1, para.35(1), (3), Sch.18, Pt 5.
  Date in force: to be appointed: see the Constitutional Reform Act 2005, s.148(1).

Tribunals of Inquiry

20.—(1) In relation to any tribunal to which the Tribunals of Inquiry (Evidence) Act 1921 applies, and the proceedings of such a tribunal, the provisions of this Act (except subsection (3) of section 9) apply as they apply in relation to courts and legal proceedings; and references to the course of justice or the administration of justice in legal proceedings shall be construed accordingly.

(2) The proceedings of a tribunal established under the said Act shall be treated as active within the meaning of section 2 from the time when the tribunal is appointed until its report is presented to Parliament.

NOTES

Initial Commencement
Specified date
Specified date: 27 August 1981: see s.21(3).

APPENDIX 1

Short title, commencement and extent

21.—(1) This Act may be cited as the Contempt of Court Act 1981.

(2) The provisions of this Act relating to legal aid in England and Wales shall come into force on such day as the Lord Chancellor may appoint by order made by statutory instrument; and the provisions of this Act relating to legal aid in Scotland and Northern Ireland shall come into force on such day or days as the Secretary of State may so appoint.

Different days may be appointed under this subsection in relation to different courts.

(3) Subject to subsection (2), this Act shall come into force at the expiration of the period of one month beginning with the day on which it is passed.

(4) Sections 7, 8(3), 12, 13(1) to (3), 14, 16, 17 and 18, Parts I and III of Schedule 2 and Schedules 3 and 4 of this Act do not extend to Scotland.

(5) This Act, except sections 15 and 17 and Schedules 2 and 3, extends to Northern Ireland.

NOTES

Initial Commencement
Specified date
Specified date: 27 August 1981: see s.21(3).

SCHEDULE 1

TIMES WHEN PROCEEDINGS ARE ACTIVE FOR PURPOSES OF SECTION 2

Preliminary

1. In this Schedule "criminal proceedings" means proceedings against a person in respect of an offence, not being appellate proceedings or proceedings commenced by motion for committal or attachment in England and Wales or Northern Ireland; and "appellate proceedings" means proceedings on appeal from or for the review of the decision of a court in any proceedings.

2. Criminal, appellate and other proceedings are active within the meaning of section 2 at the times respectively prescribed by the following paragraphs of this Schedule; and in relation to proceedings in which more than one of the steps described in any of those paragraphs is taken, the reference in that paragraph is a reference to the first of those steps.

Criminal proceedings

3. Subject to the following provisions of this Schedule, criminal proceedings are active from the relevant initial step specified in paragraph 4 [or 4A] until concluded as described in paragraph 5.

4. The initial steps of criminal proceedings are:—

(a) arrest without warrant;

(b) the issue, or in Scotland the grant, of a warrant for arrest;

(c) the issue of a summons to appear, or in Scotland the grant of a warrant to cite;

(d) the service of an indictment or other document specifying the charge;

(e) except in Scotland, oral charge.

[4A Where as a result of an order under section 54 of the Criminal Procedure and Investigations Act 1996 (acquittal tainted by an administration of justice offence) proceedings are brought against a person for an offence of which he has previously been acquitted, the initial step of the proceedings is a certification under subsection (2) of that section; and paragraph 4 has effect subject to this.]

5. Criminal proceedings are concluded—

(a) by acquittal or, as the case may be, by sentence;

(b) by any other verdict, finding, order or decision which puts an end to the proceedings;

(c) by discontinuance or by operation of law.

6. The reference in paragraph 5(a) to sentence includes any order or decision consequent on conviction or finding of guilt which disposes of the case, either absolutely or subject to future events, and a deferment of sentence under [section 1 of the Powers of Criminal Courts (Sentencing) Act 2000], section 219 or 432 of the Criminal Procedure (Scotland) Act 1975 or Article 14 of the Treatment of Offenders (Northern Ireland) Order 1976.

7. Proceedings are discontinued within the meaning of paragraph 5(c)—

(a)   in England and Wales or Northern Ireland, if the charge or summons is withdrawn or a *nolle prosequi* entered;

[(aa) in England and Wales if they are discontinued by virtue of section 23 of the Prosecution of Offences Act 1985;]

(b)   in Scotland, if the proceedings are expressly abandoned by the prosecutor or are deserted *simpliciter;*

(c)   in the case of proceedings in England and Wales or Northern Ireland commenced by arrest without warrant, if the person arrested is released, otherwise than on bail, without having been charged.

8. Criminal proceedings before a court-martial or standing civilian court are not concluded until the completion of any review of finding or sentence.

9. Criminal proceedings in England and Wales or Northern Ireland cease to be active if an order is made for the charge to lie on the file, but become active again if leave is later given for the proceedings to continue.

[9A. Where proceedings in England and Wales have been discontinued by virtue of section 23 of the Prosecution of Offences Act 1985, but notice is given by the accused under subsection (7) of that section to the effect that he wants the proceedings to continue, they become active again with the giving of that notice.]

10. Without prejudice to paragraph 5(b) above, criminal proceedings against a person cease to be active—

(a) if the accused is found to be under a disability such as to render him unfit to be tried or unfit to plead or, in Scotland, is found to be insane in bar of trial; or

(b) if a hospital order is made in his case under [section 51(5) of the Mental Health Act 1983] or [Article 57(5) of the Mental Health (Northern Ireland) Order 1986] or, in Scotland, where a transfer order ceases to have effect by virtue of [section 73(1) of the Mental Health (Scotland) Act 1984],

but become active again if they are later resumed.

11. Criminal proceedings against a person which become active on the issue or the grant of a warrant for his arrest cease to be active at the end of the period of twelve months beginning with the date of the warrant unless he has been arrested within that period, but become active again if he is subsequently arrested.

Other proceedings at first instance

12. Proceedings other than criminal proceedings and appellate proceedings are active from the time when arrangements for the hearing are made or, if no such arrangements are previously made, from the time the hearing begins, until the proceedings are disposed of or discontinued or withdrawn; and

for the purposes of this paragraph any motion or application made in or for the purposes of any proceedings, and any pre-trial review in the county court, is to be treated as a distinct proceeding.

13. In England and Wales or Northern Ireland arrangements for the hearing of proceedings to which paragraph 12 applies are made within the meaning of that paragraph—

(a) in the case of proceedings in the High Court for which provision is made by rules of court for setting down for trial, when the case is set down;

(b) in the case of any proceedings, when a date for the trial or hearing is fixed.

14. In Scotland arrangements for the hearing of proceedings to which paragraph 12 applies are made within the meaning of that paragraph—

(a) in the case of an ordinary action in the Court of Session or in the sheriff court, when the Record is closed;

(b) in the case of a motion or application, when it is enrolled or made;

(c) in any other case, when the date for a hearing is fixed or a hearing is allowed.

Appellate proceedings

15. Appellate proceedings are active from the time when they are commenced—

(a) by application for leave to appeal or apply for review, or by notice of such an application;

(b) by notice of appeal or of application for review;

(c) by other originating process,

until disposed of or abandoned, discontinued or withdrawn.

16. Where, in appellate proceedings relating to criminal proceedings, the court—

(a) remits the case to the court below; or

(b) orders a new trial or a *venire de novo*, or in Scotland grants authority to bring a new prosecution,

any further or new proceedings which result shall be treated as active from the conclusion of the appellate proceedings.

NOTES

Initial Commencement
Specified date
Specified date: 27 August 1981: see s.21(3).

Amendment
Para.3: words in square brackets inserted by the Criminal Procedure and Investigations Act 1996, s.57(4).
Para.4A: inserted by the Criminal Procedure and Investigations Act 1996, s.57(4).
Para.6: words "section 1 of the Powers of Criminal Courts (Sentencing) Act 2000" in square brackets substituted by the Powers of Criminal Courts (Sentencing) Act 2000, s.165(1), Sch.9, para.86.
Date in force: 25 August 2000: see the Powers of Criminal Courts (Sentencing) Act 2000, s.168(1).
Para.7: sub-para.(aa) inserted by the Prosecution of Offences Act 1985, s.31(5), Sch.1, Part I.
Para.9A: inserted by the Prosecution of Offences Act 1985, s.31(5), Sch.1, Part I. Para.10: first words in square brackets substituted by the Mental Health Act 1983, s.148, Sch.4, para.57; second words in square brackets substituted by SI 1986/595, art.136(1), Sch.5, Part II; final words in square brackets substituted by the Mental Health (Scotland) Act 1984, s.127(1), Sch.3, para.48.

CONTEMPT OF COURT ACT

SCHEDULE 2
AMENDMENTS

Sections 13, 14

PART I
...

...

NOTES

Amendment
Repealed by the Legal Aid Act 1988, s.45(2), (3), Sch.6.

PART II
...

...

NOTES

Amendment
Repealed by the Legal Aid (Scotland) Act 1986, s.45(3), Sch.5.

PART III
CORONERS ACT 1887, COUNTY COURTS ACT 1959, ATTACHMENT OF EARNINGS ACT 1971 AND MAGISTRATES' COURTS ACT 1980

NOTES

Initial Commencement
Specified date
Specified date: 27 August 1981: see s.21(3).

Amendment
This Part contains amendment only.
Repealed in part by the County Courts Act 1984, s.148(3), Sch.4.
Repealed in part by the Statute Law (Repeals) Act 2004.
Date in force: 22 July 2004: (no specific commencement provision).

Extent
This Part does not extend to Scotland: see s.21(4).

SCHEDULE 3

Application of Magistrates' Courts Act 1980 to Civil Contempt Proceedings under section 63(3)

Section 17

1.—(1) Where the proceedings are taken of the court's own motion the provisions of the Act listed in this sub-paragraph shall apply as if a complaint had been made against the person against whom the proceedings are taken, and subject to the modifications specified in sub-paragraphs (2) and (3) below. The enactments so applied are:—

section 51 (issue of summons)
section 53(1) and (2) (procedure on hearing)
section 54 (adjournment)
section 55 (non-appearance of defendant)
section 97(1) (summons to witness)
section 101 (onus of proving exceptions etc)
section 121(1) and (3)(a) (constitution and place of siting of court)
section 123 (defect in process).

(2) In section 55, in subsection (1) for the words "the complainant appears but the defendant does not" there shall be substituted the words "the defendant does not appear", and in subsection (2) the words "if the complaint has been substantiated on oath, and" shall be omitted.

(3) In section 123, in subsections (1) and (2) the words "adduced on behalf of the prosecutor or complainant" shall be omitted.

2.—here the proceedings are taken by way of complaint for an order, section 127 of the Act (limitation of time) shall not apply to the complaint.

3.—whether the proceedings are taken of the court's own motion or by way of complaint for an order, subsection (3) of section 55 shall apply as if the following words were added at the end of the subsection:—

[" or, having been arrested under section 47 of the Family Law Act 1996 in connection with the matter of the complaint, is at large after being remanded under subsection (7)(b) or (10) of that section."]

NOTES

Initial Commencement
Specified date
Specified date: 27 August 1981: see s.21(3).

Amendment
Para.3: words from ""or, having been arrested" to "or (10) of that section."" in square brackets substituted by the Family Law Act 1996, s.66(1), Sch.8, para.50.
Date in force: 1 October 1997: see SI 1997/1892, art.3(1)(b).

Extent
This Schedule does not extend to Scotland: see s.21(4).

SCHEDULE 4

Sections 12, 13, 14 and 16 as applied to Northern Ireland

Section 18

12.— OFFENCES OF CONTEMPT OF MAGISTRATES'S COURTS

(1), (2) . . .

13.—LEGAL AID

(1) In any case where—

(a) a person is liable to be committed or fined—

(i) by a magistrates' court under [Article 160 of the Magistrates' Courts (Northern Ireland) Order 1981];
(ii) by a county court under Article 55 of the County Courts (Northern Ireland) Order 1980; or
(iii) by any superior court for contempt in the face of that or any other court; and

(b) it appears to the court that it is desirable in the interests of justice that he should have legal aid and that he has not sufficient means to enable him to obtain that aid;

the court may order that he shall be given legal aid for the purposes of the proceedings.

(2) Unless the court orders that the legal aid to be given under this section shall consist of representation by counsel only or, in any court where solicitors have a right of audience, by a solicitor only, legal aid under this section shall consist of representation by a solicitor and counsel assigned by the court; and the court may assign for the purpose any counsel or solicitor who is within the precincts of the court at the time when the order is made.

(3) If on a question of granting a person legal aid under this section there is a doubt whether his means are sufficient to enable him to obtain legal aid or whether it is desirable in the interests of justice that he should have legal aid, the doubt shall be resolved in favour of granting him legal aid.

(4) Articles 32, 33, 36 and 40 of the Legal Aid, Advice and Assistance (Northern Ireland) Order 1981 shall apply in relation to legal aid under this section as they apply in relation to legal aid under Part III of that Order as if any legal aid under this section were given in pursuance of a certificate under Article 29 of that Order.

(5) This section is without prejudice to any other enactment by virtue of which legal aid may be granted in or for purposes of civil or criminal proceedings.

14.—Proceedings in Northern Ireland

(1) In any case where a court has power to commit a person to prison for contempt of court and (apart from this provision) no limitation applies to the period of committal, the committal shall (without prejudice to the power of the court to order his earlier discharge) be for a fixed term, and that term shall not on any occasion exceed two years in the case of committal by a superior court, or one month in the case of committal by an inferior court.

(2) In any case where an inferior court has power to fine a person for contempt of court and (apart from this provision) no limit applies to the amount of the fine, the fine shall not on any occasion exceed [£2500].

[(2A) A fine imposed under subsection (2) above shall be deemed, for the purposes of any enactment, to be a sum adjudged to be paid by a conviction.]

(3) . . .

(4) Each of the superior courts shall have the like power to make a hospital order or guardianship order under [Article 44 of the Mental Health (Northern Ireland) Order 1986 or an interim hospital order under Article 45 of that Order] in the case of a person suffering from mental disorder who could otherwise be committed to prison for contempt of court as the Crown Court has under [that Article] in the case of a person convicted of an offence.

[(4A) Each of the superior courts shall have the like power to make an order under Article 42 of the said Order of 1986 where there is reason to suspect that a person who could be committed to prison for contempt of court is suffering from mental illness or severe mental impairment as the Crown Court has under that Article in the case of an accused person within the meaning of that Article.]

[(4A) For the purposes of the preceding provisions of this section a county court shall be treated as a superior court and not as an inferior court.]

(5)–(7) . . .

16.—Enforcement of Fines Imposed by Superior Courts.

Section 35 of the Criminal Justice Act (Northern Ireland) 1945 enforcement of fines imposed by superior courts shall apply to fines imposed for contempt of court by any superior court other than the Crown Court as it applies to fines imposed by the Crown Court.

APPENDIX 1

NOTES

Initial Commencement
Specified date
Specified date: 27 August 1981: see s.21(3).

Amendment

Section 12: subs.(1) repealed by SI 1981/1675, art.170(3); subs.(2) repeals SI 1980/704, Sch.1, para.26.

Section 13: words in square brackets substituted by SI 1981/1675, art.170(2), Sch.6, para.61.

Section 14: in subs.(2) sum "£2500" in square brackets substituted by SI 1994/2795, art.3(5), Sch.1.

Date in force: 9 January 1995: see SI 1994/446, art.2.

Section 14: para.(2A): inserted by SI 1996/3160, art.29(6), Sch.3, para.4.

Date in force: 1 January 1998: see SI 1997/523, art.2(b), (h).

Section 14: subs.(3) amends the Children and Young Persons Act (Northern Ireland) 1968, s.72; in subs.(4) words in square brackets substituted, and first subs.(4A) inserted, by SI 1986/595, art.136(1), Sch.5, Part II; second subs.(4A) inserted by the County Courts (Penalties for Contempt) Act 1983, ss.1, 2; subs.(5) amends the Coroners Act (Northern Ireland) 1959, s.20; subs.(6) repealed by SI 1981/1675, art.170(3), Sch.7; subs.(7) amends SI 1980/397, art.55(2).

Section 14: subs.(6) repealed by SI 1981/1675, art.170(3), Sch.7.

Date in force: 25 December 1981: see SI 1981/1675, art.1(3).

Extent

This Schedule does not extend to Scotland: see s.21(4).

APPENDIX 2

FORMS AND PRECEDENTS

I. CIVIL PROCEDURE FORMS

18–1

APPENDIX 2

N40A(HC)

18–1 Warrant of arrest for disobedience
(order to attend court for questioning)

In the High Court of Justice
[Queen's Bench][Chancery] Division
[District Registry]

Claim No

Warrant No

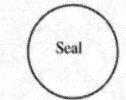

Claimant

Defendant

To the Tipstaff attending Her Majesty's Supreme Court, his deputy or assistants, and all police constables and other peace officers whom it may concern

On   20   , The Honourable [Mr]{Mrs} Justice
sitting at
found that   of
                                                                      ('the judgment debtor') had committed a
breach of the order to attend court for questioning dated   20   and is accordingly in contempt of
court and
ordered that [he][she] be committed for contempt to Her Majesty's Prison
for a period of   days
and that the order be suspended for so long as [he][she] attend court at the time and place specified in that order and
otherwise comply with the order to attend court for questioning dated   20   [and
                                                                                                                                     ]

The court is satisfied that the suspended committal order dated   20   was served on the
judgment debtor on   20   [but[he][she][failed to attend court at that time and place.][and that
[he][she] attended court but failed to comply with the order in that [he][she]

                                                                                                                                     ]

THIS WARRANT COMMANDS you and every one of you in Her Majesty's name to arrest
                          and to bring [him][her] before a judge to consider whether the committal order
should be discharged.

Dated

N40A(HC) Warrant of arrest for disobedience (order to attend court for questioning)(March 2002)
Crown Copyright. Reproduced by Sweet & Maxwell Ltd.

N40A

Warrant of arrest for disobedience
(order to attend court for questioning)

In the

County Court

Claim No.

Warrant No.

Claimant

Defendant

To the bailiffs of the court and every constable within the district of the court:

On   20   , [His] [Her] Honour Judge
sitting at
found that   of
                                                ('the judgment debtor') had
committed a breach of the order to attend court for questioning dated   20   and is accordingly
in contempt of court and

ordered that [he] [she] be committed for contempt to Her Majesty's Prison
for a period of   days
and that the order for committal be suspended so long as [he] [she] attend court at the time and
place specified in that order and otherwise comply with the order to attend court for questioning dated
                20   [and
                                                                                                            ].

The court is satisfied that the suspended commital order dated   20   was served on the
judgment debtor on   20   [but [he] [she] failed to attend court at that time and place.] [and that
[he] [she] attended court but failed to comply with the order in that [he] [she]
                                                                                                            ]

You the bailiffs and constables are therefore required to arrest the judgment debtor
and to bring [him] [her] before a judge to consider whether the committal order should be discharged.

Dated

18–2   APPENDIX 2

Bailiff's Certificate

I arrested _____
the judgment debtor, on _____ and brought [him] [her]
before the judge on _____

Signed _____
        Bailiff of the County Court

FORMS AND PRECEDENTS   18–3

N40B(HC)

Warrant of committal for disobedience
(order to attend court for questioning)

In the High Court of Justice
[Queen's Bench][Chancery] Division
[District Registry]

Claim No

18–3

Warrant No

Claimant

Defendant

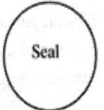
Seal

To the Tipstaff attending on Her Majesty's Supreme Court, his deputy or assistants, and all police constables and other peace officers whom it may concern;

On   20   , The Honourable [Mr][Mrs] Justice   sitting at   found that   of
                                                    ('the judgment debtor') had committed a breach of the order to attend court for questioning dated   20   and is accordingly in contempt of court and

ordered that [he][she] be committed for contempt to Her Majesty's Prison for a period of   days
and that the order be suspended for so long as [he][she] attend court at the time and place specified in that order and otherwise comply with the order to attend court for questioning dated   20   [and
                                                                                      ]

On   20   , the judgment debtor was arrested and [on   20   ] brought before [The Honourable [Mr][Mrs][Justice][[His][Her] Honour Judge][Master][District Judge]   sitting at
                                    on   20   .
The judge was satisfied that

- the judgment debtor [did not attend court][refused to take the oath][refused to answer the questions asked] as required by the order to attend court for questioning dated   20
- at the time and place mentioned in the order for committal dated   20   the judgment debtor did not [attend court][take the oath][answer the questions][
                                                                                      ]
- the conditions for suspension of that order of committal were therefore not met
- the judgment debtor persists in the contempt of court
and that the order for committal dated the   20   should not be discharged

THIS WARRANT COMMANDS you and every one of you in Her Majesty's name to covey   to the Governor of Her Majesty's Prison   to be detained there and kept in safe custody for a period of   days from the date of [his][her] arrest or until lawfully discharged if sooner.

Dated

N40B(HC) Warrant of arrest for disobedience (order to attend court for questioning)(March 2002)
Crown Copyright. Reproduced by Sweet & Maxwell Ltd.

18–4

APPENDIX 2

N40B

18–4 **Warrant of committal for disobedience**
(order to attend court for questioning)

In the High Court of Justice
[Queen's Bench][Chancery] Division
[District Registry]

Claim No

Warrant No

Claimant

Defendant

To the Tipstaff attending on Her Majesty's Supreme Court, his deputy or assistants, and all police constables and other peace officers whom it may concern;

Seal

On   20   , The Honourable [Mr][Mrs] Justice
sitting at
found that   of
                                                                    ('the judgment debtor') had committed a breach of the order to attend court for questioning dated   20   and is accordingly in contempt of court and

ordered that [he][she] be committed for contempt to Her Majesty's Prison for a period of   days
and that the order be suspended for so long as [he][she] attend court at the time and place specified in that order and otherwise comply with the order to attend court for questioning dated   20   [and
  ]

On   20   , the judgment debtor was arrested and [on   20] brought before [The Honourable [Mr][Mrs][Justice][[His][Her] Honour Judge][Master][District Judge]
            sitting at
                                                                    on   20 .
The judge was satisfied that

- the judgment debtor [did not attend court][refused to take the oath][refused to answer the questions asked] as required by the order to attend court for questioning dated   20
- at the time and place mentioned in the order for committal dated   20   the judgment debtor did not [attend court][take the oath][answer the questions][
                                                                                                                                                                        ]
- the conditions for suspension of that order of committal were therefore not met
- the judgment debtor persists in the contempt of court

and that the order for committal dated the   20   should not be discharged

THIS WARRANT COMMANDS you and every one of you in Her Majesty's name to covey
                                  to the Governor of Her Majesty's Prison   to be detained there and kept in safe custody for a period of   days from the date of [his][her] arrest or until lawfully discharged if sooner.

Dated

N40B(HC) Warrant of arrest for disobedience (order to attend court for questioning)(March 2002)
Crown Copyright. Reproduced by Sweet & Maxwell Ltd.

N79A

Suspended committal order for disobedience
(order to attend court for questioning)

In the	Claim No

Claimant

Defendant

On _____ 20 ___, [[Mr][Mrs]Justice][[His][Her]Honour Judge] _____ sitting at _____ and]

[heard
read the order made on _____ 20 , [the certificate dated _____ 20 of the bailiff,] the affidavit[s] of _____ sworn on _____ 20 [and _____ sworn on _____ 20 respectively as to service of the order and] as to the provision of travelling expenses and the certificate dated _____ 20 of the [Master][District Judge][Court Officer]

and the court is satisfied that

1. _____ was ordered to attend court on _____ 20 to be questioned
2. the order to attend was served on _____ on _____ 20 .....
3. _____ did not within seven days of the service of the order request from the judgment creditor payment of a sufficient sum for travelling expenses
4. on _____ 20 the judgment creditor _____ paid a sufficient sum for travelling expenses
5. _____ did not attend court on _____ 20 to be questioned
6. _____ , having attended court, refused to be sworn
7. _____ , having attended court, refused to answer [any question][the question _____]

And that _____ has been guilty of contempt of court by disobeying the order of _____ 20

and the court orders that

_____ be committed to Her Majesty's Prison

for a period of _____ days

N79A Suspended committal for disobedience (order to attend for questioning)(March 2002)
Crown Copyright. Reproduced by Sweet & Maxwell Ltd

and the court orders that

1. this order shall be suspended so long as   attends court at

   and complies with the order made on   20
   [and

                                                                                                                                                          ]

2. if   does not comply with these terms, a warrant of arrest
   shall be issued and   shall, when arrested, be
   brought before a judge to consider whether the committal order should be discharged

3. and that   pay the judgment creditor's costs of attending of £
       , on or before   20

Certificate of Service

I certify that a copy of this order was served by me on _____
the judgment debtor, on _____

Signed _____
      Bailiff of the County Court

II. HIGH COURT

No. 67
Writ of sequestration (Schedule 1 - RSC O.45 r.12(4), O.46 r.5)

IN THE HIGH COURT OF JUSTICE
QUEEN'S BENCH DIVISION
[   ] District Registry

Claim No.

Claimant

Defendant

ELIZABETH THE SECOND, by the Grace of God, of the United Kingdom of Great Britain and Northern Ireland and of Our other realms and territories Queen, Head of the Commonwealth, Defender of the Faith.

To (*names of not less than four commissioners*) greeting:

Whereas in this claim:
(1) it was on the (*date*) ordered that the defendant (*name*) should (*state act defendant was ordered to do or abstain from doing*),
(2) on (*date*) the defendant was found guilty of contempt of court in failing to comply with that order, and
(3) on (*date*) the Court gave the claimant permission to issue this writ of sequestration.

Take notice therefore, that we, confident of your prudence, integrity and fidelity, do by this writ authorise and command you, or any two or three of you,
(1) to enter upon and take possession of all the real and personal estate of the defendant (*name*),
(2) to collect, receive and take into your hands the rents and profits of his real estate and all his personal estate, and
(3) keep the same under sequestration in your hands until the defendant (*name*) shall comply with the order dated (*date*) and clear his contempt and the court make other order to the contrary.

Witness (*name*) Lord High Chancellor of Great Britain, the (*date*)

This writ was issued by (*name*) of (*address*) [agent for (*name*) of (*address*)] solicitor for [the claimant] [or this writ was issued by the claimant (*name*) in person] who resides at (*address*).

The defendant resides (*or as the case may be*) at (*address including county*).

No. 85
Order of committal or other penalty upon finding of contempt of court
(Schedule 1- RSC O.52)

IN THE HIGH COURT OF JUSTICE
[   ] DIVISION
[   ] District Registry

Claim No.

Before (*Judge's name and title*)

Claimant

Defendant

AN APPLICATION was made by Counsel for (*party*) and was attended by [Counsel for](*party*).

The Judge read the written evidence filed and the Order of (*title and name of Judge/Master/District Judge*) dated (*date of Order*) in which [it was ordered that (*set out details of Order(s) breached*)] [the following undertaking was given (*set out undertaking breached*)].

AND THE COURT being satisfied that the (*party*) (*name*) has been guilty of contempt of court in failing to comply with [the order dated (*date of Order*)] [paragraphs (*give paragraph numbers*) of the order dated (*date of Order*)] [the undertakings given to the court and contained in the order dated (*date of Order*)] by (*set out details of breach*).

IT IS ORDERED
(1) that for his contempt the (*party*) (*name*) stand committed to HM Prison (*name of prison*) for a period of (*number of days or as may be*) from the date of his apprehension.
[(2) that the warrant of committal remain in the court office at [the Royal Courts of Justice] and that execution of it be suspended so long as the (*party*) (*name*) (*set out terms of suspension*) until (*date or as may be*) after which the sentence and warrant of committal be discharged.]
or
(3) that for his contempt the (*party*) (*name*) pay to Her Majesty the Queen a fine of £   on or before (*date payment due*).
or

(4) that the (*party*) may issue a writ of sequestration directed to the commissioners named in it to sequester all the real and personal property of the (*party*) (*name*) for its[his] contempt of court and that the writ of sequestration shall remain in full force and operation until the (*party*) clears its[his] contempt or until further order.

(5) that the costs of the (*party*) [summarily assessed in the sum of £   ] [to be the subject of a detailed assessment] be paid by the (*party*) to the (*party*).

(6) that the contemnor has permission to apply to the Court to clear his contempt and ask for his release or discharge.

Dated

18–8

PF 87
Praecipe for Writ of Sequestration
(Schedule 1- RSC O.45 r.12(4) and O.46 r.6)

IN THE HIGH COURT OF JUSTICE
[QUEEN'S BENCH] DIVISION

Claim No.

Claimant

Defendant

Seal a writ of sequestration against (*name and address of party*) directed to (*names of Commissioners*).

Permission to issue writ of sequestration given by (*title and name of Judge*) on (*date*).

Signed

Dated

PF 102
Bench Warrant (Schedule 1 - RSC O.52)

To: The Tipstaff attending on Her Majesty's Supreme Court, his deputy or assistants, and all police constables and other peace officers whom it may concern.

IN THE HIGH COURT OF JUSTICE
[   ] DIVISION
[   ]

Claim No.

Claimant

Defendant

IT APPEARING to the satisfaction of The Honourable Mr Justice (*name*) one of the Justices of the (*name of Division*) Division of Her Majesty's High Court of Justice that (*name of contemnor*) has committed a breach of the Order dated (*date*) and is accordingly in contempt of Court.

THIS WARRANT COMMANDS you and every one of you in Her Majesty's name to apprehend (*name of contemnor*) and bring [him] before me or another of the Justices of the (*name of Division*) Division of Her Majesty's High Court of Justice at (*time*) on (*date*) or as soon as possible thereafter at the High Court in [London] to be dealt with according to law [and if you apprehend the contemnor after 4.00pm [he] shall be held in custody until such time as the Court shall next sit].

Dated

A JUSTICE OF THE HIGH COURT

PF 103
Warrant of committal (general) (Schedule 1 - RSC O.52)

To: The Tipstaff attending on Her Majesty's Supreme Court, his deputy or assistants, and all police constables and other peace officers whom it may concern.

IN THE HIGH COURT OF JUSTICE
[   ] DIVISION
[   ] District Registry

Claim No.

Claimant

Defendant

BY THE ORDER OF THIS COURT given this day it was Ordered that (*name of contemnor*) stands committed to Her Majesty's Prison (*name of prison*) for [his] contempt as set out in the Order.

THIS WARRANT COMMANDS you and every one of you in Her Majesty's name to apprehend (*name of contemnor*) and convey [him] safely to Her Majesty's Prison (*name of prison*) to be detained there and kept in safe custody for a period of (*specify period*) from the date of his apprehension.

Dated

A JUSTICE OF THE HIGH COURT

PF 104
Warrant of committal (contempt in face of court) (Schedule 1 - RSC O.52)

To: The Tipstaff attending on Her Majesty's Supreme Court, his deputy or assistants, and all police constables and other peace officers whom it may concern.

IN THE HIGH COURT OF JUSTICE
[   ] DIVISION
[   ] District Registry

Claim No.

Claimant

Defendant

A CONTEMPT IN THE FACE OF THE COURT having been committed by (*name*)

NOW BY THE ORDER OF THIS COURT given this day (*name of contemnor*) stands committed to Her Majesty's Prison (*name of prison*) for [his] contempt.

THIS WARRANT COMMANDS you and every one of you in Her Majesty's name to apprehend (*name of contemnor*) and convey [him] safely to Her Majesty's Prison (*name of prison*) to be detained there and kept in safe custody for a period of (*specify period*) from the date of his apprehension.

Dated

A JUSTICE OF THE HIGH COURT

18–12

PF 105
Bench Warrant (failure of witness to attend) (Schedule 1 - RSC O.52)

To: The Tipstaff attending on Her Majesty's Supreme Court, his deputy or assistants, and all police constables and other peace officers whom it may concern.

IN THE HIGH COURT OF JUSTICE
[   ] DIVISION
[   ] District Registry

Claim No.

Claimant

Defendant

A WITNESS SUMMONS having been issued in this Claim for the attendance of (*name and address*) as a Witness.

AND (*name of witness*) having failed personally to appear before me The Honourable Mr Justice (*name*) one of the Justices of the (*name of Division*) Division of Her Majesty's High Court of Justice on the trial of the Claim, under the Witness Summons served on [him].

THIS WARRANT COMMANDS you and every one of you in Her Majesty's name to apprehend (*name of witness*) and bring [him] before me or another of the Justices of the (*name of Division*) Division of Her Majesty's High Court of Justice at (*time*) on (*date*) or as soon as possible thereafter at the High Court in [London] to be dealt with according to law [and if you apprehend the contemnor after 4.00pm [he] shall be held in custody until such time as the Court shall next sit].

Dated

A JUSTICE OF THE HIGH COURT

PF 106

Warrant of committal (of prisoner) (Schedule 1 - RSC O.52)

To: The Governor of Her Majesty's Prison (name) or his deputy and to the Tipstaff attending on Her Majesty's Supreme Court, his deputy or assistants, and all police constables and other peace officers whom it may concern.

IN THE HIGH COURT OF JUSTICE
[   ] DIVISION
[   ] District Registry

Claim No.

Claimant

Defendant

BY THE ORDER OF THIS COURT given this day it was Ordered that (*name of contemnor*) stands committed to Her Majesty's Prison (*name of prison*) for [his] contempt as set out in the Order.

AND (*name of contemnor*) is at present a prisoner in the custody of the Governor of Her Majesty's Prison (*name of prison*).

THIS WARRANT COMMANDS you and every one of you in Her Majesty's name to detain (*name of contemnor*) and keep [him] in safe custody at Her Majesty's Prison (*name of prison*) for a period of (*specify period*) from the completion of the sentence [he] is at present detained for.

Dated

A JUSTICE OF THE HIGH COURT

PF 141
Witness Statement/Affidavit of Personal Service of Judgment or Order
(Schedule, RSC O.45, r.7)

IN THE HIGH COURT OF JUSTICE
[   ] DIVISION
[   ] District Registry

Claim No.

Claimant

Defendant

I, (*name, address and description*) state [on oath]:

1. That I did on (*date*) at (*address*) personally serve the above defendant (*or as appropriate*) with a sealed copy of the [order][judgment] dated (*date*) in these proceedings, [which I refer to] [shown to me] marked ["A"] (*recite operative part of order or judgment*).

2. The copy of the [order][judgment] I served had endorsed on it on the front page the following words; "If you, the within-named (*name*), do not comply with this order you may be held to be in contempt of court and imprisoned or fined, or [in the case of a company or corporation] your assets may be seized".

I believe that the facts stated in this witness statement are true.

Signed   Name

Dated

[Sworn, etc.]

Form CH 39
Order for an Injunction (Intended action)

[IN THE HIGH COURT OF JUSTICE]   Claim No.........
[...   ....] DIVISION]
               ] DISTRICT REGISTRY
[   ] COUNTY COURT
BEFORE the Honourable Mr Justice/Master/District Judge

..................20.........

IN AN INTENDED ACTION BETWEEN

Between
                                                    Intended Claimant
               and
                                                    Intended Defendant

ORDER FOR AN INJUNCTION BEFORE THE ISSUE OF A CLAIM FORM

IMPORTANT:-
NOTICE TO THE INTENDED DEFENDANT ("the Defendant")
  (1)   This Order [prohibits you from doing] [obliges you to do] the acts set out in this Order. You should read it all carefully. You are advised to consult a solicitor as soon as possible. You have a right to ask the Court to vary or discharge this Order.
  (2)   If you disobey this Order you may be found guilty of Contempt of Court and [any of your directors] may be sent to prison or fined [and you may be fined] or your assets may be seized.

   Include the words in square brackets in the case of a corporate defendant. This notice is not a substitute for the indorsement of a penal notice

An Application was made on the by Counsel for .... (who is to be the Claimant in a Claim against.............) to the Judge who heard the Application supported by the Witness Statements / affidavits listed in schedule 1 to this order, and accepted the undertakings in Schedule 2 at the end of this Order.
IT IS ORDERED that up to and including [.......(*date*) the ("the Return Date")] [trial of the intended action]:-
       The Defendant must/must not (*body of injunction*)
SUBSTITUTED SERVICE/SERVICE OUT OF THE JURISDICTION
1)   The Claimant may issue and serve the Claim Form on the Defendant at.......(*address*) by....... (*date*).
2)   If the Defendant wishes to defend the Claim he must acknowledge service within ....days of being served with the Claim Form.

VARIATION OR DISCHARGE OF THIS ORDER
The Defendant may apply to the Court at any time to vary or discharge this Order but if he wishes to do so he must first inform the Claimant's solicitors [in writing].

NAME AND ADDRESS OF CLAIMANT'S SOLICITORS
The Claimant's solicitors are:- (*name, address and telephone number*)

INTERPRETATION OF THIS ORDER
1) In this Order the words "he" "him" or "his" include "she" or "her" and "it" or "its".
2) Where there are two or more Defendants then (unless the contrary appears)
    (a) References to "the Defendant" mean both or all of them;
    (b) An Order requiring "the Defendant" to do or not to do anything requires each Defendant to do or not to do it;
    (c) A requirement relating to service of this Order or of any legal proceedings on "the Defendant" means on each of them.

THE EFFECT OF THIS ORDER
1) A Defendant who is an individual who is ordered not to do something must not do it himself or in any other way. He must not do it through others acting on his behalf or on his instructions or with his encouragement.
2) A Defendant which is a corporation and which is ordered not to do something must not do it itself or by its directors, officers, employees, or agents or in any other way.

SERVICE OF THIS ORDER
This Order shall be served by the Claimant on ....

SCHEDULE 1.
witness statements/Affidavits
The Claimant relied on the following Witness Statements / Affidavits:
   1)
   2)

SCHEDULE 2.
Undertakings given to the Court by the Claimant
1. To pay any damages which the Defendants (or any other party served with or notified of this Order) shall sustain which the Court considers the Claimant should pay.
2. If made without notice to any other party to serve on the Defendant Application Notice, evidence in support this Order as soon as practicable.
3. If made before filing the Application Notice to file and pay the appropriate fee on this or the next working day.
4. To issue a Claim Form and pay the appropriate fee on this or the next working day and to serve the Claim Form on the Defendant as soon as practicable.
5. To file a Witness Statement [substantially in the terms of the draft Witness Statement produced to the Court and initialled by the Judge] [confirming the substance of what was said to the Court by the Claimant's Counsel/Solicitors]

Form Ch 40
Order for Interim Injunction

[IN THE HIGH COURT OF JUSTICE]   Claim No.........
[... ....] DIVISION]
              ] DISTRICT REGISTRY
[   ] COUNTY COURT
BEFORE the Honourable Mr Justice/Master/District Judge

................20.........

BETWEEN
                              A.B
                                                    Claimant
                              And
                              C.D
                                                    Defendant

BETWEEN

                                              Claimant

                          and

                                              Defendant

ORDER FOR AN INJUNCTION

IMPORTANT:-
NOTICE TO THE DEFENDANT
    (1) This Order [prohibits you from doing] [obliges you to do] the acts set out in this Order. [You should read it all carefully. You are advised to consult a Solicitor as soon as possible]. You have a right to ask the Court to vary or discharge this Order.
    (2) If you disobey this Order you may be found guilty of Contempt of Court and [any of your directors] may be sent to prison or fined [and you may be fined] or your assets may be seized.2

Include the words in square brackets in the case of a corporate defendant. This notice is not a substitute for the indorsement of a penal notice

An Application was made .....(*date*) by Counsel for the Claimant to the Judge [and was attended by Counsel for the Defendant]. The Judge heard the Application and read the Witness Statements/Affidavits listed in Schedule 1 and accepted the undertakings in Schedule 2 of this Order.
IT IS ORDERED that:

THE INJUNCTION
(1) Until after [........(*date*)][final judgment in this Claim] the Defendant must/must not (*body of injunction*)

COSTS OF THE APPLICATION
(2) [The Defendant shall pay the Claimant's costs of this Application.] [The costs of this Application are reserved to be dealt with by the Judge who tries this Claim.] [The costs of this Application are to be costs in the case.] [The costs of this Application are to be the Claimant's costs in the case.]

VARIATION OR DISCHARGE OF THIS ORDER
The Defendant may apply to the Court at any time to vary or discharge this Order but if he wishes to do so he must first inform the Claimant's Solicitors in writing at least 48 hours beforehand.

NAME AND ADDRESS OF CLAIMANT'S SOLICITORS
The Claimant's Solicitors are: (*name address and telephone number*)

INTERPRETATION OF THIS ORDER
1) In this Order the words "he" "him" or "his" include "she" or "her" and "it" or "its".
2) Where there are two or more Defendants then (unless the contrary appears)
    (a) References to "the Defendant" mean both or all of them;
    (b) An Order requiring "the Defendant" to do or not to do anything requires each Defendant to do or not to do it;

THE EFFECT OF THIS ORDER
1) A Defendant who is an individual who is ordered not to do something must not do it himself or in any other way. He must not do it through others acting on his behalf or on his instructions or with his encouragement.
2) A Defendant which is a corporation and which is ordered not to do something must not do it itself or by its directors, officers, employees or agents or in any other way.

SERVICE OF THIS ORDER
This Order shall be served by the Claimant on ....

SCHEDULE 1.
Witness Statements/Affidavits
The Judge read the following Witness Statements / Affidavits before making this Order:
    1)
    2)

SCHEDULE 2.
Undertaking given to the Court by the Claimant
If the Court later finds that this Order has caused loss to the Defendant or any other Party served with or notified of this Order and decides that the Defendant or other Party should be compensated for that loss, the Claimant will comply with any Order the Court may make.

III. COUNTY COURT
N16(1)

Injunction Order

Between .... Claimant/Applicant/Petitioner

and .... Defendant/Respondent

In the	
	County Court
Claim No.	
Claimant	
Defendant	
Claimant's Ref.	
For completion by the court Issued on	

Seal

To (1)

of (2)

(1) The name of the person the order is directed to

(2) The address of the person the order is directed to

(3) The terms of any restraining order are to be preceeded by the words "is forbidden whether by himself or by instructing or encouraging any other person" or if the defendant is a limited company "by its servants, agents, officers or otherwise"

If you do not obey this order you will be guilty of contempt of court and you may be sent to prison

On the   of   [19][20]   the court considered an application for an injunction

The Court ordered that[1]

(3)

If you do not understand anything in this order you should go to a Solicitor, Legal Advice Centre or a Citizens' Advice Bureau

The court office at

is open between 10 am and 4 pm Monday to Friday. When corresponding with the court, please address forms or letters to the Court Manager and quote the claim number.

N16(1) General form of injunction for interlocutory application or originating application (January 2002) Crown Copyright. Reproduced by Sweet & Maxwell Ltd. (Formal Parts - See complete N16 for wording of operating clauses)

18–17 APPENDIX 2

Injunction Order - Record of Hearing   Claim No. ....

On ....the .... day of ....[19   ][20   ]
Before (H Honour) (District) Judge ....
The court was sitting at ....
....

The	☐	Claimant	☐ Applicant	☐ Petitioner	(Name)............................
was	☐	represented by Counsel			
	☐	represented by a Solicitor			
	☐	in person			
The	☐	Defendant ☐ Respondent			(Name)............................
was	☐	represented by Counsel			
	☐	represented by a Solicitor			
	☐	in person			
	☐	did not appear having been given notice of this hearing			
	☐	not given notice of this hearing			

The court read the affidavit(s) of
☐   the Claimant/Applicant/Petitioner   sworn on ....
☐   the Defendant/Respondent   sworn on ....
And of..sworn on ....

The court heard spoken evidence on oath from
....
....

The Claimant(Applicant/Petitioner) gave an undertaking (through his counsel or solicitor) promising to pay any damages ordered by the court if it later decides that the Defendant/Respondent has suffered loss or damage as a result of this order*

Delete this paragraph if the court does not require the undertaking

Signed _____   Dated _____
                (Judges Clerk)

N16(1) General form of injunction for interlocutory application or originating application under Order 47 rule 8(2) (January 2002) Crown Copyright. Reproduced by Sweet & Maxwell Ltd.
(Formal Parts - See complete N16 for wording of operative clauses)

N41

Order Suspending Warrant / Judgment

Claimant

Defendant

In the	
	County Court
Claim No.	
Warrant No.	
Local No.	
Claimant's Ref.	

Seal

On the application of

And the court being satisfied that the defendant is unable to pay and discharge the sum payable by him in this action (or the instalments due under the judgment or order in this action)

(enter name of Judge) **ordered that**

(1) delete as necessary
(2) state time
(3) delete where balance is not known to the court

The judgment or order be suspended (1)(2)
The warrant of execution issued in this action be suspended (1)
The warrant of committal issued in this action be suspended for (1)(2)
so long as the defendant do pay the claimant the outstanding sum (of £   ) (3)
(by instalments of £   for every calendar month, the first instalment) to reach the claimant by   and further payments to reach the claimant by the   day of each month

Or

(4) state terms including liability to re-arrest if so ordered

that the defendant be discharged from custody under the warrant of committal (4)

(The warrant has been returned to the   County Court
and any further correspondence should be sent there, quoting the claim number (1))

Dated

——Take Notice——

To the defendant
If you do not pay in accordance with this order, the warrant may be reissued or other enforcement proceedings may be taken against you. If your circumstances change and you cannot pay, ask at the court office about what you can do.

——Address for Payment——

——How to Pay——

- PAYMENT(S) MUST BE MADE to the person named at the address for payment quoting their reference and the claim number.
- DO NOT bring or send payments to the court. THEY WILL NOT BE ACCEPTED.
- You should allow at least 4 days for your payment to reach the applicant or his representative.
- Make sure that you keep records and can account for all payments made. Proof may be required if there is any disagreement. It is not safe to send cash unless you use registered post.
- A leaflet giving further advice about payment can be obtained from the court.
- If you need more information you should contact the applicant or his representative.

The court office at
is open between 10 am and 4 pm Monday to Friday. When corresponding with the court, please address forms or letters to the Court Manager and quote the claim number.

N41 Order suspending judgment or order and/or warrant of execution/committal (January 2002)   Crown Copyright. Reproduced by Sweet & Maxwell Ltd.

APPENDIX 2

N41A

Order Suspending Warrant (determination)

Claimant

Defendant

In the	
	County Court
Claim No.	
Warrant No.	
Local No.	
Claimant's Ref.	

seal

On the application of the defendant

And the court having considered the papers received from the parties and being satisfied that the defendant is unable to pay and discharge the sum payable by him in this action (or the instalments due under the judgment or order in this action)

It is ordered that

This warrant of execution and the judgment (or order) be suspended and not enforced so long as the defendant do pay the claimant the outstanding sum of £   (by instalments of £   for every calendar month, the first payment to reach the claimant) by   and further payments to reach the claimant by the   day of each month.

*delete as necessary

(The warrant will be returned to the   County Court after 16 days. After that date any further correspondence should be sent there, quoting the claim number)*

Dated

─── **Take Notice** ───

If you (either the claimant or defendant) object to the payment rate fixed by the court, you must write to the court with your reasons. You have 16 days from the date of the postmark to do this. A hearing will be arranged and both parties will be told when to come to court.

To the defendant
If you do not pay in accordance with this order the warrant may be reissued or other enforcement proceedings may be taken against you. If your circumstances change and you cannot pay, ask at the court office about what you can do.

─── **Address for Payment** ───

─── **How to Pay** ───

- PAYMENT(S) MUST BE MADE to the person named at the address for payment quoting their reference and the claim number.
- DO NOT bring or send payments to the court. THEY WILL NOT BE ACCEPTED.
- You should allow at least 4 days for your payment to reach the claimant or his representative.
- Make sure that you keep records and can account for all payments made. Proof may be required if there is any disagreement. It is not safe to send cash unless you use registered post.
- A leaflet giving further advice about payment can be obtained from the court.
- If you need more information you should contact the claimant or his representative.

The court office at
is open between 10 am and 4 pm Monday to Friday. Address all communications to the Court Manager quoting the claim number
N41A Order suspending warrant (determination) (January 2002)   Crown Copyright. Reproduced by Sweet & Maxwell Ltd.

N71

Order revoking an order of commitment under section 110 of the County Courts Act 1984

18–20

In the	
	County Court
Claimant	
Defendant[1]	
Claim No.	
Judgment Summons No.	
In the	

(seal)

(1) Defendant's address, description and, if known, place of employment

UPON APPLICATION made this day by the defendant,   who was

committed to prison by order dated   20 for failing to attend the adjourned

hearing of a judgment summons; and

Upon reading the affidavit [or witness statement] of the defendant showing the reasons for this failure; and

Upon the undertaking of the defendant to attend the court when next ordered or required to do so:

[His][Her] Honour Judge

has ordered that the order of commitment be revoked

[and that   , the defendant, be discharged out of the custody of the

Governor of Her Majesty's Prison at

as to the said failure].

DATED

**THE GOVERNOR
H M PRISON**

The court office at

is open between 10 am and 4 pm Monday to Friday. Address all communications to the Court Manager and quote the above claim number

N71 Order revoking an order of commitment under Section 110 of the County Courts Act 1984 (January 2002) Crown Copyright. Reproduced by Sweet & Maxwell Ltd.

APPENDIX 2

N72

Suspended committal order (judgment summons)

Claimant

Defendant

In the	
	County Court
Claim No.	
J/S No.	
Claimant's Ref.	

(seal)

On   20   [His][Her] Honour Judge
sitting at
heard

and the court orders that

1. The defendant be committed to prison for   days

(1) where judgment entered for more than £5000 on

2. This order will not be put into force if (in addition to the sum of £   paid since issue of the judgment summons) the defendant pays to the claimant the sum, including any interest$^{(1)}$,

of £

(2) delete if not applicable

by   (or by instalments of £   for every calendar month, the first instalment to reach the claimant by   and on the same date for each successive month.)

To the defendant

If you do not pay (any instalment) in accordance with this order, a warrant for your committal may be issued without further notice, and you may be imprisoned for the period shown above.

(When you have paid the sum of £   there will remain a further sum of £   payable under the original judgment or order)$^{(2)}$

——— **Address for Payment** ———

- If you cannot pay as directed by this order you should write or go to the court office immediately, stating the reasons why you cannot pay.
- The court will send you notice of a day and time to attend before the judge.
- If you satisfy the judge that you are unable to pay, he has the power to grant a further suspension on such terms as he thinks fit

——— **How to Pay** ———

- PAYMENT(S) MUST BE MADE to the person named at the address for payment quoting their reference and the claim number.
- DO NOT bring or send payments to the court. THEY WILL NOT BE ACCEPTED.
- You should allow <u>at least</u> 4 days for your payment to reach the claimant or his representative.
- Make sure that you keep records and can account for all payments made. Proof may be required if there is any disagreement. It is not safe to send cash unless you use registered post.
- A leaflet giving further advice about payment can be obtained from the court.
- If you need more information you should contact the claimant or his representative.

The court office at
is open between 10 am and 4 pm Monday to Friday. Address all communications to the Court Manager quoting the claim number.
N72 Notice to defendant where a committal order made, but directed to be suspended under Debtors Act Order 28 rule 7(1) (January 2002) Crown Copyright. Reproduced by Sweet & Maxwell Ltd.

I certify that this duplicate warrant of commital is in substitution for the original warrant dated

and numbered

and has been issued by order of the Judge by reason of the failure of the Debtor to comply with the terms imposed when the Debtor was discharged in respect of the original warrant of committal.

DATED

District Judge

N76 Certificate to be indorsed on duplicate warrant of committal issued for re-arrest of debtor.
(April 1999) Crown Copyright. Reproduced by Sweet & Maxwell Ltd.

18–23

APPENDIX 2

N77

18–23

-v-

Penal Notice

To

of

You must obey the directions
contained in this order. If
you do not, you will be guilty of
contempt of court, and you
may be sent to prison.

Date

N.77 - w3 - Notice as to consequences of disobedience to order of court
Crown Copyright. Reproduced by Sweet & Maxwell Ltd

N78

Notice to Show Good Reason why an Order for Your Committal to Prison should not be made

In the	
	County Court
Claim No	

Between

_____ **Applicant**
Claimant

and

_____ **Respondent**
Defendant

(Seal)

(1) Insert name of person against whom the committal order is sought.
(2) Insert full address.
(3) Set out the precise parts of the injunction or undertaking relevant to this committal application.

To ⁽¹⁾

of ⁽²⁾

On the   day of   [19   ][20   ] , the Court made an order [*or* you gave an undertaking] as follows:⁽³⁾

(4) Insert name of applicant.
(5) List the ways in which it is alleged that the respondent has disobeyed the order or broken the undertaking. If necessary continue on a separate sheet.

⁽⁴⁾   has applied for an order that you should be committed to prison. It is alleged that you have disobeyed the order [*or* broken the undertaking] by⁽⁵⁾

You must attend Court

at

on the   day of   [19   ][20   ], at   o'clock

to show good reason why you should not be sent to prison.

- If the Court is satisfied that any of the allegations are true, it may order that you be imprisoned for your contempt of this Court.
- **Important instructions about what you should do are set out overleaf.**

The applicant's solicitors are
Name
Address

Ref/tel no

The Court Office at
is open from 10 am to 4 pm Monday to Friday.

N78 Notice of an application to commit (January 2002)   Crown Copyright. Reproduced by Sweet & Maxwell Ltd.

Claim No.

Important notes

- The Court has the power to send you to prison if it finds that any of the allegations made against you are true. Full details of the allegations are contained in the applicant's sworn statement (the affidavit).

- You must attend court on the date shown on the front of this form. It is in your own interest to do so. You should bring any witnesses and documents with you which you think will help you put your side of the case.

- If you can show good reason why you should not be sent to prison you must tell the Court.

- If you need advice you should show this document at once to your Solicitor or go to a Citizens' Advice Bureau.

- Even if you do not seek advice you can, if you wish, file a sworn statement at the Court setting out your side of the case. The Court Office can give you a form for this purpose and it can be sworn before a Court Officer. If you have disobeyed the order you can apologise for it on this form. You must still attend court on the date shown, however.

For Court use only

I certify that the notice, of which this is a true copy, was served by me on

(date).......................................

or: the   personally,

at the address stated in the notice, or at

Or *in accordance with an order for substituted service.*

Bailiff/Officer of the Court

....

Notice of Non-Service

I certify that this notice has not been served for the following reasons:

Bailiff/Officer of the Court

N79

Committal or Other Order upon Proof of Disobedience of a Court Order or Breach of an Undertaking

In the	**County Court**
Claim No. *Always quote this*	

Between _____ Applicant Claimant Petitioner

and _____ Respondent Defendant

(seal)

Before His (Her) Honour Judge _____
Sitting at _____ on *(date)*

1. **An application having been made by**[1] _____ **for committal of**[2] _____ **to prison for disobeying the order [breach of the undertaking] dated** _____ The relevant terms of the order (undertaking) and the allegations made by the applicant are recited on the attached notice to show good reason

   or

2. **Whereas**[2] _____ has been suspected of a breach of the attached order dated _____ and has been arrested by a constable and brought before the Judge under section 47(6) of the Family Law Act 1996.

   or

3. **Whereas**[2] _____ has been suspected of a breach of the attached {u[dd]ertaking] dated _____ and has been arrested under a warrant of arrest and brought before the Judge under [section 47(8) of the Family Law Act 1996] [section 3(3) of the Protection from Harassment Act 1997].

—————————————— **IMMEDIATE CUSTODIAL ORDER** ——————————————

It is ordered that[2] _____ be committed for contempt to Her Majesty's Prison _____ for a (be detained under section 9(1) of the Criminal Justice Act 1982) at[3] _____ (total) period of[4] _____ or until lawfully discharged if sooner, and that a warrant of arrest and committal be issued forthwith.

And the contemnor can apply to the (court) (judge) to purge his contempt and ask for release.

[**And,** as the court by order dated _____ dispensed with service of the notice of application for a committal order,
It is ordered that the contemnor be brought before a judge of this court as soon as practicable.]

—————————————— **ALTERNATIVE DISPOSAL** ——————————————

It is ordered that[2] _____ be committed for contempt to prison for a (total) period of[4] _____

The order is suspended until _____ [19][20] and will not be put in force if during that time the contemnor complies with the following terms:

And it is further ordered that in the event of non compliance any application for issue of the warrant shall be made to a judge (on notice to the contemnor)

It is ordered that[2] _____ be fined the sum of £ _____
Such sum to be paid into the office of the court within 14 days of the date of this order.

It is ordered that consideration of the penalty for the contempts found proved be adjourned until _____ [19]
[20] and may be restored for decision if during that time[2] _____ does not comply with the following terms

—————————————— **PROVISION FOR COSTS** ——————————————

And it is ordered that

Date
For record of service, hearing and contempts found proved, see overleaf

18–25

APPENDIX 2

RECORD OF SERVICE, HEARING AND CONTEMPTS FOUND PROVED

At the hearing

(1)   [appeared personally] [was represented by solicitor / counsel] [did not attend]
(2)   [appeared personally] [was represented by solicitor / counsel] [did not attend]

The court read the affidavits of (Names)	Date affidavit(s) sworn

And the court heard oral evidence given by
Name(s)

And the court is satisfied having considered the facts disclosed by the evidence and/or admitted in court by him/her that⁽²⁾   has been guilty of contempt of this court by disobeying the order (breaking the undertaking) dated   by (and as set out in the attached schedule)

And for the particular contempt the court imposed the penalty of:

1.

2.

1.

2.

-----RECORD OF SERVICE-----

Service of Injunction Order with Penal Notice incorporated or indorsed
(Order dated   [19][20])
(for substituted) (dispensing with) service)
Service proved by
☐ certificate of service
     dated   [19][20]
☐ certificate of bailiff
☐ oral evidence of

Service of Notice to show good reason in form N78
(Order dated   [19][20])
(for substituted) (dispensing with) service)
Service proved by
☐ certificate of service
     dated   [19][20]
☐ certificate of bailiff
☐ oral evidence of

Arrest under warrant of arrest
respondent arrested on

by

in accordance with a warrant of arrest issued

Service of Immediate Custodial Order

I *(name of Officer)*   certify that I served the contemnor with a copy of this order by:

☐ delivery by hand to the contemnor before he was taken from the court building or other place of arrest to the place of detention
☐ delivery by hand to the contemnor at *(time)*   on *(date)*   [19][20] at *(place)*

Where a suspended committal order is made, the applicant is responsible for service. (Rules of the Supreme Court Order 52 rule 7(2).)
Where there is suspended committal order or penalty is adjourned on terms, personal service is advisable.

The court office is open from 10 am to 4 pm Monday to Friday.

When corresponding with the court, please address forms and letters to the Court Manager and quote the case number.

Notes for completion of page 1

Terms or names that may be used more than once in the order are numbered in brackets as follows:

(1) Person making application for committal
(2) Person against whom the committal order is made (contemnor)
(3) Name of prison or young offender institution
(4) Period of detention

If the respondent has been brought before the court under a power of arrest (Family Law Act 1996) delete 1 and 3.

If the respondent has been brought before the court under a warrant of arrest (Family Law Act 1996 or Protection from Harassment Act 1997) delete 1 and 2.

In all other cases delete 2 and 3.

Enter the date of order (with penal notice incorporated or indorsed) or undertaking.

Date of form N78 Notice to show good reason (applies to 1 only).

Date of the warrant of arrest (applies to 3 only).

Note: A warrant of arrest cannot be issued on an undertaking under the Protection from Harassment Act 1997.

IMMEDIATE CUSTODIAL ORDER

Complete this section if an immediate custodial order is made otherwise delete and complete section below

Section 9(1) of CJA is for persons aged less than 21 and at least 18.

The total period of detention must be specified by the Judge. The maximum period for contempt of court (including a county court) is 2 years.

If the offence is failure to do a specific act and the judge decides that the application may be made to a district judge upon proof that the act has been done delete (judge) otherwise delete (court).

Complete only if order dispensing with service of notice of application was granted otherwise delete.

ALTERNATIVE DISPOSAL

Delete this section if an immediate custodial order is made otherwise delete alternatives not selected by judge.

Enter the exact terms of any suspended committal order or adjournment of penalty.

There are further possible alternative disposals, eg under sections 35, 37 and 38 of the Mental Health Act and sequestration.

COSTS

Enter any order for costs here or show that no order for costs has been made if applicable

Date the order here

N329 Notes for guidance on completion (Form N79) (April 1999)   Crown Copyright. Reproduced by Sweet & Maxwell Ltd.

18–25   APPENDIX 2

Notes on completion of page 2
(Record of service, hearing and contempts found proved)

---REPRESENTATION---

The parties and their legal representative (advocate only)

---AFFIDAVIT EVIDENCE---

Only those affidavits which the judge has considered at the hearing. There is unlikely to be any affidavit evidence offered where the respondent has been brought to court under a power of arrest.

---ORAL EVIDENCE---

Only those witnesses sworn and examined

---CONTEMPTS FOUND PROVED---

List and give exact details of only those allegations of contempt which the judge has found proved.

If separate penalties are imposed for each contempt found proved these are to be recorded in the right-hand column showing whether or not periods of detention are to run consecutively or concurrently.

If necessary annex additional page and continue list on it. If an additional page is not used delete the words (and as set out in the attached schedule).

---JUDGE'S APPROVAL---

The Judge must be asked to initial the order here

---RECORD OF SERVICE---

Enter details of certificates of service.

Record of delivery of an undertaking need not be made on this document as it can be found on the form of undertaking.

A sealed copy of the approved order must be served on the contemnor, see Order 29 rule 1(5) recited opposite.

Where the respondent is brought before the court under a power of arrest delete record of service of form N78.
Where the respondent is brought before the court under a warrant of arrest delete record of service of form N78 and complete record of service of warrant of arrest.

Disobedience of a Court Order or Breach of an Undertaking   (Form N79)

Notes for Guidance on Completion

The Court Officer responsible for the forms completion should note the following:

- **Where the respondent is brought before the court after being arrested under a power of arrest** (Section 47(6) of the Family Law Act 1996) a sealed copy of the injunction order giving the power of arrest (not Power of Arrest form FL406) with penal notice indorsed becomes part of form N79 and must be attached to the approved order.

- **Where the respondent is brought before the court after being arrested under a warrant of arrest** (section 47(8) of the Family Law Act 1996) (section 3(3) of the Protection from Harassment Act 1997) a sealed copy of the injunction order becomes part of form N79 and must be attached to the approved order.

- **In all other cases** Form N78 (notice to show good reason why an order for committal should not be made) becomes part of form N79 and a sealed copy of N78 must be attached to the approved order.

- In all cases the warrant is in form N80.

- **When the form has been fully completed it must be passed to the judge for approval.** If the judge is available he/she should be asked to approve and initial or sign the final (typed) version. If this is not possible the judge must be asked to initial or sign the final hand-written draft. In either case the document endorsed by the judge **must be retained on the court file.**

- Before the order is served it must also be checked by an officer of no less than HEO grade.

- Before the order is served these notes should be detached, they are for the guidance of Court Staff only.

When an immediate custodial order is made:

- A copy of N79 (with attached N78 or injunction) must be sent to the Office of the Official Solicitor.

- A sealed copy of the approved order must be served on the contemnor. Order 29 rule 1(5) CCR states:

  If a committal order is made, the order shall be for the issue of a warrant of committal and unless the judge otherwise orders:-

  (a) a copy of the order shall be served on the person to be committed either before or at the time of the execution of the warrant; or
  (b) where the warrant has been signed by the Judge, the order for issue of the warrant may be served on the person to be committed at any time within 36 hours after execution of the warrant.

N79A

Suspended committal order for disobedience
(order to attend court for questioning)

In the

Claim No

Claimant

Defendant

On _____ 20 ___, [[Mr][Mrs]Justice][[His][Her]Honour Judge] sitting at

and]

[heard read the order made on   20 , [the certificate dated   20   of the bailiff,] the affidavit[s] of
sworn on   20   [and
sworn on   20   respectively as to service of the order and] as to the provision of travelling expenses and the certificate dated   20   of the [Master][District Judge][Court Officer]

and the court is satisfied that

1.   was ordered to attend court on   20   to be questioned
2. the order to attend was served on   on   20 .....
3.   did not within seven days of the service of the order request from the judgment creditor payment of a sufficient sum for travelling expenses
4. on   20   the judgment creditor   paid a sufficient sum for travelling expenses
5.   did not attend court on   20   to be questioned
6.   , having attended court, refused to be sworn
7.   , having attended court, refused to answer [any question][the question
]

And that   has been guilty of contempt of court by disobeying the order of
           20

and the court orders that

          be committed to Her Majesty's Prison

for a period of   days

N79A Suspended committal for disobedience (order to attend for questioning)(March 2002)
Crown Copyright. Reproduced by Sweet & Maxwell Ltd

and the court orders that

1. this order shall be suspended so long as   attends court at

   and complies with the order made on   20
   [and

                                                                                                                                    ]

2. if   does not comply with these terms, a warrant of arrest
   shall be issued and   shall, when arrested, be
   brought before a judge to consider whether the committal order should be discharged

3. and that   pay the judgment creditor's costs of attending of £
        , on or before   20

Certificate of Service

I certify that a copy of this order was served by me on _____
the judgment debtor, on _____

Signed _____
     Bailiff of the County Court

FORMS AND PRECEDENTS

N80

Warrant of Committal to prison

Between

_____ Applicant
                              Petitioner

and

_____ Respondent
                              Defendant

In the	
	County Court
Claim No.	
Warrant No.	

Seal

To • the District Judge and Bailiffs of the Court
    • every constable within his jurisdiction
    • the Governor (of Her Majesty's Prison at)[(1)]

(1) Name of Prison

(2) Name and
(3) address of
    person to be
    committed.

On the   day of   [19][20] ,
         (enter name of judge) has ordered that [(2)]

of [(3)]

(4) Where the
    person to
    be committed is
    aged less than
    21 years and
    at least 18 delete
    all references
    to prison
    otherwise
    delete
    reference to
    Sec 9(1)CJA

should be committed to Prison [(4)] (detained under Section 9(1) Criminal Justice Act 1982) for a period of [(5)]

You the District Judge and Bailiff are therefore required forthwith to arrest and deliver

[(2)]

to (Her Majesty's Prison at) [(1)]

(5) State term of
    imprisonment

And you, the Governor, are required to receive and keep [(2)]

safely (in prison) from the arrest under this warrant for a period of [(5)]   or until

lawfully discharged, if sooner.

(6) Add if so
    ordered
    otherwise
    delete

[[(6)] **And,** as the court by order dated   dispensed with service of the notice of

application for a committal order,

It is ordered that you, the Governor, bring [(2)]

before a judge of this court at such time and place as the court shall specify and afterwards,

return him to the prison unless the court orders his discharge.]

Date

I arrested the person named in this warrant on (date)

and delivered him into the custody of the Governor (of Her Majesty's Prison) at [(1)]

on *(date)*

Bailiff of the County Court

The Court Office is open from 10am to 4pm Monday to Friday

Address all communications to the Court Manager and quote the above claim number.

N80 Warrant for committal to prison (April 1999)   Crown Copyright. Reproduced by Sweet & Maxwell Ltd.

18–28

Notice to Solicitor to show cause why an undertaking should not be enforced by committal to prison

N81

In the	
	County Court
Claim No.	
Claimant	
Defendant	

To
of

seal

TAKE NOTICE that you are required to attend at a court to be held at

on

at   o'clock to show cause why an order should not be made committing you to prison

for failing to carry out the undertaking given by you on the   day of   20   ,

to this court to (1)

(1) Here set out terms of undertaking

DATED

Important notes

- The Court has the power to send you to prison if it finds that any of the allegations made against you are true.
- You must attend court on the day shown on the front of this form. It is in your own interest to do so. At the hearing, the judge will explain to you why this summons has been issued and why the court is considering sending you to prison. You will then have the opportunity to put your case. You should bring any witnesses and documents with you which you think will help you put your side of the case.
- If you need advice you should show this document at once to your solicitor or go to a Citizens' Advice Bureau. If you do not already have a solicitor acting for you the court can give details of local solicitors. You may be entitled to help towards the cost of legal advice.

The court office at
is open between 10 am and 4 pm Monday to Friday. Address all communications to the Court Manager quoting the above Claim Number
N81 Notice to solicitor to show cause why an undertaking should not be enforced by committal to prison (October 2000) Crown Copyright. Reproduced by Sweet & Maxwell Ltd.

N82

Order for committal for failure by solicitor to carry out undertaking

In the	**County Court**
Claim No.	
Claimant's Ref.	

Claimant

Defendant

(seal)

[19] [20]

⁽¹⁾ enter name of person against whom order is made

⁽²⁾ state terms of undertaking

By an undertaking given to this court on the   day of
⁽¹⁾   of
as solicitor for the claimant (or defendant) undertook to⁽²⁾

Now upon reading the affidavit of
dated the   day of   [19] [20], and upon hearing

⁽³⁾ add if solicitor giving the undertaking does not appear in person

⁽³⁾and being satisfied upon oath [or by the indorsement of a bailiff of this court (or the   County Court)], that a copy of the notice to show cause why⁽¹⁾
should not be committed has been served personally upon him and being satisfied that⁽¹⁾
has failed to carry out the undertaking before referred to)

(enter name of judge) **has ordered** that⁽¹⁾

⁽⁴⁾ insert name of prison used by the court

be committed for contempt to Her Majesty's Prison at⁽⁴⁾
for a period of   or until lawfully discharged if sooner and that a warrant for the arrest and committal of⁽¹⁾   be issued forthwith

And it is ordered that⁽¹⁾
do pay the costs of this application and of the committal of,   (to be assessed by the District Judge) and paid by⁽¹⁾

⁽⁵⁾ insert name of party to receive the costs and where payable

to⁽⁵⁾
on or before (within 14 days of assessment)
[And it is further ordered that any application for the release from custody of⁽¹⁾

⁽⁶⁾ delete if inapplicable

should be made to the Judge]⁽⁶⁾

Dated

Address for Payment

How to Pay

- PAYMENT(S) MUST BE MADE to the person named at the address for payment quoting their reference and the claim number.
- DO NOT bring or send payments to the court. THEY WILL NOT BE ACCEPTED.
- You should allow <u>at least</u> 4 days for your payment to reach the claimant or his representative.
- Make sure that you keep records and can account for all payments made. Proof may be required if there is any disagreement. It is not safe to send cash unless you use registered post.
- A leaflet giving further advice about payment can be obtained from the court.
- If you need more information you should contact the claimant or his representative.

The court office at
is open between 10 am and 4 pm Monday to Friday. Address all communications to the Court Manager quoting the claim number
N82 Order for committal for failure by solicitor to carry out undertaking (April 1999)   Crown Copyright. Reproduced by Sweet & Maxwell Ltd.

APPENDIX 2

N83

Order for Discharge from Custody under Warrant of Committal

Claimant

Defendant

In the	County Court
Claim No.	
Claimant's Ref.	

(seal)

Upon application made this   day of   [19   ][20   ],
by
who was committed to prison for contempt by an order of this court dated the   day of
[19   ][20   ], and upon reading the application of
attested on the   day of   [19   ][20   ], showing that he is desirous of purging his
contempt, and upon hearing

(1) or, if no one appears for him

(1)(and upon being satisfied that the notice of this application has been duly served upon the
)

(2) insert name of prison

It is ordered that
be discharged out of the custody of Her Majesty's Prison at(2)

(3) add if so ordered

(3)**And it is ordered** that
do pay the sum of £   , the costs of this application, such costs to be assessed and paid

(4) insert name of person to whom payment is to be made

to(4)
by   (or within 14 days of assessment)

Dated

─── **Address for Payment** ─── ─── **How to Pay** ───

- PAYMENT(S) MUST BE MADE to the person named at the address for payment quoting their reference and the claim number.
- DO NOT bring or send payments to the court. THEY WILL NOT BE ACCEPTED.
- You should allow <u>at least</u> 4 days for your payment to reach the claimant or his representative.
- Make sure that you keep records and can account for all payments made. Proof may be required if there is any disagreement. It is not safe to send cash unless you use registered post.
- A leaflet giving further advice about payment can be obtained from the court.
- If you need more information you should contact the claimant or his representative.

The court office at
is open between 10 am and 4 pm Monday to Friday. Address all communications to the Court Manager quoting the claim number.
N83 Order for discharge from custody under warrant of committal (January 2002)   Crown Copyright. Reproduced by Sweet & Maxwell Ltd.

N90

Summons for Assaulting an officer of the Court or rescuing goods

18–31

In the	
	County Court
Claim No.	
Claimant	
Defendant	
Claimant's Ref.	

To

(seal)

You are summoned to appear at a court to be held at

on the   at   o'clock

to answer a complaint made against you by

an Officer of this Court, and to show cause why an order should not be made against you

under the County Courts Act 1984, for payment of a fine or for your committal to prison or both,

for an assault committed by you on the   day of   [19   ][20   ],

upon the said Officer whilst in the execution of his duty [or for rescuing or attempting to rescue,

on the   day of   [19   ][20   ], certain goods seized under process of

this Court].

DATED

Note: to be served personally not less than eight days before the return date

The court office at

is open between 10 am and 4 pm Monday to Friday. Address all communications to the Court Manager quoting the above Claim Number

N90 Summons for assaulting an officer of the court or rescuing goods (January 2002)   Crown Copyright. Reproduced by Sweet & Maxwell Ltd.

18–32

APPENDIX 2

N91C

18–32 Order of Commitment and/or imposing a fine for Assaulting an Officer of the Court or Rescuing Goods

In the

County Court

seal

To the District Judge and bailiffs of the court, and every constable within his jurisdiction, and to the Governor of Her Majesty's Prison at

(1) Enter name & address of offender

IT has been proved to the satisfaction of the court that

(1)

on the   day of   [19   ][20   ], [assaulted an officer of this court, whilst in the execution of his duty] or [(and) rescued or attempted to rescue certain goods seized under process of this court]

(2) Delete as necessary

1.   (enter name of judge) **has ORDERED** (2) that

do pay a fine of £   for the offence(s)   and the sum of £   for costs, amounting together to the sum of £   and do pay that sum into the office of this court forthwith [or by instalments of £   for every   the first instalment to be paid on or before the

2.   (enter name of judge) **has ORDERED** (2) that

shall be committed to prison for

AND YOU the District Judge, bailiffs and others are therefore required to arrest

and deliver him to   Prison

AND YOU the Governor to receive

and keep him safely in prison for

from the arrest under this order or until he shall sooner be discharged by due course of law.

DATED

The court office at

is open between 10 am and 4 pm Monday to Friday. Address all communications to the Court Manager

N91 Order of commitment and/or imposing a fine for assaulting an officer of the court or rescuing goods (January 2002)   Crown Copyright. Reproduced by Sweet & Maxwell Ltd.

18–32

Claim No.

Warrant No.

Defendant

Address

Occupation

I arrested the within named person on the day of [19]20] and delivered him into the custody of the Governor of HM Prison at

on the day of [19]20].

Bailiff of the
County Court

APPENDIX 2

N110

Power of Arrest attached to injunction
under section 2 Domestic Violence and
Matrimonial Proceedings Act 1976   F.P.R. 3.9

Applicant

Respondent

(here set out the provisions of the injunction to which the power of arrest relates)

In the	
	County Court
Claim No.	
Applicant's Ref.	

(seal)

Power of Arrest

[1] Name each child   And the judge being satisfied that the respondent has caused actual bodily harm to the applicant (or and/the children)[1]
and being of the opinion that he is likely to do so again, a power of arrest is attached to this injunction whereby any constable may under the power given by section 2(3) of the Domestic Violence and Matrimonial Proceeding Act 1976 arrest without
[2] Delete as required   warrant the respondent if the constable has reasonable cause for suspecting the respondent of (using violence)(or)(entering any premises or area)[2] in breach of this injunction.

This power of arrest expires on the   day of   [19   ][20   ]

Note to Arresting Officer

Where the respondent is arrested under the power given by section 2 of the Domestic Violence and Matrimonial Proceedings Act 1976, that section requires that:

- the respondent shall be brought before the judge within the period of 24 hours beginning at the time of his arrest;
- the respondent shall not be released within that period except on the direction of the judge;
- the arresting constable shall forthwith seek the directions of the court as to the time and place at which the respondent is brought before a judge.

Nothing in section 2 authorises the detention of the respondent after the expiry of the period of 24 hours beginning at the time of his arrest.

In calculating any period of 24 hours, no account shall be taken of Christmas Day, Good Friday or any Sunday.

The court office at

is open between 10 am and 4 pm Monday to Friday. Address all communications to the Court Manager quoting the claim number

N110 Power of arrest attached to injunction under section 2 Domestic Violence and Matrimonial Proceedings Act 1976 (FPR 3.9) Crown Copyright. Reproduced by Sweet & Maxwell Ltd.

N110A

Anti-Social Behaviour Injunction Power of Arrest

In the	
	County Court
Claim No.	
Applicant's Name	
Applicant's Ref.	
Respondent's Name	

Applicant

Phone Number:

Seal

Power of Arrest

And the judge being satisfied that the respondent has

^[delete]
a) used or threatened violence against a person residing in, visiting, or otherwise engaged in a lawful activity in residential premises to which section 152 of the Housing Act 1996 applies, or in the locality of such premises

b) used or threatened violence against a person residing in, visiting, or otherwise engaged in a lawful activity in the locality of premises of which the applicant is the landlord

^[In sub-paragraph c) where the power of arrest is granted under section 153(b)]
c) allowed a sub-tenant, lodger or other person residing in or visiting the premises in which the respondent resides to use or threaten violence against a person residing in, visiting or otherwise engaged in a lawful activity in the locality of premises of which the applicant is the landlord

^[If or le will apply where the power of arrest is granted under section 153(b)]
and there is a significant risk of harm to that person or a person of similar description, a power of arrest is attached to this injunction whereby any constable may under the power given by section 155 of the Housing Act 1996 arrest without warrant the respondent if the constable has reasonable cause for suspecting the respondent of (using or threatening violence)[1a, 1b] or (allowing a sub-tenant, lodger or visitor to use or threaten violence)[1c] in breach of this injunction.

This power of arrest was ordered on	19	expires on the	day of	19

Note to Arresting Officer

Respondent

Where the respondent is arrested under the power given by section 155 of the Housing Act 1996, that section requires that:-

- the respondent shall be brought before the judge within the period of 24 hours beginning at the time of his arrest;
- the respondent shall not be released within that period except on the direction of the judge;
- a constable shall forthwith inform the person on whose application the injunction was granted.

Nothing in section 155 authorises the detention of the respondent after the expiry of the period of 24 hours beginning at the time of his arrest.

In calculating any period of 24 hours, no account shall be taken of Christmas Day, Good Friday or any Sunday.

The court office at

is open between 10am and 4pm. When corresponding with the court, please address forms or letters to the Court Manager and quote the claim number.

N110A Power of arrest attached to injunction (January 2002)   Crown Copyright. Reproduced by Sweet & Maxwell Ltd.

18–35

N112

18–35 Order and warrant for defendant to be arrested and brought before the court

Claimant

Defendant

In the	
	County Court
Claim No.	
A/E Number	
J/S Number	
Claimant's Ref.	

Seal

To the bailiffs of the court and every constable within the district of the court

(1) delete as appropriate

The defendant was ordered to attend on a specified day for the adjourned hearing of (an application for an attachment of earnings order) (a judgment summons)[(1)] and has failed to do so.

On   20   [His][Her] Honour Judge
sitting at
heard

and the court orders that the defendant be arrested and brought before this court (immediately)[(1)]
(or

on   at   o'clock

at

                                                                 .)

You, the bailiffs and others are therefore required to arrest the defendant and to bring him/her before this court

Description of defendant	Defendant's place of employment

The court office at
is open between 10 am and 4 pm Monday to Friday. When corresponding with the court, please address forms or letters to the Court Manager and quote the claim number.

N112 Order and warrant for defendant to be arrested and brought before the court (January 2002) Crown Copyright. Reproduced by Sweet & Maxwell Ltd.

Certificate of Service *(to be completed by the court)*

I certify that I arrested the person named in this order

on the   day of   20   and brought him before the court.

                                        Bailiff

                                        Date

I certify that the order has **not been executed** for the following reason:

                                        Bailiff

                                        Date

18–36

APPENDIX 2

N117

18–36 General Form of Undertaking

In the	
	County Court
Claim No.	
Claimant's Ref.	
Defendant's Ref.	

Between _____ Claimant / Applicant / Petitioner

and _____ Defendant / Respondent

This form is to be used only for an undertaking not for an injunction

On the   day of   [19   ][20   ]
(1)

[appeared in person] [was represented by Solicitor / Counsel]

(1) Name of the person giving undertaking

and gave an undertaking to the Court promising (2)

(2) Set out terms of undertaking

(3) Give the date and time or event when the undertaking will expire

(4) The judge may direct that the party who gives the undertaking shall personally sign the statement overleaf

And to be bound by these promises until (3)

The Court explained to (1)

the meaning of his undertaking and the consequences of failing to keep his promises,

And the Court accepted his undertaking (4) [and *if so ordered* directed that

(1)   should sign the statement overleaf].

And   (enter name of Judge) **ordered** that (5)

(5) Set out any other directions given by the court

(6) Address of the person giving undertaking

Dated

To (1)
of (6)

Important Notice

- You may be sent to prison for contempt of court if you break the promises that you have given to the Court.

- If you do not understand anything in this document you should go to a Solicitor, Legal Advice Centre or a Citizens' Advice Bureau

The Court Office at

is open from 10 am to 4 pm. When corresponding with the court, address all forms and letters to the Court Manager and quote the claim number.

N117 General form of undertaking (April 1999)   Crown Copyright. Reproduced by Sweet & Maxwell Ltd.

The Court may direct that the party who gives the undertaking shall personally sign the statement below.

Statement

I understand the undertaking that I have given, and that if I break any of my promises to the Court I may be sent to prison for contempt of court.

Signed

To be completed by the Court

Delivered

☐ By posting on:

☐ By hand on:

☐ Through solicitor on:

Officer:

18–37

APPENDIX 2

N118

18–37 **Suspended Committal Order (Attachment of Earnings)**

Claimant

Defendant

In the	
	County Court
Claim No.	
A/E Number	
Claimant's Ref.	

Take notice that today   (enter name of Judge) made a committal order for your imprisonment for   days

This order will not be put into force so long as you attend this court

on

at

at   **o'clock**

You must also complete the enclosed form of reply and statement of means and send it to reach the court office **within 8 days** after you receive this order

Dated

Take Notice

To the defendant

If you do not comply with this order, a **warrant for your committal may be issued without further notice and you may be imprisoned for the period shown above.**

If you cannot attend on the specified date, you should write or go to the court office immediately, stating the reason why you cannot attend. The court will send you notice of a day and time to attend before the judge

Notes to help you complete the form of reply

- If you are unemployed or self employed, you should say so on the form of reply and answer as many questions as you can.
- Read the notes on the form of reply before giving the details asked for.
- If you want an opportunity to pay voluntarily without your employer being ordered to make deductions from your pay, you should ask for a suspended order on the form of reply. You should also enclose a copy of your most recent payslip.
- You can obtain help in completing the form of reply at any county court office or Citizens' Advice Bureau.

The court office is

N118 Notice to defendant where committal order made but directed to be suspended under Attachment of Earnings Act 1971 (January 2002) Crown Copyright. Reproduced by Sweet & Maxwell Ltd.

APPENDIX 3

EXAMPLES OF PENALTIES IMPOSED SINCE 1981

I. CRIMINAL CONTEMPTS

NAME OF CASE	NATURE OF CONTEMPT	PENALTIES
Mulvaney (1982) 4 Cr.App.R. (S) 106	Approaches to witnesses in a murder trial. Said to be a prevalent offence requiring a deterrent sentence. Misguided sense of loyalty to a friend.	12 months' imprisonment, reduced to six months on appeal.
Att-Gen v News Group Newspapers Ltd (1982) 4 Cr.App.R. (S) 182	Publication by *News of the World* prejudicial to a re-trial of poisoning charges. An unfortunate error of judgment at the lower end of the scale. No previous similar offence.	Fine of £500.
Goult (1982) 4 Cr.App.R. (S) 355	Menacing female jurors. Deliberate and partially successful attempts to intimidate. The threats were "not by any means as serious as they might have been".	18 months' imprisonment, reduced to nine months.
Giscombe (1983) 5 Cr.App.R. (S) 151	Witness remaining in court after giving evidence: shouting out that a policeman was a liar. Later approaching a juror near the court.	Four months' imprisonment upheld.

NAME OF CASE	NATURE OF CONTEMPT	PENALTIES
Kohli (1983) 5 Cr.App.R. (S) 175	Failing to surrender to bail for a re-trial on a perjury charge. "A serious case": he "decided, quite simply, that he would not turn up but leave the country".	Three months' imprisonment upheld.
Sergiou (1983) 5 Cr.App.R. (S) 227	A witness, served with an unconditional witness order, arranged to be on holiday abroad when the trial was to take place. "Properly dealt with by an immediate but short custodial sentence".	14 days' imprisonment upheld.
Phillips (1983) 5 Cr.App.R. (S) 297	Witness for the Crown refusing to be sworn or give evidence in a murder trial. Not "crucial", but this had not been taken into account by the judge.	Four months' imprisonment, reduced to 14 days' detention.
Smithers and Bowen (1983) 5 Cr.App.R. 248	Spectators at a Crown Court trial saying to a witness, following her evidence, "grass" and "fucking bastard". Significant differences from *Goult*. This was a case of "casual and boorish abuse".	Six months' imprisonment, reduced to 60 days.
Davis (1983) 8 Cr.App.R. (S) 64	Failure to surrender to bail at the Crown Court. Sentenced to 30 months' imprisonment for the substantive offences with a consecutive term for the contempt. "Richly deserved", but no opportunity afforded to give an explanation.	Six months' imprisonment. Sentence quashed.

Examples of Penalties Imposed since 1981

NAME OF CASE	NATURE OF CONTEMPT	PENALTIES
Leonard (1984) 6 Cr.App.R. (S) 279	Crown witness refusing to answer questions. No "impertinent defiance", and no specially deterrent sentence required. The judge's sentence "completely out of scale". The maximum under the 1965 Act should have been the guideline.	18 months' imprisonment, reduced to 28 days.
Att-Gen v News Group Newspapers Ltd (1984) 6 Cr.App.R. (S) 418	Proprietors of *The Sun* published a photograph of a defendant, charged with assaulting a baby, gesturing at a photographer and under a headline which misrepresented the case ("Baby was Blinded by Dad"). "Not deliberate" but nevertheless serious.	Fine of £5,000 imposed.
Att-Gen v RSPCA, The Times, June 22, 1985	The Society brought disciplinary proceedings against one of its officers for not appearing to be a reluctant witness for the defence at the hearing of a private prosecution brought by the Society.	Fine of £10,000 imposed.
Moran (1985) 7 Cr.App.R. (S) 101	The appellant was serving a sentence of 30 months' imprisonment for aggravated burglary. Having implicated another man, he refused to take the oath when called for the Crown. "Everything went wrong": no opportunity to apologise or to have legal advice.	Six months' imprisonment. Sentence quashed.

NAME OF CASE	NATURE OF CONTEMPT	PENALTIES
Pittendrigh (1985) 7 Cr.App.R. (S) 221	The appellant uttered a threat to a witness and her companion during the trial of his son. A grave contempt: custodial sentence "inevitable" but it was "a single act of menace", and apparently unplanned.	18 months' imprisonment, reduced to nine months.
Maloney (1986) 8 Cr.App.R. (S) 123	The appellant threatened a witness waiting to give evidence at his brother's trial ("You're in for a seeing to")	Six months' imprisonment upheld.
Neve (1986) 8 Cr.App.R. (S) 270	The appellant was charged with conspiracy to supply and to possess controlled drugs: following release on bail he went abroad and obtained false identity documents.	Six months' imprisonment. Security of £10,000 forfeited. Appeal dismissed.
Jardine (1987) 9 Cr.App.R. (S) 41	The appellant pleaded guilty to handling stolen jewellery, and sentenced to two years' imprisonment, the judge assuming his willingness to give evidence against the robbers. He subsequently refused to give evidence. "A devious and deliberate ploy".	Six months' imprisonment upheld.
Bashir and Azam (1988) 10 Cr.App.R. (S) 76	Threats of violence to a witness waiting to give evidence in the Crown Court. "Done on the spur of the moment".	Nine months' imprisonment upheld.
James (1988) 10 Cr.App.R. (S) 392	Threat of violence to a witness and a suggestion that he give false evidence. "A very serious contempt . . . upon a man who was clearly susceptible".	Two years' imprisonment upheld.

EXAMPLES OF PENALTIES IMPOSED SINCE 1981

NAME OF CASE	NATURE OF CONTEMPT	PENALTIES
Att-Gen v News Group Newspapers plc [1989] Q.B. 110	Newspaper proprietors publishing a summary of what was likely to be the prosecution case against a doctor after the newspaper group itself had undertaken to fund a private prosecution against him for raping a child.	Fine of £75,000 imposed.
Att-Gen v Newspaper Publishing plc [1989] 1 F.S.R. 457	Spycatcher	Publishers of *The Independent, The Sunday Times* and *News on Sunday* each fined £50,000 (expressed to be by reference to the recent precedent of *Att-Gen v News Group Newspapers plc*).
Att-Gen v TVS Television Ltd, *The Times*, July 7, 1989	Television and newspaper coverage of landlords abusing public funds which led to a trial having to be aborted at a cost of £215,000.	TVS fined £25,000 and proprietors of the *Reading Standard* fined £5,000.
Smith (1989) 11 Cr.App.R. (S) 353	Approach by a defendant, indicted for wounding, to the principal prosectuion witness ("Whichever way it goes, you're dead").	Six months' imprisonment upheld.
Samuda (1989) 11 Cr.App.R. (S) 471	Refusal by the alleged victim to give evidence for the Crown against a defendant charged with attempted murder. "The appellant's evidence was vital". Immediate prison sentence rightly imposed.	15 months' imprisonment, reduced to six months.

NAME OF CASE	NATURE OF CONTEMPT	PENALTIES
Woods (1989) 11 Cr.App.R. (S) 551	Appellant sentenced to 18 months' imprisonment for various offences of dishonesty, with three months consecutive for failing to surrender. "Separate and consecutive sentence ... correct in principle and ... desirable". The procedure recommended in *Davis* not followed: no opportunity to counsel to raise a proper point on disparity.	Three months' imprisonment. Sentence quashed.
Solicitor-General v Henry and News Group Newspapers plc [1990] C.O.D. 307 (Lexis)	*News of the World* published an article ("Bride Quiz Man is Rapist") which revealed the criminal record of an arrested man currently being questioned in connection with a kidnapping and murder. This was apparently "an honest, if wholly unprofessional, mistake rather than a deliberately contumacious or risky course of conduct". Legal advice was taken before publication. Such publications "are playing with fire".	Proprietors fined £15,000 with no separate penalty on the editor.
McDaniel (1990) 12 Cr.App.R. (S) 44	The appellant had been warned about noisy conversations during the trial of his brother but, following conviction and sentence, he called the judge "a dog". He apologised shortly afterwards. The abuse was vulgar; "not of the most serious kind".	Three months' imprisonment, reduced to 14 days. Immediate release ordered.

Examples of Penalties Imposed since 1981   19–1

NAME OF CASE	NATURE OF CONTEMPT	PENALTIES
Watson (1990) 12 Cr.App.R. (S) 227	The appellant sentenced to nine months' imprisonment for burglary, with two months consecutive for failing to surrender. "Two things went wrong": it had not been explained in clear terms that he was at risk for the bail offence; nor was he given an opportunity to explain the circumstances.	Two months' imprisonment. Sentence quashed.
Att-Gen v Hislop [1991] 1 Q.B. 514	Articles published in *Private Eye* when proceedings for libel by the wife of the Yorkshire Ripper were pendng. It was held by the Court of Appeal that these exercised improper pressure on her to discontinue her action.	Proprietors and editor each fined £10,000 (in addition to a "further significant liability for costs").
Uddin (1991) 13 Cr.App.R. (S) 114	The appellant was committed for trial over hygiene offences relating to a restaurant, and then left the country for Bangladesh. He was eventually arrested on a bench warrant.	Three months' imprisonment upheld.

Appendix 3

NAME OF CASE	NATURE OF CONTEMPT	PENALTIES
Att-Gen v BBC [1992] C.O.D. 264	A broadcast news item purporting to cover the first day of a drug importation trial, mis-represented the opening speech of counsel by including certain information, deriving from an earlier police briefing, which he had deliberately omitted. Reference was made in argument to the need to reflect the waste of public time and money through the Judge having to hear submissions and seeking to avoid prejudicial consequences of the programme.	A fine of £5,000 imposed.
Osbourne (1992) 14 Cr.App.R. (S) 265	Following the imposition of a sentence upon his girlfriend for benefit frauds, the appellant followed the female prosecuting solicitor and said "you will not be smiling any more". Officers of the court ... should be free to perform their functions without being harassed by surly individuals who regard the operation of law as a personal affront".	Four months' imprisonment reduced to two. Immediate release.
Palache (1992) 14 Cr.App.R. (S) 294	A young woman advanced towards the jury following her mother's conviction of drugs offences and the imposition of custodial sentence. She brandished a water carafe. "A very grave contempt". Jurors entitled to feel that "they had the support of the law in protecting them".	28 days' imprisonment upheld.

NAME OF CASE	NATURE OF CONTEMPT	PENALTIES
Official Solicitor v News Group Newspapers plc [1994] 2 F.L.R. 174	*The Sun* published articles making extensive reference to medical opinions and other confidential material contained in a file passed to the newspaper by a husband who had only obtained the material for the purposes of contested proceedings relating to the custody of a child. There was a pressing social need to protect the privacy of proceedings under the Children Act 1989. It was accepted that it had not been done contumaciously, and that the editor had not given a thought to the possibility of contempt arising.	Proprietors fined £5,000 and the editor £1,000
Att-Gen v News International plc and McKenzie July 5, 1994 (Lexis)	*The Sun* published articles and a photograph which referred to a man already arrested and charged with murder shortly before an identification parade was to take place.	Fines of £80,000 against the proprietor and £20,000 against the editor.
Montgomery (1994) 16 Cr.App.R. (S) 274	The appellant refused to attend a Crown Court trial as a witness and, following arrest, repeated that he was afraid to give evidence.	12 months' imprisonment, reduced to three months.
Carter and Nailor (1994) 16 Cr.App.R. (S) 434	Crown witnesses failing to attend at the right time on two successive days. The accused was acquitted on the direction on the judge. They were "not unwilling witnesses, they were just witnesses who failed to come".	Six weeks' imprisonment each, reduced to 14 days.

APPENDIX 3

NAME OF CASE	NATURE OF CONTEMPT	PENALTIES
Sparks and Kingsnorth (1994) 16 Cr.App.R. (S) 480	Spectators in a public gallery making threatening gestures towards a juror, which led to the jury's discharge. "They did what they did to gratify their idea of fun, . . . frightening peaceful citizens doing their duty for the community".	Nine months' imprisonment each, reduced to six months.
Att-Gen v Jackson [1994] C.O.D. 171	Series of threatening phone calls made from person to a witness.	12 months' imprisonment upheld.
Att-Gen v Judd [1995] C.O.D. 15	After conviction by a jury the respondent approached one of the jurors and harassed her at a car boot sale, and suggested that she write to the judge to say that she had made a mistake in her support of a verdict of guilty.	42 days' imprisonment imposed for common law contempt (no separate penalty for an offence under s.8 of the 1998 Act).
Att-Gen v Stott, unreported, December 1995, Potts J.	The Attorney-General moved the court in respect of the publishers and editor of the defunct newspaper *Today* for having published extracts from the memoirs of a former royal housekeeper. This was despite their knowledge of the existence of an injunction against the housekeeper herself. The in-house legal adviser mistakenly assumed that publication could take place in England once the book was published in the United States.	Proprietors fined £50,000 and the editor £25,000.

Examples of Penalties Imposed since 1981

NAME OF CASE	NATURE OF CONTEMPT	PENALTIES
R. v Att-Gen Ex p. BBC and Jones, December 1, 1995 (Lexis)	A broadcast on BBC Radio Wales referred to a man due to appear that day at the Crown Court to plead to a charge of wounding with intent. Potential jurors were told that he had "an appalling record, including armed robbery and firearms offences".	Fine of £2,000 imposed.
Wedlock (1996) 1 Cr.App.R. (S) 391	The appellant was a defendant in the Crown Court. During the trial he drove past the principal prosecution witness (a girl aged 16), threw something at her, and made an abusive remark. Found to have intended to intimidate.	Six months' imprisonment upheld.
Re a Solicitor (Disclosure of Confidential Records) [1997] 1 F.L.R. 101	Through an oversight, a mother was sent copies of confidential records by her solicitor. Johnson J. directed the Official Solicitor to bring proceedings for contempt against the firm, because it was imperative that those who were ordered to disclose confidential information in such circumstances could be assured that the order would be obeyed.	A fine of £1,000 was imposed upon the firm, which was also ordered to pay the costs of the Official Solicitor and of the hospital on an indemnity basis.

Appendix 3

NAME OF CASE	NATURE OF CONTEMPT	PENALTIES
Att-Gen v Associated Newspapers Ltd, unreported, October 31, 1997	Feature article published during a trial identifying some of the defendants as having been convicted of terrorist offences. There had been a history of unfortunate press coverage and postponements. This article led to a permanent stay. It was accepted as being a serious error of judgment for which the editor apologised. Apparently no calculation was made of the wasted costs.	Proprietors fined £40,000 (specifically assessed at a lower level than the fine imposed in *Morgan* (see below).
Att-Gen v BBC & Hat Trick Productions Ltd [1997] E.M.L.R. 76	In a humorous and irreverent quiz programme, the presenter referred to the sons of Robert Maxwell as "heartless scheming bastards" at a time when they were due to stand trial on two counts of conspiracy to defraud. The programme was repeated after a protest from their solicitor: "a most serious contempt" following a decision "of the risk-taking variety".	The broadcaster and producer were each fined £10,000.
Cole [1997] 1 Cr.App.R. (S) 228	A Crown witness in an affray case refused to give evidence because of alleged threats. The jury was discharged, and eventually the three defendants pleaded guilty to lesser offences. The court applied *Montgomery*, regarding it as a "serious contempt" which had "a terminal effect on the process of that trial".	Four months' imprisonment upheld.

EXAMPLES OF PENALTIES IMPOSED SINCE 1981   19–1

NAME OF CASE	NATURE OF CONTEMPT	PENALTIES
Stredder [1997] 1 Cr.App.R. (S) 209	The appellant spoke to the sole prosecution witness at his trial whose car had been damaged ("That was just a warning"). He also said "I'll do you when I see you anyway". This was "unplanned, hot headed, rash but, nevertheless, severely threatening".	12 months' imprisonment upheld.
Bryan (Lloyd) [1998] 2 Cr.App.R. (S) 109	Mouthed from the public gallery at a witness at a murder trial words which were subject of dispute (but, admittedly, calling her a liar).	6 months' committal upheld.
Att-Gen v Morgan [1998] E.M.L.R. 294. Pill L.J., DC	*News of the World* published an article concerning a large scale conspiracy to distribute counterfeit money. Following the arrest of two defendants the newspaper published an account of the investigation including reference to their criminal past ("We smash £100m fake cash ring"). This led to a permanent stay. Deterrence was a factor.	Publishers fined £50,000. No additional penalty was imposed upon the editor.

NAME OF CASE	NATURE OF CONTEMPT	PENALTIES
Att-Gen v Birmingham Post and Mail Ltd, [1998] 4 All E.R. 49	A prejudicial article was published in the *Birmingham Post* which caused a trial at the Birmingham Crown Court to be halted and started afresh ten days later before a different jury at a different venue. The total additional expense was estimated at £87,000. Reference was made to the fact that this was a lesser interference with justice than had occurred in *Att-Gen v Associated Newspapers Ltd* (October 31, 1997), where a fine of only £40,000 had been imposed.	Proprietors fined £20,000.
Mitchell-Crinkley [1998] 1 Cr.App.R. (S) 368	The appellant was a friend of an accused person. He recognised a juror and telephoned him, mentioning that the previous jury had been discharged. "A grave case".	12 months' imprisonment upheld.
X v Dempster [1999] 1 F.L.R. 894	Publishing matter relating to family proceedings in private (sanctioned by legal advice).	Proprietors fined £10,000 and individual journalist, £1,000.
Att-Gen v News Group Newspapers (1999) C.O.D.	Revealing circumstances of an arrest in the context of a terrorist case in breach of a section 4(2) order made by the trial judge. A serious contempt. The trial was of the utmost gravity and was aborted.	Fine of £35,000 imposed.
HM Coroner for Kent v Terrill [2001] A.C.D. 27 (May 8, 2000)	Failure to attend an inquest when formally required to do so.	Sentenced to four days' imprisonment.

EXAMPLES OF PENALTIES IMPOSED SINCE 1981

NAME OF CASE	NATURE OF CONTEMPT	PENALTIES
R. v MacLeod (Calum Iain) (November 29, 2000, CA (Crim. Div.))	Intimidatory remarks to a female witness by the accused in the course of a trial, while on bail.	Two months' imprisonment.
R. v Hardwick (November 2, 2000, CA (Crim. Div.))	Intimidating a witness during a criminal trial.	Two months imprisonment not excessive.
Att-Gen v BBC [2001] All E.R. (D) 274 (Dec.)	Broadcasting on two successive news programmes the identity of a witness in a sexual assault case who was entitled to anonymity for life under section 1 of the Sexual Offences (Amendment) Act 1992. The Divisional Court took the view that the individual concerned would not return the next day to complete his evidence, and that other complainants might also have been deterred from giving evidence. It was aggravated by the distress caused to the witness in the midst of his evidence.	The BBC was fined £25,000 and the individual journalist £500. The corporation was ordered to pay the Attorney's costs.

Appendix 3

NAME OF CASE	NATURE OF CONTEMPT	PENALTIES
Att-Gen v Mirror Group Newspapers Ltd [2002] EWHC 907	Two Leeds United footballers were charged with assaulting an Asian student. Although the police had announced at an early stage that they were treating the crime as racially motivated, by the time of a preparatory hearing in the Crown Court it had been confirmed to the court that the Crown was not pursuing the suggestion of racial aggravation. At the trial it was submitted that a fair hearing would not be possible because of the earlier police claims and the widespread publicity they received, but the judge rejected the submission and the trial proceeded. After the jury had retired the *Sunday Mirror* published two articles. The first was an interview with the victim's father, which he had been assured would be published only after the verdicts. It included the comment that his son would have been safe if he had fled Britain at the time when he himself had "battered by racists". The other article criticised the co-defendant who had been acquitted and then had given evidence for the Crown. The jury was discharged and the cost of the aborted trial put at approximately £1 million. It was said that the gravity of the contempt was at the top end of the range of strict liability contempts,	A fine of £75,000 was imposed.

Examples of Penalties Imposed since 1981   19–1

NAME OF CASE	NATURE OF CONTEMPT	PENALTIES
	but there were mitigating factors; in particular, the company's good record and its acceptance of the fact that it had erred. Moreover, deterrence was not likely to be a significant factor in the case of a "responsible newspaper with an excellent record".	
Att-Gen v Express Newspapers [2004] EWHC 2859 (Admin)	Following a great deal of coverage and media speculation, for nearly a month, after allegations of gang rape involving professional footballers in a London hotel, one newspaper, uniquely, identified two individuals and published photographs. This was despite repeated warnings from the Attorney-General and the Metropolitan Police to the effect that identification was likely to be an issue. The Divisional Court concluded that "the publication was precisely what might cause a prosecution to be abandoned because of the tainting of the principal witness' evidence". By reason of "systemic failure" within the newspaper, the guidelines had been "overlooked". This was regarded as an aggravating feature. (It was subsequently announced that there was insufficient evidence and no criminal proceedings were instituted.)	A fine of £60,000 was imposed, together with an order for payment of the Attorney's costs.

II. Civil Contempts

NAME OF CASE	NATURE OF CONTEMPT	PENALTIES
Re British Concrete Pipe Association's agreement [1982] I.C.R. 182 [note]	Failure to comply with undertakings not to enter into agreements to which the Restrictive Trade Practices Act 1956 applied.	Redland Pipes Ltd: £100,000. A.R.C. Concrete Ltd: £75,000 Spun Concrete Ltd: £5,000 Mixconcrete Pipes Ltd: £5,000.
Re Diane (Stockport) Ltd, The Times, August 4, 1982	Wilful disobedience by a liquidator to four orders of the court requiring him to submit six half-yearly statements as to the position of liquidations.	A term of eight months' imprisonment, subsequently rescinded in the light of sworn explanation and submissions of counsel. Fine of £500 substituted.
Peart v Stewart [1983] 2 A.C. 109	Breach of non-molestation order.	Six months' imprisonment, reduced to one month.
Messenger Group Newspapers Ltd v NGA [1984] I.R.L.R. 397	NGA breaching injunctions restraining secondary picketing and using improper pressure upon advertisers to persuade them not to use Messenger Newspapers during an industrial dispute.	For the first breaches: £50,000 When mass picketing continued: £100,000 and sequestration of assets. Following violent demonstrations: £525,000.
Mirror Group Newspapers v Harrison (unreported) November 7, 1986, Mars-Jones J.	Failure to comply with an injunction in an industrial dispute by an individual. Qualified apology to which the judge did not attach much weight.	Fined £10,000.

Examples of Penalties Imposed since 1981

NAME OF CASE	NATURE OF CONTEMPT	PENALTIES
Kent Free Press v NGA [1987] I.R.L.R. 267	Breaches of injunctions restraining the NGA and others from procuring interference with Adscene's business by blacking their typesetting. Somewhere between "passive ignoring" and a "half-hearted or... colourable attempt to comply". "Well down the scale of trade union contempts, and a marked improvement on other behaviour of the union on other occasions".	Union fined £4,000.
Smith v Smith [1988] 1 F.L.R. 179	Breach of non-molestation order: admission of entering plaintiff's garden and, following an undertaking, waving papers outside her window (for which "a lying explanation" had been given).	28 days' imprisonment reduced to permit immediate release.
I v D (Access Order: Enforcement) [1988] 2 F.L.R. 286	Breach of access order in magistrates' court.	Magistrates' fine of £80 set aside, and new access arrangements to abide a High Court hearing.
Re S & A Conversions Ltd [1988] B.C.C. 384	The appellant was without qualifications or experience, but obtained appointments to act as a liquidator in respect of companies in voluntary liquidation. He failed to make returns at required intervals: "Guilty of criminal folly and pertinacious refusal to pay the least attention to what the court had said, notwithstanding the clearest of warnings".	Five consecutive sentences of six months' imprisonment quashed, on the basis that concurrent sentences would have sufficed. Immediate release ordered.

NAME OF CASE	NATURE OF CONTEMPT	PENALTIES
Mesham v Clarke [1989] 1 F.L.R. 370	Repeated breaches of a non-molestation and exclusion order, despite express warning from the judge.	Maximum sentence of two years' imprisonment upheld.
Lightfoot v Lightfoot [1989] 1 F.L.R. 414	Breach of an order not to dispose of any monies received, and to pay them into a joint account. He received £30,000, none of which was paid into the joint account.	18 months' imprisonment upheld.
Brewer v Brewer [1989] 2 F.L.R. 251	Regular breaches of a non-molestation order and an order to vacate the matrimonial home. Damaging property, shouting abuse and threats to kill. No contrition: circumstances aggravated by perjuried evidence to the effect that the wife had invited him into the home for sexual intercourse.	Two months' imprisonment upheld.
Goff v Goff [1989] 1 F.L.R. 436	Breaches of non-molestation and exclusion order: conflicting evidence. The husband's previous good character and the pressures on him following breakdown needed to be taken into account.	28 days' imprisonment reduced to 14 days, to be suspended for three months.
Wilsher v Wilsher [1989] 2 F.L.R. 187	Two sets of breaches of the non-molestation order: first, telephoning the wife and making threats and, secondly, accosting her in the street and trying to effect a reconciliation. The breaches were admitted and an apology tendered. The husband was dismissed from the army and lost a gratuity.	28 days' imprisonment varied to permit immediate release.

Examples of Penalties Imposed since 1981 — 19-2

NAME OF CASE	NATURE OF CONTEMPT	PENALTIES
Mason v Lawton [1991] 2 F.L.R. 50	A non-molestation order was breached and the appellant committed to a young offender institution for 28 days. Further orders were made with a penal notice and power of arrest. On release further breaches were committed. "Open defiance" but no actual physical violence.	Two year sentence reduced to nine months and, pursuant to s.14 of the 1981 Act, the Court of Appeal ordered early release because of an apparently sincere wish to purge his contempt.
Juby v Miller [1991] 1 F.L.R. 133	Two breaches of non-molestation order found proved, including an incident for which the appellant had already been dealt with in the magistrates' court. There is a difference between a criminal offence committed against someone not subject to the protection of a court order and one committed against a citizen so protected. The latter is to be regarded as "in a wholly special category".	Consecutive sentences of eight months' imprisonment upheld.
Duo v Osborne [1992] 2 F.L.R. 425	Two breaches of a non-molestation order, despite warnings as to the serious consequences. Insufficient opportunity given to the husband's solicitor to take instructions.	Six months' imprisonment quashed and the matter remitted to a different trial judge for a re-hearing.
Jones v Jones [1993] 2 F.L.R. 377	Breach of an ouster order found proved, the husband having entered the home and removed personal belongings and the children's birth certificates. An immediate custodial sentence was appropriate in a case of blatant and aggravated contempt so as to mark the court's disapproval and deter others.	Six months' imprisonment reduced to three months.

[1343]

NAME OF CASE	NATURE OF CONTEMPT	PENALTIES
Hudson v Hudson [1995] 2 F.L.R. 72	Husband dissipated £20,000 army gratuity in breach of an injunction. Despite previous good character, the breach was a serious one. The wife had lost all chance of recovering a lump sum.	Nine months' imprisonment upheld.
Re O (Contempt: Committal) [1995] 2 F.L.R. 767	Parents writing anonymous letters in breach of an injunction. They would apparently stop at nothing to secure the return of their "former children" who had been adopted. There was a danger of destabilising the adoption, and the parents' conduct constituted an attempt to pervert the course of justice.	12 months' imprisonment upheld.
Director General of Fair Trading v Pioneer Concrete (U.K.) Ltd [1995] 1 A.C. 456	Breaches by two companies of injunctions granted by the Restrictive Practices Court restraining them from giving effect to agreements relating to the supply of ready-mixed concrete contrary to the Restrictive Trade Practices Act 1976.	Fines of £20,000 imposed by the Restrictive Practices Court in respect of each company in September 1990. Later, on August 4, 1995, fines totalling £6.5 million were imposed on various companies for blatant disregard of rulings. These included £2,225,000 against Pioneer Mixconcrete and £1,500,000 against Tarmac.
Taylor Made Golf Co Inc v Rata & Rata [1996] F.S.R. 528	"Cynical and deliberate" failure to comply with the terms of an *Anton Piller* order.	Fine of £75,000 imposed.

EXAMPLES OF PENALTIES IMPOSED SINCE 1981   19–2

NAME OF CASE	NATURE OF CONTEMPT	PENALTIES
G v C [1998] 1 F.L.R. 43	Eighteen breaches of an injunction alleged over a three month period. The father acknowledged most incidents of contempt, but denied two of them and challenged the more serious aspects of many others. The judge rejected his evidence. The judge gave no credit for the father's admissions, or for the fact that the breaches stemmed from distress rather than malice.	13 months' imprisonment reduced to eight months.
Thorpe v Thorpe [1998] 2 F.L.R. 127	Breach of an order requiring a husband to vacate the matrimonial home and return a large quantity of missing property. Probably the only course open to the judge was to impose a custodial penalty on this "obdurate husband". He had been given two previous chances to restore the property.	Six weeks' imprisonment reduced to two weeks.
Neil v Ryan [1998] 2 F.L.R. 1068	The respondent had gone to his former partner's home, in breach of a non-molestation order and asaulted her.	The judge at Bow County Court had imposed a sentence of one month but had suspended it for three months. The Court of Appeal removed the suspension. The test was whether it was "unduly lenient".
Citadel Management Inc v Equal Ltd [1999] 1 F.L.R. 21	Solicitor failing to comply with undertaking to pay to the claimant $17.6M or with the subsequent order of the court. It as no excuse for non-compliance with an undertaking by a solicitor to make payment that, for reasons not disclosed at the time it was given, it would be difficult or impossible for him to comply.	Leave refused to appeal against committal for six months. A sentence of six months had been suspended for a month to enable him to comply with an order to pay. It was thereafter activated.

NAME OF CASE	NATURE OF CONTEMPT	PENALTIES
Cambridgeshire County Council v D [1999] 2 F.L.R. 42	The Court of Appeal held that a sentence of twelve months was manifestly excessive and wrong in principle for the sending of genuine love letters (in the context of "the tortured emotions of two immature young lovers") even though there had been an almost immediate breach of an undertaking that D should not contact S by letter or by other means.	The sentence was reduced to one of three months in a young offenders' institution.
Secretary of State for Defence v Percy [1999] 1 All E.R. 732	Nine incidents of a breach of a final injunction restraining her from entering on certain defined land at RAF Menwith Hill.	Six months' imprisonment suspended for 12 months in respect of earlier breaches. Period of suspension extended subsequently.
Raffique v Muse [2000] 1 F.L.R. 820	Breaches of an injunction to restrain a son from harassing his mother.	Six months' imprisonment upheld.
Hale v Tanner [2000] 1 W.L.R. 2377	There was clear evidence of the female respondent harassing a former boyfriend and his new partner. There were mitigating factors, in that she had not received the usual warnings at the time the order was made, because she had not attended; nor had she had the benefit of legal advice. Also, it was the first instance of a breach, and it was relevant that she was the mother of a young child (of whom she claimed that the applicant was the father).	A six-month sentence (suspended) was reduced to one of 28 days.

Examples of Penalties Imposed since 1981

NAME OF CASE	NATURE OF CONTEMPT	PENALTIES
Olk v Olk [2001] EWCA Civ 1075	Long history of breaching injunctions—attending his estranged wife's home on a daily basis, normally drunk, and shouting abuse.	Twelve months held not to be excessive.
H v H (Breach of Injunction) [2001] EWCA Civ 653; [2001] 3 F.C.R. 628	A unique and unhappy history of defiance and abuse, detailed in the various judgments of Munby J. and in the Court of Appeal judgment.	Ten months' imprisonment not excessive.
Salisbury DC v Le Roi; sub nom. *Salisbury DC v Williams* [2001] EWCA Civ 1490; [2002] 1 P. & C.R. 39; [2002] J.P.L. 700, CA (Civ Div)	Flagrant non-compliance with a demolition order imposed in respect of breach of planning control	Three months' imprisonment, suspended for 16 weeks to afford further opportunity for compliance upheld by the Court of Appeal.
Heathcote v Crackles [2002] EWCA Civ 222	Non-compliance with a non-molestation order, involving throwing a cup at a former partner and reversing a car into her vehicle as she was leaving. No apology was offered or other indication that he recognised the seriousness of the breach.	Twelve months immediate custody was not manifestly excessive. It had, however, been inappropriate to make an order under section 91(14) of the Children Act 1989, whereby the judge purported to restrict the respondent from making an application for further contact for 12 months. There was no jurisdiction to make an order in those circumstances. The provision had its own specified procedures.

NAME OF CASE	NATURE OF CONTEMPT	PENALTIES
Robinson v Robinson [2001] All E.R. (D) 144 (Feb.)	There were orders in place to prevent contact or violence but, during a [re-arranged visit for the purpose of returning the family dog, the husband tricked a child into admitting him to the home where he subjected his wife to aggressive language and threatened to slit her throat. He was arrested and the judge sentenced him to eight months imprisonment for what he considered a "bad case".	Eight months was held to be manifestly excessive and it was reduced to two months, largely because the judge was said not to have fully appreciated that the breach occurred "in the white heat of a marital breakdown".
McKnight v Northern [2001] EWCA Civ 2028	Breach of a non-molestation order. The father visited the mother, threatened to attack her and kicked her car while she was inside. The power of the arrest was exercised and he was remanded in custody for seven days.	The judge should have invited mitigation before sentencing but, since there was in fact no mitigation, there was no ground for interfering with the sentence of four months on that ground. The judge should have taken into account, however, the seven days on remand and made a corresponding reduction. This was because section 67 of the Criminal Justice Act 1967 did not apply to "committal . . . for failure to abstain from doing anything required . . . to be left undone": see section 104. Accordingly there would be no automatic deduction in such a case the Court of Appeal therefore reduced the sentence by 14 days (since he would serve only half the term in any event: see **14–32** to **14–33** of the main text).

EXAMPLES OF PENALTIES IMPOSED SINCE 1981   **19–2**

NAME OF CASE	NATURE OF CONTEMPT	PENALTIES
A-A v B-A [2001] 4 F.L.R. 1	The husband raped the wife during the currency of restraining orders. (See para.**12–11** of the main text).	12 months' imprisonment for the contempt in respect of rape. Upheld on appeal.
London Borough of Barnet v Hurst [2002] EWCA Civ 1009; W.L.R. 722; [2002] 4 All E.R. 457	Breach of an undertaking not to commit specified acts of anti-social behaviour (including assaulting, threatening, harassing, or causing nuisance to residents in a certain block of flats). A sentence of nine months was imposed on the basis of a limited admission, to the effect that the respondent had been "loud and noisy, disturbing the neighbours' sleep".	The Court of Appeal reduced the sentence to one of three months, because the circuit judge's sentence was manifestly too long for the activities encompassed by the limited admissions.

NAME OF CASE	NATURE OF CONTEMPT	PENALTIES
Horgan v Horgan [2002] EWCA Civ 1371	The judge had imposed a three-month sentence for an episode when the husband had repeatedly telephoned his wife and threatened her with words "You don't have a life. I'll make sure of it". A few days later he had uttered oblique remarks which were interpreted as a threat to use a gun. For this, and similar threats a week later, he was sentence to six months. Because the respondent had spent some time on remand (some part of it imposed illegally) it was necessary to allow for this when passing sentence (see *McKnight v Northern* above). Despite the fact that threats to kill and references to firearms were to be regarded with the utmost concern, it was held that the sentences were far too long. The respondent had spent 24 days in custody, which equated to a sentence of seven weeks. This period had, in effect, to be added to the terms of six and nine months—in order to arrive at the true sentence passed by the judge.	Ward L.J. said, at [37], that 14 days was enough for the first two breaches and one month for the others.

NAME OF CASE	NATURE OF CONTEMPT	PENALTIES
Dubarry v Dubarry [2002] EWCA Civ 1808	The defendant was "a dangerous pest". He was addicted to crack cocaine, and had been excluded from the family home by his mother after she had been harassed and terrorised by him. She remained there with her daughter and her granddaughter. He attended frequently, making threats and causing physical damage, and the mother eventually obtained orders under Part 4 of the Family Law Act 1996. He was, after further threatening behaviour, sentenced to two months' imprisonment. After release, he continued to threaten his mother and, in breach of the orders, appeared in the road outside her house. He was given six months but appealed, stating that he was willing to engage in a drug rehabilitation programme.	The sentence was said to be excessive and was halved to one of three months. It was observed, however, that suspension would not have been appropriate becuase of the seriousness of his actions.
The Coca-Cola Company v Aytacli [2003] EWHC 91 Ch D	The respondent had earlier been found liable for counterfeiting the claimant's products. On a committal application, he was held to have breached orders and made false statements in documents verified by statements of truth without any belief in the truth. He sought to allege duress but it was held that there was no evidence to support such a contention. He was also held to be in continuing breach by not revealing the identity of the printer of the offending labels.	He was sentenced to four months' imprisonment.

NAME OF CASE	NATURE OF CONTEMPT	PENALTIES
Re G (Contempt: Committal) [2003] EWCA Civ 489, [2003] 1 W.L.R. 2051	In the course of a contact dispute, G put details on the internet from which it would be possible to identify a carer.	14 days' imprisonment imposed, suspended for six months. (Overturned on appeal through lack of jurisdiction, since there had been neither a contempt in the face, nor a breach of an order.)
Kabushiki Kaisha Sony Computer Entertainment Ball (Gaynor David) [2004] EWHC 1984, Ch	A false statement under CPR 32.14.	Fine of £2,000.
Southwark LBC v Areola, 3 March 2005, Lewison J.	Breach of injunction against noise nuisance. Business already closed, and so no likelihood of repetition.	14 days suspended for six months.
Rollins v Gardener, 16 May 2005	Breach of an order to comply with the requirements of a trustee in bankruptcy.	Three months' imprisonment, suspended for two years.

APPENDIX 4

PHILLIMORE COMMITTEE: ENGLAND AND WALES

On June 8, 1971 Lord Hailsham L.C. appointed a committee under the chairmanship of **20–1**
Lord Justice Phillimore to consider whether any changes were required in the law relating
to contempt of court. They eventually reported in December 1974, in a *Report of the
Committee on Contempt of Court*, Cmnd. 5794, concluding as follows:

GENERAL CONCLUSIONS

(1) The law of contempt in England and Wales and in Scotland is required as a means of—

   (a) maintaining the rights of the citizen to a fair and unimpeded system of justice; and

   (b) protecting the orderly administration of law

(2) The operation of the law of contempt should be confined to circumstances where the achievement of its objectives require the application of a swift and summary procedure.

(3) In essentials the law of contempt, especially as it affects the press, should be the same in England and Wales and in Scotland so far as the procedural differences allow.

(4) The law as it stands contains uncertainties which impede and restrict reasonable freedom of speech. It should be amended and clarified by statute so as to allow as much freedom of speech as is consistent with the achievement of the objective set out in conclusion 1.

(5) One area of uncertainty concerns the period of operation of the law of contempt, as to whether publications are at risk when proceedings are imminent and, if so, what period that expression covers.

RECOMMENDATIONS

(6) Any conduct, including publication as described in recommendation 8, which is intended to pervert or obstruct the course of justice in particular proceedings should continue to be capable of being dealt with as a contempt of court, but only if the proceedings in question have started and have not yet been fully settled or concluded. However, such conduct should normally be dealt with as a criminal

offence unless there are compelling reasons requiring it to be dealt with as a matter of urgency by means of summary contempt procedures.

(7) A publication, as described in the following recommendation should be subject to the law of contempt if it creates a risk of serious prejudice (whether intentionally or not) but this strict liability should not apply to other conduct and should apply to publications only in accordance with recommendations 9–16 below.

(8) For the purposes of recommendations 7 and 9–16 a publication should be defined as any speech, writing, broadcast or other communication, in whatever form, which is addressed to the public at large.

(9) A publication should give rise to strict liability in the law of contempt only if it creates a risk that the course of justice will be seriously impeded or prejudiced. A definition on these lines should be provided by statute.

(10) Where the proceedings in question are criminal, strict liability for publications should only apply—

(i) in England and Wales, when the accused person is charge or a summons served;
(ii) in Scotland, when the person is publicly charged on petition or otherwise or at the first calling in court of a summary complaint

(11) Where the proceedings in question are civil, strict liability for publications should only apply:

(i) in England and Wales, when the case has been set down for trial;
(ii) in Scotland, when proof or jury trial has been ordered;
(iii) in other civil proceedings, the equivalent stage.

(12) Strict liability for publications should cease to operate when a verdict has been returned and sentence pronounced or judgment given, or an equivalent order or decree made or given. If in a jury trial a jury fails to agree, the law should continue to apply until it is clear that no retrial is to be ordered. In the event of a new trial being ordered, the law should again apply from the date when the new trial is ordered.

(13) The defence of innocent publication and distribution provided by section 11 of the Administration of Justice Act 1960 should be retained, with such modifications as will be necessary if our recommendations are implemented, for England and Wales, and should be extended to Scotland.

(14) It should be a defence to an allegation of contempt to show that the publication was a fair and accurate report of legal proceedings in open court published contemporaneously and in good faith.

(15) It should be a defence to an allegation of contempt to show that a publication formed part of a legitimate discussion of matters of general public interest and that it only incidentally and unintentionally created a risk of serious prejudice to particular proceedings.

(16) A defence that a publication is for the public benefit should not be introduced into the law of contempt.

(17) The existing law governing editorial and corporate responsibility for publications should be retained, with necessary modifications in regard to broadcasting and television organisations.

(18) In Scotland, it should continue to be a contempt of court to publish the content of the written pleadings before the record is closed.

(19) It should also be provided by statute that bringing influence or pressure to bear upon a party to proceedings shall not be held to be a contempt unless it amounts to intimidation or unlawful threats to his person, property or reputation.

(20) It should no longer be a contempt to take or threaten reprisals against a witness or juror after the conclusion of legal proceedings with the intention of punishing him for his part in them. Instead, such conduct should be made an indictable offence; with provisions for the victim to recover compensation for any loss or damage he may have suffered.

(21) "Scandalising the court" should cease to be part of the law of contempt. Instead, it should be made an indictable offence both in England and Wales and in Scotland to defame a judge in such a way as to bring the administration of justice into disrepute. Proof that the allegations were true and that publication was for the public benefit should be a defence. In England and Wales this offence should be made a branch of the law of criminal libel.

(22) All distinctions between "civil" and "criminal" contempts in England and Wales should be abolished and in particular:

(a) all rules which confer privilege from process for "civil" as opposed to "criminal" contempt of court should be abolished. Parliament may wish to review the Parliamentary aspects of these rules;
(b) the rule that waiver by an aggrieved party in civil proceedings automatically relieves the contemnor of liability should be abolished. The power of the courts to order that a breach of an order be reported to it should be confirmed;
(c) all committals to prison for contempt should be for fixed terms;
(d) the rules as to execution of process in civil contempt should be brought into line with those for criminal contempt;
(e) exercise of the Royal prerogative of mercy should not be advised in any case of contempt;
(f) the practice of the courts in requiring a breach of a court order to be proved beyond reasonable doubt should be confirmed.

(23) Certain rules of the Supreme Court which provide for committal in the event of breaches of specific court orders should be revoked, and all cases of disobedience which may be dealt with by contempt procedure left to the general provisions of Order 45, r. 5.

(24) The grounds for a motion to commit for disobedience to a court order should wherever possible be set out in detail in the supporting affidavit.

(25) Ex parte committal orders in England and Wales should in every case include a direction that the contemnor is to be brought up before the judge making the order (or another judge if he is not available) at the earliest opportunity.

(26) The right of private individuals to initiate proceedings for contempt both in England and Wales and in Scotland should continue, without prejudice to the powers of either the Attorney-General or Lord Advocate to take proceedings at his own instance should he consider it proper to do so in the public interest.

(27) In all contempt proceedings which a private individual seeks to institute, other than those for the enforcement of a court order made in his favour, he should be required to serve notice of these proceedings on the Attorney-General or Lord Advocate as the case may be.

(28) In cases of contempt in the face of the court:

(a) the judge should always ensure that the contemnor is in no doubt about the nature of the conduct complained of, and give him an opportunity of explaining or denying his conduct, and of calling witnesses;

(b) before any substantial penalty is imposed there should be a short adjournment, with power to remand the contemnor in custody. The judge should have power to obtain a background report on the contemnor, and the contemnor should be entitled to speak in mitigation of sentence;

(c) for the purpose of defending himself and of making a plea in mitigation the contemnor should be entitled to legal representation, and the court should have power to grant legal aid immediately for this purpose where appropriate;

(d) if the contempt also amounts to a criminal offence, the judge should consider referring it to the prosecuting authorities to be dealt with under the ordinary criminal law, and should so refer it in serious cases unless reasons of urgency or convenience require that it be dealt with summarily.

(29) Magistrates in England and Wales should be given power to impose penalties for contempt in the face of the court, subject to the limits proposed in recommendation 37 below.

(30) Bankruptcy Registrars in the High Court in England should be given the same powers as county court judges to punish contempts in the face of the court.

(31) For the purpose of section 41 of the Criminal Justice Act 1925 (prohibition on use of cameras in courts and their precincts) a map or plan should be displayed wherever practicable indicating the boundaries of the precincts of the court.

(32) Regulations should be made governing the unofficial use of tape recorders in court, and of recordings obtained thereby. Breach of the regulations in court should be punishable as a contempt.

(33) There should be created a right of appeal to the Court of Criminal Appeal in Scotland by way of Note of Appeal from a finding of contempt in a criminal trial on indictment.

(34) In superior courts both in England and Scotland the power to fine should remain unlimited but the power to imprison should be limited to a maximum period of two years. All courts should in addition have appropriate powers to deal with mentally disordered offenders.

(35) The powers of judges in county courts to impose penalties for contempt in the face of the court (under s. 157 of the County Courts Act 1959) should be increased to a fine of £150 or three months' imprisonment.

(36) The powers of sheriffs in Scotland to impose penalties for contempt in the face of the court should be limited to a £150 fine or three months' imprisonment.

(37) Both in England and Scotland the powers of magistrates and justices of the peace to impose penalties for contempt in the face of the court should be limited to a £20 fine or seven days' imprisonment.

(38) Powers of both sheriffs and magistrates in Scotland and of magistrates in England to certify more serious cases of contempt in the face of the court to the High Court of Justiciary or the Inner House of the Court of Session and the Divisional Court respectively should be given or confirmed as the case may be.

(39) All sentences of imprisonment for contempt of court in England and Wales should be for fixed terms, but the power to review a case and order release before the full sentence is served should be retained.

(40) Prison regulations in England and Wales should be amended to require notification to be given to the Official Solicitor of prisoners committed for contempt by county courts for fixed terms of less than six weeks, in the same way as for other contempt prisoners.

(41) The machinery for the enforcement of fines in the High Court and Restrictive Practices Court in England and Wales should be replaced by a system on the lines of that provided by the Criminal Justice Act 1967.

Appendix 5

PRACTICE DIRECTIONS

APPENDIX 5A

PRACTICE DIRECTION—COMMITTAL APPLICATIONS

This Practice Direction is Supplemental to RSC, Order 52 (Schedule 1 to the CPR) and CCR, Order 29 (Schedule 2 to the CPR)

GENERAL

1.1 Part I of this practice direction applies to any application for an order for committal of a person to prison for contempt of court (a "committal application"). Part II makes additional provision where the committal application relates to a contempt in the face of the court.

1.2 Where the alleged contempt of court consists of or is based upon disobedience to an order made in a county court or breach of an undertaking given to a county court or consists of an act done in the course of proceedings in a county court, or where in any other way the alleged contempt is a contempt which the county court has power to punish, the committal application may be made in the county court in question.

1.3 In every other case (other than one within Part II of this practice direction), a committal application must be made in the High Court.

1.4 In all cases the Convention rights of those involved should particularly be borne in mind. It should be noted that the burden of proof, having regard to the possibility that a person may be sent to prison, is that the allegation be proved beyond reasonable doubt.

(Section 1 of the Human Rights Act defines "the Convention rights")

PART I

COMMENCEMENT OF COMMITTAL PROCEEDINGS

2.1 A committal application must, subject to paragraph 2.2, be commenced by the issue of a Part 8 claim form (see paragraph 2.5).

2.2 (1) If the committal application is made in existing proceedings it may be commenced by the filing of an application notice in those proceedings.
 (2) An application to commit for breach of an undertaking or order may be commenced by the filing of an application notice in the proceedings in which the undertaking was given or the order was made.
 (3) The application notice must state that the application is made in the proceedings in question and its title and reference number must correspond with the title and reference number of those proceedings.

2.3 If the committal application is one which cannot be made without permission, the claim form or application notice, as the case may be, may not be issued or filed until the requisite permission has been granted.

2.4 If the permission of the court is needed in order to make a committal application—

(1) the permission must be applied for by filing an application notice (see CPR rule 23.2(4));
(2) the application notice need not be served on the respondent;
(3) the date on which and the name of the judge by whom the requisite permission was granted must be stated on the claim form or application notice by which the committal application is commenced;
(4) the permission may only be granted by a judge who, under paragraph 11, would have power to hear the committal application if permission were granted; and
(5) CPR rules 23.9 and 23.10 do not apply.

2.5 If the committal application is commenced by the issue of a claim form, CPR Part 8 shall, subject to the provisions of this practice direction, apply as though references to "claimant" were references to the person making the committal application and references to "defendant" were references to the person against whom the committal application is made (in this practice direction referred to as "the respondent") but:

(1) the claim form together with copies of all written evidence in support must, unless the court otherwise directs, be served personally on the respondent,
(2) the claim form must set out in full the grounds on which the committal application is made and must identify, separately and numerically, each alleged act of contempt including, if known, the date of each alleged act,
(3) an amendment to the claim form can be made with the permission of the court but not otherwise,
(4) CPR rule 8.4 does not apply, and
(5) the claim form must contain a prominent notice stating the possible consequences of the court making a committal order and of the respondent not attending the hearing. A form of notice, which may be used, is annexed to this practice direction.

2.6 If a committal application is commenced by the filing of an application notice, CPR Part 23 shall, subject to the provisions of this practice direction, apply, but:

(1) the application notice together with copies of all written evidence in support must, unless the court otherwise directs, be served personally on the respondent,
(2) the application notice must set out in full the grounds on which the committal application is made and must identify, separately and numerically, each alleged act of contempt including, if known, the date of each of the alleged acts,
(3) an amendment to the application notice can be made with the permission of the court but not otherwise, and
(4) the court may not dispose of the committal application without a hearing.
(5) the application notice must contain a prominent notice stating the possible consequences of the court making a committal order and of the respondent not attending the hearing. A form of notice, which may be used, is annexed to this practice direction.

Written evidence

3.1 Written evidence in support of or in opposition to a committal application must be given by affidavit.

3.2 Written evidence served in support of or in opposition to a committal application must, unless the court otherwise directs, be filed.

3.3 A respondent may give oral evidence at the hearing, whether or not he has filed or served any written evidence. If he does so, he may be cross-examined.

3.4 A respondent may, with the permission of the court, call a witness to give oral evidence at the hearing whether or not the witness has sworn an affidavit.

Case management and date of hearing

4.1 The applicant for the committal order must, when lodging the claim form or application notice with the court for issuing or filing, as the case may be, obtain from the court a date for the hearing of the committal application.

4.2 Unless the court otherwise directs, the hearing date of a committal application shall be not less than 14 days after service of the claim form or of the application notice, as the case may be, on the respondent. The hearing date must be specified in the claim form or application notice or in a Notice of Hearing or Application attached to and served with the claim form or application notice.

4.3 The court may, however, at any time give case management directions, including directions for the service of written evidence by the respondent and written evidence in reply by the applicant, or may hold a directions hearing.

4.4 The court may on the hearing date—

(1) give case management directions with a view to a hearing of the committal application on a future date, or
(2) if the committal application is ready to be heard, proceed forthwith to hear it.

4.5 In dealing with any committal application, the court will have regard to the need for the respondent to have details of the alleged acts of contempt and the opportunity to respond to the committal application.

4.6 The court should also have regard to the need for the respondent to be—

(1) allowed a reasonable time for responding to the committal application including, if necessary, preparing a defence;
(2) made aware of the availability of assistance from the Community Legal Service and how to contact the Service;
(3) given the opportunity, if unrepresented, to obtain legal advice; and
(4) if unable to understand English, allowed to make arrangements, seeking the assistance of the court if necessary, for an interpreter to attend the hearing.

Striking out

5. The court may, on application by the respondent or on its own initiative, strike out a committal application if it appears to the court:

(1) that the committal application and the evidence served in support of it disclose no reasonable ground for alleging that the respondent is guilty of a contempt of court,
(2) that the committal application is an abuse of the court's process or, if made in existing proceedings, is otherwise likely to obstruct the just disposal of those proceedings, or
(3) that there has been a failure to comply with a rule, practice direction or court order.

(CPR Part 3 contains general powers for the management by the court)

MISCELLANEOUS

6. CPR Rules 35.7 (Court's power to direct that evidence is to be given by a single joint expert), 35.8 (Instructions to single joint expert) and 35.9 (Power of court to direct a party to provide information) do not apply to committal applications.

7. An order under CPR rule 18.1 (Order for a party to give additional information) may not be made against a respondent to a committal application.

8. A committal application may not be discontinued without the permission of the court.

9. A committal application should normally be heard in public (see CPR rule 39.2), but if it is heard in private and the court finds the respondent guilty of contempt of court, the judge shall, when next sitting in public, state:

(1) the name of the respondent,
(2) in general terms the nature of the contempt or contempts found proved, and
(3) the penalty (if any) imposed.

10. The court may waive any procedural defect in the commencement or conduct of a committal application if satisfied that no injustice has been caused to the respondent by the defect.

11. Except where under an enactment a Master or district judge has power to make a committal order,[1] a committal order can only be made:

(1) in High Court proceedings, by a High Court Judge or a person authorised to act as such,[2]
(2) in county court proceedings by a Circuit Judge or a person authorised to act or capable by virtue of his office of acting as such.[3]

PART II

12. Where the committal application relates to a contempt in the face of the court the following matters should be given particular attention. Normally, it will be appropriate to defer consideration of the behaviour to allow the respondent time to

---

[1] See, *e.g.* sections 14 and 118 of the County Courts Act 1984.
[2] See section 9(1) of the Supreme Court Act 1981.
[3] See section 5(3) of the County Courts Act 1984.

reflect on what has occurred. The time needed for the following procedures should allow such a period of reflection.

13. A Part 8 claim form and an application notice are not required for Part II, but other provisions of this practice direction should be applied, as necessary, or adapted to the circumstances. In addition the judge should:
    (1) tell the respondent of the possible penalty he faces;
    (2) inform the respondent in detail, and preferably in writing, of the actions and behaviour of the respondent which have given rise to the committal application;
    (3) if he considers that an apology would remove the need for the committal application, tell the respondent;
    (4) have regard to the need for the respondent to be—
        (a) allowed a reasonable time for responding to the committal application, including, if necessary, preparing a defence;
        (b) made aware of the availability of assistance from the Community Legal Service and how to contact the Service;
        (c) given the opportunity, if unrepresented, to obtain legal advice;
        (d) if unable to understand English, allowed to make arrangements, seeking the court's assistance if necessary, for an interpreter to attend the hearing; and
        (e) brought back before the court for the committal application to be heard within a reasonable time.
    (5) allow the respondent an opportunity to—
        (a) apologise to the court;
        (b) explain his actions and behaviour; and,
        (c) if the contempt is proved, to address the court on the penalty to be imposed on him;
    (6) if there is a risk of the appearance of bias, ask another judge to hear the committal application;
    (7) where appropriate, nominate a suitable person to give the respondent the information.

    (It is likely to be appropriate to nominate a person where the effective communication of information by the judge to the respondent was not possible when the incident occurred.)

14. Where the committal application is to be heard by another judge, a written statement by the judge before whom the actions and behaviour of the respondent which have given rise to the committal application took place may be submitted as evidence of those actions and behaviour.

ANNEX

IMPORTANT NOTICE

The Court has power to send you to prison and to fine you if it finds that any of the allegations made against you are true and amount to a contempt of court.
You must attend court on the date shown on the front of this form. It is in your own interest to do so. You should bring with you any witnesses and documents which you think will help you put your side of the case.

21–1 APPENDIX 5A

If you consider the allegations are not true you must tell the court why. If it is established that they are true, you must tell the court of any good reason why they do not amount to a contempt of court, or, if they do, why you should not be punished.

If you need advice you should show this document at once to your solicitor or go to a Citizens' Advice Bureau.

APPENDIX 5B

FAMILY DIVISION—PRACTICE DIRECTION (FAMILY PROCEEDINGS: COMMITTAL)

Practice—Family proceedings—Contempt of court—Committal applications— Proceedings in which committal order may be made—Human Rights Act 1998 (c. 42), Sch. 1, Pt. I, art. 6—CPR Sch. 1, RSC Ord. 32, r.3(2)(a); Ord. 52, r.3; Sch. 2, CCR Ord. 13, r.1(2); Ord. 29—Family Proceedings Rules 1991 (S.I. 1991/1247), r.7.2.

1 As from the date of this direction, the Practice Direction—Committal Applications supplemental to RSC Ord. 52 (CPR Sch. 1) and to CPR Ord. 29 (CPR Sch. 2) (*Civil Procedure 2000*, vol. 1, pp. 1192–1197, 1462–1466, paras scpd52–001 to scpd52–007, ccpd29–001 to ccpd29–006) ("the CPR Direction") shall apply to all applications in family proceedings for an order of committal in the same manner and to the same extent as it applies to proceedings governed by the Civil Procedure Rules 1998 but subject to: (a) the provisions of the Family Proceedings Rules 1991 and the rules applied by those rules namely, the Rules of the Supreme Court and the County Court Rules 1981 in force immediately before 26 April 1999, and (b) the appropriate modifications consequent upon the limited application of the Civil Procedure Rules 1998 to family proceedings.

1.1 In particular, the following modifications apply. (a) Where the alleged contempt is in connection with existing proceedings (other than contempt in the face of the court) or with an order made or an undertaking given in existing proceedings, the committal application shall be made in those proceedings. (b) As required by rule 7.2 of the 1991 Rules committal applications in the High Court are to be made by summons. In county court proceedings applications are to be made in the manner prescribed by CCR Ord. 29. References in the CPR Direction to "claim form" and "application notice" are to be read accordingly. (c) In instances where the CPR Direction requires more information to be provided than is required to be provided under the Rules of the Supreme Court and the County Court Rules, the court will expect the former to be observed. (d) Having regard to the periods specified in RSC Ord. 52, r.3, Ord. 32, r.3(2)(a) and CCR Ord. 13, r.1(2), the time specified in paragraph 4.2 of the CPR Direction shall not apply. Nevertheless, the court will ensure that adequate time is afforded to the respondent for the preparation of his defence. (e) Paragraph 9 of the CPR Direction is to be read with paragraph (3) of each of *Practice Direction (Exclusion Requirement: Procedure on Arrest)* [1998] 1 W.L.R. 475 and *Practice Direction (Domestic Violence: Procedure on Arrest) (No. 2)* [1998] 1 W.L.R. 476 issued on 17 December 1997.

2 In any family proceedings (not falling within paragraph 1 above), in which a committal order may be made, including proceedings for the enforcement of an existing order by way of judgment summons or other process, full effect will be given to the Human Rights Act 1998 and to the rights afforded under that Act. In particular, article 6 of the Convention for the Protection of Human Rights and Fundamental Freedoms (as set out in Part I of Schedule 1 to the Human Rights Act 1998) is fully applicable to such proceedings. Those involved must ensure that in the conduct of the proceedings there is due observance of the Human Rights Act 1998 in the same manner as if the proceedings fell within the CPR Direction.

3 As with all family proceedings, the costs provisions in the Civil Procedure Rules apply to all committal proceedings.

4   Issued with the approval and concurrence of the Lord Chancellor.

DAME ELIZABETH BUTLER-SLOSS P.

16 March 2001

APPENDIX 5C

QUEEN'S BENCH DIVISION

PRACTICE DIRECTION (MAGISTRATES' COURTS: CONTEMPT)

54. Contempt in the face of the magistrates' court

General

54.1 Section 12 of the Contempt of Court Act 1981 gives magistrates' courts the power to detain, until the court rises, someone, whether a defendant or another person present in court, who wilfully insults anyone specified in section 12 or who interrupts proceedings. In any such case, the court may order any officer of the court, or any constable, to take the offender into custody and detain him until the rising of the court; and the court may, if it thinks fit, commit the offender to custody for a specified period not exceeding one month or impose a fine not exceeding level 4 on the standard scale or both. This power can be used to stop disruption of their proceedings. Detention is until the person can be conveniently dealt with without disruption of the proceedings. Prior to the court using the power the offender should be warned to desist or face the prospect of being detained.

54.2 Magistrates' courts also have the power to commit to custody any person attending or brought before a magistrates' court who refuses without just cause to be sworn or to give evidence under section 97(4) of the Magistrates' Courts Act 1980, until the expiration of such period not exceeding one month as may be specified in the warrant or until he sooner gives evidence or produces the document or thing, or impose on him a fine not exceeding £2,500, or both.

54.3 In the exercise of any of these powers, as soon as is practical, and in any event prior to an offender being proceeded against, an offender should be told of the conduct which it is alleged to constitute his offending in clear terms. When making an order under section 12 the justices should state their findings of fact as to the contempt.

54.4 Exceptional situations require exceptional treatment. While this direction deals with the generality of situations, there will be a minority of situations where the application of the direction will not be consistent with achieving justice in the special circumstances of the particular case. Where this is the situation, the compliance with the direction should be modified so far as is necessary so as to accord with the interests of justice.

54.5 The power to bind persons over to be of good behaviour in respect of their conduct in court should cease to be exercised.

Contempt consisting of wilfully insulting anyone specified in section 12 or interrupting proceedings

54.6 In the case of someone who wilfully insults anyone specified in section 12 or interrupts proceedings, if an offender expresses a willingness to apologise for his misconduct, he should be brought back before the court at the earliest convenient moment in order to make the apology and to give undertakings to the court to refrain from further misbehaviour.

54.7 In the majority of cases, an apology and a promise as to future conduct should be sufficient for justices to order an offender's release. However, there are likely to be certain cases where the nature and seriousness of the misconduct requires the justices to consider using their powers under section 12(2) of the Contempt of Court Act 1981 either to fine or to order the offender's committal to custody.

Where an offender is detained for contempt of court

54.8 Anyone detained under either of the provisions in paragraph 54.1 or 54.2 should be seen by the duty solicitor or another legal representative and be represented in proceedings if they so wish. Public funding should generally be granted to cover representation. The offender must be afforded adequate time and facilities in order to prepare his case. The matter should be resolved the same day if at all possible.

54.9 The offender should be brought back before the court before the justices conclude their daily business. The justices should ensure that he understands the nature of the proceedings, including his opportunity to apologise or give evidence and the alternative of them exercising their powers.

54.10 Having heard from the offender's solicitor, the justices should decide whether to take further action.

Sentencing of an offender who admits being in contempt

54.11 If an offence of contempt is admitted the justices should consider whether they are able to proceed on the day or whether to adjourn to allow further reflection. The matter should be dealt with on the same day if at all possible. If the justices are of the view to adjourn they should generally grant the offender bail unless one or more of the exceptions to the right to bail in the Bail Act 1976 are made out.

54.12 When they come to sentence the offender where the offence has been admitted, the justices should first ask the offender if he has any objection to them dealing with the matter. If there is any objection to the justices dealing with the matter a differently constituted panel should hear the proceedings. If the offender's conduct was directed to the justices, it will not be appropriate for the same bench to deal with the matter.

54.13 The justices should consider whether an order for the offender's discharge is appropriate, taking into account any time spent on remand, whether the offence was admitted and the seriousness of the contempt. Any period of committal should be for the shortest time commensurate with the interests of preserving good order in the administration of justice.

Trial of the issue where the conempt is not admitted

54.14 Where the contempt is not admitted the justices' powers are limited to making arrangements for a trial to take place. They should not, at this stage make findings against the offender.

54.15 In the case of a contested contempt the trial should take place at the earliest opportunity and should be before a bench of justices other than those before whom alleged contempt took place. If a trial of the issue can take place on the day such arrangements should be made taking into account the offender's rights under article 6 of the European Convention for the Protection of Human Rights and Fundamental Freedoms (as set out in Part I of Schedule 1 to the Human Rights Act 1998). If the trial cannot take place that day the justices should again bail the offender unless there are grounds under the Bail Act 1976 to remand him in custody.

54.16 The offender is entitled to call and examine witnesses where evidence is relevant. If the offender is found by the court to have committed contempt the court should again consider first whether an order for his discharge from custody is sufficient to bring proceedings to an end. The justices should also allow the offender a further opportunity to apologise for his contempt or to make representations. If the justices are of the view that they must exercise their powers to commit to custody under section 12(2) of the 1981 Act, they must take into account any time spent on remand and the nature and seriousness of the contempt. Any period of committal should be for the shortest period of time commensurate with the interests of preserving good order in the administration of justice.

INDEX

Abuse of process
abuse of privilege, 11–64—11–65
confidentiality
  criminal proceedings, in, 11–82—11–87
  prosecution material, 11–82
  statutory duty, 11–82
court documents
  destruction, of, 11–84
  evidential material, 11–87
  improper access, 11–79—11–80
  judgments, access to, 11–81
  leaked documents, 11–85
fair trial, and, 2–77
  and see **Fair trial**
false case
  false facts, 11–51, 11–54, 11–55
  fictitious cause, 11–52
  putting forward, 11–51—11–53
false disclosure, 11–58
false statements, 11–56—11–57
forgery
  counsel's name, 11–50
  court documents, 11–48
  statements of case, 11–50
improper collusion, 11–61—11–63
media publicity, and, 2–76
mens rea, 11–86
professional misconduct, 11–66
  see also **Professional advocates**
strict liability, and, 4–148
vexatious claims, 11–59—11–60

Access to justice
legal representation, 15–108, 15–110, 15–113, 15–114
statutory provisions, 15–110—15–111

Active proceedings
appellate proceedings, 4–178, 4–179, 4–182
common law rules, 5–67, 5–69, 5–70
criminal proceedings, 4–177
gagging writs, 4–181
imminence
  meaning, 5–87—5–89
  test, of, 5–90—5–95
  uncertainties, as to, 5–90, 5–92
intention to prejudice, 5–72, 5–74
jury trials, 4–181
non-criminal proceedings, 4–178

Active proceedings—*cont.*
press freedom, uncertainty, 5–11
proceedings
  active, 5–75
  commenced, 5–81, 5–82, 5–85, 5–86
  course of justice, 5–83, 5–93
  imminent, 5–69, 5–77, 5–85, 5–86
  in existence, 5–75
  pending, 5–69, 5–77, 5–78, 5–81, 5–82
  preliminary, 5–79
provisions determining, 4–174, 4–176
reporting restrictions, 5–67
starting point, 4–180
statutory definition, 5–67, 5–70
strict liability, and, 4–175, 4–180, 5–69
  and see **Strict liability**
summary procedures, 5–73
uncertainty, relating to, 5–67—5–76

Actus reus **(common law contempt)**
active proceedings
  see **Active proceedings**
case decisions, 5–45—5–60
criticising litigants, 5–116—5–119
degree of prejudice
  see **Prejudice**
dormant civil litigation, 5–64—5–66
human rights, and, 5–22, 5–23
identity issues, 5–112—5–113
inadmissible evidence, 5–114—5–115
interference
  administration of justice, 5–7, 5–23, 5–24, 5–28, 5–34, 5–35, 5–37, 5–70
  calculated acts, 5–28
  extraneous advocacy, 5–25
  fair trial, with, 5–31, 5–33
  real risk, 5–37, 5–38
  remote possibility, 5–33
  serious prejudice, 5–7
  serious risk, 5–37, 5–38
  statutory threshold, 5–7
  strict liability rule, 5–8
  substantial, 5–30, 5–31
  tendency to interfere, 5–39
pre-trial prejudice, examples of, 5–104, 5–107
proceedings
  active, 5–67—5–76

[1371]

INDEX

***Actus reus* (common law contempt)**—*cont.*
proceedings—*cont.*
  imminent, 5–12, 5–74, 5–163, 5–167
  "on the cards", 5–12, 5–96—5–99
  pending, 5–12, 5–62
  predicting, 5–105
publication
  confessions, 5–109
  previous convictions, 5–104, 5–115
publication contempt
  common law test, 5–5
  degree of risk, 5–10, 5–11
  intentional conduct, 5–7
  lesser prejudice, 5–12, 5–18
  nature, of, 5–8
  prior to appeal, 5–12, 5–100—5–103
  private publication, 5–12, 5–13
  risk of prejudice, 5–6, 5–8
  scope, 5–9
  serious prejudice, 5–6, 5–8, 5–9, 5–10, 5–18, 5–26
statements
  disparaging, 5–110
  guilt, 5–106
  innocence, 5–106
  prejudicial, 5–107, 5–108, 5–111
technical contempt
  see **Technical contempt**
Administration of justice
see also **Interference with administration of justice**
adverse consequences, for, 5–200
impeding, 5–200
interference
  actus reus, 5–24, 5–28, 5–34, 5–35, 5–37
  circumstances, leading to, 2–189, 5–198
  statutory provisions, 4–16, 4–51
    see also **Contempt of Court Act (1981)**
  prejudicing, 5–200
  threats to, 3–54, 3–69, 3–92
Anonymity
granting, of, 7–86, 7–98, 7–104
human rights considerations, 7–106—7–108
"psychiatric interests", 7–96, 7–105
rightly withheld, 7–96, 7–97, 7–99, 7–102
sexual offences, 7–97, 7–105, 8–17, 8–18, 8–19, 8–24
Anti-social behaviour orders (ASBOs)
breach of, 8–46
human rights, and, 8–44
nature, of, 8–44
publicity, relating to, 8–42—8–44, 8–46
statutory provisions, 8–42, 8–45
Appeals
certiorari, and, 3–132
Court of Appeal, to, 3–88, 3–131, 3–133, 3–135, 15–90–15–93
criminal cause or matter, 3–136—3–137

Appeals—*cont.*
criminal contempt, for, 3–134—3–136, 3–139
errors, on the face, 3–132
evidence
  fresh evidence, 15–100
  unsafe, 3–140
habeas corpus, and, 3–132, 3–137
High Court, to, 13–125—13–132
House of Lords, 15–103—15–106
penalties, against, 13–119
permission, for, 13–119, 13–120, 15–88
right of appeal, 13–118, 13–120, 13–122, 15–88—15–89
statutory provisions, 3–131
Appellate jurisdiction
active proceedings, 4–178, 4–179, 4–182
Administration of Justice Act (1960)
  appeal without leave, 13–119
  committal orders, 13–120
  criminal contempt, 13–119
  double jeopardy, 13–119
  orders, meaning of, 13–123
  penalties, appeal against, 13–119
  permission for appeal, 13–120
  right to appeal, 13–118, 13–120, 13–122
  written evidence, 13–119
appellate tribunals, 13–133
bail pending appeal, 13–134
Civil Procedure Rules (CPR), 13–120, 13–121
district judges, 13–121
High Court, 13–125—13–132
reversals, 13–134
variations, 13–134
Arbitration proceedings
reporting, of, 7–21—7–25
Arrest powers
family proceedings
  adjournment, 14–73, 14–74, 14–86
  bail provisions, 14–85
  co-habitees, 14–76
  discretionary powers, 14–77, 14–79, 14–80
  domestic violence, 14–71, 14–75—14–77, 14–79, 14–96
  enforcement difficulties, 14–72
  hearings, 14–73
  mandatory powers, 14–77
  non-molestation order, 14–74, 14–76—14–78, 14–81, 14–86, 14–96
  practice directions, 14–86
  remand powers, 14–88
  undertakings, 14–77
    and see **Family proceedings**
housing matters
  annoyance, causing, 14–91, 14–94
  anti-social behaviour, 14–89, 14–90, 14–92
  nuisance, causing, 14,94

INDEX

Arrest powers—*cont.*
  housing matters—*cont.*
    unlawful use, 14–95
Assault
  actions, for, 1–14
  court officers, on, 13–84—13–87
  face of court contempt, 10–93—10–96
    and see **Face of court contempt**
  judges, on, 11–173
  judicial powers, 13–85
  sexual assaults, 8–18
Attempted contempt, 11–14
Attorney-General
  accountability, 2–215
  civil contempt, and, 2–200, 12–6
  common law jurisdiction, 4–186, 4–187
  complainants, 2–204
  criminal contempt, and, 15–1
  decision to proceed, 2–204, 2–212—2–214, 2–219
  initiating proceedings, 2–199, 2–201, 4–183, 4–184, 4–187, 15–1, 15–2, 16–320
  injunction proceedings, 2–208
  judicial review, 2–212, 2–214—2–216
  public interest, and, 2–200, 2–209, 6–27, 9–239, 9–240, 9–243, 9–244, 12–6
  quia timet injunctions, 6–22, 6–27
    and see ***Quia timet*** **injunctions**
  receiving complaints, 2–200, 2–201
  referral, to, 3–170, 13–22
  refusal to give reasons, 2–217, 2–218
  statutory provisions, concerning, 4–183, 4–185—4–187
  strict liability rule, 2–203, 2–205, 2–206, 4–183
Autrefois acquit
  amended proceedings, 3–215
  civil contempt, in, 3–217
  continuing obligations, 3–222
  continuing offences, 3–220
  double jeopardy, 3–209, 3–215
  ex parte orders, and, 3–210
  fresh proceedings, 3–213—3–214
  jurisdiction, 3–210, 3–216
  principle applied, 3–209, 3–216, 3–218, 3–220
  re-committal, 3–209
  warrant for committal, 3–211
Autrefois convict
  principle applied, 3–209, 3–212, 3–218, 3–220

Bail, 13–134, 14–85
Breach of orders
  administration of justice, and, 3–96—3–98
  answering questions, 3–108—3–111
  civil proceedings, and, 3–105—3–106
  common law, 3–99—3–104

Breach of orders—*cont.*
  compliance
    committal orders, 12–124, 12–131, 12–132
    no time specified, 12–130
    sequestration, 12–124—12–125
    time specified, for, 12–124, 12–127, 12–128, 12–137
  criminal proceedings, and, 3–105
  defiance in face of court, 3–112, 3–114
  disobedience
    companies, by, 12–125
    delivery of goods, 12–135
    positive orders, 12–124, 12–127
    possession of land, 12–133—12–134
  errors
    judicial error, 12–139
    orders wrongly obtained, 12–139—12–143
    stay of order, 12–139—12–140
  freezing orders (*Mareva*)
    see **Freezing orders (*Mareva*)**
  incidental contempt, 3–122—3–114
  mens rea, 7–91—7–92
  non-parties, by, 3–105
  party, by, 3–106, 3–124
  positive orders
    companies, involving, 12–125
    costs, 12–126
    disobedience, 12–124, 12–127
    enforcement measures, 12–124—12–126
  postponement orders
    ipso facto contempt, 7–124, 7–132—7–136
    mens rea, 7–124, 7–203—7–227
    powers, relating to, 7–124, 7–228—7–234
    and see **Postponement orders**
  prohibitive orders
    committal orders, 12–136
    compliance, with, 12–137
    enforcement, 12–138
    sequestration, 12–136, 12–138
  reporting proceedings, 3–107, 3–95—3–97
  risk of prejudice, 7–91
  search and seizure orders (*Anton Piller*)
    see **Search and seizure orders (*Anton Piller*)**
  specific intention, 7–93
  statutory provisions, 7,87
  wards of court, and, 3–115—3–118
  withholding names, 3–95—3–97
Breach of undertaking
  see also **Undertakings**
  aiding and abetting, 12–198
  company directors, 12–199
  effect, 12–182, 12–184, 12–200
  injunctions, and, 12–182, 12–200
  nature, of, 12–182
  non-molestation orders, 12–186
  power of arrest, and, 14–77, 14–96

INDEX

Breach of undertaking—*cont.*
punishment, 12–188
safeguards
careful drafting, 12–192
duty explained, 12–191
proof of breach, 12–190
service of order, 12–191
solicitors
see **Solicitors**
strangers
Lord Eldon's principle, 12–241—12–245
proceedings, involving, 12–198, 12–240, 12–246—12–247

Cameras in court, 10–201—10–203
Chambers hearings
Civil Procedure Rules (CPR), 7–53—7–54
disclosure, 7–51
exclusion, from, 7–47—7–50
in camera proceedings, distinguished, 7–41, 7–46
interlocutory proceedings, 7–52
meaning, 7–42
private nature, 7–43, 7–51
public access, 7–43, 7–51
report, of, 7–44, 7–45, 7–151
Cheque-book journalism
active proceedings, involving, 11–269
contingent payments, 11–264
criminal trials, and, 11–266
effect, of, 11–264
mens rea, 11–264, 11–271
Phillimore Committee, 11–265
Press Complaints Commission, 11–266
reforms, concerning, 1–172, 11–272—11–275
victims, payment to, 11–270
witness payments, 11–266—11–268
Children
see also **Parens patriae jurisdiction**
child, meaning of, 8–94
confidentiality, 6–76—6–77
human rights protection, 6–76
identity, protection of, 8–55
media interviews, 6–75, 6–78, 6–79
privacy rights, 6–76, 6–87, 6–92, 6–105, 8–126, 8–127
removal, of, 14–130
reporting restrictions, 6–76
return, of, 14–131
welfare, of, 6–64, 6–65, 6–81, 6–82, 6–87, 6–89, 6–90, 6–102
Children and young persons
adult proceedings, in, 8–50
anti-social behaviour orders (ASBOs)
see **Anti-social behaviour orders (ASBOs)**
Children and Young Persons Act (1933)
judicial decisions, 8–60

Children and young persons—*cont.*
Children and Young Persons Act (1933)—*cont.*
provisions, of, 8–25
clearing the court, 8–71
criminal proceedings
transfers for trial, 8–91—8–94
family proceedings
newspaper reports, 8–80—8–82
reporting restrictions, 8–76—8–80
identity
jigsaw identification, 8–72—8–73
judicial discretion, 8–57, 8–62—8–64
offenders, 8–55, 8–56
protection, 8–55, 8–56
public interest considerations, 8–64—8–66
sex offences, 8–73
inherent jurisdiction, 8–51—8–52
order making procedure, 8–68—8–70
privacy
human rights, 8–83
statutory provisions, 8–83—8–85
reporting restrictions
challenges, to, 8–59
lifting, of, 8–32—8–38
provisions governing, 8–27—8–31, 8–47, 8–49
relevant proceedings, 8–39—8–41
witnesses, 8–74—8–75, 8–192—8–194
and see **Witnesses**
Youth Court proceedings, 8–26, 8–48
Youth Justice and Criminal Evidence Act (1999), 8–53—8–54
Civil contempt
administration of justice, and, 3–7, 3–79
aiding and abetting, 3–121—3–122
Attorney-General, role of, 12–6
autrefois acquit, 3–39
autrefois convict, 3–39
breach of orders
see **Breach of orders**
breach of undertaking, 3–69, 3–80
and see **Breach of undertaking**
burden of proof, 12–97
Civil Procedure Rules (CPR), 12–96—12–97
coercion, 3–12, 3–22, 3–76, 3–78
committal proceedings
see **Committal proceedings**
criminal characteristics, 3–21
criminal safeguards
human rights, 3–75
imprisonment, 3–73
joint hearings, 3–74
legal representation, 3–74
standard of proof, 3–74
criminal sanctions, 3–5
definition, 12–4
deterrent, as, 3–78
development, 1–41, 1–47—1–50

[1374]

INDEX

Civil contempt—*cont.*
  disobedience, 3–7, 3–8, 3–10, 3–11,
    3–20—3–69
  drafting of orders
    alternative construction, 12–54
    clarification, 12–59—12–63
    clarity, 12–48—12–50, 12–54, 12–55,
      12–58
    misunderstandings, over, 12–50—12–51
  duress, 3–75
  family proceedings
    enforcing compliance, 12–32
    exhaustion of remedies, 12–32
  imprisonment, 3–22, 14–7, 14–24
  injunctions, and, 3–12, 3–15, 3–17, 12–38
    and see **Injunctions**
  jurisdiction
    arbitrary nature, 12–15—12–17, 12–33
    committal proceedings, 12–18, 12–22
    criminal proceedings, 12–8—12–14
    double punishment, avoiding, 12–11
    family proceedings, 12–24—12–32
    sequestration, 12–18—12–20,
      12–96—12–97
  liability
    agents, 12–104—12–108
    corporate, 12–101—12–103
    directors, 12–109—12–115
    ministers of the crown, 12–123
    partnerships, 12–119
    servants, 12–104—12–108
    solicitors, 12–122
    trade unions, 12–116—12–117
    unincorporated bodies, 12–118—12–122
    vicarious, 12–99—12–100, 12–118
  mens rea
    acting knowingly, 12–81—12–85
    corporate liability, 12–91—12–92
    deliberate acts, 12–91
    duress, 12–94
    intentional conduct, 12–81,
      12–88—12–90, 12–98
    mental incapacity, 12–83
    mitigation, 12–94
    service of order, 12–81
    strict liability, 12–82, 12–86, 12–87
    traditional approach, 12–80—12–87
    wilful disobedience, 12–96—12–98
  misdemeanour, as, 3–78—3–80, 3–82, 3–83,
    12–44
  nature, of, 3–1, 3–12, 3–69, 3–80, 3–119,
    12–1—12–4
  penalties, 12–97, 19–2
  private injury, 3–18
  private orders, 3–19
  procedure, 12–33, 12–39, 12–96—12–97
  procedure, involving, 3–119
  proceedings
    mitigation, 3–5
    nature, of, 12–7

Civil contempt—*cont.*
  proceedings—*cont.*
    proving duress, 3–5
    quasi-criminal, 3–4
  public and private aspects, 12–5
  public injury, 3–18
  public interest, and, 3–69, 12–5, 12–6
  public policy, 3–70
  punishment, 3–12, 3–13, 3–39, 3–76, 3–79
  punitive element, 3–24
  quasi-criminal, 3–4, 3–71
  remedial function, 3–76, 3–77
  risk of prejudice, 12–10
  safeguards
    service requirements, 12–35—12–42
    standard of proof, 12–43
  service
    company service, 12–40
    judgment, of, 12–35, 12–37, 12–39
    order, of, 12–35—12–39
    personal service, 12–35, 12–37, 12–39
  standard of proof
    criminal standard, 12–43, 12–44,
      12–45—12–47, 12–52, 12–53
  summary process, 3–72, 3–75
    and see **Summary process**
  unintentional acts, 12–96
Civil Procedure Rules (CPR)
  appellate jurisdiction, and, 13–120—13–121
  chambers hearings, 7–53—7–54
  civil contempt, and, 12 96—12–97
  Crown Court, relevance to, 13–25, 13–27
  disclosure of information, 3–206
  failure to attend court, 11–91—11–93
  sequestration, and, 15–78
  undertakings
    applied, to, 12–219, 12–224—12–227
    libel proceedings, 12–228—12–236
Commonwealth jurisdictions
  civil liberties, 1–143
  development, in, 1–142, 2–71, 2–99, 2–102,
    2–110, 4–62—4–69, 5–260,
    10–11—10–28, 12–76
  freedom of information, 1–144
Committal proceedings
  abridgments, 12–41
  ambiguous orders, 12–48, 12–56
  amendments, 12–41
  applications
    application notice, 15–12, 15–19
    personal service, 15–13—15–14
    supporting evidence, 15–12, 15–19
  attachment, distinguished, 15–6—15–8
  avoiding, 12–22
  committal for trial, 8–87—8–94
  committal orders
    contents, 15–67—15–69
    defective orders, 15–70—15–76
    effect, 15–48—15–50
    form, of, 15–45—15–47

[1375]

INDEX

Committal proceedings—*cont.*
Company directors, 12–109
County court
  see **County court**
court orders
  see **Court orders**
criminal contempt
  initiating proceedings, 15–1—15–3
  jurisdiction, 15–4, 15–9
Divisional Court applications
  form, of, 15–9
  grounds, 15–9
  permission, for, 15–9—15–10
  personal service, 15–11
  supporting affidavit, 15–9
  supporting statements, 15–9
  see also **Divisional Court**
evidence
  no case to answer, 15–43
  respondent's election, 15–43—15–44
Family Division applications
  burden of proof, 5–18
  hearing in private, 15–15—15–16
  infants, involving, 15–16
  mental patients, 15–16
  summons, by, 15–15, 15–18
family proceedings, 12–24—12–32
  and see **Family proceedings**
fresh evidence, 12–65
further applications, 12–42
non-molestation orders, 12–56—12–57
penal notice
  corporate bodies, and, 15–26
  need, for, 15–24
  wording, 15–25—15–26
practice direction, 21–1
presence of contemnor, 14–59
procedural safeguards
  adjournments, 15–40
  evidential rules, 15–35, 15–36, 15–39, 15–40
  extent, of, 15–32
  human rights, 15–41—15–42
  legal representation, 15–41
  meeting charges, 15–37
sanctions, relating to, 12–23, 14–1
service of notice, 12–34
severance, 12–64
sitting in private, 15–28—15–31
undertakings, enforcement of, 15–27
use of, 12–18
vague orders, 12–48
Common law contempt
actus reus, 4–90, 5–4, 5–5
  and see **Actus reus (common law contempt)**
mens rea, 4–90, 5–1, 5–3, 5–7
  and see **Mens rea (common law contempt)**

Common law contempt—*cont.*
publication contempt
  active proceedings, 5–67—5–76
  actus reus, 1–130, 5–5—5–9
  administration of justice, and, 1–131
  Contempt of Court Act (1981), 5–1
  defences, 5–201—5–203
  intentional, 1–128, 1–129
  media publications, 5–1
  press freedom, 5–11
  technical contempt, 5–10
  uncertainties, concerning, 1–128, 5–1
  and see **Publication contempt**
Common law interference
arrest cases, and, 11–168—11–172
mens rea
  knowledge of proceedings, 11–160
  motive, 11–161—11–167
  underlying policy, 11–155—11–159
Companies
common law contempt, 4–207
criminal law, and, 4–209
doctrine of identification, 4–209—4–211
gross negligence, 4–211
liability
  attribution rules, 4–204—4–206, 4–210
  directors, 12–109, 15–24
  knowledge of proceedings, 4–207
  necessary intent, 4–207
  vicarious liability, 4–197, 4–204, 4–209
Contempt
administration of justice, and, 3–54, 3–69
attempted contempt, 11–14
categories, 2–3
criminal law, and, 2–13, 2–16
criminal nature, 3–54
evidential safeguards, 3–84
historical background
  see **Historical background**
juridical nature, 3–54
meaning, 2–10, 2–11
misdemeanour, as, 3–67—3–68, 3–78—3–80, 3–82, 3–83, 12–44
procedural safeguards, 3–84
public interest, and, 3–55
  and see **Public interest**
sui generis, 3–85—3–87
Contempt of Court Act 1981
actus reus, 4–4
administration of justice, interference with, 4–16, 4–51
anonymity
  see **Anonymity**
background influences
  administration of justice, 1–110, 1–111
  Attorney-General v Times Newspapers Ltd, 1–87—1–90, 1–92, 1–93, 1–98
  certainty, need for, 1–97, 1–98
  classification, under, 3–92
  freedom of speech, 1–110

[1376]

INDEX

Contempt of Court Act 1981—*cont.*
background influences—*cont.*
  human rights, 1–104, 1–105, 1–108,
    1–114, 1–132
  judicial authority, 1–106—1–108, 1–112
  judicial impartiality, 1–106—1–108
  Phillimore Committee, 1–86
  pre-judgment, 1–89, 1–92, 1–93, 1–98,
    1–112, 1–113
  pressurising litigants, 1–94—1–95
  protection of morals, 1–109
  public interest, 1–96, 1–112, 1–113
  risk of prejudice, 1–89
  social need, 1–110
  Sunday Times v United Kingdom,
    1–104—1–113
  technical contempt, 1–98
  trial by newspaper, 1–94, 1–113, 2–74
breach of orders
  see **Breach of orders**
civil contempt, 1–124—1–125
  and see **Civil contempt**
common law contempt, and, 1–128, 5–1
conflicting interests, under, 5–6
court
  function, 4–19
  inquiries, 4–22, 4–23
  judicial powers, 4–17—4–20
  jurisdiction, 4–21, 4–22
  meaning, 4–17, 4–18
crime prevention, 1–127, 3–3
criminal offences, and, 13–110
defences, 4–4, 4–321, 4–323, 4–335, 4–366
fair trial, 2–42, 2–43
  and see **Fair trial**
freedom of speech, and, 2–33,
  4–324—4–329
  and see **Freedom of speech**
impeding, under, 4–97—4–99, 4–103,
  4–106, 4–107, 4–151
imprisonment, and, 14–8, 16–420, 16–423,
  16–424
  and see **Imprisonment**
internet publications, 4–27, 4–28
journalists' sources
  common law, and, 9–64—9–66
  disclosure, 9–67, 9–70, 9–71, 9–75, 9–76
  factual enquiry, 9–68, 9–70
  information, 9–64—9–65, 9–97
  interests of justice, 9–55—9–57, 9–69
  internet operators, 9–58
  judicial discretion, 9–66, 9–67, 9–72,
    9–73, 9–77, 9–98
  photographs, 9–63
  prevention of crime, 9–182 — 9–192
  protection, 1–119, 1–127, 9–52—9–53
  publication, 9–54, 9–59, 9–60—9–62
  and see **Journalists' sources**
judicial assessment, 1–122
judicial consideration, 1–126

Contempt of Court Act 1981—*cont.*
jury deliberations, 1–119, 3–93, 11–358
liability for publication
  see **Liability for publication**
litigants, criticising, 4–330
mental illness reports, 14–69
postponement orders
  see **Postponement orders**
prejudice
  serious risk, 4–53, 4–96, 4–151
  substantial risk, 4–53, 4–54—4–57
provisions, of, 17–1
public interest, 2–31, 2–42, 2–43
publication contempt, 4–4
  and see **Publication contempt**
publication of names, 1–120
purposes, 1–115
re-publication, 4–29, 4–30, 4–50
restriction orders
  see **Restriction orders**
sanctions, under, 3–177
  see also **Sanctions and remedies**
saving provisions, 4–321—4–322
section of public
  communication, to, 4–38, 4–39, 4–47,
    4–48, 4–50
  comparable legislation, 4–41, 4–42, 4–44
  meaning, 4–36, 4–38, 4–41, 4–50
  numbers involved, 4–50
  private clubs, 4–43, 4–45, 4–46
  public at large, 4–36
  publication, to, 4–36
  statutory interpretation, 4–41, 4–45
serious prejudice test, 1–127
statute, terms, 17–1
strict liability rule
  application, 3–92, 3–97, 4–90
  criminal contempt, 1–116, 3–92, 3–97
  defence, 4–247, 4–248, 4–250, 4–260
  human rights, 4–91
  "included" publications, 4–31, 4–32
  intent, and, 4–1, 4–40, 4–51
  limits on, 1–118, 1–119
  meaning, 4–1
  outbursts in court, 4–37
  press freedom, 2–40
  publication, and, 4–34—4–38, 4–41
  restrictions, on, 4–52, 4–56
  wards of court, 1–116
tape recorders, use of, 1–119, 3–94
terminology
  court, meaning of, 4–17, 4–18
  "includes", meaning of, 4–31, 4–32
  legal proceedings, 4–17
  "particular legal proceedings", 4–16
  "public at large", 4–34—4–35
  publication, meaning of, 4–24—4–26
  "section of public", 4–36, 4–38, 4–41
wilful insults, 13–106
wilful interruptions, 13–106

INDEX

Contempt of Court Act 1981—*cont.*
  young persons, 13–111, 14–65
Coroner's Court
  attendance, 11–144, 14–107
  jurisdiction, 13–102
  powers, 13–100, 13–102
  strict liability, in, 13–101
Costs
  detailed assessment (taxation), 14–135
  judicial discretion, 14–136
  payment, of, 7–274, 14–135
  successful appeal, on, 7–270, 14–137
  third parties, 14–139—14–141
County court
  assaults on officers, 13–84—13–87
  committal proceedings
    arrest and detention, 15–54—15–55
    Civil Procedure Rules (CPR), 15–51—15–52, 15–77
    dispensing with service, 15–57—15–62
    family law matters, 15–56
    immediate detention, 15–53—15–54
    police involvement, 15–54
    procedural rules, 15–64—15–66
    safeguards, 15–64—15–66
    service of order, 15–65
    statutory jurisdiction, 15–77
  imprisonment powers, 14–24—14–27
    see also **Imprisonment**
  jurisdiction
    ancillary, 14–25—14–26
    companies, involving, 13–97
    inherent, 13–80
    injunctions, 13–92—13–94
    seized goods, 13–88—13–89
    statutory, 13–80
  non-attendance, 13–99
  sequestration powers, 14–116
    see also **Sequestration**
  solicitors' undertakings, 13–98
    see also **Solicitors**
  status, 13–80
  wilful insults, 13–90, 13–91
  wilful interruptions, 13–90
  witnesses, in, 13–95—13–96
    and see **Witnesses**
Court of Appeal
  appeals procedure, 15–97
  bail, granting of, 15–101—15–102
  Civil Procedure Rules (CPR), 15–97—15–98
  Criminal Division, 15–96
  fresh evidence, 15–100
  jurisdiction, 13–13—13–15
    and see **Jurisdiction**
  permission to appeal, 15–94—15–95
  right of appeal, 3–88, 3–131, 3–133, 3–135, 15–90—15–93
Court of Chancery
  civil contempt, 1–47—1–50
    and see **Civil contempt**

Court of Chancery—*cont.*
  criminal contempt, 1–42—1–46
    and see **Criminal contempt**
  interrogatories, 1–44, 1–53
  jurisdiction, 1–47, 1–51
  penalties, 1–47
  procedure, 1–48, 1–50
  strict liability, 1–64
    and see **Strict liability**
  summary process, 1–41, 1–47, 1–51—1–56
  writ of attachment, 1–41, 1–47, 1–50
Court officers
  Admiralty Marshals, 11–325
  assaults, on, 11–313, 13–84—13–87
  interference
    common law, at, 11–311, 11–312, 11–316
    execution of duty, 11–311
  liquidators, 11–323
  obstruction
    court officers, 11–315
    enforcement officers, 11–315
  privilege, and, 3–147—3–153
  process servers, 11–317
  receivers, 11–318—11–321, 11–324
  sequestrators, 11–318, 11–323, 11–324
  Sheriffs, 11–326—11–330
  statutory provisions
    assaults, 11–313
    insults, 11–314
Court orders
  anticipated contempt, 6–1, 6–29
  breaches of,
    see **Breaches of**
  disobedience, to, 3–119, 3–124
  enforcement, 3–120
  mandatory orders, 15–22
  non-parties named, 3–127—3–129
  parens patriae jurisdiction
    see **Parens patriae jurisdiction**
  penal notice, 15–24
  quia timet injunctions
    see **Quia timet injunctions**
  service
    dispensing, with, 15–22—15–23
    proof of service, 15–20
  subverting
    see **Subverting court orders**
  third parties, 3–119, 3–121, 3–125, 15–21
Court proceedings
  chambers hearings
    see **Chambers hearings**
  Criminal Procedure Rules (2005), 7–32
  exclusion powers, 7–13, 7–27—7–29, 7–47, 7–72
  in camera, 7–10—7–12, 7–27, 7–28, 7–32—7–34, 7–46, 7–74
  juries, protection of, 7–14
  open court, in, 7–36—7–40
  openness principle
    appellate proceedings, 7–66, 7–67

INDEX

Court proceedings—*cont.*
  openness principle—*cont.*
    ecclesiastical hearings, 7–72
    exceptions, to, 7–56, 7–58, 7–59, 7–62
    family proceedings, 7–63—7–65
    parens patriae cases, 7–56, 7–63
    secret technical processes, 7–57
    statutory exceptions, 7–62
  powers, relating to, 7–27
  pre-reading, 7–18, 7–19
  privacy, 7–30
  public access, 7–7—7–10, 7–42
  public and private hearings, distinguished, 7–36
  reporting, 2–72, 4–289, 4–290, 4–291
    see also **Court reporting**
  secrecy, 7–75
  withholding information, 7–76—7–80
  witnesses
    protection, 7–14, 7–68—7–71
    vulnerable witnesses, 7–13, 7–80
  written submissions, 7–18

Court reporting
  see also **Court proceedings**
  abuse of process, 2–76
  accuracy, 4–268, 4–269, 12–216
  arbitration proceedings, 7–21—7–26
  bad faith, and, 4–281
  bail applications, 2–81
  burden of proof, 4–267
  common law principles
    continuing relevance, 7–82
    human rights, 7–3—7–5
    open justice, 7–1, 7–6, 7–7, 7–16
  contemporaneous
    meaning, 4–277—4–279
    provisions governing, 4–263, 4–265, 4–269
    public interest, and, 4,275—4–276
    requirement, for, 4–274
    statutory protection, 4–275
  Contempt of Court Act (1981)
    see **Contempt of Court Act (1981)**
  Criminal Justice Act (2003)
    prosecution appeals, 8–15
    restriction on publication, 8–15—8–16
    re-trials, 8–16
  defendant, on, 2–85
  employment tribunals, 7–35
  fair and accurate, 2–94, 4–264, 4–286—4–288
  generally, 7–1, 8–1
  good faith, 4–283—4–285
  human rights, and, 4–273
  Judicial Proceedings (Regulation of Reports) Act (1926)
    see **Judicial Proceedings (Regulation of Reports) Act (1926)**
  national security, and, 7–34, 7–55, 7–60, 7–61, 7–76

Court reporting—*cont.*
  open justice, and, 4–292
  physical safety, protecting, 7–31
  postponement, 4–277, 4–280
  pre-judgment, 2–72, 4–272
  prejudicial comment, 2–72, 2–77, 2–78
  pre-trial publicity, 2–72, 2–75, 2–77, 2–80
  proceedings in private, 4–282
  public enquiries, and, 7–20
  qualified privilege, 6–17
  reforms, concerning, 1–173
  report, meaning of, 4–268
  right to be informed, 7–16
  sexual offences
    see **Sexual offences**
  special measures directions, 7–15
  statutory provisions, 4–265, 4–292
  strict liability, and, 4–265, 4–260, 8–1
  television reporting, 4–270, 4–271, 4–273
  unfair reporting, 2–75

Criminal and Civil Contempt distinguished
  appeal rights, 3–88, 3–89, 3–123
  classification
    re-classification, 3–51—3–54
    significance, of, 3–25—3–27
  common features
    administration of justice, 3–6, 3–9, 3–24
    court authority, 3–6
    public policy, 3–6
  comparison points
    appeals, 3–30, 3–88, 3–131—3–140
    autrefois acquit, 3–39, 3–209—3–222
    autrefois convict, 3–39, 3–209—3–222
    extra-territorial jurisdiction, 3–40, 3–223—3–226
    execution, 3–36
    fresh evidence, 3–42, 3–239
    hearsay evidence, 3–41, 3–227—3–238
    instituting proceedings, 3–33, 3–170
    prerogative, 3–37, 3–185
    privilege, 3–31, 3–88, 3–89, 3–141—3–156
    release *ex debito justitiae*, 3–35, 3–88, 3–89, 3–179—3–183
    sanctions, 3–34, 3–176—3–178
    self-incrimination, 3–38, 3–188—3–208
    standard of proof, 3–43, 3–241
    waiver, 3–32, 3–88, 3–89, 3–157
    writ of attachment, 3–36
  disclosure of information
    see **Disclosure of information**
  distinction
    common law development, 3–29
    criticisms, 3–48—3–50
    duress, 3–46, 3–250—3–255
    evidence on appeal, 3–42, 3–239—3–240
    maintaining, 3–3
    mens rea, 3–44, 3–90, 3–97, 3–124, 3–247—3–249
    minimised, 3–88—3–91

Index

Criminal and Civil Contempt
distinguished—*cont.*
distinction—*cont.*
nature, of, 3–1, 3–2
Phillimore Committee, 3–47
public funding, 3–45
remedial punishment, 3–1, 3–2
standard of proof, 3–43, 3–241—3–246
extra-territorial jurisdiction, 3–223—3–225
hearsay evidence
see **Evidence**
instituting proceedings
see **Instituting proceedings**
third parties
see **Third parties**
waiver
see **Waiver**

Criminal contempt
administration of justice, and, 3–54, 3–69, 3–92
characteristics
criminal offences distinguished, 3–55, 3–56
jury trial, absence of, 3–59, 3–81
right to silence, 3–64
sentencing provisions, 3–60
civil proceedings, in, 3–28
conduct, amounting to, 3–27, 3–28
criminal liability, 3–65
criminal proceedings, in, 3–28
development, 1–42—1–46
double jeopardy, 3–39
injunctions, and, 3–16
and see **Injunctions**
judicial extension, 2–177
mens rea, 1–117, 1–118, 3–66
misdemeanour, as, 3–67—3–68
nature, of, 3–1
penalties, 19–1
Police and Criminal Evidence Act (1984), 3–61—3–63
right of appeal, 1–126
strict liability, 1–116
and see **Strict liability**
summary conviction, 3–60
summary process, 3–55, 3–57, 3–75
and see **Summary process**
wardship, 3–115—3–118

Criminal Defence Service
legal representation, and, 15–111, 15–112, 15–117

Criminal law
judicial law-making, 2–191
mens rea, absence of, 2–184, 2–186
new situations, dealing with, 2–184, 2–190
principles and rules
application, 2–183, 2–184
conflict, between, 2–181
contrast, between, 2–179
vagueness, 2–180

Criminal law—*cont.*
rules
advantages, of, 2–182
compliance, with, 2–187
knowledge, of, 2–185, 2–187, 2–188
sanction, as, 2–185

Crown
immunity, 2–222, 2–223
ministers
advice given, by, 2–226
immunity, 2–224, 2–225, 2–227—2–230
non-compliance, 2–228, 2–229

Crown Court
Civil Procedure Rules (CPR), 13–25, 13–27
creation, of, 13–24
jurisdiction
concurrent, 13–26, 13–29, 13–33
overlapping, 13–28
quia timet jurisdiction, 13–36—13–37
powers
committal powers, 13–38—13–42
extent, of, 13–22, 13–25, 13–27, 13–30—13–32
status, 13–34

Damages
see also **Financial compensation**
arrest, for, 14–152
availability, 14–148—14–149
early case law, 14–150—14–151
non-compliance, for, 14–153—14–63
Phillimore Committee, 14–148

Derogatory remarks in mitigation
false assertions, 8–96
mischief, nature of, 8–95

Disclosure of documents
confidentiality, 12–209, 12–212, 12–213
counsel, reference by, 12–223
court reporter, to, 12–217
criminal proceedings, in, 12–203
documents, destruction of, 11–86
ease of access, 12–213, 12–222
freedom of information, 12–213, 12–216
full disclosure, 12–211, 12–213
implied undertaking, 12–201, 12–202, 12–210, 12–218—12–220
judicial reading, 12–221, 12–223
press freedom, and, 1,158
and see **Press freedom**
prior knowledge, and, 12–213
privacy, and, 12–209, 12–212
prohibiting use, 12–237—12–239
public interest, and, 12–209, 12–213
restricting use, 12–237—12–239

Disclosure of information
see also **Disclosure of documents**
Civil Procedure Rules (CPR), 3–206
collateral use, 3–201, 3–202
related offences, 3–197

[1380]

INDEX

Disclosure of information—*cont.*
related proceedings, 3–198—3–201
statutory provisions, 3–196
third parties, 3–203

Discussing public affairs
burden of proof, 4–318
common law, and, 4–294—4–299, 4–315
continuing debate, 4–311—4–312
defence burden, 4–303
freedom of information, 4–299
human rights, and, 4–299, 4–315
injunctions, and, 4–316
jury directions, as to, 4–303
mens rea, 4–310
prejudice
    incidental prejudice, 4–305, 4–306, 4–308
    intention to prejudice, 4–310, 4–315
    risk of prejudice, 4–303, 4–305, 4–307, 4–309, 4–310, 4–315
    and see **Prejudice**
prior discussion, 4–311
public discussion, 4–312—4–314
public interest, 4–312, 4–317
statutory provisions, 4–293, 4–303, 4–306

Distributors
common law, at, 4–235
defences, available to, 4–259
innocent dissemination, 4–234
liability, 4–234
meaning, 4–234

Divisional Court
committal proceedings
    see **Committal proceedings**
inferior courts, and, 13–43
jurisdiction
    concurrent, 13–26, 13–29, 13–33
    overlapping, 13–28
    proper forum, 13–33
    protection, of, 13–43, 13–50, 13–56, 13–81
powers, of, 13–22, 13–23, 13–25, 15–9

Double jeopardy
autrefois acquit, and, 3–209, 3–215
criminal contempt, and, 3–39, 12–11, 14–18—14–19
and see **Criminal contempt**
freezing orders (*Mareva*), and, 12–164
and see **Freezing orders (*Mareva*)**
judicial consideration, 1–152
unfairness, and, 2–47

Duress
burden of proof, 3–251
civil contempt, and, 3–5, 3–46, 3–75, 3–251, 12–94
criminal contempt, 3–251
defence, as, 3–251—3–255, 10–166
domestic violence, and, 10–169, 10–170
journalists, and, 9–119
mitigation, as, 3–250
threats of violence, 3–254—3–255

Duress—*cont.*
witnesses, and, 10–165, 10–169, 10–170

Editorial responsibility
see also **Liability for publication**
criminal responsibility, 4–214
decision to publish, 4–213
Phillimore Committee, 4–254
primary responsibility, 4–212, 4–255
publishers and, 4–215
statutory defence, 4–256
strict liability, and, 4–254
vicarious liability, 4–214, 4–254—4–256, 4–258

Employment tribunals
reporting restrictions, 7–35, 8–141—8–146, 13–63
and see **Reporting restrictions**

European Convention on Human Rights (ECHR)
see also **Human Rights Act (1998)**
access to justice, 7–1
application, 2–124
breaches of, 1–104, 1–105, 1–108, 1–132
case decisions, 2–192, 2–194, 2–195, 2–197
certainty, importance of, 1–97, 2–169—2–178, 5–160
children, protection of, 6–76, 8–83
common law
    comparisons, with, 2–163
    uncertainties, resolving, 2–138—2–164
competing objectives, 7–2
compliance, 2–125
criminal offences, and, 2–143, 2–169, 2–173
disclosure, 1–104
fair trial
    ensuring, 2–145
    fair and public hearing, 1–105, 2–143, 2–144, 2–162, 3–84, 7–1
    right to, 2–143
family life, respect for, 1–176, 2–146
freedom of expression, 1–104, 2–142, 6–11, 6–87, 7–5, 12–214
freedom of information, 1–162, 2–32, 2–36, 4–299, 7–1
hearsay evidence, 3–238
incorporation, 1–134, 2–123
individual petition, 2–166—2–167
influence, 1–132—1–133, 2–52, 2–53, 2–122, 2–196
international obligations, 2–125
judicial role issues
    authority, 2–165, 5–42, 6–9
    development, 2–169—2–178
    discretion, and, 2–133—2–137
    impartiality, 2–165, 5–42, 6–9
juries, and, 11–355—11–360
margin of appreciation, 2–159, 2–168, 5–22, 5–23, 7–2, 7–108

INDEX

European Convention on Human Rights (ECHR)—*cont.*
 ministerial discretion, and, 2–139—2–141
 morals, protection of, 8–7
 municipal law, and, 2–125
 natural justice, and, 10–36—10–37
 open justice, 2–161—2–162
 prejudicial comment, 2–144
 press freedom, 1–153, 7–108
 presumption of innocence, 2–143
 privacy, and, 1–174, 1–175, 2–36, 2–37, 2–163, 6–76, 8–83
 procedural issues, 2–193
 public statements, 1–164, 1–166—1–168, 1–171
 publishing restrictions, 2–194, 6–20
 reputation, protection of, 6–8
 restrictions on freedom, 1–104
 social need, 1–110, 5–22, 5–42, 5–217
 statutory interpretation, and, 2–127—2–132, 2–164
 strict liability, and, 4–91
 summary process, and, 2–144

Evidence
 affidavit evidence, 3–192
 answering questions, 3–108—3–111
 evidence *in camera*, 2–64—2–66
 evidence in public, 2–63
 evidence on appeal, 3–239, 3–240
 hearsay
  admissibility, 3–227, 3–229, 3–234
  civil contempt, 3–229
  Civil Evidence Act (1995), 3–236—3–237
  criminal contempt, and, 3–227
  criminal proceedings, 3–228
  human rights, and, 3–238
  interlocutory proceedings, 3–230, 3–232
  matrimonial proceedings, 3–231
  reforms proposed, 3–228
  statutory provisions, 3–228, 3–232, 3–233
 publication, of, 1–73, 1–78
 self-incrimination, and, 3–192, 3–207
 standard of proof, 3–241—3–246
 unsafe, 3–140

Face of court contempt
 breach of order, 3–112, 3–114
  and see **Breach of orders**
 disruption, 10–3, 10–22, 10–64, 10–98
 disturbing proceedings
  arrest in court, 10–109—10–111
  assault, 10–93—10–96
  background, 10–88—10–89
  County Court jurisdiction, 10–130
  insults, 10–97
  judicial approach, to, 10–98—10–105
  public gallery, from, 10–99, 10–104, 10–209, 10–211
  removal orders, 10–106—10–107

Face of court contempt—*cont.*
 disturbing proceedings—*cont.*
  serious interference, 10–102
  summary procedure, 10–98
  Treason Act (1351), 10–90—10–92
 elements
  defining elements, 10–11, 10–12, 10–15
  disruption, 10–3, 10–22, 10–64, 10–98
  external interference, 10–20, 10–22, 10–23, 10–25
  interfering with proceedings, 10–12, 10–16, 10–21
  judicial awareness, 10–17, 10–19
  judicial presence, 10–18
 improper case conduct
  litigants, 10–131—10–134
  professional advocates, 10–135—10–156
 "in the face"
  jurisdictional issues, 10–6—10–7
  significance, of, 10–5
 juries
  see **Juries**
 jurisdiction
  Divisional Court, 10–7
  inherent, 10–6
  restrictions, on, 10–27
 jurors
  see **Jurors**
 legal aid, 10–10, 15–107
 mens rea,
  calculated interference, 10–209, 10–213, 10–218
  criminal standard, 10–225
  deliberate intent, 10–216
  intention inferred, 10–212– 10–218, 10–224
  nature, of, 10–8—10–9
  necessary intent, 10–208
  positive intent, 10–217, 10–224
  recklessness, 10–220—10–223
  uncertainty, regarding, 10–208—10–219
 natural justice
  breaches, of, 10–62—10–63
  human rights, 10–36—10–37
  traditional requirements, 10–36
 nature, of, 2–19, 2–24, 10–2
 procedure
  difficult witnesses, 10–30
  emotional displays, 10–34
  imperative to act, 10–31
  summary procedure, 10–21, 10–23, 10–26, 10–98
 professional advocates
  see **Professional advocates**
 safeguards
  common law jurisdictions, in, 10–85—10–87
  cooling-off period, 10–42—10–45
  defence, preparation of, 10–56, 10–58
  guidance, on, 10–72—10–83

INDEX

Face of court contempt—*cont.*
 safeguards—*cont.*
  judicial referral, 10–46—10–50
  legal advice, 10–53—10–55
  legal representation, 10–53, 10–60, 10–62, 10–65, 10–69
  need, for, 10–38—10–42
  precise charge, need for, 10–51—10–52
  self-incrimination, 10–71
  time to reflect, 10–59
 scope, 10–4
 statutory contempt
  geographical scope, 10–121—10–125
  magistrates' powers, 10–112—10–113
  mens rea, 10–126—10–129
  recklessness, 10–126
  right of appeal, 10–114—10–118
  wilful disruption, 10–113
  wilful insults, 10–113, 10–127, 10–129
 unauthorised recordings
  court precincts, in, 10–204—10–205
  photographs, 10–201—10–203
  sketches, 10–202
  tape recorders, 10–190
  television, 10–206—10–207
 witnesses
  see **Witnesses**

Failure to attend court
 advocates, 11–88—11–89
 Coroner's Court, 11–144
 Crown Court
  breach of bail, 11–129
  enquiry procedure, 11–121
  magistrates' powers, and, 11–117
  procedural rules, 11–95, 11–116
  production of documents, 11–134
  service of notice, 11–122
  witness attendance, 11–116
  witness summons, 11–118—11–120, 11–127
 documents, production of, 11–134—11–137
 juries, 11–140 — 11–143
  and see **Juries**
 jurors, 11–138—11–139
  and see **Jurors**
 just excuse, 11–124—1–128
 magistrates' court, and, 11–34
  and see **Magistrates' court**
 mens rea, 11–111—11–112, 11–123
 procedure
  arbitration proceedings, 11–99
  Civil Procedure Rules (CPR), 11–91—11–93
  conduct money, 11–102—11–105
  County Court, 11–91, 11–93, 11–94
  Crown Court, 11–95, 11–116, 11–117
  High Court, 11–91, 11–93
  material evidence, 11–106—11–108
  parties' non-attendance, 11–96
  pre-trial depositions, 11–98

Failure to attend court—*cont.*
 procedure—*cont.*
  witness summons, 11–97, 11–100, 11–109, 11–112, 11–118
 reasonable excuse, 11–114—11–115, 11–142
 witnesses, 11–90

Fair trial
 abuse of process, and, 4–148
 ensuring, 2–72, 2–144, 2–145
 fair and public hearing, 1–105, 2–143, 2–144, 2–162, 3–84, 7–1
 freedom of expression, and, 2–71
 freedom of information, and, 2–33, 2–34, 2–155
 human rights, and, 2–143—2–145, 2–162
  see also **European Convention on Human Rights (ECHR)**
 impossibility, of, 2–76, 2–78, 2–90
 judicial direction, 2–120—2–121
 juries, and, 2–84, 2–85
  and see **Juries**
 local prejudice, 2–108, 2–109
 media publicity, 2–76, 2–77
 miscarriage of justice, 2–85, 2–86
 postponement of trial, 2–105
 prejudicial publicity, 2–75—2–77, 2–79, 2–82, 2–90, 2–92
 pre-trial publicity, 4–61—4–63
 press freedom, and, 1–153, 1–162, 2–34, 2–70, 2–73
 press reporting
  abuse of process, 2–76, 4–148
  bail applications, 2–81
  court proceedings, 2–72
  defendant, on, 2–85
  exclusion, 2–162
  fair and accurate, 2–94
  pre-judgment, 2–72
  prejudicial comment, 2–72, 2–77, 2–78
  pre-trial publicity, 2–72, 2–75, 2–77, 2–80
  unfair reporting, 2–75
 public hearing, 2–162
 public interest, 2–71
 publication bans, 2–102, 2–103
 quashed convictions, 2–73, 2–79, 2–81, 2–82
 right to silence, 2–91
 risk of prejudice, 2–79, 2–102, 2–104, 2–119
 strict liability, and, 4–1
 trial abandoned, 2–73
 unsafe convictions, 2–90
 venue, change of, 2–106, 2–107, 2–109, 2–119

Family proceedings
 arrest powers
  see **Arrest powers**
 disobedience orders, 1–138
 domestic violence, 1–152
 compliance, 12–32

[1383]

INDEX

Family proceedings—*cont.*
imprisonment, and, 14–18
  and see **Imprisonment**
minors, restrictions on, 1–139
non-molestation orders, 1–138, 1–152
  and see **Non-molestation orders**
patients, restrictions on, 1–139
reporting restrictions
  court attendance, as to, 8–76, 8–78, 8–79
  newspaper reports, 8–80—8–82
  statutory provisions, 8–77, 8–79, 8–80
  and see **Reporting restrictions**
sequestration, 14–130, 14–131
  and see **Sequestration**
undertakings, 14–77

Financial compensation
compensation orders, 14–144—14–145
damages
  see **Damages**
harassment, for, 14–147
statutory compensation, 14–143
statutory offences, for, 14–146

Fines
see also **Non-custodial sentences**
indemnifying payment, 14–108
industrial disputes, 14–126
inferior courts, 14–103—14–105, 14–107
standard scale, 14–106
superior courts, 14–101, 14–109
suspension, of, 14–102

Forms and precedents
assaulting an officer, 18–32
bench warrants, 18–9, 18–12
committal orders, 18–7, 18–25, 18–29
discharge order, 18–30
general undertaking, 18–36
notice to show good reason, 18–24
notice to solicitor, 18–28
orders for injunction, 18–15, 18–16, 18–17
orders suspending warrant, 18–18, 18–19
power of arrest, 18–33– 18–34, 18–35
rescuing goods, 18–32
revocation order, 18–20
summons for assault, 18–31
suspended committal orders, 18–5, 18–21, 18–26, 18–37
warrant of arrest, 18–1, 18–2
warrants of committal, 18–3, 18–4, 18–10, 18–11, 18–12, 18–27
witness statements, 18–14
writ of sequestration, 18–6, 18–8

Freedom of information
competing rights, 2–32, 2–33
fair trial, and, 2–33, 2–34, 2–155
freedom of speech, and, 2–38
  and see **Freedom of speech**
human rights, and, 1–162, 2–32, 2–36, 4–299, 7–1
jury deliberations, and, 2–44

Freedom of information—*cont.*
privacy, and, 2–36
  and see **Privacy**
reform needs, 1–162
reporting restrictions, and, 2–55—2–57, 2–60
  and see **Reporting restrictions**

Freedom of speech
administration of justice, and, 2–157
common law, and, 2–150, 4–324
common law jurisdictions, 2–99—2–101
convicted persons, vilification of, 2–45, 2–46
gagging writs, 4–324—4–329
human rights, 1–104, 2–142, 6–11, 6–87, 7–5, 12–214
importance of, 2–50, 2–156, 2–158
judicial attitudes, towards, 2–151—2–152
margin of appreciation, and, 2–159
restrictions, on, 2–38, 2–39, 2–159
risk of prejudice, 2–43
strict liability, and, 2–40
  and see **Strict liability**

Freezing orders (*Mareva*)
acting knowingly, 12–145, 12–146, 12–150
criminal contempt, and, 12–145, 12–146, 12–157
effect, 12–147, 12–155
financial limits, 12–170—12–174
funds
  missing, 12–173
  unidentifiable, 12–172
  withdrawal, of, 12–148—12–149
joint account holders, 12–151
nature, of, 12–146
overseas
  assets, 12–158, 12–159, 12–164, 12–166
  conflict of laws, 12–162—12–163
  double jeopardy, 12–164
  jurisdiction, 12–155, 12–157, 12–158, 12–160
  proceedings, 12–167—12–169
  seeking relief, 12–163, 12–165
  service, 12–161
penalties, 12–171
third party assets, 12–52—12–54

"Fundamental freedoms"
see also **European Convention on Human Rights (ECHR)**
balancing considerations, 2–155, 2–159, 6–43—6–44
judicial attitudes, towards, 2–151—2–153
protection, of, 2–148—2–149
recognition, of, 2–151
rights adjudication, 2–155—2–160
rule of law, and, 2–148

Government ministers
contempt, and, 1–141, 2–223

[1384]

Index

Harassment
  compensation, for, 14–147
  imprisonment, and, 14–19—14–20
  legislative development, 1–154
  restraining orders, 1–152
High Court
  appeals, to, 13–125—13–132
  jurisdiction, 13–17—13–20
  and see **Jurisdiction**
Historical background
  actions
    abuse of party, 1–12
    assault, for, 1–14
    damages, 1–10, 1–47
    distress, for, 1–47
    hindering proceedings, 1–12
    resisting a writ, 1–13—1–15
    trespass, 1–10, 1–11
  appellate jurisdiction
    civil contempt, 1–75
    Court of Appeal, 1–74, 1–75
    criminal contempt, 1–74
    right of appeal, 1–75
  attachment, demise of, 1–84
  common law courts
    court officers, 1–24—1–25
    early contempt, 1–1
    jurisdiction, 1–24—1–25
    penalties, 1–35
  Court of Chancery
    see **Court of Chancery**
  family proceedings
    see **Family proceedings**
  judicial powers, 1–85
  King's Council, 1–27—1–29
  nature of contempt
    assault, 1–3, 1–4
    breach of peace, 1–11
    hindrance, 1–1
    obstruction, 1–1
    words, 1–5
  oath, examination under, 1–32—1–34
  procedure
    complaint, 1–9
    indictment, 1–16—1–19
    informations, 1–20
    remedial claims, 1–10—1–12
    writ of attachment, 1–8
  publication contempt
    see **Publication contempt**
  Star Chamber
    see **Star Chamber**
  strict liability
    see **Strict liability**
  summary committal, 1–17, 1–21—1–23
  summary process, 1–76—1–77
  technical contempt
    see **Technical contempt**
Home Secretary
  media pressure, on, 2–48

Home Secretary—*cont.*
  prerogative power, 3–185
House of Lords
  appeals
    general public importance, 15–104—15–105
    permission, for, 15–103, 15–106
  jurisdiction, 13–12, 13–75
    and see **Jurisdiction**
  prejudicial influences, and, 4–125—4–128
Human Rights Act (1998)
  see also **European Convention on Human Rights (ECHR)**
  enactment, 1–134, 2–123, 2–124, 2–198
  freedom of expression, 6–11
  impact, 6–114
  journalists' sources, 9–3
    and see **Journalists' sources**
  principles, 2–198
  publishing restraints, 6–11

Impeding
  course of justice, 4–97, 4–151, 5–200
    see also **Committal proceedings**
Imprisonment
  civil contempt, and, 3–22, 14–7
  criminal contempt, 3–176, 14–10, 14–11
  debt, committal for, 14–22
  discharge powers
    automatic release, 14–32—14–35
    inferior courts, 14–30—14–31
    superior courts, 14–28—14–29
  domestic violence, 14–20
  family proceedings, and, 14–18
  harassment, for, 14–19—14–20
  historical use, 14–5—14–6
  magistrates' courts, and, 14–21—14–23
    and see **Magistrates' courts**
  pardons, 14–39
  prison rules, 14–37—14–38
  release, from, 14–13, 14–32—14–35
  sentencing, and, 14–9—14–11
    and see **Sentencing**
  statutory provisions, 14–8
Industrial relations
  contempt, and, 1–137, 14–125—14–129
Injunctions
  anticipated, publication, 6–1, 14–132
  breach, 1–152, 3–12, 3–15, 3–17, 12–1
  civil contempt, and, 3–12, 3–15, 3–17, 12–1
  committal, and, 14–132
  criminal contempt, and, 3–16
  non-parties
    actus reus, and, 6–131, 6–136, 6–144
    avoiding difficulties, 6–149—6–151
    confidentiality, 6–128, 6–130, 6–138, 6–141, 6–142, 6–144
    consent orders, 6–143
    contra mundum orders, 6–139, 6–146

Injunctions—*cont.*
  non-parties—*cont.*
    in personam principle, 6–119, 6–121, 6–146
    intention to interfere, 6–122, 6–132, 6–133, 6–135
    intention to prejudice, 6–129, 6–131, 6–135
    jurisdiction, 6–115—6–117, 6–120, 6–122
    knowledge of order, 6–127, 6–129, 6–130, 6–132, 6–140
    liability, 6–126, 6–127, 6–137, 6–138, 6–146
    mens rea, and, 6–127, 6–129, 6–132, 6–135, 6–144
    principles governing, 6–148
    procedural safeguards, 6–134, 11–34
    protective orders, undermining, 6–130
    restriction, of, 6–139
    wilful interference, by, 6–122, 11–34
  purpose, of, 6–147—6–148
  quia timet injunctions
    see **Quia timet injunctions**
  restraint, by, 14–134
  third parties, affected by, 6–124, 6–125, 6–146
  use, of, 14–132
Innocent publication
  burden of proof, 4–261—4–262
  journalists, and, 4–257
    and see **Journalists**
  knowledge of proceedings, 4–244 , 4–245, 4–249, 4–250, 5–91
  liability for publication, 4–203
    and see **Liability for publication**
  protection, 4–238—4–241
  standard of care, 4–242—4–251, 4–253
  statutory defence, 4–236—4–238, 4–254, 4–256, 4–260, 4–318
  statutory provisions, 4–236—4–238
  vicarious liability, 4–254—4–256, 4–258
Instituting proceedings
  Attorney-General, 2–199, 2–202, 3–170, 3–173, 3–174
    and see **Attorney-General**
  civil contempt, 3–170
  court, initiative of, 3–170—3–173
  criminal contempt, 3–170, 3–173, 3–174
  Phillimore Committee, 3–170
  political issues, involving, 3–172
  public interest, 3–173
  strict liability rule, 3–173
  United States, experience in, 3–175
Intellectual property rights
  defending, 3–196, 3–208
  disclosure of documents, 3–198—3–201
Interference with Administration of Justice
  abuse of process
    see **Abuse of process**
  attempted contempt, 11–14—11–20

Interference with Administration of Justice—*cont.*
  common law interference
    see **Common law interference**
  court officers
    see **Court officers**
  failure to attend court
    see **Failure to attend court**
  interference
    actus reus, 11–3
    circumstances, leading to, 2–189
    mens rea, 11–9, 11–11
  intimidation
    see **Intimidation**
  judges
    see **Judges**
  juries
    see **Juries**
  litigants
    see **Litigants**
  neutral acts
    intention to interfere, 11–11
    intention to prejudice, 11–7—11–10
    mere intent, 11–12—11–13
  non-publication contempt
    see **Non-publication contempt**
  omissions, 11–4—11–6
  parens patriae jurisdiction
    see **Parens patriae jurisdiction**
  subverting court orders
    see **Subverting court orders**
  summary process, 11–1, 11–2
  witnesses
    see **Witnesses**
Internet
  accessibility, 1–180
  archived material, 1–149, 4–27
  fade factor, 1–150, 1–180
  impact, 1–179
  journalists' sources, and, 9–58
    and see **Journalists' sources**
  jurisdictional issues, 1–181
  legal response, 1–145, 1–147
  overseas litigants, 1–181
  problems, associated with, 1–146
  public domain, 1–150
  publications
    prejudicial, 1–150, 1–180
    statutory provisions, 4–27, 4–28
  service providers, 1–148, 1–149
  websites, 1–148
Intimidation
  civil proceedings, 11–150
  common law, at, 11–148—11–149
  criminal proceedings
    attempt, 11–147
    harm caused, 11–151
    investigation in progress, 11–147
    mens rea, 11–152
    statutory provisions, 11–145—11–146

INDEX

Intimidation—*cont.*
  criminal proceedings—*cont.*
    unlawful actions, 11–151
    meaning, 11–153
    threats, 11–154

Journalists
  cheque-book journalism
    see **Cheque-book journalism**
  extent of liability, 4–217—4–219
  intention to publish, 4–216, 4–222
  investigative journalism, 2–59, 4–221, 5–93, 5–94, 9–19
  personal liability, 4–216, 4–221
  postponement orders
    challenges, by, 7–124, 7–235—7–243
    locus standi, 7–124, 7–244—7–257
    restrictions, relating to, 7–124, 7–149—7–152
    and see **Postponement orders**
  proceedings, against, 4–223
  reasonable care, 4–257
  reporting restrictions, 6–41—6–42
  responsibility, extent of, 9–101
  standard of care, 4–242—4–251
  statutory defence, 4–247, 4–248, 4–250
  supplying information, 4–220

Journalists' sources
  authenticity, 9–30
  case decisions, 9–147—9–150, 9–152, 9–155—9–176
  common law
    background, 9–4
    "chilling effect", 9–7—9–10, 9–126
    common law jurisdictions, 9–50—9–51
    discretionary approach, 9–13, 9–42—9–49
    duress, defence of, 9–119—9–125
    statutory provisions, and, 9–66
  competing interests, 9–15
  Contempt of Court Act (1981)
    see **Contempt of Court Act (1981)**
  credibility, 9–30
  disclosure
    human rights, and, 9–80
    interests of justice, 9–69, 9–74, 9–76, 9–81
    necessity, 9–67, 9–71, 9–75, 9–83—9–85
    peer pressure, 9–39
    press freedom, 2–154, 2–210, 2–211
    prevention of disorder, 9–193
    reasonable excuse, 9–79, 9–185, 9–186
    refusal, 9–36, 9–194
    statutory conditions, 9–70
    statutory exceptions, 9–66, 9–70, 9–75, 9–92, 9–113—9–118, 9–182—9–192
    terrorism, prevention of, 9–232, 9–234
    see also **Necessity of disclosure**
  disclosure order
    appropriateness, 9–194

Journalists' sources—*cont.*
  disclosure order—*cont.*
    compliance, 9–198, 9–237
    judicial discretion, 9–232
    jurisdiction, absence of, 9–203—9–204, 9–206, 9–207, 9–213, 9–2234, 9–226
    obedience, and, 9–201, 9–205, 9–223, 9–232
    unlimited jurisdiction, 9–214, 9–217, 9–219
    void and voidable, distinction, 9–202
  disobedience, over, 9–36
  duty of confidence, 9–14—9–15
  freedom of expression, 9–1, 9–6
  human rights, and, 9–1—9–3, 9–147—9–153
  identification, 9–104—9–106
  immunity, waiver of, 9–111—9–112
  information
    information flow, 9–20, 9–102
    nature, of, 9–64—9–65, 9–97
    photographs, 9–63
    publication, in, 9–60 — 9–62
  journalistic principles, 9–39—9–41
  jurisdiction, 9–70, 9–78
  media, role of, 9–16, 9–19
  national security, 9–177—9–181
  National Union of Journalists (NUJ), 9–37
  peer pressure, 9–39
  policy considerations, 9–16, 9–18
  Press Complaints Commission, 9–38—9–39
  press freedom, and, 1–157, 1–158, 2–67, 2–154, 2–210, 2–211, 9–22
    and see **Press freedom**
  public interest, 9–15, 9–19, 9–20, 9–102, 9–20, 9–35
  refusal to disclose
    effect, of, 9–194
    right of appeal, 9–196, 9–197, 9–236—9–238
    statutory right, 9–227, 9–235
  right to information, 9–23—9–24
  rule of law, and, 9–32—9–33, 9–35, 9–36
  sanctions, 9–39
  significance, of, 9–1, 9–20
  statutory rights, 9–34
  summary of principles, 9–245
  unnamed sources, 9–25
  whistleblowing
    see **Whistleblowing**

Judges
  assault, on, 11–173
  authority, 1–106—1–108, 1–112, 2–165, 5–42, 5–204, 5–207—5–209, 6–9
  bias, 5–229—5–231, 5–239—5–241
  bribes, 11–174—11–175
  competence, 5–207, 5–208, 5–226
  impartiality, 1–106—1–108, 2–165, 5–42, 6–9
  improper influence, on, 11–177

[1387]

INDEX

Judges—*cont.*
  integrity, 5–204
  intimidation of, 11–13
  law making, and, 2–169, 5–160
  prejudicial influences, 4–118—4–124
  private communication, with,
    11–175—11–176
Judicial Proceedings (Regulation of Reports) Act (1926)
  see also **Court reporting**
  dissolution of marriage, 8–11
  indecent material, 8–6, 8–8
  judicial proceedings, 8–3
  provisions extended, 8–13—8–14
  public morals, 8–4
  restrictions on publication, 8–2
Juries
  see also **Jurors**
  common law jurisdictions, 2–101
  confidentiality, 10–177, 10–189
  deliberations
    see **Jury deliberations**
  discharge, of, 7–162
  embracery, 11–179—11–180
  fair trial, and, 2–84, 2–85
  influences
    extraneous influences, 2–87—2–88
    improper influence, 10–182
    media influence, 2–87, 2–89, 2–93, 2–97, 2–98, 2–116
  interference, with, 11–178—11–179
  jury contamination, 11–189
  jury directions, 2–86, 4–114, 4–170, 4–171
  jury service, 10–176
  jury summons, 11–140—11–143
  jury tampering
    objectionable behaviour, 11–183
    penalties, for, 11–185
    statutory offence, 11–182
    summary jurisdiction, 11–181
  jury vetting, 2–114, 2–115
  objectivity, 2–96
  separation, of, 10–187
  susceptibility, 2–96
  verdict
    capricious conduct, 10–181
    improper influence, 10–182
    judge's directions, and, 10–180
    judge's views, contrary to, 10–179
    refusal to give, 10–179
Jurisdiction
  administration of justice, and, 2–7, 2–8, 2–10, 2–11
  appellate jurisdiction
    see **Appellate jurisdiction**
  cautious exercise, of, 2–18, 2–25
  Commissioners of Income Tax, 13–60
  Consistory Courts, 13–103
  Contempt of Court Act (1981), 13–3—13–4
    and see **Contempt of Court Act (1981)**

Jurisdiction—*cont.*
  Coroner's Court, 13–100—13–103
  County court
    see **County court**
  court authority, upholding, 2–9
  Court of Appeal, 13–13—13–15
  Courts Martial Appeal Court, 13–16
  Crown Court
    see **Crown Court**
  Divisional Court
    see **Divisional Court**
  Election Court, 13–103
  Employment tribunals, 13–21, 13–62—13–65
  General Medical Council, 13–76
  general principles, 13–1—13–4, 13–6
  High Court, 13–17—13–20, 13–125—13–132
  House of Lords, 13–12, 13–75
  inferior courts
    administrative purpose, 13–54, 13–57, 13–60
    judicial purpose, 13–54, 13–57, 13–60
    meaning, 13–44—13–47
    "non-tests", applied to, 13–51—13–55, 13–64
    valuation courts, 13–48—13–50, 13–52, 13–54, 13–57—13–59
  Lands Tribunal, 13–61
  Magistrates' courts
    see **Magistrates' courts**
  parens patriae jurisdiction
    see ***Parens patriae*** **jurisdiction**
  Queen's Bench Division, 13–77—13–78, 13–83
  rule of law, and, 2–6, 2–9
  strict liability rule, 13–3, 13–4
  summary jurisdiction
    see **Summary jurisdiction**
  tribunals
    employment, 13–21, 13–62—13–65
    inquiry, of, 13–78
    mental health, 13–66—13–69
    transport, 13–103
    and see **Tribunals**
Jurors
  see also **Juries**
  absent without leave, 10–183—10–185
  bias, 11–392
  directions, to, 4–114, 4–170, 4–171
  discussion, between, 2–112
  failure to attend
    jury summons, 11–140—11–143
    statutory provisions, 11–138—11–139
    see also **Failure to attend court**
  impersonating, 11–188
  improper behaviour, 11–392
  intimidation, 11–299
  misconduct, 10–179—10–189

[1388]

INDEX

Jurors—cont.
  prejudicial influence
    improper influence, 10–182
    prejudicial publication, 4–111
    risk of prejudice, 7–159—7–161
    susceptibility, 4–112—4–114, 4–159, 4–161, 4–169
  reprisals, against, 11–187
  separation, of, 2–112, 10–187
  sequestration, 2–110, 2–111, 2–113
  statutory offences, involving, 10–178
Jury deliberations
  confidentiality, 11–363—11–364
  disclosure
    alleged irregularities, 11–373—11–374
    common law, at, 11–349
    criminal law, and, 11–352
    deliberate, 11–378, 11–383
    exceptions, relating to, 11–362—11–364
    meaning, 11–365—11–366
    mens rea, 11–378—11–385
    offers to disclose, 11–367
    provisions governing, 3–93, 11–349—11–354
    subsequent proceedings, involving, 11–371
    verdict, affected by, 11–371, 11–376
  evidence, relating to, 11–392
  extraneous influences, 11–362—11–363, 11–392
  extrinsic matters, affecting, 11–362
  failure to deliberate, 11–392
  freedom of information, and, 2–44
  importuning jurors, 11–353
  interference
    actus reus, 11–380
    foreseeable consequences, 11–381
    inferred intent, 11–381
    intention to interfere, 11–384
    mens rea, 11–378—11–385
    specific intention, 11–381
  meaning, 11–368—11–370
  publication, 11–353
  secrecy
    Canadian Charter, and, 11–361
    human rights, 11–355—11–360, 11–389, 11–394
  miscarriage of justice, 11–386—11–395

Legal aid
  legal representation, and, 10–10, 15–107, 15–108, 15–110
Legal representatives
  see also **Professional advocates**
  information leaks, 1–169
  interference, with, 11–310
  media coverage, and, 1–171
  public statements, by, 1–164—1–168, 1–171

Legal Services Commission
  legal representation, and, 15–115
Liability for publication
  corporate liability, 4–197, 4–198, 4–204
    see also **Companies**
  defamation law
    comparisons, with, 4–224—4–225
    internal communications, 4–226, 4–228
    publication, under, 4–224, 4–226, 4–227
    re-publication, 4–228
    subordinate responsibility, 4–229
  distributors
    see **Distributors**
  editorial responsibility
    see **Editorial responsibility**
  innocent publication
    see **Innocent publication**
  journalists
    see **Journalists**
  printers
    see **Printers**
  proprietors, 4–195, 4–199
  publication
    communicating information, 4–194
    innocent publication, 4–203
    production process, 4–194
    public at large, 4–194
  publishers, 4–195
    and see **Publishers**
  statutory provisions, 4–191—4–192
  vicarious liability, 4–197—4–202
Litigants
  access to court, hindering, 11–300—11–309
  civil proceedings, 4–137
  claimants, 11–292—11–293
  criminal proceedings, 4–137
  fair criticism, 4–142
  false pleadings, 11–287
  improper pressure, 11–282—11–285, 11–292
  injurious misrepresentation, 4–141
  intimidation, 11–280—11–281
  legal rights, threat to exercise, 11–289—11–295
  media pressure, 11–277
  Phillimore Committee, 11–296—11–298
  prejudice, involving, 4–136
  pressure on, 4–135, 4–138—4–137, 4–147, 11–280
  private communications, 4–136
  private prosecutions, 4–137, 11–286
  public obloquy, 4–139, 4–144, 4–146
  public policy, and, 11–278—11–279, 11–292
  publications, influencing, 4–136
  threats, to, 4–141, 4–145
  warnings, to, 11–282
Locus standi
  contempt proceedings, 2–207
  injunctions, involving, 2–208
  quia timet injunctions, 6–22—6–29

[1389]

INDEX

Magistrates
prejudicial influences, 4–115—4–117
Magistrates' courts
absence of defendant, 13–113—13–115
adjournment, 13–113—13–115
debt, committal for, 14–22
disobedience to orders, 13–116
imprisonment, and, 14–21—14–23
   and see **Imprisonment**
jurisdiction, 13–106
   and see **Jurisdiction**
nature, of, 13–104—13–111
Phillimore Committee, 13–104
powers
   extent, 13–105, 13–112
   imprisonment, 13–108, 14–21—14–23
   statutory contempt, 10–112—10–113
production of documents, 11–134
status, 13–104
witness, attendance of, 11–134, 13–117
   and see **Witnesses**
Mens rea (common law contempt)
administration of justice
   adverse consequences, for, 5–200
   impeding, 5–200
   interference, with, 5–198
   prejudicing, 5–200
basic propositions, regarding, 5–200
criminal law
   intention, 5–120
   recklessness, 5–120, 5–129
intention
   burden of proof, 5–175, 5–178
   certain consequence, 5–125, 5–126
   foresight of consequence, 5–124, 5–127, 5–155, 5–156, 5–166
   inevitable consequence, 5–200
   inference, 5–182
   intention to interfere, 5–121, 5–163
   meaning, 5–120, 5–128
   natural consequence, 5–125, 5–156
   oblique intention, 5–123, 5–153
   prejudicial, 5–167—5–170
   purpose, as, 5–122
   recklessness, 5–178, 5–180
   risk of prejudice, 5–171, 5–174, 5–179, 5–183, 5–187, 5–199
   specific intent, 5–198
   standard of proof, 5–187—5–189, 5–198
interference
   positive intention, 5–190, 5–195
   specific intention, 5–198, 5–200
motive, distinguished from, 5–200
recklessness
   advertent, 5–131
   inadvertent, 5–130
   insufficient, 5–192, 5–193, 5–200
   intention, and, 5–195
   significance, of, 5–165, 5–166

Mens rea (common law contempt)—*cont.*
requirements
   impeding administration of justice, 5–140
   risk of prejudice, 5–140
Spycatcher Case
   see **Spycatcher Case**
strict liability rule
   common law, at, 5–133
   statutory application, 5–134—5–136
   statutory definition, 4–1, 5–133
Mobile telephones
use of, 10–203, 10–225
Murmuring
see also **Scots law**
common law, and, 16–92—16–100
breadth of publication, 16–89
false charges, 16–88
history, 16–87—16–100
meaning, 16–90
penalties, 16–91

National security
journalists' sources, and, 9–177—9–181
   and see **Journalists' sources**
protection, of, 7–34, 7–55, 7–60, 7–61, 7–76
Necessity of disclosure
commission of crime, 9–94, 9–99
concept, 9–83—9–85
interests of justice, 9–92, 9–95, 9–96, 9–99, 9–126, 9–140
interlocutory stage, at, 9–108—9–110
journalists' sources, 9–67, 9–71, 9–75, 9–76
   and see **Journalists' sources**
judicial discretion, 9–70, 9–98, 9–100, 9–104
jurisdictional issues, 9–224—9–231
national security, 9–92—9–94, 9–126
nature of information, 9–97
onus of proof, 9–90
proportionality, 9–107
public disorder, 9–94
public interest, 9–93, 9–94, 9–97, 9–103, 9–129, 9–141—9–146
residual discretion, 9–71, 9–100
Non-custodial sentences
binding over, 14–110
community sentences, 14–98—14–100
coroner's powers, 14–107
   see also **Coroner's Court**
enforcement, 14–109
fines
   see **Fines**
mental health
   guardianship orders, 14–97
   hospital orders, 14–97
sequestration
   see **Sequestration**

[1390]

INDEX

Non-molestation orders
arrest powers, 14–74, 14–76—14–78, 14–81, 14–86, 14–96
breach of undertaking, 12–186
and see **Breach of undertaking**
committal proceedings, and, 12–56—12–57
duration, 14–81—14–82
family proceedings, in, 1–138, 1–152
Non-publication contempt
criminal law, and, 1–177, 1–178
mens rea
foreseeable consequences, 11–29—11–31
intention to interfere, 11–32
judicial authority, 11–23—11–28
strict liability, 11–33
uncertainty, as to, 11–21—11–22

Oath
examination, under, 1–32—1–34

Parens patriae (inherent) jurisdiction
children
see **Children**
Children Act (1989), effect of, 6–62, 6–66, 6–63, 6–108, 6–109 criminal proceedings, 6–97—6–106
custodial jurisdiction
Children Act (1989), 6–62, 6–66, 6–63
child's welfare, 6–64—6–65
duty of confidence, 6–65
nature, of, 6–56—6–59, 6–61, 6–68—6–73
paramount interests, 6–64, 6–65, 6–68, 6–77, 6–89, 6–113
prohibited steps orders, 6–66—6–67
protection afforded, 6–56, 6–57, 6–59, 6–61
development, of, 6–46—6–50
extent, 6–42—6–44, 6–46, 6–49
High Court, and, 6–96
historical background, 6–53—6–55
human rights, 6–42—6–44, 6–52, 6–57, 6–60, 6–106, 6–106, 6–114
inter partes litigation, 6–116
interference
criminal contempt, 11–332—11–336
mens rea, 11–339—11–348
protective jurisdiction, with, 11–331—11–332
limits, on, 6–51—6–52
media rights, 6–76, 6–80, 6–86, 6–87, 6–97, 6–98
press freedom, 6–87
privacy, 6–105
proportionality, and, 6–44
protection
court process, 6–56—6–58
individual rights, 6–56—6–58
publication, from, 11–337

Parens patriae (inherent) jurisdiction—*cont.*
protection—*cont.*
publicity, from, 11–337
protective jurisdiction
administration of justice, and, 6–84, 6–86
care proceedings, 6–101
carers, 6–93
Children Act (1989), 6–92
child's welfare, 6–82, 6–87, 6–89, 6–90, 6–102
fair trial, ensuring, 6–83
freedom of expression, 6–87
freedom of speech, 6–92, 6–110
guidelines, 6–90
human rights, and, 6–90, 6–91
judicial discretion, 6–88
nature, of, 6–56—6–59, 6–68—6–73
press freedom, 6–87
privacy, and, 6–92, 6–111
publication, against, 11–337
supervisory jurisdiction, 11–337
public domain
material, in, 6–50
proviso, as to, 6–93, 6–94
public interest, 6–87, 6–90
reporting restrictions, 6–41—6–43, 6–56, 6–76, 6–80, 6–86
and see **Reporting restrictions**
topicality, recognition of, 6–95
vulnerable persons, protecting, 6–41, 6–43, 6–51, 6–56
wards of court
see **Wards of court**

Penalties (examples)
civil contempt, 19–2
criminal contempt, 19–1

Persuasion of witnesses
common law, and, 11–226
empty threats, 11–247
evidence, relating to, 11–216
improper means, 11–227, 11–229, 11–230, 11–251
improper pressure, 11–231, 11–234, 11–248
intimidation, 11–244—11–246
litigants, distinguished, 11–127
mens rea, 11–233, 11–248, 11–254
motive, 11–227—11–228
non-attendance, encouraging, 11–216
status of witness, knowing, 11–255—11–257
threatening lawful action, 11–241—11–243
timing factors, 11–218—11–225
unacceptable pressure, 11–235—11–240
unlawful means, 11–232, 11–251

Phillimore Committee
cheque-book journalism, 11–265
damages, 14–148
editorial responsibility, 4–254
instituting proceedings, 3–170
litigants, 11–296—11–298
pre-judgment test, 1–90, 1–100, 1–109

INDEX

Phillimore Committee—*cont.*
  privilege, 3–156
  public benefit defence, 1–102, 1–103
  publication, on, 4–38, 4–39, 4–44
  recommendations, 20–1
  risk of interference, 1–100
  Scots law, 16–268—16–300
  serious prejudice, 1–100
  strict liability, 1–99, 4–2
  test of contempt, 1–100, 1–101
  waiver, 3–166
Photographs
  cameras, in court, 10–192, 10–201
  identification issues, 5–112
  journalists' sources, and, 9–63
    and see **Journalists' sources**
  publication, of, 5–112
  unauthorised use, 10–201—10–203
Police
  committal proceedings, involving, 15–54
  contempt by, 2–222, 11–23, 11–28
  powers of arrest, 14–72
  public statements, by, 1–164, 16–184
Postponement orders
  appeals
    orders, against, 7–124, 7–258—7–264
    procedure, 7–124, 7–266—7–269
    spent orders, 7–124, 7–265
  breach of order
    ipso facto contempt, 7–124, 7–132—7–136
    mens rea, 7–124, 7–203—7–227
    powers, relating to, 7–124, 7–228—7–234
  challenges
    basis, for, 7–236, 7–237
    journalists, by, 7–235, 7–236, 7–239, 7–241
    procedure, 7–235
    validity of order, 7–235
  common law, at, 7–109—7–110, 7–124, 7–129—7–131
  costs, 7–124, 7–270—7–279
  criteria
    criteria analysed, 7–171
    degree of risk, 7–200
    evaluating risk, 7–177, 7–200
    judicial discretion, 7–172, 7–190—7–197
    necessity, 7–164, 7–166, 7–172, 7–185—7–189, 7–198, 7–200, 7–201
    risk of prejudice, 7–164, 7–165, 7–172
    serious prejudice, 7–165, 7–167, 7–174
    substantial risk, 7–173, 7–175, 7–176, 7–199
    tendentious coverage, 7–178—7–182
    time factors, 7–183—7–184
    uncertainty, 7–164, 7–199—7–202
  journalists
    see **Journalists**
  juries, and, 7–159—7–162

Postponement orders—*cont.*
  mens rea
    intention to interfere, 7–204, 7–221
    knowledge of order, 7–204—7–208
    nature, of, 7–203
    recklessness, 7–204, 7–209—7–220, 7–222—7–225
    strict liability, 7–204, 7–226—7–227
  practice direction, as to, 7–124, 7–153—7–158
  proceedings
    contemplated, 7–124, 7–137—7–141
    imminent, 7–124, 7–143, 7–145
    pending, 7–124, 7–143
    publication postponed, 7–124, 7–142, 7–146—7–148
  reporting restrictions
    appellate proceedings, 7–141
    judicial review, 7–118
    misuse of power, 7–116—7–117, 7–123
    restraint, as to, 7–115, 7–119—7–122
    statutory limitations, 7–113—7–114
    statutory provisions, 7–111—7–112
  revealing existence, of, 7–159
  strict liability rule, 7–124, 7–129—7–131
Practice and procedure
  access to justice
    Criminal Defence Service, 15–111, 15–112, 15–117
    legal representation, 15–113—15–114
    Legal Services Commission, 15–115
    statutory provisions, 15–110—15–111
  appeals
    see **Appeals**
  committal proceedings
    see **Committal proceedings**
  legal representation
    access to justice, 15–108, 15–110
    human rights, and, 15–108
    legal aid, 15–107, 15–108, 15–110
    need, for, 10–10, 10–53, 15–107
  sequestration
    see **Sequestration**
Pre-trial publicity
  court reports, 2–72, 2–75, 2–77, 2–80
  fair trial, 4–61—4–63
  press freedom, and, 1–154
    and see **Press freedom**
  risk of prejudice, 4–89, 4–84, 4–80
Prejudice
  see also **Risk of prejudice**
  degree of prejudice
    policy interests, 5–22—5–27
    pre-judgment test, 1–92, 1–100, 5–19, 5–20, 5–21, 5–26, 5–41, 5–44
    serious prejudice, 5–10, 5–18, 5–26
    substantial risk, 5–10, 5–15, 5–18, 5–26
    technical contempt, 1–78, 5–19, 5–26, 5–27, 5–29
  media coverage, and, 4–155—4–157

Index

Prejudice—*cont.*
pre-trial publicity, 4–155, 4–163, 4–164
prejudicial influences
  House of Lords, and, 4–125—4–128
  judges, 4–118—4–124
  jurors, 4–111—4–114
  magistrates, 4–115—4–117
  witnesses, 4–129—4–134
risk, relationship with, 4–60, 4–71
serious prejudice, 1–127, 4–53, 4–72, 4–73, 4–96
single standard, need for, 4–169—4–173
stay of proceedings, 4–149—4–152, 4–154
strict liability
  abuse of process, 4–109
  definition, 4–92
  impeding, and, 4–105, 4–107
  nature, of, 4–92—4–95
  proceedings affected, 4–95, 4–101
  scope, 4–94
  and see **Strict liability**
subsequent conviction, and, 4–150
substantial risk, 4–53—4–57, 4–72, 4–76, 4–78, 4–80
trial abandoned, 4–148
venue, change of, 4–150—4–151

Press
see also **Press freedom**
courts, relationship with, 2–51, 2–53, 2–54, 2–60, 2–62, 2–67
information packs, 2–60, 2–61
role
  constitutional significance, 2–51
  democracy, and, 2–52, 2–54
  protected role, 2–49, 2–50

Press Complaints Commission
journalists' sources, and, 9–38—9–39

Press freedom
administration of justice, 1–159, 1–165
disclosure of documents, 1–158
evidence *in camera*, 2–64—2–66
fair trial, 1–153, 1–162, 2–34, 2–70, 2–73
  and see **Fair trial**
human rights, 1–153, 2–52
importance, of, 2–49
investigative journalism, 2–59
journalists' sources, 2–67, 2–154, 2–210—2–211, 9–1
  and see **Journalists' sources**
judicial attitudes, towards, 2–54—2–57
media contempt, 1–164, 1–167
pre-trial publicity, 1–154
public comment, and, 2–34
public interest, 2–54
reporting guidelines, 1–160
responsibility, and, 2–68, 2–69
restrictions, on, 2–49, 2–40, 2–41, 2–55, 2–56, 2–57
serious prejudice, 1–160, 1–164
strict liability, and, 2–40

Press freedom—*cont.*
summary process, and, 1–153, 1–156
trial by newspaper, 2–39

Printers
common law contempt, 4–232
defences, available to, 4–232
liability
  innocent dissemination, 4–230—4–231
  mens rea, 4–232—4–233

Privacy
children, and, 6–43, 6–76, 6–87, 6–92, 6–105, 8–126—8–127
court proceedings, and, 7–30, 7–99, 7–105
freedom of information, and, 2–36
human rights, and, 1–175, 1–176, 2–146, 2–163
protection, of, 1–171, 1–174
right to privacy, 1–174

Privilege
arrest, from, 3–141—3–143
availability, 3–145—3–146
civil process, and, 3–141
court officers, 3–147—3–153
criminal conduct, 3–142
criminal process, and, 3–141, 3–152—3–155
diplomatic, 3–126
disciplinary jurisdiction, 3–147—3–150
entitlement, 3–146
Phillimore Committee, 3–156
self-incrimination, against, 3–188, 3–190, 3–193, 3–208
  and see **Self-incrimination**
witnesses, claiming, 10–173—10–174

Proceedings in private
disclosure
  Children and Family Court Advisory and Support Service, 8–111— 8–116
  defence, 8–100—8–101
  wardship papers, 8–110
practice directions, 8–108—8–110
publication
  chambers hearings, 8–124, 8–126, 8–128
  conversations, 8–103
  formal details, 8–117
  judgments, 8–122
  meaning, of, 8–102, 8–103, 8–106
  permitted, 8–117, 8–121
  proceedings-related, 8–119—8–120
  underlying policy, 8–123
  unlawful, 8–107
  wardship proceedings, 8–120
publicity, involving, 8–97
sitting *in camera*, 8–128
statutory provisions, 8–98—8–99
strict liability, 8–129—8–140

Professional advocates
abuse of process, 10–136
  and see **Abuse of process**
accusations, by, 10–147—10–148
bad points, made by, 10–155

INDEX

Professional advocates—*cont.*
  barristers, 10–143
  disclosure of documents, 11–75—11–77
  disciplinary bodies, 10–136, 10–155, 11–68
  excessive zeal, 11–71
  failure to attend, 11–69
  freedom, of, 10–135
  improper influence, 11–72
  improper questioning, 10–151
  insulting remarks, 10–140, 10–145, 10–146
  interference, by, 11–72, 11–78
  media contact, 11–73, 11–75
  misconduct, 10–136, 10–143, 11–66, 11–67, 11–70, 11–78
  negligence, 10–139
  otherwise neutral conduct, 10–154
  public policy, and, 10–150
  responsibility, of, 10–135
  summary punishment, 10–144
  trade mark actions, 11–74
  vicarious liability, 11–66
Proprietors
  liability of, 4–195, 4–199, 4–258
Public affairs
  see **Discussing public affairs**
Public interest
  journalists' sources, and, 9–141
  public law remedies, and, 2–209
  representation, of, 2–209—2–211
    see also **Attorney-General**
Public statements
  expressions of innocence, 1–170
  information leaks, 1–169
  legal representatives, by, 1–164, 1–66—1–168, 1–171
  police, by, 1–164, 16–184
  reform, suggestions for, 1–164—1–166
Publication contempt
  background
    actus reus, 1–71, 1–130
    development, 1–57
    ex parte statements, 1–71
    fair trial, 1–57, 1–61, 1–63
    intentional contempt, 1–128—1–129
    out of court, 1–61
    scandalising the court, 1–57, 1–60, 1–63
    scope, 1–62—1–63
    speaking disrespectfully, 1–57, 1–58
    uncertainties, relating to, 1–128
  course of justice, interfering with, 4–16
  defences
    fair comment, 5–203
    public interest, 5–201—5–203
  mens rea, 1–165
  publication
    court proceedings, 1–72
    evidence, 1–73, 1–78
    injunction proceedings, 1–72
    insolvency proceedings, 1–72

Publication contempt—*cont.*
  reporting restrictions, 4–16
    and see **Reporting restrictions**
  scandalising the court, 4–16
    and see **Scandalising the court**
  strict liability, 1–165
    and see **Strict liability**
Publishers
  defences, available to, 4–259
  definition, 4–196
  liability, of, 4–195, 4–200—4–202
Purging contempt
  Canadian Charter, 12–76
  coercive nature, 12–66
  compliance, 12–79
  discretion, as to, 12–67, 12–69, 12–70, 12–79
  flexible approach, 12–70, 12–73
  human rights, 12–74—12–75
  rules, as to, 12–66—12–68, 14–6, 14–28—14–29, 14–50

Quia timet **injunctions**
  applications, 6–39—6–40
  Canadian experience, 6–21
  censorship, and, 6–36—6–37
  confidentiality, 6–14
  defamation, and, 6–7, 6–17, 6–18
  freedom of speech, 6–6, 6–9, 6–11, 6–12, 6–14
  human rights, 6–8, 6–11
  jurisdiction, 6–2—6–4, 6–10, 6–24
  justification, 6–6
  locus standi, 6–22—6–26, 6–29
  media publications, 6–1
  press freedom, 6–5
  prior restraint, 6–5, 6–20
  proof
    common law contempt, 6–33
    criminal standard, 6–33, 6–38
    nature, of, 6–30, 6–35
    proceedings imminent, 6–34
    risk of prejudice, 6–31—6–33
    standard of proof, 6–38
  public interest, 6–16, 6–31
  statutory intervention, 6–12, 6–16—6–19
  success at trial, 6–12—6–15
  threshold test, 6–13—6–15

Reform
  possible scope for
    cheque-book journalism, 11–264
    court reporting, 1–173
    freedom of information, 1–162
    impartial jury trial, 1–162
    non-publication contempt, 1–177, 1–178
    privacy, 1–171, 1–174
    public statements, 1–164—1–166
    reassessing priorities, 1–161

[1394]

INDEX

Reform—*cont.*
  possible scope for—*cont.*
    standard of proof, 1–163
Release *ex debito justitiae*
  application, for, 3–182
  early release, 3–183
  fixed term sentences, and, 3–181—3–182
  judicial discretion, 3–181
  punitive sentence, relating to, 3–180
  right, of, 3–179
Reporting restrictions
  see also **Court proceedings**
  appeal, against, 2–62
  breach of, 4–16
  children, and, 6–105, 8–27—8–31, 8–47, 8–49
    see also **Children and young persons**
  contesting, 6–105
  court reporting
    see **Court reporting**
  criminal proceedings, 6–97
  criticisms, of, 4–77
  defendant's identity, 6–105
  effect, of, 6–105
  employment tribunals, 8–141—8–146
  evidence in public, 2–63
  fair and accurate reports, 6–100
  family proceedings, 8–76—8–82
    and see **Family proceedings**
  freedom of information, and, 2–55—2–57, 2–60, 7–16
  human rights, 1–140
  guidelines, 6–103
  jurisdiction, 6–101
  knowledge, of, 4–292
  minors, 1–139, 1–140
  patients, 1–139
  postponement orders
    see **Postponement orders**
  press freedom, 2–40, 2–41, 2–55—2–57
  public interest, 1–140, 6–105
  risk of prejudice, and, 4–77
    and see **Risk of prejudice**
  sexual offences
    see **Sexual offences**
  strict liability, and, 2–40, 2–41
    and see **Strict liability**
  tribunals, 8–147—8–150
Restraining orders
  harassment, for, 1–152
Restriction orders
  actual service, 5–11, 7–94
  applications, 7–90
  breach, 7–87, 7–91
  partial secrecy, 7–87
  powers, relating to, 7–84—7–85
  practice direction, on, 7–89
  statutory provisions, 7–83
Risk of prejudice
  assertion of guilt, 4–82

Risk of prejudice—*cont.*
  assessment, 4–60, 4–67—4–69, 4–72, 4–86, 4–87, 5–43
  breach of orders, 7–91
  civil contempt, 12–10
    and see **Civil contempt**
  contributory facts, 4–66
  de minimis risks, 4–58, 5–44
  fair trial, and, 2–79, 2–102, 2–104, 2–119
    and see **Fair trial**
  judicial assessment of, 5–16, 5–37, 5–38
  juries, and, 4–60, 4–68, 7–159—7–161
  lesser risk, 5–12, 5–14—5–17
  past convictions, references to, 4–61, 4–81, 4–83
  Phillimore Committee, 4–55, 4–57
  postponement orders, 7–164, 7–165, 7–172
    and see **Postponement orders**
  pre-trial publicity, 4–61—4–63, 4–80, 4–84, 4–89
  technical contempt, and, 1–78, 1–80, 1–83
  time of publication, at, 4–76
  reporting restrictions, imposed, 4–77
  sensational presentation, 4–81
  significant risk, 4–64
  substantial risk, 4–53—4–57, 4–72, 4–76, 4–78, 4–80
  time factors, affecting, 4–65, 4–71, 4–79, 4–86, 4–168—4–173
Royal prerogative
  civil contempt, 3–186
  criminal contempt, 3–185
  exercise of, 3–37, 3–185
  pardons, 3–187
Rule of law
  nature, of, 2–147
  residual rights, 2–6, 2–148

Sanctions and remedies
  arrest
    see **Arrest powers**
  attendance centres, 14–65
  costs
    see **Costs**
  damages
    see **Damages**
  double jeopardy, 14–58
  financial compensation
    see **Financial compensation**
  imprisonment
    see **Imprisonment**
  injunction
    see **Injunction**
  non-custodial sentences
    see **Non-custodial sentences**
  release *ex debito justitiae*, 3–179—3–183
    and see **Release *ex debito justitiae***

INDEX

Sanctions and remedies—*cont.*
  sanctions
    civil contempt, 3–176, 14–7, 14–14,
      14–16, 14–17
    criminal contempt, 3–176, 14–10, 14–11
    scope, of, 14–1—14–4
  sentencing
    see **Sentencing**
  sequestration
    see **Sequestration**
Scandalising the court
  actus reus
    basis, of, 5–235, 5–236
    manner of criticism, 5–236—5–237
  common law jurisdictions, other,
    5–261—5–274
  defence
    fair comment, 5–204, 5–256—5–259
    truth, 5–204, 5–253—5–255
    uncertainty, as to, 5–256—5–259
  freedom of speech, 5–235
  judicial, criticism of
    authority, 5–204, 5–207—5–209
    bias, 5–229—5–231, 5–239—5–241
    competence, 5–207, 5–208, 5–226
    integrity, 5–204
  legal development, 5–220—5–231
  legitimate criticism, 5–232—5–234
  mens rea
    nature, of, 5–246
    recklessness, 5–247, 5–249
    requirement, for, 5–204, 5–244, 5–245,
      5–248
  protection
    common law, at, 5–216, 5–219
    Commonwealth authorities, 5–219
    human rights, 5–217—5–240
    Law Commission recommendations,
      5–213—5–215
    Phillimore Committee, 5–210—5–212
  public confidence, and, 5–205, 5–206,
    5–235, 5–237, 5–238, 5–242
  public interest, and, 5–256—5–257
  publication
    affidavit, in, 5–243
    circular letters, 5–242
    extent, of, 5–242, 5–243
    good faith, lack of, 5–251
    knowledge of contents, 5–250
  scurrilous abuse, 5–204, 5–224, 5–225,
    5–236
Scots law
  appeals procedure, 16–427—16–429
  breach of interdict
    contempt, constituting, 16–244—16–248
    court orders, 16–234—16–236
    breach of undertaking, 16–237—16–240
    mental element, 16–241—16–243
    orders *ad factum praestandum*, 16–265 —
      16–267

Scots law—*cont.*
  breach of interdict—*cont.*
    presence of defendant, 16–264
    procedure, 16–260—16–26
    quasi-criminal, 16–249—16–259
    sentencing, 16–257
    standard of proof, 16–256
    wilful breach, 16–242
  contempt
    categories, 16–65—16–68
    constructive contempt, 16–67—16–68
    crimes, amounting to, 16–17—16–20
    criminal nature, 16–22—16–28
    direct contempt, 16–67, 16–84—16–85
    public policy, 16–65
    quasi-crime, as, 16–29—16–38
    sui generis, as, 16–39—16–40
  Contempt of Court Act (1981)
    abuse of process, 16–318
    clearance in advance, 16–333—16–334
    disclosure of sources, 16–383—16–386
    fair trial, 16–310
    incidental prejudice, 16–323, 16–325
    interdicts, 16–335
    jury trial, 16–304, 16–309—16–319,
      16–378, 16–387—16–396
    legal aid, 16–347
    penalties, 16–348—16–350
    pre-trial publicity, 16–309, 16–311,
      16–317, 16–320
    procedural matters, 16–304,
      16–320—16–321, 16–323, 16–360
    proceedings, under, 16–302, 16–317,
      16–338, 16–341—16–346
    public interest, 16–326, 16–400
    restraining publication, 16–328—16–332
    risk of prejudice, 16–303, 16–310,
      16–313, 16–314, 16–322, 16–371
    Scottish exclusions, 16–351
    Scottish proceedings, definition of,
      16–337
    statutory defences, 16–361—16–367
    strict liability rule, 16–302, 16–303,
      16–320, 16–338—16–340,
      16–354—16–359
    unifying objective, 16–301
  court reports
    appellate proceedings, 16–376
    confidentiality, 16–379
    contemporaneous, 16–202—16–204,
      16–373
    fair and accurate, 16–368
    fair trial, and, 16–379
    judicial decisions, as to, 16–205—16–212
    necessity test, 16–371—16–372
    postponing, 16–223, 16–373—16–375,
      16–377
    restrictions, on, 16–200
    statutory provisions, 16–368—16–371,
      16–381—16–382

INDEX

Scots law—*cont.*
  evidence, interference with,
    16–135—16–141
  human rights, and, 16–1
  internet archives, 1–149, 4–27
  judges
    abuse, of, 16–85
    assaults, on, 16–84
    complaints, against, 16–106—16–108
    criticism, of, 16–101—16–102
    murmuring, 16–85
  judicial authority, 16–2—16–10
  jurisdiction
    domestic jurisdiction, 16–14
    extent, 16–11—16–16
    summary jurisdiction, 16–44—16–53
    terminus a quo, 16–164, 16–165, 16–170
  Lord Advocate, role of, 16–64
  Lord Justice-General's Memoranda,
    16–41—16–43
  media contempt
    administration of justice, and, 16–142
    case decisions, 16–146—16–149
    editorial responsibility, 16–163
    fair trial, 16–143, 16–160–16–187
    freedom of expression, 16–42, 16–188
    police press announcements,
      16–184—16–186
    pre-judgment, 16–150—16–151
    prejudice, 16–145, 16–158—16–162,
      16–189, 16–190
    public and private interests,
      16–152—16–157
    trial by newspaper, 16–142—16–145
  mens rea
    common law, at, 16–69—16–72
    constructive contempt, 16–73—16–81
    direct contempt, 16–82—16–83
  misbehaviour in court
    insults, 6–112—6–113
    intoxication, 6–109—6–111
    non-attendance, 6–114—6–116
    refusal to be sworn, 6–117
  murmuring
    see **Murmuring**
  Phillimore Committee, 16–268—16–300
  photographs, use of, 16–410—16–413
  postponement orders, 16–370
  pre-1981
    criminal conduct, 16–17—16–20
    development, 16–1
    double jeopardy, 16–17
    judicial authority, 16–2—16–5
    sources, 16–1
    statutory provisions, 16–21
    underlying principles, 16–1
  prevarication
    constructive contempt, as,
      16–124—16–127
    meaning, 16–120

Scots law—*cont.*
  prevarication—*cont.*
    oath, on, 16–118—16–123
    perjury, distinguished, 16–128
    procedural aspects, 16–131—16–134
    statutory prevarication, 16–129—16–130
  procedure
    non-summary cases, 16–61—16–62
    summary procedure, 16–54—16–60
  proceedings
    active, 16–166, 16–177, 16–317
    concluded, 16–191
    imminent, 16–171, 16–371
    pending, 16–166, 16–187, 16–371
  public affairs, discussing, 16–192—16–199
  publication
    perverting course of justice,
      16–231—16–233
    prejudicial material, 16–224—16–229
    restrictions, on, 16–230
  summary process
    absence from court, 16–59
    justification, 16–57
    need, for, 16–54, 16–58
  trial
    bar of trial, 16–397—16–409
    change of venue, 16–406
    fair trial, 16–400
    judge sitting alone, 16–409
    jury vetting, 16–407
    risk of prejudice, 16–404—16–405
    television, use of, 16–415—16–419
    unauthorised recordings, 16–413
Search and seizure orders (*Anton Piller*)
  acting knowingly, 12–181
  compliance, 12–175
  consent to entry, 12–177
  exercise, of, 12–179
  inadequate disclosure, 12–177
  nature, of, 12–175, 12–179
  persons not bound, 12–181
  preservation of material, 12–176, 12–178
  prohibitory orders, 12–176
  self-incrimination, and, 3–194—3–198
  standard form, 12–180
  vicarious liability, 12–178
Self-incrimination
  affidavit evidence, 3–192
  civil contempt, 3–188
  civil proceedings, in, 3–190—3–191, 15–18,
    15–35
  criminal contempt, 3–189
  cross-examination, 3–192, 3–204
  disclosure of documents, 3–196—3–203
  filing evidence, 3–207
  interrogatories, 3–192
  privilege, against, 3–188, 3–190, 3–193,
    3–208
  search and seizure orders, 3–194—3–198
  witnesses, and, 3–192, 3–204

Index

Sentencing
see also **Imprisonment**
civil contempt, 14–12, 14–14, 14–16
consecutive sentences, 14–55—14–57
criminal contempt, 14–10—14–11
disability, persons with, 14–70
penalties, examples of, 19–1
postponement, 14–49—14–54
pre-sentence reports, 14–67—14–70
suspended sentences, 14–45—14–48
suspension powers, 14–40—14–44
time on remand, 14–36
young persons, 14–60—14–64

Sequestration
applications, for, 15–78
availability, 14–112—14–115, 14–124
breach of order, 14–112
  and see **Breach of order**
corporate bodies, and, 14–122
county court powers, 14–116
Crown, against, 15–84
discharge, 15–87
effect, 14–120—14–124
enforceable order, need for, 14–117—14–119
family law, in, 14–130—14–131
fines, and, 14–112
  and see **Fines**
hearings, 15–79—15–80
industrial disputes, 14–125—14–129
judgment debtors, 15–86
nature, 14–111
permission, 15–81—15–82
property, subject to, 15–85—15–86
third parties, 14–123
use, of, 14–124—14–125, 14–130
validity, 15–83

Sexual offences
anonymity
  accused, for, 8–24
  displacing restrictions, 8–20
  protection, of, 8–19, 8–73
  rape victims, 8–17
  sexual assaults, 8–18
  and see **Anonymity**
reporting
  defences, 8–21
  offences, relating to, 8–21—8–23

Solicitors
breach of undertaking
  Admiralty proceedings, 12–261—12–262
  County Court jurisdiction, 13–98
  disciplinary jurisdiction, 12–250, 12–252—12–260
  enforcement, 12–250
  liability, 12–251
  personal capacity, in, 12–254, 12–257
  professional misconduct, 12–252
  provisions governing, 12–248—12–250
  summary jurisdiction, 12–258

Solicitors—*cont.*
civil contempt, liability for, 12–122

Spycatcher Case
administration of justice
  conduct, prejudicial to, 5–144, 5–146, 5–148, 5–150
  interference, with, 5–143, 5–144, 5–146, 5–148, 5–150, 5–153– 5–161
confidential information, 1–136
freedom of speech, 5–149
human rights issues, 2–194
influence, 1–135
intention
  actual intention, 5–158
  deliberate, 5–153
  general, 5–145
  inevitable consequence, 5–154, 5–156, 5–157
  inferred, 5–146, 5–166
  recklessness, 5–151
  specific, 5–145, 5–158—5–160
liability
  intention, and, 5–147
  mens rea, 5–141, 5–147
litigation, relating to, 1–135
publication
  breach of confidence, 5–143
  intention, as to, 5–154
  protective injunctions, 5–143, 5–144
  restraints, on, 5–142
restraining orders, 1–136
subverting court orders, 6–115, 6–124, 11–34

Star Chamber
abolition, 1–38—1–40, 1–46
influence, 1–26
interrogatories, 1–44
jurisdiction, 1–26, 1–29
King's Council, and, 1–27—1–29
procedure
  fine and imprisonment, 1–35—1–37
  general writs, 1–31
  interrogatories, 1–32—1–34

Strict liability
abuse of process, 4–148
  and see **Abuse of process**
active proceedings
  see **Active proceedings**
actus reus
  common law, 4,52
  pre-judgment test, 4–91, 4–319, 4–323
  risk, associated with, 4–52
Attorney-General, and, 2–203, 2–205, 2–206, 4–183
  and see **Attorney-General**
aggregated conduct, 4–87
common law
  application, of, 4–90
  criminal libel, 4–6
  innocent dissemination, 4–5

[1398]

INDEX

Strict liability—*cont.*
  common law—*cont.*
    knowledge of proceedings, 4–5, 4–8, 4–9, 4–11, 4–13
    mens rea, 4–9, 4–10, 4–12
    prejudicing course of justice, 4–5, 4–11, 4–40
    publication contempt, 4–5—4–8
    standard of care, 4–11
    technical contempt, 4–14
    uncertain scope, 4–5, 4–9, 4–10, 4–14
    see also **Common law contempt**
  historical background
    criminal libels, 1–68, 1–69
    enforcement, 1–64
    publication contempt, 1–67
    scandalising the court, 1–70
  libel, and, 4–325
  litigants
    see **Litigants**
  parliamentary privilege, 4–332—4–334
  pre-judgment test, 4–91, 4–319, 4–323
  prejudice
    see **Prejudice**
  public benefit defence, 4–335, 4–336
  public domain information, 4–88
  public interest, and, 4–84
  restrictions, on, 5–8
  standard of proof, 4–149, 4–151, 4–164, 4–167
  statutory basis, 4–1—4–3
  statutory defence, 4–247, 4–248, 4–250, 4–260
  strict liability rule
    criminal contempt, 1–116
    limits on, 1–118, 1–119
    mens rea, 4–2, 4–35, 4–40, 4–51
    nature, of, 4–1, 4–3
    Phillimore Committee, 4–2
    wards of court, 1–116
  summary procedures, 5–73
  technical contempt, 4–93

Subverting court orders
  assault, 11–36
  defamation, 11–36
  freezing orders (*Mareva*), 11–46
    and see **Freezing orders (*Mareva*)**
  industrial disputes, 11–38
  mens rea, 11–34—11–35
  non-parties, 6–115, 11–34
  search and seizure orders (*Anton Piller*), 11–47
    and see **Search and seizure orders (*Anton Piller*)**
  subject matter destroyed
    absence of order, 11–40
    confidential information, 11–39
    joint tenancies, 11–42—11–45
    trade secrets, 11–37

Summary jurisdiction
  see also **Jurisdiction**
  exercise, of, 2–17, 2–18
  judicial resort, to, 2–15, 2–16
  purpose, 2–1
  safeguards, 2–17, 2–19
  summary procedure, 2–4

Summary process
  administration of justice, and, 2–28
  affidavit evidence, 2–19—2–21
  arbitrary nature, 12–33
  coercive nature, 12–7
  criminal contempt, and, 3–55, 3–57, 3–75
  delay and expense, avoiding, 2–29, 2–30
  disputed facts, 2–22
  human rights, 2–144, 10–39
  judicial extension, 2–175
  justification, 2–23, 2–26
  practical necessity, and, 2–26, 2–27
  press freedom, and, 1–153, 1–156
    and see **Press freedom**
  punitive nature, 12–7
  resort, to, 12–23

Tape recorders
  unauthorised use
    publication of recordings, 10–192
    statutory provisions, 10–191
    summary jurisdiction, 10–193
  use of, 1–119, 3–94, 10–196—10–198, 10–200

Technical contempt
  degree of prejudice, 4–92, 4–100, 5–19, 5–26, 5–29, 5–35
  degree of risk, 5–35
  demise, of, 5–35, 5–61
  development, 1–79, 1–80
  historical context, 5–27—5–36
  pre-judgment, and, 5–26
  reprehensible conduct, 5–31, 5–32
  risk of interference, 5–31, 5–35
  risk of prejudice, 1–78, 1–80, 1–83
  scope of contempt, 5–30
  substantial contempt, distinguished, 1–81, 1–82

Technological developments
  archived material, 1–149, 4–27
  internet, 1–145
    and see **Internet**
  satellite television, 1–145

Television
  court reporting, and, 4–270, 4–271, 4–273, 16–415—16–419
  unauthorised recordings, 10–206—10–207

Third parties
  company directors, 3–120
  court orders, 3–119, 3–121
  criminal contempt, 3–119
  liability, 3–119—3–129

INDEX

Tribunals
jurisdiction, 13–70—13–78
   and see **Jurisdiction**
protection, afforded to, 13–70
public policy, and, 13–71—13–72
reporting restrictions, 8–147—8–150
   and see **Reporting restrictions**

Undertakings
see also **Breach of undertaking**
absence of knowledge, 12–194
authority
   absence, of, 12–194—12–195
   companies, involving, 12–197
   express, 12–195—12–196
   implied, 12–195—12–196
Civil Procedure Rules (CPR)
   application, 12–219, 12–224—12–227
   libel proceedings, 12–228—12–236
disclosure of documents
   see **Disclosure of documents**
enforcement, 12–183—12–185, 15–27
family proceedings, in, 12–184—12–185, 14–77
   and see **Family proceedings**
implied undertakings
   Civil Procedure Rules (CPR), 12–219, 12–224—12–226
   disclosure of documents, 12–201—12–202
   policy considerations, 12–205—12–217
   release, 12–200
   specific rule, 12–218, 12–220
mistaken undertakings, 12–189
non-molestation orders, 12–186
payment of money, 12–187
release, 12–188
solicitors, 12–248
strangers to proceedings, 12–198
variation, 12–188

Waiver
civil contempt, 3–157
criminal contempt, 3–157
examples, of, 3–159—3–161
exclusion, of, 3–162—3–165
Phillimore Committee, 3–166
public interest, 3–158, 3–162—3–165
reform proposals, 3–166—3–169

Wards of court
breach of order, 3–115—3–118
criminal contempt, and, 3–115—3–118
jurisdiction, 6–41, 6–47, 6–48, 6–74, 6–75, 6–77, 6–85, 6–90, 11–331—11–332
   see also **Parens patriae jurisdiction**
privacy, 6–111—6–112
procedure, 6–109
wardship
   anticipation, of, 11–338
   cessation, 11–338

Wards of court—*cont.*
wardship—*cont.*
   Ignorance of, 11–339, 11–341, 11–347
   interference, with, 11–331—11–332
   notice, of, 11–342
   protective jurisdiction, 11–331—11–332
   strict liability, and, 11–344—11–346

Whistleblowing
see also **Journalists' sources**
freedom of information, 9–24
importance, of, 9–27
private objectives, 9–29
public interest, 9–27—9–29

Withholding information
anonymity, granting of, 7–86, 7–104
common law jurisdiction, 7–76, 7–84
prohibiting publication, 7–83—7–84
restriction orders, 7–83—7–85
statutory provisions, 7–83

Witnesses
advertising, for, 4–134
anonymity, 8–74—8–75
attendance, of, 10–171
blackmail victims, 7–69
child witnesses, 8–192—8–194
complainants, as, 11–222
duress, and, 10–165, 10–169, 10–170
failure to attend court, 11–90
false evidence, 10–159—10–161
informants, 7–69
interference
   deterring, 4–129, 4–130, 11–190
   improper influence, 11–190
   intention, 11–207—11–212
   mens rea, 11–190
intimidation, 1–151, 4–130, 10–167, 11–299
judicial discretion, 10–175
payment, of, 11–259—11–263, 11–266—11–268
perjury, 10–157, 10–168, 10–172
persuasion
   see **Persuasion of witnesses**
prejudicial material, 4–129—4–134
privilege, claiming, 10–173—10–174
protection, of, 7–14, 7–71, 8–192—8–194, 10–165, 11–191—11–195
publicity, affecting, 7–68, 7–70
refusal to answer, 10–162—10–164
refusal to be sworn, 10–158
remaining in court, 10–158
reprisals
   motive, 11–201—11–206
   positive intention, 11–207—11–212
   private reprisals, 11–213—11–215
   protection, against, 11–197—11–200
summons, 1–97, 11–100, 11–109, 11–112, 11–118—11–120, 11–127
threats, to, 4–131, 10–166, 10–167

Witnesses—*cont.*
  vulnerable witnesses, 7–80, 10–165
Writ of attachment
  exercise, of, 1–84, 3–184, 15–6

Young offenders
  see also **Children and young persons**
  attendance centres, 14–65
  social enquiry reports, 14–68